WEST'S
BUSINESS LAW
ALTERNATE EDITION

Text
Summarized Cases
Legal, Ethical, Regulatory,
    and International Environment

FIFTH EDITION

WEST'S
BUSINESS LAW
ALTERNATE EDITION

Text
Summarized Cases
Legal, Ethical, Regulatory,
and International Environment

FIFTH EDITION

GAYLORD A. JENTZ
Herbert D. Kelleher
Professor in Business Law
MSIS Department
University of Texas at Austin

ROGER LeROY MILLER
Department of Legal Studies
Clemson University

FRANK B. CROSS
MSIS Department
and
Associate Director, Center for Legal and Regulatory Studies
University of Texas at Austin

WEST PUBLISHING COMPANY
St. Paul   New York   Los Angeles   San Francisco

WEST'S COMMITMENT TO THE ENVIRONMENT

In 1906, West Publishing Company began recycling materials left over from the production of books. This began a tradition of efficient and responsible use of resources. Today, up to 95 percent of our legal books and 70 percent of our college texts are printed on recycled, acid-free stock. West also recycles nearly 22 million pounds of scrap paper annually—the equivalent of 181,717 trees. Since the 1960s, West has devised ways to capture and recycle waste inks, solvents, oils, and vapors created in the printing process. We also recycle plastics of all kinds, wood, glass, corrugated cardboard, and batteries, and have eliminated the use of styrofoam book packaging. We at West are proud of the longevity and the scope of our commitment to our environment.

Production, Prepress, Printing and Binding by West Publishing Company.

Two study guides have been developed to assist you in mastering the concepts in the text. Both workbooks are available from your local bookstore under the following titles:

- *Study Guide to Accompany West's Business Law* prepared by Barbara Behr

- *Mastering West's Business Law, Alternate Edition: With Programmed Review* prepared by Roger LeRoy Miller and Eric Hollowell.

For more information on the study guides, please see the preface of this text where they are explained in greater detail.

The Uniform Commercial Code is reproduced with permission of the American Law Institute and the National Conference of Commissioners on Uniform State Laws. Copyright © 1991.

Composition: Parkwood Composition
Copy Editing: Pat Lewis
Artwork: Randy Miyake, Miyake Illustration

Library of Congress Cataloging-in-Publication Data

Jentz, Gaylord A.
    West's business law: text, summarized cases, legal, ethical, regulatory, and international environment / Gaylord A. Jentz, Roger LeRoy Miller, Frank B. Cross.—Alternate ed., 5th ed.
      p. cm.
    Rev. ed. of: West's business law / Kenneth W. Clarkson et al. 5th ed. ©1992.
    Includes index.
    ISBN 0-314-00997-3
    1. Commercial law—United States—Cases. 2. Business law—United States. I. Miller, Roger LeRoy. II. Cross, Frank B. III. West's business law. 5th ed. IV. Title.
KF888.J46 1993
346.73'07—dc20
[347.3067]

92-24124
CIP

Contents in Brief

Contents

■ APPENDICES

Concept Summaries

▨ Exhibits

◼ Exhibits—continued

▦ Emerging Trends in Business Law

▦ Legal Perspectives in Business

PREFACE

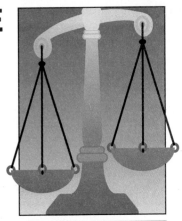

Many students preparing for a career in business, accounting, government, law, or a variety of other careers in today's world need little convincing that the legal environment is an important area of study. Now, more than ever before, a basic knowledge of law is an important part of a student's general education, for the law touches on just about every individual at one time or another. It is not an exaggeration to state that the law provides an all-encompassing framework in our society.

It is with this universal applicability of the law and the legal environment in mind that we have fashioned this text. The result is, we believe, a useful "tool for living" and a text that should satisfy the demands of students preparing for future careers. (The text also includes all areas covered by the CPA exam.)

While we cannot in any way dictate how business law and the legal environment of business should be taught, we can attempt, and have attempted, to present a text that allows maximum flexibility for the instructor. To that end, you will find this text to be extremely comprehensive. Instructors can choose those areas of the law that they wish to emphasize, rather than depending on our—the authors'—personal preferences. We have made every attempt to present the law in the most authoritative and accurate manner possible. Specifically, all case and statutory law, as well as all appendices, are current up to the date of printing.

■ Important Chapters and Special Topics

While every chapter in this text has been designed to correspond to the needs of a complete course in business law and the legal environment, some stand out as being especially timely. They are as follows:

- **Business Ethics (Chapter 2)**—This chapter stresses the importance of ethics in business decision making and focuses on the following topics: the relationship between ethics and the law, traditional ethical reasoning as it relates to business decisions and practices, and ethical issues in business today.

- **Torts and Crimes Related to Business (Chapter 7)**—Traditional torts and crimes affecting business, as well as recent trends in the liability of corporations and corporate personnel for torts and crimes committed while undertaking business activities, are singled out for special attention in this chapter.
- **Intellectual Property and Computer Law (Chapter 8)**—This chapter looks in detail at some pressing legal issues in today's business world—particularly, how to protect against infringement of rights in patented, trademarked, or copyrighted property—as well as the evolving legal framework surrounding computerized business transactions and ownership rights in computer software.
- **International Transactions (Chapter 24)**—Because business transactions have become increasingly global in nature, it is particularly important for those contemplating a career in business to understand the law governing international transactions. To fulfill this need, this chapter concentrates solely on international business activities and international sales contracts. (An additional chapter on international law is found in the last unit of the text.)
- **Electronic Fund Transfers (Chapter 30)**—This chapter summarizes the rights and liabilities of consumers and banking institutions under federal legislation covering electronic fund transfers undertaken by consumers. The chapter also discusses commercial fund transfers and Article 4A of the Uniform Commercial Code, which was recently drafted to establish uniformity in respect to commercial fund transfers.
- **Lender Liability (Chapter 34)**—Liability for the consequences of loans that they make to customers is of growing concern to lending institutions today. This chapter explores this relatively new area of legal liability and describes the common law and statutory law framework for lender liability.
- **Landlord-Tenant Relationships (Chapter 52)**—Few individuals go through life without, at one time or another, renting or leasing an apartment or house. In addition, those who invest in real estate often lease their property to others. Because the rights and liabilities of landlords and tenants are of widespread concern today, this chapter is devoted entirely to landlord-

tenant relationships and the rights and liabilities of landlords and tenants in leased property.
- **Liability of Accountants and Other Professionals (Chapter 55)**—This chapter focuses on the liability of accountants, attorneys, and other professionals to their clients and, particularly in the case of accountants, to third parties who rely on their work product.

■ Other Special Features of This Text

In addition to offering coverage of the topics of special concern discussed above, our text provides many special features for the student and the instructor.

Cases

Special attention is given in the Fifth Edition of *West's Business Law: Alternate Edition* to case selection and presentation, as well as to simplifying the task of finding and analyzing case law.

CLASSIC AND CONTEMPORARY CASES   You will find a diverse selection of summarized cases in the chapters. We have attempted to provide tried-and-true classic and landmark cases, as well as some of the most modern examples of applications of points of business law. Many of the cases in this edition are from the 1990s.

CASES FULLY INTEGRATED   Our cases are fully integrated into the surrounding text. That is, they directly follow and illustrate the points of law that are being discussed within the chapter text rather than appearing at the end of the chapter.

AN EFFECTIVE CASE FORMAT   Each case presented in this text follows a special format:

- *Case Title and Full Case Citation*—The case title and full case citation (including all parallel citations) are presented in the margin at the beginning of each case.
- *Background and Facts*—This section contains a summary, in the authors' own words, of the events leading up to the lawsuit.
- *Decision and Remedy*—In this section, the authors summarize, in their own words, the out-

come of the case. Additionally, when appropriate, the exact words of the court are given. The quotations usually consist of one or two sentences interspersed throughout this section.

- *Comments*—Special comments by the authors are added following the *Decision and Remedy* section whenever the student might benefit from additional information regarding the case or its outcome.

- *Ethical Considerations*—This section discusses ethical aspects of the law or laws under consideration. Because ethical concerns have become an increasingly important part of the legal and regulatory environment, *Ethical Considerations* are appended to numerous cases in this text.

CASE CITATIONS ARE FULLY EXPLAINED In Chapter 1, we use a comprehensive format to explain case citations. In addition to our explanatory text, we offer an exhibit in four-color graphics to lead the student to a full understanding of how to read and understand case citations in this text and in other legal references.

CASE BRIEFING ASSIGNMENTS Many professors prefer to have their students brief cases. To make these assignments more manageable for both students and professors, we provide in Appendix A a short explanation of how to brief a case, followed by twenty-five cases for briefing. Case briefing assignments, including questions that should be answered for each of the cases chosen for briefing, are found at the end of the problem sets in twenty-five of the chapters in the text. Sample answers to the questions listed in the case briefing assignments are found in the free manual, *Answers to Questions and Case Problems*.

Ethics

The teaching of ethics has become an integral part of every introductory course in business law and the legal and regulatory environment of business. To satisfy the increased interest in ethical questions, we have integrated ethics throughout this text.

ETHICAL ISSUES ARE DESCRIBED IN UNIT OPENERS At the beginning of each unit of this text, the student is introduced to some of the ethical issues that may arise concerning the materials presented in the chapters in that unit. These ethical issues tie in with three other ethically oriented features—the *Ethical Considerations* sections appended to some of the cases, the ethical problems presented at the end of the *Questions and Case Problems* sections in many of the chapters, and the *Focus on Ethics* section that concludes each unit.

AN EARLY CHAPTER ON ETHICS After students have been introduced to law and legal reasoning in Chapter 1, they immediately read Chapter 2, which deals with business ethics. This chapter sets the tone for ethical analyses throughout the remainder of the text.

CASE ETHICAL CONSIDERATIONS As already mentioned, a number of cases contain special concluding sections called *Ethical Considerations*. These sections expose and define the ethical issues brought out in the cases.

A QUESTION OF ETHICS Thirty-one chapters of the Fifth Edition of *West's Business Law: Alternate Edition* have a special problem at the end of the chapter entitled *A Question of Ethics*. A real-world case is summarized, and then ethical questions are presented for the student to answer. Suggested answers to these questions are included in the *Answers to Questions and Case Problems*.

FOCUS ON ETHICS At the end of each of the ten units in this text is a special section entitled *Focus on Ethics*. Each of these sections addresses ethical aspects of the law discussed in the preceding unit. While these sections are not intended to substitute for a course in ethics, each section is designed to elicit comments and discussion from the student-readers on ethical issues. For this reason, each *Focus* ends with a set of discussion questions. Brief suggested answers to these questions can be found in the *Instructor's Manual*. Additionally, further comments on, and references for, these sections are given in the *Instructor's Manual*.

Emerging Trends in Business Law

A number of chapters include a feature entitled *Emerging Trends in Business Law*. These two-page spreads emphasize policy issues that have arisen, or will arise, with respect to certain aspects of business law and the legal environment. Each feature concludes with the following two sections:

- *Implications for the Businessperson*—A list of the steps that businesspersons might take to prevent legal problems in the particular area being discussed.
- *For Critical Analysis*—A set of two or three questions that require the student-readers to critically analyze aspects of the emerging trend being discussed.

The following *Emerging Trends* are included in this edition:

- Codes of Ethics—Do They Work? (Chapter 2).
- Adversarial versus Nonadversarial Justice (Chapter 3).
- The Boundaries of Free Commercial Speech (Chapter 4).
- How to Imprison a Corporation (Chapter 7).
- Tort Reform (Chapter 23).
- The Growing World of Bankruptcy (Chapter 33).
- The Growing Rights of Independent Contractors (Chapter 35).
- Toward Stricter Enforcement of Antitrust Laws (Chapter 47).
- Privacy Rights versus Worker Safety and Efficiency (Chapter 48).
- Facing a United Europe (Chapter 56).

Legal Perspectives in Business

Today's law and legal environment students need to know about some of the practical aspects of the course that they are taking. To this end, we have prepared a large number of what we call *Legal Perspectives in Business*. There are seventeen of these boxed-in perspectives in this edition. They alert students to certain legal pitfalls in business relationships and frequently expand the law's application in a given situation. The following are some of the topics covered in the *Legal Perspectives*:

- Retailers and Tort Liability (Chapter 5).
- Problems with Oral Contracts (Chapter 14).
- When You Can't Perform (Chapter 16).

- Stop-Payment Orders (Chapter 29).
- Voluntary versus Involuntary Bankruptcy (Chapter 33).
- Using Independent Contractors (Chapter 35).
- The Benefits and Costs of Franchising (Chapter 37).
- Guarding against Employment Discrimination (Chapter 48).

Unit Opening Notes

Each of the ten units in this text begins with a listing of the chapters in the unit, followed by a discussion of the importance of the topics to be discussed. The student can read about the broad concepts, including traditional business practices and public-policy considerations, upon which the law covered in the unit is based. For example, in Unit Four on commercial paper, we explain how commercial paper law is essentially a codification of the traditional business practices in this area. Immediately following the introductory comments is the section on ethical issues discussed above, under ethics.

Concept Summaries

Whenever key areas of the law need additional emphasis, we provide a *Concept Summary*. These summaries have always been a popular pedagogical tool in this text. There are now thirty-nine such summaries, including the following:

- Courts and Procedures (Chapter 3).
- Common Basic Torts (Chapter 5).
- Methods by Which an Offer Can Be Terminated (Chapter 10).
- Contracts Subject to the Statute of Frauds (Chapter 14).
- The Formation of Sales Contracts (Chapter 18).
- Requirements for Negotiable Instruments (Chapter 26).
- The Priority of Claims to a Debtor's Collateral (Chapter 31).
- Suretyship and Guaranty Relationships (Chapter 32).
- Forms of Business Organization (Chapter 37).
- Rights and Duties of the Bailee and Bailor (Chapter 50).

Exhibits

When appropriate, we have illustrated important aspects of the law in graphic or summary form in exhibits. In numerous instances, to make sure that the student fully understands the concept being illustrated, we have added explanatory legends. In addition, we have included a number of sample forms for the student's reference. In all, eighty-three exhibits are now featured in *West's Business Law: Alternate Edition,* including the following:

- *Exhibit 1–6* How to Read Citations.
- *Exhibit 2–1* Ethical Decision Making.
- *Exhibit 3–5* A Typical Complaint.
- *Exhibit 8–1* Federal Legislation Relating to Privacy.
- *Exhibit 15–1* Third Party Beneficiary Contract Relationships.
- *Exhibit 17–2* Measurement of Damages— Breach of Construction Contracts.
- *Exhibit 18–2* Major Differences between Contract Law and Sales Law.
- *Exhibit 19–1* A Sample Negotiable Bill of Lading.
- *Exhibit 24–2* The "Life Cycle" of a Letter of Credit.
- *Exhibit 26–3* A Qualified Indorsement.
- *Exhibit 28–1* Time for Proper Presentment.
- *Exhibit 29–6* How a Check Is Cleared.
- *Exhibit 31–1* Secured Transactions—Concepts and Terminology.
- *Exhibit 31–2* Types of Collateral and Methods of Perfection.
- *Exhibit 35–1* Sample Power of Attorney.
- *Exhibit 37–1* Major Business Forms Compared.
- *Exhibit 37–2* Tax Aspects of Partnerships and Corporations.
- *Exhibit 43–5* Comparison of Coverage, Application, and Liabilities under Rule 10b-5 and Section 16(b).
- *Exhibit 47–1* An Index of Industrial Concentration.
- *Exhibit 51–1* A Sample Warranty Deed.
- *Exhibit 53–1* Insurance Classifications.

Vocabulary Stressed

One of the major stumbling blocks in the study of business law and the legal environment is legal vocabulary. In addition to including bracketed explanations of difficult terms and phrases within the court opinions presented in the text, this edition has been completely reedited to ensure that every important legal term used by the authors is fully defined when it is first introduced.

At the end of each chapter, all terms that were boldfaced within the chapter are listed in alphabetical order under the heading *Terms and Concepts.* The page on which the term is defined is given after each term. Students can briefly examine the list to make sure they understand all important terms introduced in the chapter and can immediately review terms that they do not completely understand by referring to the page number given. All boldfaced terms are listed and again defined in the *Glossary* at the end of the text.

"For Review" Questions

At the end of every chapter in this edition, we have added five *For Review* questions. These review questions will help your students to quickly review the most important legal concepts covered within the chapter.

Questions and Case Problems

Every chapter of this text ends with nine to fourteen questions and case problems. The first three to six of these are hypothetical questions. The remainder are actual case problems, many from the 1990s. Many of the case problems are based on cases that can be found in their entirety in the LEGAL CLERK Research Software System (which will be discussed later in this preface). Complete answers are given in a separate manual for all questions and case problems in the text, including the ethical questions and case briefing assignments. The *Answers to Questions and Case Problems* is free to adopters and can be placed on reserve in the library, if desired.

Appendices

Because the majority of students keep their business law text as a reference source, we have included a full set of appendices. They are as follows:

A. How to Brief a Case and Selected Cases.
B. The Constitution of the United States.
C. The Uniform Commercial Code (fully updated, including the 1990 amendments to Article 2A on leases, Revised Articles 3 and 4, Article 4A on funds transfers, and Article 6–Alternative B on bulk transfers).

D. The Uniform Partnership Act.

E. A Guide to Research in Business Law.

F. Spanish Equivalents for Important Legal Terms in English.

A Special Note on the Research Guide

Increasingly, business law and legal environment instructors are requiring their students to do research projects covering legal topics studied in the text. Appendix E, our research guide, is designed to let students know the sources available to help them conduct their research. Many publications deal with legal issues, and these are categorized in this appendix and tied, when appropriate, to chapters in the text.

How This Book Differs from *West's Business Law: Text, Cases, Legal and Regulatory Environment,* Fifth Edition

Basically, these two books are very similar. The major difference concerns the case presentation format. In this text, we summarize the cases, whereas in *West's Business Law: Text, Cases, Legal and Regulatory Environment* we include full case excerpts. Additionally, this text features the *Legal Perspectives in Business* and the special introductory *For Review* questions at the end of each chapter.

■ Supplements

West's Business Law has always been known as an innovator in teaching and learning supplements. This edition provides the largest and most comprehensive supplements package ever to be offered for a business law text. We understand that instructors face a difficult task in finding the time necessary to teach the material that they wish to cover during each term. Individually and in conjunction with a number of our colleagues, we have developed supplementary teaching materials that we believe are the best available today. Each component of the supplements package is described below.

A Course Planning Guide

To simplify and make more efficient the work effort of the instructor using *West's Business Law: Alternate Edition,* we have developed for the Fifth Edition a unique 200-page guide that integrates all of the print, video, and computer software supplements. The *Instructor's Course Planning Guide and Media Handbook* offers helpful suggestions on what parts of the complete learning/teaching package to use with each chapter of the text.

Printed Supplements

The printed supplements for *West's Business Law: Alternate Edition* have a single goal: to make the task of teaching and the task of learning more enjoyable and more efficient.

INSTRUCTOR'S MANUAL The *Instructor's Manual* has been written by text author Roger LeRoy Miller, together with Eric Hollowell. Having one of the co-authors of the main text write the *Instructor's Manual* has resulted in complete agreement between what is stressed in the text and what is fully outlined in the *Instructor's Manual.*

We believe that the *Instructor's Manual* for this edition is the best that has ever been presented for a business law text. Each chapter of the manual contains the following features:

● An introductory section, which highlights the main concepts and importance of the law covered in the chapter.
● A detailed, explanatory outline of the chapter contents, which is keyed very closely to the text.
● Synopses of all cases, often accompanied by additional notes and comments, as well as questions to ask in class and answers to these questions.
● Additional background on significant persons, statutes, and especially *Restatements* that are mentioned or referred to in the text.
● Teaching suggestions, including points to be stressed, hypothetical questions to elicit class discussion, and discussion questions keyed closely to the text and based on information contained within the text.
● Suggested activities and research assignments.
● Explanations of selected footnotes. Cases, statutes, and other references cited in footnotes of the chapter are briefly summarized or explained so that the relationship between the footnote and the text is clear.

A computerized version of the *Instructor's Manual* is now also available (this version is described below, under software).

TWO STUDY GUIDES WITH CPA REVIEW
For this edition of *West's Business Law: Alternate Edition,* you have the choice of ordering one of two available study guides. The first of these guides, which has been prepared by Professor Barbara E. Behr, is entitled *Study Guide to Accompany West's Business Law* and allows students to comprehend not only black-letter law but also some of the subtleties behind the legal process. This *Study Guide* contains:

● A ''Things to Keep in Mind'' section.
● A list of key terms.
● An outline of the chapter.
● A set of fill-in questions (a type of programmed learning device).
● A set of multiple-choice questions.
● The answers to the fill-in and multiple-choice questions.
● A section entitled ''Uniform C.P.A. Business Law Examination Information.''

The second study guide, entitled *Mastering West's Business Law, Alternate Edition: With Programmed Review,* has been prepared by text author Roger LeRoy Miller together with Eric Hollowell. This study guide contains an introductory study skills section, a guide to briefing cases, a chapter-by-chapter review of *West's Business Law: Alternate Edition,* and a guide to the business law portion of the Uniform AICPA Examination. The chapter-by-chapter review offers the following for each chapter of the text:

● Pre-study questions.
● Brief chapter introduction.
● Checklist of what each student should be able to do after finishing the chapter.
● Chapter outline (including helpful mnemonics).
● A list of cases excerpted in the chapter.
● True-false questions.
● Fill-in questions.
● Multiple-choice questions.
● Short essay problems (with answers in the *Instructor's Manual*).
● Programmed review.

A computerized version of the Behr study guide—called *Microguide*—is also available (see below, under software supplements).

CASE PRINTOUTS   Most of the cases in the main body of the text have been reprinted *in their entirety* and published in a separate booklet called *West's Business Law: Alternate Edition Case Printouts.* This booklet is available free to adopters. It provides readily accessible and complete information on all the cases selected for detailed discussion in the classroom. Instructors may also copy any of the cases in their entirety to hand out to their students.

ANSWERS MANUAL   A complete answers manual entitled *Answers to Questions and Case Problems* is available to all adopters. Each answer is presented in a standard format.

● *Point of Law*—The point of law to which the problem relates is first stated in boldface.
● *Page Reference*—The point of law is followed by the page number or numbers at which the point of law is discussed in the text .
● *Answer*—The specific answer to the question or the problem is then given.

WEST'S ADVANCED TOPICS AND CONTEMPORARY ISSUES: EXPANDED COVERAGE
A specially prepared paperback text entitled *West's Advanced Topics and Contemporary Issues: Expanded Coverage to Accompany West's Business Law* has been created by text author Frank B. Cross. This book adds a unique element to the total teaching/learning package for the Fifth Edition of *West's Business Law: Alternate Edition.* The book is available to students free of charge at their instructor's option. *West's Advanced Topics and Contemporary Issues: Expanded Coverage,* keyed to the text of the Fifth Edition, provides supplemental detailed coverage of the most pressing legal issues confronting business today. The chapters in this text are as follows:

1. Business Ethics
2. International Business Law
3. Individual Employee Rights
4. Employment Discrimination Law
5. Occupational Safety and Workers' Compensation
6. Accounting and the Law
7. Securities Law and Regulation
8. Mergers and Acquisitions
9. Insurance Law
10. Real Estate Finance and Liability

11. Bank Regulation and Liability
12. Unfair Competition
13. Advertising Law
14. Environmental Liability
15. Health Care Law
16. Sports and Entertainment Law
17. Hospitality Management Law
18. Communications Law
19. Government Contracts
20. Legal Representation of Business

Each chapter ends with *Ethical Perspectives* and *International Perspectives*.

HANDBOOK ON THE CIVIL RIGHTS ACT OF 1991 A thirty-two-page handbook entitled *The Civil Rights Act of 1991: Handbook to Accompany West's Business Law* is now available for your students on request.

HANDBOOK ON REVISED ARTICLES 3 AND 4 OF THE UCC A 100-page handbook entitled *Revised Articles 3 and 4 of the UCC: Handbook to Accompany West's Business Law* is available free for your students on request. This special supplement presents the revised versions of UCC Articles 3 and 4 and analyzes their significance for commercial law.

HANDBOOK ON CRITICAL THINKING AND WRITING A new booklet entitled *Handbook on Critical Thinking and Writing in Business Law,* written by text author Roger LeRoy Miller, provides students with an overview of techniques used in critical thinking. It allows students to examine and analyze legal assumptions and arguments. The *Handbook* is closely tied to some of the examples given in the chapters of the Fifth Edition of *West's Business Law: Alternate Edition.* Additionally, the student is given twelve steps to effective writing. Copies are available to adopters and their students when requested.

A COMPREHENSIVE TEST BANK Again, to ensure consistency between the teaching materials and the text, one of the authors, Roger LeRoy Miller, has co-written the examination bank. There are approximately 2,500 multiple-choice questions with answers and over 1,600 true-false questions with answers. These questions are available in booklet form or, as discussed below, on software.

WEST'S BOOK OF FORMS Professors can order for their students *West's Book of Forms,* compiled by Robert D. McNutt. The *Book of Forms* contains forty sample business forms.

TRANSPARENCY ACETATES The supplements package contains nearly 100 transparency acetates for overhead projection in the classroom. Included in this package are key actual business forms.

REGIONAL REPORTERS West's regional reporters cover all state appellate court decisions. The following reporters are available to qualified adopters: Pacific, North Western, South Western, North Eastern, Atlantic, South Eastern, and Southern.

Software Supplements

Software supplements represent an increasingly significant portion of the *West's Business Law: Alternate Edition* teaching/learning package. We now offer for adopters and students a wide variety of software supplements.

LEGAL CLERK SOFTWARE The LEGAL CLERK Research Software System is a user-friendly, interactive software package that simultaneously introduces students to the rudiments of computer-aided legal research and reinforces the underlying concepts of business law and the legal environment. LEGAL CLERK provides a valuable learning tool to help your school meet AACSB recommendations for using microcomputers in business law and legal environment courses.

To provide instructors with maximum flexibility, LEGAL CLERK covers three major subject areas of business law and the legal environment: (1) UCC/Article 2—Sales, (2) Government Regulation and the Legal Environment of Business, and (3) Contracts. Instructors may select one version or all three versions for their classes. Cases appearing in LEGAL CLERK are clearly identified in the text with a computer logo. The logos are color coded to help users easily identify which version of LEGAL CLERK contains specific cases.

 Uniform Commercial Code/Article 2—Sales (Version 1.0)

 Government Regulation and the Legal Environment of Business (Version 1.0)

 Contracts (Version 1.0)

A site license for all three versions of LEGAL CLERK is free to qualified adopters. Each version is accompanied by an *Instructor's Resource Guide* and, for student purchase, a *Student User's Guide*.

LEGAL REVIEW SOFTWARE   This new software allows students to review legal concepts found in all three LEGAL CLERK versions: Contracts, Government Regulation and the Legal Environment of Business, and Uniform Commercial Code/Article 2—Sales. LEGAL REVIEW runs on IBM PCs and compatible microcomputers and is available to qualified adopters. A *LEGAL REVIEW Student User's Manual* can be purchased by the student. The manual contains specific questions about the legal concepts covered in the software.

COMPUTERIZED INSTRUCTOR'S MANUAL For those instructors who wish to modify the *Instructor's Manual* to add their own notes, we provide a fully computerized version of the *Instructor's Manual*. You may order the manual in the following formats:

- ASCII format for IBM, on 5-inch diskettes.
- ASCII format for IBM, on 3½-inch diskettes.
- ASCII format for Macintosh, on 3½-inch diskettes.
- Microsoft Word 4.0 format for Macintosh, on 3½-inch diskettes.

This software allows the *Instructor's Manual* to be imported into any popular word-processing program, such as WordPerfect. Instructors wishing to obtain these diskettes may request them directly from their West sales representative.

COMPUTERIZED STUDY GUIDE   Your students can test their knowledge of chapter material with the new computerized study guide called *Microguide*. The questions from the Behr study guide described above are now on diskette, allowing your students to practice taking computerized tests. Multiple-choice and true-false questions are included. *Microguide* runs on IBM PCs and compatible microcomputers or Macintosh microcomputers (with Hypercard). *Microguide* is available free to qualified adopters of the text.

COMPUTERIZED TEST BANK—WESTEST The test bank is available on the latest version of WESTEST, a highly acclaimed computerized test-

ing system, which is offered for IBM PCs and compatible microcomputers (in a menu-driven environment) or the Macintosh family of microcomputers. WESTEST allows instructors to do the following:

- Import and export graphs.
- Add or edit questions, instructions, and answers.
- Select questions by previewing the question on the screen.
- Let the system select questions randomly.
- Select questions by question number.
- View summaries of the examination or the test-bank chapters.
- Set up the page layout for exams.
- Print exams in a variety of formats.

INTERACTIVE SOFTWARE—CONTRACTS AND SALES   The use of computers in many areas of learning has increased dramatically at the college level. For those students who have their own computers or who have access to computers through friends or learning labs, we have developed a unique interactive program for the teaching/learning of contracts and sales. This program uses HyperText and allows for flexibility in learning the subject matter based on each user's level of understanding.

"YOU BE THE JUDGE" SOFTWARE   This software provides case problems for ten topic areas. The user is supplied with the facts and is then asked how the issue should be decided. A word processor, integrated in the software, allows the user to key in his or her response and print it. A glossary of key legal terms is also included.

CASE PROBLEM CASES ON DISKETTE   Cases for virtually all of the case problems found at the end of all fifty-six chapters of the text are now available in ASCII format on diskette. These can be imported into any word-processing program, such as Microsoft Word or WordPerfect. The diskettes are available in the following formats:

- 5¼-inch diskettes for IBM PCs and compatible microcomputers.
- 3½-inch diskettes for IBM PCs and compatible microcomputers.
- 3½-inch diskettes for all Macintosh computers.

WESTLAW WESTLAW, the premiere computerized legal-research system, is renowned for its ability to help law professors, law students, attorneys, and paralegals do research in the law. Qualified adopters of *West's Business Law: Alternate Edition* are allowed free time on WESTLAW. Contact your West sales representative for more details.

WESTRAIN II These diskettes provide an entire tutorial to train both instructors and students in the use of West Publishing Company's computerized legal-research system, WESTLAW. The tutorial allows for mastery of search skills in a self-paced environment.

Videocassettes

No introductory business law and legal environment text would be complete without supplemental visual materials. We are proud to announce that an extensive videocassette library is now available for adopters of *West's Business Law: Alternate Edition*. These instructional videos can help you in the teaching of business law and the legal environment in a variety of areas, including ethics and social responsibility, employment law, and others.

Many of these instructional videos have specially prepared instructor's manuals, most of which were written by one of this text's authors.

THE DRAMA OF THE LAW VIDEO SERIES West is proud to announce a ten-videocassette series entitled the *Drama of the Law*. This is the first law tele-series that uses humor and wit to teach important legal concepts to today's business law and legal environment students. The scripts were written by John Jay Osborn, Jr., author of *The Paper Chase* and *The Associates*. The ten points of law are as follows:

1. Mistake
2. Offer and Acceptance
3. Negligence and Assumption of Risk
4. Conditions on a Promise
5. Risk of Loss
6. Third Party Beneficiaries
7. Breach and Remedies
8. Warranties
9. Agency and *Respondeat Superior*
10. Private Property and Bailments

Most of these videos are also available on the *West's Business Law and Legal Environment Laser Videodisc* (discussed later in this preface).

John Jay Osborn, Jr., and text author Roger LeRoy Miller have prepared a unique 100-page *Instructor's Manual* for the *Drama of the Law* video series. For each chapter, there is a complete shooting script of the video in which certain portions of the dialogue have been underlined and numbered. In the pages that follow each script, there is a section entitled "Teaching Points of Law." This section includes the following:

- A reference to the page numbers in *West's Business Law: Alternate Edition* covering the legal concepts illustrated by the video.
- A lead-in question for your students.
- One to fifteen points showing the legal implications of the underlined text in the video script.
- An answer to the lead-in question.

THE MAKING OF A CASE This is a specially prepared video hosted and narrated by *L.A. Law's* Richard Dysart. He takes the viewer on a tour of the process by which appellate decisions are published.

MOOT COURT—THE TEXACO/PENNZOIL CASE Students at Stanford University demonstrate what moot court is. This is an effective learning device to show the elements of a trial and is of special interest to students because it was done by students.

PBS ETHICS IN AMERICA SERIES Several of the highly acclaimed videos from the PBS series on ethics are now available for use in your business law and legal environment courses. Included are videos on advertising and corporate takeovers.

ANATOMY OF A TRIAL—CONTRACTS A series of videos on a hypothetical contract case prepared by the American Bar Association has been edited down to one video. The video shows each aspect of a typical trial. Additionally, much information on contract and sales law is given.

An extensive *Instructor's Manual* has been prepared to accompany this video. It gives an outline of the video as well as key points of law and civil procedure.

ANATOMY OF A TRIAL—A PRODUCTS LIABILITY CASE This video also shows many of the aspects of a typical trial. Additionally, it brings out important points in product liability law.

An *Instructor's Manual* similar to the one for the video on contracts has been prepared. It gives a summary of the video as well as key points about contract law.

A SUPREME COURT CASE While no cameras are allowed in the Supreme Court and therefore no actual Supreme Court case has ever been filmed, the American Bar Association created a hypothetical Supreme Court case. This dramatization uses famous lawyers and jurists to argue a First Amendment issue about tobacco advertising. Short of actually going to the Supreme Court to hear a case, this is probably the only exposure that students can have to how a Supreme Court case is actually argued.

An extensive *Instructor's Manual* has been prepared for this hypothetical Supreme Court case. It points out the many procedural aspects of the case and comments on the issues argued.

UNDERSTANDING THE COURTS: ANATOMY OF A CRIMINAL CASE/ANATOMY OF A CIVIL CASE These two videos, prepared exclusively by the American Bar Association, present in detail every aspect of a criminal case and of a civil case. An *Instructor's Manual* prepared by the ABA is also available.

LAW AND LITERATURE This is a videotaped lecture given by John Jay Osborn, Jr., of the University of California School of Law, Berkeley Campus (Boalt Hall). It is a lecture that he has given to business law students, law students, law professors, and state and federal judges. In this lecture, Professor Osborn attempts to relate different legal theories to great works of fiction.

West's Business Law and Legal Environment Laser Videodisc

Technology has provided instructors of business law with yet another way to present teaching materials: the laser videodisc. We have made available for this edition a complete videodisc that provides you with the latest method for presenting important topics to your students.

The *West's Business Law and Legal Environment Laser Videodisc* includes the following:

● Most of the videos from the *Drama of the Law* video series.
● Excerpts from sample trials, ethics videos, and other videos.
● Hundreds of still-frame exhibits.

THE LECTURE BUILDER SOFTWARE Those who use the *West's Business Law and Legal Environment Laser Videodisc* will find that THE LECTURE BUILDER software can allow for complete customization of each separate lecture. This software works with any Macintosh system and any IBM or compatible using the WINDOWS operating system environment. THE LECTURE BUILDER permits the instructor to pick and choose the order of the still frames and the motion videos from any part of the videodisc. Also, the motion videos can be edited by the instructor in any fashion desired. THE LECTURE BUILDER also has a fully automated mode with programmable time segments.

The Complete Supplements Package

With the addition of the *Instructor's Planning Guide*, videocassettes, laser videodisc, numerous computer software programs, two study guides, the most complete instructor's manual ever produced, and many other supplements, the Fifth Edition of *West's Business Law: Alternate Edition* has, more than ever before, the biggest and best total learning/teaching package available today. The goal in preparing all of the supplements has been twofold: to make the instructor's job efficient, enjoyable, and effective and to make the student's learning process as painless as possible with maximum results.

■ For Users of the Fourth Edition

First of all, we want to thank you for continuing to support our work efforts. Second, we want to make you aware of the numerous additions and changes we have made in this edition. The major additions and changes are summarized below.

New Chapters

To keep pace with current legal trends and developments, we have added new materials to each edition of this text. To ensure that the Fifth Edition is as up to date as possible, we have added several new chapters on topics of special interest today. These new chapters are as follows:

- Chapter 2 (Business Ethics).
- Chapter 7 (Torts and Crimes Related to Business).
- Chapter 8 (Intellectual Property and Computer Law).
- Chapter 24 (International Transactions).
- Chapter 34 (Lender Liability).
- Chapter 49 (The Nature of Property and Personalty).

In addition to these entirely new chapters, the following chapters have been completely rewritten:

- Chapter 31 (Secured Transactions).
- The following chapters in Unit Eight on government regulation:
    –Chapter 44 (Introduction and Administrative Law).
    –Chapter 45 (Consumer Law).
    –Chapter 46 (Environmental Law).
    –Chapter 47 (Antitrust Law).
    –Chapter 48 (Employment and Labor Relations Law). This chapter now includes a discussion of the Civil Rights Act of 1991.
- Chapter 56 (The International Legal Environment).

Important Chapter Revisions

- Chapter 1 (Introduction to Law and Legal Reasoning) has been substantially revised and reorganized to create a clearer, more logical, and more thorough introduction to business law. The section on schools of jurisprudential thought has been entirely rewritten to indicate to students how judicial decisions are affected by philosophical and ethical principles. A discussion on the distinction between civil law and common law systems has also been added so that students will be able to view American business law and the legal environment from a broader perspective.
- Chapter 3 (Courts and Civil Dispute Resolution) now includes an expanded section on alternative dispute resolution.

- Chapter 9 (Contracts/Nature and Terminology) presents a more thorough introduction to contracts. Sections on the interpretation of contracts and the objective theory of contracts are now included in this chapter, rather than later in the unit. A new exhibit on the law governing contracts has been added to better orient the student to the nature and function of contract law.
- Chapter 18 (Introduction to Sales Contracts and Their Formation) features a more extensive discussion of Article 2A on leases. An exhibit clarifying the relationship between sales law under the Uniform Commercial Code and general contract law has also been added.
- Chapter 26 (Negotiability and Transfer) discusses the concept of negotiability and the transfer of commercial paper in a more readable, streamlined fashion and emphasizes with greater clarity the distinction between assignment and negotiation.
- Chapter 30 (Electronic Fund Transfers) now includes a discussion of Article 4A of the Uniform Commercial Code on commercial fund transfers.
- Chapter 32 (Other Creditors' Remedies and Suretyship) contains greater coverage of, and emphasis on, the concepts of surety and guaranty. A *Concept Summary* and an exhibit clarifying these concepts have also been added.
- Chapters 38 and 39 (on partnerships) have been restructured to achieve a more logical presentation of this area of the law.
- Chapter 43 (Corporations/Financing and Investor Protection) now includes the section on corporate financing that was previously in the chapter introducing corporations. The section on insider trading has been expanded to include greater coverage of the liability of outsiders.
- Chapter 51 (Real Property) has been substantially revised and reorganized to present real property law in simpler, more understandable language. A new section on the sale of real estate covers the steps involved in the sale of real property, including the sales contract, title examination and insurance, financing, and closing procedures.
- Chapter 55 (Liability of Accountants and Other Professionals) has been revised to include the liability of attorneys and other professionals to their clients and to third parties.

New Features and Supplements

To make *West's Business Law: Alternate Edition* as useful as possible for both the instructor and the student, we have included in the Fifth Edition text a number of new pedagogical features and have expanded the supplements package. These new elements are listed below to give you a brief overview of what is new to this edition. Each item has been discussed in greater detail in the preceding sections of this preface.

NEW FEATURES IN THE TEXT
- Unit introductions.
- *Emerging Trends in Business Law.*
- *Ethical Considerations* sections in many of the cases.
- *For Review* questions.
- *Terms and Concepts.*
- Case briefing assignments.
- Ethical problems.
- Appendix A (How to Brief a Case and Selected Cases).
- Appendix C (The Uniform Commercial Code) has been updated to include the 1990 Amendments to Article 2A and Revised Articles 3 and 4.
- Appendix E (A Guide to Research in Business Law).

NEW SUPPLEMENTS—PRINTED
- *Instructor's Course Planning Guide and Media Handbook.*
- *West's Advanced Topics and Contemporary Issues: Expanded Coverage to Accompany West's Business Law.*
- *Handbook on Critical Thinking and Writing in Business Law.*
- *Mastering West's Business Law, Alternate Edition: With Programmed Review.*
- A newly written *Instructor's Manual.*
- *The Civil Rights Act of 1991: Handbook to Accompany West's Business Law.*
- *Revised Articles 3 and 4 of the UCC: Handbook to Accompany West's Business Law.*

NEW SUPPLEMENTS—SOFTWARE
- A computerized version of the *Instructor's Manual.*
- A computerized study guide (*Microguide*).

- Case problem cases on diskette.
- Interactive software—for instruction in contracts and in sales.
- "You Be the Judge" interactive software.
- WESTEST—a new computerized version of the test bank.
- LEGAL REVIEW software with *LEGAL REVIEW Student User's Manual.*
- THE LECTURE BUILDER.
- WESTrain II—WESTLAW tutorial.

NEW SUPPLEMENTS—VIDEO
- *Anatomy of a Trial: Contracts*—with *Instructor's Manual.*
- *Anatomy of a Trial: A Products Liability Case*—with *Instructor's Manual.*
- *Drama of the Law* series—with *Instructor's Manual.*
- *Law and Literature.*
- *The Making of a Case.*
- *Moot Court: The Texaco/Pennzoil Case.*
- *PBS Ethics in America* series.
- *A Supreme Court Case*—with *Instructor's Manual.*
- *Understanding the Courts: Anatomy of a Criminal Case/Anatomy of a Civil Case* (ABA videos)—with *Instructor's Manual* (available from the ABA).
- *West's Business Law and Legal Environment Laser Videodisc.*

New Exhibits

To enhance the student's understanding of concepts presented in the text, we have modified the exhibits contained in the Fourth Edition whenever necessary to achieve greater clarity or accuracy. In addition, the following entirely new exhibits have been added for the Fifth Edition of *West's Business Law: Alternate Edition:*

- *Exhibit 1–3* Criminal and Civil Law.
- *Exhibit 2–1* Ethical Decision Making.
- *Exhibit 3–4* Exclusive and Concurrent Jurisdiction.
- *Exhibit 8–1* Federal Legislation Relating to Privacy.
- *Exhibit 9–1* Law Governing Contracts.

- *Exhibit 17–1* Measurement of Damages—Breach of Construction Contracts.
- *Exhibit 17–3* Remedies Available on Breach of Contract.
- *Exhibit 18–2* Major Differences between Contract Law and Sales Law.
- *Exhibit 19–3* Void and Voidable Title.
- *Exhibit 24–1* Sample International Purchase Order Form.
- *Exhibit 25–1* Basic Types of Commercial Paper.
- *Exhibit 32–1* Classifications of Guaranty Contracts.
- *Exhibit 42–1* Merger.
- *Exhibit 42–2* Consolidation.
- *Exhibit 44–1* The Process of Administrative Adjudication.
- *Exhibit 54–1* *Per Stirpes* Distribution.
- *Exhibit 54–2* *Per Capita* Distribution.
- *Exhibit 54–3* Trust Arrangement.
- *Exhibit 56–1* Multilateral International Organizations in which the United States Participates.

New Concept Summaries

Several new *Concept Summaries* have also been added to the Fifth Edition of *West's Business Law: Alternate Edition.* These new summaries cover the following topics:

- Common Basic Torts (Chapter 5).
- Effective Time of Acceptance (Chapter 10).
- Legal Effect of Incapacity (Chapter 12).
- Suretyship and Guaranty Relationships (Chapter 32).
- Requirements for Ratification (Chapter 36).
- Forms of Business Organization (Chapter 37).
- Environmental Law (Chapter 46).

Expanded Answers Manual

The *Answers to Questions and Case Problems* for the Fifth Edition has been greatly expanded in size. Answers to all of the questions and case problems in *West's Business Law: Alternate Edition* are now presented in the uniform format described earlier in this preface.

Expanded Number of Transparencies

The Fifth Edition also includes an expanded number of transparencies. For this edition, transpar-

encies have been included for exhibits and forms that are not in the text itself.

■ Acknowledgments for the First Edition

Barbara E. Behr, Bloomsburg University of Pennsylvania; Robert Staaf, Daniel E. Murray, Richard A. Hausler, Irwin Stotsky, Patrick O. Gudridge, all of the University of Miami School of Law; William Auslen, San Francisco City College; Donald Cantwell, University of Texas at Arlington; Frank S. Forbes, University of Nebraska; Bob Garrett, American River College, California; Thomas Gossman, Western Michigan University; Charles Hartman, Wright State University, Ohio; Telford Hollman, University of Northern Iowa; Robert Jesperson, University of Houston; Susan Liebeler, Loyola University; Robert D. McNutt, California State University, Northridge; Roger E. Meiners, Texas A&M University; Gerald S. Meisel, Bergen Community College, New Jersey; James E. Moon, Meyer, Johnson & Moon, Minneapolis; Bob Morgan, Eastern Michigan University; Arthur Southwick, University of Michigan; Raymond Mason Taylor, North Carolina State; Edwin Tucker, University of Connecticut; Gary Victor, Eastern Michigan University; Gary Watson, California State University, Los Angeles.

■ Acknowledgments for the Second Edition

Robert Staaf, Kenneth Burns, Judith Kenney, Thomas Crane, all of the University of Miami; Sylvia A. Spade, David A. Escamilla, Peyton J. Paxson, and JoAnn W. Hammer, all of the University of Texas at Austin. Frank S. Forbes of the University of Nebraska, Omaha, Jeffrey E. Allen, University of Miami; Raymond August, Washington State University; David L. Baumer, North Carolina State; Barbara E. Behr, Bloomsburg University of Pennsylvania; William J. Burke, University of Lowell, Massachusetts; Robert Chatov, State University of New York, Buffalo; Larry R. Curtis, Iowa State University; Gerard Halpern, University of Arkansas; June A. Horrigan, California State University, Sacramento; John P. Huggard, North Carolina State University; John W. McGee, Southwest Texas State University; Robert D. McNutt, California State University, Northridge; Thomas

E. Maher, California State University, Fullerton; David Minars, Brooklyn College, New York; Joan Ann Mrava, Los Angeles Southwest College; Thomas L. Palmer, Northern Arizona University; Charles M. Patten, University of Wisconsin, Oshkosh; Arthur D. Wolfe, Michigan State University.

■ Acknowledgments for the Third Edition

Kristi K. Brown, Kenneth S. Culotta, Michele A. Dunkerley, Karen Kay Matson, Melinda Ann Mora, Dana Blair Smith, Marshall Wilkerson, Elizabeth Anene Wolfe, all of the University of Texas at Austin; Tamra Kempf, University of Miami; Janine S. Hiller, Virginia Polytechnic Institute and State College; Margaret Jones, Southwest Missouri State College; Carol D. Rasnic, Virginia Commonwealth University; Lorne H. Seidman, Larry Strate, and Cotton Meagher of the University of Nevada, Las Vegas; Thomas M. Apke, California State University, Fullerton; John J. Balek, Morton College, Illinois; Joseph E. Cantrell, DeAnza College, California; Frank S. Forbes, University of Nebraska, Omaha; Chris L. Hamilton, Golden West College, California; Woodrow J. Maxwell, Hudson Valley Community College, New York; David Minars, City University of New York, Brooklyn; Rick F. Orsinger, College of DuPage, Illinois; Ralph L. Quinones, University of Wisconsin, Oshkosh; Jesse C. Trentadue, University of North Dakota; Robert J. Walter, University of Texas, El Paso.

■ Acknowledgments for the Fourth Edition

Lawrence J. Bradley, University of Notre Dame; Robert J. Enders, California State Polytechnic University, Pomona; Frank Forbes, University of Nebraska at Omaha; James M. Haine, University of Wisconsin, Stevens Point, Wisconsin; Christopher L. Hamilton, Golden West College; Harry E. Hicks, Butler University, Indianapolis; Janine S. Hiller, Virginia Polytechnic Institute and State University; June A. Horrigan, California State University, Sacramento; Terry Hutchins, Pembroke State University, North Carolina; Carey Kirk, University of Northern Iowa; Nancy P. Klintworth, University of Central Florida; Kathleen M. Knutson, College of St. Catherine, St. Paul, Minnesota;

Gene A. Marsh, University of Alabama; Richard Mills, Cypress College; Alan Moggio, Illinois Central College; Violet E. Molnar, Riverside City College; Dwight D. Murphey, Wichita State University; Paula C. Murray, University of Texas; John M. Norwood, University of Arkansas; Michael J. O'Hara, University of Nebraska at Omaha; Peyton Paxson, Mesa College; S. Alan Schlact, Kennesaw College, Georgia; Lorne H. Seidman, University of Nevada at Las Vegas; Bennett D. Shulman, Lancing Community College; David Vyncke, Scott Community College.

■ Acknowledgments for the Fifth Edition

We greatly benefited from the useful criticisms, comments, and suggestions received from the following professors: Rodolfo Camacho, Oregon State University; Robert J. Cox, Salt Lake Community College; O. E. Elmore, Texas A&M University; Michael Engber, Ball State University; Marty Y. Franklin, Wilkes Community College; E. Clayton Hipp, Jr., Clemson University; James E. Holloway, East Carolina University; Bryce J. Jones, Northeast Missouri State University; Gene A. Marsh, University of Alabama; George A. Nation, III, Lehigh University; Daniel J. O'Shea, Hillsborough Community College; James Petrosino, Monroe Community College; Brad Reid, Abilene Christian University; Robert M. Rodgers, Springfield Technical Community College; Rudy Sandoval, University of Texas, San Antonio; Martha C. Santoro, Charleston Southern University; Martha Sartoris, North Hennepin Community College; Barbara P. Scheller, Temple University; Brenda Steuer, North Harris Community College, South; H. Allan Tolbert, Central Texas College; John L. Weimer, Nicholls State University; Ronald C. Young, Kalamazoo Valley Community College.

Numerous individuals spent countless hours helping with this edition. We especially wish to thank Lavina Leed Miller for her management of the entire project, as well as her superb use of her extensive editorial skills. Much of the research for this edition was masterfully undertaken and completed by Eric Hollowell, who also appropriately worked on the *Instructor's Manual* and *Mastering West's Business Law, Alternate Edition: With Programmed Review.* The copyediting services of Beverly Peavler and Mary Berry will not go unnoticed by the casual—as well as the careful—reader. Proofreading lasted many, many months. Our thanks go again to Lavina Leed Miller and Eric Hollowell for their participation, as well as to Marie-Christine Loiseau. Our appreciation also goes to Laura Lee Prather and Gina Elizabeth McVay for their tireless efforts in assisting the research and flow of materials from and through Austin. We wish to thank our long-time editor, Clyde Perlee, Jr., for his numerous suggestions for this revision. Our developmental editor, Jan Lamar, skillfully added to the planning of this project and oversaw the preparation and production of the supplements. We also thank our production manager and designer at West, John Orr, who worked many months to make sure that this project came out ahead of schedule. Our project manager, Shannon Richmond, made a difficult task as painless as possible. Bette Darwin, Production Assistant, and Bridget Neumayr, Editorial Assistant, also deserve our sincere gratitude for their help.

As always, all errors that remain in this text are solely our own responsibility. Many of you have taken the time to write us with your ideas about how we can improve this book. We welcome all comments and promise to respond. It is by incorporating your ideas that we continue to write a business law text that is best for you and for your students.

DEDICATION

Gaylord A. Jentz dedicates this edition to his wife, JoAnn; his children, Kathy, Gary, Lori, and Rory; and his granddaughter, Erin Marie.

RLM dedicates this edition to his sister, Lorraine, whose kindness knows no bounds.

Frank B. Cross dedicates this book to his parents and sisters.

UNIT ONE

The Legal Environment of Business

■ The Importance of the Legal Environment of Business

The world of business today is increasingly subject to various laws and regulations. Such rules govern all aspects of business—raising capital, marketing and the distribution of goods or services, repairing or replacing defective products, hiring and firing employees, and numerous other activities. In its broadest sense, the legal environment of business includes every topic of every chapter in this text. After all, any law that touches on business becomes part of the legal environment of business. Therefore, the legal environment of business includes contracts, sales, the formation of partnerships, corporate transactions, insurance policies, business properties, and, of course, all government regulations. No individual contemplating a career in the business world can escape the legal environment of business. A knowledge of that environment will, by necessity, aid any individual undertaking a business career.

In this unit, we discuss many of the laws and procedures affecting the legal environment of business. In Chapter 1, we look at the sources of American law, including the common law tradition. In Chapter 2, we look at an increasingly important aspect of the American legal environment—business ethics. In Chapter 3, courts, legal procedures, and alternative dispute resolution are outlined. No businessperson can realistically assume that he or she will not at some time be exposed to legal liability or the mechanics of a lawsuit. Chapter 4 examines the constitutional authority to regulate business, and Chapters 5 and 6 concern the general areas of torts (private, noncontractual wrongs committed by one party against another) and crimes (wrongs against the state). In Chapter 7, torts and crimes related to business, including white-collar crimes, are discussed at greater length. Chapter 8, which concludes the unit, looks at the laws governing intellectual property—including trademarks, patents, and copyrights—as well as issues relating to computer law.

■ Ethical Issues in the Legal Environment of Business

Ethical issues in the legal environment of business commonly arise when there is some uncertainty about whether a given action is right or wrong. Such uncertainty often exists when two fundamental ethical principles come into conflict. For example, a basic ethical precept underlying American society and expressed in the U.S. Constitution is that individuals should be free to speak and act as they like without interference from government. The First Amendment freedoms of speech and religion are zealously guarded by the government and by our courts, as are all other constitutional freedoms. Sometimes, however, the exercise of individual freedom results in harm to others, and thus the right to act freely comes into conflict with another ethical assumption operative in our society—that individuals should not harm one another. The latter principle forms the basis of tort law and criminal law. Tort law and criminal law do restrict individual freedom, but for the most part we accept those restrictions.

The thorniest ethical issues in the legal environment of business usually arise when there is no definite social consensus as to whether a given action by an individual or a business firm is *sufficiently* harmful to society to warrant the *legal* limitation of that person's or firm's freedom of expression or action.

Put another way, ethical issues frequently arise in the "gray area" that separates legally rightful from legally wrongful actions. Many "gray areas" relating to ethics and social responsibility have come about because of rapid technological changes in our society. We can be certain that as technological evolution progresses, many business actions and transactions will not immediately be defined by law as either legal or illegal, so that uncertainty will continue to exist as to which actions are "right" and which are "wrong."

Chapter 1

Introduction to Law and Legal Reasoning

Imagine living in a world without laws. The term *chaos* would perhaps best describe the state of such a society. You would not know what your rights were, and you would not know what your duties were. If something went wrong with a product that you just purchased, you would not know what redress was available to you. If there were no laws, you would not know which business agreements had any validity and which did not. Law is necessary to the smooth functioning of any modern society. Society needs certain standards to govern relationships among individuals and between the people and their government. That is why law developed. Law works within the social order, an order containing numerous activities—including business activities. The laws to be described in this text exist as an expression of the compulsory standards set by society and agreed to by society's members.

◼ What Is Law?

There have been and will continue to be different definitions of *law*. Aristotle saw law as a rule of conduct. Plato believed law was a form of social control. Cicero contended that law was the agreement of reason and nature, the distinction between the just and the unjust. The British jurist Sir William Blackstone described law as ''a rule of civil conduct prescribed by the supreme power in a state, commanding what is right, and prohibiting what is wrong.'' In America, the eminent jurist Oliver Wendell Holmes, Jr., contended that law was a set of rules that allowed one to predict how a court would resolve a particular dispute—''the prophecies of what the courts will do in fact, and nothing more pretentious, are what I mean by the law.''

Although these definitions vary in their particulars, note that all are based on the following general observation: *Law consists of enforceable rules governing relationships among individuals and between individuals and their society.* In the study of law, often referred to as **jurisprudence,** this very broad statement concerning the nature of law is the point of departure for all legal scholars and philosophers.

■ Schools of Jurisprudential Thought

The court opinions in this book show that judges often refer to logic, history, custom, or a philosophy of what is right in making their decisions. These opinions also show that different judges—for example, a trial court judge and an appellate court judge—when examining the same case, sometimes arrive at different conclusions about how the law should apply. That judges differ in their philosophies of law should come as no surprise to Americans. We frequently read or hear about the differences in legal philosophy among United States Supreme Court justices, especially when a significant, controversial case—such as one relating to abortion—is before the court. Part of the study of law, or jurisprudence, is discovering how different approaches to law affect judicial decision making.

All legal philosophers agree that ideals, logic, history, and custom have influenced the development of law in some way. They disagree, however, on the importance that each of these influences should have in shaping law, and their disagreements have produced different schools of jurisprudence. The three most influential schools of legal thought are described below and then illustrated by a hypothetical court case.

The Natural Law School

The oldest and one of the most significant schools of jurisprudence is the **natural law school.** Those who adhere to the natural law school of thought believe that government and the legal system should reflect universal moral and ethical principles that are inherent in human nature.

The natural law school traces its origins to ancient Greece. The Greek philosopher Aristotle (384–322 B.C.) made the distinction between natural law and conventional law (**positive law,** or written law). He pointed out that natural law has the same force everywhere and is not a function of individual situations, cultures, or history. A law prohibiting murder, for example, does not reflect the values accepted by a particular society at a particular time but is based on a universally accepted precept that murder is wrong. To murder someone is thus a violation of natural law.

Because natural law is universal, it takes on a higher order than positive, or conventional, law. It was this higher law to which the international tribunal of judges at Nuremburg appealed when convicting Nazi German war criminals of "crimes against humanity" at the end of World War II. Although these "criminals" may not have disobeyed any positive law of their country and may have been merely following their government's (Hitler's) orders, they were deemed by the tribunal to have violated a natural law that transcends any particular country's written laws. The natural law school of thought encourages individuals to disobey conventional, or written, laws if those individuals believe that the laws are in conflict with natural law. Protesters who felt that America's involvement in Vietnam (1964–1973) was wrong, for example, used natural law as their reason to violate written laws as they protested America's war effort.

At the basis of natural law is the concept that all persons have natural rights. John Locke, an important English political philosopher, writing in 1689, argued that no one was born with an obligation to obey rulers. He argued that all individuals were born free, equal, and independent and that they had a natural right to life, liberty, and property. The purpose of government was to secure those rights. The authors of the Declaration of Independence relied heavily on Locke's notion of natural law. In the first paragraph of the Declaration of Independence, for example, we read that people have to assume the "separate and equal Station to which the Laws of Nature and of Nature's God entitle them." In the first paragraph are also listed the "unalienable rights" of "mankind," including the right to life, liberty, and the pursuit of happiness.

In essence, the natural law tradition presupposes that the legitimacy of conventional, or positive, law derives from natural law. Whenever it conflicts with natural law, conventional law loses its legitimacy and should be changed.

The Positivist School

At the other end of the spectrum exists the **positivist school.** Those who adhere to this school believe that there can be no higher law than a nation's positive law—law created by a particular society at a particular point in time.

Thomas Hobbes, an English philosopher who lived from 1588 to 1679, is viewed by many as the founder of the positivist approach to law. Because Hobbes believed that in the original state of nature humans were no better than monkeys killing each other to get at the few bananas on the banana tree, he concluded that sovereign power was necessary for stability and peace—in fact, for survival. No rights existed prior to the creation of a sovereign power (government) that could make and enforce laws, and it was governmental authority—not nature or a deity—that conferred rights on individuals. In other words, individuals do not have any ''natural'' rights, only those acquired as a result of the existence of enforceable law. This is why, in the positivist view, positive law takes on a greater significance and finality than it does in the natural law tradition. Essentially, from the positivist perspective, the law is the law and must be obeyed on pain of punishment. Whether a particular law is bad or good is irrelevant. The merits or demerits of a given law can be discussed, and laws can be changed—in an orderly manner through a legitimate lawmaking process—but as long as a law exists, it must be obeyed.

The Legal Realists

Legal realism was a school of legal thought popular in the 1920s and 1930s, one that left a strong imprint on American jurisprudence. The legal realists were in a sense rebels. They were rebelling against some of the common assumptions of the legal theorists and jurists of their time. One such assumption was that judges, at least ideally, apply the law impartially, logically, and uniformly. Thus, in theory at least, all cases involving similar circumstances and issues should have similar outcomes. But in fact, reality rarely demonstrated such consistency—issues involving identical facts would often be decided differently by different courts, even when the same legal principles were applied. Why was this? For the legal realists, different outcomes resulted from the fact that judges are human beings with unique personalities, value systems, and intellects. It would be impossible, given this obvious fact, for any two judges to en-

gage in an identical reasoning process when evaluating the same case. In other words, it would be impossible for the law to be applied in a completely impartial, logical, and uniform manner. The task of jurists, from the legal realist's point of view, was to acknowledge this fact and become as objective as possible by becoming aware of, and clarifying, the ways in which their reasoning in particular cases was affected by their personal biases and values.

The legal realists further believed that, just as each judge is influenced by the beliefs and attitudes unique to his or her personality, so, too, is each case attended by a unique set of circumstances. That is, no two cases, no matter how similar, are ever exactly the same. Therefore, judges should tailor their decisions to take account of the specific circumstances of each case, rather than rely on some abstract rule that may not relate to those particular circumstances. Extra-legal sources, such as economic and sociological data, could also be considered in making decisions, to the extent that such sources illuminated the circumstances and issues involved in specific cases.

United States Supreme Court Justice Oliver Wendell Holmes, Jr., who lived from 1841 to 1935, was an influential proponent of legal realism. In one of his best known works, *The Common Law,* Holmes emphasized the practical nature of the law: ''The life of law has not been logic; it has been experience.'' Another proponent of this legal school of thought was Karl Llewellyn, who lived from 1893 to 1962. He, too, viewed judges' decisions as being necessarily shaped by the judges' value judgments and their interpretations of the outcomes of previous cases. Llewellyn is best known for his dominant role in drafting the Uniform Commercial Code, a set of rules for commercial transactions that will be discussed shortly. This code, which governs most contracts for the sale of goods, reflects the influence of legal realism in its emphasis on practicality, flexibility, reasonability, and customary trade practices.

The Case of the Speluncean Explorers

To illustrate how philosophies of law affect judicial decisions, Lon Fuller, a professor of law at Harvard, devised a hypothetical court case entitled *The*

Case of the Speluncean Explorers.[1] The "facts" of this hypothetical case, briefly, are as follows.

In May of the year 4299, five members of the Speluncean Society, a society of cave explorers, were exploring a deep cavern when a landslide blocked the entrance to the cave. When the men failed to return to their homes, a rescue effort was launched at the site, and for days the workers attemped to clear the entrance. Further landslides made the task extremely difficult and dangerous, and several members of the rescue team were killed during the rescue operation.

Twenty days elapsed before the explorers inside the cave discovered that they had brought a radio transmitter/receiver into the cave with them. They immediately made contact with the rescuers and asked a physician, who had come to the cave with the rescue party, whether they could survive for ten more days without food, as their provisions were now so scant. The physician said that there was little possibility of this. They then asked the physician if they could survive ten days longer if they consumed the flesh of one of their number. The physician, albeit reluctantly, said yes. The men then asked whether they should cast lots to decide who should be eaten. No one outside the cave would respond to this question. The radio was silent from that time until the thirty-second day, when the rescuers finally succeeded in clearing the entrance and reaching the men trapped inside. The rescue team then learned that the five men had cast lots by a throw of the dice, and the man who threw the losing number was put to death and eaten by the others.

The four survivors were given medical treatment and then indicted for murder and tried and sentenced to death by the Court of General Instances of the County of Stowfield. The four men petitioned the Supreme Court of Newgarth to hear the case. The relevant statute stated, "Whoever shall willfully take the life of another shall be punished by death." The decisions reached by the judges were essentially as described below. As you read them, try to relate each judge's reasoning to one of the schools of legal thought discussed above.

Judge Truepenny held that the men should be sentenced to death, in accordance with the statute—which "permits of no exception"—but suggested that the court should also petition the Chief Executive of the state of Newgarth to extend clemency. "If this is done, then justice will be accomplished without impairing either the letter or spirit of our statutes and without offering any encouragement for the disregard of law."

Judge Foster held the men to be innocent of any crime for two reasons. First, the positive law of the state of Newgarth was inapplicable to the situation in which the men found themselves. They were not in civil society but in a "state of nature." Therefore, "the law applicable to them is not the enacted and established law of this Commonwealth, but the law derived from those principles that were appropriate to their condition." In effect, the men had to create a "new charter of government," and their agreement to cast lots represented this effort. Second, even if the men's action violated the letter of the law of Newgarth, it did not violate the spirit of the law, because self-defense is permitted by the law, and the men acted in self-defense—that is, they killed so that they could survive.

Judge Tating stated that he was "wholly unable to resolve the doubts that beset me about the law of this case" and withdrew from the decision.

Judge Keen agreed with Judge Truepenny, holding that the men violated the statute and therefore should be sentenced to death accordingly. The moral rightness or wrongness of the men's action was irrelevant, he felt, "to the discharge of my office as a judge sworn to apply, not my conceptions of morality, but the law of the land." In Judge Keen's opinion, the court should not even petition the Chief Executive for clemency, as Judge Truepenny had recommended. That was a decision for the Chief Executive alone; it is not the role of the judge to make or advise on policy but simply to apply the law.

Judge Handy concluded that the men were innocent of any crime and that the lower court's ruling should be set aside. He approached the problem as follows: "The problem before us is what we, as officers of the government, ought to do with these defendants. That is a question of practical wisdom, to be exercised in a context, not of abstract theory, but of human realities." Law is a practical, "human affair," and flexibility is "essential if we are to keep our actions in reasonable accord with the sentiments of those subject to our rule." Handy based his decision largely on two "realities": First, public opinion was 90 percent in favor of pardoning the

---

1. 62 *Harvard Law Review* 616 (1949).

defendants or letting them off with only a token punishment. Second, the Chief Executive, as all on the court knew, would very likely not pardon the men or commute their sentences if the issue was left up to him.

Because the court was evenly divided, the lower court's ruling remained unchanged, and the men were put to death.

Obviously, both Judge Truepenny and Judge Keen are legal positivists. Although they differ in some of their views, both stress that the law is the law, and no exceptions are to be made. Because the explorers violated the law by killing their companion, they must pay the consequences and be sentenced to death, as the law requires. Judge Foster believes that applying the law of the Commonwealth of Newgarth would be inappropriate, because the deed occurred outside the bounds of civilized society. Given the extraordinary circumstances, the only law appropriate to the situation was natural law. From this perspective, the men's actions were reasonable and excusable, according to Judge Foster. Judge Handy's approach is that of the legal realist. If the court fails to take "human realities"—such as public opinion or the Chief Executive's predilections—into account, it will not serve the needs of society.

■ Sources of American Law— The Common Law Tradition

Because of our colonial heritage, much of American law is based on the English legal system. Without a knowledge of this legal heritage, one cannot understand the nature of our legal system today.

The English Origins of Common Law

In 1066 the Normans conquered England, and William the Conqueror and his successors began the process of unifying the country under their rule. One of the means they used to this end was the establishment of the **King's Court.** Before the conquest, disputes had been settled according to local custom. The King's Court sought to establish a common, or uniform, set of customs for the whole country. The body of rules that evolved under the King's Court, called the *Curia Regis,* was the beginning of the **common law**—law that was common to the entire realm. As the number of courts

and cases increased, the more important decisions of each year were gathered together and recorded in *Year Books.* Judges, when settling disputes similar to ones that had been decided before, used decisions recorded in the Year Books as the basis for their decisions. If a case was unique, judges had to create new laws, but they based their decisions on the general principles suggested by earlier cases. Each interpretation became part of the authoritative law on the subject and served as a legal **precedent.** Later cases that involved similar legal principles or facts would be decided with reference to that precedent. The practice of deciding new cases with reference to former decisions is called the doctrine of *stare decisis.*

Stare Decisis — ← *very important*

The practice of deciding new cases with reference to former decisions eventually became a cornerstone of the English and American judicial systems. As noted, it forms the doctrine of **stare decisis**[2] (Latin for "to stand on decided cases").

The doctrine of *stare decisis* performs many useful functions. First, it helps the courts to be more efficient. It would be very time-consuming if each judge had to reason out the policies for deciding what the law should be for each case brought before the court. If other courts have confronted the same issue and reasoned through the case carefully, their opinions can serve as guides.

Second, *stare decisis* creates a more just and uniform system. The rule of precedent tends to neutralize the prejudices of individual judges. If judges feel pressure to use precedent as the basis for their decisions, they will be less influenced by any personal biases. Different states and regions, however, often follow different precedents, and so rules of law do vary.

Third, *stare decisis* makes the law more stable and predictable. If the law on a given subject is well settled, someone bringing a case to court can usually rely upon the court to make a decision based on what the law has been.

Finally, *stare decisis* reflects the experience of the past and is based on the wisdom of the past.

Sometimes a court departs from the rule of precedent because it has decided that the precedent

---

2. Pronounced *ster*-ay dih-*si*-ses.

is incorrect. For example, if changes in technology, business practices, or society's attitudes necessitate a change in the law, courts may depart from precedent. Judges are reluctant to overrule precedent, however, and whether they will do so depends on the subject of the case, the number and prestige of prior decisions, the degree of social change that has occurred, and the identity of the deciding court.

Sometimes there is no precedent on which to base a decision, or there are conflicting precedents. In these situations, a court will: (1) refer to past decisions that involved somewhat similar issues and decide the case by reasoning through *analogy* (discussed below); (2) look at social factors—changes in the status of women, for example—that might influence the issues involved; and (3) consider what the fairest result would be.

Cases that overturn precedent often receive a great deal of publicity. In *Brown v. Board of Education*,[3] for example, the United States Supreme Court expressly overturned precedent when it concluded that separate educational facilities for African Americans were inherently unequal. Previously, in *Plessy v. Ferguson*,[4] as well as in numerous other cases, the Court had upheld as constitutional the provision of separate but equal accommodations. The Supreme Court's departure from precedent in *Brown* received a tremendous amount of publicity as people began to realize the ramifications of this change in the law. Although such cases receive the most attention, the majority of cases are decided according to precedent because of the application of the doctrine of *stare decisis*.

Stare Decisis and Legal Reasoning

When applying, overruling, or creating precedent, judges use many forms of reasoning. Generally, a judge writes an opinion in the form of a **syllogism**—that is, deductive reasoning consisting of a major premise, a minor premise, and a conclusion. For example, a **plaintiff** (a suing party) comes before the court alleging *assault* (a wrongful action, or tort, in which one person makes another fearful of immediate physical harm). The plaintiff claims that the **defendant** (the party who is sued)

threatened her while she was sleeping. Although the plaintiff was unaware that she was being threatened, her roommate heard the defendant make the threat. The judge might point out that "under the common law, an individual must be *aware* of a threat of danger for the threat to constitute civil assault" (major premise); "the plaintiff in this case was unaware of the threat at the time it occurred" (minor premise); and "therefore, the circumstances do not amount to a civil assault" (conclusion).

A second important form of commonly employed legal reasoning might be thought of as a knotted rope, with each knot tying together separate pieces of rope to form a tight length. As a whole, the rope represents a logical progression of connected points, and the last knot represents the conclusion.

For example, imagine that a tenant in an apartment building sues the landlord for damages for an injury resulting from an allegedly dimly lit stairway. The landlord, who was on the premises the evening the injury occurred, testifies that none of the other nine tenants who used the stairway that night complained about the lights. The court concludes that the tenant is not entitled to compensation on the basis of the stairway's lighting. The "pieces of rope" might be stated as follows:

1. The landlord testifies that none of the tenants who used the stairs on the evening in question complained about the lights.
2. The fact that none of the tenants complained is the same as if they had said the lighting was sufficient.
3. That there were no complaints does *not* prove that the lighting was sufficient but proves that the landlord had no reason to believe that it was not.
4. The landlord's belief was reasonable, because no one complained.
5. Therefore, the landlord acted reasonably and was not negligent in providing adequate lighting.

In the majority of cases, the two methods of legal reasoning discussed above predominate, and it is unnecessary to look beyond them. There are, however, two other important forms of reasoning that judges use in deciding cases: reasoning by *analogy* and the process of determining which rules and policies to apply.

---

3. 347 U.S. 483, 74 S.Ct. 686, 98 L.Ed. 873 (1954).
4. 163 U.S. 537, 16 S.Ct. 1138, 41 L.Ed. 256 (1896).

To reason by **analogy** is to compare the facts in the case at hand to the facts in other cases and, to the extent the *patterns* are similar, apply the same rule to the case at hand. To the extent the facts are unique, or "distinguishable," different rules may apply. For example, in case A, it is held that a driver who crosses a highway's center line is negligent. In case B, a driver crosses the line to avoid hitting a child. In determining whether case A's rule applies in case B, a judge would consider what the reasons were for the decision in A and whether B is sufficiently similar for those reasons to apply. If the judge holds that B's driver is not liable, that judge must pinpoint a policy and explain a rule that is not inconsistent with the decision in case A.

Simply put, legal reasoning means that a judge must harmonize his or her decision with decisions that have been made before. Of course, judges have a seemingly infinite array of precedential decisions from which to choose. When determining which rules and policies to apply in a given case, and in applying them, a judge may examine any or all of the following:

1. Previous case law and the legal principles and policies behind the decisions, as well as their historical setting.
2. Statutes and the policies—legal, historical, and social—underlying the legislature's decision to enact a particular statute.
3. Society's values (for example, fairness).
4. Custom (for example, when a controversial business transaction involves a contract, a judge might ask what the participants expected, based on the usual and customary practices within their trade).
5. Other sources, including data and principles from the fields of economics, psychology, sociology, and philosophy.

Which of these sources is chosen, or receives the greatest emphasis, will depend on the nature of the case being considered and the particular judge hearing the case. Although judges always strive to be free of subjectivity and personal bias in deciding cases, each judge has his or her own unique personality, set of values or philosophical leanings, and intellectual attributes—all of which necessarily frame the decision-making process.

The Common Law Today

The body of law that developed under the English system and that is still used today consists of the rules of law announced in court decisions, including court interpretations of statutes, regulations, and provisions in constitutions. Today this law is known variously as judge-made law, the common law, or **case law.**

Common law, or case law, must be distinguished from **statutory law,** which generally consists of those laws enacted by state legislatures and, at the federal level, by Congress. In all areas not covered by statutory law, common law governs and generally has the same force as statutory law. The history and circumstances of the fifty states differ, and this has given rise to differences among the courts' decisions and thus in the common law among states. Even when legislation has been substituted for common law principles, courts often rely on common law to interpret the legislation, on the theory that the people who drafted the statute intended to codify an existing common law rule.

England and the United States are not the only countries that have common law systems. Generally, those nations that were once colonies of Great Britain retained their English common law heritage once they achieved independence. Today, common law systems also exist in Ireland, Canada, Australia, New Zealand, and India. Precedents in these other common law countries can be referred to by U.S. judges even today—although the precedents are not binding.

In contrast to Great Britain and the common law countries, most of the other European nations base their legal systems on Roman civil law, or "code law." The term *civil law,* as used here, does not refer to civil as opposed to criminal law, but to *codified* law—an ordered grouping of legal principles enacted into law by a legislature or governing body. In a **civil law system,** the statutory code is the primary source of law, and case precedents are not judicially binding as they are in a common law system. This is not to say that precedents are unimportant in a civil law system. On the contrary, judges in such systems commonly refer to previous decisions as sources of legal guidance. The difference is that judges in a civil law system are not bound by precedent; the doctrine of *stare decisis* does not apply. Today, civil law systems are in effect in most continental European countries and in the Latin American, African, and Asian countries that were once their colonies. In the United States, the state of Louisiana—once a French possession—has in part a civil law system.

Islamic law represents a third major legal system in the world. At least twenty-seven countries follow Islamic law to some degree, although Islamic law is frequently mixed with civil or common law, depending on colonial prinicples. Islamic law governs all aspects of life in an Islamic nation.

■ Other Sources of American Law

In addition to case law, or common law, courts have numerous other sources of law to consider when making their decisions.

Constitutions

The U.S. Constitution is the supreme law of the land. A law in violation of the Constitution, no matter what its source, will be declared unconstitutional and will not be enforced. The U.S. Constitution delineates how federal powers are divided among the three governmental branches, establishing a system of checks and balances. Article I vests the legislative power (power to make laws) in the Congress; Article II vests the executive power (power to see that laws are carried out) in the president; and Article III vests the judicial power (power to determine what the law is and whether laws are valid) in the courts.

Each state also has its constitution which sets forth the general organization, powers, and limits of the state government. Generally, state governments are organized in the same way as the federal government. The Tenth Amendment to the U.S. Constitution, which defines the powers and limitations of the federal government, reserves all powers not granted to the federal government to the states, or to the people. Thus, each state constitution, unless it conflicts with the U.S. Constitution, is supreme within each state's borders. The U.S. Constitution, for example, gives the federal government the power to regulate *interstate* commerce (commerce between or among states), but the states retain the power to regulate *intrastate* commerce (commerce within a state).

The regulation of interstate commerce is one of the chief ways in which the U.S. Constitution affects business. This and other aspects of constitutional law as it relates to business will be discussed in detail in Chapter 4. The complete text of the U.S. Constitution is contained in Appendix B.

Statutes and Ordinances

Statutes enacted by the U.S. Congress and the various state legislative bodies constitute another source of law, which is generally referred to as *statutory law,* as noted above. The statutory law of the United States further consists of the ordinances passed by cities, counties, and other political subdivisions. None of these laws can violate the U.S. Constitution or the relevant state constitution.

Administrative Law

An administrative agency is created when the executive or legislative branch of the government delegates some of its authority to an appropriate group of persons, usually called an agency or a commission. Administrative agencies exercise legislative, executive, and judicial power. In their **rulemaking,** they use legislative power; in their regulation and supervision, they use executive power; and in their adjudication procedures, they use judicial power. Unlike legislators, presidents, governors, and many judges, however, administrative agency personnel are rarely chosen by popular elections, and many do not serve fixed terms. As a result, great power is given to people who may not be responsive to the public.

Administrative law is the branch of public law concerned with the executive power and actions of administrative agencies, their officials, and their employees. When an individual has a dispute with such an agency, administrative law applies. The scope of administrative law has expanded enormously in recent years, and the scope of administrative agencies has increased so much that their activities have come to be called **administrative process,** in contrast to **judicial process.** Administrative process involves the administration of law by nonjudicial bodies, such as the Federal Trade Commission, whereas judicial process is the administration of law by judicial bodies (the courts). Administrative law will be discussed in further detail in Chapter 44.

Commercial Law Codes

The body of law that pertains to commercial dealings is commonly referred to as commercial, or business, law. It includes most of the topics in this text—contracts, partnerships, and corporations, for example. For business students, the most important codification of commercial law is the Uniform Commercial Code (UCC). Because the UCC forms the basis of many chapters in this book, its origins will be briefly discussed here.

CODIFICATION OF COMMERCIAL LAW In the interests of uniformity and reform, in the late nineteenth century the legal profession suggested that comprehensive codes of laws concerning specific subject areas be adopted by the states. (When adopted by a state, these codes of laws become statutory law.)

The National Conference of Commissioners on Uniform State Laws started to meet in the late 1800s to draft uniform statutes. Once these uniform codes had been drawn up, the commissioners urged each state legislature to adopt them. Adoption of uniform codes is a state matter, and a state may reject all or part of a code or rewrite it as the state's legislature sees fit. Hence, even when a proposed code is said to have been adopted in many states, those states' laws may not be entirely ''uniform.''

The first uniform code, or act, was the Uniform Negotiable Instruments Law, which was finally approved in 1896 and adopted in every state by the early 1920s (though not all states used exactly the same wording). Afterwards, other acts were drawn up in a similar manner; they included the Uniform Sales Act, the Uniform Warehouse Receipts Act, the Uniform Bills of Lading Act, the Uniform Partnership Act, the Model Business Corporation Act (drafted by the American Bar Association), and the Uniform Stock Transfer Act. More recently, a Uniform Probate Code was prepared. The most ambitious uniform act of all, however, was the Uniform Commercial Code (UCC).

THE UNIFORM COMMERCIAL CODE (UCC) The National Conference of Commissioners on Uniform State Laws and the American Law Institute sponsored and directed the preparation of the Uniform Commercial Code. These two organizations were assisted by literally hundreds of law professors, businesspersons, judges, and lawyers. The official 1991 complete text of the UCC can be found in Appendix C in this book. The District of Columbia, the Virgin Islands, and forty-nine states have adopted all articles of the UCC. Louisiana is the only state that has not adopted the UCC in its entirety. Significantly, one of the articles not adopted by that state is Article 2, which covers contracts for the sale of goods.

The UCC is designed to facilitate the legal relationship of parties involved in modern commercial transactions by helping to determine the intentions of the parties to a commercial contract and by giving force and effect to their agreement. Moreover, the UCC is meant to encourage business transactions by assuring businesspersons that their contracts, if validly entered into, will be uniformly enforced.

International Doctrines and Agreements

American business is becoming increasingly global in scope, and numerous cases are brought before the courts that involve a foreign element. International doctrines, treaties, and other agreements are also sources of law that pertain to business transactions. These laws will be examined in Chapters 24 and 56.

■ Restatements of the Law

Notwithstanding the movement toward uniform, statutory laws, the common law remains a significant source of legal authority. To summarize and clarify common law rules, the American Law Institute drafted and published compilations of the common law called Restatements of the Law. There are Restatements of the Law in the areas of contracts, torts, agency, trusts, property, restitution, security, judgments, and conflict of laws. Many of the Restatements are now in their second edition. The *Restatement of the Law of Contracts,* for example, was first published in May 1932. Thirty years later, a second edition was undertaken. It was completed in 1979 and is referred to as the *Restatement (Second) of the Law of Contracts,* or, more simply, as the *Restatement (Second) of Contracts.*

The Restatements, which generally summarize the common law rules followed by most states, do not in themselves have the force of law but are an important secondary source of legal analysis and opinion to which judges often refer in making their decisions. We refer to the Restatements frequently in subsequent chapters of this text.

■ Classifications of Law

The body of law is huge. To study it, one must break it down by some means of classification. No single classification system can cover such a large mass of information; consequently, those systems that have been devised tend to overlap. Moreover, they are, of necessity, arbitrary in some respects. A discussion of the best-known systems follows.

Substantive versus Procedural Law

Substantive law includes all laws that define, describe, regulate, and create legal rights and obligations. For example, a rule stating that promises are enforced only when each party has received something of value from the other party is part of substantive law. So, too, is a rule stating that a person who has injured another through negligence must pay damages.

Procedural law establishes the methods of enforcing the rights established by substantive law. Questions about how a lawsuit should begin, what papers need to be filed, which court will hear the suit, which witnesses can be called, and so on are all questions of procedural law. In brief, substantive law tells us our rights; procedural law tells us how to exercise them.

Exhibit 1–1 classifies law in terms of its subject matter, dividing it into law covering substantive issues and law covering procedural issues. Most of this text concerns substantive law.

Public versus Private Law

Public law addresses the relationship between persons and their government, whereas **private law** addresses direct dealings between persons.

Criminal law and constitutional law, for example, are generally classified as public law because they deal with persons and their relationships to government. Criminal acts, though they may involve only one victim, are seen as offenses

■ Exhibit 1–1 Subject Matter of Substantive and Procedural Law

The importance of the distinction between substantive and procedural law is more than academic. The *result* of a case may well depend upon the determination that a rule is substantive rather than procedural.

Substantive (Policy)	Procedural (Method of Enforcement)
Administrative law	Administrative procedure
Agency	Appellate procedure
Bailments	Civil procedure
Commercial paper	Criminal procedure
Constitutional law	Evidence
Contracts	
Corporation law	
Criminal law	
Insurance	
Partnerships	
Personal property	
Real property	
Sales	
Taxation	
Torts	
Trusts and wills	

against society as a whole and are prohibited by governments for the purpose of protecting the public. Constitutional law is frequently classified as public law, because it involves questions of whether the government—federal, state, or local—has the power to act in a particular fashion; often the issue is whether a law, duly passed, exceeds the limits set on the government.

When persons deal with or affect other persons, such as in contract or tort, the law governing these relationships is classified as private law.

See Exhibit 1–2 for examples of private and public law.

Civil versus Criminal Law

Civil law is concerned with the duties that exist between persons or between citizens and their governments, excluding the duty not to commit crimes. Contract law, for example, is part of civil law. The

■ Exhibit 1–2 Examples of Public and Private Laws

Public law governs the relationship between persons and their government. Private law governs the relationships among individuals.

Public Law	Private Law
Administrative law	Agency
Civil, criminal, and appellate procedure	Commercial paper
	Contracts
Constitutional law	Corporation law
Criminal law	Partnerships
Evidence	Personal property
Taxation	Real property
	Sales
	Torts
	Trusts and wills

whole body of *tort law,* which has to do with the infringement by one person of the legally recognized rights of another, is an area of civil law. Tort law will be discussed in Chapter 5, as well as in Chapters 7 and 8, which deal with torts related to business.

Criminal law, in contrast to civil law, is concerned with wrongs committed against the public as a whole. Criminal acts are prohibited by local, state, or federal government statutes. Criminal law is always public law, whereas civil law is sometimes public and sometimes private. In a criminal case, the government seeks to impose a penalty on an allegedly guilty person. In a civil case, one party (sometimes the government) tries to make the other party comply with a duty or pay for the damage caused by failure to so comply. Criminal law is discussed in Chapters 6 and 7.

Exhibit 1–3 lists the areas of law falling within each of these classifications.

■ Remedies at Law versus Remedies in Equity

In the early English King's Courts, the kinds of **remedies** (the legal means to recover a right or redress a wrong) that the courts could grant were severely restricted. If one person wronged another in some way, the King's Courts could award as compensation one or more of the following: (1) land, (2) items of value, or (3) money. The courts that awarded this compensation became known as **courts of law,** and the three remedies

■ Exhibit 1–3 Criminal and Civil Law

An important feature distinguishing criminal and civil law is the sanction imposed on the wrongdoer. Criminal sanctions may include imprisonment while civil sanctions emphasize payment of money.

Criminal Law	Civil Law
Administrative law	Agency
Antitrust	Bailments
Constitutional law	Bankruptcy
Criminal law	Business organizations
Environmental law	Commercial paper
Labor law	Contracts
Securities law	Insurance
	Property
	Sales
	Secured transactions
	Torts
	Trusts and wills

were called **remedies at law.** Even though the system introduced uniformity in the settling of disputes, when plaintiffs wanted a remedy other than economic compensation, the courts of law could do nothing, so "no remedy, no right." When individuals could not obtain an adequate remedy in a court of law because of strict technicalities, they petitioned the king for relief. Most of these petitions were decided by an adviser to the king, called a **chancellor,** who was said to be the "keeper of the king's conscience." When the chancellor thought that the claim was a fair one, new and unique remedies were granted. In this way, a new body of rules and remedies came into being, and eventually formal courts of chancery, or **courts of equity,** were established.

Equity Courts

The distinction between law and equity courts is now primarily of historical interest, but it is still relevant to students of business law because legal and equitable remedies differ. To seek the proper remedy for a wrong, one must know what remedies are available.

Equity is that branch of law, founded on what might be described as notions of justice and fair dealing, that seeks to supply a remedy when there is no adequate remedy available at law. With the establishment of equity courts, two distinct court systems were created, each having a different set of judges. Two bodies of rules and remedies existed at the same time, remedies at law and **remedies in equity.** Plaintiffs had to specify whether they were bringing an ''action at law'' or an ''action in equity,'' and they chose their courts accordingly. Only one remedy could be granted for a particular wrong, and even in equity the wrong had to be of a type the court could recognize as remediable.

Courts of equity had the responsibility of using discretion in supplementing the common law. Even today, when the same court can award both legal and equitable remedies, such discretion is often guided by so-called **equitable principles and maxims.** Equitable maxims are propositions or general statements of rules of law that courts often invoke. Listed below are a few of the maxims of equity.

1. Whoever seeks equity must do equity. (Anyone who wishes to be treated fairly must treat others fairly.)
2. When there is equal equity, the law must prevail. (The law will determine the outcome of a controversy in which the merits of both sides are equal.)
3. One seeking the aid of an equity court must come to the court with clean hands. (Plaintiffs must have acted fairly and honestly.)
4. Equity will not suffer a right to exist without a remedy. (Equitable relief will be awarded when there is a right to relief and there is no adequate remedy at law.)
5. Equity regards substance rather than form. (Equity is more concerned with fairness and justice than with legal technicalities.)
6. Equity aids the vigilant, not those who rest on their rights. (Equity will not help those who neglect their rights for an unreasonable period of time.)

The last maxim is worthy of discussion. It has become known as the equitable doctrine of **laches,** and it can be used as a **defense** (an argument raised by the defendant to defeat the plaintiff's cause of action or recovery). The doctrine arose to encourage people to bring lawsuits while the evidence was fresh. What constitutes a reasonable time, of course, varies according to the circumstances of the case. Time periods for different types of cases are now usually fixed by **statutes of limitations.**

After the time allowed under a statute of limitations has expired, no action can be brought, no matter how strong the case was originally.

Equitable Relief

A number of equitable remedies are available. Three of them—specific performance, injunctions, and rescission—are briefly discussed here. These and other equitable remedies are discussed in more detail at appropriate points in the chapters that follow.

SPECIFIC PERFORMANCE Previously, courts of law and equity were separate. Hence, a plaintiff might come into a court of equity asking it to order a defendant to perform within the terms of a contract. A court of law could not issue such an order because its remedies were limited to payment of money or property as compensation for damages. A court of equity, however, could issue a decree of **specific performance**—an order to perform what was promised. This remedy was, and still is, only available when the dispute before the court involves a *contractual* transaction.

INJUNCTIONS If a person wanted to prevent the occurrence of a certain activity, he or she would have to go to the chancellor in equity and ask that the person doing the wrongful act be ordered to stop. The order was called an injunction. An **injunction** is usually an order to a specific person, directing that person to do or to refrain from doing a particular act.

RESCISSION Somtimes the legal remedy of the payment of money for damages is unavailable or inadequate when disputes occur over agreements. In such cases, the equitable remedy of rescission may be appropriate. **Rescission**[5] is an action to undo an agreement—to return the parties to their *status quo* prior to the agreement. If rescission is granted, all duties created by the agreement are abolished. If, for example, a person is fraudulently induced to enter into a contract and the fraud is discovered before any performance under the contract takes place, the innocent party might seek to rescind the agreement.

---

5.   Pronounced reh-*sih*-zhen.

The Merging of Law and Equity

During the nineteenth century, most states adopted rules of procedure that resulted in combined courts of law and equity—although some states, such as Arkansas, still retain the distinction. Today, a plaintiff or a petitioner in equity (the person bringing the action) may request both legal and equitable remedies in the same action, and the trial court judge may grant either or both forms of relief.

Despite the merging of the courts, it is still important to distinguish between actions at law and actions in equity. As mentioned, the primary importance is in the remedy sought. Vestiges of the procedures used when the courts were separate still exist. Today, differences in procedure depend on whether the civil lawsuit involves an action in equity or an action at law. Exhibit 1–4 is illustrative and applies to most states.

The major practical difference between law and equity today is the right to demand a jury trial in actions at law. In the old courts of equity, the chancellor heard both sides of an issue and decided what should be done. Juries were considered inappropriate. In actions at law, however, juries heard evidence and made determinations regarding questions of fact, including the amount of damages to be awarded. Today, in a case involving equitable rights, a judge may impanel a jury to serve in an advisory capacity.

■ How to Find Case Law

Laws pertaining to business consist of case law and statutory law. A substantial number of cases are presented in this text to provide you with concise, real-life illustrations of the interpretation and application of the law by the courts. Many other court decisions have been referenced in footnotes throughout the text. Because of the importance of knowing how to find these and other court opinions, this section offers a brief introduction to the case reporting system and to the legal ''shorthand'' employed in referencing court cases.

Today, computerized datasearch systems allow for computer access to both case law and statutory law. How to do legal research and the data bases, periodicals, and other publications relevant to legal research are presented in detail in Appendix F.

State Court Decisions

Most state trial court decisions are not published. Except in New York and a few other states, which publish selected opinions of their trial courts, decisions from the state trial courts are merely filed in the office of the clerk of the court; they are available there for public inspection.

Written decisions of the appellate (reviewing) courts, however, are published and distributed. At one time, each state published the decisions of its own appellate courts. Many states still publish these decisions, in consecutively numbered volumes called *Reports.*

Additionally, state court opinions appear in regional units of the *National Reporter System,* published by West Publishing Company. Most lawyers and libraries have the West reporters because they report cases more quickly and are distributed more widely than the state-published reports. In fact, many states have eliminated their own reports in favor of West's National Reporter System. The National Reporter System divides the states into geographical regions and includes the following regional reporters: *Atlantic* (A. or A.2d), *South Eastern* (S.E. or S.E.2d), *South Western* (S.W. or S.W.2d), *North Western* (N.W. or N.W.2d), *North Eastern* (N.E. or N.E.2d), *Southern* (So. or So.2d),

■ Exhibit 1–4 Procedural Differences between an Action at Law and an Action in Equity

Procedure	Action at Law	Action in Equity
Initiation of lawsuit	By filing a complaint	By filing a petition
Decision	By jury or judge	By judge (no jury)
Result	Judgment	Decree
Remedy	Monetary damages	Injunction, decree of specific performance, or rescission

and *Pacific* (P. or P.2d). The states included in each of these regional divisions are indicated in Exhibit 1–5, which illustrates West's National Reporter System. The "2d" after any of the abbreviations in the National Reporter System refers to the second series for that particular reporter.

After appellate decisions have been published, they are normally referred to (cited) by the name of the case; the volume, name, and page of the state's official report (if different from West's National Reporter System); the volume, unit, and page number of the *National Reporter;* and the volume, name, and page number of any other selected reporter. This information constitutes what is called the **citation.** For example, consider the following case: *Hoffman v. Red Owl Stores, Inc.,* 26 Wis.2d 683, 133 N.W.2d 267 (1965). We see that the opinion in this case may be found in volume 26 of the official *Wisconsin Reports, Second Series,* on page 683 and in volume 133 of the *North Western Reporter, Second Series,* on page 267. When, as in this case, two or more citations are given for the same case, they are called *parallel citations.* In reprinting appellate opinions in this text, in addition to the reporter, we give the name of the court hearing the case and the year of the court decision.

A few of the states—including those with intermediate appellate courts, such as California, Illinois, and New York—have more than one report for opinions given by courts within their states. Sample citations from these courts, as well as others, are listed and explained in Exhibit 1–6.

Federal Court Decisions

Federal trial court decisions are published unofficially in West's *Federal Supplement* (F.Supp.), and opinions from the circuit courts of appeal are reported unofficially in West's *Federal Reporter* (F. or F.2d). Cases concerning federal bankruptcy law are published unofficially in West's *Bankruptcy Reporter* (Bankr.). Opinions from the United States Supreme Court are reported in the *United States Reports* (U.S.), West's *Supreme Court Reporter* (S.Ct.), the *Lawyers' Edition of the Supreme Court Reports* (L.Ed.), and other publications.

The *United States Reports* is the official edition of all decisions of the United States Supreme Court for which there are written opinions. Published by the federal government, the series includes reports of Supreme Court cases dating from the August term of 1791, although originally many of the decisions were not reported in the early volumes.

West's *Supreme Court Reporter* is an unofficial edition dating from the Court's term in October 1882. Preceding each of its case reports are a summary of the case and *headnotes* (brief editorial statements of the law involved in the case, numbered to correspond to numbers in the report). The headnotes are also given classification numbers that serve to cross-reference each headnote to other headnotes on similar points throughout the National Reporter System and other West publications to facilitate research of all relevant cases on a given point. This is important because, as may be evident from the discussion of *stare decisis,* a lawyer's goal in undertaking legal research is to find an authority that cannot be factually distinguished from his or her case.

The Lawyers Cooperative Publishing Company of Rochester, New York, publishes the *Lawyers' Edition of the Supreme Court Reports,* an unofficial edition of the entire series of the Supreme Court reports that contains many of the decisions not reported in the early official volumes. Also, among other editorial features, the *Lawyers' Edition,* in its second series, precedes the report of each case with a full summary, includes excerpts from briefs of counsel, and discusses in detail selected cases of special interest to the legal profession.

Sample citations for federal court decisions are listed and explained in Exhibit 1–6.

Old Case Law

On a few occasions, the opinions cited in this text are from old, classic cases dating to the nineteenth century or earlier; some of these are from the English courts. The citations to these cases appear not to conform to the descriptions given above because the reports in which they were published have since been replaced. A sample citation for an English reporter is included in Exhibit 1–6. Whenever citations to old reporters are made in this text, the citations will be explained when they are presented.

Case Digests and Legal Encyclopedias

The body of American case law consists of nearly 5 million decisions, to which more than 40,000 are

■ **Exhibit 1–5 National Reporter System—Regional/Federal**

Regional Reporters	Coverage Beginning	Coverage
Atlantic Reporter (A. or A.2d)	1885	Connecticut, Delaware, Maine, Maryland, New Hampshire, New Jersey, Pennsylvania, Rhode Island, Vermont, and District of Columbia.
North Eastern Reporter (N.E. or N.E.2d)	1885	Illinois, Indiana, Massachusetts, New York, and Ohio.
North Western Reporter (N.W. or N.W.2d)	1879	Iowa, Michigan, Minnesota, Nebraska, North Dakota, South Dakota, and Wisconsin.
Pacific Reporter (P. or P.2d)	1883	Alaska, Arizona, California, Colorado, Hawaii, Idaho, Kansas, Montana, Nevada, New Mexico, Oklahoma, Oregon, Utah, Washington, and Wyoming.
South Eastern Reporter (S.E. or S.E.2d)	1887	Georgia, North Carolina, South Carolina, Virginia, and West Virginia.
South Western Reporter (S.W. or S.W.2d)	1886	Arkansas, Kentucky, Missouri, Tennessee, and Texas.
Southern Reporter (So. or So.2d)	1887	Alabama, Florida, Louisiana, and Mississippi.

Federal Reporters		
Federal Reporter (F. or F.2d)	1880	U.S. Circuit Court from 1880 to 1912; U.S. Commerce Court from 1911 to 1913; U.S. District Courts from 1880 to 1932; U.S. Court of Claims from 1929 to 1932 and since 1960; U.S. Court of Appeals since 1891; U.S. Court of Customs and Patent Appeals since 1929; U.S. Emergency Court of Appeals since 1943.
Federal Supplement (F.Supp.)	1932	U.S. Court of Claims from 1932 to 1960; U.S. District Courts since 1932; U.S. Customs Court since 1956.
Federal Rules Decisions (F.R.D.)	1939	U.S. District Courts involving the Federal Rules of Civil Procedure since 1939 and Federal Rules of Criminal Procedure since 1946.
Supreme Court Reporter (S.Ct.)	1882	U.S. Supreme Court since the October term of 1882.
Bankruptcy Reporter (Bankr.)	1980	Bankruptcy decisions of U.S. Bankruptcy Courts, U.S. District Courts, U.S. Courts of Appeals, and U.S. Supreme Court.
Military Justice Reporter (M.J.)	1978	U.S. Court of Military Appeals and Courts of Military Review for the Army, Navy, Air Force, and Coast Guard.

NATIONAL REPORTER SYSTEM MAP

Pacific
North Western
South Western
North Eastern
Atlantic
South Eastern
Southern

■ **Exhibit 1–6 How to Read Citations**

State Courts

235 Neb. 315, 454 N.W.2d 698 (1990)[a]

> *N.W.* is the abbreviation for West's publication of state court decisions rendered in the northwestern region of the National Reporter System. *2d* indicates that this case was included in the second series of those reports. The number 454 refers to the volume number of the reporter; the number 698 refers to the first page in that volume on which this case can be found.

> *Neb.* is an abbreviation for *Nebraska Reports,* Nebraska's official reports of the decisions of its highest court, the Nebraska Supreme Court.

50 Cal.3d 1118, 791 P.2d 587, 270 Cal.Rptr. 1 (1990)

> *Cal.Rptr.* is the abbreviation for West's unofficial reports—titled *California Reporter*—of the decisions of California courts.

75 N.Y.2d 175, 550 N.E.2d 919, 551 N.Y.S.2d 470 (1990)

> *N.Y.S.* is the abbreviation for West's unofficial reports—titled *New York Supplement*—of the decisions of New York courts.

> *N.Y.* is the abbreviation for *New York Reports,* New York's official reports of the decisions of its court of appeals. The New York Court of Appeals is the state's highest court, analogous to other states' supreme courts. In New York, a supreme court is a trial court.

195 Ga.App. 39, 392 S.E.2d 270 (1990)

> *Ga.App.* is the abbreviation for *Georgia Appeals Reports,* Georgia's official reports of the decisions of its court of appeals.

Federal Courts

___ U.S. ___, 110 S.Ct. 2394, 110 L.Ed.2d 243 (1990)

> *L.Ed.* is an abbreviation for *Lawyers' Edition of the Supreme Court Reports,* an unofficial edition of decisions of the United States Supreme Court.

> *S.Ct.* is the abbreviation for West's unofficial reports—titled *Supreme Court Reporter*—of United States Supreme Court decisions.

> *U.S.* is the abbreviation for *United States Reports,* the official edition of the decisions of the United States Supreme Court. Volume and page numbers are not included in this citation because they have not yet been assigned.

a.   The case names have been deleted from these citations to emphasize the publications. It should be kept in mind, however, that the name of a case is as important as the specific page numbers in the volumes in which it is found. If a citation is incorrect, the correct citation may be found in a publication's index of case names. The date of a case is also important because, in addition to providing a check on error in citations, the value of a recent case as an authority is likely to be greater than that of earlier cases.

(Figure continued on next page)

■ **Exhibit 1–6 How to Read Citations (Continued)**

Federal Courts (continued)

---

901 F.2d 1550 (11th Cir. 1990)

> *11th Cir.* is an abbreviation denoting that this case was decided in the United States Court of Appeals for the Eleventh Circuit.

744 F.Supp. 1118 (M.D.Fla. 1990)

> *M.D.Fla.* is an abbreviation indicating that the United States District Court for the Middle District of Florida decided this case.

English Courts

---

9 Exch. 341, 156 Eng.Rep. 145 (1854)

> *Eng.Rep.* is an abbreviation for *English Reports, Full Reprint*, a series of reports containing selected decisions made in English courts between 1378 and 1865.

> *Exch.* is an abbreviation for *English Exchequer Reports*, which included the original reports of cases decided in England's Court of Exchequer.

Statutory and Other Citations

---

18 U.S.C. Section 1961(1)(A)

> *U.S.C.* denotes *United States Code*, the codification of *United States Statutes at Large*. The number 18 refers to the statute's U.S.C. title number and 1961 to its section number within that title. The number 1 refers to a subsection within the section and the letter A to a subdivision within the subsection.

UCC 2-206(1)(b)

> *UCC* is an abbreviation for *Uniform Commercial Code*. The first number 2 is a reference to an article of the UCC and 206 to a section within that article. The number 1 refers to a subsection within the section and the letter b to a subdivision within the subsection.

Restatement (Second) of Torts, Section 568

> *Restatement (Second) of Torts* refers to the second edition of the American Law Institute's *Restatement of the Law of Torts*. The number 568 refers to a specific section.

17 C.F.R. Section 230.505

> *C.F.R.* is an abbreviation for *Code of Federal Regulations*, a compilation of federal administrative regulations. The number 17 is a reference to the regulation's title number and 230.505 to a specific section within that title.

added each year. Because judicial decisions are published in chronological order, finding relevant precedents would be a Herculean task if it were not for case digests, legal encyclopedias, and many other publications that classify decisions according to subject.

Case digests consist of alphabetical arrangements of legal topics. Collected under each topic heading are very short statements of relevant points of law in reported cases. Citations to the cases are included. The American Digest System, the most comprehensive in its coverage, condenses and arranges cases reported in West's National Reporter System.

Legal encyclopedias also arrange topics alphabetically and provide case citations, but legal encyclopedias include more detailed consideration of the law than digests. A legal encyclopedia editorially synthesizes rules from groups of cases and discusses majority and minority views, historical developments, and so on. The text of *Corpus Juris Secundum,* the most comprehensive legal encyclopedia, is based on all reported cases from 1658 to date.

◼ How to Find Statutory and Administrative Law

When Congress passes laws, they are collected in a publication titled *United States Statutes at Large.* When state legislatures pass laws, they are collected in similar state publications. These publications arrange laws by date of enactment. Most frequently, however, laws are referred to in their codified form—that is, the form in which they appear in the federal and state codes. These references are called citations. This section offers a brief introduction to the abbreviations used in citations to statutory and administrative law. (For information on legal data bases in which statutes and regulations can be found, see Appendix E.)

In these codes, laws are compiled by subject. For example, the *United States Code* (U.S.C.) arranges by subject all existing federal laws of a public and permanent nature. Each of the fifty subjects into which the laws have been arranged is given a title and a title number. For example, laws relating to commerce and trade are collected in Title 15, which is titled "Commerce and Trade." Within each subdivision (title), statutes are assigned numbers, which are referred to as section

numbers. A U.S.C. citation includes title and section numbers. Thus, a reference to "15 U.S.C. Section 1" means that the statute can be found in Section 1 of Title 15. ("Section" may also be designated by the symbol §.)

State codes follow the U.S.C. pattern of law arranged by subject. They may be called Codes, Revisions, Compilations, Consolidations, General Statutes, or Statutes, depending on the preference of the states. In some codes, subjects are designated by number. In others, they are designated by name. For example, "13 Pennsylvania Consolidated Statutes Section 1101" means that the statute can be found in Section 1101 of Title 13 of the Pennsylvania code. "California Commercial Code Section 1101" means that the statute can be found in Section 1101 under the commercial heading of the California Code. Abbreviations may be used. For example, "13 Pennsylvania Consolidated Statutes Section 1101" may be abbreviated to "13 Pa. C.S. § 1101," and "California Commercial Code Section 1101" may be abbreviated to "Cal. Com. Code § 1101."

Rules and regulations adopted by federal administrative agencies are compiled in the *Code of Federal Regulations* (C.F.R.). Like the U.S.C., the C.F.R. is divided into fifty titles. Rules within each title are assigned section numbers. A full citation to the C.F.R. includes title and section numbers. For example, a reference to "17 C.F.R. Section 230.504" means that the rule can be found in Section 230.504 of Title 17.

Commercial publications of these laws and regulations are available and are widely used. For example, West Publishing Company publishes the *United States Code Annotated* (U.S.C.A.). The U.S.C.A. contains the complete text of laws included in the U.S.C., as well as notes of court decisions that interpret and apply specific sections of the statutes, plus the text of presidential proclamations and executive orders. The U.S.C.A. also includes research aids, such as cross-references to related statutes, historical notes, and library references. A citation to the U.S.C.A. is similar to a citation to the U.S.C.: "15 U.S.C.A. Section 1."

◼ How to Analyze Case Law

Knowing how to read and analyze a court opinion is an essential step in undertaking accurate legal research. A further step involves "briefing" the case. Legal researchers routinely brief cases by summarizing and reducing the texts of the opinions to their essential elements. How to brief a case is discussed in Appendix A, which also includes excerpts from selected cases for briefing.

The cases presented in this text have already been analyzed and edited by the authors. For each case presented, we have provided a *Background and Facts* section so that you may quickly perceive the issue or issues before the court. These sections are strictly our own summaries—in our own words—of information given in the full written opinion of the court. We conclude each case presentation with the court's *Decision and Remedy*— again, in our own words. Occasionally, we also add *Comments* or *Ethical Considerations* at the end of a case presentation.

Case Titles

In the title of a case, such as *Adams v. Jones,* the *v.* stands for versus, which means "against." In the trial court, Adams was the plaintiff—the person who filed the suit. Jones was the defendant. If the case is appealed, however, the appellate court will sometimes place the name of the party appealing the decision first, so that the case may be called *Jones v. Adams* if Jones was the party who appealed the case. Because some appellate courts retain the trial court order of names, it is often impossible to distinguish the plaintiff from the defendant in the title of a reported appellate court decision. The student must carefully read the facts of each case to ascertain the identity of each party. Otherwise, the discussion by the appellate court will be difficult to understand.

Terminology

The following terms and phrases are frequently encountered in court opinions and legal publications. Because it is important to understand what is meant by these terms and phrases, we define and discuss them here.

DECISIONS AND OPINIONS Most decisions reached by appellate courts are explained in written **opinions.** The opinion contains the court's reasons for its decision, the rules of law that apply, and the judgment. There are four possible types of written opinions for a case decided by an appellate court.

When all judges or justices unanimously agree on an opinion, the opinion is written for the entire court and can be deemed a *unanimous opinion.* When there is not a unanimous opinion, a *majority opinion* is written, outlining the views of the majority of the judges or justices deciding the case. Often a judge or justice who feels strongly about making or emphasizing a point that was not made or emphasized in the unanimous or majority opinion will write a *concurring opinion.* That means the judge or justice agrees (concurs) with the judgment given in the unanimous or majority opinion, but for different reasons. In other than unanimous opinions, a *dissenting opinion* is usually written by a judge or justice who does not agree with the majority. The dissenting opinion is important because it may form the basis of the arguments used years later in overruling the precedential majority opinion.

JUDGES AND JUSTICES The terms *judge* and *justice* are usually synonymous and represent two designations given to judges in various courts. All members of the United States Supreme Court, for example, are referred to as justices. Justice is the formal title usually given to judges of appellate courts, although this is not always the case. In New York, a justice is a trial judge of the trial court (which is called the Supreme Court), and a member of the Court of Appeals (the state's highest court) is called a judge. The term *justice* is commonly abbreviated to J., and *justices* to JJ. A United States Supreme Court case might refer to Justice Kennedy as Kennedy, J., or to Chief Justice Rehnquist as Rehnquist, C. J.

APPELLANTS AND APPELLEES The **appellant** is the party who appeals a case to another court or jurisdiction from the court or jurisdiction in which the case was originally brought. Sometimes, an appellant who appeals from a judgment is referred to as the **petitioner** (which is also the term used to refer to a party who initiates a proceeding in equity, as previously mentioned). The **appellee** is the party against whom the appeal is taken. Sometimes, an appellee is referred to as the **respondent.**

ABBREVIATIONS In court opinions, as well as in other areas of this text, certain terms appearing in the names of firms or organizations will often be abbreviated. The terms *Company, Incorporated,* and *Limited,* for example, will frequently appear in their abbreviated forms as *Co., Inc.,* and *Ltd.,* respectively, and *Brothers* is commonly abbreviated to *Bros.* Certain organizations or legislative acts are also frequently referred to by their initials or acronyms. In all such cases, to prevent confusion, we will give the complete name of the organization or act upon first mentioning it in a given section of the text.

A Sample Court Case

To illustrate how to read and analyze a court opinion, we have annotated an actual case that was

heard by the United States Court of Appeals for the Fifth Circuit in 1991. The lawsuit was initiated by Betty Ann Ferguson, who apparently disagreed with an Internal Revenue Service determination regarding her taxes. At the hearing, she refused to ''swear'' before testifying, and that became the issue on her appeal.

---

1 **FERGUSON v. COMMISSIONER OF INTERNAL REVENUE**

2 United States Court of Appeals, Fifth Circuit, 1991.

3 921 F.2d 588.

4 **BACKGROUND AND FACTS** Betty Ann Ferguson disagreed with an Internal Revenue Service decision regarding her taxes and filed a petition for a hearing in the United States Tax Court. Her only evidence was her own testimony. But when she was asked to "swear" or "affirm" before testifying at the hearing, she refused on religious grounds. She offered to "declare that the facts I am about to give are, to the best of my knowledge and belief, accurate, correct, and complete," but the tax court judge refused to accept her testimony without an oath or affirmation and dismissed her petition. Ferguson appealed.

5 **DECISION AND RATIONALE** The United States Court of Appeals for the Fifth Circuit reversed the tax court's decision to refuse to hear Ferguson's testimony and remanded the case for further proceedings. The appellate court found the tax court's failure to accommodate Ferguson's objections to be inconsistent with the applicable Federal Rule of Evidence and the First Amendment to the United States Constitution. The court pointed out that the rule, which requires that a witness "declare that [she] will testify truthfully," was designed to afford flexibility: "[N]o special verbal formula is required." The court noted that under the First Amendment, which guarantees the right to the free exercise of religion, other courts have attempted to accommodate the objections of witnesses who would not use various words—"solemnly," references to "God," "swear," "affirm"—in their affirmations for religious reasons. The court added that the disagreement between Ferguson and the tax court judge "might have been nothing more than an unfortunate misunderstanding." Had the judge "attempted to accommodate Ms. Ferguson by inquiring into her objections and considering her proposed alternative, the entire matter might have been resolved without an appeal to this court."

■ Review of Case

1. The first entry informs us that the name of the case is *Ferguson v. Commissioner of Internal Revenue.*

2. The second entry indicates that the case was decided by the United States Court of Appeals for the Fifth Circuit in 1991.

3. A citation for the case appears as the third entry. The citation to the *Federal Reporter, Second Series,* (abbreviated to ''F.2d'') indicates that this case can be found in Volume 921 of that reporter on page 588.

4. This paragraph—the ''Background and Facts'' section—provides the setting for the controversy by describing the events that created the issue before the court. It discusses the suit's initial filing, the trial court's decision, and the case's disposition on subsequent appeals, leading up to the opinion forming the basis for this case summary.

5. The ''Decision and Rationale'' section paraphrases the court's opinion, including the court's decision and the reasons the court gave for reaching that decision. Generally, judicial decisions have two parts: findings of fact and conclusions of law. Findings of fact are determinations from the evidence concerning facts that one party asserts and another denies. A conclusion of law is a determination as to the legal effect of the facts that the parties disclosed. Conclusions of law represent a court's holding—that is, the legal principle derived from the decision that other courts rely on when using the case as precedent in subsequent lawsuits. A court's reasoning provides the basis for its findings and conclusions. Reasoned opinions make it easier to understand what the law is; a reasoned explanation of why a court decided the way it did contributes to an understanding of what the court will do when confronted with a similar situation.

■ Terms and Concepts

administrative law 9	equitable principles and	private law 11
administrative process 9	maxims 13	procedural law 11
analogy 8	injunction 13	public law 11
appellant 20	judicial process 9	remedy 12
appellee 20	jurisprudence 2	remedy at law 12
case law 8	King's Court 6	remedy in equity 13
chancellor 12	laches 13	rescission 13
citation 15	legal realism 4	respondent 20
civil law 11	natural law school 3	rulemaking 9
civil law system 8	opinion 20	specific performance 13
common law 6	petitioner 20	*stare decisis* 6
court of equity 12	plaintiff 7	statutes of limitations 13
court of law 12	positive law 3	statutory law 8
criminal law 12	positivist school 3	substantive law 11
defendant 7	precedent 6	syllogism 7
defense 13		

■ For Review

1. What is the common law?

2. What are the differences between remedies at law and remedies in equity?

3. What is the Uniform Commercial Code?

4. Dan contracts to sell ninety cases of video game cartridges to Paula. Dan delivers ninety cases of cartridges, but Paula discovers that 80 percent of the cartridges are defective. She sends all the cartridges back to Dan. A state statute provides that if goods fail in any respect to conform to a contract, the buyer can reject the goods and sue the seller for damages for breach of contract. If Paula sues Dan, how might the judge reason to conclude that Paula is entitled to damages?

5. In one case, the court holds that a grocery store that does not clean its floors is negligent. In a second case, a store's customer breaks a bottle of fruit juice, but before the store learns of the mess, another customer slips on the puddle and breaks her arm. In a suit by the injured customer against the store, how might the judge reason in determining whether the principle in the first case applies in the second case?

■ Questions and Case Problems

1-1. In the middle of the last century, the United States declared war on Mexico and levied taxes to support the war effort. Henry David Thoreau, who felt that the war was unjust, refused to pay taxes to support it and was subsequently imprisoned for violating the law. Thoreau maintained that obeying the law in these circumstances would be unethical. Which of the schools of legal philosophy discussed in this chapter would be the most sympathetic toward Thoreau's views on law? Explain.

1-2. How does statutory law come into existence? How does it differ from the common law? If statutory law conflicts with the common law, which law will govern?

1-3. What is substantive law? What is procedural law? Are there reasons for the two to exist side by side?

1-4. Courts of equity tend to follow general rules or maxims rather than common law precedents as courts of law do. Some of these maxims were listed in this chapter. Why would equity courts give more credence to such maxims than to a hard-and-fast body of law?

1-5. A student is interested in reading the entire court opinion in the case of *U.S. v. Sun and Sand Imports, Ltd.,* 725 F.2d 184 (2d Cir. 1984). The case deals with the transportation, via interstate commerce, of flammable sleepwear for children in violation of the Flammable Fabrics Act. Explain specifically where the student would locate the court's opinion.

1-6. The equitable principle "Equity aids the vigilant, not those who rest on their rights" means that courts will not aid those who do not pursue a cause of action while the evidence is fresh and while the true facts surrounding the issue can be discovered. The statute of limitations, discussed in Section 2-725 of the Uniform Commercial Code (see Appendix C), is based on this principle. Under the statute of limitations, the period of time within which a party can bring an action for breach of a contract covering the sale of goods is four years—although the parties (the seller and the buyer) can reduce this period by agreement to only one year. As a practical matter, discuss which party would benefit more by a one-year period and which would benefit more by a four-year period.

1-7. Most states hold that a manufacturer who sells a defective product that causes harm to a person is strictly liable for damages, even though the manufacturer used reasonable care in the production and sale of the product and was unaware of the defect. Most state constitutions and statutes do not provide for such liability. Where, then, does such a law come from, and on what basis can such liability be imposed?

1-8. Briefly discuss whether an action at law or an action in equity is more appropriate in the following situations:
   (a) Divorce.
   (b) Automobile accident.
   (c) Preventing future trespass on your property by a neighbor.
   (d) Bankruptcy.
   (e) Libel or slander (defaming a person's reputation).

1-9. The text of this chapter stated that the doctrine of *stare decisis* became a cornerstone of the English and American judicial systems. What does *stare decisis* mean, and why has this doctrine been so fundamental to the development of our legal tradition?

1-10. Different courts sometimes reach opposite conclusions when deciding cases involving similar, if not identical, issues. Assuming that the laws and case precedents pertaining to the issues are identical in the jurisdictions in question, how can such differences in legal reasoning and consequent decisions be accounted for?

1-11. What is the difference between a concurring opinion and a majority opinion? Between a concurring opinion and a dissenting opinion? Why do judges and justices write concurring and dissenting opinions, given that they will not affect the outcome of the case at hand, which has already been decided by majority vote?

Chapter 2

Business Ethics

Businesspersons receive more extensive media coverage today than perhaps at any other time in our history. We constantly read and hear about business improprieties relating to insider trading activities, hostile takeovers, drug testing and discrimination in the workplace, product liability suits, or investments in South Africa. Indeed, because the media often focus on the improprieties of businesspersons, rather than the *ethical* activities that occur daily in the business arena, one might easily conclude that the men and women in business today are more unethical than businesspersons were in the past. In reality, this is probably not so.

Compare today's business practices, for example, with those of the nineteenth and early twentieth centuries. Gone now is the era of robber barons, cutthroat competition, and a nation run by large business trusts. Society's concern with business ethics today stems in part from a greater awareness of the not-so-ethical practices that occur in the business world and how these business practices and business decisions generally affect our welfare as consumers, our political well-being, and the health of planet Earth. As a result of these concerns, businesspersons face increasing pressure to conduct their affairs more responsibly and ethically.

In preparing for your career in business, you may find a background in business ethics and a commitment to ethical behavior just as important as a knowledge of the specific laws that you will read about in the remainder of this text. Furthermore, if you wish to truly understand the law, you need to be aware of the ethical framework within which it operates. This chapter first examines the nature of business ethics and the relationship between ethics and the law. Then it discusses some of the traditional approaches to ethical reasoning that have guided others in their ethical decision making. No chapter in business ethics would be complete without addressing one of the major ethical issues facing every businessperson—how to justify the self-interested search for profits. Related to this question is another important ethical issue: How can businesspersons act in an ethically responsible manner and at the same time make profits for their firms or their firms' owners?

The ultimate goal of this chapter is to provide you with the basic tools necessary for analyzing ethical issues in business contexts. It cannot tell you how to decide ethical issues. That is something you alone must do—on the basis of your own ethical convictions. As you read this chapter, and this book, examine carefully the ethical dimensions of specific laws and of specific court cases or hypothetical situations. Also examine closely your own ethical standards. What are your ethical criteria? How would you apply these criteria to a particular case or business situation? How can you best adapt your personal ethical standards to the kinds of ethical issues you will face in the business world? Although you can never be fully prepared for the task of ethical decision making—because no two situations are ever exactly alike—the more you analyze ethical issues relating to business that have arisen in the past, the better prepared you will be to make any ethical decisions you may face in the future.

■ The Nature of Business Ethics

Before we can talk about ethics, we need to define it. **Ethics** can be defined as the study of what constitutes right or wrong behavior. It is the branch of philosophy that focuses on morality and the way in which moral principles are applied to daily life. Ethics has to do with fundamental questions such as What is fair? What is just? What is the right thing to do in this situation?—essentially with any question relating to the fairness, justice, rightness, or wrongness of an action. Often, ethical questions or statements contain the words ''should'' or ''ought to.'' For example, when we say that someone ''ought to'' do something, we are not saying that he or she is forced to do it; merely that the person ''should'' do it because it is the fair, just, or right thing to do.

Ethics is not an abstract or a static concept. On the contrary, ethics affects, and gives meaning to, our everyday life and the decisions we make. We constantly apply our values and moral convictions to our actions and decisions, frequently without even being aware of the fact that we are doing so. The clothes we buy, the music we prefer, the way we treat our friends, the books we choose to read— these and a thousand other everyday activities and decisions, if you analyze them carefully, ultimately relate to ethical values and goals.

Defining Business Ethics

Business ethics focuses on what constitutes right or wrong behavior in the world of business and on how moral principles are applied by businesspersons to situations that arise in their daily work and during their careers. It is important to remember that business ethics is not a different *kind* of ethics. That is, businesspersons do not necessarily adopt one set of ethical principles to guide them in their business decisions and another set to guide them in their personal lives. The ethical standards that we set up for our behavior as, say, mothers, fathers, or students apply equally well to our activities as businesspersons. Business activities are just one part of the human enterprise, and business ethics is a subset of ethics that relates specifically to the kinds of situations that arise in the everyday world of business.

The Complexity of Business Ethics

Ethical decision making in the business world is somewhat more complicated than it is in our personal lives, however. In private life, it is not always necessary to analyze your ethical convictions too closely. As mentioned, personal ethical decisions are frequently made almost unconsciously and often from sheer habit. This usually presents no problem, because you are not normally called upon to explain the ethical reasoning underlying your personal decisions to others—except possibly your family or good friends. Even then, if you said you made a certain decision because you felt it was the ''right'' thing to do at the time, this would very likely be an acceptable ''reason'' for your decision.

The business world is a little different. One decision on the part of a businessperson can have repercussions throughout the entire society. Therefore, you need to be prepared to justify—to your superiors, to your colleagues or employees, to corporate shareholders, or even in a court of law— whatever decisions you make. It is not enough to say, ''I felt that it was the best decision in the circumstances'' or ''It seemed like the right thing to do at the time.'' You will need to demonstrate the rational basis for your decision and explain why, given the alternatives facing you, you concluded that your decision was the right one. In the business context, ethical behavior requires that you decide ethical issues on the basis of clearly defined ethical standards. Clearly defined ethical standards are especially important in today's world because businesspersons are increasingly being held to higher standards of accountability for their actions and decisions than they were in the past. To assist employees in making ethical decisions, many business firms today issue ethical policy guidelines or codes of conduct. The use and effectiveness of ethical codes are discussed in the *Emerging Trends* feature in this chapter.

Reasons for Unethical Business Behavior

Unethical behavior in the business context occurs in some cases because employers or owners implicitly condone such behavior. For example, an employee may go along with an unethical decision that economically benefits the company because the employee assumes that the company will reward him or her for increasing company profits. In other situations, unethical conduct may occur because of the belief that one can ''get away with it''—that the unethical activity will not be discovered. According to some, another reason for unethical business behavior is the corporate structure itself. By its very nature, the corporate structure promotes unethical behavior because it tends to protect corporate actors from personal responsibility for what they do.

For example, if a corporation markets a product that results in a consumer's death, the corporate officer who made the decision to market the product may not be deemed a ''murderer'' in the same sense that an individual who intentionally killed another would be. Nor would that corporate officer, in all likelihood, condone the killing of others. In effect, corporate decision makers are shielded from the consequences of their decisions by the corporate entity—that is, they do not witness or deal directly with the harm or injuries generated by their decisions. To a certain extent, they are also shielded from personal responsibility for their actions by the corporate collectivity. In other words, normally no *one* individual makes a corporate decision and therefore no one individual ever has to assume total responsibility for a corporate action (although in recent years, the courts have been increasingly willing to look behind the ''corporate veil'' and hold individual corporate actors liable for actions resulting in harm to others—see Chapter 7).

It is important to realize, though, that much unethical business behavior occurs simply because it is not always clear what ethical standards and behaviors are appropriate or acceptable in the business context. How can you learn what is appropriate or inappropriate behavior in the business world? One important source is business law itself.

■ Ethics and the Law

Virtually every law you read about in this book is related in one way or another to business ethics. Why? Because the law in a broad sense is itself an expression of ethical principles; it expresses what society—through its courts and other governmental bodies—has deemed to be right and proper behavior in the marketplace.

Ethics, as stated above, involves an active process of applying values, which may range from religious principles to customs and traditions. A *social ethic* expresses the dominant ethical values, or shared beliefs, of society in general. Indeed, it is the sharing of beliefs and the desire to spread these beliefs that cause people to organize as groups—pressure groups lobbying Congress to create or amend a law, social groups urging Americans to be for or against abortion, and so on. When enough people are convinced, say, that a certain law is wrong, sufficient pressure will be exerted on government to change that law so that it more effectively represents the social ethic. Because ethics and the law go hand in hand, a careful study of business law will help you to understand what is, and is not, considered by society to be ethical behavior in business.

Business Law as a Guide to Ethical Behavior

Business law rests on the premise that businesspersons should act ethically in their dealings with one another. It requires that people in business honor their contractual commitments, cooperate with one another in the performance of contracts, act reasonably and in good faith, and exercise due care and consideration for others in their undertakings. Although a law may seem arbitrary at first glance, if you look closely, you will very likely find the connection between that particular law and the broad, underlying ethical premise on which it ultimately rests. Insofar as possible, we will help you see this connection by indicating, as we discuss particular laws in this text, how these laws relate to broad social policies and ethical principles.

The Limits of the Law

Because the law reflects and codifies our society's ethical values, many of our ethical decisions are made for us—by our laws. Our laws force us to behave ethically or face undesirable consequences—a fine or even imprisonment. But in the interest of preserving personal freedom, as well as for practical reasons, the law does not, and cannot, codify all ethical requirements. No law says, for example, that it is *illegal* to lie to one's family, but it may be *unethical* to do so. Similarly, in the business world, numerous actions might be unethical but not necessarily illegal. Mere compliance with the law does not always equate with ethical behavior.

Consider the following hypothetical example. The U.S. government has discovered that a child's toy is dangerous and has caused the deaths of some children. Consequently, the government has banned sales of the toy, leaving the manufacturer with a large unsold inventory. Although sales of the product are banned in the United States, it may be perfectly legal to export this toy to nations that have little consumer protection legislation. But would it be ethical to do so?

It is also possible that an individual may consider a particular law to be immoral. In such a situation, should the individual obey the law even if he or she thinks it would be unethical to do so? As discussed in Chapter 1, adherents of the natural law school believe that there is a higher law than that prescribed by a particular society at a particular point in time. If law accepted by courts and embodied in statutes conflicts with natural law, it loses its legitimacy and "deserves" to be disobeyed. This is the basis for the theory of civil disobedience espoused by Henry David Thoreau, Martin Luther King, Jr., Mahatma Gandhi, and others.

In short, the law has its limits—it cannot make all our ethical decisions for us. When it does not, personal ethical standards must guide the decision-making process. We now examine some of the traditional ways in which ethical standards have been derived.

■ The Derivation of Ethical Standards

Although it would be nice to think that ethical standards simply exist, just as the law of gravity does,

such is not the case. Ethical standards are not discoverable, like some universal law of nature. Indeed, the many scientific and technological achievements of the modern world offer us no guidance when it comes to establishing ethical standards of behavior. Ethical standards are by nature subjective; they are derived from basic religious beliefs or philosophical postulates concerning the nature of the good, fair, right, or just. We each have to decide what we believe in and how to translate our beliefs into action.

This is not to say that there are no resources to which we can turn for ethical guidance. On the contrary, religious and philosophical inquiry into the nature of "the good" is an age-old pursuit, and the amount written on this subject could fill a library. Broadly speaking, though, ethical reasoning relating to business has traditionally been characterized by two fundamental approaches. One approach defines ethical behavior in terms of *duty*. The other approach determines what is ethical, or good, in terms of the *consequences* of any given action. We examine each of these approaches below.

Duty-Based Ethics

Is it wrong to cheat on an examination, if nobody will ever know you cheated and if it helps you get into law school so that you can eventually represent *pro bono* (without pay) the needy? Is it wrong to lie to your parents, if the lie harms nobody but helps to keep family relations congenial? These kinds of ethical questions implicitly weigh the "end" of an action against the "means" used to attain that end. If you believe that you have an ethical *duty* not to lie or cheat, then lying and cheating can never be justified by the consequences— no matter how benevolent or desirable those consequences may be. In American culture, the dominant duty-based ethical standard derives from religious sources.

RELIGIOUS ETHICS   The Western religious tradition—more specifically, the Judeo-Christian religious tradition—is rooted in the belief that certain absolute truths have been revealed through the prophets, the Bible, and religious institutions. Who among us has not been exposed to the "Thou shalt nots" of the Ten Commandments, the "seven deadly sins," and Christ's instruction to help and care for others ("Love one another as I have loved you"; "Love thy neighbor as thyself"; "He who shall lay down his life for a friend . . . "). These teachings establish for all who believe in them an *absolute ethical duty* to act in accordance with them. It is not the consequences of an act that determine how ethical the act is, but the nature of the act itself. For example, if, like Robin Hood, an individual decides to rob the rich to help the poor, that individual's benevolent motive does not alter the fact that he or she has acted unethically ("sinned"), because stealing violates the Seventh Commandment ("Thou shalt not steal").

Religious ethical standards are *absolute*. When an act is prohibited by religious teachings, it is unethical and should not be undertaken—regardless of its consequences. Telling a lie, for example, for the sake of gaining a promotion is unethical—even though no one would be harmed by the lie and your future would be rosier. Religious ethical standards also involve an element of *compassion*. Therefore, even though it might be profitable for a firm to lay off a less productive employee, if that employee would find it difficult to find employment elsewhere and his or her family would suffer as a result, this potential suffering would be given substantial weight by the decision makers. A compassionate manager or employer might decide to keep the employee and attempt to increase profits in another way. Compassionate treatment of others is also mandated—to a certain extent, at least—by the Golden Rule of the ancients ("Do unto others as you would have them do unto you"), which has been adopted by most religions.

KANT AND DUTY-BASED ETHICS What we have been describing is an other-oriented, duty-based system of ethics. A duty-based approach to ethics is also characteristic of the philosophy of Immanual Kant (1724–1804). This philosopher identified some general guiding principles for moral behavior based on what he believed to be the fundamental nature of human beings. Kant held that it is rational to assume that human beings are qualitatively different from other physical objects occupying space, such as CD players, sofas, and computers. Persons are *moral* agents—that is, they are endowed with moral integrity and the capacity to reason and conduct their affairs rationally; therefore, their thoughts and actions should be re-

spected. When human beings are treated merely as means, they are being treated as the equivalent of objects and are being denied their basic humanity.

A central postulate in Kantian ethics is that individuals should evaluate their actions in light of the consequences that would follow if *everyone* in society acted in the same way. This "categorical imperative" can be applied to any action. For example, say that you are deciding whether to cheat on an examination. If you have adopted Kant's categorical imperative, you will decide not to cheat, because if everyone cheated, the examination would be meaningless. Similarly, you would not cut in line to purchase a ticket for a rock concert, because if everyone else did the same thing, the concept of a line would disappear and chaos would reign.

Kant's ethics impose a duty to respect the moral integrity of others at all times and to act only as we would have all others act. In its effect, Kantian ethical reasoning gives philosophical weight to the Golden Rule mentioned above, but note the distinction: The Golden Rule merely exhorts us to "do unto others as we would have them do unto ourselves." Kant's categorical imperative forces us to look at the larger picture: What would *society* be like if everybody acted as we did? It forces us to look at and evaluate, from a more objective point of view, *social* goals as well as our personal desires and welfare.

PROBLEMS WITH DUTY-BASED ETHICS Sometimes, applying religious or Kantian ethics can pose difficulties. This is especially true in the business context. For example, a business executive negotiating with another firm's representatives may feel it necessary to "stretch the truth" or "hold back" information to obtain the best "deal" for his or her employer. Is this a violation of the religious precept that one should not lie or of Kant's categorical imperative? In some absolute sense, yes, it is unethical in both religious and Kantian terms. But remember that the executive also owes an ethical duty to his or her employer to make decisions that are profitable for the firm. Furthermore, what if the executive knows that, unless the deal is struck, his or her employer will have to lay off a number of long-time employees who depend on the firm to look after their economic welfare? Would "stretching the truth" in negotiating the deal then be consistent with the religious ethical duty to be compassionate toward others? Or the Kantian imperative to act only as we would have all others act?

You can see how, in the business context, ethical decision making may involve fulfilling not just one ethical responsibility but a number of ethical responsibilities simultaneously. When one ethical duty conflicts with another, you have to decide which duty is the most fundamental and act accordingly. In the situation here, the executive may conclude that the ethical duty to be fully honest with others is more fundamental than the duty owed to the firm (even though the cost of this decision may include a personal cost, such as a future promotion or pay raise, which will affect not only the executive but also his or her family). Alternatively, the executive might decide that the ethical duty owed to the firm and its employees (and possibly to his or her family) is more fundamental than, and thus overrides, the duty to be fully honest with the other negotiators. As this example illustrates, frequently the ethical decisions faced by businesspersons are not clear cut; that is, the decisions involve choices not between good and bad alternatives but between good and less good alternatives.

Utilitarianism

''Thou shalt act so as to generate the greatest good for the greatest number.'' This is a paraphrase of the major premise of utilitarian theory. **Utilitarianism** is a philosophical theory first developed by Jeremy Bentham (1748–1832) and then advanced, with some modifications, by John Stuart Mill (1806–1873)—both British philosophers. In contrast to religious ethics and Kant's moral theory, utilitarianism is *outcome oriented*. It focuses on the consequences of an action, not on the nature of the action itself or on any set of preestablished moral values or religious beliefs.

RIGHT AND WRONG IN UTILITARIANISM Under a utilitarian model of ethics, an action is morally correct or right when, among the people it affects, it produces the greatest amount of good for the greatest number. When an action affects the majority adversely, it is morally wrong. Applying the utilitarian theory thus requires (1) a determi-

nation of what individuals will be affected by the action in question; (2) an assessment, or **cost-benefit analysis,** of the negative and positive effects of alternative actions on these individuals; and (3) a choice among alternative actions that will produce maximum societal utility—or, in other words, the greatest positive benefits for the greatest number of individuals.

How does a utilitarian determine what constitutes the general welfare or happiness of individuals? Jeremy Bentham's approach to this question was to define happiness strictly in terms of physical pleasure or pain. By thus quantifying happiness, he felt it would be possible to calculate scientifically, by a kind of moral mathematics, the human costs and benefits of any legislative decision. Mill argued that qualitative factors, such as psychological and spiritual well-being, also play a significant role in creating happiness and need to be considered in calculations of the positive and negative effects of a decision. With Mill and later followers of the utilitarian school of thought, what constitutes happiness is individually determined. Therefore, the successful application of the utilitarian welfare-maximization principle depends on the freedom—and physical, mental, social, and financial ability—of all individuals to make and express their choices.

A brief digression: Freedom of choice is at the heart of Mill's philosophy, and it stems from his libertarian outlook. Mill believed that a person should have the liberty to think and do as he or she likes, without government interference, so long as that individual's actions do not infringe on another's rights. Mill's concern with individual liberty has had a profound influence on Western political and legal thought. The right to privacy, for example, is grounded to a certain extent in Mill's philosophical principles concerning individual rights.

PROBLEMS WITH UTILITARIANISM While interesting in principle, utilitarianism suffers from a major problem: Any true calculation of overall welfare, happiness, or utility requires a knowledge of what the *actual* consequences, both negative and positive, of a given decision will be—and rarely, if ever, can all of the possible ramifications of a decision be predicted with total accuracy. This is especially true with decisions that may affect millions of people.

Another problem with utilitarianism is that it always involves both winners and losers—that is, it is impossible to satisfy everybody with a policy action based on the principle of utility. Consider the following example: Johnson, a manufacturer, owns many plants. One of the plants is much older than the others. Equipment at the old plant is outdated and inefficient, and the costs of production at that plant are now twice what they are at any of Johnson's other plants. The price of the product cannot be increased because of competition, both domestic and international. What should Johnson do? In a utilitarian analysis of the problem, the costs of closing the plant (the financial insecurity of those who would be laid off) would be weighed against the benefits of closing the plant (the future financial security of the firm and of those workers who would retain their jobs at the other plants). If Johnson decides the issue from a utilitarian perspective, he will very likely close the plant, because closing the plant will yield the greatest benefit for the greatest number of people. The winners are the majority who will be aided by the decision; the losers are the workers at the old plant, now without jobs.

Utilitarianism is often criticized because its objective, calculated approach to problems tends to reduce the welfare of human beings to plus and minus signs on a cost-benefit worksheet. Utilitarian reasoning has also been used to "justify" human costs that many find totally unacceptable.

There are other theories of moral responsibility, but all of them involve making difficult choices in a world in which information is imperfect. Frequently, ethical choices in the business context involve choosing between self-interest (of the businessperson or of the business firm) and perceived ethical obligations. In the business context, self-interest is usually equated with profit-seeking behavior. Not surprisingly, the question of profits and how to justify them ethically has been, and continues to be, a fundamental concern of the business world.

■ Ethics and the Search for Profits

Unethical and, often, illegal business behavior makes good press in America today, but businesspersons in general are respected members of Western society. Profit-making activities are not deemed unethical—so long as no laws or fundamental eth-

ical principles are violated. In fact, successful businesspersons often rank among the most admired individuals in our society. This was not always the case. Historically (and still in our time in those nations that have adopted a communist political ideology), the self-interested pursuit of profits was ethically suspect because it pitted self-gain against community-oriented behavior.

Merchants and Society: A Brief History

Two thousand years ago in ancient Greece, the businessperson ranked about the same as a slave on the social ladder. Greek society allowed businesses to exist, but business profits could only be used to serve the community. Businesspersons who did well were not allowed to display their wealth or success by altering their material standard of living. They had to live in the same manner as others in their class. Whenever a Greek businessperson was suspected of violating this strict standard of morality, the upper classes severely criticized and socially censured that person. Although merchants fared somewhat better in the Roman era, there was little significant change in social status.

In the medieval world, which was dominated by Christian institutions and ethics, merchants presented a perplexing challenge from an ethical point of view. On the one hand, the profit motive and the self-interest that it represented were considered anti-Christian *per se* (inherently; in itself)—one's duty was to serve God and others, not one's own material well-being. On the other hand, the trading activities of merchants increased social welfare by making more products available, some of which were vitally necessary. Generally, from about 700 A.D. to 1500 A.D., merchants were therefore regarded as a kind of necessary evil in society. Commerce was deemed acceptable, but only insofar as it served the public interest. And certain types of business activities that are common today were prohibited—charging interest on loans, for example, was forbidden by the Church. One was not allowed to make "profits" from loaning money. The concept of a *just price* was also established. Businesspersons accused of setting other than a just price, of using profits irresponsibly, or of acting dishonestly were severely punished.

In the wake of the social and religious activities of the sixteenth century, business activity became more respectable. The religious reformer John Calvin (1509–1564) was particularly influential in this respect. Some of the tenets of Calvinism had profound social implications. Calvin, for example, placed a high value on thrift, industry, and hard work and regarded business success as evidence of God's grace. The spread of Calvinism across Europe was accompanied by an ethical climate favorable to trade and commerce, and businesspersons for the first time began to make their way into the upper social classes. Although the Calvinist doctrine encouraged trade, it did not condone unethical business practices, but held that immoral business behavior should be punished. Also, because businesspersons achieved success only through the grace of God, they were morally obligated to make substantial contributions to the Church and to charitable causes that furthered the welfare of the needy.

From about 1800 to the Great Depression in the 1930s, during the era of the Industrial Revolution, the businessperson moved up to the highest notch on the social ladder. The corporation grew in importance and, with it, the importance of corporate leaders in the political, social, and moral life of this nation, as well as in Western Europe. Profit-seeking activity was fully justified, from an ethical point of view, not only by the Calvinist work ethic but by an economic theory in which the self-interested search for profits was firmly united with social welfare: the theory of capitalism.

Capitalism and the Ethical Justification of Profits

In 1776, Adam Smith, a Scottish economist and the so-called father of capitalism, published his *Wealth of Nations.* In this treatise, Smith firmly linked self-interest to "other-interest" by arguing that the self-interested behavior of individuals in an unfettered marketplace results in maximum social welfare.

Implicitly, the *laissez-faire*[1] ("let them do as they please") world of capitalism described by Smith was a form of utilitarianism. Adam Smith "proved" that individuals acting in their own self-interest generate the greatest social welfare for the greatest number of citizens. According to Smith, this is because an "invisible hand" (the forces of

supply and demand) regulates the free market to ensure that only socially worthwhile profit-seeking enterprises survive. In a nutshell, capitalist theory can be described as follows: The only way that businesses can sell their services or products is if people want them. People show their preferences for goods and services by agreeing to purchase them at whatever the market price is. The market price is determined by the forces of supply and demand—the actions of all suppliers taken together and all consumers taken together, interacting with each other. There is no such thing as a "just" price, only the price generated by the forces of supply and demand. Businesspersons who produce commodities that individuals want at the lowest price survive in this highly competitive marketplace; others do not. Businesses use resources to produce commodities. The difference between the cost of those resources and the revenues businesses receive from the buying public is what we define as profit.

Because consumers are not forced to purchase any particular product, they never pay more than the highest subjective valuation they place on a product. That is, if good X costs $20 but a consumer only values it at $18, the consumer will never buy it. Hence, the total revenues received by the businessperson represent the minimum valuation that society places on the commodity that the businessperson sells. The difference between those revenues and the cost of providing the commodity—profits—represents an indication of the social desirability of producing the commodity. High profits are good because they show that resources are being put to highly valued uses. Low profits and losses are bad because they indicate that businesspersons made incorrect decisions about which commodities consumers really wanted.

Presumably, we do not have to worry about high profits lasting forever because such profits encourage new producers to enter the marketplace or old producers to expand output. When output increases, prices fall, and so, too, do profits. In the long run, firms tend to make only a competitive rate of return, or a normal rate of profit. Resources are constantly moving from lower-valued uses to higher-valued uses as businesspersons constantly search for highly profitable opportunities. In the world of Adam Smith, profits are therefore good,

_____

1. Pronounced leh-say *fair.*

morally acceptable, and indeed necessary for the material well-being of society.

Today's Marketplace

Adam Smith's theory rested on a vision of a marketplace characterized by perfect competition. But in reality, we live in a world of imperfect competition. Some of the reasons for market imperfections are as follows:

1. When a firm becomes large and powerful enough to control a substantial share of the market, it need not be as sensitive to the dollar votes of consumers. This is because consumers will be unable to purchase the same product from the firm's competitors—there will be no significant competition. Therefore, high profits will not be reduced.
2. It is difficult, if not impossible, for firms to obtain perfect information about what consumers really want or about optimal production techniques. It is also difficult for consumers to obtain perfect information on product availability, price, and quality. As a result of imperfect information, profits in the marketplace do not necessarily go hand in hand with consumer welfare.
3. The existence of **externalities**—the costs or benefits of an action that are not known or properly accounted for by the parties to that action—also results in market imperfections. Environmental pollution is a good example of an externality. If a business firm releases chemicals into a river, pollution results. But the business firm does not pay the ''cost'' of that pollution; society does. Although the product produced by the firm may be a life-saving drug and thus a benefit to society, the pollution that is produced by the firm mitigates against the social welfare.

Because of market imperfections, the search for profits is not always in society's best interests. To the extent that the ethics of capitalism and the free enterprise system lead to social harm, a socially responsible firm modifies those ethics by applying other ethical standards. The business manager in today's world typically looks at more than just the profit side of the picture when making decisions. The profitability of a given action or decision is still the first consideration, to be sure—after all, the reason a business firm exists is to make profits. It goes without saying that the second primary consideration is the legality of the proposed action. The final consideration is whether the proposed action is ethically justifiable. Exhibit 2–1 illustrates graphically how these three factors—profitability, legality, and ethical considerations—interrelate in the decision-making process.

■ Tradeoffs and Ethical Decision Making

Ideally, each decision you make as a businessperson would fall readily into the center area of the diagram shown in Exhibit 2–1. Frequently, however, to ensure that a decision or action is at once profitable, legal, and ethical, some profitability or some ethical considerations must be sacrificed—or *traded off*—in the decision-making process. Thus, the concept of a **tradeoff** is intimately involved in ethical decision making.

No matter what your approach to ethics in the business world or in your personal life, you will be faced with the necessity of making tradeoffs

■ Exhibit 2–1 Ethical Decision Making

This diagram illustrates how legality, profitability, and ethical factors interrelate in the ethical decision-making process in the business context. Ideally, business decisions will fall within the shaded area in which all circles overlap. If they do not, ethically responsible decision making requires that tradeoffs be made so that all three criteria are satisfied.

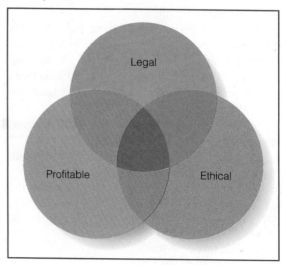

between equally desirable goals. Recognizing the nature of the tradeoff required to resolve an ethical conflict is the first step in the ethical decision-making process. The next step necessarily requires you to bring your own—or your firm's—ethical standards to bear on the decision. You must decide whether one goal is more important or fundamental than the other or others and minimize, to the extent possible, any modification or sacrificing of that goal.

It is important to stress that the ethical tradeoffs normally faced by businesspersons are not clear-cut tradeoffs between "good" and "bad" alternatives. By definition, ethical dilemmas only arise when two or more *ethical* goals come into conflict. For example, assume that a corporate executive has to decide whether to approve the sale of a new product that would be beneficial for most consumers but that might have undesirable side effects for a small percentage of its users. In this situation, the tradeoff becomes relatively obvious: expose an unknown but extremely small number of individuals to possible harm while allowing all other consumers to enjoy the benefits of the new product (and in the process, probably make higher profits) or protect that small number of individuals from possible harm and not allow all other consumers to enjoy the benefits of the new product.

In statistics, this tradeoff is known as a tradeoff between Type I and Type II errors. A *Type I error* occurs because of the sin of *commission*. When the new product is sold and there is an undesirable side effect—a customer becomes sick or is injured—the harm occurs because of the sin of commission. On the other hand, if the product is not entered into the marketplace, a *Type II error* will occur. Type II errors result from the sin of *omission*. All of the benefits that people would have derived had the product been introduced do not exist if the product is not marketed.

Let us take a specific example that involves a pharmaceutical company. The firm has developed a new medication that is very effective in the treatment of high blood pressure. The only problem is that the company estimates that one person in a million using the product may have a violent allergic reaction to the medication and might even suffer death. The tradeoff here is between the Type I error (the one-in-a-million chance that someone will suffer or even die as a result of using the med-

ication) and the Type II error (that people may die from cardiovascular disease or other problems resulting from high blood pressure if the new medication is never introduced into the marketplace).

Obviously, because Type I errors can be observed and linked directly to the new medication, they are usually the ones that make the headlines. Type II errors resulting from the nonintroduction of the new medication into the marketplace are not easily calculated, however. There is simply no accurate and widely acceptable way to measure how much suffering and dying occur because the new medication was not introduced into the marketplace.

■ Ethical Issues in Business

It would be impossible to describe all of the different kinds of ethical issues that arise in the business world. As you will discover in reading through this text, ethics relates to all aspects of business activity. Broadly speaking, ethical issues can be categorized as internal issues or external issues. Because many ethical issues internal to the firm concern the relationship between the firm and its employees, we offer here a few examples of ethical issues that have arisen in the employment relationship. Ethical issues external to the firm predominantly relate to the products or services marketed by the firm and to how marketing decisions affect the welfare of the ultimate consumers of those products and services. We also examine below some of the ethical dimensions of marketing decisions.

It is important to keep the tradeoff concept in mind as you consider the ethical issues discussed below because often what is at issue is the extent to which the employer's profit-making goals should be traded off to fulfill a perceived ethical duty toward employees or consumers.

Employment Relationships

One of the primary concerns of every employer is the ability to control the workplace environment. After all, it is the employer who is responsible for making the business firm a success, and success requires qualified, competent, loyal employees and efficient operations. But employees also have concerns. They want to earn a fair wage; they want to

EMERGING TRENDS IN BUSINESS LAW   **Codes of Ethics—Do They Work?**

One way for everyone in a company to be aware of the ethical standards expected of employees is for that company to create, print, and distribute among the employees a code of ethics. Such a code may be called a code of ethics, a code of conduct, a mission statement, a policy statement, or by some other name. In 1968, 32 percent of companies polled had ethical codes. By 1970, 75 percent had such codes, and today well over 90 percent of the Fortune 500 companies have ethical codes of conduct. Indeed, such codes have become a permanent fixture in the business policy-making landscape.

What Are Ethical Codes?

In general, ethical codes provide employees with the knowledge of what the firm expects in terms of their responsibilities and behavior. Relationships that are covered include employee-employee, employee-manager, employee-consumer, and employee-supplier relationships. Some ethical codes offer a lengthy and detailed set of guidelines for employees. Others are not really "codes" at all but summary statements of goals, policies, and priorities.

The Pro Side of Ethical Codes

Do ethical codes work? Do they really result in more ethical behavior on the part of employees? Many believe that they do. A good example of the effectiveness of an ethical policy statement is the guidance offered by such a statement to employees of Johnson & Johnson Company (J&J) when that company was faced with a crisis in 1982.

The crisis arose when some of J&J's popular nonaspirin pain reliever, marketed under the name of Tylenol, was "spiked" with cyanide, causing the deaths of several persons in Chicago. When top management at J&J was informed of the problem, it immediately formed a committee to handle the crisis. Following the company's ethical guidelines, the committee created a set of priorities, the first one being to assure the safety of its customers. To this end, the committee recalled Tylenol from the market until the company could develop tamper-resistant packaging for its product. The second priority was to communicate openly with the buying public about what had happened and why it had happened. This was done through numerous press releases, press conferences, and printed statements, as well as television and radio interviews.

The third priority was to maintain J&J's goodwill and reputation.

Some thought, at the time, that J&J would never recover its former hegemony over the pain-reliever market. The doubters were wrong. Within only a few months, Tylenol had regained its former share of that market, because of the quick and open action on the part of J&J's top management in the face of the crisis.

The Con Side of Ethical Codes

Critics of ethical codes claim that many of them are simply legalistic documents that forbid specific actions. These critics contend that most ethical codes do not provide a set of guidelines based on ethical values for employees and management. Those ethical codes that do contain more than legalistic rules, they maintain, are often filled with platitudes rather than truly important ethical guidelines because the latter may concern sensitive issues.

Other critics contend that no matter how good an ethical code is, the code itself has little effect on the ethical attitudes and behavioral patterns of the company's employees. Rather, it is the example set by top management that promotes ethical (or nonethical) conduct by other members of the corporate family. Employees learn what acceptable norms of conduct are by observing top management's behavior.

For example, if management emphasizes meeting performance objectives at any cost, then employees will know that ethical considerations are being placed, implicitly, in a secondary role. Also, whenever employees are being treated unfairly, they may doubt whether the employer takes ethical considerations seriously. In such settings, it is difficult for a code of ethics to have any effective impact on workers' behavior.

■ Implications for the Businessperson

1. Businesspersons today have to face the fact that unethical behavior will no longer be excused on the premise that ''business will be business'' or ''it's legal, so it's okay.'' Indeed, today's businessperson benefits most by *preventive measures*—that is, by looking ahead of the law and anticipating problems (including potential court judgments or legislative restraints) that could result from unethical business practices. Paying attention to the ''ethical credentials'' of potential employees is one such preventive measure; training current employees in the goals and benefits of ethical behavior is another.

2. Top management in any corporation is well advised to develop a meaningful and appropriate code of ethics, to have it printed, to give every employee a copy, and, most importantly, to explain to employees the importance of ethics and how the specific components of the code relate to the company's overall ethical goals and policies.

3. Traditionally, business managers have framed their responsibilities in response to the firm's environment— particularly in response to consumer demand for their firms' products and the actions of competitors in the marketplace. Today's managers must also evaluate their decisions from the opposite perspective—that is, by looking at how the firm affects the environment in which it operates.

■ For Critical Analysis

1. In many countries, the giving of gifts and side payments in return for political or economic favors is a normal way of doing business. American businesspersons, however, are prohibited from bribing foreign officials to obtain contracts or other favorable treatment. Also, some countries encourage—and even legally require—discrimination in employment on the basis of religion, race, or gender, while

such employment discrimination is both unethical and illegal in America. Because of the increasingly international scope of business transactions, many efforts have been directed toward the creation of an effective international code of business ethics. Do the differences in ethical standards among nations mean that a workable international code of business conduct is an impossible dream?

2. To what extent do you believe that ethical codes are adopted simply to make firms look good in the eyes of their employees, shareholders, customers, and suppliers? Is it possible that even if an ethical code was adopted for this reason, it would still be a step in the right direction?

3. Analysts of ethical codes maintain that to be effective, an ethical code should relate to the specific business activities of the firm. But what about a huge conglomerate corporation that owns and ultimately directs the activities of numerous, completely diverse subsidiary companies? Is it possible to create a code of ethics that can apply to all employees in the conglomerate and yet be specific enough to offer practical and useful guidance to the employees?

work in an environment free of health-endangering hazards; they want to be treated fairly and equally by their employers; and, increasingly in recent years, they want employers to respect their personal integrity and privacy rights.

By law, employers are required to provide a safe workplace, to pay a minimum wage, and to provide equal employment opportunities for all potential and existing employees. But does an employer have ethical obligations to employees that go beyond those duties written into the law? This question was implicitly raised by the hypothetical situation discussed earlier in this chapter—in which an employer, Johnson, had to decide whether to close down an old, inefficient plant to increase the profitability of the firm. Johnson's dilemma represents a classic conflict between profit-making goals and perceived ethical duties to employees and, according to some, to the community at large. This conflict frequently faces businesspersons today and was dramatized in the film *Roger and Me,* which concerns the decision by General Motors to close its Flint, Michigan, plant.

"PRICE DISCRIMINATION" IN EMPLOYMENT

In recent years, some firms have been criticized for firing highly paid employees who have worked for—and received annual raises from—the firms for years and then replacing those employees with younger, less experienced persons who are happy to accept lower salaries. Such actions are not necessarily illegal. If the fired employee cannot prove that the employer has breached an employment contract or violated the Age Discrimination in Employment Act (ADEA), he or she will not have a cause of action against the employer. The ADEA prohibits discrimination against workers forty years old and older on the basis of their age, but employers can always say that lack of performance or ability, not age, was the deciding factor.

Increasingly, employers who want to shed older, highly paid employees are avoiding liability for age discrimination by offering the employees early retirement plans, financial incentives, and perhaps job-placement services—in return for a written waiver of the right to sue the firm for age discrimination. To ensure that employees are fully cognizant of the rights they are waiving, the Older Workers Benefit Protection Act, which went into effect in 1990, requires that employees be given

forty-five days to consider the waiver agreement and seven days to revoke the waiver after signing it. But from an ethical viewpoint, is it fair to long-time, loyal employees to force them to make a choice between early retirement and continuing on the job when the latter choice may involve a lower salary, a demotion to a less desirable position, or even eventual dismissal on the grounds of some "manufactured" reason other than age?

In deciding this issue, remember that if employers fail to keep their eyes on their profit margins, they may place in jeopardy the financial well-being of the firm. Why should a firm retain highly paid employees if it can obtain essentially the same work output for a lower price by hiring cheaper labor? Does an employer or manager owe an ethical duty to employees who have served the firm loyally over a long period of time? Most people would say yes. Should this duty take precedence over, say, a corporate manager's duty to the firm's owners to maintain or increase the profitability of the firm? Would your answer be the same if the firm faced imminent bankruptcy if it could not lower its operational costs? What if the long-time employees were willing to take a slight reduction in pay to help the firm through its financial difficulties? What if they were not?

THE COMPARABLE WORTH CONTROVERSY

The issue of **comparable worth** also pits profit-making goals against the duty to treat employees fairly and equally. In a nutshell, proponents of comparable worth standards think that employers should pay all employees on a comparable basis—by assessing "objectively" the value of each job classification and paying everybody with the same valuation the same amount of money. Typically, a panel of experts uses a point scale to assign a value to each job category. If, for example, a secretary is valued at 200 points and a truck driver is valued at 220 points, the truck driver's salary should be only 10 percent higher than that of the secretary.

Equal pay laws require equal pay for equal work—a male nurse, for example, must be paid the same salary as a female nurse doing the same job. But equal pay laws do not address the issue of comparable worth. The notion of comparable worth involves equality in pay not just for different persons holding the *same* kind of job but for different persons holding *different* kinds of jobs that require the same degree of education or training or effort. The comparable worth doctrine aims to correct the reality that male-dominated jobs still draw higher salaries than female-dominated jobs, even though the former may not require any more expertise or effort than the latter.

Does the employer have a moral obligation to correct for past discrimination against women by correcting the current inequities in female-male pay standards that have resulted from this discrimination? Those who say yes have to face the fact that this decision may be costly to the firm in terms of profits. This is because relative pay is determined largely by overall supply and demand conditions in the labor market. The quantity supplied of typists, for example, may be so great relative to the quantity demanded that their pay scale is 50 percent lower than that of truck drivers. If an employer adopts a comparable worth standard that requires typists to be paid only 10 percent less than truck drivers, that employer will face higher costs than competing firms who do not adopt a comparable worth pay scale. These higher costs will result in lower profits, which could jeopardize the firm's financial future. If the firm is a corporation, an additional ethical issue arises: Is it fair to divert profits from the shareholders to female employees?

EMPLOYMENT DISCRIMINATION As will be discussed in Chapter 48, by law employers must offer equal employment opportunities to all job applicants and employees. Today's employers are prohibited from discriminating against existing or potential employees on the basis of race, color, national origin, sex, pregnancy, religion, or age. Discrimination against the handicapped is also prohibited. This means that employers must sometimes treat employees unfairly and unequally. For example, many companies have adopted *affirmative action* policies to make up for past discriminatory practices against protected classes, such as minority groups or women. These policies occasionally result in what has been termed "reverse discrimination"—that is, discrimination against qualified members of the "majority" group. Essentially, the ethical question here is whether it is fair to promote a less qualified employee to a position instead of a more qualified employee simply to correct for past discrimination. Some would say yes; others, no. But the question indicates how employers who are trying to fulfill a perceived ethical obligation to treat employees fairly and equally can sometimes find themselves in a no-win situation.

The following case is illustrative. Even though the employer went substantially beyond minimum legal compliance in attempting to provide a safe workplace for employees, the firm was nonetheless charged by some of its employees with having violated another ethical (and legal) duty—that of providing equal employment opportunities for women.

BACKGROUND AND FACTS In an attempt to prevent possible injuries resulting from exposure to lead, Johnson Controls, Inc., prohibited women of childbearing age from working in its Battery Division. Johnson's policy was based on scientific studies indicating that a pregnant woman's exposure to high lead levels could harm the fetus and on the failure of the company's previous voluntary policy to protect pregnant women and their unborn children from dangerously high blood lead levels. Several employees and their union (United Automobile, Aerospace, and Agricultural Implements Workers of America) sued Johnson in federal district court, claiming that the policy violated Title VII of the Civil Rights Act of 1964, which prohibits discrimination in employment on the basis of sex. Johnson won at the trial level, and the employees and the union appealed. The United States Court of Appeals affirmed the trial court's ruling. The United States Supreme Court granted *certiorari*.

Case 2.1

UNITED AUTO WORKERS v. JOHNSON CONTROLS, INC.

Supreme Court of the
United States, 1991.
____ U.S. ____ ,
111 S.Ct. 1196,
113 L.Ed.2d 158.

DECISION AND RATIONALE The United States Supreme Court reversed the judgment of the appellate court and remanded the case for further proceedings. The Supreme Court held that Johnson's policy violated Title VII of the Civil Rights Act and its amendment, the Pregnancy Discrimination Act. The Court considered whether the policy represented an instance in which sex was a "bona fide occupational qualification." To be permissible, distinctions based on sex must relate to the ability to perform a job. Under the Pregnancy Discrimination Act, unless pregnant employees differ from others in their ability to work, they must be "treated the same" as other employees. The Court concluded that "[f]ertile women, as far as appears in the record, participate in the manufacture of batteries as efficiently as anyone else."

OTHER EMPLOYMENT ISSUES An increasingly significant ethical issue in the employment context concerns the privacy rights of employees. To what extent, for example, may employers engage in drug testing, integrity testing, performance monitoring, or other procedures before violating an employee's right to privacy? Another ethical problem arises when an employee is asked to "look the other way" when faced with unethical or illegal practices in the workplace. Should the employee "blow the whistle" on the employer by informing the press or a government agency of the activity—when the consequences would, in all probability, mean losing his or her job? What if the employee's family has no other source of income? What if the employee is older and faces few prospects of finding another job with an equivalent salary? If the employee is not asked to participate directly in any illegal act, does he or she have an ethical responsibility to act? These and other employment-related issues will be discussed in Chapter 48.

Consumer Welfare

Manufacturers and sellers have not only an ethical duty to provide safe products but a legal one as well. During the course of the twentieth century, numerous laws have been enacted to protect the consumer against defective or harmful products. A manufacturer that markets a defective product that is unreasonably dangerous to users may be held liable for any resulting injury to a consumer. (Product liability is discussed in more detail in Chapter 23.)

The law, however, has its limits. For example, no law prohibits a corporation from producing and distributing a food product just because it is not nutritious. If a firm markets, say, a type of baby food that babies like and mothers buy but that is not nutritionally satisfactory for babies because of a high MSG (monosodium glutamate) or sugar content, the law will not intervene, nor could a consumer successfully sue the manufacturer for marketing an unsafe product. Thus, the decision to market the food does not violate the law, but it does raise an ethical question.

A case in point is the Nestlé controversy, which arose in the 1970s over the Nestlé Company's distribution of a baby formula in Third World countries. Mothers frequently mixed the infant formula with impure water or excessively diluted it to make it last longer. As a result, babies suffered from malnutrition, diarrhea, and in some cases even death. By 1974, Nestlé was being accused of "killing babies" by marketing its formula in Third World nations. Although other companies pulled out of the market, Nestlé continued to distribute its product to those countries. In defense of its action, Nestlé argued that the availability of the formula freed mothers from the task of breastfeeding and thus allowed them to earn money to help raise their income and standard of living. Besides, Nestlé claimed, mothers who drank impure water would pass on these impurities to the babies while breastfeeding anyway. In general, Nestlé's defense rested on a cost-benefit analysis from which Nestlé concluded that the social benefits of the formula outweighed the social costs. Nestlé's opponents were ethically outraged, not because the formula had been marketed initially, but because of Nestlé's utilitarian defense for refusing to leave the market once it was learned that the product, from ignorance or for other reasons, was being misused and harming babies.

There are other situations in which, although it may be legal to market a given product, the ethics of doing so might be called into question. In the case presented below, for example, the Honda Motor Company warned those who purchased its mini-bike of the dangers that could result if the product was not used as directed. The case is representative of numerous situations in which consumer misuse of products leads to harms and injuries. If a court concludes—as it did in this case— that the manufacturer has adequately warned consumers of the possible dangers of product misuse,

the manufacturer may escape liability for these harms. Nonetheless, there are some who feel that manufacturers should be legally compelled to withdraw from the market products that are capable of seriously injuring consumers, even if the injuries result from consumer misuse. At the least, these people would hold that Honda's continued marketing of its mini-bike violated that firm's ethical responsibility to consumers.

BACKGROUND AND FACTS Two eight-year-old boys were injured while riding a Honda trail bike on a public street. The bike had a prominent warning label stating

> READ OWNER'S MANUAL CAREFULLY. THIS VEHICLE WAS MANUFACTURED FOR OFF-THE-ROAD USE ONLY. DO NOT OPERATE ON PUBLIC STREETS, ROADS OR HIGHWAYS.

Douglas Bratz, the boy driving the bike, was operating it carelessly. He had run three stop signs and was looking behind him when the bike collided with a truck. The owner's manual urged operators to "Always Wear a Helmet." Bratz was wearing a helmet, but it was not fastened and flew off when the accident occurred. Bradley Baughn, the other boy, was not wearing a helmet. The parents of the boys sued Honda in Washington state court, claiming that the bike was unreasonably dangerous. Honda argued that it had sufficiently warned consumers of potential dangers. The trial court granted Honda's motion for summary judgment.[a] The parents appealed.

DECISION AND RATIONALE On appeal, the Washington Supreme Court affirmed. The court pointed out that "a manufacturer may be held liable for manufacturing a defective product if that product is not reasonably safe. 'This means that it must be unsafe to an extent beyond that which would be reasonably contemplated by the ordinary consumer.' " The court agreed with a comment accompanying Section 402A of the Restatement (Second) of Torts: "Where warning is given, the seller may reasonably assume that it will be read and heeded; and a product bearing such a warning, which is safe for use if it is followed, is not in defective condition, nor is it unreasonably dangerous." The court concluded that although Honda did not warn of "every conceivable danger," it did state that the bikes were intended for off-the-road use and that helmets should be worn.

Case 2.2

BAUGHN v. HONDA MOTOR CO.

Supreme Court of Washington, 1986.
107 Wash.2d 127,
727 P.2d 655.

a. A summary judgment is a judgment entered by a trial court before trial, based on the valid assertion by one of the parties that there are no disputed issues of fact that necessitate a trial.

■ International Perspectives

As American business becomes increasingly global in scope, so also do ethical considerations.

Today's business leaders and decision makers must consider such political issues as human rights in other countries. Firms must decide, for example, whether they should profit from business with—and thus lend economic support to—foreign governments that oppress their citizens. Additionally, in undertaking international transactions, business executives need to be aware of the economic and cultural differences between nations. In the Nestlé controversy discussed above, for example, the marketing of the baby formula in the United States and other economically advanced nations posed no problems. It did cause a problem in the Third World, however, because of the different economic and cultural circumstances of consumers in less-developed nations.

Another example of how differences among nations can affect business decisions is the custom of bribing government officials. In many countries, the practice of bribing officials to gain favorable treatment or lucrative business contracts is not considered unethical—indeed, in many nations it is simply considered to be another cost of doing business. In the United States, however, such bribery is deemed unethical; indeed, it was prohibited by law in 1977 with the Foreign Corrupt Practices Act (see Chapter 56). The effect of this law on Americans doing business abroad is, of course, that it places American businesspersons at a competitive disadvantage relative to foreign businesspersons who are not so constrained in their tactics.

◼ An Ever-Changing Ethical Landscape

It is important to remember that our sense of what is ethical—what is fair or just or right in a given situation—varies not only from individual to individual and from group to group but also over time. Business conduct that might have been considered socially responsible a decade or two ago might not be considered ethical today. Indeed, most of the major ethical and social issues discussed in this chapter and elsewhere in this text either did not exist or were of little public concern at the turn of this century. The ethical businessperson not only seeks to clarify his or her own personal ethical standards but also strives to be aware of the ethical concerns of others in society and to consider those concerns when making business decisions.

◼ Terms and Concepts

business ethics 25	ethics 25	*per se* 30
comparable worth 36	externalities 32	tradeoff 32
cost-benefit analysis 29	*laissez-faire* 31	utilitarianism 29

◼ For Review

1. Why is ethical decision making in the business world more complicated than decision making in one's personal life?
2. What are the three primary considerations in any business manager's decision making?
3. What are the initial steps in the ethical decision-making process?
4. Katek Electronics Company has to decide whether to take steps to correct existing inequities in pay that have resulted from past discrimination. What factors might Katek consider in making this decision?
5. LC Pharmaceutical Corp. has to decide whether to market a new headache remedy that may cause serious injury to some users. In doing so, LC may weigh the costs of the injuries against the benefits of marketing the product. If the benefits are greater than the costs, can marketing the product be ethically justified, considering the effect on the consumers who will be injured? Discuss fully.

◼ Questions and Case Problems

2-1. Coach Sharon Youngblood works as an athletic coach and recruiter for State University. Athletic competitions and the recruitment of athletes require Sharon to do a great deal of traveling. The university reimburses Sharon for her travel expenses. Sharon joined a frequent-flyer program and has been receiving credit for her business travels as athletic coach.

Solely because of the mileage accumulated from her business travels, Sharon will soon be eligible for a free trip anywhere in the continental United States. She very much wants to travel to Miami, Florida, over her Christmas vacation to visit her daughter and family. Sharon is considering using her free ticket for this personal trip but is not sure whether it would be ethical to do so. Analyze Sharon's ethical responsibilities in this situation.

2-2. John Landers works as a computer programmer for IBC—a large New York company. John is from humble beginnings and was lucky to get the job he has through an old roommate's father. John would like to be an artist, but he knows that he could never earn a living by pursuing his artistic ambitions. John has several friends who are "starving artists," and he is convinced that society oppresses talent rather than encourages it. Through his work at IBC, John learns of a proposed merger and decides to tell his artist friends about it—even though disclosing to outsiders this "inside information" is against the law—so they can make enough money to live on while pursuing their artistic careers. John views his decision as perfectly acceptable because it is simply a way for creative people to survive in an unfair society. Is John's behavior ethical? Why or why not?

2-3. Dagmar Hollifield is a scientific genius. He works for Toys 'n' Stuff creating mechanical devices. Hollifield created an entire war simulation game, complete with robot armies. Each robot can shoot its own ammunition. The game was approved by the company's board of directors, and plans were made to produce and market the game in time to profit from the Christmas rush. Just before the date on which the game was to be distributed on the market, Hollifield developed a safety mechanism for the robot. The safety mechanism would make the product much safer for children to use, and the manufacturing cost involved in adding the safety feature would be minimal. Hollifield told his immediate supervisor about the safety device, but the supervisor told him to keep quiet about it so that production and distribution could continue as planned. Should Hollifield tell someone higher on the management ladder about the safety device? What ethical considerations face Hollifield in making this decision?

2-4. Susan Whitehead serves on the City Planning Commission. The city is planning to build a new subway system and is accepting bids on the proposal. Susan's brother-in-law, Jerry, who owns the Custom Transportation Co., has submitted the lowest bid for the system. The Transportation-We-Make-It Co. has submitted a slightly higher bid. Susan knows that Jerry could complete the job for the estimated amount, but she also knows that if Jerry gets and completes this job he will have enough money to sell his company and quit working. Susan is concerned that Custom Transportation's subsequent management might not be as easy to work with if revisions need to be made on the subway system after its completion. She is torn as to whether she should tell the city about the potential changes in Custom Transportation management. If the city knew about the instability of Custom Transportation, it might prefer to give the contract to Transportation-We-Make-It, whose bid was higher than Custom Transportation's bid by only an insignificant amount. Does Susan have an ethical obligation to disclose the information about Jerry to the City Planning Commission? Discuss.

2-5. Beverly Landrine's infant daughter died after the baby swallowed a balloon while playing with a doll known as "Bubble Yum Baby." When a balloon was inserted into the doll's mouth and the doll's arm was pumped, thereby inflating the balloon, the doll simulated the blowing of a bubble gum bubble. The balloon was made by Perfect Product Co. and distributed by Mego Corp. Landrine brought a suit against the manufacturer and distributor, alleging that the balloon was defectively made or inherently unsafe when used by children and that Perfect had failed to warn of the danger associated with the balloon's use. Discuss whether the producer and distributor of the balloon should be held liable for the harm caused by its product. [*Landrine v. Mego Corp.,* 464 N.Y.S.2d 516, 95 A.D.2d 759 (1983)]

2-6. John Novosel was an employee of Nationwide Insurance Co. for almost fifteen years. He was never reprimanded or disciplined, and he rose steadily through the company's ranks. Toward the end of his tenure, the company circulated a memo requesting employees to assist Nationwide's lobbying efforts in the Pennsylvania House of Representatives. Specifically, employees were asked to collect signatures for a petition urging changes in Pennsylvania's no-fault insurance laws. Novosel refused. Privately, he told others that he did not agree with the company's position. Within a few weeks, he was fired. He filed suit. Pennsylvania law prohibits an employment discharge that "abridges a significant and recognized public policy." Novosel argued that "a significant and recognized public policy" could be derived from the important political freedoms expressed in the Pennsylvania Constitution and the First Amendment of the U.S. Constitution. May an employer's power to hire and fire be used to dictate an employee's political activities? Discuss. [*Novosel v. Nationwide Insurance Co.,* 721 F.2d 894 (3d Cir. 1983)]

2-7. George Geary was employed by the United States Steel Corp. to sell tubular products to the oil and gas industry. Geary believed that one of the company's new products, a tubular casing, had not been adequately tested and constituted a serious danger to anyone who used it. Even though Geary at all times performed his duties to the best of his ability, he continued to express his reservations with respect to the company's new product. Geary alleged that because of his complaints, he was summarily discharged without notice. Given these facts, and in view of the fact that Geary was not a safety expert and had bypassed ordinary company procedures in his complaints, address the following questions. [*Geary v. United States Steel Corp.,* 456 Pa. 171, 319 A.2d 174 (1974)]

    (a) Did the employer act wrongfully in discharging Geary?

    (b) Did Geary have an ethical duty to complain about the company's product?

    (c) Did the employer's need to maintain internal administrative order and harmony in the company outweigh its duty to do all it could to ensure product safety? Suppose that you were a manager and Geary raised the matter with you. How would you act and what ethical factors would influence your decision?

2-8. In 1984, the General Telephone Co. of Illinois, Inc., (GTE) for reasons of efficiency, decided to consolidate its nationwide operations and eliminate unnecessary job positions. One of the positions eliminated was one held by John Burnell, a fifty-two-year-old employee who had worked for GTE for thirty-four years and had always received "above average" performance ratings. GTE offered Burnell the choice of either accepting another position within the firm at the same salary or accepting early retirement with a salary continuation for a certain period of time. Burnell did not want to retire, but he was afraid that if he did accept the other position and if the other position were then also eliminated, he might not then have the choice of early retirement with the same separation benefit. Because he received no assurances that the other job would be secure in the future, he accepted the early-retirement alternative. Burnell alleged that he had been "constructively discharged" because GTE had made his working conditions so intolerable that he was forced to resign. Had GTE constructively discharged Burnell? Can GTE's actions toward Burnell be justified from an ethical standpoint? Discuss. [*Burnell v. General Telephone Co. of Illinois, Inc.,* 181 Ill.App.3d 533, 536 N.E.2d 1387, 130 Ill.Dec. 176 (1989)]

2-9. A Question of Ethics

On July 5, 1884, Dudley, Stephens, and Brooks—"all able-bodied English seamen"—and an English boy between seventeen and eighteen years of age were cast adrift in a lifeboat following a storm at sea that occurred when they were some sixteen hundred miles from the Cape of Good Hope. The lifeboat was not stocked with food and water, and all they had for sustenance were two one-pound tins of turnips. On July 24, Dudley proposed that one of the four in the lifeboat be sacrificed to save the others. Stephens agreed with Dudley, but Brooks refused to consent—and the boy was never asked for his opinion. On July 25, Dudley killed the boy, and the three men then fed upon the boy's body and blood. Four days later, the men were rescued by a passing vessel. They were taken to the port of Falmouth in England and committed for trial at Exeter for the murder of the boy. If the men had not fed upon the boy's body, they would have probably died of famine within the four-day period. The boy, who was in a much weaker condition, would likely have died before the rest. [Regina v. Dudley and Stephens, 14 Q.B.D.[Queen's Bench Division, England] 273 (1884)]

1. This problem is similar to *The Case of the Speluncean Explorers,* the hypothetical case discussed in Chapter 1. The basic question in that case, as here, is whether the survivors should be subject to penalties under the criminal law given the men's unusual circumstances. You be the judge and decide the issue. Give the reasons for your decisions.

2. Solely from an ethical point of view, had the men acted wrongfully? Evaluate their actions from the three ethical perspectives—religious, Kantian, and utilitarian—discussed in this chapter. Do the different ethical approaches yield different conclusions? If so, in what way?

Chapter 3

Courts and Civil Dispute Resolution

Today in the United States there are fifty-two separate court systems. Each of the fifty states, in addition to the District of Columbia, has its own fully developed, independent system of courts. Additionally, there is a separate federal court system. It is important to understand that the federal court system taken as a whole is not necessarily superior to the state courts. The federal courts simply are an independent system set up to handle matters of particular federal interest and authorized by Article III, Section 2, of the United States Constitution. The federal court system extends beyond the boundaries of the United States to U.S. territories such as Guam, the Virgin Islands, and Puerto Rico. (In Guam and the Virgin Islands, territorial courts serve as both federal and state courts, whereas in Puerto Rico they serve only as federal courts.) U.S. territorial courts are established by Congress, by its authority under Article I of the U.S. Constitution. As we shall see, the United States Supreme Court is the final controlling voice over all these fifty-two systems, at least when questions of federal law are involved.

This chapter examines both the state and the federal court systems and then follows a typical case through the courts. Remember that an important step in the use of the courts or in the process of adjudication is *determining which rules apply to the facts in the case.* These rules can be *substantive* or *procedural.* They may come from several sources and can cover several areas of the law.

In studying the courts and their procedures, the first question should be which courts have the power to decide a particular case—that is, which courts have jurisdiction.

■ Jurisdiction

Juris means ''law''; *diction* means ''to speak.'' Thus, ''the power to speak the law'' is the literal meaning of the term **jurisdiction.** Before any court can hear a case, it must have jurisdiction—that is, the power to hear and decide the case. Without jurisdiction, a court cannot exercise any authority in the case. For a court to exercise valid authority, it must have jurisdiction both over the person against whom the suit is brought or the property involved in the suit and over the subject matter of the case.

In personam and *In rem* Jurisdiction

Before it can consider a case, a court must have power over the *person* or the *property* involved in the action. Power over the person is often referred to as **in personam jurisdiction.** *In personam* jurisdiction is required before a court can enter a personal judgment against a party to the action. This type of jurisdiction may be contrasted with **in rem jurisdiction.** An *in rem* proceeding is taken directly against property. In an *in rem* proceeding, for example, a court may use property within a state to help satisfy a general debt.

In all cases in which a court exercises jurisdiction, the parties must be served with notice that they are involved in a suit. The parties may receive actual notice (usually by service of a summons), or, when the parties cannot be located, notice may be published in a newspaper or in some other manner if permitted by statute.

Generally, a court's power is limited to the territorial boundaries of the state in which it is located. Thus, a court has jurisdiction over the person of anyone who can be served with a summons within those boundaries. Additionally, the court has jurisdiction over a person who is a resident of the state or does business within the state. Finally, in some cases in which an individual has committed a wrong, such as causing an automobile injury or selling defective goods within the state, a court can exercise jurisdiction using the authority of a *long arm statute,* even if the individual is outside the state. A **long arm statute** is a state law permitting courts to obtain jurisdiction over nonresident defendants. A court can further exercise jurisdiction over a corporation in the state in which it is incorporated, in the state in which it has its main plant or office, and in any state in which it does business.[1]

Subject Matter Jurisdiction

Subject matter jurisdiction involves a limitation on types of cases a court can hear. **Probate courts** that handle only matters relating to wills and estates offer a common example of limited subject matter jurisdiction. The subject matter jurisdiction of a court is usually defined in the statute or constitution that created the court. A court's subject matter jurisdiction can be limited not only by the subject of the lawsuit but also by the amount of money in controversy, by whether a case is civil or criminal, and by whether the proceeding is a trial or an appeal. Courts that have limited jurisdiction are sometimes said to have "special" jurisdiction.

The distinction between courts of general jurisdiction and courts of limited jurisdiction lies in the subject matter of cases heard. A court of general jurisdiction can decide virtually any type of case, including some cases that involve matters of federal law. Every state has courts of general jurisdiction, which may be called county courts, circuit courts, district courts, or some other name. On the other hand, at both federal and state levels there are courts that hear only cases of limited subject matter. For example, one court may handle only cases dealing with divorce or child custody. Another may handle disputes over relatively small amounts of money (a small claims court). Courts of general jurisdiction will not handle cases that are appropriate for these courts of limited jurisdiction.

Original and Appellate Jurisdiction

The distinction between courts of original jurisdiction and courts of appellate jurisdiction normally lies in whether the case is being heard for the first time. Courts having original jurisdiction are those of the first instance. In other words, they are the courts in which the trial of a case begins. In contrast, courts having appellate jurisdiction act as reviewing courts. In general, cases can be brought to them only on appeal from an order or a judgment of a lower court.

■ Venue

Jurisdiction is concerned with whether a court has authority over a specific subject matter or individual. **Venue,**[2] in contrast, is concerned with the

---

1. For an example of the minimum contacts required for a court to exercise jurisdiction over a corporation that is not based within its state, see *International Shoe Co. v. State of Washington,* 326 U.S. 310, 66 S.Ct. 154, 90 L.Ed. 95 (1945). This case is presented in Chapter 40 as Case 40.1.

---

2. Pronounced *ven*-yoo.

county or city in which a court with jurisdiction may hear and determine a case. Venue is a question that arises after a determination of jurisdiction. A particular court may have jurisdiction but not venue.

Basically, the concept of venue reflects the policy that a court trying a suit should be in the geographic neighborhood in which the incident leading to the suit occurred or in which the litigating parties reside. That neighborhood is usually the county in which the incident occurred or in which the parties live. Pretrial publicity or other factors may, however, require a change of venue to another community, especially in criminal cases, if the defendant's right to a fair and impartial jury is impaired.

The proper venue for a suit is defined by statute. Sometimes the parties to a contract designate in the contract the venue in which any future contractual disputes will be heard. Improper venue does not deprive the court of power to hear a case, but a party can request a change of venue if the venue is not proper.

■ Standing to Sue

Standing is a jurisdictional issue that affects the power of courts to hear and decide cases. A party that has *standing to sue* has a sufficient "stake" in a controversy to seek judicial resolution of it. In other words, a party must have a legally protectible and tangible interest at stake in the litigation to have standing. The party must have been injured or been threatened with injury by the action about which he or she complained.

The question is whether the **litigant**—an active party in a lawsuit—is the proper party to fight the suit, not whether the matter at issue is *justiciable.* (A **justiciable controversy** is real and substantial, as opposed to hypothetical or academic.) To illustrate: A conservation organization wanted to challenge a government agency's approval of locating a ski complex near a national wilderness area. Before the court would consider whether the challenge involved justiciable issues, the organization needed to show that it was a proper party to bring the suit. To show that it was a proper party—that is, to show that it had standing—the organization alleged that some of its members used, hiked in, and enjoyed the wilderness area that the devel-

opment threatened. The organization also alleged that the ski complex compromised these members' enjoyment of the area.[3]

■ A Typical State Court System

Most state court systems are based on a three-tiered model. Any person who is a party to a lawsuit typically has the opportunity to plead the case before a trial court and then, if he or she loses, before two levels of appellate courts. Consider the typical state court system represented in Exhibit 3–1. It has three main tiers: (1) state trial courts of general or limited jurisdiction, (2) the state appellate court or courts, and (3) the state supreme court. If a federal constitutional issue is involved in the decision of the state supreme court, yet another level may be added: the decision may be appealed to the United States Supreme Court.

One can view the typical state system, then, as being made up of trial courts and appellate courts (also called courts of appeals or reviewing courts).

Trial Courts

Trial courts are exactly what their name implies—courts in which trials are held and testimony is taken. Trial courts may be courts of record, in which case a written record is taken, or courts not of record. Today, most are courts of record. Every state has trial courts that have original jurisdiction. Most states have trial courts of both limited and general jurisdiction.

Trial courts that have *limited jurisdiction* as to subject matter are often called special inferior trial courts or minor judiciary courts. Some typical courts of limited jurisdiction are **domestic relations courts,** which handle only divorce actions and child custody cases; local **municipal courts,** which handle mainly traffic cases; probate courts, which handle the administration of wills and estate settlement problems; and **small claims courts** and **justice of the peace courts.** Typically, the minor judiciary courts do not keep complete written records of trial proceedings.

Trial courts that have *general jurisdiction* as to subject matter may be called county, district,

---

3. *Sierra Club v. Morton,* 348 F.Supp. 219 (N.D.Cal. 1972).

■ **Exhibit 3–1 A Typical State Court System**

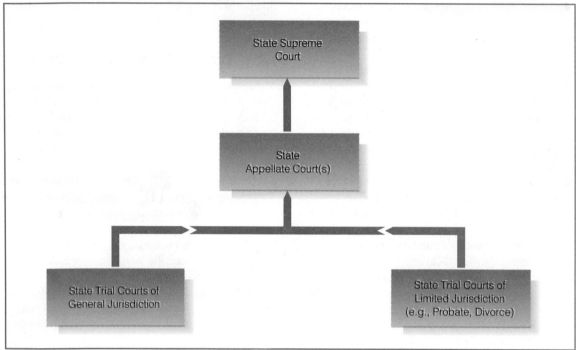

superior, or circuit courts.[4] General-jurisdiction trial courts have authority to hear and decide cases involving nearly every subject matter. These courts of general jurisdiction may be supplemented by the courts of limited jurisdiction, or minor judiciary courts, discussed above.

At the trial level, the parties to a controversy may dispute the particular facts, what law should be applied to those facts, and how that law should be applied. Generally, with some exceptions, as discussed below, it may be said that judges decide **questions of law** and juries decide **questions of fact.** If a party is entitled to and requests a trial by jury, the appropriate issues will be tried before a jury at the trial level, not on appeal. In an appeal, what is at issue is the initial tribunal's legal procedures and application of the law to the facts.

Appellate Courts

Appellate courts, or courts of review, are not usually trial courts—although in some states trial

courts of general jurisdiction also have limited jurisdiction to hear appeals from the minor judiciary (for example, small claims and traffic cases).

Every state has at least one appellate court. The jurisdiction of these courts is substantially limited to hearing appeals. Many states have intermediate reviewing courts and one court at the highest level. The intermediate appellate court is often called the court of appeals. The highest court of the state is normally called the supreme court.[5] Appellate courts try few cases. Most appellate courts have multijudge panels that examine the record of the case on appeal and determine whether the trial court committed an error. They look at questions of law and procedure, not questions of fact. The only time an appellate court looks at a trial court's finding of fact is when the finding is clearly erroneous (that is, when it is contrary to the evidence presented at trial) or when there is no evidence to support the finding. The decisions of each state's

---

4. The name in Ohio is Court of Common Pleas; the name in New York is Supreme Court, Trial Division; the name in Massachusetts is Trial Court.

5. In New York, Maryland, and the District of Columbia, it is called the Court of Appeals. In Maine and Massachusetts, it is called the Supreme Judicial Court. In West Virginia, it is called the Supreme Court of Appeals.

highest court in all questions of state law are final. It is only when questions of federal law are involved that a state's highest court can be overruled by the United States Supreme Court.

■ The Federal Court System

The federal court system is similar in many ways to most state court systems. It is also a three-tiered model consisting of (1) trial courts, (2) intermediate courts of appeals, and (3) the Supreme Court. Exhibit 3–2 shows the organization of the federal court system.

All federal judges and justices, including the nine justices of the United States Supreme Court, are appointed by the president, with the advice and consent of the Senate. Federal district and appellate court judges and United States Supreme Court justices receive lifetime appointments (because under Article III of the U.S. Constitution they "hold their Offices during good Behaviour").

U.S. District Courts

At the federal level, the equivalent of a state trial court of general jurisdiction is the district court. In fact, United States district courts are often referred to as federal trial courts. There is at least one federal

district court in every state. The number of judicial districts is determined by Congress and varies over time, primarily because of population changes and corresponding case loads. Thus, a state can comprise a single district or be divided into several districts. When there are two or more district courts within a state, the geographical jurisdiction in each court is limited. The state of Florida, for example, has district courts for northern, middle, and southern Florida.

In the Judicial Improvements Act of 1990, Congress took the opportunity to increase the total number of federal judgeships in the United States. The law provides for 629 district court judgeships within the ninety-six judicial districts.[6]

U.S. district courts have original jurisdiction in federal matters. In other words, district courts are the courts in which most federal cases originate. There are other trial courts with original, albeit limited, jurisdiction, in federal matters. These include the U.S. Tax Court, the U.S. Bankruptcy Courts, and the U.S. Claims Court (which hears suits against the United States). Certain adminis-

---

6. See Sections 44(a) and 133 of Title 28 of the United States Code.

■ Exhibit 3–2 A Simplified Organization of the Federal Court System

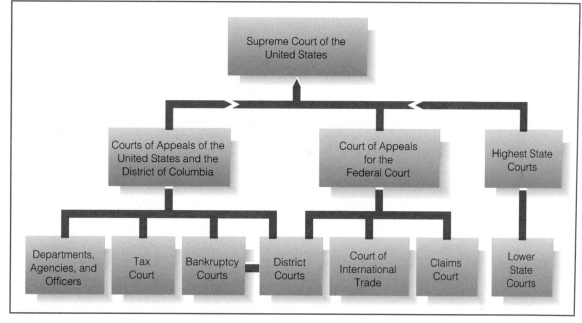

trative agencies and departments having judicial power also have original jurisdiction.

U.S. Courts of Appeals

Congress has established twelve judicial circuits. Each of the fifty states, the District of Columbia, and the territories are assigned to one of these circuits. The circuit courts (U.S. courts of appeals, or U.S. circuit courts of appeals) hear appeals from the district courts located within their respective circuits. The decisions of the courts of appeals are final in most cases, but appeal to the United States Supreme Court is possible. Appeals from federal administrative agencies, such as the Federal Trade Commission, are made directly to the U.S. courts of appeals.

There is also a thirteenth circuit, the federal circuit, which was created by the Federal Courts Improvement Act of 1982. The federal circuit court of appeals, unlike the other U.S. courts of appeals, has *national* jurisdiction over certain types of subject matter. It hears appeals involving special topics such as public contracts, patents, international trade, and other matters in which the uniform application of legal principles on a nationwide basis is highly desirable.

Judicial opinions on cases heard in one of the U.S. courts of appeals are binding on the federal courts within that jurisdiction, but they are not binding on courts in other circuits. Other circuits can use such opinions as precedents if they wish, but they are not legally bound to do so. Exhibit 3–3 shows the geographical boundaries of U.S. district courts and U.S. courts of appeals.

The law provides for 191 appellate court judgeships within the thirteen circuits, and each of the nine justices of the United States Supreme Court is a circuit justice. Courts of appeals normally hear cases in panels consisting of three judges, although the court may sit *en banc* (from the French, "on the bench"). Cases heard *en banc* require that all judges be present, rather than the usual quorum. In the federal circuit court of appeals, judges also sit in panels of three or more in each case and may also hear or rehear a case *en banc*.

The Supreme Court of the United States

The highest level of the three-tiered model of the federal court system is the United States Supreme Court. According to the language of Article III of the U.S. Constitution, there is only one Supreme Court. All other courts in the federal system are considered "inferior." Congress is empowered to create such other inferior courts as it deems necessary. Thus, according to this language, the inferior courts that Congress has created include the second tier in our model (the U.S. courts of appeals), as well as the first tier (the district courts and any other courts of limited jurisdiction).

The Supreme Court was created by the U.S. Constitution. Although it has original, or trial, jurisdiction in rare instances, set forth in Article III, Section 2, most of its work is as an appeals court. The Supreme Court can review any case decided by any of the federal courts of appeals, and it also has appellate authority over some cases decided in the state courts.

■ Judicial Review

A problem often arises as to whether a law is contrary to the mandates of the Constitution. **Judicial review** is the process for resolving such a problem. The term *judicial review* means that the judicial branch of the government has the authority and power to determine if a particular law violates the Constitution. Thus, any state or federal court may refuse to enforce a statute that it concludes is in violation of the U.S. Constitution. Assuming the jurisdictional criteria are satisfied, both state and federal courts may rule on the validity of state and federal statutes and executive acts. Also, federal courts may rule that provisions of state constitutions are unconstitutional under the U.S. Constitution.

The power of judicial review was first established in *Marbury v. Madison*. In determining that the United States Supreme Court had the power to decide that a law passed by Congress violated the Constitution, the Court stated:

> It is emphatically the province and duty of the Judicial Department to say what the law is. Those who apply the rule to a particular case, must of necessity expound and interpret that rule. If two laws conflict with each other, the courts must decide on the operation of each.
>
> So if the law be in opposition to the Constitution, if both the law and the Constitution apply to a particular case, so that the court must either decide that

■ **Exhibit 3–3 United States Courts of Appeals and United States District Courts**

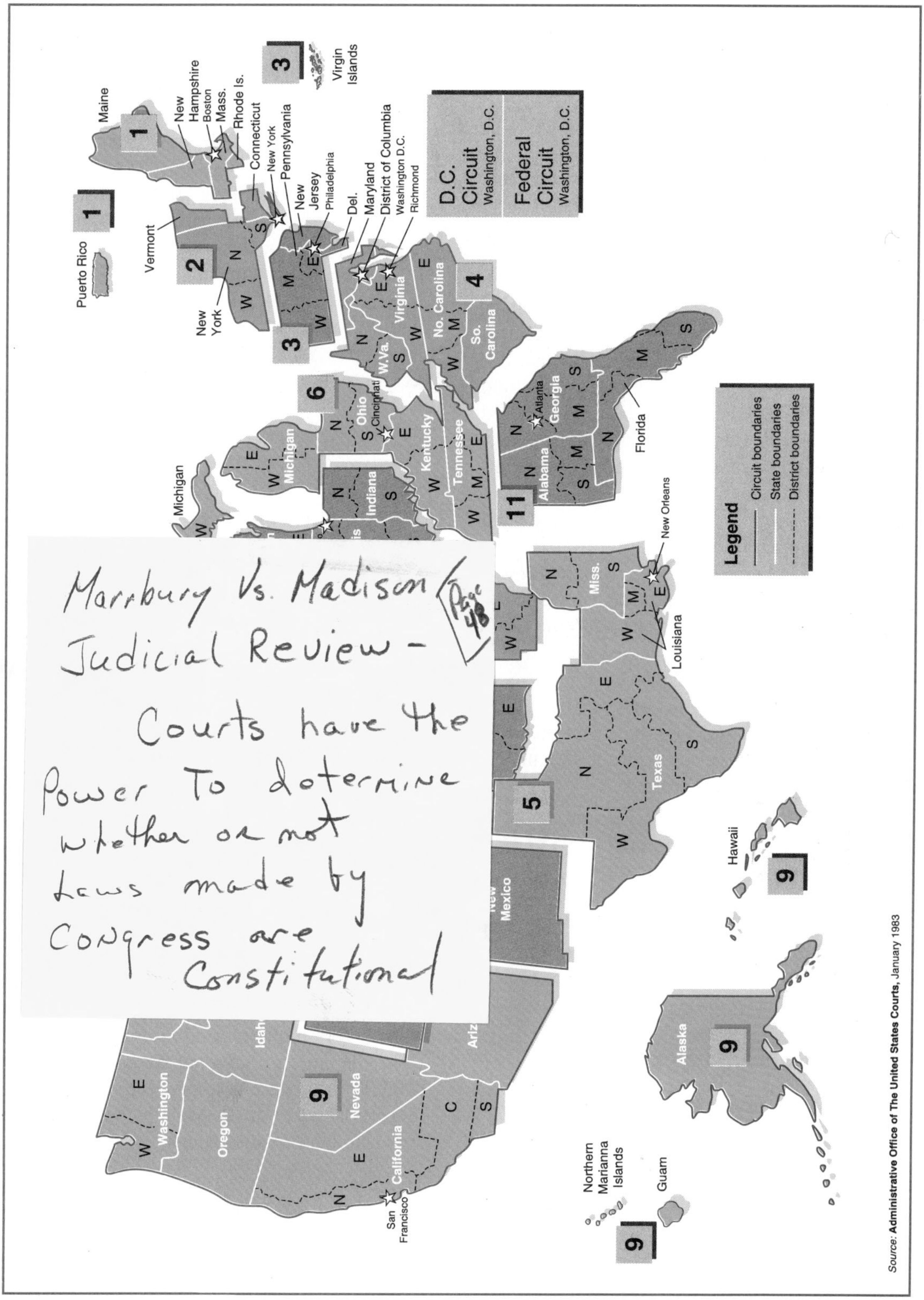

Source: Administrative Office of The United States Courts, January 1983

Marrbury Vs. Madison Page 48

Judicial Review –

Courts have the power To determine whether or not Laws made by Congress are Constitutional case conformably to the law, disregarding the Constitution; or conformably to the Constitution, disregarding the law; the court must determine which of these conflicting rules governs the case. This is of the very essence of judicial duty.

If, then, the courts were to regard the Constitution and the Constitution is superior to any ordinary Act of the Legislature, the Constitution, and not such ordinary Act, must govern the case to which they both apply.[7]

In another famous case, *United States v. Nixon*,[8] the United States Supreme Court established its power over actions of the president. In 1974, a grand jury indicted seven individuals for obstruction of justice and conspiracy to defraud (among other things). President Nixon was ordered by the special prosecutor to produce tapes, memoranda, papers, and transcripts. The president attempted to avoid the subpoena on the ground of "executive privilege," but this ground was denied him by the district court.

The president's view of the privilege was broad, and he claimed the courts lacked the power to demand the records sought. The Supreme Court subsequently heard the case, denied the claim of executive privilege that was at the heart of the controversy, and affirmed the order of the district court. Among other things, the Court balanced the president's claim against the needs of the defendants and the courts to have the records.

◼ Jurisdiction of the Federal Courts

Because the federal government is a government of limited powers, the jurisdiction of the federal courts is limited.

The Constitutional Boundaries of Federal Judicial Power

Section 1 of Article III states that "The judicial Power of the United States shall be vested in one

supreme Court and in such inferior Courts as the Congress may from time to time ordain and establish." Section 2 states that "The judicial Power shall extend to all Cases in Law and Equity arising under this Constitution, the Laws of the United States, and Treaties made, or which shall be made, under their Authority."

In line with the checks and balances system of the federal government, Congress has the power to control the number and kind of inferior courts in the federal system. Congress can also regulate the appellate jurisdiction of the United States Supreme Court. Although the Constitution sets the outer limits of federal judicial power, Congress can set other limits on federal jurisdiction. Furthermore, the courts themselves can promulgate rules that further narrow the types of cases they will hear.

Federal Questions

"The judicial Power shall extend to all cases . . . arising under this Constitution, the Laws of the United States and Treaties made . . . under their Authority." This statement from Article III, Section 2, of the Constitution defines a **federal question** as a cause of action based, at least in part, on the U.S. Constitution, a treaty, or a federal law. Such cases come under the judicial power of federal courts. People whose claims are based on rights granted by an act of Congress can sue in a federal court. People who claim that their constitutional rights have been violated can begin their suits in federal court. For example, a woman who believes that her employer has discriminated against her in violation of a federal law may sue the employer in a federal court.

Any lawsuit involving a federal question can originate in a federal court. As will be discussed below, in lawsuits involving *diversity of citizenship*, the amount in controversy must exceed $50,000 if the case is to proceed in federal court. In federal question cases, however, there is no dollar-amount requirement.

Diversity of Citizenship

Article III, Section 2 of the Constitution establishes another basis for federal district court jurisdiction:

---

7. 5 U.S. (1 Cranch) 137, 2 L.Ed. 60 (1803).
8. 418 U.S. 683, 94 S.Ct. 3090, 41 L.Ed.2d 1039 (1974); *certiorari* denied 431 U.S. 933, 97 S.Ct. 2641, 53 L.Ed.2d 250 (1977); rehearing denied 433 U.S. 916, 97 S.Ct. 2992, 53 L.Ed.2d 1103 (1977).

diversity of citizenship. Diversity of citizenship cases are those arising between (1) citizens of different states, (2) a foreign country and citizens of a state or different states, and (3) citizens of a state and citizens or subjects of a foreign country. Under Title 28 of the United States Code, Section 1332, the amount in controversy must be more than $50,000 before a federal district court can take jurisdiction, as indicated above. This amount is determined by Congress. For purposes of diversity of citizenship jurisdiction, a corporation is a citizen of the state in which it is incorporated and of the state in which it has its principal place of business. Cases involving diversity of citizenship can commence in the appropriate federal court or, if they have started in a state court, can sometimes be transferred to federal court.

Diversity jurisdiction originated in 1789. The authors of the Constitution felt that a state court might be biased toward its own citizens. Hence, the option of using the federal courts provided by the principle of diversity of citizenship is a means of protecting the out-of-state party. A large percentage of the more than 70,000 cases filed in federal courts each year are based on diversity of citizenship.

Consider an example. Ortega is driving from his home state, New York, to Florida. In Georgia he runs into a car owned by Flanders, a citizen of Georgia. Flanders's new Mercedes is demolished, and, as a result of the personal injuries she sustains in the accident, Flanders is unable to work for six months. Thus, the case in question involves more than $50,000 worth of damages. Flanders can therefore bring suit in a federal district court on the basis of diversity of citizenship.

Concurrent versus Exclusive Jurisdiction

When both federal and state courts have the power to hear a case, as when there is diversity of citizenship of the parties, **concurrent jurisdiction** exists. In contrast, when cases can be tried only in federal courts or only in state courts, **exclusive jurisdiction** exists. Federal courts have exclusive jurisdiction in cases involving federal crimes, bankruptcy, patents, and copyrights; in suits against the United States; and in some areas of

■ Exhibit 3–4 Exclusive and Concurrent Jurisdiction

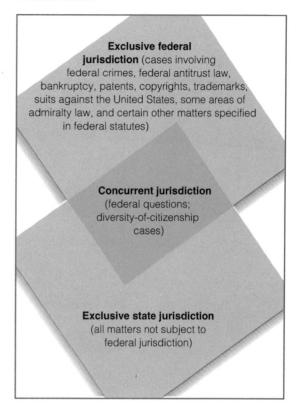

admiralty (maritime) law. States have exclusive jurisdiction in certain subject matters also—for example, in divorce and in adoption. The concepts of concurrent and exclusive jurisdiction are illustrated in Exhibit 3–4.

When concurrent jurisdiction exists, a party may choose to bring suit in either a state court or a federal court. In making that decision, the party might consider a number of factors, including the location of the courts, the procedural rules of the courts, the expertise of the respective judges, and whether the judge has a lifetime appointment (which means he or she may be subject to fewer outside pressures than a judge who is elected).

In the following case, the court considered whether state and federal courts have concurrent jurisdiction over employment discrimination claims brought under Title VII of the Civil Rights Act of 1964.

Case 3.1

**YELLOW FREIGHT
SYSTEM, INC. v.
DONNELLY**

Supreme Court of the
United States, 1990.
494 U.S. 820,
110 S.Ct. 1566,
108 L.Ed.2d 834.

BACKGROUND AND FACTS   In March 1985, Colleen Donnelly filed charges with the Equal Employment Opportunity Commission (EEOC) against Yellow Freight System, Inc. Donnelly charged that Yellow Freight had discriminated against her on the basis of sex by failing to offer her employment as a dockworker. On March 15, Donnelly received a "Notice of Right to Sue within Ninety Days" from the EEOC. This notice is required by procedures governing discrimination claims based on Title VII of the Civil Rights Act of 1964. If a plaintiff fails to initiate an action within this ninety-day period, he or she loses the right to sue. Donnelly filed suit against Yellow Freight within ninety days in an Illinois state court, alleging that Yellow Freight had violated the Illinois Human Rights Act, which prohibits employment discrimination. After the ninety-day period elapsed, the suit was moved to a federal district court, and Donnelly amended her complaint to include claims of discrimination under Title VII. Yellow Freight objected, arguing that the state court lacked jurisdiction over Title VII claims and that thus Donnelly's filing was not effected within ninety days. The district court ruled, and the appellate court agreed, that state and federal courts have concurrent jurisdiction over Title VII claims, and that therefore Donnelly's filing was timely. Yellow Freight appealed to the United States Supreme Court.

DECISION AND RATIONALE   The United States Supreme Court affirmed the appellate court's decision that actions alleging violations of Title VII may be brought in either state or federal court. The Supreme Court pointed out that unlike other federal statutes that "unequivocally stated that the jurisdiction of the federal courts is exclusive, Title VII contains no language that expressly confines jurisdiction to federal courts or ousts state courts of their presumptive jurisdiction." Unless Congress includes in a statute a statement vesting federal courts with exclusive jurisdiction, state courts may presume that they share jurisdiction concurrently with federal courts over a federal cause of action.

■ Which Cases Reach the Supreme Court?

The United States Supreme Court is given original, or trial court, jurisdiction in a small number of situations. In all other cases, its jurisdiction is appellate "with such Exceptions, and under such Regulations as the Congress shall make."

Original Jurisdiction

The United States Supreme Court has original and exclusive jurisdiction over all controversies between two or more states. In addition, the Supreme Court has original, but not exclusive, jurisdiction

over all actions or proceedings (1) to which ambassadors, other public ministers, consuls, or vice consuls of foreign states are parties; (2) involving controversies between the United States and a state; and (3) commenced by a state against the citizens of another state or against aliens.

Appellate Jurisdiction

Many people are surprised to learn that in a typical case there is no absolute right of appeal to the United States Supreme Court. Thousands of cases are filed with the Supreme Court each year; yet it hears less than two hundred. To bring a case before the Supreme Court, a party requests the Court to issue a writ of *certiorari.*[9]

A **writ of *certiorari*** is an order issued by the Supreme Court to a lower court requiring the latter to send it the record of the case for review. Parties can petition the Supreme Court to issue a writ of *certiorari,* but whether the Court will issue one is entirely within its discretion. In no instance is the Court required to issue a writ of *certiorari.*

Listed below are some of the situations in which the Supreme Court may issue a writ of *certiorari:*

1. When a state court decides a substantial federal question that has not been determined by a federal court or the Supreme Court or when a state court decides such a question in a way that is probably in disagreement with the trend of the Supreme Court's decisions.
2. When two or more federal courts of appeals disagree with each other.
3. When a federal court of appeals decides an important state question in a way that conflicts with state law, decides an important federal question not yet addressed by the Court but which should be decided by the Court, decides a federal question in a way that conflicts with applicable decisions of the Court, or departs from the accepted and usual course of judicial proceedings.
4. When a federal court of appeals holds that a state statute is invalid because it violates federal law.
5. When the highest state court of appeals holds a federal law invalid or upholds a state law that has been challenged as violating federal law.
6. When a federal court holds an act of Congress unconstitutional.

Most petitions for writs of *certiorari* are denied. A denial is not a decision on the merits of a case, nor does it indicate agreement with the lower court's opinion. Furthermore, denial of the writ has no value as a precedent.[10] The Court will not issue a writ unless at least four justices approve of it. This is called the **rule of four.** Typically, only the petitions that raise the possibility of important constitutional questions are granted.

■ Judicial Procedures: Following a Case through the Courts

American and English courts follow the *adversary system of justice.* The judge's role is viewed as nonbiased and mostly passive. The lawyer functions as the client's advocate, presenting the client's version of the facts in order to convince the judge or the jury (or both) that this version is true. Judges do not have to be entirely passive. They are responsible for the appropriate application of the law. They do not have to accept the legal reasoning of the attorneys. They can base a ruling and a decision on a personal study of the law. Judges sometimes ask questions of witnesses, sometimes limit the amount of information that can be introduced about an expert witness's qualifications, and sometimes even suggest types of evidence to be presented. For example, if a defendant chooses to act as his or her own counsel, the judge will often play a role more like that of an advocate, intervening during the trial proceedings to help the defendant.[11]

A large body of law—procedural law—establishes the rules and standards for determining disputes in courts. The rules are very complex, and they vary from court to court. There is a set of federal *rules of procedure,* and there are various sets of procedural rules in the state courts. Rules of procedure differ in criminal and civil cases.

We now present a hypothetical *civil* case. The case involves an automobile accident in which a car driven by John Jones, a resident of New Jersey, collided with a car driven by Jane Adams, a resident of New York. The accident occurred at an intersection in New York City. Adams suffered personal injuries, incurring medical and hospital expenses

---

9. Pronounced sur-shee-uh-*rah*-ree. Between 1790 and 1891, Congress allowed the United States Supreme Court almost no discretion over which cases to decide. After 1925, the Court could choose in almost 95 percent of appealed cases to decide whether to hear arguments and issue an opinion. Beginning with the term in October 1988, mandatory review was eliminated altogether.

10. *Singleton v. Commissioner of Internal Revenue,* 439 U.S. 940, 99 S.Ct. 335, 58 L.Ed.2d 335 (1978).
11. See *Faretta v. California,* 422 U.S. 806, 95 S.Ct. 2525, 45 L.Ed.2d 562 (1975).

as well as lost wages for four months. Jones and Adams are unable to agree on a settlement, and Adams sues Jones. Adams is the *plaintiff*, and Jones is the *defendant*. Both are represented by lawyers.

The Pleadings

The *complaint* and *answer* (and the *counterclaim* and *reply*)—all of which are discussed below—taken together are called the **pleadings.** The pleadings inform each party of the claims of the other and specify the issues (disputed questions) involved in the case. Pleadings remove the element of surprise from a case. They allow lawyers to gather the most persuasive evidence and to prepare better arguments, thus increasing the probability that a just and true result will be forthcoming from the trial.

COMPLAINT AND SUMMONS   Adams's suit, or action, against Jones will commence when her lawyer files a **complaint** (sometimes called a petition or declaration) with the clerk of the trial court in the appropriate geographic area (the proper venue). In most states, it will be a court having general jurisdiction; in others, it may be a court having special jurisdiction with regard to subject matter. The complaint will contain (1) a statement alleging the facts necessary for the court to take jurisdiction, (2) a short statement of the facts necessary to show that the plaintiff is entitled to a remedy, and (3) a statement of the remedy the plaintiff is seeking. A typical federal district court complaint is shown in Exhibit 3–5.

The complaint will state that Adams was driving her Ford through a green light at the specified intersection, exercising good driving habits and reasonable care, when Jones negligently drove his Cadillac through a red light and into the intersection from a cross street, striking Adams and causing serious personal injury and property damage. The complaint will go on to state that Adams is entitled to $85,000 to cover medical bills, $10,000 to cover lost wages, and $5,000 to cover property damage to the car.

After the complaint has been filed, the person empowered to do so will serve a **summons** and a copy of the complaint on the defendant, Jones. The summons notifies Jones that he is required to prepare an answer to the complaint and to file a copy of his answer with both the court and the plaintiff's

attorney within a specified time period (usually twenty to thirty days after the summons has been served). The summons also informs Jones that failure to answer will result in a **default judgment** for the plaintiff—in which case the plaintiff would be awarded the damages alleged in her complaint. The summons is not part of the pleadings. A typical federal district court summons is shown in Exhibit 3–6.

Rules governing the service of a summons vary, but usually *service* is made by handing the summons to the defendant personally or by leaving it at the defendant's residence or place of business. A summons can be served by certified or registered mail. When the defendant cannot be reached, special rules sometimes permit serving the summons by leaving it with a designated person, such as the secretary of state.

CHOICES AVAILABLE AFTER RECEIPT OF THE SUMMONS AND COMPLAINT   Once the defendant has been served with a copy of the summons and complaint, the defendant must respond by filing a *motion to dismiss* or an *answer*. If a defendant does not respond, either by choice or for some other reason, the court may enter a default judgment against him or her, as mentioned above.

MOTION TO DISMISS   If the defendant challenges the sufficiency of the plaintiff's complaint, the defendant can present to the court a **motion to dismiss** for failure to state a claim on which relief can be granted, or a *demurrer*. (The rules of civil procedure in many states do not use the term *demurrer;* they use only *motion to dismiss*.) The motion to dismiss for failure to state a claim on which relief can be granted is an allegation that even if the facts presented in the complaint are true, their legal consequences are such that there is no reason to go further with the suit and no need for the defendant to present an answer (discussed below). It is a contention that the defendant is not legally liable even if the facts are as the plaintiff alleges. If, for example, Adams's complaint had alleged facts that excluded the possibility of negligence on Jones's part, Jones can move to dismiss, and he will not be required to answer if his motion is granted.

If the court denies the motion to dismiss, the judge is indicating that the plaintiff has stated a

■ **Exhibit 3–5 A Typical Complaint**

IN THE UNITED STATES DISTRICT COURT
FOR THE ____Southern____ DISTRICT OF __New York__

CIVIL NO. 9–1047

_____Jane Adams_____ ,
Plaintiff

vs.

_____John Jones_____ ,
Defendant.

COMPLAINT

Comes now the plaintiff and for his cause of action against the defendant alleges and states as follows:

1. This action is between plaintiff, who is a resident of the State of New York, and defendant, who is a resident of the State of New Jersey. There is diversity of citizenship between parties.

2. The amount in controversy, exclusive of interest and costs, exceeds the sum of $50,000.

3. On September 10th, 1992 plaintiff, Jane Adams, was exercising good driving habits and reasonable care in driving her car through the intersection of Broadwalk and Pennsylvania Ave. when defendant, John Jones, negligently drove his vehicle through a red light at the intersection and collided with plaintiff's vehicle.

4. As a result of the collision plaintiff suffered severe physical injury, that prevented her from working, and property damage to her car. The cost she incurred included: $85,000 in medical bills, $10,000 in lost wages, $5,000 automobile repair.

WHEREFORE, plaintiff demands judgment against the defendant for the sum of $100,000 plus interest at the maximum legal rate and the costs of this action.

By _____

Joseph Roe
Attorney for Plaintiff
100 Main Street
New York, New York

1/2/93

■ **Exhibit 3–6 A Typical Summons**

SUMMONS IN A CIVIL ACTION

United States District Court

FOR THE _____Southern_____ DISTRICT OF: New York

CIVIL ACTION FILE No. __91047__

Jane Adams

Plaintiff

v.

John Jones

Defendant

SUMMONS

To the above named Defendant:

You are hereby summoned and required to serve upon   Joseph Roe

plaintiff's attorney, whose address is   100 Main Street
New York, New York

an answer to the complaint which is herewith served upon you, within 20* days after service of this summons upon you, exclusive of the day of service. If you fail to do so, judgment by default will be taken against you for the relief demanded in the complaint.

_____Tom Smith_____
Clerk of Court

_____Mary Doakes_____
Deputy Clerk.

Date: 1/10/93

[Seal of Court]

NOTE:—This summons is issued pursuant to Rule 4 of the Federal Rules of Civil Procedure.

recognized cause of action, and the defendant is given an extension of time to file a further pleading. If the defendant does not do so, a judgment will normally be entered for the plaintiff. If, on the other hand, the court grants the motion to dismiss for failure to state a claim on which relief can be granted, the judge is saying that the plaintiff has failed to state a recognized cause of action, and the plaintiff generally is given time to file an amended complaint. If the plaintiff does not file this amended complaint, a judgment will be entered against the plaintiff solely on the basis of the pleadings, and the plaintiff will not be allowed to bring suit on the matter again.

In addition to a plaintiff's failure to state a claim on which relief can be granted, a defendant's pre-answer motion to dismiss may be based on the court's lack of subject matter or personal jurisdiction, improper venue, and other specific reasons. The motion to dismiss is often used for purposes of delay.

If Adams wishes to discontinue the suit because, for example, an out-of-court settlement has been reached, she can likewise move for dismissal. The court can also dismiss on its own motion.

ANSWER AND COUNTERCLAIM If the defendant has not filed a motion to dismiss or has filed a motion to dismiss that has been denied, then an **answer** must be filed with the court. This document either admits the statements or allegations set out in the complaint or denies them and sets out any defenses that the defendant may have. If Jones admits to all of Adams's allegations in his answer, a judgment will be entered for Adams. If Jones denies Adams's allegations, the matter will proceed to trial.

Jones can deny Adams's allegations and set forth his own claim that Adams was in fact negligent and therefore owes Jones money for damages to the Cadillac. This is appropriately called a **counterclaim.** If Jones files a counterclaim, Adams will have to answer it with a pleading, normally called a **reply,** that has the same characteristics as an answer.

ANSWER AND AFFIRMATIVE DEFENSES Jones can also admit the truth of Adams's complaint but raise new facts that will result in dismissal of the action. This is called raising an **affirmative defense.**

For example, Jones could admit that he was negligent but plead that the time period for raising the claim has passed and that Adams's complaint must therefore be dismissed because it is barred by the statute of limitations (a statutory limit on the time during which one can raise a claim).

Dismissals and Judgments before Trial

Many actions for which pleadings have been filed never come to trial. There are numerous procedural avenues for disposing of a case without a trial. Many of them involve one or the other party's attempts to get the case dismissed through the use of **pretrial motions.** We have already mentioned the motion to dismiss. Another equally important motion is the motion for a judgment on the pleadings.

MOTION FOR JUDGMENT ON THE PLEADINGS After the pleadings are closed—after the complaint, answer, and any counterclaim and reply have been filed—either of the parties can file a **motion for judgment on the pleadings.** This motion may be used when no facts are disputed and, thus, only questions of law are at issue. For example, this motion would be appropriate if the facts as shown in the pleadings revealed that the time limit allowed for bringing the lawsuit has in fact run out.

Discovery

After the pleadings have been filed and while motions are being argued, the parties can use a number of procedural devices to obtain information and gather evidence about the case. Adams, for example, will want to know how fast Jones was driving, whether or not he had been drinking, whether he saw the red light, and so on. The process of obtaining information from the opposing party or from other witnesses is known as **discovery.**

Discovery serves several purposes. It preserves evidence from witnesses who might not be available at the time of the trial or whose memories will fade as time passes. It can pave the way for summary judgment (discussed below) if it is found that both parties agree on all facts. It can lead to an out-of-court settlement if one party decides that the opponent's case is too strong to challenge. (A civil case can normally be settled at any time, often without the court's permission.) Even if the case does go to trial, discovery prevents surprises by giving parties access to evidence that might otherwise be hidden, and it serves to narrow the issues so that trial time is spent on the main questions in the case. In addition, discovery procedures may serve to establish a witness's testimony so that the witness's credibility can be attacked at trial if that testimony is changed.

The federal rules of civil procedure and similar rules in the states set down the guidelines for discovery activity. Discovery includes gaining access to witnesses, documents, records, and other types of evidence.

DEPOSITIONS AND INTERROGATORIES   Discovery can involve the use of depositions or interrogatories, or both. A **deposition** is sworn testimony by either party or any witness, recorded by a court official. The person deposed appears before a court officer and is sworn. That person then answers questions asked by the attorneys from both sides. The questions and answers are taken down, sworn to, and signed. These answers will, of course, help the attorneys prepare their cases. They can also be used in court to challenge a party or a witness who changes testimony at the trial. Finally, they can be used as testimony if the witness is not available at trial. Depositions can also be taken with written questions from both sides prepared ahead of time.

Interrogatories are series of written questions for which written answers are prepared and then signed under oath. The main difference between interrogatories and depositions with written questions is that an interrogatory is directed only to a party, not to a witness, and the party can prepare answers with the aid of an attorney. The scope of interrogatories is broader, because parties are obligated to answer questions even if the answer requires disclosing information from their records and files. Interrogatories are also usually less expensive than depositions.

REQUEST FOR ADMISSIONS   A party can serve a written request to the other party for an admission of the truth of matters relating to the trial. Any matter admitted under such a request is conclusively established as true for the trial. For example, Adams can ask Jones to admit that he was driving

at a speed of forty-five miles an hour. A request for admission saves time at trial because parties will not have to spend time proving facts on which they already agree.

REQUEST FOR DOCUMENTS, OBJECTS, AND ENTRY UPON LAND   A party can gain access to documents and other items not in his or her possession in order to inspect and examine them. Likewise, a party can gain "entry upon land" to inspect the premises. Jones, for example, can gain permission to inspect and duplicate Adams's repair bills.

REQUEST FOR PHYSICAL AND MENTAL EXAMINATION   When the physical or mental condition of one party is in question, the opposing party can ask the court to order a physical or mental examination. For example, to prepare for trial, Jones would want to have his own medical professionals examine Adams. If the court is willing to make the order, the opposing party can obtain the results of the examination. It is important to note that the court will make such an order only when the need for the information outweighs the right to privacy of the person to be examined.

The rules governing discovery are designed to make sure that a witness or party is not unduly harassed, that privileged material is safeguarded, and that only matters relevant to the case at hand are discoverable.

Motion for Summary Judgment

A lawsuit can be shortened or a trial can be avoided if there are no disagreements about the facts in a case and the only question is which laws apply to those facts. Both sides can agree to the facts and ask the judge to apply the law to them. In this situation, it is appropriate for either party to move for **summary judgment.** Summary judgment will be granted when there are no genuine *questions of fact* (which, as mentioned earlier in this chapter, may be decided by judge or a jury) and the only question is a *question of law* (which only a judge, not a jury, can rule on). Motions for summary judgment can be made before or during a trial, but they will be granted only if it is clear that there are no genuine factual disputes.

When the court considers a motion for summary judgment, it can take into account evidence outside the pleadings. This distinguishes the motion for summary judgment from the motion to dismiss and from the motion for a judgment on the pleadings. To support a motion for summary judgment, one party can bring in an **affidavit** (a sworn statement) that refutes the other party's claim. Unless the second party brings in affidavits of conflicting facts, the first party will normally receive summary judgment. Jones, for example, can bring in the sworn statement of a witness that Jones was in California at the time of the accident. Unless Adams can bring in other statements raising the possibility that Jones was at the scene of the accident, Jones will normally be granted his motion for summary judgment. As mentioned above, a motion for summary judgment will be granted only if there is no dispute concerning the facts of the case.

Pretrial Hearing

Either party or the court can request a pretrial hearing. Usually the hearing consists of an informal discussion between the judge and the opposing attorneys after discovery has taken place. The purpose of the hearing is to identify the matters that are in dispute and to plan the course of the trial. The pretrial hearing is not intended to compel the parties to settle their case before trial, although judges may encourage them to settle out of court if circumstances suggest that a trial would be a waste of time.

Jury Trials

A trial can be held with or without a jury. If there is no jury, the judge determines the truth of the facts alleged in the case. The Seventh Amendment to the U.S. Constitution guarantees the right to a jury trial in federal courts in all "suits at common law" when the amount in controversy exceeds $20. Most states have similar guarantees in their own constitutions, although many states put a higher minimum dollar restriction on the guarantee. For example, Iowa requires the dollar amount of damages to be at least $1,000 before there is a right to a jury trial. If this threshold requirement is met, either party may normally request a jury trial.

The right to a trial by jury does not have to be exercised, and many cases are tried without one. In most states and in federal courts, one of the parties must request a jury or the right is presumed

to be waived. The decision to exercise the right to a jury trial usually depends on the complexity of the case, the nature of the party's legal theory, and the disposition of the judge assigned to the trial.

Jury Selection

In the case between Adams and Jones, both parties want a jury trial. Each state has a system for the selection of prospective jurors to hear cases. Once the prospective jurors have been selected, then the judge and both attorneys examine the prospective jurors to ensure that their judgment will be impartial. This examination is called *voir dire,*[12] a French phrase meaning "to speak the truth." In most jurisdictions, *voir dire* consists of oral questions that attorneys for the plaintiff and the defendant ask a group of prospective jurors (one at a time) in order to determine whether a potential jury member is biased or has any connection with a party to the action or with a prospective witness. During *voir dire,* a party may challenge *peremptorily*—that is, without providing any reason—a certain number (the number is determined by statute) of prospective jurors and ask that these individuals not be sworn in as jurors. Alternatively, a party may challenge a prospective juror *for cause*—that is, provide a reason why this individual should not be sworn in as a juror. If the judge grants the challenge, the individual is asked to step down. After the jurors have been selected, they are impaneled and sworn in, and the trial is ready to begin.

Note that there are two types of juries: the ordinary (*petit,* or small) jury and the **grand jury**. The latter is called grand because it consists of a greater number of jurors than the ordinary trial jury. A grand jury is convened in criminal cases (criminal law is discussed in Chapter 6). Potential grand jurors are usually drawn from lists of qualified residents. Minors, persons who have been convicted of a crime, and those who are biased toward the subject of the investigation are not qualified. Those who are chosen are sworn in by the court and sit to hear the evidence presented by the prosecutor. A grand jury does not determine the guilt or innocence of an accused party; rather, its function is to determine, after hearing the state's evidence,

---

12. Pronounced vwahr-*deer.*

whether probable (reasonable) cause exists to believe that a crime has been committed and whether a trial ought to be held. If the jury finds probable cause, it will return a ''bill of indictment,'' and the case will be heard by an ordinary jury; if no probable cause is found, it will return ''no bill,'' and the accused is released from the criminal charge.

The Trial

Both attorneys are allowed to make *opening statements* concerning the facts that they expect to prove during the trial. Because Adams is the plaintiff and has the burden of proving that her case is correct, Adams's attorney begins the case by calling the first witness for the plaintiff and examining (questioning) the witness. (For both attorneys, the type of question and the manner of asking are governed by the rules of evidence.) This examination is called *direct examination*. After Adams's attorney is finished, the witness will be questioned by Jones's attorney on *cross-examination*. After that, Adams's attorney has another opportunity to question the witness in *redirect examination,* and Jones's attorney can then follow with *recross-examination*. When both attorneys have finished with the first witness, Adams's attorney will call the succeeding witnesses in the plaintiff's case, each of whom is subject to cross-examination (and redirect and recross, if necessary).

The plaintiff must prove her case through a *preponderance of the evidence*. That is, she need not provide indisputable proof that she is entitled to a judgment. She need only show that her factual claim is more likely to be true than the defendant's. In a criminal trial, the prosecution has a higher standard of proof to meet—it must prove its case *beyond a reasonable doubt* (see Chapter 6). Some claims must be proved by *clear and convincing evidence*—evidence that is more than usually convincing. In these situations, the proof must show that the truth of the party's claim is highly probable. These situations include suits involving charges of fraud, suits to establish the terms of a lost will, some suits involving oral contracts, and other suits involving circumstances in which there is thought to be a particular danger of deception.

At the conclusion of the plaintiff's case in a jury trial, the defendant's attorney may ask the judge to direct a verdict for the defendant on the ground that the plaintiff has failed to present a *prima facie*[13] **case** (a case in which the plaintiff has produced sufficient evidence of his or her conclusion that the case can go to a jury) and, thus, there can be only one verdict as a matter of law— a verdict in the defendant's favor. This is called a **motion for a directed verdict.** In considering the motion, the judge will look at the evidence that is favorable to the plaintiff and the unquestionable evidence that is favorable to the defendant and will grant the motion only if he or she believes that a reasonable jury could not find for the plaintiff. (Motions for directed verdicts at this stage of trial are seldom granted.)

The defendant's attorney will then present the evidence and witnesses for the defendant's case. Witnesses are called and examined. The plaintiff's attorney has a right to cross-examine them, and there is a redirect and recross-examination if necessary. At the end of the defendant's case, either attorney can again move for a directed verdict, and the test will again be whether the jury could, under any reasonable interpretation of the evidence, find for the party against whom the motion is made.

After the defendant's attorney has finished presenting evidence, the plaintiff's attorney can present additional evidence to refute the defendant's case in a **rebuttal.**[14] The defendant's attorney can meet that evidence in a **rejoinder.** After both sides have rested their cases, each attorney presents a **closing argument,** urging a verdict in favor of his or her client. The judge instructs the jury (assuming it is a jury trial) in the law that applies to the case. The instructions to the jury are often called *charges*. Then the jury retires to the jury room to deliberate the case and return a verdict. In the *Adams v. Jones* case, the jury will not only decide for the plaintiff or for the defendant but, if it finds for the plaintiff, will also decide on the amount of money to be paid to her. Let us assume that the jury does decide for Adams, the plaintiff.

MOTION FOR NEW TRIAL At the end of the trial, a posttrial motion can be made to set aside

---

13.   Pronounced *pry*-muh *fay*-shee.
14.   A rebuttal is an attempt by any party (not just the plaintiff) to refute an adverse party's evidence.

■ **Exhibit 3–7 A Typical Lawsuit**

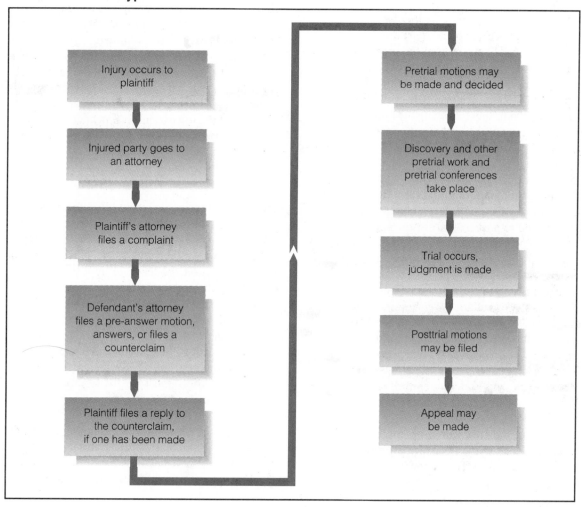

an adverse verdict and to hold a new trial. The motion will be granted if the judge is convinced, after looking at all the evidence, that the jury was in error. A new trial can also be granted on the grounds of newly discovered evidence, prejudicial misconduct by the participants during the trial, or prejudicial error by the judge.

MOTION FOR JUDGMENT *N.O.V.* (NOTWITH-STANDING THE VERDICT) If Jones's attorney previously moved for a directed verdict, this attorney can now make a posttrial motion for a **judgment *n.o.v.*** (from the Latin *non obstante ver-*

edicto, or notwithstanding the verdict). In other words, Jones can state that even if the evidence is viewed in the light most favorable to Adams, a reasonable jury should not have found a verdict in Adams's favor. If the judge finds this contention to be correct or decides that the law requires the opposite result, the motion will be granted. The standards for granting a judgment *n.o.v.* are the same as those for granting a motion to dismiss or a motion for a directed verdict. We will assume here that this motion is made and denied and that Jones appeals the case. These events are illustrated in Exhibit 3–7.

The Appeal

When a case as appealed, as it is by Jones in our example, a notice of appeal must be filed with the clerk of the trial court within the prescribed time. Jones now becomes the *appellant* or *petitioner.* His attorney files in the reviewing court (usually an intermediate court of appeals) the record on appeal, which contains the following: (1) the pleadings, (2) a transcript of the trial testimony and copies of the exhibits, (3) the judge's rulings on motions made by the parties, (4) the arguments of counsel, (5) the instructions to the jury, (6) the verdict, (7) the posttrial motions, and (8) the judgment order from which the appeal is taken. Jones may also be required to post a bond for the appeal.

In some courts, Jones's attorney will be required to prepare a condensation of the record, known as an *abstract.* The abstract and a brief are filed with the reviewing court. Generally, an appellant's **brief** contains (1) a short statement of the facts, (2) a statement of the issues, (3) the rulings by the trial court that the appellant contends are erroneous and prejudicial, (4) the grounds for reversal of the judgment, (5) a statement of the applicable law, and (6) arguments on the appellant's behalf, citing applicable statutes and relevant cases as precedent. The attorney for the *appellee,* or *respondent,* Adams, must now file an answering brief. Jones's attorney can file a reply (although this is not required). The reviewing court then considers the case.

No Evidence Heard   Appeals courts do not hear any evidence. An appeals court's decision concerning a case is based on the abstracts, the record, and the briefs. Any error that the appellant brings up on appeal must appear clearly in the trial court record, and the appellant must have objected promptly to the ruling in the trial court. After the appellate court has reviewed the records submitted to it, the attorneys can present oral arguments. The appellate court then takes the case under advisement. After the court reaches a decision, the decision is usually published. It contains the court's reasons for its decision, the rules of law that apply, and the court's ultimate decision. In general, appellate courts do not reverse findings of fact unless the findings are unsupported or contradicted by the evidence. Rather, they review the record for errors of law. If the reviewing court believes that a **reversible error** was committed during the trial or that the jury was improperly instructed, the judgment will be reversed. Sometimes the case will be **remanded** (sent back to the court that originally heard the case) for a new trial. In many cases the decision of the lower court is *affirmed,* resulting in the enforcement of that court's judgment or decree.

Higher Appeals Courts   If the reviewing court is an intermediate appellate court, the party who has lost in that court may seek a reversal of its decision by filing within the prescribed time period a petition for leave to appeal to a higher court.[15] Such a petition corresponds to a petition for a writ of *certiorari* in the United States Supreme Court. The winning party in the intermediate appellate court can file an answer to the petition for leave to appeal. If the petition is granted, the complete record is certified and forwarded to the higher court. New briefs must be filed before the state supreme court, and the attorneys may be allowed or requested to present oral arguments. If the state supreme court concludes that the judgment of the intermediate appellate court is correct, it affirms the judgment. If it decides otherwise, it reverses the appellate court's decision and enters an appropriate order of remand. At this point, unless a federal question is at issue or there is some other jurisdictional ground for an appeal to a federal court, the case has reached its end. If a new trial is ordered, it will start again at the court of origin.

It is important to know that the vast majority of disputes are settled out of court, mainly because of the time and expense of trying a case. Furthermore, of those cases that go to trial, about 97 percent are finally resolved at the trial level, as relatively few trial court decisions are changed on appeal.

---

15. In most states, the appeal from the court of original jurisdiction up to the state supreme court is a matter of right.

■ CONCEPT SUMMARY 3.1   Courts and Procedures

Types of Jurisdiction	1. *Jurisdiction over persons/property*—Power of a court over the defendant or the defendant's property; generally limited by territorial boundaries.
	2. *Jurisdiction over subject matter*—Restriction on the types of cases a court can hear.
	   a. Limited jurisdiction—Exists when a court is limited to specific subject matter, such as probate or divorce.
	   b. General jurisdiction—Exists when a court can hear any kind of case.
	3. *Original jurisdiction*—Exists with courts that have authority to hear a case first (trial courts).
	4. *Appellate jurisdiction*—Exists with courts of appeals; generally, appellate courts do not have original jurisdiction.
	5. *Federal jurisdiction*—Arises in the following situations:
	   a. When a federal question is involved (when the plaintiff's cause of action is based at least in part on the U.S. Constitution, a treaty, or a federal law).
	   b. In diversity of citizenship cases between (1) citizens of different states; (2) a foreign country and citizens of a state or different states; or (3) citizens of a state and citizens or subjects of a foreign country. The amount in controversey must exceed $50,000.
	6. *Concurrent jurisdiction*—Exists when two different courts have authority to hear the same case.
	7. *Exclusive jurisdiction*—Exists when only one court has authority to hear a case.

Types of Courts	1. *Trial courts*—Courts of original jurisdiction, in which actions are initiated.
	   a. State—Courts of general jurisdiction can hear any case; courts of limited jurisdiction include divorce courts, probate courts, traffic courts, small claims courts, etc.
	   b. Federal—The federal district court is the equivalent of the state trial court. Federal courts of limited jurisdiction include the U.S. Tax Court, the U.S. Bankruptcy Court, and the U.S. Claims Court.
	2. *Intermediate appellate courts*—Courts of appeals (reviewing courts), generally without original jurisdiction. Many states have an intermediate appellate court; in the federal court system, the U.S. circuit courts of appeals are the intermediate appellate courts.
	3. *Supreme court*—The highest court. Each state has a supreme court, although it may be called by some other name, from which appeal to the United States Supreme Court is only possible if a federal question is involved. The United States Supreme Court is the highest court in the federal court system and the final arbiter of the Constitution and federal law.

Rules of Procedure	Rules of procedure prescribe how disputes are handled in the courts. Rules differ from court to court, and separate sets of rules exist for federal and state courts, as well as for criminal and civil cases. A sample civil court procedure involves the following steps:
	1. *The pleadings:*
	   a. Complaint or petition—A statement of the cause of action and parties involved, filed with the court by the plaintiff's attorney. After the filing, a summons is delivered to the defendant.
	   b. Pre-answer motion, such as a motion to dismiss for failure to state a claim on which relief can be granted.

(Continued on next page)

■ CONCEPT SUMMARY 3.1 *(Continued)*

| Rules of Procedure (Continued) | c. Answer—Can take the form of (1) an admission; (2) an affirmative defense; (3) a counterclaim; or (4) an answer denying some or all of the allegations, which may also contain an admission, an affirmative defense, and a counterclaim.
 2. *Dismissal or judgment before trial:*
   a. Motion for judgment on the pleadings—May be made by either party; will be granted if no cause of action exists or if the defendant fails to answer.
   b. Motion for summary judgment—May be made by either party; will be granted if the parties agree on the facts. Judge applies law in rendering judgment.
 3. *Discovery*—The process of gathering evidence concerning the case; involves *depositions* (sworn testimony by either party or any witness) and *interrogatories* (in which parties to the action write answers to questions with the aid of their attorneys).
 4. *Pretrial hearing*—Either party or the court can request a pretrial hearing to identify the matters in dispute after discovery has taken place and to plan the course of the trial.
 5. *Trial*—Involves jury selection, opening statements from both parties' attorneys, and then:
   a. Plaintiff's introduction and direct examination of witnesses and cross-examination by defendant's attorney; possible redirect by plaintiff's attorney and recross-examination by defendant's attorney.
   b. Defendant's introduction and direct examination of witnesses and cross-examination by plaintiff's attorney; possible redirect by defendant's attorney and recross-examination by plaintiff's attorney.
   c. Possible rebuttal of defendant's argument by plaintiff's attorney, who presents more evidence.
   d. Possible rejoinder by defendant's attorney to meet that evidence.
   e. Closing arguments by both plaintiff's and defendant's attorneys in favor of their respective clients.
   f. Judge's instructions to the jury.
   g. Jury verdict.
 6. *Posttrial options:*
   a. Motion for a new trial—Will be granted if the judge is convinced that the jury was in error.
   b. Motion for judgment *n.o.v.* (notwithstanding the verdict)—Movant (party making the motion) must have filed a motion for a directed verdict at the close of all the evidence during the trial; motion will be granted if the judge is convinced that the jury was in error.
   c. Appeal—Either party can appeal the trial court's judgment to an appropriate court of appeals. After posting of bond(s), briefs are filed, a hearing is held, and the appellate court renders a written opinion. |

■ Alternative Dispute Resolution

Trials are costly and time consuming. Because of the logjam in the courts today (see this chapter's *Emerging Trends* feature), it may be months before a hearing can even be scheduled. Depending on the complexity of the case, the extent of discovery proceedings required, and the delaying tactics of the opposing party, years may be spent in litigation. Even in the best of situations, the civil procedures discussed above all require time—and money. For these reasons, businesspersons and other individuals are increasingly turning to **alternative dispute resolution (ADR)**—*mediation, arbitration,* or other nonjudicial settlement procedures—as an alternative to civil lawsuits.

ADR is normally a less expensive and less time-consuming process than litigation in court. It also has the advantage of being more private. No public record of ADR proceedings is created, and only the parties directly involved in the dispute resolution procedures are privy to the information presented in the ADR process. This is an important consideration when sensitive commercial information is involved or privacy is desired for some other reason.

ADR occurs in many forms, ranging from very informal negotiations between neighbors to legally binding arbitration of contractual or other types of disputes.

Negotiation and Mediation

Negotiation is a usually informal process in which the two disputing parties come together, with or without attorneys to represent them, to try to settle their differences. Negotiation is the simplest form of ADR because no third party is involved. **Mediation** is similar to negotiation; the major difference is that mediation involves a third party, called a mediator, who assists the parties in reaching a mutually acceptable agreement—but does not make the decision for them. Mediation, like negotiation, may take place in an informal atmosphere, such as a community center, church, or neighbor's home; or it may take on quite formal characteristics, as when a U.S. president acts as a mediator for disputing foreign nations.

Arbitration

A more formal method of ADR is **arbitration.** With arbitration, a third person, called an arbitrator, makes a *legally binding* decision by which both parties must abide.

THE ARBITRATION PROCESS   In the arbitration process, the arbitrator becomes a private judge, but he or she does not have to be a lawyer, even though many arbitrators are lawyers. Arbitrators decide on their own procedural rules as well as

their own rules of evidence (within certain guidelines). The decision of the arbitrator is called the **award** and is legally binding upon the parties. A losing party may appeal an arbitrator's decision to a court, but except in cases of evident error, courts are reluctant to overturn decisions arrived at through arbitration.

Virtually any commercial matter can be submitted to arbitration. Parties can agree, when a dispute arises, to settle their differences informally through arbitration rather than formally through the court system. Frequently, disputes are arbitrated because of an **arbitration clause** in a contract entered into before the dispute arose. An arbitration clause provides that any disputes arising under the contract will be resolved by arbitration. It is important to note that if parties agree in their contract to arbitrate subsequent disputes arising thereunder, they will very likely be compelled to do so by state or federal statute.

ENFORCEMENT OF ARBITRATION CLAUSES
Most states have enacted statutes (often based on the Uniform Arbitration Act of 1955) under which arbitration clauses will be enforced. At the federal level, the Federal Arbitration Act, enacted in 1925, provides for the enforcement of arbitration clauses in contracts involving maritime activity or interstate commerce and can preempt state coverage in these areas in the event of conflict between a state statute and the federal act.

Even when a claim involves a violation of statutory law, a court may determine that the parties must nonetheless abide by their agreement to arbitrate the dispute—if the court, in interpreting the relevant statute, can find no legislative intent to the contrary. For example, in *Shearson/American Express, Inc. v. McMahon,*[16] a case decided by the United States Supreme Court in 1987, customers of a brokerage firm alleged that the firm had engaged in fraudulent trading on their accounts in violation of two federal acts—the Racketeer Influenced and Corrupt Organizations Act (see Chapter 7) and the Securities Exchange Act of 1934 (see Chapter 43). When the customers sued the firm, the firm moved to compel arbitration of the claims in accordance with an arbitration clause in their contract. The Court found that when Congress en-

---

16.   482 U.S. 220, 107 S.Ct. 2332, 96 L.Ed.2d 185 (1987).

Adversarial versus Nonadversarial Justice

Frank DePalma may be dead by the time you read this. In 1989, the retired welder from Pittsburgh was diagnosed as having terminal cancer caused by asbestos exposure. He promptly filed a lawsuit against the asbestos manufacturer for damages and, in so doing, added his name to 100,000 other asbestos cases that have clogged state and federal courts. DePalma hopes to collect before he dies, but the odds do not appear to be in his favor. In addition to the massive numbers of asbestos and other tort lawsuits that are clogging the courts, a rising number of criminal, drug-related cases are also burdening the legal system. This country is now pressured to find alternative vehicles for meting out justice.

Attacking the Problem

A number of solutions have been proposed, and some have been implemented, to reduce the logjam in our court system and to reduce the litigation costs facing all members of society. The enforcement of arbitration clauses, court-referred arbitration, and the emergence of an increasing number of private forums for dispute resolution have all helped to reduce the caseload of the courts. Another solution to the problem involves putting caps on damage awards, particularly for pain and suffering. Without the probability of obtaining multimillion-dollar judgments for pain and suffering, some potential litigants will be deterred from undertaking lawsuits to obtain damages. (See the *Emerging Trends in Business Law* on tort reform in Chapter 23.)

Another avenue of attack is to penalize those who bring frivolous lawsuits. Rule 11 of the Federal Rules of Civil Procedure allows for disciplinary sanctions against lawyers and litigants who bring frivolous lawsuits in federal court. In the last few years, federal judges have issued hundreds of public opinions on motions by attorneys requesting sanctions against opposing counsel. More than 60 percent of those requests were granted. The United States Supreme Court even upheld a $21,000 fine against a Washington, D.C., law firm.

There are now proposals that would supposedly reduce delay and expenses in federal civil cases, and such proposals are being considered by the states as well. All of the proposals can be viewed as case-management plans. One such proposal, for example, would require each federal district court to appoint a local advisory committee and to put into place procedures for placing cases on different tracks, with simple cases being handled more quickly than complex ones.

Not a Painless "Cure"

Some have complained that mandatory arbitration deprives individuals of their right to trial by jury, although so far the courts have held that access to the courts is not denied because appeal of an arbitrator's decision to the courts is always possible. Others have criticized the enforcement of arbitration clauses as unfair to consumers. For example, arbitration clauses in contracts for the purchase of securities usually require investors to agree to submit any disputes arising under the contracts to arbitration. Because the arbitration forums in which these disputes must be settled are largely sponsored by the securities industry, consumer-purchasers are not given the opportunity to have their problems heard by a truly impartial arbitrator. To protect consumers, the state of Massachusetts recently enacted regulations that prohibited securities brokers from requiring individuals to enter into pre-dispute arbitration agreements when purchasing securities. The securities industry brought suit in federal court, claiming that the regulations were unconstitutional because they conflicted with the provisions of, and policies underlying, the Federal Arbitration Act. The court agreed and struck down the legislation as unconstitutional.[a] The presiding judge in that case likened the court system of today, with its swollen court calendars, to a body suffering from hypertrophy (pathologic swelling or overgrowth). Arbitration, like a medical shunt that diverts the flow of blood from one area of the body to another, is a way to relieve pressure. Although the patient often resists such treatment, it is necessary for regaining health.[b]

---

a. *Securities Industry Association et al. v. Connolly,* 883 F.2d 1114 (1st Cir. 1989).
b. Consumers gained some protection, however, in a case heard recently by the New York Court of Appeals [*In the Matter of Cowen & Co. v. Anderson,* 559 N.Y.S.2d 225, 76 N.Y.2d 318, 558 N.E.2d 27 (1990)]. In this case, the court allowed an investor to bring a dispute with a broker to an independent arbitration panel rather than the forum subsidized by the securities industry. This case will set a nationwide pattern because most brokerage firms are governed by New York laws.

A New Way of Looking at Justice

Traditionally, the English and American systems of justice have been adversarial. Alternative dispute resolution involves a totally different approach, which is geared toward finding grounds for agreement rather than grounds for disagreement. If the trend toward ADR continues, this will require a dramatic change in the attitudes of lawyers, judges, and the public. We will have to change from a litigious society with a win-lose legal philosophy to a society that looks at a broader picture that is oriented toward problem solving on a fair and equitable basis rather than an adversarial basis.

■ Implications for the Businessperson

The trend toward ADR has obvious implications for the businessperson because this trend may alter a businessperson's decision about when to sue and when not to sue. A civil suit currently may remain on the docket for years. Therefore, the cost of delays have to be examined. Other factors that must be considered are the quality of evidence, the publicity, the expense, and the risk of losing, as well as the ability to collect if a favorable judgment is rendered. Whenever

it looks as if using the judicial system will be too expensive, the businessperson owes it to himself or herself to examine the ADR procedures outlined in this chapter.

■ For Critical Analysis

1. As mentioned above, Rule 11 of the Federal Rules of Civil Procedure provides for disciplinary actions against lawyers and litigants who bring frivolous lawsuits in federal court. Critics of Rule 11 believe that these sanctions are being used disproportionately against plaintiffs in civil rights cases. Others contend that such sanctions have a ''chilling effect''—the effect of discouraging the exercise of a constitutional right. Why would Rule 11 sanctions be used more in civil rights cases than in other cases? Do you think that Rule 11 has a chilling effect? Why or why not?
2. Speedy trial acts throughout the states and at the federal level require that criminal cases be heard within a specified period of time. Because of these acts, criminal cases are placed on the dockets sooner than civil cases. The delays for civil lawsuits in some jurisdictions exceed three years. Why should criminal cases be given priority over civil cases? What logic lies behind speedy trial acts?

acted these federal acts, it did not intend to bar enforcement of all predispute arbitration agreements, and the Court thus ruled that the claims were arbitrable (capable of being decided outside a judicial forum) pursuant to the Federal Arbitration Act.

In the following case, the court had to decide whether an alleged violation of the federal Age Discrimination in Employment Act of 1967 was arbitrable.

Case 3.2

GILMER v. INTERSTATE/ JOHNSON LANE CORP.

United States Court of Appeals, Fourth Circuit, 1990. 895 F.2d 195.

BACKGROUND AND FACTS In 1981, Interstate/Johnson Lane Corporation hired Robert Gilmer as a financial manager. As a condition of his employment, Gilmer was required to register as a securities representative with the New York Stock Exchange. The application for registration contained a clause under which Gilmer agreed to the arbitration of any disputes between himself and his employer arising out of his employment. In 1987, when Interstate terminated Gilmer's employment, Gilmer sued, alleging that the termination violated the Age Discrimination in Employment Act (ADEA) of 1967. Interstate filed a motion in a federal district court to compel arbitration under the contract. The court denied the motion, ruling that arbitration procedures are inadequate for the final resolution of rights created by the ADEA and that Congress intended to protect ADEA plaintiffs from waiver of the judicial forum. Interstate appealed.

DECISION AND RATIONALE The United States Court of Appeals reversed the judgment of the district court. The appellate court noted that the United States Supreme Court "has endorsed arbitration as an effective and efficient means of dispute resolution" and that the Federal Arbitration Act "establishes a 'federal policy favoring arbitration.' " The court stated that one of the reasons for not enforcing an arbitration agreement is "if Congress has evinced an intention to preclude waiver of the judicial forum for a particular statutory right." Congressional intent may be deduced from a statute's text or legislative history, or from an inherent conflict between arbitration and the statute's purpose. The court found nothing in the text, legislative history, or purpose of the ADEA indicating a congressional intent to preclude enforcement of arbitration agreements. "Moreover, we see no conflict between arbitration and the underlying purposes of the ADEA." The appellate court remanded the case with directions to enter an order compelling the arbitration of Gilmer's claim. On appeal, the United States Supreme Court held that an ADEA claim can be subjected to compulsory arbitration.

ETHICAL CONSIDERATIONS This case illustrates the increasing tendency on the part of courts to enforce arbitration clauses, even in cases involving alleged violations of federal law enacted to protect the rights of certain classes of people (such as employees in this case). This may seem to contradict the public policy on which the federal law is based. In making their decisions, courts must weigh this public policy against two other policies: (1) freedom of contract, which means that the courts are reluctant to interfere with contracts (including arbitration clauses) voluntarily formed; and (2) the policy favoring alternative methods of dispute settlement to reduce the logjam in the courts.

Court-Annexed ADR

Alternative dispute resolution is increasingly being integrated into the legal system itself. Some states compel the arbitration of certain types of disputes, and many states and some federal court jurisdictions have adopted programs that allow them to refer certain types of cases for mediation or arbitration. Since 1984, for example, ten federal district courts have experimented with court-annexed, nonbinding arbitration for cases involving amounts less than $100,000. Only 10 percent of the cases thus far referred for arbitration have gone to trial.

Court systems in Colorado, Hawaii, Texas, and other states have adopted mandatory mediation or nonbinding arbitration programs for certain types of disputes, usually involving less than a specified threshold amount. Only if the parties fail to reach an agreement, or if one of the parties disagrees with the decision of a third party mediating or arbitrating the dispute, will the case be heard by the court. South Carolina was the first state to institute a voluntary arbitration program at the *appellate* court level. Arbitration at this level is designed to reduce the time and expense of having a case decided at the appellate level. In the South Carolina system, litigants must waive a court hearing when requesting arbitration. All decisions by the arbitrators are final and binding.

ADR Forums and Services

Services facilitating dispute resolution outside the courtroom are provided by both government agencies and private organizations. The major source of private arbitration services is the American Arbitration Association (AAA). Most of the largest law firms in the nation are members of this association. Founded in 1926, the AAA now settles more than 50,000 disputes a year in its thirty-one offices throughout the country. Cases brought before the AAA are heard by an expert or a panel of experts—about half of whom are usually lawyers—in the area relating to the dispute. To cover its costs, this nonprofit organization charges a fee, paid by the party filing the claim. In addition, each party to the dispute pays a price for each hearing day, as well as a special additional fee in cases involving personal injuries or property loss.

In addition to the AAA, there exist numerous other state and local nonprofit organizations that provide arbitration services. For example, the Arbitration Association of Florida provides ADR services in that state. The Better Business Bureau offers ADR programs to aid in the resolution of certain types of disagreements. Its latest ADR process involves a mediation program called ComputerCare, through which buyers and sellers of computer equipment and software can settle their disputes. Many industries—including the insurance, automobile, and securities industries—also now have mediation or arbitration programs to facilitate timely and inexpensive settlement of claims. In all, there exist over 600 dispute-resolution entities in the United States.

MINI-TRIALS AND SUMMARY JURY TRIALS A fairly recent development in the area of ADR is the use of mini-trials and summary jury trials to facilitate dispute settlement. A **mini-trial** is a *private* proceeding in which each party's attorney briefly argues the party's case before the other party. Often, a neutral third party, who acts as an adviser, is also present. If the parties fail to reach an agreement, the adviser renders an opinion as to how a court would likely decide the issue.

A **summary jury trial** is similar to a mini-trial, but it takes place in a courtroom before a judge and jury. After the attorneys have briefly presented their evidence and arguments, the jury renders a verdict. The difference between a summary jury trial and a real jury trial is that in a summary jury trial the jury's verdict is not binding—it is advisory only. Like the mini-trial, the summary jury trial gives the parties an idea of what they could expect if they took their case to court. At the end of the summary jury trial, the presiding judge meets with the parties and encourages them to settle their dispute.

FOR-PROFIT ALTERNATIVES Those who seek to settle their disputes quickly now have yet another alternative—they can pay private, for-profit organizations to act as mediators or arbitrators. Leading firms in the for-profit justice industry include Endispute of Washington, D.C.; Judicial Arbitration and Mediation Services of California; and Judicate, a Philadelphia-based firm that offers nationwide services and a network of approximately 450 judges—retired judges who are paid an hourly fee for their services—to assist its clients. Procedures in these private courts are fashioned to meet the desires of the clients seeking their services. With Judicate, for example, the parties decide on the date of the hearing, the presiding judge, whether the judge's decision will be legally binding, and the site of the hearing—which could be a conference room, a law-school office, or a leased court-room complete with flag and Bible. The judges follow procedures similar to those of the federal courts and use similar rules. Each party to the dispute pays a filing fee and a designated fee for a half-day hearing session or a special, one-hour settlement conference.

■ Terms and Concepts

affidavit 59
affirmative defense 57
alternative dispute
    resolution (ADR) 65
answer 57
arbitration 65
arbitration clause 65
award 65
brief 62
closing argument 60
complaint 54
concurrent jurisdiction 51
counterclaim 57
default judgment 54
depositions 58
discovery 57
diversity of citizenship 51
domestic relations
    courts 45
exclusive jurisdiction 51
federal question 50
grand jury 59
in personam jurisdiction 44
in rem jurisdiction 44

interrogatories 58
judgment *n.o.v.* 61
judicial review 48
jurisdiction 43
justice of the peace
    courts 45
justiciable controversy 45
litigant 45
long arm statute 44
mediation 65
mini-trial 69
motion for a directed
    verdict 60
motion for judgment on the
    pleadings 57
motion to dismiss 54
municipal courts 45
negotiation 65
pleadings 54
pretrial motions 57
prima facie case 60

probate courts 44
questions of fact 46
questions of law 46
rebuttal 60
rejoinder 60
remanded 62
reply 57
reversible error 62
rule of four 53
small claims courts 45
standing 45
summary judgment 58
summary jury trial 69
summons 54
trial courts 45
venue 44
voir dire 59
writ of *certiorari* 53

■ For Review

1. Before a court can hear a case, it must have jurisdiction. Over what must it have jurisdiction?

2. In what circumstances does a federal court have jurisdiction?

3. At trial, parties may dispute the facts, what law applies, and how that law should be applied. On appeal, an appellate court may examine the record of the case. What records does the appellate court examine, and what is it looking for?

4. Hawaii enacts a statute that prohibits the publication of parodies of state officials. *Aloha* magazine brings a suit against the state to prevent enforcement of the statute, alleging that the law violates the U.S. Constitution's protection against laws abridging freedom of speech. Can a Hawaii state court refuse to enforce the statute? Could a federal court for the district in which Hawaii is located? How about the United States Supreme Court?

5. In Patty's suit against Will, after the parties' opening statements, Patty calls and examines Ted, the first witness. Will cross-examines Ted, after which Patty and Will each have another chance to ask questions of Ted. After Patty presents her case, Will files a motion for a directed verdict. The judge denies the motion and tells the jury to retire to consider a verdict. On what grounds might Will object?

■ Questions and Case Problems

3-1. (a) Before two parties go to trial, an involved process called pleadings and discovery takes place. In the past, the rules of discovery were very formal, and trials often turned on elements of surprise. For example, a plaintiff would not necessarily know until the trial what the defendant's defense was going to be. Does this seem like a fair way to conduct a trial? (b) Within the last twenty-five years, new rules of discovery have substantially changed all this. Now each attorney can discover practically all the evidence that the other will be presenting at trial. Certain information, however, is still not available to a party—namely, the opposing attorney's work product. *Work product* is not a clear concept. Basically, it includes all the attorney's thoughts on the case. Can you see any reason why such information should not be made available to the opposing attorney?

3-2. Quite often, trials are concluded before they are begun. If the parties do not disagree on the facts, they simply relate those facts to the judge, and then, through a motion for judgment on the pleadings, they ask the judge to decide what the law is and how it applies to this set of facts. How is it possible that two parties can agree on the facts yet disagree as to which party is liable?

3-3. Once a case is appealed, most appellate courts do not have the power to enter judgment or to award damages to a party who should have received them at trial. Consequently, if the appellate court disagrees with the trial court's decision, it will reverse and remand for retrial and, in effect, order the trial court judge to change the judgment. Why should an appellate court not take a trial court judge's word as final?

3-4. Sometimes on appeal there are questions of whether the facts presented in a trial support the conclusion reached by the judge or the jury. The appellate court will reverse on the basis of the facts only when it concludes that no reasonable person, from the evidence presented at trial, could have reached the conclusion that the judge or jury reached. Appellate courts normally defer to a trial court's decision with regard to the facts. Can you see any reason for this?

3-5. Marya Callais, a citizen of Florida, was walking near a busy street in Tallahassee, Florida, one day when a large crate flew off a passing truck and hit her, causing her to suffer numerous injuries. She incurred a great deal of pain and suffering plus numerous medical expenses, and she could not work for six months. She wishes to sue the trucking firm for $300,000 in damages. The firm's headquarters are in Georgia, although the company does business in Florida. In what court can Marya bring her suit—in a Florida state court, a Georgia state court, or a federal court? What factors might influence her decision?

3-6. In January of 1983, Colleen Cote, a Wisconsin resident, hired a Michigan lawyer, Peter Wadel, to represent her in a medical malpractice action in a Michigan state court. Wadel scheduled a court appearance for her on February 10, 1983, and sent her a bill for $118.25 for court costs that he had paid on her behalf. She paid him the following month. In July she learned from the defendant's lawyer that the court had dismissed her case in April for lack of prosecution. On checking with Wadel's office, she was told that settlement negotiations were under way with the defendant's insurer—which Cote knew to be untrue, because the defendant was uninsured. She then contacted another lawyer to look into the matter, but the lawyer could obtain no information from Wadel or his law firm concerning the issue. Cote then brought suit in a Wisconsin federal court (there is at least one federal trial court in each state) against Wadel, alleging malpractice in handling her case. Under Wisconsin's long arm statute, jurisdiction is conferred on Wisconsin state and federal courts over nonresident defendants "in any action claiming injury to person or property within or without this state arising out of an act or omission within this state by the defendant." The federal district court in Wisconsin dismissed Cote's suit for lack of personal jurisdiction over the defendant, whose business and residence were in Michigan. Cote appealed, claiming that Wisconsin's long arm statute gave her jurisdiction or that, if it did not, the district should have transferred her case to a court with jurisdiction. Discuss her claims. [*Cote v. Wadel,* 796 F.2d 981 (7th Cir. 1986)]

3-7. A former probationary employee of the Ohio Department of Mental Retardation brought suit in the Ohio Court of Claims against her employer. The employee claimed that her discharge constituted a violation of her right to freedom of speech, guaranteed by the First Amendment, in that she was fired because she vocally disagreed about the treatment received by a particular mentally retarded person. Without ruling on her constitutional claims, the state court dismissed her action as a valid personnel decision. Following the dismissal by the Ohio court, the plaintiff brought suit in federal district court. The federal district court dismissed the constitutional claim against the state officials on the ground that the employee's previous state action constituted "a knowing, intelligent, and voluntary waiver" of her federal action. An Ohio statute provides that "filing a civil action in the Court of Claims results in a complete waiver of any cause of action, based on the same act or omission . . . against any state officer or employee." The employee appealed. The question before the appellate court is whether a state statute can limit jurisdiction granted by federal law. What should the court decide, and why? [*Leaman v. Johnson,* 794 F.2d 1148 (6th Cir. 1986)]

3-8. Gates worked for Arizona Brewing Co. and was a member of the International Union of United Brewers, Flour, Cereal, and Soft Drink Workers of America. A contract between Gates's employer and the union stated that the employer and the union were to try to settle their differences, but if the parties could not reach a settlement, the matter was to be decided by arbitration. Claiming that the arbitration clause was void under an Arizona arbitration statute, Gates brought a lawsuit against Arizona Brewing Co. to recover wages. Gates had not made any attempt to submit the dispute between him and the employer to arbitration. The employer argued that Gates could not bring a lawsuit until after arbitration had occurred. A provision in the Arizona arbitration statute, which generally enforced arbitration clauses in contracts, stated that "this act shall not apply to collective [bargaining] contracts between employers and . . . associations of employ[ees]." Must Gates undergo arbitration before bringing a lawsuit? Explain. [*Gates v. Arizona Brewing Co.,* 54 Ariz. 266, 95 P.2d 49 (1939)]

3-9. When Roger and Susan Faherty divorced, they entered into a property settlement agreement that was incorporated into the final divorce decree. The property settlement agreement contained a clause that mandated arbitration of any dispute arising out of the agreement. Roger failed to make several alimony and child support payments, and Susan sought court enforcement of the property settlement agreement. Roger's consequent motion to have the court compel arbitration was granted by the court, and the dispute was arbitrated. The arbitrator's decision required Roger to pay Susan $37,648 for back alimony payments and $12,284 for overdue child support. Roger, although he had been the one to petition the court for arbitration, now challenged the validity of the arbitration clause in alimony and child support matters. He claimed that as a matter of public policy such matters should be settled by the courts, not by arbitration. Will the court agree with Roger? Discuss. [*Faherty v. Faherty,* 97 N.J. 99, 477 A.2d 1257 (1984)]

3-10. Joseph Stout, while on the job as a construction worker, fell from a beam while he was attempting to secure the beam to a steel column. As a result of the fall, Stout sustained injuries that rendered him a paraplegic. Stout brought suit against his employer, A. M. Sunrise Construction Co., and Central Rent-A-Crane, Inc., for damages. Prior to the trial, a number of discovery motions were filed by the defendants, who sought detailed information on the nature of the accident and the injuries incurred. Stout repeatedly failed to respond to these requests, even when the

trial court ordered him to do so. Finally, the trial court dismissed the action because of Stout's failure to respond. Stout appealed the dismissal. On appeal, Stout claimed that the trial court had abused its discretion by dismissing his action against the defendants, thus depriving him of his right to be heard in court. What will the appellate court decide? Discuss. [*Stout v. A. M. Sunrise Construction Co.,* 505 N.E.2d 500 (Ind.App. 1987)]

3-11. Colorado's Mandatory Arbitration Act, which went into effect in January 1988, required that all civil lawsuits involving damages of less than $50,000 be arbitrated rather than tried in court. The statutory scheme, which was a pilot project to continue until July 1, 1990, affected eight judicial districts in the state. It provided for a court trial for any party dissatisfied with an arbitrator's decision. It also provided that if the trial did not result in more than a 10 percent improvement in the position of the party who demanded the trial, that party had to pay the costs of the arbitration proceeding. The constitutionality of the act was challenged by a plaintiff who maintained in part that it violated litigants' rights of access to the courts and to trial by jury. What will the court decide? Explain your answer. [*Firelock, Inc. v. District Court, 20th Judicial District,* 776 P.2d 1090 (Colo. 1989)]

3-12. Case Briefing Assignment

Examine Case A.2 [Goeller v. Liberty Mutual Insurance Co., 568 A.2d 176 (Pa. 1990)] in Appendix A. The case has been excerpted there in great detail. Review and then brief the case, making sure that you include in your brief answers for the following questions.

1. The Pennsylvania Supreme Court acknowledged that a strong presumption exists in favor of an arbitration panel's award. What must occur before that presumption is applied?
2. What statutory authority guided the court in its deliberations?
3. What two reasons underlie the court's decision that the arbitration panel's award was a nullity?

Chapter 4

Constitutional Authority to Regulate Business

The U.S. Constitution is the supreme law in this country.[1] Neither Congress nor any state may pass a law that conflicts with the Constitution. Laws that govern business have their origin in the lawmaking authority granted by this document.

Before the Constitution was written, a *confederal* form of government existed. The Articles of Confederation, ratified in 1778, established a confederation of independent states and a central government of very limited powers. The central government could handle only those matters of common concern expressly delegated to it by the member states, and the national congress had no ability to make laws directly applicable to individuals unless the member states explicitly supported such laws. In short, the *sovereign power* to govern rested essentially with the states.[2] The Articles of Confederation clearly reflected the central tenet of the American Revolution—that a government should not have unlimited power.

After the Revolutionary War, however, the states began to pass laws that hampered national commerce and foreign trade by preventing the free movement of goods and services. Consequently, in 1787, the Constitutional Convention convened to **amend** the Articles of Confederation to give the national government the power to address the country's commercial problems. Instead of amending the Articles of Confederation, the Convention created the Constitution and a completely new type of federal government, which they believed was much better equipped than its predecessor to resolve the problems of the nation.

■ Basic Constitutional Concepts

The U.S. Constitution delineates the structure and powers of the government, as well as the limitations on those powers.

Federalism

Federalism is the basis for the structure of the government in the United States. A *federal* form of government is one in which the states form a union

---

1. The U.S. Constitution has been included as Appendix B in this text.
2. *Sovereign power* refers to that supreme power to which no other person or authority is superior or equal.

and the sovereign power is divided between a central governing authority and the member states. The Constitution delegates certain powers to the national government, and the states retain all powers not delegated to the national government. The relationship between the national government and the state governments is a partnership—neither partner is superior to the other except within the particular area of authority granted to it under the Constitution. Hence, the concept of federalism recognizes that society may be best served by a distribution of functions among state governments and the national government on the basis of which government is better equipped to perform these functions. The Constitution reflects the belief that a national government can handle certain problems better than individual state governments can.

Conflicts frequently arise regarding the question of which government—national or state— should be exercising power in a particular area. The United States Supreme Court, as the arbiter of the Constitution, resolves such conflicts by deciding which governmental system is empowered to act under the Constitution.

Delegated Powers

The Constitutional Convention created a federal system of government in which the states delegated certain *enumerated powers* to the national government and reserved all other powers to themselves. Thus, the national government has no powers apart from those delegated to it by the states. The national government has no inherent powers (except in dealings with other nations) and can only exercise those powers that have been enumerated in the Constitution or that are necessary and proper for carrying out those powers. These delegated powers, however, are very broad, as reflected in the growth of the federal (national) government.

The Bill of Rights

For various reasons, proposals related to the rights of individuals made during the Constitutional Convention of 1787 were rejected. Yet the importance of a written declaration of the rights of individuals eventually caused the first Congress to submit ten amendments to the Constitution for the approval of the states. These amendments, commonly known as the Bill of Rights, were adopted in 1791 and embody a series of protections for the individual against various types of interference by the federal government. Among the guarantees provided for by the Bill of Rights are the First Amendment protection of the freedom of religion, speech, and assembly; the Fourth Amendment provisions regarding arrest and searches and seizures; and the Sixth Amendment rights to counsel, confrontation, and cross-examination in criminal prosecutions. Furthermore, through the Fourteenth Amendment, passed after the Civil War, most of these guarantees have been held to be so fundamental as to be applicable at the state level as well.

Also held to be so fundamental as to be applicable at both the state and the federal level is a personal right to privacy. There is no specific guarantee of a right to privacy in the Constitution. The right is derived from guarantees found in the First, Third, Fourth, Fifth, and Ninth Amendments. To date, the right to privacy has been held to apply only in cases involving matters of marriage, family relationships, and decisions on whether to bear children.

The rights secured by the Bill of Rights are not absolute. The principles enunciated in the Constitution are given form and substance by the government. Ultimately, it is the United States Supreme Court, as the interpreter of the Constitution, that gives meaning to, and determines the boundaries of, the rights guaranteed by the Constitution. For example, the freedom of speech guaranteed by the Constitution will be restrained whenever speech becomes *defamatory* (wrongfully injurious to another's reputation—see Chapter 5).

Separation of Powers

The federal government is divided into three branches—the executive branch, which enforces the laws; the legislative branch, which makes the laws; and the judicial branch, which interprets the laws. Article I of the Constitution provides for the legislative branch. The duties of the executive branch and the method of electing the president are set forth in Article II. The federal judicial system was created by Article III.

Deriving its power from the Constitution, each branch performs a separate function, and no branch may exercise the authority of another branch. Each branch, however, has some power to *limit* the actions of the other branches. In each article of the Constitution that grants specific powers to one of the three branches of the government, there is also a provision for the limitation of that power by another branch. Congress, for example, has power over spending and commerce, but the president can veto that legislation. The executive branch is responsible for foreign affairs, but treaties with foreign governments require the advice and consent of the members of the Senate. Under Article III, Congress determines the jurisdiction of the federal courts, but the United States Supreme Court has the power to hold acts of the other branches of the federal government unconstitutional.[3] Thus, with this system of checks and balances, no one branch of government can accumulate too much power.

The Commerce Clause

Article I, Section 8, of the United States Constitution expressly permits Congress "[t]o regulate Commerce with foreign Nations, and among the several States, and with the Indian tribes." This clause, referred to as the **commerce clause,** has had a greater impact on business than any other provision in the Constitution. Theoretically, the power over commerce authorizes the federal government to regulate every commercial enterprise

in the United States. This power was delegated to the federal government to ensure the uniformity of rules governing the movement of goods through the states.

For some time, the commerce power was interpreted as being limited to *interstate* commerce and not applicable to *intrastate* commerce. The United States Supreme Court, however, now recognizes that Congress has the power to regulate any activity, interstate or intrastate, that *affects* interstate commerce. Wheat production of an individual farmer intended wholly for consumption on his or her own farm, for example, was held to be subject to federal regulation, because such home consumption reduces the demand for wheat and thus may have a substantial effect on interstate commerce.[4]

The following case is illustrative. The case specifically demonstrates the United States Supreme Court's use of the commerce clause to affirm the power of Congress to pass the Civil Rights Act of 1964. The breadth of the commerce clause permits the national government to legislate in areas in which there is no explicit grant of power to Congress.

---

3. See *Marbury v. Madison,* 5 U.S. (1 Cranch) 137, 2 L.Ed. 60 (1803).

4. See *Wickard v. Filburn,* 317 U.S. 111, 63 S.Ct. 82, 87 L.Ed. 122 (1942).

BACKGROUND AND FACTS   A motel owner who refused to rent rooms to African Americans despite the Civil Rights Act of 1964 brought an action in a federal district court to have the Civil Rights Act of 1964 declared unconstitutional. The owner alleged that, in passing the act, Congress had exceeded its power to regulate commerce because his motel was not engaged in interstate commerce. The motel was accessible to state and interstate highways. The owner advertised nationally, maintained billboards throughout the state, and accepted convention trade from outside the state (75 percent of the guests were residents of other states). The court sustained the constitutionality of the act and enjoined the owner from discriminating on the basis of race. The owner appealed. The case went to the United States Supreme Court.

 Case 4.1

HEART OF ATLANTA MOTEL v. UNITED STATES
Supreme Court of the United States, 1964.
379 U.S. 241,
85 S.Ct. 348,
13 L.Ed. 2d 258.

DECISION AND RATIONALE   The United States Supreme Court upheld the constitutionality of the Civil Rights Act of 1964. The Supreme Court noted that the act was passed to correct "the deprivation of personal dignity" accompanying the denial of equal access to "public establishments." Testimony before Congress leading to the passage of the act indicated that African Americans in particular experienced substantial discrimination in attempting to secure lodging. This discrimination impeded interstate travel, thus impeding interstate commerce. As for the owner's argument that his motel was "of a purely local character," the Court said, "[I]f it is interstate commerce that feels the pinch, it does not matter how local the operation that applies the squeeze." Therefore, under the commerce clause, Congress has the power to regulate any local activity that has a harmful effect on interstate commerce.

SINCE *HEART OF ATLANTA* Actions are still brought to determine whether a local activity "substantially affects" interstate commerce and is thus subject to regulation by Congress. In *McLain v. Real Estate Board of New Orleans, Inc.,* the United States Supreme Court held that local real estate brokers, who were licensed to perform their function only in Louisiana, substantially affected financial transactions and title insurance that were clearly interstate in nature. Thus, the brokers' activities sufficiently affected interstate commerce to be regulated by federal laws. The Court acknowledged that the commerce clause had "long been interpreted to extend beyond activities actually in interstate commerce to reach other activities, while wholly local in nature, which nevertheless substantially affect interstate commerce." [5]

THE POWER OF STATES TO REGULATE Another problem that frequently arises under the commerce clause concerns a state's ability to regulate matters within its own borders. The U.S. Constitution does not expressly exclude state regulation of commerce, and there is no doubt that states have a strong interest in regulating activities within their borders. As part of their inherent sovereignty, states possess **police powers.** The term does not relate solely to criminal law enforcement but to the right of state governments to regulate private activities to protect or promote the public order, health, safety, morals, and general welfare. Fire and building codes, antidiscrimination laws, parking regulations, zoning restrictions, licensing requirements, and thousands of other state statutes covering virtually every aspect of life have been enacted under the state police power.

When state regulations impinge on interstate commerce, courts must balance the state's interest in the merits and purposes of the regulation against the burden placed on interstate commerce.[6] In *Raymond Motor Transportation, Inc. v. Rice,* for

example, the United States Supreme Court invalidated Wisconsin administrative regulations limiting the length of trucks traveling on its highways. The Court weighed the burden on interstate commerce against the benefits of the regulations and concluded that the challenged regulations "place a substantial burden on interstate commerce and they cannot be said to make more than the most speculative contribution to highway safety." [7]

Because courts balance the interests involved, it is extremely difficult to predict the outcome in a particular case. State laws enacted pursuant to a state's police powers and affecting the health, safety, and welfare of local citizens do carry a strong presumption of validity.

The Supremacy Clause

Article VI of the Constitution provides that the Constitution, laws, and treaties of the United States are "the supreme Law of the Land." This article, commonly referred to as the **supremacy clause,** is important in the ordering of state and federal relationships. When there is a direct conflict between a federal law and a state law, the state law is rendered invalid. But because some powers are shared by the federal government and the states—because they are concurrent powers—it is necessary to determine which law governs in a particular circumstance.

When concurrent federal and state powers are involved, a state law that conflicts with a federal law is prohibited. A federal action based on a power specifically delegated to the federal government by the Constitution always has the capacity to override a state law on the same matter. A federal regulatory scheme will supersede state law when there is an outright conflict between the two or when the state regulation interferes with federal objectives.

When Congress chooses to act exclusively in a concurrent area, it is said to have *preempted* the area. In this circumstance, a valid federal statute

---

5.   444 U.S. 232, 100 S.Ct. 502, 62 L.Ed.2d 441 (1980).

6.   See *Southern Pacific Co. v. Arizona,* 325 U.S. 761, 65 S.Ct. 1515, 89 L.Ed. 1915 (1945).

7.   434 U.S. 429, 98 S.Ct. 787, 54 L.Ed.2d 664 (1978).

or regulation will take precedence over a conflicting state or local law or regulation on the same general subject. Congress, however, rarely makes clear its intent to preempt an entire subject area against state regulation; consequently, the courts must determine whether Congress intended to exercise exclusive dominion over a given area. Consideration of preemption often occurs in the commerce clause context.

No single factor is decisive as to whether a court will find preemption. Generally, congressional intent to preempt will be found if the federal law is so pervasive, comprehensive, or detailed that the states have no room to supplement it. Also, when a federal statute creates an agency—such as the National Labor Relations Board—to enforce the law, matters that may come within the agency's jurisdiction will likely preempt state laws.

In the following case, the court had to determine whether federal laws preempted a county regulation.

BACKGROUND AND FACTS Bay Soaring leased a small private airport from Robert Harrison for glider operations, including gliding lessons and rides to the public. Sometimes as many as ninety flights a day took place. Harrison's neighbors, including Bernard Schwartz, protested the noise from the aircraft that towed the gliders aloft. Their protests were heard by the county zoning board, which concluded that the use of the airport had expanded substantially beyond the limits of the permit that the board had granted to Harrison several years before. The board granted a new permit but attached several conditions: Aircraft takeoffs had to be separated by intervals of at least fifteen minutes and could not be made before 9:00 A.M. or after 7:00 P.M. Bay Soaring appealed to a Maryland state court, claiming that these conditions were unconstitutional regulations by the county because federal noise and aviation laws preempted this area. The trial court agreed; the neighbors and the county appealed. The appellate court agreed with the neighbors and the county. Harrison and Bay Soaring appealed to the state's highest court, the Maryland Court of Appeals.

Case 4.2

HARRISON v. SCHWARTZ

Court of Appeals of Maryland, 1990.
319 Md. 360,
572 A.2d 528.

DECISION AND RATIONALE The Maryland Court of Appeals held that the conditions were preempted by federal law and were, therefore, unconstitutional. The court pointed out that "we are dealing with preemption by occupation of the field. Once the field is occupied by the federal government, neither state nor local government may enter it. And occupation of the field does not mean that every blade of grass within it must be subject to express federal control; it means only that Congressional intent demonstrates that the area is subject to exclusive federal control, whether potential or actual."

The Taxing Power

Article I, Section 8, further provides that Congress has the "Power to lay and collect Taxes, Duties, Imposts, and Excises . . . ; but all Duties, Imposts and Excises shall be uniform throughout the United States." The requirement of uniformity refers to uniformity among the states, and thus Congress may not tax some states while exempting others.

Traditionally, in reviewing cases related to the taxing power, the courts have examined whether Congress was actually attempting to regulate indirectly, by taxation, an area in which it had no authority to regulate directly. If the regulatory effect could have been achieved directly by Congress, then the tax would not be stricken as an invalid, disguised regulation. If Congress was attempting to regulate an area over which it had no authority, however, the tax would be invalidated.

In recent cases, the United States Supreme Court has focused less on the motives of Congress and more on whether the tax can be sustained as a valid exercise of federal regulation. The Court has upheld taxes on dealers in firearms,[8] on the transfer of marijuana,[9] and on persons engaged in the business of accepting wagers.[10] If Congress does not have the power to regulate the activity being taxed, the tax will still be upheld if it is a valid revenue-raising measure. If a tax measure bears some reasonable relationship to revenue production, it is generally held to be within the national taxing power. Moreover, the expansive interpretation of the commerce clause almost always provides a basis for sustaining a federal tax.

The Spending Power

Under Article I, Section 8, Congress has the power ''to pay the Debts and provide for the common Defence and general welfare of the United States.'' Through the spending power, Congress disposes of the revenues accumulated from the taxing power, and thus this power necessarily involves policy choices.

The requirement of *standing to sue* (discussed in Chapter 3) makes it difficult for taxpayers to use the judicial system to object to government spending, and consequently, the spending power is seldom challenged. The doctrine of standing to sue requires a litigant to demonstrate *a direct and immediate personal injury* caused by the challenged action.[11] Thus, a litigant must show that the injury suffered can be fairly traced to the challenged action and will be redressed by the judicial relief sought.[12] Communicating directly with members of Congress has proved to be a more efficient route to curbing or increasing federal allocations.

Congress can spend revenues not only to carry out its enumerated powers but also to promote any objective it deems worthwhile, so long as it does not violate the Bill of Rights. For example, Congress could not condition welfare payments on the

recipients' agreements not to criticize government policies.

■ The Bill of Rights in a Business Context

A *business* is a commercial, industrial, or professional activity engaged in for profit. Some business entities, such as corporations, exist as separate legal entities and enjoy many of the same rights and privileges as *natural* persons. A corporation is generally identified as an artificial person, or legal entity, under the law. The Bill of Rights guarantees citizens certain protections, and some constitutional protections apply to business entities as well.

The first ten amendments prohibit specific actions of the federal government, and the Fourteenth Amendment further prohibits most of the same actions by state governments. The due process clause of the Fourteenth Amendment applies certain rights guaranteed by the first ten amendments to the states. Under the doctrine of *selective incorporation,* only those guarantees of individual liberty that are fundamental to the American system of law must be protected by the states.

Freedom of Speech

All of the First Amendment freedoms of religion, speech, press, assembly, and petition have been applied to the states through the *due process clause* of the Fourteenth Amendment (discussed later in this chapter). As mentioned previously, however, none of these freedoms confers an absolute right. It is unclear what types of speech the First Amendment was designed to protect, but constitutional protection has never been afforded to certain classes of speech. In 1942, for example, the United States Supreme Court held as follows:

> There are certain well-defined and narrowly limited classes of speech, the prevention and punishment of which have never been thought to raise any Constitutional problem. These include the lewd and obscene, the profane, the libelous, and the insulting or ''fighting'' words—those which by their very utterance inflict injury or tend to incite an immediate breach of the peace. It has been well observed that such utterances are no essential part of any exposition of ideas, and are of such slight social value as a step to truth that any benefit that may be derived

---

8. *Sonzinsky v. United States,* 300 U.S. 506, 57 S.Ct. 554, 81 L.Ed. 772 (1937).

9. *United States v. Sanchez,* 340 U.S. 42, 71 S.Ct. 108, 95 L.Ed. 47 (1950).

10. *United States v. Kahriger,* 345 U.S. 22, 73 S.Ct. 510, 97 L.Ed. 754 (1953).

11. *Sierra Club v. Morton,* 405 U.S. 727, 92 S.Ct. 1361, 31 L.Ed.2d 636 (1972).

12. *Simon v. Eastern Kentucky Welfare Rights Organization,* 426 U.S. 26, 96 S.Ct. 1917, 48 L.Ed.2d 450 (1976).

from them is clearly outweighed by the social interest in order and morality.[13]

Also, governments may regulate the time, place, and manner of speech so long as they do not favor some ideas over others. In other words, two people can be prohibited from giving speeches at the same location at the same time. Otherwise, freedom of speech would belong only to the one who could shout the loudest.

Although the United States Supreme Court initially took the view that language treated as defamatory under state law was not entitled to First Amendment protection, it subsequently concluded that the First Amendment requires that a defense for honest error be allowed when statements are made about *public figures.* We will return to the distinction between private and public figures in the section on defamation in Chapter 5.

POLITICAL SPEECH   Speech that otherwise would be within the protection of the First Amendment does not lose that protection simply because its source is a corporation. For example, in *First National Bank of Boston v. Bellotti,* national banking associations and business corporations sought United States Supreme Court review of a Massachusetts statute that prohibited corporations from making political contributions or expenditures that individuals were permitted to make. The Court ruled that the Massachusetts law was unconstitutional because it violated the right of corporations to freedom of speech.[14]

Recently, a more conservative United States Supreme Court ruled that a similar Michigan statute was *not* unconstitutional. The Michigan statute prohibited corporations from using corporate funds for independent expressions of opinion about political candidates. Although the Court acknowledged that corporate spending to support candidates constitutes political speech and thus falls under the protection of the First Amendment, the limitation on political speech created by the Michigan statute was based on a compelling state interest in preserving the fairness of political debate. The Court stressed that corporations, which are creatures of state law, are given advantages that enable some of them to amass wealth. The statute ensured that the wealth of corporations would not give them a potential for unfair advantage over other voters.[15]

COMMERCIAL SPEECH   Freedom-of-speech cases generally distinguish between commercial and noncommercial messages. Although commercial speech, such as advertising, is protected by the First Amendment, its protection is not as extensive as that afforded to noncommercial speech. A restriction on commercial speech will generally be considered valid as long as it (1) seeks to implement a substantial government interest, (2) directly advances that interest, and (3) goes no further than necessary to accomplish its objective. The greater protection afforded to noncommercial speech by the First Amendment is stressed in the following case.

13.   *Chaplinsky v. New Hampshire,* 315 U.S. 568, 62 S.Ct. 766, 86 L.Ed. 1031 (1942).

14.   435 U.S. 765, 98 S.Ct. 1407, 55 L.Ed.2d 707 (1978).

15.   *Austin v. Michigan Chamber of Commerce,* 494 U.S. 652, 110 S.Ct. 1391, 108 L.Ed.2d 652 (1990).

Case 4.3

METROMEDIA, INC. v. CITY OF SAN DIEGO

Supreme Court of the United States, 1981.
453 U.S. 490,
101 S.Ct. 2882,
69 L.Ed.2d 800.

BACKGROUND AND FACTS   San Diego enacted an ordinance that imposed prohibitions on outdoor advertising displays "to eliminate hazards to pedestrians and motorists brought about by distracting sign displays" and "to preserve and improve the appearance of the City." The ordinance permitted on-site commercial advertising but forbade other commercial advertising and noncommercial advertising using fixed-structure signs. The ordinance excepted some signs, such as temporary political campaign signs. Companies that were engaged in the outdoor-advertising business sued in California state court to enjoin enforcement of the ordinance. The trial court held that the ordinance was an unconstitutional exercise of the city's police power and an abridgment of the companies' (First Amendment) free speech rights. The California Court of Appeal affirmed the decision, but the California Supreme Court reversed. The companies appealed.

DECISION AND RATIONALE The United States Supreme Court concluded that the ordinance was unconstitutional on its face and reversed and remanded the case. The Supreme Court emphasized that commercial speech could be regulated in situations in which noncommercial speech could not. The Court pointed out that San Diego's ordinance inverted this position by providing a broad exception for on-site commercial advertising but no similar exception for noncommercial speech. The Court ruled that the city could not limit the content of billboards to commercial messages. The city might prohibit or make exceptions for categories of commercial speech, but "[w]ith respect to noncommercial speech, the city may not choose the appropriate subjects for public discourse: 'To allow a government the choice of permissible subjects for public debate would be to allow that government control over the search for political truth.' "

Freedom of Religion

The First Amendment requires that the government neither establish any religion nor prohibit the free exercise of religious practices. This constitutional provision is referred to as either the **establishment clause** or the **free exercise clause.** Government action, both federal and state, must be consistent with this constitutional mandate. Federal or state regulation that does not promote, or place a significant burden on, religion is constitutional even if it has some impact on religion. ''Sunday closing laws,'' for example, make the performance of some commercial activities on Sunday illegal. These statutes, also known as ''blue laws,'' have been upheld on the ground that it is a legitimate function of government to provide a day of rest. The United States Supreme Court has held that the closing laws, although originally of a religious character, have taken on the secular purpose of promoting the health and welfare of workers.[16] Even though closing laws admittedly make it easier for Christians to attend religious services, the Court has viewed this effect as an incidental, not a primary, purpose of Sunday closing laws.

The First Amendment does not require a complete separation of church and state. On the contrary, it affirmatively mandates *accommodation* of all religions and forbids hostility toward any.[17] For

example, the United States Supreme Court held in *Lynch v. Donnelly* that a municipality could include religious symbols, such as a Nativity scene, in its annual Christmas display, as long as the religious symbols constituted just one part of a holiday display in which other, nonreligious symbols (such as reindeer and candy-striped poles) were also featured.[18] The Court applied this same reasoning in *County of Allegheny v. American Civil Liberties Union.* In this case, the presence of a Nativity scene within a county courthouse was held to be unconstitutional because it was not displayed in the same area of the courthouse as other, nonreligious holiday symbols. A menorah (a nine-branched candelabrum used in celebrating Chanukah) positioned on the courthouse steps, however, did not violate the First Amendment because it was situated next to a Christmas tree.[19]

Another freedom-of-religion issue involves the accommodation that businesses must make for the religious beliefs of their employees. Title VII of the Civil Rights Act of 1964 prohibits government employers, private employers, and unions from discriminating against persons because of their religion. The Equal Employment Opportunity Commission—the regulatory agency that interprets and applies Title VII—has required that private employers ''reasonably accommodate'' the religious practices of their employees, unless to do so would cause undue hardship to the employer's business.

16. *McGowan v. Maryland,* 366 U.S. 420, 81 S.Ct. 1101, 6 L.Ed.2d 393 (1961).

17. *Zorach v. Clauson,* 343 U.S. 306, 72 S.Ct. 679, 96 L.Ed. 954 (1952).

18. 465 U.S. 668, 104 S.Ct. 1355, 79 L.Ed.2d 604 (1984).

19. 492 U.S. 573, 109 S.Ct. 3086, 106 L.Ed.2d 472 (1989).

For example, if an employee's religion prohibits him or her from working on a certain day of the week or at a certain type of job, the employer must make a reasonable attempt to accommodate these religious requirements. Employers must reasonably accommodate an employee's religious belief even if the belief is not based on the tenets or dogma of a particular church, sect, or denomination. The only requirement is that the belief be sincerely held by the employee.[20]

---

20. *Frazee v. Illinois Department of Employment Security,* 489 U.S. 829, 109 S.Ct. 1514, 103 L.Ed.2d 914 (1989).

In the following case, the sacramental use of peyote by two employees violated both an employment policy and state law. When the employees were discharged for ''misconduct,'' the state refused to grant them unemployment benefits. Ultimately, the United States Supreme Court had to determine whether a state law prohibiting the use of peyote violated the religious rights of Native Americans whose religion required the sacramental use of this drug.

BACKGROUND AND FACTS   Two Native Americans, who worked as drug and alcohol abuse rehabilitation counselors, were discharged by their employer for ingesting peyote, a hallucinogenic drug, for sacramental purposes during a religious ceremony of the Native American church. When they applied for unemployment compensation, the state employment division denied their applications under a statute disqualifying employees who were discharged for work-connected misconduct. They appealed, claiming that the sacramental use of peyote did not constitute ''misconduct'' and that the denial of unemployment benefits violated their religious rights under the free exercise clause of the First Amendment. The Supreme Court of Oregon ruled in their favor, holding that the law prohibiting the sacramental use of peyote was unconstitutional. The state appealed the case to the United States Supreme Court.

DECISION AND RATIONALE   The United States Supreme Court reversed the Oregon court's ruling. The Supreme Court said that ''an individual's religious beliefs [do not] excuse him from compliance with an otherwise valid law prohibiting conduct that the State is free to regulate.'' That would inhibit the government's ability to enforce prohibitions of socially harmful conduct. ''To make an individual's obligation to obey such a law contingent upon the law's coincidence with his religious beliefs'' would contradict ''both constitutional tradition and common sense.'' The Court acknowledged that less common religious practices might be at a disadvantage, ''but that unavoidable consequence of democratic government must be preferred to a system in which each conscience is a law unto itself or in which judges weigh the social importance of all laws against the centrality of all religious beliefs.''

Case 4.4

EMPLOYMENT DIVISION, DEPARTMENT OF HUMAN RESOURCES OF THE STATE OF OREGON v. SMITH

Supreme Court of the United States, 1990.
494 U.S. 872,
110 S.Ct. 1595,
108 L.Ed.2d 876.

Searches and Seizures

The Fourth Amendment protects the ''right of the people to be secure in their persons, houses, papers, and effects.'' Federal, state, and local governments must obtain search warrants before searching or seizing private property. To obtain a warrant, law enforcement officers must convince a judge that they have *probable cause* to believe a search will reveal a specific illegality. **Probable cause** requires law enforcement officials to have trustworthy evidence that would convince a reasonable person that the proposed search or seizure is more likely justified than not. Furthermore, the Fourth Amendment prohibits general warrants and requires a particular description of that which is to be searched or seized. General searches through a

The Boundaries of Free Commercial Speech

 The First Amendment to the U.S. Constitution guarantees freedom of speech. However explicit this guarantee may seem, the courts have nonetheless imposed limitations on individuals' rights to free speech. For example, one does not have the right to yell "fire" in a crowded movie theater. Nor does one have the right to defame the good name or reputation of others by making false statements about them. Furthermore, there are numerous restrictions on the rights of individuals to publish obscene materials. Businesses have even more stringent restrictions on their rights to free speech.

Limitations on Commercial Speech

A distinction is often made between "normal" speech and "commercial" speech. Commercial speech—speech by business firms—consists of advertising, political endorsements, and the like. This type of speech is protected, but to a much lesser extent than speech by individuals. Whenever corporate or business speech is contrary to a "compelling state interest," it can be restrained. For example, a state has a compelling interest in seeing to it that consumers are not misled by false advertising claims. Therefore, the state can limit commercial speech if it deems that the commercial speech at issue misleads consumers. Another state interest is the beautification of roadsides, and this interest allows the state to place restraints on billboard advertising.

The point at which commercial speech passes over the boundary line that separates protected from unprotected commercial speech depends on whether a court holds that a given state interest in limiting the speech is sufficiently compelling to justify the restraint. Court decisions that limit commercial speech are often the subject of controversy.

The Regulation of Housing Advertisements

The Fair Housing Act of 1968[a] and its amendments make it unlawful to publish any advertisement with respect to the sale or rent of a dwelling that indicates any preference based on race. Publishers of newspapers and those controlling other media that accept advertisements rarely, if ever, willfully violate federal law in this regard. What happens, though, when the models used in an advertisement for a housing development do not reflect a "fair" racial make-up? This issue arose recently when the Open Housing Center, Inc., and several African-Americans in New York City brought suit against the New York Times Company (the Times), alleging that certain real estate ads in the *New York Times* communicated a "whites only" message to potential buyers of the real estate—not in the words used in the ads, but in the illustrations, in which African Americans were depicted as being subservient to whites.[b] The Times claimed that the suit should be dismissed because it would be unconstitutional to require newspapers to monitor their ads. Furthermore, the Times argued, to prohibit it from publishing advertisements for a perfectly legal activity—the selling of real estate—would infringe on its right to free speech. The federal trial court hearing the case did not agree with the Times (nor did the appellate court when the case was appealed). The court pointed out that the Times routinely monitors ads to avoid publishing ads that do not meet its "Standards of Advertising Acceptability." These standards provide, among other things, that the Times will not accept ads that fail to comply with antidiscrimination laws.

The appellate court concluded that "it strains the credibility

---

a.   42 U.S.C. Section 3604(c).

b.   *Ragin v. New York Times Co.,* 923 F.2d 995 (2d Cir. 1991).

beyond the breaking point to assert that monitoring ads for racial messages imposes an unconstitutional burden [on the Times].''

The Question of Emotional Injury

The Times pointed out that, given the court's holding, the potential for baseless claims for emotional injury exists. For example, a plaintiff may establish a *prima facie* case for punitive damages for emotional injury simply by *oral* testimony that he or she is a newspaper reader of a race different from that of the models used and was substantially insulted and distressed by a certain ad. The court sympathized with the Times but did not regard such a possibility as a reason to ''immunize publishers from any liability.'' The court stated that ''[w]here the claim of an illegal preference is based solely upon the use of models and not upon more directly offensive racial messages, we are confident that courts will be able to keep such awards within reason.''

It looks as if the newspaper publisher, rather than the real estate company placing the ads, may be held liable for racial overtones and suggestions implicit in advertisements.

■ Implications for the Businessperson

1. It is now clear that advertisements must be

monitored not only by advertisers but also by the publishers of advertisements. Advertisers and those who provide vehicles for advertisements must be careful to monitor the racial (and sexual) makeup of the models used in all advertisements. (Such monitoring has been carried out for many years by publishers of elementary and secondary school books to ensure that a fair representation of American society is presented to student readers.)

2. The issue of restrictions on commercial speech is one that will continue to create controversy within and without the courts. All businesses must be concerned with the extent to which they are abiding by the law and public policy when they express themselves in advertising and in other corporate speech, such as political speech (overtly sponsoring a particular political candidate, for example).

■ For Critical Analysis

1. Is it possible not to discriminate against any group when advertising in a nationwide publication such as the *New York Times?* In other words, because the U.S. population is made up of many ethnic groups, how does one determine what percentage of each group must be depicted in advertisements? What if a firm only places one ad, and in that

ad a white person is used as a model? Is the ad discriminatory and thus in violation of the federal Fair Housing Act? If you were the publisher of a newspaper, would you be reluctant to use any models in your advertisements for fear of insulting those among your readership who are from an ethnic background different from that of the model depicted?

2. Models are used in advertisements in television also. To what extent do the owners of television networks have to worry about liability for damages if a viewer is distressed by the fact that one of the network's advertisers consistently uses only white males in its ads?

3. Some people contend that there is an inconsistency between the protection afforded to individual speech and that afforded to commercial speech. For example, ''hate messages'' and racial slurs are counter to the public policy underlying antidiscrimination laws, yet they continue to be heard daily throughout this country. Why should individuals be allowed to engage in overtly discriminatory speech while publishers are prohibited from allowing ads that are suggestive of discrimination?

person's belongings are impermissible. The search cannot extend beyond what is described in the warrant.

There are exceptions to the requirement of a search warrant, as when it is likely that the items sought will be removed before a warrant can be obtained. For example, if a police officer has probable cause to believe an automobile contains evidence of a crime and it is likely that the vehicle will be unavailable by the time a warrant is obtained, the officer can search the vehicle without a warrant.

Constitutional protection against unreasonable searches and seizures is important to businesses and professionals. With increased federal and state regulation of commercial activities, frequent and unannounced government inspection to ensure compliance with the law would be extremely disruptive. In *Marshall v. Barlow's, Inc.,*[21] the United States Supreme Court held that government inspectors do not have the right to enter business premises without a warrant, although the standard of probable cause is not the same as that required in nonbusiness contexts. A general and neutral enforcement plan will justify issuance of the warrant. Lawyers and accountants frequently possess the business records of their clients, and inspecting these documents while they are out of the hands of their true owners also requires a warrant.

On the other hand, no warrant is required for seizures of spoiled or contaminated food. Nor are warrants required for searches of businesses in such highly regulated industries as liquor, guns, and strip mining. General manufacturing is not considered to be one of these highly regulated industries.

---

21.   436 U.S. 307, 98 S.Ct. 1816, 56 L.Ed.2d 305 (1978).

Self-Incrimination

The Fifth Amendment guarantees that no person "shall be compelled in any criminal case to be a witness against himself." Thus, in any federal proceeding, an accused person cannot be compelled to give testimony that might subject him or her to any criminal prosecution. An accused person cannot be forced to testify against himself or herself in state courts either, because the Fourteenth Amendment due process clause incorporates the Fifth Amendment provision against self-incrimination.

The Fifth Amendment's guarantee against self-incrimination extends only to natural persons. Because a corporation is a legal entity and not a natural person, the privilege against self-incrimination is inapplicable to it. Similarly, the business records of a partnership do not receive Fifth Amendment protection.[22] No artificial organization may utilize the personal privilege against compulsory self-incrimination. When it is required that records of such organizations be produced, the information must be given even if it incriminates the persons who constitute the business entity.

Sole proprietors and sole practitioners who have not incorporated cannot be compelled to produce their business records. These individuals have full protection against self-incrimination because they function in only one capacity: there is no separate business entity.

In the following case, the sole stockholder in a corporation attempted to assert his Fifth Amendment privilege to avoid having to produce his corporation's records.

---

22.   The privilege has been applied to some small family partnerships. See *United States v. Slutsky*, 352 F.Supp. 1105 (S.D.N.Y. 1972).

Case 4.5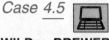

WILD v. BREWER
United States Court of Appeals,
Ninth Circuit, 1964.
329 F.2d 924.

BACKGROUND AND FACTS   Bennett Brewer, an Internal Revenue Service agent, served Albert Wild with a summons issued by a federal district court, requiring Wild to appear and testify about the tax liability of "Albert J. Wild, President, Air Conditioning Supply Company." Wild was the sole owner of the company, a corporation, and corporate records were also requested. Wild refused to produce the records on the ground that they might tend to incriminate him and hence were protected by the Fifth Amendment. Wild was cited for contempt and appealed.

DECISION AND RATIONALE   The United States Court of Appeals affirmed and ordered Wild to produce the records, indicating that a corporation does not have a constitutional privilege against self incrimination. One judge dissented. The judge pointed out that Wild "did not claim the privilege for the corporation *   *   *. He claims it for himself, and says that he, and not any artificial legal entity, will be the one to suffer the punishment if he is obliged to furnish to the Government the evidence which will bring about his conviction." As "sole owner of his corporation, the corporation does embody the 'purely private or personal interests of its [only] constituent(s),' who is Wild himself."

COMMENTS   A corporation is a legal fiction; that is, it is considered to be a person for most purposes under the law. An unsettled area of corporation law has to do with the criminal acts of a corporation. It is obvious that a corporation cannot be sent to prison even though, under law, it is a person. Most courts hold a corporation that has violated the criminal statutes liable for fines, although in recent years, other penalties have been imposed (see Chapter 7). When criminal conduct can be attributed to corporate officers or agents, those individuals, as natural persons, are held liable and can be imprisoned for their acts.

■ Other Constitutional Guarantees

Two other constitutional guarantees of great significance to Americans are mandated by the due process clauses of the Fifth and Fourteenth Amendments and the equal protection clause of the Fourteenth Amendment.

Due Process

Both the Fifth and the Fourteenth Amendments provide that no person shall be deprived "of life, liberty, or property, without due process of law." The **due process clause** of these constitutional amendments has two aspects—procedural and substantive. *Procedural* due process requires that any government decision to take life, liberty, or property must be made fairly, and thus fair procedures must be used in determining whether a person will be subjected to punishment or have some burden imposed on him or her. Fair procedure has been interpreted as requiring that the person have at least an opportunity to object to a proposed action before a fair, neutral decision maker (which need not be a judge). Thus, for example, if a driver's license is construed as a "property" interest, some sort of opportunity to object to its suspension or termination by the state must be provided.

Substantive due process focuses on the content, or substance, of legislation. In general, a law that is not compatible with the Constitution violates substantive due process. If a law or other govern-

mental action limits a *fundamental right,* it will be held to violate substantive due process unless it promotes a *compelling or overriding interest.* Fundamental rights include interstate travel, privacy, voting, and all First Amendment rights. Compelling interests could include, for example, the public's safety. Thus, laws designating speed limits may be upheld, even though they affect interstate travel, if they are shown to reduce highway fatalities because the state has a compelling interest in protecting the lives of its citizens.

In all other cases, a law or action does not violate substantive due process if it rationally relates to any legitimate governmental end. It is almost impossible for a law or action to fail the "rationality" test. Under this test, virtually any business regulation will be upheld as reasonable— the United States Supreme Court has sustained insurance regulations, price and wage controls, banking controls, and controls of unfair competition and trade practices against substantive due process challenges.

To illustrate: If a state legislature enacted a law imposing a fifteen-year term of imprisonment without allowing a trial on all businesspersons who appeared in their own television commercials, the law would be unconstitutional on both substantive and procedural grounds. Substantive review would invalidate the legislation because it abridges freedom of speech. Procedurally, the law is unfair because it imposes the penalty without giving the accused a chance to defend his or her actions. The lack of procedural due process will cause a court to invalidate any statute or prior court decision. Similarly, a denial of substantive due process requires courts to overrule any state or federal law that violates the Constitution.

Equal Protection

Under the Fourteenth Amendment, a state may not "deny to any person within its jurisdiction the equal protection of the laws." The United States Supreme Court has used the due process clause of the Fifth Amendment to make the **equal protection clause** applicable to the federal government. Equal protection means that the government must treat similarly situated individuals in a similar manner.

Both substantive due process and equal protection require review of the substance of the law or other governmental action rather than the procedures used. When a law or action limits the liberty of all persons to do something, it may violate substantive due process; when a law or action limits the liberty of some persons but not others, it may violate the equal protection clause. Thus, for example, if a law prohibits all persons from buying contraceptive devices, it raises a substantive due process question; if it prohibits only unmarried persons from buying the same devices, it raises an equal protection issue.

Basically, in determining whether a law or action violates the equal protection clause, a court will consider questions similar to those previously noted as applicable in a substantive due process review. Under an equal protection inquiry, when a law or action distinguishes between or among individuals, the basis for the distinction—that is, the *classification*—is examined. If the law or action inhibits some persons' exercise of a fundamental right, the classification must be necessary to promote a compelling interest. Also, if the classification is based on a *suspect* trait—such as race, national origin, or citizenship status—the classification must be necessary to promote a compelling interest. Compelling interests include remedying past unconstitutional or illegal discrimination but do not include correcting the general effects of "society's" discrimination. Thus, for example, if

a city gives preference to minority applicants in awarding construction contracts, the city must identify the past unconstitutional or illegal discrimination against minority construction firms that it is attempting to correct. (Discrimination and affirmative action are discussed more fully in Chapter 48.)

In matters of economic or social welfare, the classification will be considered valid if there is any conceivable *rational basis* on which the classification might relate to any legitimate government interest. It is almost impossible for a law or action to fail the rational-basis test. Thus, for example, a city ordinance that in effect prohibits all pushcart vendors except a specific few from operating in a particular area of the city will be upheld if the city proffers a rational basis—perhaps regulation and reduction of traffic in the particular area—for the ordinance. On the other hand, a law that provides unemployment benefits only to people over six feet tall would violate the guarantee of equal protection. There is no rational basis for determining the distribution of unemployment compensation on the basis of height. Such a distinction could not further any legitimate government objective.

Another approach is applied in cases involving discrimination based on gender or legitimacy. Laws using these classifications must be *substantially related to important government objectives.* For example, an important government objective is preventing illegitimate teenage pregnancies. Because males and females are not similarly situated in this circumstance—only females can become pregnant—a law that punishes men but not women for statutory rape will be upheld. On the other hand, a state law requiring illegitimate children to bring paternity suits within six years of their birth will be struck down if legitimate children are allowed to seek support from their parents at any time. An important objective behind statutes of limitations is to prevent persons from bringing stale or fraudulent claims, but distinguishing between support claims on the basis of legitimacy has no relation to this objective.

In the following case, the defendant asserted that age discrimination against a government employee was rationally related to a legitimate state interest.

BACKGROUND AND FACTS   Adela Izquierdo Prieto, age forty-two, had worked for a government-owned public television station in Puerto Rico for over a decade when, without notice, she was transferred to the station's radio affiliate. Her replacement was a less experienced woman, age twenty-eight. Agustin Mercado Rosa, the administrator of the television channel, explained to a newspaper reporter that Izquierdo was removed because "we need new faces" and Izquierdo's replacement "is young, attractive and refreshing." Izquierdo sued Mercado in a federal district court, alleging that the transfer discriminated against her on the basis of age and therefore violated her rights under the equal protection clause. Mercado claimed that the transfer was rationally related to furthering a legitimate state interest in maximizing viewership for the television channel, and therefore it was a permissible action. The trial court agreed with Izquierdo and awarded damages. Mercado appealed.

Case 4.6

IZQUIERDO PRIETO v. MERCADO ROSA

United States Court of Appeals,
First Circuit, 1990.
894 F.2d 467.

DECISION AND RATIONALE   The United States Court of Appeals reversed. Under the rational-basis test, the question was whether Mercado's actions were based on a legitimate state interest. Mercado's ostensible objective was to replace Izquierdo with someone with greater audience appeal. The court stated that "Mr. Mercado could have rationally believed that having 'new [and young] faces' would maximize audience drawing power." The purpose of public television "includes serving the public by providing increased access to information and enhanced opportunities for education. Benefit to the public as a whole is maximized the more people take advantage of the services provided. Thus, to maximize viewership by making programs as appealing as possible is a legitimate objective in the operation of government-owned television stations."

COMMENTS   The court noted that Congress intended to make age discrimination unlawful by passing the Age Discrimination in Employment Act (ADEA) of 1967. The ADEA prohibits discrimination against employees on the basis of their age. Izquierdo, however, did not bring her claim under the ADEA but under the equal protection clause. Therefore the court did not address the issue of whether Mercado's actions had violated the ADEA.

■ Terms and Concepts

amend 73	establishment clause 80	police powers 76
commerce clause 75	federalism 73	probable cause 81
due process clause 85	free exercise clause 80	supremacy clause 76
equal protection clause 86		

■ For Review

1.   What is the basic structure of the American national government?
2.   What body gives meaning to, and determines the boundaries of, the rights guaranteed by the Constitution?
3.   The first ten amendments to the Constitution—the Bill of Rights—embody protections against various types of interference by the federal government. Certain of these protections that are considered fundamental to the American system apply to the states. Under what part of the Constitution do these rights apply to the states?

4. Massachusetts enacts a statute requiring that every automobile be covered by an insurance policy as a condition of registering the vehicle. Several automobile owners bring a suit against the state, challenging the law on the ground that it violates substantive due process because it affects the right to interstate travel. The state argues that the requirement is necessary to protect the welfare of its citizens. What might the court decide?

5. New Jersey enacts a statute prohibiting all persons who are more than 50 pounds overweight from appearing in swimming suits on state beaches. Sid and Sam, who are respectively 100 pounds and 125 pounds overweight, bring a suit against the state, challenging the statute on the ground that it violates the equal protection clause. The state argues that the prohibition is necessary to protect the aesthetic sensibilities of its citizens. How might the court rule?

■ Questions and Case Problems

4-1. The U.S. Constitution, in which the people of the United States give the government the "power to govern," was written by a handful of men who represented the aristocracy of the time. Surprisingly, this group of aristocrats wrote a document giving more freedoms to common people than any other constitution in existence. Look at Appendix B. Name some of the basic guarantees found in the Constitution.

4-2. Suppose that in 1973, when the nation was suffering a fuel shortage, the Public Service Commission of the State of Illinois ordered that all "promotional advertising" by electric utilities cease. Assume that this order was based on the commission's finding that the state in all likelihood did not have sufficient fuel for the upcoming winter. If the Public Service Commission sought to enforce its ban in 1977, when the fuel shortage had eased, would such enforcement be a regulation of commercial speech in violation of the First Amendment? If so, why? (Assume that the commission's interest in conservation could not have been adequately protected by a less restrictive alternative.)

4-3. A Georgia statute requires the use of contoured rear-fender mudguards on trucks and trailers operating within Georgia state lines. The statute further makes it illegal for trucks and trailers to use straight mudguards. In approximately thirty-five other states, straight mudguards are legal. Moreover, in Florida, straight mudguards are explicitly required by law. There is some evidence that suggests that contoured mudguards might be a little safer than straight mudguards. Discuss whether this Georgia statute violates any constitutional provisions.

4-4. A mayoral election is about to be held in a large U.S. city. One of the candidates is Gregory Schumann, and his campaign supporters wish to post campaign signs on lamp posts and utility posts throughout the city. A city ordinance, however, prohibits the posting of any signs on public property. Schumann's supporters contend that the city ordinance is unconstitutional because it violates their rights to free speech. Do you agree? In your answer, discuss what factors a court might consider in determining the constitutionality of the ordinance.

4-5. Thomas worked in the nonmilitary operations of a large firm that produced both military and nonmilitary goods. When the company discontinued the production of nonmilitary goods, Thomas was transferred to a plant producing war materials. Thomas left his job, claiming that it violated his religious principles to participate in the manufacture of materials to be used in destroying life. In effect, he argued, the transfer to the war-materials plant forced him to quit his job. He was denied unemployment compensation by the state because he had not been effectively "discharged" by the employer but had voluntarily terminated his employment. Does the state's denial of unemployment benefits to Thomas violate the free exercise clause of the First Amendment? Explain. [*Thomas v. Review Board of the Indiana Employment Security Division,* 450 U.S. 707, 101 S.Ct. 1425, 67 L.Ed.2d 624 (1981)]

4-6. A 1988 Minnesota statute required all operators of slow-moving vehicles to display on their vehicles a fluorescent orange-red triangular emblem or, as an alternate, a dull black triangle with a white reflective border, plus seventy-two square inches of permanent red reflective tape. A vehicle operator who chose the alternate emblem still had to carry a regular orange-red emblem in the vehicle and display it externally during times of darkness or low visibility. The state brought charges against Hershberger and other members of the Amish religion (the defendants) because they refused to comply with the statute. The defendants claimed that the statute violated their freedom of religion under the First Amendment because displaying the "loud" colors and "worldly symbols" on their slow-moving vehicles (black, box-like buggies) compromised their religious belief that they should remain separate and apart from the modern world. The defendants stated that they would not object to displaying a sign similar to the alternate symbol, if they could use silver, instead of red, reflective tape, and if they did not have to display the "regular" emblem at night. The state argued that, although the silver tape was as effective as the red, in terms of visibility, the red tape was customarily associated with slow-moving vehicles, and therefore the Amish should comply with the statute as written. What will the court hold? Discuss. [*State v. Hershberger,* 444 N.W.2d 282 (Minn. 1989)]

4-7. The California Fair Employment and Housing Act requires employers to provide leave and reinstatement to employees disabled by pregnancy. At the federal level, Title VII of the Civil Rights Act of 1964, which prohibits employment discrimination on the basis of sex, was amended by the Pregnancy Discrimination Act (PDA) in 1978. The PDA specifies that sex discrimination includes discrimination on the basis of pregnancy. The PDA does not, though, require employers to provide pregnancy leave and reinstatement of employment. A woman employed as a receptionist by California Federal Savings and Loan Association (Cal Fed) took a pregnancy disability leave in 1982. When she notified Cal Fed that she was able to return to work, she was told that her job had been filled and that there were no similar positions available. She then filed a complaint with the California Department of Fair Employment and Housing, which charged Cal Fed with violating the Fair Employment and Housing Act. Before a hearing was held on the complaint, Cal Fed, joined by other employers, brought an action in federal court seeking a declaration that the California Fair Employment and Housing Act was inconsistent with, and preempted by, Title VII of the Civil Rights Act, as amended, and that Cal Fed was thus entitled to an injunction against its enforcement. How should the court rule? Give the reasons for your conclusion. [*California Federal Savings and Loan Association v. Guerra,* 479 U.S. 272, 107 S.Ct. 683, 93 L.Ed.2d 613 (1987)]

4-8. Eligibility and benefit levels in the Federal Food Stamp Program are determined on a household rather than an individual basis. The statutory definition of the term *household* was amended in 1981 and 1982 so that parents, children, and siblings who lived together were to be generally treated as single households but more distant relatives or groups of unrelated persons living together were not to be treated as households unless they also customarily purchased food and prepared meals together. Families that generally bought food and prepared meals as separate economic units, and not as families, would either lose benefits or have their food stamp allotments decreased as a result of the 1981 and 1982 amendments. Several of these families brought suit, claiming the statutory definition of the term *household* was unconstitutional. Did the statutory distinction between parents, children, and siblings, on the one hand, and all other groups of individuals, on the other, violate the guarantee of equal treatment in the due process clause of the Fifth Amendment? Explain. [*Lyng v. Castillo,* 477 U.S. 635, 106 S.Ct. 2727, 91 L.Ed.2d 527 (1986)]

4-9. In 1982, Philip Zauderer, an attorney practicing in Columbus, Ohio, placed a series of newspaper ads directed at women who had used the Dalkon Shield intrauterine device (IUD). In his ads, Zauderer included a drawing of the Dalkon Shield and informed women that they could still sue for any injuries or other harm to their health sustained by its use, even though the IUD was no longer being marketed. As a result of these ads, Zauderer filed lawsuits for 106 women. The Ohio Supreme Court deemed such advertisements unethical, and Zauderer was reprimanded by the court for his actions. He was further reprimanded for not having disclosed in his ads that, although his clients would owe no legal fees if they lost, they might still be faced with other costs involved in litigation. Zauderer appealed, claiming the ads were protected under the First Amendment as ''commercial speech'' and that failure to disclose other costs was not deceptive. Discuss the probable success of Zauderer's appeal. [*Zauderer v. Office of Disciplinary Counsel,* 471 U.S. 626, 105 S.Ct. 2265, 85 L.Ed.2d 652 (1985)]

4-10. In 1983, Gary Peel, an Illinois attorney, began placing on his letterhead the following statement: ''Certified Civil Trial Specialist / By the National Board of Trial Advocacy.'' In so doing, Peel violated Rule 2-105(a) of the Illinois Code of Professional Responsibility, which prohibits lawyers from holding themselves out as ''certified'' or ''specialists'' in fields other than admiralty, trademark, and patent law. The Attorney Registration and Disciplinary Commission (ARDC) censured Peel for the violation. The ARDC claimed that Peel's letterhead was misleading because it implied that Peel had special qualifications as an attorney, although in fact no such thing as a civil trial specialty existed in Illinois; because the word *certified* might be interpreted to mean ''licensed,'' and the National Board of Trial Advocacy (NBTA) did not have the authority to license lawyers; and because, given the fact that not all attorneys licensed to practice in Illinois are certified by the NBTA, Peel's assertion might erroneously be construed by some readers to mean that those who are certified by that board are superior to those who are not. Peel argued that Rule 2-105(a) violated his constitutional right to free speech and appealed the ARDC's decision to the United States Supreme Court. What will the Court decide? Discuss. [*Peel v. Attorney Registration and Disciplinary Commission,* 496 U.S. 91, 110 S.Ct. 2281, 110 L.Ed.2d 83 (1990)]

4-11. Taylor owned a bait business in Maine and arranged to have live baitfish imported into the state. The importation of the baitfish violated a Maine statute. Taylor was indicted under a federal statute that makes it a federal crime to transport fish in interstate commerce in violation of state law. Taylor moved to dismiss the indictment on the ground that the Maine statute unconstitutionally burdened interstate commerce. Maine intervened to defend the validity of its statute, arguing that the law legitimately protected the state's fisheries from parasites and nonnative species that might be included in shipments of live baitfish. Were Maine's interests in protecting its fisheries from parasites and nonnative species sufficient to justify the burden placed on interstate commerce by the Maine statute? Discuss. [*Maine v. Taylor,* 477 U.S. 131, 106 S.Ct. 2440, 91 L.Ed.2d 110 (1986)]

4-12. In 1988, as a result of a general election, Arizona added Article XXVIII to its constitution. Article XXVIII provided that English was to be the official language of the state and required all state officials and employees to use only the English language during the performance of government business. Maria-Kelly Yniguez, an employee of the Arizona Department of Administration, frequently spoke in Spanish to Spanish-speaking persons with whom she dealt in the course of her work. Yniguez claimed that Article XXVIII violated constitutionally protected free speech rights and brought an action in federal court against the state governor, Rose Mofford, and other state officials. Does Article XXVIII violate the freedom of speech guaranteed by the First Amendment to the U.S. Constitution? Why or why not? [*Yniguez v. Mofford,* 730 F.Supp. 309 (D.Ariz. 1990)]

4-13. In 1957, Rhodes and several other Georgia landowners entered into a sixty-five-year timber purchase contract with Inland-Rome, Inc. Thereafter, Inland-Rome cut timber from the landowners' land and then removed it for processing in certain Georgia facilities, after which it was shipped as lumber products to points throughout the country. In 1986, the landowners claimed that Inland-Rome had breached the contract and filed suit. Inland-Rome moved to compel arbitration because the parties had agreed, in their contract, to arbitrate any disputes arising thereunder. Georgia law enforces arbitration clauses only if they are contained in construction contracts. Arbitration clauses are enforceable under the Federal Arbitration Act only if the contracts in which they appear affect interstate commerce. Inland-Rome contended that, because lumber products from the cut timber were shipped throughout the nation, the contract related to interstate commerce, and therefore the Federal Arbitration Act should apply. Will the court agree? Discuss. [*Rhodes v. Inland-Rome, Inc.,* 195 Ga.App. 39, 392 S.E.2d 270 (1990)]

4-14. Case Briefing Assignment

 Examine Case A.3 [Austin v. Berryman, 878 F.2d 786 (4th Cir. 1989)] in Appendix A. The case has been excerpted there in great detail. Review and then brief the case, making sure that you include answers to the following questions in your brief.

1. Who were the plaintiff and defendant in this action?
2. Why did Austin claim that she had been forced to leave her job?
3. Why was she refused state unemployment benefits?
4. Did the state's refusal to give her unemployment compensation violate her rights under the free exercise clause of the First Amendment?
5. What logic or reasoning did the court employ in arriving at its conclusion?

Chapter 5

Torts

Part of doing business today and, indeed, part of everyday life is the risk of being involved in a lawsuit. A normal and ever-increasing business operating cost is that of liability insurance to protect against lawsuits. The list of circumstances in which business people can be sued is long and varied. An employee injured on the job may attempt to sue the employer because of an unsafe working environment. The consumer who is injured while using a product may attempt to sue the manufacturer because of a defect in the product. At issue in these examples is alleged wrongful conduct by one person that causes injury to another. Such wrongful conduct is covered by the law of **torts.** (The word *tort* is French for "wrong.")

Tort law covers a broad variety of injuries. Society recognizes an interest in personal physical safety, and tort law provides a remedy for acts causing physical injury or interfering with physical security and freedom of movement. Society recognizes an interest in protecting property, and tort law provides a remedy for acts causing destruction or damage to property. Society recognizes other, more intangible interests in such things as personal privacy, family relations, reputation, and dignity. Tort law provides a remedy for invasion of protected interests in these areas.

Tort law is constantly changing and growing with society. Although many torts have their origin in the old common law, new torts are recognized to protect new interests that develop with social change. For example, until recently, because of old notions of family structure, it was not a legally recognizable tort for a husband to negligently injure his wife or child. But today minors, as well as spouses, receive much more protection. Traditionally, one could not recover **damages** for psychological injury unless one had personally risked physical harm. That rule is changing, with more and more courts allowing recovery for emotional damage to those who witness traumatic injury to another.

■ Tort Law versus Criminal Law

Two notions serve as the basis of all torts: wrongs and compensation. Tort law recognizes that some acts are wrong because they cause injuries to persons. Those who commit the acts are to blame, or bear the fault, for these injuries. Of course, torts are not the only type of wrongs that exist in the law; crimes involve wrongs also. In fact, most crimes involve torts. The commission of a tort, however, is not always a crime. A crime is an act so reprehensible that it is considered to be a wrong against the state or against society as a whole. Therefore, the *state* prosecutes the criminal, and the resulting judgment imposes a jail term, a fine, or both. A tort action, in contrast, is a *civil* action in which one person brings a suit of a personal nature against another. The state is not a party to the suit, and the resulting judgment imposes damages but no jail term. In some cases, the same act can be a criminal wrong *and* a civil wrong. Intentionally threatening another, for example, could be the basis for a criminal prosecution as well as the basis of an action in tort for assault (assault will be discussed shortly).

The function of tort law is to provide the injured party with some *remedy*. The law of torts is used to decide when victims must bear the loss themselves and when the responsibility belongs to someone else. A typical tort action involves an intentional or a negligent act of one party that causes personal or property damage to another.

■ Kinds of Torts

Torts have been traditionally divided into the following three categories:

1.   Intentional torts.
2.   Negligence.
3.   Strict liability.

Intentional torts involve acts that were intended to bring about the consequences that are the basis of the tort. **Negligence** involves matters of risk—sometimes a negligent actor is unaware of the results that will follow from his or her act, and sometimes he or she considers the consequences carefully before acting, but in neither case are the consequences intended. **Strict liability** rules require someone to compensate the injured party without regard to fault.

■ Intentional Torts: Wrongs against the Person

An intentional tort, as the term implies, requires *intent*. The **tortfeasor** (the one committing the tort) must intend to commit an act, the consequences of

which interfere with the personal or business interests of another in a way not permitted by law. The underlying motive—the reason or impulse behind the intentional act—does not matter. The actor could have been joking or playing around or could even have had some benevolent motive. In tort law, intent only means that the actor intended the consequences of his or her act or knew with substantial certainty that certain consequences would result from the act. The nature of the damage ultimately caused is irrelevant in determining whether there was intent. If Johnson intentionally pushes Adams and Adams falls to the ground and breaks her arm, it does not matter that Johnson never wished to break Adams's arm. It is enough that Johnson intended to bring about harmful or offensive contact to Adams, and Johnson is thus liable for the consequences, including the injury to Adams's arm.

The law generally assumes that one intends the normal consequences of his or her actions. Thus, a push is an intentional tort because the object of the push can ordinarily be expected to go flying; however, a playful pat on the shoulder is not an intentional tort even though, in drawing away suddenly, the person touched may be injured. To recover damages, the injured person must normally prove that real harm has occurred.

Assault

Any intentional, unexcused act that creates in another person a reasonable apprehension or fear of immediate harmful or offensive contact is an **assault.** Apprehension is not the same as fear. If the contact is such that a reasonable person would want to avoid it, and if there is a reasonable basis for believing the contact is coming, then the plaintiff suffers apprehension whether or not he or she is afraid. For example, the *threat* of forceful delivery of an unwanted kiss may constitute an assault.

The interest protected by tort law concerning assault is the freedom from having to expect harmful or offensive contact. The arousal of apprehension is enough to justify compensation. Of course, the *completion* of the act that caused the apprehension, if it results in harm to the plaintiff, also constitutes a tort—a *battery*, discussed below. For example, Jones brings a gun along to an interview with Smith. There is no assault unless she threatens Smith with it, perhaps by pointing it at him and showing that all she has to do to use it is to cock it. If she fires the gun, and the bullet hits Smith, she has committed a battery.

Battery

A **battery** is an unexcused, harmful, or offensive physical contact intentionally performed. If Jones intentionally punches Smith in the nose, it is a battery. The interest protected by tort law in this case is the right to personal security and safety. The contact can be harmful, or it can be merely offensive (such as an unwelcome kiss). Physical injury does not have to occur. The contact can be to any part of the body or anything attached to it— for example, a hat or other clothing, a purse, or a chair or an automobile in which one is sitting. The contact can be made by the defendant or by some force that the defendant sets in motion—for example, a rock thrown, food poisoned, or a stick swung.

If the plaintiff shows that there was a contact, and the jury agrees that the contact was offensive, that is enough to establish a right to some compensation. Damages from a battery can be for emotional harm or loss of reputation as well as for physical harm.

Defenses to Assault and Battery

A number of legally recognized defenses can be raised by a defendant who is sued for assault or battery, or both. The defenses to be discussed here are (1) consent, (2) self-defense, (3) defense of others, and (4) defense of property.

CONSENT   When a person **consents** to the act that harms him or her, there is no liability for the damage done. A person who voluntarily signs up for a touch football team implicitly consents to the *normal* physical punishment that takes place during such activities. This defense is good only as long as the defendant remains within the boundaries of the consent given—that is, plays football by the normal rules.

SELF-DEFENSE   An individual who is defending his or her life or physical well-being may use the defense of **self-defense.** A person is privileged to use whatever force is *reasonably* necessary to prevent harmful contact. This defense extends not only to *real* danger but also to *apparent* danger. Rea-

sonable grounds must exist for believing the danger is real, however. Also, force cannot be used once the danger has passed, and revenge is always prohibited.

DEFENSE OF OTHERS   An individual can act in a reasonable manner to protect others who are in real or apparent danger.

DEFENSE OF PROPERTY   Individuals who use reasonable force in attempting to remove intruders from their homes can use defense of property to counter tort lawsuits for assault or battery, or both. The law does value life, though, more than it values property. In principle, force that is likely to cause death or great bodily injury may never be used just to protect property. Setting a mechanical device that fires a gun if an intruder enters an empty house is not considered reasonable by most courts.

False Imprisonment

False imprisonment is defined as the intentional confinement or restraint of another person without justification. It involves interference with the freedom to move without restraint. The confinement can be accomplished through the use of physical barriers, physical restraint, or threats of physical force. Moral pressure or future threats are not restraints sufficient to constitute false imprisonment. It is essential that the person being restrained not comply with the restraint willingly.

Businesspersons are often confronted with suits for false imprisonment after they have attempted to confine suspected shoplifters for questioning. Consider, for example, the case in which a store detective locks an alleged shoplifter in one of the store's offices. If the customer can prove that the detention was totally unreasonable, the customer can successfully sue the store for false imprisonment.

The loss to business from shoplifting is estimated to exceed $15 billion a year. Almost all states have adopted so-called merchant-protection legislation, which allows a merchant to detain any suspected shoplifter, provided that there is reasonable cause for suspicion and provided that the confinement is carried out in a reasonable way. Because the risk of real injury to an innocent person is great, however, educational programs should be offered to all employees; these programs explain the exact procedures to be followed when a customer is suspected of shoplifting and help to prevent unlawful detentions and consequent lawsuits. Harm to reputation and emotional distress caused by wrongful imprisonment are believed by the law to be so real that damages are presumed and need not be proved to make a case.

Under the privilege to detain granted to merchants in some states, a merchant can use the defense of *probable cause* to justify delaying a suspected shoplifter. Probable cause exists when there is more evidence for the belief that a person is guilty than against it. The detention, however, must be conducted in a *reasonable* manner and for only a *reasonable* length of time. The following case provides a good example.

Case 5.1

JOHNSON v. K-MART ENTERPRISES, INC.

Court of Appeals of Wisconsin, 1980.
98 Wis.2d 533,
297 N.W.2d 74.

BACKGROUND AND FACTS   Deborah Johnson went to the K-Mart in Madison, Wisconsin, carrying her child with her in an infant seat that she had bought at K-Mart two or three weeks before. After buying some diapers and children's clothes, Johnson approached the exit. The store's security officer stopped her and asked her to come back into the store because an employee had reported that she had seen Johnson steal the infant seat. To show ownership, Johnson pointed to cat hair, food crumbs, and stains on the seat. After twenty minutes, the officer apologized and let Johnson leave. Johnson sued K-Mart for damages in a Wisconsin state court, on grounds of false imprisonment. The trial court dismissed Johnson's action, and Johnson appealed.

DECISION AND RATIONALE   The Wisconsin Court of Appeals upheld the dismissal of Johnson's claim. The court held that "the merchant, through its security guard, had probable cause based on [its employee's] report to believe that plaintiff had shoplifted." By statute, a merchant with probable cause may detain a shoplifter for a reasonable time in a reasonable manner. There was nothing in the store's actions to "permit an inference that the detention was accomplished in an unreasonable manner." Finally, weighing the merchant's interest in detaining suspected shoplifters against the customer's "liberty interests," the court concluded that the twenty-minute delay was reasonable.

Infliction of Emotional Distress

Recently the courts have begun to recognize an interest in freedom from emotional distress as well as an interest in physical security. The tort of *infliction of emotional distress* can be defined as an intentional act that amounts to extreme and outrageous conduct resulting in severe emotional distress to another.[1] For example, a prankster telephones an individual and says that the individual's spouse has just been in a horrible accident. As a result, the individual suffers intense emotional pain or anxiety. This is deemed to be extreme and outrageous conduct that exceeds the bounds of

decency accepted by society and is therefore actionable.

As this is a relatively new tort, it poses some problems. One major problem is that it could flood the courts with lawsuits. A society in which individuals are rewarded if they are unable to endure the normal emotional stresses of day-to-day living is obviously undesirable. Therefore, the law usually focuses on the nature of the acts that come under this tort. Indignity or annoyance alone are usually not enough to support a lawsuit based on intentional infliction of emotional distress. Many times, however, repeated annoyances, coupled with threats, are enough. In a business context, for example, the repeated use of extreme methods to collect a delinquent account may be actionable.

---

1.   Restatement (Second) of Torts, Section 46, Comment d.

Also, an unusually severe emotional reaction, such as the extreme distress of a woman incorrectly informed that her husband and two sons have been killed, may be actionable. Because it is difficult to prove the existence of emotional suffering, a court may require that the emotional distress be evidenced by some physical symptom or illness or some emotional disturbance that can be documented by a psychiatric, or other, consultant.

In recent years, some courts have permitted emotional distress lawsuits for psychic damage if the emotional trauma suffered was sufficiently severe. An issue currently before the courts is whether airline passengers who endure the torture of preparing for a crash landing, or who survive a crash landing without physical injury, should have a cause of action for emotional distress. In some cases, emotional distress actions have been allowed to those who suffer emotionally and psychologically just from having witnessed a horrible accident. For example, a California court recently allowed parties to bring an emotional distress lawsuit after they witnessed the traumatic death of a passenger—a total stranger to the plaintiffs—on a Palm Springs tramway car in which the plaintiffs were riding. The accident occurred when a part of the tramway car broke loose, crashed through the overhead window, and killed the passenger.[2]

Defamation

As discussed in Chapter 4, the freedom of speech guaranteed by the First Amendment is not absolute. In interpreting the First Amendment, the courts must balance the vital guarantee of free speech against another pervasive and strong social interest—preventing and redressing attacks on reputation. When one wrongfully hurts another's good reputation, the tort of **defamation** results. Tort law imposes a general duty on all persons to refrain from making false, defamatory statements about others. Breaching this duty orally involves the tort of **slander**; breaching it in writing or in any form of communication that has ''the potentially harmful qualities characteristic of written or printed words''[3] involves the tort of **libel.** Courts have held that the forms of libelous communication include pictures, signs, statues, and films.

The common law has defined four types of false utterances that are considered slanderous *per se,* or on their face. That means that no proof of damages is required before these false utterances become actionable. They are:

1. *A statement that another has a loathsome communicable disease.* Courts have generally limited this tort to imputations that an individual has a venereal disease—although a statement that a person had AIDS has been held to be slanderous *per se.*[4]

2. *A statement that another has committed improprieties while engaging in a profession or trade.* For example, it is actionable to say of an attorney that he or she is unethical, of a merchant that his or her credit is bad, or of a person holding public office that he or she has accepted a bribe. But statements alleging that a clerk has consorted with prostitutes or is a homosexual, that a physician has committed adultery, or that a stenographer's credit is bad have not been held to be actionable—because the clerk, the physician, and the stenographer may still be competent at their work.

A statement that another has committed or has been imprisoned for a serious crime. Courts generally agree that the crime referred to in the statement must involve ''moral turpitude,'' which has been defined as ''inherent baseness or vileness of principle in the human heart.'' Beating children, for example, involves moral turpitude, while other forms of battery may not.

A statement that an unmarried woman is unchaste.

THE PUBLICATION REQUIREMENT   The basis of the tort of defamation is the *publication* of a statement or statements that hold an individual up to contempt, ridicule, or hatred. *Publication* here means that the defamatory statements are made to or within the hearing of persons other than the defamed party. If Thompson writes Andrews a private letter accusing him of embezzling funds, that does not constitute libel. If Peters calls Gordon dishonest, unattractive, and incompetent when no one else is around, that does not constitute slander. In neither case was the message communicated to a third party. Interestingly, the courts have gen-

---

2. *Ballinger v. Palm Springs Aerial Tramway,* 220 Cal.App.3d 581, 269 Cal.Rptr. 583 (Cal.App. 1990).
3. Restatement (Second) of Torts, Section 568.

---

4. See *McCune v. Neitzel,* 235 Neb. 754, 457 N.W.2d 803 (1990).

erally held that dictating a letter to a secretary constitutes publication (although a privilege could be involved in this situation—see privileged speech below). Moreover, if a third party overhears defamatory statements by chance, the courts have generally held that this also constitutes publication. Note further that any individual who republishes or repeats defamatory statements is liable even if that person reveals the source of the statements. Most radio stations have instituted seven-second delays for live broadcasts, such as talk shows, to avoid this kind of liability.

DEFENSES TO DEFAMATION   Truth is normally an *absolute* defense against a defamation charge. But the statement at issue must be true in whole, not in part, and if the statement is specific, the truth must also be specific. For instance, if the accusation is that Tony stole a stereo from Sara, it is insufficient to show that Tony is known as a bad character or that Tony stole stereos from Ruth. On the other hand, if the statement is substantially true, it is not necessary to prove every detail. For example, saying a politician has wasted $80,000 of the taxpayers' money has been held justified when it was proved that he wasted $17,500.

Other defenses to defamation may exist if the speech concerns a *public figure* or if the speech is *privileged.*

Public Figures   **Public figures** include public officials and employees who exercise substantial governmental power and any persons in the public limelight. Statements made about public figures, especially when they are made via a public medium, are usually related to matters of general public interest; they are made about people who substantially affect all of us. Furthermore, public figures generally have some access to a public medium for answering disparaging falsehoods about themselves; private individuals do not. For these reasons, public figures have a greater burden of proof in defamation cases than do private individuals. In *New York Times Co. v. Sullivan,* the United States Supreme Court held that to recover damages, a public figure must prove that a defamatory statement was made with **actual malice**— that is, *with either knowledge of its falsity or a reckless disregard of the truth.*[5]

The following case illustrates a libel case involving a public figure and the extent of liability when actual malice is proved.

---

5.   *New York Times Co. v. Sullivan,* 376 U.S. 254, 84 S.Ct. 710, 11 L.Ed.2d 686 (1964).

Case 5.2

BURNETT v. NATIONAL ENQUIRER, INC.

California Court of Appeal, Second District, 1983.
144 Cal.App.3d 991,
193 Cal.Rptr. 206.

BACKGROUND AND FACTS   Carol Burnett, the comedienne, believed that she had been libeled by an article in the *National Enquirer,* which stated that she was intoxicated and involved in a "row" with Henry Kissinger in a Washington, D.C., restaurant. Burnett sued the *Enquirer* in a California state court and was awarded $300,000 in general damages and $1,300,000 in punitive damages. The *Enquirer* moved for judgment notwithstanding the verdict and a new trial, claiming, among other things, that there was no actual malice on its part and that the damages were excessive. The trial court judge denied the *Enquirer's* motions, but reduced the general damages to $50,000 and the punitive damages to $750,000. The *Enquirer* appealed.

DECISION AND RATIONALE   The California Court of Appeal affirmed the trial court's denial of the *Enquirer's* motions and upheld the general damage reduction to $50,000 but lowered punitive damages from $750,000 to $150,000. The court pointed out that Burnett had to establish actual malice by clear and convincing evidence to recover general damages and by a preponderance of the evidence to recover punitive damages. *Actual malice* is established by proving that the defendant published the item either knowing it was false or with reckless disregard for its truth. The court concluded that Burnett had proved malice at the trial by a preponderance of the evidence and upheld the general-damages award, but also found that the amount of punitive damages was unjustifiably disproportionate to the amount of general damages.

Privileged Speech   In some circumstances, a person will not be liable for defamatory statements because he or she enjoys a **privilege,** or immunity. Privileged communications are of two types, *absolute* and *qualified.* Only in limited cases, such as in judicial proceedings and legislative proceedings, is absolute privilege granted. For example, statements made by attorneys and judges during a trial are absolutely privileged and therefore cannot be the basis for a defamation charge. Members of Congress making statements on the floor of Congress have an absolute privilege. Legislators have complete immunity from liability for false statements made in debate, even if they make such statements maliciously—that is, knowing them to be untrue. This absolute immunity is granted because judicial and legislative personnel deal with matters that are so much in the public interest that the parties involved should be able to speak out fully and freely and without restriction.

In other situations, a person will not be liable for defamatory statements because he or she has a *qualified* privilege. Qualified, or conditional, privilege is a common law concept based on the philosophy that the right to know or speak is of equal importance with the right not to be defamed. For example, a qualified privilege exists when there is a common interest between the person who makes the statement and the one who receives it. Thus, a statement concerning corporate business made by one corporate director to another is qualifiedly privileged. If a communication is conditionally privileged, to recover damages the plaintiff must show that the privilege was abused.

Another example of a qualified privilege is found in letters of recommendation and in written evaluations of employees. This privilege allows some latitude for making mistakes in the communication without defamation liability. Generally, if the communication statements are made in good faith and the publication is limited to those who have a legitimate interest in the communication, the statements fall within the area of qualified privilege.

Invasion of the Right to Privacy

A person's right to solitude and freedom from prying public eyes is the interest protected by the tort of invasion of privacy. Four different acts qualify as invasions of privacy:

1.   *The use of a person's name or picture or other likeness for commercial purposes without permission.* For example, using without permission someone's picture to advertise a product or someone's name to enhance a company name invades the person's privacy.

2.   *Intrusion upon an individual's affairs or seclusion.* For example, invading someone's home or illegally searching someone's briefcase is an invasion of privacy. This tort has been held to extend to eavesdropping by wiretap, unauthorized scanning of a bank account, compulsory blood testing, and window peeping.

3.   *Publication of information that places a person in a false light.* This could be a story attributing to a person ideas not held or actions not taken by that person. (Publishing such a story could involve the tort of defamation as well.)

4.   *Public disclosure of private facts about an individual that an ordinary person would find objectionable.* A newspaper account of a private citizen's sex life could be an actionable invasion of privacy. An example of what would *not* constitute this form of invasion of privacy is an article publicizing what a one-time child star is doing today, as long as nothing is revealed that the community would regard as highly objectionable (unless the objectionable information is truthful and contained in official records that are open to public inspection).

In the following case, the well-known consumer advocate Ralph Nader sued General Motors for the invasion of his right to privacy.

Case 5.3

NADER v. GENERAL MOTORS CORP.

Court of Appeals of New York, 1970.
25 N.Y.2d 560,
255 N.E.2d 765,
307 N.Y.S.2d 647.

BACKGROUND AND FACTS When Ralph Nader was about to publish *Unsafe at Any Speed*, a book that criticized the safety and design of vehicles manufactured by General Motors Corporation (GM), GM allegedly sought to intimidate him. Nader claimed that GM (1) asked Nader's acquaintances about his political and religious views, integrity, sexual proclivities and inclinations, and personal habits; (2) kept him under surveillance in public places for an unreasonable length of time; (3) caused him to be accosted by women for the purpose of entrapping him into illicit relationships; (4) made threatening, harassing, and obnoxious telephone calls to him; (5) tapped his telephone and eavesdropped on his private conversations with others; and (6) conducted a continuing and harassing investigation of him. Nader brought an action in a New York state court against GM, alleging, among other things, that GM had invaded his privacy by these actions. The trial court held for Nader, and GM appealed.

DECISION AND RATIONALE The New York Court of Appeals affirmed the lower court's ruling in favor of Nader, although it held that only the eavesdropping by wiretap was an invasion of Nader's right to privacy. The court pointed out that an invasion of privacy involves conduct that is "truly 'intrusive' " and "designed to elicit information which would not be available through normal inquiry." GM's inquiries of Nader's acquaintances could have revealed only information already known to others. Being accosted and receiving threatening and harassing telephone calls may have been "offensive and disturbing," but neither involved "intrusion for the purpose of gathering information of a private and confidential nature."

Fraud means "lie"

Fraudulent Misrepresentation

The tort of fraudulent misrepresentation involves the use of fraud and deceit for personal gain. It includes several elements:

1. Misrepresentation of facts or conditions with knowledge that they are false or with reckless disregard for the truth.
2. Intent to induce another to rely on the misrepresentation.
3. Justifiable reliance by the deceived party.
4. Damages suffered as a result of reliance.
5. Causal connection between the misrepresentation and the injury suffered.

In general, the reliance must be on a statement of fact. Reliance on a statement of opinion is not justified unless the person making the statement has a superior knowledge of the subject matter. A lawyer's opinion of the law, for instance, is an example of superior knowledge, and reliance on that opinion will be regarded as reliance on a statement of fact.

For fraud to occur, more than mere *seller's talk*, or **puffing**, must be involved. Fraud exists only when a person represents as a material fact something he or she knows is untrue. For example, it is fraud to claim that a building does not leak when one knows it does. Facts are objectively ascertainable, whereas seller's talk is not. "I'm the best lawyer in town" is seller's talk. The speaker is not trying to represent something as fact, because "best" is a subjective, not an objective, term. (The topic of fraud in contracts is discussed in Chapter 13.)

■ Intentional Torts: Wrongs against Property

Wrongs against property include (1) trespass to land and to personal property, (2) conversion, and (3) nuisance. The wrong is against the individual who has legally recognized rights with regard to real or personal property. The law distinguishes real property from personal property. *Real property*, also called *realty*, is land and things permanently attached thereto. *Personal property,* or *personalty,* includes things that are basically movable. Thus, a house and lot are real property, whereas the furniture inside a house is personal property. Money and securities are also personal property.

Trespass to Land

The civil tort called a **trespass to land** occurs any time a person, without permission, enters onto land that is owned by another, or causes anything or anyone to enter onto the land, or remains on the land, or permits anything to remain on it. Note that actual harm to the land is not an essential element of this tort, because tort law in respect to trespass is designed to protect the right of an owner to exclusive possession. If no harm is done, usually only nominal—in name only, not significant—damages (such as $1) can be recovered by the landowner. Examples of common types of trespass to land include walking or driving on the land, shooting across it with a gun, throwing rocks or spraying water on a building in the possession of another, building a dam across a river that causes water to back up on someone else's land, and placing part of one's building on the adjoining landowner's property.

In the past, the right to land gave exclusive possession of a space that extended from ''the center of the earth to the heavens,'' but this rule has been relaxed. Today, reasonable intrusions are permitted. Thus, aircraft can normally fly over privately owned land. The temporary invasion of the air space over such land is, in effect, considered privileged as to the aircraft owner. Society's interest in air transportation preempts the individual's interest in the air space.

TRESPASS CRITERIA, RIGHTS, AND DUTIES Before a person can be held to be a trespasser, the real property owner (the person who legally controls the realty) must establish that person as a trespasser. For example, ignoring ''posted'' trespass signs and entering onto the property anyway establish a person as a trespasser. A guest in your home is not a trespasser; if the guest becomes unruly and you *ask* the guest to leave, however, the guest will become a trespasser. Any person who enters onto another's property to commit an illegal act (such as a thief entering a lumberyard at night to steal lumber) is established as a trespasser without verbal establishment or posted signs.

Once a person is established as a trespasser, certain rights and duties are applied to both the owner of the realty and to the trespasser. Some of these rights and duties are as follows:

1. A trespasser is liable for any damage caused to the property. The owner does not have to prove negligence.

2. A trespasser assumes the risks of the premises and cannot hold the owner liable for injuries sustained. This rule does not permit the owner to lay traps with the intent to injure a trespasser. Under the ''attractive nuisance'' doctrine, infants or young persons do not assume the risks of the premises if they are attracted to the premises by some object or feature thereon. Under some circumstances an owner may even have a duty to warn of dangers on the property, such as guard dogs.

3. As previously discussed, a trespasser can be removed from the premises through the use of reasonable force without the owner being liable for assault and battery. This same basic concept allows an owner to remove, without liability, another's personal property, the presence of which constitutes a trespass, if the removal is accomplished by the exercise of reasonable care.

DEFENSES TO TRESPASS TO LAND Trespass to land involves wrongful interference with another person's real property rights. But if one can show that the trespass was warranted, as when a trespasser enters to assist someone in danger, a complete defense exists. Consent may also be implied from past behavior. Another defense is to show that the purported owner did not actually have the right to possess the land in question.

In some situations, courts can easily assess damages for trespass to land, especially when the trespasser damages or wrongfully destroys items of value on the land. For example, land purchasers can recover the value of destroyed trees when avoidable errors caused construction crews to knock them down.

Trespass to Personal Property

Whenever any individual unlawfully harms the personal property of another or otherwise interferes with the personal property owner's right to exclusive possession and enjoyment of that property, **trespass to personal property**—also called *trespass to personalty*—occurs. Trespass to personal property involves interference with a person's right to possess his or her property and, thus, may entail acts of damage, dispossession, or both. For example, if a student takes another student's business law book as a practical joke and hides it so that the owner is unable to find it for several days prior to the final examination, the student has engaged in a trespass to personal property.

If it can be shown that trespass to personal property was warranted, then a complete defense has been made. Many states, for example, allow automobile repair shops to hold a customer's car (under what is called an artisan's, or possessory, lien) when the customer has refused to pay for repairs rendered.

Conversion

Whenever personal property is taken from its rightful owner or possessor and placed in the service of one who has no legal right to it, or whenever the rightful owner of personal property is otherwise deprived of its use (due to vandalism, for example), the act of **conversion** occurs. Conversion is a trespass to personal property so serious that a converter can be forced to buy the property. A store clerk who steals merchandise from the store commits not only a crime but the tort of conversion as well. Of course, when conversion occurs, the lesser offense of trespass to personal property usually occurs as well. If the initial taking of the property was unlawful, there is trespass. Retention of the property is conversion. If the initial taking of the property was permitted by the owner or, for some other

reason, is not a trespass, failure to return it may nonetheless constitute conversion.

Even if a person mistakenly believed that he or she was entitled to the goods, a tort of conversion may take place. In other words, good intentions are not a defense against a charge of conversion, and conversion can be an entirely innocent act. To illustrate: Green loaned her lawn mower to Samuels to mow his lawn. Samuels used the lawn mower and then lent it to his neighbor, Nichols. A thief stole the lawn mower from Nichols. When Green learned what had happened to the mower, she demanded that Samuels pay for it. Samuels is guilty of conversion because he had no right to lend the mower to Nichols. His misuse of the mower renders him liable. He obviously did not intend for the mower to be stolen, but he intentionally took the mower from Green and intentionally and knowingly lent it to his neighbor.

Whoever suffers a conversion is generally entitled to recover the reasonable value of the lost goods. If Henries deliberately smashes a vase that Arts, Inc., exhibits for sale in its store, Henries is liable for the value of the vase. Deliberate destruction of the personal property of another is conversion. Henries treated the vase as if he owned it when he asserted a right to destroy it. When the goods have not been destroyed, the owner can either try to get them back through a lawsuit or ask for damages for conversion. The court will not give the owner full value for the goods and return the property as well.

The following case illustrates the concept of the tort of conversion.

Case 5.4

RUSSELL-VAUGHN FORD, INC. v. ROUSE
Supreme Court of Alabama, 1968.
281 Ala. 567,
206 So.2d 371.

BACKGROUND AND FACTS   During negotiations to buy a new car from Russell-Vaughn Ford, Inc., E. W. Rouse gave a sales representative the keys to his old car. When Rouse decided not to buy a new car, the sales representatives said that they had lost the keys. Rouse called the police, and when they arrived, a salesperson returned the keys, saying that "they just wanted to see him cry a while." Rouse sued Russell-Vaughn in an Alabama state court for conversion of his car. The trial court held for Rouse and awarded him $5,000 in punitive damages. Russell-Vaughn appealed, arguing that Rouse could have called his wife at home, who had another set of keys.

DECISION AND RATIONALE   The Supreme Court of Alabama upheld the award. The court explained that "it is the refusal, without legal excuse, to deliver a chattel, which constitutes a conversion." Withholding the keys, after Rouse demanded them and without which he could not move his car, "amounted to a conversion of the automobile." It did not matter that Rouse could have called his wife to get another set of keys—the court found no case requiring plaintiffs to exhaust all possible means of regaining possession of property being withheld from them without legal excuse, after demanding its return.

STOLEN GOODS   As mentioned above, intent to engage in a wrongdoing is not necessary for conversion to exist. Rather, it is the intent to exercise control over property when such control is inconsistent with the plaintiff's rights that constitutes conversion. Therefore, someone who *buys* stolen goods is guilty of conversion even if he or she did not know the goods were stolen—although the buyer is not guilty of a crime in this situation. If the true owner brings a tort action against the buyer, the buyer must pay the owner the full value of the property, despite having already paid some money to the thief.

DEFENSES TO CONVERSION   A successful defense against the charge of conversion is that the purported owner has no title, or right to possess, superior to the holder's rights.

Necessity is another possible defense against conversion. If Abrams takes Stephens's cat, Abrams is guilty of conversion. If Stephens sues Abrams, Abrams must return the cat or pay damages. If, however, the cat has rabies and Abrams took the cat to protect the public, Abrams has a valid defense—necessity (and perhaps even self-defense if he can prove that he was in danger from the cat).

Nuisance

It is possible to commit a tort and be liable because of unreasonable uses you make of your own property. A **nuisance** is an improper activity that interferes with another's enjoyment or use of his or her property. Nuisances can be either *public* or *private*. A public nuisance disturbs or interferes with the public in general, as when the burning of leaves causes smoke to pollute an entire neighborhood. A private nuisance interferes with the property interest of a limited number of individuals, as when a trash pile left next to a neighbor's property creates an attraction for rodents. Reasonable limitations are placed on the use of property in all situations. Such limitations prevent the owner from unreasonably interfering with the health and com-

fort of neighbors or with their right to enjoy their own private property. The usual remedy is damages for one who suffers as a result of a nuisance. When damages are unavailable or inadequate, one can have the nuisance stopped by seeking an injunction in the courts. An injunction is an equitable remedy. The court, if it grants the injunction, will prohibit the continuation of the undesirable activity.

Nuisances can also involve indecent, improper, or unlawful personal conduct. Obviously, there is an extremely subjective element in any definition of nuisance, particularly when it involves personal conduct. Moreover, a nuisance may be a crime as well as a tort, and the dividing line is difficult to ascertain. Finally, nuisances may result from intentional types of conduct as well as from negligent (careless) conduct. The defendant may even be held liable on the grounds of strict liability (discussed at the end of this chapter). The fact that there is no one, clear-cut definition of nuisance has led to difficulties in applying the doctrine. As William Prosser—a leading scholar in the area of torts—noted, nuisance "has come to mean all things to all people, and has been applied indiscriminately to everything from an alarming advertisement to a cockroach baked in a pie."[6]

■ Unintentional Torts: Negligence

Technological changes during the Industrial Revolution increased the number of injuries to people and their property. Because the injuries were generally unintended, it could not be held that they resulted from intentional torts. Also, to hold the new industries responsible for all of these injuries would have inhibited industrial progress. With these considerations in mind, the courts created negligence law. Today in the United States, negligence is the dominant cause of action for accidental injuries.

---

6.   W. Page Keeton et al., *Prosser and Keeton on Torts, 5th Ed.* (St. Paul: West Publishing Co., 1984), p. 616.

In contrast to intentional torts, in negligent torts the tortfeasor neither wishes to bring about the consequences of an act nor believes that they will occur. The actor's conduct merely creates a *risk* of such consequences. Without the creation of a risk, there can be no negligence. Moreover, the risk must be foreseeable; that is, it must be such that a reasonable person would anticipate it and guard against it. In determining what is reasonable conduct, courts consider the nature of the possible harm. A very slight risk of a dangerous explosion might be unreasonable, whereas a distinct possibility of burning one's fingers on a stove might be reasonable.

Some of the actions discussed in the preceding section on intentional torts would constitute negligence if the element of intent were missing. For instance, deliberately punching someone in the nose is an intentional tort—battery. But carelessly bumping into someone who then falls and breaks an arm constitutes negligence. Likewise, carelessly, as opposed to intentionally, flooding someone's land constitutes negligence. In a sense, negligence is a *way of committing* a tort rather than a distinct *category* of torts.

Negligence has been committed when someone has suffered an injury caused by the failure of another to live up to a required *duty of care.* Generally, the tort of negligence requires the presence of the following four elements:

1. The defendant owed a duty of care to the plaintiff.
2. The defendant breached that duty.
3. The plaintiff suffered a legally recognizable injury.
4. The defendant's breach of the duty of care caused the plaintiff's injury.

Each of these elements is examined below.

The Duty of Care

Basically, the concept of duty arises from the notion that if we are to live in society with other people, some actions can be tolerated and some cannot, some actions are right and some are wrong, and some actions are reasonable and some are not. For example, drivers of motor vehicles are required to follow certain rules of the road and to exercise care when driving. The basic principle underlying the duty of care is that people are free to act as they please so long as their actions do not infringe upon the interests of others.

If an individual has knowledge, skill, or intelligence superior to that of an ordinary person, the individual's conduct must be consistent with that status. In other words, that individual has a higher standard of care—his or her duty is that which is reasonable in light of those capabilities. For example, professionals (doctors, dentists, psychiatrists, architects, engineers, accountants, lawyers, and so on) are required to have a standard minimum level of special knowledge and ability. Consequently, the extent of their duty of care is measured by the standards acceptable within their professions.

Breach of the Duty of Care

Tort law relating to negligence measures duty by the **reasonable person standard.** In determining whether a tort has been committed, the courts ask how a reasonable person would have acted in the same circumstances. The reasonable person standard is said to be (although in an absolute sense it cannot be) objective. It is not necessarily how a particular person would act. It is society's judgment on how people should act. If the so-called reasonable person existed, he or she would be careful, conscientious, even-tempered, and honest. This hypothetical "reasonable person" is frequently used by the courts in decisions relating to other areas of law as well.

When someone fails to comply with the duty of exercising reasonable care, a potentially tortious act may have been committed. Failure to live up to the standard of care may involve an act (setting fire to a building) or an omission (neglecting to put out a fire). It may involve an intentional act, a careless act, or a carefully performed but nevertheless dangerous act that results in injury.

Whether or not a person's act or failure to act is unreasonable depends on the interaction of a number of factors. One factor is the nature of the act. Some actions—shooting off a gun in a crowd, for instance—are so outrageous and some acts, like blasting with dynamite, are so dangerous that any damage they cause should be paid for. Another factor in determining whether damages should be awarded is the manner in which an act is performed. Nearly all human acts carry some risk of harm, and individuals are expected to pay attention to their conduct and surroundings when undertaking to do something, rather than to proceed heedlessly. A third factor is the nature of the injury—whether it is serious or slight, extraordinary or simply part of everyday life. Another factor to be considered is whether the activity causing the injury was socially useful. For example, a person may be justified in darting into the path of an oncoming train to save a child, but not to save a hat. Yet another factor to consider is how easily the injury could have been guarded against. Could, for example, a simple, inexpensive warning sign have prevented the injury?

Retail businesses are particularly vulnerable to negligence lawsuits. Unless a retail firm has taken all reasonable precautions against potential injuries to its business invitees (customers), it may be held to have breached its duty of care to those invitees. The following case is illustrative.

BACKGROUND AND FACTS   Lowell Bray was about to open the door of a restaurant owned by Kate, Inc., when he slipped on some ice and fell, injuring his shoulder. He testified that he could not see the ice but felt it when he slipped. Bray sued Kate for damages in a Nebraska state court, alleging that Kate, by failing to remove the ice from in front of its door, had breached its duty of care and therefore was negligent. The trial court held for Bray, and Kate appealed.

Case 5.5

BRAY v. KATE, INC.

Supreme Court of Nebraska, 1990.
235 Neb. 315,
454 N.W.2d 698.

DECISION AND RATIONALE   The Supreme Court of Nebraska affirmed the trial court's judgment. The court pointed out that under state law a possessor of land is liable for injury caused to a business invitee by a condition on the land if (1) the possessor created the condition, knew of it, or by the exercise of reasonable care would have discovered it; (2) the possessor should have realized the condition involved an unreasonable risk of harm to the invitee; (3) the possessor should have expected that the invitee would either (a) not realize the danger or (b) fail to protect against it; (4) the possessor failed to use reasonable care to protect the invitee against the danger; and (5) the condition was a proximate cause of injury to the invitee.

The Injury Requirement and Damages

For a tort to have been committed, there must be a *legally recognizable injury* to the plaintiff. To recover damages, the plaintiff must have suffered some loss, harm, wrong, or invasion of a protected interest. The reason for the requirement of injury is obvious. Without an injury of some kind, there is nothing to "recover."

An injured plaintiff is ordinarily denied recovery for damage that he or she could have avoided by taking reasonable action after the injury occurred. That is, the plaintiff has a duty to take reasonable steps to mitigate (reduce the amount of) damages. Seeking appropriate medical treatment, for example, would be reasonable.

It is important to stress that the purpose of tort law is not to punish people for tortious acts but to compensate the injured parties for damages suffered. Because society wants to discourage some torts, however, occasionally the injured person may be given extra compensation in the form of **punitive damages.** Few negligent acts are so reprehensible that punitive damages are available.[7]

Under some circumstances, one person commits a tortious act and another person is liable to the injured party for the result. For example, an employer is liable for the negligent act of an employee if it was committed within the scope of employment. This liability involves the doctrine of *respondeat superior* (see Chapter 36).

---

7.   Although punitive damages may be awarded in tort actions, they are usually *not* available in breach of contract actions (to be discussed in the next unit). See the *Emerging Trends in Business Law* on tort reform in Chapter 23 for a discussion of current issues relating to punitive-damages awards.

Causation

The fourth element necessary to a tort is causation. If a person fails in a duty of care and someone suffers injury, the wrongful activity must have caused the harm for a tort to have been committed. In deciding whether there is causation, the court must address two questions:

1. Was there *causation in fact?*
2. Was the act the *proximate cause* of the injury?

CAUSATION IN FACT Did the injury occur because of the defendant's act, or would it have occurred anyway? If an injury would not have occurred without the defendant's act, then there is **causation in fact.** If Johnson carelessly leaves a campfire burning and the fire burns down the forest, there is causation in fact. If Johnson carelessly leaves a campfire burning, but it burns out, and then lightning causes a fire that burns down the forest, there is no causation in fact. In both cases, there is a wrongful act and damage. In the second case, however, there is no causal connection and thus no liability. Causation in fact can usually be determined by use of the *but for* test: but for the wrongful act, the injury would not have occurred.

In some cases, causation in fact is difficult to determine. What if Johnson's campfire did spread, but at the same time lightning also started a fire? In this type of situation, the courts apply the *substantial factor* test: If Johnson's conduct was a substantial factor in bringing about the damage, Johnson will normally be held liable.

Determining causation in fact entails examining the facts portrayed in evidence at a trial. The plaintiff has the burden of proving causation in fact as well as other elements, such as damages. The plaintiff must prove the case by a *preponderance of the evidence* (see Chapter 3) in a civil suit.

PROXIMATE CAUSE How far should a defendant's liability extend for a wrongful act that was a substantial factor in causing injury? For example, suppose Johnson's fire not only burns down the forest but also sets off an explosion in a nearby chemical plant that spills chemicals into a river, killing all the fish for a hundred miles downstream and ruining the economy of a tourist resort. Should Johnson be liable to the resort owners? To the tourists whose vacations were ruined? These are questions about the limitation of liability, which is the second element in the general issue of causation. The courts use the term **proximate cause** (or sometimes *legal cause*) to describe this element. Proximate cause is a question not of fact but of law and policy. The question is whether the connection between an act and an injury is strong enough to justify imposing liability.

There is probably nothing in the field of law that has caused more disagreement than the subject of proximate cause. The term is somewhat misleading, because the question is not primarily one of causation and does not arise until causation has been established. Instead, the question concerns a fundamental policy of law: Should a negligent defendant's responsibility extend to consequences that could in no way have been anticipated?

The most discussed and debated of all tort cases, the *Palsgraf* case, which follows, involves what may be called, instead of unforeseeable consequences, the unforeseeable plaintiff. The question before the court is: Does the defendant's duty of care extend only to those who may be injured as a result of a foreseeable risk, or does it extend also to a person who is outside the zone of danger and whose injury could not reasonably have been foreseen?

Case 5.6

PALSGRAF v. LONG ISLAND RAILROAD CO.

Court of Appeals of New York, 1928.
248 N.Y. 339,
162 N.E. 99.

BACKGROUND AND FACTS A man carrying a nondescript package tried to board a moving train of the Long Island Railroad Company from a crowded station platform. Railroad employees on the train and the platform tried to help him. The man dropped his package, which contained fireworks, and the package exploded. The explosion caused scales located at the other end of the platform to fall on Mrs. Palsgraf, injuring her. She sued the railroad in a New York state court. The trial court found that the railroad employees were negligent in their conduct toward Palsgraf, and the court awarded damages to her. The railroad appealed.

DECISION AND RATIONALE The New York Court of Appeals dismissed Palsgraf's complaint. The conduct of the railroad employees may have been negligent toward the man with the package, but it was not negligent in relation to Palsgraf, who was standing far away. Negligence with respect to her turns on whether her injury was reasonably foreseeable from the actions of the railroad. The court held that the railroad was not negligent toward her because "[n]othing in the situation gave notice * * * of peril to persons thus removed. * * * [N]o hazard was apparent to the eye of ordinary vigilance * * * with reference to her." In the eyes of the court, "The risk reasonably to be perceived defines the duty to be obeyed."

FORESEEABILITY Since the decision in the *Palsgraf* case, the courts have used *foreseeability* as the test for proximate cause. The railroad guards were negligent, but the railroad's duty of care did not extend to Palsgraf because she was an unforeseeable plaintiff. According to this view, a defendant's duty of care does not extend to a victim who is not located within a foreseeable zone of danger. Thus, a victim can recover damages only on proving that a reasonable person would have foreseen in the circumstances a risk of injury to him or her.

SUPERSEDING INTERVENING FORCES A superseding intervening force may break the connection between a wrongful act and injury to another. If so, it cancels out the wrongful act. For example, keeping a can of gasoline in the trunk of one's car creates a foreseeable risk and is thus a negligent act. If lightning strikes the car, exploding the gas tank *and* the can, injuring passing pedestrians, the lightning supersedes the original negligence as a cause of the damage, because it was not foreseeable. This example illustrates that the doctrine of superseding intervening forces is also a matter of proximate cause and legal duty.

In other situations, the intervention of a force may not relieve one of liability. If medical mal-treatment of an injury aggravates the injury, the person whose negligence originally caused the injury is not relieved of liability. If subsequent disease or a subsequent accident is proximately caused by the original injury, the person who caused the original injury will be liable for the injury caused by the subsequent disease or accident. When negligence endangers property and the owner is injured in an attempt to protect the property, the negligent party will be liable for the injury.

In negligence cases, the negligent party will often attempt to show that some act has intervened after his or her action and that this second act was the proximate cause of injury. Typically, in cases in which an individual takes a defensive action, such as attempting to escape by swerving or leaping from a vehicle, the original wrongdoer will not be relieved of liability even if the injury actually resulted from the escape attempt. The same is true under the "danger invites rescue" doctrine. Under this doctrine, if Smith commits an act that endangers Jones, and Brown sustains an injury trying to protect Jones, then Smith will be liable for Brown's injury, as well as for any injuries Jones may sustain. Rescuers can injure themselves, or the person rescued, or even a stranger, but the original wrongdoer will still be liable. The following case illustrates this doctrine.

BACKGROUND AND FACTS John Rooney, a New York City sewer worker, was fatally stricken by lethal gas when the protective mask he was wearing failed to operate properly. Responding to calls for help, Stephen Guarino was also killed by the gas when he entered the sewer without a mask. Mary Guarino, Stephen's widow, sued the Mine Safety Appliance Company, the manufacturer of the masks, in a New York state court. The trial court held for her, and the manufacturer appealed.

DECISION AND RATIONALE The New York Court of Appeals upheld the award. The manufacturer's negligent act was manufacturing and distribut-

 Case 5.7

GUARINO v. MINE SAFETY APPLIANCE CO.

Court of Appeals of New York, 1969.
25 N.Y.2d 460,
255 N.E.2d 173,
306 N.Y.S.2d 942.

ing the defective mask. The defective mask placed a worker in peril, which invited his rescue. Guarino, a fellow crew member, responded to Rooney's call for help reasonably: "To require that a rescuer answering the cry for help make inquiry as to the nature of the culpable act that imperils someone's life would defy all logic." The court concluded that "[t]he wrong that imperils life is a wrong to the imperilled victim; it is a wrong also to his rescuer."

ETHICAL CONSIDERATIONS   There is no law that says one person must voluntarily come to the aid of, or rescue, another person in danger. You will not be legally liable, for example, if you do not lend assistance to someone being robbed, or even threatened with death or killed, on a subway. Many believe, however, that individuals have an ethical duty to help, or rescue, others in peril. In a sense, the "danger invites rescue" doctrine implicitly recognizes this ethical duty by ensuring that a wrongdoer causing danger will be held liable for harm suffered by rescuers.

RES IPSA LOQUITUR   Generally, in lawsuits involving negligence, the plaintiff has the burden of proving that the defendant was negligent. In certain situations, when negligence is very difficult or impossible to prove, the courts may infer that negligence has occurred, in which case the burden of proof rests on the defendant—to prove he or she was *not* negligent. The inference of the defendant's negligence is known as the doctrine of *res ipsa loquitur,*[8] which translates as "the facts speak for themselves." This doctrine is applied only when the event creating the damage or injury is one that ordinarily does not occur in the absence of negligence. *Res ipsa loquitur* has been applied to such events as train derailments, wheels falling off moving vehicles, falling elevators, and bricks or window panes falling from a defendant's premises. For the doctrine to apply, the event must be caused by an agency or instrumentality within the exclusive control of the defendant, and it must not have been due to any voluntary action or contribution on the part of the plaintiff. Some courts will add still another condition—that the evidence available to explain the event be more accessible to the defendant than to the plaintiff.

Defenses to Negligence

Basic defenses in negligence cases include assumption of risk, contributory negligence, comparative negligence, and the last-clear-chance doctrine.

---

8.   Pronounced rays ihpsuh *loh*-kwuh-duhr.

ASSUMPTION OF RISK   A plaintiff who voluntarily enters into a risky situation, knowing the risk involved, will not be allowed to recover damages. This is the defense of **assumption of risk.** For example, a driver who enters a race knows that there is a risk of being killed or injured in a crash. By entering the race, the driver has thus assumed the risk of injury. The two requirements of this defense are: (1) knowledge of the risk and (2) voluntary assumption of the risk.

The risk can be assumed by express agreement, or the assumption of risk can be implied by the plaintiff's knowledge of the risk and subsequent conduct. Of course, the plaintiff does not assume a risk different from, or greater than, the risk normally carried by the activity. In our example, the race driver assumes the risk of being injured in the race but not the risk that the banking in the curves of the racetrack will give way during the race because of a construction defect.

Risks are not deemed to be assumed in situations involving emergencies. Neither are they assumed when a statute protects a class of people from harm and a member of the class is injured by the harm. For example, employees are protected by statute from harmful working conditions and therefore do not assume the risks associated with the workplace. If an employee is injured, he or she will generally be compensated regardless of fault.

CONTRIBUTORY NEGLIGENCE   All individuals are expected to exercise a reasonable degree of care in looking out for themselves. In some jurisdictions, a person who has failed to exercise such care cannot recover for an injury resulting from negligence. This is the doctrine of **contributory negligence,** according to which both parties have been negligent and their negligence has combined to cause the injury. When one party sues the other in tort for damages for negligence, the defendant can claim contributory negligence, which is a complete defense under common law rules. (Contributory negligence is not, however, a defense to intentional torts or to suits based on strict liability, a topic that will be covered later.) Over the last century, the contributory negligence doctrine has been eroded considerably. Today, most jurisdictions have developed other doctrines—including the doctrines of comparative negligence and last clear chance—to avoid the strict application of the contributory negligence rule.

COMPARATIVE NEGLIGENCE A majority of the states now allow recovery based on the doctrine of **comparative negligence.** This doctrine permits

computation of both the plaintiff's and the defendant's negligence. The plaintiff's damages are reduced by a percentage that represents the degree of his or her contributing fault. To illustrate: Jaime negligently drove through a red light and injured Teresa, who was also driving negligently. Teresa suffered damages of $200,000. The jury found that Jaime was 70 percent negligent and Teresa was 30 percent negligent, so Teresa recovered 70 percent of $200,00, or $140,000. In some states, a plaintiff's negligence must be less serious than the defendant's—that is, the plaintiff can recover only if he or she was 49 percent or less at fault. In other states, a plaintiff's negligence must be no greater than the defendant's—50 percent or less. In still other states, a plaintiff can recover no matter how negligent he or she was—if the defendant was 5 percent at fault, the plaintiff can recover 5 percent of the damages. In some cases, the plaintiff may be subject to a counterclaim by the defendant.

In the following case, an automobile accident victim was held to be comparatively negligent because he failed to wear his seat belt.

BACKGROUND AND FACTS William Burns was injured in an automobile accident with Ruth Smith and sued Smith and her insurer for damages in a Florida state court. The court awarded damages to Burns, but reduced the award on finding Burns to be 75 percent comparatively negligent, because he had not been wearing his seat belt at the time of the accident. Burns appealed, contending that the trial court could not find a causal relationship between his nonuse of a seat belt and his injuries without testimony from an accident reconstruction expert.

Case 5.8

BURNS v. SMITH
District Court of Appeal of Florida, Second District, 1985.
476 So.2d 278.

DECISION AND RATIONALE The Florida appellate court affirmed the trial court's judgment. The court concluded that it was within "the province of the jury from its common knowledge" to find that Burns's failure to use a seat belt "contributed substantially to producing at least a portion of [his] damages."

LAST CLEAR CHANCE **Last clear chance** is a doctrine that can excuse the effect of a plaintiff's contributory negligence. If applicable, the last-clear-chance rule allows the plaintiff to recover full damages despite failure to exercise care. This rule operates when, through his or her own negligence, the plaintiff is endangered (or his or her property is endangered) by a defendant who has the last clear chance to avoid the event that causes the damage. For example, if Murphy walks across the street

against the light and Lewis, a motorist, sees her in time to avoid hitting her but hits her anyway, Lewis (the defendant) is not permitted to use Murphy's (the plaintiff's) prior negligence as a defense. The defendant negligently missed the opportunity to avoid injuring the plaintiff. The adoption of the comparative negligence rule has effectively abolished the last-clear-chance doctrine in most jurisdictions.

■ Strict Liability

The final category of torts is called *strict liability,* or *liability without fault.* Intentional or negligent torts involve acts that depart from a reasonable standard of care and cause an injury. Under the doctrine of strict liability, liability for injury is imposed for reasons other than fault.

Abnormally Dangerous Activities

Strict liability for damages proximately caused by abnormally dangerous activities is one application of this doctrine. Abnormally dangerous activities have three characteristics:

1. The activity involves potential harm, of a serious nature, to persons or property.
2. The activity involves a high degree of risk that cannot be completely guarded against by the exercise of reasonable care.

3. The activity is not commonly performed in the community or area.

Strict liability is applied because of the extreme risk of the activity. Even when an activity such as blasting with dynamite is performed with all reasonable care, there is still a risk of injury. Balancing that risk against the potential for harm, it is fair to ask the person engaged in the activity to pay for injury caused by the activity. Although there is no fault, there is still responsibility because of the nature of the activity. In other words, it is reasonable to require the person engaged in the activity to carry the necessary insurance or otherwise stand prepared to compensate anyone who suffers.

The following case illustrates a type of abnormally dangerous activity.

Case 5.9

YOMMER v. McKENZIE

Court of Appeals of Maryland,
1969.
255 Md. 220,
257 A.2d 138.

BACKGROUND AND FACTS   The Yommers operated a gas station with underground storage tanks. Gasoline contaminated the well water of their neighbors, the McKenzies. The Yommers replaced one of the tanks, but the water remained contaminated. The McKenzies sued the Yommers in a Maryland state court, alleging a nuisance, and recovered damages of $3,500. The Yommers appealed, arguing that there was no proof of negligence and that a gas station is not a nuisance.

DECISION AND RATIONALE   The Maryland Court of Appeals upheld the judgment for the McKenzies. The court concluded that there was no need to prove negligence because the nature of the activity and the location of the tank subjected the Yommers to strict liability. The court reasoned that, although the operation of a gas station does not involve a high degree of risk, placing a tank close to a residence does, and placing the tank next to the McKenzies' well was "inappropriate to the locale."

Other Applications of Strict Liability

There are other applications of the strict liability principle. Persons who keep dangerous animals, for example, are strictly liable for any harm inflicted by the animals. A significant application of strict liability is in the area of *product liability.*

Retailers and Tort Liability

Retailers face a potential lawsuit not only any time a customer steps onto the retailer's property, but also any time a customer buys a product from the retailer. Retailers are faced with potential legal problems every day. Let us consider a few areas in which knowledge of the law can help a retailer prevent legal problems.

Negligence is an important area in tort law. Any retail firm, whether it be a shoe store or a hamburger stand, must take reasonable care—not be negligent—in providing a safe environment where the customer can examine products or buy goods and services. The courts have come to conclude that "the customer is always right." Therefore, to believe that customers will take reasonable care in their behavior or in the management of their small children while on your premises is to court disaster. The retailer who assumes that any person on the premises will show a complete lack of common sense is going a long way to prevent being sued for negligence. For example, even though it might be obvious that an employee is washing a section of the floor, there should be signs posted that warn customers as to what the employee is doing.

The law of trespass may seem clear to the businessperson who has invested his or her life savings in starting a small retail store. But to the courts, the law of trespass and, more specifically, the protection of property against trespassers (thieves) is not so clear. The usual methods of protecting property against trespassers, such as hiring police protection services and installing alarm systems, are well utilized and accepted, but other methods are not.

In one case, for example, a landowner had prepared a "mantrap" to protect an old, abandoned farmhouse from thieves. A spring gun was set so that it would fire when anyone entered the house. A thief lost most of his leg when the gun fired at him on his entry into the building, and the landowner was held liable for both actual and punitive damages—despite the "no trespassing" signs on the property and despite the thief's illegal presence there. In general, courts will hold that landowners cannot do mechanically what they cannot do in person—that is, use deadly force without sufficient justification.

Shrinkage, the polite word for *shoplifting,* involves both employee theft and customer theft. To what extent can you, the businessperson, detain a suspected shoplifter without being successfully sued for false imprisonment, invasion of privacy, or some other charge—such as defamation or infliction of mental distress? Suspected shoplifters can be accosted, accused, and temporarily detained if certain reasonable procedures are used. These procedures differ, depending on the jurisdiction. The word to remember is *reasonable.* Keeping a suspected shoplifter in a locked storeroom for two hours because your manager has not yet gotten around to contacting the police would usually not be considered reasonable if the individual in question sued for false imprisonment.

When apprehending and questioning a suspected shoplifter, choose your words carefully. Using abusive or accusatory words or otherwise subjecting the person to indignity may result in a lawsuit. (In one case, the words "A big fat woman like you" served as the basis for recovery for the tort of infliction of emotional distress.) If you think someone has shoplifted, act on your suspicion before the suspect leaves the store. Usually, the courts will allow detention only if the suspected shoplifter is still on your premises.

Liability here is a matter of social policy and is based on two factors: (1) the ability of the employer and manufacturer to better bear the cost of injury by spreading it out to society through an increase in the cost of goods and services and (2) the fact that the employer and manufacturer are making a profit from their activities and therefore should bear the cost of injury as an operating expense. Product liability will be considered in depth in Chapter 23.

■ CONCEPT SUMMARY 5.1   Common Basic Torts

Torts	Elements
Intentional Torts against Persons	
Assault	An intentional act that creates in another a reasonable apprehension or fear of immediate harmful or offensive contact.
Battery	An intentional act that brings about harmful or offensive contact to another.
False Imprisonment	An intentional act that confines or restrains another.
Infliction of Emotional Distress	An intentional act amounting to extreme and outrageous conduct that causes severe emotional distress to another.
Defamation	The publication of defamatory factual language concerning, and causing damage to the reputation of, another.
Torts	**Elements**
Intentional Torts against Persons	
Invasion of Privacy	1. Use of another's name, picture, or other likeness for commercial purposes without permission. 2. Intrusion into another's affairs or seclusion. 3. Publication of information that places another in a false light. 4. Public disclosure of private facts about another.
Fraudulent Misrepresentation	An intentional misrepresentation of facts or conditions, made with knowledge of their falsity or reckless disregard for their truth, to induce another's reliance. The other must have justifiably relied on the misrepresentation, and damage must have been caused by the misrepresentation.
Intentional Torts against Property	
Trespass to Land	An intentional act of physical invasion of another's real property.
Trespass to Personal Property	An intentional act that interferes with another's right to possession of his or her personal property.
Conversion	An intentional act that interferes with another's right to possession of his or her personal property resulting in the destruction of the property or the converting of the property to the tortfeasor's use or benefit.
Nuisance	An intentional act that substantially and unreasonably interferes with another's use or enjoyment of his or her property or with the community's health, safety, or property rights.

(Continued on next page)

■ CONCEPT SUMMARY 5.1 *(Continued)*

Unintentional Torts	
Negligence	A breach, with or without fault, of a duty of care owed to another, causing injury to the other or damage to the other's property.
Strict Liability	A breach of an absolute duty to make something safe, causing injury to another or damage to his or her property.

■ Terms and Concepts

actual malice 96
assault 92
assumption of risk 106
battery 93
causation in fact 104
comparative negligence 107
consent 93
contributory negligence 107
conversion 100
damages 91
defamation 95

intentional tort 92
last clear chance 107
libel 95
negligence 92
nuisance 101
privilege 97
proximate cause 104
public figure 96
puffing 98
punitive damages 103
**reasonable person
   standard** 102

res ipsa loquitur 106
self-defense 93
slander 95
strict liablity 92
tort 91
tortfeasor 92
trespass to land 99
**trespass to personal
   property** 99

■ For Review

1. What is the function of tort law?
2. One of the elements of a tort is causation. What are the two parts of the causation element?
3. What defenses are available in an action in negligence?
4. Ozzie borrows $500 from Vic. Ozzie agrees to repay the money in monthly installments of $50. When Ozzie fails to make several payments, Vic goes to Ozzie's office and asks for the money. Ozzie says that he cannot pay anything until next week. When Vic yells that Ozzie is a deadbeat, the receptionist and secretaries in the outer office start giggling. Has Vic committed a tort?
5. Gillis Oil Corp. discovers oil reserves beneath a residential area of the city of Los Angeles. Gillis drills wells and begins pumping the oil. A spill from one of the wells causes damage within a three-square-mile area. Can Gillis be held strictly liable for the damage?

■ Questions and Case Problems

5-1. Richards is an employee of the Dun Construction Corp. While delivering materials to a construction site, he carelessly runs Dun's truck into a passenger vehicle driven by Green. This is Richard's second accident in six months. When Dun learns of this latest accident, a heated discussion ensues, and Dun fires Richards. Dun is so angry that he immediately writes a letter to the union of which Richards is a member and to all other construction outfits in the community, stating that Richards is the "worst driver in the city" and that "anyone who hires him is asking for legal liability." Richards files suit against Dun, alleging libel on the basis of the statements made in the letters. Discuss the results.

5-2. It is a cold, wintry day. Ken needs to do some shopping on his way home from work. He is running late and is in a hurry. He stops at a drugstore to buy a tube of toothpaste on sale. He sticks the toothpaste in his overcoat pocket, laying the correct amount of change for the purchase on the counter. He is proceeding home when he suddenly remembers his wife's request that he pick up some much-needed groceries. He stops at a grocery store and rushes through the store picking up the groceries. He checks out and in a slow trot starts to leave the store when the checkout clerk sees the toothpaste in his overcoat pocket. Believing

Ken is attempting to leave the store without declaring the item, the clerk yells, "Stop, thief!" Two bagboys grab Ken, haul him—struggling and protesting—to a small, dark back room, and lock him in it. One hour later, the store manager gets back from dinner, learns of the events, and, after questioning a distraught Ken, lets him go. Ken starts having nightmares and backaches and becomes extremely nervous when friends and neighbors look at him. Discuss fully whether any torts have been committed against Ken.

5-3. Frank is a former employee of ABC Auto Repair Co. He enters the property of ABC, claiming the company owes him $150 in back wages. An argument ensues, and the ABC general manager, Steward, orders Frank off the property. Frank refuses to leave, and Steward orders two mechanics to throw him off the property. Frank runs to his truck, but on the way he grabs some tools valued at $150. Frank gets into his truck and, in his haste to drive away, destroys a gatepost. Frank refuses to return the tools.

(a) Discuss whether Frank has committed any torts.
(b) If the mechanics had thrown Frank off the property, would ABC be guilty of assault and battery? Explain.

5-4. John is a delivery employee for Crystal Glass, Inc. He is making a delivery when, at an intersection, his van and the passenger car of Jane collide. Jane wants to hold both John and Crystal Glass liable for the damages she has sustained. John claims that Jane was also at fault, at least as much at fault as he, and therefore neither he nor Crystal should be liable. Discuss fully these claims.

5-5. Ruth carelessly parks her car on a steep hill, leaving the car in neutral and failing to engage the parking brake. The car rolls down the hill, knocking down an electric line. The sparks from the broken line ignite a grass fire. The fire spreads until it reaches a barn one mile away. The barn has dynamite inside, and the burning barn explodes, causing part of the roof to fall on and injure a passing motorist, Jim. Can Jim recover from Ruth? Why or why not?

5-6. Professor Ronald R. Hutchinson received federal funding for animal (monkey) studies on aggression. U.S. Senator William Proxmire bestowed his Golden Fleece of the Month Award on the federal agency that funded Hutchinson's research. The purpose of the award was to publicize wasteful government spending. Senator Proxmire announced the award in a speech prepared for and given to the Senate. The speech was reprinted in a press release mailed to 275 members of the news media and in a newsletter sent to 100,000 people. Among Proxmire's critical comments was a description of the federal grants for Hutchinson's research as "monkey business." Hutchinson sued Proxmire for defamation. The U.S. district court and court of appeals confirmed Senator Proxmire's claims that his communication was privileged and that Professor Hutchinson was a public figure who had not proved that Proxmire acted with malice. Discuss whether either of Senator Proxmire's claims is a valid defense. [*Hutchinson v. Proxmire,* 443 U.S. 111, 99 S.Ct. 2675, 61 L.Ed.2d 411 (1979)]

5-7. H. E. Butt Grocery Co. (H.E.B.) has numerous retail grocery stores scattered throughout the state of Texas. Hawkins went to grocery shop at one of the H.E.B. stores. A heavy rainstorm and north wind had caused water to be tracked into the store by customers and water to be blown through the door each time it was opened. As Hawkins entered through the automatically opened door, she slipped and fell in approximately one-half inch of rain water that had accumulated on the floor. The manager knew of the weather conditions and had had employees mop the floor on numerous occasions. There was no sign posted warning customers of the water hazard. Can Hawkins recover from H.E.B. for injuries sustained from slipping on the water-covered floor? Why or why not? [*H. E. Butt Grocery Co. v. Hawkins,* 594 S.W.2d 187 (Tex.Civ.App. 1980)]

5-8. O'Neill was injured when he was struck in the eye by a softball thrown by Daniels, a teammate, during warm-up activities before an amateur softball game. O'Neill claimed that Daniels was negligent and filed suit. Discuss the probable success of O'Neill's suit in light of the fact that the injury occurred during the warm-up activities. [*O'Neill v. Daniels,* 135 A.D.2d 1076, 523 N.Y.S.2d 264 (1987)]

5-9. One night in August of 1985, Gerrit and Kay Mostert and their daughter went to a movie theater in Cheyenne, Wyoming. While they were in the theater, the National Weather Service warned the community that a severe thunderstorm was imminent and that flash floods and tornadoes could occur. Civil authorities urged citizens to stay indoors in safe areas to avoid injury or death. Although the theater managers were aware of the dangerous weather conditions and the warning that had been issued, they did not inform departing theater-goers of the perilous situation. Shortly after driving away from the theater parking lot, the Mosterts encountered a flooded area. During their attempt to escape, the daughter drowned. The Mosterts brought an action against the theater owners, CBL & Associates, claiming that the theater had been negligent in its failure to warn those leaving the theater of the danger. Discuss whether the theater had a duty to inform the Mosterts and others leaving the theater of the hazardous weather conditions. [*Mostert v. CBL & Associates,* 741 P.2d 1090 (Wyo. 1987)]

5-10. Sharon Lee Glynn, a sixteen-year-old girl, was waiting for a bus in a Peter Pan Bus Lines terminal in Springfield, Massachusetts, when a stranger approached her and stabbed her without warning or provocation. Glynn died as a result of the attack. The bus terminal was in a run-down section of the city, and homeless people and drunks frequented the area. There had been robberies in the terminal's restrooms and assaults in the terminal, and apparently the terminal's managers called the police every week or so because of a security or other problem. Although the terminal was aware that it needed a uniformed security officer to deter crime on its premises, it had not yet hired any security personnel. The administrator of Glynn's estate, Alfred Sharpe, brought an action against the terminal for damages, claiming that the terminal, by failing to have security personnel present, had breached its duty of care to the patrons of the terminal. In evaluating Sharpe's claim, the court must address the following three questions:

(a) Did the bus terminal owe a duty of care toward its patrons?

(b) If so, did it breach this duty by failing to hire a uniformed security officer?

(c) If it did breach its duty of care, was its breach the proximate cause of Glynn's death?

How will the court decide, and why? [*Sharpe v. Peter Pan Bus Lines, Inc.*, 401 Mass. 788, 519 N.E.2d 1341 (1988)]

5-11. George Giles was staying at a Detroit hotel owned by the Pick Hotels Corp. While a bellboy was removing luggage from the back seat of Giles's car, Giles reached into the front seat to remove his briefcase. As he did so, he supported himself by placing his left hand on the center pillar to which the rear door was hinged, with his fingers in a position to be injured if the rear door was closed. The bellboy closed the rear door, and a part of Giles's left index finger was amputated. Giles sued the hotel for damages. The hotel claimed that it was not liable because Giles, by placing his hand on the car as he did, contributed to the injury. (Under state law, contributory negligence was an absolute defense to liability.) Discuss whether the hotel will succeed in its defense. [*Giles v. Pick Hotels Corp.*, 232 F.2d 887, 6th Cir. 1956)]

5-12. Tony Shreve, an employee of Duke Power Co., lodged a complaint about plant safety violations at the Dan River plant. Lewis Stultz, Shreve's supervisor, reported to other Duke management personnel that Shreve had threatened him with physical violence. The management personnel discussed the matter among themselves and, believing that Stultz was telling the truth, fired Shreve. Shreve sued both Stultz and Duke Power Co. for slander, claiming that he had never threatened Stultz and that he was fired solely because he had voiced concerns about plant safety. The trial court granted the defendants' motion for a directed verdict, and Shreve appealed. The appellate court held that the trial court erred in granting the motion for a directed verdict because, if believed, Shreve's testimony would establish that Stultz had slandered Shreve both in his trade and means of livelihood and in accusing him of criminal conduct. The court then turned to Shreve's claim that Duke Power personnel, because they discussed the matter among themselves, also were liable for slander. What defense might Duke Power successfully raise against this claim? Discuss. [*Shreve v. Duke Power Co.*, 97 N.C.App. 648, 389 S.E.2d 444 (1990)]

5-13. A Question of Ethics

 George Ward entered a K-Mart department store in Champaign, Illinois, through a service entrance near the home improvements department. After purchasing a large mirror, Ward left the store through the same door. On his way out the door, carrying the large mirror in front and somewhat to the side of him, he collided with a concrete pole located just outside the door about a foot and a half from the outside wall. The mirror broke, and the broken glass cut his right cheek and eye, resulting in reduced vision in that eye. He later stated that he had not seen the pole, did not realize what was happening, and only knew that he felt "a bad pain, and then saw stars." Ward sued K-Mart Corp. for damages, alleging that the store was negligent. The Supreme Court of Illinois ultimately decided in Ward's favor and upheld the jury's award of $68,000 in damages. The court held that the store had failed in its duty to its patrons by not maintaining the premises in a reasonably safe condition. The store should have foreseen the risk to its customers posed by the poles and guarded against it. [Ward v. K-Mart Corp., 136 Ill.2d 132, 554 N.E.2d 223, 143 Ill.Dec. 288 (1990)]

1. What ethical principle underlies the common law doctrine that business owners have a duty of care toward their customers?

2. K-Mart argued that the pole was such an obvious obstacle that it did not pose any risk, and therefore no warning to customers was needed. Do you agree with this argument? Why or why not?

3. Can you think of any reasons for the court's conclusion that K-Mart should have foreseen the possibility that a customer could be injured because of the presence of the pole?

4. Does the duty of care unfairly burden business owners? Discuss.

Chapter 6

Criminal Law

Previously in this text we referred to a **crime** as a wrong defined by society and perpetrated against society. A discussion of criminal law is appropriate to a study of business law because the prevention of crime and the effort of capturing and prosecuting those accused of crimes are time-consuming and costly activities. Consequently, it is important that we understand the nature and extent of such activities and their impact on businesses.

The sanctions used to bring about a peaceful society, in which individuals engaging in business can compete and flourish, include those imposed by the civil law, such as damages for various types of tortious conduct (as discussed in the preceding chapter) and damages for breach of contract (to be discussed in Chapter 17). Chapter 1 also pointed out that courts of equity may restrain certain types of unlawful conduct or require that things done unlawfully or having certain unlawful effects be undone by issuing injunctions.

These remedies have not been sufficient deterrents in some instances. Consequently, additional sanctions have been developed for particular undesirable activities. As a result, a *criminal law element* exists within the legal environment of business. The prerequisites of *fault* or *guilt* in this area are different from those in the civil law, as are the sanctions and penalties.

A *Concept Summary* showing which types of offenses are classified as criminal law and which are classified as civil law has been included near the end of this chapter.

■ The Nature of Crime

Crimes can be distinguished from other wrongful acts in that they are *offenses against society as a whole.* Criminal defendants are prosecuted by a public official, not by their victims. In addition, those who have committed crimes are punished. Tort remedies—remedies for civil wrongs—are generally intended to compensate the injured (except when damages of a punitive nature are assessed), but criminal law is directly concerned with punishing (and, ideally, rehabilitating) the wrongdoer.

A final factor distinguishing criminal sanctions from tort remedies is that the source of criminal law is primarily statutory. Both the acts that constitute crimes and the resulting punishments are formally and very specifically set out in statutes. A crime can thus be defined as a wrong against society proclaimed in a statute and, if intentionally committed, punishable by society.

Classifications of Crimes

Crimes are classified as felonies or misdemeanors according to the punishment provided (the place or the length of confinement).

FELONIES **Felonies** are punishable by death or by imprisonment in a federal or state penitentiary for more than a year. Felonies can also be classified by type of punishment. The Model Penal Code,[1] for example, provides for four degrees of felony: capital offenses for which the maximum penalty is death, first degree felonies punishable by a maximum penalty of life imprisonment, second degree felonies punishable by a maximum of ten years' imprisonment, and third degree felonies punishable by up to five years' imprisonment. (It is important to note that these are maximum penalties. The actual sentence served can be less than the maximum.)

At common law, homicides were divided into three classifications: justifiable, excusable, and criminal. Justifiable homicides were authorized by law and included state executions and homicides by police officers in the performance of their duties. Excusable homicides were those for which there was a defense to criminal liability—killing in self-defense, for example. Criminal homicides were divided into three offenses: murder, voluntary manslaughter, and involuntary manslaughter.

Most states follow the common law classifications of criminal homicides. *Murder* is the unlawful killing of a human being with malice aforethought. *Malice aforethought* is an intent to kill, an intent to do serious bodily harm, an awareness of an unjustifiably high risk of death, or an intent

to commit a felony. (Under the **felony murder** rule, when death occurs during, or as a result of, a felonious crime, many states charge the accused person with murder in addition to the crime that was intended.) If there was sufficient provocation, an intentional killing could be reduced to *voluntary manslaughter.* The provocation must have been of a type that would produce a sudden, intense passion in the mind of an ordinary person so as to cause him or her to lose control, and there must not have been enough time to cool off. *Involuntary manslaughter* involves killing by criminal negligence or by an unlawful act. Killing by an unlawful act is killing in the course of the commission of a crime that does not qualify as felony murder.

Unlike the common law, which featured only one degree of murder, punishable by death, criminal statutes often divide murder into degrees to provide a less severe penalty for some murders. Deliberate and premeditated killing is typically classified as first degree murder. First degree murder sometimes also includes killing during the commission of a specific felony—such as arson, burglary, kidnapping, rape, or robbery. Other felony murders are classified as second degree murders. Many states do not impose the death penalty for second degree murder but instead impose a life sentence.

MISDEMEANORS **Misdemeanors** are crimes punishable by a fine or by confinement for up to a year. Misdemeanors are also sometimes defined as offenses punishable by incarceration in a local jail instead of a penitentiary. In practice, the jail confinement usually lasts no more than a year. Disorderly conduct and trespass are common misdemeanors. Some states have different classes of misdemeanors. For example, in Illinois there are Class A misdemeanors (confinement for up to a year), Class B (not more than six months), and Class C (not more than thirty days). A case concerning a crime classified as a misdemeanor may be tried before a justice of the peace, a police court judge, or some other official with limited judicial authority.

PETTY OFFENSES Another kind of wrong is termed a **petty offense** and often is not classified as a crime. Petty offenses include many traffic violations and violations of building codes. Even for petty offenses, a guilty party may be put in jail for a few days, or fined, or both.

---

1. The American Law Institute issued the Official Draft of the Model Penal Code in 1962. The Model Penal Code is not a uniform code. Rather, it is a rational and integrated body of material drafted for the purpose of assisting state legislatures in reexamining and recodifying state criminal laws. Uniformity among the states is not as important in criminal law as in other areas of the law. Crime varies with local circumstances, and it is appropriate that punishments vary accordingly. The Model Penal Code contains four parts: (1) general provisions, (2) definitions of specific crimes, (3) provisions concerning treatment and correction, and (4) provisions on the organization of correction.

FEDERAL AND STATE CRIMES   Criminal law is primarily the province of the states, but the federal government also has a criminal code. Federal crimes relate to federal government functions or involve federal personnel or institutions. Counterfeiting, unlawful immigration, spying, robbing a federally insured bank, and assaulting a federal officer are examples of federal crimes. In other instances, the federal government can use its general regulatory powers to aid state law enforcement agencies in combating crimes that have a national impact. Transportation of stolen vehicles across state lines, kidnapping, and civil rights violations are areas that fall under federal criminal law.

CLASSIFICATION BY NATURE   Crimes can be classified according to their nature. For example, there are crimes against property (theft, burglary, arson), crimes against the person (murder, assault, rape), and crimes against the government (perjury, bribery). These classifications are used to group crimes within a statutory code.

■ The Essentials of Criminal Liability

Two elements are necessary for a person to be convicted of a crime: (1) the performance of a prohibited act and (2) a specified state of mind on the part of the actor.

Performance of Prohibited Acts

Every criminal statute prohibits certain behavior. Most crimes require an act of *commission;* that is, a person must *do* something before he or she can be accused of a crime. In criminal law, a prohibited act is referred to as the *actus reus,*[2] or guilty act. In some cases an act of *omission* can be a crime, but only if what is omitted is a legal duty. Failure to file a tax return is an example of an omission that is a crime.

The *guilty act* requirement is based on one of the premises of criminal law—that a person is punished for *harm done* to society. Thinking about killing someone or about stealing a car may be wrong, but these thoughts in themselves do no harm until they are translated into action. Of course, a person can be punished for attempting murder or robbery, but normally only if substantial steps toward the criminal objective have been taken.

Even a completed act that harms society is not legally a crime unless the court finds that the required state of mind was present.

State of Mind

A wrongful mental state (*mens rea*[3]) is as necessary as a wrongful act to establish criminal liability. What constitutes such a mental state varies according to the wrongful action. Thus, for murder, the *actus reus* (act) is the taking of a life, and the *mens rea* (mental state) is the intent to take life. For theft, the *actus reus* is the taking of another person's property, and the *mens rea* involves both the knowledge that the property belongs to another and the intent to deprive the owner of it. Without the mental state required by law for a particular crime, there can be no crime.

The *mens rea* in which a particular act is committed can vary in the degree of its wrongfulness. The same act—shooting someone—can result from varying mental states. It can be done coldly, after premeditation, as in murder in the first degree. It can be done in the heat of passion, as in voluntary manslaughter. Or it can be done as the result of criminal negligence, as in involuntary manslaughter. In each of these situations, the law recognizes a different degree of wrongfulness, and the harshness of the punishment depends on the degree to which the act of shooting another was an *intentional* act.

■ Defenses to Criminal Liability

The law recognizes certain conditions that will relieve a defendant of criminal liability. These conditions are called defenses, and among the important ones are infancy, intoxication, insanity, mistake, consent, duress, justifiable use of force, entrapment, and statutes of limitations. The burden of proving one or more of these defenses lies on the defendant. A criminal defendant can also be given immunity from prosecution.

Infancy

Under the common law, children up to seven years of age were considered incapable of committing a

---

2.   Pronounced *ak*-tus *ray*-uhs.

3.   Pronounced mehns *ray*-uh.

crime because they did not have the moral sense to understand that they were doing wrong. Children between the ages of seven and fourteen were presumed to be incapable of committing a crime, but this presumption could be rebutted by a demonstration that the child understood the wrongful nature of the act. (See Exhibit 6–1.)

Today, states vary in their approaches, but all retain the defense of infancy as a bar to criminal liability. Most states retain the common law approach, although age limits vary from state to state. Other states have rejected the rebuttable presumption and simply set a minimum age required for criminal responsibility. All states have juvenile court systems that handle children below the age of criminal responsibility who commit delinquent acts. Their aim is allegedly to reform rather than to punish. In states that retain the rebuttable presumption approach, children who are beyond the minimum age but are still juveniles can be turned over to the criminal courts if the juvenile court determines that they should be treated as adults.

Intoxication

The law recognizes two types of intoxication caused by drugs or alcohol: *involuntary* and *voluntary*. Involuntary intoxication occurs when a person is physically forced to ingest or inject an intoxicating substance, is unaware that an ingested substance contains drugs or alcohol, or takes an intoxicating substance under medical advice. Involuntary intoxication is a defense to crime if its effect was to make a person either incapable of understanding that the act committed was wrong or incapable of obeying the law.

Voluntary intoxication can also be used as a defense if intoxication precludes having the required *mens rea*. Thus, if Johnson shoots Peters while too drunk to know what she is doing, she cannot be convicted of *murder* because she did not have the required *intent* to kill when she shot Peters.

Voluntary intoxication, however, does not serve as a defense for crimes of recklessness or negligence. The law requires that people understand that intoxication can prevent the intoxicated from behaving as a reasonable person. Therefore, becoming intoxicated and committing a reckless or negligent act is a crime. In the example above, Johnson could be convicted of the lesser crime of *manslaughter*.

■ Exhibit 6–1 Responsibility of Infants for Criminal Acts under the Common Law

Age 0–7	Absolute presumption of incompetence.
Age 7–14	Presumption of incompetence, but government may oppose.
Age 14 +	Presumption of competence, but infant may oppose.

Insanity

Just as a child is judged incapable of having the state of mind required to commit a crime, so also is someone suffering from mental illness. Thus, insanity is a defense to a criminal charge. Because there is a general presumption of sanity, a defendant must introduce evidence creating a reasonable doubt as to his or her sanity. If such evidence is introduced, some states then require the defendant to prove *insanity* by a preponderance of the evidence. Other states require the prosecution to prove *sanity* beyond a reasonable doubt. After all evidence has been presented, the jury is instructed on the applicable insanity test and renders a verdict— guilty, not guilty, not guilty by reason of insanity, or, in some states, guilty but insane.

The courts have had difficulty deciding what the test for legal insanity should be, and psychiatrists, as well as lawyers, are critical of the tests used. Almost all federal courts and some states use the standard in the Model Penal Code in Section 4.01:

> A person is not responsible for criminal conduct if at the time of such conduct as a result of mental disease or defect he lacks substantial capacity either to appreciate the wrongfulness of his conduct or to conform his conduct to the requirements of the law.

Other states use the *M'Naghten* test, also known as the "right from wrong" test, which excuses a criminal act if a mental defect makes a person incapable of either appreciating the nature of the act or knowing that it was wrong.[4] Some states have also adopted the irresistible impulse test. A person operating under an irresistible impulse may know that an act is wrong but may still

---

4. *M'Naghten's Case*, 8 Eng.Rep. 718 (1843).

be unable to keep from doing it. Even if a mental illness is not grave enough to serve as a complete defense, it may render a person legally incapable of certain crimes if the illness precludes the possibility of the required *mens rea.*

Mistake

Everyone has heard the saying "ignorance of the law is no excuse." It may seem harsh to presume that everyone knows or should know the law, but the result of a different rule would be unmanageable. Ordinarily, ignorance of the law or a mistaken idea about what the law requires is not a valid defense. In some states, however, that rule has been modified. A person who claims that he or she honestly did not know that a law was being broken may have a valid defense if (1) the law was not published or reasonably made known to the public, or (2) the person relied on an official statement of the law that was erroneous. An official statement is a statute, judicial opinion, administrative order, or statement by someone responsible for administering, interpreting, or enforcing the law. Statements in newspapers or textbooks are not official statements.

A *mistake of fact,* as opposed to a *mistake of law,* will operate as a defense if it negates the required *mens rea.* If, for example, Jones mistakenly drives off in Thompson's car because he thinks that it is his, there is no theft. Theft requires knowledge that the property belongs to another. (Of course, this has no bearing on a civil action for the tort of conversion, discussed in Chapter 5.)

Consent

What if a victim consents to a crime or even encourages the person intending a criminal act to commit it? The law will allow **consent** as a defense if the consent cancels the harm that the law is designed to prevent. In each case, the question is whether the law forbids an act against the victim's will or forbids the act without regard to the victim's wish. The law forbids murder, prostitution, and illicit drug use whether the victim consents to it or not. Consent operates as a defense most successfully in crimes against property, because one can always give away one's property. Of course, if the act operates to harm a third person who has not consented, there will be no escape from criminal liability. Consent or forgiveness given after a crime

has been committed is not really a defense, though it can affect the likelihood of prosecution.

Duress

A person who is asked or instructed to commit a crime is not excused from criminal liability, but committing a crime, other than homicide, under *duress* is a valid defense. **Duress** exists when the *wrongful threat* of one person induces another person to perform an act that he or she would not otherwise perform. In such a situation, duress is said to negate the *mens rea* necessary to commit a crime.

The courts use a number of requirements to determine whether duress exists. First, the threat must involve serious bodily harm or death. A person who was threatened with failing a course or losing a job cannot plead duress as a defense. Second, the harm that is threatened must be greater than the harm that will be caused by the crime. A threat to shoot a woman's husband unless she robs a bank would be sufficient; a threat to hit him might not be. The third requirement is that the threat must be immediate and inescapable. Finally, people who plead duress as a defense must have been involved in the situation through no fault of their own. If, for example, a person committing a burglary forces an accomplice to kill someone, the accomplice cannot use duress as an excuse. The act of participating in the burglary carries with it the possibility of being forced to commit a greater crime.

Justifiable Use of Force

Probably the most well-known defense to criminal liability is **self-defense.** But there are other situations that justify the use of force: the defense of one's dwelling, the defense of other property, and the prevention of a crime. In all of these situations, it is important to distinguish between the use of deadly and nondeadly force. *Deadly force* is likely to result in death or serious bodily harm. *Nondeadly force* is force that reasonably appears necessary to prevent the imminent use of criminal force. Generally speaking, people can use the amount of nondeadly force that is reasonably necessary to protect themselves, to protect their dwellings or other property, or to prevent the commission of a crime.

Deadly force can be used in self-defense if there is a *reasonable belief* that imminent death or grievous bodily harm will otherwise result, if the attacker is using unlawful force (an example of lawful force is that exerted by a police officer), and if the person has not initiated or provoked the attack.

Deadly force can be used to defend a dwelling only if the person believes that deadly force is necessary to prevent imminent death or great bodily harm or—in some jurisdictions—if the person believes deadly force is necessary to prevent the commission of a felony in the dwelling. In the defense of other property, the use of nondeadly force is justified to prevent or to end a criminal attempt to take away or otherwise interfere with the property. Deadly force usually is justifiable only when used in self-defense.

Force reasonably necessary to prevent a serious crime is permissible but, in the majority view, deadly force can be used to prevent only crimes that involve a substantial risk of death or great bodily harm.

Entrapment

Entrapment is a defense designed to prevent the police or other government agents from encouraging persons to commit criminal acts. In the typical entrapment case, an undercover agent *suggests* that a crime be committed and somehow pressures or induces an individual to commit it. The agent then arrests the individual for the crime. Both the suggestion and the inducement must take place. The defense is not intended to prevent the police from setting a trap for an unwary criminal. It is intended to prevent them from pushing an individual into it. The crucial issue is whether a person who committed a crime was *predisposed* to commit the crime or committed the crime because the agent induced it. This is often a question of fact, as illustrated by the following case.

BACKGROUND AND FACTS   Richard Clegg, a government informer, initiated a relationship with Charles Bower and encouraged him to sell cocaine to federal Drug Enforcement Administration agent Sylvestri, posing as a buyer. After Bower delivered the cocaine, Sylvestri arrested him. Bower was tried in federal district court, which found him guilty on various charges, including possession and distribution of cocaine. Bower claimed entrapment and appealed.

DECISION AND RATIONALE   The United States Court of Appeals affirmed the convictions. The court held that the evidence supported the jury's verdict that Bower was "predisposed to commit the crime" rather than induced to do so, which is necessary for the defense of entrapment. The court noted that Bower admitted he saw the sale as a source of "easy money," that he bought the cocaine from a source who trusted him enough to defer payment until he resold it, and that he assured Sylvestri he could handle Sylvestri's future cocaine needs if the amounts were not too large. The court also noted that during the exchange, Bower received a telephone call from his source and offered to produce additional cocaine for Sylvestri in thirty minutes. The court stated that "[a]lthough the record contains evidence upon which a jury might conclude that defendant was induced by a Government informer to commit a crime that he was not otherwise predisposed to commit, the evidence was not 'so overwhelming that it was "patently clear" or "obvious" that [Bower] was entrapped as a matter of law.' "

 Case 6.1

UNITED STATES v. BOWER

United States Court of Appeals, Fifth Circuit, 1978.
575 F.2d 499.

Statutes of Limitations

An individual can be excused from criminal liability by a **statute of limitations.** Such statutes provide that the state has only a certain amount of time within which to prosecute a crime. If the state does not do so within the allotted time, it has lost its opportunity, and the suspect is free from prosecution. These statutes exist to prevent stale or false claims from arising. If prosecution is delayed for too long, it becomes difficult to find out what the truth is because witnesses die or disappear and evidence is destroyed.

Time limits vary from state to state. Felonies usually have longer statutes of limitations than misdemeanors, and there is no time limitation placed on prosecution for murder. For all other crimes, the time limit runs from the time the crime is committed, unless it is a crime that is difficult to discover. In those cases, the time begins to run when the crime is discovered. A time limitation will be suspended, however, if the suspect leaves the state or cannot be found.

Immunity

At times, the state may wish to obtain information from a person accused of a crime. Such accused persons are understandably reluctant to give information, which under the Fifth Amendment they can refuse to provide on the grounds of self-incrimination, if it will be used to prosecute them. In these cases, the state can grant **immunity** from prosecution or agree to prosecute for a less serious offense in exchange for the information. Once immunity is given, the person may be compelled to answer questions. There are two types of immunity. *Use immunity* guarantees that the testimony (and evidence located as a result) will not be used against the person. The person may still be prosecuted on the basis of evidence that comes from a source independent of the person's testimony. *Transactional immunity* guarantees immunity from prosecution for any crime related to the transaction about which the person testifies.

Often a grant of immunity from prosecution for a serious crime is part of the *plea-bargaining* negotiations (discussed below) between the defense and the prosecution. The defendant may still be convicted of a lesser offense, but the state uses his or her testimony to prosecute accomplices for serious crimes carrying heavy penalties.

■ Criminal Procedure

Our criminal justice system operates on the premise that it is far worse for an innocent person to be punished than for a guilty person to go free. A person is innocent until proved guilty, and guilt must be proved beyond a reasonable doubt. The

procedure of the criminal legal system is designed to protect the rights of the individual and to preserve the presumption of innocence.

Constitutional Safeguards

Criminal law brings the weighty force of the state, with all its resources, to bear against the individual. Specific safeguards are provided in the Constitution for those accused of crimes. The United States Supreme Court has ruled that most of these safeguards apply not only in federal but also in state courts by virtue of the due process clause of the Fourteenth Amendment. The safeguards include:

1.   Fourth Amendment protection from unreasonable searches and seizures.
2.   The Fourth Amendment requirement that no warrants for a search or an arrest can be issued without probable cause.
3.   The Fifth Amendment requirement that no one can be deprived of ''life, liberty, or property without due process of law.''
4.   The Fifth Amendment prohibition against double jeopardy (trying someone twice for the same criminal offense).
5.   Sixth Amendment guarantees of a speedy trial, trial by jury, a public trial, the right to confront witnesses, and the right to legal counsel.
6.   Eighth Amendment prohibitions against excessive bails and fines and cruel and unusual punishment.[5]

In recent decades, the United States Supreme Court has been active in interpreting the constitutional rights of accused persons. Under what is known as the **exclusionary rule**, all evidence obtained in violation of the constitutional rights spelled out in the Fourth, Fifth, and Sixth Amendments must be excluded, as well as all evidence derived from the illegally obtained evidence. Illegally obtained evidence is known as the ''fruit of the poisonous tree.'' For example, if a confession is obtained after an illegal arrest, the arrest would be ''the poisonous tree'' and the confession, if ''tainted'' by the arrest, would be the ''fruit.''

Miranda v. Arizona established the rule that individuals who are arrested must be informed of certain constitutional rights, which have come to be

---

5.   See the United States Constitution in Appendix B.

called the "Miranda warnings." The *Miranda* decision, excerpts from which are presented below, has not only been cited in more court decisions than any other case in the history of American law but, through television shows and other media, has also become familiar to most of America's adult population.

BACKGROUND AND FACTS   Ernesto Miranda was arrested for kidnapping and raping an eighteen-year-old woman near Phoenix, Arizona. During the police interrogation, Miranda, who was not informed of his right to remain silent or his right to counsel, confessed to the crime. The confession was introduced at trial, and Miranda was convicted. Miranda appealed, claiming that he had not been informed of his constitutional rights. His case was consolidated with three other cases involving similar issues and reviewed by the United States Supreme Court.

DECISION AND RATIONALE   The United States Supreme Court reversed Miranda's conviction, ruling that he could not be convicted of the crime on the basis of his confession because the confession was inadmissible as evidence. As a prerequisite to the admissibility of any statement made by a defendant, the defendant must be informed, before a police interrogation, of certain constitutional rights: (1) he or she has a right to remain silent; (2) anything said can and will be used against the individual in court; (3) he or she has the right to have an attorney present during questioning; and (4) if the individual cannot afford an attorney, one will be appointed. If the accused waives his or her rights to remain silent and to have counsel present, the government must be able to demonstrate that the waiver was made knowingly and intelligently.

COMMENTS   Four of the nine justices dissented from the majority ruling in this case. The minority complained that the majority vote distorted the Constitution by placing the rights of criminal suspects above the rights of society as a whole. In the past two decades, the courts have fashioned many exceptions to the *Miranda* ruling and have on occasion—when public safety demanded it, for example—allowed into evidence confessions not given voluntarily or information gained through police interrogations conducted before a suspect was advised of his or her rights. The protection afforded accused persons by the *Miranda* ruling was strengthened, however, by a case decided by the United States Supreme Court in 1990. In *Minnick v. Mississippi,*[a] the Court held that once a defendant has requested counsel, the police cannot question the defendant unless his or her attorney is present.

a.   _____ U.S. _____, 111 S.Ct. 486, 112 L.Ed.2d 489 (1990).

Case 6.2

MIRANDA v. ARIZONA

Supreme Court of the United States, 1966.
384 U.S. 436,
86 S.Ct. 1602,
16 L.Ed.2d 694.

Criminal Process

A criminal prosecution differs significantly from a civil case in several respects. These differences reflect the desire to safeguard the rights of the individual against the state.

ARREST   Before a warrant for arrest can be issued, probable cause must exist for believing that the individual in question has committed a crime. **Probable cause** can be defined as a substantial likelihood that the individual has committed or is

■ CONCEPT SUMMARY 6.1   Criminal versus Civil Law

Issue	Criminal Law	Civil Law
Who initiates the legal action?	The government, on behalf of the people.	The plaintiff or petitioner.
Reason for the legal action.	Punishment, deterrence, rehabilitation.	Compensation for wrongful act and/or deterrence.
Burden of proof.	Beyond a reasonable doubt.	Preponderance of the evidence.
Major sanctions available.	Fines, incarceration, capital punishment.	Various equitable remedies (injunction, specific performance, etc.) and/or monetary damages.
Result of trial.	Conviction/acquittal.	Judgment or decree/dismissal.
Trial by jury.	Yes.	Yes, in actions at law; no, for actions in equity.

about to commit a crime. Note that probable cause involves a likelihood, not just a possibility. Arrests may sometimes be made without a warrant when there is no time to get one, but the action of the arresting officer is still judged by the standard of probable cause.

INDICTMENT   An individual must be formally charged with having committed a specific crime before he or she can be brought to trial. This charge is called an **indictment** if issued by a grand jury and an **information** if issued by a magistrate, such as a justice of the peace or other public officer. Before a charge can be issued, the grand jury or the magistrate must determine that there is sufficient evidence to justify bringing the individual to trial. The standard used to make this determination varies from jurisdiction to jurisdiction. Some courts use the probable cause standard. Others use the *preponderance of evidence* standard, which requires that the evidence as a whole show that it is more likely than not that the individual committed the crime. Still another standard is the *prima facie* case standard. In a *prima facie* case, the belief that the individual is guilty is based only on the prosecution's evidence.

ARRAIGNMENT   After the indictment or information is filed, the defendant is arraigned—that is, he or she is brought before the trial court judge (sitting without a jury), informed of the charges, and asked to enter a plea. By pleading guilty, a

defendant waives the right to a trial. If a defendant pleads not guilty, the case may proceed to trial.

In most criminal cases, defendants plead guilty. Usually, this occurs after the prosecutor has promised that concessions will be granted (or at least sought). This is known as plea negotiation, or **plea bargaining.** Sometimes a defendant agrees to plead guilty to a charge less serious than the evidence supports because the consequences will be less costly—a lesser penalty, for example. In other cases, a defendant pleads guilty to the original charge in exchange for the prosecutor's promise to seek leniency, or at least not to oppose the defendant's request for leniency, or to drop other charges.

Plea bargaining came about, in part, because of crowded court dockets and expensive changes in the jury process. Thus, from the prosecutor's point of view, plea bargaining helps dispose of large numbers of cases—in some cities, 80 to 95 percent of all criminal cases—quickly and simply. Critics charge that the practice has at least two negative results: serious offenders receive undeserved leniency, and innocent persons plead guilty (to avoid delays before trial and risks of conviction on greater charges).

TRIAL   At the trial, the accused person does not have to prove anything. The entire burden of proof is on the prosecution (the state). Guilt must be established **beyond a reasonable doubt.** The prosecution must show that, based on all the evidence, the defendant's guilt is clear and unquestionable. This strict standard of proof—which is higher than that required in civil proceedings—reflects a fundamental social value that it is worse to convict an innocent individual than to let a guilty person go free. The consequences to the life, liberty, and reputation of an accused from a wrong conviction for a crime are usually more serious than the effects of an erroneous judgment in a civil case. Thus, the margin of error as to criminal defendants is reduced by placing a high burden of proof on the prosecution.

A verdict of "not guilty" is not the same as a statement that the defendant is innocent. It merely means that not enough evidence was properly presented to the court to prove guilt beyond a reasonable doubt. Courts have complex rules about what types of evidence may be presented and how the evidence may be brought out, especially in jury trials. These rules are designed to ensure that evidence in trials is relevant, reliable, and not unfairly prejudicial to the defendant. The defense attorney will cross-examine the witnesses who present evidence against his or her client in an attempt to show that their evidence is not reliable. Of course, the state may also cross-examine any witnesses presented by the defendant.

■ Crimes Affecting Business

Numerous forms of crime occur in a business context. In this section, we focus on some of the important crimes affecting business. Other types of crimes relating to business, including white-collar crime and computer crime, will be discussed in Chapters 7 and 8.

Forgery

The fraudulent making or alteration of any writing that changes the legal liability of another is **forgery.** If Samson signs Brewster's name without authorization to the back of a check made out to Brewster, Samson has committed forgery. Forgery also includes changing trademarks, falsifying public records, counterfeiting, and altering any legal document.

Most states have a special statute, often called a *credit-card statute,* to cover the illegal use of credit cards. Thus, the state attorney can prosecute a person who misuses a credit card for violating either the forgery statute or the special credit-card statute.

The following case deals with a fraudulent scheme perpetrated by two individuals against a New York bank. At issue is whether the scheme involved the crime of forgery.

Case 6.3

UNITED STATES v. McGOVERN

United States Court of Appeals, Third Circuit, 1981.
661 F.2d 27.

BACKGROUND AND FACTS James McGovern bought Citibank traveler's checks in New York and agreed to let his friend John Scull cash them, by forging McGovern's name, in Pennsylvania. McGovern informed Citibank that the checks had been stolen and requested (and received) reissued checks. McGovern was convicted in federal district court of transporting forged traveler's checks across state lines. Claiming that no forgery had occurred because he had authorized Scull to sign the checks, McGovern appealed the decision.

DECISION AND RATIONALE The United States Court of Appeals upheld the conviction. The court noted the elements of common law forgery: "(a) The false making or material alteration (b) with intent to defraud (c) of a writing which, if genuine, might be of legal efficacy." As for the first element, the court reasoned that a purchaser's agreement to sign each traveler's check at the time of purchase and to countersign the checks only in the presence of the person cashing them invalidated McGovern's attempt to authorize Scull to sign his name. The second element was satisfied because McGovern knew the effect that his actions would have—in fact, defrauding the bank was the sole purpose. The third element was satisfied because the unauthorized signatures were on "otherwise legally sufficient instruments."

ETHICAL CONSIDERATIONS   The defendants' attempt to raise form over substance did not obviate the unethical nature of the scheme. Attempts to reverse criminal convictions on "technicalities" do not alter the underlying ethical issues in question.

Robbery

At common law, **robbery** was the taking of another's personal property, from his or her person or immediate presence, by force or intimidation. The use of force or fear is this crime's distinguishing characteristic. Thus, picking pockets is larceny (discussed below) and not robbery because the action is unknown to the victim. Typically, states have more severe penalties for *aggravated* robbery—robbery by use of a deadly weapon.

Burglary

At common law, **burglary** was defined as breaking and entering the dwelling of another at night with the intent to commit a felony. Originally, the definition was aimed at protecting an individual's home and its occupants. Most state statutes have eliminated some of the requirements found in the common law definition. Thus, the time at which the breaking and entering occurs is usually immaterial, and many state statutes do not require that the building that is entered need be a person's dwelling or home. Aggravated burglary, which is defined as burglary with the use of a deadly weapon, and burglary of a dwelling incur greater penalties.

Larceny

The wrongful or fraudulent taking and carrying away by any person of the personal property of another is **larceny.** It includes the fraudulent intent to permanently deprive an owner of property. Much business-related larceny, such as shoplifting, entails fraudulent conduct.

The place from which physical property is taken is generally immaterial. Statutes usually prescribe a stiffer sentence, however, when property is taken from buildings such as banks or warehouses. Larceny is differentiated from robbery by the fact that robbery involves force or fear and larceny does not. Therefore, as mentioned above, picking another's pockets is larceny, not robbery.

As society has become more complex, a question has often arisen as to what is property. In most states, the definition of the property that is subject to larceny statutes has been expanded. Stealing computer programs may constitute larceny even though the programs consist of magnetic impulses. Trade secrets can be subject to larceny statutes. Stealing the use of telephone wires by the device known as a "blue box" or the unauthorized use of cable television is subject to larceny statutes. So, too, is the theft of natural gas.

In most states, the value of the property taken determines whether the offense is a misdemeanor or a felony. Historically, if the value of the property was less than $50, the crime was a misdemeanor, or *petit larceny*. Today, the states differ as to what amount escalates the crime into a felony, or *grand larceny*. Threshold amounts range from $50 to $2,000.

Obtaining Goods by False Pretenses

It is a criminal act to obtain goods by means of false pretenses—that is, to represent as true some information or circumstance that is not true, with the intent of deceiving and with the result of defrauding an individual into relinquishing property without adequate compensation. For example, buying groceries with a check knowing that one has insufficient funds to cover it is obtaining goods by false pretenses. Statutes covering such illegal activities vary widely from state to state.

Receiving Stolen Goods

It is a crime to receive stolen goods. The recipient of such goods need not know the true identity of the owner or of the thief. All that is necessary is that the recipient know or should know that the goods are stolen, which implies an intent to deprive the owner of those goods.

Embezzlement

The fraudulent conversion of property or money owned by one person but *entrusted* to another is **embezzlement.** Typically, it involves an employee who fraudulently appropriates money. Banks face this problem, and so do a number of businesses in which corporate officers or accountants "jimmy" the books to cover up the fraudulent conversion of money for their own benefit. Embezzlement is not larceny because to commit embezzlement the wrongdoer does not need to carry away the property from the possession of another. In fact, embezzlement involves the conversion of property by a person *in lawful possession* of that property, whereas larceny involves the taking and carrying away of another's property, usually without any right to possession at all. (For example, Stevenson's taking home the company-owned typewriter that he uses in his office is embezzlement. If he gets caught and fired for it and, on the way out, takes a company-owned pocket calculator, he com-

mits larceny.) Embezzlement is not robbery because there is no taking by use of force or fear.

It does not matter whether the accused takes the money from the victim or from a third person. If, as the comptroller of a large corporation, Saunders pockets a certain number of checks from third parties that were given to her to deposit into the account of another company, she has committed embezzlement.

Often the owner of property will remit money to a contractor specifically for the contractor to use in paying various persons who worked on the owner's building. The contractor who does not use the money for this purpose commits a special form of embezzlement called *misapplication of trust funds.* The funds have been entrusted to the contractor for a specific purpose, and that trust has been violated.

An embezzler who returns what has been taken will not ordinarily be prosecuted, because the owner usually will not take the time to make a complaint, give depositions, and appear in court. The fact that the accused intended eventually to return the embezzled property, however, does not constitute a sufficient defense to the crime of embezzlement. This point is made clear in the following case.

BACKGROUND AND FACTS Glenn Slemmer controlled the account of Profit Design Group (PDG), an investment club for which he made investment decisions, but he was not authorized to withdraw money from the account. Nonetheless, he withdrew money to make payments on real estate that he owned. Slemmer eventually lost all the money in PDG's account. After a trial in a Washington state court, a jury found Slemmer guilty of theft by embezzlement. Slemmer objected to the trial court's failure to instruct the jury that an intent to deprive permanently was an element of the crime of theft by embezzlement.

 Case 6.4

STATE v. SLEMMER
Court of Appeals of
Washington, Division 1, 1987.
48 Wash.App. 48,
738 P.2d 281.

DECISION AND RATIONALE The Court of Appeals of Washington upheld Slemmer's conviction. The court stated that proof of intent to permanently deprive is not a necessary element of the crime of embezzlement. The court concluded that "[t]he facts demonstrate embezzlement. Slemmer had control of PDG's account as their agent, and was authorized to control the account by agreement. Thus, when he appropriated the funds in the account to his own use he was [embezzling]."

Arson

The willful and malicious burning of a building or some other structure (and in some states personal

property) owned by another is the crime of **arson.** At common law, arson applied only to burning down the house of another. The law was designed to protect human life. Today, arson statutes apply to other kinds of structures as well. Also, if someone is killed as a result of arson, the act is murder under the felony murder rule.

Every state has a special statute that covers burning a building for the purpose of collecting insurance. If Allison owns an insured apartment building that is falling apart and burns it himself or pays someone else to set fire to it, Allison is guilty of *burning to defraud insurers*. Of course, the insurer need not pay the claim when insurance fraud is proved.

Use of the Mails to Defraud

It is a federal crime to use the mails to defraud the public. Illegal use of the mails must involve (1) mailing or causing someone else to mail a writing for the purpose of executing a scheme to defraud and (2) a contemplated or organized scheme to defraud by false pretenses. If, for example, Johnson uses the mails to sell a cure for cancer that he knows to be fraudulent because it has no medical validity, he can be prosecuted for fraudulent use of the mails. Federal law also makes it a crime to

---

■ CONCEPT SUMMARY 6.2 Classifications of Law

Law Classifications	Types of Offense

Criminal law is concerned with acts against society for which society seeks redress in the form of punishment.	1. Felony
	  a. Homicide
	  b. Manslaughter
	  c. Robbery
	  d. Burglary
	  e. Larceny (grand)
	  f. Bribery
	  g. Arson
	
	2. Misdemeanor
	  a. Public intoxication
	  b. Vagrancy
	  c. Prostitution
	  d. Larceny (petit)
	  e. Trespass
	  f. Disturbing the peace
	  g. Assault and battery

Civil law is concerned with acts against a person for which the injured party seeks redress in the form of compensation or other relief.	1. Contract breach
	  a. Real estate
	  b. Insurance
	  c. Sales
	  d. Business organization formation
	  e. Services
	  f. Commercial paper obligations
	  g. Commercial bailments
	
	2. Tort
	  a. Defamation
	  b. Invasion of privacy
	  c. Assault and battery
	  d. Negligence
	  e. Strict liability
	  f. Trespass
	  g. Fraud

use a telegram, telephone, radio, or television to defraud. Violators may be fined up to $1,000, imprisoned for up to five years, or both. If the violation affects a financial institution, the fine may be up to $1 million and the imprisonment up to twenty years, or both.

Unlike the crime of obtaining goods by false pretenses, the crime of mail fraud does not require that the scheme succeed in defrauding anyone. The crime is committed when a person devises a scheme involving the making of a false promise and uses the mails to carry it out. Mail order frauds, dummy corporations, phony franchise schemes, and other frauds on the general public are the traditional targets of the statute. It has also been used against schemes involving the bribery of public officials and corporate employees.

In the following case, a used-car distributor's scheme to roll back odometers on the automobiles that he sold to dealers was held to constitute mail fraud.

BACKGROUND AND FACTS Wayne Schmuck bought used cars, rolled back their odometers, and sold them to Wisconsin dealers for prices that were artificially high due to the low-mileage readings. The dealers resold the cars to the public, who also paid higher prices because of the low-mileage readings. To complete the resales, the dealers had to submit a title-application form for each sale to the Wisconsin Department of Transportation. Schmuck was indicted for mail fraud. After a trial in federal district court, the court held that mailing the title-application forms constituted the mailing element of the crime of mail fraud, and Schmuck was convicted. Schmuck appealed, contending that the mailings were not made in furtherance of the fraudulent scheme and thus did not satisfy the mailing element. The appellate court affirmed the district court's ruling, and Schmuck appealed to the United States Supreme Court.

DECISION AND RATIONALE The United States Supreme Court upheld Schmuck's conviction. The Supreme Court reasoned that the scheme "did not reach fruition until the retail dealers resold the cars and effected transfers of title. * * * [A]lthough the registration-form mailings may not have contributed directly to the duping of either the retail dealers or the customers, they were necessary to the passage of title, which in turn was essential to the perpetuation of Schmuck's scheme." The Court pointed out that a mailing that is "incident to an essential part of the scheme" satisfies the mailing element of the mail fraud offense.

Case 6.5

SCHMUCK v. UNITED STATES

Supreme Court of the United States, 1989.
489 U.S. 705,
109 S.Ct. 1443,
103 L.Ed.2d 734.

■ Terms and Concepts

actus reus 116	entrapment 119	*mens rea* 116
arson 125	exclusionary rule 120	misdemeanor 115
beyond a reasonable doubt 122	felony 115	petty offense 115
burglary 124	felony murder 115	plea bargaining 122
consent 118	forgery 123	probable cause 121
crime 114	immunity 120	robbery 124
duress 118	indictment 122	self-defense 118
embezzlement 125	information 122	statute of limitations 119
	larceny 124	

■ For Review

1. What distinguishes crimes from other wrongful acts?
2. What must exist before a warrant for arrest can be issued?
3. What is excluded under the exclusionary rule?
4. As part of his job for the Refreshing Beverage Co., Bat travels to cities throughout the Midwest. Refreshing gives Bat access to a petty cash fund to withdraw money for use in his travels and issues Bat a credit card to make related

charges. When Refreshing fires Bat, he takes all the money from the petty cash fund and uses the credit card to buy a plane ticket to Belize. What crimes has Bat committed?
5. Sam's television set is stolen. While passing Jean's house one night, Sam sees a portable television left unattended on Jean's lawn. The set is the same brand and model as Sam's. Believing the television is his, Sam takes the set and carries it home. Has Sam committed a crime?

■ Questions and Case Problems

6-1. In criminal trials, the defendant must be proved guilty beyond a reasonable doubt, whereas in civil trials, the defendant need only be proved guilty by a preponderance of the evidence. Discuss why a higher standard of proof is required in criminal trials.

6-2. Crimes are classified as either felonies or misdemeanors. Determine from the facts below what type of crime has been committed and whether the crime is a felony or a misdemeanor.

(a) Allen and George become involved in a shouting argument. Allen knocks George down, causing a serious head injury to George.

(b) Darrell continually crosses Mary's backyard without permission, despite Mary's notice to Darrell to get off her land.

(c) Harold walks into a camera shop. Without force and without the owner noticing, Harold walks out of the store with a camera.

6-3. The following situations are similar to each other (in all of them, Jean's television set is stolen); yet three different crimes are described. Identify the three crimes, noting the differences among them.

(a) While passing Jean's house one night, Sam sees a portable television set left unattended on Jean's lawn. Sam takes the television set, carries it home, and tells everyone he owns it.

(b) While passing Jean's house one night, Sam sees Jean outside with a portable television set. Holding Jean at gunpoint, Sam forces her to give up the set. Then Sam runs away with it.

(c) While passing Jean's house one night, Sam sees a portable television set in a window. Sam breaks the front door lock, enters, and leaves with the set.

6-4. Jack, an undercover police officer, stops Patricia on a busy street and offers to sell her an expensive wristwatch for a fraction of its value. After some questioning, Jack admits that the watch is stolen property, although he says that he was not the thief. Patricia pays for and receives the wristwatch and is immediately arrested by Jack for receiving stolen property. At trial, Patricia contends she was a victim of entrapment. What is the result of the trial? Discuss.

6-5. Two basic elements are needed for a person to be convicted of a crime. The first element is called *actus reus,*

and the second is called *mens rea.* Explain what these terms mean, and discuss how each is applied to the following:

(a) Murder or manslaughter.

(b) Forgery.

(c) Arson.

6-6. Faulkner was a seaman on the ship *Zemindar.* One night while on duty, Faulkner went in search of the rum that he knew the ship was carrying. He found it and opened one of the kegs, but because he was holding a match at the time, he inadvertently ignited the rum and set fire to the ship. Faulkner was criminally prosecuted for setting the fire. At the trial, it was determined that even though he had not intended to set fire to the rum, he had been engaged in the unlawful act of stealing it. Does Faulkner's theft of the rum make him criminally liable for setting fire to the ship? Discuss. [*Regina v. Faulkner,* 13 Cox C.C. 550 (1877)]

6-7. In 1965, Rybicki failed to pay the complete amount of income tax he owed the federal government. Attempts by the Internal Revenue Service (IRS) to collect the tax proved fruitless. Therefore, the IRS, through lawful means, obtained a tax lien on Rybicki's personal property, which included his truck. In February 1967, Rybicki's wife, upon hearing the motor of the truck, awoke her sleeping husband. Wielding a shotgun, Rybicki went to his front door and told the two men who were attempting to take his truck to stop. Rybicki claimed that he did not know that the two men were IRS agents. Subsequently, the federal government indicted Rybicki for obstructing justice. Can Rybicki be held criminally liable if he did not know that the men were IRS agents performing their duty? Explain. [*United States v. Rybicki,* 403 F.2d 599 (6th Cir. 1968)]

6-8. Gomez, an informant for the police posing as an ex-convict, urged Saldana on several occasions to sell cocaine to make money, but Saldana, although he used cocaine, did not wish to sell any. Finally, to get Gomez to stop pestering him, Saldana agreed to sell some cocaine to one Castello, who turned out to be a police officer. May Saldana successfully claim an entrapment defense? Discuss. [*Saldana v. State,* 732 S.W.2d 701 (Tex.App.—Corpus Christi 1987)]

6-9. Britt was convicted of second degree homicide for the shooting death of his neighbor, Cavell. The victim was killed by a .44 caliber revolver that was part of a trap set by Britt to prevent forcible entry into his home from the back door. The booby trap was set to discharge if the door was opened a distance of two to four inches. The relevant Louisiana law reads: "A homicide is justifiable . . . when committed by a person lawfully inside a dwelling against a person who is attempting to make an unlawful entry into the dwelling or who has made an unlawful entry into the dwelling and the person committing the homicide reasonably believes that the use of deadly force is necessary to prevent the entry or to compel the intruder to leave the premises. The homicide shall be justifiable even though the person committing the homicide does not retreat from the encounter." Britt argued on appeal that the shooting of Cavell was justified because, had he been present, he would have been authorized to use deadly force and to use a mechanical contrivance. Will Britt's appeal be successful? Explain. [*State v. Britt*, 510 So.2d 670 (La.App. 1st Cir. 1987)]

6-10. Patterson was charged with first degree robbery for pointing a loaded gun at a man and demanding money from him. At trial, Patterson did not contest the state's proof that she committed these acts but instead relied on the defense of insanity. She claimed she was unable, as a result of mental disease or defect, to appreciate the nature and quality of her conduct. The superior court instructed the jury that to find Patterson not guilty by reason of insanity, it had to find that, because of a mental disease or defect, she did not understand that she was performing the physical acts that constitute the elements of the crime with which she was charged. In other words, the superior court read the insanity defense statute as incorporating only the first prong of the traditional *M'Naghten* insanity defense—that the defendant did not understand the basic nature and quality of his or her conduct. The jury found Patterson did not come within this interpretation. The court of appeals, however, ruled that the trial court had interpreted the insanity defense too narrowly. It held that the correct interpretation of the insanity defense included *both* prongs of the *M'Naghten* test—that the defendant could be found not guilty by reason of insanity if the defendant *either* was not aware of the physical acts he or she was performing *or* did not understand the wrongfulness of those acts. Is the appellate court right? Explain. [*State v. Patterson*, 740 P.2d 944 (Alaska 1987)]

6-11. The defendant (Faulkner), a truck driver, was hauling a load of refrigerators from San Diego to New York for the trucking com-

pany that employed him. He departed from his assigned route, stopped in Las Vegas, and attempted to display and sell some of the refrigerators to a firm. Although the refrigerators never left the truck, to display them he had to break the truck's seals, enter the cargo department, and open two refrigerator cartons. The store owner refused to purchase the appliances, and when Faulkner left the store, he was arrested. He was later convicted under federal law for the embezzlement of an interstate shipment. Faulkner appealed, claiming that there were no grounds for the charge, since he had never removed any equipment from the truck. Discuss whether the charge of embezzlement applies when the property has not been physically removed from the owner's possession. [*United States v. Faulkner*, 638 F.2d 129 (9th Cir. 1981)]

6-12. A Question of Ethics

A troublesome issue concerning the constitutional privilege against self-incrimination has to do with "jail plants"—that is, placing undercover police officers in cells with criminal suspects to gain information from the suspects. For example, in one case the police placed an undercover agent, Parisi, in a jail cellblock with Lloyd Perkins, who had been imprisoned on charges unrelated to the murder that Parisi was investigating. When Parisi asked Perkins if he had ever killed anyone, Perkins made statements implicating himself in the murder. Perkins was then charged with the murder. [Illinois v. Perkins, *496 U.S. 292, 110 S.Ct. 2394, 110 L.Ed.2d 243 (1990)*]

1. Review the discussion and case presentation of *Miranda v. Arizona* (Case 6.2). Should Perkins's statements be suppressed—that is, not be treated as admissible evidence at trial—because he was not "read his rights" as required by the *Miranda* decision prior to making his self-incriminating statements? Does *Miranda* apply to Perkins's situation?

2. Do you think that it is fair for the police to resort to trickery and deception to bring those who have committed crimes to justice? Why or why not? What rights or public policies must be balanced in deciding this issue?

Chapter 7

Torts and Crimes Related to Business

Our economic system of free enterprise is predicated on the ability of persons, acting either as individuals or as business firms, to compete for customers and for sales. Unfettered competitive behavior has been shown to lead to economic efficiency and economic progress. Businesses may, generally speaking, engage in whatever is *reasonably* necessary to obtain a fair share of a market or to recapture a share that has been lost. But they are not allowed to use the motive of completely eliminating competition to justify certain business activities. Thus, an entire area of what is called business torts has arisen. Remember that a tort is a breach of a duty owed to an individual or to a group. **Business torts** are defined as wrongful interferences with others' business rights. Included in business torts are such vaguely worded concepts as *unfair competition* and *wrongfully interfering with the business relations of others.*

Following a discussion of business torts, we address the subject of so-called *white-collar crime.* Recall from Chapter 6 that a crime is a breach of a duty owed to society as a whole. Although no official definition exists for **white-collar crime,** the term is popularly used to refer to nonviolent crimes committed by individuals or businesses to obtain a personal or business advantage. Bribery, money laundering, insider trading, and corporate crime all fall within the broad category of white-collar crime.

We conclude the chapter with a section on the application of the Racketeer Influenced and Corrupt Organizations Act (RICO) to business activities.

■ Torts Related to Business

Because the area of business torts is so broad, we restrict our discussion in this section to the following general categories of business torts: wrongful interference with the business rights of others; appropriation of another's name without permission; and defamation or disparagement of business property or reputation. Other business torts will be discussed in Chapter 8, in the context of our discussion of intellectual property and computer law.

Wrongful Interference with the Business Rights of Others

Torts involving wrongful interference with another's business rights generally fall into two categories—interference with a contractual relationship and interference with a business relationship. These two torts and the defenses that can be raised against them are discussed below.

WRONGFUL INTERFERENCE WITH A CONTRACTUAL RELATIONSHIP

The body of tort law relating to *intentional interference with a contractual relationship* has increased greatly in recent years. A landmark case in this area involved an opera singer, Joanna Wagner, who was under contract to sing for a man named Lumley for a specified period of years.[1] A man named Gye, who knew of this contract, nonetheless "enticed" Wagner to refuse to carry out the agreement, and Wagner began to sing for Gye. Gye's action constituted a tort because it interfered with the contractual relationship between Wagner and Lumley. (Wagner's refusal to carry out the agreement also entitled Lumley to sue for breach of contract.)

In principle, any lawful contract can be the basis for an action of this type. The plaintiff must prove that the defendant actually *induced* the breach of a contractual relationship, not merely that the defendant reaped the benefits of a broken contract. For example, suppose that Jones has a contract with Smith that calls for Smith to mow Jones's lawn every week for fifty-two weeks at a specified price per week. Miller, who needs gardening services, contacts Smith and offers to pay Smith a wage that is substantially higher than that offered by Jones—although Miller knows nothing about the Smith-Jones contract. Smith breaches his contract with Jones so that he can work for Miller. Jones cannot sue Miller, because Miller knew nothing of the Smith-Jones contract and was totally unaware that the higher wage he offered induced Smith to breach that contract.

Three basic elements are necessary to the existence of wrongful interference with a contractual relationship:

1. A valid, enforceable contract must exist between two parties.
2. A third party must *know* that this contract exists.
3. This third party must *intentionally* cause either of the two parties to the contract to break the contract. Whether this third party acts in bad faith or with malice (the intention to harm another) is immaterial to establishing this tort, even though in most cases bad faith or malice is in evidence. The interference, however, must be for the purpose of advancing the economic interest of the inducer.

The contract may be between a firm and its employees or a firm and its customers, suppliers, competitors, or other parties. Sometimes a competitor of a firm may attempt to draw away a key employee, even to the extent of paying the damages for breach of contract. If the original employer can show that the competitor induced the breach—that is, that the employee would not normally have broken the contract—damages can be recovered.

The following highly publicized case illustrates the requirements for the tort of wrongful interference with a contractual relationship.

---

1. *Lumley v. Gye*, 118 Eng.Rep. 749 (1853).

BACKGROUND AND FACTS Pennzoil Company agreed to buy control of Getty Oil Company. Although details of the agreement remained unsettled, on January 5, the news was announced by both companies and was reported widely in newspapers. While a formal written document was being negotiated, Texaco, Inc., made a higher bid for Getty, and on January 6, Getty's board of directors accepted it. As part of the deal, Getty insisted on full indemnity from Texaco against any claims by Pennzoil, and Getty's major shareholders insisted on a guarantee of at least "the price Pennzoil had agreed to pay." Pennzoil sued Texaco, alleging tortious interference with its contract with Getty. The trial court jury found that (1) Getty had agreed to Pennzoil's offer; (2) Texaco knowingly interfered with this agreement; (3) as a result, Pennzoil suffered damages of $7.53 billion; (4) Texaco's actions were intentional, willful, and in wanton disregard of Pennzoil's rights; and (5) Pennzoil was entitled to punitive damages of $3 billion. Texaco appealed.

 Case 7.1

TEXACO, INC. v. PENNZOIL CO.

Court of Appeals of Texas—Houston (First District), 1987.
729 S.W.2d 768.

DECISION AND RATIONALE The Texas Court of Appeals accepted the jury's findings and affirmed the trial court's decision. As to whether Pennzoil and Getty actually had a contract, the court pointed out that if "there is no understanding that a signed writing is necessary before the parties will be bound, and the parties have agreed upon all substantial terms, then an informal agreement can be binding, even though the parties contemplate evidencing their agreement in a formal document later." There was sufficient evidence to support the jury's finding that the parties intended to be bound to an agreement. Similarly, as to whether Texaco knew about the contract, the court stated that there was sufficient evidence to support the jury's inference. The court noted Pennzoil's assertion that Texaco knew about the deal from the widely reported announcement. As to whether Texaco intentionally interfered with the contract between Getty and Pennzoil, causing Getty to breach it, the court noted as an example of interference an "offering [of] better terms or other incentives" and again determined that there was sufficient evidence to support the jury's finding that "Texaco actively induced the breach of the Getty entities['] agreement with Pennzoil."

COMMENTS On a later appeal, the Supreme Court of Texas found no reversible errors. Other issues in the case were appealed as high as the United States Supreme Court. In 1988, the case was settled for $3 billion. The day of the payment, Texaco completed its reorganization and emerged from twelve months in bankruptcy proceedings.

WRONGFUL INTERFERENCE WITH A BUSINESS RELATIONSHIP Individuals devise countless schemes to attract business, but they are forbidden by the courts to interfere unreasonably with another's business in their attempts to gain a share of the market. There is a difference between *competition* and *predatory behavior*. The distinction usually depends on whether a business is attempting to attract customers in general or to solicit only those customers who have already shown an interest in the similar product or service of a specific competitor. If a shopping center contains two shoe stores, an employee of Store A cannot be positioned at the entrance of Store B for the purpose of diverting customers to Store A. This type of activity constitutes the tort of wrongful interference with a business relationship, often referred to as interference with a prospective (economic) advantage, and is commonly considered to be an unfair trade practice. If this type of activity were permitted, Store A would reap the benefits of Store B's advertising.

A salesperson cannot follow another company's salesperson through the city, soliciting the same prospective customers. Even though the people contacted may have purchased nothing from the first salesperson, that salesperson still has a business relationship with them. Courts will issue injunctions against this kind of behavior and will award damages when the business alleging interference can prove it suffered a monetary loss. In the following case a salesperson's activities exceeded the bounds of fair competition.

Case 7.2

AZAR v. LEHIGH CORP.

District Court of Appeal of Florida, Second District, 1978. 364 So.2d 860.

BACKGROUND AND FACTS Lehigh Corporation, a developer of real estate, brought prospective customers to its development and provided accommodations at its company-owned motel. Leroy Azar, a former Lehigh sales representative, followed Lehigh buyers as they entered the motel and persuaded them to rescind their contracts with Lehigh and purchase less expensive property from him. Lehigh sued in a Florida state court, asserting that Azar was tortiously interfering with the advantageous business relationship between Lehigh and its customers. Azar contended that the customers had a legal right under federal law to rescind their contracts within three days and that he was merely providing them with an opportunity to obtain comparable property for lower prices. Lehigh was granted a restraining order against Azar.

DECISION AND RATIONALE The Florida District Court of Appeal sustained the restraining order. The court noted that in cases of interference with prospective advantage, the central question is whether the conduct is considered fair according to contemporary business standards. The court stated that there are three basic elements for the tort of interference with a business relationship: "(1) the existence of a business relationship under which the plaintiff has legal rights, (2) an intentional and unjustified interference with that relationship by the defendant, and (3) damage to the plaintiff as a result of the breach of the business relationship." The court concluded that "[k]eeping in mind the trial judge's broad discretion to enter temporary restraining orders," there was sufficient evidence to support the decision to grant the restraining order. "Moreover, we believe the terms of the order are precise enough for the appellant to understand what he cannot do. * * * [W]e are confident that he will have no difficulty in ascertaining which of the motel patrons constitute appellees' guests."

DEFENSES TO WRONGFUL INTERFERENCE
A person will not be liable for the tort of wrongful interference with a contractual or business relationship if it can be shown that the interference was *permissible.*

Permissible interferences are interfering actions that the courts have not held to be tortious interferences. For example, bona fide competitive behavior is a privileged (justifiable, or permissible) interference even if it results in the breaking of a contract. If Jones Meats advertises so effectively that it induces Sam's Restaurant Chain to break its contract with Paul's Meat Company, Paul's Meat Company will be unable to recover against Jones Meats on a wrongful interference theory. After all, the public policy that favors free competition in advertising definitely outweighs any possible instability that such competitive activity might cause in contractual relations. Therefore, although luring customers away from a competitor through aggressive marketing and advertising strategies obviously interferes with the competitor's relationship with his or her customers, such activity is permitted by the courts.

Also, so long as there is no associated *illegal* activity, a businessperson will not incur tort liability for negotiating secretly behind a rival's back, refusing to do business with a competitor, or refusing to deal with third parties until they stop doing business with a rival.

PERMISSIBLE INTERFERENCES VERSUS TORTIOUS INTERFERENCES
What the courts consider normal competitive activity is not always easy to ascertain. One might ask when the normal desire to compete and obtain profits ends and when a tortious action begins. The courts often emphasize parties' bad motives, but such cases often involve conduct that would be objectionable anyway—for example, efforts that are directed toward driving a competitor out of business are objectionable for the same reasons that led to the enactment of antitrust laws (see Chapter 47). The landmark case that follows illustrates how a Minnesota court grappled with the question of malicious injury to business.

BACKGROUND AND FACTS For ten years, Edward Tuttle owned and operated a barbershop in Howard Lake, Minnesota. Cassius Buck, a banker in Howard Lake, set up a competing barbershop for no apparent business reason. Buck hired a barber to run the business and used his personal influence to attract customers from Tuttle's shop. Circulating malicious rumors about Tuttle, Buck personally persuaded many persons to stop patronizing Tuttle's shop. Using his personal power as the town's

 Case 7.3

TUTTLE v. BUCK
Supreme Court of Minnesota, 1909.
107 Minn. 145,
119 N.W. 946.

banker, Buck threatened some of the bank's customers to force them to use Buck's shop instead. Tuttle sued Buck in a Minnesota state court for malicious interference, charging that Buck undertook the entire plan with the sole design of injuring Tuttle and destroying his business, not for serving any legitimate business interest. The trial court's decision for Tuttle was affirmed by the appellate court, and the defendant appealed.

DECISION AND RATIONALE The Supreme Court of Minnesota affirmed the lower court's decision, concluding that business requires protection against abusive business practices. The court stated that "when a man starts an opposition place of business, not for the sake of profit to himself, but regardless of loss to himself, and for the sole purpose of driving his competitor out of business, and with the intention of himself retiring upon the accomplishment of his malevolent purpose, he is guilty of a wanton wrong and an actionable tort." Calling this conduct competitive, said the court, "is a perversion of terms. It is simply the application of force without legal justification, which in its moral quality may be no better than highway robbery."

Appropriation

The use of one person's name or likeness by another, without permission and for the benefit of the user, constitutes the tort of **appropriation.** Under the law, an individual's right to privacy includes the right to the exclusive use of his or her identity. A number of cases have arisen concerning the use of a famous person's name for the benefit of the user. One case involved the use of "Here's Johnny"—the opening line of the Johnny Carson show. A Michigan corporation that rented and sold portable toilets advertised them as "Here's Johnny" toilets. Carson brought suit, claiming that the Michigan corporation had violated his right to privacy by publicly appropriating his celebrity status for the corporation's commercial benefit. Even though the corporation had not used Carson's name or picture, the court held that the use of "Here's Johnny" was an appropriation of Carson's identity because the phrase was so strongly associated with Carson's public personality.[2] Other cases have involved the unauthorized use of former world heavyweight boxing champion

Muhammad Ali's appellation "The Greatest" to describe a nude male model[3] and professional football wide receiver Elroy Hirsch's moniker "Crazylegs" as the name of a shaving gel.[4]

Defamation

As we stated in Chapter 5, the tort of *defamation* occurs when an individual makes a false statement that injures another's reputation. We also divided defamation into its component parts of libel (defamatory statements in written or printed form) and slander (defamatory statements made orally). Defamation becomes a business tort when the defamatory matter injures someone in a profession, business, or trade or when it adversely affects a business entity in its credit rating and other dealings.

When erroneous information from a computer about a person's credit standing or business reputation impairs that person's ability to obtain further credit, *defamation by computer* results. The following case illustrates how this tort can occur.

---

2. *Carson v. Here's Johnny Portable Toilets,* 698 F.2d 831 (6th Cir. 1983).

3. *Ali v. Playgirl, Inc.,* 447 F.Supp. 723 (S.D.N.Y. 1978).
4. *Hirsch v. S. C. Johnson & Son, Inc.,* 90 Wis.2d 379, 280 N.W.2d 129 (1979).

BACKGROUND AND FACTS   Dun & Bradstreet, Inc., the credit-reporting agency, included false information concerning Greenmoss Builders, Inc., in a computerized letter sent to several of its subscribers. The letter stated falsely that Greenmoss had filed for bankruptcy. Greenmoss lost business and income and sued Dun & Bradstreet in Vermont state court for defamation. The trial court awarded $50,000 in compensatory damages and $300,000 in punitive damages to Greenmoss. Dun & Bradstreet appealed, claiming that its credit report was a form of speech protected by the First Amendment. Dun & Bradstreet asserted that its report involved a matter of public concern, and thus, to recover damages for defamation, Greenmoss would have to prove that Dun & Bradstreet acted with actual malice. The case was ultimately reviewed by the United States Supreme Court.

 Case 7.4

DUN & BRADSTREET, INC. v. GREENMOSS BUILDERS, INC.

Supreme Court of the United States, 1985.
472 U.S. 749,
105 S.Ct. 2939,
86 L.Ed.2d 593.

DECISION AND RATIONALE   The United States Supreme Court ruled in Greenmoss's favor, holding that the speech did not involve a public concern or issue. The Supreme Court explained that whether speech addresses a matter of public concern is determined by its content, form, and context. Under these factors, Dun & Bradstreet's credit report concerned no public issue. It was speech solely in the interest of Dun & Bradstreet and its specific audience; it was wholly false and clearly damaging to Greenmoss's business reputation. The Court also pointed out that "the credit report was made available to only five subscribers, who, under the terms of the subscription agreement, could not disseminate it further," and thus "it cannot be said that the report involves any 'strong interest in the free flow of commercial information.'"

Disparagement of Property

Disparagement of property occurs when economically injurious falsehoods are made not about another's reputation but about another's *product* or *property*. Disparagement of property is a general term for torts that can be more specifically referred to as *slander of quality* or *slander of title*.

SLANDER OF QUALITY   Publication of false information about another's product, alleging it is not what its seller claims, constitutes a tort of **slander of quality.** This tort has also been given the name **trade libel.** The plaintiff must prove that actual damages proximately resulted from the slander of quality. That is, it must be shown not only that a third person refrained from dealing with the plaintiff because of the improper publication but that the plaintiff suffered damages because the third person refrained from dealing with him or her as a result of the improper publication. The economic calculation of such damages—they are, after all, conjectural—is often extremely difficult.

It is possible for an improper publication to be both a slander of quality and a defamation. For example, a statement that disparages the quality of a product may also, by implication, disparage the character of the person who would sell such a product.

The law of trademarks has, to some extent, made it easier for companies to sue other companies on the basis of purported false advertising. In the past, courts often ruled that companies could only be liable for false advertising when they misrepresented their own products. It mattered little what such companies claimed about their competitors' brands, particularly in so-called comparative advertisements. Today, false or misleading statements about another firm's products are actionable.

In the following case, the court evaluates the advertising claims made by the two leading competitors in the U.S. puppy food market.

Case 7.5

ALPO PETFOODS, INC. v. RALSTON PURINA CO.

United States District Court, District of Columbia, 1989. 720 F.Supp. 194.

BACKGROUND AND FACTS   For more than a year, Alpo Petfoods, Inc., and Ralston Purina Company conducted extensive advertising campaigns. Ralston claimed that its Purina Puppy Chow helped reduce the incidence of canine hip dysplasia (CHD), a feared, incurable dog disease. Ralston's status as the leading puppy food seller in the United States lent the claim a high degree of credibility. Alpo, the second largest seller of puppy food in the United States, claimed that veterinarians preferred the formula in Alpo Puppy Food "2 to 1" over Ralston's puppy food. Alpo sued Ralston in federal district court, alleging that Ralston's claims were false, misleading, and deceptive in violation of federal statutes and common law. Ralston counterclaimed, alleging that Alpo's claims were false, misleading, and deceptive under the same laws. Ralston added that Alpo's statements to veterinarians and news media regarding Ralston's CHD claims constituted unfair competition, deceptive trade practices, and defamation. Each party sought damages and an injunction prohibiting the other party from further publication of its claims.

DECISION AND RATIONALE   The United States District Court entered judgment for Alpo but enjoined both parties from further publication of their respective claims and ordered both to issue corrective releases. The district court based its decision on the federal statute. The court found that CHD is hereditary and concluded that Ralston's CHD claims were clearly false. The court found that Alpo's veterinarian preference claim was also false—veterinarians overwhelmingly preferred Ralston's Purina Puppy Chow. Ralston was not awarded damages for Alpo's false advertising because the "magnitude of Ralston's misconduct" was comparable to that of Alpo. As for Alpo's statements to veterinarians and the news media, the court found that they were not defamatory and that they constituted neither unfair competition nor deceptive trade practices.

SLANDER OF TITLE   When a publication denies or casts doubt upon another's legal ownership of any property, and when this results in financial loss to that property's owner, the tort of **slander of title** may exist. Usually this is an intentional tort in which someone knowingly publishes an untrue statement about property with the intent of discouraging a third person from dealing with the person slandered. For example, it would be difficult for a car dealer to attract customers after competitors published a notice that the dealer's stock consisted of stolen autos.

■ Crimes Related to Business

Crimes such as embezzlement, robbery, burglary, larceny, arson, and so on, when directed against business property, are crimes related to business. Since those crimes have already been discussed in Chapter 6, we restrict our attention here to what is popularly designated as white-collar crime. As mentioned in this chapter's introduction, white-collar crime is nonviolent in nature. It is also usually committed in the course of a legitimate occupation and often difficult to detect. Since it is impossible to cover the vast range of what are considered to be white-collar crimes, the efforts in this section will center on four areas: (1) bribery, (2) money laundering, (3) insider trading and other financial fraud, and (4) corporate crime. Computer crime, which is also a form of white-collar crime, will be discussed in Chapter 8 in the context of computer law.

Bribery

Basically, three types of actions called *bribery* are considered crimes. They involve (1) bribery of public officials, (2) commercial bribery, and (3) bribery of foreign officials.

BRIBERY OF PUBLIC OFFICIALS The attempt to influence a public official to act in a way that serves a private interest is a crime. As an element of this crime, *intent* must be present and proved. The bribe that is offered can be anything that the recipient of the offer—that is, the public official—considers valuable. The commission of the crime of **bribery** occurs when the bribe is *tendered* (offered or given). The recipient does not have to agree to perform whatever action is desired by the person tendering the bribe; nor does the recipient have to accept the bribe.

COMMERCIAL BRIBERY In some states, so-called kickbacks and payoffs from an individual working for one company to another individual or individuals working for another company are crimes. No public official need be involved. Such commercial bribes are typically given with the intent of obtaining proprietary information, covering up an inferior product, or securing new business. Industrial espionage sometimes involves this kind of activity—for example, a payoff of some type to an employee in a competing firm in exchange for trade secrets and pricing schedules.

BRIBERY OF FOREIGN OFFICIALS Bribing foreign officials for the purpose of obtaining favorable business contracts is a crime. This crime and the Foreign Corrupt Practices Act of 1977, which was passed to curb the practice of bribery by American businesspersons securing foreign contracts, are discussed in detail in Chapter 56 in the context of international law.

Money Laundering

The profits from illegal activities amount to billions of dollars a year, particularly the profits from illegal drug transactions and, to a lesser extent, from racketeering, prostitution, and gambling. Under federal law, banks, savings and loan associations, and other financial institutions are required to report currency transactions of over $10,000. Consequently, those who engage in illegal activities face difficulties in placing their cash profits from illegal transactions. Until 1977, Switzerland was a haven for such "flight money." In that year, however, a treaty gave the United States access to Swiss bank-deposit information relating to certain white-collar crimes. Pan-

ama City then became a leading haven for such money.

As an alternative to simply placing cash from illegal transactions in bank deposits, wrongdoers and racketeers have invented ways to launder "dirty" money to make it "clean." This **money laundering** is done through legitimate businesses. For example, a successful drug dealer might become partners with a restaurateur. Little by little, the restaurant shows an increasing profit. As a shareholder or partner in the restaurant, the wrongdoer is able to report the "profits" of the restaurant as legitimate income on which federal and state taxes are paid. The wrongdoer can then spend those monies without worrying about whether his or her lifestyle exceeds the level possible with his or her reported income. The Federal Bureau of Investigation estimates that organized crime alone has invested tens of billions of dollars in as many as a hundred thousand business establishments in the United States.

The most appropriate businesses for laundering dirty money are those that are capable of absorbing large volumes of cash income, which then can be commingled with legitimate income. That is why restaurants, bars, and massage parlors are key businesses—they take in large amounts of cash, as opposed to checks and credit-card charges. Another characteristic of a favorable "laundry" is a business in which fixed expenses do not vary with sales volume. An example of such a business is a pornographic film theatre. The rent, electricity, and wages remain virtually constant regardless of the number of clients. Law-enforcement officials examining a pornographic movie theatre's transactions would have a difficult time proving that the income reportedly generated by the theatre was more than what was really taken in.

Insider Trading and Other Financial Fraud

An individual who obtains "inside information" about the plans of large corporations can often make staggering profits by using such information to engage in "inside trading." An *insider* is an individual with material information about a publicly traded corporation that is not available to the public. **Insider trading**—that is, the buying or selling of corporate securities by a person in pos-

EMERGING TRENDS IN BUSINESS LAW   How to Imprison a Corporation

Individuals who commit crimes may be sent to prison. But, as everybody knows, corporations are a different matter. How can you imprison a corporation? Traditionally, judges have not even toyed with the idea, resorting instead to other types of criminal penalties—such as the imposition of fines. But at least one judge has concluded that it is possible to imprison a corporation. On August 30, 1988, in a case heard by the United States District Court for the Eastern District of Virginia, Judge Doumar sentenced a corporation to a three-year term of imprisonment and a $1 million fine.[a] The sentence was imposed on Allegheny Bottling Company (formerly Allegheny Pepsi-Cola Bottling Company) after that firm had been convicted of conspiring with a Coca-Cola distributor to fix prices in violation of the Sherman Antitrust Act of 1890.[b]

In his decision, Judge Doumar took issue with the common assumption that a corporation cannot be imprisoned. That assumption "was made by judges, and not by Congress" and "has lingered in the legal system unexamined and without support." The judge pointed out that Webster's dictionary defines *imprisonment* not in terms of stone walls and iron bars but as a "constraint of a person either by force or by such other coercion as restrains him within limits against his will." Judge Doumar also noted that cases involving false imprisonment entailed not confinement in a jail or prison but rather a forceful restraint of a person against that person's will. Therefore, concluded the judge, corporate imprisonment would require only that a court restrain or immobilize the corporation. Restraints (such as the seizure of corporate assets) are commonly placed on corporations in bankruptcy. Why not effectively "imprison" corporations that commit crimes by applying similar restraints?

After all, the judge reasoned, why should corporations escape imprisonment for criminal offenses when individuals cannot? In no case had any court cited an authority for the proposition that corporations cannot be imprisoned, and no court had ever—to the judge's knowledge—actually held that corporate imprisonment was illegal, unconstitutional, or impossible. The judge maintained that "considerable confusion" attends the concept of corporate imprisonment only because courts mistakenly think that imprisonment "necessarily involves incarceration in jail."

The judge fashioned his sentence so that, insofar as possible, the punishment would fit the crime. After the sentencing, the judge suspended all of the imprisonment and $50,000 of the fine and placed Allegheny on probation for three years. As a special

---

a. *United States v. Allegheny Bottling Co.*, 695 F.Supp. 856 (E.D.Va. 1988).

b. Price fixing and the Sherman Antitrust Act are discussed in Chapter 47.

condition of the probation, Allegheny would not be allowed to "dispose of any of its franchises, capital assets or plants or facilities in the Norfolk, Richmond or Baltimore areas, without specific permission of this Court through the probation officer." In addition, Allegheny was to provide four high-ranking officers or employees to perform community service for forty hours each week for one or two years without compensation. The service was to be performed in the Norfolk, Richmond, and Baltimore areas—the areas affected by the price-fixing agreement. The community service was also to be performed under the direction of the probation office and subject to the approval of the court. The judge emphasized that "[i]n no event is Allegheny Bottling Company to receive any form of compensation for the community service performed."

"Stone walls do not a prison make, nor iron bars a cage"— so said Richard Lovelace well over three hundred years ago. Obviously, Judge Doumar

agrees with Lovelace's sentiment—and, very possibly, so might Allegheny Bottling Company.

■ Implications for the Businessperson

The *Allegheny* case discussed here is illustrative—albeit in the extreme—of the general trend to hold corporations and their agents liable for corporate crimes. The implication for the businessperson is that today's corporate directors, officers, and managers can no longer assume that their actions will be sheltered by the corporate veil or that yesterday's standard of reasonable care and oversight will suffice. Today, key corporate personnel must exercise great care to ensure that corporate activities do not violate any law and to avoid the cost of criminal liability. The community service required by Judge Doumar was very costly for Allegheny Bottling Company. In addition, note that the judge did not specify that the "four top-ranking officers" had to be themselves guilty of participating in the crime. Even an *innocent* high-ranking officer

or director may have to pay the price of corporate crime.

■ For Critical Analysis

1. What is the logic behind the common assumption that a corporation cannot be imprisoned?

2. Why did the judge include in his order the condition that the guilty corporation could not dispose of any of its assets or franchises in the Norfolk, Richmond, and Baltimore areas?

3. One of the major appeals of the corporation as a form of business organization is the fact that the corporate veil shields the corporation's directors and officers from personal liability. To the extent that courts strip away this veil, the corporation becomes less attractive as a form of business organization. Discuss the tradeoff faced by business and society when corporate shareholders are held personally liable for criminal actions.

session of material nonpublic information—is covered under Sections 10(b) and 16(b) of the Securities Exchange Act of 1934 and Rule 10b-5 of the Securities and Exchange Commission and is considered more fully in Chapter 43. At this point, it may be said that one who possesses inside information has a duty not to disclose it to outsiders or to profit from the purchase or sale of securities based on that information until the information is available to the public.

One of the most famous instances of insider trading involved Ivan Boesky, Dennis Levine, and others in trades that made use of inside information concerning many of the largest corporate takeover attempts in the 1980s. Boesky was sentenced to three years in a federal prison, paid $100 million in penalties, and agreed to work with the government to apprehend other offenders.

The most recent area of white-collar crime has involved scandals in the savings and loan industry. Although actual fraud was not responsible for *all* of the monumental savings and loan failures in the United States, it was evident in many of these failures. A number of heads of failed savings and loan associations have been indicted and will face criminal proceedings. The chairman of the U.S. House Judiciary Subcommittee on Criminal Justice wrote that about "half of the recent bank failures and one-quarter of the thrift failures . . . involved criminal activity by insiders, few of whom, according to a congressional survey, were adequately punished." [5]

Corporate Crime

A corporation is a legal entity created under the laws of a state. It is not a living person and therefore must act through human beings. Hence, any crime committed in the corporate name must be committed by a person or persons in control of the corporation's affairs or in the employment of the corporation.

A criminal act requires intent. Therefore, common law thinking was that a corporation, because it had no mind of its own, could not be guilty of a crime. Corporate officers or employees could and can, however, be charged for committing criminal acts. Moreover, corporations have always been

civilly liable for the acts of their officers and employees.

Today, the common law view does not prevail. Corporations may be charged with many types of crimes. (They cannot be charged with all types of crimes—for example, a corporation cannot be charged with rape.) The Model Penal Code provides that a corporation may be convicted of a crime in the following situations:

1. The criminal act by the corporation's agent or employee is within the scope of his or her employment, and the purpose of the statute defining the act as a crime is to impose liability on corporations.
2. The crime consists of a failure to perform a specific affirmative duty imposed on corporations by law.
3. The crime was authorized, requested, commanded, committed, or recklessly tolerated by one of the corporation's high managerial agents.

When a law requires intent as an element of a crime, the agent's or employee's intent may be imputed to the corporation. An important factor is how high in the corporate hierarchy the individual stands. Is he or she high enough in the management structure that his or her conduct can be interpreted without proof of authorization as the corporation's acts? This test is known as the "high managerial agent" rule.

Crimes for which corporations have been indicted or convicted include manslaughter, homicide, arson, and grand theft.

LIABILITY OF OFFICERS AND DIRECTORS Although an officer of a corporation cannot be held personally liable for crimes of the corporation or of corporate employees simply because he or she is an officer, if that officer was in a position to prevent the crime, he or she may be held liable. Normally, the court must show that the crimes were committed at the officer's direction or with his or her permission.

This does not mean that it must be proved that the officer had criminal intent. In some instances, when employees under an officer's supervision commit crimes, criminal liability may be imposed on the officer for his or her negligent failure to supervise the employees. In one case, the chief executive officer of a national supermarket chain

5. John Conyers, Jr., "Don't Water Down the Anti-Fraud Law," *New York Times,* December 27, 1987.

was held personally liable for sanitation violations in corporate warehouses in which food was exposed to contamination by rodents. The officer admitted that as president he was responsible for the entire operation of the company, including providing sanitary conditions. He testified that he had no choice, however, but to delegate duties, including sanitation, to subordinates. He said that he had no reason to suspect that these subordinates were violating the law and that when violations came to light, acting through those subordinates, he did everything possible to correct them. Evidence of earlier violations at another warehouse was introduced, however, to show that he was on notice that he could not rely on these subordinates to prevent or correct unsanitary conditions. The court concluded that he was not justified in relying on the subordinates to handle sanitation matters. On appeal, the United States Supreme Court upheld the conviction.[6]

The protection of the safety of workers is another area of potential officer and director liability. The Occupational Safety and Health Act of 1970 established specific regulations concerning safety in the workplace. Criminal penalties for willful violations of the act are, however, limited. Until very recently, even blatant violations of federal workplace guidelines have not met with serious criminal penalties under the federal law. States, however, have successfully prosecuted individual officers for criminal violations of state-imposed worker safety standards.[7]

LIABILITY OF CORPORATIONS   Corporate criminal liability is vicarious. That is, one person is punished for the act or acts of another. Thus, the corporation that is found to be criminally responsible for an act committed by an employee can be fined for that offense. Through the fine, stockholders and other employees suffer because of the vicarious liability of the corporation. The justification for such criminal liability involves a showing that the corporation could have exercised control and precluded the act or that there was authorization, consent, or knowledge of the act by persons in supervisory positions within the corporation.[8]

■ RICO

In 1970 Congress passed the Organized Crime Control Act. It included the Racketeer Influenced and Corrupt Organizations Act, otherwise known as RICO.[9] The purpose of the act was to curb the apparently increasing entry of organized crime into the legitimate business world. Under RICO, it is a federal crime (1) to use income obtained from racketeering activity to purchase any interest in an enterprise, (2) to acquire or maintain an interest in an enterprise through racketeering activity, (3) to conduct or participate in the affairs of an enterprise through racketeering activity, or (4) to conspire to do any of the preceding.

Racketeering activity is not a new type of crime created by RICO; rather, RICO incorporates by reference twenty-six separate types of federal crimes and nine types of state felonies[10] and states that if a person commits two of these offenses, he or she is guilty of ''racketeering activity.'' Recently, the statute has been rigorously enforced, and the penalties for violations are harsh. The act provides for both civil liability and criminal liability.

Civil Liability

In the event of a violation, the RICO statute permits the government to seek civil penalties, including the divestiture (selling off) of a defendant's interest in a business or the dissolution of the business. Perhaps the most controversial section of RICO is Section 1964(c), under which, in some cases, private individuals are allowed to recover three times their actual loss (treble damages), plus attorneys' fees, for business injuries caused by a violation of the statute.

The broad language of RICO has allowed it to be applied in cases that have little or nothing to do with organized crime, and an aggressive prose-

---

6.   *United States v. Park,* 421 U.S. 658, 95 S.Ct. 1903, 44 L.Ed.2d 489 (1975).

7.   See *People v. Pymm,* 76 N.Y.2d 511, 563 N.E.2d 1, 561 N.Y.S. 687 (1990). See also *People v. Chicago Magnet Wire Corp.,* 126 Ill.2d 356, 534 N.E.2d 962, 128 Ill.Dec. 517 (1989), in which five executives were held criminally liable for allowing workers to become ill from exposure to hazardous chemicals. The issue of worker safety is discussed in more detail in Chapter 48 in the context of employment law.

---

8.   Section 2.07 of the Model Penal Code: ''Liability of corporations, unincorporated associations, and persons acting, or under a duty to act, in their behalf.''

9.   18 U.S.C. Sections 1961 *et seq.*

10.   See 18 U.S.C. Section 196(1)(A).

cuting attorney may attempt to show that any business fraud constitutes ''racketeering activity.'' Plaintiffs have used the RICO statute in numerous commercial fraud cases because of the inviting prospect of being awarded triple damages if they win. The most frequent targets of civil RICO lawsuits are insurance companies, employment agencies, commercial banks, and stock brokerage firms.

In the case presented below, a plaintiff brought suit against a business firm, claiming that the firm's fraudulent business activities violated RICO. By interpreting RICO provisions very broadly, the United States Supreme Court set a significant precedent for subsequent applications of RICO.

Case 7.6

SEDIMA, S.P.R.L. v. IMREX CO.

Supreme Court of the United States, 1985. 473 U.S. 479, 105 S.Ct. 3275, 87 L.Ed.2d 346.

BACKGROUND AND FACTS   Sedima, S.P.R.L., agreed to supply a Belgian firm with electronic components. Sedima formed a joint venture with Imrex Company to ship the components and share the proceeds. Imrex had shipped approximately $8 million in orders when Sedima concluded that Imrex was fraudulently claiming extra expenses and inflating its bills to get more than its fair portion of the proceeds. Sedima sued Imrex in a federal district court, alleging, in part, that Imrex had violated RICO. Sedima claimed an injury of at least $175,000 (the amount of alleged overbilling) and asked for treble damages. The trial court dismissed Sedima's RICO claims on the ground that Sedima failed to demonstrate it had suffered injury as a result of any pattern of racketeering activity. The appellate court affirmed, and Sedima appealed to the United States Supreme Court.

DECISION AND RATIONALE   The United States Supreme Court reversed the appellate court's decision. The Supreme Court held that a plaintiff does not have to establish that a defendant has been or could be criminally prosecuted under RICO and does not have to show a separate racketeering injury to recover treble damages. The Court noted that legitimate businesses "enjoy neither an inherent incapacity for criminal activity nor immunity from its consequences." The Court admitted that under RICO private civil actions "are being brought almost solely against such defendants, rather than against the archetypal, intimidating mobster. Yet this defect—if defect it is—is inherent in the statute as written, and its correction must lie with Congress." The Court recognized that "RICO is evolving into something quite different from the original conception of its enactors." Nevertheless, "the 'extraordinary' uses to which civil RICO has been put appear to be primarily the result of the breadth of the predicate offenses, in particular the inclusion of wire, mail, and securities fraud, and the failure of Congress and the courts to develop a meaningful concept of 'pattern' " of racketeering activity.

COMMENTS   This case illustrates some of the difficulties courts face in interpreting and applying RICO. Because of the statute's broad language, it has been applied in ways not anticipated by Congress and, as the Court indicated in the opinion above, is "evolving into something quite different from the original conception of its enactors." Congress is currently considering amendments to the statute that would restrict the application of RICO to criminal racketeering cases.

Criminal Liability

Most of the criminal offenses under RICO have little, if anything, to do with normal business ac-

tivities, for they involve gambling, arson, and extortion. But securities fraud (involving the sale of stocks and bonds) and mail fraud are also criminal violations of RICO, and RICO has become an effective tool in attacking these white-collar crimes in recent years. Under criminal provisions of RICO, any individual found guilty of a violation is subject to a fine of up to $25,000 per violation or imprisonment for up to twenty years—or both.

In the following case, the owner of a motel was charged with criminal violations of RICO because the person to whom he leased the motel operated it as a place of prostitution. The owner-defendant was considered by the court to be sufficiently involved in the illegal operation to warrant conviction under the criminal provisions of RICO.

Case 7.7

UNITED STATES v. TUNNELL

United States Court of Appeals, Fifth Circuit, 1982.
667 F.2d 1182.

BACKGROUND AND FACTS   For more than thirty years, the Pines Motel at Kilgore, Texas, was known as a place of prostitution. In 1967, Perry Tunnell bought the motel and in 1974 leased it to Odessa Mae French. Tunnell was indicted for a RICO offense (prostitution) and a RICO conspiracy offense, together with French and King Russell, a justice of the peace whom Tunnell and French were charged with bribing. The government maintained that they had also bribed Dwight Watson, a local constable. Russell testified that he had an arrangement with Tunnell by which Tunnell reimbursed the sums Russell paid the prostitutes at the motel. Tunnell acknowledged the long-standing reputation of the motel and admitted knowing Russell and Watson, but he denied knowledge of any bribes and of the reimbursement scheme. Before trial, in federal district court, Russell pleaded guilty to a lesser charge. The jury found Tunnell and French guilty on both counts. Tunnell appealed his conviction, claiming that there was no bribery or conspiracy.

DECISION AND RATIONALE   The United States Court of Appeals affirmed Tunnell's conviction. Tunnell contended that furnishing the services of a prostitute free of charge does not constitute bribery. Noting that the evidence established "the economic value of the services of a prostitute" and that "[t]hese services were provided at no cost," the court reasoned that this constituted "the bestowing of an economic gain, a benefit" on Russell. As for the conspiracy charges, the court referred to testimony that "Tunnell often ran the prostitution business, even though French had leased the motel. He personally passed approval on new prostitutes, bribed the local justice of the peace and constable, [and] told others about the operation." The court concluded that the evidence showed that "Tunnell possessed active knowledge of the racketeering operations conducted on the motel premises and involved himself in these activities."

■ Terms and Concepts

appropriation 134
bribery 137
business torts 130
disparagement of
   property 135

insider trading 137
money laundering 137
slander of quality 135

slander of title 136
trade libel 135
white-collar crime 130

■ For Review

1.   What elements are necessary to establish the existence of wrongful interference with a contractual relationship?

2.   Under what circumstance will a person who interferes with a business relationship of others not be considered liable for the tort of wrongful interference?

3.   Under the Model Penal Code, in what circumstances can a corporation be convicted of a crime?

4.   The Pezz Corp. hires Betal Engineering Co. to investigate deposits of ore on Pezz's property in Idaho. Betal

discovers a rich vein of copper. Mal, a Betal employee, learns of the discovery. Before the discovery is announced to the public, Mal buys Pezz stock, planning to sell the stock after the announcement and make a large profit. Mal carries out the plan, selling some of the stock to Clif and the rest to Elain, neither of whom knew anything about the copper discovery. What crime has Mal committed?

5.   Must Mal, in the previous problem, be convicted before Clif and Elain can recover damages from Mal under RICO?

■ Questions and Case Problems

7-1. Stevens owns a bakery. He has been trying to obtain a long-term contract with the owner of Martha's Tea Salons for some time. Stevens starts a local advertising campaign on radio and television and in the newspaper. This advertising campaign is so persuasive that Martha decides to break the contract she has had with Hank's Bakery so that she can patronize Stevens's bakery. Is Stevens liable to Hank's Bakery for the tort of wrongful interference with contractual relations? Is Martha liable for this tort? For anything?

7-2. Jenny was stranded in Alaska as the result of a union strike against the airline. She had purchased a round-trip ticket before leaving her home in Dallas. She was forced to return to Dallas on another airline and incurred additional expense for her return ticket. She sued the union for tortious interference with her contract with the airline and sought to recover the additional expense. Should the union be liable to Jenny for damages? Why or why not?

7-3. After a careful study and analysis, Green Top Airlines decides to expand its operations into Harbor City. Green Top acquires the necessary regulatory authorizations and licenses, negotiates a lease at the airport terminal, and makes substantial capital expenditures renovating airport gates. Immediately thereafter, Red Stripe Airlines, Green Top's major competitor, also undertakes operations in Harbor City even though (1) Harbor City is nowhere near any of Red Stripe's major existing routes, and (2) Red Stripe will lose money by servicing Harbor City. Green Top claims that Red Stripe's entry into Harbor City constitutes a tort. Discuss fully Green Top's claim.

7-4. Assume that Red Stripe Airlines (in Problem 7-3) negotiates a lease at the airport for gates on the same concourse as Green Top Airlines. In fact, for passengers to get to Green Top's gates, they must walk past Red Stripe's gates. Red Stripe puts up a large sign that states, "Passengers of other airlines—turn in your *tickets* or cancel your *reservations,* and we will give you 25 percent off the price of your trip if you fly on Red Stripe Airlines." In addition, Red Stripe's ticket agents solicit business from travelers on their way to Green Top gates. At this time, only Red Stripe and Green Top have operative gates on the concourse. Discuss fully any business tort theories under which Green Top can re-

cover against Red Stripe for the latter's actions. (Remember: A ticket is a contract.)

7-5. Luigi owns and operates a famous Italian restaurant in New York City. Luigi hires chef Toni to prepare the pasta and other dishes on his menu. Toni also contributes a column to *Gourmet Eating* magazine in which he discusses Italian food and restaurants in the area and rates all restaurants with stars. The ratings range from one star (the lowest rating) to five stars (the highest rating). Toni is prohibited from discussing or rating Luigi's restaurant in his column as long as he is employed by Luigi. One day, Luigi and Toni have a dispute over Toni's salary, and Toni, in front of a substantial number of regular customers who are well known in New York society, accuses Luigi of watering his house wine and of not making his own pasta. Luigi has on occasion purchased some pasta from a pasta shop in the neighborhood, but he has never watered his wine. Toni quits on the spot and later, in *Gourmet Eating,* rates Luigi's restaurant with only one star, adding a notation that Luigi's wine and pasta are inferior to the wine and pasta offered by other restaurants. Under what tort theories, if any, can Luigi file suit against Toni? Discuss fully.

7-6. Duggin entered into a contract to purchase certain land from Williams. The contract specified that if the property was not rezoned by June 15, 1981, either party could cancel. Duggin invested a great deal of time and money for engineering studies and surveys that increased the value of the property. Before the June 15 rezoning deadline, Duggin made an agreement to assign the contract to Centennial Development Corp. at a profit. The land was not rezoned as of June 15, but Centennial was prepared to purchase the land without the rezoning. Williams's attorney, Adams, learned of Duggin's deal and convinced Williams to cancel on July 30, 1981, in accordance with the provision in the agreement. Adams also convinced Williams to transfer the property to Adams, after which he sold the land to Centennial. Adams claimed that he was merely working on behalf of his client, Williams. Does Duggin have a claim against Adams for intentional interference with contract rights even though Williams had the right to terminate the contract at will? Explain your answer. [*Duggin v. Adams,* 234 Va. 221, 360 S.E.2d 832 (1987)]

7-7. Dierdorff was the president of Sun Savings and Loan Association. Sun Savings claimed that over a period of time Dierdorff had received kickbacks from several of Sun's larger loan customers. In relation to the fraudulent kickback scheme, Dierdorff had written letters to four entities—the Internal Revenue Service, the Federal Home Loan Bank Board, the California Savings and Loan commissioner, and the accounting firm of Arthur Young. Sun filed a civil suit alleging that Dierdorff had violated the federal Racketeering Influenced and Corrupt Organizations Act (RICO). The federal district court decided in favor of Dierdorff, holding that the plaintiff, Sun, had failed to allege a ''pattern of racketeering activity'' and that the acts had not been conducted by an ''enterprise.'' On appeal, how should the appellate court rule on the decision of the district court? Discuss. [*Sun Savings and Loan Association v. Dierdorff,* 825 F.2d 187 (9th Cir. 1987)]

7-8. DBI Services, Inc., provided oil-field trucking services, brine water, and drilling mud to oil producers in the Seminole area of Texas. From 1983 to 1986, the major oil producer in the area, Amerada Hess Corp. (AH), regularly contracted with DBI for its services. AH learned in a 1986 audit of its contractors that DBI had engaged in lavish entertainment of certain AH employees who were responsible for awarding job contracts. Disturbed by this discovery, AH thereafter refused to deal with DBI. AH also refused to accept contract bids from any firms that planned to subcontract work out to DBI, even if the firms had submitted the lowest bids for the contracts. DBI sued AH for tortious interference with its contractual relationships with these other firms. AH claimed that it was not obligated to accept the lowest bids for contracts and that it had a right to determine with whom it would do business. How will the court decide the issue? Discuss. [*DBI Services, Inc. v. Amerada Hess Corp.,* 907 F.2d 506 (5th Cir. 1990)]

7-9. In 1963, Pacific Gas and Electric Co. (PG&E) entered into a contract with the Placer County Water Agency (Agency) under which PG&E would purchase hydroelectric power from the Agency. The contract provided that the agreement would terminate in the year 2013 or at the end of the year in which the Agency completed the retirement of its project bonds, whichever occurred first. As energy prices rose, the Agency wished it could terminate the contract and sell its hydroelectric power in a more favorable market, but it felt it could not do so without breaching its contract with PG&E. Bear Stearns & Co., an investment brokerage firm, approached the Agency and spent several years overcoming the Agency's resistance to making any

effort to terminate the contract. Finally it succeeded, and in 1983 the Agency entered into an agreement with Bear Stearns in which Bear Stearns agreed to pay for legal, engineering, and marketing studies on the feasibility of terminating the power contract, in return for 15 percent of any resulting increase in the Agency's revenues above $2.5 million for twenty years. Bear Stearns retained legal counsel to draw up a plan by which the Agency could retire its project bonds and to litigate the question of whether the Agency could terminate the contract. PG&E sued Bear Stearns for tortious interference with PG&E's contract with the Agency. What will the court decide? Explain. [*Pacific Gas and Electric Co. v. Bear Stearns & Co. et al.,* 50 Cal.3d 1118, 270 Cal.Rptr. 1, 791 P.2d 587 (1990)]

7-10. Fortner LP Gas Co., a Kentucky corporation, was sued by the Commonwealth of Kentucky when a Fortner truck struck two schoolchildren, injuring one and killing the other. The children had just gotten off a school bus and were walking across the street when the truck, unable to stop because the brakes failed to work, hit them. Later inspection of the brakes revealed them to be defective. The Commonwealth of Kentucky prosecuted the corporation, and a grand jury indicted the corporation for manslaughter in the second degree, a felony punishable by a $20,000 fine. Fortner brought a motion for dismissal of the indictment on the ground that it was a corporation and, as such, could not commit manslaughter. Can a corporation commit manslaughter? Discuss. [*Commonwealth v. Fortner LP Gas Co.,* 610 S.W.2d 941 (Ky. 1980)]

7-11. Case Briefing Assignment

Examine Case A-4 [United States v. O'Connor, *910 F.2d 1466 (7th Cir. 1990)] in Appendix A. The case has been excerpted there in great detail. Review and then brief the case, making sure that you include answers to the following questions in your brief.*

1. O'Connor was charged with having committed two crimes. What were they?
2. What kind of services did O'Connor provide for ''Bill Burns'' and the other agents? What did O'Connor receive from the agents in return for these services?
3. What was O'Connor's defense against the RICO charge?
4. What did the court decide, and why?

Chapter 8

Intellectual Property and Computer Law

Most individuals think of wealth in terms of houses, land, cars, stocks, and bonds. But wealth also includes **intellectual property,** which consists of the products of individuals' minds—products that result from intellectual, creative processes. Although it is an abstract term for an abstract concept, intellectual property is nonetheless wholly familiar to virtually everyone. *Trademarks, service marks, copyrights,* and *patents* are all forms of intellectual property. The book you are reading is copyrighted. Undoubtedly, the personal computer you use at home is trademarked and patented. Some of the resident software within that computer might be copyrighted. You see advertisements for trademarked items every day—Xerox, IBM, and the like. The study of intellectual property law is important because intellectual property has taken on an increasing importance, not only within the United States but globally as well. Much of what is sold abroad—including popular American television series, computer programs, and blockbuster films—consists of intellectual property.

The need to protect creative works was voiced by the framers of the U.S. Constitution over two hundred years ago: Article I, Section 8, of the Constitution authorized Congress ''To promote the Progress of Science and useful Arts, by securing for limited Times to Authors and Inventors the exclusive Right to their respective Writings and Discoveries.'' Laws protecting patents, trademarks, and copyrights are explicitly designed to protect and reward inventive and artistic creativity. For example, trademark law provides incentives to companies to invest in the development of goodwill by ensuring that others will not steal and profit from their trade symbols. Although intellectual property law limits the economic freedom of some individuals, it does so to protect the freedom of others to enjoy the fruits of their labors—in the form of profits.

In the last decade, computers have become dominant in the business world, and they are becoming increasingly familiar in every household in America, as well as in the rest of the economically developed world. But the many and diverse advantages brought about by the computer revolution have not been risk free. Not surprisingly, unfair trade practice issues arise constantly in this growth industry. The protection of intellectual property relating to computers—such as computer software—has posed difficulties for legislatures and the courts because computers were not envisioned by the legislators who drafted the previous patent, trademark, and copyright laws. Therefore, previous laws have had to be amended, or new laws created, to serve the needs of a computer generation. In the sections below on patent, copyright, and trademark laws, we discuss how these laws have been applied to computer software. In the final section in this chapter, we address another legal challenge presented by computers—the problem of computer crime.

■ Patents

A **patent** is a grant from the federal government that conveys and secures to an inventor the exclusive right to make, use, and sell an invention for a period of seventeen years. Patents for a lesser period are given for designs, as opposed to inventions. For either a regular patent or a design patent, the applicant must demonstrate to the satisfaction of the patent office that the invention, discovery, or design is genuine, novel, useful, and not obvious in the light of the technology of the time. A patent holder gives notice to all that an article or design is patented by placing on it the word "Patent" or "Pat.," plus the patent number.

Patent Infringement

If a firm makes, uses, or sells another's patented design, product, or process without the patent owner's permission, the tort of patent infringement exists. Patent infringement may exist even though not all features or parts of an invention are copied. (With respect to a patented process, however, all steps or their equivalent must be copied in order for infringement to exist.) Often, litigation for patent infringement is so costly that the patent holder will instead offer to sell to the infringer a license to use the patented design, product, or process. Indeed, in many cases the costs of detection, prosecution, and monitoring are so high that patents are valueless to their owners, because they cannot afford to protect them.

Patents for Computer Software

It is difficult for developers and manufacturers of software to obtain patent protection because many software products simply automate procedures that can be performed manually. In other words, the

computer programs do not meet the "novel" and "not obvious" requirements mentioned above. Also, the basis for software is often a mathematical equation or formula, which is not patentable. It is possible, however, to obtain a patent for a *process* that incorporates a computer program, providing, of course, that the process itself is patentable.[1]

Another obstacle to obtaining patent protection for software is the procedure of obtaining patents. The process can be expensive and slow. The time element is a particularly important consideration for someone wishing to obtain a patent on software: in light of the rapid changes and improvements in computer technology, the delay could undercut the product's success in the marketplace.

International Patent Issues

The scope of manufacturing and distribution is now very much international. Consequently, inventors often file for patent protection in many countries simultaneously. The international patent protection afforded a U.S. national is normally governed by the patent laws in each country in which the American inventor seeks protection. Additionally, the United States may have a treaty with another country, which may govern patents.

Patent practices in other countries normally differ substantially from those in the United States. For example, it took Texas Instruments thirty years to obtain a patent in Japan. Political and economic issues obviously were at play here, for the delay allowed the Japanese computer chip industry to flourish. In the United States, Texas Instruments was granted patent protection for the same invention within four years of the patent application.

The nature of the product for which a patent will be granted differs dramatically from country to country. A number of countries, for example, do not permit invention patents for pharmaceuticals (although some protection may be obtained by a process patent).

■ Copyrights

A **copyright** is an intangible right granted by statute to the author or originator of certain literary or artistic productions. Works created after January 1,

---

1. See *Diamond v. Diehr*, 450 U.S. 175, 101 S.Ct. 1048, 67 L.Ed.2d 155 (1981).

1978, are automatically given statutory copyright protection for the life of the author plus fifty years. Copyrights owned by publishing houses expire seventy-five years from the date of publication or a hundred years from the date of creation, whichever is first. For works by one or more authors, the copyright expires fifty years after the death of the last surviving author.

The Copyright Act provides that a copyright owner no longer needs to place a © or ℗ on the work to have the work protected against infringement. Chances are, if somebody created it, somebody owns it.

Under the "fair use" doctrine, the reproduction of copyrighted material is permitted without the payment of royalties under certain circumstances. Section 107 of the Copyright Act provides as follows:

[T]he fair use of a copyrighted work, including such use by reproduction in copies or phonorecords or by any other means specified by [Section 106 of the Copyright Act], for purposes such as criticism, comment, news reporting, teaching (including multiple copies for classroom use), scholarship, or research, is not an infringement of copyright. In determining whether the use made of a work in any particular case is a fair use the factors to be considered shall include—

(1) the purpose and character of the use, including whether such use is of a commercial nature or is for nonprofit educational purposes;

(2) the nature of the copyrighted work;

(3) the amount and substantiality of the portion used in relation to the copyrighted work as a whole; and

(4) the effect of the use upon the potential market for or value of the copyrighted work.

Because these guidelines as to what constitutes fair use are very broad, the courts determine whether a particular use is fair on a case-by-case basis. Thus, any reproduction can still make its producer subject to a violation.

Copyright Infringement

Whenever the form or expression of an idea is copied, an infringement of copyright has occurred. The reproduction does not have to be exactly the same as the original; nor does it have to reproduce the original in its entirety. If a substantial part of the original is reproduced, a copyright infringement exists. Penalties or remedies can be imposed on those who infringe copyrights. These range from actual damages plus the infringer's profits or statutory damages not exceeding $100,000 imposed at the discretion of the court, to criminal proceedings for willful violations, which may result in fines, imprisonment, or both.

The following case discusses whether recording television broadcasts on home videotape recorders constitutes a copyright infringement.

Case 8.1

SONY CORP. v. UNIVERSAL CITY STUDIOS

Supreme Court of the United States, 1984. 467 U.S. 417, 104 S.Ct. 774, 78 L.Ed.2d 574.

BACKGROUND AND FACTS   Universal City Studios, Inc., owns copyrights on some television programs, which were broadcast on public airwaves. Sony Corporation manufactures and sells Betamax videotape recorders (VTRs, or VCRs). Alleging that the public used Sony VTRs to record some of Universal's copyrighted works, Universal sued Sony for copyright infringement in federal district court. Universal maintained that Sony was liable for the infringement because Sony marketed the VTRs. The trial court denied relief, but the court of appeals held Sony liable for contributory infringement. Sony appealed to the United States Supreme Court.

DECISION AND RATIONALE   The United States Supreme Court held that Sony was not liable for contributory infringement. The Supreme Court explained that the sale of "copying equipment" is not contributory infringement "if the product is widely used for legitimate, unobjectionable purposes. Indeed, it need merely be capable of substantial noninfringing uses." Citing the fair use doctrine, the Court stated that challenging a noncommercial use of a copyrighted work requires proof that the use is harmful "or that if it should become widespread, it would adversely affect the potential market for the copyrighted work." The Court concluded that (1) a substantial number of copyright holders would not object to having their television broadcasts recorded, and (2) Universal had failed to prove that the recordings would cause more than minimal harm to the market for, or value of, its works. Thus, Sony's Betamax VTR was capable of noninfringing uses, and Sony was not liable for contributory infringement.

What Is Protected Expression?

Section 102 of the Copyright Act specifically excludes copyright protection for any "idea, procedure, process, system, method of operation, concept, principle or discovery, regardless of the form in which it is described, explained, illustrated, or embodied." Note that it is not possible to copyright an *idea*. The underlying ideas embodied in a work may be freely used by others. What is copyrightable is the particular way in which an idea is *expressed*. Whenever an idea and an expression are inseparable, the expression cannot be copyrighted.

Consider an example: A video game manufacturer develops a Thai kick-boxing game. The developer cannot prevent a competitor from producing another kick-boxing game that is based on the standard moves and rules of Thai kick-boxing. The idea for the game is not copyrightable. The developer can, however, prevent competitors from copying original graphics whenever they can be separated from the standard treatment of Thai kick-boxing.

Generally, anything that is not an original expression will not qualify for copyright protection. Facts widely known to the public are not copyrightable. Page numbers are not copyrightable because they follow a sequence known to everyone. Mathematical calculations are not copyrightable. *Compilations* of facts, however, are copyrightable. Section 103 of the Copyright Act defines a compilation as "a work formed by the collection and assembling of preexisting materials of data that are selected, coordinated, or arranged in such a way that the resulting work as a whole constitutes an original work of authorship."

Does the compilation of "facts" (names, addresses, and telephone numbers) listed in the white pages of a telephone directory qualify for copyright protection? This issue arose in the following case.

BACKGROUND AND FACTS The Rural Telephone Service Company provides telephone service to several communities in Kansas. For those communities, Rural publishes a telephone directory, for which it obtains data from subscribers, who must provide their names and addresses to obtain telephone service. Feist Publications, Inc., specializes in area-wide telephone directories covering a much larger geographic area than directories such as Rural's. To obtain listings for its directory covering northwest Kansas, Feist offered to pay each of the eleven telephone companies operating in that area for the right to use their listings. Only Rural refused. When Feist used the listings it needed from Rural's directory without Rural's consent, Rural sued Feist in federal district court for copyright infringement. The trial court granted summary judgment to Rural, holding that telephone directories are copyrightable, and the appellate court affirmed the decision. The United States Supreme Court granted *certiorari*.

DECISION AND RATIONALE The United States Supreme Court reversed the appellate court's decision, holding that Feist's use of the listings did not constitute copyright infringement. The Supreme Court acknowledged that Feist took a substantial amount of information from Rural's directory. The Court pointed out, however, that not all copying is infringement—the work that is copied must be original. The Court reasoned that names, towns, and telephone numbers are uncopyrightable facts; "they existed

Case 8.2

FEIST PUBLICATIONS, INC. v. RURAL TELEPHONE SERVICE CO.

Supreme Court of the United States, 1991.
____ U.S. ____,
111 S.Ct. 1282,
113 L.Ed.2d 358.

before Rural reported them and would have continued to exist if Rural had never published a telephone directory." The question was whether Rural "selected, coordinated, or arranged these uncopyrightable facts in an original way." The Court concluded that Rural did not. Its selection of listings "could not be more obvious"—the name, town, and telephone number of each person who applied to it for service. Observing that the directory listed the subscribers in alphabetical order, the Court said, "[T]here is nothing even remotely creative about arranging names alphabetically in a [telephone] directory."

ETHICAL CONSIDERATIONS   This case raises an obvious ethical question: Is it fair that Feist should be able to reap the fruits of Rural's labors without any penalty? In addressing this question, the Court at one point in its opinion pointed out that the "primary objective of copyright is not to reward the labor of authors, but '[t]o promote the Progress of Science and useful Arts.' To this end, copyright assures authors the right to their original expression, but encourages others to build freely upon the ideas and information conveyed by a work. This principle, known as the idea/expression or fact/expression dichotomy, applies to all works of authorship. As applied to a factual compilation, assuming the absence of original written expression, only the compiler's selection and arrangement may be protected; the raw facts may be copied at will. This result is neither unfair nor unfortunate. It is the means by which copyright advances the progress of science and art."

Copyright Protection for Computer Software

The Computer Software Copyright Act of 1980 amended the 1976 Copyright Reform Act to include computer programs in the list of creative works protected by federal copyright law. The 1980 statute defines a computer program as a "set of statements or instructions to be used directly or indirectly in a computer in order to bring about a certain result." Because of the unique nature of computer programs, the courts have had many problems in applying and interpreting the 1980 act. One of the basic problems concerns computer language.

THE LANGUAGE PROBLEM   Traditionally, copyright protection was extended only to literary works that were perceptible to humans—that is, to things written or printed in intelligible notation. But computer programs, which are classified as "literary works" under the 1980 act, are expressed in a language "readable" by machines. Should copyright protection be limited to those parts of a computer program that can be read by humans, such as the "high-level" language of a source code? Or should it also extend to the binary-

language object code of a computer program, which is readable only by the computer?

In an important 1983 decision, *Apple Computer, Inc. v. Franklin Computer Corp.,* copyright protection was extended to include both the binary object code and the source code of a computer program. In this decision, the Court of Appeals for the Third Circuit held that "a computer program, whether in object code or source code . . . is protected from unauthorized copying whether from its object or source code version."[2]

PROGRAM STRUCTURE PROTECTION   By 1983 it was fairly well established—particularly by the *Apple Computer* decision just mentioned—that a program's computer codes were copyrightable. The next issue that arose in the evolution of computer copyright law was whether copyright protection should cover other elements of computer software, such as the overall structure, sequence, and organization of a program. In a 1986 case, *Whelan Associates v. Jaslow Dental Laboratory,* the Third Circuit Court of Appeals noted that copyrights of other literary works can be infringed upon

---

2.   714 F.2d 1240 (3d Cir. 1983).

even when there is no substantial similarity between the works' *literal* elements. The copyright of a play or a book, for example, can be infringed upon if its plot or plot devices are copied. The court applied the same principle to computer programs and held that the structure, sequence, and organization of computer programs were copyrightable.[3]

PROGRAM "LOOK AND FEEL" PROTECTION
An issue addressed in *Whelan* has evolved into what is now generally called program "look and feel" protection. Should the "look and feel"—the general appearance, command structure, video images, menus, windows, and other screen displays—of computer programs also be protected by copyright? This is a significant question because the software industry is so highly competitive. If the look and feel of a program makes it easy to learn and use, the manufacturer of that program will have a competitive edge in the marketplace—an edge that will be quickly lost to competitors if such program features cannot be copyrighted. On the other hand, some argue that allowing such features as menus or other command structures or visual displays to be copyrighted would be like copyrighting the alphabet.

Program "look and feel" was at issue in a case filed in 1988 by Apple Computer, Inc., against Microsoft Corporation and Hewlett-Packard Company. Apple contended that Microsoft's Windows 2.03 program and Hewlett-Packard's New Wave program infringed Apple's copyright because the programs copied the "look and feel" of the popular Macintosh computer displays. Although the outcome of this lawsuit is not yet known, a federal district court in Boston recently addressed a very similar issue in a case brought by Lotus Development Corporation against Paperback Software International. Lotus claimed that Paperback Software had infringed its copyright in its Lotus 1-2-3 spreadsheet format design and the keystroke sequences used in manipulating information. In what many regard as a significant decision for software manufacturers, the court held that Lotus's menu command structure—including the choice of command terms, the structure and order of those terms, their presentation on the screen, and the long prompts—was copyrightable and that Paperback

Software International had infringed Lotus's copyright.[4]

PROTECTION FOR MASK WORKS The Semiconductor Chip Protection Act of 1984 provides protection for the **mask work,** which is defined as a series of images related to the pattern formed by the many layers of a semiconductor-chip product. A mask work must be fixed in the product to qualify for the protection, and within two years of initially taking commercial advantage of the mask work, the owner must register it with the U.S. Copyright Office. On registration, the owner of the protected mask work obtains the exclusive right, for ten years, to reproduce, import, or distribute the work or a semiconductor-chip product that contains it.

International Copyright Issues

To some extent, international copyright issues have become less of a problem for American copyright owners. The United States is now a party to a number of international copyright treaties, including the Berne Convention and the Universal Copyright Convention. Under the Berne Convention, if an American writes a book, his or her copyright in the book must be recognized by every country that has signed the convention. Also, if a citizen of a country that has not signed the convention first publishes a book in a country that has, all other countries that have signed the convention must recognize that author's copyright. Copyright notice is not needed to gain protection under the Berne Convention for works published after March 1, 1989.

■ Trademarks and Related Property

A **trademark** is a distinctive mark, motto, device, or emblem that a manufacturer stamps, prints, or otherwise affixes to the goods it produces, so that they can be distinguished from the goods of other manufacturers and merchants. Bestowing an exclusive trademark right on the originator of a mark yields several benefits, some of which were mentioned at the beginning of this chapter. First, exclusive trademark protection creates incentives for merchants to invest in product development and

---

3. 797 F.2d 1222 (3d Cir. 1986).

4. *Lotus Development Corp. v. Paperback Software International,* 740 F.Supp. 37 (D.Mass. 1990).

improvement. Second, trademark law permits consumers to be certain that they are obtaining the same product from the same manufacturer every time that they return to the marketplace. Trademark law therefore reduces ''search costs'' for consumers and prevents the confusion that would result in the marketplace if trademarks were not protected. Finally, trademark law prevents unjust enrichment by prohibiting unscrupulous merchants from selling inferior imitations under the same trademark as the original.

Normally, personal names, words, or places that describe an article or its use cannot be trademarked; they are available to anyone. Words that are used as part of a design or device, however, or words that are used in an uncommon or fanciful way may be trademarked. Consider an example. *English Leather* may not be trademarked to describe leather processed in England. In contrast, *English Leather* may be, and is, trademarked as a name for after-shave lotion, because this constitutes a *fanciful* use of the words. Consider also that under some circumstances, even the common name of an individual may be trademarked if purchasers associate the name with the product and not primarily with its status as a name—for example, Campbell Soups.

Trademark Infringement

Once a trademark has been registered, a firm is entitled to its exclusive use for marketing purposes. Whenever that trademark is copied to a substantial degree or used in its entirety by another, intentionally or unintentionally, the trademark has been infringed. The owner of the trademark need not register it with the state or with the federal government to obtain protection from the tort of trademark infringement, but registration does furnish proof of the date of inception of its use. Moreover, registration may prolong the life of the trademark. Registration is renewable between the fifth and sixth years after the initial registration and every twenty years thereafter, as long as the mark remains distinctive and is used.

The defendant firm in the following case was liable for trademark infringement even though it did not manufacture the article.

Case 8.3

VUITTON ET FILS, S.A. v. CROWN HANDBAGS

United States District Court, Southern District of New York, 1979.
492 F.Supp. 1071.

BACKGROUND AND FACTS Vuitton et Fils, S.A., manufactures expensive handbags and distributes them through an exclusive retail network. The handbags are of high quality and bear a registered trademark: the firm's initials and a *fleur de lis*. Crown Handbags was not a retail outlet for Vuitton handbags. Nevertheless, a Vuitton private investigator discovered Crown selling handbags bearing the Vuitton trademark. The handbags were cheap imitations of Vuitton's product. Vuitton sued Crown in federal district court for trademark infringement.

DECISION AND RATIONALE The United States District Court granted Vuitton permanent injunctive relief against Crown's violation of Vuitton's trademark, damages totaling the price of handbags offered for sale to Vuitton's investigator, and attorneys' fees. The court pointed out that to avoid infringement, a merchant "has a duty to so name and dress his product as to avoid all likelihood of consumers confusing it with [another's] product." The court found that the Vuitton trademark was a strong mark, representing a "product of perceived quality and prestige." If infringement were permitted, inferior products would undercut Vuitton's reputation and deceive consumers into believing they were getting something they were not. The court noted that although Crown did not manufacture the inferior bags, "it took an active part in their distribution and sale, making use of plaintiff's trademark in the process."

The Trademark Revision Act

In 1988, the Trademark Revision Act was passed by Congress. This act, which took effect on November 16, 1989, significantly altered the prior registration scheme. That scheme required that the mark be used before an application could be filed. The 1988 act, in contrast, allows an applicant to file on the basis either of use or of the bona fide intention to use the mark in commerce. This is the so-called "intent to use" provision, which requires that the mark be put into commerce within six months after filing with the U.S. Patent and Trademark Office. At the end of the six months, the applicant must provide proof that the mark was put into commerce and that the application was not opposed. Under extenuating circumstances, the six-month period can be extended by thirty months, giving the applicant a total of three years from the date of notice of trademark approval to make use of the mark and file the required use statement. Registration under the 1988 act is postponed until actual use of the mark. Nonetheless, during this waiting period, any applicant can legally protect his or her trademark against a third party who previously has neither used the mark nor filed an application for it. The 1988 act's new provision has considerably cut the costs in developing and marketing a new product. It has particularly benefitted small companies.

Trademarks for Computer Hardware and Software

Trademarks for computer hardware and software are protected under federal trademark law, just as trademarks for other products are. Trademark registration provides protection for twenty years and is renewable. Once a trademark has been registered with the U.S. Patent and Trademark Office, its owner has the right to its exclusive and continued use, providing the mark does not become generic (as described below). Trademark infringement occurs when an unauthorized party copies the trademark to a substantial degree or uses it in its entirety, intentionally or unintentionally.

Service, Certification, and Collective Marks

A **service mark** is similar to a trademark but is used to distinguish among services rather than goods. For example, each airline has a particular mark or symbol associated with its name. Titles and character names used in radio and television are frequently registered as service marks. Service marks are registered in the same manner as trademarks.

A **certification mark** is used by one or more persons, other than the owner, to certify the region, materials, mode of manufacture, quality, or accuracy of the owner's goods or services. When used by members of a cooperative, association, or other organization, such a mark is referred to as a **collective mark.** Examples of certification marks are the "Good Housekeeping Seal of Approval" and "UL Tested." Collective marks appear at the ends of the credits of movies to indicate the various associations and organizations that participated in the making of the movies. The union marks found on the tags of certain products are also collective marks. The same policies and restrictions that apply to trademarks and service marks normally apply to certification and collective marks.

■ Trade Names

The term **trade name** is used to indicate part or all of a business's name, whether that business be a sole proprietorship, a partnership, or a corporation. Generally, a trade name is directly related to a business and to its goodwill. As with trademarks, words must be unusual or fancifully used to be protected as trade names. The word *Safeway* was held by the courts to be sufficiently fanciful to obtain protection as a trade name.[5] The decisions of the courts do not give entirely clear guidelines as to when the name of a corporation can be regarded as a trade name. A particularly thorny problem arises when a trade name acquires generic use. For example, *aspirin, thermos, escalator, trampoline, raisin bran, dry ice, cube steak, linoleum, nylon, kerosene,* and *cornflakes* originally were used only as trade names, but they are now used to refer to those products generally. Similarly, other trade names—such as Frigidaire, Scotch Tape, Xerox, and Kleenex—have acquired secondary mean-

---

5. *Safeway Stores v. Suburban Foods,* 130 F.Supp. 249 (E.D.Va. 1955).

ings and are close to becoming generic terms. Even so, the courts will not allow other firms to use those names in such a way as to deceive a potential consumer. Consider, for example, the following case concerning Coca-Cola, decided by the United States Supreme Court.

Case 8.4

COCA-COLA CO. v. KOKE CO. OF AMERICA

Supreme Court of the United States, 1920. 254 U.S. 143, 41 S.Ct. 113, 65 L.Ed. 189.

BACKGROUND AND FACTS The Coca-Cola Company asked a federal district court to enjoin the Koke Company of America and other beverage companies from, among other things, using the word Koke for their products. Koke contended that the Coca-Cola trademark was a fraudulent representation and that Coca-Cola was thus not entitled to an injunction. Koke alleged that Coca-Cola, by its use of the Coca-Cola name, represented that the beverage contained cocaine (from coca leaves). The trial court granted the injunction against Koke, but the appellate court reversed the lower court's ruling. Coca-Cola appealed to the United States Supreme Court.

DECISION AND RATIONALE The United States Supreme Court upheld the district court's decision. The Supreme Court acknowledged that before 1900 Coca-Cola's goodwill was enhanced by the presence of a small amount of cocaine, but that the cocaine had long been eliminated from the drink. The Court emphasized that Coca-Cola was not "a medicine" and that its attraction did not lie in producing "a toxic effect." Since 1900, sales had increased. The name had come to characterize a well-known beverage to be had almost anywhere "rather than a compound of particular substances." Noting that before this suit was brought Coca-Cola had advertised that the public would not find cocaine in Coca-Cola, the Court said that "it would be going too far to deny the plaintiff relief against a palpable fraud because possibly here and there an ignorant person might call for the drink with the hope for incipient cocaine intoxication." Thus, the use of a similar-sounding name was disallowed.

■ Trade Secrets

Some business processes and information that are not, or cannot be, patented, copyrighted, or trademarked are nevertheless protected against appropriation by a competitor as **trade secrets.** Customer lists, plans, research and development, pricing information, marketing techniques, production techniques, and generally anything that makes an individual company unique and that would have value to a competitor constitute trade secrets. The most widely used definition of a trade secret is found in the Restatement of Torts, Section 757(b):

A trade secret may consist of any formula, pattern, device, or compilation of information which is used in one's business, and which gives him an opportunity to obtain an advantage over competitors who do not know or use it. It may be a formula for a

chemical compound, a process of manufacturing, treating or preserving materials, . . . or a list of customers.

Virtually all law with respect to trade secrets is common law. Identical types of information reviewed by different courts in similar factual settings have been classified differently. In an effort to reduce the unpredictability of common law with respect to trade secrets, a model act, the Uniform Trade Secrets Act, was presented to the states in 1979 for adoption. Parts of it have been adopted in over twenty states. Typically, a state that has adopted parts of the act has only adopted those parts that encompass its own existing common law.

Unlike copyright and trademark protection, protection of trade secrets extends both to ideas and to their expression. (For this reason, and because a trade secret involves no registration or filing requirements, trade secret protection may be well suited for software.) Of course, the secret formula, method, or other information must be disclosed to some persons, particularly to key employees. Businesses generally attempt to protect their trade secrets by having all employees who use the process or information agree in their contracts never to divulge it. Thus, if a salesperson tries to solicit the company's customers for noncompany business, or if an employee copies the employer's unique method of manufacture, he or she has appropriated a trade secret and has also broken a contract—two separate wrongs. Theft of confidential business data by industrial espionage, as when a business taps into a competitor's computer, is a theft of trade secrets without any contractual violation and is actionable in itself.

Under Section 757 of the Restatement of Torts, "One who discloses or uses another's trade secret, without a privilege to do so, is liable to the other if (a) he discovered the secret by improper means, or (b) his disclosure or use constitutes a breach of confidence reposed in him by the other in disclosing the secret to him." In the following case, the court had to decide whether aerial photography was an "improper means" of discovering another's trade secret.

BACKGROUND AND FACTS Rolfe and Gary Christopher, at the request of a third party, took aerial photographs of a new plant being constructed by E. I. duPont de Nemours & Company in Beaumont, Texas. Because construction was not complete, a process for making methanol, which DuPont was trying to keep secret, was visible from the air. DuPont learned that photographs had been taken. When the Christophers refused to reveal the name of the party who requested the photographs, DuPont sued in federal district court, alleging that the Christophers had wrongfully obtained photographs revealing DuPont's trade secrets. The Christophers argued that they had committed no "actionable wrong" because "they conducted all of their activities in public airspace, violated no government aviation standards, did not breach any confidential relation, and did not engage in any fraudulent or illegal conduct." The trial court held that DuPont's claim was actionable, and the Christophers appealed.

Case 8.5

E. I. duPONT de NEMOURS & CO. v. CHRISTOPHER

United States Court of Appeals, Fifth Circuit, 1970.
431 F.2d 1012.

DECISION AND RATIONALE The United States Court of Appeals affirmed the trial court's holding and remanded the case. The appellate court noted that Texas recognizes a cause of action for the discovery of a trade secret by any "improper" means. In Texas, proper means include reverse engineering applied to a finished product and independent research; proper means do not include taking a competitor's secret process without permission when the competitor is taking reasonable precautions to maintain its secrecy. The court pointed out that during DuPont's construction, its trade secret was exposed to view from the air. "To require DuPont to put a roof over the unfinished plant to guard its secret would impose an enormous expense," representing "unreasonable precautions to prevent another from doing that which he ought not do in the first place."

■ Computer Crime

The American Bar Association defines **computer crime** as any act that is directed against computers and computer parts, that uses computers as instruments of crime, or that involves computers and constitutes abuse. Generally, computer crimes are classified as white-collar crimes, since ordinarily they do not involve physical violence. Recall from the discussion earlier in this chapter the difficulties faced by the courts in applying conventional copyright law to computer software. Similar difficulties exist in attempting to apply traditional criminal law to computer crimes. In some cases, existing laws have been extended—either by amendment or through judicial interpretation—to include computer crimes. In other cases, new legislation has been enacted to specifically address crimes unique to the computer age.

Detecting and Prosecuting Computer Crime

Computer crime is often difficult to detect; and if the crime is cleverly executed, it may go undetected for some time. In some cases, victimized companies, and even the government, have discovered multimillion-dollar thefts only after a considerable lapse of time. Even when it is apparent that a computer crime has occurred, tracing the crime to the individual who committed it can be very difficult, because the individual's identity is "hidden," as it were, by the anonymous nature of the computer system. It is also frequently true that, in the case of an employee, no one with enough expertise to discover a crime is overseeing the perpetrator's activities.

Even when computer crimes are detected and reported, the complexities of the computer systems involved have often frustrated the attempts of attorneys, police officers, jurors, and others to comprehend the offenses and prosecute the offenders successfully. Computer crimes may also be difficult to prosecute because a particular form of computer-assisted abuse falls outside the traditional definition of a crime. For example, the commonly used definition of larceny (theft) does not encompass intangible property such as the data stored in a computer.

Under existing federal statutes, successful prosecutions include convictions under laws concerning theft and property offenses, transportation of stolen property, wire fraud, and mail fraud. The following case is representative of the types of problems encountered by courts in trying to apply traditional laws to situations involving computers. In this case, the court had to decide whether alterations of accounts payable documents that resulted in the issuance of checks by the computer to an improper payee constituted forgery.

Case 8.6

UNITED STATES v. JONES

United States Court of Appeals, Fourth Circuit, 1977. 553 F.2d 351.

BACKGROUND AND FACTS   Criminal indictments were returned against Amy Everston Jones, charging her with transporting in interstate and foreign commerce certain checks that she knew had been "stolen, converted or taken by fraud" in violation of federal law. The purported crime was against Inglis, Ltd., a subsidiary of Whirlpool Corporation. Michael Everston, an alleged accomplice, was the supervisor of Inglis's accounting department. Everston had an accounting clerk set up an account payable to A. L. E. Jones and, by changing computerized data, converted documents payable to Whirlpool into the Jones account. The computer ultimately issued checks to Jones, which she deposited in her account. Jones admitted that the checks were forgeries, but because forgeries are excluded as violations under the federal statutes, she moved to dismiss the indictments. The federal district court agreed. The United States appealed.

DECISION AND RATIONALE   The United States Court of Appeals reversed the decision of the district court, concluding that there was fraud (an offense covered under the federal statutes) but not forgery (an excluded offense). The appellate court agreed with the district court that the term forgery should be viewed in light of its common law meaning, noting that the United States Supreme Court has held that "[a]n essential element of the crime of forgery is making the false writing." The appellate court concluded that Everston had not made a false writing, but had created a genuine writing that contained false statements of fact. False statements in otherwise valid instruments are not forgeries within the common law meaning. The court pointed out that the checks were made payable "to the order of A. L. E. Jones," which implied the existence of an obligation running from Inglis to Jones. In fact, there was no such obligation. Everston defrauded Inglis's accounting department into believing that there was and, thus, into issuing a genuine instrument containing a false statement of fact. Jones's petition to the United States Supreme Court for a writ of *certiorari* was denied.

COMMENTS The common law definition of forgery requires that a writing falsely purport to be the writing of one other than the actual maker. In other words, the crime requires a lie about the genuineness of a document. Thus, the employee who pads a timecard does not commit forgery, because the lie does not relate to the timecard's genuineness but to the truth of the information on it. Similarly, in this case, the court reasoned that because the company actually issued the checks, the checks were genuine; it was the statements on them that were false.

Types of Computer Crime

Crimes committed with or against computers generally fall into five broad categories: financial crimes, theft of computer equipment, theft or unauthorized use of data or services, software piracy (the unauthorized copying of another's computer program), and vandalism and destructive programming.

FINANCIAL CRIMES   In addition to using computers for information storage and retrieval, businesses increasingly use computers to conduct financial transactions. This is equally true of the government, which handles many of its transactions by computer. These circumstances provide opportunities for employees and others to commit crimes that can involve serious economic losses. For example, employees of accounting and computer departments can, with little effort and without the risk involved in transactions evidenced by paperwork, transfer monies among accounts. The potential for crime in the area of financial transactions is great, and it is in this category of computer crime that most monetary losses are suffered.

With the right computer equipment—desktop-publishing or drawing programs, scanners, laser printers, and so on—checks, stock certificates, gift certificates, identification cards, college transcripts, and even currency can be (and have been) forged. To date, this "desktop forgery" has not resulted in significant financial losses—relative to losses incurred by other types of counterfeiting—but its potential is worrisome for many.

THEFT OF COMPUTER EQUIPMENT   The theft of computer equipment (hardware) has become easier and more commonplace as computer components have become smaller and thus more readily transportable. Computer-related theft may involve goods that are controlled and accounted for by means of a computer applications program. For example, an employee in a company's accounting department could manipulate inventory records to funnel orders for goods through a phony account and ship the merchandise elsewhere. Payments could also be made on the basis of dummy orders for goods that the company never received. Thefts of computer equipment and thefts of goods with computers are subject to the same criminal and tort laws as thefts of other property (see Chapters 5 and 6).

THEFT OR UNAUTHORIZED USE OF DATA OR SERVICES   Most people would agree that when an individual uses another's computer or computer information system without authorization, the individual is stealing. For example, an employee who used a computer system or data stored in a computer system for private gain and without the employer's authorization would likely be considered a thief, as would a politician who used a government computer to send out campaign brochures.

Once a computer system has been accessed, information contained in the computer's records can be altered. An individual could, for example, remove a bad credit history and obtain loans that otherwise might not be obtainable. Alternatively, an individual could create a bad credit history to prevent or delay another party's receipt of borrowed funds.

The theft or unauthorized use of computer data and services does not fit within the common law definition of larceny or its traditional statutory counterparts. At common law and under most criminal codes, larceny requires a physical taking and carrying away of property from another's possession. Under the common law, criminal statutes are to be strictly construed (that is, a criminal statute cannot be held to include offenses other than those that the statute clearly describes and provides for). Thus, because stealing computer data or services need not involve physically taking and carrying away property from another's possession, it could not be held to constitute larceny.

In a number of states, however, legislation has been passed to abolish or at least limit the application of the common law rule of strict construction of criminal statutes. For example, Model Penal Code Section 1.02(3) provides for construction "according to the fair import of [a statute's] terms." Thus, under an increasing number of revised criminal codes or broad judicial interpretations of existing statutes, the unauthorized use of computer data or services is considered larceny.

Particularly vulnerable to the theft of data or services are systems to which more than one party has access. Even systems accessible only through *passwords* (codes designed to prohibit access to all but authorized users) are often used illegally, especially when the codes are not changed for long periods of time. Breaking a computer's security code or device and perusing the information in the system's records is commonly known as *hacking*. Some instances of hacking have been widely publicized and have generated considerable alarm. Such was the case, for example, in 1983 when a group of Wisconsin high school students discovered the passwords for the computer system at the defense research center in Los Alamos, New Mexico, and thereby gained access to it. More recently, Robert Morris, Jr., a Cornell University student, paralyzed a nationwide computer research network involving six thousand computers. Morris's program unleashed a "virus" that copied itself repeatedly and used up much of the memory of the computers. The activities of these and other so-called computer "hackers" have brought to the public's attention the alarming vulnerability of computer systems—and the businesses and government agencies that rely on them.

In the following case, two employees used their employer's computer facilities, without the employer's authorization, to develop an outside business interest. As you read the case, note how an existing criminal statute (governing mail fraud) is interpreted very broadly by the court to cover computer-assisted crime.

Case 8.7

UNITED STATES v. KELLY

United States District Court, Eastern District of Pennsylvania, 1981. 507 F.Supp. 495.

BACKGROUND AND FACTS David Kelly and Matthew Palmer, Jr., employees at Sperry Univac's applications development center, developed a system, which they called the allegro system, for computerizing the generation of sheet music. Without Univac's knowledge or permission, they used substantial computer time and storage capacity within the central processing unit of the center. To market their system, they mailed promotional materials to music publishers. When Univac discovered their activities, they were indicted on five counts of mail fraud and one count of conspiracy to commit mail fraud. The indictment alleged that in using Univac's computer time and facilities without authorization, Kelly and Palmer defrauded Univac of their services as employees and used the mails to further a fraudulent scheme. After a jury trial in federal district court, the defendants were found guilty on all counts. They filed posttrial motions contending that their acts did not constitute a scheme or an attempt to defraud within the meaning of the mail fraud statute and that the mails had not been used to execute the scheme.

DECISION AND RATIONALE The district court denied their motions and upheld their convictions. The court noted that the "elements of mail fraud are (1) a scheme or artifice to defraud and (2) the use of the United States mails in execution of the scheme." The court found that the evidence was more than sufficient to sustain the jury's determination that Kelly and Palmer acted with intent to defraud. They knew of Univac's policy against the use of its facilities for personal business, but they used the company's computers for personal business anyway, took steps to conceal their activities, and failed to seek authorization. As to their contention that the mailings were unrelated to the scheme's execution, the court emphasized that Kelly and Palmer were charged with defrauding Univac by using its resources for their personal gain. The court found that the evidence clearly established that while they were utilizing Univac's facilities to develop their system, they were attempting to develop a market for it. Thus the mailing was directly related to achieving the fruits of the scheme.

ETHICAL CONSIDERATIONS Kelly and Palmer might have escaped legal liability for their unauthorized use of Univac's computer if they had not used the mails to further their scheme. A lack of legal liability would not have changed the fact that Kelly and Palmer acted unethically. They knowingly used their employer's property for personal gain—certainly in violation of their duty of loyalty to their employer. Ethically, there is no difference between using Univac's computer and using, say, Univac's trucks to run a delivery service on the side.

SOFTWARE PIRACY For the average consumer, software is expensive. It can also be expensive to produce. Often, considerable sums are invested in the research and development necessary to create new, innovative software programs. And, once marketed, new software requires that user support be provided during its life on the market. It is not surprising that, given the expense of software and the zealous competition in today's software market, many individuals and business firms have been tempted to steal software by decoding and making unauthorized copies of software programs. This is known as *software piracy*. It has been estimated that the annual loss to developers from this practice is more than $250 million.

Manufacturers have incorporated protective codes into their software to inhibit its duplication. Breaking through these security codes became little more than a game to some individuals, who then made illegal copies of the software. Consequently, some manufacturers ceased attempting to protect their software by this method, since little benefit was gained in comparison with the increased cost and software complexity required by the security measures. Many companies now take protective steps against software piracy by stressing the benefits—such as written instructions and user support—associated with using authorized copies. Others are suing the users of unauthorized copies in tort for copyright or patent infringement.

Software piracy is illegal, but the applicability of traditional criminal or tort law is made difficult by the unique nature of computer programs. For example, as with the theft of data or services, statutes designed to prohibit larceny—the taking of property without the owner's consent—may be difficult to apply. These statutes were originally enacted to prohibit the theft of *tangible* property. Computer programs, however, are *intangible*, or intellectual, property. As mentioned in Chapter 6, some states have dealt with the issue of program piracy by expanding their definitions of property to bring the theft of computer programs under their larceny statutes. At the federal level, existing laws protecting intellectual property (such as patent and copyright laws) have been amended in recent years to extend coverage to computer programs—as was discussed earlier in this chapter. In 1990, in an attempt to further control the unauthorized copying of computer programs, the federal government passed a law that prohibits, with some exceptions, the renting, leasing, or lending of computer software without the express permission of the copyright holder.

VANDALISM AND DESTRUCTIVE PROGRAM-
MING On occasion, political activists, terrorists,
and disgruntled employees have physically damaged computer hardware or ruined computer software. These acts have included such conduct as
smashing computer equipment with a crowbar,
shooting it with a pistol, and—in an attempt to
make a political point—pouring blood over a computer. In one instance, to erase a company's records, an individual merely walked past computer
storage banks with a large electromagnet.

Other destructive acts have required greater
technical awareness and facility. For example, a
computer program can be designed to rearrange,
replace, or even destroy data. Further, the program
can be time-delayed and set—much like a time-
bomb—to ''explode'' in the future. Similarly, lines
can be inserted into an existing program to damage
a system or, for example, to have funds transferred
into a phony account. Thus, a knowledgeable individual can do a considerable amount of damage.

Some software companies include in their programs mechanisms that will disable programs if,
for example, annual license fees are not paid by a
certain date. In one case, when a dispute arose
between Revlon, Inc., and its software supplier,
Logisticon, Inc., over software performance, Logisticon gained telephone access to the computer
system and activated software-disabling commands. As a result, operations at two of Revlon's
main distribution centers were brought to a standstill for three days. In its still-pending lawsuit
against Logisticon, Revlon characterized Logisticon's actions as a form of extortion. Logisticon
viewed the matter somewhat differently: it claimed
that it ''repossessed'' the software because Revlon
refused to pay the agreed price for the software.[6]

Private Protective Measures

An increasingly common practice among business
firms and government institutions is restricting access to, and use of, information in a computer system through the use of various security measures.
In some cases, the data's availability can be limited
to those with special security clearances. Establishing a system of security clearances may involve

organizing data in specific categories. The category
to which an individual is given access is related to
the information the individual needs to perform his
or her job. For example, the names of account holders can be kept separate from the accounts' balances. In this way, a party who needs to work with
the balances can be prevented from learning the
holders' identities.

Passwords may be attached to a system or to
a portion of the data within a system to preclude
unauthorized access. Considering the relative ease
with which unauthorized individuals have discovered passwords in the past, however, it is advisable
to change the passwords frequently.

Another means of limiting access to computer
information is to encode the data contained within
the system—that is, to translate the data into a secret code. Data can be encoded before it is stored
or communicated to another party. The data is de-
coded when it is taken from storage or when the
other party receives it.

As a further protective measure, a copy of the
data can be stored outside the facilities in which a
company's computer system is located. Then, if
some of the information kept in the system is destroyed or lost, it can be reproduced.

Crime Control Legislation

At the federal level, Congress has enacted legislation directed at specific computer abuses. The
most significant federal legislation relating to computer crimes is the Counterfeit Access Device and
Computer Fraud and Abuse Act of 1984. This act
prohibits the unauthorized access to, or use of,
computer systems. Under the act, it is a crime to
access a computer knowingly for any of the following reasons:

1. To obtain restricted government information—which includes information protected for
reasons of national defense or foreign relations and
information restricted under the Atomic Energy
Act—with the intent that the information be used
to the injury of the United States or the advantage
of a foreign nation.
2. To obtain information contained in a financial
institution's financial records or in a consumer reporting agency's files on consumers.

---

6. *New York Times,* October 24, 1990, pp. C1, C4.

3. To use, modify, destroy, or prevent the authorized use of a computer operated for or on behalf of the federal government or to disclose the information that it contains.

Another federal act, the Electronic Fund Transfer Act (EFTA)—discussed in more detail in Chapter 30—concerns electronic fund transfers, such as direct payroll and social security deposits and transactions conducted at automatic teller machines (ATMs). These transfers provide opportunities for theft through such means as the interception and alteration of data involved in the transfers, the counterfeiting of ATM cards, and the use of stolen code numbers to gain access to financial information and accounts.

Under the EFTA, it is a crime to use, sell, furnish, or transport in interstate commerce any counterfeit, fictitious, altered, forged, lost, stolen, or fraudulently obtained device (such as an ATM card or code number) used to conduct an electronic fund transfer to obtain money, goods, services, or anything else of value. Penalties for violations include up to ten years' imprisonment and a fine of up to $10,000.

At the state level, computer crime is being controlled both by the expansion of traditional criminal laws to cover computer abuses, as mentioned above, and by the passage of laws prohibiting specific computer uses or abuses. In Idaho, for example, accessing computer information without authorization is a misdemeanor, and illegally changing information is a felony. South Dakota has made it illegal to disclose passwords. All unauthorized computer use is a felony in Hawaii. California, Arizona, and numerous other states have also passed new legislation or revised their laws to cover the specific types of computer offenses discussed in this section.

■ Privacy Rights in a Computer Age

Although computers have greatly facilitated commercial transactions, they have also led to a tradeoff that many have found disturbing: speedier, more efficient transactions at the expense of individual privacy. Today, virtually all institutions with which an individual has dealings—including schools, doctors and dentists, insurance companies, mail-order houses, banking institutions, credit card companies, and mortgage firms—obtain information about that individual and store it in their computer files. In addition, numerous government agencies, such as the Census Bureau, the Social Security Administration, and the Internal Revenue Service, collect and store data concerning individuals' incomes, expenses, marital status, and other personal history and habits. Any time an individual applies for a driver's license, a credit card, or even telephone service, information concerning that individual is gathered and stored. Frequently, this personal information finds its way to credit bureaus, marketing departments and firms, or others without the permission or even the knowledge of the individuals concerned.

As mentioned in previous chapters, an individual's right to privacy is protected under tort law and, to a certain extent, under the U.S. Constitution. In situations involving computers, tort damages may be awarded for unauthorized intrusion into another's private records or unauthorized examination of another's bank account. But how does one demonstrate that private records have been invaded when there has been no physical intrusion into one's home or place of business? In such a case, there is no "evidence" of the invasion of privacy.

In response to society's concern over the potential abuse of personal information collected by the government and other institutions, Congress has enacted several laws (see Exhibit 8–1). In addition, many of the laws that states have enacted to address computer crime are also necessarily concerned to some extent with the issue of privacy. The Privacy Act of 1974 has served as a model for many of the state laws regulating government records and recording practices. Although this legislation has helped to control the collection and dispersal of information contained in computer files, information in computer files is still to a great extent unprotected by rules, laws, or codes of ethics. In general, how to control computer use and abuse remains a significant legal challenge of our time.

■ **Exhibit 8–1 Federal Legislation Relating to Privacy**

Title	Provisions Concerning Privacy
Freedom of Information Act (1966)	Provides that individuals have a right to obtain access to information about them collected in government files.
Fair Credit Reporting Act (1970)	Provides that consumers have the right to be informed of the nature and scope of a credit investigation, the kind of information that is being compiled, and the names of the firms or individuals who will be receiving the report.
Crime Control Act (1973)	Safeguards the confidentiality of information amassed for certain state criminal systems.
Family Educational Rights and Privacy Act (1974)	Limits access to computer-stored records of education-related evaluations and grades in private and public colleges and universities.
Privacy Act (1974)	Protects the privacy of individuals about whom the federal government has information. Specifically, the act provides the following: 1. Agencies originating, using, disclosing, or otherwise manipulating personal information must ensure the reliability of the information and provide safeguards against its misuse. 2. Information compiled for one purpose cannot be used for another without the concerned individual's permission. 3. Individuals must be able to find out what data concerning them are being compiled and how the data will be used. 4. Individuals must be given a means through which to correct inaccurate data.
Tax Reform Act (1976)	Preserves the privacy of personal financial information.
Right to Financial Privacy Act (1978)	Prohibits financial institutions from providing the federal government with access to a customer's records unless the customer authorizes the disclosure.
Electronic Fund Transfer Act (1980)	Requires financial institutions to notify an individual if a third party gains access to the individual's account.
Counterfeit Access Device and Computer Fraud and Abuse Act (1984)	Prohibits use of a computer without authorization to retrieve data in a financial institution's or consumer reporting agency's files.
Cable Communications Policy Act (1984)	Regulates access to information collected by cable service operators on subscribers to cable services.
Electronic Communications Privacy Act (1986)	Prohibits the interception of information communicated by electronic means.

■ **Terms and Concepts**

certification mark 153	intellectual property 146	trade name 153
collective mark 153	mask work 151	trade secrets 154
computer crime 156	patent 147	trademark 151
copyright 147	service mark 153	

■ **For Review**

1. What are four distinct forms of intellectual property?
2. Name three issues that courts have addressed in inter-

preting and applying the Computer Software Copyright Act of 1980.

3. What are the five broad categories of crimes committed with or against computers?

4. Max plots a new Batman adventure and carefully and skillfully imitates DC Comics' art to create an authentic looking Batman comic. Max is not affiliated with the owners of the copyright to Batman. Can Max publish the comic without infringing on the owners' copyright?

5. Max, in the previous problem, has also created an entirely original costumed crusader who battles the forces of evil. Can Max publish a comic featuring this character without infringing on the Batman copyright? In other words, do the owners of the copyright in Batman have a copyright in the concept of a costumed crusader who battles the forces of evil?

■ Questions and Case Problems

8-1. Professor Wise is teaching a summer seminar in business torts at State University. Several times during the course, he makes copies of relevant sections from business law texts and distributes them to his students. Unbeknownst to Wise, the daughter of one of the textbook authors is a member of his seminar. She tells her father about Wise's copying activities, which have been done without her father's or his publisher's permission. Her father sues Wise for copyright infringement. Wise claims protection under the "fair use" doctrine. Who will prevail? Explain.

8-2. Adams, who owns and operates a restaurant, has had an account with Uptown Bank for over twenty years. All of Uptown's banking records are computerized. Greed, a competitor of Adams, pays a sum of money to a disgruntled Uptown employee to access Uptown's computer system and provide Greed with information on the financial position and activities of Adams. In addition to giving Greed this information, the employee gives one of Adams's creditors the access code of Uptown's computer system. The creditor, using its own computer, then gathers financial information on Adams. Uptown Bank learns of these activities and discharges the employee. Discuss whether any of the federal laws mentioned in this chapter are specifically applicable to these facts.

8-3. As a college student, you are required to write a term paper. You are currently employed part-time by ABC, Inc. Without ABC's permission, you secure access to ABC's computer and use the computer to generate certain data formulations for your paper. Discuss whether you could and should be liable to ABC for theft.

8-4. One day during algebra class, Diedra, an enterprising fourteen-year-old student, began drawing designs on her shoelaces. By the end of the class, Diedra had decorated her shoelaces with the name of the school, "Broadson Junior High," written in blue and red (the school colors) and with pictures of bears, the school's mascot. After class, Mrs. Laxton, Diedra's teacher, reprimanded Diedra for not paying attention in class and asked Diedra what she had been doing during the lecture. Diedra showed Mrs. Laxton her shoelaces. When Diedra got home that night, she wrote about the day's events in her diary. She also drew her shoe-lace design in the diary. Mrs. Laxton had been trying to think of how she could build up the school spirit. She thought about Diedra's shoelaces and decided to go into business for herself. She called her business "Spirited Shoelaces" and designed shoelaces for each of the local schools, decorating the shoelaces in each case with the school's names, mascots, and colors. The business became tremendously profitable. Even though Diedra never registered her idea with the patent or copyright office, does she nonetheless have intellectual property rights in the shoelace design? Will her diary account be sufficient proof that she created the idea? Discuss fully.

8-5. Original Appalachian Artworks, Inc., (OAA) makes and distributes the very successful product called Cabbage Patch Kids—soft, sculptured dolls that were in great demand in the early 1980s. The dolls are unique in appearance, and the name is registered as a trademark to OAA. The design, too, is protected under a copyright registration. In 1986, Topps Chewing Gum, Inc., had an artist copy many of the features of the dolls for Topps's new product—stickers that depicted obnoxious cartoon characters called Garbage Pail Kids. The stickers proved very lucrative; in fact, Topps expanded the product line to include T-shirts, balloons, and school notebooks.

(a) Did Topps infringe upon OAA's trademark and copyrighted product? Why or why not?

(b) Topps claimed that its product was actually a satire of OAA's product and therefore a fair use of a protected work. Would this amount to a fair use? Discuss.

[*Original Appalachian Artworks, Inc. v. Topps Chewing Gum, Inc.,* 642 F.Supp. 1031 (N.D.Ga. 1986)]

8-6. McGraw was employed by the city of Indianapolis as a computer operator. The city leased computer services on a fixed-charge, or flat-rate, basis; hence, its expense for computer services was constant, regardless of how much computer time was used. McGraw was provided with a terminal at his desk and assigned a portion of the computer's information storage capacity, or private library. McGraw became involved in a private sales venture and began using a small portion of his assigned library to maintain records associated with the venture. At the time he was hired, he received a handbook disclosing the general prohibition against the unauthorized use of city property, and he was reprimanded several times for selling his products in the office and on ''office time.'' The relevant criminal theft statute reads: ''A person who knowingly or intentionally exerts unauthorized control over property of another person with intent to deprive the other of any part of its value or use commits theft.'' Discuss whether McGraw should be convicted of theft because of his unauthorized use of city facilities. [*State v. McGraw,* 480 N.E.2d 552 (Ind. 1985)]

8-7. Data Cash Systems, Inc., (DCS) retained an independent consultant to design and develop a program for a computerized chess game. The program was then translated into machine language and used to create an object program in the form of a read-only-memory (ROM) silicon chip, which was installed as part of the computer's circuitry. All copies of the source program contained copyright notices, but neither the marketed game nor the ROM program contained any copyright notice. After DCS had filed a copy of the source program with the Registrar of Copyrights, it was issued a certificate of copyright registration. A year after DCS began marketing the chess game, JS&A Group, a competitor, began marketing a similar game that used a ROM identical to that of DCS. Investigation revealed that the new ROM was being manufactured by a Hong Kong firm for JS&A. DCS sued JS&A for copyright infringement and unfair competition. Should the copyright of the source program be extended to the ROM? Explain. [*Data Cash Systems, Inc. v. JS&A Group, Inc.,* 628 F.2d 1038 (7th Cir. 1980)]

8-8. On September 21, 1987, Quality Inns International, Inc., announced a new chain of economy hotels to be marketed under the name ''McSleep Inns.'' The response of the owners of McDonald's Corp., the fast-food chain, was immediate. McDonald's wrote Quality Inns a letter stating that the use of ''McSleep Inns'' infringed upon the McDonald's family of marks characterized by the prefix ''Mc'' attached to a generic term. Five days later, Quality Inns filed an action seeking a declaratory judgment from the court that the mark ''McSleep Inns'' did not infringe on McDonald's federally registered trademarks or common law rights to its marks and would not constitute an unfair trade practice. McDonald's counterclaimed, alleging trademark infringement and unfair competition. McDonald's argued that the use of the name ''McSleep Inns'' by Quality Inns would confuse and mislead the public and allow Quality Inns to trade on the goodwill and reputation of McDonald's. Quality Inns claimed that ''Mc'' had come into generic use as a prefix and therefore McDonald's had no trademark rights to the prefix itself. Quality Inns further claimed that its use of the prefix for lodging accommodations would not be confusing to the public because McDonald's products were fast foods. Does the use of the prefix ''Mc'' by Quality Inns for its new ''McSleep'' chain of economy motels infringe on McDonald's trademarks? Explain. [*Quality Inns International, Inc. v. McDonald's Corp.,* 695 F.Supp. 198 (D.Md. 1988)]

8-9. Vault Corp. produces computer diskettes, under the registered trademark PROLOK, that are designed to prevent the unauthorized copying of programs placed on the diskettes by software computer companies, Vault's customers. A program placed on a PROLOK diskette can be copied onto another diskette, but the computer will not read the program from the copy unless the original PROLOK diskette is also in one of the computer's disk drives. Quaid Software, Ltd., markets the CopyWrite diskette. Quaid's diskette contains a feature called RAMKEY, which unlocks the PROLOK protective device. Individuals who purchase the CopyWrite diskette can therefore make fully functional copies of any programs placed on PROLOK diskettes. Vault alleged that Quaid's RAMKEY feature contributed to the infringement of Vault's copyright and Vault's customers' copyrights in violation of the Copyright Act. Quaid claimed that because the RAMKEY feature was capable of substantial noninfringing uses—including the making of archival copies of PROLOK diskettes to be used if the original PROLOK diskettes were damaged—Quaid should not be held responsible for any infringing uses of RAMKEY made by those who purchased the CopyWrite diskette. Review *Sony Corp. v. Universal City Studios* (Case 8.1) and discuss the merits of Quaid's claim in light of that decision. [*Vault Corp. v. Quaid Software, Ltd.,* 847 F.2d 255 (5th Cir. 1988)]

8-10. Jonathan Caven-Atack had been a member of the Church of Scientology for nine years when he decided that the church was a dangerous cult and its leader, L. Ron Hubbard, a vindictive and profoundly disturbed man. Caven-Atack spent the next several years investigating, and then writing a book about, Hubbard and the church. Caven-Atack's purpose was to expose what he believed was the pernicious nature of the church and the deceit upon which its teachings were based. Approximately 3 percent of Caven-Atack's book consisted of quotations from Hubbard's published works. When New Era Publications International, which held exclusive copyright rights in all of Hubbard's works, learned that the Carol Publishing Group planned to publish Caven-Atack's book, it sued Carol Publishing for copyright infringement. Carol Publishing claimed that Caven-Atack's use of Hubbard's works was a ''fair use'' of the copyrighted materials. What factors must the court consider in making its decision? What will its decision be? Discuss. [*New Era Publications International, ApS v. Carol Publishing Group,* 904 F.2d 152 (2d Cir. 1990)]

8-11. Mead Data Central, Inc., provides a computerized legal research service under the trademark LEXIS. LEXIS is widely known and used by the legal community, but a survey indicated that only about 1 percent of the general population recognized the name. In August of 1987, Toyota Motor Corp. announced a new line of luxury automobiles to be called Lexus. Mead Data Central sought to enjoin Toyota from using the name Lexus, claiming that Toyota's use of that name would dilute the distinctive quality of LEXIS as a mark and thus violate Section 368-d of New York's General Business Law. That statute reads, in part, as follows: ''Likelihood of injury to business reputation or of dilution of the distinctive quality of a mark or trade name shall be a ground for injunctive relief in cases of infringement of a mark registered or not registered.'' What will result in court? Discuss. [*Mead Data Central, Inc. v. Toyota Motor Sales, U.S.A., Inc.*, 875 F.2d 1026 (2d Cir. 1989)]

8-12. A Question of Ethics

 Gayle Schreier, a travel agent, has access to the computer reservation system of American Airlines (American). American's frequent-flyer program, called AAdvantage, allows American's passengers who join the program to accumulate mileage credits. When enough credits are accumulated, American issues coupons that can be used to acquire, without any cash payment, tickets for American flights. Passengers who are not members of AAdvantage can also receive mileage credits if they sign up for the program within a twenty-four-hour claim period following their flights. Gayle devised a scheme by which she could take advantage of mileage credits that were not claimed by American's passengers. She enrolled a fictitious person, G. Johnson, in the AAdvantage program. Then she accessed the computer system to replace the name of actual passengers who had made particular flights with that of G. Johnson. AAdvantage issued coupons to G. Johnson and sent them to G. Johnson's address, which Gayle had provided. Eventually, these coupons were exchanged for tickets and used. In no case did Gayle use mileage credits that any passenger of American Airlines had claimed. [United States v. Schreier, *908 F.2d 645 (10th Cir. 1990)*]

1. In light of the fact that she was not depriving any passenger of mileage credits, and assuming that she has not violated any law, was Gayle acting wrongfully from an ethical point of view? If you were in her position, would you do as she did? Why or why not?
2. Did Gayle's activities in any way harm the interests of American Airlines? Discuss.
3. Has Gayle violated any of the laws discussed in this or the two previous chapters? Explain.

Ethics and Social Responsibility

Business ethics and social responsibility are intertwined concepts, but they are not exactly the same thing. *Business ethics* involves the application of ethical standards to business activities. *Social responsibility* involves the fulfillment of social expectations concerning the relationship between business and all individuals—within or outside the firm—who are affected by business actions. What is deemed to be socially responsible business activity varies from culture to culture, from time period to time period within a given culture, and from group to group at any moment in time. For example, even though a business firm may act on the basis of what it considers to be very high ethical standards, there will probably be at least one group of individuals who question the ethical responsibility of that firm. In other words, we cannot tell you here what business actions will receive an A+ in terms of social responsibility, because there is no one definition of the term. It means different things to different people at different times.

The Debate over Social Responsibility

Traditionally in capitalist theory, profit-making activities—insofar

as they provided desired goods and services to society and violated no laws—were *per se* socially responsible. Profit making was and continues to be an essential goal of any business. But in today's world, as mentioned in Chapter 2, a businessperson needs to balance profit-seeking goals against duties owed to other groups—which may include the firm and its employees, the consumers who purchase the firm's products or services, and society as a whole. The determination of whether a given firm is acting in a socially responsible manner will ultimately depend on how the observer answers the following question: When two or more of these duties come into conflict, which duty should take precedence over the other or others?

Duty to Shareholders

At one end of the spectrum in the debate over corporate social responsibility is the notion that the corporation's primary duty is to the firm and its owners. Because the owners of any corporate business firm are the shareholders, corporate directors and officers have an ethical duty to act in the shareholders' interest and not abuse the trust placed in them by the shareholder-owners of the firm. The reason people buy

shares of stock is to make a profit, and many people contend that the primary goal of corporations should therefore be profit maximization. The Nobel-Prize-winning economist Milton Friedman effectively phrases this view:

> In a free enterprise, private property system, a corporate executive is an employee of the owners of the business [shareholders]. He has a direct responsibility to his employers. That responsibility is to conduct the business in accordance with their desires, which generally will be to make as much money as possible while conforming to the basic rules of society, both those embodied in law and those embodied in ethical custom.[1]

Those arguing for profit maximization as the primary corporate goal also point out that it would be inappropriate to use the power of the corporate business world to fashion society's goals. For example, many people refuse to invest in, or buy products produced by, firms that are engaged in certain activities—such as the construction or maintenance of nuclear plants or the production of weapons for the military—or that fail to take definitive steps

---

1. Milton Friedman, "Does Business Have Social Responsibility?" *Bank Administration*, April 1971, pp. 13–14.

toward the advancement of women and minorities in their work forces. Those who perceive profit maximization to be the primary goal of the corporation would argue that the determination as to whether military or nuclear support is in society's best interest is essentially a political question, and therefore the political process—not the corporate boardroom—is the appropriate forum for such a decision.

Duty to Consumers

Somewhere in the middle of the debate spectrum are those who contend that the corporation has an ethical duty to look beyond profit maximization to the welfare of consumers and that consumer welfare should take precedence over profit maximization if these two duties conflict. Many consumers feel that they have absolutely no effect on the pricing, quality, and nature of the products and services offered by modern-day giant corporations. Therefore, corporations have a strict ethical duty *not* to market unsafe and unhealthful products, even when it is legal to do so.

What really is at issue here? Can the corporation meet its goal of profit maximization if it willfully ignores the well-being of consumers? Some would argue that the ultimate control of the corporation actually lies in the hands of the consumer. After all, they argue, the consumer freely chooses to buy or not to buy a corporation's product. Even in the absence of effective competition, the consumer can purchase a smaller quantity of the product being offered. Thus, it is in the corporation's best interest to attempt to satisfy the consumer.

But even assuming that the consumer can exert control over corporate production decisions, the process of competition takes time. Information is costly to obtain and is never perfect. If corporate leaders know or suspect that certain of their products may have deleterious long-run effects on the consumer, do not such corporate leaders have an ethical responsibility to inform the consumer? Eli Lilly had an arthritis drug, Oraflex, approved for sale in the United States without informing the Food and Drug Administration of thirty-two overseas deaths associated with the use of this drug. The dangers of Oraflex only became apparent to the American public when an eighty-one-year-old woman died as a result of taking the drug and Lilly had to pay $6 million in punitive damages.

Although most people would agree that a corporation has an ethical duty to consumers, there is less agreement on how far that duty should extend. In other words, at what point does corporate responsibility for the safety of consumers end and consumer responsibility begin? If a consumer is harmed by a product because that consumer failed to exercise due care or did not use the product as directed by the manufacturer, who should bear the responsibility for that harm, the consumer or the manufacturer?

To illustrate: The Seven-Up Company, as part of a marketing scheme, placed two glass bottles of "Like" cola on the front entrance of the Gruenemeier residence. Russell Gruenemeier, a nine-year-old boy, began playing while holding one of the bottles. He tripped and fell, and the bottle broke and severely cut his right eye, eventually causing him to lose the eye. Russell's mother brought an action against the Seven-Up Company for damages, claiming that the proximate cause of Russell's injury was Seven-Up's negligence. She claimed that the company was negligent because it placed inherently dangerous instrumentalities— glass bottles—within the reach of small children and that the firm should have used unbreakable bottles for its marketing scheme. Had Seven-Up violated any legal or ethical duty by distributing its product in glass bottles? Are glass bottles so inherently dangerous that Seven-Up should be held liable for the boy's injury? If you were the judge, how would you decide the issue? Would you agree with the court's decision in this case that glass bottles are not inherently dangerous, and therefore Seven-Up should not be held liable?[2] Where would you draw the line between the manufacturer's duty of care in product design and distribution and the consumer's responsibility to exercise common sense and reasonable care in the use of products?

Duty to Society

At the other end of the spectrum in the debate on social responsibility are those who feel that business firms should be concerned not only with the welfare of consumers but also with the welfare of society in general. Those who stress the firm's duty to society maintain that because so much of the wealth and power of this country are controlled by business, business in turn has a

---

2. *Gruenemeier v. Seven-Up Co.*, 229 Neb. 267, 426 N.W.2d 510 (1988).

responsibility to society to use that wealth and power in socially beneficial ways. From this perspective, major corporations and business firms are in a sense trustees, or caretakers, of society. As caretakers, they are charged with a host of ethical duties. They should promote human rights, strive for equal treatment of minorities in the workplace, be concerned with environmental health, and generally not profit from activities that society has deemed unethical. They should also share some of their wealth with society in the form of charity.

Indeed, many who have adopted this view of corporate ethical responsibility claim that businesses can best maximize profits by being socially responsible. This is because individuals may be more likely to invest in, and purchase products from, business firms that act ethically in the marketplace and support socially desirable goals. The upswing in so-called ethical investing—that is, investing in firms on the basis of their corporate conduct (relating to a number of criteria, such as investments in South Africa, participation in military contracts, construction or maintenance of nuclear plants, discrimination against minorities, and so on)— in recent years would seem to confirm this assumption.

It should be stressed that business firms generally have been very responsive to social needs, and they routinely donate to hospitals, medical research, the arts, universities, and programs that benefit society. B. Dalton Bookseller, for example, put up $3 million to launch a massive drive against functional illiteracy. The Bank of America created a $10 million revolving-loan program in which funds are loaned to community development groups at a 3 percent interest rate. The Coca-Cola company established the National Hispanic Business Agenda—a major program to expand ties with the Hispanic community. And more recently, that firm announced that its private foundation will distribute $50 million over a ten-year period to support educational institutions and programs throughout the United States. As one of its many philanthropic projects, Levi Strauss & Company established an "AIDS Initiatives" program to fund public educational programs concerning AIDS and patient care for the victims of that disease. The list goes on. Indeed, today every major business firm has a branch or foundation that has been established specifically to screen charitable requests and to decide on and manage corporate charitable contributions and programs.

The Corporate Balancing Act

Obviously, it is impossible for corporations to be all things to all people at all times. Each corporate board of directors has to make numerous tradeoffs in determining corporate goals. Directors do have an ethical duty to shareholders, because they control the shareholders' wealth. Society has also deemed that corporate directors and officers have an ethical duty not to market defective or unreasonably dangerous products—this social ethic is written into warranty and product liability laws. Similarly, they have a duty to provide safe working conditions for their employees—and this also is written into law. But there is no law that says how much weight each duty should be given on the balancing scales beyond the minimum prescribed by law.

The tradeoffs become more complicated when one realizes that these duties overlap considerably. For example, for a corporation to run smoothly and productively, it must recruit qualified personnel. To attract qualified personnel in a competitive marketplace, the firm must offer a competitive salary, a good benefits package, and desirable working conditions. If this is done and the corporation is well managed by the qualified personnel, ideally profits will increase and both shareholders and employees will benefit. But this ideal result is not a certainty. What is certain is that such expenses will mean reduced profits for shareholders in the short run. Similarly, corporate philanthropic activities that receive wide publicity may benefit shareholders in the long run—if the public image of the firm entices more consumers to purchase its products—but such long-run possible benefits are difficult to calculate. In sum, ethical decision making in the business context is not easy. Ideally, each corporate decision would provide equal benefits for all individuals affected by that decision, but this is rarely possible. When it is not, difficult tradeoffs must be made.

Evaluating Social Responsibility

Now you can see why it is difficult to evaluate corporate social responsibility. First of all, no one definition of the term is acceptable to all people. Social responsibility means different things to different persons, depending on their economic and moral convictions. Second, because we live in a world of imperfect information, it is not always possible to acquire a sufficient amount of information about a given business firm's activities to make an informed decision as to whether that firm is acting ethically or not. We might read in the paper, for example, that a certain corporation has made generous contributions toward a worthy social cause and therefore assume the corporation has socially responsible goals. What we might not know is that the same corporation is marketing a product that some corporate officers have reason to suspect may be harmful to many of those who purchase it. A case in point is the A. H. Robins Company. In less than two decades, E. Claiborne Robins, the founder and chairman of the company, and his family gave away more than $100 million in support of educational and other charitable causes, and Robins became widely known for his generosity and concern for his fellow Americans. At the same time, the A. H. Robins Company continued to defend the relative safety of its Dalkon Shield intrauterine device (IUD), even though evidence allegedly known by the company indicated that the device could

harm users—and had in fact caused the deaths of several women.[3]

■ Discussion Questions

1. Assume that you are the president of a growing company. You decide to form a code of ethics to guide the firm's employees in their decision making and workplace behavior. What would your major ethical policies be in regard to each of the following areas of concern, and what ethical reasoning would you use to justify your position in each case?
(a) The advancement of women and minority groups.
(b) Military contracts.
(c) Nuclear power.
(d) Animal testing.
(e) Community outreach (involvement in community education, housing, and other projects benefiting the community).
(f) Direct or indirect investment in South Africa.
(g) Charitable contributions.

---

3. Studies released in 1991 purported to show that most IUDs may never have been harmful to users. In view of these findings, A. H. Robins is reevaluating its position in respect to the use of the Dalkon Shield.

2. In creating a code of ethics for your business firm, to what extent would you solicit input from employees? In other words, do you believe that business codes of ethics should be written by owners alone? Or should key management personnel—and perhaps all employees—have a say in the matter?
3. Many managers of so-called ethical funds believe that business firms can best maximize profits by engaging in ethical business behavior. Discuss what reasons they might give for drawing this conclusion.
4. Should business firms *ever* manufacture products that have deleterious effects on the environment? How do you weigh the benefits of a product (e.g., automobiles) against the negative environmental effects (e.g., smog) caused by the product? Should these kinds of decisions be made by the business sector, or should political bodies be left to determine such policies?

UNIT TWO

Contracts

■ The Importance of Contract Law

The noted legal scholar Roscoe Pound once said that "[t]he social order rests upon the stability and predictablity of conduct, of which keeping promises is a large item."[1] Contract law deals with, among other things, the formation and keeping of promises (in Latin, *pacta sunt servanda*—agreements shall be kept). The law encourages competent parties to form contracts for lawful objectives. No aspect of modern life is entirely free of contractual relationships. Indeed, even the ordinary consumer in his or her daily activities acquires rights and obligations based on contract law. You acquire rights and obligations, for example, when you borrow money to make a purchase or when you buy a stereo or a house. Contract law is designed to provide stability and predictability, as well as certainty, for both buyers and sellers in the marketplace.

The study of contract law is important because it is the framework for all commercial law. The law described in the following chapters is the basis for much of the law in more specialized areas, such as the sale of goods. In Chapter 9, you will be introduced to the nature and terminology of contracts. As you will see, there are many types of contracts. There are also basic requirements that must be met before a valid contract comes into existence. These basic requirements are discussed in detail in Chapters 10 through 14. Sometimes, a third party (one who is not a direct party to the contract) acquires rights under the contract. Third party rights are covered in Chapter 15. Parties to a contract need to know at what point they can reasonably assume that their duties under the contract have been fulfilled. The performance and discharge of contractual duties are covered in Chapter 16. Finally, you will learn in Chapter 17 what remedies are available to the nonbreaching party when the other party breaches the contract.

---

1. R. Pound, *Jurisprudence*, Vol. 3 (St. Paul: West Publishing Co., 1959), p. 162.

■ Ethical Issues in Contract Law

The field of contract law is rife with ethical questions. The black-letter law of contracts is not without its gray areas. *Black-letter law* is the informal term for the principles of law normally accepted by the courts. It is also the law that is embodied in statutes. One of the major ethical considerations in contract law concerns the freedom of contract. At what point should this freedom be limited to achieve justice? For example, in an era dominated by large corporations, consumers frequently have little choice but to contract for their purchases on terms dictated by the seller. At times, injustice results from this unequal bargaining power. But courts will intervene in such contracts only if the contracts are so one-sided or unfair that they "shock the conscience" of the court.

In the next nine chapters, you will read about many other areas of contract law in which questions of ethics arise. If one party makes a mistake when entering into a contract, is it ethical to force that party to perform nonetheless? What if, for example, a bidder on a construction project incorrectly calculated his costs before submitting an offer, only to have it accepted and then be faced with losses if forced to perform the contract at the bid price? Courts have become more lenient in recent years when such computational errors have crept into a business firm's offers. Oral contracts can also present ethical problems. This is because when there is no written evidence of a contract, it is easier for a party to claim that no contract existed in the first place. Denying that one has made a promise is obviously unethical. In some situations, particularly if the other party has partially performed a contract or relied on an oral promise to his or her detriment, a court might enforce the promise notwithstanding the lack of written evidence. Fairness may have no exact definition in the law, but the courts do shape what fairness means in any given situation and set ethical standards that govern all contractual activity.

Chapter 9

Nature and Terminology

In the legal environment of business, one of the most significant bodies of law deals with contracts. Contract law shows what promises or commitments our society believes should be legally binding. It shows what excuses our society will accept for the breaking of such promises. And it shows what kinds of promises will be considered as being against public policy and therefore legally void.

A **contract** may be defined as a promise enforceable at law.[1] A **promise** is an undertaking that something will or will not happen in the future. Thus, a contract may be formed when two or more parties each promise to perform or to refrain from performing some act now or in the future. The promises need not be in writing to constitute a contract, although some contracts must be in writing to be enforceable (see Chapter 14). On the contract's breach (a **breach of contract** occurs when a contractual promise is not fulfilled), the breaching party may be subject to legal or equitable sanctions. These sanctions may include a payment of money (damages) to the nonbreaching party for the *failure to perform.* Under some circumstances, the breaching party may be required to render the performance promised in the contract.

A contractual relationship involves the giving of a promise in exchange for either an act or another promise. All contractual relationships thus involve promises. All promises, however, do not establish contractual relationships. For example, if your friend promises to go to the movies with you and then decides not to go, you cannot sue your friend for breach of contract. Although promises were exchanged—to go to the movies together—the legal system will not expend resources to enforce these promises. In essence, contract law reflects society's determination of the kinds of promises that should be legally enforced.

The use of contract principles to govern the relationships of those who make promises to one another dates back thousands of years. Early in history the importance of contracts was recognized and given legal effect. The

---

1.   The American Law Institute defines a *contract* as ''a promise or set of promises for the breach of which the law gives a remedy, or the performance of which the law in some way recognizes as a duty.'' Restatement (Second) of Contracts, Section 1.

following chapters will explain how contracts are formed, how they are discharged, and what happens when they are not performed. The rules relating to the formation, discharge, and breach of enforceable promises are called the *law of contracts.*

Society as we know it today could not exist without the law of contracts. The foundation for almost all commercial activity is the contract. The purchase of goods, such as automobiles, is governed by a sales contract; the hiring of people to work for us or to make repairs, by service contracts; the sharing of risks on our property, by insurance contracts. In short, we could not order our daily activities without contracts.[2]

Contract law is based on the common law and governs all contracts except when the common law of contracts has been modified or replaced by statutory law or administrative agency regulations. Contracts relating to services, real estate, employment, insurance, and so on generally are governed by general contract law. All contracts for the sale of *goods,* however, are governed by statutory law—particularly the Uniform Commercial Code (UCC)[3]—to the extent that statutory law has modified or replaced general contract law. The relationship between general contract law and the law governing sales of goods is illustrated in Exhibit 9–1. In the discussion of general contract law in this unit, we indicate the areas in which the UCC has significantly altered common law contract principles.

■ The Function of Contracts

Contract law is necessary to ensure compliance with a promise or to entitle a nonbreaching party to some form of relief when a contract is breached. By providing procedures for enforcing private agreements, contract law provides an essential condition for the existence of a market economy. Without a legal framework within which to plan, businesspersons would be able to rely only on the good faith of others. Duty and good faith are usually sufficient, and most contractual promises are kept simply because keeping them is in the mutual self-interest of the **promisor** (the person making the promise) and the **promisee** (the person to whom the promise is made). But when price changes or adverse economic factors make it costly for one of the parties to comply with a promise, duty or good faith alone may not be enough.

Contract law provides a major part of the foundation on which more specialized areas of the law have been built. A basic understanding of the principles governing contracts facilitates an understanding of the principles involved in sales of goods (Chapters 18–24); in the negotiation and transfer of funds by check, draft, note, or electronic means (Chapters 25–30); in relations between debtors and creditors (Chapters 31–34); in relations among employers, employees, and agents (Chapters 35 and 36); in the creation, operation, and termination of partnerships and corporations (Chapters 37–43); in the regulation of trade and monopolies (Chapter 47); and in transfers of property other than goods or by means other than sales or between parties who are not merchants (Chapters 49–52).

■ Freedom of Contract and Freedom from Contract

As a general rule, the law recognizes everyone's ability to enter freely into contractual arrangements. This recognition is called *freedom of contract,* a freedom protected by the U.S. Constitution in Article I, Section 10. But as the character of institutions and society changes, the functions of contract law and its enforcement must also change.

Such change can be perceived today in the fact that certain types of agreements are no longer considered valid. For example, illegal bargains, agree-

---

2. The Soviet Union attempted to eliminate the need for contracts by dispensing with the private ordering of activities. The state required everyone to engage in certain specified activities—work, education, recreation—in the hope of redistributing wealth according to administrative standards and norms. The experiment failed, and Lenin explicitly recognized this when he wrote in 1921, "The private market proved to be stronger than we [thought]. . . . We ended up with ordinary . . . trade." Ultimately, contracts were reintroduced, and contract law was codified along traditional lines. See Loeber, "Plan and Contract Performance in Soviet Law," reprinted in *Law in the Soviet Society,* ed. Wayne R. LaFave (Urbana: University of Illinois Press, 1965).

3. See Chapter 1 and Chapter 18 for further discussions of the significance and coverage of the UCC. The UCC is presented in its entirety in Appendix C at the end of this book.

■ **Exhibit 9–1 Law Governing Contracts**
This exhibit illustrates the relationship between general contract law and the law governing sales contracts. Sales contracts are not governed exlusively by Article 2 of the Uniform Commercial Code but are also governed by general contract law whenever it is relevant and has not been modified by the UCC.

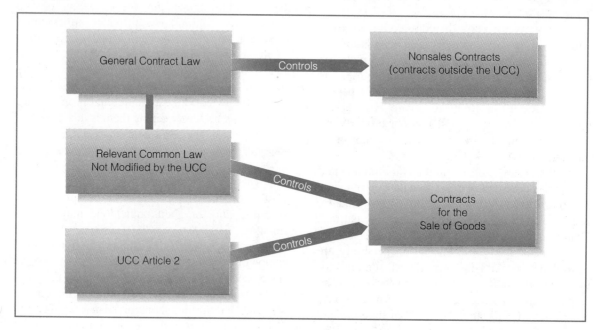

ments unreasonably in restraint of trade, and certain unfair contracts made between one party with a great amount of bargaining power and another with little power are generally not enforced. In addition, certain contracts with consumers, as well as certain clauses within those contracts, are not enforceable, because they have come to be considered incompatible with public policy, fairness, and justice (see Chapter 14 for details). The law of contracts is broadening to include new controls on the manner of contracting and on the allowable terms of agreements. These controls are meant to provide freedom *from* contract for certain members of society who heretofore may have been forced into making contracts unfavorable to themselves.

■ **Basic Requirements of a Contract**

The many topics that will be discussed in this unit on contracts require an understanding of the basic requirements of a contract and the processes by which a contract is created. The following list

briefly describes these requirements. They will be explained more fully in subsequent chapters.

1. *Agreement.* An agreement includes a valid offer and a valid acceptance. One party must voluntarily offer to enter into a legal agreement, and another party must voluntarily accept the terms of the offer.

2. *Consideration.* Generally, consideration is the inducement (reason, cause, motive, or price) to a contract. Any promises made by the parties must be supported by legally sufficient and bargained-for consideration.

3. *Contractual capacity.* Both parties entering into the contract must have the contractual capacity to do so; they must be recognized by the law as possessing characteristics that qualify them as competent parties.

4. *Legality.* The contract must be made to accomplish some goal that is legal and not against public policy.

These four requirements constitute what are formally known as the elements of a contract. Also important are possible *defenses* (that is, reasons why a party should not be awarded what he or she seeks in an action or suit) to the formation or enforcement of a contract. These include the following:

1. *Genuineness of assent.* Apparent consent of both parties must be genuine.

2. *Form.* The contract must be in whatever form the law requires, such as in writing—if any special form is required.

■ Objective Theory of Contracts

The intent or apparent intent to enter into a contract is of prime importance in the formation of the contract. This intent is determined by what is called the **objective theory of contracts,** not by the personal or subjective intent, or belief, of a party. The theory is that a party's intention to enter into a

contract is judged by outward, objective facts as they would be interpreted by a reasonable person, rather than by the party's own secret, subjective intentions. Objective facts include (1) what the party said when entering into the contract, (2) how the party acted or appeared, and (3) the circumstances surrounding the transaction.

Courts need verifiable evidence to determine whether a contract has been made, so they usually rely only on objective factors when passing judgment on a contract dispute. In other words, courts examine all the objective facts, conduct, and circumstances surrounding a particular transaction to determine whether the parties have made a contract and, if so, what its terms are.

The following case illustrates a court's use of the objective theory of contracts to review the conduct and circumstances surrounding a transaction to determine whether a contract exists, and, if so, what its terms might be.

BACKGROUND AND FACTS Purcell Tire and Rubber Company operated fifteen stores. In early 1983, Purcell discussed buying personal computers through Computer Network, Ltd. (CN). Harry Chapman, a Purcell agent, signed a CN memo that referred to twenty-one personal computers, described the equipment, and listed its price. In 1984, CN delivered nine computers to Purcell, who paid for them but refused to accept more. Chapman claimed that the memo was not a contract, that they had only talked about "possible transactions," that he had only wanted to verify a price-and-equipment configuration, and that he had intended eventually to buy only fifteen computers, one for each store. CN claimed that the memo was a contract and sued Purcell in a Missouri state court. The trial court ruled in CN's favor, and Purcell appealed.

 Case 9.1

COMPUTER NETWORK, LTD. v. PURCELL TIRE & RUBBER CO.

Missouri Court of Appeals, Eastern District, Division Five, 1988.

747 S.W.2d 669.

DECISION AND RATIONALE The Missouri Court of Appeals affirmed the lower court's decision. The court pointed out that "[i]f the parties act in a way which recognizes the existence of a contract, one may exist even though the writing does not otherwise establish a contract. Sellers usually do not ship and buyers do not receive goods unless they think they have struck a deal." The court explained that the objective theory of contracts "lays stress on the outward manifestation of assent made to the other party," that is, "what a reasonably prudent person would be led to believe from the actions and words of the parties." The court concluded that there was "mutual assent" to purchase twenty-one computers because of the terms of the memo signed by Chapman.

■ Types of Contracts

Contracts are divided into various categories. In studying these categories, it is important to re-

member that each category signifies a legal distinction regarding a contract's formation, performance, or enforceability (see the *Concept Summary* at the end of this Section).

Bilateral versus Unilateral Contracts

Every contract involves at least two parties. The **offeror** is the party making the offer, and the **offeree** is the party to whom the offer is made. The offeror always promises to do or not to do something and thus is also a promisor. Whether the contract is classified as *unilateral* or *bilateral* depends on what the offeree must do to accept the offer and to bind the offeror to a contract. If the offer requires as acceptance only that the offeree *promise* to perform, the contract formed is called a **bilateral contract.** Hence, a bilateral contract is a promise for a promise. The exchange of mutual promises (called mutuality of obligation) is the basis of the consideration for the contract and the heart of the formation of a bilateral contract. If the offer is phrased so that the offeree can accept only by complete performance, the contract formed by completion of the act (performance) is called a **unilateral contract.** Hence, a unilateral contract is a promise for an act.

The classic illustration of a unilateral contract is that in which Alan says to Barbara, ''If you walk across the Brooklyn Bridge, I'll give you $10.'' Alan promises to pay only if Barbara walks the entire span of the bridge. Only upon Barbara's complete crossing does she accept Alan's offer to pay $10 and therefore bind Alan in contract. If she chooses not to walk at all, there are no legal consequences. If Alan had said to Barbara, ''If you promise to walk across the Brooklyn Bridge, I'll give you $10,'' the offer would have requested a promise for a promise. If Barbara had made the return promise, they would have had a bilateral contract.

A problem arises in unilateral contracts when the promisor attempts to revoke the offer after the promisee has begun performance but before performance has been completed. Offers are normally revocable until accepted, and in the case of unilateral contracts, the traditional view was that acceptance could occur only on full performance. The modern view, however, is that the offer becomes irrevocable once performance has begun. Partial performance does not act as an acceptance but prohibits the offeror from revoking the offer for a reasonable period of time.

Suppose Ann offers to buy John's sailboat, moored in San Diego, upon delivery to Ann's dock in Newport Beach. John rigs the boat and sets sail.

Shortly before his arrival at Newport Beach, John receives a radio message from Ann withdrawing her offer. Ann's offer is for a unilateral contract, and only John's delivery of the sailboat at her dock is an acceptance. Under the traditional view, her revocation would terminate the offer, but since substantial performance has been completed by John, under the modern-day view her offer is irrevocable. John can deliver the boat and bind Ann to the contract.

Under a unilateral contract, only one party is obligated to perform—the promisor (because the promisee has already performed his or her part of the bargain, or the contract would not have come into existence). In contrast, under a bilateral contract, both parties are obligated to perform, because the contract reflects only the *promises* of the parties to do (or refrain from doing) some act in the future.

Express versus Implied Contracts

An **express contract** is one in which the terms of the agreement are fully and explicitly stated in words, oral or written. A signed agreement to buy a house is an express written contract. If a classmate calls you on the phone and agrees to buy your textbooks from last semester for $50, an express oral contract has been made.

A contract that is implied from the conduct of the parties is called an **implied-in-fact contract,** or an implied contract. Implied-in-fact contracts differ from express contracts in that the *conduct* of the parties, rather than their words, reveals that they *intended* to form a contract and creates and defines the terms of the contract. Generally, the following three steps are necessary to establish an implied-in-fact contract:

The plaintiff furnished some service or property.

The plaintiff expected to be paid for that service or property and the defendant knew or should have known that payment was expected. Therefore, services rendered by a family member are presumed to be performed gratuitously.

The defendant had a chance to reject the services or property and did not.

For example, suppose you enter John's Barber Shop, and John motions you to an empty chair by a nod of his head. You sit in the chair, and John proceeds to cut your hair. Although not a word has been exchanged, you have nonetheless entered into an implied-in-fact contract to pay John for his services. The contract is implied by your conduct and by John's conduct. John expects to be paid for cutting your hair, and, by allowing him to cut it, you have implied an intent to pay him for his work. As another example, suppose that, while passing a store at which you have an open account, you see a display of apples marked ''30 cents each.'' You take an apple and hold it up so that the clerk can see it. She nods, and you pocket the apple and walk on. You have promised to pay 30 cents for the apple and are obligated to pay this amount when you receive your bill at the end of the month.

Quasi Contracts
(Contracts Implied in Law)

Quasi contracts, or **contracts implied in law,** do not arise from a mutual agreement between the parties but are imposed by a court to avoid *unjust enrichment.* The doctrine of unjust enrichment holds that people should not be allowed to profit or enrich themselves inequitably at the expense of others.

The quasi contract is, in essence, a legal fiction. It is based neither on an express promise by the defendant to pay for the benefit received nor on conduct of the defendant implying such a promise. Indeed, the recipient of such a benefit (the defendant) not only has not solicited it but often may be unaware that it has been conferred. The doctrine under which the court implies such a contract is called **quantum meruit**,[4] an expression that means ''as much as he deserves.'' *Quantum meruit* essentially describes the extent of compensation owed under a contract implied in law.

For example, a doctor is driving down the highway on vacation and comes upon Smith lying on the side of the road unconscious. The doctor renders medical aid that saves Smith's life. Although the injured, unconscious Smith has not solicited the medical aid and is not aware that the aid has been rendered, Smith has received a valuable benefit, and the requirements for a quasi contract have been fulfilled: Smith has been ''enriched'' by the

actions of the doctor, and it would be unjust to allow Smith to enjoy, without payment, the benefit of the doctor's services. Smith must pay the doctor a reasonable amount for the services rendered.

The principle underlying quasi-contractual obligations, as suggested earlier, is based on the notion of unjust enrichment. Nonetheless, there are situations in which the party obtaining the ''unjust enrichment'' is not liable. To illustrate: You take your car to the local car wash and ask to have it run through the washer and to have the gas tank filled. While it is being washed, you go to a nearby shopping center for two hours. In the meantime, one of the workers at the car wash has mistakenly hand-waxed your car. When you come back, you are presented with a bill for a full tank of gas, a wash job, and a hand wax. Clearly, a benefit has been conferred on you. But this benefit has been conferred because of a mistake by the car wash employee. You have not received an *unjust* benefit under these circumstances. People cannot normally be forced to pay for benefits ''thrust'' upon them.

Also, the doctrine of quasi contract cannot normally be used when there is a contract that covers the area in controversy. For example, Gonzales contracts with Mott to deliver a furnace to a building project owned by Mitchell. Mott goes out of business without paying Gonzales. Gonzales cannot collect from Mitchell in quasi contract, because Gonzales had an existing contract with Mott.

In the following case, the defendant was totally unaware that a benefit had been bestowed upon him by a neighbor who, because of a tax assessor's mistake, paid real estate taxes that should have been paid by the defendant. Nor was the defendant in any way at fault. Nonetheless, the defendant was held liable in quasi contract for the amount by which he had been unjustly enriched by the neighbor's tax payments.

---

4. Pronounced *kwahn*-tuhm *mehr*-oo-wuht.

Case 9.2

**PARTIPILO v.
HALLMAN**

Appellate Court of Illinois, First
District, Fourth Division, 1987.
156 Ill.App.3d 806,
510 N.E.2d 8,
109 Ill.Dec. 387.

BACKGROUND AND FACTS Frank Partipilo and Elmer Hallman were neighbors. Hallman made improvements to his property, but the tax assessor mistakenly concluded that the improvements had been made to Partipilo's property. Because real estate taxes are generally increased when property is improved, Partipilo paid taxes that should have been assessed against Hallman. When Partipilo discovered the error, he brought an action against Hallman in an Illinois state court to recover the amount of the overassessment on the theory of unjust enrichment. The trial court ruled in favor of Partipilo. Hallman appealed.

DECISION AND RATIONALE The Appellate Court of Illinois held that Partipilo was entitled to recover in quasi contract some of the amount of the extra taxes paid. (The statute of limitations[a] had run for two of the tax years; thus Partipilo could not recover the additional taxes paid for those years.) The court quoted the Restatement of Restitution: "A person who has been unjustly enriched at the expense of another is required to make restitution to the other." For example, noted the court, "A receives from the collector of taxes a notification of taxes due, describing lot X which is owned by B. Believing that it describes lot Y owned by him, A pays the tax. A is entitled to restitution from B." Hallman argued that Partipilo's payment of the extra taxes was not his fault. The court pointed out that fault on his part was not required. "[T]he essence of the cause of action is that one party is enriched and it would be unjust for that party to retain the enrichment."

ETHICAL CONSIDERATIONS The doctrine of unjust enrichment, which arose centuries ago in England, reflects the ethical conviction that justice should be done, even in the absence of a contractual cause of action. Although quasi-contractual recovery is a remedy at law, in which the relief is a money judgment, it is often mistakenly regarded as an equitable remedy because it involves fundamental issues of fairness and justice.

a.   A statute of limitations prevents a party from suing on a contract after a certain period of time—five years, in this case—has elapsed.

Formal versus Informal Contracts

Formal contracts are contracts that require a special form or method of creation (formation) to be enforceable. Formal contracts include **contracts under seal,** which are formalized writings with a special seal attached. The seal may be actual (made of wax or some other durable substance) or impressed on the paper or indicated simply by the word *seal* or the letters *L.S.* at the end of the document. *L.S.* stands for *locus sigilli* and means "the place for the seal."

Informal contracts include all other contracts. Such contracts are also called *simple contracts.* No special form is required (except for certain types of contracts that must be in writing), as the contracts are usually based on their substance rather than on their form.

Executed versus Executory Contracts

Contracts are also classified according to their stage of performance. A contract that has been fully performed on both sides is called an **executed contract.** A contract that has not been fully performed on both sides is called an **executory contract.** If one party has fully performed but the other has not, the contract is said to be executed on the one side and executory on the other, but the contract is still classified as executory. For example, assume that you have agreed to buy ten tons of coal from the Wheeling Coal Company. Further assume that Wheeling has delivered the coal to your steel mill, at which the coal is now being burned, but that you have not yet paid for it. At this point, the contract is executed on the part of Wheeling and executory on your part. After you pay Wheeling for the coal, the contract will be executed on both sides.

Valid, Void, Voidable, and Unenforceable Contracts

A **valid contract** results when all of the four elements necessary to contract formation—agreement, consideration, contractual capacity, and legality—exist. In other words, the parties agreed, through an offer and an acceptance, to form a contract; the contract was supported by legally sufficient consideration; the contract was for a legal purpose; and the contract was made by parties who had the legal capacity to enter into the contract. (Each of these elements is discussed in detail in the following chapters.)

A **void contract** is no contract at all. The terms *void* and *contract* are contradictory. A void contract produces no legal obligations on the part of any of the parties. For example, a contract is void if one of the parties was adjudged by a court to be mentally incompetent at the time of contract formation or if the purpose of the contract was illegal.

A **voidable contract** is a *valid* contract in which one or both of the parties has the option of avoiding his or her legal obligations. The party having this option can elect to avoid any duty to perform or can elect to *ratify* the contract. If the contract is avoided, both parties are released from it. If it is ratified, both parties must fully perform their legal obligations.

Subject to exceptions, contracts made by minors are voidable at the option of the minor. (See Chapter 12 for details.) Contracts entered into under fraudulent conditions are voidable at the option of the defrauded party. (These are discussed in Chapter 13.) In addition, some contracts entered into because of mistakes and all contracts entered into under legally defined duress or undue influence are voidable.

An **unenforceable contract** is a valid contract that cannot be enforced because of certain legal defenses against it. For example, a valid contract barred by a statute of limitations is an unenforceable contract. Some oral contracts are also unenforceable. (See Chapter 14 for details.)

■ CONCEPT SUMMARY 9.1 Classification of Contracts

Contract Formation	1. *Bilateral*—A promise for a promise. 2. *Unilateral*—A promise for an act (acceptance is the completed performance of the act). 3. *Express*—Formed by words (oral, written, or a combination). 4. *Implied in fact*—Formed by the conduct of the parties. 5. *Quasi contract* (implied in law)—Imposed by law to prevent unjust enrichment. 6. *Formal*—Requires a special form for creation. 7. *Informal*—Requires no special form for creation.
Performance	1. *Executed*—A fully performed contract. 2. *Executory*—A contract not fully performed.
Enforceability	1. *Valid*—The contract has the necessary contractual elements of agreement (offer and acceptance), consideration, and parties with legal capacity, and it is made for a legal purpose. 2. *Void*—No contract exists, or there is a contract without legal obligations. 3. *Voidable*—One party has the option of avoiding or enforcing the contractual obligation. 4. *Unenforceable*—A contract exists, but it cannot be enforced because of a legal defense.

■ Interpretation of Contracts

When considering the rules that govern the courts' interpretation of contracts, the most important principle to keep in mind is that the law attempts not only to enforce a contract but to enforce *the contract the parties made.* The rules of contract interpretation, which emerged and developed in the common law over hundreds of years, provide the courts with guidelines for determining the meaning of, and giving effect to, the contract the parties made.

The Plain Meaning Rule

In most cases in which the meaning of a contract or its terms is in doubt, the dispute concerns the writing. When the writing is clear and unequivocal (that is, not subject to conflicting meanings), the court will enforce the writing according to its plain terms, and there is no need for the court to interpret the language of the contract. This is sometimes referred to as the *plain meaning rule.* Under this rule, the meaning of a contract's words must be determined from *the face of the instrument*—that is, the written document alone. In other words, the court cannot consider *extrinsic evidence*—evidence that is extrinsic, or external, to the contract itself. Extrinsic evidence may include prior or contemporaneous oral or written agreements, the conduct of the parties, and customs normally followed in the trade.

The following case illustrates a court's application of the plain meaning rule in interpreting a lease clause.

Case 9.3

GREAT FALLS HARDWARE CO. OF RESTON v. SOUTH LAKES VILLAGE CENTER ASSOCIATES, LIMITED PARTNERSHIP

Supreme Court of Virginia, 1989.
238 Va. 123,
380 S.E.2d 642.

BACKGROUND AND FACTS The Great Falls Hardware Company of Reston (Great Falls) signed a lease with South Lakes Village Center Associates, Limited Partnership (South Lakes), to rent space in a shopping center. The lease provided that Great Falls would pay a share of the center's common area maintenance (CAM) expenses, "so long as at least ninety-five percent (95%) of the other tenants * * * are also required to comply with the terms and conditions as herein provided." When the parties disagreed over Great Falls' payment of CAM and other charges, Great Falls asked a Virginia state court to construe the CAM provision. Great Falls contended that it was not required to pay the expenses unless 95 percent of the other tenants paid CAM expenses under lease provisions substantially the same as those in Great Falls' lease. South Lakes contended that Great Falls was obliged to pay the expenses as long as 95 percent of the other tenants complied with CAM provisions in their own leases, regardless of the provisions' differences. Both parties agreed that the language was unambiguous. The trial court considered evidence concerning the circumstances under which the lease was executed and the intent of the parties and decided in South Lakes' favor. Great Falls appealed.

DECISION AND RATIONALE The Supreme Court of Virginia reversed the trial court's decision and remanded the case. The court stated that "[w]here language is unambiguous, it is inappropriate to resort to extrinsic evidence; an unambiguous document should be given its plain meaning. * * * The guiding light in the construction of a contract is the intention of the parties as expressed by them in the words they have used, and courts are bound to say that the parties intended what the written instrument plainly declares." Turning to the contract, the court said that "as herein provided" could only refer to what the lease provided. "The language means what it says: Great Falls is required to pay CAM expenses * * * under its lease only so long as at least ninety-five percent of the other tenants comply with provisions substantially the same as those contained in Great Falls' lease."

Other Rules of Interpretation[5]

When the writing is ambiguous, a court will interpret the language to give effect to the parties' intent *as expressed in their contract*. This is the primary purpose of the rules of interpretation—to determine the parties' intent from the language used in their agreement and give effect to that intent. A court will neither make or remake a contract nor interpret the language according to what the parties claim their intent was when they made it.

As much as possible, a reasonable, lawful, and effective meaning will be given to all of a contract's terms. It is presumed that persons who make a contract intend it to be legal, reasonable, and effective rather than illegal, invalid, or unreasonable or ineffective in its provisions. A contract will be interpreted as a whole; individual, specific clauses will be considered subordinate to the contract's general intent. All writings that are part of the same transaction will be interpreted together. Nevertheless, terms that were the subject of separate negotiation will be given greater consideration than standardized terms and terms that were not negotiated separately.

A word will be given its ordinary, commonly accepted meaning, and a technical word or term will be given its technical meaning, unless the parties clearly intended something else. Specific and exact wording will be given greater consideration than general language. Written or typewritten terms prevail over printed ones.

Because a contract should be drafted in clear and unambiguous language, a party who uses ambiguous expressions is held to be responsible for the ambiguities. Thus, when the language used has more than one meaning, it will be interpreted against the party who drafted the contract.

Finally, when evidence of trade usage, prior dealings between the parties, and previous course of performance under the contract is admitted, what each of the parties does in pursuance of the contract will be interpreted as consistent with what the other does and with any relevant usage of trade and course of dealing and performance. In these circumstances, express terms are given the greatest weight, followed by course of performance, course of dealing, and usage of trade, in that order. When considering custom and usage, a court will look at the customs and usage of trade of the particular business and the locale in which the contract was made or is to be performed.

---

5.   This section paraphrases parts of the text of the Restatement (Second) of Contracts, Sections 201, 202, 203, and 206. The UCC has adopted these same principles in whole or in part; see UCC 1-205, 2-202, and 2-208.

■ Terms and Concepts

bilateral contract 176	implied-in-fact contract 176	promisor 173
breach of contract 172	informal contract 178	*quantum meruit* 177
contract 172	objective theory of	quasi contract 177
contract implied in law 177	contracts 175	unenforceable contract 179
contract under seal 178	offeree 176	nilateral contract 176
executed contract 178	offeror 176	valid contract 179
executory contract 178	promise 172	void contract 179
express contract 176	promisee 173	voidable contract 179
formal contract 178		

■ For Review

1.   What are the basic elements necessary to the formation of a contract?

2.   What is the difference between an implied-in-fact contract and an implied-in-law contract?

3.   A valid contract exists when all of the elements necessary to the formation of a contract exist. A void contract is no contract. A voidable contract is a valid contract that at least one of the parties can avoid. An unenforceable contract is a valid contract that cannot be enforced due to certain defenses. What are the obligations of the parties under each of these types of contracts?

4.   The Steel Insurance Co. issues to Mary a fire insurance policy covering inventory stored in Mary's ''warehouse.'' Mary also stores inventory in the basement of one of her stores. The store is destroyed by fire, and the inventory is lost. Steel refuses to pay for the loss. If Mary sues Steel,

and the court applies the plain meaning rule, might Steel be ordered to pay?

5. Cameron leases a restaurant from Cheese Properties, Inc. The lease provides that Cheese will pay for electricity and that Cameron will pay for "fuel used in the preparation of food." Local usage in the restaurant trade is that "fuel" includes electricity used in cooking. Should "fuel" in the parties' lease be read to include electricity?

■ Questions and Case Problems

9-1. Suppose Felix, a local businessperson, is a good friend of Miller, the owner of a local candy store. Every day at his lunch hour Felix goes into Miller's candy store and usually spends about five minutes looking at the candy. After examining Miller's candy and talking with Miller, Felix usually buys one or two candy bars. One afternoon, Felix goes into Miller's candy shop, looks at the candy, picks up a $1 candy bar and, seeing that Miller is very busy, waves the candy bar at Miller without saying a word and walks out. Is there a contract? If so, classify it within the categories presented in this chapter.

9-2. Janine was hospitalized with severe abdominal pain and placed in an intensive care unit. Her doctor told the hospital personnel to order around-the-clock nursing care for Janine. At the hospital's request, a nursing services firm, Nursing Services Unlimited, provided two weeks of in-hospital care and, when Janine was sent home, an additional two weeks of at-home care. During the at-home period of care, Janine was fully aware that she was receiving the benefit of the nursing services. Nursing Services later billed Janine $4,000 for the nursing care, but Janine refused to pay on the grounds that she had never contracted for the services, either orally or in writing. In view of the fact that no express contract was ever formed, can Nursing Services recover the $4,000 from Janine? If so, under what legal theory? Discuss.

9-3. James is confined to his bed. He calls a friend who lives across the street and offers to sell her his watch next week for $100. If his friend wishes to accept, she is to put a red piece of paper in her front window. The next morning, she places a red piece of paper in her front window. Is the contract formed bilateral or unilateral? Explain.

9-4. Burger Baby restaurants engaged Air Advertising to fly an advertisement above the Connecticut beaches. The advertisement offered $1,000 to any person who could swim from the Connecticut beaches to Long Island across Long Island Sound in less than a day. On Saturday, October 10, at 10:00 A.M., Air Advertising's pilot flew a sign above the Connecticut beaches that read: "Swim across the Sound and Burger Baby pays $1,000." Upon seeing the sign, Davison dived in. About four hours later, when he was about halfway across the Sound, Air Advertising flew another sign over the Sound that read: "Burger Baby revokes." Davison completes the swim in another six hours. Is there a contract between Davison and Burger Baby? Can Davison recover anything?

9-5. Susan contacts Joe and makes the following offer: "When you finish mowing my yard, I'll pay you $25." Joe responds by saying, "I accept your offer." Is there a contract? Is it a bilateral or unilateral contract? What is the legal significance of the distinction?

9-6. Sosa Crisan, an eighty-seven-year-old widow of Romanian origin, collapsed while shopping at a local grocery store. The Detroit police took her to the Detroit city hospital. She was admitted, and she remained there fourteen days. Then she was transferred to another hospital, in which she died some eleven months later. Crisan had never regained consciousness after her collapse at the grocery store. After she died, the city of Detroit sued her estate to recover the expenses of both the ambulance that took her to the hospital and her hospital stay. Is there a contract between Sosa Crisan and the hospital? If so, how much can the Detroit hospital recover? Explain. [*In re Estate of Crisan*, 362 Mich. 569, 107 N.W.2d 907 (1961)]

9-7. Josephine Wideman was an elderly woman who moved in with her daughter and son-in-law so that they could provide care for her. Until that time, each of Wideman's children had periodically lived with her in her own home. While Wideman lived with her daughter, other members of Wideman's family would come and care for her while the daughter was at work. Wideman always paid her family members for these services, and the evidence at trial supported the proposition that Wideman intended that everyone who cared for her should be paid. The daughter never received any such remuneration. When Wideman died, her daughter sued the estate for the reasonable value of her services and rent. Discuss whether the daughter can state a claim, and specify the theory on which such a claim would be based. [*Sturgeon v. Estate of Wideman*, 631 S.W.2d 55 (Mo.App. 1981)]

9-8. Nichols is the principal owner of Samuel Nichols, Inc., a real estate firm. Nichols signed an exclusive brokerage agreement with Molway to find a purchaser for Molway's property within ninety days. This type of agreement entitles the broker to a commission if the property is sold to any purchaser to whom the property is shown during the ninety-day period. Molway tried to cancel the brokerage agreement before the ninety-day term had expired. Nichols had already advertised the property, put up a "for sale" sign, and shown the property to prospective buyers. Molway claimed that the brokerage contract was unilateral and that she could cancel at any time before Nichols found a buyer. Nichols claimed that the contract was bilateral and that Molway's cancellation breached the contract. Discuss who should prevail at trial. [*Samuel Nichols, Inc. v. Molway*, 25 Mass.App. 913, 515 N.E.2d 598 (1987)]

9-9. Engelcke Manufacturing, Inc., planned to design and manufacture Whizball, an electronic parlor game. Engelcke asked Eaton to design the electronic schematic for it. Engelcke told Eaton that he would be paid for the reasonable value of his services upon the project's completion, but no written contract was signed. The specific amount and terms were also not discussed. Eaton had produced a plan that represented 90 percent of the finished design when Engelcke terminated his employment. Eaton sued Engelcke for breach of an implied-in-fact contract. Engelcke claimed that they had an express contract. Why did Engelcke claim an express contract rather than an implied-in-fact contract? [*Eaton v. Engelcke Manufacturing, Inc.*, 37 Wash.App. 677, 681 P.2d 1312 (1984)]

9-10. In 1973, and again in 1976, an agreement was executed between Industrial Lift Truck Service Corp. (IL) and Mitsubishi International Corp. calling for IL to purchase forklift trucks from Mitsubishi and to use its best efforts to service and sell the trucks. The agreement allowed Mitsubishi to terminate the agreement without just cause by giving ninety days' notice. From 1973 to 1977, IL allegedly became the nation's largest dealer of Mitsubishi forklift trucks. During this period, IL made design changes in the truck to better suit the American market, design changes that Mitsubishi did not request but later incorporated into the trucks it sold to other dealers. In 1978, Mitsubishi terminated the agreement. IL sued under quasi-contract principles to recover the benefits conferred upon Mitsubishi by the design changes. The suit was dismissed, and IL appealed. Discuss whether IL's quasi-contractual claim could overcome the written contract attesting to their relationship. [*Industrial Lift Truck Service Corp. v. Mitsubishi International Corp.*, 104 Ill.App.3d 357, 432 N.E.2d 999, 60 Ill.Dec. 100 (1982)]

9-11. William Greene began working for Grant Building, Inc., in 1959. Greene allegedly agreed to work at a pay rate below union scale in exchange for a promise that Grant would employ him ''for life.'' In 1975, Oliver Realty, Inc., took over the management of Grant Building. Oliver Realty's president assured former Grant employees that existing employment contracts would be honored. During that same year, Greene explained the terms of his agreement to an Oliver Realty supervisor. The supervisor stated that he would look into the matter but never got back to Greene. After twenty-four years of ser-vice, Greene was fired by the new owners of the business. Greene sued Oliver Realty for breach of a unilateral contract. Discuss fully whether Greene and Oliver Realty had a unilateral contract. [*Greene v. Oliver Realty, Inc.*, 363 Pa.Super. 534, 526 A.2d 1192 (1987)]

9-12. A Question of Ethics

In 1982, in the closing days of Minnesota's gubernatorial campaign, Dan Cohen offered a reporter from the Minneapolis Star and Tribune *some ''documents which may or may not relate to a candidate in the upcoming election.'' Cohen, who was actively promoting one of the gubernatorial candidates, agreed to give the reporter the documents—copies of two public court records of a rival party's candidate for lieutenant governor—if the reporter promised not to reveal the source of the information. The reporter promised to keep the source confidential. The editor of the* Tribune, *however, in spite of the reporter's objections, decided to name Cohen as the source of the information so as not to mislead the public into thinking that the information came from an unbiased source. On the day the newspaper article was published, Cohen was fired by his employer. Cohen sued the newspaper's owner, Cowles Media Co., for breach of contract. Given these facts, discuss the following questions.* [Cohen v. Cowles Media Co., ____ U.S. ____, 111 S.Ct. 2513, 115 L.Ed.2d 586 *(1991)*.]

1. Do you think that the editor's ethical duty to provide the reading public with unbiased news coverage should have overridden the editor's ethical duty to honor the reporter's promise to Cohen?

2. Did the reporter's promise to keep Cohen's identity confidential create solely an ethical obligation or a contract enforceable in a court of law?

3. If the court decides that an enforceable contract was formed between Cohen and the reporter, how would this affect society's valuation—as expressed in the First Amendment to the Constitution—that freedom of the press should not be constrained?

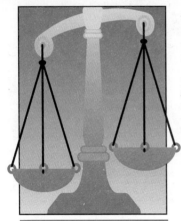

Chapter 10

Agreement

Essential to any contract is an **agreement**; that is, an offer must be made by one party and accepted or assented to by the other party. The agreement does not necessarily have to be in writing. Both parties, however, must manifest their assent to the same bargain. Once an agreement is reached, if the other elements of a contract are present (consideration, capacity, and legality—discussed in subsequent chapters), a valid contract is formed, generally creating enforceable rights and duties between the parties.

A contract must contain reasonably definite terms; otherwise, it would be impossible for a court to enforce the contract. What specific terms are required depends, of course, on the type of contract. Generally, a contract must include the following terms, either expressed in the contract or capable of being reasonably inferred from it:

1. The identification of the parties.
2. The identification of the object or subject matter of the contract (also quantity, when appropriate), including the work to be performed, with specific identification of such items as goods, services, and land.
3. The consideration to be paid.
4. The time of payment, delivery, or performance.

If these terms are expressly stated in the agreement, the contract is definite. Although terms and intent are equally important in both the offer and the acceptance, for simplicity's sake we will discuss the relevant laws only in terms of the offer.

■ Mutual Assent

Ordinarily, mutual assent is evidenced by an *offer* and an *acceptance*. One party offers a certain bargain to another party, who then accepts that bargain. The parties are required to manifest to each other their **mutual assent** to the same bargain.[1] Because words often fail to convey the precise meaning intended, the law of contracts generally adheres to the objective theory of

1. Restatement (Second) of Contracts, Section 22.

contracts, as discussed in Chapter 9. Under this theory, a party's words and conduct are held to mean whatever a reasonable person in the offeree's position would think they meant. The court will give words their usual meaning even if "it were proved by twenty bishops that [the] party . . . intended something else." [2]

■ Requirements of the Offer

The parties to a contract are the *offeror,* the one who makes an offer or proposal to another party, and the *offeree,* the one to whom the offer or proposal is made. An **offer** is a promise or commitment to do or refrain from doing some specified thing in the future. Under the common law, three elements are necessary for an offer to be effective:

1. There must be a *serious intention* by the offeror to become bound by the offer.
2. The terms of the offer must be reasonably *certain,* or *definite,* so that they can be ascertained by the parties and a court of law.
3. The offer must be communicated by the offeror to the offeree.

Once an effective offer has been made, the offeree has the power to accept the offer. If the offeree accepts, an agreement is formed (and thus a contract, if other essential elements are present).

Intention

The first element for an effective offer to exist is a serious intent on the part of the offeror. But serious intent is not determined by the *subjective* intentions, beliefs, and assumptions of the offeror. It is determined by what a reasonable person in the offeree's position would conclude the offeror's words and actions meant. Offers made in obvious anger, jest, or undue excitement do not meet the intent test. Since these offers are not effective, an offeree's acceptance would not create an agreement. For example, suppose you and three classmates ride to school each day in Jane's new automobile, which has a market value of $12,000. One cold morning the four of you get into the car, but Jane cannot get the car started. She yells in anger, "I'll sell this car to anyone for $500!" You drop $500 in her lap. Given these facts, a reasonable person, taking into consideration Jane's frustration and the obvious difference in value between the car and the purchase price, would declare that her offer was not made with serious intent and that you did not have an agreement.

The concept of intention can be further explained by distinctions between offers and various kinds of nonoffers. Consider the following:

1. Expressions of opinion.
2. Statements of intention.
3. Preliminary negotiations.
4. Certain kinds of advertisements, catalogues, and circulars.

In each of these cases, an offer (as legally defined) probably does not exist, because the legal requirement of intention has probably not been met.

EXPRESSIONS OF OPINION An expression of opinion is not an offer. It does not evidence an intention to enter into a binding agreement. Hawkins took his son to McGee, a doctor, and asked McGee to operate on the son's hand. McGee said the boy would be in the hospital three or four days and that the hand would *probably* heal within a few days afterward. The son's hand did not heal for a month, but the father did not win a suit for breach of contract. The court held that McGee did not make an offer to heal the son's hand in three or four days. He merely expressed an opinion as to when the hand would heal.[3]

STATEMENTS OF INTENTION No contract is created when Henry says "I *plan* to sell my stock in Ryder Systems for $150 per share," and Fred "accepts" and tenders (offers) to Henry the $150 per share for the stock. Henry has merely expressed his intention to enter into a future contract for the sale of the stock. No contract is formed, because

---

2. Learned Hand in *Hotchkiss v. National City Bank of New York,* 200 F. 287 (2d Cir. 1911), aff'd 231 U.S. 50, 34 S.Ct. 20, 58 L.Ed. 115 (1913). The term *aff'd* is an abbreviation for *affirmed;* an appellate court can affirm a lower court's judgment, decree, or order, thereby declaring that it is proper and must stand as rendered.

---

3. *Hawkins v. McGee,* 84 N.H. 114, 146 A. 641 (1929).

a reasonable person would conclude that Henry was only *thinking* about selling his stock, not promising to sell, even if Fred accepted and tendered the $150 per share. Henry is stating a future contractual intent, not a present one.

PRELIMINARY NEGOTIATIONS A request or invitation to negotiate is not an offer. It only expresses a willingness to discuss the possibility of entering into a contract. Included are statements such as "Will you sell Blythe Estate?" or "I wouldn't sell my car for less than $1,000." A reasonable person in the offeree's position would not

conclude that these statements evidenced an intention to enter into a binding obligation. Likewise, when construction work is done for the government and private firms, contractors are invited to submit bids. The *invitation* to submit bids is not an offer, and a contractor does not bind the government or private firm by submitting a bid. (The bids that the contractors submit *are* offers, however, and the government or private firm can bind the contractor by accepting the bid.)

Consider whether the court was dealing with preliminary negotiations or an actual offer in the following case.

Case 10.1

SOUTHWORTH v. OLIVER

Supreme Court of Oregon, 1978.
284 Or. 361,
587 P.2d 994.

BACKGROUND AND FACTS The Olivers mentioned to Southworth that they were planning to sell some of their land. When Southworth told the Olivers that he had the money to buy the property, the Olivers told Southworth that they would let him know the details concerning the sale. Later, Southworth asked the Olivers if they still planned to sell the property, and the Olivers said they did, but were awaiting the results of an appraisal. Later the Olivers sent a letter to Southworth—and (unknown to Southworth) to others—giving information about the land and the sale. Southworth sent a letter to the Olivers "accepting" their offer. The Olivers said that their letter had not been intended as an "offer" but as a starting point for negotiations. Southworth filed suit in an Oregon state court for specific performance,[a] which the trial court awarded. The Olivers appealed.

DECISION AND RATIONALE The Supreme Court of Oregon held that the Olivers' letter was an offer that Southworth accepted. The court upheld the specific performance award. The court explained that while a price quotation alone is not an offer, when considered with other circumstances it may constitute an offer that, if accepted, will result in a binding contract, even if the quotation was sent to more than one person. The court stated that "[t]he basic problem is found in the expressions of the parties. People very seldom express themselves either accurately or in complete detail. Thus, difficulty is encountered in determining the correct interpretation of the expression in question." The court held that the terms of the letter and the circumstances under which it was sent were sufficient to have led a "reasonable person" to believe the Olivers were making an offer to sell the property to Southworth.

a. Specific performance is a remedy in which a court orders a party who has breached a contract to perform as promised (see Chapter 17).

ADVERTISEMENTS, CATALOGUES, AND CIRCULARS In general, advertisements, mail order catalogues, price lists, and circular letters are treated not as *offers* to contract but as *invitations to negotiate.* Suppose that Loeser advertises a used paving machine. The ad is mailed to hundreds of

firms and reads, "Used Case Construction Co. paving machine. Builds curbs and finishes cement work all in one process. Price $21,250." If Star Paving calls Loeser and says, "We accept your offer," no contract is formed. Any reasonable person would conclude that Loeser was not promising to sell the paving machine but rather was soliciting offers to buy it. If such an ad were held to constitute a legal offer, and fifty people accepted the offer, there is no way that Loeser could perform all fifty of the resulting contracts. He would have to breach forty-nine contracts. Obviously, the law seeks to avoid such unfairness.

The same result occurs when a car dealership advertises, "New Lincoln Continentals; loaded with options; now only $27,899." The ad is intended to draw customers who will make offers. If Bill Weinberg goes to the dealership with a check for $27,899, the dealership is not legally bound to sell the Lincoln. (Note, however, that federal and state statutes prohibit "false and misleading advertising" that is intended solely to draw customers to the retail outlet—see Chapter 45.)

Most advertisements are not offers, because the seller never has an unlimited supply of goods. If advertisements were offers, then everyone who "accepted" after the retailer's supply was exhausted could sue for breach of contract. Suppose you put an ad in the classified section of your local newspaper offering to sell a guitar for $75. Suppose further that seven people called and "accepted" your "offer" before you could remove the ad from the newspaper. If the ad were truly an offer, you would be bound on seven contracts to sell your guitar. But since initial advertisements are treated as *invitations* to make offers, rather than as offers, you would have seven offers to choose from, and you could accept the best one without incurring any liability for the six you rejected.

Price lists are another form of invitation to negotiate or trade. The price list of the seller is not an offer to sell at that price. It merely invites the buyer to offer to buy at that price. As further evidence of the lack of intent to offer to sell at the listed prices, the words "prices subject to change" are usually printed somewhere on the price list.

Although most advertisements and the like are treated as invitations to negotiate, this does not mean that an advertisement can never be an offer. *If the advertisement makes a promise so definite in character that it is apparent that the offeror is binding himself or herself to the conditions stated, the advertisement is treated as an offer.* This is particularly true when the advertisement solicits performance—for example, by offering a reward for the capture of a criminal or for the return of a lost article.

Suppose an advertisement states, "To the first five persons in our store at 8:00 A.M. on May 1, we offer to sell Singer Sewing Machines, Model X, at $100." This statement invites an acceptance of the terms stated rather than an offer to buy. If you were one of the first five in the store at the time specified, your acceptance would create a contract. Another example is a reward offered in a newspaper for the return of a lost dog. The finder's return of the dog in response to the advertisement creates a unilateral contract, as the reward obviously invited an acceptance, not an offer, from the offeree.

In the following case, the court had to decide whether a newspaper advertisement announcing a "special sale" in a department store should be construed as an offer, the acceptance of which would complete a contract. (Today, the Federal Trade Commission has a set of rules governing such ads.)

BACKGROUND AND FACTS   Morris Lefkowitz saw newspaper ads in which Great Minneapolis Surplus Store, Inc., offered certain items of merchandise for sale. One of the ads read:

Saturday 9 A.M.
2 Brand New Pastel Mink 3-Skin Scarfs
Selling for $89.50
Out they go Saturday
Each .   .   . $1.00
1 Black Lapin Stole
Beautiful, worth $139.50
.   .   .   . $1.00
First Come
First Served

Case 10.2

LEFKOWITZ v. GREAT MINNEAPOLIS SURPLUS STORE, INC.

Supreme Court of Minnesota, 1957.
251 Minn. 188,
86 N.W.2d 689.

Twice, Lefkowitz was the first person to demand the goods. On both occasions, the store refused to sell the advertised goods to him, saying that the offer was intended for women only, even though the ads were directed to the general public. Lefkowitz sued the store in a Minnesota state court for breach of contract. The trial court awarded him damages. The store appealed.

DECISION AND RATIONALE   The Supreme Court of Minnesota affirmed the trial court's judgment. The state supreme court stated that the test as to whether a binding obligation originates in ads addressed to the general public is "whether the facts show that some performance was promised in positive terms in return for something requested." The court concluded that the offer in the ad was "clear, definite, and explicit, and left nothing open for negotiation." Lefkowitz, being the first to appear at the store, was entitled to performance. As for the store's claim that the offer was directed at women, the court pointed out that the ad did not say so. "[W]hile an advertiser has the right at any time before acceptance to modify his offer, he does not have the right, after acceptance, to impose new or arbitrary conditions not contained in the published offer."

OTHER NONOFFER SITUATIONS   Sometimes what appears to be an offer is not sufficient to serve as the basis for formation of a contract. Particularly problematic in this respect are "offers" to sell goods at auctions and agreements to agree.

Auctions   In an auction, a seller "offers" goods for sale through an auctioneer. This is not, however, an offer for purposes of contract. The seller is really only expressing a willingness to sell. Unless the terms of the auction are explicitly stated to be *without reserve*, the seller (through the auctioneer) may withdraw the goods at any time before the auctioneer closes the sale by announcement or by fall of the hammer. The seller's right to withdraw goods characterizes an auction *with reserve; all auctions* are assumed to be of this type unless a clear statement to the contrary is made.[4] At auctions "without reserve," the goods cannot be withdrawn and must be sold to the highest bidder.

In an auction with reserve, there is no obligation to sell, and the seller may refuse the highest bid. The bidder is actually the offeror. Before the auctioneer strikes the hammer, which constitutes acceptance of the bid, a bidder may revoke his or her bid, or the auctioneer may reject that bid or all bids. Typically, an auctioneer will reject a bid that is below the price the seller is willing to accept. When the auctioneer accepts a higher bid, he or she rejects all previous bids. Because rejection terminates an offer (as pointed out below), if the highest bidder withdraws his or her bid before the hammer falls, none of the previous bids are reinstated. If the bid is not withdrawn or rejected, the contract is formed when the auctioneer announces "Going once, going twice, sold" (or something similar) and lets the hammer fall.

Agreements to Agree   Traditionally, agreements to agree—agreements to agree to a material term of a contract at some future date—were not considered to be binding contracts. More recent cases illustrate the view that agreements to agree serve valid commercial purposes and can be enforced if the parties clearly intended to be bound by such agreements. For example, suppose Zahn Consulting leases office space from Leon Properties, Inc. Their lease agreement includes a clause permitting Zahn to extend the lease at an amount of rent to be agreed on when the lease is extended. Under the traditional rule, because the amount of rent was not specified in the lease clause itself, the clause would be too indefinite in its terms to enforce. Under the modern view, a court could hold that the parties intended the future rent to be a reasonable amount and could enforce the clause.[5]

---

4.   See UCC 2-328.

5.   Restatement (Second) of Contracts, Section 33. See also UCC 2-204, 2-305.

In other words, under the modern view the emphasis is on the parties' intent rather than on form. For example, when the Pennzoil Company discussed with the Getty Oil Company the possible purchase of Getty's stock, a Memorandum of Agreement was drafted to reflect the terms of the conversations. After more negotiations over the price, both companies issued press releases announcing an agreement in principle on the terms of the memorandum. The next day, Texaco, Inc., offered to buy all Getty's stock at a higher price. The day after that, Getty's board of directors voted to accept Texaco's offer, and Texaco and Getty signed a merger agreement. When Pennzoil sued Texaco for tortious interference with its "contractual" relationship with Getty, a jury concluded that Getty and Pennzoil had intended a binding contract before Texaco made its offer, with only the details left to be worked out. Texaco was held liable for interfering with this contract.[6]

Definiteness

A contract must have reasonably definite terms so that a court can determine if a breach has occurred and can give an appropriate remedy.[7] An offer may invite an acceptance to be worded in such specific terms that the contract is made definite. For example, assume D'Onfro contacts your corporation and offers to sell "from one to ten pizza ovens for $999 each" and further specifies that your company should "state number desired in acceptance." Your corporation agrees to buy two ovens. If the quantity had not been specified in the acceptance, the contract would have been unenforceable, because the terms of the contract would have been indefinite. But since the acceptance states that your corporation wants two ovens, the contract is definite and can be enforced.

Courts are sometimes willing to supply a missing term in a contract when the parties have clearly manifested an intent to form a contract. If, on the other hand, the parties have attempted to deal with a particular term of the contract but their expression of intent is too vague or uncertain to be given any

precise meaning, the court will not supply a "reasonable" term, since to do so might conflict with the intent of the parties. In other words, the court will not rewrite the contract.

Article 2 of the UCC has different rules relating to definiteness of terms in a contract for the sale of goods. In essence, Article 2 modifies general contract law by requiring less specificity (see Chapter 18 and UCC 2-204). It is especially important to specify with clarity and certainty the terms of international sales contracts. This topic is pursued in further detail in Chapter 24.

Communication

A third element for an effective offer is communication of the offer to the offeree, resulting in the offeree's knowledge of the offer. Ordinarily, one cannot agree to a bargain without knowing that it exists. For example, suppose that Emerman advertises a reward for the return of her lost dog. Baldwin, not knowing of the reward, finds the dog and returns it to Emerman. Baldwin cannot recover the reward, because he did not know it had been offered.[8]

A reward can be accepted only by complete performance. Thus, the contract formed by completion of the act for which the reward was offered is *unilateral,* as explained in Chapter 9. An essential element in the reward contract is that the one who claims the reward must have known that it was offered.

The following case is one of the classic reward cases in the common law dealing with the requirement of communication of the offer.

---

8.   A few states allow recovery of the reward, but not on contract principles. Because Emerman wanted her dog to be returned, and Baldwin returned it, these few states would allow Baldwin to recover on the basis that it would be unfair to deny him the reward just because he did not know about it.

---

6.   *Texaco, Inc. v. Pennzoil Co.,* 729 S.W.2d 768 (Tex.App—Houston [1st Dist.] 1987, error refused n.r.e.). This case was presented in Chapter 7 as Case 7.1.

7.   Restatement (Second) of Contracts, Section 33.

Case 10.3

GLOVER v. JEWISH WAR VETERANS OF THE UNITED STATES, POST NO. 58

Municipal Court of Appeals for the District of Columbia, 1949. 68 A.2d 233.

BACKGROUND AND FACTS The Jewish War Veterans of the United States offered a reward of $500 in a newspaper "to the person or persons furnishing information resulting in the apprehension and conviction of the persons guilty of the murder of Maurice L. Bernstein." A suspect was arrested, and the police learned that another suspect was the "boyfriend" of a daughter of Mary Glover who suggested the location at which the suspect was later found and arrested. The suspects were convicted. Glover claimed the reward, arguing that the information she gave to the police led to the arrest and conviction of the murderers. When Glover gave the information to the police, however, she had not known about the reward. The trial court denied Glover the reward, and she appealed.

DECISION AND RATIONALE The Municipal Court of Appeals for the District of Columbia affirmed the trial court's judgment. The appellate court stated the rule that no contract exists unless a party acts with the knowledge of and the intent of accepting an offer. The court reasoned that because Glover's performance had not been induced by the offer, of which she had no knowledge, no contract existed. The court added that "this rule is particularly applicable in the present case since the claimant did not herself contact the authorities and volunteer information but gave information only upon questioning by the police officers and did not claim any knowledge of the guilt or innocence of the criminal but only knew where he probably could be located."

■ Termination of the Offer

The communication of an effective offer to an offeree creates a power in the offeree to transform the offer into a binding, legal obligation—a contract. This power of acceptance, however, does not continue forever. It can be terminated by either *action of the parties* or *operation of law*.

Termination by Action of the Parties

The power of the offeree to transform the offer into a binding, legal obligation can usually be terminated by any of the following actions:

1. Revocation of the offer by the offeror.
2. Rejection of the offer by the offeree.
3. Counteroffer by the offeree.

REVOCATION OF THE OFFER BY THE OFFEROR **Revocation** is the withdrawal of the offer by the offeror. Generally, an offer may be revoked by the offeror at any time before acceptance. A revocation, like an offer, is not effective until it is received by the offeree. Revocation may be accomplished by express repudiation of the offer

(such as "I withdraw my previous offer of October 17") or by acts inconsistent with the existence of the offer that are made known to the offeree.

The revocation must be communicated to the offeree before acceptance, or it will be ineffective, and a valid contract can be formed. The general rule followed by most states is that a revocation is effective only upon actual receipt of the revocation by the offeree or the offeree's agent. Therefore, a letter of revocation that is mailed on April 1 and is delivered at the offeree's residence or place of business on April 3 becomes effective on April 3.

Alternatively, communication to the offeree exists if the offeree indirectly discovers that the offer has been revoked. This indirect discovery may occur when a third person tells the offeree that the offer has been revoked prior to the offeree's acceptance, when the offeree learns that the subject matter of the contract has been sold to a third party, or when the offeree learns that the offeror is no longer willing or able to fulfill the promise made in the offer.

Revocation of an offer made to the general public must be communicated in the same manner in which the offer was originally communicated, and the revocation must be given the same amount of publicity that was given the offer. For example, suppose Macy's offers a $10,000 reward for anyone giving information leading to the apprehension of the persons who burglarized Macy's downtown store. The offer is published in three local papers and in four papers in neighboring communities. To revoke the offer, Macy's must publish the revocation in all seven papers for the same number of days as it published the offer. The revocation will then be accessible to the general public, even if some particular offeree does not learn about it.

IRREVOCABLE OFFERS Although most offers are revocable, certain offers can be made irrevocable. Three types of **irrevocable offers** deserve discussion. They are the following:

1. Option contracts.
2. Firm offers under the UCC.
3. Offeree's detrimental reliance on the offer (promissory estoppel).

Option Contracts As a general rule, offerors may revoke their offers even if they have expressly agreed to hold them open for a specified period of time. When an offeror promises to hold an offer open for a specified period, however, and the offeree pays for the promise (gives consideration), an **option contract** is created. An option contract is a *separate* contract that takes away the offeror's power to revoke the offer for the period of time specified in the option. If no time is specified, then a reasonable period of time is implied.

For example, suppose Brennan offers to sell one hundred shares of stock in Texas Instruments to Columbus for $189 per share. Brennan promises to keep the offer open for thirty days. After fourteen days Brennan calls Columbus on the telephone and says that the offer is revoked. If Columbus has not given any consideration for the option (to keep the offer open) up to this time, Brennan may revoke the offer despite his promise to keep it open for thirty days. But if Columbus has given some consideration (say, $25 in cash) for the option, Brennan must hold the offer open for the stated thirty days. This particular option contract (for the purchase of common stock) is becoming increasingly popular, and similar options are traded publicly on numerous exchanges.

Generally, the death or incompetence of either party does not terminate a *contract*; thus, the death of the offeror or offeree does not terminate an option contract—unless the offeror's personal performance is essential to the fulfillment of the contract.[9] For example, assume Vendrick executes an option to Carney entitling Carney to purchase Vendrick's hundred-acre ranch in Costa Rica. Carney pays $750 for the option, but before she can exercise it, Vendrick dies. Carney can still exercise the option against Vendrick's estate, since Vendrick is not required to perform the act of conveying the ranch to Carney personally.

Firm Offers Under the UCC, certain offers may be irrevocable even if no consideration is given. These are called **firm offers**.[10] If a merchant[11] makes a written, signed offer to buy or sell goods and states that the offer will be held open, the offer cannot be revoked regardless of the lack of consideration. The offer will remain open for the period of time specified in the offer or, if no time is specified, for a reasonable period; but the period of irrevocability without consideration cannot exceed three months. Note the various elements necessary for a firm offer:

1. The offer must be for the purchase or sale of goods.
2. The offer must be made by a merchant dealing in those goods.
3. The offer must be written and signed by the merchant.
4. The offer must indicate that it will be held open—for example, ''This offer will be held open for ten days.''

Detrimental Reliance Increasingly, courts are refusing to allow an offeror to revoke an offer when the offeree has changed position in justifiable reliance on the offer. In such cases, revocation is considered unjust to the offeree. Consider an example. Feinberg has rented commercial property from Pfeiffer for the past thirty-three years under

---

9. Restatement (Second) of Contracts, Section 37.
10. UCC 2-205.
11. Generally, under the UCC a *merchant* is a person who deals in goods of the kind involved in the transaction or otherwise by his or her occupation holds himself or herself out as having knowledge or skill peculiar to the practices or goods involved. See Chapter 18 and UCC 2-104(1).

a series of five-year leases. Under business conditions existing as their seventh lease nears its end, the rental property market is more favorable for tenants than landlords. Feinberg tells Pfeiffer that she is going to look at other, less expensive properties as possible sites for her business. Wanting Feinberg to remain a tenant, Pfeiffer promises to reduce the rent in their next lease. In reliance on the promise, Feinberg does not look at other sites but continues to occupy and do business on Pfeiffer's property. When they sit down to negotiate a new lease, Pfeiffer says he has changed his mind and will increase the rent. Can he effectively revoke his promise?

The argument is that he normally will not be able to do so because Feinberg has been relying on his promise to reduce the rent. Had the promise not been made, she would have relocated her business. This is a case of detrimental reliance on a promise, which therefore cannot be revoked. The situation is normally called **promissory estoppel.** To **estop** means to bar or impede or to preclude. Thus, promissory estoppel means that the promisor (the offeror) is barred or prevented from revoking the offer, in this case because the offeree has already changed her actions in reliance on the offer. We cover the doctrine of promissory estoppel again in Chapter 11.

Another situation causing detrimental reliance on the part of the offeree involves *partial performance* by the offeree in response to an offer looking toward formulation of a *unilateral* contract. The offer invites acceptance only by full performance; merely promising to perform does not constitute acceptance. Obviously, injustice can result if an offeree expends time and money in partial performance, and then the offeror revokes the offer before performance is complete. Consequently, many courts will not allow the offeror to revoke after the offeree has performed some substantial part of his or her duties.[12] In effect, partial performance renders the offer irrevocable, giving the original offeree reasonable time to complete performance. Of course, when performance is complete, a unilateral contract exists. per page 176

REJECTION OF THE OFFER BY THE OFFEREE

An offer may be rejected by the offeree, in which case the offer is terminated. Any subsequent at-

tempt by the offeree to accept will be construed as a new offer, giving the original offeror (now the offeree) the power of acceptance. A rejection is ordinarily accomplished by words or conduct evidencing an intent not to accept the offer. As in the case of revocation of the offer, rejection is effective only when actually received by the offeror or the offeror's agent.

Suppose you offer to sell Procter & Gamble twenty-five tons of linseed oil at 50 cents per gallon. Procter & Gamble could expressly reject your offer by writing or telephoning you—perhaps saying, "We are sufficiently stocked in linseed oil and do not need any more." Alternatively, the company could mail your offer back to you, evidencing an intent to reject the offer. Or it could offer to buy the oil at 48.3 cents per gallon, which would operate as a counteroffer (discussed below) and as a rejection of the original offer.

Merely inquiring about an offer does not constitute rejection. For example, a friend offers to buy your bicycle for $75. If you respond, "Is this your best offer?" or "Will you pay me $100 for it?" a reasonable person would conclude not that you had rejected the offer but that you had merely made an inquiry for further consideration of the offer. You can still accept and bind your friend to the $75 purchase price. When the offeree merely inquires as to the firmness of the offer, there is no reason to presume that he or she intends to reject it.

Some responses are borderline in nature. For example, if you respond to your friend's offer with, "The price seems low. I'll bet you can do better than that," it could be argued that you are inquiring about the offer or that you are rejecting it.

COUNTEROFFER BY THE OFFEREE

A rejection of the original offer and the simultaneous making of a new offer is called a **counteroffer.** Suppose Stewart offers to sell his home to Twardy for $70,000. Twardy responds, "Your price is too high. I'll offer to purchase your house for $65,000." Twardy's response is termed a counteroffer, since it terminates Stewart's offer to sell at $70,000 and creates a new offer by Twardy to purchase at $65,000. At common law, the **mirror image rule** requires the offeree's acceptance to match the offeror's offer exactly—to mirror the offer. Any material change in, or addition to, the terms of the original offer automatically terminates

---

12.   Restatement (Second) of Contracts, Section 25.

that offer and substitutes the counteroffer, which, of course, need not be accepted. The original offeror can, however, accept the terms of the counteroffer and create a valid contract.

Variance in terms between the offer and the offeree's acceptance, violating the mirror image rule, has caused considerable problems in commercial transactions. This is particularly true when, in the sale of goods, the seller and buyer exchange different standardized purchase forms in the process of offer and acceptance. Seldom do the terms of both purchase forms match exactly. This phenomenon has been called the "battle of the forms" because of the problem of whose form will prevail. The UCC addresses this issue by providing a series of rules to determine which form will prevail under specific circumstances. Generally, the UCC substantially alters the rules on acceptance for contracts for the sale of goods. Under the UCC, an acceptance may modify the terms of the offer and still be considered a definite acceptance (see Chapter 18).

It is possible for an offeree to make a new offer without intending to reject the original offer. In such a case, two offers exist, each capable of being accepted. To illustrate, suppose Frank offers to sell his bicycle for $100. Irene's response is, "I do not have $100 but will try to raise that sum. I do have $75 and will offer to purchase your bicycle for that price." Since the offeree did not reject the $100 offer, that offer remains effective. But the offeree did offer to purchase the bicycle for $75. Thus, two offers exist, and the first to be accepted binds the parties to a contract for that amount.

The following case illustrates the rule that, under general contract law, an acceptance must mirror the terms of the offer; if it does not, it will be considered a counteroffer.

BACKGROUND AND FACTS In October 1983, James Naylor agreed to be CEAG Electric Corporation's exclusive sales representative in upstate New York for commissions of up to 7 percent. The contract provided that it could be modified only by a writing signed by both parties and that it could be terminated by either party without cause on thirty days' written notice. In September 1984, Naylor had an opportunity to sell CEAG products to IBM Corporation. On September 7, CEAG wrote Naylor a letter stating that it would pay Naylor a minimum 2 percent commission on any IBM orders within his territory. The letter told Naylor to sign both copies of the letter and return one to CEAG. Instead, Naylor wrote to CEAG, demanding higher compensation and a long-term contract. CEAG notified Naylor in writing that it was canceling the October 1983 agreement. Naylor sued CEAG in a New York state court, alleging that the September correspondence constituted a contract under which he was owed commissions. The trial court held that Naylor's letter requesting higher compensation and a long-term contract was a counteroffer, not an acceptance, and therefore no contract or contractual modification was made. Naylor appealed.

DECISION AND RATIONALE The Supreme Court of New York, Appellate Division, affirmed the trial court's ruling. The appellate court agreed with the trial court's conclusion that CEAG's September letter was an offer or proposal to modify the October 1983 agreement and Naylor's September reply was a rejection and counteroffer. The appellate court pointed out that CEAG "made its intent quite clear" in its September letter that the exclusive means of acceptance was for Naylor to sign both copies "and this did not occur. The parties had explicitly stated in their October agreement that modifications could only be made in a writing signed by both parties." Instead, Naylor rejected CEAG's September offer to modify the October 1983 agreement and made a new offer, demanding higher compensation and a longer-term contract—a counteroffer. The court concluded that "without mutuality of assent, no contract could be formed as a matter of law."

Case 10.4

NAYLOR v. CEAG ELECTRIC CORP.

Supreme Court of New York, Appellate Division, Third Department, 1990.
158 A.D.2d 760,
551 N.Y.S.2d 349.

Termination by Operation of Law

The power in the offeree to transform the offer into a binding, legal obligation can be terminated by operation of the law through the following:

1. Lapse of time.
2. Destruction of the subject matter of the offer.
3. Death or incompetence of the offeror or the offeree.
4. Supervening illegality of the proposed contract.

LAPSE OF TIME   An offer terminates automatically when the period of time specified in the offer has passed. A definite termination date may be stated in the offer (''This offer is good until 5:00 P.M. on Monday, July 15''), or the offer may specify a period of time (a number of days, weeks, or months) during which the offer will be held open. For example, suppose Anna offers to sell her boat to Bob if he accepts *within twenty days*. Bob must accept within the twenty-day period or the offer will lapse (terminate). The period of time specified in an offer begins to run when the offer is actually received by the offeree, not when it is sent or drawn up, unless the offer specifies that the time period will begin on a stated date (for example, ''Offer to expire thirty days after date of this letter''). When the offer has been delayed, the period begins to run from the date the offeree would have received the offer, but only if the offeree knows or should know that the offer was delayed.[13] For example, if Anna used improper postage when mailing the offer to Bob, but Bob knew Anna used improper postage, the offer would lapse twenty days after the day Bob would ordinarily have received the offer had Anna used proper postage.

If no time for acceptance is specified in the offer, the offer terminates at the end of a *reasonable* period of time. A reasonable period is determined by the subject matter of the contract, business and market conditions, and other relevant circumstances. An offer to sell farm produce, for example, will terminate sooner than an offer to sell farm equipment because farm produce is perishable and subject to greater fluctuations in market value.

DESTRUCTION OF THE SUBJECT MATTER
An offer is automatically terminated if the specific subject matter of the offer is destroyed before the offer is accepted.[14] For example, if Watts offers to sell her race horse to Teagle but the horse dies before Teagle can accept, the offer is automatically terminated. Watts does not have to tell Teagle that the horse died for the offer to terminate.

DEATH OR INCOMPETENCE OF THE OFFEROR OR OFFEREE   An offeree's power of acceptance is terminated when the offeror or offeree dies or is deprived of legal capacity to enter into the proposed contract.[15] An offer is personal to both parties and cannot pass to the decedent's heirs, guardian, or estate. Furthermore, this rule applies whether or not the other party had notice of the death or incompetence. For example, on June 4, Manne offers to sell Clark a rowboat for $600, telling Clark that he, Manne, needs the answer by June 20. On June 10, Manne dies. On June 18, Clark informs the executor of Manne's estate that he accepts the offer. The executor can refuse to sell the rowboat because the death of the offeror has terminated the offer.

There is an exception to the rule that the death of either the offeror or the offeree before acceptance terminates an offer. The exception applies to *irrevocable offers*—offers that legally cannot be withdrawn by the offeror once made. As previously discussed, an *option contract* is an example of an irrevocable offer. Although a few disagree, most legal scholars believe that the exception also applies to *firm offers* (irrevocable under the UCC).

SUPERVENING ILLEGALITY OF THE PROPOSED CONTRACT   A statute or court decision that makes an offer illegal will automatically terminate the offer.[16] If Barker offers to loan Jackson $20,000 at an annual interest rate of 15 percent and a law is enacted prohibiting loans at interest rates higher than 14 percent before Jackson can accept, the offer is automatically terminated. (If, in this hypothetical case, the law had been passed after Jackson accepted the offer, a valid contract would have been formed, but the contract might have been unenforceable.)

13.   Restatement (Second) of Contracts, Section 49.

14.   Restatement (Second) of Contracts, Section 36.
15.   Restatement (Second) of Contracts, Section 48.
16.   Restatement (Second) of Contracts, Section 36.

◼ CONCEPT SUMMARY 10.1
Methods by Which an Offer Can Be Terminated

Methods of Termination	Basic Rules
By Acts of the Parties:	
1. Revocation	1. An offer can be revoked at any time before acceptance without liability unless the offer is irrevocable. 2. Option contracts, firm offers under UCC 2-205, and, in some circumstances, the promissory estoppel theory render offers irrevocable. 3. Except for public offers, revocation is not effective until *known* by the offeree or the offeree's authorized agent.
2. Rejection	1. Rejection of an offer is accomplished by words or actions that demonstrate a clear intent not to accept or consider the offer further. Inquiries about an offer do not constitute a rejection. 2. A rejection is not effective until *known* by the offeror or an authorized agent of the offeror.
3. Counteroffer	1. A counteroffer is a rejection of the original offer and the making of a new offer. Inquiries are not rejections. 2. Under UCC 2-207, a definite acceptance of an offer is not a counteroffer, even if the acceptance terms modify the terms of the offer.
By Operation of Law:	
1. Lapse of Time	1. If a time period for acceptance is stated in the offer, the offer ends at the stated time. 2. If no time period for acceptance is stated, the offer terminates at the end of a reasonable period.
2. Destruction	Destruction of the specific subject matter of the offer terminates the offer.
3. Death or Incompetence	Death or incompetence of either the offeror or offeree terminates an offer, unless the offer is irrevocable.
4. Illegality	Supervening illegality terminates an offer.

◼ Acceptance

Acceptance is a voluntary act (either words or conduct) by the offeree that shows assent (agreement) to the terms of an offer. The acceptance must be unequivocal and communicated to the offeror.

Who Can Accept?

Generally, a third person cannot interpose himself or herself as a substitute for the offeree and effectively accept the offer. After all, the identity of the offeree is as much a condition of a bargaining offer as any other term contained therein. Thus, except in certain special circumstances to be discussed, only the person to whom the offer is made can accept the offer and create a binding contract. For example, Jones makes an offer to Hanley. Hanley is not interested, but Hanley's friend, Smith, accepts the offer; no contract is formed.

EXCEPTIONS The special circumstances in which a third party can accept an offer in place of the offeree are as follows:

1. If the offer is an option contract, the right to exercise the option is generally considered a contract right. As such, it is assignable or transferable to third persons (with exceptions—see Chapter 15).

2. If the offeree is an agent for a principal, the acceptance may be made by the principal, and a contract will be formed between the principal and the offeror. (An *agent* is one who acts on behalf of, and in the place of, another person called the *principal* —see Chapters 35 and 36.)

WHEN THE OFFER IS MADE TO TWO OR MORE PERSONS   If an offer is made to two or more persons, it must be accepted by all of them. If individual offers are made to two or more persons individually, then contracts are created only with those persons who accept the offer.

Unequivocal Acceptance

To accept an offer, an offeree must know of the offer, intend to accept it, and accept it *unequivocally.* Unequivocal acceptance is required by the *mirror image rule* previously discussed. If the acceptance is subject to new conditions, or if the terms of the acceptance materially change the original offer, the acceptance may be considered a counteroffer that implicitly rejects the original offer. An acceptance may be unequivocal even though the offeree expresses dissatisfaction with the contract. For example, "I accept the goods, but I wish I could have gotten a better price" will operate as an effective acceptance. So, too, will "I accept, but can you shave the price?" In contrast, the statement "I accept the goods, but only if I can pay on ninety days' credit" is not an unequivocal acceptance and normally operates as a counteroffer, rejecting the original offer.

Certain conditions, when added to an acceptance, do not qualify the acceptance sufficiently to make it a rejection of the offer. Suppose that Childs offers to sell a sixty-five-acre cotton farm to Sharif. Sharif replies, "I accept your offer to sell the farm, provided that you are the owner." This condition does not make the acceptance equivocal. The condition that a seller own the property is normally implied in every offer for the sale of land, so the condition does not add any new or different terms to the offer.

Or suppose that in response to an offer to sell a motorcycle, the offeree replies, "I accept; please send written contract." The offeree has requested a written contract but has not made it a condition for acceptance. Therefore, the acceptance is effective without the written contract. If, however, the offeree replies "I accept if you send a written con-

tract," the acceptance is expressly conditioned on the request for a writing, and the statement is not an acceptance but a counteroffer. (Notice how important *each* word is!) As noted above, under the UCC, an acceptance is still valid even if terms are added. The additional terms are simply treated as proposals for additions to the contract.[17]

Silence as Acceptance

Ordinarily, silence cannot constitute acceptance, even if the offeror states, "By your silence and inaction you will be deemed to have accepted this offer." This general rule applies because an offeree should not be obligated to act affirmatively to reject an offer when no consideration has passed to the offeree to impose such a liability.

On the other hand, silence can operate as an acceptance when an offeree takes the benefit of offered services even though he or she had an opportunity to reject them and knew that they were offered with the expectation of compensation. Suppose that Jeff gives Holmes's daughter several guitar lessons after school while Holmes is working, intending to charge Holmes for the lessons. Holmes never asked for the lessons but is aware of them and silently lets them continue, knowing that Jeff expects to be paid. Here, Holmes's silence constitutes an acceptance, and a contract is created. Holmes is bound to pay a reasonable value for the lessons. This rule applies only to services and goods from which the offeree has received a benefit.

Silence can also operate as acceptance when the parties have had prior dealings in which the offeree has led the offeror reasonably to understand that the offeree will accept all offers unless the offeree sends notice to the contrary. For example, Brodsky, a sales agent, has previously received shipments of goods from Morales and paid without notifying Morales of his acceptance. Brodsky sells the goods and simply sends Morales a check. Only if the goods are defective does he notify Morales. The last shipment has been neither paid for nor rejected. Four months have passed. Brodsky is bound on a contract and must pay Morales for this last shipment of goods.[18]

---

17. Restatement (Second) of Contracts, Sections 84, 246, and 247. The Restatement uses the term *promise* rather than *waiver.*

18. Restatement (Second) of Contracts, Section 72.

In the past, at common law, silence could constitute acceptance in the following situation: Books or magazines are sent to an individual through the mails. The individual did not order the books or magazines and is under no duty to reship them to the seller. If, however, the individual uses the books or magazines, acceptance is established, and he or she must pay reasonable value for them. Note that silence does not constitute an acceptance unless the receiver exercises control over the goods. This common law rule of contract law has been changed by statute. The Postal Reorganization Act of 1970 provides that *unsolicited* merchandise sent by U.S. mail may be retained, used, discarded, or disposed of in any manner deemed appropriate, without the individual incurring any obligation to the sender.[19] In addition, the mailing of unordered merchandise (except for free samples) constitutes an unfair trade practice and is not permitted. (Exceptions may include mailings by certain charitable agencies.)

Acceptance by silence may be provided for by agreement. This frequently occurs, for example, with such organizations as the Book-of-the-Month Club. Once an individual has agreed that his or her failure to respond will constitute acceptance, merchandise is shipped periodically (usually every month) unless the customer sends a card indicating that he or she does not want the merchandise. Failure to reject the offered merchandise in this manner operates as acceptance by silence.

Communication of Acceptance

Whether the offeror must be notified of the acceptance depends on the nature of the contract. In a unilateral contract, no notification or communication is generally necessary. Since a unilateral contract calls for the performance of some act, acceptance is not complete until the act has been substantially performed. Therefore, notice of acceptance is usually unnecessary. To illustrate: Beta offers to pay Gamma $150 to paint Beta's garage. Gamma can accept only by painting the garage. Once the garage is completely painted (and hence the acceptance is complete), notification of the acceptance is superfluous. Exceptions do exist. When the offeror requests notice of acceptance or has no adequate means of determining whether the requested act has been performed, or when the law

requires such notice of acceptance, then notice is necessary.[20]

In a bilateral contract, *communication* of acceptance is necessary because acceptance is in the form of a promise (not performance), and the contract is formed when the promise is made (rather than when the act is performed). The offeree must use reasonable efforts to communicate the acceptance to the offeror. It is possible for a bilateral contract to exist when an offer is accepted by undertaking performance. The beginning of performance by the offeree operates as an implied promise. When an offer is accepted by performance, notification to the offeror is needed to trigger the offeror's duty if the offeror would not normally be aware of the beginning of performance. Under those circumstances, however, notification of acceptance is not necessary if the offer dispenses with the requirement. In addition, if the offer can be accepted by silence, no communication or notification is necessary.

Under the UCC, an order or other offer to buy goods for prompt shipment may be treated as an offer contemplating either a bilateral or a unilateral contract and may be accepted by either a promise to ship or actual shipment.[21] Consider an example. Peters receives a telegram that he is to ship certain goods to Johnson. The UCC provides that Peters can accept by either promptly shipping the goods or sending a telegram to Johnson saying that he is going to ship the goods. (If the shipment will take a considerable amount of time, Peters would be wise to telegraph Johnson that the goods are in transit.)

Mode and Timeliness of Acceptance in Bilateral Contracts

The general rule is that an acceptance is timely if it is made before the offer is terminated. Problems arise, however, when the parties involved are not dealing face to face. In such cases, the offeree may use an authorized mode of communication. Acceptance takes effect, thus completing formation of the contract, at the time that communication is sent by whatever mode is expressly or impliedly authorized by the offeror. This is the so-called acceptance-upon-dispatch rule **(mailbox rule),** which

---

19.   39 U.S.C. Section 3009.

20.   UCC 2-206(2).
21.   UCC 2-206(1)(b).

the majority of courts uphold. What becomes an issue is the *authorized* means of communicating the acceptance. Authorized means can be either expressly stated in the offer or impliedly authorized by facts or by law. In any case, the acceptance becomes effective at the time that it is sent by an authorized means of communication, regardless of whether the offeror receives that communication.

EXPRESS MEANS OF ACCEPTANCE   When an offeror specifies an exclusive means by which acceptance should be sent (for example, first-class mail or fax), *express authorization* is said to exist, and the contract is not formed unless the offeree uses that specified means of acceptance. Moreover, both offeror and offeree are bound in contract the moment such means of acceptance are employed. If telegraph is expressly authorized as the means for acceptance, a contract is established as soon as the offeree gives his or her message to Western Union. Even if Western Union for some reason fails to deliver the message, the contract still exists.

It is important to remember that the offeror is the master of his or her offer and can fashion the terms of the offer to preclude as many pitfalls as necessary. For example, the offeror can specifically condition his or her offer on the receipt of an acceptance. In this case, the offer might be worded as follows: ''Acceptance is not binding unless received by the offeror in her office by 5:00 P.M. on May 1.'' When acceptance is conditioned on its receipt by the offeror, it is immaterial how the offeree sends the acceptance, as the acceptance is effective only if it is received before the offer expires.

IMPLIED MEANS OF ACCEPTANCE   When the offeror does not specify expressly that the offeree is to accept by a certain means, or that the acceptance will be effective only when received, the common law and statutes recognize what are called *implied authorized means of acceptance.* In the absence of expressly authorized means, three implied authorized means have been designated:

1.   The choice by the offeror of a particular means to make the offer implies that the offeree is authorized to use the *same* or a *faster* means for acceptance.

2.   When two parties are at a distance, *mailing* is impliedly authorized.[22]

3.   Under the Restatement (Second) of Contracts and the UCC, acceptance of an offer can be made by any medium that is reasonable under the circumstances.[23] Under the Restatement, a medium is reasonable if it is one used by the offeror or one customarily used in similar transactions, unless the offeree knows of circumstances that would argue against the reasonableness of the medium (for example, the need for speed because of rapid price changes).[24]

An acceptance sent by means not expressly or impliedly authorized is often not effective until it is received by the offeror. If an acceptance is timely sent and timely received, however, despite the means by which it is sent, it is considered to have been effective on its dispatch.[25]

To illustrate authorized means of acceptance, consider the following examples:

1.   On January 1, Jones makes an offer to sell Smith his motorcycle for $450, stipulating that Smith should send acceptance by telegram. On January 2, Jones mails Smith a letter of revocation. On January 3, Smith delivers to Western Union his telegram of acceptance. Smith receives Jones's letter of revocation at noon on January 4. The telegram of acceptance is incorrectly sent and is not received by Jones until January 5. Are Jones and Smith bound in contract? The answer is yes. Telegram was the expressly stated means of acceptance in the offer; therefore, acceptance is effective the moment Smith delivers his acceptance to Western Union on January 3. A revocation is not effective until it is received by the offeree, in this case on January 4, subsequent to the acceptance; so the revocation is ineffective.

2.   On January 1, Jones by telegram offers to sell Smith his motorcycle for $450. The offer contains no expressly stated means for Smith to make his acceptance. The telegram is received by Smith the

22.   *Adams v. Lindsell,* 106 Eng.Rep. 250 (K.B. 1818); Restatement (Second) of Contracts, Section 65, Comment c.
23.   Restatement (Second) of Contracts, Section 30; UCC 2-206(1)(a).
24.   Restatement (Second) of Contracts, Section 65.
25.   Restatement (Second) of Contracts, Section 67.

same day it is sent. On January 2, Smith delivers his acceptance to Western Union. The telegram is lost and is never received by Jones. Jones sells the motorcycle to Green on January 20, believing that Smith was not interested in his offer. Can Smith hold Jones liable for breach of contract? The answer is yes. Although the offer did not expressly state a means for Smith's acceptance, telegraph was impliedly authorized. The court here could use either the common law ''same or faster means''

rule of implied authorization or the UCC ''reasonable medium'' rule dealing with the sale of goods. Either way, Smith formed a contract with Jones on January 2.

The following case illustrates the principle that, when the means of acceptance is not expressly authorized by the offeror, the same or a *faster* means is impliedly the authorized means of acceptance.

BACKGROUND AND FACTS On September 5, 1987, Ralph Defeo and others offered to purchase a farm owned by Amfarms Associates. Amfarms made a counteroffer in which certain conditions in the Defeo offer were deleted. A month later, Defeo and the others submitted another offer including the previously deleted conditions. On October 9, Amfarms, using the same form, counteroffered by again deleting the conditions. Amfarms added that the offer would be valid only until 5 P.M., October 17. Amfarms's attorney sent the offer to Defeo's attorney by Federal Express. On October 16, Defeo and the others sent their acceptance to Amfarms's October 9 offer by certified mail to Amfarms's real estate broker. Amfarms received the acceptance on October 19. On October 16, however, Amfarms had accepted an offer from another party. Defeo and the others sued in a New York state court, claiming that their acceptance on October 16 was effective on the day it was sent. The trial court dismissed the complaint, holding that because the offer had been transmitted by Federal Express, the acceptance sent by certified mail was ineffective. Defeo and the others appealed.

DECISION AND RATIONALE The Supreme Court of New York, Appellate Division, affirmed the trial court's decision. The acceptance was not effective on dispatch because it was not transmitted by the impliedly authorized means of acceptance. The appellate court explained that ''[t]he reasonableness of the manner in which an offer is accepted must be viewed under the circumstances in which the offer had been made, with speed and reliability being relevant factors.'' Federal Express overnight delivery is faster than certified mail, and Amfarms had emphasized time. The receipt of the acceptance two days after the acceptance deadline ''was not operative.''

COMMENTS Had the contract involved a sale of goods, the result might have been different. Under UCC 2–206(1)(a), acceptance sent by any medium reasonable under the circumstances is presumed to be impliedly authorized. Thus, even a slower means of communication could be reasonable under the circumstances.

Case 10.5

DEFEO v. AMFARMS ASSOCIATES

Supreme Court of New York, Appellate Division, Third Department, 1990.
161 A.D.2d 904,
557 N.Y.S.2d 469.

EXCEPTIONS There are three basic exceptions to the rule that a contract is formed when acceptance is sent by authorized means:

1. If the acceptance is not properly dispatched by the offeree, in most states it will not be effective

until it is received by the offeror.[26] For example, if mail is the authorized means for acceptance, the offeree's letter must be properly addressed and have the correct postage. (There is an exception to

---

26. Restatement (Second) of Contracts, Section 66.

this exception. If acceptance is timely sent and timely received, despite carelessness in sending it, it is considered to have been effective on dispatch.[27])

2. As mentioned above, the offeror can stipulate in the offer that an acceptance will not be effective until it is received by the offeror.

3. Sometimes an offeree sends a rejection first, then later changes his or her mind and sends an

acceptance. Obviously, this chain of events could cause confusion and even detriment to the offeror, depending on whether the rejection or the acceptance arrived first. Because of this, the law cancels the rule of acceptance upon dispatch in such situations, and the *first* communication to be received by the offeror determines whether a contract is formed. If the rejection is received first, there is no contract.[28]

---

27.   Restatement (Second) of Contracts, Section 67.

28.   Restatement (Second) of Contracts, Section 40.

■ CONCEPT SUMMARY 10.2   Effective Time of Acceptance

Acceptance	Time Effective
1. By Authorized Means of Communication	Effective when communication is given to medium of transmission expressly or impliedly authorized by offeror (mailbox rule). *Exceptions:* 1. If acceptance is not properly dispatched. 2. If offeror specifically conditioned offer on receipt of acceptance.
2. By Unauthorized Means of Communication	Effective upon receipt of acceptance by offeror (if timely received, it is considered to have been effective on dispatch).
3. Acceptance after Rejection	Whichever communication is received first is given effect.
4. Revocation and Acceptance	A revocation by the offeror will be effective if received by the offeree prior to the offeree's acceptance.

■ Terms and Concepts

acceptance 195
agreement 184
counteroffer 192
estop 192
firm offer 191

irrevocable offer 191
mailbox rule 197
mirror image rule 192
mutual assent 184

offer 185
option contract 191
promissory estoppel 192
revocation 190

■ For Review

1. To have an agreement, each party must manifest mutual assent to the same bargain. What are the basic elements of "mutual assent"?

2. What basic elements are necessary for an effective offer?

3. What elements are necessary for an effective acceptance?

4. Rondi is a student. In her senior year, with graduation approaching, Rondi begins interviewing prospective employers, including Bau Engineering Corp. Bau offers Rondi

a job at a salary that is lower than Rondi would like. Bau says that the offer will remain open for one month. Three weeks later, Bau informs Rondi that the position is no longer available. Can Bau do this?

5. In the previous problem, instead of informing Rondi that the position is no longer available, Bau asks Rondi whether she will accept the job. Rondi says, "I am still thinking about it, but I can give you an answer immediately, if you'll increase the salary right now." Is Rondi's response a rejection of the job?

■ Questions and Case Problems

10-1. As a bank officer, you have been given the responsibility of purchasing word processing equipment. On May 6, the ABC Manufacturing Corp. sends you a letter offering to sell your bank some word processing equipment at a price of $10,000, to be shipped via LM Truck Lines. The letter states that the offer is to remain open until May 20. On May 12, you write ABC a letter stating, "Offer appears a little high; I am sure you can do better. I'll need presidential approval for the $10,000 offer. I have authority to purchase word processing equipment for $8,500 and will buy your products at that price." ABC receives this letter on May 16. On May 15, the president of your bank approves the $10,000 purchase. On the same date, ABC sends you a letter revoking its offer. The letter of revocation is received at your bank at 11:00 A.M. on May 19. On May 19 at 11:15 A.M. you send ABC the following telegram: "Accept your offer for $10,000." Because of a delay by the telegraph company, this message is not delivered until May 21.

(a) Discuss the legal effect of ABC's revocation sent on May 15.

(b) Discuss fully the legal effect of your response sent on May 12.

(c) Discuss whether your bank has a contract in light of the fact that the telegram was not delivered until May 21.

10-2. Ball writes Sullivan and inquires how much Sullivan is asking for a specific forty-acre tract of land Sullivan owns. In a letter received by Ball, Sullivan states, "I will not take less than $60,000 for the forty-acre tract as specified." Ball immediately sends Sullivan a telegram stating, "I accept your offer for $60,000." Discuss whether Ball can hold Sullivan to a contract for sale of the land.

10-3. Smith, operating a sole proprietorship, has a large piece of used farm equipment for sale. He offers to sell the equipment to Barry for $10,000. Discuss the legal effect of the following events on the offer.

(a) Smith dies prior to Barry's acceptance, and at the time Barry accepts, she is unaware of Smith's death.

(b) The night before Barry accepts, fire destroys the equipment.

(c) Barry pays $100 for a thirty-day option to purchase the equipment. During this period Smith dies, and later Barry accepts the offer, knowing of Smith's death.

(d) Barry pays $100 for a thirty-day option to purchase the equipment. During this period Barry dies, and Barry's estate accepts Smith's offer within the stipulated time period.

10-4. Perez sees an advertisement in the newspaper that the ABC Corp. has for sale a two-volume set of books, *How to Make Repairs around the House,* for $22.95. All Perez has to do is send in a card requesting delivery of the books for a thirty-day trial period of examination. If he does not ship the books back within thirty days of delivery, ABC will bill him for $22.95. Discuss whether or not Perez and ABC have a contract under either of the following circumstances.

(a) Perez sends in the card and receives the books in the U.S. mail. He uses the books to make repairs and fails to return them within thirty days.

(b) Perez does not send in the card, but ABC sends him the books anyway through the U.S. mail. Perez uses the books and fails to return them within thirty days.

10-5. A plaintiff is attempting to recover death benefits under a life insurance policy. The policy contained a provision that allowed the policyowner to terminate the policy and receive its so-called cash value. All that the company required was a written request received at the home office. The owner of the policy died after having sent a letter requesting the cash value of the policy (which was much less than the face value). The letter was received *after* the policyowner died. The representative of the deceased owner contended that the estate was entitled to the death benefits of the life insurance policy. What was the result? [*Franklin Life Insurance Co. v. Winney,* 469 S.W.2d 21 (Tex.Civ.App. 1971)]

10-6. John H. Surratt was one of John Wilkes Booth's alleged accomplices in the murder of President Lincoln. On April 20, 1865, the secretary of war issued and caused to be published in newspapers the following proclamation: "$25,000 reward for the apprehension of John H. Surratt and liberal rewards for any information that leads to the arrest of John H. Surratt." On November 24, 1865, President Johnson revoked the reward and published the revocation in the newspapers. Henry B. St. Marie learned of the reward but left for Rome prior to its revocation. In Rome, St. Marie discovered Surratt's whereabouts; and in April of 1866, unaware that the reward had been revoked, he reported this information to U.S. officials. Pursuant to receiving this information, the officials were able to arrest Surratt. Should St. Marie have received the reward? If so, was he entitled to the full $25,000? [*Shuey v. United States,* 92 U.S. (2 Otto) 73, 23 L.Ed. 697 (1875)]

10-7. Central Properties entered into a contract with Robbinson and Westside, a real estate development company, whereby Central Properties purchased sixty acres of land. The contract included a "right of first refusal" to purchase the water and sewage system on the remaining property of Westside. Westside wanted to sell the sewage system and over the course of three months exchanged letters with Central asking whether it wished to exercise its "right." Central Properties never affirmatively accepted in any of its responses but requested different terms, price, and so on. Central now wishes to hold Westside to a contract for the system. Westside states no contract was formed. Discuss who is right. [*Central Properties, Inc. v. Robbinson,* 450 So.2d 277 (Fla.App. 1st Dist. 1984)]

10-8. Treece, a vice-president of Vend-A-Win, Inc., was testifying before the Washington State

Gambling Commission concerning an application his firm had made for a temporary license to distribute punchboards (gambling devices). The Gambling Commission was conducting an investigation into gambling practices, and Treece's testimony was given during a televised hearing. Treece made the following statement at the hearing: "I'll pay $100,000 to anyone to find a crooked board. If they find it, I'll pay it." The audience laughed, and Treece thought no more about the offer until he received a telephone call from Barnes. Barnes had watched Treece's television appearance and later read about Treece's statement in a newspaper. Barnes asked Treece if Treece had been serious when he made the statement, and Treece affirmed that he had been serious. Barnes then brought a crooked board into Vend-A-Win's offices and delivered another crooked board to the Gambling Commission. When Vend-A-Win and Treece refused to pay Barnes $100,000, Barnes sued them for the promised amount, claiming that Treece had made an offer for a unilateral contract. What will the court decide? Explain. [*Barnes v. Treece,* 15 Wash.App. 437, 549 P.2d 1152 (1976)]

10-9. Deeco, Inc., owned a campground and had made a three-year lease with 3-M Co. in 1976 for advertising Deeco's campsite on a billboard. The lease was renewed in 1979. The billboard was destroyed by a hurricane shortly thereafter, and 3-M wanted to form another contract because the wrong form had been used in 1976. The new 1980 form, which stated that it would not be a binding contract until signed by 3-M, was signed by Deeco but never signed by 3-M, although the 3-M representative told Deeco's president that 3-M would have the new billboard up in sixty days. The billboard was never erected. 3-M did, however, send Deeco monthly bills from January until April 1981 for advertising services on the nonexistent billboard, and delinquent payment notices were also sent to Deeco. Deeco sued for breach of contract. 3-M held that no contract existed because it had not signed (accepted) the contract offered by Deeco in 1980. Deeco argued that 3-M had indicated acceptance by its subsequent conduct—especially by the monthly bills sent by 3-M to Deeco. Discuss fully whether there is a contract between Deeco and 3-M. [*Deeco, Inc. v. 3-M Co.,* 435 So.2d 1260 (Ala. 1983)]

10-10. James sent invitations to a number of potential buyers to submit bids for some timber he wanted to sell. Two bids were received as a result, the highest one being that submitted by Eames. James changed his mind about selling the timber, however, and did not accept Eames's bid. Eames claimed that a contract for sale existed and sued James for breach. Did a contract exist? Discuss. [*Eames v. James,* 452 So.2d 384 (La.App., 3d Cir. 1984)]

10-11. On July 31, 1966, Lee Calan Imports (the defendant) advertised a 1964 Volvo Station Wagon for sale in the Chicago *Sun Times.* The defendant had instructed the newspaper to advertise the price of the automobile at $1,795. Through an error of the newspaper, however, and without fault on the part of the defendant, the newspaper inserted a price of $1,095 for the automobile

in the advertisement. Christopher O'Brien (the plaintiff) visited the defendant's place of business, examined the automobile, and stated that he wished to purchase it for $1,095. One of the defendant's sales agents at first agreed, but then refused to sell the car for the erroneous price listed in the advertisement. O'Brien sued Lee Calan Imports for breach of contract, claiming the ad constituted an offer that had been accepted by O'Brien. O'Brien died before the trial, and his administrator (O'Keefe) continued the suit. Discuss whether there is a contract. [*O'Keefe v. Lee Calan Imports, Inc.,* 128 Ill.App.2d 410, 262 N.E.2d 758 (1970)]

10-12. In August 1984, James and Barbara Gibbs submitted an offer for $180,000 to American Savings & Loan Association to purchase a house. The Gibbses submitted another offer on March 27, 1985, after learning from an American Savings employee, Dorothy Folkman, that their original offer had been lost. On the morning of June 6, 1985, the Gibbses received a counteroffer from American Savings containing several additional terms and conditions, but nothing was mentioned about the purchase price. Barbara Gibbs claimed that she and her husband immediately signed the counteroffer as an acceptance and at 10 A.M. on that same day handed an envelope containing the signed counteroffer to the mail clerk (not a U.S. Postal employee) at her office, with instructions to mail it for her. An hour later, at 11 A.M., Barbara had a telephone conversation with Dorothy Folkman who said that the counteroffer was in error, since American Savings had intended to increase the sales price to $198,000. Folkman said that because of this error the counteroffer was revoked. The Gibbses insisted that they had accepted the counteroffer before it was revoked. The Gibbses contended that they had placed the acceptance in the "course of transmission" at 10 A.M. on June 6 when Barbara handed the letter to the mail clerk in her office. Does handing the counteroffer to the mail clerk in her office constitute dispatch by mail in this case? Discuss. [*Gibbs v. American Savings & Loan Association,* 217 Cal.App.3d 1372, 266 Cal.Rptr. 517 (1990)]

10-13. Case Briefing Assignment

Examine Case A.5 [Heinzel v. Backstrom, *310 Or. 89, 794 P.2d 775 (1990)*] *in Appendix A. The case has been excerpted there in great detail. Review and then brief the case, making sure that you include answers for the following questions in your brief.*

1. How did the trial court, the court of appeals, and the Supreme Court of Oregon, respectively, view the document signed by the parties on September 4, 1986?

2. Why did the court of appeals hold that specific performance should be granted?

3. How did the decision of Supreme Court of Oregon differ from that of the court of appeals?

4. Why was it significant in this case that Heinzel, and not Backstrom, had drafted the September 4 document? How did this affect the outcome of the case?

Chapter 11

Consideration

The fact that a promise has been made does not mean the promise can or will be enforced. Under Roman law, a promise was not enforceable without some sort of *causa*—that is, a reason for making the promise that was also deemed to be a sufficient reason for enforcing it. Since the beginning of the common law tradition in England, good reasons for enforcing informal[1] promises have been held to include something given as an agreed exchange, a benefit that the promisor received, and a detriment that the promisee incurred. Over time, these reasons came to be referred to legally as "consideration."

Thus, for centuries, it has been said that no informal promise is enforceable without consideration. **Consideration** may be defined as the *value* given in return for a promise. In other words, consideration is something that is exchanged for something else. A contract cannot be formed without sufficient consideration.

Often, consideration is broken into two elements: (1) the value of whatever is exchanged for the promise must be *legally* sufficient, and (2) there must be a *bargained-for* exchange. The something of "legally sufficient value" that is bargained for may consist of goods, money, performance, or a *return promise*. If it consists of *performance*, that performance may consist of the following:

1. An act (other than a promise).
2. A forbearance (refraining from doing something that one has a legal right to do).
3. The creation, modification, or destruction of a legal relation.[2]

For example, Earl says to his son, "Upon completion of your mowing my yard, I promise to pay you $25." Earl's son mows the yard. The act of mowing the yard is the consideration that creates the contractual obligation of Earl to pay his son $25. Suppose, however, that Earl says to his son, "In

[handwritten margin note: Consideration — must be Bargained For]

---

1. An example of a *formal* contract, binding because of its form alone, is the contract under seal. It has been almost entirely abolished under such provisions as UCC 2-203.
2. Restatement (Second) of Contracts, Section 71.

consideration of the fact that you are not as wealthy as your brothers, I will pay you $500.'' This promise is not enforceable because Earl's son has not given any consideration for the $500 promised.[3] Earl has simply stated his *motive* for giving his son a gift. The fact that the word *consideration* is used does not, alone, mean that consideration has been given.

In the preceding example, Earl was not bargaining for consideration. Performance or a return promise is bargained for if the promisor seeks it in exchange for his or her promise and the promisee gives it in exchange for that promise. It is not enough that the promise induces the conduct of the promisee or that the conduct of the promisee induces the making of the promise. They must induce each other, or the bargained-for exchange element does not exist.

■ Legal Sufficiency of Consideration

To create a binding contract, consideration must be legally sufficient. To be *legally sufficient,* consideration for a promise must be either legally *detrimental to the promisee*—the one receiving the promise—or legally *beneficial to the promisor*—

---

3. *Fink v. Cox,* 18 Johns. 145, 9 Am.Dec. 191 (N.Y.1820).

the one making the promise. Legal detriment occurs when one does or promises to do something that one had no prior legal duty to do. It also includes a forbearance, a refraining or promising to refrain from doing something that one has a legal right to do. Conversely, legal benefit is obtaining something that there was no prior legal right to obtain. *Legal* detriment or benefit is not synonymous with *actual* (economic) detriment or benefit. In most cases, the promisor's legal benefit is the same as the promisee's legal detriment. The existence of *either* a legal detriment to the promisee *or* a legal benefit to the promisor, however, constitutes legally sufficient consideration.

Suppose that Myers owns the right to use the name "The Brickhouse Restaurant." Bernard offers Myers $5,000 to stop using the name for her restaurant. Myers agrees. The consideration flowing from Myers to Bernard is a promise to refrain from doing something that Myers is legally entitled to do—that is, to use the name "The Brickhouse Restaurant" for her restaurant. The consideration flowing from Bernard to Myers is the promise to pay a sum of money that need not otherwise be paid.

In the following case, one of the classics of contract law, the court found that refraining from certain behavior at the request of another was sufficient consideration to support a promise to pay a sum of money.

Case 11.1

HAMER v. SIDWAY

Court of Appeals of New York, Second Division, 1891. 124 N.Y. 538, 27 N.E. 256.

BACKGROUND AND FACTS   William E. Story, Sr., was the uncle of William E. Story II. Story, Sr., promised to pay his nephew $5,000 if he would refrain from drinking, using tobacco, swearing, and playing cards or billiards for money until he became twenty-one. The nephew agreed and performed his part of the bargain. His uncle said, "[Y]ou shall have five thousand dollars, as I promised you. I had the money in the bank the day you was twenty-one years old that I intend for you, and you shall have the money certain." The nephew consented that the money should remain with his uncle accruing interest. The uncle died about twelve years later without having paid his nephew anything. Sidway, the executor of the uncle's estate, did not want to pay the $5,000 (with interest) to Hamer, a third party to whom the nephew had transferred his rights in the money; Sidway claimed there had been no valid consideration for the promise. Hamer sued Sidway in a New York state court. After a judgment for Hamer, Sidway appealed.

DECISION AND RATIONALE   The Court of Appeals of New York upheld the trial court's judgment for Hamer. The court ruled that the nephew had provided legally sufficient consideration by refraining from smoking, drinking, swearing, and playing cards or billiards for money until he became twenty-one and was therefore entitled to the money. Sidway argued that the nephew had suffered no detriment, because what he had done was in his own best interest. The court pointed out that "[i]n general a waiver of any legal right at the request of another party is a sufficient consideration for a promise." In this case, the court noted, "[T]he promisee used tobacco, occasionally drank liquor, and he had a legal right to do so. That right he abandoned for a period of years upon the strength of the promise of the testator that for such forbearance he would give him $5,000 * * *. [I]t is of no moment whether such performance actually proved a benefit to the promisor."

COMMENTS *The Hamer v. Sidway* case is a good illustration of the distinction between benefits to the promisor and detriment to the promisee. Here the court did not inquire as to whether a benefit had flowed to the promisor but required only that the promisee had suffered a legally sufficient detriment.

■ Adequacy of Consideration

Adequacy of consideration refers to the fairness of the bargain. On the surface, when the values of the items that are exchanged are unequal, fairness would appear to be an issue. If Bryant and Kowalewski make an agreement by which Bryant is to pay $100 for Kowalewski's car (which has a market value of $1,000), is the agreement supported by consideration? There is no question that $100 is legal value and that Kowalewski is giving up her legal title to the car. Thus, it appears that the requirements of legally sufficient consideration and bargained-for exchange have been met. The consideration is far from adequate, however, because Kowalewski does not appear to be getting a fair bargain. Does this unfairness negate the bargain?

In general, a court of law will not question the adequacy of consideration if the consideration is legally sufficient. Under the doctrine of freedom of contract, parties are normally free to bargain as they wish. If people could sue merely because they had entered into an unwise contract, the courts would be overloaded with frivolous suits. In extreme cases, a court of law may consider the adequacy of consideration in terms of its amount or worth, because inadequate consideration may indicate fraud, duress, undue influence, or a lack of bargained-for exchange. It may also reflect a party's incompetence (for example, an individual might have been too intoxicated, insane, or simply too young to make a contract). Suppose Lansky

has a house worth $100,000, and he sells it for $50,000. A $50,000 sale could indicate that the buyer unduly pressured Lansky into selling or that Lansky was defrauded into selling the house at far below market value.

In an equity suit, courts will more likely question the adequacy of consideration. (Remember from Chapter 1 that actions at law allow for remedies that consist of some form of compensation. Actions in equity allow for remedies that involve specific performance, injunction, or rescission.) In an equity suit, it must be shown that the transaction was not **unconscionable**[4]—that is, generally speaking, so one-sided under the circumstances as to be unfair—and that consideration was exchanged.

As a general principle of contract law, the courts will not ordinarily attempt to evaluate the adequacy of the consideration in an agreed-upon exchange, unless the consideration is so grossly inadequate as to "shock the conscience" of the court.

■ Preexisting Duty Rule

Under most circumstances, a promise to do what one already has a legal duty to do is not legally sufficient consideration, because no legal detriment or benefit has been incurred or received.[5] For ex-

---

4. Pronounced un-*kon*-shun-uh-bul.
5. *Foakes v. Beer,* 9 App.Cas. 605 (1884).

ample, if the only thing bargained for is to refrain from committing a crime or a tort against the promisor, there is no consideration. Suppose Butte often fires his rifle at squirrels in Helena's backyard in violation of a city ordinance. Helena offers to pay Butte $50 if Butte will not shoot at the squirrels for a month. Helena's promise is not supported by consideration because Butte has no legal right to do what he has been doing. Similarly, a sheriff cannot collect a reward for giving information leading to the capture of a criminal if the criminal's capture is one of the sheriff's official duties.

The preexisting duty may also arise out of a previous contract. For example, assume that Healey agrees to hire Brewster for one year at $350 per week. Brewster begins working. After two months, Healey agrees orally to increase the wages to $400 per week. Healey's promise falls under the preexisting duty rule and is generally held to be unenforceable unless the promise is supported by legally sufficient consideration. Brewster was under a preexisting contractual duty to work for one year, and the performance of that duty cannot serve as consideration for the wage increase.

The harshness of the preexisting duty rule is evident. In the last two examples above, the sheriff is denied a reward that anyone else could have received, and Brewster, the employee, can be denied his pay raise. Therefore, the courts are alert to finding any legal detriment or benefit that may exist, no matter how small or insignificant it may be, so that the promise will be enforceable. Hence, if Brewster was required to perform any extra duties, the promise modifying his employment contract normally would be enforceable.[6]

The law recognizes the following basic exceptions to the preexisting duty rule:

1. Rescission and new contract.
2. Sale of goods—modification of contract without consideration.
3. Unforeseen difficulties.

Rescission and New Contract

The law recognizes that two parties can mutually agree to rescind (nullify) their contract, at least to the extent that it is executory (not yet performed).

For example, suppose Jerry contracts with Anna to purchase Anna's watch for $100. Later Jerry tells Anna that he would prefer not to purchase the watch. As it happens, Anna no longer desires to sell it, so they call off the deal. This is called **rescission,**[7] defined as the unmaking of a contract, in which the parties to it are returned to their status quo prior to the making of the contract.

Suppose that one day later Jerry decides he really wants the watch and offers to purchase it once again. Anna is willing to sell, but this time for a price of $125. Jerry agrees, and a new contract is formed. Similarly, in the Healey-Brewster example above, to arrange a raise for Brewster before the contract expires, the parties need to rescind the first contract and agree to a new one that includes the wage increase. Note that in each of these situations there are three separate agreements—the initial agreement, the rescission agreement, and the later agreement. At the time of the later agreement, there are no preexisting duties because they were discharged by the rescission agreement.

When rescission and the making of the new contract take place at the same time, some courts apply the preexisting duty rule and refuse to enforce the new promise. To illustrate: Suppose, in the Healey-Brewster example, that Healey and Brewster had rescinded their initial agreement and made the new agreement at the same time. Some courts would hold that the new agreement was unenforceable on the grounds of insufficient consideration. Other courts would consider the timing unimportant, as long as the rescission is express, and would hold that the new promises furnish consideration for each other.[8] Still other courts would hold that the original consideration carries over into the new agreement.[9]

Sale of Goods—Modification

The UCC deals with the problem of preexisting duty or modification of an existing contract very simply: "[A]n agreement modifying a contract within this Article needs no consideration to be binding."[10]

---

6. Note, however, that in the example of the sheriff, the person taking the job as sheriff knows ahead of time that he or she will not be allowed to take rewards.

7. Pronounced re-*sih*-zhen.
8. See, for example, *Schwartzreich v. Bauman-Basch, Inc.,* 231 N.Y. 196, 131 N.E. 887 (1921).
9. See, for example, *Holly v. First National Bank,* 218 Wis. 259, 260 N.W. 429 (1935).
10. UCC 2-209(1).

To illustrate, Sachs and Jacobsen have entered into a one-year contract under which Sachs is to supply Jacobsen with all the flour she needs for her bakery at $50 per barrel. Subsequently, the price of wheat to Sachs increases so sharply that the cost of producing a barrel of flour is $56. Sachs tells Jacobsen he will not ship her any more flour unless she agrees to pay $58 per barrel. Jacobsen agrees. This modification of an existing sales contract is enforceable under the UCC even though Sachs was under a preexisting duty to supply flour at $50 per barrel. Jacobsen must pay the additional $8 per barrel. The UCC simply eliminates the consideration requirement when both parties in good faith agree to a modification.

Unforeseen Difficulties

Sometimes a party to a contract runs into unforeseen and substantial difficulties that could not have been anticipated at the time the contract was entered into. If the parties later agree to pay extra compensation for overcoming these unforeseen difficulties, the court may enforce the agreement. It should be noted that these unforeseen difficulties do not include the types of risks ordinarily assumed in business. For example, the increase in the price of wheat in the preceding example would not normally be deemed an unforeseen hardship or difficulty.

Suppose you contract with Carvelli to dig a basement on your vacant lot for $1,000. Carvelli starts to dig the basement and unexpectedly encounters a concrete slab reinforced with steel. He will now require special equipment and additional time to finish digging the basement. He asks for an additional $200 to dig the basement, and you agree. Many courts will enforce the modification, under the unforeseen-difficulty exception. Others will not.

■ Moral Obligations

Promises based on moral duty or obligation are not enforceable, because a moral obligation is not held to be legally sufficient consideration. Suppose your friend is injured in a distant city and a grocer takes care of him during his recovery. Thereafter, feeling a moral obligation to help your friend and aid the grocer, you promise the grocer to pay for your friend's expenses. The promise is unenforceable because it is supported only by your moral obligation—you have received no material benefit that would support an action by the grocer to recover from you his expenses in caring for your friend.

Sometimes people feel a moral obligation to make promises to loved ones. A father may promise to pay $10,000 to his daughter "in consideration of the love and affection that I have for you." An employer may promise to give a sum of money to a trusted employee "in consideration of your many acts of kindness and thoughtfulness over the years." Frequently, promises to pay for acts already performed (called past consideration, as will be discussed) are premised on moral obligations or on natural duty and affection. These are not legally sufficient consideration, however, and promises made in exchange for them are unenforceable.

Another example of a promise made out of a moral obligation is a promise to pay the debts of one's parents or a promise to pay for the care rendered to relatives one was under no duty to support.[11]

■ Past Consideration

Promises made with respect to events that have already taken place are unenforceable. These promises lack consideration in that the element of bargained-for exchange is missing. In short, you can bargain for something to take place now or in the future, but not for something that has already taken place. Therefore, **past consideration** is no consideration.

Suppose that an employer tells a retiring employee, "In consideration of your forty years of faithful service, you will be paid a pension of $500 per month." The promise relates to an event that has already taken place, so it is unenforceable. A similar example is a promise to pay for "past love and affection given." Although there may be strong moral obligations to fulfill those promises, there is no legal obligation to do so.

Suppose instead that an employer tells newly hired employees, "On retirement, in consideration of your years of faithful service from now until

---

11. A minority of states enforces such promises supported only by a moral obligation—but only to the extent of the actual obligation or of the services or care rendered. For an example, see California Civil Code Section 1606.

retirement age, you will be paid a pension of $500 per month." Here is a bargained-for exchange with legally sufficient consideration; so the employer is bound to pay.

In the following case, we see an illustration of how "past" and "moral" issues can be involved in consideration.

Case 11.2

LANFIER v. LANFIER

Supreme Court of Iowa, 1939.
227 Iowa 258,
288 N.W. 104.

BACKGROUND AND FACTS   Two days after his birth, August Dwayne Lanfier was named after his grandfather August Schultz. Over three months later, Schultz orally agreed with Lanfier's mother to give Lanfier certain real estate if the mother would name Lanfier after him. He also agreed to reserve to the parents a life estate (possession and use during their lives) in that same real estate. The parents, who had already named Lanfier after Schultz, accepted. Schultz gave possession of the property to the parents but never performed the rest of the agreement. Schultz died without a will, and Lanfier (a minor) through his father filed suit in an Iowa state court to obtain ownership of the property. The administrator of Schultz's estate and the other beneficiaries challenged Lanfier's claim. The trial court awarded the property to Lanfier based on the alleged oral contract between his grandfather and his mother. The estate appealed.

DECISION AND RATIONALE   The Supreme Court of Iowa reversed the trial court's decision and did not award the property to Lanfier. The state supreme court found that there was a lack of consideration on the part of Lanfier, who had been named after his grandfather months before the oral contract was made. The court stated that "past or moral consideration is not sufficient to support an executory contract." Lanfier argued that love and affection constituted sufficient consideration to support the contract, but the court held that a promise made "on the basis of mere love and affection * * * create[s] at most bare moral obligations, and a breach thereof creates no cause for redress by the court."

■ Problem Areas
Concerning Consideration

Because of the difficulty in clearly defining the requirements for consideration, numerous exceptions have been created to allow enforcement of contracts without consideration or to emphasize the intent of the parties to contract with one another, rather than to emphasize the existence or nonexistence of consideration.

Businesses face a great deal of uncertainty (risk) in the form of changing market conditions. This uncertainty makes it difficult to define the future rights and duties of parties who contract today. As a result, some output and requirements contracts (to be discussed shortly) may not call for any performance in the future under certain market conditions. Yet this does not mean that the contracts fail for lack of consideration. Problems con-

cerning the issue of consideration usually fall into one of the following categories:

1.   Situations in which promises are exchanged but total performance by the parties is uncertain.
2.   Settlement of claims.
3.   Certain promises enforceable without consideration.

The court's solutions to these types of problems offer insights into how the law views the complex concept of consideration.

Uncertain Performance—
Illusory versus Nonillusory Promises

If the terms of the contract express such uncertainty of performance that the promisor has not actually promised to do anything, the promise is said to be *illusory*—without consideration and unenforceable. For example, suppose the president and sole owner of ABC Corporation says to his employees: "All of you have worked hard, and if profits remain high, you will be given a 10 percent bonus at the end of the year—if management thinks it is warranted." The employees continue to work hard, and profits remain high, but no bonus is given. This is an illusory promise, or no promise at all, because performance depends solely on the discretion of the president. There is no bargained-for consideration. The statement declares merely that the president may or may not do something in the future. The president is not obligated (incurs no detriment) now or in the future.

Consider another example. Pepsico promises to buy from Crystal Sugar, Inc., "all sugar as Pepsico may wish to order from Crystal Sugar, Inc." Because Pepsico is still free to buy from anyone else it chooses or not to buy at all, its promise is illusory.

The following four types of business contracts have a degree of uncertainty as to the amount of performance legally required:

1. Requirements contracts.
2. Output contracts.
3. Exclusive dealing contracts.
4. Option-to-cancel clauses.

Frequently, the determination of whether the promise is illusory or nonillusory depends on all the surrounding facts, not just on the terms of the agreement.

REQUIREMENTS CONTRACTS   A contract in which the buyer agrees to purchase from the seller, and the seller agrees to sell to the buyer, all of the goods of a designated type the buyer *needs* or *requires* is called a **requirements contract.** If the buyer promises to purchase only if the buyer *wishes or desires* to do so, or if the buyer reserves the right to buy the goods from someone other than the seller, the promise is illusory (without consideration) and is unenforceable by either party.

For example, a manufacturer uses coal to operate and to heat his plant. The manufacturer agrees to purchase from a coal producer all the coal that the manufacturer will require to heat and to run his plant for one year at a set price per ton. Because the agreement is based on the *established* needs of the buyer, and because the contract requires the buyer to purchase the goods to fill those needs from this seller, the contract is nonillusory (with consideration) and enforceable, even though the exact amount of coal tonnage to be purchased is unknown. If the agreement had stated that the buyer had to buy only the coal he wanted or wished or desired, however, or if the buyer had reserved the right to purchase from any seller whose delivery price was lowest, there would have been no contract, because the buyer would not have been obligated to buy any coal from this seller and would thus have incurred no legal detriment.

But, one might ask, is there not a possibility that the manufacturer will go out of business and thus have no requirements? Where, then, is the detriment, or consideration? The detriment is that the buyer gives up the opportunity (legal right) to purchase from other sellers and the seller gives up the opportunity (legal right) to sell to other buyers (who do not have requirements contracts) until he or she has satisfied the obligation under the requirements contract.

OUTPUT CONTRACTS   An **output contract** is a contract in which the seller agrees to sell to the buyer, and the buyer agrees to purchase from the seller, all of what the seller produces.

For example, if U.S. Steel agrees to sell to Boeing Aircraft all the I-beams it produces during the month of March at an agreed-upon price per beam, a binding, nonillusory promise is made. The criteria for a nonillusory output contract are basically the same as for a requirements contract, except that the criteria are applied to the seller's obligation to produce rather than to the buyer's obligation to purchase.

Under the common law of contracts, a court may compel performance according to what it believes the implied obligation of good faith and fair dealing requires. The UCC also imposes a *good faith limitation* on output and requirements contracts. The quantity under such contracts is the amount of output produced or the amount of requirements needed during a *normal* production year. The actual quantity sold or purchased cannot be unreasonably disproportionate to normal or comparable prior output or requirements.[12]

---

12.   UCC 2-306.

EXCLUSIVE DEALING CONTRACTS A contract that gives a party the sole right to deal in or with the product of the other party is called an **exclusive dealing contract.** For example, an exclusive dealing contract may require a buyer to carry only products made by the seller. Wood agrees to market only the fabrics, millinery, and dresses upon which Lady Duff-Gordon places her endorsement. Lady Duff-Gordon receives no promise that Wood will market any dresses, but she gives Wood an exclusive right to market whatever number of items Wood deems appropriate. At first glance, Wood's promise appears illusory. He has not agreed to sell anything. As in the output and the requirements contracts, however, Wood is under a duty to use his ''best efforts'' to market the dresses.[13] This duty, or obligation, is consideration for the promise to either supply or sell.

Consider another example. A real estate broker obtains a thirty-day *exclusive* contract from the seller of a house. The broker has the duty to perform his or her best efforts in selling the house within thirty days and in dealing with potential buyers. The seller's detriments are the loss of the opportunity (legal right) to hire another broker and the duty to pay the agent if the agent finds a satisfactory buyer for the house. In return, the law imposes a legal obligation on the broker to perform according to his or her best efforts.

OPTION-TO-CANCEL CLAUSES A term, or time-limited, contract may include a clause in which one or both parties reserve the right to cancel the contract before the stated period has elapsed. For example, consider a three-year lease (a term contract) in which the tenant reserves the right to cancel, with notice, at any time after one year's occupancy. The uncertainty of performance is that the contract may or may not last for the entire three-year period.

The basic rule of law is that the contract with an option to cancel will be enforced if the party having the option has given up an opportunity (legal right). The loss of the opportunity is a detriment and thus constitutes consideration. This point will become clearer as we look at two more examples.

Suppose I contract to hire you for one year at $4,000 per month, reserving the right to cancel the

contract at any time. Upon close examination of these words, you can see that I have not actually agreed to hire you, as I could cancel without liability before you started performance. I have not given up the opportunity of hiring someone else. This contract, therefore, is illusory.

Now suppose I contract to hire you for one year at $4,000 per month, reserving the right to cancel the contract at any time after you have begun performance by giving you thirty days' notice. By saying that I will give you thirty days' notice, I am relinquishing the opportunity (legal right) to hire someone else instead of you for a thirty-day period. Therefore, if you work for one month, at the end of which I give you thirty days' notice, you will be entitled to enforce the contract for $8,000 in salary.

Settlement of Claims

An understanding of the enforceability of agreements to settle claims or discharge debts is important in the business world. The following agreements are the most frequent:

1. Accord and satisfaction.
2. Creditors' composition agreements.
3. Release.
4. Covenant not to sue.

ACCORD AND SATISFACTION The concept of **accord and satisfaction** deals with a debtor's offer of payment and a creditor's acceptance of a lesser amount than the creditor originally purported to be owed. The accord is defined as the agreement under which one of the parties undertakes to give or perform, and the other to accept, in satisfaction of a claim, something other than that which was originally agreed on. Satisfaction takes place when the accord is executed. Accord and satisfaction deal with an attempt by the obligor to extinguish an obligation. A basic rule is that there can be no satisfaction unless there is first an accord.

For accord and satisfaction to occur, the amount of the debt *must be in dispute.* If a debt is *liquidated,* accord and satisfaction cannot take place. A liquidated debt is one whose amount has been ascertained, fixed, agreed-on, settled, or exactly determined. For example, if Baker signs an installment loan contract with her banker in which she agrees to pay a specified rate of interest on a

---

13. *Wood v. Lucy, Lady Duff-Gordon,* 222 N.Y. 88, 118 N.E. 214 (1917). See also UCC 2-306(2).

specified sum of borrowed money at monthly intervals for two years, that is a liquidated debt. The amount owing is precisely known to both of the parties, and reasonable persons will not differ over the amount owed. Suppose that Baker misses her last two payments on the loan and the creditor demands that she pay the overdue debt. Baker makes a partial payment and states that she believes that is all that she should have to pay and that, if the creditor accepts the payment, the debt will be satisfied, or discharged. In the majority of states, acceptance of a lesser sum than the entire amount of a liquidated debt is not satisfaction, and the balance of the debt is still legally owed. The rationale for this rule is that no consideration is given by the debtor to satisfy the obligation of paying the balance to the creditor—because the debtor has a preexisting legal obligation to pay the entire debt.

The opposite of a liquidated debt is an *unliquidated debt*. Here, reasonable persons may differ over the amount owed. It is not settled, fixed, agreed-on, ascertained, or determined. In these circumstances, acceptance of payment of the lesser sum can operate as a satisfaction, or discharge, of the debt. For example, suppose that Devereaux goes to the dentist's office. The dentist tells him that he needs three special types of gold inlays. The price is not discussed, and there is no standard fee for this type of work. Devereaux leaves the office. At the end of the month, the dentist sends him a bill for $3,000. Devereaux, believing that this amount is grossly out of proportion with what a reasonable person would believe to be the debt owed, sends a check for $2,000. On the back of the check he writes "payment in full for three gold inlays." The dentist cashes the check. Because we are dealing with an unliquidated debt—the amount has not been agreed on—payment accepted by the dentist normally will eradicate the debt. One argument to support this rule is that the parties give up a legal right to contest the amount in dispute, and thus consideration is given.

The use of a payment-in-full check to discharge an unliquidated (disputed) debt is illustrated by the following case. This case illustrates four important concepts of the law concerning accord and satisfaction. First, it is important that the creditor receiving the tendered payment have notice that the payment is intended to satisfy the purported debt. Second, the recipient of the notice cannot negate it by scratching it off or altering it. Third, acceptance of the payment by the creditor constitutes accord. Fourth, if the debt is genuinely in dispute, accord will discharge (satisfy) the debt.

BACKGROUND AND FACTS   PLM, Inc., contracted with Quaintance Associates, Inc., an executive recruiting firm, for Quaintance to search for a new controller for PLM. After a four-month search during which Quaintance had not found a controller, Quaintance sent PLM a bill. PLM argued that it had agreed to pay only if Quaintance found a controller. PLM sent Quaintance a check for a lesser amount than that on Quaintance's bill with a letter stating, in part: "I do believe this is fair. I consider this the end of the matter but certainly would be prepared to discuss it if you so desire." PLM wrote on the back of the check: "In full payment of any claims Mr. Simpler [Quaintance's agent] has against PLM, Inc." Quaintance cashed the check but wrote on it that "negotiation does not release claim of payee against PLM, Inc." When Quaintance sued PLM in an Illinois state court for the remainder of the alleged debt, PLM argued that the cashing of the check by Quaintance constituted an accord and satisfaction. The trial court held for PLM, and Quaintance appealed.

 Case 11.3

QUAINTANCE ASSOCIATES, INC. v. PLM, INC.

Appellate Court of Illinois, First District, Fifth Division, 1981.
95 Ill.App.3d 818,
420 N.E.2d 567,
51 Ill.Dec. 153.

DECISION AND RATIONALE   The Appellate Court of Illinois affirmed the decision of the trial court. The appellate court held that the cashing of the check by Quaintance constituted an accord and satisfaction. The court pointed out that "[t]he act of negotiating a check that is offered in compromise of a disputed debt constitutes acceptance notwithstanding that the creditor added, without the debtor's knowledge or authority, words indicating a refusal to accept the offer." The court noted that Quaintance did

not allege that it did not understand that the check was offered as a compromise. The correspondence between the parties indicated that the terms
of their contract and the amount of fees were in dispute. Quaintance could
accept the check in full satisfaction or refuse it but could not cash it without
accepting it in settlement.

COMMENTS A minority of courts have held that UCC 1–207 alters the
common law of accord and satisfaction. Section 1–207 states that "[a] party
who with explicit reservation of rights * * * assents to performance in a
manner * * * offered by the other party does not thereby prejudice the
rights reserved." These courts have held that a creditor, by indorsing a
"payment in full" check with such words as "under protest" or "without
prejudice," will not jeopardize the right to recover the deficiency. A revision
to the Uniform Commercial Code presently being considered by the states,
however, specifically notes in UCC 1-207 that this section "does not apply
to accord and satisfaction." Furthermore a new section to Article 3 has been
added [RUCC 3-311], entitled "ACCORD AND SATISFACTION BY USE OF
INSTRUMENT." The combination of the two revisions fully reinstates the
common law concept of accord and satisfaction.

CREDITORS' COMPOSITION AGREEMENTS

A creditors' composition agreement is similar
to an accord. The difference is that, whereas an
accord is an agreement between a debtor and a
single creditor, a creditors' composition agreement
is an agreement between a debtor and two or more
creditors acting together to liquidate their claims.
Under this arrangement, an insolvent or financially
troubled debtor's creditors agree to accept either a
specified amount or a percentage of the full amount
owed.

As in the case of any contract, to be enforceable
the creditors' composition agreement must be supported by consideration. Each creditor's promise
to accept a proportionate share of the debtor's partial payment in lieu of full payment of whatever
amount is outstanding is his or her consideration
for the agreement. Surrender of the right to file a
petition for bankruptcy is the debtor's consideration.

RELEASE

A **release** serves to bar any further
recovery beyond the terms stated in the release.
Generally, releases are binding if three criteria are
proved:

1. The release is secured and given in good
faith—that is, in the absence of fraud and the like.

2. The release is in a signed writing. (This is a
requirement in many, but not in all, states.)

3. Consideration for the release is given. (But,
under the UCC, a written, signed waiver or renunciation by an aggrieved party discharges any further liability for a breach, even without
consideration.[14])

For example, suppose that you are involved in
an automobile accident caused by the negligence
of Jean. Jean offers you $500 if you will release
her from any further liability resulting from the
accident. You believe that the damages to your car
will not exceed $400. You agree to the release and
sign a writing to that effect. Later you discover that
the damage to your car is $600. Can you collect
the balance? The answer is no. No fraud was involved in obtaining the release; the release was in
a signed writing; and consideration was given.
Consideration in this case is Jean's promised payment of $500 in return for your promise not to bring
an action for a larger amount. You are thus limited
to the $500 specified in the release. This example
and the case below illustrate how important it is to
know the extent of injuries or damages before signing a release.

---

14. UCC 1-107.

BACKGROUND AND FACTS In August 1982, James Bennett's automobile was struck from behind by a Shinoda Floral, Inc., truck. After the collision, Bennett's physician told him that he had incurred a sprain that would only temporarily disable him. Aetna Casualty and Surety Company, Shinoda's insurance company, paid Bennett's medical expenses and lost wages until December, at which time Aetna offered Bennett $5,000 to settle his claim. Bennett accepted the offer and signed a release "of all claims of every nature and kind whatsoever * * * that are known and unknown, suspected and unsuspected." Later, Bennett's back condition worsened, and medical examinations revealed a more serious condition than originally diagnosed—Bennett was permanently and totally disabled. Bennett sued Shinoda and the employee-driver of the truck in a Washington state court. Both Shinoda and the employee-driver asserted the release as a defense, and the trial court granted their motion for summary judgment. The appellate court reversed the decision. The case was consolidated with a similar case and appealed.

DECISION AND RATIONALE The Supreme Court of Washington held that Bennett was bound by the release. The trial court's decision was affirmed. The state supreme court noted that "[o]n one hand, the law favors the just compensation of accident victims. On the other hand, the law favors the private settlement of disputes and gives releases great weight in order to support the finality of such settlements." The court pointed out that when a person signs a release with no knowledge of any personal injury, the release may be avoided if it "was not executed fairly and knowingly" because it would be "unjust to hold him to the release where it is clear that he did not contemplate the possibility that an injury would arise in the future." When a person signs a release knowing of an injury, however, he or she assumes "some risk" that the condition may worsen. The court added that avoiding the releases in these cases would "severely impair the policy favoring private settlements and promoting their finality. * * * The absence of finality would greatly reduce the incentive to settle personal injury claims, thus impeding timely compensation to injury victims and adding to the congestion crisis in our courts."

ETHICAL CONSIDERATIONS The law assumes that individuals will look after their own interests and, in the case of releases, not sign away rights without first exploring the possible consequences. Ethical questions arise, however, when an insurance company "pressures" an individual to sign a release. Certainly, the injured party should be allowed to make such a decision freely after having first been given all relevant information about the true options available.

Case 11.4

BENNETT v. SHINODA FLORAL, INC.

Supreme Court of Washington, 1987.
108 Wash.2d 386,
739 P.2d 648.

COVENANT NOT TO SUE A **covenant not to sue,** unlike a release, does not always bar further recovery. The parties simply substitute a contractual obligation for some other type of action. For example, assume that you are involved in an automobile accident caused by John's reckless driving. You allege that John was negligent and you are going to sue him in tort for damages. John and you agree that if you will refrain from bringing a tort action, he will pay for all damages to your car. Therefore, a contract is substituted for the tort action. If John fails to pay for your damages as agreed, you may pursue an action for breach of contract (you do not have to prove negligence). This does not prevent you from bringing a negligence suit; but if you do so, you have breached your contract.

The three criteria required for a binding release are also required for a valid covenant not to sue.

Promises Enforceable without Consideration

There are exceptions to the rule that only promises supported by consideration are enforceable. Other circumstances in which promises will be enforced despite the lack of what one normally considers legal consideration are as follows:

1. Promises to pay debts barred by a statute of limitations.
2. Promises to pay debts barred by discharge in bankruptcy. (Since 1984, the enforcement of these promises has been severely restricted. See Chapter 33.)
3. Detrimental reliance, or promissory estoppel.
4. Charitable subscriptions.

PROMISES TO PAY DEBTS BARRED BY A STATUTE OF LIMITATIONS   Statutes of limitations in all states require a creditor to sue within a specified period to recover debts. If the creditor fails to sue in time, recovery of the debt is barred by the statute of limitations. A debtor who promises to pay a previous debt barred by the statute of limitations makes an enforceable promise. *The promise needs no consideration.* (Some states, however, require that it be in writing.) In effect, the promise extends the limitations period, and the creditor can sue to recover the entire debt, or at least the amount promised. The promise can be implied if the debtor acknowledges the barred debt by making a partial payment.

Suppose you borrow $5,000 from First National Bank of San Jose. The loan is due in November 1990. You fail to pay, and the bank does not sue you until December 1995. If California's statute of limitations for this debt is five years, recovery of the debt is barred. If you then agree to pay off the loan, First National Bank can sue for the entire amount. This is an example of an express promise, which extends the limitations period. Likewise, you can make a monthly payment and implicitly acknowledge the existence of the debt. Again, First National Bank can sue you for the entire debt. This is an example of acknowledgment. Suppose instead that you expressly promise First National Bank to pay it $2,500. In most states, this

promise is enforceable only to the extent of $2,500 (and usually must be in writing).

PROMISES TO PAY DEBTS BARRED BY DISCHARGE IN BANKRUPTCY   A promise to pay a debt discharged in bankruptcy (called a reaffirmation) may be enforceable despite the absence of consideration for the promise, which nevertheless must be clear and explicit.

The Bankruptcy Reform Act of 1978, as amended by the Bankruptcy Amendments and Federal Judgeship Act of 1984, has made substantial changes in the law concerning reaffirmations of debts barred by a discharge in bankruptcy. Prior to the enactment of the law, a former debtor could make a promise in writing to repay a debt totally discharged by a bankruptcy decree, and that promise would be enforced without consideration. Currently, the law severely restricts such reaffirmations, which must be made before the debts are discharged in bankruptcy. (See Chapter 33 for a detailed discussion of these restrictions.)

DETRIMENTAL RELIANCE, OR PROMISSORY ESTOPPEL   The doctrine of detrimental reliance, or **promissory estoppel,** involves a promise given by one party that induces another party to rely on that promise to his or her detriment. When the promisor can reasonably have expected the promisee to act on the promise, and injustice cannot be avoided any other way, the promise will be enforced.[15] Additionally, the promisee must have acted with justifiable reliance on the promise—that is, must have been justified in relying on it—and in most instances the act must have been of a substantial nature.

The promise is enforced by refusal to allow the promisor to set up the defense of lack of consideration. That is, the promisor is *estopped* (prevented) from asserting the lack of consideration as a defense. The estoppel arises from the promise, and hence *promissory estoppel* is the term used. (This doctrine is not used in some jurisdictions.)

Imagine that your grandfather tells you, "I'll pay you $350 per week so you won't have to work

---

15.   Restatement (Second) of Contracts, Section 90, provides: "A promise which the promisor should reasonably expect to induce action or forbearance on the part of the promisee or a third person and which does induce such action or forbearance is binding if injustice can be avoided only by enforcement of the promise."

anymore." Then you quit your job, and your grandfather refuses to pay. You may be able to enforce the promise, because you have justifiably relied on it to your detriment.[16]

---

16.   *Ricketts v. Scothorn,* 57 Neb. 51, 77 N.W. 365 (1898).

Traditionally, promissory estoppel has been applied only to gratuitous promises—that is, when the parties are not bargaining in a commercial setting. The trend, however, is to apply it in any situation if justice so requires. The following classic case illustrates this point.

 Case 11.5

HOFFMAN v. RED OWL STORES, INC.

Supreme Court of Wisconsin, 1965.
26 Wis.2d 683,
133 N.W.2d 267.

BACKGROUND AND FACTS   Red Owl Stores, Inc., promised Hoffman that for $18,000 it would establish him in a Red Owl store in Chilton. Hoffman currently owned a grocery store, and he and his wife owned a bakery building in Wautoma. To make the payment, Hoffman sold his grocery store fixtures and inventory on the promise that he would be in his new store by the coming fall. After Hoffman sold his grocery store, the $18,000 figure was changed to $24,100. Later, Red Owl assured Hoffman that if the figure were increased by another $2,000, the deal would go through. To meet the new price, the Hoffmans sold their bakery building on Red Owl's assurance that this was the last necessary step. When the deal ultimately fell through because Red Owl failed to keep its promise concerning the operation of the franchise agency store, the Hoffmans sued in a Wisconsin state court to recover their losses. The trial court found in their favor, and Red Owl appealed.

DECISION AND RATIONALE   The Supreme Court of Wisconsin affirmed the trial court's judgment based on the principle of promissory estoppel. Hoffman was entitled to damages, the exact amount to be determined on the case's return to the trial court. The state supreme court quoted from Section 90 of the Restatement of Contracts: "A promise which the promisor should reasonably expect to induce action or forbearance of a definite and substantial character on the part of the promisee and which does induce such action or forbearance is binding if injustice can be avoided only by enforcement of the promise." The court noted that Red Owl made a number of promises on which the Hoffmans relied to their detriment, thus invoking the principle of promissory estoppel. The court held that "enforcement of the promise" does not necessarily require specific performance, but the damages awarded "should be only such as * * * are necessary to prevent injustice."

COMMENTS   Promissory estoppel does not mean that each and every gratuitous promise will be binding merely because the promisee has changed position. Liability is created only when there is "justifiable reliance on the promise." The promisor must have known or had reason to believe that the promisee would likely be induced to change position as a result of the promise.

CHARITABLE SUBSCRIPTIONS   Subscriptions to religious, educational, and charitable institutions are promises to make gifts and are unenforceable on traditional contract grounds because they are not supported by legally sufficient consideration. A gift is the opposite of bargained-for consideration—although there have been cases in which it was held that a promise to give money to a charity was supported by consideration. For example, the promisor may have bargained for and received a promise from the charity that the gift be used in a specific way or that it be memorialized with the promisor's name. The modern view, however, is to enforce these promises under the doctrine of promissory estoppel or to find consideration simply as a matter of public policy.

The premise for enforcement is that a promise is made and an institution changes its position because of reliance on that promise. For example, suppose a church solicits and receives donative subscriptions to build a new church. On the basis of these pledges, the church purchases land, employs architects, and makes other contracts that change its position. Courts may enforce the pledges under promissory estoppel or find consideration in the fact that each promise was made in reliance on the other promises of support or that the trustees, by accepting the subscription, impliedly promised to complete the proposed undertaking. Such cases represent exceptions to the general rule that consideration must exist for the formation of a contract. And these exceptions come about as a result of public policy.

■ Terms and Concepts

accord and satisfaction 210	exclusive dealing	release 212
consideration 203	contract 210	requirements contract 209
covenant not to sue 213	output contract 209	rescission 206
creditors' composition	past consideration 207	unconscionable 205
agreement 212	promissory estoppel 214	

■ For Review

1. What are the elements of consideration?

2. Why, under most circumstances, doesn't a promise to do what one already has a legal duty to do constitute consideration?

3. State four examples of circumstances in which promises will be enforced despite a lack of what is normally considered consideration.

4. Donna offers to buy a book from Robert for $10. Robert accepts the offer and delivers the book to Donna. Ordinarily, Robert's transfer and delivery of the book would constitute performance and consideration for Donna's promise. Does it make any difference if Donna, when she makes the offer, secretly intends to pay Robert $10 whether or not she gets the book? Does it make any difference if Robert, when he accepts, secretly intends not to collect the $10?

5. Emmanuel works for Milagro Restaurants, Inc. Milagro promises to pay Emmanuel a monthly pension when Emmanuel retires. After forty years, Emmanuel retires. For six years, Emmanuel does not work elsewhere, and Milagro pays the pension. Business has slowed, however, and Milagro would like to cut costs. Is Milagro's promise to pay the pension binding?

■ Questions and Case Problems

11-1. D'Albergo is the owner of a large bakery. He contracts to purchase from XYZ Flour, Inc., all the flour he might desire for a one-year period at $30 per barrel. Payment terms call for a billing at the end of each month for shipments made, with a 3 percent discount for payment within twenty days of the billing date. During the first month D'Albergo orders and XYZ delivers 1,000 barrels of flour. On the third day of the next month, XYZ sends D'Albergo a bill for $30,000 dated that same day. A dispute develops between the two parties. XYZ refuses to ship any more flour to D'Albergo, and on the thirtieth day of the month, D'Albergo sends XYZ a check for $27,500 marked clearly, "payment in full." Discuss whether XYZ's refusal to ship any more flour places it in breach of contract. Also, if XYZ cashes D'Albergo's check, can XYZ recover in a lawsuit the balance of $2,500?

11-2. Tabor is the buyer of widgets manufactured by Martin. Martin's contract with Tabor calls for delivery of 10,000 widgets at $1 per widget in ten equal installments. After delivery of two installments, Martin informs Tabor that because of inflation, Martin is losing money and will promise to deliver the remaining 8,000 widgets only if Tabor will pay $1.20 per widget. Tabor agrees in writing. Discuss whether Martin can legally collect the additional $200 upon delivery to Tabor of the next installment of 1,000 widgets.

11-3. Starek Furniture Co. manufactures summer lawn furniture. Its sole product consists of webbed aluminum frame furniture used mainly on outdoor patios and on beaches. As of October 1, Star Furniture was heavily indebted to its three main suppliers—Aluminum Pole, Inc.; Plastic Webbing, Ltd.; and The Little Steel Rivet Co. Starek owed each of these suppliers approximately $10,000. Starek's president met with the presidents of the three suppliers to work out some arrangement whereby the company could avoid declaring bankruptcy. Because all the parties desired that Starek Furniture not go bankrupt, an agreement was made among the four parties that Starek would pay each supplier $7,000, which would be accepted as full payment of all outstanding debts as of October 1. Discuss whether this agreement is enforceable.

11-4. Bernstein owns a lot and wants to build a house according to a specific set of plans and specifications. She solicits bids from building contractors and receives three bids: one from Carlton for $60,000, one from Friend for $58,000, and one from Shade for $53,000. She accepts Shade's bid. One month after construction of the house has begun, Shade contacts Bernstein and informs her that because of inflation and a recent price hike in materials, he will not finish the house unless Bernstein agrees to pay an extra $3,000. Bernstein reluctantly agrees to pay the additional sum. After the house is finished, however, Bernstein refuses to pay the additional $3,000. Discuss whether Bernstein is legally required to pay this additional amount.

11-5. Daniel, a recent college graduate, is on his way home for the Christmas holidays from his new job. Daniel gets caught in a snowstorm and is taken in by an elderly couple, who provide him with food and shelter. After the snowplows have cleared the road, Daniel proceeds home. Daniel's father, Fred, is most appreciative of the elderly couple's action and in a letter promises to pay them $500. The elderly couple, in need of money, accept Fred's offer. Because of a dispute between Daniel and Fred, Fred refuses to pay the elderly couple the $500. Discuss whether they can hold Fred in contract for the services rendered to Daniel.

11-6. Martino was a police officer in Atlantic City. Gray, who lost a significant amount of her jewelry during a burglary of her home, offered a reward for the recovery of the property. Incident to his job, Martino possessed certain knowledge concerning the theft of Gray's jewelry. When Martino informed Gray of his knowledge of the theft, Gray offered Martino $500 to help her recover her jewelry. As a result of Martino's police work, the jewelry was recovered and returned to Gray. Martino sued Gray for the reward he claimed she promised him. Was there a valid contract between Gray and Martino? [*Gray v. Martino,* 91 N.J.L. 462, 103 A. 24 (1918)]

11-7. Kowalsky, a contractor, was required to make periodic payments to a union pension fund administered by Kelly, trustee for the union. Kowalsky and Kelly disagreed over the amount of money Kowalsky owed the union. After a number of heated discussions Kowalsky sent Kelly four checks totaling $8,500 and enclosed them in a letter saying: "These checks are tendered with the understanding that they are full payment of all claims against Kowalsky." Immediately after receiving the checks, Kelly called Kowalsky and told him the checks were not going to be cashed but would simply be held and that Kowalsky still owed Kelly money because the $8,500 did not cover late charges on the deposited payments. Kowalsky did not ask for the return of the checks or stop payment. Kelly retained, but did not cash, the checks and sued Kowalsky for the late

charges. Kowalsky claimed that retention of the checks constituted full accord and satisfaction of the debt. Who won, and why? [*Kelly v. Kowalsky,* 186 Conn. 618, 442 A.2d 1355 (1982)]

11-8. In 1972, Thomas L. Weinsaft signed a written agreement with his son, Nicholas L. Weinsaft. Thomas agreed that during his lifetime he would not transfer any interest in his 765 shares of stock of Crane Manufacturing Co. unless he first gave Nicholas an opportunity to purchase it, and upon Thomas's death, Nicholas would have the "option and right to purchase all of the stock" from the estate. The agreement stated that it was entered into "In consideration of $10.00 and other good and valuable consideration, including the inducement of Second Party [Nicholas] to remain the chief executive officer of said company." Thomas died in 1980. Nicholas gave notice that he intended to buy the stock, but one of the beneficiaries under Thomas's will objected, contending that there was no consideration for Thomas's promises. Nicholas sued to force the estate to transfer the shares. Discuss whether this contract is supported by consideration. [*In re Estate of Weinsaft,* 647 S.W.2d 179 (Mo.App. 1983)]

11-9. Gordon Hayes and Winslow Construction Co. (Hayes) promised to hire Kathleen Hunter as a flag girl on a construction job beginning June 14, 1971. Relying on the offer, Hunter left her position with the telephone company, as Hayes had asked her to do. When Hayes failed to hire her, she was unemployed for two months—in spite of her efforts to find another job. Hunter sued Hayes for damages in the amount of $700, which she would have earned during the two months had she not left the telephone company (she had been earning $350 a month). The trial court ruled for Hunter, awarding her $700 in damages. Hayes appealed, contending that it should not be liable because no valid employment contract existed between the plaintiff and the defendant. Discuss whether Hunter should be allowed to recover damages incurred by her reliance on Hayes's offer of employment, even in the absence of a valid employment contract. [*Hunter v. Hayes,* 533 P.2d 952 (Colo.App. 1975)]

11-10. Ellen and Gabriel Fineman held MasterCards issued by Citibank. Holders of these cards paid an annual $15 fee. The issuance and use of the cards were governed by a retail installment credit agreement, which contained the following statement: "We can change this Agreement including the *finance charge* and the *annual percentage rate* at any time." The agreement did provide for thirty days' notice of any such changes, and the cardholder had a right to reject the changes in writing and return the credit card. Two months before the expiration of the Finemans' cards, Citibank notified them that it was increasing its annual fee to $20; however, Citibank was also providing its cardholders with extra services and benefits, such as "$100,000 common carrier travel insurance." The Finemans did not object in writing, nor did they return the cards. Citibank added 83 cents to the Finemans' next bill, the prorated portion of the increase for the two months remaining on their cards. The Finemans filed suit (a class-action lawsuit on behalf of all cardholders) to recover the increased charges. Among other claims, the Finemans argued that the modification failed because the travel insurance was not adequate consideration for the modification, because they never received any benefits from the insurance and its cost to Citibank was negligible. Was there adequate and legally sufficient consideration for Citibank's modification of the annual credit card fee? [*Fineman v. Citicorp USA, Inc.,* 137 Ill.App.3d 1055, 485 N.E.2d 591, 92 Ill.Dec. 780 (1985)]

11-11. The state of Connecticut offered a $20,000 reward to anyone giving information leading to the arrest and conviction of the individual responsible for the murder of a man who was killed during the course of a robbery. Robert DePretis, a private investigator hired by an attorney—Joseph Gallicchio—representing a codefendant in the case, obtained a written and signed confession from James Avis, in which Avis admitted responsibility for the murder, and delivered the confession to the state police. This information eventually led to Avis's arrest, and Avis was later convicted for the crime. When DePretis tried to obtain the reward money, the state claimed, among other things, that DePretis was not eligible to collect the reward because, as Gallicchio's private investigator, he had a preexisting duty to investigate and report information relating to the crime. DePretis argued that although he commenced his activity in this matter as a result of his relationship with the attorney, he had no duty—as a police officer would—to continue his investigations. What will the court decide? Discuss. [*State v. Avis,* 41 Conn.Supp. 385, 577 A.2d 1146 (1990)]

11-12. A Question of Ethics

Glenn Widener and Mohammed Mozumder were employed as geophysicists by Arco Oil and Gas Co. On March 31, 1986, both employees were notified by letter that they were being placed on "surplus" status—which meant that if they were not placed in another position within the company within the next sixty days, their employment would be terminated. On termination, they would become eligible for benefits, including lump-sum allowance payments, under either of two company termination and retirement programs. To be eligible for payments under either plan, the employees were required to sign release documents. The employees were given informational packets outlining each plan in detail and advising the employees to contact the company's benefits specialist, Barbara Hough, about which plan they wished to elect. The employees went to Hough's office and signed various documents, among which was a general release that read, in part: "I release

and discharge the Company . . . from all claims, liabilities, demands, and causes of action known or unknown, fixed or contingent, which I may have or claim to have against the Company as a result of this termination and do hereby covenant not to file a lawsuit to assert such claims." After signing the release, each employee received a lump-sum payment. When the employees later sued Arco, alleging wrongful discharge on the basis of age discrimination, Arco claimed that the release document signed by the employees released it from any liability. The employees contended that they had not voluntarily and knowingly given the releases. The release document was confusing because it was not entitled a release, and Hough had never informed them of the significance of what they were signing. She only told them that they had to sign the various documents before they left. The court held that the releases were valid and granted Arco's motion for summary judgment. [Widener v. Arco Oil and Gas Co., 717 F.Supp. 1211 (N.D.Tex. 1989)]

1. Widener and Mozumder were apparently genuinely surprised to learn that one of the documents that they had signed was a release. In view of their apparent "innocence" in this regard, is it fair that they should be held to what they promised in the release document?

2. If the two employees had not been highly educated men, would your answer to the above question be different?

3. A recurring problem in the area of contract law is that innocent parties sometimes suffer harmful consequences because they failed to read what they were signing. A general ethical principle underlying the law is that people should be held responsible for their own actions. But the law also seeks to prevent one party from taking undue advantage of another. How well do you think the court balanced these two fundamental ethical policies in its decision in this case? Would you have held differently if you were the judge?

4. Companies seeking to reduce or replace personnel frequently offer special retirement or termination benefits to induce employees to retire early or voluntarily terminate their employment. A company frequently will also request—as Arco did in this case—that the departing employees, in consideration for termination benefits received, sign release forms in which they promise not to hold the company liable for any future claims that the employees may have against the company. Is this practice in any way unethical?

Chapter 12

Capacity

Although the parties to a contract must assume certain risks, the law indicates that neither party should be allowed to benefit from the other party's lack of **contractual capacity**—the legal ability to enter into a contractual relationship. Courts generally presume the existence of contractual capacity, but there are some situations in which capacity is lacking or may be questionable. In some situations, a party may have the capacity to enter into a valid contract but also have the right to avoid liability under it. For example, minors usually are not legally bound by contracts. Therefore, certain contracts are *voidable*. A *voidable contract* may be either validated or avoided (canceled) at the option of the incapable or wronged party. Other contracts may be *void*. A *void contract* lacks an essential element for the formation of a legal contract, and thus, either party may ignore it.

Historically, the law has concerned itself with the relative strength of the bargaining power of each contracting party. Thus, special protection is afforded those who bargain with the inexperience of youth or those who lack the degree of mental competence required by law. *Full competence* exists when both parties have full legal capacity to enter into a contract and to have the contract enforced against them. *No competence* exists when one or both of the parties have been adjudged by a court to be mentally incompetent and therefore have no legal capacity to contract. In this event, an essential element for a valid contract is missing, and the contract is void. *Limited competence* exists when one or both of the parties are minors, intoxicated, or mentally incompetent (but not yet adjudicated officially as such). These parties have full and legal capacity to enter into a contract; but if they wish, they can normally avoid liability under the contract, which is thus voidable. The *Concept Summary* at the end of this chapter summarizes the legal effect of contracts entered into by minors, intoxicated persons, and mentally incompetent persons.

■ Minors

At common law, a minor was defined as a male who had not attained the age of twenty-one or a female who had not attained the age of eighteen. Today, in most states, the **age of majority** (the age at which a person is no longer a minor) for contractual purposes has been changed by statute to

219

eighteen years for both sexes.[1] In addition, some states provide for the termination of minority upon marriage. Subject to certain exceptions, the contracts entered into by a minor are voidable at the option of that minor. The minor may avoid legal obligations by exercising the option to *disaffirm* the contract. Note, however, that an adult who enters into a contract with a minor cannot avoid his or her contractual duties on the ground that the minor can do so. Unless the minor exercises the option to avoid the contract, the adult party is bound by it.

Minors' Rights to Disaffirm

The general rule is that a minor can enter into any contract that an adult can enter into, provided that the contract is not one prohibited by law for minors (for example, the sale of alcoholic beverages). Although minors can enter into contracts, they also have the right to disaffirm their contracts. Exceptions to this rule exist and will be discussed later in this section.

DISAFFIRMANCE IN GENERAL   For a minor to exercise the option to avoid a contract, he or she need only manifest an intention not to be bound by the contract. The minor avoids the contract by disaffirming it. The technical definition of **disaffirmance** is the legal avoidance, or setting aside, of a contractual obligation. Words or conduct may serve to express this intent. Suppose James Caldwell, a seventeen-year-old, enters into a contract to sell his car to Henry Reed, an adult. Caldwell can avoid the contract and avoid his legal duty to deliver possession of the car to Reed either by telling Reed that he refuses to abide by the contract or by selling the car to a third person. In other words, Caldwell can disaffirm the contract by expressing his intention in words or by acting inconsistently with his duties under the contract.

The contract can ordinarily be disaffirmed at any time during minority or for a reasonable time after the minor comes of age. In some states, however, a minor's disaffirmance of certain contracts is prohibited under a statute. For example, in the case of a contract for the sale of land by a minor, the rule in most states is that a minor can disaffirm only after attaining his or her majority. Other statutes include complete proscriptions of a minor's right to avoid contracts for student loans, contracts for medical care, contracts for insurance, and contracts that a minor makes pursuant to running a business. On grounds of public policy, other promises of a minor may be enforced, particularly when they entail something that the law would compel anyway—supporting an illegitimate child, for example.

If a minor fails to disaffirm a contract within a reasonable time after reaching the age of majority, the court must determine whether the conduct constitutes *ratification,* binding the minor in contract, or *disaffirmance,* allowing the minor's avoidance. Generally, if the contract is fully performed by both parties (executed), it is presumed to be ratified. If the contract is still executory (not yet fully performed by both parties), it is considered disaffirmed.

For example, assume that the age of majority in your state is eighteen. Your sister, age seventeen, contracts to purchase a bicycle from an adult for $125. Your sister then turns eighteen. If she has not taken possession of the bicycle or paid the $125 purchase price, an executory contract exists. If she fails to take possession of and pay for the bicycle within a reasonable time after her eighteenth birthday, most courts would hold her conduct to be an act of disaffirmance. On the other hand, if she has taken possession of the bicycle and paid the purchase price, an executed contract exists, and most courts would hold her failure to actively disaffirm within a reasonable time after her eighteenth birthday to be an act of ratification. A minor must disaffirm the entire contract to disaffirm it at all. For example, the minor cannot decide to keep part of the goods and return the remainder.

DUTY OF RESTITUTION   When a contract has been executed, the general rule is that minors cannot disaffirm without returning whatever goods they may have received or paying for their rea-

---

1. Although the age of majority applicable in contracts has been changed to eighteen in many states, it may still be twenty-one for some purposes, including the purchase and consumption of alcohol. The law often preserves archaic terminology. Common parlance refers to minors as "minors." The law refers to minors as "infants." If the term were changed, however, volumes of legal publications would immediately become obsolete.

sonable value. Under the majority view, the minor need only return the goods (or other consideration), provided such goods are in the minor's possession or control. Even if the goods have been used, damaged, or ruined, the minor's right to disaffirm the contract is not affected. Suppose Pat Boland, a seventeen-year-old, purchases a used Ford Taurus from Jane Crow, an adult. Boland is a bad driver and negligently runs the car into a telephone pole. The next day he returns the car to Crow and disaffirms the contract. Under the majority view, this return fulfills Boland's duty, even though the auto is now wrecked. This rule protects minors from reckless commitments because it discourages adults from dealing with them.

A few states, either by statute or by court decision, have placed an additional duty on the minor—the *duty of restitution.* This duty accords with the maxim that one's youth may be used as a shield, but not as a sword. The theory is that the adult should be returned to his or her position before the contract was made. This rule recognizes the legitimate interests of those who deal with minors. The duty of restitution requires Boland to pay Crow for the damage done to the car in addition to returning it. Some states do not require full restitution. A minor must pay only a "reasonable" amount to compensate the adult.

When a minor disaffirms, all property that he or she has transferred to the adult as consideration may be recovered, even if it is in the hands of a third party. If the property itself cannot be returned, the adult must pay the minor its equivalent value. Under UCC 2-403(1), which deals with the sale of or a contract to sell *goods,* a minor cannot recover goods transferred to a third party who is a bona fide purchaser[2] ("a good faith purchaser for value"). For example, Mary, a minor, sells her stereo to Ann, an adult, for $100. Ann immediately sells the stereo to Grant for $110. Later, Mary wishes her stereo back and notifies Ann of her intent to disaffirm the contract. Even though Mary has a legal right to disaffirm the contract with Ann, Mary cannot require Grant, a bona fide purchaser, to return the stereo to her.

MISREPRESENTATION OF AGE   Suppose a minor tells a seller that she is twenty-one years old when she is actually only seventeen. In the majority of states, the minor can disaffirm the contract even though she has misrepresented her age. Moreover, in certain jurisdictions, a minor will not be held liable under the tort theory of deceit for misrepresenting his or her age, because, indirectly, the judgment might force the minor to perform the contract.

In many jurisdictions, however, legislatures or courts have declared that under certain circumstances a minor will be bound to a contract upon his or her misrepresentation of age. First, several states have enacted statutes for precisely this purpose. In these states, misrepresentation of age is enough to prohibit disaffirmance. Other statutes prohibit a minor who has engaged in business as an adult from disaffirming contracts negotiated in carrying out the business.[3]

Second, some courts refuse to allow minors who have misrepresented their age to disaffirm executed contracts unless they can return the consideration received. In these cases, the courts reason that the combination of misrepresentation and unjust enrichment estops (prevents) minors from asserting contractual incapacity.

Third, some courts allow a misrepresenting minor to disaffirm a contract but hold the minor liable for damages in tort, and the defrauded party may sue the minor for misrepresentation or fraud. A split in authority exists on this point, because some courts, as previously pointed out, have recognized that allowing a suit in tort is equivalent to indirectly enforcing the minor's contract.

In the following case, an Ohio appellate court had to deal with the problem of a minor's false representation of her age as the inducement to a contract. At the time this case was decided, the age of majority in Ohio was twenty-one.

---

2. A bona fide purchaser is a "purchaser for a valuable consideration paid or parted with in the belief that the vender had a right to sell, and without any suspicious circumstances to put him on inquiry." [*Merritt v. Railroad Co.,* 12 Barb. 605 (N.Y.App.Div. 1852)].

3. See, for example, statutes in Iowa, Kansas, Utah, and Washington.

Case 12.1

HAYDOCY PONTIAC, INC. v. LEE

Court of Appeals of Ohio, Franklin County, 1969.
19 Ohio App.2d 217,
250 N.E.2d 898.

BACKGROUND AND FACTS   Jennifer Lee was twenty years old when she contracted to buy an automobile, but she represented to Haydocy Pontiac, Inc., that she was twenty-one. She bought the car by making a trade-in and financing the rest of the price under a promissory note with Haydocy. Immediately following delivery of the car, Lee turned it over to a third person and never retook possession. She made no attempt to make payment on the note and announced that she was disaffirming the contract. She did not return the car to Haydocy, nor did she offer to return it. Haydocy sued her in an Ohio state court. The trial court applied the general rule that a minor can avoid a transaction without being required to restore the consideration received. Haydocy appealed.

DECISION AND RATIONALE   The Court of Appeals of Ohio reversed the judgment of the trial court and allowed Haydocy to recover from Lee the car's fair market value (which the court said could not exceed the car's original purchase price). The court reasoned that "[t]o allow infants to avoid a transaction without being required to restore the consideration received where the infant has used or otherwise disposed of it causes hardship on the other party," particularly when "the contract has been induced by a false representation of the age of the infant." The court explained that "[t]he common law has bestowed upon the infant the privilege of disaffirming his contracts in conservation of his rights and interests. Where the infant, 20 years of age, through falsehood and deceit enters into a contract with another who enters therein in honesty and good faith and, thereafter, the infant seeks to disaffirm the contract without tendering back the consideration, no right or interest of the infant exists which needs protection. The privilege given the infant thereupon becomes a weapon of injustice." Disaffirmance is to be determined by equitable principles.

EMANCIPATION   Emancipation is the release of a minor by his or her parents. It involves completely relinquishing the right to the minor's control, care, custody, and earnings. It is a repudiation of parental obligations. Emancipation may be express or implied, absolute or conditional, total or partial. Several jurisdictions permit minors to petition for emancipation themselves. In those states, a grant of emancipation may also remove a minor's lack of capacity to contract, but generally emancipation does not affect a minor's contractual capacity.

LIABILITY FOR NECESSARIES   A minor who enters into a contract for *necessaries* (food, clothing, shelter, and other items, as discussed below) may disaffirm the contract but will still remain liable for the reasonable value of the goods. If the minor has a parent or guardian who is able to provide the minor with necessaries, but fails to do so, the parent or guardian will be liable for the reasonable value of any necessary goods, such as clothing, purchased by the minor. The legal duty

to pay a reasonable value does not arise from the contract itself but is imposed by law under a theory of quasi contract (implied-in-law contract). Parents' liability will be discussed later in this chapter.

The minor's right to disaffirm a contract has economic ramifications in that sellers are likely to refuse to deal with minors because of it. If minors can at least be held liable for the reasonable value of the goods, sellers' reluctance to enter into contracts with minors will be offset. This theory explains why the courts narrow the subject matter to necessaries. Without such a rule, minors might be denied the opportunity to purchase necessary goods.

Note, though, that the minor is liable only for the reasonable value of the goods based on use (in quasi contract) because with disaffirmance there is no contract and therefore no contract price to which the court can refer. Suppose Hank Olsen, a minor, purchases a suit at its list price of $150. After wearing the suit for several weeks, Olsen wants to disaffirm his contract with the clothier. He can do so, but he is liable for the reasonable value of the suit. If the court deems the value of the suit to be $115, then the clothier can recover only that amount, even if this deprives the clothier of some of the profit that he thought he would realize on the sale.

There is no firm, universally accepted definition of necessaries. At a minimum, necessaries include food, clothing, shelter, medicine, and hospital care. In some cases, however, courts have not limited necessaries to items required for physical existence but have extended the term to include whatever is believed to be necessary to maintain a person's financial and social status. Thus, what will be considered necessaries for one person may not be for another. Moreover, necessaries have been held to include education as well as services that are reasonably necessary to enable a minor to earn a living.

To be held liable for necessaries, the minor must not be under the care of a parent or guardian who is required, and able, to provide the minor with such necessaries. The philosophy is that the seller or provider of services can legally hold the parent or guardian liable for these contracted-for necessaries, and thus the minor should be allowed to disaffirm such contracts rather than be held liable for the reasonable value of the goods or services.

Generally, courts determine on a case-by-case basis what constitutes necessaries. Even housing, in the form of a leased apartment, may not constitute a necessary in certain circumstances—as the following case illustrates.

 Case 12.2

WEBSTER STREET PARTNERSHIP, LTD. v. SHERIDAN

Supreme Court of Nebraska, 1985.
220 Neb. 9,
368 N.W.2d 439.

BACKGROUND AND FACTS Webster Street Partnership, Ltd., owned apartments in Omaha, Nebraska. In September, Webster leased an apartment to Mathew Sheridan and Pat Wilwerding for a six-month term at $250 per month with a deposit of $150. Sheridan and Wilwerding were minors and had left home with the understanding that they could return at any time. Unable to pay the rent, they left the apartment in November. In January, their attorney notified Webster that Sheridan and Wilwerding would not pay the rental amount Webster claimed was owed and demanded return of the deposit. Webster sued in a Nebraska state court for the amount of the rent due under the lease. The trial court found for the minors but awarded Webster money for clean-up and repairs and rent for the month that Sheridan and Wilwerding had occupied the apartment. Webster appealed.

DECISION AND RATIONALE The Nebraska Supreme Court reversed the judgment of the trial court. The state supreme court ruled that Sheridan and Wilwerding were entitled to all the money that they had paid Webster. The court pointed out that the minors had left their parents' homes by choice. Under that circumstance, the apartment was not a necessary. Thus, they had a right to avoid the contract by disaffirmance, "either during their minority or within a reasonable time after reaching their majority," which they exercised. The court added that "[d]isaffirmance by an infant completely puts an end to the contract's existence. * * * Because the parties then stand as if no contract had ever existed, the infant can recover payments made to the adult and the adult is entitled to the return of whatever was received by the infant."

ETHICAL CONSIDERATIONS Although minors have a legal right to disaffirm their contracts, their disaffirmance can sometimes result in unfair treatment of adults. In this case, Wilwerding and Sheridan freely agreed to lease the apartment. The fact that they could legally avoid their responsibilities under the contract does not mean that it was ethical to break their contract with the landlord.

INSURANCE AND LOANS   Traditionally, insurance has not been viewed as a necessary, so minors can ordinarily disaffirm their insurance contracts and recover all premiums paid. Some jurisdictions, however, prohibit the right to disaffirm—for example, when minors contract for life or medical insurance. Other jurisdictions allow a minor to disaffirm but limit recovery to the value of premiums paid, less the insurance company's actual cost of protecting the minor under the policy. Suppose Bob Berzak, a minor, takes out an automobile insurance policy and pays $1,000 in premiums. Bob has an accident for which his insurance company, State Farm, pays a claim of $700. In states following the traditional rule, Bob's recovery upon disaffirmance will be $1,000, the full value of the premiums. In states limiting his recovery, Bob can recover only $300, the excess of the value of the premiums over State Farm's actual cost under the policy.

In and of itself, a loan is seldom viewed as a necessary, even if the minor spends the money on necessaries. If, however, the lender makes a loan for the express purpose of enabling the minor to purchase necessaries, and the lender personally makes sure the money is so spent, the minor is normally obligated to repay the loan.

Ratification

In contract law, **ratification** is the act of accepting and giving legal force to an obligation that previously was not enforceable. In relation to minors' contracts, ratification may be defined as an act or an expression in words by which a minor, upon or after reaching majority, indicates an *intention* to become bound by the contract. Ratification must occur, if at all, after the individual comes of age, because any attempt to become legally bound prior to majority is no more effective than the original contractual promise. This protects the minor and is consistent with the theory that the contracts of a minor are voidable at his or her option.

EXPRESS RATIFICATION   Suppose John Lawrence enters into a contract to sell a stereo to Carol Ogden. At the time the contract is made, Carol is a minor. Naturally, Carol can avoid her legal duty to pay for the stereo by disaffirming the contract. Imagine that instead Carol reaches majority and writes a letter to John stating that she still agrees to buy the stereo. Carol thus ratifies the contract and is now legally bound. John can sue for breach of contract if Carol refuses to perform her part of the bargain. This is an example of *express* ratification.

IMPLIED RATIFICATION   The contract can also be ratified by *conduct*. Suppose Carol takes possession of the stereo as a minor and continues to use it after reaching the age of majority. This conduct evidences an intent to abide by the contract and is a form of *implied* ratification. Again, Carol is legally bound, and John can sue her for breach of contract if she fails to perform her duty to pay the purchase price. When an individual, after reaching majority, continues to use and make payments on property purchased as a minor, the continued use and payment are inconsistent with disaffirmance and implicitly indicate an intention to be bound by the contract.

In general, any act or conduct showing an intention to affirm the contract will be deemed to be ratification. As previously suggested, however, silence after reaching the age of majority does not in and of itself constitute ratification of an executory contract in most situations. If Carol had said nothing to John and had not taken possession or made payment, she would not have ratified the contract, because she had expressed no intention to abide by it. On the other hand, the minor may have a duty to speak in some circumstances. Suppose that after coming of age, a former minor seller fails to disaffirm, knowing that the purchaser is making costly improvements on the property sold. In this case the minor cannot disaffirm the contract.

In the following case, a minor attempted to disaffirm a contract ten months after reaching the age of majority. The essential issue before the court is whether the ten months was a "reasonable time," after reaching the age of majority, within which to disaffirm a contract.

BACKGROUND AND FACTS Charles Edward Smith, Jr., bought a car on credit from Bobby Floars Toyota, Inc., a month before his eighteenth birthday. Smith made regular monthly payments for eleven months but then returned the car to the dealer and made no more payments. The dealer sold the car and sued Smith in a North Carolina state court to recover the difference between the amount obtained from the sale of the car and the money Smith still owed to the dealer. Smith refused to pay on the grounds that he had been a minor at the time of purchase and had disaffirmed the contract within a reasonable time after he had reached the age of majority. The trial court ruled that Smith had properly "disaffirmed the contractual obligation" by relinquishing the car ten months after attaining his majority, holding that ten months was a "reasonable time within which to disaffirm his contractual obligations under the circumstances of this case." The dealer appealed.

 Case 12.3

BOBBY FLOARS TOYOTA, INC. v. SMITH

Court of Appeals of North Carolina, 1980.
48 N.C.App. 580,
269 S.E.2d 320.

DECISION AND RATIONALE The Court of Appeals of North Carolina reversed the decision of the trial court and remanded the case for further proceedings consistent with the appellate court's opinion. The appellate court held that ten months was an unreasonable time within which to elect between disaffirmance and ratification. The court acknowledged that a minor may disaffirm a contract during minority or within a reasonable time after reaching majority. "[W]hat is a reasonable time depends upon the circumstances of each case." The court pointed out that this case involved a car "which is constantly depreciating in value," that Smith recognized the installment note as binding by continuing to make payments for many months, and that Smith continued to use the car until he returned it. Also, there was no evidence that he attempted to rescind the contract. The court held "that defendant's acceptance of the benefits and continuance of payments under the contract constituted a ratification of the contract, precluding subsequent disaffirmance."

Nonvoidable Contracts

Many states have passed statutes restricting the ability of minors to avoid certain contracts. For example, as previously discussed, some states prohibit minors from disaffirming certain insurance contracts. Other states hold that loans for education or medical care received by minors create binding legal duties that they cannot avoid.[4]

In addition, certain statutes specifically require minors to perform legal duties. Suppose James Dornan, a minor, wants to legally seize the property of Davis Snowden for default of a loan. In some states, Dornan is required to file a bond before the legal seizure, or attachment, can occur. After filing the bond, Dornan cannot avoid the obligations of the bonding agreement, because the bond is a legal

duty imposed by state statute. In such situations, a minor cannot rely on the common law rule that the bonding contract is voidable. Similar legal duties are imposed on minors with respect to bank accounts and transfers of stock.

Some contracts cannot be avoided, simply as a matter of law, on the grounds of public policy. For example, marriage contracts and contracts to enlist in the armed services fall into this category.

Liability for Torts

Generally, minors are liable for their torts. Courts do, however, weigh the factors of age, mental capacity, and maturity before determining a minor's liability. As has been pointed out, a breach of contract is normally not treated as a tort for which the minor is liable. When the tort is more than simply the improper execution of some lawful act in the performance of a contract, however, and when it

---

4. New York Education Law, Section 281; California Civil Code Section 36.

is independent of the contract, the court may rule against the minor. The test of whether an action against the minor can be brought is whether a basis for establishing liability exists apart from the contract. For example, suppose a minor rents a boat. The rental agreement provides that the minor will use due care to prevent damage to the boat. Nonetheless, the minor's careless use of the boat damages it. Will a court uphold an action in tort for negligence? The answer to this question depends on whether the court interprets imposing tort liability on the minor as directly or indirectly enforcing the minor's promise, which, because of a lack of contractual capacity, is voidable. The minor may be held liable, however, to any third parties injured by the minor's negligence.

Parents' Liability

As a general rule, parents are not liable for the contracts made by their minor children acting on their own. This is why businesses ordinarily require parents to sign any contract made with a minor. The parents then become personally obligated under the contract to perform the conditions of the contract, even if their child avoids liability.

Parents who have neglected the care of their minor child can be held liable for the reasonable value of necessaries supplied to the child, even when they have not signed a contract. In other words, if a child purchases shoes because his or her parents refuse to provide any shoes, the parents normally can be held liable for the reasonable value of the shoes.

Under the common law, parents were not held li ble for the torts of their minor children simply because of the parent-child relationship. In some states, the courts have adopted a rule that requires a separate determination of the parents' negligence. In those states, a parent may be liable if he or she failed to exercise proper parental control over the minor child and knew, or should have known, from the minor's habits and tendencies, that failure to exercise control posed an unreasonable risk of harm to others.

Other states have enacted statutes imposing on parents legal responsibility for the consequences of the tortious acts of their children. These statutes vary. For example, in some states, liability will be imposed on parents only for the willful, malicious, or wanton acts of their minor children.

■ Intoxicated Persons

Intoxication is a condition in which a person's normal capacity to act or think is inhibited by alcohol or some other drug. A contract entered into by an intoxicated person can be either voidable or valid.

If the person was intoxicated enough to lack mental capacity, then the transaction is voidable at the option of the intoxicated person even if the intoxication was purely voluntary. For the contract to be voidable, it must be proved that the intoxicated person's reason and judgment were impaired to the extent that he or she did not comprehend the legal consequences of entering into the contract.

If, despite intoxication, the person understands these legal consequences, the contract will be enforceable. Simply because the terms of the contract are foolish or obviously favor the other party does not mean that the contract is voidable (unless the other party *fraudulently* induced the person to become intoxicated). Problems often arise in determining whether a party was intoxicated enough to avoid legal duties. Many courts prefer to look at objective indications to determine whether the contract is voidable because of intoxication rather than inquire into the intoxicated party's mental state.

If a contract is held to be voidable because of a person's intoxication, that person has the option of disaffirming (avoiding) it—the same option available to a minor. The vast majority of courts, however, require the intoxicated person to make full restitution (fully return consideration received) as a condition of disaffirmance, except in cases involving necessaries, as discussed below. For example, suppose a person contracts to purchase a set of encyclopedias while intoxicated. If the books are delivered, the purchaser can disaffirm the executed contract (and get back the payment made) only by returning the encyclopedias.

An intoxicated person, after becoming sober, may ratify a contract expressly or implicitly, just as a minor may do upon reaching majority. Implied ratification occurs when a person enters into a contract while intoxicated and fails to disaffirm the contract within a *reasonable* time after becoming sober. Acts or conduct inconsistent with an intent to disaffirm—for example, continued use of property purchased under a voidable contract—will also ratify the contract.

In addition, contracts for necessaries are voidable (as in the case of minors), but the intoxicated person is liable in quasi contract for the reasonable value of the consideration received.

The lack of contractual capacity due to intoxication while the contract is being made must be distinguished from capacity (or the lack thereof) of an alcoholic. If an alcoholic makes a contract while sober, there is no lack of capacity.[5]

---

5. *Olsen v. Hawkins*, 90 Idaho 28, 408 P.2d 462 (1965).

The following case shows an unusual business transaction in which boasts, brags, and dares "after a few drinks" resulted in a binding sale and purchase transaction. It should be noted that avoidance due to intoxication is very rare.

 Case 12.4

LUCY v. ZEHMER

Supreme Court of Appeals of Virginia, 1954.
196 Va. 493,
84 S.E.2d 516.

BACKGROUND AND FACTS For eight years, W. O. Lucy had been anxious to buy the Ferguson Farm from A. H. Zehmer, whom he had known for at least fifteen years. One night, while visiting, Lucy said, "I bet you wouldn't take $50,000 for that place." Zehmer replied, "Yes, I would too; you wouldn't give fifty." Throughout the evening, the parties drank whiskey and talked, repeatedly returning to the subject of the farm. At different times, they discussed what would be included in the sale, the title examination, and Mrs. Zehmer's interest. Eventually, Zehmer wrote out an agreement, which the Zehmers signed, to the effect that he and Mrs. Zehmer agreed to sell the farm to Lucy for $50,000. Lucy sued Zehmer in a Virginia state court to go through with the sale. Zehmer argued that he was drunk at the time he made the agreement and that the offer had been made in jest and hence was unenforceable. The trial court agreed. Lucy appealed.

DECISION AND RATIONALE The Supreme Court of Virginia held that there was an enforceable contract and reversed the lower court's ruling. The Zehmers were ordered to carry through with the sale of the farm. Noting that Zehmer attempted to testify in detail as to what was said and done the night of the transaction, the state supreme court concluded that "Zehmer was not intoxicated to the extent of being unable to comprehend the nature and consequences of the instrument he executed, and hence that instrument is not to be invalidated on that ground." The court held that execution of the agreement was a serious business transaction, as evidenced by a number of circumstances: the contract was discussed for forty minutes or more before it was signed; it was rewritten to reflect Mrs. Zehmer's interest; Zehmer and Lucy discussed what was to be included in the sale; provision was made for examination of the title; the instrument was complete; and Lucy took possession of the instrument without Zehmer's requesting that he give it back.

■ Mentally Incompetent Persons

Contracts made by mentally incompetent persons can be either void, voidable, or valid. If a person has been adjudged mentally incompetent by a court of law and a guardian has been appointed, any contract made by the mentally incompetent person is void—no contract exists. Only the guardian can enter into binding legal duties on the incompetent person's behalf.

Mentally incompetent persons not so adjudged by a court may enter into voidable contracts if they do not know they are entering into the contract or if they lack the mental capacity to comprehend its subject matter, nature, and consequences. In such situations executory contracts are voidable at the option of the mentally incompetent person, although the other party does not have this option. Executed contracts are not voidable at the option of incompetent persons, unless they can return or pay for whatever they received. If the incompetence was obvious, however, the incompetent person need only pay for benefits that he or she retains.

Voidable contracts may be disaffirmed or ratified. Ratification must occur after the person has become mentally competent or after a guardian has been appointed and ratifies the contract. Like minors and intoxicated persons, mentally incompetent persons are liable in quasi contract for the reasonable value of necessaries they receive.

A contract entered into by a mentally incompetent person may also be valid. A person may be able to understand the nature and effect of entering into a certain contract, yet simultaneously lack capacity to engage in other activities. In such cases the contract will be valid, because the person is not legally mentally incompetent for contractual purposes.[6] Similarly, an otherwise mentally incompetent person may have a *lucid interval*—that is, a temporary restoration of sufficient intelligence, judgment, and will to enter into contracts without disqualification—during which he or she will be considered to have full legal capacity.

In the following case, a father suffering from Alzheimer's disease deeded his property over to his two sons in unequal shares. The son receiving the smaller share contested the transfer, claiming in part that his father was mentally incompetent at the time the deeds were signed. The case illustrates the general principle of law that mental competence is presumed and that the burden of proof of incompetence rests on the contesting party.

---

6. Modern courts no longer require a person to be completely irrational to disaffirm contracts on the basis of mental incompetence. A contract may be voidable if, by reason of a mental illness or defect, an individual was unable to act reasonably with respect to the transaction and the other party had reason to know of the condition. See *Ortelere v. Teachers' Retirement Board*, 25 N.Y.2d 196, 250 N.E.2d 460, 303 N.Y.S.2d 362 (1969).

Case 12.5

FEIDEN v. FEIDEN

Supreme Court of New York,
Appellate Division, Third
Department, 1989.
151 A.D.2d 889,
542 N.Y.S.2d 860.

BACKGROUND AND FACTS Frank Feiden was diagnosed as having Alzheimer's disease in 1982. In January 1986, during a hospital stay, Feiden conveyed his farm to his sons, Harry and Norman. The deeds gave Harry a larger share of the property. An earlier will had divided the property equally between them. In a New York state court, Norman sought to have the deeds set aside, alleging, among other things, that his father was not mentally competent at the time the deeds were signed. At the trial, witnesses testified that by early 1986, Feiden was unable to handle his financial affairs or understand the consequences of his actions. Others testified that he "had lucid intervals" and could not be called "wholly incompetent." The attorney who obtained Feiden's signatures on the deeds claimed that Feiden understood clearly what he was signing and was aware that he was deeding more of the property to Harry. Nursing summaries covering the period indicated that Feiden was periodically lucid. The trial court without a jury held that the deeds were valid, and Norman appealed.

DECISION AND RATIONALE The Supreme Court of New York, Appellate Division, held that Feiden might have been competent at the time of signing and deferred to the trial court's judgment. The deeds were valid. The appellate court pointed out that competence is presumed and incompetence must be proved. A person's mind must be "so affected as to render him

wholly and absolutely incompetent to comprehend and understand the nature of the transaction." Giving due deference to the trial judge, because
"he was in a better position to assess the evidence and the credibility of
the witnesses," the appellate court noted that there was "no direct proof
that [Feiden] was not lucid, alert or oriented at the time of the transaction."
Thus the "presumption of competency was not overcome."

■ CONCEPT SUMMARY 12.1   Legal Effect of Incapacity

	Intoxication	Minority	Mental Incompetence
General Rule	If an intoxicated person lacks the mental capacity to comprehend the legal consequences of entering into the contract, the contract is VOIDABLE at the option of the intoxicated person.	Contracts entered into by minors are VOIDABLE at the option of the minor.	1. Contracts made by a person adjudged to be mentally incompetent by a court of law and for whom a guardian has been appointed are VOID. 2. Contracts made by persons who lack the mental capacity to comprehend the subject matter, nature, and consequences of their actions, but who have not been adjudged by a court to be mentally incompetent, are VOIDABLE. 3. Contracts made by persons who understand the nature and effect of entering into a contract, even if the persons lack capacity to engage in other activities, are VALID.
Rules of Disaffirm-ance	An intoxicated person may disaffirm the contract at any time while intoxicated and for a reasonable time after becoming sober, but must make full restitution.	A minor may disaffirm the contract at any time while still a minor and within a reasonable time after reaching the age of majority. Most states do not require restitution.	A mentally incompetent person may disaffirm a voidable contract at any time while mentally incompetent and for a reasonable time after regaining mental competence, but must make full restitution.

(Continued on next page)

■ CONCEPT SUMMARY 12.1 *(Continued)*

	Intoxication	Minority	Mental Incompetence
Exceptions to Basic Rules of Disaffirm-ance	1. *Necessaries* Liable for the reasonable value of the necessaries. 2. *Ratification* After becoming sober, an intoxicated person can expressly or implicitly ratify the contract, becoming fully liable thereon.	1. *Necessaries* Liable for the reasonable value of the necessaries. 2. *Ratification* After reaching the age of majority, a minor can expressly or implicitly ratify the contract, becoming fully liable thereon. 3. *Fraud or Misrepresentation* Misrepresentation of age in many jurisdictions prohibits the right of disaffirmance.	1. *Necessaries* Liable for the reasonable value of the necessaries. 2. *Ratification* After regaining mental competence, an individual can expressly or implicitly ratify the voidable contract, becoming fully liable thereon.

■ Aliens

An alien is a citizen of another country who resides in this country. Generally, aliens who are legally in this country have the same contractual rights as U.S. citizens. They may be sued and they may sue in the courts to enforce their contractual rights.

Some states restrict the right of an alien to own real property. In virtually all cases, an *enemy alien* (that is, a citizen of a country with which we are at war) will not be able to enforce a contract, although the contract can be held in abeyance (temporarily set aside) until the war is over.

■ Terms and Concepts

age of majority 219   disaffirmance 220   ratification 224
contractual capacity 219

■ For Review

1. Generally, a minor can disaffirm any contract. What are some of the exceptions to this rule—that is, what are some contracts that minors cannot avoid?

2. Under what circumstance does intoxication make a contract voidable?

3. Under what circumstance does mental incompetence make a contract void?

4. Joel, who is six months short of his eighteenth birthday, contracts to buy a car from Northern Lights Motors. Five months later, Joel drives the car to Northern Lights to make the fifth monthly payment and tells Northern Lights, ''I love this car.'' Sixty days and two payments later, Joel drives the car to Northern Lights and says, ''I'm tired of this piece of junk. Take it and give me my money back.'' Is Joel too late to get any of his money back?

5. Neal, an adult, contracts to buy a car from Northern Lights Motors. Five months later, Neal drives the car to Northern Lights to make the fifth monthly payment and tells Northern Lights, ''I love this car.'' Sixty days later, Neal is adjudged by a court to be mentally incompetent. Later, Neal drives the car to Northern Lights and says, ''I'm tired of this piece of junk. Take it and give me my money back.'' What is the standard for determining whether Neal can get any of his money back?

■ Questions and Case Problems

12-1. Seling, a minor, sold her bicycle to Adam, an adult, for $100. Adam took possession and paid Seling. Two months later, Adam sold the bicycle to Bonnet, a bona fide purchaser, for value. Seling's parents became upset when they learned of her sale. Seling, who has not yet reached the age of majority, seeks to disaffirm the contract with Adam and recover the bicycle from Bonnet. Discuss whether Seling can recover the bicycle from Bonnet, and discuss Adam's liability to Seling.

12-2. Treat is a seventeen-year-old minor who has just graduated from high school. She is attending a university 200 miles from home and has contracted to rent an apartment near the university for one year at $250 per month. She is working at a convenience store to earn enough money to be self-supporting. She moves into the apartment and has paid four months' rent when a dispute arises between her and the landlord. Treat, still a minor, moves out and returns the key to the landlord. The landlord wants to hold Treat liable for the balance of the lease, $2,000. Discuss fully Treat's liability on the lease.

12-3. After Kira had several drinks one night, she sold Charlotte a valuable fur stole for ten dollars. The next day, Kira offered the ten dollars to Charlotte and requested the return of her stole. Charlotte refused to accept the ten dollars or return the stole, claiming that they had a valid contract of sale. Kira explained that she was intoxicated at the time the bargain was made, and thus the contract is voidable at her option. Is Kira correct? Explain.

12-4. Stewart, who was sixteen years old, purchased a used car at Harry Krank's Auto Lot for $300. At the time of the sale, Krank knew that Stewart was a minor. Stewart drove the car several times during the following week and discovered that the main bearing was burned out. He took the car back to the auto lot and was told by Krank that it would cost between $200 and $225 to repair the vehicle. Stewart refused to pay for any repairs, left the car on the lot, and later disaffirmed the contract and requested the return of the purchase price. Krank alleged that because Stewart's aunt had paid Krank $240 toward the purchase price of the car, she, and not Stewart, was the owner of the vehicle—notwithstanding the fact that Krank had made out the sales receipt in Stewart's name alone. Assuming the car is not a necessity for Stewart, how will the court rule? Discuss.

12-5. Two physicians, Devito and Burke, leased an office suite for five years and agreed to share the rent payments equally—even if one of them moved out or was unable to occupy his part of the premises as a result of disability or for any other reason. Two weeks later, Devito consulted a neurologist about his increasing absent-mindedness and forgetfulness and discussed the possibility of giving up his practice. A few months later, Devito was diagnosed as suffering from presenile dementia (premature deterioration of the brain). The condition had been developing slowly for a matter of years, resulting in the progressive loss of memory and other mental abilities. The following year, Devito was so impaired mentally that he had to close his practice and retire. Burke later sued Devito for his share of the remaining rent under the lease. Devito claimed that he had been mentally incompetent at the time he signed the agreement to share the rent, and hence the agreement was voidable at his option. Will Devito prevail in court? Discuss.

12-6. Allen Apfelblat began suffering from mental illness in the summer of 1983. In November of that same year, he executed three notes to his bank to purchase three automobiles. On January 6, 1984, Apfelblat was involuntarily committed to a psychiatric hospital, where he was successfully treated. Upon Apfelblat's release, the bank threatened to pursue legal recourse if Apfelblat did not pay on the notes. In response, Apfelblat agreed, at the insistence of the bank, to execute new notes to cover the accrued debts and to make several interest payments that were in arrears. Apfelblat later filed an action to discharge the notes due because of lack of capacity at the time the original notes were executed. Apfelblat also claimed that he did not intend to legally ratify the contract or to accept liability from a voidable contract when he did not have to. Discuss whether Apfelblat's contract is enforceable by the bank. [*Apfelblat v. National Bank of Wyandotte-Taylor,* 158 Mich.App. 258, 404 N.W.2d 725 (1987)]

12-7. In 1973, James Halbman, Jr., a minor, entered into an agreement to buy a 1968 Oldsmobile from Michael Lemke for $1,250. He made a $1,000 down payment and took possession of the automobile immediately. After experiencing problems with the car, Halbman took it to a garage for repairs. When he failed to pay the garage bill of $637, the garage removed the vehicle's engine and transmission. Halbman subsequently disaffirmed the sale contract with Lemke and returned the title to the Oldsmobile. Halbman also successfully sued to obtain the return of the money that he had paid to Lemke. Can Lemke countersue for restitution of the amount by which the automobile has declined in value because of the removal of the auto parts? Why or why not? [*Halbman v. Lemke,* 99 Wis.2d 241, 298 N.W.2d 562 (1980)]

12-8. Sheehan Buick, Inc., sold a 1965 Buick Riviera to Rose, a minor, for $5,176. While still a minor, Rose elected to disaffirm the purchase and notified Sheehan of his intention, offering to return the vehicle for a full refund. Sheehan refused, claiming that Rose appeared to be adult and acted and negotiated like an adult. In addition, Sheehan claimed that the vehicle was a necessary item for Rose because it was used to carry on his school, business, and social activities. Discuss whether Rose can disaffirm the sale and if so whether Sheehan is entitled to an offsetting amount for depreciation in the automobile's value. [*Rose v. Sheehan Buick, Inc.,* 204 So.2d 903 (Fla.App. 1967)]

12-9. Carol Ann White, a nineteen-year-old minor, went to Dr. Demetrios Cidis and asked him to furnish her with contact lenses. They agreed on a price of $225, and Carol gave Cidis her personal check for $100. The doctor examined Carol on Thursday evening, ordered the lenses on Friday, and received them on Saturday. The cost to the doctor for the lenses was $110. On Monday, at the insistence of her father, Carol called and canceled the contract and stopped payment on the check. At the time, Carol lived at home, had a full-time job, and paid her parents a sum each month for room and board. The lenses could be used by no one but Carol and thus had no market value. Dr. Cidis brought suit, claiming that the lenses were a necessary. Carol claimed her minority as a defense to any liability. Discuss whether contact lenses are necessaries. [*Cidis v. White*, 71 Misc.2d 481, 336 N.Y.S.2d 362 (1972)]

12-10. April Iverson's uncle, John Polachek, obtained a life insurance policy through his employer, Scholl, Inc. The policy, issued by Bankers Life and Casualty, named April as the sole beneficiary. April, the plaintiff, was eleven years old when her uncle died and when Bankers mailed the $10,000 death-benefit check to her. The check was made out in her name because Scholl had not informed Bankers that April was a minor. Subsequently, April's father misappropriated the funds by having April sign (indorse) the check. Later, April sued Bankers and Scholl for the $10,000. Bankers claimed that her indorsement discharged its obligation to her. She claimed that as a minor she did not have the capacity to discharge this contractual obligation. Who will prevail in court? Discuss. [*Iverson v. Scholl, Inc.*, 136 Ill.App.3d 962, 483 N.E.2d 893, 91 Ill.Dec. 407 (1985)]

12-11. A Question of Ethics

Kevin Green, a sixteen-year-old minor, entered into a sales agreement to purchase a Camaro from Star Chevrolet Co. for $4,642.50. The title for the car was drawn up in Kevin's name, and the money came from Kevin's personal bank account. The question of Kevin's age was not raised by him or the car dealership. He used the car daily to drive six miles to school and back and to drive about one mile to his place of part-time work. Kevin brought the car back several times for repairs, and he later discovered that the size and power of the engine were not what they were supposed to be. Finally, when the main head gasket blew, Kevin's attorney informed Star Chevrolet that Kevin was disaffirming the contract. Kevin repaired the gasket and continued to use the car until an accident destroyed the car more than a year after the purchase. He then returned the Camaro and sought a refund of the full purchase price of the car. In the lawsuit that followed, the car was not deemed a necessary by the court, and the dealer was required to refund the full purchase price of the car to Kevin. [Star Chevrolet Co. v. Green, *473 So.2d 157 (Miss. 1985)*]

1. The fact that minors are allowed by law to disaffirm contracts has often resulted in seemingly unfair treatment of the adult parties to such contracts. In view of this fact, do you think that the law has achieved a "fair" balance between the policy of protecting minors and the policy of protecting innocent parties who are harmed by the failure of others to keep their contractual promises? In other words, does the law favor minors to an unfair extent?

2. If the car had been deemed a necessary in this case, the outcome would have been different—Kevin would not have been able to avoid the contract. What ethical principle underlies the doctrine that minors cannot avoid contracts for necessaries?

Chapter 13

Genuineness of Assent

A contract has been entered into for a legal purpose between two parties, each with full legal capacity to form a contract. The contract is also supported by consideration. Nonetheless, the contract may be unenforceable if the parties have not genuinely assented to the terms. **Genuineness of assent** may be lacking because of mistakes, misrepresentation, undue influence, or duress (in other words, because there is no true "meeting of the minds"). If the law were to enforce contracts not genuinely assented to by the contracting parties, injustice would result. In this chapter, we examine problems relating to genuineness of assent.

◼ Mistakes

It is important to distinguish between mistakes *in judgment as to value or quality* and mistakes *as to facts.* Only the latter have legal significance. Suppose Jane Simpson plans to buy ten acres of land in Montana. If she believes the land is worth $100,000, and it is worth only $40,000, her mistake is one of value or quality. If she believes, however, that the land is the ten acres owned by the Boyds, and it is actually the ten acres owned by the Deweys, her mistake is one of fact. Only a mistake as to fact allows a contract to be avoided.

Mistakes occur in two forms—*unilateral* and *mutual (bilateral).* A unilateral mistake is made by only one of the contracting parties; a mutual, or bilateral, mistake is made by both.

Unilateral Mistakes

A unilateral mistake occurs when one contracting party makes a mistake as to some *material fact*—that is, a fact important to the subject matter of the contract. In general, a unilateral mistake does not afford the mistaken party any right to relief from the contract.[1] For example, John intends to sell his stereo for $550. He learns that Jane is interested in buying a used stereo. John writes a letter to Jane offering to sell his stereo, but he mistakenly types

---

1. Restatement (Second) of Contracts, Section 153, liberalizes this rule to take into account the modern trend of allowing avoidance although only one party has been mistaken.

in the price of $500. Jane immediately writes back, accepting John's offer. Even though John intended to sell his stereo for $550, his unilateral mistake falls on him. He is bound in contract to sell the stereo to Jane for $500.

There are two exceptions to the general rule. First, the rule is not applied when the *other* party to the contract knows or should have known that a mistake was made. Second, some states will not enforce the contract against the mistaken party if the error was due to a mathematical mistake in addition, subtraction, division, or multiplication and if it was done inadvertently and without gross negligence (a mistake of this nature is sometimes referred to as a *scrivener's error*—meaning a writer's, or scribe's, error).

For an example of how these exceptions are applied, consider the following case. Odell Construction Co. made a bid to install the plumbing in a proposed apartment building. When Herbert Odell, the president, added up his costs, his secretary forgot to give him the figures for the pipe fittings. Because of the omission, Odell's bid was $6,500 below that of the other bidders. The prime contractor, Sunspan, Inc., accepted Odell's bid. If Sunspan was not aware of Odell's mistake and could not reasonably have been aware of it, the contract will be enforceable, and Odell will be required to install the plumbing at the bid price. If it

can be shown that Odell's secretary mentioned her error to Sunspan, however, or if Odell's bid was so far below the others that, as a contractor, Sunspan should reasonably have known the bid was a mistake, the contract can be rescinded. Sunspan would not be allowed to accept the offer knowing it was made by mistake.[2] The law of contracts protects only *reasonable* expectations.

Mutual Mistakes of Material Fact

When both parties are mistaken as to the same material fact, the contract can be rescinded by either party at any time.[3] Again, the mistake must be about a material fact—a fact important to the subject matter of the contract. The classic case on mutual mistake of fact involved a ship named *Peerless* that was to sail from Bombay with certain cotton goods on board. More than one ship named *Peerless* sailed from Bombay that winter, however. The consequent mistake as to the identity of the subject matter of the contract was mutual, and it was about a material fact.

2. *Peerless Glass Co. v. Pacific Crockery Co.*, 121 Cal. 641, 54 P. 101 (1898).
3. Restatement (Second) of Contracts, Section 152.

Case 13.1

RAFFLES v. WICHELHAUS

Court of Exchequer, England, 1864.
159 Eng.Rep. 375.

BACKGROUND AND FACTS Wichelhaus bought a shipment of cotton from Raffles, "to arrive ex 'Peerless' from Bombay." Wichelhaus expected the goods to be shipped on the *Peerless* sailing from Bombay in October. Raffles expected to ship the goods on another *Peerless*, which sailed in December. When the goods arrived, Raffles tried to deliver them, but Wichelhaus refused to accept them. Raffles brought suit for breach of contract.

DECISION AND RATIONALE The Court of Exchequer held that there was no binding contract because each party had attached a different meaning to an essential term of the contract. The court reasoned that the mistake was mutual, based on reasonable assumptions on the part of both parties. The court concluded that when two parties have contracted under a mistaken, but reasonable, belief that a certain fact is true from an objective point of view, neither is bound to the contract. The court noted that here, "[t]here is nothing on the face of the contract to show that any particular ship called the 'Peerless' was meant."

Mutual Mistakes in Value

Value is variable. Depending on the time, place, and other circumstances, the same item may be worth considerably different amounts. When parties contract, their agreement establishes the value of the object of their transaction—for the moment. At the next moment, the value may change. Either party may be mistaken as to the shape that change will take, but a mistake as to value will almost never justify voiding a contract. Each party is considered to have assumed the risk that the value will change or prove to be different from what he or she thought. Without this rule, almost any party who did not receive what he or she considered a fair bargain could argue mistake.

Suppose Daniel Murray, after seeing Beverly Beale's violin, buys it for $250. Neither party knows that it is a Stradivarius built in 1717 and worth thousands of dollars. Although Beverly may claim a mutual mistake has been made, the mistake is not one that warrants contract rescission (cancellation). Both Murray and Beale mistook the value of that particular violin. Therefore, the contract cannot be rescinded.

As pointed out above, if the parties are mistaken as to some fact that is material to their transaction, the transaction may be avoided. This rule applies when the fact affects the value of the subject matter of the parties' deal. For example, an early Michigan case, *Sherwood v. Walker*,[4] involved two farmers who entered into a contract for the purchase of a cow. The owner told the purchaser that the cow was barren (incapable of breeding and producing calves). Based on this belief, the parties negotiated a price several hundred dollars less than it would have been had the cow been capable of breeding. Just before delivery, the owner discovered the cow had conceived a calf, and he refused to deliver the much more valuable cow to the purchaser. In a split decision, the court held that ''a barren cow is substantially a different creature than a breeding one,'' and the transaction was avoided.

The following case illustrates a situation in which the parties were mutually mistaken as to the value of the personal property being transferred. In discussing the issue, the court compares the circumstances to those in *Sherwood v. Walker*.

---

4. 66 Mich. 568, 33 N.W. 919 (1887).

Case 13.2

WILKIN v. 1ST SOURCE BANK

Court of Appeals of Indiana, Third District, 1990.
548 N.E.2d 170.

BACKGROUND AND FACTS In 1984, when Olga Mestrovic died, she owned a large number of artworks created by her husband, Ivan, an internationally known artist who had died in 1962. Under her will, all artwork not otherwise disposed of by the will was to be sold and the proceeds distributed to the Mestrovic family. Also included in Olga's estate was certain real estate. In 1985, Olga's executor, 1st Source Bank, sold the real estate to Terrence and Antoinette Wilkin. The bank and the Wilkins agreed that the Wilkins could clean the premises and keep any items of personal property that they wanted. Neither party suspected that any artwork remained, but the Wilkins found eight drawings and a plaster sculpture that had apparently been created by Ivan Mestrovic. The bank filed a petition in an Indiana probate court to determine title to the works. The probate court held that the works belonged to Mestrovic's estate. The Wilkins appealed, claiming ownership based on their agreement with the bank.

DECISION AND RATIONALE The Court of Appeals of Indiana affirmed the probate court's decision. The appellate court explained that when parties base their contract on a common assumption about ''a vital fact'' that proves false, the transaction may be avoided ''if because of the mistake a quite different exchange of values occurs from the exchange of values contemplated.'' There is no contract, the court said, ''because the minds of the parties have in fact never met." The court noted that the bank and the Wilkins considered the property that the Wilkins bought to be "cluttered" with " 'junk,' 'stuff' or 'trash.' " The court pointed out that the Wilkins "sought to retain a gain that was produced, not by a subsequent change in circumstances, nor by the favorable resolution of known uncertainties when the contract was made, but by the presence of facts quite different from those on which the parties based their bargain."

■ Fraudulent Misrepresentation

Although **fraud** is a tort, it also affects the genuineness of the innocent party's consent to the contract. Thus, the transaction is not voluntary in the sense of involving "mutual assent." When an innocent party is fraudulently induced to enter into a contract, the contract normally can be avoided, because that party has not *voluntarily* consented to its terms.[5] Normally, the innocent party can either rescind the contract and be restored to the original position or can enforce the contract and seek damages for any injuries resulting from the fraud.

The word *fraudulent* is used in various senses in the law. Generally, fraudulent misrepresentation refers only to misrepresentation that is consciously false and is intended to mislead another. That is, the perpetrator of the fraudulent misrepresentation must know or believe that the assertion is not true, or must be lacking the confidence that he or she states or implies in the truth of the assertion, or must know that he or she does not have the basis stated or implied for the assertion.[6]

What is at issue is whether the defendant believes that the plaintiff is substantially certain to be misled as a result of the misrepresentation. For example, Jones makes a statement to ABC Credit Rating Company about his financial condition that he knows is untrue. Jones realizes that ABC will publish this information for its subscribers. Marchetti, a subscriber, receives the published information. Relying on that information, Marchetti is induced to make a contract to lend money to Jones. Jones's statement is a fraudulent misrepresentation. The contract is voidable by Marchetti.

Typically, fraud consists of the following elements:

1. A misrepresentation of a material fact has occurred.
2. There exists an intent to deceive.
3. The innocent party has justifiably relied on the misrepresentation.
4. For damages, the innocent party must have been injured.

We will examine each of these elements in turn.

Misrepresentation Has Occurred

The first element of proving fraud is to show that misrepresentation of a material fact has occurred. This misrepresentation can be in words or actions. For example, the statement "This sculpture was created by Michelangelo" is an express misrepresentation of fact if the statue was sculpted by another artist. The misrepresentation as to the identity of the artist would certainly be a *material* fact in the formation of a contract.

Misrepresentation can also take place by the conduct of a party. One such form of conduct is concealment. Concealment is basically an act that keeps the other party from learning of a material fact.[7] Suppose Quid contracts to buy a new car from Ray, a dealer in new automobiles. The car has been used as a demonstration model for prospective customers to test drive, but Ray has turned back the odometer. Quid cannot tell from the odometer reading that the car has been driven nearly five hundred miles, and Ray does not tell Quid the distance the car has actually been driven. The concealment constitutes fraud because of Ray's con-

---

5. Restatement (Second) of Contracts, Sections 163 and 164.
6. Restatement (Second) of Contracts, Section 162.

7. Restatement (Second) of Contracts, Section 160.

LEGAL PERSPECTIVES IN BUSINESS	**Mistakes**

In today's world, decisions must often be made rapidly. Inevitably, mistakes will occur. But contracts require that mutual assent exist in order to be formed. Consider the following example. Acme Landscaping is asked by Extra Enterprises to bid for a landscaping job on its "lakeside property." Acme goes to Extra's facility on Lake Diamond and, after surveying the property, submits a bid for $20,000 to landscape the property, including the area to be completely sodded with grass. Extra sends Acme a contract entitled "Landscaping Contract for Extra Enterprises' Lakeside Facility." In the body of the contract, the property is described as located at 1500 Lakeside Drive. But this is not the property that Acme has surveyed. Acme's manager, however, does not carefully read the contract and signs it anyway without realizing his mistake.

When Acme begins the landscaping job a week later, the mistake is discovered. Acme's manager indicates to Extra that he is withdrawing his bid, since the 1500 Lakeside Drive property is five times bigger than the property surveyed. Extra's lawyers call Acme and assert that it would be in breach of contract if it does not perform.

Why did Acme's problem exist? Because the manager was careless and did not make sure that he and Extra Enterprises were discussing the same property. Acme will claim there was no mutuality of assent because Acme thought it was contracting for landscaping services on one property and Extra Enterprises was seeking a contract on another property. The court, however, will in most cases disallow evidence of mistaken belief, because of the presumption that Acme's manager read and understood the contents of the contract that he signed. Regardless of whether Acme ultimately prevails in court, the manager's mistake will be expensive, either in performing the contract or in defending the lawsuit.

Mistakes of this kind can be avoided. When a contract is drafted by the *other* party and presented for you to sign, it is up to *you* to verify that the contract explicitly describes the object of the contract and the obligations of each party.

---

duct. Likewise, if a salesperson shows a sample from the top of a large box but does not show the samples at the bottom, a misrepresentation by conduct has occurred if there is a marked difference in quality between the top and bottom merchandise.

Representations of future facts (predictions) or statements of opinion are generally not subject to claims of fraud. Every person is expected to exercise care and judgment when entering into contracts, and the law will not come to the aid of one who simply makes an unwise bargain. For example, statements like "This land will be worth twice as much next year" or "This car will last for years and years" are statements of opinion, not fact. Contracting parties should recognize them as such and not rely on them. An opinion is usually subject to contrary or conflicting views; a fact is objective

and verifiable. A seller of goods, then, is allowed to use *puffery* to sell his or her wares without liability for fraud.

In certain cases, however, opinions may entitle the innocent party to rescission. These cases almost always involve an "expert" giving a naive purchaser an opinion, and they are decided on equitable grounds. The courts usually hold it to be unfair to allow an expert to take advantage of a novice, especially if the expert knows the novice is relying on the expert's opinion. Thus, an expert's statement of opinion to a layperson is treated as fact.

The following case illustrates how a dance instructor with superior knowledge made statements of opinion concerning a prospective student's dance potential that were treated as misrepresentations of a material fact.

Case 13.3

VOKES v. ARTHUR MURRAY, INC.

District Court of Appeal of
Florida, Second District, 1968.
212 So.2d 906.

BACKGROUND AND FACTS Arthur Murray, Inc., operated dancing schools through local, franchised operators. Audrey Vokes, a widow without family, wished to become "an accomplished dancer" and to find "a new interest in life." In 1961, when she attended a "dance party" at J. P. Davenport's "School of Dancing," an instructor praised her for her grace, poise, and potential to become "an excellent dancer." The instructor sold Vokes eight half-hour dance lessons for $14.50 each, to be used within a month. Over the next sixteen months, Vokes bought 2,302 hours of lessons for $31,090.45, all at Davenport's school. When Vokes realized that she did not have the potential to become an excellent dancer, she filed suit in a Florida state court against the school, alleging fraudulent misrepresentation. The trial court dismissed her complaint. She appealed.

DECISION AND RATIONALE The District Court of Appeal of Florida reinstated Vokes's complaint and remanded the case to the trial court to allow Vokes to prove her case. The appellate court held that Vokes could avoid the contract because it was procured by false representations that she had a promising career in dancing. The court acknowledged that ordinarily, to be grounds for rescission, a misrepresentation must be one of fact rather than of opinion. The court concluded that "[a] statement of a party having * * * superior knowledge may be regarded as a statement of fact although it would be considered as opinion if the parties were dealing on equal terms. It could be reasonably supposed here that defendants had 'superior knowledge' as to whether plaintiff had 'dance potential.'"

COMMENTS Fraud is an ambiguous concept in law. It includes various degrees of misrepresentation, which can be separated into three tort categories: (1) intentional behavior, (2) negligent behavior, and (3) strict liability for certain behavior. In all cases involving the tort of misrepresentation and the contract defense of fraud, the defendant must misrepresent a fact or facts, and the plaintiff must reasonably believe the misrepresentation to be true and rely on it with resulting damages.

MISREPRESENTATION OF LAW Misrepresentation of law does not *ordinarily* entitle the party to relief from a contract. For example, Sarah has a parcel of property that she is trying to sell to Brad. Sarah knows that a local ordinance prohibits building anything on the property higher than three stories. Nonetheless, she tells Brad, "You can build a condominium fifty stories high if you want to." Brad buys the land and later discovers that Sarah's statement is false. Normally, Brad cannot avoid the contract because at common law people are assumed to know state and local law where they reside. Additionally, a layperson should not rely on a statement made by a nonlawyer about a point of law.

Exceptions to this rule occur when the misrepresenting party is in a profession that is known to

require greater knowledge of the law than the average citizen possesses. The courts are recognizing an increasing number of such professions. For example, the courts recognize that real estate brokers are expected by their clients to know the law governing real estate sales, land use, and so on. If Sarah, in the preceding example, were a lawyer or a real estate broker, her misrepresentation of the area's zoning status would probably constitute fraud.[8]

SILENCE Ordinarily, neither party to a contract has a duty to come forward and disclose facts. Therefore, a contract cannot be set aside because certain pertinent information is not volunteered.

---

8.   Restatement (Second) of Contracts, Section 170.

For example, suppose you have an accident that requires extensive body work on one side of your car. After the repair, the car's appearance and operation are the same as they were before the accident. One year later you decide to sell your car. Do you have a duty to volunteer the information about the accident to the seller? The answer is no. In this case, silence does not constitute misrepresentation. On the other hand, if the purchaser asks you if the car has had extensive body work and you lie, you have committed a fraudulent misrepresentation.

Some exceptions to this rule exist. If a *serious* potential problem or latent defect is known to the seller but cannot reasonably be suspected by the buyer, the seller may have a duty to speak. Expanding the example just given, suppose your car occasionally vibrates dangerously because of the earlier accident. In this case, you have a duty to speak. Similarly, if the foundation of a factory is cracked, creating a potential for serious water damage, the seller must reveal this fact. Likewise, when a city fails to disclose to bidders subsoil conditions that will cause great expense in constructing a sewer, the city is guilty of fraud.[9]

Failure to disclose important facts also constitutes fraud if the parties have a relationship of trust and confidence, called a **fiduciary relationship.** In such a relationship, if one party knows any facts that materially affect the other's interests, they must be disclosed. An attorney, for example, has a duty to disclose material facts to a client. Other such relationships include those between partners in a partnership, directors of corporations and shareholders, and guardians and wards.[10]

A seller's silence, coupled with active concealment, constitutes misrepresentation. In the Ray-Quid example discussed above, for example, Ray not only failed to disclose the true mileage to Quid but concealed the true mileage by turning back the odometer. Disclosing some, but not all, of the facts can be equally deceitful. Such would be the case if Ray had mentioned that the car actually had "a few more miles on it" than shown by the odometer—which registered three miles. In addition, if circumstances change so that what once was true is now false, the party knowing of the change has a duty to inform the other.

Statutes provide other exceptions to the general rule of nondisclosure. The Truth-in-Lending Act, for example, requires disclosure of certain facts (see Chapter 45). Statutes may even specify the type size to be used in the document providing the information.

Intent to Deceive

The second element of fraud is knowledge on the part of the misrepresenting party that facts have been falsely represented. This element, normally called *scienter,*[11] or "guilty knowledge," signifies that there was an *intent to deceive. Scienter* clearly exists if a party knows a fact is not as stated. *Scienter* also exists if a party makes a statement that he or she believes not to be true or makes a statement recklessly, without regard to whether it is true or false. Finally, this element is met if a party says or implies that a statement is made on some basis such as personal knowledge or personal investigation when it is not.

Suppose that Roper, when selling a house to Chipper, tells Chipper that the plumbing includes pipe of a certain quality. Roper knows nothing about the quality of the pipe but does not believe it to be as she is representing it to be (and in fact it is not as she says it is). Roper's statement induces Chipper to buy the house. Roper's statement is a misrepresentation because Roper does not believe the truth of what she said and because she knows that she does not have any basis for making it. Chipper can avoid the contract.

In many cases involving a seller's misrepresentation, courts have held that it is not necessary to prove fault. That is, a buyer need prove only that the seller's representation was false, without regard to the seller's state of mind. In those cases—often involving sales of land or stock—the courts reason that it is the seller's duty to know the truth of what he or she says.

---

9. *City of Salinas v. Souza & McCue Construction Co.,* 66 Cal.2d 217, 424 P.2d 921, 57 Cal.Rptr. 337 (1967). Normally, the seller must disclose only "latent" defects—that is, defects that the seller is aware of but that would not readily be discovered. Thus, termites in a house would not be a latent defect, since a buyer could readily discover their presence.

10. Restatement (Second) of Contracts, Sections 161 and 173.

11. Pronounced sy-*en*-ter.

Reliance on the Misrepresentation

The third element of fraud is *justifiable reliance* on the misrepresentation of fact. The deceived party must have a justifiable reason for relying on the misrepresentation, and the misrepresentation must be an important factor in inducing the party to enter into the contract, though it need not be the sole factor.

Reliance is not justified if the innocent party knows the true facts or relies on obviously extravagant statements. Suppose a used-car dealer tells you, ''This old Cadillac will get fifty miles to the gallon.'' You would not normally be justified in relying on the statement. Or suppose Phelps, a bank director, induces Scott, a co-director, to sign a guaranty that the bank's assets will satisfy its liabilities, stating, ''We have plenty of assets to satisfy our creditors.'' If Scott knows the true facts, he will not be justified in relying on Phelps's statement. If, however, Scott does not know the true facts *and has no way of finding them out,* he will be justified in relying on the statement. The same rule applies to defects in property sold. If the defects are of the kind that would be obvious on inspection, the buyer cannot justifiably rely on the seller's representations. If the defects are hidden or latent (that is, not apparent on the surface), the buyer is justified in relying on the seller's statements.

Injury to the Innocent Party

The final element of fraud is injury to the innocent party. The courts are divided on this issue. Some do not require a showing of injury when the action is to *rescind* (cancel) the contract. Because rescission returns the parties to the position they were in before they made the contract, showing injury to the innocent party has been held to be unnecessary.[12]

In an action to recover *damages* caused by the fraud, proof of an injury is universally required. The measure of damages is ordinarily equal to what the value of the property would have been if it had been delivered as represented, less what it is actually worth. In effect, this gives the innocent (nonbreaching) party the *benefit of the bargain* rather than reestablishing the party's position prior to the

contract. In actions based on fraud, courts often award **punitive damages,** or *exemplary damages,* which are defined as damages awarded to a plaintiff over and above the proved, actual compensation for the loss. Punitive damages are based on the public policy consideration of *punishing* the defendant or setting an example for similar wrongdoers.

■ Nonfraudulent Misrepresentation

If a plaintiff seeks to rescind a contract because of *fraudulent* misrepresentation, the plaintiff must prove that the defendant had the intent to deceive. Most courts also allow rescission in cases involving *nonfraudulent* misrepresentation—that is, innocent or negligent misrepresentation—if all of the other elements of misrepresentation exist.

Innocent Misrepresentation

If a person makes a statement that he or she believes to be true but that actually misrepresents material facts, the person is guilty only of an **innocent misrepresentation,** not of fraud. If an innocent misrepresentation occurs, the aggrieved party can rescind the contract but usually cannot seek damages. For example, Parris tells Roberta that a tract contains 250 acres. Parris is mistaken—the tract contains only 215 acres—but Parris does not know that. Roberta is induced by the statement to make a contract to buy the land. Even though the misrepresentation is innocent, Roberta can avoid the contract if the misrepresentation is material.

Negligent Misrepresentation

Sometimes a party will make a misrepresentation through carelessness, believing the statement is true. This misrepresentation is negligent if he or she fails to exercise reasonable care in uncovering or disclosing the facts or does not use the skill and competence that his or her business or profession requires. For example: An operator of a weight scale certifies the weight of Sneed's commodity, even though the scale's accuracy has not been checked in more than a year. In virtually all states, such **negligent misrepresentation** is equal to *scienter,* or to knowingly making a misrepresentation. In effect, negligent misrepresentation is treated as fraudulent misrepresentation, even though the misrepresention was not intentional. In

---

12.   See, for example, *Kaufman v. Jaffee,* 244 A.D. 344, 279 N.Y.S. 392 (1935).

negligent misrepresentation, culpable ignorance of the truth supplies the intention to mislead, even if the defendant can claim, ''I didn't know.''

■ Undue Influence

Undue influence arises from special kinds of relationships in which one party can greatly influence another party, thus overcoming that party's free will. Minors and elderly people are often under the influence of guardians. If the guardian induces a young or elderly ward to enter into a contract that benefits the guardian, undue influence may have been exerted. Undue influence can arise from a number of fiduciary relationships: attorney-client, doctor-patient, guardian-ward, parent-child, husband-wife, or trustee-beneficiary. The essential feature of undue influence is that the party being taken advantage of does not, in reality, exercise free will in entering into a contract. A contract entered into under excessive or undue influence lacks genuine assent and is therefore voidable.[13]

To determine whether undue influence has been exerted, a court must ask: To what extent was the transaction induced by domination of the mind or emotions of the person in question? It follows, then, that the mental state of the person in question will often show to what extent the persuasion from the outside influence was ''unfair.''

When a contract enriches a party at the expense of another who is in a relationship of trust and confidence with or who is dominated by the enriched party, the court will often *presume* that the contract was made under undue influence. For example, if a ward challenges a contract made by his or her guardian, the presumption will normally be that the guardian has taken advantage of the ward. To rebut this presumption successfully, the guardian has to show that *full disclosure* was made to the ward, that consideration was adequate, and that the ward received independent and competent advice before completing the transaction.

In a relationship of trust and confidence, such as between an attorney and a client, the dominant party (the attorney) is held to extreme or utmost good faith in dealing with the subservient party. Suppose that a long-time attorney for an elderly man induces him to sign a contract for the sale of some of his assets to a friend of the attorney at

below-market prices. It is presumed that the attorney has not upheld good faith in dealing with the man. Unless this presumption can be rebutted, the contract will be voidable.

■ Duress

Undue influence involves conduct of a *persuasive* nature; **duress** involves conduct of a *coercive* nature. That is, assent to the terms of a contract is not genuine if one of the parties is *forced* into agreement. Recognizing this, the courts allow that party to rescind the contract. Forcing a party to enter into a contract by threatening the party with a wrongful act is legally defined as *duress*. For example, if Piranha Loan Company threatens to harm you or your family unless you sign a promissory note for the money that you owe, Piranha is guilty of duress. In addition, threatening blackmail or extortion to induce consent to a contract constitutes duress. Duress is both a defense to the enforcement of a contract and a ground for rescission. Therefore, the party upon whom the duress is exerted can choose to carry out the contract or to avoid the entire transaction. (This is true in most cases in which assent is not real.)

Generally, the threatened act must be wrongful or illegal. Threatening to exercise a legal right is not ordinarily illegal and usually does not constitute duress. Suppose that Donovan injures Jaworski in an auto accident. The police are not called. Donovan has no automobile insurance, but she has substantial assets. Jaworski is willing to settle the potential claim out of court for $3,000. Donovan refuses. After much arguing, Jaworski loses her patience and says, ''If you don't pay me $3,000 right now, I'm going to sue you for $35,000.'' Donovan is frightened and gives Jaworski a check for $3,000. Later in the day, she stops payment on the check. Jaworski comes back to sue her for the $3,000. Donovan argues that she was the victim of duress. The threat of a civil suit is normally not duress, however.

Being in need is generally not a circumstance that will lead to a finding of duress, even when one party exacts a very high price for whatever it is the other party needs. If the party exacting the price also creates the need, however, *economic duress* may be found. For example, the Internal Revenue Service assessed a large tax and penalty against Weller. Weller retained Eyman, the accountant

---

13.   Restatement (Second) of Contracts, Section 177.

who had filed the tax returns on which the assessment was based, to resist the assessment. Two days before the deadline for filing a reply with the Internal Revenue Service, Eyman declined to represent Weller unless he signed a very high contingency fee agreement for his services. The agreement was unenforceable.[14] Although Eyman had

---

14. *Thompson Crane & Trucking Co. v. Eyman,* 123 Cal.App.2d 904, 267 P.2d 1043 (1954).

threatened only to withdraw his services, something that he was legally entitled to do, he was responsible for delaying the withdrawal until the last days. Because it would have been impossible at that late date to obtain adequate representation elsewhere, Weller was forced either to sign the contract or lose his right to challenge the IRS assessment.

In the following case, the plaintiff claimed that it had signed a release agreement under duress.

Case 13.4

ART STONE THEATRICAL CORP. v. TECHNICAL PROGRAMMING & SYSTEMS SUPPORT OF LONG ISLAND, INC.

Supreme Court of New York, Appellate Division, Second Department, 1990. 157 A.D.2d 689, 549 N.Y.S.2d 789.

BACKGROUND AND FACTS   Art Stone Theatrical Corporation bought a computer software system from Technical Programming & Systems Support of Long Island, Inc. After a dispute over the software's performance, a representative of Technical removed the source code from the system without Stone's knowledge or consent. Removing the source code made the system useless to Stone. Later the parties agreed that Technical would make the source code available and that Stone would release Technical from liability for any damages incurred by its removal of the source code. Stone signed the release but later sued Technical for damages in a New York state court, claiming that the release was void because it had been procured under duress. The trial court dismissed the action on the ground that the action was barred by the release. Stone appealed.

DECISION AND RATIONALE   The New York Supreme Court, Appellate Division, ruled the trial court's judgment improper and remanded the case for trial on the issue of duress. The appellate court pointed out that "[a] contract may be voided on the ground of economic duress where the complaining party was compelled to agree to its terms by means of a wrongful threat which precluded the exercise of its free will." The court found Stone's allegations of having to sign the release to obtain the return of the source code "sufficient to raise a factual issue with regard to the * * * claim of duress."

◼ Adhesion Contracts and Unconscionability

Modern courts are beginning to strike down terms dictated by a party with overwhelming bargaining power. **Adhesion contracts** arise in situations in which the signer must agree to certain dictated terms or go without the commodity or service in question. An adhesion contract is written *exclusively* by one party (the dominant party, usually the seller or creditor) and presented to the other party (the adhering party, usually the buyer or borrower) with no opportunity to negotiate. Adhesion

contracts usually contain copious amounts of fine print disclaiming the maker's liability for everything imaginable. Standard lease forms are often called adhesion contracts. Many automobile retailers have used contracts containing several pages of fine print when selling a car. In the past, nearly every automobile company excluded liability for personal injuries suffered as a result of using the product. The average consumer buying a car was in no position to bargain for personal injury coverage. The consumer could either go without an automobile or buy the auto, risking personal injury for which he or she could not hold the auto manufacturer liable.

Standard form contracts are used by a variety of businesses and include life insurance policies, residential leases, loan agreements, and employment agency contracts. To avoid enforcement of the contract or of a particular clause, the aggrieved party must show substantially unequal bargaining positions and show that enforcement would be manifestly unfair or oppressive. If the required showing is made, the contract or particular term is deemed *unconscionable* and not enforced. Technically, unconscionability under Section 2-302 of the UCC applies only to contracts for the sale of goods. Many courts, however, have broadened the concept and applied it in other situations.

Although unconscionability will be discussed in the next chapter, it is important to note here that the great degree of discretion permitted a court to invalidate or strike down a contract or clause as being unconscionable has met with resistance. As a result, some states have not adopted Section 2-302 of the UCC. In those states, the legislature and the courts prefer to rely on traditional notions of fraud, undue influence, and duress. In one respect, this gives certainty to contractual relationships, because parties know they will be held to the exact terms of their contracts. But on the other hand, public policy does require that there be some limit on the power of individuals and businesses to dictate the terms of contracts. The following classic case is illustrative.

Case 13.5

CAMPBELL SOUP CO. v. WENTZ

United States Court of Appeals, Third Circuit, 1949.
172 F.2d 80.

BACKGROUND AND FACTS In June 1947, Campbell Soup Company contracted with George and Harry Wentz for all Chantenay red-cored carrots to be grown on fifteen acres of their farm during the season. Prices under the contract ranged from $23 to $30 per ton according to the time of delivery. The contract price for January 1948 was $30 per ton. The contract included a liquidated-damages clause of "$50 per acre for any breach by the grower." Early in January 1948, the Wentzes told Campbell that they would not deliver their carrots at the contract price. The market price had risen to more than $90 per ton, and Chantenay red-cored carrots were virtually unobtainable. The Wentzes harvested 100 tons of the carrots and sold 62 tons to Lojeski, a neighboring farmer. Lojeski sold about half of these to Campbell on the open market. Campbell brought suit in a federal district court against the Wentzes and Lojeski to enjoin the sale of the rest of the 100 tons and to compel specific performance of the contract. The trial court denied Campbell's petition, and Campbell appealed.

DECISION AND RATIONALE The United States Court of Appeals for the Third Circuit affirmed the trial court's ruling on the ground that the contract was unconscionable and therefore did not merit enforcement by a court of equity. The appellate court held that the contract was "too hard a bargain and too one-sided * * * to entitle the plaintiff to relief in a court of conscience." The court noted that "[f]or each individual grower the agreement is made by filling in names and quantity and price on a printed form furnished by the buyer. This form has quite obviously been drawn by skilful draftsmen with the buyer's interests in mind." The court pointed out that the form contained a provision for liquidated damages for any breach of the contract by the grower but none for a breach by Campbell. Under the contract, Campbell was excused from accepting carrots under certain circumstances, but the grower was not permitted to sell them elsewhere unless Campbell agreed.

■ CONCEPT SUMMARY 13.1   Genuineness of Assent

Problems of Assent	Rule
Mistakes	1. *Unilateral*—Generally, the mistaken party is bound by the contract, *unless* (1) the other party knows or should have known of the mistake or (2) in some states, the mistake is an inadvertent mathematical error in addition, subtraction, etc., that is committed without gross negligence. 2. *Bilateral (mutual)*—If both parties are mistaken about a material fact, such as the identity of the subject matter, either party can avoid the contract. If the mistake relates to the value or quality of the subject matter, either party can enforce the contract.
Fraudulent Misrepresentation	Four elements are necessary to establish fraudulent misrepresentation: 1. A misrepresentation of a material fact has occurred. 2. There exists an intent to deceive. 3. The innocent party has justifiably relied on the misrepresentation. 4. For damages, the innocent party must have been injured.
Nonfraudulent Misrepresentation	1. *Innocent misrepresentation*—Occurs when a person makes a statement that he or she believes to be true but that actually misrepresents material facts. The aggrieved party can rescind the contract but usually cannot seek damages. 2. *Negligent misrepresentation*—Occurs when a person makes an untrue statement but, through carelessness, believes the statement to be true. The legal effect of negligent misrepresentation is the same as for fraudulent misrepresentation in virtually all states.
Influence/Coercion	1. *Undue influence*—Arises from special relationships, such as fiduciary relationships, in which one party's free will has been overcome by the undue influence of another. Usually, the contract is avoidable. 2. *Duress*—Defined as forcing a party to enter into a contract under the fear of threat—for example, the threat of violence or economic pressure. The party forced to enter the contract can rescind the contract.
Unconscionability	Concerned with one-sided bargains in which one party has substantially superior bargaining power and can dictate the terms of a contract. Unconscionability typically occurs as a result of the following: 1. "Standard form" contracts in which a fine print provision purports to shift a risk normally borne by one party to the other (for example, a liability disclaimer). 2. "Take it or leave it" adhesion contracts in which the buyer has no choice but to agree to the seller's dictated terms if the buyer is to procure certain goods or services.

■ Terms and Concepts

For Review

1. What is the difference between a mistake of judgment as to value or quality and a mistake of fact?

2. What is the difference between fraudulent misrepresentation and nonfraudulent misrepresentation?

3. To avoid an adhesion contract on grounds of unconscionability, what must a party show?

4. Asa wants to sell his house. To prevent buyers from discovering that the foundation is cracked, Asa paints the basement floor. Sandra, a potential buyer, tells Asa that the most important part of a house is a solid foundation. Asa says nothing. Sandra buys the house. Is the contract voidable by Sandra? On what ground?

5. Sample Manufacturing Co. leaves a machine with Best Repair Co. for repairs. Best fixes the machine, and Sample pays for the repairs, but Best refuses to deliver the machine unless Sample signs a service contract with Best for all future repair work. Because delay will cause Sample considerable financial loss, Sample urgently needs the machine and thus is induced by Best's threat to sign the service contract. Is the contract voidable by Sample? On what ground?

Questions and Case Problems

13-1. John is an elderly man who lives with his nephew, Samuel. John is totally dependent on Samuel's support. Samuel tells John that unless he transfers a tract of land he owns to Samuel for a price 15 percent below market value, Samuel will no longer support and take care of him. John enters into the contract. Discuss fully whether John can set aside this contract.

13-2. Martin owns a forty-room motel on Highway 100. Tanner is interested in purchasing the motel. During the course of negotiations, Martin tells Tanner that the motel netted $30,000 last year and that it will net at least $45,000 next year. The motel books, which Martin turns over to Tanner before the purchase, clearly show that Martin's motel netted only $15,000 last year. Also, Martin fails to tell Tanner that a bypass to Highway 100 is being planned that will redirect most traffic away from the front of the motel. Tanner purchases the motel. During the first year under Tanner's operation, the motel nets only $18,000. It is at this time that Tanner learns of the previous low profitability of the motel and the planned bypass. Tanner wants his money back from Martin. Discuss fully Tanner's probable success in getting his money back.

13-3. Discuss whether any of the following contracts will be unenforceable on the grounds that genuineness of assent is lacking.

(a) Simmons finds a stone in his pasture that he believes to be quartz. Jenson, who also believes that the stone is quartz, contracts to purchase it for $10. Just before delivery, the stone is discovered to be a diamond worth $1,000.

(b) Jacoby's barn is burned to the ground. He accuses Goldman's son of arson and threatens to bring criminal action unless Goldman agrees to pay him $5,000. Goldman agrees to pay.

(c) Kober, a new salesperson, innocently tells Larry that a lawn mower he is selling has a five-year manufacturer's warranty. Larry contracts to purchase the lawn mower in reliance on that information. Larry and Kober are transacting business for the first time.

At the time of delivery, it is discovered that the manufacturer warrants the lawn mower for only one year.

13-4. Lund offered to sell Steck his car and told Steck that the car had been driven only 25,000 miles and had never been in an accident. Steck hired Carvallo, a mechanic, to appraise the condition of the car, and Carvallo said that the car probably had at least 50,000 miles on it and probably had been in an accident. In spite of this information, Steck still thought the car would be a good buy for the price, so he purchased it. Later, when the car developed numerous mechanical problems, Steck sought to rescind the contract on the basis of Lund's fraudulent misrepresentation of the auto's condition. Will Steck be able to rescind his contract? Explain.

13-5. Steven Lanci was involved in an automobile accident with an uninsured motorist. Lanci was insured with Metropolitan Insurance Co., although he did not have a copy of the insurance policy. Lanci and Metropolitan entered settlement negotiations, during which Lanci told Metropolitan that he did not have a copy of his policy. Ultimately, Lanci agreed to settle all claims for $15,000, noting in a letter to Metropolitan that $15,000 was the "sum you have represented to be the . . . policy limits applicable to this claim." After signing a release, Lanci learned that the policy limits were actually $250,000, and he refused to accept the settlement proceeds. When Metropolitan sued to enforce the settlement agreement, Lanci argued that the release had been signed as the result of a mistake and was void. Should the court enforce the contract or void it? Explain. [*Lanci v. Metropolitan Insurance Co.*, 388 Pa.Super. 1, 564 A.2d 972 (1989)]

13-6. In 1982, William Schmalz was hired by the Hardy Salt Co. under an employment contract that stated that he was entitled to six months' severance pay in the event that he was laid off. The company would not have to pay in the event of any voluntary separation or involuntary termination for other reasons, such as for poor performance or for cause. In mid-1983, Schmalz was asked to resign after having an affair with the chairman's executive secretary. Schmalz was told that if he did not resign he would be fired but that if he did resign the company would keep him on the payroll for another six weeks. Schmalz resigned and signed an agreement releasing Hardy Salt from any liability for breach of the employment contract. Schmalz later claimed that he had signed the release under duress and sued Hardy Salt for the six months' severance pay under his employment contract. Discuss whether Schmalz's claim for duress should succeed. [*Schmalz v. Hardy Salt Co.*, 739 S.W.2d 765 (Mo.App.1987)]

13-7. William and Lilly Adams obtained a divorce in 1985 and began the process of dividing their property. They inventoried their worldly possessions and decided that certain property would go to Mrs. Adams and the remainder, including the debts on the community property, would remain with Mr. Adams. Mrs. Adams later testified in legal proceedings that Mr. Adams had consistently told her that she must take the property as offered and agree not to seek alimony, that Mr. Adams had threatened to declare bankruptcy and force her to accept the responsibility for her share of the community debts if she did not agree, and that Mr. Adams frequently cursed her but did not in any way threaten physical harm. Mrs. Adams also testified that she had examined the subsequent formal community property settlement and that she basically understood it. At that time, she had casually spoken to two different attorneys about the settlement contract, but because both attorneys said that they would need time to investigate before giving advice, she went ahead and signed it. She now claims that she had signed the agreement under duress and because of fraudulent misrepresentation. Discuss whether Mrs. Adams can rescind the settlement contract on these grounds. [*Adams v. Adams*, 503 So.2d 1052 (La.App.2 Cir. 1987)]

13-8. Division West Chinchilla Ranch made numerous TV advertisements that induced listeners to go into the business of raising chinchillas. The advertisements stated that, for a payment of $2,150 or more, Division would send one male and six female chinchillas and—for an additional sum—cages, feed, and supplies. Division's representations were that "chinchilla ranching can be done in the basement, [and] spare rooms, . . . with minor modifications" and that chinchillas were "odorless and practically noiseless" and "a profitable pastime that can explode into a FIVE FIGURE INCOME." All statements would lead one to believe that no special skill was needed in the raising of chinchillas. Based on these representations, Adolph Fischer and others (the plaintiffs) purchased chinchillas from Division. None of the plaintiffs was a sophisticated businessperson or highly educated. It soon became apparent that greater skill than that advertised was required to raise chinchillas and that certain statements made by Division's sales representatives as to the value of the pelts were untrue. None of the plaintiffs had financial success with their growing (ranching) of chinchillas over a three-year period. The plaintiffs sought to rescind the contracts to get their money back, claiming fraud on the part of Division. Discuss whether Division's statements constitute fraud. [*Fischer v. Division West Chinchilla Ranch*, 310 F.Supp. 424 (D.Minn. 1970)]

13-9. In July 1965, Loral Corp. was awarded a $6 million contract to produce radar sets for the Navy. For this contract Loral needed to purchase forty pre-cision gear parts. Loral awarded to Austin Instrument, Inc., a subcontract to supply twenty-three of the forty gear parts. In May of 1966 Loral was awarded a second contract to produce more radar sets. Loral solicited bids for forty more gear parts. Austin submitted a bid for all forty but was told by Loral that the subcontract would be awarded only for items for which Austin was the lowest bidder. Austin's president told Loral that it would not accept an order for less than forty gear parts and, one day later, told Loral that Austin would cease deliveries on the existing contract unless (1) Loral awarded Austin a contract for all forty gear part units and (2) Loral consented to substantial increases for the prices of all gear parts under the existing contract. Ten days later Austin ceased making deliveries. Loral tried to find other suppliers to furnish the gear parts, but none were available. Because of deadlines and liquidated damage clauses (clauses providing for money damages to be paid in the event of delays) in the Navy contract, plus the possible loss of reputation by Loral with the government, Loral agreed to Austin's terms. After Austin's last delivery, Loral filed suit to recover the increased prices Austin had charged on the grounds that the agreement to pay these prices was based on duress. Discuss Loral's claim. [*Austin Instrument, Inc. v. Loral Corp.*, 29 N.Y.2d 124, 272 N.E.2d 533, 324 N.Y.S.2d 22 (1971)]

13-10. Robert and Wendy Pfister held a hundred shares of Tracor Computing Corp. stock. The stock was no longer being traded on the New York Stock Exchange, and they thought their shares were of little value. They asked a stock brokerage firm, Foster & Marshall, Inc., to evaluate the shares for them. The brokerage firm advised the Pfisters that Tracor Computing had changed its name to Continuum Company, Inc., and that its stock was worth $49.50 a share; thus, the Pfisters' holdings were valued at $4,950. Robert Pfister suspected there might be an error in the valuation and asked Foster & Marshall to recheck the value, which was done. The Pfisters sold their shares to Foster & Marshall, which paid them the $4,950 for the hundred shares. Later, the brokerage firm discovered that the Tracor Computing stock had been exchanged for Continuum stock at a ten-to-one ratio, which meant that the Pfisters had owned only ten shares. The Pfisters refused to return the $4,455.25 overpayment they had received from the brokerage firm. Can Foster & Marshall recover the overpayment it made to the Pfisters resulting from its own unilateral mistake of fact? Discuss. [*Foster & Marshall, Inc. v. Pfister*, 66 Or.App. 685, 674 P.2d 1215 (1984)]

13-11. Nosrat, a citizen of Iran, owned a hardware store with his brother-in-law, Edwin. Edwin induced Nosrat to sign a promissory note for $11,400, payable to a third party, telling Nosrat that the document was a credit application for the hardware store. Although Nosrat could read and write English, he failed to read the note or to notice that the document was clearly entitled "PROMISSORY NOTE (SECURED) and Security Agreement." The money received from the third party in exchange for the note was spent by Edwin and others. When the third party sued for payment, Nosrat sought to void the note on the basis of Edwin's fraudulent inducement. Will Nosrat succeed in his attempt? Discuss. [*Waldrep v. Nosrat*, 426 So.2d 822 (Ala. 1983)]

13-12. A Question of Ethics

Roy Jacobsen attended Columbia University from 1951 to 1954. During his years at Columbia, Jacobsen was a difficult student and critical of his professors. He shifted his academic interests a number of times—from physics to social work to creative writing and other areas. In his last year, he attended classes only as he chose, and he rejected the university's regimen requiring examinations and term papers. Ultimately, he failed to graduate because of poor scholastic standing. When Columbia sued Jacobsen for $1,000 in tuition still owed by him, Jacobsen countered with the allegation that the university had failed to impart the "wisdom" promised—by its motto, its brochures, the inscriptions over its buildings, in its presidential addresses, and so on. Because Columbia had promised something it could not deliver, it was guilty of misrepresentation and deceit and should return to Jacobsen all the tuition he had paid—$7,016. [Trustees of Columbia University v. Jacobsen, 53 N.J.Super. 574, 148 A.2d 63 (1959)]

1. Do you agree with Jacobsen that Columbia, by implicitly promising to impart wisdom, was guilty of misrepresentation? Can "wisdom" be imparted?

2. What exactly is the nature of a university's contractual duty to its students?

3. Review the list of equitable maxims in Chapter 1. Which maxim is most appropriate to Jacobsen's behavior in this case?

Chapter 14

Legality and the Statute of Frauds

A contract, to be enforced in court, must not call for the performance of an illegal act—that is, any act that is criminal, tortious, or otherwise opposed to public policy. The first part of this chapter considers what makes a bargain illegal—being contrary to state or federal statutes or to public policy—and the *effects* of an illegal bargain. Such contracts are normally void—that is, they really are not contracts.

A contract that is otherwise valid may still be unenforceable if it is not in the proper form. For example, certain types of contracts are required to be in writing. If a contract is required by law to be in writing and there is no written evidence of the contract, it may not be enforceable. In the second part of this chapter, we examine the kinds of contracts that require a writing under what is called the *Statute of Frauds*. The chapter concludes with a discussion of the *parol evidence rule,* under which courts determine the admissibility at trial of evidence extraneous, or external, to written contracts.

■ Legality

A contract to do something that is prohibited by federal or state statutory law is illegal and, as such, void from the outset and thus unenforceable. Also, a contract that is tortious or calls for an action contrary to public policy is illegal and unenforceable. It is important to note that a contract, or a clause in a contract, may be illegal even in the absence of a specific statute prohibiting the action promised by the contract.

Contracts Contrary to Statute

Statutes often prescribe the terms of contracts. In some instances, the laws are specific, even providing for the inclusion of certain clauses and their wording. Other statutes prohibit certain contracts on the basis of their subject matter, the time at which they are entered into, or the status of the contracting parties. We now examine several ways in which contracts may be contrary to statute and thus illegal.

USURY Every state has statutes that set the maximum rates of interest that can be charged for different types of transactions, including ordinary loans. A lender who makes a loan at an interest rate above the lawful maximum is guilty of **usury.** The maximum rate of interest varies from state to state.

The maximum rate of interest should not be confused with either the **legal rate of interest** or the **judgment rate of interest.** The legal rate of interest is a rate fixed by statute when the parties to a contract intend an interest rate to be paid but do not fix the rate in the contract. This rate is frequently the same as the maximum rate of interest permitted by statute. A judgment rate of interest is a rate fixed by statute that is applied to monetary judgments from the moment the judgment is awarded by a court until the judgment is paid. In some states, the legal rate is also the *prejudgment rate.* That is, it is the rate of interest that accrues on the amount of a judgment from the time of the filing of the suit to the issuance of the judgment.

Although usury statutes place a ceiling on allowable rates of interest, exceptions have been made to facilitate business transactions. For example, many states exempt corporate loans from the usury laws. In addition, almost all states have adopted special statutes allowing much higher interest rates on small loans to help those borrowers who are in need of money but simply cannot get loans at interest rates below the normal lawful maximum.

The effects of a usurious loan differ from state to state. A number of states allow the lender to recover the principal of a loan along with interest up to the legal maximum. In effect, the lender is denied recovery of the excess interest. In other states, the lender can recover the principal amount of the loan but not the interest. In a few states, a usurious loan is a void transaction, and the lender cannot recover either the principal or the interest.

GAMBLING In general, wagers and games of chance are illegal. All states have statutes that regulate gambling—defined as any scheme for the distribution of property by chance among persons who have paid a valuable consideration for the opportunity to receive the property.[1] Gambling is the creation of risk for the purpose of assuming it. In other words, a person making a bet creates the risk that he or she may lose the bet on the happening of an uncertain event in which he or she otherwise has no interest. A few states do permit gambling, some only as long as the prizes or winnings do not exceed $100 to $500. In addition, about half of the states have recognized the substantial revenues that can be obtained from gambling and have legalized state-operated lotteries, horse racing, and lotteries arranged for charitable purposes (such as bingo).

Sometimes it is difficult to distinguish a gambling contract from the risk-sharing inherent in almost all contracts. For example, it might appear that a person selling or buying a futures contract (a contract for the future purchase or sale of a commodity, such as corn or wheat) is essentially gambling on the future price of the commodity. Because, however, the seller of the futures contract either already has a property interest in the commodity or can purchase the commodity elsewhere and deliver the commodity as required in the futures contract, courts have upheld the legality of such contracts.

Insurance contracts also involve risk but differ from gambling contracts in significant ways. First, the buyer of an insurance policy has an *insurable interest* in the subject of the policy. For example, a homeowner's insurable interest in his or her home is the benefit derived by the homeowner from the home's continued existence or the loss the homeowner would suffer from its destruction. Second, the seller of the policy agrees to compensate the buyer for loss under circumstances involving an existing risk. For example, a homeowner does not create the risk that his or her home may be lost in a fire but merely shifts this risk to the insurer. Insurance is discussed more fully in Chapter 53.

The following case illustrates a court's analysis of the difference between a contest of chance and one of skill in forecasting the results of football games to be played.

---

1. See *Wishing Well Club, Inc. v. Akron,* 66 Ohio L. Abs. 406, 112 N.E.2d 41 (Ohio Com. Pl. 1951).

Case 14.1

**SEATTLE TIMES CO. v.
TIELSCH**

Supreme Court of Washington,
En Banc, 1972.
80 Wash.2d 502,
495 P.2d 1366.

BACKGROUND AND FACTS   The *Seattle Times* ran a football forecasting contest that it named "Guest-Guesser." The Seattle chief of police claimed that the contest was illegal because it was a lottery. When the *Times* petitioned a Washington state court to determine the legality of the contest, the trial court found that the contest was an illegal lottery. The *Times* appealed.

DECISION AND RATIONALE   The Washington Supreme Court upheld the trial court's ruling. The state supreme court found that football game results are so unpredictable that the contest's dominant factor was chance rather than skill. Even the name of the contest conveyed the promoter's and participants' concept of the true nature of the contest. Thus, the "Guest-Guesser" game was held to be a lottery and illegal, even though the participants and the promoter considered it harmless.

SABBATH LAWS   Statutes called Sabbath, or Sunday, laws prohibit the formation or performance of certain contracts on Sunday. At common law, in the absence of this statutory prohibition, such contracts are legal. Most states, however, have enacted some type of Sunday statute.

Some states have statutes making all contracts entered into on Sunday illegal. Statutes in other states prohibit only the sale of merchandise, particularly alcoholic beverages, on Sunday. (These are often called *blue laws*.) A number of states have laws that forbid the carrying on of "all secular labor and business on The Lord's Day." In such states, contracts made on Sunday are normally illegal and unenforceable *as long as they remain executory* (not performed).

Exceptions to Sunday laws permit contracts for necessities, such as food, and works of charity. In addition, a contract entered into on Sunday that has been fully performed (that is, an *executed* contract) cannot be rescinded, or canceled. Active enforcement of Sunday laws varies from state to state and even among communities within a particular state. Many do not enforce the Sunday laws, and some of these laws have been held to be unconstitutional on the grounds that they are contrary to the freedom of religion.

LICENSING STATUTES   All states require members of certain professions or callings to obtain licenses allowing them to practice. Doctors, lawyers, real estate brokers, construction contractors, electricians, and stockbrokers are but a few of the people who must be licensed. When a person enters into a contract with an unlicensed individual,

the contract may be enforceable despite the lack of a license. The nature of the statute itself often tells if such a contract is enforceable. Some statutes expressly provide that the lack of a license for people engaged in certain occupations will bar enforcement of any work-related contracts they enter into.

If the statute does not expressly state this, one must look to the underlying purpose of the licensing requirements for that occupation. If the underlying purpose of the licensing statute is to raise revenues, a contract entered into with an unlicensed practitioner will normally be enforceable. The sanction instead will usually be a fine on the unlicensed practitioner. If the underlying purpose is to protect the public from unauthorized practitioners, however, then the contract will be illegal and unenforceable. For example, if you enter into a contract involving the professional services of an unlicensed chiropractor, the chiropractor cannot enforce the contract. The licensing of chiropractors is designed to protect the public from persons who are not capable (or who have not shown their capability) of practicing their trade.

CONTRACTS TO COMMIT A CRIME   Any contract to commit a crime is a contract in violation of a statute.[2] Thus, a contract to sell an illegal drug (the sale of which is prohibited by statute) is not enforceable. Should the object or performance of the contract be rendered illegal by statute *after* the

---

2.   See, for example, *McConnell v. Commonwealth Pictures Corp.*, 7 N.Y.2d 465, 166 N.E.2d 494, 199 N.Y.S.2d 483 (1960).

contract has been entered into, the contract is said to be discharged by law. (See the discussion under "Impossibility of Performance" in Chapter 16.)

Contracts Contrary to Public Policy

Although contracts are entered into by private parties, some are not enforceable because of the negative impact they would have on society. These contracts are said to be *contrary to public policy.* Numerous examples exist. Any contract to commit an immoral act falls in this category. Contracts that prohibit marriage have been held to be illegal on this basis. Suppose Dangerfield promises a young man $500 if he will refrain from marrying Dangerfield's daughter. If the young man accepts, the resulting contract is void. Thus, if he married Dangerfield's daughter, Dangerfield could not sue him for breach of contract.

CONTRACTS IN RESTRAINT OF TRADE   An example of contracts that adversely affect the public are contracts in restraint of trade. For example, competitors who agree to set the levels or ranges of the prices they will charge for their products or services inhibit competition, and public policy favors competition in the economy. Such price-fixing arrangements may be horizontal (between competitors) or vertical (between manufacturers and distributors, concerning resale prices). Contracts in restraint of trade usually violate one or more *antitrust statutes,* which have been enacted to encourage competition within the economy.[3] Prior to the adoption of antitrust statutes, however, the common law prohibited certain contracts that had the effect of restraining trade.

Although most contracts in restraint of trade are illegal, an exception is recognized for some restraints that are considered to be *reasonable* and are interpreted as being integral to certain contracts. Many such exceptions involve a type of restraint that is called a covenant not to compete, or a restrictive covenant.

Covenants Not to Compete   *Covenants not to compete* are often contained in contracts for the sale of an ongoing business. The seller agrees not to open a new store within a certain geographical area surrounding the old store for a specified period of time. When covenants, or agreements, not to compete are accompanied by the sale of an ongoing business, the agreements are usually upheld as legal if they are "reasonable," usually in terms of time and area. The purpose of these covenants is to enable the seller to sell, and the purchaser to buy, the goodwill and reputation of an ongoing business. If these covenants were not valid, then the valuable business interest of goodwill and reputation could not be transferred.

For example, suppose the seller has built up an established clientele because the business is known for its high-quality products and service. If the buyer desires to keep the opportunity to serve the established clientele, he or she will include a covenant that imposes reasonable restrictions on the seller—for example, that the seller shall not establish a similar business within a two-mile radius for a period of two years. The seller, in turn, receives consideration in return for giving up his or her legal right to compete under the conditions prescribed. In this way, the seller is prevented from opening a similar business down the block and drawing away the buyer's customers.

If the agreement not to compete is made without an accompanying sales agreement, it is void because it tends to restrain trade and is contrary to public policy. Even when ancillary to a primary agreement, an agreement not to compete can be contrary to public policy if it is unreasonably broad or restrictive as to time or geographic area. Suppose Orian Capital, doing business in San Francisco, sells its loan and finance business to Bankers Life Company. If Orian Capital agrees not to open another business in the state of California, the agreement not to compete is unreasonably broad. After all, the threat of losing customers to Orian is not very severe in San Diego. On the other hand, if the agreement covers only the San Francisco Bay area, it will probably be upheld.

Ancillary agreements not to compete can also be held contrary to public policy if they cover an unreasonably long period of time. In the preceding example, if Orian agrees not to compete for a hundred years, the contract is contrary to public policy. On the other hand, a two-year agreement is reasonable and enforceable (and in some cases, depending on the situation, up to twenty years would be reasonable).

---

3.   Some of these statutes are the Sherman Antitrust Act, the Clayton Act, and the Federal Trade Commission Act. States also have separate antitrust statutes. Antitrust and contracts in restraint of trade are discussed in Chapter 47.

Agreements not to compete can be ancillary to employment contracts. It is increasingly common for many professionals and key management personnel to agree not to work for competitors or not to start a new practice or business for a specified period of time in a specified area after terminating employment. Covenants not to compete are frequently used to prevent a competitor from pirating personnel, to limit a departing employee's disclosure of trade secrets to a competing firm, and to protect an employer's investment in training personnel by not permitting departing employees to use their training immediately with a competitor. If such an agreement is not ancillary to an employment contract, it is illegal. If the agreement is ancillary to an employment contract, it is legal as long as it is not excessive in scope or duration. Covenants not to compete that are ancillary to employment contracts are closely scrutinized by the courts.

On occasion, when a covenant not to compete has been construed to be unreasonable in its essential terms, some courts have *reformed* the covenant, converting its terms into reasonable ones. Instead of declaring the covenant illegal and unenforceable, the courts have applied the rule of reasonableness and changed the contract so that its basic, original intent could be enforced. For example, in the Orian Capital case, if Orian is forbidden to open another business anywhere in California for a period of one hundred years, the court may either declare the entire covenant null and void or reform the covenant terms to cover only the San Francisco Bay area for a period of five years. This presents a problem, however, in that the judge becomes a party to the contract. Consequently, contract reformation is usually carried out by a court only when necessary to prevent undue burdens or hardships.

In the following case, the court examines whether a covenant not to compete is reasonable as to duration and geographic area—and therefore enforceable.

Case 14.2

PARAMOUNT TERMITE CONTROL CO. v. RECTOR

Supreme Court of Virginia, 1989.
238 Va. 171,
380 S.E.2d 922.

BACKGROUND AND FACTS   In 1982, Thomas Rector and four other employees of Paramount Termite Control Company each signed a noncompetition agreement with Paramount as a condition of continued employment. In the agreement, the employees agreed that for two years after they left Paramount's employ they would not solicit business for pest control services in the same areas that they had serviced in their last two years as Paramount employees. In 1986 and 1987, Rector and the others quit Paramount and went to work for a competitor that solicited business in the prohibited areas. Paramount asked a Virginia state court to enjoin the competitive activities of its ex-employees and to award damages for breach of the noncompetition agreements. The trial court denied Paramount's petition on the ground that the restrictive covenants were "not reasonable, under the circumstances presented in the evidence and therefore [were] an unreasonable restraint of trade." Paramount appealed.

DECISION AND RATIONALE   The Virginia Supreme Court held that the agreements' restrictions on competition were reasonable in both time and geographic area. The judgment of the trial court was reversed and the case remanded for further proceedings consistent with the court's opinion. Concerning the geographic area, the state supreme court explained that because the agreement prohibited the employees from engaging in the pest control business in counties in which they were assigned by Paramount during the two-year period—and no other counties—"we find that the area is not geographically overbroad." The court also found the restraint to be "no greater than reasonably necessary to protect Paramount's legitimate business interest" in the counties in which the employees worked in the two years preceding their termination. Finally, the court found that the restraint allowed the employees to earn a livelihood because they were not prohibited from performing pest control work "in a number of areas within commuting distance. Moreover, they may engage in any other work but that of pest control in the counties in which they formerly worked for Paramount." Because "the pest control business is highly competitive, with a limited supply of customers, and an ample supply of businesses and personnel," the court did not find that the agreements constituted an unreasonable restraint of trade or otherwise violated public policy.

EXCULPATORY CLAUSES Ordinarily, a court does not look at the fairness or equity of a contract. That is, the courts generally do not inquire into the adequacy of consideration, as discussed in Chapter 11. Persons are assumed to be reasonably intelligent, and the courts will not come to their aid just because they have made an unwise or foolish bargain. In certain circumstances, however, bargains are so oppressive that the courts relieve innocent parties of part or all of their duties. Such bargains are called **unconscionable** because they are so unscrupulous or grossly unfair as to be "void of conscience" (see the discussion of unconscionability in Chapter 13).

Contracts attempting to absolve parties of negligence or other wrongs are often held to be unconscionable. For example, suppose Jones and Laughlin Steel Company hires a laborer and has him sign a contract stating:

> Said employee hereby agrees with employer, in consideration of such employment, that he will take upon himself all risks incident to his position and will in no case hold the company liable for any injury or damage he may sustain, in his person or otherwise, by accidents or injuries in the factory, or which may result from defective machinery or carelessness or misconduct of himself or any other employee in service of the employer.

This contract provision attempts to remove Jones and Laughlin's potential liability for injuries to the employee, and it is usually contrary to public policy.[4] Such clauses are called **exculpatory clauses,** which for our purposes may be defined as clauses that purport to release a party from all liability for property damage or personal injury arising within contexts related to the subject matter of the contract.

Exculpatory clauses are also sometimes found in rental agreements, ordinary sales agreements, and commercial and residential property leases. In the majority of cases involving leases for commercial property, these clauses are held to be contrary to public policy. Additionally, they are almost universally held to be illegal and unenforceable when they are included in residential property leases. Generally, an exculpatory clause is not enforced if the party seeking its enforcement is involved in a business that is important to the public as a matter of practical necessity. These businesses include public utilities, common carriers, banks, and automobile repair shops. Because of the essential nature of these services, the companies offering them have an advantage in bargaining strength and could insist that anyone contracting for their services agree not to hold them liable. This would tend to relax their carefulness and increase the number of injuries. Imagine the results, for example, if exculpatory clauses in contracts between airlines and their passengers were enforced.

Exculpatory clauses have been enforced when the parties seeking their enforcement were not involved in businesses considered important to the public interest. These businesses have included health clubs, amusement parks, horse rental concessions, golf cart concessions, and skydiving organizations. Because these services are not essential, the firms offering them are sometimes considered to have no relative advantage in bargaining strength, and anyone contracting for their services is considered to do so voluntarily.

An exculpatory clause may be enforced if it relates to harm occurring outside the party's ordinary course of business or caused by circumstances outside the party's control. For example, a school district might include an exculpatory clause in a parents' permission form to avoid being held liable for injuries to students on a field trip as a

---

4. For a case with similar facts, see *Little Rock & Fort Smith Railway Co. v. Eubanks*, 48 Ark. 460, 3 S.W. 808 (1887). In such a case the clause may also be illegal on the basis of a violation of the state workers' compensation law.

result of the negligence of someone outside the district's control. Also, a clause limiting liability—for example, in a common carrier's shipping agreement—may be enforced.

In the following case, a federation sponsoring a bicycle race claimed that an exculpatory clause released it from liability for an injury incurred by one of the cyclists during the event.

Case 14.3

BENNETT v. U.S. CYCLING FEDERATION

Court of Appeal of California, 1987.
193 Cal.App.3d 1485,
239 Cal.Rptr. 55.

BACKGROUND AND FACTS   Albert Bennett entered an amateur bicycle race conducted by the U.S. Cycling Federation. Bennett signed a document provided by the Federation that stated in part: "In consideration of the acceptance of my application for entry in the above event, I hereby waive, release and discharge any and all claims for * * * damage which I may have, or which may hereafter accrue to me, as a result of my participation in said event." The release also included a clause by which Bennett was to assume risks associated with bicycle racing. During the race, Bennett collided with an automobile driven by James Ketchum. Bennett sued the Federation in California state court, alleging that the car was allowed onto the track by a Federation agent who knew, or should have known, of the hazard it presented to the cyclists. The Federation claimed that it had no liability because of the release signed by Bennett and moved for summary judgment, which the trial court granted. Bennett appealed.

DECISION AND RATIONALE   The Court of Appeal of California ruled that summary judgment was improper and remanded the case for trial. The appellate court reasoned that it was unclear whether Bennett had assumed the risk of a car being on the race course. The court explained that when Bennett signed the release, he waived any hazards relating to the race that were obvious or might reasonably have been foreseen. But Bennett alleged that the course was "known to be and was in fact" closed to motor vehicles, in which case "it is doubtful whether he or any participant would have realistically appreciated the risk of colliding with a car traveling in any direction along the closed race course." Despite this allegation, the court recognized that the circumstances of the race might have been such that a participant should reasonably have anticipated the risk of a car on the course. Based on this possible anticipation, the release was a triable issue.

ADHESION CONTRACTS AND UNCONSCIONABILITY   Contracts entered into because of one party's vastly superior bargaining power may also be deemed unconscionable. For example, if every auto manufacturer were to insert an exculpatory clause in contracts for the sale of autos, consumers presumably would have no chance to bargain for the elimination of the clause from a given contract. (Contracts with such clauses, which were discussed in the preceding chapter, are also called *adhesion contracts*.) Essentially, the consumer's choice would be to take a contract or leave it. To combat such clauses, courts have held them to be uncon-

scionable.[5] The consumer has no choice, so the contract is contrary to public policy.

Another example of an unconscionable contract is a contract in which the terms of the agreement "shock the conscience" of the court. Suppose a welfare recipient with a fourth-grade education agrees to purchase a refrigerator for a price of $2,000, signing a two-year, nonusurious installment contract. The same type of refrigerator usually sells for $400 on the market. Some courts have

---

5. See *Henningsen v. Bloomfield Motors, Inc.*, 32 N.J. 358, 161 A.2d 69 (1960).

held this type of contract unconscionable despite the general rule that the courts will not inquire into the adequacy of consideration.[6] Typically, the cases have involved consumer transactions in which the buyer was not aware of the actual price he or she was agreeing to pay.

Both the Uniform Commercial Code (UCC) and the Uniform Consumer Credit Code (UCCC) embody the unconscionability concept—the former with regard to the sale of goods[7] and the latter with regard to consumer loans and the waiver of rights.[8]

DISCRIMINATORY CONTRACTS Contracts in which a party promises to discriminate in terms of color, race, religion, national origin, or sex are contrary to statute and contrary to public policy.[9] For example, if a property owner promises in a contract not to sell the property to a member of a particular race, the contract is unenforceable. The public policy underlying these prohibitions is very strong, and the courts are quick to invalidate discriminatory contracts. Thus, the law attempts to ensure that people will be treated equally.

CONTRACTS FOR THE COMMISSION OF A TORT Contracts that require a party to commit a civil wrong, or a tort, have been held to be contrary to public policy. Remember that a *tort* is an act that is wrongful to another individual in a private sense, even though it may not necessarily be criminal in nature (an act against society).

CONTRACTS INJURING PUBLIC SERVICE Contracts that interfere with a public officer's duties are contrary to public policy. For example, contracts to pay legislators for favorable votes are obviously harmful to the public. Often, a fine line is drawn between lobbying efforts and agreements to influence voting. When a lobbying group provides certain factual information to influence the outcome of legislation, the group is not engaging in an illegal activity. But if the group enters into a contingency-fee agreement, whereby the legislator receives a certain amount of money if a certain

bill is passed or a certain contract is awarded, the agreement is illegal because it is deemed contrary to public policy. In the United States, people are not entitled to buy and sell votes. Therefore, agreements to do so are illegal.

Agreements that involve a *conflict of interest* are often illegal. Public officers cannot enter into contracts that cause conflict between their official duties as representatives of the people and their private interests. Statutes require many public officers to liquidate their interests in private businesses before serving as elected representatives. Other statutes merely require that while they are in office they take no part in the operation of, or decisions concerning, any business in which they have an interest, so that private and public responsibilities remain separate.

Suppose Ladd is a county official in charge of selecting land for the building of a new courthouse. He makes a contract for the state to buy land that he happens to own. This is a conflict of interest. If the state discovers later that Ladd owned the land, it can normally use this information to show a conflict of interest and to void the contract.

AGREEMENTS OBSTRUCTING THE LEGAL PROCESS Any agreement that is intended to delay, prevent, or obstruct the legal process is illegal. For example, an agreement to pay some specified amount if a criminal prosecution is terminated is illegal. Likewise, agreements to suppress evidence in a legal proceeding or to commit fraud upon a court are illegal. Tampering with a jury by offering jurors money in exchange for their votes is illegal.

In a trial, most witnesses (except expert witnesses) are paid a flat fee to compensate them for their expenses. Offering to pay one witness more than another is contrary to public policy, because the extra payment can provide an incentive for the witness to lie.

A promise to refrain from prosecuting a criminal offense in return for a reward is void because it is against public policy. A reward given under the threat of arrest or prosecution is also void.

Effect of Illegality

In general, an illegal contract is void. That is, the contract is deemed never to have existed, and the courts will not aid either party. In most illegal contracts, both parties are considered to be *in pari*

---

6. *Jones v. Star Credit Corp.*, 59 Misc.2d 189, 298 N.Y.S.2d 264 (1969).
7. See, for example, UCC Sections 2-302 and 2-719.
8. See, for example, UCCC Sections 5.108 and 1.107.
9. Civil Rights Act of 1964, 42 U.S.C. Sections 2000e et seq.

delicto (equally at fault).[10] In such cases the contract is void. If it is executory, neither party can enforce it. If it has been executed, there can be neither contractual nor quasi-contractual recovery.

Suppose Sonatrach, Algeria's national oil company, contracts to sell oil to Tenneco without government approval. Algerian law prohibits the export of oil without government approval. Therefore, the contract is illegal and unenforceable. If Tenneco sues to enforce delivery of the oil, the suit will be dismissed, because the contract is void. Even if Tenneco has paid for some of the oil, the contract cannot be enforced. Tenneco cannot even get back the money it paid under the illegal contract. In general, the courts take a hands-off attitude toward illegal contracts.

That one wrongdoer who is a party to an illegal contract is unjustly enriched at the expense of the other is of no concern to the law—except under certain special circumstances that will be discussed below. The major justification for this hands-off attitude is that it is improper to place the machinery of justice at the disposal of a plaintiff who has broken the law by entering into an illegal bargain. Another justification is the hoped-for deterrent effect of this general rule. A plaintiff who suffers loss because of it should presumably be deterred from entering into similar illegal bargains.

EXCEPTIONS TO THE GENERAL RULE   There are some exceptions to the general rule that neither party to an illegal bargain can sue for breach and neither can recover for performance rendered.

Justifiable Ignorance of the Facts   When one of the parties is relatively innocent, that party can often recover any benefits conferred in a partially executed contract. In this case, the courts will not enforce the contract but will allow the parties to return to their original positions.

It is also possible for an innocent party who has fully performed under the contract to enforce the contract against the guilty party. For example, a trucking company contracts with Gillespie to carry goods to a specific destination for a normal fee of $500. The trucker delivers the goods and later finds out that the contents of the shipped crates were illegal. Although the law specifies that the shipment, use, and sale of the goods were illegal,

the trucker, being an innocent party, can still legally collect the $500 from Gillespie.

Members of Protected Classes   When a statute is clearly designed to protect a certain class of people, a member of that class can enforce a contract in violation of the statute even though the other party cannot. A statute that prohibits employees from working more than a specified number of hours per month is designed to protect those employees. An employee who works more than the maximum can recover for those extra hours of service. Flight attendants are subject to a federal statute that prohibits them from flying more than a certain number of hours every month. Even if an attendant exceeds the maximum, the airline must pay for those extra hours of service.

Most states also have statutes regulating the sale of insurance. If the insurance company violates a statute when selling insurance, *the purchaser can nevertheless enforce the policy.* For example, assume Indemnity Insurance Company is not qualified to sell insurance in Montana but does so anyway. A purchaser who buys a policy to insure his auto has an accident and seeks to recover. The insurer cannot avoid payment under the policy, even though the contract is illegal. The statutes regulating insurance companies are designed to protect policyholders, so the buyer can recover from the insurer.

Withdrawal from an Illegal Agreement   If an agreement has been only partly performed and the illegal part of the bargain has not yet been performed, the party rendering performance can withdraw from the bargain and recover the performance or its value. For example, Sam and Jim decide to wager (illegally) on the outcome of a boxing match. Each deposits money with a stakeholder, who agrees to pay the winner of the bet. At this point, each party has performed part of the agreement, but the illegal part of the agreement will not occur until the money is paid to the winner. Before such payment occurs, either party is entitled to withdraw from the agreement by giving notice of repudiation to the stakeholder.

Contract Illegal through Fraud, Duress, or Undue Influence   Often, illegal contracts involve two blameworthy parties, but one party is more at fault than the other. When a party has been induced

---

10.   Pronounced in *paa*-ree deh-*lick*-tow.

to enter into an illegal bargain by fraud, duress, or undue influence from the other party to the agreement, that party will be allowed to recover for the performance or its value.

Consider the following example: A number of creditors are threatening to file suit for debts owed by Pfeifferco, a company owned by Mildred. Mildred's financial advisor, Harry, points out to Mildred that if the creditors succeed in their lawsuit, they might be able to "get their hands on" the company's valuable investment properties. Therefore, Harry suggests, Mildred should arrange a "sale" of the properties to his firm for a nominal price, and then, after Pfeifferco has "gotten the creditors off its back," Harry will "sell" the properties back to Pfeifferco at the same price. Mildred agrees to the scheme. Believing Pfeifferco to have insufficient assets to pay its debts in full, the creditors agree to accept less than they are owed and release Pfeifferco from further liability. When Mildred demands that Harry arrange to sell the investment properties back to Pfeifferco, he says that unless his firm is paid their full market value, he will tell the creditors about the deal. Mildred decides to sue. Although Mildred arranged the original "sale" to defraud Pfeifferco's creditors—who could have had the sale set aside had they discovered it—a court would allow recovery of the properties from Harry's firm. Harry used Mildred's confidence in him to unduly influence her to participate in the first transaction. His coercion in the "resale" constitutes duress.

SEVERABLE, OR DIVISIBLE, CONTRACTS A *severable* contract consists of distinct parts that can be performed separately, with separate consideration provided for each part. If a contract is severable into legal and illegal portions, and the illegal portion does not affect the essence of the bargain, the legal portion can be enforced. This is consistent with the basic policy of courts to enforce the legal intentions of the parties wherever possible.

Suppose Norman Harrington contracts to buy ten pounds of bluegrass seed for $25 and five gallons of herbicide for $30. At the time, Harrington does not know that the Food and Drug Administration has banned sale of the herbicide and that the contract for its sale is therefore illegal. Here, the contract is severable because separate considerations were stated for the bluegrass seed ($25) and the herbicide ($30). Therefore, the portion of the contract for the sale of bluegrass seed is enforceable; the other portion is not.

In contrast, a contract is indivisible if the parties intend that each party's complete performance be essential, even if the contract contains a number of seemingly separate provisions. For instance, a contract for the sale of an entire, ongoing business might contain, as one of its clauses, a covenant not to compete—which would prevent the seller from opening a competing business nearby. Although this clause would seem to be a separate and divisible provision of the contract, in fact, it goes to the heart of the contract. Without such a clause, the buyer might not obtain the goodwill and reputation associated with the business name by the seller's former customers.

■ Statute of Frauds

Suppose I meet you on the street and orally offer to sell you my used personal computer for $800. You accept my offer. Later, upon your tender of the $800, I refuse to transfer my personal computer to you because I have had a better offer from another person. You threaten to sue me. After all, we did have an *oral* contract. The question is whether an oral contract is enforceable. In most cases, it is, but the party seeking to enforce it must establish the existence of the contract as well as its actual terms. Naturally, when the parties have no writing or memorandum about the contract, only oral testimony can be used in court to establish the existence of the terms of the contract. The problem with oral testimony is that parties are sometimes willing to perjure themselves to win lawsuits.

Therefore, at early common law, parties to a contract were not allowed to testify. This led to the practice of hiring third party witnesses. As early as the seventeenth century, the English recognized the many problems presented by this practice and enacted a statute to help deal with it. The statute, passed by the English Parliament in 1677, was known as "An Act for the Prevention of Frauds and Perjuries." The act required that certain types of contracts, to be enforceable, had to be evidenced by a writing and signed by the party against whom enforcement was sought. For example, our oral contract for the sale of my computer would fall under the act and could not be enforced by you in the appropriate court. In the United States, the descendant of the British act is called the Statute of Frauds.

Today almost every state has a statute, modeled after the English act, that stipulates what types of contracts must be in writing. In this text, we refer to these statutes—even if a particular state has more than one statute relating to the topic—as the **Statute of Frauds.** The actual name of the Statute of Frauds is misleading because it neither applies to fraud nor invalidates any type of contract. Rather, it denies *enforceability* to certain contracts that do not comply with its requirements. The primary purpose of the act is *evidentiary*—to provide reliable evidence of the existence and terms of certain classes of contracts deemed historically to be important or complex. Although the statutes vary slightly from state to state, all states require the types of contracts listed below to be in writing or evidenced by a written memorandum signed by the party against whom enforcement is sought, unless certain exceptions apply—these exceptions will be discussed later in this chapter. These contracts are said to fall ''under'' or ''within'' the Statute of Frauds and therefore require a writing.

1. Contracts involving interests in land.
2. Contracts that cannot *by their terms* be performed within one year from the date of formation.
3. Collateral, or secondary, contracts, such as promises to answer for the debt or duty of another and promises by the administrator or executor of an estate personally to pay a debt of the estate—that is, out of his or her own pocket.
4. Promises made in consideration of marriage.
5. Under the UCC, contracts for the sale of goods priced at $500 or more.

Contracts Involving Interests in Land

Under the Statute of Frauds, a contract involving an interest in land must be attested to by a writing to be enforceable. Certain exceptions to this general rule are made in some circumstances. These exceptions are discussed later in this chapter.

SALE OF LAND   A contract calling for the sale of land is not enforceable unless it is in writing or evidenced by a written memorandum. Land is real property and includes all physical objects that are permanently attached to the soil, such as buildings, fences, trees, and the soil itself. The Statute of Frauds operates as a *defense* to the enforcement of an oral contract for the sale of land. Therefore, even if both parties acknowledge the existence of an oral contract for the sale of land, under most circumstances the contract will still not be enforced. If Sam contracts orally to sell Blackacre to Betty but later decides not to sell, under most circumstances Betty cannot enforce the contract. Likewise, if Betty refuses to close the deal, Sam cannot force Betty to pay for the land.

Frequently it is necessary to distinguish between real property, which may include property affixed to the land, and personal property. A contract for the sale of land ordinarily involves the entire interest in the real property, including buildings, growing crops, vegetation, minerals, timber, and anything else affixed to the land. Therefore, a *fixture* (personal property so affixed or so used as to become a part of the realty) is treated as real property. But anything else, such as a couch, is treated as personal property.

OTHER INTERESTS   The Statute of Frauds requires contracts for the transfer of other interests in land, such as mortgages, and leases, to be in writing although most state statutes provide for the enforcement of short-term leases. These other interests will be described in detail in Chapters 49–52.

The One-Year Rule

A contract that cannot, *by its own terms,* be performed within one year from the date it was formed must be in writing to be enforceable.[11] Because disputes over such contracts are unlikely to occur until some time after the contracts have been made, resolution of these disputes is difficult unless the contract terms have been put in writing.

For a particular contract to fall under the one-year rule of the Statute of Frauds, contract performance within a year from the date of contract formation must be objectively impossible.

The one-year period begins to run *the day after the contract is made.* Suppose you graduate from college on June 1. An employer orally contracts to hire you immediately (June 1) for one year at $2,000 per month. This contract is not subject to the Statute of Frauds (and thus need not be in writ-

---

11.   Restatement (Second) of Contracts, Section 130.

ing to be enforceable) because the one-year period to measure performance begins on June 2. Because your performance of one year can begin immediately, it would take you exactly one year from the date of entering the contract to perform.

Now suppose that on March 1 the dean of your college, in your presence, orally contracts to hire your professor for the next academic year (a nine-month period) at a salary of $45,000. The academic year begins on September 1. Does this contract have to be in writing to be enforceable? The answer is yes. The one-year period used to measure whether performance by contract terms is possible begins on March 2. Because the nine-month contract could not begin until September 1 and would end on May 31 of the next year, the contract performance period exceeds the one-year measurement period by three months. Thus, this contract is within the Statute of Frauds. But if this oral contract had been entered into at any time between June 1 and September 1, the contract, by its terms, would be performed within one year of the date of contract formation (acceptance of the offer), and the oral contract would be enforceable.

Even if performance within one year is improbable, if the contract, by its terms, makes complete performance within the year *possible,* the contract is not covered by the Statute of Frauds and need not be in writing. For example, suppose that Bankers Life orally contracts to loan $40,000 to Janet Lawrence "as long as Lawrence and Associates operates its financial consulting firm in Omaha, Nebraska." The contract is not within the Statute of Frauds—no writing is required—because Lawrence and Associates could go out of business in one year or less. In this event, the contract would be fully performed within one year. Although this occurrence is unlikely, it is nevertheless possible, and that possibility removes the contract from the province of the Statute of Frauds.[12]

Suppose, on the other hand, that Bankers Life agrees to loan the money to Lawrence "for a period of two years with the provision that there will be no acceleration or prepayment for the period." Lawrence and Associates could go out of business in one year or less. Because the debtor is not allowed to accelerate payments on the loan or prepay

the remainder at any time, she cannot perform the contract within one year without breaching the contract's terms. Therefore, this contract is subject to the Statute of Frauds and must be evidenced by a writing to be enforceable. Compare the specified two years in this contract with the statement in the preceding example, where the words "as long as" were used.

Next, assume that the contract states that the loan will last for two years but may be "terminable at the end of six months, subject to review of Lawrence and Associates' financial condition." Here the contract is not subject to the Statute of Frauds because, by the terms of the contract, it can be fully performed within one year.

In summary, the test to determine whether an oral contract is enforceable under the one-year rule of the Statute of Frauds is not whether an agreement is *likely* to be performed within a year from the date of making the contract. Rather, the question revolves around whether performance within a year is *possible.* Even if performance actually takes more than one year, an oral contract is binding so long as performance was possible in less than a year. Exhibit 14–1 illustrates graphically the application of the one-year rule.

Collateral Promises

A **collateral promise,** or secondary promise, is one that is ancillary to a principal transaction or primary contractual relationship. Promises made by one person to pay the debts or discharge the duties of another if the latter fails to perform are subject to the Statute of Frauds. Three elements must be present in this collateral promise situation to require that the agreement must be in writing to be enforceable:

1. Three parties are involved.
2. Two promises are involved.
3. The secondary, or collateral, promise is to pay a debt or fulfill a duty only if the first promisor fails to do so.

This set of requirements is illustrated in Exhibit 14–2.

OBLIGATION MUST BE SECONDARY The Statute of Frauds applies only to promises made by a third party to fulfill the obligations of a principal party (debtor) to a contract if that party does not

---

12. See *Warner v. Texas & Pacific Railroad Co.,* 164 U.S. 418, 17 S.Ct. 147, 41 L.Ed. 195 (1896).

■ **Exhibit 14–1 The One-Year Rule**

Under the Statute of Frauds, contracts that by their terms are impossible to perform within one year from the date of contract formation must be in writing to be enforceable. Put another way, if it is at all possible to perform an oral contract within one year after the contract is made, the contract will fall outside the Statute of Frauds and be enforceable.

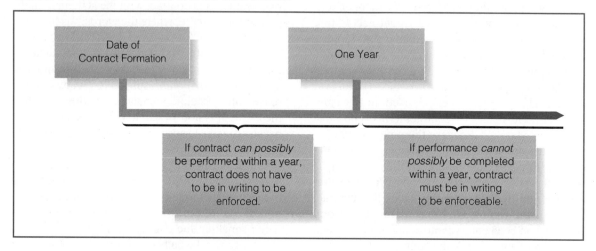

perform. Such promises are referred to as *surety-ship* or *guaranty* contracts (see Chapter 32 for a more detailed discussion of these terms). Assume, for example, that David wants to borrow $10,000 from Bancroft. Owens, David's father, forms a contract with Bancroft in which Owens promises to pay the $10,000 if David fails to pay the debt when it becomes due. Owens's promise to Bancroft is secondary (collateral) to the David-Bancroft contract and must be in writing to be enforceable. The underlying purpose behind this provision of the Statute of Frauds is to ensure that a person will not

■ **Exhibit 14–2 Collateral Promises**

A collateral (secondary) promise is one made by a third party (C, in this exhibit) to a creditor (B, in this exhibit) to pay the debt of another (A, in this exhibit), who is primarily obligated to pay the debt. Under the Statute of Frauds, collateral promises must be in writing to be enforceable.

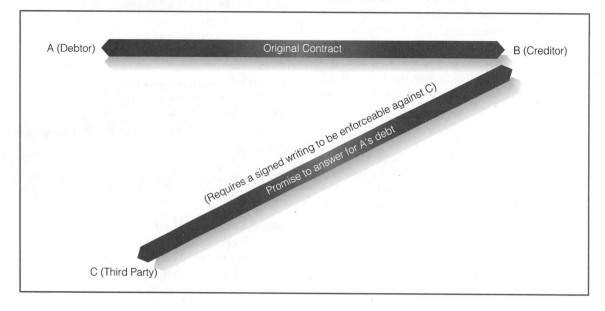

be forced to pay the debt of another on the basis of oral testimony—which could be perjured.

The key point here is that the obligation of the guarantor (Owens, in the above example) is secondary, and the guarantor's liability for the obligation is thus secondary—Owens will not become liable *unless* David is unable or unwilling to pay the $10,000. David, in contrast, is primarily liable for the obligation, and the David-Bancroft contract does not have to be in writing to be enforceable. The Statute of Frauds only applies if the guarantor's obligation is contingent on the principal debtor's refusal or inability to pay the creditor.

"MAIN PURPOSE RULE" EXCEPTION   The oral promise to answer for the debt of another is covered by the Statute of Frauds unless the guarantor is effectively a debtor because his or her main purpose in accepting secondary liability is to secure a pecuniary (monetary) benefit. This kind of contract need not be in writing.[13] The assumption is that a court can infer from the circumstances of any given case whether the "leading object" of the promisor was to secure a pecuniary advantage.

Consider an example. Oswald contracts with Machine Manufacturing Company to have some machines custom-made for her factory. She promises Materials Supply Company, Machine Manufacturing's supplier, that if Materials Supply Company continues to deliver materials to Machine Manufacturing, she will guarantee payment. This promise need not be in writing, even though the effect may be to pay the debt of another, because Oswald's main purpose is to serve her own pecuniary benefit.[14]

Another typical application of the so-called main purpose doctrine occurs when one creditor guarantees the debtor's debt to another creditor for the purpose of forestalling litigation so as to allow the debtor to remain in business long enough to generate enough profits to pay *both* creditors.

The following case illustrates an application of the main purpose doctrine. A creditor of a development complex guaranteed the general contractor's payments to a subcontractor to ensure that the development would be completed on time. Failure of the development project to be completed as contracted would have markedly decreased tenant revenue, placing the principal debtor in default on its loan to the bank.

---

13.   Restatement (Second) of Contracts, Section 116.

14.   *Kampman v. Pittsburgh Contracting and Engineering Co.*, 316 Pa. 502, 175 A. 396 (1934).

BACKGROUND AND FACTS   Wilson Floors Company contracted to provide flooring materials for a development owned by Sciota Park, Ltd., a local bank. When the general contractor for Sciota fell behind in payments to Wilson, Wilson stopped work. Sciota orally assured Wilson that he would be paid if he returned to work. When Wilson's final bill was not paid, Wilson sued Sciota in an Ohio state court. The trial court held that the bank's assurances to Wilson that he would be paid did not fall under the Statute of Frauds because the bank assumed a "direct undertaking"—not a secondary obligation—when it guaranteed payment to Wilson. Therefore the oral promise was enforceable. The appellate court reversed, finding that Sciota became only secondarily liable to Wilson when it guaranteed payment. Therefore, the oral promise was unenforceable. Wilson appealed.

DECISION AND RATIONALE   The Ohio Supreme Court held that "the bank did not become primarily liable when it guaranteed the subcontractors that they would be paid" but that "so long as the main purpose of the promisor is to further his own business or pecuniary interest, the promise is enforceable." The court reasoned that the bank's main purpose was to derive a benefit for itself by retaining the subcontractors already working on the project to keep costs down. Therefore, the oral promise to pay the general contractor's debts was outside the Statute of Frauds and thus enforceable.

 Case 14.4

WILSON FLOORS CO. v. SCIOTA PARK, LTD.

Supreme Court of Ohio, 1978.
54 Ohio St.2d 451,
377 N.E.2d 514.

ESTATE DEBTS   The administrator (or executor) of an estate has the duty of paying the debts of the deceased and distributing any remainder to the deceased's heirs. The administrator can contract orally on behalf of the estate. Under the Statute of Frauds, promises made by the administrator or executor of an estate to pay *personally* the debts of the estate must be in writing to be enforceable, even though the nature of the promise is to assume a primary obligation to pay the creditor. For example, suppose that Edward Post (an estate administrator) contracts with Martha Lynch for legal services. If Post contracts orally on behalf of the estate, the contract is valid, and the estate is bound to pay Lynch for her legal services. But if Post agrees to pay Lynch's legal fees personally out of his own pocket, the contract must be in writing. Otherwise it is not enforceable, and Lynch cannot recover.

Promises Made in Consideration of Marriage

A unilateral promise to pay a sum of money or to give property in consideration of a promise to marry must be in writing. If Bill MacAdams promises $10,000 to Bruce Coby if Coby promises to marry his daughter, Sally MacAdams, MacAdams's promise must be in writing to be enforceable. The same rule applies to *prenuptial agreements* (agreements made before marriage, sometimes called antenuptial agreements), which define the ownership rights of each partner in the other partner's property. For example, a prospective husband may wish to limit the amount his prospective wife could obtain if the marriage should end in divorce. Another common situation involving prenuptial agreements occurs when a man and woman who wish to get married both have separate assets and children from prior marriages. A prenuptial arrangement may be highly desirable in this case. Prenuptial arrangements made in consideration of marriage must be in writing to be enforceable.

Contracts for the Sale of Goods

The UCC contains several Statute of Frauds provisions that require written evidence of a contract. Section 2-201 contains the major provision, which generally requires a writing or memorandum for the sale of goods priced at $500 or more. A writing that will satisfy this requirement need only state the quantity term, and that need not be stated "accurately," as long as it adequately reflects both parties' intentions. The contract will not be enforceable, however, for any quantity greater than that set forth in the writing. In addition, the writing must have been signed by the person to be charged—that is, the person who refuses to perform or the one being sued. Beyond these two requirements, the writing need not designate the buyer or seller, the terms of payment, or the price.

Exceptions to the applicability of the Statute of Frauds are discussed in the next two sections. Here we look at two important exceptions that relate only to contracts for the sale of goods. These exceptions, contained in UCC 2-201, will be discussed in further detail in Chapter 18.

GOODS MADE SPECIALLY TO ORDER   Contracts for goods made specially for the buyer—that is, goods that cannot be resold by the seller in the ordinary course of the seller's business—are enforceable even when not in writing, provided that the seller has made a substantial beginning of manufacture or commitment for their procurement [UCC 2-201(3)(a)]. Suppose Magic Johnson orally contracts with a furniture factory for $250,000 worth of furniture specially designed on a larger-than-normal scale to accommodate his larger-than-normal physique. Once the factory has committed itself to the manufacture of, or has made a substantial beginning in manufacturing, the furniture, the oral contract is enforceable.

CONFIRMATION OF AN ORAL CONTRACT BETWEEN MERCHANTS   If one merchant sends to another a written confirmation of an oral contract, the merchant receiving the confirmation (with knowledge of its terms) must object in writing within ten days of its receipt, or the oral contract will be enforceable by either party [UCC 2-201(2)].

Suppose Rodriguez in Los Angeles calls Cohen in New York City on June 1, and an oral contract is formed for Cohen's purchase of a new $10,000 machine. The next day Rodriguez sends Cohen a fax that states, "This is to confirm our telephone contract of June 1 for your purchase of the Model 12 machine at $10,000. Thank you for your order." Cohen receives the fax the same day and makes no written response. On June 15 Cohen discovers that a similar machine can be purchased for $9,000. Cohen claims the Statute of Frauds as a defense

---

Problems with Oral Contracts

As a general rule, most business contracts should be in writing, even when the contract falls outside the Statute of Frauds requirement. Oral contracts are, however, frequently made over the telephone, particularly when the parties have done business with each other in the past.

When an oral contract is made, it is advisable for one of the parties to send either a written memorandum or confirmation of the oral contract. This accomplishes two purposes: (1) it demonstrates a clear intention to form a contract, and (2) it outlines the terms that at least one of the parties believed were agreed upon. If the party receiving the memorandum or confirmation then disagrees with the terms or with the intent, the issue can be addressed before performance begins.

In the sale of goods *between* merchants, a written confirmation received by one merchant removes the Statute of Frauds requirement of a writing unless the merchant receiving the confirmation objects in writing within ten days of its receipt. This law points out clearly the need for the merchant receiving the confirmation to review it carefully to be certain that the confirmation conforms to the oral contract. If the writing does not so conform, the merchant can object in writing (the Statute of Frauds still applies), and the parties can resolve misunderstandings without legal liability. If the merchant fails to object, the written confirmation can be used as evidence to prove the terms of the oral contract. (This ten-day rule does not apply to contracts for services and interests in realty.)

---

for his refusal of Rodriguez's tender of the machine. Cohen will lose against Rodriguez's suit for breach because he failed to object in writing within ten days of receiving Rodriguez's confirmation.

Partial Performance

As stated above, the Statute of Frauds is a defense against the enforcement of an oral contract. Executed contracts—that is, contracts that have been fully performed—are not subject to the Statute of Frauds. Problems arise when an oral contract has been partially performed. For example, a buyer may have paid part of the purchase price and taken complete or partial possession of the seller's property.

SALE OF LAND   In cases involving contracts relating to the transfer of interests in land, if the purchaser has paid part of the price, taken possession, and made permanent improvements to the property and the parties cannot be returned to their pre-contract status quo, a court may grant *specific performance* (that is, performance of the contract

according to the precise terms agreed on). Whether the courts will enforce an oral contract for an interest in land when partial performance has taken place is usually determined by the degree of injury that would be suffered if the court chose not to enforce the oral contract. In some states, mere reliance on an oral contract is enough to remove it from the Statute of Frauds.

SALE OF GOODS   Under the UCC, an oral contract is enforceable to the extent that a seller accepts payment or a buyer accepts delivery of the goods [UCC 2-201(3)(c)]. For example, Windblown Sailboats makes an oral contract with Sunset Sails to have Sunset make 750 sails for Windblown's new nineteen-foot Day Sailer. Windblown repudiates the agreement after the sails have been made and after two dozen have been delivered. The contract will be enforceable to the extent of the two dozen sails accepted by Windblown.

Admissions

In some states, if a party against whom enforcement of an oral contract is sought ''admits'' in ''pleading, testimony or otherwise in court that a contract for sale was made," the contract will be enforceable.[15] A contract subject to the UCC will be enforceable but only to the extent of the quantity admitted [UCC 2-201(3)(b)]. Thus, if the president of Windblown Sailboats admits under oath that an oral agreement was made with Sailmakers, Inc., for fifty sails, the agreement will be enforceable to that extent.

Promissory Estoppel

Recently, some courts have used the doctrine of promissory estoppel (detrimental reliance) to allow parties to recover under oral contracts that would otherwise be rendered unenforceable under the Statute of Frauds. Section 139 of the Restatement (Second) of Contracts provides that a promise that induces action or forbearance can be enforceable notwithstanding the Statute of Frauds if the reliance was foreseeable to the party making the promise and if injustice can be avoided only by enforcing the promise.

In the following case, the court considers whether the plaintiff's detrimental reliance on an oral contract should bar, or estop, the defendant from raising the Statute of Frauds as a defense.

---

15. Restatement (Second) of Contracts, Section 133.

Case 14.5

FREDERICK v. CONAGRA, INC.

United States District Court, District of Massachusetts, 1989.

713 F.Supp. 41.

BACKGROUND AND FACTS Thomas Frederick was a regional sales manager with Kahn's & Company and was not seeking any change of employment. Bernard Zilinskas, a vice-president for a division of the Armour Processed Meat Company (a subsidiary of ConAgra, Inc.), contacted Frederick about coming to work for Armour as its Northeast Regional Sales Manager. Zilinskas made numerous representations about the job, including that Armour wanted to hire Frederick for a minimum of two years. Frederick accepted the position and began work for Armour, although no employment contract was signed. He moved his family from New York to Massachusetts and arranged to have a new home constructed. Three months later, he was fired on thirty days' notice for no stated cause. Frederick sued ConAgra in a federal district court for breach of contract, and ConAgra moved to dismiss the complaint, contending, among other things, that even if there was an employment contract, an action for its enforcement was barred by the Statute of Frauds.

DECISION AND RATIONALE The United States District Court for the District of Massachusetts held that Frederick's reliance on the employment offer estopped ConAgra from raising the Statute of Frauds as a defense. ConAgra's motion to dismiss was denied. The court pointed out that in Massachusetts, when a party against whom enforcement of an oral contract is sought has made a material misrepresentation, the party may be estopped from raising the Statute of Frauds as a defense. The court concluded that "a jury would be warranted in finding that certain oral representations were made by Zilinskas for the purpose of inducing Frederick to leave his job with Kahn's and to join Armour. Sufficient facts exist to justify the conclusion that Frederick, relying on these representations, moved his family * * * and contracted for the construction of a new home * * *. A jury would also be warranted in finding that Frederick's reliance and his consequent actions, in light of his subsequent firing, worked to his detriment."

ETHICAL CONSIDERATIONS Since its inception more than three hundred years ago, the Statute of Frauds has been criticized by some because, although it was created to prevent injustice, it can also be employed as a technical defense to the enforcement of an otherwise valid oral contract. Using promissory estoppel in these circumstances is one of the ways in which courts have circumvented the problem. Nevertheless, the use of promissory estoppel in these cases is controversial. Enforcing an oral contract on the basis of a party's reliance arguably undercuts the essence of the statute.

Sufficiency of the Writing

To be safe, all contract terms should be fully set forth in a writing signed by all the parties. This assures that if any problems arise concerning performance of the contract, a written agreement can be introduced into court. The Statute of Frauds and the UCC require either a written contract or a written memorandum *signed by the party against whom enforcement is sought,* except when there is a legally recognized exception, such as partial performance. The signature need not be placed at the end of the document but can be anywhere in the writing. It can even be an initial rather than the full name. Note, however, that even if the Statute of Frauds is satisfied, the *terms* of the contract must be proved in court.

A memorandum evidencing the oral contract need only contain the essential terms of the contract. Under the UCC, for contracts evidencing sales of goods, the writing need only name the quantity term and be signed by the party to be charged. Any confirmation, invoice, sales slip, check, or telegram can constitute a writing sufficient to satisfy the Statute of Frauds. Under most other provisions of the Statute of Frauds, for contracts evidencing transactions other than sales of goods, the writing must also name the parties, the subject matter, the consideration, and the essential terms with reasonable certainty. In some states, contracts for the sale of land must state the price and describe the property with sufficient clarity to allow them to be determined without reference to outside sources.[16]

As indicated above, only the party to be held liable on the oral contract need sign the writing. In other words, the party against whom enforcement of the contract is sought must have signed it. Thus, a contract may be enforceable by one of its parties but not by the other. Suppose Ota and Warrington orally contract for the sale of Ota's lake house and lot for $55,000. Ota writes Warrington a letter confirming the sale by identifying the parties and the essential terms—price, method of payment, and legal address—and signs the letter. Ota has made a written memorandum of the oral land contract. Because she signed the letter, she can be held to the oral contract by Warrington. Because Warrington has not signed a written contract or memorandum, however, he can plead the Statute of Frauds as a defense, and Ota cannot enforce the contract against him.

---

16. *Rhodes v. Wilkins*, 83 N.M. 782, 498 P.2d 311 (1972).

■ CONCEPT SUMMARY 14.1
Contracts Subject to the Statute of Frauds

Types of Contracts	Applications
Contracts involving interests in land	Applies to any contract for an interest in realty, such as a sale of land, a mortgage, or a long-term lease. Exceptions— 1. Partial performance—When the parties cannot be restored to their pre-contract status. 2. Statute—Most states provide for the enforcement of short term oral leases.

(Continued on next page)

■ CONCEPT SUMMARY 14.1 *(Continued)*

Types of Contracts	Applications
Contracts that cannot, by their terms, be performed within one year	Applies only to contracts objectively impossible to perform fully within one year from the date of contract formation.
Collateral promises	Applies to express contracts in which one party agrees to be responsible for the debt or duty of another. Exception—Main purpose, or leading object, doctrine.
Promises made in consideration of marriage	Applies (1) to promises to pay money or give property in consideration of a promise to marry and (2) to prenuptial agreements. Exception—None.
Sale of goods priced at $500 or more	Applies to the sale of goods the purchase price (excluding taxes) of which is $500 or more [UCC 2-201(1)]. Exceptions— 1. Between merchants—When one party sends a written confirmation and the receiver does not object in writing within ten days [UCC 2-201(2)]. 2. Specially ordered goods—When the seller has made a substantial beginning of manufacture or commitment for procurement [UCC 2-201(3)(a)]. 3. Partial performance—At least to the extent that the buyer has paid for or possesses the goods [UCC 2-201(3)(c)].
Exceptions to Contracts Otherwise Unenforceable under the Statute of Frauds	
1. Memorandum	Written evidence of an oral contract signed by the party against whom enforcement is sought. Generally, the writing must name the parties, identify the subject matter of the contract, and, in contracts for the sale of goods, the quantity. In the sale of land, it must name essential terms, such as property description and price.
2. Admissions	Admission under oath, by the party against whom enforcement is sought, that a contract exists.
3. Partial performance	Applies to contracts for the sale of land, as well as to the sale of goods.

■ The Parol Evidence Rule

Before putting an agreement in writing, the parties often negotiate the terms. There may be telephone calls, conversations, memos, and other communications. Terms are put forward, haggled over, and then agreed to, rejected, or forgotten. Finally, a written draft of the contract is prepared, and the parties sign it.

In interpreting and enforcing the contract, questions may arise as to whether the written document includes everything the parties intended. If the document does include everything the parties intended,

no evidence of prior oral or written negotiations or agreements or contemporaneous oral negotiations may be used to change the terms of the writing. This is the **parol evidence rule.** Parol evidence is any evidence—oral or written—that is outside the written contract and not made a part of the contract directly or by a reference in the writing. The parol evidence rule applies to *all* written contracts, not just those governed by the Statute of Frauds.

There are two reasons for the parol evidence rule: (1) to give effect to the intent of the parties and (2) to help interpret their contract by having a single source of proof (the contract) of their agreement. Concerning the intent of the parties, the basic question is whether the parties intended the writing to be the final and complete expression of their agreement. If the writing is shown to be final but not complete, it may be supplemented by evidence of consistent additional terms.

Evidence can also be offered to show subsequent modifications of a written contract. In other words, the parties may show that they changed their agreement after putting it in writing. These and other circumstances in which parol evidence is not excluded are listed and explained in Exhibit 14–3.

■ **Exhibit 14–3 Circumstances under Which Extrinsic Evidence Is Admissible**

Circumstance	Rationale
Subsequent modification of contract	Since the parol evidence rule only applies to *prior* or *contemporaneous* negotiations, parol evidence is admissible to show changes in the written contract that occur *after* the writing. Of course, if the modification brings the contract under the Statute of Frauds, the contract as modified must be in writing to be enforceable.
Void or voidable contract	If one of the parties was deceived into agreeing to the terms of a written contract through mistake, fraud, or misrepresentation, evidence attesting to the deception should not be excluded.
Ambiguous contract terms	When the terms of a written contract are ambiguous, evidence is admissible to show the meaning of the terms.
Incomplete contract	If a written contract is incomplete because it lacks one or more essential terms, courts will allow evidence to fill in the gaps existing in the written contract.
Prior course of dealing or usage of trade	When buyers and sellers deal with each other over extended periods of time, certain customary practices develop. They are often overlooked in the writing of the contract, so courts allow the introduction of evidence to show how the parties have acted in the past or what is customary within the trade.
Contract subject to an agreed-upon condition	Extrinsic evidence is admissible if the existence of the entire agreement is subject to an orally agreed-upon condition. Proof of the condition does not *alter* or *modify* the written terms but involves the very *enforceability* of the written contract. For example, Carvelli agrees, in a written contract with Jackson, to purchase real property from Jackson for $100,000. Prior to signing the contract, the parties orally agree that the contract is binding *only on the condition* that Carvelli's attorney approve the deal. Evidence concerning this condition is admissible because what is at issue is whether the contract is enforceable.
Obvious mistake (typographical, clerical, etc.)	When an *obvious* or *gross* typographical or clerical error exists that would clearly not represent the agreement of the parties, evidence is admissible to correct the error.

■ **Terms and Concepts**

collateral promise 259
exculpatory clauses 253
in pari delicto 255–256

judgment rate of
  interest 249
legal rate of interest 249
parol evidence rule 266

Statute of Frauds 258
unconscionable 253
usury 249

■ For Review

1. Under what circumstances will a covenant not to compete be unenforceable?   *IF over 1YR.,*
2. What contracts must be in writing to be enforceable? ✓
3. If a writing that constitutes a contract includes everything that the parties intended, can evidence of earlier oral negotiations be used to change its terms?
4. Gregory promises to work for Peck Corp., and Peck promises to employ Gregory for five years at a certain salary. Do these promises fall within the Statute of Frauds— that is, must the promises be in writing to be enforceable

under the Statute of Frauds? Why or why not?
5. Connie orally agrees to buy electronic equipment from Lem for $1,000. When Lem learns that he can get a better price for the goods, he refuses to deliver them to Connie. Connie sues to enforce the contract against Lem. The only evidence of their agreement is a confirmation order initialed by Lem and sent to Connie. Is this agreement subject to the Statute of Frauds? If so, will the confirmation order initialed by Lem satisfy the writing requirement?

■ Questions and Case Problems

14-1. A famous New York City hotel, Hotel Lux, is noted for its food as well as its luxury accommodations. Hotel Lux contracts with a famous chef, Chef Perlee, to become its head chef at $6,000 per month. The contract states that should Perlee leave the employment of Hotel Lux for any reason, he will not work as a chef for any hotel or restaurant in the states of New York, New Jersey, or Pennsylvania for a period of one year. During the first six months of the contract, Hotel Lux substantially advertises Perlee as its head chef, and business at the hotel is excellent. Then a dispute arises between the hotel management and Perlee, and Perlee terminates his employment. One month later, he is hired by a famous New Jersey restaurant just across the New York state line. Hotel Lux learns of Perlee's employment through a large advertisement in a New York City newspaper. It seeks to enjoin Perlee from working in that restaurant as a chef for one year. Discuss how successful Hotel Lux will be in its action.

14-2. In State X, persons must be at least eighteen years old before they can purchase alcoholic beverages. The state also has passed a law requiring that persons who prepare and serve liquor in the form of drinks in commercial establishments be licensed. The only requirement for obtaining a yearly license is that the person be at least eighteen years old. Michael, age thirty-five, is hired as a bartender for the Lone Star Restaurant. George, a staunch alumnus of a nearby university, brings twenty of his friends to the restaurant to celebrate a football victory. George has ordered four rounds of drinks, and the bar bill exceeds $150. George learns that Michael has failed to renew his bartender's license, and George refuses to pay, claiming the contract is unenforceable. Discuss whether George is correct.

14-3. On May 1, by telephone, Yu offers to hire Benson to perform personal services. On May 5, Benson returns Yu's call and accepts the offer. Discuss fully whether this contract falls under the Statute of Frauds under the following circumstances:
   (a) The contract calls for Benson to be employed for one year, with the right to begin performance immediately.
   (b) The contract calls for Benson to be employed for

nine months, with performance of services to begin on September 1.
   (c) The contract calls for Benson to submit a written research report, with a deadline of two years for submission.

14-4. William Rowe was admitted to General Hospital, suffering from the effects of a severe gastric hemorrhage. On the day Rowe was admitted, Rowe's son informed an agent for the hospital that his father had no financial means but that he would pay for his father's medical services. Subsequently, the son stated, "Well, we want you to do everything you can to save his life, and we don't want you to spare any expense. Whatever he needs, Doctor, you go ahead and get it, and I will pay you." After Rowe was discharged from the hospital, his son refused to pay the medical bills. Can the hospital enforce the son's oral promise? Discuss fully.

14-5. Fernandez orally promised Pando that if Pando helped her win the New York state lottery, she would share the proceeds equally with him. Pando agreed to purchase the tickets in Fernandez's name, select the lottery numbers, and pray for divine intervention from a saint to help them win. Fernandez won $2.8 million in the lottery, which was to be paid over a ten-year period. When Fernandez failed to share the winnings equally, Pando sued for breach of her contractual obligation. Fernandez countered that the contract was unenforceable under the Statute of Frauds, because the contract could not be performed within one year. Could the contract be performed within a year? Explain. [*Pando by Pando v. Fernandez,* 127 Misc.2d 224, 485 N.Y.S.2d 162 (1984)]

14-6. Illinois Bell Telephone Co. (IBT) and the Reuben H. Donnelley Corp. (RHD) had by contract jointly produced telephone directories in Illinois for over sixty years. While in the process of oral negotiations to renew the contracts, IBT notified RHD by letter that the existing contracts were being canceled pursuant to contract terms. These contract terms required RHD to turn over records, to assign advertising contracts, to refrain from using certain information in any future directories RHD might publish, and so on. The termination clause under which IBT canceled stated that "either party may cancel this agreement by giving prior written notice to the other one year in advance of the effective date of cancellation.'' The requirements imposed on RHD were to take place upon ''termination.'' In anticipation that RHD's and IBT's interpretation of the contract terms and the time when RHD's obligations would become effective would differ, IBT filed suit seeking specific performance of its demand for RHD to meet the termination requirements immediately. RHD moved to dismiss the suit, claiming that the words of the contract were clear and that such demands were not effective until one year after ''the effective date of cancellation.'' Discuss who is correct. [*Illinois Bell Telephone Co. v. Reuben H. Donnelley Corp.,* 595 F.Supp. 1192 (N.D.Ill. 1984)]

14-7. Samuel DaGrossa and others were planning to open a restaurant. At some point prior to August 1985, DaGrossa orally agreed with Philippe LaJaunie that LaJaunie, in exchange for his contribution in designing, renovating, and managing the restaurant, could purchase a one-third interest in the restaurant's stock if the restaurant was profitable in its first year of operations. The restaurant opened in March 1986, and a few weeks later LaJaunie's employment was terminated. LaJaunie brought an action to enforce the stock-purchase agreement. Is the agreement enforceable? Why or why not? [*LaJaunie v. DaGrossa,* 159 A.D.2d 349, 552 N.Y.S.2d 628 (1990)]

14-8. In 1983, Doughty contracted to sell a portion of his anticipated potato crop to Idaho Frozen Foods Corp. (IFF) to secure financing for the growing of the crop. To express the terms of their agreement, the parties used a ''form'' contract that had been developed through negotiations between IFF and the Potato Growers of Idaho (PGI), of which Doughty was not a member. Under the contract, Doughty was to receive a base price if the potato crop contained a certain percentage of potatoes weighing ten ounces or more. If the crop contained a higher percentage, the price would be increased. Conversely, if the crop contained a lower percentage, the price would be reduced. These provisions in the contract reflected IFF's desire to have potatoes a certain size in order to meet its processing needs. The contract also provided IFF with the option of accepting or refusing delivery of the potatoes if less than 10 percent of them weighed ten ounces or more. Doughty contracted to sell only a portion of his crop to IFF; the rest of his crop he sold to another processor on the ''fresh pack'' market—in which potatoes are packaged in sacks and sold for whole use, such as for baking potatoes— for $4.69 per hundredweight. In the fresh pack market, no preharvest contract is used. The potatoes are sold after harvest. Because of poor weather conditions, only 8 percent of Doughty's potato crop consisted of ten-ounce potatoes. Because of the small percentage of ten-ounce potatoes, Doughty was entitled to only $2.57 per hundredweight for his potatoes under the terms of the IFF contract. After four days of delivery under the contract, Doughty refused to deliver any more potatoes to IFF. IFF brought suit for breach of contract. Doughty claimed that the contract was not enforceable because it was unconscionable and therefore void. Will the court agree? Discuss. [*Doughty v. Idaho Frozen Foods Corp.,* 112 Idaho 791, 736 P.2d 460 (1987)]

14-9. John Peck, an employee of V.S.H. Realty, Inc., asked Abdu Nessralla, his father-in-law, to act as a ''straw'' (a person who is put up in name only to take part in a deal) in V.S.H.'s acquisition of real property near Nessralla's farm. In return, Peck agreed to act as a straw to assist Nessralla in purchasing other nearby property—the Sturtevant farm. Nessralla purchased the property V.S.H. wanted and conveyed it to V.S.H. Subsequently, Peck purchased the Sturtevant farm and conveyed the property to himself and his cousin. Nessralla took no part in the purchase of the Sturtevant farm, provided none of the purchase price, and did not know that the purchase had taken place until about a month later. When Nessralla learned of the purchase and asked Peck to sell the farm to him, Peck refused. Nessralla filed a complaint seeking specific performance of Peck's oral agreement to convey the Sturtevant farm to him. The trial court dismissed Nessralla's action, concluding that the Statute of Frauds operated as a complete defense. Nessralla appealed, arguing that Peck was estopped from pleading the Statute of Frauds as a defense. Nessralla claimed that he suffered injury in reliance on the oral agreement, both because he purchased property on Peck's (V.S.H.'s) behalf and because he took no action to purchase the Sturtevant farm on his own behalf. Will the appellate court uphold the trial court's ruling? Explain. [*Nessralla v. Peck,* 403 Mass. 757, 532 N.E.2d 685 (1989)]

14-10. The plaintiffs—the Nicols, Hoerrs, Turners, and Andersons—purchased subdivision lots from Ken Nelson. The lots bordered an undeveloped tract and offered scenic views of an adjacent lake. When Nelson and his partners began taking steps to develop the previously undeveloped tract, the plaintiffs sued. The trial court found that the plaintiffs had purchased their lots only after receiving oral assurances from Nelson that (1) the tract would remain undeveloped open space, (2) the property was owned by a company that had no plans to build on the land, (3) he held an option to purchase the property if it became available, and (4) he would not develop the land if it came under his ownership. Concluding that the plaintiffs had reasonably relied on Nelson's oral promise, the trial court enjoined Nelson's development of the property. Nelson appealed, arguing that the Statute of Frauds, which requires that contracts involving interests in real property be in writing, barred enforcement of his oral promise. Will the appellate court affirm the trial court's judgment? Discuss fully. [*Nicol v. Nelson,* 776 P.2d 1144 (Colo.App. 1989)]

14-11. Case Briefing Assignment

Examine Case A.6 [Mann v. Wetter, *100 Or.App. 184, 785 P.2d 1064 (1990)*] *in Appendix A. The case has been excerpted there in great detail. Review and then brief the case,* making sure that you include answers to the following questions in your brief.

1. What were the plaintiff's contentions on appeal?
2. Why did the appellate court conclude that the release signed by Virkler, which exempted the defendant from liability, did not violate public policy?
3. Why did the appellate court declare that the release agreement was ambiguous as to whether Wetter was among those released from liability under the agreement?

Chapter 15

Third Party Rights

Once it has been determined that a valid and legally enforceable contract exists, attention can be turned to the rights and duties of the parties to the contract. Because a contract is a private agreement between the parties who have entered into it, it is fitting that these parties alone should have rights and liabilities under the contract. This idea is referred to as **privity of contract,** and it establishes the basic concept that a third party has no rights in a contract to which he or she is not a party. In other words, parties in privity are those who exchange the promissory words or those to whom the promissory words are directed.

To illustrate, suppose I offer to sell you my watch for $100, and you accept. Later, I refuse to deliver the watch to you even though you tender the $100. You decide to overlook my breach, but your close friend, Ann, is unhappy with my action and files suit. Can she receive judgment? The answer is obviously no, as she was not a party to the contract. You, as a party, have rights under the contract and could file a successful suit, but Ann has *no standing in court* (no right to sue).

There are two exceptions to this rule. The first involves a **third party beneficiary contract.** Here the parties to a contract make it with the intent to benefit a third party, and the third party has rights in the contract and may sue the promisor and, under some circumstances, the promisee to have it enforced. The second exception involves an **assignment of rights** or a **delegation of duties.** Here one of the original parties *transfers* contractual rights or obligations to a third party, giving the third party the rights or obligations of the transferor.

■ Third Party Beneficiary Contracts

When the promisee to a contract intends at the time of contracting that the contract performance benefit a third person, the third person becomes a beneficiary of the contract and as a beneficiary has legal rights in the contract.

This means that three parties, instead of the traditional two, have rights under third party beneficiary contracts: (1) the one making the promise (the promisor) that benefits the third party; (2) the one to whom the promise is made (the promisee); and (3) the third party on whom the promisee intends to confer a benefit under the contract (the third party beneficiary). If the promisor fails to keep the promise that benefits the third party, the third party normally can bring an action against the promisor to have the contract enforced.

For example, Alma, an unemployed nurse, owes Dr. Courtney, her dentist, $375. Because she is short of funds, Alma promises her friend Brady that she will provide nursing services to Brady's invalid mother for a week if Brady will pay the debt to Dr. Courtney. Brady agrees, and a third party beneficiary contract is thus formed. Dr. Courtney is a third party beneficiary (because Alma intends him to benefit from Brady's promise). The courts normally will uphold Dr. Courtney's right to enforce the contract against Brady. Exhibit 15–1 illustrates the relationships of the parties in a third party beneficiary contract.

Note that only **intended beneficiaries** have legal rights. Third parties who benefit from a contract only *incidentally* are **incidental beneficiaries** and have no legal rights under the contract; they cannot sue to have the contract enforced.

Intended Beneficiaries

In determining whether a third party beneficiary is an intended or incidental beneficiary, the best question to ask is: To whom is performance to be given according to the language of the contract? In other words, according to the language of the contract, was the promisee's primary purpose in forming the contract to obtain a benefit for himself or herself or for a third party?

The presence of one or more of the factors listed below strongly indicates an *intended* (rather than an incidental) benefit to the third party.

1. Performance rendered directly to the third party.
2. The rights of the third party to control the details of performance.
3. Express designation in the contract.

Traditionally, third party beneficiaries were divided into two types: creditor beneficiaries and donee beneficiaries. These two major categories are

■ Exhibit 15–1 Third Party Beneficiary Contract Relationships

This exhibit illustrates the nature of performance required under a third party beneficiary contract. Alma has promised to take care of Brady's invalid mother; in return, Brady has promised Alma that he will pay $375 to Dr. Courtney, who becomes a third party beneficiary of the Brady-Alma contract. If Brady fails to perform (pay Dr. Courtney the $375), Dr. Courtney may bring an action against Brady to enforce the contract.

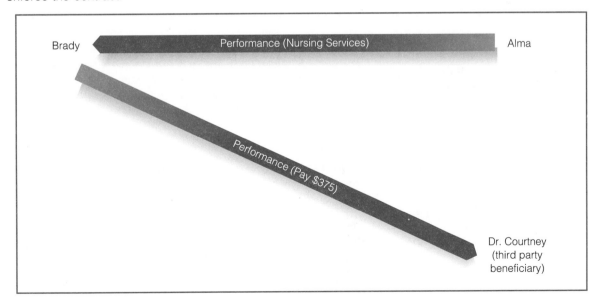

discussed below, but bear in mind that any *intended* beneficiary to a contract may sue to enforce the promise.[1]

CREDITOR BENEFICIARIES If a promisee's main purpose in making a contract is to discharge a duty or debt he or she already owes to a third party, then the third party is a **creditor beneficiary**.[2] The creditor beneficiary contract arises when another person (the promisor) promises the debtor (the promisee) to pay the debtor's debt to the creditor (the third party). Although not a party to the contract, the creditor is *intended* as the beneficiary and can thus enforce the promise against the promisor.

Allowing a creditor beneficiary to sue the promisor directly results in a reduction of the number of potential lawsuits before the courts. For example, assume that Alcott decides to sell her house to Bennett. When Alcott originally purchased the house, she financed the purchase with a mortgage loan from Centennial Bank. Her monthly payments are $650, and she still owes the bank $55,000. Bennett gives Alcott $10,000 cash and promises Alcott in writing to assume the mortgage debt and make the monthly payments to the bank. Alcott and Bennett have created a third party beneficiary contract in which Bennett is the promisor (because he made the promise benefiting the third party), Alcott is the promisee (because Bennett made the promise to Alcott), and Centennial Bank is the creditor beneficiary. If Bennett breaches his promise to Alcott and fails to make the monthly payments to the bank, the bank can, of course, bring an action against Alcott to collect the debt because, under their prior contract, Alcott owes the bank the money. Alcott, in turn, can then sue Bennett for breach of contract. Allowing the creditor beneficiary (the bank) to sue the promisor (Bennett) directly, however, renders the litigation more efficient: by circumvention of the middle person (Alcott), the same result is achieved with one legal action instead of two.

In the following case, a creditor beneficiary to a contract sued the promisor directly for payment of the debt. This case, one of the earliest in a U.S. court in which an exception to the rule of privity was allowed, is a landmark in the law governing third party beneficiary contracts and is often cited by the courts.

---

1. The Restatement (Second) of Contracts dispenses with the terms *creditor beneficiary* and *donee beneficiary* and distinguishes only between intended and incidental beneficiaries. Because the traditional terms appear in court decisions and are still occasionally used by the courts, we retain their usage here.
2. Restatement (Second) of Contracts, Section 302(1)(a).

Case 15.1

LAWRENCE v. FOX

Court of Appeals of New York, 1859.
20 N.Y. 268.

BACKGROUND AND FACTS Holly owed Lawrence $300. Fox suggested that Holly give him the money and promised to pay it to Lawrence to discharge Holly's debt. (Sufficient consideration was present to create a contract between Holly and Fox.) Fox never paid Lawrence, so Lawrence sued Fox in a New York state court, considering himself a third party beneficiary of the contract between Holly and Fox. The trial court decided that Lawrence had a legal right to sue Fox for failing to pay the $300 as promised, even though Lawrence was not a direct party to the contract. Fox appealed.

DECISION AND RATIONALE The Court of Appeals of New York affirmed the judgment and ordered Fox to pay Lawrence $300 to fulfill the contract with Holly. Recognizing Lawrence as a third party beneficiary, the court explained "[t]hat where one person makes a promise to another for the benefit of a third person, that third person may maintain an action upon it." The court noted that this was a "long recognized and clearly established" principle, resting on the ground "that the law operating on the act of the parties creates the duty, establishes a privity, and implies the promise and obligation on which the action is founded."

DONEE BENEFICIARIES If a promisee's main purpose in making a contract is to confer a gift upon a third party, then the third party is a **donee beneficiary.**[3] A donee beneficiary can enforce the promise of a promisor just as a creditor beneficiary can. The most common third party beneficiary contract involving a donee beneficiary is a life insurance contract. In a typical contract, Arthur, the promisee, pays premiums to Old Life, a life insurance company, and Old Life promises to pay a certain amount of money upon Arthur's death to anyone Arthur designates as beneficiary. The designated beneficiary, Calvin, is a donee beneficiary under the life insurance policy and can enforce payment against the insurance company upon Arthur's death.

As a further example, suppose that Anna goes to her attorney, Barton, and enters into a contract in which Barton promises to draft a will naming Anna's son, Cory, as an heir. Cory is a donee beneficiary, and if Barton does not prepare the will properly, Cory can sue Barton.[4] Or suppose that Anderson offers to paint Burke's house if Burke pays $750 to Cabot, Anderson's son. Anderson wants to give the money to Cabot as a gift. Cabot is a donee beneficiary and can enforce Burke's promise to pay $750.

Note that a donee beneficiary, unlike a creditor beneficary, cannot sue the *promisee* if the contract is breached. A donee beneficiary is essentially the recipient of a gift, and promises to give gifts are unenforceable because no consideration is given in return for the gift.

Incidental Beneficiaries

The benefit that an incidental beneficiary receives from a contract between two parties is unintentional. Therefore, an incidental beneficiary cannot enforce a contract to which he or she is not a party. Several factors must be examined to determine whether a party is an incidental beneficiary.

The following are examples of incidental beneficiaries. In each case, the third party has no rights in the contract and cannot enforce it against the promisor.

1. Jon contracts with Pat to build a factory on Pat's land. Jon's plans specify that Ad Pipe Company pipe fittings must be used in all plumbing. Ad Pipe Company is an incidental beneficiary and cannot enforce the contract against Jon by attempting to require Jon to purchase its pipe.

2. Ken contracts with Stu to build a recreational facility on Stu's land. Once the facility is constructed, it will greatly enhance the property values in the neighborhood. If Ken subsequently refuses to build the facility, Pete, a neighboring property owner, cannot enforce the contract against Ken by attempting to require Ken to build the facility.

3. Hank is an employee of Mary. Hank has been promised a promotion if his employer obtains a contract with Jones. Mary is unable to obtain the contract with Jones. Hank is an incidental beneficiary to that contract and has no right to sue Jones for being the cause of his failure to be promoted to a better-paying position. Indeed, Hank cannot sue Jones even if Hank loses his job as a result of the failure of Mary and Jones to reach an agreement.

Government contracts often benefit the public, but individual members of the public are treated as incidental beneficiaries, unless the contract provides otherwise. For example, Benningson contracts with the federal government to carry mail over a certain route. Cagney is a member of the public whose mail is to be carried over the route. Benningson fails to perform. Benningson is under no contractual duty to Cagney individually, and thus Cagney is treated as an incidental beneficiary and cannot enforce the contract.

Enforceable Rights—When The Rights of a Third Party Vest

Until the rights of a third party vest, the third party cannot enforce a contract against the original parties. When a right is *vested,* it is fixed or it takes effect. The rights of a third party vest when the original parties *cannot rescind or change the contract without the consent of the third party.*

The rights of an intended third party beneficiary vest (and the power of the original contracting parties to change, alter, or rescind the contract terminates) whenever one of the following three things happens:

---

3. Restatement (Second) of Contracts, Section 302(1)(b).
4. *Lucas v. Hamm,* 56 Cal.2d 583, 364 P.2d 685, 15 Cal.Rptr. 821 (1961).

1. The third party beneficiary learns of the contract and manifests assent to it at the request of the promisor and promisee.
2. The third party beneficiary brings suit upon the contract.
3. The third party materially alters his or her position in detrimental reliance on the contract.[5]

If the contract expressly reserves to the contracting parties the right to cancel, rescind, or modify the contract, the rights of the third party beneficiary are subject to any change that results.[6] This is particularly true in most life insurance contracts, in which the insured party reserves the right to change the beneficiary.

◼ Assignment of Rights

In every bilateral contract, the two parties have corresponding rights and duties. One party has a *right* to require the other to perform some task, and the other has a *duty* to perform it. The transfer of *rights* to a third person is known as an *assignment*.

How Assignments Function

Assignments are important because they are involved in many financing devices for businesses. Probably the most common contractual right that is assigned is the right to the payment of money. For instance, Ted sells stereo and video equipment—including compact disc players, dual cassette decks, DAT decks, camcorders, videocassette players, and television sets. To be ready for the holiday sales season, Ted needs to buy more inventory. Because he sells on credit to most of his customers (who then make small monthly payments), he does not have enough funds on hand to purchase new inventory, but he does have the *right* to receive the monthly payments from his customers. To obtain funds, Ted assigns the right to these payments to a financing agency. In return, the agency gives Ted cash.

Assignments may involve accounts receivable, as well as the proceeds from contracts not yet performed and *general intangibles* (that is, property that is a right rather than a physical object—for

example, stocks, bonds, and the goodwill of a business). Such assignments *secure* (that is, act as assurances of payment for) millions of dollars of loans daily, providing working capital without which many businesses could not continue to operate. Secured financing is subject to UCC Article 9 (discussed in Chapter 31).

A distinction must be made between an assignment and a novation. As will be discussed in Chapter 16, a *novation* is a written agreement entered into by *all* the parties in which one party is substituted for another party; that is, one party is completely dismissed from the contract, and another is substituted. The dismissed party is no longer liable under the original contract. Such is not always the case with an assignment.

Relationship of Parties

When rights under a contract are assigned unconditionally, the rights of the **assignor** (the party making the assignment) are extinguished.[7] The third party (the **assignee,** or party receiving the assignment) has a right to demand performance from the other original party to the contract (the obligor).

For example, suppose that Bolivar owes Allison $50. Allison assigns to Cartwright the right to receive the $50 and notifies Bolivar of the assignment. Here, a valid assignment of a debt exists, and Bolivar must pay the $50 to Cartwright (the assignee) or Cartwright will be entitled to enforce payment in a court of law. The relationship of the parties in an assignment relationship is illustrated in Exhibit 15–2.

The assignee takes only those rights that the assignor originally had. Furthermore, the assignee's rights are subject to the defenses that the obligor has against the assignor. To illustrate, suppose Beth contracts to sell her boat to Arne for $40,000. The contract calls for delivery of the boat to Arne upon presentation of a receipt of payment signed by Beth. Arne fraudulently gives Beth a worthless check, and Beth signs the receipt, noting thereon "payment by check." Beth, on discovering the worthless check, has a legal right to avoid the contractual obligation to deliver the boat to Arne. Arne is in debt to Cassie and in satisfaction of the debt assigns to Cassie the contract rights for the delivery of the boat, notifying Beth of the assignment. Be-

---

5. Restatement (Second) of Contracts, Section 311.
6. Defenses raised against third party beneficiaries are given in the Restatement (Second) of Contracts, Section 309.

---

7. Restatement (Second) of Contracts, Section 317.

■ **Exhibit 15–2 Assignment Relationships**

In the assignment relationship illustrated here, Allison assigns her *rights* under a contract that she made with Bolivar to a third party, Cartwright. Allison thus becomes the *assignor* and Cartwright the *assignee* of the contractual rights. Bolivar, the *obligor* (the party owing performance under the contract) now owes performance to Cartwright instead of Allison. Allison's original contract rights are extinguished after assignment.

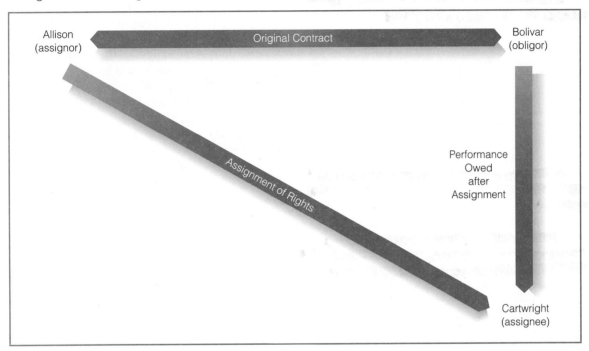

Allison (assignor) — Original Contract — Bolivar (obligor)

Assignment of Rights

Performance Owed after Assignment

Cartwright (assignee)

cause the assignee Cassie's rights are subject to Beth's defense, Cassie cannot require Beth to transfer the boat, even though she is an innocent party to these events.

Form of the Assignment

In general, an assignment can take any form, oral or written. Naturally, it is more difficult to prove the occurrence of an oral assignment, so it is practical to put all assignments in writing.

Of course, assignments covered by the Statute of Frauds must be in writing to be enforceable. For example, an assignment of an interest in land must be in writing to be enforceable. In addition, most states require contracts for the assignment of wages to be in writing.[8]

Consideration

An assignment need *not* be supported by legally sufficient consideration to be effective. A gratuitous assignment is just as effective as an assignment made for money. The absence of consideration becomes significant, however, when the assignor wants to revoke the assignment. If the assignment was made for consideration, the assignor cannot revoke it. If no consideration is involved, the assignor can revoke, thereby canceling the right of the third party to demand performance or to sue for failure to render that performance.[9] Gratuitous assignments can be revoked by:

1. The subsequent assignment of the same right to another third party.
2. The death of the assignor.
3. The bankruptcy of the assignor.
4. A notice of revocation given to the assignee.

---

8. See, for example, California Labor Code Section 300. There are other assignments that must be in writing, as well.

9. Restatement (Second) of Contracts, Section 332.

Rights That Cannot Be Assigned

As a general rule, all rights can be assigned, except in special circumstances. The following is a list of these special circumstances with examples:

1. If a statute expressly prohibits assignment, the right in question cannot be assigned. Suppose John is a new employee of Craft, Inc. Craft is an employer subject to state workers' compensation statutes, and thus John is a covered employee. John has a relatively high-risk job. In need of a loan, John borrows the money from Shady, assigning to Shady all workers' compensation benefits due him should he be injured on the job. This type of assignment of *future* workers' compensation benefits is prohibited by state statute.

2. If a contract stipulates that the rights cannot be assigned, then *ordinarily* they cannot be assigned. Antiassignment clauses in contracts are discussed in detail in the next section.

3. When a contract is uniquely *personal* in nature, the rights under the contract cannot be assigned unless all that remains is a money payment. Suppose Beasley signs a contract to be a tutor for Abby's children. Abby then attempts to assign her right in Beasley's services to Catherine. Catherine cannot enforce the contract against Beasley because the contract calls for the rendering of a unique personal service.[10]

4. Finally, a right cannot be assigned if the assignment will materially increase or alter the risk of the obligor [see UCC 2-210(2)]. Assume that Allen takes out an insurance policy on her hotel with Preventive Casualty, an insurance company. The policy insures against fire, theft, floods, and vandalism. Allen then attempts to assign the insurance policy to Cassidy, who also owns a hotel. The assignment is ineffective because it substantially alters Preventive Casualty's risk. An insurance company evaluates the particular risk associated with a certain party and tailors its policy to fit that exact risk. If the policy is assigned to a third party, the insurance risk will be materially altered. Therefore, the assignment will not operate to give Cassidy any rights against Preventive Casualty. A fire-insurance policy is also treated as a personal contract.

In the following case, the central issue was whether a covenant not to compete contained in an employment contract could be assigned.

---

10. Restatement (Second) of Contracts, Sections 317 and 318.

Case 15.2

PINO v. SPANISH BROADCASTING SYSTEM OF FLORIDA, INC.

District Court of Appeal of Florida, Third District, 1990.
564 So.2d 186.

BACKGROUND AND FACTS In October 1985, Beatriz Pino signed a five-year employment contract as a radio announcer and disc jockey with two radio stations. The contract provided that Pino would not "engage * * * in the broadcasting business * * * in Dade or Broward Counties, Florida, for a period of twelve (12) months after the termination of her employment." The contract also provided that it was assignable. In December 1986, the stations sold their assets to Spanish Broadcasting System of Florida, Inc. (SBS), and as part of the sale, Pino's contract was assigned to SBS. In October 1989, Pino contracted with Viva, a broadcasting competitor of SBS, to begin work for Viva when her SBS contract terminated in March 1990. SBS asked a Florida state court to grant a temporary injunction to enforce the noncompetition clause. Pino contended that the assignment of the covenant-not-to-compete clause was invalid. Although a Florida statute provided that covenants not to compete could be enforced, it said nothing about the covenants being assignable. The trial court held for SBS. Pino appealed.

DECISION AND RATIONALE The District Court of Appeal of Florida affirmed the trial court's ruling. The appellate court held that because the contract contained a provision permitting its assignment, the covenant not to compete was assignable. The court explained that its holding "conform[ed] with the policy of preserving the sanctity of contract and providing uniformity and certainty in commercial transactions."

Antiassignment Clauses

Antiassignment clauses in contracts are increasing in both number and importance. If the promisor makes it clear that a right is *not* to be assignable, generally no subsequent assignment will be effective. Note that restraints on the power to assign only operate against the parties themselves. They do not effectively prohibit an assignment by operation of law, such as an assignment pursuant to bankruptcy or death.

Suppose Benvenuto agrees to build a house for Atchison. The contract between Atchison and Benvenuto states: "The contract cannot be assigned by Atchison. Any assignment renders this contract void, and all rights hereunder will thereupon terminate." Atchison then attempts to assign her rights to Carvelli. Carvelli cannot enforce the contract against Benvenuto by trying to get Benvenuto to build the house, because the contract expressly prohibits the assignment of rights.

Whether an antiassignment clause is effective depends in part on how it is phrased. A contract that states that any assignment is "void" effectively prohibits any assignment. In the Carvelli example, the provision stated that any assignment would render the contract void. Therefore, when Atchison attempted to assign the contract to Carvelli, Benvenuto had an option to avoid the contract—that is why Carvelli could not enforce it.

There are several exceptions to the rule that a contract can, by its terms, prohibit any assignment of the contract. First, a contract cannot prevent an assignment of the right to receive money. For example, in the hypothetical situation discussed above, once Benvenuto has built the house, he could assign the right to receive *payment* for the construction. This exception exists to encourage the free flow of money and credit in modern business settings. Second, the assignment of rights in real estate normally cannot be prohibited, because this would be contrary to public policy. Such prohibitions are called *restraints against alienation* (to alienate, in this context, means to freely sell or transfer land interests). Third, the assignment of negotiable instruments cannot be prohibited.

Fourth, in a sale-of-goods contract, the right to receive damages for breach of contract or for payment of an account owed may be assigned even though the sales contract prohibits assignment [UCC 2-210(2)].

Antiassignment clauses have appeared in leases for many years. Now they are being used more frequently in other types of contracts as well. Recently, they have appeared in mortgage contracts and represent attempts by the mortgagee (the lending person or institution in a mortgage contract) to restrict the assumption of mortgages by new owners of real property. The typical lease or mortgage today cannot be assigned without the landlord's or mortgagee's consent.

Typical clauses in mortgages are due-on-sale (DOS) provisions. Under such provisions, a purchaser of mortgaged realty cannot assume the mortgage without the mortgagee's consent. The due-on-sale provision accelerates the entire loan, making the mortgage fully payable. Therefore the loan must be fully paid (by the buyer) or the buyer must secure a new mortgage (at the current interest rate). Under federal law, DOS clauses are generally enforceable. Some states prohibit DOS clauses.

Insurance contracts frequently stipulate that the policy rights will be forfeited if the policyholder assigns the policy. If the assignment is attempted before a loss has been incurred, the company can declare that the policy is void. (On the other hand, if the assignment is made after the loss, the claim is reduced to a monetary right, and the assignee can recover.)

In the following case, the court discussed whether an assignment of proceeds payable under an insurance policy constituted an assignment of the personal contract represented by the policy.

Case 15.3

SMITH v. BUEGE

Supreme Court of Appeals of
West Virginia, 1989.
387 S.E.2d 109.

BACKGROUND AND FACTS   Thomas Smith agreed to buy a house from James, Jackie, Terrie, and Chong Buege. The contract provided that if fire damaged the property before the sale was complete, Smith could either cancel the contract or accept the property as damaged and receive the insurance proceeds. Before the sale was completed, fire damaged the house. The Bueges notified their insurer, Prudential Insurance Company, of the contract with Smith. Smith notified the Bueges and Prudential that he still wanted the property and that he was opting to receive the insurance proceeds. Prudential sent the Bueges a check. When Smith sued the Bueges and Prudential in a West Virginia state court to recover the insurance proceeds, Prudential moved to dismiss the suit against it on the grounds that it was not a party to the contract and had met its obligations under the policy by paying the Bueges. The trial court granted the motion, and Smith appealed. Smith contended that his claim against Prudential had been improperly dismissed because the contract included an assignment of the proceeds (not the policy) and therefore Prudential should have paid him, not the Bueges. Prudential argued that the assignment was not valid because the policy provided that "[a]ssignment of this policy shall not be valid except with [Prudential's] consent," which was absent.

DECISION AND RATIONALE   The Supreme Court of Appeals of West Virginia reversed the trial court's decision, holding that the trial court improperly dismissed Smith's claim against Prudential. The appellate court acknowledged that an insurance policy is a personal contract, and therefore a provision that prohibits an assignment before a loss occurs will be enforced. The court pointed out, however, that assignment of a policy or its proceeds *after* a loss occurs is valid regardless of the provisions of the policy. The court explained that an assignment of proceeds after a loss is not an assignment of the personal contract that the policy represents but only of a claim or right of action on the policy. In this case, the court explained, there was an agreement to assign the proceeds. That agreement was not effective as an assignment until after the loss, when Smith decided to accept the property and the proceeds rather than rescind the contract. Prudential had notice of this postfire assignment before paying on the policy and therefore should have paid Smith. Instead, Prudential wrongfully paid the Bueges.

Notice of the Assignment

Once a valid assignment of rights has been made to a third party, the third party should notify the obligor of the assignment. This is not legally necessary, because an assignment is effective immediately, whether or not notice is given. Two major problems arise, however, when notice of the assignment is *not* given to the obligor:

1.   If the assignor assigns the same right to two different persons, the question arises as to which one has the right to receive performance from the obligor. Although the rule most often observed in the United States is that the first assignment in time is the first in right, some states follow the English rule, which basically gives priority to the first assignee who gives notice.[11] For example, suppose

---

11.   At common law, there were three different rules. The first rule was called the English rule. Assignees second in time to the first assignee prevailed in every case in which they had paid value, had taken the assignment without notice of the prior assignment, and had given the *obligor* notice of the assignment before the first assignee gave such notice. Another rule, called the New York rule, essentially stated that the first assignment in time is first in right. According to the third rule, the Massachusetts rule, the first assignee prevailed provided the first assignment was not revocable at the time the second assignment was made.

Berleson owes Astor $1,000 on a contractual obligation. On May 1, Astor assigns this monetary claim to Crockett. No notice of assignment is given to Berleson. On June 1, for services Dietrich has rendered to Astor, Astor assigns the same monetary claim from Berleson to Dietrich. Dietrich immediately notifies Berleson of the assignment. Although in the majority of states Crockett would have priority to receive payment, because Crockett's assignment was first in time, in some states Dietrich would have priority because Dietrich gave first notice.

Until the obligor has notice of the assignment, the obligor can discharge his or her obligation by performance to the assignor, and performance by the obligor to the assignor constitutes a discharge to the assignee. Once the obligor has received proper notice, only performance to the assignee can discharge the obligor's obligations. To illustrate, suppose Battelle owes Archer $1,000 on a contract obligation. Archer assigns this monetary claim to Crowley. No notice of assignment is given to Battelle. Battelle pays Archer the $1,000. Although the assignment was valid, Battelle's payment to Archer was a discharge of the debt, and Crowley's failure to give notice to Battelle of the assignment caused Crowley to lose the right to collect the money from Battelle. If Crowley had given Battelle notice of the assignment, Battelle's payment to Archer would not have discharged the debt, and Crowley would have had a legal right to require payment from Battelle.

■ Delegation of Duties

Just as a party can transfer rights under a contract through an assignment, a party can also transfer duties. Duties are not assigned, however. They are *delegated.* The relationship of the parties in a delegation relationship is illustrated in Exhibit 15–3.

Traditionally, when a contract provided for an "assignment of all rights," only the rights under the contract, and not the duties, were transferred. The traditional view was that the acceptance of the

■ Exhibit 15–3 Delegation Relationships

In the delegation relationship illustrated here, Bolivar delegates her *duties* under a contract that she made with Allison to a third party, Cartwright. Bolivar thus becomes the *delegator* and Cartwright the *delegatee* of the contractual duties. Cartwright now owes performance of the contractual duties to Allison (the obligee). Note that a delegation of duties does not normally relieve the delegator of liability if the delegatee fails to perform the contractual duties.

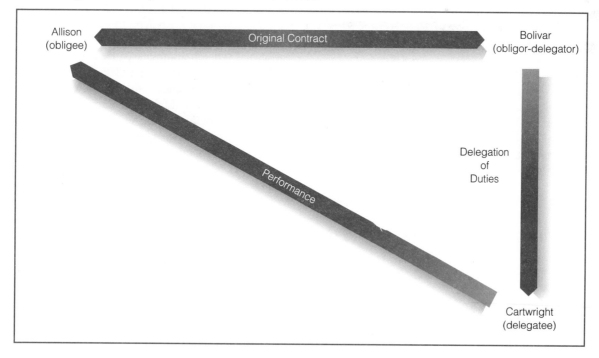

benefits of the contract was not sufficient to imply a promise to assume the duties of the contract. Modern authorities, however, take the view that the probable intention in using such general words as "assignment of all rights" is to create an assignment of rights *and* a delegation and an assumption of duties.[12] Therefore, when general words are used (for example, "I assign the contract" or "I assign all my rights under the contract"), the contract is construed as implying an assignment of rights and a delegation and an assumption of duties.

No special form is required to create a valid delegation of duties. As long as the delegator expresses a present intention to make the delegation, it is effective. The delegator need not even use the word *delegate*.

Duties That Cannot Be Delegated

As a general rule, any duty can be delegated. There are, however, some exceptions to this rule. Delegation is prohibited in the following situations:

1. When performance depends on the *personal skill* or talents of the obligor.
2. When special trust has been placed in the obligor.
3. When performance by a third party will vary materially from the performance expected by the obligee under the contract.
4. Usually, when a contract restricts either party's right to delegate duties.

Suppose that Bruckner contracts with Amati to tutor Amati in the various aspects of financial underwriting and investment banking. Bruckner is an experienced businessperson who is well known for his expertise in finance. Further, assume that Bruckner wants to delegate his duties to teach Amati to a third party, Corelli. This delegation would be ineffective, because Bruckner has contracted to render a service to Amati that is founded on Bruckner's *expertise*. It would represent a change from Amati's expectancy under the con-

tract. Therefore, Corelli cannot perform Bruckner's duties.

Suppose that Banks, an attorney, contracts with Anthony, a banker, to advise Anthony on a proposed merger with a savings and loan association. Banks wishes to delegate this duty to Claren, a partner in a law firm across town. Services of an attorney are *personal in nature*. Banks's delegation will be ineffective.

Finally, assume that Bourselan contracts with Applegate to pick up and deliver heavy construction machinery to Applegate's property. Bourselan then delegates this duty to Cantrell, who is in the business of delivering heavy machinery. The delegation is effective. The performance required is of a *routine and nonpersonal nature* and does not change Applegate's expectancy under the contract.

Liability for Performance

Normally, a valid delegation of duties does not relieve the party making the delegation—the delegator—of the obligation to perform in the event that the party who has been delegated the duty—the delegatee—fails to perform.[13] If the delegatee fails to perform, the delegator is still liable to the obligee.

If the delegatee fails to perform, whether the obligee can hold the delegatee liable comes into issue. If the delegatee has promised performance that will directly benefit the obligee, there is an assumption of duty. Breach of this duty makes the delegatee liable to the obligee. For example, suppose that Allison contracts with Clausen to build Clausen a house according to Clausen's blueprint plans. Allison becomes seriously ill and contracts to have Barnaby build the house for Clausen. Barnaby fails to build the house. Is Barnaby (the delegatee) liable to Clausen (the obligee)? The answer is yes. Clausen can sue Barnaby *or* Allison (the delegator), or both, for damages. This is an area in which the law governing third party beneficiaries overlaps with delegation law. In effect, Clausen's position here is the same as that of a third party beneficiary to the Allison-Barnaby contract.

Finally, note that the delegator has no further liability after a novation has occurred. We return to the concept of novation in the next chapter.

---

12.   UCC 2-210(1) (where there is a general assignment of a contract for the sale of goods); Restatement (Second) of Contracts, Section 328.

13.   *Crane Ice Cream Co. v. Terminal Freezing Co.,* 147 Md. 588, 128 A. 280 (1925).

■ Terms and Concepts

■ For Review

1. What factors indicate that a third party beneficiary is an intended beneficiary?
2. State four rights that can be assigned despite a contract clause expressly prohibiting assignment.
3. When a contract provides for "an assignment of all rights," will the contract be construed as implying an assignment of rights, a delegation of duties, or both?
4. Warren owes Ruth $100. Howie promises Warren to pay Ruth the money. Is Ruth an intended beneficiary of the Howie–Warren contract?
5. Simone sells her business to Tamara. As part of the sale, Simone promises not to compete in the same city for three years. Tamara sells the business to Chassidy and tells Chassidy that the sale includes an assignment of the right to have Simone refrain from competing with Chassidy for the stipulated period. Is the assignment effective?

■ Questions and Case Problems

15-1. John has been accepted as a freshman at a college 200 miles from his home for the fall semester. John's rich uncle, Michael, decides to give John a car for Christmas. In November, Michael makes a contract with auto dealer Jackson to purchase a new car for $10,000 to be delivered to John just before the Christmas holidays, in mid-December. The title to the car is to be in John's name. Michael pays the full purchase price, calls John and tells him about the gift, and takes off for a six-month vacation in Europe. Jackson never delivers the car, and John files an action against Jackson. Discuss fully whether John can recover for Jackson's breach of contract. What if Michael had agreed with Jackson to make installment payments on the car and then failed to make the payments. Could John have sued his uncle for breach of the contract? Discuss.

15-2. Five years ago, Jane purchased a house. At that time, being unable to pay the full purchase price, she borrowed money from Thrift Savings and Loan, which in turn took a 9.5 percent mortgage on the house. The mortgage contract did not prohibit the assignment of the mortgage. Then Jane secured a new job in another city and sold the house to Sylvia. The purchase price included payment to Jane of the value of her equity and the assumption of the mortgage held by Thrift. At the time the contract was made, Thrift did not know of or consent to the sale. On the basis of these facts, if Sylvia defaults in making the house payments to Thrift, what are Thrift's rights? Discuss.

15-3. Thomas is a student attending college. He signs a one-year lease agreement that runs from September 1 to August 31. The lease agreement specifies that the lease cannot be assigned without the landlord's consent. Thomas decides not to go to summer school and assigns the balance of the lease (three months) to a close friend, Fred. The landlord objects to the assignment and denies Fred access to the apartment. Thomas claims Fred is financially sound and should be allowed the full rights and privileges of an assignee. Discuss fully whether the landlord or Thomas is correct.

15-4. Diane has a specific set of plans to build a sailboat. The plans are detailed in nature, and any boat builder can build the boat. Diane secures bids, and the low bid is made by the Whale of a Boat Corp. Diane contracts with Whale to build the boat for $4,000. Whale then receives unexpected business from elsewhere. To meet the delivery date in the contract with Diane, Whale assigns (delegates) the contract, without Diane's consent, to Quick Brothers, a reputable boat builder. When the boat is ready for delivery, Diane learns of the assignment and refuses to accept delivery, even though the boat is built to specifications. Discuss fully whether Diane is obligated to accept and pay for the boat. Would your answer be any different if Diane had not had a specific set of plans but had instead contracted with Whale to design and build a sailboat for $4,000? Explain.

15-5. Christopher wrote a letter to Donald claiming that Donald owed him $3,000 for the shipment of string bikinis he had sent Donald three months before. Donald wrote back, saying that the bikinis were defective and that he therefore refused to pay. Christopher wrote back that his lawyer had advised him that it was questionable whether Donald had informed him of the defect in time and that Christopher might have a valid claim for the purchase price of $3,000 despite any defects. About a month later, Donald wrote back to Christopher informing him that Jerry, who owed Donald $3,000 from a previous contract, had agreed with Donald to make the payment to Christopher. Thereafter, Jerry failed to make the payment to Christopher. Can Christopher sue Jerry? Discuss fully.

15-6. Owens, a federal prisoner, was transferred from federal prison to the Nassau County Jail pursuant to a contract between the U.S. Bureau of Prisons and the county. The contract included a policy statement that required the receiving prison to provide for the safekeeping and protection of transferred federal prisoners. While in the Nassau County Jail, Owens was beaten severely by prison officials and suffered lacerations, bruises, and a lasting impairment that caused blackouts. Can Owens, as a third party beneficiary, sue the county for breach of its agreement with the U.S. Bureau of Prisons? Discuss fully. [*Owens v. Haas,* 601 F.2d 1242 (2d Cir. 1979)]

15-7. Clement was seriously injured in a car accident with King. Clement sued King. King retained Prestwich as her attorney. Because of the alleged negligence of Prestwich, Clement was able to obtain a $21,000 judgment on her claim against King. Clement received from King a purported written assignment of King's malpractice claim against Prestwich as settlement for the judgment against her. Can King assign her cause of action against Prestwich to Clement? Explain. [*Clement v. Prestwich,* 114 Ill.App.3d 479, 448 N.E.2d 1039, 70 Ill.Dec. 161 (1983)]

15-8. Fox Brothers Enterprises, Inc., agreed to convey to Canfield a lot, Lot 23, in a subdivision known as Fox Estates, together with a one-year option to purchase Lot 24. The agreement did not contain any prohibitions, restrictions, or limitations against assignments. Canfield paid the price of $20,000 and took title to Lot 23. Thereafter, Canfield assigned his option rights in Lot 24 to the Scotts. When the Scotts tried to exercise their right to the option, Fox Brothers refused to convey the property to them. The Scotts then brought suit for specific performance. What was the result? [*Scott v. Fox Brothers Enterprises, Inc.,* 667 P.2d 773 (Colo.App. 1983)]

15-9. Rensselaer Water Co. was under contract to the city of Rensselaer, New York, to provide water to the city, including water at fire hydrants. A warehouse owned by H. R. Moch Co. was totally destroyed by a fire, which could not be extinguished because of inadequate water pressure at the fire hydrants. Moch brought suit against Rensselaer Water for damages, claiming that Moch was a third party beneficiary to the city's contract with the water company. Will Moch be able to recover damages from the water company on the basis that the water company breached its contract with the city? Explain. [*H. R. Moch Co. v. Rensselaer Water Co.,* 247 N.Y. 160, 159 N.E. 896 (1928)]

15-10. Rogers agreed with Newton to do the plumbing work as a subcontractor on a construction project. Their contract stipulated that Rogers was to receive $22,100 in three installments. Rogers secured a loan from the Merchants & Farmers Bank of Dumas for $15,500 to pay for the necessary expenses he would incur when he began work and before he had received his first installment from Newton. In return for the borrowed money, Rogers assigned to the bank his rights in the contract he had formed with Newton. On February 11, the bank sent Newton notice of the assignment and asked Newton to make his payment checks payable to Rogers and the bank *jointly.* Newton agreed in a letter to the bank to do this. On March 12, however, Newton wrote a check for $7,085 payable to Rogers only. Rogers completed the work for Newton and had paid all his expenses except for that owed to one of his suppliers, Southern Pipe and Supply Co. Rogers eventually

defaulted on his payments to the bank, and the bank sued Newton for the balance on the note. Newton could not avoid his obligation to the assignee of the note (the bank), but he claimed that he should not be responsible for the bill to Southern Pipe and Supply. He claimed that Rogers's assignment of his contract with Newton to the bank obligated the bank to assume Rogers's duties under the contract (including payments to all suppliers) and that the bank should therefore pay the bill owed to Southern Pipe and Supply. Did Rogers's assignment of his rights in the contract with Newton include a delegation of his duties under the contract as well? Discuss. [*Newton v. Merchants & Farmers Bank of Dumas,* 11 Ark.App. 167, 668 S.W.2d 51 (1984)]

15-11. On August 8, 1978, the plaintiff, Shirley Petry, entered into a contract with the defendant, Cosmopolitan Spa International, Inc. The contract was for a spa membership that was to include ''processing, program counseling, and facilities usage.'' The written contract contained an exculpatory clause. The pertinent part of the clause stated, ''Member fully understands and agrees that in participating in one or more of the courses, or using the facilities maintained by Cosmopolitan, there is the possibility of accidental or other physical injury. Member further agrees to assume the risk of such injury and further agrees to indemnify Cosmopolitan from any and all liability to Cosmopolitan by either the Member or third party as the result of the use by the Member of the facilities and instructions as offered by Cosmopolitan.'' On or around January 1, 1980, Cosmopolitan sold the spa to Holiday Spa of Tennessee, Inc. On February 25, 1980, the plaintiff, Shirley Petry, injured her back when she sat on an exercise machine and it collapsed under her. She brought suit against both Cosmopolitan and Holiday for damages for personal injuries resulting from the defendants' negligence in properly maintaining the exercise machine. The defendants claimed that the exculpatory clause negated their liability. Petry argued that Holiday could not use the exculpatory clause as a defense because it was part of a contract for personal services, and therefore the contract was not assignable. What will the court decide? Discuss fully. [*Petry v. Cosmopolitan Spa International, Inc.,* 641 S.W.2d 202 (Tenn.App. 1982)]

15-12. Case Briefing Assignment

Examine Case A.7 [Rhodes v. United Jewish Charities of Detroit, *184 Mich.App. 740, 459 N.W.2d 44 (1990)*] *in Appendix A. The case has been excerpted there in great detail. Review and then brief the case, making sure that you include answers to the following questions in your brief.*

1. Why was this lawsuit brought?
2. Why did the appellate court hold that the trial court did not ''address the merits of the plaintiff's argument''?
3. What was the critical issue before the court on appeal?
4. What was the basis for the appellate court's conclusion that Rhodes was an intended third party beneficiary to the UJC-JVS contract?

Chapter 16

Performance and Discharge

Just as rules are necessary to determine when a legally enforceable contract exists, so also are they necessary to determine when one of the parties can justifiably say, "I have fully performed, so I am now discharged from my obligations under this contract." The legal environment of business requires the identification of some point at which the parties can reasonably know their duties are at an end.

The **discharge** (termination) of a contract is ordinarily accomplished when both of the parties perform those acts promised in the contract. For example, a buyer and seller have a contract for the sale of a bicycle for $50. This contract will be discharged upon the buyer's payment of $50 to the seller and the seller's transfer of possession of the bicycle to the buyer.

Although a contract is ordinarily discharged by the parties' performance of their contractual duties, discharge can also occur in other ways. In this chapter, we will discuss some of the more important ways in which contracts can be discharged. Broadly speaking, contracts can be discharged by the following:

1. The occurrence or failure of a *condition* upon which a contract is based.
2. *Performance* (or breach of contract, in which case the nonbreaching party is discharged from the duty of performance).
3. *Agreement of the parties* (through rescission, novation, or accord and satisfaction).
4. *Operation of law* (resulting from material alteration of the contract, the statute of limitations, bankruptcy, or impossibility or commercial impracticability of performance).

■ Conditions

Normally, promises must be performed, or the party promising the act will be in breach of contract. For example, I promise to pay you $100 on September 1. The promise is unconditional. If I do not pay you the $100, I am in breach of contract.

In some cases, however, performance is contingent on the occurrence or nonoccurrence of a certain event. Therefore, a *condition* is inserted into the contract, either expressly by the parties or impliedly by courts. If this condition is not satisfied, the obligations of the parties are discharged. Thus, a **condition** is a possible future event, the occurrence or nonoccurrence of which will trigger the performance of a legal obligation or terminate an existing obligation under a contract.[1]

For example, suppose that I offer to purchase a tract of your land on the condition that your neighbor to the south agrees to sell me her land. You accept my offer. Our obligations (promises) are conditioned on your neighbor's willingness to sell her land. Should this condition not be satisfied (for example, if your neighbor refuses to sell), our obligations to each other are discharged and cannot be enforced.

Three types of conditions can be present in contracts—conditions *precedent,* conditions *subsequent,* and *concurrent* conditions. Conditions are also classified as *express* or *implied.*

---

1. Restatement (Second) of Contracts, Section 224, defines a condition as ''an event, not certain to occur, which must occur, unless its nonoccurrence is excused, before performance under a contract becomes due.''

Conditions Precedent

A condition that must be fulfilled before a party's performance can be required is called a **condition precedent.** The condition precedes the absolute duty to perform. Real estate contracts frequently are conditioned on the buyer's ability to obtain financing. For example, Fisher promises to buy Calvin's house if Salvation Bank approves Fisher's mortgage application. The Fisher-Calvin contract is therefore subject to a condition precedent—the bank's approval of Fisher's mortgage application. If the bank does not approve the application, the contract will fail because the condition precedent was not met.

The following case concerns a condition precedent in a contract for the sale of a pharmacy.[2]

---

2. As a practical matter, the difference between conditions precedent and conditions subsequent is relatively unimportant from a substantive point of view, but very important procedurally. Normally, as in Case 16.1, the plaintiff must prove conditions precedent, because usually it is he or she who claims there is a duty to be performed. Similarly, the defendant must usually prove conditions subsequent, because it is usually he or she who claims a duty no longer exists.

Case 16.1

K & K PHARMACY, INC. v. BARTA

Supreme Court of Nebraska, 1986.
222 Neb. 215,
382 N.W.2d 363.

BACKGROUND AND FACTS   K & K Pharmacy, Inc., contracted to sell a pharmacy to James Barta. The pharmacy was in a shopping mall, and the pharmacy premises were leased from the owner of the mall, Larsen Enterprises. The contract between K & K and Barta provided: "This Agreement shall be contingent upon Buyer's ability to obtain a new lease from Larsen Enterprises, Inc., for the premises presently occupied by Seller. In the event Buyer is unable to obtain a new lease satisfactory to Buyer, this Agreement shall be null and void." Barta wanted to sell certain food in the pharmacy, as in his other stores, but another lessee in the mall had an exclusive right to sell groceries and refused to give the necessary concession. As a result, Barta refused to sign a lease with Larsen and notified K & K that he would not go through with the sale. K & K sued in a Nebraska state court to recover damages for Barta's alleged breach of contract. The trial court granted Barta's motion for summary judgment, and K & K appealed.

DECISION AND RATIONALE   The Supreme Court of Nebraska held that the contract was not enforceable, because the condition precedent had not occurred, and affirmed the lower court's decision. The state supreme court pointed out that the case turned on the meaning and effect of the "new lease" provision of the contract and interpreted the provision as a condition precedent. The contract was contingent on Barta's "obtaining a new lease that was satisfactory to him." As to satisfaction, the court stated that "[i]f the agreement leaves no doubt that honest satisfaction and no more is meant, the condition does not occur if the obligor is honestly, even though unreasonably, dissatisfied." In this case, Barta could not obtain a lease allowing him to employ his established marketing policy, and there was no evidence that Barta was anything but honestly dissatisfied with the lease.

Conditions Subsequent

When a condition operates to terminate a party's duty to perform, it is called a **condition subsequent.** The condition follows, or is subsequent to, the absolute duty to perform. If the condition occurs, the party need not perform any further. For example, if Hartman promises to work for the San Pedro Company for one year unless he is admitted to Stanford's Graduate School of Business, the absolute duty to work is conditioned on his not being admitted. Hartman's promise to work for San Pedro continues to be absolute until he is admitted to Stanford. Once Hartman is officially admitted, the absolute duty to work for San Pedro ends, and Hartman is released from the contract.

Generally, conditions precedent are common; conditions subsequent are rare. The Restatement (Second) of Contracts deletes the terms *condition subsequent* and *condition precedent* because they are confusing.

Concurrent Conditions

When each party's absolute duty to perform is conditioned on the other party's absolute duty to perform, there are **concurrent conditions.** Concurrent conditions occur only when the parties expressly or impliedly are to perform their respective duties *simultaneously.* For example, if a buyer promises to pay for goods when they are delivered by the seller, each party's absolute duty to perform is conditioned on the other party's absolute duty to perform. The buyer's duty to pay for the goods does not become absolute until the seller either delivers or tenders the goods. Likewise, the seller's duty to deliver the goods does not become absolute until the buyer tenders or actually makes payment. Therefore, neither can recover from the other for breach unless he or she first tenders his or her own performance.

Express and Implied Conditions

Conditions can also be classified as: (1) express, (2) implied in fact, or (3) implied in law.

Express conditions are provided for by the parties' agreement. An express condition is usually prefaced by the word *if, provided, after,* or *when.* Conditions *implied in fact* are similar to express conditions because they are understood to be part of the agreement, but they are not expressly found in the language of the agreement. The court infers them from the promises. For example, Kelly promises to make necessary repairs to an office building she leases to Cooper, but in their contract the parties do not expressly provide for Kelly's inspection of the premises. Therefore, Cooper's notifying Kelly of any necessary repairs of which Kelly would otherwise be unaware is an implied condition of Kelly's duty to make those repairs.

Finally, *implied-in-law,* or *constructive,* conditions are imposed by the law to achieve justice and fairness. They are not contained in the language of the contract or even necessarily implied.[3] For example, a contract in which a builder is supposed to build a house for a buyer can omit the date on which the buyer is supposed to pay the builder. Nonetheless, a court would consider it an implied condition that the buyer not be obliged to pay the builder until the house was completed, because the buyer should not be compelled to perform unless the builder has performed.

■ Discharge by Performance

The great majority of contracts are discharged by performance. The contract comes to an end when both parties fulfill their respective duties by performing the acts they have promised. Performance can also be accomplished by tender. **Tender** is an unconditional offer to perform by one who is ready, willing, and able to do so. Therefore, a seller who places goods at the disposal of a buyer has tendered delivery and can demand payment. A buyer who offers to pay for goods has tendered payment and can demand delivery of the goods. Once performance has been tendered, the party making the tender has done everything possible to carry out the terms of the contract. If the other party then refuses to perform, the party making the tender can sue for breach of contract.

---

3.   Restatement (Second) of Contracts, Section 226.

Degree of Performance Required

It is important to distinguish between *complete performance* and *substantial performance*. Courts typically use a *reasonable expectations test* for determining which of these categories a performance fits. Complete performance occurs when performance is within the bounds of reasonable expectations. Substantial performance occurs when performance is slightly below reasonable expectations. (As will be discussed in the next section, performance far below reasonable expectations constitutes a *material* breach of contract.)

A contract may stipulate that performance must meet the personal satisfaction of either the contracting party or a third party. Such a provision will also affect the degree of performance required under the contract.

COMPLETE PERFORMANCE Normally, conditions expressly stated in the contract must fully occur in all aspects for complete, or strict, performance to take place. Any deviation operates as a discharge. For example, a home building contract expressly states that *only* Fuller brand plasterboard is to be used for the walls, and no substitute brand is to be used without the owner's express permission. Suppose that the builder cannot secure the Fuller brand and, without obtaining the owner's permission, installs Honeyrock brand instead. Even though Honeyrock brand may be equivalent in quality to Fuller brand and all other aspects of construction conform to the contract, a court may hold that the failure of the contractor to meet the express contractual condition discharges the owner from his or her contractual obligation to pay for the house on completion.

SUBSTANTIAL PERFORMANCE Human nature dictates that performance will not always fully satisfy the parties. Therefore, for the sake of justice and fairness, the courts hold that a party must fulfill his or her obligation to perform as long as the other party has fulfilled the terms of the contract with *substantial performance*. To qualify as substantial, the performance must not vary greatly from the performance promised in the contract. If performance is substantial, the other party's duty to perform remains absolute, less damages, if any, for the minor deviations.

For example, what if, in the example given above, the contract had stipulated merely that Fuller brand plasterboard was to be used for the walls. The contract did not state that *only* Fuller brand was to be used and that there could be no substitution without the owner's permission. Fuller brand is unavailable, so the contractor substitutes Honeyrock brand, which the contractor knows is equivalent in quality to Fuller brand. In this case, does the contractor's deviation discharge the buyer from paying for the house on completion? The answer depends on a single question: Does the term in dispute constitute either an express or an implied-in-fact condition? If so, then only complete performance can discharge the promise. If the term of the contract is interpreted as *constructive* (that is, a promise to install plasterboard of Fuller brand quality), then *substantial,* not complete, performance is required. Obviously, if Honeyrock is of similar quality, substantial performance by the builder has taken place, and the buyer may be obligated to pay according to the contract.[4] This kind of deviation from the terms of a contract, however, must not be grossly negligent. The courts differ as to whether an intentional variation from a contract, even if made with good motives, prevents substantial performance.

Although substantial performance does not prevent discharge, a breach of contract—however slight—has occurred. If the plasterboard substituted for Fuller brand had been of a somewhat lower quality than Fuller, reducing the value of the house by $3,000, the contractor would still be allowed to recover the price agreed on in the contract, less that $3,000. Remedies will be discussed in detail in the next chapter.

The following case, also involving a contract for the construction of a house, will help to clarify when there has been substantial performance by the contractor.

---

4. For an excellent analysis of substantial performance, see Judge Cardozo's opinion in *Jacob & Youngs v. Kent*, 230 N.Y. 239, 129 N.E. 889 (1921).

BACKGROUND AND FACTS Frank and Carol Jacobs contracted with Eugene Plante for Plante to furnish the materials and construct a house on their lot, in accordance with plans and specifications, for $26,765. During construction, Plante was paid $20,000. Disputes arose concerning the work, and the Jacobses refused to make further payments. Plante did not complete the house, and an allowance of approximately $1,600 was given the Jacobses. When Plante asked a Wisconsin state court to place a lien on the house for the rest of the money, the Jacobses counterclaimed for damages, complaining that there were cracks in the living room and kitchen ceilings, that a wall between the living room and the kitchen had been located incorrectly, and that numerous other problems existed. The trial court found that the contract had been substantially performed and required the Jacobses to pay $4,152.90 plus interest and court costs. The Jacobses appealed.

DECISION AND RATIONALE The Supreme Court of Wisconsin upheld the trial court's judgment. The state supreme court held that substantial performance was evident—although there were more than twenty items of incomplete performance by Plante, none of them went to the essence of the contract. The court explained that substantial performance "does not mean that every detail must be in strict compliance with the specifications and the plans." Plante and the Jacobses based their specifications on a "stock floor plan." Problems that arose during construction were solved "on the basis of practical experience." When there is substantial performance, the measure of damages "is the difference between the value of the house as it stands * * * and the value of the house if it had been constructed in strict accordance with the plans and specifications. This is the diminished-value rule," which was applied by the trial court.

ETHICAL CONSIDERATIONS Substantial performance also looks to the good faith effort on the part of a builder to satisfy a construction contract, as well as to the good faith effort on the part of the buyer of the building services to understand the problems that occur during the construction of any structure. Indeed, it would be virtually impossible to include every detail in a building contract. When disputes concerning building contracts reach the courts, the courts must impose reasonability on the parties if they themselves fail to be reasonable in contract performance. It is clearly unethical for the buyer to use minor deviations from contract specifications to avoid a money obligation that is rightly owed to a contractor.

Case 16.2

PLANTE v. JACOBS

Supreme Court of Wisconsin, 1960.
10 Wis.2d 567,
103 N.W.2d 296.

PERFORMANCE TO THE SATISFACTION OF ANOTHER Contracts often state that completed work must personally satisfy one of the parties or a third person. The question then arises whether this satisfaction becomes a condition precedent, requiring actual personal satisfaction or approval for discharge, or whether the test of satisfaction is an absolute promise requiring such performance as would satisfy a ''reasonable person'' (substantial performance).

When the subject matter of the contract is personal, a contract to be performed to the satisfaction of one of the parties is conditioned, and performance must actually satisfy that party. For example, contracts for portraits, works of art, medical or dental work, and tailoring are considered personal. Therefore, only the personal satisfaction of the party will be sufficient to fulfill the condition. Suppose Williams agrees to paint a portrait of Hirshon's daughter for $750. The contract provides that Hirshon must be satisfied with the portrait. If Hirshon is not, she will not be required to pay for it. The only requirement imposed on Hirshon is that she act honestly and in good faith. If she expresses dissatisfaction only to avoid paying for the portrait, the condition of satisfaction is excused, and her duty to pay becomes absolute. (Of course, the jury, or the judge acting as a jury, will have to decide whether she is acting honestly.[5])

Contracts that involve mechanical fitness, utility, or marketability need only be performed to the satisfaction of a reasonable person. For example, construction contracts or manufacturing contracts are usually *not* considered to be personal, so the party's personal satisfaction is normally irrelevant. As long as the performance will satisfy a reasonable person, the contract is fulfilled. To illustrate: Assume that Finnish Furniture Company agrees to build cabinets for Garden's component sound system, to be paid "on condition of satisfactory completion." Finnish builds the cabinets, and they house the components precisely, but Garden says he is not satisfied—without giving any reason for his dissatisfaction—and refuses to pay for the cabinets. Most courts would not construe these terms as a condition; if a reasonable person would be satisfied with the cabinets, Finnish is entitled to be paid for the work.[6]

At times, contracts also require performance to the satisfaction of a third party (not a party to the contract). For example, assume you contract to pave several city streets. The contract provides that the work will be done "to the satisfaction of Phil Hopper, the supervising engineer." In this situation, the courts are divided. A minority of courts require the personal satisfaction of the third party, here Phil Hopper. If Hopper is not satisfied, you will not be paid, even if a reasonable person would be satisfied. Again, the personal judgment must be made honestly, or the condition will be excused. A majority of courts require the work to be satisfactory to a reasonable person. So even if Hopper was dissatisfied with the cement work, you would be paid, as long as a qualified supervising engineer would have been satisfied.

All of the above examples demonstrate the necessity for *clear, specific wording in contracts*. Also, one must never underestimate the importance of reading the small print in contracts.

Material Breach of Contract

A **breach of contract** is the nonperformance of a contractual duty. The breach is *material*[7] when performance is not at least substantial—in other words, when there has been a failure of consideration. In such cases, the nonbreaching party is excused from the performance of contractual duties and has a cause of action to sue for damages caused by the breach. If the breach is *minor* (not material), the nonbreaching party's duty to perform can sometimes be suspended until the breach has been remedied but is not entirely excused. Once the minor breach has been cured, the nonbreaching party must resume performance of the contractual obligations undertaken. Any breach entitles the nonbreaching party to sue for damages, but only a material breach discharges the nonbreaching party from the contract. The policy underlying these rules allows contracts to go forward when only minor problems occur but allows them to be terminated if major problems occur.

Suppose Raytheon Corporation contracts with the U.S. government to build an all-weather tactical force system that uses Hawk missiles coated with paint that will deflect defensive weapons' heat-sensor guidance systems. The total contract price is $15.2 billion, of which $1 million is the cost of obtaining and applying the paint. Raytheon builds the system on schedule and according to the contract, except that the Hawk missiles function effectively only under good weather conditions. The government will be entitled to treat the contract as breached, because the lack of the all-weather capability contracted for makes the system virtually useless. In addition, the government can sue Raytheon and recover damages caused by the system's ineffectiveness. If Raytheon builds the system on schedule and according to the contract, except for a failure to coat the Hawk missiles with the deflective paint, which is easily obtainable, the government will not be able to treat the contract as discharged, because the damage is easily curable and the breach is thus only minor. Of course, the

---

5. For a classic case, see *Gibson v. Cranage,* 39 Mich. 49 (1878).
6. If, however, the contract specifically states that it is to be fulfilled to the "personal" satisfaction of one or more of the parties, and the parties so intended, the outcome will probably be different.

---

7. Restatement (Second) of Contracts, Section 241.

government can sue Raytheon for damages that its failure to paint has caused.

A nonbreaching party need not treat a material breach as a discharge of the contract but can treat the contract as being in effect and simply sue for damages. In the above example, if Raytheon delays four months on the first stage of the project, the government can treat the contract as still being in effect and sue for damages caused by the delay.

Anticipatory Breach of Contract

Before either party to a contract has a duty to perform, one of the parties may refuse to perform his or her contractual obligations. This is called **anticipatory breach,** or *anticipatory repudiation,*[8] of the contract and can discharge the non-breaching party from performance. For example, De La Tour made a contract with Hochster in March to employ Hochster as a courier for three months—June, July, and August. On May 11, De La Tour wrote to Hochster, "I am going abroad this summer and will not need a courier." This is an anticipatory breach of the employment contract. Because De La Tour repudiated the contract, Hochster could treat the act as a present, material breach. Furthermore, he could sue to recover damages *immediately,* without having to wait until June 1 to sue.[9]

There are two reasons for treating an anticipatory breach as a present, material breach:

1. The nonbreaching party should not be required to remain ready and willing to perform when the other party has already repudiated the contract.
2. The nonbreaching party should have the opportunity to seek a similar contract elsewhere.

Thus, Hochster should not be required to remain ready to serve as De La Tour's courier until June 1, because that would be a waste of time. In the meantime, Hochster could be working elsewhere.

It is important to note that until the nonbreaching party treats this early repudiation as a breach, the breaching party can retract his or her anticipatory repudiation by proper notice and restore the parties to their original obligations.[10]

Quite often an anticipatory breach occurs when performance of the contract would be extremely unfavorable to one of the parties because of a sharp fluctuation in market prices. For example, Martin Corporation contracts to manufacture and sell 10,000 personal computers to Com-age, a retailer of computer equipment that has 500 outlet stores. Delivery is to be made six months from the date of the contract. The contract price is based on the seller's present costs of purchasing inventory parts from others. One month later, three inventory suppliers raise their prices to Martin. Based on these prices, if Martin manufactures and sells the personal computers to Com-age at the contract price, it stands to lose $500,000. Martin immediately writes Com-age that it cannot deliver the 10,000 computers at the contract price. Even though you may feel sorry for Martin, Martin's letter is an anticipatory repudiation of the contract that allows Com-age the option to treat the repudiation as a material breach and to proceed immediately to pursue remedies, even though the actual contract delivery date is still five months away.[11]

Time for Performance

If no time for performance is stated in the contract, a *reasonable time* is implied.[12] If a specific time is stated, the parties must usually perform by that time. Unless time is expressly stated to be vital, however, a delay in performance will not destroy the performing party's right to payment. When time is expressly stated to be vital, or when it is construed to be "of the essence," the time for performance must usually be strictly complied with. The time element becomes a condition.

For example, a contract for the sale of soybeans must be performed within a reasonable time, even if it does not mention time. A contract for the sale of soybeans "on or before April 1" may be performed by April 2 or 3. (But the party rendering late performance will have to pay for any damages

---

8. Restatement (Second) of Contracts, Section 253, and UCC 2-610.

9. The doctrine of anticipatory breach first arose in this landmark case [*Hochster v. De La Tour,* 2 Ellis and Blackburn Reports 678 (1853)], when the English court recognized the delay and expense inherent in a rule requiring a nonbreaching party to wait until the time for performance to sue on an anticipatory breach.

10. See UCC 2-611.

11. See *Reliance Cooperage Corp. v. Treat,* 195 F.2d 977 (8th Cir. 1952), as a further illustration.

12. See UCC 1-204.

caused by the delay.) A contract for the sale of soybeans ''on or before April 1—necessary for immediate shipment abroad on April 2'' must be performed by April 1. Time is of the essence because the buyer plans on immediate resale. Delivery after April 1 will prevent the buyer from exporting the soybeans and will constitute a material breach.

■ Discharge by Agreement

Any contract can be discharged by agreement of the parties. The agreement can be contained in the original contract, or the parties can form a new contract for the express purpose of discharging the original contract.

Discharge by Rescission

Rescission is the process by which a contract is canceled or terminated and the parties are returned to the positions they occupied prior to forming it. For **mutual rescission** to take place, the parties must make another agreement, which must also satisfy the legal requirements for a contract. There must be an *offer,* an *acceptance,* and *consideration.* Ordinarily, in an executory contract in which neither party has yet performed, if the parties agree to rescind the original contract, their promises not to perform those acts promised in the original contract will be legal consideration for the second contract.

The rescission agreement is generally enforceable even if made orally. This applies even if the original agreement was in writing except when the new agreement falls within the Statute of Frauds (discussed in Chapter 14). Another exception applies to agreements rescinding a contract for the sale of goods regardless of price under the UCC when the contract requires written rescission.[13]

When one party has fully performed, however, an agreement to call off the original contract will not normally be enforceable. Because the performing party has received no consideration for the promise to call off the original bargain, additional consideration will be necessary.

To illustrate: Suppose Alberto's Food Company contracts to buy forty truckloads of oranges

from Citrus Products, Inc. Later, representatives of Alberto's and Citrus get together and decide to call off the deal (rescind the original contract). This agreement is enforceable, because neither party has yet performed. The consideration that Citrus receives for calling off the deal is freedom from performing what it was legally bound to perform under the contract—that is, freedom from having to deliver the forty truckloads of oranges. The consideration Alberto's receives for calling off the deal is not having to pay for the oranges, an obligation it would otherwise have had to honor.

On the other hand, if Citrus had already delivered the oranges, an agreement to call off the deal would not normally be enforceable. In this case, Citrus would have received no consideration for its promise to call off the deal.

In sum, contracts that are *executory* on *both* sides (contracts on which neither party has performed) can be rescinded solely by agreement.[14] But contracts that are *executed on one side* (contracts on which one party has performed) can be rescinded only if the party who has performed receives consideration for the promise to call off the deal.

Discharge by Novation or Substituted Agreement

The process of **novation** substitutes a new party for one of the original parties. Essentially, the parties to the original contract and one or more new parties get together and agree to substitute the new party for one of the original parties. The requirements of a novation are as follows:

1. A previous valid obligation.
2. An agreement of all the parties to a new contract.
3. The extinguishment of the old obligation (discharge of the prior party).
4. A new contract that is valid.

Suppose that Union Carbide Corporation contracts to sell its petrochemical division to British

---

13. UCC 2-209(2), (4).

14. Certain sales made to consumers at their homes can be rescinded by the consumer within three days for no reason at all. This three-day ''cooling-off'' period is designed to aid consumers who are susceptible to high-pressure door-to-door sales tactics. See Chapter 45 and 15 U.S.C. Section 1635(a).

Petroleum Company. Before the transfer is completed, Union Carbide, British Petroleum, and a third company, BP Chemicals, execute a new agreement to transfer all of British Petroleum's rights and duties in the transaction to BP Chemicals. As long as the new contract is supported by consideration, the novation will discharge the original contract (between Union Carbide and British Petroleum) and replace it with the new contract (between Union Carbide and BP Chemicals).

Substitution of a new contract between the same parties expressly or impliedly revokes and discharges a prior contract.[15] The parties involved may simply want a new agreement with somewhat different terms, so they expressly state in a new contract that the old contract is now discharged. They can also make the new contract without expressly stating that the old contract is discharged. If the parties do not expressly discharge the old contract, it will be *impliedly* discharged because of the change or because of the new contract's different terms, which are inconsistent with the old contract's terms.

For example, suppose Triangle Pacific Corporation contracts to sell its lumber manufacturing facilities in Slocan, British Columbia, to a Canadian investor group for $7.9 million in cash and $800,000 in a five-year note. Before the sale is closed, however, Triangle Pacific Corporation decides that it wants to pay $6.9 million in cash and $1.8 million in a five-year note. The Canadian investor group agrees, and the parties draw up a new contract with these terms of sale. If the second agreement states, ''Our previous contract to accept payment of $7.9 million in cash, balance in a five-year note is hereby revoked,'' the original contract will be expressly discharged by substitution. If the second agreement does not state this, the original contract will nevertheless be discharged by implication. Triangle Pacific Corporation cannot sell the same lumber manufacturing facilities under two different terms of payment. Because the terms are inconsistent, a court will enforce the terms that were decided on most recently—$6.9 million in cash and $1.8 million in a five-year note.

A *compromise,* or settlement agreement, that arises out of a bona fide dispute over the obligations under an existing contract will be recognized at law. Such an agreement will be substituted as a new contract, and it will either expressly or impliedly revoke and discharge the obligations under any prior contract.

Discharge by Accord and Satisfaction

For a contract to be discharged by **accord and satisfaction,** the parties must agree to accept performance different from the performance originally promised. An *accord* is defined as an executory contract to perform some act to satisfy an existing contractual duty.[16] The duty has not yet been discharged. A *satisfaction* is the performance of the accord agreement. An accord and its satisfaction discharge the original contractual obligation.

Once the accord has been made, the original obligation is merely suspended. (This differs from substitution of a new contract, which, as pointed out above, operates to discharge the original obligation.) The obligor can discharge the obligation by performing the obligation agreed to in the accord. If the obligor refuses to perform the accord, the obligee can bring action on the original obligation or seek a decree for specific performance on the accord.

To illustrate, Matthews obtains a judgment against Brown for $3,000. Later both parties agree that the judgment can be satisfied by Brown's transfer of her stamp collection to Matthews. This agreement to accept the stamps in lieu of $3,000 in cash is the accord. If Brown transfers her collection to Matthews, the accord agreement has been fully performed, and the $3,000 debt is discharged. If Brown refuses to transfer her stamps, the accord has been breached. Because the original obligation has merely been suspended, Matthews can bring action to enforce the judgment for $3,000 in cash or, in most states, obtain a decree for specific performance for the transfer of the collection and the discharge of the debt.

As pointed out in Chapter 11 with respect to consideration, acceptance by a creditor of a debtor's payment on a disputed (unliquidated) debt operates as both accord and satisfaction of the debt claim of the creditor, resulting in a discharge.

---

15. It is this immediate discharge of the prior contract that distinguishes a substituting contract from accord and satisfaction, discussed in the next section.

16. Restatement (Second) of Contracts, Section 281.

When You Can't Perform

Understanding your rights and obligations is important with every contract. Actual litigation can be costly, time consuming, and emotionally draining. Avoidance of litigation through compromise is usually one approach that should be considered. For example, if you anticipate that you will be unable to perform a contract, you may offer a payment in exchange for being released from your obligation. Let's say that you are a builder who has contracted to build a home for Samuels, with performance to begin on March 15. On March 1, Acme Builders offers you a position that is too good to refuse—two and one-half times the salary you could earn as an independent builder. You must start on March 12 if you wish to accept. Clearly, acceptance of the new position will require that you breach the contract with Samuels.

An attempt at negotiating with Samuels for a release should be made. You can offer to find another qualified builder who will build the house instead at the same price, for the same quality. Or you can offer to pay any additional costs if another builder turns out to be more expensive. In any event, this additional cost would be the measure of damages that a court would impose upon you if you were sued by Samuels for breach of contract and he prevailed. Thus, by making the offer, you can avoid the expense of litigation if Samuels agrees.

Sometimes parties are reluctant to propose compromise settlements because they fear that what they say will be used against them in court if litigation ensues. The general rule, however, is that offers for settlement cannot be used in court to prove that you are liable for a breach of contract.

■ Discharge by Operation of Law

Under certain circumstances, contractual duties may be discharged by operation of law. These circumstances include material alteration of the contract, the running of the statute of limitations, bankruptcy, and the impossibility or impracticability of performance.

Alteration of the Contract

To discourage parties from altering written contracts, the law operates to allow an innocent party to be discharged when the other party has materially altered a written contract without consent. For example, contract terms such as quantity or price might be changed without the knowledge or consent of all parties. If so, the party who was unaware of the change can treat the contract as discharged or terminated.[17]

---

17. The contract is voidable, and the innocent party can also treat the contract as in effect, either on the original terms or on the terms as altered. A buyer who discovers that a seller altered the quantity of goods in a sales contract from 100 to 1,000 by secretly inserting a zero can purchase either 100 or 1,000 of the items.

Statutes of Limitations

Statutes of limitations limit the period during which a party can sue on a particular cause of action. (A cause of action is the basis or reason for suing or bringing an action.) After the applicable limitations period has passed, a suit can no longer be brought in a court of law or equity.

For example, the limitations period for bringing suits for breach of oral contracts is usually two to three years; for written contracts, four to five years; for recovery of amounts awarded in judgment, ten to twenty years, depending on state law.

Section 2-725 of the UCC deals with the statute of limitations applicable to contracts for the sale of goods. For purposes of applying this section, the UCC does not distinguish between oral and written contracts. Section 2-725 provides that an action for the breach of any contract for sale must be commenced within four years after the cause of that action has accrued. The cause of action accrues when the breach occurs, regardless of the aggrieved party's lack of knowledge of the breach. By original agreement, the parties can reduce this four-year period to a one-year period. They cannot, however, extend it beyond the four-year limitation period.

Technically, the running of a statute of limitations bars access only to *judicial* remedies; it does not extinguish the debt or the underlying obligation. The statute precludes access to the courts for collection. But if the party who owes the debt or obligation agrees to perform (that is, makes a new promise to perform), the cause of action barred by the statute of limitations will be revived. For the old agreement to be revived by a new promise in this manner, many states require that the promise be in writing or that there be evidence of partial performance.

For example, suppose Burlington Northern Railroad contracts for sixty-three new miles of track to be laid between Dalhart and Amarillo, Texas. Martin Marietta Corporation supplies four tons of cast iron railway for the project and is paid $22,000 of the $30,000 purchase price. Texas's statute of limitations for collection of this debt is four years, but Martin Marietta Corporation fails to collect the debt or sue for collection during that four-year period after delivery of the iron. Therefore, Martin Marietta Corporation can no longer sue. It is barred by the statute of limitations. But if Burlington Northern Railroad agrees, in writing, to pay the remaining $8,000, or if it actually pays part of the $8,000, Marietta Corporation can again sue to collect the full debt. The statute of limitations is no longer a bar, and the cause of action for recovery of the full debt is revived.

Bankruptcy

A **discharge in bankruptcy** will ordinarily bar enforcement of most of a debtor's contracts by the creditors. (Bankruptcy is fully discussed in Chapter 33.) Bankruptcy can be entered into voluntarily or involuntarily.[18] A proceeding in bankruptcy attempts to allocate the assets the debtor owns at bankruptcy to the creditors in a fair and equitable fashion. Once the assets have been allocated, the debtor receives a discharge in bankruptcy. Partial payment of a debt *after* discharge in bankruptcy will not revive the debt.

Discharge by Impossibility or Impracticability of Performance

After a contract has been made, performance may become impossible in an objective sense. This is known as *objective impossibility of performance,* or simply as **impossibility of performance,** and may discharge a contract.[19] Occasionally, if circumstances arise after the contract has been formed that make performance *extremely* difficult or costly, courts may allow the contract to be discharged under the doctrine of **commercial impracticability.** These two legal excuses from performance under a contract are discussed below.

IMPOSSIBILITY OF PERFORMANCE Certain basic types of situations generally qualify to discharge contractual obligations under the doctrine of impossibility of performance:

1. One of the essential parties to a personal contract *dies or becomes incapacitated* prior to performance.[20] To illustrate this type of impossibility, suppose Jane, a famous actress, contracts to play the leading role in a movie. Before the picture starts, she becomes ill and dies. Her personal performance was essential to the completion of the contract. Thus, her death discharges the contract and her estate's liability for her nonperformance.

2. The *specific* subject matter of the contract is destroyed.[21] For example, Pappagoras contracts to sell 10,000 bushels of apples to be harvested "from his Green Valley apple orchard in the state of Washington." Volcanic ash from Mount St. Helens destroys his apples. Because the contracted-for apples were to come specifically from his Green Valley orchard, his performance has been rendered impossible by the eruption of Mount St. Helens. Thus, this contract is discharged.

Similarly, a contract to lease a building cannot be executed if the building is destroyed by fire, and a contract to sell oil from a particular well cannot be executed if the well goes dry.

3. A change in *law* renders performance illegal.[22] For example, a contract to loan money at 20 percent

---

18. A Chapter 12 or 13 case, however, can be initiated *only* by a debtor's filing of a voluntary petition.

19. Restatement (Second) of Contracts, Section 261.
20. Restatement (Second) of Contracts, Section 262.
21. Restatement (Second) of Contracts, Section 263.
22. Restatement (Second) of Contracts, Section 264.

interest becomes illegal when the usury rate is changed to prohibit loans in excess of 12 percent, and a contract to build an apartment building at a certain location becomes illegal when the zoning laws are changed to prohibit the construction of residential rental property at that location. Both changes render the contracts impossible to perform.

In the following case, it was objectively impossible for the plaintiff to continue to take dance lessons under a contract because of a serious injury.

Case 16.3

PARKER v. ARTHUR MURRAY, INC.

Appellate Court of Illinois, Second Division, First District, 1973.
10 Ill.App.3d 1000, 295 N.E.2d 487.

BACKGROUND AND FACTS In November 1959, Ryland Parker went to the Arthur Murray Dance Studio for three free dance lessons. During the free lessons, the instructor told Parker that he had "exceptional potential to become * * * [an] accomplished dancer" and encouraged him to take more lessons. Parker signed a contract for seventy-five hours of lessons at a cost of $1,000. At the bottom of the contract, "NON-CANCELLABLE NE-GOTIABLE CONTRACT" was printed in boldface type. During the lessons, the instructors praised Parker despite his lack of progress, and he signed several more contracts, each containing similar language. Some contained the statement, "I UNDERSTAND THAT NO REFUNDS WILL BE MADE UN-DER THE TERMS OF THIS CONTRACT," also in boldface. Eventually, he contracted for 2,734 hours of lessons for which he paid $24,812.80. In September 1961, Parker was seriously injured in an accident, rendering him incapable of continuing the lessons. Despite his repeated written demands, the studio refused to return any of his money. He sued in an Illinois state court. The trial court ruled that Parker could recover his money under the impossibility of performance doctrine. Arthur Murray, Inc., and the studio appealed.

DECISION AND RATIONALE   Appellate Court of Illinois upheld the trial court's ruling entitling Parker to recover the prepaid sums of money for unused lessons. The appellate court concluded that despite the contract provisions, Parker never contemplated waiving the right to invoke the doctrine of impossibility of performance. The court said, "Although neither party to a contract should be relieved from performance on the ground that good business judgment was lacking, a court will not place upon language a ridiculous construction. We conclude that plaintiff did not waive his right to assert the doctrine of impossibility."

COMMERCIAL IMPRACTICABILITY Courts will at times excuse performance under a contract when the performance becomes much more difficult or expensive than originally contemplated at the time the contract was formed. For someone to invoke successfully the doctrine of commercial impracticability, however, the anticipated performance must become *extremely* difficult or costly.[23]

For example, the California Supreme Court held that a contract was discharged because it would cost ten times more than the original estimate to excavate a certain amount of gravel.[24] In another case, however, commercial impracticability was not found when a carrier of goods was to deliver wheat from the West Coast of the United States to a safe port in Iran.[25] The Suez Canal, the usual route, was nationalized by Egypt and closed, forcing the carrier to travel around Africa and the

---

23. Restatement (Second) of Contracts, Sections 265 and 266, and UCC 2-615.

24. *Mineral Park Land Co. v. Howard,* 172 Cal. 289, 156 P. 458 (1916).
25. *Transatlantic Financing Corp. v. United States,* 363 F.2d 312 (D.C. Cir. 1966).

Cape of Good Hope—instead of through the Mediterranean—to get to Iran. The added expense was approximately $42,000 above and beyond the contract price of $306,000, and the original journey of 10,000 miles was extended by 3,000 miles. Nevertheless, the court held that the contract was not commercially impracticable to perform, because the closing of the Suez Canal was a foreseeable event in view of the political circumstances of the time—circumstances of which businesspersons were, or should have been, fully aware.

Therefore, caution should be used in invoking commercial impracticability. The added burden of performing must be *extreme* and, more importantly, must *not* have been within the cognizance of the parties when the contract was made.

A closely allied theory is the doctrine of **frustration of purpose.** In principle, a contract will be discharged if supervening circumstances make it impossible to attain the purpose both parties had in mind when making the contract. The origins of the doctrine lie in the old English "coronation cases." A coronation procession was planned for Edward VII when he became king of England following the death of his mother, Queen Victoria. Hotel rooms along the coronation route were rented at exorbitant prices for that day. When the king became ill and the procession was canceled, the purpose of the room contracts was "frustrated." A flurry of lawsuits resulted. Hotel and building owners sought to enforce the room rent bills against would-be parade observers, and would-be parade observers sought to be reimbursed for rental monies paid in advance on the rooms. Would-be parade observers were excused from their duty of payment. It was from this situation that the court developed its theory of recovery known as *frustration of purpose.*

TEMPORARY IMPOSSIBILITY An occurrence or event that makes it temporarily impossible to perform the act for which a party has contracted will operate to *suspend* performance until the impossibility ceases. Then, ordinarily, the parties must perform the contract as originally planned. If the lapse of time and the change in circumstances surrounding the contract make it substantially more burdensome to perform the promised acts, however, the parties will be discharged.

The leading case on this subject, *Autry v. Republic Productions,*[26] involved an actor who was drafted into the army in 1942. Being drafted rendered his contract temporarily impossible to perform, and it was suspended until the end of the war. When the actor got out of the army, the value of the dollar had so changed that performance of the contract would have been substantially burdensome for him. Therefore, the contract was discharged.

---

26. 30 Cal.2d 144, 180 P.2d 888 (1947).

■ CONCEPT SUMMARY 16.1 Discharge of Contracts

Method	Types and Basic Rules
Discharge by occurrence or failure of a condition	1. *Failure of a condition precedent*—Duty to perform does not become absolute absent fulfillment of condition precedent. 2. *Occurrence of condition subsequent.*
Discharge by performance (or breach of contract)·	1. *Performance*—Complete (if terms are construed as express conditions) or substantial. 2. *Breach*—Material nonperformance discharges the nonbreaching party's performance.
Discharge by agreement	1. *Mutual rescission*—An enforceable agreement to restore parties to their precontract positions. 2. *Novation*—By valid contract, a new party is substituted for an original party, thereby terminating the old contract. 3. *Accord and satisfaction*—An agreement under which the original contract can be discharged by a different performance.

(Continued on next page)

■ CONCEPT SUMMARY 16.1 *(Continued)*

Method	Types and Basic Rules

Discharge by operation of law	1. *Alteration*—An innocent party is discharged by material alteration of the contract without consent.
	2. *Statute of limitations*—The plaintiff's delay in filing suit bars availability of judicial remedies, thus discharging the defendant's duty to perform.
	3. *Bankruptcy*—The decree discharges most of the debtor's contractual obligations.
	4. *Impossibility or impracticability of performance*—
	  a. A person whose performance is essential to completion of the contract dies or is incapacitated.
	  b. The specific subject matter of the contract is destroyed prior to transfer.
	  c. Performance is declared illegal.
	  d. Performance becomes commercially impracticable.
	  e. If performance is temporarily suspended because of events or occurrences (such as war), and subsequent circumstances make the contract substantially more difficult to perform, the parties may be discharged.

■ Terms and Concepts

accord and satisfaction 291
anticipatory breach 289
breach of contract 288
commercial
  impracticability 293
concurrent conditions 285

condition 284
condition precedent 284
condition subsequent 285
discharge 283
discharge in
  bankruptcy 293

frustration of purpose 295
impossibility of
  performance 293
mutual rescission 290
novation 290
tender 285

■ For Review

1. How are most contracts discharged?
2. Complete performance is performance within the bounds of reasonable expectations. What is substantial performance?
3. If a nonbreaching party has not treated an anticipatory repudiation as a breach, can the breaching party retract his or her repudiation? How?
4. For $250,000—paid in advance—Nico, "The Voice," contracts with Windsong Productions, Inc., to sing in each of five operettas in Windsong's summer concert series. Nico

goes to rehearsals but unjustifiably fails to perform publicly in the first two operettas. Does Windsong have a valid claim against Nico for damages for breach?

5. Lodz, Ltd., a budding enterprise in a former communist country, contracts with Transoceanic Imports, Inc., an American firm, to sell to Transoceanic the output of Lodz's factory for one year. Civil war breaks out in Lodz's country, and the government orders Lodz to sell it the factory's output instead. Lodz does so, thereby failing to deliver to Transoceanic. Is Lodz liable for breach of contract?

■ Questions and Case Problems

16-1. The Rosenbergs own a real estate lot, and they contract with Faithful Construction, Inc., to build a house on it for $60,000. The specifications list "all plumbing bowls and fixtures . . . to be Crane brand." The Rosenbergs leave on vacation, and during their absence Faithful is unable to buy and install Crane

plumbing fixtures. Instead, Faithful installs Kohler brand fixtures, an equivalent in the industry. Upon completion of the building contract, the Rosenbergs, on inspection, discover the substitution and refuse to accept the house, claiming Faithful has breached the conditions set forth in the specifications. Discuss fully the Rosenbergs' claim.

16-2. Junior owes creditor Carlton $1,000, which is due

and payable on June 1. Junior has been in a car accident, has missed a great deal of work, and consequently will not have the money on June 1. Junior's father, Fred, offers to pay Carlton $1,100 in four equal installments if Carlton will discharge Junior from any further liability on the debt. Carlton accepts. Discuss the following:

(a) Is the transaction a novation, or is it accord and satisfaction? Explain.

(b) Does the contract between Fred and Carlton have to be in writing to be enforceable? (Review the discussion of the Statute of Frauds in Chapter 14.) Explain.

16-3. ABC Clothiers, Inc., has a contract with retailer Taylor & Sons to deliver 1,000 summer suits to Taylor's place of business on or before May 1. On April 1, Taylor senior receives a letter from ABC informing him that ABC will not be able to make the delivery as scheduled. Taylor is very upset, as he had planned a big ad sale campaign. He wants to file suit against ABC immediately (April 2). Taylor's son, Tom, tells his father that a lawsuit is not proper until ABC actually fails to deliver the suits on May 1. Discuss fully who is correct, Taylor or his son Tom.

16-4. The following events take place after the formation of the contracts. Discuss which of these contracts are discharged because the events render the contracts impossible to perform.

(a) Jimenez, a famous singer, contracts to perform in your nightclub. He dies prior to performance.

(b) Raglione contracts to sell you her land. Just before title is to be transferred, she dies.

(c) Oppenheim contracts to sell you 1,000 bushels of apples from her orchard in the state of Washington. Because of a severe frost, she is unable to deliver the apples.

(d) Maxwell contracts to lease a service station for ten years. His principal income is from the sale of gasoline. Because of an oil embargo by foreign oil-producing nations, gasoline is rationed, cutting sharply into Maxwell's gasoline sales. He cannot make his lease payments.

16-5. Murphy contracts to purchase from Lone Star Liquors six cases of French champagne for $1,200. The contract states that delivery is to be made at the Murphy residence "on or before June 1, to be used for daughter's wedding reception on June 2." The champagne is carried regularly in Lone Star's stock. On June 1, Lone Star's delivery van is involved in an accident, and the champagne is not delivered that day. On the morning of June 2, Murphy discovers the nondelivery. Unable to reach Lone Star because its line is busy, Murphy purchases the champagne from another dealer. That afternoon, just before the wedding reception, Lone Star tenders delivery of the champagne at Murphy's residence. Murphy refuses tender, and Lone Star sues for breach of contract. Discuss fully the result.

16-6. John Agosta and his brother Salvatore had formed a corporation, but disagreements between the two brothers caused John to petition for voluntary dissolution of the corporation. According to the dissolution agreement, the total assets of the corporation, which included a warehouse

and inventory, would be split between the brothers by Salvatore's selling his stock to John for $500,000. This agreement was approved, but shortly before the payment was made, a fire totally destroyed the warehouse and inventory, which were the major assets of the corporation. John refused to pay Salvatore the $500,000, and Salvatore brought suit for breach of contract. Discuss whether the destruction of the major assets of the corporation affects John's required performance. [*In the Matter of Fontana v. D'Oro Foods Inc.,* 122 Misc.2d 1091, 472 N.Y.S.2d 528 (1983)]

16-7. Zilg is author of *DuPont: Behind the Nylon Curtain,* a historical account of the DuPont family in America's social, political, and economic affairs. Prentice-Hall, Inc., signed Zilg to a contract to publish the book exclusively. There was no provision to have Prentice-Hall use its best efforts to promote the book; rather, it was left up to the publisher to use its discretion as to the number of volumes printed and the level of promotion. Prentice-Hall had originally planned a first printing of 15,000 copies and an advertising budget of $15,000 for the book. Later, having had second thoughts about the sales potential of the book, Prentice-Hall decided to do a first printing of only 10,000 copies and to reduce the amount it had allocated for advertising. In all, Prentice-Hall published a total of 13,000 volumes (3,000 beyond the sales volume at which it received the highest royalties), authorized an advertising budget of $5,500, distributed over 600 copies to reviewers, and purchased ads in major newspapers. Zilg later claimed that the reductions in the number of volumes printed and in the advertising budget were evidence that Prentice-Hall had not made a "best effort" to fully promote the book. Prentice-Hall claimed that its reduction came after careful review and was based on sound and valid business decisions. Based on these facts only, discuss whether Prentice-Hall has fulfilled its contractual duty to Zilg. [*Zilg v. Prentice-Hall, Inc.,* 717 F.2d 671 (2d Cir. 1983)]

16-8. Sun Maid Raisin Growers signed a contract to buy 1,800 tons of raisins from Victor Packing Co. in 1976. Victor planned to supply the raisins by purchasing them in the market during that year but to wait until very late to get a good price. It waited too long. Because of heavy, "disastrous" rains that year, 50 percent of the crop was destroyed, and the price of raisins skyrocketed from $860 per ton to $1,600 per ton. Victor Packing could not meet Sun Maid's contract demand without sustaining equally "disastrous" losses, and it notified Sun Maid that it was repudiating the contract. Sun Maid sued for damages for breach of contract, and Victor Packing claimed, among other things, that performance was impracticable. Discuss whether Victor Packing's defense should succeed. [*Sun Maid Raisin Growers v. Victor Packing Co.,* 146 Cal.App.3d 787, 194 Cal.Rptr. 612 (5 Dist. 1983)]

16-9. Grane, a homeowner, contracted with Butkovich & Sons, Inc., to enlarge Grane's basement and build a new room over the new basement area. Butkovich was also to lay a new garage floor and construct a patio area. The parties agreed to a price of $19,290 for the work. When the construction was completed, Grane refused to pay the contractor the $9,290 balance he still owed, claiming that Butkovich had failed to install water stops and reinforcing wire in one concrete floor in accordance with Grane's specifications and that the main floor of the addition was 8-7/8 inches lower than the plans had called for. Butkovich sued Grane for recovery of the $9,290. As a mortgage holder on the property, the State Bank of St. Charles was named codefendant by Butkovich, because its interests would be affected by a judgment against Grane if the latter could not pay. Butkovich claimed that it had substantially performed the contract. Grane claimed that performance was of poor quality and that failure to follow contract specifications constituted a material breach. Discuss who should win. [*Butkovich & Sons, Inc. v. State Bank of St. Charles,* 62 Ill.App.3d 810, 379 N.E.2d 837, 20 Ill.Dec. 4 (1978)]

16-10. Larry Allen signed a contract with Weyerhaeuser, Inc., to work as a truck driver to haul timber. The contract provided: "Contractor agrees to comply with all operational safety and conservation rules and regulations promulgated by Weyerhaeuser." Billy Corey, the company's supervisor in charge of contract trucking, was responsible for informing contractors of safety regulations and ensuring that drivers complied with them. Before Allen signed the contract, Corey told him that Weyerhaeuser required its contract truckers to operate their trucks with headlights on while they were on the road. Initially, Allen complied. Occasionally, however, Corey had to remind him to turn on his lights. Allen's noncompliance became more frequent, even though Corey explained to him on several occasions that he had to comply with company policy. Finally, Allen told Corey that "he [wasn't] going to run with his lights on; that he was tired of it anyway and if [Corey] would fire him it would do him a favor." Weyerhaeuser terminated Allen's contract. Allen sued, claiming that the contract was wrongfully terminated. The trial court granted Weyerhaeuser a directed verdict in Weyerhaeuser's favor, and Allen appealed. Discuss whether Allen's conduct constituted an anticipatory breach of his contract. [*Allen v. Weyerhaeuser, Inc.,* 95 N.C.App. 205, 381 S.E.2d 824 (1989)]

16-11. Coker International, Inc., entered into a contract with Burlington Industries, Inc., under which Coker agreed to purchase 221 used textile looms from Burlington for a total price of $1,021,000. Under the contract, Coker was required to pay a 10 percent down payment, with the balance to be paid prior to the removal of the looms. Coker planned to resell the looms to a customer in Peru, but the contract was not conditioned on any resale of the looms by Coker. Because of actions of the Peruvian government, Coker's plan to resell the equipment to the Peruvian buyer fell through. Coker sought to rescind the contract with Bur-

lington and recover its down payment, asserting that it should be excused from performance under the doctrine of frustration of purpose. Discuss fully whether Coker can be excused from performance of the contract under this doctrine. [*Coker International, Inc. v. Burlington Industries, Inc.,* 747 F.Supp. 1168 (D.S.C. 1990)]

16-12. A Question of Ethics

Sharon Russell's weight varied between 280 and 305 pounds while she was enrolled in a nursing program at Salve Regina College in Newport, Rhode Island. Her weight was never an issue until her sophomore year, at which time she began to be the target of cruel remarks by school officials. In her junior year, she received a failing grade in a clinical nursing course—not on the basis of her performance but simply because she was obese. The normal consequence of failing a clinical nursing course was expulsion from the college, but Russell was offered a deal: If she signed a "contract" in which she promised to attend Weight Watchers regularly and to submit proof of her attendance, and if she managed to lose two pounds a week steadily, she would remain in good standing. Russell attended Weight Watchers regularly but failed to lose the required two pounds a week, and the following year the college requested that she withdraw from the nursing program. Russell sued the college for damages for breach of contract. The jury found that Russell's relationship to the college was essentially a contractual one in which she was required to abide by disciplinary rules, pay tuition, and maintain a good academic record (which she did— except for the course that she failed because of her obesity) and the college was required to provide her with an education until graduation. The jury also found that Russell had "substantially performed" her side of the bargain and that the college's actions prevented Russell from rendering complete performance and constituted a breach. [Russell v. Salve Regina College, 890 F.2d 484 (1st Cir. 1989)]

1. The college contended that it was inappropriate to apply the principle of substantial performance to college-student contracts. From an ethical point of view, what arguments could you make in support of the college's contention? That is, what would be some of the negative ethical ramifications of permitting such flexibility in the student-college relationship?
2. Do the circumstances of Sharon Russell's situation justify the application of the principle of substantial performance in this case?

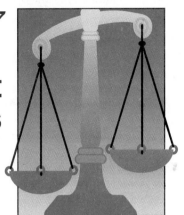

Chapter 17

Breach of Contract and Remedies

Whenever a party fails to perform part or all of the duties under a contract, that party is in breach of contract. *Breach of contract* is the failure to perform what a party is under an absolute duty to perform.[1] Once a party has failed to perform or has performed inadequately, the other party—the nonbreaching party—can choose one or more of several remedies. A *remedy* is the relief provided for an innocent party when the other party has breached the contract. It is the means employed to enforce a right or to redress an injury. Strictly speaking, the remedy is not a part of a lawsuit, but the result thereof, the object for which the lawsuit is presented and the end to which all litigation is directed.

The most common remedies available to a nonbreaching party include damages, rescission and restitution, specific performance, and reformation. As discussed in Chapter 1, a distinction is made between *remedies at law* and *remedies in equity*. An award of damages is a remedy at law. The other three remedies just mentioned are equitable remedies.

■ Damages

A breach of contract entitles the nonbreaching party to sue for money (damages). *Damages* are designed to compensate the nonbreaching party for the loss of the bargain. When a party loses the benefit of the bargain or contract, the breaching party must make up this loss to the nonbreaching party. Often, courts say that innocent parties are to be placed in the position they would have occupied had the contract been fully performed.[2] For example, in the famous case of the "hairy hand," a doctor promised to make a boy's scarred hand "a hundred percent perfect." Skin was taken from the boy's chest and grafted onto his thumb and fingers. The hand became infected, and the boy was hospitalized for three months. Use of the hand was greatly restricted, and hair grew out of the grafted skin. In hearing a suit against the doctor, the court explained that the amount of damages was to be determined by the difference between the value to the boy of the "perfect" hand that

---

1. Restatement (Second) of Contracts, Section 235(2).
2. Restatement (Second) of Contracts, Section 347, and UCC 1-106(1).

299

the doctor had promised and the value of the hand in its condition after the operation.[3]

Types of Damages

There are basically four broad categories of damages:

1. Compensatory (to cover direct losses and costs).
2. Consequential (to cover indirect and foreseeable losses).
3. Punitive (to punish and deter wrongdoing).
4. Nominal (to recognize wrongdoing when no monetary loss is shown).

We examine each of these categories below. How compensatory and consequential damages are measured is illustrated graphically in Exhibit 17–1.

COMPENSATORY DAMAGES Damages compensating the nonbreaching party for the *loss of the bargain* are known as **compensatory damages.** These damages compensate the injured party only for injuries actually sustained and proved to have arisen directly from the loss of the bargain caused

by the breach of contract. They simply replace what was lost because of the wrong or injury. To illustrate: Wilcox contracts to perform certain services exclusively for Hernandez during the month of March for $2,000. Hernandez cancels the contract and is in breach. Wilcox is able to find another job during the month of March, but can only earn $1,000. He can sue Hernandez for breach and recover $1,000 as compensatory damages. Wilcox can also recover from Hernandez the amount that he spent to find the other job. Expenses that are caused directly by a breach of contract—such as those incurred to obtain performance from another source—are known as *incidental damages.*

The measurement of compensatory damages varies by type of contract. Certain types of contracts deserve special mention. They are contracts for the sale of goods, land contracts, and construction contracts.

Sale of Goods In a contract for the sale of goods, the usual measure of compensatory damages is an amount equal to the difference between the contract price and the market price.[4] Suppose Chrysler Cor-

---

3. *Hawkins v. McGee,* 84 N.H. 114, 146 A. 641 (1929).

4. That is, the difference between the contract price and the market price at the time and place at which the goods were to be delivered or tendered. See UCC 2-708 and UCC 2-713.

■ **Exhibit 17–1 Injured Party's Damages for Breach of Contract**
The usual measure of damages for a breached contract is the value of the breaching party's promised performance (1) *less* the value of the breaching party's actual performance and any amount of loss avoided by the injured party (2) *plus* incidental damages and consequential damages.

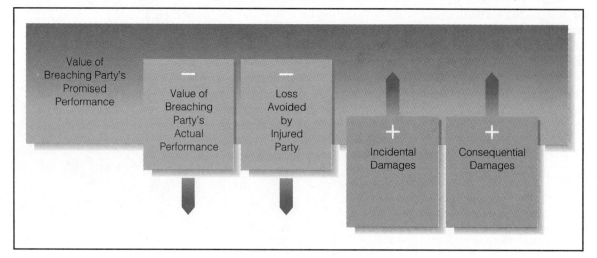

poration contracts to buy ten model UTS 400 computer terminals from Sperry Rand Corporation for $8,000 apiece. If Sperry Rand fails to deliver the ten terminals and the current market price of the terminals is $8,150, Chrysler's measure of damages is $1,500 (10 × $150). In a case in which the buyer breaches and the seller has not yet produced the goods, compensatory damages normally equal lost profits on the sale, not the difference between the contract price and the market price.

Sale of Land　Ordinarily, because each parcel of land is unique, the remedy for a seller's breach of a contract for a sale of real estate is *specific performance* (that is, the buyer is awarded the piece of property he or she bargained for). When this remedy, which is discussed more fully later in this chapter, is unavailable (for example, when the seller has sold the property to someone else), or when the breach is on the part of the buyer, the measure of damages is ordinarily the same as in contracts for the sale of goods—that is, the difference between the contract price and the market price of the land. The majority of states follow this rule. A minority of states, however, follow a different rule when the seller breaches the contract and the breach is not deliberate.[5] In such a case, these states allow the prospective purchaser to recover any down payment plus any expenses incurred (such as fees for title searches, attorneys, and escrows). This minority rule effectively places purchasers in the position they occupied prior to the sale.

Construction Contracts　The measure of damages in a building or construction contract varies depending on which party breaches and when the breach occurs. The owner can breach at three different stages of the construction:

1. Before performance has begun.
2. During performance.
3. After performance has been completed.

If the owner breaches *before performance has begun,* the contractor can recover only the profits that would have been made on the contract (that is, the total contract price less the cost of materials and labor). If the owner breaches *during performance,* the contractor can recover the profits plus the costs incurred in partially constructing the building. If the owner breaches *after the construction has been completed,* the contractor can recover the entire contract price[6] plus interest.

When the *construction contractor breaches the contract* by stopping part of the way through the project, the measure of damages is the cost of completion, which includes reasonable compensation for any delay in performance. If the contractor finishes late, the measure of damages will be the loss of use. If the contractor substantially performs, the courts may use the cost-of-completion formula, but only if there is no substantial economic waste in requiring completion. Economic waste occurs when the cost of additional resources to finish the project exceeds any conceivable value placed on the additional work done. For example, if a contractor discovers that it will cost $10,000 to move a large coral rock eleven inches as specified in the contract, and the change in the rock's position will alter the appearance of the project only a trifle, full completion will involve an economic waste.

These rules concerning the measurement of damages in breached construction projects are summarized in Exhibit 17–2.

CONSEQUENTIAL DAMAGES　Foreseeable damages that result from a party's breach of contract are called **consequential,** or *special,* **damages.** They differ from compensatory damages in that they are caused by special circumstances beyond the contract itself. They flow from the consequences, or results, of a breach.

For example, if a seller fails to deliver goods with knowledge that a buyer is planning to resell these goods immediately, consequential damages will be awarded for the loss of profit from the planned resale. The buyer will also recover com-

---

5.　The category of a deliberate breach includes the vendor's (seller's) failure to convey the land because the market price has gone up. The category of a nondeliberate breach includes the vendor's failure to convey the land because an unknown easement (right of use over another's property) has rendered title unmarketable. See Chapter 51.

6.　Actually, this is true for most contracts; the nonbreaching party is normally owed the contract profit plus the cost of performance.

■ Exhibit 17–2 Measurement of Damages—Breach of Construction Contracts

Party in Breach	Time of Breach	Measurement of Damages
Owner	Before construction has begun	Profits (contract price less cost of materials and labor)
Owner	During construction	Profits plus costs incurred up to time of breach
Owner	After construction is completed	Contract price, plus interest
Contractor	Before construction is completed	Generally, all costs incurred by owner to complete construction

pensatory damages for the difference between the contract price and the market price of the goods.

To recover consequential damages, the breaching party must know (or have reason to know) that special circumstances will cause the nonbreaching party to suffer an additional loss. The rationale here is to give the nonbreaching party the whole benefit of the bargain, provided the breaching party knew of the special circumstances when the contract was made.

For example, Leed contracts to have a specific part shipped to her—one that she desperately needs to repair her printing press. In contracting with the shipper who is to deliver the part, Leed tells the shipper that she must receive it by Monday or she will not be able to print her paper and will lose $750. If the shipper is late, Leed normally can recover the consequential damages caused by the delay (that is, the $750 in lost profits).

Similarly, when a bank wrongfully dishonors a check (does not pay on a check in violation of its contractual obligations to its customer), the drawer of the check (a customer of the bank) may recover consequential damages (such as those resulting from slander of credit or reputation) if he or she is arrested or prosecuted.[7]

A leading case on the necessity of giving notice of consequential circumstances is *Hadley v. Baxendale,* decided in England in 1854. The case involved a crankshaft used in a mill operation. In the mid-1800s, it was very common for large mills, such as the one the plaintiffs operated, to have more than one crankshaft in case the main one broke and had to be repaired, as it did in this case. Also, in those days it was common knowledge that flour mills had spares. It is against this background that the parties argued whether or not the damages resulting from profits lost while the crankshaft was out for repair were "too remote" to be recoverable.

---

7. *Weaver v. Bank of America,* 59 Cal.2d 428, 380 P.2d 644, 30 Cal.Rptr. 4 (1963). A checking account is a contractual arrangement. See UCC 4-402.

Case 17.1

HADLEY v. BAXENDALE

Court of Exchequer, 1854.
9 Exch. 341,
156 Eng.Rep. 145.

BACKGROUND AND FACTS The Hadleys ran a flour mill in Gloucester. The crankshaft attached to the steam engine in the mill broke, causing the mill to shut down. The shaft had to be sent to a foundry located in Greenwich so that the new shaft could be made to fit the other parts of the engine. Baxendale, a common carrier, transported the shaft from Gloucester to Greenwich. The Hadleys claimed that they had informed Baxendale that the mill was stopped and that the shaft must be sent immediately. The freight charges were collected in advance, and Baxendale promised to deliver the shaft the following day. It was not delivered for several days, however, during which time the mill was closed. The Hadleys sued to recover the profits lost during that time. Baxendale contended that the loss of profits was "too remote." The court ruled in the Hadleys' favor, and the jury was allowed to take the lost profits into consideration. Baxendale appealed.

DECISION AND RATIONALE The Court of Exchequer ordered a new trial. According to the court, the Hadleys had never sufficiently communicated to Baxendale the circumstances that caused the loss of profits. The court pointed out that compensation is given only for those injuries that a breaching party could reasonably have foreseen as a probable result of the course of events following the breach. If an injury is outside the usual course of events, it must be shown that the breaching party had reason to foresee the injury. In this case, the Hadleys would have to have given express notice of the circumstances to be awarded consequential damages.

COMMENTS On breach of a contract for a sale of goods, what constitutes consequential damages is stated in Section 2–715 of the Uniform Commercial Code (UCC)—see Appendix C.

PUNITIVE DAMAGES Punitive, or exemplary, damages are generally not awarded in a breach of contract action. Punitive damages are designed to punish a guilty party and to make an example of the party to deter similar conduct in the future. Such damages have no legitimate place in contract law, because they are, in essence, penalties, and a breach of contract is not unlawful in a criminal or societal sense. A contract is simply a civil relationship between the parties. The law may compensate one party for the loss of bargain, no more and no less.

In a few situations, a person's actions can cause both a breach of contract and a tort. For example, the parties can establish by contract a certain reasonable standard or duty of care. Failure to live up to that standard is a breach of contract, and the act itself may constitute negligence.

A careful review of Chapters 5, 7, and 8, which deal with torts, will indicate that some intentional torts may also be tied to a breach of the terms of a contract. In such cases it is possible for the nonbreaching party to recover punitive damages for the commission of the tort in addition to compensatory and consequential damages for breach of contract. Also, some jurisdictions—California, for instance—recognize that a breach of the implied covenant of good faith and fair dealing is actionable as a tort and may warrant an award of punitive damages.

NOMINAL DAMAGES **Nominal damages** have been defined as those awarded when only a technical injury is involved and no actual damages have been suffered. In other words, when no financial loss results from a breach of contract, the court may award nominal damages to the innocent party.

Nominal damage awards are often trifling, such as a dollar, but they do establish that the defendant acted wrongfully. For example, suppose that Jackson contracts to buy potatoes from Stanley at 50 cents a pound. Stanley breaches the contract and does not deliver the potatoes. In the meantime, the price of potatoes has fallen. Jackson is able to buy them in the open market at half the price he contracted for with Stanley. He is clearly better off because of Stanley's breach. Thus, in a breach of contract suit, Jackson may be awarded only nominal damages for the technical injury he sustained, because no monetary loss was involved. Most lawsuits for nominal damages are brought as a matter of principle under the theory that a breach has occurred and some damages must be imposed regardless of actual loss.

Mitigation of Damages

In most situations, when a breach of contract occurs, the innocent injured party is held to a duty to mitigate, or reduce, the damages that he or she suffers. Under this **mitigation of damages** doctrine, the duty owed depends on the nature of the contract. For example, some states require the lessor to use reasonable means to find a new tenant if the lessee abandons the premises and fails to pay rent. If an acceptable tenant becomes available, the landlord is required to lease the premises to this tenant to mitigate the damages recoverable from the former lessee. The former lessee is still liable for the difference between the amount of the rent under the original lease and the rent received from the new lessee. If the lessor has not taken the reasonable means necessary to find a new tenant, presumably a court can reduce the award made by the amount of rent he or she could have received had such reasonable means been taken.

In the majority of states, persons whose employment has been wrongfully terminated owe the duty to mitigate damages suffered by their employers' breach. The damages they receive are their salaries less the incomes they would have received in similar jobs that they could have obtained by reasonable means. The employer must prove both the existence of such a job and that the employee could have been hired. As the following case illustrates, however, the employee is under no duty to take a job that is not of the same type and rank.

Case 17.2

PARKER v. TWENTIETH-CENTURY FOX FILM CORP.

Supreme Court of California, 1970.
3 Cal.3d 176,
474 P.2d 689,
89 Cal.Rptr. 737.

BACKGROUND AND FACTS Twentieth-Century Fox Film Corporation contracted with Shirley MacLaine Parker to play the female lead in *Bloomer Girl*. Fox agreed to pay Parker $53,571.42 per week for fourteen weeks, for a total of $750,000. Fox later decided not to produce *Bloomer Girl* and tried to substitute for Parker's contract a contract for her to play the female lead in *Big Country, Big Man* for the same amount of money. Fox gave Parker a week to accept the new contract. Parker sued Fox in a California state court to recover the amount of compensation guaranteed in the *Bloomer Girl* contract because, she maintained, the two roles were not equivalent. *Bloomer Girl* was to have been a musical, filmed in California. *Big Country* was to be a western, produced in Australia. The trial court granted Parker's motion for summary judgment. Fox appealed.

DECISION AND RATIONALE The Supreme Court of California affirmed the trial court's ruling. Parker could not be required to accept Fox's offer of the second contract to mitigate the damages she incurred as a result of Fox's breach of contract. The state supreme court acknowledged that the measure of recovery by a wrongfully discharged employee is the amount of agreed-on salary minus the amount that the employer proves the employee earned or with reasonable effort might have earned from other employment. The court recognized, however, that first the employer must show that the other employment was comparable to the job of which the employee was deprived. The court noted that "the female lead as a dramatic actress in a western style motion picture can by no stretch of imagination be considered the equivalent of or substantially similar to the lead in a song-and-dance production."

Liquidated Damages versus Penalties

Unliquidated damages are damages that have not been calculated or determined. For example, in a lawsuit, after Jane has proved her right to recover from Dick for his breach of their contract but before she has proved the amount she is entitled to recover, the damages are unliquidated. **Liquidated damages** are damages that are certain in amount. A liquidated damages provision in a contract specifies a certain amount to be paid in the event of a future default or breach of contract. For example, a provision requiring a construction contractor to pay $100 for every day he or she is late in completing the construction is a liquidated damages provision. Liquidated damages differ from penal-

ties. **Penalties** specify a certain amount to be paid in the event of a default or breach of contract and are designed to *penalize* the breaching party. Liquidated damages provisions are enforceable; penalty provisions are not.

To determine if a particular provision is for liquidated damages or for a penalty, two questions must be answered. First, when the contract was entered into, was it apparent that damages would be difficult to estimate in the event of a breach? Second, was the amount set as damages a reasonable estimate and not excessive?[8] If both answers

---

8.   Restatement (Second) of Contracts, Section 356(1).

are yes, the provision will be enforced. If either answer is no, the provision will not be enforced. Section 2-718(1) of the UCC specifically permits the inclusion of liquidated damages clauses in contracts for the sale of goods as long as both of these tests are met. In construction contracts, it is difficult to estimate the amount of damages caused by a delay in completing construction, so liquidated damages clauses are often used.

In the following case, the court interpreted a liquidated damages clause to be in fact a penalty and refused to enforce the provision.

Case 17.3

SCHRENKO v. REGNANTE

Appeals Court of Massachusetts, Essex, 1989. 27 Mass.App. 282, 537 N.E.2d 1261.

BACKGROUND AND FACTS The Schrenkos agreed to buy a house from James and Jean Mazareas for $360,000 and paid a $16,000 deposit toward the price. Under the contract, the deposit was to be "retained by the seller as liquidated damages unless within thirty days after the time for performance of this agreement or any extension hereof, the seller otherwise notifies the buyer in writing." As the November 11 closing date approached, the buyers sought an extension, but the sellers would not offer one on terms acceptable to the buyers. When the buyers refused to close on November 11, the sellers' attorney, Theodore Regnante, who had been holding the deposit, gave it to the sellers. On December 2, Regnante advised the buyers in writing that the sellers intended to retain the deposit as liquidated damages and to hold the buyers liable for any additional damages incurred by them as a result of the buyers' breach. The sellers later calculated additional damages to be $18,831.62. On December 19, the sellers sold the house to a third party for $385,000. The Schrenkos sued the sellers in a Massachusetts state court to recover the deposit. The trial court, concluding that the buyers had transferred the deposit to the sellers under a valid liquidated damages clause, granted the sellers' motion for summary judgment, and the buyers appealed.

DECISION AND RATIONALE The Appeals Court of Massachusetts reversed the trial court's ruling. The court stated, "[A] liquidated damage clause, reasonable when agreed to, is enforceable." Given the sellers' decision to claim damages in addition to the $16,000 in liquidated damages and the fact that the sellers suffered no actual loss, the appellate court held that the liquidated damages clause was a penalty and therefore would not be enforced. The court explained that the deposit, instead of being a settlement agreed on in advance, became at the sellers' option only the minimum amount that they would receive as compensation for their loss. "Such a clause may not be enforced * * * if the amount involved is so disproportionate to the actual expenses caused by the breach as to shock the conscience of the court and make it in reality a penalty."

▪ Rescission and Restitution

Rescission is essentially an action to undo, or terminate, a contract—to return the contracting parties to the positions they occupied prior to the transaction.[9] When fraud, a mistake, duress, undue influence, misrepresentation, or lack of capacity to contract is present, unilateral rescission is available.[10] The failure of one party to perform entitles the other party to rescind the contract. The rescinding party must give prompt notice to the breaching

---

9. The rescission discussed here is *unilateral* rescission, in which only one party wants to undo the contract. In mutual rescission, both parties agree to undo the contract (see Chapter 16). Mutual rescission discharges the contract; unilateral rescission is generally available as a remedy for breach of contract.

10. The Federal Trade Commission and many states have rules or statutes allowing consumers to unilaterally rescind contracts made at home with door-to-door salespersons. Rescission is allowed within three days for any reason or for no reason at all. See, for example, California Civil Code Section 1689.5.

party. Generally, to rescind a contract, both parties must make **restitution** to each other by returning goods, property, or money previously conveyed.[11] If the goods or property received can be restored *in specie*—that is, if the actual goods or property can be returned—they must be. If the goods or property has been consumed, restitution must be made in an equivalent amount of money.

Essentially, restitution refers to the plaintiff's recapture of a benefit conferred on the defendant through which the defendant has been unjustly enriched. For example, Ann conveys $10,000 to Bob in return for Bob's promise to design a house for her. The next day Bob calls Ann and tells her that he has taken a position with a large architectural firm in another state and cannot design the house. Ann decides to hire another architect that afternoon. Ann can obtain restitution of the $10,000.

Circumstances under which rescission and restitution may be ordered are illustrated in the following case.

---

11.   Restatement (Second) of Contracts, Section 370.

Case 17.4

COX v. BISHOP

Court of Appeals of Arkansas, 1989.
28 Ark.App. 210,
772 S.W.2d 358.

BACKGROUND AND FACTS   Jimmy and Brenda Bishop contracted with Dave Cox & Company to install a swimming pool in the Bishops' yard. They paid $13,500 for the pool and installation. Six months after the pool was installed, the Bishops discovered that it had risen six inches from the hole in which it had been put, exposing a sharp edge on which, subsequently, several children were hurt. The pool developed other problems, including leaks, cracks, and bulges. Alleging that the pool was unsafe, the Bishops filed suit in an Arkansas state court for rescission of the contract. The trial court concluded that Cox had undertaken to install the pool properly but that "this was just a 'botched' job. There is a material breach of contract." The court ordered rescission of the contract and restitution of the Bishops' $13,500. Cox appealed. He argued that rescission was improper because the evidence did not support the court's conclusion and because the Bishops had not returned to Cox what they received under the contract (the pool).

DECISION AND RATIONALE   The Court of Appeals of Arkansas affirmed the trial court's judgment. The Bishops were entitled to rescind the contract and recover the money paid to Cox. The appellate court pointed out that "where there is a material breach of contract, substantial nonperformance and entire or substantial failure of consideration, the injured party is entitled to rescission of the contract and restitution and recovery back of money paid." Generally, for restitution to be awarded, the nonbreaching party must return whatever consideration he or she has received. The court noted that the Bishops had sought to return the pool by having Cox remove it, but that Cox "did not agree to this request."

ETHICAL CONSIDERATIONS   The pool company's defense—that the Bishops had not returned the pool that they had received under the contract—certainly relates to form rather than substance in the law. How could the Bishops have reasonably been able to return an improperly installed swimming pool? Ethically, the pool builder had no grounds to deny at least some payment to the Bishops for an improper installation.

■ Specific Performance

The equitable remedy of **specific performance** calls for the performance of the act promised in the contract. This remedy is quite attractive to the nonbreaching party, because it provides the exact bargain promised in the contract. It also avoids some of the problems inherent in a suit for money damages.

There are three basic reasons for the attractiveness of the remedy of specific performance. First, the nonbreaching party need not worry about collecting the judgment.[12] Second, the nonbreaching party need not look around for another contract. Third, the actual performance is more valuable than the money damages.

Although the equitable remedy of specific performance is often preferable to other remedies, specific performance will not be granted unless the party's legal remedy (money damages) is inadequate.[13] For example, contracts for the sale of goods rarely qualify for specific performance. The legal remedy, money damages, is ordinarily adequate in such situations because substantially identical goods can be bought or sold in the market. If the goods are unique, however, a court of equity will decree specific performance. For example, paintings, sculptures, or rare books or coins are so unique that money damages will not enable a buyer to obtain substantially identical substitutes in the market.

Sale of Land

Specific performance is granted to a buyer in a contract for the sale of land. The legal remedy for breach of a land sales contract is inadequate because every parcel of land is considered to be unique. Money damages will not compensate a buyer adequately because the same land in the same location obviously cannot be obtained elsewhere. Only when specific performance is unavailable (for example, when the seller has sold the property to someone else) will damages be awarded instead.

Contracts for Personal Services

Personal service contracts require one party to work personally for another party. Courts of equity normally refuse to grant specific performance of personal service contracts. If the contract is not deemed personal, the remedy at law may be ade-

quate if substantially identical service (for example, lawn mowing) is available from other persons.

In individually tailored personal service contracts, courts will not order specific performance by the party who was to be employed, because public policy strongly discourages involuntary servitude.[14] Moreover, the courts do not want to have to monitor a continuing service contract if supervision would be difficult—as it would be if the contract required the exercise of personal judgment or talent. For example, if you contracted with a brain surgeon to perform brain surgery on you, and the surgeon refused to perform, the court would not compel (and you certainly would not want) the surgeon to perform under those circumstances. A court cannot assure meaningful performance in such a situation.[15]

◼ Reformation

Reformation is an equitable remedy used when the parties have *imperfectly* expressed their agreement in writing. Reformation allows the contract to be rewritten to reflect the parties' true intentions. It applies most often when fraud or mutual mistake (for example, a clerical error) is present. Reformation is almost always sought so that some other remedy may then be pursued.

For example, if Gilge contracts to buy a certain parcel of land from Cavendish, but their contract mistakenly refers to a parcel of land different from the one being sold, the contract does not reflect the parties' intentions. Accordingly, a court of equity can reform the contract so that it conforms to the parties' intentions and accurately refers to the parcel of land being sold. Gilge can then, if necessary, show that Cavendish has breached the contract as reformed. She can then claim specific performance.

Two other examples deserve mention. The first involves two parties who have made a binding oral contract. They further agree to reduce the oral con-

---

12. Courts enter judgments as final dispositions of cases. The judgment, of course, must be collected, and collection may pose problems. For example, the judgment debtor may be broke or have only a very small net worth.

13. Restatement (Second) of Contracts, Section 359.

14. The Thirteenth Amendment to the U.S. Constitution prohibits involuntary servitude, but *negative* injunctions (that is, injunctions prohibiting rather than ordering certain conduct) are possible. Thus, whereas you may not be able to compel a person to perform under a personal service contract, you may be able to restrain that person from engaging in similar contracts for a period of time.

15. Similarly, courts often refuse to order specific performance of construction contracts because courts are not set up to operate as construction supervisors or engineers.

tract to writing, but in doing so, they make an error in stating the terms. Universally, the courts will allow into evidence the correct terms of the oral contract, thereby reforming the written contract.

The second example deals with written agreements (covenants) not to compete (see Chapter 14). If the covenant is for a valid and legitimate purpose (such as the sale of a business) but the area or time restraints of the covenant are unreasonable, some courts will reform the restraints by making them reasonable and will enforce the entire contract as reformed. Other courts, however, will throw out the entire restrictive covenant as illegal.

■ Recovery Based on Quasi Contract

As stated in Chapter 9, quasi contract is a legal theory under which an obligation is imposed in the absence of an agreement. The courts use this theory to prevent unjust enrichment. Hence quasi contract provides a basis for relief when no enforceable contract exists. The legal obligation arises because the law considers that a promise to pay for benefits received is implied by the party accepting the benefits. Generally, when one party has conferred a benefit on another party, justice requires the party receiving the benefit to pay the reasonable value for it. The party conferring the benefit can recover *in quantum meruit*, which means "as much as he deserves."

Quasi-contractual recovery is useful when one party has partially performed under a contract that is unenforceable. It can be used as an alternative to a suit for damages and will allow the party to recover the reasonable value of the partial performance, measured in some cases according to the benefit received and in others according to the detriment suffered.

To recover on a quasi contract, the party seeking recovery must show that:

1. He or she has conferred a benefit on the other party.
2. He or she conferred the benefit with the reasonable expectation of being paid.
3. He or she did not act as a volunteer in conferring the benefit.
4. The party receiving the benefit would be unjustly enriched by retaining the benefit without making payment.

For example, suppose that Raphael agrees orally to buy Donatello's house and gives Donatello $10,000 as a down payment. Because their agreement is oral and involves the sale of land, it is unenforceable under the Statute of Frauds (see Chapter 14). Raphael will be able to recover the money in a suit in quasi contract because (1) a benefit ($10,000) was conferred on Donatello, (2) Raphael paid the $10,000 reasonably expecting to get the house, (3) Raphael paid the $10,000 at Donatello's request (Raphael was not a "volunteer"), and (4) allowing Donatello to keep the $10,000 would enrich Donatello unjustly.

■ Election of Remedies

In many cases, a nonbreaching party has several remedies available. The party must choose which remedy to pursue. Exhibit 17–3 summarizes the availability and results of various remedies available to nonbreaching parties.

The purpose of the *election of remedies* doctrine is to prevent double recovery. Suppose McCarthy agrees in writing to sell his land to Tally. Then McCarthy changes his mind and repudiates the contract. Tally can sue for compensatory damages or for specific performance. If she receives damages, she should not be able to get specific performance of the sales contract, because failure to deliver title to the land was the cause of the injury for which she received damages. If Tally could seek compensatory damages in addition to specific performance, she would recover twice for the same breach of contract. The doctrine of election of remedies requires Tally to choose the remedy she wants, and it eliminates any possibility of double recovery. In other words, the election doctrine represents the legal embodiment of the adage "you can't have your cake and eat it, too."

Unfortunately, the doctrine has been applied in a rigid and technical manner, leading to some harsh results. For example, in a Wisconsin case,[16] Carpenter was fraudulently induced to buy a piece of land for $100. He spent an additional $140 moving onto the land and then discovered the fraud. Instead of suing for damages, Carpenter sued to rescind the contract. The court allowed Carpenter to recover only the purchase price of $100. The court

---

16. *Carpenter v. Mason*, 181 Wis. 114, 193 N.W. 973 (1923).

■ Exhibit 17–3 Remedies Available on Breach of Contract

There is a breach of contract. The injured party sues. The circumstances determine what relief is available.

Remedy	Availability	Result
1. Damages		
a. Compensatory damages	A party sustains and proves injury arising directly from the loss of the bargain.	The injured party is compensated for the *loss* of the bargain.
b. Consequential damages	Special circumstances, which the breaching party knows of, or has reason to know of, cause the injured party additional loss.	The injured party is given the entire *benefit* of the bargain.
c. Punitive damages	A tort is involved.	The wrongdoer is punished, and others are deterred from committing similar acts.
d. Nominal damages	There is no financial loss.	Wrongdoing is established without actual damages being suffered. Plaintiff is awarded a nominal amount (such as $1) in damages.
2. Rescission and Restitution	The injured party is entitled to recapture a benefit conferred.	The contract is terminated. The parties are returned to the positions they were in before the contract was made.
3. Specific Performance	The legal remedy (money damages) is inadequate.	The injured party gets the bargain promised in the contract.
4. Reformation	The written contract imperfectly expresses the parties' agreement.	The contract is rewritten to reflect the parties' true intention.
5. Quasi-contractual Recovery	The parties have no contract, but unjust enrichment cannot otherwise be avoided.	The party who conferred the benefit gets the reasonable value of the benefit conferred.

denied recovery of the additional $140 because the seller, Mason, did not receive the $140 and was therefore not required to reimburse Carpenter for his moving expenses. So Carpenter suffered a net loss of $140 on the transaction. If Carpenter had elected to sue for damages instead of seeking the remedy of rescission and restitution, he could have recovered the $140 as well as the $100.

Because of such problems, the doctrine of election of remedies has been eliminated in contracts for the sale of goods. The UCC expressly rejects the doctrine. (See UCC 2-703 and UCC 2-711.) Remedies under the UCC are not exclusive but cumulative in nature and include all the available remedies for breach of contract. Thus, for example, under UCC 2-721, in a suit based on fraud, the defrauded party may obtain rescission of the contract, restitution of the benefits conferred, and any damages due to the fraud. Even though the UCC rejects the doctrine of election of remedies, parties may still not recover twice for the same harm by

seeking, for example, specific performance *and* damages at the same time.

■ Waiver of Breach

Under certain circumstances, a nonbreaching party may be willing to accept a defective performance of the contract. This knowing relinquishment of a legal right (that is, the right to require satisfactory and full performance) is called a **waiver.**[17] When a waiver of a breach of contract occurs, the party waiving the breach cannot take any later action on the theory that the contract was broken. In effect, the waiver erases the past breach; the contract continues as if the breach had never occurred. Of course, the waiver of breach of contract extends only to the matter waived and not to the whole

17. Restatement (Second) of Contracts, Sections 84, 246, and 247. The Restatement uses the term *promise* rather than *waiver*.

contract. Businesspersons often waive breaches of contract to get whatever benefit possible out of the contract.

For example, a seller contracts with a buyer to deliver to the buyer 10,000 tons of coal on or before November 1. The contract calls for the buyer's payment to be made by November 10 for coal delivered. Because of a coal miners' strike, coal is scarce. The seller breaches the contract by not tendering delivery until November 5. The buyer may be well advised to waive the sellers' breach, accept delivery of the coal, and pay as contracted.

Ordinarily, the waiver by a contracting party will not operate to waive subsequent, additional, or future breaches of contract. This is always true when the subsequent breaches are unrelated to the first breach. For example, an owner who waives the right to sue for late completion of a stage of construction does not waive the right to sue for failure to comply with engineering specifications.

A waiver will be extended to subsequent defective performance if a reasonable person would conclude that similar defective performance in the future will be acceptable. Therefore, a *pattern of conduct* that waives a number of successive breaches will operate as a continued waiver. To change this result, the nonbreaching party should give notice to the breaching party that full performance will be required in the future.

To illustrate: Suppose the construction contract mentioned above was to be completed in six stages two months apart, spanning a period of one year. The question is whether the waiver of the right to object to lateness of performance of stage 1 will operate as a waiver of the time requirements for stages 2 through 6. If only the first stage's time requirements have been waived, the waiver will not extend to the other five stages. If, however, the first five stages have all been late (and the right to object to lateness has always been waived), the waivers will extend to the final stage unless the owner has given proper notice that future performance is to be on time.

The party who has rendered defective or less-than-full performance remains liable for the damages caused by the breach of contract. In effect, the waiver operates to keep the contract going. The waiver prevents the nonbreaching party from calling the contract to an end or rescinding the contract. The contract continues, but the nonbreaching party

can recover damages caused by defective or less-than-full performance.

■ Contract Provisions Limiting Remedies

A contract can include provisions stating that no damages can be recovered for certain types of breaches or that damages must be limited to a maximum amount. In addition, the contract can provide that the only remedy for breach is replacement, repair, or refund of the purchase price. Provisions stating that no damages can be recovered are called *exculpatory clauses*. (See Chapter 14.) Provisions that affect the availability of certain remedies are called *limitation of liability clauses*. Because of the importance of these clauses and their uses, some discussion and illustrative situations are offered here.

Mutual Assent to Limitation Required

Initially, a court must determine if the provision limiting remedies has been made a part of the contract by offer and acceptance. For a term or provision to become part of a contract, both parties must consent to it. Therefore, courts analyze whether the provision was noticed by the parties—whether, for example, the provision was in fine print or on the back of a lengthy contract. If either party did not know about the provision, it is not a part of the contract and will not be enforced.[18]

For example, when motorists park their cars in lots, they often receive small ticket stubs that exclude liability for damages to cars parked in the lot. If the clause is not conspicuous and a reasonable person would not have noticed it, the clause will not normally be enforced, and the motorist can sue for damage caused to his or her car.[19]

Type of Liability Excluded

Once it has been determined that the provision or clause is part of the contract, the analysis must focus on the type of breach that is excluded. For

---

18. See, for example, the discussion of the Magnuson-Moss Warranty Act in Chapter 22.
19. See *California State Auto Association Inter-Insurance Bureau v. Barrett Garages, Inc.*, 257 Cal.App.2d 71, 64 Cal.Rptr. 699 (1967).

example, a provision excluding liability for injuries that are inflicted intentionally or that occur as a result of fraud will not be enforced. Likewise, a clause excluding liability for illegal acts or violations of law will not be enforced. On the other hand, a clause excluding liability for negligence may be enforced in appropriate cases. When an *exculpatory clause* for negligence is contained in a contract made between parties with roughly equal bargaining positions, the clause usually will be enforced.

For example, assume Delta Airlines buys six DC-9s from Douglas Aircraft. In the contract for sale, a clause excludes liability for errors in design and construction of the aircraft. The clause will be upheld because both parties are large corporations with roughly equal bargaining positions. The equality of bargaining power assures that the exculpatory clause was not dictated by one of the parties and forced on the other.

Limited Remedies—UCC

Under the UCC, in a contract for the sale of goods, remedies can be limited, but rules different from those just discussed apply. If only a certain remedy is desired, the contract must state that the remedy is exclusive. Suppose you buy an automobile and the sales contract limits your remedy to repair or replacement of defective parts. Under the UCC, the sales contract must state that the *sole* and *exclusive* remedy available to the buyer is repair and/or replacement of the defective parts.[20] If the contract states that the remedy is exclusive, then the specified remedy will be the only one ordinarily

available to the buyer (provided the contract is not *unconscionable*).[21]

When circumstances cause an exclusive remedy to fail in its essential purpose, then it will not be exclusive.[22] Suppose the car you bought breaks down several times and the dealer is unable to fix or replace the defective parts. In that case, the exclusive remedy fails in its essential purpose, and all the other remedies under the UCC become available.

Under the UCC, a sales contract may also limit or exclude consequential damages, provided the limitation is not unconscionable. When the buyer is purchasing consumer goods, the limitation of liability for personal injury is *prima facie* unconscionable and will not normally be enforced. When the buyer is purchasing goods for commercial use, the limitation of liability for personal injury is not necessarily unconscionable.

Suppose that you have purchased a small printing press for your teenage son. It is a present to him for his birthday. He will be using it to print leaflets and pamphlets for his social club. The contract for purchase states that consequential damages arising from personal injury as a result of a defect in the small printing press are excluded. This exclusion or limitation of liability is *prima facie* unconscionable. It will not be enforced. On the other hand, if you buy a printing press for your business, the limitation will not necessarily be unconscionable and may be enforceable.

---

20. UCC 2-719(1).

21. Unconscionability is discussed in Chapters 14 and 18. See also UCC 2-719(3).
22. See UCC 2-719(2).

■ Terms and Concepts

■ For Review

1. What is the usual measure of damages on breach of a contract for the sale of goods?
2. Under what circumstances can a contract be unilaterally rescinded?

3. Sometimes, a nonbreaching party has several remedies available. When must a party choose which remedy to pursue to the exclusion of the others? When are remedies cumulative?

4. Tip Manufacturing Corp. contracts to sell to Garcia Products, a dealer in used machinery, a used steel separator that Garcia plans to resell. Tip refuses to deliver the separator. Garcia is unable to obtain a similar machine elsewhere. Could Garcia sucessfully sue for the net profit that Garcia would have made on resale of the separator?

5. Restitution is a party's recapture of a conferred benefit through which another party has been unjustly enriched. A party is entitled to restitution only to the extent that he or she has conferred a benefit on the other party. Perry contracts to work full-time as an accountant for Elle, Inc. Perry uses some of the time that he should be working for Elle to perform work for Crawford Stationary Co., which pays him an additional salary. If Elle sues Perry for breach of contract, can Elle recover from Perry the amount of the salary paid by Crawford?

■ Questions and Case Problems

17-1. Cohen contracts to sell his house and lot to Windsor for $100,000. The terms of the contract call for Windsor to pay 10 percent of the purchase price as a deposit toward the purchase price, or down payment. The terms further stipulate that should the buyer breach the contract, the deposit will be retained by Cohen as liquidated damages. Windsor pays the deposit, but because her expected financing of the $90,000 balance falls through, she breaches the contract. Two weeks later Cohen sells the house and lot to Ballard for $105,000. Windsor demands her $10,000 back, but Cohen refuses, claiming that Windsor's breach and the contract terms entitle him to keep the deposit. Discuss who is correct.

17-2. Under which of the following breach of contract situations would specific performance be an appropriate remedy? Discuss fully.

(a) Thompson contracts to sell her house and lot to Cousteau. Then, upon finding another buyer willing to pay a higher purchase price, she refuses to deed the property to Cousteau.

(b) Amy contracts to sing and dance in Fred's nightclub for one month, beginning May 1. She then refuses to perform.

(c) Hoffman contracts to purchase a rare coin owned by Erikson, as Erikson is breaking up his coin collection. At the last minute Erikson decides to keep his coin collection intact and refuses to deliver the coin to Hoffman.

(d) There are three shareholders of the ABC Corp.: Panozzo, who owns 48 percent of the stock; Chang, who owns another 48 percent; and Ryan, who owns 4 percent. Ryan contracts to sell her 4 percent to Chang. Later, Ryan refuses to transfer the shares to Chang.

17-3. Ken owns and operates a famous candy store and makes most of the candy sold in the store. Business is particularly heavy during the Christmas season. Ken contracts with Sweet, Inc., to purchase 10,000 pounds of sugar to be delivered on or before November 15. Ken has informed Sweet that this particular order is to be used for the Christmas season business. Because of production problems the sugar is not tendered to Ken until December 10, at which time Ken refuses it as being too late. Ken has been unable to purchase the quantity of sugar needed to meet the Christmas orders and has had to turn down numerous regular customers, some of whom have indicated that they will purchase candy elsewhere in the future. What sugar Ken has been able to purchase has cost him 10 cents per pound above the price contracted for with Sweet. Ken sues Sweet for breach of contract, claiming as damages the higher price paid for sugar from others, lost profits from this year's lost Christmas sales, future lost profits from customers who have indicated that they will discontinue doing business with him, and punitive damages for failure to meet the contracted delivery date. Sweet claims Ken is limited to compensatory damages only. Discuss who is correct.

17-4. Wallechinsky purchases an automobile from Anderson Motors, paying $1,000 down and agreeing to pay off the balance in thirty-six monthly payments of $200 each. The terms of the agreement call for Wallechinsky to make a payment on or before the first of each month. During the first six months, Anderson receives a $200 payment before the first of each month. During the next six months, Wallechinsky's payment is never made until the fifth of the month. Anderson accepts and cashes the payment check each time. When Wallechinsky tenders the thirteenth payment on the fifth of the next month, Anderson refuses to accept the check, claiming that Wallechinsky is in breach of contract, and demands the entire balance owed. Wallechinsky claims that Anderson cannot hold her in breach. Discuss the result fully.

17-5. Putnam contracts to buy a new Oldsmobile from Old Century Motors, paying $2,000 down and agreeing to make twenty-four monthly payments of $350 each. He takes the car home and, after making one payment, learns that his Oldsmobile has a Chevrolet engine in it rather than the famous Olds Super V-8 engine. Old Century never informed Putnam of this fact. Putnam immediately notifies Old Century of his dissatisfaction and tenders back the car to Old Century. Old Century accepts the car and returns to Putnam the $2,000 down payment plus the one $350 payment. Two weeks later Putnam, without a car and angry, files a suit against Old Century, seeking damages for breach of warranty and fraud. Discuss the effect of Putnam's actions.

17-6. Vrgora, a general contractor, entered into a contract with the Los Angeles Unified School District (LAUSD) to construct an "automotive service shed" and an enclosed room outfitted with an electronic vehicle performance tester. The contract specified a price of $167,195.09, a completion time of 250 days from commencement, and a liquidated damages clause of $100 per day for late completion. Vrgora began construction on January 31, 1977, with an expected completion date of July 29, 1977. Delays in the project arose when the manufacturer of the tester did not receive approval for the tester until September 23, 1977 (a delay of over six months). The tester arrived on November 15, 1977, but because of a conflict over payment, the manufacturer removed the tester. Upon payment, the manufacturer delivered the tester again on December 2, 1977, and Vrgora completed the project on May 2, 1978. LAUSD assessed $20,700 as liquidated damages and eventually brought an action against Vrgora to collect the assessed damages, which Vrgora refused to pay. Given the circumstances of this case, will the court require Vrgora to pay the liquidated damages demanded by LAUSD? [*Vrgora v. Los Angeles Unified School District,* 152 Cal.App.3d 1178, 200 Cal.Rptr. 130 (1984)]

17-7. Kerr Steamship Co. delivered to Radio Corp. of America (RCA) a twenty-nine-word coded message to be sent to Kerr's agent in Manila. The message included instructions on loading cargo onto one of Kerr's vessels. Kerr's profits on the carriage of the cargo were to be about $6,600. RCA mislaid the coded message, and it was never sent. Kerr sued RCA for the $6,600 in profits that it lost because RCA never sent the message. Can Kerr recover? Explain. [*Kerr Steamship Co. v. Radio Corp. of America,* 245 N.Y. 284, 157 N.E. 140 (1927)]

17-8. Teachers Insurance and Annuity Association of America (T.I.A.A.) agreed to lend City Centre One Associates $14.5 million for the construction of an office building in Salt Lake City. City Centre, however, refused to go through with the closing on the loan, and T.I.A.A. sued for specific performance of their contract. Courts have in the past granted specific performance of lending agreements when requested by the *borrower* if failure to go through with the loan would result in irreparable injury to the borrower, who may be unable to secure alternate financing. Should T.I.A.A., as a *lender,* succeed in its request for specific performance? Explain. [*City Centre One Associates v. Teachers Insurance and Annuity Association,* 656 F.Supp. 658 (D.Utah 1987)]

17-9. Roger and Lois Robinson bought a mobile home and lot subject to a promissory note secured by a deed of trust in favor of Delores Dorn and Elizabeth Britt. The note provided for monthly payments. The deed of trust provided that "by accepting payment of any sum secured hereby after its due date" Dorn and Britt would "not waive [their] right either to require prompt payment when due of all other sums so secured or to declare default for failure so to pay." For the first six months, none of the Robinsons' payments was more than a week late. Over the next seven months, their payments were consistently, on average, one or two weeks late. After they had missed two consecutive payments without explanation, Dorn and Britt initiated foreclosure proceedings. The Robinsons argued that since Dorn and Britt had accepted the previous late payments, they were required to give notice before filing to foreclose. Had Dorn and Britt, by their acceptance of late payments, waived their right to prompt payment, notwithstanding the non-

waiver clause in the deed of trust? Explain. [*Dorn v. Robinson,* 158 Ariz. 279, 762 P.2d 566 (1988)]

17-10. Southwestern Bell Telephone Co. executed a license agreement that gave United Video Cablevision of St. Louis, Inc., authority to construct and operate a cable television system using poles and conduits owned by Bell. The agreement specified that United Video would make a down payment for rent and telephone wire service. By law, Bell was required to locate and mark underground facilities, upon request, before any excavation so that no disruption of the telephone lines would take place. Bell had provided this service free of charge for many years, and it performed the service for United Video before United Video installed its lines. After United Video had substantially completed its installation, Bell notified the company of its intention to charge for the locating and marking service. The charge was not a part of the oral or written contract, and United Video refused to pay. Bell sought to recover based on *quantum meruit.* Discuss whether Bell should succeed in its claim. [*Southwestern Bell Telephone Co. v. United Video Cablevision of St. Louis, Inc.,* 737 S.W.2d 474 (Mo.App. 1987)]

17-11. W. A. and Lola Dunn were payees of several installment promissory notes issued by General Equities of Iowa, Ltd. Each note contained an acceleration clause that permitted the holder of the note to accelerate and demand full payment of the note should any installment not be paid when due. Over a period of time the Dunns accepted late installment payments from General Equities without invoking the acceleration clause. General Equities made a further late payment. The Dunns returned the General Equities check and demanded payment of the entire balance, with interest, in accordance with the acceleration clause. General Equities claimed that the acceptance of the previous late payments constituted a waiver of the Dunns' right to invoke the acceleration clause. Discuss whether General Equities was correct. [*Dunn v. General Equities of Iowa, Ltd.,* 319 N.W.2d 515 (Iowa 1982)]

17-12. Case Briefing Assignment

Examine Case A.8 [Potter v. Oster, *426 N.W.2d 148 (Iowa 1988)*] *in Appendix A. The case has been excerpted there in great detail. Review and then brief the case, making sure that you include answers to the following questions in your brief.*

1. Why was the plaintiff appealing the trial court's decision?
2. Why did the plaintiff assert that allowing the remedy of rescission and restitution in this case would lead to an inequitable result?
3. According to the court, what three requirements must be met before rescission will be granted?
4. Did the defendant meet these three requirements and, if so, why?
5. What reasons did the court give for its conclusion that remedies at law were inadequate in this case?
6. Why are remedies at law presumed inadequate for breach of real estate contracts?

Focus on Ethics

Contract Law and the Application of Ethics

Ethics and Freedom of Contract

In Chapter 2, we pointed out the basic tradeoffs that might exist between ethics and profitability. In general, the responsible business manager will evaluate a business transaction on the basis of three criteria—legality, profitability, and ethics. Any action that is simultaneously legal, profitable, and ethical can certainly put the decision maker's mind at ease. But what does acting ethically really mean in the area of contracts? If an individual with whom you enter into a contract fails to look after his or her own interests, is that your fault, and should you therefore be doing something about it? That is to say, if the contract happens to be to your advantage and therefore to the other party's detriment, do you have a responsibility to correct the situation?

For example, assume that a neighbor whom you have never met places a "for sale" sign on her car, offering to sell it for $2,000. You learn that she is moving to another state and needs the extra cash to help finance the move. You know that she could easily get, with

little time or effort on her part, $5,000 for the car, and you congratulate yourself on your good fortune. Even if you do not need a car, you can purchase it and then sell it at an immense (for you) profit. But you also learn that your neighbor has failed to do the preliminary research—checking blue book prices and so on—that most reasonable individuals would undertake when selling a car, and therefore she is unaware that the car is vastly underpriced.

Are you obligated to tell her that she is essentially giving away $3,000 if she sells you the car for only $2,000? Do you have an ethical responsibility toward this woman—whom you will probably never see again—simply because she failed to look after her own interests?

This kind of situation, transplanted into the world of commercial transactions, raises an obvious question: At what point should the savvy businessperson cease looking after his or her own economic welfare and become "his brother's keeper," so to speak?

The answer to this question is not simple. On the one hand, a common ethical assumption in

our society is that individuals should be held responsible for the consequences of their own actions, including their contractual promises. This principle is expressed in the legal concept called freedom of contract, a topic discussed in Chapter 9. Applying this ethical precept to the above example, you could justify not saying anything about the true value of the car to your neighbor by stating that you were upholding the principle of freedom of contract. But another common assumption in our society is that individuals should not harm one another by their actions. This is the basis of both tort law and criminal law. If you applied this ethical yardstick to the above example, would you be obligated not to harm your neighbor's interests by taking advantage of her offer? How would you balance these two ethical principles?

In the area of contract law, ethical behavior often involves just such a "balancing act." In the above example, if you purchased the car and the neighbor later learned its true value and sued you for the difference, very likely no court of law would agree that the

314

contract should be rescinded. In other words, the law would not "answer" your ethical question in this case. In all likelihood, the court would not come to the aid of the neighbor, because she could easily have prevented the injustice by learning, as a "reasonable person" would have, the market price of the car.

There are times, however, when courts will hold that the principle of freedom of contract should give way to the principle that people should not be harmed by the actions of others. We look below at some examples of how parties to contracts may be excused from performance under their contracts if that is the only way injustice can be prevented.

Impossibility

The doctrine of impossibility of performance is based to some extent on the ethical question of whether one party should suffer economic loss when it is impossible to perform a contract. The rule that one is "bound by his or her contracts" is not followed when performance is made impossible. The doctrine of impossibility of performance is applied to relieve a contracting party of liability for failure to perform. This doctrine, however, is applied only when the parties themselves did not consciously assume the risk of the events that rendered performance impossible. Furthermore, this doctrine rests on the assumption that the party claiming the defense of impossibility has acted ethically. In other words, a party cannot arrange events intentionally to make performance impossible.

A contract is discharged, for example, if performance of the contract calls for the delivery of a particular car and through no fault of either party this car is stolen and completely demolished in an accident. Yet the doctrine of impossibility of performance is not available if the party agreeing to sell his or her car either crashed the car to avoid performance of the contract or caused the car's destruction by his or her negligence.

The well-known English case of *Taylor v. Caldwell* is also illustrative of the doctrine of impossibility of performance.[1] In *Taylor,* the plaintiff entered into a contract with the defendant to rent the defendant's music hall for a series of concerts. Before the first concert, but after the contract had been entered into, the music hall was destroyed by fire. The court held that the defendant was discharged from performing. Furthermore, because performance was impossible, his failure to perform was not a breach of contract.

Prior to the late nineteenth century, courts were reluctant to discharge a contract even when it appeared that performance was literally impossible. Just as society's ethics change with the passage of time, however, law also makes a transition to reflect society's new perceptions of ethical behavior. Today, courts are much more willing to discharge a contract when its performance has become literally impossible. Holding a party in breach of contract, when performance has become literally impossible through no fault of the party claiming the defense of impossibility, no longer coincides with society's notions of fairness.

Mistake

The notion that mistake in contracts should release the contracting parties from their obligations has gained strength as the ethics of society have changed. If one were to study the cases of several hundred years ago, one would find much less acceptance of mistake as an excuse to avoid a contractual obligation than exists today.

Mistakes can arise in numerous contexts surrounding the making of a contract. A mistake may be unilateral in that it is made by only one party. In a case tried early in this century, *Steinmeyer v. Schroeppel,*[2] a bidder on a construction project incorrectly calculated his costs and therefore submitted an offer that was substantially lower than it would have been if he had correctly calculated his costs. The Illinois court held that the bidder was not entitled to rescind the contract. The court further stated that rescission based on a unilateral mistake could not be obtained when the mistake resulted from a failure to exercise reasonable care and diligence.

More recent court decisions appear to be less harsh. Some courts have concluded that rescission on account of computationerrors is permissible when the only injury to the other party is the loss of the expectancy engendered by a favorably low bid. Thus, ideas of fairness to each of the contracting parties change over time.

Unconscionability

The doctrine of unconscionability represents a good example of

---

1.   122 Eng.Rep. 309 (K.B. 1863).

2.   226 Ill. 9, 80 N.E. 564 (1907).

how the law attempts to enforce ethical behavior. This doctrine suggests that some contracts may be so unfair to one party as to be unenforceable, even though that party originally agreed to the contract's terms. Section 2-302 of the UCC provides that a court will consider the fairness of contracts and may consider a contract or any clause of a contract to have been unconscionable at the time it was made. If so, the court may refuse to enforce the contract, or it may enforce the contract without the unconscionable clause, or it may limit the application of the clause so as to avoid an unconscionable result.

The UCC does not define the term *unconscionability*. The drafters of the UCC, however, have added explanatory comments to the relevant sections of the UCC, and these comments serve as guidelines to the UCC's application. Comment 1 to Section 2-302 suggests that the basic test for unconscionability is whether, under the circumstances existing at the time of the making of the contract, the clause in question was so one-sided as to be unconscionable. This test is to be applied against the general commercial background of the contract. For example, a contract with a marginally literate consumer might be seen as unfair and unenforceable, whereas the same contract with a major business firm would be upheld by the courts. The doctrine of unconscionability could be used broadly to ensure that all contracts appeared perfectly ethical, but the courts have not used it in this way. Only contracts that are so extremely

one-sided as to "shock the conscience" of the court have been found unconscionable.

A classic case dealing with unconscionability is *Williams v. Walker-Thomas Furniture Co.*[3] This case involved a consumer who purchased over time, under an installment contract, several items of furniture from a furniture company. Under the terms of the contract, each time a new item of furniture was purchased, that item, in addition to all of the furniture purchased previously, would be used as collateral (property securing the debt). In 1962, the consumer, Williams, bought a stereo set on which she soon stopped making payments. The furniture company wanted to repossess all of the items that she had purchased from it since 1957.

Both the trial court and the intermediate appellate court, even though they felt that the contract was unconscionable, nonetheless held for the furniture company because, since the UCC had not yet been adopted by the District of Columbia (the jurisdiction in which this suit was brought), there was no legal basis on which to find the contract unenforceable. Upon review, however, the District of Columbia Circuit Court of Appeals held that there was no reason why the lower courts could not, under the common law, apply the concept of unconscionability to contracts. The appellate court then remanded the case to the trial court for an examination of whether the terms of the contract were so extreme as to be unconscionable according to business customs and practices.

_____

3.   350 F.2d 445 (1965).

It may appear that the furniture store acted unethically by including in its standard form for installment sales contracts the provision that all furniture purchased would serve as collateral for future purchases as well. But can you say with certainty that this is necessarily the case? Obviously, Walker-Thomas faced competition in the marketplace from other furniture stores. That it succeeded in using the same contract for so many years indicates that it was engaged in business practices that could not be successfully undermined by its competitors. What did this mean? It probably meant that the losses were typically so high in installment sales contracts in terms of defaults and inability to repossess collateral that Walker-Thomas found itself attempting to obtain additional collateral.

While to an outsider, such an action might seem unconscionable, to the business owner, the action may have appeared to be simply a "good business practice." That means that you cannot develop a general rule as to what constitutes unethical or unconscionable contract terms. You must look at each situation individually and examine carefully the context of each transaction.

Problems with Oral Contracts

Oral contracts are made every day. Many—if not most—of them are carried out, and no problems arise. Occasionally, however, oral contracts are not performed, and one party wishes to sue the other. Sometimes it is possible for one party to hide behind a technical defense to prevent the enforcement of a promise that he or she genuinely made to the other party. One of these technical defenses is the Statute of Frauds.

Statute of Frauds

As you learned in Chapter 14, the Statute of Frauds was originally instituted in 1677 in England to prevent harm to innocent parties by requiring written evidence of agreements concerning important transactions. The British act was created specifically to prevent further perpetration of the many frauds caused by witnesses' giving perjured testimony in cases involving breached oral agreements for which no written evidence existed. Because the British courts, until the Statute of Frauds was passed, had enforced oral contracts on the strength of oral testimony by witnesses, it was not too difficult to evade justice by alleging that a contract had been created and then breached by procuring "convincing" witnesses to support the claim. The possibility of fraud in such actions was enhanced by the fact that in seventeenth-century England, courts did not allow oral testimony to be given by the parties to a lawsuit—or by any parties with an interest in the litigation, such as husbands or wives. Defense against breach of contract actions was thus limited to written evidence or the testimony given by third parties.

Under the Statute of Frauds, if a contract is oral when it is required to be in writing, it will not, as a rule, be enforced by the courts. Since its inception over three hundred years ago, the statute has been heavily criticized because, although it was created to protect the innocent, it can also be used as

a technical defense by a party breaching a genuine oral contract. Some legal scholars have suggested that the Statute of Frauds has actually caused more fraud than it has prevented. Because the statute limits the kinds of contracts that will be enforceable and because it is frequently used as a technical defense only, it generally renders commercial transactions more cumbersome.

But does this mean that the statute should be abandoned? In the interest of promoting commerce, many nations have repealed similar statutes. Even England, the country that created the original Statute of Frauds, has repealed all of it except for the provisions relating to land and suretyship. Following the lead of other nations, in 1988 the United States agreed (in the United Nations Convention for the International Sale of Goods— see Chapter 24) that the Statute of Frauds would not apply to contracts between U.S. firms and firms in other nations. Nonetheless, it is still the law of the land for those doing business within U.S. borders. The retention of the statute in this country suggests that we are willing to accept the tradeoff that it represents. Even though the statute may be used to perpetrate injustice and even though it encumbers commercial transactions, it also serves to protect innocent parties from being held to oral contracts that they did not in fact make.

Promissory Estoppel

You learned in Chapter 11 that under the doctrine of promissory estoppel, a person who has reasonably relied on the promise of another can often obtain some measure of

recovery. Ethical standards are certainly at issue here. It just does not seem fair that one party, in reliance on another's promise, should perform when the other party does not. As individuals, we face the problem of detrimental reliance all of the time.

Suppose, for example, that you are engaged in an important research project. Your roommate agrees to pick up a book that is being held for you at the library. You need it to finish your research report. Your roommate fails to pick up the book, and when you go to the library the next day to obtain it, you find that it has been released to another student and will not be returned until after your report is due. You relied on your roommate to your detriment. Had your roommate indicated that he or she would not be able to get the book, you would have gone yourself to ensure that you had it in time. In this particular situation, the doctrine of promissory estoppel would probably not allow you to recover anything from your roommate, except perhaps a statement of "I'm sorry."

In the business world, however, a person who relies to his or her detriment on the promise of another can often recover damages, particularly when justice is better served by estopping the other party from denying that a contractual promise was made.

For example, in *Bower v. AT&T Technologies, Inc.,*[4] a number of AT&T repairpersons were laid off by AT&T when that company closed one of its Missouri plants to convert the plant into office space. AT&T

---

4. 852 F.2d 361 (1988).

promised the laid-off employees that as soon as the renovation of the plant building was completed, they would be rehired as clerical workers at a specified wage rate. AT&T also promised that the employees' seniority would be "bridged" and that their pension benefits would remain intact. For nearly five months, the workers continued to contact AT&T frequently and were always assured that as soon as AT&T began hiring clerical workers for the new plant, the laid-off employees would be notified. Relying on these assurances, the former employees refused other job offers and delayed their searches for other jobs. When the former employees learned that AT&T was hiring clerical workers and in fact did not intend to hire the laid-off workers for clerical positions in the new plant, the workers brought suit against AT&T for damages caused by their detrimental reliance on AT&T's promises.

Although the trial court held for AT&T, the appellate court, on reviewing the issue, ruled that the employees had a right to recover damages sustained in their reliance on the "clear and unambiguous promise" that AT&T had made and broken.

Quasi Contract

Quasi contracts, often referred to as contracts implied in law, arise to establish justice and fairness. The term *quasi contract* is misleading because a quasi contract is not really a contract at all. It does not arise from any agreement between two individuals. Rather, a court imposes a quasi contract on the parties when justice requires it. Quasi contracts are used to prevent unjust enrichment. The doctrine of unjust enrichment is based on the theory that individuals should not be allowed to profit or enrich themselves inequitably at the expense of others. This belief is fundamental in our society and is clearly inspired by ethical considerations.

We have said previously in this text that all ethical issues involve a tradeoff in one form or another. What tradeoff is involved here? Obviously, by imposing contractual obligations on persons who did not freely enter into those obligations, the government, by way of the courts, is interfering with the personal freedom of individuals to contract as they wish and to be responsible for only those obligations they freely undertake. To a certain extent, when quasi-contractual remedies are granted, this freedom is sacrificed to attain greater justice and fairness by preventing unjust enrichment of one person at the expense of others.

■ Discussion Questions

1. Although minors have the power to avoid contracts, the adults with whom the minors contract do not. Because of this one-sided power, some observers have suggested that the law confers on minors a privilege and that it is thus inaccurate to speak of the "limited" capacity of minors. But there is another side to consider. Adults often refuse to contract with minors, because minors cannot provide legal assurance that they will not disaffirm. From this point of view, minors are under a legal and practical disability, and their power of avoidance may work against their own best interests. As is often the case, the protection of the law limits the liberty of the protected person. Is the price of this protection too high? Would governments best serve the interests of minors by granting them full freedom of contract? Or should the law strike a different balance— perhaps by instituting a younger age of majority or permitting minors to avoid only those contracts that are not beneficial to them?

2. The courts have often relieved signatories to a valid contract from their obligations on a showing of impossibility of performance. Critics of the doctrine of impossibility argue that the price and other contract terms included in any agreement take into account the possibility that unforeseen difficulties might arise that would render the performance of the contract impossible. Therefore, these critics argue, the promisor should be held to his or her promise even when the performance called for by the contract would be excused under the doctrine of impossibility. Do you agree with this conclusion?

3. People rely to their detriment on others' promises in everyday life. Yet the doctrine of promissory estoppel is rarely, if ever, applied in these situations to enable the party who suffered a detriment to recover damages. Would society benefit if courts allowed all persons who suffered from detrimental reliance on others' promises to recover damages incurred by that reliance? If so, in what way? What would be the cost to society if such actions were permitted?

UNIT THREE

Domestic and International Sales Law

■ The Importance of Domestic and International Sales Law

Most of the chapters in this unit deal exclusively with Article 2 of the Uniform Commercial Code (UCC). The official text of the UCC in its entirety (including comments) is more than 700 pages long. It is probably the most sweeping in scope of any uniform law in the United States. As you will read in the opening chapter of this unit, the UCC contains rules that deal with all of the phases that ordinarily arise in the handling of a commercial transaction. An understanding of these fundamental rules is imperative for anyone contemplating a career in business. Because the UCC is the general and inclusive group of laws adopted by all of the states, it is impossible for a person to be in the business world without being affected by some provision of the UCC.

Chapter 18 opens the unit with a discussion of the requirements of sales contracts and how they are formed. The sometimes sticky concept of when title passes and who bears the risk of loss for goods in the process of being sold—for example, goods en route from the seller to the buyer—is examined in Chapter 19, along with the concept of insurable interest. The performance and obligations required under sales contracts are then discussed in Chapter 20. When a breach by either the buyer or the seller occurs, remedies will normally be sought, and these are outlined in Chapter 21. A sale of goods usually carries with it at least one type of warranty. Additionally, the manufacture and sale of products may subject the manufacturers and sellers to liability. These topics—sales warranties and product liability—are covered in Chapters 22 and 23. Finally, no business law text today would be complete without some coverage of the law governing international sales transactions. In Chapter 24, which concludes this unit, we address this topic and point to the ways in which the law governing domestic sales transactions differs from that governing international sales contracts.

■ Ethical Issues in Domestic and International Sales Law

The law of sales has one fundamental guiding principle—the requirement that both parties to a sales contract should act in good faith. Indeed, the UCC is permeated by the concept of good faith. A sister concept is that of commercial reasonableness. It, too, permeates the UCC. By making good faith and commercial reasonableness legal requirements in sales contracts, the UCC has attempted to prevent unethical behavior on the part of American businesspersons.

Ethical considerations lie at the heart of product liability laws and are, to a great extent, responsible for the trend toward product liability litigation in the last several decades. Courts, at least until recently, increasingly sought to compensate consumers harmed by defectively designed or improperly functioning products to balance the scales of justice. Product liability laws are attended by numerous ethical questions, one of which will probably never be answered to everyone's satisfaction: Is it necessarily fair to determine the outcome of a particular liability case simply on the basis of which party has the "deepest pockets"? In other words, should triers of fact award damages to consumers simply because the manufacturers or sellers have so much wealth?

International sales transactions give rise to numerous ethical considerations. For example, is it ethical to market pharmaceutical products in other countries when those products have not yet been approved by the U.S. Food and Drug Administration as safe? Is it ethical to sell children's toys in foreign markets when such toys might not pass muster under the watchful eye of the U.S. Consumer Product Safety Commission?

Sales transactions, whether domestic or international, are fraught with ethical considerations that cannot be ignored by the serious student of business law.

Chapter 18

Introduction to Sales Contracts and Their Formation

Almost every day of our lives we make purchases—the daily newspaper, groceries, clothes, textbooks, compact discs, a car, and so on. For this reason studying the law relating to the sale of goods is relevant to our daily lives.

The people from whom we buy our goods are, to us, sellers. But our sellers are in turn buyers from their suppliers, who are in turn buyers from manufacturers. The law of sales is the study of the rights and responsibilities of those in the purchase-and-sale-of-goods chain, from the original maker of the item to the ultimate user.

■ Historical Perspective

Today's law of sales originated centuries ago in the customs and traditions of merchants and traders. The *Lex Mercantoria* (Law Merchant) was a system of rules, customs, and usages self-imposed by early commercial traders and merchants to settle disputes and to enforce obligations among themselves. These rules were established at "fairs," at which merchants met to exchange goods and settle differences through "fair courts" established and operated by the merchants themselves.

By the end of the seventeenth century, the principles of the Law Merchant had become widely accepted. Quite naturally, they became part of the common law. From that time on, judges, not merchants, refined the principles of mercantile law into the modern commercial law of sales.

In the United States, sales law varied from state to state, and this made multistate sales contracts difficult. The difficulties became especially troublesome in the late nineteenth century as multistate contracts became the norm. For this reason, numerous attempts were made to produce a uniform body of laws relating to commercial transactions. Two major proposals, the Uniform Negotiable Instruments Law (1896) and the Uniform Sales Act (1906), were widely adopted by the states. Several other proposed "uniform acts" followed, although most were not widely adopted.

In the 1940s the need to integrate the half-dozen or so uniform acts covering commercial transactions into a single, comprehensive body of statutory law was recognized. Accordingly, the National Conference of Commissioners on Uniform State Laws developed the Uniform Commercial Code (UCC) to serve that purpose.

■ The Uniform Commercial Code

It is important to note that when we focus on sales contracts, the subject of this chapter, we move away to some extent from common law principles and into a body of statutory law. The UCC is the statutory framework we will use, because it has been adopted as law by all states (with the exception of Louisiana, which has not adopted it in its entirety). Relevant sections of the UCC are noted in the following discussion of sales contracts. You should refer to Appendix C in the back of the book while examining these notations. Many similarities to the contract law discussed in Unit Two will be apparent. Indeed, such similarities should be expected, because the UCC represents the codification of much of the existing common law of contracts.

The UCC is the single most comprehensive codification of the broad spectrum of laws involved in a total commercial transaction. The UCC views the entire "commercial transaction for the sale of and payment for goods" as a single legal occurrence having numerous facets.

As an example, first look at the titles of the articles of the UCC in Appendix C. Now consider a consumer who buys a refrigerator from an appliance store and agrees to pay for it on an installment plan. Several articles of the UCC can be applied to this single commercial transaction. Because there is a contract for the sale of goods, Article 2 will apply. If a check is given as the down payment on the purchase price, it will be negotiated and ultimately passed through one or more banks for collection. This process is the subject matter of Article 3, Commercial Paper, and Article 4, Bank Deposits and Collections. If the appliance store extends credit to the consumer through the installment plan, and if it retains a right in the refrigerator (the collateral), then Article 9, Secured Transactions, will be applicable.

Suppose, in addition, the appliance company must first obtain the refrigerator from its manufacturer's warehouse, after which it is to be delivered by common carrier to the consumer. The storage and shipment of goods is the subject matter of Article 7, Documents of Title. If the appliance company arranges to pay the manufacturer, located in another state, for the refrigerator supplied, a letter of credit, which is the subject matter of Article 5, may be used.

Thus, the UCC attempts to provide a consistent and integrated framework of rules to deal with all the phases *ordinarily arising* in a commercial sales transaction from start to finish.[1]

■ The Scope of Article 2— the Sale of Goods

No body of law operates in a vacuum removed from other principles of jurisprudence. A sales contract is governed by the same common law principles applicable to all contracts—offer, acceptance, consideration, capacity, and legality—and these principles should be reexamined when sales are studied. In regard to sales contracts, it is important to remember that when the UCC speaks, its principles will apply; when the UCC is silent on a given issue, then other state statutes and the common law of contracts will apply. The law of sales, found in Article 2 of the UCC, is a part of the law of contracts.

Two other things should be kept in mind. First, Article 2 deals with the sale of *goods,* not real property (real estate), services, or intangible property such as stocks and bonds. Second, in some cases, the rules may vary quite a bit, depending on whether the buyer or seller is a *merchant.* It is always a good idea to note the subject matter of a dispute and the kind of people involved. If the subject is goods, then the UCC will govern. If it is real estate or services, then the common law will apply.

What Is a Sale?

Section 2-102 of the UCC states that Article 2 "applies to transactions in goods." This implies a broad scope for this article, covering gifts, pur-

---

1. Two articles of the UCC seem not to apply to the "ordinary" commercial sales transaction. Article 6, Bulk Transfers, involves merchants who sell off the major part of their inventory (sometimes pocketing the money and disappearing, leaving creditors unpaid). Because bulk sales do not ordinarily arise in a commercial sales transaction, they are treated separately. Article 8, Investment Securities, deals with transactions involving certain negotiable securities (stocks and bonds), transactions that do not involve a sale of or payment for *goods.* The subject matter of Articles 6 and 8, however, was considered by the UCC's drafters to be related *sufficiently* to commercial transactions to warrant inclusion in the UCC.

chases of goods, and bailments. (A bailment involves delivery of personal property without title for a specific purpose, as when, for example, an individual drops off his or her clothes at the cleaner's. Bailments are discussed more fully in Chapter 50.) For the purposes of this chapter, we will treat Article 2 as applicable only to an actual sale. A **sale** is officially defined "as the passing of title from the seller to the buyer for a price" [UCC 2-106(1)]. The price may be payable in money or in other goods, services, or realty (real estate).

What Are Goods?

To be characterized as a *good,* an item must be *tangible,* and it must be *movable.* A tangible item has physical existence—it can be touched or seen, as can a horse, a car, or a chair. Intangible property, such as corporate stocks and bonds, promissory notes, bank accounts, patents and copyrights, and ordinary contract rights, have only conceptual existence and do not come under Article 2. A *movable* item can be carried from place to place. Hence, real estate is excluded from Article 2.

Two basic areas of dispute arise in determining whether the object of the contract is goods and thus whether Article 2 is applicable. One dispute concerns *goods associated with realty,* such as crops and timber, and the other concerns contracts involving a combination of *goods and services.*

GOODS VERSUS REALTY Goods associated with real estate fall under Article 2. Section 2-107 provides the following rules:

1. A contract for the sale of minerals or the like (including oil and gas) or of a structure (such as a building) is a contract for the sale of goods *if severance, or removal, is to be made by the seller.* If the buyer is to sever the subject of the contract from the land, the contract is considered a sale of real estate governed by the principles of real property law, not the UCC.

To illustrate: Sue agrees to sell Ben a quantity of oil that is located under her property. If Ben is to drill the wells to remove the oil, their contract is a contract for the sale of real estate. If the agreement provides that Sue is to drill the wells to obtain the oil, the transaction is a sale of goods. Similarly, if Sue agrees to sell Ben an old barn located on her farm with Ben to remove the barn, the agree-

ment is a contract for the sale of real estate. If Sue is to remove the barn, the transaction is characterized as a sale of goods under UCC Article 2.

2. A sale of growing crops or timber to be cut is a sale of goods *regardless of who severs them.*

3. Other "things attached" to realty but capable of severance without *material harm* to the land are considered goods regardless of who severs them.[2]

GOODS VERSUS SERVICES When goods and services are combined, courts have disagreed over whether a particular transaction involves the sale of goods or the rendering of a service. For example, is the blood furnished to a patient during an operation a sale of goods or the performance of a medical service? Some courts say a good; some say a service. The same kind of "mixed transaction" problem is encountered when a beautician applies hair dye to a customer in a beauty shop. The UCC does not provide the answer, and court decisions are in conflict. Whether the transaction in question involves the sale of goods or of services is important because the majority of courts treat services as being excluded by the UCC. In discussing their decisions, the courts try to determine which factor is predominant—the good or the service.

Computer software has been held to fall within the UCC's definition of goods, which includes "all things . . . which are movable at the time of the identification for sale."[3] Also, the serving of food or drink to be consumed either on or off restaurant premises involves a sale of goods, at least for the purpose of an *implied warranty of merchantability*[4] [UCC 2-314(1)]. Also, a contract for specially manufactured goods is one for goods, not services [UCC 2-105(1)]. Several other special cases are explicitly characterized as goods by the UCC, including unborn animals, rare coins, and other forms of money as a commodity.

In the following case, the court evaluates whether a mixed transaction was primarily for the sale of goods or the sale of services.

---

2. The UCC avoids using the word *fixtures* here because of the numerous definitions of this term. (See Chapter 49.)
3. See *Advent Systems, Ltd. v. Unisys Corp.,* 925 F.2d 670 (3d Cir. 1991).
4. Every merchant who deals in goods of the kind sold warrants that the goods are merchantable—that is, "reasonably fit for the ordinary purposes for which such goods are used." Implied warranties are examined in Chapter 22.

BACKGROUND AND FACTS   The Suess Brothers contracted with Aerial Farm Service, Inc., for the sale and aerial application of a herbicide on a section of farmland that they rented from Willard Grossman. During the application, the chemical drifted and damaged trees next to the field. More than two years later, Grossman sued in a Minnesota state court for damages, alleging, among other things, negligent application of the herbicide. Aerial Farm Service and others involved in the spraying operation moved for summary judgment, claiming that Grossman's action was barred by the state's two-year statute of limitations governing recovery of damages for improper application of pesticides. The trial court granted the motion. Grossman appealed, contending that the contract was for a sale of goods, not a contract for services. Under the UCC, a four-year statute of limitations applies.

Case 18.1

GROSSMAN v. AERIAL FARM SERVICE, INC.

Court of Appeals of Minnesota, 1986.
384 N.W.2d 488.

DECISION AND RATIONALE   The Court of Appeals of Minnesota affirmed the trial court's decision. The appellate court held that the contract was for services. The court explained that which law applied depended on whether the purpose of a mixed goods and services contract was "the rendition of service, with goods incidentally involved (e.g., contract with artist for painting)" or "a transaction of sale, with labor incidentally involved (e.g., installation of a water heater in a bathroom)." Because the Suess Brothers chose to apply the herbicide by a method that could only be performed by a contractor equipped to handle the specific method, "the dominant purpose and character of the contract * * * became one for services" and not one for the sale of the herbicide.

Who Is a Merchant?

Article 2 governs the sale of goods in general. It applies to sales transactions between all buyers and sellers. In a limited number of instances, however, the UCC presumes that in certain phases of sales transactions involving professional merchants, special business standards ought to be imposed because of the merchants' degree of commercial expertise.[5] Such standards do not apply to the casual or inexperienced seller or buyer. Section 2-104 defines three ways in which merchant status can be determined:

1.   A merchant is a person who deals in goods of the kind involved in the sales contract. Thus, a retailer, a wholesaler, or a manufacturer is a merchant of those goods sold in the business. A merchant for one type of goods is not necessarily a merchant for any other type. For example, a sporting equipment retailer is a merchant when buying tennis equipment but not when buying stereo equipment.

2.   A merchant is a person who, by occupation, holds himself or herself out as having knowledge and skill peculiar to the practices or goods involved in the transaction. This is a broad definition that can include banks or universities as merchants.

3.   A person who employs a merchant as a broker, agent, or other intermediary has the status of merchant in that transaction. Hence, if a "gentleman farmer" who ordinarily does not run the farm hires a broker to purchase livestock, the farmer is considered a merchant in the livestock transaction.

In summary, a person is a merchant when that person, acting in a mercantile capacity, possesses or uses an expertise specifically related to the goods being sold. This basic distinction, however, is not always clear-cut. For example, disagreement has arisen over whether a farmer is a merchant. The answer depends on the particular goods involved, the transaction, and whether, in the particular situation, the farmer has special knowledge concerning the goods involved in the transaction.

---

5.   The provisions that apply only to merchants deal principally with the Statute of Frauds, firm offers, confirmatory memoranda, warranties, and contract modification. These special rules reflect expedient business practice commonly known to merchants in the commercial setting. They will be discussed later in this chapter.

■ Formation of a Sales Contract

The policy of the UCC is to recognize that the law of sales is part of the general law of contracts. The UCC often restates general principles or is silent on certain subjects. In those situations, the common law of contracts and applicable state statutes govern. The following sections summarize how UCC provisions *change* the effect of the general law of contracts.

Offer

In general contract law, the moment a definite offer is met by an unqualified acceptance, a binding contract is formed. In commercial sales transactions, the verbal exchanges, the correspondence, and the actions of the parties may not reveal exactly when a binding contractual obligation arises. The UCC states that an agreement sufficient to constitute a contract can exist even if the moment of its making is undetermined [UCC 2-204(2)].

OPEN TERMS   According to contract law, an offer must be definite enough for the parties (and the courts) to ascertain its essential terms when it is accepted. The UCC states that a sales contract will not fail for indefiniteness even if one or more terms are left open, as long as: (1) the parties intended to make a contract and (2) there is a reasonably certain basis for the court to grant an appropriate remedy [UCC 2-204(3)].

The UCC has lessened the requirements for definiteness of essentials in contracts for sale, but it has not removed the common law requirement that the contract be at least definite enough for the court to identify the agreement so as to enforce it or award appropriate damages on its breach. Two factors should be kept in mind. First, the more terms left open, the less likely the courts will find that the parties intended to form a contract. Second, as a general rule, if the *quantity* term is left open, the courts will have no basis for determining a remedy, and the sales contract will fail unless it is either an output or a requirements contract [UCC 2-306].[6]

The quantity need not be accurately stated, but a contract will not be enforced beyond the amount stated in the writing.

Open Price Term   If the parties have not agreed on a price, the court will determine "a reasonable price *at the time for delivery*" [UCC 2-305(1)]. If either the buyer or the seller is to determine the price, the price is to be fixed in good faith [UCC 2-305(2)].

Sometimes the price fails to be fixed through the fault of one of the parties. In that case, the other party can treat the contract as canceled or fix a reasonable price. For example, Axel and Beatty enter into a contract for the sale of goods and agree that Axel will fix the price, and Axel refuses to fix the price. Beatty can either treat the contract as canceled or can set a reasonable price [UCC 2-305(3)].

Open Payment Term   When parties do not specify payment terms, payment is due at the time and place at which the buyer is to receive the goods [UCC 2-310(a)]. Generally, credit is not used when payment terms are unspecified. The buyer can tender payment in cash or a commercially acceptable substitute, such as a check or a credit card. If the seller demands payment in actual cash, the buyer must be given a reasonable time to obtain it [UCC 2-511(2)]. This is especially important when a definite and final time for performance is stated in the contract.

Open Delivery Term   When no delivery terms are specified, the buyer normally takes delivery at the seller's place of business [UCC 2-308(a)]. If the seller has no place of business, then the seller's residence is used. When goods are located in some other place and both parties know it, then delivery is made there. When the time for shipment or delivery has not been clearly specified in the sales contract, the court will infer a "reasonable" time under the circumstances for performance [UCC 2-309(1)]. The following case illustrates a court's determination of what constitutes a reasonable time for the delivery of produce to be sold at market.

---

6.   An *output contract* is a buyer's agreement to purchase a seller's entire output for a stated period; a *requirements contract* is a seller's agreement to supply a buyer with all the buyer's requirements for certain goods used in his or her operations. Output and requirements contracts are discussed in detail in Chapter 11.

BACKGROUND AND FACTS Mendelson-Zeller Company contracted orally to sell to Joseph Wedner & Son Company a truckload of mixed produce (lettuce and lemons), which was to be handled on consignment. (In a consignment sale, title remains with the seller but the buyer has the right to sell the goods.) The contract price was $1,900. As agreed, Mendelson shipped the produce to arrive, according to Wedner, for the Monday morning market. Due to winter driving conditions, however, the goods arrived Monday at 12:30 P.M. Wedner's docking superintendent refused delivery and told the driver to return Tuesday morning. On Tuesday morning, the produce was unloaded and sold. Wedner gave $1,028.93, the net proceeds, to Mendelson. Mendelson sued for $871.07, the difference between the contract price of $1,900 and the sum paid.

Case 18.2

MENDELSON-ZELLER CO. v. JOSEPH WEDNER & SON CO.
United States Department of Agriculture, 1970.
7 UCC Rep. Serv. 1045.

DECISION AND RATIONALE Mendelson prevailed. The produce was delivered and accepted; the only question was whether delivery was within a reasonable time. The court stated that under Section 2–309(1) of the Uniform Commercial Code, "the time for delivery in the absence of an agreed time shall be a reasonable time." The court held that under the circumstances—the winter driving conditions—delivery was made within a reasonable time. Thus Wedner's failure to pay the full contract price was a breach of contract. The court awarded Mendelson damages, plus interest on the amount owing.

Duration of an Ongoing Contract A single contract may specify successive performances but may not indicate how long the parties are required to deal with one another. Although either party may terminate the ongoing contractual relationship, principles of good faith and sound commercial practice call for reasonable notification before termination so as to give the other party reasonable time to seek a substitute arrangement [UCC 2-309(2), (3)].

Options and Cooperation Regarding Performance When no specific shipping arrangements have been made but the contract contemplates shipment of the goods, the *seller* has the right to make these arrangements in good faith, using commercial reasonableness in the situation [UCC 2-311].

When terms relating to the assortment of goods are omitted from a sales contract, the *buyer* can specify the assortment. For example, Harley and Babcock contract for the sale of 1,000 pens. The pens come in a variety of colors, but the contract is silent on which colors are ordered. Babcock, the buyer, has the right to take whatever colors he wishes. Babcock, however, must make the selection in good faith and must use commercial reasonableness [UCC 2-311].

MERCHANT'S FIRM OFFER The firm offer is in the special category of rules applicable only to merchants. Under common law contract principles, an offer can be revoked any time before acceptance. The major common law exception is an option contract, in which the offeree pays consideration for the offeror's irrevocable promise to keep the offer open for a stated period of time.

The UCC creates a second exception that applies only to **firm offers** for the sale of goods made *by a merchant* (regardless of whether or not the offeree is a merchant). If the merchant gives *assurances* in a *signed writing* that the offer will remain open, the merchant's firm offer is irrevocable, without consideration[7] for the stated period of time, or, if no definite period is specified, a reasonable period (neither period to exceed three months) [UCC 2-205].

To illustrate: Daniels, a used-car dealer, writes a letter to Peters on January 1 stating, "I have a 1986 Dodge Aries on the lot that I'll sell to you for $4,200. This offer will remain open until the end of the month." By January 18, Daniels has

---

7. If the offeree pays consideration, then an *option contract* rather than a *merchant's firm offer* is formed.

Direct marketing is a growing field of business activity. Indeed, it is estimated that 15 percent of all goods are sold through direct-marketing channels, such as through the mails (so-called junk mail), telephone solicitation, television home-shopping programs, and door-to-door sales. The direct marketer faces numerous problems if he or she does not understand the concept of the *firm offer*. Once a firm offer is made, it cannot be revoked. Thus, as a direct marketer, you should never, as a rule, make a firm offer unless you truly plan to keep the offer open. The Uniform Commercial Code specifies that for an offer to be considered a "firm offer," and thus irrevocable, it must (1) concern the purchase and sale of goods; (2) be made by a merchant dealing in those goods; (3) be written and signed by the merchant; and (4) give assurance that it will be held open for some period of time. If an offer you make in the course of your business meets these criteria, it will be a

firm offer, and the offeree can accept and bind you to a contract. Most legal scholars hold that even an offeree's rejection or counteroffer does not terminate a firm offer. Even if there is a lack of consideration, the offer cannot be revoked; it will remain open for the period of time specified in the offer, or, if no time is specified, for a reasonable period (although the period of irrevocability without consideration cannot normally exceed three months).

As a direct marketer, you must be able to distinguish between advertisements that a court would consider merely preliminary negotiations or solicitations to deal with buyers, and advertisements or communications that a court would consider firm offers. Say, for example, that you place the following ad in a magazine: "Classic Hits Compact Discs, $9.95 plus $2.00 shipping and handling; sale ends one month from today." The response is so great that you run out of compact discs (CDs). Are you bound in this situation to a contract with customers who accept your "offer" of the CDs at the price specified? Is

heard nothing from Peters, so he sells the Dodge Aries to another person. Later that day, he sends a notice to Peters that he is revoking his offer. On January 23, Peters tenders $4,200 to Daniels and asks for the car. When Daniels tells him that the car has already been sold, Peters claims that Daniels has breached a good contract. Peters is right. Because Daniels is a merchant of used cars, he is obligated to keep his offer open until the end of January. Because he has not done so, he is liable for breach.

It is necessary that the offer be both *written and signed* by the offeror.[8] When a firm offer is contained in a form contract prepared by the of-

feree, a *separate* firm offer assurance must be signed as well. The purpose of the merchant's firm offer rule is to give effect to a merchant's deliberate intent to be bound to a firm offer. If the firm offer is buried in one of the pages of the offeree's form contract amid copious language, the offeror might inadvertently sign the contract without realizing the firm offer is included, thus defeating the purpose of the rule.

Acceptance

Generally, acceptance of an offer to buy or sell goods may be made in any reasonable manner and by any reasonable means. If the response indicates a definite acceptance of the offer, a contract is formed, even if the response includes additional or different terms—so long as acceptance is not made expressly conditional on the offeror's assent to the new terms. An offeree's additional terms are considered proposals, and the contract is formed on

---

8. "Signed" includes any symbol executed or adopted by a party with present intention to authenticate a writing [UCC 1-201(39)]. A complete signature is not required. Therefore, initials, a thumbprint, a trade name, or any mark used in lieu of a written signature will suffice, regardless of its location on the document.

this a firm offer? No. Although it contains most of the elements necessary for a firm offer to exist—that is, the ad was placed by a merchant, was for the sale of goods, was in writing (a court could assume the ad sufficed as a writing), and was for a definite time period—the offer was not signed by you, and the recipient of the offer in this case is so vague (the general public) that a court would conclude the ad represents a solicitation to deal and not an offer.

But be careful. If, in addition to the price ($9.95 plus $2.00 shipping and handling), quantity (one CD), time period (thirty days), and place (your business address), you also specify a particular recipient (such as first come, first served), a court may consider your ad an offer.

Let's examine another situation. Say Music Retailing Stores, Inc., writes to you and inquires about the price of CDs. You write back and offer to sell CDs to Music Retailing at $9.95 each (plus $2.00 shipping and handling). You state that Music Retailing can accept your offer within thirty days, after which the CDs may not be available at the same price. In the meantime, increasing sales have decreased your inventory. You call the CD plant and learn that its price has increased 300 percent since your last order. You send notice of revocation to Music Retailing. Before the thirty-day period has lapsed, however, Music Retailing accepts your offer. Can you revoke your offer to Music Retailing? No—you are committed to a contract of sale with Music Retailing because the terms and conditions specified in your letter were sufficiently definite and met all the requirements of a firm offer under the UCC.

When determining whether an offer is present, the courts generally use the "reasonable person" test. If a recipient of a price quotation, a letter, or a catalogue ad offering goods for sale at a certain price would "reasonably" conclude that he or she is the intended offeree, and if the other terms and conditions of sale are definite enough, then the ad or announcement may be considered an offer.

the offeror's terms, unless the parties are both merchants. These points are examined in the following sections.

MEANS OF ACCEPTANCE The general common law rule is that an offeror can specify or authorize a particular means of acceptance, making that means the only one effective for the contract. The common law rule has been altered recently, however, so that even unauthorized means of communication are effective as long as the acceptance is received by the specified deadline. For example, suppose the offer states, "Answer by fax within five days." If the offeree sends a letter, and it is received by the offeror within five days, a valid contract is formed.

When the offeror does not specify a means of acceptance, the UCC provides that acceptance can be made by any means of communication reasonable under the circumstances, even if the acceptance is not received within the designated time [UCC 2-206(1)]. For example, Alpha Corporation writes Beta Corporation a letter offering to sell Beta $1,000 worth of goods. The offer states that Alpha will keep the offer open for only ten days from the date of the letter. Before the ten-day period has lapsed, Beta sends Alpha a telegram of acceptance. The telegram is misdirected by the telegraph company and does not reach Alpha until after the deadline. Is a valid contract formed? The answer is yes, because the telegraph appears to be a commercially reasonable medium of acceptance under the circumstances. Acceptance would be effective upon Alpha's delivery of the message to the telegraph office, which occurred before the offer lapsed.

PROMISE TO SHIP OR PROMPT SHIPMENT The UCC permits acceptance of an offer to buy goods for current or prompt shipment by either a *promise* to ship or *prompt shipment* of the goods to the buyer [UCC 2-206(1)(b)]. This provision of the UCC retains the common law means of acceptance of an offer (performance by delivery of conforming goods—that is, goods that are in accordance with the contract terms—to the carrier) and adds as another means of acceptance the commercial practice of sellers who send promises to ship conforming goods. These promises are effective when sent, if they meet the test of being sent by a medium that is commercially reasonable under the circumstances, as discussed above.

The UCC goes one step further and provides that if the seller does not promise to ship conforming goods but instead ships (in response to the order) *nonconforming goods,* this shipment constitutes both an *acceptance* and a *breach.* This rule does not apply if the seller seasonably (within the time agreed on or within a reasonable time) notifies the buyer that the nonconforming shipment is offered only as an *accommodation.* The notice of accommodation must clearly indicate to the buyer that the shipment does not constitute an acceptance and that, therefore, no contract has been formed.

For example, Barrymore orders 1,000 *blue* widgets from Stroh. Stroh ships 1,000 *black* widgets to Barrymore, notifying Barrymore that because Stroh has only black widgets in stock, these are sent as an accommodation. The shipment of black widgets is not an acceptance but a counteroffer, and a contract will be formed only if Barrymore accepts the black widgets.

If, however, Stroh ships 1,000 black widgets instead of blue without notifying Barrymore that the goods are being shipped *as an accommodation,* Stroh's shipment acts as both an acceptance of Barrymore's offer and a *breach* of the resulting contract. Barrymore may sue Stroh for any appropriate damages.

COMMUNICATION OF ACCEPTANCE   At common law, because a unilateral offer invites acceptance by a performance, the offeree need not notify the offeror of performance unless the offeror would not otherwise know about it. The UCC is more stringent than common law, stating that "[w]here the beginning of requested performance is a reasonable mode of acceptance an offeror who is not notified of acceptance within a reasonable time may treat the offer as having lapsed before acceptance" [UCC 2-206(2)].

To illustrate: Johnson writes the Scroll Bookstore on Monday, "Please send me a copy of *West's Business Law* for $55, COD," signed "Johnson."

Scroll receives the request on Tuesday. Scroll immediately prepares the book for shipment but does not ship it for four weeks. Upon its arrival, Johnson rejects the shipment, claiming that the book has arrived too late to be of value.

In this case, because Johnson heard nothing from Scroll for a month, he was justified in assuming that the store did not intend to deliver *West's Business Law.* Johnson could consider that the offer had lapsed because of the length of time that had passed.

ADDITIONAL TERMS   Under traditional common law, if Able makes an offer to Baker, and Baker in turn accepts but adds some slight qualification, there is no contract. This is known as the *mirror image rule* and requires that the acceptance exactly mirror the offer (see Chapter 10). Under this rule, Baker's action would constitute a rejection of, and a counteroffer to, Able's offer.

The UCC generally takes the position that if the offeree's response indicates a *definite* acceptance of the offer, a contract is formed, even if the acceptance includes terms in addition to or different from the original offer [UCC 2-207(1)]. The UCC, however, provides that the offeree's expression cannot be construed as an acceptance if the modifications are subject to (conditional upon) the offeror's assent.

For example, Trevor offers to sell Perry 500 pounds of chicken breasts at a specified price and on specified delivery terms. Perry responds, "I accept your offer for 500 pounds of chicken breasts, and I want that evidenced by a city scale weight certificate."

Perry's response constitutes a contract even though the acceptance adds the words "and I want that evidenced by a city scale weight certificate." If, however, Perry says, "I accept your offer for 500 pounds of chicken breasts on the condition that the weight be evidenced by a city scale weight certificate," there will be no contract unless Trevor so agrees.

Once it has been determined that a contract exists, the next issue to be determined is whether performance will be measured under the offeror's terms or the offeree's terms (which include modifications). The UCC addresses this issue in an attempt to solve the so-called "battle of the forms" between commercial buyers and sellers. *Battle of the forms* is an informal term describing the effect of buyers' and sellers' use of standard purchase or sales forms. If the buyer, for example, uses its standard purchase form to accept an offer contained in the seller's form, the variance in the terms of the two forms results in the problem of determining whose terms form the contract. [See UCC 2-207(2).]

Exhibit 18–1 is an example of a purchase order. The front of the form is the actual order for particular goods. The back contains standard contract clauses and terms governing the sale. These clauses are sometimes modified to meet a particular purchase requirement. The clauses will have even more meaning as you read the following materials on sales.

Rules When Seller or Buyer Is a Nonmerchant
When either the seller or the buyer is a nonmerchant, or when both are nonmerchants, the additional terms are construed as mere proposals, and do not become part of the contract. Thus, the contract is formed on the offeror's terms [UCC 2-207(2)].

For example, O'Hare offers to sell his *personal* car to Green for $1,000. Green replies, ''I accept your offer to purchase your car for $1,000. I would like a new spare tire to be included as part of the purchase price.'' Green has given O'Hare a definite expression of acceptance, creating a contract, even though Green's acceptance also suggests an added term for the offer. Because O'Hare is not a merchant, the additional term is merely a proposal, and O'Hare is not legally obligated to comply. On the other hand, if Green made the spare tire a *condition* of acceptance, then Green would be making a counteroffer and rejecting the original offer.

Rules between Merchants   The UCC rule for additional terms in the acceptance is a little different when both buyer and seller are merchants. In a transaction between merchants, the additional pro-

posed terms *automatically* become part of the contract unless:

1.   They materially alter the original contract.
2.   The offer expressly states that no terms other than those in the offer will be accepted.
3.   The offeror objects to the modified terms in a timely fashion [UCC 2-207(2)].

Suppose Vinson and Brady are merchants. Vinson offers to sell Brady 1,000 pen-and-pencil sets at $10 per set *plus* freight. Brady responds, ''I accept your offer. Price is $10.01 per set, *including* freight.'' There is a contract between Vinson and Brady because Brady made a definite expression of acceptance. Unless Vinson objects to the modification within a reasonable time after receiving notice of the change, Vinson is bound to the $10.01 price per set including freight. Such is not the case, however, if the modification is one that materially alters the contract. What constitutes a material alteration is frequently a question of fact that only a court can decide. Generally, if the modification involves no unreasonable element of surprise or hardship for the offeror, the court will hold that it did not materially alter the contract.

Now suppose that Vinson's offer states, ''1,000 pen-and-pencil sets at a price of $10 per set plus freight. Your acceptance on these terms and these terms only.'' Brady's definite expression of acceptance with the modified freight terms still constitutes a contract. Because Vinson's offer specifically restricts his obligations to the terms of the offer, however, the contract is formed on Vinson's terms of ''$10 per set plus freight.''

In the following case, the court considers the question of whether a seller's written confirmation of a buyer's oral orders for carpet was an ''acceptance expressly conditioned on the buyer's consent to additional terms'' (specifically, an arbitration provision), and whether the arbitration clause materially altered the contract.

BACKGROUND AND FACTS   Frank Dorton, a representative of the Carpet Mart, bought some carpets from Collins & Aikman Corporation, a carpet manufacturer. Collins & Aikman included in its acknowledgment form (a form confirming its acceptance of Dorton's order) a provision stating that its acceptance of Dorton's order was ''subject to all of the terms and conditions on the face and reverse side [of the acknowledgment form] including arbitration, all of which are accepted by the buyer.'' When Dorton dis-

Case 18.3

DORTON v. COLLINS & AIKMAN CORP.

United States Court of Appeals, Sixth Circuit, 1972.
453 F.2d 1161.

covered that the carpets were of a lower-quality fiber than Collins & Aikman had promised, Dorton sued Collins & Aikman in a federal district court for fraudulent misrepresentation. Collins & Aikman moved to stay (suspend) the litigation, claiming that the dispute should be arbitrated under the arbitration provision in its acceptance. The trial court denied the motion, and Collins & Aikman appealed.

DECISION AND RATIONALE   The United States Court of Appeals for the Sixth Circuit remanded the case to the trial court for further proceedings, particularly for a determination as to whether the addition of the arbitration clause in Collins & Aikman's acceptance constituted a material alteration of Dorton's offer. Under the common law, an acceptance or confirmation that added to or varied the terms of the offer constituted a counteroffer, and the parties, without acceptance of the counteroffer, were not bound in contract. UCC 2–207(1) provides for a different result; unless the acceptance expressly conditions the additional terms on the assent of the offeror, a contract is formed. In addition, if a contract is formed between merchants, the additional terms become a part of the contract unless these terms materially alter the terms of the offer [UCC 2–207(2)]. In the words of the appellate court: "We believe that the question of whether the arbitration provision materially altered the oral offer under Subsection 2–207(2)(b) is one which can be resolved only by the [trial court] on further findings of fact in the present case. If the arbitration provision did in fact materially alter The Carpet Mart's offer, it could not become a part of the contract 'unless expressly agreed to' by The Carpet Mart."

Consideration

The UCC radically changes the common law rule that contract modification must be supported by new consideration. Section 2-209(1) states that "an agreement modifying a contract needs no consideration to be binding." Of course, contract modification must be sought in good faith [UCC 1-203]. Modifications *extorted* from the other party are in bad faith and therefore unenforceable.

For example, Hal agrees to manufacture and sell certain goods to Betty for a stated price. Subsequently, a sudden shift in the market makes it difficult for Hal to sell the items to Betty at the given price without suffering a loss. Hal tells Betty of the situation, and Betty agrees to pay an additional sum for the goods. Later, Betty reconsiders and refuses to pay more than the original price. Under Section 2-209(1) of the UCC, Betty's promise to modify the contract needs no consideration to be binding. Hence, Betty is bound by the modified contract.

In the example above, a shift in the market provides an example of a *good faith* reason for contract modification. Section 1-203 states: "Every contract or duty within this act imposes an

obligation of good faith in its performance or enforcement." Good faith in a merchant is defined to mean honesty in fact and the observance of reasonable commercial standards of fair dealing in the trade [UCC 2-103(1)(b)]. But what if there really was no shift in the market, and Hal knew that Betty needed the goods immediately but refused to deliver unless Betty agreed to pay an additional sum of money? This sort of extortion of a modification without a legitimate commercial reason would be ineffective because it would violate the duty of good faith. Hal would not be permitted to enforce the higher price.

There are situations in which modification without consideration must be written to be enforceable. For example, the contract itself may prohibit its modification or rescission except by signed writing. Therefore, only those changes agreed to in the signed writing are enforceable [UCC 2-209(2)]. If a consumer (nonmerchant buyer) is dealing with a merchant, and the merchant supplies the form that contains the prohibition against oral modification, the consumer must sign a separate acknowledgment of the clause.

Also, any modification that brings the contract under the Statute of Frauds must usually be in writ-

Exhibit 18–1 An Example of a Purchase Order (Front)

IBM

Purchase Order

IBM DATA

SUPPLIER	MACH	U/M	OC	SUC	PP	REC	EXP	COMMODITY	MM	DEPT. ORDER	ALT	JOB NO.	DEPT. CHG.	APPROP.	CC	PR ORIG.	CHG. RN

NUMBER DATE

REC. NO.	B.J. S.O. OR REF. NO.	ACCOUNT NO.	COMMITMENT

REMIT TO→

NOTIFY BUYER IMMEDIATELY IF REMIT TO ADDRESS IS DIFFERENT ON INVOICE.

SHIP TO

IBM 11400 BURNET ROAD AUSTIN, TEXAS 78758 BLDG.

OTHER THAN ABOVE

CODE — TAXES

DO NOT CHARGE TEXAS SALES USE TAX SINCE WE PAY DIRECT OUR DIRECT PAY AUTHORIZATION NUMBER IS:

3-000001-7281-4

SPECIFICATION CODE

1. Print Attached.
2. Specifications Attached.
3. Sample Attached.
4. Print in Your Possession.
5. Specification in Your Possession.
6. Sample in Your Possession.

SEE CODE BELOW

SHIP VIA

IBM DATA

F.O.B. SHIP POINT DESTINATION

IBM DATA

YOUR TERMS OF PAYMENT

TRANSPORTATION ROUTING GUIDELINES
(DO NOT INSURE OR DECLARE VALUE)

- 0-99 (45kg.) United Parcel Service, if available. If not,
- 0-40 (18kg.) Parcel Post *(Zones 1-8)* up to $1000 value.
- All other Ship as indicated in "ship via" block.

IMPORTANT

1. SHOW OUR COMPLETE ORDER NUMBER, ITEM NUMBER AND IBM PART NUMBER (IF ANY) ON ALL INVOICES, SHIPPING CONTAINERS, PACKING LISTS AND CORRESPONDENCE
2. SECURELY ATTACH PACKING SLIP TO OUTSIDE OF CARTON.
3. PACKAGES WEIGHING OVER 75 LBS MUST BE PACKAGED FOR HANDLING WITH A MECHANICAL DEVICE

ITEM	PART NUMBER		E/C LEVEL	SHIP TO ARRIVE	QUANTITY	U/M	UNIT PRICE	U/M

*TOTAL QUANTITY OF ITEM ORDERED

"SUBJECT TO THE TERMS AND CONDITIONS ON THE BACK HEREOF WHICH ARE INCORPORATED AND MADE A PART HEREOF"

ADDRESS ALL INVOICES TO:
INTERNATIONAL BUSINESS MACHINES CORP.
Attn: Accounts Payable
P. O. Box 9928
Austin, Texas 78766

AUTHORIZED SIGNATURE

512-838-3300 EXT.

942-0262-4

Source: Reprinted with the permission of the IBM Corporation. © 1985. Copyright: IBM.

■ **Exhibit 18–1 (Continued) An Example of a Purchase Order (Back)**

STANDARD TERMS AND CONDITIONS

IBM EXPRESSLY LIMITS ACCEPTANCE TO THE TERMS SET FORTH ON THE FACE AND REVERSE SIDE OF THIS PURCHASE ORDER AND ANY ATTACHMENTS HERETO:

PURCHASE ORDER CONSTITUTES COMPLETE AGREEMENT	This Purchase order, including the terms and conditions on the face and reverse side hereof and any attachments hereto, contains the complete and final agreement between International Business Machines Corporation (IBM) and Seller. Reference to Seller's bids or proposals, if noted on this order, shall not affect terms and conditions hereof, unless specifically provided to the contrary herein, and no other agreement or quotation in any way modifying any of said terms and conditions will be binding upon IBM unless made in writing and signed by IBM's authorized representative.
ADVERTISING	Seller shall not, without first obtaining the written consent of IBM, in any manner advertise, publish or otherwise disclose the fact that Seller has furnished, or contracted to furnish to IBM, the material and/or services ordered hereunder.
APPLICABLE LAW	The agreement arising pursuant to this order shall be governed by the laws of the State of New York. No rights, remedies and warranties available to IBM under this contract or by operation of law are waived or modified unless expressly waived or modified by IBM in writing.
CASH DISCOUNT OR NET PAYMENT PERIOD	Calculations will be from the date an acceptable invoice is received by IBM. Any other arrangements agreed upon must appear on this order and on the invoice.
CONFIDENTIAL INFORMATION	Seller shall not disclose to any person outside of its employ, or use for any purpose other than to fulfill its obligations under this order, any information received from IBM pursuant to this order, which has been disclosed to Seller by IBM in confidence, except such information which is otherwise publicly available or is publicly disclosed by IBM subsequent to Seller's receipt of such information or is rightfully received by Seller from a third party. Upon termination of this order, Seller shall return to IBM upon request all drawings, blueprints, descriptions or other material received from IBM and all materials containing said confidential information. Also, Seller shall not disclose to IBM any information which Seller deems to be confidential, and it is understood that any information received by IBM, including all manuals, drawings and documents will not be of a confidential nature or restrict, in any manner, the use of such information by IBM. Seller agrees that any legend or other notice on any information supplied by Seller, which is inconsistent with the provisions of this article, does not create any obligation on the part of IBM.
GIFTS	Seller shall not make or offer gifts or gratuities of any type to IBM employees or members of their families. Such gifts or offerings may be construed as Seller's attempt to improperly influence our relationship.
IBM PARTS	All parts and components bailed by IBM to Seller for incorporation in work being performed for IBM shall be used solely for such purposes.
OFF-SPECIFICATION	Seller shall obtain from IBM written approval of all off-specification work.
PACKAGES	Packages must bear IBM's order number and show gross, tare and net weights and/or quantity.
PATENTS	Seller will settle or defend, at Seller's expense (and pay any damages, costs or fines resulting from), all proceedings or claims against IBM, its subsidiaries and affiliates and their respective customers, for infringement, or alleged infringement, by the goods furnished under this order, or any part or use thereof of patents (including utility models and registered designs) now or hereafter granted in the United States or in any country where Seller, its subsidiaries or affiliates, heretofore has furnished similar goods. Seller will, at IBM's request, identify the countries in which Seller, its subsidiaries or affiliates, heretofore has furnished similar goods.
PRICE	If price is not stated on this order, Seller shall invoice at lowest prevailing market price.
QUALITY	Material is subject to IBM's inspection and approval within a reasonable time after delivery. If specifications are not met, material may be returned at Seller's expense and risk for all damages incidental to the rejection. Payment shall not constitute an acceptance of the material nor impair IBM's right to inspect or any of its remedies.
SHIPMENT	Shipment must be made within the time stated on this order, failing which IBM reserves the right to purchase elsewhere and charges Seller with any loss incurred, unless delay in making shipment is due to unforeseeable causes beyond the control and without the fault or negligence of Seller.
SUBCONTRACTS	Seller shall not subcontract or delegate its obligations under this order without the written consent of IBM. Purchases of parts and materials normally purchased by Seller or required by this order shall not be construed as subcontracts or delegations.
(NON-U.S. LOCATIONS ONLY)	Seller further agrees that during the process of bidding or production of goods and services hereunder, it will not re-export or divert to others any IBM specification, drawing or other data, or any product of such data.
TAXES	Unless otherwise directed, Seller shall pay all sales and use taxes imposed by law upon or on account of this order. Where appropriate, IBM will reimburse Seller for this expense.
TOOLS	IBM owned tools held by Seller are to be used only for making parts for IBM. Tools of any kind held by Seller for making IBM's parts must be repaired and renewed by Seller at Seller's expense.
TRANSPORTATION	Routing—As indicated in transportation routing guidelines on face of this order. F.O.B.—Unless otherwise specified, ship collect, F.O.B. origin. Prepaid Transportation (when specified)—Charges must be supported by a paid freight bill or equivalent. Cartage) No charge allowed Premium Transportation) unless authorized Insurance) by IBM. Consolidation—Unless otherwise instructed, consolidate all daily shipments to one destination on one bill of lading.
COMPLIANCE WITH LAWS AND REGULATIONS	Seller shall at all times comply with all applicable Federal, State and local laws, rules and regulations.
EQUAL EMPLOYMENT OPPORTUNITY	There are incorporated in this order the provisions of Executive Order 11246 (as amended) of the President of the United States on Equal Employment Opportunity and the rules and regulations issued pursuant thereto with which the Seller represents that he will comply, unless exempt.
EMPLOYMENT AND PROCUREMENT PROGRAMS	There are incorporated in this order the following provisions as they apply to performing work under Government procurement contracts: Utilization of Small Business Concerns (if in excess of $10,000) (Federal Procurement Regulation (FPR) 1-1.710-3(a)); Small Business Subcontracting Program (if in excess of $500,000) (FPR 1-1.710-3 (b)); Utilization of Labor Surplus Area Concerns (if in excess of $10,000) (FPR 1-1.805-3(a)); Labor Surplus Area Subcontracting Program (if in excess of $500,000) (FPR 1-1.805-3 (b)); Utilization of Minority Enterprises (if in excess of $10,000) (FPR 1-1.1310-2 (a)); Minority Business Enterprises Subcontracting Program (if in excess of $50,000) (FPR 1-1.1310-2(b)); Affirmative Action for Handicapped Workers (if $2,500 or more) (41 CFR 60-741.4); Affirmative Action for Disabled Veterans and Veterans of the Vietnam Era (if $10,000 or more) (41 CFR 60-250.4); Utilization of Small Business Concerns and Small Business Concerns Owned and Controlled by Socially and Economically Disadvantaged Individuals (if in excess of $10,000) (44 Fed. Reg. 23610 (April 20, 1979)); Small Business and Small Disadvantaged Business Subcontracting Plan (if in excess of $500,000) (44 Fed. Reg. 23610 (April 20, 1979)).
WAGES AND HOURS	Seller warrants that in the performance of this order Seller has complied with all of the provisions of the Fair Labor Standards Act of 1938 of the United States as amended.
WORKERS' COMPENSATION, EMPLOYERS' LIABILITY INSURANCE	If Seller does not have Workers' Compensation or Employer's Liability Insurance, Seller shall indemnify IBM against all damages sustained by IBM resulting from Seller's failure to have such insurance.

Source: Reprinted with the permission of the IBM Corporation. © 1985. Copyright: IBM.

ing to be enforceable. Thus, if an oral contract for the sale of goods priced at $400 is modified so that the goods are priced at $600, the modification will have to be in writing to be enforceable because under that statute, contracts for the sale of goods for the price of $500 or more must be in writing to be enforceable [UCC 2-209(3)]. If, however, the buyer accepts delivery of the goods after the modification, he or she is bound to the $600 price [UCC 2-201(3)(c)].

Statute of Frauds

Section 2-201(1) of the UCC contains a Statute of Frauds provision that applies to contracts for the sale of goods. The provision requires a writing for the contract to be enforceable when the price of the goods is $500 or more. The parties can have an initial oral agreement, however, and satisfy the Statute of Frauds by having a subsequent written memorandum of their oral agreement. In each case the writing must have been signed by the party against whom enforcement is sought.

WRITTEN CONFIRMATION BETWEEN MERCHANTS   Once again the UCC provides a special rule for contracts for the sale of goods between merchants. In transactions between merchants, the requirements of a writing for the Statute of Frauds are satisfied if, after the parties have agreed orally, one of the merchants sends a signed written confirmation to the other merchant. The communication must indicate the terms of the agreement, and the merchant receiving the confirmation must have reason to know of its contents. Unless the merchant who receives the confirmation gives *written* notice of objection to its contents within ten days after receipt, the writing will be sufficient against this merchant even though he or she has not signed anything.

For example, Jonas is a Miami merchant buyer. He contracts over the telephone to purchase $5,000 worth of goods from Sarah, a New York City merchant seller. Two days later Sarah sends written confirmation detailing the terms of the oral contract, which Jonas later receives. If Jonas wishes to use the Statute of Frauds as a defense against enforcement of the contract against him, he must give Sarah written notice of objection to the contents of the written confirmation within ten days of receipt.

RELAXED REQUIREMENTS   The UCC has greatly relaxed the requirements for the sufficiency of a writing to satisfy the Statute of Frauds. A written contract or a memorandum will be sufficient as long as it indicates that a sales contract was intended and, with the exception for contracts between merchants mentioned above, as long as it is signed by the party against whom enforcement is sought. Except in the case of output and requirements contracts, a contract is not enforceable beyond the quantity of goods shown in the writing. All other terms can be proved in court by oral testimony. Often, terms that are not agreed on can be supplied by the open term provisions of Article 2 itself.

The importance of including some indication of the quantity term in the writing is illustrated by the following case. As the court indicates, if the writing is silent as to quantity, quantity cannot be created "out of thin air" by parol evidence.

BACKGROUND AND FACTS   Lorillard, Inc., orally agreed with Thomas J. Kline, Inc., to sell tobacco products to Kline and to grant Kline certain credit terms. On January 15, Lorillard wrote a letter to Kline, stating that "your request to purchase Lorillard products on a direct basis has been approved" and that credit would be extended for up to fifteen days following Kline's receipt of any goods ordered. In early February, Kline placed a $30,000 order with Lorillard. Lorillard refused to ship the goods unless Kline wired $30,000 in cash before delivery. A few weeks later, Kline and Lorillard again agreed on credit arrangements and the transaction went forward, but the delay caused serious losses for Kline. Kline sued Lorillard in a federal district court for damages, alleging, among other claims, that Lorillard had breached a contract. Lorillard contended that the contract was unenforceable under the Statute of Frauds because the only evidence of the deal

Case 18.4

THOMAS J. KLINE, INC. v. LORILLARD, INC.

United States Court of Appeals, Fourth Circuit, 1989.

878 F.2d 791.

was the January 15 confirmation letter, which contained no quantity term. The court found Lorillard's revocation of credit to be a breach of contract and awarded Kline $2,053,466 in damages. Lorillard appealed.

DECISION AND RATIONALE   The United States Court of Appeals for the Fourth Circuit reversed the district court's decision. The appellate court reasoned that because the writing signed by Lorillard contained no indication of quantity, the Statute of Frauds barred Kline's claim for breach of contract. Under Maryland law (the applicable state law) and the UCC, to be enforceable under the Statute of Frauds, a writing must evidence a contract for a sale of goods, be signed by the party against whom enforcement is sought, and specify the quantity of goods to be sold. The January 15 letter obviously evidenced the sale and was signed by Lorillard, but it did not mention the quantity of tobacco products sold. The court said, "The Statute of Frauds was enacted to avoid the potential for injustice in precisely these circumstances. Parol evidence cannot create quantity out of thin air."

EXCEPTIONS   Section 2-201 defines three exceptions to the Statute of Frauds requirement [UCC 2-201(3)]. A contract, if proved to exist, will be enforceable despite the absence of a writing, even if it involves a sale of goods for the price of $500 or more, under the following circumstances:

1.   *The oral contract is for (a) specially manufactured goods for a particular buyer; (b) these goods are not suitable for resale to others in the ordinary course of the seller's business; and (c) the seller has substantially started to manufacture the goods or made commitments for the manufacture of the goods.* In this situation, once the seller has taken action, the buyer cannot repudiate the agreement claiming the Statute of Frauds as a defense.

To illustrate: Archer orders a uniquely styled cabinet from Collins, a cabinetmaker. The price of the cabinet is $1,000, and the contract is oral. Collins finishes the cabinet and offers to deliver it to Archer. Archer refuses to pay for it even though the job is completed on time. Archer claims that he is not liable because the contract is oral. If the unique style of the cabinet makes it improbable that Collins can find another buyer, then Archer is liable to Collins. Note that Collins must have made a substantial beginning in manufacturing the specialized item prior to Archer's repudiation. Of course, the court must be convinced that there was actually an oral contract.

2.   *The party against whom enforcement of a contract is sought admits in pleadings (written answers), testimony, or other court proceedings that a contract for sale was made.* In this case the contract will be enforceable even though it was oral, but enforceability is limited to the quantity of goods admitted.

To illustrate: Archer and Collins negotiate an agreement over the telephone. During the negotiations, Archer requests a delivery price for 500 gallons of gasoline and a separate price for 700 gallons of gasoline. Collins replies that the price is the same, $1.60 per gallon. Archer verbally orders 500 gallons. Collins honestly believes that Archer has ordered 700 gallons and tenders that amount. Archer refuses the shipment of 700 gallons, and Collins sues for breach. Archer's answer and testimony admit an oral contract was made, but only for 500 gallons. Because Archer admits the existence of the oral contract, Archer cannot plead the Statute of Frauds as a defense. The contract is enforceable, however, only to the extent of the quantity admitted, 500 gallons.

3.   *Some payment has been made and accepted or some goods have been received and accepted.* This is the "partial performance" exception. The oral contract will be enforced to the extent of the amount of performance that *actually* took place.

To illustrate: Archer orally contracts to sell Collins ten chairs at $100 each. Before delivery, Collins sends Archer a check for $500, which Archer cashes. Later, when Archer attempts to deliver the chairs, Collins refuses delivery, claiming the Statute of Frauds as a defense, and demands the return of his $500. Under the UCC's partial

■ **Exhibit 18–2 Major Differences between Contract Law and Sales Law**

	Contract Law	Sales Law
Contract Terms	Contract must contain all material terms.	Open terms acceptable, if parties intended to form a contract, but contract not enforceable beyond quantity term.
Acceptance	Mirror image rule applies. If additional terms added in acceptance, counteroffer is created.	Additional terms will not negate acceptance unless acceptance is made expressly conditional on assent to the additional terms.
Contract Modification	Requires consideration.	Does not require consideration.
Irrevocable Offers	Option contracts (with consideration).	Merchants' firm offers (without consideration).
Statute of Frauds Requirements	All material terms must be included in the writing.	Writing required only for sale of goods of $500 or more but not enforceable beyond quantity specified. *Exceptions:* 1. Contracts for specially manufactured goods. 2. Contracts admitted to under oath by party against whom enforcement is sought. 3. Contracts will be enforced to extent goods delivered or paid for. 4. Confirmatory memorandum (between merchants): Contract is enforceable if merchant fails to object in writing to confirming memorandum within ten days.

performance rule, Archer can enforce the oral contract by tender of delivery of five chairs for the $500 accepted. Similarly, if Collins had made no payment but had accepted the delivery of five chairs from Archer, the oral contract would have been enforceable against Collins for $500, the price of the five chairs delivered.

These exceptions and other ways in which sales law differs from general contract law are summarized in Exhibit 18–2.

Parol Evidence

If the parties to a contract set forth its terms in a confirmatory memorandum (a writing expressing offer and acceptance of the deal) or in a writing intended as their final expression, the terms of the contract cannot be contradicted by evidence of any prior negotiations or agreements or contemporaneous oral agreements. The terms of the contract can be explained or supplemented by consistent additional terms, however, or by *course of dealing, usage of trade,* or *course of performance* [UCC 2-202].

CONSISTENT ADDITIONAL TERMS   If the court finds an ambiguity in a writing that is supposed to be a complete and exclusive statement of the agreement between the parties, it may accept evidence of consistent additional terms to clarify or remove the ambiguity. The court will not, however, accept evidence of contradictory terms. This is the rule under both the UCC and the common law of contracts.

COURSE OF DEALING AND USAGE OF TRADE

In construing a commercial agreement, the court will assume that the *course of dealing* between the parties and the *usage of trade* were taken into account when the agreement was phrased [UCC 2-202 and 1-201(3)]. The UCC states, "A course of dealing between the parties and any usage of trade in the vocation or trade in which they are engaged or of which they are or should be aware give particular meaning to [the terms of an agreement] and supplement or qualify the terms of [the] agreement" [UCC 1-205(3)]. The UCC has determined, then, that the meaning of any agreement, evidenced by the language of the parties and by their action, must be interpreted in light of commercial practices and other surrounding circumstances.

A **course of dealing** is a sequence of previous conduct between the parties to a particular transaction that establishes a common basis for their understanding [UCC 1-205(1)]. Course of dealing is restricted, literally, to the sequence of conduct between the parties that has occurred prior to the agreement in question. **Usage of trade** is defined as any practice or method of dealing having such regularity of observance in a place, vocation, or trade as to justify an expectation that it will be observed with respect to the transaction in question [UCC 1-205(2)]. The expressed terms of an agreement and an applicable course of dealing or usage of trade will be construed to be consistent with each other whenever reasonable. When such construction is *unreasonable,* however, the expressed terms in the agreement will prevail [UCC 1-205(4)].

Parol evidence of a course of dealing or usage of trade that is not inconsistent with the terms of the written agreement can be introduced in situations in which both parties knew or should have known of the existence of the particular custom or usage in that industry in that locality. Such evidence is supplemental and shows the meaning that the parties attach to the particular language. It does not alter the contract terms. Just as a previous course of dealing between parties can be regarded as establishing a common basis for interpreting their expressions and conduct [UCC 1-205(1)], so, too, can a usage of trade establish a common basis for interpreting expressions or conduct [UCC 1-205(2)]. In the following case, the court permitted the introduction of evidence of usage and custom in the trade to explain the meaning of quantity figures that the parties took for granted when the contract was formed.

Case 18.5

HEGGBLADE-MARGULEAS-TENNECO, INC. v. SUNSHINE BISCUIT, INC.

Court of Appeal of California, Fifth District, 1976. 59 Cal.App.3d 948, 131 Cal.Rptr. 183.

BACKGROUND AND FACTS Heggblade-Marguleas-Tenneco, Inc. (HMT), contracted to supply Sunshine Biscuit, Inc., with processing potatoes (potatoes to be used in the production of potato-snack foods). HMT had never marketed processing potatoes before. On October 1, HMT hired Heinie Hoffman, who had over twenty years' experience in the potato-processing industry, to obtain more marketing contracts for its potatoes and to assist in selling the potatoes HMT was planning to grow. Hoffman signed contracts with Sunshine Biscuit for HMT on October 15. The quantity mentioned in the negotiations was 100,000 sacks. It was agreed that the amount would vary somewhat with Sunshine Biscuit's needs. Subsequently, a decline in demand for Sunshine Biscuit products severely reduced its need for potatoes, and it prorated the reduced demand among its suppliers as fairly as possible. Sunshine Biscuit was able to take only 60,105 sacks from HMT. In HMT's suit in a California state court for breach of contract, Sunshine Biscuit introduced evidence that it is customary in the potato-processing industry for the number of potatoes specified in contracts to be reasonable estimates rather than exact numbers. The trial court held for Sunshine Biscuit. HMT appealed.

DECISION AND RATIONALE The Court of Appeal of California affirmed the trial court's ruling that evidence of custom in the potato-processing trade was admissible. The appellate court quoted from a comment to UCC

202(a): "[I]n order that the true understanding of the parties as to the agreement may be [reached, such] writings are to be read on the assumption that * * * the usages of trade were taken for granted when the document was phrased. Unless carefully negated they have become an element of the meaning of the words used." Sunshine Biscuit did not have to pay HMT for the difference between the 100,000 sacks of potatoes it estimated it would need and the 60,105 sacks of potatoes it actually purchased.

COURSE OF PERFORMANCE A **course of performance** is the conduct that occurs under the terms of a particular agreement. The course of performance actually undertaken is the best indication of what the parties to an agreement intended it to mean, because presumably the parties themselves know best what they meant by their words [UCC 2-208].

To illustrate: Akron Lumber Company contracts with Blauveldt to sell Blauveldt a specified number of "2 by 4s." Akron agrees to deliver the lumber in five separate deliveries. Blauveldt accepts the first three deliveries but rejects the fourth, claiming that Akron has breached the contract by delivering lumber measuring $1\frac{7}{8}$ inches by $3\frac{3}{4}$ inches rather than 2 inches by 4 inches. Akron can argue that in the trade (usage of trade) 2 by 4s are commonly $1\frac{7}{8}$ inches by $3\frac{3}{4}$ inches and that Blauveldt, by accepting the lumber without objection in the three previous deliveries under the agreement (course of performance), attested to his understanding that "2 by 4" actually means "$1\frac{7}{8}$ by $3\frac{3}{4}$."

RULES OF CONSTRUCTION The UCC provides *rules of construction* for the interpretation of contracts. Express terms, course of performance, course of dealing, and usage of trade are to be construed together when they do not contradict one another. When such construction is unreasonable, however, the following order of priority controls: (1) express terms, (2) course of performance, (3) course of dealing, and (4) usage of trade [UCC 1-205(4) and 2-208(2)].

Unconscionability

An unconscionable contract is one that is so unfair and one-sided that enforcing it would be unreasonable. Section 2-302 allows the court to evaluate a contract or any clause in a contract. If the court deems it to be unconscionable *at the time it was made,* the court can (1) refuse to enforce the contract, or (2) enforce the remainder of the contract without the unconscionable clause, or (3) limit the application of any unconscionable clauses to avoid an unconscionable result.

The court, in determining whether a contract or clause is unconscionable, must decide whether, in light of general commercial practice and the commercial needs of the particular trade involved, the contract or clause is so one-sided as to be unconscionable under the circumstances at the time the contract was made. In this day of consumer law, more and more consumer sales contracts are being attacked as unconscionable. Typical cases involve high-pressure salespersons and uneducated consumers who contract away their basic rights. In general, the courts have concluded that unequal bargaining power, coupled with unscrupulous dealings by one party, will result in an unenforceable, unconscionable contract.

It is noteworthy that the doctrine of unconscionability expressed explicitly in Section 2-302 is a codification of a pre-UCC notion. The right of the courts to refuse to enforce all of the terms agreed to by the parties to a contract has been recognized for centuries. Equity courts have refused to grant performance of a contract deemed unfair (unconscionable). One of the leading cases involved Campbell Soup Company.[9] The form contract prepared by Campbell Soup contained a clause that excused the company from accepting goods under certain circumstances. Additionally, the clause prohibited the seller of the goods from selling them elsewhere without Campbell's written consent. The court refused to grant specific performance in this classic case on the basis that this clause was unconscionable.

The inclusion of Section 2-302 in the UCC reflects an increased sensitivity to certain realities

---

9. *Campbell Soup Co. v. Wentz,* 172 F.2d 80 (3d Cir. 1948). This case is presented in Chapter 13 as Case 13.5.

of modern commercial activities. Classical contract theory holds that a contract is a bargain in which the terms have been worked out *freely* between parties that are equals. In many modern commercial transactions, this premise is invalid. Standard form contracts are often signed by consumer-buyers who understand few of the terms used and who often do not even read them. Virtually all of the terms are advantageous to the parties supplying the standard form contract. With Section 2-302, the courts have a powerful weapon for policing such transactions, as the next case illustrates.

Case 18.6

JONES v. STAR CREDIT CORP.

Supreme Court of New York, Nassau County, 1969. 59 Misc.2d 189, 298 N.Y.S.2d 264.

BACKGROUND AND FACTS   Clifton and Cora Jones, welfare recipients, agreed to buy a freezer for $900 as the result of a salesperson's visit to their home. Sales taxes, insurance, and financing charges raised the total price to $1,439.69. The Joneses sued Star Credit Corporation in a New York state court to have the purchase contract declared unconscionable under the UCC. At trial, the freezer was found to have a maximum retail value of approximately $300.

DECISION AND RATIONALE   The Supreme Court of New York (a New York trial court) entered judgment for the Joneses. The contract was reformed so that they were required to make no further payments. The court relied on UCC 2–302, which authorizes a court to "limit the application of any unconscionable clause to avoid any unconscionable result." The court considered the disparity between the purchase price and the retail value, the credit charges that alone exceeded the retail value, and the sellers' knowledge of the buyers' limited resources to render the contract unconscionable under the UCC.

ETHICAL CONSIDERATIONS   A court may be reluctant to find a contract unconscionable if the retail price and the total installment-payment purchase price differ by a reasonable amount or if credit charges are reasonable in light of current interest rates. Generally, the court has to balance two ethical premises, and the public policies based on them, in determining whether a contract is unconscionable. On the one hand, the law seeks to preserve the integrity of contracts and allow people to deal and bargain as they will. On the other hand, the law seeks to protect individuals from becoming victimized by—in this court's words—the "exploitive" and "callous" practices of those with grossly superior bargaining power.

■ Leases

The UCC also now applies to leases of goods under a separate section, Article 2A. Article 2A covers any transaction that creates a lease and includes subleases of goods [UCC 2-102, 2-103(k)]. The article defines a **lease agreement** as the lessor and lessee's bargain, as found in their language and as implied by other circumstances, including course of dealing and usage of trade or course of performance [UCC 2A-103(k)]. A **lessor** is one who sells the right to possession and use of goods under a lease [UCC 2A-103(p)]. A **lessee** is one who acquires the right to possession and use of goods under a lease [UCC 2A-103(o)].

In short, Article 2A is a repetition of Article 2, except that it applies to leases, instead of sales, of goods and thus varies to reflect differences between sale and lease transactions. Differences between the provisions of Article 2 and Article 2A include the following.

Article 2A does not provide for acceptance by shipment of goods or for additional terms in an acceptance or confirmation [UCC 2A-206]. Under Article 2, an oral contract is enforceable if the price

■ CONCEPT SUMMARY 18.1
The Formation of Sales Contracts

Offer and Acceptance	1. The acceptance of unilateral offers can be made by a promise to ship or by shipment itself [UCC 2-206(1)(b)].
	2. Not all terms have to be included for a contract to result [UCC 2-204].
	3. Particulars of performance can be left open [UCC 2-204(3), 2-311(1)].
	4. Firm written offers made by a *merchant,* the duration of which is three months or less, cannot be revoked [UCC 2-205].
	5. Acceptance by performance requires notice within a reasonable time; otherwise, the offer can be treated as lapsed [UCC 2-206(2)].
	6. The price does not have to be included for a contract to be formed [UCC 2-305].
	7. Variations in terms between the offer and the acceptance may not be a rejection but may be an acceptance [UCC 2-207(1)].
	8. Acceptance may be made by any reasonable means of communication; it is effective when dispatched [UCC 2-206(1)(a)].
Consideration	1. Contract modification does not require consideration [UCC 2-209(1)].
Requirements under the Statute of Frauds	1. All contracts for the sale of goods priced at $500 or more must be in writing. A writing is sufficient so long as it evidences a contract between the parties and it has been signed by the party against whom enforcement is sought. A contract is not enforceable beyond the quantity shown in the writing.
	2. Exceptions to the requirement of a writing exist in the following situations:
	a. When written confirmation of an oral contract *between merchants* is not objected to in writing by the receiver within ten days [UCC 2-201(2)].
	b. When the oral contract is for specially manufactured goods not suitable for resale to others, and the seller has substantially started to manufacture the goods [UCC 2-201(3)(a)].
	c. When the defendant admits in pleadings, testimony, or other court proceedings that an oral contract for the sale of goods was made. In this case the contract will be enforceable to the quantity of goods admitted [UCC 2-201(3)(b)].
	d. When payment has been made and accepted or possession taken under the terms of an oral contract. The oral agreement will be enforceable to the extent that such payment has been received and accepted or to the extent that goods have been received and accepted [UCC 2-201(3)(c)].
Parol Evidence	1. The terms of a clearly and completely worded written contract cannot be contradicted by evidence of prior negotiations or agreements or contemporaneous oral agreements [UCC 2-202].
	2. Evidence is admissible to clarify the terms of a writing:
	a. If the contract terms are ambiguous [UCC 2-202(b)].
	b. If evidence of course of dealing, usage of trade, or course of performance is necessary to learn or to clarify the intentions of the parties to the contract [UCC 2-202(a)].
Unconscionability	An unconscionable contract is one that is so unfair and one-sided that it would be unreasonable to enforce it. If the court deems a contract to be unconscionable at the time it was made, the court can (1) refuse to enforce the contract; (2) refuse to enforce the unconscionable clauses of the contract; or (3) limit the application of any unconscionable clause to avoid an unconscionable result [UCC 2-302].

of goods is less than $500 [UCC 2-201]. Under Article 2A, an oral lease is enforceable if the lease payments are less than $1,000 [UCC 2A-201]. Unlike Article 2, Article 2A does not say whether a lease as modified needs to satisfy the Statute of Frauds.

Article 2A replaces Article 2's implied warranty of title (discussed in Chapter 22) with an implied warranty of quiet possession. This is "a warranty that for the lease term no person holds a claim or interest in the goods that arose from an act or omission of the lessor . . . which will interfere with the lessee's enjoyment of its leasehold interest" [UCC 2A-211(1)].

Article 2A extends Article 2's protection against unconscionability to leases and expands it in cases concerning consumer leases. A consumer lease involves a lessor who regularly engages in the business of leasing or selling, a lessee (except an organization) who leases the goods "primarily for a personal, family, or household purpose," and total lease payments that are less than $25,000 [UCC 2A-103(1)(e)]. If unconscionable conduct induced the consumer to enter the lease or occurred in the collection of a claim under it, courts can grant relief, even if the lease itself is not unconscionable [UCC 2A-108(2)]. In cases involving consumer leases, courts can also award attorneys' fees [UCC 2A-108(4)].

One type of nonconsumer lease is a commercial finance lease. A finance lease—commercial or otherwise—involves a lessor, a lessee, and a third party: a financer who buys or leases goods from a supplier and leases or subleases them to the lessee [UCC 2A-103(g)]. The supplier manufactures or supplies the goods according to the lessee's specifications, the financer acquires the goods or the right to their possession and use in connection with the lease, and the lessee looks almost entirely to the supplier for warranties and so on. Article 2A, unlike ordinary contract law, makes the lessee's obligations under a commercial finance lease irrevocable and independent from the financer's [UCC 2A-407]. That is, the lessee must perform whether or not the financer performs.

Many leasing transactions are based on the parties' ability to provide for the measure of damages if there is a default or other act or omission. Article 2A allows greater flexibility in liquidation of damages with respect to leases than Article 2 does with respect to sales [UCC 2A-504].

Article 2A is included in the full text of the UCC in Appendix C of this book.

■ Terms and Concepts

course of dealing 338	**lease agreement** 340	**sale** 324
course of performance 339	**lessee** 340	**usage of trade** 338
firm offer 327	**lessor** 340	

■ For Review

1. What is the scope of the UCC's Article 2?
2. The UCC changes the effect of the common law of contracts in several ways. For instance, at common law, an offer must be definite enough for the parties to ascertain its essential terms when it is accepted. What happens under the UCC if some of an offer's terms—the price term, for example—are left open? What if the quantity term is left open?
3. Section 2-201 of the UCC defines three exceptions to the Statute of Frauds requirement. What are these three exceptions?
4. Mateo and Klaus attempt to negotiate a sale of electric pencil sharpeners, but they cannot agree on the quantity or the price. Later, Mateo mails to Klaus an offer to buy 700 sharpeners at $1 per sharpener, and Klaus mails to Mateo an offer to sell 800 sharpeners at $1 per sharpener. The offers cross in the mail—Klaus receives Mateo's offer at the same time that Mateo receives Klaus's offer. Klaus ships 700 sharpeners. Mateo rejects them. Do Mateo and Klaus have a contract?
5. In the previous problem, would the result be any different if Klaus had not mailed an offer but had simply shipped 700 sharpeners?

Questions and Case Problems

18-1. A. B. Zook, Inc., is a manufacturer of washing machines. Over the telephone, Zook offers to sell Radar Appliances 100 Model-Z washers at a price of $150 per unit. Zook agrees to keep this offer open for ninety days. Radar tells Zook that the offer appears to be a good one and that it will let Zook know of its acceptance within the next two to three weeks. One week later, Zook sends and Radar receives notice that Zook has withdrawn its offer. Radar immediately thereafter telephones Zook and accepts the $150-per-unit offer. Zook claims, first, that no sales contract was ever formed between it and Radar and, second, that if there is a contract, the contract is unenforceable. Discuss Zook's contentions.

18-2. Flint, a retail seller of television sets, orders 100 Model Color-X sets from manufacturer Martin. The order specifies the price and that the television sets are to be *shipped* by Humming Bird Express on or before October 30. The order is received by Martin on October 5. On October 8 Martin writes Flint a letter indicating that the order was received and that the sets will be shipped as directed, at the specified price. This letter is received by Flint on October 10. On October 28, Martin, in preparing the shipment, discovers it has only 90 Color-X sets in stock. Martin ships the 90 Color-X sets and 10 television sets of a different model, stating clearly on the invoice that the 10 are being shipped only as an accommodation. Flint claims Martin is in breach of contract. Martin claims the shipment was not an acceptance and therefore no contract was formed. Explain who is correct and why.

18-3. Shane has a requirements contract with Sky that obligates Sky to supply Shane with all the gasoline Shane needs for his delivery trucks for one year at $1.50 per gallon. A clause inserted in small print in the contract by Shane, and not noticed by Sky, states, "The buyer reserves the right to reject any shipment for any reason without liability." For six months Shane orders and Sky delivers under the contract without any controversy. Then, because of a war in the Middle East, the price of gasoline to Sky increases substantially. Sky contacts Shane and tells Shane he cannot possibly fulfill the requirements contract unless Shane agrees to pay $1.70 per gallon. Shane, in need of the gasoline, agrees in writing to modify the contract. Later that month, Shane learns he can buy gasoline at $1.60 per gallon from Collins. Shane refuses delivery of his most recent order to Sky, claiming, first, that the contract allows him to do so without liability, and, second, that he is required to pay only $1.50 per gallon if he accepts the delivery. Discuss fully Shane's contentions.

18-4. Hatter owns 360 acres of land in Bear County. Hatter makes three separate contracts, in writing, with Bean concerning the land. First, Hatter contracts to sell Bean 500 tons of gravel from a quarry located on the land for a stated price. The contract calls for Bean to remove the gravel. The second contract sells to Bean all the wheat presently grow-

breach by shipping the shirts by Dependable contrary to the contract terms. Discuss fully Bailey's claims.

18-6. Fred and Zuma Palermo contacted Colorado Carpet for a price quotation on providing and installing new carpeting and tiling in their home. In response, Colorado Carpet submitted a written proposal to provide and install the carpet at a certain price per square foot of material, *including* labor. The total was in excess of $500. The proposal was never accepted in writing by the Palermos, and the parties disagreed over how much of the proposal had been agreed to orally. After the installation of the carpet and tiling had begun, Mrs. Palermo became dissatisfied and sought the services of another contractor. Colorado Carpet then sued the Palermos for breach of the oral contract. The trial court held that the contract was one for services and was thus enforceable (that is, it didn't fall under the Statute of Frauds [UCC 2-201], which requires contracts for the sale of *goods* for the price of $500 or more to be in writing to be enforceable). Discuss fully whether the contract between the Palermos and Colorado Carpet was primarily for the sale of goods or the sale of services. [*Colorado Carpet Installation, Inc. v. Palermo,* 668 P.2d 1384 (Colo. 1983)]

18-7. Loeb & Co. entered into an oral agreement with Schreiner, a farmer, whereby Schreiner was to sell Loeb 150 bales of cotton, each weighing 480 pounds. Shortly thereafter, Loeb sent Schreiner a letter confirming the terms of the oral contract. Schreiner neither acknowledged receipt of the letter nor objected to its terms. When delivery came due, Schreiner ignored the oral agreement and sold his cotton on the open market because the price of cotton had more than doubled (from 37 cents to 80 cents per pound) since the oral agreement was made. In a lawsuit by Loeb & Co. against Schreiner, can Loeb & Co. recover? Explain. [*Loeb & Co. v. Schreiner,* 294 Ala. 722, 321 So.2d 199 (1975)]

18-8. Helvey received electricity from the Wabash County REMC, the county electrical utility. A mistake in the voltage delivered over the electrical line resulted in damage to Helvey's household appliances; households require only 110 volts, and Wabash delivered

135 volts or more. Some years later, Helvey sued Wabash County for breach of express and implied contractual warranties. Wabash County claimed that under UCC 2-725 a four-year statute of limitations existed and that Helvey had no claim because more than four years had elapsed since the accident. Indiana has a shorter statute of limitations period for sales of goods than for service contracts, however. Helvey claimed that the UCC provision did not apply because electricity is a service and not a good. Discuss whether the UCC should be applied in this case. [*Helvey v. Wabash County REMC,* 151 Ind.App. 176, 278 N.E.2d 608 (1972)]

18-9. R-P Packaging, Inc., is a manufacturer of cellophane wrapping material. The plant manager for Flowers Baking Co. decided to improve the company's packaging of cookies. The plant manager contacted R-P Packaging regarding the possible purchase of cellophane wrap imprinted with designed ''artwork.'' R-P took measurements to determine the appropriate size of the wrap and submitted to Flowers a sample of wrap conforming to the measurements, along with a sample of the artwork to be imprinted. After agreeing that the artwork was satisfactory, Flowers gave a verbal order to R-P for the designed cellophane wrap at a price of $13,000. When the wrap was tendered, although it conformed to the measurements and design, Flowers complained that the wrap was too short and the design off-center. Flowers rejected the shipment. R-P sued. Flowers contended that the oral contract was unenforceable under the Statute of Frauds. Discuss this contention. [*Flowers Baking Co. v. R-P Packaging, Inc.,* 229 Va. 370, 329 S.E.2d 462 (1985)]

18-10. Peggy Holloway, a real estate broker, guaranteed payment for a shipment of over $11,000 worth of mozzarella cheese sold by Cudahy Foods Co. to Pizza Pride in Jamestown, North Carolina. The entire arrangement was made orally. Cudahy mailed to Holloway an invoice for the order, and Holloway did not object in writing to the invoice within ten days of receipt. Later, when Cudahy demanded payment from Holloway, Holloway denied having guaranteed payment for the cheese and raised the Statute of Frauds as an affirmative defense. Cudahy claimed that the Statute of Frauds could not be used as a defense, as both Cudahy and Holloway were merchants and Holloway had failed to object in writing within ten days to Cudahy's invoice. Discuss Cudahy's argument. [*Cudahy Foods Co. v. Holloway,* 286 S.E.2d 606 (N.C.App. 1982)]

18-11. Case Briefing Assignment

Examine Case A.9 [Goldkist, Inc. v. Brownlee, 182 Ga.App. 287, 355 S.E.2d 773 (1987)] in Appendix A. The case has been excerpted there in great detail. Review and then brief the case, making sure that you include answers to the following questions in your brief.

1. What defense did the Brownlees raise against Goldkist's claim that the Brownlees had formed a contract with Goldkist for the sale of goods?
2. Why is the question as to whether the Brownlees were merchants significant?
3. What were the court's reasons for reversing the trial court's summary judgment for the Brownlees?

Chapter 19

Title, Risk, and Insurable Interest

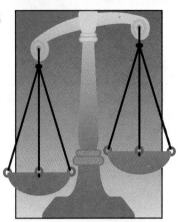

The sale of goods transfers ownership (title) from seller to buyer. Often a sales contract is signed before the actual goods are available. For example, a sales contract for oranges may be signed in May, but the oranges may not be ready for picking and shipment until October. Any number of things can happen between the time the sales contract is signed and the time the goods are actually transferred to the buyer's possession. Fire, flood, or frost may destroy the orange groves. The oranges may be lost or damaged in transit. The parties may want to obtain casualty insurance on the goods. The government may levy a tax on the oranges.

Before the creation of the Uniform Commercial Code (UCC), *title*—right of ownership—was the central concept in sales law, controlling all issues of rights and remedies of the parties to a sales contract. Frequently, however, it was difficult to determine when title actually passed from seller to buyer, and therefore it was also difficult to predict which party a court would decide had title at the time of a loss. Because of such problems, the UCC divorced the question of title as completely as possible from the question of the rights and obligations of buyers, sellers, and third persons (such as subsequent purchasers, creditors, or the tax collector).

In some situations, title is still relevant under the UCC, and the UCC has special rules for locating title. These rules will be discussed in the materials that follow. In most situations, however, the UCC replaces the concept of title with three other concepts: (1) identification, (2) risk of loss, and (3) insurable interest.

■ Identification

Before any interest in specific goods can pass from the seller to the buyer, two conditions must prevail: (1) the goods must be in existence, and (2) they must be identified to the contract. If either condition is lacking, only a *contract to sell* (not a sale) exists [UCC 2-105(2)]. Goods that are not both existing and identified to the contract are called *future goods*. For example, a contract to purchase next year's crop of hay is a contract for future goods, a crop yet to be grown.

For passage of title, the goods must be identified in a way that will distinguish the particular goods to be delivered under the sales contract from all other similar goods.[1] **Identification** is a designation of goods as the subject matter of the sales contract.

In many cases, identification is simply a matter of specific designation. For example, you contract to purchase a fleet of five cars by the serial numbers listed for the cars, or you agree to purchase all the wheat in a specific bin at a stated price per bushel. Problems usually occur only when a quantity of goods is purchased from a larger mass, such as 1,000 cases of peas from a 10,000-case lot.

There is a general rule that when a purchaser buys a quantity of goods to be taken from a larger mass, identification can be made only by separation of the contracted goods from the mass. Therefore, until the seller separates the 1,000 cases of peas from the 10,000-case lot, title and risk of loss remain with the seller.

There are a few exceptions to this general rule. For example, a seller owns approximately 5,000 chickens (hens and roosters). A buyer agrees to purchase all the hen chickens at a stated price. Most courts would hold that ''all the hen chickens'' is a sufficient identification, and title and risk can pass to the buyer without the goods identified in the contract being physically separated from the other goods (the hens from the roosters). The reasoning is that the contract identification serves as sufficient separation.

The most common exception deals with **fungible goods** [UCC 1-201(17)]. Fungible goods are goods that are alike by physical nature, by agreement, or by trade usage. Typical examples are wheat, oil, and wine. If these goods are held or intended to be held by owners in common (owners that have undifferentiated shares of the entire mass), an owner can pass title and risk of loss to a buyer without an actual separation. The buyer replaces the seller as an owner in common [UCC 2-105(4)].

For example, Abraham, Bush, and Carroll are farmers. They deposit, respectively, 5,000 bushels, 3,000 bushels, and 2,000 bushels of the same grade of grain in a bin. The three become owners in common, with Abraham owning 50 percent of the 10,000 bushels, Bush 30 percent, and Carroll 20 percent. Abraham could contract to sell 5,000 bushels of grain to Tyson and, because the goods are fungible, pass title and risk of loss to Tyson without physically separating 5,000 bushels. Tyson now becomes an owner in common with Bush and Carroll.

Identification is significant because it gives the buyer the right to obtain insurance on the goods and the right to recover from third parties who damage the goods. In certain circumstances, identification allows the buyer to take the goods from the seller. In other words, the concept of identification is easier to understand if one looks at its consequences.

Parties can agree on when identification will take place in their contract; but if they do not so specify, in addition to the preceding rules, the following rules apply [UCC 2-501(1)]:

1. Identification takes place at the time the contract is made *if the contract calls for the sale of specific and ascertained goods already existing.*
2. If the sale involves unborn animals that will be born within twelve months from the time of the contract, identification will take place when the young are conceived. If it involves crops to be harvested within twelve months (or during the next harvest season occurring after contracting, whichever is further in the future), identification will take place when the crops are planted or begin to grow.
3. In other cases, identification takes place when the goods are marked, shipped, or somehow designated by the seller as the particular goods to pass under the contract. The seller can delegate the right to identify goods to the buyer.

◼ When Title Passes

Once goods exist and have been identified, the provisions of UCC 2-401 apply to the passage of title. Parties can expressly agree to when and under what conditions title will pass to the buyer. In virtually all subsections of UCC 2-401, the words ''unless otherwise explicitly agreed'' appear, meaning that

---

1. According to UCC 2-401, each provision of Article 2 ''with respect to the rights, obligations, and remedies of the seller, the buyer, purchasers or other third parties applies irrespective of title to the goods except where the provisions refer to such title.'' These provisions referring to title include: UCC 2-312, warranty of title by seller; UCC 2-326(3), consignment sales; UCC 2-327(1)(a), sale on approval and ''risk of loss''; UCC 2-403(1), entrustment; UCC 2-501(2), insurable interest in goods; and UCC 2-722, who can sue third parties for injury to goods.

any explicit understanding between the buyer and the seller will determine when title passes.

Unless an agreement is explicitly made, title passes to the buyer at the time and place at which the seller performs the physical delivery of the goods [UCC 2-401(2)]. The delivery terms determine when this occurs.

Shipment Contracts

Under shipment contracts, the seller is required or authorized to ship goods by carrier. Here, the seller is required only to deliver the goods into the hands of a carrier (such as a trucking company), and title passes to the buyer at the time and place of shipment [UCC 2-401(2)(a)].

Destination Contracts

With destination contracts, the seller is required to deliver the goods to a particular destination, usually directly to the buyer but sometimes to another destination designated by the buyer. Title passes to the buyer when the goods are tendered at that destination [UCC 2-401(2)(b)].

Delivery without Movement of the Goods

When the contract of sale does not call for the seller's shipment or delivery (when the buyer is to pick up the goods), the passage of title depends on whether the seller must deliver a document of title, such as a bill of lading or a warehouse receipt, to the buyer. A **bill of lading** is a receipt for goods that is signed by a carrier and that serves as a contract for the transportation of the goods. A **warehouse receipt** is a receipt issued by a warehouser for goods stored in his or her warehouse. (See Exhibits 19–1 and 19–2.) When a document of title is required, title passes to the buyer *when and where the document is delivered.* Thus, if the goods are stored in a warehouse, title passes to the buyer when the appropriate documents are delivered to the buyer. The goods need not move. In fact, the buyer can choose to leave the goods at the same warehouse for a period of time, and the buyer's title to those goods will be unaffected.

When no documents of title are required, and delivery is made without the goods being moved, title passes at the time and place the sales contract was made, if the goods have already been identi-

fied. If the goods have not been identified, then title does not pass until identification occurs. Consider an example: Fein sells lumber to Ozo. It is agreed that Ozo will pick up the lumber at the yard. If the lumber has been identified (segregated, marked, or in any other way distinguished from all other lumber), title will pass to Ozo when the contract is signed. If the lumber is still in storage bins at the mill, however, title will not pass to Ozo until the particular pieces of lumber to be sold under this contract are identified [UCC 2-401(3)].

■ Risk of Loss

Under the UCC, risk of loss does not necessarily pass with title. The question of who suffers a financial risk if goods are damaged, destroyed, or lost is resolved primarily under Sections 2-509 and 2-319. Several factors determine when risk of loss passes from the seller to the buyer. We look at those factors below, as well as the effect of a breach of contract on risk of loss.

Passage of Risk of Loss Absent a Breach of Contract

Risk of loss can be assigned through an agreement by the parties, preferably in writing. Therefore, the parties can generally control the exact moment risk of loss passes from the seller to the buyer. Of course, at the agreed-on time, the goods must be in existence and identified to the contract for this contract provision to be enforceable. In the absence of agreement, risk of loss generally passes to the buyer when the seller delivers, or tenders delivery, of the goods to the buyer. The following sections discuss the basic rules governing passage of risk of loss when there has been no express agreement on the subject and no breach of contract.

CARRIER CASES Assuming that there is no specification in the agreement, the following rules apply to carrier cases (in which the goods are delivered by railroad, truck, airplane, ship, or other mode of paid transport).

Contract Terms Certain specific terms in the contract, normally used in sales price quotations, assist in determining when risk of loss passes to the buyer. Four such terms should be noted:

■ **Exhibit 19–1 A Sample Negotiable Bill of Lading**

UNIFORM MOTOR CARRIER ORDER BILL OF LADING

1st Sheet

Original—Domestic

Shipper's No._____

Agent's No._____

CENTRAL FREIGHT LINES INC.

RECEIVED, subject to the classifications and tariffs in effect on the date of the issue of this Bill of Lading,

From _____ , Date _____ 19 ____

At _____ Street, _____ City, _____ County, _____ State

the property described below, in apparent good order, except as noted (contents and condition of contents of packages unknown) marked, consigned · and destined as shown below, which said company (the word company being understood throughout this contract as meaning any person or corporation in possession of the property under the contract) agrees to carry to its usual place of delivery at said destination, if within the scope of its lawful operations, otherwise to deliver to another carrier on the route to said destination. It is mutually agreed, as to each carrier of all or any of said property over all or any portion of said route to destination, and as to each party at any time interested in all or any of said property, that every service to be performed hereunder shall be subject to all the conditions not prohibited by law, whether printed or written, herein contained, including the conditions on back hereof, which are hereby agreed to by the shipper and accepted for himself and his assigns.

The surrender of this Original ORDER Bill of Lading properly indorsed shall be required before the delivery of the property. Inspection of property covered by this bill of lading will not be permitted unless provided by law or unless permission is indorsed on this original Bill of lading or given in writing by the shipper.

Consigned to Order of _____

| Destination | Street, | City, | County, | State |

Notify _____

| At | Street, | City, | County, | State |

I. C. C. No. _____ **Vehicle No.** _____

Routing _____

No. Pack- ages	Description of Articles, Special Marks, and Exceptions	*Weight (Subject to Correction)	Class or Rate	Check Column	Subject to Section 7 of Conditions, if this shipment is to be delivered to the consignee without recourse on the consignor, the consignor shall sign the following statement:
					The carrier shall not make delivery of this shipment without payment of freight and all other lawful charges.
					(Signature of consignor.)
					If charges are to be prepaid write or stamp here, "To be Prepaid."
					Received $_____ to apply in prepayment of the charges on the property described hereon.
					Agent or Cashier.
					Per_____ (The signature here acknowledges only the amount prepaid.)
					Charges advanced: $_____

*If the shipment moves between two ports by a carrier by water, the law requires that the bill of lading shall state whether it is "carrier's or shipper's weight."

Note—Where the rate is dependent on value, shippers are required to state specifically in writing the agreed or declared value of the property.

The agreed or declared value of the property is hereby specifically stated by the shipper to be not exceeding

_____ per _____

| | Shipper | | Agent. |
| Per | | Per | |

Permanent address of Shipper _____ Street, _____ City, _____ State

MOORE BUSINESS FORMS, INC., WACO, TEX. M

Source: Reprinted with permission of Central Freight Lines Inc. © 1985 Central Freight Lines, Inc.

Note: This form is printed in yellow to warn holders that it is an order bill of lading. The back of the form permits negotiation by indorsement.

■ **Exhibit 19–2 A Sample Nonnegotiable Warehouse Receipt**

Warehouse Receipt – Not Negotiable

HART

Agreement No. _____   Vault No. _____ _____ _____ _____ _____

Service Order _____   _____ _____ _____ _____ _____

Receipt and
Lot Number_____   Date of Issue_____19____

Received for the account of and deliverable to •_____

whose latest known address is _____   SAMPLE

_____ the goods enumerated on the inside or attached schedule to be

stored in Company warehouse, located at _____
which goods are accepted only upon the following conditions set forth below:

READ CAREFULLY ▶ That the value of all goods stored, including the contents of any container, and all goods hereafter stored for Depositor's account to be not over $_____ **per pound † per article** unless a higher value is noted in the schedule, for which an additional monthly storage charge of _____¢ on each $_____ valuation in excess of $_____ **per pound † per article** or fraction thereof will be made.

If there are any items enumerated in this receipt valued in excess of the above limitations per pound per article and not so noted in the schedule, return this receipt within 10 days with proper values so indicated in writing in order that the receipt may be re-issued and proper higher storage rates assessed.

OWNERSHIP. The Customer, Shipper, Depositor, or Agent represents and warrants that he is lawfully possessed of goods to be stored and/or has the authority to store or ship said goods. (If the goods are mortgaged, notify the Company the name and address of the mortgagee.)

PAYMENT OF CHARGES. Storage bills are payable monthly in advance for each month's storage or fraction thereof. Labor charges, cartage and other services rendered are payable upon completion of work. All charges shall be paid at the warehouse location shown hereon, and if delinquent, shall incur interest monthly at the rate of _____ per cent ( ) per year.
The Depositor will pay reasonable attorney's fee incurred by The Company in collecting delinquent accounts.

LIABILITY OF COMPANY. The company shall be liable for any loss or injury to the goods caused by its failure to exercise such care as a reasonably careful man would exercise under like circumstances. The company will not be liable for loss or damage to fragile articles not packed, or articles packed or unpacked by other than employees of this company. Depositor specifically agrees that the warehouse will not be liable for contamination of or for insect damage to articles placed in drawers of furniture by the depositor. Periodic spraying of the warehouse premises shall constitute ordinary and proper care, unless the depositor requests in writing and pays for anti-infestation treatment of articles in drawers and compartments of stored furniture.

CHANGE OF ADDRESS. Notice of change of address must be given the Company in writing, and acknowledged in writing by the Company.

TRANSFER OR WITHDRAWAL OF GOODS. The warehouse receipt is not negotiable and cannot be produced and all charges must be paid before delivery to the Depositor, or transfer of goods to another person; however, a written direction to the Company to transfer the goods to another person or deliver the goods may be accepted by the Company at its option without requiring tender of the warehouse receipt.

ACCESS TO STORAGE, PARTIAL WITHDRAWAL. A signed order from the person in whose name the receipt is issued is required to enable others to remove or have access to goods. A charge is made for stacking and unstacking, and for access to stored goods.

BUILDING—FIRE—WATCHMAN. The Company does not represent or warrant that its building cannot be destroyed by fire or that the contents of said buildings including the said property cannot be destroyed by fire. The Company shall not be required to maintain a watchman or sprinkler system and its failure to do so shall not constitute negligence.

CLAIMS OR ERRORS. All claims for non-delivery of any article or articles and for damage, breakage, etc., must be made in writing within ninety (90) days from delivery of goods stored or they are waived. Failure to return the warehouse receipt for correction within ( ) days after receipt thereof by the depositor shall be conclusive that it is correct and delivery will be made only in accordance therewith.

FUTURE SERVICE. This Contract shall extend and apply to future services rendered to the Depositor by the Company and to any additional goods deposited with the Company by the Depositor.

WAREHOUSEMAN'S LIEN. The Company reserves the right to sell the goods stored, in accordance with the provisions of the Uniform Commercial Code (Business and Commerce Code if stored in Texas), for all lawful charges in arrears.

TERMINATION OF STORAGE. The Company reserves the right to terminate the storage of the goods at any time by giving to the Depositor thirty (30) days' written notice of its intention so to do, and, unless the Depositor removes such goods within that period, the Company is hereby empowered to have the same removed at the cost and expense of the Depositor, or the Company may sell them at auction in accordance with state law.

DEPOSITOR WILL PAY REASONABLE LEGAL FEES INCURRED BY WAREHOUSE IN COLLECTING DELINQUENT CHARGES.

THIS DOCUMENT CONTAINS THE WHOLE CONTRACT BETWEEN THE PARTIES AND THERE ARE NO OTHER TERMS, WARRANTIES, REPRESENTATIONS, OR AGREEMENTS OF EITHER DEPOSITOR OR COMPANY NOT HEREIN CONTAINED.

Storage per month
or fraction thereof . . . . $_____
Warehouse labor . . . . . $_____
Cartage . . . . $_____
Packing at residence . . . $_____
Wrapping and preparing
for storage . . . . $_____
Charges advanced . . . . $_____
_____ $_____
_____ $_____

*By*_____

•Insert "Mr. and/or Mrs." or, if military personnel, appropriate rank or grade.
†Delete the words "per pound" if the declared value is per article.
For goods stored for military personnel under PL 245, the contractor's liability for care of goods is as provided in Basic Agreement with U.S. Government.

**THIS PROPERTY HAS NOT BEEN INSURED BY THIS COMPANY FOR FIRE OR ANY OTHER CASUALTY
SCHEDULE OF GOODS ON FOLLOWING PAGE OR ATTACHED**

H-1 (1/81) Approved by S H H T 4 ©   Re-order from Hart Graphics, Austin, Texas

Source: Reprinted with permission of Hart Graphics, Inc. of Austin, Texas. © 1985 Hart Graphics, Inc.

1. *F.O.B.* (free on board) means that delivery is at the seller's expense to a specific location. The parties can agree that delivery be either at the place of shipment (for example, the seller's city or place of business) or at the place of destination (for example, the buyer's city or place of business). Absent a contrary agreement, when the term is F.O.B. the place of shipment, the risk of loss passes when the seller puts the goods into the carrier's possession. When the term is F.O.B. the place of destination, the risk of loss passes when the seller tenders delivery [UCC 2-319(1)].

2. *F.A.S.* (free alongside) requires the seller at his or her own expense and risk to deliver the goods alongside the ship that will transport the goods at which point risk passes to the buyer [UCC 2-319(2)].

3. *C.I.F.* or *C.&F.* (cost, insurance, and freight, or just cost and freight) requires, among other things, that the seller "put the goods in possession of a carrier" before risk can pass to the buyer [UCC 2-320(2)].

4. *Delivery ex-ship* (from the carrying vessel) means that risk of loss does not pass to the buyer until the goods leave the ship or are otherwise properly unloaded [UCC 2-322].

Shipment Contracts   In a shipment contract, the seller is required or authorized to ship goods by carrier (that is, not required to deliver them to a particular destination). Risk of loss in shipment contracts passes to the buyer when the goods are duly delivered to the carrier [UCC 2-509(1)(a)].

For example, a seller in New York sells 10,000 tons of sheet metal to a buyer in California, F.O.B. New York (free on board in New York—that is, the buyer pays the transportation charges from New York). The contract authorizes a shipment by carrier; it does not require the seller to tender the metal in California. Risk passes to the buyer when the conforming goods are properly placed in the possession of the carrier. If the goods are damaged in transit, the loss falls on the buyer. (For this reason, buyers usually insure the goods from the time they leave the seller.) Generally, all contracts are assumed to be shipment contracts if nothing to the contrary is stated in the contract.

Destination Contracts   A destination contract requires the seller to deliver the goods to a particular destination. The risk of loss in destination contracts passes to the buyer when the goods are tendered to the buyer at that destination. In the preceding example, if the contract had been F.O.B. California, risk of loss during transit to California would have fallen on the seller.

In the following case, the court reviewed UCC 2-509(1) as it relates to passage of the risk of loss. Under the UCC, an F.O.B. term indicates whether the contract is a shipment contract or a destination contract and thus indicates when the risk of loss passes. The F.O.B. terminology controls. In this case, the contract contained neither delivery terms, such as F.O.B., nor specific terms for allocation of loss while goods were in transit.

Case 19.1

PESTANA v. KARINOL CORP.

District Court of Appeal of Florida, Third District, 1979. 367 So.2d 1096.

BACKGROUND AND FACTS   Karinol Corporation contracted "to ship" watches to Pedro Pestana in Chetumal, Mexico. The contract, formed in Florida and governed by Florida's codification of the UCC, contained a "ship to" address but did not otherwise indicate it should be considered a destination contract. Pestana made a deposit, and the watches were shipped, but they were lost in transit. Pestana sought a refund for the deposit in a Florida state court, claiming that the risk of loss fell on Karinol. Karinol claimed that Pestana bore the risk and owed the balance of the purchase price. The trial court held for Karinol. Pestana appealed.

DECISION AND RATIONALE   The District Court of Appeal of Florida upheld the trial court's decision. The appellate court held that the contract was a shipment contract, not a destination contract, and that Karinol had fulfilled all of its obligations of performance. The court explained that a contract that has no specific provision allocating risk of loss while goods are in the possession of a carrier and no delivery terms "such as F.O.B. Chetumal" is a shipment contract.

| LEGAL PERSPECTIVES IN BUSINESS | Seller or Buyer—Who Has the Risk of Loss? |

A major aspect of commercial transactions involves the shipment of goods. Many issues arise when the unforeseen occurs, such as fire, theft, or other forms of damage to goods in transit.

You may recall from the discussion in this chapter that the UCC uses a three-part test to determine risk of loss. First, if the contract includes terms allocating risk of loss, those terms are binding and must be applied. Second, if the contract is silent as to risk, and either party breaches the contract, the breaching party is liable for risk of loss. Third, when a contract makes no reference to risk and neither party breaches, risk of loss is borne by the party having control over the goods.

A seller of goods to be shipped should realize that, absent any explicit agreement in the contract or any breach on the buyer's part, as long as the seller has control over the goods, the seller is liable for any loss.

When there is no explicit agreement, the Uniform Commercial Code uses the delivery terms in a contract as a basis for determining control. Thus a shipment ''F.O.B. buyer's business'' is a destination-delivery term, and risk of loss would not pass to the buyer until there was a tender of delivery at the point of destination. Any loss or damage in transit falls on the seller, because the seller has control until proper tender has been made.

From the buyer's point of view, it is important to remember that most sellers prefer ''F.O.B. seller's business'' delivery terms. Under these terms, once the goods are delivered to the carrier, the buyer has the risk of loss. Thus, if conforming goods are completely destroyed or lost in transit, the buyer not only suffers the loss, but is legally obligated to pay the seller the contract price.

At the time of contract negotiation, both the seller and buyer should determine the importance of risk of loss. In some cases, risk is relatively unimportant (such as when ten boxes of inexpensive copier paper are being sold) and the delivery terms should simply reflect costs and price. In other cases, risk is extremely important (such as when a fragile piece of equipment is being sold), and the parties will need an express agreement as to the moment risk is to pass so they can insure accordingly. The important point is that risk should be considered before the loss, not after it.

DELIVERY WITHOUT MOVEMENT OF THE GOODS Frequently, the goods are to be picked up from the seller by the buyer. In the absence of agreement, if the seller is a merchant, risk of loss passes to the buyer only on the buyer's taking physical possession of the goods. If the seller is a nonmerchant, risk passes to the buyer on the seller's tender of delivery [UCC 2-509(3)]. To illustrate: Mellor buys a stereo from Circuit Electronics on Tuesday and tells Circuit that she will pick it up on Thursday. On Wednesday, the electronics store burns down, and the stereo is lost. Because Circuit is a merchant and Mellor had not yet taken possession of the stereo, the loss falls on Circuit. If Mellor had bought the stereo from her neighbor, with Mellor agreeing to pick up the stereo at anytime within the next two days, and the neighbor's house had burned down before Mellor picked up the set, the loss would fall on Mellor—because her neighbor is a nonmerchant.

When a bailee[2] is holding goods for a person who has contracted to sell them and the goods are to be delivered without being moved, the risk of loss passes to the buyer when: (1) the buyer receives a negotiable (transferable by indorsement or delivery)[3] document of title for the goods, or

---

2. Under the UCC, a bailee is a party who by bill of lading, warehouse receipt, or other document of title acknowledges possession of goods and contracts to deliver them [UCC 7-102(1)(a)]. A warehousing company, for example, or a trucking company that normally issues documents of title for goods it receives is a bailee. Bailments are the subject of Chapter 50.
3. UCC 7-104 states what constitutes negotiable and nonnegotiable documents of title. See Chapter 50.

(2) the bailee acknowledges the buyer's right to possess the goods, or (3) the buyer receives a non-negotiable document of title *and* has had a *reasonable time* to present the document to the bailee and demand the goods. Obviously, if the bailee refuses to honor the document, the risk of loss remains with the seller [UCC 2-509(2), 2-503(4)(b)]. (See Exhibit 19-1 for a sample negotiable bill of lading and Exhibit 19-2 for a sample nonnegotiable warehouse receipt.)

To illustrate: McKee stores goods in Hardy's warehouse and takes a negotiable warehouse receipt for them. On the following day, McKee indorses the receipt (in this instance, signs his name on the document) and sells it to Byne for cash. The day after that, Hardy's warehouse burns down, and the goods are completely destroyed. The risk of loss is on Byne because it accompanied the negotiable warehouse receipt that gave him title to the goods.

In the following case, goods stored in a warehouse were destroyed by fire just a few days after they had been sold. The court had little difficulty in determining that title to the goods had passed from seller to buyer at the time the transfer was entered on the warehouse books—before the fire occurred. Because the goods were uninsured at the time of the fire, the significant issue for the parties involved was whether risk of loss had also passed to the buyer prior to the fire.

Case 19.2

JASON'S FOODS, INC. v. PETER ECKRICH & SONS, INC.

United States Court of Appeals, Seventh Circuit, 1985. 774 F.2d 214.

BACKGROUND AND FACTS   In December, Peter Eckrich & Sons, Inc., contracted to buy from Jason's Foods, Inc., 38,000 pounds of "St. Louis style" pork ribs. The ribs would be transferred from Jason's account in an independent warehouse to Eckrich's account in the same warehouse, without actual movement of the ribs. In its confirmation of the agreement, Jason's notified Eckrich that the transfer would be effected between January 10 and January 14. On January 13, Jason's asked the warehouse to make the transfer. The transfer was made on the warehouse books immediately, but a warehouse receipt was not sent to Eckrich until January 17 or 18, and Eckrich did not receive the receipt—and thus did not know the transfer had occurred—until January 24. The warehouse burned down on January 17, and Jason's subsequently sued Eckrich in a federal district court to recover the contract price. The trial court held that Eckrich was not liable because risk of loss had not passed to Eckrich before the fire. The trial court judge granted summary judgment for Eckrich, and Jason's appealed.

DECISION AND RATIONALE   The United States Court of Appeals for the Seventh Circuit, affirming the decision of the trial court, held that risk of loss passes when there is "acknowledgment" to a buyer that goods have been transferred to its account. The appellate court pointed out that an acknowledgment need not be in writing and Jason's could have instructed the warehouse supervisor to call Eckrich and acknowledge the transfer as soon as the transfer had been completed on the books. The court reasoned that because Jason's chose not to give these instructions, "acknowledgment" took place when Eckrich received the receipt on January 24, not when it was sent. Thus, when the warehouse burned down on January 17, risk of loss had not yet passed to Eckrich. As to Jason's argument that risk passed on January 14, the court explained, "By the close of business on January 14 Eckrich had a well-founded expectation that the ribs had been transferred to its account; but considering the many slips that are possible between cup and lips, we do not think that this expectation should fix the point at which the risk shifts."

Sale on Approval and Sale or Return Contracts

A **sale on approval** is not a sale until the buyer accepts (approves) the offer. A **sale or return** is a sale that can be rescinded by the buyer without liability. In each case, passage of title and risk of loss depend on the conditional event's happening or not happening, because these transactions are conditional by their very nature.

SALE ON APPROVAL When a seller offers to sell goods to a buyer and permits the buyer to take the goods on a trial basis, a sale on approval is made. The term *sale* here is a misnomer because only an *offer* to sell has been made, along with a bailment (the holding or storage of another's personal property—see Chapter 50) created by the buyer's possession.

Therefore, title and risk of loss (from causes beyond the buyer's control) remain with the seller until the buyer accepts the offer. Acceptance can be made expressly, by any act inconsistent with the *trial* purpose or seller's ownership, or by the buyer's election not to return the goods within the trial period. If the buyer does not wish to accept, the buyer may notify the seller of that fact within the trial period, and the return is at the seller's expense and risk [UCC 2-327(1)]. Goods held on approval are not subject to the claims of the buyer's creditors until acceptance.

To imagine a sale on approval, suppose that East Side Motors, a Nissan dealership, agrees to let Elena take a new 300SX home to drive for a day to see whether she wants to buy it. Under these circumstances, if Elena drives the 300SX for a day and then tells East Side Motors that she does not want to buy the car, she will be considered not to have accepted the car. If she takes the car for a week's drive along the coast, however, she will be considered to have accepted the car because she used it in a manner inconsistent with the trial purpose—that is, she used it as if she were the car's owner.

SALE OR RETURN The sale or return (sometimes called *sale and return*) is a species of contract by which the seller delivers a quantity of goods to the buyer with the understanding that if the buyer wishes to retain any portion of those goods (for use or resale), the buyer will consider the portion retained as having been sold to him or her and will pay accordingly. The balance will be returned to the seller or will be held by the buyer as a bailee subject to the seller's order. When the buyer receives possession at the time of sale, the title and risk of loss pass to the buyer. Both remain with the buyer until the buyer returns the goods to the seller within the time period specified. If the buyer fails to return the goods within this time period, the sale is finalized. The return of the goods is at the buyer's risk and expense. The goods held on a sale or return contract are subject to the claims of the buyer's creditors while they are in the buyer's possession.

To illustrate: If Sapor, a diamond wholesaler, delivers diamonds to Brande Gems, a retailer, to sell on the understanding that Brande may return any unsold diamonds at the end of six months, the transaction is a sale or return. The risk of loss falls on Brande. If none of the diamonds is returned—because Brande has sold them (or even lost them)—Brande is responsible to Sapor for their price. Brande is also responsible for the expense of returning whatever diamonds are returned. If Brande goes bankrupt, the diamonds will be subject to the claims of Brande's creditors.

It is often difficult to determine from a particular transaction which exists—a sale on approval or a contract for sale or return. The UCC states that (unless otherwise agreed) if the goods are for the buyer to use, the transaction is a sale on approval; if the goods are for the buyer to resell, the transaction is a sale or return [UCC 2-326(1)].

The UCC treats a **consignment** as a sale or return. Under a consignment, the owner of goods (the *consignor*) delivers them to another (the *consignee*) for the consignee to sell. If the consignee sells the goods, he or she must pay the consignor for them. If the goods are not sold, they may simply be returned to the consignor. While the goods are in the possession of the consignee, the consignee holds title to them, and creditors of the consignee will prevail over the consignor in any action to repossess the goods. The UCC does make an exception to this rule if the person making delivery (the consignor) does one of the following:

1. Complies with an applicable law providing for a consignor's interest or the like to be evidenced by a sign.

■ CONCEPT SUMMARY 19.1
Passage of Title and Risk of Loss Absent Agreement

Situation	Basic Rules
Contract terms call for goods to be *shipped* (i.e., F.O.B. seller's location)	1. Title and risk pass upon seller's delivery of conforming goods to the carrier [UCC 2-401(2)(a), UCC 2-509(1)(a)].
Contract terms call for goods to be delivered at *destination* (i.e., F.O.B. buyer's location)	1. Title and risk pass upon seller's *tender* of delivery of conforming goods to the buyer at the point of destination [UCC 2-401(2)(b), UCC 2-509(1)(b)].

Contract terms call for goods to be delivered *without physical movement* (i.e., the buyer must pick up the goods)	1. If the goods are not represented by a document of title—
	   a. Title passes upon the formation of the contract [UCC 2-401(3)(b)].
	   b. Risk passes to the buyer, if seller is a merchant, upon buyer's *receipt* of the goods or, if seller is a nonmerchant, upon seller's *tender* of delivery of the goods [UCC 2-509(3)].
	 2. If the goods are represented by a document of title—
	   a. If the document is negotiable, and the goods are held by a bailee, title and risk pass upon the buyer's *receipt* of the document [UCC 2-401(3)(a), UCC 2-509(2)(a)].
	   b. If document is nonnegotiable, and the goods are held by a bailee, title passes upon the buyer's receipt of the document, but risk does *not* pass until the buyer, after receipt of the document, has had reasonable time to present the document to demand the goods [UCC 2-401(3)(a), UCC 2-509(2)(c), UCC 2-503(4)(b)].
	 3. If the goods are held by a bailee and no document of title is transferred, risk passes to the buyer when the bailee acknowledges the buyer's right to the possession of the goods [UCC 2-509(2)(b)].

2. Establishes that the person conducting the business (the consignee) is generally known by his or her creditors to be substantially engaged in selling the goods of others.

3. Complies with the filing provisions of Article 9 (to be discussed in Chapter 31) [UCC 2-326(3)].

For example, suppose that Buendia operates a retail furniture store under the name of Affordable Furniture. Lindo Outdoor Furniture Company delivers some patio sets to Buendia on consignment. Lindo is the consignor, and Buendia is the consignee. If (1) no sign is posted evidencing Lindo's interest, (2) Buendia is not generally known to sell from a consigned inventory, and (3) Lindo does not comply with the filing provisions of Article 9, the patio sets are subject to the claims of Buendia's creditors.

Risk of Loss in a Breached Sales Contract

There are many ways to breach a sales contract. The transfer of risk operates differently depending on whether the seller or the buyer breaches. Generally, the party in breach bears the risk of loss.

SELLER'S BREACH If the goods are so nonconforming that the buyer has the right to reject them, the risk of loss will not pass to the buyer until the defects are cured or until the buyer accepts the goods in spite of their defects (thus waiving the right to reject). For example, a buyer orders blue widgets from a seller, F.O.B. seller's plant. The seller ships black widgets, giving the buyer the right to reject. The widgets are damaged in transit. The risk of loss falls on the seller (although the risk would have been on the buyer if blue widgets had been shipped) [UCC 2-510].

If a buyer accepts a shipment of goods and later discovers a latent defect, acceptance can be revoked. Revocation allows the buyer to pass the risk of loss back to the seller, at least to the extent that the buyer's insurance does not cover the loss [UCC 2-510(2)].

BUYER'S BREACH The general rule is that when a buyer breaches a contract, the risk of loss *immediately* shifts to the buyer. There are three important limitations to this rule:

1. The seller must already have identified the goods under the contract.

2. The buyer will bear the risk for only a *commercially reasonable time* after the seller learns of the breach.

3. The buyer will be liable only to the extent of any *deficiency* in the seller's insurance coverage [UCC 2-510(3)].

The following case is a good example of how a seller's failure to conform to the contract can result in the risk of loss remaining with the seller.

Case 19.3

MOSES v. NEWMAN

Court of Appeals of Tennessee, 1983.

658 S.W.2d 119.

BACKGROUND AND FACTS On February 7, in response to an advertisement offering a "trailer, complete set-up," Mike Moses bought a mobile home from Lakeview Mobile Homes, which was owned by Gary Newman. On February 9, the mobile home was delivered, blocked up and leveled, and sewer and water pipes were connected. Lakeview, however, failed to anchor the mobile home. Moses notified Lakeview of several problems with the home, and an installation crew was to return the following day. On February 10, a windstorm totally destroyed the home. Moses sued in a Tennessee state court, claiming that the loss fell on the seller. The trial judge concluded that Moses had not accepted the home at the time of the loss. Lakeview appealed.

DECISION AND RATIONALE The Court of Appeals of Tennessee upheld the trial court's determination that the risk of loss had not shifted from Lakeview to Moses because Lakeview had failed to conform completely to the contract. The appellate court pointed out that under the Tennessee statute corresponding to UCC 2–510(1), "[w]here a tender or delivery of goods so fails to conform to the contract as to give a right of rejection the risk of their loss remains on the seller until cure or acceptance." Under UCC 2–601, the right of rejection arises if goods "fail in any respect to conform to the contract." Under UCC 2–106(2), goods or performance "conform to the contract when they are in accordance with the obligations under the contract." The court noted that a seller cannot shift the risk of loss to a buyer unless the seller has fulfilled his or her obligations under the contract. Because the home had not been installed as provided for in the contract, Lakeview had not delivered conforming goods. Thus Lakeview had not fulfilled its contractual obligations, and the loss remained with the seller.

■ Insurable Interest

Buyers and sellers often obtain insurance coverage to protect against damage, loss, or destruction of goods. But any party purchasing insurance must have a "sufficient interest" in the insured item to obtain a valid policy. Insurance laws—not the UCC—determine sufficiency. (See Chapter 53.)

The UCC is helpful, however, because it contains certain rules regarding a buyer's and a seller's **insurable interest** in goods on a sales contract.

Buyers have an insurable interest in *identified* goods. The moment the goods are identified to the contract by the seller, the buyer has this special property interest, which allows the buyer to obtain necessary insurance coverage for the goods even before the risk of loss has passed [UCC 2-501(1)].

Consider an example: In March a farmer sells a cotton crop he hopes to harvest in October to a buyer. After the crop is planted, the buyer insures it against hail damage. In September, a hailstorm ruins the crop. When the buyer files a claim under her insurance policy, the insurer refuses to pay the claim, asserting that the buyer has no insurable interest in the crop. The insurer is not correct. The buyer acquired an insurable interest in the crop when it was planted, since she had a contract to buy it. The rule in UCC 2-501(1)(c) states that a buyer obtains an insurable interest in the goods by identification, which occurs "when the crops are planted or otherwise become growing crops . . . if the contract is . . . for the sale of crops to be harvested within twelve months or the next normal harvest season after contracting whichever is longer."

Sellers have an insurable interest in goods as long as they retain title to the goods. Even after title has passed to a buyer, however, a seller who has a "security interest" in the goods (a right to secure payment) still has an insurable interest and so can insure the goods [UCC 2-501(2)].

Hence, both a buyer and a seller can have an insurable interest in identical goods at the same time. In all cases, one must sustain an actual loss to have the right to recover from an insurance company.

■ Bulk Transfers

Special problems arise when a major portion of a business's assets are transferred. This is the subject of UCC Article 6, Bulk Transfers. A bulk transfer is defined as any transfer of a major part of the material, supplies, merchandise, or other inventory *not made in the ordinary course of the transferor's business* [UCC 6-102(1)]. Problems may arise, for example, when a business owing numerous creditors sells a substantial part of its equipment and inventories to a buyer. If the merchant uses the proceeds to pay off debts, no problems arise. But what if the merchant spends the money on a trip around the world, leaving the creditors without payment? Can the creditors lay any claim to the goods that were transferred in bulk to the buyer? To prevent this problem from arising, Article 6 lays out certain requirements for bulk transfers.

Requirements of Article 6

A party's bulk transfer of assets is ineffective against any creditor of the transferor, and thus a creditor may disregard the transfer and have the goods seized by court order to satisfy a debt, just as if they still belonged to the transferor, unless the following requirements are met:

1. The seller (transferor) must furnish to the buyer (transferee) a sworn list of the seller's existing creditors. This list must include those whose claims are disputed, stating names, business addresses, and amounts due [UCC 6-104(1)(a)].
2. The buyer and the seller must prepare a schedule of the property transferred [UCC 6-104(1)(b)].
3. The buyer must preserve the list of creditors and the schedule of property for six months. He or she must permit inspection of the list and the schedule of property by any creditor of the seller or file the list and the schedule in a designated public office [UCC 6-104(1)(c)].
4. Notice of the proposed bulk transfer must be given by the buyer to each creditor of the seller at least ten days before the buyer takes possession of the goods or makes payments for them, whichever happens first [UCC 6-105]. (Some states also require the buyer to apply the proceeds from the sale to payment of the seller's creditors.)

If all of these steps are undertaken, then the bulk transfer complies with the statutory requirements. The buyer acquires title to the goods free of all claims of the seller's creditors.

Notice to Creditors

The specific requirements for the contents of the notice to creditors are as follows:

1. A statement that a bulk transfer is about to be made.
2. Names and business addresses of the seller in bulk and buyer in bulk.
3. Information about whether all debts of the seller in bulk are to be paid in full as a result of the bulk transfer and, if so, the addresses to which creditors should send their bills [UCC 6-107(1)].

When the debts of the transferor in bulk are not to be paid in full as they fall due, the notice to creditors must also state such things as the location and general description of the property to be transferred, the address at which the schedule of property and list of creditors may be inspected, and whether the transfer is for new consideration or to pay existing debts [UCC 6-107(2)].

Failure to Comply

When the requirements of Article 6 are not complied with, goods in possession of the transferee continue to be subject to the claims of the unpaid creditors of the seller for a period of six months [UCC 6-111]. Nonetheless, a **good faith purchaser**—one who buys in good faith, for value, and without knowledge of any other claims to the goods or reason to suspect the seller's good title to the goods—of these goods acquires the goods free of any claim of the transferor's creditors.

If a creditor did not receive notice through the fault of the seller (for example, if the creditor was not on the seller's list), the seller is liable to the buyer for any loss the buyer incurs as a result of that creditor's claim against the property transferred. If the failure to receive notice is the buyer's fault and the seller's creditor satisfies his or her claim from the property transferred, the buyer can only recover from the seller the amount of the debt the seller owed to that creditor (under quasi-contractual theory).

Recommended Repeal or Revision

Article 6 has been criticized as impeding normal business transactions. For example, the article obligates *buyers* in bulk to incur costs to protect the interest of the *seller's* creditors, parties with whom buyers usually have no relationship. The article also provides creditors with a remedy against a good faith purchaser for full value who has no notice of any wrongdoing on a seller's part.

At one time, the benefits to creditors appeared to justify the costs of interfering with good faith transactions. Today, however, with changes in technology, credit reporting services are able to provide credit histories faster and more accurately than in years past. Changes in the law also provide creditors with greater opportunities to collect their debts. As a result of these changes, creditors are generally better able to make informed decisions

about whether to extend credit. Fraudulent bulk sales no longer appear to be frequent enough or to result in losses significant enough to require regulation of all bulk sales.

Because changes in the business and legal contexts in which bulk sales are conducted have made their regulation unnecessary, the National Conference of Commissioners on Uniform State Laws recently recommended that those states that have adopted Article 6 repeal it. For states disinclined to repeal Article 6, the article has been revised to provide creditors with better protection while reducing the burden imposed on good faith purchasers. The revised Article 6 limits its application to bulk sales by sellers whose principal business is the sale of inventory from stock. It does not apply to transactions involving property valued at less than $10,000 or at more than $25 million. If a seller has more than two hundred creditors, rather than requiring the buyer to send individual notice to each creditor, the buyer can give notice by public filing (for example, in the office of a secretary of state). The revised Article 6 also increases the notice period from ten to forty-five days and increases the statute of limitations from six months to one year. The text of the revised article—''Alternative B''—is included in Appendix C of this book.

■ Sales by Nonowners

Special problems arise when persons who acquire goods with imperfect titles attempt to resell them. UCC 2-402 and 2-403 deal with the rights of two parties who lay claim to the same goods, sold with imperfect titles.

Sometimes a seller of goods does not possess full ownership rights (good title) to the goods being sold. This can happen, for example, if the seller has stolen the goods or obtained them fraudulently. In such situations, does the buyer acquire title to the goods? The answer to this question depends on the circumstances, as discussed below and indicated in Exhibit 19–3. Generally, a buyer acquires at least whatever title the seller has to the goods sold.

Void Title

A buyer may unknowingly purchase goods from a seller who is not the owner of the goods. If the seller is a thief, the seller's title is *void*—legally,

■ Exhibit 19–3 Void and Voidable Title

If goods are transferred from their owner to another by theft, the thief acquires no ownership rights. Because the thief's title is *void,* a later buyer can acquire no title, and the owner can recover the goods. If the transfer occurs by fraud, the transferee acquires *voidable* title. A later good faith purchaser for value can acquire good title, and the original owner cannot recover the goods. If the buyer is aware of circumstances that would make a person of ordinary prudence ask about the seller's title to the goods, the owner can recover them.

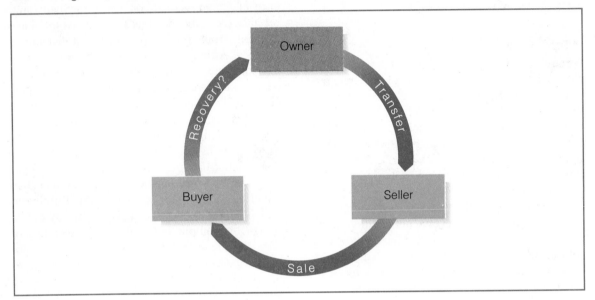

no title exists. Thus, the buyer acquires no title, and the real owner can reclaim the goods from the buyer.

For example, if Thomas steals goods owned by Carl, Thomas has *void title* (no legally recognized title) to those goods. If Thomas sells the goods to Benson, Carl can reclaim them from Benson even though Benson acted in good faith and honestly had no knowledge that the goods were stolen.

Voidable Title

A seller has a *voidable title* if the goods that he or she is selling were obtained by fraud; paid for with a check that is later dishonored; purchased on credit, when the seller was insolvent; or purchased from a minor. Purchasers of goods acquire all title that their transferors either had or had the power to transfer. A purchaser of a limited interest acquires rights only to the extent of the interest purchased. A seller with voidable title has the power, nonetheless, to transfer a good title to a good faith purchaser for value.

A good faith purchaser, as mentioned earlier, is one who buys without knowledge of circumstances that would make a person of ordinary prudence inquire about the seller's title to the goods. In other words, such circumstances may exist, but the purchaser is unaware of them. The real owner cannot recover goods from a good faith purchaser for value [UCC 2-403(1)]. If the buyer of the goods is not a good faith purchaser for value, then the actual owner of the goods can reclaim them from the buyer (or from the seller, if the goods are still in the seller's possession).

To illustrate: Martin sells his bicycle to Allen, who pays for the bicycle with a check that is later dishonored by the bank because of insufficient funds in Allen's account. Before Martin can retrieve the bicycle from Allen, Allen sells it to Peter. Peter, who has no knowledge that Allen has only voidable title to the bicycle, pays Allen with a check that is honored by the bank. Martin cannot recover his bicycle from Peter because Peter is a good faith purchaser. Peter has good title to the bicycle, and Martin's only recourse is to sue Allen for the price of the bike—if Allen is anywhere to be found.

The defendant in the following case had some warning that there was something suspicious about the transaction in which he was participating.

 Case 19.4

LANE v. HONEYCUTT
Court of Appeals of North
Carolina, 1972.
14 N.C.App. 436,
188 S.E.2d 604.

BACKGROUND AND FACTS   Fred Lane, owner of Lane's Outboard, sold boats, motors, and trailers. He sold a new boat, motor, and trailer to a person who called himself John Willis. Willis paid for the goods with a check for $6,285. The check was later dishonored. About six months later, Jimmy Honeycutt bought the boat, motor, and trailer for $2,500 from Willis (now identified as "Garrett"), who was renting a summer beach house to Honeycutt and whom Honeycutt had known for several years. Garrett purported to transfer title to the goods with a document that was not the statutorily required certificate of title. Lane sought to recover the goods from Honeycutt in a North Carolina state court. Honeycutt's defense was that he was a good faith purchaser and therefore Lane should not be able to recover from him. The trial court held for Lane, and Honeycutt appealed.

DECISION AND RATIONALE   The Court of Appeals of North Carolina affirmed the trial court's ruling. The appellate court determined that Lane was the owner and entitled to immediate possession of the boat, motor, and trailer. The court also awarded damages against Honeycutt for wrongful detention of the property. The court stated that under UCC 2–403, good faith purchasers can retain possession when they purchase from persons with a voidable title. The court recognized that Garrett had a voidable title because he bought the goods with a check that bounced (a fraudulent transaction). The court held that Honeycutt was not a good faith purchaser, however, because he paid $2,500 for goods valued at more then $6,500, and he accepted a document that was not an official certificate of title.

ETHICAL CONSIDERATIONS   The difference between "getting a good deal" and entering into a transaction clothed in suspicious trappings is usually quite obvious to a buyer. The UCC expresses a commonly held ethical precept by recognizing that those who purchase in good faith—that is, good faith purchasers—should merit more protection at law than those who know, or should know, that they are entering into a shady transaction.

The Entrustment Rule

According to Section 2-403(2), entrusting goods to a merchant *who deals in goods of that kind* gives the merchant the power to transfer all rights to a *buyer in the ordinary course of business.* **Entrustment** includes both delivering the goods to the merchant and leaving the purchased goods with the merchant for later delivery or pickup [UCC 2-403(3)]. A "buyer in the ordinary course" is a person who buys in good faith from a person who deals in goods of that kind. The buyer cannot have knowledge that the sale violates the ownership rights of a third person.

For example, Sue leaves her watch with a jeweler to be repaired. The jeweler sells both new and used watches. The jeweler sells Sue's watch to Ann, a customer, who does not know that the jeweler has no right to sell it. Ann gets *good title* against Sue's claim of ownership. Sue's only recourse in this situation is to sue the merchant for wrongfully selling her watch to Ann.

The good faith buyer, however, obtains only those rights held by the person who entrusted the goods. For example, Sue's watch is stolen by Thomas. Thomas leaves the watch with a jeweler for repairs. The jeweler sells the watch to Betty, who does not know that the jeweler has no right to sell it. Betty gets good title against Thomas, the entrustor, but not against Sue, who neither entrusted the watch to Thomas nor authorized Thomas to entrust it.

Seller's Retention of Sold Goods

Ordinarily, sellers do not retain goods in their possession or use after the goods have been sold. A seller who retained goods after they had been sold could mislead creditors into believing that the seller's assets were more substantial than they really were.

Retention of the goods, and particularly their use by the seller, is basic evidence of an intent to defraud creditors. If a creditor can prove that the retention is in fact fraud, or if the state has a statute providing that such retention creates a presumption of fraud (and if the presumption is unrebutted), the creditor can set aside the sale to the buyer.

UCC 2-402(2), however, recognizes that it is not necessarily a fraud upon creditors if a *merchant* seller retains possession in good faith for a "commercially reasonable time" to accomplish some legitimate purpose (for example, to make repairs or adjustments).

A seller can defraud creditors by selling items at something substantially less than "fair consideration," thereby depleting the seller's assets. This is fraud on the seller's creditors if the seller is insolvent at the time of the sale, is made insolvent by the sale, or actually intended to defraud or delay actions by the creditors. Assets sold at less than fair consideration often are sold to a friend or relative of the seller. Such sales are considered **sham transactions** used to conceal assets.

For example, suppose that FL Boat Company is on the verge of bankruptcy. Many of the loans that FL's owner has taken out are personally secured by him, so his creditors can go after his personal assets to recover what he owes them. Knowing this, FL's owner sells several expensive cars to his father for only $3,000 apiece, and he sells his personal yacht to his brother-in-law for $10,000 (although it is worth $110,000). He has an implicit understanding with his father and his brother-in-law that he will retain control over these assets but that they will have title. If the creditors find out about the sham transactions, they can void the sales.

Terms and Concepts

bill of lading 347	good faith purchaser 357	sale or return 353
consignment 353	identification 346	sham transaction 360
entrustment 359	insurable interest 355	warehouse receipt 347
fungible goods 346	sale on approval 353	

For Review

1. What is the significance of identifying goods to a contract?

2. If the parties to a contract do not expressly agree on when title to goods passes, what determines when title passes?

3. Risk of loss does not necessarily pass with title. If the parties to a contract do not expressly agree when risk passes, when does risk pass?

4. Bells Galore, Inc., contracts to deliver 100,000 jingle bells to Holiday Toy Manufacturing Co. in Washington, D.C., on or before December 15. Galore ships the bells by rail. En route, the train derails in an accident with a Snelling Oil Co. gas truck, and the bells are destroyed in the fire. Galore cannot otherwise deliver 100,000 jingle bells to Holiday by December 15. Which party bore the risk of loss? Is Galore excused from performing?

5. Les drops his Daytona watch off at a Burn Jewelry store for repair. After the watch is repaired, a Burn clerk sells it to Erin, who does not know that Les is the true owner. Erin gives the watch to her brother Dave for his birthday. Does Dave have good title to the watch?

■ Questions and Case Problems

Mackey orders from Pride 1,000 cases of Greenie brand peas from Lot A at list price to be shipped F.O.B. Pride's city via Fast Freight Lines. Pride receives the order and immediately sends Mackey an acceptance of the order with a promise to ship promptly. Pride later separates the 1,000 cases of Greenie peas and prints Mackey's name and address on each case. The peas are placed on Pride's dock, and Fast Freight is notified to pick up the shipment. The night before the pickup by Fast Freight, through no fault of Pride, a fire destroys the 1,000 cases of peas. Pride claims that title passed to Mackey at the time the contract was made and risk of loss passed to Mackey when the goods were marked with Mackey's name and address. Discuss Pride's contentions.

19-2. On May 1, Peale goes into Carson's retail clothing store to purchase a suit. Peale finds a suit he likes for $190 and buys it. The suit needs alteration. Peale is to pick up the altered suit at Carson's store on May 10. Consider the following separate sets of circumstances:

(a) One of Carson's major creditors obtains a judgment on the debt Carson owes and has the court issue a writ of execution (a court order to seize a debtor's property to satisfy a debt) to collect on that judgment all clothing in Carson's possession. Discuss Peale's rights to the suit on which the major creditor has levied.

(b) On May 9, through no fault of Carson, his store burns down, and all contents are a total loss. Between Carson and Peale, who suffers the loss of the suit destroyed by fire? Explain.

19-3. Zeke, who sells lawn mowers, tells Lewis, a regular customer, about a special promotional campaign. On receipt of a $50 down payment, Zeke will sell Lewis a new Universal lawn mower for $200, even though it normally sells for $350. Zeke further states to Lewis that if Lewis does not like the performance of the lawn mower, he can return it within thirty days and Zeke will refund the $50 down payment. Lewis pays the $50 and takes the mower. On the tenth day the lawn mower is stolen through no fault of Lewis. Lewis calls Zeke and demands the return of his $50. Zeke claims that Lewis should suffer the risk of loss and that he still owes Zeke the remainder of the purchase price, $150. Discuss whether Lewis or Zeke is correct.

19-4. In the following situations, two parties lay claim to the same goods sold. Discuss which of the parties would prevail in each situation.

(a) Thomas steals Dean's television set and sells the set to Bosky, an innocent purchaser, for value. Dean learns Bosky has the set and demands its return.

(b) Kerr takes her television set for repair to Martin, a merchant who sells new and used television sets. By accident, one of Martin's employees sells the set to Gale, an innocent purchaser-customer, who takes possession. Kerr wants her set back from Gale.

19-5. Benes contracts to purchase from Glover 100 cases of Knee High Corn to be shipped F.O.B. Glover's warehouse by Reliant Truck Lines. Glover, by mistake, delivers 100 cases of Green Valley Corn to the Reliant Truck Lines. While in transit, the Green Valley Corn is stolen. Between Benes and Glover, who suffers the loss?

19-6. Harold Shook agreed with Graybar Electric Co. to purchase three reels of burial cable for use in Shook's construction work. When the reels were delivered, each carton was marked "burial cable," although two of the reels were in fact aerial cable. Shook accepted the conforming reel of cable and notified Graybar that he was rejecting the two reels of aerial cable. Because of a trucker's strike, Shook was unsuccessful in arranging for the return of the reels to Graybar. He stored the reels in a well-lighted space near a grocery store owner's dwelling, which was close to his work site. About four months later, he noticed that one of the reels had been stolen. On the following day he notified Graybar of the loss and, worried about the safety of the second reel, arranged to have it transported to a garage for storage. Before the second reel could be transferred, however, it was also stolen, and Shook notified Graybar of the second theft. Graybar sued Shook for the purchase price, claiming that Shook had agreed to return to Graybar the nonconforming reels and had failed to do so. Shook contended that he had agreed only to contact a trucking company to return the reels and that, because he had contacted three trucking firms to no avail (owing to the strike), his obligation had been fulfilled. Discuss who bears the risk of loss for the stolen reels. [*Graybar Electric Co. v. Shook*, 283 N.C. 213, 195 S.E.2d 514 (1973)]

19-7. Hargo Woolen Mills had purchased bales of card waste, used in Hargo's manufacture of woolen cloth, from Shabry Trading Co. for many years. On this occasion, however, Shabry shipped twenty-four bales to Hargo without an order. Rather than pay for reshipment, both parties decided that Hargo would retain possession of the bales and pay for what it used. Hargo kept the bales separate inside its warehouse and eventually used, and was billed for, eight bales. The remaining sixteen bales were still kept separate by Hargo. Hargo went bankrupt, and everything in its warehouse was taken by the receiver, Meinhard-Commercial Corp. Shabry claimed that it was the owner and title holder of the bales and requested their return, but Meinhard refused. Discuss fully whether Shabry will be able to retake possession of the bales. [*Meinhard-Commercial Corp. v. Hargo Woolen Mills*, 112 N.H. 500, 300 A.2d 321 (1972)]

19-8. A new car owned by a New Jersey car rental agency was stolen in 1967. The agency collected the full price of the car from its insurance company, Home Indemnity Co., and assigned all its interest in the automobile to the insurer. Subsequently, a thief sold the car to an automobile wholesaler, who in turn sold it to a retail car dealer. Schrier purchased the automobile from the car dealer without knowledge of the theft. Home Indemnity sued Schrier to recover the car. Can Home Indemnity recover? Discuss. [*Schrier v. Home Indemnity Co.,* 273 A.2d 248 (D.C.App. 1971)]

19-9. Kumar Corp. agreed to sell 700 television sets to Nava, a Venezuelan wholesaler. Kumar and Nava expressly agreed that Nava would not pay for the television sets until it received and actually sold the merchandise in Venezuela. Kumar loaded the goods from its Miami warehouse into a trailer and delivered the trailer to the freight handler but failed to procure insurance. The shipping documents reflected that the goods were sold by Kumar to Nava for $144,417, C.I.F. Venezuela. Several days later, the trailer was discovered missing and was subsequently found abandoned and empty. Kumar sued the carrier. The carrier challenged Kumar's standing (right) to sue on the ground that the term C.I.F. (or its equivalent) required Kumar, the seller, to perform certain obligations with respect to the goods, including placing the goods in possession of the carrier, and that when these obligations had been properly performed, the risk of loss or damage to the goods passed to Nava, the buyer. Because Nava suffered the loss, only Nava had standing to sue. Discuss whether this argument is persuasive in light of all of the terms of the contract. [*Kumar Corp. v. Nopal Lines, Ltd.,* 462 So.2d 1178 (Fla.App. 1985)]

19-10. Samuel Porter was the owner of a Maurice Utrillo painting entitled "Chateau de Lion-sur Mer." Harold Von Maker, who called himself Peter Wertz, bought a different painting from Porter, paying $50,000 cash and giving Porter ten promissory notes for $10,000 each. At the same time, Wertz talked Porter into allowing Wertz to hang the Utrillo painting in Wertz's home while he decided whether to buy it. When the first promissory note was not paid, Porter learned that he was dealing with Von Maker, a man with a history of arrests and judgments against him. Von Maker told Porter that the Utrillo painting was on consignment and would be returned or Porter would receive $30,000. Actually, the painting had already been sold to Feigen Gallery, which had in turn sold it to Irwin Brenner, trading under the name Irwin Brenner Gallery. The painting was then taken to Venezuela. Porter filed suit against Wertz, the Feigen Gallery, and Irwin Brenner to recover either possession of the painting or its value. Feigen Gallery and Irwin Brenner claimed that they had good title under UCC 2-403 and that Porter was estopped from repossessing the painting or its value. Discuss whether Porter is entitled to repossession or the value of the Utrillo painting. [*Porter v. Wertz,* 68 A.D.2d 141, 416 N.Y.S.2d 254 (1979)]

19-11. Donald Hayward agreed to buy a thirty-foot Revel Craft Playmate Yacht from Herbert F. Postma, a yacht dealer, on February 7, 1967. The boat was to be delivered to a slip on Lake Macatawa during April 1967. Hayward signed a security agreement on March 1, 1967, and gave a promissory note for $13,095.60 to Postma's dealership. The security agreement provided clauses requiring the buyer to keep the boat in first-class order or repair and to keep the boat fully insured at all times. Prior to the delivery of the boat to Hayward, the boat was de-

stroyed by fire. Neither Postma nor Hayward had insured the boat, and Hayward requested that Postma pay off the note or reimburse him for payments made. Postma refused, and Hayward sued. Discuss whether Hayward or Postma has the risk of loss as to the boat destroyed in the fire. [*Hayward v. Postma,* 31 Mich.App. 720, 188 N.W.2d 31 (1971)]

19-12. A Question of Ethics

When Toby and Rita Kahr donated some used clothing to Goodwill Industries, Inc., they were not aware that a small bag containing their sterling silver had been accidentally included within one of the bags of donated clothing. The silverware, which was valued at over $3,500, had been given to them twenty-seven years earlier by Rita's father as a wedding present and had great sentimental value for them. The Kahrs realized what had happened shortly after Toby returned from Goodwill, but when Toby called Goodwill, he was told that the silver had immediately been sold to a customer, Karon Markland, for $15. Although Goodwill called Markland and asked her to return the silver, Markland refused to return it. The Kahrs then brought an action against Markland to regain the silver, claiming that Markland did not have good title to it. In view of these circumstances, discuss the following issues. [Kahr v. Markland, *187 Ill.App.3d 603, 543 N.E.2d 579, 135 Ill.Dec. 196 (1989)*]

1. The basic issue in this case is whether the silver was "lost property" (defined as property unintentionally separated from its owner) or property entrusted to a merchant, Goodwill Industries. If the court decides that the silver was lost, this will mean that the party in possession of the property will have good title against all parties except the true owner—in which case, the Kahrs will be able to recover the silver from Markland. If the court decides that the Kahrs entrusted the silver to Goodwill, then the entrustment rule will be applied—in which case, the Kahrs will be unable to recover the silver from Markland, a good faith purchaser. If you were the judge, how would you decide the issue? Why?

2. The entrustment rule can sometimes result in unfair treatment of the entrustor, because the entrustor cannot recover the property from a good faith purchaser (although the entrustor can recover the *value* of the property from the merchant who wrongfully sold the entrusted property). Given this potential for unfair treatment, how can the entrustment rule be justified from an ethical point of view?

3. Did Karon Markland act wrongfully in any way by not returning the silver to Goodwill when requested to do so? What would you have done in her position?

4. Goodwill argued that the entrustment rule should apply. Is this ethical behavior on the part of Goodwill? Why or why not? How might Goodwill justify its argument from an ethical point of view?

Chapter 20

Performance and Obligation

To understand the *performance* that is required of a seller and of a buyer under a sales contract, it is necessary to know the duties and obligations each party has assumed under the terms of the contract. Keep in mind that "duties and obligations" under the terms of the contract here include those specified by the agreement, the custom, and the UCC. In this chapter, after first looking at the general requirement of good faith, we will examine the basic performance obligations of the buyer and the seller under a sales contract.

■ The Good Faith Requirement

The obligations of "good faith" and "commercial reasonableness" underlie every sales contract within the UCC. These obligations can form the basis for a breach of contract suit later on. The UCC's good faith provision, which can never be disclaimed, reads as follows: "Every contract or duty within this Act imposes an obligation of good faith in its performance or enforcement" [UCC 1-203]. Good faith means honesty in fact. In the case of a merchant, it means honesty in fact *and* the observance of reasonable commercial standards of fair dealing in the trade [UCC 2-103(1)(b)]. In other words, merchants are held to a higher standard of performance or duty than nonmerchants are.

Good faith can mean that one party must not take advantage of another party by manipulating contract terms. Good faith applies to both parties, even the nonbreaching party. The principle of good faith applies through both the performance and the enforcement of all agreements or duties within a contract. Good faith is a question of fact for the jury.

The standards of good faith and commercial reasonableness are read into every contract, and they provide a framework in which the parties can specify particulars of performance. If a sales contract leaves open some particulars of performance and permits one of the parties to specify them, "[a]ny such specification must be made in good faith and within limits set by commercial reasonableness" [UCC 2-311(1)]. Thus, when one party delays specifying particulars of performance for an unreasonable period of time or fails to cooperate with the other party, the innocent party is excused from any resulting delay in performance. In addition, the innocent party can proceed to perform in any reasonable manner. If the innocent party has performed as far as is reasonably possible under the circumstances, then the other party's failure to specify particulars or failure to cooperate can be treated as a breach of contract.

The following case deals with the issue of good faith in the termination of a franchise contract.

Case 20.1

ZAPATHA v. DAIRY MART, INC.

Massachusetts Supreme Judicial Court, 1980.
408 N.E.2d 1370.

BACKGROUND AND FACTS In 1973, Bernard and Elaine Zapatha entered into a franchise agreement with Dairy Mart, Inc. The agreement permitted either party to terminate the relationship without cause on ninety days' written notice. A second agreement was executed in 1974 when the Zapathas moved their store to a new location. In 1977, the Zapathas refused to sign a new agreement submitted by Dairy Mart because they believed that the provisions were too burdensome (they required the store to be open longer hours, required the Zapathas to pay future increases in the cost of utilities, and allowed Dairy Mart to relocate the Zapathas). Dairy Mart gave written notice that the contract would be terminated in ninety days. The Zapathas brought an action in a Massachusetts state court to enjoin termination of the agreement, alleging, among other things, that Dairy Mart had not acted in good faith. The trial court held for the Zapathas, and Dairy Mart appealed.

DECISION AND RATIONALE The Massachusetts Supreme Judicial Court reversed the lower court's judgment. The state's highest court held that Dairy Mart acted in good faith in terminating the franchise agreement. The court held that the clause giving Dairy Mart the right to terminate the contract on ninety days written notice was very clear and came as no surprise to the Zapathas (who were experienced in business and knew of the clause before signing the agreement) and that Dairy Mart's exercise of its right did not create an undue burden on the franchisees to recoup their initial investment. The court pointed out that "[t]he sole test of 'honesty in fact' is whether the person was honest. We think that, whether or not termination according to the terms of the franchise agreement may have been arbitrary, it was not dishonest."

Performance of a Sales Contract

In the **performance** of a sales contract, a seller has the basic obligation to *transfer and deliver conforming goods,* and the buyer has the basic obligation to *accept and pay for conforming goods* in accordance with the contract [UCC 2-301]. Overall performance of a sales contract is controlled by the agreement between the buyer and the seller. When the contract is unclear, or when terms are indefinite in certain respects and disputes arise, the UCC provides built-in standards and rules for interpreting the agreement.

Seller's Obligation— Tender of Delivery

Tender of delivery requires that the seller have and hold **conforming goods** at the buyer's disposal and give the buyer whatever notification is reasonably necessary to enable the buyer to take delivery [UCC 2-503(1)].

Tender must occur at a *reasonable hour* and in a *reasonable manner.* What is reasonable depends in part on the subject matter of the contract. In most cases, a seller cannot call the buyer at 2:00 A.M. and say, "The goods are ready. I'll give you twenty minutes to get them.'' Unless the parties have agreed otherwise, the goods must be tendered for delivery at a reasonable time and must be kept available for a reasonable period of time to enable the buyer to take possession of them [UCC 2-503(1)(a)].

All goods called for by a contract must be tendered in a single delivery unless the parties agree otherwise [UCC 2-612] or the circumstances are such that either party can rightfully request delivery in lots [UCC 2-307]. Hence, an order for 1,000 shirts cannot be delivered two shirts at a time. If seller and buyer contemplate, though, that the shirts will be delivered in four orders of 250 each as they are produced for summer, winter, fall, and spring stock and the price can be apportioned accordingly, it may be commercially reasonable to follow this course.

Place of Delivery

The UCC provides for the place of delivery pursuant to a contract if the contract does not. Of course, the parties may agree on a particular destination, or their contract's terms or the circumstances may indicate the place.

NONCARRIER CASES If the contract does not designate the place at which the goods will be delivered, and the buyer is expected to pick them up, the place of delivery is the *seller's place of business* or, if the seller has none, the *seller's residence* [UCC 2-308]. If the contract involves the sale of *identified goods* (see Chapter 19 for a discussion of such goods) and the parties know when they enter into the contract that these goods are located somewhere other than at the seller's place of business (such as at a warehouse or in the possession of a bailee), then the *location of the goods* is the place for their delivery [UCC 2-308].

For example, Laval and Boyd live in San Francisco. In San Francisco, Laval contracts to sell to Boyd five used railroad dining cars, which both parties know are located in Atlanta. If nothing more is specified in the contract, the place of delivery for the railroad cars is Atlanta.

Suppose that the railroad cars are stored in a warehouse and that Boyd will need some type of document to show the warehouse (bailee) in Atlanta that he is entitled to take possession of the

five dining cars. The seller tenders delivery without moving the goods. The seller may deliver either by giving the buyer a *negotiable document of title* or by obtaining the *bailee's* (warehouse's) *acknowledgment* that the buyer is entitled to possession.[1]

CARRIER CASES In many instances, resulting either from attendant circumstances or from delivery terms contained in the contract, it is apparent that the parties intend that a carrier be used to move the goods. There are two ways a seller can complete performance of the obligation to deliver the goods—through a shipment contract or a destination contract.

Shipment Contracts A shipment contract requires or authorizes the seller to ship goods by a carrier. The contract does not require the seller to deliver the goods at a particular destination [UCC 2-509, 2-319]. Unless otherwise agreed, the seller must do the following [UCC 2-504]:

1. Put the goods into the hands of the carrier.
2. Make a contract for their transportation that is reasonable according to the nature of the goods and their value. (For example, certain types of goods need refrigeration in transit.)
3. Obtain and promptly deliver or tender to the buyer any documents necessary to enable the buyer to obtain possession of the goods from the carrier.
4. Promptly notify the buyer that shipment has been made.

If the seller fails to notify the buyer that shipment has been made or fails to make a proper contract for transportation, and a *material loss* of the goods or a *delay* results, the buyer can reject the shipment.

Destination Contracts Under destination contracts, the seller agrees to ensure that the goods will be duly tendered to the buyer at a particular des-

---

1. If the seller delivers a nonnegotiable document of title or merely writes instructions to the bailee to release the goods to the buyer without the bailee's *acknowledgment* of the buyer's rights, this will also be a sufficient tender, unless the buyer objects [UCC 2-503(4)]. But risk of loss will not pass until the buyer has had a reasonable time to present the document or the instructions.

tination. Once the goods arrive, the seller must tender the goods at a reasonable hour and hold conforming goods at the buyer's disposal for a reasonable length of time, giving appropriate notice. The seller must also provide the buyer with any documents of title necessary to enable the buyer to obtain delivery from the carrier.

The Perfect Tender Rule

As previously noted, the seller has an obligation to ship or tender *conforming goods,* and this entitles the seller to acceptance by and payment from the buyer according to the terms of the contract. At common law the seller was obligated to deliver goods in conformity with the terms of the contract in every detail. This was called the **perfect tender rule.** The UCC, in Section 2-601, preserves the perfect tender rule by providing that "if goods or tender of delivery fail *in any respect* to conform to the contract" (emphasis added), the buyer has the right to accept the goods, reject the entire shipment, or accept part and reject part.

For example, the buyer contracts to purchase 100 cases of Brand X peas to be delivered at the buyer's place of business on or before October 1. On September 28, the seller discovers that there are only 99 cases of Brand X in inventory but there will be another 500 cases within the next two weeks. So the seller tenders delivery of the 99 cases of Brand X on October 1, with the promise that the other case will be delivered within three weeks. Because the seller failed to make a perfect tender of 100 cases of Brand X, the buyer has the right to reject the entire shipment and hold the seller in breach.

Exceptions to the Perfect Tender Rule

Because of the rigidity of the perfect tender rule, several exceptions have been created, some of which are discussed here.

AGREEMENT OF THE PARTIES If the parties have agreed, for example, that defective goods or parts will not be rejected if the seller is able to repair or replace them within a reasonable time, then the perfect tender rule does not apply.

CURE The term **cure** is not specifically defined in the UCC, but it refers to the seller's right to repair, adjust, or replace defective or nonconforming goods [UCC 2-508].

When any tender or delivery is rejected because of nonconforming goods and the time for performance has not yet expired, the seller can notify the buyer promptly of the intention to cure and can then do so *within the contract time for performance* [UCC 2-508(1)].

For example, Horn sells Gill a white refrigerator, to be delivered on or before September 15. Horn delivers a yellow refrigerator on September 10, and Gill rejects it. Horn can cure by notifying Gill that he intends to cure and by delivering a white refrigerator on or before September 15.

Once the time for performance under the contract has expired, the seller can still exercise the right to cure if the seller had *reasonable grounds to believe that the nonconforming tender would be acceptable to the buyer.* Frequently the seller tenders nonconforming goods with some type of price allowance, but he or she may still have a reasonable belief that the goods will be accepted by the buyer for other reasons.

For example, Demsetz has been supplying auto body paint to Hall Body, an auto body paint shop, for several years. Demsetz and Hall have a contract for R-Z type paint. In the past, when Demsetz could not obtain R-Z type paint, he substituted R-Y type paint, and Hall accepted without any objection. Hall signs a new contract for R-Z type paint to be delivered on April 30. Demsetz realizes that, with the paint supply on hand, only half the order can be filled with R-Z type paint, so he completes the other half of the order with R-Y type paint. The order is delivered on April 30. Hall rejects. Demsetz, knowing from their prior course of dealing that R-Y had always been an acceptable substitute, had "reasonable grounds to believe" that R-Y would be acceptable. Therefore, Demsetz can cure within a reasonable time, even though conforming delivery will occur after the actual time for performance under the contract.

As just pointed out, the seller may offer a price allowance with the tender of nonconforming goods. This frequently creates a presumption that a buyer will accept the fortuitous offer. Suppose a buyer contracts to purchase 100 Model Z hand calculators at a price of $20 each from a seller, to be delivered on or before October 1. The seller cannot deliver 100 Model Z calculators but tenders 100 new, more sophisticated, more expensive Model

A-1 calculators at the same price as the 100 Model Z calculators contracted for on October 1. The buyer rejects the delivery. If the seller *notifies* the buyer of intent to cure, the seller has a *reasonable time* (after October 1) to substitute a conforming tender of Model Z calculators.

The seller's right to cure substantially restricts the buyer's right to reject. If the buyer refuses a tender of goods as nonconforming but does not disclose the nature of the defect to the seller, the buyer cannot later assert the defect as a defense if the defect is one that the seller could have cured. The buyer must act in good faith and state specific reasons for refusing to accept the goods [UCC 2-605].

SUBSTITUTION OF CARRIERS When an agreed-on manner of delivery (such as particular loading or unloading facilities) becomes impracticable or unavailable through no fault of either party but a commercially reasonable substitute is available, this substitute performance is sufficient tender to the buyer [UCC 2-614(1)].

For example, a sales contract calls for the delivery of a large piece of machinery to be shipped by ABC Truck Lines on or before June 1. The contract terms clearly state the importance of the delivery date. The employees of ABC Truck Lines go on strike. The seller will be entitled to make a reasonable substitute tender, perhaps by rail. Note that the seller here is responsible for any additional shipping costs, unless contrary arrangements have been made in the sales contract.

INSTALLMENT CONTRACTS An **installment contract** is a single contract that requires or authorizes delivery in two or more separate lots to be accepted and paid for separately. In an installment contract, a buyer can reject an installment *only if the nonconformity substantially impairs the value of the installment* and cannot be cured [UCC 2-612(2), 2-307]. Notice how this is a substantial limitation on the perfect tender rule.

The entire installment contract is breached only when one or more nonconforming installments *substantially* impair the value of the *whole contract*. If the buyer, after such a breach has occurred, accepts a nonconforming installment and fails to notify the seller of cancellation, then the contract is reinstated, however. Also, if the buyer brings an action with respect only to past installments or de-

mands performance as to future installments, the aggrieved party has reinstated the contract [UCC 2-612(3)].

A major issue to be determined is what constitutes *substantial* impairment of the "value of the whole." For example, consider an installment contract for the sale of twenty carloads of plywood. The first carload does not conform to the contract because 9 percent of the plywood in the car deviates from the thickness specifications. The buyer cancels the contract, and immediately thereafter the second and third carloads of plywood arrive at the buyer's place of business. The court would have to grapple with the question of whether the 9 percent of nonconforming plywood substantially impaired the value of the whole.[2]

A more clear-cut example is an installment contract that involves parts of a machine. Suppose that the first part is delivered and is irreparably defective but is necessary for the operation of the machine. The failure of this first installment will be a breach of the whole contract. Even when the defect in the first shipment is such that it gives the buyer only a "reasonable apprehension" about the ability or willingness of the seller to properly complete the other installments, the breach on the first installment may be regarded as a breach of the whole.

The point to remember is that the UCC substantially alters the right of a buyer to reject the entire contract in installment sales contracts. Such contracts are broadly defined in the UCC, which strictly limits rejection to cases of substantial nonconformity.

COMMERCIAL IMPRACTICABILITY Whenever occurrences unforeseen by either party when the contract was made make performance commercially impracticable, the rule of perfect tender no longer holds. According to UCC 2-615(a), delay in delivery or nondelivery in whole or in part is not a breach when performance has been made impracticable "by the occurrence of a contingency the nonoccurrence of which was a basic assumption on which the contract was made." The seller, however, must notify the buyer as soon as it is prac-

---

2. *Continental Forest Products v. White Lumber Sales, Inc.,* 256 Or. 466, 474 P.2d 1 (1970). The court held that the deviation did not substantially impair the value of the whole contract. Additionally, the court stated that the nonconformity could be cured by an adjustment in the price.

ticable to do so that there will be a delay or nondelivery.

The concept of **commercial impracticability** is closely allied with contract law theories of impossibility of performance and frustration of purpose (see Chapter 16). Increased costs resulting from inflation do not in and of themselves excuse performance. This is the kind of risk ordinarily assumed by a seller conducting business. The unforeseen contingency must alter the essential nature of the performance, such as would occur with a sudden, severe shortage of raw materials.

For example, a major oil company that receives its supplies from the Middle East has a contract to supply a buyer with 100,000 gallons of oil. Because of an oil embargo by the Organization of Petroleum Exporting Countries (OPEC), the seller is prevented from securing oil supplies to meet the terms of this contract. Because of the same embargo, the seller cannot secure oil from any other source. This situation comes under the commercial impracticability exception to the perfect tender doctrine.

Sometimes the unforeseen event only *partially* affects the seller's capacity to perform. As a result, the seller is able to fulfill the contract partially but cannot tender total performance. In this event, the seller is required to allocate in a fair and reasonable manner any remaining production and deliveries among the contracted customers. The buyer must receive notice of the allocation, with the obvious right to accept or reject it [UCC 2-615(b), (c)].

For example, a grower of cranberries in the state of Washington, Cran Plan, has contracted to sell this season's production to a number of customers, including the G & G grocery chain. G & G has contracted to purchase 2,000 crates of cranberries. Cran Plan has sprayed some of its bogs of cranberries with a chemical called Green. The Department of Agriculture discovers that persons who eat products sprayed with Green may develop cancer. An order prohibiting the sale of these products is effected. Cran Plan has harvested all the bogs not sprayed with Green but cannot fully meet all contract deliveries. In this case, Cran Plan is required to allocate fairly its production, notifying G & G of the amount it is able to deliver.

The following case illustrates an application of the doctrine of commercial impracticability.

Case 20.2

WALDINGER CORP. v. CRS GROUP ENGINEERS, INC.

United States Court of Appeals, Seventh Circuit, 1985. 775 F.2d 781.

BACKGROUND AND FACTS   The Clark Dietz Division of CRS Group Engineers, Inc., set specifications for two waste-water treatment facilities for the Urbana and Champaign Sanitary District. Dietz's specifications required certain performance capabilities, as well as exact conformity of mechanical components, for all equipment, including belt filter presses. The specifications were set with reference to a press manufactured by the Ralph B. Carter Company. The Waldinger Corporation, a subcontractor on the project, took bids from four press manufacturers and selected Ashbrook-Simon-Hartley, Inc., to provide the presses. Ashbrook's presses could meet the performance specifications, but the mechanical components varied from those required by Dietz. Dietz did not approve Ashbrook's machine, and Waldinger was forced to buy the presses from Carter at a higher price. Waldinger sued Ashbrook in a federal district court for breach of contract (and CRS for wrongful interference with Waldinger's contract with Ashbrook). Ashbrook claimed that Dietz had intentionally or negligently drafted restrictive specifications that made it commercially impracticable for Ashbrook to fulfill its contract. The trial court agreed and excused Ashbrook from performance. Waldinger appealed.

DECISION AND RATIONALE   The United States Court of Appeals for the Seventh Circuit affirmed the district court's decision. The appellate court agreed that a basic assumption of the contract between Waldinger and Ashbrook was that Ashbrook equipment was competitive and would comply with Dietz's specifications. That assumption was based on the belief that Dietz would interpret its specifications in a competitive and nonrestrictive manner. Because Dietz did not do so, Ashbrook's performance was rendered impracticable. The court also agreed that "it was not foreseeable at the time of contracting that Dietz would require strict compliance with all specifications." The court said that Dietz's "insistence on literal compliance with exclusionary specifications ha[d] no scientific or rational basis." The court commented that Environmental Protection Agency regulations—which prohibited exclusionary specifications and according to which the plant was to be built—and industry practice on waiver of mechanical specifications further indicated that Ashbrook could not have foreseen the possibility that Dietz would not accept its machine even if it met performance specifications.

DESTRUCTION OF IDENTIFIED GOODS The UCC provides that when a casualty occurs that totally destroys *identified goods* under a sales contract (through no fault of either party) *before risk passes to the buyer,* the seller and buyer are excused from performance [UCC 2-613(a)]. If the goods are only partially destroyed, however, the buyer can inspect them and either treat the contract as void or accept the damaged goods with àn allowance off the contract price.

Consider an example. Antioch Appliances has on display six ABC dishwashers of a discontinued model. Five are white, and one is black. No others of that model are available. Chavez, who is not a merchant, clearly specifies that he needs the black dishwasher because it fits in his kitchen's color scheme. Chavez buys the black dishwasher. Unfortunately, before Antioch can deliver it, it is destroyed by a fire. In such a case, under Section 2-613, Antioch Appliance will not be liable to Chavez for failure to deliver the black dishwasher. The goods here suffered a casualty without fault of either party before the risk of loss passed to the buyer, and the loss was complete, so the contract is avoided. Clearly, Antioch has no obligation to tender that dishwasher. Of course, Chavez has no obligation to pay for it, either.

Change the example somewhat. Chavez purchases a discount-priced dishwasher model but does not specify the color. If the black dishwasher is destroyed by fire, Antioch is still obliged to tender one of the other discontinued models, and Chavez is obligated to accept and to make payment. Only if Antioch's entire stock of the discontinued model were destroyed by the fire would it be excused from performance in this instance.

ASSURANCE AND COOPERATION Two other exceptions to the perfect tender doctrine apply equally to the seller and buyer.

The right of assurance—the right to obtain objective indications that performance will occur—stems from the concept that the essential purpose of a contract is performance by both parties, and thus when one party has reason to believe the other party will not perform, forcing the first party to perform creates an undue hardship.

The UCC provides that should a seller (or buyer) have "reasonable grounds" to believe the buyer (or seller) will not perform as contracted, he or she may "in writing demand adequate assurance of due performance" from the other party; and until such assurance is received, he or she may "suspend" further performance without liability. The grounds for such belief and action must be reasonable. Between merchants, the grounds are determined by commercial standards [UCC 2-609]. The assurances requested also must be reasonable. If such assurances are not forthcoming within a reasonable time (not to exceed thirty days), the failure to respond may be treated as a *repudiation* of the contract.

For example, Hilary has contracted to ship Jenkins 100 dozen shirts on or before October 1, with Jenkins's payment due within thirty days of delivery. Hilary has made two previous shipments, neither of which has been paid for by Jenkins. On September 20, Hilary demands in writing certain assurances of payment (such as payment of the last two orders to bring the account up to date) before she will ship the 100 dozen shirts. If these assurances are reasonable, Hilary can suspend shipment of the shirts without liability pending Jenkins's compliance. If Jenkins does not provide the assurances within a reasonable time (no longer than thirty days), Hilary can hold Jenkins in breach of contract without having made the contracted shipment.

Sometimes the performance of one party depends on the cooperation of the other. The UCC provides that when such cooperation is not forthcoming, the other party can suspend his or her own performance without liability and hold the uncooperative party in breach or proceed to perform the contract in any reasonable manner [see UCC 2-311(3)(b)].

For example, Amati is required by contract to deliver 1,200 Model Z washing machines to locations in the state of California to be specified later by Farrell. Deliveries are to be made on or before October 1. Amati has repeatedly requested the delivery locations, and Farrell has not responded. The 1,200 Model Z machines are ready for shipment on October 1, but Farrell still refuses to give Amati delivery locations. Amati does not ship on October 1. Can Amati be held liable? The answer is no. Amati is excused for any resulting delay of performance because of Farrell's failure to cooperate.

■ Buyer's Obligations

Once the seller has adequately tendered delivery, the buyer is obligated to accept the goods and pay for them according to the terms of the contract. In the absence of any specific agreements to the contrary, the buyer must:

1. Furnish facilities reasonably suited for receipt of the goods [UCC 2-503(1)(b)].
2. Make payment at the time and place the buyer *receives* the goods, even if the place of shipment is the place of delivery [UCC 2-310(a)].

Payment

When a sale is made on credit, the buyer is obliged to pay according to credit terms (for example, in 60, 90, or 120 days), *not* when the goods are received. The credit period usually begins on the *date of shipment* [UCC 2-310(d)].

Payment can be made by any means agreed on between the parties. Cash can be used, but the buyer can also use any other method generally acceptable in the commercial world. If the seller demands cash when the buyer offers a check, credit card, or the like, then the seller must permit the buyer reasonable time to obtain legal tender [UCC 2-511].

Right of Inspection

Unless otherwise agreed or for C.O.D. (collect on delivery) goods, the buyer's right to inspect the

goods is absolute. This right allows the buyer to verify, before making payment, that the goods tendered or delivered are what were contracted for or ordered. If the goods are not what the buyer ordered, there is no duty to pay. *An opportunity for inspection is therefore a condition precedent to the seller's right to enforce payment* [UCC 2-513(1)].

Unless otherwise agreed, inspection can take place at any reasonable place and time and in any reasonable manner. Generally, what is reasonable is determined by custom of the trade, past practices of the parties, and the like. The UCC also provides for inspection after arrival when goods are to be shipped.

Costs of inspecting conforming goods are borne by the buyer unless agreed otherwise [UCC 2-513(2)].

C.O.D. SHIPMENTS If a seller ships goods to a buyer C.O.D. (or under similar terms), the buyer can rightfully *reject* them (unless the contract expressly provides for a C.O.D. shipment). This is because C.O.D. does not permit inspection before payment, and the effect is a denial of the buyer's right of inspection. But when the buyer has agreed to a C.O.D. shipment in the contract or has agreed to pay for the goods on the presentation of a bill of lading, no right of inspection exists, because it was negated by the agreement [UCC 2-513(3)].

PAYMENT DUE—DOCUMENTS OF TITLE Under certain contracts, payment is due on the receipt of the required documents of title, even though the goods themselves may not have arrived at their destination. With C.I.F. and C.&F. contracts, payment is required on receipt of the documents unless the parties have agreed otherwise. Thus, payment is required *prior* to inspection, and it must be made unless the buyer knows that the goods are nonconforming [UCC 2-310(b), 2-513(3)].

Acceptance

The buyer can manifest acceptance of the delivered goods in several different ways:

1. The buyer can expressly accept the shipment by words or conduct. For example, there is an acceptance if the buyer, after having had a reason-

able opportunity to inspect, signifies agreement to the seller that either the goods are conforming or they are acceptable despite their nonconformity [UCC 2-606(1)(a)].

2. Acceptance will be presumed if the buyer has had a reasonable opportunity to inspect the goods and has failed to reject them within a reasonable period of time [UCC 2-606(1)(b), 2-602(1)].

3. The buyer can accept the goods by performing any act inconsistent with the seller's ownership. For example, any use or resale of the goods will generally constitute an acceptance. Limited use for the sole purpose of testing or inspecting the goods is not an acceptance, however [UCC 2-606(1)(c)].

Revocation of Acceptance

Acceptance does not in and of itself impair the right of the buyer to pursue remedies, although it does preclude the buyer from exercising the right of rejection. Also, if the buyer accepts nonconforming goods and fails to notify the seller of the breach when it is discovered (or when it should have been discovered), then the buyer is barred from pursuing any remedy against the seller. What is at issue here is the necessity for the buyer to inform the seller of the breach within a reasonable time. The burden is on the buyer to establish the existence of a breach of contract once the goods have been accepted [UCC 2-607(3)].

After a buyer accepts a lot or a *commercial unit*,[3] acceptance can be revoked if nonconformity *substantially* impairs the value of the unit or lot and if one of the following factors also is present:

1. Acceptance was predicated on the reasonable assumption that the nonconformity would be cured, and it has not been seasonably cured [UCC 2-608(1)(a)].

2. The buyer does not discover the nonconformity, and his or her acceptance was reasonably induced by the difficulty of discovery before acceptance or by the seller's assurances that the goods conform [UCC 2-608(1)(b)].[4]

In the following case, the court stresses the elements that must be present before a buyer can revoke acceptance after having accepted the goods.

---

3. A commercial unit is a unit of goods that, by commercial usage, is viewed as a single whole for purposes of sale and that cannot be divided without materially impairing the character of the unit, its market value, or its use [UCC 2-105]. A commercial unit can be a single article (such as a machine), a set of articles (such as a suite of furniture or an assortment of sizes), or a quantity (such as a bale, gross, or carload) or any other unit treated in the trade as a single whole.

4. Prior to the passage of state lemon laws, purchasers of automobiles that turned out to be ''lemons'' frequently had no other recourse than to revoke acceptance and request the return of the purchase price. Because of limitations on the seller's liability and the fact that an attempted revocation often led to costly litigation, consumers found it difficult to prevail against the automobile dealer in such disputes. Lemon laws, discussed in the next chapter, have to a great extent eased this problem.

BACKGROUND AND FACTS Susan Thomas visited the horse farm of George Alpert and Lee Wolfman, the owners of Raxx, a Russian Arabian stallion. She spoke to the general manager, Jon Mallory, about buying Raxx for breeding purposes. A few days later, a price of $175,000 was set. Thomas told Mallory that she wished to have a sample of Raxx's sperm to test the stallion's fertility, and Mallory assured her that he would take care of it (but never did). Thomas bought Raxx, paid part of the price, and took him to Vermont. Raxx was unable to impregnate any of Thomas's Arabian mares. Thomas contacted Mallory, who continued to assure her of Raxx's breeding soundness. Dr. Woods of the New York College of Veterinary Medicine determined that Raxx was an unsatisfactory prospective breeder. A stallion's value decreases significantly when he is not readily capable of breeding. Alpert and Wolfman filed suit in a federal district court against Thomas to recover the remaining purchase price. Thomas counterclaimed for rescission, claiming that she had revoked any acceptance (or, alternatively, for damages due to breach of express and implied warranties).

Case 20.3

ALPERT v. THOMAS

United States District Court,
District of Vermont, 1986.
643 F.Supp. 1406.

DECISION AND RATIONALE The United States District Court for the District of Vermont rejected Alpert and Wolfman's complaint and entered judgment for Thomas on her counterclaim. The court concluded that Thomas had properly revoked her acceptance of Raxx. Under UCC 2-608, there are four elements to proper revocation: "(1) the goods' non-conformity with the contract substantially impairs the value to the buyer; (2) the buyer's acceptance was (a) forthcoming on the reasonable assumption that the non-conformity would be cured (discovery at time of acceptance) or (b) reasonably induced by the difficulty of the discovery or by the seller's assurances (no discovery at the time of acceptance); (3) revocation occurred within a reasonable time after the nonconformity was discovered or should have been discovered; and (4) revocation took place before a substantial change occurred in the condition of the goods not caused by their own defects." The court determined that each element had been met. First, Raxx's status as an unsatisfactory breeder rendered him in nonconformity with the agreement's warranties that he be merchantable as a breeder, substantially impairing his value to Thomas. Second, "Thomas was induced to accept Raxx without discovering his non-conformity as a result of Mallory's assurances." Third, Thomas "formally revoked within a reasonable time after Raxx's non-conformity was discovered or should have been discovered." The court noted several facts that were relevant to its finding: "plaintiffs' assurances that they would perform a breeding soundness test rendered the timing of Thomas's discovery of Raxx's infertility reasonable; Thomas promptly notified plaintiffs that Raxx's breedability had become suspect; Thomas * * * attempted several times to discuss the problem with plaintiffs and Mallory repeatedly replied that plaintiffs would 'make it right'; and [both plaintiffs and defendant's veterinarians recommended] that Thomas should wait a few months and see if Raxx's problem would correct itself." Fourth, "there was no substantial damage in Raxx's condition not caused by his inability to breed." The court allowed Thomas to recover the $94,879.28 she had already paid for Raxx and $25,560.00 for transportation and care that she had reasonably incurred after the purchase.

NOTICE OF REVOCATION REQUIRED Revocation of acceptance will not be effective until notice is given to the seller, and that must occur within a reasonable time after the buyer either discovers or should have discovered the grounds for revocation. Also, revocation must occur before the goods have undergone any substantial change that was not caused by their own defects (such as spoilage) [UCC 2-608(2)].

PARTIAL ACCEPTANCE If some of the goods delivered do not conform to the contract and the seller has failed to cure, the buyer can make a *partial* acceptance [UCC 2-601(c)]. The same is true if the nonconformity was not reasonably discoverable before acceptance. A buyer cannot accept less than a single commercial unit, however.

■ Anticipatory Repudiation

What if, before the time for either performance, one party clearly communicates to the other the intention not to perform? Such an action is a breach of the contract by *anticipatory repudiation.* When this occurs, the aggrieved party can, according to UCC 2-610, do the following:

1. For a commercially reasonable time await performance by the repudiating parties.
2. Resort to any remedy for breach (see Chapter 21) even if the aggrieved party has notified the repudiating party that he or she awaits the latter's performance and has urged retraction.
3. In either case, *suspend performance* or proceed in accordance with the provisions of UCC

2-704 on the seller's right to identify goods notwithstanding breach or to salvage unfinished goods (see Chapter 21).

The key to anticipatory breach is that the repudiation takes place before the time that the party is required under contract to tender performance. The nonbreaching party has a choice of two responses. He or she can treat the repudiation as a final breach by pursuing a remedy; or he or she can wait, hoping that the repudiating party will decide to honor the obligations required by the contract despite the avowed intention to renege. Should the latter course be pursued, the UCC permits the breaching party (subject to some limitations) to "retract" his or her repudiation. The retraction can be made by any method that clearly indicates an intent to perform. Once retraction has been made, the rights of the repudiating party under the contract are reinstated [UCC 2-611]. The concept of anticipatory repudiation is illustrated in the following case.

Case 20.4

NEPTUNE RESEARCH & DEVELOPMENT, INC. v. TEKNICS INDUSTRIAL SYSTEMS, INC.

Superior Court of New Jersey, 1989.
235 N.J.Super.522,
563 A.2d 465.

BACKGROUND AND FACTS   Neptune Research & Development, Inc., contracted to buy a high-precision drilling machine for approximately $55,000 from Teknics Industrial Systems, Inc. The contract specified a mid-June delivery date, but said nothing about time being of the essence, and one of the standard-term paragraphs stated that shipping dates were approximate. By late August, the machine had not been delivered. On August 29, the parties agreed to a September 5 delivery date, and Dave Robertson, a Teknics representative, promised to call Neptune on September 3 to make delivery arrangements. Robertson did not call. On September 4, Neptune called Robertson, who allegedly said that under "no circumstances" would Teknics have the machine ready for pickup until September 9. Neptune canceled the contract. Later that day, Teknics told Neptune that the machine could be ready on September 5, but Neptune refused to complete the transaction and sued Teknics in a New Jersey state court to recover Neptune's $3,000 deposit. The trial court held for Neptune, concluding that Teknics had anticipatorily breached the contract on September 4, giving Neptune the right to cancel. Teknics appealed.

DECISION AND RATIONALE   The Superior Court of New Jersey affirmed the trial court's ruling. The appellate court held that Teknics's statement on September 4 that it could not deliver the machine by September 5 constituted an anticipatory repudiation of the contract, justifying Neptune's cancellation. Teknics's "retraction" of the repudiation was ineffective because Neptune had already treated the breach as final and canceled the contract. Teknics argued that the announcement that it could not deliver in time was not an anticipatory breach because it was not material. The court found that under the circumstances the repudiation went to the essence of the contract.

■ Terms and Concepts

commercial
  impracticability 368
conforming goods 364

cure 366
installment contract 367
perfect tender rule 366

performance 364
tender 364

■ For Review

1. Under the UCC, to a nonmerchant, good faith means honesty in fact. Under the UCC, what does good faith mean to a merchant?

2. At common law, a seller must comply with a contract in every detail or the buyer can hold the seller in breach. Is this rule changed by the UCC?

3. Under a contract for a sale of goods subject to the UCC, a buyer has two basic obligations. What are they?

4. Penn Electronics Corp. contracts to deliver Woo stereo speakers to Terence by May 15. On April 29, Penn delivers Moss speakers to Terence, who immediately informs Penn

by telephone: "You delivered the wrong speakers, and I don't want them." Can Penn still comply with the contract by delivering Woo speakers to Terence by May 15? If so, what must Penn do first?

5. Alpha, Inc., contracts to sell a used word processor to Lena. Alpha is in the business of selling used computer equipment, including word processors. Lena is to pick up the processor on Wednesday. Their contract says nothing about a "right of inspection." When Lena arrives to pick up the processor, can she inspect it before she accepts or pays for it?

■ Questions and Case Problems

20-1. Ames contracts to ship to Curley 100 Model Z television sets. The terms of delivery are F.O.B. Ames's city, by Green Truck Lines, with delivery on or before April 30. On April 15, Ames discovers that, because of an error in inventory control, all Model Z sets have been sold and the stock has not been replenished. Ames has Model X, a similar but slightly more expensive unit, in stock. On April 16, Ames ships 100 Model X sets, with notice that Curley will be charged the Model Z price. Curley (in a proper manner) rejects the Model X sets tendered on April 18. Ames does not wish to be held in breach of contract, even though he has tendered nonconforming goods. Discuss Ames's options.

20-2. Thal contracts to deliver to Hurwitz 1,000 bushels of corn at market price. Delivery and payment are to be made on October 1. On September 10, Hurwitz informs Thal that because of financial reverses she cannot pay on October 1. Thal immediately notifies Hurwitz that he is holding her in breach of contract. On September 15, Thal files suit for breach of contract. On October 3, Hurwitz files an answer to Thal's lawsuit. Hurwitz claims that had Thal tendered delivery on October 1, she would have paid for the corn. Because no delivery was tendered, Hurwitz claims she cannot be held liable. Discuss whether Thal can hold Hurwitz liable for breach.

20-3. Kirk has contracted to deliver to Doolittle 1,000 cases of Wonder brand beans on or before October 1. Doolittle is to specify the means of transportation twenty days prior to the date of shipment. Payment for the beans is to be made by Doolittle on tender of delivery. On September 10, Kirk prepares the 1,000 cases for shipment. Kirk asks Doolittle how he would like the goods to be shipped, but Doolittle does not respond. On September 21, Kirk demands in writing assurance that Doolittle will be able to pay on tender of the beans. Kirk's demand is that the money be placed in escrow prior to October 1 in a bank in Doolittle's city named by Kirk. Doolittle does not respond to any of the requests made by Kirk, but on October 5 he wants to file suit against Kirk for breach of contract for failure to deliver

the beans as contracted. Discuss Kirk's liability for failure to tender delivery on October 1.

20-4. Gibson contracts to deliver 100 Model X color television sets to a new retail customer, Beaver, on May 1, with payment to be made on delivery. Gibson tenders delivery in her own truck. Gibson notices that one or two cartons have scrape marks on them. Beaver inquires of Gibson whether the sets might have been damaged as they were being loaded. Gibson assures Beaver that the sets are in perfect condition. Beaver tenders Gibson a check, but Gibson refuses the check, claiming that the first delivery to new customers is always for cash. Beaver promises to have the cash within two days. Gibson leaves the sets with Beaver, who stores them in a warehouse pending an "opening sale" date. Two days later, Beaver opens some of the cartons and discovers that a number of the televisions are damaged beyond ordinary repair. Gibson claims Beaver has accepted the sets and is in breach by not paying on delivery. Discuss fully Gibson's claims.

20-5. Leemar Steel Co. manufactured counterweight inserts for CMI Corp., according to blueprints from CMI, and shipped them to CMI. CMI prepared an internal memo rejecting the shipment for nonconformance two days after it was received. CMI did not send the rejection notice to Leemar. Instead, a few weeks later, it notified Leemar by phone that there was a "problem with the inserts." CMI paid for the inserts and attempted, with Leemar's aid, to have the inserts ground to the correct tolerances during the next few months. Because this could not be accomplished, CMI filed suit to cancel the contract and to recover the money that it had paid Leemar pursuant to the contract. Discuss whether CMI had accepted the goods. Could it still revoke its acceptance and get its money back? [*CMI Corp. v. Leemar Steel Co.*, 733 F.2d 1410 (10th Cir. 1984)]

20-6. Bryant Lewis contracted to sell Ross Cattle Co. 400 head of cattle at $47.50 per hundredweight. Ross made an $8,000 down payment. Before delivery, Lewis heard a rumor that Ross was in poor financial condition, and Lewis demanded that he receive full payment before delivering the animals. Ross told Lewis the balance would be paid on delivery, based on the weight of the cattle delivered. Lewis refused to deliver the cattle and sold them to a third party. Ross filed suit. Lewis claimed that the refusal of Ross to pay was an anticipatory repudiation of the contract. Discuss whether Lewis was correct and what action Lewis could have taken on the basis of the rumor. [*Ross Cattle Co. v. Lewis,* 415 So.2d 1029 (Miss. 1982)]

20-7. Rheinberg-Kellerei GMBH, a German wine producer and export seller, sold 1,245 cases of wine to Vineyard Wine Co., a U.S. company. The contract did not specify delivery to any particular destination, and Rheinberg, through its agent, selected the port of Wilmington for the port of entry. Rheinberg delivered the wine to the boat carrier in early December 1978. On or about January 24, 1979, Vineyard learned that the wine had been lost in the North Atlantic sometime between December 12 and December 22, when the boat sank with all hands aboard. Vineyard refused to pay Rheinberg. Rheinberg filed an action for the purchase price, claiming that risk of loss had passed to the buyer, Vineyard, on delivery of the wine to the carrier. Vineyard claimed that, because of Rheinberg's failure to give prompt notice of shipment (notice had not been given until after the ship was lost at sea), risk of loss had not passed to the buyer. Discuss fully who is correct. [*Rheinberg-Kellerei GMBH v. Vineyard Wine Co.,* 281 S.E.2d 425 (N.C.App. 1981)]

20-8. In September of 1982, Kathleen Inniss purchased a 1982 Buick Skylark from Methot Buick-Opel, Inc. The car, which was a demonstrator, had nearly 6,000 miles on it but was accompanied by a new-car, twelve-month or 12,000-mile warranty. It also had a history of significant mechanical and electrical problems, which Methot failed to mention to Inniss. Shortly after Inniss took possession, she experienced problems with the car. Between September and December of 1982, she took the car back to Methot eight times for repairs. The horn, rear window defogger, throttle, and brakes were repaired, but by the end of the warranty period, several other problems still had not been. The temperature gauge continued to malfunction, intermittently the car would not start, it vibrated in the front end, and the directional indicators intermittently flashed incorrectly when in use. In addition, although the purchase agreement had provided that the car would be rustproofed, much of it had not been. Before the twelve-month warranty had lapsed, Innis sought to revoke her acceptance of the contract and asked for her money back. (The state of Maine did not have a "lemon law" at the time this case was brought.) Discuss fully whether Inniss could revoke her acceptance of the purchase contract and recover the purchase price of the automobile. [*Inniss v. Methot Buick-Opel, Inc.,* 506 A.2d 212 (Me. 1986)]

20-9. Case Briefing Assignment

Examine Case A.10 [Triad Systems Corp. v. Alsip, *880 F.2d 247 (10th Cir. 1989)*] *in Appendix A. The case has been excerpted there in great detail. Review and then brief the case, making sure that you include answers to the following questions in your brief.*

1. Why did Alsip seek to revoke his acceptance of the computer system?
2. How did the district court rule on the matter of evidence regarding statements made to Alsip by Triad's employees prior to the contract's execution?
3. Why did Triad Systems Corp. contend on appeal that Alsip's attempt to revoke acceptance was ineffective as a matter of law?
4. What other arguments did Triad Systems raise on appeal, and how did the court respond to them?

Chapter 21

Remedies of Buyer and Seller for Breach

When a sales contract is breached, the aggrieved party may have a number of remedies from which to choose [UCC 2-703, 2-711]. These remedies range from retaining the goods to requiring the breaching party's performance under the contract. The general purpose of these remedies is to put the aggrieved party "in as good a position as if the other party had fully performed." It is important not only that the nonbreaching party know what remedies are available but that he or she know which remedy is most appropriate for a given situation [UCC 1-106(1)].

■ Remedies of the Seller

The remedies available to a seller when the buyer is in breach under the UCC include:

1.   The right to withhold delivery of the goods.
2.   The right to stop a carrier or bailee from delivering the goods.
3.   A limited right to reclaim goods in the possession of an insolvent buyer.
4.   The right to identify and/or resell goods identified to the contract.
5.   The right to recover the purchase price plus incidental damages in certain cases.
6.   The right to recover damages for the buyer's wrongful repudiation or nonacceptance of the contract.
7.   The right to cancel the sales contract.

The Right to Withhold Delivery

In general, sellers can withhold or discontinue performance of their obligations under a sales contract when buyers are in breach. If the breach is due to the buyer's insolvency, the seller can refuse to deliver the goods unless the buyer pays in cash [UCC 2-702(1)]. A person is **insolvent** under the UCC when that person ceases to pay "his debts in the ordinary course of business or cannot pay his debts as they become due or is insolvent within the meaning of the federal bankruptcy law" [UCC 1-201(23)].

Consider an example. On September 1, Simpson receives an order from Bentley for ten cases of ballpoint pens to be shipped on September 13. Bentley wants the goods put on his thirty-day open account. On September 6,

Bentley files a petition in bankruptcy. On September 9, Simpson learns of Bentley's bankruptcy and therefore refuses to ship the goods on September 13. Bentley now claims that Simpson has breached his contract by not shipping the goods on September 13 as agreed. Bentley will not prevail, because Simpson was under no obligation to ship goods on credit to an insolvent buyer. Of course, Bentley could still obtain the goods by paying cash for them.

If a buyer has wrongfully rejected or revoked acceptance of the goods, failed to make proper and timely payment, or repudiated a part of the contract, the seller can withhold delivery of the goods in question. Furthermore, the seller can withhold the entire undelivered balance of the goods if the buyer's breach is material [UCC 2-703]. (Recall that a material breach is one that substantially impairs the value of the entire contract.)

The Right to Stop
Delivery of Goods in Transit

If the seller has delivered the goods to a carrier or a bailee but the buyer has not yet received them, the goods are said to be *in transit*. If the seller learns of the buyer's insolvency while the goods are in transit, the seller can stop the carrier or bailee from delivering the goods to the buyer on the basis of the buyer's insolvency, regardless of the quantity shipped.

If the buyer is not insolvent but repudiates the contract or gives the seller some other right to withhold or reclaim the goods, the seller can stop the goods in transit only if the quantity shipped is at least a carload, a truckload, a planeload, or a larger shipment[1] [UCC 2-705(1)].

Consider an example. On January 1, Beel orders a carload of onions from Sneed. Sneed is to ship them on January 8, and Beel is to pay for them on January 10. Sneed ships on time, but Beel does not pay on January 10. As soon as Sneed learns of this, she orders the carrier to stop the carload in transit. Because the carload is still on its way to Beel's city, the carrier is able to stop shipment. Beel cannot claim that Sneed and the carrier have performed a wrongful act by stopping the shipment, for a seller can always stop a carload of goods in transit when a buyer commits some breach of contract that gives the seller the right to withhold or reclaim the goods. Had the contract called for a shipment of ten bags of onions, rather than a carload, Sneed could *not* have stopped the goods in transit unless Beel was insolvent (unable to pay for the goods).

To stop delivery, the seller must *timely notify* the carrier or other bailee that the goods are to be returned or held for the seller. If the carrier has sufficient time to stop delivery, then the goods must be held and delivered according to the instructions of the seller, who is liable to the carrier for any additional costs incurred. If the carrier fails to act properly, it will be liable to the seller for any loss [UCC 2-705(3)].

The right of the seller to stop delivery is lost when:

1. The buyer obtains possession of the goods.
2. The carrier acknowledges the buyer's rights by reshipping or storing the goods for the buyer.
3. A bailee of the goods other than a carrier acknowledges that he or she is holding the goods for the buyer.
4. A negotiable document of title covering the goods has been negotiated to the buyer [UCC 2-705(2)].

Under general contract law, circumstances that make it unlikely that a party will be able to fulfill his or her contract may sometimes be treated as an anticipatory breach. As discussed in Chapter 20, under the UCC, circumstances that increase the risk of nonperformance but that do not clearly indicate that performance will not be forthcoming may not be treated as repudiation immediately. A seller may withhold performance, which includes stopping delivery, pending the buyer's assurances that performance will be forthcoming at the proper time. If adequate assurances are not given within a reasonable time (thirty days), the seller may treat the contract as repudiated. What is adequate, of course, depends on the circumstances [UCC 2-609].

---

1. This limitation of stoppage to larger shipments when the stoppage is due to reasons other than insolvency recognizes the burden that stoppage represents to carriers [UCC 2-705, Comment 1].

For example, imagine that in the Sneed-Beel onion deal described above, Sneed hears a rumor on January 9 that Beel is in financial trouble. Reasonably believing that the rumor may have a basis in fact, Sneed can order the delivery stopped in transit and demand assurance from Beel that payment will be made. A financial report from Beel's banker showing that Beel is in good financial condition would be adequate assurance, and on its receipt, Sneed must order the delivery resumed. On the other hand, if Beel provides no assurance, then Sneed normally could consider the failure a repudiation.

The Right to Reclaim the Goods

When a seller discovers that a buyer has received goods on credit while insolvent, the seller can demand return of the goods if the demand is made within ten days of the buyer's receipt of the goods. The seller can demand and reclaim the goods at any time if the buyer misrepresented his or her solvency in writing within three months prior to the delivery of the goods [UCC 2-702(2)].

The seller's right to reclaim, however, is subject to the rights of a good faith purchaser or other buyer in the ordinary course of business who purchases the goods from the buyer before the seller reclaims.[2]

It is obvious that the seller who successfully reclaims goods under the UCC receives preferential treatment over the buyer's other creditors. Because of this, the UCC provides that reclamation *bars* the seller from pursuing any other remedy as to these goods [UCC 2-702(3)].

The Right to Resell the Goods

Sometimes a buyer breaches or repudiates a sales contract while the seller is still in possession of finished or partially manufactured goods. In this event, the seller can identify to the contract the conforming goods that are still in his or her possession or control, even if they were not identified at the time of the breach. Then the seller can resell the goods and seek to recover damages from the breaching party [UCC 2-704]. Alternatively, as discussed in the following section, if the seller is unable to resell the goods, he or she can maintain an action for the price of the goods to recoup the value to the seller of the contract [UCC 2-709].

When the goods contracted for are unfinished at the time of breach, the seller can treat the unfinished goods in two ways. First, the seller can cease manufacturing the goods and resell them for scrap or salvage value. Second, the seller can complete the manufacture, identify the goods to the contract, and resell them. In choosing between these two alternatives, the seller must exercise reasonable commercial judgment to mitigate the loss and realize maximum value from the unfinished goods [UCC 2-704(2)].

When a seller possesses or controls the conforming goods at the time of the buyer's breach (because of the buyer's wrongful rejection or revocation of acceptance of the goods, failure to pay, or repudiation of the contract) or when the seller rightfully reacquires the goods by stopping them in transit, then the seller has the right to resell the goods. The resale must be made in good faith and in a commercially reasonable manner. The seller can recover any deficiency between the resale price and the contract price, along with **incidental damages,** defined as those costs to the seller resulting from stopping delivery of and transporting, caring for, and reselling the goods and other similar actions undertaken because of the breach [UCC 2-706(1), 2-710]. The seller is *not liable to the buyer* for any profits made on the resale [UCC 2-706(6)].

The resale can be private or public, and the goods can be sold as a unit or in parcels. The seller must give the original buyer reasonable notice of the resale, unless the goods are perishable or will rapidly decline in value [UCC 2-706(2), (3)]. In the latter case, the seller has a duty to resell the goods as rapidly as possible to mitigate damages. A good faith purchaser in a resale takes the goods free of any of the rights of the original buyer, even if the seller fails to comply with the resale requirements just described [UCC 2-706(5)].

---

2. A *buyer in the ordinary course of business* is a person who, in good faith and without knowledge that the sale violates the ownership rights or security interest of a third party, buys in ordinary course from a person (other than a pawnbroker) in the business of selling goods of that kind [UCC 1-201(9)].

Consider some examples. Cohen contracts on Monday to sell his car to Leuhrs for $5,000, with delivery of the car and payment for it due on the following Monday. When Cohen tenders delivery on Monday, Leuhrs refuses to accept or pay for the car. Cohen informs Leuhrs that he will resell the car at a *private* sale. Cohen sells the car to Devins for $2,000 on Tuesday. The following day, Cohen sues Leuhrs for $3,200—$3,000 being the difference between the resale price and the contract price and $200 being the value of incidental damages (the expense of arranging the sale). In this example, the seller would be unlikely to recover the $3,000 difference between the resale price and the contract price, because the resale was obviously not made in good faith or in a commercially reasonable manner.

Suppose that Cohen contracts to sell Leuhrs a prize bull for $10,000, with delivery and payment due on Monday. On Monday, Cohen tenders delivery of the prize bull, but Leuhrs refuses to accept or pay for it. Cohen tells Leuhrs that he is going to sell the bull at an area livestock auction the next day. At the auction, there are few bidders for the prize bull. Leuhrs decides to bid on the bull himself and obtains it for $9,000. Cohen then demands $1,100 in damages from Leuhrs—$1,000 for the difference between the contract price and the resale price plus $100 for incidental expenses in getting the prize bull to the auction. In this example, the total sum could probably be recovered by Cohen, assuming he can substantiate his incidental expenses. The livestock auction was a reasonable place for resale, and the resale was done in a commercially reasonable manner.

As a third example, Cohen contracts on Monday to sell 4,000 heads of romaine lettuce to Leuhrs for 30 cents per head, with delivery and payment due on Friday. On Wednesday, Cohen has 14,000 heads of romaine lettuce in his inventory, but he has not yet identified the 4,000 he intends to sell to Leuhrs. On that day, Leuhrs telephones Cohen to inform him that he will not accept or pay for the lettuce. Leuhrs claims that, because the 4,000 heads of romaine lettuce for his contract have not yet been identified, Cohen cannot resell and recover damages from him. Leuhrs is incorrect here. Cohen has the right to identify the 4,000 heads of lettuce for Leuhrs's contract and the right to resell the lettuce. Cohen can recover the difference between the resale price received and the contract price of 30 cents per head, plus any incidental damages [UCC 2-704(1), 2-706(1), 2-710].

The Right to Recover the Purchase Price

Before the UCC was adopted, a seller could not sue for the purchase price of the goods unless title had passed to the buyer. Under the UCC, an unpaid seller can bring an action to recover the purchase price and incidental damages, but only under one of the following circumstances:

1.   When the buyer has accepted the goods and has not revoked acceptance, in which case title would have passed to the buyer.
2.   When conforming goods have been lost or damaged after the risk of loss has passed to the buyer.
3.   When the buyer has breached after the goods have been identified to the contract and the seller is unable to resell the goods [UCC 2-709(1)].

If a seller sues for the contract price of goods that he or she has been unable to resell, the goods must be held for the buyer. The seller can resell at any time prior to the collection of the judgment from the buyer, but the net proceeds from the sale must be credited to the buyer. This is an example of the duty to mitigate damages.

To illustrate: Suppose Loomis has contracted to sell Zetting 200 tablecloths with the name of Zetting's restaurant inscribed on them. Loomis delivers the 200 tablecloths to Zetting, but Zetting refuses to pay. Or suppose Loomis tenders the 200 tablecloths to Zetting but Zetting refuses to accept them. In either case, Loomis has, as a proper remedy, an action for the purchase price.

In the first situation, Zetting accepted conforming goods, but he is in breach by failure to pay. In the second situation, the goods have been identified to the contract, and it is obvious that Loomis could not sell tablecloths inscribed with Zetting's restaurant's name to anyone else. Thus, both situations fall under UCC 2-709.

In the following case, the court had to determine whether a seller was entitled to recover the purchase price of specially manufactured goods after the buyer had breached the sales contract.

Case 21.1

ROYAL JONES & ASSOCIATES, INC. v. FIRST THERMAL SYSTEMS, INC.

District Court of Appeal of Florida, First District, 1990.
566 So.2d 853.

BACKGROUND AND FACTS Royal Jones & Associates, Inc., ordered three steel rendering tanks from First Thermal Systems, Inc., for use in its business of constructing rendering plants. The contract provided that First Thermal would manufacture the tanks according to Royal Jones's specifications for a price of $64,350. When the tanks were finished, Royal Jones refused to accept them and refused to pay the contract price. First Thermal sued in a Florida state court for the contract price of the tanks. The trial court, finding that Royal Jones had breached the contract and that the specially manufactured goods were not suitable for sale in the ordinary course of First Thermal's business, awarded First Thermal the full contract price as damages. Royal Jones appealed.

DECISION AND RATIONALE The District Court of Appeal of Florida affirmed the trial court's ruling: First Thermal was entitled to the full contract price of the specially manufactured tanks as damages because the evidence showed that efforts to resell the tanks would be useless. The appellate court pointed to evidence that the rendering tanks "were the only ones First Thermal ever made, the tanks were manufactured according to Royal Jones's specifications, First Thermal had no other customers to which it could resell the tanks," First Thermal did not know how to market the tanks for resale, and the "tanks were built without needed internal components and to a special size" and "could not be used as rendering tanks without special engineering to which First Thermal had no access." The court noted that the scrap value of the tanks to First Thermal was only about $700.

The Right to Recover Damages

If a buyer repudiates a contract or wrongfully refuses to accept the goods, a seller can maintain an action to recover damages. The seller may recover the difference between the contract price and the market price (at the time and place of tender of the goods) plus incidental damages [UCC 2-708(1)]. The time and place of tender are frequently given by such terms as F.O.B., F.A.S., C.I.F., and the

like, which determine whether there is a shipment or destination contract. If the market price is less than the contract price, the proper measure of damages includes the seller's lost profits [UCC 2-708(2)].

The question of wrongful repudiation of a sales contract concerning specially manufactured roller wheels for skateboards is the subject of the next case.

Case 21.2

CHICAGO ROLLER SKATE MANUFACTURING CO. v. SOKOL MANUFACTURING CO.

Supreme Court of Nebraska, 1970.
185 Neb. 515,
177 N.W.2d 25.

BACKGROUND AND FACTS Chicago Roller Skate Manufacturing Company contracted with Sokol Manufacturing Company to provide truck and wheel assemblies with plates and hangers for use in the manufacture of skateboards. When Chicago sent the goods to Sokol, there was a balance due of $12,860. Because the skateboard fad had declined, Sokol returned, without Chicago's consent, a quantity of the goods purchased and demanded full credit on the contract price. These goods were not suitable for any other use; nor could they be resold. Chicago held them for seven months, during which time Chicago offered Sokol a credit of 70 cents per unit, which Sokol neither accepted nor rejected. Finally, Chicago disassembled, cleaned, and rebuilt the units to make them suitable for use on normal roller skates. The rebuilt units had a reasonable value of between 67 cents and 69 cents. The salvage operation cost Chicago $3,540.76. Profits lost amounted to an additional $2,572. Chicago, disregarding its expense, credited Sokol with 70 cents per unit and brought suit in a Nebraska state court for the balance due of $4,285. The trial court awarded this amount to Chicago, and Sokol appealed.

DECISION AND RATIONALE   The Supreme Court of Nebraska affirmed the trial court's judgment. Sokol argued that because the goods were not resold or held for the buyer, Chicago could not maintain an action to recover the full contract price. The state supreme court noted that UCC 1-106 provides that "[t]he remedies provided * * * shall be liberally administered to the end that the aggrieved party shall be put in as good a position as if the other party had fully performed." Relying on UCC 2-708(2), the court determined that Chicago should have been awarded the profit that it would have made from full performance by Sokol, plus any incidental damages resulting from Sokol's breach and costs reasonably incurred. Using this measurement, the court arrived at an amount higher than that awarded by the trial court, but found that the trial court's award was without prejudice to Sokol, and the award was allowed to stand.

The Right to Cancel the Sales Contract

A seller can cancel a contract if the buyer wrongfully rejects or revokes acceptance of conforming goods, fails to make proper payment, or repudiates the contract in part or in whole. The contract can be canceled with respect to the goods directly involved, or the entire contract can be canceled if the breach is material [UCC 2-703].

The seller must *notify* the buyer of the cancellation, and at that point all remaining obligations of the seller are discharged. The buyer is not discharged from all remaining obligations but is in breach and can be sued under any of the subsections mentioned in UCC 2-703 and UCC 2-106(4).

If the seller's cancellation is not justified, then the seller is in breach of the contract, and the buyer can sue for appropriate damages.

Seller's Lien

Under certain circumstances, a seller's rights go beyond the remedies provided for under the UCC. One such right is a seller's common law lien in the goods being sold. A **lien** is an interest in property to secure payment of a debt or performance of an obligation. Technically, a lien is a right that is incident to the sale rather than a remedy for breach of contract. A seller's lien enables the seller to retain possession of the goods until the buyer pays for them.

The seller's lien can be waived or lost through: (1) express agreement, (2) acts inconsistent with the lien's existence, (3) payment or tender of payment by the buyer, or (4) voluntary and unconditional delivery of the goods to a carrier or other bailee or to the buyer or an authorized agent of the buyer.

If the sales agreement provides for an extension of credit to the buyer, the seller normally has no lien on the goods, because the act of extending credit is inconsistent with the existence of the lien. The seller will have a lien on the goods, however, if the buyer becomes insolvent or if the credit period expires while the goods are still in the seller's possession.

The tender of payment or the actual payment of the debt that the lien secures will ordinarily discharge the lien. This occurs when the buyer pays the full price for the goods and the seller gives up possession. When the buyer gives a promissory note, the lien ordinarily will *not* be discharged until the note is paid, even if the seller relinquishes possession of the goods.

Finally, sellers lose their liens when they voluntarily deliver possession of the goods to the buyer or to an authorized agent of the buyer. The lien is not lost, though, when delivery is qualified—that is, when the seller reserves his or her rights to the lien—or when the buyer obtains possession fraudulently.

Consider the following illustration. Williams, the plaintiff, sold his Chevrolet sedan to the Greers, the defendants. The defendants paid $6,280 by check and $600 in cash. After the Greers received

■ CONCEPT SUMMARY 21.1
Seller's Remedies for Buyer's Breach

Situations	Seller's Remedies
	The remedies available to a seller are basically determined by who has possession of the goods at the time of the buyer's breach.
Goods are in the seller's possession	1. Withhold delivery [UCC 2-703(a)]. 2. Resell [UCC 2-706]. 3. Sue for breach of contract [UCC 2-708]. 4. Cancel (rescind) [UCC 2-703]. 5. Identify goods to the contract [UCC 2-704].

Goods are in transit	1. Stoppage in transit:
	  a. Any size shipment if reason is buyer's insolvency.
	  b. Carload, truckload, planeload, or larger shipment for reasons other than buyer's insolvency [UCC 2-705].

Goods are in the buyer's possession	1. Sue for purchase price [UCC 2-709]. 2. Reclaim goods received by insolvent buyer (excludes all other remedies on reclamation) [UCC 2-702].

possession of the Chevrolet, they stopped payment on the check. Williams went to court to regain possession of the auto by enforcing his seller's lien. The court upheld his complaint, allowing him to regain possession of the auto and to keep it until the Greers paid the $6,280. Essentially, the Greers had obtained possession fraudulently; therefore, they had a voidable title. Williams could validly enforce his lien because he had the right to void the title.

■ Remedies of the Buyer

Under the UCC, the remedies available to the buyer include:

1. The right to reject nonconforming or improperly delivered goods.
2. The right to recover identified goods upon the seller's insolvency.
3. The right to obtain specific performance.
4. The right to replevy the goods.
5. The right to retain the goods and enforce a security interest in them.
6. The right to cancel the contract.
7. The right of cover.
8. The right to recover damages for nondelivery or repudiation by the seller.

9. The right to recover damages for breach in regard to accepted goods.

The Right of Rejection

If either the goods or the seller's tender of the goods fails to conform to the contract *in any respect,* the buyer can reject the goods. If some of the goods conform to the contract, the buyer can keep the conforming goods and reject the rest [UCC 2-601].

Goods must be rejected within a reasonable time and the seller must be seasonably notified [UCC 2-602]. Recall that notification is seasonable if it occurs before there is any substantial change in the goods not caused by their own defects—for example, before perishable goods perish. Furthermore, the buyer must designate particular defects that are ascertainable by reasonable inspection. Failure to do so precludes the buyer from using such defects to justify rejection or to establish breach when the seller could have cured the defects if they had been stated seasonably [UCC 2-605]. After rejecting the goods, the buyer cannot exercise any right of ownership over them. If the buyer acts inconsistently with the seller's ownership rights, the buyer will be deemed to have accepted the goods [UCC 2-606].

If a *merchant buyer* rightfully rejects goods, and the seller has no agent or business at the place of rejection, the buyer is required to follow any reasonable instructions received from the seller with respect to the goods controlled by the buyer. The buyer is entitled to reimbursement for the care and cost entailed in following the instructions [UCC 2-603]. The same requirement holds if the buyer rightfully revokes acceptance [UCC 2-608(3)].

If no instructions are forthcoming and the goods are perishable or threaten to decline in value quickly, the buyer can resell the goods in good faith, taking the appropriate reimbursement from the proceeds and is entitled under the UCC to a commission for selling the goods [UCC 2-603(1), (2)]. If the goods are not perishable, the buyer may store them for the seller's account or reship them to the seller at the seller's expense [UCC 2-604].

The Right to Recover Identified Goods

If a buyer has made a partial or a full payment for goods that remain in the possession of the seller, the buyer can recover the goods if the seller is insolvent or becomes insolvent within ten days after receiving the first payment and if the goods are identified to the contract. To exercise this right, the buyer must tender to the seller any unpaid balance of the purchase price [UCC 2-502].

The Right to Obtain Specific Performance

Under UCC 2-716(1), a buyer can obtain specific performance when the goods are unique or in other proper circumstances. Although it is not stated in this section of the UCC, an award of specific performance is usually considered inappropriate unless the buyer's remedy at law is inadequate. Ordinarily, a suit for money damages will be sufficient to place a buyer in the position he or she would have occupied if the seller had fully performed. When the contract is for the purchase of a particular work of art, patent, copyright, or similarly unique item, however, money damages may not be sufficient. Under these circumstances, equity will require the seller to perform exactly by delivering the unique goods (a remedy of specific performance).

To illustrate: Casey contracts to sell an antique car to Hammer for $30,000, with delivery and payment due on June 14. Hammer tenders payment on June 14, but Casey refuses to deliver. Can Hammer force delivery of the car? Probably, because the antique car is unique. Therefore, Hammer can obtain specific performance of the contract from Casey.

The Right to Replevy the Goods

Closely associated with a buyer's right to obtain specific performance is a buyer's right of replevin. Outside the UCC, the term **replevin** refers to a prejudgment process that permits the seizure of specific personal property in which a party claims an interest or to which a party has a right. For example, when a buyer defaults on installment payments under a contract for the purchase of an automobile, the seller might make use of replevin. Under the UCC, replevin is an action to recover goods that are identified to the contract and that are in the hands of a breaching seller. The buyer can use replevin if the seller has repudiated or breached the contract. Additionally, buyers must show that they were *unable to cover*. As will be discussed below, *cover* is the right of a buyer, after the seller's breach, to purchase goods in substitution for those due under the contract; but the purchase must be made in good faith and without unreasonable delay [UCC 2-716(3)].

Consider the following example. On July 1, Salvador contracts to sell her tomato crop to Bryan, with delivery and payment due on August 10. By August 1, it is clear that the local tomato crop will be bad and that the price of tomatoes is going to rise. Salvador contracts to sell her tomato crop to Green for a higher price and then informs Bryan that she will not deliver on August 10 as agreed. Bryan indicates that cover is unavailable and that he is therefore going to bring a replevin action against Salvador to force her to deliver her tomatoes to him on August 10.

This replevin action will normally succeed. Although a tomato crop is not unique, a buyer of goods identified to the contract for which no cover is available has a right to a replevin. In a normal tomato year, cover would probably have been available, and Bryan would have been limited to an action for damages.

The Right to Retain and Enforce a Security Interest in the Goods

Buyers who rightfully reject goods or who justifiably revoke acceptance of goods that remain in their possession or control have a security interest in the goods (basically, a lien to recover expenses, costs, and the like). The security interest encompasses any payments the buyer has made for the goods as well as any expenses incurred with regard to inspection, receipt, transportation, care, and custody of the goods [UCC 2-711(3)]. A buyer with a security interest in the goods is a ''person in the position of a seller.'' This gives the buyer the same rights as an unpaid seller. Thus, the buyer can resell, withhold delivery, or stop delivery of the goods. A buyer who chooses to resell must account to the seller for any amounts received in excess of the amount of the security interest [UCC 2-711(3), 2-706(6)].

The Right to Cancel the Contract

When a seller fails to make proper delivery or repudiates the contract, the buyer can cancel, or rescind, the contract. In addition, a buyer who has rightfully rejected or revoked acceptance of the goods can cancel, or rescind. Under these circumstances, the buyer can cancel, or rescind, that portion of the contract directly involved in the breach. If the seller's breach is material and substantially impairs the value of the whole contract, the buyer can cancel, or rescind, the whole contract. Upon notice of cancellation, the buyer is relieved of any further obligations under the contract but still retains all remedy rights that can be assessed against the seller.

The Right of Cover

In certain situations, buyers can protect themselves by obtaining **cover** (by purchasing goods in substitution for those due under the contract). This option is available to a buyer who has rightfully rejected goods or revoked acceptance. It is also available when the seller repudiates the contract or fails to deliver the goods. In obtaining cover, the buyer must act in good faith without unreasonable delay [UCC 2-712].

After purchasing substitute goods, the buyer can recover from the seller the difference between the cost of cover and the contract price, plus incidental and consequential damages less the expenses (such as delivery costs) that were saved as a result of the seller's breach [UCC 2-712, 2-715]. Consequential damages include any loss suffered by the buyer that the seller could have foreseen at the time of contract and any injury to the buyer's person or property proximately resulting from a breach of warranty[3] [UCC 2-715(2)].

Suppose Samms contracts to sell Byerly 10,000 pounds of sugar at 20 cents per pound. Delivery is to be on or before November 15. Samms knows that Byerly is going to use the sugar to make candy for Christmas sales. Byerly usually makes a $15,000 profit from these sales. Samms fails to deliver on November 15. Byerly attempts to purchase the sugar on the open market, but she must pay 30 cents per pound and take delivery on December 8. Because of this late delivery date, Byerly can prepare and sell only half as much Christmas candy as usual.

Byerly can recover from Samms the difference between the cover price and the contract price of sugar ($3,000 − $2,000 = $1,000) plus any incidental damages (costs incurred in effecting the cover). In addition, because Samms knew the reason for Byerly's purchase, Byerly normally would be entitled to consequential damages. In this case, Byerly could probably include as part of her damages against Samms the lost profits from the Christmas candy sales ($7,500—half of the $15,000 profit usually made).

Buyers are not required to cover, and failure to cover will not bar them from using any other remedies that are available under the UCC [UCC 2-712(3)]. But a buyer who fails to cover when it is reasonably possible to do so may *not* be able to collect consequential damages that he or she could have avoided by purchasing acceptable substitute goods [UCC 2-715(2)(a)]. Thus, the UCC encourages buyers to cover to mitigate damages. For example, if a wholesaler is supposed to supply a grocer with eggs for resale and the wholesaler is unable to deliver them, the grocer has the option of covering. If the grocer covers, he or she can recover any lost profits resulting from the wholesaler's breach of the contract. If the grocer does not cover and has no eggs to sell, he or she cannot recover lost profits to the extent that appropriate cover could have reasonably prevented their loss.

---

3. *Warranties,* which are discussed more fully in Chapter 22, may be defined generally as sellers' statements or representations referring to the character, quality, or title of their goods and constituting part of the contracts of sale. Under the UCC, certain warranties are implied in a sale of goods.

The Right to Recover Damages for Nondelivery or Repudiation

If a seller repudiates the sales contract or fails to deliver the goods, the buyer can sue for damages. The measure of recovery is the difference between the contract price and the market price of the goods at the time that the buyer *learned* of the breach. The market price is determined at the place at which the seller was supposed to deliver the goods. In some cases, the buyer can also recover incidental and consequential damages less the expenses that were saved as a result of the seller's breach [UCC 2-713]. Note that the damages here are based on the time and place a buyer would normally obtain cover.

Consider an example. Billings orders 10,000 bushels of wheat from Sneed for $5 a bushel, with delivery due on June 14 and payment due on June 20. Sneed does not deliver on June 14. On June 14, the market price of wheat is $5.50 per bushel. Billings chooses to do without the wheat. He sues Sneed for damages for nondelivery. Billings can recover $5,000 plus any expenses the breach may have caused him to incur. Here, the measure of damages is the market price less the contract price at the date that Billings was to have received delivery. (Any expenses Billings saved by the breach would have to be deducted from the damages.)

The Right to Recover Damages for Breach in Regard to Accepted Goods

A buyer who has accepted nonconforming goods must notify the seller of the breach within a reasonable time after the defect was or should have been discovered. Otherwise, the buyer cannot complain about defects in the goods [UCC 2-607(3)]. In addition, the parties to a sales contract can insert a provision requiring the buyer to give notice of any defects in the goods within a certain prescribed period. Such a requirement is ordinarily binding on the parties.

DAMAGES FOR BREACH OF WARRANTY When the seller breaches a warranty, the measure of damages equals the difference between the value of the goods as accepted and their value if they had been as warranted. The measure of damages under UCC 2-714 when the seller breaches a warranty is illustrated by the following case.

Case 21.3

CHATLOS SYSTEMS, INC. v. NATIONAL CASH REGISTER CORP.

United States Court of Appeals, Third Circuit, 1982.
670 F.2d 1304.

BACKGROUND AND FACTS Chatlos Systems, Inc., bought a computer from National Cash Register Corporation (NCR) for $46,020, a bargain price. The computer failed to operate as NCR had warranted, and Chatlos sued NCR in a federal district court for damages. Applying UCC 2-714(2), the trial judge found that the value of the system delivered was $6,000 and the fair market value of the system that would perform as NCR had warranted was $207,826. A judgment was rendered for Chatlos for $201,826, plus prejudgment interest (interest on the award of $201,826 calculated from the date that the system was delivered). NCR appealed, contending that basing damages on the value of computers to Chatlos rather than on the contract price was "substituting a Rolls Royce for a Ford."

DECISION AND RATIONALE The United States Court of Appeals for the Third Circuit affirmed the judgment of the trial court. The appellate court explained that Chatlos did not order and was not promised "merely a specific NCR computer model, but an NCR computer system with specified capabilities." The court pointed out that "[t]he correct measure of damages * * * is the difference between the fair market value of the goods accepted and the value that they would have had if they had been as warranted." The court also noted that this measure is not confined to instances in which there has been an increase in value between the dates of ordering and delivery. The court said that in determining fair market value, evidence of the contract price may be relevant, but it is not controlling. In this case, NCR limited its fair market value analysis to the contract price of the computer it delivered. Chatlos presented evidence of the worth of a computer with the promised capabilities. Noting that testimony by NCR's witnesses corroborated Chatlos's estimates to some extent, the court stated that "[c]redibility determinations had to be made by the [trial] judge" and concluded that "the computation of damages for breach of warranty was not clearly erroneous."

COMMENTS   The general purpose of the remedies in the UCC is to put the aggrieved party "in as good a position as if the other party had fully performed" [UCC 1-106(1)]. Chatlos was promised a system that was worth $207,826, but the system delivered was worth only $6,000. Thus, to put the company in as good a position as if NCR had performed, Chatlos would have to be awarded $201,826 [UCC 2-714(2)].

SUIT BY A BUYER'S CUSTOMER FOR BREACH OF WARRANTY   When a buyer resells defective goods that were originally sold by a breaching seller, the buyer's customer can sue the buyer. Under these circumstances the buyer has two alternatives:

1.   The buyer can notify the seller of the pending litigation. The notice should state that the seller can come into the customer's action against the buyer and defend. The notice should also point out that if, after seasonable receipt of the notice, the seller does not come in, the seller may nevertheless be bound by determinations of fact in the customer's action against the buyer. If the buyer brings a subsequent action against the seller, the seller cannot relitigate factual issues that are common to both the buyer's action against the seller and the buyer's customer's action against the buyer and that were determined in the customer's action [UCC 2-607(5)(a)].

2.   The buyer can also defend against the customer's suit and later bring an action against the original seller. This situation arises most frequently when there is a manufacturer-dealer arrangement—for example, when a car dealer sells a defective automobile and the customer sues the dealer but not the manufacturer.

OTHER MEASURES OF DAMAGES   The UCC also allows for two additional remedies for damages in accepted goods. Both can also be applied when there has been a breach of warranty.

The first applies when the buyer has accepted nonconforming goods. The buyer is entitled to recover for any loss "resulting in the ordinary course of events . . . as determined in any manner which is reasonable." Thus, this remedy is available for both a breach of warranty situation and any other failure of the seller to perform according to the contractual obligations [UCC 2-714(1)].

The second remedy is extremely important to a buyer, as the buyer not only has possession of the goods but also determines the amount of damages. The UCC permits the buyer, with proper notice to the seller, to deduct all or any part of the damages from the price still due and payable to the seller [UCC 2-717].

Suppose Reese is under contract to deliver 100 pairs of dress shoes at $50 a pair to Boone. The shoes are tendered, and upon inspection Boone discovers that 10 pairs are high-quality work shoes, not dress shoes. Boone accepts all 100 pairs and notifies Reese of the breach. At the time for contracted payment by Boone, Boone notifies Reese that she will not be able to sell the work shoes as quickly or for the same price or profit as the dress shoes and that she is tendering a check for $4,750 instead of the full $5,000 to reflect this loss. If Reese accepts and cashes Boone's check, Boone's measurement of damages is final.

▪ Contractual Provisions Affecting Remedies

The parties to a sales contract can vary their respective rights and obligations by contractual agreement. Certain restrictions are placed on the ability of parties to contract to limit their rights and remedies under the UCC, but provisions that the parties frequently include relate to the limitation

■ CONCEPT SUMMARY 21.2
Buyer's Remedies for Seller's Breach

Situations	Buyer's Remedies
	The remedies available to a buyer are basically determined by the facts of the situation.
Seller refuses to deliver, or seller tenders nonconforming goods and buyer rejects them	1. Cancel (rescind) [UCC 2-711]. 2. Cover [UCC 2-712]. 3. Sue for breach of contract [UCC 2-713].
Seller tenders nonconforming goods and buyer accepts them	1. Sue for ordinary damages [UCC 2-714(1)]. 2. Sue for breach of warranty [UCC 2-714(2)]. 3. Deduct damages from the price of the goods [UCC 2-717].
Seller refuses delivery and buyer wants the goods	1. Sue for specific performance [UCC 2-716(1)]. 2. Exercise right of replevin [UCC 2-716(3)]. 3. Recover goods from seller on seller's insolvency (when the buyer has paid part or all of the purchase price) [UCC 2-502].

of damages, the limitation of remedies, and the waiver of defenses.

Limitation of Damages

The parties can provide in the sales contract that a specified amount of damages will be paid in the event that either party breaches. These damages, called *liquidated damages,* must be reasonable in amount in view of the anticipated or actual loss caused by the breach, the difficulties of proof of loss, and the inconvenience or nonfeasibility of otherwise obtaining an adequate remedy. If the provision is valid, the aggrieved party is limited to recovering the amount of damages agreed on. If the amount of liquidated damages is unreasonably large, the provision is void, because it imposes a penalty, and the court will determine the appropriate amount of damages [UCC 2-718].

Consider as an example the sale of an uncommon antique. Seuss contracts with Barnes to sell it for $3,000. The contract contains a liquidated damages clause that holds the breaching party liable for $1,000 in case of a breach by either party. Payment and delivery of the antique are due on January 1. Barnes tenders payment on that date, but Seuss refuses to deliver for no valid reason. Can Barnes

demand $1,000 in damages instead of specific performance? Because we are dealing with an uncommon antique, Barnes will probably be able to recover. Seuss's breach might cause Barnes a loss of $1,000 in that the object in question is probably not easily acquired on the open market for the price of $3,000. If, instead, the object in question were easily obtainable for the agreed-on price, then Barnes probably would not be able to recover the $1,000. The normal measure of damages would then be the market price of the object less the contract price. The $1,000 damage clause in the contract would, in essence, be imposing a penalty on Seuss and therefore would be void under UCC 2-718(1). The court could determine that a smaller damage amount was appropriate, however.

A buyer often makes a down payment when a contract is executed. If the buyer defaults and the contract contains a liquidated damages provision, the seller retains the down payment as damages, and the buyer can recover only the part of the down payment that exceeds the amount specified as liquidated damages. The buyer is entitled to this sum as restitution. If the contract contains no provision for liquidated damages, the seller's damages are deemed to be 20 percent of the purchase price or $500, whichever is less [UCC 2-718(2)(b)]. The

LEGAL PERSPECTIVES IN BUSINESS

Breach of Contract

A contract for the sale of goods has been breached. Can such a breach be settled without going to court? The answer depends upon the willingness of the parties to agree on the appropriate remedy as a resolution for the breach. First, the parties may by contract have already agreed upon the remedy applicable in the event of a breach. This may be in the form of liquidated damages [UCC 2-718] or by a contract restricting or expanding remedies provided for under the Uniform Commercial Code [UCC 2-719].

Second, in the absence of any agreement, the UCC specifies a number of remedies available to a nonbreaching party, depending upon circumstances. In this particular situation, you need to analyze those remedies available if you were to go to court, put these remedies in order of priority, and then predict how successful you would be in pursuing the remedy. Once you have determined the most appropriate remedy or remedies, you can then look at the position of the breaching party to determine the limit and the basis for negotiating the settlement, including whether it is actually worth your trouble to go to court. Remember that the vast majority of breach of contract cases do not end up in court—they are settled beforehand.

amount by which the buyer's down payment exceeds this sum must be returned to the buyer. If the seller can prove that his or her actual damages are higher, the buyer can recover only the excess over the seller's actual damages.

For example, Rieken pays $1,250 down on a $10,000 lathe. Rieken then breaches, and Shaneyfelt, the seller, offers no proof of the actual damages. In the absence of a liquidated damages clause, Rieken is entitled to restitution of $750 ($1,250 less $500). If Rieken had put $350 down on a $500 lathe, he would have been entitled to $250 ($350 less $100, which is 20 percent of the purchase price).

Limitation of Remedies

The parties to a sales contract can vary their respective rights and obligations by contractual agreement. For example, a seller and a buyer can expressly provide for remedies in addition to those provided in the UCC. They can also provide for remedies in lieu of those provided in the UCC, or they can change the measure of damages. The seller can provide that the buyer's only remedy on breach of warranty will be repair or replacement of the item, or the seller can limit the buyer's remedy to return of the goods and refund of the purchase price. An agreed-on remedy is available in addition

to remedies provided in the UCC unless the parties expressly agree that the remedy is exclusive of all others [UCC 2-719(1)].

If the parties state that a remedy is exclusive of all other remedies, then it is the sole remedy. But when circumstances cause an exclusive remedy to fail in its essential purpose, the remedy will no longer be exclusive [UCC 2-719(2)]. For example, a sales contract that limits the buyer's remedy to repair or replacement fails in its essential purpose if the item cannot be repaired and no replacements are available. Of course, any clause limiting remedies in an unconscionable manner is void.

Suppose Bing buys a motorcycle from merchant Simple. The sales contract is accompanied by an express warranty stating that the exclusive remedy is repair or replacement of defective parts. The contract explicitly provides that Simple will not be responsible for consequential loss. Bing discovers numerous defects in her motorcycle after only a few days' use. After discovering each defect, she returns the motorcycle for repairs. Some of the parts are out of stock and will not arrive at Simple's repair station for months. Bing sues Simple. A trier of fact in this situation may return a verdict for Bing in an amount far exceeding the cost of repairs. The reason is that the exclusive remedy of repair or replacement of defective parts fails in its essential purpose, because the motorcycle cannot be repaired to make it operate as it should, free of defects.

A contract can limit or exclude consequential damages provided the limitation is not unconscionable. When the buyer is a consumer, the limitation of consequential damages for personal injuries resulting from a breach of warranty is *prima facie* unconscionable. The limitation of consequential damages is not necessarily unconscionable when the loss is commercial in nature—for example, lost profits and property damage [UCC 2-719(3)].

Waiver of Defenses

A buyer can be precluded from objecting to a breach of warranty by a seller in certain situations. For example, when a buyer purchases on credit, the seller usually assigns the note or account to a financial institution to obtain ready cash. To facilitate the assignment of these notes or accounts, the seller will include a waiver of defense clause in the sales contract. By entering into the contract, the buyer agrees not to assert against the assignee defenses that may apply to the seller. In essence, the buyer must complain directly to the seller, and the buyer cannot withhold payment for breach of warranty. Thus, this waiver—if enforceable—gives the assignee rights similar to those of a *holder in due course* (a purchaser who took the note in good faith, for value, and without notice of any claims or defenses against it, as described in Chapter 27), and no personal defense can be asserted against the assignee [UCC 9-206].

In such cases, buyers are in the same position as if they had signed a waiver. Because of this, many states, including those that have adopted the Uniform Consumer Credit Code, have invalidated such clauses in sales contracts for consumer goods. In addition, Federal Trade Commission rules provide that in consumer purchases on credit, any personal defense of the debtor-buyer against the seller is equally applicable against *any* holder, including a holder in due course. Therefore, these clauses are invalid in consumer transactions.

the UCC, after limitations had been imposed by the seller, were inadequate. In response to the frustrations of these buyers, the majority of states[4] have enacted *lemon laws*. Basically, lemon laws provide that if an automobile under warranty possesses a defect that significantly affects the vehicle's value or use, and the defect has not been remedied by the seller within a specified number of opportunities (usually four), the buyer is entitled to a new car, replacement of defective parts, or return of all consideration paid.

In most states, lemon laws require an aggrieved new-car owner to notify the dealer or manufacturer of the problem and provide the dealer or manufacturer with an opportunity to solve it. If the problem remains, the owner must then submit complaints to the arbitration program specified in the manufacturer's warranty before taking the case to court. Decisions by arbitration panels are binding on the manufacturer (that is, cannot be appealed by the manufacturer to the courts) but are not usually binding on the purchaser.

Most major automobile companies use their own arbitration panels. Ford and Chrysler, for example, have the Ford Consumer Appeals Board and the Chrysler Customer Arbitration Board, to which lemon-law disputes are submitted. Some companies, however, such as General Motors, subscribe to independent arbitration services, such as those provided by the Better Business Bureau. Although arbitration boards must meet state and/or federal standards of impartiality, industry-sponsored arbitration boards have been criticized for not being truly impartial in their decisions. In response to this criticism, some states[5] have established mandatory, government-sponsored arbitration programs for lemon-law disputes.

---

4. Currently, all states except Arkansas, South Carolina, and South Dakota have lemon laws covering the sale of new automobiles.

5. Including Connecticut, Massachusetts, Montana, New York, Texas, and Vermont, as well as the District of Columbia.

■ Lemon Laws

Some purchasers of defective automobiles—called "lemons"—found that the remedies provided by

■ Terms and Concepts

cover 384	insolvent 376	replevin 383
incidental damages 378	lien 381	

■ For Review

1. What remedies are available to a seller if a buyer wrongfully rejects or revokes acceptance of goods, fails to make proper and timely payment, or repudiates part or all of a contract?

2. What remedies are available to a buyer when a buyer rightfully rejects or revokes acceptance of goods, or when the seller repudiates the contract or fails to deliver?

3. A contract can be canceled if a breach is material. On notice of cancellation, the nonbreaching party's contractual obligations are discharged. Are the obligations of the breaching party also discharged?

4. Teddy's Bears, Inc., contracts to deliver 5,000 stuffed toy bears to the National Gift Co. on November 1. The contract price is $3.25 per bear. National Gift plans to retail the bears for $6.50 each. National Gift repudiates the contract on the day of delivery, at which time the market price for the bears is $3.00 each. Teddy's sues for damages. If Teddy's wins, what is the measure of those damages?

5. In the previous problem, if Teddy's had repudiated on the day of delivery instead of National Gift, what would be the measure of National Gift's damages?

■ Questions and Case Problems

21-1. Scopes contracts to ship Keen via Quickway Truck Line 100 cases of Knee High brand corn, F.O.B. Keen's city, at $6.50 per case. Keen is to make a 10-percent down payment. The payment is to be received at Scopes's place of business before shipment occurs. Scopes ships the corn as contracted, although he has not yet received the down payment, and the goods arrive in Keen's city. There they remain in the delivery van. Because Keen has failed to make the down payment, Scopes orders Quickway not to make the delivery to Keen's warehouse. Keen claims that the transit has ended and that Scopes has no right to stop the delivery of the corn. Discuss the validity of Keen's claim and Scopes's action.

21-2. Bullard has contracted to sell Lorwin 500 washing machines of a certain model at list price. Bullard is to ship the goods on or before December 1. Bullard produces 1,000 washing machines of this model but has not yet prepared Lorwin's shipment. On November 1, Lorwin repudiates the contract. Discuss the remedies available to Bullard.

21-3. Roy has contracted with Schnee for the purchase and delivery of 100 Model Z dryers. At the time for the contracted tender, Schnee does not have 100 Model Z dryers in stock and does not expect to acquire any for at least three months. Schnee tenders 80 Model Z dryers and 20 Model X dryers. Roy wants 100 Model Z dryers or none at all. Discuss the remedies available to Roy under these circumstances.

21-4. McDonald has contracted to purchase 500 pairs of shoes from Vetter. Vetter manufactures the shoes and tenders delivery to McDonald. McDonald accepts the shipment. Later, on inspection, McDonald discovers that 10 pairs of the shoes are poorly made and will have to be sold to customers as seconds. If McDonald decides to keep all 500 pairs of shoes, what remedies are available to her? Discuss.

21-5. Lehor is an antique car collector. He contracts to purchase spare parts for a 1938 engine from Beem. These parts are not made any more and are scarce. To get the contract with Beem, Lehor agrees to pay 50 percent of the purchase price in advance. On May 1, Lehor sends the payment, which is received on May 2. On May 3, Beem, having found another buyer willing to pay substantially more for the parts, informs Lehor that he will not deliver as contracted. That same day, Lehor learns that Beem is insolvent. Discuss fully any possible remedies available to Lehor to get these parts.

21-6. Lupofresh, Inc., contracted to sell a quantity of hops to the defendant Pabst Brewing Co. Lupofresh processed the hops and notified Pabst that the hops were ready for shipment. Pabst responded with a letter indicating acceptance of the hops but later refused to issue shipping orders, claiming that the price determination violated antitrust laws. Lupofresh sued for the full purchase price under UCC 2-709(1)(a). Pabst claimed that the goods had not been accepted but merely identified to the contract and that Lupofresh was required to attempt to resell the hops before it was entitled to recover the purchase price. Discuss fully who was correct. [*Lupofresh, Inc. v. Pabst Brewing Co.,* 505 A.2d 37 (Super.Ct.Del. 1985)]

21-7. Engineering Measurements Co. (EMCO) agreed to manufacture and deliver to International Technical Instruments, Inc., (ITI) a specified number of optical communication links (devices that allow wireless communication between two points). The links were to be delivered in stated installments. During a seven-month period, ITI continually complained that EMCO had failed to meet delivery schedules and had delivered some defective units. ITI did not refuse any shipment during this period. Eventually, ITI filed suit, claiming EMCO had breached its contract by failing to meet its delivery schedules and by delivering defective units. EMCO argued that ITI had accepted the goods and that by failing to revoke its acceptance and give notice, ITI was precluded from any remedy under UCC 2-607(3)(a). Discuss fully whether ITI was able to recover under its suit for breach of contract. [*International Technical Instruments, Inc. v. Engineering Measurements Co.,* 678 P.2d 558 (Colo.App. 1983)]

21-8. Servbest Foods, Inc., had a contract with Emessee Industries, Inc., under which Emessee was to purchase 200,000 pounds of beef trimmings from Servbest at 52.5 cents per pound. Servbest delivered to Emessee the warehouse receipts and invoices for the beef trimmings. The price of beef trimmings then fell significantly, and Emessee returned the documents to Servbest and canceled the contract. Servbest then sold the beef trimmings for 20.25 cents per pound and sued Emessee for damages (the difference between the contract price and the market price at which it had been forced to sell the trimmings) for breach of contract, plus incidental damages. Discuss whether Servbest Foods exercised a proper remedy and was entitled to the damages alleged in its lawsuit. [*Servbest Foods, Inc. v. Emessee Industries, Inc.,* 82 Ill.App.3d 662, 403 N.E.2d 1, 37 Ill.Dec. 945 (1980)]

21-9. Bigelow-Sanford, Inc., entered into a contract to buy 100,000 yards of jute at $0.64 per yard from Gunny Corp. Gunny delivered 22,228 yards to Bigelow but informed the company that no more would be delivered. Several other suppliers to Bigelow defaulted, and Bigelow was forced to go into the market one month later to purchase a total of 164,503 yards of jute for $1.21 per yard. Bigelow sued Gunny for the difference between the market price and the contract price of the amount of jute that Gunny had not delivered. Discuss whether Bigelow could recover this amount from Gunny. [*Bigelow-Sanford, Inc. v. Gunny Corp.,* 649 F.2d 1060 (5th Cir. 1981)]

21-10. A Question of Ethics

In March 1985, Bruce Young purchased from Hessel Tractor & Equipment Co., a John Deere equipment dealer, a feller-buncher to shear trees in his logging business. The only warranty in the contract was a one-year warranty against defects in the equipment with an exclusive remedy of repair and replacement for any defect in material or workmanship. All other warranties were expressly and conspicuously disclaimed. Young began to have serious problems with the equipment after less than a month of use. After over a year of continuing unsuccessful attempts at repair and after the one-year warranty had expired, Hessel, the seller, stopped repairing the machine. Given these facts, consider the following questions. [Young v. Hessel Tractor & Equipment Co., 782 P.2d 164 (Or.App. 1989)]

1. Do you think that it is fair for a seller to limit available remedies under a sales contract to just one, exclusive remedy—such as repair and replacement of parts? Is there anything unethical about this practice?

2. When an exclusive remedy leads to unfair results, as in this case, what, if anything, can be done about it?

3. What UCC provisions might Young cite to persuade the court that he is entitled to revoke his acceptance of the machine and recover the purchase price? How do these provisions reflect the UCC's attempt to balance freedom of contract against the need for fairness and justice in commercial transactions?

Chapter 22

Introduction to Sales Warranties

In the past, *caveat emptor*—let the buyer beware—was the prevailing philosophy in sales contract law. This may not have been an unrealistic approach when buyers and sellers were more or less equally capable of judging the quality (or lack of it) of the goods that were the subjects of their bargains. In twentieth-century America, however, it is unlikely that any buyer will comprehend the workings of any but a few of the goods he or she purchases, much less grasp all of the risks and be able to assume them intelligently and pay for any resulting injuries or damage. Thus, *caveat emptor* has given way to a consumer-oriented approach. Today, most goods are covered by some type of warranty designed to protect consumers. This change, of course, has not been without cost to consumers, who generally pay higher prices imposed by sellers and their insurers to cover their increased costs.

The concept of *warranty* is based on the seller's assurance to the buyer that the goods will meet certain standards. The UCC designates five types of warranties that can arise in a sales contract:

1. Warranty of title [UCC 2-312].
2. Express warranty [UCC 2-313].
3. Implied warranty of merchantability [UCC 2-314(1), (2)].
4. Implied warranty of fitness for a particular purpose [UCC 2-315].
5. Implied warranty arising from the course of dealing or trade usage [UCC 2-314(3)].

In the law of sales, because a warranty imposes a duty on the seller, a breach of warranty is a breach of the seller's promise. If the parties have not agreed to limit or modify the remedies available to the buyer on the seller's breach of warranty, the buyer can sue to recover damages against the seller. Under some circumstances, a breach can allow the buyer to rescind the agreement.[1]

---

1. Rescission can occur by rejection of goods before acceptance or by revocation by the buyer after acceptance.

■ Warranty of Title

Title warranty arises automatically in most sales contracts. UCC 2-312 imposes three types of warranties of title.

Good Title

In most cases, sellers warrant that they have good and valid title to the goods sold and that transfer of the title is rightful [UCC 2-312(1)(a)]. For example, Alice steals goods from Ophelia and sells them to Betty, who does not know that they are stolen. If Ophelia discovers that Betty has the goods, then Ophelia has the right to reclaim them from Betty. Under this UCC provision, however, Betty can then sue Alice for breach of warranty, because a thief has no title to stolen goods and thus cannot give good title in a subsequent sale. When Alice sold Betty the goods, Alice *automatically* warranted to Betty that the title conveyed was valid and that its transfer was rightful. Because this was not in fact the case, Alice breached the warranty of title imposed by UCC 2-312(1)(a) and became liable to the buyer for appropriate damages. (See Chapter 19 for a detailed discussion of sales by nonowners.)

No Liens

A second warranty of title provided by the UCC protects buyers who are *unaware* of any encumbrances (claims or liens) against goods at the time the contract is formed [UCC 2-312(1)(b)]. This warranty protects buyers who, for example, unknowingly purchase goods that are subject to a creditor's security interest (an interest in property that secures payment to the creditor—see Chapter 31). If a creditor legally repossesses the goods from a buyer who *had no actual knowledge of the security interest,* then the buyer can recover from the seller for a breach of warranty. (The buyer who has *actual knowledge* of a security interest has no recourse against a seller.)

To illustrate: Henderson buys a used boat from Sneed for cash. A month later, Reynolds repossesses the boat from Henderson, having proved that she, Reynolds, has a valid security interest in the boat and that Sneed is in default, having missed five payments. Henderson demands his money back from Sneed. Under Section 2-312(1)(b), Henderson has legal grounds to recover because the seller of goods warrants that the goods shall be delivered free from any security interest or other lien of which the buyer has no knowledge.

No Infringements

A third category of title warranty is the warranty against infringement. A merchant is deemed to warrant that the goods delivered are free from any patent, trademark, or copyright claims of a third person[2] [UCC 2-312(3)]. If this warranty is breached and the buyer is sued by the claim holder, the buyer *must notify the seller* of litigation within a reasonable time to enable the seller to decide whether to defend the lawsuit. If the seller states in writing that he or she has decided to defend and agrees to bear all expenses, including that of an adverse judgment, then the buyer must let the seller undertake litigation; otherwise the buyer loses all rights against the seller if any infringement liability is established [UCC 2-607(3)(b), (5)(b)]. If the seller refuses to defend, the buyer can do so and then, in turn, sue the seller.

This infringement warranty does not apply to buyers who furnish specifications for goods to be made in a particular way. In fact, it is the buyer who must indemnify the seller against any third person's claims of infringement arising out of goods manufactured to the buyer's specifications [UCC 2-312(3)]. Under these circumstances, the requirements of notice described above apply to a seller who is sued for breach of an infringement warranty [UCC 2-607(6)].

To illustrate: Green orders a custom-made machine from Beryl, a manufacturer of such machines. It is built strictly to Green's specifications. While the machine is being built, Patton files a suit against Beryl for patent infringement. Beryl immediately informs Green in writing of this suit and demands that Green take over the expense of the litigation. Green refuses to do so. Beryl settles with Patton out of court by paying Patton modest damages. Beryl now wishes to be reimbursed by Green. Beryl will be able to collect because a buyer who orders custom-built goods from a seller and who furnishes the seller with the specifications warrants

---

2.　Recall from Chapter 18 that a *merchant* is defined in UCC 2-104(1) as a person who deals in goods of the kind involved in the sales contract or who, by occupation, presents himself or herself as having knowledge or skill peculiar to the goods involved in the transaction.

The Creation of Warranties

Warranties are important in both commercial and consumer purchase transactions. There are three basic types of product warranties: express warranties, implied warranties of merchantability, and implied warranties of fitness for a particular purpose. If you are a seller of products, you can make or create any one of these warranties, and these are available to a consumer or commercial purchaser.

First and foremost, sellers and buyers need to know whether warranties have been created. Express warranties do not have to be labeled as such, but statements of opinion generally do not constitute express warranties. Express warranties can be made by descriptions of the goods or from purchases made from a seller's sample. Express warranties can be found in a seller's advertisement, brochure, or promotional materials, in addition to being made orally or in an express writing. The point is that a sales representative should use care in describing the merits of a product or the seller could be subject to an express warranty. If an express warranty is not intended, the sales pitch should not promise too much.

In most sales, because the seller is a merchant, the purchased goods carry the implied warranty of merchantability. You also have to remain aware of the importance of the implied warranty of fitness for a particular purpose. Assume a

customer comes to your sales representative and says, "I really need something that can do the job." (The "job" has been described in detail by the customer.) Your sales representative replies, "This product will do the job." An implied warranty that the product is fit for *that* particular purpose has been created.

Many sellers, particularly in commercial sales, try to limit or disclaim warranties. The Uniform Commercial Code permits all warranties, including express warranties, to be excluded or negated. Conspicuous statements such as "THERE ARE NO WARRANTIES WHICH EXTEND BEYOND THE DESCRIPTION ON THE FACE HEREOF" or "THERE ARE NO IMPLIED WARRANTIES OF FITNESS NOR MERCHANTABILITY WHICH ACCOMPANY THIS SALE" disclaim the implied warranties of fitness and/or merchantability respectively. Used goods sometimes are sold "as is" or "with all faults" to disclaim any implied warranties of fitness or merchantability that accompany the sale. Thus, a purchaser should be aware that his or her expectations of an average quality product will not be enforced.

Consumer purchasers under the Magnuson-Moss Act (applicable when a written express warranty is made) have implied warranty protection, as these warranties cannot be disclaimed as long as the express warranty is in effect. The key is frequently whether there is a written (express) warranty.

to the seller that the specifications do not infringe any patent.

Disclaimer of Title Warranty

In an ordinary sales transaction, the title warranty can be disclaimed or modified only by *specific language* in a contract. For example, sellers may assert that they are transferring only such rights, title, and interest as they have in the goods.

In certain cases, the circumstances of the sale are sufficient to indicate clearly to a buyer that no

assurances as to title are being made. The classic example is a sheriff's sale, when buyers know that the goods have been seized to satisfy debts and it is apparent that the goods are not the property of the person selling them [UCC 2-312(2)].

■ Express Warranties

A seller can create an **express warranty** by making representations concerning the quality, condition, description, or performance potential of the goods.

Under UCC 2-313, express warranties arise when a seller indicates that:

1. The goods will conform to any *affirmation or promise* of fact that the seller makes to the buyer about the goods. Such affirmations or promises are usually made during the bargaining process. Statements such as "These drill bits will *easily* penetrate stainless steel—and without dulling" constitute express warranties.
2. The goods will conform to any *description* of them—for example, a label that states that a "crate contains one 150-horsepower diesel engine" or a contract that calls for delivery of a "camel's hair coat" creates an express warranty.
3. The goods will conform to any *sample* or *model*. For example, an express warranty arises when the sales representative of a textile firm says to a prospective customer, "The bolts of cloth we deliver will match this swatch."

Express warranties can be found in a seller's advertisement, brochure, or promotional materials, in addition to being made orally or in an express warranty provision in a sales contract. If an express warranty is not intended, the marketing agent or salesperson should not promise too much. According to Section 2-313(2), "It is not necessary to the creation of an express warranty that the seller use formal words such as 'warrant' or 'guarantee' or that he have a specific intention to make a warranty." It is necessary only that a reasonable buyer would regard the representation as part of the basis of the bargain.

Basis of the Bargain

The UCC requires that for any express warranty to be created, the affirmation, promise, description, or sample must become part of the "basis of the bargain." To become part of the basis of the bargain, an affirmation, promise, description, or sample must come at such a time that the buyer could have relied on it when he or she agreed to the contract. The buyer does not have to prove that he or she actually did rely on it, but the seller can nullify the warranty by proving that the buyer did not rely on it. It does not matter whether the seller intended the statement, sample, or model to create a warranty. Each case presents a question of fact whether a representation came at such a time and in such a way that it induced the buyer to enter the contract.

Are certain vague telephone statements part of the basis of the bargain? That is the question addressed in the following case.

BACKGROUND AND FACTS Riegle sold a racehorse to Sessa for $25,000. Before the sale, Sessa sent his friend Maloney to examine the horse. Maloney reported that he "liked him." During a telephone conversation, Riegle told Sessa that Sessa would like the horse and that he was a "good one" and "sound." After delivery, the horse almost immediately went lame in the hind legs. Experts were unable to determine the cause or whether the condition had been present before Riegle shipped the horse. Although the horse was later able to race, Sessa sued in a federal district court for damages for breach of express warranties.

Case 22.1

SESSA v. RIEGLE

United States District Court,
Eastern District of
Pennsylvania, 1977.
427 F.Supp. 760.

DECISION AND RATIONALE The United States District Court for the Eastern District of Pennsylvania decided in Riegle's favor. The court considered three fundamental express warranty issues under UCC 2-313. The first issue centered on whether Riegle's statements constituted an "affirmation of fact or promise" or were "merely the seller's opinion or commendation of the goods." If they were opinions, they would not constitute express warranties. The court pointed out that whether statements constitute express warranties depends on the circumstances. Because it is not common to guarantee a horse (unless expressly agreed), the court considered Riegle's statements to be opinions. The second issue dealt with whether the statements, even if express warranties, served as part of the basis of the bargain. Because the statements were "largely collateral to the sale rather than an essential part of it," and Sessa relied primarily on Maloney's advice rather than on Riegle's statements, the court concluded that the statements were not part of the basis of the bargain. The third issue was whether there was a breach of warranty. The court found that even if there had been express warranties, Sessa failed to prove a breach as to the soundness of the horse at the time of the sale.

Statements of Opinion and Value

As stated above, according to Section 2-313(2), it is not necessary that a seller use formal words such as "warrant" or "guarantee" to make an express warranty. It is necessary only that a reasonable buyer would regard the representation as part of the basis of the bargain.

On the other hand, if the seller merely makes a statement that relates to the value or worth of the goods or makes a statement of opinion or recommendation about the goods, the seller is not creating an express warranty [UCC 2-313(2)]. For example, a seller claims, "This is the best used car to come along in years; it has four new tires and a 200-horsepower engine just rebuilt this year." The seller has made several *affirmations of fact* that can create a warranty: the automobile has an engine; it is a 200-horsepower engine; it was rebuilt this year; there are four tires on the automobile; the tires are new. But the seller's *opinion* that it is "the best used car to come along in years" is known as *puffing* and creates no warranty. (Puffing is the expression of an opinion by a seller that is not made as a representation of fact.) A statement relating to the value of the goods, such as "it's worth a fortune" or "anywhere else you'd pay $10,000 for it," will not normally create a warranty.

The ordinary seller can give an opinion that is not a warranty. If the seller is an expert and gives an opinion as an expert, however, then a warranty can be created. For example, Saul is an art dealer and an expert in seventeenth-century paintings. If Saul states to Lauren, a purchaser, that in his opinion a particular painting is a Rembrandt, Saul has warranted the accuracy of his opinion.

The question of what constitutes an express warranty and what constitutes puffing is not easy to resolve. Merely recognizing that some statements are not warranties does not tell us where one should draw the line between puffs and warranties. The reasonableness of the buyer's reliance appears to be the controlling criterion in many cases. For example, a salesperson's statements that a ladder "will never break" and will "last a lifetime" are so clearly improbable that no reasonable buyer should rely on them. Also, the context within which a statement is made might be relevant in determining the reasonableness of the buyer's reliance. For example, any statement made in a written advertisement is more likely to be relied on by a reasonable person than a statement made orally by a salesperson. Another factor is the specificity of the statements made. For example, a car dealer's statement that a vehicle is in "excellent" or "mint" condition may be too nonspecific for a court to deem it an express warranty—as is illustrated by the following case.

Case 22.2

WEB PRESS SERVICES CORP. v. NEW LONDON MOTORS, INC.

Supreme Court of Connecticut, 1987.
203 Conn. 342,
525 A.2d 57.

BACKGROUND AND FACTS Web Press Services Corporation purchased a used 1980 Ford Bronco from New London Motors, Inc., in July 1984. During the sale, the New London salesperson told Web Press's agent that the truck was "excellent" and in "mint condition." The agent test drove the truck before buying it. Mechanical troubles developed almost immediately after Web Press purchased the vehicle. Many problems were minor and were fixed by New London. The Bronco had a major structural defect in the rear axle, however, and New London did not fix it. In October, Web Press tendered the Bronco back to New London and revoked its acceptance of the vehicle. Web Press requested the return of the purchase price, but New London refused. Web Press sued in a Connecticut state court for breach of express warranties, among other claims. The trial court found that New London had not made any express warranties, and Web Press appealed.

DECISION AND RATIONALE The Supreme Court of Connecticut upheld the trial court's decision that the salesperson's statements about the car's condition did not create an express warranty. The court acknowledged that drawing the line between puffing and the creation of a warranty is often difficult, but mentioned two factors that have been identified as helpful in making that determination. "One such factor is the specificity of the statements made." Saying that a truck will not give less than 15.1 miles to the gallon when driven at a steady 60 miles per hour is more likely to be found to create an express warranty than saying that the truck is "top-notch," "in good condition," or "in perfect running order." Another factor is "whether a statement * * * was written or oral, the latter more likely to be considered puffing." The court concluded that the dealer's statements could not be considered specific. The court also found it significant that the plaintiff had been allowed to examine and test drive the truck before purchasing it.

■ Implied Warranties

An **implied warranty** is one that *the law derives* by implication or inference from the nature of the transaction or the relative situations or circumstances of the parties. For example, Kaplan buys an axe at Enrique's Hardware Store. No express warranties are made. The first time she chops wood with it, the axe handle breaks, and Kaplan is injured. She immediately notifies Enrique. Examination shows that the wood in the handle was rotten but that the rottenness could not have been noticed by either Enrique or Kaplan. Nonetheless, Kaplan notifies Enrique that she will hold him responsible for the medical bills. Enrique is responsible because a merchant seller of goods warrants that the goods he or she sells are fit for the ordinary purposes for which such goods are used. This axe was obviously not fit for those purposes.

Under the UCC, merchants impliedly warrant that the goods they sell are merchantable and, in certain circumstances, fit for a particular purpose. In addition, an implied warranty may arise from a course of dealing or usage of trade. We examine these three types of implied warranties in the following subsections.

Implied Warranty of Merchantability

An **implied warranty of merchantability** automatically arises in every sale of goods made *by a merchant* who deals in such goods [UCC 2-314(1)].

Thus, a retailer of ski equipment makes an implied warranty of merchantability every time the retailer sells a pair of skis, but a neighbor selling skis at a garage sale does not.

Goods that are *merchantable* are "reasonably fit for the ordinary purposes for which such goods are used" [UCC 2-314(2)]. They must at least:

1. Be of average, fair, or medium-grade quality.
2. Pass without objection in the trade or market for goods of the same description.
3. Be adequately packaged and labeled as provided by the agreement.
4. Conform to the promises or affirmations of fact made on the container or label.
5. Be of an even quality and quantity in each unit and among all units.

Some examples of nonmerchantable goods include light bulbs that explode when switched on, pajamas that burst into flames on slight contact with the heating elements of an electric room heater, high heels that break off shoes under normal use, and shotgun shells that explode prematurely. It makes no difference whether the merchant knew of or could have discovered a defect that makes the product unsafe. (Of course, merchants are not absolute insurers against *all* accidents arising in connection with the goods. For example, a bar of soap is not unmerchantable merely because a user can slip and fall by stepping on it.) In an action based on breach of warranty, it is necessary to show that an implied warranty existed, that the warranty was broken, and that the breach of warranty was the proximate cause of the damage sustained.

The serving of food or drink to be consumed on or off the premises is recognized as a sale of goods subject to the warranty of merchantability [UCC 2-314(1)]. Merchantable food means food that is fit to eat. What is food that is fit to eat? It might be argued that a food containing cholesterol is nonmerchantable because cholesterol may cause heart disease. But if that food is exactly like all other food of the particular brand and virtually the same as other brands on the market, it is unlikely that a court would agree. In such cases, consumers can reasonably expect the product to contain cholesterol.

Similarly, the courts assume that consumers should reasonably expect to find on occasion bones in fish fillets, cherry pits in cherry pies, nut shells in packages of shelled nuts, and so on—because such substances are natural incidents of the food.

Even a chicken bone in a chicken enchilada did not render the food unmerchantable, according to a recent California court decision, because the bone was "natural" to the food served.[3] Cases in which courts have found breaches of the implied warranty of merchantability have involved food containing substances that consumers would not reasonably expect to find there, such as an inchworm in a can of peas or a piece of glass in a soft drink.

The following classic case gives a court's interpretation of whether a fish bone in fish chowder is a foreign substance rendering the chowder unwholesome or not fit to be eaten.

---

3. *Mexicali Rose v. Superior Court,* 214 Cal.App.3d 238, 262 Cal.Rptr. 750 (1989). But see *Evart v. Suli,* 211 Cal.App.3d 605, 259 Cal.Rptr. 535 (1989), in which another California appellate court held that a jury might find that a hamburger containing a bone fragment large enough to break a consumer's tooth was unmerchantable because consumers do not reasonably expect to find bone fragments of such a size within ground meat. (These cases are both scheduled for review by the California Supreme Court.)

Case 22.3

WEBSTER v. BLUE SHIP TEA ROOM

Supreme Judicial Court of Massachusetts, 1964.
347 Mass. 421,
198 N.E.2d 309.

BACKGROUND AND FACTS Priscilla Webster ordered a cup of fish chowder at the Blue Ship Tea Room, Inc. After a few spoonfuls, she felt something lodged in her throat and could not swallow. In the second of two esophagoscopies at Massachusetts General Hospital, a fish bone was found in her throat and removed. Webster brought an action for breach of implied warranty of merchantability against the Blue Ship Tea Room in a Massachusetts state court. A jury rendered a verdict for her. Blue Ship Tea Room appealed.

DECISION AND RATIONALE The Supreme Judicial Court of Massachusetts "sympathized with a plaintiff who has suffered a peculiarly New England injury" but entered a judgment for Blue Ship Tea Room. To recover under a breach of implied warranty of merchantability, the injured party must prove that the goods were unfit "for the ordinary purposes for which such goods are used." The court reasoned that no breach of warranty had occurred. The court stated that the question was whether a fish bone made chowder unfit for eating. In the court's opinion, "the joys of life in New England include the ready availability of fresh fish chowder. We should be prepared to cope with the hazards of fish bones, the occasional presence of which in chowders is, it seems to us, to be anticipated, and which, in the light of a hallowed tradition, do not impair their fitness or merchantability."

Implied Warranty of Fitness for a Particular Purpose

The **implied warranty of fitness for a particular purpose** arises when *any seller* (merchant or non-merchant) knows the particular purpose for which a buyer will use the goods *and* knows that the buyer is relying on the seller's skill and judgment to select suitable goods [UCC 2-315].

A "particular purpose of the buyer" differs from the "ordinary purpose for which goods are used." Goods can be merchantable—suitable for the use to which such goods are ordinarily put— but still not fit for the buyer's particular purpose. For example, house paints suitable for painting ordinary walls are not suitable for painting stucco walls.

A contract can include both a warranty of merchantability and a warranty of fitness for a particular purpose, which relates to a specific use or to a special situation in which a buyer intends to use the goods. For example, a seller recommends a particular pair of shoes, *knowing* that a customer is looking for mountain climbing shoes. The buyer purchases the shoes *relying* on the seller's judgment. If the shoes are found to be not only improperly made but suitable only for walking, not for mountain climbing, the seller has breached both the warranty of fitness for a particular purpose and the warranty of merchantability.

A seller does not need "actual knowledge" of the buyer's particular purpose. It is sufficient if a seller "has reason to know" the purpose. However, the buyer must have relied on the seller's skill or judgment in selecting or furnishing suitable goods for an implied warranty of fitness to be created.

For example, Josephs buys a shortwave radio from Hi-Tech Electronics, telling the salesperson that she wants a set strong enough to pick up Radio Luxembourg, which is 8,000 miles away. Hi-Tech Electronics sells Josephs a Model XYZ set. The set works, but it will not pick up Radio Luxembourg. Josephs wants her money back. Here, because Hi-Tech Electronics is guilty of a breach of implied warranty of fitness for the buyer's particular purpose, Josephs will be able to recover. The salesperson knew specifically that she wanted a set that would pick up Radio Luxembourg. Furthermore, Josephs relied on the salesperson to furnish a radio that would fulfill this purpose. Because the salesperson did not do so, the warranty was breached.

In the next case, a seller helped a buyer solve a painting problem and became the defendant in a lawsuit for breach of an implied warranty of fitness.

BACKGROUND AND FACTS Charles Brown was engaged in the retail paint business. Michael Catania asked Brown to recommend a paint to cover the exterior stucco walls of his house. Brown recommended and sold to Catania a certain brand of paint called "Pierce's Shingle and Shake" paint. Brown also advised Catania how to prepare the walls before applying the paint and how to mix the paint in proper proportion to the thinner. Catania followed Brown's instructions, but the paint blistered and peeled soon after it was applied. Catania sued Brown in a Connecticut state court for breach of the implied warranty of fitness for a particular purpose, and the trial court rendered a judgment in Catania's favor. Brown appealed.

 Case 22.4

CATANIA v. BROWN
Circuit Court of Connecticut,
Appellate Division, 1967.
4 Conn.Cir.Ct. 344,
231 A.2d 668.

DECISION AND RATIONALE The Appellate Division of the Circuit Court of Connecticut affirmed the trial court's decision. The appellate court held that Brown created and breached a warranty of fitness for a particular purpose by recommending the particular paint as suitable for stucco walls. The court found that Catania relied on Brown's advice. The court stated, "[T]he buyer, being ignorant of the fitness of the article offered by the seller, justifiably relied on the superior information, skill and judgment of the seller and not on his own knowledge or judgment, and under such circumstances an implied warranty of fitness could properly be claimed by the purchaser."

Implied Warranty Arising from Course of Dealing or Trade Usage

The UCC recognizes in Section 2-314(3) that implied warranties can arise from a course of dealing, course of performance, or usage of trade. In the absence of evidence to the contrary, when both parties to a sales contract have knowledge of a well-recognized trade custom, the courts will infer that they both intended that custom to apply to their contract. For example, in the sale of a new car, when the industry-wide custom includes lubricating the car before delivery, a seller who fails to do so can be held liable to a buyer for resulting damages for breach of implied warranty. This failure, of course, also constitutes negligence on the part of the dealer.

Overlapping Warranties

Sometimes two or more warranties are made in a single transaction. An implied warranty of merchantability or of fitness for a particular purpose, or both, can exist in addition to an express warranty. For example, when a sales contract for a new car states that "this car engine is warranted to be free from defects for 12,000 miles or twelve months, whichever comes first," there is an express warranty against all defects and an implied warranty that the car will be fit for normal use.

The rule of UCC 2-317 is that express and implied warranties are construed as cumulative if they are consistent with one another. If the warranties are inconsistent, the courts will usually hold that:

1. Express warranties displace inconsistent implied warranties except implied warranties of fitness for a particular purpose.
2. Samples take precedence over inconsistent general descriptions.
3. Technical specifications displace inconsistent samples or general descriptions.

Suppose that when Josephs buys a shortwave radio at Hi-Tech Electronics, the contract expressly warrants that the radio will receive radio waves transmitted from as far as 4,000 miles away. She tries to pick up Radio Luxembourg—the stated purpose of her purchase—which is 8,000 miles away. The set cannot perform that well. Josephs claims that Hi-Tech Electronics is guilty of breach of warranty of fitness. The express warranty takes precedence over any implied warranty of merchantability (that a shortwave set should pick up any station anywhere in the world). Josephs does have a good claim for breach of implied warranty of fitness for a particular purpose, however, because she made it clear that she was buying the set to pick up Radio Luxembourg. In cases of inconsis-

tency between an express warranty and a warranty of fitness for a buyer's particular purpose, the warranty of fitness for the buyer's particular purpose normally prevails [UCC 2-317(c)].

Warranties and Third Parties

One of the general principles of contract law is that a person who is not one of the parties to a contract has no rights under the contract. (Notable exceptions are assignments and third party beneficiary contracts. See Chapter 15.) As discussed in Chapter 15, the connection that exists between the contracting parties is called *privity of contract*. It was established at common law that privity must exist between a plaintiff and a defendant for any action based on a contract to be maintained.

For example, I purchase a ham from retailer Ralph. I invite you to my house that evening. I prepare the ham properly. You are served first, because you are my guest, and you become severely ill because the ham is spoiled. Can you sue retailer Ralph for breach of the implied warranty of merchantability? Because warranty is based on a contract for the sale of goods, under the common law you would normally have warranty rights only if you were a party to the purchase of the ham. Therefore, the warranty would extend only to me, the purchaser.

In the past, this hardship was sometimes resolved by court decisions removing privity as a requirement to hold manufacturers and sellers liable for certain defective products (notably food, drugs, and cosmetics) that were sold. The UCC, reflecting some of these decisions, has addressed the problem of privity, at least to the extent of including three optional, alternative provisions eliminating privity in various circumstances. All three alternatives are intended to eliminate the privity requirement with respect to certain enumerated types of injuries (personal versus property) for certain beneficiaries (for example, household members versus bystanders). Each state may adopt one of these three alternatives [UCC 2-318].

Warranty Disclaimers

Courts view warranty disclaimers with disfavor, especially when consumers are involved. As discussed below, even when sellers have adhered exactly to the methods of disclaimer specified by the UCC, courts have sometimes held that the disclaimers are unconscionable. Also, there are other federal and state statutes (for example, the Magnuson-Moss Warranty Act, which is considered below) that may make disclaimers of a particular warranty unenforceable. A buyer prevented from claiming breach of warranty may be able to sue successfully on a theory of negligence or strict liability (each of which is discussed in more detail in Chapter 23).

Obviously, then, the seller's best protection from being held accountable for affirmations of fact or promises is not to make them in the first place. Of course, a contract normally involves a sale of something describable and described. A clause purporting to disclaim all warranties cannot negate the seller's obligation with respect to this description and therefore cannot be given literal effect [UCC 2-313, Comment 4]. Thus, the manner in which a seller can disclaim or qualify any warranty varies with the way the warranty is created. For example, a seller's description of his or her merchandise as an "automobile" creates an express warranty that what will be delivered to a buyer is an automobile. Stating that goods are being sold "as is" cannot disclaim this warranty; and thus, a seller cannot deliver a car without wheels or a motor and avoid liability.

Express Warranties

Any affirmation of fact or promise, description of the goods, or use of samples or models by a seller creates an express warranty. Obviously, then, express warranties can be excluded if the seller has carefully refrained from making any promise or affirmation of fact relating to the goods, or describing the goods, or selling by means of a sample or model [UCC 2-313].

The parol evidence rule protects the seller from a buyer's false claims that an oral warranty was created. Under this rule, if the parties intended the written contract to be the complete expression of their agreement, the buyer cannot offer evidence of an oral warranty. Nevertheless, a court may conclude that the contract was not a complete expression of the parties' intentions and permit proof of oral terms.

The UCC does permit express warranties to be negated or limited by specific and unambiguous language, provided this is done in a manner that protects the buyer from surprise. Therefore, a written disclaimer in language that is clear and conspicuous, and called to a buyer's attention, could negate all oral express warranties not included in the written sales contract [UCC 2-316(1)].

Implied Warranties

Generally speaking, and unless circumstances indicate otherwise, implied warranties (of merchantability and fitness for a particular purpose) are disclaimed by the expression "as is," or "with all faults," or some other similar phrase that in common understanding for *both* parties calls the buyer's attention to the fact that there are no implied warranties [UCC 2-316(3)(a)].

The UCC also permits a seller to specifically disclaim the implied warranty either of fitness for a particular purpose or of merchantability [UCC 2-316(2)]. To disclaim the implied warranty of fitness for a particular purpose, the disclaimer *must* be in writing and conspicuous. The word *fitness* does not have to be mentioned in the writing; it is sufficient, for example, for the disclaimer to state: "There are no warranties that extend beyond the description on the face hereof."

A merchantability disclaimer must be more specific; it must mention *merchantability*. It need not be written; but if it is, the writing must be conspicuous. According to UCC 1-201(10):

> A term or clause is conspicuous when it is so written that a reasonable person against whom it is to operate ought to have noticed it. A printed heading in capitals . . . is conspicuous. Language in the body of a form is "conspicuous" if it is in larger or other contrasting type or color.

To illustrate: Merchant Logan sells Breen a particular lawn mower selected by Logan with the characteristics clearly requested by Breen. At the time of the sale, Logan orally tells Breen that he does not warrant the merchantability of the mower, as it is last year's model. The mower proves to be defective and will not work. Breen wishes to hold Logan liable for breach of implied warranty of merchantability and of fitness for a particular purpose.

Breen can hold Logan liable for breach of the warranty of fitness for a particular purpose but not of the warranty of merchantability. Logan's oral disclaimer mentioning the word *merchantability* is a proper disclaimer. For Logan to have disclaimed the implied warranty of fitness for a particular purpose, a conspicuous writing would have been required. Because no written disclaimer was made, Logan can still be held liable.

The court's opinion in the following case focuses on the conspicuousness requirement.

Case 22.5

CATE v. DOVER CORP.

Supreme Court of Texas, 1990.
790 S.W.2d 559.

BACKGROUND AND FACTS Edward Cate, doing business as Cate's Transmission Service, bought from Beech Tire Mart three lifts manufactured and designed by Dover Corporation to elevate vehicles for maintenance. Despite repairs by Beech and Dover, the lifts never functioned properly. When Cate brought an action against Dover in a Texas state court for breach of the implied warranty of merchantability, Dover contended that the claim was barred by a disclaimer. The disclaimer of implied warranties, which was contained in a separate paragraph within a written, express warranty, in the same typeface, size, and color as the rest of the warranty, read, "This warranty is exclusive and is in lieu of all other warranties expressed or implied including any implied warranty of merchantability or any implied warranty of fitness for a particular purpose, which implied warranties are hereby expressly excluded." The trial court and court of appeals upheld the disclaimer, and Cate appealed to the Supreme Court of Texas.

DECISION AND RATIONALE The Supreme Court of Texas reversed the judgment of the appellate court and remanded the case to the trial court for further proceedings consistent with its opinion. To specifically disclaim in writing the implied warranties of merchantability and fitness for a particular purpose, the written disclaimer must be conspicuous or the buyer must have actual knowledge of the disclaimer. The state supreme court pointed out that whether a disclaimer was conspicuous was a question of law. Dover argued that a lesser standard of conspicuousness should apply to a disclaimer made to a merchant. The court concluded, however, that conspicuousness was subject to an objective standard. In this case, there was nothing to distinguish the disclaimer from the rest of the warranty text in the contract. The court held that "a disclaimer contained in text undistinguished in typeface, size or color within a form purporting to grant a warranty is not conspicuous, and is unenforceable unless the buyer has actual knowledge of the disclaimer." Actual knowledge overrides inconspicuousness, because the purpose of the requirement is to protect a buyer from surprise. The court concluded, however, that Dover failed to establish that, as a matter of law, Cate knew of the disclaimer.

Buyer's Examination of the Goods

If the buyer refuses to examine the goods or if the buyer actually examines the goods (or a sample or model) as fully as desired before entering a contract, *there is no implied warranty with respect to defects that a reasonable examination will reveal.*

Suppose, in the earlier illustration concerning Kaplan's purchase of an axe from Enrique's Hardware Store, that the defect in Kaplan's axe could have been easily spotted by normal inspection. Kaplan, even after Enrique asked, refused to inspect the axe before buying it. After being hurt by the defective axe, she will not be able to hold Enrique liable for breach of warranty of merchantability because she could have spotted the defect during an inspection [UCC 2-316(3)(b)].

Failure to examine the goods is not refusal to examine them; it is not enough that the goods were available for inspection and the buyer failed to examine them. A refusal can occur only when the seller *demands* that the buyer examine the goods. Of course, the seller always remains liable for latent (hidden) defects that ordinary inspection would not reveal. What the examination ought to reveal depends on a particular buyer's skill and method of examination. Therefore, an auto mechanic purchasing a car should be responsible for the discovery of some defects that a nonexpert would not be expected to find. The circumstances of each case determine what defects a so-called reasonable inspection should reveal.

In the following case, the buyer conducted tests on samples of an adhesive product before purchasing large quantities of it for use in its business. The court considers the question of whether these tests excluded all implied warranties.

BACKGROUND AND FACTS In its business of converting automotive vans into recreational vehicles, Trans-Aire International, Inc., installed carpeting and ceiling fabrics using an adhesive manufactured by 3M Company. Because the adhesive often failed at warmer temperatures, Trans-Aire sought a replacement. Trans-Aire's chief engineer tested several samples of Northern Adhesive Company's Adhesive 7448 and determined that it was better than the 3M product. Because the tests were conducted in a cool plant, rather than under the warm weather conditions that caused the 3M product to fail, the engineer suggested to Trans-Aire's president that they test the adhesive under summer-like conditions. The president stated that he was satisfied without the test and bought several shipments of the product. A Northern representative made it clear that there was no warranty other than that the product shipped would be like the samples. Adhesive 7448 led to the same problems as the 3M product, and Trans-Aire was forced to repair more than 500 vans. Trans-Aire sued Northern in a federal district court for, among other claims, breach of the implied warranty of fitness for a particular purpose and breach of the implied warranty of merchantability. The trial court granted Northern's motion for summary judgment on the issue, and Trans-Aire appealed.

DECISION AND RATIONALE The United States Court of Appeals for the Seventh Circuit affirmed the trial court's decision. Trans-Aire was precluded from bringing an action for breach of any implied warranty. The court held that under UCC 2-316, "implied warranties are excluded when a party examines a product or sample 'as fully as it desires' or 'refuses to examine' the product or sample in a reasonable manner given the circumstances of the case." Trans-Aire argued that it did not have the means to discover the "latent defects" of the adhesive because of the cool plant conditions at the time the tests were performed, and that the UCC does not exclude implied warranties under these circumstances. But Trans-Aire offered no evidence as to why the tests were not done, other than that the company's president did not feel that they were necessary. The court concluded that Trans-Aire waived reliance on the implied warranties.

ETHICAL CONSIDERATIONS This case offers a specific illustration of the ethical premise underlying both the UCC and the common law of contracts—that the law should not be used as a shield to protect those who fail to look after themselves. In this case, Trans-Aire did not rely on Northern's judgment concerning the adhesive but on its own testing of the product. It would therefore be unfair to hold Northern responsible for damages that essentially were caused by Trans-Aire's failure to test the adhesive under conditions similar to those in which the 3M adhesive had failed.

Case 22.6

TRANS-AIRE INTERNATIONAL, INC. v. NORTHERN ADHESIVE CO.

United States Court of Appeals, Seventh Circuit, 1989. 882 F.2d 1254.

Unconscionability

The UCC sections dealing with warranty disclaimers do not refer specifically to unconscionability as a factor. Eventually, however, the courts will test warranty disclaimers with reference to the unconscionability standards of Section 2-302. Such things as lack of bargaining position, ''take it or leave it'' choices, and failure of a buyer to understand or know of a warranty disclaimer provision will become relevant to the issue of unconscionability.

■ Statute of Limitations

An action brought by a buyer or seller for breach of contract must be commenced under the UCC *within four years after the cause of action accrues.* In addition to filing suit within the four-year period, an aggrieved party must ordinarily notify the breaching party of a defect within a reasonable time [UCC 2-607(3)(a)]. By agreement in the contract, the parties can reduce this period to not less than one year, but they cannot extend the period beyond the stated four years [UCC 2-725(1)].

A cause of action accrues for breach of warranty when the seller makes *tender* of delivery. This is the rule even if the aggrieved party is unaware that the cause of action has accrued [UCC 2-725(2)]. Remember, tender of delivery takes place under a shipment contract on delivery of the goods to the carrier and under a destination contract on tender of the goods at the specified destination delivery location. The statute of limitations in these cases may have a tremendous impact if the goods purchased are going to be stored primarily for future use. To avoid this impact, the UCC provides that when a warranty explicitly extends to future performance, discovery of its breach must await the time of that performance [UCC 2-725(2)]. The statute of limitations also begins to run at that time. For example, Hoover purchases a central air-conditioning unit for his restaurant. The unit is warranted to keep the temperature below a certain level during the summer months. The unit is installed in the winter, but when summer comes, the restaurant does not stay cool. Therefore, discovery of the warranty's breach is made in the summer and not when the unit was delivered in the winter. The statute of limitations does not begin to run until the summer.

When a buyer or seller brings suit on a legal theory unrelated to the UCC, the limitations periods specified above do not apply, even though the claim relates to goods. For example, Nilsson buys tires for his automobile. The tires prove to have an inherently dangerous defect. Four years and one month after purchasing the tires, Nilsson loses control of the car and injures several passengers as well as himself. Nilsson can bring a suit against the tire manufacturer based on strict liability in tort (see Chapter 5). The suit will not be governed by the UCC's statute of limitations but rather by the state's tort statute of limitations.

The following case illustrates how the expectation of the parties extends the time of warranty performance to a future date for statute of limitation purposes.

Case 22.7

MOORE v. PUGET SOUND PLYWOOD, INC.

Supreme Court of Nebraska, 1983.
214 Neb. 14,
332 N.W.2d 212.

BACKGROUND AND FACTS   Puget Sound Plywood, Inc., manufactured lauan wood siding that Dennis and Lois Moore bought during the construction of their house in 1970–71. By October 1977, the Moores noticed some problems with the appearance of the siding. Delamination had occurred because the species of lauan tree used in making the siding was not susceptible to being glued with the resin that Puget Sound used. The Moores began investigating a remedy for the situation in 1979, but they had difficulty determining who manufactured the siding. Alleging damages of $4,550, the Moores filed an action in a Nebraska state court in April 1981 against Puget Sound. Two lower courts dismissed the case, holding that the statute of limitations had run. The Moores appealed.

DECISION AND RATIONALE   The Supreme Court of Nebraska agreed with the Moores that the lower courts were in error. The state supreme court remanded the case with instructions that a judgment be entered in favor of the Moores for $4,550. The court explained "that an oral representation concerning the origin of goods, made in the course of a sale, constitutes an express warranty. * * * [A]ny description of goods which becomes a part of the basis of the bargain creates an express warranty that the goods shall conform to the description." In this case, the parties agreed that the description of the goods as "siding" carried with it a representation that the siding would last the lifetime of the house. The court reasoned that the breach of the warranty did not occur on tender of delivery because, in light of the expectations of the parties that the siding would last for the life of the house, the warranty extended to future performance. In other words, discovery of the defect could occur at any time between installation and the end of the life of the house. Thus, the court concluded that the Moores acted within a reasonable time (within the statute of limitations) after they discovered the defect.

■ Magnuson-Moss Warranty Act

The Magnuson-Moss Warranty Act[4] (enacted in 1975) was designed to prevent deception in warranties by making them easier to understand. The act is mainly enforced by the Federal Trade Commission (FTC). Additionally, the Attorney General or a consumer who has been injured can enforce the act if informal procedures for settling disputes prove to be ineffective. The Magnuson-Moss Warranty Act modifies UCC warranty rules to some extent when *consumer* sales transactions are involved. The UCC, however, remains the primary codification of warranty rules for industrial and commercial transactions.

No seller is *required* to give a written warranty for consumer goods sold under the Warranty Act. But if a seller chooses to make an express written warranty and the cost of the consumer goods is more than $10, the warranty must be labeled as either full or limited. In addition, if the cost of the goods is more than $15 (by FTC regulation), the warrantor is required to make certain disclosures fully and conspicuously in a single document in "readily understood language." This disclosure states the names and addresses of the warrantors, what specifically is warranted, procedures for enforcement of the warranty, any limitations on warranty relief, and that the buyer has legal rights.

Although a *full warranty* may not cover every aspect of the consumer product sold, what it covers ensures some type of buyer satisfaction in case the product is defective. Full warranty requires free repair or replacement of any defective part; if it

cannot be repaired within a reasonable time, the consumer has the choice of either a refund or a replacement without charge. The full warranty frequently does not have a time limit. Any limitation on consequential damages must be *conspicuously* stated. Also, the warrantor need not perform warranty services if the problem with the product was caused by unreasonable use or damage by the consumer.

A *limited warranty* arises when the written warranty fails to meet one of the minimum requirements for a full warranty. The fact that a seller is giving only a limited warranty must be conspicuously designated. If only a time limitation would distinguish a limited warranty from a full warranty, then the Warranty Act allows the seller to designate the warranty as full by such language as "full twelve-month warranty."

Although, under the UCC, express warranties can be created by description or sample or model, only written promises or affirmations of fact are covered by the Magnuson-Moss Warranty Act. Thus, for purposes of the Warranty Act:

1. An express warranty is *any written promise* or *affirmation of fact* made by the seller to a consumer indicating the quality or performance of the product and affirming or promising that the product is either free of defects or will meet a specific level of performance over a period of time—for example, "this watch will not lose more than one second a year."

2. An express warranty is a written agreement to refund, repair, or replace the product if it fails to meet written specifications. This is typically a service contract.

---

4. 15 U.S.C. Sections 2301–12.

■ CONCEPT SUMMARY 22.1   Warranties under the UCC

Type of Warranty	How Created	Possible Defenses
Warranty of title [UCC 2-312]	Upon transfer of title, the seller warrants— 1. That he or she has the right to pass good and rightful title. 2. That the goods are free from unstated liens or encumbrances. 3. When the seller is a merchant, that the goods are free from infringement claims.	Specific language or circumstances excluded or modified warranty [UCC 2-312(2)].
Express warranty [UCC 2-313]	As part of a sale or bargain, a seller may create an express warranty by— 1. An affirmation of fact or promise. 2. A sale by description. 3. A sample shown as conforming to bulk.	1. Statement that is purported to create warranty was an opinion. 2. Specific language or conduct negated or limited warranty [UCC 2-316(1)].
Implied warranty of merchantability [UCC 2-314]	This warranty arises when the seller is a merchant who deals in goods of the kind sold.	1. Warranty was specifically disclaimed (disclaimer can be oral or in writing, but must mention *merchantability* and, if in writing, must be conspicuous) [UCC 2-316(2)]. 2. Sale was stated to be "as is" or "with all faults" [UCC 2-316(3)(a)]. 3. The buyer examined the goods and is therefore bound by all defects that were found or should have been found. If the buyer refused or failed to examine, the buyer is bound by obvious defects [UCC 2-316(3)(b)]. 4. Course of dealing, performance, or usage of trade [UCC 2-316(3)(c)].
Implied warranty of fitness for a particular purpose [UCC 2-315]	This warranty arises when— 1. The buyer's purpose or use is known or should be known by the seller, and 2. The buyer purchases in reliance on the seller's selection.	1. Specific disclaimer excluded or modified warranty (disclaimer must be in writing and be conspicuous. "There are no warranties which extend beyond the description on the face hereof.") [UCC 2-316(2)]. 2. Same as items 2–4 under merchantability, above.
Implied warranty arising from course of dealing or trade usage [UCC 2-314(3)]	This warranty is created by prior dealings and/or custom of trade.	Warranty was excluded by specific language or as provided under UCC 2-316.

The Magnuson-Moss Warranty Act does not deal with implied warranties. They continue to be created according to the UCC provisions. When an express warranty is made in a sales contract or a combined sales and service contract (when the service contract is undertaken within ninety days of the sale), the Magnuson-Moss Warranty Act prevents sellers from disclaiming or modifying the implied warranties of merchantability and fitness for a particular purpose. Sellers can impose a time limit on the duration of an implied warranty, but the time limit has to correspond to the duration of the express warranty.[5]

---

5. The time limit on an implied warranty occurring by virtue of the seller's express warranty must, of course, be reasonable, conscionable, and set forth in clear and conspicuous language on the face of the warranty.

■ Terms and Concepts

express warranty 394
implied warranty 397

implied warranty of fitness for a particular purpose 398

implied warranty of merchantability 397

■ For Review

1. Express warranties arise under the UCC when a seller indicates that goods will conform to what? Are particular words required?

2. What are factors to consider in determining whether a seller's statement is an express warranty or puffing?

3. Implied warranties arise by implication or inference from the nature of a transaction or the circumstances of the parties. What are the three implied warranties that arise under the UCC?

4. In negotiating a sale of a bottling machine to the Ruby Soda Bottling Co., the sales representative for Orr Machines, Inc., points to a paragraph in the contract that states the machine consumes specific, very low, amounts of energy. Ruby's buyer says, "That's all I needed to know. We'll take it." The contract also includes a provision in large red capital letters that the machine is sold "as is." In using the machine, Ruby discovers that it consumes more than three times the energy than the amount claimed by Orr. What effect does the "as is" provision have on Orr's express representation about the machine's consumption of energy?

5. In the previous problem, imagine that Ruby said it needed the machine to fill and cap 3,000 bottles an hour, and Orr said, "No problem," but that in using the machine, Ruby found that it filled and capped no more than 1,400 bottles an hour. What effect would the "as is" provision have on Orr's representation?

■ Questions and Case Problems

22-1. Quid contracted to purchase a used car from Johnson's Quality Used Cars. During the oral negotiations for the sale, Johnson told Quid that this used car was in "A-1 condition" and would get sixteen miles to the gallon. Quid asked if the car used a lot of oil. Johnson replied that he had personally checked the car, and in his opinion the car did not use a lot of oil. Since delivery, Quid has used the car for one month (400 miles of driving) and is unhappy with it. The car needs numerous repairs, does not get sixteen miles to the gallon, and has used two quarts of oil. Quid claims Johnson is in breach of express warranties as to the condition of the car, gas mileage, and oil use. Johnson claims no express warranties were made. Discuss who is correct.

22-2. Jeremy is a farmer who needs to place a 2,000-pound piece of equipment in his barn. This will require lifting the equipment 30 feet up into a hayloft. Jeremy goes to Davidson Hardware and tells Davidson that he needs some heavy-duty rope to be used on his farm. Davidson recommends a one-inch-thick nylon rope, and Jeremy purchases 200 feet of the rope. Jeremy ties the rope around the piece of equipment, puts it through a pulley, and, with a tractor, lifts the equipment off the ground. Suddenly the rope breaks. In the crash to the ground the equipment is severely damaged. Jeremy files suit against Davidson for breach of implied warranty of fitness for a particular purpose. Discuss how successful Jeremy will be in his suit.

22-3. Darrow purchases a new car from Slippery Motors. The retail installment contract states immediately above the buyer's signature in large, bold type: "There are no warranties that extend beyond the description on the face hereof" and "There are no express warranties that accompany this sale unless expressly written in this contract." Before purchasing the car, Darrow specifically informed Slippery's salesperson that he wanted a car that could be driven in a dusty area without needing mechanical repairs. Slippery's salesperson said to Darrow, "Nothing will go wrong with this car, but if it does, return it to us, and we will repair it without cost to you." Neither this statement nor any similar statement appears in the retail sales contract. Darrow drives the car into a dust storm. The air filter gets plugged up and the car engine overheats, causing motor damage. Slippery Motors refuses to repair the engine under any warranty. Darrow claims that Slippery is liable for breach of the implied warranty of fitness for a particular purpose, that the Magnuson-Moss Warranty Act prohibits disclaiming this implied warranty, and that the salesperson's express warranty has also been breached. Discuss Darrow's claims.

22-4. Terry has a used television set that she wishes to sell. Howard contracts to purchase the set. At the time of the making of the contract, Terry demands that Howard inspect the set to be sure it is exactly what he wants. Howard tells Terry that he does not have the time to do so. The set is delivered and paid for. Howard, on using the set, discovers that the picture has a tendency to "jump" and that the vertical control does not always correct that tendency. The cost to repair the set is $50. Howard claims that the set is neither merchantable nor fit for its purpose. Terry claims she has no liability. Discuss who is correct.

22-5. John buys a one-karat diamond ring from Shady Sailor for $500. John is assured by Shady that the ring belonged to his deceased mother and that the only reason the price is so low is that he is behind in making payments on his car. John has no reason to believe differently. Bekins, a neighbor, admires the ring and offers to purchase it for $1,000. John agrees to sell the ring to Bekins, stating that he is transferring only such right and title as he has. Two months later, the police confiscate the ring as property stolen in a burglary of Owen's home. Bekins seeks to hold John liable. Discuss Bekins's action under warranty laws.

22-6. Vertis Smith was considering buying a used car from Fitzner Pontiac-Buick-Cadillac, Inc. He particularly liked a 1982 Olds Cutlass on the lot and took it for a test drive. Smith then told Fitzner's sales representative that if Fitzner would fix a rattle he had heard and paint the car, he would purchase it for $7,475. The salesperson agreed to have these things done and assured Smith that when the car was delivered it would be in "first class shape." Fitzner performed as agreed, and the car was delivered shortly thereafter to Smith. During the next few months, Smith had to install a new intake gasket, a new transmission, and a new radiator—repairs that were made by others, not Fitzner. Fitzner repaired a broken taillight and adjusted a window mechanism. In addition, Smith claimed that the car stalled frequently in traffic and got only eleven miles per gallon of gas. Nine months after he had purchased the car, Smith returned it to Fitzner and requested a refund of the purchase price plus the cost of the repairs, alleging, among other things, that Fitzner had breached an express warranty. Discuss fully whether Fitzner's statement that the car would be delivered in "first class shape" constituted an express warranty. [*Fitzner Pontiac-Buick-Cadillac, Inc. v. Smith,* 523 So.2d 324 (Miss. 1988)]

22-7. Myrtle Carpenter purchased hair dye from a drugstore. The use of the dye caused an adverse skin reaction. She sued the local drugstore and the manufacturer of the dye, Alberto Culver Co. She claimed that a sales clerk had indicated that several of Myrtle's friends used the product and that their hair came out "very nice." The clerk purportedly also told Myrtle that she would get very fine results. On the package, there were cautionary instructions telling the user to make a preliminary skin test to determine if the user was sensitive in any unusual way to the product. Myrtle stated that she had not made the preliminary skin test. Did the seller make an express warranty about the hair dye? Explain. [*Carpenter v. Alberto Culver Co.,* 28 Mich.App. 399, 184 N.W.2d 547 (1970)]

22-8. In 1984, the Lindemann farm's cotton crop fared poorly because of lack of weed control. That year, and every year since the early 1960s, the Lindemanns (plaintiffs) had used Treflan, an herbicide manufactured by the defendants, Eli Lilly and Co. The label specifically stated that Treflan would control weeds when used according to label instructions. The Treflan label recommended that the herbicide be incorporated into the soil twice after it had been sprayed. The purpose of the double incorporation was to provide greater uniformity in the herbicide's distribution. The Lindemanns, in an effort to create still greater uniformity in the distribution of the Treflan, made an application by spraying half the amount of a normal application in one direction and half in the opposite direction. Each spraying was incorporated into the soil after it had been applied. If the directions did not contain a specific directive calling for a single application, could the Lindemanns recover for breach of express warranty of the herbicide to control weeds? Discuss. [*Lindemann v. Eli Lilly and Co.,* 816 F.2d 199 (5th Cir. 1987)]

22-9. On December 22, 1980, Jack M. Crothers purchased a used 1970 Dodge from Maurice Boyd, a sales agent employed by Norman Cohen, the owner of Norm's Auto Sales. On December 23, 1980, Crothers was seriously injured when the Dodge he had just purchased went out of control and crashed into a tree. Crothers filed suit, asserting breach of an express warranty based on Boyd's representation to Crothers that the 1970 Dodge had a rebuilt carburetor and was a "good runner." Did Boyd's representations amount to an express warranty? [*Crothers by Crothers v. Cohen,* 384 N.W.2d 562 (Minn.App. 1986)]

22-10. On March 13, 1980, Judith Roth went to the hairdresser she had been using for the last seven years to have her hair bleached. The hair stylist used a new bleaching product, manufactured by Roux Laboratories, on Mrs. Roth's hair. Although other Roux products had been used previously with excellent results, the use of the new product resulted in damage to Mrs. Roth's hair that caused her embarrassment and anguish for the next several months as her hair grew back. The product's label had guaranteed it would not cause damage to a user's hair. Roth sued Ray-Stel's Hair Stylists, Inc., and Roux Laboratories, Inc., alleging, among other claims, breach of express warranty resulting in personal injuries to her. Discuss whether there was a breach of express warranty. [*Roth v. Ray-Stel's Hair Stylists, Inc.,* 18 Mass.App. 975, 470 N.E.2d 137 (1984)]

22-11. While passing by the American Kennels pet store, owned by defendant George Rosenthal, Ruby Dempsey, the plaintiff, decided to purchase a pedigreed white poodle. Dempsey told the salesperson that she wanted a dog suitable for breeding purposes. She purchased the poodle, whom she named Mr. Dunphy. Five days later, the dog was examined by a veterinarian and discovered to have a congenital defect. Dempsey returned to the store and demanded a refund of the purchase price. The store refused, and Dempsey filed suit. Dempsey claimed that the defendant was guilty of breach of the implied warranties of merchantability and fitness for a particular purpose. The defendant claimed that the poodle was still capable of breeding and thus no warranties had been breached. Discuss fully whether Dempsey was successful. [*Dempsey v. Rosenthal,* 121 Misc.2d 612, 468 N.Y.S.2d 441 (1983)]

22-12. Robert Levondosky was a patron at Harrah's Marina Hotel Casino, an Atlantic City casino owned by Marina Associates. While playing at one of the casino's tables, he ordered a cocktail, which was served free of charge—it was the casino's custom to give complimentary drinks to patrons at the gambling tables. Levondosky alleged that he swallowed a few thin chips of glass from the rim of the glass in which the drink was served and, as a result, suffered internal injuries. Levondosky sued the casino, contending that the casino had breached an implied warranty of merchantability. In evaluating this claim, the court had to determine (1) whether a "sale" had in fact occurred, which is prerequisite to the creation of an implied warranty of merchantability; and (2) whether the casino gave an implied warranty as to the glass as well as to the drink within it. Review UCC 2-314 and discuss how the court should rule on both issues. [*Levondosky v. Marina Associates,* 731 F.Supp. 1210 (D.N.J. 1990)]

22-13. Case Briefing Assignment

Examine Case A.11 [Travel Craft, Inc. v. Wilhelm Mende GmbH & Co., *552 N.E.2d 443 (Ind. 1990)*] *in Appendix A. The case has been excerpted there in great detail. Review and then brief the case, making sure that you include answers to the following questions in your brief.*

1. What were the three issues before the appellate court?
2. Why did the state supreme court hold that the implied warranty of merchantability was effectively disclaimed, even though the word *merchantability* was not mentioned, as required under the UCC?
3. The state supreme court agreed with the trial court that the written warranty was a "final expression of the parties' agreement on warranties." Why, then, did the state supreme court hold that parol evidence was admissible?
4. How might the admissibility of parol evidence affect Travel Craft's chances of recovery?
5. Why did the state supreme court reverse the trial court's decision as to the express warranty?

Chapter 23

Product Liability

Often, retailers serve simply as go-betweens, selling manufacturers' goods to consumers in prepackaged, sealed containers. Even so, retailers may be liable to purchasers on express or implied warranties despite the fact that they cannot always examine the goods prior to resale. In the past, courts frequently addressed the question of whether the injured party should recover from the manufacturer, the processor, or the retailer for damages caused by the manufacture and marketing of a defective product. Today, liability has been extended to manufacturers and processors through the application of new and old principles of the law.

Manufacturers and sellers of goods can be held liable to consumers, users, and bystanders for physical harm or property damage that is caused by the goods. This is called **product liability,** and it encompasses the contract theory of *warranty* and tort theories of *negligence, misrepresentation,* and *strict liability.*

■ Warranty Law

Today, warranty law is an important part of the entire spectrum of laws relating to product liability. Consumers, purchasers, and even users of goods can recover *from any seller* for losses resulting from breach of implied and express warranties. A manufacturer is a *seller.* Therefore, a person who purchases goods from a retailer can recover from the retailer or the manufacturer if the goods are not merchantable, because in most states *privity of contract* (the connection that exists between contracting parties) is no longer a prerequisite for breach-of-warranty recovery for personal injuries. That is, a product purchaser may sue not only the firm from which he or she purchased a product but also a third party, the manufacturer of the product, in product liability.

Because warranty laws were discussed in Chapter 22, the balance of this chapter will deal with the tort theories of recovery for damages and injuries caused by defective products.

■ Negligence

Negligence is generally defined as the failure to use that degree of care that a reasonable, prudent person would have used under the circumstances. Recall from Chapter 5 that an action in negligence requires the plaintiff to prove that (1) a duty of care existed, (2) this duty was breached, (3) the plaintiff suffered a legally recognizable injury, and (4) the injury was proximately caused by the breach of due care. If the failure to exercise reasonable care in the creation or marketing of a product causes an injury, the basis of product liability is negligence. Thus, the manufacturer of a product must exercise ''due care'' to make that product safe to be used as intended. Due care must be exercised in designing the product, in selecting the materials, in using the appropriate production process, in assembling and testing the product, and in placing adequate warnings on the label informing the user of dangers of which an ordinary person might not be aware. The duty of care extends to the inspection and testing of products purchased by the manufacturer for use in the final product. The failure to exercise due care is negligence. Failure to exercise due care must be proved in actions based on the theory of negligence—in contrast to actions based on the doctrine of strict liability (discussed below), in which liability does not depend on proof of negligence.

Privity of Contract Not Required

An action based on negligence does not require privity of contract between the injured plaintiff and the negligent defendant-manufacturer. Section 395 of the Restatement (Second) of Torts states:

A manufacturer who fails to exercise reasonable care in the manufacture of a chattel [movable good] which, unless carefully made, he should recognize as involving an unreasonable risk of causing substantial physical harm to those who lawfully use it for a purpose for which the manufacturer should expect it to be used and to those whom he should expect to be endangered by its probable use, is subject to liability for physical harm caused to them by its lawful use in a manner and for a purpose for which it is supplied.

Simply stated, a manufacturer is liable for its failure to exercise due care to any person who sustains an injury proximately caused by a negligently made (defective) product. (The analysis of whether a product is so defective as to be *unreasonably dangerous* applies equally to actions based on strict tort liability and is discussed below.)

In the following landmark case, the New York court dealt with the liability of a manufacturer that failed to exercise reasonable care in manufacturing a finished product. The *MacPherson* case is the classic negligence case in which privity of contract was not required between the plaintiff and the defendant to establish liability. This is a forerunner to product liability, although it does not use product liability theory. Its subject matter, defectively manufactured wooden wheels for automobiles, is dated, but the principles involved are not.

 Case 23.1

MacPHERSON v. BUICK MOTOR CO.
Court of Appeals of New York, 1916.
217 N.Y. 382,
111 N.E. 1050.

BACKGROUND AND FACTS Buick Motor Company was sued in a New York state court by Donald MacPherson, who suffered injuries while riding in a Buick that suddenly collapsed because one of the wheels was made of defective wood. The spokes crumbled into fragments, throwing MacPherson out of the vehicle and injuring him. The wheel had not been made by Buick but had been bought from another manufacturer. There was evidence, however, that the defects could have been discovered by reasonable inspection and that no such inspection had taken place. Although there was no charge that Buick knew of the defect and willfully concealed it, MacPherson charged Buick with negligence for putting a human life in imminent danger. MacPherson sued Buick directly, although the automobile was bought from a retail Buick dealer. The trial court rendered a judgment in MacPherson's favor, and Buick appealed.

DECISION AND RATIONALE The Court of Appeals of New York, the highest court in the New York state system, affirmed the judgment of the trial court and the intermediate review court that Buick was liable to MacPherson for the injuries he sustained when he was thrown from the vehicle. The state's highest court held that Buick's duty of care extended to MacPherson even though Buick and MacPherson were not in privity of contract. The court held that Buick's duty lay in tort and extended to any person who could foreseeably be injured as a result of a defect in an automobile that it manufactured. The duty arose because of the potential danger that a defectively manufactured automobile poses to anyone who rides in it. The court stated, "Because the danger is to be foreseen, there is a duty to avoid the injury. * * * If the nature of a thing is such that it is reasonably certain to place life and limb in peril when negligently made, it is then a thing of danger. Its nature gives warning of the consequences to be expected. If to the element of danger there is added knowledge that the thing will be used by persons other than the purchaser, and used without new tests, then, irrespective of contract, the manufacturer of this thing of danger is under a duty to make it carefully."

COMMENTS   This case has been interpreted to cover all articles that imperil life when negligently made. Before *MacPherson,* manufacturers escaped liability to consumers when their contractual dealings were with distributors or retailers. Since *MacPherson,* that has no longer been the case.

Violation of Statutory Duty

Numerous federal and state laws impose duties on manufacturers of cosmetics, drugs, foods, toxic substances, and flammable materials. These duties involve appropriate description of contents, labeling, branding, advertising, and selling. For example, federal statutes include the Flammable Fabrics Act, the Federal Food, Drug and Cosmetic Act, and the Hazardous Substances Labeling Act. In a tort action for damages, a violation of statutory duty is often held to constitute *negligence per se.*

Consider an example: Jason Manufacturing Company produces pipe fittings *specifically* for use in the construction of homes in Monroe County. The fittings do not comply with county building codes. One of the pipe fittings bursts in a home, allowing hot water to spray on the homeowner. The homeowner can bring a negligence action for personal damages on the ground that failure to comply with the building codes is in and of itself an automatic breach of the manufacturer's duty of reasonable care. Of course, the homeowner has to show proximate cause—that is, he or she must relate the injury to the careless act.

Defenses to Negligence

Any manufacturer, seller, or processor who can prove that due care was used in the manufacture of its product has an appropriate defense against a

negligence suit, because failure to exercise due care is one of the major elements of negligence.

But there are other defenses, and their use and application vary from state to state. One area of variation is the tying of the breach (failure to exercise reasonable care) to the injury, referred to as causation (see Chapter 5). Numerous events, involving different people, take place between the time a product is manufactured and the time of its use. If any of these events can be shown to have caused or contributed to the injury, the manufacturer will claim, on the basis of this intervening cause, that it has no liability.

Two other defenses are contributory negligence and, when recognized, assumption of risk (both also discussed in Chapter 5). For example, assume that the manufacturer of an industrial grinder states in its instruction manual that the grinder's operator should wear safety goggles. The owner of a machine tool repair shop purchases a grinder, has her employees read the manufacturer's instructions, and reminds them to wear safety goggles when they use the machine. Employee Joe Kidd chooses to ignore the warnings. As Kidd begins using the grinder to sharpen a sawblade's cutting edge, a tiny spark of hot metal flies into and causes the loss of his right eye. Kidd files suit, claiming the manufacturer was negligent in failing to warn that the grinder might throw off hot metal sparks. The manufacturer-defendant would claim that Kidd's own knowledge of the risk and voluntary use of the product with such knowledge was a reasonable assumption of risk and that his failure to wear the goggles was the proximate cause of the injury.

Likewise, any time a plaintiff misuses a product or fails to make a reasonable effort at preserving his or her own welfare, the manufacturer or seller will claim that the plaintiff contributed to causing the injuries. The claim is that the plaintiff's negligence offsets the negligence of the manufacturer or seller. In some states, the contributory negligence of the plaintiff is an absolute defense for the defendant-manufacturer or seller. In many others, the negligence of both these parties is compared (under the theory of comparative negligence), and damages are based on the proportion of negligence attributed to the defendant.

■ Misrepresentation

When a fraudulent misrepresentation has been made to a user or consumer and that misrepresentation ultimately results in an injury, the basis of liability may be the tort of fraud. In this case, the misrepresentation must have been made knowingly or with reckless disregard for the facts. Examples are the intentional mislabeling of packaged cosmetics and the intentional concealment of a product's defects.

Nonfraudulent misrepresentation, which occurs when a merchant *innocently* misrepresents the character or quality of goods, can also provide a basis of liability. In this situation, it does not have to be proved that the misrepresentation was made knowingly. A famous example involved a drug manufacturer and a victim of addiction to a pre-

scription medicine called Talwin. The manufacturer, Winthrop Laboratories, a division of Sterling Drug, Inc., innocently indicated to the medical profession that the drug was not physically addictive. Using this information, a physician prescribed the drug for his patient, who developed an addiction that turned out to be fatal. Even though the addiction was a highly unusual reaction resulting from the victim's unusual susceptibility to this product, the drug company was still held liable.[1]

Whether fraudulent or nonfraudulent, the misrepresentation must be of a material fact (a fact concerning the quality, nature, or appropriate use of the product on which a normal buyer may be expected to rely). There must also have been an intent to induce the buyer's reliance. Misrepresentation on a label or advertisement is enough to show an intent to induce the reliance of anyone who may use the product. The buyer must rely on the misrepresentation—if the buyer is not aware of it or if it does not influence the transaction, there is no liability.

In contrast to actions based on negligence and strict liability, in a suit based on fraudulent misrepresentation the plaintiff does not have to show that the product was defective or malfunctioned in any way. This is clearly illustrated in the following case, in which the court stressed that in an action based on fraud, it is only necessary that the plaintiff have suffered a legally recognizable injury as a result of relying on the seller's misrepresentations concerning the product.

---

1. *Crocker v. Winthrop Laboratories, Division of Sterling Drug, Inc.*, 514 S.W.2d 429 (Tex. 1974).

BACKGROUND AND FACTS Judy Khan had a mechanical heart valve implanted in her heart to replace a diseased valve, after having been told that she would die without the implant. Khan later stated that she had been thoroughly advised of the risks associated with mechanical heart valves, but that she had never been told that there was a risk that the valve might fracture. A little over two years after the valve was implanted, Khan learned that the valve was being recalled because of numerous reports that the valves were "falling apart and malfunctioning without notice resulting in death to the patients." Khan was also told that the risk of open-heart surgery to remove the valve was even greater than the risk of a malfunction. Khan sued the valve's manufacturer, Shiley, Inc., and its parent company, Pfizer, Inc., in a California state court, alleging numerous causes of action—including negligence, fraud and misrepresentation, breach of warranty, strict

Case 23.2

KHAN v. SHILEY, INC.

California Court of Appeal, Fourth District, Division 3, 1990.
217 Cal.App.3d 848, 266 Cal.Rptr. 106.

liability in tort, and intentional infliction of emotional distress—and seeking compensatory and punitive damages. The trial court entered summary judgment for Shiley, holding that no liability could exist because Khan's valve had not yet malfunctioned and she could not demonstrate that it was defective. Khan appealed.

DECISION AND RATIONALE   The California Court of Appeal reversed the trial court's decision, concluding that Khan had stated a cause of action for fraud and the case should proceed to trial. The appellate court acknowledged and stated that there is no cause of action "under any theory premised on the risk the valve may malfunction in the future. This includes negligence, i.e., failure to warn, and breach of warranty. Allegations of fraud, however, are in a class by themselves." The court then found the elements of fraudulent misrepresentation in Khan's allegations: Shiley and Pfizer misrepresented the valve's propensity to fail and omitted material facts showing that the valve had a history of failure; they did so knowing of the risk of death and without providing adequate warnings, with the intent that Khan rely on the misrepresentations, which she did.

ETHICAL CONSIDERATIONS   Shiley and Pfizer asserted that to allow a plaintiff to sue a manufacturer of a mechanical heart valve that had not yet malfunctioned—and had in fact prolonged the plaintiff's life—was contrary to public policy and essentially unfair. The court responded, "We recognize the role public policy has played, and continues to play, in the torts arena. However, our decision neither establishes a new cause of action nor drastically extends existing law. It merely confirms that a manufacturer of a product may be liable for fraud when it conceals material product information from potential users. This is true whether the product is a mechanical heart valve or frozen yogurt."

■ Strict Liability

A fairly recent development of tort law is the revival of the old doctrine of *strict liability*. Under this doctrine, people may be held liable for the results of their acts regardless of their intentions or their exercise of reasonable care. For example, a company that uses dynamite in constructing a road is strictly liable for any damages that it causes, even if it takes reasonable and prudent precautions to prevent such damages. In essence, the blasting company becomes liable for any personal injuries it causes and thus is an absolute insurer—that is, the company is liable for damages regardless of fault.

The English courts accepted the doctrine of strict liability for many years. Often, persons whose conduct resulted in the injury of another were held liable for damages, even if they had not intended to injure anyone and had exercised reasonable care. This approach was abandoned around 1800 in favor of the *fault* approach, in which an action was con-

sidered tortious only if it was wrongful or blameworthy in some respect.

Strict liability was reapplied in several landmark cases involving manufactured goods in the 1960s and has since become a common method of holding manufacturers liable. Section 402A of the Restatement (Second) of Torts, promulgated in 1965 and now adopted by most of the states, clearly espouses the doctrine of strict liability in tort.

The Restatement of Torts

The Restatement (Second) of Torts designates how the doctrine of strict product liability should be applied. It is a precise and widely accepted statement of the liabilities of sellers of goods (including manufacturers, processors, assemblers, packagers, bottlers, wholesalers, distributors, and retailers) and deserves close attention. Section 402A of the Restatement (Second) of Torts states:

(1) One who sells any product in a defective condition unreasonably dangerous to the user or con-

sumer or to his property is subject to liability for physical harm thereby caused to the ultimate user or consumer or to his property, if

(a) the seller is engaged in the business of selling such a product, and

(b) it is expected to and does reach the user or consumer without substantial change in the condition in which it is sold.

(2) The rule stated in Subsection (1) applies although

(a) the seller has exercised all possible care in the preparation and sale of his product, and

(b) the user or consumer has not bought the product from or entered into any contractual relation with the seller.

Under this doctrine, liability does not depend on privity of contract. The injured party does not have to be the buyer or a third party beneficiary, as required under contract warranty theory [UCC 2-318]. Indeed, this type of liability in law is not governed by the provisions of the UCC. Under this doctrine, a plaintiff does not have to prove that there was a failure to exercise due care, as he or she does in an action based on negligence. If certain requirements (discussed in the following section) are met, the seller's liability to an injured party may be virtually unlimited.

Strict liability is imposed by law as a matter of public policy. This public policy rests on the three-fold assumption that (1) consumers should be protected against unsafe products; (2) manufacturers and distributors should not escape liability for faulty products simply because they are not in privity of contract with the ultimate users of those products; and (3) manufacturers and sellers of products are in a better position to bear the costs associated with injuries caused by their products—costs that they can ultimately pass on to all consumers in the form of higher prices.

California was the first state to impose strict liability in tort on manufacturers. In the landmark decision that follows, the Supreme Court of California sets out the reasons for applying tort law rather than contract law to cases in which consumers are injured by defective products.

BACKGROUND AND FACTS William Greenman wanted a Shopsmith, a combination power tool that could be used as a saw, drill, and wood lathe, after seeing the tool demonstrated by a retailer and studying a brochure prepared by Yuba Power Products, Inc., the manufacturer. Greenman's wife bought him a Shopsmith for Christmas. More than a year later, a piece of wood flew out of the lathe attachment while Greenman was using the Shopsmith, inflicting serious injuries on him. About ten and a half months later, Greenman sued Yuba and the retailer in a California state court for breach of warranties and negligence. The jury returned a verdict for Greenman against Yuba and for the retailer against Greenman. The court entered a judgment on the verdict. Greenman and Yuba appealed.

 Case 23.3

GREENMAN v. YUBA POWER PRODUCTS, INC.

Supreme Court of California, 1962.
59 Cal.2d 57,
377 P.2d 897,
27 Cal.Rptr. 697.

DECISION AND RATIONALE The Supreme Court of California upheld the jury verdict for Greenman and held Yuba strictly liable. The court concluded that Greenman had proved that the design and construction of the Shopsmith were defective, that "statements in the manufacturer's brochure were untrue, that they constituted express warranties, and that plaintiff's injuries were caused by their breach." Yuba argued that Greenman had waited too long to give notice of the breach of warranty, but the court held that it was not necessary for recovery for Greenman to establish an express warranty or its breach. The court stated that "[a] manufacturer is strictly liable in tort when an article he places on the market, knowing that it is to be used without inspection for defects, proves to have a defect that causes injury to a human being." The court pointed out that the "purpose of such liability is to insure that the costs of injuries resulting from defective products are borne by the manufacturers that put such products on the market rather than by the injured persons who are powerless to protect themselves."

Requirements of Strict Product Liability

Just because a person is injured by a product does not mean he or she will have a cause of action against the manufacturer of the product. A cause of action will exist only if the following six basic requirements of strict product liability are met:

1. The product must be in a defective condition when the defendant sells it.
2. The defendant must normally be engaged in the business of selling that product.
3. The product must be unreasonably dangerous to the user or consumer because of its defective condition.[2]
4. The plaintiff must incur physical harm to self or property by use or consumption of the product.
5. The defective condition must be the proximate cause of the injury or damage.
6. The goods must not have been substantially changed from the time the product was sold to the time the injury was sustained.

Thus, in any action against a manufacturer or seller, the plaintiff does not have to show why or in what manner the product became defective. The plaintiff does, however, have to show that at the time the injury was sustained, the condition of the product was essentially the same as when it left the hands of the defendant manufacturer or seller.

The plaintiff normally must also show that the product was so defective as to be an **unreasonably dangerous product.** A court may consider a product so defective as to be unreasonably dangerous if either (1) the product was dangerous beyond the expectation of the ordinary consumer or (2) a less dangerous alternative was economically feasible for the manufacturer, but the manufacturer failed to produce it.

Under the feasible-alternative approach, courts will consider a product's utility and desirability;

the availability of other, safer products; the dangers that have been identified prior to an injured user's suit; the dangers' obviousness; the normal expectation of danger, particularly for established products; the probability of injury and its likely seriousness; the avoidability of injury by care in the product's use, including the contribution of instructions and warnings; and the viability of eliminating the danger without appreciably impairing the product's function or making the product too expensive. For example, people often cut themselves on knives, but a court would consider that knives are very useful. Reasoning that there is no way to avoid injuries without making the product useless and that the danger is obvious to users, a court normally would not find a knife to be unreasonably dangerous and would not hold a supplier of knives liable.

On the other hand, a court may consider a snowblower without a safety guard over the opening through which the snow is blown to be in a condition that is unreasonably dangerous, even if it carries warnings to stay clear of the opening. The danger may be within the user's expectations, but the court will also consider the likelihood of injury and its probable seriousness, as well as the cost of putting a guard over the opening and the guard's effect on the blower's operation.

Some products are safe when used as their manufacturers and distributors intend but not safe when used in other ways. Suppliers are generally required to expect reasonably foreseeable misuses and to design products that are either safe when misused or marketed with some protective device, for example, a childproof cap.

The following case represents a plaintiff's attempt to recover damages for her son's death which resulted from a dangerous "product"—a handgun. Although unusual, the case clearly illustrates that a fundamental requirement in a strict product liability action is that the product causing the injury must be defective in some way.

---

2. This element is no longer required in some states—for example, California.

Case 23.4

PATTERSON v. ROHM GESELLSCHAFT

United States District Court, Northern District of Texas, Dallas Division, 1985. 608 F.Supp. 1206.

BACKGROUND AND FACTS   James Patterson, who worked as a clerk in a "7-Eleven" store in Dallas, was shot and killed during a robbery of the store in 1980. The revolver used by the robber was a .38 caliber "Saturday Night Special" manufactured by a West German company, Rohm Gesellschaft. Jett Patterson, James's mother, brought a product liability action in a federal district court against Rohm and R. G. Industries, Inc., the Florida distributor of the handgun, claiming that the gun was "defective and unreasonably dangerous" in design because its potential for injury and death far outweighed any social utility it might have. Rohm moved for summary judgment, contending that it could not be liable for Patterson's death because the handgun was not defective—the gun did not malfunction nor did it lack any essential safety features.

DECISION AND RATIONALE The United States District Court for the Northern District of Texas, Dallas Division, granted Rohm's motion for summary judgment, holding that Patterson had no cause of action under Texas product liability law. The court pointed out that although a manufacturer is not required to ensure that its products are completely safe or that they will not injure anyone, a manufacturer is liable for injuries resulting from products that are defective. To determine whether a product is defective because its design is unsafe, a court will "weigh the risks involved in the defective product against the feasibility and cost of an improved design." In this case, Patterson offered no alternatives or safer designs, "[n]or can [she] do so—because a gun, by its very nature, must be dangerous and must have the capacity to discharge a bullet with deadly force." The court explained that if Patterson's "unconventional" theory were correct, it would apply equally to other products to the extent that "the manufacturer of a match would be liable for anything burned by a fire started by a match produced by him, * * * and a purchaser of food with high calories would have an action for his overweight condition and for an ensuing heart attack."

ETHICAL CONSIDERATIONS If gun manufacturers were held liable for all crimes committed with handguns, in effect handguns would be "banned"— because no gun manufacturer could profitably produce them. But, as the judge in this case pointed out, such an expansion of product liability law would essentially ban all other products, including automobiles, that can cause harm. Moreover, it is not the function of the courts to write the law. The judge in this case stressed the latter precept: "As an individual, I believe, very strongly, that handguns should be banned and that there should be stringent, effective control of other firearms. However, as a judge, I know full well that the question of whether handguns can be sold is a political one, not an issue of products liability law—and that this is a matter for the legislatures, not the courts."

Liability Sharing

As with other theories of product liability, a plaintiff using a theory of strict liability in tort has been required to prove that the defective product that caused his or her injury was the product of a specific defendant. In recent years, however, in cases in which plaintiffs could not prove which of many distributors of a harmful product supplied the particular product that caused the plaintiffs' injuries, courts have dropped this requirement. This has occurred in several cases involving DES (diethylstilbestrol), a drug administered in the past to prevent miscarriages. DES's harmful character was not realized until, a generation later, daughters of the women who had taken DES developed health problems, including vaginal carcinoma, that were linked to the drug. Partly because of the passage of time, a plaintiff-daughter often could not prove which pharmaceutical company—of as many as 300—had marketed the DES her mother ingested.

In these cases, some courts applied **industry-wide liability,** holding that all firms that manufactured and distributed DES during the period in question were liable for the plaintiffs' injuries in proportion to the firms' respective shares of the market.[3] In 1989, the New York Court of Appeals went still further and held that even if a firm can prove that it did not manufacture the particular

---

3. This theory of liability was first set out by the California Supreme Court in a 1980 case, *Sindell v. Abbott Laboratories,* 26 Cal.3d 588, 607 P.2d 924, 163 Cal.Rptr. 132 (1980).

product that caused injuries to the plaintiff, the firm can be held liable based on its share of the national market.[4]

---

4. *Hymowitz v. Eli Lilly and Co.*, 73 N.Y.2d 487, 539 N.E.2d 1069, 541 N.Y.S.2d 941 (1989).

The following case is illustrative of the market-share approach to liability and the application of the rule of apportionment used by the courts in determining each firm's respective liability to the plaintiff.

Case 23.5

MARTIN v. ABBOTT LABORATORIES

Supreme Court of Washington, 1984.
102 Wash.2d 581,
689 P.2d 368.

BACKGROUND AND FACTS   Rita Martin was born in October 1962. Her mother, Shirley, had obtained a prescription for DES, which she took from May 1962 until the date Rita was born. In 1980, Rita was diagnosed as suffering from vaginal carcinoma and underwent a radical hysterectomy and a partial vaginectomy. Because of the passage of time and because DES had been marketed generically, Shirley could not remember which company had manufactured or marketed the DES she ingested, nor could her physician or pharmacist. The Martins filed suit in a Washington state court against numerous drug companies, on theories of negligence, strict liability, and breach of warranty, for personal injuries, pain, suffering, and destruction of the parent-child relationship. The Martins alleged that all the companies were liable because of their concerted action to gain FDA approval and to market DES. The companies contended that none of them had been identified as the actual manufacturer or distributor of the DES ingested by Shirley and that thus the Martins had failed to state a cause of action for which relief could be granted. The trial court ruled that the Martins stated a valid cause, and the companies appealed.

DECISION AND RATIONALE   The Supreme Court of Washington agreed that the Martins had stated a valid cause of action and remanded the case to the trial court for further proceedings. The state supreme court reasoned that all companies that produced or marketed DES contributed to the risk of injury, even though they may not have contributed to the actual injury of a particular plaintiff. Although the companies did not act together, they all participated either in gaining approval of DES or in producing or marketing the drug, and they thus contributed to the risk of injury to the public and, consequently, the risk of injury to individuals. The court added: "Moreover, as between the injured plaintiff and the possibly responsible drug company, the drug company is in a better position to absorb the cost of the injury. The drug company can either insure itself against liability, absorb the damage award, or pass the expense along to the consuming public as a cost of doing business." As to apportionment of liability, the court ruled that companies that could not clear themselves of potential liability were members of the DES market, "defined by the specificity of the evidence as to geographic market area, time of ingestion, and type of DES." Each was presumed to have an equal share of the market, but could rebut the presumption and reduce its potential liability by establishing its actual market share in a particular plaintiff's geographic market. Each company's presumed market share would then be adjusted "so that 100 percent of the market is accounted for."

Limitations on Recovery

Some courts have limited the application of the strict liability doctrine to cases in which personal injuries have occurred. Thus, when a defective product causes only *property damage*, the seller may not be liable under a theory of strict liability, depending on the law of the particular jurisdiction. In addition, until recently, recovery for *economic loss* was not available in an action based on strict liability (and even today it is rarely available). Note, however, that recovery for *breach of warranty* may be available, depending on the type of injury and which alternative section of UCC 2-318 is in effect.

Statutes of limitations restrict the time within which an action may be brought. A typical statute of limitations provides that an action must be brought within a specified period of time after the cause of action accrues. Generally, a cause of action is held to accrue when some damage occurs. Sometimes the running of the prescribed period is tolled (that is, suspended) until the party suffering an injury has discovered it (or should have discovered it).

Many states have passed laws placing outer time limits on some claims so that the defendant will not be left vulnerable to lawsuits indefinitely. These **statutes of repose** may limit the time within which a plaintiff can file a product liability suit. Typically, a statute of repose begins to run at an earlier date and runs for a longer time than a statute of limitations. For example, a statute of repose may proscribe any claims not brought within twelve years from the date of *sale* or *manufacture* of the defective product. Therefore, it is immaterial that the product is defective or causes an injury if the

injury occurs after this statutory period has lapsed. In addition, some of these legislative enactments have limited the application of the doctrine of strict liability to new goods. Some states, such as Massachusetts, have refused to recognize strict product liability. In these states, recovery is gained mainly through breach of warranty or negligence theory.

Strict Liability to Bystanders

All courts extend the strict liability of manufacturers and other sellers to injured **bystanders,** although the drafters of Restatement (Second) of Torts, Section 402A, did not take a position on bystanders. For example, the manufacturer of an automobile was held liable for injuries caused by the explosion of the car's motor while the car was in traffic. A cloud of steam that resulted from the explosion caused multiple collisions because it kept other drivers from seeing well.[5]

In the following case, the court extends the protections of Section 402A to bystanders whose injuries from defective products are reasonably foreseeable. Thus, someone injured by an exploding bottle in a supermarket was able to seek damages from the manufacturer for an injury caused by the defective product.

---

5. *Giberson v. Ford Motor Co.,* 504 S.W.2d 8 (Mo. 1974).

BACKGROUND AND FACTS Janice Embs was buying groceries at Stamper's Cash Market, Inc. Unnoticed by her, a carton of 7-Up was sitting on the floor at the edge of the produce counter about one foot from where she was standing. Several of the 7-Up bottles exploded. Embs's leg was injured severely enough that Embs had to be taken to the hospital by Mrs. Stamper, one of the store's managers. Embs brought an action in a Kentucky state court against Arnold Vice, the local 7-Up distributor, and Pepsi-Cola Bottling Co. of Lexington, Kentucky, Inc., the local 7-Up bottler. The trial court directed a verdict against Embs. Embs appealed.

 Case 23.6

EMBS v. PEPSI-COLA BOTTLING CO. OF LEXINGTON, KENTUCKY, INC.
Court of Appeals of Kentucky, 1975.
528 S.W.2d 703.

DECISION AND RATIONALE The Court of Appeals of Kentucky reversed the trial court's directed verdict and remanded the case to the lower court for a new trial. The appellate court extended the protection of the Restatement (Second) of Torts, Section 402A, "to bystanders whose injury from the defective product is reasonably foreseeable." The court based this extension on the policy that "the loss for injuries resulting from defective products should be placed on those members of the marketing chain best able to pay the loss, who can then distribute such risk among themselves by means of insurance and indemnity agreements."

EMERGING TRENDS IN BUSINESS LAW   **Tort Reform**

The percentage of total national income devoted to tort costs is higher in the United States than anywhere else on earth. It is five times what it is in Canada, France, Britain, and Japan. The cost of liability insurance alone is fifteen times higher than in Japan and twenty times higher than in European nations. While tort costs in other nations have remained relatively stable, they have risen dramatically in the United States. For example, medical malpractice costs soared from $1.1 billion in 1978 to $4.2 billion in 1987. Then these costs dropped by $100 million in 1988 and have since continued to fall a little each year. As a consequence, some of the nation's largest underwriters of medical malpractice coverage dropped their rates.

Tort litigation and insurance to protect against tort liability have proved increasingly costly to manufacturers. In 1970 there were seven multimillion-dollar verdicts in tort cases; it is estimated that there will be six hundred in 1992. As mentioned in the chapter text, tort liability has gone to such an extreme in some areas that even when a company proves that it could not have provided a product to an injured party, it can nonetheless be forced to pay part of the award under a theory of liability sharing.[a] While the costs associated with tort litigation may be assumed to be borne by manufacturers, ultimately these costs fall on consumers. Consider, for example, that approximately 20 percent of the cost of a $40 stepladder goes to insurance. Because federal, state, and local governments are increasingly the objects of lawsuits, taxpayers also find themselves paying for tort litigation.

Caps on Noneconomic Damages

Noneconomic damages traditionally have been awarded in personal-injury actions for the pain and suffering associated with physical injuries. Such damages are also recovered in wrongful-death actions brought by spouses or family members for the pain and suffering and loss of consortium (companionship) associated with the untimely death of loved ones.

Reform measures in state legislatures have sought not to bar recovery of noneconomic damages but rather to limit the extent of damage awards. The state caps range from $100,000 to $1,000,000. The types of lawsuits in which the caps are applied are also restricted. For example, caps in California are applied only to negligence and

malpractice actions involving health-care providers and other professionals, such as lawyers. Because juries are not allowed to know about the caps, if the jury award exceeds the legislative cap, the judge is required to reduce the award by a procedure known as *remittitur*.

Although some state cap laws have been challenged as unconstitutional, more states are imposing such legislative limits in an attempt at tort reform.

Pending Federal Reform Legislation

Approximately 20,000 companies are named as lead defendants in product liability suits each year, and they are subject to a product liability system consisting of different, changing, and often conflicting state product liability laws. To establish consistency, some have argued for federal legislation creating uniform product liability laws. A bill that has been reintroduced on several occasions is the Product Liability Reform Act, sponsored by Senator Robert W. Kasten, Jr., of Wisconsin. If such a bill were enacted, it would supersede state laws on virtually all established issues. Here are some of the provisions of the pending federal tort reform legislation:

■ A two-year statute of limitations after the injury occurs.

---

a.   *Hymowitz v. Eli Lilly and Co.,* 73 N.Y.2d 487, 539 N.E.2d 1069, 541 N.Y.S.2d 941 (1989).

■ A twenty-five-year statute of repose.

■ A requirement that a party rejecting settlement must pay part of the other party's attorneys' fees if the final judgment is not better than the settlement offer.

■ A requirement that to obtain punitive damages, a claimant must prove conscious and flagrant indifference to the safety of those harmed by the product.

■ A limitation on manufacturers' liability in lawsuits involving products that were approved by the Food and Drug Administration (FDA) or the Federal Aviation Administration (FAA) prior to distribution.

■ The elimination of joint and several liability (sometimes called "deep pocket" liability) for noneconomic damages, making each defendant liable only according to its share of responsibility for harm.

Some tort reform advocates recommend that all product liability cases at the state court level be reviewed by federal judges. Occasionally, during the reviewing process, the federal judiciary could proclaim a broad new principle or correct a particularly bad state decision. One tort reform proponent suggests that manufacturers be allowed to disclaim liability in certain states. If a manufacturer does not want to take a chance in a state notorious for its high

product liability awards, it could stamp on its product "not for sale or use in _____" (with the blank filled in with the appropriate state name). If passed at the federal level, such tort reform legislation would allow manufacturers to escape state laws.

Finally, many tort reformers want to put a limit on lawyers' contingency fees—fees that are based on a percentage of the final awards. Personal injury and product liability attorneys, among others, have vociferously argued against such a reform, however.

■ Implications for the Businessperson

1. If one tort reform suggested above—the limitation on lawyers' contingency fees—is instituted, the number of suits brought against business firms and professionals may decline. This would obviously benefit businesspersons and business profit margins.

2. If the continuing trend toward capping punitive damages and noneconomic damages continues, liability insurance rates will fall, and this too will have a beneficial effect on business firms.

3. If the proposed federal Product Liability Reform Act is passed in its current form, businesses may still face punitive damages in product liability suits, but such damages will be harder for plaintiffs to

obtain and will be automatically limited for products approved by the FDA and the FAA.

■ For Critical Analysis

1. Limiting or eliminating attorneys' contingency fees may seem a step in the right direction, at least for beleaguered manufacturers and professionals. On the other hand, the benefit of a contingency-fee system is that it motivates attorneys to take on cases that poorer plaintiffs might not otherwise be able to pay for. On balance, then, will a limitation on contingency fees benefit the nation as a whole?

2. Under the proposed federal tort reform bill, damages awarded for injuries caused by FDA-approved products would be limited. Yet according to one study by consumer groups, over 1,300 deaths and thousands of life-threatening illnesses and permanent injuries have resulted from the use of products approved by the FDA. In view of the fact that FDA approval does not infallibly ensure that a product is safe, is it fair to allow manufacturers to use FDA approval as a defense? A similar question might be raised concerning FAA-certified aircraft.

Crashworthiness Doctrine

Certain courts have adopted the **crashworthiness doctrine**, which imposes liability for defects in the design or construction of motor vehicles that increase the extent of injuries to passengers if an accident occurs. The doctrine holds even when the defects do not actually cause the accident.[6] By accepting the crashworthiness doctrine, the courts reject the argument of automobile manufacturers that involving a car in a collision does not constitute "ordinary use" of the car. There are, however, strong differences of opinion among the courts on this issue.

Other Applications of Strict Liability

Under the rule of strict liability in tort, the basis of liability has been expanded to include suppliers of component parts and lessors of movable goods. Thus, if General Motors buys brake pads from a subcontractor and puts them in Chevrolets without changing their composition, and if those pads are defective, both the supplier of the brake pads and General Motors will be held strictly liable for the damages caused by the defects.

Liability for personal injuries caused by defective goods extends to those who lease such goods. Section 408 of the Restatement (Second) of Torts states that:

> One who leases a chattel as safe for immediate use is subject to liability to those whom he should expect to use the chattel, or to be endangered by its probable use, for physical harm caused by its use in a manner for which, and by a person for whose use, it is leased, if the lessor fails to exercise reasonable care to make it safe for such use or to disclose its actual condition to those who may be expected to use it.

Some courts have held that a leasing agreement gives rise to a contractual *implied warranty* that the leased goods will be fit for the duration of the lease. Under this view, if Hertz Rent-a-Car leases a Chevrolet that has been improperly maintained and a passenger in the Chevrolet is injured in an accident, the passenger can sue Hertz. (Liability here is based on the contract theory of warranty, not tort.)

---

6. *Turner v. General Motors Corp.*, 514 S.W.2d 497 (Tex. Civ.App. 1974).

Defenses

Frequently, negligent misconduct or misuse of the product by the harmed person or a third party, coupled with the product's defect, causes damage or injury. If the misconduct or misuse can be charged to a claimant, it may be a defense to reduce the claimant's recovery or bar it altogether.

ASSUMPTION OF RISK   In some states, assumption of risk is a defense in an action based on strict liability in tort. For such a defense to be established, the defendant must show the following basic elements:

1.   That the plaintiff voluntarily engaged in the risk while realizing the potential danger.
2.   That the plaintiff knew and appreciated the risk created by the defect.
3.   That the plaintiff's decision to undertake the known risk was unreasonable.

MISUSE OF THE PRODUCT   Similar to the defense of voluntary assumption of risk is that of **product misuse**. Here the injured party did not know that the product was dangerous for a particular use, but the use was not the one for which the product was designed. (Contrast this with assumption of risk.) This defense has been severely limited by the courts, however. If the misuse is reasonably foreseeable, the seller must take measures to guard against it.

COMPARATIVE FAULT   As pointed out in Chapter 5, at common law, in any action based on negligence, contributory negligence of the injured party either completely barred recovery or reduced the amount of recovery under the rule of comparative negligence. In principle, contributory negligence is immaterial in any action based on the theory of strict liability in tort and in fact has been abolished as a defense by most courts.

Recent developments in the area of comparative negligence are affecting the doctrine of strict liability. Whereas previously the plaintiff's conduct was not a defense to strict liability, today a growing number of jurisdictions considers the negligent or intentional actions of the plaintiff in the apportionment of liability and damages. This "comparing" of the plaintiff's conduct to the defendant's strict liability results in an application of the doctrine of comparative negligence. Thus, for example, failure to take precaution against a known defect will reduce a plaintiff's recovery. The majority of states have adopted this doctrine, either legislatively or through court decisions. Its recent growth may have a pervasive effect on strict liability as well.

■ CONCEPT SUMMARY 23.1 Comparison of Negligence and Strict Liability in the Area of Product Liability

	Negligence	Strict Liability
Applicability	All products.	Products dangerously defective in design or manufacture.
Basic test	Considering all of the circumstances, was reasonable care exercised?	Is there a defect making the product unreasonably dangerous?[a]
Elements	1. Duty of care. 2. Breach of the duty. 3. Breach causes injury or damage.	1. Unreasonably dangerous defect. 2. Defect causes[b] injury or damage.[c]

Defenses	1. Exercise of reasonable care.
	2. Intervening or superseding event caused injury or damage.
	3. Claimant unreasonably assumed risk.
	4. Claimant was also negligent:
	  a. Contributory-negligence jurisdiction—absolute defense.
	  b. Comparative-negligence jurisdiction—damages apportioned.
		1. Defect did not exist when product was in defendant's hands.
		2. Claimant misused product in an unforeseeable way.
		3. Claimant unreasonably assumed risk.
		4. Claimant was also negligent:[d]
		  a. Contributory-negligence jurisdiction—absolute defense.
		  b. Comparative-negligence jurisdiction—damages apportioned.

a. As mentioned, some jurisdictions do not require that a defect render a product unreasonably dangerous.
b. In a few jurisdictions, under the crashworthiness doctrine, the defect need not have caused the accident that resulted in an injury. It need only have increased the extent of the injury.
c. Some jurisdictions limit awards to cases involving personal injuries. A few jurisdictions permit recovery of economic losses.
d. This defense is available in only a few states.

■ Terms and Concepts

■ For Review

1. Under what contract theory can a seller be held liable to a consumer for physical harm or property damage that is caused by the goods sold? Under what tort theories can the seller be held liable?

2. Can a manufacturer be held liable to *any* person who suffers an injury proximately caused by the manufacturer's negligently made product? If the product was not negligently made but is nevertheless so defective as to be un-

reasonably dangerous, does liability extend to any person who suffers an injury proximately caused by the product?

3. What are the elements of a cause of action based on a strict liability theory in a product liability suit?

4. The Ace Cord Co. manufactures bungee cords. Rollo buys one of the cords, fastens one end to a bridge over a 1,500-foot gorge, fastens the other end to a car, and drives the car off the bridge into the gorge. The car drops until it

reaches the end of the cord, the cord snaps, and the car plunges the rest of the distance to the bottom of the gorge. Rollo is injured in the crash. If Rollo brings a product liability suit against Ace based on a negligence theory, what are Ace's possible defenses?

Matador Industries, Inc., manufactures lawn mowers. Matador sells mowers to Wilson Supplies Co., a wholesaler of mowers and related products. Wilson sells mowers to Carlton Distributors, a firm that sells largely to retailers. Carlton sells one of the Matador mowers to Rent-All, a consumer leasing company. Rent-All leases the mower to Darryle. The mower is defective and injures Darryle. Who might be held liable to Darryle for the injury?

■ Questions and Case Problems

 **23-1.** Susan buys a television set manufactured by Quality TV Appliance, Inc. She is going on vacation, so she takes the set to her mother's house for her mother to use. Because the set is defective, it explodes, causing considerable damage to her mother's house. Susan's mother sues Quality for the damages to her house. Discuss the theories under which Susan's mother can recover from Quality.

23-2. Perfect Drug Co. manufactures and has placed on the market a drug for airsickness. Jacob purchases the drug from Green's Drug Store. Jacob is going on a trip and takes two of the tablets as directed. Jacob loses consciousness because of the side effects of the drug, and he falls down a flight of stairs at the airport, breaking an arm and a leg. Perfect knew of the possible side effects but did not place any warning on the label. Also, it is learned that Perfect failed to meet minimum federal drug standards in the manufacture of the drug—standards that would have reduced the side effects. Jacob wants to file an action based on Perfect's negligence.

  (a) Discuss Jacob's burden of proof.
  (b) Discuss how the situation would be different if a warning had been placed on the package and minimum standards had been met.

23-3. Colt manufactures a new pistol. Firing of the pistol is dependent on an enclosed high-pressure device. The pistol has been thoroughly tested in two laboratories in the Midwest, and it has been designed and manufactured according to current technology. Wayne purchases one of the new pistols from Hardy's Gun and Rifle Emporium. When he uses the pistol in the high altitude of the Rockies, the difference in pressure causes the pistol to misfire, resulting in serious injury to Wayne. Colt can prove that all due care was used in the manufacturing process, and it refuses to pay for Wayne's injuries. Discuss Colt's liability in tort.

23-4. Baxter manufactures electric hair dryers. Julie purchases a Baxter dryer from her local Ace Drug Store. Green, a friend and guest in Julie's home, has taken a shower and wants to dry her hair. Julie tells Green to use the new Baxter hair dryer that she has just purchased. As Green plugs in the dryer, sparks fly out from the motor and continue to do so as she operates it. Despite this, Green begins drying her hair. Suddenly, the entire dryer ignites into flames, severely burning Green's scalp. Green sues Baxter on the basis of the torts of negligence and strict liability. Baxter admits the dryer was defective but denies liability, particularly because Green did not purchase the dryer. Discuss the validity of any defense claimed by Baxter.

23-5. Gina is standing on a street corner waiting for a ride to work. Barney has just purchased a new car manufactured by Optimal Motors. Barney is driving down the street when suddenly the steering mechanism breaks, causing him to run over Gina. Gina suffers permanent injuries. Barney's total income per year has never exceeded $15,000. Gina files suit against Optimal under the theory of strict liability in tort. Optimal pleads no liability because (1) due care was used in the manufacture of the car, (2) Optimal is not the manufacturer of the steering mechanism (Smith is), and (3) the Restatement governing strict liability applies only to users or consumers, and Gina is neither. Discuss the validity of the defenses claimed by Optimal.

23-6. A two-year-old child lost his leg when he became entangled in a grain auger on his grandfather's farm. The auger had a safety guard that prevented any item larger than 4⅝ inches from coming into contact with the machine's moving parts. The child's foot was smaller than the openings in the safety guard. Was such an injury reasonably foreseeable? Discuss. [*Richelman v. Kewanee Machinery & Conveyor Co.,* 59 Ill.App.3d 578, 375 N.E.2d 885, 16 Ill.Dec. 778 (1978)]

23-7. During the 1960s, Aluminum Co. of America (Alcoa) designed, patented, manufactured, and marketed a closure system for applying aluminum caps to carbonated soft-drink bottles. In 1969, Alcoa sold a capping machine to Houston 7-Up Bottling Co. On June 3, 1976, James Alm suffered a severe eye injury when an aluminum bottle cap exploded off a thirty-two-ounce bottle of 7-Up that had come from the Houston 7-Up Bottling Co. Alm sued Alcoa, alleging that, as the manufacturer, Alcoa had a duty to warn consumers of the dangers of a possible bottle-cap explosion. Alcoa argued that it had not had a duty to warn Alm because it had not manufactured or sold any component part or the final product that injured Alm. Alcoa had mentioned possible cap explosions in the machine users' manual, wall charts, and technical information that it had provided to the Houston 7-Up Bottling Co. Which allegation is correct? Explain. [*Alm v. Aluminum Co. of America,* 717 S.W.2d 588 (Tex. 1986)]

23-8. Frances Ontai entered the Straub Clinic and Hospital to have an x-ray examination of the colon. Ontai was placed in a vertical position on a table manufactured by General Electric. The footrest on the table broke, and Ontai fell to the floor of the examination room, suffering injuries. Ontai filed suit against Straub and General Electric. Ontai's suit against General Electric was based on strict liability in tort, negligence, and implied warranties. Discuss briefly each of these theories of liability. [*Ontai v. Straub Clinic and Hospital, Inc.,* 66 Hawaii 237, 659 P.2d 734 (1983)]

23-9. William Mackowick, who had worked as an electrician for thirty years, was installing high-voltage capacitors in a switchgear room in a hospital when he noticed that a fellow electrician had removed the cover from an existing capacitor manufactured by Westinghouse Electric Corp. Westinghouse had placed a warning label inside the cover of the metal box containing the capacitor on which users were instructed to ground the electricity before handling. Nothing was said on the label about the propensity of electricity to "arc." (Arcing occurs when electricity grounds itself by "jumping" to a nearby object or instrument.) Mackowick walked over to warn the other electrician of the danger associated with the exposed capacitor, and, while talking, pointed his screwdriver toward the capacitor box. The electricity flowing through the fuses arced to the screwdriver and sent a high-voltage electric current through Mackowick's body. As a result, he sustained severe burns and was unable to return to work for three months. Should Westinghouse be held liable because it failed to warn users of arcing—a principle of electricity? Discuss. [*Mackowick v. Westinghouse Electric Corp.,* 575 A.2d 100 (Pa. 1990)]

23-10. Case Briefing Assignment

Examine Case A.12 [Bernal v. Richard Wolf Medical Instruments Corp., *221 Cal.App.3d 1326, 272 Cal.Rptr. 41 (1990)*] *in Appendix A. The case has been excerpted there in great detail. Review and then brief the case, making sure that you include answers to the following questions in your brief.*

1. What product malfunction brought about this product liability suit?
2. What instructions did the trial court judge give the jury on the design-defect issue, and why did they become the central issue on appeal?
3. According to the appellate court, which party bore the burden of proving that a safer alternative design was feasible, the plaintiff or the defendant?
4. Why did the appellate court state that it "would not hesitate to affirm the jury's verdict" if correct instructions had been given to the jury?

Chapter 24

International Transactions

At the end of the 1950s, only about 3 or 4 percent of the nation's gross national product involved imports or exports. Since then, that percentage has doubled and at times tripled. This increase is due to technological improvements in communications and transportation as well as the ongoing globalization of American business as international trade barriers are being removed on a continuing basis. What happens in other parts of the world now affects virtually every business in this country, whether it operates only domestically or in international markets.

◼ Doing Business Internationally

There are a number of ways in which a U.S. domestic firm can engage in international business transactions. The simplest way is to seek out foreign markets for domestically produced products (or services). In other words, U.S. firms can look abroad for **export** markets for their goods and services. Alternatively, a U.S. firm can establish foreign production facilities so as to be closer to the foreign market or markets in which its products are sold. The advantages may include lower labor costs, fewer government regulations, and lower taxes and trade barriers. It is also possible to obtain business from abroad by licensing technology developed and owned by the domestic firm to an existing foreign company. Finally, it is possible to expand abroad by selling franchises to overseas entities. The presence of McDonald's, Burger King, and Holiday Inns throughout the world attests to the popularity of franchising.

Exporting

The initial foray into international business by most U.S. companies is through exporting—that is, selling their products to buyers located in other countries. Exporting can take two forms: direct exporting or indirect exporting. In *direct exporting,* a U.S. company signs a sales contract with a foreign purchaser that provides for the conditions of shipment and payment for the goods. (How payments are made in international transactions is discussed later in this chapter.) If business develops sufficiently in foreign countries, a U.S. corporation may develop a specialized marketing organization in the foreign market itself. Such *indirect exporting* can be undertaken by the appointment of a foreign agent or a foreign distributor.

FOREIGN AGENT   When a U.S. firm desires a limited involvement in an international market, it will typically establish an *agency relationship* with a foreign firm. In an agency relationship, one person (the agent) agrees to act on behalf of, or instead of, another (the principal)—see Chapter 35. The foreign agent is thereby empowered to enter into contracts in the agent's country on behalf of the U.S. principal.

FOREIGN DISTRIBUTOR   When a substantial market exists in a foreign country, a U.S. firm may wish to appoint a distributor located in that country. The U.S. firm and the distributor enter into a **distribution agreement**, which is a contract between the seller and the distributor setting out the terms and conditions of the distributorship—for example, price, currency of payment, guarantee of supply availability, and method of payment. The terms and conditions primarily involve contract law. Disputes concerning distribution agreements may involve jurisdictional or other issues that are treated in detail later in this chapter. In addition, some **exclusive distributorships** have raised antitrust problems. The application of antitrust laws to international transactions is discussed in Chapter 56.

A distributor is not normally the same as a foreign agent because the distributor takes title to the merchandise when it is received. Thus the distributor bears the risk connected with commercial sales.

Manufacturing Abroad

An alternative to direct or indirect exporting is the establishment of foreign manufacturing facilities. Typically, U.S. firms desire to establish manufacturing plants abroad if they believe that by doing so they will reduce costs—particularly for labor, shipping, and raw materials—and thereby be able to compete more effectively in foreign markets. As pointed out above, foreign manufacturing facilities may lead to fewer trade restrictions and a lowering of taxes, particularly import taxes, in the country involved. Apple Computer, IBM, General Motors, and Ford are some of the many U.S. companies

that have established manufacturing facilities abroad. Foreign firms have done the same in the United States. Sony, Nissan, and other Japanese manufacturers have established U.S. plants to avoid possible import duties that the U.S. Congress may impose on Japanese products entering this country.

There are several ways in which an American firm can manufacture in other countries. They include licensing and franchising, as well as investing in a wholly owned subsidiary or a joint venture.

LICENSING   It is possible for U.S. firms to license their technologies to foreign manufacturers. **Technology licensing** may involve a process innovation that lowers the cost of production, or it may involve a product innovation that generates a superior product. Technology licensing may be an attractive alternative to establishing foreign production facilities, particularly if the process or product innovation has been patented, because the patent protects—at least to some extent—against the possibility that the innovation might be pirated. Firms may be able to acquire parallel patents in a foreign country, depending on the patent laws of that country, and international agreements protecting intellectual property rights may allow for patent or copyright protection in the countries abiding by such agreements. (International protection for intellectual property rights is discussed in Chapter 8.) As with any licensing agreement, a licensing agreement with a foreign-based firm calls for a payment of royalties on some basis—such as so many cents per unit produced or a certain percentage of profits from units sold in a particular geographical territory.

In certain circumstances, even in the absence of a patent, a firm may be able to license the "know-how" associated with a particular manufacturing process—for example, a plant design or a secret formula. The foreign firm that agrees to sign the licensing agreement further agrees to keep the know-how confidential and to pay royalties. For example, the Coca-Cola Bottling Company licenses firms worldwide to use (and keep confidential) its secret formula for the syrup used in that soft drink, in return for a percentage of the income gained from the sale of Coca-Cola by those firms.

The licensing of technology benefits all parties to the transaction, in that those who receive the license can take advantage of an established reputation for quality, and firms that grant the license receive income from the foreign sales of the firm's products, as well as the establishment of a worldwide reputation. Also, once a firm's trademark is known worldwide, the demand for other products manufactured or sold by that firm may increase—an obviously important consideration.

FRANCHISING   Franchising is a well-known form of licensing. A **franchise** can be defined as an arrangement in which the owner of a trademark, a trade name, or a copyright (the **franchisor**) licenses another (the **franchisee**) to use the trademark, trade name, or copyright under certain conditions or limitations in the selling of goods or services in exchange for a fee, usually based on a percentage of gross or net sales. Examples of international franchises include McDonald's, the Coca-Cola Bottling Company, Holiday Inn, Avis, and Hertz. Because of their franchising arrangements, these firms are known throughout the world.

INVESTING IN A WHOLLY OWNED SUBSIDIARY OR A JOINT VENTURE   One way to expand into a foreign market is to establish a wholly owned subsidiary firm in a foreign country. The European subsidiary would likely take the form of the *société anonyme* (S.A.), which is similar to a U.S. corporation. In German-speaking nations, it would be called an *Aktiengesellschaft* (A.G.). When a wholly owned subsidiary is established, the parent company, which remains in the United States, retains complete ownership of all of the facilities in the foreign country, as well as complete authority and control over all phases of the operation.

The expansion of a U.S. firm into international markets can also take the form of a joint venture. In a **joint venture,** the U.S. company owns only a part of the operation—the rest is owned either by local owners in the foreign country or by another foreign entity. In a joint venture, responsibilities, as well as profits and liabilities, are shared by all of the firms involved in the venture. A joint venture is the only way in which U.S. companies are allowed to have manufacturing facilities in many developing countries. Often, U.S. ownership of joint ventures in these countries cannot exceed 49 percent. Additionally, some less-developed countries require that Americans constitute a minority of the management of the joint venture.

■ Contracting for the International Sale of Goods

Many of the same contractual issues that you have examined in earlier chapters also apply to international contracts. There are of course additional issues, such as differences in currency and legal systems, that must be considered. The necessity of addressing such issues when forming contracts for international transactions cannot be overstated.

Contracts for the international sale of goods between firms or individuals located in different countries are governed by the United Nations Convention on Contracts for the International Sale of Goods (CISG) if the countries of the parties to the contract have ratified the CISG. Essentially, the CISG is to international sales contracts what Article 2 of the Uniform Commercial Code (UCC) is to domestic sales contracts. Recall that in domestic transactions the UCC applies when the parties to a contract for a sale of goods have failed to specify in writing some important term concerning price, delivery, or the like. Similarly, whenever the parties to international transactions have failed to specify in writing the precise terms of a contract, the CISG will be applied. The provisions of the CISG, while similar for the most part to those of the UCC, differ from them in some respects. In the event that the CISG and the UCC are in conflict, the CISG applies (because it is a treaty of the national government and therefore is supreme—see the discussion of the supremacy clause of the U.S. Constitution in Chapter 4).

The Convention for the International Sale of Goods

Although international trade has taken place since at least the beginning of recorded history, the emergence of multinational and global business enterprises is a twentieth-century phenomenon. As early as the 1930s, a number of nations saw the need for, and began to develop, uniform laws to cover contracts for the international sale of goods to facilitate international transactions. The end result of this important legal development was the 1980 Vienna Convention on Contracts for the International Sale of Goods, which applies to all contracts between firms located in the countries that have adopted the convention.

By the beginning of the 1990s, the following countries had ratified the CISG: Argentina, Australia, Austria, the Byelorussian S.S.R., Denmark, Egypt, Germany, Finland, France, Hungary, Italy, Lesotho, Mexico, Norway, the People's Republic of China, Sweden, the Syrian Arab Republic, the Ukrainian S.S.R., the United States, Yugoslavia, and Zambia. While the current list of signatories is small, it is expected to grow rapidly. The United States ratified the convention in 1987, and it became effective for this country on January 1, 1988. As of that date, the CISG, and not Article 2 of the UCC, became the governing law for all international sales transactions carried out by U.S. firms.

When the CISG Applies

Technically speaking, the CISG applies only to contracts between entities located in countries that have ratified the CISG. The application of the provisions of the CISG is not mandatory because any U.S. company dealing with a firm located in a signatory country can, by contractual agreement, provide that another law, and not the CISG, will apply. The specific language used in such a provision would have to be as follows:

> The provisions of the Uniform Commercial Code as adopted by the state of [say] California, and *not* the Convention for the International Sale of Goods, apply.

The CISG does not apply to domestic sales or noncommercial sales—that is, it does not apply to consumer sales of goods bought for family, household, or personal use. Nor does it apply to the sale of services. In situations in which the contract calls for both services and goods, if the sale of goods outweighs the sale of services, then the CISG will apply. In these respects, the CISG is very similar to the UCC.

How the CISG Differs from the UCC

The provisions of the CISG are very similar to those of the UCC, but there are some significant differences. The major differences concern the following:

1. The mirror image rule.
2. Irrevocable offers.
3. The Statute of Frauds.

4. The price term.
5. The time of contract formation.

THE MIRROR IMAGE RULE   In Chapter 10, you learned that under the common law of contracts an acceptance had to be the mirror image of the offer. You later learned, in Chapter 18, that the UCC did away with this requirement. In contracts between merchants, often the contractual conditions stipulated on the buyer's standard order forms do not agree with the seller's contractual conditions as stipulated on the seller's standard forms. A "battle of the forms" then ensues to determine which party's terms should prevail. The UCC implicitly acknowledges the fact that in the ordinary course of business, sellers and buyers rarely read the backs of their sale or purchase forms. Accordingly, the UCC relaxed substantially the rules governing contractual agreement. Under the UCC, an acceptance that contains additional terms can still result in the formation of a contract, unless the additional terms constitute a material alteration of the contract (see Chapter 18).

Article 19 of the CISG provides the rules governing additional terms in international sales contracts. Article 19(1) provides that if the terms of the acceptance vary from those of the offer, there is no contract: "A reply to an offer which purports to be an acceptance, but contains additions, limitations, or other modifications is a rejection of the offer and constitutes a counter-offer." But Article 19(2) then stipulates that an acceptance containing additional terms may still bind the offeror in contract:

> However, a reply to an offer which purports to be an acceptance but contains additional or different terms which do not materially alter the terms of the offer constitutes an acceptance, unless the offeror, without undue delay, objects orally to the discrepancy or dispatches a notice to that effect. If he does not so object, the terms of the contract are the terms of the offer with the modifications contained in the acceptance.

Do not get the mistaken impression, however, that Article 19(2) of the CISG is the same in effect as UCC 2-207(2). The definition of "material alteration" under the CISG involves virtually any differences in the terms relating to payment, quality, quantity, price, time and place of delivery, extent of one party's liability to the other, or how disputes under the contract will be settled. In effect, then, Article 19 requires—more or less—that the terms of the acceptance mirror those of the offer. As a practical matter, businesspersons undertaking international sales transactions therefore should not use the sale or purchase forms that they customarily use for transactions within the United States. Although the sample form shown in Exhibit 24–1 illustrates the typical terms and conditions that might be contained in an international purchase order, it is important to remember that international purchase and sale forms need to be specially drafted to suit the needs of the specific transaction.

IRREVOCABLE OFFERS   UCC 2-205 requires that an irrevocable offer without consideration must be in writing. In contrast, Article 16(2) of the CISG provides that an offer will be irrevocable if it simply states that it is irrevocable or if the offeree reasonably relies on the offer as being irrevocable. In both of these situations, the offer will be irrevocable even without a writing and without consideration.

STATUTE OF FRAUDS   The UCC requires, as a general rule, a writing for contracts for the sale of goods priced at $500 or more [UCC 2-201]. The writing must be signed by the party against whom enforcement is sought and must be sufficient to show that a contract has been made. Article 11 of the CISG, however, does not include the formal requirements imposed by the Statute of Frauds:

> A contract of sale need not be concluded in or evidenced by writing and is not subject to any other requirements as to form. It may be proved by any means, including witnesses.

The difference between the UCC and the CISG in respect to writing requirements should not be overstated, however. The UCC allows for many exceptions to the Statute of Frauds requirements, and as a result oral contracts are often enforceable. In particular, whenever partial or complete performance has occurred, the plaintiff to a dispute need not produce a writing to demonstrate that a contract was made. Because the majority of contractual disputes occur after some degree of performance, the difference between the UCC and the CISG with respect to writing requirements may seem more significant than it actually is.

Article 11 accords with the legal customs of most nations, in which contracts no longer need to meet certain formal or writing requirements to be enforceable. Ironically, even England, the nation that created the original Statute of Frauds in 1677, has repealed all of it but the provisions relating to land and suretyship. Many other countries that once had such a statute have also repealed all or parts of it. Civil law countries, such as France, never had a writing requirement. Although countries that wish to retain the applicability of the Statute of Frauds to international sales contracts are allowed to exclude Article 11 when ratifying the CISG, the American Bar Association recommended that the United States follow the practice of the majority of nations and *not* exclude the provision.

THE NECESSITY OF A PRICE TERM   Under the UCC, if the parties to a contract have not agreed on a price, the contract will not fail if the parties intended to form a contract (had a ''meeting of the minds''). If the price term is left open, the court will determine ''a reasonable price at the time for delivery'' [UCC 2-305(1)]. Under the CISG, the price term must be specified, or at least provisions for its specification must be included in the agreement; otherwise, no contract exists.

The CISG does not specifically require that the exact price be calculated in the offer, but the contract must include an *express* provision that allows for an exact determination of the price. For example, if the contract states that the price of wheat to be delivered in two months will be its price at the Chicago Board of Trade on that day, that is a sufficient price term under the CISG.

TIME OF CONTRACT FORMATION   Under the common law of contracts, an acceptance is effective on dispatch, and thus a contract is created when the acceptance is transmitted. The UCC does not alter this so-called ''mailbox rule.'' Under the CISG, however, a contract is created not at the time the acceptance is transmitted but only on its *receipt* by the offeror. Article 18(2) states that an acceptance by return promise ''becomes effective at the moment the indication of assent reaches the offeror.'' Under Article 18(3), the offeree may also bind the offeror by performance even without giving any notice to the offeror. The acceptance becomes effective ''at the moment the act is performed.'' The rule is therefore that it is the

■ Exhibit 24-1 Sample International Purchase Order Form (Front)

Caution: This form contains a typical set of terms written from the buyer's point of view, but it is not applicable to all factual situations and the laws of all states. Terms and conditions of sale or purchase must be custom-drafted to be appropriate to the type of business and type of goods involved.

Sample International Purchase Order Terms & Conditions*

The _____ Company, Inc.
International Terms and Conditions of Purchase

1. *Acceptance.* Acceptance of this order is expressly limited to the terms and conditions contained herein, including all terms and conditions set forth on the face hereof. Acceptance of this order by Seller may be made by signing and returning the attached acknowledgement copy hereof, by other express acceptance, or by shipment of goods hereunder. If Seller uses its own order acknowledgement or other form to accept this order, it is understood that said form shall be used for convenience only and any terms or conditions contained therein inconsistent with or in addition to those contained herein shall be of no force or effect whatsoever between the parties hereto.

2. *Warranty.* Seller warrants the goods covered by this Agreement and their packaging and labelling shall be in merchantable condition and shall be free from defects in workmanship and materials and shall be in conformity with the specifications, drawings, samples and descriptions attached hereto or referred to on the face hereof, if any. Seller warrants that the goods covered by this Agreement shall be fit for such particular purposes and uses, if any, as specified by BUYER or otherwise known to Seller. Seller warrants that the goods shall be free and clear of any lien or other adverse claim against title, and to the extent not manufactured to detailed designs furnished by BUYER shall be free from defects in design. All warranties contained herein shall survive inspection, test and acceptance by BUYER. Seller agrees, at its own costs and expense, to defend and hold BUYER harmless from and against any and all claims made against BUYER based upon, relating to, or arising out of any claimed defects in the goods or services ordered hereunder. Seller's warranties (and any consumer warranties, service policies, or similar undertakings of Seller) shall be enforceable by BUYER'S customers and any subsequent owner or operator of the goods as well as by BUYER.

3. *Shipping Instructions.* No charge shall be made to BUYER for draying and packaging unless authorized by BUYER. Merchandise shipped by freight or express shall be packed, marked and described and the carrier shall be selected, so as to obtain the lowest rate possible under freight or express classifications or regulations except when otherwise specified by BUYER, and penalties or increased charges due to failure so to do will be charged to Seller. The foregoing notwithstanding, Seller shall comply with all instructions of BUYER as to packaging, marking, shipping and insurance. Prior to passage of title to BUYER the goods shall be held by Seller without risk or expense to BUYER.

4. *Invoices, Other Documents and Charges.* Seller shall invoice in duplicate. Originals of all invoices, government and commercial bills of lading and air express receipts shall be air mailed to the Purchasing Department of BUYER when goods are shipped. Packing slips must accompany item number, and a complete description of its contents. Except as otherwise provided on the face hereof, the contract price includes all costs and charges to be paid or reimbursed to Seller by BUYER, including without limitation, all applicable taxes and duties and all charges for packing, loading and transportation. Transportation charges and taxes and duties, when applicable, and when agreed on the face hereof to be borne by BUYER shall be billed as separate items on Seller's invoices.

5. *Inspection—Nonconformity.* BUYER may inspect the goods and, with respect to nonconforming goods, may return them or hold them at the Seller's risk and expense, and may in either event charge the Seller with cost of transportation, shipping, unpacking, examining, repacking, reshipping, and other like expense. Promptly upon BUYER's written request, and without expense to BUYER, Seller agrees to replace or correct defects of any rejected goods or other goods not conforming to the warranty set forth above. In the event of failure of Seller to replace or correct defects in nonconforming goods promptly, BUYER after reasonable notice to Seller, may make such corrections or replace such goods and charge Seller for the costs incurred by BUYER in doing so. Time is of the essence in this transaction. In addition to its remedies for breach of contract, BUYER reserves the right to return any or all goods in unopened original packing to Seller if delivered to BUYER more than five (5) days after the delivery date shown in shipping instructions. If the delivery date shown in shipping instructions is revised by BUYER by notification to Seller, then such five (5) day period shall not commence to run until such revised delivery date. Also, BUYER reserves the right to refuse goods delivered contrary to instructions or not in recognized standard containers. BUYER shall be under no duty to inspect goods prior to BUYER's use or resale, and neither retention, use nor resale of such goods shall be construed to constitute an acceptance of goods not in compliance with the requirements of this order.

6. *Changes.* Unless agreed in writing by BUYER, Seller shall not purchase materials, or make material commitments, or production arrangements, in excess of the amount, or in advance of the time necessary to meet BUYER'S delivery schedule. BUYER shall have the right at any time to make changes in drawings, designs, specifications, materials, packaging, time and place of delivery and method of transportation. If any such changes cause an increase or decrease in the cost, or the time required for the performance, an equitable adjustment shall be made and this agreement shall be modified in writing accordingly. Seller agrees to accept any such changes subject to this paragraph. This right to an adjustment shall be deemed waived unless asserted within thirty (30) days after the change is ordered. BUYER reserves the right to terminate this order or any part hereof for its sole convenience. In the event of such termination, Seller shall immediately stop all work hereunder, and shall immediately cause any of its suppliers or subcontractors to cease such work. Seller shall be paid a reasonable termination charge consisting of a percentage of the order price reflecting the percentage of the work performed prior to the notice of termination. Such charge shall be Seller's only remedy for such termination. Seller shall not be paid for any work done after receipt of the notice of termination nor for any work done by Seller's suppliers or subcontractors which Seller could reasonably have avoided.

7. *Default.* BUYER may also terminate this order or any part hereof for cause in the event of any default by the Seller or if the Seller fails to comply with any of the terms and conditions of this offer. Late deliveries, deliveries of goods which are defective or which do not conform to this order, and failure to provide BUYER, upon request, reasonable assurances of future performance shall all be causes allowing BUYER to terminate this order for cause. In the event of termination for cause, BUYER shall not be liable to Seller for any amount and Seller shall be liable to BUYER for any and all damage sustained by reason of the default which gave rise to the termination.

Copyright 1988, Barry A. Sanders. All rights reserved. Reprinted with permission. These sample terms and conditions were used in connection with a presentation with the 21st Annual Uniform Commercial Code Institute. Mr. Sanders is with Latham & Watkins in Los Angeles, CA.

■ **Exhibit 24–1** *(Continued)* **Sample International Purchase Order Form (Back)**

8. *Indemnity.* Seller will defend and indemnify BUYER, upon demand, against all claims, actions, liability, damage, loss and expense (including investigative expense and attorney's fees incurred in litigation or because of threatened litigation) as the result of BUYER'S purchase and/or use of the goods and arising or alleged to arise from patent, trademark or copyright infringement; unfair competition; the failure or alleged failure of the goods to comply with specifications or with any express or implied warranties of Seller; the alleged violation by such goods or in its manufacture or sale of any statute, ordinance, or administrative order, rule or regulation; defects, whether latent or patent, in material or workmanship; defective design; defective warnings or instructions; or Seller's negligence.

9. *Price Reductions.* Seller will give BUYER the benefit of any price reductions occurring before the specified shipping date or to actual time of shipment, whichever is later. Likewise, if Seller accepts this order as a commission merchant, Seller shall obtain for BUYER from the manufacturer of such goods the benefit of price reductions to the specified date or to actual time of shipment, whichever is later. Seller warrants that the price for the articles sold BUYER hereunder are not less favorable than those currently extended to any other customer for the same or similar articles in similar quantities.

10. *Information.* Seller shall consider all information furnished by BUYER to be confidential and shall not disclose any such information to any other person, or use such information itself for any purpose other than performing this order unless Seller obtains written permission from BUYER to do so. This confidential requirement shall also apply to drawings, specifications, or other documents prepared by Seller for BUYER in connection with this order. Seller shall provide confidential information only to those of its agents, servants and employees who have been informed of the requirements of this paragraph and have agreed to be bound by them. Upon completion or termination of this order, Seller shall make such disposition of all such information and items as may be directed by BUYER. Seller shall not advertise or publish the fact that BUYER has ordered goods from Seller nor shall any information relating to this order be disclosed without BUYER'S written permission. Unless otherwise agreed in writing, no commercial, financial or technical information disclosed in any manner or at any time by Seller to BUYER shall be deemed secret or confidential and Seller shall have no rights against BUYER with respect thereto except such rights as may exist under patent laws.

11. *Tools, Dies, Etc.* Seller agrees that the information, tools, jigs, dies, etc., drawings, patterns and specifications supplied or paid for by BUYER shall be and remain BUYER'S property, shall be used only on BUYER'S orders, and shall be held by Seller for BUYER unless directed otherwise. Seller will account for such items and keep them in good working condition and fully covered by insurance at all times without expense to BUYER. In the event Seller devises and incorporates any new features design into any goods made under this order, Seller grants to BUYER the right of reproduction of such goods, together with a royalty-free, nonexclusive, irrevocable license to use such new features of design.

12. *General Provisions.*

(a) Seller and BUYER shall be independent contractors. This transaction does not create a principal-agent or partnership relationship between them, and neither one may legally commit the other in any matter.

(b) BUYER may deduct from any payment due to Seller or set-off against any claim by Seller any amount which is due to BUYER by Seller for any reason, including, among other reasons, any excess transportation charges caused by deviations from BUYER'S shipping instructions or the shipping of partial shipments.

(c) Seller shall comply with all laws, regulations and policies applicable to it by any jurisdiction and shall obtain all permits needed to complete this transaction under the laws of the country from which the shipment is made, including among other things, any required export permits and Central Bank approvals.

(d) All billings and payments shall be made in U.S. Dollars.

(e) In the event the importation of the goods results in the assessment of a countervailing duty on BUYER as the importer, Seller shall reimburse such countervailing duty to BUYER, provided such reimbursement is permitted under U.S. laws and regulations,

(f) Goods ordered hereunder to be made with use of BUYER'S confidential information, BUYER'S designs, BUYER'S trademarks or tradenames or BUYER'S customer's trademarks or tradenames shall be furnished by Seller exclusively to BUYER. Any excess of such inventory shall be destroyed by Seller at its own expense.

(g) Seller warrants that it has accepted no gratuities of any kind from any employee of BUYER in connection with placement of this order.

(h) Seller shall cooperate fully with BUYER at Seller's expense in obtaining approvals of the goods requested by BUYER from certifying organizations such as Underwriters Laboratories.

(i) Any goods that are hazardous will be packaged, marked and shipped by Seller to comply with all U.S. federal, state and local regulations and will further comply with all special BUYER requirements. Seller shall furnish BUYER a Material Hazard Data Sheet covering all such goods.

(j) BUYER shall not be liable to Seller for any loss incurred by Seller due to strikes, riots, storms, fires, explosions, acts of God, war, embargo, government boycott or other governmental action or any other causes similar thereto beyond the reasonable control of BUYER. Any failure or delay in performance of any of the foregoing shall not be a default hereunder.

(k) BUYER may waive performance of any condition, but waiver by BUYER of a condition shall not be considered a waiver of that condition for succeeding performance. None of BUYER'S remedies hereunder shall exclude its pursuit of its other legal remedies.

(l) This document and any other documents mentioned on the face hereof, constitute the entire agreement between the parties on this subject. All prior representations, negotiations or arrangements on this subject matter are superseded by these terms and shall not form a basis for interpretation of these terms. All amendments to these terms must be agreed to in writing by BUYER.

(m) If any manufacturer's excise tax, value added tax or other tax measured by selling price is included in or added to the price of the goods paid by BUYER, then, in the event all or any part of that tax shall be refunded to Seller, Seller shall promptly remit such refund in full to BUYER.

(n) This order is nonassignable. Any attempt to assign without BUYER'S written consent is void.

(o) This transaction and all its terms shall be construed in accordance with and all disputes shall be governed by the laws of the State of _____ , U.S.A., specifically including the provisions of the Uniform Commercial Code, as adopted by that state, and excluding the provisions of the Convention on the International Sale of Goods. Seller submits to the jurisdiction of the courts located in the State of _____ in the event of any proceedings therein in connection herewith.

(p) Any and all disputes arising between BUYER and Seller in connection with this transaction (other than actions for contribution or indemnity with respect to court actions involving third parties) shall be exclusively and finally decided by arbitration in _____ under the rules of the American Arbitration Association. The arbitration award shall be final and nonappealable. There shall be three arbitrators, one chosen by each party and the third chosen by the first two, or in the event of their failure to agree, by the _____ state court of general jurisdiction. The arbitrators shall reach their decision, and state it in writing with reason for it, within twelve months after the appointment of the third arbitrator.

(q) This order shall expire in thirty (30) days from the date of issuance by BUYER, unless earlier revoked by BUYER or accepted by Seller. ■

offeree's reliance, rather than the communication of acceptance to the offeror, that creates the contract.

Special Provisions in International Contracts

Language and legal differences among nations can create special problems for parties to international contracts when disputes arise. It is possible to avoid these problems by including in a contract special provisions designating the official language of the contract, the legal forum in which disputes under the contract will be settled, and the substantive law that will be applied in settling any disputes. These contractual provisions will be examined in the following sections. It is also important to indicate in the contract whether disputes under the contract will be arbitrated or litigated, and what acts or events will excuse the parties from performance under the contract. In provisions for arbitration, it is important that the forum, choice of law, and expertise of the arbitrator be specified in the contract.

CHOICE OF LANGUAGE   A deal struck between a U.S. company and a company in another country normally involves two languages. The complex contractual terms involved may not be understood by one party in the other party's language. Typically, many phrases in one language are not readily translatable into another. To make sure that no disputes arise out of this language problem, an international sales contract should have a **choice-of-language clause** designating the official language by which the contract will be interpreted in the event of disagreement. Such a clause might state that the agreement is being written in English,

which is to be regarded as the authoritative and official language of the contract's text. The clause may further allow that the agreement is to be translated into, say, Spanish; that the translation is to be ratified by both parties; and that the foreign company can rely on the translation. If arbitration is anticipated, an additional clause must be added to indicate that the arbitration will be in, say, English, Spanish, or French—or whatever the case may be.

CHOICE OF FORUM   In international contracts, it is especially important to include a **forum-selection clause**. When several countries are involved, litigation may be sought in courts in different nations. There are no universally accepted rules regarding the jurisdiction of a particular court over subject matter or parties to a dispute. Consequently, parties to an international transaction should always include in the contract a forum-selection clause designating the forum in which a dispute will be litigated. A forum-selection clause should specifically indicate the court that will have jurisdiction. The forum does not necessarily have to be within the geographical boundaries of either of the parties' nations.

Under certain circumstances, a forum-selection clause will not be valid. Specifically, if the clause denies one party an effective remedy, is the product of fraud or unconscionable conduct, causes substantial inconvenience to one of the parties to the contract, or violates public policy, the clause will not be enforced.

In the following case, the United States Supreme Court made it clear that wide latitude should be granted the parties in selecting the forum in which a contractual dispute would be settled.

BACKGROUND AND FACTS   Zapata Off-Shore Company, an American corporation, contracted with Unterweser, a German corporation, to tow Zapata's drilling rig from Louisiana to Italy. The contract contained a forum-selection clause: "Any dispute arising must be treated before the London Court of Justice." Unterweser's ship, the *M/S Bremen*, began the towing operation, but a storm in the Gulf of Mexico severely damaged the drilling rig. Zapata, ignoring the contract's forum-selection clause, sued in a federal district court in Florida, seeking damages for allegedly negligent towage. Unterweser filed a motion to dismiss the case, arguing that the U.S. court lacked jurisdiction under the contract. The court rejected Unterweser's motion, and Unterweser appealed. The appellate court affirmed the district court's decision. Unterweser appealed to the United States Supreme Court.

Case 24.1

M/S BREMEN v. ZAPATA OFF-SHORE CO.

Supreme Court of the United States, 1972.
407 U.S. 1,
92 S.Ct. 1907,
32 L.Ed.2d 513.

DECISION AND RATIONALE   The United States Supreme Court held that the contract provision controlled and that consequently U.S. courts lacked jurisdiction. The Supreme Court expressed concern that the expansion of American business and industry would be harmed if, despite legal contracts, American courts insisted that all disputes must be resolved under American law and in American courts. Although the Court acknowledged the traditional reluctance of American courts to accept forum-selection clauses, it ruled that the clauses should be enforced unless shown to be unreasonable under the circumstances. The Court concluded that the courts of England would provide a suitably neutral forum for resolution of the dispute. The Court stated that "the choice of that forum was made in an arm's-length negotiation by experienced and sophisticated businessmen, and absent some compelling and countervailing reason it should be honored by the parties and enforced by the courts." The Court vacated the appellate court's decision and remanded the case for further proceedings consistent with its opinion.

CHOICE OF LAW   A contractual provision designating the applicable law, called a **choice-of-law clause,** is typically included in every international contract. At common law (and in European civil law systems), parties are allowed to choose the law that will govern their contractual relationship provided that the law chosen is the law of a jurisdiction that has a substantial relationship to the parties and to the international business transaction. Under Section 1-105 of the UCC, parties may choose the law that will govern the contract as long as the choice is ''reasonable.'' Article 6 of the CISG, however, imposes no limitation on the parties in their choice of what law will govern the contract, and the 1986 Hague Convention on the Law Applicable to Contracts for the International Sale of Goods—often referred to as the ''Choice-of-Law Convention''—allows unlimited autonomy in the choice of law. Whenever a choice of law is not specified in a contract, the Hague Convention indicates that the governing law is that of the country in which the *seller's* place of business is located.

FORCE MAJEURE   Every contract, particularly those involving international transactions, should have a *force majeure* **clause.** The definition of the French term *force majeure* is ''impossible or irresistible force''—which sometimes is loosely identified as ''an act of God.'' In international business contracts, *force majeure* clauses commonly stipulate that a number of other eventualities, in addition to acts of God, may excuse a party from

liability for nonperformance. Consider, for example, the following typical *force majeure* clause:

> The parties hereto shall not be liable for failure of performance hereunder if occasioned by undeclared or declared war, flood, fire, embargo, governmental orders, regulations, restrictions, governmental expropriation, fire, flood, accident, interruptions of transportation facilities, labor strikes and disputes, shortages of materials, or production facilities, or any other causes beyond the control of the parties.

■ Making Payment on International Transactions

Currency differences between nations and the geographic distance between parties to international sales contracts add a degree of complexity to international sales that does not exist within the domestic market. Because international contracts involve greater financial risks, special care should be taken when drafting the contract to specify both the currency in which payment is to be made and the method of payment. Additionally, there may be difficulties in repatriating profits made in businesses in wholly owned subsidiaries or joint ventures abroad.

Monetary Systems

While it is true that our national currency, the U.S. dollar, is one of the primary forms of international money, any U.S. firm undertaking business transactions abroad must be prepared to deal with one or more other currencies. After all, just as a U.S. firm wants to be paid in U.S. dollars for goods and services sold abroad, so too does, say, a Japanese firm want to be paid in Japanese yen for goods and services sold outside of Japan. Both firms therefore must rely on the convertibility of currencies.

FOREIGN EXCHANGE MARKETS Currencies are convertible when they can be freely exchanged one for the other at some specified market rate in a **foreign exchange market**. The foreign exchange market is a worldwide system for the buying and selling of foreign currencies. At any particular point in time, the foreign exchange rate is set by the forces of supply and demand in unrestricted foreign exchange markets. The **foreign exchange rate** is simply the price of a unit of one country's currency in terms of another country's currency. For example, if today's exchange rate is 100 yen for $1, that means that anybody with 100 yen can obtain $1, and vice versa.

CORRESPONDENT BANKING Many times, a U.S. company can deal directly with its domestic bank, which will take care of the international money flow problem. Commercial banks sometimes have correspondent branches or banks in other countries, which are called **correspondent banks**. For example, Citicorp might open an account in French francs in *Credit Lyonnais* in Paris. At the same time, *Credit Lyonnais* will open an account in Citibank by depositing U.S. dollars with Citibank. Citibank and *Credit Lyonnais* are correspondent banks.

Correspondent banking is a major means of transferring funds internationally. Suppose, for example, that a customer of Citibank wishes to pay a bill in French francs to a company in Paris. Citibank can draw a bank check payable in francs on its account in *Credit Lyonnais* and then send it to the French company to whom its customer owes the money. Alternatively, Citibank's customer can request a **wire transfer** of the funds to the French company. Citibank instructs *Credit Lyonnais* by wire to pay the necessary amount in French francs. Wire transfers are a major part of electronic fund transfer systems (to be discussed in Chapter 30). Fedwire, which is operated by the U.S. Federal

Reserve System, is available for wire transfers between banks within the United States. The Clearinghouse Interbank Payment Systems (CHIPS) handles about 90 percent of both national and international interbank transfers of U.S. funds. Finally, the Society for Worldwide International Financial Telecommunications (SWIFT) is a communication system that provides banks with messages concerning transactions. The funds do not, however, accompany the message and therefore must be transferred by some other means.

Letters of Credit

Because buyers and sellers engaged in international business transactions are often separated by thousands of miles, special precautions are often taken to ensure performance under the contract. Sellers want to avoid delivering goods for which they might not be paid. Buyers desire the assurance that sellers will not be paid until there is evidence that the goods have been shipped. Thus, **letters of credit** are frequently used to facilitate international business transactions. In a simple letter-of-credit transaction, the *issuer* (a bank) agrees to issue a letter of credit and to ascertain the occurrence of certain acts by the *beneficiary* (seller). In return, the *account party* (buyer) promises to reimburse the issuer for the amount paid to the beneficiary. There may also be an *advising bank* that transmits information, and a *paying bank* may be involved to expedite payment under the letter of credit. See Exhibit 24–2 for the "life cycle" of a letter of credit.

Under a letter of credit, the issuer is bound to pay the beneficiary (seller) when the beneficiary has complied with the terms and conditions of the letter of credit. The beneficiary looks to the issuer, not to the account party (buyer), when it presents the documents required by the letter of credit. Typically, the letter of credit will require that the beneficiary deliver a *bill of lading* (a document that evidences the transportation of goods—see Chapter 19) to prove that shipment has been made. Letters of credit assure beneficiaries (sellers) of payment while at the same time assuring account parties (buyers) that payment will not be made until the beneficiaries have complied with the terms and conditions of the credit.

■ Exhibit 24–2 The "Life Cycle" of a Letter of Credit

Although the letter of credit appears quite complex at first, it is not difficult to understand. This exhibit depicts the steps involved in a letter-of-credit procurement cycle. This cycle merely involves the exchange of documents (and money) through intermediaries.

Step 1: The buyer and seller agree on the terms of sale. The sales contract dictates that a letter of credit is to be used to finance the transaction.

Step 2: The buyer completes an application for a letter of credit and forwards it to the buyer's bank, which will issue the letter of credit.

Step 3: The issuing (buyer's) bank then forwards the letter of credit to a correspondent bank in the seller's country.

Step 4: The correspondent bank relays the letter of credit to the seller.

Step 5: Having received assurance of payment, the seller makes the necessary shipping arrangements.

Step 6: The seller prepares the documents required under the letter of credit and delivers them to the correspondent bank.

Step 7: The correspondent bank examines the documents. If it finds them in order, it sends them to the issuing bank and pays the seller in accordance with the terms of the letter of credit.

Step 8: The issuing bank, having received the documents, examines them. If they are in order, the issuing bank will charge the buyer's account and send the documents on to the buyer or the buyer's customs broker. The issuing bank also will reimburse the correspondent bank.

Step 9: The buyer or broker receives the documents and picks up the merchandise from the shipper (carrier).

THE VALUE OF A LETTER OF CREDIT The basic principle behind letters of credit is that payment is made against the documents presented by the beneficiary and not against the facts that the documents purport to reflect. Thus, in a letter-of-credit transaction, the issuer does not police the underlying contract: *a letter of credit is independent of the underlying contract between the buyer and the seller.* Eliminating the need for banks (issuers) to inquire into whether actual conditions have been satisfied greatly reduces the cost of letters of credit and encourages the free flow of commerce. Moreover, as mentioned above, the use of a letter of credit protects both buyers and sellers.

COMPLIANCE WITH A LETTER OF CREDIT In a letter-of-credit transaction, generally at least three separate and distinct contracts are involved: the underlying contract between the account party (buyer) and the beneficiary (seller), the contract between the issuer (bank) and the account party (buyer), and finally the letter of credit itself, which involves the issuer and the beneficiary. Given the fact that these contracts are separate and distinct, the issuer's obligations under the letter of credit do not concern the underlying contract between the

buyer and the seller. Rather, it is the issuer's duty to ascertain whether the documents presented by the beneficiary (seller) comply with the terms of the letter of credit.

If the documents presented by the beneficiary comply with the terms of the letter of credit, the issuing bank must honor the letter of credit. Sometimes, however, it is difficult to determine exactly what a letter of credit requires. Moreover, the courts are divided as to whether *strict* or *substantial* compliance with the terms of the letter of credit is required. Traditionally, courts required strict compliance with the terms of a letter of credit, but in recent years some courts have moved to a standard of *reasonable* compliance.[1]

If the issuing bank refuses to pay the seller (beneficiary) even though the seller has complied with all the requirements of the letter, the seller can bring an action to enforce payment. In the international context, the fact that the issuing bank may be thousands of miles distant from the seller's business location can pose difficulties for the seller—as the following case illustrates.

---

1. See, for example, *Crocker Commercial Services v. Countryside Bank,* 538 F.Supp. 1360 (N.D. Ill., 1981).

BACKGROUND AND FACTS Pacific Reliant Industries, Inc., an Oregon corporation, sold building materials to Paradise Development Company, a corporation located in American Samoa. Because Pacific was reluctant to make several large deliveries (totaling more than $1 million) without some protection against nonpayment, representatives from Pacific, Paradise, and Amerika Samoa Bank (ASB) met in American Samoa to discuss the supply contract and the letter of credit. Following these negotiations, ASB issued a letter of credit in favor of Pacific on Paradise's account. Pacific later brought suit in the United States District Court for the District of Oregon against ASB to recover payment, alleging that ASB had wrongfully dishonored the letter of credit. The court dismissed the suit for lack of personal jurisdiction, holding that ASB lacked sufficient "minimum contacts" with Oregon to subject it to a lawsuit in that state. Pacific appealed, contending that this case was not typical of other letter of credit cases because ASB had participated in forming the underlying contract, had had personal contact with the beneficiary (Pacific), and had known that Pacific would not extend credit or ship goods from Oregon without the letter of credit.

Case 24.2

PACIFIC RELIANT INDUSTRIES, INC. v. AMERIKA SAMOA BANK

United States Court of Appeals, Ninth Circuit, 1990.
901 F.2d 735.

DECISION AND RATIONALE The United States Court of Appeals for the Ninth Circuit affirmed the lower court's ruling. The appellate court ruled that Pacific could not bring suit against ASB in Oregon because ASB lacked sufficient minimum contacts with Oregon to satisfy jurisdictional requirements: ASB did not initiate the transactions between itself, Paradise, or Pacific, nor did ASB take any significant actions in Oregon. The court noted that "both the negotiations for the underlying contract and the letter of credit occurred in American Samoa." Furthermore, ASB did not invoke the benefits and protections of Oregon law. The court reasoned that ASB could not have reasonably expected to be hauled into court in Oregon and "that ASB's conduct as an issuing bank of a letter of credit does not subject it to suit in Oregon."

▪ Resolving International Contract Disputes

It goes without saying that disputes will arise with international contracts just as they do with domestic ones. Indeed, it might be argued that more disputes will arise internationally, because of cultural differences among nations. Differences in language and custom certainly contribute. Countries may differ distinctly in their attitudes toward contracts. In Japan, for example, it is customarily assumed that the relationship between contracting parties will be long term in nature. This leads to lengthy negotiations and short contracts. The opposite expectation characterizes businesspersons in the United States, and this leads to short negotiation periods and lengthy contracts. In any event, when contract disputes do arise, contractual parties need to decide whether to undertake litigation or arbitration as a method of dispute settlement.

Litigation

If no arbitration clause is contained in the sales contract, litigation may be the method by which a dispute is settled. If forum-selection and choice-of-law clauses were included in the contract, the lawsuit will be heard by a court in the specified forum country, and the specified substantive law will be applied. If no forum and choice of law were specified in the contract, however, legal proceedings will be more complex and attended by much more uncertainty. For example, litigation may take place in two or more countries, with each country applying its own choice-of-law rules to determine which substantive law will be applied to the particular transactions. Furthermore, even if a plaintiff wins a judgment in a lawsuit litigated in the plaintiff's country, there is no guarantee that the court's judgment will be enforced by judicial bodies in the defendant's country. Under the *principle of comity*, an international principle of law founded in the need for courteous interaction among nations (see Chapter 56), the judgment may be enforced in the defendant's country. This is particularly true if the defendant's country is the United States and the foreign court's decision is consistent with U.S. national law and policy. Other nations, however, may not be as accommodating as the United States, and the plaintiff may be left empty-handed.

Arbitration

As discussed in Chapter 3, the arbitration of civil disputes is becoming an increasingly attractive alternative to costly litigation through the court system. This is true on the international level as well. Arbitration clauses are frequently found in contracts governing the international sale of goods. By means of such clauses, the parties agree in advance to be bound by the decision of a specified third party in the event a dispute should arise. The third party may be a neutral entity such as the International Chamber of Commerce, a panel of individuals representing both parties' interests, or some other group or organization. The 1958 United Nations Convention on the Recognition and Enforcement of Foreign Arbitral Awards[2]—which has been implemented in more than fifty countries, including the United States—assists in the enforcement of arbitration clauses, as do provisions in specific treaties between nations.

In the following case, the plaintiff alleged that the defendant had violated U.S. securities laws and that therefore, in accordance with a ruling case precedent on a similar issue, the arbitration clause should not be enforced. The United States Supreme Court had to decide whether the precedent should apply to an international contractual dispute.

---

2. 21 U.S.T. 2518, T.I.A.S. No. 6997, 330 U.N.T.S. 38, implemented in the United States by 9 U.S.C. Sections 201-208.

Case 24.3 **SCHERK v. ALBERTO-CULVER CO.** Supreme Court of the United States, 1974. 417 U.S. 506, 94 S.Ct. 2449, 41 L.Ed.2d 270.	**BACKGROUND AND FACTS** Alberto-Culver Company, an American corporation with its principal office in Illinois, manufactured and sold toiletry products in the United States and abroad. Alberto-Culver bought from Fritz Scherk, a German citizen, three interrelated toiletry-business entities, organized under the laws of Germany and Liechtenstein, that were engaged, in part, in the licensing of trademarks. The contract stated that Scherk's ownership of the trademarks was unencumbered and provided that any dispute arising out of the agreement would be referred for arbitration to the International Chamber of Commerce in Paris. On learning that the trademark rights were subject to substantial encumbrances, Alberto-Culver brought an action for damages and other relief in a federal district court in Illinois, contending that Scherk's fraudulent representations concerning the status of the trademark rights violated the Securities Exchange Act of 1934 (see Chapter 43). Scherk filed a motion to dismiss the action, contending, among other things, that the dispute should be arbitrated under the contract. The court denied Scherk's motion on the basis of a 1953 United States Supreme Court ruling that an agreement to arbitrate could not preclude a buyer of a security from seeking a judicial remedy under U.S. securities laws.[a] Scherk appealed. The appellate court affirmed the district court's order, and Scherk appealed to the United States Supreme Court.

DECISION AND RATIONALE The United States Supreme Court reversed the judgment of the district court, holding that the arbitration clause was enforceable. The Supreme Court pointed out that the transaction was an international agreement and that thus there was considerable uncertainty as to the law applicable to the resolution of disputes arising out of the contract. The Court reasoned that this uncertainty, which "will almost inevitably exist with respect to any contract touching two or more countries," supported its view that the arbitration clause should be enforced. The Court saw the parties' specifying in advance the forum in which a dispute was to be heard as "an almost indispensable precondition" for carrying out orderly business transactions while avoiding the danger that the dispute might be decided in a forum hostile to the interests of one of the parties. The Court remanded the case for further proceedings consistent with its opinion.

a. The United States Supreme Court has since ruled that claims alleging violations of securities laws can be arbitrated pursuant to a contractual arbitration clause. See, for example, *Shearson/American Express, Inc. v. McMahon*, 482 U.S. 220, 107 S.Ct. 2332, 96 L.Ed.2d 183 (1987).

■ Terms and Concepts

choice-of-language clause 433	*force majeure* **clause** 434	**franchisee** 428
choice-of-law clause 434	**foreign exchange market** 435	**franchisor** 428
correspondent banks 435	**foreign exchange rate** 435	**joint venture** 428
distribution agreement 427	**forum-selection clause** 433	**letter of credit** 435
exclusive distributorship 427	**franchise** 428	**technology licensing** 427
export 426		**wire transfer** 435

■ For Review

1. At common law, an acceptance must mirror the offer, or there is no contract. Under the UCC, an acceptance containing additional terms may still result in the formation of a contract. What does the CISG provide?

2. When does the CISG apply? Is its application mandatory?

3. On what grounds might a forum-selection clause be held invalid?

4. Mena Overseas Sales, an American company, wants to do business with Odessa Imports, Ltd., a Ukrainian firm. Because of the recent economic changes in former communist countries, Mena is reluctant to do business with Odessa without some assurance of Odessa's ability to pay. What might Mena require Odessa to do to reassure Mena?

5. Luna Industries, a Chilean firm, sues the Sunn Co., an American firm, in a Chilean court. Luna wins. Sunn is uncooperative in paying the judgment, however. To collect, Luna must seek enforcement of the Chilean court's judgment in an American court. On what ground might an American court refuse to enforce the Chilean court's judgment?

■ Questions and Case Problems

24-1. There are rumors throughout Hollywood that Work Hard Ethic Media Group, a People's Republic of China company, is planning to purchase the Cartoon King movie film library. Management personnel of both companies have had talks on several occasions, but no written contracts have yet been signed. You have just learned that the president of Work Hard Ethic and the president of Cartoon King have agreed upon a sales price of $1.2 million for the film library. Following the Chinese custom, the two corporate leaders shook hands to consummate the deal (still no writings were signed). Later, before delivery of the film library, Cartoon King learned that Titus Industrus, the owner of a U.S. television superstation, would have paid $1.5 million for the films. Cartoon King refuses to deliver the film library to Work Hard Ethic, claiming that the contract is unenforceable. Discuss fully Cartoon's contention under both the UCC and the CISG.

24-2. The U.S. government and the Mexican government enter into an agreement for the special sale of Mexican oil to be shipped to oil reserve storage areas along the Gulf Coast. Provisions for the total quantity of oil, the price, and the place of delivery have been agreed on, and all appropriate government documents have been exchanged. The contract is created through the use of two forms—a seller's form as an offer from the Mexican government and a purchase order form as an acceptance by the U.S. government. Three weeks later, Congress passes an energy policy bill that allocates most of the energy funds to support new breakthroughs in solar energy. The bill is signed into law by the president. Because of this legislation, the United States wants to cancel its agreement with Mexico. A U.S. government official notices that there are some differences between the Mexican offer and the U.S. acceptance. For example, the Mexican offer was for equal monthly shipments over a one-year period, while the U.S acceptance called for larger shipments during the first six months and smaller shipments during the last six months. The United States claims that its form, with the shipment quantity changes, constitutes a rejection of Mexico's offer and is a counteroffer. Mexico claims that the terms on the form used by the United States was an acceptance forming a binding contract. Discuss fully which party would be correct if the UCC were applied and which party would be correct if the CISG applied.

24-3. McBride's, a U.S. retail jewelry store, contacted Lanslow's Gemology Laboratory, a Brazilian jewelry manufacturer, about the possibility of entering into a requirements contract. It was proposed that Lanslow's would supply McBride's with precious and semiprecious stones on a monthly basis, the quantity to be determined by McBride's needs. Lanslow's sent a contract to McBride's by Federal Express for McBride's signature. McBride's signed the contract, without making any changes to it, and faxed it back to Lanslow's headquarters in Rio de Janeiro. Unfortunately, the fax transmission was never received. Discuss whether a contract has been created under the UCC or under the CISG—or under both.

24-4. The Swiss Credit Bank issued a letter of credit in favor of Antex Industries to cover the sale of 92,000 electronic integrated circuits manufactured by Electronic Arrays. The letter of credit specified that the chips would be transported to Tokyo by ship. Antex shipped the circuits by air. Payment on the letter of credit was dishonored because the shipment by air did not fulfill the precise terms of the letter of credit. Should a court compel payment? Discuss. [*Board of Trade of San Francisco v. Swiss Credit Bank,* 728 F.2d 1241 (9th Cir. 1984)]

24-5. DBM Drilling Corp. contracted to purchase a drilling rig from GATX Leasing Corp. DBM arranged to have Frost National Bank issue an irrevocable letter of credit to GATX to pay for the rig. GATX complied with all the provisions of the letter of credit. DBM argued, however, that the oil rig itself did not comply with the terms of the underlying contract between DBM and GATX. DBM therefore sued to enjoin the bank from paying GATX under the letter of credit. Discuss whether the court should issue such an injunction. [*GATX Leasing Corp. v. DBM Drilling Corp.,* 657 S.W.2d 178 (Tex.App. 1983)]

24-6. In a contract between Arthur Young & Co., a New York corporation with a branch office in Hawaii, and Robert Leong, whose only office was in Hawaii, the parties included a forum-selection clause stating that any dispute arising under the contract would be heard before a New York court and New York law would apply. When a dispute did eventually arise, Leong claimed that the forum-selection clause should not be enforced, on the grounds of inconvenience. Not only had the dispute arisen in Hawaii, but all of the relevant records and witnesses were located there,

and to transport the records and witnesses to New York would entail a major inconvenience. Discuss whether the court should enforce the forum-selection clause in these circumstances. [*Arthur Young & Co. v. Leong,* 53 A.D.2d 515, 383 N.Y.S.2d 618 (1976)]

24-7. Royal Bed and Spring Co., a Puerto Rican distributor of furniture products, entered into an exclusive distributorship agreement with Famossul Industria e Comercio de Moveis Ltda., a Brazilian manufacturer of furniture products. Under the terms of the contract, Royal Bed was to distribute in Puerto Rico the furniture products manufactured by Famossul in Brazil. The contract contained choice-of-forum and choice-of-law clauses, which designated that the judicial district of Curitiba, State of Parana, Brazil, as the judicial forum and the Brazilian Civil Code as the law to be applied in the event of any dispute. Famossul terminated the exclusive distributorship and suspended the shipment of goods without just cause. Puerto Rican law refuses to enforce forum-selection clauses providing for foreign venues as a matter of public policy. In what jurisdiction should Royal Bed bring suit? Discuss fully. [*Royal Bed and Spring Co. v. Famossul Industria e Comercio de Moveis Ltda.,* 906 F.2d 45 (5th Cir. 1990)]

24-8. Panhandle Eastern Pipe Line Co. (PEPL) and another party entered into a contract for the purchase of liquified natural gas (LNG) from the Algerian National Oil & Gas Co. A *force majeure* clause in the contract stated that ''chance events affecting the facilities used for the performance of the contract'' could reduce the quantities of LNG that PEPL was obligated to purchase. If the purchaser were to claim that full performance under the contract was impossible because of the nationwide recession, the enactment of energy conservation legislation, the warm winter season, the unprecedented reduction in the price of crude oil, and the emergence of increased competition in the sales market, would the purchaser's contractual performance be excused under the *force majeure* clause? Discuss fully. [*United States v. Panhandle Eastern Corp.,* 693 F.Supp. 88 (D.Del. 1988)]

24-9. Case Briefing Assignment

Examine Case A.13 [China Resource Products (U.S.A.), Ltd. v. Fayda International, Inc., 747 F.Supp. 1101 (D.Del. 1990)] *in Appendix A. The case has been excerpted there in great detail. Review and then brief the case, making sure that you include answers to the following questions in your brief.*

1. Why was this lawsuit initiated, and who was the plaintiff?
2. The court stated that the defendant apparently believed that this case was ''actually the story of Little Red Riding Hood''? Did the court agree with this depiction?
3. On what grounds did the plaintiff seek to have the court stay (suspend) the defendant's counterclaim?
4. What evidence did the defendant offer to support its claim that the arbitration clause in the 1987 contract did not apply to the present action?
5. What federal statutes guided the court's reasoning?

Focus on Ethics

Domestic and International Sales Law

Transactions involving the sale of goods constitute a major portion of business activity in the commercial and manufacturing sectors of this economy. Since the 1960s, the sale of goods has been governed by the Uniform Commercial Code (UCC) in virtually every state. Many of the UCC provisions express our ethical standards.

Good Faith and Commercial Reasonableness

"Good faith" and "commercial reasonableness" are two key concepts that permeate the UCC and help to prevent the success of unethical behavior by businesspersons. These two concepts are read into every contract and impose certain duties on all parties. Section 2-311(1) indicates that when parties leave the particulars of performance to be specified by one of the parties, "[a]ny such specification must be made in good faith and within limits set by commercial reasonableness." The requirement of commercial reasonableness means that the term subsequently supplied by one party should not come as a surprise to the other. The party filling in the missing term may not take advantage of the opportunity to add a contractual

term that will be beneficial to himself or herself (and detrimental to the other party) and then demand contractual performance of the other party that was totally unanticipated. Under the UCC, in this situation the party filling in the missing term may not deviate from what is commercially reasonable in the context of the transaction. Courts frequently look to course of dealing, usage of trade, and the surrounding circumstances in determining what is commercially reasonable in a given situation.

Good Faith

The concept of good faith implies that one party will not take advantage of another party by manipulating contract terms. The obligation of good faith is particularly important in so-called requirements and output contracts. UCC 2-306 states "quantity" in these contracts "means such actual output or requirements as may occur in good faith." For example, if General Motors contracts with Smith's Carburetors to purchase all of Smith's output, Smith's cannot then increase its production from one eight-hour shift per day to three eight-hour shifts per day to make greater profits under the contract. As another example, assume that

Mary's Machines has fifty employees assembling IBM clones. Mary has a requirements contract with Advanced Tech Circuit Boards under which Advanced Tech is to supply Mary with all of the circuit boards she needs. If all of a sudden Mary quadruples the size of her business, she cannot insist that Advanced Tech supply her with all her requirements as per the original contract.

In many situations, parties may find it advantageous (profitable) to avoid a legal obligation. Without the counterobligation of good faith, the potential for abuse in the area of sales contracts is tremendous. Suppose, for example, that the market price of the good subject to a requirements contract rises rapidly and dramatically because of a shortage of materials necessary to its production. The buyer could claim that his or her needs are equivalent to the entire output of the seller. Then, after buying all of the seller's output at the contract price, which is substantially below the market price, the buyer could turn around and sell the goods that he or she does not need at the higher market price. Under the UCC, this type of unethical

441

behavior is prohibited—even though the buyer in this instance has not technically breached the contract. Actual requirements must be determined in good faith. No speculation is allowed under requirements contracts.

Commercial Reasonableness

Under the UCC, the concept of good faith is closely linked to commercial reasonableness. All commercial actions—including the performance and enforcement of contract obligations—must exhibit commercial reasonableness. A merchant is expected to act in a reasonable manner according to reasonable commercial customs. Indeed, the words *reasonable, reasonability,* and *reasonableness* appear again and again in the UCC. The concept of commercial reasonableness is clearly expressed in the doctrine of commercial impracticability. Under this doctrine, which is related to the common law doctrine of impossibility, a party's nonperformance of a contractual obligation may be excused when, because of unforeseen difficulties, performance of the contract becomes extremely difficult and burdensome. But the UCC makes it clear that the nonperformance must result from difficulties that could not *reasonably* have been foreseen or contemplated at the time of contract formation.

As an example, consider the case of *Maple Farms, Inc. v. City School District of Elmira.*[1] In June of 1973, Maple Farms, Inc., formed an agreement with the school district to supply the

school district with milk for the 1973–1974 school year. The agreement was in the form of a requirements contract, under which Maple Farms would sell to the school district all the milk the district required at a fixed price—which was the June market price of milk. By December of 1973, however, the price of raw milk had increased by 23 percent over the price specified in the contract. This meant that if the terms of the contract were fulfilled, Maple Farms would lose $7,350. Because it had similar contracts with other school districts, Maple Farms stood to lose a great deal if it was held to the price stated in the contracts.

Maple Farms sought to be released from its contractual obligations on the grounds of commercial impracticability, but did not succeed. The court noted that an increase in the price of milk should not have been totally unexpected, given the fact that the price of milk had traditionally varied and in the previous year had risen 10 percent. Also, the general inflation of prices in the United States should have alerted Maple Farms to the possibility of an increased milk price. According to the court, Maple Farms had reason to know these facts and could have placed a clause in its contract with the school district to protect itself from its present situation. Maple Farms could not be excused from performance because it should reasonably have anticipated the possibility that the price of milk might rise at least 10 percent, and possibly more because of the general inflation. In the court's eyes, a price rise of 23 percent was within the range of possibilities that Maple Farms should have anticipated.

The ethical principle expressed in the doctrine of commercial impracticability is that of fairness. In the *Maple Farms* case, essentially the court held that it would not be fair to the school district to excuse Maple Farms from its contractual obligation—because the price rises were not totally unexpected or unreasonable in view of the known facts at the time of contract formation. Maple Farms, in short, had failed to look after its own interests by not including in the contract a clause that would have prevented its financial difficulties. But what about the school district? Was it acting reasonably—or ethically—when it refused to release Maple Farms from the contract? The court, at least, found no problem here. It did not escape the court's attention that the primary purpose of the contract, on the part of the school district, was to protect itself (for budgetary reasons) against price fluctuations. Therefore, it would make no sense to expect the school district to release Maple Farms from performance when such fluctuations did, in fact, occur.

The Concept of the Good Faith Purchaser

The UCC defines a good faith purchaser as a person who buys without knowledge of circumstances that would cause a person of ordinary prudence to inquire about the seller's title to the goods. That means that even though such circumstances may exist, the purchaser must be unaware of them if he or she is to acquire the status of a good faith purchaser. Under a voidable contract, the real owner cannot recover goods from a good faith

---

1. 76 Misc.2d 1080, 352 N.Y.S.2d 784 (1974).

purchaser who has given value for the goods [UCC 2-403(1)].

Here we see the UCC's emphasis on protecting innocent parties. If you innocently and in good faith purchase a boat, for example, from someone who appears to have good title and who demands and receives from you a fair market price, then the UCC believes that you should be protected from the possibility that the real owner—from whom the seller may have fraudulently obtained the boat—may later appear and demand his or her boat back. (Nothing, however, prevents the true owner from bringing suit against the party who defrauded him or her.)

Ethical questions arise in situations in which the purchaser has reason to suspect that the seller may not have good title to the goods being sold but nonetheless lets the transaction go forward because it is a "good deal." At what point does the buyer, in such a situation, cross over the boundary that separates the good faith purchaser from one who purchases in bad faith? This boundary is a significant one in the law of sales because the UCC will not be a refuge for those who purchase in bad faith. The term *good faith purchaser* means just that—one who enters into a contract for the purchase of goods without knowing, or having any reason to know, that there is anything shady or illegal about the deal.

Warranties

A seller has not only a legal obligation to provide safe products but also an ethical one. When faced with the possibility of providing additional safety at no extra cost, every ethical businessperson will indeed opt for a safer product. An ethical issue arises,

however, when the production of a safer product means higher costs and therefore higher consumer prices. Also at issue is the extent to which manufacturers should be responsible for repairing products that fail or that are broken in the course of normal use. To some extent, our warranty laws have been deemed necessary to protect consumers from sellers who choose, perhaps, to neglect ethical concerns if what they are doing is both legal and profitable. We see, for example, that the use of the term "warranty" in the UCC reflects a promise or a guarantee made by a seller of goods that the goods will have certain characteristics. Both express and implied warranties are recognized by the UCC. Under UCC 2-314(2), goods sold by a merchant must be fit for the ordinary purposes for which such goods are used, be of proper quality, and be properly labeled and packaged. A description of goods is an express warranty, and hence a seller of goods may be held to have breached a contract if the goods fail to conform to the seller's description. The UCC injects greater fairness into contractual situations by recognizing descriptions as express warranties. The UCC acknowledges the fact that a buyer may often reasonably believe that a seller is warranting his or her product, even though the seller may not use formal words such as *warrant* or *guarantee*. Thus, the law imposes an ethical obligation on merchants in a statutory form.

The Magnuson-Moss Warranty Act, which was discussed in Chapter 22, as well as lemon laws and the creation of the Consumer Product Safety

Commission, all have had the effect of imposing higher and higher standards on manufacturers of goods. Nonetheless, numerous ethical issues continue to arise over warranties, especially in regard to warranty disclaimers.

Warranty Disclaimers
The UCC requirement that warranty disclaimers must be sufficiently conspicuous to catch the eye of a reasonable purchaser is based on the ethical premise that sellers of goods should not take advantage of unwary consumers who may not—in the excitement of making a new purchase—always read the "fine print" on standard purchase order forms. As discussed in Chapter 22, if a seller, when attempting to disclaim warranties, fails to meet the specific requirements imposed by the UCC, the warranties will not effectively be disclaimed.

The ethical significance of the UCC rules on warranty disclaimers can best be illustrated by looking at the situation that existed prior to the implementation of the UCC. Before the UCC was adopted by the states, purchasers of automobiles, for example, frequently signed standard-form purchase agreements, drafted by the auto manufacturer, without learning until later what all the fine print meant. *Henningsen v. Bloomfield Motors, Inc.*,[2] a case decided in New Jersey before the UCC was in effect in that state, involves just such a situation. Henningsen had purchased a new Chrysler from Bloomfield Motors for his wife. Subsequently, his wife suffered severe injuries as a result of an

---

2. 32 N.J. 358, 161 A.2d 69 (1960).

apparent defect in the steering wheel mechanism. The standard-form purchase order used in the transaction contained an express ninety-day/4,000-mile warranty and, in fine print, a disclaimer of any and all other express or implied warranties. Thus Bloomfield Motors and Chrysler Corporation refused to pay for Mrs. Henningsen's injuries, asserting that the sales contract, which warranted that Bloomfield Motors would repair defects at no charge, disclaimed warranty liabilities for injuries suffered. The case was eventually heard by the Supreme Court of New Jersey, which expressed outrage at the fact that the automobile manufacturer had used its grossly disproportionate bargaining power, as well as the unfair surprise of fine print, to relieve itself from liability and to impose on the buyer, who in effect had no real freedom of choice, the grave danger of injury that is posed by a defectively made automobile. In a landmark decision, the court held that the disclaimer was unconscionable and allowed the Henningsens to recover from the auto dealer and manufacturer.

While freedom of contract reflects a basic ethical principle in our society, courts—including the New Jersey court mentioned above—have made it clear that when such freedom leads to gross unfairness, it should be curbed. (Several examples of the kinds of exceptions to freedom of contract that courts will make were offered in the *Focus on Ethics* at the end of Unit Two.) But in regard to warranty disclaimers in fine print or otherwise "hidden" in a standard purchase order form, a court, before the UCC was in effect, would not intervene unless, as in the Henningsen

case, the resulting unfairness "shocked the conscience" of the court. By obligating merchants to meet specific requirements when disclaiming warranties, the UCC has made dealing fairly with buyers—an already ethical obligation of all sellers of goods—a legal obligation as well. Today, if a warranty disclaimer unfairly "surprises" a purchaser, chances are that the disclaimer was not sufficiently conspicuous; and the unfairness of the bargain will not have to be so great as to shock the court's conscience before a remedy will be granted.

Product Liability

Ethical questions abound in the area of product liability. As the courts have imposed higher and higher damages on manufacturers in product liability lawsuits, so, it would seem, are more consumers bringing lawsuits to obtain damages when they are harmed by a product. In some cases, lawsuits are brought even though it is essentially the consumer who is at fault—if anyone is—and not the manufacturer. Such litigation raises an obvious ethical question: Is it fair that consumers should recover damages for harm caused by their own carelessness or product misuse or for simple accidents for which no one is really at fault?

Consider, for example, the case of *Kemp v. Beneke*, a 1990 Nevada district court case[3] that involved a nine-month-old child, Ryan Kemp, who fell through a toilet seat and suffocated in the water. The Kemp family sued the toilet-seat manufacturer, arguing that a

warning sticker should have been placed on the toilet-seat lid to tell parents to take protective measures, such as buying a so-called "potty lock" to attach to the lid or installing self-closing hinges on the bathroom door. Should the toilet-seat manufacturer be required to warn against the obvious? Although in this case the manufacturer agreed to pay $90,000 to the Kemps, many persons might question the ethics of requiring a manufacturer to warn parents of such an obvious household danger.

In a similar vein, should tobacco companies and liquor companies be held liable for the numerous premature deaths of persons who purchase tobacco or liquor products because they are addicted to these psychoactive drugs? No one forces individuals to become nicotine addicts or alcoholics. Indeed, at least today, virtually no individual can be ignorant of the detrimental effects of consuming tobacco products and alcoholic beverages on a regular basis. Nonetheless, courtrooms in America are still faced with plaintiffs who are suing tobacco companies, and sometimes manufacturers of alcoholic beverages, for the premature deaths of loved ones. To date, no tobacco company has lost a suit, but the fact that such suits can be brought—in spite of the common knowledge of the detrimental effects of cigarette smoking and in spite of the warning labels on cigarette packages—does indicate that the courts are still receptive to a strict liability standard for consumer products.

At the other end of the spectrum is the need to impose strict liability standards on manufacturers to ensure that they will do all they can, within

_____

3. No. A 267563 (Clark Co.).

reason, to prevent unsafe products from entering the marketplace. There is a fine line, however, between an imposition of ethical standards on manufacturers to benefit society and one that has the effect of overprotecting consumers—in the sense that it opens the door to the possibility that consumers may recover damages that are essentially incurred by their own carelessness or product misuse.

International Considerations

The problem of diversity of interests and values faced by large corporations is magnified in the international arena. Multinational corporations need to consider not only ethical values of Americans but also those values of the host countries within which they do business. In the event of a conflict, which values should prevail? For example, in some countries discrimination on the basis of race, sex, or religion is required by law. Also, in many countries labor is cheaper and the legal standards for employee health and safety are much lower. U.S. employment laws do not apply abroad, but should U.S firms nonetheless, for ethical reasons, abide by U.S. standards?

The United Nations recently drafted a code of conduct for multinational corporations that, if accepted, would impose specific ethical requirements on firms involved in foreign business operations. Among other things, these firms would be required to consider the health and safety of consumers and the environment of the host country, to respect human rights and fundamental freedoms, and to disclose whether their products have been banned in other countries. The proposed code has come under much criticism, however. According to officials within the U.S. Department of State, the code will probably not be accepted in its present form by this country because it is "unbalanced." While multinational corporations face numerous restrictions under the code, the host countries are not required to abide by equally restrictive guidelines.

■ Discussion Questions

1. Do you think customer satisfaction is as important an element today as it once was in the success and profitability of business firms? Why or why not?

2. In what ways might a competitive marketplace foster ethical behavior on the part of businesspersons? How might competition lead to the opposite result—that is, to unethical business behavior? On the whole, do you believe that a competitive economic system promotes more ethical behavior or more unethical behavior in the business world?

3. To what extent should economic considerations be taken into account in the determination of product safety standards? For example, suppose that a proposed regulation requires all commercial airlines to use aircraft that have two additional emergency exit doors. Given the average number of airline crashes per year and the average number of individuals injured or killed in such crashes, it is estimated that the new safety standard will save an additional ten lives per year. But the total cost of implementing the new regulation will be $50 million. This means that it will cost an estimated $5 million to save one life per year. Is this too much to pay for one human life? Too little? What if it cost $300 million to implement the regulation? The point is, can a human life be subjected to a cost-benefit analysis by having a "price tag" attached to it? If not, how can it be determined whether a product safety standard is "reasonable" or "unreasonable"?

4. Although the UCC good faith provisions hold merchants to a standard of honesty in fact, such honesty is weighed in the context of commercial customs and habitual practices—course of dealing, usage of trade, commercial reasonableness, and so on. Puffing is a case in point. Merchants may "huff and puff" their wares as they traditionally have and still not—in most instances—violate their duty of dealing honestly and in good faith with the buyers of their products. Do you think that the customary practice of puffing is a fundamentally dishonest practice that should be abandoned? Is there anything the law can, or should, do to ensure that buyers will not be taken in by sellers' statements of opinion?

UNIT FOUR

Commercial Paper and Banking

■ The Importance of Commercial Paper and Banking

The law governing commercial paper, such as checks and promissory notes, is important because checks, notes, and other commercial paper affect the lives of nearly everyone in this country and in the world. For convenience and safety, debtors use commercial paper instead of currency. People often pay their debts by check. Indeed, in just about every transaction in which currency is not used as a payment for goods or services purchased, or to be purchased, some form of commercial paper is used, and it is therefore related to the underlying sales transaction.

In some cases, commercial paper may represent an extension of credit. For example, when a buyer gives a seller a promissory note, the terms of which, say, provide that it is payable within sixty days, the seller has extended sixty days of credit to the buyer. The credit aspect of commercial paper was developed in the Middle Ages and has continued since.

In an ideal world in which dishonesty and unforeseen events did not exist, there would be little need for commercial paper law. In the real world, however, parties do breach contracts. In addition, some contracts are obtained through fraud and duress, and some contracts are simply illegal. In such circumstances, it is important to know what rights you, as a buyer or seller, have under commercial paper law.

Much of commercial paper law involves a specialized terminology, and that is what we present in Chapter 25, along with some of the important basic concepts in commercial paper law. In Chapter 26, you will be introduced to what is and what is not negotiable commercial paper and how commercial paper is transferred from one person or entity to another. Who is or is not a holder in due course is examined in Chapter 27. The liability of parties with respect to commercial paper, as well as how parties can be discharged from that liability, is examined in Chapter 28. The most common examples of commercial paper—checks—are discussed, along with the banking system, in Chapter 29. Finally, electronic fund transfers are examined in Chapter 30.

■ Ethical Issues in Commercial Paper and Banking

The area of commercial paper and banking is permeated with possibilities for fraud and the like. For example, passing bad checks, while usually a criminal action in most states, is also unethical and costly to the banking system. Forgery of checks and other instruments will probably be a problem as long as negotiable instruments continue to exist. Even if we move into a so-called cashless, paperless world, electronic fund transfers are also possible targets for unethical individuals. Every year, literally millions of dollars are illegally transferred within the banking system by individuals both in and out of the industry who use their computer knowledge and inside information for illegal personal gain. Many of these issues are not ethical issues—because no one believes they are anything but unethical—but rather criminal problems. But an ethical issue certainly arises when fraud perpetrated by an imposter or through other false representation results in economic losses to two or more innocent parties: Who, in such a situation, should bear the loss?

In electronic fund transfer systems, errors occasionally occur. What if you discover that an error has occurred in your favor. Is it ethical for you to keep silent? Electronic fund transfers also can give rise to problems that cannot really be addressed very successfully by the law. For example, what if you receive your bank statement and notice that several withdrawals were made from your account on a certain date and you are certain that you did not make the withdrawals? If you have no witnesses who can testify that you could not possibly have made the withdrawals at that time and the bank's computer printout shows that the withdrawals were definitely made with your ATM access card, essentially, it will be your word against that of the computer. This is a legal problem, to be sure, but it also has ethical dimensions when it leads to unfair treatment of bank customers.

Chapter 25

Basic Concepts of Commercial Paper

Commercial paper can be defined as any written promise or order to pay a sum of money. Drafts, checks, certificates of deposit, and promissory notes are typical examples. The development of the law concerning commercial paper grew from commercial necessity. As early as the thirteenth century, merchants dealing in foreign trade were using commercial paper to finance and conduct their affairs. Problems in transportation and in the safekeeping of gold or coins had prompted this practice. In medieval England, the free flow of money was inhibited because the common law courts of those times did not permit the assignment of a contractual right to receive payment to a third party. As a consequence, the merchants had to develop their own rules governing commercial paper, and these rules were enforced by "fair" or "borough" courts. For this reason, the early law governing commercial paper was part of the Law Merchant (see Chapter 18).

Later, the Law Merchant was codified in England in the Bills of Exchange Act of 1882. In 1896, in the United States, the National Conference of Commissioners on Uniform State Laws drafted the Uniform Negotiable Instruments Law. This law was reviewed by the states, and by 1920 all the states had adopted it. The Uniform Negotiable Instruments Law was the forerunner of Article 3 of the Uniform Commercial Code (UCC).[1]

■ The Significance of Article 3

To understand the significance of Article 3 of the UCC, it is necessary first to distinguish between *negotiable* and *nonnegotiable* commercial paper. To qualify as a **negotiable instrument,** commercial paper must meet special requirements relating to form and content. These requirements, which are imposed by UCC 3-104, are discussed at length in the next chapter. When an instrument is negotiable, its transfer from one person to another is governed by Article 3 of the UCC. Indeed, UCC 3-102(e) defines *instrument* as a

---

1. In 1990, the National Conference of Commissioners on Uniform State Laws and the American Law Institute approved amendments to Articles 3 and 4 of the Uniform Commercial Code. As of May 15, 1992, sixteen states have adopted the "Revision" and it was introduced in a number of other states. The text of revised Articles 3 and 4 is included in Appendix C, and some of the major changes will be footnoted in the following chapters.

"negotiable instrument." For that reason, whenever the term *instrument* is used in this book, it refers to a negotiable instrument. Although the terms *commercial paper* and *negotiable instruments* are frequently used interchangeably, commercial paper also includes *nonnegotiable* paper. Transfers of nonnegotiable commercial paper are governed by the rules of assignment of contract rights. A negotiable instrument can be transferred by assignment or negotiation. When a transfer fails to qualify as a negotiation, it becomes an assignment and is governed by the rules of assignment under contract law. Whether an instrument is negotiable or nonnegotiable can be very important for the parties involved in terms of the applicable law and of the legal consequences attending the transfer of commercial paper, as the examples in the sections below illustrate.

Transfer by Assignment

When commercial paper is transferred by assignment, the basic principles of contract law govern the transaction. Recall from the discussion of assignments in Chapter 15 that persons who transfer or assign contractual rights pass on only the rights that they had under the contract. Furthermore, the assignee (the party to whom the contract rights are assigned) is subject to any defenses or claims that exist against the party assigning the contract (the assignor). In other words, under the common law of contracts, the assignee stands "in the shoes of the assignor" and is burdened with every legal defense that exists between the original parties to the contract, regardless of the assignee's knowledge of that defense.

To illustrate: Suppose that Martin contracts in writing to purchase a used word processor from Francis for $600. Martin needs the word processor in his business. He pays $200 down and agrees to pay the balance, plus 10 percent interest, in six equal installments. Francis, as part of the sale, makes certain assertions as to the amount of prior use and the condition of the word processor. Shortly after the sale and transfer, Francis sells and assigns the contract and the balance due to Arlene. Martin learns that Francis has lied about the prior use and the condition of the processor. He refuses to make any further payments on the contract, claiming fraud and breach of warranty. Arlene in-

sists that she has no knowledge of the deceit, is an innocent party, and wants to sue Martin to collect the debt. Because as an assignee Arlene is subject to any defense Martin has against the assignor (Francis), Arlene is subject to Martin's claims and defenses. (Of course, if Martin's claim or defense proves unsuccessful, the debt is still collectible.)

Transfer by Negotiation

One of the key differences between a transfer of commercial paper by assignment and a transfer by negotiation is that with the latter, the **transferee** (the party to whom the instrument is transferred) not only receives the rights of the **transferor** (the party transferring the instrument) but also may receive even *more* rights in the instrument. Under Article 3 of the UCC, a person who acquires an instrument for value, in good faith, and without notice that it is defective or overdue or that any person has a claim to it or defense against it acquires the special status of a *holder in due course* (HDC). If a transferee has met the requirements for HDC status, he or she takes the instrument free of most defenses to payment on the instrument or adverse claims to it.

For example, assume that in the hypothetical situation discussed above, instead of creating an installment contract, Martin pays Francis with a $600 check. Francis, who owes Arlene $600, indorses the check to Arlene in payment of the debt. Before Arlene cashes the check, however, Martin requests his bank to stop payment on the check because he has learned of Francis's fraud and breach of warranty. In this situation, because a check is a *negotiable* instrument, Arlene may be entitled to payment notwithstanding Martin's stop-payment order. If Arlene can demonstrate that she took the check for value, in good faith, and without notice that it is defective or overdue or that any person has a claim to it or a defense against it, she will qualify as an HDC and, as such, will not be subject to Martin's defenses against payment. (Of course, if Arlene knows that Francis lied to Martin about the word processor, she will not qualify as an HDC and will not be entitled to payment.) Because the HDC doctrine of Article 3 is particularly important in the law governing commercial paper, all of Chapter 27 is devoted to a discussion of that doctrine.

■ Functions and Purposes of Commercial Paper

Commercial paper has two functions—to serve as a substitute for money and as a credit device. Debtors sometimes use currency, but for convenience and safety they often use commercial paper instead. For example, commercial paper is being used when a debt is paid by check. The substitute-for-money function of commercial paper developed in the Middle Ages. Merchants deposited their precious metals with goldsmiths to avoid the dangers of loss or theft. When a merchant needed funds to pay for goods, he gave the seller a written order addressed to the goldsmith. This authorized the ''bank'' to deliver part of the precious metals to the seller. These orders, called *bills of exchange,* were sometimes used as a substitute for money. Today people use checks the same way. They also use drafts, promissory notes, and certificates of deposit that are payable either on demand or on some specified date in the future.

Commercial paper may represent an extension of credit. When a buyer gives a seller a promissory note, the terms of which provide that it is payable within sixty days, the seller has essentially extended sixty days of credit to the buyer. The credit aspect of commercial paper was developed in the Middle Ages soon after bills of exchange began to be used as substitutes for money. Merchants were able to give sellers bills of exchange that were not payable until a future date. Because the seller would wait until the maturity date to collect, this was a form of extending credit to the buyer. The holder of a promissory note payable in sixty or ninety days who wishes to sell this instrument to a third party may do so for immediate cash. Typically, banks buy these instruments and wait until their maturity date to receive payment. To induce a bank to buy a promissory note, the holder of the instrument accepts a discount of, say, 5, 10, or 15 percent of the face amount. In effect, the bank pays less than the amount it will eventually collect as a way of making a profit.

For commercial paper to operate practically as a substitute for money or as a credit device, it is essential that the paper be easily transferable without danger of being uncollectible. This is the function that characterizes *negotiable* commercial paper. Each rule studied in this chapter can be examined in light of this function.

■ Types of Commercial Paper

UCC 3-104 specifies four types of instruments—drafts, checks, notes, and certificates of deposit. These instruments are defined and described below and summarized briefly in Exhibit 25–1.

Drafts

A **draft** (bill of exchange) is an unconditional written order. The party creating it (the **drawer**) orders another party (the **drawee**) to pay money, usually to a third party (the **payee**). The drawee must be obligated to the drawer either by agreement or through a debtor-creditor relationship for the drawee to be obligated to the drawer to honor the order. A *time draft* is a draft that is payable at a definite future time. A *sight* (or demand) *draft* is payable on sight—that is, when the holder presents it for payment—or at a stated time after sight.[2] Exhibit 25–2 shows a typical time draft.

A *trade acceptance* is a draft that is frequently used in the sale of goods. The seller is both the drawer and the payee on this draft. Essentially, the draft orders the buyer to pay a specified sum of money to the seller, usually at a stated time in the future. A *banker's acceptance* is a draft commonly used by persons or businesses involved in international trade. A banker's acceptance is drawn by a creditor against his or her debtor, who must pay the draft at maturity. Typically, the term is short.

Checks

A **check** is a distinct type of draft, *drawn* on a *bank* and payable on *demand.* Checks are discussed more fully in Chapter 29. Note here, however, that with certain types of checks the bank is both the drawer and the drawee. For example, *cashier's checks* drawn by the bank on itself are payable on demand when issued. In addition, a check can be drawn by a bank on another bank. This instrument is known as a **bank draft.**[3]

---

2. A sight draft may be payable on **acceptance,** the drawee's written promise (engagement) to pay the draft when it comes due. The usual manner of accepting is by writing the word *accepted* across the face of the instrument, followed by the date of acceptance and the signature of the drawee.

3. Revised Article 3 defines a bank draft as a ''teller's check'' [RUCC 3-104(h)].

■ **Exhibit 25–1 Basic Types of Commercial Paper**

Instruments	Characteristics	Parties
Orders to Pay Draft Check	An order by one person to another person to pay money to a third person or to bearer [UCC 3-104(2)(a)]. A draft drawn on a bank and payable on demand [UCC 3-104(2)(b)].[a]	Drawer—the person who makes the order to pay. Drawee—the person to whom the order to pay is made. Payee—the person to whom payment is ordered.
Promises to Pay Note Certificate of deposit	A promise by one party to pay money to another party or to bearer [UCC 3-104(2)(d)]. A note made by a bank acknowledging a deposit of funds made payable to the holder of the note [UCC 3-104(2)(c)].[b]	Maker—the person who promises to pay. Payee—the person to whom the promise is made.

a. Under federal law, "banks" on whom checks are drawn includes other financial institutions [see also RUCC 4-105(1)].

b. A certificate of deposit is a note with a special characteristic. A bank cannot be sued on a certificate of deposit unless and until a demand for payment has been made. Usually, a maker is liable with or without a demand.

When *traveler's checks* are drawn on a bank, they are checks, but they require the purchaser's authorized signature before becoming payable. (Technically, most traveler's checks are not checks but drafts, because the drawee—for example, American Express—is ordinarily not a bank.)[4]

Promissory Notes

The **promissory note** is a written promise between two parties. One party is the **maker** of the promise to pay, and the other is the payee, or the one to whom the promise is made. A promissory note, commonly referred to as a **note,** can be made payable at a definite time or on demand. It can name a specific payee or merely be payable to bearer. A sample promissory note is shown in Exhibit 25–3.

Notes are used in a variety of credit transactions and often carry the name of the transaction in-volved. For example, a note payable in installments, such as for payment for a color television set over a twelve-month period, is called an *installment note*. A note that is secured by personal property is called a *collateral note*. In real estate transactions, a promissory note for the unpaid balance on a house, secured by a mortgage on the property, is called a *mortgage note*. And a note that calls for minimum payments (consisting mostly of interest) at regular intervals and a large ("balloon") payment of the entire principal at the end of the term is called a *balloon note*.

Certificates of Deposit

A **certificate of deposit (CD)** is an acknowledgment by a bank of the receipt of money with an engagement to repay it [UCC 3-104(2)(c)]. Certificates of deposit in small denominations are often sold by savings and loan associations, savings banks, and commercial banks. They are called small CDs and are for amounts up to $100,000. Certificates of deposit for amounts of $100,000 or more are called large or jumbo CDs. Exhibit 25–4 shows a typical small CD.

---

4. Under Revised Article 3, any designated "traveler's check" is an instrument if "drawn on or payable through a bank" [RUCC 3-104(i)]. In addition, an instrument may be a check even though it is described on its face "as a money order" [RUCC 3-104(f)].

■ **Exhibit 25–2 A Typical Time Draft**

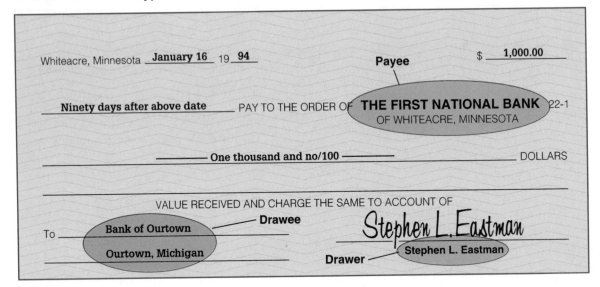

Large and small certificates of deposit pay interest, and most large and some small CDs are negotiable. Their negotiability allows them to be sold, to be used to pay debts, or to serve as security (collateral) for loans.

■ **Other Ways of Classifying Commercial Paper**

The preceding classifications of commercial paper follow the language of the UCC. There are numerous other ways to classify commercial paper, including those discussed below.

Demand Instruments and Time Instruments

Commercial paper can be classified as demand instruments or time instruments. A demand instrument is payable on demand, that is, whenever the holder chooses to present it to the maker in the case of a note or to the drawee in the case of a draft.

■ **Exhibit 25–3 A Typical Promissory Note**

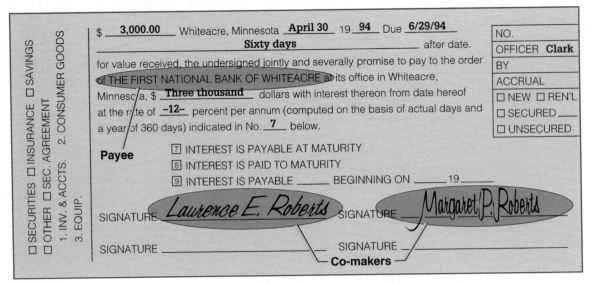

■ **Exhibit 25–4 A Typical Small CD**

THE FIRST NATIONAL BANK OF WHITEACRE $\frac{22\text{-}1}{960}$ **13992**
NEGOTIABLE CERTIFICATE OF DEPOSIT

WHITEACRE, MINN. _____ **February 15** _____ 19 __94__

THIS CERTIFIES to the deposit in this Bank the sum of $ __5,000.00__

——————— **Five thousand and no/100** ——————— **DOLLARS**

Payee (Bearer)
which is payable to (bearer) on the __15th__ day of __August__, 19 __94__ against presentation and surrender of this certificate, and bears interest at the rate of __7 ½__ % per annum, to be computed (on the basis of 360 days and actual days elapsed) to, and payable at, maturity. No payment may be made prior to, and no interest runs after, that date. Payable at maturity in federal funds, and if desired, at Manufacturers Hanover Trust Company, New York.

THE FIRST NATIONAL BANK OF WHITEACRE

By ___*John Doe*___
                                        SIGNATURE
Maker

(Instruments payable on demand include those payable on sight or on presentation and those in which no time for payment is stated [UCC 3-108].) All checks are demand instruments because, by definition, they must be payable on demand; therefore, checking accounts are called **demand deposits.** Time instruments are payable at a future date.

Orders to Pay and Promises to Pay

Commercial paper involving the payment of money must contain either a *promise* to pay or an *order* to pay. Thus, commercial paper can be classified as either promises to pay or orders to pay. Accordingly, a check and a draft are orders to pay. On the other hand, a certificate of deposit and a promissory note are promises to pay.

■ Parties to Commercial Paper

To review, a note or a certificate of deposit has two original parties—the maker and the payee. A draft or a check has three original parties—the drawer, the drawee, and the payee. Sometimes two of the parties to a draft can be the same person (drawer-drawee or drawer-payee). Once an instrument is issued, additional parties can become involved. **Issue** is defined as the "first delivery of an instru-

ment to a holder'' [UCC 3-102(1)(a)]. The liability of these parties is discussed in Chapter 28.

Maker

A *maker* is the person who issues a promissory note or a CD promising to pay a certain sum of money to a payee or bearer. The maker's signature must appear on the face of the promissory note or CD for the maker to be liable on the note.

Drawer, Drawee, and Payee

When a check or other draft is issued, the person who issues it, known as the *drawer,* orders the *drawee* (who is a bank in the case of a check) to pay a certain sum of money to a *payee* (or to the bearer of the instrument).

To illustrate: Smith has a checking account with West Wind Bank. At the end of the month, Smith receives his utility bill of $152 from the Tower Power and Light Corporation. Smith writes a check payable to the order of the utility, signing it in the lower right-hand corner. Smith is the drawer of the check. The West Wind Bank, which has been ordered to pay the check, is the drawee. Tower Power and Light, to which Smith has issued the check, is the payee.

Indorser and Indorsee

The payee of a note or draft may transfer it by signing (indorsing[5]) it and delivering it to another person. By doing this, the payee becomes an **indorser.** For example, Carol receives a graduation check for $250. She can transfer the check to her mother (or anyone) by signing her name on the back of the check. Carol is an indorser, and Carol's mother is entitled to the $250 payment by virtue of Carol's indorsement. If Carol's indorsement states that her mother is the specific person to whom the check is payable, her mother is the **indorsee.**

Bearer and Holder

A **bearer** is any person who has physical possession of an instrument that either is payable to anyone without specific designation or is indorsed in blank (an indorsement consisting of the indorser's signature only—see Chapter 26). A *bearer instrument* is payable to whoever possesses it. If a note is expressly made "payable to bearer" or if a check that already is imprinted with "pay to the order of" is made to read "pay to the order of bearer," the person who possesses that note or check is the bearer. One of the most common methods of creating bearer paper is to make a check read "pay to the order of cash." A check payable to the order of a named person and indorsed by that named person in blank on the back makes its possessor a bearer also.

The term **holder** includes any person in possession of an instrument drawn, issued, or indorsed to him or her or to his or her order or to bearer or in blank.[6] To illustrate: If John Doe has in his possession a check made payable to the order of John Doe, John Doe is a holder of the check. Alternatively, a promissory note written by Sarah Smith promises to pay a sum of money to the order of Tom Jones. While the note is in Jones's possession, Jones is a holder. If Jones signs (indorses) the back of the note—which, because it is indorsed in blank,

becomes bearer paper—and transfers (negotiates) it to Adam White, White becomes the holder.

Under these definitions, all bearers are holders, but not all holders are bearers (because not all commercial paper is bearer paper). All holders are owners—an *owner* is defined as a person who has the right to possess and use a thing to the exclusion of others—to the extent that they are in rightful possession of instruments to which they technically have good title. Not all owners are holders, however, because a person who has the right to a thing may not be in *possession* of it.

Holder in Due Course

As mentioned earlier in this chapter, under UCC 3-302, a holder in due course (HDC) is a person who acquires an instrument for value, in good faith, and without notice that it is defective or overdue or that any person has a claim to or defense against it. HDCs are discussed fully in Chapter 27. At this point, the most important concept to remember, and one of the reasons a holder would want to become an HDC, is that it is easier for an HDC to collect payment on an instrument, because the HDC is protected from all but a few defenses to payment on the instrument.

Accommodation Party

An **accommodation party** is one who signs an instrument in any capacity to lend "his name to another party to it" [UCC 3-415(1)]. The accommodation party actually lends his or her credit to the party to whom the accommodation is made and is classified according to the accommodated party's status (that is, if the accommodated party is, for example, the drawer, the accommodation party is liable on the instrument as if he or she were the drawer). The commonly used term for accommodation party is *cosigner.*

For example, Barrow seeks a loan from the West Wind Bank. The bank will make the loan only if Barrow will get a third party with a good credit rating to cosign the note. Able qualifies and agrees to accommodate Barrow by signing the note below Barrow's signature. Barrow is the *maker,* and Able, by cosigning the note, becomes the *accommodation maker.* If, prior to the instrument's due date, Smith acquires it through the negotiation process, Able is still liable in the capacity in which

---

5. We should note here that because the UCC uses the spelling *indorse* (*indorsement,* etc.), rather than *endorse* (and so on), we adopt that spelling here and in other chapters within this text.

6. UCC 1-201(20) defines a *holder* as "a person who is in possession of a document of title or an instrument or an investment security drawn, issued, or indorsed to him or to his order or to bearer or in blank."

she signed, even though Smith knows of the accommodation [UCC 3-415(2)].

In any case, Able, as the accommodation party, is not liable to Barrow. Able is liable to Smith, who took the note for value. But if Able pays the instrument, she has the right to recover from Barrow [UCC 3-415(5)].

■ Terms and Concepts

acceptance 452
accommodation party 456 454
bank draft 452
bearer 456
certificate of deposit
  (CD) 453
check 452
commercial paper 450

demand deposits 455
draft 452
drawee 452
drawer 452
holder 456 — 454
indorsee 456
indorser 456
issue 455

maker 453
negotiable instrument 450
note 453
payee 452
promissory note 453
transferee 451
transferor 451

■ For Review

1. What are the four types of commercial paper with which Article 3 of the UCC is concerned? Which of these are *orders* to pay and which are *promises* to pay?
2. A note has two original parties. Who are they? A check has three original parties. Who are they?
3. To whom is a bearer instrument payable?
4. Ralph makes out a check to Fonzie. Fonzie signs the back of the check and transfers the check to Richie by negotiation. Is Ralph the drawer or the drawee of the check? While the check is in Fonzie's possession, is Fonzie a holder? When Fonzie signs the check, does it become bearer paper? After Fonzie negotiates the check to Richie, is Richie a holder?
5. In the previous problem, imagine that Ralph has a defense to payment on the check. In acquiring the check, what would Richie have to do to put himself in the best position to collect payment on the check despite Ralph's defense—that is, what would Richie have to do to become a holder in due course?

■ Questions and Case Problems

25-1. Adam Smith, a college student, wished to purchase a new component stereo system from John Locke Stereo, Inc. Because Smith did not have the cash to pay for the entire stereo system, he offered to sign a note promising to pay $150 per month for the next six months. Locke Stereo, anxious to sell the system to Smith, agreed to accept the promissory note as long as Smith had one of his professors sign it. Smith did this and tendered a note to John Locke Stereo that stated, ''I, Adam Smith, promise to pay John Locke Stereo or its order the sum of $150 per month for the next six months.'' The note was signed by Adam Smith and his business law professor. About a week later, John Locke Stereo, which was badly in need of cash, signed the back of the note and sold it to Fidelity Bank. Give the specific designation of each of the four parties on this note.

25-2. A partnership called Larson and Adkins is a law firm. Larson won a case for her client, Brown, against Bill Bucks. When Larson went to collect the judgment from Bucks, Bucks wrote out a check that read: ''Pay to the order of Larson and Adkins $60,000 [Signed] Bill Bucks.'' On the top of the check were the words ''Hanover Trust.'' When Larson went to deposit the check in the trust account that she had set up for her client, she signed the back of the check ''L. Larson.'' How are each of these parties designated in commercial paper law?

25-3. Negotiable instruments play an important part in commercial transactions. Different needs can be fulfilled by various uses of different types of instruments. For instance, many insurance companies use a form of draft instead of a check to remit insurance benefits. The insurance company is both the drawer and the drawee; the beneficiary (the person receiving the money) is the payee; and the draft is made payable through a named bank in which the insurance company maintains a large account. Discuss fully the advantages of using such a draft.

25-4. Often, when two parties to a sale are strangers to each other and the sale is for a substantial amount of money, the selling party will insist that the purchaser make payment with a cashier's check. A cashier's check is a check for which the bank is both the drawer and the drawee. To purchase a cashier's check, a person goes to a bank teller, tenders the amount of money for which the check is to be payable, and supplies the teller with the name of the person who is to be the payee of the check. Once the payee's name is inscribed on the check, only the payee (or a person to whom the payee negotiates the check) will be able to receive money for the check. What problem might arise if a seller asked a prospective buyer of goods to make payment with a cashier's check, and the buyer purchased the check, naming the seller as the payee? How might this problem be avoided?

25-5. Identify the following types of commercial paper or parties involved in the use of commercial paper.

   (a) A draft drawn on a bank payable to a payee on demand.

   (b) A written acknowledgment by a bank of a receipt of money with an obligation to repay it.

   (c) A written promise to pay another (or holder) a certain sum of money.

   (d) An instrument drawn by a bank on itself payable on demand.

   (e) Any person who acquires the instrument as a payee, by indorsement, or by delivery.

   (f) A person who issues a promissory note payable to a named payee.

   (g) A payee who transfers an order instrument by signing the instrument.

25-6. A California statute makes possession of a check with intent to defraud a crime. Norwood had in his possession an instrument that had the following title in the upper right-hand corner: "AUDITOR CONTROLLER'S GENERAL WARRANT COUNTY OF LOS ANGELES." Below this, the instrument stated, "The treasurer of the County of Los Angeles will pay to the order of John Norwood $5,000."

At trial the district attorney proved that Norwood had intended to defraud the County of Los Angeles of $5,000 while in possession of the instrument. You are Norwood's attorney, and you are now appealing the case. What argument would appear to offer the strongest means of overturning Norwood's conviction? [*People v. Norwood,* 26 Cal.App.3d 148, 103 Cal.Rptr. 7 (1972)]

25-7. Case Briefing Assignment

Examine Case A.14 [Lawton v. Walker, 231 Va. 247, 343 S.E.2d 335 (1986)] in Appendix A. The case has been excerpted there in great detail. Review and then brief the case, making sure that you include answers to the following questions in your brief.

1. What was the underlying transaction in this case?
2. Why did Walker refuse to pay the remaining balance on the promissory note?
3. Why is the holder-in-due-course (HDC) doctrine of Article 3 central to this case?
4. What requirements must Lawton meet to acquire the status of a holder in due course?
5. Did he meet those requirements? If so, in what way or ways? If not, why not?
6. How does Lawton's status—as an HDC or an ordinary holder—affect Walker's chances of successfully defending against payment on the note?

Chapter 26

Negotiability and Transfer

For business and commerce to operate smoothly, commercial paper must be generally accepted as money and freely transferable from one person to another. The law governing commercial paper is designed primarily to ensure that it will be readily accepted as a substitute for money. Under Article 3 of the Uniform Commercial Code (UCC), commercial paper must meet specific requirements to qualify as a *negotiable instrument.*[1]

We open this chapter with an examination of those requirements and then look at the process of *negotiation*—that is, the transfer of negotiable instruments from one person to another. Recall from the previous chapter that commercial paper can also be transferred by assignment—in which case contract law governs the transaction. Article 3 of the UCC applies only to negotiable instruments.

■ The Requirements for a Negotiable Instrument

UCC 3-104(1) specifies that for an instrument to be negotiable, it must meet the following requirements:

1. Be in writing.
2. Be signed by the maker or the drawer.
3. Be an unconditional promise or order to pay.
4. State a specific sum of money.
5. Be payable on demand or at a definite time.
6. Be payable to order or to bearer.

A Writing

Negotiable instruments must be in *written form.* Clearly, an oral promise can create the danger of fraud or make it difficult to determine liability. Negotiable instruments must possess the quality of certainty that only formal written expression can give.

---

1. Except for checks, an instrument that, at the time it is issued or first comes into possession of a holder, contains a conspicuous statement to the effect that it is NONNEGOTIABLE renders the instrument nonnegotiable even if it meets all requirements to qualify as a negotiable instrument.

There are certain practical limitations concerning the writing and the substance on which it is placed.

1. The writing must be on material that lends itself to *permanence*. A carved block of ice or a writing in the sand, for example, would be too impermanent to qualify as a negotiable instrument. Thus, if Mary writes in the sand, "I promise to pay $100 to the order of Tom," this is not a writing, because it lacks permanence. Using the shirt off your back as the medium on which you make out a check to the IRS to pay your taxes would probably be acceptable, however.

2. The writing must have *portability*. This is not a legal requirement, but if an instrument is not movable, it cannot meet the requirement that it be freely transferable. A promise to pay written on the side of a building, for example, is technically correct, but a building cannot easily be transferred in the ordinary course of business.

Signed by the Maker or the Drawer

For an instrument to be negotiable, it must be signed by the maker if it is a note or a certificate of deposit or by the drawer if it is a draft or a check [UCC 3-104(1)(a)].

Extreme latitude is granted in determining what constitutes a **signature.** UCC 1-201(39) defines the word *signed* as including "any symbol executed or adopted by a party with present intention to authenticate a writing." UCC 3-401(2) expands upon this: "A signature is made by use of any name, including any trade or assumed name, upon an instrument, or by any word or mark used in lieu of a written signature." Thus, initials, an X, or a thumbprint will suffice (usually, such signatures must be witnessed, however). A trade name or an assumed name is sufficient even if it is false. A rubber stamp bearing a person's signature is permitted and frequently used in the business world. If necessary, parol evidence (evidence not contained on the instrument itself—see Chapter 14) is admissible in identifying the signer. When the signer is identified by parol evidence, the signature becomes effective.

PLACEMENT OF THE SIGNATURE   The location of the signature on the document is unimportant. The usual place is the lower right-hand corner, but this is not required. A *handwritten* statement on the body of the instrument, such as "I, Mary Jones, promise to pay to the order of John Doe," is sufficient to act as Mary's signature.

There are virtually no limitations on the manner in which a signature can be made, but it is necessary to be careful when receiving an instrument that has been signed in an unusual way. Furthermore, an unusual signature clearly decreases the marketability of an instrument because it creates uncertainty.

If the signature's genuineness is denied, the signature is nevertheless presumed valid. The party against whom it operates must provide some evidence of the signature's invalidity. The party asserting the signature's validity must then provide proof of the signature's genuineness.

SIGNATURE BY AUTHORIZED REPRESENTATIVE   If a person with the *authority* to do so signs an instrument as the agent for the maker or drawer, the maker or drawer has effectively signed the instrument. No particular form of appointment as an agent is necessary to show such authority; all that is needed is proof that the agent has such authority [UCC 3-403].

If the agent has authority, the maker or drawer is liable on the instrument, just as if he or she had actually signed it. If the agent has authority and clearly has signed the instrument in a representative capacity, he or she will not be personally liable. If the agent has no such authority, or if the agent did not clearly sign in a representative capacity, the agent is personally liable. The importance of the liability of the parties in these situations will be discussed briefly in Chapter 28 and in more detail, in the context of agency law, in Chapter 36.

Unconditional Promise or Order to Pay

The terms of a promise or order must be included in the writing on the face of a negotiable instrument. These terms must not be conditioned on the occurrence or nonoccurrence of some other event or agreement. Nor can the promise state that it is to be paid only out of a particular fund or source [UCC 3-105(2)].[2]

---

2. Under the revised Article 3, a promise that states an instrument is to be paid only out of a particular fund or source is not conditional [RUCC 3-106(b)].

PROMISE OR ORDER For an instrument to be negotiable, it must contain an express order or promise to pay. A mere acknowledgment of the debt, which might logically *imply* a promise, is not sufficient under the UCC because the promise must be an *affirmative* undertaking [UCC 3-102(1)(c)].

For example, the traditional I.O.U. is only an acknowledgment of indebtedness, not a negotiable instrument. But if such words as *to be paid on demand* or *due on demand* are added, the need for an affirmative promise is satisfied. For example, if a buyer executes a promissory note using the words, ''I promise to pay $1,000 to the order of the seller for the purchase of goods X, Y, Z,'' then the requirement for a negotiable instrument is satisfied.

A certificate of deposit (CD) is different. Here, the requisite promise is satisfied because the bank's acknowledgment of the deposit and the other terms of the instrument clearly indicate a promise.

An *order* is associated with three-party instruments, such as trade acceptances, checks, and drafts. An order directs a third party to pay the instrument as drawn. In the typical check, the word *pay* (to the order of a payee) is a command to the drawee bank to pay the check when presented, and thus it is an order. The order is mandatory even if it is written in a courteous form with such words as *please pay* or *kindly pay*. Precise language must be used, however. An order stating, ''I wish you would pay,'' does not fulfill the requirement of precision.

In addition to being precise, an effective order must specifically identify the drawee (the person who must pay) [UCC 3-102(1)(b)]. A bank's name printed on the face of a check, for example, sufficiently designates the bank as drawee.

UNCONDITIONAL A negotiable instrument's utility as a substitute for money or as a credit device would be dramatically reduced if the promises attached to it were conditional. Investigating such conditional promises would be expensive and time-consuming, and therefore, the free transferability of the negotiable instrument would be greatly reduced. Substantial administrative costs would be associated with processing conditional promises. Furthermore, the payee would risk the possibility that the condition would not occur. If Martin promises to pay Paula $10,000 only if a certain ship reaches port safely, for example, anyone interested

in purchasing the promissory note would have to investigate whether the ship arrived. The facts that the investigation disclosed might be incorrect. To avoid such problems, the UCC provides that only unconditional promises or orders can be negotiable [UCC 3-104(1)(b)].

The UCC expands the definition of *unconditional,* however, to make sure that certain conditions commonly used in business transactions do *not* render an otherwise negotiable instrument nonnegotiable.[3] These are resolved by UCC 3-105(1). Some of these conditions are very common and are discussed briefly here.

Implied Conditions If the rule did not allow implied conditions, no instrument could be negotiable. Implied conditions, such as good faith and commercial reasonableness, appear in virtually every example of a negotiable instrument. For instance, every check implies that in the bank on which the check is drawn, there is an account containing sufficient funds to pay the check.

Statements of Consideration Many instruments state the terms of the underlying agreement as a matter of standard business practice. Somewhere on its face, such an instrument refers to the transaction or agreement for which it is being used in payment. The policy of the UCC is to integrate standard trade usages into its provisions. For example, the words ''as per contract'' or ''this debt arises from the sale of goods X and Y'' do not render an instrument nonnegotiable.

If James Quinta writes, ''On July 14, 1994, I promise to pay to the order of Louis Sneed $300 in full payment for the television set that Louis Sneed delivered to me on July 2, 1994, [signed] James Quinta,'' this promissory note is a negotiable instrument. The statement concerning the television set is not a condition. It describes the consideration for which the note was given. On the other hand, if the following words were added, the instrument would become nonnegotiable: ''If this television set fails to suit my tastes and preferences in any way whatsoever on July 13, then the maker's obligation hereunder shall be null and void.''

---

3. Revised Article 3 provides that the required FTC Rule 433 notice, found at the end of Chapter 27, does not make a note evidencing a consumer credit transaction conditional [RUCC 3-106(d)].

Reference to Other Agreements The UCC provides that mere reference to another agreement does not affect negotiability. If, on the other hand, the instrument is made *subject* to the other agreement, it will be nonnegotiable [UCC 3-105(2)(a)]. A reference to another agreement (such as, "In accordance with a security agreement of [a specified date]") is normally inserted for the purpose of keeping a record or giving information to anyone who may be interested. Notes frequently refer to separate agreements that give special rights to a creditor for an acceleration of payment or to a debtor for prepayment. References to these rights do not destroy the negotiability of the instrument.

For example, an instrument states, "On January 23, 1994, I promise to pay to the order of Patricia Senior $1,000, this note being secured under a security agreement and lien upon my 1992 Chevy Caprice, noted upon the title certificate thereof, [signed] Henry Winn." This instrument is negotiable. A statement that an instrument's payment is secured by collateral will not render an otherwise negotiable instrument nonnegotiable [UCC 3-112(1)(b)]. In fact, this statement adds to the salability and marketability of the instrument.

In the following case, a promissory note that incorporated another agreement was rendered nonnegotiable.

Case 26.1

MITCHELL v. RIVERSIDE NATIONAL BANK

Court of Civil Appeals of Texas—Houston (14th District), 1981.
613 S.W.2d 802.

BACKGROUND AND FACTS To make improvements to his property, Larfavor Mitchell signed a builder's and mechanic's lien contract (which permits a claim against the property if the note is not paid) and a note in the amount of $4,435 payable to the contractor who was to perform the work. The note provided that it was secured by a lien contract and "subject to and governed by said contract, which is hereby expressly referred to, incorporated herein and made a part hereof." The contract provided that if the improvements were not completed, the owner and holder of the note would have a lien against the property for the contract price less the cost to complete the improvements. Before the note matured, the contractor assigned it to Riverside National Bank for a discounted price of $3,548. The contractor began the improvements but never finished them, forcing Mitchell to hire another contractor to complete the job at a cost of $3,400. When the note came due, Mitchell refused to pay. Riverside filed suit in a Texas state court for the face amount of the note and for a lien against the property to force payment. Mitchell claimed that the note was nonnegotiable and that the bank's remedy was limited to the lien contract. The trial court awarded the bank the amount it had paid for the note and gave it a lien on Mitchell's property. Mitchell appealed.

DECISION AND RATIONALE The Court of Civil Appeals of Texas affirmed the trial court's decision in Riverside's favor, but reformed the judgment to reduce the award to an amount representing the improvements that the contractor actually completed. Mitchell contended that the language in the note referring to the contract burdened the note with the conditions of the contract, making the note nonnegotiable and subjecting recovery on the note to defenses available under the contract. The appellate court agreed. The court explained that use of the terms "subject to and governed by" to refer to "an extrinsic contract in an otherwise negotiable instrument destroys the negotiability of the instrument." The court held that Riverside had a lien against Mitchell's property for $1,035—the face amount of the note ($4,435) less the cost of completion ($3,400)—plus interest at a 10 percent annual rate.

Secured by a Mortgage A simple statement in an otherwise negotiable note indicating that the note is secured by a mortgage does not destroy its negotiability. Actually, such a statement might make the note even more acceptable in commerce. Realize, however, that the statement that a note is secured by a mortgage must not stipulate that the maker's promise to pay is *subject* to the terms and conditions of the mortgage.

Indication of Particular Funds or Accounts In many instruments, it is indicated expressly or impliedly that payment should come from a particular fund or that a particular account is to be debited. For example, a check is drawn impliedly on funds in a particular checking account.

Generally, mere reference to the account to be debited or to the fund from which payment is preferred will not affect the negotiability of the instrument. If, however, payment is expressly limited to payment *only* from a particular fund, the instrument is rendered nonnegotiable [UCC 3-105(2)(b)]. The condition obviously restricts the acceptability of the instrument as a substitute for money, as a holder's payment depends on whether such a fund exists and whether it is sufficient to pay the instrument.

For example, a note dated March 3, 1994, reads, "Gilbert Corporation promises to pay to the order of the *Miami Herald* $150 on demand, charged to advertising expense, [signed] Harold Henry, Treasurer, Gilbert Corporation." This note is negotiable. The phrase "charged to advertising expense" is merely a posting instruction to the corporation's accounting department. If a note states that "Jones plans to liquidate real estate to pay this obligation," the note is still considered negotiable.[4] On the other hand, if a note reads "payment to be made within the next thirty days from jobs now under construction," the note will be held nonnegotiable, because it does not contain an unconditional promise.

Consider another example. A note states that "payment of said obligation is restricted to payment from accounts receivable." In this case, payment is conditioned from one particular source—accounts receivable—and this renders the instrument nonnegotiable. It does not make the note uncollectible,

however. The contract may still be assigned under contract rules of assignment.

The two exceptions to this rule are instruments issued by government agencies that are payable out of particular revenue funds and instruments limited to partnership, unincorporated association, estate, or trust assets [UCC 3-105(1)(g), (h)].

Sum Certain in Money

Negotiable instruments must state the amount to be paid in a *sum certain in money*. This requirement promotes clarity and certainty in determining the value of the instrument [UCC 3-104(1)(b)]. Any promise to pay in the future is risky because the value of money (purchasing power) fluctuates. Nonetheless, the present value of such an instrument can still be estimated with a reasonable degree of accuracy by financial experts. If the instrument's value were stated in terms of goods or services, it would be too difficult to ascertain the market value of those goods and services at the time the instrument was to be discounted.

The UCC mandates that negotiable commercial paper be paid wholly in money. For example, a promissory note that provides for payment in diamonds or in 1,000 hours of services is not payable in money. Thus, the note is nonnegotiable.

SUM CERTAIN The term *sum certain* means an amount that is ascertainable from the instrument itself without reference to an outside source.[5] A demand note payable with 12 percent interest meets the requirement of sum certain because its amount can be determined at the time it is payable. UCC 3-106(1) states that the sum is not rendered uncertain by the fact that it is to be paid:

(a) with stated interest or by stated installments; or
(b) with stated different rates of interest before and after default or a specified date; or
(c) with a stated discount or addition if paid before or after the date fixed for payment.

The basic test is whether any holder who receives the instrument can determine by calculation

---

4. *Southern Baptist Hospital v. Williams,* 89 So.2d 769 (La.App. 1956).

5. Under revised Article 3, the amount or rate of interest may be determined with reference to information not contained in the instrument [RUCC 3-112(b)].

the amount required to be paid when the instrument is due. Thus, instruments that provide simply for payment of interest at prevailing bank rates are generally nonnegotiable, because interest rates fluctuate. An adjustable-rate mortgage (a note tied to a variable rate of interest that fluctuates as a result of market conditions) is not negotiable.[6] Similarly, a note is nonnegotiable if it indexes the amount to be paid to the consumer price index in an attempt to avoid the effects of inflation. But a note that states, "If paid before maturity, maker will pay $50 less than promised," is negotiable because the exact amount of payment can be determined from the face of the instrument. Also, when an instrument is payable at the legal rate or at a judgment rate (see Chapter 14) or as fixed by state law, the instrument can be negotiable.

In international trade, notes that are to be paid in another currency satisfy the sum certain requirement. If Pierre promises in a note to pay 1,000 French francs, this note meets the certainty requirement even though the parties must refer to foreign exchange rates that are not embodied in the instrument. The UCC, therefore, makes an exception to its own general rule because of the realities of international trade [UCC 3-107(2)].

Often, instruments have provisions authorizing collection costs and attorneys' fees in the event of the maker's default. UCC 3-106(1)(e) indicates that an instrument with such provisions still meets the sum certain requirement and therefore is still negotiable. Providing for collection costs and attorneys' fees lessens some of the costs and risks that a bank (or other institution) dealing in commercial paper would otherwise incur. Note, though, that a few states have invalidated such provisions either by statute or by judicial decision. In states in which such provisions are legal, the fees must be reasonable, or the clause will be voided as being against public policy.

MONEY AND NO OTHER PROMISE UCC 3-104(1)(b) provides that a sum certain is to be payable in "money and no other promise." The UCC defines money as "a medium of exchange authorized or adopted by a domestic or foreign government as a part of its currency" [UCC 1-201(24)].

Suppose that the maker of a note promises "to pay on demand $1,000 in U.S. gold." Because gold is not a medium of exchange adopted by the U.S. government, the note is not payable in money and is thus not negotiable. The same result would occur if the maker promised "to pay $1,000 *and* fifty liters of 1964 Chateau Lafite-Rothschild wine," as the instrument is not payable *entirely* in money.

An instrument "payable in $1,000 U.S. currency or an equivalent value in gold" would be nonnegotiable, if the *maker* reserved the option of paying in money or gold. If the option were left to the *payee,* some legal scholars argue that the instrument would be negotiable.

Under UCC 3-107(2), any instrument payable in the United States with a face amount stated in a foreign currency can be paid in the equivalent in U.S. dollars at the due date, unless the paper expressly requires payment in the foreign currency.

To summarize, only instruments payable in money are negotiable. An instrument payable in U.S. government bonds or in shares of IBM stock is not negotiable, because neither bonds nor stocks are a medium of exchange recognized by the U.S. government.

Payable on Demand or at a Definite Time

UCC 3-104(1)(c) requires that a negotiable instrument "be payable on demand or at a definite time." Clearly, to ascertain the value of a negotiable instrument, it is necessary to know when the maker, drawee, or acceptor is required to pay. It is also necessary to know when the obligations of secondary parties—drawers, indorsers, and accommodation parties—will arise. Futhermore, it is necessary to know when an instrument is due to calculate when the statute of limitations may apply. And finally, with an interest-bearing instrument, it is necessary to know the exact interval during which the interest will accrue to determine the present value of the instrument.

---

6.   Variable-interest loans have become popular because lenders are protected when rates rise and borrowers benefit when rates decline. Some states (including Arizona, Iowa, Mississippi, Missouri, New York, Tennessee, and Virginia) have amended UCC 3-106 to make these notes negotiable. Under revised Article 3, a variable interest rate note can be negotiable. The requirement that to be negotiable a writing must contain a promise or order to pay a fixed sum applies only to principal [RUCC 3-104(a)]. Interest may be stated as a variable amount [RUCC 3-112(b)].

PAYABLE ON DEMAND Instruments that are payable on demand include those that contain the words "payable at sight" or "payable upon presentment" and those that say nothing about when payment is due. The very nature of the instrument may indicate that it is payable on demand. For example, a check, by definition, is payable on demand [UCC 3-104(2)(b)]. If no time for payment is specified and the person responsible for payment must pay upon the instrument's presentment, the instrument is payable on demand [UCC 3-108]. A drawee contracts to pay an instrument on presentment, and an indorser contracts to pay an instrument on sight.

PAYABLE AT A DEFINITE TIME To be negotiable, time instruments must be payable at a definite time that is specified on the face of the instrument. The maker or drawee is under no obligation to pay until the specified time.

Often, instruments contain additional terms that seem to conflict with the definite time requirement. UCC 3-109 attempts to clear up some of these potential problems:

(1) An instrument is payable at a definite time if by its terms it is payable
   (a) on or before a stated date or at a fixed period after a stated date; or
   (b) at a fixed period after sight; or
   (c) at a definite time subject to any acceleration; or
   (d) at a definite time subject to extension at the option of the holder, or to extension to a further definite time at the option of the maker or acceptor or automatically upon or after a specified act or event.
(2) An instrument which by its terms is otherwise payable only upon an act or event uncertain as to time of occurrence is not payable at a definite time even though the act or event has occurred.

To illustrate: An instrument dated June 1, 1993, states, "One year after the death of my grandfather, James Taylor, I promise to pay to the order of Henry Winkler $500. [Signed] Mary Taylor." This instrument is nonnegotiable. Because the date of the grandfather's death is uncertain, the maturity date is uncertain, even though the event is bound to occur. Even if the grandfather has already died, the note does not specify the time for payment.

When an instrument is payable on or before a stated date, it is clearly payable at a definite time, although the maker has the option of paying before the stated maturity date. This uncertainty does not violate the definite time requirement. Suppose Lee gives Zenon an instrument dated May 1, 1993, that indicates on its face that it is payable on or before May 1, 1994. This instrument satisfies the requirement. On the other hand, an instrument that is undated and made payable "one month after date", is clearly nonnegotiable. There is no way to determine the maturity date from the face of the instrument.

Drafts stating that they are payable within a fixed period after sight are considered payable at a definite time [UCC 3-109(1)(b)]. The term *sight* means the moment that the draft is presented by the holder for payment or for acceptance by the drawee. The UCC further requires that such instruments be presented for acceptance to the drawee to determine the maturity date [UCC 3-501(1)(a)]. Presenting an instrument to the drawee for acceptance establishes the sight and the time period, which run from the date the instrument is presented.

ACCELERATION CLAUSES An **acceleration clause** allows a payee or other holder of a time instrument to demand payment of the entire amount due, with interest, if a certain event occurs, such as a default in payment of an installment when due. There must be, of course, a good faith belief that payment will not be made before an acceleration clause is invoked.

For example, Carl lends $1,000 to Debra. Debra makes a negotiable note promising to pay $100 per month for eleven months. The note may contain a provision that permits Carl or any holder to accelerate all the payments plus interest if Debra fails to pay an installment in any given month. If, for example, Debra fails to make the third payment, the note will be due and payable in full. If Carl accelerates the unpaid balance, Debra will owe Carl the remaining principal plus interest.

Under UCC 3-109(1)(c), instruments that include acceleration clauses (regardless of the stated reason for the acceleration) are negotiable because the exact value of the instrument can be ascertained, and the instrument will be payable on a fixed date if the event allowing acceleration does not occur. Thus, the fixed date is the outside limit used to determine the value of the instrument.

Furthermore, as noted, the payee or holder cannot accelerate the instrument even if it contains an acceleration clause unless it is done in good faith. Section 1-208 indicates that the acceleration clause "shall be construed to mean that [the holder of the instrument] shall have power to [accelerate] only if he [or she] in good faith believes that the prospect of payment or performance is impaired." But the burden of proving a *lack* of good faith is on the borrower—the maker of the note.

EXTENSION CLAUSES The reverse of an acceleration clause is an **extension clause,** which allows the date of maturity to be extended into the future. To keep the instrument negotiable, the interval of the extension must be specified if the right to extend is given to the maker of the instrument. If, on the other hand, only the holder of the instrument can extend it, the maturity date does not have to be specified.

Suppose a note reads, "The maker [obligor] has the right to postpone the time of payment of this note beyond its definite maturity date of January 1, 1994. This extension, however, shall be for no more than a reasonable time." A note with this language is not negotiable because it does not satisfy the definite time requirement. The right to extend is the maker's, and the maker has not indicated when the note will become due after the extension.

A note that reads "The holder of this note at the date of maturity, January 1, 1994, can extend the time of payment until the following June 1 or later, if the holder so wishes" is a negotiable instrument. The length of the extension does not have to be specified because the option to extend is solely that of the holder. After January 1, 1994, the note is, in effect, a demand instrument.

Payable to Order or to Bearer

Because one of the functions of a negotiable instrument is to substitute for money, freedom to transfer is an essential requirement. To ensure that a proper transfer can be made, one of the requirements of a negotiable instrument is that it be "pay-

able to order or to bearer" [UCC 3-104(1)(d)].[7] These required words indicate that at the time of issuance it is expected that unknown persons—not just the immediate party—will eventually be the owners.

ORDER INSTRUMENTS UCC 3-110(1) defines an instrument as an order to pay "when by its terms it is payable to the order . . . of any person therein specified with reasonable certainty." This section goes on to state that an **order instrument** can be payable to the order of:

    (a) the maker or drawer; or
    (b) the drawee; or
    (c) a payee who is not maker, drawer or drawee; or
    (d) two or more payees together or in the alternative; or
    (e) . . . the representative of [an] estate, trust, or fund or his successors; or
    (f) an office or officer by his [or her] title [such as a tax assessor] . . . ; or
    (g) a partnership or unincorporated association.

The purpose of order paper is to allow the maker or drawer to transfer the instrument to a specific person. In turn, that person may transfer the instrument to whomever he or she wishes. Thus, the maker or drawer agrees to pay the person specified or to pay whomever that person designates. In this way, the instrument retains its transferability.

Suppose an instrument states, "payable to the order of Sam Smith" or "pay to Sam Smith or order." The maker or drawer has indicated that a payment will be made to Smith or to whomever Smith designates. The instrument is negotiable.

If the instrument states, "payable to Sam Smith" or "pay to Sam Smith only," however, the instrument loses its negotiability because it does not state "to the order of" or "to bearer." The maker or drawer has indicated only that Smith will be paid.

---

7. Revised Article 3 states that any instrument payable to order or bearer at time of issue or when it first comes into possession of a holder may be a negotiable instrument (those that are not so payable to order or bearer are definitely not negotiable instruments except for a check). A check is a negotiable instrument even if the traditional word order ("Pay to the order of") is deleted [RUCC 3-104(a),(c)].

In addition, except for bearer paper, the person specified must be named with *certainty,* because the transfer of an order instrument requires an indorsement (indorsements will be discussed shortly). If an instrument is "payable to the order of my kissing cousin," the instrument is nonnegotiable, as a holder could not be sure which cousin was intended to indorse and properly transfer the instrument.

BEARER INSTRUMENT UCC 3-111 defines a **bearer instrument** as one that does not designate a specific payee. The term *bearer* means the person in possession of an instrument that is payable to bearer or indorsed in blank [UCC 1-201(5)]. Here, the maker or drawer agrees to pay anyone who presents the instrument for payment, and complete transferability is implied.

Any instrument containing the following terms is a bearer instrument: "Payable to the order of bearer," "Payable to Sam Sneed or bearer," "Payable to bearer," "Pay cash," or "Pay to the order of cash." In addition, an instrument that contains "any other indication which does not purport to designate a specific payee" is bearer paper [UCC 3-111(c)]. The use of the above designations can cause problems and should be avoided. A check made payable to the order of "Uncle Sam" would probably be considered to designate a payee, the U.S. government, and would thus be an order instrument. An instrument "payable to the order of one case of beer" would not designate a specific payee and would be a bearer instrument.

When an instrument is made payable to order *and* to bearer, the instrument is a bearer instrument if the bearer words are handwritten or typewritten but an order instrument if the bearer words are in a printed form [UCC 3-110(3)].

■ Factors That Do Not Affect Negotiability

Article 3 of the UCC provides that the omissions and terms included in the list below will not affect an instrument's negotiability. In addition, certain UCC rules come into play when the terms on the face of a negotiable instrument are ambiguous or otherwise present difficulties in interpretation. These rules are also included in the following list.

1. The omission of a statement of any consideration will not affect an instrument's negotiability [UCC 3-112].
2. The omission of the name of the bank or other institution on which the instrument is drawn or payable will not render the instrument nonnegotiable [UCC 3-112].
3. The promise or power to maintain or protect collateral or to give additional collateral will not affect negotiability [UCC 3-112].
4. The term in a draft indicating that the payee, by indorsing or cashing the draft, acknowledges full satisfaction of the obligation of the drawer will not affect negotiability [UCC 3-112].
5. Unless the date of an instrument is necessary to determine a definite time for payment, the fact that an instrument is undated does not affect its negotiability. A typical example is an undated check [UCC 3-114(1)].
6. Postdating or antedating an instrument does not affect negotiability [UCC 3-114(1)].
7. Handwritten terms outweigh typewritten and printed terms, and typewritten terms control those that are printed [UCC 3-118(b)]. For example, if your check is printed "Pay to the order of," and in handwriting you insert in the blank "John Smith or bearer," the check is a bearer instrument. An instrument reading "Pay to the order of John Smith or bearer" is payable to order *unless* the bearer words are handwritten or typewritten [UCC 3-110(3)].
8. Words outweigh figures unless the words are ambiguous [UCC 3-118(c)]. This is important when the numerical amount and written amount on a check differ.
9. Unless otherwise specified, when interest is provided for, the rate is the *judgment rate* (that is, the rate provided by law for a judgment) at the place of payment and runs from the date of the instrument or, if undated, from the date of its issue [UCC 3-118(d)].

■ The Process of Negotiation

Negotiation is the transfer of an instrument in such form that the transferee becomes a holder [UCC 3-202(1)]. Strictly speaking, negotiation occurs at the first delivery of a negotiable instrument to a holder, when the maker or drawer *issues* the in-

■ CONCEPT SUMMARY 26.1
Requirements for Negotiable Instruments

Requirements	Basic Rules
Must be in writing UCC 3-104(1)	1. A writing can be on anything that is readily transferable and that has a degree of permanence. [See also UCC 1-201(46).]
Must be signed by the maker or drawer UCC 3-104(1)(a) UCC 3-401(2) UCC 1-201(39) UCC 3-403(1)	1. The signature can be anyplace on the instrument. 2. It can be in any form (such as a word, mark, or rubber stamp) that purports to be a signature and authenticates the writing. 3. It can be signed in a representative capacity.
Must be a definite promise or order UCC 3-104(1)(b)	1. A promise must be more than a mere acknowledgement of a debt. 2. The words "I/We promise" or "Pay" meet this criterion.
Must be unconditional UCC 3-104(1)(b) UCC 3-105	1. Payment cannot be expressly conditional on the occurrence of an event. 2. Payment cannot be made subject to or governed by another agreement. 3. Payment cannot be paid only out of a particular fund (with some exceptions, including government-issued instruments).
Must be an order or promise to pay a sum certain UCC 3-104(1)(b) UCC 3-106	1. An instrument may state a sum certain even if payable in installments, with interest, at a stated discount, or at an exchange rate. 2. Inclusion of costs of collection and attorneys' fees does not disqualify the statement of a sum certain.
Must be payable in money UCC 3-104(1)(b) UCC 3-107	1. Any medium of exchange recognized as the currency of a government is money. 2. The maker or drawer cannot retain the option to pay the instrument in money or something else.
Must be payable on demand or at a definite time UCC 3-104(1)(c) UCC 3-108 UCC 3-109	1. Any instrument payable on sight, presentation, or issue is a demand instrument. 2. An instrument is still payable at a definite time even though it is payable on or before a stated date or within a fixed period after sight or the drawer or maker has an option to extend time for a definite period. 3. Acceleration clauses, even if unenforceable, do not affect the negotiability of the instrument.
Must be payable to order or bearer UCC 3-104(1)(d) UCC 3-110 UCC 3-111	1. An order instrument must name the payee with reasonable certainty. 2. An instrument whose terms intend payment to no particular person is payable to bearer.

strument [UCC 3-102(1)(a)]. Typically, however, in commercial practice, the term *negotiation* is used to identify transfers occurring in a particular way *after* the instrument has been issued.

Recall from Chapter 25 that the method of transfer—by assignment or by negotiation—determines the rights and duties that are passed with the negotiable instrument. A transfer by assignment transfers only the rights of the previous possessor [UCC 3-201(1)]. Under UCC principles, a transfer by negotiation can make it possible for a holder to receive *more* rights in the instrument than the prior possessor [UCC 3-305]. (A holder who receives greater rights is known as a *holder in due course*—a concept discussed at length in Chapter 27.) Furthermore, whether the instrument is an order or bearer instrument determines how one *initially* negotiates it.

NEGOTIATING ORDER PAPER *Order paper* contains the name of a payee capable of indorsing, as in "pay to the order of Jane Smith." Order paper is also paper that has as its last or only indorsement a *special* indorsement, as in "Pay to Smith.

[Signed] Jones." If the instrument is order paper, it is negotiated by delivery with any necessary indorsements. For example, the Transco Company issues a payroll check "to the order of Jane Smith." Smith takes the check to the supermarket, signs her name on the back (an indorsement), gives it to the cashier (a delivery), and receives cash. Smith has negotiated the check to the supermarket [UCC 3-202(1)].

Whether a transfer of order paper met the requirement of delivery is at issue in the following case.

BACKGROUND AND FACTS Richard Caliendo, an accountant, prepared tax returns for various clients. To satisfy their tax liabilities, the clients issued checks payable to various state taxing entities and gave them to Caliendo. Between 1977 and 1979, Caliendo forged·indorsements on the checks, deposited them in his own bank account, and subsequently withdrew the proceeds. In 1983, after learning of these events and after Caliendo's death, the state of New York brought an action in a New York state court against Barclays Bank of New York, N.A., the successor to Caliendo's bank, to recover the amount of the checks. Barclays moved for dismissal on the ground that because the checks had never been delivered to the state, the state never acquired the status of holder and therefore never acquired any rights in the instruments. The trial court ruled in the state's favor. Barclays appealed. The appellate court reversed the trial court's ruling. The state appealed.

DECISION AND RATIONALE The New York Court of Appeals affirmed the appellate court's dismissal of the claim. The state's highest court ruled that the state could not recover the amount of the checks from the bank because the checks had never been delivered to the payee. The court explained that "[i]t has long been held that a check has no valid inception until delivery. Further, a payee must have actual or constructive possession of a negotiable instrument in order to attain the status of a holder and to have an interest in it. * * * Permitting a payee who has never had possession to maintain an action * * * would have the effect of enforcing rights that do not exist."

Case 26.2

STATE v. BARCLAYS BANK OF NEW YORK, N.A.

Court of Appeals of New York, 1990.
561 N.Y.2d 533,
563 N.E.2d 11,
561 N.Y.S.2d 697.

NEGOTIATING BEARER PAPER If an instrument is payable to bearer, it is negotiated by delivery—that is, by transfer into another person's possession. Indorsement is not necessary [UCC 3-202(1)]. The use of *bearer paper* involves more risk through loss or theft than the use of order paper.

Assume Bob Robles writes a check "payable to cash" and hands it to Debbie Myers (a delivery). Robles has negotiated the check (a bearer instru-

ment) to Myers. Myers places the check in her wallet, which is subsequently stolen. The thief has possession of the check. At this point, negotiation has not occurred, because delivery must be voluntary on the part of the transferor. If the thief "delivers" the check to an innocent third person, however, negotiation will be complete. All rights to the check will be passed *absolutely* to that third person, and Myers will lose all right to recover the proceeds of the check from the third person [UCC 3-305]. Of course, she can recover her money from the thief if the thief can be found.

CONVERTING ORDER TO BEARER PAPER AND VICE VERSA   The method used for negotiation depends on the character of the instrument at the time the negotiation takes place. For example, a check originally payable to ''Cash'' but subsequently indorsed ''Pay to Salk'' must be negotiated as order paper (by indorsement and delivery), even though it was previously bearer paper [UCC 3-204(1)].

An instrument payable to the order of a named payee and indorsed in blank (by signature only) becomes a bearer instrument [UCC 3-204(2)]. To illustrate: A check is made payable to the order of Axel Amundsen. The check is issued to Amundsen, and Amundsen indorses it by signing his name on the back. The instrument can now be negotiated by delivery only. Amundsen can negotiate the check to whomever he wishes by delivery, and that person in turn can negotiate by delivery without indorsement. If Amundsen, after such indorsement, loses the check, then a finder can negotiate it further.

Indorsements

Indorsements are required whenever the instrument being negotiated is classified as an order instrument. (Many transferees of bearer paper require indorsement for identification purposes, even though the UCC does not require it.) An **indorsement** is a signature with or without additional words or statements. It is most often written on the back of the instrument itself. If there is no room on the instrument, indorsements can be written on a separate piece of paper called an **allonge.** The allonge must be ''so firmly affixed'' to the instrument ''as to become a part thereof'' [UCC 3-202(2)]. Attachment by pins or paper clips will not suffice. Most courts hold that staples are sufficient.

One purpose of an indorsement is to effect the negotiation of order paper. Sometimes the transferee of bearer paper will request the holder-transferor to indorse. This is done to impose liability on the indorser. The liability of indorsers will be discussed later, in Chapter 28.

Once an instrument qualifies as a negotiable instrument, the form of indorsement will have no effect on the character of the underlying instrument. Indorsement relates to the right of the holder to negotiate the paper and the manner in which negotiation must be done.

Types of Indorsements

We will examine four categories of indorsements—blank, special, qualified, and restrictive. A negotiable instrument may have one or more of these types of indorsements on it.

BLANK INDORSEMENTS   A **blank indorsement** specifies no particular indorsee and can consist of a mere signature [UCC 3-204(2)]. Hence, a check payable ''to the order of Rosemary White'' can be indorsed in blank simply by having her signature written on the back of the check. Exhibit 26–1 shows a blank indorsement.

■ **Exhibit 26–1 A Blank Indorsement**

As mentioned, an instrument payable to order and indorsed in blank becomes payable to bearer and can be negotiated by delivery alone [UCC 3-204(2)]. In other words, a blank indorsement converts an order instrument to a bearer instrument. If De Wert indorses in blank a check payable to her order and then loses it on the street, Ketchum can find it and sell it to Lucas for value without indorsing it. This constitutes a negotiation, because Ketchum makes delivery of a bearer instrument (which was an order instrument until it was indorsed).

SPECIAL INDORSEMENTS   An indorsement that indicates the specific person to whom the indorser intends to make the instrument payable is a **special indorsement**; that is, it names the indorsee [UCC 3-204(1)]. No special words of negotiation are needed. Words such as ''pay to the order of Wilson'' or ''pay to Wilson'' followed by the signature of the indorser are sufficient. When an instrument is indorsed in this way, it is order paper.

To avoid the risk of loss from theft, one may convert a blank indorsement to a special indorsement. This reconverts the bearer paper to order paper. UCC 3-204(3) allows a holder to "convert a blank indorsement into a special indorsement by writing over the signature of the indorser in blank any contract consistent with the character of the indorsement."

For example, a check is made payable to Arthur Engles. He indorses his name by blank indorsement on the back of the check and negotiates the check to Sam Wilson. Sam, not wishing to cash the check immediately, wants to avoid any risk should he lose the check. He therefore writes "pay to Sam Wilson" above Arthur's blank indorsement. (See Exhibit 26–2.) In this manner Sam has converted Arthur's blank indorsement into a special indorsement. Further negotiation now requires Sam Wilson's indorsement plus delivery.

■ **Exhibit 26–2 A Special Indorsement**

Pay to Sam Wilson
Arthur Engles

QUALIFIED INDORSEMENTS   Generally, an indorser, *merely by indorsing*, impliedly promises to pay the holder or any subsequent indorser the amount of the instrument in the event that the drawer or maker defaults on the payment [UCC 3-414(1)]. A **qualified indorsement** is used by an indorser to disclaim or limit this liability on the instrument. In this form of indorsement, the notation *without recourse* is commonly used. A sample is shown in Exhibit 26–3.

■ **Exhibit 26–3 A Qualified Indorsement**

Without recourse
Jeremy Myers

A qualified indorsement is often used by persons acting in a representative capacity. For instance, insurance agents sometimes receive checks payable to them that are really intended as payment to the insurance company. The agent is merely indorsing the payment through to the principal and should not be required to make good on the check if it is later dishonored. The "without recourse" indorsement absolves the agent. If the instrument is dishonored, the holder cannot obtain recovery from the agent who indorsed "without recourse" unless the indorser has breached one of the warranties listed in UCC 3-417(2), (3).

Usually, blank and special indorsements are *unqualified* indorsements. That is, the blank or special indorser is guaranteeing payment of the instrument *in addition to* transferring title to it. The qualified indorser is not guaranteeing such payment. Nonetheless, the qualified indorsement ("without recourse") still transfers title to the indorsee; an instrument bearing a qualified indorsement can be further negotiated.

Qualified indorsements are accompanied by either a special or a blank indorsement that determines further negotiation. Therefore, a special qualified indorsement makes the instrument an order instrument, and it requires an indorsement plus delivery for negotiation. A blank qualified indorsement makes the instrument a bearer instrument, and only delivery is required for negotiation.

To illustrate: A check is made payable to the order of Maggie Mede. Maggie wants to negotiate the check specifically to Harold Hollis with a qualified indorsement. Maggie would indorse the check, "Pay to Harold Hollis, without recourse. [Signed] Maggie Mede." For Harold to further negotiate the check to George Green, he would have to indorse and deliver the check to George.

RESTRICTIVE INDORSEMENTS   Prior to the existence of the UCC, a **restrictive indorsement** was thought to prohibit the further negotiation of an instrument. Although some who indorse in this manner still believe the restrictive indorsement prevents any further transfer, the UCC holds to the contrary. UCC 3-206(1) states that "no restrictive indorsement prevents further transfer or negotiation of the instrument." The restrictive indorsement requires indorsees to comply with certain instructions regarding the funds involved.[8]

---

8. Under UCC 3-206(3), any transferee taking under a conditional or "for collection, for deposit, or pay any bank" indorsement must "apply any value given . . . consistently with the indorsement." Revised Article 3 provides that a conditional indorsement does "not effect the right of the indorsee to enforce the instrument" and that persons paying or giving value may disregard the condition without liability [RUCC 3-206(b)].

Restrictive indorsements come in many forms. UCC 3-205 categorizes the four separate types discussed below.

Conditional Indorsements   When payment is dependent on the occurrence of some specified event, the instrument has a conditional indorsement [UCC 3-205(a)]. It is important to note that a conditional indorsement does not prevent further negotiation of the instrument. If the conditional language had appeared *on the face* of the instrument, however, the instrument would not have been negotiable because it would not have met the requirement that it contain an unconditional promise to pay.

Indorsements Prohibiting Further Indorsement   An indorsement such as "Pay to Bill Jones only. [Signed] Sue Wong" does not prevent further negotiation. Jones can negotiate the paper to a holder just as if it read "Pay to Bill Jones. [Signed] Sue Wong" [UCC 3-206(1)]. This type of restrictive indorsement, which is rarely used, has the same legal effect as a special indorsement [UCC 3-205(b)].

Indorsement for Deposit or for Collection   A common type of restrictive indorsement is one that makes the indorsee (almost always a bank) a collecting *agent* of the indorser. Exhibit 26–4 illustrates such indorsements of a check payable and issued to Mary Smith.

■ **Exhibit 26–4 For Deposit—For Collection Indorsements**

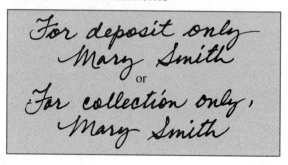

In particular, an indorsement of "Pay any bank or banker" or "For deposit only" has the effect of locking the instrument into the bank collection process. Only a bank can acquire rights of a holder following this indorsement until the item has been specially indorsed by a bank to a person who is not a bank [UCC 4-201(2)]. A bank's liability for payment of an instrument with a restrictive indorsement is discussed in Chapter 29.

In the following case, the indorser of a check, instead of writing the indorsee's name on the back of the check, attached a removable sticker containing the indorsee's name, signed his name, and wrote under his name his mortgage account number. When the check reached the bank, the sticker was no longer attached. The issue before the court was whether the indorser, by these actions, had created a blank indorsement, a special indorsement, or a restrictive indorsement.

Case 26.3

WALCOTT v. MANUFACTURERS HANOVER TRUST

Civil Court of the City of New York, Kings County, Trial Part 31, 1986. 133 Misc.2d 725, 507 N.Y.S.2d 961.

BACKGROUND AND FACTS   Kenneth Walcott filed suit in a New York state court against Bilko Check Cashing Corporation and Manufacturers Hanover Trust. Walcott alleged that he had mailed his paycheck and a money order to Midatlantic Mortgage Company in payment of his mortgage. He claimed he had signed (indorsed) his name in blank on the back of the check and placed his mortgage number and the Midatlantic mailing sticker on the back of the check. Shortly thereafter, Midatlantic notified Walcott that his mortgage payment was late. Walcott investigated and discovered that his paycheck had been cashed at Bilko by a third party. Bilko had deposited the check into its account at Manufacturers Hanover Trust. The payroll check had cleared and been charged to Walcott's employer's account. A copy of the back of the check showed Walcott's indorsement and his mortgage number but no sign of the sticker. Walcott claimed that his indorsement was either special or restrictive and that thus Bilko had cashed the check improperly. Bilko and Manufacturers claimed that the indorsement was in blank and that thus Bilko had cashed the check properly.

DECISION AND RATIONALE The Civil Court of the City of New York dismissed the complaint. The court found no evidence that Walcott specified any particular indorsee on the back of the check, "thus failing to meet the indorsement requirements under the UCC to constitute a special indorsement." The court reviewed UCC 3-205, which states what constitutes a restrictive indorsement. The court explained that "[t]his section of the Uniform Commercial Code is very specific. The series of numbers [alone] was insufficient to restrict negotiation of plaintiff's check." Because the sticker that had been attached to the back of the check had apparently fallen off, the court ruled that Walcott's failure to limit his blank indorsement meant that the check was properly negotiated by delivery to Bilko and properly cashed.

Trust, or Agency, Indorsements Indorsements that state that they are for the benefit of the indorser or a third person are trust, or agency, indorsements. Samples are shown in Exhibit 26-5.

■ Exhibit 26-5 Trust Indorsements

Pay to Ann North
in trust for
Johnny North
          R. P. North

or

Pay to Ann North
as agent for
R. P. North
          R. P. North

The indorsement results in legal title vesting in the original indorsee. To the extent that the original indorsee pays or applies the proceeds consistently with the indorsement (for example, "in trust for Johnny North"), the indorsee is a holder and can become a holder in due course, described in Chapter 27 [UCC 3-205(d), 3-206(4)].

The fiduciary restrictions on the instrument do not reach beyond the original indorsee.[9] Any subsequent purchaser can qualify as a holder in due course unless he or she has actual notice that the instrument was negotiated in breach of the fiduciary duty.[10]

Miscellaneous Indorsement Problems

Of course, a significant problem in relation to indorsements occurs when an indorsement is forged or unauthorized. The UCC rules concerning unauthorized or forged indorsements will be discussed in Chapter 28 in the context of signature liability and again in Chapter 29 in the context of the bank's liability for payment of an instrument over an unauthorized signature. Here we look at some other kinds of problems that may arise with indorsements.

NO STANDARD CATEGORY Sometimes an indorsement does not seem to fit into any of the standard categories. For example, an indorsement can read: "I hereby assign all my right and title and interest in this note. [Signed] Beverly Hatch." The signature is an effective blank indorsement despite the additional language of transfer. Use of the word *assign* does not change the negotiation into a mere assignment. Clearly, Beverly Hatch did not intend to limit the rights of the person to whom she was transferring the instrument [UCC 3-202(4)].

CORRECTION OF NAME An indorsement should be identical to the name that appears on the instrument. The payee or indorsee whose name is misspelled can indorse with the misspelled name, or the correct name, or both [UCC 3-203].

---

9. Compare this with the rule governing conditional indorsements. A conditional indorsement binds all subsequent indorsers (except certain banks) and primary parties to see that the money is applied consistently with the condition. Agency, or trust, indorsements limit this responsibility to the original indorsee. Subsequent parties are not encumbered with this restriction.

10. See *In re Quantum Development Corp.*, 397 F.Supp. 329 (D.V.I. 1975).

■■ CONCEPT SUMMARY 26.2
Types of Indorsements and Their Consequences

Words Constituting the Indorsement	Type of Indorsement	Indorser's Signature Liability[a]
"Rosemary White"	Blank	Unqualified signature liability on proper presentment and notice of dishonor.[b]
"Pay to Sam Wilson, Rosemary White"	Special	Unqualified signature liability on proper presentment and notice of dishonor.
"Without recourse, Rosemary White"	Qualified (blank for further negotiation)	No signature liability. Transfer warranty liability if breach occurs.[c]
"Pay to Sam Wilson, without recourse, Rosemary White"	Qualified (special for further negotiation)	No signature liability. Transfer warranty liability if breach occurs.
"Pay to Sam Wilson on condition he completes painting my house at 23 Elm Street by 9/1/93, Rosemary White"	Restrictive— conditional (special for further negotiation)	Signature liability only if condition is met. If condition is met, signature liability on proper presentment and notice of dishonor.
"Pay to Sam Wilson only, Rosemary White"	Restrictive— prohibitive (special for further negotiation)	Signature liability only on Sam Wilson receiving payment. If Wilson receives payment, signature liability on proper presentment and notice of dishonor.
"For deposit, Rosemary White"	Restrictive—for deposit (blank for further negotiation)	Signature liability only on White having amount deposited in her account. If deposit is made, signature liability on proper presentment and notice of dishonor.
"Pay to Ann South in trust for John North, Rosemary White"	Restrictive—trust (special for further negotiation)	Signature liability only on payment to Ann South for John North's benefit. If restriction is met, signature liability on proper presentment and notice of dishonor.

a. *Signature liability* refers to the liability of a party who signs an instrument. The basic questions include whether there is any liability and, if so, whether it is unqualified or restricted. Signature liability is discussed in more detail in Chapter 28.

b. When an instrument is dishonored—that is, when, for example, a drawer's bank refuses to cash the drawer's check on proper presentment—an indorser of the check may be liable on it if he or she is given proper *notice of dishonor*. Dishonor and notice of dishonor are discussed in Chapter 28.

c. The transferor of an instrument makes certain warranties to the transferee and subsequent holders, and thus, even if the transferor's signature does not render him or her liable on the instrument, he or she may be liable for breach of a transfer warranty. Transfer warranties are discussed in Chapter 28. See also UCC 3-417(2), (3).

For example, Susan Lock receives a check payable to the order of "Susan Locke." She can indorse the check either "Susan Locke" or "Susan Lock." The usual practice is to indorse the name as it appears on the instrument and follow it by the correct name.[11]

---

11. *Watertown Federal Savings and Loan v. Spanks,* 346 Mass. 398, 193 N.E.2d 333 (1963).

BANK INDORSEMENTS When a customer deposits a check with a bank and fails to indorse it, the bank has the right to supply any necessary indorsement for its customer unless the instrument *specifically prohibits it* [UCC 4-205(1)].

For example, Morty Adams deposits his government check with First National Bank and forgets to indorse it. Because government checks typically state "Payee's indorsement required," the bank will not supply the indorsement. The check will be returned to Adams for his signature.

Ordinarily, checks do not specifically require the payee's indorsement. The bank merely stamps or marks the check, indicating that it was deposited by the customer or credited to the customer's account [UCC 4-205].

Commercial paper must move rapidly through banking channels. In the process of clearing through collection, a check can be transferred between banks by use of any agreed-on method of indorsement that identifies the transferor bank [UCC 4-206]. For example, a bank can indorse using its Federal Reserve number instead of its name.

MULTIPLE PAYEES An instrument payable to two or more persons *in the alternative* (for example, "Pay to the order of Capron or Baker") requires the indorsement of only one of the payees [UCC 3-116(a)]. If an instrument is payable to two or more persons *jointly* (for example, "Pay to the order of Carl and Doris" or "Pay to the order of Glenda, Harold"), then all the payees' indorsements are necessary for negotiation [UCC 3-116(b)].

AGENTS OR OFFICERS A negotiable instrument can be drawn payable to a legal entity such as an estate, a partnership, or an organization. For example, a check may read "Pay to the order of the Red Cross." An authorized representative of the Red Cross can negotiate this check.

Similarly, negotiable paper can be payable to a public officer. For example, checks reading "Pay to the order of the County Tax Collector" or "Pay to the order of Larry White, Receiver of Taxes" can be negotiated by whoever holds the office [UCC 3-110(1)(b)].

■ Terms and Concepts

acceleration clause 465	extension clause 466	qualified indorsement 471
allonge 470	indorsement 470	restrictive indorsement 471
bearer instrument 467	negotiation 467	signature 460
blank indorsement 470	order instrument 466	special indorsement 470

■ For Review

1. What requirements must an instrument meet to be negotiable?
2. What is the difference between an indorsement in blank and a special indorsement?
3. What distinguishes order paper from bearer paper?
4. Don gives to Dan an instrument that states "I will pay you $50 if the Dolphins win the Super Bowl." Is this instrument negotiable? If not, why not?
5. Sam gives to Pam an instrument that states "Payable thirty days after the Cubs win the Series." Is this instrument negotiable? If not, why not?

■ Questions and Case Problems

26-1. A check drawn by Daniel for $200 is made payable to the order of Paula. The check is issued to Paula. Paula owes her landlord $200 in rent and transfers the check to her landlord with the following indorsement: "For rent paid. [Signed] Paula." Paula's landlord has contracted to have Peter Plumber repair a number of apartment leaks. The plumber insists on immediate payment. The landlord transfers the check to Peter without indorsement. Later, to pay for plumbing supplies at Facet's Store, Peter transfers the check with the following indorsement: "Pay to Facet's Store, without recourse. [Signed] Peter Plumber." Facet sends the check to its bank indorsed "For deposit only. [Signed] Facet's Store."

(a) Classify each of these indorsements.
(b) Was the transfer from Paula's landlord to Peter Plumber, without indorsement, an assignment or a negotiation? Explain.

26-2. The following note is written by Mary Ellen on the back of an envelope: "I, Mary Ellen, promise to pay to Kathy Martin or bearer $100 on demand." Discuss fully whether this constitutes a negotiable instrument.

26-3. A promissory note is signed by Peter Paul. The note is dated May 1, 1994. Assuming that all other terms in the note meet the requirements for negotiability, discuss fully whether the following clause would render the note non-negotiable: "This note is payable 100 years from date, but payment of principal plus interest is due and payable immediately upon the death of the maker."

26-4. You have signed a year's lease for an apartment near campus. The October rent is due and payable. You write a check for the rent due. On the check you write the following, "Payment for October rent as per lease agreement."

(a) Does this statement render the instrument nonnegotiable? Explain.

(b) Would your answer be any different if the written clause read, "Payment subject to the terms of a signed lease dated September 1, 1994"?

26-5. Martin Moss needs a loan. He borrows $500 from his friend Paula Peters, signing a promissory note. Two clauses in the note are as follows:

(a) "On or before July 1, 1994, I promise to pay to Paula Peters or bearer $550 in cash or title to my 1982 car, at the holder's option."

(b) "The maker hereof reserves the right to extend the time of payment of said note for six months; however, the holder reserves the right to extend the time of payment indefinitely."

Explain whether either clause or both clauses render Martin's note nonnegotiable.

26-6. On or about November 15, 1979, Warnock purchased a cashier's check for $53,541.93, payable to her order and drawn on the Pueblo Bank and Trust Co. Between November 15, 1979, and November 30, 1979, Warnock indorsed "Katherine Warnock" on the reverse side of the check, and Warnock's attorney, Jerry Quick, wrote the words "deposit only" under Warnock's indorsement. On November 30, 1979, Quick deposited the check into the Marquez Trust account, which was an account maintained by Quick at La Junta State Bank. Warnock did not at any time maintain an account with the bank. Warnock died on November 10, 1981. Robert Travis, a personal representative of the estate of Warnock, filed an action against La Junta State Bank seeking recovery of the amount of the cashier's check. Travis alleged that the words "deposit only" constituted a restrictive indorsement placed on the check by Quick for the benefit of Warnock and that, consequently, the bank had a duty to either deposit the item into an account for Warnock or to undertake further investigation of the indorsement before crediting the sum to any account other than to an account for Warnock. Is Travis correct? Discuss fully. [*La Junta State Bank v. Travis,* 727 P.2d 48 (Colo. 1986)]

26-7. In January of 1973, Keith and Joyce Alves loaned Joyce Alves's parents, Beatrice and William Baldaia, $15,000. In return, the Baldaias executed a promissory note payable to Joyce Alves. In February of 1978, Keith and Joyce Alves divorced. The separation agreement contained the following provision: "Wife agrees to assign to Husband any and all right, title, and interest she may have in a certain note, executed by her parents, dated January 3, 1973 on or before date of final hearing." Joyce Alves later wrote on the promissory note, "Pay to the order of Keith R. Alves. [Signed] Joyce Ann Alves." Some time later, Keith Alves tried to collect payment on the note from the Baldaias, who refused to pay it. Alves then sought payment from his former wife, who had since remarried and taken the name of Schaller. Schaller claimed

that her transfer of the promissory note to Alves, pursuant to the separation agreement, constituted an "assignment" of her rights and interests in the note and not a formal "negotiation" of the note. Was the transfer of the promissory note an assignment or a negotiation? Explain. [*Alves v. Baldaia,* 14 Ohio App.3d 187, 470 N.E.2d 459 (1984)]

26-8. In October 1970, Hall issued a draft that included the following: "Pay to L. Westmoreland and B. Bridges or order $1,000 on demand." Before he handed it to Bridges, Hall scratched out the words *or order* with his pen. Does the fact that the draft is payable to two payees destroy its negotiability? Does the scratching out of the words *or order* destroy the draft's negotiability? Explain. [*First Federal Savings and Loan Association v. Branch Banking and Trust Co.,* 282 N.C. 44, 191 S.E.2d 683 (N.C. 1972)]

26-9. McDonald, the personal representative of the Marion Cahill estate, made out a check to himself on the estate checking account. The payee and the amount of the check read: "Pay to the order of Emmett E. McDonald $10,075.00 Ten hundred seventy-five . . . Dollars." The bank paid to McDonald and charged the estate account $10,075—the numerical rather than the written amount. McDonald then absconded with the money. Yates, who succeeded McDonald as the personal representative of the estate, sued the bank to recover the $9,000 difference between $1,075 and $10,075, alleging that the bank should have paid only the smaller amount, which had been written on the check in words. The trial court dismissed the claim, and Yates appealed. Should Yates prevail on appeal? Discuss fully. [*Yates v. Commercial Bank & Trust Co.,* 432 So.2d 725 (Fla.App. 1983)]

26-10. Appliances, Inc., performed electrical heating and plumbing work for Yost Construction totaling approximately $7,000 during a three-year period. Appliances, Inc., was never paid by Yost Construction for any of these jobs. Yost, in both his capacity as president of the construction company and in his individual capacity, signed an undated ninety-day promissory note in favor of Appliances to reduce Yost Construction's debt and to have Appliances perform services for Yost as an individual. Neither Yost in his individual capacity nor Yost Construction paid the note, and Appliances filed suit. The trial court held that the undated note was totally unenforceable. Should Appliances prevail on appeal by arguing that the note was negotiable? Discuss fully. [*Appliances, Inc. v. Yost,* 181 Conn. 207, 435 A.2d 1 (Conn. 1980)]

26-11. Higgins, a used-car dealer, sold a 1977 Corvette to Holsonback, the defendant. Holsonback paid for the car with a draft drawn on First State Bank of Albertville, the plaintiff. On the draft were the following words: "ENCLOSED—TITLE ON 77 CHEV. VETT. FREE OF ALL LIENS AND ENCUMBRANCE." The bank paid Higgins. First State presented the draft to Holsonback for payment, but Holsonback refused to pay, claiming that Higgins was in breach of contract. First State Bank filed suit against Holsonback on his draft. Holsonback claimed that the draft was nonnegotiable because the draft's reference to the title rendered the draft conditional. Discuss Holsonback's contention. [*Holsonback v. First State Bank of Albertville,* 394 So.2d 381 (Ala.Civ.App. 1980)]

26-12. Gilbert Ramirez claimed that he had purchased a winning lottery ticket, the prize for which was approximately $1.5 million. Unfortunately, Ramirez had lost the ticket itself and therefore could not claim the prize. Even though the evidence indicated that he very likely was indeed the purchaser of the winning ticket, under the state lottery rules, he could not claim the prize unless he produced the winning ticket. In a legal action brought by Ramirez against the state lottery bureau, Ramirez claimed, among other things, that the lottery ticket was a negotiable instrument because on the back of each lottery ticket were the following words: "THIS TICKET IS A BEARER INSTRUMENT SO TREAT IT AS IF IT WERE CASH." Because under UCC 3-804 the owner of a lost negotiable instrument can collect on the instrument if certain requirements are met—such as establishing proof of ownership, the terms of the instrument, and so on—Ramirez argued that he should be allowed to claim the prize if he could meet these requirements. Discuss fully whether Ramirez will succeed in his claim that the lottery ticket was a negotiable instrument. [*Ramirez v. Bureau of State Lottery,* 186 Mich.App. 275, 463 N.W.2d 245 (1990)]

26-13. Case Briefing Assignment

Examine Case A.15 [Knauf v. Bank of LaPlace, 567 So.2d 182 (La.App. 1990)] in Appendix A. The case has been excerpted there in great detail. Review and then brief the case, making sure that you include answers to the following questions in your brief.

1. Why did BLP dishonor LPM's checks payable to Knauf when the checks were presented through the banking system for payment?
2. What was the trial court's ruling, and which party appealed the decision?
3. Why did the appellate court hold that Martin's bank had wrongfully dishonored the checks?
4. Despite the fact that the appellate court ruled that a bank is not liable to a payee for the wrongful dishonor of a check, the court reversed the trial court's holding that Knauf had no cause of action. Why?
5. What provisions of the UCC did the court cite in its opinion, and how did those provisions bear on this case?

Chapter 27

Holder in Due Course and Defenses

Commercial paper is not money; rather, it is an instrument that is payable in money. The body of rules contained in Article 3 of the Uniform Commercial Code governs a party's right to payment of a check, draft, note, or certificate of deposit.[1] Problems arise when a holder seeking payment of a negotiable instrument learns that a defense to payment exists or that another party has a prior claim to the instrument. In such situations, for the person seeking payment, it becomes important to have the rights of a *holder in due course* (HDC). As mentioned in Chapter 25, a holder in due course takes a negotiable instrument free of all claims and most defenses of other parties. Of course, the maker or drawer of the instrument might prefer that an instrument not be negotiable if he or she has a defense to payment on it that would not be good against a holder in due course.

We open this chapter by distinguishing between an ordinary holder and an HDC. We then examine the requirements for HDC status and look at the two types of defenses to payment that can be raised against holders of negotiable instruments. These defenses fall into two categories: *universal defenses* and *personal defenses*. Universal defenses, also referred to as *real defenses*, defeat payments to all holders, including HDCs. Personal defenses can only be successfully asserted against ordinary holders.

Our discussion of holders in due course is concerned primarily with negotiable instruments that have been *negotiated*.

■ Holder versus Holder in Due Course

As pointed out in Chapter 25, a *holder* is a person who possesses a negotiable instrument "drawn, issued, or indorsed to him or his order or to bearer or in blank" [UCC 1-201(20)]. To be a holder, a person must have possession and good title (free of forgeries of those names necessary to the chain of title). The holder is the person who, by the terms of the instrument, is legally

---

1. The rights and liabilities on checks, drafts, notes, and certificates of deposit are determined under Article 3 of the UCC. Other kinds of commercial paper, such as stock certificates and bills of lading and other documents of title, meet the requirements of negotiable instruments, but the rights and liabilities of the parties on these documents are covered by Articles 7 and 8 of the UCC. See Chapter 50 on bailments for information on Article 7.

entitled to payment. The holder of an instrument need not be its owner to transfer it, negotiate it, discharge it, or enforce payment of it in his or her own name [UCC 3-301].

A holder has the status of an assignee of a contract right. A transferee of a negotiable instrument who is characterized merely as a holder (as opposed to an HDC) obtains only those rights that the predecessor-transferor had in the instrument. In the event that there is a conflicting, superior claim to or defense against the instrument, an ordinary holder will not be able to collect payment.

A **holder in due course (HDC)** is a special-status transferee of a negotiable instrument who, by meeting certain acquisition requirements, takes the instrument *free* of most defenses or adverse claims to it. Stated another way, an HDC can normally acquire a higher level of immunity to defenses against payment on the instrument or claims of ownership to the instrument by other parties.

■ Requirements for HDC Status

The basic requirements for attaining HDC status are set forth in Section 3-302 of the UCC. First, the instrument must be negotiable, and whoever seeks HDC status must be a holder. The holder must take the instrument (1) for value, (2) in good faith, and (3) without notice that it is overdue, or that it has been dishonored, or that any person has a defense against it or a claim to it.

The underlying requirement for HDC status is that a person must first be a holder of that instrument. Regardless of other circumstances surrounding acquisition, only a holder has a chance to become an HDC.

Taking for Value

An HDC must have given *value* for the instrument [UCC 3-303]. A person who receives an instrument as a gift or who inherits it has not met the value requirement. In such a situation, the person becomes an ordinary holder and does not possess the rights of an HDC.

Article 3 of the UCC provides that a holder can take an instrument for value in one of three ways. Basically, a holder gives value:

1. To the extent that the agreed-on consideration has been paid or a security interest or lien acquired.

2. By payment of, or as security for, an *antecedent,* or prior, *claim.*

3. By giving a negotiable instrument or irrevocable commitment as payment.

AGREED-ON CONSIDERATION PERFORMED The concept of value in the law of negotiable instruments is not the same as the concept of consideration in the law of contracts. An executory promise (a promise to give value in the future) is clearly valid consideration to support a contract [UCC 1-201(44)]. It does not, however, normally constitute value sufficient to make a holder an HDC. UCC 3-303 provides that a holder takes the instrument for value only to the extent that the agreed-on consideration has been performed. Therefore, if the holder plans to pay for the instrument later or plans to perform the required services at some future date, the holder has not yet given value. In that case, the holder is not yet an HDC.

Do not be confused when the value of the agreed-on consideration differs from the face amount of the instrument. When a time instrument is sold, it is usually discounted to allow for transfer costs, collection costs, and interest charges. Thus, a $1,000 note due in ninety days may be sold for $950 cash to a financial institution. The requirement of agreed-on consideration is satisfied by the $950 payment. And when the instrument comes due, the holder will collect the full $1,000. If the discrepancy between the purchase amount and the face value is great, however, this discrepancy can be considered along with other factors to indicate either that the purchaser lacks good faith or that only a partial payment is being made, reducing the HDC status to this amount. The good faith element is discussed later in this chapter.

A holder also takes an instrument for value to the extent that the holder acquires a security interest in or a lien on the instrument. It is not unusual for an instrument to be given as security for a loan or other obligation. If, for example, Norris issues a $1,000 note payable to Lomond, Lomond can use the note to secure a $700 loan from Hilton. (Lomond gets $700 cash; Hilton holds the note as security.) Hilton's $700 loan qualifies her as a holder for value. If Lomond does not repay the $700, Hilton can collect on the note. But what if Norris has a personal defense (such as breach of contract or fraud in the inducement) against Lomond? Hilton, as an HDC, is free and clear of the defense, but *only to the extent of $700*. Hence, the rule is: "A purchaser of a limited interest can be a holder in due course only to the extent of the interest purchased" [UCC 3-302(4)].

A holder can also take for value by acquiring a lien on the instrument through an agreement rather than through operation of law. For example, a payee of a note pledges it to a bank as security for a loan. The terms of the pledge agreement give the bank a lien on the instrument. The bank is a holder for value to the extent of its lien.

ANTECEDENT CLAIM When an instrument is given in payment of (or as security for) an **antecedent claim,** the value requirement is met [UCC 3-303(b)]. Here again, commercial law and contract law produce different results. An antecedent claim is not valid consideration under general contract law, but it does constitute value sufficient to satisfy the requirement for HDC status in commercial law.

Assume Cary owes Dwyer $2,000 on a past due account. If Cary negotiates a $2,000 note to Dwyer and Dwyer accepts it to discharge the overdue account balance, Dwyer has given value for the instrument.

NEGOTIABLE INSTRUMENT AS VALUE UCC 3-303(c) provides that a holder takes the instrument for value "when he gives a negotiable instrument for it or makes an irrevocable commitment to a third person."

To illustrate: Martin has issued a $500 negotiable promissory note to Paula. The note is due six months from the date issued. Paula's financial circumstances are such that she does not want to wait for the maturity date to collect. Therefore, she negotiates the note to her friend Susan, who pays her $200 in cash and writes her a negotiable check for the balance of $300. Susan has given full value for the note by paying $200 in cash and issuing Paula the check for $300.

A negotiable instrument has value when issued, not when the underlying obligation is finally paid. In the preceding example, assume that before Paula cashes Susan's check, Susan learns that the maker of the note has a personal defense against Paula. In this event, Susan has the protection of HDC status. Commercial practicality requires this

rule because a negotiable instrument, by its nature, carries the possibility that it might be negotiated to an HDC. If it is, the party that issued it generally cannot refuse to pay [UCC 3-303].

CHECK DEPOSITS AND WITHDRAWALS On occasion, a commercial bank can become an HDC when honoring other banks' checks for its own customers. In this situation, the bank becomes an "involuntary" HDC, in that at the time of giving value the bank has no intention of becoming an HDC.

Assume that on Monday morning at the end of the month Pat Stevens has $400 in her checking account at the First National Bank. That morning Stevens deposits her payroll check for $300, drawn by her employer on the Second National Bank. During her lunch hour she issues a check to her landlord for $425. The landlord cashes the check at the First National Bank. Later, the Second National Bank returns the payroll check marked "insufficient funds." In most cases, First National would charge this check against Stevens's account. If that cannot be done, however, is the First National Bank an HDC of the employer's check? The answer is yes. According to what is referred to as the *first-money-in, first-money-out rule*, First National Bank has paid to the landlord $25 of its own funds [UCC 4-208(2)]. Therefore, First National is an HDC to the extent it has given value—$25.

SPECIAL CASES In a few exceptional circumstances, a holder can take an instrument for value but still not be accorded HDC status. UCC 3-302(3) specifies the following situations:

1. Purchase at a judicial sale (for example, a bankruptcy sale) or by taking under legal process.
2. Acquisition when taking over an estate (as administrator).
3. Purchase as part of a bulk transfer (as when a corporation buys the assets of another corporation).

In these situations, the UCC limits the rights of the holder to those of an ordinary holder.

Taking in Good Faith

Another requirement for HDC status is that the holder take the instrument in good faith [UCC 3-302(1)(b)]. This means that the purchaser-holder must have acted honestly in the process of acquiring the instrument. *Good faith* is defined in UCC 1-201(19) as "honesty in fact in the conduct or transaction concerned."[2]

Because of the good faith requirement, one must ask whether the purchaser, when acquiring the instrument, honestly believed the instrument was not defective. If a person purchases a $10,000 note for $100 from a stranger on a street corner, the issue of good faith can be raised on the grounds of the suspicious circumstances *and* the grossly inadequate consideration. The UCC does not provide clear guidelines to determine good faith. Thus, each situation will be examined separately.

Taking without Notice

The final requirement for HDC status involves notice [UCC 3-304]. A person will not be afforded HDC protection if he or she knew or should have known at the time the instrument was acquired that it was defective in any one of the following ways [UCC 3-302(1)(c)]:

1. It was overdue.
2. It had been dishonored.
3. There was a defense against it.
4. There was another claim to it.

The main provisions of UCC 3-304 spell out the common circumstances that, as a matter of law, constitute notice of a claim or defense and notice of an overdue instrument. A person has notice of a fact when he or she has: (1) actual knowledge of the fact, (2) receipt of notice of the fact, or (3) reason to know that the fact exists, given all the facts and circumstances known at the time in question [UCC 1-201(25)].

UCC 3-304(4) contains a list of specific facts that do not in themselves constitute notice of a defense or claim. The list can be reviewed in the full text of the UCC contained in Appendix C. In short, the UCC's position is that certain kinds of information about the instrument or about parties to it can raise some suspicion regarding the ultimate enforceability of the paper, but the information falls short of indicating a defense or claim. Also, knowl-

edge from a public notice—for example, through newspapers or official records—is not automatically imputed to a purchaser; it must be shown that the information was read [UCC 3-304(5)]. Recall that the basic test of good faith is honesty in fact. The key concern is whether this particular purchaser honestly knew something was wrong with a particular instrument at the time it was acquired.

OVERDUE INSTRUMENTS All negotiable paper is either payable at a definite time (time instrument) or payable on demand (demand instrument). What will constitute notice that an instrument is overdue or has been dishonored will vary depending on whether it is demand or time paper.

Time Instruments A holder of a time instrument who takes the paper the day after its expressed due date is "on notice" that it is overdue. Nonpayment by the due date should indicate to any purchaser that the primary party who is obligated to pay has a defense to payment. Thus, a promissory note due on May 15 must be acquired before midnight on May 15. If it is purchased on May 16, the purchaser will be an ordinary holder, not an HDC.

Sometimes instruments read, for example, "Payable in thirty days." A note dated December 1 that is payable in thirty days is due by midnight on December 31(generally, the time period begins to run on the day *after* the date of the instrument). But what if a note is dated December 2 and is payable in thirty days? When is it due? Because the payment date falls on January 1, a holiday, the instrument is payable on the next business day. This is also the case when the payment date falls on Sunday.

A large debt is often broken down into successive payments. The debt can be evidenced by a single, large-denomination note payable in installments; or a series of notes in smaller denominations can be issued, each identified as part of the same indebtedness. In the case of an installment note, notice that the maker has defaulted on any installment of principal (but not interest payments) will prevent a purchaser from becoming an HDC [UCC 3-304(3)(a)]. Most installment notes provide specifically that any payment made on the note is applied first to interest, with the balance to principal. Thus, any payment that is less than the amount due on that installment will put a holder on notice that some of the principal is overdue.

---

2.   Under Revised Article 3, good faith is defined as "honesty in fact and the observance of reasonable commercial standards of fair dealing [RUCC 3-103(a)(4)].

The same result occurs when a series of notes with successive maturity dates is issued at the same time for a single indebtedness. Default in payment of any one note of the series will constitute overdue notice for the entire series. Prospective purchasers who know of the default then know that they cannot qualify as HDCs.

Suppose a note reads, "Payable May 15, but may be accelerated if the holder feels insecure." A purchaser, unaware that a prior holder has elected to accelerate the due date on the instrument, buys the instrument prior to May 15. UCC 3-304(3)(b) provides that such a purchaser can be an HDC unless he or she has reason to know that the acceleration has occurred.

Demand Instruments A purchaser has notice that a demand instrument is overdue if he or she takes the instrument knowing that demand has been made or takes it an unreasonable length of time after its *issue.* "A reasonable time for a check

drawn and payable within the states and territories of the United States and the District of Columbia is *presumed* to be thirty days" [UCC 3-304(3)(c)]. [Emphasis added.][3]

Obviously, what constitutes a reasonable time period depends on the circumstances. Except for a domestic check, in which a reasonable time is presumed to be thirty days, there are no exact measurements for determining a reasonable time. Past cases indicate, however, that a reasonable time for payment of an interest-bearing demand instrument is longer than for one payable without interest.

In the following case, the court held that a one-year-old check was an overdue instrument. This fact precluded the holder from attaining HDC status, even though the holder had checked with the drawer of the check before depositing it.

---

3. Revised Article 3 extends the thirty-day period to "90 days after its date" [RUCC 3-304(a)(2)].

Case 27.1

AMERICAN STATE BANK OF PIERRE v. NORTHWEST SOUTH DAKOTA PRODUCTION CREDIT ASSOCIATION

Supreme Court of South Dakota, 1987.
404 N.W.2d 517.

BACKGROUND AND FACTS On October 25, 1983, in payment for cattle sold at auction, Fort Pierre Livestock Auction, Inc., issued check number 19074 for $31,730.23 to Gene Hunt. Later, Fort Pierre discovered that it had miscounted the cattle, and on October 31, it issued check number 19331 for $36,343.95 to Hunt. This check was meant to replace check 19074, but Fort Pierre made no notation to that effect on the check and did not ask Hunt to return check 19074. Fort Pierre tried to stop payment on check 19074, but its bank (American State Bank of Pierre) later could find no record of the attempt. On October 26, 1984, a representative of the Northwest South Dakota Production Credit Association (PCA) met with Hunt to arrange repayment of a delinquent loan. Hunt agreed to give PCA checks 19074 and 19331 in exchange for forgiveness of his remaining debt. PCA did not know that one check had replaced the other or that Fort Pierre had attempted to stop payment on check 19074. PCA told Fort Pierre that a couple of old "Hunt" checks would be deposited. Fort Pierre called its bank and warned it not to accept the checks without full indorsements. On discovering in January 1985 that both checks had cleared, Fort Pierre informed PCA that one check was meant to replace the other and demanded repayment for check 19074. PCA refused, asserting HDC status. Fort Pierre and its bank sued PCA in a South Dakota state court. The trial court found that PCA was an HDC and denied recovery. Fort Pierre and its bank appealed.

DECISION AND RATIONALE The Supreme Court of South Dakota held that PCA was not a holder in due course, because it had sufficient notice that the checks were overdue, and reversed the lower court's judgment. The state supreme court said that it could imagine instances when a delay of more than thirty days may be legitimate in the ordinary course of commerce. But in this case, the court noted, PCA offered no justification for a one-year delay. The court concluded that "PCA's warning to Fort Pierre that it was about to deposit Hunt's 'old checks' was insufficient to negate what was plainly visible on the check's face: a year-old date."

DISHONORED INSTRUMENTS Actual knowledge that an instrument has been dishonored or knowledge of facts that would lead a holder to suspect that such has happened puts a holder on notice. Thus, a person who takes a check clearly stamped "insufficient funds" is put on notice. No notice exists without this knowledge. For example, Burton holds a demand note dated March 1 on Kayto, Inc., a local business firm. On March 19, she demands payment, and Kayto refuses (that is, dishonors the instrument). On March 20, Burton negotiates the note to Reynolds, a purchaser who lives in another state. Reynolds does not know and has no reason to know that the note has been dishonored, so Reynolds is not put on notice and can therefore become an HDC.

DEFENSES AGAINST OR CLAIMS TO AN INSTRUMENT Knowledge of claims or defenses can be imputed to the purchaser if they are apparent on the face of the instrument—if the instrument is incomplete or irregular in any way, for example—or if the purchaser otherwise had reason to know of them from facts surrounding the transaction.

Incomplete Instruments A purchaser cannot expect to become an HDC of an instrument so incomplete on its face that an element of negotiability is lacking (for example, the name of the payee on order paper is missing or the amount is not filled in). Minor omissions are permissible because these do not call into question the validity of the instrument. For example, omission of connective words, such as the "or" in "Pay to Johnson or order," does not affect negotiability, and neither does omission of the date from a check that has the month and year [UCC 3-304(1)(a), 3-114(1)].

Similarly, when a person accepts an instrument that has been completed without knowing that it was incomplete when issued, the person can take it as an HDC [UCC 3-304(4)(d)]. To illustrate: Stuart Morgan asks Joan Nelson to buy a textbook for him when she goes to the campus bookstore. Morgan writes a check payable to the campus store,

leaves the amount blank, and tells her to fill in the price of the textbook. The cost of the textbook is $35.00. If Nelson fills in the check for $75.00 before she gets to the bookstore, the bookstore cashier sees only a properly completed instrument. Therefore, he or she will take the check as an HDC and the store can enforce it for the full $75.00. The unauthorized completion is not a sufficient defense against the store in this situation [UCC 3-407, 3-115].

Irregular Instruments Any irregularity on the face of an instrument that calls into question its validity or terms of ownership, or creates an ambiguity as to the party to pay, will bar HDC status [UCC 3-304(1)(a)].

A difference between the handwriting used in the body of a check and that used in the signature will not in and of itself make an instrument irregular. Postdating or antedating a check or stating the amount in digits but failing to write out the numbers will not make a check irregular [UCC 3-114(2)].

Visible evidence of forgery of a maker's or drawer's signature or alterations to material elements of negotiable paper will disqualify a purchaser from HDC status. Conversely, a careful forgery of a maker's or drawer's signature or a careful alteration can go undetected by reasonable examination; and therefore, the purchaser can qualify as an HDC [UCC 3-304(1)(a)]. Losses that result from careful forgeries, however, usually fall on the party to whom the forger transferred the instrument (assuming, of course, that the forger cannot be found). Also, a forged indorsement (see Chapter 28) does not transfer title, and thus a person obtaining an instrument that has a forged indorsement of a name necessary to title cannot normally become a holder or an HDC.

In the case presented below, the court focuses on the question of whether the obliteration of the restrictive words "for deposit only" in check indorsements constituted notice to the bank of irregularity, thus precluding the bank from HDC status.

Case 27.2

**J. M. HEINIKE
ASSOCIATES, INC. v.
LIBERTY NATIONAL
BANK**

Supreme Court of New York,
Appellate Division,
Fourth Department, 1990.
560 N.Y.S.2d 720.

BACKGROUND AND FACTS   An employee of J. M. Heinike Associates, Inc., on several occasions obliterated the restrictive words "for deposit only" from indorsements made by Heinike on checks. The checks thus became bearer instruments, which the employee cashed at the Liberty National Bank. When Heinike learned of these activities, it sued Liberty in a New York state court to recover the amount of the converted funds. Heinike contended that Liberty lacked HDC status because obliteration of the restrictive words served as notice that the indorsement had been materially altered. Liberty filed a motion for summary judgment. The trial court found Liberty to be an HDC and granted the motion. Heinike appealed.

DECISION AND RATIONALE   The New York Supreme Court, Appellate Division, affirmed the lower court's judgment. It ruled that Liberty was a holder in due course of the checks because obliteration of the words "for deposit only" in the indorsements did not constitute notice of a claim to or defense against the instruments. In particular, the court concluded that obliteration of the restrictive indorsements on the checks did not satisfy the test of "crude alteration" required by the statute. That is, that "the instrument bears such visible evidence of alteration, or is otherwise so irregular that it calls into question its validity or ownership." Because it is not an uncommon occurrence for a payee initially to decide to deposit a check and then decide to cash it, the court held that obliteration of the "for deposit only" indorsements is not the kind of alteration that would normally put the bank on notice that the instrument has been altered.

ETHICAL CONSIDERATIONS   Although it is natural to sympathize with the "victim" in this case, Heinike, the court offered a sound reason for its holding—that people do frequently change their minds about depositing checks and should not be forced to go through with a deposit simply because they have indorsed a check "for deposit only." The law governing commercial paper generally attempts to place liability for fraudulent or otherwise illegal acts on those who are in the best position to prevent such actions. After all, it was not the bank's fault that Heinike's employee breached her duty of loyalty to her employer. Nor, perhaps, was it Heinike's fault. Nonetheless, Heinike entrusted the employee with the checks and was in the best position to judge her trustworthiness.

Voidable Obligations   It stands to reason that a purchaser who knows that a party to an instrument has a defense that entitles that party to avoid the obligation cannot be an HDC. At the very least, good faith requires *honesty in fact* of the purchaser in a transaction. For example, a potential purchaser who knows that the maker of a note has breached the underlying contract with the payee cannot thereafter purchase the note as an HDC [UCC 3-304(1)(b)].

Knowledge of one defense precludes a holder from asserting HDC status in regard to all other defenses. For example, Litchfield, knowing that the note he has taken has a forged indorsement, presents it to the maker for payment. The maker re-

fuses to pay on the grounds of breach of the underlying contract. The maker can assert this defense against Litchfield even though Litchfield had no knowledge of the breach, because Litchfield's knowledge of the forgery alone prevents him from being an HDC in *all* circumstances.

Knowledge that a fiduciary has wrongfully negotiated an instrument is sufficient notice of a claim against the instrument to preclude HDC status. Suppose Jordan, a trustee of a university, improperly writes a check on the university trust account to pay a personal debt. Farley knows that the check has been improperly drawn on university funds, but she accepts it anyway. Farley cannot claim to be an HDC. When a purchaser knows that a fiduciary is acting in breach of trust, HDC status is denied [UCC 3-304(2)].

Payee as HDC

Under certain circumstances, a payee may qualify as an HDC [UCC 3-302(2)]. To be an HDC, a payee must exercise good faith, give value, and take the instrument without notice of a defense against it or claim to it.

To illustrate: Marshall Reed is an attorney for Dana Smith. Marshall recently had minor office surgery performed by Dr. Peters and owes Dr. Peters $600. Marshall has agreed to draft a land sales contract for Dana next week, on condition that Dana issue a check payable to Dr. Peters for $600. Dana sends the check to Dr. Peters with a note, ''in payment of medical services rendered to Marshall Reed.'' Marshall leaves town and never performs the services for Dana. Dana stops payment on the check. Can Dr. Peters enforce payment as an HDC? The answer is yes. Although Dr. Peters is the payee, she gave value (medical services), took the check in good faith, and took without notice of dishonor, of defense, of claim, or that the check was overdue.

Logic dictates that in the majority of instances, if there are defenses to the instrument, the payee will know or have reason to know about them. To illustrate: Baker Painters contracts with Amex Company to paint the exterior of its new office building for $4,000. Amex issues a negotiable promissory note to Baker Painters for $4,000, due thirty days later. When the note comes due, Baker tries to collect the $4,000 from Amex. Amex refuses to pay the note, claiming that the paint was defective; it washed off during a rainstorm. Because Baker Painters obviously knows, or should know, about the defective paint, Baker Painters is not an HDC. Amex can disavow liability on the note based on the breach of the underlying contract.

■ Holder through an HDC

A person who does not qualify as an HDC but who derives his or her title *through an HDC* can acquire the rights and privileges of an HDC. According to UCC 3-201(1):

> Transfer of an instrument vests in the transferee such rights as the transferor has therein, except that a transferee who has himself been a party to any fraud or illegality affecting the instrument or who as a prior holder had notice of a defense or claim against it cannot improve his position by taking from a later holder in due course.

This is sometimes referred to as the **shelter principle.** This rule seems to detract from the basic HDC philosophy. It is, however, in line with the concept of marketability and free transferability of commercial paper, as well as with contract law, which provides that assignees acquire the rights of assignors. The transfer rule extends the holder-in-due-course benefits, and it is designed to aid the HDC in disposing of the instrument readily.

Anyone, no matter how far removed from an HDC, who can trace his or her title ultimately back to an HDC comes within the shelter principle. Normally, a person who acquires an instrument from an HDC or from someone with HDC rights acquires HDC rights on the principle that the transferee of an instrument gets at least the rights that the transferor had. For example, Traci D'Alemberte signs a promissory note payable to Richfield DeBenedictus, who negotiates it to Maria Morocco, who acquires it for value, in good faith, and without notice of any claim to or defense against it. In other words, Maria is an HDC. Maria makes a gift of the note to Stephan Marcotte, who gives it to Don Abello. Neither Stephan nor Don pays value for the note, and thus neither qualifies for HDC status in his own right. Nevertheless, under the shelter principle, Stephan obtains Maria's HDC rights, and when Stephan gives the note to Don, Don takes shelter in Stephan's status, which includes Maria's HDC rights.

UCC 3-201(1) explicitly indicates, however, that in certain circumstances, persons who have held and transferred instruments cannot improve their positions by later reacquiring the instruments from HDCs. Thus, a holder who was a party to fraud or illegality affecting the instrument or who, as a prior holder, had notice of a claim or defense against an instrument, is not allowed to improve his or her status by repurchasing from a later HDC. In other words, a person is not allowed to ''launder'' the paper by passing it into the hands of an HDC and then buying it back.[4]

---

4. Of similar effect is a Federal Trade Commission rule that effectively abolishes the HDC doctrine in consumer credit transactions. Any holder who acquires commercial paper resulting from a consumer credit contract is subject to all claims and defenses that the consumer could assert against the original party to the contract. This rule is discussed later in this chapter.

To illustrate: Bailey and Zopa collaborate to defraud Manor. Manor is induced to give Zopa a negotiable note payable to Zopa's order. Zopa then specially indorses the note for value to Adams, an HDC. Bailey and Zopa split the proceeds. Adams negotiates the note to Stanley, another HDC. Stanley then negotiates the note for value to Bailey.

Bailey, even though he got the note through an HDC, cannot acquire HDC rights, for he participated in the original fraud.

The following case demonstrates the importance of establishing a prior transferor as an HDC to gain the rights of an HDC under the shelter principle.

Case 27.3

ROZEN v. NORTH CAROLINA NATIONAL BANK

United States Court of Appeals, Fourth Circuit, 1978. 588 F.2d 83.

BACKGROUND AND FACTS North Carolina National Bank (NCNB) made a long-term loan to Sharpe Hosiery Mill. In October 1974, NCNB issued a $20,000 certificate of deposit (CD) to Sharpe. A few days later, Allen Stein bought Sharpe. As a result of the sale, NCNB called for payment of the long-term loan and said that it was going to apply the CD, as well as Sharpe's checking account balance, toward the unpaid balance. Stein refused to return the CD and instead used it as partial collateral for a personal loan from Manufacturers Hanover Bank and Trust, which did not know of the NCNB claim. When the CD matured, Manufacturers sent it to NCNB for collection. NCNB dishonored and retained the CD. After paying the balance owed on the personal loan, Stein had Michael Rozen, his brother-in-law, purchase all Manufacturers' rights in the CD from Manufacturers. Claiming the rights of an HDC, Rozen sued NCNB in a federal district court for the value of the CD. The trial court held that Rozen was not protected by the shelter principle. Rozen appealed.

DECISION AND RATIONALE The United States Court of Appeals for the Fourth Circuit affirmed the trial court's decision. The appellate court found little merit in Rozen's argument that Manufacturers enjoyed HDC status and thus under the "shelter principle" had transferred this protection to Rozen with its assignment of rights in the CD. The court reasoned that any HDC rights that Manufacturers enjoyed were terminated when Stein paid Manufacturers the money that he owed: "Thus at the time that Manufacturers executed the purported assignment to Rozen, the only rights it had in the NCNB certificate of deposit were those of a secured creditor which had been paid in full, and those rights are nothing." Because Manufacturers held the CD as collateral on Stein's loan, Stein was the true assignor of the CD. Stein was not an HDC, however, so Rozen could not become an HDC under the shelter principle.

■ Defenses

When the holder of a negotiable instrument seeks payment from its drawer or maker, there are certain defenses that will be effective to bar collection. As a matter of public policy, certain defenses are assertable against all parties, including an HDC. Others, which constitute most of the traditional defenses to contract actions generally, cannot be used against an HDC unless the individual asserting the defense dealt personally with the HDC.

As mentioned in this chapter's introduction, defenses fall into two general categories—universal defenses and personal defenses. **Universal defenses,** which are sometimes referred to as *real defenses,* are used to avoid payment to all holders of a negotiable instrument, including an HDC or a holder through an HDC (under the shelter principle) [UCC 3-305(2)]. **Personal defenses** are used to avoid payment to an ordinary holder of a negotiable instrument [UCC 3-306].

Universal (Real) Defenses

UCC 3-305(2) specifically sets forth the very limited number of universal defenses that defeat payments to an HDC. We look at each of these defenses below. As noted above, universal defenses are valid against *all* holders, including HDCs or holders through HDCs.

FORGERY   A forgery of a maker's or a drawer's signature cannot bind the person whose name is used (unless that person ratifies the signature or is precluded from denying it) [UCC 3-404 and 3-401(1)]. Thus, when a person forges an instrument, the person whose name is used has no liability to pay any holder or any HDC the value of the forged instrument. In addition, a principal can assert the defense of unauthorized signature against any holder or HDC when an agent has exceeded his or her authority in signing negotiable paper on behalf of the principal [UCC 3-404]. For example, Harvey Huddleson is an executive with Files, Inc., a tool manufacturer, but has no authority to sign corporate checks. Harvey signs a check ''Files, Inc., by Harvey Huddleson, vice president.'' Files can assert the defense of unauthorized signature. Because the corporate signature is unauthorized, it does not bind the corporation—Harvey is personally liable. (Unauthorized signatures and indorsements are discussed in greater detail in Chapter 28.)

FRAUD IN THE EXECUTION   If a person is deceived into signing a negotiable instrument, believing that he or she is signing something other than a negotiable instrument (such as a receipt), fraud in the execution or inception—also known as fraud *in factum*—is committed against the signer. For example, suppose a consumer unfamiliar with the English language signs a paper that is presented by a salesperson as a request for an estimate but that is in fact a promissory note. Even if the note is negotiated to an HDC, the consumer has a valid defense against payment. This defense cannot be raised, however, when a reasonable inquiry would have revealed the nature and terms of the instrument.[5] Thus, the signer's age, experience, and intelligence are relevant, because they fre-

quently determine whether the signer should have known the nature of the transaction before he or she signed.

MATERIAL ALTERATION   An alteration is material if it changes the contract terms between any two parties in any way. Examples of material alterations are [UCC 3-407(1)]:

1.   A change in the number or relations of the parties.
2.   The completion of an instrument in an unauthorized manner.
3.   An addition to the writing as signed or the removal of any part of it.

Thus, cutting off part of the paper of a negotiable instrument, adding clauses, or changing in any way the amount, the date, or the rate of interest—even if the change is only one penny, one day, or 1 percent—is material. But it is not a material alteration to correct the maker's address, to have a red line drawn across the instrument to indicate that an auditor has checked it, or to correct the total final payment due when a mathematical error is discovered in the original computation. If the alteration is not material, any holder is entitled to enforce the instrument according to its original terms.

Material alteration is a *complete* defense against an ordinary holder but is at best only a *partial* defense against an HDC. An ordinary holder can recover nothing on an instrument if it has been materially altered—unless the alteration was caused by the negligence of another party, who may then be liable on the instrument as changed [UCC 3-407(2)].

If an original term, such as the monetary amount payable, has been altered, an HDC can enforce the instrument against the maker or drawer according to the original terms. If the instrument was incomplete and was later completed in an unauthorized manner, alteration cannot be claimed as a defense against an HDC, and the HDC can enforce the instrument as completed [UCC 3-407(2), (3)]. If the alteration is readily apparent, then obviously the holder has notice of some defect or defense, and such a holder cannot be an HDC [UCC 3-302(1)(c), 3-304(1)(a)]. In regard to checks, if a material alteration results from a drawer's negligence, the liability of a bank that pays the

---

5.   *Burchett v. Allied Concord Financial Corp.*, 74 N.M. 575, 396 P.2d 186 (1964).

■ CONCEPT SUMMARY 27.1
Rules and Requirements for HDC Status

1. Must be a *holder*	A *holder* is defined as a person who is in possession of an instrument "drawn, issued or indorsed to him or his order or to bearer or in blank" [UCC 1-201(20)].
2. Must take for *value*	A holder gives value: a. To the extent agreed-on consideration has been paid or a security interest or lien acquired. b. By payment of or as security for an antecedent claim. c. By giving a negotiable instrument or irrevocable commitment as payment [UCC 3-303].
3. Must take in *good faith*	*Good faith* is defined as "honesty in fact in the conduct or transaction concerned" [UCC 1-201(19)].
4. Must take without *notice* a. That instrument is *overdue*	1. Time instruments are overdue the moment after due date for payment. 2. Demand instruments are overdue after a reasonable time has lapsed from issue. 3. Domestic checks are *presumed* overdue after thirty days from issue. 4. A note is overdue if any part of the *principal* is not paid when due. 5. If any acceleration of a time instrument has taken place, the instrument is overdue [UCC 3-304(3)].
b. That instrument has been *dishonored*	1. Actual knowledge or knowledge of facts that would lead a person to suspect an instrument has been dishonored is notice of dishonor [UCC 3-302(1)(c)].
c. That a *claim* or *defense* exists	1. Notice exists if a person has actual knowledge of a claim or defense against an instrument. 2. Notice exists if an instrument is so incomplete, bears such visible evidence of forgery or alteration, or is so irregular that a reasonable person would be put on notice from examination or from facts surrounding the transaction [UCC 3-304(1)].
Special Situations	**Rules**
1. Shelter principle—holder through a holder in due course	A holder who cannot qualify as a holder in due course has the *rights* of a holder in due course if he or she derives title through a holder in due course [UCC 3-201].
2. Payee	A payee who meets the requirements can be a holder in due course [UCC 3-302(2)].
3. Purchasers not holders in due course	The following acquisitions cannot result in a holder's having HDC status: a. Purchase at a judicial sale. b. Acquisition as part of an estate. c. Purchase of a bulk transfer [UCC 3-302(3)].

altered instrument may be shifted back to the customer (see Chapter 29).

DISCHARGE IN BANKRUPTCY Discharge in bankruptcy is an absolute defense on any instrument regardless of the status of the holder because the purpose of bankruptcy is to settle finally all of the insolvent party's debts [UCC 3-305(2)(d)].

MINORITY Minority, or infancy, is a universal defense only to the extent that state law recognizes it as a voidable right. [UCC 3-305(2)(a)]. (See

Chapter 12.) Thus, this defense renders the instrument voidable rather than void. Because state laws on minority vary, so do determinations of whether minority is a universal defense against an HDC.

For example, in some states, when a minor misrepresents his or her age, the minor is prohibited from exercising the right of disaffirmance. In those states, minority is not allowed as a universal defense if a minor who signs a negotiable instrument misrepresents his or her age. In other states, a minor is allowed to disaffirm (and is liable only for a tort of deceit) despite the misrepresentation of age, and therefore minority is a universal defense.

ILLEGALITY When the law declares that an instrument is *void* because it has been executed in connection with illegal conduct, then the defense of illegality is absolute against both an ordinary holder and an HDC. If the law merely makes the instrument *voidable,* as in the personal defense of illegality (discussed below), then it is still a defense against a holder but not against an HDC. The courts are sometimes prone to treat the word *void* in a statute as meaning ''voidable'' to protect an HDC [UCC 3-305(2)(b)].

MENTAL INCAPACITY There are various types and degrees of incapacity. Incapacity is ordinarily only a personal defense. If, however, the maker or drawer has been declared mentally incompetent by a court, a guardian has been appointed, and then the instrument is written, many courts hold the obligation null and void and unenforceable by any holder, including an HDC [UCC 3-305(2)(b)].

EXTREME DURESS When a person signs and issues a negotiable instrument under such extreme duress as an immediate threat of force or violence (for example, at gunpoint), the instrument is void and unenforceable by any holder, including an HDC [UCC 3-305(2)(b)]. (Ordinary duress, to be discussed shortly, is only a personal defense.)

Personal Defenses

As mentioned above, personal defenses are used to avoid payment to an ordinary holder of a negotiable instrument. Personal defenses include every defense available in ordinary contract actions.

BREACH OF CONTRACT When there is a breach of the underlying contract for which the negotiable instrument was issued, the maker of a note can refuse to pay it or the drawer of a check can stop payment. Breach of the contract can be claimed as a defense to liability on the instrument. For example, Thieu and Price contract for the sale of Price's land. As part of the deal, Thieu signs a note for $35,000, payable to Price in monthly installments. The contract provides that Price will deliver a deed to Thieu after the third monthly payment and that Thieu can cancel the purchase within 120 days if he is not satisfied. Price transfers the note to his daughter as a gift. Price fails to give Thieu a deed after the third payment. When Thieu attempts to cancel, Price refuses. If Price's daughter sues to recover the unpaid balance of the note, Thieu can raise Price's breach of contract as a personal defense against payment.

BREACH OF WARRANTY Breach of warranty is a form of breach of contract that occurs when goods do not conform to a seller's statement or promise. For example, Peter purchases several cases of imported wine from Walter. The wine is to be delivered in four weeks. Peter gives Walter a promissory note for $1,000, which is the price of the wine. The wine arrives, but many of the bottles are broken, and several bottles that are tested have turned to vinegar. Peter refuses to pay the note on the basis of breach of warranty. (Under the law of sales, a seller impliedly promises that the goods are at least merchantable; see Chapter 22.) If the note is no longer in the hands of the payee seller but is presented for payment by an HDC, the maker buyer will not be able to plead breach of contract as a defense against liability on the note.

LACK OR FAILURE OF CONSIDERATION The absence of consideration may be a successful defense in instances involving commercial paper [UCC 3-306(c), 3-408]. For example, if, without more, Tony says to Cleo, ''I will sign a note promising to pay you $100,000,'' and Cleo says, ''Okay,'' there is no consideration for Tony's promise to sign the note, and a court will not enforce the promise.

Similarly, if delivery of goods becomes impossible, a party who has agreed to issue or has issued a draft or note under the contract has a defense for not issuing the note or for not paying the note if it has been issued. Thus, in the hypothetical wine transaction just described, if delivery of the wine became impossible due to its loss in an accident, Walter could not subsequently sue successfully to enforce Peter's promise to pay the $1,000 promissory note.

FRAUD IN THE INDUCEMENT A person who issues a negotiable instrument based on false statements by the other party will be able to avoid payment on that instrument. To illustrate: Peter agrees to purchase Sam's used tractor for $24,500. Sam, knowing his statements to be false, tells Peter that the tractor is in good working order and that it has been used for only one harvest. In addition, he tells Peter that he owns the tractor free and clear of all claims. Peter pays Sam $4,500 in cash and issues a negotiable promissory note for the balance. As it turns out, Sam still owes the original seller $10,000 on the purchase of the tractor, and the tractor is subject to a filed security interest (discussed in detail in Chapter 31). In addition, the tractor is three years old and has been used in three harvests. Peter can refuse to pay the note if it is held by an ordinary holder; but if Sam has negotiated the note to an HDC, Peter must pay the HDC. (Of course, Peter can then sue Sam.)

ILLEGALITY As mentioned above, if a statute makes an illegal transaction *void*, the defense of illegality is a universal defense and can successfully be asserted against an HDC. If, however, a statute provides that an illegal transaction is *voidable*, then illegality can only be successfully raised as a personal defense and will not be good against an HDC. A statute may provide that a given transaction is illegal and yet not state that payments associated with the transaction are void. In that case, instruments involved in the transaction will be voidable. For example, if a state makes gambling contracts illegal and void but is silent on instruments given in payment under gambling contracts, the instruments are voidable.

MENTAL INCAPACITY If a maker drafts a negotiable instrument while mentally incompetent but before a formal court hearing has declared (adjudicated) him or her to be mentally incompetent, many courts declare the obligation on the instru-

---

■ CONCEPT SUMMARY 27.2
Valid Defenses against Holders of Negotiable Instruments

Defenses	Types
Universal (real) defenses UCC 3-305 Valid against all holders, including holders in due course and holders with the rights of holders in due course (through the shelter principle).	1. Forgery. 2. Fraud in the execution. 3. Material alteration. 4. Discharge in bankruptcy. 5. Minority, if the contract is voidable. 6. Illegality, incapacity, or duress, if the contract is void under state law.
Personal defenses UCC 3-306 Valid against ordinary holders but not against holders in due course or holders with the rights of holders in due course.	1. Breach of contract (including breach of contract warranties). 2. Lack or failure of consideration. 3. Fraud in the inducement. 4. Illegality, incapacity (other than minority), or duress, if the contract is voidable. 5. Previous payment of the instrument. 6. Unauthorized completion of an incomplete instrument. 7. Nondelivery of the instrument.

ment to be voidable, in which case mental incapacity may be successfully asserted as a personal defense.

ORDINARY DURESS OR UNDUE INFLUENCE

Duress involves threats of harm or force. Ordinary duress—for example, the threat of a boycott—is a personal defense. As stated before, when the threat of force or harm becomes so violent and overwhelming that a person is deprived of his or her free will (comprising extreme duress), it becomes a universal defense, good against all holders, including HDCs [UCC 3-305]. Thus, for example, an instrument signed at the point of a gun is void, even in the hands of an HDC, but one signed under a threat to prosecute the son or daughter of the maker for theft may be merely voidable, so that the defense is not good against an HDC.

DISCHARGE BY PAYMENT OR CANCELLATION

If commercial paper is paid before its maturity date, the maker will ordinarily demand the return of the instrument itself or will note on the face of the instrument that payment has been made. Otherwise, the instrument may continue circulating. If it comes into the hands of an HDC who demands payment at maturity, the defense of discharge by payment, which is merely a personal defense, will not allow the maker to avoid paying a second time on the same note [UCC 3-601(1)(a), 3-602]. (But in a quasi-contract action—see Chapter 9—the maker should be able to pass the additional liability on to the party who received the payment and continued the instrument's circulation.)

UNAUTHORIZED COMPLETION OF AN INCOMPLETE INSTRUMENT

It is unwise for a maker or drawer to sign any negotiable instrument that is not complete. For example, Daniel signs a check, leaves the amount blank, and gives it to Dorman, an employee, instructing Dorman to make certain purchases and to complete the check "for not more than $500." Dorman fills in the amount as $5,000 *contrary to instructions*. If Daniel can stop payment in time, Daniel *may* be able to assert the defense of unauthorized completion and avoid liability to an ordinary holder. If the check is negotiated to an HDC, however, the instrument is payable as completed [UCC 3-115, 3-407, 3-304(4)(d), 4-401(2)(b)].

NONDELIVERY If a bearer instrument is lost or stolen, the maker or drawer of the instrument has the defense of nondelivery against an ordinary holder. Recall that delivery means "voluntary transfer of possession" [UCC 1-201(14)]. This defense, however, is not good against an HDC [UCC 3-305, 3-306(c)].

■ Federal Limitations on HDC Rights

The HDC doctrine has been abused in consumer transactions. For example, a merchant would sell shoddy goods on credit, sell the promissory notes to a finance company, and cease doing business. When the goods proved to be defective, consumers would discover the empty storefront and stop paying on the notes. Consequently, the finance company would sue. Because the finance company was an HDC, consumers could not successfully assert personal defenses, such as breach of warranty, and would be held liable on the notes.

To protect consumers, the Federal Trade Commission (FTC) promulgated Rule 433,[6] which effectively abolished the HDC doctrine in consumer transactions. Rule 433 limits the rights of an HDC in an instrument that evidences a debt arising out of a *consumer credit* transaction. (Payment by check is not a credit transaction.) Rule 433, entitled "Preservation of Consumers' Claims and Defenses," attempts to prevent a situation in which a consumer is required to make payment for a defective product to a third party who is an HDC of a promissory note that formed part of the contract with the dealer who sold the defective good.

FTC Rule 433 requires that any seller or lessor of goods or services who takes or receives a consumer credit contract or who accepts as full or partial payment for such sale or lease the proceeds of any purchase-money loan made in connection with any consumer credit contract include in the contract the following provision:

NOTICE
ANY HOLDER OF THIS CONSUMER CREDIT
CONTRACT IS SUBJECT TO ALL CLAIMS

---

6. 16 C.F.R. Section 433.2. The rule was enacted pursuant to the FTC's authority under the Federal Trade Commission Act, 15 U.S.C. Section 41 *et seq.*

AND DEFENSES WHICH THE DEBTOR COULD ASSERT AGAINST THE SELLER OF GOODS OR SERVICES OBTAINED PURSUANT HERETO OR WITH THE PROCEEDS HEREOF. RECOVERY HEREUNDER BY THE DEBTOR SHALL NOT EXCEED AMOUNTS PAID BY THE DEBTOR HEREUNDER.

Obviously, the purpose of this notice is to inform any holder that, upon acquisition of a negotiable commercial paper, he or she is subject to all claims and demands that the debtor could assert against the promisee or payee named in the paper. In essence, FTC Rule 433 places an HDC of the paper or of the negotiable instrument in the position of a contract assignee. FTC Rule 433 clearly reduces the degree of transferability of commercial paper resulting from consumer credit contracts.[7]

---

7. Revised Article 3 provides that a negotiable instrument that contains this notice or a similar statement required by law may remain negotiable [see RUCC 3-106(d) in Appendix C], but the new section adds that there cannot be an HDC of such an instrument.

■ Terms and Concepts

antecedent claim 480	personal defenses 486	universal defenses 486
holder in due course (HDC) 479	shelter principle 485	

■ For Review

1. What are the three requirements for attaining HDC status?

2. A person will not be afforded HDC protection if he or she knew or should have known at the time the instrument was acquired that it was defective. What are the four ''defects'' spelled out in the UCC?

3. How can a person who does not qualify as an HDC acquire the rights and privileges of an HDC?

4. Martin sells to Avery a car that Martin says was driven by his grandmother only on Sundays. Avery pays for the car with a check, then discovers that the car was used as a delivery vehicle for Speedy Pizza. If Avery's check is now held by an HDC, can Avery assert the defense of fraud to avoid payment?

5. Freda signs a promissory note for $5,000 and negotiates the note to Ivan. Ivan fraudulently alters the amount of the note to $15,000. Ivan transfers the note to Winnie. Winnie is an HDC. Can either Ivan or Winnie enforce the note against Freda for $15,000? For $5,000?

■ Questions and Case Problems

27-1. Janice Kurtz issues a ninety-day negotiable promissory note payable to the order of Dennis Nolan. The amount of the note is left blank, pending a determination of the amount of money Nolan will need to purchase a bull for Kurtz. Kurtz authorizes any amount not to exceed $2,000. Nolan, without authority, fills in the note in the amount of $5,000 and thirty days later sells the note to the First National Bank of Texas for $4,500. Nolan not only does not buy the bull but leaves the state. The First National Bank has no knowledge that the instrument was incomplete when issued or that Nolan had no authority to complete the instrument in the amount of $5,000.

(a) Does the bank qualify as a holder in due course? If so, for what amount? Explain.

(b) If Nolan had sold the note to a stranger in a bar for $500, would the stranger qualify as a holder in due course? Explain.

27-2. Dana draws and issues a $100 check payable to the order of Peter. The check is dated and issued on May 1. On May 25, Peter indorses the check by special indorsement to his son, Sam, as a gift. On June 5, Sam negotiates the check for value by blank indorsement to Helen. Meanwhile, Dana has stopped payment on the check, claiming that Peter is in breach of contract. Helen claims that she has the rights of a holder in due course. Discuss Helen's contention.

27-3. Daniel is a well-known industrialist in the community. He has agreed to purchase a rare coin from Helen's Coin Shop. The purchase price is to be determined by independent appraisal. Payment is to be by Daniel's check. Daniel is going out of town and informs Helen that his agent will bring her a check during his absence. Daniel draws up a check payable to Helen, leaves the amount blank, and gives the check to his agent, Max. Max, without authority, fills in the amount for $10,000 and presents it to Helen, who now has the appraisal. The appraisal price is $7,000. Max tells Helen that Daniel wanted to be sure the check would cover the appraisal and that he (Max) is authorized to receive the coin plus the balance in cash. Helen gives Max the coin plus $3,000. When Daniel discovers Max's fraud, Daniel stops payment on the check and offers Helen $7,000 for the coin. Helen claims she is a holder in due course and is entitled to the face value of the check, $10,000. Discuss whether Helen is an HDC and can therefore successfully pursue her claim.

27-4. Jerry Foster is a recent college graduate. A stranger comes to his door with a package. The stranger tells Jerry that the package is a gift from an anonymous friend and asks Jerry to sign a delivery receipt. Jerry, without reading what he is signing, signs at the place designated by the stranger and marked with an X. Jerry opens the package, and inside are two recently published novels. Jerry does not give the incident a second thought until six months later, when an HDC demands $1,000 from Jerry. Jerry now learns that he signed a six-month, negotiable promissory note instead of a delivery receipt. He is the victim of fraud. Discuss fully whether Jerry is obligated to pay the HDC $1,000.

27-5. Erwin has received from dishonest payees through negotiation two checks with the following histories:

(a) The drawer issued a check to the payee for $7. The payee cleverly altered the numeral on the check from $7 to $70 and the written word from *seven* to *seventy*.

(b) The drawer issued a check to the payee without filling in the amount. The drawer authorized the payee to fill in the amount for no more than $70. The payee filled in the amount of $700.

Discuss whether Erwin, by giving value to the payees, can qualify as a holder in due course of these checks.

27-6. Dennis Bowling was a friend and neighbor of David Dabney. Bowling had no indication that Dabney was financially troubled. Indeed, by all evidence, Dabney was quite well off: he owned four grocery stores; he drove a Cadillac; his wife owned a new sports car; he had race horses and lived in an expensive home. In the fall of 1983, Dabney admitted to Bowling that he had "cash flow" problems and borrowed $40,000 from Bowling. At the same time, Dabney proposed they become partners in his grocery business, and discussions concerning this prospect ensued over the following weeks. At one point, Dabney asked Bowling for a signed blank check that would be deposited with a new grocery supplier as "security" and would never be used without Bowling's consent. If it was, Dabney promised, he would reimburse Bowling's account appropriately. Shortly thereafter, Dabney dated and filled out Bowling's blank check for $10,606.79 and gave the check to his major supplier and creditor, E. Bierhaus & Sons. Dabney owed Bierhaus more than $400,000 for past deliveries; and after having received ten to twenty bad checks from Dabney, Bierhaus required cash or cashier's checks from Dabney for any deliveries. Dabney had told Bierhaus about the supposedly imminent partnership with Bowling, and under those circumstances, Bierhaus's agent accepted the $10,606.79 check from Bowling in payment for a delivery of groceries. Bowling's check was returned to Bierhaus, as there were insufficient funds in Bowling's account to cover

it. By this time, Dabney had filed for bankruptcy protection. Bierhaus sought to collect the amount of the check from Bowling. Is Bierhaus a holder in due course? [*E. Bierhaus & Sons v. Bowling,* 486 N.E.2d 598 (Ind.App. 1 Dist. 1985)]

27-7. In the fall of 1980, the Williams Brothers Asphalt Paving Co. contracted with two local communities in Michigan to resurface some of their streets. During the course of the jobs, Williams incurred debts to its supplier, Rieth-Riley Construction Co., in the amount of $45,960. When the work was completed, Williams received a total of $188,433 from the two communities and deposited the funds into its checking account at First Security Bank. Although the amount owed to Rieth-Riley ($45,960) was to have been set aside by the communities in a special trust (the Michigan Builders Trust Fund), it was not. Williams owed a secured debt to First Security Bank and so immediately paid to the bank the entire amount it had received. The payment was in the form of checks drawn on Williams's checking account at the bank and made payable to the bank's order. Williams later filed for bankruptcy, and Rieth-Riley sought to get its money from the bank, contending that Williams Brothers had no right to the $45,960 still owed to Rieth-Riley and thus could not negotiate it to the bank (via the checks Williams Brothers had made payable to the bank). Is the bank a holder in due course in this instance? [*In re Williams Brothers Asphalt Paving Co.,* 59 Bankr. 71 (Bankr.W.D.Mich. 1986)]

27-8. James Balkus died without leaving a will. A few days later, Ann Vesely, his sister, discovered in his personal effects two promissory notes made payable to her in the amount of $6,000. She presented the notes to the Security First National Bank of Sheboygan Trust Department, the personal representative for the estate of Balkus, for payment. The personal representative refused, claiming that Vesely was not an HDC and that nondelivery of the notes to her was a proper defense. The trial court upheld the personal representative's claim, and Vesely appealed. Discuss whether nondelivery is a proper defense against Vesely. [*Vesely v. Security First National Bank of Sheboygan Trust Department,* 128 Wis.2d 246, 381 N.W.2d 593 (App. 1985)]

27-9. Gary Culver, a Missouri farmer, made a business arrangement in 1984 with Nasib Ed Kalliel. Kalliel was to manage the business end of the farming enterprise, while Culver did the actual farming. Culver was to receive a salary and a percentage of the profits. In the summer of 1984, Culver notified Kalliel that he urgently needed money to prevent foreclosure. One week later, Culver received $30,000 from the Rexford State Bank of Rexford, Kansas. Culver thought that the money had come from Kalliel and that Kalliel was responsible for repayment. About a week later, a representative from the Rexford Bank, Jerry Gilbert, approached Culver and requested Culver's signature on a blank promissory note form, stating that "Rexford State Bank wanted to know where the $30,000.00 went, . . . for their records." Apparently, Gilbert led Culver to believe that the document was merely a receipt for the $30,000. The maturity date, interest rate, and amount of the promissory note were later filled in, only the amount read $50,000 instead of $30,000. It was later verified that $50,000 had been deposited in Kalliel's Rexford Bank account, from which the $30,000 sent to Culver had been drawn. Subsequent to these events, the Rexford Bank became insolvent, and the Federal Deposit Insurance Corp. (FDIC) purchased the bank's outstanding notes, including the one signed by Culver. The FDIC sought recovery on the note, because the note had matured and no money had ever been paid on it, and moved for summary judgment against Culver. Culver claimed that he should not be liable on the note because Gilbert's misrepresentations of the nature of the note constituted fraud in the execution. Can Culver successfully raise the universal defense of fraud in the execution to avoid liability on the note? [*Federal Deposit Insurance Corp. v. Culver,* 640 F.Supp. 725 (D.Kan. 1986)]

27-10. Pamela Haas, an employee of Trail Leasing, Inc., had access to her employer's blank checks. Over a period of about two and a half years, Haas used the firm's checks to fraudulently obtain cash from the firm's bank, Drovers First American Bank. She carried out her scheme by writing checks payable to Drovers First, having the checks signed by an authorized officer of Trail Leasing, and then taking the checks to the bank. There she would fill out a "change order form"—a form used by bank customers to specify the coins and bill denominations in which they wished to take cash for business operations—and pocket the cash that she received. By the time the scheme was discovered (through a discrepancy in one of the change orders), Haas had negotiated fifty-five checks for a total of nearly $40,000. Trail Leasing sued the bank to recover the funds paid to Haas without its authorization, and the issue turned on whether the bank was a holder in due course of the checks delivered to it by Haas. The court had no trouble deciding that the bank took the checks in good faith and without notice of any claim. The issue thus became whether the bank met the remaining requirement for HDC status—taking for value. Trail Leasing argued that because the bank essentially paid Haas from Trail Leasing's funds (by debiting Trail Leasing's bank account), the bank had not given value for the instruments and therefore could not be an HDC. Will the court concur in this argument? Discuss. [*Trail Leasing, Inc. v. Drovers First American Bank,* 447 N.W.2d 190 (Minn. 1989)]

27-11. A Question of Ethics

Timothy Kirkman was involved in the horse business. He formed a business arrangement with an acquaintance, John Roundtree, who worked as a loan officer for American Federal Bank. Under the arrangement, Kirkman would locate buyers for horses, and the buyers could seek financing from American Federal. Roundtree gave Kirkman blank promissory notes and security agreements from American Federal, and Kirkman was to locate potential purchasers, take care of the paperwork, and bring the documents to the bank for approval of the purchaser's loan. Eventually, Kirkman entered into a purchase agreement with Gene Parker, a horse dealer. Parker agreed with Kirkman that they would jointly purchase a certain horse for $35,000. Parker signed a blank American Federal promissory note, with the understanding that Kirkman would cosign the note and complete the details of the transaction with the bank. Parker also signed a form authorizing the bank to release the funds to the seller of the collateral (the horse). Kirkman did not cosign the note and completed it for $85,000 instead of $35,000. He then took the note and authorization form to Roundtree, told Roundtree that he was the seller, and received from Roundtree checks totaling $85,000. After paying the actual seller of the horse the agreed-on $35,000 and seeing to it that Parker received the horse, Kirkman skipped town with the remaining $50,000. Parker paid American Federal $35,000 but refused to pay any more, claiming that he had agreed to pay only $35,000 and that the other $50,000 was unauthorized by him. In the subsequent action brought by the bank to collect the $50,000, the bank prevailed. The court found that the bank was a holder in due course of the promissory note and had not been negligent in the way it handled the transaction. [American Federal Bank, FSB v. Parker, *392 S.E.2d 798 (S.C. 1990)*]

1. Parker contended that the bank was negligent because it did not contact him to make sure that everything was correct before disbursing the proceeds of the loan to Kirkman. Do you agree with the court's finding that the bank was not negligent in this regard? Even if the bank had been negligent, would its negligence have outweighed Parker's negligence in signing a blank promissory note?

2. Because the bank was deemed a holder in due course and Parker had signed an incomplete instrument, Parker was prohibited under UCC 3-407(3) from asserting successfully the universal defense of material alteration. What ethical premise underlies this rule?

3. Overall, from an ethical point of view, do you think that the court's holding in this case was fair? Would it be fairer to hold the bank liable for the loss instead of Parker? If you were the judge, how would you decide the issue?

Chapter 28

Liability and Discharge

Two kinds of liability are associated with negotiable instruments: signature liability and warranty liability. *Signature liability* relates to signatures on instruments. Those who sign commercial paper are potentially liable for payment of the amount stated on the instrument. *Warranty liability,* on the other hand, extends to both signers and nonsigners. A breach of warranty can occur when the instrument is transferred or presented for payment.

The following sections cover the liability of the parties who sign the instrument—for example, drawers of drafts and checks, makers of notes and certificates of deposit, and indorsers. They also cover the liability of accommodation parties and the warranty liability of those who transfer instruments and present instruments for payment. Note that the focus is on liability *on the instrument itself or on warranties connected with transfer or presentment of the instrument* as opposed to liability for the underlying contract. The final section in the chapter then looks at the some of the ways in which parties can be *discharged* from liability on negotiable instruments.

■ Signature Liability

The key to liability on a negotiable instrument is a *signature.* The parties to a negotiable instrument are bound by all of the terms implied by their signatures by operation of law. Once it is established that a party signed an instrument (or that it was signed by that party's authorized agent), the UCC defines the party's liability. The liability is contractual in the sense that each party voluntarily incurs it and thus can modify it.

UCC 3-401(2) defines a **signature** as ''any name, including any trade or assumed name, upon an instrument, or . . . any word or mark used in lieu of a written signature.'' A signature can be handwritten, typed, or printed; or it can be made by mark, by thumbprint, or in virtually any manner. According to UCC 1-201(39), ''signed'' refers to any symbol executed or adopted by a party with the ''present intention to authenticate a writing.''

The requirement of a signature on an instrument has its origin in the Law Merchant (the early law governing commercial transactions—see Chapter 18) and is based simply on the need to know whose obligation the instrument represents. The critical element with any signature is a ''present intention to authenticate a writing.'' Parol evidence can be used to identify the signer, and, once identified, the signature is effective against the signer no matter how it is made. UCC 3-401(1) states the general rule: ''No person is liable on an instrument unless his signature appears thereon.'' There are a few exceptions to this general rule under UCC 3-404. These exceptions are discussed later in this section.

Primary and Secondary Liability

Every party, except a *qualified indorser,*[1] who signs a negotiable instrument is either primarily or secondarily liable for payment of that instrument when it comes due.

PRIMARY LIABILITY   A person who is primarily liable on a negotiable instrument is absolutely required to pay the instrument, subject to certain real defenses [UCC 3-305]. Unless a real defense exists, a party who is primarily liable on an instrument will remain subject to that obligation until the applicable statute of limitations runs out. Only *makers* and *acceptors* are primarily liable [UCC 3-413(1)].

The maker of a note promises to pay the note. The words ''I promise to pay'' embody the maker's obligation to pay the instrument according to the terms as written at the time of the signing. If the instrument is incomplete when the maker signs it, then the maker's obligation is to pay it as completed, assuming that the instrument is properly completed [UCC 3-413(1), 3-115].

A maker guarantees that certain facts are true by signing a promissory note. In particular, Section 3-413(3) specifies that a maker admits to all subsequent parties that the payee in fact exists and that the payee has current capacity to indorse the note (for example, that the payee is not a minor at the time the note is signed). Primary liability is unconditional. The primary party's liability is immediate when the note becomes due. No action by the holder of the instrument is required.

The drawee-acceptor is in virtually the same position as the maker of a note [UCC 3-413(1), (3)]. An **acceptor** is a drawee of a draft or check who has, by signing the instrument, manifestly agreed to pay the draft when due. A drawee who does not accept owes a contractual duty to the drawer to pay in accordance with the drawer's orders, but a drawee owes no duty to either the payee or any holder [UCC 3-409].

For example, Pope buys from Whitney goods costing $2,000. The goods will be shipped to arrive on September 1. Instead of giving Whitney cash, Pope draws a draft on Fairweather Finance Company for $2,000 payable to Whitney on September 1. At this point, Fairweather is not liable on the draft, and it will not become liable on the draft unless and until it accepts the draft.

A holder must present the instrument to a drawee for acceptance in three situations:

1.   When the instrument requires such presentation.
2.   When the draft is to be payable at an address different from that of the drawee.
3.   When the draft's payment date is dependent on such presentment—for example, when the draft is payable thirty days after acceptance or sight.

Presentment in these situations is required in order for the drawer and indorsers to be charged with secondary liability (see below) [UCC 3-501(1)(a)].

If the drawee accepts the instrument as presented, the drawee becomes an acceptor and is primarily liable to all subsequent holders. A drawee who refuses to accept such a draft has dishonored the instrument. In refusing to accept, the drawee retains his or her original status and owes no duty to the payee or any holder.

A check is a special type of draft that is drawn on a bank and is payable on demand. Acceptance of a check is called *certification* (discussed in Chapter 29). Certification by a bank is not required on checks, and thus a bank is under no obligation to certify. (Indeed, an increasing number of banks will not certify checks.) Upon certification, however, the drawee bank occupies the position of an acceptor and is primarily liable on the check to holders [UCC 3-411].

SECONDARY LIABILITY   Secondary liability on a negotiable instrument is similar to the liability of a guarantor in a simple contract. Recall from Chapter 14 that a guarantor becomes liable under a con-

---

1.   Recall from Chapter 26 that a qualified indorser is one who indorses without recourse—in other words, he or she undertakes no obligation to pay. A qualified indorser merely assumes warranty liability, which is discussed later in this chapter.

tract only if the primarily liable party does not or cannot fulfill his or her obligations under the contract. Secondary liability is thus ''contingent liability.'' *Drawers* and *indorsers* have secondary liability. In the case of notes, an indorser's secondary liability does not arise until the maker, who is primarily liable, has defaulted on the instrument [UCC 3-413(1), 3-414].

With regard to drafts and checks, a drawer's secondary liability does not arise until the drawee fails to pay or to accept the instrument, whichever is required. Note, however, that the drawee is not primarily liable. Makers of notes promise to pay, but drawees are ordered to pay. Therefore, drawees are not primarily liable unless they promise to pay—for example, by certifying a check. Nor are drawees even secondarily liable on an instrument. As stated in UCC 3-409, ''[a] check or other draft does not of itself operate as an assignment of any funds in the hands of the drawee available for its payment.'' Thus, unless a drawee *accepts,*[2] the drawee's only obligation is to honor the drawer's orders.

Dishonoring an instrument triggers the liability of secondarily liable parties on the instrument—that is, the drawer, unqualified indorsers, and accommodation indorsers. Parties who are secondarily liable on a negotiable instrument promise to pay on that instrument only if the following events occur:

1. The instrument is properly and timely presented.
2. The instrument is dishonored.
3. Notice of dishonor is timely given to the secondarily liable party.[3]

These requirements are necessary for a secondarily liable party to have signature liability on a negotiable instrument, but they are not necessary for a secondarily liable party to have warranty liability (to be discussed later in this chapter) [UCC 3-414, 3-501, 3-502].

UCC 3-413(2) provides that ''upon dishonor of the draft and any necessary notice of dishonor

... [the drawer] will pay the amount of the draft to the holder or to any indorser who takes it up.'' For example, Nancy Oliver writes a check on her account at Third National Bank payable to the order of Joel Andrews. If Third National does not pay the check when Andrews presents it for payment, then Oliver is liable to Andrews on the basis of her secondary liability. Drawers are secondarily liable on drafts unless they disclaim their liability by drawing the instruments without recourse [UCC 3-413(2)].

Because drawers are secondarily liable, their liability does not arise until presentment and notice of dishonor have been made *properly* and in a *timely* way. If a draft (or check) is payable at a bank, improper presentment or notice relieves the drawer from secondary liability only when the drawee bank is insolvent and the drawer is thereby deprived of funds that would have covered the draft [UCC 3-502].

An *unqualified indorser* promises that in the event of presentment, dishonor, and notice of dishonor he or she will pay the instrument. Thus, the liability of an indorser is much like that of a drawer, with one major exception: indorsers are *relieved* of their contractual liability to the holder of the instrument by (1) improper (late) presentment or (2) late notice or failure to notify the indorser of dishonor [UCC 3-414, 3-501, 3-502].

When an indorser has actively caused an instrument to be dishonored, the requirements of presentment and notice of dishonor are excused [UCC 3-511(2)(b)].

The next three subsections define what constitutes proper presentment, dishonor, and proper notice of dishonor under the UCC.

Proper Presentment

The UCC spells out what constitutes a proper presentment. Basically, presentment by a holder must be made to the proper person, must be made in a proper manner, and must be timely [UCC 3-503, 3-504].

A note or CD must be presented to the maker for payment. A draft is presented by the holder to the drawee for acceptance or payment, or both, whichever is required. A check is presented to the drawee for payment [UCC 3-504].

Presentment can be properly made in any one of the following three manners, depending on the type of instrument [UCC 3-504(2)]:

---

2. To accept a draft, the drawee must place his or her signature on it [UCC 3-410].
3. An instrument can be drafted to provide a waiver of the presentment, dishonor, and notice of dishonor requirements. Presume for simplicity's sake that no such waivers have been incorporated into the instruments described in this chapter.

1. By mail (but presentment is not effective until the instrument is received).
2. Through a clearinghouse procedure, as for deposited checks.
3. At the place specified in the instrument for acceptance or payment—or, if the instrument is silent as to place, at the place of business or the residence of the person required to accept or pay.

One of the most crucial criteria for proper presentment is timeliness [UCC 3-503]. Failure to present on time is the most prevalent reason for improper presentment and consequent discharge of unqualified indorsers from secondary liability. See Exhibit 28–1, bearing in mind that its contents are somewhat oversimplified.

Dishonor

An instrument is dishonored when presentment is properly made and acceptance or payment is refused or cannot be obtained within the prescribed time, or when presentment is excused and the instrument is not properly accepted or paid [UCC 3-507(1)]. Payment can be postponed without dishonor to determine whether an instrument is properly payable, but not beyond the close of business on the day of presentment [UCC 3-506(2)]. Returning an instrument because it lacks a proper indorsement is not dishonor [UCC 3-507(3)].

Proper Notice

Once an instrument has been dishonored, proper notice must be given for secondary parties to be held liable. The rules of proper notice are basically as follows [UCC 3-508]:

1. Notice operates for the benefit of all parties who have rights on an instrument against the party notified [UCC 3-508(8)]. For example, assume there are four indorsers on a note that its maker dishonors, and the holder gives timely notice to the first and the fourth. If the holder collects payment from the fourth indorser, this indorser does not have to give notice to the first indorser again to collect from the first indorser.

It is important to remember that if more than one indorsement appears on an instrument, each indorser is liable for the full amount to any later indorser or to any holder. For example, imagine a note (Ernest's) indorsed by four indorsers (Hadley, Pauline, Martha, and Mary) before coming into the possession of a holder (Jack). If Ernest, the maker, dishonors the note at maturity, Jack, the holder, may demand and recover payment from Mary, the fourth indorser, who may then recover the full amount from any prior indorser. If Mary collects from Pauline (the second indorser), Pauline gets the note and may seek payment from Hadley. But Pauline cannot sue Martha, who is a later indorser, because liability moves only *up* the indorsement chain.

2. Except for dishonor of foreign drafts (drafts drawn in one country and payable in another country), notice may be given in any reasonable manner. This includes oral or written notice and notice written or stamped on the instrument itself [UCC 3-508(3)]. To give notice of dishonor of a foreign

■ **Exhibit 28–1 Time for Proper Presentment [UCC 3-503]**

Type of Instrument	For Acceptance	For Payment
Time	On or before due date	On due date
Demand	Within a reasonable time (after date or issue or after secondary party becomes liable thereon)	
Check (domestic)	Not applicable	Presumed to be:[a] Within thirty days (of date on the instrument or the issue date, whichever is later) to hold drawer secondarily liable Within seven days (of indorsement) to hold indorser secondarily liable
a. In the case of a domestic, uncertified check, these are the time periods within which to present for payment *or* to initiate the bank collection process. Revised Article 3 extends the seven-day period to hold an indorser secondarily liable to thirty days, but this thirty-day period is absolute [RUCC 3-415(e)].		

draft, a formal notice called a *protest* is required [UCC 3-509].

3. Any necessary notice must be given by a bank before its midnight deadline (midnight of the next banking day after receipt) [UCC 4-104(1)(h)] and by all others before midnight of the third *business* day after either dishonor or receipt of notice of dishonor [UCC 3-508(2)]. Written notice is effective when sent, not when received [UCC 3-508(4)].

4. Notice to a partner is notice to a partnership [UCC 3-508(5)]. Similarly, when a party is deceased, incompetent, or bankrupt, notice may be given to his or her representative [UCC 3-508(6), (7)].

Accommodation Parties

Recall from Chapter 25 that an *accommodation party* is one who signs an instrument for the purpose of lending his or her name to that of another party to the instrument [UCC 3-415(1)]. Accommodation parties are one form of security against nonpayment on a negotiable instrument.

For example, a bank about to lend money, a seller taking a large order for goods, or a creditor about to extend credit to a prospective debtor all want some reasonable assurance that the debts will be paid. A party's uncertain financial condition or the fact that the parties to a transaction are complete strangers can make a creditor reluctant to rely solely on the prospective debtor's ability to pay. To reduce the risk of nonpayment, the creditor can require the joining of a third person as an accommodation party on the instrument.

If the accommodation party signs on behalf of a maker, he or she will be an *accommodation maker* and will be primarily liable on the instrument. If the accommodation party signs on behalf of a payee or other holder (usually to make the instrument more marketable), he or she will be an *accommodation indorser* and will be secondarily liable. Any indorsement not in the ordinary chain of title gives notice of its accommodation character [UCC 3-415(2), (4)]. For example, a signature that appears on an instrument above that of the payee, who would normally be the first indorser, is outside the chain of title. An accommodation party is never, however, liable to the party accommodated, and if the accommodation party pays the instrument, he or she has a right of recourse against the party accommodated [UCC 3-415(5)].

Agents' Signatures

The general law of agency covered in Chapters 35 and 36 applies to negotiable instruments. Agents can sign negotiable instruments and thereby bind their principals [UCC 3-403(1)]. Without such a rule, all corporate commercial business would stop. As Chapter 41 will show, every corporation can and must act through its agents. Because of the critical function the signature plays in determining liability on a negotiable instrument, however, we will go into some detail here concerning the potential problems of agents' signatures.

Generally, an authorized agent must indicate that he or she is signing an instrument on behalf of a *clearly named* principal to bind the principal on the instrument. The agent must write out the principal's name (by signature, mark, or some symbol) and his or her own name, or the agent can supply only the principal's signature.[4] To illustrate: The following signatures by Henry Yokum as agent for Peter Barnam would bind Peter on the instrument:

1. ''Peter Barnam, by Henry Yokum, agent.''
2. ''Peter Barnam.''
3. ''Peter Barnam, Henry Yokum'' (by parol evidence).

If an authorized agent signs just his or her own name, the principal will not be bound on the instrument. Under UCC 3-403(2)(a), when an agent carelessly signs only his or her own name, the agent is *personally* liable on the instrument even though the parties know of the agency relationship. In addition, parol evidence is not admissible to establish that the signature was made for a principal. In such situations, form prevails over intent.

Under UCC 3-403(2)(b), two other situations in which an agent is held personally liable on a negotiable instrument can arise. If the instrument is signed in both the agent's name and the principal's name—''Peter Barnam, Henry Yokum''—but nothing on the instrument indicates the agency relationship, both parties can be liable. Because inclusion of both the agent's and the principal's names without indication of their relationship is

---

4. If the agent signs the principal's name, the UCC presumes that the signature is authorized and genuine [UCC 3-307(1)(b)].

ambiguous, parol evidence is admissible in controversies arising *between the immediate parties* to prove the agency relationship.

Another situation envisioned under UCC 3-403(2)(b) occurs when an agent signs a negotiable instrument and indicates agency status but fails to name the principal—for example, "Barry Scott, agent." Against any subsequent holder the agent is *personally* liable, but the unnamed principal cannot be held liable on the instrument. Because the indication of agency status without naming of the principal is ambiguous, parol evidence is admissible in controversies arising *between the immediate parties* to prove the agency relationship and to establish the liability of the unnamed principal [UCC 3-403(2)(b)].[5]

When a negotiable instrument is signed in the name of an organization (any legal or commercial entity [UCC 1-201(28)]) and the organization's name is preceded or followed by the name and office of an authorized individual, the organization will be bound; the individual who has signed the instrument in the representative capacity will not be bound [UCC 3-403(3)].[6]

If the agent has no authority, either apparent or implied, to sign the principal's name on an instrument, then the agent's signature will be unauthorized and subject to the UCC rules governing unauthorized signatures—which are discussed in the next section.

In the following case, an agent who signed a check without disclosing that he was signing in a representative capacity was held personally liable.

---

5.   Revised Article 3 retains the same personal liability of the agent as does the present UCC when a holder in due course is involved. For others, however, the agent can escape liability if the agent can prove the original parties did not intend the agent to be liable on the instrument [RUCC 3-402(b)(2)].

---

6.   Under Revised Article 3, if an organization requires more than one signature on a check, the signature of the organization is considered unauthorized if one of the required signatures is lacking [RUCC 3-403(b)].

Case 28.1

GRIFFIN v. ELLINGER

Supreme Court of Texas, 1976.
538 S.W.2d 97.

BACKGROUND AND FACTS   Percy Griffin, the president of Greenway Building Company, issued three checks to O. B. Ellinger, doing business as Ellinger Paint and Dry Wall. The checks, totaling $3,950, were drawn on Greenway's account and signed by Griffin, without corporate officer designation, as payment for labor and materials furnished to Greenway for a construction project. Greenway was the prime contractor for the project, and Griffin was authorized to sign checks as president of the company. The bank refused to honor the checks because of insufficient funds in the Greenway account. Ellinger sued in a Texas state court to recover from Griffin personally. The trial court ruled in Ellinger's favor. Griffin appealed, and the appellate court affirmed the ruling. Griffin then appealed to the state's highest court. The major question before the court was whether Griffin's signature on a corporate check, without any indication of his representative capacity, obligated him personally and individually for the amount of the check.

DECISION AND RATIONALE   After examining the checks, the Supreme Court of Texas concluded that Griffin was individually liable on the three checks because there was no indication that he signed only in his capacity as president of Greenway. The court acknowledged that it is unusual to demand the individual obligation of a corporate officer on checks drawn on a corporate account but explained that Griffin's use of corporate checks only indicated that the account was a corporate account—it did not give any information as to the capacity in which Griffin signed the instruments. The court noted that under UCC 3-403, one signing an instrument "is personally liable thereon even though he is authorized to and does in fact bind his principal, if he does not disclose that he is signing only in a representative capacity. In short, the burden is on the signer to relieve himself of personal liability by disclosing his agency."

COMMENTS Although this case represents the majority rule, there are differences among states on the issue of personal liability. When the question of personal liability arises, and the instrument either names the principal or shows the fact of representation, the signer can offer evidence to prove that he or she acted in a representative capacity and may thus overcome the presumption that he or she is personally obligated.

Unauthorized Signatures

People are not normally liable to pay on negotiable instruments unless their signatures appear on the instruments. Hence, a forged or an unauthorized signature is wholly inoperative and will not bind the person whose name is forged.[7] There are exceptions to this rule, found in UCC 3-404(1):

1. Any unauthorized signature is wholly inoperative as that of the person whose name is signed unless the person whose name is signed ratifies it or is precluded from denying it [UCC 3-404(1)]. For example, a signature made by an agent exceeding the scope of actual, implied, or apparent authority can be ratified by the principal. If a person fails to repudiate an unauthorized signature, this may constitute ratification. For example, Richard Eutsler was held to have ratified his brother's forgery of Richard's signature on checks cashed at a bank when Richard asked the bank not to prosecute, entered into a repayment agreement with his brother, and did not sue the bank until his brother disappeared six months later.[8]

Moreover, a person who writes and signs a check, leaving blank the amount and the name of the payee, and who then leaves the check in a place available to the public can be estopped (prevented), on the basis of negligence, from denying liability for its payment [UCC 3-115, 3-406, 4-401(2)(b)]. Acts that usually constitute negligence include incompletely filling out an instrument (that is, leaving blanks that can be filled in by someone else, fraudulently or otherwise), mailing an instrument to a person who has the same name as the payee, failing to follow internal procedures designed to thwart forgery, failing to examine the bank's monthly statement, and carelessness in the issuance of an instrument.

2. An unauthorized signature operates as the signature of the unauthorized signer in favor of an HDC [UCC 3-404(1)]. In other words, if Michel Vuillard signs "Paul Richaud" without Richaud's authorization, Vuillard is personally liable just as if he had signed his own name. Vuillard's liability is limited, however, to persons who take or pay the instrument in good faith. One who knew the signature was unauthorized would not qualify as an HDC and thus could not recover from Vuillard on the instrument.

Unauthorized Indorsements

Generally, when there is a forged or unauthorized *indorsement,* the burden of loss falls on the first party to take the forged indorsement. In other words, a forged indorsement does not transfer title; and thus, whoever takes an instrument with a forged indorsement cannot become a holder. In effect, for purposes of negotiation and transferring title, a forged indorsement is no indorsement at all. For example, if Doc's Check Cashing Service cashes Carol's alimony check for Ed, who has forged Carol's signature on the check, Doc's is not legally entitled to payment from Carol's ex-husband's bank account. (A bank's liability for payment over a forged indorsement is discussed in Chapter 29.) In two situations involving forged indorsements, however, the resulting loss falls on the drawer or maker. These situations, which will be discussed in more detail in the following subsections, are as follows:

1. When an imposter induces the maker or drawer of an instrument to issue it to the imposter.
2. When a person signs as or on behalf of a maker or drawer, intending that the payee have no interest in the instrument, or when an agent or employee of the maker or drawer has supplied him or her

---

7. On the other hand, a drawee is charged with knowledge of the *drawer's* signature. The drawee cannot recover money it pays out to a holder in due course on a negotiable instrument bearing a forged drawer's signature (see UCC 3-418).
8. *Eutsler v. First National Bank, Pawhuska,* 639 P.2d 1245 (Okla. 1982).

with the name of the payee, also intending the payee to have no such interest [UCC 3-405(1)]. This is frequently referred to as the *fictitious payee rule* and often involves an employee who wishes to swindle an employer by padding bills or payrolls.

IMPOSTERS   An **imposter** is one who, by use of the mails, telephone, or personal appearance, induces a maker or drawer to issue an instrument in the name of an impersonated payee. The maker or drawer honestly believes that the imposter is actually the named payee and issues the instrument to the imposter. Because the maker or drawer did issue and intend the imposter to receive the instrument, the indorsement by the imposter is not treated as unauthorized when the instrument is transferred to an innocent party.

In such situations, the unauthorized indorsement of a payee's name can be as effective as if the real payee had signed. The *imposter rule* of UCC 3-405 provides that an imposter's indorsement will be effective—that is, not a forgery— insofar as the drawer goes.

For example, a man walks into John Green's clothing store and purports to be Jerry Lewis soliciting contributions for his annual fund raising for muscular dystrophy. John Green has heard of the Lewis Telethon but has never met or seen Jerry Lewis. Wishing to support a worthy cause, Green writes out a check for $500 payable to Jerry Lewis and hands it to the imposter. The imposter forges the signature of Jerry Lewis and negotiates the check to a Stop and Shop convenience store. Green discovers the fraud and stops payment on the check, claiming the payee's signature is forged. Because the imposter rule is in effect, Green cannot claim a forgery against Stop and Shop, and he must seek redress from the imposter. If Green had sent the check to the real Jerry Lewis but the check had been stolen and negotiated to the store by a forged indorsement, the imposter rule would not apply, and Stop and Shop would have to seek redress against the forger. In either instance, the party who assumes the risk of loss is the party in the best position to guard against an instrument's transfer to an imposter or forger.

FICTITIOUS PAYEES   The so-called **fictitious payee rule** deals with an instrument issued in the name of a payee with the intention that the payee have no interest in the instrument. The payee need not be fictitious (that is, the payee may be a real person). The determining factor is that the maker or drawer, or another party who has supplied the payee's name to the maker or drawer, intends that the payee have no interest in the instrument to entitle the party to receive the proceeds when payment is made on the instrument. This most often takes place when (1) a dishonest employee deceives the employer, the maker or drawer, into signing an instrument payable to a party with no right to receive the instrument, or (2) a dishonest employee or agent has the authority to so issue the instrument on behalf of the maker or drawer. In these situations, the payee's indorsement is not treated as a forgery, and the maker or drawer is held liable on the instrument by an innocent holder.

Assume that the Revco Company gives its bookkeeper, Sam Snyde, general authority to issue checks in the company name drawn on Second Federal Bank so that Snyde can pay employees and pay other corporate bills. Snyde decides to cheat Revco out of $10,000 by issuing a check payable to Fanny Freid, an old acquaintance of his. Snyde does not intend Freid to receive any of the money, and Freid is not an employee or creditor of the company. Snyde indorses the check in Freid's name, naming himself as indorsee. Snyde cashes the check with a local bank, which collects payment from the drawee bank, Second Federal. Second Federal then charges Revco's account $10,000. Revco discovers the fraud and demands that its account be recredited.

In this situation, who bears the loss? Neither the local bank that first accepted the check nor Second Federal is liable. The rule of UCC 3-405 provides the answer. Because Snyde's indorsement in the name of a payee with no interest in the instrument is effective, there is no forgery. Hence, the collecting bank is protected in paying on the check, and the drawee bank is protected in charging Revco's account. It is the employer-drawer, Revco, that bears the loss.[9] Of course, Revco has recourse against Snyde, who, however, has most likely spent the money or absconded with it.

Whether a dishonest employee actually signs the check or merely supplies his or her employer with names of fictitious creditors (or with true names of creditors having fictitious debts), the

---

9. *May Department Stores Co. v. Pittsburgh National Bank,* 374 F.2d 109 (3rd Cir. 1967).

UCC makes no distinction in result. For example, Ned Norris draws up the payroll list from which employee checks are written. Norris fraudulently adds the name of his friend Sue Swift (a fictitious person) to the payroll, thus causing checks to be issued to her. Again, it is the employer-drawer who bears the loss, because the employer is in the best position to prevent such fraud.

In the following case, the court must determine whether a bank should bear the loss for forged indorsements on checks payable to fictitious payees.

Case 28.2

RETAIL SHOE HEALTH COMMISSION v. MANUFACTURERS HANOVER TRUST CO.

Supreme Court of New York, Appellate Division, First Department, 1990.
160 A.D.2d 47,
558 N.Y.S.2d 949.

BACKGROUND AND FACTS Jerome Simon was an administrator of the Retail Shoe Health Commission, an employee welfare fund ("the Fund"). Over a period of eight years, Simon, who was an authorized signatory to the Fund's checking account at Manufacturers Hanover Trust Company, embezzled approximately $675,000 from the Fund by preparing duplicate vouchers and signing checks payable to fictitious payees for medical benefit claims submitted by the Fund's beneficiaries. Simon would indorse the fictitious payees' names on the backs of the checks and deposit the checks primarily into a bank account at Bankers Trust Company. Simon's scheme was not discovered until after his death, when various discrepancies in check vouchers surfaced. After discovering the embezzlement, the Fund's insurer sued Manufacturers Hanover and Bankers Trust in a New York state court to recover the full amount of the checks, on the ground of forged indorsements. The trial court denied the banks' motion for summary judgment, and the banks appealed.

DECISION AND RATIONALE The Supreme Court of New York, Appellate Division, reversed the lower court's ruling. The appellate court held that any recovery by the Fund against the banks on a claim of forged indorsements was barred by the fictitious payee rule of UCC 3-405(1). This rule provides that an indorsement by any person in the name of a named payee is effective if "an agent or employee of the maker or drawer has supplied him with the name of the payee intending the latter to have no such interest." Simon was the Fund's administrator and prepared checks in the names of payees, intending that those payees have no interest in the checks. Thus, Simon's indorsement in the names of the payees were not forgeries, and the indorsements were effective. The court ruled that the allocation of risk of loss to the Fund—Simon's employer—was the most appropriate solution to the issue of liability, because the Fund was in the best position to detect Simon's unauthorized actions.

ETHICAL CONSIDERATIONS The court noted that the principle underlying the fictitious payee rule rests on a fundamental public policy determination that losses arising from unauthorized checks payable to fictitious payees are "more business risks than banking risks." As a general rule, the employer—in this case the Fund—is in a better position to prevent such forgeries by reasonable care in the selection and supervision of its employees. Furthermore, employers often obtain insurance (called fidelity insurance) to cover losses sustained as a result of the malfeasance (wrongdoing) of employees entrusted with the handling of funds. Revised Article 3 recognizes this ethical concern and reduces the maker or drawer's liability for any loss caused by negligence on the part of the person paying the instrument or taking it for value or collection [RUCC 3-404(d)]. This is a comparative negligence standard.

■ Warranty Liability

In addition to the signature liability discussed in the preceding sections, transferors make certain implied warranties regarding the instruments that they are negotiating. Liability under these warranties is not subject to the conditions of proper presentment, dishonor, and notice of dishonor. These warranties arise even when a transferor does not indorse the instrument (as in delivery of bearer paper) [UCC 3-417]. Warranties fall into two categories, those that arise upon the *transfer* of a negotiable instrument and those that arise upon *presentment.*[10]

Transfer Warranties

Five **transfer warranties** are described in UCC 3-417(2). They provide that any person who *indorses* an instrument and *receives consideration* warrants to *all* subsequent transferees and holders who take the instrument in good faith that:

1. The transferor has good title to the instrument or is otherwise authorized to obtain payment or acceptance on behalf of one who does have good title.
2. All signatures are genuine or authorized.
3. The instrument has not been materially altered.
4. No defense of any party is good against the transferor. For example, Ariman defrauded Braun into giving her a promissory note. Ariman negotiated the note to Chelsea Loan Company. When Ariman transferred the note to Chelsea, she breached the warranty that there was no defense good against her, because Braun could successfully defend against a suit on the note by Ariman.
5. The transferor has no knowledge of any insolvency proceedings against the maker, the acceptor, or the drawer of an unaccepted instrument.

A qualified indorser who indorses an instrument without recourse limits the fourth warranty to a warranty that he or she has no knowledge of

such a defense rather than that there is no defense [UCC 3-417(3)].

The manner of transfer and the negotiation that is used determine how far and to whom a transfer warranty will run. Transfer by indorsement and delivery of order paper extends warranty liability to any subsequent holder who takes the instrument in good faith. The warranties of a person who transfers without indorsement (by delivery of bearer paper), however, extend only to the immediate transferee [UCC 3-417(2)].

For example, Asher forges Martin's name as maker of a promissory note. The note is made payable to Asher. Asher indorses the note in blank, negotiates it to Paula, and leaves the country. Paula, without indorsement, delivers the note to Bill. Bill, in turn without indorsement, delivers the note to Helen. On Helen's presentment of the note to Martin, the forgery is discovered. Helen can hold Bill (the immediate transferor) liable for breach of warranty that all signatures are genuine. Helen cannot hold Paula liable, because Paula is not Helen's immediate transferor but is a prior nonindorsing transferor. This example shows the importance of the distinction between transfer by indorsement and delivery of order paper and transfer by delivery of bearer paper without indorsement.

Presentment Warranties

Any person who seeks payment or acceptance of a negotiable instrument impliedly warrants to any other person who in good faith pays or accepts the instrument that:

1. The party presenting has good title to the instrument or is authorized to obtain payment or acceptance on behalf of a person who has good title.
2. The party presenting has no knowledge that the signature of the maker or the drawer is unauthorized.
3. The instrument has not been materially altered.

These warranties exist under UCC 3-417(1) and are often referred to as **presentment warranties** because they protect the person to whom the instrument is presented.

The second and third warranties do not apply in certain cases in which the presenter is a holder in due course. It is assumed, for example, that a

---

10. Revised Article 3 separates the two warranties into two sections [RUCC 3-416 and 3-417]. In addition, these warranties cannot be disclaimed with respect to checks, and any claim for breach must be made on the warrantor "within thirty days" after the claimant has reason to know of the breach and the identity of the warrantor. Failure to give notice discharges the warrantor "to the extent of any loss caused by the delay" [RUCC 3-416(c), 3-417(e)].

■ CONCEPT SUMMARY 28.1 Transfer Warranty Liability for Transferors Who Receive Consideration

Types	Persons to Whom Warranties Extend
General indorsers	The five transfer warranties listed below extend to *all* subsequent holders: 1. Transferor has good title or is otherwise authorized to obtain payment or acceptance on behalf of one who does have good title. 2. All signatures are genuine or authorized. 3. Instrument has not been materially altered. 4. No defense of any party is good against transferor. 5. Transferor has no knowledge of insolvency proceedings against the maker, acceptor, or drawer of an unaccepted instrument.
Nonindorsers	Same as for the general indorser, but warranties extend *only* to the *immediate transferee.*
Qualified indorsers	Same as for the general indorser, except that a qualified indorsement (without recourse) limits the fourth warranty to a warranty that indorser has no knowledge of such a defense rather than that there is no defense. The warranties extend to *all* subsequent holders.

drawer or maker will recognize his or her own signature and that a maker or acceptor will recognize whether an instrument has been materially altered.

Both transfer and presentment warranties attempt to shift liability back to a wrongdoer or to the person who dealt face to face with a wrongdoer and thus was in the best position to prevent the wrongdoing.

The following case illustrates an accommodation indorser's possible signature and warranty liability.

BACKGROUND AND FACTS John Bugay came into the possession of a check drawn on the American National Bank to the order of Henry Sherman, Inc. He fraudulently indorsed "Henry Sherman" on the back of the check and asked James Maropoulos to help him cash it. Maropoulos took Bugay to the Oak Park Currency Exchange, Inc., because Maropoulos was known by the personnel of that company. While on the company premises, Maropoulos identified himself and induced the company to cash the check. Oak Park agreed to cash the check only if Maropoulos would indorse it. He did so, received the money, and immediately gave it to Bugay. When Oak Park subsequently indorsed the check and deposited it in the Belmont National Bank, the "Henry Sherman" indorsement was found to be a forgery. Belmont recovered full payment from Oak Park. Oak Park sought reimbursement in an Illinois state court from Maropoulos on his indorsement and for breach of the transfer warranty of good title. At trial, the court directed a verdict in favor of Maropoulos. Oak Park appealed.

Case 28.3

OAK PARK CURRENCY EXCHANGE, INC. v. MAROPOULOS

Appellate Court of Illinois, First District, First Division, 1977.
48 Ill.App.3d 437,
363 N.E.2d 54,
6 Ill.Dec. 525.

DECISION AND RATIONALE The Appellate Court of Illinois affirmed the trial court's verdict in favor of Maropoulos. The court held that Maropoulos was an accommodation indorser under the UCC but that he was not liable because he did not receive timely notice that the check had been presented and dishonored. He was also discharged from liability because American National, the drawee bank, did not dishonor, but paid, the check containing the forged indorsement. The statutory transfer warranty of good title did not apply to Maropoulos as an accommodation indorser. Transfer warranties only apply to transferors who receive consideration, and Maropoulos "received no consideration for his endorsement."

ETHICAL CONSIDERATIONS Because of the relationship between Maropoulos and Oak Park, the latter placed its faith in the former. One might argue that Maropoulos acted unethically.

◼ Discharge

Discharge from liability on an instrument can come from payment, cancellation, or, as previously discussed, material alteration. Discharge can also occur if a party reacquires an instrument, if a holder impairs another party's right of recourse, or if a holder surrenders collateral without consent [UCC 3-601].

Discharge by Payment

According to UCC 3-601(1)(a) and 3-603, all parties to a negotiable instrument will be discharged when the party primarily liable on it pays to a holder the amount due in full.[11] The same is true if the drawee of an unaccepted draft or check makes payment in good faith to the holder. In these situations, all parties on the instruments are usually discharged. By contrast, such payment made by any other party (for example, an indorser) will discharge only the indorser and subsequent parties on the instrument. The party making such a payment still has the right to recover on the instrument from any prior parties.

A party will not be discharged when paying in bad faith to a holder who acquired the instrument by theft or who obtained the instrument from someone else who acquired it by theft (unless, of course, the person has the rights of a holder in due course) [UCC 3-603(1)(a)]. A party who pays on a restric-

tively indorsed instrument cannot claim that he or she is discharged if the payment is made in a manner inconsistent with the terms of the restrictive indorsement [UCC 3-603(1)(b)].

Discharge by Cancellation

The holder of a negotiable instrument can discharge any party to the instrument by cancellation. UCC 3-605(1)(a) explains how cancellation can occur: "The holder of an instrument may even without consideration discharge any party in a manner apparent on the face of the instrument or the indorsement, as by intentionally cancelling the instrument or the party's signature by destruction or mutilation, or by striking out the party's signature." For example, writing the word "Paid" across the face of an instrument constitutes cancellation. Tearing up a negotiable instrument cancels the instrument. Crossing out a party's indorsement cancels that party's liability and the liability of subsequent indorsers who have already indorsed the instrument, but not the liability of any prior parties.

Destruction or mutilation of a negotiable instrument is considered cancellation only if it is done with the intention of eliminating obligation on the instrument [UCC 3-605(1)(a)]. Thus, if destruction or mutilation occurs by accident, the instrument is not discharged, and the original terms can be established by parol evidence [UCC 3-804].

Discharge by Reacquisition

A person who reacquires an instrument that he or she held previously discharges all intervening indorsers against subsequent holders who do not qualify as holders in due course [UCC 3-208, 3-601(3)(a)]. Of course, the person reacquiring the instrument may be liable to subsequent holders.

---

11. This is true even if the payment is made "with knowledge of a claim of another person to the instrument unless prior to such payment or satisfaction the person making the claim either supplies indemnity deemed adequate by the party seeking the discharge or enjoins payment or satisfaction by order of a court of competent jurisdiction in an action in which the adverse claimant and the holder are parties" [UCC 3-603(1)].

Discharge by Impairment of Recourse or of Collateral

Sometimes a party to an instrument posts or gives collateral to secure that his or her performance will occur. When a holder surrenders that collateral without consent of the parties who would benefit from the collateral in the event of nonpayment, those parties to the instrument are discharged [UCC 3-606(1)(b)].

■ Terms and Concepts

acceptor 496

fictitious payee rule 502

imposter 502

presentment warranties 504

signature 495

transfer warranties 504

■ For Review

1. What is the key to liability on a negotiable instrument?
2. Which parties to an instrument are primarily liable?
3. What is the significance of proper presentment, dishonor, and notice of dishonor?
4. Eddie, an employee in the Movietime Concessions Co. accounting department, draws forty checks on Movietime payable to phony suppliers. Eddie forges the names of the suppliers and cashes the checks at River Bank, Movietime's drawee bank. Does Movietime have any recourse against River Bank for the amounts paid?

5. Micky tells Bart that she is Madonna, collecting money for a charity. Bart draws a check payable to "Madonna." Micky forges Madonna's name and cashes the check at Jackson Bank. Is Micky's forgery of Madonna's name effective to pass good title to Jackson? Would it make any difference if Micky had represented instead that she was only working for Madonna?

■ Questions and Case Problems

28-1. On December 1, Daniel drew a check payable to Peter for $100 for services to be rendered on or before January 1. Peter indorsed the check in blank to Smith on December 15 as payment of a debt. Smith was unable to cash the check during the Christmas holidays. Finally, on January 5, he negotiated the check to Harold, without indorsement, as payment for a cord of wood delivered. Peter never performed the services, and Daniel had stopped payment on the check by the time Harold attempted to cash it. Harold contended that he could hold Daniel liable on the check. Daniel claimed that his defense was good against Harold. Discuss the contentions of Daniel and Harold.

28-2. Martin makes out a negotiable promissory note payable to Peter. Peter indorses the note "without recourse, Peter" and transfers it for value to Susan. Susan, in need of cash, negotiates the note to Helen by indorsing it "Pay to Helen, Susan." On the due date, Helen presents the note to Martin for payment, only to learn that Martin has filed for bankruptcy and will have all debts (including the note) discharged in bankruptcy. With these facts, discuss fully whether Helen can hold Martin, Peter, and Susan liable on the note.

28-3. Martin makes out a $500 negotiable promissory note payable to Peter. By special indorsement, Peter transfers the note for value to Susan. By blank indorsement, Susan transfers the note for value to Martha. By special indorsement, Martha transfers the note for value to Harold. In need of cash, Harold transfers the instrument for value by blank indorsement *back* to Susan. When told that Peter has left the country, Susan strikes out Peter's indorsement. Later she learns that Peter is a wealthy restaurant owner in Miami and that Martin is financially unable to pay the note. Susan contends she can hold either Peter, Martha, or Harold liable on the note as an HDC. Discuss fully Susan's contentions.

28-4. Julie Willsted is a purchasing agent for Greenville, Inc., a manufacturer of video tape recorders. Julie has authority to sign checks in payment of purchases made by Greenville. Julie makes out three checks to suppliers and signs each one differently, as follows:

   (a) Greenville, Inc., by Julie Willsted, purchasing agent.

   (b) Julie Willsted, purchasing agent.

   (c) Julie Willsted.

Discuss briefly whether Julie is personally liable on each signature and whether parol evidence is admissible to hold Greenville, Inc., liable.

28-5. Lonny Ledger has been Ann Green's employee accountant for five years. During that time, Green has relied more and more on Ledger to prepare payment checks for suppliers, payroll checks, and the like. Unknown to Green, Ledger is a compulsive gambler and is deeply in debt. Ledger, believing that his life is at stake, prepares two checks payable to nonexistent suppliers. Green signs both checks without knowledge of these events. Ledger indorses both suppliers' names and adds "Pay to Lonny Ledger" above both names. Ledger takes the checks and deposits them at his bank without indorsement. Later, he withdraws the funds from his bank. His bank sends the checks through the collection process. The checks are paid by Green's bank, the drawee. Green discovers Ledger's action after Ledger has left town. Green claims that Ledger's indorsement of the suppliers' names constituted a forgery, that Ledger's bank did not have Ledger's indorsement, and that the bank must therefore recredit her account. Discuss Green's contentions.

28-6. F. Mitchell, assistant treasurer of Travco Corp., caused two checks payable to a fictitious company, L. and B. Distributors, to be drawn on the corporation's account. Mitchell took both checks to his personal bank, indorsed them "F. Mitchell," and gave them to the teller. The teller cashed them. When Travco learned of the embezzlement, it demanded reimbursement from the bank. The bank contended that under the rule concerning fictitious payees and imposters, Mitchell's indorsement was valid and that therefore the bank should be allowed to collect. Discuss whether the bank's contention is true. [*Travco Corp. v. Citizens Federal Savings & Loan Association,* 42 Mich.App. 291, 201 N.W.2d 675 (1972)]

28-7. Mowatt worked as a bookkeeper for the law firm of McCarthy, Kenney & Reidy, P.C., which had several branch offices in the Boston area. Part of Mowatt's job involved preparing checks payable to the partners in other offices for the authorized signature of a partner of the firm. On numerous occasions, Mowatt wrote such checks with no intention of transmitting them to the payee-partners. Instead, after they had been signed by an authorized partner, Mowatt would forge indorsements on the checks and then either cash them or deposit them in one of three bank accounts that he had opened for this purpose. The fraudulent scheme went on for a year and a half, and when the forgeries were finally discovered, the law firm demanded that the bank credit its account with the full amount of loss that it had sustained as a result of the forgeries. The bank refused to do so, and the law firm brought an action against the bank. Which party had to bear the loss arising from the forgeries, the law firm or the drawee bank? Discuss. [*McCarthy, Kenney & Reidy, P.C. v. First National Bank of Boston,* 402 Mass. 630, 524 N.E.2d 390 (1988)]

28-8. Jay Maisel was employed by the city of Phoenix under a program to assist ex-convicts. After five months in a nonsensitive position, Maisel was promoted to a position in which he was responsible for preparing documentation for issuance of warrants (orders authorizing payment from the municipal treasury) to vendors. Six months later, Maisel prepared duplicate claims for which the city issued warrants, each in the amount of $514,320.40, to the order of Duncan Industries. One warrant was sent to the vendor in Chicago, and the other was sent to Maisel's partner, Gary Hann, in Tucson. In the meantime, Hann had set up a checking account at Great Western Bank & Trust in the name of Duncan Industries, telling the bank that the company was a sole proprietorship involved in investments. Hann provided a taxpayer identification number for the business, his social security number, a local telephone number, a local

business address, a post office box number, his driver's license number, and his hospital patient card. Four days after the account had been opened, Hann deposited the fraudulent warrant, which was accepted with a four-day hold to prevent withdrawals prior to payment by the drawee bank. Four days after the warrant had been deposited, Hann began making withdrawals from the account. Within ten days, he had withdrawn over $441,000. Later, the city of Phoenix sued Great Western Bank & Trust to recover for payment of the check, claiming that the bank had been negligent and had acted in bad faith in accepting such a large amount and allowing such a large withdrawal within ten days. The bank claimed that it was protected by the fictitious payee rule. What should the court decide? Discuss. [*City of Phoenix v. Great Western Bank & Trust,* 148 Ariz. 53, 712 P.2d 966 (1985)]

28-9. James Liddell, the president of JHL & Associates, Inc., persuaded Clifford Marston and his wife to invest in Fidelity, a company that Liddell said he represented. To execute the transaction, Liddell had the Marstons issue a check for $15,000 payable to Seattle-First National Bank (Sea-First) for the purpose of obtaining cashier's checks, which would then be sent to Fidelity. Liddell, in Clifford Marston's presence, obtained three cashier's checks payable to "JHL & Associates, Trust." Liddell did not send the checks to Fidelity, but indorsed them to different individuals as part of a fraudulent Ponzi scheme (a scheme in which the perpetrator uses funds of recent investors to pay previous investors—often referred to as pyramiding), signing the indorsements "JHL & Associates." The Marstons sued Sea-First to recover their money, alleging that the bank was liable for the loss because the checks were indorsed by entities other than the named payee (JHL & Associates, Trust). Discuss fully whether Liddell's indorsements were ineffective and whether the bank should be liable to the Marstons. [*Marston Enterprises, Inc. v. Seattle-First National Bank,* 57 Wash.App. 662, 789 P.2d 784 (1990)]

28-10. Case Briefing Assignment

Examine Case A.16 [State v. Skorpen, 57 Wash.App. 144, 787 P.2d 54 (1990)] in Appendix A. The case has been excerpted there in great detail. Review and then brief the case, making sure that you include answers to the following questions in your brief.

1. Why did the issue in this case turn on the value of the forged check?
2. Why did the appellate court hold that the forged check had no value?
3. If the check had no value, how could Skorpen be guilty of theft in any degree? What element of criminal liability had he satisfied, if any?
4. If Skorpen had succeeded in his attempt to cash the forged check at the bank and then disappeared, would Anthony have suffered the $375 loss? Explain.

Chapter 29

Checks and the Banking System

Checks are the most common kind of commercial paper regulated by the Uniform Commercial Code (UCC). Checks, credit cards, and charge accounts are rapidly replacing currency as a means of payment in almost all transactions for goods and services. It is estimated that sixty billion personal and commercial checks are written each year in the United States. Checks are more than a daily convenience; checking account balances are an integral part of the economic system.

This chapter identifies the legal characteristics of checks and the legal duties and liabilities that arise when a check is issued. Then it considers the check deposit-and-collection process—that is, the actual procedure by which checkbook money moves through banking channels, causing the underlying cash dollars to be shifted from bank account to bank account.

Checks are governed by both Article 3 and Article 4 of the UCC. The extent to which any party is either charged with or discharged from liability on a check is established according to the provisions of Article 3. Article 4 is a statement of the principles and rules of modern bank deposit-and-collection procedures. It governs the relationship of banks with one another as they process checks for payment, and it establishes a framework for deposit and checking agreements between a bank and its customers. A check can therefore fall within the scope of Article 3 and yet be subject to the provisions of Article 4 while it is in the course of collection. In the case of a conflict between Articles 3 and 4, Article 4 controls [UCC 4-102(1)].[1]

■ Checks

Recall from Chapter 25 that a **check** is defined as a special type of draft drawn on a *bank*, ordering the bank to pay a sum of money on *demand* [UCC 3-104(2)(b)]. The person who writes the check is called the *drawer* and is

---

1. In 1990, the National Conference of Commissioners on Uniform State Laws and the American Law Institute approved amendments to Article 4. Among those amendments is a definition of the term *bank* as "a person engaged in the business of banking, including a savings bank, savings and loan association, credit union or trust company" [RUCC 4-105(1)]. If one of these institutions does not handle a check for payment or collection, the check is not covered by revised Article 4. As with revised Article 3 (mentioned in Chapter 26), many state legislatures are considering revised Article 4 for adoption. The text of revised Article 4 is included in Appendix C.

usually a depositor in the bank on which the check is drawn. The person to whom the check is payable is the *payee*. The bank or financial institution on which the check is drawn is the *drawee*. If Anne Gordon writes a check from her checking account to pay her school tuition, she is the drawer, her bank is the drawee, and her school is the payee.

The payee can indorse the check to another person, thereby making that receiver a holder. Recall that a holder is a person who is in rightful possession of an instrument that is drawn to that person's order (or drawn to bearer) or that is indorsed to that person (or in blank) [UCC 1-201(20)]. The *payee as a holder* of a check has the right to transfer or negotiate it or to demand its payment in his or her own name, *as does any subsequent holder.*

A check does not, in and of itself, operate as an assignment of funds [UCC 3-409(1)]. The drawee bank is not liable to a payee or holder who presents the check for payment, even though the drawer has sufficient funds to pay the check. The payee's, or holder's, only recourse is against the drawer. (The drawer, however, may subsequently hold the bank liable for its wrongful refusal to pay.)

Between the time a check is drawn and the time it reaches the drawee, the effectiveness of the check may be altered by some event—for example, the drawer may die or order payment not to be made, or the account on which the check is drawn may

be depleted. To avoid this problem, a payee may insist on payment by an instrument that has already been accepted. Such an instrument may be a cashier's check, a traveler's check, or a certified check.

Cashier's Checks

Checks are usually three-party instruments, but on certain types of checks, the bank can serve as both the drawer and the drawee. For example, when a bank draws a check on itself, the check is called a **cashier's check** and is a negotiable instrument on issue. (See Exhibit 29–1.) In effect, with a cashier's check, the bank lends its credit to the purchaser of the check, thus making it available for immediate use in banking circles. A cashier's check is therefore an acknowledgment of a debt drawn by the bank on itself.

Traveler's Checks

A **traveler's check** has the characteristics of a cashier's check. It is an instrument on which a financial institution is both the drawer and the drawee. The institution is directly obligated to accept and pay its traveler's check according to the instrument's terms. The purchaser must provide his or her authorized signature on the traveler's check at the time it is bought and when it is used. (See Exhibit 29–2.)

■ **Exhibit 29–1 A Cashier's Check**

■ **Exhibit 29–2 A Traveler's Check**

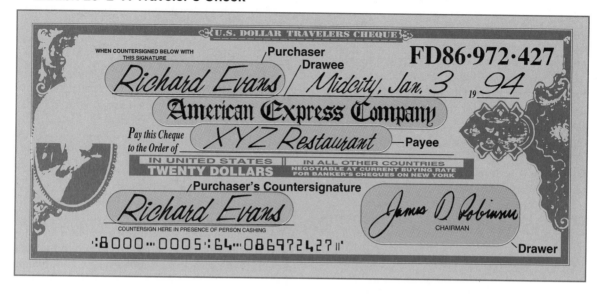

Certified Checks

A **certified check** is sometimes used to ensure against dishonor for insufficient funds. When a drawee bank agrees to certify a check, it immediately charges the drawer's account with the amount of the check and transfers those funds to its own certified check account. In effect, the bank is agreeing in advance to accept that check when it is presented for payment and to make payment from those funds reserved in the certified check account [UCC 3-411(1)]. Essentially, certification prevents the bank from denying liability. It is a promise that sufficient funds are on deposit and *have been set aside* to cover the check. A drawee bank is not obligated to certify a check, and failure to do so is not a dishonor of the check [UCC 3-411(2)]. Sometimes, certified checks (or cashier's checks) are the required form of payment under state law—for example, in purchases at a sheriff's sale. Exhibit 29–3 illustrates a sample certified check.

Certification can be requested by a holder, as well as the drawer. The legal liability of the drawer

■ **Exhibit 29–3 A Certified Check**

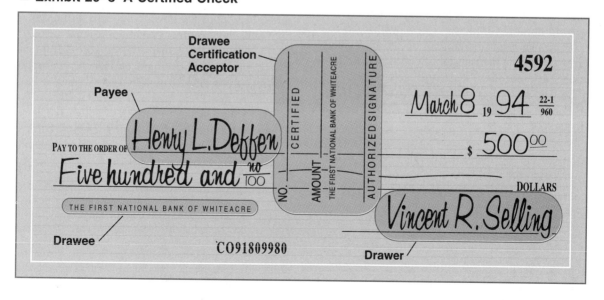

varies on the basis of whether the certification is requested by the drawer or the holder. The drawer who obtains certification remains *secondarily liable* on the instrument if for some reason the certifying bank cannot or does not honor the check when it is presented for payment. If the check is certified at the request of the holder, then the drawer and any indorsers prior to certification are completely discharged. A holder's request for certification is viewed as a choice of the bank's promise to pay over the drawer's and any indorser's promises. In this situation, the holder can look only to the bank for payment.[2]

■ The Bank-Customer Relationship

The bank-customer relationship begins when the customer opens a checking account and deposits money that will be used to pay for checks written. The rights and duties of the bank and the customer are contractual and depend on the nature of the transaction.

A creditor-debtor relationship is created between a customer and a bank when, for example, the customer makes cash deposits into a checking account or when final payment is received for checks drawn on other banks. (Creditor-debtor relationships generally are discussed in Chapters 31–34.)

A principal-agent relationship underlies the check collection process. A check does not operate as an immediate legal assignment of funds between the drawer and the payee [UCC 3-409]. The money in the bank represented by that check does not move from the drawer's account to the payee's account; nor is any underlying debt discharged until the drawee bank honors the check and makes final payment. In the transfer of checkbook dollars among different banks, each bank acts as the agent of collection for its customer [UCC 4-201(1)]. (Agency relationships generally are discussed in Chapters 35 and 36.)

A commercial bank serves its customers primarily in the following two ways, each of which is discussed in detail below:

1. By honoring checks for the withdrawal of funds on deposit in its customers' accounts.

2. By accepting deposits in U.S. currency and collecting checks written to or indorsed to its customers that are drawn on other banks.

■ Honoring Checks

When a commercial bank provides checking services, it agrees to honor the checks written by its customers with the usual stipulation that there be sufficient funds available in the account to pay each check. When a drawee bank *wrongfully* fails to honor a check, it is liable to its customer for damages resulting from its refusal to pay. The UCC does not attempt to specify the theory under which the customer may recover for wrongful dishonor; it merely states that the drawee is liable. Thus, the drawer-customer does not have to prove that the drawee bank breached its contractual commitment, or slandered the customer's credit, or was negligent [UCC 4-402]. When the bank properly dishonors a check for insufficient funds, it has no liability to the customer.[3]

On the other hand, a bank may charge against a customer's account an *overdraft*—that is, a check that is paid from that account even though the account contains insufficient funds to cover the check [UCC 4-401(1)]. Once a bank makes special arrangements with its customer to accept overdrafts on an account, the payor bank can become liable to its customer for damages proximately caused by its wrongful dishonor of overdrafts. Overdrafts are discussed later in this chapter.

The customer's agreement with the bank includes a general obligation to keep sufficient money on deposit to cover all checks written. In a civil suit, the customer is liable to the payee or to the holder of a check that is not honored. If intent to defraud can be proved, the customer can also be subject to criminal prosecution for writing a bad check.

The following case illustrates that when a bank agrees with a customer to pay overdrafts, the bank's refusal to honor checks on an overdrawn account is a wrongful dishonor.

---

2. A number of legal issues have arisen over cashier's, teller's, and certified checks that are lost, stolen, or destroyed and the liability of a drawee who wrongfully refuses to make payment. Revised Article 3 addresses some of the issues in RUCC 3-312 and 3-411.

3. Banks usually determine whether an account has sufficient funds to pay an item at the end of the banking day. What if a customer deposits sufficient funds to pay the check before the check is returned dishonored (before the bank's midnight deadline)? Revised Article 4 makes it clear that the bank does not need to make a second determiniation of a customer's account balance and thus is not liable for wrongful dishonor [RUCC 4-402(c)].

BACKGROUND AND FACTS Lawrence and Linda Kendall were officers and principal shareholders of Kendall Yacht Corporation, which built yachts on special order from customers. The corporation, which had never issued stock, needed operating funds. The corporation had a payroll checking account and a general business checking account with United California Bank. Mr. Kendall spoke with Ron Lamperts, a loan officer at the bank, to obtain financing. The bank agreed to honor overdrafts on the corporate accounts until the corporation was financially more stable. The Kendalls continued to write checks for supplies, payroll, and other corporate operating expenses from about mid-October through December. The corporate accounts were by then badly overdrawn, and a number of checks had been dishonored, resulting in several criminal prosecutions against them. The Kendalls' business failed, and they sued the bank in a California state court, charging that the bank's wrongful dishonor of checks that it had initially agreed to accept as overdrafts had damaged the Kendalls' personal and credit reputation. The trial court issued a judgment in the Kendalls' favor, and the bank appealed.

Case 29.1

KENDALL YACHT CORP. v. UNITED CALIFORNIA BANK

Court of Appeal of California, Fourth District, Division 2, 1975.
50 Cal.App.3d 949,
123 Cal.Rptr. 848.

DECISION AND RATIONALE The Court of Appeal of California affirmed the trial court's ruling, awarding the Kendalls $26,000 each as compensatory damages for the bank's wrongful dishonor of the checks. The court rejected the bank's argument that the wrongful dishonor of a corporate check does not give rise to a cause of action for damages to individual officers and shareholders of the corporation. The court focused on UCC 4-402, which states: "A payor bank is liable to its customer for damages proximately caused by the wrongful dishonor of an item. When the dishonor occurs through mistake liability is limited to actual damages proved." The court declared that, after the bank agreed to accept overdrafts, it "was entirely foreseeable that the Bank's dishonoring of the Corporation's checks would reflect on the personal credit and reputation of the Kendalls and that they would suffer the adverse personal consequences which resulted when the Bank reneged on its commitments."

Stale Checks

The bank's responsibility to honor its customers' checks is not absolute. A bank is not obliged to pay an uncertified check presented more than six months from its date [UCC 4-404]. Commercial banking practice regards a check outstanding for longer than six months as a **stale check.** UCC 4-404 gives a bank the option of paying or not paying on a stale check. The usual banking practice is to consult the customer, but if a bank pays in good faith without consulting the customer, it has the right to charge the customer's account for the amount of the check. In the following case, a bank's payment of a stale check is at issue. The court's discussion of this issue is illustrative.

BACKGROUND AND FACTS Granite Equipment Leasing Corporation issued a check to Overseas Equipment Company. After five days, Overseas indicated that the check had not been received. Granite ordered payment on the check stopped and wired the funds to Overseas. Approximately one year later, the check cleared, and Granite's account was charged. Granite sued the bank in a New York state court for return of the funds to its account, maintaining that the bank had a duty to inquire into the circumstances of the stale check. The bank argued that the stop-payment order had expired and that it had acted in good faith in honoring the check.

Case 29.2

GRANITE EQUIPMENT LEASING CORP. v. HEMPSTEAD BANK

Supreme Court of New York, Trial Term, Nassau County, Part VII, 1971.
68 Misc.2d 350,
326 N.Y.S.2d 881.

DECISION AND RATIONALE The New York Supreme Court, Trial Term, ruled that the bank had acted in good faith even though the check was clearly stale and the stop-payment order was properly given at the outset. The court noted that UCC 4-403 provides that a written stop order is effective for only six months unless renewed in writing. Because more than a year had passed and the stop-payment order had not been renewed in writing, it was no longer effective. As to the payment of a stale check, the court reasoned that the bank was not required to "inquire into the circumstances of that stale check." Granite had failed to renew the stop-payment order, and the bank was not obligated to search its records to discover old, lapsed stop-payment orders. Thus, "[i]n the absence of any facts which could justify a finding of dishonesty, bad faith, recklessness, or lack of ordinary care," the court ruled that payment was made in good faith.

Missing Indorsements

Banking institutions are allowed to supply any necessary indorsements of a customer. (This rule does not apply if the item expressly requires the payee's indorsement.) The bank places a statement on the item to the effect that it was deposited by a customer or credited to that customer's account [UCC 4-205(1)].

Death or Incompetence of a Customer

UCC 4-405 provides that if, at the time a check is issued or its collection has been undertaken, a bank does *not know* of the death of its customer or of an adjudication of incompetence, a check can be paid and the bank will not incur liability. Neither death nor incompetence revokes the bank's authority to pay an item until the bank knows of the situation and has had reasonable time to act. Even when a bank *knows* of the death of its customer, for ten days after the date of death, it can pay or certify checks drawn on or prior to the date of death—unless a person claiming an interest in that account, such as an heir or an executor of the estate, orders the bank to stop all payment. Without this provision, banks would constantly be required to verify the continued life and competence of their drawers.

Stop-Payment Orders

Only a customer—or, if a customer is deceased, any person claiming an interest in the account—can order the customer's bank to pay a check, and only a customer can order payment to be stopped. This right does not extend to holders—that is, payees or indorsees—because the drawee bank's contract is only with its drawers. A customer has no right to stop payment on a check that has been certified or that has been accepted by a bank.[4] A **stop-payment order** must be received within a reasonable time and in a reasonable manner to permit the bank to act on it [UCC 4-403(1)].

A stop-payment order can be given orally, usually by phone.[5] An oral order is binding on the bank for only fourteen calendar days unless confirmed in writing. (See Exhibit 29–4.) A written stop-payment order or an oral order confirmed in writing is effective for six months only, unless renewed in writing [UCC 4-403(2)]. If the stop-payment order is not renewed, the check can be properly cashed, even though it is a stale check.

Should the drawee bank pay the check over the customer's properly instituted stop-payment order, the bank will be obligated to recredit the account of the drawer customer. The bank, however, is liable for no more than the actual loss suffered by the drawer because of the wrongful payment.

For example, suppose Pat Davis orders one hundred used typewriters at $50 each from Jane Greer. Davis pays in advance for the goods with her check for $5,000. Later that day, Greer tells Davis that she is not going to deliver any typewriters. Davis immediately calls her bank and stops payment on the check. Two days later, in spite of this stop-payment order, the bank inadvertently honors Davis's $5,000 check to Greer for the undelivered typewriters. The bank will be liable to Davis for the full $5,000.

---

4. See RUCC 4-405(b).
5. Some states do not recognize oral stop-payment orders; they must be in writing.

■ **Exhibit 29–4 A Stop-Payment Order**

Bank of America

Checking Account
Stop Payment Order

BANK USE ONLY

To: Bank of America NT&SA
I want to stop payment on the following check(s).

ACCOUNT NUMBER: ☐☐☐☐☐ — ☐☐☐☐

SPECIFIC STOP

*ENTER DOLLAR AMOUNT: _____   *CHECK NUMBER: _____

THE CHECK WAS SIGNED BY: _____

THE CHECK IS PAYABLE TO: _____

THE REASON FOR THIS STOP PAYMENT IS: _____

STOP RANGE (Use for lost or stolen check(s) only.)

DOLLAR AMOUNT: 000

*ENTER STARTING CHECK NUMBER: _____   *END CHECK NUMBER: _____

THE REASON FOR THIS STOP PAYMENT IS: _____

I agree that this order (1) is effective only if the above check(s) has (have) not yet been cashed or paid against my account, (2) will end six months from the date it is delivered to you unless I renew it in writing, and (3) is not valid if the check(s) was (were) accepted on the strength of my Bank of America courtesy-check guarantee card by a merchant participating in that program. I also agree (1) to notify you immediately to cancel this order if the reason for the stop payment no longer exists or (2) that closing the account on which the check(s) is (are) drawn automatically cancels this order.

(Optional—please circle one: Mr., Ms., Mrs., Miss)   CUSTOMER'S SIGNATURE X _____ DATE _____

TRANCODE:
☐ 21—ENTER STOP PAYMENT (SEE OTHER SIDE TO REMOVE)

NON READS: _____
UNPROC. STMT HIST: _____
PRIOR STMT CYCLE: _____
HOLDS ON COOLS: _____
REJECTED CHKS: _____
LARGE ITEMS: _____
FEE COLLECTED: _____
DATE ACCEPTED: _____
TIME ACCEPTED: _____

IF ANOTHER BRANCH OF THIS BANK OR ANOTHER PERSON OR ENTITY BECOMES A "HOLDER IN DUE COURS" OF THE ABOVE CHECK, I UNDERSTAND THAT PAYMENT MAY BE ENFORCED AGAINST THE CHECK'S MAKER (SIGNER).

*I CERTIFY THE AMOUNT AND CHECK NUMBER(S) ABOVE ARE CORRECT.
☐ I have written a replacement check (number and date of check).

The result would be different if Greer had delivered ninety-nine typewriters. Because Davis would have owed Greer $4,950 for the goods delivered, she would have been able to establish actual losses of only $50 resulting from the bank's payment over her stop-payment order. The bank would be liable to Davis for only $50.

A stop-payment order has its risks for a customer. The drawer must have a *valid legal ground* for issuing such an order; otherwise the holder can sue the drawer for payment. Moreover, defenses sufficient to prevent payment against a payee may not be valid grounds to prevent payment against a subsequent holder in due course [UCC 3-305]. A person who wrongfully stops payment on a check will not only be liable to the payee for the amount of the check but may also be liable for *special damages* resulting from the wrongful order. Special damages, however, must be separately pleaded and proved at trial.

Cashier's checks, which were defined earlier in this chapter, are sometimes used in the business community as nearly the equivalent of cash. Except in very limited circumstances, payment will not be stopped on a cashier's check—once it has been issued by a bank, the bank must honor it when it is presented for payment.[6] But what if, after issuing a cashier's check, the bank learns that the check was procured from the purchaser through fraud? May the bank stop payment on its check in such circumstances? This is the issue before the court in the following case.

6. Revised Article 3 considerably increases the acceptability of cashier's, certified, and teller's checks by allowing a holder to recover from a bank for wrongful dishonor all expenses incurred, interest, and consequential damages [RUCC 3-411].

BACKGROUND AND FACTS   Clara Lamstein owned a business firm, the primary "business" of which was an illegal pyramid scheme (in which payments made by current investors are used to pay previous investors and no bona fide business exists). The business was closed by the state of Florida and placed in the hands of a receiver (a person appointed by a court to wind up the affairs of a business), William Rishoi. When the business was closed, Lamstein had in her possession $100,000 in uncashed cashier's checks, which had been delivered to her by the Crosbys—who

Case 29.3

FIRST AMERICAN BANK AND TRUST v. RISHOI

District Court of Appeal of Florida, Fifth District, 1990.
553 So.2d 1387.

had been fraudulently induced by Lamstein to make a number of investments. The Crosbys requested the issuing bank, First American Bank and Trust, to stop payment on the outstanding checks. When the checks were presented for payment and dishonored, Rishoi sued First American in a Florida state court, claiming that the bank had improperly refused to honor the checks. The trial court granted summary judgment in favor of Rishoi, and the bank appealed.

DECISION AND RATIONALE   The District Court of Appeal of Florida ruled that Rishoi was a holder in due course and thus took the checks subject only to the bank's defenses against payment and not to the Crosbys' personal defenses against payment. Only the drawer of a check has a right to stop payment, and the drawer must have a legal reason for doing so. A cashier's check is a check drawn by a bank on itself. Thus, only the bank has a right to stop payment. The court held that "upon presentment of payment by a holder, a bank may only assert its real and personal defenses in order to refuse payment on a cashier's check issued by the bank," not the defenses of third parties. The court concluded that Rishoi was a legitimate holder and affirmed the trial court's ruling, finding that the bank had wrongfully dishonored its own obligation and was, as a result, liable for payment to Rishoi.

ETHICAL CONSIDERATIONS   The issue raised by this case is an ethically perplexing one because it brings into conflict two fundamental ethical principles underlying commercial paper law—to protect against fraud on the one hand and to encourage the free flow of commerce on the other. The bank argued in this case that, on public policy grounds, it should be able to assist its customer by stopping payment on a cashier's check that had been obtained from the customer by a criminal act. A minority of courts would agree, on the theory that a cashier's check (because the bank draws it on itself) is a note. The court in the case above represents the majority view—that cashier's checks, as the next-best thing to cash, play a significant role in the business community by furthering certainty in commercial transactions. To preserve their cash-equivalent function, cashier's checks should be considered analogous to certified checks (which prohibit customers from issuing stop-payment orders) and dishonored only in extremely limited circumstances.

Overdrafts

As mentioned previously, when the bank receives an item properly payable from its customer's checking account but there are insufficient funds in the account to cover the amount of the check, the bank can either dishonor the item or pay the item and charge the customer's account, creating an overdraft [UCC 4-401(1)].[7] The bank can subtract the difference from the customer's next deposit because the check carries with it an enforceable implied promise to reimburse the bank.

---

7.   Revised Article 4 only permits payments creating overdrafts if the customer has authorized the payment and it does not violate any bank-customer agreement [RUCC 4-401(a)]. Also, if there is a joint account, the bank cannot hold any joint-account customer liable for payment of an overdraft unless the customer has signed the item or has benefitted from the proceeds of the item [RUCC 4-401(b)]. Lastly, a bank can pay a postdated check without liability unless the customer has properly notified the bank not to do so until the stated date. This is necessary because the automated check-collection system cannot accommodate the postdating of checks [RUCC 4-401(c)].

When a check "bounces," a holder can resubmit the check, hoping that at a later date sufficient funds will be available to pay it. The holder must notify any indorsers on the check of the first dishonor; otherwise they will be discharged from their signature liability.

Payment on a Forged Signature of the Drawer

A forged signature on a check has no legal effect as the signature of a drawer [UCC 3-404(1)]. Banks require signature cards from each customer who opens a checking account. The bank is responsible for determining whether the signature on a customer's check is genuine. The general rule is that the bank must recredit the customer's account when it pays on a forged signature.

The bank has no right to recover from a holder who, without knowledge, cashes a check bearing a forged drawer's signature. The holder merely guarantees that he or she has no knowledge that the signature of the drawer is unauthorized. Unless the bank can prove that the holder has such knowledge, its only recourse is against the forger [UCC 3-418, 4-207(1)(b)].

CUSTOMER NEGLIGENCE   When the customer's negligence substantially contributes to the forgery, the bank will not normally be obliged to recredit the customer's account for the amount of the check. Suppose Axelrod Corporation uses a mechanical check-writing machine to write its payroll and business checks. Axelrod discovers that one of its employees used the machine to write himself a check for $10,000 and that the bank subsequently honored it. Axelrod requests the bank to recredit $10,000 to its account for incorrectly paying on a forged check. If the bank can show that Axelrod failed to take reasonable care in controlling access to the check-writing equipment, Axelrod cannot require the bank to recredit its account for the amount of the forged check [UCC 3-406].[8]

TIMELY EXAMINATION REQUIRED   A customer has an *affirmative duty* to examine monthly statements and canceled checks promptly and with reasonable care and to report any forged signatures promptly [UCC 4-406(1)].[9] This includes forged signatures of indorsers, to be discussed later [UCC 4-406].

Failure to examine and report, or any carelessness by the customer that results in a loss to the bank, makes the customer liable for the loss [UCC 4-406(2)(a)]. Even if the customer can prove that reasonable care was taken against forgeries, the UCC provides that unless discovery of such forgeries and notice to the bank takes place within specific time frames the customer cannot require the bank to recredit his or her account.

Suppose a series of forgeries of the same signature is committed by the same wrongdoer. The UCC provides that the customer, to recover for all the forged items, must discover and report the forgery to the bank within fourteen calendar days of the receipt of the bank statement and canceled checks that contain the first forged item [UCC 4-406(2)(b)].[10] Failure to notify within this period of time discharges the bank's liability for all similar forged checks that were paid by the bank prior to notification, unless the customer can establish that the bank failed to exercise ordinary care in paying the checks.[11]

For example, Middletown Bank sends out monthly statements and canceled checks on the last day of each month. Bradley, owner of a small store,

---

8.   Under Revised Article 3, this liability may be reduced by any amount of loss caused by the negligence on the part of a person paying the instrument or taking it for value or for collection [RUCC 3-406(b)].

9.   Revised Article 4 recognizes modern automated check-clearing procedures by truncation (presentment by electronic means). All that is required is that either the items (canceled checks) be returned or that the bank provide the customer with information to reasonably identify the items paid (item number, amount, date of payment) and maintain ability to furnish legible copies of the items upon the request of the customer for a period of seven years [RUCC 4-406(a),(b)].

10.   Revised Article 4 extends the fourteen-day requirement for examining and reporting to *thirty* days [RUCC 4-406(d)(2)].

11.   Under Revised Article 4, when both the customer failed to report promptly and the bank failed to exercise ordinary care in paying the check(s), a comparative-negligence allocation for the loss will be made [RUCC 4-406(e)]. Revised Articles 3 and 4 define *ordinary care* to mean the "observance of reasonable commercial standards, prevailing in the area in which [a] person is located, with respect to the business in which that person is engaged" [RUCC 3-103(a)(7), 4-104(c)]. In the case of a bank, reasonable commercial standards do not require the bank to examine all customers' checks if the failure to examine does not violate the bank's prescribed procedures and the procedures do not vary unreasonably from general banking usage.

Stop-payment orders should not be misused by a drawer for a variety of reasons. There is clearly the monetary reason because banks charge for your stop-payment order. These charges are not small in relation to checks written for small amounts.

There are other risks attached to the issuing of a stop-payment order for any drawer-customer. First, the bank is entitled to take a reasonable amount of time to enforce your stop order before it has liability for improper payment. Hence, it is possible that although you have made an oral or written stop-payment order, the payee or holder may still be able to cash the check if he or she acts quickly. Indeed, you could be writing out a stop order in the bank lobby and have the payee or holder cash the check in the drive-in facility next door at the same time.

Second, each drawer must have a legal reason for issuing a stop-payment order. Any wrongful stop order subjects the drawer to liability to the payee or a holder. This liability may include special damages that resulted because of the order.

When all is considered, care must be taken before rushing to the telephone or to the bank to stop payment on a check because of a minor dispute with the payee.

---

unknowingly has had a number of his blank checks stolen by employee Harry. On April 20, Harry forges Bradley's signature and cashes check number 1. On April 22, Harry forges Bradley's signature and cashes check number 2. The checks canceled in April (including the forged ones) and the April statement from the Middletown Bank are received on May 1. Bradley sets aside the statement and does not reconcile his checking account. On May 20 Harry forges Bradley's signature and cashes check number 3. The checks canceled in May and the May statement are received by Bradley on June 1. Bradley immediately examines both statements, discovers the forgeries, and demands that the bank recredit his account for *all* forged checks.

Must the bank do so? The answer is no, assuming the bank was not negligent in paying the forged checks [UCC 4-406(3)]. The two forged checks in April were made available to Bradley for inspection on May 1. Liability for any forged check in this series fell on Bradley after May 15 (fourteen days after receipt of the April statement). In addition, if Bradley's negligence in failing to examine his April statement promptly resulted in a loss to the Middletown Bank, the bank's liability to re-credit Bradley's account for any forged item would be reduced by the amount of this loss.

Had Bradley examined his April statement immediately on receipt and reported the two April forgeries, the bank would have been obligated to fully recredit Bradley's account. If the bank could have proved that Bradley's carelessness in permitting the blank checks to be stolen substantially contributed to the forgery, however, Bradley—not the bank—would have been liable [UCC 3-406, 4-406].

Regardless of the degree of care exercised by the customer or the bank, the UCC places an absolute time limit on the liability of a bank for forged customer signatures. UCC 4-406(4) provides that a customer who has not reported his or her forged signature one year from the date that the statement and canceled checks were made available for inspection loses the legal right to have the bank re-credit his or her account.

In the following case, the customer's duty to discover and report an unauthorized signature was at issue.

BACKGROUND AND FACTS Ossip-Harris Insurance Company maintained a checking account with Barnett Bank of South Florida, N.A., during 1980 and 1981. From May 1980 through June 1981, Ossip's bookkeeper, Dorothy Edgerly, used a facsimile signature stamp to forge the name of Ossip's president, Edward Harris, to ninety-nine checks totaling $19,711.90. When the canceled checks came back to Ossip, Edgerly would replace the payee name (her own name or the name of one of her creditors) with one that represented a legitimate Ossip business expense. Throughout this period, Harris periodically reviewed the monthly statements and canceled checks but did not detect the forgeries until June 1981. At that time, Harris notified Barnett, and no further forged instruments were paid by Barnett. In its suit against Barnett in a Florida state court, Ossip alleged that Barnett wrongfully paid the ninety-nine checks drawn on Ossip's account, but the trial court entered a summary judgment in favor of Barnett. Ossip appealed the summary judgment.

DECISION AND RATIONALE The District Court of Appeal of Florida sustained the summary judgment entered by the trial court, holding that Ossip could not recover the $19,711.90 paid out of its account by Barnett Bank. The appellate court focused on UCC 4-406(1) through (3) regarding a customer's duty to "exercise reasonable care and promptness" in examining bank statements to discover any unauthorized signatures or alterations and report the unauthorized signatures to the bank. In particular, the court noted that under UCC 4-406(2)(b), a reasonable period for a series of forgeries by the same wrongdoer is fourteen calendar days from the time the first item and statement were made available to the customer. Unless the bank is negligent, the customer's failure to examine the statement and items or to notify the bank of any discovered unauthorized signatures discharges the bank of liability. Although Ossip received bank statements from Barnett each month, Harris admitted that he did not actually review the signatures on all canceled checks but was more concerned with the amounts and purposes for which the checks were issued. Consequently, Harris did not comply with the state statute requiring prompt and reasonable examination for unauthorized signatures, and Harris failed to give Barnett reasonable notice of any wrongdoing after the first statement and canceled unauthorized checks were returned to Ossip. The court concluded that Ossip's argument that Barnett was negligent in not discovering the forgery was offset by the fact that Harris failed to discover the forgery of his own signature.

ETHICAL CONSIDERATIONS This case illustrates a basic ethical precept underlying the UCC—that parties who are themselves negligent should not look to the law for protection. In this case, Ossip-Harris might have prevented the problem by more selective hiring policies or by more careful monitoring of employee performance. Ossip-Harris also could have limited its losses by exercising greater care in reviewing the bank statements and canceled checks. Needless to say, this case also illustrates the importance of reconciling your bank statement promptly and notifying your bank of any alterations or unauthorized signatures.

Case 29.4

OSSIP-HARRIS INSURANCE CO. v. BARNETT BANK OF SOUTH FLORIDA, N.A.
District Court of Appeal of Florida, Third District, 1983.
428 So.2d 363.

Payment on a Forged Indorsement

A bank that pays a customer's check bearing a forged indorsement must recredit the customer's account or be liable to the drawer-customer for breach of contract. For example, Baker issues a $50 check "to the order of Thelma Posner." Larry steals the check, forges Posner's indorsement, and cashes the check. When the check reaches Baker's bank, the bank pays it and debits Baker's account. Under UCC 4-401, the bank must recredit Baker's account $50 because it failed to carry out Baker's order to pay "to the order of Thelma Posner." Baker's bank will in turn recover—under breach of warranty principles—from the bank that cashed the check [UCC 4-207(1)(a)].

Eventually, the loss usually falls on the first party to take the instrument bearing the forged indorsement because, as discussed in Chapter 28, a forged indorsement does not transfer title. Thus, whoever takes an instrument with a forged indorsement cannot become a holder.

The customer, in any case, has a duty to examine the returned checks and statements received by the bank and to report forged indorsements upon discovery or notice. Failure to report forged indorsements within a three-year period after the items containing the forgeries have been made available to the customer relieves the bank of liability [UCC 4-406(4)].[12]

Payment on an Altered Check

The customer's instruction to the bank is to pay the exact amount on the face of the check to the holder. The bank must examine each check before making final payment. If it fails to detect an alteration, it is liable to its customer for the loss because it did not pay as the drawer-customer ordered. The loss is the difference between the original amount of the check and the amount actually paid. Suppose a check written for $11 is altered to read $111 and the drawee bank fails to detect the alteration and pays the $111. The bank may charge the customer's account for only $11 (the amount the customer ordered it to pay) [UCC 4-401(2)(a)].

The bank may recover the remaining $100 from the party who presented the check for payment[13] on the ground of breach of the presentment warranty that the instrument has not been altered. If the bank is the drawer, however, it cannot recover on this ground from the presenting party, if the party is an HDC acting in good faith [UCC 3-417(1)(c), 4-207(1)(c)]. The reason is that an instrument's drawer is in a better position than an HDC to know whether the instrument has been altered.

Similarly, when an HDC, acting in good faith, presents a certified check for payment to the certifier of the check, the HDC does not warrant that it was not altered before the HDC acquired it, whether the alteration occurred before or after the certification [UCC 3-417(1)(c), 4-207(1)(c)]. For example, Selling, the drawer, draws a check for $500 payable to Deffen, the payee. Deffen alters the amount to $5,000. The First National Bank of Whiteacre, the drawee, certifies the check for $5,000. Deffen negotiates the check to Evans, an HDC. The drawee-bank pays Evans $5,000. On discovering the mistake, the bank cannot recover from Evans the $4,500 paid by mistake, even though the bank was not in a superior position to detect the alteration. This is in accord with the purpose of certification, which is to obtain the definite obligation of a bank to honor a definite instrument. If it is the HDC who obtains certification, however, the HDC gives the same warranties as anyone else and may be held liable if the instrument is altered before it is presented for payment.

A customer's negligence can shift the risk of loss. A common example occurs when a person carelessly writes a check, leaving large gaps around the numbers and words so that additional numbers and words can be inserted. (See, for example, Exhibit 29–5.)

Similarly, a person who signs a check and leaves the dollar amount for someone else to fill in is barred from protesting when the bank unknowingly and in good faith pays whatever amount is shown [UCC 4-401(2)(b)]. Finally, if the bank

---

12. Revised Article 4 deletes the three-year limitation for reporting unauthorized indorsements [RUCC 4-406]. Revised Article 4, however, has added a new section [RUCC 4-411], called "Statute of Limitations," which provides that "[a]n action to enforce an obligation, duty, or right arising under this Article must be commenced within three years after the [cause of action] accrues." Thus, the drawer or customer still has a three-year period to seek credit for an instrument bearing an unauthorized indorsement that was paid by the bank.

---

13. Usually, the party presenting an instrument for payment is a bank's customer or a collecting bank. A bank's customers include its account holders, which may include other banks [UCC 4-104(1)(e)]. A collecting bank is any bank handling an item for collection except the payor bank [UCC 4-105(d)].

■ **Exhibit 29–5 A Poorly Filled Out Check**

XYZ CORPORATION
10 INDUSTRIAL PARK
ST. PAUL, MN 55165

2206

June 8 19 94   22-1
960

Pay to the order of   *John Doe* $ *100.00*

One hundred and no/100 ———————— DOLLARS

THE FIRST NATIONAL BANK OF MYTOWN
332 MINNESOTA STREET
MYTOWN, MINNESOTA 55555

Stephanie Roe

⑂94⑂77577⑂ 0885

can trace its loss on successive altered checks to the customer's failure to discover the initial alteration, then the bank can alleviate its liability reimbursing the customer's account[14] [UCC 4-406]. The law governing the customer's duty to examine monthly statements and canceled checks and to discover and report alterations to the drawee bank is the same as that applied to forged customer signatures.

In every situation involving a forged drawer's signature or an alteration, a bank must observe reasonable commercial standards of care in paying on a customer's checks [UCC 4-406(3)]. The customer's contributory negligence can be asserted only if the bank has exercised ordinary care.

■ **Accepting Deposits**

A second fundamental service a commercial bank provides for its checking account customers is to accept deposits of cash and checks. Cash deposits made in U.S. currency are received into the customer's account without being subject to further collection procedures. As a matter of routine, banks

provisionally credit a customer's account for an item when it is first deposited. More than 99 percent of these items are paid, and the credits become final. In cases in which items are not finally paid, banks are allowed to charge back to customers' accounts the amounts that were provisionally paid [UCC 4-212].

This section focuses on what happens to checks after they have been deposited. In most situations, deposited checks have come from parties who do business at different banks, but sometimes checks are written between customers of the same bank. Either situation brings into play the bank collection process as it operates within the statutory framework of Article 4 of the UCC.

Definitions

The first bank to receive a check for payment is the **depositary bank.**[15] When a person deposits his or her IRS tax refund check into a personal checking account at the local bank, that bank acts as a depositary bank. The bank on which a check is drawn (the drawee bank) is called the **payor bank.** Any bank except the payor bank that handles a check during some phase of the collection process is a **collecting bank.** Any bank except the payor bank or depositary bank to which an item is trans-

---

14.   The bank's defense is the same whether successive payments were made on a forged drawer's signature or an altered check. The bank must prove that prompt notice would have prevented its loss. For example, notification might have alerted the bank not to pay further items or enabled it to catch the forger.

---

15.   All definitions in this section are found in UCC 4-105 and RUCC 4-105.

■ CONCEPT SUMMARY 29.1   Bank-Customer Relationships

Situation	Basic Rules
Bank's charge against customer's account [UCC 4-401]	The bank has the right to charge a customer's account for any item properly payable even if the charge results in an overdraft.
Wrongful dishonor [UCC 4-402]	The bank is liable to its customer for wrongful dishonor due to mistake for actual damages proved. Damages can include those proximately caused by consequent arrest or prosecution, as well as other consequential damages.
Stop-payment order [UCC 4-403]	The customer must make a stop-payment order in time for the bank to have a reasonable opportunity to act. Oral orders are binding for only fourteen days unless they are confirmed in writing. Written orders are effective for only six months, unless renewed in writing. The bank is liable for wrongful payment over a timely stop-payment order.
Stale check [UCC 4-404]	The bank is not obligated to pay an uncertified check presented more than six months after its date, but it may do so in good faith without liability.
Death or incompetence of customer [UCC 4-405]	As long as the bank does not know of the death or incompetence of a customer, the bank can pay an item without liability. Even with knowledge of a customer's death, a bank can honor or certify checks (in the absence of a stop-payment order) for ten days after the date of the customer's death.
Unauthorized signature or alteration [UCC 4-406]	The customer has a duty to examine account statements with reasonable care upon receipt and to notify the bank promptly of any unauthorized signatures or alterations. On a series of unauthorized signatures or alterations by the same wrongdoer, examination and report must be given within fourteen calendar days of receipt of the statement. Failure to comply releases the bank from liability unless the bank failed to exercise reasonable care. Regardless of care or lack of care, the customer is estopped from holding the bank liable after one year for unauthorized customer signatures or alterations and after three years for unauthorized indorsements.

ferred in the course of this collection process is called an **intermediary bank.**

The Collection Process

During the collection process, any bank can take on one or more of the above roles. For example, a buyer in New York writes a check on her New York bank and sends it to a seller in San Francisco. The seller deposits the check in her San Francisco bank account. The seller's bank is both a *depositary bank* and a *collecting bank.* The buyer's bank in New York is the *payor bank.* As the check travels from San Francisco to New York, any collecting bank (other than the depositary bank) hold-

ing the item in the collection process is an *intermediary bank.*

BANK'S LIABILITY FOR RESTRICTIVE INDORSEMENTS   A bank is not bound by any restrictive indorsements of any person except the immediate holder who transfers or presents the instrument for payment [UCC 3-206(2)]. This means that *only the first bank to which the item is presented for collection must pay in a manner consistent with any restrictive indorsement* [UCC 3-206(3)]. This bank is the depositary bank [UCC 4-105(a)].

To illustrate: Elliott writes a check on his New York bank account and sends it to Barton. Barton indorses the check with a restrictive indorsement that reads, ''For deposit into account #4921 only.'' A Miami bank is the first bank to which this check is presented for payment (the depository bank), and it must act consistently with the terms of the restrictive indorsement. Therefore, it must credit account #4921 with the money or be liable to Barton for conversion. Elliot's check leaves the Miami bank indorsed ''for collection.'' As the check moves through the collection network of intermediary banks to Elliot's New York bank for payment, each intermediary bank is only bound by the preceding bank's indorsement to collect.

The division of responsibility between types of banks is necessary. Collecting banks process huge numbers of commercial instruments, and there is no practical way for them to examine and comply with the effect of each restrictive indorsement. Therefore, the only reasonable alternative is to charge the depositary bank with the responsibility of examining and complying with any restrictive indorsements.

CHECK COLLECTION BETWEEN CUSTOMERS OF THE SAME BANK

An item payable by the depository bank that receives it is called an ''on-us item.'' If the bank does not dishonor the check by the opening of the second banking day following its receipt, it is considered paid [UCC 4-213(4)(b)]. For example, Harriman and Goldsmith have checking accounts at First National Bank. On Monday morning, Goldsmith deposits into his own checking account a $300 check from Harriman. That same day, First National issues Goldsmith a ''provisional credit'' for $300. When the bank opens on Wednesday, Harriman's check is considered honored and Goldsmith's provisional credit becomes a final payment.

CHECK COLLECTION BETWEEN CUSTOMERS OF DIFFERENT BANKS

Once a depositary bank receives a check, it must arrange to present it either directly or through intermediary banks to the appropriate payor bank. Each bank in the collection chain must pass the check on before midnight of the next banking day following its receipt [UCC 4-202(2)]. Thus, for example, a collecting bank that receives a check on Monday must forward it to the next collection bank before midnight on Tuesday. Unless the payor bank dishonors the check or returns it by midnight on the next banking day following receipt, the payor bank is accountable for the face amount of the check [UCC 4-302].[16]

To facilitate an even flow of the many items handled by banks daily, the UCC permits what is called *deferred posting,* or delayed return. Deferred posting permits posting (recording) of checks received after a certain time (say, 2:00 P.M.) to be deferred until the next day. Thus, a check received by a payor bank at 3:00 P.M. on Monday would be deferred for posting until Tuesday. In this case, the payor bank's deadline would be midnight Wednesday [UCC 4-301(1)].

THE FEDERAL RESERVE SYSTEM CLEARS CHECKS

The Federal Reserve System serves as the central bank of the nation by transferring funds, handling government deposits, and supervising and regulating banks. The twelve Federal Reserve banks act as clearinghouses and agents in the collection of checks and other instruments. This has greatly simplified the clearing of checks—that is, the method by which checks deposited in one bank are transferred to the banks on which they were written. Suppose Samuel Evans of Chicago writes a check to John Lucky of San Francisco. When Lucky receives the check in the mail, he deposits it in his bank. His bank then deposits the check in the Federal Reserve Bank of San Francisco, which sends the check to the Federal Reserve Bank of Chicago. That Federal Reserve Bank then sends the check to Evans's bank, where the amount of the check is deducted from Evans's account. Exhibit 29–6 illustrates this process.

EXPEDITED FUNDS AVAILABILITY ACT

The Expedited Funds Availability Act of 1987[17] requires that any local check deposited must be available for withdrawal by check or as cash within one business day from the date of deposit. The Federal Reserve Board of Governors has designated check processing regions, and if the depositary and payor banks are located in the same region, the check is

---

16. Revised Article 4 recognizes that most checks are cleared by a computerized process and that communication and computer facilities may fail due to weather, equipment malfunction, or other conditions. If such conditions arise and a bank fails to meet its midnight deadline, the bank is ''excused'' from liability if the bank has exercised ''such diligence as the circumstances require'' [RUCC 4-109(d)].

17. 12 U.S.C. Sections 4001 *et seq.*

■ **Exhibit 29–6 How a Check Is Cleared**

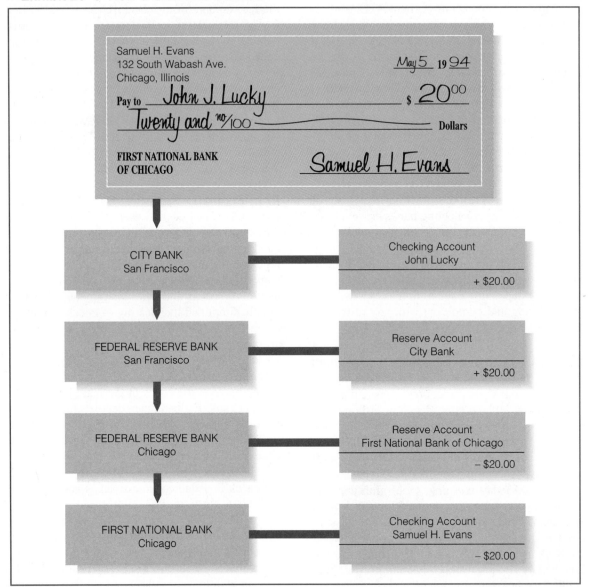

classified as a local check. For nonlocal checks, the funds are to be available for withdrawal within four business days.

   In addition, the act requires the following:

1.   That funds be available on the *next business day* for cash deposits and wire transfers, government checks, the first $100 of a day's check deposits, cashier's checks, certified checks, and checks for which the depositary and payor banks are branches of the same institution.

2.   That the first $100 of any deposit be available for cash withdrawals on the opening of the next business day after deposit. If the deposit is a local check, the next $400 is to be available for withdrawal by no later than 5:00 P.M. the next business day. If, for example, you deposit a local check for $500 on Monday, you can withdraw $100 in cash at the opening of the business day on Tuesday, and an additional $400 must be available for withdrawal by no later than 5:00 P.M. on Wednesday.

There is a different availability schedule for deposits made at *nonproprietary* automated teller machines (ATMs)—ATMs that are not owned or operated by the banking institution. Basically, a six-day hold is permitted on all deposits, including cash deposits, made at nonproprietary ATMs. Also, a banking institution has eight days to make funds available in new accounts (those open less than thirty days) and an extra four days on deposits over $5,000 (except deposits of government and cashier's checks), on accounts with repeated overdrafts, and on checks of questionable collectibility (but only if the institution tells the depositor it suspects fraud or insolvency).

■ Terms and Concepts

cashier's check 510
certified check 511
check 509
collecting bank 521

depositary bank 521
intermediary bank 522
payor bank 521

stale check 513
stop-payment order 514
traveler's check 510

■ For Review

1. Checks are usually three-party instruments. On what type of check, however, does a bank serve as both drawer and drawee? What type of check does a bank agree in advance to accept when the check is presented for payment?
2. When may a bank properly dishonor a customer's check without liability to the customer?
3. Could a holder successfully sue a drawee bank for honoring a stop-payment order when the drawer had no valid legal ground for requesting that payment be stopped?
4. Markie steals one of Aretha's checks, forges Aretha's signature on the check, and cashes the check at First American Bank. First American presents the check for payment to Bank of Menlo Park, the drawee bank, which cashes the check. Aretha timely discovers the forged signature and requires Menlo Park to recredit her account for the amount of the check. Could Menlo Park recover the amount of the check from First American?
5. Holly makes a check out to Willy. Tara steals the check, forges Willy's signature on the check, and cashes the check at Executive Bank. Executive presents the check for payment to Fidelity National Bank, the drawee bank, which cashes the check. Holly notifies Fidelity of the loss of the check and requires Fidelity to recredit her account for the amount of the check. Could Fidelity recover the amount of the check from Executive?

■ Questions and Case Problems

29-1. Daniel drafts a check for $1,000 payable to Paula and drawn on the West Bank. After issue of the check, Paula, by blank indorsement, negotiates the check to Fred. Fred finds an ideal real estate lot for sale, but to close the deal he needs to make a $1,000 down payment by certified check. Fred takes the check to West Bank and requests West Bank to certify Daniel's check.
(a) If West Bank refuses to certify Daniel's check, can either Daniel or Fred hold the bank liable? Explain.
(b) If West Bank certifies the check, explain fully the liability of Daniel as drawer to Fred and to Paula as indorser.

29-2. On January 5, Daniel drafts a check for $3,000 drawn on the East Bank and payable to his secretary, Sylvia. Daniel puts last year's date on the check by mistake. Sylvia has not yet cashed the check at the East Bank when, on January 7, Daniel is killed in an automobile accident. The East Bank is aware of Daniel's death. On January 10, Sylvia presents the check to the East Bank, and the bank honors the check by payment to Sylvia. Daniel's widow, Martha, claims that the East Bank has wrongfully paid Sylvia, because it knew of Daniel's death and because the check was by date over one year old. Martha, as executor of Daniel's estate and sole heir by his will, demands that East Bank recredit Daniel's estate for the check paid Sylvia. Discuss fully East Bank's liability in light of Martha's demand.

29-3. Daniel goes grocery shopping and carelessly leaves his checkbook in his shopping cart. His checkbook, with two blank checks remaining, is stolen by Thomas. On May 5, Thomas forges Daniel's name on a check for $100 and cashes the check at Daniel's bank, the First Bank of Jonestown. Daniel has not reported the theft to his bank. On June 1, Daniel receives his monthly bank statement and canceled checks from Jonestown Bank, including the check forged by Thomas. Daniel does not reconcile his checking account. On June 20, Thomas forges Daniel's last check. This check is for $1,000 and is cashed at the West Bank, a bank with which Thomas has previously done business. The West Bank sends the check through the collection process, and the Jonestown Bank honors it. On July 1, upon receipt of Jonestown Bank's statement and canceled checks, Daniel discovers both forgeries and immediately notifies Jonestown Bank. Thomas cannot be found. Daniel claims that Jonestown must recredit his account for both checks, as his signature was forged. Discuss fully Daniel's claim.

29-4. Diana takes her television set to Honest John's TV Service Store for repairs. The set is supposedly repaired, at a cost of $125. On Saturday, Diana writes out a check payable to Honest John drawn on the First Greenville Bank. Diana takes the set home and discovers that virtually no repairs have been made. On Monday, Diana calls Honest John to complain about his lack of performance. Honest John insists the repairs were made and refuses even to look at the television set. Diana immediately calls the First Greenville Bank and issues a stop-payment order over the phone. Three weeks later, Honest John cashes Diana's check at a drive-in window of the First Greenville Bank. Diana is furious when she discovers the bank's payment to Honest John and wants the bank to recredit her account. Discuss fully the First Greenville Bank's liability in this matter.

29-5. Daniel has $5,000 in his checking account with the Second Bank of Fielder. Daniel writes a check for $500 payable to Peter in settlement of a long-standing dispute between the two. Peter deposits the check in his bank. Peter's bank sends the check through the collection process. The Second Bank, by mistake, returns the check to Peter's bank marked "insufficient funds." Peter's bank returns the check to Peter, charging his account for $500, plus the bank's service charge of $10 for returned checks. Peter is furious and files criminal charges against Daniel. Discuss fully the Second Bank of Fielder's liability for wrongful dishonor of Daniel's check.

29-6. Edward and Christine McSweeney opened a joint checking account with the United States Trust Co. of New York in September 1976. Between April and July of 1978, 195 checks totaling $99,063 were written. In July 1978, activity in the account ceased. Ninety-five of the 195 checks, totaling $16,811, were written by Christine, and the balance were written by Edward. After crediting of deposits during the period, the checks amounted to a cumulative overdraft of $75,983. Can a bank knowingly honor a check when payment creates an overdraft, or must the bank dishonor the check? If the bank pays a check creating an overdraft, can the bank collect the amount of overdraft from its customer? Explain. [*United States Trust Co. of New York v. McSweeney,* 91 A.D.2d 7, 457 N.Y.S.2d 276 (1982)]

29-7. 🖥 Susan Wolf forged her employer's name on more than ninety checks drawn on the employer's bank account. The bank cashed the checks, debiting the employer's account, and Wolf wrongfully received a total of more than $22,500. When the forgeries were discovered, the employer brought a criminal action against Wolf but later dropped the charges and settled out of court. The employer also demanded that the bank credit its account for the amount of the forged checks. The bank refused. Assuming there was no evidence that the employer's negligence had substantially contributed to the forgery, discuss whether the employer was entitled to have the bank

credit its account. [*SCCI, Inc. v. United States National Bank of Oregon,* 78 Or.App. 176, 714 P.2d 1113 (1986)]

29-8. In July of 1979, Read & Read, Inc., a corporation owned by Thomas and Emerson Read, hired Judy Bode as a sales secretary. She was promoted to executive secretary shortly thereafter and worked primarily for Emerson Read. Bode eventually assumed responsibility for overseeing nearly all of Read's checking accounts, including his personal account. She also reviewed the bank statements for each account and reconciled them to the corresponding checkbooks. As a result of a hunting accident, Emerson Read lost one of his hands and, to facilitate check signing, had a rubber signature stamp made. Bode had easy access to the stamp. From September 1980 until January 1981, she used the rubber stamp to forge a total of fourteen checks for her own purposes on Read's accounts, including one check for over $8,000. Read, who did not review any bank statements during this entire period of time, was unaware of the forgeries. When the forgeries were discovered in January of 1981, Read sued his bank, the South Carolina National Bank, to recover the amount of the forged checks, which he alleged had been wrongfully honored by the bank. The trial court held for the bank, and Read appealed. Can Read recover from the bank the funds lost as a result of Judy Bode's forgeries? Discuss fully. [*Read v. South Carolina National Bank,* 286 S.C. 534, 335 S.E.2d 359 (1985)]

29-9. Robert Parrett was the principal shareholder, president, and chief operating officer of P & P Machinery, Inc., a farm machinery business located in Nebraska. On March 1, 1984, Parrett signed and delivered a check from P & P Machinery to a South Dakota firm. The check was dishonored by the bank even though P & P Machinery had sufficient funds in its account to cover the check. In addition, Parrett had a long-standing relationship with the bank as personal guarantor of corporate obligations to the bank and had never had any previous problems with the bank. As a result of the dishonored check, Parrett was charged with felony theft in South Dakota and extradited for trial in South Dakota. On learning that the bank had dishonored the check erroneously, the trial court dismissed the charge against Parrett. Parrett sued the bank for damages. The trial court held that Parrett had no standing to sue the bank because he was not the bank's "customer"—the corporation was. Will the appellate court agree that Parrett lacked standing to sue the bank? Discuss fully. [*Parrett v. Platte Valley State Bank & Trust Co.,* 236 Neb. 139, 459 N.W.2d 371 (1990)]

29-10. A Question of Ethics

 Dan Palmer, representing himself as an agent of Monarch Investment of Colorado, sold a used backhoe to Ryan Neibaur for $6,500. Neibaur paid for the backhoe with a check drawn on his account at Valley Bank in Idaho Falls, Idaho, and payable to Monarch Investment. Palmer then exchanged the check at a Valley Bank branch in Pocatello, Idaho, for a cashier's check payable to Monarch Investment. Palmer used the cashier's check to purchase

$6,500 worth of gold coins from Monarch Coin Corp. (also known as Monarch Investment Co.) of Salt Lake City and then disappeared. In the meantime, Neibaur, learned that he had purchased a stolen backhoe. He informed Valley Bank of the fraudulent transactions and requested the bank to stop payment on the check he had issued to Palmer. Two days later, when the cashier's check arrived at Valley Bank for payment, the bank refused to honor the check. Monarch Coin sought to recover $6,500 from the bank on the grounds that the bank had wrongfully dishonored the cashier's check. Neibaur sought recovery of $6,500 from the bank on the grounds that the bank had wrongfully paid his check over a forged indorsement. The court held that Valley Bank was liable on both claims. [Valley Bank v. Monarch Investment Co., 800 P.2d 634 (Idaho 1990)]

1. The court's decision in this case meant that Valley Bank had to pay $6,500, plus attorneys' fees, to each of the claimants—in other words, it suffered a loss of more than $13,000. Does this result seem fair? On the basis of the UCC provisions discussed in this and in previous chapters, would you have arrived at the same conclusion?

2. This case involved one "scoundrel"—to use the court's term—and three (relatively) innocent parties—Neibaur, Valley Bank, and Monarch Coin. Do you think that the court's decision accords with the general policy adopted by the drafters of the UCC that, between innocent parties, the party in the best position to prevent the fraud should bear the loss? Was Valley Bank in a better position to prevent the fraud than Neibaur?

Chapter 30

Electronic Fund Transfers

The application of computer technology to banking, in the form of **electronic fund transfer systems (EFTS),** promises to relieve banking institutions of the burden of having to move mountains of paperwork to process fund transfers. An **electronic fund transfer** is a transfer of money made by the use of an electronic terminal, a telephone, a computer, or magnetic tape. Automatic payments, direct deposits, and other fund transfers are now made electronically; no physical transfers of cash, checks, or other negotiable instruments are involved. Through the use of EFTS, transactions that would otherwise take days can now be completed in minutes. For example, Hannah in New York can pay a debt to Barbara in Los Angeles by entering into a computer a bank order to pay it. Chase Manhattan, the drawee bank, can instantly debit Hannah's account and transfer the credit to the Bank of America, Barbara's bank, which can immediately credit her account. EFT transactions eliminate the **float time** that the drawer of a check currently enjoys. A drawer uses float time by retaining the use of the funds on which the check is written during the period between the check's issuance and final payment.

Commercial electronic fund transfers are governed by contract law and tort law. Consumer transactions utilizing EFTS, however, are subject to the Electronic Fund Transfer Act (EFTA),[1] which is Title IX of the Consumer Credit Protection Act. To cover fund transfers that the EFTA and other federal and state laws do not cover, the National Conference of Commissioners on Uniform State Laws and the American Law Institute approved a draft of a new UCC article—Article 4A. Article 4A, discussed later in this chapter, is primarily intended to cover fund transfers between businesses and financial institutions.

■ Types of Electronic Transfers

There are four principal types of EFTS in use: (1) automated teller machines, (2) point-of-sale systems, (3) systems handling direct deposits and withdrawals of funds, and (4) pay-by-telephone systems. To initiate a transaction on one of the machines involved, a consumer often uses a card that provides access to the computer system. Each card has an accompanying

---

1.   15 U.S.C. Sections 1693 *et seq.*

personal identification number (PIN) that is given only to the account holder—a number that is meant to be kept secret so as to inhibit others' use of the card. A sample access card is shown in Exhibit 30–1.

Automated Teller Machines

A major EFTS development has involved the **automated teller machine (ATM),** also called a customer-bank communication terminal or a remote service unit. ATMs are located on banks' premises as well as at convenient locations such as supermarkets, drugstores, and shopping centers. Once the access card activates an ATM, the ATM can receive deposits, dispense funds from checking or savings accounts, transfer funds between accounts, make credit card advances, and receive payments on loan accounts. ATMs are usually connected on-line to the bank's computers.

Point-of-Sale Systems

Point-of-sale systems allow consumers to transfer funds to merchants to pay for purchases. On-line terminals are located at checkout counters in, for example, grocery stores. Instead of receiving cash or a check from the customer, the checkout person inserts the customer's card into a terminal, which reads the data encoded on the card. The computer at the customer's bank verifies that the card and identification code are valid and that there are enough funds in the customer's account to cover the purchase. After the payment is made, the customer's account is debited for the amount of the purchase.

For the merchant, direct payment from customers by means of point-of-sale systems involves, under current law, less risk of nonpayment or ''bounced'' checks. For the customer, the electronic transfer makes bills and check writing unnecessary.

Direct Deposits and Withdrawals

Automated clearinghouses are similar to the ordinary clearinghouses in which checks are cleared between banks. The main difference is that entries are made in the form of electronic signals; no checks are used. Thus, these systems do not further automate the handling of checks; they replace checks. This type of EFTS allows a bank to complete a transaction for less than the cost of clearing a check.

A direct deposit may be made to a customer's account through an electronic terminal when the customer has authorized the deposit in advance. The federal government often uses this EFTS to deposit Social Security payments directly into beneficiaries' accounts. Similarly, an employer may agree to make payroll and pension payments directly into an employee's account at specified intervals.

A customer may also authorize a bank (or other financial institution at which the customer's funds

■ **Exhibit 30–1 A Sample Access Card**

a. Front Side

b. Back Side

are on deposit) to make automatic payments at regular, recurrent intervals to a third party. For example, insurance premiums, utility bills, and home mortgage and automobile installment loan payments may sometimes be made automatically. Additionally, a customer may authorize its bank to make a payment or payments to the Internal Revenue Service for taxes due.

Pay-by-Telephone Systems

When it is undesirable to arrange in advance for an automatic payment—as, for example, when the amount of a regular payment varies—some financial institutions permit their customers to pay bills through a pay-by-telephone system. This allows the customer to access the institution's computer system by telephone and direct a transfer of funds. Utility bills sometimes are paid directly by customers using pay-by-telephone systems. Customers may also be permitted to transfer funds between accounts—for example, to withdraw funds from a savings account and make a deposit in a checking account—in this way.

■ Consumer Transfers: The Electronic Fund Transfer Act

In 1978, Congress passed the Electronic Fund Transfer Act (EFTA) "to provide a basic framework establishing the rights, liabilities, and responsibilities of participants in electronic fund transfers." The EFTA is essentially a disclosure law designed to benefit consumers; it requires financial institutions to inform consumers of their rights with respect to EFTS. The EFTA is not concerned with *commercial* electronic fund transfers—transfers between businesses or between businesses and financial institutions.

Under the EFTA, the Federal Reserve System's board of governors is authorized to administer the act and to promulgate regulations to carry out the purposes of the act. The board of governors has issued a set of rules, called **Regulation E,** to protect users of EFTS; this regulation should be consulted for a complete understanding of the EFTA. Also, the board has drafted model clauses for financial institutions to use in disclosing information about their electronic systems.

Institutions and Transactions Covered

The EFTA governs financial institutions that offer electronic fund transfers involving customer accounts. The EFTA defines **financial institutions** to include banks, savings and loan institutions, credit unions, and any other business entities that directly or indirectly hold accounts belonging to consumers. Thus, securities brokerage houses that permit consumers to make electronic transfers to and from money market fund accounts are included.

The types of accounts covered include demand accounts, savings accounts, and other asset accounts established for personal, family, or household purposes. All electronic fund transfers involving such accounts are covered by the EFTA. Note that, although telephone transfers are included in the definition of an electronic fund transfer, they are only covered by the EFTA if they are made *pursuant to a prearranged plan under which periodic or recurring transfers are contemplated.*

In the following case, the court examines the purposes of the EFTA and stresses the fact that the act covers only electronic fund transfers made by *consumers.* Transfers between financial institutions are not covered by the act.

Case 30.1

SHAWMUT WORCESTER COUNTY BANK v. FIRST AMERICAN BANK & TRUST

United States District Court, District of Massachusetts, 1990.
731 F.Supp. 57.

BACKGROUND AND FACTS   Shawmut Worcester County Bank, a Massachusetts bank, transferred $10,000 to First American Bank & Trust of Palm Beach, Florida, through an EFTS system known as Fedwire. Shawmut's payment order stated that the beneficiary of the transfer was Fernando Degan and that First American should credit account number 100 205 001 633. It turned out that the First American account under that number was held jointly by Degan and Joseph Merle. When Shawmut discovered its error 106 days after the mistaken transfer, it credited the account of its customer who had requested the transfer with the $10,000 and then asked First American to "reverse" the transfer. First American asked Merle, its customer, if he would authorize the reversal. Merle refused. Accordingly, First American told Shawmut it would not reverse the transfer. Shawmut sued First American in a federal district court to recover the $10,000, alleging, among other claims, that the transaction fell under the EFTA, which prescribes specific requirements that must be followed in the event of error in a funds transaction. First American moved for a summary judgment in its favor.

DECISION AND RATIONALE The United States District Court for the District of Massachusetts determined that the EFTA "was primarily created for the especial benefit of consumers" to provide them with legal protection "against financial institutions in electronic funds transfers." Because this dispute was between two financial institutions and there was no evidence that First American "directly or indirectly holds an account belonging to a consumer," the court held that it was "a garden-variety wire transfer between financial institutions" and thus not covered by the EFTA. The court granted First American's motion for summary judgment.

Disclosure of Terms and Conditions

The EFTA requires that the terms and conditions of electronic fund transfers involving a customer's account must be disclosed in readily understandable language at the time the customer contracts for the services. Included among the required disclosures are:

1. The customer's liability for unauthorized transfers resulting from the loss or theft of the card, code, or other access device.
2. Whom and what phone number to call to report a theft or loss.
3. The charges for using the EFTS.
4. What systems are available and the limits on frequency of use and dollar amounts.
5. The customer's right to see evidence of transactions in writing.
6. How errors can be corrected.
7. The customer's right to stop payments.
8. The financial institution's liability to the customer.
9. Rules concerning disclosure of account information to third parties.

Exhibit 30–2 shows a disclosure form containing the requisite information.

Documentation Regarding Transactions

The EFTA considerably reduces the amount of paper used in transferring funds. Financial institutions are required to provide the customer with written documentation—a receipt—of each transfer made from an electronic terminal at the time of the transfer. (Receipts are not required for telephone transfers, even when a telephone transfer is otherwise subject to the EFTA.) The receipt must clearly state the date, the type of transfer, the amount, the identity of the customer's account, the identity of any third party involved (such as a merchant accepting the customer's card as a means of paying for purchased goods), and the location of the terminal involved. Exhibit 30–3 shows an automatic teller machine (ATM) transaction receipt.

In addition, financial institutions must give customers periodic statements describing types, amounts, dates, transferees, and locations of transfers for each account through which an EFTS provides access. The type of account and the frequency with which the customer uses it determine the timing of the statements. Monthly statements are required for every month in which there is an electronic transfer of funds. Otherwise, statements must be provided quarterly.

The statement must show the amount and date of the transfer, the fees charged, the location or identification of the terminal, and the name of the retailer or third party, if any, involved. Also, the statement must provide an address and phone number for inquiries and error notices.

Financial institutions must also notify customers if an automatic deposit is not made as scheduled. This helps customers to avoid overdrawing their accounts.

Exhibit 30–2 A Sample Form Disclosing Terms and Conditions Required under the EFTA

This disclosure contains the terms and conditions for all Home Federal electronic banking services, in addition to specific information about pre-authorized electronic payments and deposits.

As someone who uses these services, you should read this information, as it pertains to your rights and responsibilities, as well as the terms and conditions of their use.

Electronic transactions may be payments or deposits, authorized by you, to or from your checking or savings account(s) or loan(s), or to or from a third party. They include:

- Anytimeteller℠ transactions
- STAR SYSTEM® network transactions
- EXPLORE℠ point-of-sale network (participating gas stations, grocery stores, and other merchants) transactions
- Pre-authorized debits and credits (includes Automatic Payroll Deposit)
- Direct Deposit service
- Telephone Transfer service
- SurePay (automatic loan payments and electronic deposit or payment transactions to or from your checking or savings account)
- Electronic payment or deposit transactions to or from your checking or savings account through an Automated Clearing House (ACH)

Business Days

Our business days are Monday through Friday, except holidays. When allowing processing time, it is important to only count business days. Weekends and holidays are not considered business days.

Privacy

Home Federal may disclose account information to third parties under any of the following conditions:
1. Where it is necessary for completing transfers;
2. To verify the existence and condition of your account for a third party, such as a credit bureau or merchant;
3. To comply with a legitimate request from a government agency, or a court order;
4. With your written permission.

Home Federal Liability/Change of Terms

If Home Federal does not complete a transfer to or from your account at the specified time, or in the specified amount, according to our Agreement with you, we will be liable for any losses or damages to you, with these exceptions:

Home Federal will not be liable if:
1. There are insufficient funds in your account to make a transfer or payment, for reasons beyond the control of this Association;
2. A transfer would exceed the credit limit on your line of credit;
3. The electronic banking system or terminal was not working properly at the time you initiated a transfer, and you were aware of this malfunction.

Home Federal may cease to offer any electronic banking service at any time. Service users will be given prior notice of any such change in policy.

Home Federal may change any term of the Agreement, including changes which will affect your cost or liability, by giving you at least 21 days written notice.

NOTE: There may be additional exceptions which apply, as stated in our Agreement with you.

Errors and Questions

In case of errors or questions about your electronic transactions, please contact your branch of account.

Home Federal must hear from you within 60 days from the date of the first statement on which the problem or error appears. Failure to do so may result in your being held fully liable for the amount of the error.

Notification by phone or in person requires a written follow-up within 10 working days.

To Resolve an Error

When notifying Home Federal in writing of a suspected error:
1. Include your name, address, and account number.
2. Describe in detail the transaction in question and explain as clearly as you can why you believe it is an error or why you need more information.
3. Indicate the dollar amount of the suspected error.

Home Federal will investigate the error and report to you, usually within 10 business days.

Point-of-sale transactions, however, may take up to 20 business days to investigate.

We may take up to 45 days to investigate a reported error. If so, Home Federal will provisionally recredit your account within 10 business days (or 20 days for point-of-sale transactions) for the amount in question, so that you may have use of the money during the investigation period. This recrediting to your account may not occur if we have not received your notification in writing within the 10 business days.

If it is determined that no error occurred, we will notify you in writing within 3 business days following the investigation. Any amounts recredited to your account during the course of the investigation will be debited from your account. Copies of documents used in our investigation will be available to you upon request.

Anytimecard℠ Safety

For your protection, please:
1. Be sure to keep your Anytimecard in a safe place, and don't allow anyone to use it.
2. Keep your Personal Identification Number (PIN) a secret. Do not write it on your Anytimecard or otherwise make it available to anyone.
3. Notify Home Federal immediately of any loss, theft, or unauthorized use of your Anytimecard or PIN. Lost or stolen Anytimecards can be reported 24 hours a day, 7 days a week.

Anytimecard Consumer Liability

1. It is your responsibility to notify Home Federal immediately if your Anytimecard and/or Personal Identification Number (PIN) has been lost or stolen. Provided you notify Home Federal within 2 business days after you discover the possible loss or theft, your loss will be limited to a maximum of $50 if your Anytimecard and PIN are used without your permission.
2. If you fail to notify Home Federal within 2 business days of the possible loss or theft of your Anytimecard or PIN, and it can be proven that such notification could have prevented the unauthorized use of your Anytimecard or PIN, your loss could be as much as $500.
3. If you fail to notify Home Federal within 60 days, and it can be proven that such notification could have prevented the unauthorized use of your Anytimecard or PIN, you may not be able to recover

Preauthorized Transfers

A **preauthorized transfer** is a transaction authorized in advance to recur at substantially regular intervals. For example, an employee may be able to arrange with an employer and a bank for the direct deposit of payroll checks into his or her checking account. Similarly, an individual might authorize a monthly transfer from his or her account to pay insurance premiums or installments on a home mortgage or automobile loan.

A situation in which a credit to a customer's account from the same payor is made at least once in each successive sixty-day period requires the financial institution to notify the customer when the credit is made, if the payor does not make the notification. As noted in the preceding section, the financial institution must also notify the customer if the deposit is not made as scheduled. The parties can agree on the manner of notice when the service is contracted for. In other words, if an employee has arranged with his or her employer for the direct deposit of weekly payroll checks, the bank handling the receipt of the checks must notify the employee weekly, if the employer does not, whether a check has been deposited as arranged.

As its name implies, a preauthorized transfer must be authorized by the customer in advance. The authorization must be in writing, and a copy of it must be provided to the customer when it is made. To stop payment of a preauthorized EFT, a customer may notify the financial institution orally or in writing at any time up to three business days before the scheduled date of the transfer. The institution may require the customer to provide written confirmation within fourteen days of an oral notification. For example, suppose Temple has arranged with his bank, Manufacturers Hanover Trust, to have the bank make automatic payments on his automobile installment loan. If Temple wishes to make a given payment on the loan personally, he must order the bank more than three days before the automatic payment is scheduled to be made not to make the payment.

Stopping Payment and Reversibility

Under the EFTA, then, a customer may cancel a *preauthorized* transfer before the transfer is made, just as a drawer—the person who signs a check—may stop payment on a check before it is paid. For other EFT transactions, however, the EFTA does not provide for the reversal of an electronic transfer of funds, once it has occurred. This is because the uniquely instantaneous nature of an electronic transfer of funds provides no float time during which an effective reversal of an order to pay can be made.

Mistakes and Corrections

Under the EFTA, a customer has a duty to examine the periodic—monthly or quarterly—statements provided by the financial institution handling his or her account or accounts. Within sixty days after the institution has sent a statement, the customer must notify the institution of any errors that appear on it. Whether oral or written, the notice must contain the following information:

1. The customer's name and account number.
2. A sentence stating that an error has been made and its alleged amount.
3. Why the customer believes an error has been made.

The institution is required to investigate and report the results within ten business days. If the institution needs more than ten days, it may take up to forty-five, but it must recredit the customer's account for the amount alleged to be in error until the problem is resolved. If it determines that an error did occur, it has one business day to adjust the customer's account. Even if no mistake has

■ **Exhibit 30–3 An ATM Receipt**

AnytimeTeller^{SM}

TRANSACTION RECEIPT

YOUR IDENTIFICATION   TRANSACTION CODE

AMOUNT   DATE   TIME

FROM ACCOUNT   TO ACCOUNT   LOCATION

PRESENT BALANCE   AVAILABLE BALANCE   DAILY LIMIT

All deposits and payments subject to verification. Please retain receipt for your records.

EP-012 (1/88)

HOME FEDERAL

©1988 Home Federal. Reprinted with permission.

been made, the institution has to give the customer a full written report with conclusions. Failure to investigate in good faith makes the institution liable to the customer for **treble damages**—three times the amount of provable damages.

Banks are held to strict compliance with the terms of the EFTA, and if they fail to adhere to the letter of the law of the EFTA they will be held liable for violation, as is illustrated in the following case.

Case 30.2

BISBEY v. D.C. NATIONAL BANK

United States Court of Appeals, District of Columbia Circuit, 1986. 793 F.2d 315.

BACKGROUND AND FACTS   Sandra Bisbey opened a checking account with the District of Columbia National Bank in January 1981. Bisbey subsequently authorized the bank to debit her checking account for fund transfer directives that were submitted monthly by the New York Life Insurance Company (NYLIC) for payment of her insurance premiums. In September 1981, Bisbey's account lacked sufficient funds to cover the insurance directive, and no transfer was made. NYLIC resubmitted the September directive in October, with the October monthly directive. Bisbey's funds were insufficient to satisfy either submission, but the bank covered the premiums. As a result, two overdraft notices were sent to Bisbey, each in the amount of her monthly insurance premium. Bisbey, having forgotten her nonpayment in September, believed that the bank had erroneously made two payments in October. At this point, Bisbey informed a customer representative of the bank that she believed that an error had occurred with regard to the preauthorized transfers. Approximately ten days later, an official of the bank telephoned Bisbey and orally explained that there had been no improper duplication of her insurance premiums. Bisbey, however, still considered the matter unresolved, and she filed suit under the EFTA in a federal district court, alleging that the bank had unlawfully failed to advise her properly about the result of its investigation into the alleged duplication error in the transfers from her checking account. Under the EFTA, a bank's notification to a customer that no error has been made must be in writing. The trial court ruled in favor of the bank, and Bisbey appealed.

DECISION AND RATIONALE   The United States Court of Appeals for the District of Columbia Circuit found that the EFTA imposes a duty on a bank to "deliver or mail" a written report of the results of its investigation to its customer and to advise him or her of the right to request reproductions of all documents that the bank relied on to conclude that no error occurred. The court held that the bank's oral notice to Bisbey "was insufficient with respect to the [statute's] required 'explanation,' and it did not even purport to give 'notice of the right to request reproductions.'" The court emphasized that under the EFTA, civil liability attaches to *all* failures of compliance with respect to *any* provision. The court acknowledged that "it may seem odd" that the bank is liable for a transaction that benefited Bisbey—she had no overdraft agreement, but the bank did not charge her an overdraft fee, and on her inquiry, the bank gave her a correct report, neglecting only to send it in writing as the EFTA requires. Bisbey conceded that she suffered no damage. "Despite this, the litigation has continued for nearly three years, and the statute compels a finding that the [b]ank is liable."

ETHICAL CONSIDERATIONS   Although it may seem unfair that Bisbey should succeed in her suit against the bank, given that she in fact benefited from the bank's error, the reasoning behind holding banks to strict compliance with the requirements of the EFTA is clear: overall, strict compliance will ensure more fairness to consumers. As with any consumer protection statute, there will be occasional consumers who take unfair advantage of the letter of the law for personal gain.

Customer Liability for Unauthorized Transfers

Under the EFTA, before a customer can be held liable for any unauthorized transfer, it must be established that the transfer resulted from the use of an accepted means of access and that the customer had been provided with a means of identifying himself or herself to that means of access. For example, a bank's customer will not be held liable for unauthorized withdrawals from the customer's checking account unless the bank has provided the customer with a card (such as the one illustrated in Exhibit 30–1) and a secret number for access to the bank's EFTS.

In the event that the access card or other device is lost, stolen, or misplaced, the EFTA limits the customer's liability for any unauthorized transfers of funds to $50 if the customer notifies the financial institution within two business days of learning of the loss or theft. If the customer does not inform the institution until after the second day, his or her liability climbs to $500. The customer's liability may be unlimited if notification does not occur within sixty days of the customer's receipt of a periodic statement that reflects an unauthorized transfer.

In any action involving a customer's liability for an unauthorized transfer, the institution must prove first that the customer and the institution had an agreement under which the customer agreed to this liability and second that the customer knew that the access device had been lost, stolen, or misplaced. When an unauthorized transfer has appeared on a statement, the institution must show that any loss of funds due to the unauthorized transfer would not have occurred but for the customer's failure to report the unauthorized transfer's appearance on the statement within sixty days of the statement's transmittal.

To illustrate: On May 1, Wistful goes to an automatic teller machine belonging to Citicorp, his bank, to make a withdrawal from his checking account. He discovers that his access card is missing but fails to tell Citicorp until May 15. Meanwhile, on May 12, Warp, a thief, has made a $100 withdrawal from the account using Wistful's card and number. Wistful, as the account's owner, is liable for the full $100 because he did not notify Citicorp that the card had been stolen or lost prior to Warp's illegal withdrawal. If Wistful had failed to tell Citicorp at all that the card was missing and Warp had continued to use it to withdraw funds, Wistful could have been held liable for the entire amount withdrawn.

Unauthorized use of EFTS access devices constitutes a federal felony. Unauthorized users of EFTS are subject to sanctions, including a $10,000 fine and ten years' imprisonment.

The following case involves a bank customer who, trying to do a good deed, allowed another person (an alleged bank representative) to use his access card. The alleged bank representative, who had earlier surreptitiously observed the customer enter his PIN into the ATM, withdrew funds from the customer's account. The issue before the court is whether these actions resulted in an authorized or an unauthorized transfer of funds.

BACKGROUND AND FACTS Frederick Ognibene sought to recover from Citibank $400 that had been withdrawn from his account at the bank by an unauthorized person using an automated teller machine. Ognibene claimed that he was the victim of a scam that the bank had been aware of for some time. On August 16, 1981, Ognibene went to the ATM area at one of the bank's branches and activated one of two ATMs—which were located side by side with a telephone situated between them—with his Citibank card. He pressed in his personal identification code and withdrew $20. While he did this, a person who was using the telephone situated between the

Case 30.3

OGNIBENE v. CITIBANK, N.A.

Civil Court of the City of New York, New York County, Small Claims Part, 1981. 112 Misc.2d 219, 446 N.Y.S.2d 845.

machines, after observing the number punched in by Ognibene, said loudly into the telephone, "I'll see if his card works in my machine." The stranger, purporting to be a bank representative, asked Ognibene if he could use Ognibene's card to check whether the other machine was working. Ognibene handed the card to him and saw him insert it into the adjoining machine at least two times while stating into the telephone, "Yes, it seems to be working." The bank's computer records showed that two withdrawals of $200 each were made from Ognibene's account on August 16, 1981, on the machine adjoining the one Ognibene used for his $20 withdrawal. The two $200 withdrawals were made at 5:42 P.M. and 5:43 P.M.; Ognibene's $20 withdrawal was made at 5:41 P.M. At the time, Ognibene was unaware that any withdrawals from his account were being made on the adjoining machine. After later learning that $400 had been withdrawn from his checking account, Ognibene filed suit against the bank under the EFTA in a New York state court, alleging that, because the withdrawals were not authorized by him, the bank should bear the loss.

DECISION AND RATIONALE The Civil Court of the City of New York concluded that the transfer was unauthorized and that the bank was liable. Ognibene was awarded $400. Under the EFTA, a transaction is unauthorized if (1) a person other than the consumer initiates it without actual authority to do so, (2) the consumer receives no benefit from it, and (3) the consumer did not furnish the person "with the card, code, or other means of access" to his or her account. The court pointed out that merely providing a card does not furnish the "means of access" because a person must use both a card and a PIN to obtain access to an account via an ATM. As for the PIN in this case, the court found that Ognibene did not furnish it to the unauthorized person. The court concluded that the person obtained it due to the bank's negligence. Because the bank knew of the scam and how it was perpetrated—including the use of the customer service telephone—the court found that the bank "was negligent in failing to provide [the] plaintiff customer with information sufficient to alert him to the danger when he found himself in the position of a potential victim." Because the bank established the ATMs and had the ability to tighten their security, the responsibility for the observation and use of Ognibene's PIN rested with the bank.

ETHICAL CONSIDERATIONS Clearly, the scam artist was acting unethically, as well as illegally. The ethical question here is whether the bank was in a better position than the customer to protect against fraud. Is it fair to hold the bank liable? Might a customer be less motivated to act responsibly if he or she knows that the bank will be liable for losses resulting from these kinds of fraudulent scams?

Liability of the Financial Institution

A financial institution is liable to a customer for all damages *proximately caused* by its failure to make an electronic fund transfer according to the terms and conditions of an account, in the correct amount, or in a timely manner when the customer properly instructs it to do so.

There are exceptions. The institution will not be liable if:

1. The customer's account has insufficient funds through no fault of the financial institution.
2. The funds are subject to legal process, such as attachment (see Chapter 32).

3. The transfer would exceed an established credit limit.
4. An ATM has insufficient cash.
5. Circumstances beyond the institution's control prevent the transfer.

The institution is also liable for failure to stop payment of a preauthorized transfer from a customer's account when instructed to do so under the account's terms and conditions.

For an institution's violation of EFTA, a consumer may recover actual damages as well as punitive damages of not more than $1,000 or less than $100. (Unlike actual damages, punitive dam-

ages are assessed to punish a defendant or to set an example for similar wrongdoers.) In a class action suit, the punitive damage limit is the lesser of $500,000 or 1 percent of the institution's net worth.

It is a federal misdemeanor to violate the EFTA. Criminal sanctions for violations of the EFTA by banking institutions may subject an institution or its officials to a $5,000 fine and up to one year's imprisonment.

■ Commercial Fund Transfers

Nearly all commercial electronic fund transfers are excluded from coverage under the UCC and

■ CONCEPT SUMMARY 30.1
Electronic Fund Transfer Act of 1978

Area of Coverage	Essential Provisions
Disclosure	Terms and conditions must be disclosed in readily understandable language.
Documentation	1. The customer must be provided with a written receipt for each transfer made from an electronic terminal at the time of the transfer. 2. Financial institutions must provide customers with periodic statements of each account to which an electronic fund transfer system provides access.
Preauthorized transfers	*Deposits*—Banks·must notify the customer when the account is credited if the payor does not notify the customer or if the credit is not made as scheduled. *Transfers*—Authorization must be in writing; three business days' notice is required to stop a preauthorized transfer.
Mistakes and corrections	1. The customer must notify the institution of a mistake within sixty days after the statement has been mailed. 2. The institution is required to investigate and report the results within ten business days; it can have up to forty-five days but must recredit the customer's account until the problem has been resolved. 3. The institution must give the customer a full written report, even if no mistake occurred.
Customer liability for unauthorized transfers	1. Liability is limited to $50 if the customer notifies the financial institution within two business days of learning of loss or theft of access card or device. 2. Liability limit is $500 if the customer fails to notify the institution within two business days but notifies within sixty days. 3. Liability may be unlimited if the customer fails to notify the bank within sixty days of receipt of the bank statement reflecting an unauthorized transfer.
Liability of financial institution	1. The institution is liable for all damages proximately caused by its failure to make electronic fund transfers according to the terms and conditions of an account. Punitive damages may be assessed against the institution. 2. The institution is liable for failure to stop payment of a preauthorized transfer when instructed to do so under the terms and conditions of the EFTA. 3. Violation of the EFTA constitutes a federal misdemeanor.

federal and state electronic fund transfer statutes. Currently, contract and tort common law and, indirectly, federal and state laws that regulate the financial institutions involved govern these transfers.

Generally, the contracts or customary courses of dealing on which commercial electronic fund transfer systems are based allocate the risk of error, fraud, and loss among the systems' users. When parties utilizing commercial electronic fund transfer systems are unable to resolve disputes on their own and choose to litigate, the courts apply common law contract or tort principles. Thus, when a transfer is not effected as ordered, when a transfer is made to the wrong party, or when it is uncertain whether a transfer has been received or completed, a court may take into consideration the facts of the particular case.

In the future, commercial wire transfers and other types of transfers (including payments by mail) may be subject to Article 4A of the UCC—when the provisions of that article are adopted by all of the states. Article 4A is mainly intended to cover payments between businesses or financial institutions—generally, transfers of funds that are not covered by the EFTA. The primary focus is a type of payment commonly referred to as a *wholesale wire transfer.* The dollar volume of payments made by wire transfer far exceeds the dollar volume of payments made by other means. For example, the dollar volume of payments by wire transfer over the two principal wire payment systems—the Federal Reserve wire transfer network (Fedwire) and the New York Clearing House Interbank Payment Systems (CHIPS)—is about a trillion dollars a day.

The type of funds transfer that Article 4A covers is illustrated in the following example. Agar, Inc., owes $5 million to Paragon, Inc. Instead of sending Paragon a check or some other instrument that would enable Paragon to obtain payment, Agar tells its bank, West Bank, to credit $5 million to Paragon's account in East Bank. West Bank instructs East Bank to credit $5 million to Paragon's account. In more complex transactions, additional banks would be involved.

In these and similar circumstances, ordinarily a financial institution's instruction is transmitted electronically. Any means may be used, however, including first class mail. To reflect this fact, Article 4A uses the term "funds transfer" rather than "wire transfer" to describe the overall payment transaction. The full text of Article 4A is included in Appendix C, following Article 4 of the UCC.

■ Future Developments

With the enactment of the EFTA and the drafting of Article 4A, major steps have been taken toward establishing uniform laws to govern electronic and other fund transfers. Will this trend toward uniformity continue? Some observers hold that consumer interests are better served if the rules vary with the payment system, because the relationships among the parties involved often vary among systems. For example, the holder or presenter of a check may not be known to the bank on which the check is drawn; and thus, the reversibility of a transaction might not be possible. On the other hand, a retailer who accepts a credit card in payment for goods may have an ongoing relationship with the financial institution that issued the card. In that situation, permitting reversibility could protect consumers against flawed merchandise, if the merchandise could be charged back against the merchant.

Others argue that it is premature to establish a uniform set of rules for EFTS because the technology is still developing. Among the newer developments are systems that use personal computers and television monitors to allow customers to pay bills, buy merchandise, and conduct banking transactions from home.

There is little doubt that the expense of processing checks and credit card paperwork has caused financial institutions to turn increasingly to the use of EFTS. We can expect that in the future, as computerized banking systems continue to develop and expand, serious attention will also have to be given to defining the rights, obligations, and liabilities of parties utilizing these systems.

■ Terms and Concepts

automated teller machine
 (ATM) 529
electronic fund transfer 528
electronic fund transfer
 system (EFTS) 528

financial institutions 530
float time 528
personal identification
 number (PIN) 529

point-of-sale system 529
preauthorized transfer 533
Regulation E 530
treble damages 534

■ For Review

1. Consumer transactions using electronic fund transfer systems are subject to what federal act?
2. What law governs electronic fund transfers between businesses and between businesses and financial institutions?
3. The Electronic Fund Transfer Act is essentially a disclosure law. Basically, it requires financial institutions to do what, as regards consumers?
4. On January 1, Maria goes to an automatic teller machine to make a withdrawal from her bank account and discovers that her access card is missing. On January 15, Enrique uses the card to withdraw $500 from Maria's ac-

count. On January 30, Maria tells the bank that the card is missing. On February 4, Enrique uses the card to withdraw an additional $250. How much of the amount that Enrique withdrew could Maria be liable for?
5. Doug authorizes First Bank of Hopkins to transfer funds automatically from his account to pay his automobile insurance premiums. Due to a computer glitch, the bank fails to make the transfers for several months. Doug's insurance is canceled, and consequently, he is forced to pay for minor damage to his automobile sustained in a subsequent accident. If Doug sues First Bank, could First Bank be held liable for the cost of the repairs?

■ Questions and Case Problems

30-1. Kim has a checking account at First National Bank. She has had this bank account for over five years and has never had a check returned for insufficient funds. Kim works at Monmouth Medical Center and has arranged with her employer for direct deposit of her monthly paycheck into her checking account at First National. For an unexplained reason, Kim's July 1 paycheck is not deposited in her checking account. On July 15, Kim receives four notices from the bank stating that four of her checks have not been honored because her account is overdrawn. She incurs late charges from her creditors and charges from the bank for the overdrawn checks. Kim files suit against her bank. Can she recover any money from the bank? If so, under what theory and how much?

30-2. Sandy has a checking account at Texas Bank. She frequently uses her access card to obtain money from the automatic teller machines. She always withdraws $50 when she makes a withdrawal, but she never withdraws more than $50 in any one day. When she received the April statement on her account, she noticed that on April 13 two withdrawals for $50 each had been made from the account. Believing this to be a mistake, she went to her bank on May 10 to inform the bank of the error. A bank officer told her that the bank would investigate and inform her of the result. On May 26, the bank officer called her and said that bank personnel were having trouble locating the error but would continue to try to find it. On June 20, the bank sent her a

full written report advising her that no error had been made. Sandy, unhappy with the bank's explanation, filed suit against the bank, alleging that it had violated the Electronic Fund Transfer Act. What was the outcome of the suit? Would it matter if the bank could show that on the day in question it had deducted $50 from Sandy's account to cover a check that Sandy had written to a local department store and that had cleared the bank on that day?

30-3. On August 23, 1983, Robert Porter tried to withdraw $100 from his checking account at an automatic teller machine. When no money was dispensed from the machine after the necessary buttons had been pushed, he reported the incident to a bank official. A few weeks later, on September 5, Robert tried to withdraw $200. When no money appeared after two tries, he again reported the problem to a bank official. As a result of these two incidents, Robert's next bank statement showed one withdrawal of $100 and two of $200 each (for a total of $500). Robert filed suit against the bank to recover the $500 debit on his checking account for money he never received. Discuss whether Robert was able to recover the $500. [*Porter v. Citibank, N.A.,* 123 Misc.2d 28, 472 N.Y.S.2d 582 (1984)]

30-4. Parviz Haghighi Abyaneh and Iran Haghighi were co-owners of a savings account at First State Bank. On May 23, 1984, a person identifying himself as Abyaneh entered the Raleigh, North Carolina, office of Citizens Savings and Loan Association of Rocky Mount and opened a savings account. He then called the First State Bank and asked a bank employee to transfer funds from Abyaneh's First State account into the newly created account. As a result,

$53,825.66 was transferred to the new account, and subsequently, the funds were withdrawn. When the true owners of the First State Bank account learned of the transfer, they filed suit against Merchants Bank, North, successor by merger to First State Bank, for violating the Electronic Fund Transfer Act. Discuss whether Abyaneh will be able to recover the $53,825.66. [*Abyaneh v. Merchants Bank, North,* 670 F.Supp. 1298 (M.D.Pa. 1987)]

30-5. Melanie Curde went to the ATM at her bank, Tri-City Bank & Trust Co., checked her account balance, withdrew some funds, and attempted to deposit a $200 check that she had received. She inserted the check and a deposit slip into the ATM slot labeled ''Deposit.'' She later testified that the check and deposit slip disappeared into the slot and were not seen again. Several months later, when the front covering of the ATM was removed for servicing, Curde's check and deposit slip were found between the covering and the machine itself, in an area near the bottom of the machine away from the deposit slot. Although Curde was unable to present any receipts for the ATM transactions of that day, the bank's ATM tape reflected that Curde had indeed checked her account balance, withdrawn funds, and attempted a third transaction that resulted in an error and was canceled by the customer. Curde filed suit against the bank for damages, alleging, in part, that the bank had violated the Electronic Fund Transfer Act (EFTA). The bank claimed, in part, that it could not be liable under the EFTA

because the EFTA governs only when electronic fund transfers are made, and in this case no actual transfer of funds had ever taken place. How should the court decide this issue? Discuss fully. [*Curde v. Tri-City Bank & Trust Co.,* 826 S.W.2d 911 (Tenn. 1992)]

30-6. Case Briefing Assignment

Examine Case A.17 [Mellon Bank, N.A. v. Securities Settlement Corp., *710 F.Supp. 991 (D.N.J. 1989)*] *in Appendix A. The case has been excerpted there in great detail. Review and then brief the case, making sure that you include answers to the following questions in your brief.*

1. Who brought this lawsuit, and why?
2. What was the threshold issue in this case, according to the court?
3. What did the court mean by its statement that it ''must sail between the Scylla of common law and the Charybdis of statute in an attempt to predict what Pennsylvania's highest court would do if confronted with this situation''?
4. What law governed the resolution of this case? Did the provisions of the UCC play a significant role in the court's reasoning?
5. What law or legal duty had Mellon violated?

Commercial Paper and Banking

Articles 3 and 4 of the Uniform Commercial Code (UCC), which deal with commercial paper, constitute an important part of the law governing commercial transactions. These articles reflect two fundamental ethical principles: (1) that individuals should be protected against harm caused by the misuse of commercial paper and (2) that the free flow of commerce should be encouraged by practical and reasonable laws governing the use of commercial paper. These twin goals of protecting individuals against wrongdoing and encouraging commerce are reflected throughout the UCC, particularly in its emphasis on good faith and commercial reasonability.

We illustrate below how both of these principles underlie specific provisions governing commercial paper law. We also examine some ethical dimensions of transactions not envisioned when Articles 3 and 4 were drafted—electronic fund transfers.

Good Faith and the HDC Concept

In the UCC articles covering commercial paper, the first principle—protecting innocent parties—is perhaps nowhere so clearly evident as in the rules relating to holders in due course (HDCs). Just as disputes arise in the law of sales and contracts when innocent purchasers end up with, say, property to which the seller did not have good title, so, too, do disputes arise when innocent third parties end up with commercial paper that they cannot collect on because of fraud or illegality in the underlying transaction or because someone else has a superior claim to ownership. In the interest of protecting these parties, the UCC provides that a person who takes an instrument for value, in good faith, and without knowledge that a claim to or defense against the instrument exists acquires the special status of an HDC—which brings with it a higher level of immunity to claims to or defenses against payment on the instrument.

The drafters of Article 3 did not create out of thin air the concept that third parties who take instruments in good faith should be protected against all but a relatively few defenses. Indeed, under the common law, courts had often restricted the extent to which defenses could successfully be raised against a good faith holder of a negotiable instrument. As an example,

consider a classic 1884 case, *Ort v. Fowler*.[1] In this case, Ort, a farmer who was working alone in his field one day, was approached by a stranger who claimed to be the state agent for a manufacturer of iron posts and wire fence. The two men conversed for some time, and eventually the stranger persuaded the farmer to accept a township-wide agency for the same manufacturer. The stranger then completed two documents for Ort to sign, telling Ort that they were identical copies of an agency agreement. Because the farmer did not have his glasses with him and could read only with great difficulty, he asked the stranger to read what the document said. The stranger then purported to read the document to Ort, not mentioning that it was a promissory note. Both men signed each document, the farmer assuming that he was signing an agency agreement. The stranger later negotiated the promissory note he had fraudulently obtained from Ort to an HDC. When the HDC brought suit against the farmer, the farmer attempted to defend on the basis of fraud in the execution.

---

1. 31 Kan. 478, 2 P. 580 (1884).

The Kansas court deciding the issue entertained three possible views. One was that because Ort never *intended* to execute a note, he should not be held liable for the act. A second view was that the jury should decide, as a question of fact, whether Ort was guilty of negligence under the circumstances. The third view was that because Ort possessed all of his faculties and was able to read the English language, signing a promissory note solely in reliance on a stranger's assurances that it was a different instrument constituted negligence. This third view was the one adopted by the court in 1884. The court held that Ort's negligence had contributed to the fraud and that such negligence precluded Ort from raising fraud as a defense against payment on the note. Today, UCC 3-305(2)(c) expresses essentially the same reasoning: fraud is only a defense against an HDC if the injured party signed the instrument "with neither knowledge nor a reasonable opportunity to obtain knowledge of its character or essential terms."

While it may not seem fair that an innocent victim (in this case Ort) should have to suffer the consequences of another's fraudulent or illegal act, the UCC assumes that it would be even less fair if an HDC could not collect payment. The reasoning behind this assumption is that an HDC, as a third party, is less likely to have been responsible for—or to have had an opportunity to protect against—the fraud in the underlying transaction. In general, the HDC doctrine, like other sections of the UCC, reflects the philosophy that

when two or more innocent parties are at risk, the burden should fall on the party that was in the best position to prevent the loss. For businesspersons, the HDC doctrine means that caution must be exercised in the issuance and acceptance of commercial paper to protect against the risk of loss through fraud.

Efficiency versus Due Care

A major problem faced by today's banking institutions is how to verify customer signatures on the billions of checks that are processed through the banking system each month. If a bank fails to verify a signature on a check it receives for payment and the check turns out to be forged, the bank will normally be held liable to its customer for the amount paid. But how can banks possibly examine, item by item, each signature on every check that they pay?

The banks' solution to this problem is simply not to examine all signatures. Instead, computers are programmed to verify all signatures only on checks exceeding a certain threshold amount, such as $1,000 or $2,500 or perhaps some higher amount. Checks for less than the threshold amount are selected for signature verification only on a random basis. In other words, serious attention is restricted to serious matters. The result is that many checks, if not most, are paid without signature verification. This practice, which has become an acceptable standard within the banking industry of today, is economically efficient for banks: even though liability costs are sometimes incurred—when forged checks are paid—the

costs involved in verifying the authenticity of each and every signature would be far higher.

From an ethical standpoint, some have claimed that this banking practice is not fair to small depositors, who normally do not write checks exceeding the threshold amount. Although the UCC permits a bank customer to recover from the bank any amounts paid over the customer's forged signature, recovery will be precluded if the customer was negligent in his or her duty to examine canceled checks promptly and then report any forgeries to the bank within the time prescribed by the UCC. But it is the small depositor—and not those whose checks usually exceed the threshold amount—who is more likely to delay in examining canceled checks and who therefore is more likely to suffer losses as a result of random signature verification.

In view of the effect of random signature verification on small depositors, some people have alleged that banks using such procedures are not exercising due care in the handling of the customers' accounts. Under the UCC, banks are held to a standard of "ordinary care." At one time in the banking industry, ordinary care normally was interpreted to mean that a bank had a duty to inspect *all* signatures on checks. The question is, what constitutes ordinary care in the context of today's world? Does a bank exercise ordinary care if it follows the prevailing industry practice of examining signatures on only a few, randomly selected checks under a certain amount? Or does ordinary care still mean that a bank should examine each signature?

This became a critical issue in a case involving the Rhode

Island Trust National Bank and one of its customers, Zapata Corporation.[2] Zapata found itself the victim of a series of check forgeries ranging in amount from $150 to $800. In all, over a three-month period, more than $100,000 in forged checks were paid by the bank. None of the checks was examined by the bank, which only verified all signatures on checks for $1,000 or more. Unfortunately, Zapata failed to promptly inspect its canceled checks and report the forgeries to the bank, as required by UCC 4-406(1). Under UCC 4-406(2), Zapata's negligence precluded recovery of the funds from the bank—unless Zapata could show that the bank had failed to exercise ordinary care. Under UCC 4-406(3), if the customer establishes lack of ordinary care on the part of the bank in paying the checks, the customer can recover from the bank regardless of the customer's own negligence.

Zapata alleged that the bank itself was negligent because it did not examine the signatures on all the checks it paid, but the court was not convinced that the bank had violated its duty of care. The First Circuit Court of Appeals ruled that, indeed, the $1,000 signature-verification threshold was within the limits of ordinary care, and therefore the bank was not liable. Not all courts would agree with the First Circuit's conclusion, but that provided no consolation to Zapata, which was left out in the cold. While we may sympathize with Zapata, the other side of the story also deserves to be considered: if

banks were required to examine the signature on every $2 or $10 or $150 check that came through the banking system, the system would probably screech to a grinding halt and make everybody worse off. What we see here is a cost imposed on the few—those who are victims of forgeries similar to the one just described above and who do not inspect their canceled checks—for the benefit of the whole. The tradeoff here can be phrased as follows: the stricter the rule of liability to which banks are held for paying checks over forged signatures, the more expensive banking activities become, and therefore the slower the rate of growth of banking and commerce in the nation.[3]

Fund Transfers

Everybody knows that we live in the age of the computer, and the use of computers in the banking industry is probably just short of overwhelming. As more and more of the work of the banking system is handled by computers, fewer and fewer transactions are evidenced by a "paper trail." Needless to say, electronic fund transfer systems (EFTS) have posed legal—and

ethical—problems, just as computers and computerized transactions have created problems in other areas of the law such as torts and crimes.

Electronic Fund Transfer Act

The Electronic Fund Transfer Act (EFTA) addressed many of the issues that involve the customer's liability with respect to EFTS and the bank's duty of care to the customer. Not all issues have been resolved, however—particularly those that involve disagreement between the customer and the bank's computer. Consider, for example, the following situation.

Mrs. Judd and her husband had a joint checking account at a Citibank branch in New York. They also had Citicards that gave them access to the computer via the bank's automated teller machines (ATMs) located throughout the city. Each card, before it could access the computer, had to be first "validated" by the bank. Although Mrs. Judd had gone into the bank to receive her personal identification number (PIN) and have her card validated, her husband had not yet done so. Thus, only Mrs. Judd's card could be used to obtain cash or make any other transaction via the ATM, and then only if the user knew her PIN—which she said she had given to no one and which she had not even written down, but memorized.

The Judds were thus stunned to learn that $800 had been charged to their checking account as a result of two transactions, one made on February 26, 1980, between 2:13 and 2:14 P.M., and the other on March 28, 1980, between 2:30 and 2:32 P.M. The

2. *Rhode Island Hospital Trust National Bank v. Zapata Corp.,* 848 F.2d 291 (1st Cir. 1988).

3. Revised Articles 3 and 4 essentially codify the result in the *Zapata* case. As mentioned in Chapter 29, under the revisions, ordinary care is defined as the "observance of reasonable commercial standards, prevailing in the area in which [a] person is located, with respect to the business in which that person is engaged" [RUCC 3-103(a)(7), 4-104(c)]. Thus, if a bank's failure to verify check signatures does not violate its own procedures or general banking procedures, it is likely complying with "reasonable commercial standards."

bank maintained that there was no way the funds could have been withdrawn without the use of Mrs. Judd's card and PIN. But Mrs. Judd was convinced the bank had made an error—or, rather, that the computer had. She could not have withdrawn the funds at those times, she contended, because she had been at work on both days at those times; a letter from her employer confirmed her statement.

Eventually, the case came before the Civil Court of New York City, and Judge John Marmarellis was faced with the problem of deciding the issue. Whom was he to believe? Mrs. Judd, whom he described as a "credible witness"? Or the bank's computer printout, which, as "translated" by the bank's manager, verified that the amounts could have been withdrawn from her account only by the use of her card and PIN? He opted to believe Mrs. Judd and awarded her $800 plus interest and disbursements, having stated in his opinion the following: "It is too commonplace in our society that when faced with the choice of man or machine, we readily accept the 'word' of the machine every time. This, despite the tales of computer malfunctions that we hear daily."[4]

Stories similar to that of the Judds do not always have happy endings, but courts recognize that machines can err and have shown a willingness, as in the Judds' case, to take the word of a credible witness over that of a computer. Nonetheless, in the absence of paper evidence of fund transactions, there is no foolproof guarantee that truth and fair play will win out in these kinds of situations. Although it is natural to sympathize with a person who loses money at the hands of an erring and uncaring machine, banks can also be victimized by unethical individuals who falsely, but convincingly, allege computer mistakes and seek recovery from the bank.

Fraudulent Wire Transfers

The EFTA covers only consumer transfers. Commercial wire transfers between banking and other institutions are not covered by the act. In the event of an erroneous or fraudulent commercial wire transfer, the courts must therefore wade through a jungle of legal principles and precedents to determine the issue. Article 4A of the UCC was drafted to fill the need for a uniform law with respect to wire transfers, but until it is adopted by all of the states, courts will still have to rely on tort and contract law in settling disputes between parties to commercial wire transfers.

Unfortunately, it is relatively easy for a technologically sophisticated and well-placed individual to commit fraud using an EFTS. Unless, however, specific requirements are met, the transfer will not fall under the EFTA, and the bank will not be liable. For example, telephone transfers are covered by the EFTA only if they are made pursuant to a prearranged plan under which periodic or recurring transfers are contemplated. Therefore, if an imposter, posing as an account holder, calls a bank official and requests him or her to transfer funds, the true owner of the account cannot hold the bank liable under the EFTA. The owner may be able to recover the fradulently transferred funds in a tort or contract lawsuit, but the action will not lie under the EFTA.[5]

A fraudulent wire transfer was central to a scheme cleverly executed by two con artists, aliases Hank and David Friedman. The Friedmans arranged to buy $800,000 worth of bullion and rare gold coins from Colonial Coins, Inc., in Houston. They told Colonial that they would arrange to have the funds transferred from their Boston bank to Colonial's account at the Texas American Bank, and Colonial agreed. The Friedmans then wrote a letter to Bradford Trust Company in Boston and, over the forged signature of Frank Rochefort, one of Bradford's account holders, authorized Bradford to liquidate $800,000 worth of mutual funds in Rochefort's account and wire the proceeds to his account at the Texas American Bank of Houston. Although the letter stated that the funds should be transferred to the account of Frank S. Rochefort, the account number given in the request was that of Colonial Coins. To expedite the transfer, the Friedmans also included in the letter the acount number of the Houston bank. The agent at Bradford that handled the transaction saw nothing unusual or unduly suspicious about the letter and arranged for the $800,000 to be transferred by wire to the Texas bank. When the money arrived at Texas American, the bank failed to investigate the discrepancy between the account number and the

---

4. *Judd v. Citibank,* 107 Misc.2d 526, 435 N.Y.S.2d 210 (1980).

---

5. *Kashanchi v. Texas Commerce Medical Bank. N.A.,* 703 F.2d 936 (5th Cir. 1983).

account holder's name. Instead, because it had been advised by Colonial to expect the transfer, it immediately deposited the funds into the account number given on the wire and telephoned Colonial to let the merchant know that the funds had been received. At that point, the Freidmans received the gold and coins and left, not to be heard from again.

The matter went unnoted by Bradford Trust until an astonished Frank Rochefort noted the withdrawal on his statement and informed Bradford Trust that he had not authorized the transfer. Bradford credited Rochefort's account with $800,000 and then turned to the Texas bank to recover. Unfortunately for Bradford, it never did retrieve its money. The court would not agree that the Texas bank had been more at fault than Bradford Trust, and Bradford was thus left holding the proverbial bag—in this case, a very empty one.[6]

Until Article 4A is uniformly in effect, courts will have to continue to apply laws that were drafted before the computer age to disputes involving wire transfers. But sometimes this is difficult. Often, courts will look to Articles 3 and 4 for guidance and apply, by analogy, rules governing transfers via paper to

---

6. *Bradford Trust Co. v. Texas American Bank—Houston,* 790 F.2d 407 (5th Cir. 1986).

a transfer of funds via an EFTS. In the case just described, the court's conclusion reflected the reasoning implicit in the UCC provisions governing commercial paper: that between two innocent parties, the party in the best position to prevent the fraud should bear the loss. Although the court found the Texas American bank to have been negligent, it held that Bradford Trust should bear the loss because it had dealt more directly with the imposter.

■ Discussion Questions

1. One often hears about individuals who complain that "the system" is unfair to "the little person." This complaint is nowhere more evident than within the world of commercial paper and banking. The small depositor who is lax about reviewing his or her canceled checks may find out too late that he or she has been the victim of forgery. The customer's negligence in failing to discover the forgery typically gets the bank off the hook, particularly if the forgery involves an amount so small that it clearly falls under any threshold level the bank might have set for examination of checks for unauthorized signatures. Furthermore, it is the less well educated and experienced individual who often is taken in by a scam

artist or otherwise becomes an innocent victim of fraud. Yet because the UCC offers special protection to HDCs, an innocent party to a fraudulent transaction often has no legal recourse. From an ethical standpoint, how could you justify to the "losers" in the above situations the provisions of the UCC that fail to protect them? How would you explain the tradeoffs involved? Can you think of a way in which such problems could be handled more fairly or ethically than they are under the UCC?

2. What do you think would result if a change in the law allowed personal defenses to be successfully raised against HDCs? Who would lose, and who would gain? What would happen to economic efficiency?

3. It would be possible to eliminate an imposter's ability to effectuate telephone fund transfers by simply making it illegal for banks to act on transfer requests made by telephone. If this were done, no one would have to worry about innocent parties being hurt because of fraudulent fund transfers that do not fall under the EFTA. It is clear, then, who the beneficiaries of such a change in the law would be. What would be the costs to society, though, of such a change in the law? Who would pay those costs? What might the ultimate outcome of such a law be?

UNIT FIVE

Creditors' Rights, Bankruptcy, and Lender Liability

■ **The Importance of Debtor-Creditor Relationships**

The world of business is a world of credit. Without credit, our advanced economy would come to a standstill. Indeed, without credit, we would not have an advanced economy. Business firms would be unable to purchase most equipment for production if they could not purchase it on credit. Big-ticket items, such as houses and automobiles, would be out of the reach of most consumers without the ability to purchase those items on credit. Credit—in the form of automobile loans, business loans, mortgage loans, credit-card transactions, and other lending arrangements—affects virtually everyone's everyday life. It is not surprising, therefore, that the rights of creditors must be protected by law. If this were not the case, virtually no one would be willing to loan money.

On the debtor's side, the easy availability of credit has allowed some debtors to become perilously indebted. Bankrupty law developed to protect such debtors, while at the same time protecting creditors' rights—at least, to the extent possible under the debtor's circumstances. Additionally, other laws had to be developed to limit the rights of creditors so that they could not use harassment and duress as tactics to ensure the payment of their claims.

Because of the increasing trend toward lender liability, lending institutions in recent years have had to be particularly careful in their relationships with debtors to avoid lawsuits by debtors seeking damages for the institutions' improper actions. Indeed, a lending institution today may be liable not only to debtors but also for the costs incurred for toxic waste clean-up efforts on property on which the lending institution has foreclosed because of a debtor's default.

In this unit, you will examine various aspects of credit. Secured transactions are described in Chapter 31. Chapter 32 discusses other creditors' remedies and the concept of suretyship, which involves a way of guaranteeing payment of another's debt. Chapter 33 covers bankruptcy and reorganization. The last chapter in the unit, Chapter 34, gives an overview of lender liability law.

■ Ethical Issues in Debtor-Creditor Relationships

The ethical issues that concern debtor-creditor relationships stem from the obvious tradeoff: whenever a creditor is protected, the debtor may not receive what seems to be "fair" treatment; conversely, whenever a debtor is protected, the creditor may not receive what seems to be "fair" treatment. In a sense, the law with respect to debtors' and creditors' rights is a zero-sum game. One party in a credit transaction may believe that he or she is receiving unfair treatment whenever the other party is treated favorably by a particular law, and vice versa.

Creditors may often have the legal right to take specific actions against debtors, but those legal actions may not be ethically appropriate. This is particularly the case when defaulting debtors have little income and have been borrowing money for necessities. In a similar vein, a debtor who uses the law as a shield for avoiding a genuine obligation is clearly acting unethically.

Bankruptcy law necessarily favors debtors and thus gives rise to issues of fairness. Is it ethical, for example, to take advantage of protection under bankruptcy law when that law was originally designed as the "last resort"? Should debtors be allowed to avoid permanently the debts they owe by taking refuge under bankruptcy law, even when they are solvent? These are ethical questions that must be faced by our society.

With respect to lender liability, the commonplace notion that "the big banks" can do whatever they want has been turned on its head. Lending institutions, no matter what their size, now frequently face a barrage of defenses, as well as lawsuits, when they attempt to collect on loans in default.

Remember, when you are reading this unit, that for every creditor's right discussed, there is a corresponding debtor's duty; and for every debtor's right discussed, there is a corresponding creditor's duty. In other words, the mirror image of a creditor's right is a debtor's duty, and vice versa.

Chapter 31

Secured Transactions

The concept of a secured transaction is as basic to modern business practice as the concept of credit. Few purchasers—be they manufacturers, wholesalers, retailers, or consumers—have the resources to pay cash for all the goods they purchase. Lenders are reluctant to lend money to a debtor solely on the debtor's promise to repay the debt. Therefore, to minimize the risk of loss, the creditor often requires the debtor to provide some type of security beyond the mere promise that the debt will be paid. When this security takes the form of personal property owned by the debtor or in which the debtor has a legal interest, the transaction becomes known as a **secured transaction.**

The importance of being a secured creditor cannot be overemphasized. Business as we know it today could not exist without the presence of secured transaction law. Secured creditors are generally not hampered by certain state laws favorable to debtors (such as exemption laws), and secured creditors have a favored position should the debtor become bankrupt.

A key to understanding this area of the law is to consider a transaction from a creditor's point of view. From this perspective, the basic questions are the following:

1. If the debtor defaults, does the creditor have an enforceable security interest in the debtor's property?
2. If an enforceable security interest in the debtor's property does exist, will the creditor's security interest take *priority* over other security interests and creditors' claims?

The answers to these two questions form the basis for the law of secured transactions and involve two important concepts: *attachment* and *perfection.* A security interest is not enforceable unless the creditor's rights have attached to the *collateral* (the property the debtor offered as security). What has to be done for a security interest to attach is considered in this chapter, following a brief introduction to Article 9 of the UCC and the key terminology of secured transactions. The chapter then discusses the process of perfection and its importance in establishing priority over other creditors' and some purchasers' claims. Basically, perfection is what the creditor must do in the way of giving legal notice to make his or her security interest effective against the debtor's other creditors and purchasers.

Article 9 of the UCC

Prior to adoption of the UCC, creditors used a great number of security devices, each of which had its own rules and terminology. Article 9 of the UCC has eliminated the distinctions among the various forms of financing, simplified the terminology, and provided a framework for the law of secured transactions.

Article 9 applies to any transaction that is intended to create a security interest in personal property, accounts, chattel paper, and fixtures. (See Exhibit 31–2 on pages 548–549 for definitions of these terms.) Debtor-creditor transactions that are not covered under Article 9 are discussed in the next chapter.

As will become evident, the law of secured transactions tends to favor the rights of creditors; but, to a lesser extent, it offers debtors some protection, too.

Definitions

The terminology established under the UCC is now uniformly used in all documents drawn in connection with a secured transaction. A brief summary of the UCC's definitions follows.

1. A **security interest** is any interest ''in *personal property or fixtures* [emphasis added] which secures payment or performance of an obligation'' [UCC 1-201(37)].
2. A **secured party** is a lender, seller, or any person in whose favor there is a security interest, including a person to whom accounts or chattel paper have been sold [UCC 9-105(1)(m)].
3. A **debtor** is the party who owes payment or performance of the secured obligation, whether or not that party actually owns or has rights in the collateral. The term *debtor* includes sellers of accounts or chattel paper. When the debtor and owner of the collateral are not the same person, the term *debtor* refers to the actual owner of the collateral or describes the obligor on an obligation, or both, depending on the context in which the term is used [UCC 9-105(1)(d)].
4. A **security agreement** is an agreement that creates or provides for a security interest between the debtor and a secured party [UCC 9-105(1)(l)].
5. **Collateral** is the property subject to a security interest, including accounts and chattel paper that have been sold [UCC 9-105(1)(c)].

Exhibit 31–1 illustrates how these terms and concepts frame the debtor-creditor relationship in the context of a secured transaction.

Classification of Collateral

There are basically two types of collateral, tangible and intangible. *Tangible* collateral is movable; *intangible* collateral is nonphysical property. The various types of tangible and intangible collateral are defined in Exhibit 31–2, as well as the method of perfection required for each type.

Creating Security Interests

To become a secured party, the creditor must acquire a security interest in the collateral of the debtor. Three requirements must be met for a creditor to have an enforceable security interest:

1. Unless the creditor has possession of the collateral, there must be an agreement in writing.

■ Exhibit 31–1 Secured Transactions–Concepts and Terminology

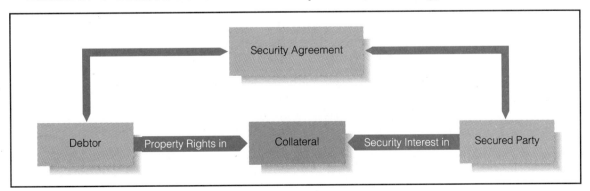

■ Exhibit 31–2 Types of Collateral and Methods of Perfection

Type of Collateral	Definitions	Perfection Method	UCC Sections
Tangible	All things that are *movable* at the time the security interest attaches or that are *fixtures* [UCC 9-105(1)(h)]. This includes timber to be cut, growing crops, and unborn animals.		
1. Consumer goods	Goods used or bought primarily for personal, family, or household purposes—for example, household furniture [UCC 9-109(1)].	For purchase-money security interest, attachment is sufficient; for boats, motor vehicles, and trailers, filing or compliance with a certificate of title statute is required; for other consumer goods, general rules of filing or possession apply.	9-302(1)(d), 9-302(3), 9-302(4), 9-305
2. Equipment	Goods bought for or used primarily in business—for example, a delivery truck [UCC 9-109(2)].	Filing or possession by secured party.	9-302(1), 9-305
3. Farm products	Crops, livestock, and supplies used or produced in a farming operation in the possession of a farmer-debtor. This includes products of crops or livestock—for example, milk, eggs, maple syrup, and ginned cotton [UCC 9-109(3)].	Filing or possession by secured party.	9-302(1), 9-305
4. Inventory	Goods held for sale or lease and materials used or consumed in the course of business—for example, raw materials or the floor stock of a retailer [UCC 9-109(4)].	Filing or possession by secured party.	9-302(1), 9-305
5. Fixtures	Goods that become so affixed to realty that an interest in them arises under real estate law—for example, a central air conditioning unit [UCC 9-313(1)(a)].	Filing only.	9-313(1)
Intangible	Nonphysical property that exists only in connection with something else.		
1. Chattel paper	Any writing that evidences both a *monetary obligation* and a *security interest*—for example, a thirty-six-month-payment retail security agreement signed by a buyer to purchase a car [UCC 9-105(1)(b)].	Filing or possession by secured party.	9-304(1), 9-305
2. Documents of title	Paper that entitles the person in possession to hold, receive, or dispose of the paper or goods the document covers—for example, bills of lading, warehouse receipts, and dock warrants [UCC 9-105(1)(f), 1-201(15), 7-201].	Filing or possession by secured party.	9-304(1), (3); 9-305

■ **Exhibit 31–2 Types of Collateral and Methods of Perfection (Continued)**

Type of Collateral	Definitions	Perfection Method	UCC Sections
3. Instruments	Any writing that evidences a right to payment of money and that is not a security agreement or lease, and any negotiable instrument or certificated security that in the ordinary course of business is transferred by delivery with any necessary indorsement or assignment—for example, stock certificates, promissory notes, and certificates of deposit [UCC 9-105(1)(i), 3-104, 8-102(1)(a)].	Unless temporary perfected status, possession only.	9-304(1), (4), (5); 9-305
4. Accounts	Any right to payment for goods sold or leased or services rendered that is not evidenced by an instrument or chattel paper—for example, accounts receivable and contract right payments [UCC 9-106].	Filing (with exceptions).	9-302(1)(e), (g)
5. General intangibles	Any personal property other than that defined above—for example, a patent, a copyright, goodwill, or a trademark [UCC 9-106].	Filing only.	9-302(1)

2. The creditor must give value to the debtor.
3. The debtor must have rights in the collateral.

Once these requirements have been met, the creditor's rights are said to *attach* to the collateral. This means that the creditor has an *enforceable* security interest against the debtor. **Attachment** ensures that the security interest between the debtor and the secured party is effective [UCC 9-203].

Written Agreement

Unless the collateral is in the possession of the secured party (the creditor), there must be a *written security agreement* describing the collateral and signed by the debtor. (The creditor's signature is not required.) See Exhibit 31–3 for a sample security agreement. The security agreement creates or provides for a security interest. For example, it might read "Debtor hereby grants to secured party a security interest in the following goods." The description must reasonably identify the collateral [UCC 9-203(1), 9-110]. For example, the description "my 1993 Ford truck" is sufficient if the debtor has only one 1993 Ford truck.

Value Given to Debtor

The secured party must give *value* to the debtor. Under UCC 1-201(44), value is any consideration that supports a simple contract. In addition, value can be security given for a preexisting (antecedent) obligation or any binding commitment to extend credit. Normally, the value given by a secured party involves a direct loan or a commitment to sell goods on credit.

Debtor Has Rights in Collateral

The debtor must have *rights* in the collateral; that is, the debtor must have some ownership interest in, or right to obtain possession of, the collateral. The debtor's rights can represent either a current or a future legal interest in the collateral. For example, a retailer-debtor can give a secured party a security interest not only in existing inventory owned by the retailer but also in future inventory to be acquired by the retailer.

■ Perfecting a Security Interest

As mentioned in this chapter's introduction, a creditor has two primary concerns if the debtor defaults—satisfaction of the debt out of certain predesignated property and priority over other creditors who have claims against the debtor. The concept of *attachment,* which establishes the criteria for creating an enforceable security interest, deals with the former concern; the concept of *perfection*

■ **Exhibit 31–3 A Sample Security Agreement**

SECURITY AGREEMENT

DEBTOR_____

DEBTOR'S RESIDENCE _____
        OR
PLACE OF BUSINESS _____

SECURED PARTY_____

SECURED PARTY'S ADDRESS_____

SECURITY INTEREST In order to secure the payment of the Debt described below and the obligations of this Security Agreement, Debtor gives Secured Party a security interest in the following Collateral under Article 9 of the Uniform Commercial Code (UCC):

COLLATERAL_____

_____

_____

_____

AFTER-ACQUIRED PROPERTY AND PROCEEDS The Collateral includes: all proceeds, increases, substitutions, replacements, additions, improvements and accessions to the Collateral, all proceeds from insurance on the Collateral, and all refunds of unearned premiums for insurance; but does not include any consumer goods (other than accessions) acquired by Debtor more than 10 days after the loan proceeds are advanced. This provision shall not be construed to mean that Debtor is authorized to sell, lease, or dispose of the Collateral without the consent of Secured Party.

DEBT $_____ Note dated _____ , 19____ payable to Secured Party.

FUTURE ADVANCES AND OTHER DEBTS The debt includes: any renewals or extensions of the Note; any amounts advanced by Secured Party to protect its security interest in the Collateral; any future amounts advanced by Secured Party at its option to Debtor; any and all other liabilities of Debtor to Secured Party, now existing or later incurred, matured or unmatured, direct or contingent; any costs or expenses that may be lawfully assessed against Debtor for the collection of the Debt, including attorney's fees;

LOCATION OF COLLATERAL Debtor agrees to keep the Collateral
[ ] at the Debtor's address stated above;
[ ] at the following location: _____

REAL ESTATE If marked here [ ], the Collateral is either [ ] a fixture that is, or will be, attached to the following described real estate; or [ ] crops growing or to be grown upon the following described real estate: _____

whose record owner is: _____

FARM PRODUCTS If marked here [ ], the Collateral is farm products and includes the offspring and increase of any livestock or crops given as such Collateral and all feed, seed, fertilizer and other supplies now owned or later acquired in connection with such farming operations, all of which is located upon the above described real estate.

LOCATION OF RECORDS If marked here [ ], the Collateral consists of accounts, instruments, chattel paper, documents or other general intangibles and the records concerning such Collateral are kept at _____

POSSESSION BY SECURED PARTY If marked here [ ], the Collateral will be retained in the possession of Secured Party, and the following provisions in this section shall be applicable. Secured Party's duty with reference to the Collateral shall be solely to use reasonable care in the custody and preservation of the Collateral in its possession and to receive collections, earnings, dividends, remittances and payments on such Collateral as and when made. Secured Party shall have the option of applying the amounts so received, after deduction for any collection costs that may be lawfully charged, as payment of any debt secured by this Security Agreement, or holding such amounts for the benefit of Debtor. Secured Party shall not be responsible in any way for any depreciation in value of the Collateral, nor shall Secured Party have any duty or responsibility to take any steps to preserve rights against other parties or to enforce collection of the Collateral.

USE OF COLLATERAL The Collateral will be used primarily for the purposes checked below:
[ ] Personal, family, or household purposes
[ ] Business operations (other than farming)
[ ] Farming operations

OWNERSHIP OF COLLATERAL Debtor is the owner of the Collateral, or if marked here [ ], Debtor is purchasing the Collateral with the proceeds of the Note described above. Except for the security interest created by this Security Agreement, the Collateral is free from any lien, security interest, encumbrance, or claim. With respect to any instruments, chattel paper, documents or other general intangibles given as Collateral, Debtor warrants and represents that: they are genuine, free from adverse claims, default, prepayment or defenses; all persons appearing to be obligated thereon have authority and capacity to contract and are bound thereon; and they comply with applicable laws concerning form, content, and manner of preparation and execution. Debtor will, at Debtor's cost and expense, defend any action which may affect Secured Party's security interest in, or Debtor's title to, the Collateral.

FINANCING STATEMENT No Financing Statement covering the Collateral or any part thereof or any proceeds thereof is on file in any public office and, at Secured Party's request, Debtor will join in executing all necessary Financing Statements in forms satisfactory to Secured Party and will pay the cost of filing and will further execute all other necessary instruments deemed necessary by Secured Party and pay the cost of filing.

SALE OR ENCUMBRANCE OF COLLATERAL Debtor will not, without the written consent of Secured Party, sell, contract to sell, lease, encumber, or dispose of the Collateral or any interest therein until this Security Agreement and all debts secured thereby have been fully satisfied.

■ Exhibit 31–3 A Sample Security Agreement (Continued)

INSURANCE If the Collateral is tangible property and is insurable, Debtor will insure the Collateral with companies acceptable to Secured Party against such casualties and in such amounts as Secured Party shall reasonably require with a loss payable clause in favor of Debtor and Secured Party as their interest may appear, and Secured Party is hereby authorized to collect sums which may become due under any of said policies and apply the same to the obligations hereby secured.

PROTECTION OF COLLATERAL If the Collateral is tangible property, Debtor will keep the Collateral in good order and repair and will not waste or destroy the Collateral or any part thereof. Debtor will not use the Collateral in violation of any statute or ordinance and Secured Party will have the right to examine and inspect the Collateral at any reasonable time.

TAXES Debtor will pay promptly when due all taxes and assessments on the Collateral or for its use and operation.

DECREASE IN VALUE OF COLLATERAL If in Secured Party's judgment the Collateral has materially decreased in value or if Secured Party shall at any time deem that Secured Party is insecure, Debtor shall either provide enough additional Collateral to satisfy Secured Party, or shall reduce the total indebtedness by an amount sufficient to satisfy Secured Party.

REIMBURSEMENT OF EXPENSES At the option of Secured Party, Secured Party may discharge taxes, liens, interest, or perform or cause to be performed for and on behalf of Debtor any actions and conditions, obligations, or covenants which Debtor has failed or refused to perform, and may pay for the repair, maintenance, and preservation of the Collateral, including, to the extent but only to the extent such amounts may be lawfully collected, attorney's fees, court costs, agent's fees, or commissions, or any other costs or expenses. All sums so expended shall bear interest from the date of payment at the rate of interest stated in the Note described above, if such rate of interest can be lawfully collected and if not then at the maximum legal rate, and shall be payable on demand at the place designated in the Note and shall be secured by this Security Agreement.

CHANGE OF RESIDENCE OR PLACE OF BUSINESS Debtor will promptly notify Secured Party of any change of the Debtor's residence, place of business, or place where records are kept.

TIME OF PERFORMANCE AND WAIVER In performing any act under this Security Agreement and the Note secured thereby, time shall be of the essence. Secured Party's acceptance of partial or delinquent payments, or the failure of Secured Party to exercise any right or remedy shall not be a waiver of any obligation of Debtor or right of Secured Party or constitute a waiver of any other similar default subsequently occurring.

DEFAULT Debtor shall be in default under this Security Agreement on the happening of any of the following events or conditions:
(1) Default in the payment or performance of any obligation, covenant, or liability contained or referred to in the Note or in this Security Agreement;
(2) Any warranty, representation, or statement made or furnished to Secured Party by or on behalf of Debtor proves to have been false in any material respect when made or furnished;
(3) Loss, theft, substantial damage, destruction, sale, or encumbrance to or of any of the Collateral, or the making of any levy, seizure, or attachment thereof or thereon;
(4) Any time Secured Party believes that the prospect of payment of any indebtedness secured hereby or the performance of this Security Agreement is impaired;
(5) Death, dissolution, termination of existence, insolvency, business failure, appointment of a receiver for any part of the Collateral, assignment for the benefit of creditors or the commencement of any proceeding under any bankruptcy or insolvency law by or against Debtor or any guarantor or surety for Debtor.

REMEDIES Upon the occurrence of any such event of default, and at any time thereafter, Secured Party may declare all obligations secured immediately due and payable and may proceed to enforce payment of the same and exercise any and all of the rights and remedies provided by the Uniform Commercial Code as well as other rights and remedies either at law or in equity possessed by Secured Party.

Secured Party shall have the right to remove the Collateral from the premises of Debtor and, for purposes of removal and possession, Secured Party or its representatives may enter any premises of the Debtor without legal process and the Debtor hereby waives and releases Secured Party of and from any and all claims in connection therewith or arising therefrom.

Secured Party may require Debtor to assemble the Collateral and make it available to Secured Party at any place to be designated by the Secured Party which is reasonably convenient to both parties. Unless the Collateral is perishable or threatens to decline speedily in value or is of a type customarily sold on a recognized market, Secured Party will give the Debtor reasonable notice of the time and place of any public sale thereof or of the time after which any private sale or any other intended disposition thereof is to be made. The requirements of reasonable notice shall be met if such notice is mailed, postage prepaid, to the address of Debtor shown at the beginning of this Security Agreement at least five days before the time of the sale or disposition. Expenses of retaking, holding, preparing for sale, selling, or the like shall include Secured Party's reasonable attorney's fees and legal expenses, to the extent but only to the extent such amounts may be lawfully collected.

TEXAS LAW TO APPLY This Agreement shall be construed under and in accordance with the Uniform Commercial Code and other applicable laws of the State of Texas and all obligations of the parties created hereunder are performable in the County of the Secured Party's address stated above.

PARTIES BOUND This Agreement shall be binding on and inure to the benefit of the parties hereto and their respective heirs, executors, administrators, legal representatives, successors, and assigns. If there is more than one Debtor, their obligations shall be joint and several.

LEGAL CONSTRUCTION In case any one or more of the provisions contained in this Agreement shall for any reason be held to be invalid, illegal, or unenforceable in any respect, such invalidity, illegality, or unenforceability shall not affect any other provision thereof and this Agreement shall be construed as if such invalid, illegal, or unenforceable provision had never been contained herein. Notwithstanding anything else herein to the contrary, if the Debt secured by this Security Agreement is a loan made under any chapter of the Texas Credit Code that limits charges and expenses that may be collected by Secured Party, the provisions of such Code shall govern in the event of any conflict between the provisions of this Security Agreement and the provisions of such Code.

Executed _____ ,19_____.

Secured Party: Debtor:

_____   _____

_____   _____

Source: Reprinted with permission of Hart Graphics Inc. of Austin, Texas. © 1985 Hart Graphics Inc.

deals with the latter. Even though a security interest has attached, the secured party must take steps to protect his or her claim to the collateral over claims that may be brought by third parties, such as other secured creditors, general creditors, trustees in bankruptcy, and purchasers of the collateral that is the subject matter of the security agreement. **Perfection** represents the legal process by which a secured party is protected against some of the claims of third parties who may wish to have their debts satisfied out of the same collateral.

The methods by which security interests can be perfected under Article 9 are described below. Which method is appropriate depends on how the collateral is classified—see Exhibit 31–2. The creditor who fails to perfect by the prescribed method may lack a perfected security interest. Although the usual means of perfecting a security interest is by filing, this is not the exclusive means of perfection. In specific situations, perfection by possession and automatic perfection serve as alternatives to the filing of a financing statement.

Perfection by Filing

The most common method of perfecting a security interest under Article 9 is to file a *financing statement* with the appropriate public office.

THE FINANCING STATEMENT A **financing statement** gives notice that the secured party claims an interest in collateral belonging to a certain named debtor. A public filing is required so that potential creditors can learn what claims already exist to certain property. Under Article 9, a financing statement must meet certain requirements. It must (1) be signed by the debtor, (2) contain the addresses of both the debtor and secured party, and (3) describe the collateral by type or item

[UCC 9-402(1)].[1] A sample financing statement is shown in Exhibit 31–4.

The financing statement must contain a description of the collateral in which the secured party has a security interest. The purpose of including a description of the collateral in a financing statement is to put persons who might later wish to lend to the debtor on notice that certain goods in the debtor's possession are already subject to a perfected security interest.

Sometimes the description given in the security agreement varies from that given in the financing statement, with the description in the security agreement being more precise and the description in the financing statement more general. For example, a security agreement drafted as part of a loan to a manufacturer may list all of the manufacturer's equipment subject to the loan by serial number, whereas the financing statement may simply describe it as ''all equipment owned or hereafter acquired.'' To avoid problems that might be caused by such differences, a secured party may repeat exactly the security agreement's description in the financing statement; file the security agreement as a financing statement, assuming it meets the previously discussed criteria; or, when permitted, file a combination security agreement–financing statement form. If the financing statement is too general or vague, a court may find it insufficient to perfect a security interest. This occurred in the following case.

---

1. For certain types of collateral—crops, timber to be cut, minerals, accounts, and goods that are to become fixtures—the financing statement must include more than a description of the collateral itself. For example, a description of the real estate concerned is also required in some of these cases [UCC 9-402(1), (5); 9-103(5); 9-313].

Case 31.1
_____

IN RE BECKER[a]

United States District Court,
Western District of Wisconsin,
1985.
53 Bankr. 450.

BACKGROUND AND FACTS On September 5, 1974, Dwight and Irene Becker entered into a loan agreement with the Bank of Barron. To secure the loan, the agreement provided the bank with a security interest in all the Beckers' assets. On September 11, the bank filed a financing statement with the Barron County Register of Deeds. The statement claimed an interest in "[a]ll the Becker farm's personal property and feed now owned and

a. *In re* means concerning or regarding. It is a way to refer to judicial proceedings—such as bankruptcy proceedings—in which there are no adversarial parties but only some matter on which action is taken.

hereafter acquired. 25% dairy assignment." When the Beckers later filed for bankruptcy, the bank claimed that the statement gave it the status of a perfected secured creditor in the bankruptcy proceedings. The Beckers claimed that the statement was too general and therefore insufficient to give the bank a perfected security interest. The bankruptcy court agreed with the Beckers, and the bank appealed.

DECISION AND RATIONALE The United States District Court for the Western District of Wisconsin held that the description in the financing statement was not sufficiently specific in regard to the property subject to the security interest—with the exception of the description of the feed and the 25 percent milk assignment—to perfect the bank's security interest in the collateral. The bankruptcy court's decision was thus affirmed. The district court pointed out that the purpose of perfection by filing was to give "notice to third parties of the possible claims of others." The court stated, "[I]t is clear that the description 'all farm personal property' * * * provides little more notice to third parties than if no description at all were included. * * * Even if livestock and farm equipment might be considered farm personal property, the breadth of the term destroys the intended purpose of the filing."

WHERE TO FILE Depending on the classification of the collateral, filing is done either centrally with the secretary of state or locally with a county official, or both, according to state law. According to UCC 9-401, a state may choose one of three proposed alternative systems.[2] In general, financing statements for consumer goods or for any collateral used or arising from a farmer's business should be filed locally with the county clerk. Other kinds of collateral require filing with the secretary of state [UCC 9-401].

The correct place of filing will depend on how the collateral is classified, as mentioned above. Tangible property is classified as consumer goods, equipment, farm products, inventory, or fixtures; and intangible property is classified as chattel paper, documents of title, instruments, accounts, or general intangibles. The classes of goods are mutually exclusive; for example, *the same property cannot at the same time and to the same person be both equipment and inventory.* How do you determine the appropriate classification? How do you decide, for example, whether a physician's car or a farmer's jeep should be classified as equipment or a consumer good? The answer is provided by UCC 9-109. The principal *use* to which the property is put by the debtor determines its classification. If the physician puts the car primarily to personal use, then it is a consumer good; if it is used primarily for his or her medical practice, then it is equipment. If a farmer's jeep is necessary for farming operations and is used primarily for that, then the jeep is classified as farm equipment. But the car and jeep can never be categorized as *both* equipment and consumer goods.

Goods can fall into different classes at different times. For example, a CB radio is inventory when it is in the hands of a dealer [UCC 9-109(4)]. But when it is purchased by a consumer for use in a private car, it becomes a consumer good [UCC 9-109(1)]. When it is bought and installed in a police patrol car, it is equipment [UCC 9-109(2)]. Under the UCC, the majority rule is that the classification and filing are based on the *primary use* being made of the collateral at the time of filing. According to UCC 9-401, once the security agreement is properly filed, any change in the use of the collateral will not endanger the security interest of the secured party.

If a secured party fails to perfect properly, the perfection is void. This means that a later, properly perfected security interest has priority. For example, suppose that a state has adopted the second alternative offered by UCC 9-401. This alternative provides for central filing (usually with the secretary of state) if the collateral is inventory. West

---

2. See UCC 9-401 in Appendix C for these three alternatives. Approximately half of the states have adopted the second alternative. Filing fees range from as low as $3 to as high as $25.

■ **Exhibit 31–4 A Sample Financing Statement**

This FINANCING STATEMENT is presented for filing pursuant to the California Uniform Commercial Code.

1. DEBTOR (LAST NAME FIRST—IF AN INDIVIDUAL)			1A. SOCIAL SECURITY OR FEDERAL TAX NO.	
1B. MAILING ADDRESS		1C. CITY, STATE	1D. ZIP CODE	
2. ADDITIONAL DEBTOR (IF ANY) (LAST NAME FIRST—IF AN INDIVIDUAL)			2A. SOCIAL SECURITY OR FEDERAL TAX NO.	
2B. MAILING ADDRESS		2C. CITY, STATE	2D. ZIP CODE	
3. DEBTOR'S TRADE NAMES OR STYLES (IF ANY)			3A. FEDERAL TAX NUMBER	

4. SECURED PARTY	4A. SOCIAL SECURITY NO., FEDERAL TAX NO. OR BANK TRANSIT AND A.B.A. NO.
NAME MAILING ADDRESS CITY STATE ZIP CODE	

5. ASSIGNEE OF SECURED PARTY (IF ANY)	5A. SOCIAL SECURITY NO., FEDERAL TAX NO. OR BANK TRANSIT AND A.B.A. NO.
NAME MAILING ADDRESS CITY STATE ZIP CODE	

6. This FINANCING STATEMENT covers the following types or items of property **(Include description of real property on which located and owner of record when required by Instruction 4).**
As security for and in consideration of all present and any future advances or other obligations debtor hereby grants United California Bank a security interest in all of the following types or items of property ("Collateral" herein) in which the debtor now has or hereafter acquires any right, title, or interest, or rights present and future, wheresoever located and whether in the possession of the debtor, a warehouseman, bailee, trustee or any other person, and all increases, therein and replacements, products, and proceeds thereof. Proceeds include but are not limited to inventory, returned merchandise, accounts, chattel paper, general intangibles, insurance proceeds, documents, money, goods, equipment, instruments, and any other tangible or intangible property arising under the sale, lease or other disposition of collateral:

7. CHECK IF APPLICABLE [X]	7A. ☐ PRODUCTS OF COLLATERAL ARE ALSO COVERED	7B. DEBTOR(S) SIGNATURE NOT REQUIRED IN ACCORDANCE WITH INSTRUCTION 5(c) ITEM: ☐ (1) ☐ (2) ☐ (3) ☐ (4)

8. CHECK IF APPLICABLE [X]	☐ DEBTOR IS A "TRANSMITTING UTILITY" IN ACCORDANCE WITH UCC § 9105 (1) (n)

9.	DATE:	C O D E	10. THIS SPACE FOR USE OF FILING OFFICER (DATE, TIME, FILE NUMBER AND FILING OFFICER)
▶ SIGNATURE(S) of DEBTOR(S)			
TYPE OR PRINT NAME(S) OF DEBTOR(S)		1	
▶		2	
SIGNATURE(S) OF SECURED PARTY(IES)		3	
		4	
TYPE OR PRINT NAME(S) OF SECURED PARTY(IES)		5	
11. *Return copy to:*		6	
NAME		7	
ADDRESS		8	
CITY		9	
STATE		0	
ZIP CODE			

(1) *FILING OFFICER COPY*	FORM UCC-1—FILING FEE $3.00 *Approved by the Secretary of State*

MS-336 10-78

Bank loans retail seller Alger $5,000, and Alger puts up all existing inventory and any inventory she might later acquire as collateral. Alger signs a security agreement and a financing statement. By error, West files the financing statement locally (with the county clerk). Later, Alger, in need of working capital, secures a loan from Friendly Savings and Loan. Alger puts up as collateral some newly acquired inventory she paid for with cash. Alger signs a security agreement and a financing statement. Friendly Savings perfects its security interest by filing centrally. If Alger goes into default on both loans, Friendly's proper perfection gives priority to its interest in the newly acquired inventory because West Bank's perfection, although prior in time, was improperly filed and therefore void.

There is an exception. A financing statement filed in an improper place is effective against any party who has actual knowledge of the contents of the improperly filed statement [UCC 9-401(2)]. Thus, in the example just given, if, in a search of financing statements filed locally, Friendly had discovered West Bank's statement, Friendly's properly filed statement would not have had priority over West Bank's defectively filed statement.

Perfection by Possession

An alternative to perfection by filing is perfection by the secured party's possession of the collateral. Consider an example: Ulster borrows $2,000 from Levine, giving Levine possession of three antique guns as collateral for the loan. Several months later, before Ulster has repaid the loan, a creditor obtains a judgment against Ulster. The creditor seeks to have the sheriff take the valuable antique guns away from Levine. Even though no financing statement has been filed, the creditor cannot touch the antique guns because Levine perfected his security interest in them when he took possession of them.

Perfection by possession is impractical in many cases because it denies the debtor the right to use, sell, or derive income from the property to pay off the debt secured by the collateral. Security interests in some types of collateral, however, can *only* be perfected by possession of the collateral. If the collateral consists of negotiable instruments or certificated securities—such as stocks and bonds—the only way proper perfection can be attained is through possession of the instruments or securities.

The transfer of collateral subject to a security interest to the secured party is called a **pledge** [UCC 9-302(1)(a), 9-304(1), 9-305]. The pledge is the oldest form of secured transaction, dating back to at least the days of the Roman Empire, when debtors pledged (gave to a creditor) certain property to assure the creditor that the debt would be paid. If the debt was not paid, the creditor could sell or keep the property in satisfaction of the debt.

Automatic Perfection

In certain circumstances, a security interest can be perfected automatically at the time of a credit sale—that is, at the time the security interest is created under a written security agreement. Situations in which perfection is automatic are listed in UCC 9-302(1) and described below.

PURCHASE-MONEY SECURITY INTEREST The automatic-perfection rule is sometimes called *perfection by attachment*. It applies when there is a purchase-money security interest and the goods are *consumer goods* (defined as goods bought or used by the debtor primarily for personal, family, or household purposes). The seller in this situation need do nothing more to protect his or her interest.

One of the ways in which a **purchase-money security interest** comes into being is when a business selling consumer durable goods agrees to lend much of the purchase price for the goods purchased. Formally, such an interest is created in the following situations:

1. When a seller retains or takes a security interest in collateral to secure part or all of the purchase price of the property serving as collateral.
2. When some other party takes a security interest in the collateral to secure the party's advances or other obligation that is actually used by the debtor to acquire rights in or to use the collateral. For example, a financing agency takes a purchase-money security interest when it makes advances to a buyer to enable him or her to buy goods from a seller, and the buyer uses the money for that purpose [UCC 9-107].

In either of the above-listed situations, a lender or seller has essentially provided a buyer with the purchase money to buy goods and therefore, under Article 9, has an automatically perfected security interest in the goods purchased. To illustrate: Suppose that Barbara wants to purchase a stereo from Sounds Unlimited. The purchase price is $900. Not being able to pay cash, Barbara signs a security agreement to pay $100 down and $50 per month until the balance plus interest is fully paid. Sounds Unlimited will retain a perfected security interest in the purchased stereo until full payment has been made.

The same result would occur if Barbara went to West Bank and borrowed the $900 to buy the stereo from Sounds Unlimited. If Barbara signs a security agreement with West Bank, with the yet-to-be-purchased stereo as collateral, West Bank will have a purchase-money security interest the moment that the stereo is actually purchased from Sounds Unlimited with the money provided by the bank. To protect its investment of the purchase money and thereby its security interest, West Bank might arrange to pay the $900 directly to Sounds Unlimited.

Exceptions to this rule exist for security interests in fixtures and in motor vehicles [UCC 9-302(1)(d)]. Also, in states that have not adopted the 1972 UCC amendments[3] or that have decided to retain certain pre-1972 sections, a purchase-money security interest in farm equipment under a certain value is also automatically perfected by attachment.

ACCOUNTS RECEIVABLE Another instance of automatic perfection occurs when a person assigns a small portion of his or her accounts receivable to a collecting agent. Perfection is automatic as long as the assignment does not by itself, or in conjunction with other assignments to the same assignee, constitute a transfer of a significant part of the outstanding accounts of the debtor. Other less common situations in which perfection is automatic are listed in UCC 9-302(1).

Exceptions to Perfection under Article 9

There are sources of law other than Article 9 that deal with perfection of security interests. The three most important sources are federal law, such as the Federal Aviation Act; UCC Article 8, which deals with investment securities; and state certificate of title laws that deal with motor vehicles.

Most states require a certificate of title for any motor vehicle, boat, or motor home. The normal methods described above for perfection of a security interest typically do not obtain where such vehicles are concerned. Rather, perfection of a security interest only occurs when a notation of such interest appears on the certificate of title that covers the vehicle.

As an example, suppose that your commercial bank lends you 80 percent of the money necessary to purchase a new BMW. You live in a state that requires certificates of title for all automobiles. If your bank fails to have its security interest noted on the certificate of title, its interest is not perfected. That means that a good-faith purchaser of your BMW would take it free of the bank's interest. In most states, purchasers of motor vehicles can either buy or extend credit on those vehicles with the confidence that no security interest exists that is not disclosed on the certificate of title.[4]

Collateral Moved to Another Jurisdiction

Obviously, collateral may be moved by the debtor from one jurisdiction (state) to another. When this occurs, a problem arises in that only parties who check the records in the county (local filing) or state (central filing) in which perfection properly took place are actually aware of the secured party's filing, even though the law imputes constructive notice to all. Frequently, the secured party is not even aware that the collateral has been moved out of the jurisdiction. A subsequent lender who perfects his or her security interest in the same collateral could wrongly believe that he or she has first priority on the debtor's default.

The UCC addresses these problems. In general, a properly perfected security interest in collateral moved into a new jurisdiction continues to be perfected in the new jurisdiction for a period of up to four months from the date it was moved or for the period of time remaining under the perfection in the original jurisdiction, whichever expires first [UCC 9-103(1)(d), 9-103(3)(e)]. Collateral moved from county to county *within* a state when *local* filing is required, however, may not have a four-

---

3. Only Vermont has not adopted the 1972 amendments.

4. In the few states that do not require title registration of motor vehicles, one must examine the appropriate statutes to determine the priority of conflicting security interests.

Perfecting Your Security Interest

The importance of perfecting your security interest cannot be overemphasized, particularly when the debt is large and you wish to maximize your priority over the debtor's other creditors to the collateral covered by your security interest. Failure to perfect or to perfect properly may result in your becoming the equivalent of an unsecured creditor.

The filing of a financing statement, either locally or centrally with the secretary of state, is the most common method of perfection. Generally, the moment the filing takes place, your priority over other creditors—as well as some purchasers of the collateral and a subsequent trustee in bankruptcy—is established.

Sometimes credit transactions occur outside normal business relationships. You may be asked, for example, to aid an associate, a relative, or a friend. At that moment, you should reflect on your need for security for any debt that will be owed to you. If there is a need for security, then your security interest should be perfected, even if you believe this is an unnecessary action because the debtor is a friend or a relative. That particular relationship is irrelevant if he or she is forced into bankruptcy. Bankruptcy law does not allow friends or relatives to be paid ahead of nonfriends or nonrelatives. You will end up standing in line with the other unsecured creditors if you have not perfected your security interest in the collateral. The best method to protect your security interest by perfection is to have your friend, relative, or associate transfer to your possession the collateral. The collateral may be stocks, bonds, or jewelry, for example. Possession of such collateral by the secured party is a method of perfection that permits the transaction to be kept private, but still allows you to have security for the loan.

month limitation, and the original filing may have continuous priority [see UCC 9-403(3)].

To illustrate: Suppose that on January 1 Calvin secures a loan from a Kansas bank by putting up all his wheat-threshing equipment as security. The Kansas bank files a financing statement centrally with the secretary of state. In June, Calvin has an opportunity to harvest wheat crops in South Dakota and moves his equipment into that state on June 15. Under the UCC, the Kansas bank's perfection remains effective in South Dakota for a period of four months from June 15. If the equipment remains in South Dakota, and the Kansas bank wishes to retain its perfection priority longer than four months, it must perfect properly in South Dakota during this four-month period. Should it fail to do so, its perfection will be lost after four months, and subsequent perfected security interests in the same collateral in South Dakota will prevail.

Among mobile goods, automobiles pose one of the biggest problems. If the original jurisdiction does not require a certificate of title as part of its perfection process for an automobile, perfection automatically ends four months after the automobile is moved into another jurisdiction.

When a security interest exists on an automobile in a state in which title registration is required, and when the security interest is noted on the certificate of title, the perfection of the security interest continues after the automobile is moved to another state requiring a certificate of title until the automobile is registered in the new state [UCC 9-103(2)]. Such a rule protects the secured party against anyone purchasing the car in a new state prior to the new registration. Moreover, because each title state requires that the old certificate of title be surrendered to obtain a new one, and because the secured party typically holds the certificate, the secured party usually is able to ensure that the security interest is noted on the new certificate of title.

Effective Time of Perfection

A filing statement is effective for five years from the date of filing [UCC 9-403(2)]. If a continuation statement is filed *within six months* prior to the expiration date, the effectiveness of the original statement is continued for another five years following the expiration date of the first five-year period [UCC 9-403(3)]. The effectiveness of the statement can be continued in the same manner indefinitely.

■ Enlarging Security Interests

In addition to collateral already in the debtor's possession, a security agreement can cover various other types of property, including the proceeds from the sale of the collateral, after-acquired property, and future advances.

Proceeds

A secured party has an interest in the **proceeds** (whatever is received) from the sale, exchange, or other disposal of the collateral [UCC 9-203(3), 9-306(2)]. To illustrate: Suppose that a bank has a perfected security interest in the inventory of a retail seller of television sets. The retailer sells a television set out of this inventory to you, a buyer in the ordinary course of business. Because you cannot pay cash, you sign a retail security agreement under which you agree to pay for the television set on the installment plan, in twenty-four monthly payments. If the retailer should default on the loan from the bank, the bank is entitled to the remaining payments that you owe to the retailer as proceeds.

A security interest in proceeds perfects automatically on perfection of the secured party's security interest and remains perfected for ten days after receipt of the proceeds by the debtor. One way to extend the ten-day period is to provide for such extended coverage in the original security agreement. This is typically done when the collateral is of the type that is likely to be sold.

The UCC provides three methods by which a security interest in proceeds may remain perfected for longer than ten days after the receipt of the proceeds by the debtor. They are as follows:

1. When a filed financing statement covers the original collateral and the proceeds are collateral in which a security interest may be perfected by filing in the office or offices in which the financing · statement has been filed. Furthermore, a secured creditor's interest automatically perfects in property that the debtor acquires with cash proceeds if the original filing would have been effective as to that property and the financing statement indicates the types of property constituting those proceeds [UCC 9-306(3)(a)]. (See Exhibit 31–4 for an example of the appropriate phrasing.)

2. When there is a filed financing statement that covers the original collateral and the proceeds are identifiable cash proceeds [UCC 9-306(3)(b)].

3. When the security interest in the proceeds is perfected before the expiration of the ten-day period [UCC 9-306(3)(c)].

After-acquired Property

After-acquired property of the debtor is property acquired after the execution of the security agreement. In other words, after-acquired property is property that a debtor does not own or have the rights to at the time the debtor enters into a security agreement but that he or she will acquire at some time in the future.

The security agreement itself may provide for coverage of after-acquired property [UCC 9-204(1)]. This is particularly useful for inventory financing arrangements because a secured party whose security interest is in existing inventory knows that the debtor will sell that inventory, thereby reducing the collateral subject to the security interest. Generally, the debtor will purchase new inventory to replace the inventory sold. The secured party wants this newly acquired inventory to be subject to the *original* security interest. Thus, the after-acquired property clause extends the secured party's claim to any inventory acquired thereafter.

Consider a typical example. Anderson buys factory equipment from Blonsky on credit, giving as security an interest in all of her equipment— both what she is buying and what she already owns. The security interest contains an after-acquired property clause. Six months later, Anderson pays cash to another seller for more equipment. Six months after that, Anderson goes out of business before she has paid off her debt to Blonsky. Blonsky has a security interest in *all* of Anderson's equipment, even the equipment bought from the other seller.

An after-acquired property clause normally does not allow for attachment of a security interest in consumer goods "unless the debtor acquired rights in them within ten days after the secured party gives value" [UCC 9-204(2)]. Presumably, this protects consumers from encumbering all their present and future property.

Future Advances

Often a debtor has a continuing *line of credit* under which the debtor can borrow intermittently. Advances against lines of credit can be subject to a properly perfected security interest in certain collateral.

The security agreement may provide that any future advances made against the line of credit are subject to a security interest in the same collateral. For example, Tobrun is the owner of a small manufacturing plant with equipment valued at $1,000,000. Tobrun is in immediate need of $50,000 of working capital. Tobrun secures a loan from West Bank, signing a security agreement putting up all his equipment as security. In the security agreement Tobrun can borrow up to $500,000 in the future, using the same equipment as collateral for future advances. In such cases, it is not necessary to execute a new security agreement and perfect a security interest in the collateral each time an advance is made to the debtor [UCC 9-204(3)].

The Floating Lien Concept

When collateral is sold, exchanged, or otherwise disposed of, a security interest shifts automatically to the proceeds. Under most circumstances, a creditor may also take a security interest in a debtor's after-acquired property; and the obligations a security agreement covers may include future advances. Because Article 9 provides for these possibilities, it is often referred to as a **floating lien** statute. A floating lien is a lien on inventory that changes over time. Floating liens commonly arise in the financing of inventories. A creditor is not interested in specific pieces of inventory, because they are constantly changing.

Consider the following example. Sound Components, a stereo dealer, has a line of credit with Interstate Bank to finance its inventory. Sound Components and Interstate enter into a security agreement that provides for coverage of: (1) proceeds, (2) after-acquired property, (3) inventory, and (4) future advances. Interstate perfects its security interest in Sound Components' inventory.

Suppose that Sound Components sells a new digital tape deck for which it receives a used cassette deck in trade plus cash. The same day, Sound Components purchases two new digital decks from the local wholesaler with money obtained from Interstate. Interstate gets a perfected security interest in the used cassette deck under the proceeds clause, and has a perfected security interest in the two new digital decks purchased from the local wholesaler under the after-acquired property clause. Furthermore, the additional amount of money Interstate advanced to Sound Components to purchase the two new digital decks is secured by the future-advances clause. All of this is accomplished under the original perfected security agreement. The various items in Sound Components' inventory have changed, but Interstate still has a perfected security interest in Sound Components' inventory, and hence it has a floating lien on that inventory.

Similarly, the concept of the floating lien can apply to a stock of goods as it is processed and sold. Under Section 9-205, the lien can start with raw materials and follow them as they become finished goods and inventories and as they are sold, turning into accounts receivable, chattel paper, or cash.

Commingled Goods

When grapes are processed into wine, their identity is lost in the wine product. When flour is processed into bread, its identity is lost in the bread product. These are commingled or processed goods as defined under UCC Section 9-315(1). Even though commingling occurs, the security interest that attaches to the goods before they are commingled or processed continues in the product or mass.

A question may arise as to when the security interest in the original goods has priority over the security interest in the whole. To ensure that no problems arise, the financing statement could cover both the original goods and the product that results from their commingling. Whenever more than one security interest attaches to the finished product or mass, according to UCC 9-315(2), all rank equally. The share associated with each component is determined according to the ratio of the component's contribution to the total *cost* of the resultant product or mass.

■ Resolving Priority Disputes

What happens when several creditors claim a security interest in the same collateral of a debtor? This important issue is addressed by the UCC with a set of rules for determining which of the conflicting security interests has priority—or the best claim to the collateral. The question of priority is most common in bankruptcy situations, for unless a creditor has a perfected security interest in the debtor's property, that creditor may end up with little or nothing.

Secured versus Unsecured Parties

In general, secured creditors prevail over unsecured creditors and over creditors who have obtained judgments against the debtor but who have not begun the legal process to collect on those judgments [UCC 9-301]. In other words, once a security interest attaches, it has priority over the claims of other creditors who do not have a security interest. This priority does not depend on whether the security interest has been perfected.

Secured Party versus Lien Creditor

A **lien creditor** is one who has a lien in the property because of a judgment.[5] Any security interest that is perfected has priority over lien creditors who acquired their lien after perfection. In contrast, a lien creditor has priority over a security interest that has not yet been perfected. A so-called ten-day exception to this rule, however, provides as follows: if a secured party files with respect to a purchase-money security interest during a ten-day period after the debtor receives possession of the collateral, the secured party has priority over the lien creditor's rights that arise between the time the security interest attaches and the time of filing [UCC 9-301(2)]. In many states, this so-called grace period has been extended to twenty days.

When More Than One Party Is Secured

When more than one party has a secured interest in the collateral of a defaulting debtor, the issues of perfection and timing become critical, as does the type of collateral involved. There are several general rules and, of course, exceptions to those rules.

THE GENERAL RULE   Among secured parties, the general rule of priority is as follows: The first security interest to be filed or perfected has priority over other filed or perfected security interests. If, however, none of the conflicting security interests has been perfected, the first security interest to attach has priority [UCC 9-312(5)].

For example, suppose that West Bank filed a financing statement covering Alger's inventory on March 1, and Friendly Savings and Loan filed a financing statement covering the same inventory on April 1. West Bank's interest would have priority over Friendly's interest. It would not matter which lender made its loan and attached its security interest first. If West Bank failed to perfect its security interest, however, and Friendly perfected its interest, then Friendly's interest would have priority as the *only* perfected security interest. If both failed to perfect their interests, then the first to attach would have priority. Thus, if West Bank had a security agreement covering Alger's inventory on March 1 and advanced money to Alger on the same day, and Friendly's agreement and advance were made on April 1, West Bank would have priority over Friendly.

AN EXCEPTION—PURCHASE-MONEY SECURITY INTEREST   The general rule, as previously stated, is that the first in time to file or perfect is first in priority rights to the collateral. This rule is always applicable when the first in time to perfect is a purchase-money security interest. The UCC provides, however, that under certain conditions a purchase-money security interest, properly perfected, will prevail over a non-purchase-money security interest in after-acquired collateral, even though the non-purchase-money security interest was the first in time to perfect.

If the collateral is *inventory*, a perfected purchase-money security interest will prevail over a previously perfected non-purchase-money security interest, provided (generally) that the purchase-money secured party perfects *and* gives the non-purchase-money secured party written notice of his or her interest *before* the debtor takes

---

5.   This definition also includes a receiver in equity, a trustee in bankruptcy, and an assignee for the benefit of creditors.

possession of the newly acquired inventory [UCC 9-312(3)].

If the collateral is other than inventory, a purchase-money security interest will have priority over a previously perfected non-purchase-money security interest provided that the purchase-money security interest is perfected either before or within ten days *after* the debtor takes possession. No notice is required [UCC 9-312(4)].

To illustrate: Retailer Mary needs a loan of money to be used as working capital. On May 1, she obtains a one-year installment loan from West Bank, signing a security agreement and putting up her present inventory plus any after-acquired inventory as collateral. That same date, West Bank perfects by filing a financing statement centrally. On August 1, Mary learns that she can purchase directly from Martin, a manufacturer, $10,000 worth of new inventory, which is a bargain. Because she cannot pay this amount in cash, she signs a security agreement with Martin, giving Martin a security interest in the newly purchased inventory.

The new inventory is delivered on September 1, as ordered. On September 7, a fire destroys most of Mary's store and warehouse. There remains only a part of the new inventory, and its value is insufficient to cover both debts. Who has priority with regard to the remaining inventory, West Bank or Martin?

If Martin perfected by filing and gave West Bank written notice of its security interest prior to September 1, the date Mary received possession, Martin prevails. If Martin did not meet these conditions, West Bank prevails.

Suppose the collateral is equipment, rather than inventory, and Martin perfected on September 8, after the fire. Because Martin properly perfected its purchase-money security interest within ten days after Mary received delivery, Martin prevails over West Bank for the remaining after-acquired equipment.

Secured Party versus Buyer

In general, a security interest in collateral continues even after the collateral has been sold unless the secured party has authorized the sale [UCC 9-306(2)]. There are exceptions, however, and they allow the buyers of collateral sold without the secured party's authorization to take that collateral free of the security interest, even in some situations when the security interest has been perfected. We examine those situations now.

BUYERS IN THE ORDINARY COURSE OF BUSINESS   To require buyers to find out if there is an outstanding security interest on, for example, a merchant's inventory would impose a time-consuming restriction and would certainly inhibit commerce. Therefore, the UCC provides that a person who buys "in the ordinary course of business" will take the goods free from any security interest attached to those goods, even if the security interest is perfected and even if the buyer knows of its existence [UCC 9-307(1)]. A *buyer in the ordinary course of business* is defined as any person who, in good faith and without knowledge that the sale is *in violation* of the ownership rights or security interest of a third party in the goods, buys in ordinary course from a person in the business of selling goods of that kind [UCC 1-201(9)].

Suppose retail seller Carl secures a loan from West Bank and puts up his existing appliance inventory and any appliance inventory thereafter acquired as collateral. Carl signs a security agreement and a financing statement, which West Bank properly perfects. Later Carl sells an appliance from inventory covered by the security agreement to a consumer, Lee, with Lee paying cash. If Carl goes into default on the loan, West Bank's prior perfected security interest has no effect on Lee. Lee took the appliance completely free of West Bank's security interest, even though perfected, and West Bank loses this item of collateral for satisfaction of the debt. (Of course, West Bank has rights in any identifiable cash proceeds.)

In the following case, the court must determine at what point a buyer becomes a buyer in the ordinary course of business.

Case 31.2

BIG KNOB VOLUNTEER FIRE CO. v. LOWE & MOYER GARAGE, INC.

Superior Court of Pennsylvania, 1985.
338 Pa.Super. 257,
487 A.2d 953.

BACKGROUND AND FACTS The Big Knob Volunteer Fire Department Company agreed to buy a fire truck from Hamerly Custom Productions, Inc., which was in the business of assembling component parts into fire trucks. Big Knob paid Hamerly $48,000 of the $51,836 purchase price. Hamerly agreed to deliver the truck within twenty to seventy days of receiving the chassis from a third-party supplier. The contract provided that title to the truck would not pass to Big Knob until the price was paid in full. Hamerly ordered and received the chassis from Lowe & Moyer Garage, Inc. Hamerly began working on the truck and painted "Big Knob Volunteer Fire Department" on the cab. The chassis was subject to a security interest. Hamerly neither paid Lowe & Moyer for the chassis nor completed the truck and delivered it to Big Knob. Big Knob and Lowe & Moyer sued Hamerly in a Pennsylvania state court. Hamerly surrendered the truck to Lowe & Moyer, which dropped its suit. Big Knob obtained a default judgment against Hamerly for specific performance and then sued Hamerly and Lowe & Moyer to replevy (repossess) the truck. The trial court found in favor of Lowe & Moyer for the chassis or its value, reasoning that because title had not passed, Big Knob was not a buyer in the ordinary course of business. Big Knob appealed.

DECISION AND RATIONALE The Superior Court of Pennsylvania overruled the trial court, holding that identification of goods to the contract rather than passing of title is the point at which a person becomes a buyer in the ordinary course of business. The appellate court recognized that "[t]he modern trend in contests between a buyer without possession and a secured creditor, typically the inventory financer, is to ignore or deemphasize the concept of 'sale.' Instead of focusing on passage of title (delivery), courts * * * increasingly favor identification as the critical moment that determines when a buyer becomes a buyer in the ordinary course." The court stated that it agreed with the modern trend and held that, because the truck was identified to the contract, Big Knob was a buyer in the ordinary course of business. The court explained that in this case, "[u]pon entrusting the goods to Hamerly, which dealt in goods of that kind, Lowe & Moyer gave Hamerly the power to transfer its rights to a buyer in the ordinary course of business, and Hamerly exercised that power when it painted the Volunteer Fire Department's name on the cab of the fire truck."

BUYERS OF FARM PRODUCTS Under the UCC, a buyer of farm products takes the products subject to a security interest, even if the buyer knows nothing about the existence of a security agreement [UCC 9-307(1)]. Under the Food Security Act of 1985,[6] however, buyers in the ordinary course of business include buyers of farm products from farmers. Under the Food Security Act, a secured party is not protected against a buyer of farm products from a farmer unless one of the following events occurs:

1. The buyer has received notice of the security interest within one year before the purchase.
2. The buyer fails to register with the secretary of state before the purchase, and the secured party has properly perfected his or her interest centrally.
3. The buyer has received notice from the secretary of state that the farm products being sold are subject to an *effective financing statement* (EFS). An EFS is a form that a secured party must file in addition to an Article 9 financing statement to protect his or her interest in a farmer's products in those states with EFS filing systems.

BUYERS OF CONSUMER GOODS FROM CONSUMERS Carla, a consumer, purchases a re-

---

6. 7 U.S.C. Section 1631.

frigerator on credit because she cannot pay the full purchase price. A written security agreement exists in which the seller takes a purchase-money security interest in the consumer goods under this type of credit plan. Further, the seller need not file a financing statement because, when a purchase-money security interest is taken in consumer goods, *perfection occurs automatically* [UCC 9-302(1)(d)]. Later, Carla sells the refrigerator to her next-door neighbor, Nan, who purchases it—as a purchaser not in the ordinary course of business—for home use without any knowledge of the credit arrangements between Carla and the original seller. Subsequently, Carla defaults on the credit payments to the seller. What are the seller's rights? The seller had a perfected purchase-money security interest in the refrigerator when it was held by Carla. Under UCC 9-307(2), however, the perfection is not good against the next-door neighbor.

UCC 9-307(2) requires that a person in the position of this next-door neighbor must purchase (give value for) the goods for personal, family, or household use, and without knowledge of the original seller's security interest, and that the purchase must take place *before* the secured party has filed a financing statement. In this case, recall that the seller took a purchase-money security interest, which is perfected automatically. No filing was required. Hence, the next-door neighbor purchased the refrigerator free and clear before the seller had filed a financing statement. The seller could have avoided this possibility simply by *filing* a financing statement, even though a purchase-money security interest had been perfected.

BUYERS OF CHATTEL PAPER AND INSTRUMENTS   Another purchaser who may not be subject to a secured party's interest despite perfection is the purchaser of chattel paper and instruments. This protection is provided by UCC 9-308. As previously defined, *chattel paper* is a writing or writings that evidence both a monetary obligation and a security interest in specific goods. *Instrument* means a negotiable instrument as defined in UCC 3-104, or a certificated security as defined in UCC 8-102, or basically any other writing that evidences a right to the payment of money and is not itself a security agreement or lease transferred in the ordinary course of business [UCC 9-105(1)(i)]. Security interests in instruments can be perfected only by possession.

Chattel paper is a very important class of collateral used in financing arrangements, especially in automobile financing. When it is sold by a creditor, the creditor can deliver it over to the assignee, who is then responsible for collecting the debt directly from the debtor. This arrangement is known as *notification* or *direct collection.* As an alternative, a creditor can sell chattel paper to an assignee with the understanding that the creditor will retain the chattel paper, make collections from the debtor, and then remit the money to the assignee. This kind of transaction is *nonnotification* or *indirect collection.* The widespread use of both methods of dealing with chattel paper is recognized by the UCC, and hence the UCC permits perfection of a chattel paper security interest either by filing or by taking possession of the chattel paper.

Problems arise when perfection of chattel paper is made by filing only. If the chattel paper is thereafter sold to another purchaser who gives *new value* and takes *possession* of the paper in the *ordinary course of business, without knowledge* that it is subject to a security interest, the new purchaser will have priority over the secured creditor. (Of course, the creditor has rights in the proceeds.)

■ The Rights and Duties of Debtors and Creditors under Article 9

The security agreement itself determines most of the rights and duties of the debtor and the creditor. The UCC, however, imposes some rights and duties that are applicable in the absence of a security agreement to the contrary.

Information Request by Creditors

Under UCC 9-407(1), a creditor has the option, when making the filing, of asking the filing officer to make a note of the file number, the date, and the hour of the original filing on a copy of the financing statement. The filing officer must send this copy to the person making the request. Under UCC 9-407(2), a filing officer must also give information to a person who is contemplating obtaining a security interest from a prospective debtor. The filing officer must give a certificate that provides information on possible perfected financing statements involving the named debtor.

The filing officer will charge a fee for copies provided.

Assignment, Amendment, and Release

At any time, a secured party of record can release part or all of the collateral described in a filed financing statement. This ends his or her security interest in the collateral [UCC 9-406]. A secured party can assign part or all of the security interest to another, called the assignee. That assignee becomes the secured party of record if, for example, he or she either makes a notation of the assignment

---

■ CONCEPT SUMMARY 31.1
The Priority of Claims to a Debtor's Collateral

Parties	Priority
Unperfected secured party	Prevails over unsecured creditors and creditors who have obtained judgments against the debtor but who have not begun the legal process to collect on those judgments [UCC 9-301].
Perfected secured parties to same collateral	Between two perfected secured parties to the same collateral, the general rule is that first to file or perfect is first in right to the collateral [UCC 9-312(5)]. An exception is a purchase-money security interest. Even if second in time of perfection (when first in time of perfection is a non-purchase-money security interest), it has priority providing: a. In the case of inventory, that the purchase-money security interest is perfected and proper notice is given to non-purchase-money perfected security interest holder *on* or *before* time that debtor takes possession [UCC 9-312(3)]. b. In the case of other collateral, that the purchase-money security interest has been perfected within ten days after debtor receives possession [UCC 9-312(4)].

Purchaser of debtor's collateral	1. Goods purchased in the ordinary course of business: Purchaser prevails over a perfected secured party even if the purchaser knows of the security interest [UCC 9-307(1)].
	2. Farm products purchased in the ordinary course of business: Purchaser prevails unless purchaser:
	  a. Received notice of the security interest within one year before the purchase.
	  b. Fails to register with the secretary of state before the purchase, and the secured party has properly perfected his or her interest centrally.
	  c. Received notice from the secretary of state that the farm products being sold are subject to an effective financing statement.
	3. Consumer goods purchased out of the ordinary course of business: Purchaser prevails over a perfected secured party, providing the purchaser purchased:
	  a. For value.
	  b. Without actual knowledge of the security interest.
	  c. For use as a consumer good.
	  d. Prior to secured party's perfection by *filing* [UCC 9-307(2)].
	4. The chattel paper purchaser prevails over a perfected secured party, providing the purchaser:
	  a. Gave new value.
	  b. Took possession.
	  c. Took in the ordinary course of business.
	  d. Took without *actual* knowledge of secured party's perfection [UCC 9-308].
	5. The purchaser of negotiable instruments, documents, and securities prevails over a perfected secured party, particularly if the purchaser is a holder in due course, a holder to whom the document has been duly negotiated, or a bona fide purchaser of a security [UCC 9-308, 9-309].

somewhere on the financing statement or files a written statement of assignment [UCC 9-405(2)].

It is also possible to amend a financing statement that has already been filed. The amendment must be signed by *both* parties. The debtor has to sign the security agreement, the original financing statement, and the amendments [UCC 9-402(4)]. All other secured transaction documents, such as releases, assignments, continuations of perfection, perfections of collateral moved into another jurisdiction, and termination statements, need only be signed by the secured party.

Reasonable Care of Collateral

If a secured party is in possession of the collateral, he or she must use reasonable care in preserving it. Otherwise, the secured party is liable to the debtor [UCC 9-207(1), (3)]. If the collateral increases in value, the secured party can hold this increased value or profit as additional security unless it is in the form of money, which must be remitted to the debtor or applied toward reducing the secured debt [UCC 9-207(2)(c)]. Additionally, the collateral must be kept in identifiable condition unless it is fungible [UCC 9-207(2)(d)]. Finally, the debtor must pay for all reasonable charges incurred by the secured party in preserving, operating, and taking care of the collateral in possession [UCC 9-207(2)(a)].

The Status of the Debt

While the secured debt is outstanding, the debtor may wish at times to know its status. If so, the debtor need only sign a statement that indicates the aggregate amount of the unpaid debt at a specific date (and perhaps a list of the collateral covered by the security agreement). The secured party must then approve or correct this statement in writing. The creditor must comply with the request within two weeks of receipt; otherwise, the creditor is liable for any loss caused to the debtor by the failure to do so [UCC 9-208(2)]. One such request is allowed without charge every six months. For each additional request, the secured party can require a fee not exceeding $10 [UCC 9-208(3)].

■ Enforcing Security Agreements

When a debtor breaches the terms of the security agreement, the debtor is in default. Article 9 defines the rights, duties, and remedies of a secured party and of the debtor upon a debtor's default. Should the secured party fail to comply with its duties, the debtor is afforded particular rights and remedies.

Default

The topic of default is one of great concern to secured lenders and to the lawyers who draft security agreements. What constitutes default is not always clear. In fact, Article 9 does not define the term. Thus, parties are encouraged in practice and by the UCC to include in their security agreements certain standards to be applied in the event that default actually comes about. Consequently, parties can stipulate the conditions that will constitute a default [UCC 9-501(1)].

Typically, because of the disparity in bargaining position between a debtor and a creditor, these critical terms are shaped with exceeding breadth by the creditor to give some sense of security. The ultimate terms, however, are not allowed to go beyond the limitations imposed by the good faith requirement of UCC 1-208 and the unconscionability doctrine.

Although any breach of the terms of the security agreement can constitute default, default occurs most commonly when the debtor fails to meet the scheduled payments that the parties have agreed on or when the debtor becomes bankrupt. If the security agreement covers equipment, the debtor may have warranted that he or she is the owner of the equipment or that no liens or other security interests are pending on that equipment. Breach of any of these representations can also result in default.

Note that a secured party's rights on the debtor's default go beyond merely obtaining the collateral. They also include accelerating the secured debt and stopping all other credit. The latter occurs, typically, because the secured party is the debtor's principal source of credit. Hence, the fact that a creditor obtains the collateral on default is not normally what kills a debtor's business, but the exercise of other rights just mentioned.

Repossessing Collateral

The secured party has the right to take possession of the collateral on default unless the security agreement states otherwise. As long as there is no breach of the peace, the secured party can simply repossess the collateral. Otherwise the secured party must resort to the judicial process [UCC 9-503].

What constitutes a breach of the peace is of prime importance to both parties, for such an act can open the secured party to tort liability. The UCC does not define *breach of the peace.* Therefore, parties must resort to state law to determine it.

Generally, neither the creditor nor the creditor's agent can enter a debtor's home, garage, or place of business without permission. Consider a situation in which an automobile is collateral. A repossessing party who walks onto the debtor's premises, proceeds up the driveway, enters the vehicle without entering the garage, and drives off will probably not be considered to have breached the peace. In some states, however, satisfying the elements of an action for wrongful trespass could provide the grounds necessary to initiate an action for breach of the peace. (Most car repossessions occur when the car is parked on a street or in a parking lot.)

In the following case, vehicles were repossessed while on a third party's premises. The issue before the court is whether the trespass to the third party's land constituted a breach of the peace.

Case 31.3

SALISBURY LIVESTOCK CO. v. COLORADO CENTRAL CREDIT UNION

Supreme Court of Wyoming, 1990.
793 P.2d 470.

BACKGROUND AND FACTS George Salisbury III borrowed $13,000 from Colorado Central Credit Union, giving as collateral several vehicles that he owned. Salisbury defaulted on the loan, and Colorado Central hired a repossession company to repossess the vehicles. The repossession crew towed away one of the vehicles from Salisbury's property in Slater, Colorado, near the Wyoming border. The crew found two other vehicles on a ranch just across the Wyoming border, after following a private roadway with a large "Salisbury" sign near the entrance. It was early in the morning, and although the crew could hear people stirring in a nearby building, they encountered no one while towing the vehicles away. The ranch was owned by Salisbury's father. The father, doing business as Salisbury Livestock Company, brought an action for trespass against Colorado Central in a Wyoming state court. The trial court, holding that the trespass was privileged and did not result in any breach of the peace, entered a directed verdict for Colorado Central. Salisbury Livestock appealed, contending that the trespass itself—onto land owned by a third party—constituted a breach of the peace.

DECISION AND RATIONALE The Supreme Court of Wyoming reversed the trial court's decision and remanded the case for trial. The state supreme court concluded that whether Colorado Central's entry onto Salisbury Livestock's property was reasonable or breached the peace was a question for the jury, and therefore the trial court's directed verdict was inappropriate. The court stated that "[a] trespass breaches the peace only if certain types of premises are invaded, or immediate violence is likely," but neither confrontation nor violence is necessary to find a breach of the peace. The court noted two elements of the case that could lead jurors to conclude that the trespass was a breach of the peace: there was an entry onto the premises of a third party not privy to the loan agreement, and those premises were residential—"the secluded ranchyard of an isolated ranch where the vehicles sought [were] not even visible from a public place. * * * [T]he location and setting * * * is sufficiently distinct, and the privacy expectations of rural residents sufficiently different, that a jury should weigh the reasonableness of this entry, or whether the peace may have been breached by a real possibility of imminent violence, or even by mere entry into these premises."

Disposing of Collateral

Once default has occurred and the secured party has obtained possession of the collateral, the secured party is faced with several alternatives to satisfy the debt. The party can retain the collateral [UCC 9-505(2)] or sell, lease, or otherwise dispose of it in any commercially reasonable manner [UCC 9-504(1)]. Any sale is always subject to procedures established by state law.

RETENTION OF THE COLLATERAL   The UCC recognizes that parties are sometimes better off if they do not sell the collateral. Therefore, a secured party can retain collateral, but this general right is subject to several conditions. The secured party must send written notice of the proposal to the debtor if the debtor has not signed a statement renouncing or modifying his or her rights after default. With consumer goods, no other notice has to be given. In all other cases, notice must be sent to any other secured party from whom the secured party has received written notice of a claim of interest in the collateral in question. If within twenty-one days after the notice has been sent the secured party receives an objection in writing from a person entitled to receive notification, then the secured party must dispose of the collateral under UCC 9-504. If no such written objection is forthcoming, the secured party can retain the collateral in full satisfaction of the debtor's obligation [UCC 9-505(2)].

CONSUMER GOODS   When the collateral is *consumer goods* in which the creditor has a *purchase-money security interest,* and the debtor has paid *60 percent* of the *cash price* or *loan,* then the secured party must dispose of the collateral under UCC 9-504 within ninety days. Failure to comply opens the secured party to an action for conversion or other liability under UCC 9-507(1) unless the consumer-debtor signed a written statement *after default* renouncing or modifying the right to demand the sale of the goods [UCC 9-505(1)].

DISPOSITION PROCEDURES   A secured party who does not choose to retain the collateral must resort to the disposition procedures prescribed under UCC 9-504. The UCC allows a great deal of flexibility with regard to disposition. The only real limitation is that it must be accomplished in a commercially reasonable manner. UCC 9-507(2) supplies some examples of what does and does not meet the standard of commercial reasonableness:

> The fact that a better price could have been obtained by a sale at a different time or in a different method from that selected by the secured party is not of itself sufficient to establish that the sale was not made in a commercially reasonable manner. If the secured party either sells the collateral in the usual manner in any recognized market therefor or if he sells at the price (current) in such a market at the time of his sale or if he has otherwise sold in conformity with reasonable commercial practices among dealers in the type of property sold he has sold in a commercially reasonable manner.

A secured party is not compelled to resort to public sale to dispose of the collateral. The party is given the latitude under the UCC to seek out the best terms possible in a private sale. Generally, no specific time requirements must be met; however, the time must ultimately meet the standard of commercial reasonableness.

Generally, for a sale to be classified as a sale conducted in a commercially reasonable manner, notice of the place, time, and manner of sale is required. Notice must be sent by the secured party to the debtor if the debtor has not signed a statement renouncing or modifying the right to notification of sale after default. For consumer goods, no other notification need be sent. In all other cases, notification must be sent to any other secured party from whom the secured party has received written notice of claim of an interest in the collateral [UCC 9-504(3)]. No such notice is necessary, however, when the collateral is perishable or threatens to decline speedily in value or when it is of a type customarily sold on a recognized market.

Whether a debtor received sufficient notice of a private sale of collateral and whether the sale was conducted in a commercially reasonable manner are the questions presented in the following case.

Case 31.4

**CONNECTICUT BANK
& TRUST CO., N.A. v.
INCENDY**

Supreme Court of Connecticut,
1988.
207 Conn. 15,
540 A.2d 32.

BACKGROUND AND FACTS   Connecticut Electric Products, Inc. (CEP), took out a loan with Connecticut Bank & Trust Company, N.A. (CBT). CEP placed among other things all its machinery and equipment as security for a loan. Victor and Jeanette Incendy, the sole owners of CEP, personally guaranteed repayment. CEP defaulted, and CBT had a liquidator, Thomas Industries, Inc., dispose of the collateral by public auction. The sale was conducted in a commercially reasonable manner, held on CEP's premises and attended by the Incendys. Thomas consigned some machines that were not auctioned to Gavlick Machinery Corporation for private resale. Eventually, the machines were sold, but the Incendys never received notice of the private sales. The amounts received from all sales did not cover the debt to CBT, so CBT sued in a Connecticut state court for a deficiency judgment against the Incendys on their personal guaranties. The Incendys claimed they were not liable for the deficiency because of their lack of notice of the private sales. CBT argued that the Incendys were aware that not all the equipment had been sold at the public auction and that notice of an unsuccessful public sale is sufficient for a subsequent private sale. The trial court agreed with the Incendys and held that CBT was not entitled to a deficiency judgment because (1) notice to the Incendys of the public sale did not constitute sufficient notice of the private sales, and (2) CBT could not demonstrate to the court's satisfaction that the private sales had been conducted in a commercially reasonable manner. CBT appealed.

DECISION AND RATIONALE   The Supreme Court of Connecticut affirmed the trial court's ruling. The state supreme court held that notice to the Incendys of the public sale did not suffice as notice of the subsequent private sales, nor were the private sales proved to have been conducted in a commercially reasonable manner. Therefore, CBT was not entitled to a deficiency judgment against the Incendys. The court explained that to ensure that a sale is conducted in a commercially reasonable manner, notice to the debtor of the time, place, and manner of the sale is required. The evidence indicated that the Incendys had received no notice at all of the private sales and did not even know that the machines had been sold until the bank brought its action for a deficiency judgment. The court noted that in some situations, such as when goods are perishable or may rapidly decline in value, exceptions are made, but the circumstances in this case did not fall within the exceptions. As for the bank's argument, the court pointed out that it was "clear from a reading of [UCC 9-504(3)] that a debtor must be given reasonable notice of 'any private sale,' and not just private sales that occur in the absence of a prior unsuccessful public sale of the same collateral."

COMMENTS   In some jurisdictions, failure to comply with the notice requirements of Article 9 would absolutely bar a creditor's recovery of a deficiency judgment—even if the disposition of the collateral was otherwise made in a commercially reasonable manner. The court in this case rejected this rule in favor of what is known as the "rebuttable presumption" rule. Under this rule, the failure of a creditor to comply strictly with the notice requirements may not bar the creditor from recovering a deficiency judgment if the creditor can prove that the sale of collateral was conducted in a commercially reasonable manner.

PROCEEDS FROM DISPOSITION   Proceeds from the disposition must be applied in the following order:

1.   Reasonable expenses stemming from retaking, holding, or preparing for sale are covered first. When authorized by law and if provided for in the agreement, these can include reasonable attorneys' fees and legal expenses.
2.   Satisfaction of the balance of the debt owed to the secured party must then be made.
3.   Subordinate security interests whose written demands have been received prior to the completion of distribution of the proceeds are covered third [UCC 9-504(1)].
4.   Any surplus generally goes to the debtor.

DEFICIENCY JUDGMENT   Often, after proper disposition of the collateral, the secured party has not collected all that was owed by the debtor. Unless otherwise agreed, the debtor is liable for any deficiency. If the underlying transaction was a sale of accounts or of chattel paper, however, the secured party can collect a **deficiency judgment** only if the security agreement so provides [UCC 9-504(2)].

REDEMPTION RIGHTS   At any time before the secured party disposes of the collateral or enters into a contract for its disposition or before the debtor's obligation has been discharged through the secured party's retention of the collateral, the debtor or any other secured party can exercise the right of **redemption** of the collateral. The debtor or other secured party can do this by tendering performance of *all* obligations secured by the collateral, by paying the expenses reasonably incurred by the secured party, and by retaking the collateral and maintaining its care and custody [UCC 9-506].

■ Termination

When a debt is paid, the secured party generally must send to the debtor or file with the filing officer to whom the original financing statement was given a termination statement. If the financing statement covers consumer goods, the termination statement must be filed by the secured party within one month after the debt has been paid or within ten days of the debtor's requesting a filing in writing after the debt has been paid, whichever is earlier [UCC 9-404(1)]. In all other cases, the termination statement must be filed or furnished to the debtor within ten days after a written request has been made by the debtor. If the affected secured party fails to file such a termination statement, as required by UCC 9-404(1), or fails to send the termination statement within ten days after proper demand, the secured party will be liable to the debtor for $100. Additionally, the secured party will be liable for any loss caused to the debtor.

■ Terms and Concepts

after-acquired property 560
attachment 551
collateral 549
debtor 549
deficiency judgment 571
financing statement 554

floating lien 561
lien creditor 562
perfection 554
pledge 557
proceeds 560
purchase-money security interest 557

redemption 571
secured party 549
secured transaction 548
security agreement 549
security interest 549

■ For Review

1.   What is a security interest? Who is a secured party? What is a security agreement? What is a financing statement?
2.   What are the three requirements for an enforceable security interest?
3.   What rights does a secured creditor have upon the debtor's default?

4.   On July 1, Barber Credit Co. loans money to Rita Cosmetics Stores, a merchant, and obtains a security agreement covering Rita's inventory. Barber files a financing statement covering the collateral on July 6. On August 1, the Bank of Kingston loans money to Rita and obtains a security agreement covering the same collateral. On August 3, Kingston files a financing statement covering the collateral.

If Rita defaults on both loans, whose interest has priority? Would the priority be different if Barber had not filed a financing statement? What would determine priority if neither party had filed a financing statement?

5.   In the previous problem, imagine that Rita sells an item from its inventory to Liz, a buyer in the ordinary course of business. Does Barber or Kingston have priority to the item on Rita's default? Would the priority be different if Liz bought the item knowing of Barber's interest, but not Kingston's?

■ Questions and Case Problems

31-1.   Ray is a seller of electric generators. He purchases a large quantity of generators from manufacturer Martin Corp. by making a down payment and signing a security agreement to make the balance of payments over a period of time. The agreement gives Martin Corp. a security interest in the generators and the proceeds. Martin Corp. files a financing statement on its security interest centrally. Ray receives the generators and immediately sells one of them to Green on an installment contract, with payment to be made in twelve equal installments. At the time of sale, Green knows of Martin's security interest. Two months later Ray goes into default on his payments to Martin. Discuss Martin's rights against purchaser Green in this situation.

31-2.   Marion has a prize horse named Thunderbolt. Marion is in need of working capital. To secure it, she borrows $5,000 from Rodriguez, with Rodriguez taking possession of Thunderbolt as security for the loan. No written agreement is signed. Discuss whether, in the absence of a written agreement, Rodriguez has a security interest in Thunderbolt *and* whether Rodriguez can be a perfected secured party without filing a financing statement.

31-3.   Discuss how each secured party would properly perfect his or her security interest in the following cases.
   (a)   Martin is a manufacturer of refrigerators. Ray, a retailer, buys a number of these refrigerators. Ray signs a security agreement giving Martin a security interest in the refrigerators.
   (b)   Mary sells a refrigerator to Carla, to be used in Carla's home. Carla signs a security agreement giving Mary a security interest in the refrigerator.
   (c)   Ray sells a refrigerator to Dr. Dodd, to be used in his office to store medicines. Dr. Dodd signs a security agreement giving Ray a security interest in the refrigerator.
   (d)   Mary sells a refrigerator to farmer Ames, who needs it to store eggs not sold at market. Ames signs a security agreement giving Mary a security interest in the refrigerator.

31-4.   Martin is a manufacturer of washing machines. On September 1, in need of working capital, Martin's president contacts Smith, a loan officer for the First Bank. He asks to borrow $200,000, and offers to put up all Martin's equipment as security. Smith agrees to make the loan. In the security agreement signed by Martin's president is a clause stating that this loan is secured not only by the existing equipment presently located at Martin's plant but by any equipment acquired in the future by Martin. The First Bank files a financing statement centrally on *September 5*. On *November 1*, Martin has an opportunity to purchase from Daniel Equipment Corp. some newly manufactured Daniel equipment at a bargain price of $50,000. On that same date, Martin contracts by a security agreement to purchase the equipment from Daniel, paying $20,000 down and the balance in monthly payments over a three-year period, with Daniel having a security interest in the purchased equipment. The new equipment is delivered on *December 1*. On *December 7*, Daniel perfects its security interest in the newly delivered equipment by filing a financing statement centrally. Later Martin goes into default to both parties. Discuss whose interest in the new equipment has priority, First Bank's or Daniel's.

31-5.   Ray is a retail seller of television sets. Ray sells a color television set to Clara for her apartment for $600. Clara cannot pay cash and signs a security agreement, paying $100 down and agreeing to pay the balance in twelve equal installments of $50 each. The security agreement gives Ray a security interest in the television set. Clara makes six payments on time; then she goes into default because of unexpected financial problems. Ray repossesses the set and wants to keep it in full satisfaction of the debt. Discuss Ray's rights and duties in this matter.

31-6.   Calcote obtained an automobile loan from Citizens & Southern National Bank, with the Bank maintaining a security interest in the car. On March 28, 1984, after Calcote had defaulted on the loan, the bank repossessed the vehicle. On the following day, the bank sent a certified letter, return receipt requested, to Calcote informing her of the repossession, of the bank's plans to sell the auto at a private sale in May of 1984, and of her right to demand a public sale of the vehicle. Although the letter was sent to the address on the bank's records and at which the bank had repossessed the car, Calcote never received the letter. On April 19, 1984, it was returned to the bank stamped "unclaimed." On May 11, 1984, the car was sold at a private sale to which over 150 dealers had been invited. When Calcote learned that the car had been sold, she brought an action against the bank, claiming she had not been properly notified of the repossession and sale and that the private sale was not a commercially reasonable method of disposition. Discuss fully her claims. [*Calcote v. Citizens & Southern National Bank*, 179 Ga.App. 132, 345 S.E.2d 616 (1986)]

31-7.   On June 12, 1985, Edward Dye purchased a 1985 Buick Riviera from his close friend of over thirty years, Gordon McGrath, d/b/a (doing business as) McGrath Auto Sales. Under the terms of the sale, Dye purchased the vehicle for the price that the dealer had paid for it. Dye used a set of dealer's license plates, and no certificate of title was assigned to him. McGrath on several occasions asked to use the vehicle to show other clients. The Bank of Illinois provided "floor plan" (inventory) financing to McGrath's automobile dealership and had a perfected security interest in all McGrath's new automobiles. When McGrath defaulted on his loan, the bank sought to gain possession of the automobile from Dye. Did the bank have a claim to the automobile? Discuss. [*Bank of Illinois v. Dye,* 163 Ill.App.3d 1018, 517 N.E.2d 38, 115 Ill.Dec. 73 (1987)]

31-8. McGovern Auto Specialty, Inc., the debtor, granted Kay Automotive Warehouse, Inc., a security interest in various personal property that it owned. Both the security agreement and the financing statement listed the name of the debtor as McGovern Auto and Truck Parts, Inc. Later, the debtor filed a petition to reorganize its capital structure under Chapter 11 of the Bankruptcy Code. Under the Bankruptcy Code, the debtor in possession is given the powers and rights of a trustee in bankruptcy. A trustee can void any unperfected security interest. The debtor claimed that the erroneous listing of the debtor's name in the filing caused the security interest to be unperfected. Kay claimed that the error was minor and that it held a perfected security interest in the personal property with rights superior to those of unsecured creditors and the debtor. Discuss whether Kay was a properly perfected secured party. [*In re McGovern Auto Specialty, Inc.,* 51 Bankr. 511 (Bkrtcy.E.D.Pa. 1985)]

31-9. The First National Bank of North Dakota loaned Freddie Mutschler, a prominent farmer in Jamestown, North Dakota, $3 million. Mutschler gave the bank a lien on his crops as partial security for the loan. The loan agreement provided that when Mutschler sold his grain, he would be obligated to turn over the proceeds to cover the indebtedness. Mutschler was also the owner, but not the manager, of the Jamestown Farmers Elevator, which bought and sold various farmers' grain. In the fall of 1982, Mutschler sold his crop to the Jamestown Farmers Elevator but did not apply the proceeds to the debt at the bank. The elevator in turn sold some of the grain to the Pillsbury Co., which knew of the bank's security interest but did not know the terms of the security agreement. The bank did not discover these events until Mutschler and the Jamestown Farmers Elevator filed for bankruptcy in early 1983. The bank sued Pillsbury for conversion of the collateral. Which party prevailed? Discuss. [*First Bank of North Dakota v. Pillsbury Co.,* 801 F.2d 1036 (8th Cir. 1986)]

31-10. For several years, Hugh Meyer had financial dealings with the First National Bank of Midland. On one occasion, Meyer delivered some stock certificates to the bank as security for a loan. The security agreement defined the collateral to include any "profits, interest and income from the listed property." Although the securities were in the bank's possession, the bank never registered the stock in its name, nor did it take other steps to ensure that any stock dividends would be sent to the bank instead of to Meyer. Meyer eventually received a stock dividend of $500,000 and turned over the dividend to his law firm as security for a debt he owed to the firm for legal services. Meyer went bankrupt, and the bank's successor, the Federal Deposit Insurance Corp., laid claim to the $500,000 as a perfected secured creditor. The law firm claimed that it, and not the bank, had a perfected security interest in the dividend because the dividend was in the law firm's possession. Which party had a perfected security interest in the $500,000 dividend? Explain. [*Federal Deposit Insurance Corp. v. W. Hugh Meyer & Associates, Inc.,* 864 F.2d 371 (5th Cir. 1989)]

31-11. In 1982 Charline Gail Keaton and Kenneth Keaton purchased a used mobile home and entered into a retail installment contract with the seller. The contract designated "Gail Keaton and Kenneth C. Keaton" as the purchasers, but the signatures on the contract read "Charline Gail Keaton" and "Kenneth Keaton." The seller subsequently assigned the contract to First Manufactured Housing Credit Corp. On a financing statement filed with the proper officials, First Manufactured listed Charline's name as "Gail Keaton." Later, Charline Keaton moved the home to a lot in the Clarkson Mobile Home Park, where she was known as "Charlene Keaton." When she fell behind in her rent, Clarkson obtained a judgment for the rent due and levied against the mobile home, ultimately taking title to the home. Charlene also defaulted on her loan payments, and First Manufactured brought an action to recover the amount due under its security agreement or possession of the mobile home or its market value. Clarkson contended that because First Manufactured had erroneously filed its financing statement under "Gail Keaton," its security interest was unperfected. Discuss whether Clarkson will succeed in this claim. [*First Manufactured Housing Credit Corp. v. Clarkson Mobile Home Park,* 148 A.D.2d 901, 539 N.Y.S.2d 529 (1989)]

31-12. Case Briefing Assignment

Examine Case A.18 [All Valley Acceptance Co. v. Durfey, *800 S.W.2d 672 (Tex.App.— Austin 1990)*], *in Appendix A. The case has been excerpted there in great detail. Review and then brief the case, making sure that you include answers to the following questions in your brief.*

1. Why did the Durfeys cease making payments on the manufactured home that they had purchased from All Valley Acceptance Co.?

2. Why did All Valley claim that the trial court's decision to grant summary judgment in the Durfeys' favor was improper?

3. On what grounds did All Valley allege that the Durfeys had waived their rights to notice of sale of the mobile home?

4. Why did the court hold that All Valley's subsequent sale of the mobile home did not comply with Article 9 requirements regarding disposition of repossessed collateral?

5. What was the appellate court's ruling, and how did it justify its decision?

Chapter 32

Other Creditors' Remedies and Suretyship

The law of debtor-creditor relations has undergone various changes over the years. Historically, debtors and their families have been subjected to punishment for their inability to pay debts, including involuntary servitude and imprisonment. The modern legal system has moved away from a punishment philosophy in dealing with debtors. In fact, many observers say that it has moved too far in the other direction, to the detriment of creditors. Today, consumer protection is emphasized, and the legal system is designed to aid and protect the debtor and the debtor's family.

This chapter deals with various rights and remedies available through statutory laws, common law, and contract law to assist the debtor and creditor in resolving their disputes without the debtor's having to resort to bankruptcy. The next chapter discusses bankruptcy as a last resort to resolve debtor-creditor problems.

■ Laws Assisting Creditors

As pointed out in Chapter 31, if a debtor defaults, a secured creditor's priority can determine whether the creditor recoups complete, partial, or no payment of amounts he or she is owed. Creditors with no priority are paid last, of course—if at all.

A perfected security interest, in the case of personal property, or a mortgage, in the case of real estate, may be referred to as a *consensual lien.* A **lien** is a claim or charge on a debtor's property that must be satisfied before the property (or its proceeds) is available to satisfy the claims of other creditors. Referring to the lien as *consensual* indicates that its basis is the parties' agreement. Consensual liens on personal property are the subject of Article 9 of the UCC and were discussed in Chapter 31. Enforcing payment under a consensual lien on real estate is discussed later in this chapter.

A lien may also arise under a statute or the common law or through a judicial proceeding. Statutory liens include *mechanic's liens.* Liens created at common law include *artisan's liens* and *innkeeper's liens. Judicial liens* include those that represent a creditor's efforts to collect on a debt before a judgment (for example, through *prejudgment attachment*) or after it (for example, through a *writ of execution*). These terms are defined in the discussion of remedies that follows.

It is important to remember that a lien creditor has priority only to the extent of the value of his or her collateral. To illustrate, imagine that McInerney owns property worth $100,000, including a cache of furs worth $40,000. McInerney owes Bret $40,000, Easton $50,000, and Ellis $60,000. Bret has a lien on the furs. On McInerney's default, Bret has the first right to the furs or the proceeds from their sale. If the furs turned out to be worth only $20,000, Bret's claim for the other $20,000 would have no greater priority than the claims of Easton and Ellis.

Generally, a lien creditor has priority over an unperfected security interest but not over a perfected security interest. Thus, a person who becomes a lien creditor before another security interest in the same property is perfected has priority, but one who acquires the lien after perfection does not. Mechanic's and artisan's liens, however, have priority over perfected security interests unless a statute provides otherwise. These types of liens are discussed below.

Mechanic's Lien

When a person contracts for labor, services, or material to be furnished for the purpose of making improvements on real property but does not immediately pay for the improvements, a creditor can place a **mechanic's lien** (also known as a *materialman's lien*) on the property. This creates a special type of debtor-creditor relationship wherein the real estate itself becomes security for the lien (debt).

For example, a roofer repairs a leaky roof at the request of a homeowner. The homeowner owes the roofer the agreed-on price for the materials, labor, and services performed. If the homeowner cannot pay or pays only a portion of the charges, a mechanic's lien against the property can be created. The roofer is the lienholder, and the real property is encumbered with a mechanic's lien for the amount owed. If the homeowner does not pay the lien, the property can be sold to satisfy the debt.

The procedures by which a mechanic's lien is created are controlled by state law. Generally, the lienholder must file a written notice of lien against the particular property involved. The notice of lien must be filed within a specific time period, mea-

sured from the last date on which materials or labor were provided (usually within 60 to 120 days). Failure to pay the debt entitles the lienholder to foreclose on the real estate on which the improvements were made and to sell it to satisfy the amount of the debt. Of course, the lienholder is required by statute to give notice to the owner of the property prior to foreclosure and sale. The sale proceeds are used to pay the debt and the costs of the legal proceedings; and the surplus, if any, is paid to the former owner.

Artisan's Lien

An **artisan's lien** is a security device created at common law through which a creditor can recover payment from a debtor for labor and materials furnished in the repair of personal property. For example, Ann leaves her watch at the jeweler's to be repaired and to have her initials engraved on the back. In absence of agreement, the jeweler can keep the watch until Ann pays for the repairs and services that the jeweler provides. Should Ann fail to pay, the jeweler has an artisan's lien on Ann's watch for the amount of the bill and can sell the watch in satisfaction of the lien.

In contrast to a mechanic's lien, an artisan's lien is *possessory*. The lienholder ordinarily must have retained possession of the property and have expressly or impliedly agreed to provide the services on a *cash, not a credit, basis*. Usually, the lienholder retains possession of the property. In this case, the lien remains in existence as long as the lienholder maintains possession and is terminated once possession is voluntarily surrendered—unless the surrender is only temporary. When the surrender is temporary, there must be an agreement that the property will be returned to the lienholder. Even with such an agreement, if a third party obtains rights in that property while it is out of the lienholder's possession, the lien is lost. The only way a lienholder can protect a lien and surrender possession at the same time is to record notice of the lien in accordance with state lien and recording statutes.

Modern statutes permit the holder of an artisan's lien to foreclose and sell the property subject to the lien to satisfy payment of the debt. As with the mechanic's lien, the lienholder is required to give notice to the owner of the property prior to foreclosure and selling. The sale proceeds are used to pay the debt and the costs of the legal proceedings, and the surplus, if any, is paid to the former owner.

Can towing and storage services give rise to an artisan's lien? The court deals with this issue in the following case.

Case 32.1

CHRYSLER CREDIT CORP. v. KEELING

Missouri Court of Appeals, 1990.
793 S.W.2d 222.

BACKGROUND AND FACTS Chrysler Credit Corporation had a perfected security interest in a 1988 Dodge pickup that had been bought by Robert Keeling. When Keeling defaulted on his payments, Chrysler attempted to repossess the truck but could not locate it for some time. Finally, the pickup was found in a lot operated by Joe Booth, doing business as Highway Tow Service. Booth had towed the pickup from an apartment complex parking lot to his lot at the request of the apartment manager and had stored the pickup on his auto lot for over two months. Chrysler asked Booth to give the pickup to Chrysler, but Booth refused unless he was paid for towing and storage. Chrysler sued Booth in a Missouri state court to gain possession of the pickup. Booth contended that he had a common law artisan's lien on the truck that took priority over Chrysler's perfected security interest. The trial court held for Chrysler, and Booth appealed.

DECISION AND RATIONALE The Missouri Court of Appeals affirmed the trial court's holding that Chrysler was entitled to possession of the pickup. The appellate court acknowledged that under Missouri law, an artisan's lien would be superior to a duly perfected security interest, such as Chrysler's, but found that Booth did not have an artisan's lien because he had furnished no labor or materials for the repair of the vehicle. "[T]owing a vehicle does not constitute the furnishing of labor or materials for the repair of a vehicle." The court concluded that Booth had a statutory lien for storage. The court cited a Missouri statute "which provides that a storage lien shall not take precedence over or be superior to any prior lien duly perfected * * * without the written consent of the holder of such prior lien."

Innkeeper's Lien

An **innkeeper's lien** is another security device created at common law. An innkeeper's lien is given on the baggage of guests for the agreed-on charges that remain unpaid. If no express agreement was made on those charges, then the lien will be the reasonable value of the accommodations furnished. The innkeeper's lien is terminated either by the guest's payment of the hotel's charges or by surrender of the baggage to the guests, unless such surrender is temporary. Also, the lien is terminated by *conversion* (that is, simply the assumption of ownership) of the guest's baggage by the innkeeper. Although state statutes permit conversion by means of a public sale, there is a trend toward

requiring that the guest first be given an impartial judicial hearing.[1]

In some states, if a tenant does not pay rent, the landlord may take and keep or sell whatever of the tenant's personal property is on the leased premises. Different states have different requirements regarding landlord's liens. Landlord's liens are discussed in more detail in Chapter 52.

Judicial Liens

A debt must be past due before a creditor may commence legal action against a debtor. Once legal

---

1. *Klim v. Jones,* 315 F.Supp. 109 (N.D.Cal. 1970).

action is brought, the debtor's property may be seized to satisfy the debt. If the property is seized prior to trial proceedings, the seizure is referred to as an *attachment* of the property. If the seizure occurs following a court judgment in the creditor's favor, the court's order to seize the property is referred to as a *writ of execution.*

ATTACHMENT *Attachment* under Article 9 of the UCC, as discussed in Chapter 31, refers to the process through which a security interest becomes enforceable against a debtor with respect to the debt's collateral [UCC 9-203]. In the present context, **attachment** refers to a prejudgment, court-ordered seizure and taking into custody of property that is in controversy because of a debt. In many cases, the creditor will want this done to assure that there will be some assets of the debtor against which to execute the judgment. Attachment is normally a *prejudgment* remedy. It occurs either at the time of or immediately after the commencement of a lawsuit but before the entry of a final judgment.

Attachment rights are created by state statutes. To use attachment as a remedy, the creditor must

have an enforceable right to payment of the debt under law and must follow certain procedures. Otherwise, the creditor can be liable for damages for wrongful attachment. He or she must file with the court an affidavit stating that the debtor is in default and stating the statutory grounds under which attachment is sought. A bond must be posted by the creditor to cover court costs, the value of the loss of use of the good suffered by the debtor, and the value of the property attached. When the court is satisfied that all the requirements have been met, it issues a **writ of attachment.** This writ is similar to a writ of execution in that it directs the sheriff or other officer to seize property belonging to the debtor. If the creditor prevails at trial, the seized property can be sold to satisfy the judgment.

The following case illustrates that strict compliance with every specific procedure established by the state's attachment statute is required for the property to be subject to an enforceable writ of attachment, because a writ of attachment operates against a debtor's property simply on the strength of the creditor's sworn statement that a debt is owed.

BACKGROUND AND FACTS Topjian Plumbing and Heating, Inc., sought prejudgment writs of attachment to satisfy an anticipated judgment in a contract action in a New Hampshire state court against Bruce Topjian, Inc. Topjian Plumbing did not petition the court for permission to effect the attachments but merely completed the forms, served them on Bruce Topjian and on the Fencers—the owners of a parcel of land that had previously belonged to Bruce Topjian—and recorded them at the registry of deeds. The Fencers objected to the attachment of their property, and in the course of the hearing on their objection, the court invalidated all of the attachments, holding that they were not in compliance with the New Hampshire prejudgment attachment statute, which requires application to the court for an order to attach property. Topjian Plumbing appealed.

DECISION AND RATIONALE The Supreme Court of New Hampshire affirmed the lower court's decision. The state supreme court pointed out that it had previously "determined that the standard requirements of due process, such as notice and hearing, must be adhered to before property interests can be encumbered by a pre-judgment attachment." The court noted that the proper procedure is to petition the court for permission to obtain an attachment order before serving it on the defendant and recording it at the registry of deeds. The court added that plaintiffs must file the petition "prior to service or entry of any writ of summons or other pleading."

Case 32.2

TOPJIAN PLUMBING AND HEATING, INC. v. BRUCE TOPJIAN, INC.

Supreme Court of New Hampshire, 1987.
129 N.H. 481,
529 A.2d 391.

WRIT OF EXECUTION   A debt must be past due for a creditor to commence legal action against a debtor. If the creditor is successful, the court awards the creditor a judgment against the debtor (usually for the amount of the debt plus any interest and legal costs incurred in obtaining the judgment). Attorneys' fees are not included in this amount unless provided for by statute or contract.

Frequently, it is easy to secure a judgment, but this is only half the battle. If the debtor does not or cannot pay the judgment, the creditor is entitled to go back to the court and obtain a **writ of execution.** This writ is an order, usually issued by the clerk of the court, directing the sheriff or other officer to seize (levy) and sell any of the debtor's nonexempt real or personal property (exemptions are described below) that is within the court's geographic jurisdiction, which is usually the county in which the courthouse is located. The proceeds of the sale are used to pay the judgment and the costs of the sale. Any excess is paid to the debtor. The debtor can pay the judgment and redeem the non-exempt property at any time before the sale takes place. Because of exemption and bankruptcy laws, many judgments are virtually uncollectible.

DEBTOR'S EXEMPT PROPERTY   In most states, certain types of real and personal property are exempt from levy of execution or attachment. Probably the most familiar of these exemptions is the **homestead exemption.** Each state permits the debtor to retain the family home, either in its entirety or up to a specified dollar amount, free from the claims of unsecured creditors or trustees in bankruptcy. The purpose is to ensure that the debtor will retain some form of shelter.

For example, Daniels owes Carey $40,000. The debt is the subject of a lawsuit, and the court awards Carey a judgment of $40,000 against Daniels. The homestead of Daniels is valued at $50,000. The state statute permits a homestead exemption of $25,000. There are no outstanding mortgages or other liens on his homestead. To satisfy the judgment debt, Daniels's family home is sold at public auction for $45,000. The proceeds of the sale are distributed as follows:

1.   Daniels is paid $25,000 as his homestead exemption.
2.   Carey is paid $20,000 toward the judgment debt, leaving a $20,000 deficiency judgment (that

is, "leftover debt") that can be satisfied (paid) from any other nonexempt property (personal or real) that Daniels may have, if allowed by state law.

In some states, statutes permit the homestead exemption only if the judgment debtor has a family. The policy behind this type of statute is to protect the family. If a judgment debtor does not have a family, a creditor may be entitled to collect the full amount realized from the sale of the debtor's home.

State exemption statutes usually include both real and personal property. Personal property that is most often exempt from satisfaction of judgment debts includes:

1.   Household furniture up to a specified dollar amount.
2.   Clothing and certain personal possessions, such as family pictures or a Bible.
3.   A vehicle (or vehicles) for transportation (at least up to a specified dollar amount).
4.   Certain classified animals, usually livestock but including pets.
5.   Equipment the debtor uses in a business or trade, such as tools or professional instruments, up to a specified dollar amount.

Garnishment

Garnishment is similar to attachment except that it is a collection remedy directed not at the debtor but at the debtor's property or rights held by a third person. The third person, the garnishee, owes a debt to the debtor or has property that belongs to the debtor, such as wages or a bank account (such as a checking account, a savings account, or a certificate of deposit). It is important to remember that garnishment is available against any money owed by a third person to the debtor, not just wages. Typically, a garnishment judgment is served on a person's employer so that part of the person's usual paycheck will be paid to the creditor. Under federal law, garnishment of an employee's wages for any one indebtedness cannot be grounds for dismissal of the employee.

Both federal laws and state laws limit the amount of money that can be garnished from a debtor's weekly take-home pay.[2] Federal law provides a minimal framework to protect debtors from

---

2.   A few states (for example, Texas) do not permit garnishment of wages, except under a child-support order.

losing all their income to the payment of judgment debts.[3] State laws also provide dollar exemptions, and these amounts are often larger than those provided by federal law. State and federal statutes can be applied together to help create a pool of funds sufficient to enable a debtor to continue to provide for family needs while also reducing the amount of the judgment debt in a reasonable way.

The legal proceeding for a garnishment action is governed by state law. As a result of a garnishment proceeding, the debtor's employer is ordered by the court to turn over a portion of the debtor's wages to pay the debt. Garnishment operates differently from state to state, however. According to the laws in some states, the judgment creditor need obtain only one order of garnishment, which will then continuously apply to the judgment debtor's weekly wages until the entire debt has been paid. In other states, the judgment creditor must go back to court for a separate order of garnishment for each pay period.

Creditors' Composition Agreements

As discussed in Chapter 11, creditors may contract with a debtor for discharge of the debtor's debts on payment of a sum less than that owed. (The contract discharges only those debts of creditors who agree to be bound.) These agreements are called compositions or creditors' composition agreements and are usually held to be enforceable. Note, however, that they may be superseded by the debtor's bankruptcy.

Foreclosure

A real estate mortgage agreement provides that when the **mortgagor** (debtor/borrower) *defaults* in making payments, the **mortgagee** (creditor/lender) can declare the entire mortgage debt due immediately. The mortgagee can enforce this provision of the agreement through a legal action called **foreclosure.**

There are four statutory methods of foreclosure: strict foreclosure, entry, power of sale, and foreclosure sale. A few states allow strict foreclosure. Under this method, after a specified period of time following default, the mortgagee acquires absolute title to the property. A few states provide for entry, or writ of entry. With this method, on default, the mortgagee obtains a writ entitling him or her to possession, and after a specified period of time, the mortgagee receives absolute title. Most states permit power of sale, according to which a sale can follow guidelines stated in the mortgage agreement instead of statutory guidelines. The usual method of foreclosure, however, is by a foreclosure sale.

A foreclosure sale is a judicial sale at which the mortgaged real estate is sold.[4] If the proceeds of the sale cover the mortgage debt and the foreclosure costs, the debtor receives any surplus. If the proceeds do not cover the mortgage debt and foreclosure costs, the mortgagee can seek to recover the difference from the mortgagor through a *deficiency judgment.* A deficiency judgment, which is obtained in a separate action after the foreclosure, entitles the creditor to recover this difference from a sale of the debtor's other nonexempt property. Some states do not permit deficiency judgments for some types of real estate interests.

Before the foreclosure sale, a defaulting mortgagor can redeem the property by paying the full amount of the debt, plus any interest and costs that have accrued. This right is known as the **equity of redemption.** In some states, a mortgagor may even redeem the property within a certain period of time—called a **statutory period of redemption**—after the sale. In these states, the deed to the property is not usually delivered to the purchaser until the statutory period has expired.

Assignment for Benefit of Creditors

Both common law and statutes may provide for a debtor's assignment of assets to a trustee or assignee for the benefit of the debtor's creditors. In these situations, the debtor voluntarily transfers title to assets owned to a trustee or assignee, who in turn sells or liquidates these assets, tendering payment to the debtor's creditors on a *pro rata* (proportionate) basis. Each creditor may accept

---

3. The federal Consumer Credit Protection Act, 15 U.S.C. Sections 1601 *et seq.,* provides that a debtor can retain either 75 percent of the disposable earnings per week or the sum equivalent to thirty hours of work paid at federal minimum wage rates, whichever is greater. In 1991, a federal law was enacted that permits garnishment of wages to repay guaranteed student loans.

4. A mortgage is a debt that is not subject to the statutory homestead exemption.

■ CONCEPT SUMMARY 32.1   Remedies Available to Creditors

Remedy	Definition
Mechanic's lien	A nonpossessory, filed lien on an owner's real estate for labor, services, or materials furnished to or made on the realty.
Artisan's or innkeeper's lien	A possessory lien on an owner's personal property for labor performed, value added, or care of the personal property (in many states) for which no payment was received.
Attachment	A court-ordered seizure of property (generally prior to full resolution of the creditor's rights resulting in judgment). Attachment is only available upon posting of bond and in strict compliance with the applicable state statutes.
Writ of execution	In cases of unsatisfied judgments, a court order directing the sheriff or other officer to seize and sell sufficient nonexempt property of the judgment debtor to satisfy the judgment.
Garnishment	A collection remedy that allows the creditor to attach a debtor's money (such as wages owed or bank accounts) or other property that is held by a third person.
Creditors' composition agreement	A contract between the debtor and creditors whereby the debtor's debts are discharged by payment of a sum less than that owed in the original debt.
Mortgage foreclosure	The creditor's selling or taking title to realty to satisfy the mortgage debt upon the debtor's default on the mortgage payments.
Assignment for benefit of creditors	The debtor's assignment of certain assets to a trustee or assignee, who sells or liquidates these assets and tenders payments to creditors on a *pro rata* basis. Acceptance of this payment by a creditor is discharge of the debt.

the tender (and discharge the debt owed to him or her) or reject it (and attempt to collect the debt in another way).

The flexibility and informality of an assignment for the benefit of creditors may save creditors time and expense and result in better prices when a debtor's property is liquidated. Nevertheless, creditors may decide that this option does not adequately protect their rights. Under the bankruptcy laws, creditors of a certain number with a certain amount of claims may have administration of the debtor's property transferred to the bankruptcy court—in other words, force the debtor into involuntary bankruptcy (see Chapter 33). Thus, like a creditors' composition agreement, a debtor's bankruptcy may supersede an assignment for the benefit of creditors—even if the bankruptcy is initiated by creditors.

■ Suretyship and Guaranty

When a third person promises to pay a debt or perform an obligation owed by another in the event that the debtor does not pay or perform, a suretyship or guaranty relationship is created. The third person's credit becomes the security for the debt owed. We look below at the nature of the third party's liability in suretyship and guaranty contracts and then at the defenses available to sureties and guaranties. The liabilities and rights arising in suretyship and guaranty contracts are also briefly described in the *Concept Summary* at the end of this section.

Suretyship

A contract of **suretyship** is a promise to a creditor made by a third person (the surety) to be respon-

■ **Exhibit 32–1 Classifications of Guaranty Contracts**

Type of Guaranty	Extent of Liability
Absolute	No conditions—the guarantor is liable on the debtor's default.
Conditional	The guarantor is liable only if a specified event occurs.
Continuing	The guarantor is liable for a series of transactions.
Unlimited	The guarantor is liable for an unlimited time or amount.
Limited	The guarantor is liable only for a limited time or amount.
General	The guarantor is liable to the public generally—as under a letter of credit, for example.
Special	The guarantor is liable only to specified persons.

sible for the debtor's obligation. The **surety** is *primarily* liable. In other words, the creditor can hold the surety responsible for payment of the debt the moment the debt is due, without first exhausting all legal remedies against the debtor. A surety agreement does not have to be in writing to be enforceable—as, for example, when the surety makes the promise directly to the obligee—but it usually is.

For example, David Brown wants to borrow money from the bank to buy a used car. Because David is still in college, the bank will not lend him the money unless his father will cosign the note. When his father cosigns the note, his father becomes primarily liable to the bank. On the note's due date, the bank can, without first making an effort to collect from David, seek payment from his father or, without attempting to collect from his father, seek payment from David, or seek payment from both.

Guaranty

A guaranty contract is similar to a suretyship contract—it also includes a promise to answer for the principal's obligation. Unlike a surety, who is primarily liable, however, a **guarantor** (the person making the guaranty) is *secondarily* liable. When the contract involves a debt, for instance, the guarantor can be required to answer for the obligation only after the principal has defaulted. Usually, the creditor must also have attempted to collect from the principal, because usually a debtor would not otherwise be declared to be in default.

To illustrate: AB Corporation approaches Norwest Bank to borrow money to meet its payroll. Doubting AB's creditworthiness, Norwest asks Merrimack, the company's president and owner of 70 percent of its stock, to sign an agreement making him personally liable if AB does not pay off the loan. If Merrimack signs, he becomes the loan's guarantor, but Norwest cannot hold him liable until AB is in default.

The contract between the guarantor and the creditor must be in writing to be enforceable unless the "main purpose" exception applies. That is, if the guaranty agreement's main purpose is to benefit the guarantor, the contract will be enforceable even if it is not in writing. (See Chapter 15 for a more detailed discussion.)

The guaranty contract's terms determine the extent and duration of the guarantor's liability. For example, a guaranty can cover only a single transaction or be *continuing* (that is, cover a series of transactions). Similarly, a guaranty can be *limited* or *unlimited* as to time or amount, *absolute* or *conditional,* or *general* or *special.* Exhibit 32–1 indicates the liability of the guarantor under each of these types of guaranty contracts.

In the following case, the defendant claimed that he was a guarantor, not a surety, on a contract for the purchase of an automobile. The case illustrates that a guarantor who cosigns a note will incur primary liability as a surety unless specific precautions—such as a separate contractual writing or other objective indication of guaranty status—are taken.

Case 32.3

**GENERAL MOTORS
ACCEPTANCE CORP.
v. DANIELS**

Court of Appeals of Maryland,
1985.
303 Md. 254,
492 A.2d 1306.

BACKGROUND AND FACTS   In June 1981, John Daniels agreed to buy a used car from Lindsay Cadillac Company. Because John had a poor credit rating, his brother, Seymoure, agreed to cosign the installment sales contract. Seymoure signed the contract on the line designated "Buyer," and John signed on the line designated "Co-Buyer." Lindsay assigned the contract to General Motors Acceptance Corporation (GMAC). In May 1982, GMAC declared the contract in default. After attempting to locate the car for several months, GMAC found it in a condition of total loss. GMAC brought an action in a Maryland state court for damages, but because service of process was never effected on John, the action proceeded only against Seymoure. The trial court found that Seymoure was a guarantor of the contract between John and GMAC and held that GMAC would have to attempt to bring suit against John before it could proceed against Seymoure. GMAC appealed the ruling.

DECISION AND RATIONALE   The Court of Appeals of Maryland reversed the lower court's ruling. The appellate court reasoned that although Seymoure intended to be a guarantor liable only on John's default, Seymoure's failure to make his subjective intent evident in any writing rendered him primarily liable as a surety. The court applied the "objective law of contracts" to determine the interpretation and construction of the contract. The court held that "when the language of the contract is plain and unambiguous * * * a court must presume that the parties meant what they expressed." Thus the court held that "the true test of what is meant is not what the parties to the contract intended it to mean, but what a reasonable person in the position of the parties would have thought it meant." All objective evidence indicated that Seymoure had cosigned the contract as a surety and not as a guarantor—Seymoure signed the line designated "buyer," the contract clearly said that all buyers agreed to be jointly and severally liable, and there was no evidence of a collateral agreement.

Defenses of the Surety and Guarantor

The defenses of the surety and the guarantor are basically the same. Therefore, for the sake of simplicity, we use the term *surety* throughout this section to mean both the surety and the guarantor.

A creditor must try to prevent certain actions that will release the surety from the obligation. Any material change in the terms of the original contract between the principal debtor and the creditor without the prior consent of the surety may discharge the surety completely. Even a material change that does not affect the surety's risk could effect a discharge. Such changes include extensions of time for making payment, providing the extension agreement is binding on the creditor and (for a compensated surety) the surety suffers a loss.

A release of the principal debtor without the surety's consent releases the surety unless the creditor expressly reserves his or her rights against the surety. A release with a reservation is treated as a covenant not to sue (discussed in Chapter 11) rather than a release.

Naturally, if the principal obligation is paid by the debtor or by another person on behalf of the debtor, the surety is discharged from obligation. Similarly, if valid tender of payment is made and the creditor for some reason rejects it with knowledge of the surety's existence, then the surety is released from any obligation on the debt.

Generally, any defenses available to a principal debtor can be used by the surety to avoid liability on the obligation to the creditor, except that the surety cannot use defenses personal to the debtor, such as the debtor's incapacity (due to minority, intoxication, or mental incompetence) or bankruptcy. The ability of the surety to assert any defenses the debtor may have against the creditor is the most important concept in suretyship, because most defenses available to the surety are those of the debtor.

Obviously, a surety may have his or her own defenses—for example, incapacity or bankruptcy. Another defense is available when the creditor has fraudulently induced the surety to guarantee the debt of the debtor. In most states, prior to formation of the suretyship contract, the creditor has a legal duty to inform the surety of material facts known by the creditor that would materially increase the surety's risk. Failure to so inform is fraud and makes the suretyship obligation voidable.

In addition, if a creditor surrenders or impairs the value of the debtor's collateral while knowing of the surety and without the surety's consent, the surety is released to the extent that the surety would suffer a loss from the creditor's actions—as the following case illustrates. The primary reason for this principle of suretyship law is to protect the surety who agreed to become obligated only because the debtor's collateral was in the possession of the creditor.

BACKGROUND AND FACTS Hallmark Cards, Inc., sued Edward Peevy, who had guaranteed an obligation owed to Hallmark by Garry Peevy. At the time of Edward's guaranty, Hallmark had in its possession property pledged as security by Garry. Before the suit was filed, Hallmark sold the pledged property without giving notice to Edward. Because the property sold did not cover the loan balance, Hallmark sued for the balance in an Arkansas state court, seeking a deficiency judgment. Edward contended that Hallmark was not entitled to a deficiency judgment against him because he had not been notified before Hallmark sold the property pledged by Garry as security for the obligation. Hallmark contended that Edward was not entitled to notice of the sale of the collateral. The court granted Edward's motion for summary judgment, holding that notice to a guarantor of a sale of the collateral was a necessary prerequisite to seeking a deficiency judgment against the guarantor. Hallmark appealed.

Case 32.4

HALLMARK CARDS, INC. v. PEEVY

Supreme Court of Arkansas, 1987.
293 Ark. 594,
739 S.W.2d 691.

DECISION AND RATIONALE The Supreme Court of Arkansas affirmed the lower court's holding that Hallmark's failure to notify the guarantor of the sale of property securing an obligation precluded Hallmark's recovery of the remainder of the debt from the guarantor. The state supreme court noted that state law requires a secured party to notify a debtor "of the time after which any private sale or other intended disposition is to be made." Hallmark argued that Edward was not a debtor. The court pointed out that other jurisdictions have held—"virtually unanimously"—that a guarantor is a debtor for purposes of the notice requirement. The court reasoned that "simple fairness" requires that the term debtor include one who is responsible for payment on default of a principal obligor.

Rights of the Surety and Guarantor

The rights of the surety and the guarantor are basically the same. Therefore, as in the preceding section, we use the term *surety* here to refer to both the surety and the guarantor.

When the surety pays the debt owed to the creditor, the surety is entitled to certain rights. First, the surety has a legal **right of subrogation.** Simply stated, this means that any right the creditor had against the debtor now becomes the right

of the surety. Included are creditor rights in bankruptcy, rights to collateral possessed by the creditor, and rights to judgments secured by the creditor. In short, the surety now stands in the shoes of the creditor. For example, if the creditor is in possession of collateral pledged by the debtor, the surety's payment of the debt on the debtor's default entitles the surety to the collateral in proportion to the surety's liability.

■ CONCEPT SUMMARY 32.2
Suretyship and Guaranty Relationships

	Types of Liability	Right of Subrogation	Right of Reimbursement
Strict Suretyship	*Primary liability*—The surety is liable as a co-debtor the moment the debt is due. The contract need not be in writing to be enforceable.	The surety has the right of subrogation on payment.	The surety has the right to be reimbursed by the co-debtor for the full amount paid.
Guaranty	*Secondary liability*—The guarantor is liable only if the debtor defaults or as provided in the contract. The contract must be in writing to be enforceable.	The gurantor has the right of subrogation on payment.	The guarantor has the right to be reimbursed by the principal for the full amount paid.

Second, the surety has a right to be reimbursed by the debtor. This **right of reimbursement** stems from either the suretyship contract or equity. Basically, the surety is entitled to receive from the debtor all outlays the surety has made on behalf of the suretyship arrangement. These can include expenses incurred as well as the actual amount of the debt paid the creditor.

Third, if there are *co-sureties* (two or more sureties on the same obligation owed by the debtor), a surety who pays more than his or her proportionate share on a debtor's default is entitled to recover from the co-sureties the amount paid above the surety's obligation. This is referred to as the surety's **right of contribution.** Generally, a co-surety's liability either is determined by agreement or, in absence of agreement, is set at the maximum liability under the suretyship contract.

For example, suppose two co-sureties are obligated under a suretyship contract to guarantee the debt of a debtor. One surety's maximum liability is $15,000, and the other's is $10,000. The debtor owes $10,000 and is in default. The surety with the $15,000 maximum liability pays the creditor the entire $10,000. In the absence of other agreement, this surety can recover $4,000 from the other surety ($10,000/$25,000 × $10,000 = $4,000, the other surety's obligation).

■ Terms and Concepts

■ For Review

1. What is prejudgment atttachment? What is a writ of execution? How does a creditor use these remedies?
2. What property is exempt from attachment and execution?

3. What is garnishment? How does a creditor use garnishment?
4. Ramsey takes out a mortgage on his house. When he fails to make the payments, Home Savings Bank, the mort-

gagee, declares the entire debt due immediately. On September 1, Home Savings announces that a foreclosure sale will be held October 1. What could Ramsey do before October 1 to retain an interest in the property? If the property sells for more than the mortgage debt, who gets the surplus? If the property sells for less than the mortgage debt, what could Home Savings do to recover the difference?

5. Sara wants to buy a new car. To obtain the money to buy the car, she approaches Quarles National Bank about a loan. Quarles refuses to lend the money to Sara unless Bev, Sara's mother, cosigns the note. When Sara and Bev cosign the note, Sara and Bev are each primarily liable on it. Is this a suretyship or guaranty arrangement? Can Quarles seek payment from Bev on the note's due date without first attempting to collect from Sara? If Bev pays the note, can Bev collect the amount of the payment from Sara?

■ Questions and Case Problems

32-1. Sylvia takes her car to Crank's Auto Repair Shop. A sign in the window states that all repairs must be paid for in cash unless credit is approved in advance. Sylvia and Crank agree that Crank will repair Sylvia's car engine and put in a new transmission. No mention is made of credit. Because Crank is not sure how much engine repair will be necessary, he refuses to give Sylvia an estimate. He repairs the engine and puts in a new transmission. When Sylvia comes to pick up her car, she learns that the bill is $795. Sylvia is furious, refuses to pay Crank that amount, and demands possession of her car. Crank demands payment. Discuss the rights of the parties in this matter.

32-2. James is employed by the Cross-Bar Packing Corp. and earns take-home pay of $400 per week. He is $2,000 in debt to the Holiday Department Store for goods purchased on credit over the past eight months. Most of this property is nonexempt and is presently located in James's apartment. James is in default on his payments to Holiday. Holiday learns that James has a girlfriend in another state and that he plans on giving her most of this property for Christmas. Discuss what actions are available and should be taken by Holiday to resolve the debt owed by James.

32-3. Ann is a student at Slippery Stone University. In need of funds to pay for tuition and books, she attempts to secure a short-term loan from West Bank. The bank agrees to make a loan if Ann will have someone financially responsible guarantee the loan payments. Sheila, a well-known businesswoman and a friend of Ann's family, calls the bank and agrees to pay the loan if Ann cannot. Because of Sheila's reputation, the loan is made. Ann is making the payments, but because of illness she is not able to work for one month. She requests that West Bank extend the loan for three months. West Bank agrees, raising the interest rate for the extended period. Sheila is not notified of the extension (and therefore does not consent to it). One month later Ann drops out of school. All attempts to collect from Ann fail. West Bank wants to hold Sheila liable. Discuss West Bank's claim against Sheila.

32-4. Higgins is the owner of a relatively old home valued at $45,000. He notices that the bathtubs and fixtures in both bathrooms are leaking and need to be replaced. He contracts with Plumber to replace the bathtubs and fixtures. Plumber replaces them, and on June 1 she submits her bill of $4,000 to Higgins. Because of financial difficulties, Higgins does not pay the bill. Higgins's only asset is his home, which, under state law, is exempt up to $40,000 as a homestead. Discuss fully Plumber's remedies in this situation.

32-5. Kloster-Madsen, Inc., a general contractor, entered into a contract with the owner of a building to do certain remodeling work. About a month later, pursuant to the contract, an electrical subcontractor removed several light fixtures from one of the ceilings, cutting four holes in the ceiling and placing the removed light fixtures in the holes. Immediately after this work was begun, a new owner, Tafi's, Inc., purchased the building. Material and labor worth several thousand dollars were expended before Tafi's informed the general contractor that it did not wish to have the building remodeled. Discuss whether Kloster-Madsen can impose a mechanic's lien on the building even though it entered into the building contract with a different owner. [*Kloster-Madsen, Inc. v. Tafi's, Inc.,* 303 Minn. 59, 226 N.W.2d 603 (1975)]

32-6. John Shumate parked his car in a vacant lot where he had left it several times previously. When he returned, he was informed that the car had been towed at the property owner's request. Thomas Younger had a collision with another car. His car was towed from the scene of the accident at the request of the police while Younger was discussing the accident with the police. The towing companies informed both car owners that they must pay towing and storage charges before their autos would be returned. The car owners sued to challenge the towing companies' claim of a possessory lien. Could the owners be prevented from removing their cars until payment was made? Discuss fully. [*Younger v. Plunkett,* 395 F.Supp. 702 (E.D.Pa. 1975)]

32-7. Harmony Unlimited obtained a judgment against John Chivetta and his company, JMC Enterprises. At the time of the judgment, John lacked sufficient funds to pay. Just before Harmony obtained the judgment, John had transferred $126,000 to his mother, Nettie, who had signed a promissory note. The note for $126,000 was payable on demand, carried no interest, and contained a provision that barred John from obtaining a money judgment against his mother. Nettie paid some of John's bills after the transfer of money from her son to her. Harmony served a garnishment summons on Nettie, claiming that she was a party to a fraudulent scheme by her son to conceal his assets and was holding funds that belonged to her son. Nettie argued that Harmony's rights against her could not be any greater than John's rights against her and that because John could not obtain a judgment against her for the money, Harmony could not do so either. Discuss Harmony's right of garnishment against Nettie. [*Harmony Unlimited, Inc. v. Chivetta,* 743 S.W.2d 884 (Mo.App. 1987)]

32-8. In February of 1973, Gladys Schmidt borrowed $4,120 from the National Bank of Joliet to finance the purchase of a Cadillac. The bank held a security interest in the automobile and perfected this interest by filing in the office of the secretary of state. In August of 1973, Schmidt took the car to Bergeron Cadillac, Inc., for repairs, which cost approximately $2,000. When Schmidt failed to pay for the repairs, Bergeron Cadillac retained possession of the car and placed an artisan's lien on it. In September, Schmidt defaulted on her payments to the bank, and the bank later filed an action to gain possession of the Cadillac from Bergeron. Discuss which party had a right to possession of the vehicle—Bergeron Cadillac or the National Bank. [*National Bank of Joliet v. Bergeron Cadillac, Inc.,* 66 Ill.2d 140, 361 N.E.2d 1116, 5 Ill.Dec. 588 (1977)]

32-9. Levinson and Johnson, who had both signed a promissory note, did not pay the note when it was due. Instead, American Thermex, Inc., a corporation in which Johnson had a controlling interest, voluntarily paid the note. American Thermex later brought suit against Levinson, seeking reimbursement for the payment. American Thermex argued, among other things, that because it had paid the note

it had the legal right of subrogation against the note's co-maker, Levinson. Will the court agree that American Thermex has a legal right of subrogation? Why or why not? [*Levinson v. American Thermex, Inc.,* 196 Ga.App. 291, 396 S.E.2d 252 (1990)]

32-10. Case Briefing Assignment

Examine Case A.19 [Allison-Bristow Community School District v. Iowa Civil Rights Commission, *461 N.W.2d 456 (Iowa 1990)*] *in Appendix A. The case has been excerpted there in great detail. Review and then brief the case, making sure that you include answers to the following questions in your brief.*

1. Why did Rowland claim that the back pay, plus interest, that the Civil Rights Commission ordered his employer to pay him were exempt earnings, not subject to garnishment under Iowa law?
2. How did the relevant Iowa statute define *earnings*?
3. On what grounds did the district court rule against Rowland?
4. What arguments were advanced by the judgment creditor, Willow Tree, to convince the court that Rowland's award of back pay, plus interest, should be subject to garnishment?
5. What was the reasoning behind the state supreme court's conclusion on the issue? In what way did the supreme court's ruling differ from that of the district court?

Chapter 33

Bankruptcy and Reorganization

Article I, Section 8, of the U.S. Constitution provides that "The Congress shall have the power . . . to establish . . . uniform laws on the subject of bankruptcies throughout the United States." Bankruptcy proceedings are rooted in federal laws; bankruptcy courts are special federal courts; and bankruptcy judges are federally appointed.

■ Federal Bankruptcy Law—Historical Background

Bankruptcy law is designed to accomplish two main goals. The first is to provide relief and protection to debtors who have "gotten in over their heads." The second is to provide a fair means of distributing a debtor's assets among all creditors. Thus, the law attempts to protect the rights of both the debtor and the creditor.

The original Bankruptcy Act was enacted in 1898 and was amended by the 1938 Chandler Act. A major overhaul of the federal bankruptcy law occurred in 1978 with the passage of the Bankruptcy Reform Act of 1978. The 1978 act was amended in 1984, basically to correct what many felt to be deficiencies brought about by the 1978 major overhaul, and again in 1986 to increase the number of bankruptcy judgeships, provide for U.S. trustees, and create a new Chapter 12 in bankruptcy to aid the family farmer.

Bankruptcy proceedings are held in bankruptcy courts. The bankruptcy courts' primary function is to hold *core proceedings*[1] dealing with the procedures required to administer the estate of the debtor in bankruptcy. Bankruptcy courts are under the authority of U.S. district courts, and rulings from bankruptcy courts can be appealed to the district courts. Fundamentally, a bankruptcy court fulfills the role of an administrative court for the district court concerning matters in bankruptcy. Decisions on personal injury, wrongful death, and other civil proceedings affecting the debtor are now resolved in other federal or state courts.

Although the Bankruptcy Act is a federal law, state laws on secured transactions, liens, judgments, and exemptions also play a role in a federal bankruptcy proceeding.

---

1. Core proceedings are procedural functions, such as allowance of claims, decisions on preferences, automatic stay proceedings, confirmation of bankruptcy plans, discharge of debts, and so on.

■ The Bankruptcy Reform Act of 1978 as Amended

The Bankruptcy Reform Act of 1978, as amended—hereinafter called the Bankruptcy Code, or simply the Code—is contained in Title 11 of the U.S. Code and has eight chapters. Chapters 1, 3, and 5 include general definitional provisions and provisions governing case administration, creditors, the debtor,[2] and the estate. These three chapters apply generally to all kinds of bankruptcies. The next five chapters set forth the different types of relief that debtors may seek. Chapter 7 provides for **liquidation** (the selling of all remaining nonexempt assets for cash). Chapter 9 governs the adjustment of debts of a municipality. Chapter 11 governs reorganizations. Chapter 12 (family farmers) and Chapter 13 (individuals) provide for adjustment of debts by parties with regular incomes.[3]

The following sections deal with Chapter 7 liquidations, Chapter 11 reorganizations, and Chapter 12 and 13 plans. The latter three chapters have been referred to as "rehabilitation" chapters.

To fully inform a consumer-debtor of the various types of relief available, the Code requires the clerk of the court to give all **consumer-debtors** (defined as individuals whose debts are primarily consumer debts) written notice of each chapter under which they may proceed prior to the commencement of a filing.

■ Chapter 7 Liquidations

Chapter 7 liquidation is the most familiar type of bankruptcy proceeding and is often referred to as an ordinary or "straight" bankruptcy. Put simply, a debtor in a straight bankruptcy states his or her debts and turns his or her assets over to a **trustee.** The trustee sells the nonexempt assets and distributes the proceeds to creditors. With certain exceptions, the balance of the debts is then discharged (extinguished), and the debtor is relieved of his or her obligation to pay the debts. Any "person"—defined as including individuals, partnerships, and corporations[4]—may be a debtor under Chapter 7. Railroads, insurance companies, banks, savings and loan associations, and credit unions cannot be Chapter 7 debtors, however. Other chapters of the Code, or federal or state statutes, apply to them.

Debtors are allowed to have their debts discharged under Chapter 7 only once within a six-year period.

Filing the Petition

A straight bankruptcy may be commenced by the filing of either a voluntary or an involuntary petition.

VOLUNTARY BANKRUPTCY   When a voluntary **petition in bankruptcy** is brought by the debtor, he or she files official forms designated for that purpose in the bankruptcy court. The Code requires a consumer-debtor who has selected Chapter 7 to state in the petition, at the time of filing, that he or she understands the relief available under other chapters of the Code and has chosen to proceed under Chapter 7. If the consumer-debtor is represented by an attorney, the attorney must file an affidavit stating that he or she has informed the debtor of the relief available under each chapter. A debtor does not have to be insolvent to file or petition in bankruptcy. Anyone liable to a creditor can declare bankruptcy.[5]

The voluntary petition contains the following schedules:

1. A list of both secured and unsecured creditors, their addresses, and the amount of debt owed to each.
2. A statement of the financial affairs of the debtor.

---

2. It is noteworthy that the term *bankrupt* no longer exists under the Code. Those who were *bankrupts* under bankruptcy law prior to the Bankruptcy Reform Act of 1978 are now merely *debtors* under the Code.

3. There are no Chapters 2, 4, 6, 8, or 10 in Title 11. Such "gaps" are not uncommon in the U.S.C. This is because chapter numbers (or other subdivisional unit numbers) are sometimes reserved for future use when a statute is enacted. (A gap may also appear if a law has been repealed.)

4. The definition of *corporation* includes unincorporated companies and associations. It also covers labor unions.

5. The inability to pay debts as they become due is known as *equitable* insolvency. A *balance sheet* insolvency, which exists when a debtor's liabilities exceed assets, is not the test. Thus, it is possible for debtors to voluntarily petition for bankruptcy or to be thrown into involuntary bankruptcy even though their assets far exceed their liabilities. This may occur when a debtor's cash flow problems become severe.

3. A list of all property owned by the debtor, including property claimed by the debtor to be exempt.

4. A listing of current income and expenses. (This schedule provides creditors and the court with relevant information on the debtor's ability to pay creditors a reasonable amount from future income. This information *could* permit a court, on its own motion, to dismiss a debtor's Chapter 7 petition after a hearing, and to encourage the filing of a Chapter 13 petition, when that would substantially improve the chances that creditors would be paid.)[6]

---

6. For example, Marcy has recently graduated from a school of law and earns an annual salary of $50,000. She has few assets. While attending school, she acquired numerous debts. To silence her creditors, she files for Chapter 7 bankruptcy. Her creditors will be better off if the court denies her petition for Chapter 7 bankruptcy. Note, however, that the law does give the debtor a presumption in favor of granting an order for relief under whatever chapter in the Code is requested by the debtor.

The official forms must be completed accurately, sworn to under oath, and signed by the debtor. To conceal assets or knowingly supply false information on these schedules is a crime under the bankruptcy laws. If the voluntary petition for bankruptcy is found to be proper, the filing of the petition will itself constitute an **order for relief.** (An order for relief is a court's grant of assistance to a complainant. In the context of bankruptcy, relief consists of discharging a complainant's debts.) Once a consumer-debtor's voluntary petition has been filed, the clerk of the court or other appointee must give the trustee and creditors mailed notice of the order for relief not more than twenty days after entry of the order. A new feature allows a husband and wife to file jointly for bankruptcy under a single petition.

As mentioned above, debtors do not have to be insolvent to file for voluntary bankruptcy. Debtors do not have unfettered access to Chapter 7 bankruptcy proceedings, however, as the following case illustrates.

Case 33.1

IN RE WALTON
United States Court of Appeals, Eighth Circuit, 1989. 866 F.2d 981.

BACKGROUND AND FACTS In 1985, Ronald Walton voluntarily petitioned for Chapter 7 bankruptcy. The bankruptcy court ordered a hearing at which it was determined that Walton's monthly income exceeded his monthly expenses by an amount sufficient to pay off at least a substantial portion of his debts under a sixty-month Chapter 13 reorganization plan. The court concluded that granting Walton relief under Chapter 7 would constitute substantial abuse of Chapter 7 and dismissed his petition. Chapter 7 expressly prohibits "substantial abuse" of its provisions, but it does not indicate what constitutes substantial abuse. Walton appealed, arguing, among other things, that Congress intended "substantial abuse" to mean nothing more than "bad faith" and that because he had filed in good faith, he was not abusing Chapter 7.

DECISION AND RATIONALE The United States Court of Appeals for the Eighth Circuit affirmed the lower court's ruling. The appellate court stressed that most bankruptcy commentators agree that "[t]he primary factor that may indicate substantial abuse is the ability of the debtor to repay the debts out of future disposable income." In this case, Walton's total unsecured debt was $26,484. Because Walton's monthly income exceeded his monthly expenses by an estimated $497, the court reasoned that Walton would very likely be able to pay his debts over a five-year period under Chapter 13. The court dismissed Walton's contention that Congress intended substantial abuse to mean nothing more than bad faith by stating that "the cramped interpretation * * * that Walton advances would drastically reduce the bankruptcy courts' ability to dismiss cases filed by debtors who are not dishonest, but who also are not needy."

ETHICAL CONSIDERATIONS By its very nature, bankruptcy law favors debtors' interests over those of creditors. As this case shows, however, the rights of creditors are very much of concern to a bankruptcy court, and a debtor who can pay debts rightfully owed without undue hardship will rarely be offered refuge under bankruptcy law.

INVOLUNTARY BANKRUPTCY   An involuntary bankruptcy occurs when the debtor's creditors force the debtor into bankruptcy proceedings. An involuntary case cannot be commenced against a farmer[7] or a charitable institution. For an involuntary action to be filed against other debtors, the following requirements must be met. If the debtor has twelve or more creditors, three or more of these creditors having unsecured claims totaling at least $5,000 must join in the petition. If a debtor has fewer than twelve creditors, one or more creditors having a claim of $5,000 may file.

If the debtor challenges the involuntary petition, a hearing will be held and the bankruptcy court will enter an order for relief if it finds either of the following:

1.   The debtor is generally not paying debts as they become due.
2.   A general receiver, assignee, or custodian took possession of or was appointed to take charge of substantially all of the debtor's property within 120 days before the filing of the petition.

If the court grants an order for relief, the debtor will be required to supply the same information in the bankruptcy schedules as in a voluntary bankruptcy.

An involuntary petition should not be used as an everyday debt-collection device, and the Code provides penalties for the filing of frivolous petitions against debtors. Judgment may be granted against the petitioning creditors for the costs and attorneys' fees incurred by the debtor in defending against an involuntary petition that is dismissed by the court. If the petition is filed in bad faith, damages can be awarded for injury to the debtor's reputation. Punitive damages may also be awarded.

---

7.   The definition of *farmer* includes persons who receive more than 80 percent of their gross income from farming operations, such as tilling the soil, dairy farming, ranching, or the production or raising of crops, poultry, or livestock. Corporations and partnerships may qualify under certain conditions.

Automatic Stay

The moment a petition, either voluntary or involuntary, is filed, there exists an **automatic stay,** or suspension, of virtually all litigation and other action by creditors against the debtor or the debtor's property. In other words, once a petition has been filed, creditors cannot commence or continue most legal actions, such as foreclosure of liens, execution on judgments, trials, or any action to repossess property in the hands of the debtor. A secured creditor, however, may petition the bankruptcy court for relief from the automatic stay in certain circumstances.

Underlying the Code's automatic stay provision for a secured creditor is a concept known as *adequate protection.* The **adequate protection doctrine**, among other things, protects secured creditors from losing their security as a result of the automatic stay. The bankruptcy court can provide adequate protection by requiring the debtor or trustee to make periodic cash payments or a one-time cash payment (or to provide additional collateral or replacement liens) to the extent that the stay may actually cause the value of the property to decrease. Or the court may grant other relief that is the ''indubitable equivalent'' of the secured party's interest in the property, such as a guaranty by a solvent third party to cover losses suffered by the secured party as a result of the stay.

For example, suppose Speedy Express, a delivery service, owns three delivery trucks in which First Bank has a security interest. Speedy Express has failed to make its monthly payments for two months. Speedy Express files a petition in bankruptcy, and the automatic stay prevents First Bank from repossessing the trucks. Meanwhile, the trucks (whose collective value is already less than the balance due) are depreciating at a rate of several hundred dollars a month. First Bank's inability to repossess and immediately resell the trucks is harming the bank to the extent of several hundred dollars per month. The bankruptcy court may protect First Bank from being harmed by requiring Speedy Express to make a one-time cash payment or periodic cash payments (or to provide additional collateral or replacement liens) to the extent that the delivery trucks are depreciating in value. If the debtor is unable to provide adequate protection, the court may vacate (remove) the stay as applied to First Bank and allow it to repossess the trucks.

The Code provides that if a creditor *knowingly* violates the automatic stay (a willful violation), any party injured, including the debtor, is entitled to recover actual damages, costs, and attorneys' fees and may be entitled to recover punitive damages.

The Trustee

Promptly after the order for relief in a Chapter 7 proceeding has been entered, an interim or provisional trustee is appointed by the **U.S. Trustee** (a government official who performs appointing and other administrative tasks that a bankruptcy judge would otherwise have to perform). The interim or provisional trustee presides over the debtor's property until the first meeting of creditors. At this first meeting, either a permanent trustee is elected or the interim trustee becomes the permanent trustee. The trustee's principal duty is to collect and reduce to money the ''property of the estate'' and to close up the estate as expeditiously as is compatible with the best interests of the parties.

Creditors' Meeting

Within a reasonable time after the order for relief has been granted (not less than ten days nor more than thirty days) the bankruptcy court must call a meeting of creditors listed in the schedules filed by the debtor. The bankruptcy judge does not attend this meeting.

The debtor is required to attend the meeting (unless excused by the court) and to submit to examination under oath by the creditors and the trustee. Failing to appear when required or making false statements under oath may result in the debtor's being denied a discharge of bankruptcy.

Proof of claims by creditors must normally be filed within ninety days of the meeting.[8]

Property of the Estate

Upon the commencement of a Chapter 7 proceeding, an *estate in property* is created. The estate consists of all the debtor's legal and equitable interests in property presently held, wherever located, together with community property, property transferred in a transaction voidable by the trustee, proceeds and profits from the property of the estate, and certain after-acquired property. Interests in certain property—such as gifts, inheritances, property settlements (divorce), and life insurance death proceeds—to which the debtor becomes entitled *within 180 days after filing* may also become part of the estate. Thus, the filing of a bankruptcy petition generally fixes a dividing line: property acquired prior to the filing of the petition becomes property of the estate, and property acquired after the filing of the petition, except as just noted, remains the debtor's.

Exemptions

The trustee takes control over the debtor's property, but an individual debtor is entitled to exempt certain property from the bankruptcy. Prior to the enactment of the Code, state law exclusively governed the extent of the exemptions. (See Chapter 32.) The Code establishes a federal exemption scheme, however. An individual debtor (or a husband and wife who file jointly) now may choose between the exemptions provided under the applicable state law and the federal exemptions. Individual states have the power to pass legislation precluding the use of the federal exemptions by debtors residing within their borders, however.

The Bankruptcy Code exempts the following property:

1. Up to $7,500 in equity in the debtor's residence and burial plot (the homestead exemption).
2. Interest in a motor vehicle up to $1,200.
3. Interest, up to $200 for a particular item, in household goods and furnishings, wearing apparel, appliances, books, animals, crops, and musical instruments (the aggregate total of all items is limited, however, to $4,000).
4. Interest in jewelry up to $500.
5. Interest in any other property up to $400, plus any unused part of the $7,500 homestead exemption up to $3,750.[9]

---

8. This same ninety-day rule applies in Chapter 12 and Chapter 13 bankruptcies as well. In Chapter 11 bankruptcies, the court fixes the time within which proof of claims may be filed.

9. The Code places a cap of $3,750 on the unused part of the homestead exemption to prevent some debtors from receiving a windfall.

6. Interest in any tools of the debtor's trade up to $750.

7. Any unmatured life insurance contract owned by the debtor.

8. Certain interests in accrued dividends and interest under life insurance contracts owned by the debtor.

9. Professionally prescribed health aids.

10. The right to receive Social Security and certain welfare benefits, alimony and support, and certain pension benefits.

11. The right to receive certain personal injury and other awards.

Trustee's Powers

The basic duty of the trustee is to collect the debtor's available estate and reduce it to money for distribution, preserving the interests of both the debtor and unsecured creditors. This requires that the trustee be accountable for administering the debtor's estate. To enable the trustee to accomplish this duty, the Code gives the trustee certain powers, stated in both general and specific terms.

General powers are described by the statement that the trustee occupies a position *equivalent* in rights to that of certain other parties. For example, the trustee has the same rights as a *lien creditor* who could have obtained a judicial lien on the debtor's property or who could have levied execution on the debtor's property. This means that a trustee has priority over an unperfected secured party to the debtor's property. A trustee also has power equivalent to that of a *bona fide purchaser* of real property from the debtor.

Nevertheless, a creditor with a purchase-money security interest may prevail against a trustee, if the creditor files within ten days of the debtor's receipt of the collateral, even if the bankruptcy petition is filed before the creditor perfects. For example, Jill loaned Jack $20,000 on January 1, taking a security interest in the machinery Jack purchased with the $20,000 on that same date. On January 27, before Jill perfected her security interest, Jack filed for bankruptcy. The trustee can invalidate Jill's security interest, because it was unperfected when Jack filed the bankruptcy petition. Jill can only assert a claim as an unsecured creditor. But if Jack had filed for bankruptcy on January 7, and Jill had perfected her security interest on January 8, she would have prevailed, because she perfected her purchase-money security

interest within ten days of Jack's receipt of the machinery.

The trustee has specific *powers of avoidance*— that is, the trustee can set aside a sale or other transfer of the debtor's property, taking it back as a part of the debtor's estate. These powers include any voidable rights available to the debtor, preferences, certain statutory liens, and fraudulent transfers by the debtor. Each is discussed in more detail below.

The debtor shares most of the trustee's avoiding powers. Thus, if the trustee does not take action to enforce one of his or her rights (for example, to recover a preference), the debtor in a Chapter 7 bankruptcy can nevertheless enforce that right.[10]

The trustee has the power to require persons holding the debtor's property at the time the petition is filed to deliver the property to the trustee.

VOIDABLE RIGHTS A trustee steps into the shoes of the debtor. Thus, any reason that a debtor can use to obtain the return of his or her property can be used by the trustee as well. These grounds include fraud, duress, incapacity, and mutual mistake.

For example, Ben sells his boat to Frank. Frank gives Ben a check, knowing that there are insufficient funds in his bank account to cover the check. Frank has committed fraud. Ben has the right to avoid that transfer and recover the boat from Frank. Once an order for relief under Chapter 7 of the Code has been entered for Ben, the trustee can exercise the same right to recover the boat from Frank, and it becomes a part of the debtor's estate.

PREFERENCES A debtor is not permitted to transfer property or to make a payment that favors—or gives a **preference** to—one creditor over others. The trustee is allowed to recover payments made both voluntarily and involuntarily to one creditor in preference over another.

To have made a preferential payment that can be recovered, an *insolvent* debtor *generally* must have transferred property, for a *preexisting* debt, within *ninety days* of the filing of the petition in bankruptcy. The transfer must give the creditor more than the creditor would have received as a

---

10. Under Chapter 11 (to be discussed later), for which no trustee generally exists, the debtor has the same avoiding powers as a trustee under Chapter 7. Under Chapters 12 and 13 (also to be discussed later) a trustee must be appointed.

result of the bankruptcy proceedings. The trustee does not have to prove insolvency, as the Code provides that the debtor is presumed to be insolvent during this ninety-day period.

For example, suppose that Connally borrows $10,000 from the First National Bank of Texas on January 1, repays the loan on June 1 as promised, and files a bankruptcy petition on July 1. The bankruptcy trustee can recover the $10,000 payment because Connally made it within ninety days of filing. If Connally had not filed until September 1, however, the trustee could not have recovered the $10,000. If a friend of Connally's had paid off the loan, the payment could not have been recovered, regardless of whether it was made within ninety days, because it was not made with Connally's money or other property. If, on February 1, at the bank's insistence that the loan be secured, Connally had provided a mortgage on the Connally ranch and then had not repaid the loan before declaring bankruptcy, the trustee could have avoided the mortgage if it had given the bank more than the bank would have received in the Chapter 7 proceeding.

Sometimes the creditor receiving the preference is an **insider**—an individual, partner, partnership, officer, or director of a corporation (or a relative of one of these) who has a close relationship with the debtor. If such is the case, the avoidance power of the trustee is extended to transfers made within *one year* before filing; however, the *presumption* of insolvency is confined to the ninety-day period. Therefore, the trustee must prove that the debtor was insolvent at the time of earlier transfer.

Not all transfers are preferences. To be a preference, the transfer must be made for something other than current consideration. Therefore, it is generally assumed by most courts that payment for services rendered within ten to fifteen days prior to the payment of the current consideration is not a preference. If a creditor receives payment in the ordinary course of business, such as payment of last month's telephone bill, the payment cannot be recovered by the trustee in bankruptcy. To be recoverable, a preference must be a transfer for an antecedent debt, such as a year-old printing bill. In addition, the Code permits a consumer-debtor to transfer any property to a creditor up to a total value of $600, without the transfer's constituting a preference.

If a preferred creditor has sold the property to an innocent third party, the trustee cannot recover the property from the innocent party, but the creditor generally can be held accountable for the value of the property.

LIENS ON DEBTOR'S PROPERTY The trustee is permitted to avoid the fixing of certain statutory liens, such as a landlord's lien, on property of the debtor. Liens that first become effective on the bankruptcy or insolvency of the debtor are voidable by the trustee. Liens that are not perfected or enforceable on the date of the petition against a bona fide purchaser are voidable.

FRAUDULENT TRANSFERS The trustees may avoid fraudulent transfers or obligations if they are made within one year of the filing of the petition or if they are made with actual intent to hinder, delay, or defraud a creditor. Transfers made for less than a reasonably equivalent consideration are also vulnerable if by making them the debtor became insolvent, was left engaged in business with an unreasonably small amount of capital, or intended to incur debts that he or she could not pay.

The following case illustrates fraudulent transfers made by a debtor to his daughters. The transfers involved no consideration, and after the transfers the debtor retained control and derived benefits from the property. The trustee in bankruptcy sought to set aside the transfers, and the creditors and wife of the debtor filed actions to deny the debtor a discharge in bankruptcy.

BACKGROUND AND FACTS While a suit in a New York state court against Ralph Lazar for wrongful interference with a contractual relationship was pending, Lazar transferred his interest in a note and mortgage ($180,000) to his daughters, Arlene and Betty, who deposited the funds in certificates of deposit. After four months, Arlene used the funds, Lazar's personal funds, and $104,000 transferred from his solely owned pension trust fund to buy a yacht. Title was held by Arbet Enterprises, Inc., a closely held corporation formed solely to take title to the yacht. The daughters were

Case 33.2

IN RE LAZAR

United States Bankruptcy Court, Southern District of Florida, 1988. 81 Bankr. 148.

the sole shareholders. The yacht was sold, another was bought (title held by Arbet) with half the proceeds, and the rest of the proceeds was deposited for the use of Lazar and his daughters. Lazar used the yacht as his place of residence and for his personal benefit and enjoyment. Lazar lost the suit for wrongful interference with a contractual relationship, resulting in a $2 million judgment against him. When execution of the judgment was attempted, Lazar filed a Chapter 7 petition in a bankruptcy court. The trustee filed a claim against Lazar for fraudulent transfer and sought to have the money held by Arbet and the yacht turned over as part of the debtor's estate. Lazar's creditors and his wife filed separate actions seeking to deny him a discharge in bankruptcy.

DECISION AND RATIONALE   The United States Bankruptcy Court for the Southern District of Florida held that the transfers Lazar made to his daughters were fraudulent and that the trustee could set them aside, and denied Lazar the right to a discharge in bankruptcy. The court stated that the transfers of the note and mortgage and the pension trust funds were marked by several of the "badges of fraud" that courts identify as factors tending to indicate the presence of a fraudulent transfer. They "were made to family members for no consideration," and afterward "the debtor retained full control over, and derived the primary benefit from, the use of the funds and the assets subsequently purchased" with them. The court concluded that Lazar's intent in making the transfers, as well as their legal effect, was "to hinder, delay, and defraud the creditors." As a separate basis for turning the yacht over to the trustee, the court found that Arbet Enterprises, Inc., was Lazar's alter ego—a "mere instrumentality" created to aid in defrauding creditors and concealing ownership of the yachts. Finally, the court found that Lazar engaged "in the continuous concealment of his assets during the one year period prior to the filing of the bankruptcy petition, which satisfie[d] the requirements" for denying a discharge under Chapter 7.

ETHICAL CONSIDERATIONS   A debtor, knowing that he or she will be in bankruptcy proceedings, has an incentive to transfer assets to favored parties before or after the petition for bankruptcy is filed. For example, an automobile or a valuable coin collection can be "sold" at a bargain price to a trusted friend or relative to remove it from the estate in bankruptcy. In the interests of fairness to creditors, the law provides that the bankruptcy trustee can set aside such transfers, as was done in this case.

Claims of Creditors

Generally, any legal obligation of the debtor is a claim. In the case of a disputed or unliquidated claim, the bankruptcy court will set the value of the claim. Any creditor holding a debtor's obligation can file a claim against the debtor's estate. These claims are automatically allowed unless contested by the trustee, the debtor, or another creditor. A creditor who files a false claim commits a crime.

The Code, however, does not allow claims for breach of employment contracts or real estate leases for terms longer than one year. Such claims are limited to one year's rent or wages, despite the remaining length of either contract in breach.

Distribution of Property

Creditors are either secured or unsecured. The rights of secured creditors were discussed in Chapter 31. A *secured* creditor has a security interest in collateral that secures the debt. The Code provides that a consumer-debtor, within thirty days of filing a Chapter 7 petition or before the date of the first meeting of the creditors (whichever is first), must file with the clerk a statement of intention with respect to the secured collateral. The statement must indicate whether the debtor will retain or surrender the collateral to the secured party.[11] The trustee is obligated to enforce the debtor's statement within forty-five days after it is filed.

If the collateral is surrendered to the secured party, the secured creditor can enforce the security interest either by accepting the property in full satisfaction of the debt or by foreclosing on the collateral and using the proceeds to pay off the debt. Thus, the secured party has priority over unsecured parties as to the proceeds from the disposition of the collateral. Indeed, the Code provides that if the value of the collateral exceeds the secured party's claim, the secured party also has priority as to the proceeds in an amount that will cover reasonable fees and costs incurred because of the debtor's default. Any excess over this amount is used by the trustee to satisfy the claims of unsecured creditors. Should the collateral be insufficient to cover the secured debt owed, the secured creditor becomes an unsecured creditor for the difference.

Bankruptcy law establishes an order of priority for classes of debts owed to *unsecured* creditors, and they are paid in the order of their priority. Each class must be fully paid before the next class is entitled to any of the remaining proceeds. If there are insufficient proceeds to pay fully all the creditors in a class, the proceeds are distributed *proportionately* to the creditors in the class, and classes lower in priority receive nothing. The order of priority among classes of unsecured creditors is as follows:

1. Administrative expenses—including court costs, trustee fees, and attorneys' fees.
2. In an involuntary bankruptcy, expenses incurred by the debtor in the ordinary course of business from the date of the filing of the petition up to the appointment of the trustee or the issuance by the court of an order for relief.
3. Unpaid wages, salaries, and commissions earned within ninety days of the filing of the petition, limited to $2,000 per claimant. Any claim in excess of $2,000 is treated as a claim of a general creditor (listed as number 8 below).

4. Unsecured claims for contributions to be made to employee benefit plans, limited to services performed during 180 days prior to the filing of the bankruptcy petition and $2,000 per employee.
5. Claims by farmers and fishermen, up to $2,000, against debtor operators of grain storage or fish storage or processing facilities.
6. Consumer deposits of up to $900 given to the debtor before the petition was filed in connection with the purchase, lease, or rental of property or purchase of services that was not received or provided. Any claim in excess of $900 is treated as a claim of a general creditor (listed as number 8 below).
7. Certain taxes and penalties due to government units, such as income and property taxes.
8. Claims of general creditors.

If any amount remains after the priority classes of creditors have been satisfied, it is turned over to the debtor.

In a bankruptcy case in which the debtor has no assets, creditors are notified of the debtor's petition for bankruptcy but are instructed not to file a claim. In such a case, the unsecured creditors will receive no payment and most, if not all, of these debts will be discharged.

Discharge

From the debtor's point of view, the primary purpose of a Chapter 7 liquidation is to obtain a fresh start through the discharge of debts.[12] Certain debts, however, are not dischargeable in bankruptcy. Also, certain debtors may not qualify to have all debts discharged in bankruptcy. These situations are discussed below.

EXCEPTIONS TO DISCHARGE Discharge of a debt may be denied because of the nature of the claim or the conduct of the debtor. Claims that are not dischargeable under Chapter 7 include the following:

1. Claims for back taxes accruing within three years prior to bankruptcy.

---

11. Also, if applicable, the debtor must specify whether the collateral will be claimed as exempt property and whether the debtor intends to redeem the property or reaffirm the debt secured by the collateral.

12. Discharges are granted only to *individuals* who are debtors under Chapter 7, not to corporations or partnerships. The latter may use Chapter 11, or they may terminate under state law.

2. Claims against property or money obtained by the debtor under false pretenses or by false representations.

3. Claims by creditors who were not notified of the bankruptcy; these claims did not appear on the schedules the debtor was required to file.

4. Claims based on fraud or misuse of funds by the debtor while he or she was acting in a fiduciary capacity or claims involving the debtor's embezzlement or larceny.

5. Alimony and child support.

6. Claims based on willful or malicious conduct by the debtor toward another or the property of another.

7. Certain fines and penalties payable to governmental units.

8. Certain student loans, unless payment of the loans imposes an undue hardship on the debtor and the debtor's dependents.

9. Consumer debts of more than $500 for luxury goods or services owed to a single creditor incurred within forty days of the order for relief. This denial of discharge is a rebuttable presumption (that is, the denial may be challenged by the debtor), however, and any debts reasonably incurred to support the debtor or dependents are not classified as luxury goods or services.

10. Cash advances totaling more than $1,000 that are extensions of open-end consumer credit obtained by the debtor within twenty days of the order for relief. A denial of discharge of these debts is also a rebuttable presumption.

11. Judgments or consent decrees awarded against a debtor as a result of the debtor's operation of a motor vehicle while legally intoxicated.

In the following case, the question of the discharge of a student loan is at issue.

Case 33.3

IN RE BAKER

United States Bankruptcy
Court,
Eastern District of Tennessee,
1981.
10 Bankr. 870.

BACKGROUND AND FACTS Mary Lou Baker attended the University of Tennessee at Chattanooga, Cleveland State Community College, and the Baroness Erlanger School of Nursing, receiving educational loans of $6,635. After graduation, Baker's monthly take home pay was less than $650. Monthly expenses for herself and her three children were approximately $925. Her husband provided no financial support. She received no public aid and had no other income. One of her children had reading difficulty, and another required expensive shoes. Baker had not been well and had been unable to pay her medical bills. Just before filing for bankruptcy, her church paid her gas bill so that she and her children could have heat in their home. In her petition for bankruptcy, she sought a discharge of the student loans based on the hardship provision.

DECISION AND RATIONALE The United States Bankruptcy Court for the Eastern District of Tennessee granted Baker's petition and discharged the student loans. The court pointed out that the purpose of the prohibition against discharging student loans was "to remedy an abuse by students who, immediately upon graduation, would file for bankruptcy to secure a discharge of educational loans." In this case, Baker did not file for bankruptcy to secure a discharge only from her student loans. The court found that Baker could reduce her expenses somewhat, but that her reasonable expenses each month far exceeded her income. The court noted that Baker's husband had deserted her, that she had been ill, and that two of her children had physical problems. The court thus found that forcing payment of Baker's debts would create an undue hardship and that the Bankruptcy Code was drafted to provide a "fresh start" for those such as Baker "who have truly fallen on hard times."

OBJECTIONS TO DISCHARGE In addition to the exceptions to discharge previously listed, a bankruptcy court may also deny the discharge of the *debtor* (as opposed to the debt). In the latter situation, the assets of the debtor are still distributed to the creditors, but the debtor remains liable for the unpaid portion of all claims. Some grounds for the denial of discharge of the debtor include:

1. The debtor's concealment or destruction of property with the intent to hinder, delay, or defraud a creditor.
2. The debtor's fraudulent concealment or destruction of financial records.
3. The debtor's refusal to obey a lawful order of a bankruptcy court.
4. The debtor's failure to satisfactorily explain the loss of assets.
5. The granting of a discharge to the debtor within six years of the filing of the petition.
6. The debtor's written waiver of discharge approved by the court.

To encourage legitimate objections, the Code provides that even if the creditor loses on the challenge, the creditor is liable for costs and attorneys' fees only if the challenge was not *substantially justified.*

EFFECT OF DISCHARGE The primary effect of a discharge is to void any judgment on a discharged debt and enjoin any action to collect a discharged debt. A discharge does not affect the liability of a co-debtor.

REVOCATION OF DISCHARGE The Code provides that a debtor may lose his or her bankruptcy discharge by revocation upon petition by the trustee or a creditor. The bankruptcy court may within one year revoke the discharge decree if it is discovered that the debtor acted fraudulently or dishonestly during the bankruptcy proceedings. The revocation renders the discharge null and void, allowing creditors not satisfied by the distribution of the debtor's estate to proceed with their claims against the debtor.

REAFFIRMATION OF DEBT A debtor may voluntarily wish to pay a debt—such as, for example, a debt owed to a family member, family doctor,

close friend, or some other party—notwithstanding the fact that the debt could be discharged in bankruptcy. An agreement to pay a debt dischargeable in bankrtupcy is called a **reaffirmation agreement.** To be enforceable, reaffirmation agreements must be made before the debtor is granted a discharge. The agreement must be filed with the court. Approval by the court is required unless the debtor's attorney files an affidavit stating that the reaffirmation agreement is voluntarily made and that the agreement will not result in an undue hardship on the debtor or the debtor's family.

The debtor can rescind, or cancel, the agreement at any time prior to discharge or within sixty days of the filing of the agreement, whichever is later. This rescission period must be stated *clearly* and *conspicuously* in the reaffirmation agreement.

■ Chapter 11 Reorganizations

The type of bankruptcy proceeding used most commonly by a corporate debtor is the Chapter 11 reorganization. In a reorganization, the creditors and the debtor formulate a plan under which the debtor pays a portion of his or her debts and is discharged of the remainder. The debtor is allowed to continue in business. Although this type of bankruptcy is commonly a corporate reorganization, any debtor (except a stockbroker or a commodities broker) who is eligible for Chapter 7 relief is eligible for Chapter 11 relief. In addition, railroads are eligible for Chapter 11 relief.

The same principles that govern the filing of a Chapter 7 petition apply to Chapter 11 proceedings. The case may be brought either voluntarily or involuntarily. The same principles govern the entry of the order for relief. The automatic stay and adequate protection provisions are applicable in reorganizations.

In some instances, creditors may prefer private, negotiated adjustments of creditor-debtor relations, also known as **workouts,** to bankruptcy proceedings. Often these out-of-court workouts are much more flexible and thus more conducive to a speedy settlement. Speed is critical, because delay is one of the most costly elements in any bankruptcy proceeding.

Another advantage of workouts is that they avoid the various administrative costs of bankruptcy proceedings. Thus, under Section 305(a) of the Bankruptcy Code, a court, after notice and a hearing, may dismiss or suspend all proceedings in a case at any time if dismissal or suspension would better serve the interests of the creditors. Section 1112 also allows a court, after notice and a hearing, to dismiss a case under Chapter 11 "for cause." Cause includes the absence of a reasonable likelihood of rehabilitation, the inability to effec-

tuate a plan, and an unreasonable delay by the debtor that is prejudicial to creditors.[13]

In the following case, creditors of the Johns-Manville Corporation sought to dismiss, under Section 1112, a voluntary petition filed by Manville.

13. See 11 U.S.C. Section 1112(b).

Case 33.4

IN RE JOHNS-MANVILLE CORP.
United States Bankruptcy Court,
Southern District of New York,
1984.
36 Bankr. 727.

BACKGROUND AND FACTS   When Johns-Manville Corporation, a major producer of asbestos, filed for protection under Chapter 11, the filing surprised some of Manville's creditors, as well as other corporations that were being sued, with Manville, for injuries caused by asbestos exposure. Manville asserted that the approximately 16,000 lawsuits pending as of the filing date and the potential lawsuits of people who had been exposed but would not manifest asbestos-related diseases until later necessitated the filing. Manville's creditors, including people harmed by asbestos exposure who had won lawsuits or settlements, contended that Manville had not filed in good faith and that its Chapter 11 petition should thus be dismissed under Section 1112(b) of the Bankruptcy Code.

DECISION AND RATIONALE   The United States Bankruptcy Court for the Southern District of New York denied the motions to dismiss the Manville petition, concluding that bankruptcy was appropriate. Regarding voluntary petitions, the court noted that "it is no longer necessary for a petitioner for reorganization to allege or show insolvency or inability to pay debts as they mature." Thus, Manville met all of the eligibility requirements for filing a voluntary petition. Furthermore, in determining whether to dismiss under Section 1112(b), a court is not necessarily required to consider a debtor's good faith in filing because "good faith" is not a specified predicate for filing. Rather, good faith is a requirement for confirmation of the plan; that is, good faith is required to come out of Chapter 11, but not to get into it. A "principal goal" of the Code is to provide open and easy access to the bankruptcy process. Here, liquidation would be inefficient and wasteful, destroying the utility of Manville's assets as well as jobs, and, more importantly, it would preclude compensation of future asbestos claimants. Ultimately, the court concluded that Manville needed the protection of the Bankruptcy Code and should not be required to wait until its economic picture deteriorated beyond salvation to file for reorganization.

ETHICAL CONSIDERATIONS   The court's decision in this case has aroused much controversy. Many critics have argued that Manville, as a solvent corporation, was not deserving of the "fresh start" it achieved through Chapter 11 proceedings. This topic is explored more fully in the *Focus on Ethics* at the end of this unit.

Debtor in Possession

Upon entry of the order for relief, the debtor generally continues to operate his or her business as a **debtor in possession.** The court, however, may

appoint a trustee to operate the debtor's business if gross mismanagement of the business is shown or if for some other reason appointing a trustee is in the best interests of the estate.

LEGAL PERSPECTIVES IN BUSINESS

Voluntary versus Involuntary Bankruptcy

 Chapter 7 and Chapter 11 bankruptcies can be entered into voluntarily or involuntarily. A Chapter 13 (for adjustment of the debts of an individual) or a Chapter 12 (family farmer) bankruptcy can be initiated only by a voluntary petition. Most experts believe that involuntary bankruptcy should rarely occur. Indeed, it is only when a debtor is completely uncooperative that creditors may wish to use involuntary bankruptcy as a last resort.

Most debtors, particularly owners of businesses, know about their financial troubles well before creditors need to force the debtor into bankruptcy. As an owner of a business, it would be up to you to analyze your financial position and ask yourself some questions when considering which chapter in bankruptcy is preferable, and if there is no other solution to your financial problems.

For example, if you are relieved of some of your debts, could you continue in business making a profit in the future, or would your financial troubles continue? If you believe that your business could operate at a profit by reorganizing, readjusting, and eliminating some debts, you probably would want to voluntarily ask for relief under Chapter 11, Chapter 13, or, when appropriate, Chapter 12. These chapters will allow you to continue to stay in business, with some relief from the claims of your creditors.

Alternatively, if you realize that even with debt elimination your financial problems will not be resolved because of changing markets and economic conditions, you may wish to voluntarily file a Chapter 7 petition and liquidate your business. When you do so, it is you who may choose the time of such liquidation, rather than having it forced upon you. Later you will have a ''fresh start'' in pursuing another business venture if you so choose.

Creditors' Committees

As soon as practicable after entry of the order for relief, a creditors' committee of unsecured creditors is appointed. (Additional creditors' committees may be appointed to represent special-interest creditors.) The committee may consult with the debtor in possession (or the trustee) concerning the administration of the case or the formulation of the plan. Orders affecting the estate generally will not be entered without either the consent of the committee or a hearing in which the judge hears the position of the committee.

The Plan

A Chapter 11 plan of rehabilitation is a plan to conserve and administer the debtor's assets in the hope of an eventual return to successful operation and solvency. The plan must be fair and equitable and must:

1. Designate classes of claims and interests.

2. Specify the treatment to be afforded the classes. (The plan must provide the same treatment for each claim in a particular class.)
3. Provide an adequate means for execution.

FILING THE PLAN   Only the debtor may file a plan within the first 120 days after the date of the order for relief. If the debtor does not meet the 120-day deadline, however, or if the debtor fails to obtain the required creditor consent within 180 days, any party may propose a plan.

ACCEPTANCE OF THE PLAN   Once the plan has been developed, it is submitted to each class of creditors for acceptance. Each class must accept the plan unless the class is not adversely affected by the plan. A class has accepted the plan when a majority of the creditors, representing two-thirds of the amount of the total claim, vote to approve it.

CONFIRMATION OF THE PLAN   Each plan submitted is almost a case history in itself, and each plan varies from others. Each plan, however, must be "in the best interests of the creditors." Even when all classes of creditors accept the plan, the court may refuse to confirm it if it fails to meet this requirement. Conversely, even if only one class accepts the plan, the court may still confirm it under the Code's so-called *cram down* provision.

The plan is binding once it has been confirmed. On confirmation, the debtor is given a Chapter 11 discharge from all claims not protected under the plan. This discharge, however, does not apply to any claims that would be denied discharge under Chapter 7 (as previously discussed).

Collective Bargaining Agreements

Under the Bankruptcy Reform Act of 1978, questions arose as to whether a Chapter 11 debtor could reject a recently negotiated collectively bargained labor contract. In *National Labor Relations Board v. Bildisco and Bildisco,* the United States Supreme Court held that a collective bargaining agreement subject to the National Labor Relations Act is an "executory contract" and thus subject to *rejection* by a debtor in possession.[14] The Court emphasized that such a rejection should not be permitted unless there is a finding that the policy of Chapter 11 (successful rehabilitation of debtors) would be served by the action. Hence, when the bankruptcy court determines that a rejection of a collective bargaining agreement should be permitted, it must make a reasoned finding *on the record* as to *why* it has determined that a rejection should be permitted.

The Code attempts to reconcile federal policies favoring collective bargaining with the need to allow a debtor company to reject executory labor contracts while trying to reorganize under Chapter 11. The Code sets forth standards and procedures under which collective bargaining contracts can be assumed or rejected under a Chapter 11 filing.

In general, a collective bargaining contract can be rejected if the debtor has first proposed necessary contractual modifications to the union and the union has failed to adopt them without good cause. The company is required to provide the union with the relevant information needed to evaluate this proposal and to confer in good faith in attempting to reach a mutually satisfactory agreement on the modifications.

■ Chapter 13 Plans

Chapter 13 of the Bankruptcy Code provides for "Adjustment of Debts of an Individual with Regular Income." Individuals (not partnerships or corporations) with *regular income* who owe fixed unsecured debts of less than $100,000 or fixed secured debts of less than $350,000 may take advantage of Chapter 13. This includes salaried employees, individual proprietors and individuals who live on welfare, Social Security, fixed pensions, or investment income. Many small business debtors have a choice of filing a plan under Chapter 11 or Chapter 13. There are several advantages in filing a Chapter 13 plan. One advantage is that it is less expensive and less complicated than a Chapter 11 proceeding or even a Chapter 7 liquidation.

Filing the Petition

A Chapter 13 case can be initiated only by the filing of a voluntary petition by the debtor. Certain Chapter 7 and Chapter 11 cases may be converted to Chapter 13 cases with the consent of the debtor.[15] A trustee, who will make payments under the plan, must be appointed.

Automatic Stay

Upon the filing of a Chapter 13 petition, the automatic stay previously discussed takes effect. It enjoins creditors from taking action against co-obligors of the debtor. Although the stay applies to all or part of a consumer debt, it does not apply to any business debt incurred by the debtor. A creditor has the right to seek relief from the automatic stay. To save the creditor time and money in seeking court approval to vacate (remove) the stay and recover from the co-debtor, the law provides that on the creditor's request to vacate the stay against the co-debtor, unless written objection is filed, twenty days later the stay against the co-debtor is automatically terminated without a hearing.

---

14.   465 U.S. 513, 104 S.Ct. 1188, 79 L.Ed.2d 482 (1984).

15.   A Chapter 13 case may be converted to a Chapter 7 case at the request of either the debtor or, under certain circumstances denominated "for cause," a creditor. A Chapter 13 case may be converted to Chapter 11 after a hearing.

The Plan

A Chapter 13 plan of rehabilitation must:

1. Provide for the turnover to the trustee of such future earnings or income of the debtor as is necessary for execution of the plan.
2. Provide for full payment in deferred cash payments of all claims entitled to priority.
3. Provide for the same treatment of each claim within a particular class. (The Code permits the debtor to list co-debtors, such as guarantors or sureties, as a separate class.)

FILING THE PLAN   Only the debtor may file a plan under Chapter 13. This plan may provide either for payment of all obligations in full or for payment of a lesser amount. The time for payment under the plan may not exceed three years unless the court approves an extension. The term, with extension, may not exceed five years.

The Code requires the debtor to make "timely" payments, and the trustee is required to ensure that the debtor commence these payments. The law now provides that the debtor must commence making payments under the proposed plan within thirty days after the plan has been *filed*. If the plan has not been confirmed, the trustee is instructed to retain the payments until the plan is confirmed and then distribute them accordingly. If the plan is denied, the trustee will return the payments to the debtor less any costs. Failure of the debtor to make timely payments or to commence payments within the thirty-day period will allow the court to convert the case to a Chapter 7 bankruptcy or to dismiss the petition.

CONFIRMATION OF THE PLAN   After the plan is filed, the court holds a confirmation hearing at which interested parties may object to the plan. The court will confirm a plan with respect to each claim of a secured creditor under any of the following circumstances:

1. If the secured creditors have accepted the plan.
2. If the plan provides that creditors retain their liens and if the value of the property to be distributed to them under the plan is not less than the secured portion of their claims.
3. If the debtor surrenders the property securing the claim to the creditors.

OBJECTION TO THE PLAN   Unsecured creditors do not have a vote to confirm a Chapter 13 plan, but they can object to it. The court can approve a plan over the objection of the trustee or any unsecured creditor only in either of the following situations:

1. When the value of the property to be distributed under the plan is at least equal to the amount of the claims.
2. When all the debtor's projected disposable income to be received during the three-year plan period will be applied to making payments. Disposable income is all income received *less* amounts needed to support the debtor and dependents and/or amounts needed to meet ordinary expenses to continue the operation of a business.

MODIFICATION OF THE PLAN   Prior to completion of payments, the plan may be modified at the request of either the debtor, the trustee, or an unsecured creditor. If there is an objection by any interested party to the modification, the court must hold a hearing to determine approval or disapproval of the modified plan.

Discharge

After completion of all payments under a Chapter 13 plan, the court grants a discharge of all debts provided for by the plan. Except for allowed claims not provided for by the plan, certain long-term debts provided for by the plan, and claims for alimony and child support, all other debts are dischargeable. A Chapter 13 discharge is sometimes referred to as a "super-discharge." One of the reasons for this is that the law allows a Chapter 13 discharge to include fraudulently incurred debt and claims resulting from malicious or willful injury. Therefore, a Chapter 13 discharge is much more beneficial to some debtors than a Chapter 7 discharge.

Even if the debtor does not complete the plan, a hardship discharge may be granted if failure to complete the plan was due to circumstances beyond the debtor's control and if the value of the property distributed under the plan was greater than would have been paid in a Chapter 7 liquidation. A discharge can be revoked within one year if it was obtained by fraud.

The Growing World of Bankruptcy

What do the following corporations have in common: Johns-Manville, A. H. Robins, Texaco, Eastern Airlines, Continental Airlines, Pan American Airlines, Drexel-Burnham, and Greyhound? Besides being multibillion-dollar companies, all have filed for bankruptcy in recent years.

Look at the following table. You can see that the number of all bankruptcies has skyrocketed in the past thirty years. In 1992, an estimated 968,000 debtors filed for bankruptcy, and experts believe that the worst is yet to come.

There is no question that the 1978 Bankruptcy Reform Act made bankruptcy more attractive both for companies and for consumers. As pointed out in the chapter, the 1978 act increased the amount of exempt assets that a debtor is allowed to keep. Most (approximately 90 percent) of the petitions for bankruptcy relief are filed by consumers. Personal bankruptcy filings jumped from 193,000 in 1976 to 409,000 in 1980 to over 965,000 today. According to the International Credit Association, currently about 30 million consumers are in financial trouble, and 3 million of these are on the verge of filing for bankruptcy.

The Uses of Chapter 11

In 1992, approximately 24,300 business firms and individuals petitioned for Chapter 11 reorganization, representing an increase of 25 percent in just two years. Under current bankruptcy law, a corporation does not even need to be insolvent to go into Chapter 11—as you saw in the Johns-Manville case presented in this chapter. While Johns-Manville is a company that will continue to operate under Chapter 11, the same cannot be said for 90 percent of all other corporations that choose Chapter 11.

In most countries, a trustee is imposed on a bankrupt company, but under Chapter 11 of the U.S. Bankruptcy Code there is normally no trustee to watch out for creditors' interests. Chapter 11 is supposed to be the "hospital for sick companies," but, as one observer pointed out, it is more like a morgue. Only about 10 percent of the companies that have undertaken Chapter 11 reorganizations have emerged healthy, and firms that do so are the biggest ones with the most cash. The remainder are liquidated via Chapter 7, usually years later, after running down their cash position to zero and incurring huge legal expenses. A case in point is Eastern Airlines. When Eastern first filed for Chapter 11, it had enough assets to pay off all of its secured creditors. By the time it was forced into liquidation, anywhere from a

Bankruptcy Filings per Decade		
Decade	**Total Filings**	**Filings per 1,000 People**
1900–1909	173,298	1.88
1910–1919	215,296	2.03
1920–1929	410,475	3.33
1930–1939	614,938	4.65
1940–1949	296,021	1.96
1950–1959	584,272	3.26
1960–1969	1,695,416	8.34
1970–1979	2,086,189	9.21
1980–1989	4,583,391	18.36

half billion to a billion dollars in assets had been eaten up—assets that could have gone to pay creditors.

Prepackaged Plans

Chapter 11 cases seem to drag on forever. Half of the Chapter 11 cases filed since the Bankruptcy Reform Act took effect in 1979 are still pending. In some mega-cases, such as those of Eastern Airlines and Johns-Manville, legal and professional fees can run to over $1 million a month. To avoid some of these fees, a number of businesses have used "prepackaged bankruptcies," in which the debtors and certain required majorities of each class of equity holders and creditors accept a reorganization plan prior to the company's filing for protection under Chapter 11. Because the bankruptcy judge receives a full plan that needs only the court's approval, prepackaged plans often result in relatively speedy reorganizations. Such prepackaged plans are not only for small companies. The Taj Mahal Casino, owned by Donald Trump, has attempted to use one, as has the Southland Corporation (7/11 stores).

Besides saving time and money, the debtor also benefits from another important aspect of a prepackaged plan. Once the debtor's plan has won support from certain majorities of creditors and equity holders, the plan can be forced on minority creditors and equity holders. This obviates the need to get all creditors to agree voluntarily to a company's plan. Not all companies are candidates for prepackaged bankruptcies, though. The financial structure of the company has to be relatively uncomplicated and not disputed for such plans to work.

■ Implications for the Businessperson

1. Because the 1978 Bankruptcy Reform Act made bankruptcy a more attractive alternative for financially distressed debtor-consumers, businesspersons clearly have to take into account the increased probability of not being able to collect consumer debts. The businessperson must now take additional precautions by making sure that his or her claims have priority in bankruptcy. In other words, businesspersons are well advised to perfect their security interests in accordance with the rules stated in Article 9 of the UCC to guard against losses should a debtor petition for bankruptcy relief.

2. Every businessperson should be aware of the advantages of Chapter 11, and, in particular, of the advantages of a "prepackaged plan" for reorganization under Chapter 11. It is almost always better for businesses in trouble to initiate Chapter 11 proceedings themselves, rather than wait until creditors force them into bankruptcy. The one caveat is, of course, that because only 10 percent of Chapter 11 filings succeed in restoring firms to financial health, bankruptcy should be considered only as a last resort. In other words, every alternative solution should be fully explored before petitioning for Chapter 11 reorganization.

■ For Critical Analysis

1. Contrast the protection afforded to creditors by Article 9 of the UCC and by such common law protections as liens with the protection, including liquidations and reorganizations, afforded debtors under bankruptcy law. Is it possible to protect both debtors and creditors at the same time? Can a better balance than that achieved under existing laws be attained?

2. Current bankruptcy law allows debtors to seek relief in bankruptcy more than once. Debtors whose debts have been discharged in bankruptcy need only wait a certain amount of time before again seeking protection under bankruptcy law. Should debtors be further limited in the number of times they can file for bankruptcy? Would it be more appropriate to limit debtors to only one voluntary Chapter 7 bankruptcy, say, every twenty years, instead of every six years? What would be the costs and benefits of such a law?

■ CONCEPT SUMMARY 33.1
Bankruptcy—A Comparison of Chapters 7, 11, 12, and 13

Issue	Chapter 7	Chapter 11	Chapters 12 and 13
Purpose	Liquidation.	Reorganization.	Adjustment.
Who can petition	Debtor (voluntary) or creditors (involuntary).	Debtor (voluntary) or creditors (involuntary).	Debtor (voluntary) only.
Who can be a debtor	Any "person" (including partnerships and corporations) except railroads, insurance companies, banks, savings and loan institutions, and credit unions. Farmers and charitable institutions cannot be involuntarily petitioned.	Any debtor eligible for Chapter 7 relief; railroads are also eligible.	*Chapter 12*—Any family farmer whose gross income is at least 50 percent farm-dependent and whose debts are at least 80 percent farm-related or any partnership or closely held corporation at least 50 percent owned by a farm family, when total debt does not exceed $1,500,000. *Chapter 13*—Any individual (not partnerships or corporations) with regular income who owes fixed unsecured debt of less than $100,000 or secured debt of less than $350,000.
Procedure leading to discharge	Nonexempt property is sold with proceeds to be distributed (in order) to priority groups. Dischargeable debts are terminated.	Plan is submitted; and if it is approved and followed, debts are discharged.	Plan is submitted (must be approved if debtor turns over disposable income for three-year period); and if it is approved and followed, debts are discharged.
Advantages	Upon liquidation and distribution, most debts are discharged, and debtor has opportunity for fresh start.	Debtor continues in business. Creditors can accept plan, or it can be "crammed down" on them. Plan allows for reorganization and liquidation of debts over plan period.	Debtor continues in business or possession of assets. If plan is approved, most debts are discharged after a three-year period.

■ Chapter 12 Plans

On November 27, 1986, the Family Farmer Bankruptcy Act became law. To help relieve economic pressure on small farmers, Congress created a new chapter (Chapter 12) in the Bankruptcy Code. The new law defines a *family farmer* as one whose gross income is at least 50 percent farm-dependent and whose debts are at least 80 percent farm-related. The total debt must not exceed $1,500,000. A partnership or closely held corporation (at least 50 percent owned by the farm family) can also take advantage of this new law.

A Chapter 12 filing is very similar in procedure to a Chapter 13 filing. The farmer-debtor must file a plan not later than ninety days after the order for relief. The filing of the petition acts as an automatic stay against creditors' and co-obligors' actions against the estate.

A secured creditor can petition to lift the automatic stay for adequate protection of his or her interest if the value of the collateral is less than the amount of the secured debt owed the creditor. Before the enactment of Chapter 12, some courts held that ''adequate protection'' required the farmer-debtor, like other debtors under other chapters of the Code, to compensate the secured creditor for so-called ''lost opportunity costs.'' Lost opportunity costs represent a sum equal to the interest that the undercollateralized secured creditor might earn on an amount of money equal to the value of the collateral securing the debt. The rationale behind requiring these payments as part of adequate protection is that the Code's automatic stay provisions preclude the creditor from foreclosing its interest and reinvesting the proceeds.

Because farmland values have dropped substantially, family farmers are usually unable to pay lost opportunity costs. Thus, family farm reorganizations were often throttled on a creditor's motion to lift the automatic stay. Chapter 12 adds a different means for providing adequate protection—payment of reasonable market rental payments—to protect the value of the property and thereby the operation of a farm as a going concern. Generally, the amount of reasonable market rental has been based on the gross rental value of the farmland and its income potential, considering crop requirements, government payments, and so on.

The content of a Chapter 12 plan is basically the same as that of a Chapter 13 filing. The plan can be modified by the farmer-debtor but, except for cause, must be confirmed or denied within forty-five days of the filing of the plan.

Court confirmation of the plan is the same as for a Chapter 13 plan. In summary, the plan must provide for payment of secured debts at the value of the collateral. If the secured debt exceeds the value of the collateral, the remaining debt is unsecured. For unsecured debtors, the plan must be confirmed if either the value of the property to be distributed under the plan equals the amount of the claim or the plan provides that all of the farmer-debtor's disposable income to be received in a three-year period (longer by court approval) will be applied to making payments.

Disposable income is all income received less amounts needed to support the farmer-debtor and family and to continue the farming operation. Completion of payments under the plan discharges all debts provided for by the plan.

The new law also allows a farmer who has already filed under Chapter 11 or 13 to convert to Chapter 12. Chapter 12, like Chapters 11 and 13, allows for the farmer-debtor to convert to liquidation under Chapter 7.

■ Terms and Concepts

adequate protection doctrine 588	insider 591	reaffirmation agreement 595
automatic stay 588	liquidation 586	trustee 586
consumer-debtors 586	order for relief 587	U.S. Trustee 589
debtor in possession 596	petition in bankruptcy 586	workout 595
	preference 590	

■ For Review

1. What is a debtor's estate in property?
2. What is a trustee? What does a trustee do?
3. Are all creditors' claims allowed in a bankruptcy proceeding? In what order are unsecured creditors' claims paid?
4. Black & Red, Inc., files a petition for bankruptcy under Chapter 7. Black & Red's debts include a month of unpaid wages to its employees, contributions to the employees' benefit plans, federal income taxes, and the claims of seven creditors secured by Black & Red's inventory. Which of these debts is not dischargeable under Chapter 7?
5. Webster Corp. files a petition for bankruptcy under Chapter 11. Webster's debts include a month of unpaid wages to its employees, the claims of six creditors secured by its inventory, and $10,000 in fraudulently incurred debt. Which of these debts is not dischargeable under Chapter 11?

■ Questions and Case Problems

33-1. Carlton has been a rancher all his life, raising cattle and crops. His ranch is valued at $500,000, almost all of which is exempt under state law. Carlton has eight creditors and a total indebtedness of $70,000. Two of his largest creditors are Samson ($30,000 owed) and Greed ($25,000 owed). The other six creditors have claims of less than $5,000 each. A drought has ruined all of Carlton's crops and forced him to sell many of his cattle at a loss. He cannot pay off his creditors.

(a) Under the Code, can Carlton, with a $500,000 ranch, voluntarily petition himself into bankruptcy? Explain.

(b) Could either Samson or Greed force Carlton into involuntary bankruptcy? Explain.

33-2. Sam is a retail seller of television sets. He sells Martha a $900 set on a retail installment security agreement in which she pays $100 down and agrees to pay the balance in equal installments. Sam retains a security interest in the set, and he perfects that interest by filing a financing statement locally. Two months later, Martha is in default on her payments to Sam and is involuntarily petitioned into bankruptcy by her creditors. Sam wants to repossess the television set as provided for in the security agreement, and he wants to have priority over the trustee in bankruptcy as to any proceeds from the disposal of the set. Discuss fully Sam's right to repossess and whether he has priority over the trustee in bankruptcy as to any proceeds from disposal of the set.

33-3. Green is not known for his business sense. He started a greenhouse and nursery business two years ago and because of his lack of experience, he soon was in debt to a number of creditors. On February 1, Green borrowed $5,000 from his father to pay some of these creditors. On May 1, Green paid back the $5,000, depleting his entire working capital. One creditor, the Cool Springs Nursery Supply Corp., extended credit to Green on numerous purchases. Cool Springs pressured Green for payment, and on July 1, Green paid Cool Springs half the money owed. On September 1, Green voluntarily petitioned himself into bankruptcy. The trustee in bankruptcy claimed that both Green's father and Cool Springs must turn over to the debtor's estate the amounts Green paid to them. Discuss fully the trustee's claims.

33-4. Gordon petitioned himself into voluntary bankruptcy. There were three major claims against his estate. One was made by Carlton, a friend who held Gordon's negotiable promissory note for $2,500; one was made by Elmer, an employee who was owed three months' back wages of $4,500; and one was made by the United Bank of the Rockies on an unsecured loan of $5,000. In addition, Dietrich, an accountant retained by the trustee, was owed $500, and property taxes of $1,000 were owed to Rock County. Gordon's nonexempt property was liquidated, with proceeds of $5,000. Discuss fully what amount each party will receive and why.

33-5. The East Bank was a secured party on a $5,000 loan it made to Sally. Sally experienced financial difficulty, and creditors other than the East Bank petitioned her into involuntary bankruptcy. The value of the secured collateral had substantially decreased in value. On its sale, the debt to East Bank was reduced to $2,500. Sally's estate consisted of $100,000 in exempt assets and $2,000 in nonexempt assets. After the bankruptcy costs and back wages to Sally's employees had been paid, nothing was left for unsecured creditors. Sally received a discharge in bankruptcy. Later she decided to go back into business. By selling a few exempt assets and getting a small loan, she would be able to buy a small but profitable restaurant. She went to East Bank for the loan. East Bank claimed that the balance of its secured debt had not been discharged in bankruptcy. Sally signed an agreement to pay East Bank the $2,500, as the bank had not been a party to petitioning her into bankruptcy. Because of this, East Bank made the new unsecured loan to Sally.

(a) Discuss East Bank's claim that the balance of its secured debt had not been discharged in bankruptcy.

(b) Discuss the legal effect of Sally's agreement to pay East Bank $2,500 after the discharge in bankruptcy.

(c) If one year after buying the restaurant Sally went into voluntary bankruptcy, what effect would the bankruptcy proceedings have on the new unsecured loan?

33-6. Tracey Service Co. filed a petition for a Chapter 11 reorganization. Acar Supply Co., one of Tracey's creditors, filed a motion to convert the case to a Chapter 7 liquidation. The court found that the debtor corporation had no place of business, no inventory, no equipment, no employees, and no business phone. Should Tracey Service be permitted to reorganize under Chapter 11? Explain. [*In re Tracey Service Co.,* 17 Bankr. 405 (Bankr.E.D.Pa. 1982)]

33-7. Donald Lewis filed a voluntary petition for bankruptcy. One of the debts on which he sought discharge was a $1,500 judgment that had been entered against him for assault on Betty Dunson. Lewis testified in the bankruptcy court that he put both hands around Dunson's neck and told her to leave his wife alone or he would break her neck. Discuss whether the court will grant a discharge of the judgment claim. [*In re Lewis,* 17 Bankr. 341 (Bankr.S.D.Ohio 1982)]

33-8. Prior to filing for bankruptcy, Bray was making loan payments to his company's credit union through payroll deductions. Bray's employer continued to deduct the loan payments from Bray's paychecks after being notified of the bankruptcy petition. Is this a violation of the Bankruptcy Code? Discuss. [*In re Bray,* 17 Bankr. 152 (Bankr.N.D.Ga. 1982)]

33-9. In 1983, Beech Acceptance Corp. financed the sale of three airplanes to Gull Air, Inc. Approximately three years later, Gull Air defaulted on its obligations to Beech Acceptance, and Beech filed suit. Before the trial, Gull Air and Beech negotiated a workout agreement that provided for large monthly payments over a certain period. Despite the workout agreement, Gull Air filed a Chapter 11 petition in bankruptcy. Gull Air claimed that payments made under the workout agreement during the ninety days prior to the filing of the Chapter 11 petition amounted to a preference and must be returned to the debtor in possession (Gull Air). There was no question that Beech had received more than it would have under a Chapter 7 liquidation. Beech claimed that the payments had been made in the ordinary course of business. Discuss who is correct. [*In re Gull Air, Inc.,* 82 Bankr. 1 (Bankr.D.Mass. 1988)]

33-10. In 1985, the United States, under the Comprehensive Environmental Response, Compensation and Liability Act, filed suit for costs in connection with the cleaning up of asbestos released from a facility owned and operated by Nicolet, Inc. Before the lawsuit was completed, Nicolet filed a petition for Chapter 11 bankruptcy. Nicolet argued that the petition in bankruptcy operated as an automatic stay of the government's right to continue civil proceedings against it to recover the cleanup costs. The Bankruptcy Code provides an exception to the automatic stay order when the debtor has filed the petition. This exception provides that the stay is not available against a governmental unit exercising its police and regulatory powers. Discuss whether the civil action by the United States to recover clean-up costs falls under the automatic stay order or under the exception of a governmental unit exercising its police and regulatory powers. [*United States v. Nicolet, Inc.,* 81 Bankr. 310 (E.D.Pa. 1988)]

33-11. John Patrick Goulding filed for Chapter 7 bankruptcy relief in 1987. In his schedules, he listed assets of

$62,000 and debts of over $670,000. The majority of these debts were unsecured and were not consumer debts. The Federal Deposit Insurance Corp. (FDIC), as successor to two banks, was the largest unsecured creditor ($379,000). The FDIC and the trustee learned that Goulding was the beneficiary of three irrevocable spendthrift trusts (the assets of which cannot be reached by creditors) that provided him with $12,000 per month, and that he would receive from the corpus (principal) of one trust $200,000 on January 30, 1988. The trustee and the FDIC filed a joint motion requesting the court to dismiss Goulding's Chapter 7 petition. Discuss whether the court should have dismissed Goulding's petition and whether any payments made from the trusts were part of the debtor's estate. [*In re Goulding,* 79 Bankr. 874 (Bankr.W.D.Mo. 1987)]

33-12. A Question of Ethics

In September 1986, Edward and Debora Davenport pleaded guilty in a Pennsylvania court to welfare fraud and were sentenced to probation for one year. As a condition of their probation, the Davenports were ordered to make monthly restitution payments to the county probation department, which would forward the payments to the Pennsylvania Department of Public Welfare, the victim of the Davenports' fraud. In May 1987, the Davenports filed a petition for Chapter 13 relief and listed the restitution payments among their debts. The bankruptcy court held that the restitution obligation was a dischargeable debt. On appeal, the district court reversed, holding that state-imposed criminal restitution obligations cannot be discharged in a Chapter 13 bankruptcy. The Court of Appeals for the Third Circuit reversed the district court's decision, concluding that "the plain language of the chapter" demonstrated that restitution orders are debt within the meaning of the Code and hence dischargeable in proceedings under Chapter 13. Ultimately, the case was reviewed by the United States Supreme Court, which affirmed the Third Circuit's ruling. The Court noted that under the Bankruptcy Code a debt is defined as a liability on a claim and a claim is defined as a right to payment. Because the restitution obligations clearly constituted a right to payment, the Court held that the obligations were dischargeable in bankruptcy. [Pennsylvania Department of Public Welfare v. Davenport, 495 U.S. 552, 110 S.Ct. 2126, 109 L.Ed.2d 588 (1990)]

1. Critics of this decision contend that the Court adhered to the letter, but not the spirit, of bankruptcy law in arriving at its conclusion. In what way, if any, did the Court not abide by the "spirit" of bankruptcy law?

2. Do you think that Chapter 13 plans, which allow nearly all types of debts to be discharged, tip the scales of justice too far in favor of debtors?

Chapter 34

Lender Liability

Twenty-five years ago, in any litigation involving financial institutions, the lender was normally the plaintiff and the borrower the defendant. Generally, the litigation centered on merely determining the rights of the parties on the debtor's default. The court system provided numerous procedural devices that allowed lenders to collect, often without much difficulty, from their debtors.

About fifteen years ago, the lender was still the plaintiff, but the borrower had started to assert affirmative defenses against the lender's attempt at collecting on a debt when the borrower defaulted. Occasionally, a borrower would assert a counterclaim, but rarely would that borrower prevail.

In the last eight to ten years, the tables have been turned, as it were. Financial institutions have become the targets of numerous lawsuits, and the days when financial institutions seemed invulnerable are now in the past. For example, Crocker National Bank was the target of a class-action suit in which the plaintiffs claimed that the fees charged for returned checks—checks returned to account holders when there were insufficient funds in the accounts to cover them—were unconscionable.[1] This case has been cited in numerous other class-action suits against lenders on the grounds that the fees charged for returned checks were unconscionable, as well as in class-action suits challenging other fees that financial institutions charge. The area of **lender liability** has now grown to such an extent that there are even monthly newsletters on the subject.[2]

Typically, lawsuits that are brought against lending institutions involve the following types of claims:

1. The lender failed to lend sufficient funds to the borrower because of negligence in processing the loan.
2. The lender failed to renew short-term loans when the borrower was experiencing financial difficulties.

---

1. *Perdue v. Crocker National Bank,* 38 Cal.3d 913, 702 P.2d 503, 216 Cal.Rptr. 345 (1985). Although Crocker National Bank had not been held liable after ten years of litigation, in 1985 the bank agreed to a settlement. The bank apparently did not want to risk a jury verdict.
2. See, for example, Helen Chaitman, ed., *Lender Liability Law Report* (Boston, Mass.: Warren, Gorham & Lamont, Inc.).

3. The lender failed to advance funds under a line of credit when the borrower was in a weakened financial situation.

4. The lender failed to solve environmental problems created by the borrower—even though the cost of the clean-up operations exceeded the amount of the loan.

In this chapter, we examine the potential liability of lenders under both the common law and statutory law.

■ Potential Common Law Liability

Lenders can be potentially liable under the entire body of common law with respect to contracts. To the extent that the borrower can assert and prove breach of contract, the borrower may be able to avoid liability for unpaid debt. Liability of a lender may also be based on the tort theories of misrepresentation, duress, wrongful interference, and negligence. Finally, lender liability may be established if the lender breaches the duty of good faith. We discuss these theories below.

Liability for Breach of Contract

A business relationship between a borrower and a lender comes into existence at the instant when a potential borrower begins to make inquiries about a loan. At any time during the business relationship—from the moment of initial contact to the point at which all of the terms of the loan agreement (if one is formed) have been satisfied—the lender faces potential liability for breach of contract. Credit is the lifeblood of many businesses. A lender's failure to provide credit in a sufficient amount and at the right time may result in the demise of a business. So long as the lender has this ability to determine the financial fate of the borrower, the lender is required to exercise due care and act in good faith at all times.

LOAN APPLICATIONS AND NEGOTIATIONS
A loan application is an offer by the borrower, but it is the lender who furnishes the form. Any lender who does not indicate on such an application that it is only seeking information and making no commitment whatsoever to extend credit faces a potential breach of contract suit by an applicant who is turned down.

Lenders have a duty to process all loan applications with due care,[3] and this duty extends to all actions undertaken by the lender in regard to loan negotiations and the processing of loan applications. All procedures relating to loan negotiations and applications should be clearly spelled out by the lender in a loan manual or other written statement of the lending policies. Potential for liability occurs whenever lending practices and procedures undertaken during loan application and negotiation phases are not consistent with what is laid out in written lending policy documents.

The borrower also has an obligation of due care when filling out the loan application and financial statement. If, for example, there is a material change in the borrower's financial statement after the date on which the loan application was submitted, the borrower is normally under an obligation to alert the potential lender to this change in financial circumstances.

During loan negotiations, any attempt by a lender to induce a potential borrower to leave another lender may create liability. In responding to a potential borrower's loan inquiries, a loan officer will often engage in a certain amount of "puffery" and thereby perhaps inflate the services and potential benefits that his or her financial institution can offer to the borrower. If the subsequent actions of the financial institution do not live up to the loan officer's puffery, liability may be created.

LOAN COMMITMENTS While normally one would think that the commitment for a loan must be reduced to writing to be enforceable, this is not always the case. In many states, a lender who makes an oral agreement must honor that agreement or be subject to a breach of contract suit.[4] Some states do require, however, that a commitment to loan more than a set amount must be in writing to be enforceable. In any event, the prudent loan officer should never make an oral loan commitment. Furthermore, any written letter or document pertaining to loan negotiations should clearly state whether the document is merely a proposal specifying con-

---

3. *Jacques v. First National Bank of Maryland,* 307 Md. 527, 515 A.2d 756 (1986). This case is presented as Case 34.3 in this chapter.
4. *Delcon Group, Inc. v. Northern Trust Corp.,* 187 Ill.App.3d 635, 453 N.E.2d 595, 135 Ill.Dec. 212 (1989).

ditions that must be met before a loan can be obtained or an actual, binding commitment to make the loan. Whenever a letter is simply meant to be a proposal, rather than a commitment, this information should be stated obviously and immediately.

A lender may attempt to back out of a loan commitment by subsequently adding conditions to that commitment that it knows the borrower cannot meet. Normally, once a lender has entered into a loan commitment, it may not add new conditions. In one case, a savings and loan association made a loan commitment for the construction of a hotel and gambling casino. The lender sought participation by other financial institutions but was unable to obtain any. To avoid its commitment, the lender required the borrower to meet additional conditions and delayed the closing of the loan, thus causing the deal to fall through. In the lawsuit that followed, the lender was ordered to pay more than $129 million in damages.[5]

When the loan commitment is for a line of credit, the terms and conditions of the commitment must be defined clearly. Even if a clause appears to grant a lender complete discretion over the termination of funding for the line of credit, the lender does not have absolute right to refuse funding. Discretion must be exercised reasonably and in good faith. Indeed, good faith must permeate the entire loan relationship with respect to the terms of the loan contract. When a lender agrees to a certain credit limit, it may not arbitrarily decide to terminate funding before reaching that limit unless it can be shown that the borrower has not performed according to the terms of the loan agreement.[6]

Liability under a theory of promissory estoppel is also possible in unfulfilled loan commitments, whether they be implied or express. The Restatement (Second) of Contracts, Section 90(1), states as follows:

A promise which the promisor should reasonably expect to induce action or forbearance on the part of the promisee or a third person and which does induce such action or forbearance is binding if injustice can be avoided only by enforcement of the promise.

In a well-known Texas case, Ellis Wheeler sought financing from S. E. White to construct a shopping center on a specific site. White assured Wheeler that the money would be available and urged him to demolish the existing building on the site to make way for the construction of the center. White promised that if Wheeler could not obtain the money elsewhere, White would make the loan himself. After Wheeler had razed the old building, White told him that there would be no loan. Wheeler made reasonable efforts to obtain the loan himself but was unsuccessful. The court stated that ''where one party has by his words or conduct made to the other a promise or assurance which was intended . . . to be acted on accordingly, then, once the other party has taken him at his word and acted on it, the party who gave the promise cannot afterward be allowed to revert to the previous relationship as if no such promise had been made.''[7]

TERMINATING LOAN AGREEMENTS Many loan agreements have **acceleration clauses** and other devices that permit the lender to terminate the loan agreement if a debtor fails to meet certain conditions specified in the agreement. An acceleration clause was defined in Chapter 26 as a clause that allows the holder of a time instrument to demand payment of the entire amount due on the happening of a certain event—for example, on a debtor's failure to make an installment payment when due.

Acceleration clauses in all time notes are subject to the good faith requirement of UCC 1-208. To avoid liability, the lender should accelerate a loan only with valid justification, and there should be clear evidence of default. In other words, the debtor's breach of the loan agreement should be obvious to the reasonable person.

A lender's termination of a loan agreement requires (1) a declaration that the borrower is in default and (2) foreclosure and repossession of the collateral given as security for the loan.

The lender has the ability to declare the borrower in default only if the breach of contract is

5. *Penthouse International, Inc. v. Dominion Federal Savings and Loan Association*, 665 F.Supp. 301 (S.D.N.Y 1987). On appeal, this order was reversed, and the complaint was dismissed. See 855 F.2d 963 (2d Cir. 1988).

6. *Carrico v. Delp*, 141 Ill.App.3d 684, 490 N.E.2d 972, 95 Ill.Dec. 880 (1986).

7. *Wheeler v. White*, 398 S.W.2d 93 (Tex. 1965).

material. Moreover, the lender must undertake all reasonable means to allow the borrower to avoid default before declaring that the loan is in default. The borrower must be presented with a written notice that a default will be declared, and the reasons for the declaration must be included in the notice. These reasons must be tied to specific provisions in the written loan agreement. If a default is declared for an action that does not constitute a default according to the loan agreement, then the lender may be held liable.[8]

Foreclosure or repossession of the collateral given as security for the loan may subject the lender to liability under certain circumstances. For example, if an officer of the lending institution assured the borrower that foreclosure or repossession would not occur, and it does, the lender may be liable. In one case, a bank brought an action to recover on a delinquent promissory note. The borrowers had negotiated the loan to purchase equipment and pay taxes for a restaurant that they were leasing with an option to buy. When they failed to exercise the option, the lease was terminated. Facing unemployment, the borrowers were assured by the bank officer who had arranged the loan that the payment schedule would be adjusted. Because of these assurances, the borrowers were awarded damages when the bank failed to keep its word and sued to collect the debt.[9]

LOAN WORKOUTS When a borrower is in default, the lender typically attempts to establish a loan workout plan. A **loan workout** is defined as any attempt to simultaneously satisfy the lender and the borrower when the borrower is in default. Typical loan workout plans involve extending time periods for repayment of the loan, accepting payments of only interest for a defined period of time before the principal is paid off, forgiving a part of the loan if the rest is paid off within a specified time period, repossessing only a part of the collateral, or some other arrangement. A loan workout often calls for a settlement of the claim by means of accord and satisfaction, a concept covered in Chapters 11 and 16.

The lending institution typically has a **workout team** negotiate the terms of the workout arrangement when a major borrower is in default. The team normally does not include the loan officer who approved the loan that is in default.

Negotiations surrounding a workout can provide opportunities for fraud, duress, or other misconduct. For example, suppose that a borrower cannot meet a loan repayment schedule. During workout negotiations, the lender offers to extend the repayment period if the borrower puts up additional collateral. The borrower agrees, on the condition that the lender will give notice before taking possession of the additional collateral if the borrower defaults. The lender orally agrees. If the lender fails to give the notice, the lender could be liable for damages for wrongful repossession.

BASIC CONTRACT REMEDIES The basic remedies for breach of contract are available to both lenders and borrowers. These remedies, which were discussed in Chapter 17, include (1) compensatory damages, (2) consequential damages, (3) punitive damages, (4) liquidated damages, and (5) specific performance.

Briefly, compensatory damages compensate the nonbreaching party for the loss caused by the breach. For example, if Vallejos borrows $1,000 from Mayta on terms that include payment of $100 interest, and Vallejos makes payments totaling only $500, Mayta can sue for breach and recover $600 as compensatory damages.

Consequential damages, which are defined as foreseeable damages that result from a party's breach, are important for large judgments. In the example above, if Vallejos fails to repay the loan knowing that Mayta plans to reinvest the money immediately, consequential damages may be awarded for the lost profits from the planned reinvestment. Mayta can also recover compensatory damages.

Punitive damages are designed to punish a wrongdoer and deter misconduct. They are normally not awarded in a breach of contract action. If the breach includes an independent tort, however, punitive damages may be awarded. For example, suppose that a borrower needs funds to finance a project involving property that the borrower does not own but that she has an option to purchase until a certain date. If the lender prolongs loan negotiations beyond that date so as to

---

8. *In re Werth,* 37 Bankr. 979 (Bankr. D. Colo. 1984); aff'd 54 Bankr. 619 (D.Colo. 1985).

9. *First National Bank of Libby v. Twombly,* 213 Mont. 66, 689 P.2d 1226 (1984).

accommodate another borrower who wants to purchase the property, the lender may be liable for fraud. If so, the borrower may be awarded punitive damages.

Liquidated damages are amounts specified in a contract to be paid in the event of a default or breach.

Specific performance is a remedy by which the court orders the breaching party to complete the specific performance promised in the contract. This remedy is rarely granted, but occasionally it will be—as it was in a 1979 New Jersey case. In that case, a lender who had financed the construction of a shopping mall sued a savings and loan association for breach of its commitment to provide permanent mortgage financing for the mall. The court listed a number of reasons why specific performance was appropriate, including the following: (1) the mall was not successful, and as a result, it would be nearly impossible to obtain alternative permanent financing; (2) because an accurate calculation of damages was impracticable, imposing the burden of owning the mall on the savings and loan association would be more just than choosing one of various estimates of market value; and (3) placing the risk of the project's nonviability on the permanent lender was more appropriate than placing it on the construction lender.[10]

Liability in Tort

Many lender liability cases are based on tort theories. As pointed out in Chapter 5, a tort is a wrongful action by one party that causes injury to another. In general, lenders are more concerned with tort liability than with liability for breach of contract because punitive damages can be, and have been, assessed against lenders when a tort has been committed.

---

10. *First National State Bank of New Jersey v. Commonwealth Savings and Loan Association of Norristown*, 610 F.2d 164 (3d Cir. 1979).

MISREPRESENTATION AND FRAUD The tort of misrepresentation occurs when fraud or deceit is employed for personal gain. Actual fraud has four elements: (1) material misrepresentation of fact (not opinion), (2) intentional deceit (involving either knowledge that the misrepresentation is false or reckless disregard for the truth), (3) justifiable reliance on the misrepresentation by the deceived party, and (4) resulting injury or damage.

As noted in Chapters 5 and 13, misrepresentation can be accomplished by words or by actions. Intent to deceive can be inferred from circumstances. Reliance on the misrepresentation may be justified if the person to whom the misrepresentation is made does not know the true facts and has no way of finding them out. To recover damages for misrepresentation, proof of injury is universally required—although some courts do not require a showing of injury when the remedy sought is rescission.

Potential acts of fraud on the part of a lender include providing misleading or false information about the borrower to a third party and misrepresenting the effects of legal documents to induce a borrower to execute them. For example, stating that a mortgage is a mere technicality that would not place the mortgaged property at risk of loss through foreclosure could amount to fraud.

Innocent misrepresentation, or constructive fraud, can also be used as a theory on which to base lender liability. Innocent misrepresentation, which occurs without any actual intention to deceive, can be asserted against a lender who has entered into a fiduciary relationship with the borrower. A fiduciary relationship is one of trust and confidence in which one party has a duty to disclose material facts relevant to the relationship to the other. In a fiduciary relationship, therefore, the failure to disclose a material fact can constitute misrepresentation—as the following case illustrates.

Case 34.1 **BARNETT BANK OF WEST FLORIDA v. HOOPER** Supreme Court of Florida, 1986. 498 So.2d 923.	**BACKGROUND AND FACTS** Richard Hooper began doing business with Barnett Bank of West Florida in 1973. In June 1981, Hooper met with Joe Hosner, a customer of the bank, to discuss investments. Hosner took Hooper to see Edwin Riffel, the loan officer in charge of Hosner's accounts at the bank. Riffel said that Hosner's investments were sound. Hooper borrowed $50,000 from the bank to invest with Hosner. Less than a year later, Harry Stump, an assistant vice-president of the bank, began to suspect that Hosner was involved in a check-kiting scheme.[a] He told Riffel. By May

14, Stump—believing that the bank was at risk and wishing to protect it—returned all Hosner checks presented on May 13 as drawn against uncollected funds. Late on May 14, Hooper returned a call from Hosner, who came on the line with Riffel. During the conversation, Hooper asked to borrow $90,000 to invest with Hosner. A promissory note and a check for $89,863 were delivered to Hooper after banking hours. Hooper indorsed the check, and it was deposited in Hosner's account. By May 24, the check-kiting scheme had been confirmed, but because of Hooper's deposit into Hosner's account, the bank lost nothing. Without Hooper's check, Hosner's account would have been overdrawn in the amount of $87,000. Hooper sued in a Florida state court to cancel the note on grounds that the bank had a duty to disclose facts material to the loan transaction or, alternatively, a duty to disclose knowledge of Hosner's fraudulent activity. Based on the rule that a bank owes an implied duty to its depositors not to disclose information to third parties concerning a depositor's account, the trial court directed a verdict against Hooper. The appellate court reversed and remanded for a new trial. The bank appealed.

DECISION AND RATIONALE The Supreme Court of Florida affirmed the appellate court's decision, and the case was remanded for a new trial. The state supreme court reasoned that "[w]hen a bank enters into a transaction with a customer with whom it has established a confidential or fiduciary relationship, and the transaction is one from which the bank stands to benefit at the expense of the customer, * * * the bank assume[s] a duty to disclose information material to the transaction which is peculiarly within the bank's knowledge and not otherwise available to the customer." The court explained that "[s]uch 'special circumstances' may be found where a bank, having actual knowledge of fraud being perpetrated upon a customer, enters into a transaction with that customer in furtherance of the fraud, or where a bank has established a confidential or fiduciary relationship with a customer." The court pointed out that "[w]here the bank defends its breach of duty on the ground that it owes a conflicting duty of confidentiality to a second customer, the jury is entitled to weigh the one duty against the other."

a. A check-kiting scheme involves multiple checking accounts in which, say, a check is written on account number one and deposited in overdrawn account number two, and then a check drawn on account number three is deposited in account number one to cover the "bad" check previously written—and so on.

DURESS Duress includes the following three elements: (1) an unlawful threat, (2) a destruction of free will, and (3) a loss. A threat is unlawful if what is threatened is a crime or a tort. Note, however, that a threat to exercise a legal right, such as a threat to initiate a civil suit, is normally acceptable. Destruction of free will can be established by showing that assent occurred under circumstances that presented no reasonable alternative. For example, a lender who promises to lend funds to a certain borrower at a specified interest rate, but that subsequently threatens to refuse to lend the funds unless the borrower agrees to a higher interest rate, may be found guilty of duress if the borrower is in urgent need of the funds and is unable to obtain them elsewhere.

Hard bargaining between experienced parties of relatively equal bargaining power does not establish duress. For example, insisting on a condition that is commonly bargained for would not constitute duress. In cases in which agreements have been invalidated because of duress, the conduct of the party obtaining the advantage is tainted with some degree of fraud or wrongdoing.

WRONGFUL INTERFERENCE AND EXCESSIVE CONTROL When a borrower misses payments on a loan or indicates that payments may be missed, a lender may offer to help the borrower out of its financial difficulties. Alternatively, the lender may exercise economic power over the troubled borrower to obtain the required payments. The issue then becomes whether such control and interference is tortious.

For example, a lender that requires a financially troubled corporate borrower to take actions that should be decided on only by the officers or directors of the company may be liable. Whenever it can be shown that the lender's influence on the borrower's business will have, or did have, a detrimental effect on the borrower and a beneficial effect on the lender, the lender may be liable.

Sometimes, a lender may become entangled in the business affairs of the borrower to the extent that the lender becomes liable to third parties. At some point, the lender may be considered a joint venturer with the borrower or an agent of the borrower. The extreme case of lender liability under the theory of interference and control occurs when the operation of a borrower's business is so controlled by the lender that the lender becomes liable for the borrower's debts.[11]

Excessive interference and control can also create fiduciary responsibilities between a lender and a borrower. Fiduciary duties can arise if a lender becomes a borrower's financial advisor. A fiduciary relationship imposes on a lender the duties of disclosure and loyalty as well as the duty not to take unfair advantage of the borrower. Once a fiduciary relationship has been established, the lender is no longer able to act in its own best interest but must act in the best interest of the borrower.

In the following landmark case, the principles of wrongful interference and control were applied. This case also marked a turning point in the law of lender liability in general.

---

11. *A. Gay Jenson Farms Co. v. Cargill*, 309 N.W.2d 285 (Minn. 1981).

Case 34.2

STATE NATIONAL BANK OF EL PASO v. FARAH MANUFACTURING CO.

Court of Appeals of Texas—
El Paso, 1984.
678 S.W.2d 661.

BACKGROUND AND FACTS In 1964, William Farah became chief executive officer (CEO) of Farah Manufacturing Company (FMC), a successful apparel manufacturer. From 1972 through 1974, FMC was the target of a strike and national boycott. By 1976, the company had lost almost $44 million. FMC's board of directors replaced Farah, and FMC's banks renegotiated their loan agreements. The new agreements permitted the banks to call in the loans if a management change occurred that the banks opposed. In 1977, Farah tried to regain the CEO position, but the board of directors thwarted the attempt, fearing that otherwise the banks would declare a default under the management-change clause. Over the next year, representatives of the banks became members of FMC's board of directors, and one representative became CEO. The new CEO sold off assets at low prices to make loan prepayments. In 1978, Farah regained control of FMC and sued the banks in a Texas state court, alleging fraud, duress, and wrongful interference with business relations. The interference allegations were based on charges that the banks had used undue influence (threatening to exercise the management-change clause) to keep out competent management loyal to FMC instead of to the banks. The jury awarded FMC more than $18.9 million in damages for lost profits and for losses and damages related to the selling of FMC's assets. One bank—State National Bank of El Paso—appealed.

DECISION AND RATIONALE The Court of Appeals of Texas affirmed the trial court's judgment but reduced the amount of the damages by $300,105. The appellate court pointed out that the banks could have chosen to exercise or not to exercise the management-change clause, but when they threatened to exercise it to force FMC to act against FMC's interests, they committed wrongful interference. The court stated that "[t]o maintain the action for interference, it must be established that (1) there was a contract subject to interference, (2) the act of interference was willful and intentional, (3) such intentional act was a proximate cause of Plaintiff's damage, and (4) actual damage or loss occurred." The court explained that "[a] justifiable business interest does not grant absolute privilege to interfere with a contractual relationship between others. In determining the propriety of interference, * * * [t]he principal issue [is] whether the social benefits derived in permitting acts of intervention outweigh the harm to be expected therefrom." The court concluded that the banks' "conduct failed to comport with the standards of fair play. * * * [T]he social benefits derived from permitting the lenders' interference are clearly outweighed by the harm." The banks' "interference compelled the election of directors and officers whose particular business judgment and inexperience and whose divided loyalty proximately resulted in injury to FMC."

NEGLIGENCE   Negligence exists when someone suffers injury because another fails to live up to a required duty of care. To the extent that courts have expanded the areas in which a duty of care is owed by the lender to the borrower, negligence has become an increasingly important theory on which lender liability cases have been based.

In the following case, the court considered whether a lender has a duty to a borrower to process the borrower's loan application with reasonable care.

BACKGROUND AND FACTS   Robert and Margaret Jacques applied to The First National Bank of Maryland for a loan to buy a house. The loan was approved for an amount substantially less than what the Jacques had applied for. The Jacques sued the bank in a Maryland state court, alleging that it had failed to evaluate their qualifications for the loan properly. The allegations were based on five legal theories, including negligence. The Jacques offered testimony in support of the negligence claim on several points. The bank's loan officer had averaged two years of the Jacques' income, while the usual practice was to average three years of an applicant's income. The officer had known that because of illness the Jacques' income for those two years was lower than usual and thus distorted their financial status. Payments on the Jacques' current home had been included in the calculation, although the usual practice was to review only unsecured consumer debts. Income from stock investments had not been considered; if it had been, it would have bolstered the Jacques' income. Finally, the officer had given too much weight to the Jacques' debt-to-income ratio and too little weight to their favorable credit history and substantial net worth. The trial court entered a judgment for the Jacques on the negligence count and for the bank on the rest of the complaint, and both parties appealed. The reviewing court reversed the judgment for the Jacques. They appealed.

DECISION AND RATIONALE   The Court of Appeals of Maryland reversed the lower court's judgment and remanded the case. The appellate court held that, in processing a customer's loan application, a bank owes the customer a duty of reasonable care. The court reasoned that there is "a tort duty of due care arising from contractual dealings with professionals

Case 34.3
─────

JACQUES v. FIRST NATIONAL BANK OF MARYLAND

Court of Appeals of Maryland, 1986.
307 Md. 527,
515 A.2d 756.

such as physicians, attorneys, architects, and public accountants" and that "in those occupations requiring peculiar skill, a tort duty to act with reasonable care will be imposed on those who hold themselves out as possessing the requisite skill." Also, imposition of the duty was "reasonable in light of the nature of the banking industry and its relation to public welfare." As for a standard regarding the duty of care, the court stated that "[a]s in any other negligence case, an industry standard" was applicable. The court pointed to guidelines issued by the Federal Home Loan Mortgage Corporation and the Federal National Mortgage Association. The court noted that these guidelines are widely followed by banks in underwriting loans and that in this case the bank conceded that it made loans based on the guidelines.

COMMENTS   In some negligence cases, a finding of liability is based on a breach of the trust and dependence that develops from a long-term relationship. In this case, however, the Jacques and The First National Bank of Maryland had no previous relationship—liability was held to arise from a breach of the fiduciary duty of financial institutions in general. Some commentators have argued that this case is part of a trend toward imposing on lenders absolute liability (that is, strict liability—see Chapter 5).

Liability for Breach of the Duty of Good Faith

The requirement of good faith in business dealings applies also to lender-borrower relationships. Good faith and fair dealing are required in the creation and performance of all contracts subject to the Uniform Commercial Code [UCC 1-201(19), 1-203, 1-208]. The concept is also expressed in the Restatement (Second) of Contracts, Section 205. Now, in most states, the duty to act in good faith is implied in all contracts. Good faith requires that both parties to an agreement treat each other honestly, reasonably, and fairly.

The difficulty arises over the extent of the duty, particularly the extent of the duty owed on the part of the lender. The good faith test has not been uniformly applied. In some states, courts apply the good faith doctrine to all aspects of the lender-borrower relationship; in others, to only part of it. In many instances, even loan negotiations—which may include oral commitments and agreements—are included among actions subject to the good faith requirement.

The leading case in this area in regard to lender liability is *K.M.C. Co. v. Irving Trust Co.*[12] K.M.C. Company and Irving Trust Company entered into a revolving credit agreement in 1979. In 1982,

without warning, Irving Trust refused to advance $800,000 to K.M.C. under the agreement, effectively terminating K.M.C.'s account. The termination seemed, on its face, to accord with the agreement, which provided that all advances by Irving Trust were to be made at the discretion of its loan officers. Further, the agreement stated that all outstanding loans were payable on demand by Irving Trust. K.M.C. brought suit, arguing that Irving Trust's action resulted in the failure of K.M.C.'s business. At trial, the jury awarded $7.5 million to K.M.C. On appeal, the award stood. The appellate court reasoned that although the lender had the right to terminate the financing under the agreement, the lender also owed K.M.C. a duty to act in good faith. This duty reasonably required advance notice to the borrower so that it could obtain financing elsewhere.

The following year, a Florida court criticized the K.M.C. decision and in essence repudiated it.[13] More recently, courts have recognized in a number of cases that a lender owes a duty of good faith to a borrower, but in the situations presented by those cases no violation of that duty has been found.[14]

---

12.   757 F.2d 752 (6th Cir. 1985).

13.   *Flagship National Bank v. Gray Distribution Systems Inc.*, 485 So.2d 1336 (Fla.App. 1986).

14.   See, for example, *Kruse v. Bank of America*, 202 Cal.App.3d 38, 248 Cal.Rptr. 217 (1988).

■ Potential Statutory Liability

Whenever a lender becomes entangled in the business affairs of the borrower, that lender may be subject to statutory liability on a variety of grounds, including violation of federal securities law, racketeering law, tax law, and environmental law. In this section, we examine the potential liability of lenders under environmental laws.

Financial institutions currently face direct and indirect liability under federal and state environmental statutes. Under certain circumstances, because of lender liability, lenders face the same responsibilities as companies that handle, generate, or dispose of hazardous materials. There are over twenty-five major federal environmental laws. Many more state and local laws, which usually impose stricter penalties on polluters, are also important. (See Chapter 46 for a more detailed treatment of environmental law.)

At the federal level, the most important environmental legislation affecting lenders has been the Comprehensive Environmental Response, Compensation and Liability Act (CERCLA) of 1980.[15] Lenders taking ownership of real property that served as security for their loans may find themselves liable for the cost of cleaning up toxic waste or chemicals located on the property. Often the liability exceeds by many times the value of the original loan and certainly the value of the profits that were to be realized from the loan.

Liability under CERCLA

CERCLA exempts banks and other lenders that have made loans to polluters if the banks or lenders do not partake in the firms' management. But how far can a lender go in protecting its interests before it will be considered to be participating in management? A landmark case in this area was heard in 1986.[16] Maryland Bank and Trust Company had foreclosed on real estate in which it held a security interest and had then purchased the property at the foreclosure sale. Approximately a year later, the Environmental Protection Agency (EPA) discovered hazardous waste on the site. The EPA sued the bank for the clean-up costs, which exceeded the value of the loan. The court held that the bank was responsible. Under CERCLA, the EPA has the power to finance toxic waste site clean-up by billing polluters. The court reasoned that whenever a lender qualifies as an owner or operator of a polluted site, the lender can also be deemed responsible.

The scope of lender liability for environmental clean-up costs was greatly expanded in the following case.

---

15. 42 U.S.C. Sections 9601 *et seq.*

16. *United States v. Maryland Bank and Trust Co.,* 632 F.Supp. 573 (D.Md. 1986).

BACKGROUND AND FACTS Swainsboro Print Works, Inc. (SPW), operated a cloth-printing facility. In 1976, Fleet Factors Corporation acquired security interests in SPW's assets, including its printing facility and accounts receivable. In 1979, SPW filed for bankruptcy under Chapter 11. Fleet continued its arrangement with SPW, advancing funds and paying for services, until Fleet determined that the value of the funds advanced exceeded the value of SPW's accounts receivable. In 1981, SPW shut down. During the winding up of SPW's affairs, Fleet continued to check the credit of SPW's customers and to collect receivables. Chapter 7 proceedings were begun. In 1982, Fleet foreclosed on its security interests, selling some of SPW's assets at an auction through a liquidator. Fleet allowed unsold equipment to be removed. After 1983, Fleet had no contact with the site. In 1987, it was sold in a tax foreclosure sale. The federal government filed an action in a federal district court under CERCLA, seeking to impose liability on Fleet for costs associated with the removal of hazardous chemicals and asbestos from the site. The government alleged that after SPW ceased operations, Fleet became involved in the management of SPW by establishing prices, directing and approving shipments, supervising and laying

Case 34.4

UNITED STATES v. FLEET FACTORS CORP.

United States Court of Appeals, Eleventh Circuit, 1990.
901 F.2d 1550.

off employees, processing government forms, and controlling access to the facility. Thus, Fleet was liable either as the "owner or operator" of the facility from 1982 until the tax foreclosure sale or as a participant in management. The court held that only if the government could prove that Fleet's liquidator disturbed the site's hazardous substances, and thereby "operated" the site, could Fleet be held liable. Fleet's motion for summary judgment was denied. Fleet appealed.

DECISION AND RATIONALE   The United States Court of Appeals concluded that the district court had properly denied Fleet's motion for summary judgment. The appellate court also concluded, however, that the district court had erred in construing the secured creditor exemption to insulate Fleet from CERCLA liability for its conduct before 1982, but the court upheld the ruling that Fleet was liable for its subsequent activities if the government could establish its allegations. The case was remanded. The appellate court stated that "a secured creditor may incur [CERCLA] liability, without being an operator, by participating in the financial management of a facility to a degree indicating a capacity to influence the corporation's treatment of hazardous wastes." A creditor need not to involve itself in daily operations nor participate in management decisions relating to hazardous waste. "Rather, a secured creditor will be liable if its involvement with the management of the facility is sufficiently broad to support the inference that it could affect hazardous waste disposal decisions if it so chose." Fleet argued that it was only protecting its security interest. The court said that "[w]hat is relevant is the nature and extent of the creditor's involvement with the facility, not its motive."

Since the *Fleet Factors* Decision

More recently, a different circuit court put some limitations on lender liability with respect to environmental clean-up costs in *The East Asiatic Co. v. Port of St. Helens (In re Bergsoe Metal Corp.).*[17] The court held that a lender cannot be held liable under CERCLA unless it exercises "actual management authority" that results in the discharge of hazardous waste. The court further held that the lender cannot be held liable simply because it has the power to get involved in management. The court stated that a secured creditor must participate in the actual management of the facility before liability will be imposed. Some observers have argued that this decision will limit the effectiveness of the *Fleet Factors* decision in future lender liability cases involving CERCLA.

In response to the uncertainty in the lending community concerning when a lender may be held liable under CERCLA, bills have been introduced in Congress to exempt lenders from liability unless they cause or contribute to a hazardous waste release. Also, the EPA has proposed a new rule that would allow a creditor to engage in a broad range of activities without incurring liability. Under the proposed rule, "participation in management" would include only a lender's actual participation in business operations. The test would be whether the lender divested the borrower of decision-making control, particularly in regard to hazardous substance disposal. A lender would not be liable simply for monitoring a borrower's business, providing financial advice, or restructuring the terms of a loan. Even temporary acquisition of a hazardous waste site through foreclosure would not result in liability as long as the acquisition was reasonably necessary to ensure performance of the terms of the loan.

---

17.   910 F.2d 668 (9th Cir. 1990).

■ Terms and Concepts

acceleration clauses 608   loan workout 609   workout team 609
lender liability 606

■ For Review

1. Because a lender's failure to provide credit in a sufficient amount and at the right time can lead to the demise of a business, what duty does a lender have? What does this duty require?

2. What are the two steps in a lender's termination of a loan agreement? In each step, how might a lender be subject to liability for breach of contract?

3. Why would a lender be more concerned with liability in tort than liability for breach of contract?

4. Habro Grain Co. is a grain dealer—Habro buys grain from farmers and sells to cereal companies and other food processors. AllFoods, Inc., finances Habro's operations. Habro offers all the grain that it buys to AllFoods, under a right of first refusal. AllFoods advises Habro in its business, conducts periodic audits, and limits Habro's power to mortgage its property and to pay dividends. Habro defaults on several contracts with farmers. If the farmers sue AllFoods on grounds of wrongful interference and excessive control, how might the court rule?

5. Pryor Waste Management Co. secures a loan from Washawski Bank with Pryor's real estate, which includes a waste disposal site. When Pryor defaults on the loan, Washawski forecloses on the property. V. I. Properties Corp. buys the property at a foreclosure sale. When hazardous waste is discovered leaking at the site, the Environmental Protection Agency sues Pryor, Washawski, and V. I. for the clean-up costs. What is Washawski's best argument that it should not be held liable?

■ Questions and Case Problems

34-1. Arkon Corp. and First Bank of Springfield are negotiating a loan for $300,000 to finance Arkon's purchase of a new piece of equipment from Make-It Co. The equipment is usually priced at $350,000, but Make-It is willing to sell the equipment for $300,000 if cash is paid on delivery. Make-It has also agreed that if Arkon cannot pay the full cash price on delivery, Arkon can purchase the equipment for $330,000, payable with a 10 percent down payment and the rest in twelve equal installments, and Make-It will hold a security interest in the equipment until the debt is fully paid. Arkon and First Bank meet to discuss the loan. Substantial progress is made, but no loan contract is signed by the parties. Arkon is led to believe, however, that when the loan negotiation process is concluded, it will receive the loan. Based on this assumption, Arkon agrees with Make-It to purchase the equipment. Three days later, First Bank, after further evaluation, denies approval of Arkon's loan application. Make-It delivers the equipment, but Arkon cannot pay the full cash price and cannot even raise enough money for the 10 percent down payment that would allow it to retain possession under the terms of the alternative contract. The equipment is repossessed and sold by Make-It for $310,000, leaving a deficiency of $20,000 that Arkon must pay. Arkon claims that First Bank should be liable for the loss because it led Arkon to believe that the loan would be forthcoming. Will Arkon be able to hold First Bank liable under any of the theories of lender liability presented in this chapter? Discuss fully.

34-2. MMM Co. markets its products in a growing and highly competitive market. Because of cash-flow problems, MMM seeks a loan from West Bank. The bank makes the loan. The loan contract provides that because of MMM's history of cash-flow problems, all purchases by MMM of inventory or equipment will require West Bank's approval. MMM has an opportunity to purchase a new piece of equipment that would increase its productivity. West Bank, however, refuses to approve the purchase. Within six months, MMM cannot fulfill its orders, and its customers consequently shift their business to other producers. One year later, MMM has lost so many customers that it is insolvent. MMM seeks to hold West Bank liable for its failure. Discuss fully whether MMM has a cause of action under any of the theories of lender liability discussed in this chapter.

34-3. Genetop Corp. seeks a loan from Best Bank. Genetop prepares an accurate financial statement showing its poor financial status as well as the fact that two rather large lawsuits are pending against it. Even though Genetop is clearly not a good credit risk, Best Bank makes the loan. Within six months, a judgment of $1 million is levied against Genetop in one of the lawsuits. Genetop cannot make the payments due on the loan and goes into default. Discuss fully the specific theory of lender liability that Genetop would use to hold Best Bank liable.

34-4. Electrotech, Inc., obtained financing from the Bank of the West. Paul and Jean Burke, the principal shareholders of Electrotech, personally guaranteed the loan, which was secured by their home and other property that they owned. Less than a month after funding the loans, the bank informed the Burkes that they were in "technical default" because their most recent financial statement revealed that Electrotech's net worth and liability-to-asset ratios no longer conformed with the bank's requirements. A loan officer at the bank told the Burkes that if Electrotech wanted to improve its financial position by a merger, the company that merged with Electrotech would be responsible for the loans, and the bank would release the Burkes from their personal guaranties. Electrotech merged with Allright Corp., and the bank extended financing to Allright after the merger. Because of business losses during the first quarter after the merger, Allright defaulted on the loan payments and shortly thereafter filed for bankruptcy. Foreclosure proceedings were then initiated against the Burkes' property. Will the Burkes succeed in a lawsuit against the bank for breach of contract, based on the bank's failure to honor its promise to release the Burkes' personal guaranties upon the merger of Electrotech and Allright? Discuss.

34-5. Central States Stamping Co. contracted to purchase a $200,000 custom-made machine from Terminal Equipment Co. Before signing the contract, Wayne Scheer, the president of Central States, contacted Jim Martin, vice-president of Terminal's bank, for information on Terminal's financial status. Among other things, Scheer asked Martin whether Terminal's officers could be trusted and whether the firm kept its commitments to the bank. Although Martin knew that Terminal was heavily indebted to the bank and had defaulted on its payments, Martin did not disclose this information to Scheer. Instead, Martin gave generally positive responses to Scheer's questions. Relying on Martin's assurances, Central States then signed the contract with Terminal and over the next few months paid a total of $50,000 toward the purchase price of the machine. A few months later, Scheer learned that Terminal had closed its doors and would not be completing the machine; nor could Terminal refund the $50,000 to Central States. Scheer also learned that $30,000 of Central States' $50,000 payment to Terminal was not spent for labor and materials necessary for the machine's production (as Terminal had told Scheer it would be) but was instead applied to Terminal's outstanding debt at the bank. Central States then sued the bank for damages, alleging that Martin had fraudulently misrepresented Terminal's financial status. Discuss fully whether Martin had a duty to disclose to Scheer the bank's knowledge of facts suggestive of Terminal's financial instability. [*Central States Stamping Co. v. Terminal Equipment Co.,* 727 F.2d 1405 (6th Cir. 1984)]

34-6. East Bay Limited Partnership purchased a shopping center for the purpose of renovating the center and reselling it to a third party. The purchase was financed through a loan from American General Life & Accident Insurance Co. The parties agreed in writing that during the first six months of the loan, the property could be sold to a buyer approved by the lender and the loan assumed without payment of any fee, but after six months a 1 percent fee would be required. Prepayment of the loan was precluded during the first six years. The written agreement specifically provided that American had the right to approve a proposed buyer based on the buyer's "net worth, credit worthiness and management expertise." About one and a half years into the loan, East Bay requested American's approval to sell the shopping center to the James W. Hall Corp. In a letter to East Bay, American stated that it would not allow

Hall to assume the loan because of the "lack of experience of the company buying the property." East Bay wished to pay off the loan in full so that it could then sell the shopping center without American's approval. American told East Bay that the latter could pay the loan in full only if a prepayment fee of 24.25 percent was paid. In the end there was no sale and no prepayment. East Bay went into default, and American obtained ownership rights in the shopping center, which had been given as security for the loan. East Bay sued American for, among other things, intentional interference with a business relationship and breach of its duty to act in good faith and deal fairly with East Bay. Will the court hold for East Bay on either of these counts? Discuss. [*East Bay Limited Partnership v. American General Life & Accident Insurance Co.,* 744 F.Supp. 1118 (M.D.Fla. 1990)]

34-7. Neal Boge, a dairy farmer, entered into a loan agreement with the United States National Bank of Oregon, giving the bank a security interest in his cows. When Boge fell into arrears on his payments and was unable to meet the bank's subsequent demand for full payment of the loan, the bank sent Boge's file to Portland for foreclosure. Boge and the Rileys, from whom he had purchased the cows, tentatively agreed that the Rileys would repurchase the cows and that Boge would use the proceeds to pay the loan in full and redeem the collateral (the cows). The Rileys would then resell the cows to Boge and finance the purchase themselves. The Rileys and Boge met with a bank representative to obtain information about the specifics of Boge's indebtedness and to make sure that the Rileys could obtain clear title to the cows. The bank representative stated that he could not furnish the information immediately because the file was in Portland. There was evidence, however, that the information was readily available in computers that were at the bank representative's disposal. There was also evidence that the bank representative was hostile and uncooperative. A few days later, the bank demanded that Boge surrender the cows, plus other equipment subject to the bank's security interest, which Boge did shortly thereafter. The cows were then sold by the bank at auction. In the lawsuit that followed, Boge claimed that the bank had breached the implied covenant of good faith and fair dealing by failing to provide promptly the information requested by Boge. Because this information was not provided in time, the Boge-Riley refinancing plan fell through and Boge was unable to pay the loan (and redeem the collateral) before the cows were sold at auction. Had the bank breached the implied covenant of good faith and fair dealing? Discuss fully. [*United States National Bank of Oregon v. Boge,* 102 Or.App. 262, 794 P.2d 801 (1990)]

34-8. Ranjit Ghura, through a corporation he had set up, Runnemede Owners, Inc., sought a mortgage loan from Crest Mortgage Corp. The purpose of the loan was to finance the purchase of a Holiday Inn in Runnemede, New Jersey. On April 10, 1986, Crest (in a limited "commitment letter") agreed to lend Runnemede $5.5 million, but only if a number of specified conditions were met. Among other things, the loan was conditioned on the loan committee's approval of the loan following its investigation of the hotel's financial status. Another condition was that the borrower pay a commitment fee, which would be refunded if the loan, through no fault of the borrower, was not approved. Before signing the letter, Ghura talked to Steven Rayman, the chairman of Crest's board of directors, about the chances of the loan being approved by the loan committee. Rayman told Ghura, ''Don't worry about the committee, I am the committee. What I say, goes. We have a deal.'' Ghura then signed the letter, indicating his agreement to its terms, and paid the commitment fee. On May 8 and 9, just prior to the scheduled closing date, Crest's president advised Ghura orally and in writing that Crest had decided not to make the loan. The decision was based on a review of the hotel's financial data, which indicated that the cash flow from the hotel would be insufficient to carry a $5.5 million debt. Ghura sued Crest, alleging, among other things, that Rayman, Crest's chairman, had fraudulently misrepresented to Ghura that the loan would be approved and that Rayman had committed this fraud for the purpose of obtaining the use of Ghura's $89,500 commitment fee for a period of time. Discuss fully whether Ghura will succeed in this claim. [*Runnemede Owners, Inc. v. Crest Mortgage Corp.*, 861 F.2d 1053 (7th Cir. 1988)]

34-9. A Question of Ethics

 On December 8, 1981, Judico Enterprises, Inc., executed a $460,000 promissory note payable in one year to the First National Bank of Midland, Texas. Willie Coleman and Dwayne Powell, Judico's president and secretary, personally guaranteed the note, giving certain real estate as security for the loan. The guaranty contract contained express waivers of bank obligations regarding the collateral—the bank could obtain a judgment against Coleman and Powell for the full amount of the debt, even if the collateral had been sold to satisfy part of the debt. On October 26, 1982, Judico filed for Chapter 11 bankruptcy. The bank sued Coleman and Powell on their guaranties and moved in the bankruptcy court for relief from the automatic stay to foreclose on the property securing the note. Shortly thereafter, the bank became insolvent, and it was taken over by the Federal Deposit Insurance Corp. (FDIC) in October 1983. In November 1983, the guarantors' attorney sent a letter to the FDIC stating that the property was worth approximately the amount of the debt at that time. The FDIC officer assigned to the Judico account was aware that property prices in the surrounding geographic area were declining. The FDIC obtained from the bankruptcy court an order lifting the automatic stay

in August 1984 but did not sell the property until June 1985. By that time, the value of the property had declined substantially, so that after the sale, a deficiency of $500,000 still existed on the debt. The FDIC sued Coleman and Powell to collect the deficiency, and in the litigation that followed, the focal issue was whether the FDIC had breached its duty of good faith by delaying foreclosure and sale of the collateral in a period of declining property prices. Ultimately, the Supreme Court of Texas held that the FDIC had not breached its duty of good faith. The court noted that good faith is defined in the Uniform Commercial Code as ''honesty in fact''—and the guarantors did not allege that the FDIC was dishonest. Furthermore, the court said, the UCC ''does not require diligence for good faith.'' [*FDIC v. Coleman, 795 S.W.2d 706 (Tex. 1990)*]

1. The Texas Supreme Court pointed out that charging creditors with a good faith obligation to consider market factors—such as declining property prices—in timing the sale of collateral would impose an unfair burden. Creditors would have to be closely attuned to changes in the market prices of any repossessed collateral to be sold. For example, in an era of *rising* property prices, creditors could be held to have violated their duty of good faith if they failed to *delay* in selling the collateral so as to obtain the best price— and so on. Do you believe that this argument justifies the court's decision in this case?

2. In view of the guarantors' waiver of the bank's obligation to sell the collateral at all, would it be fair to hold the FDIC liable for the deficiency? Should the waiver extend to the *timeliness* of the sale, as well as to the sale itself?

3. Solely from an ethical point of view, do you think that the FDIC acted in any way wrongfully in delaying the foreclosure sale? The court maintained that it did not have a legal obligation to sell the collateral as soon as possible, but did it have an ethical duty to do so?

4. If you believe that the FDIC should have been legally obligated to sell the collateral promptly because property values were declining, how would you define ''promptly''? In other words, should the FDIC have held the sale at the very earliest possible moment? What if it delayed a week, or a month? At what point would the FDIC be liable for breaching its duty? Do such definitional difficulties constitute a sufficient basis for holding that good faith should not be imposed on the creditor in timing the sale of collateral?

Focus on Ethics

Creditors' Rights, Bankruptcy, and Lender Liability

We are certainly many years away from that period in our history when debtors' prisons existed. Today, debtors are in a much more favorable position. If a creditor fails to exercise care in all aspects of the creditor-debtor relationship, the creditor may end up being accused of fraud, negligence, breach of contract, breach of the duty of good faith, or some other claim that may render the debt uncollectible. If worse comes to worst, the debtor can file for protection under bankruptcy law. Indeed, some now say that we have proceeded too far in the direction of protecting debtors and have made it too easy for debtors to avoid paying what they legally owe. Clearly, it is difficult to ensure the rights of both debtors and creditors at the same time, and laws governing debtor-creditor relationships are frequently perceived by at least one public group as being unfair to either creditors or debtors.

For example, to protect the legitimate interests of creditors, creditors are given numerous remedies under both the common law and statutory law. When these rights and remedies are invoked, however, the creditor is often considered by the general public to be

employing unfair tactics. For many, the question of fairness revolves around the purpose for which the debt was incurred. If the debt was incurred for a needed item, such as a refrigerator, then common opinion seems to be that the debtor should be dealt with leniently. On the other hand, if the debt was incurred for a trip to the Bahamas, the issue appears to be significantly different.

In contrast, when a debtor is relieved of the obligation to pay a legitimate debt because the creditor technically violated a statutory law, many would claim that this is unfair to the creditor. It also seems unfair to many that creditors who loan money in good faith are frequently precluded from collecting their debts because of the ease with which debtors can now enter into bankruptcy proceedings. In such situations, the law seems unfair to creditors.

There is obviously no way in which the law can protect both debtors and creditors at all times under all circumstances. Tradeoffs must be made in attempting to balance the rights of both groups, and the tradeoffs made often lead to questions of fairness and justice. We look now at several

aspects of debtor-creditor relationships that frequently pose ethical questions.

Who Pays When the Debtor Defaults?

Although there is clearly a distinction in people's minds between the failure to pay a loan and the theft of a creditor's personal property, the result is the same—the wealth of the creditor-seller is reduced. Whatever the ethical issue may be when a debtor fails to perform, the economic consequence is clear: the cost of debtors' nonperformance is imposed on all of those debtors who do perform. This cost takes the form of higher average interest rates. That is, the greater the percentage of loan agreements not consummated according to the agreement, the larger the risk factor added to normal interest rates. Creditors deal in a highly competitive market. They expect to earn a normal rate of return for investment in such an industry. If costs increase because of nonperformance by debtors, those costs will have to be recouped somewhere. In general, the only way to recoup them is to charge all debtors a higher interest rate.

This means that it is not only creditors who are harmed economically when debtors default but ultimately all other debtors, or potential debtors, also. Therefore, laws protecting debtors who default may, in fact, not be protecting the interests of debtors in the long run.

"Self-Help" Repossession

UCC 9-503 states that, "[u]nless otherwise agreed, a secured party has on default the right to take possession of the collateral. In taking possession, a secured party may proceed without judicial process if this can be done without breach of the peace." The underlying rationale for this "self-help" provision of Article 9 is that it simplifies the process of repossession for creditors and reduces the burden on the courts. Because the UCC does not define "breach of the peace," it is not always easy to predict what will or will not constitute a breach of the peace. And from the debtor's point of view, it is not always clear what is happening when agents of the creditor appear to repossess collateral. Often, to avoid confrontation with the debtor and any potential violence or breach of the peace, collateral will be repossessed during the night or in the early-morning hours when the repossession effort is least likely to be observed. And yet it is just at these times that the presence of strangers on a debtor's property could justifiably alarm the debtor. This can lead to distressful situations, at least from the debtor's point of view.

Consider, for example, the plight of Mr. and Mrs. Massengill. They had borrowed money from Indiana National Bank (INB) to purchase a van. Toward the end of the loan period, the Massengills were notified by mail that they were delinquent on their last two loan payments. Mrs. Massengill called INB on a Saturday and said that she did not agree with the amount that INB said was due. It was arranged that Mr. Massengill would go to the bank the first thing the following Monday and take care of the matter. In the meantime, INB had made arrangements for the van to be repossessed. At 1:30 A.M. Sunday morning, two men appeared on the Massengills' driveway and began to hook up the van to a tow truck. Mr. Massengill, assuming that the van was being stolen, went outside to intervene and did so vociferously. During the course of events, Massengill became entangled in machinery at the rear of the tow truck and was dragged down the street and then run over by his towed van. The "repo men"—those hired by the creditor to repossess the van—knew of Mr. Massengill's plight but sped away.[1] Obviously, the peace was breached in this case, and Massengill will very likely recover damages for the injuries he sustained.

The point here is that the incident—and others similar to it—would not have happened were it not for the self-help provision. And yet, there is no way to ensure that such confrontations will not occasionally result from repossession attempts. The tradeoff here is clear: debtors are exposed to occasional abuse and violence resulting from self-help repossessions so that the rights of creditors to collect on their debts quickly and without legal proceedings may be protected.

Bankruptcy

The first goal of bankruptcy law is to provide relief and protection to debtors who have "gotten in over their heads." But consider the concept of bankruptcy from the point of view of the creditor. The creditor has extended a transfer of purchasing power from himself or herself to the debtor. That transfer of purchasing power represents a transfer of an asset for an asset. The debtor obtains the asset of money, goods, or services; and the creditor obtains the asset called a *secured* or *unsecured* legal obligation to pay. Once the debtor is in bankruptcy, voluntarily or involuntarily, the asset that the creditor owns most often has a diminished value. Indeed, in many circumstances, that asset has no value. Bankruptcy law attempts to provide a fair means of distributing to creditors the assets remaining in the debtor's possession.

Society has generally concluded that everyone should be given the chance to start over again. Thus, bankruptcy law is a balancing act between providing such a chance and ensuring that creditors are given "a fair shake." But the question of "moral hazard" arises with bankruptcy law just as it does in other areas. The easier it becomes for debtors to hide behind bankruptcy laws, the greater will be the incentive for debtors to use such laws to avoid payment of legally owed sums of money. That also means that the more easily a debtor can hide behind bankruptcy laws, the more a

---

1. *Massengill v. Indiana National Bank,* 550 N.E.2d 97 (Ind.App. 1st Dist. 1990).

creditor will charge, because of the increased degree of risk. The fact is that the total number of bankruptcies has increased since the enactment of the Bankruptcy Reform Act of 1978. What this phenomenon means is that creditors incur higher risks in making loans. To compensate for these higher risks, creditors will do one or more of the following: increase the interest rates charged to everyone, require more security (collateral), or be more selective in the granting of credit. Thus, a tradeoff exists: the more lenient bankruptcy laws are, the better off will be those debtors who find themselves in bankruptcy; but those debtors who will never be in bankruptcy will be worse off. Ethical concerns here must be matched with the economic concerns of other groups of individuals affected by the law.

Chapter 11 Filing

Particularly controversial are questions concerning at what point and in what circumstances companies should be entitled to file a Chapter 11 petition for reorganization under the Bankruptcy Code. Filing a Chapter 11 petition automatically stays the commencement, continuation, or enforcement of proceedings against the debtor. As previously stated, the bankruptcy law attempts to provide a refuge to the honest debtor who is unable to pay his or her debts. The rehabilitation of the debtor, rather than the liquidation of the debtor's estate (Chapter 7), is the primary purpose of Chapter 11.

The Johns-Manville Corporation's Chapter 11 filing[2]

_____
2. _In re Johns-Manville Corp.,_ 36 Bankr. 727 (Bankr.S.D.N.Y. 1984). This case is presented in Chapter 33 as Case 33.4.

raises many ethical issues. Many critics argue that the Johns-Manville filing was an abuse of the federal bankruptcy law, because the company was still earning profits. Manville filed for Chapter 11 reorganization on August 26, 1982, and at that time the corporation's reported assets were valued at $2.2 billion. The fact that Manville was solvent when it filed for Chapter 11 reorganization led many people to question the fairness behind Chapter 11. Should a bankruptcy court be used by a solvent company facing potential tort liability? Do companies such as Manville deserve the fresh start available under Chapter 11—which allows debtors to escape the pressures that drove them into bankruptcy?

Manville officials contended that the petition for reorganization was the only way to save the corporation from the pending 16,500 lawsuits for asbestos-related diseases. A research firm commissioned by Manville in 1982 estimated that the company would incur liability as high as $4.8 billion by the year 2009. Furthermore, the Bankruptcy Code is drafted so as to allow the filing for Chapter 11 reorganization by a solvent debtor. The theory behind allowing solvent debtors to file is that creditors will be better protected if debtors file for reorganization while their assets are still available to pay creditors' claims. As long as a debtor is "honest," bankruptcy courts have been willing to discharge the debtor from pre-petition debts and some post-petition debts.

Yet even though the filing by Manville was consistent with the letter of the Bankruptcy Code, questions still arise as to whether Manville filed in good faith and deserved a fresh start. There is no doubt that Manville

knew that exposure to asbestos resulted in asbestos-related diseases such as asbestosis, lung cancer, and cancer of the stomach, colon, and rectum. Court cases also resulted in findings that Manville withheld this knowledge from its employees. Given this evidence, is Manville truly deserving of a fresh start?

Competition and Chapter 11

Competition often induces manufacturers to take risks that may subsequently harm society, thus precipitating the manufacturer's own economic downfall. Some critics argue, however, that the imposition of punitive damages in product liability cases may in effect be "overkill." In other words, punitive damages administered to punish the offender and to deter this type of conduct in the future may make the difference between a company's filing or not filing a petition for Chapter 11 reorganization. Thus, the economic consequences of our punishment and deterrence objectives appear much more complex than on first glance. How can we punish and deter unethical conduct by a company that has done much good in the past and has the potential to do much good in the future without inviting it to file for Chapter 11? Remember, the filing of a petition in bankruptcy automatically stays the commencement of proceedings against the debtor. What then happens to potential plaintiffs?

Another aspect of Chapter 11 also raises ethical considerations (and is controversial as well). In recent years competition in many industries has increased dramatically. After the deregulation of the airline industry, for example, some airlines overexpanded and eventually became insolvent. Furthermore, as the industry grew from 36 to over 150 airlines, fare wars began to characterize the industry. Some companies—such as Braniff and Air Florida—were unsuccessful under deregulation and ultimately declared bankruptcy. Others—such as Eastern and Pan American—later followed suit. In this type of situation, a company may be tempted not to deal in good faith because it knows that resort to Chapter 11 is always available. Chapter 11 may also become a bargaining chip for management to use against labor during wage negotiations. The threat of Chapter 11 can leave employees in a very vulnerable position as they try to predict whether a company is actually considering Chapter 11 as a viable alternative or is merely bluffing.

Lender Liability

Lender liability is an issue that has become important only in the last ten or fifteen years. Today, lenders find that they are often liable for more than the size of the loan. In particular, lenders may find themselves held liable by the U.S. government for all costs of cleaning up toxic wastes from real estate on which they have foreclosed. Many have questioned the fairness of holding lenders liable in these circumstances.

Lender liability also poses a long-run tradeoff for society: To the extent that more lenders are held liable for improper repossession of collateral, improper foreclosure, or toxic waste clean-up costs, the amount of total lending will decrease. That is, the higher the total cost of lending, the smaller the amount of credit that will be offered to business firms. This will reduce the amount of commerce in America. The tradeoff is thus relatively obvious.

■ Discussion Questions

1. Is it unethical to avoid paying one's debts by going into bankruptcy? Does a person have a moral responsibility to pay his or her debts? After his haberdashery went bankrupt in the 1930s, President Harry S Truman went on to pay all his creditors over the next decade, even though he had no legal obligation to do so. Should all bankrupt individuals acknowledge their responsibilities as President Truman did?

2. Do you think that the law favors debtors at the expense of creditors, or vice versa? Is there any way a better balance between creditors' and debtors' interests could be achieved?

3. Although filing for bankruptcy is now much easier than it used to be and many more debtors are choosing bankruptcy as a solution to their financial difficulties, bankruptcy also has its negative side: those who go through bankruptcy have a difficult time reestablishing credit because of the "black mark" on their credit record. Is it ethical for a business to refuse to deal with a customer simply because that person once went into bankruptcy, even though that person is now a good credit risk in every other way? Is it consistent with bankruptcy law—the whole purpose of which is to rehabilitate debtors—for debtors to be burdened by this consequence? Can it be avoided?

4. Assume that all lending institutions are held liable for environmental clean-up costs on properties on which they foreclose. What businesses would be affected by such a development, and how would they be affected? [Hint: Dry cleaners; print shops.]

UNIT SIX

Agency

■ The Importance of Agency Law

Agency is a relationship between two persons in which one of them, called the *agent,* is authorized to act for and on behalf of the other, called the *principal.* Within the scope of the agency agreement, the agent may negotiate contracts with third parties and bind principals to those contracts.

The majority of all goods in the United States are manufactured and provided by large corporations. None of these corporations could exist without agents. That is to say, no business could be operated only by its owners. The owners of businesses must be able to delegate authority to their agents for business firms to grow and thrive. If there were no law establishing the rights of agents and principals, the corporate world would not exist as we know it today. Nor would the world of partnerships. Nor would a host of other relationships and entities that we take for granted.

Indeed, it is difficult to fully understand how business associations, such as partnerships and corporations, actually function without understanding the law of agency. Much of what is written in the next unit on business organizations, including partnerships and corporations, finds its basis in the two chapters on agency that you are about to read. Because the agent has the power to bind the principal to contracts, the law of agency imposes many obligations on the agent, including the duties of loyalty, obedience, and diligence. Agents, for example, normally must devote their actions exclusively to the principal and promote the interests of the principal.

In this unit, we divide the law of agency into two chapters. Agency formation and the duties of agents and principals are presented in Chapter 35. In Chapter 36, we discuss the liability of agents and principals to third parties and agency termination.

■ Ethical Issues in Agency Law

The agent has a duty of loyalty to the principal. This duty requires the agent to promote the interests of the principal. But what if the principal is engaged in unlawful conduct, such as generating pollution along with its production process? Does the agent's duty of loyalty to the principal dictate that the agent say or do nothing? Or is there a greater duty owed to society that transcends the duty owed to the principal? If, in such a situation, the agent decides to disclose to the authorities the pollution activities of the principal, does the principal have the right to fire the agent? What about a situation in which the principal is not engaged in illegal activities, but simply in activities that the agent finds to be ethically inappropriate? What rights does the agent have in such situations to refuse to be loyal to the principal? What rights does the principal have if the principal wishes to dismiss the agent?

Numerous ethical issues arise when third parties are involved. If an agent injures a third party while engaged in work for the principal, who should be responsible for the loss? The principal might reasonably argue that he or she was not the cause of the harm and therefore the agent should bear all of the liability. The agent may assert that, had he or she not been working for the principal, the harm to the third party would never have occurred. A tradeoff is obviously involved here. Societal considerations typically require that the principal who controls the activities of the agent be held liable for injuries to third parties caused by the agent, because the principal normally has "deeper pockets" than the agent. If the law were not such, then injured third parties might find themselves unable to collect damages when they in fact had nothing to do with causing the injury to themselves. But how far should this logic go when the agent engages in unauthorized criminal acts? Should the principal still remain liable for those acts? Clearly, societal and ethical precepts are involved in answering such a question.

Chapter 35

Agency Formation and Duties

One of the most common, important, and pervasive legal relationships is that of agency. In an **agency** relationship between two parties, one of the parties, called the **agent,** agrees to represent or act for the other, called the **principal.** The principal has the right to control the agent's conduct in matters entrusted to the agent. More formally, the Restatement (Second) of Agency[1] defines *agency* as "the fiduciary relation[2] which results from the manifestation of consent by one person to another that the other shall act in his behalf and subject to his control, and consent by the other so to act." In general, the law of agency is based on the maxim that "one acting by another is acting for himself."

■ The Nature of Agency

An agent acts for his or her principal. By using agents a principal can conduct multiple business operations simultaneously in various locations. Thus, for example, contracts that bind the principal can be made at different places with different persons at the same time. A familiar example of an agent is a corporate officer, who serves in a representative capacity for the owners of the corporation. In this capacity, the officer has the authority to bind the principals to a contract. Indeed, agency law is essential to the existence and operation of a corporate entity, because only through its agents can a corporation function and enter into contracts.

■ Kinds of Agency Relationships

The first step in analyzing an agency relationship is to determine whether such a relationship exists. Traditional analysis in the law of agency distinguishes three categories of relationships:

---

1. Restatement (Second) of Agency, Section 1(1). The Restatement (Second) of Agency is an authoritative summary of the law of agency. It is often referred to by jurists in decisions and opinions.
2. A fiduciary relationship involves a high degree of trust and a duty to act for someone else's benefit.

1. Principal and agent.
2. Employer and employee.
3. Employer and independent contractor.

It is important to note that at times an employee or an independent contractor may be acting in the capacity of an agent.

Principal–Agent

In a principal–agent relationship, the parties have agreed that the agent will act *on behalf of and instead of* the principal in negotiating and transacting business with third persons. The agent has *derivative authority* in carrying out the principal's business. This relationship will affect the principal's rights and duties. Thus, an agent is empowered to perform legal acts that are binding on the principal.

For example, Earl is hired as a booking agent for a rock group—Harry and the Rockets. As the group's agent, Earl can negotiate and sign contracts for the rock group to appear at concerts. The contracts will be binding and thus legally enforceable against the group.

Employer–Employee

Prior to the industrial revolution, the terms *employer* and *employee* had no significance in common law rules of agency. The original term used to denote an employer–employee relationship was *master–servant relationship.* The terms *master* and *servant* are now archaic and outdated; but because they have been traditionally used in the law governing agency relationships, they are still encountered occasionally.

Today, a *servant* is considered to be an employee and a *master* an employer. An **employee** is defined as one whose physical conduct is *controlled,* or subject to control, by the employer. An employee can be an agent if the employee has an appointment or contract for hire with authority to represent the employer.[3]

For example, Dana owns a dress shop. She employs Sandy, Sheila, and Sue as salespeople and Sara as a janitor. Dana is the employer (master);

the other women are the employees (servants). The key feature of the employer–employee relationship is that the employer has the right to control the employee in the performance of the tasks involved in the employment. The employees do not have *independent* business discretion. Dana can thus tell her salespeople not only to sell the dresses but also how to sell them. In selling the dresses, however, they are agents as well as employees. They have been given the authority by Dana to contract for and represent Dana in creating sales with customers. Sara, however, because she is not a salesperson, has no authority with respect to selling dresses and thus is not an agent in that respect. In fact, she may have no authority to represent Dana in any dealings with others, including receiving deliveries of janitorial supplies.

All employment laws (state and federal) apply only to the employer–employee relationship. Statutes governing Social Security, withholding taxes, workers' compensation, unemployment compensation, workplace safety laws, and the like are applicable only when there is employer–employee status. *These laws do not apply to the independent contractor.*

Employer–Independent Contractor

Independent contractors are not employees, because the person for whom they have agreed to perform some undertaking has no control over the details of their physical performance. The Restatement (Second) of Agency, Section 2, defines an **independent contractor** as follows:

> An independent contractor is a person who contracts with another to do something for him but who is not controlled by the other nor subject to the other's right to control with respect to his physical conduct in the performance of the undertaking. He may or may not be an agent.

The relationship between an employer and an independent contractor may or may not involve an agency relationship. Courts usually determine whether a person is an employee or an independent contractor by asking the following questions:

1. How much control can the employer exercise over the details of the work?

---

3. According to the Restatement (Second) of Agency, Sections 2, 14N and 25, employees are always agents.

2. Is the employed person engaged in an occupation or business distinct from that of the employer?

3. Is the work usually done under the employer's direction, or is it done by a specialist without supervision?

4. Does the employer supply the tools at the place of work?

5. For how long is the person hired or retained?

6. What is the method of payment—by time period or at the completion of the job?

7. What is the degree of skill required to do whatever it is the person was hired or retained to do?

Building contractors and subcontractors are independent contractors because a property owner does not control the acts of these professionals.

Truck drivers who own their equipment and hire out on an *ad hoc* basis are independent contractors. A collection agency is another example of an independent contractor. In contrast, truck drivers who drive company trucks on a regular basis are usually deemed employees. An owner of real estate who hires a real estate broker to negotiate a sale of his or her property has not only contracted with an independent contractor (the real estate broker) but has also established an agency relationship for the specific purpose of assisting in the sale of the property.

The following case illustrates a court's application of the above-mentioned criteria in deciding whether an employer–employee or principal–independent contractor relationship existed between the parties.

Case 35.1

AMEAR v. HALL

Court of Appeals of Georgia,
1982.
164 Ga.App. 163,
296 S.E.2d 611.

BACKGROUND AND FACTS   Dr. George Hall hired Ivan Davey, who was Tom Amear's partner, to do landscaping and other household maintenance. Hall would tell Davey what needed to be done, and Davey, Amear, or others would do the work. Davey and Amear controlled their own hours and methods. Hall asked Davey to install fiberglass over four spaces formed by exposed beams connecting the carport and the house, but did not instruct Davey how to do the job—it was Amear's idea to climb out on a beam to install the fiberglass. But the beams were purely decorative with no structural purpose, and the beam collapsed under Amear, who fell and severely injured himself. In a suit against Hall in a Georgia state court, Amear claimed that he was an employee and that Hall had failed to provide and maintain safe working conditions. Hall claimed that Amear was an independent contractor. The trial court entered judgment in favor of Hall, and Amear appealed.

DECISION AND RATIONALE   The Court of Appeals of Georgia found Davey and Amear to be independent contractors. Therefore, Hall was not liable for the injury to Amear, and the judgment of the trial court was affirmed. The appellate court held that the test of "whether a person employed is a servant or an independent contractor is whether the employer, under the contract, * * * has the right to direct the time, the manner, the methods, and the means of the execution of the work * * *." This is distinguished "from the right to insist upon the contractor producing results according to the contract, or whether the contractor in the performance of the work contracted for is free from any control by the employer of the time, manner, and method in the performance of the work." Hall was free of liability because an independent contractor is expected to determine for himself or herself whether a place of employment is safe or unsafe and ordinarily may not recover against the owner for injuries sustained in performance of a contract. Moreover, the employer normally does not have to take affirmative steps to safeguard the "contractor's employees against the consequences of the contractor's negligence, or to provide for their safety."

Using Independent Contractors

Using independent contractors is beneficial because it *may* reduce your susceptibility to tort liability. There are other reasons for hiring independent contractors. For example, you are not required to pay or deduct Social Security and unemployment taxes on behalf of such individuals. You simply pay those individuals a fee for their services. The independent contractor is responsible for paying self-employment taxes, if any.

Each independent contractor can usually deduct many of his or her expenses incurred while providing services to you, which would not be deductible as an employee. Thus, the personal income tax burden of the independent contractor is often reduced, and that may result in your being able to hire him or her for less than if you were to hire that person as an employee to do the same services. Additionally, for the purposes of any retirement or medical plans or other fringe benefits that you have for yourself and other employees, the independent contractor is not eligible, and this is a cost saving for you.

A word of caution, though: Simply designating a person as an independent contractor does not necessarily make him or her one. Under Internal Revenue Service rules, any individual will still be treated as an employee if he or she is "in fact" an employee, regardless of the classification that you might have made. It is difficult, for example, to justify calling a secretary an independent contractor simply by designating him or her as such. (You can, however, contract with a secretarial service; the secretary is an employee of the service and not your employee directly.) If you improperly designate an employee as an independent contractor, the penalty you pay might be high. Usually you would be liable for back Social Security and unemployment taxes, plus interest and penalty. In addition, if you have a pension plan, it might be disqualified. When in doubt, seek professional assistance in such matters.

■ Formation of the Agency Relationship

The following discussion emphasizes the usual form that an agency relationship takes. An agency relationship is a *consensual* relationship; that is, it comes about by voluntary consent and agreement between the parties. It is a consensual relationship because it must be based on some affirmative indication that the agent agrees to act for the principal and the principal agrees to have the agent so act.

■ CONCEPT SUMMARY 35.1 Agency—Legal Relationships

Type of Legal Relationship	Description
Principal–agent	An agent has the authority to act on behalf of and instead of the principal, using a certain degree of his or her own *discretion.*
Employer–employee	The employer has the right to *control* the physical conduct of the employee.
Employer–independent contractor	The contractor is not an employee, and the principal has *no control* over the details of physical performance. Except for real estate and certain other agencies, the contractor is not usually an agent.

EMERGING TRENDS IN BUSINESS LAW

The Growing Rights of Independent Contractors

Under copyright law, any work created by an employee during the scope of his or her employment at the request of the employer is called a "work for hire." The employer owns and holds the copyright to such works. But what about the free-lance artist or writer or other worker who is not really an employee in the usual sense? What happens, for example, when a sculptor is commissioned by an organization to create a statue? Who owns the copyright—the sculptor/creator or the organization that commissioned and paid for the work of art? Prior to passage of the Copyright Act of 1976, the courts generally presumed that the commissioning individual or firm held the copyright in such cases. In other words, free-lancers were assumed to be employees, and their works were considered to be "works for hire." If a publishing firm, for example, hired a free-lance photographer to take specifically designated types of photographs for a book the firm was publishing, the presumption would be that the publishing house owned the photographs—unless, of course, the parties had agreed otherwise in writing. The 1976 act changed the rules governing commissioned works and, in effect, reversed the

presumption operative prior to 1976. Under the Copyright Act of 1976, the free-lancer who is commissioned to do a work will be the owner of the work created *unless* the parties agree in writing that the work is "for hire" *and* the work falls into one of nine categories stipulated by the act, such as audiovisual works, translations, supplementary works, and others. For publishing houses, advertising agencies, and other firms that routinely farm out work to free-lancers, this change in copyright law obviously has serious consequences.

It takes awhile for the business world to adjust to new laws governing its practices. In the case of the provisions of the Copyright Act of 1976 concerning commissioned works, not until June 1989 did the United States Supreme Court face the task of definitively interpreting the 1976 act in this respect and setting guidelines for determining who owns the copyright to a commissioned work done by a free-lancer. In deciding the case, the crucial issue was whether the party commissioned to do the work was an employee or an independent contractor.

The case before the Supreme Court[a] involved a copyright

dispute over a sculpture created by James Earl Reid for the Community for Creative Non-Violence (CCNV), a Washington, D.C., organization dedicated to eliminating homelessness. CCNV conceived of the idea of a modern nativity scene in which, in lieu of the traditional Holy Family, the two adult figures and the infant would appear as contemporary homeless people huddled over a streetside steam grate. The title of the work was to be "Third World America," and the legend on the pedestal would read "and still there is no room at the inn."

CCNV paid Reid $15,000 to cover the actual expenses Reid incurred in creating the statue. Reid donated his services. There was no written contract, and the question of copyright or ownership rights had not been discussed. Initially, the federal district court ruled that the statue was a work for hire, reasoning that Reid had been an employee of CCNV because CCNV was the motivating force in the statue's production. Furthermore, members of CCNV continuously gave Reid direction and suggestions on how to proceed with the statue. In the end, reasoned the court, Reid had produced what CCNV wanted, not what he wanted.[b]

The Court of Appeals for the District of Columbia reversed and remanded the case back to

---

a. *Community for Creative Non-Violence v. Reid,* 490 U.S. 730, 109 S.Ct. 2166, 104 L.Ed.2d 811 (1989).

b. 652 F.Supp. 1453 (D.D.C. 1987).

the district court. The appellate court's decision hinged on "a simple dichotomy in fact between employees and independent contractors."[c] Under agency law, Reid was an independent contractor. The United States Supreme Court agreed. Even though CCNV members directed part of the work to ensure that the statue met their specifications, all other relevant circumstances pointed in the direction of Reid's being an independent contractor. He was already engaged in a skilled occupation; he supplied his own tools; he worked in Baltimore without daily supervision from CCNV members in Washington, D.C.; and he had absolute freedom in deciding when and how long to work to meet his deadline. Additionally, he had total discretion in hiring and paying assistants. Reid was also paid as independent contractors are paid. CCNV did not take out payroll or Social Security taxes, nor did it provide any employee benefits or contribute to unemployment insurance or workers' compensation funds.

CCNV was not left totally empty-handed by the decision—as yet, anyway. The Court indicated that CCNV may still be considered a co-owner of the sculpture, and thus hold copyright jointly with Reid, if on remand the lower court determines that CCNV and Reid

c. 846 F.2d 1485 (D.C. Cir. 1988).

prepared the work "with the intention that their contributions be merged into inseparable or independent parts of a unitary whole."

■ Implications for the Businessperson

1. Any businessperson who subcontracts with free-lance artists, writers, designers, and others who create "artistic" works must now take special care in crafting appropriate contracts for these subcontractual arrangements. Specifically, contracts with such independent contractors must clearly spell out who has ownership rights in the creative works generated by the free-lancer. Otherwise, the businessperson may find that he or she has paid for a work but does not have property rights in that work.

2. The independent contractor/free-lancer must examine the issue from the other side. Although the *Reid* decision described above would seem to favor free-lancers, companies hiring free-lancers now routinely include in their contracts provisions that specifically deny the free-lancers any copyright or other property interest in the works created.

■ For Critical Analysis

1. When an individual has a house built, that person may hire a subcontractor to lay

bricks. The bricklayer is an independent contractor creating a work. Why is the bricklayer not viewed in the same way a sculptor is viewed with respect to rights in the work created? Should there be any distinction made? Indeed, what would be the result if no distinction were made between the work created by a bricklayer and the work created by a sculptor?

2. In the *Reid* case, a distinction was made between an employee working for hire and a free-lancer/independent contractor. If the type of work generated is substantially the same, is it logical to make a distinction between the work product of the employee and the work product of an independent contractor? In other words, is it logical that the employee should have no property rights in the product produced but the independent contractor—absent contractual terms indicating the contrary—should? Does this distinction create a differential incentive structure with respect to employees and independent contractors? What reasons underlie the law's distinction in this regard?

3. Analyze the following statement: The *Reid* decision did not help free-lancers; rather, publishing firms and advertising agencies simply rewrote their free-lance contracts to specifically make all free-lance work "work for hire," in which the free-lancer agrees to give up all rights.

The Agency Agreement

Generally, no formalities are required to create an agency. An agency relationship can be created by oral agreement or by written contract. An agency agreement can also be implied from conduct. For example, a hotel expressly allows Jack Andrews to park cars, but Andrews has no employment contract there. The hotel's conduct amounts to a manifestation of its willingness that Jack park its customers' cars, and Jack can infer from the hotel's conduct that he has authority to act as a valet. It can be implied that for that purpose he is an agent for the hotel.

There are two main exceptions to oral agency agreements. In many states, the Statute of Frauds (discussed in Chapter 14) requires that whenever agency authority empowers the agent to enter into a contract that the Statute of Frauds requires to be in writing, the agent's authority from the principal must also be in writing. This is known as the **equal dignity rule.** It applies most frequently to contracts for the sale of an interest in land or contracts that cannot be performed within one year. An exception to the equal dignity rule exists in modern business practice. An executive of a corporation, when acting for the corporation in an ordinary business situation, is not required to obtain written authority from the corporation.

Another agency agreement that must be in writing is a power of attorney. A **power of attorney** grants an agent either full or restricted authority to act in the principal's behalf and often is executed in a notarized writing.[4] The power of attorney can be special—permitting the agent to do specified acts only—or it can be general—permitting the agent to transact all business dealings for the principal. Of course, if the appointment comes within the Statute of Frauds, it must be in writing to be enforceable. Exhibit 35–1 shows a power of attorney.

The following case illustrates the formalities required for a power of attorney to give the holder the right to convey real estate.

---

4. An agent who holds the power of attorney is called an *attorney in fact* for the principal. Despite the use of the word *attorney* here, *an agent does not have to be an attorney at law to hold a power of attorney.*

Case 35.2 **BLOOM v. WEISER** District Court of Appeal of Florida, Third District, 1977. 348 So.2d 651.	**BACKGROUND AND FACTS** Joseph Weinberg and Rachela Weiser bought a condominium unit as joint tenants.[a] Thereafter, Weinberg executed a general power of attorney making his son, Arthur Winters, his agent. Winters conveyed Weinberg's one-half interest in the condominium to Weinberg's daughter, Miriam Bloom. After Weinberg's death, Bloom wanted to sell the condominium, but Weiser claimed complete ownership by right of survivorship on the ground that the agent had no authority to transfer the real estate to Bloom. In Bloom's suit against Weiser in a Florida state court, the trial court held for Weiser, and Bloom appealed. **DECISION AND RATIONALE** The District Court of Appeal of Florida affirmed the trial court's ruling. The appellate court found that the established rule "is that a power of attorney must be strictly construed and * * * will be held to grant only those powers which are specified." The power of attorney Weinberg granted to Winters failed to authorize him to convey real estate. Therefore, the court held that the deed executed by Winters was void, and full title in the condominium belonged to Weiser. a. As will be discussed in Chapter 49, in a *joint tenancy* each tenant owns an undivided interest in the property; on the death of a tenant, his or her interest becomes the property of the surviving tenant. This is called the right of survivorship.

Legal Capacity and Purpose

A principal must have legal capacity to enter into contracts. The logic is simple. A person who cannot legally enter into contracts directly should not be allowed to do it indirectly through an agent. An agent derives the authority to enter into contracts from the principal, and a contract made by an agent

■ **Exhibit 35–1 Sample Power of Attorney**

POWER OF ATTORNEY
GENERAL

Know All Men by These Presents: That I, _____

_____

the undersigned (jointly and severally, if more than one) hereby make, constitute and appoint _____

_____

as true and lawful Attorney for me and in my name, place and stead and for my use and benefit:

(a)   To ask, demand, sue for, recover, collect and receive each and every sum of money, debt, account, legacy, bequest, interest, dividend, annuity and demand (which now is or hereafter shall become due, owing or payable) belonging to or claimed by me, and to use and take any lawful means for the recovery thereof by legal process or otherwise, and to execute and deliver a satisfaction or release therefor, together with the right and power to compromise or compound any claim or demand;

(b)   To exercise any or all of the following powers as to real property, any interest therein and/or any building thereon: To contract for, purchase, receive and take possession thereof and of evidence of title thereto; to lease the same for any term or purpose, including leases for business, residence, and oil and/or mineral development; to sell, exchange, grant or convey the same with or without warranty; and to mortgage, transfer in trust, or otherwise encumber or hypothecate the same to secure payment of a negotiable or non-negotiable note or performance of any obligation or agreement;

(c)   To exercise any or all of the following powers as to all kinds of personal property and goods, wares and merchandise, choses in action and other property in possession or in action: To contract for, buy, sell, exchange, transfer and in any legal manner deal in and with the same; and to mortgage, transfer in trust, or otherwise encumber or hypothecate the same to secure payment of a negotiable or non-negotiable note or performance of any obligation or agreement;

(d)   To borrow money and to execute and deliver negotiable or non-negotiable notes therefor with or without security; and to loan money and receive negotiable or non-negotiable notes therefor with such security as he shall deem proper;

(e)   To create, amend, supplement and terminate any trust and to instruct and advise the trustee of any trust wherein I am or may be trustor or beneficiary; to represent and vote stock, exercise stock rights, accept and deal with any dividend, distribution or bonus, join in any corporate financing, reorganization, merger, liquidation, consolidation or other action and the extension, compromise, conversion, adjustment, enforcement or foreclosure, singly or in conjunction with others of any corporate stock, bond, note, debenture or other security; to compound, compromise, adjust, settle and satisfy any obligation, secured or unsecured, owing by or to me and to give or accept any property and/or money whether or not equal to or less in value than the amount owing in payment, settlement or satisfaction thereof;

(f)   To transact business of any kind or class and as my act and deed to sign, execute, acknowledge and deliver any deed, lease, assignment of lease, covenant, indenture, indemnity, agreement, mortgage, deed of trust, assignment of mortgage or of the beneficial interest under deed of trust, extension or renewal of any obligation, subordination or waiver of priority, hypothecation, bottomry, charter-party, bill of lading, bill of sale, bill, bond, note, whether negotiable or non-negotiable, receipt, evidence of debt, full or partial release or satisfaction of mortgage, judgment and other debt, request for partial or full reconveyance of deed of trust and such other instruments in writing of any kind or class as may be necessary or proper in the premises.

Giving and Granting unto my said Attorney full power and authority to do and perform all and every act and thing whatsoever requisite, necessary or appropriate to be done in and about the premises as fully to all intents and purposes as I might or could do if personally present, hereby ratifying all that my said Attorney shall lawfully do or cause to be done by virtue of these presents. The powers and authority hereby conferred upon my said Attorney shall be applicable to all real and personal property or interests therein now owned or hereafter acquired by me and wherever situate.

My said Attorney is empowered hereby to determine in his sole discretion the time when, purpose for and manner in which any power herein conferred upon him shall be exercised, and the conditions, provisions and covenants of any instrument or document which may be executed by him pursuant hereto; and in the acquisition or disposition of real or personal property, my said Attorney shall have exclusive power to fix the terms thereof for cash, credit and/or property, and if on credit with or without security.

The undersigned, if a married woman, hereby further authorizes and empowers my said Attorney, as my duly authorized agent, to join in my behalf, in the execution of any instrument by which any community real property or any interest therein, now owned or hereafter acquired by my spouse and myself, or either of us, is sold, leased, encumbered, or conveyed.

When the contest so requires, the masculine gender includes the feminine and/or neuter, and the singular number includes the plural.

WITNESS my hand this _____ day of _____ , 19_____

_____   _____

_____   _____

State of California,
    County of _____   } SS.

On _____ , before me, the undersigned, a Notary Public in and for said
State, personally appeared _____

_____

known to me to be the person _____ whose name _____ subscribed
to the within instrument and acknowledged that _____ executed the same.

Witness my hand and official seal.   (Seal) _____

                                                                          Notary Public in and for said State.

is legally viewed as a contract of the principal. It is immaterial whether the agent personally has the legal capacity to make that contract. Any person can be an agent, then, regardless of whether he or she has the capacity to contract. Even a person who is legally incompetent can be appointed an agent. A minor can be an agent but cannot be a principal appointing an agent.[5] In the few states that permit a minor to be a principal, any resulting contracts will be voidable by the minor principal but not by the adult third party.

An agency relationship can be created for any *legal* purpose. One created for an illegal purpose or contrary to public policy is unenforceable. If Jones (as principal) contracts with Smith (as agent) to sell narcotics illegally, the agency relationship is unenforceable, because selling narcotics illegally is a felony and therefore against public policy. It is also illegal for medical doctors and other licensed professionals to employ unlicensed agents to perform professional acts.

Agency by Ratification and Estoppel

On occasion, a person who is in fact not an agent, or who is an agent acting outside the scope of his or her authority, may make a contract on behalf of another (a principal). If the principal approves or affirms that contract by word or by action, an agency relationship is created by *ratification.* Ratification is a matter of intent, and intent can be expressed by either words or conduct.

An agency relationship can also be created by **estoppel.** When a *principal* causes a third person to believe that another person is his or her agent, and the third person deals with the supposed agent, the principal is "estopped to deny" the agency relationship.

Ratification and estoppel, because they pertain to relationships between principals and agents and third parties, will be discussed more fully in the following chapter.

Agency by Operation of Law

In certain situations, an agency relationship may be created by operation of law as a result of statutory requirements. Many state statutes make state officials agents of the government for the service

of process. Service of process is delivery of a summons or other legal papers to the person who is required to respond to them. In most states, a corporation is required to designate an agent for the service of process. Some states require that this agent be the state's secretary of state.[6]

Sometimes agency by operation of law is created to give an agent emergency power to act under unusual circumstances that are not covered by the agreement when failure to act would cause a principal substantial loss. If the agent is unable to contact the principal, the courts will often grant this emergency power.

In some cases, an agency relationship by operation of law may occur when family relationships are involved. For example, suppose one spouse purchases certain basic necessaries and charges them to the other spouse's charge account. The courts will often rule that the latter is liable for payment for such necessaries. Such rulings may be based on a social policy of promoting the general welfare of the spouse who made the purchases or on the assumption that the other spouse has a legal duty to supply necessaries to family members.

■ Duties of Agents and Principals

Once the principal–agent relationship has been created, both parties have duties that govern their conduct. The principal–agent relationship is *fiduciary*—a relationship based on trust. In it, each party owes the other the duty to act with the utmost good faith. Neither party may keep from the other information that has any bearing on their agency relationship.

Agent's Duties to Principal

The duties that an agent owes to a principal are set forth in the agency agreement or arise by operation of law. They are implied from the agency relationship *whether or not the identity of the principal is disclosed to a third party.* Generally, the agent owes the principal the following five duties:

1. Performance.
2. Notification.
3. Loyalty.
4. Obedience.
5. Accounting.

---

5. Exceptions have been granted by some courts to allow a minor to appoint an agent for the limited purpose of contracting for the minor's necessities of life. See, for example, *Casey v. Kastel,* 237 N.Y. 305, 142 N.E. 671 (1924).

6. See, for example, New York Business Corporation Law Section 402(a)(7).

■ **CONCEPT SUMMARY 35.2**
Formation of Principal–Agent Relationship

Method of Formation	Description
By agreement	Formed through express consent (oral or written) or implied from conduct.
By ratification	Principal either by act or agreement ratifies conduct by a person who is not in fact an agent or who acted outside his or her scope of authority.
By estoppel	Principal causes a third person to believe that another person is his or her agent, and the third person acts to his or her detriment in reasonable reliance on that belief.
By operation of law	Based on a social duty (such as the need to support family members) or formed in emergency situations when the agent is unable to contact the principal.

DUTY OF PERFORMANCE An implied condition in every agency contract is the agent's agreement to use reasonable diligence and skill in performing the work. When an agent fails to perform his or her duties entirely, he or she will generally be liable for breach of contract.

The degree of skill or care required of an agent is usually that expected of a reasonable person under similar circumstances. Although in most cases this is interpreted to mean ordinary care, an agent may have presented himself or herself as possessing special skills (such as those that an accountant or attorney possesses). In these situations, the agent is expected to exercise the skill or skills claimed. Failure to do so constitutes a breach of the agent's duty.

For example, an insurance agent who fails to obtain the insurance coverage requested by a principal is guilty of breach of contract. When an agent performs carelessly or negligently, the agent can be liable in tort as well.

In many situations, an agent who does not act for money (a gratuitous, or free, agent) can be subject to the same standards of care and duty to perform as other agents. A gratuitous agent cannot be liable for breach of contract, because there is no contract. A gratuitous agent is subject only to tort liability. Once the agent has begun to act in an agency capacity, however, he or she has the duty to continue to perform in this capacity in an acceptable manner.

For example, Alex Paul's friend Amy Foster is a real estate broker. She (the agent) gratuitously offers to sell Paul's (the principal's) farm, Black Acres. If she never attempts to sell Black Acres, Paul has no legal cause of action to force her to do so. But assume that Foster finds a buyer. She keeps promising the buyer a sales contract but fails to provide one within a reasonable period of time. The buyer becomes disgruntled and seeks another property, and the sale ultimately falls through. Paul has a cause of action in tort for negligence—because Foster failed to use the degree of care reasonably expected of real estate brokers.

The following case raises an interesting question: Did an agent breach his duty to perform by failing to procure a life insurance policy notwithstanding the fact that no life insurance company would have insured the principal anyway—because he used drugs?

BACKGROUND AND FACTS Leonard Bias agreed with Advantage International, Inc., that Advantage would advise and represent Bias in his affairs. On June 17, 1986, the Boston Celtics picked Bias in the first round of the National Basketball Association draft. On June 19, Bias died of cocaine intoxication. Bias's estate sued Advantage in a federal district court, alleging, among other things, that Advantage had failed to procure a $1 million ("jumbo") life insurance policy on Bias, as it had been directed to do. Bias's parents maintained that Advantage had represented to them that

Case 35.3

BIAS v. ADVANTAGE INTERNATIONAL, INC.
United States Court of Appeals, District of Columbia Circuit, 1990.
905 F.2d 1558.

it had secured the policy, and in reliance on the assurances, Bias's parents had not independently sought to buy a policy. The trial court granted summary judgment for Advantage, holding that, in effect, the estate had not suffered any damage from Advantage's failure to obtain the policy because even if Advantage had tried to obtain the policy, it would not have been able to do so because of Bias's cocaine use. The estate appealed, arguing that whether Bias was a drug user and was uninsurable were triable issues of fact and should have gone to the jury.

DECISION AND RATIONALE The United States Court of Appeals affirmed the trial court's judgment. The appellate court stated that the testimony of Bias's former teammates "clearly tends to show that Bias was a cocaine user." The court pointed out that the estate did not attempt to impeach or counter the teammates' testimony. Bias's parents' testimony that they did not know Bias to be a drug user did not rebut the testimony about Bias's drug use on particular occasions. Similarly, drug tests showing that Bias had no cocaine in his system indicated only that Bias had abstained from drug use during the periods preceding the tests. The court concluded that the estate was "not entitled to reach the jury merely on the supposition that the jury might not believe the defendants' witnesses." The court also pointed out that the estate "failed to name a single particular company or provide other evidence that a single company existed which would have issued a jumbo policy in 1986 without inquiring about the applicant's drug use." Thus, there was also "no genuine issue of material fact as to the insurability of a drug user."

DUTY OF NOTIFICATION There is a maxim in agency law that "all the agent knows, the principal knows." This maxim means that a principal will be presumed to know of any statement made by an agent to a third party—because the principal may be bound by it or be liable for any damages resulting from it. Thus, it is only logical that the agent is required to notify the principal of all significant or material matters that come to his or her attention concerning the subject matter of the agency. This is the duty of notification.

For example, Able is Paula's agent for the purchase of a certain property from Tom. In the course of dealing, Able discovers that many years ago Green obtained subsurface mineral rights in this property. Thinking that this is unimportant, Able neglects to tell Paula. The purchase of the land takes place subject to Green's right to mine and remove the minerals. Paula does not have recourse against Tom; that is, Paula cannot rescind the sale or use the existence of Green's right to remove minerals as a defense to avoid going through with the sale. Able had the duty to notify Paula. The fact that he failed to do so and breached his fiduciary duty cannot be allowed to prejudice the rights of the innocent third party, Tom. Paula, however, does have recourse against Able for damages.

DUTY OF LOYALTY Loyalty is one of the most fundamental duties in a fiduciary relationship. Basically stated, the agent has the duty to act solely for the benefit of his or her principal and not in the interest of the agent or a third party.

Numerous principles result from this duty. For example, an agent cannot represent two principals in the same transaction unless both know of the dual capacity and consent to it. Thus, a real estate agent cannot represent both the seller and the buyer, unless the seller and the buyer so agree. A salesperson representing Avon cannot sell products of a competing line at the same time unless Avon consents. In addition, an agent who owns property cannot sell the property to the principal without indicating that ownership prior to the sale. Furthermore, an agent cannot make "secret" profits—that is, an agent employed by a principal to buy cannot buy from himself or herself, and an agent employed to sell cannot become the purchaser without the principal's consent. In short, the agent's loyalty must be undivided. The agent's actions must be strictly for the benefit of the principal and must not result in any secret profit for the agent.

The duty of loyalty means that any information or knowledge acquired through the agency relationship is considered confidential. It would be a breach of loyalty to disclose such information either during the agency relationship or after its termination. Typical examples of confidential information are trade secrets and customer lists compiled by the principal. Note, however, that an agent has the right to use skills and basic knowledge acquired during the course of agency employment in his or her own behalf (such as sales techniques learned during the agency relationship) so long as such actions do not violate confidentiality.

DUTY OF OBEDIENCE When an agent is acting on behalf of the principal, a duty is imposed on the agent to follow all lawful and clearly stated instructions of the principal. The agent violates this duty whenever he or she deviates from such instructions. For example, an automobile salesperson may be liable to the dealer (the salesperson's principal) if, in an effort to close a sale, he or she makes a more extensive warranty than the dealer has indicated it is willing to make and if the buyer subsequently takes advantage of that warranty.

During emergency situations, however, when the principal cannot be consulted, the agent may deviate from instructions without violating the duty of obedience if the circumstances so warrant. When instructions are not clearly stated, the agent can fulfill the duty of obedience by acting in good faith and in a manner reasonable under the circumstances.

DUTY OF ACCOUNTING Unless an agent and a principal agree otherwise, the agent has the duty to keep and make available to the principal an account of all property and money received and paid out on behalf of the principal. This includes gifts from third persons in connection with the agency. For example, a gift from a customer to a salesperson for prompt deliveries made by the salesperson's firm belongs to the firm. The agent has a duty to maintain separate accounts for the principal's funds and for personal funds, and no *commingling* (mixing) of these accounts is allowed. When a licensed professional violates this duty to account, he or she may be subject to disciplinary proceedings by the appropriate regulatory institution. In addition, the agent is liable to the principal for failure to account.

Principal's Duties to Agent

The principal also has certain duties to the agent. Generally these duties include the following:

1. Compensation.
2. Reimbursement and indemnification.
3. Cooperation.
4. Provision of safe working conditions.

The principal's duties to an agent may be express, or they may be implied by law.

DUTY OF COMPENSATION In general, when a principal requests certain services from an agent, the agent reasonably expects payment. A duty is therefore implied for the principal to pay the agent for services rendered. For example, when an accountant or an attorney is asked to act as an agent, compensation is implied. The principal has the duty to pay that compensation in a timely manner.

Except in a gratuitous agency relationship, the principal must pay the agreed-on value (or reasonable value) for an agent's services. When the amount of compensation has been agreed on by the parties, the principal owes the duty to pay it on completion of the agent's specified activities. If no amount has been expressly agreed on, then the principal owes the agent the customary compensation for such services. If no amount has been established either by custom or by law, the principal owes the agent the reasonable value of his or her services.

DUTY OF REIMBURSEMENT AND INDEMNIFICATION Whenever an agent disburses sums of money at the request of the principal, and whenever the agent disburses sums of money to pay for necessary expenses in the course of a reasonable performance of his or her agency duties, the principal has the duty to reimburse. Agents cannot, however, recover for expenses they incur through their own misconduct or negligence.

The principal has the duty to reimburse an agent for authorized payments and to **indemnify** (compensate) an agent for liabilities incurred because of authorized and lawful acts and transactions and also for losses suffered because of the principal's failure to perform his or her duties.

The amount of indemnification is usually specified in the agency contract. If it is not, the courts will look to the nature of the business and the type of loss to determine the amount.

Authorized subagents can recover from either the principal or the agent who hires them, because the subagent is in a fiduciary relationship to both. If the authorized subagent obtains indemnification from the agent who does the hiring, the agent can then seek indemnification from the principal.

DUTY OF COOPERATION A principal has a duty both to cooperate with and to assist an agent in performing his or her duties. The principal must do nothing to prevent such performance. For example, when a principal grants an agent an exclusive territory, the principal cannot compete with the agent or appoint or allow another agent to so compete in violation of the *exclusive agency*. Such competition would expose the principal to liability for the agent's lost sales or profits.

DUTY TO PROVIDE SAFE WORKING CONDITIONS The common law requires the principal to provide safe premises, equipment, and conditions for all agents and employees. The principal has a duty to inspect working conditions and to warn agents and employees about any unsafe areas. If the relationship is one of employment, the employer's liability is frequently covered by workers' compensation insurance, which is the primary remedy for an employee's injury on the job.

■ Remedies and Rights of Agents and Principals

It is said that every wrong has its remedy. In business situations, disputes between agents and principals may arise out of either contract or tort laws and carry corresponding remedies. These remedies include monetary damages, termination of the agency relationship, injunction, and required accountings.

Agent's Rights and Remedies against Principal

For every duty of the principal, the agent has a corresponding right. Therefore, the agent has the right to be compensated, reimbursed, and indemnified and to work in a safe environment. An agent also has the right to perform agency duties without interference by the principal.

Remedies of the agent for breach of duty by the principal follow normal contract and tort remedies. For example, under appropriate circumstances, an agent can lawfully withhold further performance and demand that the principal give an accounting.

When the principal–agent relationship is not contractual, an agent has no right to specific performance. An agent can recover for past services and future damages but cannot force the principal to allow him or her to continue acting as an agent.

Principal's Rights and Remedies against Agent

In general, a principal has contract remedies for an agent's breach of fiduciary duties. The principal also has tort remedies for fraud, misrepresentation, negligence, deceit, libel, slander, and trespass committed by the agent. In addition, any breach of a fiduciary duty by an agent may justify the principal's termination of the agency. The main actions available to the principal are constructive trust, avoidance, and indemnification.

CONSTRUCTIVE TRUST Anything an agent obtains by virtue of the employment or agency relationship belongs to the principal. It is a breach of an agent's fiduciary duty to retain secretly benefits or profits that, by right, belong to the principal. Courts in this case will impose a **constructive trust.** The agent actually holds the money on behalf of the principal, and the principal can recover it in a lawsuit. For example, Andrews, a purchasing agent, gets cash rebates from a customer. If Andrews keeps the rebates, he violates his fiduciary duty to his principal, Metcalf. On finding out about the cash rebates, Metcalf can sue Andrews and recover them.

An agent is also prohibited from taking advantage of the agency relationship to obtain goods or property that the principal wants to purchase. For example, Peterson (the principal) wants to purchase property in the suburbs. Cox, Peterson's agent, learns that a valuable tract of land has just become available. Cox cannot buy the land for herself. Peterson gets the right of first refusal. If Cox purchases the land for her own benefit, the courts will impose a constructive trust on the land; that is, the land will be held for and on behalf of the principal despite the fact that the agent attempted to buy it in her own name.

AVOIDANCE   When an agent breaches the agency agreement or agency duties under a contract, the principal has a right to avoid any contract entered into with the agent. This right of avoidance is at the election of the principal.

In the following case, a real estate agent was supposedly acting on behalf of a landowner for the sale of real estate. The trial court decided that the agent had breached his fiduciary duties, and therefore the principal could avoid the contract.

BACKGROUND AND FACTS   Sid Ramsey was a licensed real estate broker and was also in the business of buying and holding land for resale. John Gordon, the owner of approximately 181 acres of land, engaged Ramsey's services as a broker to find a buyer. When Ramsey learned that the land was rapidly appreciating in value, he told Gordon that he would buy the land himself. Gordon agreed to sell Ramsey the tract for $800 per acre. A contract of sale was drawn up, but before it was executed, Gordon conveyed the property to a third party for the same price ($800 per acre). Meanwhile, Ramsey, acting for himself, had begun negotiating for the resale of the property to another customer for a price of $1,250 per acre. When Ramsey learned that Gordon had conveyed the property to another buyer, he blamed Gordon for his lost profits. Claiming that he had lost over $90,000 in profits on the resale of the property, Ramsey sued Gordon in a Texas state court. Gordon maintained that Ramsey had breached his fiduciary duties as Gordon's agent by not finding a buyer at the best price. The trial court held for Gordon, and Ramsey appealed.

DECISION AND RATIONALE   The Court of Civil Appeals of Texas affirmed the judgment of the trial court. Ramsey could not recover damages from Gordon because he breached the duty he owed as Gordon's agent. Ramsey was obliged to disclose to Gordon anything he knew that might affect Gordon. Ramsey knew that the value of the land far exceeded $800 per acre, because he was in the midst of negotiating a resale to another purchaser for more than $1,000 per acre. Because Ramsey did not tell Gordon about the actual value of the land, agency law dictates that Gordon could void his contract with Ramsey. The court said, "Whenever an agent breaches his duty to his principal by becoming personally interested in an agency agreement, the contract is voidable at the election of the principal without full knowledge of all the facts surrounding the agent's interest."

Case 35.4

RAMSEY v. GORDON

Court of Civil Appeals of Texas—Waco, 1978.
567 S.W.2d 868.

INDEMNIFICATION   A principal can be sued by a third party for an agent's negligent conduct, and in certain situations the principal can sue the agent for an equal amount of damages. This is called *indemnification*. The same holds true if the agent violates the principal's instructions. For example, Lewis (the principal) tells his agent, Moore, who is a used car salesman, to make no warranties for the used cars. Moore is eager to make a sale to Walters, a third party, and makes a warranty for the car's engine. Lewis is not absolved from liability to Walters for engine failure, but if Walters sues Lewis, Lewis normally can then sue Moore for indemnification for violating his instructions.

Sometimes it is difficult to distinguish between instructions of the principal that limit an agent's authority and those that are merely advice. For example, Willis (the principal) owns an office supply company; Jones (the agent) is the manager. Willis tells Jones, "Don't order any more inventory this month." Willis goes on vacation. A larger order comes in from a local business, and the present inventory is insufficient to meet it. What is Jones to do? In this situation, Jones probably has the inherent authority to order more inventory despite Willis's statement. It is unlikely that Jones would be required to indemnify Willis in the event that the local business subsequently canceled the order.

■ Terms and Concepts

agency 626
agent 626
constructive trust 638
employee 627

equal dignity rule 629
estoppel 633
indemnify 637

independent contractor 627
power of attorney 629
principal 626

■ For Review

1. What formalities are required to create an agency relationship?
2. What is the general nature of the duties that agents and principals owe each other? What are specific duties that an agent owes to his or her principal?
3. What are specific duties that a principal owes to his or her agent?
4. First Nation Insurance Co. hires Patrice to open offices for First Nation in California. Patrice is to select the cities in which the offices will be located and hire persons to staff the offices. She will receive a salary and a commission. Is Patrice an employee or an independent contractor? Is Patrice an agent?
5. In the previous problem, if Patrice fails to open offices for First Nation in California, on what legal theory might she be held liable to First Nation? If Patrice opens the offices but hires inexperienced, untrained, and incompetent persons to staff them, on what legal theory might she be held liable to First Nation?

■ Questions and Case Problems

35-1. Paul Gett is a well-known, wealthy financier living in the city of Torris. Adam Wade, a friend of Gett, tells Timothy Brown that he is Gett's agent for the purchase of rare coins. Wade even shows Brown a local newspaper clipping mentioning Gett's interest in coin collecting. Brown, knowing of Wade's friendship with Gett, contracts with Wade to sell a rare coin valued at $25,000 to Gett. Wade takes the coin and disappears with it. On the date of contract payment Brown seeks to collect from Gett, claiming Wade's agency made Gett liable. Gett does not deny that Wade was a friend, but he claims that Wade was never his agent. Discuss fully whether an agency was in existence at the time the contract for the rare coin was made.

35-2. Alice is hired by Peter as an agent to sell a piece of property owned by Peter. The price to be obtained is to be at least $30,000. Alice discovers that because a shopping mall is planned for the area of Peter's property, the fair market value of the property will be at least $45,000 and could be higher. Alice forms a real estate partnership with her cousin Carl, and she prepares for Peter's signature a contract for $32,000 for sale of the property to Carl. Peter signs the contract. Just before closing and passage of title, Peter learns about the shopping mall and the increased fair market value of his property. Peter refuses to deed the property to Carl. Carl claims that Alice, as agent, solicited a price above that agreed on in the creation of the agency and that the contract is therefore binding and enforceable. Discuss fully whether Peter is bound to this contract.

35-3. John Paul Corp. made the following contracts:
(a) A contract with Able Construction to build an addition to the corporate office building.
(b) A contract with a CPA, a recent college graduate, to head the cost accounting section.

(c) A contract with a salesperson to travel a designated area to solicit orders (contracts) for the corporation.
Able contracts with Apex for materials for the addition; the CPA hires an experienced accountant to advise her on certain accounting procedures; and the salesperson contracts to sell a large order to Green, agreeing to deliver the goods in person within twenty days. Later, Able refuses to pick up the materials, the CPA is in default in paying the hired consultant, and the salesperson does not deliver on time. Apex, the accountant, and Green claim John Paul Corp. is liable under agency law. Discuss fully whether an agency relationship was created by John Paul with Able, the CPA, or the salesperson.

35-4. Able is hired by Peters as a traveling salesperson. Able not only solicits orders but delivers the goods and collects payments from his customers. Able places all payments in his private checking account and at the end of each month draws sufficient cash from his bank to cover the payments made. Peters is totally unaware of this procedure. Because of a slowdown in the economy, Peters tells all his salespeople to offer 20 percent discounts on orders. Able solicits orders, but he offers only 15 percent discounts, pocketing the extra 5 percent paid by customers. Able has not lost any orders by this practice, and he is rated one of Peters's top salespersons. Peters learns of Able's actions. Discuss fully Peters's rights in this matter.

35-5. L.M.T. Steel Products, Inc., contracted with a school to install numerous room partitions. To accomplish this work, L.M.T. hired a man named Webster. Webster was not a regular employee of L.M.T., and it was stipulated that he was to be paid by the number of feet of partitions installed. Webster did not have a contractor's license. He hired other workers to do the installing, and these workers were paid by L.M.T. Webster was given blueprints by L.M.T., but he was not otherwise at any time actively supervised by L.M.T. on the job. Needing to place a telephone call to L.M.T., Webster drove his own personal vehicle to a public telephone. On the way, he negligently collided with another car, and an occupant of that car, Peirson, was injured. Peirson sued L.M.T., claiming that Webster was an employee. L.M.T. claimed that Webster was an independent contractor. Who was correct? Explain. [*L.M.T. Steel Products, Inc. v. Peirson,* 47 Md.App. 633, 425 A.2d 242 (1981)]

35-6. Evan Smith experienced a heart attack in the emergency room of Baptist Memorial Hospital after being given a dose of penicillin for a sore throat. Smith sued the attending physician as well as the hospital. The hospital called itself a full-service hospital with emergency room facilities. Baptist Memorial considered the doctors as independent contractors, not agents. For example, for tax and accounting purposes the doctors were not treated as employees of the hospital. Based on this information, discuss whether the doctors who treated patients in the emergency room were independent contractors or agents. [*Smith v. Baptist Memorial Hospital System,* 720 S.W.2d 618 (Tex. App.–San Antonio 1986)]

35-7. Howard and Virginia Bankerd were having marital difficulties. In 1968 Howard decided to leave ''for the west,'' but before he did so, he executed a power of attorney to his lawyer, Arthur King. Virginia continued to reside in their home in Maryland and assumed all expenses for the home. In 1975 Howard gave King an updated power of attorney and asked King to sell the property ''on such terms as to him [King] seem best.'' In 1977 Virginia asked the lawyer to exercise his power of attorney and transfer her husband's interest in the property to her. She wished to sell the property and retire. After three letters failed to elicit any response from Howard, King concluded that Howard ''didn't give a damn'' about the property. King therefore transferred the property to Virginia by deed in 1978. Virginia paid no consideration for the transfer. Howard subsequently sued King, claiming that King had breached his duty of loyalty and trust by transferring the property gratuitously to Virginia. King argued that he had acted reasonably under the circumstances. The trial court held for Howard Bankerd, and King appealed. Had King breached his fiduciary duty of loyalty and trust by transferring the property gratuitously to Virginia? Discuss fully. [*King v. Bankerd,* 303 Md. 98, 492 A.2d 608 (1985)]

35-8. Broyles signed a sales representative's agreement with NCH Corp. that included covenants not to compete and not to solicit NCH customers after termination of the agreement. NCH maintained detailed and costly records of its routes and customers. It considered this information to be valuable and sensitive, although all the data was readily ascertainable from other sources. Broyles transcribed the names and information with intent to use this material after he left NCH's employ. He later voluntarily terminated his employment with NCH and went to work for a competing firm. Based on the information he had transcribed while an employee of NCH, he solicited business from some of his former customers. NCH sued Broyles, claiming that the use of his list was a breach of his employment contract and a breach of his fiduciary duty to NCH. Discuss whether NCH

was successful in its claim that Broyles had breached his fiduciary duty. [*NCH Corp. v. Broyles,* 749 F.2d 247 (5th Cir. 1985)]

35-9. Aztec Petroleum Corp. arranged to have Douglas buy oil and gas leases for Aztec. In return for his services, Douglas was to receive an initial $5,000 plus a royalty interest in the leases he obtained. Douglas obtained a number of leases for Aztec but represented to Aztec that the prices paid for the leases were higher than they actually were. By sending Aztec photocopies of checks altered both as to payee and amount, along with forged receipts, Douglas was able to keep for himself a substantial amount of the money that Aztec had entrusted to him for payment of the leases. This money was used by Douglas for personal purchases, including two new cars, a boat, and other personal items. When Aztec refused to grant Douglas the promised royalty interest in the leases, Douglas brought suit to obtain it. The trial court held for Aztec, and Douglas appealed. In view of Douglas's deceptive activities, is Aztec required to grant the royalty interest? Discuss fully. [*Douglas v. Aztec Petroleum Corp.,* 695 S.W.2d 312 (Tex.App. 1985)]

35-10. Brenda Tarver worked as an independent contractor with Dianne Landers's real estate agency. The agents in the firm worked on a commission basis, and Tarver's contract read that she would receive 30 percent of the agency's commissions to which she was ''entitled as either listing and/or selling agent'' in connection with a sale. In the spring of 1984 Charles Smith and his wife contacted the agency concerning some property for sale listed by the agency and advertised in the local newspaper. The Smiths were referred to Tarver, who showed them the property and handled their offer to purchase the property and the seller's counteroffer. In all, Tarver negotiated three offers and three counteroffers between the seller and the buyer. Later, however, the Smiths returned to the agency and, because Tarver was out of the office negotiated with Dianne Landers concerning the last counteroffer they had rejected. After some modifications were made, they reached an agreement with the seller and purchased the property. Landers would not pay Tarver a commission for the sale because Tarver had not negotiated the final purchase. Tarver sued to recover her commission on the grounds that it was customary in the real estate office that the initial selling agent would be paid the commission and that when the initial selling agent was absent from the office, another agent would handle negotiations—but not receive the commission if a sale resulted. Who will prevail in court? Explain. [*Tarver v. Landers,* 486 So.2d 294 (La.App. 1986)]

35-11. A Question of Ethics

Mallie Brackens consulted Dr. Floyd Jones in April 1983 because of stomach pains. Dr. Jones admitted her to the Detroit Osteopathic Hospital for the purpose of performing a gastrojejunostomy (a surgical joining of the stomach with the middle section of the small intestine). After the surgery Brackens was readmitted to the hospital twice because of dehydration and other problems and was seen by Drs. Taras and Tobes—whom she had never met before—for

upper gastrointestinal examinations. Her problems persisted and finally, in December 1983, she learned from physicians at another hospital that instead of a gastrojejunostomy, Dr. Jones had performed a gastroileostomy, which is a bypass procedure performed on obese persons. Brackens sued the Detroit Osteopathic Hospital, alleging that it was liable for the negligence of its agents. Drs. Taras and Tobes, who had failed to detect the improperly performed gastrojejunostomy when they examined her. Both the trial court and the appellate court in this case held that, generally speaking, a hospital is not liable for the negligence of a physician who is an independent contractor and merely uses the hospital's facilities to render treatment to his or her patients. Although the trial court granted the hospital's motion for summary judgment, the appellate court remanded the case for trial. The appellate court reasoned that if an individual looked to the hospital

to provide medical treatment and there was a representation by the hospital that medical treatment would be performed by physicians working therein, an agency by estoppel can be found. [Brackens v. Detroit Osteopathic Hospital, *174 Mich.App. 290, 435 N.W.2d 472 (1989)*]

1. Brackens testified that during her confinement in the hospital, she at all times believed that Drs. Taras and Tobes were hospital physicians employed by the hospital. Do you think that, in this case, an agency by estoppel should be found? In your opinion, would such a finding be a fair solution? Why or why not?

2. What general ethical principle or principles underlie the theory of agency by estoppel.

3. Why must the *principal* in some way be responsible for creating the appearance of an agency before agency by estoppel will be found? What ethical considerations underlie this requirement?

Chapter 36

Liability to Third Parties and Termination

Once the principal–agent relationship has been created, attention often focuses on the rights of third persons who deal with the agent. The first part of this chapter is concerned with the rights of these third parties when they *contract* with agents. Such contracts will make an agent's principal liable to the third party only if the agent had authority to make the contract or if the principal ratified, or was estopped from denying, the agent's acts.

The second part of the chapter will deal with an agent's liability to third parties in contract and tort and the principal's liability to third parties because of an agent's torts. The chapter concludes with a discussion of how agency relationships are terminated.

■ Scope of Agent's Authority

A principal's liability in a contract with a third party arises from the authority given the agent to enter legally binding contracts on the principal's behalf. An agent's authority to act is of two types:

1. Actual (express or implied).
2. Apparent (or by estoppel).

If an agent contracts outside the scope of his or her authority, the principal may still become liable by ratifying the contract.

Actual Authority

Actual authority can be either *express* or *implied.* **Express authority** is embodied in that which the principal has engaged the agent to do. Express authority can be given orally or in writing. In some cases, as mentioned in Chapter 35, express authority must be given in writing. For example, the express authority granted by a *power of attorney* must be in writing. In addition, the *equal dignity rule* in most states requires that if the contract being executed is or must be in writing, then the agent's authority must also be in writing. A principal may, however, ratify in writing an act done originally without written authority. For example, Palmer (the principal) orally asks Larkins (the agent) to sell a ranch that Palmer owns. Larkins finds a buyer and signs a sales contract (a contract for an interest in realty must be

643

in writing) on behalf of Palmer to sell the ranch. The buyer cannot enforce the contract unless Palmer subsequently ratifies Larkins's agency status *in writing*. Once the contract has been ratified, either party can enforce rights under the contract.

Implied authority is conferred by custom, can be inferred from the position the agent occupies, or is implied by virtue of being reasonably necessary to carry out express authority. For example, Adams is employed by Packard Grocery to manage one of its stores. Packard has not specified (expressly stated) Adams's authority to contract with third persons. In this situation, authority to manage a business implies authority to do what is reasonably required (as is customary or can be inferred from a manager's position) to operate the business. This includes making contracts for obtaining employee help, for buying merchandise and equipment, and even for advertising the products sold in the store.

Because implied authority is conferred on the basis of custom, it is important for third persons to be familiar with the custom of the trade. The list of rules that have developed to determine what authority is implied based on custom or on the agent's position is extensive. In general, implied authority is authority customarily associated with the position occupied by the agent or authority that can be inferred from the express authority given to the agent to fully perform his or her duties. The test is whether it was reasonable for the agent to believe that he or she had the authority to enter the contract in question.

Apparent Authority and Estoppel

Actual authority (express or implied) arises from what the principal manifests *to the agent*. An agent has **apparent authority** when the principal, by either word or action, causes a *third party* reasonably to believe that an agent has authority to act, even though the agent has no express or implied authority. If the third party changes his or her position in reliance on the principal's representations, the principal may be *estopped* from denying that the agent had authority.

For example, a traveling salesperson has no express authority to collect for orders solicited from customers. Because the agent neither possesses the goods ordered nor delivers them, the agent also has no implied authority to collect. As-

sume that a customer, Carla, pays an agent, Adam, for a solicited order. Adam then takes the payment to the principal's accounting department. An accountant accepts payment and sends Carla a receipt. This procedure is thereafter followed for other orders solicited and paid for by Carla. Later Adam solicits an order, and Carla pays Adam as before. This time, however, Adam absconds with the money. Can Carla claim that the payment to Adam was authorized and thus, in effect, a payment to the principal? The answer is yes, because the principal's *repeated* acts of accepting Carla's payment led Carla reasonably to believe that Adam had authority to receive payments for goods solicited. Although Adam did not have express or implied authority, the principal's conduct gave Adam apparent authority to collect. The principal would be estopped from claiming that the agent had no authority to collect in this particular case.

Sometimes a principal will go beyond mere statements or actions that convince a third party that a certain person is the principal's agent. If, for example, the principal has "clothed the agent" with both possession and apparent ownership of the principal's property, the agent has very broad powers and can deal with the property as if he or she were the true owner.

For example, to deceive certain creditors, Baker (the principal) and Hunter (the agent) agree verbally that Hunter will hold certain stock certificates for Baker. Because the certificates are bearer paper (that is, they do not require indorsement to be transferred), Hunter's possession and apparent ownership of the stock certificates are such strong indications of ownership that a reasonable person would conclude that Hunter was the actual owner. If Hunter negotiates the stock certificates to a third person, Baker will be estopped from denying Hunter's authority to transfer the stock.

When land is involved, courts have held that possession alone is not a sufficient indication of ownership. (See Chapter 51 for details.) If, on the other hand, the agent also possesses the deed to the property and sells the property against the principal's wishes to an unsuspecting buyer, the principal normally cannot cancel the sale or assert a claim to title.

The following case illustrates a situation in which an agency was deemed to exist on the basis of apparent authority.

BACKGROUND AND FACTS Red River Commodities, Inc. (RRC), contracted to buy 250,000 pounds of sunflowers from Kelby Eidsness. Because of a drought, Kelby delivered only 75,084 pounds. The contract stated that if Kelby could not deliver as promised due to an event unanticipated at the time that the contract was formed, Kelby would be excused from performance only if he seasonably notified RRC. Kelby told Richard Frith, RRC's contracting representative, about his poor crop before the harvest. The contract said, "The contracting representative * * * does not have the authority to alter or vary the terms of this agreement. He is not an agent of RRC." Nevertheless, Frith often contacted growers for RRC to help with their production problems and reported to RRC. Kelby assumed that Frith was an RRC agent and that notice to Frith would suffice as notice to RRC. In RRC's suit against Kelby in a North Dakota state court for breach of contract, RRC's manager testified that Frith was his "go between" with growers. RRC insisted that Frith was not an RRC agent and had no authority to bind RRC. The trial court directed a verdict for RRC, holding, among other things, that Kelby failed to give notice of his inability to perform because Frith was "an independent sales representative" and "not an agent * * * insofar as production, acts of God, waivers, and the like are concerned." Kelby appealed.

DECISION AND RATIONALE The Supreme Court of North Dakota reversed the trial court's decision. The state supreme court explained that how a principal and agent describe their relationship between themselves does not determine what their relationship is to others. The court pointed out that agency is apparent when "the conduct of the supposed agent is consistent with an agency, and where, in a particular transaction, someone is justified in dealing with the supposed agent." An apparent agency "must rest upon conduct or communications of the principal which, reasonably interpreted, causes a third person to believe that the agent has authority to act for and on behalf of the principal." Noting evidence that Frith knew of Kelby's production problems, the court stated that "[n]otice to an agent is ordinarily notice to the principal." The court remanded the case for further proceedings consistent with its opinion, telling the trial court to reconsider Kelby's notice to Frith "with a correct understanding of the law of agency."

ETHICAL CONSIDERATIONS RRC admittedly relied on Frith to perform a variety of agent's duties. One could argue that it was unethical for RRC to deny the agency relationship when the denial favored RRC to the detriment of Kelby.

Case 36.1

RED RIVER COMMODITIES, INC. v. EIDSNESS

Supreme Court of North Dakota, 1990.
459 N.W.2d 805.

Emergency Powers

When an unforeseen emergency demands action by the agent to protect or preserve the property and rights of the principal, but the agent is unable to communicate with the principal, the agent has emergency power.

For example, Fisher (the agent) is an engineer for Pacific Railroad (the principal). While Fisher is acting within the scope of his employment, he falls under the train many miles from home and is severely injured. Davis, the conductor (also an agent), directs Thompson, a doctor, to give medical aid to Fisher and to charge Pacific for the medical services. Davis has no express authority to bind Pacific Railroad for the services of Thompson. Yet, because of the emergency situation, the law recognizes him as having authority to act appropriately under the circumstances.

Ratification

Ratification is the affirmation of a previously unauthorized contract or act. Ratification can be either express or implied. Generally, only a principal can ratify. The principal must be aware of all material facts; otherwise, the ratification is not effective. Ratification binds the principal to the agent's acts and treats the acts or contracts as if they had been authorized by the principal *from the outset*. If the principal does not ratify, there is no contract binding the principal, and the third party's agreement with the agent is viewed merely as an unaccepted offer. Because the third party's agreement is treated as an unaccepted offer, the third party can revoke the offer (rescind the agreement) at any time before the principal ratifies, without liability. The agent, however, may well be liable to the third party for misrepresenting his or her authority.

The principal's acceptance (that is, the ratification) is binding only if the principal *knows* all the terms of the contract. If not, the principal can thereafter rescind ratification unless, of course, the third party has proceeded to change position in reliance on the contract.

Suppose an agent, without authority, contracts with a third person on behalf of a principal for repair work to the principal's office building. The principal learns of the contract from the agent and agrees to "some repair work," thinking that it will involve only patching and painting the exterior of the building. In fact, the contract includes resurfacing the parking lot, which the principal does not want done. On learning of the additional provision, the principal rescinds the contract. If the third party has made no preparations to do the work (such as purchasing materials, hiring additional workers, or renting equipment), then the principal can still re-

scind. But if the third party has, to his or her detriment, relied on the principal's ratification by making preparations, the principal must reimburse the third party for the cost of the preparations.

Two important points must be stressed. First, it is immaterial whether the principal's lack of knowledge results from the agent's fraud or is simply a mistake on the principal's part. If the third party has not changed position in reliance on the principal, the principal can repudiate the ratification. The unauthorized contract remains an offer, and the principal's acceptance is not valid, because contract law provides that one cannot accept terms one does not know about. Second, the entire transaction must be ratified; a principal cannot affirm the desirable parts of a contract and reject the undesirable parts.

Death or incapacity of the third party *before* ratification will void an unauthorized contract. Most courts will also recognize an intervening and extraordinary change of circumstances as a basis for setting aside a principal's ratification to permit a third party to revoke.

Assume that Able, without authority, enters into a contract with a third party who wants to purchase Paula's shopping center. The following night the shopping center is destroyed by fire. Paula's subsequent ratification will not be effective to bind the third party. The courts will reason that it is unjust to hold a third party liable in such a case and will permit the transaction to be avoided despite ratification.

The requirements for ratification are summarized in *Concept Summary 36.1*.

EXPRESS RATIFICATION If a principal's statements or conduct express an intent to be bound,

---

■ CONCEPT SUMMARY 36.1   Requirements for Ratification

1. The presumptive agent must have purportedly acted on behalf of a principal who subsequently ratifies.
2. The principal must know of all material facts involved in the transaction.
3. The agent's act must be affirmed in its entirety by the principal.
4. The principal must have the legal capacity to authorize the transaction at the time the agent engages in the act and at the time the principal ratifies.
5. The principal's affirmance must occur prior to the withdrawal of the third party from the transaction or prior to a change in circumstances that would make holding the third party to the transaction unjust.
6. The principal must observe the same formalities when he or she approves the act purportedly done by the agent on his or her behalf as would have been required to authorize it initially.

the prior unauthorized act will be ratified, and the principal will become a party to the contract.

For example, Smith (the agent) negotiates the sale of a shipment of oranges to World Markets without the authorization of Samuelson (the principal). Samuelson sees the completed paperwork and tells Smith to go ahead with it. Samuelson thus expressly ratifies the sale and is now bound to the terms of the sales contract.

IMPLIED RATIFICATION Implied ratification occurs most commonly when a principal decides to accept the benefits of a previously unauthorized transaction. In the preceding example, if Samuelson had said nothing to Smith but had known of the unauthorized acts and failed to repudiate or object to them within a reasonable time, the contract would have been ratified. In addition, if World Markets had paid for the oranges and if Samuelson, on learning that World Markets had paid, did not object or repudiate, Samuelson would have impliedly ratified the contract.

The following case illustrates the need of the principal to promptly repudiate unauthorized acts of an agent, once he or she knows about them, to avoid ratification.

BACKGROUND AND FACTS Charles Theis maintained an investment account with the brokerage firm of duPont, Glore Forgan Inc. Theis discovered that Craig Benjamin, a duPont account executive, was making unauthorized transactions in his account and reprimanded him. Theis closed the account when Benjamin directly contravened Theis's order not to buy on May 24, 1968. Theis filed suit against duPont in a Kansas state court for all unauthorized trading by Benjamin from the inception of the Theis account. The trial court allowed recovery on only the May 24 transaction. DuPont appealed.

Case 36.2

THEIS v. duPONT, GLORE FORGAN INC.

Supreme Court of Kansas, 1973.
212 Kan. 301,
510 P.2d 1212.

DECISION AND RATIONALE The Supreme Court of Kansas affirmed the trial court's judgment. Although the court concluded that Theis had ratified Benjamin's earlier unauthorized actions, duPont, Glore Forgan was held liable for the May 24 unauthorized act. The court held that "[r]atification is the adoption or confirmation by a principal of an act performed on his behalf by an agent [who performed the act] without authority. * * * On acquiring knowledge of the unauthorized act of an agent, the principal should promptly repudiate the act, otherwise it will be presumed he has ratified and affirmed the act." Thus, Theis's failure to promptly repudiate Benjamin's earlier unauthorized actions constituted ratification. On discovery of the unauthorized May 24 transaction, however, Theis immediately closed his account. The court considered this to be an immediate, express repudiation of the unauthorized transaction and held duPont liable.

Liability for Contracts

Principals are classified as disclosed, partially disclosed, or undisclosed.[1] A **disclosed principal** is a principal whose identity is known by the third party at the time the contract is made by the agent. A **partially disclosed principal** is a principal whose identity is not known by the third party, but the third party knows that the agent is or may be acting for a principal at the time the contract is made. An **undisclosed principal** is a principal whose identity is totally unknown by the third party, and the third party has no knowledge that the agent is acting in an agency capacity at the time the contract is made.

Disclosed and Partially Disclosed Principals

If an agent acts within the scope of his or her authority, a disclosed or partially disclosed principal is liable to a third party for a contract made by the agent. Ordinarily, if the principal is disclosed, an

---

1. Restatement (Second) of Agency, Section 4.

■ CONCEPT SUMMARY 36.2
Authority of Agent to Bind Principal and Third Party

Authority of Agent	Definition	Effect on Principal and Third Party
Express authority	Authority expressly given by the principal to the agent.	Principal and third party are bound in contract.
Implied authority	Authority implied by custom, from the position in which the principal has placed the agent, or because it is necessary to carry out expressly authorized duties and responsibilities.	
Apparent authority	Authority created when the conduct of the principal leads a third party to believe the principal's agent has authority.	
Unauthorized acts	Acts committed by an agent that are outside the scope of his or her express, implied, or apparent authority.	Principal and third party are not bound in contract—*unless* the principal ratifies prior to the third party's withdrawal.

agent has no contractual liability for the nonperformance of the principal or of the third party.

If the agent has no authority but nevertheless contracts purportedly on behalf of a disclosed principal, the principal cannot be held liable in contract by a third party, but the agent is liable on a warranty theory (discussed below).

In most states, if the principal is partially disclosed, the principal and agent are both treated as parties to the contract, and the third party can hold either liable for contractual nonperformance.[2]

Undisclosed Principals

When neither the fact of agency nor the identity of the principal is disclosed, a third party is deemed to be dealing with the agent personally, and the agent is liable as a party on the contract.

For example, in a contract for the sale of a horse, a third party knows only that Scammon (the agent) wants to purchase the horse. The third party does not know that Scammon is actually negotiating for Johnson (the principal). Scammon signs a written contract in her own name, not indicating any agency relationship. She delivers the horse to Johnson, who is in fact the principal, but Johnson refuses to pay her. Scammon tries to return the

horse to the third party, who refuses to take it. The third party is entitled to hold Scammon liable for payment. The agent's subjective intent is not relevant. The third party contracted with the agent on the basis of the *agent's* credit and reputation, not the undisclosed principal's. Therefore, the agent is liable.

In contrast, if the agent has acted within the scope of authority, the undisclosed principal is fully bound to perform just as if the principal had been fully disclosed at the time the contract was made. Exceptions to this rule are made in the following circumstances:

1. The undisclosed principal was expressly excluded as a party in the contract. For example, an agent contracts for a lease of a building with a landlord. The landlord does not know of the agency, and the lease specially lists the agent as tenant, with no right of assignment without the landlord's consent. The undisclosed principal cannot enforce the lease.

2. The contract is a negotiable instrument. Here, the UCC provides that only the agent is liable if the instrument neither names the principal nor shows that the agent signed in a representative capacity.[3]

---

2.   Restatement (Second) of Agency, Section 321.

3.   UCC 3-401(1), 3-403(2)(a). Extrinsic evidence to show an agency relationship is not normally admissible.

3. The performance of the agent is personal to the contract, allowing the third party to refuse the principal's performance. Typical examples involve extensions of credit and highly personal service contracts.

4. The third party would not have entered into a contract with the principal had the third party known the principal's identity, the agent or the principal knew this, and the third party rescinds the contract.

If the agent is forced to pay the third party, and if the agent has contracted within the scope of authority granted, the agent is entitled to indemnifi-

cation by the principal. It was the principal's duty to perform even though his or her identity was undisclosed.[4] Once his or her identity is revealed, in *most* states, the third party has a right to elect to hold *either* the principal or the agent liable on the contract.

In the following case, the undisclosed principal creates a liability problem for the travel agent.

---

4. If Ann is a gratuitous agent, and the principal accepts the benefits of Ann's contract with a third party, then the principal will be liable to Ann on the theory of quasi contract (see Chapter 9).

BACKGROUND AND FACTS Steven Rosen bought a package tour for an African safari from Deporter-Butterworth Tours, Inc. Deporter-Butterworth failed to disclose that it was a special agent for the tour's sponsor, World Trek. Before buying the package, Rosen had contact with Deporter-Butterworth but not with World Trek (making World Trek an undisclosed principal). Rosen planned to travel through Europe and join the tour in Egypt. Before leaving the United States, Rosen told Deporter-Butterworth where he could be reached in Europe and in Egypt before joining the tour. When the tour itinerary had to be changed, Deporter-Butterworth failed to contact Rosen, leaving him stranded in Egypt for a week. Rosen sued Deporter-Butterworth, which claimed that it was not liable because it was an agent for World Trek, which was thus the proper party to sue. The trial court entered a judgment for Rosen, and Deporter-Butterworth appealed.

Case 36.3

ROSEN v. DEPORTER-BUTTERWORTH TOURS, INC.

Appellate Court of Illinois, 1978.
62 Ill.App.3d 762,
379 N.E.2d 407,
19 Ill.Dec. 743.

DECISION AND RATIONALE The Appellate Court of Illinois affirmed the trial court's judgment. The evidence was conclusive that Deporter-Butterworth acted negligently in not informing Rosen of the change in the tour. The record also revealed that Deporter-Butterworth was an agent for World Trek. Although generally only a principal is liable for a breach of contract by an agent, an agent is liable when the agency relationship is undisclosed. Therefore, Deporter-Butterworth, and not World Trek, was liable to Rosen. The court concluded: "The legal principle that an agent is liable as a principal [to] a third party in the case of an undisclosed agency relationship is well established and needs no citation for authority. * * * [I]f an agent does not disclose the existence of an agency relationship and the identity of his principal, he binds himself to the third party with whom he acts as if he, himself, were the principal."

Warranties of Agent

When the agent lacks authority or exceeds the scope of authority, the agent's liability to a third party is based on the theory of breach of implied warranty of authority, not on breach of the contract itself.[5]

The agent's implied warranty of authority can be breached intentionally or by a good faith mistake.[6] The agent's liability remains, as long as the third party has relied on the agency status. Conversely, when the third party knows at the time the contract is made that the agent is mistaken about

---

5. The agent is not liable on the contract because the agent was never intended personally to be a party to the contract.

6. If the agent intentionally misrepresents his or her authority, then the agent can also be liable in tort for fraud.

the extent of his or her authority, or when the agent indicates to the third party *uncertainty* about the extent of authority, the agent is not personally liable for breach of warranty.

Liability for Agent's Torts

Obviously, an agent is liable for his or her own torts. A principal may also be liable for an agent's torts if they result from:

1. The principal's own tortious conduct.
2. The principal's authorization of a tortious act.
3. The agent's unauthorized but tortious misrepresentation.

If the agent is an employee, whose conduct the principal–employer controls, the employer may also be liable for torts committed by the employee in the course of employment under the doctrine of *respondeat superior,* as discussed below.

Principal's Tortious Conduct

A principal conducting an activity through an agent may be liable for harm resulting from the principal's own negligence or recklessness, which may include giving improper instructions, authorizing the use of improper materials or tools or the like, establishing improper rules, or failing to prevent others' tortious conduct while they are on the principal's property or using the principal's equipment, materials, or tools.

For instance, if Jack knows that Jill cannot drive but nevertheless authorizes her to take the company truck to pick up water pails for his business inventory, he will be liable for his own negligence to anyone injured by her negligent driving.

Principal's Authorization of Agent's Tortious Conduct

Similarly, a principal who authorizes an agent to commit a tortious act may be liable to persons or property injured thereby, because the act is considered to be the principal's. For example, if John directs Warren, an agent he retained to oversee the harvest of crops he bought, to cut the corn on specific acreage, which neither of them has the right to, the harvest is a trespass, and John is liable to whoever owns the corn.

In the same light, if Victoria instructs Albert, her real estate agent, to tell prospective purchasers that there is oil beneath her property, when she knows there is not, she will be liable to anyone who buys the property in reliance on the statements.

Misrepresentation

A principal is exposed to tort liability whenever a third person sustains loss due to the agent's misrepresentation. The keys to a principal's liability are whether the agent was actually or apparently authorized to make representations and whether such representations were made within the scope of the agency.

FRAUDULENT MISREPRESENTATION   Assume that Lewis is a demonstrator for Moore's products. Moore sends Lewis to a home show to demonstrate products and to answer questions from consumers. Moore has given Lewis authority to make statements about the products. If Lewis makes only true representations, all is fine; but if he makes false claims, Moore will be liable for any injuries or damages sustained by third parties in reliance on Lewis's false representations.

An interesting series of cases has arisen on the theory that when a principal has placed an agent in a position to defraud a third party, the principal is liable for the agent's fraudulent acts. For example, Pratt is a loan officer at First Security Bank. In the ordinary course of the job, Pratt approves and services loans and has access to the credit records of all customers. Pratt falsely represents to a borrower, McMillan, that the bank feels insecure about McMillan's loan and intends to call it in unless McMillan provides additional collateral, such as stocks and bonds. McMillan gives Pratt numerous stock certificates, which Pratt keeps in her own possession and later uses to make personal investments. The bank is liable to McMillan for losses sustained on the stocks even though the bank had no direct role in or knowledge of the fraudulent scheme.

The legal theory used here is that the agent's position conveys to third persons the impression that the agent has the authority to make statements and perform acts consistent with the ordinary duties that are within the scope of the position. When an agent appears to be acting within the scope of the authority that the position of agency confers but is actually taking advantage of a third party, the principal who placed the agent in that position is liable. In the example above, if a bank teller or a security guard had told McMillan that the bank required additional security for a loan, McMillan would not have been justified in relying on either person's authority to make that representation. McMillan, however, could reasonably expect that the loan officer was telling the truth.

INNOCENT MISREPRESENTATION   Tort liability based on fraud requires proof that a material misstatement was made knowingly and with the intent to deceive. An agent's innocent mistakes occurring in a contract transaction or involving a warranty contained in the contract can provide grounds for the third party's rescission of the contract and the award of damages. Moreover, justice dictates that when a principal knows that an agent is not accurately advised of facts but does not correct either the agent's or the third party's impressions, the principal is directly responsible to the third party for resulting damages. The point is that the principal is always directly responsible for an agent's misrepresentation made within the scope of authority.

Doctrine of *Respondeat Superior*

Under the doctrine of ***respondeat superior,***[7] the principal–employer is liable for any harm caused to a third party by an agent–employee in the scope of employment. This doctrine imposes **vicarious liability** on the employer—that is, liability without regard to the personal fault of the employer for torts committed by an employee in the course or scope of employment.[8]

SCOPE OF EMPLOYMENT   The Restatement (Second) of Agency, Section 229, indicates the following general factors that courts will consider in determining whether or not a particular act occurred within the course and scope of employment:

1.   Whether the act was authorized by the employer.
2.   The time, place, and purpose of the act.
3.   Whether the act was one commonly performed by employees on behalf of their employers.
4.   The extent to which the employer's interest was advanced by the act.
5.   The extent to which the private interests of the employee were involved.
6.   Whether the employer furnished the means or instrumentality (for example, a truck or a machine) by which an injury was inflicted.
7.   Whether the employer had reason to know that the employee would do the act in question and whether the employee had done it before.
8.   Whether the act involved the commission of a serious crime.

LIABILITY FOR EMPLOYEE'S NEGLIGENCE   Third persons injured through the negligence of an employee can sue either the employee who was negligent or the employer, if the employee's negligent conduct occurred while the employee was acting within the scope of employment.

At early common law, a servant (employee) was viewed as the master's (employer's) property. The master was deemed to have absolute control over the servant's acts and was held strictly liable for them no matter how carefully the master supervised the servant. The rationale for the doctrine of *respondeat superior* is based on the principle of social duty that requires every person to manage his or her affairs, whether accomplished by the person or through agents or servants, so as not to injure another. Liability is imposed on employers because they are deemed to be in a better financial position to bear the loss. The superior financial position carries with it the duty to be responsible for damages.

Today the doctrine continues, but employers carry liability insurance and spread the cost of risk over the entire business enterprise. Public policy requires that an injured person be afforded effective relief, and recovery from a business enterprise provides far more effective relief than recovery from an individual employee. Liability rights exist under law because of public policy protections of third parties. Thus, a master (employer) cannot contract with a servant (employee) to disclaim responsibilities for injuries resulting from the servant's acts, because such disclaimers are against public policy.

---

7.   Pronounced ree-*spahn*-dee-uht soo-*peer*-ee-your. The doctrine of *respondeat superior* applies not only to employer–employee relationships but also to principal–agent relationships as long as the principal has the right of control over the agent.

8.   The theory of *respondeat superior* is similar to the theory of strict liability covered in Chapters 5 and 23. This doctrine may not apply if the employer has sovereign or charitable-organization immunity. The practice of granting such immunity is diminishing in most states.

For the employer to be liable, the act causing injury must have occurred within the scope of the employee's employment. For example, Sutton (the employee) is a delivery driver for Schwartz (the employer). Schwartz provides Sutton with a vehicle and instructs him to use it for making company deliveries. Nevertheless, one day Sutton drives his own car instead of the company vehicle and negligently injures Walker. Even though Sutton's act (driving the car) was unauthorized, the negligence occurred as part of Sutton's regular duties of employment (making deliveries). Hence, Schwartz is still liable to Walker for the injuries caused by Sutton, even though Sutton used his own car contrary to Schwartz's instructions. Only if Sutton's acts had exceeded the scope of employment duties in a way that the employer could not reasonably have expected would Schwartz have been relieved of liability.

An employee going to and from work or to and from meals is usually considered outside the scope of employment. All travel time of a traveling salesperson, however, is normally considered within the scope of employment for the duration of the business trip, including the return trip home.

When an employee goes off on his or her own—that is, departs from the employer's business to take care of personal affairs—is the employer liable? It depends. If the employee's activity is a substantial departure akin to an utter abandonment of the employer's business, then the employer is not liable.

For example, a traveling salesperson is driving the employer's vehicle to call on a customer for a possible sales order. On the way to the customer's place of business, the employee deviates one block to mail a letter at the post office. As the employee approaches the post office, she negligently runs into a parked vehicle owned by Ann. The departure of the employee from the employer's business to take care of a personal affair is not substantial. The employee is still within the scope of employment, and the employer is liable to Ann. If the employee had decided to pick up a few friends for cocktails in another city, and in the process had negligently run her vehicle into Ann, Ann could not have held the employer liable, only the employee.

The following case is a classic in master–servant law. Although it is over 150 years old, the legal principle for which it stands is still viable in employment law today.

Case 36.4

JOEL v. MORISON

Court of Exchequer,
England, 1834.
172 Eng. Rep. 1338.

BACKGROUND AND FACTS   Joel was walking across Bishopsgatestreet when he was knocked down by a cart driven negligently by Morison's servant. Joel suffered a fractured leg and multiple injuries. In the subsequent suit, Joel took the position that Morison was liable for his injuries because Morison's servant was driving the cart that caused the injuries. Morison argued that his cart was never driven in the neighborhood in which Joel was injured. Moreover, it was suggested that Morison's servant had gone out of his way for his own purposes and might have taken the cart at a time when it was not wanted for business purposes to pay a visit to some friends.

DECISION AND RATIONALE   The Court of Exchequer awarded Joel damages of £30. The court held the master liable for the negligent acts of his servant, as the servant's actions were committed while the servant was "in the course of his employment" rather than "on a frolic of his own."

Borrowed Servants   Employers can lend the services of their employees to other employers. Suppose that an employer leases ground-moving equipment to another employer and sends along an employee to operate the machinery. Who is liable for injuries caused by the employee's negligent actions on the job site? Liability turns on *which employer had the primary right to control* the em-

Employer Liability for Employee Torts

At some point in your business career, you may well be involved in a basic tort lawsuit—even though you yourself are not negligent and have caused no harm to any other individual or business firm. This is because, as an employer, you are also subject to liability for your employees' torts—if the torts are committed within the scope of employment. For example, if your employer-driver has a collision with another vehicle that results in injury to the other driver, you may also be liable for the damages if it is determined that your employee was negligent.

This liability is founded on the doctrine of *respondeat superior*. One reason for imposing this liability on employers is to provide them with an incentive to prevent employee torts by careful selection and supervision of their employees.

Most businesses carry liability insurance to cover the wide breadth of basic tort claims to which they may be subjected. The cost of this insurance, however, is constantly on the rise. To keep liability insurance premiums to a minimum, the successful manager will reduce as far as possible the number of tort claims that the insurance firm must pay. This can be done by acquiring a knowledge of the kinds of torts that may arise and by taking action to prevent their occurrence.

Taking preventive action involves more than just telling employees to be careful. Preventive action entails taking specific and definite steps toward preventing employee torts—such as by forming a list of basic company rules. Supervisors and employees of the company should be carefully instructed in both the importance of these rules and the consequences—up to and including discharge—of rule violations. For example, an employer might establish a rule that any employee who incurs two moving traffic violations while driving a company car will be discharged immediately. This may inspire more careful driving habits on the part of employees. Successful preventive action also involves positive rewards—which can range from special mention in the company newsletter to a salary bonus—to those employees who perform carefully and lawfully.

---

ployee at the time the injuries occurred. Generally, the employer who rents out the equipment is presumed to retain control over his or her employee. If the rental is for a relatively long period of time, however, control may be deemed to pass to the employer who is renting the equipment and presumably controlling and directing the employee.

Notice of Dangerous Conditions

The employer is charged with knowledge of any dangerous conditions discovered by an employee and pertinent to the employment situation. To illustrate: A maintenance employee in Martin's apartment building notices a lead pipe protruding from the ground in the building's courtyard. The employee neglects either to fix it or to inform the employer of the danger. Sam falls on the pipe and is injured. The employer is charged with knowledge of the dangerous condition regardless of whether or not the employee actually informed the employer. That knowledge *is imputed to the employer* by virtue of the employment relationship.

LIABILITY FOR EMPLOYEE'S INTENTIONAL TORTS Most intentional torts that employees commit have no relation to their employment; and thus, their employers will not be held liable. Under *respondeat superior,* however, the employer is liable for intentional torts of the employee committed within the scope of employment, just as the employer is liable for negligence. For example, an employer is liable when an employee commits assault and battery or false imprisonment while acting within the scope of employment.

An employee acting at the employer's direction can be liable as a **tortfeasor** (one who commits a wrong, or tort), along with the employer, for committing the tortious act even if the employee was unaware of the wrongfulness of the act. For example, an employer directs an employee to burn out a field of crops. The employee does so, assuming that the field belongs to the employer, which it does not. Both can be found liable to the owner of the field for damages.

An employer who knows or should know that an employee has a propensity for committing tortious acts is liable for the employee's acts even if they would not ordinarily be considered within the scope of employment. For example, the Blue Moon employs Joe Green as a bouncer, knowing that he has a history of arrests for assault and battery. While he is working one night, and within the scope of his employment, he viciously attacks a patron who ''looks at him funny.'' The Blue Moon will bear the responsibility for Green's acts because it knew that he had a propensity for committing tortious acts.

Also, an employer is liable for permitting an employee to engage in reckless acts that can injure others. For example, an employer observes an employee smoking while filling containerized trucks with highly flammable liquids. Failure to stop the employee will cause the employer to be liable for any injuries that result.

To reduce the likelihood of liability losses, employers set up stringent work rules. For example, employees who drive company vehicles may be prohibited from giving rides to other passengers. Employees who violate these rules by being careless or committing unlawful or tortious acts may be subject to discipline, including discharge. Almost without exception, employers purchase liability insurance to cover the actions of certain employees.

■ Liability for Independent Contractor's Torts

The general rule concerning liability for the acts of independent contractors is that the employer is not liable for physical harm caused to a third person by the negligent act of an independent contractor in the performance of the contract. An employer who has no legal power to control the details of the physical performance of a contract cannot be held liable. Here again the test is the *right to control*. Because an employer bargains with an independent contractor only for results and retains no control over the manner in which those results are achieved, the employer is generally not expected to bear the responsibility for torts committed by an independent contractor. A collection agency is a typical example of an independent contractor. The creditor is generally not liable for the acts of the collection agency because collection is a distinct business occupation.

Generally, an exception to this doctrine prevails when exceptionally hazardous activities are involved. Typical examples of such activities include blasting operations, the transportation of highly volatile chemicals, and the use of poisonous gases. In these cases, an employer cannot be shielded from liability merely by using an independent contractor. Strict liability is imposed upon the employer–principal as a matter of law. Also, in some states, strict liability is imposed by statute.

In the following case, one of the issues before the court is whether the repossession of collateral is an inherently dangerous activity, in which case the secured creditor could be held liable for the damages caused by the independent contractor's tortious actions.

Case 36.5

SANCHEZ v. MBANK OF EL PASO

Court of Appeals of Texas—
El Paso, 1990.
792 S.W.2d 530.

BACKGROUND AND FACTS MBank of El Paso contracted with El Paso Recovery Service (El Paso) for El Paso to repossess Yvonne Sanchez's car, which had been purchased through MBank financing. El Paso employees went to Sanchez's home and proceeded to hook the car, which was in the driveway, to their tow truck. Sanchez asked them what they were doing and demanded that they stop and leave. When they ignored her, she locked herself in the car. When they got the car in the street, they identified their purpose and told her to get out of the car. She refused. They took the vehicle with Sanchez locked in it on a high-speed ride from her home to the repossession lot and parked the car in a fenced yard with a loose guard dog. She was rescued by her husband and the police. Sanchez sued

MBank in a Texas state court, alleging that El Paso and its employees were MBank's agents and that they had willfully breached the peace in violation of UCC 9-503. The trial court granted the bank's motion for summary judgment, holding that the bank could not be liable because El Paso was an independent contractor. Sanchez appealed.

DECISION AND RATIONALE The Court of Appeals of Texas reversed the trial court's decision and remanded the case for trial. The appellate court pointed out that two situations represent exceptions to the general rule that an employer is not liable for the tortious acts of an independent contractor: "(1) where the employer is by the statute * * * under a duty to provide specific safeguards for the safety of others," and "(2) where the employer employs an independent contractor to do work involving a special or inherent danger to others." The court concluded that MBank had a nondelegable duty under UCC 9-503 to avoid breaching the peace when repossessing collateral and thus could be liable to Sanchez for a breach of the peace by El Paso. The court also concluded that self-help repossession—"always bordering on the edge of illegality if not carried out carefully"—is an inherently dangerous activity.

ETHICAL CONSIDERATIONS Had the court ruled differently, MBank would have been able to use any repossession company without ever worrying about the methods used to repossess collateral. One might ask whether such a situation would be fair to MBank's loan customers. Indeed, one could argue that MBank's use of an overly aggressive "repo company" could constitute unfair commercial behavior in any event.

■ Liability for Agent's Crimes

Obviously, an agent is liable for his or her own crimes. A principal or employer is not liable for an agent's or employee's crime simply because the agent or employee committed the crime while otherwise acting within the scope of authority or employment, unless the principal or employer participated by conspiracy or other action.

In some jurisdictions, under specific statutes, a principal may be liable for an agent's violating, in the course and scope of employment, such regulations as those governing sanitation, prices, weights, and the sale of liquor.

■ Liability for Subagent's Acts

There are three instances in which an agent can hire a subagent:

1. To perform simple, definite duties.
2. When it is the business custom.
3. For unforeseen emergencies.

If an agent is authorized to hire subagents for the principal under any one of these circumstances, then the principal is liable for the acts of the subagents. There is a slight difference in result if the agent hires for an *undisclosed principal.* In that case, the agent is responsible for the subagent in contract law for such things as wages. The undisclosed principal, however, is generally held to be liable for tort injuries. The doctrine of *respondeat superior* imposes liability on the true "master." An agent's unauthorized hiring of a subagent generally does not create any legal relationship between the principal and the subagent.

■ Termination of an Agency

Agency law is similar to contract law in that both an agency and a contract terminate by an act of the parties or by operation of law. Once the relationship between the principal and the agent has ended, the agent no longer has actual authority to bind the principal—that is, he or she lacks the principal's consent to act in the principal's behalf. Under some circumstances, third persons may also need to be notified when the agency has been terminated.

Termination by Act of the Parties

The parties may terminate the authority by including in their agreement some express or implied condition or limitation, the occurrence of which will terminate the agency. This may consist of a certain date or some particular event. Furthermore, at any time, the parties may simply agree to end their relationship.

LAPSE OF TIME   An agency agreement may specify the time period during which the agency relationship will exist. If so, the agency ends when that time expires. For example, Able signs an agreement of agency with Paula ''beginning January 1, 1992, and ending December 31, 1994.'' The agency is automatically terminated on December 31, 1994. Of course, the parties can agree to continue the relationship, in which case the same terms will apply.

If no definite time is stated, then the agency continues for a reasonable time and can be terminated at will by either party. What constitutes a reasonable time depends on the circumstances and the nature of the agency relationship. For example, Paula asks Able to sell her car. If after two years Able has not sold Paula's car and there has been no communication between Paula and Able, it is safe to assume that the agency relationship has terminated. Able no longer has the authority to sell Paula's car.

PURPOSE ACHIEVED   An agent can be employed to accomplish a particular objective, such as the purchase of stock for a cattle rancher. In that case, the agency automatically ends after the cattle have been purchased.

If more than one agent is employed to accomplish the same purpose, such as the sale of real estate, the first agent to complete the sale automatically terminates the agency relationship for all the others.

OCCURRENCE OF A SPECIFIC EVENT   An agency can be created to terminate upon the happening of a certain event. For example, Paula appoints Able to handle her business affairs while she is away. When Paula returns, the agency automatically terminates.

Sometimes one aspect of the agent's authority terminates on the occurrence of a particular event, but the agency relationship itself does not terminate. For example, Paula, a banker, permits Able, the credit manager, to grant a credit line of $1,000 to certain depositors who maintain a balance of $1,000 in a savings account. If any customer's savings account balance falls below $1,000, Able can no longer make the credit line available to that customer. But Able's right to extend credit to the other customers maintaining the minimum balance will continue.

MUTUAL AGREEMENT   Recall from basic contract law that parties can cancel (rescind) a contract by mutually agreeing to terminate the contractual relationship. The same holds true in agency law regardless of whether the agency contract is in writing or whether it is for a specific duration. For example, Paula no longer wishes Able to be her agent, and Able does not want to work for Paula any more. Either party can communicate to the other the intent to terminate the relationship. Agreement to terminate effectively relieves each of the rights, duties, and powers inherent in the relationship.

TERMINATION BY ONE PARTY   As a *general* rule, either party can terminate the agency relationship. The agent's act is said to be a renunciation of authority. The principal's act is a revocation of authority. Although both parties may have the *power* to terminate—because agency is a consensual relationship, and thus neither party can be compelled to continue in the relationship—they may not possess the *right* to terminate and may therefore be liable for breach of contract. Wrongful termination can subject the canceling party to a suit for damages.

For example, Able has a one-year employment contract with Paula to act as her agent for $18,000. Paula can discharge Able before the contract period expires (Paula has the *power* to breach the contract); however, Paula will be liable to Able for money damages because Paula has no *right* to breach the contract.

Even in an agency at will (that is, an agency that either party may terminate at any time), the principal who wishes to terminate must give the agent a reasonable notice—that is, at least sufficient notice to allow the agent to recoup his or her expenses and, in some cases, to make a normal profit.

AGENCY COUPLED WITH AN INTEREST   An agency *coupled with an interest* (also referred to as a *power coupled with an interest* or a *power given as a security*) is a relationship created for the benefit of the agent. The agent actually acquires a beneficial interest in the subject matter of the agency. Under these circumstances, it is not equitable to permit a principal to terminate at will. Hence, this type of agency is irrevocable.

Because, in an agency coupled with an interest, the interest is not created for the benefit of the principal, it is not really an agency in the usual sense. Therefore, any attempt by the principal to revoke an agency coupled with an interest normally has no legal force or effect. Also, an agency coupled with an interest is not terminated by the death of either the principal or the agent.

For example, Sarah Roberts needs $10,000. John Hartwell agrees to lend her the money, but not without security. Consequently, Roberts delivers some of her jewelry to Hartwell and signs a letter giving him the power, in case she fails to repay the loan, to sell the jewelry as her agent for the best price that can be obtained and to pay out of the proceeds the unpaid amount of the loan, giving any surplus to her. Having obtained the money, Roberts tells Hartwell that she revokes the power to sell. Under the law of agency, the power is not revoked. Subsequently, Roberts dies. The power is still not affected.

An agency coupled with an interest should not be confused with a situation in which the agent merely derives proceeds or profits from the sale of the subject matter. For example, an agent who merely receives a commission from the sale of real property does not have a beneficial interest in the property itself. Likewise, an attorney whose fee is a percentage of the recovery (a **contingency fee**) merely has an interest in the proceeds. These agency relationships are revocable by the principal, subject to any express contractual arrangements between the principal and the agent.

Termination by Operation of Law

Certain events will terminate agency authority automatically, because their occurrence makes it impossible for the agent to perform or improbable

that the principal would continue to want performance. These events include death or insanity, loss of the agency's subject matter, changed circumstances, bankruptcy, and war.

DEATH OR INSANITY   The general rule is that death or insanity of either the principal or the agent automatically and immediately terminates the ordinary agency relationship. Knowledge of the death is not required. For example, Paula sends Able to the Far East to purchase a rare book. Before Able makes the purchase, Paula dies. Able's agent status is terminated at the moment of death, even though Able does not know that Paula has died. (Some states, however, have changed this common law by statute.)

An agent's transactions that occur after the death of the principal are not binding on the principal's estate. Assume Able is hired by Paula to collect a debt from Tom (a third party). Paula dies, but Able still collects the money from Tom, not knowing of Paula's death. Tom's payment to Able is no longer legally sufficient to discharge Tom's debt to Paula, because Able no longer has Paula's authority to collect the money. If Able absconds with the money, Tom must pay the debt again, to Paula's estate.

IMPOSSIBILITY   When the specific subject matter of an agency is destroyed or lost, the agency terminates. For example, Paula employs Able to sell Paula's house. Prior to any sale, the premises are destroyed by fire. Able's agency and authority to sell Paula's house terminate. Similarly, when it is impossible for the agent to perform the agency lawfully, because of war or because of a change in the law, the agency terminates.

CHANGED CIRCUMSTANCES   When an event occurs that has such an unusual effect on the subject matter of the agency that the agent can reasonably infer that the principal will not want the agency to continue, the agency terminates. Paula hires Able to sell a tract of land for $10,000. Subsequently, Able learns that there is oil under the land and that the land is therefore worth $1 million. The agency and Able's authority to sell the land for $10,000 are terminated.

BANKRUPTCY   Bankruptcy of the principal or the agent *usually* terminates the agency relationship. Insolvency, as distinguished from bank-ruptcy, does not necessarily terminate the relation-ship. Third parties, however, should be wary of forming contracts, through an agent, with a prin-cipal whose financial condition is unstable because bankruptcy—and the termination of the agency—may be imminent.

WAR   When the principal's country and the agent's country are at war with each other, the agency is terminated. .

Notice Required for Termination

When an agency terminates by operation of law because of death, insanity, or some other unfore-seen circumstance, there is no duty to notify third persons, unless the agent's authority is coupled with an interest.[9] If, however, the parties them-selves have terminated the agency, it is the prin-cipal's duty to inform any third parties who know of the existence of the agency that it has been ter-minated. The reason for the notice requirement is generally to prevent fraud. Fairness requires that third parties who have relied on the agent's con-tinuing authority be given notice of the termination of the agent's authority.

---

9.   There is an exception to this rule in banking. UCC 4-405 provides that the bank as the agent can continue to exercise specific types of authority even after the customer's death or insanity unless it has knowledge of the death or insanity. When it has knowledge of the customer's death, it has authority for ten days after the death to pay checks (but not notes or drafts) drawn by the customer unless it receives a stop-payment order from someone who has an interest in the account, such as an heir. (This rule does not apply to insanity.)

An agent's *actual authority* continues until the agent receives some notice of termination. Notice to third parties, however, follows the general rule that an agent's *apparent authority* continues until the third person is notified (from any source of information) that such authority has been terminated.

The principal is expected to notify *directly* any third person who the principal knows has dealt with the agent. For third persons who have heard about the agency but have not dealt with the agent, *con-structive* notice is sufficient.[10]

No particular form of notice is required. The principal can actually notify the agent, or the agent can learn of the termination through some other means. For example, Marshall bids on a shipment of steel, and Smith is hired as an agent to arrange transportation of the shipment. When Smith learns that Marshall has lost the bid, Smith's authority to make the transportation arrangement terminates.

If the agent's authority is written, it must be revoked in writing, and the writing must be shown to all people who saw the original writing that es-tablished the agency relationship. Otherwise, the principal may still be bound by the agent's apparent authority. Sometimes a written authorization (like that granting power of attorney) contains an ex-piration date. The passage of the expiration date is sufficient notice of termination for third parties.

---

10.   *Constructive notice* is information or knowledge of a fact imputed by law to a person if he or she could have discovered the fact by proper diligence. Constructive notice is often ac-complished pursuant to a statute by newspaper publication.

■ CONCEPT SUMMARY 36.3   Termination of an Agency

Method of Agency Termination	Rules	Termination of Agent's Authority
		Notice to Third Persons Required
Act of the Parties		1. Direct to those who have
1. Lapse of time	Automatic at end of stated time.	dealt with agency.
2. Purpose achieved	Automatic upon completion of purpose.	2. Constructive to all others.
3. Mutual rescission	Need mutual consent or acceptance of consideration.	
4. Termination by one party	At will agencies—generally no breach.	
a. Revocation by principal	Cannot revoke an agency coupled with	
b. Renunciation by agent	an interest. Specified time agencies— breach unless legal cause.	

■ CONCEPT SUMMARY 36.3 *(Continued)*

Method of Agency Termination	Rules	Termination of Agent's Authority
Operation of Law		
1. Death or insanity	Automatic upon death or insanity of either principal or agent (except when agency is coupled with an interest).	
2. Impossibility—destruction of the specific subject matter	Applies any time agency cannot be performed because of event beyond parties' control.	NO NOTICE REQUIRED—AUTOMATIC UPON THE HAPPENING OF THE EVENT
3. Changed circumstances	Events so unusual, it would be inequitable to allow agency to continue to exist.	
4. Bankruptcy	Bankruptcy decree terminates—not mere insolvency.	
5. War between principal's and agent's countries	Automatically suspends or terminates—no way to enforce legal rights.	

■ Terms and Concepts

apparent authority 644
contingency fee 657
disclosed principal 647
express authority 643

implied authority 644
partially disclosed
  principal 647
ratification 646

respondeat superior 651
tortfeasor 653
undisclosed principal 647
vicarious liability 651

■ For Review

1. A principal's liability for an agent's act starts with the agent's authority to act on the principal's behalf. What are the two types of an agent's authority? If an agent acts outside the scope of his or her authority, how might a principal still be held liable for the act?

2. Under what circumstances is a principal liable for a subagent's acts?

3. Does either party to an agency have an absolute right to terminate an agency at any time?

4. Naomi contracts with Victor for the sale of a motorcycle. Naomi contracts in her own name, and Victor reasonably believes that she is contracting for herself, but after they sign the contract, Naomi reveals that she acted for Phil. Is Phil a disclosed principal, a partially disclosed principal, or an undisclosed principal? If, before they sign the contract, Naomi tells Victor that she is acting for Phil but signs the contract with her own name, is Phil a disclosed principal, a partially disclosed principal, or an undisclosed principal? If, before they sign the contract, Naomi tells Victor that she is acting for another but does not reveal Phil's name, is Phil a disclosed principal, a partially disclosed principal, or an undisclosed principal?

5. Wolf Construction Co. tells its workers to excavate a certain tract to begin laying the foundation for a new sports arena. Claude, one of the workers, mistakenly excavates a neighboring tract, negligently injuring Mel, who fell into the pit and broke his arm. Can Wolf be held liable to Mel?

■ Questions and Case Problems

36-1. Adam is a traveling salesperson for Peter Petri Plumbing Supply Corp. Adam has express authority to solicit orders from customers and to offer a 5 percent discount if payment is made within thirty days of delivery. Petri has said nothing to Adam about extending credit. Adam calls on a new prospective customer, John's Plumbing Firm. John tells Adam that he will place a large order for Petri products if Adam will give him a 10 percent discount with payment due in equal installments thirty, sixty, and ninety days from delivery. Adam says he has authority to make such a contract. John calls Petri and asks if Adam is authorized to make contracts giving a discount. No mention is made of payment terms. Petri replies that Adam has authority to make discounts on purchase orders. On the basis of this information, John orders $10,000 worth of plumbing supplies and fixtures.

The goods are delivered and are being sold. One week later John receives a bill for $9,500, due in thirty days. John insists he owes only $9,000 and can pay it in three equal installments, at thirty, sixty, and ninety days from delivery. Discuss the liability of Petri and John only.

36-2. Alice Adams is a purchasing agent–employee for the A & B Coal Supply partnership. Adams has authority to purchase the coal needed by A & B to satisfy the needs of its customers. While Adams is leaving a coal mine from which she has just purchased a large quantity of coal, her car breaks down. She walks into a small roadside grocery store for help. While there, she runs into Will Wilson. Wilson owns 360 acres back in the mountains with all mineral rights. Wilson, in need of money, offers to sell Adams the property at $1,500 per acre. On inspection of the property, Adams forms the opinion that the subsurface contains valuable coal deposits. Adams contracts to purchase the property for A & B Coal Co., signing the contract "A & B Coal Supply, Alice Adams, agent." The closing date is August 1. Adams takes the contract to the partnership. The managing partner is furious, as A & B is not in the property business. Later, just before closing, both Wilson and the partnership learn that the value of the land is at least $15,000 per acre. Discuss the rights of A & B and Wilson concerning the land contract.

36-3. Paula Development Enterprises hires Able to act as its agent to purchase a 1,000-acre tract of land from Thompson for $1,000 per acre. Paula Enterprises does not wish Thompson to know that it is the principal or that Able is its agent. Paula wants the land for a new country housing development, and Thompson may not sell the land for that purpose or may demand a premium price. Able makes the contract for the purchase, signing only Able's name as purchaser and not disclosing to Thompson the agency relationship. The closing and transfer of deed are to take place on September 1.
   (a) If Thompson learns of Paula's identity on August 1, can Thompson legally refuse to deed the property on September 1? Explain.
   (b) Paula gives Able the money for the closing, but Able absconds with the money, causing a breach of Able's contract at the date of closing. Thompson then learns of Paula's identity and wants to enforce the contract. Discuss fully Thompson's rights under these circumstances.

36-4. Able is hired as a traveling salesperson for the ABC Tire Corp. Able has a designated geographic area and time schedule within which to solicit orders and service customers. Able is given a company car to use in covering the territory. One day, Able decides to take his personal car to cover part of his territory. It is 11:00 A.M., and Able has just finished calling on all customers in the city of Tarrytown. Able's next appointment is in the city of Austex, twenty miles down the road, at 2:00 P.M. Able starts out for Austex, but halfway there he decides to visit a former college roommate who runs a farm ten miles off the main highway. Able is enjoying his visit with his former roommate when he realizes that it is 1:45 P.M. and that he will be late for the appointment in Austex. Driving at a high speed down the country road to reach the main highway, Able crashes his car into Thomas's tractor, severely injuring Thomas, a farmer. Thomas claims he can hold the ABC Tire Corp. liable for his injuries. Discuss fully ABC's liability in this situation.

36-5. Adam is an agent for Fish Galore, Inc. Adam has express authority to solicit orders and receive payments in advance of shipment. He is well known as an agent in the region. One of his customers, Seafood Quality, has been a regular customer for five years, has usually made large orders, and has always paid Adam in advance to get the discount offered by Fish Galore. Fish Galore learns that Adam has incurred large gambling debts and has recently used some of the customers' payments to pay off these debts. When Adam cannot reimburse Fish Galore, he is fired. Fish Galore hires a new agent and publishes in regional newspapers the fact that the new agent will be covering the territory. Desperately in need of cash, Adam solicits a large order from Seafood Quality and receives payment. Then he calls on a new customer, Catfish Heaven, which also gives Adam an order and payment. Adam absconds with the money. Fish Galore refuses to honor either order. Seafood Quality and Catfish Heaven claim Fish Galore is in breach of contract. Discuss fully their claims.

36-6. The City of Delta Junction (Delta) in Alaska decided to purchase a fire tanker and sought bids from several truck dealers. The city eventually purchased a truck from Alaska Mack, Inc., a Mack truck dealer in Fairbanks. Alaska Mack modified a Mack chassis to carry a 5,000-gallon tank, but the truck exceeded the manufacturer's specified weight limits and was dangerously unbalanced and difficult to drive. When subsequent modifications failed to remedy these problems, the city brought suit for breach of warranty against Alaska Mack and against Mack Trucks, Inc., of Allentown, Pennsylvania, as principal, under the theory of apparent agency, or apparent authority. Mack Trucks, Inc., the manufacturer of Mack trucks, claimed that Alaska Mack was not its agent and that it was not responsible for any actions undertaken by Alaska Mack. Delta argued that Alaska Mack was listed in trade journals and the Fairbanks telephone directory under the heading "Mack Trucks" and that its advertisements carried the familiar Mack bulldog trademark. On the basis of these representations, both Delta's mayor and fire chief, at the time of the purchase, believed that Alaska Mack was an agent for the manufacturer of Mack trucks. Alaska Mack's bid was accepted by the city council, even though it was the highest bid received for the truck, because of the manufacturer's reputation. The trial court granted a directed verdict for Mack Trucks, Inc. What will happen on appeal? Discuss fully. [*City of Delta Junction v. Mack Trucks, Inc.,* 670 P.2d 1128 (Alaska 1983)]

36-7. Richard Lanno worked for the Thermal Equipment Corp. as a project engineer. Lanno was allowed to keep a company van and tools at his home because he routinely drove to work sites directly from his home and because he was often needed for unanticipated trips during his off hours. The arrangement had been made for the convenience of Thermal Equipment, even though Lanno's managers permitted him to make personal use of the van. Lanno was involved in a collision with Lazar while driving the van home from work. At the time of the accident, Lanno had taken a detour to stop at a store—he had intended to purchase a few items and then go home. Lazar sued Thermal Equipment, claiming that Lanno had acted while within the scope of his employment. Discuss whether Lazar was able to recover and why. Can employees act on behalf of their employers and themselves at the same time? Explain. [*Lazar v. Thermal Equipment Corp.,* 148 Cal.App.3d 458, 195 Cal.Rptr. 890 (1983)]

36-8. Fred Hash worked for Van Stavern Construction Co. as a field supervisor in charge of constructing a new plant facility. Hash entered into a contract with Sutton's Steel & Supply, Inc., to supply steel to the construction site in several installments. Hash gave the name of B. D. Van Stavern, the president and owner of the construction firm, instead of the firm name as the party for whom he was acting. The contract and the subsequent invoices all had B. D. Van Stavern's name on them. Several loads were delivered by Sutton. All of the invoices were signed by Van Stavern employees, and corporate checks were made out to Sutton. When Sutton Steel later sued Van Stavern personally for unpaid debts totaling $40,437, it claimed that Van Stavern had ratified the acts of his employee, Hash, by allowing payment on previous invoices. Although Van Stavern had had no knowledge of the unauthorized arrangement, had he legally ratified the agreement by his silence? Explain. [*Sutton's Steel & Supply, Inc. v. Van Stavern,* 496 So.2d 1360 (La.App. 3d Cir. 1986)]

36-9. Garcia was an employee of Van Groningen & Sons, Inc., which operated an orchard, and one of Garcia's duties was to drive a tractor through the orchard pulling machinery behind. On one particular occasion, Garcia invited his nephew Perez to accompany him on the job as he drove the tractor through the orchard. Perez had to sit on the tool box because there was only one seat on the tractor. Perez was knocked off by a tree branch and was severely injured when the tractor machinery ran over his leg. Perez sued Van Groningen & Sons under the theory of *respondeat superior.* Van Groningen testified that the company forbade anyone but the driver to ride on the tractor because of the danger and that Garcia had personally been advised of this rule. Discuss what chance Perez has of recovering under the doctrine of *respondeat superior.* [*Perez v. Van Groningen & Sons, Inc.,* 41 Cal.3d 962, 719 P.2d 676, 227 Cal.Rptr. 106 (1986)]

36-10. Amax Nickel Refining Co. hired Louisiana Industrial Coatings (LIC), an independent contractor, to do some painting at the Amax plant. LIC was instructed that the painting had a high priority and that it should not stop painting in any given work area unless instructed to do so by an Amax supervisor. At one point, a LIC employee, Gregory Dixon, was spray painting the surface above the work area of an Amax employee, Kenneth Johnson, and accidentally sprayed coal tar on Johnson. An argument ensued when Johnson told Dixon to stop painting in Johnson's work area. Johnson believed that Amax employees had priority and could stop LIC painters if they interfered with

Amax work. Dixon said that he had been told that the LIC work took priority and that he would not stop unless a supervisor told him to. Words and threats ensued, including racial slurs against Dixon, and eventually Johnson was injured when Dixon shoved him against a steel beam. Johnson sued Dixon and LIC for injuries caused by Dixon's battery under the doctrine of *respondeat superior.* LIC argued that it could not be held liable for Dixon's tort because the tort had been committed outside the scope of Dixon's employment. According to LIC, the argument was personal in nature and stemmed from Dixon's desire to punish Johnson for racial taunts and to "appease his own machismo." The issue turned on whether Dixon was acting within the scope of his employment when he injured Johnson. If he was, then LIC would be liable for Dixon's tort under the doctrine of *respondeat superior.* How will the court decide? Discuss fully. [*Johnson v. Dixon,* 457 So.2d 79 (La.App. 4th Cir. 1984)]

36-11. Port Ship Service, Inc., a water taxi service, ferried crew members, customs agents, supplies, and the like between ships and the shore at the Port of New Orleans. Norton, Lilly & Co. acted as an agent for various ships entering the harbor that required water taxi services. Ships needing water taxi services would call Norton, and Norton would communicate the names of the vessels needing such services to Port Ship. Although Norton never informed Port Ship of the names of the vessels' owners, such information was readily available to Port Ship in publications commonly used by port authorities, and in addition, Norton maintained a twenty-four-hour telephone service through which Port Ship could ascertain the identities of any of the ship owners. Port Ship sought to hold Norton liable for unpaid taxi services, and the issue turned on whether the ship owners were fully disclosed principals (in which case Norton could not be held liable) or only partially disclosed principals (in which case Norton could be held liable). The Court stated that the Restatement (Second) of Agency, Section 4, "makes . . . clear" that "it is the agent's duty to disclose the principal's identity, and not a third party's duty to ascertain that identity." Had Norton disclosed the principals' identities by giving Port Ship the names of the vessels? Discuss fully. [*Port Ship Service, Inc. v. Norton, Lilly & Co.,* 883 F.2d 23 (5th Cir. 1989)]

36-12. Case Briefing Assignment

Examine Case A.20 [Green v. Shell Oil Co., 181 Mich.App. 439, 450 N.W.2d 50 (1989)] in Appendix A. The case has been excerpted there in great detail. Review and then brief the case, making sure that you include answers to the following questions in your brief.

1. Green sued Shell and Lanford on two grounds. What are they?
2. Why did the court hold that summary judgment on the issue of Lanford's agency status was inappropriate?
3. Why did the court hold that the service station attendant was not acting within the scope of his employment while he was participating in the assault and battery?

Focus on Ethics

Agency

Agency law is concerned with rights, duties, and liabilities of principals and agents. Foremost in the area of agency is the nature of duty. Significantly, most of the duties discussed below are negotiable at law. In forming a contract, the principal and the agent can extend or abridge many of the ordinary duties owed in such a relationship. Legal rules generally come into play when the contract is silent or ambiguous on a point. Allowing the parties to negotiate their relative duties seems ethically fair, so long as the parties are able to understand their rights and make informed decisions.

The Duty of the Agent to the Principal

What is the nature of the duty that an agent owes to a principal in an employment situation? Does the agent have the duty to disclose all favorable information that could be used by the principal to increase the principal's profits? Or does the agent have the right to use some of the information gleaned during the course of normal employment for his or her own benefit? To understand the answers to these questions, we must understand the kind of relationship that exists between

a principal and an agent.

The very nature of the principal–agent relationship is one of trust, which we call a fiduciary relationship. Because of this, it is expected that an agent owes certain duties to the principal. These duties include being loyal and obedient, informing the principal of important facts concerning the agency, accounting to the principal for property or money received, and performing with reasonable diligence and skill.

Thus, ethical conduct would prevent an agent from representing two principals in the same transaction, or making a secret profit from the agency relationship, or failing to disclose the interest of the agent in property the principal was purchasing. The expected ethical conduct of the agent has evolved into rules that, if breached, cause the agent to be held liable.

What about looking beyond the duty to the principal and considering one's duty to society? Those employees of Firestone who knew of the company's defective tires in the early 1980s presumably could have divulged that information to the public (at the risk of losing their jobs, of course). Furthermore, employees aware of deliberate and fraudulent cost

overruns on government contracts could make this information public, once again at the risk of losing their jobs. Some scholars have argued that many of the greatest "evils" in the past twenty-five years have been accomplished in the name of "duty" to the principal. Duty in this context means placing the well-being of the principal above that of the public.

The Duty of the Principal to the Agent

Assuming that agents owe certain fiduciary duties to their principals, do principals have corresponding ethical duties to agents? In the law, principals have certain defined duties, such as compensation and reimbursement of certain expenses.

Principals also owe their agents a duty of cooperation. One might expect most principals to cooperate with their agents out of self-interest, but this is not universally the case. Suppose a principal hires an agent on commission to sell a building, and the agent puts considerable time and expense into the process. If the principal changes his or her mind and decides to retain the building, he or she might want to prevent the agent from completing a sale. Is such action ethical, or does it violate a principal's duty of cooperation? What alternatives would such a principal have?

Another duty of principals is to provide safe working conditions. The principal therefore should not expose agents to unreasonable hazards as they go about their work. The definition of *safe* remains a difficult one, however, as every job probably entails some degree of unavoidable risk. Suppose an employer hires a delivery person and supplies a truck. Must the truck contain seat belts to ensure safe working conditions? What about airbags or special safety glass?

Although a principal is legally obligated to fulfill certain duties to the agent, these duties do not include any specific duty of loyalty. Some argue that the lack of employer loyalty to employees leads to a reduction of employee loyalty to employers. After all, they maintain, why should an employee be loyal to an employer's interests over the years when the employee knows that there is no corresponding legal duty on the part of the employer to be loyal to the employee's interests. Employers who do show a sense of loyalty to employees— for example, by not laying off long-time, faithful employees when business is slow or when those employees could be replaced by younger workers at lower cost—base that sense of loyalty primarily on ethical, not legal, considerations.

Employee versus Independent Contractor

There is a distinction between an employer–employee

relationship and the relationship that exists between an employer and an independent contractor. Is it fair, when two parties contract to create an employer–independent contractor relationship, that in spite of what the parties stated in their contract, a court holds that an employer–employee relationship exists instead? Consider the case of Christopher Heard, who was hired by a pizza franchise, Numero Uno No. 12, to deliver pizza. Heard signed an independent contractor agreement with Numero Uno, which explicitly stated that Heard was being hired not as an employee but as an independent contractor. The agreement read, in part, as follows: "Independent Contractor [Heard] acknowledges that he is not being hired by the Client [Numero Uno], but the Client is strictly contracting services." The agreement also stated, "Independent Contractor agrees that the Client shall be held harmless against any lawsuits which may result from any act of the Independent Contractor's services." The term *independent contractor* is mentioned no less than ten times in the agreement.

When Heard's truck hit another vehicle while he was on the way to deliver pizza to a customer, the driver of the other car sustained $14,000 in medical and property damages. The driver-plaintiff sued Heard and the owners of Numero Uno.[1] In determining whether the owners of Numero Uno should be liable to the plaintiff, the court had to determine

---

1.   *Toyota Motor Sales U.S.A., Inc. v. Superior Court,* 220 Cal.App.3d 864, 269 Cal.Rptr. 647 (1990). (The plaintiff also sued Toyota, alleging that the seatbelt in the Toyota she was driving was defective.)

whether Heard, as a pizza deliverer, was an employee of Numero Uno or an independent contractor. The trial court concluded that Heard was an independent contractor. On review, however, the appellate court held that employer control "is clearly the most important" of the numerous factors to be weighed in determining whether an individual is an employee or an independent contractor. The appellate court in this case used the same logic that the Internal Revenue Services uses when it examines independent contractor situations. That Heard had a certain amount of freedom of action and provided his own vehicle, expenses, and insurance did not outweigh the amount of control that Numero Uno had over Heard's actions. Numero Uno "determined what would be delivered, when and to whom and what price would be charged."

In regard to determinations of employee or independent contractor status, it is not what parties say about their relationship that counts but what they actually do. This rule seems to fly in the face of social and ethical principles underlying the doctrine of freedom of contract. But it does reflect other social and ethical values, particularly the principle that those who are harmed should be compensated. Given the fact that employers are liable under the doctrine of *respondeat superior,* would it be fair to let some employers "off the hook" simply because they contracted with individuals as independent contractors rather than as employees? Would it be fair to victims who are harmed by so-called independent contractors not to allow them to be compensated by the principal–employers?

Agency by Estoppel

Sometimes a third person may be led to believe that an individual is acting in the capacity of an agent. For the most part, agency law seems to follow ethical considerations in such situations; the notion of agency by estoppel is one in which the harm that could be caused by the apparent agency relationship to the innocent third party is either prevented altogether or minimized.

Respondeat Superior

The doctrine of *respondeat superior* raises a significant ethical question: Why should innocent employers be required to pay for the tortious actions of others? This question becomes particularly relevant in the context of employment relationships within the world of sports. Traditionally, the doctrine of assumption of risk has prevented plaintiffs from recovering damages for sports injuries. In other words, because the players voluntarily participated in the sport, knowing the risks involved, they could not recover damages if they indeed were injured. In recent decades, some courts have allowed plaintiffs to recover damages from sports team owners, under the doctrine of *respondeat superior,* for intentional torts committed by professional sports players.

For example, in a game between the Denver Broncos and the Cincinnati Bengals in 1973, Dale Hackbart was playing safety for the Broncos and Charles Clark was playing fullback for the Bengals. When Hackbart attempted to block Clark to make room for a teammate to run with an intercepted pass, Clark hit Hackbart in the back of the head with his right forearm. This blow resulted in a severe neck injury, which forced Hackbart to end his career. The trial court dismissed Hackbart's lawsuit against Clark on the ground that Hackbart had assumed the risk of such an injury by participating in the sport. On appeal, however, the Tenth Circuit Court of Appeals reversed the trial court's decision and held that the owner of the team (as well as Clark) could be liable under the doctrine of *respondeat superior.*[2]

The main prevailing rationale for retaining the doctrine of *respondeat superior* in our laws is based on the employer's assumed ability to pay. Our collection of shared beliefs suggests that an injured party should be afforded the most effective relief possible. Thus, even though an employer may be absolutely innocent, the employer has a "deeper pocket" and will be more likely to have the funds necessary to make the injured party whole. Yet this rationale begins to weaken in the area of professional sports. Professional athletes are currently among the highest-paid employees in our society, and they frequently have the ability to pay substantial damage claims. In this context, does it seem ethical to apply the doctrine of *respondeat superior* and impose liability on team owners without fault?

Another rationale for the doctrine of *respondeat superior* is based on the theory of deterrence. This rationale proposes that employers will take greater precautions to deter wrongful acts by their employees if they know that they may be liable for their employees' wrongful conduct. Yet wouldn't holding a player liable for his or her own wrongful conduct be more effective in deterring this type of undesirable behavior? Is it not reasonable to assume that deterrence might be better served if a player knew that he or she, and not the team owner, would be held solely liable for such conduct?

◼ Discussion Questions

1. How much obedience and loyalty does an employee owe an employer? What if the employer engages in an activity—or requests the employee to engage in an activity—that violates the employee's ethical standards but does not necessarily violate any public policy or law? In such a situation, does an employee's duty to abide by his or her own ethical standards override the employee's duty of loyalty to the employer?

2. If an agent injures a third party during the course of employment, to what extent should the employer be held liable for the agent's actions? Does the amount of negligence on the part of the agent have any bearing on your answer? Is there any situation in which the agent alone should be held personally liable for his or her actions that harm third parties?

3. The preceding question relates to the doctrine of *respondeat superior.* What ethical considerations generated this doctrine?

4. Agency by estoppel occurs when the presumed principal's actions create the appearance of authority in a presumed agent. Do you think that agency

---

2. *Hackbart v. Cincinnati Bengals, Inc.,* 601 F.2d 516 (10th Cir. 1979).

by estoppel should be allowed under all circumstances? Or, rather, do you believe that the third person should be required to prove that he or she reasonably believed that the agent had authority?

5. The termination of an agency agreement can occur by operation of law. In particular, when unforeseen circumstances (such as impossibility of performance or bankruptcy) occur, termination by operation of law may take place. What ethical considerations are involved here?

6. When an agency is terminated by an act of the parties, the law requires that third parties who have dealt with the agency be notified of the termination. What purpose does notification serve? Are the reasons for this requirement based on any ethical considerations?

UNIT SEVEN

Business Organizations

■ The Importance of Business Organizations

Every business activity involves—implicitly or explicitly—a form of business organization, whether it be a sole proprietorship, a partnership, a corporation, or some hybrid form. Each form provides different degrees of flexibility and different rights and liabilities, and it is important to be aware of these differences when choosing and structuring one's business organization.

There is a great variety in the sizes and functions of business organizations even within the same category. For example, businesses conducted as sole proprietorships can range from a business run out of one's garage to a multimillion-dollar manufacturing company. In a similar vein, partnerships can range from a very informal arrangement between two individuals to a huge accounting firm with hundreds of partners. And, although most of the wealthiest U.S. business firms are organized as corporations, the majority of corporations are quite small. It has been estimated that over 90 percent of corporations have ten or fewer shareholders.

Even though the sizes across firms may be quite dissimilar within one category of business organizational forms, tax liabilities and other obligations faced by the firms within each category typically are constant. A sole proprietorship doing $22,000 worth of business faces the same basic federal tax laws as another sole proprietorship doing $10 million worth of business.

This unit begins with Chapter 37, which introduces the various forms of business organization available to entrepreneurs, as well as the law governing franchising relationships. The nature, formation, and operation of partnerships are then discussed in Chapter 38. A description of how partnerships are terminated and a discussion of a special type of partnership—the limited partnership—are offered in Chapter 39. Chapters 40 through 43 deal with corporations, including the regulation of corporate financing in the United States.

■ Ethical Issues in Business Organizations

A sole proprietor, as the sole owner of the business, has only himself or herself to deal with. When more than one owner is involved, however, as is the case with partnerships and corporations, ethical considerations arise. In a partnership, for example, each partner is considered an agent of the partnership and of the other partners. Therefore, as an agent, each partner is obligated by the fiduciary duties of agents that were discussed in the previous unit. In other words, being a partner requires one to abide by fairly strict moral and ethical standards in all actions relating to the partners or to the partnership. Similarly, corporate directors, officers, managers, and major shareholders are bound by fiduciary ties to the corporate entity. Shareholders place trust in the directors, officers, and managers of the corporation. When fiduciary duties are breached, lawsuits may result, and the breaching party may be liable for civil penalties and, under some circumstances (such as when securities laws are violated), for criminal penalties. In the extreme, improper behavior of the partners in a partnership or of majority shareholder shareholders in a corporation may result in a court's dissolution of the partnership or corporation.

To some extent, therefore, ethical conduct is mandated by law with respect to certain partnership and corporate relationships and activities. But a large "gray area" exists between unethical behavior that is within the bounds of legality and behavior that is so unethical that it will be considered illegal. In other words, the familiar question again rears its head: How unethical must a person's actions be before those actions will be deemed illegal? A corporate director may make an improper business decision that damages the corporation but still be excused from liability because he or she acted in good faith and in what seemed, at the time, to be the best interests of the corporation. The issue of good faith, however, is not always easy to prove; nor are the "best interests of the corporation" always totally clear. The gray area between ethical behavior and that which is outright illegal is the area in which complex ethical issues arise.

Chapter 37

Forms of Business Organization and Private Franchises

An **entrepreneur** is by definition one who initiates and *assumes the financial risks* of a new enterprise and who undertakes to provide or control its management. One of the questions faced by any entrepreneur who wishes to start a business is what form of business organization should be chosen for the business endeavor. In this chapter, we examine the basic features of the three major business forms: sole proprietorships, partnerships, and corporations. We also touch on joint ventures, syndicates, joint stock companies, business trusts, and cooperatives. A discussion of private franchises concludes the chapter.

■ Sole Proprietorships

A **sole proprietorship** is the simplest form of business. In this form, the owner is the business; thus, anyone who does business without creating a separate business entity, such as a partnership or corporation, has a sole proprietorship. Sole proprietorships are very common and constitute over two-thirds of all American businesses. They are also usually small enterprises—less than 1 percent of the sole proprietorships existing in the United States earn over $1 million per year. Sole proprietors can own and manage any type of business from an informal, home-office undertaking to a huge restaurant or construction firm.

Advantages of Sole Proprietorships

A major advantage of the sole proprietorship is that the proprietor receives all the profits (because he or she takes all the risk). In addition, it is often easier and less costly to start a sole proprietorship than to start any other kind of business, as few legal forms are involved. This business form also entails more flexibility than does a partnership or a corporation. The sole proprietor is free to make any decision he or she wishes concerning the business—whom to hire, when to take a vacation, what kind of business to pursue, and so on. A sole proprietor also pays only personal income taxes on profits. This means that, depending on the amount earned, the applicable tax rate may be lower than the corporate tax rate. Sole proprietors are also allowed to establish tax-exempt retirement accounts in the form of Keogh plans.

Disadvantages of Sole Proprietorships

The major disadvantage of the sole proprietorship is that the proprietor alone, as sole owner, bears the burden of any losses or liabilities incurred by the business enterprise. In other words, the sole proprietor has unlimited liability, or legal responsibility, for all obligations incurred in doing business. The unlimited liability of the sole proprietor, in contrast to the limited liability of the limited partner or corporate shareholder (discussed below), is a major factor to be considered when choosing a business form.

Another disadvantage is that the proprietor's opportunity to raise capital is limited to personal funds and the funds of those who are willing to make loans. The sole proprietorship also has the disadvantage of lacking continuity of business upon the death of the proprietor. When the owner dies, so does the business—it is automatically dissolved. If the business is to be transferred to family members or other heirs, a new proprietorship is created.

■ Partnerships

Partnerships can take the form of general partnerships or limited partnerships. The two forms of partnership differ considerably in regard to legal requirements and the rights and liabilities of partners.

General Partnerships

A **partnership** is a joint undertaking that arises from an agreement, express or implied, between two or more persons to carry on a business for profit. Partners are co-owners of a business and have joint control over its operation and the right to share in its profits. No particular form of partnership agreement is necessary for the creation of a partnership, although it is desirable that the agreement be in writing. Both partnerships and sole proprietorships are creatures of the common law rather than of statute. Basically, the partners may agree to almost any terms when establishing the partnership so long as they are not illegal or contrary to public policy.

A partnership is a legal entity only for limited purposes, such as the partnership name and title of ownership and property. The personal net worth of the partners is subject to partnership obligations, and the partnership itself is not subject to levy for federal income taxes, although an **information return** must be filed. That is, the partnership as an entity only *reports* (does not pay taxes on) the income received by the partnership. A partner's profit from the partnership (whether distributed or not) is taxed as individual income to the individual partner.

The nature, formation, operation, and termination of general partnerships are discussed in further detail in Chapters 38 and 39.

Limited Partnerships

A special and quite popular form of partnership is the **limited partnership,** which consists of at least one general partner and one or more limited partners. One of the major benefits of becoming a limited partner is limited liability, both with respect to lawsuits brought against the partnership and money at risk. The maximum money at risk is defined by the limited partnership agreement, which specifically states how much each limited partner must contribute to the partnership.

Unlike a general partnership, a limited partnership is completely a creature of statute. If the statute is not followed almost to the letter, the courts will hold that a general partnership exists instead. Then those who thought their liability was limited by their investment in a limited partnership will be held generally liable to the full extent of their personal net worth. Limited partnerships are discussed in more detail in Chapter 39.

■ Corporations

A third and widely used type of business organizational form is the **corporation**. Corporations consist of shareholders, who are the owners of the business. A board of directors, elected by the shareholders, manages the business. The board of directors normally employs officers to oversee day-to-day operations. One of the key features of a corporation is that the liability of its owners is limited to their investments. Their personal estates are usually not liable for the obligations of the corporation.

The corporation is a creature of statute, and it is therefore a legal entity. Its existence depends generally upon state law, although some corporations, especially public organizations, can be created under federal law. The law governing the formation, management and operation, liability, and termination of corporations will be discussed in detail in Chapters 40 through 43.

Major Business Forms Compared

Exhibit 37–1 lists the essential advantages and disadvantages of each of the three major forms of business organization. We select for further discussion here four important concerns for anyone starting a business—the ease of creation, the liability of the owners, tax features, and the need for capital—and then offer some suggestions on which business form is the most appropriate for different types of business situations.

Ease of Creation

No formalities are required in starting a business as a sole proprietorship. A partnership can be organized easily and inexpensively. A corporation must be organized according to specific statutory procedures, must have sufficient capitalization, and must pay other costs of formal incorporation. In fact, throughout its life, a corporation is subject to more governmental supervision and reporting requirements than is a partnership.

Liability of Owners

The form of the organization does not always in and of itself determine the liability of the owners. Generally, sole proprietors and general partners have personal liability, while the liability of limited partners and shareholders of corporations is limited to their investment. The issue of liability is an important one for creditors in deciding whether to extend credit to a business. For example, a bank may be unwilling to lend money to a corporation that is relatively small and has only a few shareholders.

Just because the business is a corporation does not guarantee that it is a better credit risk than, say, a sole proprietorship. Typically, in corporations with relatively few shareholders, the shareholders must personally sign for any loans made to the corporation. That is, the shareholders agree to be-

come personally liable for the loan if the corporation goes under or cannot meet its debts. In essence, the shareholders become guarantors for the corporation's debt. Hence, the corporate form of business does not prevent the shareholders from having personal liability in such a situation, because they have assumed the liability voluntarily.

Tax Considerations

Various tax considerations must be taken into account when one decides how best to organize a business. As discussed earlier, taxes on income earned by a sole proprietor are simply taxed as personal income. Tax aspects of partnerships and corporations are summarized in Exhibit 37–2.

Need for Capital

One of the most common reasons for changing from a sole proprietorship to a partnership or a corporation is the need for additional capital to finance expansion. A sole proprietor can seek partners who will bring capital with them. The partnership might be able to secure more funds from potential lenders than could the sole proprietor. But when a firm wants to expand greatly, simply increasing the number of partners can result in too many partners and make it difficult for the firm to operate effectively. Therefore, incorporation might be the best choice for an expanding business organization. There are many possibilities for obtaining more capital by issuing shares of stock. The original owners will find that, although their proportion of the company is reduced, they are able to expand much more rapidly by selling shares in the company.

The Appropriate Organizational Form

If a business is relatively small, is not diversified, employs relatively few people, has modest profits, and is not likely to expand significantly or require extensive financing in the immediate future, the most appropriate form for doing business may be a sole proprietorship. If the business is larger with greater capital needs, the most appropriate form may be a partnership. When business is expanding, becoming more profitable and diversified, or in need of a more institutional framework, it may be most advantageous to do business in the corporate form.

■ **Exhibit 37–1 Major Business Forms Compared**

Characteristic	Sole Proprietorship	Partnership	Corporation
1. Method of Creation	Created at will by owner.	Created by agreement of the parties.	Charter issued by state—created by statutory authorization.
2. Legal Position	Not a separate entity; owner is the business.	Not a separate legal entity in many states.	Always a legal entity separate and distinct from its owners—a legal fiction for the purposes of owning property and being a party to litigation.
3. Liability	Unlimited liability.	Unlimited liability (except for limited partners in a limited partnership).	Limited liability of shareholders—shareholders are not liable for the debts of the corporation.
4. Duration	Determined by owner; automatically dissolved on owner's death.	Terminated by agreement of the partners, by the death of one or more of the partners, by withdrawal of a partner, by bankruptcy, etc.	Can have perpetual existence.
5. Transferability of Interest	Interest can be transferred, but individual's proprietorship then ends.	Although partnership interest can be assigned, assignee does not have full rights of a partner.	Share of stock can be transferred.
6. Management	Completely at owner's discretion.	Each general partner has a direct and equal voice in management unless expressly agreed otherwise in the partnership agreement. (Limited partner has no rights in management in a limited partnership.)	Shareholders elect directors who set policy and appoint officers.
7. Taxation	Owner pays personal taxes on business income.	Each partner pays *pro rata* share of income taxes on net profits, whether or not they are distributed.	Double taxation—corporation pays income tax on net profits, with no deduction for dividends, and shareholders pay income tax on disbursed dividends they receive.
8. Organizational Fees, Annual License Fees, and Annual Reports	None.	None.	All required.
9. Transaction of Business in Other States	Generally no limitation.	Generally no limitation.[a]	Normally must qualify to do business and obtain certificate of authority.

a. A few states have enacted statutes requiring that foreign partnerships qualify to do business there—for example, 3 N.H.Rev.Stat.Ann. Chapter 305-A in New Hampshire.

■ Exhibit 37–2 Tax Aspects of Partnerships and Corporations[a]

Tax Aspect	Partnership	Corporation
1. Federal Income Tax	Partners are taxed on proportionate shares of partnership income, even if not distributed; the partnership files information returns only.	Income of the corporation is taxed; stockholders are also taxed on distributed dividends. The corporation files corporate income tax forms.
2. Accumulation	Partners are taxed on accumulated as well as distributed earnings.	Corporate stockholders are not taxed on accumulated earnings. There is, however, a penalty tax, in some instances, that the corporation must pay for unreasonable accumulations of income.
3. Capital Gains	Partners are taxed on their proportionate share of capital gains, which are taxed at ordinary income rate.	The corporation is taxed on capital gains and losses.
4. Exempt Income	Partners are not taxed on exempt income received from the firm.	Any exempt income distributed by a corporation is fully taxable income to the stockholders.
5. Pension Plan	Partners can adopt a Keogh plan, an IRA, or a 401-K plan.	Employees and officers who are also stockholders can be beneficiaries of a pension trust. The corporation can deduct its payments to the trust.
6. Social Security	Partners must pay a self-employment tax (in 1991, 12.4 percent on income up to $53,400, plus 2.9 percent Medicare tax on income up to $125,000).	All compensation to officers and employee stockholders is subject to Social Security taxation up to the maximum.
7. Death Benefits (excluding those provided by insurance)	There is no exemption for payments to partners' beneficiaries.	Benefits up to $5,000 can be received tax-free by employees' beneficiaries.
8. State Taxes	The partnership is not subject to taxes. State income taxes are paid by each partner.	The corporation is subject to state income taxes (although these taxes can be deducted on federal returns).

a.   As of 1991.

■ Other Organizational Forms

A business venture does not have to be organized as a sole proprietorship, a partnership, or a corporation. Several other organizational forms exist, although for the most part they are hybrid organizations—that is, they have characteristics similar to those of partnerships or corporations, or they combine features of both. We look at several of these forms here.

Joint Venture

When two or more persons or entities combine their interests in a particular business enterprise and agree to share in losses or profits jointly or in proportion to their contributions, they are engaged in a **joint venture.** The joint venture is treated much like a partnership and is taxed like a partnership, but it differs in that its creation is in contemplation of a limited activity or a single transaction. Also, members of a joint venture usually have limited powers to bind their co-venturers. A joint venture is normally not a legal entity and therefore cannot be sued as such, but its members can be sued individually. Joint ventures range in size from very small activities to huge, multimillion-dollar joint actions engaged in by some of the world's largest corporations.

Syndicate

A group of individuals getting together to finance a particular project, such as the building of a shopping center or the purchase of a professional basketball franchise, is called a **syndicate** or an *investment group*. The forms of such groups vary considerably. They may exist as corporations or as general or limited partnerships. In some cases, the members merely own property jointly and have no legally recognized business arrangement.

Joint Stock Company

A **joint stock company** is a true hybrid of a partnership and a corporation. It has many characteristics of a corporation in that (1) its ownership is represented by transferable shares of stock, (2) it is usually managed by directors and officers of the company or association, and (3) it can have a perpetual existence. Most of its other features, however, are more characteristic of a partnership, and it is usually treated like a partnership. As with a partnership, a joint stock company is formed by agreement (not statute), property is usually held in the names of the members, shareholders have personal liability, and generally the company is not treated as a legal entity for purposes of a lawsuit. In a joint stock company, however, shareholders are not considered to be agents of one another, as would be the case if the company were a true partnership.

Business Trust

A **business trust** is created by a written trust agreement that sets forth the interests of the beneficiaries and the obligations and powers of the trustees. With a business trust, legal ownership and management of the property of the business stay with one or more of the trustees, and the profits are distributed to the beneficiaries. The business trust resembles a corporation in many respects. Death or bankruptcy of a beneficiary, for example, does not terminate the trust, and beneficiaries are not personally responsible for the debts or obligations of the business trust. In fact, in a number of states business trusts must pay corporate taxes.

Cooperative

A **cooperative** is an association that is organized to provide an economic service without profit to its members (or shareholders). An incorporated cooperative is subject to state laws governing non-profit corporations. It will make distributions of dividends, or profits, to its owners on the basis of their transactions with the cooperative rather than on the basis of the amount of capital they contributed. Unincorporated cooperatives are often treated like partnerships. The members have joint liability for the cooperative's acts.

This form of business is generally adopted by groups of individuals who wish to pool their resources to gain some advantage in the marketplace. Consumer purchasing cooperatives are formed to obtain lower prices through quantity discounts. Seller marketing cooperatives are formed to control the market and thereby obtain higher sales prices from consumers. Credit cooperatives and farmers' cooperatives are other examples of this form of business enterprise. Cooperatives are often exempt from certain federal laws—for example, antitrust statutes—because of their special status.

■ Private Franchises

Times have changed dramatically since Ray Kroc, the late founder of McDonald's, launched the franchising boom over thirty years ago. Today, over a third of all retail sales and an increasing part of the gross national product of the United States are generated by private franchises. A **franchise** is any arrangement in which the owner of a trademark, a trade name, or a copyright has licensed others to use it in selling goods or services. A **franchisee** (a purchaser of a franchise), is generally legally independent, but economically dependent on the integrated business system of the **franchisor** (the seller of the franchise). In other words, a franchisee can operate as an independent businessperson but still obtain the advantages of a regional or national organization. Well-known franchises include McDonald's, Hilton Hotels, Holiday Inns, and Burger King.

The Law of Franchising

The growth in franchise operations has outdistanced the law of franchising. There has yet to be developed a solid body of appellate decisions under federal or state laws relating to franchises. In the absence of case law precisely addressed to franchising, the courts tend to apply general common law principles and appropriate federal or state statutory definitions and rules. Characteristics associated with a franchising relationship are similar in some respects to those of principal-agent, employer-employee, and employer–independent contractor relationships—yet a franchising relationship does not truly fit into any of these traditional classifications.

Some statutory requirements specifically relating to franchising have been enacted at the federal level. Automobile dealership franchisees are protected from automobile manufacturers' bad faith termination of their franchises by the Automobile Dealers' Franchise Act (enacted in 1956), also known as the Automobile Dealers' Day in Court Act.[1] If a manufacturer-franchisor terminates a franchise because of a dealer-franchisee's failure to comply with unreasonable demands (for example, failure to attain an unrealistically high sales quota), the manufacturer is liable for damages.

Another federal statute is the Petroleum Marketing Practices Act (PMPA),[2] which was adopted in 1979 to protect gasoline station franchisees' reasonable expectations in the continuation of their franchises. Before the PMPA's passage, gasoline franchisors were notorious for imposing high minimum rents and gallonage requirements, and the situation only worsened during the energy crisis in the early 1970s. The PMPA prescribes the grounds and conditions under which a franchisor may terminate or decline to renew a franchise. Federal antitrust laws (discussed in Chapter 48) may also apply if there is an illegal price-fixing agreement affecting the relationship between a franchisor and franchisee.

In 1979, the Federal Trade Commission (FTC) issued regulations that require franchisors to disclose material facts necessary to a prospective franchisee's making an informed decision concerning the purchase of a franchise.

Many states currently have statutes dealing with franchise law. State legislation tends to be similar to federal statutes and the FTC regulations. That is, state laws are generally designed to protect prospective franchisees from dishonest franchisors and to prohibit franchisors from terminating franchises without good cause. For example, a law might require the disclosure of information that is material to making an informed decision regarding the purchase of a franchise. This could include such information as the actual costs of operation, recurring expenses, and profits earned, along with facts substantiating these figures.

When a franchise exists primarily for the sale of products manufactured by the franchisor, the law governing sales as expressed in Article 2 of the UCC (discussed in Unit Three) applies.

In response to the need for a uniform franchise law, the National Conference of Commissioners on Uniform State Laws drafted a model law that standardizes the various state franchise regulations. Because the uniform law represents a compromise of so many diverse interests, it has met with little success in being adopted as law by the various states.

Types of Franchises

Franchises can take the form of distributorships, chain-style business operations, or manufacturing or processing-plant arrangements. We briefly describe each of these forms below.

1. A **distributorship** is established when a manufacturing concern (franchisor) licenses a dealer (franchisee) to sell its product. Often, a distributorship covers an exclusive territory. An example of this type of franchise is an automobile dealership.

2. A **chain-style business franchise** results when a franchise operates under a franchisor's trade name and is identified as a member of a select group of dealers that engages in the franchisor's business. The franchisee is generally required to follow standardized or prescribed methods of operations. Often, the franchisor requires that minimum prices and standards of operation be maintained. In addition, sometimes the franchisee is obligated to deal exclusively with the franchisor to obtain materials and supplies. An example of this type of franchise is McDonald's or most other fast-food chains.

3. A **manufacturing or processing-plant franchise** is created when the franchisor transmits to the franchisee the essential ingredients or formula to make a particular product. The franchisee then markets it either at wholesale or at retail in accordance with the franchisor's standards. Examples of this type of franchise are Coca-Cola and other soft-drink bottling companies.

---

1. 15 U.S.C. Section 1221 *et seq.*
2. 15 U.S.C. Section 2801 *et seq.*

Franchise Agreement

The franchise relationship is defined by a contract between the franchisor and the franchisee. Each franchise relationship and each industry has its own characteristics, so it is difficult to describe the broad range of details a franchising contract may include. The following sections, however, will define the essential characteristics of the franchise relationship.

PAYING FOR THE FRANCHISE   The franchisee ordinarily pays an initial fee or lump-sum price for the franchise license (the privilege of being granted a franchise). This fee is separate from the fee for the various products that the franchisee purchases from or through the franchisor. In some industries, the franchisor relies heavily on the initial sale of the franchise for realizing a profit. In other industries, the continued dealing between the parties brings profit to both.

In most situations, the franchisor will receive a stated percentage of the annual sales or annual volume of business done by the franchisee. The franchise agreement may also require the franchisee to pay a percentage of advertising costs and certain administrative expenses incurred under the franchise agreement.

LOCATION OF THE FRANCHISE   Typically, the franchisor will determine the territory to be served. The franchise agreement may specify whether the premises for the business must be leased or purchased outright. In some cases, construction of a building is necessary to meet the terms of the franchise agreement.

Certainly the agreement will specify whether the franchisor supplies equipment and furnishings for the premises or whether this is the responsibility of the franchisee. When the franchise is a service operation, such as a motel, the contract often provides that the franchisor will establish certain standards for the facility and will make inspections to ensure that the standards are being maintained in order to protect the franchise name and reputation.

One area of franchises that causes a great deal of conflict is the territorial exclusivity of the franchise. Many franchise agreements, while they do define the territory allotted to a particular franchise, specifically state that the franchise is nonexclusive. The ramifications of nonexclusivity can be severe, because it allows the franchisor to establish additional franchises in the same territory as the existing franchisee. The following case illustrates this problem.

BACKGROUND AND FACTS   In 1976, Imperial Motors, Inc., entered into direct dealer agreements for Chrysler and Plymouth dealerships with Chrysler Corporation. The direct dealer agreements explicitly provided that Imperial would not have the exclusive right to purchase Chrysler's cars for resale in a four-town area of South Carolina. The Chrysler district manager, however, told Imperial that Imperial's Chrysler-Plymouth dealership would be the only one in these four towns. In August 1976, Chrysler allowed another Chrysler-Plymouth dealer, Carroll Motors, to move to a new showroom seven miles from Imperial's location. Imperial filed suit in a federal district court, claiming that Chrysler had violated the Automobile Dealers' Day in Court Act by approving the relocation of Carroll Motors. Chrysler moved for summary judgment.

 Case 37.1

IMPERIAL MOTORS, INC. v. CHRYSLER CORP.

United States District Court, District of Massachusetts, 1983.
559 F.Supp. 1312.

DECISION AND RATIONALE   The United States District Court for the District of Massachusetts granted Chrysler's motion for summary judgment, reasoning that the act covers only those actions of a franchisor that amount to a "failure to act in good faith in performing or complying with any of the terms or provisions of the franchise, or in terminating, cancelling, or not renewing the franchise with a dealer." The court pointed out that good faith is narrowly defined as "the duty of each party to act in a fair and equitable manner." The court further stated that a "failure to abide by the terms of a franchise agreement could not by itself constitute a violation of the act" and that the act's explicit definition of a franchise as a written agreement precluded any oral promises from being considered as part of the franchise agreement and thus forming the basis of a claim of bad faith.

COMMENTS The franchisee in this case was left unprotected by the franchise agreement as far as territorial exclusivity was concerned. The same denial of relief resulted from a suit filed under the Unfair Trade Practices Act by a Ford automobile dealer (with a nonexclusive franchise agreement) after Ford Motor Company granted another Ford dealership near his. [See *McLaughlin Ford, Inc. v. Ford Motor Co.,* 192 Conn. 558, 473 A.2d 1185 (1984).] Franchisees must obtain exclusivity rights in their contracts to be protected.

PRICE CONTROLS Franchises provide the franchisor with an outlet for the firm's goods and services. Depending on the nature of the business, the franchisor may require the franchisee to purchase certain supplies from the franchisor at an established price.[3] Of course, a franchisor cannot set the prices at which the franchisee will resell the goods, as this is a violation of state antitrust laws, federal antitrust laws, or both. A franchisor can suggest retail prices but cannot insist on them.

BUSINESS ORGANIZATION AND QUALITY CONTROLS The business organization of the franchisee is of great concern to the franchisor. Depending on the terms of the franchise agreement, the franchisor may specify particular requirements for the form and capital structure of the business. The franchise agreement can provide that standards of operation, such as sales quotas, quality standards, or record keeping, be met by the franchisee. Furthermore, a franchisor may wish to retain stringent control over the training of personnel involved in the operation and over administrative aspects of the business. Although the day-to-day operation of the franchise business is normally left up to the franchisee, the franchise agreement may provide for whatever amount of supervision and control the parties agree upon.

As a general rule, the validity of a provision permitting the franchisor to enforce certain quality standards is unquestioned. Because the franchisor has a legitimate interest in maintaining the quality of the product or service in order to protect its name and reputation, it can exercise greater control in this area than would otherwise be tolerated.

TERMINATION OF THE FRANCHISE The duration of the franchise is a matter to be determined between the parties. Generally, a franchise will start out for a short period, such as a year, so that the franchisee and the franchisor can determine whether they want to stay in business with one another. Usually the franchise agreement will specify that termination must be ''for cause,'' such as death or disability of the franchisee, insolvency of the franchisee, breach of the franchise agreement, or failure to meet specified sales quotas. Most franchise contracts provide that notice of termination must be given. If no set time for termination is given, then a reasonable time with notice will be implied. A franchisee must be given reasonable time to wind up the business—that is, to do the accounting and return the copyright, trademark, or any other property of the franchisor.

Much franchise litigation has arisen over termination provisions. Because the franchise agreement is normally a form contract drawn and prepared by the franchisor, and because the bargaining power of the franchisee is rarely equal to that of the franchisor, the termination provisions of contracts are generally more favorable to the franchisor. This means that the franchisee, who normally invests a substantial amount of time and money in the franchise operation to make it successful, may receive little or nothing for the business upon termination. The franchisor owns the trademark and hence the business.

It is in this area that the lack of statutory law and case law is felt most keenly by the franchisee.

---

3. Requiring a franchisee to purchase *exclusively* from the franchisor may violate federal antitrust laws. See Chapter 47.

| LEGAL PERSPECTIVES IN BUSINESS | **The Benefits and Costs of Franchising** |

A franchise arrangement appeals to many prospective businesspersons who want independence, yet feel more comfortable with an established product or service and a management network that is regional or national in scope and that has been in place for some time. Franchises also have a high survival rate (90 percent)—at least relative to small businesses (20 percent). Franchise agreements and operations may, nonetheless, lead to difficulties, as well as financial loss to the actual or prospective franchisee.

Consider the franchise fee. Virtually all franchise contracts require a franchise fee payable up front or in installments. Some franchise arrangements hide franchise-fee payments as part of the price charged to the franchisee for goods or services that have to be purchased from the franchisor. In other words, if you as a franchisee are required to purchase paper napkins with a logo from the franchisor at a 20 percent premium over the bona fide wholesale price, then you are implicitly paying a franchise fee. Additionally,

your required contribution to advertising monies administered by the franchisor may be in excess of your bona fide pro rata share. The difference again is an implicit franchise fee.

A major economic consequence, usually of a negative nature, will occur if your franchise agreement is terminated by the franchisor. The courts have not made a clear statement as to what a franchisee's rights are on termination. Some courts, for example, have held that if a franchise investment is substantial and the relationship between the parties has been established, it cannot be terminated until after a reasonable period of time has elapsed. What is considered to be a reasonable time period depends on the circumstances in each case, such as the amount of preliminary promotional expenditures made, the length of time in operation, the prospects of forfeiting profits, and the actual profitability of the franchise during its operation.

To avoid many economic, as well as legal, problems, it is imperative that you as a potential franchisee, before paying for the franchise, obtain all of the relevant details of the business and of the franchise agreement.

Automobile dealerships and gasoline stations subject to franchise contracts now have some statutory protection, however, under the Automobile Dealers' Franchise Act and the Petroleum Marketing Practices Act (PMPA), respectively. Whether a franchise agreement had been unfairly terminated by the franchisor under the provisions of the PMPA is the subject of the following case.

BACKGROUND AND FACTS In June 1985, Retseig Corporation entered into a franchise agreement with Arco Petroleum Products Company under which Retseig would operate an Arco minimarket and gas station in Monterey, California. Retseig was authorized to sell only "Arco branded motor fuels"—which were designated as fuels containing a special Arco additive known as R-585. The required percentage of R-585 in Arco fuels was never made too clear by Arco in its interrogatories before trial but apparently ranged between 0.05 and 0.12 percent. In October 1986 Retseig, after informing Arco of its plans, began to purchase Arco gas (gas containing the R-585 additive) from a cheaper supplier, Caljet. Tests conducted by Arco on the Caljet gas sold by Retseig showed that the regular gas was "at the high end" of the required R-585 content, but that the unleaded gas and super unleaded gas contained only 0.02 percent and 0.03 percent,

Case 37.2

RETSEIG CORP. v. ARCO PETROLEUM PRODUCTS CO.

United States Court of Appeals, Ninth Circuit, 1989.
870 F.2d 1495.

respectively, of R-585. In November, Arco terminated Retseig's franchise by written notice on the ground that Retseig had willfully misbranded the gas in violation of the Petroleum Marketing Practices Act (PMPA). Retseig claimed that it had not misbranded the gas, willfully or otherwise, and brought an action against Arco in a federal district court for wrongful termination of the franchise. The court granted Arco's motion for summary judgment, holding that there was no triable issue of fact. The court reasoned that under the PMPA, "willful" does not require proof of a bad motive; it requires only an intentional act. The court further found it to be "undisputed" that the Caljet gas did not qualify as Arco gas. Because Retseig "willfully" bought the Caljet gas, it violated the franchise agreement, which Arco could terminate under the PMPA. Retseig appealed.

DECISION AND RATIONALE   The United States Court of Appeals for the Ninth Circuit reversed, holding that the district court's stated reasons for the grant of summary judgment were insufficient. The appellate court noted that the factual dispute regarding whether Caljet sold Arco gasoline had not been satisfactorily resolved. Moreover, the court found that the definition of Arco gasoline offered during the trial was "not so clear as to allow us to find that Arco established misbranding (whether willful or not) to the satisfaction of any rational jury." The court also held that "willful" under the PMPA required not only a voluntary act, but "an intentional disregard of, or plain indifference to, the requirements of the franchise agreement." Because R-585 was present in all the fuels, Arco had not conclusively shown that Retseig had willfully misbranded the fuel.

◼ CONCEPT SUMMARY 37.1   Forms of Business Organization

Form	Essential Characteristics
Sole Proprietorship	1. The simplest form of business; used by anyone who does business without creating an organization. The owner is the business. 2. The owner pays personal income taxes on all profits. 3. The owner is personally liable for all business debts.
General Partnership	1. Created by agreement of the parties. 2. Not treated as an entity except for limited purposes. 3. Partners have unlimited liability for partnership debts. 4. Each partner has an equal voice in management, unless otherwise provided for in the partnership agreement. 5. Capital contribution of each partner is determined by agreement. 6. Each partner pays a *pro rata* share of income taxes on the net profits of the partnership, whether or not they are distributed; the partnership files an information return only.
Limited Partnership	1. Must be formed in compliance with statutory requirements. 2. Consists of one or more general partners, and one or more limited partners.

(Continued on next page)

■ CONCEPT SUMMARY 37.1 *(Continued)*

Form	Essential Characteristics
Limited Partnership (continued)	3. Only general partners can participate in management. Limited partners have no voice in management. 4. General partners have unlimited liability for partnership losses; limited partners are liable only to the extent of their contribution.
Corporation	1. Created by state-issued charter. 2. A legal entity separate and distinct from its owners. 3. Shareholders have limited liability—that is, they are not personally liable for the debts of the corporation. 4. Shareholders elect directors who set policy and appoint officers to manage corporate affairs. 5. The corporation pays income tax on net profits; shareholders pay income tax on disbursed dividends. 6. Can have perpetual existence.
Other Business Forms	1. *Joint venture*—An organization created by two or more persons in contemplation of a limited activity or a single transaction. Otherwise, similar to a partnership. 2. *Syndicate*—An investment group that undertakes to finance a particular project; may exist as a corporation or as a general or limited partnership. 3. *Joint stock company*—A business form similar to a corporation in some respects (perpetual existence, transferable shares of stock, management by directors and officers) but otherwise resembles a partnership. 4. *Business trust*—Created by a written trust agreement that sets forth the interests of the beneficiaries and obligations and powers of the trustee(s). Similar to a corporation in many respects. Beneficiaries are not personally liable for the debts or obligations of the business trust. 5. *Cooperative*—An association organized to provide an economic service, without profit, to its members. May take the form of a corporation or a partnership.

Private Franchises	1. *Types of franchises*—
	  a. Distributorship (e.g., an automobile dealership).
	  b. Chain-style operation (e.g., fast-food chains).
	  c. Manufacturing/processing-plant arrangement (e.g., soft-drink bottling companies such as Coca-Cola).
	
	2. *The franchise agreement*—
	  a. Ordinarily requires the franchisee (purchaser) to pay a price for the franchise license.
	  b. Specifies the territory to be served by the franchisee's firm.
	  c. May require the franchisee to purchase certain supplies from the franchisor at an established price.
	  d. May require the franchisee to abide by certain standards of quality relating to product or service offered but cannot set retail resale price.
	  e. Usually provides for the date and/or conditions of termination of the franchise arrangement.

■ Terms and Concepts

business trust 673
chain-style business
   franchise 674
cooperative 673
corporation 669
distributorship 674
entrepreneur 668

franchise 673
franchisee 673
franchisor 673
information return 669
joint stock company 673
joint venture 672
limited partnership 669

manufacturing or
   processing-plant
   franchise 674
partnership 669
sole proprietorship 668
syndicate 673

■ For Review

1. Which form of business is the simplest? Which form arises from an agreement between two or more persons to carry on a business for profit? Which form consists of shareholders and is managed by a board of directors?

2. Generally, the liability of a limited partner or a corporate shareholder is limited to the amount of his or her investment. Under what circumstances might a limited partner or a shareholder be held liable for the obligations of his or her partnership or corporation?

3. Assuming a franchisor is agreeable, can a franchise be a sole proprietorship? A general partnership? A limited partnership? A corporation?

4. Howard, Patty, and Boyle agree to engage in a software marketing business. They each provide one-third of the initial capital and assume one-third of the management responsibilities. When their business loses a copyright infringement suit, they are each held personally liable for the damages. What form is their business?

5. In the previous problem, after the lawsuit, Howard, Patty, and Boyle develop a unique software product, and their business expands, becoming larger and more profitable. They diversify to market a variety of computer products and office and school supplies. Outside investors express interest in investing in the firm. What business form might Howard, Patty, and Boyle find most advantageous?

■ Questions and Case Problems

37-1. Suppose that Ann, Betty, and Carla are college graduates, and Ann has come up with an idea for a new product that she believes could make the three of them very rich. Her idea is to manufacture beer dispensers for home use, and her goal is to market them to consumers throughout the Midwest. Ann's personal experience qualifies her to be both first-line supervisor and general manager of the new firm. Betty is a born salesperson. Carla has little interest in sales or management but would like to invest a large sum of money that she has inherited from her aunt. Discuss fully what factors Ann, Betty, and Carla should consider in deciding which form of business organization to adopt.

37-2. In the situation described in Question 37-1, assume that Carla is willing to put her inherited money in the business but does not want any further liability should the beer dispenser manufacturing business fail. Alternatively, the bank is willing to lend some capital at a 12 percent interest rate, but it will do so only if certain restrictions are placed on management decisions. The bank's plan is not satisfactory to Ann or Betty, and the two decide to bring Carla into the business. Under these circumstances, discuss which types of business organizations are best suited to meet Carla's needs.

37-3. The limited liability of corporate shareholders is one of the most important reasons that firms choose to organize as corporations rather than as partnerships or sole proprietorships. Limited liability means that if a corporation is not able to meet its obligations with corporate assets, creditors will not be allowed to look to the owners (stockholders) of the corporation to satisfy their claims. Assume that Ann and Betty (in Question 37-1) do not have a wealthy friend like Carla who wishes to go into business with them and they therefore must borrow money to start their business. Ann and Betty decide to incorporate. What do you think a lender will ask them when they seek a loan? What effect does this have on the "advantage" of limited liability under incorporation?

37-4. Assume that Bateson Corp. is considering entering into two contracts—one with a joint stock company that distributes home products east of the Mississippi River and the other with a business trust formed by a number of sole proprietors who are sellers of home products on the West Coast. Both contracts involve large capital outlays for Bateson to supply each business with restaurant equipment. In both business organizations, at least two shareholders or beneficiaries are personally wealthy, but each business organization has limited financial resources. The owner-managers of Bateson are not familiar with either form of business organization. Because each form resembles a corporation, they are concerned with the possibility of liability in the event that either business organization breaches the contract by failing to make the deferred payments. Discuss fully Bateson's concern.

37-5. Otmar has been interested in securing a particular high-quality ice cream franchise. The franchisor is willing to give him a franchise. A franchise agreement is made that calls for Otmar to sell the ice cream only at a specific location, to buy all the ice cream from the franchisor, to order and sell all the flavors produced by the franchisor, and to refrain from selling any ice cream stored for more than two weeks after delivery by the franchisor, as this ice cream decreases in quality after that period. After two months of operation, Otmar believes that he can increase his profits by moving the store to another part of the city. He also refuses to order even a limited quantity of the "fruit delight" flavor because of its higher cost, and he has sold ice cream that has been stored longer than two weeks without customer complaint. Otmar claims that the franchisor has no right to restrict him in these practices. Discuss his claims.

37-6. H. C. Blackwell Co. was a truck dealership owned by the Blackwell family. In 1961 they purchased a franchise from Kenworth Truck Co. to sell Kenworth trucks. The franchise agreement had been renewed several times. In November 1975 the Blackwells began negotiations with Kenworth to renew the recently expired franchise, and disagreements arose concerning the franchise. On February 4, 1976, Kenworth wrote to Blackwell that the franchise would be terminated in ninety days unless Blackwell met twelve specific demands made by Kenworth. In trying to meet these demands—which included increased sales, a better method of keeping business records, and capital improvements at its dealership—Blackwell spent approximately $90,000. By the end of the ninety-day period, however, the demands had not been met, so Kenworth terminated the franchise. Blackwell sued Kenworth for damages on the grounds that Kenworth had wrongfully terminated the franchise agreement and, in so doing, had violated the Automobile Dealers' Franchise Act. During the trial, Kenworth's own regional sales manager stated that the demands imposed by Kenworth upon Blackwell would have taken at least a year to meet. Has Kenworth wrongfully terminated the franchise under the Automobile Dealers' Franchise Act? Discuss fully. [*H. C. Blackwell Co. v. Kenworth Truck Co.*, 620 F.2d 104 (5th Cir. 1980)]

37-7. In 1981 the Huangs entered into a franchise agreement with Holiday Inns, Inc., under which the Huangs agreed to adhere to the quality standards established by Holiday Inns and to comply in every respect with the Holiday Inns Standards Manual. In November 1983 the district director of Holiday Inns made a courtesy inspection that revealed cracked windows, damaged and discolored walls, inoperative smoke detectors, broken light fixtures, poultry being stored at room temperature, and numerous other indications that the Huangs were not maintaining the estab-

lished Holiday Inn quality standards in accordance with the franchise agreement. A formal inspection in February 1984 revealed no significant improvement in quality standards, and the hotel was given an official rating of "unacceptable." The Huangs, who had been given detailed reports concerning the findings of both inspections, were advised that if the noted deficiencies were not remedied within sixty days, Holiday Inns would have grounds to terminate the franchise. When an inspection in April 1984 revealed that the deficiencies had not been cured, Holiday Inns notified the Huangs that the franchise would be terminated on July 30 unless the deficiencies were remedied by June 28. The Huangs, who in May had begun hotel renovations costing $55,000, requested a ninety-day extension to the June 28 deadline, which Holiday Inns refused to grant. The Huangs then petitioned the court for a preliminary injunction against the termination of the franchise by Holiday Inns, claiming that Holiday Inns had acted "capriciously and arbitrarily" by (1) not stating precisely the nature of the deficiencies and what was required to make repairs and improvements and (2) not giving the Huangs a reasonable time in which to remedy the deficiencies. Discuss fully whether Holiday Inns should be enjoined from terminating the franchise, given these circumstances. [*Huang v. Holiday Inns, Inc.*, 594 F.Supp. 352 (C.D.Cal.1984)]

37-8. In 1953, Atlantic Richfield Co. (Arco) and Razumic signed a printed form titled a "Dealer Lease." The agreement referred to the parties as lessor and lessee. It authorized Razumic to operate an Arco service station and provided, among other things, for Arco's signs and trade name to be prominently displayed at the service station and for gasoline and other related products to be sold. The agreement detailed other aspects of the parties' business relationship, including Razumic's obligation to operate the service station in such a manner as to reflect favorably on Arco's goodwill. These basic terms were in all renewal agreements made by the parties over the years. In 1973, Arco notified Razumic that the agreement was being terminated and gave him thirty days to vacate the premises. Razumic refused, and Arco filed suit to force termination of the agreement. Did the "Dealer Lease" constitute a franchise agreement? If so—in view of the fact that the Petroleum Marketing Practices Act had not yet been passed when this case was decided—on what grounds might the court hold that Arco could not terminate the franchise at will? Discuss. [*Atlantic Richfield Co. v. Razumic*, 480 Pa. 366, 390 A.2d 736 (1978)]

37-9. Gustave Peterson contacted his family doctor, Leland Reichelt, complaining of abdominal pain. The doctor recommended gallbladder surgery. Dr. George Fortier performed the surgery, and Dr. Reichelt assisted. It was Dr. Reichelt's normal practice to refer patients to Dr. Fortier for surgery, and each doctor charged the patient separately for his services. During the operation, a metal clip was inadvertently left inside Peterson's abdominal cavity. It eventually formed a stone, which later caused Peterson chest and gastric pain. Peterson repeatedly complained to

Dr. Reichelt, who diagnosed the problem as related to either a hernia or stress. Peterson finally sought the advice of another physician, who, upon performing surgery, discovered the metal clip. Peterson filed suit against both Dr. Reichelt and Dr. Fortier for malpractice under the theory that Fortier and Reichelt were engaged in a joint enterprise (joint venture). Discuss fully whether the two doctors were joint venturers. [*Peterson v. Fortier,* 406 N.W.2d 563 (Minn.App. 1987)]

37-10. Ernst and Barbara Larese entered into a ten-year franchise agreement with Creamland Dairies, Inc., in 1974. The agreement provided that the franchisee ''shall not assign, transfer or sublet this franchise, or any of [the] rights under this agreement, without the prior written consent of Area Franchisor [Creamland] and Baskin Robbins, any such authorized assignment, transfer or subletting being null and without effect.'' The Lareses attempted to sell their franchise rights in February and August of 1979, but Creamland refused to consent to the sales. The Lareses brought suit, alleging that Creamland had interfered with their contractual relations with the prospective buyers by unreasonably withholding its consent; they held that Creamland had a duty to act in good faith and in a commercially reasonable manner when a franchisee sought to transfer its rights under the franchise agreement. Creamland contended that the contract gave it an unqualified right to refuse to consent to proposed sales of the franchise rights. Which party prevailed? Explain. [*Larese v. Creamland Dairies, Inc.,* 767 F.2d 716 (10th Cir. 1985)]

37-11. A Question of Ethics

H. Eugene Anderson, an attorney, had been a partner of a law firm in Burlington, Iowa, for thirteen years when he decided to withdraw from the firm and establish his own tax law practice. Many of the firm's clients, as well as one of his associates and two secretaries, chose to follow Anderson. Relations were fairly congenial during Anderson's departure, but tension later arose over the buy-out price of Anderson's partnership interest, which the partnership determined to be worth $114,243.99. Of that amount, $38,743 represented the cash Anderson had initially invested in the firm (his net purchase price), and the remainder signified the growth in the value of his partnership interest. Under the terms of the partnership agreement in effect at the time of Anderson's departure, *the firm was obligated to pay a departing partner the net purchase price but could reduce (or eliminate entirely) payment for the growth value of the partner's partnership interest if the remaining partners determined that the withdrawing partner ''committed an act which is detrimental to the partnership which affects the value of the remaining partners' interest in the partnership.'' After his departure, the firm paid Anderson $38,743 but refused to pay him for his interest in the firm above the net purchase price on the grounds that Anderson had committed acts detrimental to the partnership. The detrimental acts cited were Anderson's continued practice in Burlington in competition with the firm, his taking of an associate and two secretaries with him, and the substantial number of clients retained by Anderson and the resulting loss to the firm. Given these facts, consider the following questions. [Anderson v. Aspelmeier, Fisch, Power, Warner & Engberg, 461 N.W.2d 598 (Iowa 1990)]*

1. In Anderson's lawsuit against the firm to recover the remainder of his partnership interest, the trial court held that the ''detriment'' clause of the partnership agreement was in effect a covenant not to compete (see Chapter 14). Do you agree with this conclusion?

2. The Iowa Code of Professional Responsibility (an ethical code of conduct by which attorneys must abide) prohibits the inclusion of covenants not to compete in partnership or employment agreements. The purpose of this rule is to protect the client's freedom to choose or replace a lawyer at will. Does the law firm's attempt to ''punish'' Anderson (by refusing to pay him the full value of his partnership interest)—because he continued to practice law in the same city and the clients chose to follow him to his new practice—counter the policy that clients should have freedom of choice?

3. Do you think that it is fair to law partnerships not to allow them to include covenants not to compete in their partnership agreements? How can a law partnership protect itself against the losses that are incurred when a partner, such as Anderson in this case, withdraws from the partnership and is followed by a significant number of the firm's clients? How would you argue in favor of the law firm in this case? What social or ethical considerations, if any, are being traded off to ensure freedom of the choice on the part of clients?

Chapter 38

PARTNERSHIPS
Nature, Formation, and Operation

To a great extent, partnership law derives from agency law, which was presented in Chapters 35 and 36. Because each partner is considered an agent of the partnership, agency concepts apply—specifically, the imputation of knowledge of, and responsibility for, acts done within the scope of the partnership relationship. In their relationship to one another, partners are bound by the fiduciary ties that bind an agent and principal under agency law.

Partnership law is distinct from agency law in one significant way, however. A partnership is based on a voluntary contract between two or more competent persons who agree to place some or all of their money, effects, labor, and skill in a business with the understanding that profits and losses will be proportionately shared. In a nonpartnership agency relationship, the agent usually does not have an ownership interest in the business, nor is he or she obligated to bear a portion of the ordinary business losses.

The Uniform Partnership Act (UPA) governs the operation of partnerships *in the absence of express agreement* and has done much to reduce controversies in the law relating to partnerships. Except for Louisiana, the UPA has been adopted in all of the states, as well as in the District of Columbia. The entire text of the UPA is presented in Appendix D at the end of this text.

■ Definition of Partnership

Parties commonly find themselves in conflict over whether their business enterprise is a legal partnership, especially in the absence of a formal, written partnership agreement. Under the UPA, a *partnership* is defined as "an association of two or more persons to carry on as co-owners a business for profit" [UPA 6(1)]. In resolving disputes over whether partnership status exists, courts will usually look for the following three essential elements of partnership implicit in this definition:

1. A sharing of profits or losses.
2. A joint ownership of the business.
3. An equal right in the management of the business.

A problem arises when evidence is insufficient to establish all three factors. The UPA provides a set of guidelines to be used in this event. For

683

example, the sharing of profits and losses from a business is considered *prima facie* evidence that a partnership has been created. No such inference is made, however, if the profits were received as payment of the following:

1. A debt by installments or interest on a loan.
2. Wages of an employee.
3. Rent to a landlord.
4. An annuity to a widow or representative of a deceased partner.
5. A sale of goodwill of a business or property [UPA 7(4)].

To illustrate: Suppose that debtor owes a creditor $5,000 on an unsecured debt. To repay the debt, the debtor agrees to pay (and the creditor, to accept) 10 percent of the debtor's monthly business profits until the loan with interest has been paid. Although the creditor is sharing profits from the business, the debtor and creditor are not presumed to be partners.

Joint ownership of property, obviously, does not in and of itself create a partnership. Therefore, the fact that, say, MacPherson and Bunker own real property as joint tenants or as tenants in common (a form of joint ownership) does not establish a partnership. In fact, the sharing of gross returns and even profits from such ownership is usually not enough to create a partnership [UPA 7(2), (3)]. Thus, if MacPherson and Bunker jointly owned a piece of rural property and leased the land to a farmer, the sharing of the profits from the farming operation by the farmer in lieu of set rental payments would ordinarily not make MacPherson, Bunker, and the farmer partners.

■ Nature of Partnerships

A partnership is sometimes called a *firm* or a company, terms that connote an entity separate and apart from its aggregate members. Sometimes the law of partnership recognizes the independent entity, but for certain other purposes, the law treats the partnership as an aggregate of individual partners. At common law, a partnership was never treated as a separate legal entity. Thus, a common law suit could never be brought by or against the firm in its own name; each individual partner had to sue or be sued.

Partnership as an Entity

Many states today provide specifically that the partnership can be treated as an entity for certain purposes. These usually include the capacity to sue or be sued, to collect judgments, and to have all accounting procedures in the name of the partnership. In addition, the UPA recognizes that partnership property may be held in the name of the partnership rather than in the names of the individual partners. Finally, federal procedural laws frequently permit the partnership to be treated as an entity in such matters as suits in federal courts, bankruptcy proceedings, and filing of informational federal tax returns. These matters will be discussed here in some detail.

LEGAL CAPACITY States vary on how a partnership is viewed as a party in a legal suit. Some permit a partnership to sue and be sued in the firm name; others allow a partnership to be sued as an entity but not to sue others in its firm name (that is, the partnership must use the names of the individual partners). Federal courts recognize the partnership as an entity that can sue or be sued when a federal question is involved. Otherwise, federal courts follow the practice adopted by the state in which the federal court is located.

JUDGMENTS Partnership liability is first paid out of partnership assets when a judgment is rendered *against the firm name*. In a general partnership, the personal assets of the individual members are subject to liability if the partnership's assets are inadequate. Even in limited partnerships, at least one of the partners—the general partner—subjects his or her personal assets to liability for the partnership's obligations. Good legal practice dictates that when state law permits a firm to be sued, the partners should be joined as parties to the suit. This ensures that a wide range of assets will be available for paying the judgment.

The general rule is that a judgment creditor of a partnership (a creditor in whose favor a money judgment has been entered by a court) can execute the judgment against the partners either jointly or severally. In some states, however, the judgment creditor must exhaust the remedies against partnership property before proceeding to execute against the individual property of the partners. This is referred to as the doctrine of **marshalling assets.** Marshalling assets is a common law equitable doctrine; it is not statutory.

MARSHALLING ASSETS   The arrangement or ranking of assets in a certain order toward the payment of debts outstanding is involved in marshalling assets. In particular, when there are two classes of assets and some creditors can enforce their claims against both whereas others can enforce their claims against only one, then the creditors of the former class are compelled to exhaust the assets against which they alone have a claim before they can have recourse to the other assets. This provides for the settlement of as many claims as possible.

As applied to a partnership, the doctrine of marshalling assets requires that the partnership's creditors have first priority to the partnership's assets and that personal creditors of the individual partners have first priority to the individual assets of each partner. When the partnership's assets are insufficient to satisfy a partnership creditor, that creditor does not have access to the assets of any individual partner until the personal creditors of that partner have been satisfied from such assets. This doctrine does not apply to partnerships that are in Chapter 7 proceedings in bankruptcy (see Chapter 33).

BANKRUPTCY   In federal court, an adjudication of bankruptcy *in the firm name* applies only to the partnership entity. It does not constitute personal bankruptcy for the partners. Similarly, the personal bankruptcy of an individual partner does not bring the partnership entity or its assets into bankruptcy.

The doctrine of marshalling assets is modified when a partnership is granted an order of relief in bankruptcy. In such situations, if partnership assets are insufficient to cover debts owed to partnership creditors, each general partner becomes *personally* liable to the bankruptcy trustee for the amount of the deficiency.

CONVEYANCE OF PROPERTY   The title to real or personal property can be held in the partnership's firm name. In other words, the partnership as an entity can own property apart from that owned by its individual members [UPA 8(3)]. Thus, the property held in the firm name can be conveyed (trans-

ferred) without each individual partner's joining in the transaction.

At common law, title to real estate could not be held in a partnership's firm name. Each partner was regarded as a co-owner (known in legal terminology as a *tenant in partnership*).[1] Each partner had to join in all conveyances (transfers of rights in the real estate). Although the modern rule of partnership property ownership disregards the need for aggregate action to convey property, there are some practical difficulties to consider.

Most states do not require that public records keep lists of members of a partnership. Hence, in determining the validity of a conveyance in a partnership's name, it may be impossible to tell whether the person executing the deed is actually a partner and has authority to convey. Some states, however, have passed laws requiring firms to file a statement of partnership. This list names members of the firm authorized to execute conveyances on behalf of the firm.

Aggregate Theory of Partnership

When the partnership is not regarded as a separate legal entity, it is treated as an *aggregate* of the individual partners. For example, for federal income tax purposes, a partnership is not a tax-paying entity. The income or losses incurred by it are "passed through" the partnership framework and attributed to the partners on their individual tax returns. The partnership as an entity has no tax liability. It is an entity only for the filing of an informational return with the IRS, indicating the profit and loss that each partner will report on his or her individual tax return.

■ Partnership Formation

A partnership is a voluntary association of individuals. The *intent* to associate is a key element of a partnership, and one cannot join a partnership unless all other partners consent [UPA 18(g)]. A partnership is generally based on an agreement among the parties that reflects their intention to create a partnership, contribute capital, share prof-

---

1.   The UPA retained this concept in UPA 25(1). Although property may be held in the name of the partnership, as tenants in partnership, partners are still regarded as co-owners. Tenancy in partnership will be discussed later in this chapter.

its and losses, and participate in management. The partnership relationship involves a high degree of trust and reliance. Each partner is an agent for the other partners.

Formalities

As a general rule, agreements to form a partnership can be *oral, written,* or *implied by conduct.* Some partnership agreements, however, must be in writing to be legally enforceable within the Statute of Frauds (see Chapter 14 for details). For example, a partnership agreement that, by its terms, is to continue for more than one year or one that authorizes the partners to deal in real property transfers must be evidenced by a sufficient writing. As pointed out in the preceding chapter, a partnership agreement can include virtually any terms that the partners wish, unless they are illegal or contrary to public policy. A sample partnership agreement is shown in Exhibit 38–1.

Practically speaking, it is better if the provisions of any partnership agreement are in writing. The terms of an oral agreement are difficult to prove, because a court must evaluate oral testimony given by persons with an interest in the eventual decision. In addition, in the course of drafting a written agreement, the partners may see potential problems that they would not have seen otherwise.

For instance, Tomkins and Fredericks plan to enter into a partnership agreement to sell tires. Among the provisions to be included is that Tomkins is to provide two-thirds of the capital to start up the business and is to receive two-thirds of the profits in return. The agreement is made orally. Tomkins now sues because Fredericks claims that one-half of the profits should be his. Without a writing, Tomkins may have a hard time overcoming the presumption that he is entitled to only one-half of the profits of a two-person partnership.[2] A partnership agreement, called **articles of partnership,** usually specifies each partner's share of the profits and is binding regardless of how uneven the distribution appears to be.

Duration of Partnership

The partnership agreement can specify the duration of the partnership in terms of a date or the completion of a particular project. This is called a *partnership for a term.* A dissolution without the consent of all the partners prior to the expiration of the partnership term constitutes a breach of the agreement, and the responsible partner can be liable for any losses resulting from it.

If no fixed duration is specified, the partnership is a *partnership at will.* Any partner can dissolve this type of partnership at any time without violating the agreement and without incurring liability for losses to other partners that result from the termination.

Capacity

Any person having the capacity to enter a contract can become a partner. A partnership contract entered into with a minor as a partner is voidable and can be disaffirmed by the minor (see Chapter 12 for details). Lack of legal capacity due to insanity at the time of the agreement likewise allows the purported partner either to avoid the agreement or to enforce it. If a partner is adjudicated mentally incompetent during the course of the partnership, the partnership is not automatically dissolved, but dissolution can be decreed by a court upon petition.

The Corporation as Partner

General partners are personally liable for the debts incurred by the partnership. But if one of the general partners is a corporation, then what does personal liability mean? Basically, the capacity of corporations to contract is a question of corporation law. The Revised Model Business Corporation Act (see Appendix E) allows corporations generally to make contracts and incur liabilities. The UPA specifically permits a corporation to be a partner. By definition, ''a partnership is an association of two or more persons,'' and the UPA defines a person as including corporations [UPA 2].

Many states restrict the ability of corporations to become partners, though such restrictions have become less common over the years. Many decisions in jurisdictions that do not permit corporate partners nevertheless validate the arrangements by characterizing them as joint ventures rather than as partnerships.

---

2. The law assumes that members of a partnership share profits equally and losses in the same ratio as profits unless a partnership agreement provides otherwise [UPA 18(a)].

■ **Exhibit 38–1 Sample Partnership Agreement**

PARTNERSHIP AGREEMENT

This agreement, made and entered into as of the _____, by and among _____
_____ (hereinafter collectively sometimes referred to as "Partners").

WITNESSETH:

Whereas, the Parties hereto desire to form a General Partnership (hereinafter referred to as the "Partnership"), for the term and upon the conditions hereinafter set forth;

Now, therefore, in consideration of the mutual covenants hereinafter contained, it is agreed by and among the Parties hereto as follows:

Article I
BASIC STRUCTURE

Form. The Parties hereby form a General Partnership pursuant to the Laws of _____
_____.

Name. The business of the Partnership shall be conducted under the name of _____
_____.

Place of Business. The principal office and place of business of the Partnership shall be located at _____, or such other place as the Partners may from time to time designate.

Term. The Partnership shall commence on _____, and shall continue for _____ years, unless earlier terminated in the following manner: (a) By the completion of the purpose intended, or (b) Pursuant to this Agreement, or (c) By applicable _____ law, or (d) By death, insanity, bankruptcy, retirement, withdrawal, resignation, expulsion, or disability of all of the then Partners.

Purpose—General. The purpose for which the Partnership is organized is _____

Article II
FINANCIAL ARRANGEMENTS

Each Partner has contributed to the initial capital of the Partnership property in the amount and form indicated on Schedule A attached hereto and made a part hereof. Capital contributions to the Partnership shall not earn interest. An individual capital account shall be maintained for each Partner. If at any time during the existence of the Partnership it shall become necessary to increase the capital with which the said Partnership is doing business, then (upon the vote of the Managing Partner(s)): each party to this Agreement shall contribute to the capital of this Partnership within _ days notice of such need in an amount according to his then Percentage Share of Capital as called for by the Managing Partner(s).

The Percentage Share of Profits and Capital of each Partner shall be (unless otherwise modified by the terms of this Agreement) as follows:

Names	Initial Percentage Share of Profits and Capital

No interest shall be paid on any contribution to the capital of the Partnership. No Partner shall have the right to demand the return of his capital contributions except as herein provided. Except as herein provided, the individual Partners shall have no right to any priority over each other as to the return of capital contributions except as herein provided.

Distributions to the Partners of net operating profits of the Partnership, as hereinafter defined, shall be made at _____. Such distributions shall be made to the Partners simultaneously.

For the purpose of this Agreement, net operating profit for any accounting period shall mean the gross receipts of the Partnership for such period, less the sum of all cash expenses of operation of the Partnership, and such sums as may be necessary to establish a reserve for operating expenses. In determining net operating profit, deductions for depreciation, amortization, or other similar charges not requiring actual current expenditures of cash shall *not* be taken into account in accordance with generally accepted accounting principles.

(Continued on the next page)

■ **Exhibit 38–1 Sample Partnership Agreement (Continued)**

No Partner shall be entitled to receive any compensation from the Partnership, nor shall any Partner receive any drawing account from the Partnership.

Article III
MANAGEMENT

The Managing Partner(s) shall be _____.

The Managing Partner(s) shall have the right to vote as to the management and conduct of the business of the Partnership as follows:

Names   **Vote**

Article IV
DISSOLUTION

* In the event that the Partnership shall hereafter be dissolved for any reason whatsoever, a full and general account of its assets, liabilities and transactions shall at once be taken. Such assets may be sold and turned into cash as soon as possible and all debts and other amounts due the Partnership collected. The proceeds thereof shall thereupon be applied as follows:

(a) To discharge the debts and liabilities of the Partnership and the expenses of liquidation.

(b) To pay each Partner or his legal representative any unpaid salary, drawing account, interest or profits to which he shall then be entitled and in addition, to repay to any Partner his capital contributions in excess of his original capital contribution.

(c) To divide the surplus, if any, among the Partners or their representatives as follows: (1) First (to the extent of each Partner's then capital account) in proportion to their then capital accounts. (2) Then according to each Partner's then Percentage Share of [*Capital/Income*].

No Partner shall have the right to demand and receive property in kind for his distribution.

Article V
MISCELLANEOUS

The Partnership's fiscal year shall commence on January 1st of each year and shall end on December 31st of each year. Full and accurate books of account shall be kept at such place as the Managing Partner(s) may from time to time designate, showing the condition of the business and finances of the Partnership; and each Partner shall have access to such books of account and shall be entitled to examine them at any time during ordinary business hours. At the end of each year, the Managing Partner(s) shall cause the Partnership's accountant to prepare a balance sheet setting forth the financial position of the Partnership as of the end of that year and a statement of operations (income and expenses) for that year. A copy of the balance sheet and statement of operations shall be delivered to each Partner as soon as it is available.

Each Partner shall be deemed to have waived all objections to any transaction or other facts about the operation of the Partnership disclosed in such balance sheet and/or statement of operations unless he shall have notified the Managing Partner(s) in writing of his objectives within thirty (30) days of the date on which such statement is mailed.

The Partnership shall maintain a bank account or bank accounts in the Partnership's name in a national or state bank in the State of _____. Checks and drafts shall be drawn on the Partnership's bank account for Partnership purposes only and shall be signed by the Managing Partner(s) or their designated agent.

Any controversy or claim arising out of or relating to this Agreement shall only be settled by arbitration in accordance with the rules of the American Arbitration Association, one Arbitrator, and shall be enforceable in any court having competent jurisdiction.

Witnesses   **Partners**

_____   _____

_____   _____

Dated: _____

Partnership by Estoppel

Parties who are not partners can hold themselves out as partners and make representations that third persons rely on in dealing with the alleged partners. In such a situation, a court may conclude that a **partnership by estoppel** exists in which case liability is imposed on the alleged partner or partners (although partnership rights are not conferred on these persons).

There are two aspects of liability. The person representing himself or herself to be a partner in an actual or alleged partnership is liable to any third person who extends credit in good faith reliance on such representations. Similarly, a person who expressly or impliedly *consents* to such misrepresentation of an alleged partnership relationship is also liable to third persons who extend credit in good faith reliance [UPA 16].

For example, Moore owns a small shop. Knowing that the Midland Bank will not make a loan on his credit alone, Moore represents that Lewis, a financially secure businessperson, is a partner in Moore's business. Lewis knows of Moore's misrepresentation but fails to correct the bank's information. Midland Bank, relying on the strength of Lewis's reputation and credit, extends a loan to Moore. Moore will be liable to the bank for the loan repayment. In many states, Lewis would also be held liable to the bank in such a loan transaction. Lewis has impliedly consented to the misrepresentation and will normally be estopped from denying that she is a partner of Moore. She will be regarded as if she were in fact a partner in Moore's business to the extent that this loan is concerned.

When a real partnership exists and a partner represents that a nonpartner is a member of the firm, the nonpartner is regarded as an agent whose acts are binding on the partner (but normally not on the partnership). For example, Middle Earth Movers has three partners—Johnson, Mathews, and Huntington. Mathews represents to the business community that Thompson is also a partner. If Thompson negotiates a contract in the name of Middle Earth Movers, the contract will be binding on Mathews but normally not on Johnson and Huntington (unless, of course, Johnson and Huntington knew about, and consented to, Mathews's representation about Thompson).

Again, partnership by estoppel requires that a third person reasonably and detrimentally rely on the representation that a person was part of the partnership.

■ Partnership Operation

The rights and duties of partners are governed largely by the specific terms of their partnership agreement. In the absence of provisions to the contrary in the partnership agreement, the law imposes the rights and duties discussed in this chapter. The character and nature of the partnership business generally influence the application of these rights and duties.

Rights among Partners

The rights held by partners in a partnership relate to the following areas: management, interest in the partnership, compensation, inspection of books, accounting, and property rights.

MANAGEMENT   "All partners have equal rights in the management and conduct of partnership business" [UPA 18(e)]. Management rights belong to all partners in an ordinary partnership.[3] Unless the partners agree otherwise, each has one vote in management matters *regardless of the proportional size of his or her interest in the firm.* Often, in a large partnership, partners will agree to delegate daily management responsibilities to a management committee made up of one or more of the partners.

The majority rule controls decisions in ordinary matters connected with partnership business, unless otherwise specified in the agreement. Unanimous consent of the partners is required, however, to bind the firm in any of the following actions, which significantly affect the nature of the partnership:

1.   To alter the essential nature of the firm's business as expressed in the partnership agreement or to alter the capital structure of the partnership.
2.   To admit new partners or to enter a wholly new business [UPA 18(g), (h)].
3.   To assign partnership property into a trust for the benefit of creditors.

---

3.   In limited partnerships, limited partners may not generally participate in management without affecting their limited-liability status. See Chapter 39.

4.   To dispose of the partnership's goodwill.

5.   To confess judgment against the partnership or submit partnership claims to arbitration. (A **confession of judgment** is the act of a debtor in permitting a judgment to be entered against him or her by a creditor, for an agreed sum, without the institution of legal proceedings.)

6.   To undertake any act that would make further conduct of partnership business impossible [UPA 9(3), various subsections].

7.   To amend the articles of the partnership agreement.

INTEREST IN THE PARTNERSHIP   Each partner is entitled to the proportion of business profits and losses that is designated in the partnership agreement. If the agreement does not apportion profits or losses, the UPA provides that profits are to be shared equally and losses are to be shared in the same ratio as profits [UPA 18(a)].

COMPENSATION   Devoting time, skill, and energy to partnership business is a partner's duty and generally not a compensable service. Partners can, of course, agree otherwise. For example, the managing partner of a law firm often receives a salary in addition to his or her share of profits for performing special administrative duties in office and personnel management. UPA 18(f) provides that on the death of a partner, a surviving partner is entitled to compensation for services in winding up partnership affairs (and reimbursement for expenses incurred in the process) above and apart from his or her share in the partnership profits.

INSPECTION OF BOOKS   Partnership books and records must be kept accessible to all partners. Each partner has the right to receive (and the corresponding duty to produce) full and complete information concerning the conduct of all aspects of partnership business [UPA 20]. Each firm retains books in which to record and secure such information. Partners contribute the information, and a bookkeeper typically has the duty to preserve it. The books must be kept at the firm's principal business office unless the partners agree otherwise [UPA 19]. Every partner, whether active or inactive, is entitled to inspect all books and records upon demand and can make copies of the materials. The personal representative of a deceased partner's estate has the same right of access to partner-ship books and records that the decedent would have had.

ACCOUNTING   An accounting of partnership assets or profits is done to determine the value of each partner's proportionate share in the partnership. An accounting can be called for voluntarily, or it can be compelled by the order of a court in equity.[4] Formal accounting occurs by right in connection with dissolution proceedings, but under UPA 22, a partner also has the right to a formal accounting in the following situations:

1.   When the partnership agreement provides for a formal accounting.

2.   When a partner is wrongfully excluded from the business, from access to the books, or from both.

3.   When any partner is withholding profits or benefits belonging to the partnership in breach of the fiduciary duty.

4.   When circumstances "render it just and reasonable."

PROPERTY RIGHTS   A partner has the following three basic property rights:

1.   An interest in the partnership.

2.   A right in specific partnership property.

3.   A right to participate in the management of the partnership, as previously discussed [UPA 24].

There is an important legal distinction between a partner's rights in specific property belonging to the firm to be used for business purposes and a partner's right to share in the firm's earned profits to the extent of his or her interest in the firm. No individual partner has an absolute right to specific property of the firm. A partner is co-owner with his or her partners of specific partnership property, holding the property as a tenant in partnership. A specific asset may constitute partnership property even when title to it is in an individual partner's

---

4.   The principal remedy of a partner against co-partners is an equity suit for dissolution, an accounting, or both. With minor exceptions, a partner cannot maintain an action against other firm members for damages until partnership affairs are settled and an accounting is done. This rule is necessary because legal disputes among partners invariably involve conflicting claims to shares in the partnership. Logically, the value of each partner's share must first be determined by an accounting.

name. Among factors courts may consider in determining whether a specific asset is partnership property is how closely the asset is connected to the partnership's operation.

The rights of creditors in regard to partnerships were discussed earlier in this chapter. A judgment creditor of an individual partner has no right to execute or attach specific partnership property, but he or she can obtain the partner's share of profits. A creditor of the firm can levy directly upon partnership property.

Partner's Interest in the Firm   A partner's interest in the firm is a personal asset consisting of a proportionate share of the profits earned [UPA 26] and a return of capital after dissolution and winding up. A partner's interest is susceptible to assignment or to a judgment creditor's lien. Judgment creditors can attach a partner's interest by petitioning the court that entered the judgment to grant the creditors a **charging order.** This order entitles the creditors to profits of the partner and to any assets available to the partner upon dissolution [UPA 28]. Neither an assignment nor a court's charging order entitling a creditor to receive a share of the partner's money will cause dissolution of the firm [UPA 27].

Partnership Property   UPA 8(1) provides that "all property originally brought into the partnership's stock or subsequently acquired, by purchase or otherwise, *on account of the partnership,* is partnership property" (emphasis added). Indications that an asset was acquired with the intention that it be a partnership asset is the heart of the phrase *on account of the partnership.* Thus, the more

closely an asset is associated with the business operations of the partnership, the more likely it is to be a partnership asset. Moreover, when such an asset is purchased with partnership funds, it will belong to the partnership unless a contrary intention is shown. If, for example, a piece of property is purchased with partnership funds, it is presumed to be partnership property even if title is taken in the name of one of the partners.

Partners are *tenants in partnership* of all firm property [UPA 25(1)]. Tenancy in partnership has several important effects. If a partner dies, the surviving partners, not the heirs of the deceased partner, have the right of survivorship to the specific property. Although surviving partners are entitled to possession, they have a duty to account to the decedent's estate for the *value* of the deceased partner's interest in said property [UPA 25(2)(d), (e)].

A partner has no right to sell, assign, or in any way deal with a particular item of partnership property other than for partnership purposes [UPA 25(2)(a), (b)]. Nor is a partner's personal credit related to partnership property; creditors cannot use partnership property to satisfy the personal debts of a partner. Partnership property is available only to satisfy partnership debts, to enhance the firm's credit, or to achieve other business purposes.

Every partner is a co-owner with all other partners of specific partnership property, such as office equipment, paper supplies, and vehicles. Each partner has equal rights to possess partnership property for business purposes or in satisfaction of firm debts, but not for any other purpose without the consent of all the other partners.

The following case deals with an attempt by a deceased partner's widow to claim, as her husband's heir, an interest in partnership property.

BACKGROUND AND FACTS   James Cates and three other persons formed two partnerships, SanJac International (SJI) and SanJac Association (SJA). The partnerships provided group life, health, and accident insurance to small-business employers who could not obtain the lower rates charged to bigger businesses. To facilitate their program, the partnerships contracted with insurance providers, including ITT Life Insurance Company and Lloyds of London. The partnerships were later dissolved, but while Cates was still in the process of winding up their affairs, he died. At the time of his death, Cates was involved in a lawsuit in a federal district court against ITT Life and Lloyds of London for, among other things, failure to pay claims promptly and entering into contracts with the fraudulent intent not to perform them. On Cates's death, his wife intervened in the suit, claim-

Case 38.1
———
**CATES v.
INTERNATIONAL
TELEPHONE AND
TELEGRAPH CORP.**
United States Court of Appeals,
Fifth Circuit, 1985.
756 F.2d 1161.

ing, as Cates's heir, an interest in partnership property (that is, the damages to be awarded in the lawsuit). The court decided in favor of ITT Life and Lloyds of London, and Mrs. Cates appealed.

DECISION AND RATIONALE   The United States Court of Appeals for the Fifth Circuit held that Mrs. Cates could not bring an action on behalf of the partnership solely because she was the widow of one of the partners. Partnership property rights pass to the remaining partner(s). The court held that "the widow, heirs, legatees, or personal representatives of a deceased partner have neither any interest in or right to possess specific partnership property nor any right to the management or administration of partnership affairs, all such interest and rights vesting in the remaining partner or partners."

Duties and Powers of Partners

The duties and powers of partners consist of a fiduciary duty of each partner to the others and general agency powers.

FIDUCIARY DUTY   Partners stand in a fiduciary relationship to one another just as principals and agents do—see Chapter 35. It is a relationship of extraordinary trust and loyalty. The fiduciary duty imposes a responsibility upon each partner to act in utmost good faith for the benefit of the partnership. It requires that each partner subordinate his or her personal interests to the mutual welfare of the partners. Thus, a partner cannot engage in any independent competitive activities without the other partners' consent.

This fiduciary duty underlies the entire body of law pertaining to partnership and to agency. From it, certain other duties are commonly implied. Thus, a partner must account to the partnership for any personal profits or benefits derived without the

consent of all of the partners in any partnership transaction.[5] These include transactions among partners or with third parties connected with the formation, conduct, or liquidation of the partnership or with any use of partnership property [UPA 21].

Upon the death of a partner, the surviving partner is under a fiduciary duty to liquidate partnership assets without delay and to credit the estate of the deceased partner for the value of the decedent's interest in the partnership. The fiduciary duty of good faith owed the deceased partner extends by implication to the personal representative of the deceased partner's estate as well. The principles of fiduciary duty and property rights are illustrated in the next case.

---

5.   In this sense, to account to the partnership means not only to divulge the information but also to determine the value of any benefits or profits derived and to hold that money or property in trust on behalf of the partnership.

Case 38.2

ESTATE OF WITLIN v. RIO HONDO ASSOCIATES

California Court of Appeal, Second District, Division 3, 1978.
83 Cal.App.3d 167, 147 Cal.Rptr. 723.

BACKGROUND AND FACTS   About forty-five doctors, including Dr. Witlin, owned and operated a health center as partners. When Witlin died, the other doctors, under their partnership agreement, bought his share of the center, paying his widow $65,228. The partnership agreement provided that on Witlin's death a management committee of the partnership was required to make a good faith determination of the fair market value of Witlin's share. The partnership had the option to offer this amount to Witlin's widow. The $65,228 offer, however, was based only on the book value of the partnership's assets. (Book value is the value at which assets are carried on the books—that is, cost less depreciation. It does not include the goodwill or the ongoing business value of a successful business, factors that are likely to be considered in determining fair market value.) In addition, although the partnership was in the process of bargaining to sell the health center at a price that would have doubled Mrs. Witlin's proportionate share, the partnership did not inform her of that fact. Later, Mrs. Witlin sought a greater amount for her husband's share, even though she had accepted the partnership's offer. In a suit against the partnership in a California state court, the trial court ruled in favor of Witlin's widow, and the doctors appealed.

DECISION AND RATIONALE The California Court of Appeal affirmed the trial court's judgment, ruling that the surviving doctors owed a fiduciary duty to Mrs. Witlin as the widow and executor of their deceased partner to act toward her "in the highest good faith." The appellate court stated that the surviving partners "were forbidden to obtain any advantage over her in the matter by, among other things, the slightest concealment" or nondisclosure. This fiduciary duty was breached, according to the appellate court, because the partnership's management committee never revealed to Mrs. Witlin (1) that "the basic value in their formula for determining the fair market value of the partnership was book value alone" (and thus neglecting goodwill and other factors that would enhance the amount due to her) and (2) that "the management committee did not mention * * * the possibility that the hospital might be shortly sold," resulting in at least double the value of each partner's interest.

ETHICAL CONSIDERATIONS This case provides a clear illustration of why the law imposes on partners fiduciary duties, including the duty to act in good faith when dealing with a deceased partner's beneficiary or personal representative.

GENERAL AGENCY POWERS Each partner is an *agent* of every other partner and acts as both a principal and an agent in any business transaction within the scope of the partnership agreement. Each partner is a general agent of the partnership in carrying out the usual business of the firm. Thus, every act of a partner concerning partnership business and every contract signed in the partnership name bind the firm [UPA 9(1)].

The UPA affirms general principles of agency law that pertain to the authority of a partner to bind a partnership in contract. Under the same principles, a partner may subject a partnership to liability in tort. When a partner is apparently carrying on partnership business with third persons in the usual way, both the partner and the firm share liability. It is only when third persons *know* that the partner has no such authority that the partnership is not liable. For example, Patricia, a partner in the partnership of Heise and Green, applies for a loan on behalf of the partnership without authorization from the other partners. The bank manager knows that Patricia has no authority. If the bank manager grants the loan, Patricia will be personally bound, but the firm will not be liable.

Joint Liability In most states, partners are subject to joint liability on partnership debts and contracts [UPA 15(b)]. **Joint liability** means that if a third party sues a partner on, for example, a partnership debt, the partner has the right to insist that the other partners be sued with him or her. In fact, if the third party does not sue all of the partners, those partners sued cannot be required to pay a judgment, and the assets of the partnership cannot be used to satisfy the judgment. (Similarly, the third party's release of one partner releases all partners.) In other words, to bring a successful claim against the partnership on a debt or contract, a plaintiff must name all the partners as defendants. To simplify this rule, some states have enacted statutes providing that a partnership may be sued in its own name and a judgment will be binding on the partnership and the individual partners even though not all the partners are named in the complaint.[6]

If the third party is successful, he or she may collect on the judgment against the assets of one or more of the partners. In other words, each partner

---

6. California is an example of such a state.

is liable and may be required to pay the entire amount of the judgment. When one partner pays the entire amount, the partnership is required to indemnify that partner [UPA 18(b)]. If the partnership cannot do so, the obligation falls on the other partners.

Joint and Several Liability   In some states,[7] partners are jointly and severally liable for partnership debts and contracts. In all states, partners are jointly and severally liable for torts and breaches of trust [UPA 15(a)].

Joint and several liability means a third party may sue any one or more of the partners without suing all of them or the partnership itself. (That is, a third party may sue one or more of the partners separately or all of them together, at his or her option.) This is true even if the partner did not participate in, ratify, or know about whatever it was that gave rise to the cause of action.

A judgment against one partner on his or her several liability does not extinguish the others' liability. (Similarly, a release of one partner dis-

---
7.   Alabama, Arizona, Colorado, Missouri, North Carolina, Tennessee, and Texas.

charges the partners' joint, but not several, liability.) Thus, those not sued in the first action may be sued subsequently. The first action, however, may have been conclusive on the question of liability. If, for example, in an action against one partner, the court held that the partnership was in no way liable, the third party cannot bring an action against another partner and succeed on the issue of the partnership's liability.

If the third party is successful, he or she may collect on the judgment only against the assets of those partners named as defendants. The partner who committed the tort, though, is required to indemnify the partnership for any damages it pays.

Liability of Incoming Partner   A newly admitted partner to an existing partnership has limited liability for whatever debts and obligations the partnership incurred *prior* to the new partner's admission. UPA 17 provides that the new partner's liability can be satisfied only from partnership assets. This means that the new partner has no personal liability for these debts and obligations, but any capital contribution made by him or her is subject to them. This principle is illustrated in the following case.

Case 38.3

MOSELEY v. COMMERCIAL STATE BANK

Supreme Court of Alabama, 1984.
457 So.2d 967.

BACKGROUND AND FACTS   Southern Distilleries was a general partnership created in 1980 to produce and sell gasohol, a fuel for internal combustion engines made of a mixture of gasoline and ethyl alcohol. The partnership agreement contained a provision stating that any three partners having a combined 60 percent interest in the partnership could borrow money on behalf of the partnership, thereby binding the other partners to liability on the loan. In December 1980, Southern Distilleries, through three partners, borrowed $140,184 from Commercial State Bank and executed two promissory notes, which were due on March 19, 1981. In July 1981, Southern Distilleries paid the interest on its overdue notes held by Commercial State Bank and executed a new promissory note in the amount of $140,000. The bank marked the December notes as "paid." Southern Distilleries failed to pay the July note when it came due, and the bank sued the partnership as an entity and each of the partners jointly and severally in an Alabama state court. The trial court held that the partnership and the partners were jointly and severally liable on the note. One of the partners, Julius Moseley, had joined the partnership in April 1981. Moseley appealed, claiming that he was not personally liable on the July note, because the note represented the renewal of a preexisting obligation of the partnership. Under the UPA, an incoming partner assumes liability for preexisting obligations of the partnership, but his or her liability can be satisfied only out of partnership assets; the incoming partner cannot be held personally liable for the obligations.

DECISION AND RATIONALE The Supreme Court of Alabama affirmed the trial court's decision, holding that the partnership's debt to the bank was not a preexisting obligation but a new obligation, because the obligation created by the old note terminated when the bank accepted the new note. The court concluded that after the bank "accepted the new note and satisfied the old one, there was no obligation which was due and payable to the bank until the new note matured. * * * Since the contract sued on was entered into by a partnership which included Moseley," the court ruled that the bank was entitled to enforce the contract against Moseley.

ETHICAL CONSIDERATIONS It might appear that the court's decision in this case was unfair to Moseley, who did not find out about the note until the bank brought this action. But given the fact that Moseley was an experienced businessperson, would it be fair not to hold him liable for the consequences of his own actions? The court stressed this perspective in its concluding comments: "The parties are competent business men dealing at arm's length, who presumably have ample access to counsel. If Moseley had wished to limit his exposure to liability he should have taken steps to do so when he chose to become involved in the enterprise."

Authority of Partners Agency concepts relating to apparent authority, actual authority, and ratification are also applicable to partnerships. The extent of *implied authority* is generally broader for partners than for ordinary agents. The character and scope of the partnership business and the customary nature of the particular business operation determine the scope of implied powers. For example, each partner in a trading partnership—essentially, any partnership business that has goods in inventory and makes profits buying and selling those goods—has a wide range of implied powers to borrow money in the firm name and to extend the firm's credit in issuing or indorsing negotiable instruments.

In an ordinary partnership, firm members can exercise all implied powers reasonably necessary and customary to carry on that particular business. Some customarily implied powers include the authority to make warranties on goods in the sales business, the power to convey real property in the firm name when such conveyances are part of the ordinary course of partnership business, the power to enter contracts consistent with the firm's regular course of business, and the power to make admissions and representations concerning partnership affairs [UPA 11].

If a partner acts within the scope of authority, the partnership is bound to third parties. For example, a partner's authority to sell partnership products carries with it the implied authority to transfer title and to make usual warranties. Hence, in a partnership that operates a retail tire store, any partner negotiating a contract with a customer for the sale of a set of tires can warrant that "each tire will be warranted for normal wear for 40,000 miles."

This same partner, however, does not have the authority to sell office equipment, fixtures, or the partnership office building without the consent of all the other partners. In addition, because partnerships are formed for profit, a partner does not generally have the authority to make charitable contributions without the consent of the other partners. No such action is binding on the partnership unless it is ratified by all of the other partners.

Like the law of agency, the law of partnership imputes one partner's knowledge of all matters pertaining to partnership affairs to all other partners, because members of a partnership stand in a fiduciary relationship to one another. In other words, it is presumed that each partner discloses to every other partner all relevant information pertaining to the business of the partnership.

■ Terms and Concepts

articles of partnership 686   joint and several   marshalling assets 685
charging order 691   liability 694   partnership by estoppel 689
confession of judgment 696   joint liability 693

■ For Review

1. What are the three essential elements of partnership?
2. Are the rights and duties of partners governed largely by the specific terms of their partnership agreement or by the UPA?
3. Generally, the majority rule controls the decisions in ordinary matters connected with partnership business. Under what circumstances is the unanimous consent of the partners required?
4. Keel, Haul, and Linch are investment counselors and partners. Keel advises Meg, one of the firm's clients, to invest in Faux Co., which is a fictitious firm that Keel created to siphon investors' funds into his own pockets. After Keel absconds with the funds, Meg sues Haul and Linch. Can Haul and Linch be held liable for Keel's action?
5. In an ordinary partnership, each partner can exercise all implied powers reasonably necessary to carry on the business. Pete and Paul are partners in the paper products business. Does Pete have the power to sell paper products in the firm's name? Does Pete have the power to sell the firm's office equipment without Paul's consent?

■ Questions and Case Problems

38-1. Daniel is the owner of a chain of shoe stores. He hires Martin as the manager of a new store, which is to open in Grand Rapids, Michigan. Daniel, by written contract, agrees to pay Martin a monthly salary. In addition, Daniel and Martin have agreed to an 80-20 percent split in profits. Without Daniel's knowledge, Martin represents himself to Carlton as Daniel's partner, showing Carlton the agreement to share profits. Carlton extends credit to Martin. Martin defaults. Discuss whether Carlton can hold Daniel liable as a partner.

38-2. Agatha wishes to purchase some real property owned by Tropical Gardens. She learns that Tropical Gardens is a partnership owned by Waldheim, Berry, and Lamont. She also learns that the partnership needs capital and that the need for capital is one of the major reasons the partners are selling their real property. Because Tropical Gardens is a partnership, Agatha has the following concerns:
(a) Can the partnership convey the land in the name of Tropical Gardens?
(b) If there is a breach of contract, against whom must Agatha file a lawsuit?
(c) If Agatha obtains a judgment against Tropical Gardens, against whom can she execute it?
Discuss fully each of Agatha's concerns.

38-3. Meyer, Knapp, and Cavanna formed a partnership to operate a window washing service. Meyer contributes $10,000 to the partnership, and Knapp and Cavanna contribute $1,000 each. The partnership agreement is silent on how profits and losses will be shared. One month after the partnership has begun operation, Knapp and Cavanna vote, over Meyer's objection, to purchase another truck for the firm's operation. Meyer believes that because he contributed $10,000, no major commitment to purchase by the partnership can be made over his objection. In addition, Meyer claims that, in absence of agreement, profits must be divided in the same ratio as capital contributions. Discuss Meyer's contentions.

38-4. Lisa, Betty, and Carla form a partnership to operate a hairstyling salon. After one year's operation, the salon has become very busy and profitable. Most customers have a preference as to which partner's services they use. Lisa becomes ill, and Betty and Carla start working sixty-hour weeks. It appears that Lisa will not return to work for at least two months. Betty and Carla want to bring in Dana as a new partner. Lisa objects to Dana and refuses to consent to Dana's admission into the partnership. Betty and Carla insist that they be paid extra compensation for having to work additional hours because of Lisa's illness. Discuss whether Betty and Carla are entitled to the compensation claimed and whether Dana can be admitted as a new partner by majority vote.

38-5. Oddo and Ries entered into a partnership agreement in March 1978 to create and publish a book describing how to restore F-100 pickup trucks. Oddo was to write the book and Ries was to provide the capital. Oddo supplied Ries with the manuscript, but Ries was dissatisfied and hired someone else to revise it. The book Ries finally published contained substantial amounts of Oddo's work. Can Oddo require Ries to formally account for the profits on the book? Explain. [*Oddo v. Ries*, 743 F.2d 630 (9th Cir. 1984)]

38-6. Two brothers, Eugene and Marlowe Mehl, operated their family farm as a partnership. Property held by the partnership consisted primarily of farming equipment and machinery. The partnership did not own any real property but leased land from the family and other people. The brothers had agreed to split all profits on an equal basis, but there had never been a written partnership agreement. In 1973, Eugene withdrew $7,200 from the partnership bank account and bought the Dagmar Bar, located in Dagmar, Montana. The warranty deed and the liquor license to the bar were held in the names of Eugene Mehl and his wife, Bonnie.

In 1980, Eugene and Bonnie were divorced, and Bonnie received the bar and liquor license as part of the property settlement. In 1983, Marlowe gave written notice to Eugene that he was dissolving the partnership. Eventually a district court in Montana distributed the assets of the partnership. The court concluded that the Dagmar Bar was a partnership asset. On appeal, Eugene contended that the bar was not partnership property and entered into evidence a number of documents that tended to indicate that he was the owner of the bar. What should the appellate court decide? Discuss fully. [*Mehl v. Mehl*, 241 Mont. 310, 786 P.2d 1173 (1990)]

38-7. Pat McGowan, Val Somers, and Brent Roberson were general partners in Vermont Place, a limited partnership formed to construct duplexes on a tract of land in Fort Smith, Arkansas. In 1984 the partnership mortgaged the property so that it could build there. McGowan owned a separate company, Advance Development Corp., that was hired by the partnership to develop the project. On September 3, 1984, Somers and Roberson discovered that McGowan had not been paying the suppliers to the project, including National Lumber Co., nor making the mortgage payments. The suppliers and the bank sued the partnership and the general partners individually. Discuss whether Somers and Roberson could be held individually liable for the debts incurred by McGowan. [*National Lumber Co. v. Advance Development Corp.*, 293 Ark. 1, 732 S.W.2d 840 (1987)]

38-8. B. Darryl Clubb and Jeffere F. Van Liew formed a partnership to develop North Coast Park in northern San Diego County, California. The two were to share equally in the ownership and profits, and Clubb was to receive a 6 percent development fee. Later, Clubb claimed, he was forced to accept R. W. Wortham III as a partner, thereby reducing his interest to one-third. Subsequently, Wortham and Van Liew formed a new partnership called North Coast Park II, in which Clubb had no interest. Without Clubb's consent, Van Liew and Wortham transferred by sale improved North Coast property to the new partnership. Clubb sued Wortham and Van Liew, claiming—among other things—that the sale (transfer) of the North Coast property was in breach of the partnership agreement. To prove this and other information concerning the two partnerships, Clubb, during the discovery phase of the trial, moved for a court order requiring Lawrence T. Dougherty, an attorney for both partnerships, to disclose certain information. Dougherty refused, claiming attorney-client privilege. Clubb claimed that information known by one partner must be made available to all partners. Discuss whether Dougherty could be compelled to give Clubb the information. [*Wortham & Van Liew v. Superior Court (Clubb)*, 188 Cal.App.3d 927, 233 Cal.Rptr. 725 (1987)]

38-9. Three brothers, James, John, and Claude, purchased several parcels of land, taking title to the land either in their names or in their partnership name, Strother Brothers. The brothers never executed a written partnership agreement. After James died, John and Claude, along with their mother, Minnie, brought suit to have Minnie declared owner of a one-fourth interest in the lands. This would leave James's heirs with only a one-fourth interest in the partnership instead of a one-third interest. Before trial Minnie died, leaving all her property to John and Claude. Discuss whether John and Claude succeeded in their attempt to increase their share of the partnership's property at the expense of their deceased brother's estate. [*Strother v. Strother*, 436 So.2d 847 (Ala. 1983)]

38-10. A Question of Ethics

David Murphy and James Canion formed a general partnership to conduct real estate business. A provision in their partnership agreement provided that both partners would devote their full-time efforts to conducting partnership business, that all personal earnings from personal services would be included as partnership income, and that any real estate or other partnership business conducted by either partner during the term of the partnership agreement should be for the joint account of the partnership. Through his business associates and contacts, Canion learned of several profitable real estate opportunities. Canion never informed Murphy of these opportunities but, instead, secretly took advantage of them for his own gain. When Murphy found out about Canion's activities, he told Canion that he was canceling the partnership under a clause in the partnership agreement that allowed termination by a partner with ninety days' notice. In the lawsuit that followed, Murphy alleged that Canion had breached the partnership agreement and his fiduciary duty to the partnership. The trial court agreed with Murphy and awarded him damages, which the court held to be proximately caused by Canion's wrongful appropriation of partnership business opportunities. On appeal, Canion contended, among other things, that his breach of his fiduciary duty did not proximately cause any damages to Murphy, because the income generated by Canion's "secret" projects was received after the partnership had terminated. [Murphy v. Canion, 797 S.W.2d 944 (Tex.App.–Houston [14th Dist.] 1990)]

1. Should Murphy be entitled, in the form of damages, to a share of the profits made by Canion by his secret dealings, in view of the fact that Canion received the income *after* the partnership terminated? If you were the judge, how would you decide this issue, and on what legal basis? From an ethical point of view, what solution would be the fairest?

2. What ethical considerations are involved in the rule that partners have a fiduciary duty to subordinate their personal interests to the mutual welfare of all of the partners? Do you think that a partnership would be a viable form of business organization if partners were not held to such a fiduciary duty?

Chapter 39

PARTNERSHIPS
Termination and
Limited Partnerships

All things must eventually come to an end. Partnerships can be terminated in a variety of ways, all of which are discussed in this chapter. The formalities attending partnership termination are also discussed. We then look at a special partnership form called a limited partnership, which is an important enough form of business organization to warrant a special section in this chapter.

■ Partnership Termination

Any change in the relations of the partners that demonstrates unwillingness or inability to carry on partnership business dissolves the partnership, resulting in termination [UPA 29]. If any of the partners wishes to continue the business, he or she is free to reorganize into a new partnership with the remaining partners.

The termination of a partnership has two stages—dissolution and winding up. Both must take place before termination is complete. **Dissolution** occurs when any partner ceases to be associated with the carrying on of partnership business. **Winding up** is the actual process of collecting and distributing the partnership's assets. Dissolution terminates the right of a partnership to exist as a going concern, but the partnership continues to exist long enough to wind up its affairs. When winding up is complete, the partnership's *legal* existence is terminated.

Dissolution

Dissolution begins the process of the termination of the partnership. Dissolution of a partnership can be brought about by acts of the partners, by operation of law, or by judicial decree.

DISSOLUTION BY ACTS OF THE PARTNERS   Dissolution of a partnership may come about through the following acts of the partners: by agreement, by the withdrawal of a partner, by the addition of a partner, or by the transfer of a partner's interest.

By Agreement   A partnership can be dissolved when certain events stipulated in the partnership agreement occur. For example, when a partnership agreement expresses a fixed term or a particular business objective to be accomplished, the passing of the date or the accomplishment of the project dissolves the partnership. Partners do not have to abide by the stipulations in the agreement, however. They can mutually agree to dissolve the partnership early or to extend it. If they agree to continue in the partnership, they become *partners at will*—meaning that any partner can dissolve the partnership at any time by withdrawing from the firm.

Partner's Power to Withdraw   A partnership is a personal legal relationship among co-owners. No person can be compelled either to become a partner or to remain one. Implicit in a partnership is each partner's *power* to disassociate from the partnership at any time and thus dissolve the partnership. Note that although a partner always has the *power* to withdraw from the partnership, he or she may not always have the *right* to do so. In a partnership for a specified term or for a specified purpose, a partner does not have the right to withdraw until the term has lapsed or the purpose has been fulfilled. If a partner withdraws in contravention of the partnership agreement, he or she will be liable to the other partners for damages resulting from wrongful dissolution of the partnership.

Admission of a New Partner   A change in the composition of the partnership, whether by the withdrawal of a partner or by the *admission of a new partner* (without the consent of all the partners), results in dissolution. If the remaining or new partners agree to continue in the firm's business, a new partnership arises. The new partnership carries the debts of the dissolved partnership. Creditors of the prior partnership become creditors of the one that is continuing the business [UPA 41].

Transfer of a Partner's Interest   The UPA provides that neither a voluntary transfer of a partner's interest[1] nor an involuntary sale of a partner's interest for the benefit of creditors [UPA 28] by itself

dissolves the partnership. (A transferee acquires the right to the transferring partner's profits but does not become a partner; thus, a transferee has no say in the management or administration of the partnership affairs nor a right to inspect the partnership books.) Either occurrence, however, can ultimately lead to judicial dissolution of the partnership, as will be discussed.

DISSOLUTION BY OPERATION OF LAW   A partnership is dissolved by operation of law in the event of death, bankruptcy, or illegality.

Death   A partnership is dissolved upon the death of any partner, even if the partnership agreement provides for carrying on the business with the executor of the decedent's estate. Any change in the composition among partners results in a new partnership. (But there is always the possibility of a reformation of the partnership upon the death of a partner.)

Bankruptcy   The bankruptcy of a partner will dissolve a partnership. Insolvency alone will not result in dissolution. Naturally, bankruptcy of the firm itself will result in dissolution of the partnership.

Illegality   Any event that makes it unlawful for the partnership to continue its business or for any partner to carry on in the partnership will result in dissolution. Even if the illegality of the partnership business is a cause for dissolution, however, the partners can decide to change the nature of their business and continue in the partnership. When the illegality applies to an individual partner, the dissolution *must* occur. For example, suppose the state legislature passes a law making it illegal for magistrates to engage in the practice of law. If an attorney in a law firm is appointed a magistrate, the partnership must be dissolved. The next case deals with dissolution of a partnership due to illegality.

---

1.   A single partner cannot make another person a partner in a firm merely by transferring his or her interest to that person [UPA 27].

Case 39.1

WILLIAMS v. BURRUS

Court of Appeals of
Washington, Division 1, 1978.
20 Wash.App. 494,
581 P.2d 164.

BACKGROUND AND FACTS Paul Williams sued Richard Burrus in a Washington state court for an accounting and dissolution of their partnership. To form the partnership, Williams had provided property to serve as collateral so that Burrus could obtain a bank loan to assist in the purchase of a restaurant. The partnership agreement, in addition to providing that Williams would supply the collateral, stated that the business would be in Burrus's name and that Burrus alone would apply for a liquor license without mentioning Williams. At the time, Williams was an unacceptable licensee, according to the Washington State Liquor Control Board. To receive a license issued to a partnership, all members of the partnership have to be qualified to obtain a license. The trial court found the partnership agreement illegal and unenforceable and dismissed Williams's complaint. Williams appealed.

DECISION AND RATIONALE The Court of Appeals of Washington affirmed the trial court's dismissal of Williams's case, ruling that the partnership had been illegally formed. Therefore, the court would hear neither a suit to enforce the partnership nor one to dissolve it. "Courts will not assist in the dissolution of an illegal partnership or entertain an action for an accounting or distribution of its assets. * * * Under the general rule that the courts will not aid either party to an illegal agreement where a partnership is formed to carry out an illegal business or to conduct a business in an illegal manner, the courts will refuse to aid any of the parties thereto in an action against the other."

DISSOLUTION BY JUDICIAL DECREE Dissolution of a partnership can result from judicial decree. For dissolution to occur, an application or petition must be made in an appropriate court. The court then either denies the petition or grants a decree of dissolution. Under UPA 32, a court can dissolve a partnership for the reasons discussed below or whenever circumstances render it equitable.

Insanity A partnership can obtain a judicial declaration of dissolution when a partner is adjudicated insane or is shown to be of unsound mind. This action often involves a series of complex tests and standards.

Incapacity When it appears that a partner has become incapable of performing his or her duties under the partnership agreement, a decree of dissolution may be required. It must appear that the incapacity is permanent and will substantially affect the partner's ability to discharge his or her duties to the firm.

Business Impracticality When it becomes obvious that the firm's business can be operated only at a loss, judicial dissolution may be ordered.

Improper Conduct A partner's impropriety involving partnership business (for example, fraud perpetrated upon the other partners) or improper behavior reflecting unfavorably upon the firm (for example, habitual drunkenness resulting in gross neglect of the partnership's business) will provide grounds for a judicial decree of dissolution.

Other Circumstances Dissolution may also be granted in other circumstances when the court finds it equitable to do so. (In general, courts are reluctant to allow partners to sue each other except for dissolution.) For example, a court might order dissolution when personal dissension between partners becomes so persistent and harmful as to undermine the confidence and cooperation necessary to carry on the firm's business. The following case is illustrative.

BACKGROUND AND FACTS Wayne Taurman was an employee of John Felton's Felton Construction Company (FCC). In 1969, Felton formed Felton Investment Group (FIG) as a general partnership consisting of deserving employees of FCC. Each member of FIG made weekly contributions—deducted from the employee's paycheck—to the investment fund. The money was placed in investments agreed on by all partners. Taurman was a charter member of FIG. In 1974, Felton began to promote the idea that FIG should become a limited partnership with Felton in charge as general partner. Taurman opposed Felton's idea. The company later terminated Taurman's employment on the ground that he had refused to renounce his union membership to work on a nonunion job. Shortly after his termination, Taurman received a check for $21,448.98 from FIG. The check represented Taurman's contributions to FIG, plus 4 percent annual interest. In the FIG partnership agreement, this was the amount payable in situations in which employees were discharged for misconduct. Taurman did not feel he had been guilty of misconduct and wanted his full share of the partnership assets on withdrawing from the partnership. Felton disagreed. Taurman, joined by Derrold Paige, another employee and FIG member who had received similar treatment, brought an action in a Montana state court to have the partnership dissolved, its assets sold, and the proceeds distributed to its partners. The trial court granted the dissolution, and Felton appealed.

DECISION AND RATIONALE The Supreme Court of Montana affirmed the trial court's judgment. The court found that Taurman's termination was wrongful in that he should not have been fired for refusing to renounce his union membership. Therefore, the provision in the partnership agreement concerning dispersal of contributions when termination is due to misconduct was inapplicable. Because the agreement did not cover wrongful discharge, the court applied Montana's adaptation of the Uniform Partnership Act: "Each partner shall be repaid his contributions whether by way of capital or advances to the partnership property and share equally in the profits and surplus remaining after all liabilities * * * are satisfied." The court held that Taurman was entitled to repayment of contributions and a pro rata share of partnership assets.

Case 39.2

FELTON INVESTMENT GROUP v. TAURMAN

Supreme Court of Montana, 1986.
222 Mont. 238,
722 P.2d 1135.

NOTICE OF DISSOLUTION The intent to dissolve or to withdraw from a firm must be communicated to each partner. This notice of intent can come from the words of a partner (actual notice) or from the actions of a partner (constructive notice). All partners will share liability for the acts of any partner who continues to conduct business for the firm without knowing that the partnership has been dissolved. For example, Ann, Doreen, and Carlo have a partnership, Ann tells Doreen of her intent to withdraw. Before Carlo learns of Ann's intentions, he enters into a contract with a third party. The contract is equally binding on Ann, Doreen, and Carlo. Unless the other partners have notice, the withdrawing partner will continue to be bound as a partner to all contracts created for the firm.

To avoid liability for obligations a partner incurs after dissolution of a partnership, notice must be given to all affected third persons. The manner of giving notice depends on the third person's relationship to the firm. Any third person who has extended credit to the partnership must receive *actual notice*. For all others, a newspaper announcement or similar public notice is sufficient.

Winding Up

Once dissolution has occurred and partners have been notified, they cannot create new obligations on behalf of the partnership. Their only authority is to complete transactions begun but not finished at the time of dissolution and to wind up the business of the partnership. Winding up includes collecting and preserving partnership assets, discharging liabilities (paying debts), and accounting to each partner for the value of his or her interest in the partnership.

When dissolution is caused by a partner's act that violates the partnership agreement, the innocent partners may have rights to damages resulting from the dissolution. Also, the innocent partners have the right to buy out the offending partner and to continue the business instead of winding up the partnership. A partner who has committed a wrongful act is barred from participating in the winding up of partnership business.

Dissolution resulting from the death of a partner vests all partnership assets in the surviving partners. The surviving partners act as fiduciaries in settling partnership affairs in a quick, practicable manner and in accounting to the estate of the deceased partner for the value of the decedent's interest in the partnership. The surviving partners are entitled to payment for their services in winding up the partnership, as well as to reimbursement for any costs incurred in the process [UPA 18(f)].

The court stresses in the following case that a partnership is not terminated until the winding up of partnership affairs is completed and all obligations of the partnership are discharged.

Case 39.3

LENKIN v. BECKMAN

District of Columbia Court of Appeals, 1990.
575 A.2d 273.

BACKGROUND AND FACTS In May 1983, the partnership of Beckman, Farmer & Kirstein (B, F & K) entered into a ten-year lease agreement with Melvin Lenkin to lease office space from Lenkin in a building in Washington, D.C. The lease included a clause—clause 23(b)—that released the individual partners, as well as their successors in interest, from any personal liability under the lease. B, F & K was dissolved in May 1984, and a new partnership, Beckman & Kirstein (B & K), was formed. The parties disagreed as to whether Robert Beckman had personally assumed the lease obligation (as Beckman contended) or B & K had assumed the lease obligation (as Lenkin contended). In October 1985, almost eight years before the lease was to expire, Beckman informed Lenkin by letter that the lease was being terminated effective November 30, 1985. Lenkin later filed suit in a District of Columbia court against Beckman and Kirstein, "on behalf of Beckman & Kirstein, a partnership," seeking damages under the lease. The trial court granted Beckman and Kirstein's motion to dismiss, holding that Beckman and Kirstein, as individuals, were released from all liability by the provision in the lease agreement. The court further concluded that, as a matter of law, because a partnership entity cannot be sued in the District of Columbia, Lenkin could not obtain a judgment against the firm of B & K. Therefore, there could be neither personal nor partnership liability for the lease obligation. Lenkin appealed.

DECISION AND RATIONALE The District of Columbia Court of Appeals reversed the trial court's decision, ruling that the trial court had improperly assumed that all partnership property automatically became personal property on dissolution of the partnership and was thus insulated against Lenkin's claim. The appellate court pointed out that "dissolution of a partnership affects only future obligations of the business. As to past transactions the partnership continues until it shall have satisfied all of its pre-existing obligations" and the winding up of partnership affairs is completed. The court concluded that Lenkin's permitting the partners to contract out of personal liability so that there was no obligation to contribute to satisfying Lenkin's claims did not necessarily eliminate Lenkin's access to partnership property. The court consequently held that the partnership assets did not become unreachable personal property owned by the partners and remanded the case for further proceedings.

Distribution of Assets

Creditors of the partnership as well as creditors of the individual partners can make claims on the partnership's assets. Creditors of the partnership have priority over creditors of individual partners in the distribution of partnership assets; the converse priority is followed in the distribution of individual partner assets—except under bankruptcy law, which provides that a partner's individual assets may be utilized to pay claims against a partnership involved in certain bankruptcy proceedings.[2] (Bankruptcy law in general is discussed in Chapter 33.)

The distribution of a partnership's assets is made *after* third party debts have been paid. The priorities, after third party debts, are as follows [UPA 40(b)]:

1. Refund of advances (loans) made to or for the firm by a partner.
2. Return of capital contribution to a partner.
3. Distribution of the balance, if any, to partners in accordance with the relative proportions of their respective shares in the profits.

If the partnership's liabilities are greater than its assets, the partners bear the losses—in the absence of a contrary agreement—in the same proportion in which they shared the profits (rather than, for example, in proportion to their contributions to the partnership's capital). If the partnership is insolvent, the partners must still contribute their respective shares. If one of the partners does not contribute, the other or others must provide the additional amounts necessary to pay the liabilities; but he, she, or they have a **right of contribution** against whoever has not paid his or her share.[3]

The distribution of partnership assets begins with the subtraction of the partnership's total liabilities from its total assets (or vice versa, in the case of an insolvent partnership). Liabilities include amounts owed to creditors, to partners for their capital contributions, and to partners for other than capital and profit. Amounts that remain after payment of the liabilities are distributed to the partners according to the profit-sharing ratio. If, however, the partnership has suffered an aggregate loss, the total loss is shared as agreed or in the same ratio as the partners share profits.

Partnership Buy-Sell Agreements

Usually, when people enter into partnerships, they are getting along with one another. To prepare for the possibility that the situation may change and they may become unable to work together amicably, the partners should make express arrangements during the formation of the partnership to provide for its smooth dissolution. An agreement may be made for one or more partners to buy out the other or others should the situation warrant. Such an agreement is called a **buy-sell agreement,** or simply a buy-out agreement. To agree beforehand on who buys what, under what circumstances, and if possible, at what price, may eliminate costly negotiations or litigation later. Alternatively, it may be agreed that one or more partners will determine the value of the interest being sold and the other or others can decide whether to buy or sell.

A similar agreement can be formed for the transfer of a partner's interest on his or her death to the surviving partners. The partners can agree that the survivors will pay the value of the deceased partner's interest in the partnership to his or her representative. To fund the payment of the value of each partner's interest on his or her death, partnership funds can be used to purchase insurance.

■ Limited Partnerships

Limited partnerships consist of at least one **general partner** and one or more **limited partners** [RULPA 101(7)]. The general partner (or partners) assumes management responsibility of the partnership and, as such, has full responsibility for the

---

2. 11 U.S.C. Section 723.
3. If an individual partner is insolvent and for that reason cannot pay his or her share of the loss, however, the solvent partner or partners will be unable to recover their additional contributions from the insolvent partner.

partnership and for all debts of the partnership. The limited partner (or partners) contributes cash (or other property) and owns an interest in the firm but does not undertake any management responsibilities and is not personally liable for partnership debts beyond the amount of his or her investment. A limited partner can forfeit limited liability by taking part in managing the business. In many ways, limited partnerships are like general partnerships. They are sometimes referred to as *special partnerships,* in contrast to *general partnerships.* A comparison of the basic characteristics of general partnerships and limited partnerships appears in Exhibit 39–1.

Until 1976, the law governing limited partnerships in all states except Louisiana was the Uniform Limited Partnership Act (ULPA). Since 1976, most states and the District of Columbia have adopted its revision, the Revised Uniform Limited Partnership Act (RULPA). Because the RULPA is the dominant law governing limited partnerships in the United States, references within this section will be to the RULPA.

Formation of a Limited Partnership

Compared with the informal, private, and voluntary agreement that usually suffices for a general partnership, the formation of a limited partnership is a public and formal proceeding that must follow statutory requirements. A limited partnership must have at least one general partner and one limited partner, as mentioned previously, and the partners must sign a **certificate of limited partnership,** which requires information similar to that found in a corporate charter. The certificate must be filed with the designated state official—under RULPA, the secretary of state. The certificate is usually open to public inspection. In essence, the content of the certificate and the method of filing are similar to those for the corporate charter.

Rights and Liabilities of Limited Partners

General partners, unlike limited partners, are personally liable to the partnership's creditors; thus, at least one general partner is necessary in a limited partnership so that someone has personal liability. This policy can be circumvented in states that allow a corporation to be the general partner in a part-

nership. Because the corporation has limited liability by virtue of corporate laws, no one in the limited partnership in this case has personal liability.

RIGHTS OF LIMITED PARTNER   Subject to the limitations that will be discussed here, limited partners have essentially the same rights as general partners, including the right of access to partnership books and the right to other information regarding partnership business. Upon dissolution, they are entitled to a return of their contributions in accordance with the partnership certificate [RULPA 201(a)(10)]. They can also assign their interests subject to specific clauses in the certificate [RULPA 702, 704].

RULPA provides a limited partner with the right to sue on behalf of the firm if the general partners with authority to do so have refused to file suit [RULPA 1001]. In addition, investor protection legislation, such as securities laws (discussed in Chapter 43), may give some protection to limited partners.

LIABILITIES OF LIMITED PARTNER   A limited partner is liable to creditors to the extent of any contribution that had been promised to the firm or any part of a contribution that was withdrawn from the firm [RULPA 502]. If the firm is organized in an improper manner and the limited partner fails to renunciate (withdraw from the partnership) on discovery of the defect, the partner can be held personally liable by the firm's creditors. Note, though, that RULPA allows people to remain limited partners regardless of whether they comply with statutory technicalities. Liability for false statements in a partnership certificate runs in favor of persons relying on the false statements and against members who sign the certificate knowing of the falsity [RULPA 207]. A limited partnership is formed by good faith compliance with the requirements for signing and filing the certificate, even if it is incomplete or defective. When a limited partner discovers a defect in the formation of the limited partnership, he or she can obtain shelter from future liability by causing an appropriate amendment or certificate to be filed or by renouncing an interest in the profits of the partnership, thereby avoiding any future reliance by third parties [RULPA 304].

◼ **Exhibit 39–1 A Basic Comparison of Types of Partnerships**

Characteristic	General Partnership (UPA)	Limited Partnership (RULPA)
Creation	By agreement of two or more persons to carry on a business as co-owners for profit.	By agreement of two or more persons to carry on a business as co-owners for profit. Must include one or more general partners and one or more limited partners. Filing of certificate with secretary of state is required.
Sharing of Profits and Losses	By agreement, or in the absence thereof, profits are shared equally by partners, and losses are shared in the same ratio as profits.	Profits are shared as required in certificate agreement, and losses are shared likewise, up to their capital contribution. In the absence of provision in certificate agreement, profits and losses are shared on the basis of percentages of capital contributions.
Liability	Unlimited personal liability of all partners.	Unlimited personal liability of all general partners; limited partners only to extent of capital contributions.
Capital Contribution	No minimal or mandatory amount; set by agreement.	Set by agreement; may be cash, property, services or any obligation.
Management	By agreement, or in the absence thereof, all partners have an equal voice.	General partners by agreement, or else each has an equal voice. Limited partners have no voice, or else are subject to liability as a general partner, but *only* if a third party has knowledge of such involvement. Limited partner may act as agent or employee of the partnership, and vote on amending certificate or sale or dissolution of the partnership.
Duration	By agreement, or can be dissolved by action of partner (withdrawal), operation of law (death or bankruptcy), or court decree.	By agreement in certification, or by withdrawal, death, or mental incompetence of general partner in absence of right of other general partners to continue the partnership. Death of a limited partner, unless he or she is the only remaining limited partner, does not terminate the partnership.
Assignment	Interest can be assigned, although assignee does not have rights of substituted partner without consent of other partners.	Same as general partnership; if partners consent to assignee's becoming a partner, certificate must be amended. Upon assignment of all interest, the partner ceases to be a partner.
Priorities (order) upon Liquidation	1. Outside creditors. 2. Partner creditors. 3. Partners, according to capital contribution. 4. Partners, according to profits.	1. Outside creditors and partner creditors. 2. Partners and former partners entitled to distributions before withdrawal under the agreement or RULPA. 3. Partners, according to capital contributions. 4. Partners, according to profits.

The liability of a limited partner is limited to the capital that he or she contributes or agrees to contribute to the partnership. By contrast, the liability of a general partner for partnership indebtedness is virtually unlimited.

LIMITED PARTNERS AND MANAGEMENT

The exemptions from personal liability of the limited partners rest on their not participating in management [RULPA 303]. The surname of a limited partner cannot be included in the partnership name [RULPA 102]. A violation of this provision renders the limited partner just as liable as a general partner to any creditor who does not know that he or she is a limited partner. Note that no law expressly bars the participation of limited partners in the management of the partnership. Rather, the threat of

personal liability normally deters their participation.

Under RULPA, a limited partner will be liable as a general partner only if the third party had knowledge of the limited partner's management activities [RULPA 303]. How much actual review and advisement a limited partner can engage in before being exposed to liability is an unsettled question.[4]

In the following case, a limited partner was alleged to have participated in the control of the business by interceding on the partnership's behalf to secure credit.

---

4. It is an unsettled question partly because there are differences among the laws in different states. Factors to be considered under RULPA are listed in RULPA 303(b), (c).

Case 39.4

PITMAN v. FLANAGAN LUMBER CO.

Supreme Court of Alabama, 1990.
567 So.2d 1335.

BACKGROUND AND FACTS   Robert Pitman was one of two limited partners in Ramsey Homebuilders, a limited partnership that engaged in the business of residential construction. Michael Ramsey was the sole general partner in the partnership. Because Ramsey had a poor credit history, he was unable to borrow the money or obtain the credit that was needed to sustain the partnership's business. Pitman, who had a personal account with Flanagan Lumber Company, contacted Flanagan's credit manager and secured an account in the partnership's name. After the partnership failed to pay the account, Flanagan sued Pitman in an Alabama state court, alleging that although Pitman was a limited partner in Ramsey Homebuilders, he was responsible for the partnership's debt under RULPA 303. Pitman argued that, if anything, he was operating within the waters of the "safe harbor" provided by RULPA 303(b)(3), which states that a limited partner does not participate in the control of the partnership solely by acting as a surety or guarantor for any liabilities incurred by the partnership. The trial court found that Pitman had participated in the control of the business by securing credit for the partnership, that Flanagan had reasonably relied on that participation in extending credit, and that Pitman was therefore liable to Flanagan for the debt subsequently incurred by the partnership. Pitman appealed.

DECISION AND RATIONALE   The Supreme Court of Alabama affirmed the trial court's decision, ruling that Pitman's action of securing credit that was vitally necessary to the partnership meant that he had exercised a degree of "control" over partnership affairs sufficient to hold him liable as a general partner for the debt to Flanagan. The court held that control is defined as "the [p]ower or authority to manage, direct, superintend, restrict, regulate, govern, administer, or oversee." The appellate court pointed out that "[t]he trial court could have found * * * that Pittman participated in the 'control' of the partnership's business by securing one of the things that the partnership needed to survive—a source of building materials that would be provided on credit." Moreover, the court found that Flanagan reasonably relied on Pitman's participation in the partnership's business in deciding to extend credit to the partnership.

Dissolution of a Limited Partnership

A limited partnership is dissolved in much the same way as an ordinary partnership. The retirement, death, or mental incompetence of a general partner can dissolve the partnership, but not if the business can be continued by one or more of the other general partners in accordance with their certificate or by consent of all members [RULPA 801]. The death or assignment of interest of a limited partner does not dissolve the limited partnership [RULPA 702, 704, 705]. A limited partnership can be dissolved by court decree [RULPA 802].

Illegality, expulsion, and bankruptcy of the general partners dissolve a limited partnership.

Bankruptcy of a limited partner, however, does not dissolve the partnership unless it causes the bankruptcy of the firm. The retirement of a general partner causes a dissolution unless the members consent to a continuation by the remaining general partners or unless this contingency is provided for in the certificate.

Upon dissolution, creditor's rights, including those of partners who are creditors, take first priority. Then partners and former partners receive unpaid distributions of partnership assets and, except as otherwise agreed, amounts representing a return on their contributions and amounts proportionate to their share of the distributions [RULPA 804].

■ Terms and Concepts

buy-sell agreement 703
certificate of limited
   partnership 704

dissolution 698
general partner 703
limited partner 703

right of contribution 703
winding up 698

■ For Review

1. Under the UPA, what initiates the process that results in the termination of a partnership? What are the two stages that must occur before termination is complete?

2. Can a partner continue the business of a terminated partnership if he or she wishes to do so? How does a withdrawing partner avoid liability for contracts incurred after dissolution of a partnership?

3. What are the essential differences between the rights and liabilities of general partners and limited partners?

4. On dissolution of a general partnership between Nikki, Noel, and Adam, $100,000 in partnership assets are available for distribution. Each partner initially invested $10,000 in the partnership, and they agreed to share profits equally; Nikki later loaned the firm another $10,000. The firm owes outside creditors $20,000. Claims against the firm's assets include $10,000 owed by Noel individually. Under the UPA, how should the firm's assets be distributed? If only $50,000 in partnership assets were available for distribution, how would the assets be distributed?

5. In the previous problem, if the firm had been a limited partnership, with Nikki the sole general partner, how would the $100,000 in partnership assets be distributed? How would the $50,000 be distributed?

■ Questions and Case Problems

39-1. Alister, Bentley, and McCoy have formed a twenty-year partnership to purchase land, develop it, manage it, and then sell the property. The partnership agreement calls for the partners to devote their full time to the business. Discuss fully which of the following acts will constitute a dissolution of the partnership and whether there is any ensuing liability of Alister.

(a) After two years, Bentley and McCoy agree that the working hours of the partnership will be from 8:00 A.M. to 6:00 P.M. rather than the previously established schedule of 9:00 A.M. to 5:00 P.M. Alister refuses to come to work before 9:00 A.M. and quits promptly at 5:00 P.M.

(b) After two years, Alister quits the partnership and walks out.

(c) After two years, Alister becomes insolvent.

(d) After two years, Alister dies.

39-2. Susan and Dominic formed a partnership. At the time of formation, Susan's capital contribution was $10,000, and Dominic's was $15,000. Later, Susan made a $10,000 loan to the partnership when it needed working capital. The partnership agreement provided that profits were to be shared, with 40 percent for Susan and 60 percent for Dominic. The partnership was dissolved by Dominic's death. At the end of the dissolution and the winding up of the partnership, the partnership's assets were $50,000, and the partnership's debts were $8,000. Discuss fully how the assets should be distributed.

39-3. Karen, Doug, and Charlie were partners in a partnership at will. Karen and Doug excluded Charlie from partnership management affairs and then sought a dissolution of the partnership. A trial court dissolved the partnership and ordered a sale of the partnership asset, a shopping center. Karen and Doug were the highest bidders at the court-ordered sale and were therefore able to retain the shopping center. Will the courts protect Charlie from this type of "freeze-out"? Discuss.

39-4. Asner and Burton form a limited partnership with Asner as the general partner and Burton as the limited partner. Burton puts up $15,000, and Asner contributes some office equipment that he owns. A certificate of limited partnership is properly filed, and business is begun. One month later, Asner becomes ill. Instead of hiring someone to manage the business, Burton takes over complete management himself. While Burton is in control, he makes a contract with Thomas involving a large sum of money. Asner returns to work. Because of other commitments, the Thomas contract is breached. Thomas contends that he can hold Asner and Burton personally liable if his judgment cannot be satisfied out of the assets of the limited partnership. Discuss this contention.

39-5. Elsie, Liz, and Elena form a limited partnership. Elsie is a general partner, and Liz and Elena are limited partners. Consider each of the separate events below, and discuss fully which constitute a dissolution of the limited partnership.
 (a) Liz assigns her partnership interest to Diana.
 (b) Elena is petitioned into involuntary bankruptcy.
 (c) Elsie dies.

39-6. Carola and Grogan were partners in a law firm. The partnership began business in 1974 and was created by an oral agreement. On September 6, 1976, Carola withdrew from the partnership some of its files, furniture, and books, along with various other items of office equipment. The next day, Carola informed Grogan he had withdrawn from the partnership. Discuss whether Carola's actions on September 6, 1976 constituted effective notice of dissolution to Grogan. [*Carola v. Grogan,* 102 A.D.2d 934, 477 N.Y.S.2d 525 (1984)]

39-7. In 1964, Alex Gershunoff and Lawrence Silk formed a partnership to syndicate and manage apartment houses. Jacob Oliker served the partnership as legal counsel. In 1969, Oliker joined the partnership, known as the Alex Co., as an equal partner. Oliker paid $5,000 to the partnership and gave up his legal practice as consideration for entering the partnership, but there was never a written partnership agreement. The partnership functioned smoothly from 1969 until 1974. The partnership bought apartment houses and called itself a "development company." At one point, the partnership organized two limited partnerships: an "ownership company" to buy the property from the development company and a "leasing company" to lease the property to another leasing company. This second leasing company operated the apartment complexes under a management contract with a corporation, PIC, in which Gershunoff, Silk, and Oliker were the sole shareholders. In March 1974, Oli-

ker withdrew from the partnership. After Oliker's withdrawal, the value of land owned by the partnership greatly appreciated. For two and a half years, the parties failed to agree on the amount of Oliker's interest. In November 1976, Gershunoff and Silk sent Oliker a "final accounting," which Oliker rejected. Oliker filed suit, requesting a formal accounting and a court-supervised winding up of affairs, with his interest to be determined as of its value at the time of the court-ordered accounting. Discuss whether Oliker was entitled to an equal share in the increased value of partnership assets. [*Oliker v. Gershunoff,* 195 Cal.App.3d 1288, 241 Cal.Rptr. 415 (2d Dist. 1987)]

39-8. In January 1987, Westbrook Pharmacy and Surgical Supply (doing business as Canter's Pharmacy, Inc.), Orrie Rockwell, Jr., and another business entity entered into a partnership agreement for the purpose of operating a personal care facility in Elizabeth, Pennsylvania. The partnership agreement provided that any disputes among the partners were to be submitted to arbitration. Two years later, the partnership sued Westbrook to recover capital contributions allegedly owed by Westbrook to the partnership. Westbrook filed a counterclaim against the partnership, seeking an accounting and a dissolution of the partnership. Subsequently, Westbrook brought a separate action alleging various breaches of the partnership agreement. The trial court granted Westbrook's petition to consolidate the actions. The partnership filed a motion to stay the consolidated proceedings pending arbitration pursuant to the arbitration provision in the partnership agreement. The trial court granted the partnership's motion. The question on appeal is whether the arbitration provision—or any provision of the partnership agreement—was enforceable, given the fact that Westbrook had sought an accounting and dissolution of the firm. Did Westbrook's action dissolve the partnership, thus rendering the provisions of the partnership—including the arbitration provision—ineffective? Discuss fully. [*Canter's Pharmacy, Inc. v. Elizabeth Associates,* 396 Pa.Super. 505, 578 A.2d 1326 (1990)]

39-9. Combat Associates was formed as a limited partnership to promote an exhibition boxing match between Lyle Alzado (a professional football player) and Muhammad Ali. Alzado and others had formed Combat Promotions; this organization was to be the general partner and Blinder, Robinson & Co. (Blinder), the limited partner, in Combat Associates. The general partner's contribution consisted of assigning all contracts pertaining to the match, and the limited partner's contribution was a $250,000 letter of credit to ensure Ali's compensation. Alzado personally guaranteed to repay Blinder for any amount of loss if the proceeds of the match were less than $250,000. In preparation for the match, at Alzado's request, Blinder's president participated in interviews and a promotional rally, and the company sponsored parties and allowed its local office to be used as a ticket sales outlet. The proceeds of the match were insufficient, and Blinder sued Alzado on his guaranty. Alzado counterclaimed by asserting that Blinder took an active role in the control and management of Combat Associates and should be held liable as a general partner. How did the court rule on Alzado's counterclaim? Discuss. [*Blinder, Robinson & Co., Inc. v. Alzado*, 713 P.2d 1314 (Colo.App. 1985)]

39-10. Elfon Realty Co. was a limited partnership in which Harry Macklowe was the sole general partner and 42nd Street Development Corp. was the sole limited partner. The limited partner assigned its right to receive partnership distributions to a third party, in violation of the express conditions of the partnership agreement. In the litigation that followed, a central issue was whether 42nd Street Development Corp. should be entitled to an accounting in view of the fact that it had breached the partnership agreement. Discuss fully whether 42nd Street's assignment was sufficient misconduct to bar it from viewing partnership records and an accounting of partnership assets and profits. [*Macklowe v. 42nd Street Development Corp.*, 157 A.D.2d 566, 550 N.Y.S.2d 309 (1990)]

39-11. A Question of Ethics

Mt. Hood Meadows Oregon, Ltd., was a limited partnership established to carry on the business of constructing and operating a winter sports development in the Hood River area of Oregon. Elizabeth Brooke and two of the other limited partners were dissatisfied because, for all the years in which profits were earned after 1974, the general partner distributed only 50 percent of the limited partners' taxable profits. The remaining profits were retained and reinvested in the business. Each of the limited partners was taxed on his or her distributable share of the profits, however, regardless of whether the cash was actually distributed. Brooke and the others brought an action to compel the general partner to distribute all of the limited partnership's profits. The court held that, in the absence of a limited partnership agreement concerning the distribution of profits, the decision to reinvest profits was strictly a managerial one. Unless the limited partners could prove that the general partner's conduct was inappropriate or violated a fiduciary duty, the decision of the general partner was binding on the limited partners. [Brooke v. Mt. Hood Meadows Oregon, Ltd., 81 Or.App. 387, 725 P.2d 925 (1986)]

1. The major attraction of limited partnerships is that the investors, as limited partners, are not liable for partnership obligations beyond the amount that they have invested. The "price" paid for this limited liability, however, is that limited partners have no say in management—as is well illustrated by the case described above. What ethical considerations are expressed in the rule that limited partners cannot participate in management? Do you think such a rule is fair?

2. The case discussed above also illustrates how relatively helpless the limited partners are when faced with a general partner whose actions do not correspond to the limited partners' wishes. Apart from selling their partnership shares to others (and at times, buyers are hard to find) or participating in management (and losing their limited liability as a result), limited partners have little recourse against the decisions of general partners so long as the general partners have not violated their fiduciary duties or the partnership agreement. Do you think that, because limited partners cannot participate in management, general partners have ethical duties to limited partners that go beyond those prescribed by law? If not, why not? If so, how would you describe or define such duties?

Chapter 40

CORPORATIONS
Introduction, Formation, and Management Powers

The corporation is a creature of statute. A corporation is an artificial being, existing in law only and neither tangible nor visible. Its existence depends generally upon state law, although some corporations, especially public organizations, can be created under federal law. Each state has its own body of corporate law, and these laws are not entirely uniform. The Model Business Corporation Act (MBCA) is a codification of modern corporation law that has been influential in the codification of corporation statutes in many states. Today, the majority of state statutes are guided by the revised MBCA, known as the Revised Model Business Corporation Act (RMBCA). It should be kept in mind, however, that there is considerable variation among the statutes of the states that have used the MBCA or the RMBCA as a basis for their statutes, and several states do not follow either act. Because of this, individual state corporation laws should be relied on rather than the MBCA or RMBCA.

As stated in the introduction to this unit, the corporation is an important form of business organization in the United States and has been for over one hundred years. In this chapter, after a brief look at the history of the corporation, we examine the nature of this form of business enterprise and the various classifications of corporations. We then discuss how a corporation is formed. In the final sections of this chapter, we discuss corporate powers, as well as the responsibilities of corporate directors, officers, and shareholders.

■ Nature of the Corporation

A *corporation* is a legal entity created and recognized by state law. It can consist of one or more persons identified under a common name.

The Corporation as a Legal "Person"

A corporation is recognized under state and federal law as a "person," and it enjoys many, but not all, of the same rights and privileges that U.S. citizens enjoy. The Bill of Rights guarantees to "persons" certain protections, and corporations are considered persons in most instances. Accordingly, a corporation has the same right as a natural person to equal protection of the laws under the Fourteenth Amendment. A corporation has the right of access to the courts as an entity that can sue or be sued. It also has the right of due process before denial of life, liberty, or property, as well as freedom from unreasonable search and seizure and from double jeopardy.

Under the First Amendment, corporations are entitled to freedom of speech, just as individuals are. In addition to freedom of commercial speech (advertising), corporations may express their political viewpoints on particular issues. The right of corporations to free political speech has been challenged in the past by those who assert that news-publishing corporations should give equal space to opposing points of view. Recently, however, the United States Supreme Court has made it clear that no such restrictions should be placed on a corporation's freedom of speech.[1]

Only the corporation's individual officers and employees possess the Fifth Amendment right against self-incrimination, however.[2] And the privileges and immunities clause of the Constitution (Article IV, Section 2) does not protect corporations, nor does it protect an unincorporated association.[3] This clause requires each state to treat citizens of other states equally with respect to access to courts, travel rights, and so forth.

An unsettled area of corporation law has to do with the criminal acts of a corporation. Because obviously a corporation cannot be sent to prison—even though, under law, it is a person—most courts hold a corporation that has violated the criminal statutes liable for fines. When criminal conduct can be attributed to corporate officers or agents, those individuals, as *natural* persons, are held liable and can be punished for their acts. The criminal liability of corporations and corporate personnel is discussed in detail in the section on corporate crime in Chapter 7.

---

1. *Pacific Gas & Electric Co. v. Public Utilities Commission of California*, 475 U.S. 1, 106 S.Ct. 903, 89 L.Ed.2d 1 (1986). See Chapter 4 for a more detailed discussion of the constitutional protection given to commercial and political speech.
2. *In re Grand Jury No. 86-3 (Will Roberts Corp.)*, 816 F.2d 569 (11th Cir. 1987).
3. *W. C. M. Window Co. v. Bernardi*, 730 F.2d 486 (7th Cir. 1984).

Characteristics of the Corporate Entity

A corporation is a legal entity with rights and responsibilities. The corporation substitutes itself for its shareholders in conducting corporate business and in incurring liability, yet its authority to act and the liability for its actions are separate and apart from the individuals who own it. Responsibility for the overall management of the corporation is entrusted to a board of directors, which is elected by the shareholders [RMBCA 8.01, 8.03]. Corporate officers and other employees are hired by the board of directors to run the daily business operations of the corporation. Officers are agents of the corporation. They answer to the board of directors rather than to the shareholders directly.

When an individual purchases a share of stock in a corporation, that person becomes a shareholder and an owner of the corporation. As a general rule, a shareholder is not personally liable for the corporation's business debts; nor is the corporation responsible for a shareholder's personal debts. Each shareholder's liability is limited to the amount of the investment (that is, the money actually paid when the stock was acquired) [RMBCA 6.22]. Unlike the members in a partnership, the body of shareholders can change constantly without affecting the continued existence of the corporation. A shareholder can sue the corporation, and the corporation can sue a shareholder. Also, under certain circumstances, a shareholder can sue on behalf of a corporation. These rights, as well as the rights and duties of all corporate personnel, will be discussed in the following chapter.

Because a corporation is a separate legal entity, corporate profits are taxed by state and federal governments. Corporations can do one of two things with corporate profits—retain them or pass them on to shareholders in the form of dividends. The corporation receives no tax deduction for dividends distributed to shareholders. Dividends are again taxable (except when they represent distributions of capital) as ordinary income to the shareholder receiving them. This **double taxation** of corporate income is one of its major disadvantages. Retained earnings, if invested properly, will yield higher corporate profits in the future and thus cause the price of the company's stock to rise. Individual shareholders can then reap the benefits of these retained earnings in the gains they receive when they sell their shares.

■ Classification of Corporations

The classification of a corporation depends upon its purpose, ownership characteristics, or location.

Domestic, Foreign, and Alien Corporations

In its home state (the state in which it incorporates), a corporation is referred to as a **domestic corporation.** A corporation formed in one state but doing business in another is referred to in that other state as a **foreign corporation.** A corporation formed in another country (say, Mexico) but doing business within the United States is referred to in the United States as an **alien corporation.**

A foreign corporation does not have an automatic right to do business in a state other than its state of incorporation. It must obtain a *certificate of authority* in the states in which it plans to do business. Once the certificate has been issued, the powers conferred upon a corporation by its home state generally can be exercised in the other state. Should a foreign corporation do business without

obtaining a certificate, the state can fine it, deny it the privilege of using state courts, and even hold its officers, directors, or agents personally liable for corporate obligations incurred in that state.[4]

Before a state court can hear a dispute in which a foreign corporation is the defendant, the state court must have *jurisdiction* over the defendant; this requires that the foreign corporation have sufficient *contacts* with the state. A foreign corporation that has its home office within the state or has manufacturing plants in the state meets this **minimum-contacts requirement.** A foreign corporation whose only contact with the state is the fact that one of its directors resides there does not have sufficient contact with the state for the state court to exercise jurisdiction over it. This modern view that jurisdiction over foreign corporations is determined by a minimum-contacts standard was established in the following landmark case.

---

4. *Robertson v. Levy,* 197 A.2d 443 (D.C.Ct.App. 1964).

Case 40.1

INTERNATIONAL SHOE CO. v. STATE OF WASHINGTON

Supreme Court of the United States, 1945. 326 U.S. 310, 66 S.Ct. 154, 90 L.Ed. 95.

BACKGROUND AND FACTS The state of Washington sought to collect unemployment contributions from the International Shoe Company based on commissions paid by the company to its sales representatives who lived in Washington. In Washington's suit against International Shoe in a Washington state court, International Shoe asserted that its activities within the state were not sufficient to manifest its "presence" there, and thus the state courts could not constitutionally exercise jurisdiction over it. International Shoe argued that (1) it had no office in the state of Washington; (2) although it employed eleven to thirteen Washington sales representatives to market its product in Washington, no actual sales or purchase contracts were made in that state; and (3) it maintained no stock of merchandise in Washington. Consequently, International Shoe argued that it was a denial of due process for the state to subject it to suit. The Supreme Court of Washington held for the state, and International Shoe appealed.

DECISION AND RATIONALE The United States Supreme Court upheld the decision by the Supreme Court of Washington, ruling that International Shoe had sufficient contacts with the state of Washington to allow the state to exercise jurisdiction over the company. The Supreme Court found that International Shoe's activities in the state of Washington were "systematic and continuous throughout the years in question. They resulted in a large volume of interstate business." These ties with the state of Washington made it reasonable for the state to attempt to enforce International Shoe's obligations under Washington law by filing suit against it.

COMMENTS In this case, the United States Supreme Court established a new test for jurisdiction over foreign corporations. For a state to exercise jurisdiction constitutionally over a foreign corporation, the corporation must have minimum contacts with the foreign state.

Public and Private Corporations

A public corporation is one formed by the government to meet some political or governmental purpose. Cities and towns that incorporate are common examples. In addition, many federal government organizations, such as the U.S. Postal Service, the Tennessee Valley Authority, and Amtrak, are public corporations. Private corporations, in contrast, are created either wholly or in part for private benefit. Most corporations are private. Although they may serve a public purpose, as a public utility does, they are owned by private persons rather than by the government.

Nonprofit Corporations

Corporations that are formed without a profit-making purpose are called *nonprofit, not-for-profit,* or *eleemosynary* (charitable) corporations. Usually (although not necessarily) private corporations, they can be used in conjunction with an ordinary corporation to facilitate making contracts with the government. Private hospitals, educational institutions, charities, religious organizations, and the like are frequently organized as nonprofit corporations. The nonprofit corporation is a convenient form of organization that allows various groups to own property and to form contracts without the individual members' being personally exposed to liability.

Close Corporations

A **close corporation** is one whose shares are held by members of a family or by relatively few persons. Close corporations are also referred to as *closely held, family,* or *privately held* corporations. Usually, the members of the small group that is involved in a close corporation are personally known to each other. Because the number of shareholders is so small, there is no trading market for the shares. In practice, a close corporation is often operated like a partnership. A few states recognize this in special statutory provisions that cover close corporations.

CLOSE CORPORATION STATUTES   To be eligible for close corporation status, a corporation has to have a limited number of shareholders, the transfer of corporation stock must be subject to certain restrictions, and the corporation must not make any public offering of its securities.[5] Close corporation statutes provide greater flexibility by expressly permitting close corporations to vary significantly from those subject to traditional corporation law.[6]

A Statutory Close Corporation Supplement to the MBCA was promulgated in 1982. In those states that have adopted this supplement, it applies only to eligible corporations that elect close corporation status. To be eligible, a corporation must have fewer than fifty shareholders. As under some states' statutes, the supplement relaxes most of the nonessential formalities to the operation of a closely held corporation.

This prevents a court from holding the shareholders individually liable for the debts and torts of the corporation simply because the corporation is closely held. Nevertheless, if the circumstances would justify imposing liability on the shareholders of a large corporation, a court may still pierce the corporate veil of a close corporation.

MANAGEMENT OF CLOSE CORPORATIONS Management of a close corporation resembles that of a sole proprietorship or a partnership, although, as a corporation, the firm must meet the same legal requirements as other corporations—except when special statutes have been enacted, as mentioned previously.

The Statutory Close Corporation Supplement was designed to reduce management formalities. Under these statutes, shareholders have unlimited power to restrict decisions of the board of directors. In fact, there need not even be a board of directors; the corporation can be managed by the sharehold-

---

5.   See, for example, Delaware Code Annotated, Title 8, Section 342, which provides that close corporations can have no more than thirty shareholders.

6.   For example, in some states (such as Maryland), the close corporation need not have a board of directors.

ers. In that circumstance, the shareholders have the same fiduciary duties as directors.

To prevent a majority shareholder from dominating a close corporation, the corporation may require that action can be taken by the board only on approval of more than a majority of the directors. Typically, this would not be required for ordinary business decisions but only for extraordinary actions—such as changing the amount of dividends or dismissing an employee-shareholder.

TRANSFER OF SHARES IN CLOSE CORPORATIONS Because a close corporation, by definition, has a small number of shareholders, the transfer of shares of one shareholder to someone else can cause serious management problems. In other words, the other shareholders can find themselves required to share control with someone they may not know or like. To avoid this problem, a few states provide statutes prohibiting the transfer of close corporation shares unless certain persons—including shareholders, family members,

and the corporation—have been given the opportunity to purchase the shares for the same price first. These statutes do not apply if shareholders have otherwise specified restrictions. Thus, it may be advisable for the close corporation with several shareholders to specify restrictions on the transferability of stock in its articles of incorporation.

Another way that control of a close corporation can be stabilized is through the use of a shareholder agreement. Agreements among shareholders to vote their stock in a particular way are generally upheld.[7] Shareholder agreements can also provide that when one of the original shareholders dies, his or her shares of stock in the corporation will be divided in such a way that the proportionate holdings of the survivors, and thus their proportionate control, will be maintained. The court evaluated such a shareholder agreement in the following case.

---

7. An important case upholding the validity of shareholder agreements is *Ringling Bros.–Barnum and Bailey Combined Shows v. Ringling,* 29 Del.Ch. 610, 53 A.2d 441 (1947).

Case 40.2

RENCH v. LEIHSER

Appellate Court of Illinois,
Fifth District, 1986.
139 Ill.App.3d 889,
487 N.E.2d 1201,
94 Ill.Dec. 324.

BACKGROUND AND FACTS In February 1955, Robert Leihser, Elbert Rench, and Claude Mullen bought the Loyd Trucking Corporation. They divided the fifty corporate shares equally and signed an agreement in 1956 that should any of them die or wish to sell his shares, the remaining stockholder or stockholders would buy the shares. The agreement provided a specific procedure for transferring the shares in such an event. In 1961, Mullen sold his stock, and Leihser and Rench each bought half of Mullen's shares. Mullen did not follow the specific procedure outlined in the 1956 agreement when he sold his shares, however. Leihser and Rench also violated the 1956 agreement by assigning one share of stock each to their respective spouses. In 1981, Leihser died. Rench sought to buy Leihser's shares from Leihser's wife, Leora, under the shareholder agreement. Leora Leihser was willing to sell, but they could not agree on a price. Finally, Rench initiated an action in an Illinois state court to compel her to sell him the shares. The trial court granted Rench specific performance. Leora Leihser appealed.

DECISION AND RATIONALE The Appellate Court of Illinois reversed the decision of the trial court, finding that the conduct of Leihser and Rench after their purchase of Mullen's stock terminated the agreement in 1961. The court noted that although agreements imposing "restrictions upon the right to transfer shares of corporate stock are permissible provided that those restrictions are reasonable" and may be enforced by specific performance, the validity of the agreements is dependent on their continuing to be followed by the parties. The parties' failure to follow the agreement's procedures when Mullen sold out led the court to conclude that the agreement was no longer in force. In the absence of an agreement, the court could not grant specific performance.

S Corporations

In 1982, Congress enacted the Subchapter S Revision Act, the purpose of which was "to minimize the effect of federal income taxes on choices of the form of business organizations and to permit the incorporation and operation of certain small businesses without the incidence of income taxation at both the corporate and shareholder level."[8] Additionally, Congress decreed that all corporations are divided into two groups: **S corporations** (formerly *Subchapter S corporations*), which have elected Subchapter S treatment, and *C corporations,* which are all other corporations.

Certain corporations can choose to qualify under Subchapter S of the Internal Revenue Code to avoid the imposition of income taxes at the corporate level while retaining all the advantages of a corporation, particularly limited liability. Although the S corporation has the advantages of the corporate form without the double taxation of income (corporate income is generally not taxed separately), it does have some disadvantages. One of the most important disadvantages relates to the fact that an S corporation's fringe-benefit payments to employee-shareholders who own more than 2 percent of the stock are nondeductible.

REQUIREMENTS FOR S-CORPORATION STATUS Among the numerous requirements for S-corporation qualification are the following, more important ones:

1. The corporation must be a domestic corporation.
2. The corporation must not be a member of an affiliated group of corporations.
3. The shareholders of the corporation must be individuals, estates, or certain trusts. Corporations, partnerships, and nonqualifying trusts cannot be shareholders.
4. The corporation must have thirty-five or fewer shareholders.
5. The corporation can have only one class of stock. Not all shareholders need have the same voting rights.
6. No shareholder of the corporation can be a nonresident alien.

BENEFITS OF S CORPORATIONS At times it is beneficial for a regular corporation to elect S-corporation status, as detailed in the following checklist:

1. When the corporation has losses, the S election allows the shareholders to use such losses to offset other income.
2. Whenever the stockholders are in a lower tax bracket than that applied to a C corporation, the S election causes the corporation's entire income to be taxed in the shareholders' bracket, whether or not it is distributed. This is particularly attractive when the corporation wants to accumulate earnings for some future business purpose.
3. Only a single tax on corporate income is imposed at individual income tax rates at the shareholder level (taxable to shareholders whether or not the income is actually distributed).

Professional Corporations

Professional corporations are relatively new in corporate law. In the past, professional persons such as physicians, lawyers, dentists, and accountants could not incorporate. Today they can, and their corporations are typically called *professional service associations* or *professional corporations.* They can be identified by the letters S.C. (service corporation), P.C. (professional corporation), Inc. (incorporated), or P.A. (professional association). In general, the laws governing the formation of professional corporations are similar to those governing the formation of ordinary business corporations.

The professional corporation equalized the tax burden on professionals who, due to occupational ethics codes, could not incorporate their businesses. By 1981, however, this form of enterprise had come to be widely viewed as permitting unacceptable tax avoidance through many tax-deductible investments, including certain kinds of pension plans. Since 1981, stringent limitations enacted by Congress have helped stop the growth of professional corporations and eliminate the tax loopholes available through them.

Subject to certain exceptions, the shareholders of a professional corporation have limited liability. Three basic areas of liability deserve brief attention. First, a shareholder in a professional association may be liable for the malpractice liability of

---

8. Senate Committee Report No. 97-640.

Selling Shares in a Close Corporation

Sometimes friends, relatives, or a few close business associates form a close corporation. They intend to have management control and ownership by only a few individuals. At the time of forming of the close corporation, it is therefore important to address certain possibilities, such as each shareholder's future sale or gift of his or her stock, or the disposition of the stock upon a shareholder's death.

To prevent outsiders from becoming shareholders and to preserve management control, the articles of incorporation normally provide that the shares must first be offered for sale to the remaining shareholders, who have the right of "first refusal." Such right of first refusal must be accompanied by a method for determining the price of the stock. There exist numerous possibilities. An appraiser can be hired to value the business. Alternatively, the price can be made a multiple of the net, after-tax earnings of the business. If the parties are hostile toward each other, one solution is to let one party set the price and the other decide whether to buy or to sell. The point is that the method or methods used to determine a price must be established when the business is formed, rather than in the throes of a heated dispute among shareholders.

---

a member. Under normal corporate law, no member of a corporation is liable for the malpractice of another member. A court, however, might, for liability purposes, regard the professional corporation as a partnership in which each partner can be held liable for whatever malpractice liability is incurred by the others within the scope of the partnership. Second, a shareholder in a professional corporation is protected from the liability imposed because of torts (unrelated to malpractice) committed by other members. Third, although any shareholder of a professional corporation who engages in a negligent action and who is guilty of malpractice is *personally* liable for the damage caused, many professional corporation statutes retain personal liability of professional persons for their acts and the professional acts performed under their supervision.

■ Formation of Corporations

The formation of a corporation involves two steps: (1) preliminary organizational and promotional undertakings—particularly, obtaining capital for the future corporation—and (2) the legal process of incorporation.

Promotional Activities

Before a corporation becomes a reality, people invest in the proposed corporation as subscribers, and contracts are frequently made by **promoters** on behalf of the future corporation. Promoters are those who, for themselves or others, take the preliminary steps in organizing a corporation. They issue the *prospectus*[9] for the proposed organization and secure a charter.

PROMOTER'S LIABILITY   It is not unusual for a promoter to purchase or lease property with a view to selling it to the corporation when the corporation is formed. In addition, a promoter may enter into contracts with attorneys, accountants, architects, or other professionals whose services will be needed in planning for the proposed corporation. Finally, a promoter induces people to purchase stock in the corporation.

Some interesting legal questions arise in regard to promoters' activities, the most important centering on whether the promoter is personally liable for contracts made on behalf of a corporation that does not yet have any legal existence. In addition, once the corporation is formed, does it assume liability on these contracts, or is the promoter still personally liable?

---

9. A *prospectus* is a document required by federal or state securities laws and regulations (see Chapter 43) that contains material facts concerning the financial operations of the corporation, thus allowing an investor to make an informed decision.

As a general rule, a promoter is held personally liable on preincorporation contracts. Courts simply hold that promoters are not agents when a corporation has yet to come into existence. If, however, the promoter secures the contracting party's agreement to hold only the corporation (not the promoter) liable on the contract, the promoter will not be liable in the event of any breach of contract.

Basically, the same rule of personal liability of the promoter continues even after incorporation unless the third party *releases* the promoter. In most states, this rule is applied whether or not the promoter made the agreement in the name of, or with reference to, the proposed corporation.

Once the corporation is formed (the charter issued), the promoter remains personally liable until the corporation assumes the preincorporation contract by *novation* (see Chapter 16). Novation releases the promoter and makes the corporation liable for performing the contractual obligations. In some cases the corporation *adopts* the promoter's contract by undertaking to perform it. Most courts hold that adoption in and of itself does not discharge the promoter from contractual liability. Obviously, a corporation cannot normally *ratify* a preincorporation contract, as no principal was in existence at the time the contract was made.

SUBSCRIBERS AND SUBSCRIPTIONS   Prior to the actual formation of the corporation, the promoter can contact potential individual investors, and they can agree to purchase capital stock in the future corporation. This agreement is often called a *subscription agreement,* and the potential investor is called a *subscriber.* Depending on state law, subscribers become shareholders as soon as the corporation is formed or as soon as the corporation accepts the agreement. This way, if the corporation becomes insolvent, the trustee in bankruptcy can collect the consideration for any unpaid stock from a preincorporation subscriber.

Most courts view preincorporation subscriptions as continuing offers to purchase corporate stock. On or after its formation, the corporation can choose to accept the offer to purchase stock. Many courts also treat a subscription as a contract between the subscribers, making it irrevocable except with the consent of all of the subscribers. A subscription is irrevocable for a period of six months unless otherwise provided in the subscription agreement or unless all the subscribers agree to the revocation of the subscription [RMBCA 6.20]. In some courts and jurisdictions, however, the preincorporation subscriber can revoke the offer to purchase before acceptance without liability.

Incorporation

Exact procedures for incorporation differ among states, but the basic requirements are similar.

STATE CHARTERING   Because state incorporation laws differ, individuals have found some advantage in looking for the states that offer the most advantageous tax or incorporation provisions. Delaware has historically had the least restrictive laws. Consequently, many corporations, including a number of the largest, have incorporated there. Delaware's statutes permit firms to incorporate in Delaware and carry out business and locate operating headquarters elsewhere. (Most other states now permit this.) In contrast, closely held corporations, particularly those of a professional nature, generally incorporate in the state in which their principal stockholders live and work.

ARTICLES OF INCORPORATION   The primary document needed to begin the incorporation process is called the *articles of incorporation* (see Exhibit 40–1). The articles include basic information about the corporation and serve as a primary source of authority for its future organization and business functions. The person or persons who execute the articles are called *incorporators* and are discussed below. Generally, the following should be included in the articles of incorporation.

Corporate Name   Choice of a corporate name is subject to state approval to ensure against duplication or deception. Fictitious-name statutes usually require that the secretary of state run a check on the proposed name in the state of incorporation. Some states require that the incorporators, at their own expense, run a check on the proposed fictional name for the newly formed corporation. Once cleared, a name can be reserved for a short time, for a fee, pending the completion of the articles of incorporation. All corporate statutes require the corporation name to include the word *Corporation, Incorporated,* or *Limited,* or an abbreviation of one of these terms.

A corporate name is prohibited from being the same as, or deceptively similar to, the name of an existing corporation doing business within the state. For example, if an existing corporation is named General Dynamics, Inc., the state will not allow another corporation to be called General Dynamic, Inc., because that name is deceptively similar to the first, and it impliedly transfers a part of the goodwill established by the first corporate user to the second corporation.

Nature and Purpose   The intended business activities of the corporation must be specified in the articles, and naturally, they must be lawful. A general statement of corporate purpose is usually sufficient to give rise to all of the powers necessary or convenient to the purpose of the organization. The corporate charter can state, for example, that the corporation is organized "to engage in the production and sale of agricultural products." There is a trend toward allowing corporate charters to state that the corporation is organized for "any legal business," with no mention of specifics, to avoid unnecessary future amendments to the corporate charter.

Some states prohibit the incorporation of certain professionals, such as doctors or lawyers, except pursuant to a professional incorporation statute. Also, in some states, certain industries, such as banks, insurance companies, or public utilities, cannot be operated in the general corporate form and are governed by special incorporation statutes.

Duration   A corporation can have perpetual existence under most state corporate statutes. A few states, however, prescribe a maximum duration after which the corporation must formally renew its existence.

Capital Structure   The capital structure of the corporation is generally set forth in the articles. A few state statutes require a relatively small capital investment (for example, $1,000) for ordinary business corporations but a greater capital investment for those engaged in insurance or banking. The number of shares of stock authorized for issuance; their par value; the various types or classes of stock authorized for issuance; and other relevant information concerning equity, capital, and credit must be outlined in the articles.

Internal Organization   Whatever the internal management structure of the corporation, it should be described in the articles, although it can be included in bylaws adopted after the corporation is formed. The articles of incorporation commence the corporation; the bylaws are formed after commencement by the incorporators or the board of directors. Bylaws are subject to, and cannot conflict with, the incorporation statute or the corporation's charter [RMBCA 2.06]. Under the RMBCA, shareholders may amend or repeal bylaws. The board of directors may also amend or repeal bylaws unless the articles of incorporation or provisions of the incorporation statute reserve the power to the shareholders exclusively [RMBCA 10.20]. Typical bylaw provisions describe the quorum and voting requirements for shareholders, the election of the board of directors, the methods of replacing directors, and the manner and time of scheduling shareholder and board meetings.

Registered Office and Agent   The corporation must indicate the location and address of its registered office within the state. Usually, the registered office is also the principal office of the corporation. The corporation must give the name and address of a specific person who has been designated as an *agent* and who can receive legal documents on behalf of the corporation. These legal documents include service of process (the delivery of a court order requiring an appearance in court) if the corporation is named in a lawsuit.

Incorporators   Each incorporator must be listed by name and must indicate an address. An incorporator is a person who applies to the state on behalf of the corporation to obtain its corporate charter. The incorporator need not be a subscriber and need not have any interest at all in the corporation. Many states do not impose residency or age requirements for incorporators. States vary on the required number of incorporators; it can be as few as one or as many as three. Incorporators are required to sign the articles of incorporation when they are submitted to the state; often this is their only duty. In some states, they participate at the first organizational meeting of the corporation.

CERTIFICATE OF INCORPORATION   Once the articles of incorporation have been prepared, signed, and authenticated by the incorporators, they are sent to the appropriate state official, usually the secretary of state, along with the appropriate filing

■ **Exhibit 40–1 Articles of Incorporation**

ARTICLE ONE

The name of the corporation is _____.

ARTICLE TWO

The period of its duration is perpetual (may be a number of years or until a certain date).

ARTICLE THREE

The purpose (or purposes) for which the corporation is organized is (are) _____
_____.

ARTICLE FOUR

The aggregate number of shares that the corporation shall have authority to issue is _____ of the par value of _____ dollar(s) each (or without par value).

ARTICLE FIVE

The corporation will not commence business until it has received for the issuance of its shares consideration of the value of $1,000 (can be any sum not less than $1,000).

ARTICLE SIX

The address of the corporation's registered office is _____,
New Pacum, and the name of its registered agent at such address is _____.

(Use the street or building or rural route address of the registered office, not a post office box number.)

ARTICLE SEVEN

The number of initial directors is _____ , and the names and addresses of the directors are
_____
_____.

ARTICLE EIGHT

The name and address of the incorporator is _____
_____.

(signed) _____
Incorporator

Sworn to on _____ by the above-named incorporator.
(date)

_____
Notary Public _____ County, New Pacum

(Notary Seal)

fee. In many states, the secretary of state then issues a *certificate of incorporation* representing the state's authorization for the corporation to conduct business. (This may be called the *corporate charter.*) The certificate and a copy of the articles are returned to the incorporators, and then the initial organizational meeting is held to complete the details of incorporation.

FIRST ORGANIZATIONAL MEETING The first organizational meeting is provided for in the articles of incorporation but is held after the charter is actually granted. At this meeting, the incorporators elect the first board of directors and complete the routine business of incorporation (pass bylaws, issue stock, and so forth). Sometimes, the meeting is held after the election of the board of directors.

The business to be transacted depends upon the requirements of the state's incorporation statute, the nature of the business, the provisions made in the articles, and the desires of the promoters.

Adoption of bylaws—the internal rules of management for the corporation—is probably the most important function of the first organizational meeting. The shareholders, directors, and officers must abide by the bylaws in conducting corporate business; but corporation employees and third persons dealing with the corporation are not bound by the bylaws unless they have reason to be familiar with them.

CORPORATE FINANCING   Corporations are financed by the issuance and sale of corporate securities—bonds and stock. A detailed description of the types of securities that can be issued and the difference between stocks and bonds are given in Chapter 43.

Improper Incorporation

The procedures for incorporation are very specific. If they are not followed precisely, others may be able to challenge the existence of the corporation. Errors in the incorporation procedures can become important when, for example, a third person who is attempting to enforce a contract or bring suit for a tort injury fortuitously learns of them. On the basis of improper incorporation, the plaintiff could seek to make the would-be shareholders personally liable. To prevent the windfall that would occur in giving a plaintiff the benefit of the stockholders' personal liability, courts will sometimes attribute corporate existence to an improperly formed corporation by holding it to be a *de jure* corporation or a *de facto* corporation, as discussed below. In some cases, corporation by estoppel may also occur.

In the event of substantial compliance with all conditions precedent to incorporation, the corporation is said to have *de jure* existence in law. In most states the certificate of incorporation is viewed as evidence that all mandatory statutory provisions have been met. This means that the corporation is properly formed, and neither the state nor a third party can attack its existence. If, for example, an incorporator's address was incorrectly listed, this would mean that the corporation was improperly formed; but the law does not regard such inconsequential procedural defects as detract-

ing from substantial compliance, and courts will uphold the *de jure* status of the corporate entity.

Sometimes there is a defect in complying with statutory mandates—for example, the corporation charter may have expired. Under such circumstances, if the parties have made a good faith attempt to comply with a statute (under which the corporation can be incorporated validly) and the enterprise has already undertaken to do business as a corporation, the corporation may have a *de facto* status—meaning that its existence cannot be challenged by third persons (except for the state).

Corporation by Estoppel

If an association that is neither an actual corporation nor a *de facto* or *de jure* corporation holds itself out as being a corporation, it will be estopped from denying corporate status in a lawsuit by a third party. This usually occurs when a third party contracts with an association that claims to be a corporation but does not hold a certificate of incorporation. When the third party brings suit naming the so-called corporation as the defendant, the association may not escape from liability on the ground that no corporation exists. When justice requires, the courts treat an alleged corporation as if it were an actual corporation for the purpose of determining the rights and liabilities involved in a particular situation. Corporation by estoppel is thus determined by the situation. It does not extend recognition of corporate status beyond the resolution of the problem at hand.

Disregarding the Corporate Entity

In some unusual situations, a corporate entity is used by its owners to perpetrate a fraud, circumvent the law, or in some other way accomplish an illegitimate objective. In these cases, the court will ignore the corporate structure by ''piercing the corporate veil,'' exposing the shareholders to personal liability.

The following are some of the factors that frequently cause the courts to pierce the corporate veil:

1.   A party is tricked or misled into dealing with the corporation rather than the individual.
2.   The corporation is set up never to make a profit or always to be insolvent, or it is too ''thinly'' capitalized.

3. The shareholder or director unconditionally guarantees to be personally liable for corporate obligations, corporate debts, or both.

4. Statutory corporate formalities, such as calling required corporation meetings, are not followed.

5. Personal and corporate interests are commingled to the extent that the corporation has no separate identity.

To elaborate on the fifth factor in the preceding list, consider a close corporation that is formed according to law by a single person or by a few family members. In such a case, the corporate entity and the sole stockholder (or family-member stockholders) must carefully preserve the separate status of the corporation and its owners. Certain practices invite trouble for the one-person or family-owned corporation: the commingling of corporate and personal funds; the failure to hold, and record minutes of, board of directors' meetings; or the shareholders' continuous personal use of corporate property (for example, vehicles). When the corporate privilege is abused for personal benefit and the corporate business is treated in such a careless manner that the corporation and the shareholder in control are no longer separate entities, the court will require an owner to assume personal liability to creditors for the corporation's debts. In short, when the facts show that great injustice would result from the use of a corporation to avoid individual responsibility, a court of equity will look behind the corporate structure to the individual stockholder.

General corporation law has no specific prohibition against a stockholder's lawfully lending money to his or her corporation. When an officer or director lends the corporation money and takes back security in the form of corporate assets, however, the courts will scrutinize the transaction closely. Any such transaction must be made in good faith and for fair value.

In the following case, two shareholders made a lawful loan of money to a corporation (which later became insolvent) and in return took a security interest in certain pieces of corporate property. When the corporation became insolvent, some creditors charged that the shareholders' loan transaction had not been made in good faith and that their security interest therefore should be set aside.

BACKGROUND AND FACTS InterTherm, Inc., was a creditor of Olympic Homes Systems, Inc. Two of Olympic's shareholders, Langley and Clayton, made a sizable loan to Olympic. In return, they took a security interest in certain corporate property. When Olympic became insolvent, the general creditors asked a Tennessee state court to set aside the priority of Langley and Clayton's security interest. Langley and Clayton argued that the general creditors failed to show either that there was any fraud involved in the loan or that the loan was not a legitimate transaction. Moreover, according to Langley and Clayton, the general creditors had not established that Langley and Clayton's relationship to Olympic was fiduciary or that they showed a lack of good faith in the loan transaction. The trial court entered judgment for the general creditors, and Langley and Clayton appealed.

DECISION AND RATIONALE The Supreme Court of Tennessee reversed the lower court's decision and held that Langley and Clayton held a valid security interest in the property of Olympic and were entitled to priority over the general creditors. The state supreme court explained that "courts will closely scrutinize the transactions of a majority, or dominant, or controlling shareholder with his corporation, and will place the burden of proof upon the shareholder when the good faith and fairness of such a transaction is challenged." In this case, the court concluded that the loan should not be subjected to close scrutiny and declined to put the burden of justifying the transaction on Langley and Clayton, because there was no evidence that they owned a majority of Olympic stock or otherwise dominated the corporation in such a way as to justify imposing fiduciary responsibilities on them.

Case 40.3

INTERTHERM, INC. v. OLYMPIC HOMES SYSTEMS, INC.

Court of Appeals of Tennessee, 1978.

569 S.W.2d 467.

■ Corporate Powers

Corporations have both express and implied powers. These are distinguished and defined below.

Express Powers

The express powers of a corporation are found in its articles of incorporation, in the law of the state of incorporation, and in the state and federal constitutions. The following order of priority is used when conflicts arise among documents involving corporations:

1. The U.S. Constitution.
2. State constitutions.
3. State statutes.
4. The certificate of incorporation (charter).
5. Bylaws.
6. Resolutions of the board of directors.

Implied Powers

Certain inherent powers attach when a corporation is created. Barring express constitutional, statutory, or charter prohibitions, the corporation has the implied power to perform all acts reasonably appropriate and necessary to accomplish its corporate purposes. For this reason, a corporation has the implied power to borrow money within certain limits, to lend money or extend credit to those with whom it has a legal or contractual relationship, and to make charitable contributions.[10]

To borrow money, the corporation acts through its board of directors to authorize the execution of negotiable paper. Most often, the president or chief executive officer of the corporation will execute the necessary papers on behalf of the corporation. In so doing, corporate officers have the implied power to bind the corporation in matters directly connected with the *ordinary* business affairs of the enterprise. A corporate officer does not have the authority to bind the corporation in matters of great significance to the corporate purpose or undertaking, however, as the following case illustrates.

---

10. A corporation is prohibited from making political contributions in federal elections by the Federal Elections Campaign Act [18 U.S.C. Section 321].

Case 40.4

BOSTON ATHLETIC ASSOCIATION v. INTERNATIONAL MARATHONS, INC.

Supreme Judicial Court of Massachusetts, 1984.
392 Mass. 356,
467 N.E.2d 58.

BACKGROUND AND FACTS William Cloney was the president of the Boston Athletic Association (BAA), a nonprofit corporation whose principal purpose was to present the annual Boston Marathon. At a 1981 BAA board of directors' meeting, Cloney was "authorized and directed to negotiate and to execute in the name of and in behalf of [the BAA] such agreements as he deems in the best interest of the Association for the perpetuation, sponsorship, or underwriting of the Boston A. A. Marathon." For past marathons, Cloney himself had undertaken to secure contracts with individual sponsors, and the BAA had full control over the presentation of the marathon. This time, however, Cloney contracted with International Marathons, Inc. (IMI), for IMI to be the exclusive promoter of the race. Under the terms of the contract, (1) BAA transferred all rights to use the Boston Marathon name and logos to IMI, (2) the agreement was to be automatically renewable from year to year, and (3) IMI was entitled to keep any profits beyond the first $400,000, which would be paid to BAA. In short, the contract with IMI prevented BAA from having any significant control over the sponsorship or presentation of the race, which was essentially the reason for its corporate existence. When the board learned of Cloney's agreement with IMI, it brought an action in a Massachusetts state court to have the agreement set aside on the ground that Cloney had exceeded the authority vested in him by the board. IMI claimed that Cloney had been given the authority to make the contract, and therefore it should be enforced. The trial court held for BAA, and IMI appealed.

DECISION AND RATIONALE The Supreme Judicial Court of Massachusetts affirmed the judgment of the trial court, ruling that Cloney had exceeded his authority by granting IMI excessive and perpetual control over the Boston Marathon. The court noted that even though "[c]orporate officers are generally empowered, by delegation of authority of the board of directors, with general managerial functions" to oversee the day-to-day operations of the corporation, "certain powers cannot be delegated generally. Certain transactions require specific authorization by the board in order to be valid." The court stated that a delegation of authority by the board broad enough to permit Cloney to conclude the contract with IMI would have meant giving up control of the very essence of BAA's corporate existence. The court concluded that authority to make such a contract was even beyond the power of the board to delegate.

Ultra Vires Doctrine

The term *ultra vires* means "beyond the powers." In corporate law, acts of a corporation that are beyond the authority given to it under its charter or under the statutes by which it was incorporated are *ultra vires* acts. In other words, acts in furtherance of the corporation's expressed purposes are within the corporate power; acts beyond the scope of corporate business as described in the charter are *ultra vires* acts. Thus, *ultra vires* acts can be understood only within the context of the particular stated purpose for which the corporation was organized.

The stated purposes in the articles of incorporation set the limits of the activities the corporation can legally pursue. Any time the corporation takes on activities outside the stated purpose or purposes, the corporation can be charged with committing an *ultra vires* act. Because of this, corporations are increasingly aware of the benefit of adopting a very broad statement of purpose in their articles of incorporation to include virtually all conceivable activities.

The current trend in dealing with *ultra vires* contracts is embodied in statutory enactments similar to Section 3.04 of the RMBCA, which upholds the validity and enforceability of an *ultra vires* contract as between the parties involved. The right of shareholders on behalf of the corporation to bring an action to obtain an injunction and damages, the right of the corporation itself to recover damages from the officers and directors who caused the transactions, and the right of the attorney general of the state to institute a proceeding to obtain an injunction against the transaction or to institute dissolution proceedings against the corporation for *ultra vires* acts, however, have been upheld. Although still of some importance, the *ultra vires* doctrine is of declining significance in corporate law because courts have held that any legal action that a corporation undertakes to profit its shareholders is allowable and proper.

■ Corporate Management—Shareholders

The acquisition of a share of stock makes a person an owner and shareholder in a corporation. As a shareholder, that person acquires certain powers in the corporation. These powers are discussed here, along with the relationship of the shareholders to the corporation.

Shareholders' Powers

Shareholders must approve fundamental changes affecting the corporation before the changes can be effected. Hence, shareholders are empowered to amend the articles of incorporation (charter) and bylaws, approve the merger or dissolution of the corporation, and approve the sale of all or substantially all of the corporation's assets. Some of these powers are subject to prior board approval.

Election and removal of the board of directors are accomplished by a vote of the shareholders. The first board of directors is either named in the articles of incorporation or chosen by the incorporators to serve until the first shareholders' meeting. From that time on, selection and retention of directors are exclusively shareholder functions.

Directors usually serve their full term; if they are unsatisfactory, they are simply not reelected. Shareholders have the inherent power, however, to remove a director from office *for cause* (breach of duty or misconduct) by a majority vote.[11] Some

---

11. A director can often demand court review of removal for cause.

state statutes even permit removal of directors *without cause* by the vote of a majority of the holders of outstanding shares entitled to vote.[12] Some corporate charters expressly provide that shareholders, by majority vote, can remove a director at any time *without cause.*

Relationship between Shareholders and Corporation

As a general rule, shareholders have no responsibility for the daily management of the corporation, although they are ultimately responsible for choosing the board of directors, which does have such control. Ordinarily, corporate officers and other employees owe no direct duty to *individual* stockholders. Their duty is to the corporation as a whole. A director, however, is in a fiduciary relationship to the corporation and therefore serves the interests of the shareholders as a whole.

Generally, there is no legal relationship between shareholders and creditors of the corporation. Shareholders can, in fact, be creditors of the corporation and have the same rights of recovery against the corporation as any other creditor. The rights and liabilities of shareholders are discussed in detail in the following chapter.

Shareholders' Forum

Shareholders' meetings must occur at least annually, and additional special meetings can be

called to take care of urgent matters. Because it is usually not practical for owners of only a few shares of stock of publicly traded corporations to attend the shareholders' meetings, they normally give third persons a written authorization to vote their shares at the meeting. This authorization, called a **proxy,** is often solicited by management, as will be discussed later.

NOTICE OF MEETINGS   The notice and time of meetings, including the day and the hour, are announced in writing to each shareholder at a reasonable length of time prior to the date of the shareholders' meeting.[13] Special-meeting notices must include a statement of the purpose of the meeting; business transacted at a special meeting is limited to that purpose.

In the following case, shareholders objected to the fact that they had not been properly notified as to the purpose of a shareholder meeting and to the fact that a director participated, as a shareholder, in a vote to determine whether the business should be sold.

---

12.   Most states allow *cumulative voting* (which will be discussed shortly) with respect to the removal of directors without cause. See, for example, California Corporations Code Section 303A. Also see Section 8.08(c) of the RMBCA.

---

13.   The shareholder can waive the requirement of written notice by signing a waiver form. A shareholder who does not receive written notice, but who learns of the meeting and attends without protesting the lack of notice, is said to have waived notice by such conduct. State statutes and corporate bylaws typically set forth the time within which notice must be sent, what methods can be used, and what the notice must contain.

Case 40.5

SOLOMON v. ATLANTIS DEVELOPMENT, INC.

Supreme Court of Vermont, 1986.
145 Vt. 349,
516 A.2d 132.

BACKGROUND AND FACTS   Dennis Solomon was one of four shareholders of Atlantis Development, Inc. All shareholders held an equal number of shares. Initially, there were only three shareholders, but poor sales forced Atlantis to take on an additional one, Malloy, who supplied additional capital. Malloy's role was at first that of financier, but because of continued mismanagement of the firm, he assumed active control over business operations. In spite of Malloy's efforts, however, Atlantis continued to suffer financially until finally the shareholders considered bankruptcy. Bankruptcy was eventually rejected in favor of selling the company to Malloy for one dollar. The shareholders approved the deal by a three-to-one vote. Malloy assumed Atlantis's liabilities with the intention of liquidating the firm. He managed to turn the business around and make a profit, however, after changing the firm's name and investing a considerable amount of his money into the business. Solomon brought an action against Malloy and Atlantis in a Vermont state court, claiming that the vote to sell the corporation to Malloy should be invalidated because proper notification of the purpose of the meeting had not been given to the shareholders. Solomon further claimed that Malloy had breached his fiduciary duty to the corporation by voting to sell the firm to himself. The trial court ruled in Solomon's favor, and Malloy appealed.

DECISION AND RATIONALE The Supreme Court of Vermont reversed the decision of the trial court, ruling that the sale of the firm to Malloy could not be invalidated on the basis of improper notification to the shareholders: The court stated that "[u]nder [state] law, the sale of all or substantially all corporate assets must be authorized at a shareholders' meeting duly called for that purpose by a vote of two-thirds of the outstanding shares entitled to vote thereon." The court found that the shareholders' attendance and participation at the meeting constituted a waiver of their right to object to the business considered at that meeting. The court pointed out that "[a]s a general rule, a director should refrain from voting on matters where a conflict is apparent." In the court's opinion, that Malloy had voted in favor of selling the company to himself did not constitute a breach of his fiduciary duty to the other shareholders, because he voted as a shareholder in approving the sale of the corporation's assets as required by state law. The court did not find any evidence that there had been a breach of good faith or loyalty. It concluded that the sale of the corporation's assets was a legitimate and reasonable business decision—given its dire financial situation and poor prospects for recovery.

CONDUCT OF MEETINGS Corporate articles or bylaws may provide for the conduct of shareholders' meetings. Typically, the company president or the chairperson of the board of directors presides, and the corporate secretary records the minutes of the meeting. The agenda may include reports of management, the amendment or repeal of bylaws, resolutions submitted on behalf of management or shareholders, extraordinary corporate matters or decisions that require shareholder approval, and other subjects. Shareholders can offer and respond to proposals and resolutions. For example, shareholders concerned about social and political issues have used shareholders' meetings to propose changes in corporate activities that pertain to those issues.

SHAREHOLDER VOTING In order for shareholders to act, a minimum number of them (in terms of number of shares held) must be present at a meeting. This minimum number, called a *quorum,* is generally more than 50 percent. Corporate business matters are presented in the form of *resolu-*

tions, which shareholders vote to approve or disapprove. Some state statutes have set forth voting limits, and corporations' articles or bylaws must remain within these statutory limitations. Some states provide that obtaining the unanimous written consent of shareholders is a permissible alternative to holding a shareholders' meeting.

Once a quorum is present, a majority vote of the shares represented at the meeting is usually required to pass resolutions. At times, a larger-than-majority vote will be required either by statute or by corporate charter. Extraordinary corporate matters, such as merger, consolidation, or dissolution of the corporation (to be discussed in Chapter 42), require the approval of a higher percentage of the representatives of all corporate shares entitled to vote, not just a majority of those present at that particular meeting.

Voting Lists Voting lists are prepared by the corporation prior to each shareholders' meeting. Persons whose names appear on the corporation's stockholder records as owners are the ones ordinarily entitled to vote.[14] The voting list contains the name and address of each shareholder as shown on the corporate records on a given cutoff date, or record date. (RMBCA 7.07 allows a record date to be as much as seventy days before the meeting.) The voting list also includes the number of voting shares held by each owner. The list is usually kept at the corporate headquarters and is available for shareholder inspection.

Cumulative Voting   Most states permit or require shareholders to elect directors by **cumulative voting,** a method of voting designed to allow minority shareholders representation on the board of directors.[15] Cumulative voting operates as follows: The number of members of the board to be elected is multiplied by the total number of voting shares held. The result equals the number of votes a shareholder has, and this total can be cast for one or more nominees for director. All nominees stand for election at the same time. When cumulative voting is not required either by statute or under the articles, the entire board can be elected by a majority of shares at a shareholders' meeting.

To illustrate: A corporation has 10,000 shares issued and outstanding. The minority shareholders hold only 3,000 shares, and the majority shareholders hold the other 7,000 shares. Three members of the board are to be elected. The majority shareholders' nominees are Mott, Gregory, and Dunsworth. The minority shareholders' nominee is Diamond. Can Diamond be elected by the minority shareholders?

If cumulative voting is allowed, the answer is yes. The minority shareholders have 9,000 votes among them (the number of directors to be elected times the number of shares equals 3 times 3,000, which equals 9,000 votes). All of these votes can be cast to elect Diamond. The majority shareholders have 21,000 votes (3 times 7,000 equals 21,000 votes), but these votes have to be distributed among their three nominees. The principle of cumulative voting is that no matter how the majority shareholders cast their 21,000 votes, they will not be able to elect all three directors if the minority shareholders cast all of their 9,000 votes for Diamond, as illustrated in Exhibit 40–2.

Other Voting Techniques   A group of shareholders can agree in writing prior to the meeting to vote their shares together in a specified manner. Such *shareholder voting agreements* are usually held to be valid and enforceable. A shareholder can also appoint a voting agent and vote by proxy. A *proxy* is a written authorization to cast the shareholder's vote, and a person can solicit proxies from a number of shareholders in an attempt to concentrate voting power.

Another technique is for shareholders to enter into a **voting trust,** which is an agreement (a trust contract) by which legal title (record ownership on the corporate books) is transferred to a trustee who is responsible for voting the shares. The agreement can specify how the trustee is to vote, or it can allow the trustee to use his or her discretion. The trustee takes physical possession of the actual stock certificate and in return gives the shareholder a *voting trust certificate*. The shareholder retains all of the rights of ownership (for example, the right to receive dividend payments) except for the power to vote.

---

14.   When the legal owner is deceased, bankrupt, incompetent, or in some other way under a legal disability, his or her vote can be cast by a person designated by law to control and manage the owner's property.

15.   See, for example, California Corporations Code Section 708. RMBCA Section 7.28, however, states that no cumulative voting rights exist unless the articles of incorporation so provide.

■ **Exhibit 40–2 Results of Cumulative Voting**

Ballot	Majority Shareholder Votes			Minority Shareholder Votes	Directors Elected
	Mott	*Gregory*	*Dunsworth*	*Diamond*	
1	10,000	10,000	1,000	9,000	Mott, Gregory, Diamond
2	9,001	9,000	2,999	9,000	Mott, Gregory, Diamond
3	6,000	7,000	8,000	9,000	Gregory, Dunsworth, Diamond

A voting trust is not the same thing as a proxy, for the latter can be revoked more easily. The holder of a proxy has neither legal title to the stock nor possession of the certificates, whereas voting trustees have both.[16]

◼ Corporate Management— Directors

Every corporation is governed by directors. Subject to statutory limitations, the number of directors is set forth in the corporation's articles or bylaws. Historically, the minimum number of directors has been three, but today many states permit fewer. Indeed, the RMBCA, in Section 8.01, permits corporations with fewer than fifty shareholders to eliminate the board of directors.

Directors' Election and Term of Office

The first board of directors is normally appointed by the incorporators upon the creation of the corporation, or directors are named by the corporation itself in the articles. The first board serves until the first annual shareholders' meeting. Subsequent directors are elected by a majority vote of the shareholders.

The term of office for a director is usually one year—from annual meeting to annual meeting. Longer and staggered terms are permissible under most state statutes. A common practice is to elect one-third of the board members each year for a three-year term. In this way, there is greater management continuity.

A director can be removed *for cause,* either as specified in the articles or bylaws or by shareholder action. Even the board of directors itself may be given power to remove a director for cause, subject to shareholder review. In most states, unless the shareholders have reserved the right at the time of election, a director cannot be removed without cause.

When vacancies occur on the board of directors due to death or resignation, or when a new position is created through amendment of the articles or bylaws, either the shareholders or the board itself can fill the position, depending on state law or on the provisions of the bylaws.

Directors' Qualifications and Compensation

Few legal qualifications exist for directors. Only a handful of states retain minimum age and residency requirements. A director is sometimes a shareholder, but this is not a necessary qualification unless, of course, statutory provisions or corporate articles or bylaws require ownership.

Compensation for directors is ordinarily specified in the corporate articles or bylaws. Because directors have a fiduciary relationship to the shareholders and to the corporation, an express agreement or provision for compensation is necessary for them to receive money from the funds they control or for which they have responsibilities.

Directors' Management Responsibilities

Directors have responsibility for all policy-making decisions necessary to the management of all corporate affairs. Just as shareholders cannot act individually to bind the corporation, the directors must act as a body in carrying out routine corporate business. One director has one vote, and generally the majority rules.

The general areas of responsibility of the board of directors include the following:

1. Financial decisions such as the declaration and payment of dividends to shareholders or the issuance of authorized shares or bonds.
2. Authorization for major corporate policy decisions—for example, the initiation of proceedings for the sale or lease of corporate assets outside the regular course of business, the determination of new product lines, and the overseeing of major contract negotiations and major management-labor negotiations.
3. Appointment, supervision, and removal of corporate officers and other managerial employees and the determination of their compensation.

Board of Directors' Forum

The board of directors conducts business by holding formal meetings with recorded minutes. The date on which regular meetings are held is usually established in the articles and bylaws or by board

---

16. In most states, the term of a voting trust cannot exceed ten years. RMBCA 7.30 provides that it may be extended for an additional term of up to ten years. In contrast, proxies are typically limited to no more than eleven months, unless a proxy specifically provides otherwise [RMBCA 7.22].

resolution, and no further notice is customarily required. Special meetings can be called, with notice sent to all directors.

Quorum requirements can vary among jurisdictions. Many states leave the decision to the corporate articles or bylaws. In the absence thereof, most states provide that a quorum is a majority of the number of directors authorized in the articles or bylaws. Voting is done *in person* (unlike voting at shareholders' meetings, which can be done by proxy).[17] The rule is one vote per director. Ordinary matters generally require a majority vote; certain extraordinary issues may require a greater-than-majority vote.

Delegation of Board of Directors' Powers

The board of directors can delegate some of its functions to an executive committee or to corporate officers. In doing so, the board is not relieved of its overall responsibility for directing the affairs of the corporation, but corporate officers and managerial personnel are empowered to make decisions relating to ordinary, daily corporate affairs within well-defined guidelines.

Most states permit the board of directors to elect an executive committee from among the directors to handle the interim management decisions between board of directors' meetings, as provided in the bylaws. The executive committee is limited to making management decisions about ordinary business matters.

The officers and other executive employees are hired by the board of directors or, in rare instances, by the shareholders. In addition to carrying out the duties articulated in the bylaws, corporate and managerial officers act as agents of the corporation, and the ordinary rules of agency apply or have been applied to their employment (unlike the board of directors, whose powers are conferred by the state). Qualifications are determined at the discretion of the corporation and are included in the articles or bylaws. In most states, a person can hold more than one office and can be both an officer and a director of the corporation. Corporate officers can be removed by the board of directors at any time with or without cause and regardless of the terms of the employment contract, although it is possible for the corporation to be liable for breach of contract damages.

---

17.   Except in Louisiana, where a director can vote by proxy under certain circumstances. Some states, such as Michigan and Texas, and Section 8.20 of the RMBCA permit telephone conferences for board of director meetings.

■ Terms and Concepts

alien corporation   712
close corporation   713
cumulative voting   726
domestic corporation   712
double taxation   711

foreign corporation   712
minimum-contacts
  requirement   712
professional corporation   715
promoter   716

proxy   724
S corporation   715
ultra vires   723
voting trust   726

■ For Review

1.   A corporation is a legal entity that, in conducting business and incurring liability, substitutes itself for whom? Who has responsibility for the overall management of a corporation? Who runs the daily corporate business?
2.   Generally, liability for acts undertaken on behalf of a corporation is separate from ownership of the corporation. What are some of the exceptions to this rule?
3.   What are the steps for bringing a corporation into existence? What are circumstances in which an association that is not an actual corporation might be treated as a corporation?
4.   Juanita, Luis, Leo, and Kirk are shareholders of the Trilby Microwave Foods Corp. Trilby has 100,000 shares outstanding with Juanita holding 30,000 of the shares.

Trilby is to have its first election for the board of directors at its first annual meeting. Juanita disagrees with the other shareholders over who the directors should be and comes to you for advice about the upcoming meeting and election. What do you tell Juanita to expect regarding the notice and conduct of the meeting and voting requirements? If three directors are to be chosen, and there are four candidates, can Juanita's votes alone elect at least one of them?
5.   To respond to a downturn in business, the directors of the Kickback Tennis Shoe Corp. vote to appoint new officers to the corporation, change the company's product lines, and delegate the making of future ordinary business decisions to an executive committee made up of three directors. Do any of these acts exceed the board's power?

■ Questions and Case Problems

40-1. Jonathan, Gary, and Rob are active members of a partnership called Swim City. The partnership manufactures, sells, and installs outdoor swimming pools in the states of Texas and Arkansas. The partners want to continue to be active in management and to expand the business into other states as well. They are concerned about rather large recent judgments entered against swimming pool companies throughout the United States. Based on these facts only, discuss whether the partnership should incorporate.

40-2. Cummings, Marvin, and Taft are recent college graduates who want to form a corporation to manufacture and sell personal computers. Peterson tells them he will set in motion the formation of their corporation. First, Peterson makes a contract for the purchase of a piece of land for $20,000 with Owens. Owens does not know of the prospective corporate formation at the time of the signing of the contract. Second, Peterson makes a contract with Babcock to build a small plant on the property being purchased. Babcock's contract is conditional on the corporation's formation. Peterson secures all necessary subscription agreements and capitalization, and he files the articles of incorporation. A charter is issued.

   (a) Discuss whether the newly formed corporation, Peterson, or both are liable on the contracts with Owens and Babcock.

   (b) Discuss whether the corporation is automatically liable to Babcock upon being formed.

40-3. As a promoter forming a new corporation, Peterson enters into three pre-incorporation subscription agreements with Mary, Anne, and Harry. The three subscribers each agree to purchase 1,000 shares of stock of the future corporation for $2,000. Two months later, just prior to the issuance of the corporate charter, Mary tells Peterson she is withdrawing from the agreement. The charter is issued the next week. Just before the first organizational meeting of the corporation, Harry also withdraws from the agreement. Discuss fully whether Mary, Harry, or both can withdraw from their subscription agreements without liability.

40-4. Sarah owns 10 shares of Monmouth Corp. Monmouth Corp. has 100,000 outstanding issued common shares. Sarah believes that many decisions of the board of directors do not consider the preservation of the environment. Two pending proposals approved by the board deal with the purchase of timberland for conversion into condominiums. Both proposals require an amendment to the corporate charter and need a two-thirds shareholder vote. Sarah knows other shareholders who she believes would oppose these proposals. Unfortunately, most shareholders live a considerable distance from the site of the shareholders' meeting and will be unable to attend. Discuss any techniques Sarah can use to oppose these proposals.

40-5. Carter Corp. has issued, and has outstanding, 100,000 shares of common stock. Four stockholders own 60,000 of these shares, and for the past six years their entire slate of nominees for membership on the board has been elected. John and twenty other shareholders, who own 20,000 shares, are dissatisfied with corporate management and want a representative on the board who shares their views. Explain the circumstances under which John and the minority shareholders can elect their representative to the board.

40-6. Harvey's is a group of New York corporations. Five of these entered into an agreement with Flynt Distributing Co. for Flynt to distribute their magazines. Following this agreement, Harvey's failed to pay Flynt or to ship the magazines to Flynt, causing Flynt injury. Two of Harvey's shareholders converted the assets of the five corporations to their own use, which left the corporations undercapitalized. Discuss whether this conduct amounted to an abuse of corporate business, allowing Flynt to pierce the corporate veil to obtain recovery. [*Flynt Distributing Co. v. Harvey,* 734 F.2d 1389 (9th Cir. 1984)]

40-7. Charles Wolfe was the sole shareholder and president of Wolfe & Co., a firm that leased tractor-trailers. The corporation had no separate bank account. Banking transactions were conducted through Wolfe's personal accounts, and employees were paid from them. Wolfe never consulted with any other corporate directors. During the tax years 1974 through 1976, the corporation incurred $114,472.91 in federal tax liabilities for employment, fuel, and highway-use taxes and for penalties, fees, and interest. The government held Wolfe personally liable. Wolfe paid the tax bill and then brought an action against the government for disregarding his corporate entity. Discuss whether the government can disregard the corporate entity in Wolfe's case and hold Wolfe personally liable for corporate taxes. [*Wolfe v. United States,* 798 F.2d 1241 (9th Cir. 1961)]

40-8. Skandinavia, Inc., manufactured and sold polypropylene underwear. In 1981, following two years of poor sales, Skandinavia entered into negotiations to sell the business to Odilon Cormier, an experienced textile manufacturer. On June 15, 1981, Skandinavia and Cormier agreed that Cormier would take Skandinavia's polypropylene underwear inventory and use it in a new corporation, which would be called Polypro, Inc. In return, Skandinavia would receive a commission on future sales from Polypro, Inc. Polypro was established and began selling the underwear. Skandinavia, however, never received any commissions from the sales. It therefore brought suit against Polypro, Inc., and Cormier to recover its promised commissions. The suit against Polypro, Inc., was dismissed by the trial court. In the suit against Cormier, the trial court found Cormier to be personally liable for the commissions owed. Cormier appealed to the Supreme Court of New Hampshire. Is Cormier personally liable for the contract he signed in the course of setting up a new corporation? Explain. [*Skandinavia, Inc. v. Cormier,* 128 N.H. 215, 514 A.2d 1250 (1986)]

40-9. On October 7, 1980, the defendant, Cohen, Stracher & Bloom, P.C., a legal firm organized as a professional corporation under New York law, entered into an agreement with the plaintiff, We're Associates Co., for the lease of office space located in Lake Success, New York. The lease was signed for the landlord by one of the partners of the plaintiff company and for the defendant professional corporation by Paul J. Bloom, as vice-president. Bloom and the two other defendants, Cohen and Stracher, were the sole officers, directors, and stockholders of the professional corporation. The professional corporation became delinquent in paying its rent, and the plaintiff brought an action in May 1983 to recover rents and other charges of approximately $9,000 alleged to be due and owing under the lease. The complaint was filed against the professional corporation and each individual shareholder of the corporation. The individual shareholders moved to dismiss the action against them individually. Will the court grant their motion? Discuss fully. [*We're Associates Co. v. Cohen, Stracher & Bloom, P.C.,* 103 A.D.2d 130, 478 N.Y.S.2d 670 (1984)]

40-10. Pat Daniels, John Daniels, and Bill Mandell (the defendants) planned to purchase a tavern and restaurant business in St. Charles, Illinois, and to organize their business in the form of a corporation under the name of D&M, Inc. The defendants negotiated with Howard Realty Group to lease the premises on which the tavern and restaurant were located. While the sale of the business and the negotiation of the lease were proceeding, neither the seller of the business nor Howard contemplated personal guarantees from the defendants. On January 18, 1987, although D&M had not yet been incorporated, the lease was signed in the name of D&M, Inc., by Pat Daniels and Bill Mandell, in their capacity as president and secretary, respectively, of the future corporation. On February 11, 1987, the defendants filed the articles of incorporation for D&M with the secretary of state. The articles were returned by the secretary of state's office because the name "D&M, Inc." was already in use by another Illinois corporation. The defendants then decided to file the articles of incorporation under the name of The Lodge at Tin Cup Pass, Inc. (the Lodge). They first checked with the landlord to see if they could use that name, because it was similar to the name of the property, Tin Cup Pass. The Lodge was duly incorporated on March 5, 1987. In late 1988, when the Lodge defaulted on its lease payments, Tin Cup Pass Limited Partnership, to whom Howard had assigned the lease, sued the defendants personally to recover the lease payments due, alleging that the defendants should be held liable as corporate promoters for D&M, Inc., a corporation that was never formed. What will result in court? Discuss fully. [*Tin Cup Pass Limited Partnership v. Daniels,* 195 Ill.App.3d 847, 553 N.E.2d 82, 142 Ill.Dec. 732 (1990)]

40-11. Kay Bell, a vice-president of 20th Century Insurance Co., had been employed by that firm for over eleven years when her employment was terminated without notice or justifiable cause in January 1988. Throughout her length of service with the company, she was continually praised for performance of her duties; received a promotion; and was rewarded with continued salary increases, bonuses, and stock grants. 20th Century had agreed to compensate her accordingly and to deal fairly with her in her employment by not terminating her except for justifiable cause. Bell brought an action against 20th Century, alleging that the company had breached an implied employment contract. 20th Century argued that state corporation law barred a corporate officer from claiming breach of an implied contract for wrongful termination. The relevant state statute read, in part, as follows: "Except as otherwise provided by the articles or bylaws, officers shall be chosen by the board and serve at the pleasure of the board, subject to the rights, if any, of an officer under any contract of employment." Did an implied employment contract exist, and if so, could the company be held liable for breaching that contract? Discuss fully. [*Bell v. Superior Court,* 215 Cal.App.3d 1103, 263 Cal.Rptr. 787 (1989)]

40-12. A Question of Ethics

On November 3, 1981, Garry Fox met with a representative of Coopers & Lybrand (Coopers), a national accounting firm, to obtain tax advice from Coopers and other accounting services on behalf of a corporation Fox was in the process of forming. Coopers agreed to perform the services. The new corporation, G. Fox and Partners, Inc., was incorporated on December 4, 1981. Coopers completed its work by mid-December and billed G. Fox and Partners for $10,827 for its accounting services. When neither the new corporation nor Fox paid the bill, Coopers sued Garry Fox personally for the amount. Coopers claimed that Fox had breached express and implied contracts and that, as a corporate promoter, Fox was liable for the unpaid debt. Fox argued that Coopers had agreed to look solely to the corporation for payment. The trial court found that there was no agreement, either express or implied, that would obligate Fox individually to pay Coopers's fee, because Coopers failed to prove the existence of any such agreement. On appeal, however, the trial court's judgment was reversed. Fox was held liable as a corporate promoter for the unpaid debt. [Coopers & Lybrand v. Fox, 758 P.2d 683 (Colo. 1988)]

1. In view of the fact that Coopers & Lybrand knew that Fox was acting on behalf of a future corporation, do you think that it is fair that Fox should be held personally liable for the contract?

2. Undertaking preliminary corporate organization and promotion is an essential step in the process of corporate formation. Do you think that the risks imposed on promoters by holding them personally liable for preincorporation contracts counter the public policy of promoting business enterprises?

3. What might result if corporate promoters could never be held personally liable for preincorporation contracts? Would such a law also pose a barrier to commerce by increasing the difficulty in obtaining necessary preincorporation contracts, such as for office space, equipment, credit, and so on?

Chapter 41

CORPORATIONS
Rights and Duties
of Directors, Managers,
and Shareholders

No one individual shareholder or director bears sole responsibility for the corporation and its actions. Rather, a corporation joins the efforts and resources of a large number of individuals for the purpose of producing greater returns than those persons could have obtained individually.

Sometimes actions that benefit the corporation as a whole do not coincide with the separate interests of the individuals making up the corporation. In such situations, it is important to know the rights and duties of all participants in the corporate enterprise. This chapter focuses on the rights and duties of directors, managers, and shareholders and the ways in which conflicts between and among them are resolved.

■ Duties of
Officers and Directors

A director occupies a position of responsibility unlike that of other corporate personnel. Directors are sometimes inappropriately characterized as agents because they act for and on behalf of the corporation. No individual director, however, can act as an agent to bind the corporation, and as a group, directors collectively control the corporation in a way that no agent can control a principal. Directors are often incorrectly characterized as trustees because they occupy positions of trust and control over the corporation. Unlike trustees, however, they do not own or hold title to property for the use and benefit of others.

Directors manage the corporation through the officers who are selected by the board; these officers are agents of the corporation. Directors and officers are deemed *fiduciaries* of the corporation. Their relationship with the corporation and its shareholders is one of trust and confidence. The fiduciary duties of the directors and officers include the duty of care and the duty of loyalty.

Duty of Care

Directors are obligated to be honest and to use prudent business judgment in the conduct of corporate affairs. Directors must exercise the same degree of care that reasonably prudent people use in the conduct of their own personal business affairs.

731

Directors can be held answerable to the corporation and to the shareholders for breach of their duty of care. When directors delegate work to corporate officers and employees, the directors are expected to use a reasonable amount of supervision. Otherwise, they will be held liable for negligence or mismanagement of corporate personnel. For example, assume that a corporate bank director did not attend any board of directors' meetings in five and one-half years and never inspected any of the corporate books or records. Meanwhile, the bank president made various improper loans and permitted large overdrafts. The corporate director could be held liable to the corporation for any losses resulting from the unsupervised actions of the bank president and the loan committee.

The standard of due care has been variously described and codified in many corporation codes and by judicial decisions.[1] The impact of the standard is to require that directors carry out their responsibilities in an informed, businesslike manner.

Directors and officers are expected to act in accordance with their own knowledge and training. Most states and RMBCA 8.30, however, allow a director to make decisions based on information furnished by competent officers or employees, professionals such as attorneys and accountants, or even an executive committee of the board without being accused of acting in bad faith or failing to exercise due care if such information turns out to be faulty.

Directors are expected to attend board of directors' meetings, and their votes should be entered into the minutes of corporate meetings. Unless a dissent is entered, the director is presumed to have assented. Directors who dissent are rarely held individually liable for mismanagement of the corporation. For this reason, a director who is absent from a given meeting sometimes registers, with the secretary of the board, a dissent to actions taken at the meeting.

Directors are expected to be informed on corporate matters and to understand legal and other professional advice rendered to the board. In *Smith v. Van Gorkom*, for example, directors were held liable for accepting an offer for the purchase of a corporation because they failed to investigate the value of the business and whether a higher price could be obtained.[2] A director who is unable to carry out such responsibilities must resign. Even when the required duty of care has not been exercised, directors and officers are liable only for the damages caused to the corporation by their negligence.

Duty of Loyalty

One can define loyalty as faithfulness to one's obligations and duties. The essence of the fiduciary duty requires the subordination of self-interest to the interest of the entity to which the duty is owed. It presumes constant loyalty to the corporation on the part of the directors and officers. In general, the duty of loyalty prohibits directors from using corporate funds or confidential corporate information for their personal advantage. It requires officers and directors to disclose fully any corporate opportunity or any possible conflict of interest that might occur in a transaction involving the directors of the corporation. Cases dealing with fiduciary duty typically involve one or more of the following:

1. Competing with the corporation.
2. Usurping a corporate opportunity.
3. Having an interest that conflicts with the interest of the corporation.
4. Engaging in insider trading (using information that is not public to make a profit trading securities).
5. Authorizing a corporate transaction that is detrimental to minority shareholders.
6. Selling control over the corporation.

In the following case, the Alabama Supreme Court reviewed a situation in which officers, directors, and shareholders attempted to secure advantages for themselves at the expense of the corporation.

---

2. 488 A.2d 858 (Del. 1985).

---

1. See, for example, RMBCA 8.30(a).

BACKGROUND AND FACTS   Joseph Morad and Joseph Thomson were officers, directors, and shareholders of Bio-Lab, Inc. Bio-Lab had one additional shareholder, George Coupounas. While serving as officers and directors of Bio-Lab, Morad and Thomson incorporated and operated a competing business, Med-Lab, Inc. Coupounas brought a derivative suit in an Alabama state court on behalf of Bio-Lab against Morad, Thomson, and Med-Lab, alleging that, in opening the competing business, Morad and Thomson had usurped a corporate opportunity of Bio-Lab. The trial court agreed with Coupounas. Morad, Thomson, and Med-Lab appealed.

 Case 41.1

MORAD v. COUPOUNAS

Supreme Court of Alabama, 1978.
361 So.2d 6.

DECISION AND RATIONALE   The Supreme Court of Alabama affirmed the trial court's decision that Morad and Thomson had misappropriated a corporate opportunity from Bio-Lab. Corporate officers and directors may in some instances seize on an opportunity that they discover as a result of their positions. If the opportunity is available both to an officer or director personally and to the corporation, however, the officer or director must make others in the company aware of the opportunity and may not surreptitiously exploit it. The court decided that the appropriate remedy for Morad and Thomson's breach of the duty of loyalty was for the court to impose a "constructive trust," which would require all profits of Med-Lab to be paid to Bio-Lab.

Conflicts of Interest

Corporate directors often have many business affiliations, and they can even sit on the board of more than one corporation. Of course, they are precluded from entering into or supporting any business that operates in direct competition with the corporation. The fiduciary duty requires them to make a full disclosure of any potential conflicts of interest that might arise in any corporate transaction.

Sometimes a corporation enters into a contract or engages in a transaction in which an officer or director has a material interest. The director or officer must make a full disclosure of that interest and must abstain from voting on the proposed transaction. The various state statutes contain different standards, but a contract will generally not be voidable if it was fair and reasonable to the corporation at the time the contract was made, there was a full disclosure of the interest of the officers or directors involved in the transaction, and the contract is approved by a majority of the disinterested directors or shareholders.

Often contracts are negotiated between corporations having one or more directors who are members of both boards. Such transactions require great care, as they are closely scrutinized by courts. Section 8 of the Clayton Act of 1914 specifically states that no person shall be a director in any two or more competing corporations if any one of them has capital surplus and undivided profits aggregating more than $1 million (other than banks, banking associations, trust companies, and common carriers).

The Business Judgment Rule

Directors are expected to use their best judgment in guiding corporate management, but they are not insurers of business success. Honest mistakes of judgment and poor business decisions on their part do not make them liable to the corporation for resulting damages. This is the **business judgment rule.** The rule immunizes directors—and officers—from liability when a decision is within managerial authority, as long as the decision complies with management's fiduciary duties and as long as acting on the decision is within the powers of the corporation. Consequently, if there is a reasonable basis for a business decision, it is unlikely that the court will interfere with that decision, even if the corporation suffers thereby.

To benefit from the rule, directors and officers must act in good faith, in what they consider to be the best interests of the corporation, and with the care that an ordinarily prudent person in a like position would exercise in similar circumstances. This requires an informed decision, with a rational basis and with no conflict between the decision maker's personal interest and the interest of the corporation.

To be informed, the director or officer must do what is necessary to become informed: attend presentations, ask for information from those who have it, read reports, review other written materials such as contracts—in other words, carefully study a situation and its alternatives. To be free of conflicts of interest, the director must not engage in self-dealing. For instance, a director should not oppose a *tender offer* (an offer made by another company directly to the shareholders to purchase shares in the company) in the corporation's best interest because its acceptance may cost the director his or her position. For a decision to have an apparently rational basis, the decision itself must appear to have been made reasonably. For example, a director should not accept a tender offer with only a moment's consideration based solely on the market price of the corporation's shares.

Whether a defendant's actions could be protected by the business judgment rule was at issue in the following case.

Case 41.2

McKNIGHT v. MIDWEST EYE INSTITUTE OF KANSAS CITY, INC.

Missouri Court of Appeals, Western District, 1990.
799 S.W.2d 909.

BACKGROUND AND FACTS Scott McKnight, an ophthalmologist, was employed by Midwest Eye Institute of Kansas City, Inc. The employment contracts for 1987 and 1988 contained a covenant not to compete, which prohibited McKnight from practicing medicine within a defined area for a period of three years after his term of employment expired. When the parties failed to agree on the terms of a proposed 1989 contract, Midwest invoked the restrictive covenant before the termination of the existing employment contract and notified all hospitals and patients served by McKnight that he would be leaving the Kansas City area at the expiration of the contract term. Midwest also terminated all McKnight's on-call duties; prohibited his treatment of, and consultation with, patients; canceled surgeries that he was scheduled to perform; and locked his office. In effect, Midwest consigned McKnight to a compulsory vacation for the rest of the contract term. McKnight asked a Missouri state court to enjoin Midwest from enforcing the restrictive covenant. The trial court held that Midwest had breached the employment contract and that, because of the breach, McKnight had no duty under the restrictive covenant. Midwest appealed.

DECISION AND RATIONALE The Missouri Court of Appeals upheld the trial court's ruling and barred Midwest from enforcing the restrictive covenant against McKnight, because Midwest had breached the employment contract. The appellate court disagreed with Midwest's contention that its decision to idle McKnight fell within the ambit of the business judgment rule and that it was therefore protected from any breach of contract claim. The court reasoned that the business judgment rule does not "relieve a corporation of an obligation of contract merely because the managers hold the honest and disinterested belief that the action benefits the corporation. * * * A suit in equity to enforce a restrictive covenant partakes of a petition for specific performance. Such a redress is not a matter of right, but of discretion. A court of equity will not aid a party who resorts to unjust and unfair conduct."

ETHICAL CONSIDERATIONS An interesting aspect of this case involved medical ethics. Among other things, Midwest argued that it would violate medical ethics to allow McKnight to undertake new surgeries and consultations with patients in view of the fact that McKnight would soon be leaving the area and thus would not be able to give his patients follow-up care. The court responded to this argument as follows: "In circumstances where the employment may not exceed even the period needed for complete care, to adopt the premise that Midwest proposes would be to supplant opinions on medical ethics for the contract terms as the basis for the obligation to perform. The more satisfactory accommodation to any ethical concerns for patient care, rather, is to provide for the contingency of non-renewal by contract provisions that address them."

Rights of Directors

A director of a corporation has a number of rights, including the rights of participation, inspection, indemnification, and in some circumstances, compensation.

Participation and Inspection

Among the rights that a corporate director must have to function properly in that position, the main right is one of participation—meaning that the director must be notified of board of directors' meetings so as to participate in them. As pointed out in Chapter 40, regular board meetings are usually established by the bylaws or by board resolution, and no additional notice of these meetings is required. If special meetings are called, however, notice is required unless waived by the director.

A director must have access to all corporate books and records in order to make decisions and to exercise the necessary supervision. This right of inspection is virtually absolute and cannot be restricted.

Compensation and Indemnification

Historically, directors have had no inherent right to compensation for their services as directors. Nominal sums are often paid as honoraria to directors, and in many cases, directors are also chief corporate officers and receive compensation in their managerial positions. Most directors, however, gain through indirect benefits, such as business contacts, prestige, and other rewards. There is a trend toward providing more than nominal compensation for directors, especially in large corporations in which directorships can be enormous burdens in terms of time, work, effort, and risk. Many states permit the corporate articles or bylaws to authorize compensation for directors, and in some cases the board can set its own compensation unless the articles or bylaws provide otherwise.

It is not unusual for corporate directors to become involved in lawsuits by virtue of their position and their actions as directors. Most states (and RMBCA 8.51) permit a corporation to indemnify a director for legal costs, fees, and judgments involved in defending corporation-related suits. Many states specifically permit a corporation to purchase liability insurance for the directors and officers to cover indemnification. When the statutes are silent on this matter, the power to purchase such insurance is usually considered to be part of the corporation's implied power.

Rights of Officers and Managers

As noted earlier, corporate officers' duties are the same as the duties of directors, because their respective corporate positions involve both of them in decision making and place them in similar positions of control. Hence, officers are viewed as having the same fiduciary duties of care and loyalty in their conduct of corporate affairs. Also, they are subject to the same obligations concerning corporate opportunities and conflicts of interest as directors are.

The rights of corporate officers and other high-level managers are defined by employment contracts, because they are employees of the company.

Rights of Shareholders

As stated in Chapter 40, the acquisition of a share of stock makes a person an owner and shareholder in a corporation. Shareholders thus own the corporation. Although they have no legal title to corporate property vested in the corporation, such as buildings and equipment, they do have an equitable interest in the firm. The rights of shareholders are established in the articles of incorporation and under the state's general incorporation law.

Stock Certificates

A **stock certificate** is a certificate issued by a corporation that evidences ownership of a specified number of shares in the corporation. In jurisdictions that require the issuance of stock certificates, shareholders have the right to demand that the corporation issue a certificate and record their names and addresses in the corporate stock record books. In most states (and under RMBCA 6.26), boards of directors may provide that shares of stock be uncertificated (that is, that actual, physical stock certificates need not be issued). In that circumstance, it may be required that the corporation send the holders of uncertificated shares letters or some other form of notice containing the same information required to be included on the face of stock certificates.

Stock is intangible personal property—the ownership right exists independently of the certificate itself. A stock certificate may be lost or destroyed, but ownership is not destroyed with it. A new certificate can be issued to replace one that has been lost or destroyed.[3] Notice of shareholder meetings, dividends, and operational and financial reports are all distributed according to the recorded ownership listed in the corporation's books, not on the basis of possession of the certificate. Of course, to sell or otherwise transfer the shares, indorsement and delivery of the actual certificate to the transferee are required.

Preemptive Rights

A **preemptive right** is a common law concept in which a preference is given to a shareholder over all other purchasers to subscribe to or purchase a prorated share of a new issue of stock. This allows the shareholder to maintain his or her portion of control, voting power, or financial interest in the corporation. Most statutes either (1) grant preemptive rights but allow them to be negated in the corporation's articles or (2) deny preemptive rights except to the extent that they are granted in the articles. The result is that the articles of incorporation determine the existence and scope of preemptive rights. Generally, preemptive rights apply only to additional, newly issued stock sold for cash and must be exercised within a specified time period (usually thirty days). Preemptive rights are far more significant in a close corporation because of the relatively few number of shares and the substantial interest each shareholder controls.

Stock Warrant Rights

When preemptive rights exist and a corporation is issuing additional shares, each shareholder is usually given **stock warrants,** which are transferable options to acquire a given number of shares from the corporation at a stated price. Warrants are often publicly traded on securities exchanges. When the warrant option is for a short period of time, the stock warrants are usually referred to as *rights.*

✝ Dividend Rights

A **dividend** is a distribution of corporate profits or income *ordered by the directors* and paid to the shareholders in proportion to their respective shares in the corporation. Dividends can be paid in cash, property, stock of the corporation that is paying the dividends, or stock of other corporations.[4] Once declared, a cash dividend becomes a corporate debt enforceable at law like any other debt.[5]

State laws vary, but every state determines the general circumstances and legal requirements under which dividends are paid. State laws also control the sources of revenue to be used; only certain funds are legally available for paying dividends, including the following:

1. *Retained earnings.* All states allow dividends to be paid from the undistributed net profits earned by the corporation, including capital gains from the sale of fixed assets. The undistributed net profits are called *earned surplus* or retained earnings.
2. *Net profits.* A few state statutes allow dividends to be issued from current net profits without regard to deficits in prior years.
3. *Surplus.* A number of state statutes allow dividends to be paid out of any kind of surplus.

---

3. For a lost or destroyed certificate to be reissued, a shareholder normally must furnish an indemnity bond to protect the corporation against potential loss should the original certificate reappear at some future time in the hands of a bona fide purchaser [UCC 8-302, 8-405(2)].

4. Technically, dividends paid in stock are not dividends. They maintain each shareholder's proportional interest in the corporation. On one occasion, a distillery declared and paid a ''dividend'' in bonded whiskey.
5. An insolvent corporation cannot declare a dividend.

Sometimes dividends are improperly paid from an unauthorized account, or their payment causes the corporation to become insolvent. Generally, in this case, shareholders must return illegal dividends only if they knew that the dividends were illegal when they received them. Whenever a dividend is paid while the corporation is insolvent, it is automatically an illegal dividend, and shareholders may be liable for returning the payment to the corporation or its creditors. In all cases of illegal and improper dividends, the board of directors can be held personally liable for the amount of the payment. When directors can show that a shareholder knew a dividend was illegal when it was received, however, the directors are entitled to reimbursement from the shareholder.

When directors fail to declare a dividend, shareholders can ask a court of equity for an injunction to compel the directors to meet and to declare a dividend. For the injunction to be granted, it must be shown that the directors have acted so unreasonably in withholding the dividend that their conduct is an abuse of their discretion.

Often large money reserves are accumulated for a bona fide purpose, such as expansion, research, or other legitimate corporate goals. The mere fact that sufficient corporate earnings or surplus is available to pay a dividend is not enough to compel directors to distribute funds that, in the board's opinion, should not be paid. The courts are circumspect about interfering with corporate operations and will not compel directors to declare dividends unless abuse of discretion is clearly shown. Thus, directors are not ordinarily forced to declare dividends to shareholders. A striking exception to this rule was made in the following classic case.

Case 41.3

DODGE v. FORD MOTOR CO.

Supreme Court of Michigan, 1919.
204 Mich. 459,
170 N.W. 668.

BACKGROUND AND FACTS Ford Motor Company was formed in 1903. Henry Ford, the president and owner of most of the firm's stock, attempted to run the corporation as if it were a one-person operation. The firm expanded rapidly and, in addition to regular quarterly dividends, often paid special dividends. Originally, the Ford car sold for more than $900. From time to time, the price was reduced, and in 1916 it sold for $440. For the year beginning August 1, 1916, the price was reduced again, to $360. In the interest of setting aside money for future investment and expansion, the firm announced that it would pay no special dividends after October 1915, even though surplus capital in 1916 exceeded $110,000,000. The minority stockholders, who owned one-tenth of the shares of the corporation, petitioned a Michigan state court to compel the directors to declare a dividend. The court issued the order, and Ford appealed.

DECISION AND RATIONALE The Supreme Court of Michigan affirmed the order that Ford Motor Company declare a dividend. The court acknowledged that "[i]t is a well-recognized principle of law that the directors of a corporation, and they alone, have the power to declare a dividend of the earnings of the corporation and to determine its amount." The court determined, however, that a declaration of a dividend would not be detrimental to Ford's business and that continued failure to declare a dividend in view of the large capital surplus could "amount to such an abuse of discretion as would constitute a fraud, or breach of that good faith which they are bound to exercise towards the stockholders." Thus, to withhold a dividend would violate the directors' duty to the shareholders.

Voting Rights

Shareholders exercise ownership control through the power of their votes. Each shareholder is entitled to one vote per share, although the voting techniques discussed in Chapter 40 all enhance the power of the shareholder's vote. The articles can exclude or limit voting rights, particularly to certain classes of shares. For example, owners of preferred shares are usually denied the right to vote.

Inspection Rights

Shareholders in a corporation enjoy both common law and statutory inspection rights.[6] The shareholder's right of inspection is limited, however, to the inspection and copying of corporate books and records for a proper purpose, provided the request is made in advance. Either the shareholder can inspect in person or an attorney, agent, accountant, or other type of assistant can do so. RMBCA 7.20 requires the corporation to maintain an alphabetical voting list of shareholders with addresses and num-

---

6. See, for example, *Schwartzman v. Schwartzman Packing Co.*, 99 N.M. 436, 659 P.2d 888 (1983).

ber of shares owned. This list must be kept open at the annual meeting for inspection by any shareholder of record.

The power of inspection is fraught with potential abuses, and the corporation is allowed to protect itself from them. For example, a shareholder can properly be denied access to corporate records to prevent harassment or to protect trade secrets or other confidential corporate information. Some states require that a shareholder must have held his or her shares for a minimum period of time immediately preceding the demand to inspect or must hold a minimum number of outstanding shares. RMBCA 16.02 provides that every shareholder is entitled to examine specified corporate records. The following case illustrates a court's dilemma in determining whether a stockholder-competitor could inspect the corporate books for limited purposes.

Case 41.4

ULDRICH v. DATASPORT, INC.

Court of Appeals of Minnesota, 1984.
349 N.W.2d 286.

BACKGROUND AND FACTS   John Uldrich was a shareholder and former director, officer, and employee of Datasport, Inc. Datasport had terminated Uldrich's directorship, office, and employment. Aside from maintaining his status as shareholder, Uldrich was also a competitor of Datasport. While Uldrich was still a director and an officer, he was prohibited from marketing his competing product for one year by a court order on Datasport's request. After his dismissal, Uldrich was denied access to Datasport's records and books. Uldrich was concerned that other shareholders of Datasport were running other businesses using Datasport assets, such as leasing office space to, and sharing it with, Datasport. Uldrich felt that Datasport's revenues were being eaten up by operating expenses. In three and one-half years, Datasport had received income of over $1,500,000 from sales, yet Uldrich, over the same period, received less than $1,000 in return on his investment. Uldrich filed a petition in a Minnesota state court for a writ of mandamus (an order issued from a court and directed to a private or municipal corporation or any of its officers commanding the performance of a particular act), which would permit him to inspect Datasport's records and books. His purpose was to place a monetary value on his shares and to evaluate the conduct and affairs of the other shareholders, directors, and officers. The trial court awarded Uldrich a writ of mandamus compelling Datasport to permit inspection. Although the writ enjoined Uldrich from making competitive use of such information, Datasport appealed the order.

DECISION AND RATIONALE   The Court of Appeals of Minnesota affirmed the trial court's issuance of the writ of mandamus, ordering Datasport to allow Uldrich to exercise his right to inspect company records and books. The appellate court explained that a state statute guarantees this right of inspection to all shareholders "at any reasonable time or times, for any proper purpose." The court concluded "that Uldrich has good faith reasons for seeking access to the records and books." In particular, the court noted that Uldrich's return on his investment was "trivial" compared to the company's substantial sales record.

The Right to Transfer Shares

Corporate stock represents an ownership right in intangible personal property. The law generally recognizes the right of an owner to transfer property to another person unless there are valid restrictions on its transferability. Although stock certificates are negotiable and freely transferable by indorsement and delivery, transfer of stock in closely held corporations is generally restricted by contract, the bylaws, or a restriction stamped on the stock certificate. The existence of any restrictions on transferability must always be noted on the face of the stock certificate, and these restrictions must be reasonable.

Sometimes corporations or their shareholders restrict transferability by reserving the option to purchase any shares offered for resale by a shareholder. This **right of first refusal** remains with the corporation or the shareholders for only a specified time or reasonable time. Variations on the purchase option are possible. For example, a shareholder might be required to offer the shares to other shareholders or to the corporation first.

When shares are transferred, a new entry is made in the corporate stock book to indicate the new owner. Until the corporation is notified and the entry is complete, voting rights, notice of shareholders' meetings, dividend distribution, and so forth are all held by the current record owner.

Rights on Dissolution

When a corporation is dissolved and its outstanding debts and the claims of its creditors have been satisfied, the remaining assets are distributed on a *pro rata* basis among the shareholders. Certain classes of preferred stock (see Chapter 43) can be given priority to the extent of their contractual preference. If no preferences to distribution of assets upon liquidation are given to any class of stock, then the stockholders share the remaining assets.

Suppose a minority shareholder knows that the board of directors is mishandling corporate assets or is permitting a deadlock to threaten or irreparably injure the corporation's finances. The minority shareholder is not powerless to intervene. He or she can petition a court to appoint a receiver and to liquidate the business assets of the corporation.

RMBCA 14.30 permits any shareholder to institute such an action in any of the following circumstances:

1. The directors are deadlocked in the management of corporate affairs, shareholders are unable to break that deadlock, and irreparable injury to the corporation is being suffered or threatened.
2. The acts of the directors or those in control of the corporation are illegal, oppressive, or fraudulent.
3. Corporation assets are being misapplied or wasted.
4. The shareholders are deadlocked in voting power and have failed, for a specified period (usually two annual meetings), to elect successors to directors whose terms have expired or would have expired with the election of successors.

Shareholder's Derivative Suit

When those in control of a corporation—the corporate directors—fail to sue in the corporate name to redress a wrong suffered by the corporation, shareholders are permitted to do so "derivatively," or "secondarily," in what is known as a **shareholder's derivative suit.** Some wrong must have been done to the corporation, and any damages recovered by the suit usually go into the corporation's treasury. The right of shareholders to bring a derivative action is especially important when the wrong suffered by the corporation results from the actions of corporate directors or officers, because in such cases the directors and officers would probably want to prevent any action against themselves.

The shareholder's derivative suit is singular in that those suing are not pursuing rights or benefits for themselves personally but are acting as guardians of the corporate entity. This derivative nature of this type of lawsuit is stressed in the following case.

Case 41.5

GLENN v. HOTELTRON SYSTEMS, INC.

Court of Appeals of New York,
1989.
74 N.Y.2d 386,
547 N.E.2d 71,
547 N.Y.S.2d 816.

BACKGROUND AND FACTS   Jacob Schachter and Herbert Kulik, the founders of Ketek Electric Corporation, each owned 50 percent of the corporation's shares and served as the corporation's only officers. Arnold Glenn, as trustee, and Kulik brought a shareholder's derivative suit against Schachter in a New York state court, alleging that Schachter had diverted Ketek assets and opportunities to Hoteltron Systems, Inc., a corporation wholly owned by Schachter. The trial court held that neither Schachter nor Kulik had proved a breach of duty by the other. The appellate court reversed this decision. The trial court later determined damages and also decided that the damages should be paid to Kulik, not to Ketek. Schachter appealed, and the appellate court ruled that the damages should be awarded to the injured corporation, Ketek, rather than to the injured shareholder, Kulik. Kulik argued that awarding damages to the corporation was inequitable, because Schachter, as a shareholder of Ketek, would ultimately share in the proceeds of the award. Eventually, the case was heard by the New York Court of Appeals.

DECISION AND RATIONALE   The New York Court of Appeals affirmed the lower court's decision. The court stated, "It is the general rule that, because a shareholder's derivative suit seeks to vindicate a wrong done to the corporation through enforcement of a corporate cause of action, any recovery obtained is for the benefit of the injured corporation." Thus the court ruled that damages should be paid to Ketek Electric Corporation and not to Kulik, because the injury Kulik suffered was derivative, or secondary to the corporate injury, and not direct (personal to the shareholder). The court ruled that Schachter's diversion of Ketek's corporate assets for his own profit was a corporate injury, because it deprived Ketek of those profits. Kulik, the innocent shareholder, was injured only to the extent that he was entitled to share in those profits.

ETHICAL CONSIDERATIONS   The court acknowledged that the prospect of an inequitable result exists "in any successful derivative action in which the wrongdoer is a shareholder of the corporation." But, the court pointed out, if exceptions were made because of that prospect, the general rule that damages for a corporate injury should be awarded to the corporation would effectively be nullified. The court stated that "[w]hile awarding damages directly to the innocent shareholder may seem equitable with respect to the parties before the court," there were other interests to consider—particularly those of the corporation's creditors whose claims might be superior to those of innocent shareholders.

◼ Liabilities of Shareholders

One of the hallmarks of the corporate organization is that shareholders are not personally liable for the debts of the corporation. If the corporation fails, shareholders can lose their investment, but that is generally the limit of their liability. In certain instances of fraud, undercapitalization, or careless observance of corporate formalities, a court will pierce the corporate veil (disregard the corporate entity) and hold the shareholders individually liable. But these situations are the exceptions, not the rule. Although rare, there are certain other instances when a shareholder can be personally liable. One relates to illegal dividends, which were discussed previously. Two others relate to *stock subscriptions* and *watered stock.*

Sometimes stock-subscription agreements—which are written contracts by which one agrees to buy capital stock of a corporation—exist prior to incorporation. Normally, these agreements are treated as continuing offers and are usually irrevocable (for up to six months under RMBCA 6.20).

Once the corporation has been formed, it can sell shares to shareholder investors. In either case, once the subscription agreement or stock offer is accepted, a binding contract is formed. Any refusal to pay constitutes a breach resulting in the personal liability of the shareholder.

Shares of stock can be paid for with any tangible or intangible property, or by services rendered, instead of with cash. In some states, the rule is that for **par-value shares** sold (that is, shares that have a specific face value, or formal cash-in value, written on them, such as one penny or one dollar), the corporation must receive a value at least equal to the par-value amount. For any **no-par shares** sold (that is, shares that have no face value—no specific amount printed on their face), the corporation must receive the value of the shares as determined by the board of directors or by the shareholders. When shares are issued by the corporation for less than these stated values, the shares are referred to as **watered stock.** In most cases, the shareholder who receives watered stock must pay the difference to the corporation (the shareholder is personally liable). In some states, the shareholder who receives watered stock may be liable to creditors of the corporation for unpaid corporate debts.

■ Duties of Major Shareholders

In some cases, a majority shareholder is regarded as having a fiduciary duty to the corporation and to the minority shareholders. This occurs when a single shareholder (or a few shareholders acting in concert) owns a sufficient number of shares to exercise *de facto* control over the corporation. In these situations, majority shareholders, when they sell their shares, owe a fiduciary duty to the minority shareholders and creditors, because such a sale would be, in fact, a transfer of control of the corporation. See Chapter 42 for a more detailed discussion of the role of majority shareholders when control of a corporation is transferred.

■ Terms and Concepts

business judgment rule 733	**preemptive rights** 736	**stock certificate** 736
dividend 736	**right of first refusal** 739	**stock warrant** 736
no-par shares 741	**shareholder's derivative**	**watered stock** 741
par-value shares 741	**suit** 739	

■ For Review

1. Directors are expected to use their best judgment in managing the corporation. What must directors do to avoid liability for honest mistakes of judgment and poor business decisions?

2. What is a shareholder's preemptive right and what determines its existence and scope? What is the difference between a preemptive right and a right of first refusal?

3. From what sources may dividends be paid legally? In what circumstances is a dividend illegal? What happens if a dividend is paid illegally?

4. Tommy, Arno, and Joe are directors of the Northside Corp., which owns valuable lakefront property in Chicago. Tommy, Arno, and Joe are also shareholders of Lake Michigan Development Corp. Lake Michigan offers to buy the Northside property for a low price. Before selling the property to Lake Michigan, Tommy, Arno, and Joe sell the property to themselves for a lower price. Katherine is a Northside shareholder. On what grounds might Katherine sue Tommy, Arno, and Joe?

5. In the previous problem, on what ground might Katherine bring an action to dissolve Northside?

■ Questions and Case Problems

41-1. Otts Corp. is negotiating with the Wick Construction Co. for the renovation of the Otts corporate headquarters. Wick, owner of the Wick Construction Co., is also one of the five members of the board of directors of Otts. The contract terms are standard for this type of contract. Wick has previously informed two of the other directors of his interest in the construction company. The contract is approved by Otts's board on a three-to-two vote, with Wick voting with the majority. Discuss whether this contract is binding on the corporation.

41-2. Rheingold, Inc., has a board of directors consisting of three members (Evans, Goodrich, and Mortimer) and approximately five hundred shareholders. At a regular meeting of the board, the board selects Green as president of the corporation by a two-to-one vote, with Evans dissenting. The minutes of the meeting do not register Evans's dissenting vote. Later, upon an audit, it is discovered that Green is a former convict and has openly embezzled $500,000 from Rheingold, Inc. This loss is not covered by insurance. The corporation wants to hold directors Evans, Goodrich, and Mortimer liable. Evans claims no liability. Discuss the personal liability of the directors to the corporation.

41-3. Ann owns 10,000 shares (10 percent) of Superal Corp. Superal authorized 100,000 shares and issued all of them during its first six months in operation. Later, Superal reacquired 10,000 of these shares. With shareholder approval, Superal amended its articles so as to authorize and issue another 100,000 shares and also, by a resolution of the board of directors, to reissue the 10,000 shares of treasury stock (the shares required by the corporation). There is no provision in the corporate articles dealing with shareholders' preemptive rights. Because of her previous ownership of 10 percent of Superal, Ann claims that she has the preemptive right to purchase 10,000 shares of the new issue and 1,000 shares of the stock being reissued. Discuss her claims.

41-4. Lucy has acquired one share of common stock of a multimillion-dollar corporation with over 500,000 shareholders. Lucy's ownership is so small that she is questioning what her rights are as a shareholder. For example, she wants to know whether this one share entitles her to (1) attend and vote at shareholder meetings, (2) inspect the corporate books, and (3) receive yearly dividends. Discuss Lucy's rights in these three matters.

41-5. Riddle has made a preincorporation subscription agreement to purchase 500 shares of a newly formed corporation. The shares have a par value of $100 per share. The corporation is formed, and Riddle's subscription is accepted by the corporation. Riddle transfers a piece of land he owns to the corporation, and the corporation issues 250 shares for it. One year later, with the corporation in serious financial difficulty, the board declares and pays a dividend of $5 per share. It is now learned that the land transferred by Riddle had a market value of $18,000. Discuss any liability that shareholder Riddle has to the corporation or to creditors of the corporation.

41-6. Air Engineered Systems and Services, Inc., had three shareholders, Naquin, Dubois, and Hoffpauir. Each of the shareholders owned one-third of the corporation's outstanding shares. Naquin was fired after he had worked six years as an employee of the firm. He then formed a competing business, hired away one of Air Engineered's employees, tried to hire another, and obtained a job for his own business that he had originally solicited for Air Engineered. Under Louisiana law, any shareholder who is also a business competitor is entitled to inspect the corporate records if he or she owns 25 percent of the outstanding shares for six months prior to the demand. When Naquin requested Air Engineered to allow him to inspect the corporate records, however, Air Engineered denied his request because Naquin refused to sign an indemnity agreement protecting Air En-

gineered from any damages it might suffer as a result of Naquin's use of the information contained in the corporate records. Shortly thereafter, Dubois and Hoffpauir voted to increase the capital stock of the corporation, and then they each purchased additional shares. This reduced Naquin's percentage to less than 25 percent—which meant that he was not entitled under Louisiana law to inspect Air Engineered's records. Naquin filed suit to require the corporation to permit him to inspect the books, because at the time his request had been made, he owned more than 25 percent of the outstanding shares of Air Engineered. What was the result? Explain. [*Naquin v. Air Engineered Systems and Services, Inc.,* 463 So.2d 992 (La.App. 3d Cir. 1985)]

41-7. Midwest Management Corp. was looking for investment opportunities. Morris Stephens, one of Midwest's directors and chairman of the investment committee, proposed that Midwest provide financing for Stephens's son and his business colleagues, who were in need of financing to open a broker-dealer business. Midwest agreed to propose to the shareholders for their approval an investment of $250,000 in the new business on the condition that Stephens would manage the business and would purchase 100,000 shares of stock in the new firm. At each of two shareholder meetings, the directors informed the shareholders that Stephens agreed to the condition. Stephens was present at both meetings and did not deny that he had agreed to purchase the 100,000 shares of stock and manage the new corporation. Upon the shareholders' approval, the $250,000 investment was made, and later another $150,000 was invested when the new business suffered losses. About a year after it had opened, the business closed, and Midwest ended up losing over $325,000. Midwest then learned that Stephens had not kept his agreement to purchase stock in, or manage, the corporation. Midwest sued Stephens for breaching his fiduciary duties and asked for compensatory and punitive damages. Did Midwest succeed? Explain. [*Midwest Management Corp. v. Stephens,* 353 N.W.2d 76 (Iowa 1984)]

41-8. Frederick Valerino and his family owned 50 percent of the stock in Electrical-Mechanical of America, Inc., (EMA) and the remaining 50 percent was owned by Charles Little. Both Valerino and Little participated actively in operating the corporation until 1979, when a dispute arose, resulting in a stalemate. For two years no shareholders' meeting was held, and no board of directors could be elected. Little held a shareholders' meeting in 1981 and sent a telegram to Valerino stating that the purpose of the meeting was "[f]or the sale and purchase of the Capital Stock of EMA." Valerino did not attend and sent a reply letter indicating that he did not wish to sell any of his stock. Actually, Little held the meeting with the intention of issuing more stock to himself and his family, thus reducing Valerino's ownership to 25 percent. Valerino sued to enforce his preemptive rights in the corporation and to set aside the new stock issuance because of fraud. Discuss whether Valerino should succeed in his claim. [*Valerino v. Little,* 62 Md.App. 588, 490 A.2d 756 (1985)]

41-9. Abe Schultz, Sol Schultz, and Lawrence Newfeld were the managing directors and officers of Chemical Dynamics, Inc., a close corporation. In 1967, the corporation leased a building in which to house its offices and operations. Included in the lease agreement was a provision giving Chemical Dynamics an option to purchase the property for $300,000. In 1970, because the corporation was experiencing financial problems and could not pay its rent, it assigned the lease and the purchase option to Newfeld in return for Newfeld's loan to the corporation of approximately $21,500. In 1973, Newfeld purchased the property. Eventually, when the corporation's financial situation had improved and its debts were paid, Abe Schultz sued Newfeld on behalf of the corporation, claiming that Newfeld had breached his fiduciary duty by usurping a corporate opportunity to purchase the property. Evaluate Schultz's claim. [*Chemical Dynamics, Inc. v. Newfeld,* 728 S.W.2d 590 (Mo.App. 1987)]

41-10. Arthur Modell was the president and an 80 percent shareholder of the Cleveland Stadium Corp. (CSC). Modell also served on the board of directors of the Cleveland Browns Football Co. and owned 53 percent of its stock. Aside from Modell, several other members of the board of directors of the Browns also served on the CSC board. At a March 16, 1982, meeting of the Browns' board of directors, the board voted to purchase all of the stock of CSC for $6,000,000. The one person who did not stand to benefit by the purchase of CSC by the Browns was Robert Gries, who, jointly with his business firm, Gries Sports Enterprises, Inc., owned 43 percent of the Browns and was also a director on the board. Gries felt the purchase price was far too high, based on other appraisals that valued CSC at no more than $2,000,000. Not only did the purchase for the price of $6,000,000 increase the debt load of the Browns to a point higher than necessary, but also the sale of CSC directly—and, according to Gries, unfairly—benefited Modell. Gries had objected to the purchase at the March meeting but was outvoted by the other Browns' directors. Gries then filed a shareholder's derivative action seeking the rescission of the CSC acquisition. Had Modell breached his fiduciary duty, as a director of the Browns, to the other Browns' shareholders, including Gries? Discuss fully. [*Gries Sports Enterprises, Inc. v. Cleveland Browns Football Co.,* 26 Ohio St.3d 15, 496 N.E.2d 959 (1986)]

41-11. The Federal Deposit Insurance Corp., in an action against the officers and directors of a bank (the defendants),

alleged that the defendants had breached their duty of care by failing to exercise reasonable supervision over officers of the bank. Apparently, the bank had suffered losses particularly due to the negligence of one of the defendants, Russell Greenwood, an officer of the bank. The other defendants asserted that they should not be liable for Greenwood's negligence. They argued that no facts were ever brought to their attention that would have led them to believe that Greenwood was not properly discharging his duties, and in the absence of such information, they were entitled to rely on the judgments of Greenwood and on the appearance that he was properly discharging his duties. The question before the court is whether the directors breached their duty of care because they failed to supervise the actions of one of the bank's officers, Greenwood. How should the court rule? Discuss fully. [*Federal Deposit Insurance Corp. v. Greenwood,* 739 F.Supp. 450 (C.D.Ill. 1989)]

41-12. Case Briefing Assignment

Examine Case A.21 [Maschmeier v. Southside Press, Ltd., *435 N.W.2d 377 (Iowa App. 1989)*] *in Appendix A. The case has been excerpted there in great detail. Review and then brief the case, making sure that you include answers to the following questions in your brief.*

1. What was the primary reason for this lawsuit?
2. What restriction did the corporate bylaws place on the transfer of corporate shares? Upon transfer, how was the price of shares to be determined?
3. How did the majority shareholders (the parents) effectively ''freeze out'' or ''squeeze out'' the minority shareholders (the sons)?
4. Why was it necessary for the court to determine the fair value of shares, given the fact that the shareholders had agreed in the bylaws on a method for accomplishing this?
5. Why was it necessary to establish that the majority shareholders had acted oppressively toward the minority shareholders or wasted corporate assets before the court could fashion its particular remedy in this case?

Chapter 42

CORPORATIONS
Merger, Consolidation, and Termination

Corporations increase their holdings for a number of reasons. They may wish to enlarge their physical plant; increase their property or investment holdings; or acquire the assets, know-how, or goodwill of another corporation. Sometimes acquisition is motivated by a desire to eliminate a competitor, to accomplish diversification, or to ensure adequate resources and markets for the acquiring corporation's product. Whatever the reason, the corporation typically extends its operations by combining with another corporation through a merger, a consolidation, a purchase of assets, or a purchase of a controlling interest in the other corporation. This chapter will examine these four types of corporate events. The last part of this chapter will discuss the typical reasons for, and methods used in, terminating a corporation.

■ Merger and Consolidation

The terms *merger* and *consolidation* are often used interchangeably, but they refer to two legally distinct proceedings. Whether a combination is in fact a merger or a consolidation, however, the rights and liabilities of shareholders, the corporation, and its creditors are the same.

Merger

A **merger** involves the legal combination of two or more corporations. After a merger, only one of the corporations continues to exist. For example, Corporation A and Corporation B decide to merge. It is agreed that A will absorb B; so upon merger, B ceases to exist as a separate entity, and A continues as the **surviving corporation.** This process is illustrated in Exhibit 42–1.

After the merger, A is recognized as a single corporation possessing all the rights, privileges, and powers of itself and B. A automatically acquires all of B's property and assets without the necessity of formal transfer. A becomes liable for all B's debts and obligations. Finally, A's articles of incorporation are deemed *amended* to include any changes that are stated in the *articles of merger*.

In a merger, the surviving corporation is vested with the disappearing corporation's preexisting legal rights and obligations. For example, if the disappearing corporation had a right of action against a third party, the

■ Exhibit 42–1 Merger

In this illustration, Corporations A and B decide to merge. They agree that A will absorb B, so on merging, B ceases to exist as a separate entity, and A continues as the surviving corporation.

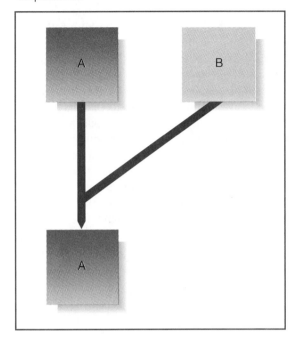

■ Exhibit 42–2 Consolidation

In this illustration, Corporations A and B consolidate to form an entirely new organization, Corporation C. In the process, A and B terminate, and C comes into existence as an entirely new entity.

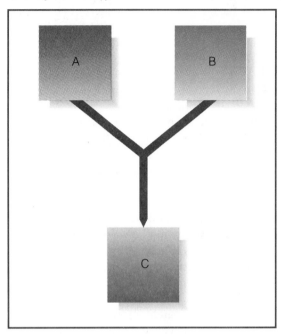

surviving corporation could bring suit after the merger to recover the disappearing corporation's damages.

Consolidation

In the case of a **consolidation,** two or more corporations combine so that each corporation ceases to exist and a new one emerges. Corporation A and Corporation B consolidate to form an entirely new organization, Corporation C. In the process, A and B both terminate. C comes into existence as an entirely new entity. This process is illustrated in Exhibit 42–2.

The results of consolidation are essentially the same as the results of merger. C is recognized as a new corporation and a single entity; A and B cease to exist. C accedes to all the rights, privileges, and powers previously held by A and B. Title to any property and assets owned by A and B passes to C without formal transfer. C assumes liability for all debts and obligations owed by A and B. The articles of consolidation *take the place of* A's and

B's original corporate articles and are thereafter regarded as C's corporate articles.

When a merger or consolidation takes place, the surviving corporation or newly formed corporation will issue shares or pay some fair consideration to the shareholders of the corporation that ceases to exist.

The Merger and Consolidation Procedure

All states have statutes authorizing mergers and consolidations for *domestic* corporations, and most states allow the combination of domestic (in-state) and foreign (out-of-state) corporations. Although the procedures vary somewhat among jurisdictions, in each case the basic requirements are as outlined below:

1. The board of directors of *each* corporation involved must approve a merger or consolidation plan.
2. The shareholders of *each* corporation must

vote approval of the plan at a shareholders' meeting. Most state statutes require the approval of two-thirds of the outstanding shares of voting stock, although some states require only a simple majority, and others require a four-fifths vote. Frequently, statutes require that each class of stock approve the merger; thus, the holders of nonvoting stock must also approve. A corporation's bylaws can dictate a stricter requirement.

3. Once approved by *all* the directors and the shareholders, the plan (articles of merger or consolidation) is filed, usually with the secretary of state.

4. When state formalities are satisfied, the state issues a certificate of merger to the surviving corporation or a certificate of consolidation to the newly consolidated corporation.

The RMBCA provides a simplified procedure for the merger of a substantially owned subsidiary corporation into its parent corporation. Under these provisions, a **short-form merger**—also referred to as a *parent-subsidiary merger*—can be accomplished *without approval of the shareholders* of either corporation. The short-form merger can be used only when the parent corporation owns at least 90 percent of the outstanding shares of each class of stock of the subsidiary corporation. The simplified procedure requires that a plan for the merger be approved by the board of directors of the parent corporation before it is filed with the state. A copy of the merger plan must be sent to each shareholder of record of the subsidiary corporation.

Appraisal Rights

The law recognizes that a dissenting shareholder should not be forced to become an unwilling shareholder in a corporation that is new or different from the one in which the shareholder originally invested. The shareholder has the right to dissent and may be entitled to be paid *fair value* for the number of shares held on the date of the merger or consolidation. This right, which is referred to as the shareholder's **appraisal right,** is given by state statute and is available only when the statute specifically provides for it. It is normally extended to regular mergers, consolidations, short-form mergers, sales of substantially all the corporate assets not in the ordinary course of business, and in certain states, adverse amendments to the articles of incorporation.

The appraisal right may be lost if the elaborate statutory procedures are not precisely followed. Whenever the right is lost, the dissenting shareholder must go along with the objectionable transaction.

One of the basic procedures usually followed requires that a written notice of dissent be filed by the dissenting shareholder or shareholders prior to the vote of the shareholders on the proposed transaction. This notice of dissent is also basically a notice to all shareholders of costs that may be imposed by dissenting shareholders should the merger or consolidation be approved. In addition, after the merger or consolidation has been approved, the dissenting shareholders must make a written demand for payment and for fair value.

Valuation of shares is often a point of contention between the dissenting shareholder and the corporation. RMBCA 13.01 provides that the "fair value of shares" is the value on the day prior to the date on which the vote was taken.[1] The corporation must make a *written* offer to purchase a dissenting shareholder's stock, accompanying the offer with a current balance sheet and income statement for the corporation. If the shareholder and the corporation do not agree on the fair value, a court will determine it.

Once a dissenting shareholder elects appraisal rights under statute, in some jurisdictions, the shareholder loses his or her shareholder status. Without that status, a shareholder cannot vote, receive dividends, or sue to enjoin whatever action prompted his or her dissent. In some of those jurisdictions, statutes provide, or courts have held, that shareholder status may be reinstated during the appraisal process (for example, if the shareholder decides to withdraw from the process and the corporation approves). In other jurisdictions, the status may not be reinstated until the appraisal has concluded. Even if the status is lost, courts may allow an individual to sue on grounds of fraud or other illegal conduct associated with the merger.

The following case illustrates the frequently encountered problem of determining the fair value of shares under appraisal rights.

---

1. Any appreciation or depreciation of the stock in anticipation of the approval is excluded.

BACKGROUND AND FACTS In 1976, Getty Oil Company began negotiating a merger with Skelly Oil Company. Both companies acknowledged
the desirability of a merger and agreed that an exchange of common stock
would be the best method for achieving it. An engineering firm, D & M, and
several investment banking and accounting firms were hired to assist in
estimating asset values. Eventually, Skelly agreed to an exchange ratio of
0.5875 shares of Getty stock for 1 share of Skelly stock. The boards of
directors of both companies agreed to the merger and submitted the question to their respective shareholders. Once the necessary shareholder approvals were obtained, the companies were merged in 1977. Emmanuel
Rosenblatt, a minority shareholder in Skelly, brought a class-action suit in
a Delaware state court on behalf of himself and other Skelly shareholders
who disapproved of the merger. They challenged the fairness of the price
and asset valuations and sought a review by the court. Part of their claim
was based on the valuation of Skelly assets according to the Delaware
Block method, which resulted in a price substantially below the liquidation
price that the minority shareholders' appraisers had determined. The minority shareholders claimed that, given the lower price offered by Getty,
liquidation would be the only fair course for Skelly. The court of chancery
(court of equity), however, held that the exchange ratio was fair to all shareholders. The minority shareholders appealed.

Case 42.1

**ROSENBLATT v.
GETTY OIL CO.**

Supreme Court of Delaware,
1985.
493 A.2d 929.

DECISION AND RATIONALE The Delaware Supreme Court affirmed the
decision of the lower court, ruling that the exchange ratio was fair to the
shareholders of both corporations. The court recognized that the Delaware
Block valuation technique used by Skelly to estimate asset value, market
value, and earnings potential had yielded a price that was arguably below
what could be obtained by liquidating the company's assets. The court
pointed out, however, that although the Delaware Block method was no
longer the exclusive method of valuation, it was "the only valuation technique permitted at that time." The court noted that "[i]n Delaware a company is valued as a going concern, not on what can be obtained by its
liquidation." Moreover, the court determined that both companies had employed leading investment bankers and engineering firms to help calculate
the value of their assets, especially their respective oil reserves. Consequently, the court ruled that Getty had dealt fairly with Skelly's minority
shareholders through the course of the merger and that the share price
was fair.

Shareholder Approval

Shareholders invest in a corporate enterprise with
the expectation that the board of directors will manage the enterprise and will approve ordinary business matters. Actions taken on extraordinary matters must be authorized by the board of directors
and the shareholders. Often, modern statutes require that certain types of extraordinary matters be
approved by a vote of the shareholders. Typically,
matters requiring shareholder approval include the
sale, lease, or exchange of all or substantially all
corporate assets outside of the corporation's regular course of business. Other examples include
amendments to the articles of incorporation, transactions concerning merger or consolidation, and
dissolution.

The following case involves a sale of corporate
assets that was negotiated without the shareholders' approval. The shareholders opposing the sale
sought injunctive relief from the court.

Case 42.2

**SCHWADEL v.
UCHITEL**

District Court of Appeal of
Florida, Third District, 1984.
455 So.2d 401.

BACKGROUND AND FACTS Mike and Peter Schwadel were major shareholders in HJU Sales & Investments, Inc. Over several years, the assets of the corporation had been sold off until only one asset remained—a restaurant called "The Place for Steak." The Schwadels sued the president and third major shareholder of the corporation, Hy Uchitel, in a Florida state court, when Uchitel entered into a contract to sell this remaining asset. Florida state law prohibits the sale of all or substantially all of a corporation's assets without shareholder approval. The Schwadels sought an injunction to prevent the sale of the restaurant, but the lower court denied the request. The Schwadels appealed.

DECISION AND RATIONALE The District Court of Appeal of Florida reversed the decision of the lower court, ruling that the sale of the restaurant constituted a sale of substantially all of the corporation's assets and therefore required shareholder approval under Florida law. The court stated that "the purpose of a shareholder 'consent' provision is 'to protect the shareholders from fundamental change, or more specifically * * * from the destruction of the means to accomplish the purposes or objections for which the corporation was incorporated and actually performs.' " The court found that the shareholder-consent provision was applicable in this case because the sale of the restaurant destroyed the purpose for which the corporation was originally created—operating restaurants. The court held that Uchitel's decision to enter into a contract for the sale of the last remaining corporate asset "deprived shareholders of their statutory rights to notice and to vote" on a transaction that would fundamentally change the nature of the corporation. Because the court concluded that "[a]n award of damages would not compensate the shareholders for the destruction of the corporation," it issued an injunction preventing the sale of the restaurant.

■ Purchase of Assets

When a corporation acquires all or substantially all of the assets of another corporation by direct purchase, the purchasing corporation, or *acquiring corporation,* simply extends its ownership and control over more physical assets. Because no change in the legal entity occurs, the acquiring corporation is not required to obtain shareholder approval for the purchase.[2]

Although the acquiring corporation may not be required to obtain shareholder approval for such an acquisition, the U.S. Department of Justice has issued guidelines that significantly constrain and often prohibit mergers that could result from a purchase of assets, including takeover bids. These guidelines are part of the federal antitrust laws to enforce Section 7 of the Clayton Act (discussed in Chapter 47).

Note that the corporation that is *selling* all its assets is substantially changing its business position and perhaps its ability to carry out its corporate purposes. For that reason, the corporation whose assets are *acquired* must obtain both board of director and shareholder approval. In most states and under the RMBCA, a dissenting shareholder of the selling corporation can demand appraisal rights.

Generally, a corporation that purchases the assets of another corporation is not responsible for the liabilities of the selling corporation. Excep-

---

2. If the acquiring corporation plans to pay for the assets with its own corporate stock and not enough authorized unissued shares are available, the shareholders must vote to approve issuance of additional shares by amendment of the corporate articles. Also, acquiring corporations whose stock is traded in a national stock exchange can be required to obtain their own shareholders' approval if they plan to issue a significant number of shares, such as a number equal to 20 percent or more of the outstanding shares.

tions to this rule are made in the following circumstances:

1. When the purchasing corporation impliedly or expressly assumes the seller's liabilities.
2. When the sale amounts to what in fact is a merger or a consolidation.
3. When the purchaser continues the seller's business and retains the same personnel (same shareholders, directors, and officers).

4. When the sale is fraudulently executed to escape liability.

In any of these situations, the acquiring corporation will be held to have assumed both the assets and the liabilities of the selling corporation. The following case addresses the issue of whether a corporation that purchased the assets of another firm could be subject to liability for an injury caused by a product manufactured by the selling firm.

Case 42.3

MILLER v. NISSEN CORP.

Court of Special Appeals of Maryland, 1990.
83 Md.App. 448,
575 A.2d 758.

BACKGROUND AND FACTS In January 1981, Frederick Brandt, a surgeon, purchased a Tredex treadmill from Atlantic Fitness Products. The treadmill was manufactured by American Tredex Corporation. In July 1981, Nissen Corporation purchased all the assets of American Tredex, as well as its goodwill and the name, American Tredex. Subsequently, Brandt obtained replacement parts for the treadmill from Nissen. In the fall of 1986, Brandt was injured when he caught one of his fingers in the treadmill's operating mechanism while adjusting the treadmill. Brandt and his wife sued Nissen and Atlantic in a Maryland state court to recover damages, alleging, among other things, negligence and breach of warranty. Nissen moved for summary judgment, contending that it was not responsible for any injuries involving equipment sold or manufactured by American Tredex before the date of the asset purchase agreement (July 1981). Atlantic filed a cross-claim against Nissen for indemnity and contribution, as well as a memorandum in opposition to Nissen's motion for summary judgment. Atlantic claimed that Nissen was liable as a successor in interest to American Tredex, because Nissen essentially continued American Tredex's business. The trial court granted Nissen's motion for summary judgment, and Atlantic (through Warren Miller) and Brandt appealed.

DECISION AND RATIONALE The Court of Special Appeals of Maryland reversed the trial court's ruling and remanded the case for further proceedings. In particular, the court noted that there were a number of clauses in the asset purchase agreement from which inferences could be drawn that Nissen would continue the business of American Tredex. The court referred to terms that included what was purchased under the agreement (the "business good-will, total inventory, patents and trademarks, customer lists, contract rights, prepaid receivables, warranties, and the continued employment of two previous high level employees of the predecessor corporation"). In addition, the selling corporation agreed to " 'indemnify, reimburse, and hold [Nissen] harmless' from liability" for five years. Thus the court held that summary judgment for Nissen was inappropriate because, based on the evidence presented, a jury could conclude that Nissen continued the business of its predecessor.

▪ Purchase of Stock

An alternative to the purchase of another corporation's assets is the purchase of a substantial number of the voting shares of its stock. This enables the acquiring corporation to control the acquired corporation, or **target corporation.** The acquiring corporation deals directly with the shareholders in seeking to purchase the shares they hold.

Tender Offers

When the acquiring corporation makes a public offer to all shareholders of the target corporation, it is called a *tender offer* (an offer that is publicly advertised and addressed to all shareholders of the target company). The price of the stock in the tender offer is generally higher than the market price of the target stock prior to the announcement of the tender offer. The higher price induces shareholders to tender (offer to sell) their shares to the acquiring firm. The tender offer can be conditional upon the receipt of a specified number of outstanding shares by a specified date. The offering corporation can make an *exchange* tender offer in which it offers target stockholders its own securities in exchange for their target stock. In a cash tender offer, the offering corporation offers the target stockholders cash in exchange for their target stock.

Federal securities laws strictly control the terms, duration, and circumstances under which most tender offers are made. In addition, a majority of states have passed takeover statutes that impose additional regulations on tender offers when in-state companies are involved.

Leveraged Buy-outs (LBOs)

In the last decade, a number of corporations have arranged to "go private" through so-called **leveraged buy-outs (LBOs).** In an LBO, the management of a corporation—or any other group, but management is usually included—purchases all outstanding corporate stock held by the public and in this way gains control over the corporate enterprise. The LBO is financed by borrowing money against the assets of the corporation, which may include real estate or plant and equipment. The borrowing may take the form of the issuance of bonds, a straight bank loan, or a loan from an investment bank. Because an LBO often results in a high debt load for the corporation, the interest payments on the debt may become so burdensome that the corporation cannot survive. Some corporations have failed to survive following LBOs for this reason.

Target Responses

As discussed in Chapter 41, the directors of a corporation owe a fiduciary duty to the shareholders. In the context of a tender offer, this requires that, after full consideration, the directors of the target firm make a good faith decision as to whether the shareholders' acceptance or rejection of the offer would be most beneficial. In making any recommendation, the directors must fully disclose all *material facts.* A fact is material if there is a substantial likelihood that a reasonable shareholder would consider it important in deciding how to vote. For example, information indicating a good price for the stock would be considered material.

Sometimes, a target firm's board of directors will see a tender offer as favorable and recommend to the shareholders that they accept it. Alternatively, to resist a takeover, a target company may make a *self-tender,* which is an offer to acquire stock from its own shareholders and thereby retain corporate control. Alternatively, a target corporation might resort to one of several other tactics, many of which are denoted by colorful names, to resist a takeover (see Exhibit 42–3).

A target may also seek an injunction against an acquiring corporation on grounds that the attempted takeover violates antitrust laws (the subject of Chapter 47), which are intended to prevent the illegal restraint of competition. This defense may succeed if the takeover would, in the eyes of a court, result in a substantial increase in the acquiring corporation's market power.

■ Termination

Termination of a corporate life, like termination of a partnership, has two phases—dissolution and liquidation. **Dissolution** is the legal death of the artificial "person" of the corporation. **Liquidation** is the process by which corporate assets are converted into cash and distributed among creditors and shareholders according to specific rules of preference.[3]

---

3. Upon dissolution, the liquidated assets are first used to pay creditors. Any remaining assets are distributed to shareholders according to their respective stock rights; preferred stock has priority over common stock, generally by charter.

■ Exhibit 42–3 The Terminology of Takeover Defenses

Crown Jewel Defense	When threatened with a takeover, management makes the company less attractive to the raider by selling to a third party the company's most valuable asset (hence the term *crown jewel*).
Golden Parachute	When a takeover is successful, top management is usually changed. With this in mind, a company may establish special termination or retirement benefits that must be paid to top management if they are "retired." In other words, a departing high-level manager's parachute will be "golden" when he or she is forced to "bail out" of the company.
Greenmail	To regain control, a target company may pay a higher-than-market price to repurchase the stock that the acquiring corporation bought. When a takeover is attempted through a gradual accumulation of target stock rather than a tender offer, the intent may be to get the target company to buy back the accumulated shares at a premium price—a concept similar to blackmail.
Lobster Trap	Lobster traps are designed to catch large lobsters but allow small lobsters to escape. In the "lobster trap" defense, holders of convertible securities (corporate bonds or stock that is convertible into common shares) are prohibited from converting the securities into common shares if the holders already own, or would own after conversion, 10 percent or more of the voting shares of stock.
Pac-man Defense	Named after the Atari video game, this is an aggressive defense by which the target corporation attempts its own takeover of the acquiring corporation.
Poison Pill	The target corporation issues to its stockholders shares that can be turned in for cash if a takeover is successful. This makes the takeover undesirably or even prohibitively expensive for the acquiring corporation.
Scorched Earth Tactic	The target corporation sells off assets or divisions or takes out loans that it agrees to repay in the event of a takeover, thus making itself less financially attractive to the acquiring corporation.
Shark Repellant	To make a takeover more difficult, a target company may change its articles of incorporation or bylaws. For example, the bylaws may be amended to require that a large number of shareholders approve the firm's combination. This tactic casts the acquiring corporation in the role of a shark that must be repelled.
White Knight	The target corporation solicits a merger with a third party, which then makes a better (often simply a higher) tender offer to the target's shareholders. The third party that "rescues" the target is the "white knight."

Dissolution

Dissolution can be brought about in any of the following ways:

1. An act of a legislature in the state of incorporation.
2. The expiration of the time provided in the certificate of incorporation.
3. The voluntary approval of the shareholders and the board of directors.
4. Unanimous action by all shareholders.

5. Court decree brought about by the attorney general of the state of incorporation for any of the following reasons: (a) failure to comply with administrative requirements (for example, failure to pay annual franchise taxes, submit an annual report, or have a designated registered agent), (b) the procurement of a corporate charter through fraud or misrepresentation upon the state, (c) the abuse of corporate powers (*ultra vires* acts), (d) the violation of the state criminal code after the demand to discontinue has been made by the secretary of

state, (e) the failure to commence business operations, or (f) the abandonment of operations before starting up [RMBCA 14.20].

The Statutory Close Corporation Supplement to the MBCA provides that the articles of incorporation of a close corporation may empower any shareholder to dissolve the corporation at will or on the occurrence of a specified event—such as the death of another shareholder. This provides a shareholder in a close corporation with the same power to dissolve his or her business organization as a partner in a partnership.

Sometimes an involuntary dissolution of a corporation is necessary—for example, when a board of directors is deadlocked. Courts hesitate to order involuntary dissolution in such circumstances unless there is specific statutory authorization to do so, but if the deadlock cannot be resolved by the shareholders and if it will irreparably injure the corporation, the court will proceed with an involuntary dissolution. Courts can also dissolve a corporation for mismanagement [RMBCA 14.30].

In the following case, a minority shareholder—one of the two shareholders in a close corporation—sued to have the corporation dissolved because he had been "frozen out" of the business by the allegedly oppressive tactics of the majority shareholder. Note the court's reluctance to grant the extreme remedy of dissolution, even though it deemed that a freeze-out had occurred.

Case 42.4

BALVIK v. SYLVESTER

Supreme Court of
North Dakota, 1987.
411 N.W.2d 383.

BACKGROUND AND FACTS   In 1984, Elmer Balvik and Thomas Sylvester decided to turn their partnership into a corporation because of the tax benefits that would result. The new Weldon Corporation carried on the partnership's old business of electrical contracting. Sylvester received 70 percent of the stock of the new corporation and Balvik received the remaining 30 percent, in proportion to the capital that each had contributed. Both took positions as directors and officers of the corporation, and each was entitled to one vote per share of stock. Balvik was at all times a minority voice in the company. Although Sylvester and Balvik had had no problems during their years as partners, difficulties emerged soon after incorporation. Sylvester believed that excess profits should be reinvested in the corporation, while Balvik wanted them withdrawn and paid out as bonuses or dividends. Balvik was fired from his job, allegedly because of poor performance, and he began working for another company. He was unable to take any of his capital contribution in the corporation with him and no longer received a salary from the corporation. Balvik sued in a North Dakota state court to have the corporation dissolved under North Dakota law, which allows dissolution for illegal, oppressive, or fraudulent acts toward minority shareholders by corporate directors or those in control of the corporation. The court found Balvik had been "frozen out" of the corporation, ordered dissolution, and appointed a receiver. Sylvester appealed.

DECISION AND RATIONALE   The Supreme Court of North Dakota agreed that Balvik had been frozen out, but refused to dissolve the corporation, remanding the case to the trial court for entry of an order granting a different remedy. Noting the limited market for stock in a close corporation, the state supreme court acknowledged that potential investors might be reluctant to purchase a noncontrolling interest in a close corporation marked by dissension. The court recognized that this "can result in a minority shareholder's interest being held 'hostage' by the controlling interest, and can lead to situations where the majority 'freeze out' minority shareholders by the use of oppressive tactics." The court defined freeze-outs as "actions taken by the controlling shareholders to deprive a minority shareholder of [his or] her interest in the business or a fair return on [his or] her investment." The court identified withholding dividends as the most common technique, often combined with the minority shareholder's discharge from employment and removal from the board of directors. But the court explained that "forced dissolution of a corporation is a drastic remedy which should be invoked with extreme caution and only when justice requires it." The court concluded that Weldon appeared to be an ongoing business and that ordering its dissolution and liquidation would be unduly harsh.

ETHICAL CONSIDERATIONS Attempts by majority shareholders to "freeze out" minority shareholders are not looked on kindly by the courts, which on occasion will, as a remedy, order dissolution and liquidation of the corporation. When faced with such situations, courts must balance the ethical policy of protecting minority shareholders from the allegedly unfair or oppressive tactics wielded by majority shareholders against the policy of promoting commercial enterprise. For that reason, if an acceptable alternative exists, courts hesitate to dissolve an ongoing business such as Weldon Corporation.

Liquidation

When dissolution takes place by voluntary action, the members of the board of directors act as trustees of the corporate assets. As trustees, they are responsible for winding up the affairs of the corporation for the benefit of corporate creditors and shareholders. This makes the board members personally liable for any breach of their fiduciary trustee duties.

Liquidation can be accomplished without court supervision unless the members of the board do not wish to act in this capacity or unless shareholders or creditors can show cause to the court why the board should not be permitted to assume the trustee function. In either case, the court will appoint a **receiver** to wind up the corporate affairs and liquidate corporate assets. A receiver is always appointed by the court if the dissolution is involuntary.

■ Terms and Concepts

appraisal right 746	liquidation 750	short-form merger 746
consolidation 745	merger 744	surviving corporation 744
dissolution 750	receiver 753	target corporation 749
leveraged buy-outs (LBOs) 750		

■ For Review

1.   What are the four steps of the merger or consolidation procedure?

2.   Under what circumstances is a corporation that buys the assets of another corporation responsible for the liabilities of the selling corporation?

3.   Directors of a corporation owe a fiduciary duty to the corporation's shareholders. What does this require in the context of a tender offer?

4.   Petroelectric, Inc., plans a merger with Navitronics Corp. Ian is a minority Petroelectric shareholder, and Ann is a minority Navitronics shareholder. Although the majority of shareholders of both companies favor the merger, neither Ian nor Ann do. Does Petroelectric need Ian's approval of the merger? Does Navitronics need Ann's approval? Would Ian or Ann's approval be necessary if, instead of merging, the firms were consolidating? Would Ian or Ann's approval be necessary if Petroelectric were buying substantially all the assets of Navitronics? Are there other circumstances in which Petroelectric or Navitronics would need Ian or Ann's approval?

5.   In the previous problem, whether or not Petroelectric or Navitronics needs Ian or Ann's approval to proceed with an extraordinary matter, can Ian or Ann be forced to become unwilling shareholders in their changed corporations? Assuming that their states provide for appraisal rights, what procedure might they follow to be paid the fair value for their shares?

■ Questions and Case Problems

42-1. Gretz is chairman of the board of directors of Faraday, Inc., and Williams is chairman of the board of directors of Firebrand, Inc. Faraday is a manufacturing corporation, and Firebrand is a transportation corporation. Gretz and Williams meet to consider the possibility of combining their corporations and activities into a single corporate entity. They consider two alternative courses of action: acquisition by Faraday of all the stock and assets of Firebrand or combination of the two corporations to form a new corporation, Farabrand, Inc. Both chairmen are concerned about the necessity of formal transfer of property, liability for existing debts, and the problem of amending articles of incorporation. Discuss what the two proposed combinations are called and what legal effect each has on the transfer of property, the liabilities of the combined corporations, and the need to amend the articles of incorporation.

42-2. Ann owns 10,000 shares of Ajax Corp. Her shares represent a 10 percent ownership in Ajax. Zeta Corp. is interested in acquiring Ajax in a merger, and the board of directors of each corporation has approved the merger. The shareholders of Zeta have already approved the acquisition, and Ajax has called for a shareholders' meeting to approve the merger. Ann disapproves of the merger and does not want to accept Zeta shares for the Ajax shares she holds. The market price of Ajax shares is $20 per share the day before the shareholder vote and drops to $16 on the day the shareholders of Ajax approve the merger. Discuss Ann's rights in this matter, beginning with notice of the proposed merger.

42-3. Green Corp. wants to acquire all the assets of Red Dot Corp. Green plans to pay for the assets by issuing its own corporate stock. Green's board of directors has already approved the merger. Discuss whether shareholder approval is required for this merger.

42-4. Alitech Corp. is a small midwestern business that owns a valuable patent. Alitech has approximately 1,000 shareholders with 100,000 authorized and outstanding shares. Block Corp. would like to have use of the patent, but Alitech refuses to give Block a license. Block has tried to acquire Alitech by purchasing Alitech's assets, but Alitech's board of directors has refused to approve the acquisition. Alitech's shares are presently selling for $5 per share. Discuss how Block Corp. might proceed to gain the control and use of Alitech's patent.

42-5. Saunders Corp. has been losing money for several years but still has valuable fixed assets. The shareholders see little hope that the corporation will ever make a profit. Another corporation, Topway Corp., has failed to pay state taxes for several years or to file annual reports required by statute. In addition, Topway is accused of being guilty of gross and persistent *ultra vires* acts. Discuss whether these corporations will be terminated and how the assets of each would be handled upon dissolution.

42-6. I. Burack, Inc., was a family-operated close corporation that sold plumbing supplies in New York. The founder and president, Israel Burack, transferred his shares in the corporation to other family members; and when Israel died in 1974, the position of president passed to his son, Robert Burack. Robert held a one-third interest in the company, and the remainder was divided among Israel's other children and grandchildren. All shareholders participated in the corporation as employees or officers and thus relied on salaries and bonuses, rather than dividends, for distribution of the corporation's earnings. In 1976, several of the family-member employees requested a salary increase from Robert, who claimed that company earnings were not sufficient to warrant any employee salary increases. Shortly thereafter, a shareholders' meeting was held (the first in the company's fifty-year history), and Robert was removed from his position as president and denied the right to participate in any way in the corporation. Robert sued to have the company dissolved because he had been frozen out. Discuss whether Robert should succeed in his suit or whether the court would choose another alternative. [*Burack v. I. Burack, Inc.,* 137 A.D.2d 523, 524 N.Y.S.2d 457 (1988)]

42-7. On March 6, 1981, Carolyn Hamaker lost three fingers from her left hand while operating a notcher machine (lathe) at her place of employment in South Dakota, Pallets and Wood Products. The notching machine had been manufactured by Kenwel Machine Co. On December 31, 1975, Kenwel sold its assets to John and Rosemary Jackson, who created a new company called Kenwel-Jackson Machine Co. Kenwel Machine Co. terminated its existence in August 1977. Kenwel-Jackson Machine Co. continued to manufacture notchers, but it made several design changes and was in fact producing a different machine from the one that injured Carolyn Hamaker. As a result of her injuries, Hamaker brought a suit for damages against Kenwel-Jackson, because Kenwel Machine Co. no longer existed. Discuss whether Kenwel-Jackson is liable for injuries caused by a machine manufactured by a company it purchased. [*Hamaker v. Kenwel-Jackson Machine Co.,* 387 N.W.2d 515 (S.D. 1986)]

42-8. In 1946, Fred Gunzberg helped his father form Art-Lloyd Metal Products Corp., and together they built it into a successful company. In 1955, Fred's brother Lloyd joined the business, and the two brothers were responsible for the day-to-day running of the firm—although the father had the final say in business matters until a stroke incapacitated him. In 1961 another brother, Arthur, joined the firm. This lawsuit arose as a result of a falling out among the brothers in 1979, when Arthur was elected president of the corporation, and another brother and sister were elected as officers on the board of directors. After the election, Fred and Lloyd were fired as employees of the corporation, after which they sought judicial dissolution of the corporation based upon the majority faction's oppression. Discuss fully whether dissolution of the corporation should be permitted. [*Gunzberg v. Art-Lloyd Metal Products Corp.,* 112 A.D.2d 423, 492 N.Y.S.2d 83 (1985)]

42-9. Edward Antar and William Markowitz were the sole stockholders and directors of E.B.M., Inc., a corporation formed for the purpose of buying and managing real estate. Antar and Markowitz were also the controlling shareholders and directors of Acousti-Phase, Inc., a corporation that manufactured and sold stereo speakers. In 1982, Acousti-Phase was effectively shut down when a fire destroyed the manufacturing and storage facility that it was renting from E.B.M. Shortly after the fire, E.B.M. contracted with a New York firm to assemble the speakers, affix the Acousti-Phase name, and sell the final product, primarily to former customers of Acousti-Phase. At the time of the fire, Acousti-Phase owed Cab-Tek, Inc.,—a corporation that supplied it with cabinet housings for its stereo speakers—$26,470. In 1985, Cab-Tek sued E.B.M. to recover the debt owed by Acousti-Phase. Discuss fully whether E.B.M. can be held liable for Acousti-Phase's debt. [*Cab-Tek, Inc. v. E.B.M., Inc.,* 153 Vt. 432, 571 A.2d 671 (1990)]

42-10. Case Briefing Assignment

Examine Case A.22 [Greenlee v. Sherman, *142 A.D.2d 472, 536 N.Y.S.2d 877 (1989)] in Appendix A. The case has been excerpted there in great detail. Review and then brief the case, making sure that you include answers to the following questions in your brief.*

1. What is the issue raised on appeal in this case?
2. The appellate court held that the successor liability theory did not apply in this case for two basic reasons. What were they?

Chapter 43

CORPORATIONS
Financing and
Investor Protection

After the great stock market crash of 1929, various studies showed a need for regulating securities markets. Basically, legislation for such regulation was enacted to provide investors with more information to help them make buying and selling decisions and to prohibit deceptive, unfair, and manipulative practices. Today, the sale and transfer of securities are heavily regulated by federal and state statutes and by government agencies. This is a complex area of the law. This chapter will first look at corporate financing and the sale of corporate securities, and then at the nature of federal securities regulations and their effect on the business world.

■ Corporate Financing

To obtain financing, corporations issue **securities**—evidence of the obligation to pay money or of the right to participate in earnings and the distribution of corporate trusts and other property. The principal method of long-term and initial corporate financing is the issuance of stocks (equity) and bonds (debt), both of which are sold to investors. **Stocks,** or *equity securities,* represent the purchase of ownership in the business firm. **Bonds** (debentures), or *debt securities,* represent the borrowing of money by firms (and governments). Of course, not all debt is in the form of debt securities. Some is in the form of accounts payable, some is in the form of commercial paper, and some is in the form of lease-back. Bonds are simply a way for the corporation to split up its long-term debt so that it can market it more easily.

Bonds

Bonds are issued by business firms and by governments at all levels as evidence of the funds they are borrowing from investors. Bonds almost always have a designated *maturity date*—the date when the principal or face amount of the bond (or loan) is returned to the investor—and are sometimes referred to as *fixed-income securities,* because their owners receive a fixed-dollar interest payment during the period of time prior to maturity.

The characteristics of corporate bonds vary widely, in part because corporations differ in their ability to generate the earnings and cash flow necessary to make interest payments and to repay the principal amount of the bonds at maturity. Furthermore, corporate bonds are only a part of the total debt and the overall financial structure of corporate business.

Stocks

Issuing *stocks* is another way corporations obtain financing. The ways in which stocks differ from bonds are summarized in Exhibit 43–1. Basically, stocks represent ownership in a business firm, whereas bonds represent borrowing by the firm. Exhibit 43–2 summarizes the types of stocks issued by corporations. The two major types are *common stock* and *preferred stock*.

COMMON STOCK   The true ownership of a corporation is represented by **common stock.** It provides a proportionate interest in the corporation with regard to (1) control, (2) earning capacity, and (3) net assets. A shareholder's interest is generally in proportion to the number of shares owned out of the total number of shares issued.

Voting rights in a corporation apply to the election of the firm's board of directors and to any proposed changes in the ownership structure of the firm.[1] For example, a holder of common stock generally has the right to vote in a decision on a proposed merger, because mergers can change the proportion of ownership.

Firms are not obligated to return a principal amount per share to each holder of common stock, because no firm can ensure that the market price per share of its common stock will not go down over time. Nor does the issuing firm have to guarantee a dividend; indeed, some business firms never pay dividends.

Holders of common stock are a group of investors who assume a *residual* position in the overall financial structure of a business. In terms of receiving payment for their investment, they are last in line. The earnings to which they are entitled also depend on all the other groups—suppliers, employees, managers, bankers, governments, bondholders, and holders of preferred stock—being paid what is due them first. Once those groups are paid, however, the owners of common stock may be entitled to *all* the remaining earnings. (But the board of directors is not normally under any duty to declare the remaining earnings as dividends.) This return-and-risk pattern is the central feature of ownership in any corporation. The owners of common stock occupy the riskiest position, but they can expect a correspondingly greater return on their investment.

PREFERRED STOCK   Stock with *preferences* is called **preferred stock.** Usually, holders of preferred stock have priority over holders of common stock as to dividends and payment upon dissolution of the corporation. Preferred-stock shareholders may or may not have the right to vote.

From an investment standpoint, preferred stock is more similar to bonds than to common stock. Preferred shareholders receive periodic dividend payments, usually established as a fixed percentage of the face amount of each preferred share. A 9 percent preferred stock with a face amount of $100

---

1.   State corporation law specifies the types of actions for which shareholder approval must be obtained.

■ **Exhibit 43–1 How Do Stocks and Bonds Differ?**

Stocks	Bonds
1. Stocks represent ownership.	1. Bonds represent owed debt.
2. Stocks (common) do not have a fixed dividend rate.	2. Interest on bonds must always be paid, whether or not any profit is earned.
3. Stockholders can elect a board of directors, which controls the corporation.	3. Bondholders usually have no voice in, or control over, management of the corporation.
4. Stocks do not have a maturity date; the corporation does not usually repay the stockholder.	4. Bonds have a maturity date on which the bondholder is to be repaid the face value of the bond.
5. Most corporations issue, or offer to sell, stocks. This is the usual definition of a business corporation.	5. Corporations do not necessarily issue bonds.
6. Stockholders have a claim against the property and income of a corporation after all creditors' claims have been met.	6. Bondholders have a claim against the property and income of a corporation that must be met before the claims of stockholders.

■ Exhibit 43–2 Stocks

Type	Definition
Common Stock	Voting shares that represent ownership interests in a corporation with lowest priorities with respect to payment of dividends and distribution of assets upon the corporation's dissolution.
Preferred Stock	Shares of stock that have priority over common stock shares as to payment of dividends and distribution of assets upon corporate dissolution. Dividend payments are usually a fixed percentage of the face value of the share.
Cumulative Preferred Stock	Shares whose required dividends not paid in a given year must be paid in a subsequent year before any common stock dividends are paid.
Participating Preferred Stock	Shares whose owners are entitled to receive the preferred stock dividend and additional dividends after payment of dividends on common stock.
Convertible Preferred Stock	Preferred shares whose owners have the option to convert their shares into a specified number of common shares either in the issuing corporation or, sometimes, in another corporation.
Redeemable, or Callable, Preferred Stock	Preferred shares issued with the express condition that the issuing corporation has the right to repurchase the shares as specified.
Authorized Shares	Shares allowed to be issed by the articles of incorporation.
Issued Shares	Shares that are actually transferred to shareholders.
Outstanding Shares	Authorized and issued shares still held by shareholders.
Treasury Shares	Shares that are authorized and issued, but are not outstanding (reacquired by the corporation).
No Par Shares	Shares issued with no stated face value. The price is usually fixed by the board of directors or shareholders.
Par-Value Shares	Shares issued and priced at a stated value per share.
Watered Shares	Shares issued (as fully paid) for transfer of property or services rendered, when in fact the value of such property or services is less than the par value or price for no par value shares.

per share would pay its owner a $9 dividend each year. This is not a legal obligation on the part of the firm. Preferred stock is not included among the liabilities of a business, because it is equity. Preferred stock appears in the ownership section of the firm's balance sheet (financial statement). Like other equity securities, preferred shares have no fixed maturity date for when they must be retired by the firm. Although occasionally firms retire preferred stock, they are not legally obligated to do so. A sample cumulative convertible preferred-stock certificate is shown in Exhibit 43–3.

Holders of preferred stock are investors who have assumed a rather cautious position in their relationship to the corporation. They have a stronger position than common shareholders with respect to dividends and claims on assets, but, as a result, they will not share in the full prosperity of the firm if it grows successfully over time.

■ Investor Protection—The SEC

The stock market crash of October 29, 1929, and the ensuing economic depression caused the public to focus on the importance of securities markets for the economic well-being of the nation. The feverish trading in securities during the preceding decade became the subject of widespread attention, and numerous reports were circulated concerning the speculative, manipulative, and at times unscrupulous trading that occurred in the stock markets.

The public, outraged by such practices, pressured Congress into action. As a result, in 1931 the Senate passed a resolution calling for an extensive investigation of securities trading. The investigation led, ultimately, to the passage by Congress of the Securities Act of 1933, which is also known as the *truth-in-securities* bill. In the following year,

■ Exhibit 43-3 A Sample Cumulative Convertible Preferred-Stock Certificate

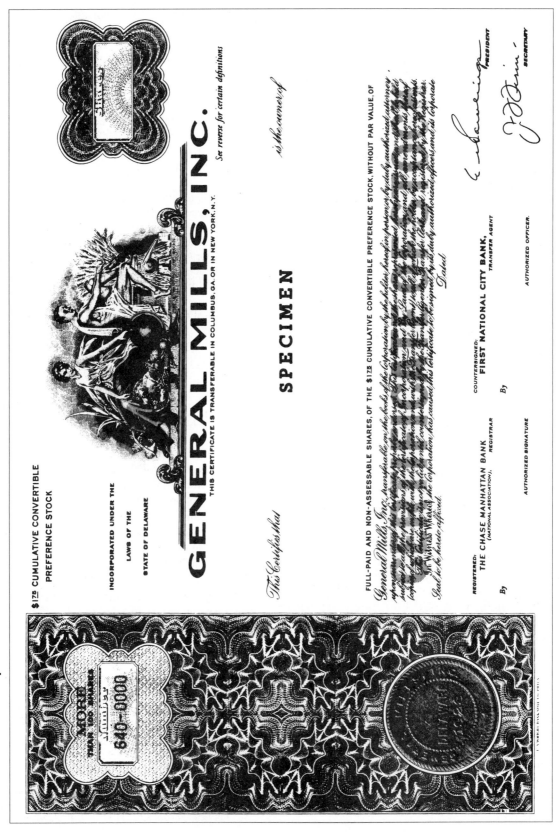

the Securities Exchange Act was passed by Congress. This 1934 act created the Securities and Exchange Commission (SEC) as an independent regulatory agency whose function was to administer the 1933 and 1934 acts. Its major responsibilities in this respect are as follows:

1. Requiring disclosure of facts concerning offerings of securities listed on national securities exchanges and offerings of certain securities traded over the counter (OTC).
2. Regulating the trade in securities on the thirteen national and regional securities exchanges and in the OTC markets.
3. Investigating securities frauds.
4. Regulating the activities of securities brokers, dealers, and investment advisers and requiring their registration.
5. Supervising the activities of mutual funds.
6. Recommending administrative sanctions, injunctive remedies, and criminal prosecution against those who violate securities laws. (The Fraud Section of the Criminal Division of the Department of Justice prosecutes violations of federal securities laws.)

From the time of its creation until the present, the SEC's regulatory functions have gradually been increased by legislation granting it authority in different areas. In recent years the SEC has been active in promoting stiffer penalties for *insider trading* and in effecting regulatory changes addressing the problem of the proliferation of hostile takeovers and corporate-control contests, in which outsiders attempt to wrest control of the corporation from its current board of directors. Another current major concern of the SEC is to effect fundamental changes in the basic regulatory framework applying to the financial services industry. Under the Securities Enforcement Remedies Act of 1990, the SEC was granted substantial new powers, increasing the range of SEC enforcement options to include new cease-and-desist powers and increased penalties.

■ Securities Act of 1933

The Securities Act of 1933[2] was designed to prohibit various forms of fraud and to stabilize the

securities industry by requiring that all essential information concerning the issuance of securities be made available to the investing public. Essentially, the purpose of this act is to require disclosure.

Definition of a Security

Generally, a *security* is any document evidencing a debt or a property interest. Under Section 2(1) of the Securities Act, securities include the following:

> any note, stock, treasury stock, bond, debenture, evidence of indebtedness, certificate of interest or participation in any profit-sharing agreement, collateral-trust certificate, preorganization certificate or subscription, transferable share, investment contract, voting-trust certificate, certificate of deposit for a security, fractional undivided interest in oil, gas, or other mineral rights, or, in general, any interest or instrument commonly known as a ''security,'' or any certificate of interest or participation in, temporary or interim certificate for, receipt for, guarantee of, or warrant or right to subscribe to or purchase, any of the foregoing.[3]

Basically, the courts have interpreted this definition to mean that a security exists in any transaction in which a person (1) invests (2) in a common enterprise (3) reasonably expecting profits (4) derived *primarily* or *substantially* from others' managerial or entrepreneurial efforts.

For our purposes, it is probably most convenient to think of securities in their most common form—stocks and bonds issued by corporations. Bear in mind, however, that securities can take many forms and have been held to include whiskey, cosmetics, worms, beavers, boats, vacuum cleaners, muskrats, and cemetery lots, as well as investment contracts in condominiums, franchises, limited partnerships, oil or gas or other mineral rights, and farm animals accompanied by care agreements.

In determining what constitutes a security under the 1933 act, courts have often cited *SEC v. W. J. Howey Co.*[4] In this classic case, in which citrus groves qualified as securities, the United States Supreme Court held that for a security to

---

2. 15 U.S.C. Sections 77a–77aa.

3. 15 U.S.C. Section 77b(1). The 1982 amendments added stock options.
4. 328 U.S. 293, 66 S.Ct. 1100, 90 L.Ed.1244 (1946).

exist, an investor's profits must be derived *solely* from others' efforts. Later court decisions, however, have required only that the profits be derived *primarily* or *substantially* from the efforts of others.[5]

Registration Requirements

Section 5 of the Securities Act of 1933 broadly provides that if a security does not qualify for an exemption, that security must be *registered* before it is offered to the public either through the mails or through any facility of interstate commerce, including securities exchanges. Issuing corporations must file a *registration statement* with the SEC. Investors must be provided with a *prospectus* that describes the security being sold, the issuing corporation, and the investment or risk attaching to the security. In principle, the registration statement and the prospectus supply sufficient information to enable unsophisticated investors to evaluate the financial risk involved.

The registration statement must include the following:

1. A description of the significant provisions of the security offered for sale, including the relationship between that security and the other capital securities of the registrant. Also, the corporation must disclose how it intends to use the proceeds of the sale.
2. A description of the registrant's properties and business.

3. A description of the management of the registrant and its security holdings, remuneration, and other benefits, including pensions and stock options. Any interests of directors or officers in any material transactions with the corporation must be disclosed.
4. A financial statement certified by an independent public accounting firm.
5. A description of pending lawsuits.

Before filing the registration statement and the prospectus with the SEC, the corporation is allowed to obtain an underwriter who will monitor the distribution of the new issue. There is a twenty-day waiting period after registration before the sale can take place. During this period, oral offers between interested investors and the issuing corporation concerning the purchase and sale of the proposed securities may take place; very limited written advertising is allowed. At this time, the so-called **red herring** prospectus may be distributed. It gets its name from the red legend printed across it stating that the registration has been filed but has not become effective.

After the waiting period, the registered securities can be legally bought and sold. Written advertising is allowed in the form of a so-called **tombstone ad,** so named because the format resembles a tombstone. Such ads simply tell the investor where and how to obtain a prospectus. Normally, any other type of advertising is prohibited.

Registration violations of the 1933 act are not treated lightly. In the following case, the BarChris Construction Corporation was sued by the purchasers of the corporation's debentures under Section 11 of the Securities Act of 1933. Section 11 imposes liability when a registration statement or a prospectus contains material false statements or material omissions.

---

5. See, for example, *SEC v. Glenn W. Turner Enterprises, Inc.,* 474 F.2d 476 (9th Cir. 1973), cert denied 414 U.S. 821, 94 S.Ct. 117, 38 L.Ed.2d 53 (1973), in which pyramid sales arrangements were held to involve investment contracts and securities, because the profits realized were due primarily or substantially to others' efforts.

BACKGROUND AND FACTS BarChris Construction Corporation came to be recognized as a significant factor in the bowling construction industry when its sales increased dramatically between 1956 and 1960. To finance its operations, BarChris was in constant need of cash, a need that grew more pressing as operations expanded. In 1959, BarChris sold over a half-million shares of its common stock to the public. By early 1961, to obtain additional working capital, BarChris decided to sell debenture bonds. BarChris filed a registration statement for the debentures with the SEC. The statement became effective May 16, 1961. BarChris received the proceeds

Case 43.1

ESCOTT v. BARCHRIS CONSTRUCTION CORP.

United States District Court, Southern District of New York, 1968.

283 F.Supp. 643.

of the financing but nevertheless experienced increasing financial difficulties, which in time became insurmountable. In October 1962, BarChris filed a petition for bankruptcy. In November, BarChris defaulted on the interest due on the debentures. Barry Escott and other buyers of the debentures filed suit in a federal district court under Section 11 of the Securities Act of 1933. Escott and the others challenged the accuracy of the registration statement and charged that the text of the prospectus—including many of the figures—was false and that material information had been omitted. The defendants fell into three categories: (1) persons who signed the registration statement, (2) underwriters (consisting of eight investment banking firms), and (3) BarChris's auditors—Peat, Marwick, Mitchell & Company. Among those who signed the statement were (1) BarChris's nine directors, (2) BarChris's controller, (3) one of BarChris's attorneys, (4) two investment bankers who were later named as directors of BarChris, and (5) numerous other persons participating in the preparation of the statement. The court reviewed all the figures and statements included in the prospectus.

DECISION AND RATIONALE The United States District Court for the Southern District of New York held BarChris and all signers of the registration statement, the underwriters, and the corporation's auditors liable. The court found that the registration statement contained false statements of fact or omitted facts that should have been included to prevent the statement from being misleading. The misstatements included overstatement of sales and gross profits, understatement of contingent liabilities, overstatement of orders on hand, and failure to disclose true facts regarding officers' loans, customers' delinquencies, application of proceeds, and the prospective operation of several bowling alleys. The facts that were falsely stated or omitted were "material" within the meaning of the Securities Act of 1933. The court found that "[t]he average prudent investor is not concerned with minor inaccuracies or with errors as to matters which are of no interest to him. The facts which tend to deter him from purchasing a security are facts which have an important bearing upon the nature or condition of the issuing corporation or its business. * * * Judged by this test, there is no doubt that many of the misstatements and omissions in this prospectus were material."

Exemptions under the 1933 Act

A corporation can avoid the high cost and complicated procedures associated with registration by taking advantage of certain exemptions. SEC regulations provide that the following offerings are exempt:

1. Private, noninvestment company offerings up to $500,000 in any twelve-month period are exempt if no general solicitation or advertising is used, the SEC is notified of the sales, and precaution is taken against nonexempt, unregistered re-

sales.[6] The limits on advertising and unregistered resales do not apply if the offering is made solely in states that provide for registration and disclosure and the securities are sold in compliance with those provisions.[7]

---

6. Precautions to be taken against nonexempt, unregistered resales include asking the investor whether he or she is buying the securities for others; before the sale, disclosing to each purchaser in writing that the securities are unregistered and thus cannot be resold, except in an exempt transaction, without first being registered; and indicating on the certificate that the securities are unregistered and restricted.
7. SEC Regulation D, 17 C.F.R. Section 230.504.

2. Noninvestment company offerings up to $5 million in any twelve-month period are exempt, regardless of the number of **accredited investors** (banks, insurance companies, investment companies, the issuer's executive officers and directors, and persons whose income or net worth exceeds certain limits), so long as there are no more than thirty-five unaccredited investors; no general solicitation or advertising is used; the SEC is notified of the sales; and precaution is taken against nonexempt, unregistered resales. If the sale involves *any* unaccredited investors, *all* investors must be given material information about the offering company, its business, and the securities before the sale. The issuer is not required to believe that each unaccredited investor "has such knowledge and experience in financial and business matters that he is capable of evaluating the merits and the risks of the prospective investment."[8]

3. Private offerings in unlimited amounts that are not generally solicited or advertised are exempt if the SEC is notified of the sales; precaution is taken against nonexempt, unregistered resales; and the issuer believes that each unaccredited investor has sufficient knowledge or experience in financial matters to be capable of evaluating the investment's merits and risks. There may be no more than thirty-five unaccredited investors, although there may be an unlimited number of accredited investors. If there are *any* unaccredited investors, the issuer must provide to *all* purchasers material information about itself, its business, and the securities before the sale.[9]

This last exemption is perhaps most important to those who want to raise funds through the sale of securities without registering them. It is often referred to as the *private placement* exemption, because it exempts "transactions not involving any public offering."[10] This provision applies to private offerings to a limited number of persons who are sufficiently sophisticated and in a sufficiently strong bargaining position so as to be able to assume the risk of the investment (and who thus have no need for federal registration protection); it also

applies to private offerings to similarly situated institutional investors.

Also exempt are *intra*state transactions involving purely local offerings.[11] This exemption applies to offerings restricted to residents of the state in which the issuing company is organized and doing business. The exemption requires that 80 percent of the issuer's assets be located in the state of issue, 80 percent of the issuer's gross revenue be from business conducted within the state, and 80 percent of the net income from the sale of the issue be used in the state. Also, for nine months after the last sale, no resale may be made to a nonresident, and precautions must be taken against this possibility. (Precautions include obtaining a statement of residence in writing from each investor, as well as indicating on the securities certificates that they are unregistered and subject to resale only to state residents.) These offerings remain subject to applicable laws in the state of issue.

Among securities exempt from the registration requirement in consideration of the "small amount involved,"[12] other than those mentioned above, is an issuer's offer of up to $1.5 million in securities in any twelve-month period. Under the SEC's Regulation A,[13] the issuer must file with the SEC notice of the issue and an offering circular, which must also be provided to investors before the sale; but this is a much simpler and less expensive process than the procedures associated with registration.

Also, an offer made *solely* to accredited investors is exempt if its amount is not more than $5 million in any twelve-month period. Any number of accredited investors may participate, but no unaccredited investors may do so. No general solicitation or advertising may be used; the SEC must be notified of all sales; and precaution must be taken against nonexempt, unregistered resales (because these are restricted securities and may be resold only by registration or in an exempt transaction).[14] The exemptions under the Securities Act of 1933 and SEC regulations are summarized in Exhibit 43–4.

---

8.   SEC Regulation D, 17 C.F.R. Section 230.505.
9.   SEC Regulation D, 17 C.F.R. Section 230.506.
10.   15 U.S.C. Section 77d(2).
11.   15 U.S.C. Section 77c(a)(11).
12.   15 U.S.C. Section 77c(b).
13.   17 C.F.R. Sections 230.251–230.264.
14.   15 U.S.C. Section 77d(6).

■ **Exhibit 43–4**
Exemptions Under the 1933 Act for Securities Offerings by Businesses

Type of Offering	Required Conditions
Private, noninvestment company offerings up to $500,000 in any twelve-month period	1. No general solicitation or advertising (unless state provides for registration and disclosure). 2. SEC is notified of sales. 3. Precaution is taken against nonexempt, unregistered resales.
Noninvestment company offerings up to $5 million in any twelve-month period	1. Unlimited number of accredited investors. 2. No more than thirty-five unaccredited investors. 3. If *any* unaccredited investors, material information about offering firm must be disclosed. 4. No general solicitation or advertising. 5. SEC is notified of sales. 6. Precaution is taken against nonexempt, unregistered resales.
Private placement (private offerings in unlimited amounts that are generally not solicited or advertised)	1. Unlimited number of accredited investors. 2. No more than thirty-five unaccredited investors. 3. If *any* unaccredited investors, (a) material information about offering firm must be disclosed, and (b) issuer must reasonably believe that each unaccredited investor is experienced in financial matters and capable of evaluating risks involved in investment. 4. SEC is notified of sales. 5. Precaution is taken against nonexempt, unregistered resales.
Intrastate transactions (offerings restricted to residents of the state in which issuing company is organized and doing business)	1. 80 percent of issuer's assets are located in the state of issue. 2. 80 percent of issuer's gross revenue is from business conducted within the state. 3. 80 percent of net income from the sale of the issue is used in the state. 4. No resale is made to a nonresident for nine months after last sale, and precautions are taken to prevent such resale.
Offerings up to $1.5 million in any twelve-month period (under SEC Regulation A)	Notice of the issue and an offering circular are filed with the SEC and provided to investors.
Offerings up to $5 million in any twelve-month period	1. Unlimited number of accredited investors. 2. No unaccredited investors. 3. No general solicitation or advertising. 4. SEC is notified of sales. 5. Precaution is taken against nonexempt, unregistered resales.

Additional Exempt Securities

The following securities are also exempt:[15]

1. All bank securities sold prior to July 27, 1933.
2. Commercial paper if a maturity date does not exceed nine months.
3. Securities of charitable organizations.
4. Securities resulting from a corporate reorganization issued for exchange with the issuer's existing security holders, as well as certificates issued by trustees, receivers, or debtors in possession under the Bankruptcy Act (bankruptcy is discussed in Chapter 33).
5. Securities issued exclusively for exchange with the issuer's existing security holders, provided no commission is paid (for example, stock dividends and stock splits).
6. Securities issued to finance the acquisition of railroad equipment.
7. Any insurance, endowment, or annuity contract issued by a state-regulated insurance company.

---

15. 15 U.S.C. Section 77c.

8. Government-issued securities.

9. Securities issued by banks, savings and loan associations, farmers' cooperatives, and similar institutions subject to supervision by governmental authorities.

■ Securities Exchange Act of 1934

The Securities Exchange Act of 1934[16] is concerned primarily with the *resale* of securities. The act provides for the regulation and registration of security exchanges, brokers, and dealers, as well as national securities associations, such as the National Association of Securities Dealers (NASD). The 1934 act regulates the markets in which securities are traded by maintaining a continuous disclosure system for all corporations with securities on the securities exchanges and for those companies that have assets in excess of $5 million and five hundred or more shareholders. These corporations are referred to as Section 12 companies, because they are required to register their securities under Section 12 of the 1934 act. The act regulates proxy solicitation for voting, and it allows the SEC to engage in market surveillance to regulate undesirable market practices such as fraud, market manipulation, misrepresentation, and stabilization. (*Stabilization* is a market-manipulating technique in which securities underwriters bid for securities to stabilize their price during their issuance.)

Insider Trading—
Section 10(b) and SEC Rule 10b-5

One of the most important parts of the 1934 act relates to so-called **insider trading.** Because of their positions, corporate directors and officers often obtain advance inside information that can affect the future market value of the corporate stock. Obviously, their positions can give them a trading advantage over the general public and shareholders. Section 10(b) of the 1934 Securities Exchange Act and SEC **Rule 10b-5** define inside information and extend liability to officers and directors in their personal transactions for taking advantage of such information when they know it is unavailable to the person with whom they are dealing.

---

16. 15 U.S.C. Sections 77a–78jj.

APPLICABILITY OF RULE 10b-5 Rule 10b-5 applies in virtually all cases concerning the trading of securities, whether on organized exchanges, in over-the-counter markets, or in private transactions. The rule covers notes, bonds, certificates of interest and participation in any profit-sharing agreement, agreements to form a corporation, and joint-venture agreements; in short, it covers just about any form of security. It is immaterial whether a firm has securities registered under the 1933 act for the 1934 act to apply.

Rule 10b-5 is applicable only when the requisites of federal jurisdiction, such as the use of the mails, of stock exchange facilities, or of any instrumentality of interstate commerce, are present. Virtually no commercial transaction, however, can be completed without such contact. In addition, the states have corporate securities laws, many of which include provisions similar to Rule 10b-5.

Rule 10b-5 covers not only corporate officers, directors, and majority shareholders but also certain "outside" persons having access to, or receiving information of, a nonpublic nature on which trading is based. Those persons to whom the material information is transmitted are known as *tippees.* (The liability of tippees and other outsiders will be discussed shortly.)

DISCLOSURE UNDER RULE 10b-5 Any material omission or misrepresentation of material facts in connection with the purchase or sale of a security may violate Section 10(b) and Rule 10b-5. The key to liability (which can be civil or criminal) under this rule is whether the insider's information is *material.* Following are some examples of material facts calling for a disclosure under the rule:

1. A new ore discovery.
2. Fraudulent trading in the company stock by a broker-dealer.
3. A dividend change (whether up or down).
4. A contract for the sale of corporate assets.
5. A new discovery of a process or product.
6. A significant change in the firm's financial condition.

Courts have struggled with the problem of when information becomes public knowledge. Clearly, when inside information becomes public knowledge, all insiders should be allowed to trade without disclosure. The courts have suggested that insiders should refrain from trading for a "reasonable waiting period" when the news is not readily translatable into investment action. Presumably, this gives the news time to filter down to, and be evaluated by, the investing public.

The following is one of the landmark cases interpreting Rule 10b-5. The SEC sued Texas Gulf Sulphur Company for issuing a misleading press release. The release underestimated the magnitude and value of a mineral discovery. The SEC also sued several of Texas Gulf Sulphur's directors, officers, and employees under Rule 10b-5 after these persons had purchased large amounts of the corporate stock prior to the announcement of the corporation's rich ore discovery.

Case 43.2

SEC v. TEXAS GULF SULPHUR CO.

United States Court of Appeals, Second Circuit, 1968. 401 F.2d 833.

BACKGROUND AND FACTS   On November 12, 1963, Texas Gulf Sulphur Company (TGS) drilled an exploratory hole near Timmins, Ontario, that appeared to yield a core with an exceedingly high mineral content. Keeping the results of the test drilling secret, TGS officers, directors, and employees made substantial purchases of company stock or accepted stock options.[a] Test drilling continued. On April 11, 1964, an unauthorized report of the discovery appeared in the newspapers. On April 12, TGS issued a press release that played down the find and stated that it was too early to tell whether it would be significant. On April 16, after the completion of test drilling, TGS announced a strike of at least 25 million tons of ore, substantially driving up the price of TGS stock. The Securities and Exchange Commission filed suit in a federal district court against TGS and several of its officers, directors, and employees for violating Rule 10b-5. Included in the complaint were charges that the April 12 press release was deceptive. The trial court decided that the drilling results were not "material" until April 9 and that the insider-trading activity before that date was thus not illegal. The trial court also held that the press release was not "misleading, or deceptive on the basis of the facts then known." The SEC appealed.

DECISION AND RATIONALE   The United States Court of Appeals for the Second Circuit reversed and remanded the case to the trial court, holding that the employees and officers violated Rule 10b-5's prohibition against insider trading. Under Rule 10b-5, the test of materiality is not whether a company would be permitted to disclose the information if it were selling securities. Rather, the test is whether the information would affect the judgment of reasonable investors. Reasonable investors include speculative as well as conservative investors. "[A] major factor in determining whether the * * * discovery [of the ore] was a material fact is the importance attached to the drilling results by those who knew about it. * * * The timing by those who knew of it of their stock purchases and their purchases of short-term calls[b]—purchases in some cases by individuals who had never before purchased calls or even TGS stock—virtually compels the inference that the insiders were influenced by the drilling results. * * * We hold, therefore, that all transactions in TGS stock or calls by individuals apprised of the drilling results * * * were made in violation of Rule 10b-5."

COMMENTS   Investors who had sold their TGS stock in reliance on the representations in the April 12 press release also sued TGS. Eventually,

---

a.   A stock option is a contract that gives the holder the right to buy a set number of shares of stock at a fixed price on demand. Stock options are often used by corporations as bonuses to employees.

b.   A call is an option to buy a certain amount of stock at a fixed price within a certain time.

they were awarded damages representing the difference between the price at which they sold their stock and the price at which they could have reinvested in TGS after they learned of the April 16 press release.

OUTSIDERS AND RULE 10b-5   The traditional insider-trading case involves true insiders—corporate officers, directors, and majority shareholders who have access to, and trade on, inside information. Increasingly, liability under Section 10(b) of the 1934 act and SEC Rule 10b-5 has been extended to include certain ''outsiders''—those who trade on inside information acquired *indirectly*. Two theories have been developed in recent years under which outsiders may be held liable for insider trading: the *tipper/tippee theory* and the *misappropriation theory*.

Tipper/tippee Theory   Anyone who acquires inside information as a result of a corporate insider's breach of his or her fiduciary duty can be liable under Rule 10b-5. This liability extends to **tippees** (those who receive ''tips'' from insiders) and even remote tippees (tippees of tippees).[17] The key to liability under this theory is that inside information was obtained as a result of someone's breach of a fiduciary duty to the corporation whose shares are traded. Unless there has been a breach of a duty not to disclose inside information, and the tippee knows of this breach (or should know of it), liability under this theory cannot result.

For example, in *Chiarella v. United States,*[18] the United States Supreme Court considered the role Rule 10b-5 plays when there was not breach of duty and no use of interstate commerce, the mails, or any of the facilities of any national securities exchange. Chiarella was a printer who worked at a New York composing room and handled announcements of corporate takeover bids. Even though the documents that were delivered to the printer concealed the identity of the target corporations by blank spaces and false names, Chiarella was able to deduce the names of the target companies. Without disclosing his knowledge, he purchased stock in the target companies and sold the shares immediately after the takeover attempts

were made public. He realized a gain of slightly more than $30,000 in the course of fourteen months.

In 1978, Chiarella was indicted on seventeen counts of violating Section 10(b) of the Securities Exchange Act of 1934 and SEC Rule 10b-5. The trial court convicted him on all counts, and the court of appeals affirmed that conviction. The United States Supreme Court, however, reversed the trial court's decision. The Supreme Court held that Chiarella could not be convicted for his failure to disclose his knowledge to stockholders or to target companies because he was under no duty to disclose his knowledge. Chiarella was under no duty to disclose because he had no prior dealing with the stockholders and was not their agent, nor was he a person in whom sellers had placed their trust and confidence. Thus, the Court held that Chiarella was not liable as a tippee.[19]

Misappropriation Theory   Liability for insider trading may also be established under the misappropriation theory. This theory of liability holds that if an individual wrongfully obtains—misappropriates—inside information and trades on it to his or her personal gain, then the individual should be held liable, because in essence, he or she stole information rightfully belonging to another. This theory has significantly expanded the range of persons who can be held liable for insider trading. (Courts will normally hold that some fiduciary duty must have been violated and some harm to the defrauded party must have occurred for liability to exist.) The following case illustrates an application of the misappropriation theory.

---

17. See the discussion of *SEC v. Musella,* 678 F.Supp. 1060 (S.D.N.Y. 1988), in the *Focus on Ethics* at the end of this unit.
18. 445 U.S. 222, 100 S.Ct. 1108, 63 L.Ed.2d 348 (1980).

19. Note, though, that Chiarella might not have escaped liability if the jury had been instructed to find liability under the misappropriation theory discussed in the next section. Under that theory, it could be argued that Chiarella violated his duty of loyalty to his employer, the printing firm, by engaging in actions that could foreseeably be harmful to the printing firm's reputation. Note also that after *Chiarella,* the SEC adopted Rule 14e-3 (17 C.F.R. Section 240.14e-3), which makes it unlawful for a person who acquires advance knowledge of a tender offer to use that information in securities transactions.

Case 43.3

UNITED STATES v. CARPENTER

United States Court of Appeals, Second Circuit, 1986. 791 F.2d 1024.

BACKGROUND AND FACTS   R. Foster Winans, a reporter for the *Wall Street Journal*, coauthored an influential daily financial column called "Heard on the Street." The column discussed selected stocks, and after its publication, the market price of the stock that was the subject of the column often underwent a noticeable change. Winans entered into a scheme with Kenneth Felis and another stockbroker at Kidder Peabody to give the brokers advance information as to the timing and contents of the "Heard on the Street" column. The brokers would then buy or sell stock based on the probable impact of the column on the market and share the resulting profits. David Carpenter, a news clerk at the *Journal,* also participated in the scheme, acting primarily as a messenger between the conspirators. Over a four-month period, the net profits resulting from this trading activity were about $690,000. Correlations between the "Heard on the Street" articles and trading in the Felis account were noted at Kidder Peabody, and inquiries began. Later, the SEC began an investigation. Eventually, Winans and Carpenter revealed the entire scheme to the SEC. Winans and Felis were convicted for participating in an insider-trading scheme based on information misappropriated from the *Journal,* as well as for mail and wire fraud. Carpenter was convicted of aiding and abetting in the commission of securities fraud and mail and wire fraud. On appeal, Winans and the others contended that they could not be held liable under Rule 10b-5 because they were not corporate insiders and did not misappropriate material nonpublic information from corporate insiders.

DECISION AND RATIONALE   The United States Court of Appeals for the Second Circuit upheld the convictions, ruling that Winans and the others had violated insider-trading laws when Winans "breached a duty of confidentiality to his employer by misappropriating from the *Journal* confidential prepublication information, regarding the time and content of certain newspaper columns, about which he learned in the course of his employment." The court brushed aside the defendants' argument that the misappropriation theory may be applied only when corporate insiders who owe the corporation and its shareholders a fiduciary duty are involved, stating that "the misappropriation theory more broadly proscribes the conversion by 'insiders' or others of material nonpublic information in connection with the purchase or sale of securities."

COMMENTS   This decision was later reviewed by the United States Supreme Court [*Carpenter v. United States,* 484 U.S. 19, 108 S.Ct. 316, 98 L.Ed.2d 275 (1987)]. Because the Supreme Court was evenly divided on the issue of liability under the misappropriation theory (the vote was four to four), the lower court's decision on the issue was upheld "by default." The Court, however, unanimously affirmed the convictions for mail and wire fraud.

Insider Reporting and Trading—Section 16(b)

Officers, directors, and certain large stockholders[20] of Section 12 corporations are required to file re-

ports with the SEC concerning their ownership and trading of the corporation's securities.[21] To discourage such insiders from using nonpublic information about their company to their personal benefit in the stock market, Section 16(b) of the 1934

---

20.   Those stockholders owning 10 percent of the class of equity securities registered under Section 12 of the 1934 act [15 U.S.C. Section 78*l*].

---

21.   15 U.S.C. Section 78*l*.

act provides for the recapture by the corporation of all profits realized by the insider on any purchase and sale or sale and purchase of the corporation's stock within any six-month period.[22] It is irrelevant whether the insider actually uses inside information; all such *short-swing* profits must be returned to the corporation. In other words, Section 16 is a strict liability provision.

Section 16(b) applies not only to stock but to warrants, options, and securities convertible into

---

22.   15 U.S.C. Section 78p(b). In a declining stock market, one can realize profits by selling at a high price and repurchasing at a later time at a lower price.

stock. In addition, the courts have fashioned complex rules for determining profits. Corporate insiders are wise to seek competent counsel prior to trading in the corporation's stock. Exhibit 43–5 compares the effects of Rule 10b-5 and Section 16(b).

If an individual is an ''officer'' of a corporation, such as a vice-president, but has no access to inside information, should this individual be subject to the provisions of Section 16(b) if he or she realizes short-swing profits by trading in the company's stock? This question arose in the following case, in which the central issue concerned the definition of a corporate officer.

BACKGROUND AND FACTS   Joseph Crotty was employed by United Artists (UA) in 1969, and by 1980 he had become UA's head film buyer for its western division, which encompassed six western states. Crotty's duties mainly involved negotiating and signing agreements to obtain movies for exhibition, distributing the movies to UA theaters, and supervising the advertising in his division. In 1982, UA made Crotty a vice-president. The appointment was essentially honorary and was accompanied by no change in duties or raise in pay. At no time was Crotty a director of the company, nor did he ever attend any board meetings or receive any information from the directors that was not available to the general public. Between December 19, 1984, and July 24, 1985, Crotty realized a large profit from the purchase and sale of UA shares. C.R.A. Realty Corporation, an organization incorporated to act as a private attorney general and commence actions against corporate officials for violations of federal securities law, sought in a federal district court to recover Crotty's short-swing profits on behalf of UA. The court dismissed the action, holding that Crotty's transactions were not subject to Section 16(b) because Crotty at no time had access to inside information. C.R.A. Realty appealed.

Case 43.4

C.R.A. REALTY CORP. v. CROTTY

United States Court of Appeals, Second Circuit, 1989.
878 F.2d 562.

DECISION AND RATIONALE   The United States Court of Appeals for the Second Circuit upheld the district court's decision, ruling that Crotty's actual functions as an employee—particularly his access to inside information—and not his corporate title should determine whether he was an officer subject to Section 16(b). The appellate court noted that the SEC had not invariably applied Section 16(b) to anyone who was an ''officer'' of a corporation. In an earlier case, the court had declared that ''it is an employee's duties and responsibilities—rather than his actual title—that determine whether he is an officer within the purview of [Section] 16(b).'' Consequently, the court concluded that Crotty's title of vice-president alone did not make him an officer for Section 16(b) purposes.

COMMENTS   In January 1991, the SEC agreed to adopt revisions to the requirements under Section 16 of the 1934 act. The revised rules define ''officer'' in such a way as to make clear that a person's functions—not simply his or her title—determine the applicability of Section 16.

■ **Exhibit 43–5**
**Comparison of Coverage, Application, and
Liabilities under Rule 10b-5 and Section 16(b)**

	Rule 10b-5	**Section 16(b)**
1. What is the subject matter of the transaction?	Any security (does not have to be registered).	Any security (does not have to be registered).
2. What transactions are covered?	Purchase or sale.	Short-swing purchase and sale or short-swing sale and purchase.
3. Who is subject to liability?	Virtually anyone with inside information under a duty to disclose—including officers, directors, controlling stockholders, and tippees.	Officers, directors, and certain 10 percent stockholders.
4. Is omission, scheme, or misrepresentation necessary for liability?	Yes.	No.
5. Are any transactions exempt?	No.	Yes, there are a variety of exemptions.
6. Is direct dealing with the party necessary?	No.	No.
7. Who can bring an action?	A person transacting with an insider, or the SEC, or a purchaser or seller damaged by a wrongful act.	Corporation and shareholder by derivative action.

Insider-Trading Sanctions

The Insider Trading Sanctions Act of 1984[23] permits the SEC to bring suit in a federal district court against anyone violating, or aiding in a violation of, the 1934 act or SEC rules by purchasing or selling a security while in the possession of material nonpublic information. The violation must occur on or through the facilities of a national securities exchange or from or through a broker or dealer. Transactions pursuant to a public offering by an issuer of securities are excepted.

The court may assess as a penalty as much as triple the profits gained or the loss avoided by the guilty party. For purposes of the act, profit or loss is defined as "the difference between the purchase or sale price of the security and the value of that security as measured by the trading price of the security at a reasonable period of time after public dissemination of the nonpublic information." [24]

The Insider Trading and Securities Fraud Enforcement Act of 1988 enlarged the class of persons who may be subject to civil liability for insider trading violations, gave the SEC authority to award bounty payments to persons providing information leading to the prosecution of insider-trading violations, gave the SEC rulemaking authority to require specific policies and procedures to prevent insider trading, and increased the criminal penalties for violations. Maximum jail terms were increased from five to ten years; fines were increased to $1 million for individuals and to $2.5 million for partnerships and corporations.[25] Neither act has any effect on other actions the SEC or private investors may take.

---

23. 15 U.S.C. Section 78u(d)(2)(A).

24. 15 U.S.C. Section 78u(d)(2)(C).
25. 15 U.S.C. Section 78ff(a).

Proxy Statements

Section 14(a) of the Securities Exchange Act of 1934 regulates the solicitation of proxies from shareholders of Section 12 companies.[26] The SEC regulates the content of proxy statements sent to shareholders by corporate managers who are requesting authority to vote on behalf of the shareholders in a particular election on specified issues. Whoever solicits a proxy must fully and accurately disclose all facts that are pertinent to the matter to be voted on. SEC Rule 14a-9 is similar to the antifraud provisions of Rule 10b-5. Remedies for violation are extensive, ranging from injunctions to prevent a vote from being taken to monetary damages.

■ Regulation of Investment Companies

Investment companies, and mutual funds in particular, grew rapidly after World War II. **Investment companies** act on behalf of many smaller shareholder-owners by buying a large portfolio of securities and managing that portfolio professionally. A **mutual fund** is a specific type of investment company that continually buys or sells to investors shares of ownership in a portfolio. Such companies are regulated by the Investment Company Act of 1940,[27] which provides for SEC regulation of their activities. It was expanded by the Investment Company Act Amendments of 1970. Further minor changes were made in the Securities Act Amendments of 1975.

The 1940 act requires that every investment company register with the SEC, and it imposes restrictions on the activities of such companies and persons connected with them. For the purposes of the act, an investment company is defined as any entity that (1) "is . . . engaged primarily . . . in the business of investing, reinvesting, or trading in securities" or (2) is engaged in such business and more than 40 percent of the company's assets consist of investment securities. Excluded from coverage of the act are banks, insurance companies, savings and loan associations, finance companies, oil and gas drilling firms, charitable foundations, tax-exempt pension funds, and other special types of institutions, such as closely held corporations.

To register with the SEC, the investment company files a notification of registration. Each year registered companies must file reports with the SEC. In order to safeguard company assets, all securities must be held in the custody of a bank or stock-exchange member, and that bank or stock-exchange member must follow strict procedures established by the SEC.

No dividends may be paid from any source other than accumulated, undistributed net income. Furthermore, there are some restrictions on investment activities. For example, investment companies are not allowed to purchase securities on the margin (pay for only part of the total price, borrowing the rest), sell short (sell shares not yet owned), or participate in joint trading accounts.

■ State Securities Laws

Today, all states have their own corporate securities laws that regulate the offer and sale of securities within individual state borders.[28] Often referred to as **blue sky laws,** they are designed to prevent "speculative schemes which have no more basis than so many feet of blue sky."

Since the adoption of the 1933 and 1934 federal securities acts, the state and federal governments have regulated securities concurrently. Indeed, both acts specifically preserve state securities laws. Certain features are common to all state blue sky laws. They have antifraud provisions, many of which are patterned after Rule 10b-5. Also, most state corporate securities laws regulate securities brokers and dealers.

Typically, these laws also provide for the registration or qualification of securities offered or issued for sale within the state. Unless an applicable exemption from registration is found, issuers must register or qualify their stock with the appropriate state official, often called a *corporations commissioner.* There is a difference in philosophy among state statutes. Many are like the Securities Act of 1933 and mandate certain disclosures before registration is effective and a permit to sell the securities is issued. Others have fairness standards that a corporation must meet to offer or sell stock in the state. The Uniform Securities Act, which has been adopted in part by several states, was drafted to be acceptable to states with differing regulatory philosophies.

---

26. 15 U.S.C. Section 78n(a).
27. 15 U.S.C. Sections 80a-1 to 80a-64.

28. These laws are cataloged and annotated in the Commerce Clearing House's *Blue Sky Law Reporter,* a loose-leaf service.

■ Terms and Concepts

accredited investors 763	investment company 771	securities 756
blue sky laws 771	mutual fund 771	stocks 756
bonds 756	preferred stock 757	tippee 767
common stock 757	red herring 761	tombstone ad 761
insider trading 765	Rule 10b-5 765	

■ For Review

1. What are the four elements in the definition of a security? What is the most common form that securities take?
2. What is a registration statement? What must it include? What is a prospectus?
3. What is the essential purpose of the Securities Act of 1933? What is the essential purpose of the Securities Exchange Act of 1934?
4. Ron is an officer of Berry Clear Spring Water Corp. Ron is aware that Berry's financial condition has improved so dramatically in the last month that there will be a hefty increase in Berry's next stock dividend. Before Berry's improved financial situation is revealed to the public, Ron telephones his broker and buys 500 shares of Berry stock. Three months later, when the situation is revealed, Ron sells the stock for a considerably higher price to Martha. After the next stock dividend is paid, Martha sells the shares to Crystal, realizing a profit on her investment. Did Ron violate SEC Rule 10b-5? Did Martha violate Rule 10b-5?
5. In the previous problem, did Ron violate Section 16(b) of the Securities Exchange Act of 1934? Did Martha?

■ Questions and Case Problems

43-1. Langley Brothers, Inc., a corporation incorporated and doing business in Kansas, decides to sell $1 million worth of its no par value common stock to the public. The stock will be sold only within the state of Kansas. Joseph Langley, the chairman of the board, says the offering need not be registered with the His brother, Harry, disagrees. Who is right? Explain.
43-2. Huron Corp. had 300,000 common shares outstanding. The owners of these outstanding shares lived in several different states. Huron decided to split the 300,000 shares two for one. Will Huron Corp. have to file a registration statement and prospectus on the 300,000 new shares to be issued as a result of the split? Explain.
43-3. Leston Nay owned 90 percent of the stock of First Securities Co. Between the years 1942 and 1966, Hochfelder sent large sums of money to Nay to be invested in *escrow accounts*—accounts belonging to one entity but held by another entity—of First Securities. The whole investment scheme was a fraud, and Nay converted the money sent by Hochfelder to his own use. When Hochfelder discovered the fraud, he sued Ernst & Ernst, the auditor of First Securities, for failing to use proper auditing procedures and thus negligently failing to discover the fraudulent scheme. Was the firm of Ernst & Ernst found guilty of violating Section 10(b) of the 1934 Securities Exchange Act and SEC Rule 10b-5? Explain. [*Ernst & Ernst v. Hochfelder*, 425 U.S. 185, 96 S.Ct. 1375, 47 L.Ed.2d 668 (1976)]
43-4. American Breeding Herds, Inc., (ABH) offered a cattle-breeding plan for which Ronnett contracted to buy thirty-six Charolais cows at $3,000 per head and a one-quarter interest in a Charolais bull at $5,000, totaling $113,000. The ABH agreement described itself as a "tax shelter program . . . unlike the purchase of securities such as stocks and bonds." Ronnett entered into the agreement after receiving investment advice from Shannon, an investment counselor. The cows were tagged and sent to an ABH-approved breeding ranch. Ronnett signed a maintenance agreement and paid a monthly maintenance fee. Was the ABH plan a security, and should it have been registered under Illinois securities law? Explain. [*Ronnett v. American Breeding Herds, Inc.,* 124 Ill.App.3d 842, 464 N.E.2d 1201, 80 Ill.Dec. 218 (1984)]

43-5. Campbell was a financial columnist for a Los Angeles newspaper owned by Hearst Corp. He often bought shares in companies on which he was about to give a favorable report, and then he would sell the shares at a profit after the columns appeared. In June 1969, Campbell interviewed the officers of American Systems, Inc. (ASI). The ASI officers did not disclose to Campbell adverse information concerning its financial condition, and Campbell relied on the officers' presentation of ASI's financial status and made no independent investigation. Planning to write a favorable report, Campbell purchased 5,000 shares of ASI stock for $2 per share. Following the publication of Campbell's favorable, and misleading, article, ASI's stock rose rapidly, and on June 5, Campbell sold 2,000 of his shares at $5 per share. ASI had made plans with another corporation, RGC, in February 1969 whereby RGC would merge with ASI, and ASI would pay RGC stockholders enough ASI stock to equal a market value of $1.8 million on the closing date of June 10, 1969. Zweig and Bruno, who each owned one-third of RGC shares, brought suit against Hearst Corp., alleging that because of the artificial rise in ASI stock due to Campbell's column, they ended up with a smaller percentage of the total outstanding shares of ASI than they would have otherwise received. Discuss whether Hearst is liable under Rule 10b-5. [*Zweig v. Hearst Corp.*, 594 F.2d 1261 (9th Cir. 1979)]

43-6. Ronald Rodeo's investment group purchased limited partnership interests in certain Illinois apartment buildings and separately, by contract, acquired an option to buy out the remaining interests of the general partners. According to the arrangement, the general partners would operate the apartments, and the limited partners would provide essential capital while retaining their limited liability. Rodeo could not actively intervene in the business without losing his limited liability. He therefore had to rely solely upon the general partners for the enterprise's profitability. Two years later, Rodeo became disenchanted with the operation of the apartment enterprise and sued R. Dean Gillman and the other general partners under the Illinois blue sky act. In his claim, Rodeo stated that material misrepresentations and omissions had been made during the negotiation of the limited partnership contracts in violation of the state securities act. The general partners responded that no securities were involved and that, because of the buy-out option, the limited partners actually had ultimate control over the management of the apartments. Discuss the definition of a *security* and whether the limited partnership contracts meet this definition. [*Rodeo v. Gillman*, 787 F.2d 1175 (7th Cir. 1986)]

43-7. U.S. News & World Report, Inc., set up a profit-sharing plan in 1962 that allotted to certain employees specially issued stock known as bonus or anniversary stock. The stock was given to the employees for past services and could not be traded or sold to anyone other than the corporate issuer, U.S. News. This special stock was issued only to employees and for no other purpose than as bonuses. Because there was no market for the stock, U.S. News hired an independent appraiser to estimate the fair value of the stock so that the employees could redeem the shares. Charles Foltz and several other employees held stock through this plan and sought to redeem the shares with U.S. News, but Foltz disputed the value set by the appraisers. Foltz sued U.S. News for violation of securities regulations. What defense would allow U.S. News to resist successfully Foltz's claim? [*Foltz v. U.S. News & World Report, Inc.*, 627 F.Supp. 1143 (D.D.C. 1986)]

43-8. In early 1985, FMC Corp. made plans to buy some of its own stock as part of a restructuring of its balance statement. Unknown to FMC management, the brokerage firm FMC employed—Goldman, Sachs & Co.—disclosed information on the stock purchase that found its way to Ivan Boesky. FMC was one of the seven major corporations in whose stock Boesky allegedly traded using inside information. Boesky made purchases of FMC's stock between February 18 and February 21 and between March 12 and April 4. Boesky's purchases amounted to a substantial portion of the total volume of FMC stock traded during these periods. The price of FMC stock increased from $71.25 on February 20, 1986, to $97.00 on April 25, 1986. As a result, FMC paid substantially more for the repurchase of its own stock than anticipated. Upon the discovery of Boesky's knowledge of FMC's recapitalization

plan, FMC sued him for the excess price it had paid—approximately $220 million. Discuss whether FMC should recover under Section 10(b) of the Securities Exchange Act and SEC Rule 10b-5. [*FMC Corp. v. Boesky*, 673 F.Supp. 242 (N.D.Ill. 1987)]

43-9. Emerson Electric Co. purchased 13.2 percent of Dodge Manufacturing Co.'s stock in an unsuccessful take-over attempt in June 1967. Later, when Dodge merged with Reliance Electric Co., Emerson decided to sell its shares. To avoid being subject to the restrictions of Section 16 of the Securities Exchange Act of 1934, which pertain to any purchase and sale by any owner of 10 percent or more of a corporation's stock, Emerson decided on a two-step selling plan. First, it sold off sufficient shares to reduce its holdings to 9.96 percent, and then it sold the remaining stock—all within a six-month period. Because under Section 16(b) of the act, the owner must be a 10 percent owner "both at the time of the purchase and sale . . . of the security involved," Emerson in this way succeeded in avoiding Section 16(b) requirements. Reliance demanded that Emerson return the profits made on both sales. Emerson sought a declaration from that court that it was not liable, arguing that because at the time of the second sale it had not owned 10 percent of Dodge stock, Section 16 did not apply. Does Section 16 of the Securities Exchange Act of 1934 apply to Emerson's transactions, and is Emerson liable to Reliance for its profits? Discuss fully. [*Reliance Electric Co. v. Emerson Electric Co.*, 404 U.S. 418, 92 S.Ct. 596, 30 L.E.2d 575 (1972)]

43-10. The W. J. Howey Co. owned large tracts of citrus acreage in Lake County, Florida. For several years, it planted about five hundred acres annually, keeping half of the groves itself and offering the other half to the public to help finance additional development. Howey-in-the-Hills Service, Inc., was a service company engaged in cultivating and developing these groves, including the harvesting and marketing of the crops. Each prospective customer was offered both a land sales contract and a service contract, after being told that it was not feasible to invest in a grove unless service arrangements were made. Of the acreage sold by Howey, 85 percent was sold with a service contract with Howey-in-the-Hills Service. Howey did not register with the SEC or meet the other administrative requirements that issuers of securities must fulfill. The SEC sued to enjoin Howey from continuing to offer the land sales and service contracts. Howey responded that no SEC violation existed because no securities were issued. Which party will prevail in court, Howey or the SEC? For what reasons? [*SEC v. W. J. Howey Co.*, 328 U.S. 293, 66 S.Ct. 1100, 90 L.Ed. 1244 (1946)]

43-11. Energy Resource Group, Inc., (ERG) entered into a written agreement with Ivan West for West to find an investor willing to purchase ERG stock. West later formed a partnership, called Investment Management Group (IMG), with Don Peters and another person. According to the terms of the partnership agreement, West's consulting work for ERG was excluded from the work of the IMG partnership. West learned through his consulting position with ERG that ERG was to be acquired by another corporation for $6.00 per share. At the time West learned of the acquisition, ERG stock was trading at $3.50 per share. Apparently, Peters learned of the acquisition from papers on West's desk in the IMG office and then shared the information with Ken Mick, his stockbroker. Mick then encouraged several clients to buy ERG stock prior to the public announcement of the acquisition. Mick, in return for leaking this inside information to clients, received a special premium from the enriched investors. Mick then paid a portion of the premium to Peters. The SEC brought an action against Peters for violating Rule 10b-5. Under what theory might Peters be held liable for insider trading in violation of Rule 10b-5? Discuss fully. [*SEC v. Peters*, 735 F.Supp. 1505 (D.Kans. 1990)]

43-12. A Question of Ethics

Between 1970 and 1981, Sanford Weill had served as the chief executive officer (CEO) of Shearson Loeb Rhodes and several of its predecessor entities (collectively "Shearson"). In 1981, Weill sold his controlling interest in Shearson to the American Express Co. and between 1981 and 1985 served as president of that firm. In 1985, Weill developed an interest in becoming CEO for BankAmerica and secured a commitment from Shearson to invest $1 billion in BankAmerica if he was successful in his negotiations with that firm. In early 1986, Weill met with BankAmerica directors several times, but these contacts were not disclosed publicly until February 20, 1986, when BankAmerica announced that Weill had sought to become its CEO but that BankAmerica was not interested in his offer. The day after the announcement, BankAmerica stock traded at prices higher than they had been during the five weeks preceding the announcement. Weill discussed his efforts to become CEO of BankAmerica with his wife, who discussed the information with her psychiatrist, Dr. Willis, prior to BankAmerica's public announcement of February 20. She also told Dr. Willis about Shearson's decision to invest in BankAmerica if Weill succeeded in becoming its CEO. Willis disclosed to his broker this ma-

terial, confidential information and purchased BankAmerica common stock. After BankAmerica's public announcement and the subsequent increase in the price of its stock, Willis sold his shares and realized a profit of approximately $27,475.79. The court held that Willis was liable for insider trading under the misappropriation theory. [United States v. Willis, *737 F.Supp. 269 (S.D.N.Y. 1990)*]

1. The court stated in its opinion in this case that "[i]t is difficult to imagine a relationship that requires a higher degree of trust and confidence than the traditional relationship of physician and patient" and then quoted the concluding words of the Hippocratic oath: "Whatsoever things I see or hear concerning the life of men, in my attendance on the sick or even apart therefrom, which ought not be noised abroad, I will keep silence thereon, counting such things to be as sacred secrets." The court held that Willis had violated his fiduciary duty to Mrs. Weill, his patient, by investing in BankAmerica stock. Do you agree that Willis's private investments, which were based on information learned through his sessions with Mrs. Weill, constituted a violation of his duty to his patient? After all, Willis had not "noised abroad" Mrs. Weill's secrets—that is, he had not told others (except for his stockbroker) about the information. If you had been in Willis's shoes, would you have felt ethically restrained from trading on the information?

2. Can you think of any ways in which Willis's trading could have been harmful to Mrs. Weill's interests? Does your answer to this question have a bearing on how you would answer Question 1 above?

3. Do you think that Willis's liability for his breach of duty should extend only to Mrs. Weill? In other words, do you think that the misappropriation theory of liability imposes too great a burden on outsiders, such as Willis? Why or why not? How might you justify, from an ethical point of view, the application of the misappropriation theory to "outsider trading"?

Focus on Ethics

Business Organizations

Because all business activities take place in one of the types of business organizations discussed within this unit, all ethical issues relate, in one way or another, to the relationships that exist within these forms of business organization. In this *Focus on Ethics,* we examine selected areas in which ethical problems relate to the specific form in which business takes place—particularly, partnerships and corporations. We leave to the next unit the discussion of employer–employee ethical issues.

Fiduciary Duties—Revisited

In the introduction to this unit, we discussed the fiduciary duties of partners to each other and to the partnership, as well as the fiduciary duties of corporate directors, officers, and major shareholders to the corporate entity. In essence, the law of agency, as outlined in Unit Six of this book, permeates virtually all relationships within any partnership or corporation. An important duty that arises in the law of agency, and that applies to all partners and corporate directors, officers, and management personnel, is the duty of loyalty. As trustees of the shareholders' wealth,

corporate directors and officers also have a fiduciary duty to exercise care when making decisions affecting the corporate enterprise.

Duty of Loyalty

Every individual has his or her own personal interests, which may at times conflict with the interests of the partnership or corporation with which he or she is affiliated. In particular, a partner or a corporate director may face a conflict between personal interests and the interests of the business entity. Corporate officers may find themselves in a position to acquire assets that would also benefit the corporation if acquired in the corporation's name. In one landmark case, *Guth v. Loft, Inc.,*[1] Charles G. Guth, the president and a director of Loft, Inc., a soft-drink bottling company, negotiated with the Coca-Cola Company for a discount on its syrups. When negotiations with Coca-Cola failed to result in a discount for Loft, Guth decided to see what Pepsi-Cola could offer. During his investigation of this possibility, Guth set up a new corporation to acquire the secret formula and trademark

for the manufacture of Pepsi-Cola. He did so without offering the opportunity to Loft. A shareholder brought a suit against Guth, arguing that the shares of the new corporation should belong to Loft, and not to Guth personally. The shareholder prevailed. The court ruled that Guth had *usurped* a corporate opportunity in violation of his duty of loyalty to the corporation.

Duty of Care

In addition to the duty of loyalty, every corporate director or officer has a duty of care, which clearly involves a duty to make informed decisions. That means that the partner, director, or officer must take sufficient care to make sure that decisions reached are based on an appropriate amount of information. This issue arises when directors of a corporation accept too hastily a merger offer and submit that offer to the shareholders without taking the time to discover whether the offer is fair—that is, whether the offered price for the shares in the company is fair. One such case, *Smith v. Van Gorkom,*[2] occurred in Delaware when the chairman of the board of Trans

1.   5 A.2d 503 (Del. 1939).

2.   488 A.2d 858 (Del. 1985).

Union Corporation, Jerome W. Van Gorkom (who was about to retire), asked his chief financial officer (CFO) to work out a per-share value at which a leveraged buy-out by the current management could take place. The CFO hastily came up with a $55-per-share figure, compared with the current stock market value of $37 per share. Van Gorkom then called a board meeting on one day's notice to obtain approval for a merger that he had worked out at $55 per share. A merger agreement was delivered to the board members only a few hours before the next day's board meeting. At that meeting, Van Gorkom gave a twenty-minute oral presentation. The board approved the deal. At trial, the shareholders who were suing lost, but on appeal the court ruled that the directors were grossly negligent in reaching an "informed" decision. In spite of the fact that there had been no bad faith, no conflict of interests, and no fraud, the directors were not protected by the business judgment rule. They could not have reasonably based their decision on the CFO's reports; they should have had an independent valuation of the company prior to accepting the leveraged buy-out offer. Note here that the court's ruling was in spite of the fact that the merger offer was at a price per share of stock that was at a substantial premium over the market price of the stock.[3]

In *Van Gorkom,* the Delaware Supreme Court held that the directors were personally liable

"to the extent that the fair value of Trans Union [exceeded] $55 per share." The action was ultimately settled for $23.5 million. Part of this liability was covered by the insurance company that Trans Union used for directors' and officers' insurance—otherwise known as D&O insurance. The D&O insurance carried by the company provided $10 million of coverage.

Many corporations find that the cost of D&O coverage is prohibitive, and therefore they carry only a small amount or none whatsoever. Consequently, many individuals are reluctant to become directors of public corporations because of their exposure. It is risky business to be on a corporate board these days, and many corporate directors and officers have become increasingly cautious. Generally, unless they own a substantial percentage of shares in their corporations, directors have little to gain by taking business risks. The increasing lack of D&O insurance protection acts as a further incentive to be even more cautious. In many cases, when a corporation loses a substantial part of its D&O insurance, directors have little choice but to leave the corporation, just to protect themselves from potentially ruinous liability claims.

Business Judgment Rule

In some situations, directors and officers can escape liability for decisions that are ultimately detrimental to the corporation's interests if they can show that they used their best business judgment in reaching their decisions. A director will normally not be held to have breached his or her fiduciary

duty to the corporation or its shareholders for any business judgment that was made in good faith and that seemed reasonable at the time, under the circumstances, and with the information then available. Unless fraud, bad faith, gross overreaching, or abuse of discretion is present, the judgment of directors is conclusive, and courts are reluctant to interfere, even if a bad decision harms the corporation. The rationale for this rule is that directors are in a better position than either the courts or the shareholders to make business judgments concerning their corporations and that a certain flexibility is necessary if directors are to fulfill their responsibility as the ultimate managers of a corporate enterprise.

Consider, for example, the case of *Shlensky v. Wrigley,*[4] in which the question before the court was whether the director and controlling shareholder of the corporation that owned the Chicago Cubs major league baseball team had exercised sound business judgment when he decided not to install lights for nighttime baseball games. Shlensky, a minority shareholder of the corporation, sued Wrigley and other directors on behalf of the corporation. Schlensky asked the court to force the board of directors to install lights at Wrigley Field and to hold night games, because the Cubs were supposedly losing profits by not doing so, to the detriment of shareholders in the corporation. The reason Wrigley had refused to install the lights and initiate night games was because he felt

---

3. Van Gorkom wrote a scathing criticism of the appellate court's decision. See "Van Gorkom's Response: The Defendant's Side of the Trans Union Case," *Mergers and Acquisitions,* January/February 1988.

---

4. 95 Ill.App.2d 173, 237 N.E.2d 776 (1968).

such a step would result in a deterioration of the surrounding neighborhood and thus in a reduction in the property value of Wrigley Field. In this case, the court stated that it was "not their function to resolve for corporations questions of policy and business management. The directors are chosen to pass upon such questions and their judgment unless shown to be tainted with fraud is accepted as final."

Other courts, however, will not accept the judgment of directors as final, even though it is not "tainted with fraud." Such courts maintain that the business judgment rule, in some circumstances, can be used as a defensive tool by directors to avoid their responsibilities to stockholders. Those who share this attitude feel that there are times when directors' decisions should be closely scrutinized according to the benefit or detriment they cause to the stockholders and the specific conflict of interest involved.

Ethics and Hostile Takeovers

Merger mania, targets, poison pills, golden parachutes, greenmail, white knights. The shenanigans of corporate raiders, arbitrageurs, boards of directors, and investment banking firms have caught the attention of the press, politicians, and laypersons alike. It is true that in the United States (and now in Europe) the amount of corporate takeover activity seems to have increased. A number of corporate raiders have become famous—some because they have gone to jail for resorting to illegal activities. The unethical nature of actions that violate the law is clear. But what about corporate raiders and

arbitrageurs who do not violate the law? Are they acting ethically?

To answer this thorny question, let's take one example. A corporate raider learns, through diligent research and personal contacts, that a certain publicly traded company seems to be undervalued in the marketplace. That is to say, the public, or market, value of the company appears to be less than its true value. The corporate raider starts to acquire shares of the company's stock. Eventually, word gets out that she is doing this, and typically the market value of the stock rises. At some point, the corporate raider may make a tender offer to purchase a certain percentage of the outstanding shares of stock at a price that exceeds the current market price. If the corporate raider succeeds, she will acquire voting control of the corporation, oust the board of directors, put in her own people, and take over the corporation. Often, after this is done, the new board of directors will sell off certain parts of the company and restructure other parts. In the process, the lives of the previous managers and employees are altered—many of them are fired. The corporate raider is viewed as a greedy scoundrel. There was even a movie about this called *Wall Street,* in which the character played by Michael Douglas was portrayed as evil incarnate as he went about taking over corporations and then restructuring them.

As always, the ethical question here involves a tradeoff. The corporate raider typically will only go after control of a corporation that is poorly managed. If a corporation is well managed, its profits and its

profit potential will be high and therefore will be reflected in a high market value, thus making it an unlikely candidate for a takeover. When a corporate raider chooses a poorly managed company as a target, a certain group of individuals will gain—current shareholders. Another group will lose—current management and some employees.

What about arbitrageurs, those persons who have no true interest in actually taking over corporations but rather engage in buying and selling the stock of companies that are, or will be, the targets of takeover attempts? Is it ethical for these individuals to bid up the price of stock in a company that is a takeover target only to sell that stock at an inflated price? Again, the answer to this question depends on whom you want to benefit. If the arbitrageurs correctly predict what is going to happen, they will make a profit. If they predict incorrectly, a loss will be incurred. At the same time, because of increased buying pressure on the company's stock, current shareholders in the target corporation will gain more than they would have if an arbitrageur had never entered the marketplace.

Sometimes, corporate raiders may go past any well-reasoned ethical boundary. This occurs in the case of greenmail. In a greenmail situation, a so-called corporate raider has no intention of actually making a raid on the corporation, but he or she gives the impression that a takeover attempt is going to occur. A large block of stock is purchased, and a threat is brandished in front of current management. Often, the board of directors, in an attempt to make sure that no corporate raid occurs, will agree to buy back this large block of stock at an inflated price. The purported corporate raider obtains a handsome profit. The shareholders in the company actually lose. The only beneficiaries, besides the raider, seem to be current management, who have made sure that their jobs are protected.

The Plight of Minority Shareholders

Minority shareholders, particularly those in close corporations, often find themselves the victims of "freeze-outs" or "squeeze-outs" via mergers and other tactics. In such situations, they feel that fairness has been dealt a cruel blow, and in some cases, it has. As a remedy, the law allows minority shareholders to have their shares appraised by a court of law when, for example, a merger at a specific price per share is approved by a majority of shareholders, and a minority of shareholders believe that the price per share is too low. But it is not always certain whether a court's appraisal will be any higher—and it may be lower— than the price per share in the merger agreement. Thus, dissatisfied shareholders face an uncomfortable option when deciding whether they should elect to have the value of their shares appraised by a court.

Consider, for example, the decision facing minority shareholders of Kirby Lumber Corporation when, as a result of a short-form merger between Kirby and another corporation, minority shareholders were given notice that they could either accept the offered price of $150 per share or elect a judicial appraisal hearing. Some

of the minority shareholders opted to accept the $150-per-share offer, whereas others elected an appraisal. The appraisal proceeding resulted in a determination that the fair market value of a Kirby share was $254.40.[5] The minority shareholders who had accepted the $150 payment were, understandably, upset about their decision. They brought suit against Santa Fe Industries, Inc., (Kirby's parent corporation, which had arranged the merger), alleging that the merger was a "self-motivated" takeover that fraudulently enriched the majority at the expense of the minority.

The court, however, disagreed. The minority shareholders had the option of the judicial appraisal. The fact that they did not elect to choose that option was nobody's fault but their own. The only other alternative for the minority shareholders was to fight the merger, but because the minority shareholders controlled only 5 percent of Kirby stock, that would have been a patently useless endeavor.[6]

Insider Trading

Only in the last few years have Americans seen rich, successful financiers end up in jail because of some violation of securities laws. One law prohibits the use of inside information to profit in the trading of shares of stock in the corporation from which the information is gleaned. Even a *tippee* (an outsider) can be liable for insider trading under securities law if the tippee's acquisition of inside information

followed from an officer's or director's breach of his or her fiduciary duties. Tippees of tippees (remote tippees) can also be held liable if they knew, or should have known, that they were trading on improperly obtained inside information. For example, in *SEC v. Musella,*[7] a manager of a law firm passed inside information about corporate mergers and acquisitions planned by the firm's clients to a friend and the friend's stockbroker. The stockbroker passed the information on to a third party. That third party then shared the information with his brother, a police officer. The police officer then recommended to two other police officers that they purchase certain securities. All parties involved, including the latter two police officers, profited substantially from their investments, and other tips and investments followed. Could the two police officers, who never were told (and never inquired about) the source of the information, be held liable for insider trading as remote tippees? Yes, according to the court. Their liability was not founded on the fact that they *knew* that they were trading on improperly acquired inside information but on the fact that they *should have known* that such was the case. The court held that the two police officers "did not ask because they did not want to know," and just because they consciously avoided knowledge about the source of the information did not mean that they were not guilty under laws prohibiting insider trading.

Outsiders trading on inside information are normally held

---

5. *Bell v. Kirby Lumber Corp.*, 413 A.2d 137, (Del. 1980).
6. See *Loengard v. Santa Fe Industries, Inc.*, 639 F.Supp. 673 (S.D.N.Y. 1986).

---

7. 678 F.Supp. 1060 (S.D.N.Y. 1988).

liable for violating securities laws only if the trading is related to a breach of some duty. Recall from Chapter 43 that in *Chiarella v. United States*,[8] Chiarella was not held liable for trading on information obtained in the course of his work as a printer because the court held that no fiduciary duty had been breached. As mentioned in Case 43.4 in Chapter 43, however, had the jury been instructed to find liability under the misappropriation theory, Chiarella may well have been held liable for violating insider trading laws on the basis that he had violated a duty of loyalty to his employer. In a sense, the development of the misappropriation theory of liability has allowed courts to address more directly the simple ethical question: "Is such behavior right?"

Partnership or Corporation?

One of the major advantages of the corporate form of business is the limited liability of shareholders. No matter how indebted a corporation may become, shareholders will only be liable for corporate debts to the extent of their investment in the corporation. This limited liability does not apply to partners in a general partnership. If necessary, the personal assets of partners may be reached to satisfy partnership debts. Physicians, lawyers, and other professionals can now take advantage of the limited liability offered by corporations by incorporating as a professional corporation instead of doing business as a partnership. By doing business in the corporate form, the

shareholders' personal assets are not placed at risk when the firm incurs extensive debts or liabilities.

Even though this advantage of limited liability is a major consideration in a professional group's decision to incorporate, the corporate form does not absolutely guarantee that the shareholders will not be treated as partners by a court of law. Because the professional corporation is so similar to a partnership, courts will sometimes disregard the corporate form and apply partnership law.[9] At other times, corporate law will be applied. As an example of how different courts approach this issue, consider the case of *Hyland v. New Haven Radiology Associates, P.C.*[10] The plaintiff, Dr. Hyland, was one of four radiologists who had formed a professional corporation in 1972. In 1980, after hearing numerous complaints about Hyland's services—that he was often unavailable, was often uncooperative, indulged in abusive conduct, and so on— the corporation requested that he resign from the firm. Hyland, then fifty-one years old, brought suit against the corporation on the grounds that his requested resignation violated the Age Discrimination in Employment Act (ADEA), which makes it unlawful for an employer to discharge an employee forty years old or older because of the individual's age.

Because a corporate director can be both an employer and an employee at the same time, if the professional corporation were deemed by the court to be

a corporation, Hyland, as an employee of that corporation, would be covered by laws (including the ADEA) prohibiting employment discrimination. If the organization were deemed by a court to be a partnership, however, Hyland, as a partner, would not be considered an employee and thus would not come under the protection of legislation prohibiting age discrimination in employment. The court's decision as to whether partnership or corporate law should be applied was thus crucial to the outcome of Hyland's case.

The district court applied an "economic realities" test—that is, it looked at how the business actually was operated. The court noted that the firm closely resembled a partnership in the way in which it was structured and managed: each of the radiologists contributed the same amount of capital for equal shares in the corporation and an equal voice in management; they each served as a corporate officer or director; they divided the profits and losses of the business evenly among themselves; and stock was held only by shareholder-members, who were required to be licensed physicians. Therefore, the district court concluded that the shareholders were in fact partners and applied partnership law. As a partner, Hyland could not claim protection under the ADEA. The appellate court, however, took a different approach. That court reversed the district court's ruling, holding that the professional corporation was a corporation. In justifying its conclusion, the appellate court stated that "the use of the corporate form precludes any examination designed to determine whether the entity is

---

8. 445 U.S. 222, 100 S.Ct. 1108, 63 L.Ed.2d 348 (1980).

9. See, for example, *EEOC v. Dowd & Dowd, Ltd.*, 736 F.2d 1177 (7th Cir. 1984).

10. 794 F.2d 793 (2d Cir. 1986).

in fact a partnership. . . . The fact that certain modern partnerships and corporations are practically indistinguishable in structure and operation is no reason for ignoring a form of business organization freely chosen and established. Having made the election to incorporate, the professional corporation should not now be heard to say that it is essentially a medical partnership among co-equal radiologists."

Both approaches to the issue are grounded in ethical considerations. On the one hand, when a professional corporation operates essentially as a partnership, is it fair to let the shareholders escape the liability that attends the partnership form of business? On the other hand, when a court holds that a professional corporation is in fact a partnership and applies partnership law, the shareholders lose one of the essential benefits—that of limited liability—that prompted them to organize as a corporation in the first place. Such treatment obviously raises questions of fairness as well.

Ethics and Franchising

There is, as yet, no uniform law adopted by all of the states with respect to franchising. Therefore, the necessity of all parties, particularly the franchisor, to act in good faith is especially important. Many ethical issues arise when franchisees believe that they have been improperly treated by larger, more powerful franchisors—particularly when the franchisor decides to terminate the franchise arrangement to the economic detriment of the franchisee.

In franchise relationships, there is typically a wide disparity

in the bargaining power of the two parties to the franchise contract, and the franchisor holds most of the bargaining chips. This situation is particularly characteristic of dealership franchises in the oil and gas industry, in which the economic and legal power of a large oil company such as Shell or Amoco could easily be used to overwhelm an individual operating one of its service stations through a franchise agreement. A leading commentator in the area of franchise law wrote in 1971 that "the major oil firms have the gasoline station dealers in virtual bondage, hinged on the constant threat that their short-term contracts will not be renewed unless they submit to burdensome franchisor-imposed practices. . . . It is generally conceded that the gasoline station situation is almost hopeless and offers a prime example of the worst abuses in franchising."[11]

Such franchising abuses led Congress to enact the Petroleum Marketing Practices Act (PMPA) of 1979, which regulates the conditions and grounds for which a franchise relationship between franchisors and franchisees in the oil and gas industry can be terminated. The act requires that the franchisor give the franchisee reasonable notice of nonrenewal of the contract, and it provides that a franchisor may sell a service station or otherwise withdraw from a market area so long as the determination is "made in good faith and in the normal course of business." If a franchisor decides to sell the station, however, in the case of leased premises, the franchisor,

---

11. Brown, "Franchising—A Fiduciary Relationship," 49 *Texas Law Review* 650 (1971).

during the ninety-day period after notification to the franchisee that the franchise contract will not be renewed, must "(1) [have] made a bona fide offer to sell, transfer, or assign to the franchisee such franchisor's interest in such premises; or (2) if applicable, offered the franchisee a right of first refusal of at least 45 days duration of an offer, made by another, to purchase such franchisor's interest in such premises." The PMPA thus addressed the disparity in bargaining power between franchisors and franchisees in this industry by establishing certain rights for the franchisee in cases in which the franchisor wants to terminate the relationship.

People and business firms, however, do (or try to) circumvent the law on occasion, especially if they have the legal resources of a firm such as Amoco at their disposal—as Don Roberts of Des Moines, Iowa, learned through first-hand experience.[12] Roberts had operated an Amoco station in Des Moines for fifteen years, leasing the premises under a franchise arrangement with Amoco. His last lease had been for five years and was due to expire January 31, 1982. In early August 1981, Amoco sent Roberts a letter notifying him that Amoco was not going to renew the lease and that it intended to sell the premises. Soon thereafter, Amoco sent Roberts the offer to sell him the premises—in accordance with PMPA requirements—for $66,500. But there was a catch: the offer specifically excluded "the gasoline pumps, dispensers, storage tanks, and piping or other equipment"—in

---

12. *Roberts v. Amoco Oil Co.*, 740 F.2d 602 (8th Cir. 1984).

short, the essence of the business.

Roberts vacated the premises on October 1, 1981, and brought suit against Amoco for violating the PMPA. Roberts alleged that Amoco had violated the PMPA's requirement that the franchisor make a "bona fide offer to sell" the leased premises to the franchisee. Amoco, Roberts argued, had not made a "bona fide" offer, because the offer excluded equipment essential to the leased premises. The district court did not agree. Instead, it concluded that "nothing in the plaintiff's brief or the exhibits indicates that defendant's decision to sell the premises and not renew the lease was less than a good faith business decision." The court accepted Amoco's argument that the replacement cost of the pumps and tanks had been deducted from the selling price in the offer, and it granted Amoco's request for summary judgment.

"Trial courts search for truth, and appellate courts search for error"—so goes the anonymous saying. In this case, the appellate court found what it considered to be an error in the trial court's reading of the pertinent clause in the PMPA. In Section 2801(9) of the PMPA, the term "leased marketing premises" is defined as "marketing premises owned, leased, or in any way controlled by a franchisor and which the franchisee is authorized or permitted, under the franchise, to employ in connection with the sale, consignment, or distribution of motor fuel." The appellate court felt the language of the act was quite clear and that it clearly applied to this case: "When Congress required a franchisor to make a bona fide offer to sell the leased marketing premises to its

franchisee, Congress certainly intended the offer to include more than the real property. It explicitly required that the offer include the property controlled by the franchisor and used by the franchisee to distribute motor fuel. . . . We thus conclude that the district court erred in granting summary judgment for Amoco on Roberts' claim."

■ Discussion Questions

1. There are laws against "interlocking directorates," in which one individual serves on the boards of directors of competing companies. Normally, however, there is no law against a major shareholder in one corporation purchasing the securities of a competing corporation. If a law were passed making such a purchase illegal, who would benefit? Who would lose? Would society be better or worse off, on net, if such a law were passed?

2. One of the major disadvantages of the partnership form of business organization is that each partner's personal assets can, under many circumstances, be reached by creditors if the partnership assets are insufficient to satisfy a partnership debt. In view of this fact, why would anyone choose to do business using the partnership form? In other words, what advantages does a partnership offer to offset the major disadvantage of the personal liability of partners?

3. Many ethical issues involved in a franchising relationship are unique to that relationship—compared with, say, the relationship between an employee and an employer or between a corporate officer and the shareholders. What are the

unique ethical concerns in franchising relationships? To what extent does current law address these concerns? Why do you think it has been so difficult to create an acceptable uniform law of franchising?

4. The securities industry is heavily regulated not only by the Securities and Exchange Commission but also by numerous state securities commissions. In spite of such regulation, unwary investors lose millions of dollars each year due to the deceptive tactics of corporations, stockbrokers, and others involved in the sale of securities. Does this mean that more regulation and enforcement should be required? Why or why not? Alternatively, is "the nature of the beast" such that no amount of regulation will ever fully protect *all* investors? In either case, what are the tradeoffs involved with increased securities regulations that are created to protect investors? In other words, what are the costs and benefits of the securities laws and regulations that are enacted or created for the purpose of protecting investors?

5. There are those who argue that hostile takeovers injure employees, officers, and directors of the target companies. Others contend that such injuries inure to the benefit of the shareholders of target corporations. After all, the latter group would argue, such corporations would not be "targets" if they were properly managed. Discuss the pros and cons of hostile takeovers. What are the costs and benefits of laws that restrict—or make exceedingly difficult—hostile takeovers?

UNIT EIGHT

Government Regulation

■ Importance of Government Regulation

If this text had been written a hundred years ago, it would have had little to say about government regulation. In the 1890s, the beginnings of federal antitrust law were manifested in the form of the Interstate Commerce Commission Act and the Sherman Act, but there was little or no legislation affecting consumer protection or environmental issues. And the right of unions to organize had not yet been fully exercised.

Today, in contrast, government regulation permeates the entire business community. Administrative agencies today generate voluminous rules by which businesses must abide. Indeed, no businessperson can expect to understand fully how business works in America without understanding administrative agencies and regulation. State and federal regulations with respect to packaging and labeling, advertising, and the dumping of toxic waste affect numerous businesses. A knowledge of what is and is not anticompetitive behavior is critical to the decision making of many businesspersons; and the issues of employment discrimination, sexual harassment, and religious discrimination affect virtually every employer in this nation.

Chapter 44, which opens this unit on government regulation, examines the role of administrative agencies and their regulatory functions. Next, an introduction to consumer protection law is presented in Chapter 45. The important area of environmental law is covered in Chapter 46, followed by antitrust law in Chapter 47 and employment and labor relations law in Chapter 48.

■ Ethical Issues in Government Regulation

From a very broad perspective, ethical issues in government regulation arise because regulation, by its very nature, means that some traditional rights and freedoms have to be given up to ensure other rights and freedoms. Essentially, government regulation brings two ethical principles into conflict. On the one hand, deeply embedded in American culture is the idea that the government should play a limited role in directing our lives. Indeed, this nation was founded so that Americans could be free from the "heavy hand of government" experienced by the colonists under English rule. On the other hand, one of the basic functions of government is to protect the constitutional rights of individuals and, in the business community, the "little guy" from the "big guy." Therefore, Americans have pressured Congress to regulate business activities that result in harm to consumers and employees or that thwart competition in the marketplace.

Questions of fairness inevitably arise. Has the government gone too far in regulating a certain industry? Is the way in which regulation is carried out a little too arbitrary? Are the costs of compliance too burdensome for businesses—and for society—to bear? At what point, for example, is increased environmental protection simply too costly? If manufacturers ceased all production and Americans returned to the rural life of earlier times, the environment would certainly benefit. Obviously, Americans do not want to pay that high a cost. Certainly, we want to enjoy the fruits of our advanced economy. But environmental protection means that some sacrifices will have to be made. How much are we willing to sacrifice today to ensure that future generations have a more healthful world in which to live? These are very broad questions, but they are ethical in nature, because they ultimately relate to notions of what is right, just, or good.

Chapter 44

Introduction and Administrative Law

Hardly a day passes that one does not hear someone inveigh against the government's intrusion into our daily lives. A good part of Ronald Reagan's appeal as a candidate for president in 1980 was his promise to get "government off the backs of the people." The "government" in this and similar usage sentiments, more often than not, is the myriad bureaucratic agencies that we encounter in some form or other in almost every facet of our lives. Although the era of deregulation ushered in with the Reagan administration (actually it began, albeit somewhat hesitantly, during the latter part of the Carter administration) has lessened somewhat the *rate of growth* of government regulation, federal agencies continue each year to issue tens of thousands of pages of regulatory fine print. Whether as consumers or as suppliers of some factor of production, each of us is affected in profound and often subtle ways by the regulations promulgated by federal and state agencies.

Firms, both private and public, have been particularly affected by the regulations established by **administrative agencies.** A variety of agencies administer rules covering virtually every aspect of a business's operation. The Securities and Exchange Commission regulates the firm's capital structure and financing, as well as its financial reporting. The National Labor Relations Board governs its hiring and firing of employees and oversees relations between the firm and any unions with which it may deal. The Environmental Protection Agency and the Occupational Safety and Health Administration may affect the way it manufactures its products. The Federal Trade Commission may affect the way it markets these products. Added to this plethora of federal regulation is a second layer of state regulation that, when not preempted by federal legislation, may cover many of the same activities or regulate independently those activities not covered by federal regulation. Because state and local rules vary widely among the various jurisdictions, even a cursory examination of those rules would present an almost insurmountable task. Hence, this chapter will focus exclusively on federal administrative law.

Administrative agencies occupy an unusual niche in the Anglo-American legal scheme. In one light they may be viewed as quasi-administrative in form and function. In another light they are more aptly viewed as being quasi-legislative. And in yet another light they are more correctly viewed as being quasi-judicial in nature. Most agencies are considered part of the executive branch. Some, however, exist as **independent regulatory agencies.**[1] The significant difference between the two types of agencies lies in the accountability of the regulators. Agencies that are considered part of the executive branch are subject to the authority of the president; independent regulatory agencies are not, and their officials cannot be removed without cause. Notwithstanding this distinction, virtually all agencies have a range

of authority so broad as to make that authority seem legislative and judicial, as well as executive, in nature. This range of authority is at the heart of much of the controversy surrounding the regulatory process.

Federal administrative agencies are created by Congress. Statutes define the limits within which an agency operates, but any statutory delegation of power gives some discretion to the agency. Opponents of the administrative process argue that Congress may not totally delegate its legislative responsibility to an agency, however, without abdicating its responsibility under the U.S. Constitution to make the laws. In the following case, the United States Supreme Court considered whether Congress had delegated too much of its legislative power.

---

1. Most economic regulation is administered by independent agencies (the Interstate Commerce Commission, the Federal Communications Commission, the Federal Maritime Commission, and others). More recently established social regulatory agencies (the Occupational Safety and Health Administration, the Environmental Protection Agency, the Food and Drug Administration, and others) are within the executive branch.

BACKGROUND AND FACTS The National Industrial Recovery Act (NIRA) of 1933 provided that trade associations could issue their own codes of "fair competition" that, on the approval of the president, would have the force of law. A trade group in the poultry industry proposed a "poultry code," and President Roosevelt approved it. Aaron and Alex Schechter were wholesale kosher poultry dealers in Brooklyn, New York. They refused to comply with the code and consequently were charged with violating it. At their trial in federal district court, they argued, among other things, that the code system of the NIRA violated the Constitution by providing for the delegation of legislative power by Congress. The court held that the NIRA was not an unconstitutional delegation of power, reasoning that Congress was simply exercising its traditional authority to establish a general standard and to delegate authority to enforce it. The Schechters were convicted on eighteen counts; they appealed. The appellate court sustained the convictions on all counts but one. Both parties appealed to the United States Supreme Court.

Case 44.1

SCHECHTER POULTRY CORP. v. UNITED STATES

Supreme Court of the United States, 1935.
295 U.S. 495,
55 S.Ct. 837,
79 L.Ed. 1570.

DECISION AND RATIONALE The United States Supreme Court held that the NIRA's delegation of legislative power was unconstitutional and that thus the Schechters could not be found liable for violations of the poultry code. The Supreme Court characterized the NIRA as "a sweeping delegation of legislative power," in which trade associations "may roam at will, and the President may approve or disapprove their proposals as he may see fit." The Court explained that the statute did not prescribe standards for any trade or industry "to be applied to particular states of fact determined by appropriate administrative procedure." Instead the statute only authorized the making of codes to prescribe rules of conduct and did not provide adequate standards for the making of the codes. The court concluded, "We think that the code-making authority thus conferred is an unconstitutional delegation of legislative power."

The Creation of Regulatory Agencies

To create an administrative agency, Congress passes **enabling legislation,** which specifies the name, composition, and powers of the agency being created. The Federal Trade Commission (FTC), for example, was created in 1914 by the Federal Trade Commission Act.[2] The act prohibits unfair and deceptive trade practices. It also describes the procedures the agency must follow to charge persons or organizations with violations of the act, and it provides for judicial review of agency orders. Other portions of the act grant the agency powers to ''make rules and regulations for the purpose of carrying out the Act,'' to conduct investigations of business practices, to obtain reports from interstate corporations concerning their business practices, to investigate possible violations of federal antitrust statutes,[3] to publish findings of its investigations, and to recommend new legislation. The act also empowers the FTC to hold trial-like hearings and to adjudicate certain kinds of trade disputes that involve FTC regulations or federal antitrust laws. Notice that, as described earlier with regard to agencies in general, the FTC's grant of power incorporates functions associated with the legislature (*rulemaking*), the courts (*adjudication*), and the executive branch (*investigation* and *prosecution*).

The Operation of Administrative Agencies

The three operations—enforcement, rulemaking, and adjudication—make up the basic functions of most administrative agencies. Taken together, and supplemented by broad investigative powers, these three functions constitute what may be termed the **administrative process.**

Combining these functions into a single governmental entity creates the institutional flexibility that provides the salient rationale for creating any administrative agency; but it also concentrates considerable power in a single organization, however. For example, the Securities and Exchange Commission imposes rules regarding what disclosures must be made in a stock prospectus; under its enforcement authority, it also prosecutes alleged violations of these regulations; and finally, it sits as judge and jury in deciding whether its rules have been violated, and if so, what punishment to impose on the offender. Given this concentration of authority, one major policy objective of administrative law is to control the risks of bureaucratic arbitrariness and overreaching without hampering the effective use of agency power to deal with a particular problem area.

The two broad categories of control over the administrative process are (1) judicial control exercised through the courts' review of administrative agency actions and (2) political controls exercised by Congress and the executive branch. The other significant limitation to agency power is found in the Administrative Procedure Act (APA),[4] which imposes procedural requirements on an agency formulating policy under its rulemaking authority[5] or adjudicating the application of general statutory commands or established rules in a formal hearing.[6] The APA is such an integral part of the administrative process that its application will be examined as we go through the various functions carried out by an administrative agency.

Other legal restraints found in the U.S. Constitution and recognizable from earlier chapters are also applicable and will be examined in this section. The broad controls exercised by the legislature, the judiciary, and the executive branch will be reserved for a subsequent section. Note, however, that most of the legal challenges to agency action discussed in this section are those that are usually brought before an independent court for review. It also should be noted that the APA does not apply to all aspects of the administrative process, but rather only to those that are characterized as being formal in nature—a distinction that will be made clear later. The bulk of administrative decisions, however, are made informally, and to these actions, the provisions of the APA do not apply directly.

Enforcement

The enforcement function of an administrative agency has two aspects. An agency has investigative powers and prosecutorial powers.

---

2. 15 U.S.C. Sections 45 *et seq.*
3. The FTC shares this task with the Antitrust Division of the U.S. Justice Department.

4. 5 U.S.C. Sections 551–706.
5. 5 U.S.C. Section 553.
6. 5 U.S.C. Section 554.

COLLECTING FACTS—THE INVESTIGATIVE POWER Virtually every aspect of the administrative process requires that agencies obtain a wide array of information concerning the activities and organizations that they are charged with overseeing. Agencies, for example, frequently hold hearings before drafting new regulations and thus must have knowledge of facts and circumstances pertinent to the proposed rules. Agencies must obtain information and investigate conduct to ascertain whether the enabling statute or the agency's rules are being violated.

Sometimes the information needed may be provided voluntarily by an interested source such as a public interest group, a dissatisfied consumer, or a disgruntled competitor. When necessary information is not readily available, however, agencies have been accorded wide latitude in compelling its disclosure. The two most important investigative tools available to an administrative agency are **subpoenas** and **searches and seizures.**

Subpoenas There are two basic types of subpoenas: the subpoena *duces tecum* and the subpoena *ad testificandum*. The subpoena *duces tecum* may be used in any investigation. It is a writ, or order, compelling an individual or organization to hand over specified books, papers, records, or documents. The subpoena *ad testificandum* may be issued as part of an agency's adjudicative function. An *ad testificandum* subpoena compels a witness to appear before an *administrative law judge* in a controversy involving an administrative agency.

Searches and Seizures Many agencies gather information through on-site inspections. Sometimes a search of a home, an office, or a factory is the only means of obtaining evidence needed to prove a regulatory violation. At other times, physical inspections or testing are used in place of a formal hearing to correct or prevent an undesirable condition. Inspection and testing cover a wide range of activities, including safety inspections of underground coal mines, safety tests of commercial equipment and automobiles, and environmental monitoring of factory emissions.

CHALLENGES TO AGENCY INVESTIGATIVE POWERS—LEGAL REQUIREMENTS The intrusive nature of an agency's investigatory actions brings into play several legal safeguards against agency abuse in exercising its investigatory powers.

Legal Authorization and Legitimate Purpose First, Section 555(c) of the APA incorporates the general principle that an agency can exercise only such powers as have been delegated to it by Congress. Thus an agency's power to conduct a particular investigation must be based in some way on the powers conferred on the agency by the enabling legislation creating the agency. Generally, this limitation is easy to satisfy in practice, because the grant of regulatory power and investigative authority is usually drafted in broad terms by the legislature. The limitation is also easy to satisfy due to the fact that courts usually decide to let an investigation proceed because a possibly injured party will have the opportunity to challenge the investigation when and if the party challenges a final agency action. More likely to be scrutinized is an investigation that appears to have no legitimate purpose, or that appears to have been pursued for an improper purpose, such as harassment.

Information Sought Must Be Relevant The Fourth Amendment also provides a limitation on an agency's investigatory powers. Even if the investigation is carried out with legal authorization and for a legitimate purpose, any information sought must be relevant to that purpose. An investigating agency, however, does not need to meet the traditional "probable cause" standard in obtaining an administrative subpoena; rather than needing a good faith belief that a violation has occurred, the agency's investigation is justifiable "merely on suspicion that the law is being violated, or even just because it wants assurance that it is not." [7] This is a lesser standard, more akin to the standard applied to the investigative powers of a grand jury.

Investigative Demands Must Be Specific and Not Unreasonably Burdensome The Fourth Amendment stricture on unreasonable searches and seizures is also a barrier to abuse of agency investigative powers. But it, too, has been modified in the context of the administrative process. The

---

7. *United States. v. Morton Salt Co.*, 338 U.S. 632, 70 S.Ct. 357, 94 L.Ed. 401 (1950).

United States Supreme Court has held that, although an administrative subpoena must adequately describe the material sought, "the sufficiency of the specifications is variable in relation to the nature, purposes, and scope of [the agency's] inquiry." [8] Although claims of unreasonable burden are often raised, seldom are they successful, despite the substantial costs of assembling and copying materials, the disruption to an organization or individual's business activities, and the like. Through the use of protective court orders and other procedural devices, however, a business generally will be protected from the dissemination of proprietary information and trade secrets.

Privileged Information May Be Protected   The common law recognized certain communications, such as those between husband and wife and between lawyer and client, as being privileged. There has also been a trend, at least at the state level, to extend the protection to other types of communications, such as protecting accountant-client communications and news reporters' confidential sources. These protections, however, have seldom been tested in connection with administrative agency investigations, and it is unclear how and to what extent they apply in the administrative law context. One problem is that there is no general federal law governing the application of protections not directly derived from the U.S. Constitution. Another problem is that enabling legislation and agency regulations seldom address these questions.

The Privilege against Self-Incrimination   More substantial than the preceding privileges is the protection against compelled, self-incriminating testimony afforded by the Fifth Amendment. This too is limited in the context of the administrative process. First, with some limitation, an agency has fairly broad power to require that certain records be kept by an individual or organization and that the records be made available to the agency on demand as part of a regulatory program. Second, the privilege against self-incrimination is available only to the person asserting it; it cannot be asserted on behalf of another individual or an organization. [9]

The privilege can be lost if the person asserting it is given immunity from prosecution based on evidence obtained solely from that individual's testimony. Finally, and perhaps most important in the context of administrative law, the privilege is only available if the penalty that might be imposed on the individual as a result of the testimony is criminal rather than civil in nature. For many regulatory regimes, the sanctions imposed for violations of administrative regulations are termed "civil penalties" or "forfeitures." Only those sanctions that are designed to effect some retribution or promote deterrence are likely to be deemed criminal penalties.

The Warrant Requirement   The Fourth Amendment protects against unreasonable searches and seizures by requiring that, in most instances, a physical search for evidence must be conducted under the authority of a warrant. Although it was once thought that administrative inspections were exempt from the warrant requirement, the United States Supreme Court, noting the anomaly of affording protection only in cases of suspected criminal activity, has held that the requirement does apply to the administrative process.

With regard to administrative searches, as in other areas of administrative law, however, the standard principles have been significantly modified. First, the standard of probable cause is different: "it may be based not only on specific evidence of an existing violation *but also on a showing that 'reasonable legislative or administrative standards for conducting an . . . inspection are satisfied with respect to a particular [establishment].' "* [10] [Emphasis added.]

Second, although the United States Supreme Court has recognized a legitimate expectation of privacy in commercial, as well as private, dwellings, it has continued to allow warrantless searches of commercial premises that are part of a "pervasively regulated" industry, provided that (1) there is a substantial government interest in the regulatory scheme under which the search is conducted, (2) a warrantless scheme is necessary to further that regulatory scheme, and (3) the terms of the search program are defined so as to limit the

---

8.   *Oklahoma Press Publishing Co. v. Walling*, 327 U.S. 186, 66 S.Ct. 494, 90 L.Ed. 614 (1946).

9.   A corporation is not a "person" under the Fifth Amendment.

10.   *Marshall v. Barlow's, Inc.*, 436 U.S. 307, 98 S.Ct. 1816, 56 L.Ed.2d 305 (1978).

risk that inspectors will abuse their discretion in conducting the search.

The "open field" doctrine is also applicable to administrative searches. It provides an exception to the warrant requirement by allowing searches of areas so open to plain view that no reasonable expectation of privacy could be entertained. In a recent case, the Environmental Protection Agency (EPA), when denied access to make a ground inspection, took an aerial photograph of a Dow Chemical plant without Dow's permission. When

Dow brought suit against the EPA, alleging a violation of the Fourth Amendment, the Supreme Court upheld the search under the "open field" doctrine.[11]

In the following case, the court considers the extent of an agency's investigative powers.

---

11. *Dow Chemical Co. v. United States,* 476 U.S. 227, 106 S.Ct. 1819, 90 L.Ed.2d 226 (1986).

BACKGROUND AND FACTS The Federal Home Loan Bank Board (FHLBB) operated the Federal Savings and Loan Insurance Corporation (FSLIC). The FHLBB's duties included examining all FSLIC-insured institutions to determine whether they were being operated properly under applicable laws and regulations. As part of an investigation of Texas-based Vision Banc Savings and Loan, the FHLBB became suspicious of a large loan made to Sandsend Financial Consultants, Ltd. Hoping to trace the proceeds of the loan, the FHLBB subpoenaed Sandsend's financial records from a second bank, West Belt. Sandsend asked a federal district court to quash the subpoena, which, for reasons not fully articulated, the court did. The FHLBB appealed. Although the government's ability to subpoena bank records is circumscribed by procedures of the Right to Financial Privacy Act, the central issue before the appellate court was the scope of the FHLBB's investigatory authority.

Case 44.2

SANDSEND FINANCIAL CONSULTANTS, LTD. v. FEDERAL HOME LOAN BANK BOARD

United States Court of Appeals, Fifth Circuit, 1989.

878 F.2d 875.

DECISION AND RATIONALE The United States Court of Appeals for the Fifth Circuit reversed the district court's decision and directed the court to enforce the subpoena. The appellate court held that "[t]he FHLBB's subpoena power extends to Sandsend's financial records; it is not limited to parties directly associated with the target of an investigation." The court noted that an "agency's power to issue subpoenas is a broad-ranging one which courts are reluctant to trammel." Also, the court saw its role in reviewing an administrative subpoena as "strictly limited" to asking only "(1) whether the investigation is for a proper statutory purpose and (2) whether the documents the agency seeks are relevant to the investigation." The court found that the FHLBB's examination of Vision Banc was a legitimate law-enforcement inquiry and that Sandsend's records were relevant to the inquiry. The court explained that as long as material "touches a matter under investigation," an administrative subpoena will survive a challenge that the material is not relevant. The court acknowledged that Sandsend had only a tangential relationship to Vision Banc but pointed out that Sandsend's financial records touched on a matter under investigation—the misuse of Vision Banc's funds.

CORRECTING VIOLATIONS—THE PROSECUTORIAL POWERS Having undertaken and concluded an investigation, an agency may bring an administrative action against an individual or or

ganization by issuing a **complaint**, the first step in an administrative action. Complaints also are brought by private citizens and organizations, but are prosecuted by the agency having authority over the particular subject matter. Because the agency is acting as prosecutor, judge, and jury, certain procedural devices have been devised to safeguard against an agency's abuse of authority. These will be discussed in the subsequent subsection on adjudication. At this juncture, however, it is useful to note that the majority of such actions are resolved at their initial stage, without resorting to the formal adjudicatory process. The fact that regulated industries often want to avoid the appearance of being uncooperative with the regulating agency, the fact that regulators are likely to have acquired pertinent information over a prolonged period of regulation, and the cost of litigation make settlement an appealing option to firms. Because settlements also conserve agency resources, agencies devote a great deal of effort to advising and negotiating so as to avoid formal actions.[12]

Rulemaking

The second major function of an administrative agency is the formulation of new regulations—the so-called **rulemaking** function. The power an agency has to make rules is conferred on it by Congress in the agency's enabling legislation. Enabling legislation is almost always written in very broad terms, but Congress is constitutionally limited in how much power to promulgate regulations it can delegate to an agency. The standards that are applied in testing whether or not a delegation is too broad to meet constitutional demands have changed over the years from being rather slight initially to being very stringent during the early 1930s and then progressively becoming less stringent again. The most demanding standard was the one applied in the famous "Sick Chicken Case," *Schechter Poultry Corp. v. United States.*[13] Another principle is worth mentioning at this point. Only Congress can establish that certain violations of agency regulations will incur criminal sanctions; it cannot delegate the authority to the agency to decide which regulations will be treated as criminal offenses.

---

12.   One way in which an agency advises on questions of how it interprets a statute and how it will respond to certain actions by private parties is through issuing "interpretative rules." See the discussion of interpretative rules in the subsection on rulemaking below. See also the subsection on the adjudication process.

13.   See Case 44.1.

One of the most significant developments in administrative law since the 1970s has been the increased importance of agency rulemaking as a means of formulating public policy. The major advantage of rulemaking is that it can resolve in one proceeding issues that might remain unsettled for years if case-by-case adjudication were the only means of effecting agency policy.

TYPES OF AGENCY RULES   There are three types of rules that an agency may create: (1) *legislative rules,* (2) *interpretative rules,* and (3) *procedural rules.*

Legislative Rules   **Legislative rules** carry the same weight as congressionally enacted statutes. Their validity, though, depends on certain strict requirements being met. First, a legislative rule will be struck down by the courts if it violates any provision of the U.S. Constitution (for example, if it violates due process or denies equal protection). Second, the rule must not involve an impermissible delegation of legislative authority to the agency; that is, there are certain powers that the U.S. Constitution grants exclusively to Congress and that cannot be delegated by Congress to the judiciary or executive branch of government or to an independent agency. Third, the rule must not operate in a way that exceeds the power conferred on the agency by its enabling legislation. Also important is that the enabling statute itself provide reasonable standards to guide the agency in carrying out its administrative tasks. Finally, unless Congress expressly provides an exemption, legislative rules enacted must be promulgated in accordance with provisions of the APA.

The other two types of agency rules, interpretative and procedural rules, need not be enacted in accordance with the provisions of the APA. Nor do they carry the same force as legislative rules, which, as already noted, carry the same weight as a statutory rule of law enacted by the legislature.

Interpretative Rules   **Interpretative rules** are simply statements and opinions issued by an agency explaining how the agency interprets and intends to apply the statutes it enforces. Such an opinion might be rendered by the Securities and Exchange Commission, for example, about whether a particular security is subject to its registration requirements and, if so, what information must be disclosed in a public offering. Because interpretative rules do not have the force of rules of law, they are not automatically binding on private individuals or organizations. They also are not binding on the courts in the way that rules of law are. In practice, however, the courts tend to give considerable weight to interpretative rules when deciding cases involving other agency regulations.

Procedural Rules **Procedural rules** describe an agency's methods of operation and establish procedures for dealings with the agency in and through hearings, negotiations, settlements, presentation of evidence, and other activities.

THE RULEMAKING PROCESS As the number and significance of policy objectives carried out through legislative rules have grown, so too have the rulemaking procedures that must be followed. Under the APA, there are three types of agency rulemaking procedures: (1) *"notice-and-comment" rulemaking, or informal rulemaking*; (2) *"rulemaking-on-a-record," or formal rulemaking*; and (3) *exempted rulemaking*.[14] The third is of limited applicability and applies in special circumstances such as military matters or foreign affairs; thus, it will not be discussed here. Dissatisfaction with aspects of both informal and formal types of procedures has been the impetus for the development of another type of procedural form called *hybrid rulemaking* which is not covered by provisions of the APA.

Notice-and-Comment Rulemaking **Notice-and-comment rulemaking,** also characterized as **informal rulemaking**, is the most common type. Although termed informal, it is nonetheless governed by the provisions of the APA. There are three requirements imposed by the APA: (1) notice, (2) opportunity for comment, and (3) a general statement of basis and purpose. These requirements parallel the sequence of events that must occur before a rule is adopted. The informal process begins with publication of a **Notice of Proposed Rulemaking** in the *Federal Register*. The notice must state the time and place for which agency proceedings on the proposed rule will be held, as well as a description of the nature of the proceedings. The notice also must state the legal authority

for the proceedings, which is usually the agency's enabling legislation. Finally, the notice must either state the terms of the proposed rule or the subject matter of the proposed rule.

Publication of notice of the proposed rule is followed by a **comment period.** The purpose of publication of notice is to allow private parties to comment in writing on the agency proposal in an effort to influence agency policy. After having received and reviewed the comments, the agency takes them into account in drafting the regulation's final version, which is usually modified from the proposed rule. If the final version of the regulation is dramatically different, it must be reproposed. The agency publishes the final version of the regulation in the *Federal Register*. The regulation does not become binding until at least thirty days after final publication unless there is ''good cause'' for its becoming effective sooner. There is also an exemption to the notice requirement whenever such is unnecessary, impractical, or contrary to the public's interest.

Rulemaking-on-a-Record **Rulemaking-on-a-record,** or **formal rulemaking,** also begins with publication of a notice of proposed rulemaking in the *Federal Register*. In this procedure, though, the announced proceedings are much more extensive, amounting to a public hearing and being conducted in the manner of a trial. At the hearing, the agency presents evidence intended to justify the proposed rule. Anyone opposing the proposed rule may present evidence to counter the agency's claims. Both sides are permitted to examine the evidence presented and to cross-examine each other's witnesses. After the hearing is concluded, the agency is required to prepare a formal written statement describing its findings based on the evidence presented by both sides.

Hybrid Rulemaking Informal and formal rulemaking both offer special advantages, but each also has distinct disadvantages. Informal rulemaking is efficient in its simplicity. Yet its streamlined procedures afford little opportunity to interested parties to learn and contest the basis of a proposed legislative rule. Formal rulemaking, although providing ample opportunity to interested parties to participate in the formulation of agency rules, is torturously slow in producing public policy responses to pressing problems. A famous example

---

14. 5 U.S.C. Section 533.

is that of the Food and Drug Administration's attempts to establish a rule setting the minimum peanut content for peanut butter. The agency attempted to set the minimum at 90 percent. When industry countered with a proposal of 87 percent, it produced a series of formal proceedings that delayed regulation for nearly ten years.

As rulemaking became an increasingly important part of agency decision making, and as frustration over the shortcomings of APA procedures increased, the courts and later the legislature began a search for alternatives. The result has been a set of ill-defined procedures referred to as **hybrid rulemaking**. These procedures incorporate advantages of both the formal and informal procedures. Like formal rulemaking, there is an opportunity for direct participation through a public hearing. The right of interested parties to cross-examine witnesses is much more restricted, however. Also, as we will see in the subsection on judicial review, the standard applied by an independent court in reviewing an agency's procedures is different.

Adjudication

As noted already, an agency not only sets the rules pursuant to its enabling statute but also enforces its own rules through its investigatory powers. Moreover, its enforcement entails prosecuting alleged offenders of agency rules in trial-like proceedings before an **administrative law judge (ALJ)** or, in some instances, before the appointed heads of the agency, its board of commissioners. Thus the agency acts as police officer, prosecutor, judge, and jury in agency **adjudication.**

ADMINISTRATIVE LAW JUDGES   Formally, an ALJ is a member of the very agency prosecuting the case. Certain safeguards exist, however, to promote fairness in the proceedings. The ALJ is separated in the agency's organization from the investigative and prosecutorial staff, according to provisions of the APA. The APA also prohibits private communication (*ex parte*) between the ALJ and anyone who is party to an agency proceeding. Finally, provisions of the APA protect the ALJ from agency discipline except on a clear showing of good cause for such action.

THE PROCESS OF ADJUDICATION   After conducting its own investigation of a suspected rule

violation, an agency may decide to take action against specific parties. In some cases (for example, FTC action on alleged false advertising), an agency's actions may be prompted by private individuals or interest groups. Procedures vary among the various agencies, but a typical scenario of adjudication might proceed as follows. (This process is illustrated in Exhibit 44–1.)

The initial investigatory phase might involve taking statements under oath by one of the agency's staff attorneys. (To promote fairness, an agency's investigative and prosecutorial staff is formally separate from the members of its commission. In fact, if these members were to take a prosecutorial role at this stage, they would likely be disqualified from ruling on the case at a later stage.) Alternatively, the agency might request documents or records of some kind. In most instances, the agency's requests are enforceable by an order from a federal court ordering that a party comply with the agency's request; failure to comply with the court order can result in fines or even jail sentences for contempt of court.

During this phase of the process, the agency may make an offer to negotiate and reach some settlement, or agreement, concerning the action with which the agency is concerned. If no settlement between the agency and the parties under investigation is reached, then the agency staff could seek approval of the agency head or commissioners to issue a formal complaint. The complaint is issued as a public document and may be accompanied by a press release. The party charged in the complaint responds by filing an answer. The case then is presented before an ALJ in an administrative hearing.

The Administrative Hearing   An administrative adjudication is very much like that of an ordinary trial court proceeding. The charged party may be represented by counsel, cross-examine agency witnesses, and present its own evidence to counter the agency's. There are significant differences, however. Significantly, the ALJ decides both questions of law and fact; there is no jury. Also important is the nature of the evidence: it may be evidence of general circumstances rather than relating solely to the charged party. The ALJ, cognizant of the role that the agency's adjudicative function plays in determining the broader aspects of agency policy, takes into consideration the impact of any decision on the public interest and not just its effect on the individual parties involved in the case.

■ **Exhibit 44–1 The Process of Administrative Adjudication**

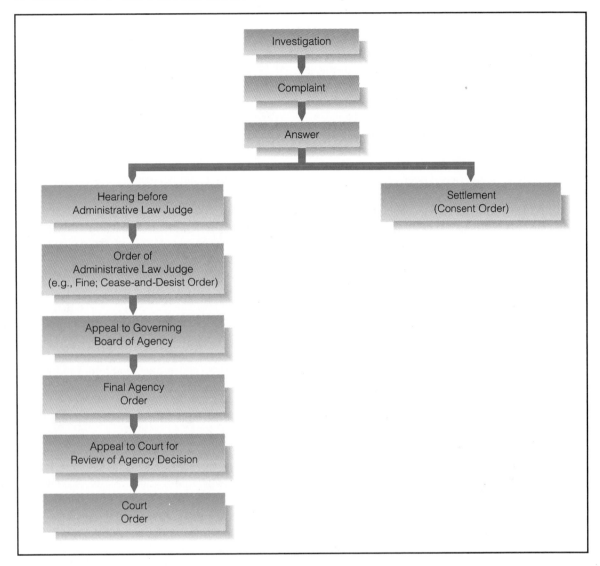

Initial Order   After the case is concluded, the ALJ renders an **initial order.** Either side may appeal the ALJ's initial order. An appeal is usually taken to a federal circuit court, though some intermediate decisions may be appealed to a federal district court. It is also possible in some cases that the commission that governs the agency will decide on its own to review the case. If it does so, it may consider all aspects of the case freshly, as though no prior decisions had been rendered.

Final Order   If no appeal is taken, or if the case is not reviewed or considered anew by the agency

commission, the ALJ's initial order becomes the **final order** of the agency. Otherwise, the final order must come from the commission's decision or that of the reviewing court.

Cease-and-Desist Orders   The final order may compel the charged party to pay damages, or it may forbid the party from carrying on some specified activity. The latter is referred to as a **cease-and-desist order** and in effect is identical to an ordinary court's injunction.

■ Control over Administrative Agencies

Agency authority is held in check by several sources of limitation. Some of these we have already encountered. The U.S. Constitution limits agency authority, and the APA significantly affects the formal administrative process. Additionally, the source of agency authority, the enabling legislation of the agency, is by implication a source of limitation as well.

There remains, however, the task of looking at the broader scheme of control over agency power, that is, the political and judicial control over agency power. Political control over agency power is found in both the executive and legislative branches of government. Judicial control is exercised by the independent review of agency action by the United States Supreme Court, the federal courts of appeal, and in more limited instances, the federal district courts.

Executive Control

Executive control over agency power is exercised through several means. First, the president may exercise veto power over any enabling legislation or subsequent modifications to agency authority that Congress may seek to enact. Another important power over agency affairs is the president's authority to appoint and remove federal officers. In theory, this power is less pronounced in the case of independent agencies whose officers serve for fixed terms and who cannot be removed without just cause. In practice, however, the president's power to exert influence over independent agencies is often considerable.

Typically, agencies that are headed by a set of commissioners have the commissioners' terms of appointment staggered. Because many commissioners do not serve out their full terms, newly elected presidents often are given the opportunity to appoint new commissioners. Moreover, the president generally has the statutory power to designate who among the commissioners will serve as chairperson; a new appointment demotes a sitting commission chairperson to the status of ordinary commissioner. The chairperson generally has the primary responsibility for managing agency operations, including the hiring of personnel. Thus this power affords the president a means of indirectly influencing the policies of an independent agency.

Legislative Control

As Congress gives power to an agency, so too, through subsequent legislation, can it take away power or even abolish an agency altogether. Congress has often moved quickly to counter agency decisions that have inflamed public ire. In the wake of public furor over a controversial National Highway Traffic Safety Administration seat belt requirement, for example, Congress amended the act creating the agency. The amendment prohibited the agency from instituting regulations requiring that cars not start unless the seat belts are fastened or that cars have a warning buzzer that sounds continuously until the seat belts are fastened. Congress's power of the purse (the constitutional taxing and spending powers) also gives it considerable power to influence agency policy. First, there must be legislative authorization for appropriation of government funds to a specific agency. This is usually contained in the enabling legislation and may set certain time and monetary limits for funding particular programs. Congress, of course, can always revise these limits.

In addition to the formal legislating and funding powers that Congress exercises, it has authority to investigate the implementation of its statutory laws and the agencies that it has created. It may also affect agency policy through its "casework" activities. This involves individual legislators' attempts to assist their constituents in dealings with agency staff and officers. Ostensibly, the legislator is performing the role of an "ombudsman" watching over the agency and helping to ensure that the agency treats his or her clients fairly. Performing this role also provides the legislator with an opportunity to identify problem areas that can be corrected through congressional action. There is a fine line, though, between what is considered proper casework and what is construed as an attempt to pressure an agency into making an improper decision in favor of a constituent.

Judicial Review

Through the political process, both the legislative and executive branches exercise considerable influence over the regulatory policies of administrative agencies. The courts, in deciding individual controversies rather than broad policy initiatives, also exercise a considerable amount of control over the regulatory process. The political process requires time and effort in building coalitions entertaining a uniform objective before action is likely to be effective. In contrast, the courts provide a direct avenue for the review of agency action. As will be seen, however, not all agency action is subject to judicial review, nor is every individual entitled to challenge an agency's actions.

THE SCOPE OF JUDICIAL REVIEW   The APA provides for judicial review of most agency action. In its exercise of control over agency actions, a court may compel agency action it deems to have been unlawfully withheld, or it may prevent action it determines to have exceeded agency authority. In reviewing administrative actions, the courts are reluctant to review questions of fact; in most cases, deference is given to the facts found in the initial agency proceeding. This stems partly from the general judicial attitude that those who hear and see the evidence presented firsthand are more suited to judge its value. In the context of administrative process, this attitude is reinforced by the courts' deference to the expertise of the agency involved. The courts, however, will conduct a hearing to make an independent finding of facts, a *de novo review,* if (1) such a review is required by statute, (2) inadequate fact-finding proceedings were employed by the agency initially adjudicating the case, or (3) new facts are raised in a proceeding to enforce a nonadjudicatory action. Nor are courts generally interested in the merits of policy determinations; thus, review of policy issues is generally limited to ascertaining whether the agency is carrying out the will of Congress as enunciated in the enabling legislation. The court is primarily concerned with the legal issues raised in a controversy over agency actions. But here too there are limits to the scope of its review.

DEFENSES TO AGENCY ENFORCEMENT   It is never a defense to an agency action that an individual or organization believes the action to be unlawful. In some cases an intermediate appeal to avoid irreparable harm from delay may be taken to avoid agency action. In other cases, however, the only course available is not to comply and then seek judicial review of the agency's enforcement. The following are the bases to any defense of

agency action. The court will review (1) whether the agency has exceeded the authority conferred by the agency's enabling legislation; (2) whether the agency has properly interpreted laws applicable to the agency action under review; (3) whether the agency has violated any constitutional provisions; (4) whether the agency has acted in accordance with procedural requirements of the law; (5) whether the agency's actions were arbitrary, capricious, or an abuse of discretion; and (6) whether any conclusions drawn by the agency are not supported by substantial evidence.

CONDITIONS TO REVIEW OF ENFORCEMENT ACTION   Agency enforcement actions are not automatically subject to review. Parties seeking to have an action reviewed must satisfy several preliminary requirements.

Reviewability   First, the challenger, or plaintiff, must show that the action is of a nature that is reviewable. This is generally quite easy in that the APA creates a presumption in favor of reviewability. To overcome the statutory presumption, the opponent must be able to show either that Congress has enacted a statute that precludes review, thus negating the APA presumption, or that the agency's action is committed to agency discretion as a matter of law. The latter is often difficult to show even apart from the APA because the functioning of the three equal branches of government generally implies the authority of judicial review. Congress does have authority, however, to establish the scope of jurisdiction of the federal courts. Moreover, the judiciary is deferential to the proper functions of the other branches of government. For example, problems of a strictly political nature or involving foreign affairs are generally viewed as being outside the proper scope of judicial review.

Standing   A second requirement for review is that the challenging party have "standing to sue." Challengers must have a direct stake in the outcome of the judicial proceeding by showing their interests have been substantially affected by the agency's action. This requirement, though perhaps not quite as easy to meet as the first requirement, has become more liberalized in recent years. The injury suffered must be to an interest within the range of interests protected by the statute or constitutional provision that provides the basis of the challenge.

An injury to an economic interest, or even in some cases to an emotional, environmental, or aesthetic interest, is sufficient to show standing to sue.

Exhaustion of Available Remedies   Courts are reluctant to interfere with the regulatory process, hoping to allow the agencies to correct their own mistakes and to develop fully the regulatory scheme before subjecting the scheme to independent judicial review. Courts, therefore, will not generally review an action until the challenging party has exhausted all possible alternative means of resolving the controversy with the agency.

Ripeness   The final requirement for review is that an actual case or controversy be at issue. This requirement is based on Article III, Section 2, of the U.S. Constitution, which, as interpreted by the United States Supreme Court, prohibits advisory opinions. When considering whether a dispute meets this requirement, courts have been willing to weigh the benefits of allowing time to refine the controversy against the harm of delaying review.

THE STANDARD OF REVIEW   There are two standards of review. Which one is applied depends on whether the procedure under review is a formal agency adjudication or rulemaking, or an informal agency adjudication or rulemaking.

Substantial Evidence Test   In reviewing formal agency adjudications or rulemaking, courts, under the APA, must apply the "substantial evidence" test. Under this test, only those findings that are unsupported by substantial evidence may be overturned. In applying this test, the reviewing courts determine the reasonableness of the challenged agency action as juxtaposed with the facts before the court that could be used to justify the action. Note that this is a different exercise than the *de novo* review described above in which the court conducts a hearing to make an independent finding of fact.

Arbitrary and Capricious Test   A different standard of review is applied with regard to informal agency adjudications and rulemaking. It is the "arbitrary and capricious" test and is the least rigorous standard of judicial review. In applying the test, the court seeks to avoid substituting its judgment for that of the agency's, seeking instead to look for merely an adequate factual basis for the agency's action. Unless the court can point to a "clear error of judgment," it will not strike down the agency's decision. The following case involved an application of the arbitrary and capricious test.

Case 44.3

MARSH v. OREGON NATURAL RESOURCES COUNCIL

Supreme Court of the United States, 1989. 490 U.S. 360, 109 S.Ct. 1851, 104 L.Ed.2d 377.

BACKGROUND AND FACTS   Four nonprofit organizations sued the Army Corps of Engineers in a federal district court. The organizations claimed that the Corps had violated the National Environmental Policy Act (NEPA) of 1969 by failing to prepare a supplemental Environmental Impact Statement (EIS) based on information contained in two studies—an Oregon Department of Fish and Wildlife (ODFW) memorandum and a U.S. Soil Conservation Service (SCS) survey—regarding a three-dam project that the Corps had begun along Oregon's Rogue River Basin. The Corps contended that the EIS was unnecessary; the Corps claimed that on the basis of its own analysis, as well as that of independent research it had commissioned, the two studies were not indisputable and in any event were of exaggerated importance in assessing the project. The court denied the organizations' request that the Corps be enjoined from completing the project. On appeal, the appellate court affirmed part of the district court's decision, reversed part of the decision, and remanded the case to the district court. The Corps petitioned for *certiorari,* which was granted.

DECISION AND RATIONALE   The United States Supreme Court reversed the appellate court's decision and remanded the case for further proceedings. The Supreme Court concluded that the issue before the reviewing court, whether the Corps's determination not to prepare an EIS should be set aside, was controlled by the arbitrary and capricious standard. The Court characterized the question as "a classic example of a factual dispute the resolution of which implicates substantial agency expertise." The Court reasoned that "[b]ecause analysis of the relevant documents 'requires a high level of technical expertise,' we must defer to 'the informed discretion of the responsible federal agencies.' " The Court explained that under the arbitrary and capricious standard, a reviewing court "must consider whether the decision was based on a consideration of the relevant factors and whether there has been a clear error of judgment." The Court concluded that "[e]ven if another decisionmaker might have reached a contrary result, it was surely not 'a clear error of judgment' for the Corps to have found that the new and accurate information in the documents was not significant and that the significant information was not new and accurate. * * * [T]he Corps conducted a reasoned evaluation of the relevant information and reached a decision that, although perhaps disputable, was not 'arbitrary or capricious.' "

■ Public Accountability

Over the last two decades, there has been a growing concern over the powers exercised by administrative agencies. As a result, Congress has passed several laws to make agencies more accountable through public scrutiny. The most significant of these laws are the Freedom of Information Act, the Government-in-the-Sunshine Act, and the Regulatory Flexibility Act.

Freedom of Information Act

Enacted in 1966, the Freedom of Information Act (FOIA) requires the federal government to disclose certain "records" to "any person" on request, even without that person's disclosing the reason for the request.[15] Although the FOIA exempts certain types of records, a request that complies with the FOIA procedures need only contain a reasonable description of the information sought. An agency's failure to comply with a request may be challenged in a federal district court.

The FOIA is utilized by the media, industry trade associations, public interest groups, and even companies seeking information about competitors.

Note that although the FOIA allows agencies to deny requests for exempted information, it does not compel them to do so, and a person cannot compel an agency to refuse disclosure of exempted information about that person.

Government-in-the-Sunshine Act

The Government-in-the-Sunshine Act, or "open meeting law," was passed in 1976. It requires that "every portion of every meeting of an agency" that is headed by a "collegial body" must be open to "public observation."[16] The act also requires procedures to ensure that the public is provided with adequate advance notice of the agency's scheduled meeting and agenda. Like the FOIA, the Sunshine Act contains certain exceptions. There are exceptions that permit closed meetings when (1) the subject of the meeting concerns the accusing of any person of a crime, (2) open meetings would frustrate implementation of future agency actions, or (3) the subject of the meeting involves matters relating to future litigation or rulemaking. Courts interpret these exceptions strictly so as to allow open access whenever possible, as the following case illustrates.

---

15.   5 U.S.C. Section 552.

16.   5 U.S.C. Section 552(b).

BACKGROUND AND FACTS   The National Economic Commission (NEC) and the General Services Administration sought to close meetings at which the NEC was to hear expert testimony and discuss national economic issues, including "economic assumptions" regarding growth, inflation, interest rates, and unemployment, as well as "budget options," such as revenue sources and budget cuts. The NEC feared that participants would not speak candidly if the meetings were open to the public. The NEC also feared that information obtained at open meetings would lead to unwar-

Case 44.4

PUBLIC CITIZEN v. NATIONAL ECONOMIC COMMISSION

United States District Court, District of Columbia, 1989. 703 F.Supp. 113.

ranted speculation about future economic policy, which in turn might disrupt national markets. Public Citizen, a public interest group, and others, including the *Washington Post* and the *Wall Street Journal,* asked a federal district court to prevent the closure of the meetings.

DECISION AND RATIONALE   The United States District Court for the District of Columbia permanently enjoined the NEC from closing its meetings. The court noted a previous case in which it was concluded that there "is no blanket exemption for agency meetings at any stage of the budget preparation process." The court acknowledged that specific items discussed at budget meetings might be exempt from the open-meeting requirement and might justify closing portions of the meetings. The court pointed out, however, that "[r]ather than singling out discrete portions of some meetings on an individual and particularized basis with justification for such limited closure, defendants assert a sweeping and broad deliberative process privilege, shielding their internal debate and operation from the public. The legislative history of the Sunshine Act as well as the relevant case law prohibits this."

COMMENTS   Is it possible that the court's reliance on the previous case was misplaced? After all, the NEC was not discussing its or any particular agency's budget, but rather was seeking to gain information about the nation's economic problems and the overall federal deficit. Moreover, the agency was not establishing policy, but only seeking to set the stage for later congressional action by soliciting a number of independent views. If it were true that the witnesses and participants would be reticent in public meetings, was not closure necessary for the NEC to fulfill its apparent function?

Regulatory Flexibility Act

Concern over the effects of regulation on the efficiency of businesses, particularly smaller ones, led Congress to pass the Regulatory Flexibility Act in 1980. Under this act, whenever a new regulation will have a "significant impact upon a substantial number of small entities," the agency must conduct a regulatory flexibility analysis. The analysis must measure the cost imposed by the rule on small businesses and must consider less burdensome alternatives. The act also contains provisions to alert small businesses about forthcoming regulations. The act has relieved some record-keeping burdens for small businesses, especially with regard to hazardous waste management.

■ Terms and Concepts

adjudication 792
administrative agencies 784
administrative law judge
  (ALJ) 792
administrative process 786
cease-and-desist order 793
comment period 791
complaint 789
enabling legislation 786

final order 793
formal rulemaking 791
hybrid rulemaking 792
independent regulatory
  agencies 785
informal rulemaking 791
initial order 793
interpretative rules 790
legislative rules 790

Notice of Proposed
  Rulemaking 791
notice-and-comment
  rulemaking 791
procedural rules 791
rulemaking 790
rulemaking-on-a-record 791
searches and seizures 787
subpoena 787

■ For Review

1. What constitutes the administrative process—that is, what are the three operations that make up the basic functions of most administrative agencies?

2. What are the two aspects of the enforcement function of an administrative agency?

3. What are the three types of rules that an administrative agency may create?

4. The National Engineering Standards Agency (NESA) suspects that Ricorn Engineering, Inc., has violated a NESA rule. NESA investigates. Its attorneys take statements under oath and request documents from Ricorn. NESA offers to negotiate a settlement, but Ricorn refuses. The agency issues a formal complaint, Ricorn responds, and the case is presented before an administrative law judge. After the

hearing, the judge issues an initial order against Ricorn. Can Ricorn appeal this order? If so, to whom? How does an initial order become a final order?

5. Investigative officers from the U.S. Mining Commission (USMC) raid the offices of *Precious Metals Digest*. Without a warrant, the officers search the *Digest's* files and confiscate several cartons of documents and floppy disks. After a brief hearing, the USMC orders the *Digest* not to publish certain information that the agency believes would damage its ability to conduct future investigations. What course might the *Digest* take to obtain judicial review of this order? What defenses might the *Digest* have against enforcement of the order? What preliminary requirements must the *Digest* satisfy before the order may be reviewed?

■ Questions and Case Problems

44-1. Assume that the Securities and Exchange Commission (SEC) has a policy not to enforce rules prohibiting insider trading except when the insiders make monetary profits for themselves. Then the SEC modifies this policy by a determination that the agency has the statutory authority to bring an enforcement action against an individual even if he or she does not personally profit from the insider trading. In modifying the policy, the SEC does not conduct a rulemaking but simply announces its new decision. A securities organization objects and says that the policy was unlawfully developed without opportunity for public comment. In a lawsuit challenging the new policy, should the policy be overruled under the Administrative Procedure Act? Discuss.

44-2. Assume that the Food and Drug Administration (FDA), using proper procedures, adopts a rule describing its future investigations. This new rule covers all future cases in which the FDA wants to regulate food additives. Under the new rule, the FDA says that it will not regulate food additives without giving food companies an opportunity to cross-examine witnesses. Some time later, the FDA wants to regulate methylisocyanate, a food additive. In doing so, the FDA conducts a normal notice-and-comment rulemaking, without cross-examination, and regulates methylisocyanate. Producers protest, saying that the FDA promised cross-examination. The FDA responds that the Administrative Procedure Act does not require such cross-examination and that its promise could simply be withdrawn. Discuss fully how the court should rule.

44-3. For decades, the Federal Trade Commission (FTC) resolved fair trade and advertising disputes through individual adjudications. In the 1960s, the FTC began promulgating rules that defined fair and unfair trade practices. In cases involving violations of these rules, the due process rights of participants were more limited and did not include cross-examination. This was because, although anyone found violating a rule would receive a full adjudication, the

legitimacy of the rule itself could not be challenged in the adjudication. If a party had violated a rule, it was almost certain to lose the adjudication. Affected parties complained, arguing that their rights before the FTC were unduly limited by the new rules. Were the rules illegal? Explain.

44-4. The Department of Commerce issued a flammability standard that required all mattresses, including crib mattresses, to pass a test that involved contact with a burning cigarette. The manufacturers of crib mattresses petitioned the court to exempt their product from the test procedure, but the department refused to do so. The crib manufacturers sued the department and argued that applying such a rule to crib mattresses was arbitrary and capricious because infants do not smoke. Discuss fully whether this rule should be overturned. [*Bunny Bear, Inc. v. Peterson,* 473 F.2d 1002 (1st Cir. 1973)]

44-5. In 1982, the president of the United States appointed Matthew Chabal, Jr., to the position of U.S. marshal. U.S. marshals are assigned to the federal courts. In the fall of 1985, Chabal received an unsatisfactory annual performance rating, and he was fired shortly thereafter by President Reagan. Given the fact that U.S. marshals are assigned to the federal courts, are these appointees still members of the executive branch? Did President Reagan have the right to fire Chabal without consulting Congress about the decision? [*Chabal v. Reagan,* 841 F.2d 1216 (3d Cir. 1988)]

44-6. A state statute required vehicle dismantlers—that is, persons whose business includes dismantling automobiles and selling the parts—to be licensed and keep records regarding the vehicles and parts in their possession. The statute also authorized warrantless administrative inspections; that is, without first obtaining a warrant, agents of the state department of motor vehicles or police officers could inspect a vehicle dismantler's license, records, and vehicles on the premises. Pursuant to this statute, police officers entered an automobile junkyard and asked to see the owner's license and records. The owner replied that he did not have the documents. The officers inspected the premises and discovered stolen vehicles and parts. Charged with possession of stolen property and unregistered operation as a vehicle dismantler, the junkyard owner argued that the warrantless inspection statute was unconstitutional under the Fourth Amendment. The trial court disagreed, reasoning that the junkyard business was a highly regulated industry. On appeal, the highest state court concluded that the statute had no truly administrative purpose and impermissibly authorized searches only to discover stolen property. The state appealed to the United States Supreme Court. Should the Court uphold the statute? Discuss. [*New York v. Burger*, 482 U.S. 691, 107 S.Ct. 2636, 96 L.Ed.2d 601 (1987)]

44-7. Congress passed legislation in 1966 that required the National Highway Traffic Safety Administration (NHTSA) to adopt automobile safety standards. Among the standards required by Section 203 of the act are rules for grading the quality of automobile tires. In 1975, the NHTSA adopted tread-wear regulations based on certain road-testing procedures. In 1983, as part of the Reagan administration's program of deregulation, the NHTSA indefinitely suspended the tire-quality regulations. The NHTSA contended that the standards were too costly for the economically troubled U.S. automobile industry and that the test procedures were not sufficiently reliable. Public Citizen, a public-interest group, sued the NHTSA, claiming that the suspension of the tire-quality standards was arbitrary and capricious. Will the court agree? Discuss. [*Public Citizen v. Steed*, 733 F.2d 93 (D.C.Cir. 1984)]

44-8. In 1977, the Department of Transportation (DOT) adopted a passive-restraint standard (known as Standard 208) that required new cars to have either air bags or automatic seat belts. By 1981, it became clear that all the major auto manufacturers would install automatic seat belts to comply with this rule. The DOT determined that most purchasers of cars would detach their automatic seat belts, thus making them ineffective. Consequently, the department repealed the regulation. State Farm Mutual Automobile Insurance Co. and other insurance companies sued in the District of Columbia Circuit Court of Appeals for a review of the DOT's repeal of the regulation. That court held that the repeal was arbitrary and capricious because the DOT had reversed its rule without sufficient support. The motor vehicle manufacturers then appealed this decision to the United States Supreme Court. What will result? Discuss. [*Motor Vehicle Manufacturers Association v. State Farm Mutual Automobile Insurance Co.*, 463 U.S. 29, 103 S.Ct. 2856, 77 L.Ed.2d 443 (1983)]

44-9. Lawrence Penny applied for a home loan guaranty with the Veterans Administration (VA) on a home located in Cleveland County, Oklahoma, just outside the city limits of Norman, Oklahoma. Kenneth Bridges, an insurance agent, mistakenly believed that the house was located inside the city limits of Norman and therefore—because the VA required flood insurance for homes within the city limits—informed Penny that he would need flood insurance to qualify for a VA-guaranteed loan. Bridges, who was authorized to prepare applications for flood insurance policies issued by the Federal Emergency Management Agency (FEMA), prepared Penny's application for flood insurance coverage in the amount of $35,000. On the application, Bridges described the house as being within the city limits of Norman.

FEMA issued the policy, and Penny paid the annual premiums from 1978 through 1982. In May 1982, Penny's home was flooded, resulting in damage of over $35,000. FEMA refused to pay on the policy because the flood insurance only covered properties in Cleveland County that were also within the city limits of Norman. Penny sued FEMA and its director, Louis Guiffrida, claiming that Bridges, as FEMA's agent, had misrepresented VA requirements to him and that the agency should be estopped from denying liability under the policy. Is FEMA liable for the amount of the policy? Discuss fully. [*Penny v. Guiffrida*, 897 F.2d 1543 (10th Cir. 1990)]

44-10. A Question of Ethics

The Marine Mammal Protection Act was enacted in 1972 to reduce the number of incidental killings of, and injuries to, marine mammals during commercial fishing operations. Pursuant to the act, commercial fishing vessels are required to allow an employee of the National Oceanic and Atmospheric Administration (NOAA) to accompany the vessels to conduct research and observe operations. In December 1986, after the NOAA had adopted a new policy of recruiting female as well as male observers, the NOAA notified Caribbean Marine Services Co. that female observers would be assigned to accompany two of their fishing vessels on their next voyages. The owners and crew of the ships (the plaintiffs) moved for an injunction against the implementation of the NOAA directive. The plaintiffs contended that the presence of a female on board a fishing vessel would be very awkward because the female would have to share the crew's quarters, and crew members enjoyed little or no privacy with respect to bodily functions. Further, they alleged that the presence of a female would be disruptive to fishing operations because some of the crew members were "crude" men with little formal education and might harass or sexually assault a female observer, and the officers would therefore have to devote time to protecting the female from the crew. Finally, the plaintiffs argued that the presence of a female observer could destroy morale and distract the crew, thus affecting the crew's efficiency and decreasing the vessel's profits. [Caribbean Marine Services Co. v. Baldrige, 844 F.2d 668 (9th Cir. 1988)]

1. In general, do you think that the public policy of promoting equal employment opportunity should override the concerns of the vessel owners and crew? If you were the judge, would you grant the injunction? Why or why not?

2. The plaintiffs pointed out that fishing voyages could last three months or longer. Would the length of a particular voyage affect your answer to the above question?

3. The plaintiffs contended that even if the indignity of sharing bunk rooms and toilet facilities with a female observer could be overcome, the observer's very presence in the common areas of the vessel, such as the dining area, would unconstitutionally infringe on the crew members' right to privacy in these areas. Evaluate this claim.

Chapter 45

Consumer Law

Many of the agencies and administrative regulatory processes described in the preceding chapter are geared toward what has become a vast area of government regulation: consumer protection. Consumer transactions take a variety of forms but broadly include those that involve an exchange of value for the purpose of acquiring goods, services, land, or credit for personal or family use. Traditionally in disputes involving consumers, it was assumed that the freedom to contract carried with it the obligation to live by the deal made. Therefore, the watchword in most such transactions was *caveat emptor*—"let the buyer beware." Over time, this attitude has changed considerably. Today myriad federal and state laws protect consumers from unfair trade practices, unsafe products, discriminatory or unreasonable credit requirements, and other problems related to consumer transactions.

In this chapter, we focus primarily on federal legislation, partly because of its wider applicability and partly because much state legislation closely parallels the federal laws. As a general rule, state consumer protection is more stringent. An important source of consumer protection on the state level is provided by those portions of the Uniform Commercial Code—adopted by virtually all of the states—that deal with unconscionable sales practices and warranties.

■ Advertising

The earliest federal consumer protection law was the Federal Trade Commission Act, and it is still one of the most important. As discussed in the preceding chapter, the act created the Federal Trade Commission (FTC) to carry out the broadly stated goal of preventing unfair and deceptive trade practices.[1]

Unfair and Deceptive Advertising

Advertising will be deemed deceptive if a consumer would be misled by the advertising claim. Vague generalities and obvious exaggerations are permissible. These claims are known as **puffing.** When a claim takes on the

---

1. 15 U.S.C. Section 45.

appearance of literal authenticity, however, it may create problems. Advertising that would *appear* to be based on factual evidence but that in fact is scientifically untrue will be deemed deceptive. A classic example is provided by a 1944 case in which the claim that a skin cream would restore youthful qualities to aged skin was deemed deceptive.[2] An-

---

2. *Charles of the Ritz Distributing Corp. v. Federal Trade Commission,* 143 F.2d 676 (2d Cir. 1944).

other advertising practice that has been attacked by the FTC as deceptive involves misleading price claims. For example, advertising to sell two cans of paint for the price of one and then setting a very high unit price has been held to be deceptive. The FTC also regulates advertising that contains the endorsements of celebrities. An advertisement may be deemed deceptive if the celebrity actually makes no use of the product. In the following case, advertisements of a sunburn treatment were alleged to be deceptive.

Case 45.1

IN RE PFIZER, INC.
Federal Trade Commission,
1972.
81 F.T.C. 23.

BACKGROUND AND FACTS The Federal Trade Commission staff's advertising substantiation rule provided that advertisements must be substantiated by well-controlled scientific studies or the claims would be considered deceptive. The staff brought an action against Pfizer, Inc., because the claims made by Pfizer in its advertisements for a sunburn treatment were allegedly unsupported by direct studies on humans. Pfizer argued that it had other forms of evidence sufficient to support its advertising claims—assurance from Pfizer's ''medical people'' that the claims could be supported by the product's ingredients, assurance from all available literature of the ingredients' effectiveness, and a review of competitors' claims for products with the same ingredients. The administrative law judge who heard the case dismissed the complaint against Pfizer, holding that no controlled scientific studies should be required. The FTC staff appealed the dismissal to the commission.

DECISION AND RATIONALE The FTC affirmed the administrative law judge's decision and dismissed the complaint against Pfizer, ruling that the staff had not met its burden of proof of demonstrating that Pfizer's advertising was insufficiently substantiated. The FTC stated that ''it is an unfair practice in violation of the Federal Trade Commission Act to make an affirmative product claim without a reasonable basis for making the claim.'' The FTC noted that it is more economically rational and far less expensive to require a manufacturer to confirm its affirmative product claims than to impose a burden on each individual consumer to test the product personally. In this case, however, it was unclear whether the tests used by Pfizer actually supported the claims made in its advertisements because the product had not been tested on humans. Although the FTC acknowledged that Pfizer had failed to demonstrate the existence of a reasonable basis for its product advertising, the commission admitted that the evidence was ''not sufficient to prove that [Pfizer] in fact *lacked* a reasonable basis for its advertising claims.''

Bait-and-Switch Advertising

The FTC has promulgated specific rules to govern some advertising techniques. One of the most important rules is contained in the FTC's *Guides on*

Bait Advertising.[3] The rule is designed to prevent **bait-and-switch advertising**—that is, advertising

---

3. 16 C.F.R. Part 238.

a very low price for a particular item that will likely be unavailable to the consumer, who will then be encouraged to purchase a more expensive item. The low price is the ''bait'' to lure the consumer into the store. The salesperson is instructed to ''switch'' the consumer to a different item. Under the FTC guidelines, bait-and-switch advertising occurs if the seller refuses to show the advertised item, fails to have in stock a reasonable quantity of the item, fails to promise to deliver the advertised item within a reasonable time, or discourages employees from selling the item.

FTC Actions against Deceptive Advertising

As described in the last chapter in regard to agency enforcement generally, an FTC action begins with an investigation after the commission receives a complaint. The investigation may lead to a hearing and ultimately a *cease-and-desist order*—an order that the business cease and desist its advertising practice. Under certain circumstances, the FTC

may also recover civil penalties. The FTC has also employed three other remedies relating to advertising. First, the FTC may compel **affirmative advertising,** which requires a firm to provide specific information in its advertisement so as to prevent consumers from being misled. Second, the FTC may require **counteradvertising**—or corrective advertising—in which the advertiser admits that prior claims about a product were untrue. Finally, the FTC may institute **multiple product orders,** which require a firm to cease and desist from false advertising not only in regard to the product that was the subject of the action but also in regard to all the firm's other products.

Counteradvertising is a harsh remedy and can be a particularly costly one for sellers. But, as the case below indicates, if an advertiser has made false claims about a product for years and years, simply ceasing from making the false claims may not be enough to dispel the illusions created about the product from consumers' minds.

BACKGROUND AND FACTS The Warner-Lambert Company began making Listerine in 1879, using the same formula employed today. As early as 1921, the firm began claiming that Listerine prevented colds and sore throats or lessened their severity. After medical testing conducted by the FTC revealed these claims to be false, the commission filed a complaint that charged Warner-Lambert with misrepresenting the efficacy of Listerine against colds. On the basis of the evidence obtained through the testing, the administrative law judge sustained the complaint. The FTC affirmed the judge's findings and ordered Warner-Lambert to cease and desist from making the claims. The FTC further ordered Warner-Lambert to "cease and desist from disseminating any advertisement for Listerine unless it is clearly and conspicuously disclosed in each such advertisement, in the exact language below that: 'Contrary to prior advertising, Listerine will not help prevent colds or sore throats or lessen their severity.' This requirement extends only to the next ten million dollars of Listerine advertising." Warner-Lambert appealed the FTC's ruling.

 Case 45.2

WARNER-LAMBERT CO. v. FEDERAL TRADE COMMISSION

United States Court of Appeals, District of Columbia Circuit, 1977.

562 F.2d 749.

DECISION AND RATIONALE The United States Court of Appeals for the District of Columbia affirmed the FTC's ruling, holding that the corrective advertising was necessary and that the duration of the corrective advertising—for the next $10 million worth of advertising for Listerine—was reasonable. The only modification the court made to the ruling was that Warner-Lambert did not have to include the words "contrary to prior advertising" in its corrective advertising. The court interpreted the FTC's standard for imposing corrective advertising as requiring two inquiries: "(1) did Listerine's advertisements play a substantial role in creating or reinforcing in the public's mind a false belief about the product? and (2) would this belief linger on after the false advertising ceases?" The court responded by repeating the findings that "Warner-Lambert has, over a long period of time, worked a substantial deception upon the public" and that a simple cease-and-desist order would not be enough to correct the false impression that Listerine could prevent common colds.

ETHICAL CONSIDERATIONS The court briefly considered the argument that corrective advertising orders, such as the one issued to Warner-Lambert, could have a "chilling effect" on (act as a disincentive to) free commercial speech—that is, on truthful advertising. A firm might be less likely to engage in advertising, given the possibility that it might be forced, at some future date, to include specific disclaimers in its advertising. The court was not worried. Not only did a substantial government interest—protecting citizens against deception—exist to justify any restraint placed on commercial speech by the requirement of corrective advertising, but the court believed that no significant chilling effect would likely result from the restraint. Quoting from an opinion of the United States Supreme Court on a similar issue, the court of appeals held that "[s]ince advertising is the *sine qua non* of [essential to] commercial profits, there is little likelihood of its being chilled by proper regulation and forgone entirely."

Labeling and Packaging Laws

In addition to the broad restrictions on advertising, a number of federal and state laws deal specifically with the information given on labels and packages. The restrictions are designed to provide accurate information about the product and to warn about possible dangers from its use or misuse. In general, labels must be accurate. That is, they must use words as those words are understood by the ordinary consumer. For example, a box of cereal cannot be labeled "giant" if it would exaggerate the amount of cereal contained in the box. In some instances, labels must specify the raw materials used in the product, such as the percentage of cotton, nylon, or other fibers used in a garment. In other instances, the products must carry a warning. Cigarette packages and advertising, for example, must include one of several warnings about the health hazards associated with smoking.[4]

The numerous federal laws include the Fur Products Labeling Act of 1951, the Wool Products Labeling Act of 1939, the Flammable Fabrics Act of 1953, the Smokeless Tobacco Health Education Act of 1986, and the Fair Packaging and Labeling Act of 1966. The Smokeless Tobacco Health Education Act, for example, requires that producers, packagers, and importers of smokeless tobacco la-

bel their product with one of several warnings about the health hazards associated with the use of smokeless tobacco similar to those contained on ordinary tobacco product packages. The Fair Packaging and Labeling Act requires that products possess labels that identify the product; the net quantity of the contents, as well as the quantity of servings, if the number of servings is stated; the manufacturer; and the packager or distributor. The act also provides authority to add requirements concerning words used to describe packages, terms that are associated with savings claims, information disclosures for ingredients in nonfood products, and standards for the partial filling of packages. The most recent standard requires that food products bear labels detailing nutrition, including how much fat a product contains and what kind of fat it is. These restrictions are enforced by the Department of Health and Human Services, as well as the Federal Trade Commission.

Sales

Many of the laws that protect consumers concern the disclosure of certain terms in sales transactions and provide rules governing the various forms of sales, such as door-to-door sales, mail-order sales, referral sales, and the unsolicited receipt of merchandise. Much of the federal regulation of sales is conducted by the FTC under its regulatory authority to curb unfair trade practices. Other federal

---

4. 15 U.S.C. Sections 1331 *et seq.*

agencies, however, are involved to various degrees. For example, the Federal Reserve Board of Governors has issued Regulation Z, which governs credit provisions associated with sales contracts. Numerous state laws are also relevant. Many states, for example, have enacted laws governing home sale transactions. Moreover, as noted earlier, states have provided a number of consumer protection provisions through the adoption of the Uniform Commercial Code. Also important is the Uniform Consumer Credit Code,[5] which has been adopted by some states.

Door-to-Door Sales

A door-to-door sale is any transaction that is initiated by a visit to, and concluded at, the buyer's home—as distinct from some other place such as the seller's showroom or office. Certain features of this type of sales activity have prompted concern. For one thing, because repeat purchases are less likely than with store sales, sellers are less constrained by the need to build up goodwill with regular customers. Additionally, individuals may feel more pressure when cornered in their own home by a persistent salesperson; they may simply buy to get rid of an obnoxious salesperson standing at the front door.

For these reasons, door-to-door sales are regulated both at the state level and by the federal government. States have enacted "cooling-off" legislation, which permits a buyer to rescind a door-to-door purchase if the election is made within a certain period of time. The FTC has also mandated a three-day cooling-off period, but when state legislation is more favorable to the buyer, the latter will govern the sale. In addition, the FTC requires the seller to notify the buyer of the right to cancel the sale within the specified time, and if the sale is originally conducted in Spanish, notice must also be given in Spanish.

Telephone and Mail-Order Sales

Sales made by either telephone or mail order are the greatest source of complaints to the nation's Better Business Bureaus. Many mail-order houses are far removed from the buyers to whom the

houses sell, thus making the burden greater in bringing a complaint against the seller. Many states, therefore, have enacted consumer protection laws that parallel and supplement the federal laws against mail fraud. In addition, the Postal Reorganization Act of 1970 provides that *unsolicited* merchandise sent by U.S. mail may be retained, used, discarded, or disposed of in any manner deemed appropriate, without the recipient incurring any obligation to the sender.

FTC Regulation of Specific Industries

Over the last decade, the FTC has begun to target certain sales practices on an industry-wide basis. Two examples are the used-car business and the funeral-home trade. In 1981 the FTC enacted a rule that requires used-car dealers to affix a "Buyers Guide" label to all cars sold on their lots. The label must disclose the following: (1) the car's warranty or a statement that the car is being sold "as is," (2) information regarding any service contract or promises being made by the dealer, and (3) a suggestion that the purchaser obtain both an inspection of the car and a written statement of any promises made by the dealer.

In 1984 the FTC also enacted rules requiring that funeral homes provide customers with itemized prices of all charges incurred for a funeral. In addition, the regulations prohibit funeral homes from requiring specific embalming procedures or specific types of caskets for bodies that are to be cremated.

Real Estate Sales

Various federal and state laws apply to consumer transactions involving real estate. These laws are designed to prevent fraud and to provide buyers with certain types of information. In some cases, these protections mirror those provided in non–real estate sales. The disclosure requirements of the Truth-in-Lending Act, which will be discussed in detail shortly, apply to a number of real estate transactions. Differences exist, however, between the disclosure requirements for real estate and for non–real estate transactions. For example, in certain real estate transactions, consumer buyers are given a right to rescind their purchase contract if certain disclosures are not made to them. Moreover, under certain circumstances, the Truth-in-Lending Act provides the consumer with a right to rescind even

---

5. Regulation Z and the Uniform Consumer Credit Code, as well as consumer credit laws generally, are discussed more fully in a subsequent section.

though a creditor has made all of the required disclosures.[6]

INTERSTATE LAND SALES FULL DISCLOSURE ACT The Interstate Land Sales Full Disclosure Act[7] was passed by Congress in 1968, and it is administered by the Department of Housing and Urban Development (HUD). The purpose of the act is to ensure disclosure of certain information to consumers so that they can make intelligent decisions about land purchases. The act is similar to the Securities Act of 1933 in both purpose and design. The act requires any seller or lessor of one hundred or more lots of unimproved land, if the sale or lease is part of a common promotional plan, to file an initial "statement of record" with HUD's Office of Interstate Land Sales Registration. The act only applies if the promotional plan can be deemed part of interstate commerce. But, as in cases involving securities, this is generally an easy requirement to meet. For example, even strictly local sales might be considered interstate commerce if transacted in part over the phone; although the calls might be local, the phone lines traverse state boundaries. For the same reason, use of the mail system is likely to ensure that a promotional plan is in the stream of interstate commerce.

Once the initial statement is filed, it must be approved by HUD before the developer can begin to offer the land for sale or lease. The act also provides purchasers with a private right of action for the land promoter's fraud, misrepresentation, or noncompliance with pertinent provisions of the act. Criminal penalties are provided under the act, and HUD is given certain rights with regard to inspections, injunctions, and prosecution of offenses. Three provisions of the act provide purchasers with rights of rescission (cancellation).

REAL ESTATE SETTLEMENT PROCEDURES ACT For many individuals, purchasing a home involves a bewildering array of settlement procedures and requirements. Settlement may require title insurance, attorneys' fees, appraisal fees, taxes, insurance, and brokers' fees. To aid home buyers, federal legislation requires specific disclosures regarding settlement procedures. The 1976

revisions of the Real Estate Settlement Procedures Act make the following stipulations:

1. Within three business days after a person applies for a mortgage loan, the lender must send a booklet prepared by HUD that explains the settlement procedures, describes the costs to the potential buyer, and outlines the applicant's legal rights.
2. Within the three-day period, the lender must give an estimate of most of the settlement costs.
3. The lender must clearly identify individuals or firms that the applicant is required to use for legal or other services, including title search and insurance.
4. If the loan is approved, the lender must provide a truth-in-lending statement that shows the annual percentage rate on the mortgage loan.
5. Lenders, title insurers, and others involved in the transaction cannot pay kickbacks for business referred to them.

■ Credit Protection

Because credit has assumed such an important role in consumer transactions, it is not surprising that some of the most important consumer protection laws have to do with credit. We look now at some of the most significant laws regulating consumer credit transactions.

The Truth-In-Lending Act

The Truth-in-Lending Act (TILA), as Title I of the Consumer Credit Protection Act (CCPA) is frequently called, is basically a disclosure law. Administered by the Federal Reserve Board, it requires sellers and lenders to disclose credit or loan terms to debtors so that the latter may shop around for the best available financing terms.

The TILA applies to creditors who, in the ordinary course of business, lend money or either sell on credit or arrange for the extension of credit. Thus sales between two consumers are not subject to the act. Only debtors who are *natural* persons are protected by the TILA; corporations and other entities created by law are not.

DISCLOSURE REQUIREMENTS The disclosure requirements are found in **Regulation Z**, promulgated by the Federal Reserve Board. If the contracting parties are subject to the TILA, the re-

---

6. 15 U.S.C. Section 1635. For example, see Case 45.3.
7. 15 U.S.C. Sections 1701 *et seq.*

quirements of Regulation Z apply to any trans-action involving an installment sales contract in which payment is to be made in more than four installments. These transactions typically include installment loans, retail and installment sales, car loans, home improvement loans, and certain real estate loans if the amount of financing is less than $25,000. Some of the disclosure requirements that may apply to these contracts include the specific dollar amount being financed; the annual percent-age rate of interest; any financing charges, pre-miums, or points; the number, amounts, and due dates of payments; and any penalties imposed on delinquent payments or prepayment.

VIOLATIONS OF THE TILA Various penalties apply to creditors who violate the TILA by either failing to provide the disclosure statement or failing

to discover an error in the statement provided. The act confers a *private right of action* on consumers who have been injured by a creditor's violation. If the suit is brought within one year of the date of the violation, the creditor will be liable for twice the amount of the finance charge, plus attorneys' fees. No more than $1,000 in damages may be recovered, but in no event will the penalty be less than $100. Federal agencies, including the De-partment of Justice and the FTC, may sue violators for criminal, as well as civil, violations. The crim-inal penalties include as much as a $5,000 fine and up to one year in jail.

The TILA also provides for contract rescission if a creditor fails to follow exactly the procedures required by the act. The following case illustrates how strictly TILA requirements will be enforced.

BACKGROUND AND FACTS In February 1986, Max and Jacquelyn Elsner met with a representative of Diamond Mortgage to discuss the pos-sibility of obtaining a loan to pay the balance on their land contract and to pay for home improvements. The representative asked the Elsners to sign some preliminary documents, including a loan application, and allegedly advised the Elsners that they would not sign the final binding papers until they received the money. The representative also gave each of the Elsners one copy of a "Notice of Right to Cancel." In fact, the documents signed by the Elsners included a mortgage contract and a promissory note, which Diamond shortly thereafter assigned to Harley and Donna Albrecht for $26,500. The Elsners never received the money. When the Albrechts sought payment on the note, the Elsners brought an action in a Michigan state court to rescind the contract, claiming that Diamond had violated the TILA because the representative gave them each only one copy of the "Notice of Right to Cancel"—instead of two copies, as required under the act. The trial court granted rescission, and the Albrechts appealed. The Albrechts argued that, as holders in due course, they were entitled to pay-ment of the note, and therefore the contract could not be rescinded.

Case 45.3

ELSNER v. ALBRECHT

Court of Appeals of Michigan, 1990.
185 Mich.App. 72,
460 N.W.2d 232.

DECISION AND RATIONALE The Court of Appeals of Michigan affirmed the decision of the trial court, ruling that the Elsners were entitled to re-scission, notwithstanding the fact that the mortgage contract and note had been transferred to a good faith purchaser for value. The court stated that the "TILA and Reg. Z provide for rescission until three days after the latest of the following events: (1) consummation of the transactions, (2) delivery of two copies to each borrower of the notice of right to cancel, or (3) deliv-ery of all 'material disclosures.' " The court's strict interpretation of the TILA and Regulation Z enabled it to conclude that the Elsners were entitled to rescind the mortgage contract because Diamond Mortgage failed to give each of them two copies of the notice of the right to cancel as required by statute. The court stated that the fact that the Elsners were husband and wife was irrelevant as each was a borrower. The court held that the TILA's rescission remedy preempts the holder-in-due-course doctrine, and therefore the Albrechts' status as holders in due course did not prevent the Elsners from rescinding their mortgage agreement.

ETHICAL CONSIDERATIONS It is important to realize that the courts generally assume that the best way to protect the greatest number of consumers is by strict enforcement of consumer protection legislation, such as the TILA, even though occasional injustices are bound to result and even, in this case, at the expense of the holder-in-due-course doctrine—which itself rests on the ethical conviction that innocent third parties should be protected.

EQUAL CREDIT OPPORTUNITY ACT In 1974, Congress enacted the Equal Credit Opportunity Act (ECOA) as part of the earlier enacted Truth-in-Lending Act. The ECOA prohibits the denial of credit solely on the basis of race, religion, national origin, color, sex, marital status, or age. The act also prohibits credit discrimination on the basis of whether an individual receives certain forms of income, such as public assistance benefits. Under the ECOA, a creditor may not require the signature of an applicant's spouse, other than a joint applicant, on a credit instrument if the applicant qualifies under the creditor's standards of creditworthiness for the amount and terms of the credit request. Creditors are permitted to request any information from a credit applicant except that which would be used for the type of discrimination covered in the act or its amendments.

FAIR CREDIT BILLING ACT In 1974, Congress also enacted the Fair Credit Billing Act as a part of the Truth-in-Lending Act. Under the terms of the act, a purchaser can withhold payment for a product that was purchased with a credit card and that is alleged to be defective. It is up to the credit card issuer to intervene and attempt to settle the dispute. A purchaser does not have an unlimited right to stop payment, however. The purchaser must first exercise a good faith effort to get satisfaction from the seller. Other provisions of the act relate to disputes over billing. If the debtor believes there is an error in a bill, the debtor may suspend payment until the credit card company investigates the complaint. The credit card holder, within sixty days of receipt of the disputed bill, must write to the company that issued the card and explain the basis of the alleged error. The com-

pany must resolve the dispute within ninety days, during which time it can neither close the account or issue additional financing charges. If, however, the error is unfounded and is resolved against the debtor, the creditor may seek to collect finance charges for the entire period for which payments were not made.

LOST AND UNAUTHORIZED CREDIT CARDS The TILA contains other provisions regarding credit cards. One of these provisions limits the liability of the cardholder to $50 per card for unauthorized charges made before the credit card issuer is notified that the card has been lost. Another provision prohibits a credit card company from billing a consumer for any unauthorized charges if the credit card was improperly issued by the company.

The Fair Credit Reporting Act

To protect consumers against inaccurate credit reporting, Congress enacted the Fair Credit Reporting Act in 1970. Under the act, consumers can determine and correct any misinformation about their credit standing that is being given out by a credit agency. The act requires that consumers be notified when reporting activities are undertaken, that they be given access to information contained in a consumer report, and that any erroneous information that leads to a denial of credit, employment, or insurance be corrected. Consumers may also request the source of any information being given out by a credit agency, as well as the identity of anyone who has received an agency's report.

The following case illustrates the liability exposure of companies that maintain credit reports and ratings.

Case 45.4

THOMPSON v. SAN ANTONIO RETAIL MERCHANTS ASSOCIATION

United States Court of Appeals, Fifth Circuit, 1982.
682 F.2d 509.

BACKGROUND AND FACTS The San Antonio Retail Merchants Association (SARMA) maintained credit reports on consumers. In 1974, William *Daniel* Thompson allowed his account at a jewelry store to become delinquent. SARMA placed a derogatory credit rating into Thompson's file but failed to include his Social Security number. In 1978, William *Douglas* Thompson applied for credit with Gulf Oil Corporation and Montgomery Ward in San Antonio. SARMA erroneously reported to both firms the bad-debt record of William *Daniel* Thompson. As a result, Gulf and Montgomery Ward denied credit to William *Douglas* Thompson. Initially, William *Douglas* Thompson believed he had been denied credit because of his 1976 burglary conviction. In 1979, however, he learned the true reason. After discovering the error, William *Douglas* Thompson attempted to get SARMA to correct the error. SARMA, however, repeatedly sent him letters addressed to William *Daniel* Thompson and failed to correct the erroneous credit report. William *Douglas* Thompson sued SARMA in a federal district court, and the court ruled in his favor. The court awarded Thompson $10,000 in damages for mental distress, plus attorneys' fees of $4,485. SARMA appealed.

DECISION AND RATIONALE The United States Court of Appeals for the Fifth Circuit upheld the district court's ruling and award of damages and attorneys' fees. The Fair Credit Reporting Act provides that "[w]hen a consumer reporting agency prepares a consumer report, it shall follow reasonable procedures to assure maximum possible accuracy of information concerning the individual about whom the report relates." The appellate court pointed out that the provision "does not impose strict liability for any inaccurate credit report, but only a duty of reasonable care in preparation of the report." The court found no error in the district court's conclusion that SARMA was liable for negligent failure to comply with this provision. First, SARMA failed to exercise reasonable care in programming its computer to accept information in a consumer's file without requiring "points of correspondence" between the consumer and the file or having an adequate auditing procedure to foster accuracy. Second, SARMA failed to employ reasonable procedures designed to learn the disparity in Social Security numbers for the two Thompsons. As for damages, SARMA argued that Thompson proved none or at best only minimal damages for humiliation. The appellate court disagreed, referring to Thompson's testimony indicating that the repeated denial of credit "really hurt" efforts "to get back on my feet again." As for attorneys' fees, the court noted that the Fair Credit Reporting Act specifically authorizes the payment of attorneys' fees.

The Fair Debt Collection Practices Act

In 1977, Congress enacted the Fair Debt Collection Practices Act in an attempt to curb what were perceived to be abuses by collection agencies. The act applies only to specialized debt-collection agencies that, usually for a percentage of the amount owed, regularly attempt to collect debts on behalf of someone else. Creditors who attempt to collect a debt are not covered by the act unless, by misrepresenting themselves to the debtor, they cause the debtor to believe they are a collection agency. The act explicitly prohibits a collection agency from using any of the following tactics:

1. Contacting the debtor at the debtor's place of employment if the debtor's employer objects.
2. Contacting the debtor during inconvenient or unusual times (for example, calling the debtor at

3 o'clock in the morning) or at any time if the debtor is being represented by an attorney.

3. Contacting third parties other than the debtor's parents, spouse, or financial advisor about payment of a debt unless a court authorizes such action.

4. Using harassment or intimidation (for example, using abusive language or threatening violence), or employing false and misleading information (for example, posing as a police officer).

5. Communicating with the debtor at any time after receiving notice that the debtor is refusing to pay the debt, except to advise the debtor of further action to be taken by the collection agency.

Enforcement of the act is primarily the responsibility of the FTC. The act allows debtors to recover civil damages, as well as attorneys' fees, in an action against a collection agency that violates provisions of the act.

Garnishment of Wages

Despite the increasing number of protections afforded debtors, creditors are not without their own means of securing payment on a debt. One of these is the right to garnish a debtor's wages after the debt has gone uncollected for a prolonged period. **Garnishment** is the legal procedure by which a creditor may collect on a debt by directly attaching, or seizing, a portion of the debtor's wages. State law provides the basis for a process of garnishment, but the law varies among the states as to how easily garnishment may be obtained. Indeed, a few states prohibit garnishment of wages altogether. In addition to state law requirements, the Constitution and, more recently, federal legislation under the TILA provide additional protections against abuse. In general, the debtor is entitled to notice and an opportunity to be heard in a process of garnishment. Moreover, wages cannot be garnished beyond 25 percent of the debtor's after-tax earnings and must leave the debtor with at least a specified minimum income.

■ Consumer Health and Safety

Laws discussed earlier regarding the labeling and packaging of products go a long way toward promoting consumer health and safety. These laws enable consumers to make informed choices about the products they choose to consume. But there is

a significant distinction between regulating the information dispensed about a product and regulating the content of the actual product. The classic example is tobacco products. Tobacco products have not been altered by regulation nor banned outright despite their obvious hazards (or perhaps because of that obviousness). What has been regulated are the warnings about the hazards of tobacco that producers are required to give consumers.[8] This section focuses on laws that regulate the actual products made available to consumers.

The Federal Food, Drug, and Cosmetic Act

The first federal legislation regulating food and drugs was enacted in 1906 as the Pure Food and Drug Act. That law, as amended in 1938, exists presently as the Federal Food, Drug, and Cosmetic Act. The original act, and the subsequent amendment strengthening its provisions, was intended to protect consumers against adulterated and misbranded foods and drugs. More recent amendments have added additional substantive and procedural requirements to the act. In its present form, the act establishes food standards, specifies safe levels of potentially hazardous food additives, and sets classifications of food and food advertising. Most of these statutory requirements are monitored and enforced by the Food and Drug Administration (FDA). Under an extensive set of procedures established by the FDA, drugs must be shown to be effective as well as safe before they may be marketed to the public, and the use of some food additives suspected of being carcinogenic is prohibited. In general, the food and drug laws make manufacturers responsible for ensuring that the food and drugs that they offer for sale are free of any substances that could be injurious to the consumer.

The Consumer Product Safety Act

Consumer product safety legislation began in 1953 with enactment of the Flammable Fabrics Act, which prohibits the sale of highly flammable clothing or materials. Over the next two decades, Congress enacted legislation for specific classes of

---

8. We are ignoring recent civil litigation concerning the liability of tobacco product manufacturers for injuries that arise from the use of tobacco.

CHAPTER 45: CONSUMER LAW

products regarding the design or composition of the products. Then in 1972, Congress, by enacting the Consumer Product Safety Act, created a comprehensive scheme of regulation over matters concerning consumer safety. The act also established far-reaching authority over consumer safety under the Consumer Product Safety Commission (CPSC). The CPSC conducts research on how safe individual products are, and it maintains a clearinghouse on the risks associated with different consumer products. Under the Consumer Product Safety Act, the CPSC is authorized to set standards for consumer products and to ban the manufacture and sale of any product it deems to be potentially hazardous to consumers. The CPSC also has authority to remove from market shelves any products it believes to be imminently hazardous and to require manufacturers to report on any products already sold or intended for sale if the products have proved to be hazardous. The CPSC also has authority to administer other product safety legislation, such as the Child Protection and Toy Safety Act of 1966, the Hazardous Substances Labeling Act of 1960, and the Flammable Fabrics Act.

The CPSC's authority is sufficiently broad to allow it to ban any product that the CPSC believes poses merely an ''unreasonable risk'' to the consumer. Some of the products that the CPSC has banned include various types of fireworks, cribs, toys, and many products containing asbestos or vinyl chloride.

■ State Consumer Protection Laws

Thus far our primary focus has been federal legislation. Our task would be incomplete, however, if at least brief mention were not made of the state laws affecting consumer transactions. Although variation among the state laws prevents making any broad generalizations, it should be noted that state laws often provide more sweeping and significant protections for the consumer than do federal laws. Precisely because of the variation among the states, a businessperson is well-advised to consider all aspects of the laws of the states in which he or she does business. Even remote connections with a state may bring a transaction within the authority of a particular state's laws. Furthermore, basic principles of contract law include the considerable discretion of the contracting parties to

choose to have the laws of a particular state govern the terms of their agreement.[9]

The Uniform Commercial Code

Consumers are afforded the protections offered by the sections in the Uniform Commercial Code (UCC) on express and implied warranties. These were covered in detail in Unit Three, and the reader should consider the importance of these protections in the context of our present discussion. The UCC also restricts the ability of sellers to limit their liability for personal injuries caused by defective products. Perhaps the most significant UCC consumer protection, however, is the principle of unconscionability based on UCC 2-302. This section, as interpreted by the courts, prohibits enforcing any contracts that are so one-sidedly unfair that they ''shock the conscience'' of the court. In discussing consumer protections under the UCC, it is important to recall the Magnuson-Moss Warranty Act, which was also discussed in Unit Three. This federal legislation supplements the UCC provisions in cases involving both a consumer transaction of at least $10 and an express written warranty.

The Uniform Consumer Credit Code

Far less widely adopted than the UCC is the Uniform Consumer Credit Code (UCCC). Promulgated in 1968 by the National Conference of Commissioners on the Uniform State Laws, the UCCC is an attempt to draft a comprehensive body of rules governing the most important aspects of consumer credit. The UCCC includes sections on truth in lending, maximum credit ceilings, door-to-door sales, and referral sales. The UCCC also contains provisions concerning fine-print clauses and creditor remedies, including provisions regarding deficiency judgments[10] and garnishments. In states that have adopted it, the UCCC applies to most sales, including those involving real estate. Its adoption also displaces the adopting state's consumer credit laws, as well as laws governing installment loans, usury, and retail installment sales. The UCCC is controversial, and it has been adopted

---

9. So-called conflicts of law may arise in any transaction that crosses state boundaries.

10. A deficiency judgment is a judgment for the portion of a debt not recovered from the forced sale of property securing that debt.

in only a handful of states. Even those states that have adopted the UCCC have adopted only portions. Moreover, substantial differences in the various state versions remove much of the uniformity from the act among the various adopting states.

Other State Consumer Protection Laws

Despite the variation among state laws generally, there is a common thread running through most of the consumer protection laws. Most are typically directed at deceptive trade practices, such as a seller's providing false or misleading information to the consumer. As mentioned earlier, some of the legislation is quite broad. A prime example is the Texas Deceptive Trade Practices Act of 1973, which forbids a seller from selling to a buyer anything that the buyer does not need or cannot afford. The California Civil Code permits consumers to keep unsolicited goods without remitting any payment for them.

California is one state that has enacted a broad statute dealing with consumer product warranties generally, but a majority of states—forty-seven at last count—have statutes dealing with warranties on specific types of goods such as new automobiles and new mobile homes. These so-called lemon laws are discussed in depth in Unit Three, but they should be noted for the sake of completeness when considering consumer protection laws. Also discussed in detail in Unit Three are the protections against personal injury and property losses provided by product liability laws based on principles of contract and tort law. Indeed, most consumer disputes are settled by contract law, personal injury being the exception; there are advantages to a plaintiff's bringing a suit on the basis of strict liability under tort law for personal injury from a defective product. Nonetheless, the appearance of government regulators as a kind of third party protector in consumer transactions is an unmistakable trend in recent years.

■ Terms and Concepts

affirmative advertising 803	**counteradvertising** 803	**puffing** 801
bait-and-switch	**garnishment** 810	**Regulation Z** 806
advertising 802	**multiple product orders** 803	

■ For Review

1. When will advertising be deemed deceptive?
2. What does the TILA require sellers and lenders to do?
3. What does the Federal Food, Drug, and Cosmetic Act provide?
4. Hank owes $1,000 to Doehr Sales Co. Doehr sends several letters to Hank under the Doehr logo, but Hank does not pay. A Doehr credit representative tells Hank that she represents Fitz Collection Agency, but Hank still does not pay. Doehr sells the account to Hardball Credit Services, an actual collection agency. Hardball contacts Hank at his workplace, despite the objection of Hank's employer, and

one evening threatens Hank with physical violence if he does not pay. Did Doehr violate the Fair Debt Collection Practices Act? Did Hardball violate the act?
5. Bobby suffers from emphysema and throat cancer. He had smoked thirty cigarettes a day for thirty years. Believing that his smoking caused the injuries, Bobby sues Gold Tobacco Co., for manufacturing the cigarettes, and the federal government, for failing to ban them. What might Gold argue in its defense? What might the government argue in its defense?

■ Questions and Case Problems

45-1. Andrew, a California resident, received a flyer in the U.S. mail announcing a new line of regional cookbooks distributed by the Every-Kind Cookbook Co. Andrew was not interested and threw the flyer away. Two days later, Andrew received in the mail an introductory cookbook entitled *Lower Mongolian Regional Cookbook,* as announced in the flyer, on a "trial basis" from Every-Kind. Andrew was not interested but

did not go to the trouble to return the cookbook. Every-Kind demanded payment of $20.95 for the *Lower Mongolian Regional Cookbook.* Discuss whether Andrew can be required to pay for the cookbook.

45-2. Fireside Rocking Chair Co. advertised in the newspaper a special sale price of $159 on machine-caned rocking chairs. In the advertisement was a drawing of a natural-wood rocking chair with a caned back and seat. The average person would not be able to tell from the drawing whether the rocking chair was machine caned or hand caned. The hand-caned rocking chairs sold for $259. Lowell and Celia Carlisle went to Fireside because they had seen the ad for the machine-caned rocking chair and were very interested in purchasing one. The Carlisles arrived on the morning the sale opened. Fireside's agent said the only machine-caned rocking chairs he had were painted lime green and were priced at $159. He immediately turned the Carlisle's attention to the hand-caned rocking chairs, praising their quality and pointing out that for the extra $100, the hand-caned chairs were surely a good value. The Carlisles, preferring the natural-wood, machine-caned rocking chair for $159 as pictured in the advertisement, said they would like to order the one in the ad. The Fireside agent said he could not order a natural-wood, machine-caned rocking chair. Discuss fully whether Fireside has violated any consumer protection laws.

45-3. On June 28, a sales representative for Renowned Books called on the Petersons at their home. After a very persuasive sales pitch on the part of the sales agent, the Petersons agreed in writing to purchase a twenty-volume set of historical encyclopedias from Renowned Books for a total of $299. An initial down payment of $35 was required, with the remainder of the price to be paid in monthly payments over a one-year period. Two days later the Petersons, having second thoughts, contacted the book company and stated they had decided to rescind the contract. Renowned Books said this would be impossible. Has Renowned Books violated any consumer law by not allowing the Petersons to rescind their contract? Explain.

45-4. Michael and Patricia Jensen purchased a new 1989 Ford Tempo from Ray Kim Ford. The Jensens signed a retail installment contract that provided for an estimated trade-in value of $800 for their old car. When the traded-in car turned out to be worth $1,388.08, Ray Kim prepared a second retail installment contract, without the Jensens' knowledge. The second contract, although it credited the increased trade-in value of the car, compensated for this credit by increasing the interest rate, increasing the sales price of the car, and making other adjustments so that the second contract basically called for future cash payments by the Jensens of about the same amount as the first contract. In effect, the second contract gave the Jensens almost no benefit for the increased value of their traded-in car. The Jensens made payments under the contract until they noticed the five-cent difference in monthly payments, asked for a copy of the contract, and realized that it was not the contract that they had signed. The Jensens sued Ray Kim, alleging that the second contract was a forgery and that Ray Kim had violated the Truth-in-Lending Act by not disclosing to them the credit terms of the second contract. Has Ray Kim violated the Truth-in-Lending Act? If the Jensens choose to adopt the terms of the second contract, despite the forgery, has the act been violated? Discuss fully. [*Jensen v. Ray Kim Ford, Inc.,* 920 F.2d 3 (7th Cir. 1990)]

45-5. Thompson Medical Co. marketed a new cream called Aspercreme that was supposed to help arthritis victims and others suffering from minor aches. Aspercreme contained no aspirin. Thompson's television advertisements stated that the product provided "the strong relief of aspirin right where you hurt" and showed the announcer holding up aspirin tablets as well as a tube of Aspercreme. The FTC held that the advertisements were misleading, because they led consumers to believe that Aspercreme contained aspirin. Thompson Medical Co. appealed this decision and argued that the advertisements never actually stated that its product contained aspirin. How should the court rule? Discuss. [*Thompson Medical Co. v. Federal Trade Commission,* 791 F.2d 189 (D.C. Cir. 1986)]

45-6. Sears, Roebuck & Co. adopted a new advertising program to boost sales of its Lady Kenmore dishwashers. The new ads claimed that these dishwashers "completely eliminated" the need for rinsing dishes before placing them in the dishwasher. The owner's manuals accompanying the machines, however, recommended pre-rinsing. Interviews with consumers indicated that pre-rinsing was still required for truly clean dishes. In an action against Sears, the FTC held that the advertising was misleading. The FTC's remedial order required that Sears keep records to support all future advertising claims for all "major home appliances" and submit them to the FTC. Sears conceded that its dishwasher advertising was misleading but argued that the remedial order, which covered other appliances, was overly broad and unfair. Discuss fully whether the FTC's broad order is legal. [*Sears, Roebuck & Co. v. Federal Trade Commission,* 676 F.2d 385 (9th Cir. 1982)]

45-7. Dennis and Janice Geiger saw an advertisement in a newspaper for a Kimball Whitney spinet piano on sale for $699 by McCormick Piano & Organ Co. Because the style of the piano drawn in the advertisement matched their furniture, the Geigers were particularly interested in the Kimball. When they went to McCormick Piano & Organ, however, they learned that the drawing closely resembled another, more expensive Crest piano, and that the Kimball spinet looked quite different than the piano sketched in the drawing. The salesperson told the Geigers that she was unable to order the spinet piano of the style requested by the Geigers. When the Geigers asked for the names of other customers who had purchased the advertised pianos, the salesperson became hysterical and said she would not, under any circumstances, sell the Geigers a piano. The Geigers then brought suit against the piano store, alleging that the store had engaged in deceptive advertising in violation of Indiana law. Was the McCormick Piano & Organ Co. guilty of deceptive advertising? Explain. [*McCormick Piano & Organ Co. v. Geiger,* 412 N.E.2d 842 (Ind.App. 1980)]

45-8. Branigar Organization, Inc., began a residential development in the 1970s. The development included a large country club with golf courses and tennis courts. The purchase price of a house or lot, however, did not include the initiation fees and dues required for club membership—although all residents could join the club if they paid these fees. Branigar later transferred the ownership and management of the club, and according to the plan of the new ownership, all members of the club were told that they would lose their usage rights as of December 31, 1990.

After that date, only members owning an equity interest in—that is, members who had purchased shares in—the club would be allowed to use the facilities. All non-equity members were offered the right to become equity members. Shirley Rice and others who had purchased lots or houses in the development claimed that Branigar's failure to disclose that the non-equity club members would eventually be required to buy equity membership to use the club violated the Interstate Land Sales Full Disclosure Act. The act requires developers to furnish prospective subdivision-lot purchasers with a property report that includes, among other things, information regarding recreational facilities associated with the subdivision. Will Rice and the others succeed in their claim? Discuss fully. [*Rice v. Branigar Organization, Inc.,* 922 F.2d 788 (11th Cir. 1991)]

45-9. Josephine Rutyna was a sixty-year-old widow who, in late 1976 and early 1977, had incurred a debt for medical treatment of her high blood pressure and epilepsy. She assumed that the cost of the services had been paid by either Medicare or her private insurance company. In July 1978, however, she was contacted by an agent of Collection Accounts Terminal, Inc., who stated that Rutyna still owed a debt of $56 for those services. She denied that she owed the debt and the following month received a letter from the collection agency threatening to contact her neighbors and employer concerning the debt if the $56 was not paid immediately. Discuss fully whether the collection agency's letter violates any consumer protection law. [*Rutyna v. Collection Accounts Terminal, Inc.,* 478 F.Supp. 980 (N.D.Ill. 1979)]

45-10. Sebastian and Maria Shaumyan entered into a home improvement contract with Sidetex Co. Sidetex agreed to install siding, replace windows, and perform other related work at the Shaumyan's home, and the Shaumyans agreed to pay Sidetex a total of $14,800 according to the following schedule: $3,000 as a deposit; $4,000 when Sidetex began the work; $3,900 when the work was half completed; $1,950 on completion of the installation of the siding; and $1,950 on completion of the work on the storm doors and shutters. Although a clause in the agreement referred to the contract as a "consumer credit contract," the Shaumyans' payments were not subject to any finance charges. Sidetex commenced work under the contract, and the Shaumyans made the scheduled progress payments of $3,000, $4,000, and $3,900. Performance was not completed, however, because a dispute arose concerning the quality of the windows that Sidetex was to install. The Shaumyans brought an action against Sidetex to recover damages, claiming that Sidetex violated the antidiscrimination provision of the Equal Credit Opportunity Act (ECOA) by requiring the signature of Mrs. Shaumyan on the home improvement contract. The central issue before the court was whether the home improvement contract, which provided for progress payments by the Shaumyans, constituted a "credit transaction" subject to the antidiscrimination provisions of the ECOA. How should the court rule? Discuss fully. [*Shaumyan v. Sidetex Co.,* 900 F.2d 16 (1990)]

45-11. Mr. and Mrs. Roberts, both African Americans, went shopping at a Walmart store in St. Charles, Missouri, and presented a check to the Walmart cashier to pay for several items that they wanted to purchase. When the Robertses noticed that the cashier was recording their race on the check, they returned the merchandise and retrieved the check. The Robertses then sued the store, claiming in part that the cashier's recording of their race on the check violated the Equal Credit Opportunity Act (ECOA), which prohibits discrimination in consumer credit transactions. The Robertses alleged that the transaction fell under the ECOA because "the exchange of goods and merchandise for a check issued by a customer creates a valid debit or obligation on the part of the purchaser and defers payment until such time as the check is presented for payment to the debtor's bank and thereafter paid." Walmart brought a motion to dismiss the complaint for failure to state a claim upon which relief could be granted. Will the court grant Walmart's motion? Discuss fully. [*Roberts v. Walmart Stores, Inc.,* 736 F.Supp. 1527 (E.D.Mo. 1990)]

45-12. A Question of Ethics

On July 16, 1982, the Semars signed a loan contract with Platte Valley Federal Savings & Loan Association, offering a second mortgage on their home as collateral. Under the Truth-in-Lending Act (TILA), borrowers are allowed three business days to rescind, without penalty, a consumer loan that uses their principal dwelling as security. The TILA requires lenders in such situations to state specifically the last *date on which the borrower can rescind the loan agreement, and if they fail to include this date, the borrower may rescind the loan within* three years *after it was made. Platte Valley's form omitted the exact expiration date of the three-day period, although it stated that the rescission right expired three business days after July 16. The Semars ceased making monthly payments on the loan in September 1983 and sent a Notice of Rescission to Platte Valley on February 15, 1984. The Semars claimed that Platte Valley had violated the TILA by failing to specify in the loan contract the exact date of the expiration of the three-day rescission period. Because of this violation, the Semars maintained they had three years in which to rescind the contract. Although the court found the Semars to be "unsympathetic plaintiffs," it nevertheless held that rescission was appropriate for the technical violation of the TILA. [Semar v. Platte Valley Federal Savings & Loan Association, 791 F.2d 699 (9th Cir. 1986)]*

1. Do you think that the court, by adhering so strictly to the letter of the law, violated the spirit of the law?
2. When deciding issues involving alleged violations of consumer protection legislation, such as the TILA, should courts balance the equities of the cases? That is, should the ethical (or unethical) behavior of the parties to a particular transaction be taken into consideration?
3. How might you justify, on ethical grounds, the court's decision in this case?

Chapter 46

Environmental Law

When the human population was small and dispersed and industry was limited, the earth was relatively unspoiled. Environmental degradation was not a significant problem. People assumed that the environment would absorb whatever they put into it. As the world became more populated, urbanized, and industrialized, however, concerns over the degradation of the environment increased. Industrial society's generation of waste threatened—and continues to threaten—the very existence of human life. The urban industrial society in this century has apparently strained the environment's capacity to handle the pollution discharged into the air and water. In the last two decades, **environmental law**—all law pertaining to environmental protection—has expanded in attempts to control this waste.

■ Common Law Actions

Common law remedies against environmental pollution originated centuries ago in England. Operations that belched dirt, smoke, noxious odors, noise, or toxic substances were sometimes held liable under common law theories of nuisance or negligence. Today, injured individuals continue to rely on the common law to obtain damages and injunctions against business polluters. (Statutory remedies are also available, a topic that we treat later.)

Nuisance

Under the common law doctrine of nuisance, persons may be held liable if they use their property in a manner that unreasonably interferes with others' rights to use or enjoy their property. In these situations, it is common for courts to balance the equities between the harm caused by the pollution and the costs of stopping it.

On the grounds that the hardships to be imposed on the polluter and on the community are relatively greater than the hardships to be suffered by the plaintiff, courts have often denied *injunctive relief.* For example, a factory that causes neighboring landowners to suffer from smoke, dirt, and vibrations may be left in operation if it is the core of a local economy. The injured parties may be awarded only their money damages. These damages may include compensation for the neighbors' total economic loss to their properties, present and future, caused by the factory's operation.

As indicated by the factory example, a property owner may be given relief from pollution in situations in which he or she can identify a distinct harm separate from that affecting the general public. This is referred to as a "private" nuisance. Under the common law, however, citizens were denied *standing* (access to the courts) unless they suffered harm distinct from the harm to the public at large. Some states still require this. Therefore, a group of citizens who wished to stop a new development that would cause significant water pollution were denied access to the courts on the ground that the harm to them did not differ from the harm to the general public.[1] A public authority (such as a state's attorney general) can sue to abate a "public" nuisance.

---

1. *Save the Bay Committee, Inc. v. Mayor of City of Savannah*, 227 Ga. 436, 181 S.E.2d 351 (1971).

Negligence and Strict Liability

An injured party may sue a business polluter in a common law negligence action. The basis for the action is the business's alleged failure to use reasonable care toward the party whose injury was foreseeable and, of course, caused by the failure. For example, employees might sue an employer whose failure to use proper pollution controls contaminated the air, causing the employees to suffer respiratory illnesses.

Injured parties might also recover under a theory of strict liability. Businesses that engage in ultrahazardous activities—such as the transportation of radioactive materials—are liable for whatever injuries the activities cause. In a strict liability action, the injured party does not need to prove that the business failed to exercise reasonable care. In the following case, the court outlines reasons for holding a particular polluter liable under theories of common law negligence and strict liability.

Case 46.1

STERLING v. VELSICOL CHEMICAL CORP.

United States District Court, Western District of Tennessee, 1986. 647 F.Supp. 303.

BACKGROUND AND FACTS   In 1964, Velsicol Chemical Corporation began operating a chemical waste burial site on a farm in Tennessee, eventually burying more than 300,000 fifty-five-gallon drums and hundreds of boxes filled with chemical waste. In 1973, Tennessee determined the site to be hazardous and closed it. Local residents sued Velsicol in a federal district court on a number of legal theories, including negligence and strict liability, claiming that the aquifer from which they drew drinking water was contaminated with chemicals that leaked from the farm. They sought damages for physical and emotional injuries and property damage.

DECISION AND RATIONALE   Finding that Velsicol's chemicals had proximately caused the residents harm, the United States District Court for the Western District of Tennessee held Velsicol liable under the doctrine of strict liability and the common law theory of negligence. The court concluded that "Velsicol's activity on the farm was not only ultrahazardous activity, but also abnormally dangerous activity and therefore [Velsicol] is strictly liable for any damages that have occurred." The court based its conclusion on the following reasons: (1) there was a high degree of risk of harm; (2) there was a likelihood that the harm would be great; (3) exercising reasonable care could not eliminate the risk; (4) the activity was not a common means of disposal and violated the state of the art; (5) the dump's location was inappropriate; and (6) the dump's dangerous attributes outweighed its value to the community. As to Velsicol's negligence, the court concluded that the firm had a duty to protect others from unreasonable harm arising from the dumping of chemicals on its property. The court stated that the firm had breached its duty by failing to (1) investigate, or hire knowledgeable persons to investigate, the geological and hydrological makeup under the site; (2) install proper monitoring procedures; (3) investigate, or hire knowledgeable persons to investigate, the situation after the U.S. Geological Survey warned the firm that its chemicals were contaminating the local water supply; (4) cease dumping after the warning; (5) select, locate, operate, maintain, and close the site according to the state of the art (including containing chemicals and fumes within the site's boundaries); (6) halt leaks that it knew about; (7) timely register with and respond to government agencies; and (8) warn residents to watch for any chemical taste or odor in the water. The court awarded the residents more than $5.2 million in compensatory damages, $7.5 million in punitive damages, and prejudgment interest (interest that accrues on the amount of a judgment from the date of the filing of the suit to the date the judgment is issued) at 8 percent per year on the compensatory damages.

State and Local Regulation

Many states regulate the degree to which the environment may be polluted. Thus, for example, even when state zoning laws permit a business's proposed development, the proposal may have to be altered to change the development's impact on the environment. State laws may restrict a business's discharge of chemicals into the air or water, or regulate its disposal of toxic wastes. States may also regulate the disposal or recycling of other wastes, including glass, metal, and plastic containers and paper. Additionally, states may restrict the emissions from motor vehicles.

City, county, and other local governments control some aspects of the environment. For instance, local zoning laws control some land use. These laws may be designed to inhibit or direct the growth of cities and suburbs or to protect the natural environment. Other aspects of the environment may be subject to local regulation for other reasons. Methods of waste and garbage removal and disposal, for example, can have a substantial impact on a community. The appearance of buildings and other structures, including advertising signs and billboards, may affect traffic safety, property values, or local aesthetics. Noise generated by a business or its customers may be annoying, disruptive, or damaging to its neighbors. The location and condition of parks, streets, and other public uses of land subject to local control affect the environment and can also affect business.

Federal Regulation

Congress has passed a number of statutes to control the impact of human activities on the environment. The major federal environmental statutes discussed in this chapter are listed and summarized in Exhibit 46–1. Some of these statutes have been passed to improve the quality of air and water. Some of them specifically regulate toxic chemicals—including pesticides, herbicides, and hazardous wastes. Some are concerned with radiation.

National Environmental Policy Act

The National Environmental Policy Act (NEPA) of 1969 imposes environmental responsibilities on all agencies of the federal government. NEPA requires that all agencies consider environmental factors when making significant decisions. For every major federal action that significantly affects the quality of the environment, an **environmental impact statement (EIS)** must be prepared. An action qualifies as "major" if it involves a substantial commitment of resources (monetary or otherwise). An action is "federal" if a federal agency has the power to control it. For example, building a new nuclear reactor involves federal action because a federal license is required.

An EIS must analyze (1) the impact on the environment that the action will have, (2) any adverse effects to the environment and alternative actions that might be taken, and (3) irreversible effects the action might generate. If an agency decides that an EIS is unnecessary, it must issue a statement supporting this conclusion. EIS's have become instruments for private citizens, consumer interest groups, businesses, and others to challenge federal agency actions on the basis that the actions improperly threaten the environment. Today, almost all environmental litigation under NEPA involves disputes with governmental agencies rather than disputes between private parties.

Complementary Federal Laws

Federal law contains a number of mandates that supplement the obligations expressed in the Na-

■ **Exhibit 46–1 Federal Environmental Statutes**

Popular Name	Purpose	Statute Reference
Rivers and Harbors Act (1886)	To regulate the discharge and deposit of refuse in navigable waterways.	33 U.S.C. Sections 407 *et seq.*
Federal Insecticide, Fungicide, and Rodenticide Act (FIFRA) (1947)	To control the use of pesticides and herbicides.	7 U.S.C. Sections 135 *et seq.*
Federal Water Pollution Control Act (FWPCA) (1948)	To eliminate the discharge of pollutants from major sources into navigable waters.	33 U.S.C. Sections 1251 *et seq.*
Atomic Energy Act (1954)	To limit environmental harm from the private nuclear industry.	42 U.S.C. Sections 2011 *et seq.*
Clean Air Act (1963)	To control air pollution from mobile and stationary sources.	42 U.S.C. Sections 7401 *et seq.*
National Environmental Policy Act (NEPA) (1969)	To limit environmental harm from federal government activities.	42 U.S.C. Sections 4321 *et seq.*
Marine Protection, Research, and Sanctuaries Act of 1972 (Ocean Dumping Act)	To regulate the transporting and dumping of material into ocean waters.	16 U.S.C. Sections 1431 *et seq.*
Noise Control Act (1972)	To regulate noise pollution from transportation and nontransportation sources.	42 U.S.C. Sections 4901 *et seq.*
Endangered Species Act (1973)	To protect species that are threatened with extinction.	16 U.S.C. Sections 1531 *et seq.*
Safe Drinking Water Act (1974)	To regulate pollutants in public drinking water systems.	42 U.S.C. Sections 300f *et seq.*
Resource Conservation and Recovery Act (RCRA) (1976)	To establish standards for hazardous waste disposal.	42 U.S.C. Sections 6901 *et seq.*
Toxic Substances Control Act (1976)	To regulate toxic chemicals and chemical compounds.	15 U.S.C. Sections 2601 *et seq.*
Comprehensive Environmental Response, Compensation, and Liability Act (CERCLA) (Superfund) (1980)	To regulate the clean-up of hazardous waste disposal sites.	42 U.S.C. Sections 9601 *et seq.*
Low Level Radioactive Waste Policy Act (1980)	To assign to the states responsibility for nuclear power plants' low-level radioactive waste.	42 U.S.C. Sections 2021b *et seq.*
Nuclear Waste Policy Act (1982)	To provide for the designation of a permanent radioactive waste disposal site.	42 U.S.C. Sections 10101 *et seq.*

tional Environmental Policy Act to protect environmental values in agency decision making. For example, the Federal Insecticide, Fungicide, and Rodenticide Act (discussed in more detail later in this chapter) requires that an agricultural economy

impact analysis be prepared in connection with a suspension or cancellation of the use of any pesticide.

Among the most important of the complementary federal laws are protections for fish and wildlife. Under the Fish and Wildlife Coordination Act,[2] federal agencies proposing to approve the impounding or diversion of the waters of a stream must consult with the Fish and Wildlife Service with a view to preventing the loss of fish and wildlife resources. An important provision is found in the Endangered Species Act of 1973. Under this act, all federal agencies are required to take steps to ensure that their actions "do not jeopardize the continued existence of endangered species" or the habitat of an endangered species. An action may jeopardize the continued existence of a species if it sets in motion a chain of events that reduces the chances that the species will survive.

Environmental Protection Agency

In 1970, the Environmental Protection Agency (EPA) was created to coordinate federal environmental responsibilities. The EPA administers most federal environmental policies and statutes. Other federal agencies with authority for regulating specific environmental matters include the Department of the Interior, the Department of Defense, the Department of Labor, the Food and Drug Administration, and the Nuclear Regulatory Commission.

■ Air Pollution

Federal involvement with air pollution goes back to the 1950s, when Congress authorized funds for air-pollution research. In 1963 the federal government passed the Clean Air Act, which focused on multistate air pollution and provided assistance to states. Various amendments, particularly in 1970, 1977, and 1990, strengthened the government's authority to regulate the quality of air.

These laws provide the basis for issuing regulations to control pollution coming primarily from mobile sources (motor vehicles) and stationary sources (electric utilities and industrial plants, among others). The EPA sets air quality standards for major pollutants. General guidelines set out requirements for protecting vegetation, climate, visibility, and certain economic conditions. The 1977 amendments to the Clean Air Act establish multilevel standards. For example, they attempt to prevent the deterioration of air quality even in areas where the existing quality exceeds that required by federal law.

Mobile Sources

Regulations governing air pollution from automobiles and other mobile sources specify pollution standards and time schedules. For example, the 1970 Clean Air Act required a reduction of 90 percent in the amount of carbon monoxide and other pollutants emitted by automobiles by 1975. (This did not happen, however, and the 1977 amendments extended the deadline to 1983. Generally, automobile manufacturers have met the 90 percent reduction goal by installing catalytic converters on automobiles.)

An automobile purchased today emits only about 4 percent of the pollutants that a new 1970 model did. Nevertheless, there are so many more automobiles being driven today that urban ground-level ozone, which decreased between the late 1970s and the late 1980s, has risen to former levels. Under the 1990 amendments, automobile manufacturers must cut new automobiles' exhaust emission of nitrogen oxide by 60 percent and emission of other pollutants by 35 percent. Beginning in 1994, increasing percentages of new vehicles must meet these standards. By 1998, all new automobiles must do so. Alternative-fuel vehicles will be introduced in California. Another set of emission controls may be ordered after 2000. To ensure compliance, the EPA certifies the prototype of a new automobile whose emission controls are effective up to 50,000 miles. The EPA may also inspect production models. If a vehicle does not meet the standards in actual driving, the EPA can order a recall and the repair or replacement of pollution-control equipment at the manufacturers' expense.

Service stations are also subject to environmental regulations. The 1990 amendments required that in 1992 service stations had to sell gasoline with a higher oxygen content in forty-one cities with winter carbon monoxide pollution. This could be accomplished by selling fuel containing corn ethanol. Beginning in 1995, service stations must sell even cleaner-burning gasoline in Los Angeles and another eight of the most polluted urban areas.

Present regulations are meant to eliminate lead completely in gasoline. In the following case, the court reviewed an EPA order regulating the lead content of gasoline, the validity of which had been challenged by Ethyl Corporation.

---

2. 16 U.S.C. Sections 661 *et seq.*

Case 46.2

ETHYL CORP. v. ENVIRONMENTAL PROTECTION AGENCY

United States Court of Appeals,
District of Columbia Circuit,
1976.
541 F.2d 1.

BACKGROUND AND FACTS   The Clean Air Act authorized the EPA to regulate gasoline additives that are a danger to public health and welfare. Ethyl Corporation, a leading producer of antiknock compounds for increasing gasoline octane ratings, filed for judicial review of the EPA order that required annual reductions in the lead content of gasoline. (Review of agency actions under the Clean Air Act are heard in the U.S. Court of Appeals for the District of Columbia Circuit.)

DECISION AND RATIONALE   The United States Court of Appeals for the District of Columbia Circuit upheld the EPA regulations. The EPA did not abuse its discretion in requiring the Ethyl Corporation to reduce the lead compounds in its gasoline. The record in this case was massive—over 10,000 pages. The EPA relied on this evidence in its decision, and, although the evidence was not wholly unassailable, it did provide a reasonable basis on which to base a decision. The court defined the scope of its review as follows: "Our [scope] requires us to strike 'agency action, findings and conclusions' [only if] we find [them] to be 'arbitrary, capricious, an abuse of discretion, or otherwise not in accordance with the law *   *   *.' This standard of review is a highly deferential one. It presumes agency action to be valid. Moreover, it forbids the court's substituting its judgment for that of the agency."

Stationary Sources

The Clean Air Act provides the EPA with authority to establish air quality standards but recognizes that the primary responsibility for preventing and controlling air pollution rests with state and local governments. The EPA sets two levels (primary and secondary) of ambient standards—that is, the maximum level of certain pollutants—and the states formulate plans to achieve those standards. The plans are to provide for the attainment of primary standards within three years and secondary standards within a reasonable time. For economic, political, or technological reasons, however, the deadlines are often subject to change.

Different standards apply to existing sources of pollution and major new sources. Different standards also apply to sources in clean areas and sources in polluted areas. Major new sources include existing sources modified by a change in a method of operation that increases emissions. Performance standards for these sources require use of the best available technology to reduce emissions from the combustion of fossil fuels.

Under the 1990 amendments, 110 of the oldest coal-burning power plants in the United States must cut their emissions by 40 percent by the year 2001 to reduce acid rain. Utilities were granted "credits" to emit certain amounts of sulfur dioxide, and those that emit less than required can sell their credits to other polluters. Controls on other factories and businesses are intended to reduce ground-level ozone pollution in ninety-six cities to healthy levels by 2005 (except Los Angeles, which has until 2010). Industrial emissions of 189 hazardous air pollutants must be reduced by 90 percent by 2000. By 2002, production of chlorofluorocarbons, carbon tetrachloride, and methyl chloroform—used in air conditioning, refrigeration, and insulation and linked to depletion of the ozone layer—must stop.

Hazardous air pollutants are those likely to cause an increase in mortality or in serious irreversible or incapacitating illness. As noted, there are 189 of these pollutants, including asbestos, benzene, beryllium, cadmium, mercury, radiation, vinyl chloride, and other cancer-causing materials. These pollutants may also cause neurological and reproductive damage. They are emitted by a variety of business activities, including smelting, dry cleaning, house painting, and commercial baking. Instead of establishing specific emissions standards for each hazardous air pollutant, the new law requires industry to use the best available technology to limit those emissions. The EPA may strengthen this requirement if necessary to protect public health.

The following case was decided before the 1990 amendments, when uniform national standards were provided for air pollutants emitted from any source. The standards included ''an ample mar-

gin of safety to protect the public health.'' The case concerns the standard for vinyl chloride (a cancer-causing chemical used in manufacturing plastic) and whether the cost of complying with that standard should be considered in setting it.

Case 46.3

NATURAL RESOURCES DEFENSE COUNCIL, INC. v. ENVIRONMENTAL PROTECTION AGENCY

United States Court of Appeals, District of Columbia Circuit, 1987.

824 F.2d 1146.

BACKGROUND AND FACTS In 1976, the EPA established emission standards for vinyl chloride (a cancer-causing chemical used in manufacturing plastic). The Clean Air Act provides for standards to be set at a level that "provides an ample margin of safety to protect the public health." The standards reduced emissions by 95 percent, leaving a risk that 1 of every 100,000 exposed individuals would develop cancer. Environmental groups protested that the standard was not strict enough to protect the public health. In 1977, the EPA responded by starting another rulemaking investigation. No action was taken until 1985, when the EPA determined that a further reduction in emissions would be unreasonably costly for the polluters. The Natural Resources Defense Council, an environmental group, sued the EPA, arguing that the standard did not provide "an ample margin of safety to protect the public health."

DECISION AND RATIONALE The United States Court of Appeals for the District of Columbia Circuit held that the EPA had not considered the appropriate factors in setting the vinyl chloride emission limits and remanded the case to the EPA for reconsideration of those limits. The court found that Congress's mandate to provide "an ample margin of safety to protect the public health" required the EPA to make an initial determination of what is "safe." The court held that in making that determination the EPA could consider only the risk to health at a particular emission level, not cost and technological feasibility. Thus, the court concluded that in this case the EPA had failed to use the proper standards.

Penalties

For violations of emission limits under the Clean Air Act, the EPA can assess civil penalties of up to $25,000 per day. To penalize those for whom this amount makes a violation more cost-effective than compliance, the EPA can obtain a penalty equal to the violator's economic benefits from noncompliance. Private citizens can also sue violators. Those who knowingly violate the act may be subject to criminal fines.

■ Water Pollution

Federal regulations governing the pollution of water can be traced back to the Rivers and Harbors Act of 1886, as amended in 1899. These regulations

required a permit for discharging or depositing refuse in navigable waterways.

Navigable Waters

Once limited to waters actually used for navigation, the term *navigable waters* is today interpreted to include coastal and freshwater wetlands and swamps, as well as intrastate lakes and streams used by interstate travelers and industries. In 1948, Congress passed the Federal Water Pollution Control Act (FWPCA), but its regulatory system and enforcement proved inadequate. In 1972, amendments to the FWPCA—known as the Clean Water Act—established a new system of goals and standards. These amendments established goals to (1) make waters safe for swimming, (2) protect fish and wildlife, and (3) eliminate the discharge of pollutants into the water. They set forth specific time schedules, which were extended by amendment in 1977 and by the Water Quality Act of 1987. Under these schedules, the EPA establishes limitations for discharges of types of pollutants based on the technology available for controlling them. Regulations for the most part specify that the best available technology be installed.

Municipal and industrial polluters must apply for permits before discharging wastes into navigable waters. Under the act, violators are subject to a variety of civil and criminal penalties. Civil penalties for each violation range from as low as a maximum of $10,000 per day, and not more than $25,000 per violation, to as much as $25,000 per day. Criminal penalties range from a fine of $2,500 per day and imprisonment of up to one year to a fine of $1 million and fifteen years' imprisonment. Injunctive relief and damages can also be imposed. The polluting party can be required to clean up the pollution or pay for the cost of doing so. In most cases, explicit penalties are also imposed on parties that pollute the water, as illustrated by the following case.

Case 46.4

UNITED STATES v. ATLANTIC RICHFIELD CO.

United States District Court, Eastern District of Pennsylvania, 1977. 429 F.Supp. 830.

BACKGROUND AND FACTS Atlantic Richfield Company (Arco) and other oil companies owned or operated vessels or facilities from which oil was discharged in harmful quantities into navigable waters. The discharges were accidental but violated the Clean Water Act. Arco and the others reported the spills to the Coast Guard and cleaned them up. When the Coast Guard assessed monetary civil penalties, Arco refused to pay. In the government's suit in a federal district court to enforce the penalties, Arco argued that the imposition of penalties, over and above clean-up costs, for an accidental oil spill when the reporting and cleaning requirements had been satisfied constituted a criminal action. Arco contended that because the spills were accidental, it was not at fault. Therefore there was nothing Arco could have done to avoid the spills, and the penalties could only be punishment. Arco believed that on that basis it had a right to a jury trial.

DECISION AND RATIONALE The United States District Court for the Eastern District of Pennsylvania held that the penalty was civil, not criminal. Therefore, the government could continue to assess and collect fines under the Clean Water Act against oil companies for accidental oil spills. Arco argued that it was not negligent and that therefore it was not at fault, but the court reasoned that although the facts would not support an action in negligence, the statute did not make fault an element in imposing the penalty. The court explained that "the principal goal of [the penalty] is to deter spills. * * * Additionally, the Congress obviously believed: (a) that no clean up effort could be complete because, after discharge, it is impossible to guarantee against residual harm from quantities of oil too small or too well dispersed to be detectable; and (b) that even the transitory pollution of waters was deleterious to the environment." The court concluded that "even where defendants are not at fault, the penalty does not act only as a punishment but serves the ends of civil regulation."

Drinking Water

Another statute governing water pollution is the Safe Drinking Water Act. Passed in 1974, this act requires the EPA to set maximum levels for pollutants in public water systems. Public water supply system operators must come as close as possible to meeting the EPA's standards by using the best available technology that is economically and technologically feasible. The EPA is particularly concerned with contamination from underground sources. Pesticides and wastes leaked from landfills or disposed of in underground injection wells are among the more than 200 pollutants known to exist in groundwater used for drinking in at least thirty-four states. Many of these substances are associated with cancer and damage to the central nervous system, liver, and kidneys.

Ocean Dumping

The Marine Protection, Research, and Sanctuaries Act of 1972 (known popularly as the Ocean Dumping Act), as amended in 1983, regulates the transportation and dumping of material into ocean waters. (The term *material* is synonymous with the term *pollutant* used in the Federal Water Pollution Control Act.) The Ocean Dumping Act prohibits entirely the ocean dumping of radiological, chemical, and biological warfare agents and high-level radioactive waste. The act establishes a permit program for transporting and dumping other materials. There are specific exemptions—materials subject to the permit provisions of other pollution legislation, wastes from structures regulated by other laws (for example, offshore oil exploration and drilling platforms), sewage, and other wastes. Each violation of any provision or permit may result in a civil penalty of not more than $50,000 or revocation or suspension of the permit. A knowing violation is a criminal offense that may result in a $50,000 fine, imprisonment for not more than a year, or both. Acts amounting to violations can also be enjoined. The Ocean Dumping Act also authorizes the designation of marine sanctuaries for ''preserving or restoring such areas for their conservation, recreational, ecological, or esthetic values.''

■ Noise Pollution

Regulations concerning noise pollution include the Noise Control Act of 1972. This act requires the establishment of noise emission standards (maximum noise levels below which no harmful effects occur due to interference with speech or other activity). The standards must be achievable by the best available technology, and they must be economically within reason. The act prohibits, among other things, distributing products manufactured in violation of the noise emission standards and tampering with noise control devices. Either of these activities can result in an injunction or whatever other remedy ''is necessary to protect the public health and welfare.'' Illegal product distribution

can also result in a fine and imprisonment. Violations of provisions of the Noise Control Act can result in penalties of not more than $50,000 per day and imprisonment for not more than two years.

■ Toxic Chemicals

Originally, most environmental clean-up efforts were directed toward reducing smog and making water safe for fishing and swimming. Over time, however, it became clear that chemicals released into the environment in relatively small amounts may pose a considerable threat to human life and health. Control of these toxic chemicals has become an important part of environmental law.

Pesticides and Herbicides

The first toxic chemical problem to receive widespread public attention was that posed by pesticides and herbicides. The federal statute regulating pesticides and herbicides is the Federal Insecticide, Fungicide, and Rodenticide Act (FIFRA) of 1947. Under FIFRA, pesticides and herbicides must be (1) registered before they can be sold, (2) certified and used only for approved applications, and (3) used in limited quantities when applied to food crops. If a substance is identified as harmful, the EPA can cancel its registration after a hearing. If the harm is imminent, the EPA can suspend registration pending the hearing. The EPA may also inspect factories in which these chemicals are manufactured.

Toxic Substances

The first comprehensive law covering toxic substances was the Toxic Substances Control Act, passed in 1976 to regulate chemicals and chemical compounds that are known to be toxic, as well as to institute investigation of any possible harmful effects from new chemical compounds, such as asbestos and polychlorinated biphenyls (popularly known as PCBs). The regulations authorize the EPA to require that manufacturers, processors, and other organizations planning to use chemicals first determine their effect on human health and the environment. The EPA can regulate substances that potentially pose an imminent hazard or an unreasonable risk of injury to health or the environment. The EPA may require special labeling, limit the use of a substance, set production quotas, or prohibit the use of a substance altogether.

Hazardous Wastes

Some industrial, agricultural, and household wastes pose more serious threats. If not properly disposed of, these toxic chemicals may present a substantial danger to human health and the environment. If released into the environment, they may contaminate public drinking water resources. A well-known example of the improper disposal of toxic and hazardous waste involved Hooker Electrochemical Company. Between 1942 and 1953, Hooker dumped more than 20,000 tons of chemical waste in an abandoned canal, known as the Love Canal, near Niagara Falls, New York. Hooker filled in the canal and sold the property to the local school board. An elementary school was built on it, and houses crowded around. In the 1970s, toxic residue bubbled to the surface. The community was abandoned.

RESOURCE CONSERVATION AND RECOVERY ACT In 1976, Congress passed the Resource Conservation and Recovery Act (RCRA) in reaction to an ever-increasing concern with the effects of hazardous waste materials on the environment. The RCRA required the EPA to establish regulations to monitor and control hazardous waste disposal and to determine which forms of solid waste should be considered hazardous and thus subject to regulation. Under the authority granted by this act, the EPA has promulgated various technical requirements for limited types of facilities for storage and treatment of hazardous waste. It also requires all producers of hazardous waste materials to properly label and package any hazardous waste to be transported.

The RCRA was amended in 1984 and 1986 to add several new regulatory requirements to those already monitored and enforced by the EPA. The basic aims of the amendments were to decrease the use of land containment in the disposal of hazardous waste and to require compliance with the act by some generators of hazardous waste—such as those generating less than 1,000 kilograms (2,200 pounds) a month—that had previously been excluded from regulation under the RCRA. In 1990, the EPA stiffened its RCRA enforcement policy. Under the new policy, a company may be assessed a civil penalty based on the seriousness of the violation, the probability of harm, and the extent to which the violation deviates from RCRA requirements. The assessment may be up to $25,000 per violation per day. Criminal penalties range from fines of $25,000 per day to $50,000 per day and imprisonment of not more than one year to not more than two years.

SUPERFUND In 1980, Congress passed the Comprehensive Environmental Response, Compensation, and Liability Act (CERCLA), commonly known as Superfund. The basic purpose of Superfund, which was amended in 1986 by the Superfund Amendments and Reauthorization Act, is to regulate the clean-up of leaking hazardous waste disposal sites. A special federal fund was created for that purpose. Superfund provides that when a release or a threatened release from a site occurs, the EPA can clean up the site and recover the cost of the clean-up from (1) the person who generated the wastes disposed of at the site, (2) the person who transported the wastes to the site, (3) the person who owned or operated the site at the time of the disposal, or (4) the current owner or operator. Liability is usually joint and several—that is, for example, a person who generated only a fraction of the hazardous waste disposed of at the site may nevertheless be liable for all of the clean-up costs.

Recently, courts have focused on the meaning of the words "owner or operator" to determine who is a potentially responsible party. A parent company has been held liable as an "operator" for clean-up costs for a chemical spill at a plant owned by its subsidiary. The court pointed out that the parent company controlled the subsidiary's finances, real estate transactions, and contact with the government, and that the parent company's personnel held most of the subsidiary's officer and director positions.[3] In other cases, courts have held officers and shareholders liable based on their authority to exercise control over their corporations.[4] A secured creditor of an operator of a facility has also been held liable on the basis that the creditor participated in the financial management of the facility to a degree indicating a capacity to control the corporation's handling of hazardous waste.[5] In the following case, the court considers whether a successor corporation can be held liable under CERCLA.

---

3. *United States v. Kayser-Roth Corp.,* 910 F.2d 24 (1st Cir. 1990).
4. See, for example, *State of New York v. Shore Realty Corp.,* 759 F.2d 1032 (2d Cir. 1985).
5. *United States v. Fleet Factors Corp.,* 901 F.2d 1550 (11th Cir. 1990). This case is discussed more fully in Chapter 34.

BACKGROUND AND FACTS The Anspec Company bought some land from Ultraspherics, Inc. After the sale, Ultraspherics merged into the Hoover Group, which was designated as the surviving corporation. Johnson Controls, Inc., is the sole shareholder of the Hoover Group and of Hoover Universal, which was the sole shareholder of Ultraspherics. Before the sale, Ultraspherics stored hazardous waste on the property. The waste contaminated the soil and groundwater. Anspec asked the Hoover Group to pay for a clean-up. When the Hoover Group refused, Anspec sued Ultraspherics and its successors in a federal district court. The trial court held that Ultraspherics could not be liable because it no longer existed. The other defendants—the Hoover Group, Hoover Universal, and Johnson Controls—moved for dismissal on the grounds that none of them had ever owned, occupied, or stored chemicals on the property and that CERCLA did not provide that successor corporations were liable for clean-up costs. The trial court granted the motion for dismissal. Anspec appealed.

DECISION AND RATIONALE The United States Court of Appeals for the Sixth Circuit reversed the trial court's judgment and remanded the case. The court noted that CERCLA clearly states liability for clean-up costs are imposed on "any person who at the time of disposal of any hazardous substance owned or operated any facility at which such hazardous substances were disposed of." The appellate court concluded that Congress included successor corporations with other entities that are potentially liable under CERCLA for clean-up costs. The court pointed out that "although the separate existence of every corporation except the surviving corporation in a merger ceases, the surviving corporation has all liabilities of every corporation that was a party to the merger. For purposes of liability, the surviving corporation and the merged corporation are one and the same." Construing CERCLA "in light of [this] universally accepted principle of private corporation law," the court said that "when Congress wrote 'corporation' in CERCLA it intended to include a successor corporation." Thus, "[i]f Ultraspherics is not liable for cleanup costs, it is only because Hoover Group stands in its shoes as the surviving party that became liable for its obligations."

Case 46.5

ANSPEC CO. v. JOHNSON CONTROLS, INC.

United States Court of Appeals, Sixth Circuit, 1991.
922 F.2d 1240.

■ Radiation

At the beginning of its development, nuclear energy was regarded as a cleaner and less expensive alternative to fossil fuels (coal and oil). During the production of nuclear energy, plutonium, uranium, and other radioactive materials emit dangerous levels of radiation. Radiation at these levels is believed to cause cancer and other diseases. The waste produced by a nuclear power plant remains dangerously radioactive for thousands of years. Despite continuing research, a method for permanent disposal of nuclear waste has not been developed.

Nuclear power plants are built and operated by private industry. The private nuclear industry is regulated almost exclusively by the federal government under the Atomic Energy Act of 1954.

The Nuclear Regulatory Commission (NRC) is the federal agency responsible for regulating the private nuclear industry. The NRC reviews the plans for each proposed nuclear plant and issues a construction permit only after preparing an environmental impact statement that considers the impact of an accidental release of radiation. After construction, the NRC licenses the plant's operation.

The Environmental Protection Agency sets standards for radioactivity in the overall environment and for the disposal of some radioactive waste. Low-level radioactive waste generated by private facilities is the responsibility of each state under the Low Level Radioactive Waste Policy Act of 1980, as amended in 1986. The NRC regulates the use and disposal of other nuclear materials and

■ CONCEPT SUMMARY 46.1 Environmental Law

Common Law Actions	1. *Nuisance*—Persons may be held liable if they use their property in a manner that unreasonably interferes with others' rights to use or enjoy their property. In nuisance suits, courts often balance the equities between the harm caused by the pollution and the costs of stopping it.
	2. *Negligence*—Parties may recover damages for injuries sustained as a result of pollution-causing activities of a firm if it can be demonstrated that the harm was a foreseeable result of the firm's failure to exercise reasonable care.
	3. *Strict liability*—Businesses engaging in ultrahazardous activities are liable for whatever injuries the activities cause, regardless of whether the firms exercise reasonable care.
Government Regulation	1. *Local and state regulation*—Activities affecting the environment are controlled at the local and state levels through regulations relating to land use, the disposal and recycling of garbage and waste, and pollution-causing activities generally.

	2. *Federal regulation*—
	   a. National Environmental Policy Act (1969)—NEPA imposes environmental responsibilities on all federal agencies and requires for every major federal action the preparation of an environmental impact statement (EIS). An EIS must analyze the action's impact on the environment, its adverse effects and possible alternatives, and its irreversible effects on environmental quality.
	   b. Complementary federal laws—Federal law contains a number of provisions that supplement the obligations expressed in the National Environmental Policy Act to protect environmental values in agency decision making. Among the most important of these are protections for fish and wildlife.
	   c. Environmental Protection Agency—Created in 1970 to coordinate federal environmental programs, the EPA administers most federal environmental policies and statutes.

	3. *Air pollution*—Six main classes of pollutants emitted from mobile and stationary sources are regulated under the authority of the Clean Air Act of 1963 and its amendments, particularly those of 1970, 1977, and 1990.

	4. *Water pollution*—
	   a. Pollution of navigable waters—Regulated under the authority of the Rivers and Harbors Act of 1886, as amended, and the Federal Water Pollution Control Act of 1948, as amended by the Clean Water Act of 1972, by additional amendments in 1977, and by the Water Quality Act of 1987.
	   b. Contamination of public drinking water systems—This contamination is regulated under the authority of the Safe Drinking Water Act of 1974.
	   c. Ocean dumping—Transporting and dumping of material into ocean waters are subject to the Marine Protection, Research, and Sanctuaries Act of 1972.

	5. *Noise pollution*—Noise pollution is regulated under the authority of the Noise Control Act of 1972.

	6. *Toxic chemicals*—
	   a. Pesticides and herbicides—These are regulated under the authority of the Federal Insecticide, Fungicide, and Rodenticide Act of 1947.
	   b. Toxic chemicals and chemical compounds—These are regulated under the authority of the Toxic Substances Control Act of 1976.
	   c. Hazardous wastes—These are regulated under the authority of the Resource Conservation and Recovery Act of 1976, as amended in 1984 and 1986, and the Comprehensive Environmental Response, Compensation, and Liability Act of 1980, as amended in 1986.

■ CONCEPT SUMMARY 46.1 *(Continued)*

Government Regulation (Continued)	7. *Radiation*—Private nuclear industry is regulated under the authority of the Atomic Energy Act of 1954. Each state is responsible for low-level radioactive waste under the Low Level Radioactive Waste Policy Act of 1980, as amended in 1986. The government is looking for a permanent radioactive waste disposal site pursuant to the Nuclear Waste Policy Act of 1982.

radioactive waste. Some radioactive waste is buried, burned, or dumped in the ocean. Currently, however, most of it is stored at the plants in which it is produced. Under the Nuclear Waste Policy Act of 1982, the government is looking for a permanent disposal site scheduled to be opened sometime in the year 2000.

There is a possibility of injury from exposure to radioactive substances in other forms. The potential for liability for injuries caused by radiation exposure begins with the mining of uranium ore. Hundreds of uranium miners have sued their employers and the federal government, alleging that they suffered lung cancer or other diseases as a result of exposure in the mines. The processing of uranium ore has also resulted in lawsuits. In one case, for example, it was claimed that exposure to uranium tailings caused the deaths of seven children in Monticello, Utah.[6]

Liability may be predicated on some of the same grounds discussed in other sections of this chapter. A common law theory may serve as the basis for a radiation suit. For example, Safety Light Corporation was held liable under a strict liability theory for the acts of its predecessor company, the United States Radium Company (USRC). USRC had extracted radium from uranium ore and deposited radioactive tailings from the process on vacant portions of its property in New Jersey be-

tween 1917 and 1926. T&E Industries, Inc., bought the property in 1974. In 1979, the state advised T&E that radiation levels on the property were excessive. In T&E's suit against Safety Light, the court held that the party creating a radiation hazard is strictly responsible for its clean-up and any damages.[7]

Liability for injury resulting from radiation may also arise under one of the statutes discussed elsewhere in this chapter. In 1986, the state of Ohio sued the Department of Energy and private contractors who had operated a nuclear weapons facility at Fernald, Ohio, alleging, among other things, that they improperly released radioactive materials into the environment in violation of the Clean Water Act, the Resource Conservation and Recovery Act, and the Comprehensive Environmental Response, Compensation, and Liability Act. In 1988, energy officials admitted that an operator of the facility had been ordered to continue dumping radioactive material at the site over a period of years. Officials agreed to pay Ohio more than $1 million to settle two suits and agreed to allow the state to oversee the clean-up of the site. In 1990, a federal appeals court ordered the Department of Energy to pay $250,000 in civil penalties to Ohio.[8]

---

6. *Maughan v. S. W. Servicing, Inc.*, 758 F.2d 1381 (10th Cir. 1985). Ultimately, it was determined that the children had not received biologically significant doses.

7. *T&E Industries v. Safety Light Corp.*, 123 N.J. 371, 587 A.2d 1249 (1991).

8. *Ohio v. Department of Energy*, 904 F.2d 1058 (6th Cir. 1990).

■ Terms and Concepts

■ For Review

1. What are the common law theories under which polluters may be held liable?

2. How do states regulate the degree to which the environment may be polluted?

3. In terms of federal environmental protection legislation, what does the National Environmental Policy Act provide? What is an environmental impact statement, and who must file one? What does the Environmental Protection Agency do?

4. Russ owns and operates a service station in Miles City, a city with winter carbon monoxide pollution and one of the eight most polluted urban areas in the United States. Russ's gasoline is stored in underground tanks, one of which has been leaking for seven years into the aquifer from which the city draws some of its drinking water. What federal environmental protection legislation is Russ's busi-

ness subject to? Specifically, what does this legislation require Russ to do regarding (1) the gasoline that he sells and (2) the leaking tank? If Russ fails to comply with these laws, what are the penalties?

Sherman Paint Co. is a subsidiary of Grant International, Inc., which controls Sherman's operations. Sherman's manufacturing process generates chemical wastes. Sherman contracts with Thomas Trucking Co. to transport the wastes to Butler Waste Management Co.'s disposal site. Butler sells the site to Franz, who secures the mortgage on the site with the property itself. When Franz defaults on the payments, Franz's mortgagee, Bank of New Ulm, repossesses the site. When the site is discovered to be leaking hazardous waste, the Environmental Protection Agency (EPA) cleans it up. From whom can the EPA recover the cost of the clean-up operations?

■ Questions and Case Problems

46-1. The EPA has set ambient standards for several pollutants, including sulfur dioxide, specifying the maximum concentration allowable in the outdoor air. One way to meet these standards is to reduce emissions. Companies discovered, however, that they could also meet the standards at less cost by building very high smokestacks. When emitted from such high stacks, pollutants were more widely dispersed and remained below the concentration level specified by the ambient standards. Environmental groups claimed that the Clean Air Act was designed to reduce pollution, not disperse it, and argued that industry should not be allowed to rely on tall stacks. Are the environmental groups correct, or should industry be allowed to use the less expensive dispersal method? Discuss.

46-2. Current scientific knowledge indicates that there is no safe level of exposure to a cancer-causing agent. In theory, even one molecule of such a substance has the potential for causing cancer. Section 112 of the Clean Air Act requires that all cancer-causing substances be regulated to ensure a margin of safety. Some environmental groups have argued that all emissions of such substances must be eliminated in order for such a margin of safety to be reached. Such a total elimination would likely shut down many major U.S. industries. Should the EPA totally eliminate all emissions of cancer-causing chemicals? Discuss.

46-3. Moonbay is a development home building corporation that primarily develops retirement communities. Farmtex owns a number of feedlots in Sunny Valley. Moonbay purchased 20,000 acres of farmland in the same area and began building and selling homes on this acreage. In the meantime, Farmtex continued to expand its feedlot business, and eventually only 500 feet separated the two operations. Because of the odor and flies from the feedlots, Moonbay found it difficult to sell the homes in its development. Moonbay wants to enjoin Farmtex from operating

its feedlots in the vicinity of the retirement home development. Discuss under what theory Moonbay would file this action. Discuss fully whether Farmtex has violated any federal environmental laws.

46-4. Fruitade, Inc., is a processor of a soft drink called Freshen Up. Fruitade uses returnable bottles, as well as a special acid to clean its bottles for further beverage processing. The acid is diluted by water and then allowed to pass into a navigable stream. Fruitade crushes its broken bottles and throws the crushed glass into the stream. Discuss fully any environmental laws that Fruitade has violated.

46-5. The EPA canceled the registration of the pesticide diazinon for use on golf courses and sod farms because of concern about the effects of diazinon on birds. The Federal Insecticide, Fungicide, and Rodenticide Act authorizes cancellation of the registration of product's that "generally cause unreasonable adverse effects on the environment." The statute further defines "unreasonable adverse effects on the environment" to mean "any unreasonable risk to man or the environment, taking into account the . . . costs and benefits." Thus, in determining whether a pesticide should continue to be used, one must balance the risks and benefits of the use of the pesticide. Does this mean that one must find that the pesticide killed birds more often than not before its use can be prohibited? Or, to prohibit the pesticide's use, is it sufficient to find only that the use of the pesticide results in recurrent bird kills? [*CIBA-Geigy Corp. v. Environmental Protection Agency*, 874 F.2d 277 (5th Cir. 1989)]

46-6. The EPA promulgated water-pollution discharge limits for several mining industries. These standards authorized variances exempting mining operations from coverage by the standards if the operations could show that they used special processes or facilities that made the standards inapplicable. Cost was not a consideration in granting the variances. An industry trade association sued, claiming that the EPA should consider costs in granting variances, and the Fourth Circuit Court of Appeals agreed. Discuss whether the United States Supreme Court should overturn this decision or affirm it and let costs be considered in the granting of variances under the Clean Water Act. [*Environmental Protection Agency v. National Crushed Stone Association,* 449 U.S. 64, 101 S.Ct. 295, 66 L.Ed.2d 268 (1980)]

46-7. The Resource Conservation and Recovery Act gives the EPA authority to require a company to clean up a hazardous-waste site that presents an "imminent and substantial endangerment" to public health or to the environment. A company disposed of dioxin by discharging it into a pond located on its property. The EPA ordered that the company stop the disposal and clean up the site. The company argued that the EPA had no evidence of any actual harm to the health of nearby residents. Should the company be compelled to clean up the dioxin even in the absence of evidence of actual harm? Discuss. [*United States v. Vertac Chemical Corp.,* 489 F.Supp. 870 (E.D.Ark. 1980)]

46-8. Taylor Bay Protective Association is a nonprofit corporation established for the purpose of restoring and improving the water quality of Taylor Bay. Local water districts began operating a flood control project in the area. As part of the project, a pumping station was developed. Testimony at trial revealed that the pumps were operated contrary to the instructions provided in the Operation and Maintenance Manual. The pumps acted as vacuums, sucking up increased amounts of silt and depositing the silt in Taylor Bay. Thus, the project resulted in sedimentation and turbidity problems in the downstream watercourse of Taylor Bay. The association sued the local water districts, alleging that the pumping operations created a nuisance. Do the pumping operations qualify as common law nuisance? Who should be responsible for the clean-up costs? Discuss both questions fully. [*Taylor Bay Protective Association v. Environmental Protection Agency,* 884 F.2d 1073 (8th Cir. 1989)]

46-9. Portland General Electric Co. maintained a turbine facility. Nearby residents complained that the facility emitted low-frequency sound waves that caused them to suffer loss of sleep, emotional distress, and mental strain. Consequently, these residents sued the company, claiming that it was creating a nuisance. The defendant contended that the plaintiffs had suffered no special harm. The district court dismissed the plaintiffs' complaint, and the plaintiffs appealed the decision. Should the appellate court affirm the dismissal? Explain. [*Frady v. Portland General Electric Co.,* 55 Or.App. 344, 637 P.2d 1345 (1981)]

46-10. Asarco, Inc., had a copper smelter at Ruston, Washington. As part of its operations, Asarco produced a by-product called "slag," a hard, rocklike substance. Industrial Mineral Products (IMP) sold the slag for Asarco to Louisiana-Pacific Corp. and other businesses, which used the slag as a ballast to stabilize the ground at log-sorting yards in the Tacoma, Washington, area. About nine months after IMP stopped selling the slag, it sold substantially all of its

assets to L-Bar Products, Inc. Government agencies later discovered that the slag reacted with the acidic wood waste in the log-sorting yards, causing heavy metals from the slag to leach into the groundwater and soil. Louisiana-Pacific and the Port of Tacoma sued Asarco under CERCLA, claiming that Asarco was liable for clean-up costs. Asarco brought a third party claim against L-Bar as corporate successor to IMP. L-Bar moved for summary judgment, claiming that it was not the successor to IMP and could not be liable under CERCLA for IMP's actions. Will the court agree with L-Bar? Discuss fully. [*Louisiana-Pacific Corp. v. Asarco, Inc.,* 909 F.2d 1260 (9th Cir. 1990)]

46-11. A Question of Ethics

In the 1970s, South Carolina Recycling and Disposal, Inc., (SCRDI) ran a hazardous waste disposal and recycling operation. A number of chemical companies (so-called generators) brought their wastes to the SCRDI facility. Handling of wastes at the site was itself hazardous; 7,200 fifty-five-gallon drums of hazardous substances—including materials that were toxic, carcinogenic, mutagenic, explosive, and highly flammable—accumulated. Stacked without regard to the source or the compatibility of the substances within, many drums deteriorated to the point that their contents spilled onto other drums, mixed with other leaking substances, and oozed into the ground. This caused noxious and toxic fumes and a number of fires and explosions. The EPA began clean-up operations and sued some of the generators (plus others) for the costs. The generators argued that they should not have to pay because there was no evidence linking their specific wastes to the problems. The court granted summary judgment for the EPA, ruling that the EPA needed to show only that the generators sent waste to the site at some time. [United States v. South Carolina Recycling and Disposal, Inc., *653 F.Supp. 984 (D.S.C. 1986)*]

1. The liability imposed on business firms under CERCLA has led to controversy because sometimes it seems unfair that certain businesses should be held liable. In this case, the generators argued that it would be unfair to hold them liable for clean-up costs in the absence of any evidence that their wastes caused any of the problems. In response, the court held that to require specific proof of causation "would . . . effectively 'eviscerate the statute' because of the technological infeasibility of 'fingerprinting' a given generator's substances at a site." What two broad ethical policies or principles are in conflict here?

2. The court also held that the generators were jointly and severally liable for clean-up costs. Joint and several liability under CERCLA means that a company that is responsible for only a fraction of the waste may nonetheless be liable for all of the clean-up costs. From an ethical point of view, evaluate the arguments for and against joint and several liability for the costs associated with environmental clean-up operations.

Chapter 47

Antitrust Law

In free and open competition, businesses attempt to develop and sell products that are more attractive to customers than are the products of rival firms. Competition among sellers therefore promotes the development of appealing products. When products sold by different firms are similar, firms compete by trying to sell at the lowest price possible while still earning enough after costs to make it worthwhile to remain in that particular endeavor. For example, if Acme, Inc., develops a new laser-printing facsimile transmission machine (laser fax) that has broad appeal among consumers, it will begin to earn profits greater than those of its rivals—profits commensurate with the appeal of its new product.

■ Market Power and Antitrust Law

To encourage such innovative behavior, we might feel justified in allowing Acme to have a *monopoly* over the sale of the laser fax—at least for a while anyway, say, seventeen years.[1] The term **monopoly** is generally used to describe a market for which there is a single seller. In that respect, Acme would be a monopolist, albeit for a limited time, in the laser fax market. In legal terms, monopoly may also describe a firm that, although not being the sole seller in the market, can nonetheless substantially ignore rival firms in setting a selling price for its product or can in some way limit rivals from competing in the market (possibly by preventing rivals from entering the market altogether). Acme's monopoly would give it such **market power** (that is, power to affect the market price of its product). Acme would have the power during the term of its monopoly to prevent other firms from selling the laser fax. Acme would be free to charge whatever price it chose to, and it would choose a price that made its profits as large as possible.

Another firm might seek to develop a different type of unique fax with equal or greater appeal. If it succeeded, it would draw customers away from Acme. If its product were sufficiently dissimilar from Acme's, it too might seek a monopoly over its product. There would then be two monopolies rather than one, but society would have the benefit of *two* unique and valued

---

1. Acme would be given a patent on its newly developed laser fax.

products. Moreover, Acme would be concerned with losing laser fax consumers to its rival if Acme charged too high a price. Acme's rival would have the same concern over the price of its fax. Eventually, after the allowed monopolies expired, numerous firms would be allowed to market these products. Each firm would seek to attract customers by charging a price that appealed to consumers. The only thing that would prevent prices from falling ever lower is that at some point the price of a laser fax would be so low that new firms would quit trying to enter the market to compete for fax consumers. They would instead devote their efforts and resources to alternative, more profitable efforts.

Our scenario, simplistic though it may be, should make clear an often overlooked point: market power is not inherently bad. Market power correlates to high profits, and large profits are the reward for innovation, foresight, and good management. Market power is the prize that motivates firms to benefit society with innovative products and competitive prices. What is at issue is not market power *per se* but how firms go about acquiring market power and what firms do with that power once they acquire it. **Antitrust law** is that body of statutes and principles that regulates business conduct so as to promote the forms of competition that benefit society, while it simultaneously seeks to rein in the exercise of market power that often is the fruit of such competition.

■ Origins of Federal Antitrust Legislation

After the Civil War ended, the nation renewed its drive westward. With the movement westward came the expansion of the railroads and the further integration of the economy. The growth of national markets also witnessed the efforts of a number of small companies to combine into large business organizations—called **trusts**—many of which gained considerable market power. The most famous—or infamous—trust was John D. Rockefeller's Standard Oil Trust. In general, a trust is an arrangement in which some party, referred to as a trustee, holds legal title to property for the benefit of another. As used by Standard Oil and others around the turn of the century, trusts were a device used to amass market power. The participants

transferred their stock to a trustee and in return received trust certificates. The trustee then made decisions fixing prices, controlling output, and allocating geographic markets in which specified members could compete free from competition with other members.

In some cases, an entire industry was dominated by a single organization. The public perception was that the trusts used their market power to drive small competitors out of business, leaving the trusts then free to raise prices virtually at will.[2] Congress initially dealt with the railroad monopolies by attempting regulation rather than an outright assault on monopoly power. The result was the Interstate Commerce Act of 1887, which created the Interstate Commerce Commission to regulate the railroad industry.

Congress next attempted to deal with trusts in a direct, unified way by passing the Sherman Act in 1890. The Sherman Act, however, failed to end public concerns. Much market power continued unabated. The United States Supreme Court initially construed the statute too narrowly to give it much effect and subsequently applied it so rigorously as to make the act unworkable. Lackluster enforcement also contributed to the public's dissatisfaction. Concern over the trust problem continued to the point that it dominated the 1912 presidential election and eventually, in 1914, led to enactment of the Clayton Act and the Federal Trade Commission Act. The Clayton Act and the Federal Trade Commission Act sought to deal with the monopoly problem by proscribing certain acts and providing for more aggressive means of enforcement.

In the following sections we discuss in turn the major provisions of the Sherman Act and the Clayton Act. The Sherman Act is a broadly worded pronouncement concerning certain agreements between competitors that restrain trade and general conduct leading to, or tending to produce, monopoly power. The Clayton Act (as amended by the Robinson-Patman Act in 1936 and the Celler-Kefauver Act of 1950) addresses specific acts that

---

2. There is now a considerable amount of literature that questions whether predatory tactics (such as pricing products at below-market levels to drive competitors from the market) are economically viable and whether they in fact accurately characterize the activities of the old robber barons such as Rockefeller.

are considered to be anticompetitive. The Federal Trade Commission Act created the Federal Trade Commission and invested it with broad enforcement powers to prevent, as well as correct, anticompetitive practices.

■ The Sherman Act

The main provisions of the Sherman Act are contained in Sections 1 and 2 of the act. Both sections broadly describe two areas of illegal conduct. Section 1 requires a concerted activity on the part of two or more persons to restrain trade:

> Section 1: Every contract, combination in the form of trust or otherwise, or conspiracy, in restraint of trade or commerce among the several States, or with foreign nations, is hereby declared to be illegal [and is a felony punishable by fine or imprisonment].

Section 2 applies to both unilateral and concerted actions:

> Section 2: Every person who shall monopolize, or attempt to monopolize, or combine or conspire with any other person or persons, to monopolize any part of the trade or commerce among the several States, or with foreign nations, shall be deemed guilty of a felony [and is similarly punishable].

Although the term *antitrust* is commonly perceived as involving "trustbusting"—that is, breaking up a single, dominant firm—the major thrust of the Sherman Act has been directed at various anticompetitive agreements between rival firms to fix prices, restrict output, divide markets, exclude other competitors, or otherwise impede the dynamics of a free market. Such joint actions have been prosecuted under Section 1 as restraints of trade and, if firms possess substantial market power, under Section 2 as conspiracies to monopolize. It is Section 2, however, that is aimed at the monopolies characterized by single, dominant firms.

Both restraint of trade and monopoly power are fundamental concepts in antitrust law. A *restraint of trade* is any agreement between firms that has the effect of reducing competition in the marketplace. The most direct, and perhaps the most useful, way of thinking of *monopoly power* is to recall our initial discussion of Acme's market power in the scenario in which the company was given, for a time, exclusive control over the laser fax market;

specifically, Acme had the ability to ignore the effect of raising its product price on the ability of competitors to enter the laser fax market. Such extreme market power is an example of monopoly power. **Monopoly power** is simply an extreme amount of market power. Any firm, even if it is not the sole supplier, that is not completely constrained by the potential response of a rival in deciding what price to charge for its product has some degree of market power. Whether such power is of a magnitude to warrant calling it monopoly power is one of the most difficult tasks encountered in the application of antitrust law.

Section 1: Overview

The underlying assumption of Section 1 of the Sherman Act is that society's welfare is harmed if rival firms are permitted to join in an agreement that consolidates their market power or otherwise restrains competition. Not all agreements between rivals, however, result in enhanced market power or *unreasonably* restrain trade. It is virtually inconceivable that an agreement to fix prices or restrict output could be designed for any purpose other than to diminish interfirm competition. Yet there are numerous instances when agreements between rivals might actually increase social welfare by making firms more efficient, by making information more readily available, or by creating joint incentives to undertake risky research and development projects. An agreement that at first glance may appear to be anticompetitive may actually provide legitimate benefits to society. Others are so blatantly and substantially anticompetitive that they are deemed *per se* **violations** of Section 1. If an agreement is found to be of a type that is deemed a *per se* violation, a court is precluded from inquiring whether it should nonetheless be upheld on the ground that it provides benefits that outweigh the anticompetitive effects. Characterization of the agreement, however, does not complete the antitrust analysis. If an agreement is not one that is a *per se* violation of Section 1, then the courts proceed to analyze its legality under what is referred to as a **rule of reason.**

In determining whether a specific agreement that is not a *per se* violation should nonetheless be condemned as a Section 1 offense, a court will consider several factors. The court must evaluate the purposes the parties have in effecting the agreement, determine whether the parties have power to implement the agreement's purposes, and assess what the effect or potential effect of the agreement is. Some antitrust scholars maintain that case law suggests that courts will also consider a fourth element: whether the parties could have relied on less restrictive means to achieve their goals.

The dividing line between *per se* violations and agreements judged under a rule of reason is seldom clear. Moreover, in some cases, the United States Supreme Court has stated it is applying a *per se* rule, and yet a careful reading of its analysis suggests that it is weighing benefits against harms under a rule of reason. Some have termed this a ''soft,'' or ''limited,'' *per se* rule. Others have termed it a ''narrow'' rule of reason. Perhaps the most that can be said with certainty is that although the distinction between the two rules seems clear in theory, in the actual application of antitrust laws, the distinction has not always been so clear.

Section 1: Horizontal Restraints

The term **horizontal restraint** is encountered frequently in antitrust law. A horizontal restraint is any agreement that in some way restrains competition between rival firms competing in the same market. Whenever firms at the same level of operation and in direct competition with one another (for example, retailers of a common product that are located in the same geographical market) agree to operate in a way that restricts their market activities, they are said to have imposed a horizontal restraint on trade. Some horizontal restraints are per se violations of Section 1, but others may be permissible; those that are not *per se* violations are tested under the rule of reason, which was described above.

PRICE FIXING Suppose in our introductory example, Acme had sought its reward of large profits by some means other than arduous and financially risky research into laser fax technology. Assume that laser technology has not yet been invented, so we are in the pre–laser fax era. Suppose that Acme's managers had decided to make life easy for themselves. Suppose that they had gone to other fax machine producers who, like Acme, were making nonlaser fax machines and said, ''Let's not work to one another's disadvantage. There's enough of a demand for fax machines for all of us to charge higher prices if we don't undercut one another's prices.'' Acme's plan called for each pro-

ducer to charge a price higher than an established minimum. The minimum price was set as the total cost of the least productive producer plus a 10 percent margin. More efficient firms (that is, those firms that could produce at lower cost), of course, enjoyed higher profits. This is the essence of **price fixing.**

Perhaps the definitive case regarding price-fixing agreements remains the 1940 case of *United States v. Socony-Vacuum Oil Co.,* also known as the *Madison Oil* case.[3] In the case, a group of independent oil producers in Texas and Louisiana were caught between falling demand due to the Great Depression and increasing supply from newly discovered oil fields in the region. In response, a group of the major refining companies agreed to buy ''distress'' gasoline (excess supplies) from the independents so as to dispose of it in an ''orderly manner.'' Although there was no explicit agreement as to price, it was clear that the purpose of the agreement was to limit the supply of gasoline on the market, thereby raising prices.

There may have been good reasons for such an agreement. Nonetheless, as demonstrated by our example of the fax producers' price-fixing scheme, the dangers of such agreements to open and free competition are enormous. The United States Supreme Court recognized these dangers in the *Socony-Vacuum* case. The Court held that the asserted reasonableness of a price-fixing agreement is never a defense; any agreement that restricts output or artificially fixes price is a *per se* violation of Section 1. The rationale of the *per se* rule was best stated in what is now the most famous portion of the Court's opinion: footnote 59 of Justice William O. Douglas's opinion. In it, Douglas compared a freely functioning price system to a body's central nervous system, condemning price-fixing agreements as threats to ''the central nervous system of the economy.''

HORIZONTAL MARKET DIVISIONS As illustrated by the *Socony-Vacuum* case, prices can be controlled indirectly through agreements to restrict output, as well as by explicitly agreeing to fix prices. Because the former type of agreement operates so as to decrease the supplies available to consumers, it has the same effect as a direct agree-

---

3. 310 U.S. 150, 60 S.Ct. 811, 84 L.Ed.2d 1129 (1940).

ment to raise prices. Similar controls can be effected by **horizontal market divisions,** that is, by agreements to divide the market up among rival firms. The allocation may be geographical (for example, letting one firm serve the Midwest, another the East Coast, and so on), or it may be by functional class of customer (for example, having one firm deal exclusively with retailers and a second firm deal solely with wholesalers). In some respects, market divisions may have an even greater impact on competition than do price-fixing agreements. Each firm has a complete monopoly over its allocated share of the market—it is the sole supplier. The sole supplier is free not only from price competition but from competition regarding quality, customer service, and all other dimensions of competition as well. Such agreements are generally treated as *per se* violations of Section 1.

The *per se* rule regarding market divisions has been criticized in certain circumstances, and its future status is uncertain. Some actual cases involved circumstances very dissimilar to those presented in our hypothetical scenario. In one instance, a group of small- and medium-sized groceries agreed to market a common brand of grocery products by allocating regional territories to members of the group. The group accounted for only about 6 percent of sales in their market and directly competed with such large chain stores as A&P and Safeway, which carried their own name-brand products.[4] A similar venture using territorial restrictions involved a group of small firms attempting to market mattresses under the trademark Sealy.[5] In both these cases the individual firms did not have resources to create their own brands individually and joined together so as to compete with larger, established firms selling their own brand-name products. Nonetheless, both cases were treated as *per se* violations of Section 1. It is possible that such considerations will ultimately lead to the United States Supreme Court's adopting a rule of reason for judging such horizontal restraints. As seen in some of the cases considered below, the Court has been more willing in recent years to consider economic factors rather than re-

lying solely on mechanical characterizations in judging business conduct.

TRADE ASSOCIATIONS   The common interests of firms or individuals within an industry or profession are frequently promoted by trade associations or professional organizations. These organizations may provide for the exchange of information among the members, the enhancement of the public image of the trade or profession, the setting of industry or professional standards, or the pooling of resources to represent the members' interests to various governmental bodies. Some of these activities benefit society as well as the individual members. Even those activities that benefit the members' general economic well-being may not necessarily be anticompetitive.

For example, lumber producers might be concerned about whether or not they are cutting more trees than expected future demand would warrant, given the cutting levels of rival firms. The market for lumber might be widely dispersed over the whole nation, making it especially difficult for small firms to get a handle on the overall demand conditions in the lumber market. Lumber firms might thus decide to form a trade association that could amass data on the output and price levels of its members in various markets.[6] The association would be of economic benefit to lumber firms by reducing the costs of projecting market demand. Such knowledge could also benefit society, however, by making the lumber market function more smoothly, dampening cycles of oversupply and undersupply of lumber output. Even if it did not make the industry function more smoothly, it would be unlikely to harm competition in the industry unless the industry were *concentrated.*

A **concentrated industry** is one in which either a single firm or a small number of firms control a large percentage of market sales. In such concentrated industries, trade associations can be, and have been, used to facilitate other anticompetitive actions, such as fixing prices, allocating markets, or, as discussed in the next section, conducting boycotts—all with the clear objective of lessening competition. Again, for example, con-

---

4.   See *United States v. Topco Associates, Inc.,* 405 U.S. 596, 92 S.Ct. 1126, 31 L.Ed.2d 515 (1972).

5.   See *United States v. Sealy, Inc.,* 388 U.S. 350, 87 S.Ct. 1847, 18 L.Ed.2d 1238 (1967).

6.   See, for example, *American Column & Lumber Co. v. United States,* 257 U.S. 377, 42 S.Ct. 114, 66 L.Ed.2d 284 (1921).

sider the lumber association. Such an association would be providing information that members could use to determine whether a secret agreement to fix a minimum price was being adhered to by the conspirators. Thus, such associations offer possibilities of both great benefits and substantial harm.

In most instances, the rule of reason is applied to these activities. If a court finds that a particular practice or agreement restrains trade but is without an apparent intent to fix prices or limit output, and if the arrangement also is beneficial to the public as well as the association, then the court will weigh those benefits against the harms to competition under the rule of reason. As in all cases, however, if the harm to competition is substantial, a trade association's activities will be condemned as a Section 1 violation. As shown in the following case, not even an action undertaken by a health-care professional group allegedly for the sole purpose of protecting the public will escape scrutiny if it is likely to harm market competition.

Case 47.1

WILK v. AMERICAN MEDICAL ASSOCIATION

United States Court of Appeals, Seventh Circuit, 1990.
895 F.2d 352.

BACKGROUND AND FACTS In 1966, the American Medical Association (AMA) passed a resolution labeling chiropractic an unscientific cult. (Chiropractors attempt to cure or relieve bodily ailments by making skeletal adjustments.) In effect, this label prevented physicians from associating with chiropractors, because Principle 3 of the Principles of Medical Ethics—the AMA's code of ethical conduct—provided that a "physician should practice a method of healing founded on a scientific basis; and he should not voluntarily associate with anyone who violates this principle." Medical doctors used Principle 3 to justify their refusal to have anything to do with chiropractors or to allow chiropractors to use hospital diagnostic services or become members of hospital medical staffs. Despite the AMA's efforts, chiropractic became licensed in all fifty states, and in a 1980 revision of the ethical code, Principle 3 was eliminated. Chester Wilk and four other chiropractors brought an action against the AMA in a federal district court, claiming that the boycott violated Section 1 of the Sherman Act and seeking injunctive relief from the boycott's "lingering effects" on chiropractors. The trial court, holding that the AMA had violated Section 1 of the Sherman Act by conducting an illegal boycott in restraint of trade, granted an injunction that required that the AMA, among other things, widely publish the trial court's order. The AMA appealed.

DECISION AND RATIONALE The United States Court of Appeals for the Seventh Circuit affirmed both the trial court's ruling that the AMA had violated Section 1 of the Sherman Act by conducting an illegal boycott of chiropractors and the trial court's decision to grant an injunction against the AMA. The appellate court noted that "the AMA failed to establish that * * * their concern for scientific methods in patient treatment had been objectively reasonable" and "failed to show that it could not adequately have satisfied its concern for scientific method in patient care in a manner less restrictive of competition than a nationwide conspiracy to eliminate a licensed profession." The court concluded that the AMA's illegal boycott, though ended a decade before, continued to have adverse lingering effects that threatened the livelihood of licensed chiropractors. That the AMA characterized its exclusionary tactics as motivated by a desire to inform the public to deal only with "scientific" health-care professionals—not "unscientific" chiropractors—was not enough to relieve it of liability for its anticompetitive behavior to " 'destroy a competitor,' namely chiropractors."

GROUP BOYCOTTS   A **group boycott**, or concerted refusal to deal, is any agreement by which two or more buyers or sellers refuse to engage in any transactions with a particular person or organization who is the object of the boycott. An obvious, and indeed frequent, purpose of a boycott is to eliminate or discipline a competitor of the boycotting group. Boycotts are thus a powerful tool for enforcing anticompetitive arrangements among firms. Sometimes, however, group boycotts are intended to promote economic efficiency, moral or social causes, or the general well-being of the group without intending to injure competition. For example, a professional organization or a trade association might seek to promote its public image by sponsoring a program to prevent its members from engaging in deceptive advertising or employing pressure sales tactics. A member's failure to abide by the program guidelines could be punished by expulsion from the organization or association or by a denial of the group's endorsement, such as withholding the association's "seal of approval."

Despite the possibility of a procompetitive intent or some other socially valuable objective, concerted refusals to deal—group boycotts—are generally said to be *per se* violations of Section 1. A more accurate statement is that a court will treat a group boycott as a *per se* violation of Section 1 only in cases in which the group possesses market power and the boycott is intended to restrict or exclude a competitor. If, however, these elements are missing, the court may be inclined to weigh the benefits of the group's efforts against the harm inflicted by the boycott; that is, it will apply a rule of reason analysis, as in the following case.

Case 47.2

FEDERAL TRADE COMMISSION v. INDIANA FEDERATION OF DENTISTS

Supreme Court of the United States, 1986.
476 U.S. 447,
106 S.Ct. 2009,
90 L.Ed.2d 445.

BACKGROUND AND FACTS   In an attempt to control costs, dental health insurers adopted a policy that required dentists to submit diagnostic dental X-rays to the insurance company for review before the company would approve payment for treatment. The Indiana Federation of Dentists objected to this policy and adopted a resolution not to submit X-rays as requested by the insurers. The federation's membership was small, but it succeeded in enforcing its policy of refusal to cooperate with insurers. In 1978, the Federal Trade Commission (FTC) issued a complaint against the federation and found that the joint refusal to submit X-rays was a violation of antitrust laws. According to the FTC, the policy of not submitting X-rays had the effect of encouraging unnecessary dental procedures and raising costs. The FTC ordered the federation to cease organizing dentists to refuse to submit X-rays to insurers. The federation appealed this order, and the United States Court of Appeals overturned the FTC's ruling. The court concluded that the FTC had not shown that the federation's policy had an anticompetitive effect. The FTC appealed to the United States Supreme Court.

DECISION AND RATIONALE   The United States Supreme Court reversed the lower court's decision and approved the FTC's order. The Supreme Court held that the FTC's findings were supported by substantial evidence that the Indiana Federation of Dentists had violated Section 1 of the Sherman Act. The Court stated that "[t]he question remains whether * * * the Federation's collective refusal to cooperate with the insurer's requests for x-rays constitutes an 'unreasonable' restraint of trade" through application of the rule of reason. The Court viewed the agreement as obviously anticompetitive. The Court found that the dentists' "refusal to compete with respect to the package of services offered to customers * * * impaired the ability of the market to advance social welfare by ensuring the provision of desired goods and services to consumers at a price approximating the marginal cost of providing them." In the absence of any countervailing procompetitive virtue such as the creation of greater market efficiencies, the Court concluded that the agreement could not be sustained under the rule of reason analysis.

JOINT VENTURES A **joint venture** is any undertaking by two or more firms or individuals who, while maintaining their distinct identities, come together for the limited purpose of achieving a specific goal. Antitrust analysis of joint ventures involves two issues: first, whether the joining together is itself a violation of antitrust laws; and second, whether the purpose or means of the joint venture are impermissible. The first issue is covered by Section 7 of the Clayton Act, as well as Section 1 of the Sherman Act. Discussion of this issue will be taken up in the section on the Clayton Act later in this chapter. Here we limit our focus to the legality of the joint venture's purpose and actions.

Unlike price-fixing agreements or market divisions, joint ventures are not necessarily anticompetitive. Indeed, many are likely to provide economic efficiencies. For example, a joint venture may be beneficial to society, as well as individual firms, if resources are pooled to undertake substantial research and development (R&D) efforts. Pooling R&D resources prevents firms from duplicating one another's efforts. Once the R&D phase has been completed, the firms will compete along other dimensions, such as price, quality, and consumer services. A joint venture also allows the firms to share the risk that the initial efforts may be fruitless. Some ventures that are desirable from society's point of view may involve risks so substantial that no single firm would want to undertake the venture alone. By spreading the risk among many firms, individual risk is reduced, and the venture is more appealing.

If a joint venture does not involve price fixing or market divisions, the agreement will be analyzed under the rule of reason. Whether the venture will then be upheld under Section 1 depends on an overall assessment of the purposes of the venture, a strict analysis of the potential benefits relative to the likely harms, and in some cases an assessment of whether there are less restrictive alternatives for achieving the same goals.[7]

---

7. See, for example, *United States v. Morgan*, 118 F.Supp. 621 (S.D.N.Y. 1953). This case is often cited as a classic example of how to judge joint ventures under the rule of reason.

Section 1: Vertical Restraints

Another distinct set of restraints involves those imposed by the seller on the buyer (or vice versa), as distinct from those imposed *among* sellers or buyers. These restraints involve what is termed the vertical relationship. Horizontal relationships occur at the same level of operations. Vertical relationships, by comparison, encompass the entire chain of production: the purchase of inputs, basic manufacturing, distribution to wholesalers, and eventual sale of a product at the retail level. For some products, it is possible that these distinct phases are carried on by different firms. In other instances, a single firm may carry out two or more of the different functional phases. Such firms are considered to be **vertically integrated firms.**

Even though firms operating at different functional levels are not in direct competition with one another, they are in competition with other firms operating at their own respective level of operation. Thus agreements between firms standing in a vertical relationship do significantly affect competition. For example, a contractual agreement between tire manufacturer Firestone and Billy Ray's Automotive Supplies, an independent retailer, conditioning Billy Ray's future supply of Firestone tires on the retailer's willingness to resell only at a price set by Firestone is a form of vertical restraint and a *per se* violation of Section 1. Other types of vertical restraints are often encountered, not all of which necessarily harm competition. Indeed, many are procompetitive. Marketing decisions within a vertically integrated firm are not subject to attack under Section 1. The legality of certain other classes of vertical restraints are judged under a rule of reason. Still others are deemed per se violations of Section 1.

TERRITORIAL OR CUSTOMER RESTRICTIONS In arranging for the distribution of its product, a manufacturing firm may seek to insulate its dealers or retailers from direct competition with one another. As discussed earlier in the context of the joint promotion by separate firms of a certain brand of product, there may be legitimate, procompetitive reasons for doing so. One such reason is to prevent a dealer from cutting costs and undercutting rivals by providing the product without promotion or customer service, while relying on a nearby dealer to provide these services. This is an example of the "free rider" problem. One way of addressing the problem is to restrict dealers to selling in specific markets or to certain classes of customers. These restrictions are judged under a rule of reason. The following case, *Continental T.V., Inc. v. GTE Sylvania, Inc.*, overturned the United States Supreme Court's earlier stance, which had been set out in *United States v. Arnold, Schwinn & Co.*[8] In *Schwinn,* the Court had held such restrictions to be *per se* violations. The *Continental* case has been heralded as one of the most important antitrust cases since the 1940s. It represents a definite shift away from rigid characterization to a more flexible approach emphasizing economics and efficiency. It also indicates that the rule of reason may again become the primary tool of antitrust analysis.

---

8.   388 U.S. 365, 87 S.Ct. 1856, 18 L.Ed.2d 1249 (1967).

Case 47.3

CONTINENTAL T.V., INC. v. GTE SYLVANIA, INC.

Supreme Court of the
United States, 1977.
433 U.S. 36,
97 S.Ct. 2549,
53 L.Ed.2d 568.

BACKGROUND AND FACTS   Before 1962, like most other television manufacturers, GTE Sylvania, Inc., sold its televisions to independent or company-owned distributors, who in turn resold to a large and diverse group of retailers. In 1962, Sylvania phased out its wholesale distributors and began to sell its televisions directly to franchised retailers. Sylvania limited the number of franchises granted for any given area and required each franchisee to sell the Sylvania products from only the franchise locations. A franchise did not constitute an exclusive territory, and Sylvania retained sole discretion to increase the number of retailers in an area, depending on the existing retailers' success or failure in developing their market. Continental T.V., Inc., a Sylvania franchisee, withheld all payments due for Sylvania products after a dispute over additional locations sought by Continental. John P. Maguire & Company, the finance company that handled the credit arrangements between Sylvania and its franchisees, sued Continental in a federal district court for payment and for the return of secured merchandise. Continental claimed that Sylvania had violated Section 1 of the Sherman Act by entering into and enforcing franchise agreements that permitted the sale of Sylvania products only in specified locations. The trial court ruled in favor of Continental. Sylvania appealed, and the appellate court reversed the trial court's decision. Continental filed an appeal with the United States Supreme Court.

DECISION AND RATIONALE   The United States Supreme Court affirmed the appellate court's decision that Sylvania's vertical restrictions had not violated Section 1 of the Sherman Act, ruling that in the future the legality of all such restraints would be tested under a rule of reason. The Supreme Court found that while "[v]ertical restrictions reduce intrabrand competition by limiting the number of sellers of a particular product competing for the business of a given group of buyers," the restrictions "promote interbrand competition by allowing the manufacturer to achieve certain efficiencies in the distribution of his products." The Court noted that if manufacturers were unable to impose any vertical restrictions, market imperfections might otherwise prevent the development of useful services, such as service and repair facilities and promotional activities.

RESALE PRICE MAINTENANCE AGREEMENTS

A **resale price maintenance agreement,** also referred to as a *fair trade agreement,* occurs whenever the manufacturer seeks to establish a minimum price that the retailer or wholesaler may charge for the manufacturer's product. Under these agreements, the manufacturer conditions sales to the retailer or wholesaler on the latter's reselling only at a price allowed by the manufacturer. Although authorized for many years under so-called *fair trade laws*, such agreements are today condemned as per se violations of Section 1. This seems anomalous for at least two reasons. First, the economic justifications for resale price maintenance agreements are often identical to those that supported the Court's holding in the *Sylvania* case, which established that vertical territorial and customer restrictions would be judged under a rule of reason. Second, manufacturers can achieve the same result by simply *integrating forward;* that is, by simply selling through their own, rather than through independent, dealers. Moreover, manufacturers are legally entitled to *suggest* to dealers a retail price. Furthermore, manufacturers may be able to refuse to deal with dealers who do not follow that suggestion.

REFUSALS TO DEAL As discussed above, group boycotts are subject to sharp scrutiny under Section 1. In contrast, basic freedom of contract has been held to support the rule that manufacturers, acting unilaterally rather than in concert (as in a group boycott), are free to deal—or not to deal— with whomever they choose. There are instances, however, when a refusal to deal will violate antitrust laws. These instances involve offenses proscribed under Section 2 of the Sherman Act and occur only if (1) the firm refusing to deal has, or is likely to acquire, monopoly power and (2) the refusal is likely to have an anticompetitive effect on a particular market.[9]

Section 2: Overview

As noted above, Section 1 of the Sherman Act proscribes certain concerted activities in the restraint of trade. In contrast, Section 2 condemns "every person who shall monopolize or attempt to monopolize." Therefore, Section 2 may be violated by a single entity. The essence of a single entity's violation of Section 2 is the entity's willful acquisition or maintenance of monopoly power, or its specifically intended *attempt* to do so, provided the attempt has a reasonable chance of success.

Section 2: Monopolization

In *United States v. Grinnell Corp.,*[10] the United States Supreme Court defined the offense of **monopolization** as involving the following two elements: "(1) the possession of monopoly power in the relevant market and (2) the willful acquisition or maintenance of the power as distinguished from growth or development as consequence of a superior product, business acumen, or historic accident." A violation of Section 2 requires that both these elements be established.

MONOPOLY POWER The Sherman Act does not define *monopoly*. In economic parlance, monopoly refers to control by a single entity. It is well established in antitrust law, however, that a firm may be a monopoly even though it is not the sole seller in a market. Nor is monopoly a function of size alone (for example, a "mom and pop" grocery located in an isolated desert town is a monopolist if it is the only grocery serving that particular market). Size in relation to the market is what matters because monopoly involves power to affect prices and output. The United States Supreme Court has defined *monopoly power* as "the power to control prices or exclude competition." This definition is of limited help, though, and most scholars generally consider monopoly power to be simply a considerable degree of market power, or otherwise stated, a significant degree of freedom from competitive pressure regarding output and pricing decisions. This generally is the way in which the Court has applied the concept.

As difficult as it is to define market power precisely, it is even more difficult to measure it. As a workable proxy, courts often look to the firm's percentage share of the "relevant market." This is the so-called **market share test**.[11] The relevant market consists of two elements: (1) a relevant product market and (2) a relevant geographic market. A firm generally is considered to have monopoly power if its share of the relevant market is 70 percent or more. This is not an absolute, however. It is only a loose rule of thumb; in some cases,

---

9. A good example is provided by the *Aspen Skiing* case discussed in the next section on Section 2 offenses.

10. 384 U.S. 563, 86 S.Ct. 1698, 16 L.Ed.2d 778 (1966).
11. Other measures of market power have been devised, but the market share test is the most widely used.

a smaller share may be held to constitute market power.[12]

No doubt the relevant product market should include all products that, although produced by different firms, nonetheless have identical attributes. But in determining the relevant market, it must be remembered that products that are not identical may be substituted for one another. Coffee may substitute for tea, cellophane may substitute for wax paper, and so on. In defining the relevant product market, the key issue is the degree of interchangeability between products. If one product is a sufficient substitute for another, the two are considered to be part of the same product market.

In *United States v. E. I. du Pont de Nemours & Co.*,[13] du Pont was sued for monopolizing the cellophane market. Du Pont controlled about 75 percent of cellophane production but contended that it had no monopoly power because the relevant market included not only cellophane but rather all flexible packaging materials. The United States Supreme Court found that there was indeed a sufficient degree of interchangeability between cellophane and alternatives such as wax paper and aluminum foil. The Court noted, for example, that although 35 percent of the snack food industry used cellophane, an even larger percent used some other packaging material. Consequently, the Court concluded that du Pont did not control a share of the relevant market sufficient to constitute market power.

The second component of the relevant market is the geographical boundaries of the market. For products that are sold nationwide, the geographical boundaries encompass the entire United States. If transportation costs are significant, or if a producer and its competitors sell in only a limited area (one in which customers have no access to other sources for the product), then the geographical market is limited to that area. In this sense a national firm may compete in several distinct areas, having mo-

nopoly power in one but not another. Generally, the geographical market is that section of the country within which a firm can increase its price without attracting new sellers or without losing many customers to alternative suppliers outside that area.

THE INTENT REQUIREMENT Monopoly power is not in and of itself illegal. Recall that there are two elements to the monopolization offense. In addition to monopoly power, there is the requirement of ''willful acquisition or maintenance of the power.'' A dominant market share may be the result of business acumen or the development of a superior product. It may be simply the result of a historical accident. None of these should give rise to antitrust concerns. Indeed, it would be counter to society's interest to condemn a firm that acquired its position on the basis of the first two reasons. If, however, a firm possesses market power as a result of some purposeful act to acquire or to maintain that power through anticompetitive means, then it is a violation of Section 2. The United States Supreme Court has interpreted this second element as requiring some conduct, coupled with intent, to diminish competition.

Some conduct diminishes competition but is not necessarily anticompetitive. Devising new low-cost production methods or developing and producing better products all hurt rival competitors. But they do not injure competition; they are the result of competition. In our initial scenario, even without receiving an exclusive monopoly, Acme's laser fax breakthrough would have given Acme market power for a period of time until rival firms had had sufficient time to develop and market products that could effectively compete. But ultimately, Acme's innovation led to increased competition. Thus, only certain acts are condemned under Section 2, even if the acting firm possesses market power. The hallmark of an action that does violate Section 2 is that, without providing better production or products, the firm's action makes it more difficult for a firm's rivals to compete in the relevant market.

The qualifier that the sanctioned action must have been ''willful'' is said to require an intent, but the intent requirement is difficult to formulate. In most monopolization cases, intent may be inferred from evidence that the firm had monopoly power and engaged in anticompetitive behavior. For example, in *United States v. Aluminum Co.*

---

12. This standard was first articulated by Justice Learned Hand in the famous *Alcoa* case discussed below. A 90 percent share was held to be clear evidence of monopoly power. Anything less than 64 percent, said Justice Hand, made monopoly power doubtful, and anything less than 30 percent was clearly not monopoly power. This is merely a rule of thumb, however; it is not a binding principle of law.

13. 351 U.S. 377, 76 S.Ct. 994, 100 L.Ed.2d 1264 (1956).

of America,[14] the seemingly innocent act of expanding production demand ran Alcoa afoul of Section 2. The court found that Alcoa had intentionally and artificially stimulated demand and then increased its own capacity to meet that increased demand. The Court of Appeals for the Second Circuit[15] relied on the fact that Alcoa clearly possessed a market share sufficient to give it monopoly power (90 percent of what the court determined to be the relevant market),[16] and that the only apparent rea-

son for its expansion was to prevent competitors from entering the aluminum market. This factual conclusion is often criticized, but the principle set out is now well established. Market domination that results from legitimate competitive behavior—such as foresight, innovation, skill, and good management—will not be condemned unless that market power is abused or acquired through behavior that harms, rather than flows from, competition.

In the following case, a skiing company's refusal to participate in a joint marketing venture was sufficient to evidence willful conduct violating Section 2. As discussed in the section above on Section 1 offenses, unilateral refusals to deal are generally permissible. In the following case, however, the refusal to deal was made by a firm possessing monopoly power, and its apparent intent was to injure competition in the relevant market.

---

14.   148 F.2d 416 (2d Cir. 1945).

15.   The Second Circuit acted as the court of final appeal in place of the Supreme Court because the latter could not muster a quorum of six qualified justices to hear the case. The case was referred to the court of appeals of the circuit from which the case came under a specially drawn statute (28 U.S.C. Section 2109).

16.   The court also mentioned that monopoly power would be doubtful if the market share were as much as 64 percent and that monopoly power clearly would be lacking if the share were 33 percent or less. Hence the general rule of thumb is often said to be that 70 percent of the relevant market implies monopoly power.

 Case 47.4

ASPEN SKIING CO. v. ASPEN HIGHLANDS SKIING CORP.

Supreme Court of the United States, 1985. 472 U.S. 585, 105 S.Ct. 2847, 86 L.Ed.2d 467.

BACKGROUND AND FACTS   Aspen, Colorado, is a leading ski resort, and private investors developed four major facilities there for downhill skiing: Ajax, Aspen Highlands, Buttermilk, and Snowmass. The facilities, which were owned by independent investors, jointly offered an "all-Aspen ticket" that could be used for skiing at any of the facilities. Receipts from the ticket were paid to the various facilities in a manner proportionate to their use, as based on surveys of skiers. By 1977, Aspen Skiing Company (Ski Co.) had acquired ownership of Ajax, Buttermilk, and Snowmass, while Aspen Highlands was owned by the Aspen Highlands Skiing Corporation. At this time, the two companies were engaged in a dispute over the proper distribution of receipts from the all-Aspen ticket. Ski Co. discontinued the all-Aspen ticket and replaced it with a three-area ticket that covered only its own facilities. Aspen Highlands' share of the local downhill skiing market declined from over 20 percent in 1976–1977 to 11 percent in 1980–1981. Aspen Highlands filed an antitrust complaint in a federal district court against Ski Co., alleging that Ski Co. had monopolized the market for downhill skiing services at Aspen, in violation of Section 2 of the Sherman Act. Aspen Highlands argued that the discontinuation of the all-Aspen ticket was a purposeful act with intent to monopolize the market. The district court issued a judgment in favor of Aspen Highlands, and the Tenth Circuit Court of Appeals affirmed in all respects. Ski Co. appealed to the United States Supreme Court.

DECISION AND RATIONALE   The United States Supreme Court affirmed the decision of the lower courts. The Supreme Court noted as most significant that Ski Co.'s action did not merely reject an offer to participate in a cooperative venture but chose "to make an important change in a pattern of distribution that had originated in a competitive market and had persisted for several years." This conduct was not "justified by any normal business purpose"—Ski Co.'s decision to stop using the interchangeable four-mountain ticket entailed costs in the form of lost revenue. The Court concluded that Ski Co.'s decision to forgo these short-term benefits was motivated by its desire to reduce competition in the Aspen market over the long run by harming its smaller competitor. The original jury had found that Aspen Highlands had suffered $2.5 million in actual damages, which were trebled under the Sherman Act to an award of $7.5 million. The Court affirmed this award.

Section 2: Attempts to Monopolize

Section 2 also prohibits attempted monopolization of a market. The challenged action must be specifically intended to exclude competitors and garner monopoly power. In addition, a majority of lower courts hold that an attempted violation also requires that the attempt have a "dangerous" probability of success; that is, actual monopolization is not required, but only serious threats of monopolization are condemned as attempted violations. Many courts hold that the probability cannot be dangerous unless the alleged offender possesses at least some degree of market power.

■ The Clayton Act

In contrast to the Sherman Act's broad proscriptions set out in Sections 1 and 2, the Clayton Act's provisions deal with specific practices that are considered to reduce competition or lead to monopoly power but that are not expressly covered by the Sherman Act.

Section 2: Price Discrimination

Price discrimination occurs when sellers charge different buyers different prices for identical goods. Section 2 of the Clayton Act prohibits certain classes of price discrimination that cannot be justified by differences in production or transportation costs. The Clayton Act was amended in 1936 by the Robinson-Patman Act as Congress sought to make it more difficult for businesses to evade the terms of Section 2. To violate Section 2, the seller must be engaged in interstate commerce, and the effect of the price discrimination must be to substantially lessen competition. Under the Robinson-Patman Act, sellers are prohibited from reducing prices to levels substantially below those charged

by their competitors unless the reduction can be justified by demonstrating that the lower price was charged "in good faith to meet an equally low price of a competitor." [17]

Section 3: Exclusionary Practices

Section 3 of the Clayton Act prohibits sellers and lessors from selling or leasing "on the condition, agreement or understanding that the . . . purchaser or lessee thereof shall not use or deal in the goods . . . of a competitor or competitors of the seller." Section 3, in effect, prohibits two types of vertical arrangements involving exclusionary tactics: exclusive dealing contracts and tying arrangements.

EXCLUSIVE DEALING CONTRACTS Contracts under which a seller forbids the buyer from purchasing products from the seller's competitors are called **exclusive dealing contracts.** Such contracts are prohibited under Section 3 if the effect of the contract will "substantially lessen competition or tend to create a monopoly."

The leading decision on exclusive dealing contracts remains the 1949 case of *Standard Oil Co. of California v. United States,* [18] in which the then-largest gasoline seller in the United States was challenged by the government under Section 3 for making exclusive dealing contracts with independent stations in seven western states. The United States Supreme Court, in assessing the impact of the exclusive dealing agreement on competition in the retail market, noted that the independents covered under the arrangement constituted 16 percent of all retail outlets and 7 percent of all retail gas sales in

---

17. *United States v. United States Gypsum Co.,* 438 U.S. 422, 98 S.Ct. 2864, 5 L.Ed.2d 854 (1978).
18. 337 U.S. 293, 69 S.Ct. 1051, 93 L.Ed. 1371 (1949).

CHAPTER 47: ANTITRUST LAW

the area. The Court also noted that the market was substantially concentrated because the seven largest suppliers all used exclusive dealing contracts with their independent retailers and together controlled 65 percent of the market. Looking at market conditions after the arrangements were instituted, the Court noted that market shares were extremely stable, and entry into the market was apparently restricted. Thus, the Court found that Section 3 had been violated because competition was ''foreclosed in a substantial share'' of the relevant market.

TYING ARRANGEMENTS   When the seller conditions the sale of a product (the tying product) on the buyer's agreeing to purchase another product (the tied product) produced or distributed by the same seller, a **tying arrangement**, or *tie-in sales agreement*, results. The legality of such agreements depends on many factors, especially on consideration of the purpose and likely effect of the arrangement on competition in the relevant markets (consider that there are two, because the agreement involves both the tying and the tied product). In 1936, the United States Supreme Court held that International Business Machines' (IBM's) and Remington Rand's practice of requiring the purchase of their own machine cards as a condition to leasing their tabulation machines violated Section 3 of the Clayton Act. The two firms were the only ones in the market with completely automated tabulation machines, and the Court concluded that they each possessed market power sufficient to ''substantially lessen competition'' through their respective tying arrangements.[19]

The Clayton Act provisions in Section 3 have been held to apply only to commodities, not to services. But tying arrangements also can be considered agreements that restrain trade in violation of Section 1 of the Sherman Act. Thus those cases involving tying arrangements of services have been brought under Section 1 of the Sherman Act. Although the United States Supreme Court has never overruled those cases that apply a different legal test to cases brought under the Sherman Act than the one applied in cases brought under the Clayton Act, most lower courts now apply a single test in both instances. Moreover, although the Court con-

tinues to state that tying arrangements are *per se* illegal, it nonetheless has shown a willingness to look at factors that are important in a rule of reason analysis. This is another example of the so-called soft *per se* rule referred to above in discussing group boycotts.

In a more recent case, for example, the United States Supreme Court held that U.S. Steel Corporation's practice of tying its attractive credit services for home builders to the builders' purchase of U.S. Steel's prefabricated houses did not violate antitrust laws because U.S. Steel did not possess market power in either the credit market or the prefabricated housing market.[20] A similar result was reached in *Jefferson Parish Hospital District No. 2 v. Hyde.*[21] Most courts today generally judge the legality of tying arrangements involving services or commodities by looking at both the firm's market power in the tying product market and the amount of commerce affected in the tied product market. The firm must have sufficient market power in the tying product to coerce the purchase of the tied product, and the tying arrangement must affect a substantial amount of commerce in the market for the tied product.

Section 7: Mergers

Mergers are a means of entering a new market or expanding operations without a firm's expanding internally. Mergers are of two kinds: asset acquisition and stock acquisition. Both types are covered by Section 7 of the Clayton Act. Under Section 7, a person or business organization cannot hold stock or assets in another business ''where the effect . . . may be to substantially lessen competition.'' Section 7 is statutory authority for preventing mergers that might result in monopoly power or adversely affect competition in a relevant market.

A crucial consideration in most merger cases is **market concentration.** Market concentration roughly translates into the allocation of percentage market shares among the various firms in the relevant market. For example, if the four largest grocery stores in Chicago accounted for 80 percent of all retail food sales, the market clearly would be concentrated in those four firms. Competition,

---

19.   *International Business Machines Corp. v. United States,* 298 U.S. 131, 56 S.Ct. 701, 80 L.Ed.2d 1085 (1936).

20.   *United States Steel Corp. v. Fortner Enterprises, Inc.,* 429 U.S. 610, 97 S.Ct. 861, 51 L.Ed.2d 80 (1977).
21.   466 U.S. 2, 104 S.Ct. 1551, 80 L.Ed.2d 2 (1984).

however, is not necessarily diminished solely as a result of market concentration, and other factors are considered.[22]

Another concept of particular importance is that of **barriers to entry.** Simply stated, this refers to the ability of firms to enter a market. Barriers arise in many forms. For example, entry into the industry of medical education has significant barriers aside from the investment in plant and staff; most, if not all, states require approval from the American Medical Association before granting permission to anyone seeking to open a school that can offer the M.D. degree to its graduates.

HORIZONTAL MERGERS Mergers between firms that compete with each other in the same market are called **horizontal mergers.** If a horizontal merger creates an entity with anything other than a small percentage market share, the merger will be presumed illegal. This is because of the United States Supreme Court's interpretation that Congress, in amending Section 7 of the Clayton Act in 1950, intended to prevent mergers that increase market concentration.[23] Three other factors are also considered: overall concentration of the relevant market, the relevant market's history of tending toward concentration, and whether the apparent design of the merger is to establish market power or restrict competition.

The Court's intense focus on market share in horizontal merger decisions has made the definition of relevant markets especially critical in most Section 7 cases. This has also prompted one government agency charged with antitrust enforcement, the Department of Justice (DOJ),[24] to establish guidelines in determining which mergers it will challenge. Note that these guidelines are only used to determine which mergers are challenged. The courts are in no way bound to follow the guidelines.

The guidelines employ the Herfindahl-Hirschman Index (HHI).[25] See Exhibit 47–1.

The HHI is computed by summing the squares of each of the percentage market shares of firms in the relevant market. For example, if there are four firms with shares of 30 percent, 30 percent, 20 percent, and 20 percent, respectively, then the HHI equals 2,600 ($30^2 + 30^2 + 20^2 + 20^2 = 2,600$).

Under the guidelines, if the pre-merger HHI is less than 1,000, then the market is unconcentrated, and the merger will not likely be challenged. If the pre-merger HHI is between 1,000 and 1,800, the industry is moderately concentrated, and the DOJ will likely challenge the merger only if it increases the HHI by 100 or more.[26] If the HHI is greater than 1,800, the market is highly concentrated. If the market is already highly concentrated, but the increase in the HHI is between 50 and 100, the DOJ will consider ''non-HHI'' factors before challenging a merger. These include the market's history of past collusion and the barriers to entry in the market. If a firm is a leading one—having at least a 35 percent share and twice that of the next leading firm—any merger with a firm having as little as a 1 percent share will be challenged.

Even firms that do not possess significant market shares have been prevented from merging. For example, Alcoa was prevented from merging with a competitor in the aluminum conductor industry even though Alcoa possessed only 27.8 percent of the aluminum conductor market and the other firm, only 1.3 percent. The United States Supreme Court stated that Alcoa was an ''important competitive factor'' and an unusually aggressive competitor,

---

22. As discussed below, simple market concentration ratios are now considered to be too simplistic a means of evaluating the competitive effects of mergers.

23. *Brown Shoe v. United States,* 370 U.S. 294, 82 S.Ct. 1502, 8 L.Ed.2d 510 (1962).

24. Agency enforcement, as well as private party enforcement, is discussed in detail in a separate section below.

---

25. The HHI was first used in the 1982 Justice Department Merger Guidelines and continues to be used in the 1984 revision. Prior guidelines established in 1968 used the four-firm concentration ratio, which consists of the sum of the percentage market shares of the four largest firms in the relevant market. The Federal Trade Commission, which also oversees merger activities, employs the HHI as a guideline measure. The HHI is used because many believe that simple concentration ratios are too simplistic to be good predictors of competition in an industry or good measures of the economic impact of mergers.

26. Compute the change in the index by doubling the product of the merging firms' pre-merger market shares. For example, a merger between a firm with a 5 percent share and one with a 6 percent share will increase the HHI by 2 x (5 x 6) = 60.

■ Exhibit 47–1 An Index of Industrial Concentration

The traditional way to measure concentration has been to add the market shares of the four largest companies, A, B, C, and D. Their combined 50 percent market share would make this a fairly concentrated industry. If D and F wanted to merge, creating the industry's largest producer with 17 percent of the market, the merger would be suspect.

Under the new guidelines, the Justice Department assures that any merger that does not raise the Herfindahl Index above 1000 is legal. Antitrusters would look at the makeup of the industry after the merger. Combining D's 10 percent and F's 7 percent, and squaring them, raises the index to 997, virtually assuring legality.

Companies	Old Method (Market Share)	Herfindahl Index (Share Squared)
A	16%	256
B	13	169
C	11	121
D	10	100
E	8	64
F	7	49
G	6	36
H	5	25
I	4	16
Others (24)	20	(Est.) 21[a]
Total	100%	857

Industrial Sectors with the Highest Herfindahl Indexes

Military tanks	5823
Telephone and telegraph equipment	5026
Sewing machines	4047
Cellulosic synthetic fibers	3189
Turbines	2443

. . . and the Lowest

Specialty dies & tools	11
Concrete blocks	27
Metal plating & polishing	31
Commercial lithography	32
Ready-mix concrete	32

a. The summation of the squares of the market shares of each of the remaining twenty-four firms.

Source: John E. Kwoka, using 1972 data from Economic Informations Systems, Inc. Reprinted by permission of McGraw-Hill from *Business Week,* May 17, 1982, p. 20.

and it voided the merger as likely to lessen competition in that market.[27]

As noted, mergers that create entities that possess anything but very small shares are presumed illegal. Evidence is allowed to rebut this presumption, however. In *United States v. General Dynamics,*[28] the Court allowed a merger between a firm and a coal supplier by noting several factors that showed that market share alone overstated the firms' importance in the relevant market: coal sup-

27. *United States v. Aluminum Co. of America (Rome Cable),* 377 U.S. 271, 84 S.Ct. 1283, 12 L.Ed.2d 314 (1964).

28. 272 U.S. 476, 47 S.Ct. 192, 71 L.Ed.2d 362 (1974).

pliers utilized very long-term contracts with their buyers; the merging firm's market share was based on contracts entered into many years earlier; and its coal reserves made it unlikely that new contracts would be sparse. Other than rebutting the presumption of illegality, there are no ways to defend a horizontal merger. Defenses that are allowed in vertical and conglomerate mergers are not valid in horizontal mergers.

Some scholars believe that there is a trend toward accepting horizontal mergers among firms that have large shares of the market to enhance competition with firms that have even larger shares. In contrast, under the Bush administration, the FTC and the DOJ seem to be reverting to a more strict view of antitrust law and mergers.

VERTICAL MERGERS A **vertical merger** occurs when a company at one stage of the chain of production and distribution acquires another company at a higher or lower stage along the chain of production and distribution. Courts in the past have almost exclusively focused on ''foreclosure'' in assessing vertical mergers. Foreclosure occurs because competitors of the merging firms lose opportunities to either sell or buy from the merging firms. For example, in *United States v. E. I. du Pont de Nemours & Co.,*[29] du Pont was challenged for acquiring a considerable amount of General Motors (GM) stock. In ruling the transaction illegal, the United States Supreme Court noted that it would enable du Pont to foreclose other sellers of fabrics and finishes from selling to GM, which then accounted for 50 percent of all auto fabric and finishes purchases. More recently, whether a merger will be illegal depends on several considerations, including the definition of the relevant market and the probable effects on competition in that market should the merger occur. Specifically considered are market concentration, barriers to entry into the market, and the apparent intent of the merging parties. Mergers that do not prevent competitors of either of the merging firms from competing in a segment of the market will not be condemned as ''foreclosing'' competition and are legal.

---

29.   353 U.S. 586, 77 S.Ct. 872, 1 L.Ed.2d 1057 (1957).

CONGLOMERATE MERGERS There are three general types of **conglomerate mergers:** market extension, product extension, and diversification. Market extension occurs when a firm seeks to sell its product in a new market by merging with a firm already established in that market. Product extension occurs when a firm seeks to add a closely related product to its existing line by merging with a firm already producing that product. For example, a manufacturer might seek to extend its product line of household products to include bleach by acquiring a leading manufacturer of bleach. Diversification occurs when a firm merges with another firm that offers a product or service wholly unrelated to the first firm's existing activities. International Telephone and Telegraph might, for example, seek to diversify by acquiring the Holiday Inn hotel chain or the Marietta Bread Company, both of which involve activities and products far removed from the telephone equipment and service industry.

These differences in the nature of various mergers are not legal distinctions, but they are apparent in the case law and often give a good indication of how a court is likely to view a particular merger. Diversification, for instance, seldom affects individual market concentration. As such, it is now least likely to be challenged. Some earlier cases express concern for what might be called a concentration-of-wealth effect and a resulting aggregation of political power, but this consideration is not a factor in modern cases.

Several theories have been applied at various times by the courts in judging the legality of the other two types of mergers. Of these, only the **potential competition doctrine** remains viable in modern courts. Potential competition is the competitive effect that a firm has on a market even though the firm does not operate in the market. The firm's effect is felt by its ''waiting in the wings'' so to speak, ready to enter the market if firms already in the market begin to earn supranormal profits by charging noncompetitive prices. This potential competition is lost if the firm that is waiting in the wings, rather than entering the market on its own (*de novo* entry) or merging with a small firm already in the market (*foothold* entry), merges with a dominant firm in the industry. For example, a national brewer was prevented from merging with a dominant regional brewer because, even though the national did not compete in that regional market, its competitive effect from waiting in the wings was lost by the merger.[30] A foothold or *de novo* entry would have been as procompetitive as the waiting in the wings effect had been. The case refines the doctrine by setting out the factors considered: whether the pre-merger market is concentrated, whether there are barriers to entry, whether the firm would be able to enter the market without the merger, whether there would still be other firms waiting in the wings after the merger, and whether the merger would nonetheless make the relevant market more competitive.

◼ Enforcement of the Antitrust Laws

The federal agencies that enforce the federal antitrust laws are the Department of Justice and the Federal Trade Commission. The DOJ can prosecute violations of the Sherman Act as either criminal or civil violations. Violations of the Clayton Act are not crimes, and the DOJ can enforce that statute only through civil proceedings. The various remedies that the DOJ has asked the courts to impose include **divestiture** (making a company give up one or more of its operating functions) and **dissolution** (the formal disbanding of a partnership or corporation). A group of meat packers, for example, can be forced to divorce itself from controlling or owning butcher shops.

The FTC enforces the Clayton Act and has sole authority to enforce the only substantive provision of the Federal Trade Commission Act, Section 5. FTC actions are effected through administrative cease-and-desist proceedings, but the FTC can seek court sanctions for violations of its administrative orders.

A private party can sue for treble damages and attorneys' fees under Section 4 of the Clayton Act if the party is injured as a result of a violation of any of the federal antitrust laws except Section 5 of the Federal Trade Commission Act (which, as noted, is that act's only substantive provision, and its enforcement is delegated solely to the FTC). In some instances, private parties may also seek injunctive relief to prevent antitrust violations. The

courts have determined that the test of ability to sue depends on the directness of the injury suffered by the would-be plaintiff. Thus, a person wishing to sue under the Sherman Act must prove (1) that the antitrust violation either directly caused, or was at least a substantial factor in causing, the injury that was suffered and (2) that the unlawful actions of the accused party affected business activities of the plaintiff that were protected by the antitrust laws.

◼ Exemptions

There are many legislative and constitutional limitations on antitrust enforcement. Most are statutory and judicially created exemptions applying to the following areas:

1. *Labor.* Section 6 of the Clayton Act generally permits labor unions to organize and bargain without violating antitrust laws. Section 20 of the Clayton Act specifies that strikes and other labor activities are not violations of any law of the United States. But a union can lose its exemption if it combines with a nonlabor group rather than acting simply in its own self-interest.

2. *Agricultural associations and fisheries.* Section 6 of the Clayton Act (along with the Capper-Volstead Act of 1922) exempts agricultural cooperatives from the antitrust laws. The Fisheries Cooperative Marketing Act of 1976 exempts from antitrust legislation individuals in the fishing industry who collectively catch, produce, and prepare for market their products. Both exemptions allow members of such co-ops to combine and set prices for a particular product, but they do not allow them to engage in exclusionary practices or restraints of trade directed at competitors.

3. *Insurance.* The McCarran-Ferguson Act of 1945 exempts the insurance business from the antitrust laws whenever state regulation exists. This exemption does not cover boycotts, coercion, or intimidation on the part of insurance companies.

4. *Foreign trade.* Under the provisions of the 1918 Webb-Pomerane Act, U.S. exporters may engage in cooperative activity to compete with similar foreign associations. Such cooperative activity may not, however, restrain trade within the United States or injure other U.S. exporters. In 1982 the Export Trading Company Act was passed, broadening the Webb-Pomerane Act by permitting the

---

30. *United States v. Falstaff Brewing Co.,* 410 U.S. 526, 93 S.Ct. 1096, 35 L.Ed.2d 475 (1973).

Toward Stricter Enforcement of Antitrust Laws

During the late 1970s, and for virtually the whole decade of the 1980s under the Reagan administration, the "new" antitrust view in Washington could be summarized, in the words of one official in the Justice Department, as "hands off." The pursuit of alleged antitrust violaters by both the Federal Trade Commission and the Antitrust Division of the Justice Department was, in principle, only to be undertaken if true economic damages were incurred by society. Otherwise, little was done, even if a business was technically violating an antitrust statute. In contrast, the 1990s are seeing increasing attention to antitrust enforcement. Those who make policy in the Justice Department and the FTC have given clear signals, through both their words and their actions, that the current approach to antitrust enforcement is, and will continue to be, more vigorous than in the past.

Court Challenges to Mergers on the Rise

One indication of this more vigorous enforcement of antitrust law has come from the Justice Department's interference with proposed mergers. At the beginning of this decade, for example, court challenges to mergers brought by the Justice Department's Antitrust Division increased by 100 percent within one year. The current policy of the Justice Department is that a merger will be challenged if it is anticompetitive and if potential entry into the same industry will not be likely, timely, or sufficiently effective to overcome the negative effects of the merger.

The Federal Trade Commission (FTC) similarly has increased its interest in supposed anticompetitive mergers. In 1990, the FTC made thirty-nine requests for information about proposed mergers—up from twenty-five such requests during the previous year. The request for additional information is the first step taken by the FTC toward blocking a merger. The FTC's Bureau of Competition has also added more than 10 percent to the number of attorneys in the Antitrust Enforcement Division.

Professional Associations under Fire

As further evidence of the federal government's renewed interest in antitrust enforcement, a number of professional organizations have recently been under attack. One of the most prominent cases was brought by the Justice Department against three Arizona dentists and two professional corporations for felonious price fixing.[a] The defendants were accused of conspiring to fix and raise the co-payment fees paid by patient members of four prepaid dental plans.

The Justice Department, speaking through Assistant Attorney General James F. Rill, said that physicians and other medical professionals "enjoy no immunity" from the well-settled rule that price fixing among competitors is a crime. They will be "pursued and prosecuted for the crime." The dentists face eighteen-month prison sentences, as well as monetary penalties, and will be subject to the new, higher maximum penalties for individuals convicted of a felony under the Sherman Act.

On July 5, 1990, the Justice Department took aim at another professional group: the American Institute of Architects (AIA). The government alleged that the trade group illegally restrains competition. The AIA decided not to fight to the bitter end and agreed to establish an antitrust compliance program and to pay $50,000 in costs to the government.

Justice Department antitrust lawyer Robert E. Bloch said that "competition is pretty important in any industry, and professionals are no different." He and others are pursuing antitrust actions against

---

a.   *United States v. Alston,* 1990 W.L. 284741 (D.Ariz. 1990).

obstetricians in Boston. The *Alston* case in Arizona concerning dentists and the case concerning obstetricians in Boston represent the first health-care criminal antitrust cases in fifty years.

Stiffer Penalties

The Comprehensive Crime Control Act of 1990 was passed by Congress on October 27 of that year and approved by the president. New maximum fines for criminal violation of the Sherman Act were included. Any individual convicted of a felony under the Sherman Act now faces a maximum of three years in prison, plus the greatest of three alternatives:

1. A $350,000 fine.
2. Twice the pecuniary gain that the individual derived from the crime.
3. Twice the pecuniary loss suffered by the victims of the crime.

For a corporation, the new maximum penalty is the greatest of three alternatives:

1. A $10 million fine.
2. Twice the pecuniary gain that the corporation derived from the crime.
3. Twice the pecuniary loss suffered by the victims of the crime.

Additionally, the government may collect treble damages for antitrust violations when it is the injured party. Although the Justice Department expressed satisfaction at the increased antitrust penalties, it stated that the Antitrust Division's "first and foremost objective" is to seek jail sentences for those violating antitrust laws.

■ Implications for the Businessperson

1. On the positive side, stricter enforcement of antitrust laws will benefit certain businesspersons because they gain protection against competitors' unfair trade practices that are prohibited by antitrust laws. Those companies that are not involved in anticompetitive practices will definitely gain.
2. In contrast, stricter enforcement of antitrust laws and the imposition of stiffer penalties mean that businesspersons must take greater care in their dealings to ensure that they are not engaging in prohibited practices. More time and resources must be spent with attorneys to determine, ahead of time, whether proposed business actions will be challenged by the Justice Department or the Federal Trade Commission.
3. Those who are members of professional groups or associations must be particularly careful about their policies and practices. Some codes of conduct may be scrutinized by the federal government because of their implicit or explicit anticompetitive requirements. Every professional today is now considered "fair game" by the federal government.

■ For Critical Analysis

1. A distinction can be made between focusing on consumers' interests, as opposed to competitors' interests. Is it appropriate, for example, for the United States to begin to flex its legal muscle on behalf of exporters against foreign companies that collude to exclude U.S. firms from a particular market, when this means that the government's attention is focused on the interests of competitors, as opposed to the interests of consumers?
2. The Robinson-Patman Act, which was originally designed to protect the small businessperson from the buying power of chain stores, has often been used by small stores to extort "tribute" from large firms. In other words, if a large operation was able to undercut the price of a smaller operation in the same line of business, the smaller firm could enter into antitrust litigation, citing violation of the Robinson-Patman Act. Is it possible that some antitrust laws actually end up being anticompetitive?

Department of Justice to certify properly qualified export trading companies. Any activity within the scope described by the certificate authorizing the business venture is exempt from public prosecution under the antitrust laws.

5. *Baseball.* In 1922 the United States Supreme Court held that professional baseball was not within the reach of federal antitrust laws, because it was not "interstate commerce." Under modern interpretations of the Constitution's commerce clause, this decision is clearly wrong. Nonetheless, professional baseball retains its antitrust exemption; but this exemption applies only to baseball, not to other sports.

6. *Oil marketing.* The 1935 Interstate Oil Compact allows states to determine quotas on oil that will be marketed in interstate commerce.

7. *Other exemptions.* Other activities exempt from antitrust laws include the following:

(a) Activities approved by the president in furtherance of the defense of our nation (under the Defense Production Act of 1950 as amended).

(b) Cooperative research among small business firms (under the Small Business Administration Act of 1958 as amended).

(c) Research by consortiums of competitors to cooperate in the development of new computer technology (under special federal legislation, including the National Cooperative Research Act of 1984).

(d) State actions, when the state policy is clearly articulated and the policy is actively supervised by the state.[31]

---

31. See *Packer v. Brown*, 317 U.S. 341, 63 S.Ct. 307, 87 L.Ed. 315 (1943).

(e) Activities of regulated industries (such as the transportation, communication, and banking industries) when federal commissions, boards, or agencies (such as the Federal Communications Commission, the Federal Maritime Commission, or the Interstate Commerce Commission) have primary regulatory authority.

(f) Some joint efforts by businesspersons to obtain legislative or executive action, which may be protected as promoting legitimate participation in the political process even though such action may be selfishly motivated. This is often referred to as the Noerr-Pennington doctrine.[32] Although supposedly permitting selfish rather than purely public-minded conduct, there is an exception that increasingly appears to be ready to swallow the rule: conduct that is asserted to be political but that is merely a sham deserves no protection, if it is clear the action is not pursued through legitimate means. The exception, however, is limited to abuse of the political process. If legitimate political means are employed, it is irrelevant that the result of the process hinders competition or that the efforts were motivated by a self-serving objective such as injuring a competitor.[33]

---

32. *United Mine Workers of America v. Pennington,* 381 U.S. 657, 89 S.Ct. 1585, 14 L.Ed.2d 626 (1965), and *Eastern Railroad Presidents Conference v. Noerr Motor Freight,* 365 U.S. 127, 81 S.Ct. 523, 5 L.Ed.2d 464 (1961).

33. *City of Columbia and Columbia Outdoor Advertising, Inc. v. Omni Outdoor Advertising, Inc.,* ___ U.S. ___, 111 S.Ct. 1344, 113 L.Ed.2d 382 (1991).

■ Terms and Concepts

antitrust law 831
barriers to entry 844
concentrated industry 834
conglomerate merger 846
dissolution 847
divestiture 847
exclusive dealing
  contracts 842
group boycott 836
horizontal market
  division 834
horizontal merger 844

horizontal restraint 833
joint venture 837
market concentration 843
market power 830
market share test 839
monopolization 839
monopoly 830
monopoly power 832
per se violations 832
potential competition
  doctrine 846

price discrimination 842
price fixing 833
resale price maintenance
  agreement 838
rule of reason 832
trust 831
tying arrangement 843
vertical merger 846
vertically integrated
  firm 837

■ For Review

1. What is a monopoly? What is market power? How do they relate?

2. An agreement that is blatantly and substantially anticompetitive is deemed a *per se* violation of Section 1 of the Sherman Act. Under what rule is an agreement analyzed if it appears to be anticompetitive but is not a *per se* violation? In making this analysis, what factors will a court consider?

3. The Clayton Act deals with specific practices that are considered to reduce competition or lead to monopoly power but are not expressly covered by the Sherman Act. What are these practices?

4. SuperStyles, Inc., and Dura-Wear Clothing Co. sell discount clothing. SuperStyles and Dura-Wear want to merge. Together, they would cover 7 percent of the national discount clothing market, but in cities between 30,000 and 100,000 in population, their joint market share would be nearly 30 percent. Casual Clothes, Inc., a competitor, challenges the merger as a violation of Section 7 of the Clayton Act. How might the court rule?

5. Over a period of ten years, a number of automobile parts manufacturers merge and sign agreements until they control 80 percent of the auto parts market in the United States. In an antitrust suit brought by the Department of Justice against the manufacturers, the firms argue that they are only attempting to compete more effectively with international firms and that consumers also benefit from their practices—prices have fallen since the firms began "cooperating." What might the court say?

■ Questions and Case Problems

47-1. Novo Appliance Store was a new retail seller of appliances in Sunwest City. Novo's innovative sales techniques and financing caused a substantial loss of sales from the appliance department of Luckluster Department Store. Luckluster was a large department store and part of a large chain with substantial buying power. Luckluster told a number of appliance manufacturers that if they continued to sell to Novo, Luckluster would stop purchasing from them. The manufacturers immediately stopped selling appliances to Novo. Novo filed suit against Luckluster and the manufacturers, claiming that their actions constituted an antitrust violation. Luckluster and the manufacturers could prove that Novo was a small retailer with a small portion of the market. Because the relevant market was not substantially affected, they claimed they were not guilty of restraint of trade. Discuss *fully* whether there was an antitrust violation.

47-2. Discuss *fully* whether each of the following situations violates the Sherman Act.

(a) Trujillo Foods, Inc., is the leading seller of frozen Mexican foods in three southwestern states. The various retail outlets that sell Trujillo products are in close competition, and customers are very price conscious. Trujillo has conditioned its sales to retailers with the agreement that the retailers will not sell below a minimum price nor above a maximum price. The retailers are allowed to set any price within these limits.

(b) Franklin, Inc., Green, Inc., and Fill-It, Inc., are competitors in the manufacture and sale of microwave ovens sold primarily east of the Mississippi River. As a patriotic gesture and to assist the unemployed, the three competitors agree to lower their prices on all microwave models by 20 percent for a three-month period that includes the Fourth of July and Labor Day.

(c) Foam Beer, Inc., sells its beer to distributors all over the United States. Foam sends each of its distributors a recommended price list, explaining that past records indicate that selling beer at those prices should ensure the distributor a reasonable rate of return. The price list clearly states that the sale of beer by Foam to the distributor is not conditioned upon the distributor's reselling the beer at the recommended price and that the distributor is free to set the price.

47-3. Quick Photo, Inc., is a manufacturer of photographic film. At present, Quick Photo has approximately 50 percent of the market. Quick Photo launches a campaign whereby the purchase price of Quick Photo film includes photo processing by Quick Photo, Inc. The company claims that its film processing is specially designed to improve the quality of the finished photos when Quick Photo's film is used. Discuss *fully* whether Quick Photo's combination of film purchase and film processing is an antitrust violation.

47-4. Bock Brewery, Inc., is a regional producer and seller of Suds Beer. In its five-state area, Bock has 15 percent of the beer market. Barrel Tap, Inc., is a corporation that has exclusive beer sales concessions in taverns in all major airports in a twenty-state area. Barrel Tap purchases beer from Bock, Miller, and Anheuser-Busch, Inc. Bock acquires the stock and assets of Barrel Tap, Inc. What type of merger is this? Discuss *fully* whether this merger is in violation of the Clayton Act, Section 7.

47-5. Super-Tech Industries presently controls 55 percent of the market in the manufacture and sale of computers. The balance of the market is controlled by Alcan Corp., which has 25 percent of the market, and five other manufacturers. Alcan has an innovative research staff, but every time Alcan introduces a faster, more powerful and efficient computer in the market, Super-Tech immediately informs its customers of the upcoming development of a competing computer that it will sell at 30 percent below the Alcan price. Alcan claims that these activities on the part of Super-

Tech are an antitrust violation. Discuss fully whether this unilateral action by Super-Tech violates antitrust law.

47-6. Radial keratotomy is a relatively new surgical procedure to correct myopia (nearsightedness). In 1980, at the recommendation of the National Eye Institute, the American Academy of Ophthalmology, Inc., issued a press release urging "patients, ophthalmologists and hospitals to approach [radial keratotomy] with caution until additional research is completed." Schacher and several other ophthalmologists who specialized in radial keratotomy claimed that the demand for their services declined following the press release. They brought an action against the Academy, contending that the press release constituted an illegal horizontal trade restraint. The district court held that the Academy had not violated any antitrust law. What will result on appeal? [*Schacher v. American Academy of Ophthalmology, Inc.,* 870 F.2d 397 (7th Cir. 1989)]

47-7. Dr. Beard, an osteopathic physician specializing in radiology, worked for G. S. Bucholz, Inc. Bucholz is the exclusive provider of radiological services to Parkview Hospital. When Dr. Beard resigned from his position at Bucholz, he had every intention of providing radiological services himself to the patients at Parkview, but the Parkview administration informed him that the hospital had an exclusive contract with Bucholz for the provision of radiological services and that Dr. Beard would no longer be permitted to work in Parkview's radiology department. Dr. Beard sued Parkview, alleging that the exclusive contract between the hospital and Bucholz was a tying arrangement in violation of Section 1 of the Sherman Act. Parkview claimed that its arrangement with Bucholz ensured responsibility and accountability for the radiology department and guaranteed the availability of services when needed. Under the terms of the agreement between Bucholz and Parkview, Bucholz bills patients directly for the services it provides; Parkview does not get a portion of any fees charged by Bucholz. Does the exclusive contract between Parkview and Bucholz violate Section 1 of the Sherman Act? Discuss fully. [*Beard v. Parkview Hospital,* 912 F.2d 138 (6th Cir. 1990)]

47-8. Hartwell and Business Electronics Corp. were both authorized by Sharp Electronics to sell Sharp electronic products in the Houston, Texas, area. Business Electronics continuously sold Sharp products at below suggested retail prices. Hartwell complained to Sharp about its rival's price-cutting tactics, and Sharp eventually terminated the dealership of Business Electronics. Business Electronics sued Sharp and Hartwell, claiming that the two firms had conspired together to create a vertical restraint of trade that was illegal *per se* under Section 1 of the Sherman Act. Does Sharp's termination of the Business Electronics dealership constitute a *per se* violation of Section 1, or should the rule of reason apply? [*Business Electronics Corp. v. Sharp Electronics Corp.,* 485 U.S. 717, 108 S.Ct. 1515, 99 L.Ed.2d 806 (1988)]

47-9. Harcourt Brace Jovanovich Legal and Professional Publications (HBJ), the nation's largest provider of bar review materials and lecture services, began offering a Georgia bar review course in 1976 and was in direct, and often intense, competition with BRG of Georgia, Inc., the other main provider of bar review courses in Georgia, from 1977 to 1979. In early 1980, HBJ and BRG entered into an agreement that gave BRG the exclusive right to market HBJ's materials in Georgia and to use its trade name, Bar/Bri. The parties agreed that HBJ would not compete with BRG in Georgia and that BRG would not compete with HBJ outside of Georgia. Immediately after the 1980 agreement, the price of BRG's course was increased from $150 to over $400. Jay Palmer, a former law student, brought an action against the two firms, alleging that the 1980 agreement violated Section 1 of the Sherman Act. What will the court decide? Discuss fully. [*Palmer v. BRG of Georgia, Inc.,* —— U.S.——, 111 S.Ct. 401, 112 L.Ed.2d 349 (1990)]

47-10. A Question of Ethics

A group of lawyers in the District of Columbia regularly acted as court-appointed attorneys for indigent defendants in District of Columbia criminal cases. At a meeting of the Superior Court Trial Lawyers Association (SCTLA), the attorneys agreed to stop providing such representation until the district increased their compensation. Their subsequent boycott had a severe impact on the district's criminal justice system, and the District of Columbia gave in to the lawyers' demands for higher pay. After the lawyers had returned to work, the Federal Trade Commission filed a complaint against the SCTLA and four of its officers and, after an investigation, ruled that the SCTLA's activities constituted an illegal group boycott in violation of antitrust laws. [Federal Trade Commission v. Superior Court Trial Lawyers Association, *493 U.S. 411, 110 S.Ct. 768, 107 L.Ed.2d 851 (1990)]*

1. The SCTLA obviously was aware of the negative impact their decision would have on the district's criminal justice system. Given this fact, do you think the lawyers behaved ethically?

2. On appeal, the SCTLA claimed that their boycott was undertaken to publicize the fact that attorneys were underpaid and that their boycott thus constituted an expression protected by the First Amendment. Do you agree with this argument?

3. Labor unions have the right to strike when negotiations between labor and management fail to result in agreement. Do you think that it is fair for members of the SCTLA to be prohibited from "striking" against their employer, the District of Columbia, simply because the SCTLA was a professional organization and not a labor union?

Chapter 48

Employment and Labor Relations Law

Traditionally, employment relationships in the United States were governed by contract, tort, and agency law. Most employer-employee contracts were considered to be ''at will.'' Under the **employment-at-will doctrine,** either party may terminate an employment contract at any time and for any reason, unless the contract specifies a particular time period. Generally, this meant that employers could fire workers for good, bad, or no cause in response to changing economic conditions. If an employee was injured on the job, it was difficult for him or her to recover from the employer, because an employee was considered to have assumed the risks of employment when he or she accepted the job.

With increasing industrialization, the size of corporate employers and the number of workplace hazards increased. Workers came to believe that to counter the power of corporations and to protect themselves, they needed to organize. As labor gained political influence, legislators responded with minimum wage, maximum hour, child labor, and other laws. Initially, the courts sided with business and struck down many of these laws as unconstitutional. Collective activities such as unions were discouraged—sometimes forcibly—by employers. Also, early legislation that protected the rights of employees was often restricted to a particular industry. The Railway Labor Act of 1926,[1] for example, required railroads and their employees to attempt to make employment agreements through representatives chosen by each side.

Beginning in 1932, however, a number of statutes were enacted that greatly increased employees' rights to join unions, to engage in collective bargaining, to receive retirement and income security benefits, to be protected against various discrimination practices, and to have a safe place to work. At the heart of labor rights is the right to unionize and bargain with management for improved working conditions, salaries, and benefits. The ultimate weapon of labor is, of course, the strike.

In this chapter, we look at some of the significant laws that regulate labor and the workplace. Drug testing, lie-detector tests, and the general issue of employees' privacy rights, which were mentioned briefly in Chapter 2 in the context of ethics, will be discussed more fully here.

---

1. 45 U.S.C. Sections 151 *et seq.*

■ Unions and Collective Bargaining

Most of the early legislation to protect employees focused on the rights of workers to join unions and to engage in collective bargaining. These early laws ensured that workers could form unions and that the unions could negotiate with employers over wages and other terms of employment. In this way, workers were better able to defend their own interests against employers.

Norris-LaGuardia Act

Congress protected peaceful strikes, picketing, and boycotts in 1932 in the Norris-LaGuardia Act.[2] The statute restricted federal courts in their power to issue injunctions against unions engaged in peaceful strikes. In effect, this act declared a national policy permitting employees to organize.

National Labor Relations Act

The National Labor Relations Act of 1935 (NLRA),[3] also called the Wagner Act, established the rights of employees to engage in collective bargaining and to strike. The act also created the National Labor Relations Board (NLRB) to oversee union elections and to prevent employers from engaging in unfair and illegal union-labor activities and unfair labor practices.

The purpose of the NLRA was to secure for employees the rights to organize, to bargain col-

---

2. 29 U.S.C. Sections 101 *et seq.*
3. 20 U.S.C. Sections 151 *et seq.*

lectively through representatives of their own choosing, and to engage in concerted activities for that and other purposes. The act specifically defined a number of employer practices as unfair to labor:

1. Interference with the efforts of employees to form, join, or assist labor organizations or to engage in concerted activities for their mutual aid or protection.
2. An employer's domination of a labor organization or contribution of financial or other support to it.
3. Discrimination in the hiring or awarding of tenure to employees for reason of union affiliation.
4. Discrimination against employees for filing charges under the act or giving testimony under the act.
5. Refusal to bargain collectively with the duly designated representative of the employees.

Another purpose of the act was to promote fair and just settlements of disputes by peaceful processes and to avoid industrial warfare. The NLRB was granted investigatory powers and was authorized to issue and serve complaints against employers in response to employee charges of unfair labor practices. The NLRB was further empowered to issue cease-and-desist orders—which could be enforced by a federal court of appeals if necessary—when violations were found.

Arguments over alleged unfair labor practices are first decided by the NLRB and may then be appealed to federal court. The following case, which involved an allegedly unfair labor practice, illustrates this process.

Case 48.1 **KENRICH PETROCHEMICALS, INC. v. NATIONAL LABOR RELATIONS BOARD** United States Court of Appeals, Third Circuit, 1990. 907 F.2d 400.	**BACKGROUND AND FACTS** Salvatore Monte was president of Kenrich Petrochemicals, Inc. Helen Chizmar had been Kenrich's office manager since 1963. Among the staff that Chizmar supervised were her sister, daughter, and daughter-in-law. In 1987, Chizmar's relatives and four other staff members designated the Oil, Chemical and Atomic Workers International Union as their bargaining representative. Chizmar was not involved, but when Monte was notified that his office was unionizing, he told Chizmar that someone else could do her job for "$20,000 less" and fired her. He told another employee that one of his reasons for firing Chizmar was that he "was not going to put up with any union bullsh___ ." During negotiations with the union, Monte said that he planned to "get rid of the whole family." Chizmar's family complained to the NLRB that the firing was an unfair labor practice. The NLRB agreed and ordered that Chizmar be reinstated with back pay. Kenrich appealed.

DECISION AND RATIONALE The United States Court of Appeals for the Third Circuit concluded that the reinstatement and back pay order was reasonably calculated to dispel the intimidation caused by Chizmar's firing and ruled that the order be enforced. Kenrich argued that the NLRA does not protect a supervisor who engages in union activity. The court agreed but pointed out that Chizmar was not fired for pro-union activity—she was fired in an effort by Kenrich to "thwart the exercise of * * * rights by protected rank-and-file employees." The court stated that "such a discharge must communicate to rank-and-file employees that the employer is willing to go to any lengths to crush [unionizing] activity." If the discharge was allowed to stand, the court reasoned, "a powerful message will be sent out to the supervisors and employees of Kenrich that the company may, without fear of redress, use family member supervisors as hostages." By reinstating and compensating Chizmar, the NLRB's order assured employees that they need not fear that an exercise of their rights would result in harm to their families.

Labor-Management Relations Act

The Labor-Management Relations Act of 1947 (the Taft-Hartley Act)[4] was passed to proscribe certain unfair union practices, such as the *closed shop*. A **closed shop** is a firm that requires union membership by its workers as a condition of employment. The closed shop was made illegal under the Taft-Hartley Act. The act preserved the legality of the **union shop,** which does not require membership as a prerequisite for employment but can, and usually does, require that workers join the union after a specified amount of time on the job. The act also allowed individual states to pass their own **right-to-work laws**—laws making it illegal for union membership to be required for *continued* employment in any establishment. Thus, union shops are technically illegal in states with right-to-work laws.

One of the most controversial aspects of the Taft-Hartley Act was the **eighty-day cooling-off period**—a provision allowing federal courts to issue injunctions against strikes that would create a national emergency. The president of the United States can obtain a court injunction that will last for eighty days, and presidents have occasionally used this provision. For example, President Eisenhower applied the eighty-day injunction order to striking steelworkers in 1959, President Nixon applied it to striking dock workers in 1971, and President Carter applied it to striking coal miners in 1978.

Labor-Management Reporting and Disclosure Act

The Labor-Management Reporting and Disclosure Act of 1959 (the Landrum-Griffin Act)[5] established an employee bill of rights and reporting requirements for union activities. The Landrum-Griffin Act strictly regulated internal union business procedures. Union elections, for example, are regulated by the Landrum-Griffin Act, which requires that regularly scheduled elections of officers occur and that secret ballots be used. Ex-convicts and communists are prohibited from holding union office. Moreover, union officials are made accountable for union property and funds. Members have the right to attend and to participate in union meetings, to nominate officers, and to vote in most union proceedings.

The Landrum-Griffin Act also outlawed certain agreements—called **hot-cargo agreements**—in which employers voluntarily agreed with unions not to handle, use, or deal in non-union-produced goods of other employers. In principle, the Taft-Hartley Act had made all such boycotts (called **secondary boycotts**) illegal. This particular type of secondary boycott was not made illegal by the Taft-Hartley Act, however, because that act only prevented unions from inducing *employees* to strike or otherwise act to force the employer not to handle these goods. The Landrum-Griffin Act addressed this problem:

---

4. 29 U.S.C. Sections 141 *et seq.*

5. 29 U.S.C. Sections 401 *et seq.*

It shall be [an] unfair labor practice for any labor organization and any employer to enter into any contract or any agreement . . . whereby such employer . . . agrees to refrain from handling, using, selling, transporting or otherwise dealing in any of the products of any other employer, or to cease doing business with any other person.

▪ Employment Discrimination

At common law, employment was terminable at will. Any employer could establish all terms and conditions of employment. Labor unions were deemed private associations, so they could determine all membership requirements without oversight of the courts. In the past several decades, however, as a result of judicial decisions, administrative agency actions, and legislation, both employers and unions have been restricted in their ability to discriminate on the basis of race, religion, nationality, age, or sex. Perhaps the most important statute relating to employment discrimination is Title VII of the Civil Rights Act of 1964.[6]

Title VII of the Civil Rights Act of 1964

Basically, Title VII of the Civil Rights Act of 1964 prohibits job discrimination against employees, applicants, and union members on the basis of race, color, national origin, religion, and sex *at any stage of employment.*

A class of persons defined by one or more of these criteria is known as a **protected class.** Title VII prohibits discrimination on the part of employers with fifteen or more employees; labor unions with fifteen or more members; labor unions that operate hiring halls (where members go regularly to be rationed jobs as they become available); employment agencies; and state and local governments, government agencies, political subdivisions, and departments. A special section forbids discrimination in most federal government employment.

Discrimination on the basis of religion and the requirement that employers reasonably accommodate the religious needs of their employees were discussed in Chapter 4. We look here at other types of discrimination prohibited by Title VII.

PROCEDURES AND REMEDIES A person who has suffered discrimination may not simply file a lawsuit under Title VII. Compliance with Title VII is monitored by the Equal Employment Opportunity Commission (EEOC). The EEOC has the power to issue guidelines for interpreting the law and to bring lawsuits against organizations that violate the law. Thus, first, the victim must file a claim with the EEOC, which investigates the facts and seeks to achieve a voluntary conciliation through which the employer and employee settle the dispute. If conciliation does not occur, the EEOC may sue the employer under Title VII. If the EEOC chooses not to sue—for example, if it does not believe that the complaining individual was discriminated against—the victim may bring his or her own suit.

Employer liability under Title VII may be extensive. If the plaintiff successfully proves that unlawful discrimination occurred, he or she may be awarded reinstatement, back pay, and retroactive promotions. The court may also grant an injunction prohibiting future violations and correcting for past discrimination.

DISPARATE-TREATMENT DISCRIMINATION When one thinks of employment discrimination, one is likely to imagine a job supervisor who is overtly racist or sexist. Blatant discrimination is known as **disparate-treatment discrimination.**

One of its elements is the employer's intent to discriminate. Because intent may sometimes be difficult to prove, courts have established certain procedures for resolving disparate-treatment cases. Suppose a woman applies for employment with a construction firm and is rejected. If she sues on grounds of disparate-treatment discrimination in hiring, she must meet the following four requirements:

1. The plaintiff is a member of a protected class.
2. The plaintiff applied and was qualified for the job in question.
3. The plaintiff was rejected by the employer.
4. The employer continued to seek applicants for the position or filled the position with a person not in a protected class.

If the plaintiff can meet these relatively easy tests, she makes out a *prima facie* case of illegal discrimination. Making out a *prima facie* case of

---

6. 42 U.S.C. Sections 2000e *et seq.*

discrimination means that the plaintiff has met her initial burden of proof and will win in the absence of an employer response. The burden then shifts to the employer-defendant to articulate a legal reason for not hiring the plaintiff. For example, the employer might say that the plaintiff was not hired because she lacked sufficient experience or training. The plaintiff must then show that the employer's reason is a pretext (not the true reason) and that discriminatory intent actually motivated the employer's decision. The following case involved allegations of disparate-treatment discrimination.

BACKGROUND AND FACTS As a senior manager and officer with the accounting firm of Price Waterhouse, Ann Hopkins succeeded in terms of technical skills and client relations, securing a multimillion dollar contract for the firm. She was proposed for partnership in 1982. Evaluations compiled by the partnership committee described Hopkins as abrasive, overbearing, and "macho," sometimes "bullying" subordinates when she was under pressure. It was suggested that these characteristics were inappropriate in a woman. One partner advised that she "take a course in charm school." Her promotion was placed on hold, and she was advised to "walk more femininely, talk more femininely, dress more femininely, wear makeup, have her hair styled and wear jewelry." She was not reproposed for partnership. Hopkins sued in a federal district court, alleging sex discrimination. She claimed that words such as "macho" indicated underlying sexism and that her manner would have been overlooked if she had been a man. The trial court held the firm liable, finding that the partnership decision was infused with stereotypical notions about how women should behave on the job. The firm appealed. The appellate court agreed with the trial court. The firm appealed to the United States Supreme Court.

DECISION AND RATIONALE The United States Supreme Court concluded that the trial court's findings were not clearly erroneous. The Supreme Court pointed out that "Hopkins showed that the partnership * * * generally relied very heavily on [the] evaluations in making its decision; that some of the partners' comments were the product of stereotyping; and that the firm in no way disclaimed reliance on those particular comments." The Court noted that "Price Waterhouse appears to think that we cannot affirm the factual findings of the trial court without deciding that, instead of being overbearing and aggressive and curt, Hopkins is in fact kind and considerate and patient." The Court explained that "[i]t is not our job to review the evidence and decide that the negative reactions to Hopkins were based on reality * * *. We sit not to determine whether Ms. Hopkins is nice, but to decide whether the partners reacted negatively to her personality because she is a woman." The Court also concluded, however, that the trial court had applied the wrong standard to the employer's burden of proof and remanded the case for a determination under the correct standard as to whether Hopkins would have been denied partnership even in the absence of discrimination. On remand, the trial court again held Price Waterhouse liable and ordered the firm to give Hopkins her partnership, retroactive to 1982, and $371,000 in back pay and interest. Price Waterhouse appealed again. The appellate court affirmed the award.

Case 48.2

PRICE WATERHOUSE v. HOPKINS

Supreme Court of the United States, 1989.
490 U.S. 228,
109 S.Ct. 1775,
104 L.Ed. 2d 268.

DISPARATE-IMPACT DISCRIMINATION Employers often find it necessary to use interviews and testing procedures to choose from among a large number of applicants for job openings. Consequently, personnel tests have been used as devices for screening applicants. Minimum educational requirements are also common. Employer practices such as those involving educational or job requirements may have an unintended discriminatory impact on a protected class. **Disparate-impact discrimination** occurs when, as a result of educational or other job requirements or hiring procedures, an employer's work force does not reflect the same percentage of nonwhites, women, or members of other protected classes that character-izes qualified individuals in the local labor market. If a person challenging an employment practice having a discriminatory effect can show a connection between the practice and the disparity, he or she makes out a *prima facie* case, and no evidence of disciminatory intent needs to be shown. In the following case, the United States Supreme Court evaluated a claim of disparate-impact discrimination in two Alaskan canneries.

Case 48.3

WARDS COVE PACKING CO. v. ATONIO

Supreme Court of the United States, 1989.
490 U.S. 642,
109 S.Ct. 2115,
104 L.Ed.2d 733.

BACKGROUND AND FACTS   At two Alaskan salmon canneries, there are "cannery jobs" (unskilled positions filled largely by local nonwhites, Filipi-nos, and Alaska natives) and "noncannery jobs" (mostly skilled positions filled largely by whites hired from the companies' offices in Washington and Oregon). Most noncannery jobs pay more than cannery jobs. Frank Atonio and other cannery workers brought a Title VII action against the canneries in a federal district court, asserting that hiring and promotion practices—including an English-language requirement and not promoting from within—caused racial stratification of the work force and denied cannery workers the opportunity to work at noncannery jobs. The trial court ruled in the employers' favor, but the appellate court held that the workers had made out a *prima facie* case of disparate-impact discrimination. The em-ployers, challenging the use of the numbers of nonwhites in cannery and noncannery positions to measure discrimination, appealed to the United States Supreme Court.

DECISION AND RATIONALE   The United States Supreme Court held that comparing the numbers of nonwhites in cannery and noncannery positions was not sufficient to establish a *prima facie* case of disparate-impact dis-crimination. The Supreme Court acknowledged that "statistical proof can alone make out a *prima facie* case," but stated that measuring discrimi-nation in the selection of skilled workers "by comparing the number of nonwhites occupying these jobs to the number of nonwhites filling cannery worker positions is nonsensical." The Court pointed out that "the vast ma-jority of these cannery workers did not seek jobs in unskilled noncannery positions; there is no showing that many of them would have done so even if none of the arguably 'deterring' practices existed." The Court explained that the "proper comparison [is] between the racial composition of [the at-issue jobs] and the racial composition of the qualified * * * population in the relevant labor market." The case was remanded to the lower court for further proceedings. On remand, the court held that the nonwhite work-ers failed to establish that the company's practices had a disparate impact on their job opportunities.

After an employee makes out a *prima facie* case of discrimination, the employer has an opportunity to respond. The employer may attempt to disprove the case, or the employer may use cer-tain defenses to justify employment practices.

Business Necessity Defense In a disparate-impact case, an employer may assert a **business necessity defense**—that is, the employer may offer a good business reason for a practice that has a discriminatory effect. For example, if requiring a high school diploma is shown to have a discriminatory effect, an employer might argue that a high school education is required for workers to do a good job. Courts have held that educational requirements are a business necessity for some jobs, but they have rejected educational requirements for positions that require primarily manual labor. In one case, a company required certain scores on standardized ability tests as prerequisites for employment in the company's skilled positions. Use of the tests had a discriminatory effect, because African-Americans consistently scored lower than whites. When the company asserted a business necessity defense, the court found no relation between the tests and job performance, and thus the requirement did not qualify as a business necessity.[7]

The employer only has to state the business reason that it believes justifies an allegedly discriminatory practice. The person challenging the practice has to show that it is not justified by business necessity.[8]

BFOQ Defense Another defense applies when discrimination against a protected class is essential to a job—that is, when a particular trait is a **bona fide occupational qualification (BFOQ).** For example, a men's fashion magazine might legitimately hire only male models. Under Title VII, race cannot be a BFOQ. The defense applies only to the traits of other protected classes. Much controversy has arisen over this defense, particularly in sex-discrimination cases. Some companies have argued that being male is a BFOQ for jobs requiring heavy lifting,[9] whereas others have contended that being female is a BFOQ for flight attendants.[10]

Courts have rejected both these arguments and have generally restricted the BFOQ defense to instances in which the employee's gender is essential to the job. In 1991, the United States Supreme Court held that even a fetal-protection policy is an unacceptable BFOQ.[11]

Seniority System Defense Another defense protects bona fide seniority systems. An employer with a history of discrimination may have no members of protected classes in upper-level positions. Even if the employer now seeks to be unbiased, it may face a lawsuit seeking an order for minorities to be promoted ahead of schedule to compensate for the past discrimination. If a present intent to discriminate is not shown, and promotions or other job benefits are distributed according to a fair seniority system, the employer has a good defense against the suit.

AFFIRMATIVE ACTION Title VII and equal opportunity regulations were designed to reduce or eliminate discriminatory practices with respect to hiring, retaining, and promoting employees. Affirmative action programs go a step further and attempt to atone for past discrimination by giving qualified minorities and women preferential treatment in hiring and promotions. Affirmative action programs are controversial, especially when they are seen as resulting in what is often called ''reverse discrimination''—discrimination against members of non-protected classes, particularly white males. Generally, affirmative action programs that are designed to correct existing imbalances in a work force have been upheld as long as employers considered factors in addition to race or gender when making employment decisions. In determining whether a challenged plan is legitimate, the United States Supreme Court looks at the circumstances surrounding the case. In the following case, a male employee who was a candidate for promotion alleged that his employer had engaged in reverse gender discrimination by promoting a less-qualified female.

---

7. *Albemarle Paper Co. v. Moody,* 422 U.S. 405, 95 S.Ct. 2362, 45 L.Ed.2d 280 (1975).

8. *Wards Cove Packing Co. v. Atonio,* 490 U.S. 642, 109 S.Ct. 2115, 104 L.Ed.2d 733 (1989).

9. *Rosenfeld v. Southern Pacific Co.,* 444 F.2d 1219 (9th Cir. 1971).

10. *Diaz v. Pan American World Airways, Inc.,* 442 F.2d 385 (5th Cir. 1971).

11. *United Auto Workers v. Johnson Controls, Inc.,* ____ U.S. ____, 111 S.Ct. 1196, 113 L.Ed.2d 158 (1991). This case was presented in Chapter 2 as Case 2.1.

Case 48.4

**JOHNSON v.
TRANSPORTATION
AGENCY, SANTA
CLARA COUNTY,
CALIFORNIA**

Supreme Court of the
United States, 1987.
480 U.S. 616,
107 S.Ct. 1442,
94 L.Ed.2d 615.

BACKGROUND AND FACTS   Paul Johnson, a male employee of the
Transportation Agency of Santa Clara County, California, challenged the
promotion of a female employee, Diane Joyce, who had a lower total score
on the qualifying test and interviews than he did. Johnson and Joyce were
among the final seven candidates for the position of road dispatcher, and
a factor in awarding the job to Joyce was that she was a woman. The
agency had adopted an affirmative action plan designed to increase the
number of women in positions in which they "have not been traditionally
employed in significant numbers." At the time of Joyce's promotion, not
one of the 238 positions in the job classification was held by a woman.
Johnson sued the agency in a federal district court, contending that the
promotion violated Title VII. The trial court agreed, but the appellate court
reversed, maintaining that the promotion was a lawful effort to remedy long-
standing imbalances in the work force. Johnson appealed to the United
States Supreme Court.

DECISION AND RATIONALE   The United States Supreme Court affirmed
the appellate court's judgment. The Supreme Court held that the agency
appropriately took into account gender in determining that Joyce should
be promoted, "[g]iven the obvious imbalance in the [job] category, and
given the [a]gency's commitment to eliminating such imbalances." The
Court also reasoned that the agency's affirmative action plan did not unnecessarily trammel the rights of male employees or create an absolute bar
to their advancement—"the [p]lan requires women to compete with all other
qualified applicants." Besides, Johnson "had no absolute entitlement to the
road dispatcher position. *   *   * [T]he Agency Director was authorized to
promote any of the [candidates]." Furthermore, Johnson "retained his employment with the [a]gency, at the same salary and with the same seniority,
and remained eligible for other promotions."

ETHICAL CONSIDERATIONS   At the center of the debate over affirmative
action programs is an ethical question: To what extent, and in what ways,
should the government regulate employment conditions to ensure equal
opportunity? How much should employees who have not been discriminated against have to pay for those who have been subject to discrimination? In 1989, the United States Supreme Court held that a city ordinance
requiring primary contractors on city construction projects to subcontract
at least 30 percent of the dollar value of the projects to minority-owned
businesses violated the equal protection clause.[a] The Court said that the
ordinance was tailored to no goal but "outright racial balancing." The Court
added, "While there is no doubt that the sorry history of both private and
public discrimination in this country has contributed to a lack of opportunities for black entrepreneurs, this observation *   *   * cannot justify a rigid
racial quota in the awarding of public contracts."

a. *City of Richmond v. J. A. Croson Co.*, 488 U.S. 469, 109 S.Ct. 706, 102 L.Ed.2d 854
(1989).

SEXUAL HARASSMENT   Workers have some
protection against sexual harassment in the workplace under Title VII provisions against sex discrimination. Sexual harassment occurs when job
opportunities, promotions, and the like are doled

out on the basis of sexual favors or when an employee is subjected to a work environment in which
the employee must put up with sexual comments,
jokes, or physical contact that is perceived to be
sexually offensive.

In a sexual harassment case, the employer may be liable even though an employee did the harassing. If the employee is in a supervising position, the employer will usually be held automatically liable for the behavior. If a lower-level employee is responsible for the harassment, the employer will be held liable only if it knew, or should have known, about the harassment and failed to take corrective action. The following case is a leading example of the law as applied to sexual harassment and employer liability.

 Case 48.5

MERITOR SAVINGS BANK, FSB v. VINSON

Supreme Court of the United States, 1986.
477 U.S. 57,
106 S.Ct. 2399,
91 L.Ed.2d 49.

BACKGROUND AND FACTS In 1974, Mechelle Vinson began working at Meritor Savings Bank. Vinson later sued the bank in a federal district court, claiming that she had "constantly been subjected to sexual harassment." She claimed that Sidney Taylor, a vice-president and branch manager, made sexual advances toward her, to which she acquiesced out of fear of losing her job. Vinson testified that Taylor fondled her in front of other employees and forcibly raped her. Taylor denied the charges. The trial court concluded that any sexual relationship between Vinson and Taylor had no relationship to Vinson's continued employment and ruled in favor of the bank. Vinson appealed, and the appellate court ruled in her favor, finding that she had made out a case of harassing-environment discrimination. The bank appealed to the United States Supreme Court.

DECISION AND RATIONALE The United States Supreme Court affirmed the appellate court's decision. The Supreme Court rejected the bank's argument that in prohibiting discrimination under Title VII, Congress was concerned with "tangible loss" of "an economic character" and not "purely psychological aspects of the workplace environment." The Court pointed out that courts have uniformly held that "a plaintiff may establish a violation of Title VII by proving that discrimination based on sex has created a hostile or abusive work environment. * * * 'Sexual harassment which creates a hostile or offensive environment for members of one sex is every bit the arbitrary barrier to sexual equality at the workplace that racial harassment is to racial equality.' " Requiring an individual to "run a gauntlet of sexual abuse in return for the privilege of being allowed to work and make a living can be as demeaning and disconcerting as the harshest racial epithets." Holding that the bank's liability for the actions of its supervisory employees should be determined according to common law principles of agency (see Chapter 36), the Court remanded the case to the district court for further proceedings.

PREGNANCY DISCRIMINATION The Pregnancy Discrimination Act of 1978,[12] which amended Title VII, prohibits discriminatory treatment of employees on the basis of pregnancy. Women affected by pregnancy, childbirth, or related medical conditions must be treated—for all employment-related purposes, including the receipt of benefits under employee benefit programs—the same as other persons not so affected but similar in ability to work.

An employer is required to treat an employee temporarily unable to perform her job due to a pregnancy-related condition in the same manner as the employer would treat other temporarily disabled employees. The employer can change work assignments, grant paid disability leaves, or grant leaves without pay, if that is how the employer would treat other temporarily disabled employees. Policies concerning an employee's return to work, accrual of seniority, pay increases, and so on must also result in equal treatment.

---

12. 42 U.S.C. Section 2000e(k).

Age Discrimination

The Age Discrimination in Employment Act (ADEA) of 1967,[13] as amended, prohibits employment discrimination on the basis of age against individuals forty years of age or older. The act was recently amended to prohibit mandatory retirement for nonmanagerial workers. For the act to apply, an employer must have twenty or more employees, and interstate commerce must be affected by the employer's business activities.

The act is similar to Title VII in that it offers protection against both intentional (disparate-

treatment) age discrimination and unintentional (disparate-impact) age discrimination. If a plaintiff can prove that his or her age was a determining reason for an employer's discriminatory treatment, the employer will be held liable under the ADEA unless the allegedly discriminatory practice is justified by some legitimate and nondiscriminatory business reason.

In the following case, the plaintiff alleged age discrimination when an employer refused to hire him because he was "overqualified" for the position. The question before the court is whether the employer's refusal to hire the plaintiff for such a reason is merely age discrimination in disguise.

---

13. 29 U.S.C. Sections 621–634.

Case 48.6

TAGGART v. TIME, INC.

United States Court of Appeals, Second Circuit, 1991.
924 F.2d 43.

BACKGROUND AND FACTS In 1982 Preview Subscription Television, Inc., a subsidiary of Time, Inc., hired Thomas Taggart as a print manager. Taggart was fifty-eight years old and had worked in the printing industry for over thirty years. In 1983, Time notified Preview employees that Preview would be dissolved, but that they would receive special consideration for any available positions at Time and its subsidiaries. Taggart applied for over thirty positions but was not offered employment. Taggart noted that younger applicants were chosen for positions for which he had applied and was better qualified, but for which he had been told he was "overqualified." Claiming that the real reason he was not hired was his age, Taggart sued Time in a federal district court. The trial court granted Time's motion for summary judgment. The court found it reasonable that an employer might reject an applicant whose qualifications are excessive in the belief that the individual would not find the job challenging and would therefore continue to seek other employment. Taggart appealed.

DECISION AND RATIONALE The United States Court of Appeals for the Second Circuit held that refusing to hire Taggart for the reason that he was overqualified refuted Time's assertion that it was not discriminating on the basis of age. The summary judgment was reversed and the case remanded for trial. The Court stated that "[t]o make out a *prima facie* case of age discrimination, plaintiff must show that (1) he belongs to the protected age group, (2) he applied for and was qualified for the position sought, (3) he was not hired despite his qualifications, and (4) the position was ultimately filled by a younger person." Noting that Taggart had established a *prima facie* case, the court said that the issue was thus whether Taggart was rejected "because of circumstances which give rise to an inference of unlawful discrimination." The court reasoned that characterizing Taggart as overqualified "has a connotation that defies common sense: How can a person overqualified by experience and training be turned down for a position given to a younger person deemed better qualified?" The court concluded that *overqualified* "is simply * * * a euphemism to mask the real reason for refusal, namely, in the eyes of the employer the applicant is too old." The court pointed out that younger individuals might seek other employment from positions for which they were overqualified, but older individuals were unlikely to do so because for them other employment opportunities were "mostly non-existent" and "loss of employment late in life ordinarily is devastating economically as well as emotionally."

ETHICAL CONSIDERATIONS In the wake of a corporate merger, takeover, acquisition, consolidation, or other corporate reorganization and the consequent reshuffling of job positions and personnel, many employees may find themselves "out in the cold." Older employees, such as Taggart, suffer particularly because they have more difficulty finding other employment, ostensibly because they are "overqualified." Although one cannot help sympathizing with Taggart and others in his position, the statutory protection against age discrimination—like the protections against other forms of employment discrimination—involves a trade-off. In selecting potential employees, employers cannot be totally objective. Job interviewers also rely, at least to some extent, on their subjective appraisal of a job candidate's personality, energy level, apparent willingness to cooperate with others, and numerous other, often quite subtle, factors when making hiring decisions. For the most part, these factors are difficult to document with any specificity and will not hold up in court as sufficient reasons not to hire a member of a protected class. In a sense, antidiscrimination laws attempt to force employers to forgo these subjective appraisals or risk being sued for discriminatory hiring practices.

Americans with Disabilities Act

The Americans with Disabilities Act (ADA) of 1990 prohibits employment discrimination against differently abled persons by businesses with twenty-five or more employees (and after July 1994, businesses with fifteen or more employees). Differently abled persons are persons with a physical or mental impairment that substantially limits "one or more major life activities." Disabilities include blindness, paralysis, heart disease, cancer, acquired immune deficiency syndrome (AIDS), emotional illness, and learning impairments.

Under the ADA, an employer cannot exclude arbitrarily a person who, with reasonable accommodation, could perform all that is required to do a particular job. This includes employees who become disabled while on the job. A differently abled person who cannot perform a job, however, may be lawfully rejected from employment. For example, a totally blind person who would be required to drive a truck as part of his or her duties would be unqualified for the job.

What constitutes "reasonable accommodation" is difficult to determine. Under the ADA, ramps must be installed for employees who use wheelchairs, and in some circumstances readers are required for blind employees and interpreters for the hearing-impaired. Not every employer is required to accommodate all differently abled employees, however. If an employer can show that an accommodation is an undue hardship, it is unlikely that the employer will be ordered to employ a particular differently abled individual.

What constitutes "undue hardship" depends on the employer's size, budget, and profitability and the financial impact of the accommodation on the employer. For example, a small employer may not be required to hire a blind applicant and a reader to fill a single opening, but a large employer may be obligated to do so.

Procedures and remedies under the ADA are the same as under Title VII. If the Equal Employment Opportunity Commission decides not to pursue an individual's complaint, the individual has the right to sue an employer for reinstatement, back pay, and other relief, including reasonable accommodation. If the employer wins the suit or other action, however, the employer can recover attorney's fees.

The Civil Rights Act of 1991

Our nation's courts have generally been at the forefront of efforts to expand the legal rights and protections afforded to members of ethnic, racial, and other minorities. During the 1960s and 1970s, the courts interpreted laws such as Title VII of the Civil Rights Act of 1964 broadly to uphold affirmative action programs that some commentators argued discriminated against members of the majority. In the 1980s, however, the courts became increasingly conservative. In the area of civil rights, this judicial conservatism culminated in 1989 in a series of United States Supreme Court rulings[14] that civil rights activists argued made it difficult for victims of discrimination to prevail in employment-discrimination cases. Believing that the courts could not be counted on to expand civil rights protections, some activists turned to Congress, requesting that it enact legislation that would in effect overrule the conservative 1989 rulings.

ENACTING THE LEGISLATION   In response to this lobbying effort, Congress passed the Civil Rights Act of 1990. President Bush vetoed the bill, however, and, despite strong support for the bill, Congress did not override Bush's veto. Much of the discussion of the proposed law concerned arguments about whether it was a ''quota bill'' that would force employers to hire persons based on racial considerations instead of merit. Some critics feared that the law would encourage suits by unqualified job applicants, in part because it would have allowed jury trials and punitive damages in federal discrimination cases. Also generating controversy was a provision that was designed to reduce prospective plaintiffs' burden of persuasion (that is, the degree to which all elements of a case must be proved).

The vetoed Civil Rights Act of 1990 was modified to obtain President Bush's approval and passed by Congress as the Civil Rights Act of 1991. This time President Bush signed it. Despite the changes that were made to obtain the president's approval, the new law in effect reversed many of the controversial 1989 Supreme Court employment-discrimination decisions. The law altered the civil rights landscape, particularly for women seeking to redress discrimination. The law makes it possible for women to obtain more damages, including higher compensatory damages and punitive damages, for a variety of discriminatory practices. These practices include sexual harassment and rules limiting jobs available to fertile women.

PROVING BUSINESS NECESSITY   Many of the sponsors of the Civil Rights Act of 1991 saw the legislative reversal of the conservative Supreme Court decisions as a key element in bolstering the legal protections available to women and minorities in the workplace. Although the Civil Rights Act of 1991 does not expressly encourage quotas, it does require companies whose business practices may appear to be neutral to prove the business necessity of those practices if they have a disparate impact on women and minorities. In other words, after an employee or job applicant has identified an employer's business practice that has an allegedly disparate impact on the individual, the employer must do more than simply state the reason for the practice: the employer must justify the practice. The person challenging the practice no longer has to prove that it is not a business necessity, which was required after the Supreme Court's ruling in *Wards Cove Packing Co. v. Atonio* (see Case 48.3). The employer must demonstrate that the particular practice is necessary to the position. For example, a construction company's requirement that all employees be over six feet tall would have a disparate impact on women—far more men than women are over six feet tall. After the Supreme Court's ruling in *Wards Cove* and before the Civil Rights Act of 1991, a woman challenging the height requirement would have had to prove that the requirement was not necessary for her to perform the job in a competent manner. Under the Civil Rights Act of 1991, the company would have to prove that the height requirement is necessary.

OBTAINING DAMAGES   Under the Civil Rights Act of 1991, women and differently abled persons are permitted to sue employers for increased compensatory damages and punitive damages. Before the Civil Rights Act of 1991, only persons succeeding in racial-discrimination suits against employers could recover punitive damages. The amounts of damages available to women and the differently abled are not unlimited. Also, the amounts of awards allowed by the law are directly related to the number of employees in a defendant-employer's company—from $50,000 for companies with 15 to 100 employees to $300,000 for those with more than 500 employees. For example,

---

14.   The cases included *Wards Cove Packing Co. v. Atonio,* 490 U.S. 642, 109 S.Ct. 2115, 104 L.Ed.2d 733 (1989) [Case 48.3 above]; *Lorance v. AT&T Technologies, Inc.,* 490 U.S. 900, 109 S.Ct. 2261, 104 L.Ed.2d 961 (1989); *Martin v. Wilks,* 490 U.S. 755, 109 S.Ct. 2180, 104 L.Ed.2d 835 (1989); and *Patterson v. McClean Credit Union,* 491 U.S. 164, 109 S.Ct. 2363, 105 L.Ed.2d 132 (1989).

Guarding against Employment Discrimination

If you are an employer, it is usually wise to review your personnel practices and analyze your workforce to guard against potential charges of employment discrimination. Take an objective look at how many women and minorities you have hired and what positions they hold. Examine your recruiting practices to be certain that there is no inadvertent discrimination. If, for example, you are only recruiting by word of mouth through your employees and friends, your workforce is more likely to be homogeneous than to reflect the available workforce in your community. Even if such an imbalance is unintentional, its existence may be used against you in employment discrimination litigation.

If you have supervisors, are they aware of your policy to *not* discriminate in employment? Such supervisory employees are responsible for implementing *your* policies because you are the one who will be liable if they fail to do so. It is up to you to establish objective procedures for your supervisors to use in evaluating employees or applicants.

It is normally appropriate to have a formal procedure by which your employees can bring to your attention complaints of unfair treatment. That way, you can detect and solve problems with your personnel policies or with your supervisors who implement them before such policies result in charges of employment discrimination. It is also advisable to have a formal procedure for the resolution (due process) of employment-discrimination complaints. Such a formal procedure frequently allows you to resolve the complaint before it becomes a lawsuit. Even if a lawsuit is filed, courts often give considerable weight to properly conducted internal due process.

---

if Sue Ellen prevailed in an employment-discrimination suit against Acme, Inc., a company employing 600 workers, she could recover up to $300,000 in damages. Sponsors of the Civil Rights Act of 1991 have indicated that future legislation will be introduced in Congress to remove these damages caps, thus bringing sexual-discrimination remedies in line with those available in racial-discrimination suits.

Those who believe that they have been discriminated against may find it easier to obtain more damages in discrimination suits for another reason—the new law allows them to present their cases to juries. Previously, plaintiffs' claims were heard exclusively by judges, who tend to be less generous in their damages awards. The new law also authorizes judges to order a losing party to pay the expert-witness fees of the winning party.

■ Rights of Privacy

In the 1980s, the law began to protect the privacy of employees in a number of areas. Lie-detector tests, drug tests, electronic monitoring of work and the workplace, and other practices have been challenged as violations of employees' rights of privacy.

Lie-Detector Tests

At one time, many employers required employees or job applicants to take polygraph examinations in connection with their employment. The results of these lie-detector tests are not admissible as evidence in criminal trials, and many persons consider the tests to be an invasion of privacy.

In 1988, Congress passed the Employee Polygraph Protection Act.[15] The act prohibits certain employers from (1) requiring or causing employees or job applicants to take lie-detector tests or suggesting or requesting that they do so; (2) using, accepting, referring to, or asking about the results of lie-detector tests taken by employees or applicants; and (3) taking or threatening negative employment-related action against employees or ap-

---

15. 29 U.S.C. Sections 2001 *et seq.*

plicants based on results of lie-detector tests, or because they refused to take the tests.

Employers excepted from these prohibitions include federal, state, and local government employers, certain security service firms, and companies manufacturing and distributing controlled substances. Other employers may use polygraph tests when investigating losses attributable to theft—including embezzlement and stealing of trade secrets.

Drug Testing

Drug and alcohol use has been estimated to cost industry $50 billion to $100 billion in absenteeism, impaired performance, and accidents each year. Employers are concerned with preventing the deterioration of job performance and other harm that can result from the use of drugs. Some employers have begun testing employees to uncover drug use. In many instances, the tests have proved to be unreliable. Even if their accuracy is unquestionable, however, there is the question as to whether the tests violate employees' privacy rights.

Constitutional limitations apply to the testing of government employees. The tests have been held constitutional when there was a reasonable basis for suspecting a government employee's use of drugs. Also, when drug use in a particular government job could threaten public safety, testing has been upheld. For example, a Department of Transportation rule that requires employees engaged in oil and gas pipeline operations to submit to random drug testing was upheld, even though the rule did not require that before being tested the individual must be suspected of drug use.[16] The court held that the government's interest in promoting public safety in the pipeline industry outweighed the employees' privacy interests.

These constitutional limitations do not always restrict private employers, however. Some state constitutions may apply to inhibit private employers' testing for drugs. Some state statutes may restrict private drug testing in any of a number of ways. A collective bargaining agreement may provide protection against testing. In other cases, employees may bring an action for invasion of privacy.

---

16. *Electrical Workers Local 1245 v. Skinner,* 913 F.2d 1454 (9th Cir. 1990).

Monitoring Performance

Overseeing employees' performance by electronic means has become more common in the last decade. Today, some employers electronically monitor employees' use of computer terminals or company telephones. In some situations, employers use video cameras to evaluate employees' performance.

Listening to employees' telephone conversations may violate the Omnibus Crime Control Act of 1968 or a state statute. Otherwise, there is little specific government regulation of these activities, and an employer may be able to avoid these laws by simply informing employees that they are subject to monitoring. Nevertheless, in all cases, an employer should consider carefully the need to monitor employees, especially in areas such as restrooms. An employee may bring an action for invasion of privacy, and a court may decide that the employee's reasonable expectation of privacy outweighs the employer's need for surveillance.

Similarly, an employer should consider alternatives before searching an employee's desk, filing cabinet, or office. If a search is conducted and the employee sues, a court may balance the purposes of the search against its intrusiveness. The court may also consider the availability of less intrusive alternatives that would have accomplished the same purposes.

■ Employment at Will

Federal statutes have modified the employment-at-will doctrine (this doctrine was discussed in this chapter's introduction). Over the last two decades, the doctrine has also been eroded through a series of court rulings that restrict the right of employers to fire workers. Because this is a common law issue, the rules vary from state to state. The trend is to recognize exceptions to the at-will doctrine, however, and some courts have awarded punitive damages against employers in wrongful-discharge litigation. Wise employers will discharge employees only for good cause and will obtain documentation to support their position, in accordance with published company policies.

Statutory Limitations

Whistleblowing occurs when an employee tells the government or the press that his or her employer is engaged in some unsafe or illegal activity. For example, an employee might tell the Environmental Protection Agency (EPA) that his employer has been violating pollution laws.

Employees who blow the whistle often find themselves disciplined or even out of a job. In a state that protects whistleblowers, the employer could not discharge the employee for informing the EPA. Federal law may also protect a whistleblower. For example, if an employee of a defense contractor reveals overcharges on weapons, the employee is protected. In one case, when trucking-company employees were fired for reporting safety violations, the Department of Labor ordered that the employees be reinstated.[17] In situations in which neither a whistleblowing statute nor an employment contract protects the worker, the case must be decided on the basis of common law doctrine.

Exceptions Based on Contract Theory

Some courts have used contract theory to protect employees from arbitrary discharge. Many of these courts have held that an implied employment contract exists between the employer and the employee. If the employee is fired outside the terms of the implied contract, he or she may succeed in a breach-of-contract action.

For example, an employer's handbook or personnel bulletin may state that, as a matter of policy, workers will be dismissed only for good cause. If the employee is aware of this policy and continues to work for the employer, a court may find that there is an implied contract based on the terms stated in the handbook or bulletin. If an employer makes promises to employees regarding discharge policy, those promises may also be considered part of an implied contract. If the employer fires the worker in a manner contrary to the manner promised, a court may hold that the employer has violated the implied contract and is liable for damages. Most state courts will consider this claim and judge it by traditional contract standards.

A few states have gone further and held that all employment contracts contain an implied covenant of good faith. This means that both sides promise to abide by the contract in good faith. If an employer fires an employee for an arbitrary or unjustified reason, the employee can claim that the covenant of good faith was breached and the contract violated.

Exceptions Based on Public Policy

The most widespread common law exception to the employment-at-will doctrine is the public policy exception. Under this rule, an employer may not fire a worker for reasons that violate a fundamental public policy of the jurisdiction. For example, a court may prevent an employer from firing a worker who serves on a jury and therefore cannot work scheduled hours. Sometimes, an employer will direct an employee to do something that violates the law. If the employee refuses to perform the illegal act, the employer might decide to fire the worker. Most states have held that firing the worker under these circumstances violates public policy. The public policy theory generally protects employees from being required to violate the law but does not always protect employees when no legal violation is involved.

Whistleblowers may be protected from wrongful discharge for public policy reasons. For example, a bank was held to have wrongfully discharged an employee who pressured the employer to comply with state and federal consumer credit laws.[18] In another case, an at-will employee—a probation officer with the police department of the city of Globe, Arizona—discovered that a man had been arrested for vagrancy under an obsolete statute, had been sentenced to ten days in prison, and had been in jail for twenty-one days. The officer pointed out to a magistrate that this was illegal. The magistrate informed the police chief, the chief fired the officer, and the officer sued the city for wrongful discharge. Holding that the discharge violated public policy, the court said, ''So long as employees' actions are not merely private or proprietary, but instead seek to further the public good, the decision to expose illegal or unsafe practices should be encouraged . . . . There is no public policy more important or fundamental than the one favoring the effective protection of the lives, liberty, and property of the people. The officer's successful attempt to free the arrestee from illegal con-

---

17. See *Brock v. Roadway Express, Inc.,* 481 U.S. 252, 107 S.Ct. 1740, 95 L.Ed.2d 239 (1987).

18. *Harless v. First National Bank in Fairmont,* 162 W.Va. 116, 246 S.E.2d 270 (1978).

finement was a refreshing and laudable exercise that should be protected, not punished."[19]

Exceptions Based on Tort Theory

In a few cases, the discharge of an employee may give rise to a tort cause of action. Abusive discharge procedures may result in intentional infliction of emotional distress or defamation. In one case, a restaurant had suffered some thefts of supplies, and the manager announced that he would start firing waitresses alphabetically until the thief was identified. The first waitress fired said that she suffered great emotional distress as a result. The state's highest court upheld her claim as stating a valid cause of action.[20]

■ Compensation for Injuries and Employee Safety

Numerous state and federal statutes are designed to protect employees and their families from the risks and effects of accidental injury, death, or disease resulting from their employment. This section discusses state workers' compensation acts and the Occupational Safety and Health Act of 1970, which are specifically designed to protect employees and their families.

State Workers' Compensation Acts

Workers' compensation laws establish an administrative procedure for compensating workers injured on the job. Instead of suing, an injured worker files a claim with the administrative agency or board that administers the local workers' compensation claims. These agencies have quasi-judicial powers. All of their rulings are subject to review by the courts.

In general, the right to recover under workers' compensation laws is determined without regard to the existence of negligence or of fault in the traditional sense. Rather, it is predicated wholly on the employment relationship and the fact that the injury was *accidental, arose out of, or in the course of, employment.* Intentionally inflicted self-injury, for example, would not be considered ac-

cidental and hence would not be covered under the workers' compensation laws. If an injury occurs while an employee is commuting to or from work, most workers' compensations schemes would not consider it to have arisen out of, or in the course of, employment and hence would not cover it. In the past, heart attacks or other medical problems arising out of preexisting disease or physical conditions were not covered, but recently some states have allowed recovery.

In exchange for compensation under these statutes, workers give up the right to sue in court for on-the-job injuries. Even if an injury is caused by an employer's negligence, the injured worker must accept workers' compensation as the sole remedy. On average, recoveries under these statutes are less than half what those in comparable tort suits would be.

Health and Safety Protection

At the federal level the primary legislation for employee health and safety protection is the Occupational Safety and Health Act of 1970.[21] This act was passed to ensure safe and healthful working conditions for practically every employee in the country. The act requires that businesses be maintained free from recognized hazards. All employers affecting commerce who have one or more employees are covered by the act.

Employees can file complaints of violations of the Occupational Safety and Health Act to the Occupational Safety and Health Administration (OSHA), which is part of the Department of Labor. Under the act, an employer cannot discharge an employee who files a complaint or who, in good faith, refuses to work in a high-risk area (where bodily harm or death might result). Employers with eleven or more employees are required to keep occupational injury and illness records for each employee. Each record must be kept and updated for a continuous five-year period and be made available for inspection by an OSHA inspector. Whenever a work-related injury or disease occurs, employers are required to report it to OSHA. Whenever an employee is killed in a work-related accident, or if five or more employees are hospitalized in one accident, the Department of Labor must be notified within forty-eight hours. If it is

---

19. *Wagner v. City of Globe,* 150 Ariz. 82, 722 P.2d 250 (1986).
20. *Agis v. Howard Johnson Co.,* 371 Mass. 140, 355 N.E.2d 315 (1976).

21. 29 U.S.C. Sections 553, 651–678.

not, the company is fined. Following the accident, a complete inspection of the premises is mandatory.

Three federal agencies were created to develop and enforce the standards set by this act. OSHA has the authority to promulgate standards, make inspections, and enforce the act. The National Institute for Occupational Safety and Health is part of the Department of Health and Human Services. Its main duty is to conduct research on safety and health problems and to recommend standards for OSHA administrators to adopt. Finally, the Occupational Safety and Health Review Commission is an independent agency set up to handle appeals from actions taken by OSHA administrators.

OSHA-compliance officers may enter and inspect facilities of any establishment covered by the act. In the past, warrantless inspections were conducted. It is now recognized that such inspections violate the warrant clause of the Fourth Amendment.[22] Nevertheless, OSHA inspectors can and do conduct surprise inspections. If a violation is discovered, a citation may be issued directing an employer to correct a situation. Civil penalties may also be assessed.

As mentioned in Chapter 7, criminal penalties for willful violation of the federal Occupational Safety and Health Act are very limited. Employers may be prosecuted under state laws, however. In 1988, the Justice Department stated its view that criminal penalties in the act did not preempt state and local criminal laws.[23] In other words, the act could no longer be used to shield employers from state criminal prosecution if they showed willful disregard for worker safety.

■ Retirement and Security Income

Federal and state governments participate in insurance programs designed to protect employees and their families by covering the financial impact of retirement, disability, death, hospitalization, and unemployment. The key federal law on this subject is the Social Security Act of 1935.[24]

Old Age, Survivors, and Disability Insurance (OASDI)

The Social Security Act provides for old-age retirement, survivors, disability, and hospital insurance (OASDI). Both employers and employees must contribute under the Federal Insurance Contributions Act (FICA)[25] to help pay for Social Security benefits. The basis for the employee's contribution is his or her annual wage base—the maximum amount of an employee's wages that are subject to the tax. Benefits are fixed by statute but increase automatically with increases in the cost of living if they exceed a certain minimum amount.

Medicare

Medicare, a health insurance program, is administered by the Social Security Administration for people sixty-five years of age and older and for some under sixty-five who are disabled. It has two parts, one pertaining to hospital costs and the other to nonhospital medical costs, such as visits to doctors' offices. People who have Medicare hospital insurance can also obtain additional federal medical insurance if they pay small monthly premiums that increase as the cost of medical care increases.

Private Retirement Income Security

There has been significant legislation to regulate retirement plans set up by employers to supplement Social Security benefits. The major piece of this legislation is the Employee Retirement Income Security Act (ERISA) of 1974.[26] This act empowers the Labor Management Services Administration of the Department of Labor to enforce its provisions to regulate individuals who operate private pension funds. ERISA does not require an employer to establish a pension plan. When a plan exists, however, ERISA establishes standards for its management.

A key provision of ERISA concerns **vesting.** Vesting gives an employee a legal right to receive pension benefits at some future date when he or she stops working. Before ERISA, some employees who had worked for companies for as long as thirty years received no pension benefits when their employment terminated, because those benefits

---

22. *Marshall v. Barlow's, Inc.,* 436 U.S. 307, 98 S.Ct. 1816, 56 L.Ed.2d 305 (1978).
23. Letter to Chairman, House Committee on Government Operations, 100th Cong., 2d Sess. (1988).
24. 42 U.S.C. Sections 301 *et seq.*

25. 26 U.S.C. Sections 3101 *et seq.*
26. 29 U.S.C. Sections 1001 *et seq.*

Privacy Rights versus Worker Safety and Efficiency

 A major employment issue today concerns perceived intrusions into employees' rights to privacy. This issue arises when employers feel that they are required to undertake certain actions, such as drug testing, to ensure safety and efficiency in the workplace. The tradeoff here is obvious: employees' privacy rights versus worker safety and efficiency. The trend is obviously toward more intrusion into workers' privacy rights. Today, of businesses with 5,000 or more employees, over 60 percent have some type of drug-testing program. A fourth of those companies test their workers randomly at the job site. The trend is clear, because a mere five years ago, only 3 percent of all private-sector employers had drug-screening programs in progress.

The Issue of Fourth Amendment Rights

To protect the safety of consumers and other employees, does the government have the right to violate the Fourth Amendment's stricture against unreasonable searches and seizures? The question, of course, turns on whether drug testing constitutes an "unreasonable" intrusion upon the rights of employees to be secure in their persons. The United States Supreme Court has ruled, on at least one occasion, that suspicionless testing of train workers following a train accident or other railroad mishap is a reasonable search and seizure.[a] For employers in the private sector, the guidelines are not quite so clear. Private drug-testing programs are governed by state law, which varies widely. Some states have statutes that restrict such testing; others do not.

Blanket, or random, drug testing has posed the greatest challenge to the courts. In 1988, for example, the Justice Department issued a plan that required certain of its employees to submit to random drug testing. Several Justice Department employees challenged the requirement as a violation of the Fourth Amendment. The United States Court of Appeals for the District of Columbia Circuit handed down a decision that said yes for some employees and no for others. Random drug testing was justified only for those employees having access to top-secret classified information; for all others, random drug testing was not justified.[b]

Recently, the Department of Transportation adopted final rules for drug testing applicable to the aviation, rail, mass transit, trucking, and pipeline industries, as well as to the U.S. Coast Guard. Employees in safety-sensitive positions are to be tested for drugs on a random basis. Drug testing is also required for job applicants and upon any reasonable suspicion after an accident.

Wiretapping and Employee Rights

Employers believe that it is necessary to monitor the phone conversations and electronic mail (e-mail) activities of their employees. In a plea-bargaining agreement between the Pennsylvania attorney general's office and R. A. Security Company, the company agreed to pay a $1 million fine for its involvement in the wiretapping of employees' telephone conversations at a western Pennsylvania oil refinery. Pennsylvania state law prohibits the secret tape-recording of

---

a.   *Skinner v. Railway Labor Executives Association,* 489 U.S. 602, 109 S.Ct. 1402, 103 L.Ed.2d 639 (1989).

---

b.   *Harmon v. Thornburgh,* 878 F.2d 484 (D.C.Cir. 1989).

conversations. R. A. Security monitored over four hundred telephone calls made by employees of United Refining Company and recorded at least one hundred of those conversations. The calls were monitored and recorded as part of a probe by the owner of the company, who suspected executives of engaging in theft. Current federal law recognizes the right of employers to listen in on telephone conversations to monitor employees' performance, but state laws vary.

The issue is even more clouded with respect to e-mail. More than ten million people in the United States use e-mail systems, and most users assume that electronic messages are just as private as letters sent through the U.S. Postal Service. The administrator of the e-mail system for Epson America was fired from her job when she questioned why her supervisors were reading employees' e-mail without their knowledge. The ex-employee's attorney maintained that Epson was reading and printing out e-mail and doing so in violation of California state law, which makes it a crime for a person or a company to eavesdrop on or record confidential communication without the consent of both the sender and the receiver. Colorado and Florida have similar legislation.

■ Implications for the Businessperson

1. Employers need to be careful in their drug-testing or monitoring practices to avoid lawsuits for violation of employee privacy rights. Therefore, all employers who decide to engage in such activities must first become familiar with the laws of the particular jurisdiction in which they are located. Private drug testing, eavesdropping on employees' telephone conversations, and e-mail and other types of surveillance are governed by widely varying state statutes.

2. Drug testing in the public sector is becoming increasingly accepted and upheld in recent court cases. Such increased acceptability may be a harbinger for the private sector. That means that employers may find themselves freer in the future to take measures that will protect the safety of those affected by employees who use drugs. Again, knowledge of state law is important in this area.

■ For Critical Analysis

1. To what extent should employers have the right to impose drug testing on employees when there is no evidence of job impairment due to drug use?

2. The costliest psychoactive drug, in terms of lost productivity, absenteeism, and so on, is alcohol. Estimates of the cost of alcohol abuse by employees exceed $50 billion a year. There appear to be more alcohol-related accidents than accidents caused by all other psychoactive drugs combined. Therefore, why is there so much emphasis on testing for the use of illegal drugs as opposed to testing for alcohol abuse and addiction?

3. Are there less intrusive and less personally offensive ways of attaining the same results gained through drug testing? Some argue, for example, that the way to measure performance is by measuring output. The performance of assembly-line workers, for example, can be tested by using time and motion studies, and pilots' performance can be tested at computerized flight simulators. Salespersons can be tested by volume of sales and typists, by words typed per minute. Would such tests truly be alternatives to drug testing?

had not vested. ERISA establishes complex vesting rules. Generally, however, all employee contributions to pension plans vest immediately, and employee rights to employer pension-plan contributions vest after five years of employment.

To prevent mismanagement of pension funds, ERISA has established rules on how they must be invested. Pension managers must be cautious in their investments and refrain from investing more than 10 percent of the fund in securities of the employer. ERISA also contains detailed record-keeping and reporting requirements.

Unemployment Compensation

The United States has a system of unemployment insurance in which employers pay into a fund that is used to pay qualified unemployed workers. The major piece of federal legislation involved is the Federal Unemployment Tax Act of 1939.[27] This act created a state system that provides unemployment compensation to eligible individuals. Employers who fall under the provisions of the act are taxed quarterly. Taxes are typically collected by the employers and submitted to the states, which then deposit them with the federal government. The federal government maintains an Unemployment Insurance Fund, in which each state has an account.

■ Other Employment Laws

Among numerous other employment laws affecting workers and their employers are the Fair Labor Standards Act, the Davis-Bacon Act, and the Walsh-Healey Act.

---

27.   26 U.S.C. Sections 3301 *et seq.*

Fair Labor Standards Act

The Fair Labor Standards Act of 1938 (FLSA),[28] also known as the Wage-Hour Law, covers employers engaged in interstate commerce. The FLSA is concerned with child labor, maximum hours, and minimum wages.

CHILD LABOR   The act prohibits oppressive child labor. Children under sixteen years of age cannot be employed full-time except by a parent under certain circumstances; nor can children between the ages of sixteen and eighteen be employed in hazardous jobs or in jobs detrimental to their health and well-being. Most states require children under sixteen years of age to obtain work permits.

MAXIMUM HOURS   Under the FLSA, any employee who agrees to work more than forty hours per week must be paid no less than one and a half times his or her regular pay for all hours over forty. An exception exists for employees (1) whose duties necessitate irregular working hours, (2) who are employed pursuant to a bona fide individual contract or collective bargaining agreement, (3) whose contracts specify a regular rate of pay for up to forty hours a week and one and a half times that rate for hours over forty, and (4) whose contracts provide a weekly pay guarantee for not more than sixty hours. If all four of these elements are present, the employee is exempt. The following case illustrates a court's consideration of these elements.

---

28.   29 U.S.C. Sections 201 *et seq.*

Case 48.7

CRENSHAW v. QUARLES DRILLING CORP.

United States Court of Appeals, Tenth Circuit, 1986. 798 F.2d. 1345.

BACKGROUND AND FACTS   Quarles Drilling Corporation hired Fred Crenshaw as a drilling-equipment mechanic to do routine maintenance and emergency repairs on Quarles's drilling equipment located in several states. Crenshaw was paid a biweekly salary based on a forty-hour regular workweek and twenty hours of overtime per week. Crenshaw often worked more than sixty hours per week but was not given overtime pay for the additional hours. Hours of travel time between job sites were not included as "working" hours. After leaving Quarles's employment, Crenshaw sued in a federal district court for overtime compensation, claiming that Quarles had violated the FLSA. The trial court awarded Crenshaw $34,082.85 in overtime compensation and an equal amount in liquidated damages. Quarles appealed.

DECISION AND RATIONALE The United States Court of Appeals for the Tenth Circuit affirmed the trial court's decision. The appellate court noted that Crenshaw's employment agreement came within the FLSA exception only if there were "irregular hours of work." For hours to be considered irregular, they must fluctuate above and below forty in a significant number of weeks. Because only 6.7 percent of the weeks that Crenshaw worked involved less than forty hours of work, the court concluded that Crenshaw did not work irregular hours and that his agreement was not within the FLSA exception. The court agreed that travel time should be included in the hours worked. "Employees who transport equipment without which well servicing could not be done, are performing an activity which is so closely related to the work which they and other employees perform, that it must be considered an integral and indispensable part of their principal activities." Because of a discrepancy concerning the hours worked during certain weeks, the court remanded the case for determination of the exact number of hours to be compensated.

MINIMUM WAGE The Fair Labor Standards Act provides that a minimum wage of a specified amount ($4.25 per hour as of April 1, 1991) must be paid to employees in covered industries. Congress periodically revises such minimum wages. The term *wages* is meant to include the reasonable cost of the employer in furnishing employees with board, lodging, and other facilities if they are customarily furnished by that employer.

Other Government-Enforced Minimum-Wage Laws

In 1931, during the Great Depression, the president signed the Davis-Bacon Act,[29] which requires the

---

29. 40 U.S.C. Sections 276a *et seq.*

payment of "prevailing wages" to employees of contractors or subcontractors working on government construction projects. In 1936 an act that extended the Davis-Bacon Act was put into effect— the Walsh-Healey Act.[30] This act requires a minimum wage as well as overtime pay of time and a half to employees of manufacturers or suppliers entering into contracts with agencies of the federal government.

---

30. 41 U.S.C. Sections 35 *et seq.*

■ **Terms and Concepts**

bona fide occupational
   qualification (BFOQ) 859
business necessity
   defense 859
closed shop 855
disparate-impact
   discrimination 858
disparate-treatment
   discrimination 856

eighty-day cooling-off
   period 855
employment-at-will
   doctrine 853
hot-cargo agreement 855
protected class 856
right-to-work laws 855

secondary boycott 855
union shop 855
vesting 869
whistleblowing 866
workers' compensation
   laws 868

■ **For Review**

1. What is the employment-at-will doctrine?
2. Under labor laws, what acts are considered to be unfair labor practices on the part of employers? What acts are

considered to be unfair labor practices on the part of unions?
3. Generally, what does Title VII of the Civil Rights Act of 1964 prohibit? What does the Age Discrimination in

Employment Act prohibit? What does the Americans with Disabilities Act prohibit?

4. Delta Manufacturing Co. employs 100 workers, 33 percent of whom are members of the minority that makes up 75 percent of the area workforce. Delta requires all applicants to pass a mechanical aptitude test before being hired. Employees at the plant are promoted on the basis of seniority and merit. Simone, a minority applicant who was denied employment at the plant when she failed the aptitude test, and Desmond, a minority worker at the plant who has been denied a promotion, file a suit against Delta, alleging

discrimination. What are some of Delta's possible defenses in the suit?

5. Pilar works for Executives Bank. Executives tells its employees not to comply with certain disclosure requirements of the Consumer Credit Protection Act when dealing with loan applicants and credit-card customers. Pilar tells her supervisor that noncompliance is illegal. The supervisor tells her to forget about it. When Pilar persists and complains to the bank manager, she is fired. What might be Pilar's best ground for a suit against Executives?

■ Questions and Case Problems

48-1. Suppose that Consolidated Stores is undergoing a unionization campaign. Prior to the election, management says that the union is unnecessary to protect workers. Management also provides bonuses and wage increases to the workers during this period. The employees reject the union. Union organizers protest that the wage increases during the election campaign unfairly prejudiced the vote. Should these wage increases be regarded as an unfair labor practice? Discuss.

48-2. Discuss fully which of the following constitutes a violation of the 1964 Civil Rights Act, Title VII, as amended:

(a) Tennington, Inc., is a consulting firm and has ten employees. These employees travel on consulting jobs in seven states. Tennington has an employment record of hiring only white males.

(b) Novo Films, Inc., is making a film about Africa and needs to employ approximately one hundred extras for this picture. Novo advertises in all major newspapers in southern California for the hiring of these extras. The ad states that only African-Americans need apply.

(c) Chinawa, a major processor of cheese sold throughout the United States, employs one hundred employees at its principal processing plant. The plant is located in Heartland Corners, whose population is 50 percent white, 25 percent black, and the balance Hispanic, Asian, and other minorities. Chinawa requires a high school diploma as a condition of employment for its cleaning crew. Three-fourths of the white population complete high school, as compared with only one-fourth of the minority groups. Chinawa has an all-white cleaning crew.

48-3. Calzoni Boating Co. is an interstate business engaged in manufacturing and selling boats. The company has five hundred nonunion employees. Representatives of these employees are requesting a four-day, ten-hours-per-day work-week, and Calzoni is concerned that this would require paying time and a half after eight hours per day. Which federal act is Calzoni thinking of that might require this? Will the act in fact require paying time and a half for all

hours worked over eight hours per day if the employees' proposal is accepted? Explain.

48-4. Denton and Carlo were employed at an appliance plant. Their job required them to do occasional maintenance work while standing on a wire mesh twenty feet above the plant floor. Other employees had fallen through the mesh, one of whom had been killed by the fall. When Denton and Carlo were asked by their supervisor to do work that would likely require them to walk on the mesh, they refused due to their fear of bodily harm or death. Because of their refusal to do the requested work, the two employees were fired from their jobs. Was their discharge wrongful? If so, under what federal employment law? To what federal agency or department should they turn for assistance?

48-5. Wise, a female employee of Mead Corp., became involved in a dispute in the lunchroom of her place of employment with another employee, Pruitt. A fight ensued, and Wise kicked and scratched Pruitt and used "abusive and uncivil" language. Because of this behavior, Wise's employment at Mead was terminated by her employer. Wise brought suit, alleging sex discrimination on the part of Mead Corp. in violation of Title VII of the Civil Rights Act of 1964, on the grounds that at least four other fights at Mead had occurred under similar circumstances and none of the participants had been fired. None of the other fights had involved a female. Did Wise's employment termination constitute sex discrimination by Mead Corp.? Discuss. [*Wise v. Mead Corp.*, 614 F.Supp. 1131 (M.D.Ga. 1985)]

48-6. Dennis Fountain, a white police officer, sued the City of Waycross when he was passed over for promotion in favor of an African-American police officer, Whitfield, who ranked lower on the promotion list. The City of Waycross had a policy of promoting its employees on the basis of merit. In accordance with this policy, police officers were promoted on the basis of a "promotional process" that involved consideration of written examinations, oral interviews, record evaluations, and longevity of service. Fountain had accumulated more points in the promotional process than Whitfield had. Before Whitfield was promoted, there had been only one African-American sergeant on the Waycross police force. In addition, although African Americans constituted 21.6 percent of the Waycross labor pool, they constituted only 2.5 percent of the Waycross police force. Given these facts, discuss whether Fountain will succeed in his suit against the City of Waycross for reverse discrimination. [*Fountain v. City of Waycross, Georgia,* 701 F.Supp. 1570 (S.D.Ga. 1988)]

48-7. Fleming Tullis was hired as a bus driver by a private school in Dade County, Florida, in September 1982. Tullis turned sixty-five on January 1, 1986. On January 3, 1986, because the insurance company would no longer insure drivers over the age of sixty-five, Tullis's employment was terminated. Tullis sued the school, alleging age discrimination in violation of the Age Discrimination in Employment Act (ADEA). Can the school successfully defend against the age discrimination charge by stating that an age of sixty-four years or younger was a bona fide occupational qualification? Is the increased cost of insurance a factor that would exempt the school from compliance with the ADEA? Discuss fully. [*Tullis v. Lear School, Inc.,* 874 F.2d 1489 (11th Cir. 1989)]

48-8. In June 1979, Castaways Management, Inc., purchased the Castaways Motel in Miami Beach, Florida. The general manager of Castaways actively supported one of the two union locals that sought to represent the motel's employees. Employees were told that voting for the other union could result in demotions, transfers, and pay reductions, and a number of employees who supported the other union were fired for asserted nonunion-related reasons prior to a union election. Both unions eventually filed unfair labor practice charges against Castaways, and the National Labor Relations Board (NLRB) found that Castaways had violated federal labor provisions by discharging employees for supporting union activity. Castaways was ordered to reinstate the discharged employees, award them back pay with interest, conduct a new election, and post notice of its violations on motel premises. By the time the initial order was affirmed by an NLRB panel in 1987, the motel had been demolished—although Castaways still existed as a business entity. On appeal, Castaways argued, among other things, that the NLRB's order was rendered moot (of no legal significance) because the motel no longer existed. Under these circumstances, is the NLRB's order unenforceable? Discuss. [*National Labor Relations Board v. Castaways Management, Inc.,* 870 F.2d 1539 (11th Cir. 1989)]

48-9. Duke Power Co. was sued by a number of its African-American employees for practicing racial discrimination in the hiring and assigning of employees at its Dan River plant. The plant was organized into five operating departments: (1) labor, (2) coal handling, (3) operations, (4) maintenance, and (5) laboratory testing. African Americans were employed only in the labor department, where the highest-paying jobs paid less than the lowest-paying jobs in the other four departments (which employed only whites). Promotions were normally made within each department on the basis of seniority. Transferees into a department usually began in the lowest position. In 1955 the company began to require a high school education for an initial assignment into any department except the labor department. In addition, it required a high

school education for any transfer from the coal handling department to any inside department (operations, maintenance, or laboratory). For ten years, this company-wide policy was enforced. In 1965, when the company abandoned its policy of restricting African Americans to the labor department, a high school diploma or equivalency test was nevertheless made a prerequisite to transfer from the labor department into any other department. This requirement rendered a markedly disproportionate number of African Americans ineligible for employment advancement in the company. Discuss fully whether these employer practices violated Title VII of the Civil Rights Act. [*Griggs v. Duke Power Co.,* 401 U.S. 424, 91 S.Ct. 849, 28 L.Ed.2d 158 (1971)]

48-10. Patricia Jackson, an African-American female and an experienced waitress, applied for a job as a part-time waitress at a restaurant owned by Jackie McCleod in Foley, Alabama. An interview was arranged for the afternoon of June 2, 1989, which was a Friday. During the course of the interview, Jackson and McCleod entered into a verbal contract for Jackson to be hired as a part-time waitress, beginning Monday, June 5. Jackson was to work her first two days in the kitchen and following that orientation period would start working as a waitress. On Sunday, June 4, McCleod made up the work schedule for the period June 5 through June 11. Jackson was scheduled to work four days during the week and on each of those days would be doing kitchen work. Jackson appeared for work on Monday, June 5, as agreed. When she discovered that she had been scheduled to work in the kitchen for four days, as opposed to the two-day orientation period she expected, she confronted McCleod and asked to be put on the floor as a waitress. When her request was not granted, Jackson left the restaurant. On that same day, McCleod hired a white female for the position of waitress. Jackson sued McCleod for discrimination on the basis of race in McCleod's hiring procedures, and the issue turned on whether any discrimination occurred during the ''hiring'' of Jackson. Will Jackson prevail in court? Discuss fully. [*Jackson v. McCleod,* 748 F.Supp. 831 (S.C.Ala. 1990)]

48-11. Case Briefing Assignment

Examine Case A.23 [Johnston v. Del Mar Distributing Co., 776 S.W.2d 768 (Tex.App.— Corpus Christi 1989)] *in Appendix A. The case has been excerpted there in great detail.* Review and then brief the case, making sure that you include answers to the following questions in your brief.

1. Why did Del Mar Distributing Co. terminate Nancy Johnston's employment?

2. What defense did Del Mar raise against Johnston's claim of wrongful discharge?

3. On what case precedent did the appellate court base its reasoning?

4. Why did the appellate court conclude that, given the circumstances of this case, it was irrelevant whether the act itself that Johnston was asked to perform was legal or illegal?

Government Regulation

Government regulation is pervasive in our economic and legal systems. It includes consumer protection, environmental protection, antitrust law, employment and labor relations law, and other issues. In all areas of government regulation, one can ask the question, Why does government regulation exist? Pure capitalist ideology has as its basis a belief that government intervention in the economic system should be minimal. Yet today virtually every area of economic activity is regulated by government. Is this increased government regulation due to a change in the capitalist ideology or to a change in the ethical concerns of society?

Employment Discrimination

Society has definitely changed its thinking with respect to employment. In the past, employers were not required to hire, retain, and promote employees with equality. Equal opportunity regulations were therefore designed to reduce or eliminate discriminatory practices. Attempts at "making up" for past patterns of discrimination have resulted in affirmative action programs. Many of these programs have

876

resulted in what has been termed "reverse discrimination" against majority groups. Such reverse discrimination raises the ethical issue of how far society should go in trying to remedy the effects of past discrimination against minorities.

Laws prohibiting employment discrimination can also come into conflict with other societal goals. Should women, for example, be hired as fire fighters by a fire department if they cannot perform fire-fighting jobs with the same strength and agility as males? Would employing female fire fighters jeopardize—to even a small extent—the safety of a city's citizens? What is the tradeoff here? This very question arose in *Evans v. City of Evanston*.[1] Thirty-nine women failed to pass an agility test that was required of all candidates for employment as fire fighters. The women brought a class-action suit against the city. They claimed that the agility test clearly had a "disparate impact" on women, because 85 percent of the women who took the test failed it, whereas only 7 percent of the men failed. Consequently, there were no women among Evanston's 106 fire fighters (although at one time there

1. 88 F.2d 382 (7th Cir. 1989).

were two women). Because the test had a disparate impact, it was in violation of Title VII—unless the employer could demonstrate that the test served a legitimate interest of the fire department. At trial, the court agreed that the test related to the employer's need for physically strong fire fighters. Certain technicalities in the scoring were noted at trial, however, which led to a judgment in favor of the plaintiffs. On appeal, the case was remanded to the trial court for consideration. One of the points made by the appellate court was that the initial agility test prevented most female candidates from taking the other two tests—of intelligence and psychological stability—required of all job candidates.

The ethical issue here is, of course, a touchy one. What if, in fact, the women who could not pass the agility test—but presumably could pass the other two tests—were nonetheless employed as fire fighters? Would their employment endanger the safety of the city's citizens? Would it be more reasonable for the fire department to allow all candidates to take all three tests and allocate available jobs on the basis of a combined score?

Whistleblowing

Employees face a major dilemma when they are forced to choose between ignoring unethical, unsafe, or illegal activities in their workplace or "blowing the whistle" on their employer. Choosing the first alternative compromises their own ethical standards and perhaps requires their participation in the unethical, unsafe, or illegal actions. Choosing the second alternative, however, may lead to undesirable results—employees who blow the whistle often find themselves disciplined or even out of a job.

Whistleblowers who bring suits against their employers for wrongful discharge can also pose special problems for the courts. In situations in which neither an employment contract nor a whistleblowing statute protects the worker, the case must be decided on the basis of common law and the employment-at-will doctrine. Employment at will means that an employee can be hired and discharged *at will* by an employer. The modern trend by the courts, however, has been to modify the employment-at-will doctrine by finding exceptions to its operation.

One such exception is created when a court construes that an "implied" contract exists between an employer and an employee. An increasing number of courts, for example, have held that an employer that discharges an employee who entered a good faith agreement with the employer is in breach of an implied employment contract—unless the employer can prove that the discharge was a reasonable action.

A second exception is based on public policy. Under this exception, an employee should not be discharged because he or she performed an act encouraged by public policy—or because he or she refused to perform an act counter to public policy. For example, in a recent case, Roger Balla sued Gambro, Inc., for wrongful discharge from his job as the in-house attorney for the firm.[2] Gambro, a maker of medical equipment, was the distributor of kidney dialysis equipment manufactured in Germany. Among the products distributed are dialyzers, which filter excess fluid and toxic substances from the blood of patients with impaired or no kidney function. Among other jobs, Balla managed the firm's regulatory affairs, which made him responsible for compliance with federal, state, and local laws and regulations affecting the company's operations and products.

In a letter written in July 1985, the parent company in Germany informed Gambro that it was going to ship some defective dialyzers to Gambro. The parent company informed Gambro of the risks associated with using the defective equipment for patients with acute or chronic kidney disease. When Balla learned of the shipment, he informed the company that the sale of the dialyzers would have to be reported to the Food and Drug Administration (FDA). Several months after the incident, Balla's employment was terminated. On the day of his termination, the company shipped some of the defective dialyzers to customers. The following day, Balla reported the

shipment of the defective equipment to the FDA, which then seized it.

The appellate court pointed out that "retaliatory discharge is an exception to the general rule that an at-will employment relationship may be terminated at any time for any or no cause. Notwithstanding the at-will employment relationship, the law recognizes a cause of action when it is alleged that the employee was discharged in retaliation for his activities, and that the discharge was in contravention of a clearly mandated public policy."

Competition and Antitrust Laws

Antitrust policy expresses American attitudes toward big business and government. Current antitrust law stems from public concern in the 1880s over the large corporate mergers resulting from new technology and improved transportation links. Indeed, in 1888, the major political parties for the first time put antitrust planks in their presidential campaign platforms. From 1889 to 1891, eighteen states enacted antitrust laws. It was not until 1890 that an antitrust bill, which was introduced by John Sherman for the third time, was passed by Congress. A key feature of the Sherman Act is that it allows private individuals to bring suit and allows those individuals to recover treble damages if they prevail. In some sense, the Sherman Act and subsequent antitrust laws have tried to grapple with the problem of the "little person" versus the "big company," which faces our society at all times today.

In the eyes of many, antitrust law has been a hindrance to international competitiveness.

---

2. *Balla v. Gambro, Inc.*, 203 Ill. App.3d 57, 560 N.E.2d 1043, 148 Ill.Dec. 446 (1990).

Although antitrust laws have been relaxed, and some areas—for example, certain cooperative research and development projects—are now exempt from antitrust laws, some argue that such relaxation should go even further. These critics of U.S. antitrust law favor a change that would allow industry rivals to jointly produce goods such as high-definition television sets and robotics so as to compete effectively in the world market. The basis of this concept is that today companies face skyrocketing development costs, a high cost of capital, and a very short product life cycle. That means that only the largest companies can afford to go it alone. It is probably for these reasons, more than anything else, that large production consortiums are common both in Europe and in Japan. They are prevented in the United States by antitrust law, however.

Defaulting on Student Loans

Defaulting on student loans seems to be a national epidemic. In recent years, the government has monitored the repayment of these loans more closely than in the past because of the loss in revenues caused by so many defaulting debtors. Occasionally, colleges and universities fight back, too. They do something to try to force former students to pay their government-guaranteed student loans. One such case involved a student, Mr. Juras, who attended Montana State University and took out a student loan to help foot the educational bill.

As it turned out, Juras defaulted on his loan. When the university eventually assigned Juras's loan to a collection agency, the university agreed

that it would not release Juras's transcript until he repaid the loan. In other words, the university would deny Juras the major benefit derived from the loan—proof of his degree. When Juras later requested a copy of his transcript, the university kept its word and refused to give it to him.

Juras sued the university, claiming that such a practice was illegal. He reasoned that the university was treating the transcript as a form of security until the loan was paid. Because the National Defense Student Loan Act required lenders to make student loans on an unsecured basis, the university's retention of the transcript was illegal under that act. The withholding of his transcript was therefore, in essence, an unfair, coercive, and unconscionable debt-collection practice that violated the Fair Debt Collection Practices Act.

The court did not agree with Juras's claims. The university was not acting counter to the National Defense Student Loan law by withholding Juras's transcript. The transcript belonged to the university, not to Juras, and therefore it could not be considered the secured property of another. A security interest cannot arise in property in which the debtor has no interest, and Juras had no ownership rights or other legal interest in the transcript. Nor did the court find that the university had violated any of the provisions of the Fair Debt Collection Practices Act by withholding the transcript. Juras lost on both counts. He would have to pay the loan if he wanted his transcript.[3]

---

3. *Juras v. Aman Collection Service, Inc.*, 829 F.2d 739 (9th Cir. 1987).

Protecting the Environment

Business enterprises generally have emphasized the maximization of profits and thus have observed the minimal environmental protections required by law. But the effect of large corporations' activities on the environment has now become a subject of public concern. The fact is, however, that companies typically cannot protect the environment without incurring higher production costs. This result is generally not happily received by stockholders—even those having environmentalist leanings. For example, pollution control clearly involves costs that must be absorbed somewhere—by shareholders, in the form of smaller dividends; by consumers, in the form of higher prices; or by employees, in the form of lower wages.

In a competitive economic system, companies normally cannot be socially responsible alone. If an individual firm tries to accept this responsibility and other firms do not, the results may be lower profits for the socially responsible firm and its eventual demise. Consequently, we can argue that it is because of our competitive system that we require government regulation and that this need is particularly great in the environmental protection area.

But does this mean that it is only through government regulation of all competitors that we will achieve a reduction in the amount of environmental destruction caused by production processes? Is it possible to combine profit-making activities *and* environmental protection programs? Dow Chemical thought so. That firm devised and implemented a massive program of pollution control directed toward waste reduction and the conservation of raw materials. Manufacturing processes were closely scrutinized to increase operating efficiency, to recycle raw materials formerly vented into the air or lost to the sewer, and to use waste products. Although in its press releases Dow emphasized its good citizenship, it nonetheless profited by these programs. Pollution control meant savings that could be transformed directly into higher company profits.

The Economics of Regulation

Most regulation is motivated by government's concern for the social welfare. Corporations may be criticized for using technicalities or loopholes to escape the letter of the law while violating its spirit. Yet regulation is not always an unmitigated blessing, even for its intended beneficiaries.

Consider the example of rent control. Local governments have placed regulations on landlords to prevent them from raising rents and thereby driving out low-income tenants. Most people are sympathetic to this concern, but the long-run

implications of rent control must still be considered. Rent control restricts the profitability of residential housing and discourages the construction of new rental units, which may be needed by the community. Some have suggested that rent control shares some responsibility for the now-major problem of homelessness. Thus, though rent control may have benefits, its full consequences should be explored.

■ Discussion Questions

1. Some government regulation, such as antitrust law, may be enforced by private corporations. Are private suits always ethical and proper, or should we consider the motives of the plaintiff company? For example, when MCI won a large antitrust award from AT&T, some suggested that federal courts were being used as part of market competition. Might not companies be using antitrust laws to enhance their own market share and to restrict competition?

2. In view of the many consumer protection laws that exist, should corporations have any ethical obligations to

consumers beyond the letter of the law? Don't consumers have the responsibility to bargain for any additional protections?

3. Both environmental and occupational safety laws strive to protect the public health from hazardous substances. Should standards in these two contexts be the same? Or should employees be allowed to voluntarily accept some greater risk in return for a higher wage scale?

4. An employer's affirmative-action policy may conflict with the interests of its current employees and their union. How should such a company balance its duties under labor law with those under discrimination law?

5. The traditional doctrine of employment-at-will allows employers to fire whomever they choose for any or no cause. Developments in both statutory and common law have eroded the effectiveness of this doctrine. Do you believe that society has gone too far in the direction of protecting the interests of employees as opposed to the interests of employers? How can these often-conflicting interests most appropriately be balanced?

UNIT NINE

Property

■ The Importance of the Law of Property

The private ownership of property, both real and personal, is at the heart of our economic and political system. Indeed, a major distinguishing feature between decentralized, capitalist systems and centralized, socialist systems is that in a capitalist nation, individuals may own—with some limitations, of course—land, houses, cars, factories, patents, copyrights, and the like. Given that the right to own, control, and dispose of property as one wishes is a right prized by virtually all Americans, the law of property can be considered to have a somewhat special status. Understanding how rights in property are protected is essential.

Property can be either movable, in which case it is called *personal property* (or *chattel*), or not movable, in which case it is called *real property*. You have already examined the laws concerning a particular type of personal property, for intellectual property was discussed in Chapter 8. You also have been introduced to the law governing the sale of personal property ("goods") in all of Unit Three. Two further aspects of personal property will be examined in this unit. In Chapter 49, you will see how ownership rights in personal property can be held and how they can be acquired. In Chapter 50, you will examine the law governing *bailments* of personal property. A bailment arises when personal property is temporarily delivered by its owner into the care of another.

In Chapter 51, you will be introduced to real property law and the formalities and legal requirements that apply to the sale and transfer of interests in real property. Not everyone needs to own real property to benefit from it. Much real property is *leased*. Consequently, we devote Chapter 52 to landlord-tenant relationships. Although few of us are or ever will be landlords, almost all of us, at one time or another, are renters. We rent apartments or houses when we are students or just starting out as a newly formed household. Therefore, it is useful for each of us to know our rights as tenants in a leased apartment or house.

◼ Ethical Issues in the Law of Property

In the area of personal property, ethical issues frequently arise whenever it is unclear who has property rights in, say, a videotape, a software program, or a human body tissue from which research is conducted. In the area of bailments, there are specific rules designating the duty of care of the bailee—the one who has temporary control over someone else's personal property. It is possible for a bailee to be negligent in the care of another's property but not sufficiently negligent to breach legally the duty of care.

Real property is another area in which ethical issues arise. They may have to do with the fairness of zoning laws or with a "taking" of private property by the government for public use, often by exercising its power of eminent domain. Sales of real property may also give rise to ethical issues. Contracts for the sale of real property fall under the Statute of Frauds and therefore must be in writing to be enforceable. This means that oral promises to buy or sell real property interests may be broken without legal liability, but breaking such promises may not always be ethical.

Some particularly difficult ethical questions arise in the area of landlord-tenant relationships. Landlords who find some pretext for keeping security or cleaning deposits may not be dealing fairly with tenants, even though their actions are often within the letter of the law. Tenants also may act unethically. Consider a tenant who, before the lease expires and without telling the landlord, moves to another city, thereby making it extremely difficult for the landlord to locate the tenant and recover damages. Such behavior is far from ethical.

Chapter 49

The Nature of Property and Personalty

Property consists of the legally protected rights and interests a person has in anything with an ascertainable value that is subject to ownership. Property would have little value if the law did not define the right to use it, to sell or dispose of it, and to prevent trespassing upon it. In the United States, the ownership of property receives special protection under the law. For example, the Fifth Amendment to the U.S. Constitution states that ''no person shall . . . be deprived of life, liberty, or property, without due process of law; nor shall private property be taken for public use, without just compensation.''

Property may be divided into real property and personal property. **Real property** (sometimes called *realty* or *real estate*) means the land and everything permanently attached to it. When structures are permanently attached to the land, then everything attached permanently to the structures is also realty. Everything else is **personal property,** or **personalty**. Attorneys sometimes refer to all personal property as **chattel,** a more comprehensive term than *goods* because it includes living as well as inanimate property.

In this chapter, we first examine the basic attributes of personal and real property and then look at the ways in which ownership rights in both of these forms of property can be held. The remainder of the chapter focuses on ownership rights in personal property, as well as the laws governing rights in mislaid, lost, or abandoned property.

■ The Nature of Personal Property

Personal property can be tangible or intangible. *Tangible personal property,* such as a television set, heavy construction equipment, or a car, has physical substance. *Intangible personal property* represents some set of rights and interests, but it has no real physical existence. Stocks and bonds are intangible personal property. So, too, are patents, trademarks, and copyrights, as discussed in Chapter 8.

Because we live in a dynamic society, new types of personal property—and therefore new types of ownership rights in personal property—emerge over time. For example, gas, water, and telephone services are now considered personal property for the purpose of criminal prosecution when they are stolen or used without payment. Federal and state statutes protect against the copying of musical compositions. It is a crime now to engage in the "bootlegging"—illegal copying for resale—of records and tapes. The theft of computer programs and services is considered in many states to be a theft of personal property.

The Nature of Real Property

Real property consists of land and the buildings, plants, and trees that it contains. Whereas personal property is movable, real property is immovable. Real property usually means land, but it also includes subsurface and air rights, plant life and vegetation, and fixtures.

Land

Land includes the soil on the surface of the earth and the natural products or artificial structures that are attached to it. It further includes all the waters contained on or under its surface and the air space above it (subject, of course, to the legal use of aviators). In other words, absent a contrary statute or case law, a landowner has the right to everything existing permanently below the surface of his or her property to the center of the earth and above it to the heavens.

Air Space and Subsurface Rights

The owner of real property has relatively exclusive rights to the air space above the land as well as the soil and minerals underneath it. Significant limitations on either air rights or subsurface rights normally have to be indicated on the document transferring title at the time of purchase. When no such encumbrances are noted, a purchaser can expect to have an unfettered right to possession of the property. The ways in which real property can be encumbered will be examined in detail in Chapter 51.

AIR RIGHTS   Until fifty years ago, the right to use air space was not too significant, but today, commercial airlines and high-rise office buildings and apartments use the air space regularly. Early cases involving air rights dealt with matters such as whether a telephone wire could be run across a person's property when the wire did not touch any

of the property[1] and whether a bullet shot over the person's land constituted trespass.[2]

Today, cases involving air rights present questions such as the right of commercial and private planes to fly over property and the right of individuals and governments to seed clouds and produce artificial rain. Flights over private land do not normally violate the property owners' rights unless the flights are low and frequent, causing a direct interference with the enjoyment and use of the land.[3]

SUBSURFACE RIGHTS   Ownership of the surface of land can be separated from ownership of its subsurface. Subsurface rights can be extremely valuable when minerals, oil, or natural gas are located beneath the surface. But a subsurface owner's rights would be of little value if he or she could not use the surface to exercise those rights. Hence, a subsurface owner will have a *profit* to, for example, find and remove minerals. (A profit is a right to go onto the property of another and remove some part or product of the land. Profits are discussed in Chapter 51.)

Of course, conflicts may arise between surface and subsurface owners when attempts are made to excavate below the surface. At common law, a landowner has the right to have the land supported in its natural condition by the owners of the interests under the surface. If the owners of the subsurface rights excavate, they are absolutely liable if their excavation causes the surface to subside, even if the excavation is done without negligence.

If the excavation causes the collapse of, or damage to, structures on the land, the excavators are liable at common law if the landowner shows that the excavation would have caused the land in its natural state to have collapsed. If the land would not have collapsed in its natural state, the excavator may still be liable on negligence or other tort

---

1. *Butler v. Frontier Telephone Co.,* 186 N.Y. 486, 79 N.E. 716 (1906). Stringing a wire across someone's property violates the air rights of that person. Leaning walls, buildings, and projecting eave spouts and roofs also violate the air rights of the property owner.
2. *Herrin v. Sutherland,* 74 Mont. 587, 241 P. 328 (1925). Shooting over a person's land normally constitutes trespass.
3. *United States v. Causby,* 328 U.S. 256, 66 S.Ct. 1062, 90 L.Ed. 1206 (1946).

grounds. Today, many states have statutes that extend excavators' liability to include damage to structures on the property. Typically, these statutes provide exact guidelines as to the support requirements for excavations of various depths.

Plant Life and Vegetation

Plant life, both natural and cultivated, is also considered to be real property. In many instances, the natural vegetation, such as trees, adds greatly to the value of the realty. When a parcel of land is sold and the land has growing crops on it, the sale includes the crops, unless otherwise specified in the sales contract. When crops are sold by themselves, however, they are considered to be personal property or goods. Consequently, the sale of crops is a sale of goods, and it is governed by the Uniform Commercial Code rather than by real property law [UCC 2-107(2)].

Fixtures

Certain personal property can become so closely associated with the real property to which it is attached that the law views it as real property. Such property is known as a **fixture**—a thing affixed to realty. A thing is *affixed* to realty when it is attached to it by roots; embedded in it; or permanently attached by means of cement, plaster, bolts, nails, or screws. The fixture can be physically attached to real property, be attached to another fixture, or even be without any actual physical attachment to the land, as long as the owner *intends* the property to be a fixture.

Fixtures are included in the sale of land if the sales contract does not provide otherwise. The sale of a house includes the land and the house and garage on it, as well as the cabinets, plumbing, and windows. Because these are permanently affixed to the property, they are considered to be a part of it. Unless otherwise agreed, however, the curtains and throw rugs are not included. Items such as drapes and window-unit air conditioners are difficult to classify. Thus, a contract for the sale of a house or commercial realty should indicate which items of this sort are included in the sale.

To determine whether or not a certain item is a fixture, the *intention* of the party who placed the property must be examined. If the facts indicate that the person intended the item to be a fixture, then it will be a fixture. When the intent of the party

who placed the fixture on the realty is in dispute, the courts usually determine the intent based on either or both of the following factors:

1. If the property attached cannot be removed without causing substantial damage to the remaining realty, it is usually deemed a fixture.
2. If the property attached is so adapted to the rest of the realty as to become a part thereof, it is usually deemed a fixture.

Certain items can only be attached to property permanently; such items are fixtures. It is assumed that the owner intended them to be fixtures, because they had to be permanently attached to the property. A tile floor, cabinets, and carpeting are examples. Also, when an item of property is custom-made for installation on real property, such as storm windows, the property is usually classified as a fixture. Again, it is assumed that the owner intended the item of property to become part of the real property.

◼ Property Ownership

Property ownership can be viewed as a bundle of rights. These rights include the right to possession of the property and the right to dispose of the property—by sale, gift, rental, lease, and so on.

Fee Simple

A person who holds the entire bundle of rights is said to be the owner in **fee simple.** The owner in fee simple is entitled to use, possess, and dispose of the property as he or she chooses during his or her lifetime; and upon death, the owner's interest in the property descends to his or her heirs. We will look further at ownership in fee simple in Chapter 51, in the context of real property ownership.

Concurrent Ownership

Persons who share ownership rights simultaneously in particular property are said to be *concurrent* owners. There are two principal types of **concurrent ownership:** *tenancy in common* and *joint tenancy.* Concurrent ownership rights can also be held in a *tenancy by the entirety* or as *community property,* although these latter two types of concurrent ownership are less common.

TENANCY IN COMMON   The term **tenancy in common** refers to a form of co-ownership in which each of two or more persons owns an undivided fractional interest in the property. Upon one tenant's death, that interest passes to his or her heirs. For example, suppose Reband and Charnock own a rare stamp collection as tenants in common. If Reband died before Charnock, one-half of the stamp collection would become the property of Reband's heirs. If Reband had sold her interest to French before she died, French and Charnock would have become co-owners as tenants in common. If French died, his interest in the personal property would pass to his heirs, and they in turn would own the property with Charnock as tenants in common.

JOINT TENANCY   In a **joint tenancy,** each of two or more persons owns an undivided interest in the whole (personal property), and a deceased joint tenant's interest *passes to the surviving joint tenant or tenants.* Joint tenancy can be terminated at any time before the joint tenant's death by gift or by sale. If no termination occurs, then upon the death of a joint tenant, his or her interest transfers to the remaining joint tenants, not to the heirs of the deceased joint tenant. The fact that the surviving joint tenant or tenants acquires the deceased tenant's interests—instead of the interest passing to the deceased tenant's heirs—is the main feature distinguishing a joint tenancy from a tenancy in common. To illustrate: If Reband and Charnock from the preceding example were joint tenants and if Reband died before Charnock, the entire collection would become the property of Charnock. Reband's heirs would receive absolutely no interest in the collection. If, prior to Reband's death, she had sold her interest to French, French and Charnock would have become co-owners. Reband's sale, however, would have terminated the joint tenancy, and French and Charnock would have become owners as tenants in common.

A joint tenancy can also be transferred by *partition;* that is, the tenants can physically divide the property into equal parts. Because a joint tenant's interest is capable of being conveyed without the consent of the other joint tenants, it can be levied against (seized by court order) to satisfy the tenant's judgment creditors. This characteristic is also true of the tenancy in common.

At common law, unless a clear intention to create a tenancy in common was shown, there was a presumption that any co-tenancy was a joint tenancy. Modern statutes, however, reverse this presumption. Most statutes now presume that a co-tenancy is a tenancy in common unless there is a clear intention to establish a joint tenancy. Thus, language such as ''to Jerrold and Eva as joint tenants with right of survivorship, and not as tenants in common'' would be necessary to create a joint tenancy.

In the following case, the issue before the court is whether certain certificates of deposit (CDs) were held in joint tenancy. Note how, in addition to specific words on the CDs, a state statute regarding banking institutions controls the decision.

BACKGROUND AND FACTS   Between 1986 and 1988, B. C. Benson bought several CDs from the First National Bank of De Queen. Before he died in 1989, Benson added the names of his neighbors and good friends, Kevin and William Gray, to three of the CDs and the name of his niece, Mary Warrengton, to two of the CDs. On their faces, the CDs stated, ''If more than one of you are named above, you will own the certificate as joint tenants with right of survivorship (and not as tenants in common).'' After Benson's death, a dispute arose as to the ownership of the CDs, and the executors of Benson's estate asked an Arkansas state court to resolve the dispute. The Grays and Warrengton claimed that, as joint tenants, they had a right of survivorship to the funds represented by the CDs. The executors claimed that no right of survivorship existed and that the funds rightfully belonged to Benson's estate. The court held that the Grays and Warrengton were owners of the CDs by virtue of joint survivorship, and the executors appealed.

Case 49.1

B. C. BENSON ESTATE v. FIRST NATIONAL BANK OF De QUEEN

Court of Appeals of Arkansas, 1991.
33 Ark.App. 87,
801 S.W.2d 58.

DECISION AND RATIONALE   The Court of Appeals of Arkansas affirmed the lower court's decision. The appellate court found that the CDs clearly came within the language of the relevant state statute, which stated that a CD purchased in the names of two or more persons and payable to any of the named persons or their survivors "shall become the property of those persons as joint tenants with right of survivorship." This statute and the legend on the faces of the CDs declaring that those named on the CDs owned them as joint tenants with the right of survivorship convinced the court to rule in favor of the Grays and Warrengton.

TENANCY BY THE ENTIRETY   A **tenancy by the entirety** is less common today than it once was. Typically, it is created by a conveyance (transfer) to a husband and wife. It is distinguished from joint tenancy by the inability of either spouse to transfer separately his or her interest during his or her life. Because neither can voluntarily convey his or her interest, the creditors of one spouse cannot levy on the property. In some states where statutes give the wife the right to convey her property, this form of concurrent ownership has been effectively abolished. A divorce, either spouse's death, or mutual agreement will terminate a tenancy by the entirety.

COMMUNITY PROPERTY   Only a limited number of states[4] allow property to be owned as **community property.** If property is held as community property, each spouse technically owns an *undivided* one-half interest in property. This type of ownership applies to most personal property acquired by the husband and/or wife during the course of marriage. It generally does not apply to property acquired prior to the marriage or to property acquired by gift or inheritance during the marriage. After a divorce, community property is divided equally in some states and according to the discretion of the court in other states.

■ Acquiring Ownership of Personal Property

The ownership of personal property can be acquired by possession, purchase, production, gift, will or inheritance, and accession. Each action is discussed below.

Possession

One example of acquiring ownership by possession is the capture of wild animals. Wild animals belong to no one in their natural state, and the first person to take possession of a wild animal normally owns it. The killing of a wild animal amounts to assuming ownership of it. Merely being in hot pursuit does not give title, however. There are two exceptions to this basic rule. First, any wild animals captured by a trespasser are the property of the landowner, not the trespasser. For instance, the fish in a pond on a farmer's land are the farmer's property, not the property of a trespasser who fishes for and catches them. Second, if wild animals are captured or killed in violation of wild game statutes, the capturer does not obtain title to the animals; rather, the state does. Those who find lost or abandoned property also can acquire ownership rights through mere possession of the property, as will be discussed later in this chapter.

Purchase

Purchase is one of the most common means of acquiring and transferring ownership of personal property. The purchase and sale of personal property (called goods) are covered in depth in Chapters 18 through 24.

Production

Production—the fruits of one's labor—is another means of acquiring ownership of personal property. For example, writers, inventors, and manufacturers all produce personal property and thereby acquire title to it. (In some situations, however, as when researchers are hired for that purpose, the producer does not usually own what is produced. Rather, the employer owns the rights in the work

---

4.   These states include Arizona, California, Idaho, Louisiana, Nevada, New Mexico, Texas, Washington, and Wisconsin, as well as Puerto Rico.

generated—which might be a new product design, for example.)

Gift

A **gift** is another fairly common means of acquiring or transferring ownership of property. A gift is essentially a *voluntary* transfer of property ownership. It is not supported by legally sufficient consideration, because the very essence of a gift is giving without consideration. Gifts can be made during a person's lifetime, or they can be made in a last will and testament. A gift made by will is referred to as a *testamentary gift*.

There are three requirements for an effective gift—delivery, donative intent, and acceptance by the donee (the one receiving the gift). Each of these requirements is discussed below. Until these three requirements are met, no effective gift has been made. For example, suppose that your aunt tells you that she is going to give you a new Mercedes-Benz for your next birthday. This is simply a *promise* to make a gift. It is not considered a gift until the Mercedes-Benz is delivered.

DELIVERY Delivery is obvious in most cases, but some objects cannot be relinquished physically. Then the question of delivery depends upon the surrounding circumstances. When the physical object cannot be delivered, a symbolic delivery, or **constructive delivery,** will be sufficient. Constructive delivery does not confer actual possession of the object in question. It is a general term for all those acts that the law holds to be equivalent to acts of real delivery. Suppose that you want to make a gift of various old rare coins that you have stored in a safe-deposit box. You certainly cannot deliver the box itself to the donee, and you do not want to take the coins out of the bank. Instead, you can simply deliver the key to the box to your donee. This constitutes symbolic, or constructive, delivery of the contents of the box.

Delivery of intangible personal property *must* be accomplished by symbolic or constructive delivery. For example, ownership interests in firms are often represented by stock certificates, and delivery of the certificate entitles the holder to dividends. Other examples of intangible personal property that must be constructively delivered include insurance policies, contracts, promissory notes, and chattel mortgages.

An effective delivery also requires giving up *complete dominion and control* (ownership rights) over the subject matter of the gift. The outcome of disputes often turns on the retaining or relinquishing of control over the subject matter of the gift. The Internal Revenue Service scrutinizes transactions between relatives when one relative has given away to another relative income-producing property. A relative who does not relinquish complete control over a piece of property will have to pay taxes on the income from that property. Under the tax laws, it may be illegal to assign or give away income while retaining control over the property that produces the income (unless a special trust is set up).

Delivery can be accomplished by means of a third person. The third person may be the agent of the donor (the one making the gift) or donee. If the person is the agent of the donor, the gift is effective when the agent delivers the property to the donee. If, in contrast, the third person is the agent of the donee, the gift is effective when the donor delivers the property to the donee's agent.[5] When there is doubt as to whose agent the third party is, he or she is generally presumed to be the agent of the donor. Naturally, no delivery is necessary if the gift is already in the hands of the donee. All that is necessary to complete the gift in such a case is the required intent and acceptance by the donee.

DONATIVE INTENT Donative intent (the intent to make a gift) is determined from the language of the donor and the surrounding circumstances. For example, when a gift is challenged in court, the court may look at the relationship between the parties and the size of the gift in relation to the donor's other assets. Donative intent might be questioned by a court if the gift was made to an archenemy. Likewise, when a person has given away a large portion of his or her assets, the court will scrutinize the transactions to determine whether the donor was mentally competent or whether fraud or duress was involved. In the following case, the court looks at the intent of the donor and the question of delivery.

---

5. *Bickford v. Mattocks,* 95 Me. 547, 50 A.894 (1901).

Case 49.2

ESTATE OF PIPER

Missouri Court of Appeals,
1984.
676 S.W.2d 897.

BACKGROUND AND FACTS   Gladys Piper died intestate (without a will) in 1982. At the time of her death, she owned personal property consisting of household goods, two old automobiles, farm machinery, and "miscellaneous" items totaling $5,150. This did not include jewelry or cash. When Gladys died, she had $206.75 in cash and her two diamond rings, known as the "Andy Piper" rings, in her purse. The contents of Gladys's purse were taken by her niece Wanda Brown on Gladys's death, allegedly to preserve them for the estate. Clara Kauffman, a friend of Gladys Piper, filed a claim against the estate for $4,800 in Missouri state court. From October 1974 until Gladys's death in 1982, Clara had taken Gladys to the doctor, beauty shop, and grocery store; written her checks to pay her bills; and helped her care for her home. Clara maintained that Gladys had promised to pay her for these services and that the diamond rings were a gift to her. The trial court denied Clara's request for payment of $4,800 on the basis that the services had been voluntary. Clara then filed a petition for delivery of personal property, the rings, which was granted by the trial court. Gladys's heirs and her estate by the administrator appealed.

DECISION AND RATIONALE   The Missouri Court of Appeals reversed the judgment of the trial court, ruling that no effective gift of the rings had been made because Gladys had never delivered the rings to Clara. Clara claimed that the rings belonged to her by reason of a "consummated gift long prior to the death of Gladys Piper." Two witnesses testified for Clara at trial that Gladys had told them that the rings belonged to Clara but that she was going to wear them until she died. The appellate court found "no evidence of any actual delivery." The court held that "[t]he essentials of such a gift are (1) a present intention to make a gift on the part of the donor, (2) a delivery of the property by donor to donee, and (3) an acceptance by donee." Because the evidence showed only an intent to make a gift, and there had been no delivery—either actual or symbolic—a valid gift was not made. For Gladys to have made a gift, she would have had to execute her intention by either a complete and unconditional delivery of the property or a delivery of a proper written instrument evidencing the gift. Because no delivery occurred, the court found that there had been no gift.

ACCEPTANCE   The final requirement of a valid gift is acceptance by the donee. This rarely presents any problems because most donees readily accept their gifts. The courts generally assume acceptance unless shown otherwise.

GIFTS *INTER VIVOS* and GIFTS *CAUSA MORTIS*   A gift made during the donor's lifetime is called a **gift *inter vivos*.** A **gift *causa mortis*** is made in contemplation of imminent death. Gifts *causa mortis* do not become absolute until the donor dies from the contemplated illness or disease. A gift *causa mortis* is revocable at any time up to the death of the donor and is automatically revoked if the donor recovers.

Suppose that Stevens is to be operated on for a cancerous tumor. Before the operation, he delivers an envelope to a close business associate. The envelope contains a letter saying, "I realize my days are numbered, and I want to give you this check for $1 million in the event of my death from this operation." The business associate cashes the check. The surgeon performs the operation and removes the tumor. Stevens recovers fully. Several months later, Stevens dies from a heart attack that is totally unrelated to the operation. If Stevens's personal representative (the party charged with administering Stevens's estate) tries to recover the $1 million, normally she will succeed. The gift *causa mortis* is automatically revoked if the donor recovers. The *specific event* that was contemplated in making the gift was death from a particular operation. Because Stevens's death was not the result of this event, the gift is revoked, and the $1 million passes to Stevens's estate.[6]

---

6. *Brind v. International Trust Co.*, 66 Colo. 60, 179 P. 148 (1919).

Although a gift *causa mortis* is revocable at any time prior to the donor's death, to be effective, the gift must meet the three requirements discussed above. The question of whether a gift *causa mortis* had been effectively delivered is at issue in the following case.

BACKGROUND AND FACTS James Wilson learned that he had terminal cancer in 1983 or 1984. At about that time, he arranged for a friend, Harold Buell, to have joint access to Wilson's safe-deposit box. Wilson gave Buell a key. The box contained, among other things, a copy of a promissory note for $65,000 from Michael Cronan. Wilson told Buell that the debt represented by the note was to be forgiven when Wilson died and that on Wilson's death, Buell was to deliver the copy of the note to Cronan. In 1984, Cronan learned of Wilson's illness, and Wilson told Cronan on at least two occasions that Cronan's debt was to be forgiven on Wilson's death. In the meantime, Cronan continued to make payments on the note. Wilson died in July 1987. On the day after Wilson died, Buell delivered the copy of the note to Cronan, as directed. Wilson's personal representative (a person appointed to look after the deceased's affairs), Carol Kesterson, sought in an Oregon state court to recover from Cronan the balance owing on the $65,000 note, the original of which was found among Wilson's personal effects after his death. Cronan claimed that the debt had been forgiven, as a gift to Cronan. The trial court held that the gift had not been adequately delivered before Wilson's death, and therefore Cronan was liable on the debt. Cronan appealed.

DECISION AND RATIONALE The Court of Appeals of Oregon affirmed the decision of the trial court, ruling that Wilson's gift to Cronan—the forgiveness of Cronan's debt—was never adequately delivered to Cronan during Wilson's lifetime. The Court stated, "[f]or a gift of personal property * * * to be valid, there must be a donative intent, coupled with the delivery of the subject of the gift to the donee with the intent that the donee have a present interest in it and an acceptance by the donee. * * * The one claiming a gift has the burden to prove the elements by clear and convincing evidence." Even though Cronan argued that Wilson had delivered the copy of the note to Buell, who was acting as Cronan's agent, the court noted that the evidence did not support the finding that an agency relationship between Buell and Cronan existed. The court found "no evidence that [Cronan] knew that Buell had the key to the safe deposit box or that he had possession of the envelope" that contained the copy of the note or even that Cronan had given instructions to Buell. Because Buell acted on Wilson's instructions and essentially served as Wilson's agent, the court found that there was no delivery of the note to Cronan before Wilson died. Because Wilson's attempted testamentary gift was not accompanied by a writing executed with the formalities of a will, the attempted testamentary gift also failed.

ETHICAL CONSIDERATIONS Sometimes an aging or ill person intends to make a gift to another, but the gift fails because the proper legal requirements of a gift were not met. Here, Wilson intended that on his death

Case 49.3

KESTERSON v. CRONAN

Court of Appeals of Oregon, 1991.
105 Or.App. 551,
806 P.2d 134.

Cronan's debt should be forgiven. Yet Cronan never received this "gift" because, as the court pointed out, in essence it was a testamentary gift—to be given on Wilson's death—and Wilson failed to provide for the gift in his will. Although it may seem unfair that the law should prevent a donor's intention from being realized, strict legal requirements are imposed in such cases to ensure that the donor did indeed intend to make a gift. Effective delivery of a gift by the donor to the donee is an objective indication of the donor's intent, as is a specific provision in a will that a gift is to be made.

Will or Inheritance

Ownership of property may be transferred by will or by inheritance under state statutes. These types of transfers are dealt with at length in Chapter 54.

Accession

Accession means "something added." It occurs when someone adds value to a piece of personal property by use of either labor or materials. Generally, there is no dispute about who owns the property after accession has occurred, especially when the accession is accomplished with the owner's consent. For example, a Corvette-customizing specialist comes to Sam's house. Sam has all the materials necessary. The customizing specialist uses them to add a unique bumper to Sam's Corvette. Sam simply pays the customizer for the value of the labor, obviously retaining title to the property.

Ownership can be at issue after the occurrence of an accession if (1) a party has wrongfully caused the accession or (2) the materials added or labor expended greatly increase the value of the property or change the identity of the property. Some general rules can be applied when these situations occur.

If the accession was caused wrongfully (without the owner's consent) and in bad faith, the courts will generally favor the owner over the improver, even if the value of the property was increased substantially. In addition, many courts will deny the improver (wrongdoer) any compensation for the value added; for example, a car thief who put new tires on the stolen car would obviously not be compensated for the value of the new tires.

If the accession is performed in good faith, however, even without the owner's consent, ownership of the improved item most often depends on the actual increase in the value of the property or change of identity of the property. The greater the increase, the more likely that ownership will pass to the improver. Obviously, when this occurs,

the improver must compensate the original owner for the value the property had prior to the accession. If the increase in value is not sufficient for ownership to be passed to the improver, most courts require the owner to compensate the improver for the value added.

Confusion

Confusion is defined as the commingling of goods so that one person's personal property cannot be distinguished from another's. It frequently involves goods that are fungible.[7] *Fungible goods* are goods of which each particle is identical to every other particle, such as grain and oil. For example, if two farmers put their number 2 grade winter wheat into the same silo, confusion will occur. If the confusion of goods is caused by a person who wrongfully and willfully mixes his or her goods with those of another to render them indistinguishable, the innocent party acquires title to the total.

This rule does not apply when confusion occurs by agreement, honest mistake, or the act of some third party. When any of these three events occurs, the owners all share ownership as tenants in common. Suppose that you enter into a cooperative arrangement with five other farmers in your local community of Midway, Iowa. Each fall everyone harvests the same amount of number 2 yellow corn. The corn is stored in silos that are held by the cooperative. Each of you owns one-sixth of the total corn in the silos. If anything happens to the corn, each of you will bear the loss in equal proportions of one-sixth.

But suppose you share ownership in some other proportion. Often, owners do not have equal interests. In such a case, the owners must keep careful records of their respective proportions. If a dispute

---

7. See UCC 1-201(17).

over ownership or loss arises, the courts will presume that everyone has an equal interest in the goods. So you must be prepared to prove that you own more or less than an equal part.

Suppose you own two-thirds of the corn in the Midway co-op silos. Further assume that the silos are damaged by a tornado and thunderstorm. How much have you lost if one-half of the corn is blown away by the storm? You have lost one-half of your two-thirds, or one-third of the total. When corn is stored by several owners, each owning a different proportion of the total, loss is shared proportionally.

Confusion that results from negligent conduct creates a different problem. When there is a loss by fire, theft, or destruction, the person responsible for the commingling must bear the entire loss. If the wrongdoer can show that no injury occurred, however, and can prove what portion he or she contributed to the whole, then the wrongdoer can recover that portion.

■ Mislaid, Lost, or Abandoned Property

As already noted, one of the methods of acquiring ownership of property is to possess it. Simply finding something and holding onto it, however, does not *necessarily* entitle the finder to it. If the property has been *mislaid,* the finder does not have first claim to it. Its true owner does, and if the owner does not assert this claim, the owner of the premises on which it was discovered may claim it. If it has been *lost,* the finder has first claim to it—after its true owner. If it has been intentionally *abandoned,* the finder's possession entitles him or her to its title.

Mislaid Property

Property that has been voluntarily placed somewhere by the owner and then inadvertently forgotten is **mislaid property.** Suppose you go to the theater and leave your gloves on the concession stand. The gloves are mislaid property, and the theater owner is entrusted with the duty of reasonable care for the goods. When mislaid property is found, the finder does not obtain title to, or possession of, the goods.[8] Instead, the owner of the

place where the property was mislaid becomes the caretaker of the property because it is highly likely that the true owner will return.[9]

Lost Property

Property that is *involuntarily* left is **lost property.** A finder of lost property can claim title to the property against the whole world, *except the true owner.* If the true owner demands that the lost property be returned, the finder must return it. If a third party attempts to take possession of lost property from a finder, the third party cannot assert a better title than the finder.

When a finder knows who the true owners of property are and fails to return it to them, that finder is guilty of a tort known as *conversion* (see Chapter 5). Finally, many states require the finder to make a reasonably diligent search to locate the true owner of lost property.

Suppose Arnolds works in a large library at night. After work, as she is walking through the courtyard of the library, she finds a piece of gold jewelry that contains several apparently precious stones. Arnolds decides to take it to a jewelry store to have it appraised. While pretending to weigh the jewelry, an employee of the jeweler removes several of the stones. If Arnolds brings an action to recover the stones from the jeweler, she will win, because she found lost property and holds valid title against everyone *except the true owner.* Because the property was *lost* and not *mislaid,* the owner of the library is not the caretaker of the jewelry. Instead, Arnolds acquires title good against the whole world (except the true owner).[10]

Many states have **estray statutes** to encourage and facilitate the return of property to its true owner and then to reward the finder for honesty if the property remains unclaimed. Such statutes provide an incentive for finders to report their discoveries by making it possible for them, after passage of a specified period of time, to acquire legal title to the

---

8. The finder is an involuntary bailee. See Chapter 50.

9. The owner of the place where property is mislaid is a bailee with right of possession against all except the true owner.
10. See *Armory v. Delamirie,* 93 Eng. Rep. 664 (K.B. 1722). If Arnolds had found the jewelry during the course of her employment, however, her employer would be the involuntary bailee. Further, many courts now say that lost property recovered in a private place allows the owner of the place, *not* the finder, to become the bailee (even if the finder is not a trespasser).

property they have found. Such statutes usually require the county clerk to advertise the property in an attempt to enhance the opportunity of the owner to recover what has been lost.

There are always some preliminary questions to be resolved before the estray statute can be employed. The item must be *lost property*, not mislaid or abandoned property. When the situation indicates that the property was probably lost and not mislaid or abandoned, as a matter of public policy, loss is presumed, and the estray statute applies.

Abandoned Property

Property that has been *discarded* by the true owner, who has *no intention* of claiming title to it, is **abandoned property.** Someone who finds abandoned property acquires title to it, and such title is good against the whole world, *including the original owner.* The owner of lost property who eventually gives up any further attempt to find the lost property is frequently held to have abandoned the property.

For example, assume that Starr is driving with the windows down in her car. Somewhere along her route, a valuable scarf blows out the window. She retraces her route and searches for the scarf but cannot find it. She finally decides that further search is futile and proceeds to her destination five hundred miles away. Six months later, Frye, a hitchhiker, finds the scarf. Frye has acquired title, which is good even against Starr. By giving up her search, Starr had abandoned the scarf just as effectively as if she had intentionally discarded it.

A trespasser who finds an item of abandoned personal property does not acquire title to it, however. The owner of the real property on which it was found does. The same rule applies if the property was lost. Similarly, if, for example, a landowner employs a crew to install an underground septic tank and the crew digs up a cache of pioneer relics, the landowner has first claim to the relics, because they were buried in his or her ground.

In contrast, if the crew had unearthed money, gold, silver, or bullion (instead of pewter dishes, tin cups, brass buttons, and old muskets), the find could be classified as **treasure trove** (treasure that is found), and the crew might be able to keep it. In the United States, in the absence of a statute, a finder has title to treasure trove against all but the true owner. (In Great Britain, the Crown gets it.) Generally, to constitute treasure trove, property need not have been buried—it could have been hidden in some other private place, such as behind loose bricks in an old chimney—but its owner must be unknown, and its finders must not have been trespassing.[11]

In the following case, an enterprising discovery group succeeded in the near impossible: locating a gold-laden ship that had sunk in the Atlantic Ocean in the mid-1800s. Whether the discovery group could claim ownership to the find is the issue before the court.

---

11.   *Danielson v. Roberts,* 44 Or. 1008, 74 P. 913 (1904).

Case 49.4	**BACKGROUND AND FACTS** In September 1857, the *S.S. Central America,* a luxury passenger ship making a voyage from Panama to New York, sank in the Atlantic Ocean some 160 miles east of Charleston, South Carolina. Many of the passengers on the ship were gold miners returning from California to the East to invest their findings. Surviving passengers told stories of vast amounts of gold that had been aboard the ship. Using high-tech equipment and the services of numerous experts, the Columbus-America Discovery Group (Columbus) began to search the ocean floor for the vessel in 1986. When Columbus succeeded in locating what it was sure was the *Central America,* it sought in a federal district court to establish ownership rights in the gold, which was estimated to be worth millions. Several insurance companies that had covered losses incurred by the sinking of the *Central America* intervened, claiming that they were the true owners of the gold.
COLUMBUS-AMERICA DISCOVERY GROUP, INC. v. UNIDENTIFIED, WRECKED AND ABANDONED SAILING VESSEL	
United States District Court, Eastern District of Virginia, 1990. 742 F.Supp. 1327.	

DECISION AND RATIONALE The United States District Court for the Eastern District of Virginia held that the Columbus group, as finders of abandoned property, acquired ownership of the vessel. Accordingly, the court dismissed the claims of the insurance companies. That the insurance companies asserting the claims had all destroyed their records a century before made it difficult, in the eyes of the court, to believe that they still intended to assert claims of ownership to the gold. The court concluded that the destruction of the documents showed that none of these companies believed that the ship could be located or its treasure recovered. Moreover, none of the companies had ever undertaken any exploratory activity to ascertain the location of the wreck once investigation had become scientifically feasible. The court concluded that "their actions—and failure of actions—speak louder than words [and confirmed] the fact they abandoned any intention to retain any interest in the gold."

■ Terms and Concepts

abandoned property 892
accession 890
chattel 882
community property 886
concurrent ownership 884
confusion 890
constructive delivery 887
estray statutes 891

fee simple 884
fixture 884
gift 887
gift *causa mortis* 888
gift *inter vivos* 888
joint tenancy 885
lost property 891
mislaid property 891

personal property 882
personalty 882
property 882
real property 882
tenancy by the entirety 886
tenancy in common 885
treasure trove 892

■ For Review

1. What is personal property? What is real property?
2. What does it mean to own property in fee simple? What is the difference between a joint tenancy and a tenancy in common?
3. What three elements are required for an effective gift? How else can property be acquired?
4. Which of the following parties owns the deer? Jake trespasses onto Sherwood's private property and hunts and kills a deer. David hunts in a public marsh where he kills a deer out of season. Barry buys a stuffed toy deer in a downtown store. Teri tells Pine Hills Children's Zoo that someday she will donate a deer to the zoo.
5. Olaf finds a gold coin on the floor in the safe-deposit-box vault of the Bank of West Bend. Who has the right of possession to the coin?

■ Questions and Case Problems

49-1. John has a severe heart attack and is taken to the hospital. He is not expected to live, and he knows it. Because he is a bachelor without close relatives nearby, John gives his car keys to his close friend, Fred, telling Fred that he is expected to die and that the car is Fred's. John survives the heart attack, but two months later he dies from pneumonia. Uncle Sam, the executor of John's estate, wants Fred to return the car. Fred refuses, claiming the car was given to him by John as a gift. Discuss whether Fred will be required to return the car to John's estate.

49-2. Sally goes into Meyer's Department Store to do some Christmas shopping. She becomes engrossed in looking over a number of silk blouses but suddenly realizes she has a dinner engagement. She hastily departs from the store, inadvertently leaving her purse on a sales counter. Julie, a sales clerk at the store, notices the purse on the counter but leaves it there, expecting Sally to return for it. Later, when Sally returns, the purse is gone. Sally files an action against Meyer's Department Store for the loss of her purse. Discuss the probable success of her suit.

49-3. Bill Heise is a janitor for the First Mercantile Department Store. While walking to work, Bill discovers an expensive watch lying on the curb. Bill gives the watch to his son, Gordon. Two weeks later, Martin Avery, the true owner of the watch, discovers that Bill found the watch and demands it back from Gordon. Discuss who is entitled to the watch and why.

49-4. Fred McDuff has a son named Don. Fred wants to give his son a new car that he has recently purchased. Fred and his son have been on bad terms during the past few years, and Fred feels part of this is his fault. He goes to his son's house, wanting to make amends by giving the car to Don. When Fred arrives at Don's house, his daughter-in-law (Don's wife) tells Fred that Don is out of town and will return the next day. Fred gives the keys to the new car to his daughter-in-law, tells her to hold the keys for his son, and says that he will return the next day. Two hours later, Fred has second thoughts about giving Don the car. He retrieves the keys from his daughter-in-law before she can turn them over to Don. Don returns from his trip, learns of the events, and demands possession of the car, claiming a gift was made. Is Don entitled to the car? Explain.

49-5. Jill DeCante owns a 1967 Chevy. The car has had continual mechanical problems, and Jill's repair expenses have been considerable. One day, in disgust, Jill parks the car on a city-owned vacant lot two blocks from her house. The car sits there for four months. During this period, Sam Green observes the car, which has been unattended by Jill. Sam takes the car and makes improvements and repairs valued at $500. Later, Jill learns that Sam has the car, has it running smoothly, and is treating it as if it were his. Jill demands the car, claiming title. Sam refuses to surrender the car, claiming that he has title. Discuss who is correct and what rights, if any, each person has against the other.

49-6. In June 1983, the First National Bank of Chicago (First Chicago) sold some of its used office furniture to Walter Zibton, a dealer in new and secondhand office supplies and furniture. Included among the items of furniture were some file cabinets that were locked and presumed to be empty. Keys for the file cabinets were unavailable. Zibton sold one of the file cabinets to Charles Strayve and included three other file cabinets free of charge. Strayve later gave one of the cabinets to his friend Richard Michael, the plaintiff in this case. About six weeks after Michael had received the cabinet, it fell over in his garage, burst open, and exposed the contents—$6,687,948.85 worth of certificates of deposit. Michael took the certificates to the Federal Bureau of Investigation for safekeeping and brought action to determine ownership of the certificates, claiming that they were abandoned property and that he, as the finder, was thus the rightful owner. First Chicago claimed that the certificates were lost property. Discuss who was correct. [*Michael v. First Chicago Corp.,* 139 Ill.App.3d 374, 487 N.E.2d 403, 93 Ill.Dec. 736 (1985)]

49-7. Lawrence Reeves was a landowning farmer whose land was being foreclosed upon by his mortgage holder, Metropolitan Life Insurance Co. Prior to the foreclosure, Reeves had contracted with Production Sale Co. to erect a grain-storage facility on the farm. Its total cost was $171,185.30. Prior to the foreclosure, Reeves had paid only $16,137.77. When Metropolitan brought the foreclosure proceedings, the question arose as to whether the grain-storage facility was a fixture to the realty or personal property. If it was considered to be a fixture, Metropolitan would receive the proceeds from the sale; if it was considered to be personal property, the proceeds would go to

Production Sale Co. Discuss whether the facility was a fixture to the real property or personal property. [*Metropolitan Life Insurance Co. v. Reeves,* 223 Neb. 299, 389 N.W.2d 295 (1986)]

49-8. For some time before she died, Merle Zimmerman allowed her good friend, Joan Robertson, to assist her with her financial affairs. Robertson was given access to Zimmerman's funds, through joint bank accounts, and to Zimmerman's safe-deposit box. At one point, Zimmerman gave Robertson a number of municipal bonds to "put . . . in safekeeping." Robertson noticed that the bonds had been placed in a series of manila envelopes, and each envelope contained a piece of paper on which was written the name of a relative. One envelope, which contained bonds with a face value of $22,000, had Robertson's name in it. When Zimmerman died, Robertson distributed the bonds to the people whose names were in the envelopes and retained the bonds in the envelope with her own name in it. Zimmerman's estate claimed ownership of the bonds. Robertson asserted that Zimmerman had made a gift to her of the bonds. Discuss whether an effective gift had been made. [*Robertson v. Estate of Zimmerman,* 778 S.W.2d 805 (Mo.App. 1989)]

49-9. Leonard Charrier, an amateur archaeologist in Louisiana, uncovered artifacts from an Indian burial ground that was several hundred years old. The artifacts had been made by the ancestors of the present-day Tunica Indian tribe of Louisiana. The Tunica tribe asked the court to award it custody of the property, which included burial pots, ornaments, and pottery. Charrier claimed that the property had been abandoned and that he had the right to title because he had taken possession of the property. Discuss whether the Tunica tribe, as heirs to the former owners of the property, should succeed in their claim to the artifacts, or whether the property was abandoned. [*Charrier v. Bell,* 496 So.2d 601 (La.App.1st Cir. 1986)]

49-10. Before her death, Melanie McCarthy had written and sent or otherwise delivered nine $3,000 checks intended as gifts to various relatives. None of the checks had been cashed prior to Melanie's death. Melanie's son, Daniel, who was one of the administrators of her estate, claimed that the Internal Revenue Service (IRS) should not levy estate taxes on the $27,000 still in Melanie's bank account to cover these checks because the checks were completed gifts. The IRS contended that the gifts had not been effectively delivered prior to Melanie's death, because Melanie could have ordered the bank to stop payment on the uncashed checks and therefore had not relinquished complete dominion and control over the checks sufficient to establish a completed gift. What should the court decide? Discuss. [*McCarthy v. United States,* 806 F.2d 129 (7th Cir. 1986)]

49-11. Paul was the owner of real estate located in Putnam County, Florida. In 1982, while Paul was living with Lucille, he executed a deed conveying the property to himself and Lucille as joint tenants with right of survivorship. In 1985, Paul and Lucille stopped living together, and three months later Lucille conveyed her interest in the property to her daughter, Sandra. What type of interest does Sandra possess in the property, and why? [*Foucart v. Paul,* 516 So.2d 1035 (Fla.App. 1987)]

49-12. A Question of Ethics

On August 19, 1985, as she was picking berries, Wanda Thayer discovered loose coins on the ground in an area near Hill City, South Dakota. Thayer and members of her family conducted a search and eventually found coins worth approximately $10,500. The Thayers did not report the find to the authorities but instead proceeded to spend $1,079 of the coins for food, rent, and other expenses. When the county sheriff's office learned of the find and queried the Thayers about the money, Thayer's son-in-law initially lied and said that the coins had belonged to his mother. Later, however, they gave the remaining coins to the authorities. After a two-day trial to determine the ownership of the coins, the court found that Marvin Kjerstad was the true owner; that Marvin was unaware that his coin collection had been stolen several years earlier by his brother, Kendall; and that Kendall, who confessed to the theft only after the coins were found, would probably not have admitted the theft if the coins had not been found. The trial court awarded the Thayers a reward of 30 percent of the coins recovered, less the $1,079 previously spent. On appeal, the appellate court evaluated whether it was appropriate to reward the Thayers for finding the coins and, if a reward was appropriate, whether the amount of the reward was too high. In view of these facts, answer the following questions. [In the Matter of Unknown Silver Coins, *418 N.W.2d 317 (S.D. 1988)*]

1. Given the fact that the Thayers did nothing to find the true owner of the coins prior to being contacted by the sheriff's office, spent approximately one-tenth of the money recovered, and initially lied about the source of the coins, should the Thayers be entitled to any amount of the find as a reward? Explain your answer.

2. In South Dakota and several other states, by statute, a finder of lost property is entitled to a "reasonable reward." South Dakota's neighboring states, Nebraska and Iowa, mandate a 10 percent finder's fee by statute. Even assuming that the Thayers had immediately tried to locate the owner of the coins, do you think that the 30 percent reward awarded to them by the trial court was an unreasonable amount? Why or why not?

3. What public policy is served by state statutes that allow persons who find lost property to be rewarded? Do you think that the trial court's holding in this case was consistent with that policy? Why or why not?

Chapter 50

Bailments

Virtually every individual and business is affected by the law of *bailments* at one time or another (and sometimes even on a daily basis). For example, doing any of the following creates a bailment relationship: shipping goods via public or private means, storing goods in a warehouse, renting a car, leaving a car in a public garage, or leaving a watch or typewriter to be repaired. When individuals deal with bailments, whether they realize it or not, they are subject to the obligations and duties that arise from the bailment relationship. A **bailment** is formed by the delivery of personal property, without transfer of title, by one person (called a **bailor**) to another (called a **bailee**), usually under an agreement for a particular purpose—for example, to loan, store, repair, or transport the property. Upon completion of the purpose, the bailee is obligated to return the bailed property in the same or better condition to the bailor or a third person, or to dispose of it as directed.

Most bailments are created by agreement, but not necessarily by contract law, because in many bailments not all of the elements of a contract (such as mutual assent or consideration) are present. For example, if you loan your business law text to a friend so that your friend can read tomorrow's assignment, a bailment is created, but not by contract, because there is no consideration. In contrast, many commercial bailments, such as the delivery of your suit or dress to the cleaners for dry cleaning, are based on contract.

A bailment is distinguished from a sale or a gift in that possession is transferred without passage of title or intent to transfer title. In a sale or a gift, title is transferred from the seller or donor to the buyer or donee.

The number, scope, and importance of bailments created daily in the business community and in everyday life make it desirable to understand the elements necessary for the creation of a bailment and to know what rights, duties, and liabilities flow from bailments.

■ Elements of a Bailment

Not all transactions involving the delivery of property from one person to another create a bailment. The required elements for the creation of a bailment are as follows:

1. Personal property.
2. Delivery of possession (without title).

3. Agreement that the property be returned to the bailor or otherwise disposed of according to its owner's directions.

Personal Property Requirement

Bailment involves only personal property. A bailment of persons is not possible. Although a bailment of your luggage is created when it is transported by an airline, as a passenger you are not the subject of a bailment. Also, you cannot bail realty; thus, leasing your house to a tenant is not bailment. Bailments involving *tangible* items—jewelry, cattle, automobiles, and the like—are more frequent than bailments of *intangible* personal property, such as promissory notes and shares of corporate stock.

Delivery of Possession

Delivery of possession means transfer of possession of property to the bailee in such a way that

1. The bailee is given exclusive possession and control over the property.
2. The bailee *knowingly* accepts the personal property.[1] In other words, the bailee *intends* to exercise control over it.

If either delivery of possession or knowing acceptance is lacking, there is no bailment relationship. For example, suppose that Stevenson is in a hurry to catch his plane. He has a package he wants to check at the airport. He arrives at the airport check-in station, but the person in charge has gone on a coffee break. Stevenson decides to leave the package on the counter. Even though there has clearly been physical transfer of the package, the person in charge of the check-in station has not knowingly accepted the personal property. Therefore, there has been no effective delivery. The same result would occur in the following example:

Delacroix checks her coat at a restaurant. In the coat pocket is a $20,000 diamond necklace. By accepting the coat, the bailee does not *knowingly* also accept the necklace.

ACTUAL DELIVERY   A distinction is made between a restaurant patron who checks a coat with an attendant and a patron who hangs a coat on a coatrack. Giving the coat to the attendant constitutes an actual, physical delivery and thereby creates a bailment. The attendant (hence the restaurant) has exclusive possession and control over the retention and removal of the coat. By contrast, the self-hung coat can be removed at any time by the patron or anyone else so inclined. The restaurant does not have substantial control over the property and normally is not considered a bailee.

CONSTRUCTIVE DELIVERY   Constructive delivery is an implied or symbolic delivery. What is physically delivered to the bailee is not the actual property bailed but something so related to the property that the requirement of delivery is satisfied. For example, Lyssenko owns a boat that she wishes to loan to Brady for the weekend. It is moored at a municipal marina. Lyssenko gives Brady the boat registration papers so that the harbormaster will allow Brady to board the boat. Lyssenko has made constructive delivery of the boat to Brady.

In certain unique situations, a bailment is found despite the apparent lack of the requisite elements of control and knowledge. In particular, safe-deposit box rental is usually held to constitute a bailor-bailee relationship between the bank and its customer, despite the bank's lack of knowledge of the contents and its inability to have exclusive control of the property.[2]

Another example of such a situation occurs when the bailee acquires the property accidentally or by mistake, as when someone finds lost or mislaid property (see Chapter 49 for definitions of lost and mislaid property). A bailment is created even though the bailor did not voluntarily deliver the property to the bailee. Such bailments are called *involuntary* bailments.

---

1. We are dealing here with *voluntary* bailments. Under some circumstances, regardless of whether a person *intentionally* accepts possession of someone else's personal property, the law imposes on him or her the obligation to redeliver it. For example, if property is *accidentally* left in another's possession without negligence on the part of its owner, the person in whose possession it has been left may be responsible for its return. This is referred to as *involuntary* bailment.

---

2. By statute or by express contract, however, a safe-deposit box may be a lease of space or license, depending on the jurisdiction, the facts, or both.

The Bailment Agreement

A bailment agreement can be *express* or *implied.* Although no written agreement is required for bailments of less than one year (that is, the Statute of Frauds does not apply), it is a good idea to have one, especially when valuable property is involved.

The bailment agreement expressly or impliedly provides for the return of the bailed property to the bailor or to a third person or provides for disposal by the bailee. The agreement presupposes that the bailee will return the identical goods originally given by the bailor. In a bailment of *fungible goods*[3]—uniform, identical goods—or a bailment with the *option to purchase,* however, only equivalent property must be returned.

For example, Sanchez, Baskin, and Corley each store 1,000 pounds of grain of the same type and grade in Hansen's Warehouse every year, and each receives receipts. When Sanchez returns to reclaim "his grain," Hansen's Warehouse is obligated to give him 1,000 pounds of wheat grain—but not necessarily the particular kernels he originally deposited. Sanchez cannot claim that Hansen's Warehouse is guilty of conversion (see Chapter 5) by not returning to him the exact wheat that he put into storage. As long as it returns goods of the same *type, grade,* and *quantity,* Hansen's Warehouse—the bailee—has performed its obligation.

A bailment with an option or offer to purchase allows the prospective buyer the right to hold or use the property while deciding whether to purchase. At the end of an agreed-upon period, the bailee must either return the property to the bailor-seller or agree to purchase the property (such as by paying cash to the seller). If he or she agrees to purchase the property, the bailee-buyer returns to the bailor-seller "equivalent" property (a promise or payment of money), terminating the bailment and creating a sale.

A typical example is a *sale on approval.* Suppose Rand is interested in buying a lawn mower. The seller gives him possession of a new model, telling him to take it home and try it out. The sales price is $280. If Rand does not like the lawn mower, he can bring it back within two weeks. If he does not bring it back within this period or if he approves

the offer, the seller will bill him. Thus, a bailment is created, and Rand has the duty either to return the lawn mower or to approve the offer and return the equivalent in the form of the purchase price.

■ Ordinary Bailments

There are three types of ordinary bailments. The distinguishing feature among them is *which party receives a benefit from the bailment.* Ultimately, the courts may use this factor to determine the standard of care required of the bailee while in possession of the personal property, and this factor will dictate the rights and liabilities of the parties. The three types of ordinary bailments are as follows:

1. *Bailment for the sole benefit of the bailor.* This is a type of gratuitous bailment (one that involves no consideration) for the convenience and benefit of the bailor. The bailee is liable only for gross negligence. (Negligence is discussed in Chapter 5.)

2. *Bailment for the sole benefit of the bailee.* This is typically a loan of an article to a person (the bailee) solely for that person's convenience and benefit. The bailee is liable for even slight negligence.

3. *Bailment for the mutual benefit of the bailee and the bailor.* This is the most common kind of bailment and involves some form of compensation for storing items or holding property. It is a contractual bailment. The bailee is liable for ordinary negligence, or the failure to observe ordinary care, which is the care that a reasonably prudent person would use under the circumstances.

The degree of care that was traditionally required of the bailee in each of these three types of bailments is indicated in Exhibit 50–1. Recently, however, most courts have tended to impute a *standard of reasonable care* regardless of the type of bailment arrangement in effect.

■ Rights and Duties of the Bailee

In a bailment situation, both the bailee and the bailor have rights and duties. The rights and duties of the bailee are discussed below. A bailor's rights and duties will be discussed in the following section.

---

3. Fungible goods are defined in UCC 1-201(17) and discussed in Chapter 19. UCC 7-207(1) states clearly, "Fungible goods may be commingled."

■ Exhibit 50–1 Degree of Care Required of a Bailee

Bailment for the Sole Benefit of the Bailor	Mutual-Benefit Bailment	Bailment for the Sole Benefit of the Bailee
	DEGREE OF CARE	
SLIGHT	REASONABLE	GREAT

Rights of the Bailee

The bailee takes possession of personal property for a specified purpose, after which that property is returned (in the same or a *pre*specified altered form). Thus, implicit in the bailment agreement is the right of the bailee to take possession, to utilize the property in accomplishing the purpose of the bailment, and to receive some form of compensation (unless the bailment is intended to be gratuitous). Depending upon the nature of the bailment and the terms of the bailment agreement, these bailee rights are present (with some limitations) in varying degrees in all bailment transactions.

RIGHT OF POSSESSION   Temporary control and possession of property that ultimately is to be returned to the owner is the hallmark of a bailment. The meaning of *temporary* depends upon the terms of the bailment agreement. If a specified period is expressed in the bailment agreement, then the bailment is continuous for that time period. Earlier termination by the bailor is a breach of contract (if the bailment involves consideration), and the bailee can recover damages from the bailor. If no duration is specified, the bailment ends when either the bailor or the bailee so demands and possession of the bailed property is returned to the bailor.

A bailee's right of possession, even though temporary, permits the bailee to recover damages from any third persons for damage or loss to the property. For example, No-Spot Dry Cleaners sends all suede leather garments to Cleanall Company for special processing. If Cleanall loses or damages any leather goods, No-Spot has the right to recover against Cleanall.

If the personal property is stolen from the bailee during the bailment, the bailee has a legal right to regain possession of (to recapture) the goods or to obtain damages from any third person who has wrongfully interfered with the bailee's possessory rights.

RIGHT TO USE BAILED PROPERTY   Naturally, the extent to which bailees can use the personal property entrusted to them depends upon the terms of the bailment contract. When no provision is made, the extent of use depends upon how necessary it is for the goods to be at the bailee's disposal for the ordinary purpose of the bailment to be carried out. For example, when leasing drilling machinery, the bailee is expected to use the equipment to drill. In contrast, when providing long-term storage for a car, the bailee is not expected to use the car, because the ordinary purpose of a storage bailment does not include use of the property (unless an emergency dictates such use to protect the car).

RIGHT OF COMPENSATION   A bailee has a right to be compensated as provided for in the bailment agreement, to be reimbursed for costs and services rendered in the keeping of the bailed property, or both. In mutual-benefit bailments, the amount of compensation is often expressed in the bailment contract. For example, in a rental (bailment) of a car, the contract provides for charges on the basis of time, mileage, or a combination of the two, plus other possible charges. In nonrental bailments, such as when a car is left at a service station for an oil change, the bailee makes a service charge.

Even in a gratuitous bailment, a bailee has a right to be reimbursed or compensated for costs incurred in the keeping of the bailed property. For example, Ann loses her pet dog, which is found by Jesse. Jesse takes Ann's dog to his home and feeds it. Even though he takes good care of the dog, it becomes ill, and a veterinarian is called. Jesse pays the bill for the veterinarian's services and the medicine. He is normally entitled to be reimbursed by Ann for these reasonable costs incurred in the keeping of her dog.

To enforce the right of compensation, the bailee has a right to place a *possessory* lien (claim) on the specific bailed property until he or she has been fully compensated. This lien on specific bailed property is sometimes referred to as an **artisan's lien.** The lien is effective only as long as the bailee has not agreed to extend credit to the bailor and the bailee retains possession over the bailed property.

If the bailor refuses to pay or cannot pay the charges (compensation), the bailee is entitled in most states to foreclose on the lien. This means that the bailee can sell the property and be paid out of the proceeds for the amount owed from the bailment, returning any excess to the bailee.

For example, Peter takes his car to the garage and enters into an agreement for repairs. The repairs are to be paid for in cash. Upon completion of the repairs, the garage tenders Peter his car, but because of unexpected bills he cannot pay the garage. The garage has a right to retain possession of Peter's car, exercising a *bailee's lien.* Unless Peter can make arrangements for payment, the garage will normally be entitled to sell the car to be compensated for the repairs.

RIGHT TO LIMIT LIABILITY In "ordinary" bailments, bailees have the right to limit their liability by type of risk, by monetary amount, or both, as long as (1) the limitations are called to the attention of the bailor, and (2) the limitations are not against public policy.

Any enforceable limitation imposed by the ordinary bailee must be brought to the bailor's attention. Although the bailee is not required to read orally or interpret the limitation for the bailor, it is essential that the bailor in some way know of the limitation. Thus, a sign in Joe's garage stating that Joe will not be responsible "for loss due to theft, fire, or vandalism" may or may not be held to be notice to the bailor. Whether the notice will be effective will depend on the size of the sign, its location, and any other circumstances affecting the likelihood of its being noticed by Joe's patrons. The same holds true with limitations placed on the back of identification receipts (stubs) for parked cars, checked coats, or stored bailed goods. Most courts require additional notice, because the bailor rarely reads the receipt and usually treats it merely as an identification number to be used when reclaiming the bailed goods.

Even if the bailor has received notice, certain types of disclaimers of liability are considered to be against public policy and therefore illegal. Clauses, called *exculpatory clauses,* that limit a person's liability for his or her own wrongful acts are carefully scrutinized by the courts, and in bailments they are often held to be illegal. The classic illustration of an exculpatory clause is found on parking receipts: "We assume no risk for damage to or loss of automobile or its contents regardless of cause. It is agreed that the vehicle owner assumes all such risks." Even though the language may vary, if the bailee attempts to exclude liability for the bailee's own negligence, the result is the same—the clause is unenforceable as being against public policy. This is especially true in the case of bailees providing quasi-public services, such as warehousers or innkeepers (discussed later in this chapter).

Duties of the Bailee

The bailee has two basic responsibilities: (1) to take proper care of the property and (2) to surrender or dispose of the property at the end of the bailment. The bailee's duties are based on a mixture of tort law and contract law. The duty of care involves the standards and principles of tort law discussed previously and in Chapter 5. A bailee's failure to exercise appropriate care in handling the bailor's property results in tort liability. The duty to relinquish the property in a mutual-benefit bailment at the end of the bailment is grounded both in contract law principles and tort law. Failure to return the property is a breach of contract, and with one exception, the bailee is liable for damages. The exception exists when the obligation is excused because the goods or chattel have been destroyed, lost, or stolen through no fault of the bailee (or claimed by a third party with a superior claim). Failure to return bailed property may also result in the tort of conversion.

DUTY OF CARE As previously discussed, bailees must exercise proper care over the property in their possession to prevent its loss or damage. The three types of bailments demand different degrees of care (although the trend is toward enforcement of standards of reasonable care). When a bailment exists for the sole benefit of the bailee, great care, or the highest level of care, is required. When the bailment exists for the mutual benefit of the bailor and the bailee, reasonable care is the standard. When the bailment exists for the sole benefit of the bailor, slight care, or something less than ordinary or reasonable care, is expected.

DUTY TO RETURN BAILED PROPERTY   At the end of the bailment, the bailee normally must re-

linquish the identical undamaged property (unless it is fungible) to either the bailor or someone the bailor designates, or must otherwise dispose of it as directed. This is usually a *contractual* duty arising from the bailment agreement (contract). Failure to give up possession at the time the bailment ends is a breach of contract and could result in the tort of conversion.

In the following case, the question arises as to whether a bailee's duty to return bailed property to the bailor applies if the bailee is a valet parking service and the bailor is intoxicated.

BACKGROUND AND FACTS   On June 2, 1983, Bonnie Vanderwerff drove her Mercedes-Benz into the parking lot of a restaurant owned and operated by El Torito Restaurants, Inc. Vanderwerff left the car with a valet service, Sam's Parking Valet (Valet), which was under contract with El Torito. Vanderwerff remained in the restaurant for some time, bought a number of drinks, and became increasingly intoxicated, to the point that she was clearly unfit to drive. On some previous occasions, El Torito and Valet had withheld vehicles and keys from intoxicated patrons. When Vanderwerff went to reclaim her car, however, Valet turned over the car and the keys, although the personnel of both Valet and El Torito were aware of Vanderwerff's condition. Vanderwerff drove out of the parking lot and hit the Knightens, who were standing in front of another restaurant. The Knightens sued El Torito and Valet in a California state court to recover damages. The trial court dismissed the action, and the Knightens appealed.

DECISION AND RATIONALE   The California Court of Appeal affirmed the decision of the trial court, ruling that El Torito and Valet, as bailees, fulfilled their duties by returning the bailed property to its owner on demand. The appellate court noted that "a number of other jurisdictions have held that a bailee who returns a dangerous instrumentality to a drunken bailor may not be held liable of negligent entrustment" because "[a] bailee does not entrust a chattel when returning it to the bailor." The court was careful to point out that while either El Torito or Valet had the "right" to refuse to give the car back to Vanderwerff, they were not under any "duty" to do so by virtue of their status as bailees.

Case 50.1

KNIGHTEN v. SAM'S PARKING VALET
California Court of Appeal, Fourth District, 1988.
253 Cal.App.3d 69,
253 Cal.Rptr. 365.

DELIVERY OF GOODS TO THE WRONG PERSON   A bailee may be liable if the goods being held or delivered are given to the wrong person. Hence, a bailee must be satisfied that the person to whom the goods are being delivered is the actual owner or has authority from the owner to take pos-

session of the goods. Should the bailee deliver in error, particularly when the bailee knows that the goods are stolen or that there is another claim of ownership against the goods, then the bailee may be liable for conversion or misdelivery. The following case presents an example of this principle.

Case 50.2

**CAPEZZARO v.
WINFREY**

Superior Court of New Jersey,
1977.
153 N.J.Super. 267,
379 A.2d 493.

BACKGROUND AND FACTS Michael Capezzaro, a robbery victim, sued the city and its police officers in a New Jersey state court after the police had arrested a person who Capezzaro claimed had stolen his money. During their apprehension of the suspect, the police removed the money from the suspect's clothing, and the police department kept it. When the suspect was released from custody, she went to the police station and demanded the return of the money. The police officers gave it to her. Capezzaro claimed to be the rightful owner of the money and sued the city for negligence because police officers in the city's employ had released the money. The jury found in favor of Capezzaro, and the police officers and the city appealed.

DECISION AND RATIONALE The Superior Court of New Jersey affirmed the trial court's judgment. Capezzaro was able to recover from the police and the city. Even though he did not enter into an express agreement with the police, a bailment relationship existed. By operation of law, an ordinary bailment arose when the police seized the money, because they were holding it for their own benefit as well as for the benefit of the rightful owner. In a bailment, the bailee (the police in this case) is held to a standard of reasonable care. In this case, the release of the suspect did not damage the credibility of Capezzaro's claim or establish the suspect's right to the money. Thus, the police were negligent in giving the money to the suspect without determining the validity of Capezzaro's claim. The court found "no error in the trial judge's * * * instruct[ing] the jury on negligence, i.e., what a reasonable man would have done as custodian of the fund."

PRESUMPTION OF NEGLIGENCE Sometimes the duty to return and the duty of care are combined to determine bailee liability. At the end of the bailment, a bailee has the duty to return the bailor's property in the condition in which it was received (allowing for ordinary wear and aging). In some cases, the bailor can sue the bailee in tort for damage to, or loss of, goods on the theory of *negligence* or *conversion.* But often it is not possible for the bailor to discover and prove what specific acts of negligence or conversion committed by the bailee caused damage or loss to the property.[4] Thus, the law of bailments recognizes a rule whereby a bailor's proof that damage or loss to the property has occurred will, in and of itself, raise a *presumption* that the bailee is guilty of negligence or conversion. Once this is shown, the bailee must prove that he

or she was not at fault. A bailee who is able to *rebut* (contradict) the presumption is not liable to the bailor. When damage to goods is of the type that normally results only from someone's negligence, and when the bailee had full control of the goods, it is more likely than not that the damage was caused by the bailee's negligence. Therefore, the bailee's negligence is presumed.

Determining whether a bailee exercised an appropriate degree of care is usually a question of fact. This means that the trier of fact (a judge or a jury) weighs the facts of a particular situation and concludes that the bailee did or did not exercise the requisite degree of care at the time the loss or damage occurred. The failure to exercise appropriate care is negligence, and the bailee is liable for the loss or damage in tort.

The following case illustrates that once a bailment is created, failure of the bailee to return the bailed property to the bailor upon demand results in a presumption of conversion (or negligence).

---

4. The basic formula for finding negligence requires proof that (1) a duty exists, (2) a breach of that duty occurred, and (3) the breach is the proximate cause of damage or loss.

BACKGROUND AND FACTS   Marvin Mueller, the president of Vin-Mar Supply, Inc., bought approximately 1,150 railroad luggage carts from the Missouri Pacific Railroad. Mueller made an oral contract with Larry Soffer to store the luggage carts in Soffer's warehouse. Subsequently, a fire destroyed the warehouse, and the carts were either destroyed or severely damaged. Without Mueller's consent, the damaged carts were removed in the clean-up operation as scrap metal. Mueller demanded that Soffer return to him all the carts in their postfire condition. When no carts were returned, Mueller and Vin-Mar filed suit in an Illinois state court, alleging that Soffer and the warehouse were negligent in the care they exercised over the bailed property. The trial court held that Mueller and Vin-Mar had established a *prima facie* case of bailment and that failure to return the bailed property on demand raised a presumption of negligence. The court also concluded that Soffer had failed to rebut the presumption of negligence. Thus, the decision was in favor of Mueller and Vin-Mar. Soffer appealed.

Case 50.3

MUELLER v. SOFFER

Appellate Court of Illinois,
Fifth District, 1987.
160 Ill.App.3d 699,
513 N.E.2d 1198,
112 Ill.Dec. 589.

DECISION AND RATIONALE   The Appellate Court of Illinois affirmed the trial court's findings that failure to return the bailed property on demand had raised a presumption of negligence (that reasonable care had not been exercised). The court explained that to establish a *prima facie* case and raise a presumption of negligence "the following elements must be alleged: an agreement *   *   * to create a bailment; delivery of the property in good condition; acceptance of the items *   *   * by the bailee; and nonreturn or redelivery of the property in a damaged condition." The court found that Mueller "had established a *prima facie* case and raised a presumption of *   *   * negligence." Because Soffer had failed to rebut this presumption, he was liable for damages. The court was apparently influenced by the fact that the bailee had made no effort to determine whether the carts were salvageable before authorizing the carts' removal without seeking Mueller's permission and without accounting to Mueller and Vin-Mar for the scrap value of the carts. This conduct indicated to the court that the bailee had failed to exercise reasonable care and should be held responsible for negligence.

▪ Rights and Duties of the Bailor

As explained below, a bailee's duties and a bailor's rights are complementary. A bailor's basic duty is to provide a bailee with property free from latent defects that could injure the bailee.

Rights of the Bailor

The bailor's rights are essentially a complement to the bailee's duties. A bailor has the right to expect the following:

1.   The property will be protected with reasonable care while in the possession of the bailee.

2.   The bailee will utilize the property as agreed in the bailment agreement (or not at all).

3.   The property will be relinquished at the conclusion of the bailment according to directions given by the bailor.

4.   The bailee will not convert (alter) the goods except as agreed.

5.   The bailor will not be bound by any limitations on the bailee's liability unless such are known and are enforceable by law.

6.   Repairs or service on the property will be completed without defective workmanship.

Duties of the Bailor

A bailor has a single, all-encompassing duty to provide the bailee with goods or chattels that are free from hidden defects that could injure the bailee. This duty translates into two rules:

1. In a *mutual-benefit bailment,* the bailor must notify the bailee of all known defects and any hidden defects that the bailor knew of or could have discovered with reasonable diligence and proper inspection.

2. In a *bailment for the sole benefit of the bailee,* the bailor must notify the bailee of any known defects.

The bailor's duty to reveal defects is based on a negligence theory of tort law. A bailor who fails to give the appropriate notice is liable to the bailee and to any other person who might reasonably be expected to come into contact with the defective article.

To illustrate: Rentco (the bailor) leases four tractors to Hopkinson. Unknown to Rentco (but discoverable by reasonable inspection), the brake mechanism on one of the tractors is defective at the time the bailment is made. Hopkinson uses the defective tractor without knowledge of the brake problem and is injured along with two other field-workers when the tractor rolls out of control. Rentco is liable on a negligence theory for injuries sustained by Hopkinson and the two others.

This is the analysis: Rentco has a mutual-benefit bailment and a *duty* to notify Hopkinson of the discoverable brake defect. Rentco's failure to notify is the *proximate cause* of injuries to farm workers who might be expected to use, or have contact with, the tractor. Therefore, Rentco is *liable* for the resulting injuries.

A bailor can also incur *warranty liability* based on contract law for injuries resulting from bailment of defective articles. Property leased by a bailor must be *fit for the intended purpose of the bailment.* The bailor's knowledge of, or ability to discover, any defects is immaterial. Warranties of fitness arise by law in sales contracts and have been applied by judicial interpretation in the case of bailments "for hire." Article 2A of the UCC extends implied warranties of merchantability and fitness for a particular purpose to bailments whenever those bailments include rights to use the bailed goods [UCC 2A-212, 2A-213].

■ Termination of Bailments

Bailments for a specific term end when the stated period lapses. When no duration is specified, the bailment can be terminated at any time by the following events:

1. The mutual agreement of both parties.
2. A demand by either party.
3. The completion of the purpose of the bailment.
4. An act by the bailee that is inconsistent with the terms of the bailment.
5. The operation of law.

■ Special Features of Specific Bailments

Most of this chapter has concerned itself with ordinary bailments, in which bailees have a duty, as regards property entrusted to them, to use ordinary care. Some bailment transactions warrant special consideration. These include bailments in which the bailee's duty of care is extraordinary—that is, his or her liability for loss or damage to the property is absolute—as is generally true in cases involving common carriers and innkeepers. Warehouse companies have the same duty of care as ordinary bailees; but like carriers, they are subject to extensive coverage of federal and state laws, including the UCC's Article 7.

Documents of Title and Article 7

Any commercial transaction may involve a shipment or storage of goods covered by a *bill of lading,* a *warehouse receipt,* or a *delivery order.* These documents of title are subject to Article 7 of the UCC.[5] To be a **document of title,** a document "must purport to be issued by or addressed to a bailee and purport to cover goods in the bailee's possession which are either identified or are fungible portions of an identified mass" [UCC 1-201(15), 7-102(1)(e); see also UCC 7-401].

A **bill of lading** is a document verifying the receipt of goods for shipment issued by a person engaged in the business of transporting or forwarding goods [UCC 1-201(6)]. A **warehouse receipt** is a receipt issued by a person engaged in

---

5. Of course, where applicable, federal law is paramount [see UCC 7-103]. For example, the Federal Bills of Lading Act [49 U.S.C. Sections 81–124], enacted in 1916, applies to bills of lading issued by a common carrier for goods shipped in interstate or foreign commerce, and the United States Warehouse Act [7 U.S.C. Sections 241–243], also enacted in 1916, applies to receipts covering agricultural products stored for interstate or foreign commerce.

■ CONCEPT SUMMARY 50.1
Rights and Duties of the Bailee and Bailor

Rights of a Bailee (Duties of a Bailor)	1. A bailee has the right to be compensated or reimbursed for keeping bailed property. This right is based in contract or quasi contract.
	2. Unpaid compensation or reimbursement entitles the bailee to a lien (usually possessory) on the bailed property and the right of foreclosure.
	3. A bailee has the right to limit his or her liability. An ordinary bailee can limit types of risk, monetary amount, or both, provided proper notice is given and the limitation is not against public policy. In special bailments, limitations on types of risk are usually not allowed, but limitations on the monetary amount at risk are permitted by regulation.
	4. The right of possession allows actions against third persons who damage or convert the bailed property and allows actions against the bailor for wrongful breach of the bailment.
	5. The right to an insurable interest in the bailed property allows the bailee to insure and recover under the insurance policy for loss or damage to the property.
Duties of a Bailee (Rights of a Bailor)	1. A bailee must exercise reasonable care over property entrusted to him or her. A common carrier (special bailee) is held to a standard of care based on *strict liability* unless the bailed property is lost or destroyed due to (a) an act of God, (b) an act of a public enemy, (c) an act of a governmental authority, (d) an act of a shipper, or (e) the inherent nature of the goods.
	2. Bailed goods in a bailee's possession must be returned to the bailor or disposed of according to the bailor's directions. Failure of return gives rise to a presumption of negligence.
	3. A bailee cannot use or profit from bailed goods except by agreement or in situations in which the use is implied to further the bailment purpose.

the business of storing goods for hire [UCC 1-201(45); see also UCC 7-201, 7-202].[6] A **delivery order** is a written order to deliver goods directed to a warehouser, carrier, or other person who, in the ordinary course of business, issues warehouse receipts or bills of lading [UCC 7-102(1)(d)].

Simply put, a document of title is a receipt for goods in the charge of a bailee-carrier or a bailee-warehouser and a contract for the shipment or storage of identified goods.

Negotiability of Documents of Title

Negotiability is a concept that applies to documents of title when—as in situations involving commer-

cial paper[7]—they contain the words "bearer" or "to the order of" [UCC 7-104(1)]. If a document of title is negotiable—that is, if it specifies that the goods are to be delivered to bearer or to the order of a named person—the following are also possible:

1. The possessor of the document of title is entitled to receive, hold, and dispose of the document and the goods it covers.

2. A good faith purchaser of the document may acquire greater rights to the document and the goods it covers than the transferor had or had the authority to convey (that is, a good faith purchaser may take free of the claims and defenses of prior parties).

---

6. UCC 7-102(h) defines the person engaged in the storing of goods for hire as a *warehouseman*.

7. Commercial paper is the subject of UCC Article 3, which is discussed in detail in Chapters 25 through 29.

If a document of title is nonnegotiable—that is, if it is not made payable to the order of any named person or to bearer—it may be transferred by assignment but not negotiation [UCC 7-104(2)].

In other words, documents of title constitute a class of commercial paper representing commodities in storage or transportation. Thus, for example, just as—under Article 3—the holder in due course of a negotiable promissory note prevails over prior ownership claims, so—under Article 7—the holder of a negotiable warehouse receipt who takes by *due negotiation* does the same.[8]

The concepts of Articles 3 and 7 are similar.[9] There are important distinctions between them, however. Article 7 relates to paper that purports to cover specific goods, but Article 3 paper does not cover or represent any particular money. Also, Article 7 refers to the negotiability process as **due negotiation.** Due negotiation requires not only that the purchaser of a document of title take it in good faith, for value, and without notice of a defense against or claim to it, but also that he or she do so in the regular course of business or financing and not in the settlement or payment of a money obligation [UCC 7-501(4)]. In other words, even if all other requirements are met, transfer of a negotiable document of title to a nonbusinessperson is *not* due negotiation. In such situations, the transferee acquires only those rights the transferor had or had the authority to convey [UCC 7-504].[10]

Upon due negotiation, however, a transferee can acquire greater rights in a document of title than the transferor had. The transferee obtains title to the document and to the goods, including rights to goods delivered to the bailee after the document was issued, and takes free of all prior claims and defenses of which he or she had no notice. The document's issuer remains obligated to store or deliver the goods according to the document's

terms [UCC 7-502]. Under this provision, businesspersons can extend credit on documents of title without concern for adverse claims of third parties.

To prevent a thief or a finder of goods from defeating the rights of the true owner (by, for example, taking them to a warehouse and subsequently negotiating the warehouse receipt to a third party who would otherwise take free of the claims of others), the goods must be delivered to the issuer of the document of title by their owner or the owner's agent [UCC 7-503(1)]. Otherwise, the document does not represent title to the goods. Even if the document does not represent title, however, the bailee will not be liable if he or she acts in good faith and observes reasonable commercial standards in receiving and delivering the goods [UCC 7-404].

In other words, a carrier or warehouser who receives goods from a thief or finder and delivers them according to that individual's instructions is not liable to the goods' true owner. The reason for this rule is that carriers and warehousers are not links in the chain of title and do not represent the owner in transactions affecting title but simply furnish a service necessary to trade and commerce.

Common Carriers

Common carriers are publicly licensed to provide transportation services to the general public. They are distinguished from private carriers, which operate transportation facilities for a select clientele. A private carrier is not bound to provide service to every person or company making a request. The common carrier, however, must arrange carriage for all who apply, within certain limitations.[11]

The common-carrier contract of transportation creates a *mutual-benefit bailment.* But, unlike the bailee in ordinary mutual-benefit bailments, the common carrier is held to a standard of care based on *strict liability,* rather than reasonable care, in protecting the bailed personal property. This means that the common carrier is absolutely liable, regardless of negligence, for all loss or damage to

---

8. Compare UCC 3-305 and 7-502.

9. For example, a delivery order under Article 7 is analogous to a draft under Article 3. A draft is an order by a drawer to a drawee to pay money to a payee. A delivery order is an order by a bailor to a bailee to deliver goods to a deliveree.

10. And until the bailee is notified of the transfer, the transferee's rights may be defeated by certain creditors of the transferor; by a buyer from the transferor in the ordinary course of business, if the bailee has delivered the goods to the buyer; or by the bailee who has dealt with the transferor in good faith [UCC 7-504(2)].

---

11. A common carrier is not required to take any and all property anywhere in all instances. Public regulatory agencies, such as the Interstate Commerce Commission, govern common carriers, and carriers may be restricted to geographical areas. They may also be limited to carrying certain kinds of goods or to providing only special types of transportation equipment.

goods except for loss or damage caused by one of the five common law exceptions:

1. An act of God.
2. An act of a public enemy.
3. An order of a public authority.
4. An act of the shipper.
5. The inherent nature of the goods.

UCC 7-309(1) provides that the UCC "does not repeal or change any law or rule of law which imposes liability on a common carrier for damages not caused by its negligence."

Common carriers are treated as if they were absolute insurers for the safe delivery of goods to the destination, even though they are not. They cannot contract away this liability for damaged goods; subject to government regulations, they are permitted, however, to limit their dollar liability to an amount stated on the shipment contract.[12]

---

12. UCC 7-309(2). Federal laws and Interstate Commerce Commission regulations require common carriers to offer shippers the opportunity to obtain higher dollar limits for loss by paying a higher fee for the transport. For interstate rail transportation, the matter is settled by the Carmack Amendment to the Interstate Commerce Act [49 U.S.C. Section 20(11)], which is discussed in Case 50.4.

Except for the five exceptions given, the common carrier is liable for any damage to goods in shipment, even that caused by the willful acts of third persons or by sheer accident. Thus, a common-carrier trucking company moving cargo is liable for acts of vandalism, mechanical defects in refrigeration units, or a dam bursting, if any of these acts results in damage to the cargo. But damage caused by acts of God—an earthquake or lightning, for example—is the shipper's loss.

SHIPPER'S LOSS   The shipper bears any loss occurring through its own faulty or improper crating or packaging procedures. For example, if a bird dies because its crate was poorly ventilated, the shipper bears the loss, not the carrier.

In the following case, the United States Supreme Court deals with the question of whether a common carrier that has exercised reasonable care and has complied with the instructions of the shipper is nonetheless liable to the shipper for spoilage in transit of an interstate shipment of perishable commodities.

BACKGROUND AND FACTS   Elmore & Stahl, a fruit shipper, contracted with the Missouri Pacific Railway Company to ship melons from Rio Grande City, Texas, to Chicago. At trial, the jury found that Missouri Pacific and its connecting carriers performed all the required transportation services without negligence even though the melons arrived in Chicago in a defective condition not due solely to an inherent defect in the melons. The trial judge ruled against the carrier, and the court of appeals affirmed the decision, as did the Texas Supreme Court. The ground for affirmation was, basically, that Missouri Pacific did not show that the spoilage or decay was due entirely to the inherent nature of the goods—in other words, it did not prove that the damage was caused solely by natural deterioration. Missouri Pacific appealed the case to the United States Supreme Court.

Case 50.4

MISSOURI PACIFIC RAILWAY CO. v. ELMORE & STAHL

Supreme Court of the United States, 1964.
377 U.S. 134,
84 S.Ct. 1142,
12 L.Ed.2d 194.

DECISION AND RATIONALE   The United States Supreme Court upheld the judgment of the Texas courts. The Supreme Court found that the federal statute at issue, part of the Interstate Commerce Act, codifies the common law rule that a carrier, though not an absolute insurer, is liable for damages to goods transported by it unless it can show that the damage was caused by "(a) the act of God; (b) the public enemy; (c) the act of the shipper himself; (d) public authority; (e) or the inherent vice [defect or imperfection] or nature of the goods." The Court also read the statute as prohibiting a carrier from limiting its liability for damages due to any event or condition other than these. Even if a common carrier exercises reasonable care, it is liable for spoilage in transit unless it can prove that the cause of the spoilage was the natural tendency of the commodities to deteriorate. The railroad failed to prove that the loss was due to this natural tendency.

CONNECTING CARRIERS   A bill of lading that specifies one or more connecting carriers is called a *through bill of lading*. When connecting carriers are involved in transporting goods under a through bill of lading, the shipper can recover from the original carrier or any connecting carrier [UCC 7-302]. Normally, the *last* carrier is presumed to have received the goods in good condition.

Warehouse Companies

Warehousing is the business of providing storage of property for compensation. Like ordinary bailees, warehouse companies are liable for loss or damage to property resulting from *negligence*. UCC 7-204(1) provides that a warehouser must "exercise such care ... as a reasonably careful [person] would exercise under like circumstances but unless otherwise agreed he is not liable for damages which could not have been avoided by the exercise of such care." Under UCC 7-204(2), a warehouse company can limit the dollar amount of liability, but the bailor must be given the option of paying an increased storage rate for an increase in the liability limit.

Innkeepers

At common law, innkeepers, hotel owners, and similar operators were held to the same strict liability as common carriers with respect to property brought into the rooms by guests. Today, only those who provide lodging to the public for compensation as a *regular* business are covered under this rule of strict liability. Moreover, the rule applies only to those who are *guests,* as opposed to *lodgers*. A lodger is a permanent resident of the hotel or inn, whereas a guest is a traveler.

In most states, innkeepers can avoid strict liability for loss of guests' valuables and money by providing a safe in which to keep them. Each guest must be clearly notified of the availability of such a safe. For articles that are not kept in the safe or articles of such a nature that they are not normally kept in a safe, statutes will often limit innkeepers' liability. These statutes vary from state to state. In many states, the monetary damages for which the innkeeper is liable are limited in amount. Indeed, these statutes may even provide that the innkeeper has no liability in the absence of negligence. Many statutes require these limitations to be posted or the guest to be notified. The posting (notice) is frequently found on the inside of the door of each room in the motel or hotel.

Normally, the innkeeper assumes no responsibility for the safety of a guest's automobile, because the guest usually retains possession and control. If, however, the innkeeper provides parking facilities, and the guest's car is entrusted to the innkeeper or to an employee, the innkeeper will be liable under the rules that pertain to parking lot bailees (ordinary bailments).

In the following case, a motel employee absconded with a bag full of cash found in a guest's room. Whether the motel should be liable to the guest is at issue.

Case 50.5

GOODEN v. DAY'S INN

Court of Appeals of Georgia,
1990.
196 Ga.App. 324,
395 S.E.2d 876.

BACKGROUND AND FACTS   Marvin Gooden checked into a Day's Inn in Atlanta, Georgia, on March 3, 1988, paying in advance for two days' lodging. The next day, Gooden temporarily left his room, in which he had a paper bag allegedly containing $9,000 in U.S. currency. Shortly after Gooden left the room, Mary Carter, a housekeeper, went into the room to clean it. She found the bag of money and, seeing no other personal effects, concluded that Gooden had checked out. Accordingly, she turned the bag and its contents over to her supervisor, Vivian Clark, who in turn gave the bag to another employee, Dempsey Wilson, to take to the motel office. Wilson had worked for the motel for about three years and had always before returned items of value to the office when asked to do so. This time, however, he decided to abscond with the bag of money. A safe was located on the premises of Day's Inn, and the motel had posted a notice concerning the availability of the safe on the inside of the door of the room occupied by Gooden. In the notice, Day's Inn disclaimed liability for guests' valuables unless they were placed in the safe. Gooden at no time asked to use the safe. Gooden sued the motel and its employees Carter and Clark in a Georgia state court to recover the $9,000. The trial court granted the defendants' motion for summary judgment, and Gooden appealed.

DECISION AND RATIONALE   The Court of Appeals of Georgia affirmed the lower court's decision to grant summary judgment for the defendants, ruling that the defendants had acted with ordinary diligence and care concerning the bag of money. The appellate court noted that the hotel had complied with the state statute, which states, "The innkeeper may provide a safe or other place of deposit for valuable articles and, by posting a notice thereof, may require guests of the innkeeper to place such valuable articles therein or the innkeeper shall be relieved from responsibility for such articles." The hotel posted the notice and Gooden had failed to request that the money be kept in the safe, thus relieving the hotel of liability for the theft. The court pointed out that the statute did not provide a basis for holding the hotel liable for negligence or for the intentional torts of its employees. The court also found that even if a bailment had existed, the defendants took reasonable steps under the circumstances to take care of the money. That Wilson absconded with the money did not reflect adversely on the actions of the defendants nor did it render the hotel liable under a theory of *respondeat superior* (because Wilson acted outside the scope of his authority).

■ Terms and Concepts

artisan's lien 900	**bailor** 896	**document of title** 904
bailee 896	**bill of lading** 904	**due negotiation** 906
bailment 896	**delivery order** 905	**warehouse receipt** 904

■ For Review

1.   What are the three elements of a bailment?
2.   What was the degree of care that was traditionally required of a bailee in each of the three types of bailments? What is the standard of care that most courts tend to impute today regardless of the type of bailment arrangement in effect?
3.   What are the two basic responsibilities of the bailee? What is the basic duty of the bailor?
4.   Finch Audio & Video, Inc., contracts with Normal Warehouse Co. to store 600 pair of name-brand stereo speakers from October until late November, when Finch plans to hold a preholiday sale. After a number of storms in October, it is discovered that Normal's roof developed a leak and half the speakers were damaged. Finch sues Normal. Who determines whether Normal exercised the appropriate degree of care? If Normal is found not to have exercised the appropriate degree of care, what tort will Normal have committed? Will this finding mean that Normal is liable for the damage?
5.   Borger Foods, Inc., contracts with Commons Shipping Co. to transport five railroad carloads of yogurt. When the yogurt arrives, Borger discovers that the yogurt has spoiled. If Borger sues Commons, is Commons likely to be held liable for the damage?

■ Questions and Case Problems

50-1. Curtis is an executive on a business trip to the West Coast. He has driven his car on this trip and checks into the Hotel Ritz. The hotel has a guarded underground parking lot. Curtis gives his car keys to the parking lot attendant but fails to notify the attendant that his wife's $10,000 fur coat is in a box in the trunk. The next day, upon checking out, he discovers that his car has been stolen. Curtis wants to hold the hotel liable for both the car and the coat. Discuss the probable success of his claim.

50-2. Discuss the standard of care required from the bailee for the bailed property in the following situations, and determine whether the bailee breached that duty:

(a) Adam borrows Tom's lawn mower because his own lawn mower needs repair. Adam mows his front yard. In order to mow the backyard, he needs to move some hoses and lawn furniture. He leaves the mower in front of his house while doing so. When he returns to the front, he discovers the mower has been stolen.

(b) Mary owns a valuable speedboat. She is going on vacation and asks her neighbor, Regina, to store the boat in one stall of Regina's double garage. Regina consents, and the boat is moved into the garage. Regina, in need of some grocery items for dinner, drives to the store. In doing so, she leaves the garage door open, as is her custom. While she is at the store, the speedboat is stolen.

50-3. Lee owns and operates a service station. Walter's car needs some minor repairs. Walter takes his car to Lee's station. Lee tells Walter that he will be unable to do the work until the next day and that Walter can either bring the car back at that time or leave it overnight. Walter leaves the car with Lee. The next afternoon Walter comes to pick up his car. Lee presents Walter with a bill for $220 and refuses to return the car until he is paid. Upon inspecting the car, Walter discovers that the mileage indicator shows 150 more miles on the car than when he brought it in. Lee claims he was legally allowed to let one of his employees road test the car by taking it to his home on the preceding evening and driving it. Discuss Walter's and Lee's legal rights under these circumstances.

50-4. Paul borrows from his neighbor, Max, a gasoline-driven lawn edger. Max has not used the lawn edger for two years. Paul is not familiar with using a lawn edger, because he has never owned one. Max previously used this edger often, and if he had made a reasonable inspection, he would have discovered that the blade was loose. Paul is injured when the blade becomes detached while he is edging his yard.

(a) Can Paul hold Max liable for his injuries?

(b) Would your answer be any different if Paul had rented the edger from Max and paid a fee? Explain.

50-5. Franklin Washer, Inc., delivered to the Western Central Railroad one hundred crated washing machines to be shipped to Rocky High Appliance Store in Denver, Colorado. Western Central received the goods on Thursday and stored them in its warehouse pending loading into boxcars the next day. On the Western Central shipping invoice was a clause printed in big, bold type that excluded the carrier from liability resulting from loss of goods under control of the carrier because of acts of vandalism, fire, or theft. The clause also limited liability to $500 per shipment unless a higher evaluation was declared and a fee paid. That evening a riot broke out. Some of the one hundred crated washing machines were stolen, some were damaged by the rioters, and some were destroyed by fire. Franklin wants to hold the carrier liable for the entire value of the one hundred machines. Western claims, first, that it has no liability by virtue of the contractual limitation against liability for loss by fire, theft, or vandalism; and second, that if it were liable, its damage cost responsibility would be only $500. Discuss the validity of Western's claims.

50-6. In her will, Rena bequeathed her jewelry to her daughter Linda. Upon Rena's death, Edward, Rena's husband and Linda's stepfather, gave Linda one ring, a gift to Rena from a prior husband, but put the other jewelry in his home in a dresser drawer. While Edward was in the hospital with a heart ailment, the jewelry was stolen from the dresser drawer. Edward never told Linda, nor did he file an insurance claim or a police report. When Linda found out, she sued her stepfather for negligence for failure to exercise reasonable care over her bailed property. What was the result? [*Estate of Murrell v. Quin,* 454 So.2d 437 (Miss. 1984)]

50-7. Robert Freeman owned a broken Bulova watch. Its band was encrusted with gold nuggets and contained two jade stones. He took the watch to John Garcia's jewelry store for repairs. Garcia did not have the necessary equipment to make all the repairs, so he sent the watch to Douglas Viers Base Watch Repair Lab. While it was at Viers's shop, the watch, along with several others, was stolen. Viers did not have insurance, nor did he have any burglar alarm or other safeguards on the premises. Freeman, claiming the watch had been worth $25,000, sued both Garcia and Viers for the value of the watch. Discuss whether Garcia, Viers, or both are liable for the loss of the watch. [*Freeman v. Garcia,* 495 So.2d 351 (La.App. 2d Cir. 1986)]

50-8. Obadiah and Rose Simmons, the plaintiffs, purchased a bedroom suite on layaway from Max's Discount Furniture, a store owned by Max Yelverton, the defendant. As part of the bargain, Yelverton's salesperson agreed that after the purchase price had been paid, Yelverton would continue to hold the furniture in storage until the Simmonses wanted to claim it or until Yelverton needed the warehouse space. Two years after the final payment had been made, the Simmonses attempted to pick up the furniture, only to discover that Yelverton had gone out of business and that the furniture was nowhere to be found. Discuss Yelverton's liability, assuming that there is no evidence that the loss of the furniture was due to lack of care on the part of Max's Discount Furniture. [*Simmons v. Yelverton,* 513 So.2d 504 (La.App. 2d Cir. 1987)]

50-9. K-2 Petroleum, Inc., and El Dorado Oil and Gas, Inc., were engaged in a joint-venture drilling project. They operated under an agreement whereby El Dorado provided a working electric generator for K-2's working interest in the well. The generator became nonfunctional, and K-2 sought to have El Dorado replace or repair it. El Dorado refused. K-2 subsequently contracted with Stewart & Stevenson Services, Inc., (S & S) for the repair of the generator. Shortly after receiving the generator for repair, S & S was notified by El Dorado that it was the true owner of the generator. El Dorado identified it by model and serial number and demanded its return upon completion of repairs. Because S & S knew of the common practice among oil field companies of switching, loaning, and borrowing equipment among themselves, it allowed El Dorado to take possession of the generator after El Dorado had paid for the repair. Before K-2 received any notice of S & S's delivery to El Dorado, K-2 and El Dorado terminated their joint venture and agreed that all salvageable equipment and supplies from the project were the property of K-2. K-2 later filed suit against S & S, claiming that S & S's failure to return the generator to K-2 and its delivery of the generator to El Dorado constituted the tort of conversion. Discuss K-2's claim. [*Stewart & Stevenson Services, Inc. v. Kratochvil,* 737 S.W.2d 65 (Tex.App.–San Antonio 1987)]

50-10. Several individuals placed personal property in a storage facility offered by the Winnebago County Fair Association, Inc. All who stored property in the building were required by the Winnebago County Fair Association to sign a storage agreement that included the following provision: "No liability exists for damage or loss to the stored equipment from the perils of fire." The storage building burned down, and all the property within was destroyed. A number of the people who had stored their property in the building brought suit against the fair association, claiming that the fire resulted from its negligence. Allstate Insurance Co., which had paid a number of claims for losses incurred due to the fire, joined the plaintiffs in the lawsuit. The Winnebago County Fair Association claimed that the excul-

patory clause in its contract relieved it from any and all liability. The issue before the court was whether the bailee (the fair association) could validly contract away *all* liability for fire damage. What was the result? [*Allstate Insurance Co. v. Winnebago County Fair Association, Inc.,* 131 Ill.App.3d 225, 475 N.E.2d 230, 86 Ill.Dec. 233 (1985)]

50-11. Wanda Perry, who had an account with Farmers Bank of Greenwood, wanted to rent a safe-deposit box from the bank. The boxes were available only to bank customers, and no rent was charged. When renting the box, Wanda was asked to sign a signature card that stated the following: "The undersigned customer holds the Farmers Bank harmless for loss of currency or coin left in the box." A little over four years later, the bank was burglarized, and most of the safe-deposit boxes were broken into. Wanda's box was among those burglarized, and she lost all the currency and coins contained therein. At trial, evidence showed that the bank had been negligent in failing to restore a burglar alarm system that had been inoperative for more than a week prior to, and including, the day the bank was burglarized. Wanda sued the bank to recover the currency and coins, alleging negligence on the part of the bank. Discuss fully whether the bank should be held liable for the loss. [*Farmers Bank of Greenwood v. Perry,* 301 Ark. 547, 787 S.W.2d 645 (1990)]

50-12. Case Briefing Assignment

 Examine Case A.24 [Strang v. Hollowell, *387 S.E.2d 664 (N.C.App. 1990)*] *in Appendix A. The case has been excerpted there in great detail. Review and then brief the case, making sure that you include answers to the following questions in your brief.*

1. Are there any facts in dispute in this case?
2. What was the only issue presented on appeal?
3. How was the bailment contract breached?
4. Why did the defendant, Hollowell, contend that he should not be held personally liable for the damages to the plaintiff's automobile?

Chapter 51

Real Property

From earliest times, property has provided a means for survival. Primitive peoples lived off the fruits of the land, eating the vegetation and wildlife. Later, as the wildlife was domesticated and the vegetation cultivated, property provided pasturage and farmland. In the twelfth and thirteenth centuries, the power of feudal lords was exemplified by the amount of land that they held; the more land they held, the more powerful they were. After the age of feudalism passed, property continued to be an indicator of family wealth and social position. In the Western World, the protection of an individual's right to his or her property has become one of the most important rights of citizenship.

In this chapter, we first look at the nature of ownership rights in real property. We then examine the legal requirements involved in the transfer of real property, including the kinds of rights that are transferred by various kinds of deeds; the procedures used in the sale of real estate; and a way in which real property can, under certain conditions, be transferred merely by possession.

It is important to realize that real property rights are never absolute, even for owners in fee simple absolute. There is a higher right—that of the government to take, for compensation, private land for public use. The concluding section in this chapter will discuss this right, called *eminent domain,* as well as zoning laws and other restrictions on the absolute ownership of property.

■ Ownership Interests in Real Property

Ownership of property is an abstract concept that cannot exist independently of the legal system. No one can actually possess or *hold* a piece of land, the air above, the earth below, and all the water contained on it. One can only possess *rights* in real property. Numerous rights are involved in real property ownership. As discussed in Chapter 49, one who holds the entire bundle of rights owns in *fee simple absolute.* A person holding property in fee simple is free to do with the property whatever he or she wishes. The owner can give the property away, sell the property for a price, or transfer the property by will to another. The owner can also transfer only certain of the rights that he or she holds to another, in which case the other party does not acquire absolute ownership or control over the property. We look below first at the fee simple absolute and then at the various types of limited property interests that can come into existence when an owner in fee simple absolute parts with some, but not all, of his or her rights in real property.

The Fee Simple Absolute

In feudal times, a *fee* (also called a *fief* or a *feud*) was an estate in land held from a feudal lord on the condition that the one holding the land remained loyal to, and performed services for, the lord. Similarly, the lords held their land subject to the king's ownership rights. The only true landowner, in the sense we think of land ownership today, was the king. The medieval ancestry of American property law is reflected in the legal terminology used today to describe certain types of property rights or interests.

In a **fee simple absolute,** the owner has the greatest aggregation of rights, privileges, and power possible. The fee simple absolute is limited absolutely to a person and his or her heirs and is assigned forever without limitation or condition. The rights that accompany a fee simple absolute include the right to use the land for whatever purpose the owner sees fit, subject to laws that prevent the owner from unreasonably interfering with another person's land and subject to applicable zoning laws.

A fee simple absolute is potentially infinite in duration and can be disposed of by deed or by will (by selling or giving away). When the owner of a fee simple absolute dies without a will, the fee simple passes to the owner's legal heirs. The owner of a fee simple absolute also has the rights of *exclusive* possession and use.

At early common law, a fee simple absolute could be conveyed to A only by the statement that the conveyance was "to A and his heirs." The words "and his heirs" denoted the fee simple absolute as infinite in duration and distinguished it from other estates, such as the *fee simple defeasible*. In the United States today, these so-called words of limitation have been eliminated, and a conveyance "to A" as well as "to A and his heirs" will convey a fee simple absolute.

The Fee Simple Defeasible

The term **fee simple defeasible** encompasses a number of estates that *almost* constitute absolute ownership. The word *defeasible* means something that can be avoided or annulled. In the context of property law, the term refers to an owner's ability to lose ownership of property, whether the loss is voluntary or involuntary. Generally, it may be said these are fee simple estates that are *conditionally* held—that is, the estates terminate or may terminate upon the occurrence of a specified condition or event.

A conveyance, for example, "to A and his heirs as long as the land is used for charitable purposes" creates a fee simple defeasible. In this type of conveyance, the original owner retains a *partial* ownership interest. As long as the specified condition occurs, A has full ownership rights. If the specified condition does not occur and the land ceases to be used for charitable purposes, however, then the land reverts, or returns, to the original owner. If the original owner is not living at the time, the land passes to his or her heirs. In other words, once the condition fails, A is divested of rights regardless of whether the original owner to (or through) whom the land reverts is alive.

The Life Estate

A **life estate** is a possessory (use) estate that lasts for the life of some specified individual. A conveyance "to A for his life" creates a life estate. A less common type of life estate is created by the conveyance "to A for the life of B." This is known as an estate *pur autre vie,* or an estate for the life of another.

In a life estate, the life tenant has fewer rights of ownership than the holder of a fee simple defeasible. The life tenant has the right to use the land provided no waste (injury to the land) is committed. In other words, the life tenant cannot injure the land in a manner that would adversely affect the owner of the future interest in it. The life tenant can use the land to harvest crops, or if mines and oil wells are already on the land, can extract minerals and oil from it. But the life tenant cannot further exploit the land by creating new wells or mines.

The life tenant has the right to mortgage the life estate and create liens, easements, and leases;

but none can extend beyond the life of the tenant. In addition, the owner of a life estate has the right to exclusive possession during his or her life. Exclusive possession, however, is subject to the rights of the future interest holder to come onto the land and protect the future interest.

Along with these rights, the life tenant also has some *duties*—to keep the property in good repair and to pay property taxes. In short, the owner of the life estate has the same rights as a fee simple owner except that the value of the property must be kept intact for the future interest holder (less the decrease in value resulting from normal use of the property allowed by the life tenancy).

Future Interests

When an owner in fee simple absolute conveys the estate conditionally to another (such as with a fee simple defeasible) or for a limited period of time (such as with a life estate), the original owner still retains an interest in the land. The owner retains the right to repossess ownership of the land if the conditions of the conveyance are not met or when the life of the life-estate holder ends. The residuary interest, or right, in the property that the owner retains is called a **future interest,** because if it arises, it will only arise in the future. An owner need not own property in fee simple absolute to retain a future interest in the property when some rights to the property are conveyed to another. An owner of a life estate, for example, would retain a future interest if the property were conveyed to another for a lesser period of time.

Future interests, or future estates, take different forms. Basically, however, future interests fall into two broad categories: (1) *reversionary* interests, which are created when the future interest is retained by the original owner or his or her heirs; and (2) *nonreversionary* interests, which are created when the future interest is held by someone other than the original owner or his or her heirs.

REVERSIONARY INTERESTS   If an owner in fee simple absolute conveys the estate to another in fee simple defeasible, the interest retained by the original owner is called a **possibility of reverter**—because if the conditions of the conveyance are not met, ownership of the estate will *revert* (be returned) to the original owner. Similarly, if an owner in fee simple conveys the estate to another as a life

estate, the interest retained by the original owner is called a **reversion.**

Suppose, for example, that Owen conveys Blackacres "to Ann and her heirs." It is clear that Owen now holds no future interest in Blackacres, because he has conveyed his entire estate to Ann as a fee simple absolute. If, in contrast, Owen conveys a fee simple defeasible (such as "to Ann and her heirs as long as the property is used for educational purposes"), Owen has retained a *possibility of reverter*. The conveyance of a fee simple defeasible that gives rise to a possibility of reverter usually includes the words "as long as," "until," "while," or "during."

Now suppose that Owen owns a fee simple estate and conveys a life estate in Blackacres to Ann. Owen has not disposed of the interest in the land remaining after Ann's life. Thus, Owen has automatically retained a *reversion* that will become possessory, upon Ann's death, in Owen or his heirs. Ann's life estate is an estate in possession (for she physically controls it), whereas Owen has a nonpossessory estate that will become possessory at some time in the future.

NONREVERSIONARY INTERESTS   Even though the original owner holds a future interest, this interest exists in the present in the sense that the owner can sell or otherwise transfer the future interest. When an owner sells or otherwise transfers the future interest, then the interest in the property held by the buyer or receiver is known as either a **remainder** or an **executory interest.** A remainder differs from an executory interest in that a remainder occurs *immediately* upon the *natural termination* of a preceding estate—such as a life estate. Executory interests, however, take effect either *before* or *after,* rather than immediately on, the natural termination of a preceding estate. For example, Papinian, an owner in fee simple, conveys land "to Paul for life and then to Johnson." Johnson's future interest takes the form of a remainder because when Paul dies, Johnson will have all remaining rights in the property. Now assume that Papinian conveys the property "to Paul for life and one year after Paul's death to Johnson." In this example, Paul is given a life estate, the property reverts to Papinian for one year, and then Johnson takes possession. Johnson's future interest is an executory interest because the interest will not become possessory immediately on Paul's death, but rather one year later.

A remainder must be created *in the same instrument* that creates the prior estate (simultaneous delivery of two deeds will satisfy this requirement). An executory interest does not have to be created simultaneously, but it usually is.

Nonpossessory Interests

Some interests in land do not include any rights of possession. These interests, known as nonpossessory interests, include easements, profits, and licenses. Because easements and profits are similar and the same rules apply to both, they will be discussed together.

EASEMENTS AND PROFITS   An **easement** is the right of a person to make limited use of another person's real property without taking anything from the property. An easement, for example, can be the right to walk across another's property. In contrast, a **profit** is the right to go onto land in possession of another and take away some part of the land itself or some product of the land. For example, Owen, the owner of Sandy View, gives Ann the right to go there and remove all the sand and gravel that she needs for her cement business. Ann has a profit. The difference between an easement and a profit is that an easement merely allows a person to use land without taking anything from it, whereas a profit allows a person to take something from the land. Easements and profits can be classified as either *appurtenant* or *in gross.*

Easement (or Profit) Appurtenant   An easement or profit appurtenant arises when the owner of one piece of land has a right to go onto (or remove things from) an adjacent piece of land owned by another. Suppose Owen, the owner of Whiteacres, has a right to drive his car across Green's land, Greenacres, which is adjacent to Whiteacres. This right-of-way over Greenacres is an easement appurtenant to Whiteacres and can be used only by the owner of Whiteacres. Owen can convey the easement when he conveys Whiteacres. Now imagine that the highway is on the other side of Black's property, Blackacres, which is on the other side of Greenacres. To reach the highway, Owen has an easement across both properties. Whiteacres and Blackacres are not adjacent, but Owen has an easement appurtenant nonetheless.

Easement (or Profit) in Gross   An easement or profit in gross exists when the right to use or take things from another's land is not dependent upon the owner of the easement or profit owning an adjacent tract of land. Suppose Owen owns a parcel of land with a marble quarry. Owen conveys to XYZ Corporation, which owns no land, the right to come onto his land and remove up to five hundred pounds of marble per day. XYZ Corporation owns a profit in gross. When a utility company is granted an easement to run its power lines across another's property, it obtains an easement in gross. An easement or profit in gross requires the existence of only one parcel of land, which must be owned by someone other than the owner of the easement or profit in gross.

Effect of Sale of Property   When a parcel of land that is *benefited* by an easement or profit appurtenant is sold, the property carries the easement or profit along with it. Thus, if Owen sells Whiteacres to Thomas and includes the appurtenant right-of-way across Greenacres in the deed to Thomas, Thomas will own both the property and the easement that benefits it.

When a parcel of land that has the *burden* of an easement or profit appurtenant is sold, the new owner must recognize its existence only if he or she knew or should have known of it or if it was recorded in the appropriate office of the county. Thus, if Owen records his easement across Greenacres in the appropriate county office before Green conveys the land, the new owner of Greenacres will have to allow Owen, or any subsequent owner of Whiteacres, to continue to use the path across Greenacres.

Creation of an Easement (or Profit)   Profits and easements can be created by *deed* or *will* or by *implication, necessity,* or *prescription.* Creation by *deed* or *will* simply involves the delivery of a deed or a disposition in a will by the owner of an easement stating that the grantee (the person receiving the profit or easement) is granted the rights in the easement or profit that the grantor had. An easement or profit, however, may be created by *implication* when the circumstances surrounding the division of a parcel of property imply its creation. If Barrow divides a parcel of land that has only one well for drinking water and conveys the half without a well to Dan, a profit by implication arises, because Dan needs drinking water. An easement may also be created by necessity. An easement by *necessity* does not require division of property for its existence. A person who rents an apartment, for example, has an easement by necessity in the private road leading up to it.

Easements and profits by *prescription* are created in much the same way as title to property is obtained by *adverse possession* (discussed later in this chapter). An easement arises by prescription when one person exercises an easement, such as a right-of-way, on another person's land without the landowner's consent, and the use is apparent and continues for a period of time equal to the applicable statute of limitations.

Termination of an Easement (or Profit) An easement or profit can be terminated or extinguished in several ways. The simplest way is to deed it back to the owner of the land that is burdened by it. Another way is to abandon it and create evidence of intent to relinquish the right to use it. Mere nonuse will not extinguish an easement or profit *unless it is accompanied by an intent to abandon*. Finally, when the owner of an easement or profit becomes the owner of the property burdened by it, then it is merged into the property.

LICENSES   A **license** is the revocable right of a person to come onto another person's land. It is a personal privilege that arises from the consent of the owner of the land and that can be revoked by the owner. A ticket to attend a movie at a theater is an example of a license. Assume that a Broadway theater owner issues to Ann a ticket to see a play. If Ann is refused entry into the theater because she is improperly dressed, she has no right to force her way into the theater. The ticket is only a revocable license, not a conveyance of an interest in property.

Leasehold Estates

A **leasehold estate** is created when a real property owner or lessor (landlord) agrees to convey the right to possess and use the property to a lessee (tenant) for a certain period of time. In every leasehold estate, the tenant has a *qualified* right to exclusive possession (qualified by the right of the landlord to enter upon the premises to assure that no waste is being committed). The tenant can use the land—for example, by harvesting crops—but

cannot injure the land by such activities as cutting down timber for sale or extracting oil. The respective rights and duties of the landlord and tenant that arise under a lease agreement will be discussed in greater detail in Chapter 52. Here we look at the types of leasehold estates, or tenancies, that can be created when real property is leased.

TENANCY FOR YEARS   A **tenancy for years** is created by an express contract (which can sometimes be oral) by which property is leased for a specified period of time, such as a month, a year, or a period of years. For example, signing a one-year lease to occupy an apartment creates a tenancy for years. At the end of the period specified in the lease, the lease ends (without notice), and possession of the apartment returns to the lessor. If the tenant dies during the period of the lease, the lease interest passes to the tenant's heirs as personal property. Often, leases include renewal or extension provisions.

PERIODIC TENANCY   A **periodic tenancy** is created by a lease that does not specify how long it is to last but does specify that rent is to be paid at certain intervals. This type of tenancy is automatically renewed for another rental period unless properly terminated. For example, a periodic tenancy is created by a lease that states, ''Rent is due on the tenth day of every month.'' This provision creates a tenancy from month to month. This type of tenancy can also be from week to week or from year to year. A periodic tenancy sometimes arises when a landlord allows a tenant under a tenancy for years to hold over and continue paying monthly or weekly rent.

At common law, to terminate a periodic tenancy, the landlord or tenant must give one period's notice to the other party. If the tenancy is month to month, one month's notice must be given. If the tenancy is week to week, one week's notice must be given. State statutes often require a different period for notice of termination in a periodic tenancy, however.

TENANCY AT WILL   Suppose a landlord rents an apartment to a tenant ''for as long as both agree.'' In such a case, the tenant receives a leasehold estate known as a **tenancy at will**. At common law, either party can terminate the tenancy without notice (that is, ''at will''). This type of estate usually arises when a tenant who has been under a tenancy for years retains possession after the termination date of that tenancy with the landlord's consent. Before the tenancy has been converted into a periodic tenancy (by the periodic payment of rent), it is a tenancy at will, terminable by either party without notice. Once the tenancy is treated as a periodic tenancy, a termination notice must conform to the one already discussed. The death of either party or the voluntary commission of waste by the tenant will terminate a tenancy at will.

TENANCY AT SUFFERANCE   The mere possession of land without right is called a **tenancy at sufferance.** It is not a true tenancy. A tenancy at sufferance is not an estate, because it is created by a tenant *wrongfully* retaining possession of property. Whenever a life estate, tenancy for years, periodic tenancy, or tenancy at will ends and the tenant continues to retain possession of the premises without the owner's permission, a tenancy at sufferance is created.

■ Transfer of Ownership

Ownership of real property can pass from one person to another in a number of ways. Ownership rights in real property are commonly transferred through a sale of the property or by will or inheritance. Real property ownership can also be transferred by gift, by possession, or (as will be discussed later in the chapter) by eminent domain. When ownership rights in real property are transferred, the type of interest being transferred and the conditions of the transfer normally are set forth in a *deed* executed by the one who is conveying the property.

Deeds

Possession and title to land are passed from person to person by means of a **deed**—the instrument of conveyance of real property. A deed is a writing signed by an owner of property by which title to it is transferred to another. Deeds must meet certain requirements.

Unlike a contract, a deed does not have to be supported by legally sufficient consideration. Gifts of real property are common, and they require deeds even though there is no consideration for the

gift. The necessary components of a valid deed are the following:

1. The names of the *grantor* (the giver or seller) and the *grantee* (the donee or buyer).
2. Words evidencing an intent to convey (for example, ''I hereby bargain, sell, grant, or give'').
3. A legally sufficient description of the land.
4. The grantor's (and usually the spouse's) signature.
5. Delivery of the deed.

TYPES OF DEEDS   Deeds may be classified according to the interests they convey and the consequent degree of protection they offer against defects of title. Four types of deeds are discussed below.

Warranty Deed   The **warranty deed** makes the greatest number of warranties and thus provides the most extensive protection against defects of title. A sample warranty deed is illustrated in Exhibit 51–1. In most states, special language is required to make a warranty deed. Thus, if a contract calls for ''a warranty deed'' without specifying the covenants to be included in the deed, or if a deed states that the seller is providing the ''usual covenants,'' most courts will infer from this language all of the following covenants (warranties) of title:

1. A **covenant of seisin**[1] and a **covenant of the right to convey** warrant that the seller has title and the power to convey the estate that the deed describes. The *covenant of seisin* specifically assures the buyer that the grantor has the property in the quantity and quality that the grantor purports to convey. For example, if Lawson, the owner of a life estate in Whiteacres, attempts to convey a fee simple to Capron, Lawson has breached the covenant of seisin. If Capron incurs damages because of Lawson's breach, then Capron is entitled to recover from Lawson.
2. A **covenant against encumbrances** guarantees that the property being sold or conveyed is not subject to any outstanding rights or interests that will diminish the value of the land, except as explicitly stated. Examples of common encumbrances include mortgages, liens, profits, easements, and private deed restrictions on the use of

---

1.   Pronounced *see*-zuhn.

■ CONCEPT SUMMARY 51.1
Ownership Interests in Real Property

Type of Interest or Ownership	Definitions
Fee Simple Absolute	The most complete form of real property ownership; owner holds all rights in the property and can transfer or sell them to another as he or she wishes. On the owner's death, the property can be transferred to the legal heirs by will or by inheritance laws.
Fee Simple Defeasible	Ownership is not absolute but conditional. The fee simple can be terminated if the condition fails—i.e., if a specified action or event occurs (or fails to occur).
Life Estate	A possessory or use ownership that lasts for the life of a specified individual, after which time ownership rights revert to the original owner or to a party designated by the original owner.
Future Interests	1. *Reversionary interests*—Residuary interests that are retained by the original owner when he or she conveys a lesser estate. 2. *Nonreversionary interests*—Residuary interests that are transferred by the owner to someone else when the future interest comes into existence. Remainders and executory interests are nonreversionary interests.
Nonpossessory Interests	1. *Easement*—The right of a person to make limited use of another person's property without taking anything from the property (e.g., a roadway or pathway across another's property). 2. *Profit*—The right of a person to go onto land in another's possession and remove some part of the land or products of the land. 3. *License*—The revocable right of a person to come onto another person's property (e.g., a ticket to attend a movie).
Leasehold Estates	1. *Tenancy for years*—Tenancy for a period of time stated by express contract. 2. *Periodic tenancy*—Tenancy for a period determined by frequency of rent payments. 3. *Tenancy at will*—Tenancy for as long as both parties agree; no notice of termination is required. 4. *Tenancy at sufferance*—Possession of real property without legal right.

land. Unless the deed expressly states that the conveyance is subject to a particular encumbrance, a covenant against encumbrances will be breached if the buyer discovers an undisclosed encumbrance. Again, as in the case of a covenant of seisin, the buyer is entitled to recover for any damage caused by the breach of this covenant.

3. A **covenant of quiet enjoyment** guarantees that the grantee or buyer will not be disturbed in his or her possession of the land by the grantor or any third persons. For example, suppose Janet Parker sells a two-acre lot and office building by warranty deed. Subsequently, a third person shows better title than Janet had and proceeds to evict the buyer. Here, the covenant of quiet enjoyment has been breached, and the buyer can recover the purchase price of the land plus any other damages incurred in being evicted.

■ Exhibit 51–1 A Sample Warranty Deed

Date: May 31, 1993

Grantor: GAYLORD A. JENTZ AND WIFE, JOANN H. JENTZ

Grantor's Mailing Address (including county):
    4106 North Loop Drive
    Austin, Travis County, Texas

Grantee: DAVID F. FRIEND AND WIFE, JOAN E. FRIEND AS JOINT TENANTS
    WITH RIGHT OF SURVIVORSHIP
Grantee's Mailing Address (including county):
    5929 Fuller Drive
    Austin, Travis County, Texas

Consideration:
For and in consideration of the sum of Ten and No/100 Dollars ($10.00) and other
valuable consideration to the undersigned paid by the grantees herein named, the
receipt of which is hereby acknowledged, and for which no lien is retained, either
express or implied.

Property (including any improvements):
Lot 23, Block "A", Northwest Hills, Green Acres Addition, Phase 4, Travis County,
Texas, according to the map or plat of record in volume 22, pages 331-336 of the
Plat Records of Travis County, Texas.

Reservations from and Exceptions to Conveyance and Warranty:

This conveyance with its warranty is expressly made subject to the following:

Easements and restrictions of record in Volume 7863, Page 53, Volume 8430,
Page 35, Volume 8133, Page 152 of the Real Property Records of Travis County,
Texas, Volume 22, Pages 335-339, of the Plat Records of Travis County, Texas;
and to any other restrictions and easements affecting said property which are
of record in Travis County, Texas.

Grantor, for the consideration and subject to the reservations from and exceptions to conveyance and warranty, grants, sells,
and conveys to Grantee the property, together with all and singular the rights and appurtenances thereto in any wise belonging, to
have and hold it to Grantee, Grantee's heirs, executors, administrators, successors, or assigns forever. Grantor binds Grantor
and Grantor's heirs, executors, administrators, and successors to warrant and forever defend all and singular the property to
Grantee and Grantee's heirs, executors, administrators, successors, and assigns against every person whomsoever lawfully
claiming or to claim the same or any part thereof, except as to the reservations from and exceptions to conveyance and warranty.

When the context requires, singular nouns and pronouns include the plural.

BY: _____
    Gaylord A. Jentz

BY: _____
    JoAnn H. Jentz

(Acknowledgment)

STATE OF TEXAS
COUNTY OF

    This instrument was acknowledged before me on the   31st day of May, 1993
by Gaylord A. and JoAnn H. Jentz

_____
Notary Public, State of Texas
Notary's name (printed): Rosemary Potter

                                          Notary's commission expires: 1/31/1996
Notary Seal

The following case raises the question of what exactly constitutes an encumbrance upon land and who has standing to sue for recovery when a covenant against encumbrances is breached.

Case 51.1

COMMONWEALTH LAND TITLE INSURANCE CO. v. STEPHENSON

Court of Appeals of North Carolina, 1991.
101 N.C.App. 379,
399 S.E.2d 380.

BACKGROUND AND FACTS   The Stephensons conveyed a parcel of land to Dennis O'Neal by way of a standard warranty deed in which the Stephensons transferred all privileges and appurtenances to O'Neal and covenanted that title was marketable and free and clear of all encumbrances. Unknown to the parties, the septic tank system servicing the house was located off the property, buried in the property of the adjoining landowner. O'Neal discovered this when he applied for a Veterans Administration (VA) loan to refinance his mortgage on the property. O'Neal ended up paying $1,400 to have the septic tank removed from the neighbor's property and to install another septic tank on his own property. As a result of the mislocation of the septic tank, the VA loan was not approved, and the refinancing did not take place. O'Neal filed a claim with Commonwealth Land Title Insurance Company, which paid him $3,000 to resolve the claim pursuant to the purchased title insurance. Subsequently, in a North Carolina state court, Commonwealth demanded reimbursement from the Stephensons on the ground that the Stephensons had breached their warranty against encumbrances, which was contained in their warranty deed to O'Neal. The trial court decided in favor of the Stephensons, and O'Neal and Commonwealth appealed.

DECISION AND RATIONALE   The Court of Appeals of North Carolina affirmed the trial court's decision, ruling that the location of a septic tank on adjoining property did not constitute an encumbrance against the fee conveyed by the general warranty deed. The court defined an encumbrance as "a claim, lien, charge, or liability attached to and binding real property." This includes as encumbrances such things as "judgment liens, mortgages, attachments, [and] covenants that run with the land"; each of these can provide the basis for a cause of action for breach of the covenant against encumbrances. Mislocation of a septic tank on a neighbor's property could not be characterized as an encumbrance on title. Because the neighbor's property, in which the septic tank was located, was not part of the land that the deed described or conveyed to O'Neal, he could not claim that title to that property—the neighbor's property—was encumbered.

Special Warranty Deed   In contrast to the warranty deed, the **special warranty deed** warrants only that the grantor or seller has not previously done anything to lessen the value of the real estate. If the special warranty deed discloses all liens or other encumbrances, the seller will not be liable to the buyer if a third person subsequently interferes with the buyer's ownership. If the third person's claim arises out of, or is related to, some act of the seller, however, the seller will be liable to the buyer for damages.

Both the special warranty deed and the warranty deed warrant that the seller has "marketable" title. Common defects that may render a title unmarketable include variations in the names of grantors and grantees, breaks in the chain of title, outstanding liens, and defectively executed deeds in the chain of title.

Quitclaim Deed   A **quitclaim deed** warrants less than any other deed. Essentially, it simply conveys to the grantee whatever interest the grantor had. In other words, if the grantor had nothing, then the grantee receives nothing. Naturally, if the grantor had a defective title, or no title at all, a conveyance by warranty deed or special warranty deed would not cure the defects. Such deeds, however, will give the buyer a cause of action to sue the seller. A quitclaim deed gives no cause of action unless the seller conveyed rights that would give rise to a cause of action.

A quitclaim deed can and often does serve as a release of the grantor's interest in a particular parcel of property. For instance, suppose Sandor owns a strip of waterfront property on which he wants to build condominiums. Lanz has an interest in a section of the property, which he might assert either to prevent the development or to insist on a share of its earnings. Sandor can negotiate with Lanz for a release of the claim. Lanz's signing of a quitclaim deed would constitute such a release.

Grant Deed　With a **grant deed,** the grantor simply states, ''I grant the property to you'' or ''I convey, or bargain and sell, the property to you.'' By state statute, grant deeds may carry with them an implied warranty that the grantor owns the property being transferred and has not previously encumbered it or conveyed it to someone else.

RECORDING STATUTES **Recording statutes** are in force in every jurisdiction. The purpose of these statutes is to provide prospective buyers with a way to check whether there have been earlier transactions creating interests or rights in specific parcels of real property. Hence, recording a deed gives constructive notice to the world that a certain person is now the owner of a particular parcel of real estate.[2] Placing everyone on notice as to the true owner is intended to prevent the previous owners from fraudulently conveying the land to a subsequent purchaser.

Properly notarized deeds are generally recorded in the county where the property is located. Many state statutes require that the grantor sign the deed in the presence of two attesting witnesses before it can be recorded. There are three basic types of recording statutes:

1. A *race statute* provides that the first purchaser to record a deed has superior rights to the property,

regardless of whether he or she knew that someone else had already bought it but had failed to record the deed.[3] Under these statutes, recording is a ''race,'' and whoever files first ''wins.''

2. A *pure notice statute* provides that, regardless of who files first, a person who knows that someone else has already bought the property cannot claim priority. In contrast, a subsequent good faith purchaser who, at the time he or she acquires a deed, has no notice of a previous deed—because, for example, it has not been recorded—may successfully assert a superior claim to the property. (A *good faith purchaser* is one who purchases for value, in good faith, and without notice.)

3. A *notice-race statute* protects a purchaser who does not know that someone else has already bought the property and who records his or her deed first.

Irrespective of the particular type of recording statute adopted by a state, recording a deed involves a fee. The grantee typically pays this fee, because he or she is the one who will be protected by recording the deed.

The Sale of Real Estate

Transfers of ownership interests in real property are frequently accomplished by means of a sale. The sale of real estate is similar to the sale of goods, because it involves a transfer of ownership, often with specific warranties. In the sale of real estate, however, certain formalities are observed that are not required in the sale of goods. For example, to meet the requirements of law, a deed must be signed and delivered.[4]

Several steps are involved in any sale of real property. The first step is the formation of the land sales contract. Then a title search (to verify that the seller has good title to the property and no other claims to the property exist) follows, along with, usually, negotiations to obtain financing for the purchase. The final step is the closing. We examine each of these steps below, as well as other require-

---

2.　In this situation, constructive notice operates to impute to a person knowledge of the ownership, regardless of whether the individual actually knows about it. This is because he or she is in a position that involves a duty to inquire; and proper diligence—for example, searching the public records—would reveal the fact of the ownership.

3.　Only two states use a race statute. Usage in the rest of the states is split about evenly between the pure notice statute and the notice-race statute.

4.　The phrase *signed, sealed, and delivered* once referred to the requirements for transferring title to real property by deed. The seal has fallen from use, but signature and delivery are still required.

ments relating to the sale of real property. First, however, we look at the important role of real estate agents, or brokers, in the sale of real property.

BROKERS Buyers and sellers of real property frequently enlist the services of a *real estate agent,* or broker. Real estate agents are information brokers. They provide buyers and sellers of real estate with information and specialize in matching the wants of buyers with the property being offered for sale by sellers.

Normally, the broker is retained by the seller and acts as the seller's agent in the sale of the property. In compensation for their services, brokers usually receive a commission (which can vary between 1 to 10 percent of the purchase price) from the seller when the sale is concluded. A broker can also act as an agent of the buyer, in which case a dual agency exists. Generally, a broker may not act as an agent for more than one party without the consent of all parties involved. Most states require real estate brokers to be licensed, and in some states, brokers may be required to meet continuing-education or other requirements.

A seller engages the services of a broker through a written *listing agreement.* In an *open* listing, the seller contracts for the services of more than one broker, and the first broker to produce a buyer receives the commission. In an *exclusive* listing, the seller contracts with just one broker, who receives the exclusive right to find a buyer and receive the commission from the seller. Under an exclusive listing agreement, the broker is entitled to a commission even if another broker sells the property.

THE SALES CONTRACT Generally, when someone decides to purchase real estate, he or she makes a written offer to purchase the property and puts up *earnest money* to show that an earnest, or serious, offer is being made. (If the offeror decides to withdraw the offer, the earnest money, or deposit binder money, will often be forfeited to the seller.) The offer states in some detail the exact offering price for the property and lists any other conditions that may be appropriate. The offer may be conditioned on the offeror's ability to obtain financing, for example. Within a specified time period, the seller of the property either accepts or rejects the offer. If the offer is accepted, then a contract of sale is drawn up. Usually, the signing of the sales

contract is accompanied by a deposit, which may be 10 percent of the purchase price paid to the seller. Usually, the buyer merely adds to the existing earnest money to bring it up to the desired amount.

Deposits toward the purchase price normally are held in a special account, called an **escrow account,** until all of the conditions of sale have been met and the closing takes place, at which time the money is transferred to the seller. The *escrow agent,* which may be a title company, bank, or special escrow company, acts as a neutral party in the sales transaction and facilitates the sale by allowing the buyer and seller to close the transaction without having to exchange documents and funds. An escrow agent is an agent of all of the parties involved in the sales transaction. When a conflict between the parties results in conflicting duties on the part of the agent, normally the agent will have a court resolve the conflict.

Sometimes, an arrangement is made in which a potential buyer is given the right to purchase property in the future, within a specified period of time and for a specific price. This is called an *option contract.* To be enforceable, the contract must be in writing, and consideration must be given to the seller. Essentially, payment to the seller compensates the seller for taking the property off the market until the end of the time specified in the option contract. Potential buyers may also obtain a *right of first refusal.* Frequently, those who lease property with the intention of possibly buying it in the future will have such a clause added to the lease contract. This right means that the lessee, or tenant, has first priority if the seller decides to sell the property. In other words, if the seller receives an offer from a third party, the seller cannot accept the offer until the tenant indicates that he or she does not intend to purchase the property.

TITLE EXAMINATION After the sales contract has been negotiated, the buyer or buyer's attorney (or the broker, escrow agent, title insurance company, or lending institution from which the purchase price is being borrowed) will begin the *title examination,* which entails examining at the county recording office the history of all past transfers of, liens on, and sales of the property in question. The title examiner will generally obtain an *abstract* from a private abstract company. This document lists all the records relating to a particular parcel of land. After reading the abstract, the examiner will give an opinion as to the validity of the title.

Title examinations are not foolproof, and buyers of real property generally purchase **title insurance** to protect their interests in the event that some defect in the title was not discovered during the examination. A title insurance policy insures against loss resulting from any defects in the title and guarantees that, if any defects do arise, the title company issuing the policy will defend the owner's interests and pay all legal expenses involved.

FINANCING Unless a buyer pays cash for the property, the buyer must obtain financing for the purchase with a mortgage loan. A **mortgage** loan is a loan made by a financial institution or trust company for which the property is given as security. In some states, the *mortgagor* (the borrower) holds title to the property; in others, the *mortgagee* (the lender) holds title until the loan is completely repaid. In several states, a trustee—a third party—holds title on behalf of the lender. The trustee then deeds the property back to the borrower when the loan is repaid. If the payments are not made, the trustee can deed the property to the lender or dispose of it by auction, depending on state law.

Types of Financing There are numerous ways of financing the purchase of real property, some of them quite creative. Here we look only at a few of the more commonly used methods. Frequently, financing is obtained through a conventional long-term mortgage loan in which the payment schedule extends over a period of twenty-five to thirty years. Traditionally, the interest rate for long-term loans was fixed—that is, the interest rate did not change over the period of the loan. Today, long-term loans often have variable rates of interest. In a variable-rate loan, the interest rate is pegged to a specified standard, such as the prime rate—the rate of interest offered by lending institutions to their most creditworthy customers—and adjusted at specified intervals, such as six months or a year.

In some situations, the seller may be willing to finance the purchase for a buyer. That is, the buyer will pay, say, 10 percent of the price as a down payment and make periodic (usually monthly) payments to the seller until the balance of the purchase price is paid. In other situations, a *wraparound mortgage* may be used. For example, suppose that a seller, Riedl, has an assumable mortgage (that is,

a mortgage that could be assumed by a purchaser of the property) with a below-market interest rate: a five-year-old $33,000, 9 percent loan now paid down to $31,631 with twenty-five years remaining on the repayment schedule. The monthly payment on the mortgage is $265.53. Riedl sells Benton the house for $70,000, and Benton makes a 20 percent down payment of $14,000. A lender (who could be the seller) gives Benton a wraparound mortgage in the amount of $56,000 at 11 percent for twenty-five years. Benton makes a monthly payment of $548.86 on the $56,000 loan. The lender in turn makes the $265.53 payment for Benton on the original loan, which Benton has assumed. The lender pockets the $283.33 difference. Because, in effect, the lender loaned Benton only $24,369 ($56,000 − $31,631), the lender's return is about 14 percent ($283.33 × 12 ÷ $24,369), not the 11 percent for the wraparound.

Mortgage Terminology Several terms used in mortgage transactions merit special mention and clarification. Obtaining a mortgage normally involves paying a fee to the lender in the form of *points.* A point is a charge of 1 percent on the amount of a loan. Therefore, if the lender's fee is two points and the amount of the loan is $80,000, the fee amounts to $1,600. This charge may be assessed against the buyer, the seller, or both.

If the mortgage terms allow for *prepayment privileges,* then the borrower can prepay the mortgage before the maturity date without penalty. Prepayment privileges may be especially important if market interest rates fall below the interest rate of the mortgage loan—in which case the loan could be refinanced to the advantage of the borrower.

An *amortization schedule* shows what portions of each monthly payment on a long-term loan, such as a mortgage loan, go to the interest and to the principal on the loan, respectively. In the first several years of the loan, the borrower pays primarily interest on the mortgage, so the amount owing on the principal of the loan declines very slowly. By the end of the payment schedule, the payments are mostly on the principal. An amortization schedule is usually given to the borrower by the lending institution; if not, the borrower can request one.

CLOSING The final step in the sale of real estate is the **closing**—also called settlement or closing escrow. The escrow agent coordinates the closing with the recording of deeds, the obtaining of title insurance, and other concurrent closing activities. Several costs must be paid, in cash, at the time of closing. These costs comprise fees for services, including those performed by the lender, escrow agent, and title company, and they can range from several hundred to several thousand dollars, depending on the amount of the mortgage loan and other conditions of sale. As discussed in Chapter 45 in the context of consumer protection, the Real Estate Settlement Procedures Act of 1976 requires lending institutions to notify—within a specified time period—each applicant for a mortgage loan of the specific costs that must be paid at the closing.

WARRANTY OF HABITABILITY The common law rule of *caveat emptor* (''let the buyer beware'') held that the seller of a home made no warranties with respect to its soundness or fitness unless such a warranty was specifically included in the deed or contract of sale. Although *caveat emptor* is still the rule of law in a minority of states, there is currently a strong trend against it and in favor of an **implied warranty of habitability.** Under this new approach, the courts hold that the seller of a new house warrants that it will be fit for human habitation regardless of whether any such warranty is included in the deed or contract of sale. This warranty is similar to the UCC's implied warranty of merchantability for sales of personal property. In recent years, some states, such as Virginia, have passed legislation creating such warranties for newly constructed residences.

Essentially, under an implied warranty of habitability, the seller warrants that the house is in reasonable working order and is of reasonably sound construction. To recover damages for breach of the implied warranty of habitability, the purchaser is required only to prove that the home he or she purchased was somehow defective and to prove the damages caused by the defect. Thus, under the warranty of habitability theory, the seller of a new home is in effect a guarantor of the home's fitness.

SELLER'S DUTY TO DISCLOSE Traditionally, under the rule of *caveat emptor,* a seller had no duty to disclose to the buyer defects in the property, even if the seller knew about the defects and the buyer had no reasonable way to discover them. Currently, in many jurisdictions, courts have placed on sellers a duty to disclose any known defect that materially affects the value of the property and that the buyer could not reasonably discover. Under these circumstances, nondisclosure is similar to representing that the defect does not exist, and the buyer may have grounds for a successful lawsuit based on fraud or misrepresentation.

For example, Nick sells Nora a five-year-old house that he knows has roof problems. Nick does not tell Nora about these problems. During the first rain after the sale, water gushes from the house's ceilings and light fixtures. Nora contacts a roofing contractor, who tells her that repair would be a temporary solution and that only a new roof would be watertight. Nora might sue Nick for breach of contract, fraud, and misrepresentation, seeking rescission of their contract and a return of whatever amount she paid Nick toward the purchase price of the house.

Transfer by Inheritance

Property that is transferred on an owner's death is passed either by will or by inheritance laws. If the owner of land dies with a will, that land passes according to the terms of the will. If the owner dies without a will, state statutes prescribe how and to whom the property will pass. The transfer of property by inheritance is the subject of Chapter 54.

Adverse Possession

Adverse possession is a means of obtaining title to land without delivery of a deed. Essentially, when one person possesses the property of another for a certain statutory period of time (three to thirty years, with ten years being most common), that person, called the adverse possessor, acquires title to the land and cannot be removed from it by the original owner. The adverse possessor is vested with a perfect title just as if there had been a conveyance by deed.

For property to be held adversely, four elements must be satisfied:

1.   Possession must be actual and exclusive; that is, the possessor must take sole physical occupancy of the property.
2.   The possession must be open, visible, and notorious, not secret or clandestine. The possessor must occupy the land for all the world to see.

3. Possession must be continuous and peaceable for the required period of time. This requirement means that the possessor must not be interrupted in the occupancy by the true owner or by the courts.
4. Possession must be hostile and adverse. In other words, the possessor must claim the property as against the whole world. He or she cannot be living on the property with the permission of the owner.

There are a number of public policy reasons for the adverse possession doctrine. These reasons include society's interest in resolving boundary disputes, in quieting (determining) title when title to property is in question, and in assuring that real property remains in the stream of commerce. More fundamentally, policies behind the doctrine include punishing owners who sit on their rights too long and rewarding possessors for putting land to productive use.

In the following case, the question before the court is whether a couple had obtained title to a certain portion of land by adverse possession.

Case 51.2

KLOS v. MOLENDA

Superior Court of Pennsylvania, 1986.
355 Pa.Super. 399,
513 A.2d 490.

BACKGROUND AND FACTS In September 1950, Michael and Albina Klos purchased part of some property owned by John and Anne Molenda. The Kloses' lot was 50 feet wide and 135 feet deep. Rather than surveying the property, the seller and buyer paced off the lot and placed stakes in the ground as boundary markers. The Kloses built a house on the lot in 1952 and put in a sidewalk along the full front. They also put in a driveway 30 inches from the stake line. They planted grass and a hedge in that 30 inches and maintained it until 1984. In 1983, Mr. Molenda died, and his widow hired a surveyor to inventory the landholdings. The survey located the rightful property line between the Molendas' and Kloses' land as being 30 inches closer to the Kloses' house than had been believed; this placed the property line right along the Kloses' driveway, instead of 30 inches to the side of the driveway. On learning of the surveyor's findings, Mrs. Molenda dug up the grass strip and the hedgerow and erected a fence right along the Kloses' driveway, marking the property line. The Kloses brought an action in a Pennsylvania state court, challenging Mrs. Molenda's conduct and claiming that they held title to the land by adverse possession. The trial court held that the Kloses had title to the land, and Mrs. Molenda appealed.

DECISION AND RATIONALE The Superior Court of Pennsylvania affirmed the decision of the trial court, ruling that the Kloses had acquired title to the land by adverse possession. The court rejected Mrs. Molenda's argument that the Kloses' possession of the land was sporadic rather than continuous and permissive rather than hostile or adverse. The court found the Kloses had maintained the land for over thirty years before the erection of the fence by Mrs. Molenda. Moreover, the court concluded that "[t]he hostile nature of the Klos possession was not destroyed because the stake line may have been placed along a property line mistakenly located by the adjoining landowners." The court concluded that the parties had implicitly agreed that the Kloses should have title to that land and that "[t]heir possession, open, notorious and exclusive for more than twenty-one years," satisfied the requirements for acquisition of title by adverse possession.

■ Limitations on the Rights of Property Owners

As mentioned earlier in this chapter, no ownership rights in real property can ever be absolute. That is, an owner of real property cannot always do whatever he or she wishes on or with the property. Nuisance and environmental laws, for example, restrict certain types of activities. Holding the property is also conditional on the payment of property taxes. If these taxes are not paid, ownership of the property will be forfeited to the state. In addition, if a property owner fails to pay debts, the property may be seized to satisfy judgment creditors. In a word, the rights of every property owner are subject to certain conditions and limitations. In this final section of the chapter, we look at some of the important ways in which owners' rights in real property may be limited.

Eminent Domain

Even if ownership in real property is in fee simple absolute, there is still a superior ownership that limits the fee simple absolute. Just as in medieval England, the king was the ultimate landowner, so in the United States, the government has an ultimate ownership right in all land. This right is known as **eminent domain,** and it is sometimes referred to as the condemnation power of the government to take land for public use. It gives a right to the government to acquire possession of real property in the manner directed by the Constitution and the laws of the state whenever the public interest requires it. Property may not be taken for private benefit, but only for public use.

For example, when a new public highway is to be built, the government must decide where to build it and how much land to condemn. The power of eminent domain is generally invoked through condemnation proceedings. After the government determines that a particular parcel of land is necessary for public use, it brings a judicial proceeding to obtain title to the land. Then, in another proceeding, the court determines the *fair value* of the land, which is usually approximately equal to its market value. Under the Fifth Amendment, private property may not be taken for public use without "just compensation."

Zoning

The state's power to control the use of land through legislation is derived from two sources: eminent domain and police power. Through eminent domain, the government can take land for public use, but it must pay just compensation. Consequently, eminent domain is an expensive method of land-use control. Under its police power, however, the state can pass laws aimed at protecting public health, safety, morals, and general welfare. These laws can affect owners' rights and uses of land

without the state's having to compensate the landowner. If, however, a state law restricts a landowner's property rights too much, the state's regulation will be deemed a *confiscation,* or a *taking,* and may be subject to the eminent domain requirement that just compensation be paid.

Suppose Perez owns a large tract of land, which she purchased with the intent to subdivide it and develop it into residential properties. At the time of the purchase, there were no zoning regulations restricting use of the land. If the government attempts to zone Perez's entire tract of land as "public parkland only" and thus to prohibit her from developing any part of it, the action will be deemed confiscatory; this is because the government will be denying her the ability to use her property for any reasonable income-producing or private purpose for which it is suited and because she had reasonable, investment-backed expectations in her development plans. The regulation normally will be held unconstitutional and void, or the government will have to compensate Perez, because it has effectively confiscated her land. Suppose, however, that the government zones Perez's parcel of land as "three-fourths residential, one-fourth park area" after her purchase. This zoning regulation is not confiscatory, because she will be able to use most of the property for building residences.

The state's power to regulate the use of land is limited in two other ways, both of which arise from the Fourteenth Amendment. First, the state cannot regulate the use of land arbitrarily or unreasonably, because this would be taking property without due process. There must be a *rational basis* for the classifications that the state imposes on property. Any act that is reasonably related to the health or general welfare of the public is deemed to have a rational basis.

Second, a state's regulation of land-use control cannot be discriminatory. A zoning ordinance is considered discriminatory if it affects one parcel of land in a way in which it does not affect surrounding parcels and if there is no rational basis for the difference. Placing a single parcel or a limited number of parcels in a classification that does not accord with a general zoning scheme or comprehensive plan (referred to as *spot zoning,* discussed below) is often held invalid on grounds of unreasonable discrimination.

Also, a zoning ordinance cannot be racially discriminatory. For example, a small community near a large metropolitan area may not zone itself so as to exclude all low-income housing if the effect is racial discrimination. If the community could prove that other tracts within its limits were suitable for integrated housing, the ordinance might be allowed to stand, however. Similarly, a zoning ordinance cannot prohibit churches or otherwise burden the exercise of religion, but a community can reasonably regulate the churches' location sites.

FLOATING ZONES   Generally, the state agency charged with the responsibility of land-use planning can take one of two approaches. The first is to designate, all at one time, use restrictions on each parcel of land located within the entire area to be zoned (usually a city or town). Alternatively, the agency can use "floating zones," deciding initially how much land should be designated for each of a variety of particular uses (commercial, residential, park, and farming) and later assigning such designations at the request of landowners. The floating zone concept allows for flexibility in zoning and reduces arbitrariness.

SPOT ZONING   One method that the agency charged with zoning an area may not use is **spot zoning.** Zoning ordinances are to apply to all property within the zone. Spot zoning occurs when an agency grants a parcel of land a classification different from the one it grants to surrounding property, if the difference between the classifications neither falls within the comprehensive zoning plan nor can be justified on the basis of health, safety, morals, or the community's general welfare. For example, spot zoning might involve granting an owner the right to construct a smelter in a residential neighborhood or limiting an owner to erecting a structure no higher than two stories when its neighbors are fifty-story skyscrapers.

VARIANCE   A landowner whose land has been limited by a zoning ordinance to a particular use cannot make an alternative use of the land unless he or she first obtains a zoning variance. A landowner must meet three criteria to be entitled to a variance:

1.   The landowner must find it impossible to realize a reasonable return on the land as zoned.
2.   The adverse effect of the zoning ordinance must be particular to the person seeking the variance and not one that has a similar effect on the other landowners within the same zone.
3.   A granting of the variance must not substantially alter the essential character of the zoned area.

By far the most important criterion used in granting a variance is whether it will substantially alter the character of the neighborhood. Courts tend to be rather lenient about the first two requirements. As the following case illustrates, courts also tend to defer to the discretion of zoning boards unless a board has abused its authority.

BACKGROUND AND FACTS   The city of Moline planned to build a new firehouse on land that was appropriately zoned for the construction of a firehouse. The proposed firehouse, however, was slightly larger than the zoning ordinances permitted. In April 1963, Moline filed applications with the Board of Zoning Adjustment of St. Louis County for variances from the setback and building line provisions in the ordinance. Alfred and Marie Conner, who owned property adjacent to the site of the new construction, objected to the variance. The variance was granted, and the Conners appealed the board's ruling to a Missouri state court. The trial court affirmed the action of the board, and the Conners appealed.

DECISION AND RATIONALE   The Court of Appeals of Missouri affirmed the judgment of the trial court, holding that the zoning board had enough evidence to grant the variance under the zoning ordinance. The court explained that the zoning board's primary function is to see that zoning ordinances are strictly followed, but, on occasion, due to changing community needs or simply to the irregular shape of a particular lot, the board

Case 51.3

CONNER v. HERD

Court of Appeals of Missouri, 1970.
452 S.W.2d 272.

must consider and weigh the propriety of granting a variance. The court pointed out that the board should grant a variance only if it has heard substantial evidence that the variance would not seriously affect any adjoining property or the general welfare of the community. "Neither this court nor the trial court can substitute its judgment on the evidence for that of the Board. We may only determine whether the Board could reach the conclusion it did upon the evidence before it. We hold it could. * * * The Board could find here that in the absence of a variance Moline would be confronted with substantial additional expense, interruption of fire protection service during the period of construction, and unnecessary inconvenience if not outright danger to the residents of the district."

Covenants Running with the Land

A **covenant running with the land** goes with the land and cannot be separated from it. A covenant runs with the land when the original parties *and* their successors, as opposed to the original parties alone, will be entitled to its benefit or burdened with its obligation. In other words, its benefit or obligation passes with the land's ownership.

Consider an example. Owen is the owner of Grasslands, a twenty-acre estate whose northern half contains a small reservoir. Owen wishes to convey the northern half to Arid City, but before he does, he digs an irrigation ditch connecting the reservoir with the lower ten acres, which he uses as farmland. When Owen conveys the northern ten acres to Arid City, he enters into an agreement with the city. The agreement, which is contained in the deed, states, "Arid City, its heirs and assigns, promises not to remove more than five thousand gallons of water per day from the Grasslands reservoir." Owen has created a *covenant running with the land* under which Arid City and all future owners of the northern ten acres of Grasslands are limited as to the amount of water they can draw from its reservoir.

The four requirements listed below must be met for a covenant running with the land to be enforceable. If they are not met, the covenant will apply to the two original parties to a contract only and will not run with the land to future owners.

1. The covenant running with the land must be created in a written agreement (covenant). It is usually contained in the document that conveys the land.

2. The parties must intend that the covenant *run with the land.* In other words, the instrument that contains the covenant must state not only that the promisor is bound by the terms of the covenant but that all the promisor's "successors, heirs, or assigns" will be bound.

3. The covenant must *touch and concern* the land. The limitations on the activities of the owner of the burdened land must have some connection with the land. For example, a purchaser of land cannot be bound by a covenant requiring him or her to drive only Ford pickups, because such a restriction has no relation to the land purchased.

4. The original parties to the covenant must be in *privity of estate* at the time the covenant is created. This requirement means that the relationship between them must be that of landlord and tenant, vendor and purchaser, or the like.

Equitable Servitudes

Because of the confusion over the meaning and application of the privity of estate requirement, covenants running with the land have not always been an effective device for guiding the development of residential and commercial land. Therefore, courts of equity have utilized an alternative means of private land-use control known as **equitable servitudes.** The most significant difference between covenants running with the land and equitable servitudes is that privity of estate is not required for enforcement of an equitable servitude.

An equitable servitude is created by an instrument that complies with the Statute of Frauds, an intention that the use of land be restricted, and *notice* of the restriction to the person acquiring the burdened land. The notice may be constructive.

For example, in the course of developing a fifty-lot suburban subdivision, Levitt records a declaration of restrictions that effectively limits construction on each lot to one single-family house. In each lot's deed is a reference to the declaration with a provision that the purchaser and his or her successors are bound to those restrictions. Thus, each purchaser assumes ownership with notice of the restrictions. If an owner attempts to build a duplex (or any structure that does not comply with the restrictions) on a lot, the other owners may obtain a court order enjoining the construction.

In fact, Levitt might simply have included the restrictions on the subdivision's map, filed the map in the appropriate public office, and included a reference to the map in each deed. In this way, each owner would also have been held to have constructive notice of the restrictions.

Equitable servitudes are usually upheld; however, equitable servitudes and covenants running with the land have sometimes been used to perpetuate neighborhood segregation, and in these cases they have been invalidated by the courts. In the United States Supreme Court case of *Shelley v. Kraemer*,[5] restrictive covenants proscribing resale to minority groups were declared unconstitutional and could no longer be enforced in courts of law. In addition, the Civil Rights Act of 1968 (also known as the Fair Housing Act) prohibits all discrimination based on race, color, religion, or national origin in the sale and leasing of housing.

In the following case, the court has to decide whether a restrictive covenant prohibiting any ''outside radio, television, Ham broadcasting, or other electronic antenna or aerial'' intended to prohibit satellite dishes, even though such dishes were not in use at the time the covenant was drafted.

---

5. 334 U.S. 1, 68 S.Ct. 836, 92 L.Ed. 1161 (1948).

BACKGROUND AND FACTS Claudia Churchill installed a satellite dish in the backyard of her residence, which was located in a residential subdivision called the Piedmont Subdivision. The Piedmont Subdivision was subject to a restrictive covenant that provided in part as follows: "No outside radio, television, Ham broadcasting, or other electronic antenna or aerial shall be erected or placed on any structure or on any lot. If used, any such antenna or aerial shall be placed in the attic of the house or in any other place in the house where it will be concealed from public view from any side of the house." Roy Breeling and a number of other homeowners in the subdivision filed an action in a Nebraska state court, asking that Churchill be required to remove the satellite dish. The trial court held that the covenant applied to the satellite dish, even though such dishes were not in use in the early 1970s when the covenant was drafted. The court therefore granted the homeowners' request and ordered Churchill to remove the dish from her property. Churchill appealed.

DECISION AND RATIONALE The Supreme Court of Nebraska upheld the decision of the trial court. The court stated that "[t]he restrictive covenants * * * read as a whole, not only specifically prohibit all outdoor antennas, they evidence a broad concern for aesthetics and prohibit many uses of the property within the subdivision which would detract from the appearance of the area as a whole." Based on the covenants' specific prohibition of certain types of electronic antenna, the court concluded that the covenants also prohibited the erection of satellite dishes.

Case 51.4

BREELING v. CHURCHILL

Supreme Court of Nebraska, 1988.
228 Neb. 596,
423 N.W.2d 469.

◼ Terms and Concepts

adverse possession **924**
closing **923**
covenant against
  encumbrances **917**

covenant of quiet
  enjoyment **918**
covenant of seisin **917**

covenant of the right to
  convey **917**
covenant running with the
  land **928**

■ For Review

1. What can a person who holds property in fee simple absolute do with the property? Can a person who holds property "for her life" do the same? If a person who holds property as long as the land is used for a certain purpose violates that restriction, what happens to the property?

2. What must a buyer prove to recover damages for a breach of the implied warranty of habitability? On what grounds might a buyer bring a suit against a seller who fails to reveal a known defect that materially affects the value of the property (and that the buyer could not reasonably discover)?

3. What are the requirements for acquiring property by adverse possession?

4. Tony's driveway runs the length of his property and connects to Mario's property. Mario has a right-of-way over the driveway, which is obviously Mario's only access to his property. Mario records his right-of-way in the county office. Mario sells his property to Olivia. Can Olivia use the driveway?

5. To avoid congestion on county highways and roads, the Diamond County Zoning Board wants to redesignate uses to which certain suburban property can be put. That is, the board wants to increase the size of housing lots, increase the amount of parkland, and dedicate more land to be used as a nature preserve and more land to be used to widen roads. What limits are there on the board's power?

■ Questions and Case Problems

51-1. Elkins owned a tract of land, but he was not sure that he had full title to the property. When Maves expressed an interest in buying the property, Elkins sold Maves the land and executed a quit-claim deed. Maves properly recorded the deed immediately. Several months later, Elkins learned that he had had full title to the tract of land. He then sold the land to Jones by warranty deed. Jones knew of the earlier purchase by Maves but took the deed anyway and later sued to have Maves evicted from the land. Jones claimed that because he had a warranty deed, his title to the land was better than that of Maves's quitclaim deed. Will Jones succeed in claiming title to the land? Explain.

51-2. Robert and Maria are neighbors. Robert's lot is extremely large, and his present and future use of it will not involve the entire area. Maria wants to build a single-car garage and driveway along the present lot boundary. Because of ordinances requiring buildings to be set back fifteen feet from an adjoining property line, and because of the placement of her existing structures, she cannot build the garage. Maria contracts to purchase ten feet of Robert's property along their boundary line for $3,000. Robert is willing to sell but will give Maria only a quitclaim deed, whereas Maria wants a warranty deed. Discuss the differences between these deeds as they would affect the rights of the parties if the title to this ten feet of land later proved to be defective.

51-3. Harold was a wanderer twenty-two years ago. It was at that time that he decided to settle down on a vacant three-acre piece of land, which he did not own. People in the area indicated to him that they had no idea who owned it. Harold built a house on the land, got married, and raised three children while living there. He fenced in the land; placed a gate with a sign, "Harold's Homestead," above it; and had trespassers removed. Harold is now confronted by Joe Moonfeld, who has a deed in his name as owner of the property. Moonfeld orders Harold and family off the property, claiming his title ownership. Discuss who has best "title" to the property.

51-4. Anthony is the owner of a lakeside house and lot. He deeds the house and lot to "my wife, Sylvia, for life, with remainder to my son, David, providing he graduates from college with a B or better average during Sylvia's lifetime." Discuss fully the following questions:

    (a) Does Anthony have any interest in the deeded lakeside house?

    (b) What is Sylvia's interest called?

    (c) What is David's interest called?

51-5. Murray owns 640 acres of rural land. A new highway is being built nearby by Ajax Corporation, Inc. Ajax purchases from Murray the rights to build and use a road across Murray's land. Construction vehicles will pass over the road and will remove sand and gravel required to build the highway. A deed is prepared and filed in the county by Ajax. Later, a dispute arises between Murray and Ajax, and Murray refuses Ajax the right to use the road or to remove sand and gravel. Ajax claims its property rights cannot be revoked by Murray. Discuss fully what property rights Ajax has in this matter.

51-6. In 1961, Mary Schaefers divided her real property and conveyed it to her children, William, Elfreda, Julienne, and Rosemary. The deed from Mary Schaefers to her daughter Rosemary contained the following language: "It is further mutually agreed by and between the grantor and the grantee that as part of the consideration set out above, the grantee agrees to provide a permanent home for my daughter, Elfreda, should she desire or request one, and for my son, William Schaefers, should he desire or request one. Failure to perform the above will be considered a material breach of the consideration set out herein." In 1974, Rosemary conveyed her portion of her mother's property to Edward and Arthur Apel. Subsequently, William Schaefers attempted to prevent the sale to the Apels from taking place by telling them that the house was encumbered by a covenant running with the land and that if they purchased the house, they would be bound to provide a home for William and Elfreda Schaefers. Is Rosemary's promise to provide a home for William and Elfreda (should they demand one) a covenant running with the land? Explain. [*Schaefers v. Apel,* 295 Ala. 277, 328 So.2d 274 (1976)]

51-7. In 1882, Moses Webster owned a parcel of land that extended down to the Atlantic Ocean. He conveyed the strip of the property fronting the ocean to another party. The deed included the following statement: "Reserve being had for said Moses Webster the right of way by land or water." The strip of property is now owned by Margaret Williams, and the portion retained by Webster now belongs to Thomas O'Neill. Williams is denying O'Neill access to the ocean. O'Neill has brought an action to establish his title to an easement over Williams's property. What should the court decide? Discuss fully. [*O'Neill v. Williams,* 527 A.2d 322 (Me. 1987)]

51-8. As the result of a survey in 1976, the Nolans discovered that their neighbor's garage extended more than a foot onto their property. As a result, Nolan requested that his neighbor, Naab, tear down the garage. The Naabs refused to do this, stating that the garage had been built in 1952 and was on the property when the Naabs purchased it in 1973. In West Virginia, there is a ten-year statute of limitations covering adverse possession of property. Were the Naabs able to claim title to the land on which the garage was situated by adverse possession? Explain. [*Naab v. Nolan,* 327 S.E.2d 151 (W.Va.1985)]

51-9. Paul and Barbara Sue Flanagan owned property in Alma, Arkansas, which was being purchased by the Smiths under an installment land contract. It was assumed by all owners of the property since 1946 that a fence located at the southern end of the property was in fact the southern boundary of the property. Over the years, all owners had maintained and generally exercised dominion over the property up to the fence. In 1985, when Jerry and Mildred Hicks purchased a lot bordering the southern side of the Flanagan property, a survey showed that the true boundary

was approximately eleven feet north of the existing fence. The Hicks asked the Smiths to remove the fence, but they refused to do so. The Hicks then brought an action to compel their neighbors to remove the fence. What will the court decide? Discuss fully. [*Hicks v. Flanagan,* 30 Ark.App. 53, 782 S.W.2d 587 (1990)]

51-10. A Question of Ethics

The Stanards have owned lakeshore property since 1963. In 1969, the Urbans purchased lakeshore property adjoining the Stanards' lot and used the property for a summer cabin from 1969 through 1974. In 1975, the Urbans converted the summer cabin into a year-round home and moved there permanently. Since 1969, the Urbans have used a grassy area of land—part of which belonged to the Stanards—up to a wooded area between the two houses. Between 1969 and 1988, the Urbans mowed the grassy area up to the woodsline and kept the weeds down, let their children and grandchildren play in the grassy area, and stored their boat dock on the grassy area each winter. In 1981, the Urbans constructed a white tin storage shed—mounted on a concrete slab—on the grassy area. Most of the shed was located on the Stanards' property. In 1988, the Stanards brought a lawsuit against the Urbans for trespass and sought removal of the white shed. The Urbans claimed that they acquired ownership of the property by adverse possession because they had used the property since 1969 (the state's statutory requirement for adverse possession was fifteen years). The Stanards claimed that the measurement of the statutory period should begin in 1981, when the permanent storage shed was constructed. Given these circumstances, consider the following questions. [Stanard v. Urban, *453 N.W.2d 733 (Minn.App. 1990)*]

1. Do you think that the Urbans' use of the Stanards' property *prior* to 1981 (when the shed was built) met the requirements for adverse possession? That is, was the use actual, open, hostile, continuous, and exclusive during those years? Or is this situation similar to many others in which there are no fences between neighboring lots and the respective owners and their families occasionally trespass on the others' property?

2. Would the fact that the Urbans, sometime between 1980 and 1982, offered to purchase the parcel of property in question from the Stanards affect your answer to the above question?

3. At what point should trespass on another's property constitute adverse possession? For example, if your neighbors customarily store their boat partially on your property, and you do not object, should this circumstance trigger a statutory period for adverse possession? What if your neighbors' children also customarily play on your side of the boundary line between your property and your neighbors' property?

4. Why do you think that state statutes permit people to acquire title to property by adverse possession? What public policy is reflected in these statutes?

Chapter 52

Landlord-Tenant Relationships

In the past century—and particularly in the past two decades—landlord-tenant relationships have become much more complex than they were before, as has the law governing them. Generally, the law has come to apply such contract doctrines as implied warranties, unconscionability, and so on to the landlord-tenant relationship. Increasingly, in recent years, landlord-tenant relationships have become subject to specific state and local statutes and ordinances as well. In 1972, in an effort to create more uniformity in the law governing landlord-tenant relationships, the National Conference of Commissioners on Uniform State Laws proposed the Uniform Residential Landlord and Tenant Act (URLTA).

■ Creation of the Landlord-Tenant Relationship: The Lease

When a landowner transfers temporary, exclusive possession of his or her property to another party in exchange for the payment of rent, a *landlord-tenant relationship* is created. The owner is the landlord, or **lessor;** the party assuming temporary possession is the tenant, or **lessee;** and their rental agreement is the **lease.** (For an explanation of the types of tenancies the parties may create, see Chapter 51.)

The *temporary* nature of possession, under a lease, is what distinguishes a tenant from a purchaser, who acquires title to the property. The *exclusivity* of possession distinguishes a tenant from a licensee, who acquires the temporary right to a *nonexclusive* use, such as sitting in a theater seat.

Leases may be oral or written. At common law, an oral lease is valid. As is the case with most oral agreements, however, a party who seeks to enforce an oral lease may have difficulty proving its existence. In most states, statutes mandate that leases be in writing for some tenancies (such as those exceeding one year).

The Lease Form

To create a landlord-tenant relationship, a document must do the following:

1. Express an intent to establish the relationship.
2. Provide for transfer of the property's possession to the tenant at the beginning of the term.

3. Provide for the landlord's *reversionary* (future) interest, which entitles the property owner to retake possession at the end of the term.

4. Describe the property—for example, give its street address.

5. Indicate the length of the term, the amount of the rent, and how and when it is to be paid.

In the drafting of commercial leases, sound business practice dictates that the leases be written carefully and that the parties' rights and obligations be clearly defined in the lease agreements.

Illegality

A property owner cannot legally discriminate against prospective tenants on the basis of race, color, religion, national origin, or sex. Similarly, a tenant cannot legally promise to do something counter to laws prohibiting discrimination. A tenant, for example, cannot legally promise to do business only with members of a particular race. The public policy underlying these prohibitions is to treat all people equally.

State or local law often dictates permissible lease terms. The URLTA, for example, prohibits the inclusion in a lease agreement of a clause under which the tenant agrees to pay the landlord's attorneys' fees in a suit to enforce the lease. Also, a statute or ordinance might prohibit leasing a structure that is in a certain physical condition or is not in compliance with local building codes.

Similarly, a statute may prohibit the leasing of property for a particular purpose. For example, a state law might prohibit gambling houses. Thus, if a landlord and tenant intend that the leased premises be used only to house an illegal betting operation, their lease is unenforceable.

Zoning ordinances present a special situation. Some courts have not invalidated leases made for purposes that violate zoning laws, when these ordinances provide for exceptions under certain circumstances. Sometimes, the courts reason that the parties drafted their lease with the understanding that the property would qualify for an exception to the zoning laws. When property is subject to zoning laws that may inhibit a tenant's intended use, the tenant should reserve an option to terminate the lease agreement if the intended use cannot be accomplished. Otherwise, of course, the tenant will be responsible for the performance of his or her obligation under the lease regardless of whether the intended use can be accomplished.

Unconscionability

The *unconscionability* concept is one of the most important of the contract doctrines applied to leases. Basically, as applied to leases in some jurisdictions (and under URLTA 1.303), the concept follows the provision of UCC 2-302. Under this provision, a court may declare an entire contract or any of its clauses unconscionable and thus illegal, depending on the circumstances surrounding the transaction and the parties' relative bargaining positions. For example, in a residential lease, a clause claiming to absolve a landlord from responsibility for interruptions in such essential services as central heating or air-conditioning will not shield a landlord from liability if the systems break down when they are needed the most.

■ Parties' Rights and Duties

At common law, the parties to a lease had relative freedom to include whatever terms they chose in the lease. Currently, the trend is to base the rights and duties of the parties on the principles of real estate law and contract law. These rights and duties generally pertain to the four broad areas of concern for landlords and tenants—the possession, use, maintenance and, of course, rent of the leased property.

Possession

Possession involves the obligation of the landlord to deliver possession to the tenant at the beginning of the lease term and the right of the tenant to obtain possession and retain it until the lease expires.

LANDLORD'S DUTY TO DELIVER POSSESSION A landlord is obligated to give a tenant possession of the property that the tenant has agreed to lease. The "English" rule, followed in many states, requires the landlord to provide actual *physical possession* to the tenant. If, for example, a previous tenant is still living on the premises on the date the new tenant is entitled to possession, the landlord must remove the previous tenant or breach the obligation to the new tenant.

The "American" rule, followed in other states, requires the landlord to transfer only the *legal right to possession.* Under this rule, the new tenant in the preceding example would have been responsible for removing the previous tenant, who no longer had the legal right to possession.

The URLTA follows the English rule and requires the landlord to provide the tenant with actual physical possession of the leased property, unless the parties agree otherwise.

TENANT'S RIGHT TO RETAIN POSSESSION
After obtaining possession, the tenant retains it exclusively until the lease expires, unless the lease provides otherwise or the tenant defaults under the terms of the lease. Most leases expressly give the landlord the right to come onto the property for the purpose of inspecting it, making necessary repairs, or showing the property to prospective purchasers or (toward the end of an expiring term) to possible future tenants.

COVENANT OF QUIET ENJOYMENT   Under the *covenant of quiet enjoyment,* the landlord promises that during the lease term neither the landlord nor anyone having a superior title to the property will disturb the tenant's use and enjoyment of the property. This covenant forms the essence of the landlord-tenant relationship. If the covenant is breached, the tenant can terminate the lease and sue for damages.

EVICTION   If the landlord deprives the tenant of the tenant's possession of the leased property or interferes with his or her use or enjoyment of it, an **eviction** occurs. This is the case, for example, when the landlord changes the lock and refuses to give the tenant a new key. A *partial eviction* occurs if the landlord deprives the tenant of the use of a part—one room, for example—of the leased premises. Assuming the tenant has a legal right to possession of the property, he or she may either sue for damages or possession, or consider the eviction a breach of condition and cease paying rent or terminate the lease.

Constructive Eviction **Constructive eviction** occurs when the landlord wrongfully performs, or fails to perform, any of the undertakings the lease requires, thereby making the tenant's further use and enjoyment of the property exceedingly difficult or impossible. To claim that a constructive eviction has occurred, the tenant must first notify the land-

lord of the interference. If the landlord fails to remedy the situation within a reasonable period of time, the tenant must then abandon the premises. On vacating the premises, the tenant's obligation to pay further rent ceases. As in cases of wrongful eviction generally, the tenant may sue to move back onto the property or terminate the lease and seek damages. Examples of constructive eviction include a landlord's failure to provide heat in the winter, light, or other essential utilities.

Retaliatory Eviction   When a landlord evicts a tenant for complaining to a government agency about the condition of leased premises, a **retaliatory eviction** occurs. Under some statutes, a retaliatory motive will be presumed if eviction proceedings are begun within a certain time after a tenant has complained. If a tenant can prove that a landlord's primary purpose in evicting or attempting to evict the tenant is retaliation for reporting violations—of a housing or sanitation code, for example—regardless of the time elapsed, the tenant may be entitled to stop the eviction proceedings or collect damages.

Using the Premises

If the parties do not limit the uses to which the property may be put, the tenant may make any use of it, so long as the use is legal and reasonably relates to the purpose for which the property is adapted or ordinarily used and does not injure the landlord's interest.

Also, the tenant is not entitled to create a *nuisance* by substantially interfering with others' quiet enjoyment of their property rights. To constitute a nuisance, conduct must be more than simply aggravating. For example, arguing with the neighbors may be annoying behavior, but it would probably not qualify as a nuisance, unless it took the form of harassment. Consistently playing drums in the middle of the night in an apartment complex, however, probably would constitute a nuisance.

TENANT'S DUTY NOT TO COMMIT WASTE
The tenant has no right to remove or otherwise damage leased property without the landlord's consent. The duty of a tenant not to damage the premises is a duty not to commit **waste,** which is the abuse or destructive use of property by one in rightful possession. For example, a tenant cannot knock

out an inside wall in a leased house to enlarge a living room or remove a fence or a grove of trees to accommodate grazing livestock unless he or she first obtains the landlord's permission to do so.

The tenant is responsible for all damage he or she causes, intentionally or negligently, and the tenant may be held liable for the cost of returning the property to the physical condition it was in at the lease's inception. Unless the parties have agreed otherwise, however, the tenant is not responsible for ordinary wear and tear and the property's consequent depreciation in value.

If, at some time during the lease term, the tenant decides to stop using the property but to continue paying the rent, the lease may require the tenant to give the landlord notice of the nonuse. There is a greater chance of vandalism, fire, or some other cause of damage to property when it is not being used, and the nonuse may affect insurance coverage.

ALTERING THE PREMISES   In most states, the tenant may make no alterations to the leased premises without the landlord's consent. In other jurisdictions, the tenant may make alterations, without being liable for the expense of their removal, if they were necessary for the tenant's use of the property and did not reduce its value. **Alterations** include improvements or changes that materially affect the condition of the property. Thus, for example, erecting additional structures probably would (and painting interior walls would not) be considered making alterations. Unless the parties have agreed otherwise, neither the landlord nor the tenant is required to make specific alterations or otherwise improve the property.

Once a residential tenant affixes an item of personal property—such as a storage cabinet—to real property, it becomes a *fixture* (see Chapter 49). In some jurisdictions, fixtures become the landlord's property and may not be removed at the end of the lease term. In other jurisdictions, fixtures can be removed at the end of the lease period if they can be taken without damage to the landlord's property.

Maintaining the Premises

At common law the landlord was under no duty to repair the leased premises or to warrant that they were habitable or suitable for the tenant's purposes. The tenant took the property "as is." Today, this common law rule has generally been replaced with statutes mandating a landowner's compliance with certain safety, health, and fire-protection standards. Also, in most states, statutes or judicial decisions impose a duty on a landlord who leases residential property to furnish premises that are *habitable*— that is, in a condition fit for human occupancy— and to make repairs not caused by the tenant's actions. Nevertheless, under a long-term commercial lease, a tenant may still assume the responsibility of making all necessary repairs, including, for example, rebuilding a structure after its destruction in a fire.

STATUTORY REQUIREMENTS   Usually, the landlord must comply with state statutes and city ordinances that delineate specific standards for the construction and maintenance of buildings. Typically, these codes contain structural requirements common to the construction, wiring, and plumbing of residential and commercial buildings. In some jurisdictions, landlords of residential property are required by statute to maintain the premises in good repair.

The landlord is also responsible for maintaining **common areas**—halls, stairways, elevators, and so on. This duty relates not only to defects of which the landlord has actual knowledge but to those that the landlord should reasonably know about. A landlord, for example, cannot avoid responsibility for repairing a dilapidated but little-used back stairway by asserting that he or she never used it and did not know it needed to be fixed.

OBLIGATIONS UNDER THE LEASE   In a long-term lease for the use of commercial property, the parties may choose to designate in the lease which of them has the responsibility to maintain the leased premises and to what extent. Generally, an express promise to repair is legally binding.

Under most circumstances, a residential tenant is not required to make such major repairs as replacing an old roof or laying a new foundation. And without a lease provision under which the tenant assumes a duty to maintain the leased property, the tenant is under no obligation to do so. Ordinarily, however, the tenant is liable for repairs required as a result of his or her intentional or negligent actions.

IMPLIED WARRANTY OF HABITABILITY   The *implied warranty of habitability* requires that a landlord who leases residential property furnish premises in a habitable condition—that is, in a condition that is safe and suitable for people to live in—at the beginning of a lease term and to maintain them in that condition for the lease's duration. Some state legislatures have enacted this warranty into law. In other jurisdictions, courts have based this warranty on the existence of a landlord's statutory duty to repair or simply have applied it as a matter of public policy.

Generally, this warranty applies to major—or *substantial*—physical defects that the landlord knows or should know about and has had a reasonable time to repair—for example, a big hole in the roof. In deciding whether a defect is sufficiently substantial to be in violation of the warranty, courts may consider the following factors:

1. Whether the tenant caused the defect or is otherwise responsible for it.
2. How long the defect has existed.
3. The age of the building, because a newer dwelling would be expected to have fewer problems.

4. The defect's impact—potential and real—on the tenant's health, safety, and activities such as sleeping and eating.
5. Whether the defect contravenes applicable housing, building, or sanitation statutes.

An unattractive or annoying feature, such as a crack in the wall, may be unpleasant, but unless the crack is a structural defect or affects the residence's heating capabilities, it is probably not sufficiently substantial to make the place uninhabitable.

In the following case, the Supreme Court of Missouri departs from its former rulings based on the common law doctrine of *caveat emptor* ("let the buyer beware") in regard to leased property. The court's reasons concerning why and when the implied warranty of habitability should apply are illustrative of the public policy considerations behind the warranty.

Case 52.1

DETLING v. EDELBROCK

Supreme Court of Missouri,
1984.
671 S.W.2d 265.

BACKGROUND AND FACTS Several tenants, including Dorothy Detling, sued their landlord, C. E. Edelbrock, in a Missouri state court for damages as a result of the landlord's breach of the implied warranty of habitability. The tenants asserted that the property they leased exhibited "material and substantial" violations of the local municipal housing code, including rodent and roach infestation, missing screens, exposed wiring, boiler malfunctions, rubbish strewn in passageways, water leakage, and unstable steps. Missouri courts did not universally recognize an implied warranty of habitability, however, and the lower court dismissed the petition for failure to state a cause of action. The tenants appealed the dismissal to the Supreme Court of Missouri.

DECISION AND RATIONALE The Supreme Court of Missouri reversed the lower court's dismissal of the tenants' petition and remanded the case for a trial on the merits, ruling that the common law rule of *caveat emptor* should no longer govern residential leases. Instead, the court held that a landlord impliedly "warrants that the dwelling is habitable and fit for living at the inception of the [lease] and that it will remain so during the entire term." The court added that "[h]abitability is to be measured by community standards, reflected in most cases in local housing and property maintenance codes."

REMEDIES FOR LANDLORD'S FAILURE TO MAINTAIN LEASED PROPERTY The tenant's remedies for the landlord's failure to maintain the leased premises vary with the circumstances and with state laws.

Withholding Rent   Rent withholding is a remedy that is generally associated with the landlord's breach of the warranty of habitability. When rent withholding is authorized under a statute (sometimes referred to as a "rent strike" statute), the tenant must usually put the amount withheld into an *escrow account.* This account is held in the name of the depositor (in this case, the tenant) and an *escrow agent* (in this case, usually the court or a government agency), and the funds are returnable to the depositor if the third person (in this case, the landlord) fails to fulfill the escrow condition.

Generally, the tenant may withhold an amount equal to the amount by which the defect rendering the premises unlivable reduces the property's rental value. How much that is may be determined in different ways, and the tenant who withholds more than is legally permissible is liable to the landlord for the excessive amount withheld.

In the following case, the tenant withheld rent because the landlord failed to maintain the premises in a habitable condition.

BACKGROUND AND FACTS   Paula Sheets rented residential premises from Betty Light in October 1988. In September 1989, Sheets notified Light that the plumbing was deficient and that mold was gradually destroying her belongings. Because Light failed to remedy the problem over the next several months, Sheets withheld the rent for January 1990, although she occupied the premises during that month. Light served Sheets with a notice of eviction and brought this action in an Oregon state court to recover the unpaid January rent. Sheets counterclaimed, alleging that Light had failed to maintain the dwelling in a habitable condition. Sheets sought damages and an injunction ordering Light to comply with statutory habitability requirements. The trial court, concluding that the plumbing problems reduced the monthly rental value of the premises by $60, awarded Sheets $240 in damages ($60 for each month from September 1989, when Sheets notified Light of the plumbing problems, through December 1989). Possession of the premises, however, was given to the landlord. Sheets appealed, seeking possession of the premises and contending that the trial court should also have awarded $60 for the month of January 1990.

DECISION AND RATIONALE   The Court of Appeals of Oregon reversed the trial court's decision and remanded the case, ruling that Sheets was entitled to possession of the premises, to $300 in damages for the diminished rental value of the premises, and to an award of attorneys' fees. The court stated, "A tenant is entitled to damages for the entire period during which the landlord fails to maintain the premises in a habitable condition after notice." Thus Sheets was entitled to receive a reduced rental rate for the month of January, because the repairs had still not been made, even though she had remained in possession. The $300 award completely offset the amount of rent owed for the month of January so that Sheets owed nothing at the time of trial. "Because no rent remained due *   *   *, 'judgment shall be entered for the tenant in the action for possession,' " which also entitled her—as the prevailing party—to recover attorneys' fees.

Case 52.2

LIGHT v. SHEETS
Court of Appeals of Oregon, 1991.
105 Or.App. 298,
804 P.2d 1197.

Repairing and Deducting   Under **repair-and-deduct statutes** or judicial recognition of a right to repair and deduct, the tenant pays for the repairs and deducts their cost from the rent. As in the case of rent withholding, this remedy is usually associated with the landlord's breach of the warranty of habitability.

Before a tenant can use this remedy, the problem—which in some states must concern a basic service, such as heat or water—must be the landlord's responsibility, and the landlord must be notified and fail to do anything about the problem within a reasonable time. Under some statutes, the deductible amount is restricted to a month's rent or some other fixed amount.

Canceling the Lease Terminating the lease is a remedy available to the tenant only when the landlord's failure to repair amounts to either constructive eviction or a breach of the warranty of habitability.

Suing for Damages Although a lawsuit for damages is always a possible course of action, it is not always economical. The amount a tenant can negotiate or be awarded may be based on the cost of a defect's repair or on the difference between the defective property's and the repaired property's rental values.

Rent

Rent is the tenant's payment to the landlord for the tenant's occupancy or use of the landlord's real property. Generally, the tenant must pay the rent even if he or she refuses to occupy the property or moves out, as long as the refusal or the move is unjustifiable and the lease is in force. Rent is payable according to an applicable statute, to custom, or to what the parties decide. The amount may be subject to a legislated ceiling—as in Berkeley, California, and New York City—or it may be as much or as little as the market will bear. Usually, rent is payable in advance or periodically throughout the lease term, but rent payable in crops may not be due until the end of a term.

Some states provide that the landlord must wait for as many as ten days after the rent's due date before initiating proceedings to terminate the lease for failure on the part of the tenant to pay rent. Notice may be required before a suit can be filed. Also, the landlord may impliedly waive the right to prompt payment if in the past he or she has accepted late payments.

SECURITY DEPOSITS At the lease's inception, the landlord may require a deposit to secure the tenant's obligation to fulfill the lease. If the tenant fails to pay the rent or damages the property, the landlord may retain the deposit.

Under the URLTA (for residential leases only), the amount of the deposit is limited to one month's

rent and must be returned—less any amounts owed for damages or unpaid rent—at the end of the lease term within fourteen days of the tenant's request for the return of the deposit. Some states permit larger deposits and longer periods before their return. Under the URLTA and some state laws, if the landlord withholds any amount from the deposit to cover damages, the tenant must be given an itemized list of the damages. In some states, the landlord must also pay interest on the deposit, less an appropriate sum as compensation for the effort involved in meeting this obligation. If the landlord fails to meet these requirements, the tenant may recover at least the amount due. In some states, the tenant may recover triple the amount due and attorneys' fees.

LATE CHARGES Legally, late charges can be imposed if a tenant does not pay rent when it is due. In general, the amount of a late charge may not be excessive, and it must bear some logical relation to the amount of the rent or to how long the payment has been overdue.

RENT ESCALATION Unless there is a clause in the lease providing otherwise, the amount of the rent cannot be increased during the lease term. If there is a clause allowing for the rent to be increased in the future—a **rent escalation** clause—the amount may be linked to the landlord's operating costs, indexed to increases in the cost of living, or subject to a real or anticipated increase in a commercial tenant's business activity.

PROPERTY TAXES In most jurisdictions, the tenant is not obligated to pay assessments and taxes on leased property. The responsibility of paying those charges may be transferred from the landlord to the tenant in the lease, however, or the lease may provide that the rent will be raised if the taxes increase. The tenant may be liable for the amount of the increase if the increase is due to improvements (such as the installation of trade fixtures in commercial premises) made by the tenant.

LANDLORD'S REMEDIES FOR TENANT'S FAILURE TO PAY RENT Under the common law and in many states, when a tenant vacates leased property unjustifiably (not as a result of constructive eviction or the landlord's breach of the warranty of habitability), the tenant remains obligated to pay the rent for the remainder of the lease term—however long that might be. The landlord may refuse to lease the premises to an acceptable new tenant and let the property stand vacant.

In a growing number of jurisdictions, however, the landlord is required to *mitigate* his or her damages—that is, the landlord is required to make a reasonable attempt to lease the property to another party. In those jurisdictions, the tenant's liability for unpaid rent is restricted to the period of time that it would reasonably take for the landlord to lease the property to another tenant. Damages may also be allowed for the landlord's costs in re-letting the property.

What is considered a reasonable period of time with respect to re-letting the property varies with the type of lease and the location of the leased premises. Under a long-term residential lease, for example, this period might be three months. In some jurisdictions, if reasonable—but unsuccessful—attempts are made to re-let, the tenant remains liable for the rent for the remainder of the lease.

Depending on the jurisdiction, if a tenant fails to pay rent or refuses to give up wrongful possession of leased property, the landlord can resort to one of three actions: a landlord's lien, a lawsuit, or recovery of possession.

Landlord's Lien   Under the common law, when a tenant did not pay the rent, the landlord could simply take and keep or sell whatever of the defaulting tenant's personal property was on the leased premises. Today, the landlord does not have this alternative unless the parties have contracted for it or it is permitted under a statute.

Among states that by statute preserve this remedy, known as a **landlord's lien,** some states grant the landlord a lien on all of the tenant's personal property but require the landlord to initiate court proceedings to exercise the lien. Typically, the court will authorize a sheriff to seize the tenant's property. Other states allow the landlord to seize specific items of the tenant's property and hold them as *security* for unpaid rent (that is, as protection or assurance that the landlord will recoup something on the tenant's obligation), but the landlord must obtain a court order to sell the property.

Lawsuit   Just as the landlord may sue the responsible tenant for damaging leased property, the landlord may also sue the defaulting tenant to collect unpaid rent.

Recovery of Possession   Under the common law, on the tenant's breach of the lease, the landlord could—with force, if necessary—evict the tenant and recover possession of the leased property without legal proceedings. Today, the landlord must use legal process, even if the parties have stipulated in the lease that the landlord has, and may exercise without legal proceedings, a **right of entry** (a right to retake possession peaceably).

There are two procedures to which the landlord may resort to evict the tenant. One is the common law remedy of **ejectment,** which requires the landlord to appear in court and show that the defaulting tenant is in wrongful possession. An action in ejectment does not take priority over other proceedings and, consequently, may be delayed for a long time. During the delay, the tenant can remain in possession. Thus, this action is used infrequently.

The remedy of ejectment has been modified under statutes that provide for a summary procedure often referred to as **unlawful detainer.** The landlord must show that the tenant is in breach of the lease or that the lease has expired and the tenant has not moved out. The court makes a decision quickly and, if the landlord prevails, orders a sheriff to remove the tenant.

■ Liability for Injuries on the Premises

Under the common law, whether a party in possession of property was liable to an individual who was injured on the property depended in part on that individual's classification as an invitee, a licensee, or a trespasser. An **invitee** is one whom the party in possession invites onto the premises for the possessing party's benefit, such as a customer. A **licensee** is one whom the party in possession invites or allows onto the premises for the licensee's benefit, such as a salesperson. A **trespasser** is one whom the party in possession does not invite and who has no other right to be on the premises. Each classification might require a different standard of care on the part of the person in possession of the property. Also, under certain circumstances, if the injured trespasser was a very young child who might be expected to be attracted onto the property, the **attractive nuisance**

doctrine could apply to require yet a different standard of care.

These distinctions have not been entirely done away with, but today liability is more likely to depend on who controls the area where the injury occurred, and the governing standard is one of **reasonable care** under all circumstances. Applying the standard of reasonable care requires taking into consideration the predictability of a particular event (that is, applying the principle of **foreseeable risk**). The person who has responsibility for a particular part of the premises must take the same precautions regarding the area's safety as would a person of ordinary prudence in the same circumstances. Essentially, this is the same standard of care that is applied in cases of negligence.

Landlord's Liability

Traditionally, when the landlord surrendered possession of his or her property to the tenant, the landlord also relinquished responsibility for injuries occurring on the property. This was true regardless of whether the injury was caused by a condition that existed at the time the property was leased or a condition that developed later. Today, however, in recognition of the policies underlying the warranty of habitability, the landlord bears greater responsibility for the conditions of the premises and for injuries resulting from those conditions.

Currently, the landlord is generally liable for injuries occurring on the part of the property within the landlord's control—that is, common areas such as basements, hallways, and elevators. Also, when the landlord assumes an obligation to repair, the landlord's liability may extend to injuries attributable to failure to make repairs or to negligently made repairs. Thus, the landlord may be responsible for injuries that occur on the part of the premises subject to the tenant's control—that is, the apartment, the house, or the store that the tenant leased from the landlord—when that responsibility is based on the landlord's duty to repair.

INJURIES CAUSED BY DEFECTS ON THE PREMISES   The landlord's liability extends to injuries resulting from a dangerous condition that the landlord knew about or should have known about, when the landlord fails to tell the tenant about it or actually conceals it. The landlord need not believe that the condition is unsafe; the situation need only be one that would lead a reasonable person to conclude that there is an unreasonable risk of harm. For example, the landlord may be liable if he or she knows that the mortar is very loose in a brick wall, and a brick subsequently falls and injures a tenant.

In most states, the landlord is not under a duty to inspect residential premises before leasing them, unless there is reason to suspect that a potentially harmful defect exists. Also, the landlord is under no obligation to tell the tenant about conditions that the tenant knows about when he or she signs the lease or that are obvious, such as a lumpy carpet in the hall.

COMMERCIAL PROPERTY   When property is leased for public purposes, including commercial activities, the landlord does have an obligation to inspect the property and make repairs before the tenant takes possession to prevent unreasonable risks to members of the public. This does not include obvious conditions, which people can be expected to avoid. The landlord's liability covers only that part of the leased premises that is open to the public. If, for example, a customer disregards a sign reading "Employees Only," goes through the door, and is somehow injured on the other side, the landlord may not be liable. Similarly, the landlord is normally not liable for the tenant's negligence in maintaining the premises, assuming they were in good condition when the tenant moved in.

The liability of a landlord of leased commercial property is at issue in the following case. Note the importance of the distinction between obvious and latent conditions in the court's determination of whether the landlord should be held liable.

Case 52.3

ALABAMA POWER CO. v. DUNAWAY

Supreme Court of Alabama, 1987.
502 So.2d 726.

BACKGROUND AND FACTS   Alabama Power Company (APCO) leased property to David Garner, who operated Real Island Marina. The land was located on the waterfront of Lake Martin in Alabama, and under the lease APCO had no duty to repair or maintain the land. Garner built a seawall without guardrails at the edge of the lake and a picnic pavilion thirty feet from the water. Garner did not designate any swimming areas, hired no lifeguards, and put up a sign—"Danger, swim at your own risk." David

Dunaway and his family, who had been to the marina before, camped near the water overnight. The next day, Dunaway took his sons swimming. Later, the family attended a picnic held at the pavilion by Dunaway's employer. Dunaway's son Daniel disappeared and a few minutes later was discovered floating in the lake. He had drowned. No direct evidence existed as to how the accident occurred. Mrs. Dunaway sued APCO, Real Island Marina, and the company that sponsored the picnic for the wrongful death of her son, claiming that the property was unsafe and that lifeguards and guardrails on the seawall by the lake should have been provided. At the trial, in an Alabama state court, APCO was the only defendant—Real Island Marina settled out of court, and summary judgment was granted to the employer. The court ruled in favor of Dunaway, and APCO appealed.

DECISION AND RATIONALE The Supreme Court of Alabama reversed the lower court's decision, holding that APCO, as landlord, was under no duty to warn the public of obvious hazards and thus was not liable for Daniel's death. The court stated that "as to the tenant, his servant, guest or others entering under his title, in the absence of a covenant to repair, the landlord is only liable for injuries resulting from latent defects, known to him at the time of the leasing, and which he concealed from the tenant." The court pointed out that Garner had built the pavilion, and if there was a defect in its proximity to the water, "it was obvious to any observer." Testimony showed that the Dunaways were aware of the pavilion's location and the absence of guardrails on the seawall. Similarly, noting that Garner had erected the sign, the court reasoned that because Garner's invitees could have discovered the lack of lifeguards by reasonable inspection, that lack was not a latent defect. The court concluded that because none of the defects were latent, it did not matter what APCO knew.

COMMON AREAS The landlord is responsible for—and liable for any injuries resulting from—the condition of common areas, as long as the areas are under his or her control. This responsibility includes a duty to inspect and repair such conditions as peeling lead-based paint, rotting stair railings, burned-out or dim lighting, and defective water heaters. It also includes a duty to otherwise correct such conditions as wet steps or a loose mat placed over the slippery surface of a polished floor.

When the landlord retains control over part of the premises leased to the tenant—for example, an apartment's walls—the landlord may be liable for injuries caused by that part's disrepair. The landlord is not, however, liable for injuries occurring on parts of his or her residential property where people could not be reasonably expected to go—for example, a roof or a closed basement.

REPAIRS In many jurisdictions, under building, housing, or sanitation codes or the warranty of habitability, the landlord is required to put or keep premises for lease in good repair. The breach of this duty may constitute negligence and establish the landlord's liability for any injuries caused thereby.

The landlord's express agreement to repair may be a basis for the landlord's liability if an injury is caused by the landlord's failure to fulfill the agreement. Ordinarily, the landlord has a reasonable time, after discovering or being told that a condition requires repair, within which to do the repair work or see that it is done. Regardless of whether the landlord has agreed to make repairs, once the landlord undertakes them, he or she is liable for injuries attributable to negligence in the repair work.

INJURIES CAUSED BY CRIMES OF THIRD PERSONS The landlord is not normally required to set up an elaborate security system to protect tenants from criminals. But when crimes are reasonably foreseeable and the landlord takes no steps to prevent them, he or she may be liable if an injury results.

Courts consider several factors in determining whether a crime is foreseeable and preventable. It is logical to assume that some prior criminal activity in the geographical area in which the property is located is required to make future crimes reasonably predictable. Similarly, it is reasonable to base an expectation of future crime on how recently the previous crime occurred. Court decisions have varied as to what constitutes "recently" (possibly less than six months) and "area" (perhaps several blocks, or perhaps no more than the leased property's parking lot or the building in which the leased premises are located).

Also, courts may consider the type of crime. For example, a series of thefts from automobiles in an apartment complex's parking garage may make subsequent apartment break-ins foreseeable, and a few assaults on tenants could indicate that steps should be taken before an assault escalates into rape. The automobile break-ins, however, would not necessarily make murder a foreseeable risk.

In the following case, the heir to a victim of a crime that occurred on leased premises brought suit against the lessors, the tenants, and the subtenants for the wrongful death of the victim, claiming that the defendants had failed to provide sufficient security in a common area. Whether the crime was a significant, foreseeable possibility is the major factor in the court's determination.

Case 52.4

IANNELLI v. POWERS

New York Supreme Court,
Appellate Division,
Second Department, 1986.
114 A.D.2d 104,
498 N.Y.S.2d 377.

BACKGROUND AND FACTS Victor Iannelli entered a commercial office building in downtown Manhattan to keep a business appointment on March 17, 1976. The appointment was with the New York Typographical Union #6. The labor union leased several floors of the building from the owner and sublet part of the leased premises to the Graphic Arts Federal Credit Union, whose president was Bertram Powers. On that morning, an employee of the credit union entered the building and was held up by several masked robbers. Iannelli was shot and killed when he chanced to encounter the robbers on their way out. Iannelli's heir sued the building's owners, the labor union, and the credit union in a New York state court for the wrongful death of Iannelli, alleging that they had been negligent in not providing better security—such as guards, alarms, and surveillance cameras. The heir claimed that the robbery was a foreseeable risk because the building was near a "bad neighborhood," and the credit union—a banking institution—was thus a likely target of crime. The trial court held that the defendants were liable, and they appealed.

DECISION AND RATIONALE The New York Supreme Court, Appellate Division, reversed the lower court's decision and held that the defendants were not liable for Iannelli's death. The appellate court recognized that a person in possession of realty has "an obligation to take minimal precautions to protect the public from the reasonably foreseeable criminal acts of third persons." The court explained that the possessor of realty is not an insurer of the safety of those who enter on such realty; to establish the existence of a duty on his or her part to take minimal protective measures, it must be shown "that he [or she] either knows or has reason to know from past experience 'that there is a likelihood of conduct on the part of third persons * * * which is likely to endanger the safety of the visitor.' " The court found little evidence of criminal conduct before the day of the shooting and concluded that the evidence did not establish that the defendants "could have reasonably foreseen the robbery and ensuing homicide, so as to give rise to a corresponding duty on their part to adopt security measures."

EXCULPATORY CLAUSES   A lease may contain a clause that claims to relieve the landlord from any liability for injuries or other damages, including those caused by the landlord's own negligence. Known as **exculpatory clauses,** these provisions are unenforceable if injury or damage results from the landlord's failure to fulfill a statutory duty, such as compliance with a state's building code. When included in a lease for residential property, an exculpatory clause releasing a landlord from liability for his or her negligence is unenforceable, in part because of the essential nature of housing.

Tenant's Liability

A tenant has a duty to maintain in a reasonably safe condition those areas under his or her control. When commercial property is involved, this duty extends to all parts of the premises onto which a customer or other member of the public might be expected to go—such as the aisles in a grocery store. The grocer's duty includes using care in displaying his or her wares so that they present no threat to customers' safety. For example, the goods should not be stacked so as to block an aisle or to fall onto a customer taking an item for purchase. Similarly, the grocer may be liable if a customer slips on the spilled contents of a broken jar and is injured.

In some situations—particularly when property is leased for commercial purposes—the tenant's duty may coincide with the landlord's duty, and thus both the landlord and the tenant may be liable for a third party's injuries. In the following case, for example, the plaintiff was injured in the parking lot of a shopping center when her shopping cart overturned. She had purchased the groceries in the cart from a grocer who had leased the premises from the owner of the shopping center. Although the landlord had agreed in the lease contract to maintain the parking lot, this provision did not relieve the tenant from liability for a customer's injury resulting from inadequate maintenance of the parking lot.

Case 52.5

WILSON v. ALLDAY
Supreme Court of Mississippi,
1986.
487 So.2d 793.

BACKGROUND AND FACTS   National Tea Company operated a grocery store inside a shopping center in Ocean Springs, Mississippi. National Tea leased the building from Chrisler Properties, the owner of the center and parking lot. The lease provided in part that "[t]he premises under this lease include the free use of properly paved, lighted * * * parking lot * * * for the parking * * * by Lessee, its customers, agents, and employees. * * * Said parking lot to be used in conjunction with other customers of Lessees in this development, if any, and Lessor agrees to maintain, light and remove snow from all parking area." James Allday was the manager of National Tea's grocery store. Romain Wilson bought some groceries at the store and carried them in a cart through the parking lot. The cart wheel hit a pothole in the pavement, and the cart overturned, pulling Wilson to the ground. Wilson severely injured her back in the fall and sued Allday and the grocery store in a Mississippi state court for damages. Wilson argued that National Tea exercised control over the parking lot, because the store had erected a cart corral there, its employees went onto the lot at least twelve times a day to gather the carts, and its customers were told to park in the lot in front of the store while employees were told to park in other areas of the lot. Wilson argued that the store was thus in a position to know of the dangers and had a duty to at least warn its invitees of them. The jury returned a verdict of $32,000 for Wilson. The judge entered an order for a judgment notwithstanding the verdict for Allday and National Tea. Wilson appealed.

DECISION AND RATIONALE   The Supreme Court of Mississippi reversed the trial court's judgment and entered a judgment for Wilson for $32,000. The state supreme court noted that under state law the "person in charge of premises owes to an invitee or business visitor a duty of exercising reasonable or ordinary care to keep the premises in reasonably safe or suitable condition or of warning invitee of dangerous conditions not readily apparent which [the person] knows or should know of." The court stated that this rule applies to a lessee in charge or in control of the premises, notwithstanding a maintenance agreement with the lessor. The court explained that the person in charge is not an insurer of an invitee's safety, however. If the invitee knows or should know of an apparent danger, no warning is required. The court pointed out that whether there was a known, obvious danger was a question for the jury to resolve. The court concluded that in this case, the jury decided that the store controlled the property and therefore owed a duty to Wilson.

■ Transferring Rights to Leased Property

Either the landlord or the tenant may wish to transfer his or her rights to the leased property during the term of the lease.

Transferring the Landlord's Interest

Just as any other real property owner can sell, give away, or otherwise transfer his or her real property (see Chapter 51), so can a landlord—who is, of course, the leased property's owner. Furthermore, the landlord may make a deal involving only the lease, only the landlord's reversionary interest in the property after the lease has been terminated, only the rent accruable under the lease, or any of these property rights in combination.

If complete title—that is, the landlord's reversionary interest—to the leased property is transferred, the tenant becomes the tenant of the new owner. The new owner may collect subsequent rent but must then abide by the terms of the existing lease agreement.

Transferring the Tenant's Interest

The tenant's transfer of his or her entire interest in the leased property to a third person is an **assignment** of the lease. The tenant's transfer of all or part of the premises for a period shorter than the lease term is a **sublease.** Under neither an assignment nor a sublease can the assignee's or sublessee's rights against the landlord be *more* than those of the original tenant.

ASSIGNMENTS   A controlling statute or a clause in the lease may require the landlord's consent to the tenant's assignment of his or her interest in the lease. If the statute or lease does not also require that consent not be unreasonably withheld, some courts will impose that condition. Typically, clauses that require the landlord's consent to assignment are written as forfeiture restraints—that is, they provide that the landlord may terminate the tenancy if the tenant attempts to assign the lease without consent. This restriction is meant to protect the landlord from an assignee-tenant who might damage the property, fail to pay the rent, or otherwise be irresponsible. The landlord's knowing acceptance of rent from an assignee, however, may constitute a waiver of the consent requirement.

When an assignment is valid, the assignee acquires all of the tenant's rights under the lease. But an assignment does not release the assigning tenant from the obligation to pay rent should the assignee default. Also, if the assignee exercises an option under the original lease to extend the term, the assigning tenant remains liable for the rent during the extension, unless the landlord agrees otherwise.

SUBLEASES   The restrictions that apply to an assignment of the tenant's interest in the leased premises apply to a sublease. For example, if the landlord's consent is required, a sublease without such permission is ineffective. Also, a sublease does not release the tenant from his or her obligations under the lease any more than an assignment does.

To illustrate: A student, Ann, leases an apartment for a two-year period. Ann has been planning to attend summer school, but she is offered a job in Europe for the summer months, and she accepts. To avoid paying three months' rent for an unoccupied apartment, she can sublease the apartment to another student, unless the lease requires the landlord's permission, in which case the landlord's consent will have to be obtained. The sublessee will take the apartment under the same lease terms as Ann. The landlord can hold Ann liable should the sublessee violate those terms.

■ Termination or Renewal of the Lease

Usually a lease terminates when its term ends. The tenant surrenders the property to the landlord, who retakes possession. If the lease does not contain an option for renewal and the parties have not agreed that the tenant may stay on, the tenant has no right to remain. If the lease is renewable and the tenant decides to exercise the option, the tenant must comply with any conditions requiring notice to the landlord of the tenant's decision.

Termination

In addition to the expiration of the lease term, a lease can be terminated in several other ways.

TERMINATION BY NOTICE   If the lease states the time it will end, the landlord is not required to give the tenant notice—that is, to remind the tenant the lease is going to expire—even as the time approaches. The lease terminates automatically. The lease may require that notice be given, however, or notice may be required under a statute. The procedures and time periods vary, but usually one or two months' notice is enough to end a tenancy for a year, and a week will suffice to end a tenancy for a shorter period.

On the other hand, a *periodic tenancy* will renew automatically unless one of the parties gives timely notice of termination. A periodic tenancy is a tenancy from week to week, month to month, or year to year. (Periodic tenancies are discussed in Chapter 51.)

RELEASE AND MERGER   A lease may give the tenant the opportunity to purchase the leased property during the term or at its end. Regardless of whether the lease provides this option, the landlord can convey his or her interest in the property to the tenant. This transfer is a **release,** and the tenant's interest in the property merges into the title to the property that he or she now holds. Of course, a release effectively relieves the tenant of his or her obligations under the lease while bestowing on him or her title to the property, as well as all of the

former landlord's responsibilities regarding the property. Because a release is a transfer of real property, it is subject to the Statute of Frauds (discussed in Chapter 14) and thus must be in writing.

SURRENDER BY AGREEMENT   The parties may agree to end a tenancy before it would otherwise terminate. If the lease was subject to the Statute of Frauds, surrender of the property by agreement must be in writing, because technically, the tenant is conveying his or her interest in the property to the landlord. Surrender of the property by operation of law, however, does not require a writing. A surrender by operation of law is sometimes held to occur when the tenant abandons the property.

ABANDONMENT   A landlord may treat a tenant's **abandonment** of the property—that is, the tenant's moving off the premises completely with no intention of returning—before the end of term as an offer of surrender, and the landlord's retaking of possession of the property will relieve the tenant of the obligation to pay rent. Sometimes, actions that the landlord takes to mitigate his or her damages—for example, refinishing an abandoned apartment's floors when preparing to lease it to another party—may be interpreted as accepting the tenant's offer of surrender, thereby absolving the tenant of responsibility for future rent payment.

FORFEITURE   The termination of a lease, according to its terms or the terms of a statute, when one of the parties fails to fulfill a condition under the lease and thereby breaches it, is called **forfeiture**. For instance, if the lease provides that the tenant will forfeit his or her interest in the leased property on failing to pay rent when it is due, the tenant's late payment of rent could prompt the lease's forfeiture. Generally, the courts do not favor forfeiture, and when neither the lease nor a statute provides for it, the landlord may only claim damages.

DESTRUCTION OF THE PROPERTY   Under statutes in most states, destruction of the leased property brought about by a fire, flood, or other cause beyond the landlord's control can terminate a residential lease. Usually, the landlord is under no obligation to restore the premises.

Similarly, the destruction of an entire building leased for business purposes may release the commercial tenant from any responsibility for continued payment of rent. (Terms vary among leases. If there is, for example, a fire, a commercial tenant's rent may only be reduced proportionally, according to how much property has been destroyed. The responsibility for restoring the property may rest on the tenant.)

Renewal

The lease may provide for renewal, or the landlord and the tenant may simply agree to renew it. When the lease provides for an option to renew, there is typically a requirement that the tenant notify the landlord within a specific period of time—usually days or months—before the lease expires as to whether the tenant will exercise the option. The tenant must comply with any particulars regarding the notice's form (for example, that it be in writing) or the renewal will be invalid, even if the tenant stays on the property. The tenant's attempt to alter other terms to which the renewal is subject can be interpreted as a choice not to exercise the option.

If a tenant neither renews a lease in accordance with its terms nor moves off the leased premises, but stays on without the landlord's consent, he or she can be treated as a trespasser. The tenant may be held liable to the landlord for damages.

■ Terms and Concepts

abandonment 945	foreseeable risk 940	rent escalation 938
alterations 935	forfeiture 945	repair-and-deduct
assignment 944	invitee 939	statutes 937
attractive nuisance	landlord's lien 939	retaliatory eviction 934
doctrine 939–940	lease 932	right of entry 939
common areas 935	lessee 932	sublease 944
constructive eviction 934	lessor 932	trespasser 939
ejectment 939	licensee 939	unlawful detainer 939
eviction 934	reasonable care 940	waste 934
exculpatory clauses 943	release 945	

■ For Review

1. What are a landlord's and a tenant's duties and rights concerning the *possession* of leased property? If the landlord fails to provide heat in the winter, what might the tenant do?

2. What are a landlord's and a tenant's duties and rights concerning *use and maintenance* of leased property? Is the tenant responsible for all damage that he or she causes, intentionally or negligently? What are a tenant's remedies if a landlord fails to maintain leased premises?

3. If a tenant vacates leased property unjustifiably, what limits are there on the tenant's obligation to pay rent? If a tenant remains on the premises but does not pay rent, what are the landlord's options?

4. Rosemary owns a Victorian-style apartment house. The building is decorated with plaster figures and other brass, iron, and marble ornamentation. A cupid figure falls from the wall in the lobby and injures Willard. What are the issues involved in determining liability for Willard's injury?

5. Gus rents an apartment to Stan. The lease contains a clause prohibiting an assignment without the landlord's consent. Stan assigns his interest in the lease to Cheryl. Gus accepts a rental payment from Cheryl. Can Gus now terminate the tenancy? If not, is Stan absolved of all responsibility under the lease?

■ Questions and Case Problems

52-1. Turner owns an apartment building. She contracts with Alvarez for one year to place coin-operated washing machines and dryers in laundry rooms in the building complex. The contract requires Alvarez to service the washers and dryers within twenty-four hours after notice is given that service is necessary. Some of the apartment leaseholders complain to Turner that Alvarez's service is poor and that Alvarez does not promptly refund money lost in the machines. After an argument, Turner orders Alvarez to remove all the machines within one week and not to come on the property again. Alvarez claims that he has a lease of the laundry rooms for one year. Turner claims that Alvarez has a revocable license (see Chapter 51). Discuss fully the property rights of the parties in this matter.

52-2. James owns a three-story building. He leases the ground floor to Juan's Mexican restaurant. The lease is to run for a five-year period and contains an express covenant of quiet enjoyment. One year later, James leases the top two stories to the Upbeat Club, a discotheque. The club's hours run from 5:00 P.M. to 11:00 P.M. The noise from the Upbeat Club is so loud that it is driving away customers from Juan's Mexican restaurant. Juan has notified the landlord of the interference and has called the police on a number of occasions. The landlord refuses to talk to the owners of the Upbeat Club or to do anything to remedy the situation. Juan abandons the premises. James files suit for breach of the lease agreement and for the rental payments still due under the lease. Juan claims that he was constructively evicted and has filed a countersuit for damages. Discuss who will be held liable.

52-3. Thomas has been a tenant of the Crestview Apartments for more than ten years. His tenancy is a month-to-month tenancy. During the ten years of his tenancy, the building's condition has steadily deteriorated. Indeed, the deterioration has reached the point at which the premises are in violation of city health and housing ordinances. Thomas has repeatedly complained to the landlord, but no repairs have been made. Thomas helps to organize a tenants' council, and the council reports numerous housing, building, and health violations to the authorities. The authorities bring actions against the landlord.

(a) Assume that immediately after the authorities bring their actions, Thomas is given notice of termination of his lease. Thomas wants to prevent his eviction. Discuss how successful he will be.

(b) Assume Thomas and the other tenants want to withhold rent payments until the premises are repaired. Discuss whether the tenants may withhold the rent payments and, if so, to what extent and on what grounds.

52-4. Sarah has rented a house from Franks. The house is only two years old. Sarah's roof leaks every time it rains. The water that has accumulated in the attic has caused plaster to fall off ceilings in the upstairs bedrooms, and one ceiling has started to sag. Sarah has complained to Franks and asked him to have the roof repaired. Franks says he caulked the roof, but the roof still leaks. Franks claims that because Sarah has sole control of the leased premises, she has the duty to repair the roof. Sarah insists that the repair of the roof is Franks's responsibility. Discuss fully who is responsible for repairing the roof and, if the responsibility belongs to Franks, what remedies are available to Sarah.

52-5. You are a student in college and plan to attend classes for nine months. You sign a twelve-month lease for an apartment and pay a security deposit of $150. Discuss fully each of the following situations:

(a) You have a summer job in your hometown and wish to assign the balance of your lease (three months) to a fellow student who will be attending summer school. Can you do so?

(b) You are graduating in May. The lease will have three months remaining. Can you terminate the lease without liability by giving a thirty-day notice to the landlord?

(c) The lease period has expired. Are you entitled to the return of your $150 security deposit?

52-6. Spirn, a shopping-mall tenant, sustained injuries when he fell while on the property of Joseph, the mall's owner. At the time of the injury, Spirn was on his way to a furnace room in the mall to check the furnace, which seemed to be malfunctioning. The furnace room was only accessible by an outside door, approximately twelve feet from the street. There was no paved walkway leading to the door, but a "trodden path" had been created in the snow by persons who had been called earlier by Joseph to repair the furnace. The repairpersons' footprints had made depressions in the snow, which had subsequently been iced over. Spirn slipped and injured himself. He filed suit against Joseph, alleging that the path was an unnatural (or aggravated natural) condition of the premises created by agents of Joseph and that Joseph had a duty to maintain safe premises. Joseph had therefore been negligent in failing to warn Spirn of the condition of the path. Discuss whether Spirn was successful. [*Spirn v. Joseph,* 144 Ill.App.3d 127, 493 N.E.2d 1197, 98 Ill.Dec. 176 (1986)]

52-7. Tachtronic Instruments, Inc., leased office and warehouse space in a building owned by Provident Mutual Life Insurance Co. The three-year lease ran until October 31, 1985, and specified monthly payments to Provident in the amount of $2,463. Within the first year of the lease term, Tachtronic defaulted on its payments. When Provident brought an action to evict Tachtronic, the small firm paid a portion of the rent due, and the action was dismissed. By February 1984, Tachtronic had largely vacated the premises. On March 1, 1984, Tachtronic met with representatives of Provident at the "leased" premises. The premises were inspected by Provident, and Tachtronic removed its remaining possessions, swept the floor with a broom, and turned over the keys to Provident. Immediately thereafter, Provident sought a new tenant for the premises. A new tenant was found, and a more lucrative lease beginning November 1, 1984, was created between Provident and the new tenant. In June 1984, Provident commenced an action to recover the rent due from Tachtronic prior to its departure from the leased premises and also the rent due and payable for the remainder of the lease. Discuss whether Provident could collect. [*Provident Mutual Life Insurance Co. v. Tachtronic Instruments, Inc.,* 394 N.W.2d 161 (Minn.App. 1986)]

52-8. Inwood North Professional Group—Phase I leased medical office space to Joseph Davidow, a physician. The terms of the five-year lease specified that Inwood would provide electricity, hot water, air-conditioning, janitorial and maintenance services, light fixtures, and security services. During his tenancy, Davidow encountered a number of problems. The roof leaked, and the air-conditioning did not function properly. The premises were not cleaned and maintained by Inwood as promised in the lease agreement, and as a consequence, rodents and pests infested the premises and trash littered the parking area. There was frequently no hot water, and at one point Davidow was without electricity for several days because Inwood had not paid the bill. About a year prior to the lease's expiration, Davidow moved to another office building and refused to pay the remaining rent due under the lease. Inwood sued for the unpaid rent. Must Davidow pay the remaining rent due under the lease? Discuss. [*Davidow v. Inwood North Professional Group—Phase I*, 747 S.W.2d 373 (Tex. 1988)]

52-9. MCM Ventures, II, Inc., leased premises from Rushing Construction Co. on which to operate a restaurant. The lease term was for two years, January 1, 1987, to December 31, 1988. The lease agreement stated in part that MCM "shall have a continuing option for a period of eight (8) consecutive years to renew this lease." Before the lease term expired on December 31, 1988, MCM did nothing to renew the lease and, after the lease expired, continued to make monthly rent payments in the same amount as before in January and February 1989. Then, on February 28, 1989, MCM notified Rushing by mail that it wanted to exercise its option to renew the lease. Rushing refused to renew the lease, contending that MCM had forfeited the option by not exercising it prior to the expiration of the lease agreement in which the option had been given. Discuss fully whether MCM still had a right to exercise the lease renewal option as late as February 28, 1989. [*Rushing Construction Co. v. MCM Ventures, II, Inc.*, 100 N.C.App. 259, 395 S.E.2d 130 (1990)]

52-10. A Question of Ethics

 C.S. lived in a rented apartment owned and operated by James Sophir. One night, while at her car in the parking lot provided for tenants, she was sexually assaulted by a male assailant. Evidence at trial showed that the person in charge of managing the apartment complex had knowledge of an earlier sexual assault occurring in the same area two months previously. C.S. brought an action against the landlord for damages, alleging that he had breached his duty to warn the female tenants about the danger of being sexually assaulted in the parking lot. Ultimately, the court held that the landlord had no duty to warn female tenants about the possibility of being sexually assaulted in the parking lot. [C.S. v. Sophir, 220 Neb. 51, 368 N.W.2d 444 (1985)]

1. The court held that a landlord should be liable for crimes on the premises only if there is a sufficient number of prior criminal acts on the premises to render a crime foreseeable. In the court's eyes, it would be unfair to impose a duty on the landlord based on a single prior assault at the complex. The court pointed out that no courts have ever imposed liability on a landlord based on a single prior criminal act perpetrated on a tenant. Do you agree that one prior criminal act is insufficient to create a foreseeable occurrence of a similar crime on the premises? Explain.

2. The court also pointed out that even if the landlord had warned the tenants of the danger, there was no guarantee that such a warning would have averted the crime. Do you think that this factor should be given any weight in deciding the issue of whether the landlord had a duty to warn?

3. The court further stated that a parking lot is a "known danger." That is, the ordinary, reasonable person should be aware that open parking lots provide an optimum place for crime to occur. Even if you agree with this conclusion, would the fact that a parking lot is a known danger relieve landlords at all times of any duty to warn tenants of possible criminal acts on the premises?

Focus on Ethics

Property

The legal structures that support our ideas about property are crucial to the continuation of the basically capitalist economic system in which we live and at times thrive. Private property is at the heart of pure capitalist ideology. That does not prevent ethical issues from arising over the control, sale, and use of private property.

Problems with New Forms of Personal Property

Most of our laws were written to deal with traditional, tangible forms of property, such as a car or a book. In the modern economy, however, intangible personal property is increasingly important. The protection of rights in intangible property raises new difficulties.

For example, a company may expend tremendous amounts of time and money in developing a new and improved software program. But a consumer, after buying one copy of the program, can duplicate the software innumerable times on new diskettes at very little expense. The company gets relatively little economic benefit from developing the software. As a consequence, the incentives for innovation in software development are diminished.

The consumer who copies software without permission is in a sense stealing the intangible personal property of the company. Yet many individuals do not even consider the ethics of copying intangible personal property. Even if this copying is deemed a civil or criminal wrong, the legal system can do little about it. Such small-scale and frequent theft could not be practicably prevented. We must depend largely upon the ethics of individuals in protecting property rights in many new forms of intangible property.

Defining Rights in Personal Property

Who owns what becomes a serious question many times. One of these times, for many people, is during divorce proceedings.

Who Owns That Degree?

Family law judges constantly have to decide which spouse is entitled to what assets after the dissolution of a marriage. In community property states, most property acquired after marriage is owned equally by each spouse. In virtually all other states, upon dissolution of the marriage, there is an "equitable" distribution of the household's property. The term *equitable,* of course, has no objective definition. And even if it did,

numerous questions still remain about what actually is an asset that is subject to division during a divorce proceeding. Is the value of a professional license, say, to practice psychotherapy, part of marital property to be divided? In a majority of states, no. But a few states, including California and New York, have held that professional licenses are marital property.[1] What about simply an academic degree earned during marriage by one party with the financial assistance of the other? Is such a degree to be considered distributable marital property? Yes again, said the Appellate Division of the New York Supreme Court in *McGowan v. McGowan.*[2] If, in contrast, the property is a teaching certificate that a spouse earned shortly after marriage, this would not be treated as marital property. Why not? Because the certificate was the result of the person's educational achievements completed prior to marriage.

Notice that the discussion of distributable marital property in these cases centers around something completely intangible. Personal property can be

---

1. See, for example, *O'Brien v. O'Brien,* 66 N.Y.2d 576, 489 N.E.2d 712, 498 N.Y.S.2d 743 (1985).
2. 142 A.D.2d 355, 535 N.Y.S.2d 990 (1988).

intangible; it does not have to be something that you can feel or even something that you are able to sell. After all, you cannot offer a professional license for sale, only your services as a licensed professional.

Who Owns Your Body Tissue?

Let us say that you are a patient in a research hospital because you have a rare disease. Do you own the rights to your body tissues that might be used by researchers to develop a cure for that rare disease? Such was the issue in *Moore v. Regents of the University of California.*[3] John Moore was a patient at the medical center of the University of California at Los Angeles. He was being treated for leukemia. His physician, Dr. David Golde, discovered that some of Moore's cells greatly overproduced a chemical that boosted his body's immune system.

Golde recommended surgery to reduce an enlarged spleen. He then used the spleen in his research. Golde and another researcher were able to grow a viable cell line that produced an anticancer compound. They patented the line in 1984 and contracted with two drug companies to develop an experimental drug. Upon learning this, Moore sued Golde, the other researcher, the university, and the two drug companies. In 1990, the California Supreme Court threw out Moore's complaint, holding that Moore could not sue for conversion because he did not have a property right in his body cells after they had been taken from his body.

The ethical question here, of course, is, at a minimum, whether Moore's doctor, Golde, had a duty to inform Moore about what he was doing. According to testimony, from 1976 through 1984, Moore continued to receive treatment from Golde, but Golde denied to Moore that he had discovered anything of value during his research on Moore's spleen cells.

Finder's Rights

The well-known children's adage "finders keepers, losers weepers" is actually written into law—provided that the loser (the rightful owner) cannot be found, that is. A finder may acquire good title to found personal property *against everyone except the true owner.* A number of landmark cases have made this principle clear. An early English case, *Armory v. Delamirie,*[4] is considered to be a landmark in Anglo-American jurisprudence concerning so-called actions in trover—an early form of recovery of damages for the conversion of property. The plaintiff in this case was Armory, a chimney sweep who found a jewel in its setting during the course of his work. He took the jewel to a goldsmith to have it appraised.

The goldsmith refused to return the jewel to Armory, claiming that Armory was not the rightful owner of the property. The court held that the finder, as prior possessor of the item, had rights to the jewel superior to all others except the rightful owner. The court said, "The finder of a jewel, though he does not by such finding acquire an absolute property or ownership, yet . . . has such a property as will enable him to keep it against all but the

rightful owner, and consequently maintain trover." The *Armory* case illustrates the doctrine of the *relativity of title.* Under this doctrine, if two contestants are before the court, neither of whom can claim absolute title to the property, the one who can claim prior possession will likely have established sufficient rights to the property to win the case.

A curious situation arises when goods wrongfully obtained by one person are in turn wrongfully obtained by another, and the two parties contest their rights to possession. In such a case, does the *Armory* rule still apply—that is, does the first (illegal) possessor have more rights in the property than the second (illegal) possessor?

In a case that came before the Minnesota Supreme Court in 1892, *Anderson v. Gouldberg,*[5] the court said yes. In the *Anderson* case, the plaintiffs had trespassed on another's land and wrongfully cut timber. The defendants later took the logs from the mill site, allegedly in the name of the owner of the property where the timber had been cut. The evidence at trial indicated that both parties had illegally acquired the property. The court instructed the jury that even if the plaintiffs were trespassers when they had cut the logs, they were entitled to recover them from later possessors—except the true owner or an agent of the true owner. The jury found for the plaintiffs, a decision affirmed later by the Minnesota Supreme Court. The latter court held that the plaintiffs' possession, "though wrongfully obtained," justified an action to repossess against another who took it from them.

3. 51 Cal.3d 120, 793 P.2d 479, 271 Cal.Rptr. 146 (1990).

4. 93 Eng.Rep. 664 (K.B. 1722).

5. 51 Minn. 294, 53 N.W. 636 (1892).

The Question of Land-Use Control

Legislation and regulation to control land use are prevalent throughout the United States. Often, such land-use control is undertaken in the name of "the public." But one must realize the consequences of such actions. Consider the effect of legislation altering property owners' rights in coastal sections of the United States. Suppose that prior to passage of the legislation, owners of land in coastal areas could use that land in any way they wanted. They could build condominiums, create golf courses, or do nothing. After the legislation goes into effect, a committee is formed that passes judgment on each requested change in the current use of the land. Suppose that a large amount of unaltered land is desired for coastal areas, even though that land is private property. If the committee routinely does not allow condominiums and housing developments to be built on the land, its market value will fall. Now we are entering into a taking issue, which is covered by the Fifth Amendment to the U.S. Constitution. Under this amendment, private property cannot be taken for public use without "just compensation." Government agencies maintain that land-use control does not involve a taking because the physical possession of the land remains in the hands of the private owner. From an economic point of view, however, a taking of potential income has occurred, because the net worth of the property owner subsequently falls when the land-use controls restrict the way in which the land can be used.

In recent years, cases have arisen concerning the passage of state laws that allow the public to come onto private beaches. For example, in Maine, firmly established rules of property law had long dictated that the owners of beachfront property held title to intertidal lands—the part of the beach that is submerged at high tide but not at low tide. That intertidal land was subject to an easement permitting public use only for fishing, fowling, and navigation and any other uses reasonably incidental or related to those activities. In 1986, however, the Public Trust and Intertidal Land Act was passed. This act gave the public the right to use, essentially without limitation, the intertidal land for recreation. Members of the public in unrestricted numbers were given the right to come onto this "private property" for boating, sunbathing, walking, ball games or other athletic events, camping, nighttime beach parties, and horseback riding.

One of the beachfront property owners decided to sue, claiming that the new law constituted an unconstitutional taking of private property without compensation and was therefore in violation of the Fifth Amendment. The court, when faced with this question, agreed with the property owner.[6] The court cited a similar case that arose in California and was decided in favor of the landowner.[7] In that case, the United States Supreme Court found that a permanent physical occupation occurs whenever the public is given a permanent and continuous right to pass to and fro on real property. Such permanent physical possession constitutes a taking.

The ethical considerations at issue here are whether the public's right to use the intertidal lands is superior to that of the property owner. Some contend that the public should have access to virtually all beaches because such beaches are a gift from nature. Here we are again faced with a tradeoff. To what extent should private property rights be given up for the benefit of the rest of society? Which weighs more heavily on the scales: maintaining the integrity of private property rights or ensuring public enjoyment of a natural resource—the beaches? Moreover, if private property owners are indeed required to allow their private property to benefit others, to what extent should the state compensate those private property owners?

The Question of Bailments

As indicated in the introduction to this unit, ethical issues arise with respect to the duty of care of the bailee. Both legal and ethical questions sometimes arise when one party claims a bailment existed and the other party disagrees. Take, for example, the common practice of hanging one's coat on a coatrack inside or outside a dining room, classroom, or hotel seminar room. In what circumstances does this action give rise to a bailment? This question arose when Timothy Augustine attended a seminar at a Marriott Hotel. Augustine was wearing a cashmere coat, which he placed on a rack outside the seminar room. At the noon recess, he discovered that the rack had been moved some distance down the lobby, to a position near an exit, and that his coat was missing. He sued

---

6. *Bell v. Town of Wells,* 557 A.2d 168 (Me. 1989).
7. *Nollan v. California Coastal Commission,* 483 U.S. 825, 107 S.Ct. 3141, 97 L.Ed.2d 677 (1987).

the hotel to recover the value of his coat. The court ruled against him, holding that a bailment never existed because there had been no delivery to the hotel, nor was the hotel ever in actual or constructive custody of the coat. Additionally, Augustine was not even a guest of the hotel. The court concluded that "a reasonable man would have wondered about the safety of his coat which he hung on a rack in a public lobby of a hotel, without ascertaining if there were a guard."[8]

An interesting question arises here: What if a sign had been placed above the coatrack that read, "Hotel not responsible for coats left here"? Would Augustine still have felt that the hotel had an ethical obligation to protect his personal property?

Landlord-Tenant Relationships

How much freedom should renters have? This question raises both legal and ethical issues. Numerous restraints are imposed on landlords by federal and state antidiscrimination laws, but sometimes these laws conflict with other constitutional rights, such as the freedom of religion.

This conflict arose in a Minnesota case, *Cooper v. French*.[9] Layle French owned a two-bedroom house in Marshall, Minnesota, which he put up for rent when he decided to move to the country. French advertised the house and agreed to rent it to Susan Parsons. He accepted a $250 check from her as a security deposit. French then realized that Parsons planned to share

the house with her fiancé, Wesley Jenson, and that the two would likely engage in sexual relations before they were married while inhabiting French's house. French, a member of the Evangelical Free Church, told Parsons that he had changed his mind because the living together of unmarried adults of the opposite sex violated his religious beliefs. Parsons sued French, alleging that French was in violation of the Minnesota Human Rights Act, which prohibited discrimination on the basis of marital status.

Minnesota's Department of Human Rights agreed with Parsons; so, too, did an administrative law judge, as well as an appellate court's panel of justices. The Supreme Court of Minnesota, however, did not agree. That court argued, among other things, that the landlord's right to exercise his religion under the Freedom of Conscience provision of the Minnesota constitution outweighed any interest of the tenant to cohabit with her fiancé in rented property prior to her marriage.

Two fundamental ethical principles—one promoting freedom from discrimination and the other promoting freedom of religion—had to be weighed against each other in this case. It is simply not possible to develop an objective rule to determine which principle should prevail in all cases.

■ Discussion Questions

1. Why are we willing to grant property rights in such intangibles as computer software programs but unwilling to grant property rights in ideas?
2. Should individuals have a

property right in their particular jobs? In other words, once a person obtains a job, should that person be given the right to continue working in that job, no matter what? How would such a right affect the doctrine of at-will employment?
3. Land-use control involves winners and losers. The losers are obviously those whose land is decreased in value because of a new rule, regulation, or law that eliminates some of the possible uses of that land. Who are the winners? Should the winners compensate the losers? What does it mean when it is said that land-use control is in the "best interests of society"?
4. What limits can be placed on a person's use of private property? Consider an owner of oceanfront property who wants to develop a resort. What if such development would threaten the habitat for an endangered species? Should the individual defer to species protection? Should government intervene to compel species protection?
5. Suppose that you own a wooded lot in an uninhabited wilderness in a distant state. You have not visited your lot for twenty-five years. One day, you decide that you would like to retire there. You go to the lot to start building a cabin. You discover that someone has "settled" on the lot and now has good title to the property as an "adverse possessor." Is it fair to you that this person received title to your land? What public policies or ethical principles are in conflict here? Should the adverse possessor at least be required to pay you the fair value of the land, or some portion thereof?

8. *Augustine v. Marriott Hotel,* 132 Misc.2d 180, 503 N.Y.S.2d 498 (1986).
9. 460 N.W.2d 2 (Minn. 1990).

UNIT TEN

Special Topics

■ Unit Contents

■ The Importance of This Unit

In the last unit, we discussed the law of property. The first two chapters in this unit—Chapter 53 on insurance and Chapter 54 on wills, trusts, and estates—are logical corollaries to that discussion. The ownership of property usually entails the need to insure that property. Ownership of property also often requires that arrangements be made for its orderly transfer on the death of the owner.

In the insurance area, we cannot stress too strongly the necessity of being familiar with the terms of each insurance contract that insures your personal property or that of your business. You might assume that your policy covers certain property when in fact it does not. For example, businesses operated in a home may not be covered by a homeowners' liability provision. You may only become fully aware of this when a client trips on your doorsill, breaks a leg, and then sues you.

The proper arrangements for the transfer of property upon death should be made when death is the furthest thing from one's mind. When proper arrangements have *not* been made, then property may be transferred according to law in a way that you, the owner, did not intend. In some instances, property may even revert to the state if there is no proper will and no heirs exist.

We treat the liability of accountants and other professionals in Chapter 55. This is an increasingly important area of the law because of the large number of successful lawsuits that have been brought against accountants for malpractice. Those going into accounting or other professions must understand their liability, and those who are in the business world must understand that liability, too.

Finally, because we live in an increasingly international economic community, the last chapter in this unit, Chapter 56, is devoted entirely to the international law. This topic was treated to a certain extent in Chapter 24, which concerned international sales contracts. In Chapter 56, we look at international transactions from a slightly different perspective, emphasizing in particular the legal environment within which international transactions take place.

■ Ethical Issues in This Unit

Each area of the law covered within the four chapters of this unit raises specific kinds of ethical problems. For example, with respect to insurance contracts, ethical issues often surround an insurer's attempt to avoid payment on a policy—particularly when the basis for avoiding payment is only a technical or trivial mistake made by the insured on the insurance application form? On the other side of the picture are those people who lie on their insurance applications. They are acting unethically and also illegally. Whatever the lie may be, in most circumstances an insurance company that does not discover the lie within two or three years cannot refuse to pay on the policy. The individual who "got away with" lying on the application did not suffer— but all other parties insured by that company's policies will face higher premiums as a result of such lying.

Ethical and legal issues in the area of wills can arise when a will is executed under the undue influence of another. It is difficult to prove undue influence; consequently, heirs may be deprived of their rightful inheritance because of the unethical actions of someone who was close to the deceased at the time the will was executed. Similarly, ethical and legal issues can arise when the mental competence of the testator—the one who made the will—is in question. In the area of accountants' liability, issues of fairness arise when accountants are held liable to third parties. Ethical issues in the international business arena frequently have to do with cultural and political differences between nations. For example, many other countries do not have such extensive consumer protection laws as does the United States. That means that U.S. business firms may export products that might be banned outright in the United States. The decision to distribute such products abroad turns on ethical considerations.

Chapter 53

Insurance

Insurance is a contract by which the insurance company (insurer) promises to pay a sum of money or give something of value to another (to either the insured or the beneficiary) in the event that the insured dies, is injured, or sustains damage as a result of particular, stated contingencies. Basically, insurance is an arrangement for *transferring and allocating risk.* In many cases, **risk** can be described as a prediction concerning potential loss based on known and unknown factors. Insurance, however, involves much more than a game of chance.

There are many precautions that may be taken to protect against the hazards of life. For example, an individual may wear a seat belt to guard against the risk of automobile accidents or install smoke detectors to guard against the risk of fire. Of course, no one can predict whether an accident or a fire will ever occur, but individuals and businesses must establish plans to protect their personal and financial interests should some event threaten to undermine their security. This concept is known as **risk management.** The most common method of risk management is the transfer of certain risks from the individual to the insurance company.

■ Insurance Concepts and Terminology

As with other areas of law, the area of insurance has its own special concepts and terminology, a knowledge of which is essential to an understanding of insurance law.

The Concept of Risk Pooling

All types of insurance companies use the principle of risk pooling; that is, they spread the risk among a large number of people—the pool—to make the premiums small compared with the coverage offered. Life insurance companies, for example, know that only a small proportion of the individuals in any particular age group will die in any one year. If a large percentage of this age group pays premiums to the company in exchange for a benefit payment in case of premature death, there will be a sufficient amount of money to pay the beneficiaries of the policyholders who die. Through the extensive correlation of data over a period of time, insurers can estimate fairly accurately the total amount they will have to pay if they insure a particular group, as well as the rates they will have to charge each member of the group so they can make the necessary payments and still show a profit.

Classifications of Insurance

Insurance is classified according to the nature of the risk involved. For example, fire insurance, casualty insurance, life insurance, and title insurance apply to different types of risk. Furthermore, policies of these types differ in the persons and interests that they protect. This is reasonable because the types of losses that are expected and the types that are foreseeable or unforeseeable vary with the nature of the activity. See Exhibit 53–1 for a list of various insurance classifications.

Insurance Terminology

An insurance contract is called a **policy;** the consideration paid to the insurer is called a **premium;** and the insurance company is sometimes called an **underwriter.** The *parties* to an insurance policy are the *insurer* (the insurance company) and the *insured* (the person covered by its provisions). Insurance contracts are usually obtained through an *agent,* who ordinarily works for the insurance company, or through a *broker,* who is ordinarily an independent contractor. When a broker deals with an applicant for insurance, the broker is, in effect, the *applicant's* agent. In contrast, an insurance agent is an agent of the insurance company, not an agent of the applicant. As a general rule, the insurance company is bound by the acts of its agents when they act within the scope of the agency relationship (see Chapters 35 and 36). In most situations, state law determines the status of all parties writing or obtaining insurance.

Insurable Interest

A person can insure anything in which he or she has an **insurable interest**—an interest either in a person's life or well-being or in property that is sufficiently substantial that insuring against injury to the person or damage to the property does not amount to a mere wagering (betting) contract.

LIFE INSURANCE In the case of life insurance, one must have a reasonable expectation of benefit from the continued life of another to have an insurable interest in that person's life. The benefit may be pecuniary (related to money), or it may be founded upon the relationship between the parties (by blood or affinity).

Close family relationships give a person an insurable interest in the life of another. Generally, blood or marital relationships fit this category. A husband can take out an insurance policy on his wife and vice versa; parents can take out life insurance policies on their children; brothers and sisters, on each other; and grandparents, on grandchildren—as all these are close family relationships.

Key-person insurance (sometimes referred to as business insurance) involves an organization's insuring the life of a person who is important to that organization. Because the organization expects to receive some pecuniary gain from the continuation of the key person's life or some financial loss from the key person's death, the organization has an insurable interest. Typically, a partnership will insure the life of each partner, because the death of any one partner will legally dissolve the firm and cause some degree of loss to the partnership. Similarly, a corporation has an insurable interest in the life expectancy of a key executive whose death would result in financial loss to the company.

The insurable interest in life insurance must exist *at the time the policy is obtained.* Because of this rule, in most states a divorce will not affect a policy. Similarly, under a key-person life insurance policy, it will not matter if the key person is no longer in the business's employ at the time of the loss—that is, the key person's death.

PROPERTY INSURANCE In the case of real and personal property, an insurable interest exists when the insured derives a pecuniary benefit from the preservation and continued existence of the property. That is, one has an insurable interest in property when one would sustain a pecuniary loss from its destruction. For example, a mortgagor and a mortgagee both have an insurable interest in the mortgaged property. So do a landlord and a tenant in leased property, a secured party in the property in which he or she has an interest, a partner in

■ **Exhibit 53–1 Insurance Classifications**

Type of Insurance	Coverage
Accident	Covers expenses, losses, and suffering incurred by the insured because of accidents causing physical injury and consequent disability; sometimes includes a specified payment to heirs of the insured if death results from an accident.
All-risk	Covers all losses that the insured may incur except those resulting from fraud on the part of the insured.
Automobile	May cover damage to automobiles resulting from specified hazards or occurrences (such as fire, vandalism, theft, or collision); normally provides protection against liability for personal injuries and property damage resulting from the operation of the vehicle.
Casualty	Protects against losses that may be incurred by the insured as a result of being held liable for personal injuries or property damage sustained by others.
Credit	Pays to a creditor the balance of a debt upon the disability, death, insolvency, or bankruptcy of the debtor; often offered by lending institutions.
Decreasing-term	Provides life insurance; requires uniform payments over the life (term) of the policy, but with a decreasing face value.
Employer's Liability	Insures employers against liability for injuries or losses sustained by employees during the course of their employment; covers claims not covered under workers' compensation insurance.
Fidelity or Guaranty	Provides indemnity against losses in trade or losses caused by the dishonesty of employees, the insolvency of debtors, or breaches of contract.
Fire	Covers losses caused to the insured as a result of fire.
Floater	Covers movable property, as long as the property is within the territorial boundaries specified in the contract.
Group	Provides individual life, medical, or disability insurance coverage but is obtainable through a group of persons, usually employees; the policy premium is paid either entirely by the employer or partially by the employer and partially by the employee.
Health	Covers expenses incurred by the insured resulting from physical injury or illness, as well as other expenses relating to health and life maintenance.
Homeowners'	Protects homeowners against some or all of the risks of loss to their residences and the residences' contents or liability related to such property.
Key-person	Protects a business in the event of the death or disability of a key employee.
Liability	Protects against liability imposed on the insured resulting from injuries to the person or property of another.
Life	Covers the death of the policyholder. Upon the death of the insured, an amount specified in the policy is paid by the insurer to the insured's beneficiary.
Major Medical	Protects the insured against major hospital, medical, or surgical expenses.
Malpractice	Protects professionals (doctors, lawyers, and others) against malpractice claims brought against them by their patients or clients; a form of liability insurance.
Marine	Covers movable property (ships, freight, or cargo) against certain perils or navigation risks during a specific voyage or time period.

■ **Exhibit 53–1 Insurance Classifications (Continued)**

Type of Insurance	Coverage
Mortgage	Covers a mortgage loan; the insurer pays the balance of the mortgage to the creditor upon the death or disability of the debtor.
No-fault Auto	Covers personal injury and (sometimes) property damage resulting from automobile accidents. The insured submits his or her claims to his or her own insurance company, regardless of who was at fault. A person may sue the party at fault or that party's insurer only in cases involving serious medical injury and consequent high medical costs. Governed by state ''no-fault'' statutes.
Term	Provides life insurance for a specified period of time (term) with no cash surrender value; usually renewable.
Title	Protects against any defects in title to real property and any losses incurred as a result of existing claims against or liens on the property at the time of purchase.

partnership property, and a stockholder in corporate property. But John or Jane Doe cannot obtain fire insurance on the White House or auto insurance on the Andrettis' racing cars.

The existence of an insurable interest is a primary concern in determining liability under an insurance policy. The insurable interest in property must exist *when the loss occurs*. In the following case, the insurance company claimed that the insured possessed no insurable interest in her former husband's house, because she had deeded her interest to him one year before his death.

Case 53.1

MOTORISTS MUTUAL INSURANCE CO. v. RICHMOND
Court of Appeals of Kentucky, 1984.
676 S.W.2d 478.

BACKGROUND AND FACTS Linda Richmond and Eddie Durham were married, the parents of two children, and homeowners in Kentucky. When Richmond and Durham divorced, Richmond deeded her legal interest in the title to their home to Durham and moved out with their children. Shortly thereafter, Durham died, leaving the two children as his only legal heirs. Richmond returned to the home with the children. She had been living there, making the mortgage payments, for more than one year when the home was totally destroyed by fire. Ten months before the fire, Richmond had secured fire insurance with Motorists Mutual Insurance Company. She sought payment from Motorists for the destruction of the house, but Motorists refused to pay, claiming that she had no insurable interest in the house. Richmond sued Motorists in a Kentucky state court. The trial court awarded Richmond, her children, and the mortgage company $29,000. Motorists appealed.

DECISION AND RATIONALE The Court of Appeals of Kentucky affirmed the trial court's judgment. Although Richmond held no legal title to the home, the court determined that she had an insurable interest in the residence for which Motorists was required to pay. Motorists characterized Richmond as a ''trespassing squatter'' who fraudulently represented her true lack of ownership interest. But the court found that she had made substantial monetary contributions to the maintenance and improvement of the house. Furthermore, as natural guardian, she was bound to care for her children, who owned the house in fee simple. Thus, she was not a trespasser and held an insurable interest in the residence. Moreover, Richmond had made no claim of ownership to the house. In fact, an agent of Motorists filled out the paperwork indicating Richmond's ownership. The agent could have easily checked on the title to the house. Because an insurer is bound by the acts of its agent within the scope of his or her apparent authority, Motorists bore the burden of any error in the nature of Richmond's insurable interest. Finally, the policy defined the "insured" to include "any person under 21 who is in the care of any person named above [Richmond]." Because both children were under the age of fifteen, the court had no trouble finding that "Motorists undertook exactly the risk it bargained for and should not now be able to successfully deny payment."

■ The Insurance Contract

An insurance contract is governed by the general principles of contract law, although the insurance industry is heavily regulated by each state. Policies generally are in standard form; and in some states, standardization of forms is required.

Application for Insurance

The filled-in application form for insurance is usually attached to the policy and made a part of the insurance contract. Thus, an insurance applicant is bound by any false statements that appear in the application (subject to certain exceptions). Because the insurance company evaluates the risk factors based on the information included in the insurance application, misstatements or misrepresentations can void a policy, especially if the insurance company can show that it would not have extended insurance if it had known the facts.

Effective Date

The effective date of an insurance contract is important. In some instances, the insurance applicant is not protected until a formal written policy is issued. In other situations, the applicant is protected between the time an application is received and the time the insurance company either accepts or rejects it. Four facts should be kept in mind:

1. A broker is merely the agent of an applicant. Therefore, if the broker fails to procure a policy, the applicant is not insured. According to general principles of agency law, if the broker fails to obtain policy coverage and the applicant is damaged as a result, then the broker is liable to the damaged applicant/principal for the loss.

2. A person who seeks insurance from an insurance company's agent will usually be protected from the moment the application is made, provided that some form of premium has been paid. Between the time the application is received and either rejected or accepted, the applicant is covered (possibly subject to certain conditions, such as passing a physical examination). Usually, the agent will write a memorandum, or **binder,** indicating that a policy is pending and stating its essential terms.

3. If the parties agree that the policy will be issued and delivered at a later time, the contract is not effective until the policy is issued and delivered or sent to the applicant, depending upon the agreement. Thus, any loss sustained between the time of application and the delivery of the policy is not covered.

4. Parties may agree that a life insurance policy will be binding at the time the insured pays the first premium, or the policy may be expressly contingent upon the applicant's passing a physical examination. (If the applicant pays the premium and passes the examination, then the policy coverage is continuously in effect.) If the applicant pays the premium but dies before having the physical examination, then, in order to collect, the applicant's estate must show that the applicant would have passed the examination had he or she not died.

Coverage on an insurance policy can begin when a binder is written; when the policy is issued; or, depending on the terms of the contract, after a certain period of time has elapsed. The following case illustrates the kinds of problems that can arise concerning the effective date of coverage of an insurance policy.

BACKGROUND AND FACTS   On October 22, 1981, the partnership of Davis and Landry, Inc., mailed two applications to Guaranty Income Life Insurance Company for $500,000 life insurance policies and a check for two years' advance premiums to insure the lives of the two principals, Davis and Landry. Davis and Landry believed that pending delivery of the policy they would receive $100,000 coverage under specific terms stated in a premium receipt. On October 27, 1981, Guaranty received the remainder of Davis's application package, a form entitled "Answers Made to the Medical Examiner," executed by a doctor. Based on the answers given in this form, Guaranty decided that it needed to obtain an "attending physician's statement" (APS) from the doctor. The request for the statement was mailed to the doctor on November 2, 1981, and had not been returned by November 10, 1981, when Davis died. The partnership sued Guaranty in a Louisiana state court to recover benefits under the insurance policy for Davis's death. The trial court granted a summary judgment for the insurance company, from which the partnership appealed.

DECISION AND RATIONALE   The Court of Appeal of Louisiana affirmed the lower court's grant of summary judgment for Guaranty. The appellate court held that "[a]n insurance company is under a duty to act upon an application for insurance within a reasonable time." What is a reasonable period depends on the facts in each case. Here, the court found that Guaranty breached no duty when it did not notify the partnership that the doctor had not returned Davis's APS. At most, the doctor held the APS for a week, a time period the court viewed as "simply not an unreasonable amount of time." Moreover, even if Guaranty did breach a duty to the partnership, there was no way for the partnership to show that the policy would have been issued immediately, because certain symptoms of Davis would have required a neurosurgeon's opinion. Because it could not be established how long the neurosurgeon's report would have taken, the partnership could not show that "but for" Guaranty's negligence the application would have been approved. The premium receipt allowed for limited coverage, after particular conditions had been fulfilled but before the policy had been delivered. One condition, however, mandated that Davis was acceptable "after" investigation. Because the investigation was ongoing at his death, Davis was not acceptable "after" the investigation, notwithstanding the fact that the report as eventually received would have established his acceptability. Furthermore, the policy required that the company "actually approve" the application for the limited coverage to be effective. Thus, because no policy had been issued, and the receipt coverage was not yet in effect because all the necessary conditions had not been fulfilled, the partnership was left with no coverage.

COMMENTS   This case illustrates the predicament of the "hopefully insured" waiting for the insurance application to be approved. The courts have granted insurance companies a "reasonable time" to act on an application. What is a "reasonable time" depends on the facts of each case. The premium receipt proved to be inadequate in protecting the plaintiff, so the plaintiff was left without any coverage.

Case 53.2

DAVIS AND LANDRY, INC. v. GUARANTY INCOME LIFE INSURANCE CO.

Court of Appeal of Louisiana, First Circuit, 1983.
442 So.2d 621.

Provisions and Clauses

Some of the important provisions and clauses contained in insurance contracts are defined and discussed in the following subsections.

PROVISIONS MANDATED BY STATUTE   If a statute mandates that a certain provision be included in insurance contracts, a court will deem that an insurance policy contains the provision regardless of whether the parties actually included it in the language of their contract. If a statute requires that any limitations regarding coverage be stated in the contract, a court will not allow an insurer to avoid liability for a claim through reliance on an unexpressed restriction.

INCONTESTABILITY CLAUSES Statutes commonly require that a life or health insurance policy provide that after the policy has been in force for a specified length of time—often two or three years—the insurer cannot contest statements made in the application. This is known as an *incontestability clause.* Once a policy becomes incontestable, the insurer cannot later avoid a claim on the basis of, for example, the insured's fraud, unless the clause provides an exception for that circumstance. The clause does not prohibit an insurer's refusal or reduction of payment for a claim due to nonpayment of premiums, failure to file proof of death within a certain period, or lack of an insurable interest.

COINSURANCE CLAUSES Often, when taking out fire insurance policies, property owners insure their property for less than full value. Part of the reason for this is that most fires do not result in a total loss. To encourage owners to insure their property for an amount as close to full value as possible, a standard provision of fire insurance policies is a *coinsurance clause.* Typically, a coinsurance clause provides that if the owner insures the property up to a specified percentage—usually 80 percent—of its value, he or she will recover any loss up to the face amount of the policy. If the insurance is for less than the fixed percentage, the owner is responsible for a proportionate share of the loss. Coinsurance applies only in instances of partial loss. For example, if the owner of property valued at $100,000 took out a policy in the amount of $40,000 and suffered a loss of $30,000, the recovery would be $15,000. The formula for calculating the recovery amount is as follows:

$$\frac{\text{Amount of insurance}\ (\$40{,}000)}{\text{Coinsurance percent}\ (80\%) \times \text{property value}\ (\$100{,}000)} = \begin{matrix}\text{recovery} \\ \text{percent} \\ (50\%)\end{matrix}$$

Recovery percent (50%) × amount of loss ($30,000) = recovery amount ($15,000)

If the owner had taken out a policy in the amount of $80,000, then, according to the same formula, the full loss would have been recovered.

APPRAISAL AND ARBITRATION CLAUSES Most fire insurance policies provide that if the parties cannot agree on the amount of a loss covered under the policy or the value of the property lost, an *appraisal* can be demanded. An appraisal is an estimate of the property's value determined by suitably qualified individuals who have no interest in the property. Typically, two appraisers are used—one being appointed by each party. A third party, or *umpire,* may be called on to resolve differences.

Other types of insurance policies also contain provisions for appraisal and arbitration when the insured and insurer disagree as to the value of a loss.

MULTIPLE INSURANCE COVERAGE If an insured has *multiple insurance coverage*—that is, policies with several companies covering the same insurance interest—and the amount of coverage exceeds the loss, the insured can collect from each insurer only the company's proportionate share of the liability to the total amount of insurance. Many fire insurance policies include a *pro rata* clause, which requires any loss to be shared proportionately by all carriers. For example, if Grumbling insured $50,000 worth of property with two companies, each of whose policies had a liability limit of $40,000, on the property's total destruction Grumbling could collect only $25,000 from each insurer.

ANTILAPSE CLAUSES A life insurance policy may provide, or a statute may require a policy to provide, that it will not automatically lapse if no payment is made on the date due. Ordinarily, under an *antilapse provision,* the insured has a *grace period* of thirty or thirty-one days within which to pay an overdue premium. If the insured fails to pay a premium altogether, there are alternatives to cancellation. The insurance company may:

Non- Forfeiture

1. Be required to extend the insurance for a period of time.
2. Issue a policy with less coverage to reflect the amount of the payments made.
3. Pay to the insured the policy's **cash surrender value**—the amount the insurer has agreed to pay

on the policy's cancellation before the insured's death. (In determining this value, the following factors are considered: the period that the policy has already run, the amount of the premium, the insured's age and life expectancy, and amounts to be repaid on any outstanding loans taken out against the policy.)

When the insurance contract states that the insurer cannot cancel the policy, these alternatives are important.

Interpreting Provisions of an Insurance Contract

The courts are increasingly cognizant of the fact that most people do not have the special training necessary to understand the intricate terminology used in insurance policies. The words used in an insurance contract have their ordinary meaning and are interpreted by courts in light of the nature of the coverage involved. When there is an ambiguity in the policy, the provision is interpreted against the insurance company. When it is unclear whether an insurance contract actually exists because the written policy has not been delivered, the uncertainty will be determined against the insurance company. The court will presume that the policy is in effect unless the company can show otherwise.

The following case concerns a disputed phrase in an insurance policy.

BACKGROUND AND FACTS   Richard Stanley was covered by an accidental death and dismemberment policy with Safeco Insurance Company of America. The policy provided payment for "loss of a foot if the loss was by actual severance at or above the ankle joint." Stanley was struck by an automobile while jogging. He suffered an immediate loss of motor power and sensation in both legs and up to the abdominal area. An undisputed medical report revealed a dislocation of the twelfth thoracic vertebra. The report concluded that Stanley had a functional severance of the spinal cord with resulting permanent paralysis, including paralysis of the feet. Safeco denied payment. Stanley sued in a Washington state court. Safeco claimed that the policy required amputation of the foot, as indicated by the language in the caption at the top of the policy's coverage page: "Accidental Death and *Dismemberment* Insurance" (emphasis added). The lower court granted a summary judgment in favor of Safeco, and Stanley appealed. The court of appeals reversed the lower court's decision, and Safeco appealed.

Case 53.3

STANLEY v. SAFECO INSURANCE CO. OF AMERICA

Supreme Court of Washington, 1988.
109 Wash.2d 738,
747 P.2d 1091.

DECISION AND RATIONALE   The Supreme Court of Washington affirmed the decision of the court of appeals. The state supreme court pointed out that "an insurance policy should be given a practical and reasonable rather than a literal interpretation;" that is, an interpretation "such as would be given by the average person purchasing insurance. If the policy is ambiguous, a meaning and construction most favorable to the insured must be applied. A policy provision is ambiguous when it is fairly susceptible to two different interpretations, both of which are reasonable." The court noted that in this case "the language in the body of the policy provides what must occur (loss of foot) and how or where the loss is sustained (actual severance at or above the ankle joint)." Although the policy did not define "actual severance" or "loss of a foot," the court stated that its holding in a previous case established that a "loss" can occur as the result of a loss of use or function. The court concluded that "the language in the body of the policy is not ambiguous; it covers the plaintiff's loss." The court reasoned that Safeco's interpretation—taking from the caption the word "dismemberment" and inserting it in the coverage language—would make the language of the body of the policy ambiguous. The court explained that thus, even if the caption was taken to be a controlling part of the coverage language, the provision would be construed against Safeco.

Cancellation

When an insurance company can cancel its insurance contract, the policy or a state statute usually requires that the insurer give advance written notice of the cancellation. Any premium paid in advance and not yet earned may be refundable. The insured may also be entitled to a life insurance policy's *cash surrender value.*

Cancellation of an insurance policy can occur for various reasons, depending on the type of insurance. For example, automobile insurance can be canceled for nonpayment of premiums or suspension of the insured's driver's license. Property insurance can be canceled for nonpayment of premiums or for other reasons, including the insured's fraud or misrepresentation, conviction for a crime

that increases the hazard insured against, or gross negligence that increases the hazard insured against. Life and health policies can be canceled due to false statements made by the insured in the application, but cancellation can only take place before the effective date of an incontestability clause. An insurer cannot cancel—or refuse to renew—a policy because of the national origin or race of an applicant or because the insured has appeared as a witness in a case against the company.

The following case involves a group life insurance plan that was canceled because the employer failed to pay the premiums. The question before the court was whether the employer could be held liable for not notifying its employees that the coverage was canceled.

Case 53.4

McCARTHY v. LOUISVILLE CARTAGE CO.

Court of Appeals of Kentucky, 1990.
796 S.W.2d 10.

BACKGROUND AND FACTS   Ronald McCarthy was employed by Louisville Cartage Company as a truck driver. As part of his employment benefits, McCarthy was covered by a group life insurance plan that was paid for entirely by his employer. When McCarthy died and his wife sought to collect on the policy as her husband's beneficiary, she learned that the employer had let the policy lapse without notifying the employees that they were no longer covered by the life insurance plan. Mrs. McCarthy sued the employer in a Kentucky state court to recover the proceeds under the policy, alleging that the employer was estopped from canceling coverage without notice to the employees, even though the life insurance plan was voluntary on the part of the employer. The trial court held that the employer did not have a legal duty to notify employees of the lapsed coverage, and therefore Mrs. McCarthy could not establish an action based on promissory estoppel. Mrs. McCarthy appealed.

DECISION AND RATIONALE   The Court of Appeals of Kentucky reversed the judgment of the trial court, holding that there was sufficient evidence presented for a jury determination of the issues. The court stated, "The whole theory of a promissory estoppel action is that detrimental reliance becomes a substitute for consideration under the facts," and thus the absence of a contract between McCarthy and the company was irrelevant. It was reasonable for the employer to expect that the employee's continued employment would be induced by virtue of its promise to provide insurance coverage. An unjust result could be avoided only by giving effect to that promise. Consequently, the court found that the true issue in this case was not whether the company should have given notice that the policy was being terminated but instead whether Mrs. McCarthy had "set forth a *prima facie* case of estoppel sufficient to preclude the directed verdict rendered below." The court declared that it was not unreasonable to conclude that the McCarthys would rely on the supposed existence of the coverage. Accordingly, the court remanded the case for trial.

Basic Duties and Rights

Essentially, the parties to an insurance contract are responsible for the obligations the contract imposes. These include the basic contractual duties discussed in Unit Two of this text.

When applying for insurance, for example, the obligation to act in good faith means that a party must reveal everything necessary for the insurer to evaluate the risk. In other words, the applicant must disclose all **material facts.** Where insurance is concerned, these include all facts that would influence an insurer in determining whether to charge a higher premium or to refuse to issue a policy altogether.

Once the insurer has accepted the risk, and on the occurrence of an event giving rise to a claim, the insurer has a duty to investigate to determine the facts. When a policy provides insurance against third party claims, the insurer is obligated to make reasonable efforts to settle such a claim. If a settlement cannot be reached, then, regardless of the claim's merit, the insurer must defend any suit against the insured. Usually, a policy provides that in this situation the insured must cooperate. A policy provision may expressly require the insured to attend hearings and trials, to assist in obtaining evidence and witnesses, and to assist in reaching a settlement.

Defenses against Payment

An insurance company can raise any of the defenses that would be valid in any ordinary action on a contract, as well as some defenses that do not apply in ordinary contract actions. If the insurance company can show that the policy was procured by fraud, misrepresentation, or violation of warranties, it may have a valid defense for not paying on a claim. (The insurance company may also have the right to disaffirm or rescind an insurance contract.) Improper actions, such as those that are against public policy or that are otherwise illegal, can also give the insurance company a defense against the payment of a claim or allow it to rescind the contract. In the following case, an inaccurate answer to a pertinent question on an application for a life insurance policy was successfully used by the insurance company to deny a claim following the policyowner's death.

BACKGROUND AND FACTS Kirk Johnson applied for life insurance with New York Life Insurance Company on October 7, 1986. One of the questions on the application form required Johnson to provide information about his past and present smoking habits. In answering the question, Johnson represented that he had not smoked in the past twelve months and that he had never smoked cigarettes. In fact, Johnson had smoked for thirteen years, and during the month before the insurance application he was smoking approximately ten cigarettes per day. Johnson died on July 17, 1988, for reasons unrelated to smoking. Johnson's father, Lawrence Johnson, who was the beneficiary of the policy, filed a claim for the insurance proceeds. While investigating the claim, New York Life discovered that Kirk Johnson had misrepresented his smoking habit on the application. The company denied the claim and sought to cancel the policy by returning to Lawrence Johnson a check for the premiums paid under the policy. Lawrence Johnson refused to accept the check, and New York Life undertook an action for declaratory judgment [a court determination of a plaintiff's rights] in a federal district court. The trial court dismissed the action, and New York Life appealed.

Case 53.5

NEW YORK LIFE INSURANCE CO. v. JOHNSON

United States Court of Appeals, Third Circuit, 1991.
923 F.2d 279.

DECISION AND RATIONALE The United States Court of Appeals for the Third Circuit reversed the trial court's decision and remanded the case for entry of a judgment declaring that the policy in question was void *ab initio* (from the beginning). The appellate court noted that state law provides "an insurance policy is void for misrepresentation when the insured establishes three elements: (1) that the representation was false; (2) that the insured knew that the representation was false when made or made it in bad faith; and (3) that the representation was material to the risk being insured." Because the representation was false, Johnson knew it was false, and smoking habits are clearly material to the risk being assumed by the insurer, the policy was void because the insurer was not able to evaluate fully the risks involved in insuring the insured.

ETHICAL CONSIDERATIONS At another point in its opinion, the court sympathized with the plight of Kirk Johnson's father and other beneficiaries who are unable to receive life insurance proceeds because of misrepresentations on the application forms. But it also pointed to the public policy underlying its decision: "If the only consequence of a fraudulent misrepresentation in a life insurance application is to reduce the amount paid under the policy, there is every incentive for applicants to lie. If the lie is undetected during the two-year contestability period, the insured will have obtained excessive coverage for which he has not paid. If the lie is detected during the two-year period, the insured will still obtain what he could have had if he had told the truth. In essence, the applicant has everything to gain and nothing to lose by lying. The victims will be the honest applicants who tell the truth and whose premiums will rise over the long run to pay for the excessive insurance proceeds paid out as a result of undetected misrepresentations in fraudulent applications."

Rebuttal of the Defenses of the Insurance Company

The insurance company can be prevented from asserting some defenses that are normally available. State statutes and case law provide for such estoppel. For example, if a company tells an insured that information requested on a form is optional and the insured provides it anyway, the company cannot use the information to avoid its contractual obligation under the insurance contract. Similarly, incorrect statements as to the age of the insured normally do not provide the insurance company with a way to escape payment upon the death of the insured. In the following case, the court evaluates whether a false statement made on an application for a life insurance policy and the backdating of the application and policy should allow the insurer to avoid payment on the policy.

Case 53.6

ROBERTS v. NATIONAL LIBERTY GROUP OF COMPANIES

Appellate Court of Illinois, Fourth District, 1987.
159 Ill.App.3d 706,
512 N.E.2d 792,
111 Ill.Dec. 403.

BACKGROUND AND FACTS In the spring of 1982, Paul Roberts, then fifty-nine years of age, applied to the National Liberty Group of Companies for a $30,000 life insurance policy available only to individuals under sixty years of age. National lost or misplaced his application, and Roberts submitted a second application in November 1982. Because Roberts had by then had his sixtieth birthday, the second application was backdated to April 11, 1982 (a date before his birthday), as was the ensuing policy. Although Roberts had suffered slight hypertension in 1979 and had been seen and treated by a physician for this condition for a short time thereafter, he marked "no" to the question on the application concerning treatment for high blood pressure. In October 1982, Roberts was diagnosed as having cancer, and he died from the disease in June 1983. Roberts, although he knew of the cancer diagnosis when he submitted the second application, did not indicate this on the application form because the diagnosis had not been made at the time of his original application. On Roberts's death, his wife submitted a claim to National for $30,000. National denied the claim on the ground that the false statement concerning hypertension and the failure to mention the cancer diagnosis constituted misrepresentation. Mrs. Roberts sued National in an Illinois state court for the proceeds plus interest. The trial court found for Mrs. Roberts, and National appealed.

DECISION AND RATIONALE   The Appellate Court of Illinois affirmed the trial court's judgment, holding that National could not avoid payment on the policy. The appellate court noted that under state law, "a false statement in an application for insurance is not in itself a ground for avoiding the insurance policy. The insurer must prove that the statements were made with intent to deceive or involved matters materially affecting the acceptance of the risk." As to the claim that the false statement concerning hypertension constituted misrepresentation allowing National to avoid the policy, the court noted that in this case, "there was testimony *   *   * that high blood pressure such as indicated here did not usually result in the defendant refusing insurance." As to the contention that the failure to disclose the cancer before issuance of the policy voided the policy, the court noted that the policy that was issued predated by six months the date that the cancer was diagnosed. The court held that the backdating of the policy estopped National from asserting the defense of nondisclosure. The court explained that the test of estoppel is whether, considering all of the circumstances, equity requires that a party be estopped. In this case, the court barred National from adopting a position inconsistent with its previous conduct.

Types of Insurance

There are four general types of insurance coverage: life insurance, fire and homeowners' insurance, automobile insurance, and business liability insurance. We will examine briefly the coverage available under each of these types of insurance. Then special features and provisions will be pointed out, with special emphasis on life and fire insurance policies as they relate to the law.

Life Insurance

There are five basic types of life insurance:

1.   **Whole life** is sometimes referred to as straight life, ordinary life, or cash-value insurance. This type of insurance provides protection with a cumulated cash surrender value that can be used as collateral for a loan. Premiums are paid by the insured during the insured's entire lifetime, with a fixed payment to the beneficiary upon death.

2.   **Limited-payment life** might be a twenty-payment life policy. Premiums are paid for a stated number of years, after which the policy is paid up and fully effective during the insured's life. Naturally, premiums are higher than for whole life. This insurance has a cash surrender value.

3.   **Term insurance** is a type of policy for which premiums are paid for a specified term. Payment on the policy is due only if death occurs within the term period. Premiums are less expensive than for whole life or limited-payment life, and there is usually no cash surrender value. Frequently, this type of insurance can be converted to another type of life insurance.

4.   **Endowment insurance** involves fixed premium payments that are made for a definite term. At the end of the term, a fixed amount is to be paid to the insured or, upon the death of the insured during the specified period, to a beneficiary. Thus, this type of insurance represents both term insurance and a form of **annuity** (the right to receive

fixed, periodic payments for life or—as in this case—for a term of years). Endowment insurance has a rapidly increasing cash surrender value, but premiums are high, as payment is required at the end of the term even if the insured is still living.

5. **Universal life** is a newer type of insurance that combines some aspects of term insurance and some aspects of whole life insurance. Every payment, usually called a "contribution," involves two deductions made by the issuing life insurance company. The first one is a charge for term insurance protection; the second is for company expenses and profit. The money that remains after these deductions earns interest for the policyholder at a rate determined by the company. The interest-earning money in the policy is called the policy's cash value, but that term does not mean the same thing as it does for a traditional whole life insurance policy. With a universal life policy, the cash value grows at a variable interest rate rather than at a predetermined rate.

The rights and liabilities of the parties in life insurance are basically dependent upon the insurance contract. A few features deserve special attention.

LIABILITY   The insurance contract determines not only the extent of the insurer's liability but, generally, whether the insurer is liable upon the death of the insured. Most life insurance contracts exclude liability for death caused by suicide, military action during war, execution by a state or federal government, or even something that occurs while the insured is a passenger in a commercial vehicle. In the absence of exclusion, most courts today construe any cause of death to be one of the insurer's risks.

ADJUSTMENT DUE TO MISSTATEMENT OF AGE   The insurance policy constitutes the agreement between the parties. The application for insurance is part of the policy and is usually attached to the policy. When the insured misstates his or her age in the application, an error takes place particularly as to the amount of premiums paid. Misstatement of age is not a material error sufficient to allow the insurer to void the policy. Instead, upon discovery of the error, the insurer will adjust the premium payments and/or benefits accordingly.

ASSIGNMENT   Most life insurance policies permit the insured to change beneficiaries. When this is the case, in the absence of any prohibition or notice requirement, the insured has a right to assign the rights to the policy (for example, as security for a loan) without the consent of the insurer or the beneficiary. If the beneficiary right is vested—that is, has become absolute, entitling the beneficiary to payment of the proceeds—the policy cannot be assigned without the consent of the beneficiary. The vast majority of life insurance contracts permit assignment and only require notice to the insurer to be effective.

CREDITORS' RIGHTS   Unless insurance proceeds are exempt under state law, the insured's interest in life insurance as an asset is subject to the rights of judgment creditors. These creditors generally can reach insurance proceeds payable to the insured's estate, proceeds payable to anyone if the payment of premiums constituted a fraud on creditors, and proceeds payable to a named beneficiary if the insured has reserved the right to change beneficiaries. Creditors, however, cannot compel the insured to make available the cash surrender value of the policy or to change the named beneficiary to that of the creditor. Almost all states exempt at least a part of the proceeds of life insurance from creditors' claims.

TERMINATION   Although the insured can cancel and terminate the policy, the insurer generally cannot do so. Therefore, termination usually takes place only upon the occurrence of the following:

1. Default in premium payments that causes the policy to lapse.
2. Death and payment of benefits.
3. Expiration of the term of the policy.
4. Cancellation by the insured.

Fire and Homeowners' Insurance

There are basically two types of insurance policies for a home—standard fire insurance policies and homeowners' policies.

STANDARD FIRE INSURANCE POLICIES   The standard fire insurance policy protects the homeowner against fire and lightning, as well as damage from smoke and water caused by the fire or the fire

Life Insurance for Partners and Shareholders

Life insurance on the lives of partners or shareholders may be a valuable tool for you as part of a partnership or a closely held corporation. There is always the question of what to do when one partner or co-shareholder dies. Typically, the others will want to buy that partner's interest, particularly if the remaining partners wish to continue in the business. The partnership or corporation may wish to purchase life insurance on each partner or co-shareholder to help fund the buy-out. Problems arise when the partners or co-shareholders are not all the same age or do not all have the same financial interest in the partnership or corporation. How does one arrange an insurance and buy-out agreement so as to be fair to everyone?

First, you must determine the current value of the business and then provide a method for determining the value of the business when one of the owners dies. There are numerous ways to accomplish such a valuation. The important point is that you need to agree to the method to be used. Each of you must be satisfied that, if you were the first to die, the valuation method would provide a fair and equitable way to buy your interest from your estate.

Now you must determine how much life insurance to purchase. Insurance can be used to fund the entire amount of the purchase price of the deceased's share or it can be used to pay just a part of that purchase price. In fact, given that the premiums for some of the owners will cost more (because they are older or not in good health), an agreement may be reached to buy less insurance for them in order to reduce the current cost of the life insurance policy. The remaining part of the buy-out purchase price will presumably be made in installments that draw current interest rates.

Owners can negotiate a variety of payment plans to fit each partner's or co-shareholder's individual needs in the event a buy-out becomes necessary. For example, for an older partner, the payments may be spread over only a few years; for younger partners, the payments may be spread over a longer period of time. All these points are negotiable. What is important is that you should attempt to draft an agreement that provides for insurance and/or a buy-out purchase plan that protects your own interest.

department. Paying slightly more will extend the coverage to damage caused by hail, windstorms, explosions, and so on. Personal theft insurance and a comprehensive liability policy can also be added.

Most fire insurance policies are classified according to the type of property covered and the extent (amount) of the issuer's liability. Exhibit 53–2 lists typical fire insurance policies.

As with life insurance, certain features and provisions of fire insurance deserve special mention. In reading the following, it is important to note some basic differences in the treatment of life and fire policies.

Liability As with all forms of insurance, with fire insurance the insurer's liability is determined from the terms of the policy. Most policies, however,

limit recovery to losses resulting from *hostile* fires—basically, those that break out or begin in places where no fire was intended to burn. A *friendly* fire—one burning in a place where it was intended to burn—is not covered. Therefore, smoke from a fireplace is not covered, but smoke from a fire caused by a defective electrical outlet is. Sometimes, owners add ''extended coverage'' to the fire policy to cover losses from ''friendly'' fires.

If the policy is a *valued* policy (see Exhibit 53–2) and the subject matter is completely destroyed, the insurer is liable for the amount specified in the policy. If it is an *open* policy, then the extent of actual loss must be determined, and the insurer is liable only for the amount of the loss or for the maximum amount specified in the policy, which-

■ **Exhibit 53–2 Typical Fire Insurance Policies**

Type of Policy	Coverage
Blanket	Covers a class of property rather than specific property, because the property is expected to shift or vary in nature. A policy covering the inventory of a business is an example.
Specific	Covers a specific item of property at a specific location. An example is a particular painting located in a residence or a piece of machinery located in a factory or business.
Floater	Usually supplements a specific policy. It is intended to cover property that may change in either location or quantity. To illustrate, if the painting mentioned under "specific policy" were to be exhibited during the year at numerous locations throughout the state, a floater policy would be desirable.
Valued	A policy in which, by agreement, a specific value is placed on the subject to be insured to cover the eventuality of its total loss.
Open	A policy in which the value of the property insured is not agreed upon. The policy usually provides for a maximum liability of the insurer, but payment for loss is restricted to the fair market value of the property at the time of loss or to the insurer's limit, whichever is less.

ever is less. For partial losses, actual loss must always be determined, and the insurer's liability is limited to that amount. Most insurance policies permit the insurer either to restore or replace the property destroyed or to pay for the loss.

Proof of Loss   Fire insurance policies require the insured to file with the insurer, within a specified period or immediately (within a reasonable time), a proof of loss as a condition for recovery. Failure to comply *could* allow the insurance carrier to avoid liability. Courts vary somewhat on the enforcement of such clauses. So that this does not become a legal issue, the insured should always report a loss immediately to the insurer and file the proper statements covering the loss.

Occupancy Clause   Most standard policies require that the premises be occupied at the time of loss. The relevant clause states that if the premises become vacant or unoccupied for a given period, unless consent by the insurer is given, the coverage is suspended until the premises are reoccupied. Persons going on extended vacations should check their policies on this matter.

Assignment   Before a loss has occurred, a fire insurance policy is not assignable without the consent of the insurer. The theory is that the fire insurance policy is a personal contract between the insured and the insurer. The nonassignability of the

policy is extremely important in the purchase of a house. The purchaser must procure his or her own insurance. If the purchaser wishes to assume the remaining insurance coverage period of the seller, consent of the insurer is essential.

To illustrate, Ann is selling her home and lot to Sam. Ann has a one-year fire policy with Ajax Insurance Company, with six months of coverage remaining at the date on which the sale is to close. Ann agrees to assign the balance of her policy, but Ajax has not given its consent. One day after passage of the deed, a fire totally destroys the house. Can Sam recover from Ajax?

The answer is no, as the policy is actually voided upon the closing of the transaction and the deeding of the property. The reason the policy is voided is that Ann no longer has an insurable interest at the time of loss, and Sam has no rights in a nonassignable policy.

HOMEOWNERS' POLICIES   A homeowners' policy provides protection against a number of risks under a single policy, allowing the policyholder to avoid the cost of buying each protection separately. There are two basic types of homeowners' policy coverage:

1. *Property coverage* includes garage, house, and other private buildings on the policyholder's lot. It also includes the personal possessions and property of the policyholder at home, in travel, or

at work. It pays additional living expenses for living away from home because of a fire or some other covered peril.

2. *Liability coverage* is for personal liability in case someone is injured on the insured's property, the insured damages someone else's property, or the insured injures someone else who is not in an automobile. It generally does not cover liability for professional malpractice.

Similar to liability coverage is coverage for the medical payments of others who are injured on the policyholder's property and coverage for property of others that is damaged by a member of the policyholder's family.

Forms of Homeowners' Policies There are five forms of homeowners' and condominium owners' policies. The essential difference among the five forms is the number of perils insured against. For example, one form (called the basic form) covers eleven perils, or risks; another (the broad form) covers eighteen; and another (the comprehensive form) covers those eighteen and all others.

Renters, too, take out insurance policies to cover losses to personal property. Renters' insurance, called "residence contents broad form," covers personal possessions against the eighteen perils and includes additional living expenses and liability coverage.

Adding a Personal Articles or Personal Effects Floater Policy An insured may wish to pay a slightly higher premium to insure specific personal articles—for example, cameras, musical instruments, works of art, jewelry, and other valuables. This is accomplished by the addition of a *personal articles floater* to a homeowners' policy. The insured submits a list of the things to be covered and some affidavits giving their current market value. Insuring under a floater provides all-risk insurance, and the covered property can therefore be omitted from fire and theft policies.

A *personal effects floater* policy covers personal items that accompany the insured when he or she is traveling. In most cases, this coverage is not necessary, because a regular homeowners' policy provides sufficient coverage. The personal effects floater covers articles only when they are taken off the insured's property. It does not cover theft from an unattended automobile unless there

is evidence of forced entry. Even then, the company's liability is generally limited to 10 percent of the amount of insurance and no more than a specified amount, such as $250 or $500, for all property in any one loss. This restriction can be removed by payment of an additional premium, however.

Automobile Insurance

There are two basic kinds of automobile insurance: liability insurance and collision and comprehensive insurance.

LIABILITY INSURANCE Automobile liability insurance covers bodily injury and property damage liability. Liability limits are usually described by a series of three numbers, such as 100/300/50. This means that the policy, for one accident, will pay a maximum of $100,000 for bodily injury to one person, a maximum of $300,000 for bodily injury to more than one person, and a maximum of $50,000 for property damage. Many insurance companies offer liability up to $500,000 and sometimes higher.

Individuals who are dissatisfied with the maximum liability limits offered by regular automobile insurance coverage can purchase separate coverage under an *umbrella* policy. Umbrella limits sometimes go as high as $5 million. They also cover personal liability in excess of a homeowners' policy's liability limits.

COLLISION AND COMPREHENSIVE INSURANCE Collision insurance covers damage to the insured's car in any type of collision. Usually, it is not advisable to purchase full collision coverage (otherwise known as zero deductible). The price per year is quite high, because it is likely that small but costly repair jobs will be required each year. Most people prefer to take out $100, $250, or $500 deductible coverage, which costs substantially less than zero deductible coverage.

Comprehensive insurance covers loss, damage, and destruction by fire, hurricane, hail, vandalism, and theft. It can be obtained separately from collision insurance.

OTHER AUTOMOBILE INSURANCE Other types of automobile insurance coverage include the following:

1. *Uninsured motorist coverage.* Uninsured motorist coverage insures the driver and passengers against injury caused by any driver without insurance or by a hit-and-run driver. Certain states require that it be included in all insurance policies sold to drivers.

2. *Accidental death benefits.* Sometimes called *double indemnity,* accidental death benefits provide a lump sum to named beneficiaries if the policyholder dies in an automobile accident. This coverage generally costs very little, but it may not be necessary if the insured has a sufficient amount of life insurance.

3. *Medical payment coverage.* Medical payment coverage provided by an auto insurance policy pays hospital and other medical bills and sometimes funeral expenses. This type of insurance protects all the passengers in the insured's car when the insured is driving.

4. *Other-driver coverage.* An **omnibus clause,** or *other-driver clause,* protects the vehicle owner who has taken out the insurance and anyone who drives the vehicle with the owner's permission. This coverage may be held to extend to a third party who drives the vehicle with the permission of the person to whom the owner gave permission.

5. *No-fault insurance.* Under no-fault statutes, claims arising from an accident are made against the claimant's own insurer, regardless of whose fault the accident was. In some cases—for example, when injuries involve expensive medical treatment—an injured party may seek recovery from another party or insurer. In those instances, the injured party may collect the maximum amount of no-fault insurance and still sue for total damages from the party at fault, although usually, on winning an award, the injured party must reimburse the insurer for its no-fault payments.

Business Liability Insurance

A business may be vulnerable to all sorts of risks. A key employee may die or become disabled; a customer may be injured when using a manufacturer's product; the patron of an establishment selling liquor may leave the premises and injure a third party in an automobile accident; or a professional may overlook some important detail, causing liability for malpractice. Should the first situation arise (for instance, if the company president dies), the business may have some protection under a key-person insurance policy, discussed previously.

In the other circumstances, other types of insurance may apply.

GENERAL LIABILITY Comprehensive general liability insurance can cover virtually as many risks as the insurer agrees to cover. For example, among the types of coverage that a business might wish to acquire is protection from liability for injuries arising from on-premises events not otherwise insured against, such as company social functions.

Some specialized establishments may be subject to liability in individualized circumstances, and policies can be drafted to meet their needs. For example, in many jurisdictions, statutes impose liability on a seller of intoxicating liquor when a buyer of the liquor, intoxicated as a result of the sale, injures a third party. Legal protection may extend not only to immediately consequent injuries, such as quadriplegia in an automobile accident, but also to the loss of support suffered by a family because of the injuries. Insurance can provide coverage for these injuries and losses.

PRODUCT LIABILITY Manufacturers may be subject to liability for injuries that their products cause, and product liability insurance can be written to match specific products' risks. Coverage can be procured under a comprehensive general liability policy or under a separate policy. The coverage may include expenses involved in recalling and replacing a product that has proved to be defective. (For a comprehensive discussion of product liability, see Chapter 23.)

PROFESSIONAL MALPRACTICE In recent years, professionals—attorneys, physicians, architects, and engineers, for example—have increasingly become the targets of negligence suits. Professionals may purchase malpractice insurance to protect themselves against such claims. The large judgments in some malpractice suits have received considerable publicity and are sometimes cited in what has been termed "the insurance crisis," because they have contributed to a considerable increase in malpractice insurance premiums in recent years.

WORKERS' COMPENSATION Workers' compensation insurance covers payments to employees who are injured in accidents arising out of and in the course of employment (that is, on the job). Workers' compensation, which was discussed in detail in Chapter 48, is governed by state statutes.

■ Terms and Concepts

annuity 967
binder 960
cash surrender value 962
endowment insurance 967
insurable interest 957
insurance 956

limited-payment life 967
material facts 965
omnibus clause 972
policy 957
premium 957
risk 956

risk management 956
term insurance 967
underwriter 957
universal life 968
whole life 967

■ For Review

1. What is an insurable interest? To obtain life insurance, when must an insurable interest exist—at the time the policy is obtained, at the time the loss occurs, or both? To obtain property insurance, when must an insurable interest exist—at the time the policy is obtained, at the time the loss occurs, or both?

2. Is an insurance broker the agent of an insurance applicant or the agent of an insurer? If the broker accepts an applicant's initial premium but fails to obtain coverage and the applicant is damaged as a result, who may be liable for the damage?

3. Generally, to avoid payment under a policy, an insurer can raise any defenses that would be valid in an ordinary contract action. Under what circumstances might an insurer be estopped from asserting a defense that would otherwise normally be available?

4. While Warren and Annette were married, Warren took out a life insurance policy with Annette as the beneficiary. After Warren and Annette are divorced, Warren dies. When Annette attempts to collect on the policy, the insurer refuses to pay, on the ground that Warren did not pay the most recent premium, which was due fifteen days before his death. In Warren and Annette's state, a statute requires a life insurance policy to provide that an insured has thirty days within which to pay an overdue premium. Warren's policy did not contain this provision. If Annette sues the insurer, what will the court likely rule?

5. Lamont owns Safety Ladder Manufacturing Co. Lamont is aware that no matter how carefully Safety manufactures a ladder, Safety may be subject to liability for injuries resulting from the ladder's use. Can Safety obtain insurance to cover this risk? If so, what might the coverage include?

■ Questions and Case Problems

53-1. Ann owns a house and has an elderly third cousin living with her. Ann decides she needs fire insurance on the house and a life insurance policy on her third cousin to cover funeral and other expenses that will result from her cousin's death. Ann takes out a fire insurance policy from Ajax Insurance Co. and a $10,000 life insurance policy from Beta Insurance Co. on her third cousin. Six months later, Ann sells the house to John and transfers title to him. Ann and her cousin move into an apartment. With two months remaining on the Ajax policy, a fire totally destroys the house; at the same time, Ann's third cousin dies. Both insurance companies tender back premiums but claim they have no liability under the insurance contracts, as Ann did not have an insurable interest. Discuss their claims.

53-2. Peter contracts with an Ajax Insurance Co. agent for a $50,000 ordinary life insurance policy. The application form is filled in to show Peter's age as thirty-two. In addition, the application form asks whether Peter has ever had any heart ailments or problems. Peter answers no, forgetting that as a young child he was diagnosed as having a slight heart murmur. A policy is issued. Three years later Peter becomes seriously ill. A review of the policy discloses that Peter was actually thirty-three at the time of application and issuance of the policy and that he erred in answering the question about a history of heart ailments. Discuss whether Ajax can void the policy and escape liability upon Peter's death.

53-3. Sarah has an ordinary life insurance policy on her life and a fire insurance policy on her house. Both policies have been in force for a number of years. Sarah's life insurance names her son, Rory, as beneficiary. Sarah has specifically removed her right to change beneficiaries, and the life policy is silent on right of assignment. Sarah is going on a one-year European vacation and borrows money from Leonard to finance the trip. Leonard takes an assignment of the life insurance policy as security for the loan, as the policy has accumulated a substantial cash surrender value. Sarah also rents out her house to Leonard and assigns to him her fire insurance policy. Discuss fully whether Sarah's assignment of these policies is valid.

53-4. Frank has an open fire insurance policy on his home for a maximum liability of $60,000. The policy has a number of standard clauses, including the right of the insurer to restore or rebuild the property in lieu of a monetary payment, and it has a standard coinsurance clause. A fire in Frank's house virtually destroys a utility room and part of the kitchen. The fire was caused by an electric water heater's overheating. The total damage to the property is $10,000. The property at the time of loss is valued at $100,000. Frank files a proof of loss claim for $10,000. Discuss the insurer's liability in this situation.

53-5. Lori has a large house. She secures two open fire insurance policies on the house. Her policy with the Ajax Insurance Co. is for a maximum of $100,000, and her policy with Beta Insurance Co. is for a maximum of $50,000. Lori's house burns to the ground. The value of the house at the time of the loss is $120,000. Discuss the liability of Ajax and Beta to Lori.

53-6. James and Hazel Gray signed a joint application for health insurance coverage with Great American Reserve Insurance Co. The application was taken by John L. Sides, who at the time was not an agent for Great American but an independent insurance broker. Upon signing the application, the Grays gave Sides $188.50, the first month's premium, and later alleged that Sides had told them the policy would become effective when the first payment was made. Sides then sent the application to Great American, along with his own application to become a salesperson for Great American. Sides subsequently was allowed to sell Great American insurance policies. After several initial problems, Great American received the Grays' policy application two and a half months after they had signed it, and only then did the company begin to process the application. Two days before Great American received the policy application, Mr. Gray was thrown from a horse and injured. Mrs. Gray notified Sides of the injury, but Sides learned from Great American that the Grays were not covered as of the date of the injury. James Gray then brought suit against Great American and Sides for breach of an insurance contract. Did the Grays have a valid insurance policy with Great American on the date of Mr. Gray's injury? Explain. [*Gray v. Great American Reserve Insurance Co.*, 495 So.2d 602 (Ala. 1986)]

53-7. Martin A. Gurrentz applied for life insurance from Federal Kemper Life Assurance Co. through an insurance agent named Alfrey. In September 1982, Gurrentz filled out an application but paid no premiums. Between the submission of the application and the delivery of the policy, Gurrentz sought medical advice from a physician relative to an ear problem. A biopsy was done and he was advised that he had a throat malignancy, for which he subsequently received radiation treatments. Upon delivery of the policy, Gurrentz signed a statement stating that there had been no changes in his health status and he had not seen a doctor since filing the application for insurance. In April 1983, Federal learned of Gurrentz's throat problem when he filed a claim under a separate medical health policy. After an investigation, Federal notified Gurrentz in February 1984 that it was canceling the life insurance policy and refunding all premiums paid. Was Federal able to rescind successfully Gurrentz's life insurance policy? Explain. [*Gurrentz v. Federal Kemper Life Assurance Co.*, 513 So.2d 241 (Fla.App. 4th Dist. 1987)]

53-8. On April 16, 1982, Frances and Michael Berthiaume made a written application for life insurance with the Minnesota Mutual Life Insurance Co. The policy sought was to provide $44,308.37 in insurance coverage to cover the amount of the Berthiaumes' loan balance on the mortgage for their house, for a monthly premium of $12.42. Mr. Berthiaume did not take a physical examination for the policy, but in filling out the application he answered "no" to a question asking whether he had ever been treated for, or had ever been advised that he had, high blood pressure. The answer Mr. Berthiaume gave was incorrect; in fact, he had been diagnosed as having hypertension four months before the application was made. In October 1982, Mr. Berthiaume became ill, and he died two months later. When his widow submitted a claim for the mortgage insurance, the insurance company denied payment, citing Mr. Berthiaume's inaccurate answer on the application. Minnesota Mutual sought summary judgment, which was granted by the trial court. Mrs. Berthiaume appealed. Discuss whether Mr. Berthiaume's inaccurate answer on the insurance policy application voided Minnesota Mutual's obligation to pay on the policy. [*Berthiaume v. Minnesota Mutual Life Insurance Co.*, 388 N.W.2d 15 (Minn.App. 1986)]

53-9. Claude and Mildred owned their home in Lexington and had a fire insurance policy on it. Claude and Mildred contracted with Benjamin to build a new home for them in exchange for cash and transfer of their present home. After conveying the home to Benjamin, Claude and Mildred continued living there and paid both rent and the insurance premium. The fire insurance policy was never assigned to Benjamin. While Claude and Mildred were still living in their old home, a fire damaged it. The insurance company would not pay, claiming that Claude and Mildred had no insurable interest in the property at the time of the loss. Discuss fully how a court will rule. [*O'Donnell v. MFA Insurance Co.*, 671 S.W.2d 302 (Mo.App. 1984)]

53-10. The insured brought an action to recover losses in excess of $100,000 sustained because of employee theft. The thefts occurred during the terms of two different policies but were not discovered until the second policy had replaced the first. Each policy limited recovery to $50,000 for employee dishonesty and provided that for a loss "which occurs partly during the Effective Period of this endorsement and partly during the period of other policies, the total liability of the Company shall not exceed in the aggregate the amount of this endorsement." The insured maintained that he was entitled to recover $50,000 on each policy. What should the court decide? Discuss fully. [*Davenport Peters Co. v. Royal Globe Insurance Co.*, 490 F.Supp. 286 (Mass. 1980)]

53-11. Robert Gladney applied for disability insurance from Paul Revere Life Insurance Co., enclosing with the application a check for $3,100, which represented the first semiannual premium. The issuance of the policy was conditional upon the insurance company's receipt of a medical form that was to be completed by Gladney's doctor following a physical examination. Gladney was a busy man and kept putting off the physical examination. Over a month later, Gladney submitted a second application, because the first one was too old. The insurance agent advised Gladney to leave the application undated so that if Gladney failed to have the physical examination within a month, he would not have to submit yet a third application. Gladney told the agent that he would notify him when the examination was completed. Soon thereafter, Gladney fell ill. His doctor examined him but did not conduct all the tests normally required by Paul Revere for disability insurance. A month later, Gladney was hospitalized and underwent heart surgery. Gladney never told the insurance agent about his visit to the doctor and the fact that the doctor had examined him. Gladney now claims that he is entitled to disability benefits under the policy because he paid the premium and would have been approved for insurance had he notified the insurance company of his examination. Will the court agree? Discuss fully. [*Gladney v. Paul Revere Life Insurance Co.*, 895 F.2d 238 (5th Cir. 1990)]

53-12. A Question of Ethics

Alma McMillan worked as a sales and reservations supervisor in a Trans World Airlines, Inc., (TWA) office located in Philadelphia. At 10:00 P.M. one evening, after she had completed her work shift, McMillan left her office and exited the building onto a covered walkway. While she stood on this walkway, her estranged husband fatally stabbed her. As a TWA employee, McMillan was covered by a group life insurance policy issued by State Mutual Life Assurance Co. of America. A provision of the policy, marked "Hazard F," provided for a payment of $100,000 to the insured's beneficiaries in the event of death resulting from "a felonious assault while on authorized business of [TWA]." The term "felonious assault" was defined to include murder. State Mutual refused to pay the proceeds of the policy to McMillan's beneficiaries (her children) on the grounds that McMillan had not been "on authorized business" at the time of her death. The beneficiaries then sued State Mutual to recover the proceeds. [McMillan v. State Mutual Life Assurance Co. of America, 922 F.2d 1073 (3d Cir. 1990)]

1. One of the questions posed by this case was at what instant following the conclusion of an employee's work shift should separation from the employer's authorized business be complete? The trial court held that this instant occurred when McMillan left the employer's premises. Although she had left the building in which she worked, she was still on her employer's premises at the time of the fatal stabbing. The appellate court agreed. One appellate court judge dissented, however, concluding that at the time of the tragedy, McMillan was on her own business, not on the business of her employer. Argue the merits of each conclusion. Which one do you think is the fairer? Why?

2. Is the phrase "on authorized business" sufficiently ambiguous for the court to construe the phrase against the insurer, State Mutual? Do you discern any ethical principle underlying the rule that ambiguous terms and phrases will be construed *against* the insurance company? Given the fact that both parties to an insurance contract must agree to the terms contained therein or no contract will be formed, do you think that it is fair to hold just one of the parties responsible for ambiguous terms or phrases?

Chapter 54

Wills, Trusts, and Estates

The laws of succession of property are a necessary corollary to the concept of private ownership of property. The law requires that upon death, title to the decedent's property must vest (full possession must be delivered) somewhere. The decedent can direct the passage of property after death by *will*, subject to certain limitations imposed by the state. If no valid will has been executed, the decedent is said to have died **intestate,** and state law prescribes the distribution of the property among heirs or next of kin. If no heirs or kin can be found, the property **escheats** (title is transferred to the state).

In addition, a person can transfer property through a *trust.*[1] The owner (settlor) of the property transfers legal title to a *trustee,* who has a duty imposed by law to hold the property for the use or benefit of another (the beneficiary).

■ Purposes of Inheritance Laws

State regulation of inheritance has developed in response to certain social and political goals. Three principles underlie U.S. inheritance and succession laws:

1. *The concept of private property.* Any system of laws to regulate the passage of a decedent's estate must do so in the context of a firmly rooted tradition of private ownership of property.

2. *The effectuation of the individual's testamentary intent.* The right to direct the distribution of one's own property to whomever one chooses (subject to the rights of the surviving spouse and children) is often taken as a basic tenet of U.S. jurisprudence. Many formalities surround the court's duty to ensure that when a will is offered for authentication, it is in fact the genuine and final expression of the decedent's wishes.

---

1. A trust can be set up by the property owner *during his or her life* (by a deed accompanied by a trust document) or *at his or her death* (by a will containing or accompanied by a trust document). This chapter discusses both types of trusts.

3. *The policy favoring family.* The protection of the family has been a cornerstone of inheritance laws throughout history. As noted earlier, intestate succession is inheritance by the heirs of the deceased. In contemporary law, this goal is reinforced by state statutes guaranteeing that an absolute portion of the decedent's estate will be allotted to the surviving spouse and children.

Wills

A **will** is the final declaration of the disposition that a person desires to have made of his or her property after death. A will is referred to as a *testamentary disposition* of property. It is a formal instrument that must follow exactly the requirements of the appropriate state's statutes to be effective. The reasoning behind such a strict requirement is obvious. A will becomes effective only after death. No attempts to modify it after the death of the maker are allowed because the court cannot ask the maker to confirm the attempted modifications. (But sometimes the wording in the will must be "interpreted" by the courts.)

A will can serve other purposes besides the distribution of property. It can appoint a guardian for minor children or incapacitated adults. It can also appoint a personal representative to settle the affairs of the deceased.

Vocabulary of Wills

Every area of law has its own special vocabulary, and the area of wills is no exception. A person who makes out a will is known as a **testator** (from the Latin *testari,* "to make a will"). The court responsible for administering any legal problems surrounding a will is called a **probate court.** When a person dies, a *personal representative* settles the affairs of the deceased. An **executor** is the personal representative named in the will; an **administrator** is the personal representative appointed by the court for a decedent who dies without a will, who fails to name an executor in the will, who names an executor lacking the capacity to serve, or who writes a will that the court refuses to admit to probate. A gift of real estate by will is generally called a **devise,** and a gift of personal property under a will is called a **bequest** or **legacy.**

Types of Gifts

Gifts by will can be specific, general, or residuary. A *specific* devise or bequest (legacy) describes particular property that can be distinguished from all the rest of the testator's property. For example, Johnson's will provides, "I give my nephew, Tom, my gold pocket watch with the initials MTJ on it." Should the gold watch not be part of Johnson's property at the time of Johnson's death (if, for example, it has been sold, destroyed, or given away), the legacy is extinguished, or canceled.

A *general* devise or bequest (legacy) does not single out any particular item of property to be transferred by will. For example, "I give to my daughter, Dana, $10,000" is a general bequest. Usually, general legacies specify a sum of money.

On occasion, assets are insufficient to pay in full all of the bequests provided for in a will, as well as the taxes, debts, and expenses of administering the estate. When this happens, an *abatement,* by which the **legatees** (the recipients of legacies) receive reduced benefits, takes place. For example, Johnson's will leaves "$15,000 each to my children, Mary and Sam." Upon Johnson's death, only $10,000 is available to honor these bequests. By abatement, each child will receive $5,000. If bequests are more complicated, abatement may be more complicated. The testator's intent, as expressed in the will, controls.

If the legatee dies prior to the death of the testator or before the legacy is payable, a *lapsed legacy* occurs. At common law, the legacy failed. Today, under an antilapse statute, a legacy may not lapse if the legatee is in a certain blood relationship to the testator—such as a child, grandchild, brother, or sister—and if the legatee also left a child or other surviving heir.

Sometimes a will provides that any assets remaining after specific gifts are made and debts are paid are to be distributed through a *residuary* clause. A residuary provision is used because the exact amount to be distributed cannot be determined until all other gifts and payouts are made. A residuary estate can pose problems, however, when the will does not specifically name the beneficiaries to receive the residue. In such a case, if the court cannot determine the testator's intent, the remainder of the residuary estate passes according to state laws of intestacy. In the following case, the court had to decide whether the residual assets of an estate should go to the only named beneficiary in the testator's will or should be distributed under intestacy laws to all of the legal heirs of the deceased.

Case 54.1

ESTATE OF CANCIK

Appellate Court of Illinois, First District, Fifth Division, 1984. 121 Ill.App.3d 113, 459 N.E.2d 296, 76 Ill.Dec. 659.

BACKGROUND AND FACTS   Edward Cancik died with a net estate valued at more than $200,000. Edward had intentionally omitted all his relatives from his will except his cousin, Charles Cancik. Edward specifically willed all his personal and household goods to Charles and placed the residue in a testamentary trust for the maintenance of the Cancik family mausoleum. After Edward's death, Charles filed a complaint alleging that the value of the trust corpus (that is, the capital or principal, as distinguished from the interest) vastly exceeded the amount necessary to accomplish its purpose (to maintain the mausoleum), and he asked that the residue be distributed to him as the testator's only heir-at-law. Thomas, another relative of Edward, acting for any unknown heirs as guardian *ad litem* (a person appointed to protect the interests of parties unable to represent themselves), filed a petition in a Illinois state court to have the residue distributed to all the testator's heirs by intestacy. (Twelve heirs were later found to be living in Czechoslovakia.) The trial court held that the residue passed to all the heirs by the laws of intestacy. Charles appealed.

DECISION AND RATIONALE   The Appellate Court of Illinois held that the residual assets of Edward's estate must go to his heirs rather than to Charles, who was merely the beneficiary of Edward's personal property. The court held that "[t]he object of testamentary construction is to ascertain the intention of the testator" through the language of the will. "Although there is a presumption against intestacy, it * * * may not be used to overcome the language of the will or to supply language which has been omitted." Moreover, the court will not rewrite the will for the testator. A testator cannot disinherit heirs by a simple declaration that they are excluded from the will, but must give the property specifically to someone else. The testator is thus presumed to know that when a testamentary gift fails for any reason, and no alternate gift is made, the property passes by intestacy to his or her heirs. A gift by implication will be recognized only if there is no reasonable doubt that it is necessary to effectuate the intent of the testator. Therefore, in this case, Edward's statement that he had intentionally omitted the names of his heirs from his will did "not give rise to an implication so strong as to leave no reasonable doubt that [he] intended Charles to inherit the entire excess residuum." The court found Edward's major concern to be the care of the family mausoleum. Even though the division of property between Charles and the trust was "vastly disproportionate," the court declined to write into the will an alternate residuary bequest to Charles.

Probate versus Nonprobate

To **probate** (''prove'') a will means to establish its validity and to carry the administration of the estate through a special court, which, as mentioned above, is called a *probate court*. Probate laws vary from state to state. In 1969, the American Bar Association and the National Conference of Commissioners on Uniform State Laws approved the Uniform Probate Code (UPC). The UPC codifies general principles and procedures for the resolution of conflicts in settling estates and relaxes some of the requirements for a valid will contained in earlier state laws. Fifteen states have adopted some form of the UPC. References to its provisions will be included in the remainder of this chapter where general practice in most states is consistent. Because succession and inheritance laws vary widely among the states, one should always check the particular laws of the state involved.[2]

The process of probate is time-consuming and costly, and the court is involved in every step of the proceedings. Attorneys and personal representatives of decedents' estates often become involved in probate.

Many states have statutes that allow for the distribution of assets without probate proceedings. Faster and less expensive methods are then used. For example, property can be transferred by affidavit (a written statement taken before a person who has authority to affirm it),[3] and problems or questions can be handled during an administrative hearing. In addition, some state statutes provide that title to cars, savings and checking accounts, and certain other property can be passed merely by filling out forms. This is particularly true when most of the property is held in joint tenancy with right of survivorship or when there is only one heir.

FAMILY SETTLEMENT AGREEMENTS   A majority of states provide for *family settlement agreements,* which are private agreements among the beneficiaries. Once a will is admitted to probate, the family members can agree to settle among themselves the distribution of the decedent's assets. Although a family settlement agreement speeds the settlement process, a court order is still needed to protect the estate from future creditors and to clear title to the assets involved.

SUMMARY PROCEDURES   The use of summary procedures in estate administration can save time and money. Summary procedures are simpler and less formal than normal probate procedures. The expenses of a personal representative's commission, attorneys' fees, appraisers' fees, and so forth can be eliminated or at least minimized if the parties utilize summary administration procedures. But in some situations—for example, when a guardian for minor children or for an incompetent person must be appointed, and a trust has been created to protect the minor or the incompetent person—probate procedures cannot be avoided. In the ordinary situation, a person can employ various will substitutes to avoid the cost of probate—for example, *inter vivos* trusts (discussed later in this chapter), life insurance policies with named beneficiaries, or joint-tenancy arrangements. Not all methods are suitable for every estate, but there are alternatives to a complete probate administration.

Testamentary Capacity

Not everyone who owns property necessarily qualifies to make a valid disposition of that property by will. *Testamentary capacity* requires the testator to be of legal age and sound mind *at the time the will is made.* The legal age for executing a will varies, but in most states and under the UPC, the minimum age is eighteen years [UPC 2-501]. Thus, a will of a twenty-one-year-old decedent written when the person was sixteen is invalid.

The concept of *sound mind* refers to the testator's ability to formulate and comprehend a personal plan for the disposition of property. Further, a testator must intend the document to be his or her will. Courts have grappled with the requirement of sound mind for a long time, and their decisions have been inconsistent. Mental incapacity is a highly subjective matter and thus is not easily measured. The general test for testamentary capacity has the following provisions:

1.   The testator must comprehend and remember the "natural objects of his or her bounty" (usually family members and persons for whom the testator has affection).
2.   The testator must comprehend the kind and character of the property being distributed.
3.   The testator must understand and formulate a plan for disposing of the property.

---

2.   For example, California law differs *substantially* from the UPC.

3.   For example, under the Virginia Small Estates Act (Va. Code Ann. Sections 64.1-132.1 to 64.1-132.4), modeled after UPC 3-1201 and 3-1202, a decedent's successor may collect the decedent's personal property by presenting an affidavit stating that (1) the value of the decedent's total personal property does not exceed $5,000, (2) sixty or more days have passed since the death, (3) no one has applied to be personal representative, (4) any will has been probated and a list of the heirs filed, and (5) the successor is entitled to payment or delivery of the property for the reason stated in the affidavit. The affidavit discharges a party paying, delivering, or transferring property in reliance on the affidavit, just as if the party had dealt with a personal representative.

Less mental ability is required to make a will than to manage one's own business affairs or to enter into a contract. Thus, a testator may be feeble, aged, eccentric, or offensive in behavior and still possess testamentary capacity. Moreover, a person can be adjudged mentally incompetent or have delusions about certain subjects and yet, during lucid moments, still be of sound mind and make a valid will.

Formal Requirements of a Will

A will must comply with statutory formalities designed to ensure that the testator understood his or her actions at the time the will was made. These formalities are intended to help prevent fraud. Unless they are followed, the will is declared void, and the decedent's property is distributed according to the laws of intestacy of the state. The requirements are not uniform among jurisdictions. Most states, however, uphold the following basic requirements for executing a will:

1. *A will must be in writing.* A written document is generally required, although in some cases oral wills, called *nuncupative wills* (to be discussed later), are found valid [UPC 2-502]. The writing itself can be informal as long as it substantially complies with the statutory requirements. In some states, a will can be handwritten in crayon or ink. It can be written on a sheet or scrap of paper, on a paper bag, or on a piece of cloth. A will that is completely in the handwriting of the testator is called a **holographic** (or olographic) **will.**

A will also can refer to a written memorandum that itself is not a will but that contains information necessary to carry out the will. For example, Thelma's will provides that a certain sum of money be divided among a group of charities named in a written memorandum that Thelma gave to the trustee *the same day the will was signed.* The written list of charities will be "incorporated by reference" into the will only if it was in existence when the will was executed (signed) and if it is sufficiently described so that it can be identified.
2. *A formal (nonholographic) will must be signed by the testator.* It is a fundamental requirement in almost all jurisdictions that the testator's signature be made with the requisite intent to validate the will; but so long as the signature is in the body of the will, it need not be at the end of the will. Each jurisdiction dictates by statute and court

decision what constitutes a signature. Initials, an "X" or other mark, and words like "Mom" have all been upheld as valid when it was shown that the testators intended them to be signatures.
3. *A formal (nonholographic) will must be witnessed.* A will must be attested by two, and sometimes three, witnesses. The number of witnesses, their qualifications, and the manner in which the witnessing must be done are generally set out in a state's statute.

A witness can be required to be disinterested— that is, not a beneficiary under the will. By contrast, the UPC provides that a will is valid even if it is attested by an interested witness [UPC 2-505]. There are no age requirements for witnesses, but they must be mentally competent.

Witnesses function to verify that the testator actually executed (signed) the will and had the requisite intent and capacity at the time. A witness does not have to read the contents of the will. Usually, the testator and witnesses must all sign in the sight or the presence of one another, but the UPC deems it sufficient if the testator acknowledges his or her signature to the witnesses [UPC 2-502]. The UPC does not require all parties to sign in the presence of one another.
4. *A will may be required to be "published."* Publication is an oral declaration by the maker to the witnesses that the document they are about to sign is his or her "last will and testament." Publication is becoming an unnecessary formality in most states, and it is not required under the UPC.

In general, strict compliance with the preceding formalities (except the one relating to witnesses and the one relating to publication) is required before a formal document is accepted as the decedent's will. Holographic wills constitute another exception in some jurisdictions. A holographic will must be signed by the decedent, however, and its material provisions must be in the testator's handwriting for the will to be probated (validated) [UPC 2-503].

Nuncupative Wills

A **nuncupative will** is an oral will made before witnesses. It is not permitted in most states. When authorized by statute, such wills are valid only if made during the last illness or in expectation of the imminent death of the testator, and usually before at least three witnesses. They are sometimes referred to as deathbed wills. Generally, only personal property can be transferred by a nuncupative will. Statutes frequently permit soldiers and sailors to make nuncupative wills when on active duty.

Undue Influence

A valid will is one that represents the maker's intention to transfer and distribute his or her property. When it can be shown that the decedent's plan of distribution was the result of improper pressure by another person overriding the maker's intent, the will is declared invalid.

Undue influence may be inferred by the court if the testator ignores blood relatives and names as beneficiary a nonrelative who is in constant close contact and in a position to influence the making of the will. For example, if a nurse or friend caring for the deceased at the time of death is named as beneficiary to the exclusion of all family members, the validity of the will might well be challenged on the basis of undue influence.

Revocation of Wills

An executed will is revocable by the maker at any time during the maker's lifetime. Wills can also be revoked by operation of law. Revocation can be partial or complete, and it must follow certain strict formalities.

ACT OF THE MAKER   Revocation of an executed will by the maker can be effected in either of two ways—by physical act or in writing.

Revocation by Physical Act   The testator may revoke a will by intentionally burning, tearing, canceling, obliterating, or destroying it or by having someone else do so in the presence of the maker and at the maker's direction. In some states, partial revocation by physical act of the maker is recognized. Thus, those portions of a will lined out or torn away are dropped, and the remaining parts of

the will are valid.[4] In no case, however, can a provision be crossed out and an additional or substitute provision written in. Such altered portions require reexecution (re-signing) and reattestation (rewitnessing).

To revoke a will by physical act, it is necessary to follow the mandates of a state statute exactly. When a state statute prescribes the exact methods for revoking a will by physical act, those are the only methods that will revoke the will.

Revocation in Another Writing   A **codicil** is a written instrument separate from the will that amends or revokes provisions in the will. It eliminates the necessity of redrafting an entire will merely to add to it or amend it. A codicil can also be used to revoke an entire will. The codicil must be executed with the same formalities required for a will. It must refer expressly to the will. In effect, it updates a will, because the will is "incorporated by reference" into the codicil.

A *second will* can be executed that may or may not revoke the first or a prior will, depending upon the language used. The second will must use specific language such as "This will hereby revokes all prior wills." If the second will is otherwise valid and properly executed, it will revoke all prior wills. If the express *declaration of revocation* is missing, then both wills are read together. If any of the dispositions made in the second will are inconsistent with the prior will, the second will controls.

When a state statute details the requirements for revoking a will with another writing, those requirements must be strictly complied with, as illustrated by the following case.

---

4.   The destruction cannot be inadvertent. The maker's intent to revoke must be shown. When a will has been burned or torn accidentally, it is normally recommended that the maker have a new document created so that it will not falsely appear that the maker intended to revoke the will.

BACKGROUND AND FACTS   Frances Maude Thompson executed a will on September 2, 1964, in Nebraska. On her death, Victor E. Thompson, her husband, filed a petition in a Nebraska state court for the probate of her will. John E. Finley, son of the decedent through a prior marriage, filed a petition seeking a formal adjudication of his deceased mother's estate by intestacy. Finley's petition claimed that his mother executed a subsequent will that revoked the 1964 document offered for probate by the husband even though Finley could not find the subsequent will. Finley's petition was dismissed, and the will was admitted to probate. Finley appealed.

Case 54.2

ESTATE OF THOMPSON

Supreme Court of Nebraska, 1983.
214 Neb. 899,
336 N.W.2d 590.

DECISION AND RATIONALE   The Supreme Court of Nebraska held that the testator did not revoke her validly executed will by writing a second will because, as far as the alleged second will was concerned, she did not adhere strictly to the state formalities of a properly executed will. In Nebraska, a person can revoke a will by writing a new one, which revokes the prior will entirely or to the extent it is inconsistent with the new will. Evidence of the revocation must be "clear, unequivocal, and convincing." Finley testified that he had seen a new will containing a clause revoking all prior wills. But the court looked to Nebraska law and stated that "[i]f revocation is by a subsequent will, it must be properly executed." At trial, no evidence was presented as to where the second will was executed, if the testator signed it, if the required witnesses observed the formalities in affixing their signatures to the document, or what role, if any, a notary public played in the process. It was not shown clearly, convincingly, and unequivocally that the second will was properly executed. Therefore, the husband's petition for the probate of the 1964 will governed the disposition of the decedent's estate.

REVOCATION BY OPERATION OF LAW

Revocation by operation of law occurs when marriage, divorce or annulment, or the birth of children takes place after a will has been executed.

Marriage   In the vast majority of states, when a testator marries *after* executing a will that does not include the new spouse, the spouse upon the testator's death can receive the amount he or she would have taken had the testator died intestate. In effect, this revokes the will to the extent of providing the spouse with an intestate share. The rest of the estate is passed under the will [UPC 2-301, 2-302]. If, however, the omission of a new spouse is intentional in the existing will or the spouse is otherwise provided for in the will (or by transfer of property outside of the will), the omitted spouse will not be given an intestate share.

Divorce or Annulment   At common law and under the UPC, divorce does not necessarily revoke the entire will. A divorce or an annulment occurring after a will has been executed will revoke those dispositions of property made under the will to the former spouse [UPC 2-508].

Children Born after a Will Has Been Executed
If a child is born after a will has been executed and if it appears that the testator would have made a provision for the child, then the child is entitled to

receive whatever portion of the estate he or she is allowed under state intestate laws. Most state laws allow a child to receive some portion of the estate if no provision is made in a will, unless it appears from the terms of the will that the testator intended to disinherit the child. Under the UPC, the rule is the same. The effect is to partially revoke the parent's will [UPC 2-302].

Rights under a Will

The law imposes certain limitations on the way a person can dispose of property in a will. For example, a married person who makes a will generally cannot avoid leaving a certain portion of the estate to the surviving spouse. In most states this is called a "forced share," "widow's share," or "elective share," and it is often one-third.

Beneficiaries under a will have rights as well. A beneficiary can renounce (disclaim) his or her share of the property given under a will. Further, a surviving spouse can renounce the amount given under a will and elect to take the "forced share" if the forced share is larger than the amount of the gift. State statutes provide the methods by which a surviving spouse accomplishes renunciation. The purpose of these statutes is to allow the spouse to obtain whichever distribution would be most advantageous. The UPC gives the surviving spouse an elective right to take one-third of the total estate [UPC 2-201].

■ CONCEPT SUMMARY 54.1 Wills

Type of Will	Definition
Holographic	A will completely in the handwriting of the testator; valid where permitted by state statute.
Attested	A written will, signed by the testator, properly witnessed, and, where required, published; one that meets formal statutory requirements for a valid will.
Nuncupative	An oral will made before witnesses during the deathbed illness of the testator; it is only valid to transfer personal property, not real property.
Method of Revocation or Modification	**Definition**
By Act of the Maker:	
Physical act	Tearing up, canceling, obliterating, or deliberately destroying part or all of a will.
Codicil	A formal separate document to amend or revoke an existing will.
New will	A new, properly executed will that expressly revokes the existing will.
By Operation of Law:	
Marriage	Generally revokes a will written before the marriage. (Under the UPC, marriage does not revoke a previously executed will. The spouse takes as he or she does under intestacy laws.)
Divorce or annulment	Revokes dispositions made under a will to a former spouse.
Subsequently born children	It is *implied* that the child is entitled to receive the portion of the estate granted under intestate distribution laws.
Type of Gift	**Definition**
Specific	A devise or bequest of a particular piece of property in the testator's estate.
General	A devise or bequest that does not single out a particular item in the testator's estate; usually a sum of money.
Residuary	A devise or bequest of any properties left in the estate after all specific and general gifts have been made.

■ Intestacy Laws

Each state regulates by statute how property will be distributed when a person dies without a will. These statutes, which are called statutes of descent and distribution—or more simply, **intestacy laws**—attempt to carry out the likely intent and wishes of the decedent. Intestacy laws assume that deceased persons would have intended that their natural heirs—spouses, children, grandchildren, or other family members—should inherit their property. Therefore, intestacy statutes set out rules and priorities under which these heirs inherit the property. If no heirs exist, then the property will revert to the state; that is, the state will assume ownership of the property.

Surviving Spouse and Children

The rules of descent vary widely from state to state, but there is usually a special statutory provision for the rights of the surviving spouse and children. In addition, the law provides that first the debts of the decedent must be satisfied out of his or her estate, and then the remaining assets can pass to the surviving spouse and to the children.

A surviving spouse usually receives a share of the estate—one-half if there is also a surviving child and one-third if there are two or more children. Only when no children or grandchildren survive the decedent will a surviving spouse succeed to the *entire estate.*

Assume that Foley dies intestate and is survived by his wife, Barbara, and his children, Carl and Diane. Foley's property passes according to intestacy laws. After Foley's outstanding debts have been paid, Barbara will receive the homestead (either in fee simple or as a life estate) and ordinarily a one-third to one-half interest in all other property. The remaining real and personal property will pass to Carl and Diane in equal portions.

Order of Distribution

State statutes of descent and distribution specify the order in which heirs of an intestate share in the estate. When there is no surviving spouse or child, then grandchildren, brothers and sisters, and—in some states—parents of the decedents are the next in line to share. These relatives are usually called *lineal descendants.* Generally, on the testator's death, title will descend before it will ascend. For example, property will pass to the deceased's children before it will pass to his or her parents. (In either case, title by inheritance is called title by descent.) But because state statutes differ so widely, few other generalizations can be made about the laws of descent and distribution. It is extremely important to refer to the exact terms of the applicable state statutes when addressing any problem of intestacy distribution.

If there are no lineal descendants, then *collateral heirs* are the next group to share. Collateral heirs include nieces, nephews, aunts, and uncles of the decedent. If there are no survivors in any of those groups of people related to the decedent, most statutes provide that the property is to be distributed among the next of kin of any of the collateral heirs. Stepchildren and other relatives by marriage are not considered kin. Legally adopted children, however, are recognized as lawful heirs of their adoptive parents.

Whether an illegitimate child inherits depends on state statutes. In all states, intestate succession between the mother and the child exists. In some states, intestate succession between the father and the child can occur only when the child is "legitimized" by ceremony or the child has been "acknowledged" by the father.

In the following case, the constitutionality of an illegitimacy statute was affirmed by the Supreme Court of Ohio. The United States Supreme Court has allowed state illegitimacy statutes to stand upon concluding that legitimate state purposes were served by the statutes.[5]

---

5. *Labine v. Vincent,* 401 U.S. 532, 91 S.Ct. 1017, 28 L.Ed.2d 288 (1971). In *Trimble v. Gordon,* 430 U.S. 762, 97 S.Ct. 1459, 52 L.Ed.2d 31 (1977), the United States Supreme Court ruled that an Illinois illegitimacy statute was unconstitutional because it did not bear a rational relationship to a legitimate state purpose.

Case 54.3
———
WHITE v. RANDOLPH
Supreme Court of Ohio, 1979.
59 Ohio St.2d 6,
391 N.E.2d 333.

BACKGROUND AND FACTS Clarence Jackson died on January 17, 1975. His will left everything to his wife in the event she survived him. Because she had died earlier, the Ohio court appointed an administrator for his estate. The administrator, White, brought an action in probate court for a determination of the decedent's heirs-at-law. Alice Marie Jackson, who claimed to be the decedent's illegitimate daughter, was among the defendants in the action. The probate court denied Alice Marie Jackson status to inherit as an heir-at-law, based on an Ohio statute that only permitted legitimate children to inherit from the father. Because the father had failed to "legitimize" her by acknowledgment, adoption, or other stated means, she could not inherit by law. Ohio did permit illegitimate children to inherit from the mother. Jackson appealed.

DECISION AND RATIONALE The Supreme Court of Ohio affirmed the probate court's ruling denying Jackson her inheritance rights and declared the Ohio statute to be constitutional. The court found that Ohio has a sufficient state interest in the disposition of property at death to justify different laws regarding intestate succession for legitimate and illegitimate children. The court pointed out that "[i]t has long been recognized in Ohio that proof of paternity, especially after the death of the alleged father, is difficult, and particularly subject to abuse. One of the resultants of such abuse would be the instability of land titles to real estate." The court held that "[c]learly, the Ohio classification scheme is rationally related to the legitimate state purpose of assuring efficient disposition of property at death while avoiding spurious claims." In addition, the court concluded that the law did not discriminate *per se,* as all children may inherit from their mothers, and some illegitimate children may inherit from their fathers. The only group discriminated against was the "class of illegitimate children whose fathers did not formally acknowledge them or designate them as heirs-in-law."

COMMENTS Most states have amended their intestacy statutes dealing with illegitimate children to provide a more liberal test for establishing inheritance rights. These states allow paternity to be established by evidence that the parents married after the child's birth, by an adjudication before the death of the father, or by clear and convincing proof after the father's death [UPC 2–109].

Distribution to Grandchildren

When a person who dies intestate is survived by descendants of deceased children, a question arises as to what share the grandchildren of the intestate will receive. *Per stirpes* is a method of dividing an intestate share by which a class or group of distributees (for example, grandchildren) take the share that their deceased parent would have been entitled to inherit had that parent lived.

Assume that Michael, a widower, has two children, Scott and Jonathan. Scott has two children (Becky and Holly), and Jonathan has one child (Paul). At the time of Michael's death, Scott and Jonathan have predeceased their father. If Michael's estate is distributed *per stirpes,* the following distribution would take place:

1. Becky and Holly: one-fourth each, taking Scott's share.
2. Paul: one-half, taking Jonathan's share.

Exhibit 54–1 illustrates the *per stirpes* method of distribution.

An estate may also be distributed on a *per capita* basis. This means that each person takes an equal share of the estate. Assume that Michael, a widower, has two children, Scott and Jonathan. Scott has two children (Becky and Holly), and Jonathan has one child (Paul). At the time of Michael's death, Scott and Jonathan have predeceased their father. If Michael's estate is distributed per capita, Becky, Holly, and Paul will each receive a one-third share. Exhibit 54–2 illustrates the *per capita* method of distribution.

In most states and under the UPC, in-laws do not share in an estate. If a child dies before his or her parents, the child's spouse will not receive an inheritance as a result of the child's parents' death. Assume that Michael, a widower, has two married children, Scott and Jonathan, and no grandchildren. If Scott predeceases his father, Michael's entire estate will go to Jonathan. Scott's surviving wife will not inherit.

■ Trusts

A trust involves any arrangement by which legal title to property is transferred from one person to be administered by a trustee for another's benefit. It can also be defined as a right of property, real or personal, held by one party for the benefit of another. A trust can be created for any purpose that is not illegal or against public policy. The essential elements of a trust follow:

1. A designated beneficiary.
2. A designated trustee.
3. A fund sufficiently identified to enable title to pass to the trustee.

■ **Exhibit 54–1** *Per Stirpes* **Distribution**

Under this method of distribution, an heir takes the share that his or her deceased parent would have been entitled to inherit, had the parent lived. This may mean that a class of distributees—the grandchildren, in this example—will not inherit in equal portions. (Note that Becky and Holly only receive one-fourth of Michael's estate, whereas Paul inherits one-half.)

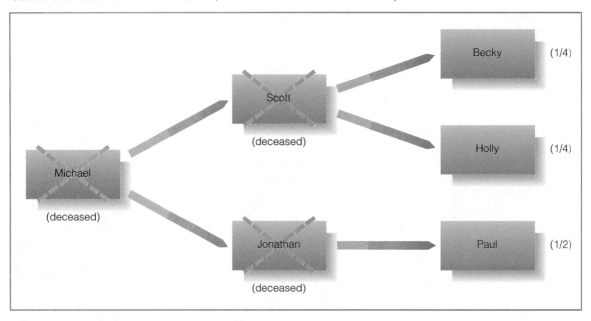

■ **Exhibit 54–2** *Per Capita* **Distribution**

Under this method of distribution, all heirs in a certain class—in this case, the grandchildren—inherit equally. Note that Becky and Holly in this situation each inherit not one-fourth of Michael's estate (as they do under the *per stirpes* method of distribution), but one-third.

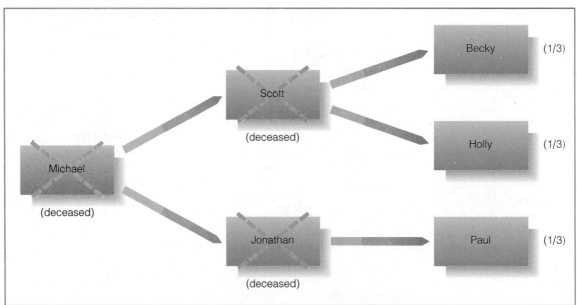

4.　Actual delivery to the trustee with the intention of passing title.

If James conveys his farm to First Bank of Minnesota to be held for the benefit of his daughters, James has created a trust. James is the settlor (the one creating the trust, or grantor), First Bank of Minnesota is the trustee, and James's daughters are the beneficiaries. This arrangement is illustrated in Exhibit 54–3.

Express Trusts

An express trust is one created or declared in expressed terms, usually in writing. It differs from a trust that is inferred by the law from the conduct or dealings of the parties (an implied trust, to be discussed later). The two types of express trusts that will be discussed here are *inter vivos* trusts and testamentary trusts.

INTER VIVOS TRUSTS　　An ***inter vivos* trust** is a trust executed by a grantor during his or her lifetime. The grantor executes a ''trust deed,'' and legal title to the trust property passes to the named trustee. The trustee has a duty to administer the property as directed by the grantor for the benefit and in the interest of the beneficiaries. The trustee must preserve the trust property; make it produc-

tive; and if required by the terms of the trust agreement, pay income to the beneficiaries, all in accordance with the terms of the trust. Once the *inter vivos* trust is created, the grantor has, in effect, given over the property for the benefit of beneficiaries.

TESTAMENTARY TRUSTS　　A trust created by will to come into existence upon the settlor's death is referred to as a **testamentary trust.** Although a testamentary trust has a trustee who maintains legal title to the trust property, actions of the trustee are subject to judicial approval. The trustee of a testamentary trust can be named in the will or be appointed by the court; thus, a testamentary trust will not fail because no trustee has been named in the will. The legal responsibilities of the trustees are the same in both an *inter vivos* and a testamentary trust. If the will setting up a testamentary trust is invalid, then the trust will also be invalid. The property that was supposed to be in the trust will then pass according to intestacy laws, not according to the terms of the trust.

Implied Trusts

Sometimes a trust is imposed by law, even in the absence of an express trust. Customarily, these implied trusts are divided into constructive and resulting trusts.

■ Exhibit 54–3 Trust Arrangement

In a trust, there is a separation of interests in the trust property. The trustee takes *legal* title, which appears to be complete ownership and possession but which does not include the right to receive any benefits from the property. The beneficiary takes *equitable* title, which is the right to receive all benefits from the property.

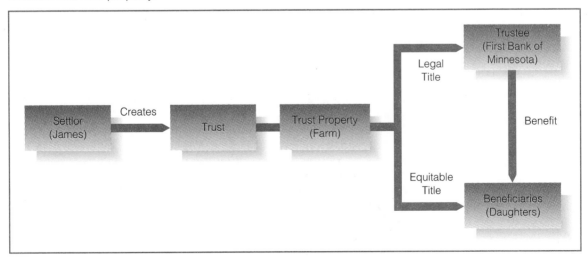

CONSTRUCTIVE TRUST   A **constructive trust** differs from an express trust in that it arises by operation of law as an equitable remedy that enables plaintiffs to recover property (and sometimes damages) from defendants who would otherwise be unjustly enriched. In other words, when a transaction takes place in which the person who takes the legal estate in property cannot also enjoy the beneficial interest without violating some established principle of equity, the court will create a constructive trust. The legal owner is declared to be a trustee for the parties who, in equity, are actually entitled to the beneficial enjoyment that flows from the trust. One source of a constructive trust is a wrongful action, such as violation of a fiduciary relationship.

To illustrate: Jules and Spring are partners in buying, developing, and selling real estate. Jules learns through the staff of the partnership that 200 acres of land will soon come on the market and that the staff will recommend that the partnership purchase the land. Jules purchases the property secretly in his own name, violating his fiduciary relationship. When these facts are discovered, a court will determine that Jules must hold the property in trust for the partnership. The following case illustrates the concept of a constructive trust.

Case 54.4

THOMAS v. FALES

Supreme Judicial Court of
Maine, 1990.
577 A.2d 1181.

BACKGROUND AND FACTS   Paula Thomas was formerly married to Charles Fales, the brother of Steven Fales. During their marriage, Charles sold illegal drugs and frequently had large amounts of cash resulting from those transactions. To avoid the increasing scrutiny of a neighbor (a police officer), Charles decided to purchase a home (the Winslow property) in another area in September 1983. To avert suspicion concerning his drug activity, Charles allegedly had his brother Steven purchase the property in Steven's name. Charles, however, provided Steven with the money for the down payment, and Charles and Paula lived in the home and paid the mortgage payments and all other expenses. Paula eventually separated from Charles and left the home, which was later rented to a third party. In 1988, Paula and Charles were divorced; the divorce judgment awarded her all of their right, title, and interest in the Winslow property. Steven refused to convey the property to Paula, contending that he was the legal owner. Paula then brought an action in a Maine state court, seeking the imposition of a constructive trust on the Winslow property and an order that legal title be conveyed to her. The trial court imposed a constructive trust on the property for the benefit of Paula and ordered that it be conveyed to her. Steven appealed.

DECISION AND RATIONALE   The Supreme Judicial Court of Maine affirmed the judgment of the trial court, ruling that it could find no clear error in the lower court's findings of fact and no abuse of discretion in its imposition of a constructive trust on the Winslow property for the benefit of Paula. The court held that "[a] constructive trust may be imposed when a party holding legal title to property stands in a fiduciary relation to another, resulting in an 'equitable duty to convey [the property] on the ground that he would be unjustly enriched if he were permitted to retain it.' " The court held that Steven stood in a fiduciary relation to Charles and Paula and would be unjustly enriched if allowed to retain the house. Because the house was bought by Charles for his own benefit, Steven was under an equitable duty to convey the property to Paula, who had been awarded Charles's interest in the house. As to the argument that Paula should not be entitled to the house because it was bought with the proceeds from an illegal activity, the court noted that there was no evidence that Paula had actively participated in the illegal activity.

RESULTING TRUST   A **resulting trust** arises from the conduct of the parties. Here the trust results or is created when circumstances raise an inference that the party holding legal title to the property does so for the benefit of another, unless the inference is rebutted or the beneficial interest is otherwise disposed of.

To illustrate: Thor purchases one acre of land from Lassen. Thor is going out of the country for two years and will be unable to attend the closing. She asks Lassen to deed the property, at the closing, to Thor's good friend, Crenshaw. Lassen does indeed convey the property to Crenshaw. If it is proved that Thor did not intend to make a gift of the land to Crenshaw, the property may be considered to be held in trust (a resulting trust), with Crenshaw as the trustee, for the benefit of Thor.

Other Kinds of Trusts

Certain trusts are created for special purposes. Three such trusts are charitable, spendthrift, and totten trusts.

CHARITABLE TRUST   A trust designed for the benefit of a segment of the public or for the benefit of the public in general is a **charitable trust.** It differs from a private trust in that the identities of the beneficiaries are uncertain. Usually, to be deemed a charitable trust, a trust must be created for charitable, educational, religious, or scientific purposes.

SPENDTHRIFT TRUST   A trust that contains a provision for the maintenance of a beneficiary by prevention of his or her improvidence with the bestowed funds is a **spendthrift trust.** Essentially, the beneficiary is not permitted to transfer his or her right to future payments of income or capital. The majority of states allow spendthrift trust provisions that prohibit creditors from subjecting the beneficiary's interest in future distributions from the trust to the payment of debts.

TOTTEN TRUST   A special type of trust created when one person deposits money in his or her own name as a trustee for another is a **totten trust.** This trust is tentative in that it is revocable at will until the depositor dies or completes the gift in his or her lifetime by some unequivocal act or declaration (for example, delivery of the funds to the intended

beneficiary). If the depositor should die before the beneficiary dies and if the depositor has not revoked the trust expressly or impliedly, a presumption arises that an absolute (a binding, irrevocable) trust has been created for the benefit of the beneficiary. At the death of the depositor, the beneficiary obtains property rights to the balance on hand.

The Trustee

The trustee is the person holding the trust property. Anyone legally capable of holding title to, and dealing in, property can be a trustee. If the settlor of a trust fails to name a trustee, or if a named trustee cannot or will not serve, the trust does not fail—an appropriate court can appoint a trustee.

TRUSTEE'S DUTIES   As obvious as it may sound, a trustee's basic duty is one of trust. Specifically, a trustee must act with honesty, good faith, and prudence in administering the trust and exercise a high degree of loyalty toward the trust beneficiary. The standard of care is the degree of care a prudent person would exercise in his or her personal affairs.[6] The duty of loyalty requires that the trustee act in the *exclusive* interest of the beneficiary.

Among specific duties, a trustee must keep clear and accurate accounts of the trust's administration and furnish complete and accurate information to the beneficiary. A trustee must keep trust assets separate from his or her own assets. A trustee has a duty to pay to an income beneficiary the net income of the trust assets at reasonable intervals. A trustee has a duty to distribute the risk of loss from investments by reasonable diversification and a duty to dispose of assets that do not represent prudent investments. Investments in federal, state, or municipal bonds; corporate bonds; and shares of preferred or common stock may be prudent investments under particular circumstances.

TRUSTEE'S POWERS   When a settlor creates a trust, he or she may prescribe the trustee's powers

---

6. Revised Uniform Principal and Income Act Section 2(a)(3); Restatement (Second) of Trusts, Section 227 (1959). This rule is in force in the majority of states by statute and in a small number of states under the common law.

and performance. Generally, state law[7] applies only to the extent that it does not conflict with the terms of the trust.[8] When state law does apply, it is most likely to restrict the trustee's investment of trust funds. Typically, statutes confine trustees to investments in conservative debt securities such as government, utility, and railroad bonds and first-mortgage loans on realty. It is common, however, for a settlor to grant a trustee discretionary investment power. In that circumstance, any statute may be considered only advisory, with the trustee's decisions subject in most states to the prudent person rule.

A difficult question concerns the extent of a trustee's discretion to ''invade'' the principal and distribute it to an income beneficiary, if the income is found to be insufficient to provide for the beneficiary in an appropriate manner. A similar question concerns the extent of a trustee's discretion to retain trust income and add it to the principal, if the income is found to be more than sufficient to provide for the beneficiary in an appropriate manner. Generally, the answer to both questions is that the income beneficiary should be provided with a somewhat predictable annual income, but with a view to the safety of the principal. Thus, a trustee may make individualized adjustments in annual distributions.

Of course, a trustee is responsible for carrying out the purposes of the trust. If the trustee fails to comply with the terms of the trust or the controlling statute, he or she is personally liable for any loss.

ALLOCATIONS BETWEEN PRINCIPAL AND INCOME Frequently, a settlor will provide one beneficiary with a life estate and another beneficiary with the remainder interest in a trust. For example, a farmer may create a testamentary trust providing that the farm's income be paid to his or her surviving spouse and that on the surviving spouse's death, the farm be given to their children. Among the income and principal beneficiaries, questions may arise concerning the apportionment of receipts and expenses for the farm's management, as well as the trust's administration between income and principal. Even when income and principal beneficiaries are the same, these questions may occur.

To the extent that a trust instrument does not provide instructions, a trustee must refer to applicable state law. The general rule is that ordinary receipts and expenses are chargeable to the income beneficiary, whereas *extraordinary* receipts and expenses are allocated to the principal beneficiaries.[9] For example, the receipt of rent from trust realty would be ordinary, as would the expense of paying the property's taxes; but the cost of long-term improvements and proceeds from the property's sale would be extraordinary.

Trust Termination

The terms of a trust should expressly state the event on which the settlor wishes it to terminate—for example, the beneficiary's or the trustee's death. If the trust instrument does not provide for termination on the beneficiary's death, the beneficiary's death will not end it. Similarly, without an express provision, a trust will not terminate on the trustee's death.

Typically, a trust instrument specifies a termination date. For example, a trust created to educate the settlor's child may provide that the trust ends when the beneficiary reaches the age of twenty-five. If the trust's purpose is fulfilled before that date, a court may order the trust's termination. If no date is specified, a trust will terminate when its purpose has been fulfilled. Of course, if a trust's purposes become impossible or illegal, the trust will terminate.

■ Estate Administration

The orderly procedure used to collect assets, settle debts, and distribute the remaining assets when a person dies is the subject matter of estate administration. The rules and procedures for managing

---

7. In ten states, the law consists, in part, of the Uniform Principal and Income Act, published in 1931. The Revised Uniform Principal and Income Act, issued in 1962, has been adopted in twenty-nine states. There are other uniform acts that may apply—for instance, about a third of the states have enacted the Uniform Trustees' Powers Act, promulgated in 1964. In addition, most states have their own statutes covering particular procedures and practices. In other words, as in other areas of estate planning, the laws concerning trusts differ among the states. Common law principles have been collected in the Restatement (Second) of Trusts (1959).

8. Revised Uniform Principal and Income Act Section 2(a)(1); Restatement (Second) of Trusts, Section 164 (1959).

9. Revised Uniform Principal and Income Act Sections 3, 6, 8, 13; Restatement (Second) of Trusts, Section 233 (1959).

the estate of a deceased are controlled by statute. Thus, they vary from state to state. In every state, there is a special court, often called a probate court, that oversees the management of estates of decedents.

The first step after a person dies is usually to determine whether or not the decedent left a will. In most cases, the decedent's attorney will have that information. If there is uncertainty as to whether a valid will exists, the personal papers of the deceased must be reviewed. If a will exists, it probably names a personal representative (executor) to administer the estate. If there is no will, or if the will fails to name a personal representative, then the court must appoint an administrator. Under the UPC, the term *personal representative* refers to either an executor (person named in the will) or an administrator (person appointed by the court) [UPC 1-201(30)].

The personal representative has a number of duties. The first duty is to inventory and collect the assets of the decedent. If necessary, the assets are appraised to determine their value. Both the rights of creditors and the rights of beneficiaries must be protected during the estate administration proceedings. In addition, the personal representative is responsible for managing the assets of the estate during the administration period and for not allowing them to be wasted or unnecessarily depleted.

The personal representative receives and pays valid claims of creditors and arranges for the estate to pay federal and state income taxes and estate taxes (or inheritance taxes, depending on the state). A personal representative is required to post a bond to ensure honest and faithful performance. Usually, the bond exceeds the estimated value of the personal estate of the decedent. Under most state statutes, the will can specify that the personal representative need not post a bond.

When the ultimate distribution of assets to the beneficiaries is determined, the personal representative is responsible for distributing the estate pursuant to the court order. Once the assets have been distributed, an accounting is rendered to the court, the estate is closed, and the personal representative is relieved of any further responsibility or liability for the estate.

■ Estate Taxes

The death of an individual may result in tax liabilities at both the federal and state levels.

Federal Estate Tax

At the federal level, a tax is levied upon the total value of the estate after debts and expenses for administration have been deducted and after various exemptions have been allowed. The tax is on the estate itself rather than on the beneficiaries. Therefore, it does not depend on the character of any bequests or on the relationship of the beneficiary to the decedent, unless a gift to charity that is recognized by the Internal Revenue Service as deductible from the total estate for tax purposes is involved. Estate planning for larger estates also considers other deductions available under federal law. And an entire estate can pass free of estate tax if the estate is left to the surviving spouse.

State Inheritance Taxes

The majority of states assess a death tax in the form of an inheritance tax imposed on the recipient of a bequest rather than on the estate. Some states also have a state estate tax similar to the federal estate tax. In general, inheritance tax rates are graduated according to the type of relationship between the beneficiary and decedent. The lowest rates and largest exemptions are applied to a surviving spouse and the children of the decedent.

■ Terms and Concepts

administrator 977
bequest 977
charitable trust 989
codicil 981
constructive trust 988

devise 977
escheat 976
executor 977
holographic will 980
inter vivos trust 987

intestacy laws 983
intestate 976
legacy 977
legatee 977
nuncupative will 980

■ For Review

1.   Who can make a will? That is, what is the minimum age for executing a will, and what are the other elements of testamentary capacity? What are the basic requirements for executing a will? How may a will be revoked?
2.   What are the three types of gifts that may be made by will? What happens to a gift if the heir has predeceased the testator?
3.   What are the four essential elements of a trust?
4.   Lucille owns a home as a tenant in common with Ricky, her husband. Lucille also owns a thousand acres of farmland from a previous marriage. Lucille and Ricky have a joint checking account and separate savings accounts. Lucille dies intestate. She is survived by Ricky and by their three children. Under intestacy laws, after Lucille's debts have been paid, who will receive how much of Lucille's property?

5.   In the previous problem, imagine that instead of dying intestate, Lucille left a will setting up a trust, in which the farmland was to be held for the benefit of her children. If the will did not designate a trustee, would the trust fail? If the will was ruled invalid, would the trust be invalid? If so, what would happen to the farmland?

■ Questions and Case Problems

54-1. John is a widower who has two married children, Frank and Amy. Amy has two children, Phil and Paula. Frank has no children. John dies, leaving a typewritten will that gives all his property equally to his children, Frank and Amy, and provides that should a child predecease him, leaving grandchildren, the grandchildren are to take *per stirpes.* The will was witnessed by Amy and John's lawyer and signed by John in their presence. Amy has predeceased John. Frank claims the will is invalid.
   (a) Discuss whether the will is valid.
   (b) Discuss the distribution of John's estate if the will is invalid.
   (c) Discuss the distribution of John's estate if the will is valid.

54-2. James was a bachelor. While single, he made out a will naming his mother, Carol, as sole beneficiary. Later, James married Lisa.
   (a) If James died while married to Lisa without changing his will, would the estate go to his mother, Carol? Explain.
   (b) Assume James made out a new will upon his marriage to Lisa, leaving his entire estate to Lisa. Later he divorced Lisa and married Sue, but he did not change his will. Discuss the rights of Lisa and Sue to his estate after his death.
   (c) Assume James divorced Lisa, married Sue, and changed his will leaving his estate to Sue. Later, a daughter, Lori, was born. James died without having included Lori in his will. Discuss fully whether Lori had any rights in the estate.

54-3. Ann has drafted and properly executed a will. Assume the following clauses in her will and the following events:

   (a) Ann's will provides, "I leave my two-carat diamond ring to my sister, Sylvia." At the time of Ann's death, Sylvia has already died, leaving one child, Lindsay.
   (b) Ann's will provides, "I leave $5,000 to each of my nieces, Fern and Dorothy." At the time of Ann's death, only $4,000 remains in her estate.
   (c) Ann's will provides, "I leave to my nephew, Donald, my $10,000 Cadillac or equivalent value." Just prior to Ann's death, she sold the Cadillac.
Discuss fully each situation, giving its name and describing its effect on the legatees.

54-4. Sam, an eighty-three-year-old invalid, employs a nurse, Sarah, to care for him. Prior to Sarah's employment, Sam executed a will leaving his entire estate to his only living relative—his great-grandson, Fred. Sarah convinces Sam that Fred is dead and gets Sam to change his will, naming Sarah as his sole beneficiary. After Sam's death, Fred appears and contests the will. Discuss the probable success of Fred's action.

54-5. The following transfers and events take place:
   (a) John lives in Europe. He transfers $20,000 to his good friend, Kate, and orally instructs her to invest and distribute the $20,000 and whatever it accrues so as to finance the MBA education of his daughter, JoAnn.
   (b) Fred is on the board of directors of the ABC Corp. and is the chairman of its research policy committee. Through his chairmanship he learns that ABC has come up with a cure for cancer. Fred purchases on the open market 20,000 shares of ABC stock at $10 per share. When the announcement of the cure is made, the market value of ABC's stock increases to $200 per share.
   (c) Sue is a successful businesswoman. She is engaged to marry John, a man of modest means who has ambitions to be an inventor. Sue creates a $20,000

joint savings account in the name of "Sue, in trust for John." Sue tells John that the purpose of the account is to encourage him to move forward in his business ventures.

Discuss fully whether a valid trust has been created in each situation; what each trust is called; and when applicable, what its effect is.

54-6. Robert and Everett Kling, two brothers, purchased rental property in Fenton, Missouri. Robert contributed $5,544 and Everett $5,624 toward the purchase price of $19,005. Title to the property was taken in the name of Everett's wife, Nancy. The brothers maintained an account in which they made deposits and from which they paid expenses related to the rental property. Although each brother had agreed to contribute $20 per month toward the remaining purchase price, Robert never did do so, and Everett consequently increased his contribution to $40 per month. When Robert died, Everett and Nancy claimed 100 percent ownership of the Fenton property. Robert's children, John and Janet, filed suit, claiming that Everett and Nancy held the property as a resulting trust and that they (John and Janet) were entitled to half of the property. Discuss whether a resulting trust had been created and, if so, what the distribution should be. [*Estate of Kling*, 736 S.W.2d 65 (Mo.App. 1987)]

54-7. Myrtle Courziel executed a valid will that provided for the establishment of a scholarship fund designed to encourage the study of corrosion as it affects metallurgical engineering. The recipients were to be students in the upper half of their class at the University of Alabama. Subsequently, Myrtle died. John Calhoun, the eventual administrator of her estate, obtained access to Myrtle's safe-deposit box to search for her will. He found the will intact, except that the last page of the will, which had contained Myrtle's signature and the signatures of the witnesses, had been removed from the document and was not in the safe-deposit box or anywhere else to be found. Because Myrtle had had sole control over the will, should it have been presumed that her removal of the last page (or her having allowed it to be removed) effectively revoked the will? [*Board of Trustees of University of Alabama v. Calhoun*, 514 So.2d 895 (Ala. 1987)]

54-8. Tennie Joyner was eighty years old and about to be hospitalized for an illness. In order to provide for her son, Calvin, Joyner wrote a will and took it to her neighbors for them to type and witness. In the document, she stated that she was giving all her possessions to Calvin because he had taken care of her for years. The will was contested on the basis that Joyner had not met the formal requirement of publication, because she did not tell her neighbors explicitly that the document was her "last will and testament." Joyner had merely told her neighbors that she wanted "a piece of paper fixed up so I can sign it and Calvin will have a place to live." Joyner intended the document to dispose of her property, and the neighbors were fully aware of her intention. Does Joyner's failure to state "this is my last will and testament" invalidate the will?

Explain. [*Faith v. Singleton*, 286 Ark. 403, 692 S.W.2d 239 (1985)]

54-9. In 1956, Jack Adams executed a will, the terms of which established a charitable trust. The trust income was to go to Prince Edward School Foundation as long as the foundation continued to operate and admitted to its schools "only members of the White Race." If the foundation admitted nonwhites to its schools, the trust income was to go to the Miller School, under the same limitation, and so on to two other educational institutions. If all of the successively named educational beneficiaries violated the limitation, the income would go to Hermitage Methodist Homes of Virginia, Inc., without any limitation attending the bequest. In 1968, Adams died. Subsequent to the execution of the will, all of the educational beneficiaries enrolled black students. The trustee, uncertain as to how to distribute the trust income under these circumstances, sought counsel from the court. Assuming that the racially discriminatory provisions are unconstitutional and void, which, if any, of the named beneficiaries should receive the trust income? Discuss. [*Hermitage Methodist Homes of Virginia, Inc. v. Dominion Trust Co.*, 387 S.E.2d 740 (Va. 1990)]

54-10. Edwin Fickes died in 1943. His will provided for the creation of a trust, half of which was to be divided, upon the death of Fickes's last surviving child, "in equal portions between [the testator's] grandchildren then living." At the time of the death of Fickes's last surviving child, there were four biological grandchildren and four adopted grandchildren living. Two of the adopted grandchildren, both boys, had been adopted prior to Fickes's death. The other two, both girls, had been adopted after Fickes died. The trustee, Connecticut National Bank and Trust Co., sought a court determination of whether the adopted grandchildren were entitled to share in the trust distribution. The trial court found that the testator, Fickes, had intended to include his adopted grandsons as "grandchildren" within the meaning of his will but could not have intended to include his adopted granddaughters as "grandchildren," so they were not entitled to a share of the trust. What will happen on appeal? Discuss fully. [*Connecticut National Bank and Trust Co. v. Chadwick*, 217 Conn. 260, 585 A.2d 1189 (1991)]

54-11. A Question of Ethics

 James Heber Burke (Heber) and his wife Evelyn spent most of their lives in Ohio and had jointly accumulated a substantial amount of property there. The Burkes, who had been married for fifty-three years, had two children, four grandchildren, and four great-grandchildren. Evelyn died in February 1985. Heber had originally hailed from Pike County, Kentucky, and in June 1985, he returned to Pike County and bought a house there. In the same month, he told his children that he was going to marry Lexie Damron, a widow who attended his church. Lexie and Heber were married on July 20. On July 27, Heber executed a will, which was drawn up by Lexie's attorney, in which

he left all of his property to Lexie. Heber died three weeks later. Heber's children, Donald Burke and Beatrice Bates, contested the will, alleging that Heber lacked testamentary capacity and that Heber's will resulted from Lexie's undue influence over him. Friends and relatives of Heber in Pike County testified that they had never known Heber to drink and that, although he seemed saddened by his first wife's death, he was not incapacitated by it. According to the children's witnesses, however, after Evelyn's death, Heber allegedly drank heavily and constantly; had frequent crying spells; repeatedly visited his wife's grave; tried to dig her up so that he could talk to her; and had hallucinations, talking to people who were not present and claiming that Evelyn visited him regularly at night, which frightened him into sleeping in the attic. The jury found the will to be invalid on the grounds of undue influence, and Lexie appealed. [Burke v. Burke, 801 S.W.2d 691 (Ken.App. 1990)]

1. The appellate court had to weigh two conflicting policies in deciding this issue. What two policies are in conflict here, and what criteria should be used in resolving the issue?

2. Given the circumstances described above, would you infer undue influence on the part of Lexie if you were the judge? Would you conclude that Heber lacked testamentary capacity? What would be the fairest solution, in your opinion?

3. In the above case, Heber's first wife, Evelyn, contributed substantially to the acquisition of the property subject to Heber's will. A natural assumption would be that Evelyn would want their children to inherit the jointly acquired property. Yet if Heber were found to be of sound mind and not the victim of any undue influence, the court would allow him to totally disregard the children, if he wished, in his will. Is this fair to Evelyn's presumed intentions? To the children? Is there any solution to the possible unfairness that can result from giving people the right to disregard natural heirs in their wills?

Chapter 55

Liability of Accountants and Other Professionals

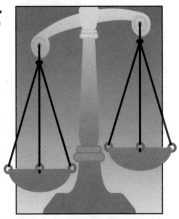

Accountants, attorneys, physicians, and other professionals have found themselves increasingly subject to liability in the past decade or so. This more extensive liability has resulted in large part from a greater public awareness of the fact that professionals are required to deliver competent services and are obligated to adhere to standards of performance commonly accepted within their professions.

Considering the many potential sources of legal liability that may be imposed upon them, accountants, attorneys, and other professionals should be well aware of their legal obligations. In the first part of this chapter, we look at the potential common law liability of professionals and then examine the potential liability of accountants under securities laws and the Internal Revenue Code. The chapter concludes with a brief examination of the relationship of professionals, particularly accountants and attorneys, with their clients.

■ Potential Common Law Liability to Clients

Under the common law, professionals may be liable to clients for breach of contract, negligence, or fraud.

Liability for Breach of Contract

Accountants and other professionals face liability for any breach of contract under the common law. A professional owes a duty to his or her client to honor the terms of the contract and to perform the contract within the stated time period. If the professional fails to perform as agreed in the contract, then he or she has breached the contract, and the client has the right to recover damages from the professional. A professional may be held liable for expenses incurred by his or her client in securing another professional to provide the contracted-for services, for penalties imposed on the client for failure to meet time deadlines, and also for any other reasonable and foreseeable monetary losses that arise from the professional's breach.

Liability for Negligence

Accountants and other professionals may also be held liable under the common law for negligence in the performance of their services. As with any negligence claim, the elements that must be proved to establish negligence on the part of a professional are as follows:

1. A duty of care existed.
2. That duty of care was breached.
3. The plaintiff suffered an injury.
4. The injury was proximately caused by the defendant's breach of the duty of care.

All professionals are subject to standards of conduct established by codes of professional ethics, by state statutes, and by judicial decisions. They are also governed by the contracts they enter into with their clients. In their performance of contracts, they must exercise the established standard of care, knowledge, and judgment generally accepted by members of that professional group. We look below at the duty of care owed by two groups of professionals that frequently perform services for business firms: accountants and attorneys.

ACCOUNTANT'S DUTY OF CARE Accountants play a major role in a business's financial system. Accountants have the necessary expertise and experience in establishing and maintaining accurate financial records to design, control, and audit record-keeping systems; to prepare reliable statements that reflect an individual's or a business's financial status; and to give tax advice and prepare tax returns.

In the performance of their services, accountants must comply with **generally accepted accounting principles (GAAP)** and **generally accepted auditing standards (GAAS).** The Federal Accounting Standards Board determines what accounting conventions, rules, and procedures constitute GAAP at a given point in time. GAAS are standards concerning an auditor's professional qualities and the judgment that he or she exercises in performing an examination and report. GAAS are established by the American Institute of Certified Public Accountants. As long as an accountant conforms to generally accepted accounting principles and acts in good faith, he or she will not be held liable to the client for incorrect judgment. As

a general rule, an accountant is not required to discover every impropriety, defalcation (embezzlement), or fraud in his or her client's books. If, however, the impropriety, defalcation, or fraud has gone undiscovered because of an accountant's negligence or failure to perform an express or implied duty, the accountant will be liable for any resulting losses suffered by his or her client. Therefore, an accountant who uncovers suspicious financial transactions and fails to investigate the matter fully or to inform his or her client of the discovery can be held liable to the client for the resulting loss. Typically, the amount of the loss resulting from an accountant's failure to exercise reasonable care according to generally accepted standards is substantially higher than the fee the client was to have paid the accountant.

A violation of generally accepted accounting principles and generally accepted auditing standards will be considered *prima facie* evidence of negligence on the part of the accountant. Compliance with generally accepted accounting principles and generally accepted auditing standards, however, does not *necessarily* relieve an accountant from potential legal liability. An accountant may be held to a higher standard of conduct established by state statute and by judicial decisions.

If an accountant is deemed guilty of negligence, the client may collect damages for losses that arose from the accountant's negligence. An accountant, however, is not without possible defenses to a cause of action for damages based on negligence. Possible defenses include the following allegations:

1. The accountant was not negligent.
2. If the accountant was negligent, this negligence was not the proximate cause of the client's losses.
3. The client was negligent (depending on whether state law allows contributory negligence as a defense).

Sometimes accountants are hired to prepare unaudited financial statements. Although a lesser standard of care is typically required for a "write-up," accountants may still be held liable in this situation. Accountants may be subject to liability for failing, in accordance with standard accounting procedures, to delineate a balance sheet as "unaudited." An accountant will also be held liable for failure to disclose to a client facts or circumstances that give reason to believe that misstatements have been made or that a fraud has been committed.

ATTORNEY'S DUTY OF CARE   The conduct of attorneys is governed by rules established by each state and by the American Bar Association's Model Rules of Professional Conduct. All attorneys owe a duty to provide competent and diligent representation. In judging an attorney's performance, the standard used will normally be that of a reasonably competent general practitioner of ordinary skill, experience, and capacity. Attorneys are required to be familiar with well-settled principles of law applicable to a case and to discover law that can be found through a reasonable amount of research. The lawyer also must investigate and discover facts that could materially affect the client's legal rights.

When an attorney fails to exercise reasonable care and professional judgment, he or she breaches the duty of care. The plaintiff must then prove that the breach actually caused him or her some injury. For example, if the lawyer allows the statute of limitations to lapse on a client's claim, the attorney can be held liable for malpractice—because the client can no longer file a cause of action in this case and has lost a potential award of damages. In recent years, malpractice claims against attorneys have increased dramatically. All attorneys are encouraged to keep calendars for their cases so that they will not carelessly miss crucial deadlines, such as the expiration of the statute of limitations. In the following case, an attorney was sued for legal malpractice because he failed to inform his client of a settlement offer.

BACKGROUND AND FACTS   Ralph Moores, a dockworker, was injured on the job. After collecting $43,000 in workers' compensation benefits, Moores brought a third party liability suit in a federal district court against the shipowners. The shipowners informed Nathan Greenberg, Moores's attorney, that they would settle the suit, at one point offering $90,000. Greenberg did not inform Moores of the offer because he did not consider it sufficiently significant. When Moores lost the case in court, he sued Greenberg, alleging that Greenberg had a duty to inform him of the offers and had breached that duty by not doing so. The trial court awarded Moores $12,000 in damages ($90,000 less $35,000 owed to Greenberg and $43,000 recovered in workers' compensation). Neither party was satisfied, and the case was appealed.

Case 55.1

MOORES v. GREENBERG

United States Court of Appeals, First Circuit, 1987.
834 F.2d 1105.

DECISION AND RATIONALE   The United States Court of Appeals for the First Circuit affirmed the trial court's judgment. Greenberg had breached his duty to Moores to inform him of the settlement offers and was thus liable to Moores for the damages Moores suffered as a result—which the court found to be $12,000. The appellate court explained that in representing a client, "an attorney has a duty to use that degree of skill, diligence, and judgment ordinarily to be expected of a member of the bar practicing in the same (or a similar) locale. As part and parcel of this duty, a lawyer must keep his client seasonably apprised of relevant developments, including opportunities for settlement." To Greenberg's argument that the $90,000 offer was "too niggardly to be relayed," the court responded that the offer "could not be said, as a matter of law, to be a patently ridiculous one," and concluded that the trial court "did not err in permitting the jury to determine whether reasonably competent counsel would have informed Moores of the *   *   * offer." As for the amount of damages, "it was 'reasonably foreseeable' that, by failing to communicate the offer, Greenberg would effectively deprive his client of the net benefit of the tendered bargain—nothing more."

Liability for Fraud

Actual fraud and constructive fraud present two different circumstances under which an accountant may be found liable. Recall from Chapter 13 that fraud, or misrepresentation, consists of the following elements:

1. A misrepresentation of a material fact has occurred.
2. There exists an intent to deceive.
3. The innocent party has justifiably relied on the misrepresentation.
4. For damages, the innocent party must have been injured.

A professional may be held liable for *actual fraud* when he or she intentionally misstates a material fact to mislead his or her client and the client justifiably relies on the misstated fact to his or her injury. A material fact is one that a reasonable person would consider important in deciding whether to act. In contrast, a professional may be held liable for *constructive fraud* whether or not he or she acted with fraudulent intent. For example, constructive fraud may be found when an accountant is grossly negligent in the performance of his or her duties. The intentional failure to perform a duty in reckless disregard of the consequences of such a failure would constitute gross negligence on the part of a professional. Both actual and constructive fraud are potential sources of legal liability under which a client may bring an action against an accountant or other professional.

When a client is dissatisfied with the performance of an accounting firm, he or she will often sue on several theories. In the following case, the court had to sift through claims for negligence, constructive fraud, and breach of contract. Notice how the court disposes of the latter two counts by its treatment of the negligence claim.

Case 55.2

IN RE THE HAWAII CORP.

United States District Court,
District of Hawaii, 1983.
567 F.Supp. 609.

BACKGROUND AND FACTS   The American Pacific Group (APG) was planning a merger with one of its subsidiaries, The Hawaii Corporation (THC). APG engaged Peat, Marwick, Mitchell & Company (PMM) to prepare financial statements for the companies and to express opinions as to the most advantageous means of combining them. When the merger resulted in an arguably unnecessary loss of $22 million, the trustee in reorganization sued PMM in a federal district court on grounds of, among others, accountant malpractice, based on the unusual method PMM had used in restructuring the companies. The trustee contended that had PMM used the accounting method generally applied in such transactions, its financial statements would have reflected a more negative picture, and the merger would not have occurred.

DECISION AND RATIONALE   The United States District Court for the District of Hawaii issued a judgment in PMM's favor. The court found that the accounting method employed by PMM, although "creative," did not violate the negligence standard because it produced a result essentially similar to that of the standard method. Further, the court concluded that even though the accounting was not done according to the usual method, it was arrived at by careful reasoning. An accountant is not a guarantor but must act honestly, in good faith, and with reasonable care. Thus, PMM was not guilty of negligence, breach of contract, or fraud. The court noted that an accountant's exercise of "that degree of skill and competence reasonably expected of persons in those professions is implied in a contract for professional services. Liability follows for breach of contract if there is negligence." As for THC's claims of fraudulent misrepresentation in the comfort letter,[a] financial statements, and pro forma statements, the court held that

---

a.   A letter from PMM stating that the informal procedures used did not reveal any material changes in the financial statements and that only an audit with certain established procedures could reliably supply that information.

THC needed to show (1) a false misrepresentation of material fact, (2) an intent to induce THC to act, (3) PMM's knowledge that the representations were false and THC's reasonable belief as to their truth, and (4) detrimental reliance on THC's part. Reckless disregard for the truth would have satisfied the knowledge requirement, but the court determined that the documents contained no material misrepresentations.

◼ Potential Common Law Liability to Third Persons

Traditionally, an accountant or other professional did not owe any duty to a third person with whom he or she had no direct contractual relationship—that is, to any person not in **privity of contract** with the professional. A professional's duty was only to his or her client. Violations of statutory laws, fraud, and other intentional or reckless acts of wrongdoing were the only exceptions to this general rule.

In regard to accountants' liability, Chief Judge Benjamin Cardozo's 1931 decision in *Ultramares Corp. v. Touche*[1] was the leading authority for this traditional view. In *Ultramares,* a lender alleged that its reliance on the accountants' negligently prepared statements had caused it to lose money on loans made to the client. The court, however, refused to impose liability upon the accountants and concluded that they owed a duty of care only to those persons for whose ''primary benefit'' the statements were intended. In this case, the client was the only person for whose ''primary benefit'' the statements were intended. The court held that in the absence of privity or a relationship ''so close as to approach that of privity,'' a party could not recover from an accountant.

In the past several years, the *Ultramares* rule has been severely criticized. Accountants perform much of their work for use by persons who are not parties to the contract; and thus, it is asserted that they owe a duty to these third parties. Consequently, there has been an erosion of the *Ultramares* rule, and accountants have been exposed to potential liability to third parties. Understanding an accountant's common law liability to third parties is critical, because often, when a business fails, its independent auditor (accountant) may be one of the few potentially solvent defendants.

Today, the majority of courts hold that accountants can be held liable to third parties for negligence, but the standard for imposition of this liability varies. Most courts have adopted the position taken by the Restatement (Second) of Torts, which states that accountants are subject to liability for negligence not only to their clients but also to *foreseen,* or *known,* users—or class of users—of their reports or financial statements. For example, if an accountant prepares a financial statement for a client and knows that the client will submit that statement to a bank to secure a loan, the accountant may be held liable to the bank for negligent misstatements or omissions—because the accountant knew that the bank would rely on the accountant's work product when deciding whether to make the loan. A minority of courts, however, extend accountants' liability even further to include liability to any users whose use of, and reliance on, an accountant's statements or reports was *reasonably foreseeable.* For example, in *Bily v. Arthur Young & Co.,*[2] a California court held that an auditor had a duty to all those persons and entities who reasonably relied on negligently prepared reports and whose reliance was reasonably foreseeable by a professionally sophisticated auditor.

In the following case, the court considers the question of the extent of an accountant's liability to a third party. Note the court's reliance on the Restatement (Second) of Torts in determining the issue.

---

1.   255 N.Y. 170, 174 N.E. 441 (1931).

2.   222 Cal.App.3d 289, 271 Cal.Rptr. 470 (1990).

Case 55.3

FIRST FLORIDA BANK, N.A. v. MAX MITCHELL & CO.

Supreme Court of Florida, 1990.
558 So.2d 9.

BACKGROUND AND FACTS In April 1985, Max Mitchell, a certified public accountant (CPA), went to First Florida Bank to negotiate a $500,000 unsecured line of credit for C. M. Systems, Inc. Mitchell introduced himself to Stephen Hickman, the bank's vice-president, and presented audited financial statements of C. M. Systems for fiscal years ending October 31, 1983, and October 31, 1984. The 1984 statement did not show that C. M. Systems owed money to any bank, and Mitchell said that as of April 16, 1985, C. M. Systems was not indebted to any bank nor was he aware of any material change in the company's financial condition since October 31, 1984. After the bank approved the loan, C. M. Systems borrowed $500,000 and never repaid it. The bank later discovered that the audit for the year ending October 31, 1984, had substantially overstated C. M. Systems' assets, understated its liabilities, and overstated its net income. The audit did not reflect that the company owed at least $750,000 to several banks. Also, material changes had occurred in the company's balance sheet after the audit but before approval of the line of credit. The bank sued Mitchell and his firm in a Florida state court, on grounds of negligence and gross negligence. Because of the absence of privity between Mitchell or his firm and the bank, the trial court granted Mitchell summary judgment. The bank appealed.

DECISION AND RATIONALE The Supreme Court of Florida ruled that because of the special role played by Mitchell in the bank's decision to give credit to C. M. Systems, he could be held liable. The court held that it was not necessary for an accountant "to have any particular person in mind as the intended, or even the probable, recipient of the information" in the accountant's statements or reports. It is sufficient if the accountant "intends it to reach and influence either a particular person or persons, known to him, or a group or class of persons, distinct from the much larger class who might reasonably be expected sooner or later to have access to the information and foreseeably to take some action in reliance upon it." The court explained that "[b]ecause of the heavy reliance upon audited financial statements in the contemporary financial world, we believe permitting recovery only from those in privity or near privity is unduly restrictive." But the court said that this rule only applied to those whom the accountant knew would rely on the statements or reports, because "an accountant controls neither his client's accounting records nor the distribution of his reports." In this case, Mitchell could not be held liable merely because he prepared the audit. He was liable because he negotiated the loan and personally delivered the statements, knowing that the bank would rely on them. The case was remanded.

Potential Statutory Liability

Both civil and criminal liabilities against accountants may be imposed by the Securities Act of 1933 and the Securities Exchange Act of 1934.

Liability under the Securities Act of 1933

Registration statements are required to be filed with the Securities and Exchange Commission (SEC) prior to an offering of securities (see Chapter 43). Accountants frequently prepare and certify the issuer's financial statements that are included in the registration statement. Section 11 of the Securities Act of 1933 imposes liability upon accountants for misstatements and omissions of material facts in registration statements. Therefore, an accountant may be found liable if he or she prepared any financial statements included in the registration statement that "contained an untrue statement of a material fact or omitted to state a material fact required to be stated therein or necessary to make the statements therein not misleading.''[3]

Under Section 11 of the 1933 act, an accountant may be held liable for his or her misstatement or omission of a material fact in a registration statement by anyone who acquires a security covered by the registration statement. A purchaser of a security need only demonstrate that he or she has suffered a loss on the security. Proof of reliance upon the materially false statement or misleading omission is not usually required. Nor is there a requirement of privity between the accountant and the security purchasers.

Section 11 imposes a duty upon accountants to use ''due diligence'' in the preparation of financial statements included in the filed registration statements. After the purchaser has proved the loss on the security, the accountant bears the burden of showing that he or she exercised **due diligence** in the preparation of the financial statements. To avoid liability, the accountant must show that he or she had, ''after reasonable investigation, reasonable grounds to believe and did believe, at the time such part of the registration statement became effective, that the statements therein were true and that there was no omission of a material fact required to be stated therein or necessary to make the statements therein not misleading.''[4] Further, the failure to follow generally accepted accounting principles and generally accepted auditing standards is also proof of a lack of due diligence.

In particular, the due diligence standard places a burden upon accountants to verify information furnished by a corporation's officers and directors. The burden of proving due diligence requires an accountant to demonstrate that he or she is free from negligence or fraud. For example, the accountants in *Escott v. BarChris Construction Corp.*[5] were held liable for a failure to detect danger signals in materials that, under generally accepted accounting standards, required further investigation under the circumstances. Merely asking questions is not always sufficient to satisfy the requirement of due diligence.

Besides proving that he or she has acted with due diligence, an accountant may raise the following defenses:

1. There were no misstatements or omissions.
2. The misstatements or omissions were not of material facts.
3. The misstatements or omissions had no causal connection to the plaintiff's loss.
4. The plaintiff purchaser invested in the securities knowing of the misstatements or omissions.

A purchaser bringing a suit under Section 11 of the Securities Act of 1933 may recover the difference between the amount paid for the security and one of the following:

1. The value of the security at the time the suit was brought.
2. The price at which the security was disposed of in the market before the suit.
3. The price at which the security was disposed of after the suit but before judgment, if such damages are less than the damages representing the difference between the amount paid for the security and its value at the time the suit was brought.[6]

Liability under the Securities Exchange Act of 1934

Under Sections 10(b) or 18 of the Securities Exchange Act of 1934 or SEC Rule 10b-5, an accountant may be found liable for fraud. A plaintiff has a substantially heavier burden of proof under the 1934 act than under the 1933 act. Unlike the 1933 act, the 1934 act provides that an accountant need not prove due diligence to escape liability. Section 18 of the 1934 act imposes civil liability on an accountant who makes or causes to be made in any application, report, or document a statement that at the time and in light of the circumstances was false or misleading with respect to any material fact.[7]

Section 18 liability is narrow in that it applies only to applications, reports, documents, and registration statements filed with the SEC. This remedy is further limited in that it applies only to sellers and purchasers. Under Section 18, a seller or purchaser must prove one of the following:

1. That the false or misleading statement affected the price of the security.

---

3. 15 U.S.C. Section 77k(a).
4. 15 U.S.C. Section 77k(b)(3).
5. 283 F.Supp. 643 (S.D.N.Y. 1968).

6. 15 U.S.C. Section 77k(e).
7. 15 U.S.C. Section 78r(a).

2. That the purchaser or seller relied upon the false or misleading statement in making the purchase or sale and was not aware of the inaccuracy of the statement.

Even if a purchaser or seller proves these two elements, an accountant can be exonerated of liability upon proof of "good faith" in the preparation of the financial statement. To demonstrate good faith, an accountant must show that he or she had no knowledge that the financial statement was false and misleading. Acting in good faith requires the total absence of an intention on the part of the accountant to seek an unfair advantage over, or to defraud, another party. Proving a lack of intent to deceive, manipulate, or defraud is frequently referred to as proving a lack of *scienter.* Absence of good faith can also be demonstrated by the accountant's reckless conduct and gross negligence. (Note that "mere" negligence in the preparation of a financial statement does not constitute liability under the 1934 act. This differs from provisions of the 1933 act, under which an accountant is liable for all negligent acts.) In addition to the good faith defense, accountants have available as a defense the buyer's or seller's knowledge that the financial statement was false and misleading.

A court, under Section 18 of the 1934 act, also has the discretion to assess reasonable costs, including attorneys' fees, against accountants.[8] Sellers and purchasers may maintain a cause of action "within one year after the discovery of the facts constituting the cause of action and within three years after such cause of action accrued."[9]

The Securities Exchange Act of 1934 further subjects accountants to potential legal liability in its antifraud provisions. Section 10(b) of the 1934 act and SEC Rule 10b-5 contain the antifraud provisions. As stated in *Herman & MacLean v. Huddleston,* "a private right of action under Section 10(b) of the 1934 act and Rule 10b-5 has been consistently recognized for more than 35 years."[10]

Section 10(b) makes it unlawful for any person, including accountants, to use, in connection with the purchase or sale of any security, any manipulative or deceptive device or contrivance in contravention of SEC rules and regulations.[11] Rule 10b-5 further makes it unlawful for any person, by use of any means or instrumentality of interstate commerce,

1. To employ any device, scheme, or artifice to defraud.
2. To make any untrue statement of a material fact or to omit to state a material fact necessary to make the statements made, in light of the circumstances, not misleading.
3. To engage in any act, practice, or course of business that operates or would operate as a fraud or deceit upon any person, in connection with the purchase or sale of any security.[12]

Accountants may be held liable only to sellers or purchasers under Section 10(b) and Rule 10b-5.[13] The scope of these antifraud provisions is extremely wide. Privity is not necessary for a recovery. Under these provisions, an accountant may be found liable not only for fraudulent misstatements of material facts in written material filed with the SEC but also for any fraudulent oral statements or omissions made in connection with the purchase or sale of any security.

For a plaintiff to recover from an accountant under the antifraud provisions of the 1934 act, he or she must, in addition to establishing status as a purchaser or seller, prove *scienter,*[14] a fraudulent action or deception, reliance, materiality, and causation. A plaintiff who fails to establish these elements cannot recover damages from an accountant under Section 10(b) or Rule 10b-5.

In the following case, the court wrestles with the reliance requirement on finding an accounting firm liable under Rule 10b-5. Ask yourself as you read the case if any evidence exists that actually shows reliance by the plaintiffs.

---

8.   15 U.S.C. Section 78r(a).
9.   15 U.S.C. Section 78r(c).
10.   459 U.S. 375, 103 S.Ct. 683, 74 L.Ed.2d 548 (1983).

11.   15 U.S.C. Section 78j(b).
12.   17 C.F.R. Section 240.10b-5.
13.   See *Blue Chip Stamps v. Manor Drug Stores,* 421 U.S. 723, 95 S.Ct. 1917, 44 L.Ed.2d 539 (1975).
14.   See *Ernst & Ernst v. Hochfelder,* 425 U.S. 185, 96 S.Ct. 1375, 47 L.Ed.2d 668 (1976).

BACKGROUND AND FACTS Westland Minerals Corporation (WMC) was the promoter of a venture in which multiple limited partnerships were formed for the purpose of drilling for oil and gas. WMC asked the accounting firm of Coopers & Lybrand (C&L) to prepare an opinion letter on behalf of one of WMC's investors, Muhammad Ali, who desired reassurance concerning the benefits offered by the tax shelter. WMC showed copies of the letter to other potential investors. C&L concluded that, to encourage potential investors, a more complete letter should be drafted and presented WMC with a revised document. When the Internal Revenue Service denied deductions taken by the investors, 210 of them sued C&L in a federal district court, partially on the basis that they had relied on the revised document, under Rule 10b-5. The trial court ruled in the investors' favor, and C&L appealed.

Case 55.4

SHARP v. COOPERS & LYBRAND

United States Court of Appeals, Third Circuit, 1981.
649 F.2d 175.

DECISION AND RATIONALE The United States Court of Appeals for the Third Circuit held that C&L had violated Rule 10b-5, basing the finding on a presumption of reliance: Because C&L knew that the letter was going to potential investors, it could assume that they would rely on it. The second letter went out under the partnership name, and C&L had full knowledge of its intended use. Consequently, the court held that C&L put itself "into a position in which the investing public would place their trust and confidence in it." Reliance is an element of an action for damages under Rule 10b-5, but in securities cases reliance may be difficult to prove. As a result, the court stated, there is a distinction between cases of alleged omission and cases of alleged misrepresentation. The presumption favoring the plaintiff operates in the former but not in the latter. In this case, the court found both "omissions and misrepresentations" of material facts—facts that a reasonable investor would consider important. For example, there was evidence that C&L did not disclose the affiliation between a putative lender and WMC. Although in a strict sense the presumption should operate only as to the omissions, the court decided that this bifurcation, of "great appeal to graduate logicians in a classroom," would not be practical in the courtroom. Thus, C&L had the burden of rebutting the presumption of reliance, a burden that C&L failed to carry.

■ Potential Criminal Liability

An accountant may be found criminally liable for violations of the Securities Act of 1933, the Securities Exchange Act of 1934, the Internal Revenue Code, and both state and federal criminal codes. Under both the 1933 act and the 1934 act, accountants may be subject to criminal penalties for *willful* violations—imprisonment of up to five years and/or a fine of up to $10,000 under the 1933 act and up to $100,000 under the 1934 act.

The Internal Revenue Code, Section 7206(2),[15] makes aiding or assisting in the preparation of a false tax return a felony punishable by a fine of $100,000 ($500,000 in the case of a corporation) and imprisonment for up to three years. Those who prepare tax returns for others may face liability under the Internal Revenue Code. Note that one does not have to be an accountant to be subject to liability for tax-preparer penalties. The Internal Revenue Code defines a tax preparer as any person who prepares for compensation, or who employs one or more persons to prepare for compensation, all or a substantial portion of a tax return or a claim for a tax refund.[16]

---

15. 26 U.S.C. Section 7206(2).

16. 26 U.S.C. Section 7701(a)(36).

■ CONCEPT SUMMARY 55.1   Civil Liability of Accountants

Type of Liability	When Liable
Common Law	
1. Liability to Client:	
a. Breach of contract	An accountant who fails to perform according to his or her contractual obligations can be held liable for breach of contract and resulting damages.
b. Negligence	An accountant in performance of his or her duties must use the care, knowledge, and judgment generally used by accountants under the same or similar circumstances. Failure to do so is negligence. Violating generally accepted accounting principles and generally accepted auditing standards is *prima facie* evidence of negligence.
c. Fraud	Actual intent to misrepresent a material fact to a client, when the client relies on the misrepresentation, is fraud. Gross negligence in performance of duties is constructive fraud.
2. Liability to Third Parties:	
a. Negligence	An accountant's duty of care to the client flows to any third person the accountant knows or should have known will benefit from the accountant's work.
b. Fraud	An accountant is liable for actual or constructive fraud perpetrated on a third person, the same as for a client.
Statutory Law	
1. Securities Act of 1933, Section 11	An accountant who makes a false statement or omits a material fact in audited financial statements required for registration of securities under the law may be liable to anyone who acquires securities covered by the registration statement. The accountant's defense is basically the use of due diligence and the reasonable belief that the work was complete and correct. The burden of proof is on the accountant.
2. Securities Exchange Act of 1934, Sections 10(b) and 18	Accountants are held liable for false and misleading applications, reports, and documents required under the act. The burden is on the plaintiff, and the accountant has numerous defenses, including good faith and lack of knowledge that what was submitted was false.

Section 6694[17] of the Internal Revenue Code imposes on tax preparers a penalty of $250 per return for negligent understatement of his or her client's tax liability and a penalty of $1,000 for willful understatement of tax liability or reckless or intentional disregard of rules or regulations. Tax preparers may also be subject to penalties under Section 6695[18] if they fail to furnish the taxpayer with a copy of the return, fail to sign the return, or fail to furnish the appropriate tax identification numbers.

Section 6701[19] of the Internal Revenue Code imposes a penalty of $1,000 per document for aiding and abetting an individual's understatement of tax liability (the penalty is increased to $10,000 in corporate cases). The tax preparer's liability is limited to one penalty per taxpayer per tax year. Note that if this penalty is imposed, no penalty can be imposed under Section 6694 with respect to the same document.

In most states, criminal penalties may be imposed for such actions as knowingly certifying

---

17. 26 U.S.C. Section 6694.
18. 26 U.S.C. Section 6695.

19. 26 U.S.C. Section 6701.

false or fraudulent reports; falsifying, altering, or destroying books of account; and obtaining property or credit through the use of false financial statements.

■ Working Papers

Performing an audit for a client involves an accumulation of **working papers**—the various documents used and developed during the audit. These include notes, computations, memoranda, copies, and other papers that make up the work product of an accountant's services to a client. Under the common law, which in this instance has been codified in a number of states, working papers remain the accountant's property. It is important for accountants to retain such records in the event that they need to defend against a lawsuit for negligence or other actions in which an accountant's competence is challenged. But because an accountant's working papers reflect his or her client's financial situation, the client has a right of access to them. (An accountant must return to his or her client any of the client's records or journals upon the client's request, and failure to do so may result in liability.)

The client must give permission before working papers can be transferred to another accountant. Without the client's permission or a valid court order, their contents are not to be disclosed. Disclosure would constitute a breach of the accountant's fiduciary duty to the client. On grounds of unauthorized disclosure, the client could initiate a malpractice suit. The accountant's best defense would be that the client gave permission for the papers' release.

■ Confidentiality and Privilege

Professionals are restrained by the ethical tenets of their professions to keep all communications with their clients confidential. The confidentiality of attorney-client communications is also protected by law, which confers a *privilege* on such communications. This privilege is granted because of the need for full disclosure to the attorney of the facts of a client's case. To encourage frankness, all attorney-client communications relating to representation are held in strictest confidence and protected by law. The attorney and his or her employees may not discuss the client's case with anyone—even under court order—without the client's permission.

In a few states, accountant-client communications are privileged by state statute. In these states, accountant-client communications may not be revealed even in court or in court-sanctioned proceedings without the client's permission. The majority of states, however, abide by the common law, which provides that, if a court so orders, an accountant must disclose information about his or her client to the court. Physicians and other professionals may similarly be compelled to disclose in court information given in confidence by patients or clients to the professionals.

Professional-client communications—other than those between an attorney and his or her client—are not privileged under federal law. In cases involving federal law, state-provided rights to confidentiality of accountant-client communications are not recognized. Thus, in those cases, in response to a court order, an accountant must provide the information sought.

■ Terms and Concepts

■ For Review

1. An accountant's violation of GAAP and GAAS may be considered *prima facie* evidence of what? Does that mean that compliance with GAAP and GAAS relieves an accountant of liability? What are an accountant's possible defenses against allegations by a client that the accountant was negligent?

2. Can an accountant be held liable for negligence to a party with whom he or she is not in privity of contract?

3. Under what circumstances may an accountant disclose the contents of working papers?

4. Pat tells Ryan, an accountant, that Pat needs a financial statement to present to Cork County Bank to secure a loan. Ryan prepares the statement but negligently understates Pat's liabilities. With the statement, Pat secures the loan. Pat fails to repay the loan. Could Ryan be held liable for the bank's loss?

5. In the previous problem, Pat also uses the statement in a stock transaction with Dubliner Corp. Under what circumstances might Ryan be held liable on grounds of negligence for Dubliner's loss? Under what circumstances might Ryan be held liable for the loss under the Securities Act of 1934?

■ Questions and Case Problems

55-1. Larkin, Inc., retains Howard Perkins to manage its books and prepare its financial statements. Perkins, a certified public accountant, lives in Indiana and practices there. After twenty years, Perkins has become a bit bored with the format of generally accepted accounting principles and has become creative in his accounting methods. Now, though, Perkins has a problem, as he is being sued by Molly Tucker, one of Larkin's creditors. Tucker alleges that Perkins either knew or should have known that Larkin's financial statements would be distributed to various individuals. Furthermore, she asserts that these financial statements were negligently prepared and seriously inaccurate. What are the consequences of Perkins's failure to adopt generally accepted accounting principles? Under the traditional *Ultramares* rule, can Tucker recover damages from Perkins? Explain.

55-2. The accounting firm of Goldman, Walters, Johnson & Co. prepared financial statements for Lucy's Fashions, Inc. After reviewing the various financial statements, Happydays State Bank agreed to loan Lucy's Fashions $35,000 for expansion. When Lucy's Fashions declared bankruptcy under Chapter 11 six months later, Happydays State Bank promptly filed an action against Goldman, Walters, Johnson & Co., alleging negligent preparation of financial statements. Assuming that the court has abandoned the *Ultramares* approach, what is the result? What are the policy reasons for holding accountants liable to third parties with whom they are not in privity?

55-3. In early 1989, Bennett, Inc., offered a substantial number of new common shares to the public. Harvey Helms had a long-standing interest in Bennett because his grandfather had once been president of the company. Upon receiving a prospectus prepared and distributed by Bennett, Helms was dismayed by the pessimism it embodied. After much debate, Helms decided to delay purchasing stock in the company. A few months later, Helms asserted that the prospectus prepared by the accountants was overly pessimistic. Moreover, Helms alleged that the prospectus contained materially misleading statements. Discuss fully how successful Helms would be in bringing a cause of action under Rule 10b-5 against the accountants of Bennett, Inc.

55-4. The plaintiffs, Harry and Barry Rosenblum, brought an action against Touche Ross & Co., a prominent accounting firm. The plaintiffs alleged that they had relied upon the correctness of audits in acquiring Giant common stock in conjunction with the sale of their business to Giant.

The financial statements of Giant were found to be fraudulent, and the stock that the Rosenblums had acquired proved to be worthless. The plaintiffs alleged that Touche's negligence in conducting the audits was the proximate cause of their loss. Does an auditor owe a duty to third persons known and intended by the auditor to be recipients of the audit? Furthermore, does an independent auditor owe a duty to anyone when the opinion he or she furnishes does not include a statement limiting the dissemination of the information contained in the financial statements? Explain. [*H. Rosenblum, Inc. v. Adler,* 93 N.J. 324, 461 A.2d 138 (1983)]

55-5. An accounting firm was engaged by two car rental companies to determine the net worth of those businesses by preparing an audited statement. At the request of their clients, the accountants did not audit the accounts receivable, made appropriate exceptions to the accounts receivable in the balance sheet, and qualified their accountants' opinion with a similar caveat. After the audit had been performed and on the basis of the figures reflected in the balance sheet, Stephens Industries, Inc., purchased two-thirds of the car rental companies' stock. The car rental businesses thereafter failed, and Stephens Industries brought an action against the accounting firm for allegedly having misrepresented the status of the accounts receivable in the audit. What was the result? [*Stephens Industries, Inc. v. Haskins & Sells,* 438 F.2d 357 (10th Cir. 1971)]

55-6. The plaintiffs were the purchasers of all the stock in companies owned by the defendant sellers. Alleging fraud under the federal securities law and under the New York common law of fraud, the plaintiffs sued the defendant sellers and their accounting firm. What should be the result with respect to the accounting firm, assuming that the treatment of shipping costs, expenses, and factoring charges was not in accordance with generally accepted accounting principles and hence created an inaccurate financial picture in the financial statement? [*Berkowitz v. Baron,* 428 F.Supp. 1190 (S.D.N.Y. 1977)]

55-7. Credit Alliance Corp. is a major financial service company engaged primarily in financing the purchase of capital equipment through installment sales and leasing agreements. As a condition of extending additional major financing to L. B. Smith, Credit Alliance required an audited financial statement. Smith provided Credit Alliance with an audited financial statement prepared by the accounting firm of Arthur Andersen & Co. Later, upon Smith's petitioning for bankruptcy, it was discovered that Smith, at the time of the audit, was in a precarious financial position.

Credit Alliance filed suit against Arthur Andersen, claiming that Andersen had failed to conduct investigations in accordance with proper auditing standards and that Andersen's recklessness had resulted in misleading statements that caused Credit Alliance to incur damages. In addition, it was claimed that Andersen knew, or should have known, that Credit Alliance would rely on these statements in issuing credit to Smith. Discuss whether Credit Alliance, as a third party, could hold Arthur Andersen liable in a negligence action. [*Credit Alliance Corp. v. Arthur Andersen & Co.*, 65 N.Y.2d 536, 483 N.E.2d 110, 493 N.Y.S.2d 435 (1985)]

55-8. Toro Co. was a major supplier of equipment and credit to Summit Power Equipment Distributors. Toro required audited reports from Summit to evaluate the distributor's financial condition. Summit supplied Toro with reports prepared by Krouse, Kern & Co., an accounting firm. The reports allegedly contained mistakes and omissions regarding Summit's financial condition. Toro alleged that it had extended and renewed large amounts of credit to Summit in reliance on the audited reports. Summit was unable to repay these amounts, and Toro brought a negligence action against the accounting firm and the individual accountants. Evidence produced at the trial showed that Krouse knew that the reports it furnished to Summit were to be used by Summit to induce Toro to extend credit, but no evidence was produced to show either a contractual relationship between Krouse and Toro or a link between these companies evidencing Krouse's understanding of Toro's actual reliance on the reports. Indiana follows the *Ultramares* rule. What was the result? [*Toro Co. v. Krouse, Kern & Co.*, 827 F.2d 155 (7th Cir. 1987)]

55-9. The accounting firm of Arthur Young & Co. was employed by DMI Furniture, Inc., to conduct a review of an audit prepared by Brown, Kraft & Co., certified public accountants, for Gillespie Furniture Co. DMI planned to purchase Gillespie and wished to determine its net worth. Arthur Young, by letter, advised DMI that Brown, Kraft had performed a high-quality audit and that Gillespie's inventory on the audit dates was fairly stated on the general ledger. Allegedly as a result of these representations, DMI went forward with its purchase of Gillespie. Subsequently, DMI charged Brown, Kraft & Co., Arthur Young, and Gillespie's former owners with violations of Section 10(b) of the Securities Exchange Act and SEC Rule 10b-5. DMI complained that Arthur Young's review had proved to be materially inaccurate and misleading, primarily because the inventory reflected in the balance sheet was grossly overstated. Arthur Young was charged "with acting recklessly in failing to detect, and thus failing to disclose, material omissions and reckless conduct on the part of Brown, Kraft, and in making affirmative misstatements in its letter" to DMI. DMI sought $8 million in compensatory damages and $8 million in punitive damages from the accounting firms. Did DMI have a valid cause of action under either Section 10(b) or Rule 10b-5? Discuss. [*DMI Furniture, Inc. v. Brown, Kraft & Co.*, 644 F.Supp. 1517 (C.D.Cal. 1986)]

55-10. Sheila Simpson and the other two shareholders in H. P. Enterprises Corp. decided to sell the corporation and turned to Ed Oliver, an attorney, for assistance. Oliver formed a corporation, Tide Creek, for a group of investors interested in purchasing the company and arranged for Tide Creek to purchase the assets of Enterprises for $500,000, of which $100,000 was paid at the time of the sale in November 1983. As security for the sellers, Oliver provided a lien on the stock of Tide Creek and personal guarantees of the buyers on the corporation's $400,000 note to the sellers. Oliver was the sole source of legal advice for both parties. About six months after the sale, a fire destroyed Tide Creek's inventory. In October 1984, Oliver left the firm, and one of his former law partners, David James, took over the Simpson and Tide Creek accounts. In January 1985, James advised Simpson that Tide Creek was having financial difficulties and suggested that the note be restructured; this was done. When Simpson asked James what he would do if her interests and those of Tide Creek diverged, James replied: "We would have to support you." Tide Creek later filed for bankruptcy, as did the individuals who had personally guaranteed the note, and Simpson and the others received nothing. Will the sellers succeed in a lawsuit against James for negligence? Discuss fully. [*Simpson v. James*, 903 F.2d 372 (5th Cir. 1990)]

55-11. A Question of Ethics

 Harry Crawford, a certified public accountant, prepared a financial statement for Erps Construction Co., which was seeking a loan from the First National Bank of Bluefield. Crawford knew at the time he prepared the statement that the bank would rely on the statement in making its decision on whether to extend credit to Erps. The bank later sued Crawford, alleging that he had been professionally negligent in preparing the financial statement, upon which the bank had relied in determining whether to give the construction company a loan. Crawford defended against the suit by asserting that he could not be liable to the bank because of lack of privity. The trial court ruled that in the absence of contractual privity between the parties, the bank could not recover from the accountant. On appeal, the appellate court adopted the rule enunciated by the Restatement (Second) of Torts in regard to a professional's liability to third parties. [First National Bank of Bluefield v. Crawford, *386 S.E.2d 310 (W.Va. 1989)*]

1. What is the standard of an accountant's liability to third parties under the Restatement (Second) of Torts? What ethical reasoning underlies this standard?
2. Do you think that the standard of liability under the Restatement adequately balances the rights of accountants and the rights of third parties? Can you think of a fairer standard?
3. A few courts have adopted the principle that accountants should be liable for negligence to all persons who use and rely on their work products, provided that this use and reliance was foreseeable by the accountants at the time they prepared the documents relied on. Does such a standard of liability impose too great a burden on accountants and accounting firms? Why or why not?

Chapter 56

The International Legal Environment

Nearly every major business considers the potential of international markets for its products or services. The simplest way to conduct international business is to seek customers abroad. It may be more profitable, however, to manufacture a product in the same country as its market, if access to raw materials is better and labor is less expensive, because customers are closer and barriers to trade may be avoided. One way to arrange production abroad is for a firm to invest in its own facilities; another method is to license the technology associated with a product to an existing foreign company.

Over the last decade, countries competing for international trade have become more evenly matched competitors than in earlier years. In part, this is due to the increased use and success of regional international organizations such as the European Community (EC). Another factor has been the ebbing economic strength of the United States relative to that of the EC, Japan, and the countries of the Middle East.

Transacting business on an international level is considerably different from transacting business within the boundaries of a single nation. Buyers and sellers in the international marketplace face laws that are more complex and uncertain. In competing for international trade, countries regulate more closely foreign investment within their borders; they also provide incentives to stimulate exports to (and foreign investment in) other countries and to inhibit imports. For example, a country may limit ownership of real property by foreigners. Similarly, a country may prohibit the importation of goods that contain an ingredient commonly found in certain exports, thereby keeping those foreign goods from entering the country. For example, in 1988 the European Economic Community banned beef imports from the United States because of concerns over the effect of growth hormones (added to beef by U.S. cattle farmers) on consumers. In contrast, a country may provide tax incentives for domestic firms engaged in export activities.

Because the exchange of goods, services, and ideas on a global level is now a more common phenomenon, it is important for the student of business law to be familiar with the laws pertaining to international business transactions. In this chapter we examine the legal context of international business transactions and then look at U.S. and international regulation of specific international business activities. The chapter concludes with a discussion of the application of U.S. antitrust, patent, and discrimination laws in a transnational setting.

◼ The Legal Context of International Business Transactions

National law is law that pertains to a particular nation. Because the legal system of each country reflects its own unique cultural, historical, economic, and political background, the laws of each nation differ. When disputes arise that cannot be settled by national law, *international law* may come into play.

What Is International Law?

International law can be defined as a body of written and unwritten laws observed by otherwise independent nations and governing the acts of individuals as well as states. The key difference between national law and international law is the fact that national law can be enforced by government authorities. But what government can enforce international law? By definition, a *nation* is a sovereign entity—which means that there is no higher authority to which that nation must submit. If a nation violates an international law, the most that other countries or international organizations can do (if persuasive tactics fail) is resort to coercive actions—from severance of diplomatic relations and boycotts to, at the last resort, war—against the violating nation.

In essence, international law is the result of centuries-old attempts to reconcile the traditional need of each nation to be the final authority over its own affairs with the desire of nations to benefit economically from trade and harmonious relations with one another. Although no sovereign nation can be compelled to obey a law external to itself, nations can, and do, voluntarily agree to be governed in certain respects by international law for the purpose of facilitating international trade and commerce, as well as civilized discourse.

Sources of International Law

One important source of international law consists of international customs that have evolved among nations in their relations with one another. Under Article 38(1) of the Statute of the International Court of Justice, international custom is referred to as "evidence of a general practice accepted as law." Even though customary law serves as an independent form of law, it is subject to challenges on various applications. When, for example, does a particular custom evolve into a general practice constituting a law? Conversely, when does a custom traditionally accepted as law become so outdated or impractical in a modern context that it should no longer be considered law? Just as customs within a nation change, often necessitating changes in that nation's laws, so do customs among nations change, thus affecting international law.

Treaties and other explicit agreements between or among foreign nations provide another important source of international law. A *treaty* is an agreement or contract between two or more nations that must be authorized and ratified by the supreme power of each nation. Under Article II, Section 2, of the U.S. Constitution, the president has the power "by and with the Advice and Consent of the Senate, to make Treaties, provided two-thirds of the Senators present concur." A *bilateral* agreement, as the term implies, occurs when only two nations form an agreement that will govern their commercial exchanges or other relations with one another. *Multilateral* agreements are those formed by several nations. For example, the European Community (EC), or Common Market, which regulates commercial activities among its European member nations, is the result of a multilateral trade agreement. Other multilateral agreements have led to the formation of regional trade associations, such as the Association of Southeast Asian Nations (ASEAN) and the Andean Common Market (ANCOM).

International organizations and conferences further contribute to what is known as international law. In international law, the term **international organization** generally refers to organizations composed mainly of nations and usually established by treaty. The United States is a member of more than one hundred multilateral and bilateral organizations, including at least twenty through the United Nations (see Exhibit 56–1). These organizations adopt resolutions, declarations, and other types of standards that often require a particular behavior of nations. The General Assembly of the

■ **Exhibit 56–1**
Multilateral International Organizations in which the United States Participates

Name	Purpose
Customs Cooperation Council	Established in 1950. Supervises the application and interpretation of an international code classifying goods and customs tariffs.
General Agreement on Tariffs and Trade (GATT)	Created in 1947, this was the first global commercial agreement in history and currently the principal instrument for regulating international trade. Limits tariffs and other barriers to world trade on particular commodities and other items.
International Bank for Reconstruction and Development	Popularly known as the World Bank, a specialized agency of the United Nations since 1947. Promotes growth, trade, and balance of trade by facilitating investment and providing technical assistance, particularly in agriculture, energy, transportation, and telecommunications.
International Center for the Settlement of Investment Disputes	Established in 1966. Conciliates and arbitrates disputes between private investors and governments of other countries.
International Civil Aviation Organization	Established in 1947 and became a specialized agency of the United Nations seven months later. Develops international civil aviation by issuing rules and policies for safe and efficient airports and air navigation.
International Court of Justice (World Court)	Established in 1922 and became one of the principal organs of the United Nations in 1945. Jurisdiction comprises all cases that are referred to it. Decides disputes in accord with the rules of international law.
International Maritime Organization	Established in 1948. Promotes cooperation in the areas of government regulation, practices and technical matters of all kinds affecting shipping in international trade, the adoption of standards of maritime safety and efficiency, and the abolition of discrimination and unnecessary restrictions.
International Monetary Fund (IMF)	Created in 1944 at the United Nations Monetary and Financial Conference. Promotes economic stability by aiding the growth of international trade and the stability of currency exchange rates, as well as by providing for a system of international monetary assistance.
International Telecommunications Satellite Organization	Established in 1964. Operates an international public communications satellite system on a commercial, nondiscriminatory basis.
Permanent Court of Arbitration	Established in 1899 to facilitate the settlement of international disputes. The court has jurisdiction over all cases that it is requested to arbitrate.
United Nations (UN)	Established in 1945 to maintain international peace and security. Promotes international cooperation.
World Intellectual Property Organization	Established in 1967 and became a specialized agency of the United Nations in 1974. Promotes protection of intellectual property throughout the world.

United Nations, for example, has adopted numerous nonbinding resolutions and declarations that embody principles of international law. Disputes with respect to these resolutions and declarations may be brought before the International Court of Justice. In general, however, that court has jurisdiction to settle legal disputes only when nations voluntarily submit to its jurisdiction.

In the past decade, the United Nations Commission on International Trade Law (UNCITRAL) has made considerable progress in establishing more uniformity in international law as it relates to trade and commerce. One of its most significant creations to date is the 1980 Convention on Contracts for the International Sale of Goods (CISG). The CISG is similar to Article 2 of the Uniform Commercial Code in that it is designed to settle disputes between parties to sales contracts. It spells out the duties of international buyers and sellers that will apply if the parties have not agreed otherwise in their contract. The CISG only governs sales contracts between trading partners in nations that have ratified the CISG. These nations include the United States. The CISG is discussed in more detail in Chapter 24 in the context of international contracts for the sale of goods.

Legal Principles and Doctrines

Over time a number of legal principles and doctrines have evolved and have been employed—to a greater or lesser extent—by the courts of various nations to resolve or reduce conflicts that involve a foreign element. The three important legal principles discussed below are based primarily on courtesy and respect and are applied in the interests of maintaining harmonious relations among nations.

THE PRINCIPLE OF COMITY Under what is known as the principle of **comity,** one nation will defer and give effect to the laws and judicial decrees of another country, so long as those laws and judicial decrees are consistent with the law and public policy of the accommodating nation. This recognition is based primarily on courtesy and respect. For example, assume that a Swedish seller and an American buyer have formed a contract, which the buyer breaches. The seller sues the buyer in a Swedish court, which awards damages. But the buyer's assets are in the United States and cannot be reached unless the judgment is enforced by a U.S. court of law. In such a case, if it is determined that the procedures and laws applied in the Swedish court were consistent with U.S. national law and policy, a court in the United States would likely defer to, and enforce, the foreign court's judgment.

THE ACT OF STATE DOCTRINE The **act of state doctrine** is a judicially created doctrine that provides that the judicial branch of one country will not examine the validity of public acts committed by a recognized foreign government within its own territory. This doctrine is premised on the theory that the judicial branch should not "pass upon the validity of foreign acts when to do so would vex the harmony of our international relations with that foreign nation."[1]

The act of state doctrine can have important consequences for individuals and firms doing business with, and investing in, other countries. For example, this doctrine is frequently employed in cases involving **expropriation,** which occurs when a government seizes a privately owned business or privately owned goods for a proper public purpose and awards just compensation. When a government seizes private property for an illegal purpose and without just compensation, the taking is referred to as a **confiscation.** The line between these two forms of taking is sometimes blurred because of differing interpretations of what is illegal and what constitutes just compensation. To illustrate: Tim Flaherty, an American businessperson, owns a mine in Brazil. The government of Brazil seizes the mine for public use and claims that the profits Tim has realized from the mine in preceding years constitute just compensation. Tim disagrees, but the act of state doctrine may prevent Tim's recovery in a U.S. court of law.

When applicable, both the act of state doctrine and the doctrine of *sovereign immunity,* which we discuss in the next section, tend to immunize foreign nations from the jurisdiction of U.S. courts. What this means is that, generally, firms or individuals who own property overseas have little legal protection against government actions in the countries in which they operate.

The applicability of the act of state doctrine is at issue in the following case.

---

1. *Libra Bank Ltd. v. Banco Nacional de Costa Rica, S.A.,* 570 F.Supp. 870 (S.D.N.Y. 1983).

Case 56.1

**W. S. KIRKPATRICK &
CO. v.
ENVIRONMENTAL
TECTONICS CORP.,
INTERNATIONAL**

Supreme Court of the
United States, 1990.
493 U.S. 400,
110 S.Ct. 701,
107 L.Ed.2d 816.

BACKGROUND AND FACTS   W. S. Kirkpatrick & Company learned that
the Republic of Nigeria was interested in contracting for the construction
and equipment of an aeromedical center in Nigeria. Kirkpatrick, with the
aid of a Nigerian citizen, secured the contract as a result of bribing Nigerian
officials. Nigerian law prohibits both the payment and receipt of bribes in
connection with the awarding of government contracts, and the U.S. Foreign Corrupt Practices Act (FCPA) of 1977 expressly prohibits U.S. firms
and their agents from bribing foreign officials to secure favorable contracts.
Environmental Tectonics Corporation, International (ETC), an unsuccessful
bidder for the contract, learned of the bribery and sued Kirkpatrick in a
U.S. federal district court for damages. The court granted summary judgment for Kirkpatrick because resolution of the case in favor of ETC would
require imputing to foreign officials an unlawful motivation (the obtaining of
bribes) and accordingly might embarrass the sovereign or interfere with
the conduct of U.S. foreign policy. ETC appealed. The court of appeals
reversed the judgment of the district court and remanded the case for trial.
Kirkpatrick appealed to the United States Supreme Court.

DECISION AND RATIONALE   The United States Supreme Court affirmed
the judgment of the court of appeals. The Supreme Court ruled that in this
case the act of state doctrine did not apply because there was no issue
as to the validity of an act by a foreign government within its own territory.
The Court noted that "[t]he act of state doctrine does not establish an exception for cases and controversies that may embarrass foreign governments." Consequently, the Court determined that "neither the claim nor any
asserted defense requires a determination that Nigeria's contract with Kirkpatrick *   *   * was, or was not, effective."

THE DOCTRINE OF SOVEREIGN IMMUNITY
When certain conditions are satisfied, the doctrine
of **sovereign immunity** immunizes foreign nations
from the jurisdiction of the U.S. courts. In 1976,
Congress codified this rule in the Foreign Sovereign Immunities Act (FSIA). The FSIA also modified previous applications of the doctrine in certain
respects by expanding the rights that plaintiff creditors have against foreign nations.

The FSIA exclusively governs the circumstances in which an action may be brought in the
United States against a foreign nation, including
attempts to attach a foreign nation's property. One
of the primary purposes of the FSIA was to have
federal courts, rather than the Department of State,
determine claims of foreign sovereign immunity.
It was thought that a determination of such an immunity by the courts would increase the degree of
certainty in the law of sovereign immunity.

Section 1605 of the FSIA sets forth the major
exceptions to the jurisdictional immunity of a foreign state. A foreign state is not immune from the
jurisdiction of the courts of the United States when
the state has "waived its immunity either explicitly

or by implication" or when the action is "based
upon a commercial activity carried on in the United
States by the foreign state."[2]

Issues frequently arise as to what entities fall
within the category of *foreign state*. The question
of what is a *commercial activity* has also been the
subject of dispute. Under Section 1603 of the FSIA,
a *foreign state* is defined to include both a political subdivision of a foreign state and an instrumentality of a foreign state. A *commercial activity*
is broadly defined under Section 1603 to mean a
commercial activity that is carried on by the foreign
state having substantial contact with the United
States. But the particulars of what constitutes a
commercial activity are not defined in the act.
Rather, it is left up to the courts to decide whether
a particular activity is governmental or commercial
in nature.

In the following case, the court had to determine whether the defense of sovereign immunity
was available under the FSIA.

---

2.   28 U.S.C. Section 1605(a)(1), (2).

Case 56.2

CHISHOLM & CO. v. BANK OF JAMAICA

United States District Court, Southern District of Florida, 1986.

643 F.Supp. 1393.

BACKGROUND AND FACTS The Bank of Jamaica, which is wholly owned by the government of Jamaica, contracted with Chisholm & Company in January 1981 for Chisholm to arrange for lines of credit from various U.S. banks and to obtain $50 million in credit insurance from the Export-Import Bank of the United States. Chisholm made the necessary arrangements, but the deals it had struck were subsequently refused by the Bank of Jamaica. The bank had decided to do its own negotiating while continuing to permit Chisholm to work on its behalf. When the bank refused to pay Chisholm for its services, Chisholm sued the bank in a U.S. federal district court for breach of the implied contract. The Bank of Jamaica filed a motion to dismiss, asserting, among other things, that it was immune from the jurisdiction of U.S. courts under the doctrine of sovereign immunity.

DECISION AND RATIONALE The United States District Court for the Southern District of Florida denied the bank's motion to dismiss because the suit was concerned with Chisholm's claim for payment for its services under its contract with the bank. The court examined the "commercial activity" exception to sovereign immunity in the FSIA and ruled that the bank's effort to secure lines of credit was a commercial activity "in which private entities generally engage." The court brushed aside the bank's argument that its actions were governmental in nature (because the bank claimed it was acting to further the Jamaican Economic Recovery Program), reasoning that "a contract, implied or otherwise, is inherently commercial, even when the ultimate purpose behind it is government regulation." Accordingly, the court ruled that the bank's implied contract with Chisholm constituted commercial activity and that the bank could not raise the defense of sovereign immunity to defeat Chisholm's claim for payment.

■ Regulation of Specific Business Activities

Doing business abroad can affect the economies, foreign policy, domestic politics, and other national interests of the countries involved. For this reason, nations impose laws to restrict or facilitate international business. Controls may also be imposed by international agreement.

Exporting

As explained in Chapter 24, *exporting* is selling products manufactured in one country to buyers in other countries. The U.S. Constitution provides in Article I, Section 9, that "No Tax or Duty shall be laid on Articles exported from any State." Thus Congress cannot impose any export taxes. Congress can, however, use a variety of other devices to control exports. Congress may set export quotas on, for example, grain being sold abroad. Under the Export Administration Act of 1979, restrictions can be imposed on the flow of technologically advanced products and technical data. Other export control provisions to inhibit development of the military potential of other countries are found in the Atomic Energy Act of 1954 and the Nuclear Non-proliferation Act of 1978.

Devices to stimulate exports and thereby aid domestic businesses include export incentives and subsidies. The Revenue Act of 1971, for example, gave tax benefits to firms marketing their products overseas through certain foreign sales corporations, exempting income produced by the exports. Under the Export Trading Company Act of 1982, U.S. banks are encouraged to invest in export trading companies. An export trading company consists of exporting firms joined to export a line of goods. The export trading company concept is modeled after a Japanese practice. The Export-Import Bank provides financial assistance, consisting primarily of credit guarantees given to commercial banks. Based on those guarantees, the banks loan funds to U.S. exporting companies.

Importing

Importing is buying products manufactured in a foreign country. All nations have restrictions on imports, and the United States is no exception. Restrictions include strict prohibitions, quotas, and tariffs. Under the Trading with the Enemy Act of 1917, for example, no goods may be imported from nations that have been designated enemies of the United States. Other laws prohibit the importation of illegal drugs, books that urge insurrection against the United States, and agricultural products that pose dangers to domestic crops or animals. Quotas are limits on the amounts of goods that can be imported. For example, at one time, the United States had quotas on the numbers of automobiles that could be imported from Japan. Currently, Japan voluntarily restricts the numbers of automobiles exported to the United States. Tariffs are taxes on imports. Generally, a tariff is a percentage of the value of the imports or is a flat-rate per unit (such as a barrel of oil). Tariffs raise the prices of goods, causing some consumers to purchase less expensive, domestically manufactured goods.

These restrictions are also known as trade barriers. The elimination of trade barriers is sometimes seen as essential to the world's economic well-being. To minimize trade barriers among nations, most of the world's leading trade nations abide by the General Agreement on Tariffs and Trade (GATT). The GATT has become the principal instrument for regulating international trade. Originally negotiated in 1947, the GATT has gone through seven major tariff and trade renegotiations. Between 1964 and 1967, for example, forty-eight countries negotiated tariff reductions of 50 percent on a broad range of products. Between 1973 and 1979, one hundred countries negotiated nearly a dozen agreements relating to other trade barriers. An eighth round of negotiations began in 1986 to consider intellectual property rights, investment policies, dispute resolution, and other topics.

Under Article I of the GATT, each member country agrees to grant most-favored-nation treatment to other member countries. This obligates each GATT member to treat other GATT members at least as well as it treats that country that receives its most favorable treatment with regard to imports or exports.

The United States has specific laws directed at what it sees as unfair international trade practices.

Dumping, for example, is the sale of imported goods at "less than fair value" (LTFV). "Fair value" is usually determined by the price of those goods in the exporting country. Dumping is designed to undersell U.S. businesses to obtain a larger share of the U.S. market. To prevent this, an extra tariff—known as an antidumping duty—may be assessed on the imports.

The procedure for imposing antidumping duties involves two U.S. government agencies: the International Trade Commission (ITC) and the International Trade Administration (ITA). The ITC is an independent agency that makes recommendations to the president concerning temporary import restrictions. The ITC assesses the effects of dumping on domestic businesses. The ITA is part of the Department of Commerce and decides whether import sales were at LTFV. The ITA determination establishes the amount of antidumping duties, which are set to equal the difference between the price charged in the United States and the price charged in the exporting country. A duty may be retroactive to cover past dumping.

Investing

Investing in foreign nations involves a risk that the foreign government may take the investment property. As explained above, expropriation occurs when property is taken and the owner is paid just compensation for what is taken. This does not violate generally observed principles of international law. Confiscation occurs when property is taken and no (or inadequate) compensation is paid. International law principles are violated when property is confiscated.

Generally, few remedies for confiscation of property by a foreign government are available. In many cases, claims are resolved by lump-sum settlements after negotiations between the United States and the taking nation. For example, investors whose claims arose out of confiscations following the Russian Revolution in 1917 were offered a lump-sum settlement by the Union of Soviet Socialist Republics in 1974. Still outstanding are $2 billion of claims against Cuba for confiscations that occurred in 1959 and 1960.

To counter the deterrent effect that the possibility of confiscation may have on potential investors, many countries guarantee compensation to foreign investors if property is taken. A guarantee can be in the form of national constitutional or statutory laws or provisions in international treaties. As further protection for foreign investments, some countries provide insurance for their citizens' investments abroad. In the United States, for example, the Overseas Private Investment Corporation (OPIC), a government agency, insures U.S. citizens and businesses against losses incurred as a result of confiscation of their assets by foreign governments, war, or other causes. The premium charged by OPIC for coverage depends on the nature and extent of the business risk covered. In addition to OPIC, several private firms offer international investment insurance.

Bribing Foreign Officials

Giving payments in cash or in-kind benefits to foreign government officials to obtain business contracts and other favors is often considered normal practice. To reduce the amount of these bribes given to foreign government officials by representatives of U.S. corporations, Congress enacted the Foreign Corrupt Practices Act[3] (FCPA) in 1977.

The FCPA is divided into two major parts. The first part applies to all U.S. companies and their directors, officers, shareholders, employees, and agents. As noted in Case 56.1, this part of the FCPA prohibits bribery of most officials of foreign governments if the purpose of the payment is to get the official to act in his or her official capacity to provide business opportunities.

The second part of the FCPA is directed toward accountants, because in the past, bribes were often concealed in corporate financial records. All companies must keep detailed records that "accurately and fairly" reflect the company's financial activities. In addition, they must have an accounting system that provides "reasonable insurance" that all transactions entered into by the company are accounted for and legal. These requirements assist in detecting illegal bribes.

The FCPA further prohibits any person from making false statements to accountants or false entries in any record or account. Businesses in violation of the FCPA may be fined up to $1 million. Individual officers or directors who violate the

FCPA may be fined up to $10,000 (the fine cannot be paid by the company) and be imprisoned for up to five years.

The FCPA does not prohibit payment of substantial sums to minor officials, whose duties are ministerial. These payments are often referred to as "grease," or facilitating payments. They are meant to ensure that administrative services that might otherwise be performed at a slow pace are sped up. Thus, for example, if a firm makes a payment to a minor official to speed up an import licensing process, the FCPA has not been violated.

■ U.S. Laws in a Transnational Setting

The internationalization of business raises questions of the extraterritorial effect of a nation's laws. Extraterritorial effect refers to the effect of a country's laws outside the country. To what extent do U.S. domestic laws affect other nations' businesses? To what extent are U.S. businesses affected by domestic laws when doing business abroad? The following sections discuss these questions in the context of U.S. antitrust, patent, and discrimination laws.

Antitrust Laws

U.S. antitrust laws (see Chapter 47) have a wide application. They may *subject* persons in foreign nations to their provisions, as well as *protect* foreign consumers and competitors from antitrust-violation acts committed by U.S. citizens. Consequently, *foreign persons,* a term that by definition includes foreign governments, may sue under U.S. antitrust laws in U.S. courts.

Section 1 of the Sherman Act provides for the extraterritorial effect of the U.S. antitrust laws. The United States is a major proponent of free competition in the global economy, and thus any conspiracy that has a substantial effect on U.S. commerce is within the reach of the Sherman Act. The act of violation may even occur outside the United States, and foreign governments as well as persons can be sued in violation of U.S. antitrust laws. Yet before U.S. courts will exercise jurisdiction and apply antitrust laws, it must be shown that the alleged violation had a *substantial effect* on U.S.

---

3. 15 U.S.C. Sections 78 *et seq.*

Facing a United Europe

 On December 31, 1992, many of the trade barriers among the twelve European Community (EC) countries[a] may have been eliminated.

A united Europe began in 1951 with the establishment of the European Coal and Steel Community (ECSC), consisting of Belgium, West Germany, France, Italy, Luxembourg, and The Netherlands. In 1957, the European Atomic Energy Community (Euratom) was established, and at the same time the Treaty of Rome[b] formally established the European Economic Community (EEC). The Treaty of Rome outlined three goals: (1) to preserve European peace; (2) to establish a European common market—that is, a market in which goods, capital, and labor could move freely from one country to another; and (3) to form a politically unified Europe.

Common Institutions

Originally, the ECSC, Euratom, and the EEC functioned separately. Under the Merger Treaty signed in 1965, however, the three now have common institutions: the European Council of Ministers, the European Commission, the European Parliament, and the European Court of Justice. Reference is now typically made to the European Community, or the EC.

The European Council, to which each EC country appoints one member, has both legislative and executive powers. The votes of the members are weighted to prevent the large countries from outvoting the small countries.

The European Commission is the principal executive body and may exercise legislative power delegated to it by the European Council. Its seventeen members, who are appointed by the European Council, do not take orders from member countries—they act only in the best interests of the EC. The European Commission proposes and drafts EC legislation, which is then submitted to the European Council for adoption. The European Council may amend the proposals only by unanimous vote. Before enacting EC legislation, the European Council must consult with the European Parliament.

The European Parliament, whose 518 members are elected directly by citizens of the EC countries, has no legislative authority, but it must be heard in an advisory capacity.[c] It may vote European Commission members out of office.

The European Court of Justice has thirteen justices appointed by the European Council. The court enforces EC and other international law (for example, the General Agreement on Tariffs and Trade) and analyzes "general principles of law common to Member States." The court has jurisdiction over EC matters throughout the EC. Its opinions have authority but no means of enforcement—national courts and law enforcement agencies must implement its judgments. Nevertheless, noncompliance has rarely been a problem.

The Single European Act

By 1968, most tariffs within the EC were eliminated. Other trade barriers continued to restrict trade among EC countries, however, preventing achievement of the goal of a real common market. By the

---

a. Belgium, Denmark, France, Germany, Greece, Ireland, Italy, Luxembourg, The Netherlands, Portugal, Spain, and the United Kingdom.
b. Treaty Establishing The European Economic Community, U.K.T.S. 15 (1979), 298 U.N.T.S. 11 (concluded at Rome March 25, 1957; entered into force Jan. 1, 1958).

---

c. In 1980, the European Court of Justice held that the European Council acts illegally if it legislates without waiting for the European Parliament's opinion. See *S.A. Roquette Freres v. Council,* 1980 Eur.Comm.Rep. 3333.

mid-1980s, it was clear that a Europe of relatively small, protected national economies was incapable of competing with the United States and Japan.

In June 1985, the European Commission set out a program of nearly three hundred EC-wide legislative measures needed to remove the financial, technical, and physical barriers that obstructed the operation of a true common market in Europe. To implement the program, EC countries ratified the Single European Act in February 1986 as an amendment to the Treaty of Rome. The act took effect in July 1987.

The objective of a unified European market is to make European businesses more competitive in Europe and the rest of the world. A unified market will give European-based companies a larger home market, which will make it possible for larger European-based companies to form. In turn, these companies will be able to undertake research and development on a larger scale. The effect of a unified European market on U.S. businesses may be profound.

■ Implications for the Businessperson

1. The EC is the largest market for exports from the United States, but no other international organization rivals the EC in its detailed rulemaking. Anyone doing business with EC countries will have contact with EC law, which is vast and intricate. There are law school courses devoted entirely to the study of EC law. Businesspersons contemplating doing business with the EC must invest in mastering the new "rules of the game."

2. U.S. businesspersons may have to invest directly in business operations in EC countries to take maximum advantage of expanding economic opportunities because of new licensing rules and other regulations under the Single European Act. For example, previously, each EC member separately licensed the sale of regulated products and services within its territory. Now a company licensed in any member country is permitted to sell its products or provide its services in all the other member countries without meeting further licensing requirements. But this privilege is extended only to individuals and legal entities that are citizens of, and licensed by, another member country. "Third-country" businesses (such as U.S. firms) will need to obtain separate licensing in each EC country in which they wish to do business.

■ For Critical Analysis

1. The Treaty of Rome states that a company organized under the laws of any EC country and "having its registered office, central administration or principal place of business within the Community" is entitled to EC status, regardless of the home country of the EC company's parent company. As noted above, "EC status" means that a company permitted to sell its products or provide its services in one EC country can do so in all member countries without meeting further licensing requirements. Should the mere formality of organizing a company in an EC country entitle the company to EC status when the company is owned and controlled by non-EC persons?

2. Even within a unified European market, there will still remain many differences compared with the U.S. market. What are they, and how will they affect the amount of trade within the EC?

commerce. U.S. jurisdiction is automatically invoked, however, when a *per se* violation occurs.[4]

A *per se* violation may consist of resale price fixing and tying, or tie-in, contracts. If a domestic firm, for example, joins a foreign *cartel* (a group of firms organized to control the market for their products) to control the production, price, or distribution of goods, and this cartel has a *substantial restraining effect* on U.S. commerce, a *per se* violation may exist. Hence, both the domestic firm and the foreign cartel have the potential to be sued in violation of the U.S. antitrust laws. Likewise, if foreign firms doing business in the United States

enter into a price-fixing or other anticompetitive agreement to control a portion of U.S. markets, a *per se* violation may exist.

In 1982, the United States amended the Sherman Act and the Federal Trade Commission Act to limit their application when unfair methods of competition are involved in U.S. export trade or commerce with foreign nations. The acts are not limited, however, when there is a ''direct, substantial, and reasonably foreseeable effect'' on U.S. domestic commerce that results in a claim for damages.

An alleged conspiracy on the part of Japanese television manufacturers to gain control of the electronic products market in the United States—in violation of the Sherman Act and other antitrust and tariff legislation—is considered by the United States Supreme Court in the following case.

---

4. Certain types of restrictive contracts are deemed inherently anticompetitive and thus in restraint of trade as a matter of law. These contracts are said to be *per se* violations of the antitrust laws. See Chapter 47.

Case 56.3

MATSUSHITA ELECTRIC INDUSTRIAL CO. v. ZENITH RADIO CORP.

Supreme Court of the United States, 1986.
475 U.S. 574,
106 S.Ct. 1348,
89 L.Ed.2d 538.

BACKGROUND AND FACTS Zenith Radio Corporation and several other U.S. manufacturers of television sets filed suit in a U.S. federal district court, alleging that Matsushita Electric Industrial Company (Matsushita) and other Japanese firms ''illegally conspired to drive American firms from the consumer electronic products market'' by means of a ''scheme to raise, fix and maintain artificially high prices for television receivers sold by [Matsushita and others] in Japan and, at the same time, to fix and maintain low prices for television receivers exported to and sold in the United States.'' The alleged conspiracy began, according to Zenith, in 1953. The American firms claimed that the Japanese were engaged in a ''predatory pricing'' arrangement whereby the losses sustained by selling at such low prices in the United States were offset by monopoly profits obtained in Japan. Once the Japanese gained control over an overwhelming portion of the American market for electronic products, their monopoly power would enable them to recover their losses by charging artificially high prices in the United States as well. The district court granted summary judgment in favor of the Japanese firms, and the case was appealed. The court of appeals reversed the judgment of the district court, and the case was appealed to the United States Supreme Court.

DECISION AND RATIONALE The United States Supreme Court reversed the decision of the court of appeals and remanded the case. The Supreme Court found little evidence to support the argument that Japanese electronic products manufacturers were engaged in a conspiracy to drive American competitors out of business by charging artificially low prices. The court stated that ''[t]he alleged conspiracy's failure to achieve its ends in the two decades of its asserted operation is strong evidence that the conspiracy does not in fact exist.'' Also, the Court noted that the American firms that brought the suit had seen their collective market share increase substantially during the same period of time.

Patent Laws

In the United States, inventions are protected by patent law, which is intended to prevent others from copying the invention (see Chapter 8). U.S. patent laws provide no direct protection overseas, however. To be protected in another country, an invention must be patented under the laws of that country. Internationally, the Paris Convention[5]

_____

5. See International Convention for Protection of Industrial Property, March 20, 1883, 21 U.S.T. 1583, T.I.A.S. No. 6923.

guarantees nondiscriminatory treatment under the laws of other nations, but it does not provide independent international patent protection.

The United States may prohibit the importation of products that infringe on patents registered in the United States. The following case addresses the issue of whether a U.S. firm, barred from marketing its product within the United States because of a competitor's superior patent claim, could nonetheless legally market the product abroad.

BACKGROUND AND FACTS Laitram Corporation held U.S. patents for machinery used in the process of deveining shrimp. (Deveined shrimp are easier and more pleasing to eat.) Under U.S. patent law, only the owner of a patent may "make" or "sell" an item patented in the United States. Deepsouth Packing Company began shipping components of deveining machinery similar to Laitram's patented machinery to foreign customers. The components were shipped in three separate boxes, but the entire machine could be assembled in less than an hour. Laitram sought an injunction in a U.S. federal district court against Deepsouth, arguing that this practice violated its exclusive rights under U.S. patent law. The court ruled in Deepsouth's favor, but the court of appeals reversed and ruled that Deepsouth's foreign sales violated Laitram's patent. Deepsouth appealed the court of appeals' decision to the United States Supreme Court.

DECISION AND RATIONALE The United States Supreme Court reversed the decision of the court of appeals, holding that Deepsouth's practice did not violate U.S. patent laws. The Supreme Court noted that under U.S. patent laws, Laitram's patent foreclosed Deepsouth and its customers from making, selling, or using Deepsouth's deveiners "throughout the United States" without Laitram's authority. The Court pointed out that the patent code and related provisions "are intended to grant a patentee a monopoly only over the United States market [and not] the bonus of a favored position as a flagship company free of American competition in international commerce." The Court concluded that "[t]o the degree that the inventor needs protection in markets other than those of this country," he or she must "seek it abroad through patents secured in countries where his [or her] goods are being used."

Case 56.4

DEEPSOUTH PACKING CO. v. LAITRAM CORP.

Supreme Court of the United States, 1972.
406 U.S. 518,
92 S.Ct. 1700,
32 L.Ed.2d 273.

Discrimination Laws

There are laws in the United States against discrimination on the basis of race, color, national origin, religion, and sex. Specifically, Title VII of the 1964 Civil Rights Act regulates employment practices of businesses and covers employees who are employed in any industry affecting commerce. The term *commerce* is defined as "trade, traffic,

commerce, transportation, transmission, or communication among the several states; or between a state and anyplace outside thereof." A central question for some employees is whether the Civil Rights Act covers U.S. citizens working abroad for U.S. employers.

This question faced the court when a naturalized U.S. citizen, Ali Boureslan, who was employed in Saudi Arabia by a U.S. corporation, Aramco, claimed that his supervisor at Aramco had undertaken a "campaign of harassment" against him when he first began working in Saudi Arabia in 1980. From then until he was fired in 1984, Bourselan alleged, he had been continually victimized by his supervisor's racial, religious, and ethnic slurs. Following his employment termination, Boureslan filed a Title VII action, in which he alleged discrimination based on race, religion, and national origin. Boureslan claimed that Congress intended the Civil Rights Act to apply to U.S. citizens working abroad for U.S. employers. The district court held to the contrary, and on appeal, the U.S. Court of Appeals for the Fifth Circuit agreed with the district court that Title VII could not be applied extraterritorially. The court stated that contrasting religious and social customs abroad "could

well leave American corporations a difficult choice of either refusing to employ U.S. citizens in such countries or discontinuing business."[6] The United States Supreme Court affirmed the lower courts' decisions in March 1991, holding that the plaintiff failed to demonstrate any clearly expressed congressional intent that Title VII should apply extraterritorially. The Court pointed out that Congress on numerous occasions has legislated extraterritorially and that Congress may similarly amend Title VII to apply abroad. In other words, any extraterritorial application of Title VII will have to be undertaken by the legislature, not the courts.[7]

_____

6. *Boureslan v. Aramco*, 892 F.2d 1271 (5th Cir. 1990).
7. *Equal Employment Opportunity Commission v. Arabian American Oil Co.*, ___ U.S., ___,111 S.Ct. 1227, 113 L.Ed.2d 274 (1991).

■ Terms and Concepts

act of state doctrine 1011
comity 1011
confiscation 1011

dumping 1014
expropriation 1011
international law 1009

international
  organization 1009
national law 1009
sovereign immunity 1012

■ For Review

1. Under the principle of comity, on what basis does one nation give effect to the laws of another country? Under the act of state doctrine, on what basis does the judicial branch of one country refuse to examine the validity of public acts committed by a foreign government within its own territory?
2. A foreign state is not immune from the jurisdiction of U.S. courts if the state waives its immunity. Under the Foreign Sovereign Immunities Act, on what other basis might a foreign state be considered subject to the jurisdiction of U.S. courts?
3. What is the GATT?
4. Osage Automobile Corp. is an American automobile manufacturer whose U.S. market share has been slipping

over the past fifteen years. Osage believes that its losses are due entirely to aggressive marketing practices on the part of Japanese automobile manufacturers, including what Osage believes to be unfair international trade practices. Specifically, Osage believes that Japanese automobile manufacturers have conspired to dump their products in the U.S. market. To what U.S. federal agencies might Osage complain, and what might those agencies do in considering Osage's complaint?
5. In the previous problem, if Osage sues the foreign manufacturers in U.S. federal court on the grounds that the manufacturers violated the Sherman Act, what might the court rule?

■ Questions and Case Problems

56-1. Air Flight is a U.S. manufacturer of helicopters. Heise, vice-president in charge of sales, wants to sell one hundred helicopters to North Zin, a foreign country. Secretary of Defense Zoro in North Zin has complete authority to purchase helicopters for his country. Zoro usually relies on evaluations made by his subordinates. Air Flight's main competition in the sale of these

helicopters is from Top Flight, a European firm. The president of Top Flight has given Zoro his own personal helicopter and deposited $100,000 into Zoro's account. Heise immediately offers Zoro $200,000 in cash, and in addition, gives $10,000 to each of Zoro's subordinates to induce them to process Air Flight's evaluation before they process Top Flight's. ABC accountants, when auditing Air Flight's accounts, discover these payments that have been made to Zoro and his subordinates. Heise and Air Flight claim that without these payments, Air Flight cannot compete in foreign markets. Discuss whether these payments made by Air Flight are illegal.

56-2. Section 1610(d)(1) of the Foreign Sovereign Immunities Act (FSIA) provides that the property of a foreign state that is used for commercial activity in the United States is not immune from attachment prior to the entry of a judgment if the foreign state has "explicitly waived its immunity from attachment prior to judgment." Banco Nacional, an instrumentality of the government of Costa Rica, entered into a written agreement with Libra Bank, Ltd., the plaintiffs. In the agreement, Banco Nacional stated that it did not have "any right of immunity from suit with respect to the Borrower's obligations" under this particular agreement. Did Banco Nacional, the defendant, "explicitly" waive its immunity from prejudgment attachment as required by the FSIA? [*Libra Bank, Ltd. v. Banco Nacional de Costa Rica, S.A.*, 676 F.2d 47 (2d Cir. 1982)]

56-3. Both Mannington Mills and Congoleum Corp. are American producers of carpets and other floor coverings. Mannington alleged that Congoleum had fraudulently obtained foreign patents through false statements and misrepresentation of data. Mannington sued Congoleum, arguing that these actions violated U.S. antitrust laws. Congoleum argued that the U.S. courts had no jurisdiction. Congoleum contended that issuance of foreign patents came under the act of state doctrine or, at least, required deference to foreign nations. Should the United States exercise jurisdiction over this dispute? [*Mannington Mills, Inc. v. Congoleum Corp.*, 595 F.2d 1287 (3d Cir. 1979)]

56-4. ICC Industries was an importer of potassium permanganate from the People's Republic of China. The International Trade Administration (ITA) of the Department of Commerce conducted an antidumping investigation and concluded that this potassium permanganate was being imported at less than fair value (LTFV), in violation of U.S. law. Fair value is an estimate of the value of the product in the home market—in this case, the People's Republic of China. As a consequence of its investigation of ICC, the ITA imposed retroactive antidumping duties on its imports of potassium permanganate for the period 1981 to 1983. Imposition of these duties required a finding that ICC had known or should have known that the product was being imported at less than fair value. ICC argued that it was unaware of this fact. ICC emphasized that because the People's Republic of China had a nonmarket economy, the company was unable to ascertain a home market value for potassium permanganate. ICC therefore appealed the ITA's order to the Court of Appeals for the Federal Circuit. What will result? Discuss fully. [*ICC Industries, Inc. v. United States*, 812 F.2d 694 (Fed.Cir. 1987)]

56-5. Harris Corp., the plaintiff, entered into a contract with the defendant, National Iranian Radio and Television (NIRT), to manufacture and deliver 144 FM broadcast transmitters to Teheran, Iran. Due to the revolution in Iran, the plaintiff was unable to complete delivery of the transmitters. NIRT attempted to collect on a letter of credit that had been set up to guarantee performance. The plaintiff subsequently brought an action against the defendant, seeking to enjoin receipt of payment on the letter of credit. Bank Melli Iran, the issuer, was also made a defendant. Both defendants alleged that the district court lacked jurisdiction over them. From 1969 to 1982, Melli maintained an office in New York City, where it carried out significant business transactions. Moreover, NIRT had entered into this contract that required performance by Harris in the United States and also the training of NIRT personnel in the United States. Was this action consistent with due process? Was the "minimum contacts" standard established for foreign jurisdiction (discussed in Chapter 40) satisfied? [*Harris Corp. v. National Iranian Radio and Television*, 691 F.2d 1344 (11th Cir. 1982)]

56-6. Texas Trading & Milling Corp. and other companies brought an action for breach of contract against the Federal Republic of Nigeria and its central bank. Nigeria, a rapidly developing and oil-rich nation, had overbought huge quantities of cement from Texas Trading and others. Unable to accept delivery of the cement, Nigeria repudiated the contract, alleging immunity under the Foreign Sovereign Immunities Act of 1976. Because the buyer of the cement was the Nigerian government, does the doctrine of sovereign immunity remove the dispute from the jurisdiction of U.S. courts? [*Texas Trading & Milling Corp. v. Federal Republic of Nigeria*, 647 F.2d 300 (2d Cir. 1981)]

56-7. Billy Lamb and Carmon Willis (the plaintiffs) are tobacco growers in Kentucky. Phillip Morris and B.A.T. Industries, PLC, routinely purchase tobacco not only from Kentucky but also from producers in several foreign countries. In 1982, subsidiaries of Phillip Morris and B.A.T. (the defendants) entered into an agreement with *La Fundacion Del Nino* (the Children's Foundation) of Caracas, Venezuela. The president of the Children's Foundation was the wife of the then president of Venezuela. The agreement provided that the two subsidiaries would donate a total of approximately $12.5 million to the Children's Foundation, and in exchange, the subsidiaries were to obtain price controls on Venezuelan tobacco, elimination of controls on retail cigarette prices in Venezuela, tax deductions for the donations, and assurances that existing tax rates applicable to tobacco companies would not be increased. The plaintiffs brought this action, alleging that the Venezuelan arrangement was an inducement designed to restrain trade in violation of U.S. antitrust laws. Such an arrangement, the plaintiffs contended, would result in the artificial depression of tobacco prices to the detriment of domestic tobacco growers, while ensuring lucrative retail prices for tobacco products sold abroad. The trial court held that the plaintiffs' claim was barred by the act of state doctrine. What will result on appeal? Discuss. [*Lamb v. Phillip Morris, Inc.*, 915 F.2d 1024 (6th Cir. 1990)]

56-8. While in the United States, Scott Nelson was hired as a monitoring systems engineer for the King Faisal Specialist Hospital in Riyadh, Saudi Arabia. Nelson alleged that in the course of performing his duties under his employment contract with the hospital, he was detained and tortured by agents of the Saudi government in Saudi Arabia for reporting safety violations at the hospital. Nelson brought suit for his injuries against Saudi Arabia, the hospital, and Royspec, a corporation owned and controlled by the government of Saudi Arabia (collectively, Saudi Arabia). Saudi Arabia claimed immunity under the doctrine of sovereign immunity. Nelson contended that because his detention and torture resulted from his recruitment within the United States by an agent of the Saudi government as part of a commercial activity, the district court had subject matter jurisdiction under the Foreign Sovereign Immunities Act. What should the court decide? Discuss fully. [*Nelson v. Saudi Arabia,* 923 F.2d 1528 (11th Cir. 1991)]

56-9. Case Briefing Assignment

 Examine Case A.25 [Trans-Orient Marine Corp. v. Star Trading & Marine, Inc., *731 F.Supp. 619 (S.D.N.Y. 1990)] in Appendix A. The case has been excerpted there in great detail. Review and then brief the case, making sure that* you *include answers to the following questions in your brief.*

1. What specific circumstances led to this lawsuit?
2. What was the central international legal issue addressed by the court?
3. How did the court distinguish a ''succession of state'' from a ''succession of government,'' and what was the effect of the distinction on executory contracts of the state?
4. What ''seminal decision'' on this issue was referred to by the court? What other cases did the court rely on in its reasoning?

Special Topics

Unique situations present special ethical problems. In this final *Focus on Ethics,* we consider a few special legal and ethical situations.

Insurance

In the area of insurance, one of the major ethical concerns involves *moral hazard.* In the insurance industry, moral hazard occurs when individuals or companies have an incentive to act negligently or to engage in activities that will result in payment by an insurance company. For example, the businessperson who takes out a large insurance policy on a building has less incentive to make sure that the building is protected from fire than an individual without an insurance policy. What is the ethical responsibility of the owner of the building when insurance is in effect? Is he or she exempt from taking precautions against a fire?

The same issue arises for insurance policies that cover losses due to theft. The smaller the deductible in such policies, the less incentive the property owner has to prevent loss due to theft. For example, with insurance in effect, the property owner may have less incentive to install alarm systems, to pay for private patrol service, and so

on. Of course, the more claims made on such insurance policies, the higher the average insurance rate per dollar amount insured. Thus, those individuals who are careless about protecting their own property impose costs on *all* individuals who buy property insurance.

Moral hazard exists with medical insurance as well. The smaller the deductible, the greater the incentive for the individual to neglect the practice of preventive medicine. What is the ethical responsibility of the individual citizen in terms of providing for his or her own well-being? Does the fact that health insurance is available for most individuals in the United States mean that these individuals should not be concerned about smoking, being overweight, and so on? Indeed, it is argued that in the United States, too many resources are devoted to the care of those who are already sick and too few resources to preventive medicine.

Sometimes, insurance companies attempt to avoid payment on a policy when the policyholder has committed a minor technical error either on the application or in the payment for the policy. A landmark case in this area involved an agent of Pacific

Mutual Life Insurance Company. The plaintiff, Cleopatra Haslip, had a medical policy with that company. The company refused to pay a medical bill of $3,800, arguing that the company had no record of the policy because a dishonest insurance agent had pocketed the premiums. Certainly, from an ethical point of view, there is little question that Pacific Mutual had a duty to pay the medical bill. From a business point of view, it also seems clear that Pacific Mutual should have paid the $3,800. It did not, however, and suffered accordingly. An Alabama jury awarded Haslip $1.04 million, including $840,000 in punitive damages—more than 200 times the plaintiff's out-of-pocket expenses. The United States Supreme Court upheld the trial court's decision in 1991.[1]

The "Living Will"

In recent years, ethical and legal issues surrounding the "right to die" have received considerable attention. In a California episode, for example, a father had terminal cancer of the esophagus and lacked the capacity to act. His son, acting on previously expressed wishes

---

1. *Pacific Mutual Life Insurance Co. v. Haslip,* ___U.S.___, 111 S.Ct. 1032, 113 L.Ed.2d 1 (1991).

1023

of the father, forced a nurse at gunpoint to disconnect the mechanical ventilator that was keeping his comatose father alive. The son was subsequently charged with murder. This is an extreme example of a recurring problem, and the law has developed the "living will" to try to deal with it.

Wills generally deal solely with the distribution of property and take effect *only* upon a client's death. The living will, however, takes effect during the client's lifetime and concerns the *person,* rather than the *estate,* of the client. The living will permits the client's physician to withhold or terminate medical care when such care does not appear to be in the patient's interest and, moreover, is simply prolonging life.

Questions arise as to how and to what extent we want to give effect to living wills. At what point should life-sustaining procedures be terminated? Wisconsin allows life-sustaining procedures to be terminated only if two physicians agree that death will occur within thirty days. The Wisconsin statute also permits some kinds of life-support systems to be terminated, but not others. Yet why should we draw the lines here? Some people have suggested that we should ask whether the brain is functioning and whether there is any expectation that the patient will continue to enjoy what is truly life in determining who among us should live or die. Drawing these types of lines is extremely difficult.

Testamentary Capacity

What does one do when a person who decides to make a will is at times mentally competent and at other times obviously not? Testamentary capacity is often difficult to establish in such situations. Consider, for example, a case involving Lena Unger,[2] who executed a last will and testament while she was confined to a nursing home and while, according to the testimony of the nursing home staff, in a state of mental confusion at the time the will was executed. The probate court found that Unger had sufficient testamentary capacity, but the court of appeals reversed the judgment. Consequently, Unger was deemed to have died intestate, and the property passed as though there had never been any will.

Inheritance Laws and Illegitimacy

In the ancient world, illegitimacy was often dealt with expeditiously by simply destroying the mother of the future illegitimate child. In biblical days, an adulteress was stoned to death—unless, as in the case of David and Bathsheba, a marriage could be arranged. In Bathsheba's case, David saved her life at the expense of her husband, Uriah, whom David arranged to have killed in battle so he could then marry Bathsheba. Under Islamic law, stoning was also the proper punishment for adultery. In the Christian world, illegitimate children and their mothers were always allowed to live, even though they were usually regarded as outcasts and pariahs until fairly recently.[3]

At common law, the illegitimate child was regarded as a *filius nullius* (Latin for "child of no one") and had no right to inherit. Today, statutes vary from state to state in regard to the inheritance laws governing illegitimate offspring. Generally, an illegitimate child is treated as the child of the mother and can inherit from her and her relatives. The child is usually not regarded as the legal child of the father unless paternity is established through some legal proceeding. Many state statutes permit the illegitimate child to inherit from the father, however, if paternity has been established prior to the father's death.

A landmark case in establishing the rights of illegitimate children was decided by the United States Supreme Court in 1977. In *Trimble* v. *Gordon,*[4] an illegitimate child sought to inherit property from her deceased natural father on the grounds that an Illinois statute prohibiting inheritance by illegitimate children in the absence of a will was unconstitutional. The child was Deta Mona Trimble, daughter of Jessie Trimble and Sherman Gordon. The paternity of the father had been established before a Cook County, Illinois, circuit court in 1973. Gordon died intestate in 1974. The mother filed a petition on behalf of the child in the probate division of the county circuit court, which was denied by the court on the basis of an Illinois law disallowing the child's inheritance because she was illegitimate. Had she been legitimate, she would have been her father's sole heir. The

---

2. *In re Estate of Unger,* 47 Or.App. 951, 615 P.2d 1115 (1980).
3. Jenny Teichman, *Illegitimacy: A Philosophical Examination* (Oxford: Blackwell, 1982), pp. 53–55.

---

4. 430 U.S. 762, 97 S.Ct. 1459, 52 L.Ed.2d 31 (1977).

Illinois Supreme Court in 1975 affirmed the petition's dismissal.

When the case came before the United States Supreme Court in 1977, the Court acknowledged that the "judicial task here is the difficult one of vindicating constitutional rights without interfering unduly with the State's primary responsibility in this area. . . . and the need for the States to draw 'arbitrary lines . . . to facilitate potentially difficult problems of proof.' " The Court found it hard to perceive any justification for the Illinois statute or for the lower court's insistence that the father could have avoided the problem had he just made a will. In reversing the Illinois Supreme Court decision, the high court stated that the section of the Illinois Probate Act that forbade Deta Mona from inheriting her father's property "cannot be squared with the command of the equal protection clause of the Fourteenth Amendment." Even though the Illinois statute rested to some extent on public policy supporting the family unit, the United States Supreme Court "expressly considered and rejected the argument that a State may attempt to influence the actions of men and women by imposing sanctions on the children born of their illegitimate relationships."

Accountants and Other Professionals

Traditionally, accountants have been considered to be professionals—much like doctors or lawyers. Members of these professions have always considered their clients' welfare to be their foremost responsibility. Thus, a lawyer will zealously defend even a client whom he or she believes to be guilty. A doctor will exert his or her greatest efforts on behalf of any human being without considering the external social consequences of treatment. Similarly, accountants have acted at the behest of their clients.

This client-centered ethic has spawned conflicts in the accounting profession. Third parties frequently rely on accounting statements to help them make essential investment decisions. The accountant who prepares misleading statements, at the request of a client, is participating in the fraud perpetrated on these individuals. Moreover, such an extreme devotion to clients threatens the credibility of the entire accounting profession. The law has recognized to some extent an accountant's liability to third parties.

Placing limits on accountants' representation of clients is not inconsistent with profession-alism. Even lawyers face limits in their defense of their clients. For example, a lawyer cannot steal or destroy evidence to advance a client's interest. Similarly, in some circum-stances, ethical duties to third parties may supersede an accountant's responsibility to his or her client.

Recognition of an accountant's responsibility to third parties is an important step, but an incomplete one. Accountants remain confidential advisors and advocates for their clients. Fairness to third parties may demand the disclosure of negative facts or future prospects about the client. Although accountants may not participate in fraud, deciding what facts must be disclosed on statements can be difficult. Frequently, the significance or materiality of financial facts or future prospects is debatable.

Must the accountant undertake a complete and independent evaluation of all such facts before deciding whether disclosure is necessary?

Ethics in International Trade

The American government has become increasingly active in protecting consumers and the environment from hazardous products and industrial processes. Many foreign governments, however, lack the capability or the will to provide similar protections. As a consequence, U.S. firms may sell seemingly hazardous products overseas with little or no regulation.

Suppose that the U.S. government discovers that a pesticide causes cancer and prohibits the use of the chemical in this nation. The pesticide producer may have large stocks of the chemical in inventory. Moreover, sales of the chemical may be quite profitable for the company. Suppose that the producer elects to sell its inventory overseas or even to continue producing the pesticide for foreign sales. Is this action ethical? Should not the company at least warn the foreign buyers of the cancer risk? Or should the company simply leave the matter in the hands of the foreign government?

Some persons have suggested that the United States should prohibit exports of any products banned for domestic use. Bear in mind, however, that foreign circumstances may differ from those in the United States. For example, the United States banned the pesticide DDT, primarily because of its adverse effects on wildlife. In Asia, however, DDT was a critical component of the mosquito control necessary to combat malaria. Perhaps foreign citizens would conclude that the benefits of a hazardous product outweigh the risks that it presents.

The Foreign Corrupt Practices Act

Congress has attempted to legislate international ethics in the Foreign Corrupt Practices Act (FCPA). Broadly speaking, this act prohibits U.S. companies from bribing foreign governments for contracts or other favors. Prior to passage of the act, such payments were relatively commonplace and an accepted cost of doing business.

American firms have voiced frustration with the act. Foreign officials in some countries have traditionally expected payments for consideration in doing business. Such payments are not always considered unethical behavior in some countries but rather a supplemental tax for the use of official services. Higher-level officials may be fully aware of such payments and implicitly authorize them.

The FCPA only prohibits U.S. firms from making such payments—it cannot prevent foreign officials from expecting or demanding them. Thus, the act may not prevent overseas bribery but may merely shift such actions from U.S. to foreign corporations, thus placing American corporations at a competitive disadvantage in international trade. This disadvantage is especially undesirable in view of the ongoing U.S. balance-of-payments deficit.

Business officials have experienced an additional ethical dilemma. An employee of a U.S. corporation has a fiduciary duty to the corporation's shareholders. Yet the FCPA may prevent the employee from making sure the company competes effectively. The problem is further complicated when the U.S. firm can provide the best products or services to the foreign country. In this instance, the FCPA may injure the U.S. company, its workers, and the foreign purchaser as well. Congress recently has amended the FCPA to reduce record-keeping requirements, but the fundamental proscription on bribery remains. Is bribery always unethical, or can it be justified by the benefits that may result?

■ Discussion Questions

1. An accounting firm is hired to prepare statements for a major company. A group of employees has recently sued the company, claiming sex discrimination and asking for millions of dollars in damages. The company and its lawyers assure the accountants that the lawsuit is frivolous and need not be disclosed as a future potential liability. Should the accountants seek an outside, independent assessment of the litigation to determine whether the potential liability should be disclosed?

2. What are the broader ethical implications of living wills? Is there a risk that withdrawing medical care will lead to less respect for human life? If so, might this precedent

endanger other relatively powerless groups, such as the mentally disabled?

3. Suppose a foreign government official demands that a U.S. company make a payment to him before the company can be granted a contract to provide water-supply facilities for the foreign nation. This payment would violate the Foreign Corrupt Practices Act. Company officials know that their company's bid is the lowest and believe that their company can do the best job of constructing the facilities. These officials further believe that the payment can be made secretly. Failure to make the payment will mean that the job will be given to a higher bidder from a European nation. Should the officials make the payment if they are unlikely to be caught?

4. Cigarette consumption in the United States has declined in the face of fears about the effects of smoking on health. Cigarette companies may, however, increase sales in foreign countries, where the health risks of smoking are less well known. Should cigarette companies include health warnings on all packs of cigarettes sold overseas, even though that country's law does not require this action? Is the warning alone enough to fulfill the companies' ethical obligations?

5. Suppose an applicant for insurance unknowingly makes a false statement concerning a material fact on the application form. Should an insurer have any responsibility to pay out on the subsequently issued insurance?

Appendix A

How to Brief a Case and Selected Cases

How to Brief a Case

To fully understand the law with respect to business, you need to be able to read and understand court decisions. To make this task easier, you can use a method of case analysis that is called *briefing*. There is a fairly standard procedure that you can follow when you "brief" any court case. You must first read the case opinion carefully. When you feel you understand the case, you can prepare a brief of it.

Although the format of the brief may vary, typically it will present the essentials of the case under headings such as those listed below.

1. **Citation.** Give the full citation for the case, including the name of the case, the date it was decided, and the court that decided it.
2. **Facts.** Briefly indicate (a) the reasons for the lawsuit; (b) the identity and arguments of the plaintiff(s) and defendant(s), respectively; and (c) the lower court's decision—if appropriate.
3. **Issue.** Concisely phrase, in the form of a question, the essential issue before the court. (If more than one issue is involved, you may have two—or even more—questions here.)
4. **Decision.** Indicate here—with a "yes" or "no," if possible—the court's answer to the question (or questions) in the *Issue* section above.

5. **Reason.** Summarize as briefly as possible the reasons given by the court for its decision and the case or statutory law relied on by the court in arriving at its decision.

When you prepare your brief, be sure you include all of the important facts. But remember that, by definition, the result should be brief.

Selected Cases for Briefing

Court opinions can run from a few pages to hundreds of pages in length. For reasons of space, only the essential parts of the opinions are presented in the cases that follow. As with the cases presented in the chapters of this text, a series of three asterisks indicates that a portion of the text—other than citations and footnotes—has been omitted. Four asterisks indicate the omission of at least one paragraph.

We have already briefed Case A.1; it was presented as the sample court case in Chapter 1. By comparing the actual court opinion with our briefed version, you can see how a court case appears both before and after the briefing process. The other cases in this appendix have been referred to within the text at the end of the chapters to which they topically relate.

This section indicates the parties to the lawsuit, the court rendering the opinion on the issue, the date the decision was made, and that the decision can be found in volume 921 of West's *Federal Reporter, Second Series,* on page 588.

Per curiam means "by the court."

The U.S. Tax Court is a federal court that hears disputes between taxpayers and the Internal Revenue Service.

This paragraph opens with a statement of the issue to be decided by the court. An *issue* is a disputed point of fact or law (such as a constitutional right). The rest of this paragraph explains the point of view of the party appealing the lower court's ruling.

A Latin term [pronounced *proh say*] meaning for himself or herself. In lawsuits, one who represents himself or herself without an attorney.

This paragraph describes the events that created the issue before the court.

This paragraph sets forth the general boundaries of the First Amendment rights as applied to religious beliefs. It does not address the specific facts or issue before the court but serves as a foundation for the decision.

FERGUSON v. COMMISSIONER OF INTERNAL REVENUE

United States Court of Appeals, Fifth Circuit, 1991.
921 F.2d 588.

PER CURIAM

* * * *

I.

This First Amendment case ironically arose out of a hearing in Tax Court. Although the government's brief is replete with references to income, exemptions, and taxable years, the only real issue is Betty Ann Ferguson's refusal to "swear" or "affirm" before testifying at the hearing. Her objection to oaths and affirmations is rooted in two Biblical passages, Matthew 5:33-37 and James 5:12. The passages refer only to oaths and swearing, but Ms. Ferguson explains her objection to affirmations in her brief to this court: Appellant is forbidden to swear as evidenced by the Bible directive from her God, and * * * the word "oath" has become synonymous and interchangeable with the word "affirmation," and the word "swear" [has] become synonymous and interchangeable with the word "affirm," as is evidenced in 1 U.S.C. 1 and many other authorities. * * * Also, "affirmation" is the chosen form of those who denounce the very existence of God. Because of these things, "swear" and "affirm" are very repugnant to appellant.

Ms. Ferguson, proceeding pro se, requested that Judge Korner consider the following statement set forth by the Supreme Court of Louisiana in *Staton v. Fought* as an alternative to an oath or affirmation:

I, [Betty Ann Ferguson], do hereby declare that the facts I am about to give are, to the best of my knowledge and belief, accurate, correct, and complete.

Judge Korner abruptly denied her request, commenting that "[a]sking you to affirm that you will give true testimony does not violate any religious conviction that I have ever heard anybody had" and that he did not think affirming "violates any recognizable religious scruple." Because Ms. Ferguson could only introduce the relevant evidence through her own testimony, Judge Korner then dismissed her petition for lack of prosecution. She now appeals to this court.

II.

The right to [the] free exercise of religion, guaranteed by the First Amendment to the Constitution, is one of our most protected constitutional rights. The Supreme Court has stated that "only those interests of the highest order and those not otherwise served can overbalance legitimate claims to the free exercise of religion." The protection of the free exercise clause extends to all sincere religious beliefs; courts may not evaluate religious truth.

Fed.R.Evid. 603, applicable in Tax Court under the Internal Revenue Code, requires only that a witness "declare that [she] will testify truthfully, by oath or affirmation administered in a form calculated to awaken the witness' conscience and impress the witness' mind with the duty to do so." As evidenced in the advisory committee notes accompanying Rule 603, Congress clearly intended to minimize any intrusion on the free exercise of religion: The rule is designed to afford the flexibility required in dealing with religious adults, atheists, conscientious objectors, mental defectives, and children. Affirmation is simply a solemn undertaking to tell the truth; no special verbal formula is required.

> This is a citation to Rule 603 of the Federal Rules of Evidence. These rules govern the admissibility of facts and testimony to establish or disprove an issue in lawsuits brought in federal courts. (These rules are the model followed by states in their own rules of evidence.)

The courts that have considered oath and affirmation issues have similarly attempted to accommodate free exercise objections. In *Moore v. United States*, for example, the Supreme Court held that a trial judge erred in refusing the testimony of witnesses who would not use the word "solemnly" in their affirmations for religious reasons.

> This paragraph provides a more specific backdrop against which to evaluate the issue by setting out the rule under which all witnesses in federal court must state that they will testify truthfully and the intent underlying the rule.

In *United States v. Looper*, the Fourth Circuit held that the trial judge erred in refusing the testimony of a defendant who would not take an oath that referred to God. Specifically, Looper had told the trial judge, "I can't [take the oath] if it has God's name in it. If you ask me if I'll tell the truth, I can say that." The Fourth Circuit concluded that any form or statement that impressed on the mind and conscious[ness] of the witness the necessity for telling the truth would suffice as an oath, citing proposed Rule 603. The opinion closed by advising trial judges faced with religious objections to an oath or affirmation "to make inquiry as to what form of oath or affirmation would not offend defendant's religious beliefs but would give rise to a duty to speak the truth."

> These paragraphs note what a number of courts have done when confronted with similar issues.

In *Gordon v. State of Idaho*, the Ninth Circuit cited both *Moore* and *Looper* in reaching a similar conclusion.

* * * Like Ms. Ferguson, Gordon objected to using either the word "swear" or "affirm" and offered an alternative statement. The Ninth Circuit held that the trial judge abused his discretion by refusing to even consider Gordon's proposed alternative.

The cases cited by the government, *United States v. Fowler* and *Kaltenbach v. Breaux*, are not contrary. In both cases, the witnesses completely refused to cooperate. Fowler would not accept even the simple statement, "I state that I will tell the truth in my testimony." And Kaltenbach's witness refused the very alternative proposed by Ms. Ferguson, the statement set forth in *Staton*.

> The "government" here means the Internal Revenue Service.

The government offers only two justifications for Judge Korner's refusal to consider the *Staton* statement. First, the government contends that the Tax Court was not bound by a Louisiana decision. This argument misses the point entirely; Ms. Ferguson offered *Staton* as an alternative to an oath or affirmation and not as a precedent.

> These paragraphs present the court's consideration of the point of view on appeal of the party who was successful in the lower court proceeding.

A *brief* is a document that concisely states the (1) issues in a lawsuit, (2) facts that bring the parties to court, (3) laws that can affect the subject of the dispute, and (4) arguments that explain how the law applies to the facts so that the case will be decided in favor of the party submitting the brief.

These paragraphs represent the final conclusions and decision of the court. The court of appeals reversed the lower court's decision, holding that the failure of that court to accommodate the appellant's beliefs, in regard to the oath to be taken before testifying, was inconsistent with the First Amendment and with the Federal Rules of Evidence.

Send back.

The government also claims that the *Staton* statement is insufficient because it does not acknowledge that the government may prosecute false statements for perjury. The federal perjury statute makes the taking of ''an oath'' an element of the crime of perjury. However, Ms. Ferguson has expressed her willingness to add a sentence to the *Staton* statement acknowledging that she is subject to penalties for perjury. *   *   *

The parties' briefs to this court suggest that the disagreement between Ms. Ferguson and Judge Korner might have been nothing more than an unfortunate misunderstanding. *   *   *

*   *   *   *

If Judge Korner had attempted to accommodate Ms. Ferguson by inquiring into her objections and considering her proposed alternative, the entire matter might have been resolved without an appeal to this court. Instead, however, Judge Korner erred not only in evaluating Ms. Ferguson's religious belief, and concluding that it did not violate any ''recognizable religious scruple,'' but also in conditioning her right to testify and present evidence on what she perceived as a violation of that belief. His error is all the more apparent in light of the fact that Ms. Ferguson was proceeding pro se at the hearing.

We therefore REVERSE the decision of the Tax Court and REMAND this case for further proceedings not inconsistent with this opinion.

Case A.2

GOELLER v. LIBERTY MUTUAL INSURANCE CO.

Supreme Court of Pennsylvania, 1990.
568 A.2d 176.

McDERMOTT, Justice.

This is an appeal from an order of the Superior Court which reversed an order of the Court of Common Pleas of Philadelphia County. The latter order denied appellee's petition to confirm a decision of a panel of arbitrators. It also mandated the convention [a convening; bringing together] of a new panel and re-hearing of appellant's claim under the uninsured motorist provision of an insurance policy. The facts and procedural history of the case are set forth below.

Appellant was injured in an automobile mishap in Connecticut while removing the driver from an overturned automobile. Involved in the accident were two other drivers, one of whom was allegedly un-insured. He entered a claim against appellee, the carrier of his employer's insurance policy, for coverage under an uninsured motorist provision which appellee disputed. The contract provided that disputes would be resolved by arbitration conducted in accordance with the Pennsylvania Arbitration Act *   *   *.

A panel of three arbitrators was assembled, as provided in the agreement, and presided over hearings on September 12 and 25, 1986. On July 28, 1987, the neutral arbitrator mailed a letter to the attorneys of the parties and each of the other panel members. It stated simply to the effect that appellee's arbitrator and the neutral arbitrator found for appellee and that appellant's arbitrator dissented and found for appellant. The neutral arbitrator's was the solitary signature to the letter. The following day, the letter was filed with the Prothonotary [principal court clerk].

Also on the following day, appellant's arbitrator[,] by certified mail, responded with a letter to the neutral arbitrator. In it he made a number of complaints. He stated that he had not agreed to the letter nor had he been consulted. He maintained in effect that the letter misrepresented his opinion. Regarding the deliberations of the panel members, he went on to express shock on learning that the other arbitrators had discussed the case out of his presence. In summary he stated that the letter was absolutely incorrect. He suggested further that the panel withdraw their purported findings and withdraw as the arbitrators in order to allow another panel to take over the matter. He sent courtesy copies to the other addressees of the neutral arbitrator's letter. On August 3, 1987, the neutral arbitrator responded by letter. Its entire text stated, "Because of (sic) you have impugned my integrity, I am withdrawing my award and I am withdrawing from the panel of arbitrators in this case."

On August 7, 1987, appellee filed a petition to confirm the award. On August 24, 1987, appellant answered, and filed new matter, petitioning, *inter alia* [among other things], for an order to convene a new arbitration panel. The court found adequate grounds to conclude that all of the panel members had not participated in the deliberations and that the award was not final in nature. The court therefore denied appellee's petition to confirm the award and ordered the parties to convene a new arbitration panel to try the case.

On appeal, the Superior Court reversed, determining that the lower court erred in its resolution of both the question of whether the panel had issued a final award and that of whether the award was the product of misconduct or other gross irregularity. Appellant petitioned this Court and we granted leave to appeal in order to review the Superior Court's determinations.

With respect to appellant's first contention, he asserts * * * that there was no final award by the arbitrators. The [Pennsylvania Arbitration] Act states in appropriate part:

Award of Arbitrators
General Rule—The award of the arbitrators shall be in writing and signed by the arbitrators joining in the award. The arbitrators shall deliver a copy of the award to each party personally or by registered or certified mail or as prescribed in the agreement to arbitrate.

In reply, appellee argues that the neutral arbitrator was without the power to withdraw the award of the arbitrators after it had been issued. We are impressed that the latter argument is non-responsive to the issue

raised: whether there was an award in the first instance. We conclude that there was not.

First we note that this arbitration, as agreed by the parties, was to be regulated by the provisions of the Act. The reviewing court is bound to construe the words of the Act according to rules of grammar and according to their common and approved usage. The object of the Court's interpretation is to ascertain and effectuate the intention of the General Assembly [the Pennsylvania legislature]. The word "shall," in the section relied on by appellant, is clearly mandatory [authoritative; compelling] in effect. But it is manifest that a purported award signed by no more than one of the three members of the panel, as herein, does not comply with the plain wording of the Act. The purported award in this case, in failing the formal statutory requirement, failed the requirement of their agreement as well. The "award" was a nullity.

Furthermore we are persuaded that there was no award in this case for another, more substantive, reason. This Court long ago voiced the principle that, "The opportunity to deliberate, and, if possible, to convince their fellows is the right of the minority, of which they cannot be deprived by the arbitrary will of the majority." * * *

The record indicates, and it is not disputed, that one of the members of the panel in this case was denied his opportunity to deliberate. When an arbitrator, properly appointed and entitled to act, is denied access to the deliberations of the other arbitrators, their decision is not a decision. It matters not whose arbitrator he or she may be. What is important is that all viewpoints must at least be heard. Each must be entitled to the opportunity to persuade the others, be permitted to dissent and to maintain his voice in the decision. It is manifest that that principle was violated in this case.

We recognize, as the Superior Court admonishes, that a strong presumption exists in favor of an arbitration panel's final award. However, before the award is paid such deference [courteous submission to another's opinion or judgment] by the courts it must come into existence as a corporate act of the panel. For the reasons set forth above, we conclude that in this case it did not.

Furthermore, the mandate of the trial court, that a new panel be convened and the matter retried, is necessary to afford the parties no less than that to which they agreed, an award by an arbitration panel.

Since we resolve appellant's first contention as we do, it is not necessary to pierce the veil of the panel's deliberations and pass on whether the award was a product of misconduct or other grave irregularity in terms of the Act.

The order of the Superior Court is reversed. The order of the Court of Common Pleas of Philadelphia County is reinstated.

Case A.3

AUSTIN v. BERRYMAN

United States Court of Appeals, Fourth Circuit, 1989.
878 F.2d 786.

MURNAGHAN, Circuit Judge:

We have before us for *en banc* reconsideration an appeal taken from an action successfully brought by Barbara Austin in the United States District Court for the Western District of Virginia against the Virginia Employment Commission, challenging a denial of unemployment compensation benefits. * * *

In brief, Austin charged, *inter alia* [among other things], that the denial of her claim for unemployment benefits, based on a Virginia statute specifically precluding such benefits for any individual who voluntarily quits work to join his or her spouse in a new location, was an unconstitutional infringement upon the incidents of marriage protected by the fourteenth amendment and an unconstitutional burden on her first amendment right to the free exercise of her religion. Her religion happened to command that she follow her spouse wherever he might go and the sincerity of her religious belief was not questioned. The district court found in Austin's favor and awarded injunctive relief and retroactive benefits.

On appeal, Judge Sprouse, writing for a panel majority, found that the denial of benefits did not implicate Austin's fourteenth amendment rights, but that it did unconstitutionally burden Austin's right to the free exercise of her religion. The panel also found, however, that any award of retroactive benefits was barred by the eleventh amendment. One panel member concurred with the panel majority as to the fourteenth and eleventh amendment issues, but dissented as to the existence of a free exercise violation. The panel opinion now, of course, has been vacated by a grant of rehearing *en banc.*

After careful consideration of the additional arguments proffered by both sides, the Court, *en banc,* is convinced that the panel majority correctly concluded that denying Austin unemployment benefits did not infringe upon fundamental marital rights protected by the fourteenth amendment. To this extent, we adopt the majority panel opinion. We also find,

however, that the denial of benefits did not unconstitutionally burden Austin's first amendment right to the free exercise of her religion. We are persuaded that the views expressed on the first amendment, free exercise of religion claim in the opinion dissenting in part from the panel majority are correct, and we hereby adopt that opinion as that of the *en banc* court. As we find that Austin is not entitled to any relief, we need not address whether the eleventh amendment bars an award of retroactive benefits.

The decisive consideration, as we see it, is that the proximate cause of Austin's unemployment is geographic distance, not her religious beliefs. There is no conflict between the circumstances of work and Austin's religious precepts. Austin's religious beliefs do not "require" her "to refrain from the work in question." Austin is unable to work simply because she is now too far removed from her employer to make it practical. In striking contrast, if one, for genuine religious beliefs, moves to a new residence in order to continue to live with a spouse, and that residence is not geographically so removed as to preclude regular attendance at the worksite, no unemployment, and hence no unemployment benefits, will arise. That amounts to proof that extent of geographical non-propinquity, not religious belief, led to Austin's disqualification for unemployment benefits.

Austin voluntarily decided to quit her job and join her spouse in a new geographic location 150 miles away. Virginia has stated that every individual who follows such a course, no matter what the reason, religious or non-religious, is disqualified for unemployment benefits. To craft judicially a statutory exception only for those individuals who profess Austin's religious convictions, particularly in the absence of a direct conflict between a given employment practice and a religious belief, would, in our view, result in a subsidy to members of a particular religious belief, impermissible under the Establishment Clause.

Accordingly, the judgment of the district court is REVERSED.

Case A.4

UNITED STATES v. O'CONNOR

United States Court of Appeals, Seventh Circuit, 1990.
910 F.2d 1466.

EASTERBROOK, Circuit Judge.

Daniel J. O'Connor, a crooked policeman, got caught in a sting operation. Federal agents posing as shady auto parts dealers—not above buying stolen cars to satisfy their customers' wants or cannibalize for parts—approached O'Connor and asked for notice of any potential investigations that might affect their business. At the initial meeting O'Connor described the tips he had provided to David Gorzellaney, operator of a bowling emporium cum gambling house, who introduced O'Connor to the agents. Gorzellaney was by then cooperating with the FBI. O'Connor boasted to "Bill Burns" (the lead agent's *nom de guerre*) that he had not only tipped Gorzellaney off to raids but also once took part in a raid and hid from fellow police officers evidence that Gorzellaney had overlooked.

Burns told O'Connor that he needed similar aid and also wanted security for legitimate used-parts sales. O'Connor generously offered to use his patrol car to help Burns transport stolen merchandise and to wear a beeper so that Burns could reach him as needed. O'Connor did not come cheap. He asked Burns: "What wouldn't hurt you?", to which the agent replied "Well, three bills [$300 per month] won't hurt me." O'Connor replied: "Maybe we should start at five." Burns agreed, provided the monthly payments were in installments. O'Connor got $300 on the spot. During the next two months he received another $650 in four installments. In exchange O'Connor agreed to give Burns news pronto, to "put a little feeler out" to potential buyers of stolen merchandise, and to obtain information about the addresses of the owners of cars whose license plate numbers Burns would furnish. Burns's "customers" would "shop" for cars by cruising the streets to find models they liked, then furnishing license plate numbers; Burns needed to track down the cars and arrange for their "appropriation." During the two months in which payments continued, O'Connor learned and told Burns that Gorzellaney had become a "pigeon" for the FBI and should be avoided. O'Connor also furnished computer printouts showing registration information for cars to be stolen.

Burns stopped paying O'Connor after two months, pleading ill health and poor business. O'Connor tried to get in touch with Burns, paging him and even once following him in a patrol car. Burns promised to resume payments. He never did; instead a grand jury indicted O'Connor, charging him with engaging in a pattern of racketeering, in violation of the Racketeer Influenced and Corrupt Organizations Act (RICO). Convicted after a bench trial, O'Connor has been sentenced to 2½ years' imprisonment, to be followed by 3 years' probation.

O'Connor contends that the evidence is insufficient to establish a "pattern" of racketeering, a necessary ingredient of the RICO offense. He emphasizes that "Burns" and the other agents determined the number and timing of payments that would be made, and he maintains that there must be a "pattern" from his side as well as from the agents'. True enough, but the trier of fact was entitled to conclude that O'Connor was prepared to (and did) undertake an extended series of criminal acts (taking bribes, providing information and protection) that would continue indefinitely, so long as Burns needed his services. Fences do not pay all the money up front; reciprocity—a "pattern" of money for information in increments—is important to maintain trust and loyalty.

Although the inference of a pattern was by no means open and shut (given the leading role played by the FBI), the evidence permitted a reasonable trier of fact to conclude beyond a reasonable doubt that O'Connor had committed himself to an enduring series of criminal acts, sufficient to establish a "pattern" * * *. O'Connor points to other cases in which this court has concluded that the evidence did not make out a pattern. There are many such cases—perhaps there is even a pattern of using the "pattern" requirement to trim off the excesses in civil RICO suits. [A previous case] emphasizes the impossibility of fitting all RICO cases to a single pattern, and nothing of moment could be achieved by surveying and attempting (probably vainly) to reconcile the many cases. Once a case has been tried, the evidence and reasonable inferences must be taken in the light favorable to the verdict. That perspective, when added to our holding in [another previous case], requires affirmance.

As for extortion: * * * [T]his court, in common with several other circuits, * * * has held that a public employee in a position to dole out or withhold official favors who solicits or accepts bribes under color of official right commits the crime of extortion. * * *

AFFIRMED. _____

Case A.5

HEINZEL v. BACKSTROM

Supreme Court of Oregon, 1990.
310 Or. 89,
794 P.2d 775.

VAN HOOMISSEN, Justice.

Plaintiffs Rodger and Judith Heinzel brought this action for specific performance of an agreement for the sale of real property owned by defendant Backstrom. The first and dispositive issue is whether the agreement is a contract. The trial court found the agreement to be a contract; but it also found that because the Heinzels had not tendered performance by the agreed closing date, Backstrom had been free to sell the property to the defendants Johnson. The Court of Appeals reversed. It found the agreement to be a contract, that the Heinzels had tendered performance within a "reasonable time" after the agreed closing date and, therefore, that they are entitled to specific performance. On *de novo* review [reviewing a case as if it had not been heard and no decision had been rendered before], we find the agreement to be a mere offer to sell which by its own terms expired before the Heinzels tendered performance. Accordingly, we reverse the decision of the Court of Appeals.

The relevant facts are uncontested. The real property which is the subject of this action consists of one commercial building and lot and two contiguous vacant lots that Backstrom had inherited from her father. After her husband died in 1984, Mrs. Backstrom decided to sell this property.

In August, 1986, the Heinzels contacted Backstrom expressing their interest in buying her property. * * *

* * * *

On September 4, 1986, after verifying the amount of taxes owing on Backstrom's property, Mr. Heinzel drafted the following document:

> September 4, 1986
> Sales agreement between Rodger and Judith Heinzel and Grace Backstrom.
> I Grace Backstrom hereby agree to sell to Rodger and Judith Heinzel my properties described as, Lt. 8 Bl 2 Everests and lt 1 & 2 Bl 2 Everests in the City of Newberg. The property to be free of encumbrances except Yamhill County property taxes both past-due and present. The purchase price to be $45,000 for Lt 8 Bl 2 Everests and $5,000 each for Lt 1 & 2 Bl 2 Everests, the total value for all properties being $55,000. Escrow to be closed on October 1, 1986.

The document was signed by all the parties. The Heinzels paid Backstrom no money at that time.

That same day, Mr. Heinzel opened an escrow for the consummation of the sale. * * *

After signing the agreement, Backstrom had become concerned about the transaction. On September 9, 1986, she consulted her attorney, who told her that he would examine the document. He advised her not to communicate with the Heinzels thereafter and to refer any inquiries about the matter to him.

On September 11, a realtor notified Backstrom that the defendants Johnson wanted to buy her property. Backstrom again consulted her attorney, who told her that her agreement with the Heinzels probably was binding until October 1. He again advised her to refer any inquiries about the matter to him. He also arranged for the Johnsons' offer to remain open until after October 1. Neither Backstrom nor her attorney communicated with the Heinzels. When the October 1 deadline passed with no word from the Heinzels, Backstrom's attorney told her that any agreement she had with them had expired. On October 16, Backstrom sold the property to the Johnsons.

On October 28, 1986, the escrow holder asked the Heinzels to inform Backstrom that the escrow documents on her sale to the Heinzels were ready for her signature. Mr. Heinzel conveyed this information to Backstrom that same day, at which time Backstrom told him that she already had sold the property to the Johnsons. That was the Heinzels' first notice of Backstrom's sale to the Johnsons.

On October 29, 1986, the Heinzels deposited the purchase price in escrow. Backstrom refused to accept it. On November 3, the escrow holder mailed Backstrom the escrow documents on her sale to the Heinzels. When Backstrom did not sign the documents, the Heinzels commenced this action for specific performance * * *

* * * *

Two facts support the Heinzels' argument that the document they signed obligated them to buy Backstrom's property. First, its caption reads: "Sales agreement between Rodger and Judith Heinzel and Grace Backstrom." That language could support an inference that the document was intended to be an agreement between the parties to sell and to buy the property. However, use of the words "sales agreement" in the caption is not determinative. The meaning of those words must be determined by reading them in the context of the entire document.

Second, the fact that the Heinzels signed the document could support an inference that the Heinzels intended to bind themselves to buy Backstrom's property. On the other hand, the Heinzels' signatures also could be interpreted as being nothing more than their acknowledgment of the terms and conditions of Backstrom's offer. More importantly, the document, which reads: "I Grace Backstrom hereby agree to sell * * *," contains no concomitant unequivocal promise by the Heinzels to buy Backstrom's property. As the Court of Appeals correctly noted, the document "does not contain express mutual promises. Although Backstrom promised to sell, [the Heinzels] did not expressly promise to buy."

Thus, the document provides support for both the Heinzels' and Backstrom's interpretations. Hence, the document is ambiguous. Given this ambiguity, the fact that Mr. Heinzel, who had previous experience in commercial real estate matters, drafted the agreement becomes legally significant. Any ambiguity in an agreement is resolved against the party who drafted it.

As the drafter of the document, Mr. Heinzel had the opportunity to include language which would have clearly shown the parties' intentions. He easily could have included the Heinzels' express promise to buy Backstrom's property, but he did not do so. Application of the rule that any ambiguity in an agreement is to be resolved against the party who drafted it weighs in favor of Backstrom's argument that the document here does not show that the Heinzels intended to bind themselves to buy her property.

On *de novo* review, we find that Backstrom offered to sell her property to the Heinzels on specific terms and conditions. We find further that the Heinzels did not obligate themselves to buy Backstrom's property.

The document here specifically provided: "Escrow to be closed on October 1, 1986." We find that to be a condition of Backstrom's offer, and that the offer terminated after that date. Any attempt by the Heinzels to accept Backstrom's offer after October 1, 1986, was a counter-offer because such "acceptance" necessarily would have involved a closing date different from that specifically stated in Backstrom's offer. We conclude that the trial court correctly determined that the equities were with defendants.

The decision of the Court of Appeals is reversed. The judgment of the circuit court is affirmed.

————

Case A.6

MANN v. WETTER

Court of Appeals of Oregon, 1990.
100 Or.App. 184,
785 P.2d 1064.

DEITS, Judge.

Plaintiff, as personal representative [a person designated in a will to handle estate matters upon the death of the maker of the will] of the estate of Bruce E. Virkler, brought this wrongful death action [a lawsuit, brought on behalf of a deceased person's beneficiaries, that alleges that the deceased person's death was attributable to the willful or negligent act of another] against defendants, alleging negligence in conducting a scuba diving instructional program. The trial court granted defendants' motion for summary judgment, based on a release signed by Virkler. Plaintiff appeals. We reverse as to defendant Wetter.

Horizon Water Sports, Inc. (Horizon) operates a diving school and is a member of NASDS, a nationwide standardized scuba instruction program. Horizon employed Wetter as a NASDS certified diving instructor. Virkler enrolled in one of Horizon's diving instruction programs. He completed a Total Information Card form, supplied by NASDS. The form requires personal and medical information and includes a clause respecting liability. The clause includes a release that states in pertinent part:

> [T]he Undersigned does for him/herself, his/her heirs, executors [persons appointed in wills to carry out the wills' directions] administrators [persons appointed by the court to manage a deceased person's estate] and assigns [those to whom property is or may be assigned (transferred)] hereby release, waive, discharge and relinquish any action or causes of action, aforesaid, which may hereafter arise for him/herself for his/her estate, and agrees that under no circumstances will he/she or his/her heirs, executors, administrators and assigns prosecute, present any claim for personal injury, property damage or wrongful death against N.A.S.D.S. or its member school, or any of its officers, agents, servants or employees for any of said causes of action, whether the same shall arise by the negligence of any of said persons, or otherwise. IT IS THE INTENTION OF THE ABOVE NAMED STUDENT

BY THIS INSTRUMENT, TO EXEMPT AND RE-
LIEVE N.A.S.D.S. AND ITS MEMBER SCHOOL
FROM LIABILITY FOR PERSONAL INJURY,
PROPERTY DAMAGE OR WRONGFUL DEATH
CAUSED BY NEGLIGENCE. (Emphasis supplied.)

After Virkler had completed six to eight weeks
of classroom and pool instruction, he participated in
a required open-water certification dive, which was
conducted by Horizon and supervised by Wetter. He
died during the dive.

Plaintiff asserts that the trial court erred in granting defendants' motion for summary judgment. She
first contends that the release should be held invalid
as a matter of public policy because of the parties'
unequal bargaining power, particularly because decedent [a deceased person; one who has recently died]
was asked to sign the release after he had already
attended some of the classes, had paid his fees and
was fully committed to the program.

Although agreements to limit liability are not favored, neither are they automatically void. An agreement limiting liability is governed by principles of
contract law and will be enforced in the absence of
some consideration of public policy derived from the
nature of the subject of the agreement or a determination that the contract was adhesionary [a contract
in which the terms are dictated by a party having
clearly superior bargaining power]. The [Oregon]
Supreme Court has stated:

> There is nothing inherently bad about a contract
> provision which exempts one of the parties from lia-
> bility. The parties are free to contract as they please,
> unless to permit them to do so would contravene the
> public interest.

Here, there are no public policy considerations
that prevent a diving school from limiting liability for
its own negligence. The diving school does not provide an essential public service, as was the case in
Real Good Food v. First National Bank, where the
court held that a bank could not limit its liability for
the negligence of its own employees. The economic
advantage, if any, that a small business that provides
a non-essential service may have over its customers
will not create unequal bargaining power, because the
customers have a multitude of alternatives. Further,
although decedent may not have signed the release
until after he had paid for and started the program,
that did not create unequal bargaining power between
the parties that would require us to invalidate the

release. He remained free not to continue the diving
program.

Plaintiff also argues that the trial court erred when
it granted summary judgment for Wetter, because, as
a matter of law, the language of the release did not
include him. Wetter contends that the language of the
release clearly did include him.

As a general rule, the construction of a contract
is a question of law for the court. The exception to
that rule is that, if the language in a contract is ambiguous, evidence may be admitted as to the intent
of the parties, and the determination of the parties'
intent then is a question of fact. *   *   * A contract
provision is ambiguous if it is capable of more than
one sensible and reasonable interpretation *   *   *.

The disputed language in the release agreement
provides that the release applies to actions ''against
N.A.S.D.S. or its member school or any of its officers,
agents, servants or employees.'' The reference to ''its
officers, agents, servants or employees'' could be read
to refer to the officers, agents, servants or employees
of NASDS or to those of Horizon. The language of
the agreement is ambiguous, and so the parties are
entitled to present evidence as to the intention of the
drafters and of those who executed the release agreement. Accordingly, summary judgment in favor of
Wetter was error.

Plaintiff also contends that the summary judgment in favor of Wetter should not have been granted,
because there was a material question of fact whether
Wetter was an officer, agent, servant or employee of
NASDS. We agree that, depending on the construction of the language of the release agreement, that
may be a material question of fact. Defendant presented evidence that Wetter was a nonvoting member
of NASDS. Although it may not necessarily follow
that, because of that, he may be an officer, agent,
servant or employee of NASDS, plaintiff is entitled
to present evidence concerning Wetter's status with
NASDS.

Judgment for respondent Wetter reversed and remanded; otherwise affirmed.

Case A.7

RHODES v. UNITED JEWISH CHARITIES OF DETROIT

Court of Appeals of Michigan, 1990.
184 Mich.App. 740,
459 N.W.2d 44.

PER CURIAM.

Plaintiff appeals as of right from an order of the Wayne Circuit Court granting defendants' motions for summary disposition. We reverse and remand for trial.

Plaintiff alleges she was assaulted by defendant Anthony King in a fenced and guarded parking lot owned by defendant United Jewish Charities of Detroit (UJC). UJC owns the building east of the parking lot and leases space in the building to defendant Jewish Vocational Services and Community Workshop (JVS) and Michigan Rehabilitation Services, plaintiff's employer. By its lease agreement, UJC required JVS to provide guard service for the parking lot. JVS in turn contracted with defendant Guardian Guard Services to provide on-site security.

Defendants UJC and JVS filed a joint motion for summary disposition pursuant to MCR [Michigan Court Rules] 2.116(C)(8), asserting that Michigan law did not impose an affirmative duty upon them to provide armed security personnel to prevent or deter criminal acts of third parties. Defendant Guardian brought a motion for summary disposition pursuant to MCR 2.116(C)(8) and (10), asserting that Michigan law does not recognize a duty to protect an individual against the criminal conduct of a third party and that there was no evidence that could substantiate a claim that Guardian failed to comply with the terms of its contract with JVS.

In granting summary disposition to these defendants, the trial court held that the parking lot was not within the common area of the building and found that defendants did not owe a duty to plaintiff. The trial court did not, however, address the merits of plaintiff's argument that, since defendants had undertaken to provide security services, they had a responsibility to insure it was not done in a negligent manner. In passing, the trial court did express its opinion that it was not going to penalize defendants for their efforts in "attempting to cut down the criminal situation."

Plaintiff first assigns error to the trial court's finding that the relationship between plaintiff and UJC and JVS was that of business invitee rather than that of landlord/tenant. We will not address this issue since it is not dispositive of the appeal before us. Regardless of the characterization given the relationship of the parties, Michigan does not impose a duty upon a landlord or a merchant to provide police protection, in the form of armed guards, to deter the criminal acts of third parties. As the [Michigan] Supreme Court reasoned in [a previous case], police protection is properly a governmental function and to shift the function of providing that protection to the private sector would be in contravention of longstanding public policy.

The critical issue before us is whether a party, having voluntarily assumed to perform a duty, is required to perform that duty in a non-negligent manner. Stated another way, once UJC and JVS assumed the duty of providing police protection and contracted with Guardian for guard services, are the parties then liable for the negligent performance of that duty?

When a person voluntarily assumes the performance of a duty, that person is required to perform it carefully, not omitting to do what an ordinarily prudent person would do in accomplishing the task.

We hold that, when UJC and JVS voluntarily assumed the duty of providing police protection in the form of guards from Guardian, it became incumbent upon them to provide that protection in a non-negligent manner. The question whether the guard was negligent in the performance of his duties is a question for the jury. The grant of summary disposition was therefore erroneous.

Lastly, plaintiff assigns error to the trial court's refusal to allow her leave to amend her complaint to allege that she was a third-party beneficiary of the contract between JVS and Guardian. MCR 2.118(A)(2) provides that leave to amend a pleading "shall be freely given when justice so requires" so long as the amendment is not futile.

For a plaintiff to sue on a contract to which he is not a party, it must be determined that the plaintiff was an intended third-party beneficiary of the contract which suit is brought on. To be an intended beneficiary, the promisor must have undertaken to do something to or for the benefit of the party asserting status as an intended beneficiary.

Plaintiff's assertion that she is a third-party beneficiary of the contract is based upon the provision of the contract listing the guard's specific duties: "Guard to act as a deterrent against possible acts of theft, vandalism, fire and trespass—safety of staff and clients."

When UJC required JVS to provide guard service for the parking lot, it must be assumed that the guard service was intended for the protection of all who were to use the parking lot. As an employee of one of the tenants, it is clear that plaintiff would fall into the class of individuals for which UJC required JVS to provide protection. Plaintiff is, arguably, an intended third-party beneficiary of JVS's contract with Guardian and, upon remand, should be granted leave to amend her pleadings to state such a claim.

Reversed and remanded.

Case A.8

POTTER v. OSTER

Supreme Court of Iowa, 1988.
426 N.W.2d 148.

NEUMAN, Justice.

This is a suit in equity brought by the plaintiffs to rescind an installment land contract based on the seller's inability to convey title. The question on appeal is whether, in an era of declining land values, returning the parties to the status quo works an inequitable result. We think not. Accordingly, we affirm the district court judgment for rescission and restitution.

The facts are largely undisputed. Because the case was tried in equity, our review is *de novo*. We give weight to the findings of the trial court, particularly where the credibility of witnesses is concerned, but we are not bound thereby.

The parties, though sharing a common interest in agribusiness, present a study in contrasts. We think the disparity in their background and experience is notable insofar as it bears on the equities of the transaction in issue. Plaintiff Charles Potter is a farm laborer and his wife, Sue, is a homemaker and substitute teacher. They have lived all their lives within a few miles of the real estate in question. Defendant Merrill Oster is an agricultural journalist and recognized specialist in land investment strategies. He owns Oster Communications, a multimillion dollar publishing concern devoted to furnishing farmers the latest in commodity market analysis and advice on an array of farm issues.

In May 1978, Oster contracted with Florence Stark to purchase her 160-acre farm in Howard County, Iowa, for $260,000 on a ten-year contract at seven percent interest. Oster then sold the homestead and nine acres to Charles and Sue Potter for $70,000. Potters paid $18,850 down and executed a ten-year installment contract for the balance at 8.5% interest.

Oster then executed a contract with Robert Bishop for the sale of the remaining 151 acres as part of a package deal that included the sale of seventeen farms for a sum exceeding $5.9 million.

These back-to-back contracts collapsed like dominoes in March 1985 when Bishop failed to pay Oster and Oster failed to pay Stark the installments due on their respective contracts. Stark commenced forfeiture proceedings [proceedings to retake the property because Oster failed to perform a legal obligation—payment under the contract—and thus forfeited his right to the land]. Potters had paid every installment when due under their contract with Oster and had included Stark as a joint payee [one of two or more payees—persons to whom checks or notes are payable; see Chapter 25] with Oster on their March 1, 1985, payment. But they were financially unable to exercise their right to advance the sums due on the entire 160 acres in order to preserve their interest in the nine acres and homestead. As a result, their interest in the real estate was forfeited along with Oster's and Bishop's and they were forced to move from their home in August 1985.

Potters then sued Oster to rescind their contract with him, claiming restitution damages for all consideration paid. * * *

Trial testimony * * * revealed that the market value of the property had decreased markedly since its purchase. Expert appraisers valued the homestead and nine acres between $27,500 and $35,000. Oster himself placed a $28,000 value on the property; Potter $39,000. Evidence was also received placing the reasonable rental value of the property at $150 per month, or a total of $10,800 for the six-year Potter occupancy.

The district court concluded the Potters were entitled to rescission of the contract and return of the consideration paid including principal and interest, cost of improvements, closing expenses, and taxes for a total of $65,169.37. From this the court deducted

$10,800 for six years' rental, bringing the final judgment to $54,369.37.

On appeal, Oster challenges the judgment. * * * [H]e claims Potters had an adequate remedy at law for damages which should have been measured by the actual economic loss sustained * * *.

* * * *

Rescission is a restitutionary remedy which attempts to restore the parties to their positions at the time the contract was executed. The remedy calls for a return of the land to the seller, with the buyer given judgment for payments made under the contract plus the value of improvements, less reasonable rental value for the period during which the buyer was in possession. The remedy has long been available in Iowa to buyers under land contracts when the seller has no title to convey.

Rescission is considered an extraordinary remedy, however, and is ordinarily not available to a litigant as a matter of right but only when, in the discretion of the court, it is necessary to obtain equity. Our cases have established three requirements that must be met before rescission will be granted. First, the injured party must not be in default. Second, the breach must be substantial and go to the heart of the contract. Third, remedies at law must be inadequate.

The first two tests are easily met in the present case. Potters are entirely without fault in this transaction. They tendered their 1985 installment payment to Oster before the forfeiture, and no additional payments were due until 1986. On the question of materiality, Oster's loss of equitable title [ownership rights protected in equity] to the homestead by forfeiture caused not only substantial, but total breach of his obligation to insure peaceful possession [an implied promise made by a landowner, when selling or renting land, that the buyer or tenant will not be evicted or disturbed by the landowner or a person having a lien or superior title] and convey marketable title under the Oster-Potter contract.

Only the third test—the inadequacy of damages at law—is contested by Oster on appeal. * * *

Restoring the status quo is the goal of the restitutionary remedy of rescission. Here, the district court accomplished the goal by awarding Potters a sum representing all they had paid under the contract rendered worthless by Oster's default. Oster contends that in an era of declining land values, such a remedy goes beyond achieving the status quo and results in

a windfall to the Potters. Unwilling to disgorge the benefits he has received under the unfulfilled contract, Oster would have the court shift the "entrepreneural risk" [the risk assumed by one who initiates, and provides or controls the management of, a business enterprise] of market loss to the Potters by limiting their recovery to the difference between the property's market value at breach ($35,000) and the contract balance ($27,900). In other words, Oster claims the court should have awarded * * * damages. * * *

* * * *

* * * [L]egal remedies are considered inadequate when the damages cannot be measured with sufficient certainty. Contrary to Oster's assertion that Potters' compensation should be limited to the difference between the property's fair market value and contract balance at time of breach, * * * damages are correctly calculated as the difference between contract price and market value at the time for performance. Since the time of performance in this case would have been March 1990, the market value of the homestead and acreage cannot be predicted with any certainty, thus rendering such a formulation inadequate.

Most importantly, the fair market value of the homestead at the time of forfeiture is an incorrect measure of the benefit Potters lost. It fails to account for the special value Potters placed on the property's location and residential features that uniquely suited their family. For precisely this reason, remedies at law are presumed inadequate for breach of a real estate contract. Oster has failed to overcome that presumption here. His characterization of the transaction as a mere market loss for Potters, compensable by a sum which would enable them to make a nominal down payment on an equivalent homestead, has no legal or factual support in this record. * * *

* * * *

In summary, we find no error in the trial court's conclusion that Potters were entitled to rescission of the contract and return of all benefits allowed thereunder, less the value of reasonable rental for the period of occupancy * * *.

AFFIRMED. _____

Case A.9

GOLDKIST, INC. v. BROWNLEE

Court of Appeals of Georgia, 1987.
182 Ga.App. 287,
355 S.E.2d 733.

BEASLEY, Judge.

The question is whether the two defendant farmers, who as a partnership both grew and sold their crops, were established by the undisputed facts as not being "merchants" as a matter of law, according to the definition in OCGA [Section] 11-2-104(1) [Official Code of Georgia Annotated; Section 11-2-104(1) corresponds to UCC 2-104(1)]. We are not called upon here to consider the other side of the coin, whether farmers or these farmers in particular are "merchants" as a matter of law.

In November 1983, Goldkist sued under OCGA [Section] 11-2-712 for losses arising out of the necessity to cover [a remedy of the buyer in a breached sales contract; if the seller fails to deliver the goods contracted for, the buyer can purchase them elsewhere and recover any additional price paid from the breaching seller (see Chapter 21)] a contract for soybeans. It produced a written confirmation dated July 22 for 5,000 bushels of soybeans to be delivered to it by defendants between August 22 and September 22 at $6.88 per bushel. A defense was that there was no writing signed by either of the Brownlees, as required by OCGA [Section] 11-2-201(1).

* * * [T]he court agreed with the Brownlees that the circumstances did not fit any of the exceptions provided for in Section 201 and granted summary judgment. On appeal, Goldkist asserts that defendants came within subsection (2), relating to dealings "between merchants."

Appellees admit that their crops are "goods" as defined in OCGA [Section] 11-2-105. The record establishes the following facts. The partnership had been operating the row crop farming business for 14 years, producing peanuts, soybeans, corn, milo, and wheat on 1,350 acres, and selling the crops.

It is also established without dispute that Barney Brownlee, whose deposition was taken, was familiar with the marketing procedure of "booking" crops, which sometimes occurred over the phone between the farmer and the buyer, rather than in person, and a written contract would be signed later. He periodically called plaintiff's agent to check the price, which fluctuated. If the price met his approval, he sold soy-

beans. At this time the partnership still had some of its 1982 crop in storage, and the price was rising slowly. Mr. Brownlee received a written confirmation in the mail concerning a sale of soybeans and did not contact plaintiff to contest it but simply did nothing. In addition to the agricultural business, Brownlee operated a gasoline service station.

In dispute are the facts with respect to whether or not an oral contract was made between Barney Brownlee for the partnership and agent Harrell for the buyer in a July 22 telephone conversation. The plaintiff's evidence was that it occurred and that it was discussed soon thereafter with Brownlee at the service station on two different occasions, when he acknowledged it, albeit reluctantly, because the market price of soybeans had risen. Mr. Brownlee denies booking the soybeans and denies the nature of the conversations at his service station with Harrell and the buyer's manager.

In this posture, of course, the question of whether an oral contract was made would not yield to summary adjudication, as apparently recognized by the trial court, which based its decision on the preliminary question of whether the Brownlee partnership was a "merchant."

Whether or not the farmers in this case are "merchants" as a matter of law, which is not before us, the evidence does not demand a conclusion that they are outside of that category which is excepted from the requirement of a signed writing to bind a buyer and seller of goods. * * *

* * * *

Defendants' narrow construction of "merchant" would, given the booking procedure used for the sale of farm products, thus guarantee to the farmers the best of both possible worlds (fulfill booking if price goes down after booking and reject it if price improves) and to the buyers the worst of both possible worlds. On the other hand, construing "merchants" in OCGA [Section] 11-2-104(1) as not excluding as a matter of law farmers such as the ones in this case, protects them equally as well as the buyer. If the market price declines after the booking, they are assured of the higher booking price; the buyer cannot renege, as OCGA [Section] 11-2-201(2) would apply.

* * * *

We believe this is the proper construction to give the two statutes, OCGA [Sections] 11-2-104(1) and 11-2-201(2), as taken together they are thus further branches stemming from the centuries-old simple legal idea *pacta servanda sunt*—agreements are to be kept. So construed, they evince the legislative intent

to enforce the accepted practices of the marketplace among those who frequent it.

Judgment reversed.

_____

Case A.10

TRIAD SYSTEMS CORP. v. ALSIP
United States Court of Appeals, Tenth Circuit, 1989.
880 F.2d 247.

PER CURIAM.

This is a case arising out of the sale of a computer system by Triad Systems Corporation, the appellant, to Mr. Dale Alsip, the appellee, for use in Mr. Alsip's automotive parts supply store, Mr. Automotive of Duncan. Triad brought this action seeking to recover the full purchase price for the system plus payment for its maintenance and service of the system. Mr. Alsip counterclaimed, seeking a refund of the purchase price based on his alleged revocation of acceptance of the system.

After a six-day trial, the jury returned a verdict for Mr. Alsip, awarding him a refund of the amount paid to Triad, less a setoff for the value of his use of the equipment prior to revocation of acceptance. Triad appeals, arguing that Mr. Alsip's attempted revocation of acceptance was ineffective as a matter of law, that the contract for the sale of the system further limited Mr. Alsip's ability to revoke acceptance, and that the court erroneously permitted parol evidence regarding certain statements of Triad's personnel made prior to execution of the contract. We affirm.

Triad's first assertion of error concerns the propriety of submitting the issue of Mr. Alsip's purported revocation of acceptance to the jury. Triad contends that the uncontroverted facts demonstrated, as a matter or law, that Mr. Alsip's revocation was ineffective under [Section] 2-608 of California's Uniform Commercial Code (U.C.C.), because of substantial changes in the equipment prior to revocation and because of Mr. Alsip's pre- and post-revocation use of the equipment. We disagree.

Whether a party's revocation of acceptance is effective in any given case is dependent upon the facts and circumstances surrounding the revocation, and is normally a question for the trier of fact. In order for us to conclude that submission of this case to the jury was improper, we would have to find that reasonable minds could not differ as to whether Mr. Alsip's re-

vocation was proper. Based on the evidence in this case, such a conclusion would be clear error.

Viewing the facts in the light most favorable to Mr. Alsip, there is sufficient evidence to show that Mr. Alsip's use of the Triad system for more than two years after it was first delivered was not unreasonable. The record indicates that the System 5 which Mr. Alsip received never operated as expected. In addition, certain components of it were completely replaced only six months after installation. Further evidence suggests that Mr. Alsip's delay in revoking his acceptance of the system was based on Triad's assurances that certain newly developed software would meet Mr. Alsip's reporting and information requirements, but that Mr. Alsip would have to replace the System 5 with a System 7. Mr. Alsip then purchased the System 7 approximately one year after receiving the original system from Triad, and again certain software malfunctioned or was completely inoperable. Only when Mr. Alsip concluded that the new system simply would not generate the reports he required, after repeated attempts by Triad to correct the problem, did he revoke his acceptance. We think on the basis of this evidence that the jury could conclude that Mr. Alsip's revocation was reasonable under all the circumstances.

Triad also asserts that revocation was barred by Mr. Alsip's continued use of the system after notice of revocation and by certain changes in the condition of the system. The fact that Mr. Alsip may have used the system for certain purposes subsequent to revocation does not as a matter of law bar revocation, as long as such use is reasonable. Based on our review of the record, there is little evidence suggesting unreasonable use. As to Triad's allegations that a substantial change in the condition of the system had occurred, this, too, is an issue for the jury's determination. We believe that the jury could properly conclude that rodent droppings and debris in the equipment and one stolen display terminal was not such a substantial change in the condition of the equipment as to prevent revocation, especially when there is evidence that some of this damage could have been prevented had Triad diligently pursued collection of the equipment.

Triad next contends that express language in its contract with Mr. Alsip precluded his revocation of acceptance of the system. Such language provided, *inter alia* [among other things] that ''[a]t any time during the 60-day System Evaluation Period, the Customer may notify Triad in writing of Customer's intent to revoke its purchase of the System. . . . Upon timely receipt by Triad of such notice of revocation, Customer shall promptly return the System to Triad, and Triad shall then promptly refund all sums paid hereunder by Customer to Triad.'' The contract contained no limitation of basis for revocation during this period; it appears that the customer could return the system for any reason if it were dissatisfied.

In response to Triad's argument that this provision limited Mr. Alsip's right to return the system to only the first 60 days after delivery, the district court ruled that the System Evaluation Period was not a limitation of Mr. Alsip's U.C.C. [Section] 2-608 right to revoke, but an expansion of that right. We are in full agreement. Section 2-608 provides that ''[t]he buyer may revoke his acceptance of a lot or commercial unit whose nonconformity substantially impairs its value to him. . . .'' The Triad contract does not require a nonconformity impairing value to justify revocation of acceptance, only a desire on the part of the customer to return the system. Consequently, we view this contract language as simply expanding upon the customer's normal remedies under the U.C.C., in line with the presumption that clauses prescribing remedies are cumulative rather than exclusive.

Triad's final argument in this appeal is that the district court erred in permitting Mr. Alsip to introduce evidence of pre-contract oral representations and warranties made by Triad salespersons, and that such testimony violated the parol evidence rule. The district court permitted this testimony on the grounds that it was simply an explanation of the equipment and software purchased by Mr. Alsip and that it could be introduced for the purpose of explaining or supplementing the contract's terms, a purpose expressly sanctioned by the rule. We concur with this reasoning.

The judgment of the United States District Court for the Western District of Oklahoma is AFFIRMED.

Case A.11

TRAVEL CRAFT, INC. v. WILHELM MENDE GmbH & CO.

Supreme Court of Indiana, 1990.
552 N.E.2d 443.

SHEPARD, Chief Justice.
* * * *

In 1982, Wilhelm Mende GmbH & Co., a West German Corporation, directed a sales campaign toward Travel Craft, Inc., a manufacturer of motor homes and recreational vehicles. Mende representatives traveled to Travel Craft's plant in Elkhart to persuade Travel Craft to purchase Alu-span, an aluminum-type material. The record indicates that the sales campaign was the first contact between the companies. Travel Craft did not have any prior knowledge of Alu-span.

Travel Craft decided to buy Alu-span for use in constructing its motor homes. After the initial purchase, Travel Craft and Mende negotiated a warranty. Travel Craft drafted the warranty, which stated in pertinent part:

Seller [Mende] agrees for a period of three (3) years from the date of delivery that product manufactured by it will be free under normal use from substantial defects in materials or workmanship. There are no other warranties, express or implied.

On finished motor homes, Alu-span cracked and separated from its base. As a result, Travel Craft recalled more than 100 motor homes. The cracks and separations apparently resulted from Alu-span's inherent inability to withstand the structural stress associated with its use in motor homes, rather than from any flaw in the material or manufacture.

Travel Craft sued Mende for breach of express and implied warranties. The trial court granted Mende's motions for summary judgment. The Court of Appeals affirmed. Because it appears that this Court has not interpreted the sales provisions of the Uniform Commercial Code since Indiana adopted them in 1963, we grant transfer.
* * * *

I. Exclusion of Implied Warranties
* * * Travel Craft argues that the disclaimer of the implied warranty of merchantability it drafted

in this case * * * was ineffective because it did not contain the word merchantability.

     * * * *

The disclaimer in this transaction would normally be inadequate because it does not mention the word merchantability. After reading [Indiana Code Section] 26-1-2-316 [the Indiana equivalent of UCC 2-316] and the Uniform Commercial Code's commentary, however, we conclude that this case is an exception to the rule. The commentary states that U.C.C. [Section] 2-316(2) seeks to:

> [P]rotect a buyer from unexpected and unbargained language of disclaimer by denying effect to such language when inconsistent with language of express warranty and permitting the exclusion of implied warranties only by conspicuous language or other circumstances which protect the buyer from surprise.

Applying [Indiana Code Section] 26-1-2-316(2) in favor of Travel Craft, the buyer and the drafter of the warranty, would subject the seller to the same type of surprise the provision is intended to prevent. Accepting Travel Craft's argument would turn a buyer's shield against surprise into a buyer's sword of surprise. We conclude, consequently, if the buyer drafts the disclaimer it cannot in good faith claim surprise or unexpected and unbargained for language. Our construction follows the drafter's intent that the Code be construed to promote its underlying purposes and policies, and leads us to hold in this case that the implied warranty of merchantability was effectively disclaimed, even though the word ''merchantability'' was not mentioned.

As for the implied warranty of fitness for a particular purpose, [Indiana Code Section] 26-1-2-316(2) provides the opportunity to disclaim simply by a conspicuous writing. We conclude that the words of this disclaimer were adequate. The trial court properly granted Mende's motion for summary judgment aimed at implied warranties.

II. Use of Parol Evidence

In ruling on the adequacy of the disclaimer and on Mende's motion for summary judgment on the express warranty, the trial court barred all parol evidence. It treated the written warranty, drafted by Travel Craft and executed by Mende, as a complete and exclusive statement of all of the terms of the agreement. Travel Craft says that this treatment was error; it argues that the trial court should have admitted parol evidence. Mende claims that ''the series of communications and final writing between the parties was only a final expression of their agreement as to warranties.'' It says parol evidence could not be admitted with respect to that agreement on warranties.

     * * * *

. We conclude that the written warranty was a final expression of the parties' agreement on warranties, but we believe that the trial court erred in treating the agreement as a final expression on all terms and thus barring all parol evidence. We read U.C.C. s 2-202 to provide that when parties create a complete and exclusive agreement on limited terms, parol evidence is still admissible if it is explanatory or supplemental. We hold that parol evidence was admissible to explain and supplement the warranty words ''normal use'' and ''defects.''

III. Summary Judgment on Express Warranty

Travel Craft argues that the trial court erred in finding that there were no genuine issues of material fact and granting summary judgment to Mende. The trial court focused on whether Alu-span was defective, and Mende urges us that there is no evidence of defect.

     * * * *

The trial court's summary judgment order states:

> A substantial difference exists between a product that is not merchantable or fit for a particular purpose and one that is defective. If it is defective it is highly unlikely it could be merchantable or fit for the particular purpose. However, it could be unmerchantable or unfit for the particular purpose without being defective. With implied warranties it is only necessary that some malfunction exist[s] that makes it unmerchantable or unfit for the particular purpose rather than showing the existence of some specific dereliction by the manufacturer that constitutes a breach. Whereas the express warranty is that the product is free under normal use from substantial defects in material or workmanship, a specific defect must be shown to constitute a breach or warranty.

We disagree with the trial court's interpretation of the express warranty terms ''normal use'' and ''defect.''

The facts before the trial court on summary judgment are subject to conflicting inferences. Who would ''normally use'' this product and for what purpose would they use it? Was Alu-span ''defective'' within the meaning of the express warranty? The black-letter definition of ''defective'' suggests that a good may be defective as the result of some sort of imperfection or dereliction, and it may also be "defective" when the product is not fit for the ordinary purposes for which it was sold or used.

When the facts are viewed most favorably for non-movant Travel Craft, the express warranty may be interpreted as tantamount to an express warranty of fitness for a particular purpose.

We affirm the trial court's decision on implied warranties. We reverse its grant of summary judgment on the express warranty and remand the case for further proceedings, to be conducted in accord with our holding on the admission of parol evidence.

Case A.12

BERNAL v. RICHARD WOLF MEDICAL INSTRUMENTS CORP.

California Court of Appeal, Fourth District, 1990.
221 Cal.App.3d 1326,
272 Cal.Rptr. 41.

TAYLOR, Associate Justice.

Plaintiffs Morris and Rosie Bernal appeal from a judgment for Richard Wolf Medical Instruments Corporation ("Wolf") in their action for personal injuries. During Morris' knee surgery, arthroscopic scissors distributed and warranted by Wolf broke, causing the injury. Plaintiffs' case was predicated, in part, on a strict products liability theory for an allegedly defectively designed instrument * * *. On appeal, they raise instructional error. We reverse.

I.

In March 1980, Wolf sold a pair of arthroscopic scissors to Mercy Hospital. In November 1984, Morris Bernal underwent arthroscopic knee surgery at Mercy.

During the surgical procedure, a scissor blade broke off inside the knee joint, "floated away," and it became imperative to open up the entire knee joint to find it. As a result of the failure of the scissors during surgery, and the subsequent arthrotomy, Bernal developed sympathetic dystrophy. His condition will continue to deteriorate and he will probably require a future total knee replacement. Medical testimony indicated Bernal's problems were proximately caused by complications arising from the failure of the scissors during surgery.

Bernal and his wife sued Wolf on several theories, including strict products liability based on design defect * * *.

Bernal's experts testified at trial the scissors broke due to a condition known as "stress corrosion cracking," resulting from a combination of design considerations. The experts did not testify to a "defect" as

such, nor did they testify that a reasonable alternative design was possible. * * *

In instructing the jury on Bernal's burden of proof with respect to the alleged design defect, the court gave the version submitted by Wolf, which read in toto as follows: "With respect to the existence of a defect in the design of the scissors, plaintiff must show by a preponderance of the evidence that a reasonable alternative design was possible, which would have avoided the breakage complained of."

Bernal contends this instruction is erroneous, in that it impermissibly places the burden on him to prove a safer alternative design. He further contends, although Wolf's manager testified the company warranted the scissors to be completely free of defects in material and workmanship, the trial judge refused to give any of Bernal's proffered jury instructions on warranty.

II.

In a case of strict products liability based on a design defect, does the plaintiff have the burden of proving a reasonable alternative design was feasible? We conclude one does not.

We begin with *Baker v. Chrysler Corp.* There the court stated: "Requiring an injured plaintiff who seeks damages against a manufacturer on the basis of strict liability in tort for a defective design to show that alternative designs for the product could reasonably have been developed does not enlarge plaintiff's burden of proof. An injured plaintiff has always had the burden to prove the existence of the defect. The reasonableness of alternative designs, where a design defect is claim, is part of that burden." Thus, held the court, the burden was upon the injured plaintiff to establish that reasonable alternative designs are possible.

Two years later, however, our [California] Supreme Court decided *Barker v. Lull Engineering Co.* There, the Court articulated a two-pronged definition of a design defect. The tests subsequently have become known as the ''consumer expectation'' test, and the ''risk-benefit'' test. The court stated: ''[A] product may be found defective in design . . . under either of two alternative tests. First a product may be found defective in design if the plaintiff establishes that the product failed to perform as safely as an ordinary consumer would expect when used in an intended or reasonably foreseeable manner. Second, a product may alternatively be found defective in design if the plaintiff demonstrates that the product's design proximately caused his injury and the defendant fails to establish, in light of the relevant factors, that, on balance, the benefits of the challenged design outweigh the risk of danger inherent in such design.''

Noting that past authorities had generally not devoted much attention to the appropriate allocation of the burden of proof, the [California] Supreme Court remarked that the ''burden is particularly significant [in that] one of the principal purposes behind the strict product liability doctrine is to relieve an injured plaintiff of many of the onerous evidentiary burdens inherent in a negligence cause of action. Because most of the evidentiary matters which may be relevant to the determination of the adequacy of a product's design under the 'risk benefit' standard—e.g., the feasibility and cost of alternative designs—are similar to issues typically presented in a negligent design case and involve technical matters peculiarly within the knowledge of the manufacturer, we conclude that once the plaintiff makes a *prima facie* showing that the injury was proximately caused by the product's design, the burden should appropriately shift to the defendant to prove, in light of the relevant factors, that the product is not defective.'' * * *

* * * *

* * * [T]here is no question Bernal presented a *prima facie* case that the design of the scissors was

a proximate cause of their failure during the surgical procedure, causing disability and the need for future surgery. That is all he had to prove. At that point, Wolf had the burden of proof to show that, on balance, the benefits of the design of the product as a whole outweigh the danger inherent in such design considering, among other enumerated ''relevant factors,'' the feasibility of a safer alternate design. We hold it was error to instruct the jury in the context of design defect that ''plaintiff must show by preponderance of the evidence that a reasonable alternative design was possible, which would have avoided the breakage complained of.''

Wolf complains to so hold renders it an insurer of its surgical instruments. Not so. Strict liability does not equate with absolute liability. Under the risk-benefit test, the defendant has the burden, and thus the opportunity, to highlight all of the benefits of its product's design before the jury. This would, of course, involve technical information peculiarly within its knowledge, and certainly more readily available to it. Among other things, the defense may show any alternate design would entail unreasonable costs, be uneconomic or impractical, interfere with the product's performance, or create other or increased risks. The case before us is a prime example. Here, the defense produced strong evidence the surgical instrument was made with the best steel available and was reasonably safe for its intended use, but had inherent dangers no human skill or knowledge has yet been able to eliminate. But for the erroneous burden of proof instruction, we would not hesitate to affirm the jury's verdict on this record.

* * * *

Judgment reversed and remanded for retrial on the [issue] of strict liability * * *. Costs awarded to appellant.

Case A.13

CHINA RESOURCE PRODUCTS (U.S.A.), LTD. v. FAYDA INTERNATIONAL, INC.

United States District Court, District of Delaware, 1990. 747 F.Supp. 1101.

LATCHUM, Senior District Judge.

This contract dispute, which involves hundreds of thousands of dollars and the shipment of goods in international commerce, is actually the story of Little

Red Riding Hood. Or so the defendant in this case apparently believes. The defendant describes itself as a small, American trading company. The plaintiff, on the other hand, although masquerading as a mere New York corporation, is in reality allegedly an arm of the People's Republic of China. The latter, ''one of the largest governments on earth,'' stars as the current dispute's Big Bad Wolf.

Presently before the Court is a motion by the plaintiff, brought pursuant to the Federal Arbitration

Act ("FAA" or "the Act"), to stay pending arbitration of a counterclaim filed by the defendant. * * * For the reasons noted below, the Court will grant the plaintiff's motion.

FACTUAL BACKGROUND

Plaintiff, China Resource Products (U.S.A.) Ltd. ("China Products"), initiated this lawsuit against defendant, Fayda International, Inc. ("Fayda"), for allegedly breaching a contract pursuant to which Fayda had agreed to purchase from China Products 187 metric tons of Chinese aluminum (hereinafter "the 1989 contract"). Fayda responded by denying liability and filing a counterclaim. This counterclaim alleges injury resulting from China Products' tardy performance of an earlier and different contract between the parties for the purchase of 200 metric tons of Chinese aluminum (hereinafter "the 1987 contract").

China Products maintains that the 1987 contract between it and Fayda contains a clause which requires Fayda to submit its counterclaim to arbitration. According to China Products, the 1987 contract consists of a written sales contract, which is dated July 13, 1987 and numbered "87MBN-010" (hereinafter "the July '87 writing"). This July '87 writing is signed by both parties and contains a broad arbitration clause on which China Products relies in its current motion to stay Fayda's counterclaim * * *.

Fayda describes its 1987 contract with China Products rather differently. It contends that the parties' sale agreement for these two hundred metric tons of aluminum was first concluded on August 21, 1987, and is contained in a writing dated as such (hereinafter "the August '87 writing"). This August '87 writing, which is signed by the parties, is labeled at the top as a "CONTRACT Amendment" and states that it is a letter meant to "confirm the agreement between . . . [Fayda and China Products] to amend contract No. 87MBN-010, dated July 13, 1987, as follows. . . ." Below these words are listed, *inter alia* [among other things], price, quantity, and delivery terms. The delivery terms state that 17 metric tons were to be shipped first, with the remaining 183 metric tons to follow a few weeks later.

Fayda maintains that after the 183-metric ton balance was not shipped in October of 1987 as agreed, the parties entered into a new contract for the purchase the same 183 metric tons of aluminum. * * *

Apparently, the 183 metric tons were never shipped pursuant to this alleged, second contract because Fayda argues that the parties entered into yet another agreement for the same shipment of aluminum [in May 1988] * * *.

Following this * * * agreement, the parties purportedly entered into yet another, now fourth, contract for the purchase of the 183 metric tons at issue. * * *

In sum, Fayda contends that the parties entered into no less than four different contracts for the purchase of the 183 metric tons of aluminum that were initially contracted for in the August '87 writing but were never shipped. Fayda maintains that the arbitration clause contained in the July '87 writing did not become part of these subsequent contracts. * * *

According to China Products, the parties entered into only one agreement, the July '87 writing. What Fayda calls subsequent contracts, China Products characterizes as at most merely modifications of the July '87 writing. Hence, China Products contends that the arbitration agreement contained in the July '87 writing remained in effect and, consequently, is still part of the parties' modified 1987 contract. Accordingly, China Products now moves, pursuant to section 3 of the FAA, to stay Fayda's counterclaim pending arbitration.

* * * *

Fayda's first argument against China Products' motion for stay is that the final contract between the parties did not contain an arbitration clause. That is, Fayda contends that there was a novation which eliminated the arbitration provision. The court rejects this argument.

Viewing the record in a light most favorable to Fayda, the Court concludes that there is absolutely no evidence to suggest there was a novation. In fact, the record suggests quite the opposite. The August '87 writing, for example, specifically refers to the parties' written sales agreement (the July '87 writing). Furthermore, the August '87 writing is plainly labeled at the top as a "CONTRACT amendment." The contract which allegedly followed the August '87 writing also specifically refers to the parties' July '87 writing. Moreover, the terms of the July '87 writing itself clearly contemplate price and possibly even shipping modifications.

* * * *

Fayda's second defense to arbitration is that the arbitration provision should not be given effect because it is unconscionable. * * *

Unconscionability is judged at the time the parties entered into the contract. It is undisputed on the record before the Court that at the time the parties entered into their sales agreement (the July '87 agreement) Fayda knew it was purchasing aluminum that was to be shipped from the People's Republic of China. Furthermore, the arbitration clause at issue in this motion, which is located directly above the signature of Fayda's representative clearly states that the parties will submit to arbitration under the auspices of the Foreign Trade Arbitration Commission of the China Council for the Promotion of International Trade ("the China Council"). Counsel for Fayda argues that pursuant to this clause arbitration "will probably take place in China or a third country, and the defendant will have to go there at great expense of time and money...." Needless to say, this is something Fayda should have considered before it signed the contract. "[T]he fact that a bargain is a hard one does not entitle a party to be relieved therefrom if he assumed it fairly and voluntarily."

*   *   *   *

The Court concludes that the arbitration provision in the July '87 writing is not unconscionable. Fayda has failed to raise a genuine issue of fact regarding unconscionability, and hence it is not entitled to an evidentiary hearing on this point.

*   *   * Fayda argues that China Products waived the parties' arbitration agreement by engaging in negotiations and subsequent agreements instead of seeking arbitration when problems with the contract first arose. The arbitration clause itself, however, specifically provides that "[a]ll disputes arising in connection with this Sales Contract or the execution thereof shall be settled amicably by negotiation." If "no settlement can be reached, the case under dispute shall then be submitted for arbitration...."

Fayda has not shown or even alleged that China Products has attempted to litigate any claims under the parties' 1987 contract. In fact, China Products' response to Fayda's counterclaim on this contract was the instant motion for stay under the FAA. Furthermore, Fayda has not alleged any prejudice from what it alleges is China Products' waiver of the arbitration remedy. Bearing in mind that a "waiver of the right to arbitration is not to be lightly inferred," the Court concludes that as a matter of law no waiver has been shown on this record.

*   *   *   *

Having considered and rejected all of Fayda's arguments against arbitration and having found that Fayda has raised no factual issues requiring an evidentiary hearing, the Court is satisfied from the present record that China Products is entitled to a stay under section 3 of the FAA. The parties' arbitration agreement is clearly broad enough to cover Fayda's counterclaim. China Products' motion to stay this counterclaim pending arbitration will therefore be granted.

———————

Case A.14

LAWTON v. WALKER

Supreme Court of Virginia, 1986.
231 Va. 247,
343 S.E.2d 335.

COMPTON, Justice.

In this appeal of a commercial law case, the main issue is whether the purchaser of a promissory note was a holder in due course.

In December 1981, appellant Charles Lawton sued appellee Emily Walker for $4,950 on a bearer note made by Walker in 1976 and held by Lawton, who claimed to be a holder in due course. Following a bench trial, the court below entered judgment for the defendant. We awarded the plaintiff this appeal. Lawton, a retired welder, purchased the note in question on April 15, 1980 from Martin Swersky, an acquaintance who had been in the aluminum siding business. *   *   *

Lawton paid Swersky approximately $5,000 for the note which, at the time of Lawton's purchase, had a balance due of $7,050. As part of the transaction, Lawton received from Swersky a title certificate issued to "Emily V. Walker" for a 1976 Ford automobile and a payment book in Walker's name with the notation, "Terms: $100 for 120 months. Amount of Note $12,000.00 (car)." *   *   *

Lawton further testified he was unaware of any "problems" with the note when he acquired it. He said he knew that the note was for purchase of an automobile from Swersky by Walker. He stated that the transaction between Swersky and Walker was "a straight cash sale'' without interest in which Swersky ''allowed her to pay over the period of ten years.'' Lawton did not know the actual cost of the vehicle when Swersky sold it to Walker.

According to the evidence, Walker made regular monthly payments to Swersky from February 1, 1976 to the date of the Swersky-Lawton deal and thereafter to Lawton. Walker ceased paying in October 1981, leaving a balance due of $4,950.

* * * According to defendant, in 1976 she bought a used 1976 Ford automobile from Swersky, agreeing to pay him $7,200 for the vehicle over a period of five years. She produced at trial the original new-car invoice for the vehicle which showed the price to be $5,671. She denied agreeing at any time to pay Swersky the sum of $12,000.

Walker admitted that her signature appeared on the note in question but denied signing the document. She testified, ''I haven't signed anything.'' Walker claimed that she had paid a total of $7,250 through October 1981, thus fulfilling her original bargain with Swersky. Neither Swersky nor Miller, the purported witness to Walker's signature on the note, testified.

In remarks from the bench following the trial, the court below ruled that Lawton was not a holder in due course. The basis for the ruling is not clear. At several points during his comments, the judge seemed to decide that Lawton was not a holder in due course because a bulk transaction was involved. The court concluded that because Lawton was not a holder in due course, he was ''subject to the defenses.'' Accordingly, the court determined that Walker had ''satisfied'' her contract with Swersky. The judgment order subsequently entered in favor of the defendant does not assign a reason for the decision.

Pertinent to our decision are the following * * * portions of Code [Section] 8.3-302, a part of the Uniform Commercial Code (UCC): * * * (1) A holder in due course is a holder who takes the instrument (a) for value; and (b) in good faith; and (c) without notice that it is overdue or has been dishonored or of any defense against or claim to it on the part of any person. * * *

On appeal, the parties do not dispute that the document in question is an ''instrument,'' meaning a ''negotiable instrument,'' nor do they dispute that Lawton took the instrument for ''value.'' However, the plaintiff insists he also took the note ''in good faith'' and ''without notice.''

The defendant asserts the plaintiff did not act in good faith and had notice of certain defenses to the payment of the note. The defendant also argues that the trial court ''did not err in finding that the plaintiff purchased the note in question as part of a bulk transaction not in the regular course of business of the transferor.''

* * * *

In the present case, the evidence dealing with the circumstances of the Lawton-Walker transaction is insufficient to raise an inference of lack of good faith on Lawton's part. He testified that the instant transaction was his ''first try'' at the business of purchasing commercial paper. He stated he was unaware of any ''problems'' with the note. Lawton thought the Swersky-Walker transaction was ''a straight cash sale,'' without interest, in which Swersky allowed Walker to pay for the automobile over a period of ten years. Nothing in the evidence suggests, and the trial court did not find, that Lawton's subjective intent was dishonest.

* * * *

In arguing the plaintiff took the note with ''notice,'' defendant contends that, from all the facts and circumstances known to Lawton at the time he purchased the note, he is deemed to have been aware of the ''rotten'' transaction between Walker and Swersky. * * * Walker also contends that the underlying obligation ''was at a minimum voidable in part,'' under [Section] 8.3-304(1)(b), because it should have been obvious to Lawton that the loan was made at a usurious rate of interest. The ''irregularities,'' the argument continues, demonstrate a scheme ''detrimental'' to Walker, and Lawton's ''protestations of ignorance . . . were nothing more than an effort to take advantage of an obviously shady transaction.'' Again, the difficulty with defendant's argument on this issue is that the record fails to support her conclusions.

According to paragraph 2 of the UCC Official Comment, the irregularity contemplated in [Section] 8.3-304(1)(a) is ''notice to the purchaser of something wrong.'' More specifically, the fact that the purchaser may have acted negligently or may have been affected with notice of suspicious circumstances is insufficient under [Section] 8.3-304 to deny him the status of holder in due course. Under the UCC and the cases, the holder must have either actual knowledge of the infirmity in the instrument or knowledge of such facts that his action in taking the instrument amounts to bad faith.

Even though Lawton may have been negligent and even though the circumstances may have been suspicious, we cannot say from this evidence that he acted in bad faith. Lawton's actual knowledge of the underlying transaction was limited to an awareness of a note with no ''problems'' which had been given in connection with a ''straight cash sale,'' payments to be made over an extended period. Under these circumstances, Lawton cannot be charged with knowledge that an exorbitant amount of interest was concealed within the sum due or that the Swersky-Walker transaction was ''rotten,'' especially when the evidence requires pure speculation to reach such conclusions. A naked denial by Walker that she executed the instrument or that she agreed to pay Swersky $12,000 furnishes no basis for a contrary finding. And, significantly, the trial court did not find that Lawton acted in bad faith and with notice of a claim or defense.

* * * *

Therefore, we will reverse the judgment in favor of the defendant and enter final judgment for the plaintiff in the amount of $4,950.

Reversed and final judgment.

Case A.15

KNAUF v. BANK OF LaPLACE

Court of Appeal of Louisiana, Fifth Circuit, 1990.
567 So.2d 182

GOTHARD, Judge.

This suit is against a bank for wrongful dishonor of a check by the drawee bank. The plaintiff payee appeals judgment dismissing his claim on an exception of no cause of action.

On or about April 15, 1988 the defendant, Lynn Paul Martin doing business as LPM Enterprises, issued two checks payable to Richard Knauf and drawn on the Bank of LaPlace. Knauf endorsed the two checks, ''For Deposit Only'' and ''A/C 12216967,'' and deposited them into his personal account at the First National Bank of Jefferson Parish. The Hibernia National Bank of New Orleans then stamped the back of the checks, ''credit to the account of the named payee, Hibernia National Bank of New Orleans.'' The Bank of LaPlace received them on or before April 18, 1988 and dishonored them, stamping them, ''endorsements missing.'' When the checks were presented again, the Bank of LaPlace returned them marked ''NSF''.

On September 7, 1988 Knauf filed suit against the Bank of LaPlace, alleging wrongful dishonor and seeking damages. The Bank filed a peremptory exception of no cause of action. [The trial court dismissed Knauf's suit.]

The issue before this court is whether or not [Knauf's] petition failed to state a cause of action.

[Knauf's] petition makes the following allegations:

9.

Defendant, BLP's, actions in the handling of LPM's account were not within ordinary and customary banking practices; BLP and LPM did not have an ordinary banking relationship. BLP permitted LPM to maintain a constant overdraft in his checking account, the daily overdraft generally exceeding $1,000,000.00. BLP benefitted significantly from this relationship, as they were charging the LPM account with significant NSF fees daily. LPM was permitted to maintain an overdraft in his account as long as he ''covered'' the overdraft with certified checks the following day.

10.

LPM had tried to conduct this type of operations with another bank prior to going to BLP, but was asked to leave the other bank because the other bank considered the activities of LPM to go beyond the scope of customary banking practices and questioned the activities of LPM.

11.

Ultimately, LPM was indicted and [pled] guilty to federal violations of law for which this account was used.

12.

On or about April 18, 1988, employees and/or officers of BLP determined to dishonor the checks because BLP claimed plaintiff's ''endorsement'' was missing.

13.

BLP, however, paid other checks in the month of April which contained the same or similar endorsements as the Knauf checks, numbers 1379 and 1875.

14.

It is a common practice in the banking industry to endorse a check with ''For Deposit Only'' with the account number.

15.

It is also an ordinary and customary banking practice for a bank to supply its customers' missing endorsement. The purpose of this provision is to facilitate the negotiation of these instruments.

16.

As long as the bank supplies the endorsement, the check can be negotiated through normal and customary banking channels. The Hibernia endorsement accomplished this.

17.

BLP policy went beyond the ordinary and customary banking practice by allowing LPM to write checks on an account that did not have proper funds and selectively determining which checks were to be paid. Check numbers 1379 and 1875 were selected not to be paid by means of the endorsement missing stamp.

Other checks drawn on LPM's account, endorsed in the same manner, were paid. This is further evidence of the peculiar banking relationship between BLP and LPM which allowed LPM to conduct his illegal activities.

18.

BLP, through the actions of its employees and/or officers deliberately rejected both properly endorsed checks number 1379 and number 1875, for the reason of, but not limited to, selective disbursal of monies deposited in LPM account for the improper benefit of BLP in earning enormous fees and/or for the benefit of LPM and his scheme.

19.

The actions of employees and/or officers of the defendant, BLP, caused the untimely delays in processing and/or payment of both LPM accounts checks, number 1379 and 1875, totalling $150,131.00.

20.

Had BLP had a proper and customary banking relationship with LPM, the checks would have been properly processed allowing Knauf to receive the funds represented by the checks when originally presented. Instead, the checks were reprocessed and returned NSF.

Knauf argues in brief that had the checks not been dishonored initially and if the Bank of LaPlace had had an ordinary relationship with its customer, Martin, then he would have received the funds represented by the checks.

At the outset we agree with Knauf that the checks were sufficiently endorsed with his First National Bank of Jefferson account number and should not have been dishonored on grounds of insufficient endorsement. * * *

However, as argued by the bank, under the Louisiana statute regarding commercial paper, the duty of the bank runs to its customer, i.e., the depositor, rather than to the third party payee. LSA-R.S. 10:4-402 [the Louisiana equivalent of UCC 4-402] provides that, ''A payor bank is liable to its customer for damages proximately caused by the wrongful dishonor of an item.'' * * * As there is no allegation that the payor bank had made a specific promise to pay Martin's checks to Knauf, R.S. 10:4-402 does not apply to his claim of wrongful dishonor.

* * * *

In our judgment, the plaintiff's allegations regarding the bank's erroneous return of Knauf's check and its selective payment of checks drawn by Martin are sufficient to make out a cause of action in tort against the bank.

LSA-R.S. 10:4-103 requires that a bank be responsible for ''its own lack of good faith or failure to exercise ordinary care.'' * * *

Under this Article banks come under the general obligations of the use of good faith and the exercise of ordinary case. * * * The term ''ordinary care'' is not defined and is here used with its normal tort meaning and not in any special sense relating to bank collections.

* * * *

* * * Although the drawee on a draft is not liable on the instrument until it is accepted, this does not preclude liability on the part of the drawee to the holder arising apart from the instrument, i.e., in tort or upon some other basis because of the drawee's representation that the instrument will be accepted. Furthermore, La.R.S. 10:4-103 imposes upon banks a duty to exercise ordinary care in the handling of commercial paper and provides for damages in the event of the violation of that duty.

* * * *

Accordingly, for the reasons assigned above, the judgment appealed from is reversed and the case is remanded for further proceedings not inconsistent with this opinion.

REVERSED AND REMANDED.

Case A.16

STATE v. SKORPEN

Court of Appeals of Washington, Division 2, 1990.
57 Wash.App. 144,
787 P.2d 54.

PHILIP H. FARIS, Judge Pro Tem [*pro tempore,* or temporarily].

David Skorpen appeals his conviction of theft in the second degree. Skorpen found and attempted to pass a check that had been forged previously by another in the amount of $375. Skorpen requested a jury trial on an amended two-count information that charged forgery and theft in the second degree by appropriating lost or misdelivered property. The court ruled, as a matter of law, that a forged check has a value equal to its face amount.

Following the court's ruling, the parties stipulated to the following facts: While on a street in the Longview-Kelso area on April 19, 1988, Skorpen found the driver's license of Greg Harris together with a document that purported to be a check that was payable to Harris in the amount of $375. The check was drawn on the First Interstate Bank account of R.K. Anthony, whom Skorpen knew. The check was complete; Skorpen did not write upon or otherwise alter it. Although Skorpen believed the check to be genuine, the check was actually forged. It was not, however, forged by Skorpen, and it was not endorsed by Harris. Using Harris' driver's license for identification, Skorpen unsuccessfully attempted to pass the check at First Interstate Bank.

Based upon this stipulation, the trial court found Skorpen guilty of theft in the second degree by appropriating lost or misdelivered property. On the State's motion, the trial court dismissed the forgery count. Skorpen appeals, and we reverse.

The parties agree that Skorpen committed a theft but disagree as to the degree of that theft. At a minimum, Skorpen committed theft in the third degree, which is a gross misdemeanor. If the forged check that Skorpen found had a value equal to its face amount, however, Skorpen committed theft in the second degree, which is a class C felony.

Thus, the disposition of this case turns upon whether the value of the forged check was its face amount, which in turn depends upon the construction of a statutory definition:

(a) "Value" means the market value of the property or services at the time and in the approximate area of the criminal act.

(b) Whether or not they have been issued or delivered, written instruments, except those having a readily ascertained market value, shall be evaluated as follows:

    (i) The value of an instrument constituting an evidence of debt, such as a check, draft, or promissory note, shall be deemed the amount due or collectible thereon or thereby, that figure ordinarily being the face amount of the indebtedness less any portion thereof which has been satisfied;

    . . . .

    (iii) The value of any other instrument that creates, releases, discharges, or otherwise affects any valuable legal right, privilege, or obligation shall be deemed the greatest amount of economic loss which the owner of the instrument might reasonably suffer by virtue of the loss of the instrument.

    . . . .

(e) Property or services having value that cannot be ascertained pursuant to the standards set forth above shall be deemed to be of a value not exceeding two hundred and fifty dollars; . . .

Because no evidence was adduced as to market value, its value must be determined under either subsection (b)(i), subsection (b)(iii), or subsection (e). If the value is not determined under subsections (b)(i) or (b)(iii), then subsection (e) applies, and the conviction must be reversed.

The State argues that the value of the check "shall be deemed the amount due or collectible thereon or thereby, that figure ordinarily being the face amount. . . ." In interpreting the predecessor statute that defined value, the [Washington] Supreme Court held that the value of a stolen check is its face amount. * * *

* * * *

In the present case, we conclude that the owner of the forged check that Skorpen stole did not lose anything of value. In [a previous case], the court stated that a "forged check has no value as a chose in action and if there was a theft of the check the only thing stolen was a piece of paper having little, if any, intrinsic value."

The statutory construction that is urged by the State requires that the check be "an instrument constituting an evidence of debt. . . ." This requirement is readily satisfied in the usual maker-payee relationship. The check itself evidences an obligation from the maker to the payee in an amount equal to that stated upon the face of the check. When that check is stolen, the payee loses something of prima facie value, i.e., the right to proceed against the maker in the event that the drawee dishonors it, even if the payee did not take the check for value.

When the check is forged by means of an unauthorized signature of the maker, however, that maker-payee relationship does not exist. The payee may recover from the forger, but only if the payee in good faith pays the check or takes it for value. Thus, a forged check does not by itself constitute evidence of a debt; extrinsic evidence is necessary to show that the payee in good faith paid the check or took it for value. Such evidence is completely lacking in the present case.

An accepted rule of statutory construction suggests a different result than that urged by the State. Statutes are construed wherever possible so that no portion is superfluous. The State argues that the value of the check "shall be deemed the amount due or collectible thereon or thereby, that figure ordinarily being the face amount. . . ." In order to avoid rendering part of this phrase superfluous, it must be construed so as to recognize the possibility of situations in which the amount due or collectible on a written instrument is not its face amount.

An obvious example of such a situation is where the instrument does not satisfy the statutory requirements of an instrument under the Uniform Commercial Code. " 'Instrument' means a negotiable instrument." "Any writing to be a negotiable instrument within this Article must (a) be signed by the maker or drawer; and contain an unconditional promise or order to pay a sum certain in money. . . ." An instrument that is forged by means of an unauthorized signature of the maker is not signed by the maker. Therefore, it is not negotiable. We conclude that the statute is not ambiguous. Subsection (b)(i) speaks of the "amount due or collectible." Clearly, nothing is due or collectible on a forged check.

* * * *

Skorpen committed a theft. He had the intent to commit the theft of $375. He believed that the check was genuine and worth $375; however, the check was forged and worth nothing or nearly nothing. He tried to commit the harm that the Legislature sought to prevent in enacting the theft statutes, i.e., economic loss to the owners of property. Skorpen's attempt to commit theft in the second degree, however, failed. * * *

* * * *

Reversed.

_____

Case A.17

MELLON BANK, N.A. v. SECURITIES SETTLEMENT CORP.

United States District Court, District of New Jersey, 1989. 710 F.Supp. 991.

CLARKSON S. FISHER, District Judge.

Before the court are the motions of plaintiff, Mellon Bank ("Mellon"), and defendant, Securities Settlement Corporation ("SSC"), for summary judgment. At oral argument, the parties agreed that the facts are not in dispute. The transaction underlying this case is relatively simple. SSC performed clearing services in connection with securities transactions in the accounts of one of its customers, Kobrin Securities ("Kobrin"). One of Kobrin's clients was another entity, Barrett Consultants ("Barrett"), to whom SSC sent monthly statements regarding Barrett's account with Kobrin. On the morning of June 4, 1985, SSC,

at Kobrin's request, instructed Mellon to wire transfer $113,080.50 to Barrett's account with the Franklin State Bank ("FSB"). Within several hours after Mellon had sent the wire, SSC learned that Kobrin was incapable of paying the securities' purchase price. Although SSC instructed Mellon to cancel the wire transfer, the money went through to Barrett's account. Mellon filed the instant complaint in October of 1987 in the Superior Court of New Jersey, Law Division, Somerset County, seeking reimbursement for the funds it had sent to FSB. SSC removed the case to this court in November of the same year.

* * * *

The threshold issue is whether Pennsylvania's version of the U.C.C. applies to this action. [Mellon and SSC agreed that Pennsylvania law governed their rights and liabilities.] SSC has cited several cases for the proposition that the U.C.C. does not govern wire transfers and contends that this case must be decided without reference to the statute. Mellon counters that the U.C.C. has been applied by analogy in other jurisdictions and urges the court to do the same. Unfortunately neither party has cited, nor has the court found, decisions from the Pennsylvania state courts which address this question.

There are merits to both positions. On one hand it might be noted that the U.C.C. covers only "items," which 13 Pa.C.S.A. [Pennsylvania Consolidated Statutes Annotated] section 4104 [Pennsylvania's version of UCC 4-104] defines as "any instrument for the payment of money even though it is not negotiable." With this definition as a starting point, it might be added that an instrument is a signed writing which expresses an agreement regarding rights, while the instant case involves an unsigned and electronically-transmitted instruction. It could be asserted that this difference is not merely semantic; it illustrates that the U.C.C. was designed to address paper transactions rather than high-speed financial distributions. According to this argument Pennsylvania's trial courts would not adjudicate this case under 13 Pa.C.S.A. section 4101 *et seq.*

On the other hand, a "check is no more than an order on the bank to pay a stated amount . . . from the maker's account." Although checks are negotiable instruments, it could be argued that Thomas 's definition exactly fits a wire transfer, which is nothing more than an order directing the bank to pay money from one account to another. Moreover, it could be argued that the total exclusion of the U.C.C. from this case would leave the court with little current law upon which to base its decision.

Thus the court must sail between the Scylla of common law and the Charybdis of statute in an attempt to predict what Pennsylvania's highest court would do if confronted with this situation. * * * The court concludes that it should follow those decisions which have applied the common law while at the same time borrowing appropriate rules from the governing version of the U.C.C.

* * * *

SSC had a right to stop the * * * wire transfer, and Mellon was under a corresponding duty to use ordinary care in handling SSC's request. * * * Before the court can determine * * * whether Mellon actually used ordinary care, it must examine the wire transfer at issue here.

The transfer was made under BankWire, a system maintained by Mellon and roughly 100 other banks. BankWire procedure requires a customer's autho-

rized representative to instruct Mellon to transfer money from the customer's account to the recipient's account in another bank. After receiving and verifying an instruction, Mellon personnel would when necessary select a "correspondent" bank. The correspondent bank would then serve as a conduit for the transfer to the recipient's bank.

This process does not transmit the funds themselves; rather, upon making the transfer Mellon would debit the customer for the the amount of the transfer, and credit the correspondent bank's account with Mellon. * * * BankWire funds become available on the day following the transfer.

Because BankWire funds are not immediately obtainable, a cancellation does not require the bank to recapture the wired funds. Essentially, a BankWire cancellation requires two steps. First, Mellon sends a cancellation notice to the "correspondent" bank, which in turn instructs the recipient bank to disregard the transfer. Second, Mellon reverses the credit/debit notation which it made upon receiving the transfer order; the customer's account is recredited and the correspondent bank's account is debited, thereby returning the balances to their pre-transfer sums. * * *

* * * *

SSC instructed Mellon to cancel the wire on the same day it learned that the funds were not covered. * * * Within several hours * * *, Mellon sent a notice to MHT [the correspondent bank] instructing them to cancel the transaction * * *. Shortly after this message was sent Mellon reversed its account entries; it restored the transferred amount to SSC's account, and debited MHT's account with Mellon to the same amount.

Mellon's notice contained two errors. First, it referred to "YR BK WIRE," i.e., a wire transfer sent by MHT rather than one received by it. Second, the notice gave a transaction number of "184B." Transaction numbers are assigned by BankWire to each transfer request. The wire's true number was "06040184B."

* * * SSC heard nothing from Mellon regarding the transfer. Mellon, however, heard from MHT on several occasions. On June 6, 1985, MHT telephoned Mellon to inform the bank that MHT had not received the June 4, 1985 wire. * * * The next day MHT again contacted Mellon and informed the bank that MHT had no record of receiving a wire transfer denominated by [the transaction number] 184B.

Mellon replied to neither of these correspondences. * * *

On July 12, 1985, MHT wired Mellon that it intended to credit FSB with $113,080.50. In the same communication MHT asked Mellon to wire them in return should Mellon not want the transaction to be completed. MHT also asked that Mellon credit MHT's account with $113,080.50. Four days later Mellon wired MHT that cancellation instructions had already been issued by Mellon on June 4, 1985. Mellon's wire contained, for the first time, the correct transaction number. Two days after this, on July 18, 1985, MHT requested that FSB authorize a reversal of the June 4 transfer. The next day FSB informed MHT that Barrett had already withdrawn the money.

No reasonable fact finder could conclude that Mellon acted with ordinary care regarding the cancellation. Mellon incorrectly identified the transaction to be cancelled, both by omitting five digits from the transaction number and by indicating that it sought to cancel a wire sent by MHT. The latter error might be considered inconsequential; after all, MHT did respond to Mellon within forty-eight hours to ask about Mellon's wire. But the inaccurate transaction number persisted throughout MHT's attempts to comply with Mellon's instructions; this error tainted such attempts for over one month.

Mellon's error easily ranks with those considered sufficient to constitute a breach of a bank's duty of ordinary care. The record demonstrates that Mellon inaccurately carried out SSC's instructions and that, even though it was twice given notice of MHT's corresponding inability to cancel the wire, Mellon failed to take prompt remedial action. Indeed, the court notes that Mellon's failures transgressed its own internal guidelines.

* * * *

Upon examining the record and the parties' arguments, the court concludes that no reasonable finder of fact could grant Mellon the relief it seeks. Rather, it is SSC who is entitled to judgment as a matter of law. Summary judgment is granted for SSC against all Mellon's claims.

————

Case A.18

ALL VALLEY ACCEPTANCE CO. v. DURFEY

Court of Appeals of Texas—Austin, 1990.
800 S.W.2d 672.

PER CURIAM.

Appellees Earl and Bonnie Durfey sued appellant All Valley Acceptance Company in the district court of Travis County asserting that All Valley breached the parties' "Manufactured Home Retail Installment Sales Contract and Security Agreement." The district court rendered partial summary judgment that the Durfeys recover $37,752.87 from All Valley and, after a bench trial, that the Durfeys recover attorney's fees. This Court will affirm the judgment.

The summary judgment proof showed that in October 1986, the Durfeys entered into an installment sales contract with Thomas Homes of Texas to purchase a manufactured home which had been built by Fleetwood Homes of Texas, Inc. After moving into the home, the Durfeys and their son suffered allergic reactions to formaldehyde which had been used in the manufacture of the home. As a result, the Durfeys vacated the home in March 1987.

After moving out, the Durfeys retained an attorney who wrote All Valley of the formaldehyde problems the family had experienced. Counsel's letter informed All Valley of the Durfeys' monetary damages and indicated that the matter could be settled if their existing home was replaced with a formaldehyde-free one and their medical, hotel, and legal expenses were paid. The Durfeys did not sign the letter.

In April 1987, after notifying All Valley of the problems with the home, the Durfeys stopped making the monthly payments to All Valley. As a result, in June 1987, All Valley sent the Durfeys a notice of default and right to cure letter, citing the Durfeys' failure to make payments for April, May and June. The Durfeys received All Valley's letter but did not respond. In early August 1987, All Valley repossessed the home with the consent of the Durfeys.

After repossessing the home, All Valley sent the Durfeys a "Notice of Private Sale" dated August 24, 1987. The notice stated that the home would be sold at a private sale "on or after the 3rd day of September,

1987.'' The notice was sent by certified mail, return receipt requested. All Valley never received the return receipt and the certified letter was eventually returned unclaimed.

Two days after this notice was sent to the Durfeys, on August 26, All Valley entered into a contract of sale with a third party and on August 28, the contract was funded by All Valley and the repossessed home sold to that party. This sale, conducted before the date indicated in the notice of sale sent to the Durfeys, gave rise to this lawsuit.

The district court rendered partial summary judgment as to liability on the breach of contract and [Section] 9.504 claims. By several points of error, All Valley complains of the judgment. We first address All Valley's claim that summary judgment was improper because the Durfeys had renounced or modified their right to notice of the resale.

In regard to a secured party's right to dispose of collateral after the debtor defaults, Texas Business and Commerce Code [Section] 9.504 [The Texas equivalent of UCC 9-504], provides:

> Unless collateral is perishable or threatens to decline speedily in value or is of a type customarily sold on a recognized market, reasonable notification of the time and place of any public sale or reasonable notification of the time after which any private sale or other intended disposition is to be made shall be sent by the secured party to the debtor, if he has not signed after default a statement renouncing or modifying his right to notification of sale.

All Valley complains that the letter written by the Durfeys' attorney, in which he informed All Valley that the home had been vacated and the Durfeys were seeking compensation, constituted a renunciation or modification of their right to notice of the resale. Section 9.504 provides, however, that a debtor may waive his right to notice only by executing a written statement after default which is signed by the debtor. This provision of [Section] 9.504 has been strictly construed to require a specific, knowing waiver of the right to notice, in writing and actually bearing the signature of the debtor. These opinions are consistent with those in other states which have adopted the same provision of the Uniform Commercial Code.

In the instant appeal, the letter from the Durfeys' attorney to All Valley was not signed by the Durfeys nor did it ever mention a waiver of their right to notice of sale of the mobile home. Accordingly, the letter

does not constitute a modification or renunciation of the type that is contemplated by [Section] 9.504.

All Valley claims, also, that summary judgment was improper because the Durfeys waived their right to notice of the sale by agreeing to the repossession of the home by All Valley. All Valley suggests, as well, that the Durfeys should be estopped from asserting their right to notice under [Section] 9.504 for the same reason. We do not agree. In Texas, and in many other states which have adopted the same U.C.C. provision, voluntary surrender of the collateral does not constitute waiver of the debtor's right to notice of resale of the collateral.

This Court also disagrees with All Valley's suggestion that summary judgment was improper because the Durfeys failed to prove they had suffered any actual damages by not receiving notice of the resale. When a creditor fails to comply with [Section] 9.504 of the Texas Business and Commerce Code, damages are specifically provided for in [Section] 9.507 of the Code. The debtor need not prove any other damages in order to recover under the statute.

All Valley further attacks the partial summary judgment on the basis that the Durfeys' summary judgment evidence did not establish that there was no genuine issue of fact with regard to lack of proper notification and breach of cor ract. Section 9.504 requires that ''reasonable notification'' be given such that the debtor will have sufficient time to take steps to protect his or her interest. What constitutes ''reasonable notification'' is not otherwise defined in the statute; instead, it is left to the contracting parties to establish the parameters of that term within their particular agreement.

In the instant appeal, the contract of sale specifically stated that should a sale of the collateral take place, the creditor may comply with the statutory requirement of reasonable notification by mailing notice of the sale ''at least ten days before such event. . . .'' This contract of sale was a part of the summary judgment proof as was the notification of sale sent by All Valley, dated August 24, 1987, which indicated that a sale would take place ''on or after September 3, 1987.'' The uncontroverted summary judgment proof showed that All Valley sold the home on August 28, 1987, only four days after the notice was sent. No other effort to notify the Durfeys was made nor did the Durfeys have actual notice of the August 28th sale.

Notice of the September 3rd sale, mailed ten days before that date, cannot serve as reasonable notice of a sale conducted on August 28th. The result of All Valley's actions was that the Durfeys had no notice of the August 28th sale, and the summary judgment evidence plainly established that fact. Accordingly, there was no genuine issue of material fact as to whether the Durfeys received reasonable notification of the resale as required by [Section] 9.504.

The same summary judgment proof established that All Valley breached the terms of the contract of sale. All Valley is correct in its assertion that the notice provision of the contract did not mandate that it give at least ten days notice to the Durfeys. The contract did, however, provide that if All Valley chose to satisfy the reasonable notice of sale requirement of [Section] 9.504 by sending such by mail, the notice was to be mailed "at least ten days before such event." The uncontroverted summary judgment evidence established that notice was mailed on August 24th and

the sale occurred on August 28th. Given that no other means of notice was attempted by All Valley, this conclusively establishes that All Valley breached the notice provision of the contract.

* * * *

During oral argument and by way of post submission brief, All Valley claimed that the Durfeys were not entitled to notice of the sale of the manufactured home because the letter written by their attorney, requesting replacement of the home and payment for damages, constituted a revocation of acceptance of the home. The matter of revocation of acceptance was never presented to the trial court, and this Court cannot consider an issue not expressly presented to the trial court.

The judgment is affirmed.

Case A.19

ALLISON-BRISTOW COMMUNITY SCHOOL DISTRICT v. IOWA CIVIL RIGHTS COMMISSION

Supreme Court of Iowa, 1990.
461 N.W.2d 456.

SCHULTZ, Justice.

In this appeal the issue is whether back pay and interest awarded to an employee in a civil rights action qualifies as personal earnings which are exempt from garnishment by a judgment creditor under Iowa Code section 642.21 (1989). The district court held that back pay and interest on the award were not exempt under section 642.21 and could be garnished by a judgment creditor. We hold that the exemption applies to the back pay, but not to the interest.

In 1981, Bernard W. Rowland filed a civil rights complaint against his employer for unlawful discrimination in terminating his employment. The Civil Rights Commission held in favor of Rowland and ordered the employer to pay him $65,377, less appropriate deductions for federal and state income taxes and social security. It further ordered that attorney fees and interest be paid by the employer. On April 26, 1989, following appeals, the employer filed a satisfaction of judgment and deposited money for payment of the judgment with the clerk of the district court. It is agreed by the parties that the tax withholdings amounted to $19,838 and that the net back-pay award plus interest amounted to $80,248.

In independent actions, Willow Tree Investment Co. (Willow Tree) obtained judgments against Rowland in state and federal courts. It caused a writ of execution to be issued and garnished the clerk of court for the funds held on behalf of Rowland for back pay and interest. On June 9, 1989, Rowland received notice of the garnishment and promptly resisted, claiming that the funds deposited for back pay and interest were personal earnings which fell within the exemption contained in section 642.21. The district court allowed the garnishment.

* * * *

I. Earnings. Throughout this appeal the underlying issue is whether the civil rights award of back pay qualifies as earnings that fall within the exemption in section 642.21. This section defines "earnings" as "compensation paid or payable for personal services, whether denominated as wages, salary, commission, bonus or otherwise. . . ." The district court relied upon federal cases interpreting the federal Consumer Credit Protection Act and upon language in *Mid-America Savings Bank v. Miehe* in concluding that the purpose of this legislation is to facilitate an employee's payment of living expenses and support. We agree with this broad assertion of purpose, but cannot agree with the district court's next conclusion.

The district court concluded that the legislature did not intend an amount subsequently received for back pay to be exempt earnings. It reasoned that the back pay was received too late to allow an employee to apply it toward day-to-day living expenses incurred during the time period when the back wages were earned. This conclusion ignores the fact that Rowland had living expenses during the period he was wrongfully unemployed. Exemption laws are to be liberally construed to allow debtors and their families assurance that necessary living expenses can be covered. Rowland should be in a position to use the judgment in his favor to replenish the source from which his living expenses were paid during the period he was deprived of earnings. In other words, a judgment creditor should not gain an advantage caused by the wrongful acts of an employer.

Willow Tree urges that the underlying intent of the exemption section is to provide a continuing means of support for a debtor. Willow Tree emphasizes that the Supreme Court found that the legislative intent behind passage of the federal Consumer Credit Protection Act was to prevent personal bankruptcy filings, to preserve a debtor's employment, and to provide an ongoing means of support for a debtor and his family. We concede that one of the purposes of the federal Act is to ensure a continued means of support for the debtor. In this case, however, the exemption is derived from the additional protection given the debtor under state law. Our state law determines the amount of the exemption on the basis of an individual's expected annual income. This method of annual calculation is less attuned to provide a continued means of support for a debtor than the federal Act, which calculates the amount of disposable income that can be garnished on a weekly basis.

* * * Consideration of the relevant Iowa legislation as a whole demands a broader view than the trial court's narrow focus upon an exemption that is conditioned only on the payment of current living expenses. We believe the more appropriate focus should be upon the true nature of the award in question to determine if it falls within the term ''earnings'' as defined in section 642.21. A civil rights award is unlike a damage award in a typical contract or tort action. The underlying purpose of allowing damages in a civil rights award is compensation for the injury sustained. In civil rights actions, the legislature gave the courts power to provide a wide variety of relief, most of which is equitable in nature. In unfair employment practices remedial action includes ''[h]iring, reinstatement or upgrading of employees with or without pay. . . .'' Although part of a civil rights award may be compensation, the real purpose behind a civil rights award is to make the person whole for an injury suffered as a result of unlawful employment discrimination.

In this case, the award not only allowed back pay, but also required the employer to pay the tax withholdings to place the employee in the same position he would have occupied if the wages were received during the period of wrongful discharge. Under these circumstances, we conclude that the judgment entered in Rowland's favor for back pay is an award of earnings paid for personal services as defined in subsection 642.21(3)(a).

Willow Tree * * * claims that Rowland's award of back wages was extinguished and replaced by a judgment debt. Thus, it urges that the back-pay award lost its character as wages and may be garnished as any other judgment. It cites *Stephen O. Cook v. Valentine W. Holbrook* for the proposition that a claim for wages merges into a judgment and becomes a separate and distinct debt losing its character as wages. It also argues that our language in *Chader v. Wilkins* supports the proposition that a judgment is a debt regardless of the nature of the original cause of action.

We cannot agree that the entry of a judgment for back pay resulted in Rowland's losing the exemption provided in section 642.21. *Cook* is distinguishable from this case because the creditor sought to garnish a fund arising from a judgment that was held by an attorney. Likewise, our decision in *Chader* is not controlling. The language in *Chader* does not persuade us to determine that a judgment extinguishes the entire character of the original claim. More important, we believe that stronger authority can be found in those cases holding that an employee's wages remain exempt when he sues an employer and recovers a judgment. We believe that these cases are more consistent with the purposes of Iowa's exemption and civil rights statutes.

* * * *

Willow Tree also urges that time has destroyed the exempt character of the wages. It cites our decision in *Miehe* for authority that the exemption only lasts for a ninety-day period after the wages are paid if the wages can be traced to a checking or savings account in a financial institution. In this case, the funds have not been transferred to Rowland nor has he exercised any control over the funds. He has not been permitted ''a reasonable opportunity to negotiate the paycheck [earnings represented by the judgment] and spend the fund.'' Under these circumstances it would be premature to establish a ninety-day limit as we did in *Miehe*.

II. Interest. We address Rowland's claim that he is entitled to an exemption in the interest due on the judgment for back pay wages. He urges that the interest should be construed as "earnings" for the purposes of section 642.21. We do not agree. Interest is allowed for the use of money or as damages for its detention. We hold that the interest is not exempt under section 642.21.

III. Conclusion. In summary, we hold that the amount of Rowland's judgment against his employer for back pay is exempt earnings under section 642.21, but that the amount awarded for interest on the judgment is not exempt. We remand for the district court to determine the amount of the exemption and render judgment accordingly.

AFFIRMED IN PART AND REVERSED IN PART.

Case A.20

GREEN v. SHELL OIL CO.

Court of Appeals of Michigan, 1989.
181 Mich.App. 439,
450 N.W.2d 50.

FITZGERALD, Justice.

* * * *

At approximately 6:00 P.M. on December 21, 1981, plaintiff drove into a Shell service station owned and operated by defendant Lanford and leased from defendant Shell Oil Company. Plaintiff filled his gas tank and, as he walked from the self-service island to the station's office to pay for the gasoline, was struck by a slow-moving vehicle plaintiff alleges was driven by Monica Gottwald. Plaintiff slapped the hood of the vehicle with his hand and yelled for Gottwald to stop and to be more careful. Immediately thereafter, Leslie Salgado, an occupant of the Gottwald vehicle and employee of the station, exited from the vehicle and began striking plaintiff. An unidentified station attendant joined Salgado in his attack on plaintiff.

On January 2, 1982, plaintiff filed a complaint in Oakland Circuit Court against defendants and Salgado, as well as others no longer parties to the instant action, alleging [among other things] vicarious liability [indirect liability] of defendants for * * * assault and battery and negligence by defendants in failing to provide a safe place for doing business. The case was remanded to district court after mediation.

Defendants moved for and were granted summary disposition. The district court held that defendants could not be held liable for an intentional tort committed by the service station attendant. The court also held that the attendant owed no duty to stop an assault by a third party. * * *

Plaintiff appealed * * * to circuit court. The circuit court reversed the district court's grant of summary disposition * * *.

* * * *

We believe that * * * defendant Lanford's employees were in a position to control the unruly situation, to eject the instigator from the premises and to refrain from increasing plaintiff's injuries. On these facts, a jury could find that defendant Lanford failed to exercise reasonable care for his invitees' protection.

The question * * * becomes whether Shell Oil had apparent authority over the service station so as to make it liable for the assault on plaintiff. In *Johnston v. American Oil Co.,* the plaintiff's decedent was shot during an altercation with the proprietor of a Standard service station, who refused to serve him and his companions. The trial court granted defendant American Oil Company's summary judgment motion based on the proprietor's status as an independent contractor. The plaintiff had pointed to the service station's use of American Oil's trademark and its sale of supplies and products obtained from American Oil. On appeal, the panel concluded:

> American Oil's national advertising campaign promoting the Standard Oil name and products, including the slogans "As you travel ask us" and "You expect more from Standard and you get it," would seem to raise a sufficient question of fact as to the existence of agency by estoppel or by apparent authority to defeat the granting of summary judgment.
>
> * * * * *
>
> We believe the trial court herein likewise erred in granting the motion for summary judgment. The question, of course, is not whether Murphy is, in fact, an agent of American Oil, the question is whether plaintiff has raised a material issue of fact that requires further proofs before the finding of fact. Here plaintiff has carried that burden.

In his affidavit [a written or printed statement confirmed by oath or affirmation], plaintiff stated:

> I always assumed that a Shell gas station was operated by Shell Oil. I cannot state whether I ever actually considered whether the operators of gas stations

have an ownership interest in the business or not, but it was my belief at the time of the assault upon me, and prior, that Shell Oil either owned the facilities and operated them directly, or exercised active control over the operations of the gas station so as to ensure uniform standards of quality, reliability and conduct of the employees at the stations.

According to defendants, Shell Oil exercised no control over the hiring, firing and supervision of the service station employees and had no authority over the supervision, management and control of the station. In addition, defendant Lanford was not required to purchase any parts from Shell Oil. As defendants state on appeal, ''the most that can be said is that '[Wayne Lanford] displayed [Shell's] brand signs, that he honored [Shell's] credit cards, [and that Shell's] agents from time to time made suggestions as to operation of the station.' ''

In light of the foregoing, we cannot say with any degree of certainty that further factual development of plaintiff's theory of apparent authority would be futile. Accordingly, we believe that plaintiff should be given the opportunity to show that Shell Oil had apparent authority over defendant Lanford's employees.

Defendants also argue that they cannot be held vicariously liable for the attendant's participation in the assault. We agree.

An employer is liable for the intentional tort of his employee if the tort is committed in the course and within the scope of the employment. An employer is not liable if the employee's tortious act is committed while the employee is working for the employer but the act is outside his authority, ''as where he steps aside from his employment to gratify some personal animosity or to accomplish some purpose of his own.''

An employer's liability may also be based upon a finding that the employee acted within the scope or apparent scope of his employment. Generally, the trier of fact determines whether an employee was acting within the scope or apparent scope of his employment. Summary disposition is appropriate, however, where it is apparent that the employee is acting to accomplish a purpose of his own.

Plaintiff testified at a deposition that Salgado struck him on the left side of the head. Plaintiff fell to the ground, dazed by the blow. The next thing he remembered was being kicked, while laying on the ground, by a man in a brown uniform, allegedly the unidentified station attendant. On this testimony, we conclude that the attendant's violent conduct was engaged in for the purpose of assisting Salgado and not for any purpose in furtherance of the employer's business interests. This is not a situation where the employee was attempting to collect plaintiff's payment on behalf of his employer. Nor is it a situation where the attendant's conduct can be reasonably construed as an attempt to end the altercation or eject plaintiff from the employer's establishment in order to restore order. Accordingly, summary disposition on plaintiff's vicarious liability claim was appropriate. The attendant's action could only be construed as an attempt to accomplish his own purpose, not to further his employer's business interests.

* * * *

We affirm in part, reverse in part and remand.

_____

Case A.21

MASCHMEIER v. SOUTHSIDE PRESS, LTD.

Court of Appeals of Iowa, 1989.
435 N.W.2d 377.

HABHAB, Judge.

Defendant Kenneth E. Maschmeier and Charlotte A. Maschmeier created a corporation, Southside Press, Ltd., that did business at 1220 Second Avenue North in Council Bluffs. This building is owned by Kenneth and Charlotte and was leased by them to the corporation.

Kenneth and Charlotte are the majority shareholders, with each having 1300 shares. They are the only officers and directors of the corporation.

They gifted to their two sons [Marty and Larry] each 1200 shares of stock. All the parties were employed by Southside Press until the summer of 1985 when, because of family disagreements, Marty and Larry were terminated as employees. * * *

The parents on August 2, 1985, created a new corporation, Southside Press of the Midlands, Ltd. They are its only officers and directors. As individuals they terminated the lease of their building * * *

with Southside and leased the same premises to Midlands. In addition, Kenneth, as president of Southside, entered into a lease with himself as president of Midlands whereby the printing equipment and two of the vehicles were leased to Midlands for $22,372 per year for five years, with an option to buy such assets at the end of the lease term at their fair market value but not to exceed $20,000. In addition, the inventory and two other vehicles owned by Southside were sold by it to Midlands. Notwithstanding the fact that a substantial part of the assets of Southside had been disposed of, the parents still received an annual salary from it of more than $20,000.

After Marty and Larry's employment with Southside had terminated, each obtained employment with other printing companies in the same metropolitan area. The family disagreement continued. All stockholders were employed by companies that were competitive to Southside. Ultimately, the parents, as majority shareholders, offered to buy the sons' shares of stock for $20 per share. Their sons felt that this amount was inadequate. Thus, this lawsuit.

In 1985, Southside Press had gross sales of more than $600,000. The trial court found that in 1985 the corporate assets had a fair market value of $160,745. Shareholders' equity was found to be $236,502.92, and divided by the number of shares equals $47.30 per share. The court found that the majority shareholders had been abusive and oppressive to the minority shareholders by wasting the corporate assets and leaving Southside Press only a shell of a corporation. The court ordered the majority shareholders to pay $47.30 per share to the sons, or $56,760 to each son, plus interest at the maximum legal rate from the date of the filing of the petition.

* * * *

* * * [D]efendants state that the shares were valued at $20 pursuant to the corporate bylaws and should be enforced as an agreement of the shareholders. * * *

* * * *

Whenever a situation exists which is contrary to the principles of equity and which can be redressed within the scope of judicial action, a court of equity will devise a remedy to meet the situation though no similar relief has been granted before. The district court has the power to liquidate a corporation under [Iowa Code] section 496A.94(1). This statute also allows the district court to fashion other equitable relief.

It is contended that, in order for the trial court to have properly invoked the powers under section 496A.94(1), it had to find either the majority shareholders were oppressive in their conduct towards the minority shareholders, or that the majority shareholders misapplied or wasted corporate assets.

* * * The alleged oppressive conduct by those in control of a close corporation must be analyzed in terms of "fiduciary duties" owed by majority shareholders to the minority shareholders and "reasonable expectations" held by minority shareholders in committing capital and labor to the particular enterprise, in light of the predicament in which minority shareholders in a close corporation can be placed by a "freeze-out" situation.

* * * The trial court found * * * here [that] the majority shareholders attempted to "freeze out" or "squeeze out" the minority shareholders by terminating their employment and not permitting them to participate in the business.

* * * *

We concur with the trial court's findings that the majority shareholders acted oppressively toward the minority shareholders and wasted corporate assets. In this respect, we further determine that the trial court properly invoked Iowa Code section 496A.94 when it fashioned the remedy requiring the majority shareholders to purchase the shares of the minority.

But that does not resolve the problem, for as stated above * * * [t]he appellant challenges the method fashioned by the trial court in fixing the value of the stock and payment thereof by asserting it should be governed by the bylaws.

The articles of incorporation of Southside vested in the directors of the corporation the "authority to make provisions in the Bylaws of the corporation restricting the transfer of shares of this corporation." This the board of directors did when they adopted the following bylaw that relates to restrictions on the transferability of stock. * * *

* * * *

Section 3 [of the corporate bylaws] is a restriction on stock transfer. If a shareholder intends to sell his stock, he must first offer it to the corporation at a price "agreed upon by the shareholders at each annual meeting." The shareholders must agree on the value of the stock and if they are unable to do so, each has a right to select an appraiser and the appraisers shall appoint another and in this instance the five appraisers are to act as a Board of Appraisers to value the stock.

* * * Since none of the shareholders requested appraisers, we deem this, as the trial court did, to be a waiver. We concur with this statement from the trial court's ruling: "All parties have left the Court with the burden of evaluating the corporate stock."

* * * *

We agree with the defendants that a contractual formula price is enforceable even if the formula price is less than its fair market value. But here the parties were unable to agree to a price, i.e., at the last meeting of the stockholders. Thus the trial court was called upon to do so.

Courts have generally held that no one factor governs the valuation of shares; but that all factors, such as market value, asset value, future earning prospects, should be considered. In this case, the parties relied rather heavily on what is referred to in the record as book value (shareholders' equity) in arriving at stock value. The trial court likewise used shareholder equity but adjusted that amount by the present day fair market value of corporate assets.

* * * *

We determine that under the circumstances here the valuation per share as fixed by the trial court and the method it employed in arriving at value is fair and reasonable. However, we further conclude that the amount Larry and Marty are to receive must be reduced by the total amount of loans made to them as they appear on the corporate books.

* * * *

We affirm and modify.

_____

Case A.22

GREENLEE v. SHERMAN

New York Supreme Court, Appellate Division, Third
Department, 1989.
142 A.D.2d 472,
536 N.Y.S.2d 877.

CASEY, Justice Presiding.

[This action arises] out of a 1980 transaction between Horace and Annie Greenlee, plaintiffs * * * and Philip Sherman, the sole proprietor of Sherman Fuel and Oil Burner Service, whereby Sherman installed a combination wood/oil furnace in the basement of the Greenlees' house. The Greenlees used the furnace until March 30, 1984, when a fire substantially destroyed their house. It is alleged that the fire was caused by the improper installation of the flue pipe from the furnace, which resulted in the exposure of a wooden joist to intense radiant heat while the furnace was operating. This exposure to intense heat allegedly caused a chemical process, known as pyrolyisis, in the wooden joist which ultimately lowered the ignition temperature of the wood to the point where it was ignited by the flue pipe.

* * * [T]he Greenlees seek [among other things] to recover damages based upon Sherman's negligent installation of the furnace. Named as defendants * * * are the executor of Sherman's estate and Main Care Heating Service, Inc. (hereinafter Main Care), as the successor in interest to Sherman Fuel and Oil Burner Service. * * * Main Care moved * * * for summary judgment dismissing the Greenlees' complaint and Supreme Court granted the motion. * * * The Greenlees have appealed * * *.

The issue raised by the appeal in [this action] is whether there exists a triable issue of fact on the question of Main Care's liability as a successor in interest to Sherman's business, pursuant to an agreement between Sherman and Main Care, dated November 19, 1980.

It is the general rule that a corporation which acquires the assets of another is not liable for the torts of its predecessor. * * * There are exceptions. * * * A corporation may be held liable for the torts of its predecessor if (1) it expressly or impliedly assumed the predecessor's tort liability, (2) there was a consolidation or merger of seller and purchaser, (3) the purchasing corporation was a mere continuation of the selling corporation, or (4) the transaction is entered into fraudulently to escape such obligations.

Main Care relies upon this general rule, while the Greenlees contend that the second and third exceptions are applicable. In *Grant-Howard Assoc. v. General Housewares Corp.*, the Court of Appeals noted that these two exceptions "are based on the concept that a successor that effectively takes over a company in its entirety should carry the predecessor's liabilities as a concomitant [something that exists concurrently with something else] to the benefits it derives from the good will purchased." But the court prefaced this remark with the following explanation of the genesis of the successor liability theory:

> Allowing recovery in tort against a successor corporation is merely an extension of the concept of products liability, which calls for the burden of consumer injuries to be borne by the manufacturer, who can transfer the costs to the general public as a component of the selling price. Strict liability assures that a responsible source is available to compensate the injured party.

The case at bar does not involve the concept of products liability. The Greenlees' action is based upon the negligence of Sherman in the installation of the furnace; there is no claim that Sherman manufactured or sold a defective product. The Greenlees contracted directly with Sherman for certain services to be performed by him, and their claim for damages is based upon Sherman's negligence in performing those services. In these circumstances, the public policy considerations underlying the concept of products liability are not present. Therefore, based upon the previously quoted language of the Court of Appeals in *Grant-Howard Assoc. v. General Housewares Corp., supra* ["above—meaning in this instance the case cited above; the full citation for this case was omitted by the authors when editing this case], it appears that the successor liability theory is not applicable in this case.

In any event, we find no proof in the record to support the Greenlees' contention that there was a consolidation or merger of Main Care and Sherman's business or that Main Care is a mere continuation of Sherman's business. As to the consolidation or merger claim, Sherman, the sole proprietor of the selling business, did not become involved with Main Care, either as a shareholder or as an employee; Main Care did not acquire either the cash on hand or the accounts receivable of Sherman's business; Main Care did not hire any employee of Sherman's business; and Main Care did not install furnaces, which was at least a part of Sherman's business. As to the "mere continuation" claim, that exception refers to corporate reorganization, which did not occur here. Main Care had been in existence for at least 12 years prior to its purchase of Sherman's business and it continued in substantially the same form thereafter, with the addition of Sherman's assets. In short, Main Care cannot be viewed as a "mere continuation" of Sherman's business. Thus, assuming that the successor liability theory is applicable outside the context of products liability, the Greenlees' proof was inadequate to defeat Main Care's motion for summary judgment.

* * * *

ORDERS AND JUDGMENT AFFIRMED.

Case A.23

JOHNSTON v. DEL MAR DISTRIBUTING CO.

Court of Appeals of Texas—Corpus Christi, 1989.
776 S.W.2d 768.

BENAVIDES, Justice.

Nancy Johnston, appellant, brought suit against her employer, Del Mar Distributing Co., Inc., alleging that her employment had been wrongfully terminated. Del Mar filed a motion for summary judgment in the trial court alleging that appellant's pleadings failed to state a cause of action. After a hearing on the motion, the trial court agreed with Del Mar and granted its motion for summary judgment.

* * * *

In her petition, appellant alleged that she was employed by Del Mar during the summer of 1987. As a part of her duties, she was required to prepare shipping documents for goods being sent from Del Mar's warehouse located in Corpus Christi, Texas to other cities in Texas. One day, Del Mar instructed appellant to package a semi-automatic weapon (for delivery to a grocery store in Brownsville, Texas) and to label the contents of the package as "fishing gear." Ultimately, the package was to be given to United Parcel Service for shipping. Appellant was required to sign her name to the shipping documents; therefore, she was concerned that her actions might be in violation of some firearm regulation or a regulation of the United Postal Service. Accordingly, she sought the advice of the United States Treasury Department Bureau of Alcohol, Tobacco & Firearms * * *. A few days after she contacted the Bureau, appellant was fired. Appellant brought suit for wrongful termination alleging that her employment was terminated solely in retaliation for contacting the Bureau.

* * * *

Del Mar asserted in its motion that, notwithstanding the above described facts, appellant's cause of action was barred by the employment-at-will doctrine. Specifically, Del Mar asserted that since appellant's employment was for an indefinite amount of time, she was an employee-at-will and it had the absolute right to terminate her employment for any reason or no reason at all.

It is well-settled that Texas adheres to the traditional employment-at-will doctrine. The Texas Supreme Court [has] held that absent a specific contractual provision to the contrary, either the employer or the employee may terminate their relationship at any time, for any reason.

Today, the absolute employment-at-will doctrine is increasingly seen as a "relic of early industrial times" and a "harsh anachronism." Accordingly, our Legislature has enacted some exceptions to this doctrine * * *.

Recently, the Texas Supreme Court, recognizing the need to amend the employment-at-will doctrine, invoked its judicial authority to create a very narrow common law exception to the doctrine. In [*Sabine Pilot Service, Inc. v. Hauck*] the Texas Supreme Court was faced with a narrow issue for consideration, i.e., whether an allegation by an employee that he or she was discharged for refusing to perform an illegal act stated a cause of action. The Court held that

> public policy, as expressed in the laws of this state and the United States which carry criminal penalties, requires a very narrow exception to the employment-at-will doctrine * * * [t]hat narrow exception covers only the discharge of an employee for the sole reason that the employee refused to perform an illegal act.

Justice Kilgarlin noted in his concurring opinion to *Sabine Pilot* that it is against public policy to allow an employer "to require an employee to break a law or face termination. . . ." He elaborated that to hold otherwise "would promote a thorough disrespect for the laws and legal institutions of our society."

* * * *

On appeal, appellant alleges that her petition did state a cause of action pursuant to the public policy exception announced in *Sabine Pilot*. In her brief, appellant contends that since Texas law currently provides that an employee has a cause of action when she is fired for refusing to perform an illegal act, it necessarily follows that an employee states a cause of action where she alleges that she is fired for simply inquiring into whether or not she is committing illegal acts. To hold otherwise, she argues, would have a chilling [inhibiting, discouraging] effect on the public policy exception announced in *Sabine Pilot*. We agree.

It is implicit that in order to refuse to do an illegal act, an employee must either know or suspect that the requested act is illegal. In some cases it will be patently obvious that the act is illegal (murder, robbery, theft, etc.); however, in other cases it may not be so apparent. Since ignorance of the law is no defense to a criminal prosecution, it is reasonable to expect that if an employee has a good faith belief that a required act might be illegal, she will try to find out whether the act is in fact illegal prior to deciding what course of action to take. If an employer is allowed to terminate the employee at this point, the public policy exception announced in *Sabine Pilot* would have little or no effect. To hold otherwise would force an employee, who suspects that a requested act might be illegal, to (1) subject herself to possible discharge if she attempts to find out if the act is in fact illegal; or (2) remain ignorant, perform the act and, if it turns out to be illegal, face possible criminal sanctions.

We hold that since the law recognizes that it is against public policy to allow an employer to coerce its employee to commit a criminal act in furtherance of its own interest, then it is necessarily inferred that the same public policy prohibits the discharge of an employee who in good faith attempts to find out if the act is illegal. It is important to note that we are not creating a new exception to the employment-at-will doctrine. Rather, we are merely enforcing the narrow public policy exception which was created in *Sabine Pilot*.

* * * *

Furthermore, it is the opinion of this Court that the question of whether or not the requested act was in fact illegal is irrelevant to the determination of this case. We hold that where a plaintiff's employment is terminated for attempting to find out from a regulatory agency if a requested act is illegal, it is not necessary to prove that the requested act was in fact illegal. A plaintiff must, however, establish that she had a good faith belief that the requested act might be illegal, and that such belief was reasonable. * * *

* * * *

The judgment of the trial court is reversed and remanded for trial. _____

Case A.24

STRANG v. HOLLOWELL

Court of Appeals of North Carolina, 1990.
387 S.E.2d 664.

[WELLS, Judge.]

On 2 January 1987 plaintiff met with defendants Hollowell and Jones in Cary, North Carolina to negotiate a consignment agreement for the sale of plaintiff's 1974 Pantera automobile which had an estimated value of $23,000 to $25,000. A written consignment contract was executed between plaintiff and Hollowell Auto Sales. Defendant Jones, then employed by Hollowell Auto Sales, signed the contract on behalf of Hollowell Auto Sales. Plaintiff gave defendants the keys to his automobile and they transported it by flatbed trailer to the Hollowell Auto Sales lot in Morehead City. Defendants Jones and Hollowell were unable to sell the Pantera and it was returned to plaintiff in August 1987. At that time plaintiff discovered that the automobile had been damaged to an extent which reduced its value to between $10,000 and $12,000.

On 23 December 1987 plaintiff sued defendants Jones and Hollowell for negligence in their bailment of his automobile. Plaintiff was unaware that Hollowell Auto Sales was a trade name for Solar Center, Inc., whose principal place of business is in Carteret County. Plaintiff was under the impression that Hollowell Auto Sales was a sole proprietorship operated by defendant Hollowell. On motion of defendant Hollowell in open court, defendant Solar Center, Inc. was added as an additional party prior to trial.

Defendant Jones did not file an answer to plaintiff's complaint and default judgment was subsequently entered against him. At a non-jury trial, judgment in the amount of $11,000 was entered against defendants Jones and Hollowell, jointly and severally. Defendant Gene Hollowell appeals.

* * * *

The only issue presented in this appeal is whether defendant Hollowell can be held individually liable for plaintiff's damages. Defendant contends that he was acting as an agent of Hollowell Auto Sales and therefore cannot be held personally liable. Defendant further asserts that, regardless of the fact that plaintiff was unaware that Hollowell Auto Sales was a trade name for Solar Center, Inc., defendant is nevertheless shielded from individual liability because Solar Center, Inc. fulfilled its legal obligation to disclose its relationship with Hollowell Auto Sales by filing an assumed name certificate in [the appropriate county office]. For the following reasons, we disagree.

When plaintiff gave possession of his automobile to defendant under the consignment contract a bailment for the mutual benefit of bailor and bailee was created. This bailment continued until the automobile was returned to plaintiff in August 1987. Defendant was therefore a bailee of plaintiff's automobile while it was in his custody in Morehead City. A bailee is obligated to exercise due care to protect the subject of the bailment from negligent loss, damage, or destruction. His liability depends on the presence or absence of ordinary negligence. While this obligation arises from the relationship created by the contract of bailment, breach of this contractual duty results in a tort. It is well settled that one is personally liable for all torts committed by him, including negligence, notwithstanding that he may have acted as agent for another or as an officer for a corporation. Furthermore, the potential for corporate liability, in addition to individual liability, does not shield the individual tortfeasor from liability. Rather, it provides the injured party a choice as to which party to hold liable for the tort.

Here there is no dispute that plaintiff's automobile was returned to him in a damaged condition. Defendant does not except to the trial court's findings and conclusions that a bailment was created between plaintiff and defendant and that "defendants were negligent in their care and control of the vehicle while it was in their possession." We therefore hold that the trial court correctly ruled that by failing to exercise due care and allowing the automobile to be damaged while in his custody, defendant committed a tort for which he can be held individually liable.

Because the resolution of this case is in tort for negligence, rather than in contract for breach, we need not reach the issue of whether defendant had sufficiently disclosed his agency with Hollowell Auto Sales or with Solar Center, Inc. However, we note that our Supreme Court has said that use of a trade name is not sufficient as a matter of law to disclose the identity of the principal and the fact of agency. Likewise, the existence of means by which the fact of agency might be discovered is also insufficient to disclose agency.

* * * *

Affirmed.

Case A.25

TRANS-ORIENT MARINE CORP. v. STAR TRADING & MARINE, INC.

United States District Court, Southern District of New York, 1990.
731 F.Supp. 619.

WILLIAM C. CONNER, District Judge:

Defendant Republic of the Sudan moves this Court to dismiss the complaint for failure to state a claim or for summary judgment. It claims that the new Republic of the Sudan, as successor state, is not liable for the alleged breach of a five-year exclusive agency contract entered into by the prior sovereign state of Sudan. Defendant further asserts that a fundamental change in circumstances relieves it of any prior contractual obligations.

FACTS

Plaintiff's cause of action for breach of contract arises from an alleged five-year exclusive agency agreement to represent the Sudan in the United States P.L. 480 program [an agricultural trade development and assistance program]. The alleged October 14, 1983 agreement was effective from October 1, 1984 through September 30, 1989. In April 1985, a military coup deposed the then head of state, declaring a state of emergency and suspending the constitution. A twelve-month transitional military regime followed, which was then replaced by a civilian coalition government. The name of the state was changed from the Sudan to the Republic of Sudan. In June 1989, there was another military coup in which the present military regime overthrew the former civilian administration and suspended the constitution. Both parties agree that the Republic of the Sudan is a foreign sovereign state.

On January 3 and 4, 1985, the then Sudanese government sent letters advising plaintiff that a new agent, CIDCO, had been appointed to handle the contracts under P.L. 480 and that CIDCO would select the shipping agent. This alleged termination of the then-executory contract did not provide the one-year termination notice required under the original contract. Since January 1985, the Sudan has awarded CIDCO a continuing series of contracts to handle the wheat and wheat flour transportation under P.L. 480, in alleged violation of plaintiff's exclusive agency contract. No additional facts are relevant to the present motion.

DISCUSSION

The present Sudanese government asserts that it is not liable for the contractual obligations of the prior sovereign, pointing to the two military coups of 1985 and 1989 to sustain its position that both the 1985 military regime and the present administration are successor states and that there has been a fundamental change in circumstances. Plaintiff contends that neither the 1985 regime nor the present regime is a successor state but that they represent mere changes in government which do not relieve the present regime from the prior government's contractual obligations. Plaintiff further argues that even if either regime is a successor state, they have ratified the prior government's contract. For the following reasons, summary judgment is denied.

Whether a new administration may terminate the executory portions of its predecessor's contracts is based on the succession of state theory. International law sharply distinguishes the succession of state, which may create a discontinuity of statehood, from a succession of government, which leaves statehood unaffected. It is generally accepted that a change in government, regime or ideology has no effect on that state's international rights and obligations because the state continues to exist despite the change. * * *

However, where one sovereign succeeds another, and a new state is created, the rights and obligations of the successor state are affected. The rule with regard to contracts with private foreign individuals involves a balancing of competing interests. While the successor state is permitted to terminate existing contracts originally executed by the former sovereign and the private party, the successor state is liable to that party only for any amount due him as of the date of the change of sovereignty. But if the contract is totally executory, the successor state is released from the contract.

The Restatement of Foreign Relations Law describes a successor state to include: a state that wholly absorbs another state, that takes over part of the territory of another state, that becomes independent of another state of which it had formed a part, or that arises because of the dismemberment of the state of which it had been a part.

Careful study of defendant's submission reveals that the state of Sudan has not (1) wholly absorbed or been wholly absorbed by another state; (2) partly taken over or been partly taken over by another state; (3) become independent from another state of which

it had formed a part; or (4) arisen out of dismemberment of a state of which it had been a part since the
date of plaintiff's contract. Under the Restatement's
definition, the state of Sudan has remained the same
entity since its independence in 1956. Defendant's
own exhibit in support of its motion substantiates that
only a change in government was effected by the two
military coups *   *   *.

Accordingly, the only changes in the Sudan since
its independence in 1956 have been in the government, with seven distinct successive administrations.
But there has been only one state.

Defendant unpersuasively emphasizes various aspects of the relevant transitions to reflect the creation
of a new state: that the transitions resulted by way of
military coups as opposed to routine, constitutional
processes, the re-naming of the nation, the suspension
of the constitution, the closing of the borders and the
declaration of a state of emergency. Treatises, as well
as applicable case law, demonstrate that such features
do not effect a succession of state. *   *   *

Furthermore, the Restatement's comparative
chart in a Recognition of States section illustrates that
a change in government by armed force or fraud, as
well as institution of another regime following a civil
war, leaves "no question of the existence of the
state." It offers as contemporary examples of mere
changes in government: Pinochet's 1973 ouster of
Allende in Chile, Franco's 1936-39 takeover of Spain,
and the Communist revolution in China.

The seminal decision on the distinction between
a succession of state versus a change in government
is the U. S. Supreme Court decision in *The Sapphire.*
In *The Sapphire,* the Supreme Court considered
whether a lawsuit begun by the French Emperor, Na-
poleon III, was abated by the overthrow of the Emperor during the course of litigation. In holding that
the action was not extinguished, the Supreme Court
stated that, "on the [Emperor's] deposition the sovereignty does not change, but merely the person or
persons in whom it resides. . . . A change in such
representative works no change in the national sovereignty or its rights."

*   *   *   *

*   *   * In *United States v. National City Bank
of New York,* the district court held the post-revolu-
tionary State of Russia liable on the treasury notes of
the pre-revolutionary state. Similarly, in *Jackson v.
People's Republic of China,* the district court determined that the People's Republic, as successor government to the Imperial Chinese Government, was
successor to its obligations, specifically, payment of
principal due on the prior government-issued bonds.
The law is clear that the obligations of a state are
unaffected by a mere change in government. It is of
no consequence that the Sudan allegedly breached an
executory contract. The distinction between executed
and executory contracts only applies where there has
been a succession of state. The military coups of 1985
and 1989 did not effect a succession of state of the
Sudan but merely changed the state's governing body,
leaving the state's obligations undisturbed.

Defendant's alternative claim that a fundamental
change of circumstances has occurred since October,
1983 relieving it of any prior contractual obligations
is unsubstantiated. Defendant presents no explanation
as to what "circumstances constituted an essential
basis of the consent of the parties to be bound by the
agreement" or what changes have "radically transform[ed] the extent of obligations still to be performed
under the agreement." Having failed to demonstrate
a fundamental change in circumstances, the present
government is therefore contractually obligated to
plaintiff under the October 14, 1983 five-year extension of agency contract if its predecessor indeed
breached that agreement.

CONCLUSION

For the reasons discussed above, summary judgment is denied. Plaintiff is directed to brief the additional grounds for dismissal or summary judgment
raised in defendant's motion papers by March 19,
1990. Defendant shall reply by March 26, 1990.

SO ORDERED.

Appendix B

The Constitution of the United States

PREAMBLE

We the People of the United States, in Order to form a more perfect Union, establish Justice, insure domestic Tranquility, provide for the common defence, promote the general Welfare, and secure the Blessings of Liberty to ourselves and our Posterity, do ordain and establish this Constitution for the United States of America.

ARTICLE I

Section 1. All legislative Powers herein granted shall be vested in a Congress of the United States, which shall consist of a Senate and House of Representatives.

Section 2. The House of Representatives shall be composed of Members chosen every second Year by the People of the several States, and the Electors in each State shall have the Qualifications requisite for Electors of the most numerous Branch of the State Legislature.

No Person shall be a Representative who shall not have attained to the Age of twenty five Years, and been seven Years a Citizen of the United States, and who shall not, when elected, be an Inhabitant of that State in which he shall be chosen.

Representatives and direct Taxes shall be apportioned among the several States which may be included within this Union, according to their respective Numbers, which shall be determined by adding to the whole Number of free Persons, including those bound to Service for a Term of Years, and excluding Indians not taxed, three fifths of all other Persons. The actual Enumeration shall be made within three Years after the first Meeting of the Congress of the United States, and within every subsequent Term of ten Years, in such Manner as they shall by Law direct. The Number of Representatives shall not exceed one for every thirty Thousand, but each State shall have at Least one Representative; and until such enumeration shall be made, the State of New Hampshire shall be entitled to chuse three, Massachusetts eight, Rhode Island and Providence Plantations one, Connecticut five, New York six, New Jersey four, Pennsylvania eight, Delaware one, Maryland six, Virginia ten, North Carolina five, South Carolina five, and Georgia three.

When vacancies happen in the Representation from any State, the Executive Authority thereof shall issue Writs of Election to fill such Vacancies.

The House of Representatives shall chuse their Speaker and other Officers; and shall have the sole Power of Impeachment.

Section 3. The Senate of the United States shall be composed of two Senators from each State, chosen by the Legislature thereof, for six Years; and each Senator shall have one Vote.

Immediately after they shall be assembled in Consequence of the first Election, they shall be divided as equally as may be into three Classes. The Seats of the Senators of the first Class shall be vacated at the Expiration of the second Year, of the second Class at the Expiration of the fourth Year, and of the third Class at the Expiration of the sixth Year, so that one third may be chosen every second Year; and if Vacancies happen by Resignation, or otherwise, during the Recess of the Legislature of any State, the Executive thereof may make temporary Appointments until the next Meeting of the Legislature, which shall then fill such Vacancies.

No Person shall be a Senator who shall not have attained to the Age of thirty Years, and been nine Years a Citizen of the United States, and who shall not, when elected, be an Inhabitant of that State for which he shall be chosen.

The Vice President of the United States shall be President of the Senate, but shall have no Vote, unless they be equally divided.

The Senate shall chuse their other Officers, and also a President pro tempore, in the Absence of the Vice President, or when he shall exercise the Office of President of the United States.

The Senate shall have the sole Power to try all Impeachments. When sitting for that Purpose, they shall be on Oath or Affirmation. When the President of the United States is tried, the Chief Justice shall preside: And no Person shall be convicted without the Concurrence of two thirds of the Members present.

Judgment in Cases of Impeachment shall not extend further than to removal from Office, and disqualification to hold and enjoy any Office of honor, Trust, or Profit under the United States: but the Party convicted shall nevertheless be liable and subject to Indictment, Trial, Judgment, and Punishment, according to Law.

Section 4. The Times, Places and Manner of holding Elections for Senators and Representatives, shall be prescribed in each State by the Legislature thereof; but the Congress may at any time by Law make or alter such Regulations, except as to the Places of chusing Senators.

The Congress shall assemble at least once in every Year, and such Meeting shall be on the first Monday in December, unless they shall by Law appoint a different Day.

Section 5. Each House shall be the Judge of the Elections, Returns, and Qualifications of its own Members, and a Majority of each shall constitute a Quorum to do Business; but a smaller Number may adjourn from day to day, and may be authorized to compel the Attendance of absent Members, in such Manner, and under such Penalties as each House may provide.

Each House may determine the Rules of its Proceedings, punish its Members for disorderly Behavior, and, with the Concurrence of two thirds, expel a Member.

Each House shall keep a Journal of its Proceedings, and from time to time publish the same, excepting such Parts as may in their Judgment require Secrecy; and the Yeas and Nays of the Members of either House on any question shall, at the Desire of one fifth of those Present, be entered on the Journal.

Neither House, during the Session of Congress, shall, without the Consent of the other, adjourn for more than three days, nor to any other Place than that in which the two Houses shall be sitting.

Section 6. The Senators and Representatives shall receive a Compensation for their Services, to be ascertained by Law, and paid out of the Treasury of the United States. They shall in all Cases, except Treason, Felony and Breach of the Peace, be privileged from Arrest during their Attendance at the Session of their respective Houses, and in going to and returning from the same; and for any Speech or Debate in either House, they shall not be questioned in any other Place.

No Senator or Representative shall, during the Time for which he was elected, be appointed to any civil Office under the Authority of the United States, which shall have been created, or the Emoluments whereof shall have been increased during such time; and no Person holding any Office under the United States, shall be a Member of either House during his Continuance in Office.

Section 7. All Bills for raising Revenue shall originate in the House of Representatives; but the Senate may propose or concur with Amendments as on other Bills.

Every Bill which shall have passed the House of Representatives and the Senate, shall, before it become a Law, be presented to the President of the United States; If he approve he shall sign it, but if not he shall return it, with his Objections to the House in which it shall have originated, who shall enter the Objections at large on their Journal, and proceed to reconsider it. If after such Reconsideration two thirds of that House shall agree to pass the Bill, it shall be sent together with the Objections, to the other House, by which it shall likewise be reconsidered, and if approved by two thirds of that House, it shall become a Law. But in all such Cases the Votes of both Houses shall be determined by Yeas and Nays, and the Names of the Persons voting for and against the Bill shall be entered on the Journal of each House respectively. If any Bill shall not be returned by the President within ten Days (Sundays excepted) after it shall have been presented to him, the Same shall be a Law, in like Manner as if he had signed it, unless the Congress by their Adjournment prevent its Return in which Case it shall not be a Law.

Every Order, Resolution, or Vote, to which the Concurrence of the Senate and House of Representatives may be necessary (except on a question of Adjournment) shall be presented to the President of the United States; and before the Same shall take Effect, shall be approved by him, or being disapproved by him, shall be repassed by two thirds of the Senate and House of Representatives, according to the Rules and Limitations prescribed in the Case of a Bill.

Section 8. The Congress shall have Power To lay and collect Taxes, Duties, Imposts and Excises, to pay the Debts and provide for the common Defence and general Welfare of the United States; but all Duties, Imposts and Excises shall be uniform throughout the United States;

To borrow Money on the credit of the United States;

To regulate Commerce with foreign Nations, and among the several States, and with the Indian Tribes;

To establish an uniform Rule of Naturalization, and uniform Laws on the subject of Bankruptcies throughout the United States;

To coin Money, regulate the Value thereof, and of foreign Coin, and fix the Standard of Weights and Measures;

To provide for the Punishment of counterfeiting the Securities and current Coin of the United States;

To establish Post Offices and post Roads;

To promote the Progress of Science and useful Arts, by securing for limited Times to Authors and Inventors the exclusive Right to their respective Writings and Discoveries;

To constitute Tribunals inferior to the supreme Court;

To define and punish Piracies and Felonies committed on the high Seas, and Offenses against the Law of Nations;

To declare War, grant Letters of Marque and Reprisal, and make Rules concerning Captures on Land and Water;

To raise and support Armies, but no Appropriation of Money to that Use shall be for a longer Term than two Years;

To provide and maintain a Navy;

To make Rules for the Government and Regulation of the land and naval Forces;

To provide for calling forth the Militia to execute the Laws of the Union, suppress Insurrections and repel Invasions;

To provide for organizing, arming, and disciplining, the Militia, and for governing such Part of them as may be employed in the Service of the United States, reserving to the States respectively, the Appointment of the Officers, and the Authority of training the Militia according to the discipline prescribed by Congress;

To exercise exclusive Legislation in all Cases whatsoever, over such District (not exceeding ten Miles square) as may, by Cession of particular States, and the Acceptance of Congress, become the Seat of the Government of the United States, and to exercise like Authority over all Places purchased by the Consent of the Legislature of the State in which the Same shall be, for the Erection of Forts, Magazines, Arsenals, dock-Yards, and other needful Buildings;—And

To make all Laws which shall be necessary and proper for carrying into Execution the foregoing Powers, and all other Powers vested by this Constitution in the Government of the United States, or in any Department or Officer thereof.

Section 9. The Migration or Importation of such Persons as any of the States now existing shall think proper to admit, shall not be prohibited by the Congress prior to the Year one thousand eight hundred and eight, but a Tax or duty may be imposed on such Importation, not exceeding ten dollars for each Person.

The privilege of the Writ of Habeas Corpus shall not be suspended, unless when in Cases of Rebellion or Invasion the public Safety may require it.

No Bill of Attainder or ex post facto Law shall be passed.

No Capitation, or other direct, Tax shall be laid, unless in Proportion to the Census or Enumeration herein before directed to be taken.

No Tax or Duty shall be laid on Articles exported from any State.

No Preference shall be given by any Regulation of Commerce or Revenue to the Ports of one State over those of another: nor shall Vessels bound to, or from, one State be obliged to enter, clear, or pay Duties in another.

No Money shall be drawn from the Treasury, but in Consequence of Appropriations made by Law; and a regular Statement and Account of the Receipts and Expenditures of all public Money shall be published from time to time.

No Title of Nobility shall be granted by the United States: And no Person holding any Office of Profit or Trust under them, shall, without the Consent of the Congress, accept of any present, Emolument, Office, or Title, of any kind whatever, from any King, Prince, or foreign State.

Section 10. No State shall enter into any Treaty, Alliance, or Confederation; grant Letters of Marque and Reprisal; coin Money; emit Bills of Credit; make any Thing but gold and silver Coin a Tender in Payment of Debts; pass any Bill of Attainder, ex post facto Law, or Law impairing the Obligation of Contracts, or grant any Title of Nobility.

No State shall, without the Consent of the Congress, lay any Imposts or Duties on Imports or Exports, except what may be absolutely necessary for executing its inspection Laws: and the net Produce of all Duties and Imposts, laid by any State on Imports or Exports, shall be for the Use of the Treasury of the United States; and all such Laws shall be subject to the Revision and Controul of the Congress.

No State shall, without the Consent of Congress, lay any Duty of Tonnage, keep Troops, or Ships of War in time of Peace, enter into any Agreement or Compact with another State, or with a foreign Power, or engage in War, unless actually invaded, or in such imminent Danger as will not admit of delay.

ARTICLE II

Section 1.   The executive Power shall be vested in a President of the United States of America. He shall hold his Office during the Term of four Years, and, together with the Vice President, chosen for the same Term, be elected, as follows:

Each State shall appoint, in such Manner as the Legislature thereof may direct, a Number of Electors, equal to the whole Number of Senators and Representatives to which the State may be entitled in the Congress; but no Senator or Representative, or Person holding an Office of Trust or Profit under the United States, shall be appointed an Elector.

The Electors shall meet in their respective States, and vote by Ballot for two Persons, of whom one at least shall not be an Inhabitant of the same State with themselves. And they shall make a List of all the Persons voted for, and of the Number of Votes for each; which List they shall sign and certify, and transmit sealed to the Seat of the Government of the United States, directed to the President of the Senate. The President of the Senate shall, in the Presence of the Senate and House of Representatives, open all the Certificates, and the Votes shall then be counted. The Person having the greatest Number of Votes shall be the President, if such Number be a Majority of the whole Number of Electors appointed; and if there be more than one who have such Majority, and have an equal Number of Votes, then the House of Representatives shall immediately chuse by Ballot one of them for President; and if no Person have a Majority, then from the five highest on the List the said House shall in like Manner chuse the President. But in chusing the President, the Votes shall be taken by States, the Representation from each State having one Vote; A quorum for this Purpose shall consist of a Member or Members from two thirds of the States, and a Majority of all the States shall be necessary to a Choice. In every Case, after the Choice of the President, the Person having the greater Number of Votes of the Electors shall be the Vice President. But if there should remain two or more who have equal Votes, the Senate shall chuse from them by Ballot the Vice President.

The Congress may determine the Time of chusing the Electors, and the Day on which they shall give their Votes; which Day shall be the same throughout the United States.

No person except a natural born Citizen, or a Citizen of the United States, at the time of the Adoption of this Constitution, shall be eligible to the Office of President; neither shall any Person be eligible to that Office who shall not have attained to the Age of thirty five Years, and been fourteen Years a Resident within the United States.

In Case of the Removal of the President from Office, or of his Death, Resignation or Inability to discharge the Powers and Duties of the said Office, the same shall devolve on the Vice President, and the Congress may by Law provide for the Case of Removal, Death, Resignation or Inability, both of the President and Vice President, declaring what Officer shall then act as President, and such Officer shall act accordingly, until the Disability be removed, or a President shall be elected.

The President shall, at stated Times, receive for his Services, a Compensation, which shall neither be increased nor diminished during the Period for which he shall have been elected, and he shall not receive within that Period any other Emolument from the United States, or any of them.

Before he enter on the Execution of his Office, he shall take the following Oath or Affirmation: ''I do solemnly swear (or affirm) that I will faithfully execute the Office of President of the United States, and will to the best of my Ability, preserve, protect and defend the Constitution of the United States.''

Section 2.   The President shall be Commander in Chief of the Army and Navy of the United States, and of the Militia of the several States, when called into the actual Service of the United States; he may require the Opinion, in writing, of the principal Officer in each of the executive Departments, upon any Subject relating to the Duties of their respective Offices, and he shall have Power to grant Reprieves and Pardons for Offenses against the United States, except in Cases of Impeachment.

He shall have Power, by and with the Advice and Consent of the Senate to make Treaties, provided two thirds of the Senators present concur; and he shall nominate, and by and with the Advice and Consent of the Senate, shall appoint Ambassadors, other public Ministers and Consuls, Judges of the supreme Court, and all other Officers of the United States, whose Appointments are not herein otherwise provided for, and which shall be established by Law; but the Congress may by Law vest the Appointment of such inferior Officers, as they think proper, in the President alone, in the Courts of Law, or in the Heads of Departments.

The President shall have Power to fill up all Vacancies that may happen during the Recess of the Senate, by granting Commissions which shall expire at the End of their next Session.

Section 3. He shall from time to time give to the Congress Information of the State of the Union, and recommend to their Consideration such Measures as he shall judge necessary and expedient; he may, on extraordinary Occasions, convene both Houses, or either of them, and in Case of Disagreement between them, with Respect to the Time of Adjournment, he may adjourn them to such Time as he shall think proper; he shall receive Ambassadors and other public Ministers; he shall take Care that the Laws be faithfully executed, and shall Commission all the Officers of the United States.

Section 4. The President, Vice President and all civil Officers of the United States, shall be removed from Office on Impeachment for, and Conviction of, Treason, Bribery, or other high Crimes and Misdemeanors.

ARTICLE III

Section 1. The judicial Power of the United States, shall be vested in one supreme Court, and in such inferior Courts as the Congress may from time to time ordain and establish. The Judges, both of the supreme and inferior Courts, shall hold their Offices during good Behaviour, and shall, at stated Times, receive for their Services a Compensation, which shall not be diminished during their Continuance in Office.

Section 2. The judicial Power shall extend to all Cases, in Law and Equity, arising under this Constitution, the Laws of the United States, and Treaties made, or which shall be made, under their Authority;—to all Cases affecting Ambassadors, other public Ministers and Consuls;—to all Cases of admiralty and maritime Jurisdiction;—to Controversies to which the United States shall be a Party;—to Controversies between two or more States;—between a State and Citizens of another State;—between Citizens of different States;—between Citizens of the same State claiming Lands under Grants of different States, and between a State, or the Citizens thereof, and foreign States, Citizens or Subjects.

In all Cases affecting Ambassadors, other public Ministers and Consuls, and those in which a State shall be a Party, the supreme Court shall have original Jurisdiction. In all the other Cases before mentioned, the supreme Court shall have appellate Jurisdiction, both as to Law and Fact, with such Exceptions, and under such Regulations as the Congress shall make.

The Trial of all Crimes, except in Cases of Impeachment, shall be by Jury; and such Trial shall be held in the State where the said Crimes shall have been committed; but when not committed within any State, the Trial shall be at such Place or Places as the Congress may by Law have directed.

Section 3. Treason against the United States, shall consist only in levying War against them, or, in adhering to their Enemies, giving them Aid and Comfort. No Person shall be convicted of Treason unless on the Testimony of two Witnesses to the same overt Act, or on Confession in open Court.

The Congress shall have Power to declare the Punishment of Treason, but no Attainder of Treason shall work Corruption of Blood, or Forfeiture except during the Life of the Person attainted.

ARTICLE IV

Section 1. Full Faith and Credit shall be given in each State to the public Acts, Records, and judicial Proceedings of every other State. And the Congress may by general Laws prescribe the Manner in which such Acts, Records and Proceedings shall be proved, and the Effect thereof.

Section 2. The Citizens of each State shall be entitled to all Privileges and Immunities of Citizens in the several States.

A Person charged in any State with Treason, Felony, or other Crime, who shall flee from Justice, and be found in another State, shall on Demand of the executive Authority of the State from which he fled, be delivered up, to be removed to the State having Jurisdiction of the Crime.

No Person held to Service or Labour in one State, under the Laws thereof, escaping into another, shall, in Consequence of any Law or Regulation therein, be discharged from such Service or Labour, but shall be delivered up on Claim of the Party to whom such Service or Labour may be due.

Section 3. New States may be admitted by the Congress into this Union; but no new State shall be formed or erected within the Jurisdiction of any other State; nor any State be formed by the Junction of two or more States, or Parts of States, without the Consent of the Legislatures of the States concerned as well as of the Congress.

The Congress shall have Power to dispose of and make all needful Rules and Regulations respecting the Territory or other Property belonging to the United States; and nothing in this Constitution shall be so construed as to Prejudice any Claims of the United States, or of any particular State.

Section 4. The United States shall guarantee to every State in this Union a Republican Form of Government, and shall protect each of them against Invasion;

and on Application of the Legislature, or of the Executive (when the Legislature cannot be convened) against domestic Violence.

ARTICLE V

The Congress, whenever two thirds of both Houses shall deem it necessary, shall propose Amendments to this Constitution, or, on the Application of the Legislatures of two thirds of the several States, shall call a Convention for proposing Amendments, which, in either Case, shall be valid to all Intents and Purposes, as part of this Constitution, when ratified by the Legislatures of three fourths of the several States, or by Conventions in three fourths thereof, as the one or the other Mode of Ratification may be proposed by the Congress; Provided that no Amendment which may be made prior to the Year One thousand eight hundred and eight shall in any Manner affect the first and fourth Clauses in the Ninth Section of the first Article; and that no State, without its Consent, shall be deprived of its equal Suffrage in the Senate.

ARTICLE VI

All Debts contracted and Engagements entered into, before the Adoption of this Constitution shall be as valid against the United States under this Constitution, as under the Confederation.

This Constitution, and the Laws of the United States which shall be made in Pursuance thereof; and all Treaties made, or which shall be made, under the Authority of the United States, shall be the supreme Law of the Land; and the Judges in every State shall be bound thereby, any Thing in the Constitution or Laws of any State to the Contrary notwithstanding.

The Senators and Representatives before mentioned, and the Members of the several State Legislatures, and all executive and judicial Officers, both of the United States and of the several States, shall be bound by Oath or Affirmation, to support this Constitution; but no religious Test shall ever be required as a Qualification to any Office or public Trust under the United States.

ARTICLE VII

The Ratification of the Conventions of nine States shall be sufficient for the Establishment of this Constitution between the States so ratifying the Same.

AMENDMENT I [1791]

Congress shall make no law respecting an establishment of religion, or prohibiting the free exercise thereof; or abridging the freedom of speech, or of the press; or the right of the people peaceably to assembly, and to petition the Government for a redress of grievances.

AMENDMENT II [1791]

A well regulated Militia, being necessary to the security of a free State, the right of the people to keep and bear Arms, shall not be infringed.

AMENDMENT III [1791]

INVASION OF PRIVACY

No Soldier shall, in time of peace be quartered in any house, without the consent of the Owner, nor in time of war, but in a manner to be prescribed by law.

AMENDMENT IV [1791]

The right of the people to be secure in their persons, houses, papers, and effects, against unreasonable searches and seizures, shall not be violated, and no Warrants shall issue, but upon probable cause, supported by Oath or affirmation, and particularly describing the place to be searched, and the persons or things to be seized.

AMENDMENT V [1791]

SELF INCRIMINATION   _Due Process_

No person shall be held to answer for a capital, or otherwise infamous crime, unless on a presentment or indictment of a Grand Jury, except in cases arising in the land or naval forces, or in the Militia, when in actual service in time of War or public danger; nor shall any person be subject for the same offence to be twice put in jeopardy of life or limb; nor shall be compelled in any criminal case to be a witness against himself, nor be deprived of life, liberty, or property, without due process of law; nor shall private property be taken for public use, without just compensation.

AMENDMENT VI [1791]

In all criminal prosecutions, the accused shall enjoy the right to a speedy and public trial, by an impartial jury of the State and district wherein the crime shall have been committed, which district shall have been previously ascertained by law, and to be informed of the nature and cause of the accusation; to be confronted with the witnesses against him; to have compulsory process for obtaining witnesses in his favor, and to have the Assistance of Counsel for his defence.

AMENDMENT VII [1791]

In Suits at common law, where the value in controversy shall exceed twenty dollars, the right of trial by jury shall be preserved, and no fact tried by jury, shall be otherwise re-examined in any Court of the United States, than according to the rules of the common law.

AMENDMENT VIII [1791]

Excessive bail shall not be required, nor excessive fines imposed, nor cruel and unusual punishments inflicted.

Prohibits excessive bail.
Prohibits cruel and unusual punishment

AMENDMENT IX [1791]

The enumeration in the Constitution, of certain rights, shall not be construed to deny or disparage others retained by the people.— *Individual rites vs Group Rites. i.e. Smoking*

AMENDMENT X [1791]

Power Delegated To States
The powers not delegated to the United States by the Constitution, nor prohibited by it to the States, are reserved to the States respectively, or to the people.

AMENDMENT XI [1798]

The Judicial power of the United States shall not be construed to extend to any suit in law or equity, commenced or prosecuted against one of the United States by Citizens of another State, or by Citizens or Subjects of any Foreign State.

AMENDMENT XII [1804]

Electoral College
The Electors shall meet in their respective states, and vote by ballot for President and Vice-President, one of whom, at least, shall not be an inhabitant of the same state with themselves; they shall name in their ballots the person voted for as President, and in distinct ballots the person voted for as Vice-President, and they shall make distinct lists of all persons voted for as President, and of all persons voted for as Vice-President, and of the number of votes for each, which lists they shall sign and certify, and transmit sealed to the seat of the government of the United States, directed to the President of the Senate;—The President of the Senate shall, in the presence of the Senate and House of Representatives, open all the certificates and the votes shall then be counted;—The person having the greatest number of votes for President, shall be the President, if such number be a majority of the whole number of Electors appointed; and if no person have such majority, then from the persons having the highest numbers not exceeding three on the list of those voted for as President, the House of Representatives shall choose immediately, by ballot, the President. But in choosing the President, the votes shall be taken by states, the representation from each state having one vote; a quorum for this purpose shall consist of a member or members from two-thirds of the states, and a majority of all states shall be necessary to a choice. And if the House of Representatives shall not choose a President whenever the right of choice shall devolve upon them, before the fourth day of March next following, then the Vice-President shall act as President, as in the case of the death or other constitutional disability of the President.—The person having the greatest number of votes as Vice-President, shall be the Vice-President, if such number be a majority of the whole number of Electors appointed, and if no person have a majority, then from the two highest numbers on the list, the Senate shall choose the Vice-President; a quorum for the purpose shall consist of two-thirds of the whole number of Senators, and a majority of the whole number shall be necessary to a choice. But no person constitutionally ineligible to the office of President shall be eligible to that of Vice-President of the United States.

AMENDMENT XIII [1865]

Elimination of Slavery
Section 1. Neither slavery nor involuntary servitude, except as a punishment for crime whereof the party shall have been duly convicted, shall exist within the United States, or any place subject to their jurisdiction.

Section 2. Congress shall have power to enforce this article by appropriate legislation.

AMENDMENT XIV [1868]

State Due Process

Section 1. All persons born or naturalized in the United States, and subject to the jurisdiction thereof, are citizens of the United States and of the State wherein they reside. No State shall make or enforce any law which shall abridge the privileges or immunities of citizens of the United States; nor shall any State deprive any person of life, liberty, or property, without due process of law; nor deny to any person within its jurisdiction the equal protection of the laws.

Section 2. Representatives shall be apportioned among the several States according to their respective numbers, counting the whole number of persons in each State, excluding Indians not taxed. But when the right to vote at any election for the choice of electors for President and Vice President of the United States, Representatives in Congress, the Executive and Judicial officers of a State, or the members of the Legislature thereof, is denied to any of the male inhabitants of such State, being twenty-one years of age, and citizens of the United States, or in any way abridged, except for participation in rebellion, or other crime, the basis of representation therein shall be reduced in the proportion which the number of such male citizens shall bear to the whole number of male citizens twenty-one years of age in such State.

Section 3. No person shall be a Senator or Representative in Congress, or elector of President and Vice President, or hold any office, civil or military, under the United States, or under any State, who having previously taken an oath, as a member of Congress, or as an officer of the United States, or as a member of any State legislature, or as an executive or judicial officer of any State, to support the Constitution of the United States, shall have engaged in insurrection or rebellion against the same, or given aid or comfort to the enemies thereof. But Congress may by a vote of two-thirds of each House, remove such disability.

Section 4. The validity of the public debt of the United States, authorized by law, including debts incurred for payment of pensions and bounties for services in suppressing insurrection or rebellion, shall not be questioned. But neither the United States nor any State shall assume or pay any debt or obligation incurred in aid of insurrection or rebellion against the United States, or any claim for the loss or emancipation of any slave; but all such debts, obligations and claims shall be held illegal and void.

Section 5. The Congress shall have power to enforce, by appropriate legislation, the provisions of this article.

AMENDMENT XV [1870]

Right To Vote

Section 1. The right of citizens of the United States to vote shall not be denied or abridged by the United States or by any State on account of race, color, or previous condition of servitude.

Section 2. The Congress shall have power to enforce this article by appropriate legislation.

AMENDMENT XVI [1913]

Collect Taxes

The Congress shall have power to lay and collect taxes on incomes, from whatever source derived, without apportionment among the several States, and without regard to any census or enumeration.

AMENDMENT XVII [1913]

Section 1. The Senate of the United States shall be composed of two Senators from each State, elected by the people thereof, for six years; and each Senator shall have one vote. The electors in each State shall have the qualifications requisite for electors of the most numerous branch of the State legislatures.

Section 2. When vacancies happen in the representation of any State in the Senate, the executive authority of such State shall issue writs of election to fill such vacancies: *Provided*, That the legislature of any State may empower the executive thereof to make temporary appointments until the people fill the vacancies by election as the legislature may direct.

Section 3. This amendment shall not be so construed as to affect the election or term of any Senator chosen before it becomes valid as part of the Constitution.

AMENDMENT XVIII [1919]

18 Repealed

Section 1. After one year from the ratification of this article the manufacture, sale, or transportation of intoxicating liquors within, the importation thereof into, or the exportation thereof from the United States and all territory subject to the jurisdiction thereof for beverage purposes is hereby prohibited.

Section 2. The Congress and the several States shall have concurrent power to enforce this article by appropriate legislation.

Section 3. This article shall be inoperative unless it shall have been ratified as an amendment to the Constitution by the legislatures of the several States, as provided in the Constitution, within seven years from the date of the submission hereof to the States by the Congress.

AMENDMENT XIX [1920]

Women Rite To Vote

Section 1. The right of citizens of the United States to vote shall not be denied or abridged by the United States or by any State on account of sex.

Section 2. Congress shall have power to enforce this article by appropriate legislation.

AMENDMENT XX [1933]

Term of president

Section 1. The terms of the President and Vice President shall end at noon on the 20th day of January, and the terms of Senators and Representatives at noon on the 3d day of January, of the years in which such terms would have ended if this article had not been ratified; and the terms of their successors shall then begin.

Section 2. The Congress shall assemble at least once in every year, and such meeting shall begin at noon on the 3d day of January, unless they shall by law appoint a different day.

Section 3. If, at the time fixed for the beginning of the term of the President, the President elect shall have died, the Vice President elect shall become President. If the President shall not have been chosen before the time fixed for the beginning of his term, or if the President elect shall have failed to qualify, then the Vice President elect shall act as President until a President shall have qualified; and the Congress may by law provide for the case wherein neither a President elect nor a Vice President elect shall have qualified, declaring who shall then act as President, or the manner in which one who is to act shall be selected, and such person shall act accordingly until a President or Vice President shall have qualified.

Section 4. The Congress may by law provide for the case of the death of any of the persons from whom the House of Representatives may choose a President whenever the right of choice shall have devolved upon them, and for the case of the death of any of the persons from whom the Senate may choose a Vice President whenever the right of choice shall have devolved upon them.

Section 5. Sections 1 and 2 shall take effect on the 15th day of October following the ratification of this article.

Section 6. This article shall be inoperative unless it shall have been ratified as an amendment to the Constitution by the legislatures of three-fourths of the several States within seven years from the date of its submission.

AMENDMENT XXI [1933]   21

Section 1. The eighteenth article of amendment to the Constitution of the United States is hereby repealed.

Section 2. The transportation or importation into any State, Territory, or possession of the United States for delivery or use therein of intoxicating liquors, in violation of the laws thereof, is hereby prohibited.

Section 3. This article shall be inoperative unless it shall have been ratified as an amendment to the Constitution by conventions in the several States, as provided in the Constitution, within seven years from the date of the submission hereof to the States by the Congress.

AMENDMENT XXII [1951]

Terms /Lenght of Presidency

Section 1. No person shall be elected to the office of the President more than twice, and no person who has held the office of President, or acted as President, for more than two years of a term to which some other person was elected President shall be elected to the office of President more than once. But this Article shall not apply to any person holding the office of President when this Article was proposed by the Congress, and shall not prevent any person who may be holding the office of President, or acting as President, during the term within which this Article becomes operative from holding the office of President or acting as President during the remainder of such term.

Section 2. This article shall be inoperative unless it shall have been ratified as an amendment to the Constitution by the legislatures of three-fourths of the several States within seven years from the date of its submission to the States by the Congress.

AMENDMENT XXIII [1961]

Section 1. The District constituting the seat of Government of the United States shall appoint in such manner as the Congress may direct:

A number of electors of President and Vice President equal to the whole number of Senators and Representatives in Congress to which the District would be entitled if it were a State, but in no event more than the least populous state; they shall be in addition to those appointed by the states, but they shall be considered, for the purposes of the election of President and Vice President, to be electors appointed by a state; and they shall meet in the District and perform such duties as provided by the twelfth article of amendment.

Section 2. The Congress shall have power to enforce this article by appropriate legislation.

AMENDMENT XXIV [1964]

Right to vote w/o paying Poll TAX

Section 1. The right of citizens of the United States to vote in any primary or other election for President or Vice President, for electors for President or Vice President, or for Senator or Representative in Congress, shall not be denied or abridged by the United States, or any State by reason of failure to pay any poll tax or other tax.

Section 2. The Congress shall have power to enforce this article by appropriate legislation.

AMENDMENT XXV [1967]

Section 1. In case of the removal of the President from office or of his death or resignation, the Vice President shall become President.

Section 2. Whenever there is a vacancy in the office of the Vice President, the President shall nominate a Vice President who shall take office upon confirmation by a majority vote of both Houses of Congress.

Section 3. Whenever the President transmits to the President pro tempore of the Senate and the Speaker of the House of Representatives his written declaration that he is unable to discharge the powers and duties of his office, and until he transmits to them a written declaration to the contrary, such powers and duties shall be discharged by the Vice President as Acting President.

Section 4. Whenever the Vice President and a majority of either the principal officers of the executive departments or of such other body as Congress may by law provide, transmit to the President pro tempore of the Senate and the Speaker of the House of Representatives their written declaration that the President is unable to discharge the powers and duties of his office, the Vice President shall immediately assume the powers and duties of the office as Acting President.

Thereafter, when the President transmits to the President pro tempore of the Senate and the Speaker of the House of Representatives his written declaration that no inability exists, he shall resume the powers and duties of his office unless the Vice President and a majority of either the principal officers of the executive department or of such other body as Congress may by law provide, transmit within four days to the President pro tempore of the Senate and the Speaker of the House of Representatives their written declaration and the President is unable to discharge the powers and duties of his office. Thereupon Congress shall decide the issue, assembling within forty-eight hours for that purpose if not in session. If the Congress, within twenty-one days after receipt of the latter written declaration, or, if Congress is not in session, within twenty-one days after Congress is required to assemble, determines by two-thirds vote of both Houses that the President is unable to discharge the powers and duties of his office, the Vice President shall continue to discharge the same as Acting President; otherwise, the President shall resume the powers and duties of his office.

AMENDMENT XXVI [1971]

Section 1. The right of citizens of the United States, who are eighteen years of age or older, to vote shall not be denied or abridged by the United States or by any State on account of age. *Right To Vote – 18 yrs old*

Section 2. The Congress shall have power to enforce this article by appropriate legislation.

AMENDMENT XXVII [1992]

No law, varying the compensation for the services of the Senators and Representatives, shall take effect, until an election of Representatives shall have intervened.

Is this saying congress can not give themselves a raise?

Appendix C

The Uniform Commercial Code

(Adopted in 52 jurisdictions; all 50 States, although Louisiana has adopted only Articles 1, 3, 4, 7, 8, and 9; the District of Columbia, and the Virgin Islands.)

The Code consists of the following articles:

Art.

1. General Provisions
2. Sales
2A. Leases
3. Commercial Paper
4. Bank Deposits and Collections
4A. Funds Transfers
5. Letters of Credit
6. Bulk Transfers (including Alternative B)
7. Warehouse Receipts, Bills of Lading and Other Documents of Title
8. Investment Securities
9. Secured Transactions: Sales of Accounts and Chattel Paper
10. Effective Date and Repealer
11. Effective Date and Transition Provisions

Article 1
GENERAL PROVISIONS

Part 1 Short Title, Construction, Application and Subject Matter of the Act

§ 1—101. **Short Title.**

This Act shall be known and may be cited as Uniform Commercial Code.

§ 1—102. **Purposes; Rules of Construction; Variation by Agreement.**

(1) This Act shall be liberally construed and applied to promote its underlying purposes and policies.

(2) Underlying purposes and policies of this Act are

(a) to simplify, clarify and modernize the law governing commercial transactions;

(b) to permit the continued expansion of commercial practices through custom, usage and agreement of the parties;

(c) to make uniform the law among the various jurisdictions.

(3) The effect of provisions of this Act may be varied by agreement, except as otherwise provided in this Act and except that the obligations of good faith, diligence, reasonableness and care prescribed by this Act may not be disclaimed by agreement but the parties may by agreement determine the standards by which the performance of such obligations is to be measured if such standards are not manifestly unreasonable.

(4) The presence in certain provisions of this Act of the words "unless otherwise agreed" or words of similar import does not imply that the effect of other provisions may not be varied by agreement under subsection (3).

(5) In this Act unless the context otherwise requires

(a) words in the singular number include the plural, and in the plural include the singular;

(b) words of the masculine gender include the feminine and the neuter, and when the sense so indicates words of the neuter gender may refer to any gender.

§ 1—103. Supplementary General Principles of Law Applicable.

Unless displaced by the particular provisions of this Act, the principles of law and equity, including the law merchant and the law relative to capacity to contract, principal and agent, estoppel, fraud, misrepresentation, duress, coercion, mistake, bankruptcy, or other validating or invalidating cause shall supplement its provisions.

§ 1—104. Construction Against Implicit Repeal.

This Act being a general act intended as a unified coverage of its subject matter, no part of it shall be deemed to be impliedly repealed by subsequent legislation if such construction can reasonably be avoided.

§ 1—105. Territorial Application of the Act; Parties' Power to Choose Applicable Law.

(1) Except as provided hereafter in this section, when a transaction bears a reasonable relation to this state and also to another state or nation the parties may agree that the law either of this state or of such other state or nation shall govern their rights and duties. Failing such agreement this Act applies to transactions bearing an appropriate relation to this state.

(2) Where one of the following provisions of this Act specifies the applicable law, that provision governs and a contrary agreement is effective only to the extent permitted by the law (including the conflict of laws rules) so specified:

Rights of creditors against sold goods. Section 2—402.

Applicability of the Article on Leases. Sections 2A—105 and 2A—106.

Applicability of the Article on Bank Deposits and Collections. Section 4—102.

Governing law in the Article on Funds Transfers. Section 4A—507.

Bulk sales subject to the Article on Bulk Sales. Section 6—103.

Applicability of the Article on Investment Securities. Section 8—106.

Perfection provisions of the Article on Secured Transactions. Section 9—103.

§ 1—106. Remedies to Be Liberally Administered.

(1) The remedies provided by this Act shall be liberally administered to the end that the aggrieved party may be put in as good a position as if the other party had fully performed but neither consequential or special nor penal damages may be had except as specifically provided in this Act or by other rule of law.

(2) Any right or obligation declared by this Act is enforceable by action unless the provision declaring it specifies a different and limited effect.

§ 1—107. Waiver or Renunciation of Claim or Right After Breach.

Any claim or right arising out of an alleged breach can be discharged in whole or in part without consideration by a written waiver or renunciation signed and delivered by the aggrieved party.

§ 1—108. Severability.

If any provision or clause of this Act or application thereof to any person or circumstances is held invalid, such invalidity shall not affect other provisions or applications of the Act which can be given effect without the invalid provision or application, and to this end the provisions of this Act are declared to be severable.

§ 1—109. Section Captions.

Section captions are parts of this Act.

Part 2 General Definitions and Principles of Interpretation

§ 1—201. General Definitions.

Subject to additional definitions contained in the subsequent Articles of this Act which are applicable to specific Articles or Parts thereof, and unless the context otherwise requires, in this Act:

(1) "Action" in the sense of a judicial proceeding includes recoupment, counterclaim, set-off, suit in equity and any other proceedings in which rights are determined.

(2) "Aggrieved party" means a party entitled to resort to a remedy.

(3) "Agreement" means the bargain of the parties in fact as found in their language or by implication from other circumstances including course of dealing or usage of trade or course of performance as provided in this Act (Sections 1—205 and 2—208). Whether an agreement has legal consequences is determined by the provisions of this Act, if applicable; otherwise by the law of contracts (Section 1—103). (Compare "Contract".)

(4) "Bank" means any person engaged in the business of banking.

(5) "Bearer" means the person in possession of an instrument, document of title, or certificated security payable to bearer or indorsed in blank.

(6) "Bill of lading" means a document evidencing the receipt of goods for shipment issued by a person engaged

in the business of transporting or forwarding goods, and includes an airbill. "Airbill" means a document serving for air transportation as a bill of lading does for marine or rail transportation, and includes an air consignment note or air waybill.

(7) "Branch" includes a separately incorporated foreign branch of a bank.

(8) "Burden of establishing" a fact means the burden of persuading the triers of fact that the existence of the fact is more probable than its non-existence.

(9) "Buyer in ordinary course of business" means a person who in good faith and without knowledge that the sale to him is in violation of the ownership rights or security interest of a third party in the goods buys in ordinary course from a person in the business of selling goods of that kind but does not include a pawnbroker. All persons who sell minerals or the like (including oil and gas) at wellhead or minehead shall be deemed to be persons in the business of selling goods of that kind. "Buying" may be for cash or by exchange of other property or on secured or unsecured credit and includes receiving goods or documents of title under a pre-existing contract for sale but does not include a transfer in bulk or as security for or in total or partial satisfaction of a money debt.

(10) "Conspicuous": A term or clause is conspicuous when it is so written that a reasonable person against whom it is to operate ought to have noticed it. A printed heading in capitals (as: NON-NEGOTIABLE BILL OF LADING) is conspicuous. Language in the body of a form is "conspicuous" if it is in larger or other contrasting type or color. But in a telegram any stated term is "conspicuous". Whether a term or clause is "conspicuous" or not is for decision by the court.

(11) "Contract" means the total legal obligation which results from the parties' agreement as affected by this Act and any other applicable rules of law. (Compare "Agreement".)

(12) "Creditor" includes a general creditor, a secured creditor, a lien creditor and any representative of creditors, including an assignee for the benefit of creditors, a trustee in bankruptcy, a receiver in equity and an executor or administrator of an insolvent debtor's or assignor's estate.

(13) "Defendant" includes a person in the position of defendant in a cross-action or counterclaim.

(14) "Delivery" with respect to instruments, documents of title, chattel paper, or certificated securities means voluntary transfer of possession.

(15) "Document of title" includes bill of lading, dock warrant, dock receipt, warehouse receipt or order for the delivery of goods, and also any other document which in the regular course of business or financing is treated as adequately evidencing that the person in possession of it is entitled to receive, hold and dispose of the document and the goods it covers. To be a document of title a document must purport to be issued by or addressed to a bailee and purport to cover goods in the bailee's possession which are either identified or are fungible portions of an identified mass.

(16) "Fault" means wrongful act, omission or breach.

(17) "Fungible" with respect to goods or securities means goods or securities of which any unit is, by nature or usage of trade, the equivalent of any other like unit. Goods which are not fungible shall be deemed fungible for the purposes of this Act to the extent that under a particular agreement or document unlike units are treated as equivalents.

(18) "Genuine" means free of forgery or counterfeiting.

(19) "Good faith" means honesty in fact in the conduct or transaction concerned.

(20) "Holder" with respect to a negotiable instrument, means the person in possession if the instrument is payable to bearer or, in the cases of an instrument payable to an identified person, if the identified person is in possession. "Holder" with respect to a document of title means the person in possession if the goods are deliverable to bearer or to the order of the person in possession.

(21) To "honor" is to pay or to accept and pay, or where a credit so engages to purchase or discount a draft complying with the terms of the credit.

(22) "Insolvency proceedings" includes any assignment for the benefit of creditors or other proceedings intended to liquidate or rehabilitate the estate of the person involved.

(23) A person is "insolvent" who either has ceased to pay his debts in the ordinary course of business or cannot pay his debts as they become due or is insolvent within the meaning of the federal bankruptcy law.

(24) "Money" means a medium of exchange authorized or adopted by a domestic or foreign government and includes a monetary unit of account established by an intergovernmental organization or by agreement between two or more nations.

(25) A person has "notice" of a fact when

   (a) he has actual knowledge of it; or

   (b) he has received a notice or notification of it; or

   (c) from all the facts and circumstances known to him at the time in question he has reason to know that it exists.

A person "knows" or has "knowledge" of a fact when he has actual knowledge of it. "Discover" or "learn" or a word or phrase of similar import refers to knowledge rather than to reason to know. The time and circumstances under which a notice or notification may cease to be effective are not determined by this Act.

(26) A person "notifies" or "gives" a notice or notification to another by taking such steps as may be reasonably required to inform the other in ordinary course whether or not such other actually comes to know of it. A person "receives" a notice or notification when

    (a) it comes to his attention; or

    (b) it is duly delivered at the place of business through which the contract was made or at any other place held out by him as the place for receipt of such communications.

(27) Notice, knowledge or a notice or notification received by an organization is effective for a particular transaction from the time when it is brought to the attention of the individual conducting that transaction, and in any event from the time when it would have been brought to his attention if the organization had exercised due diligence. An organization exercises due diligence if it maintains reasonable routines for communicating significant information to the person conducting the transaction and there is reasonable compliance with the routines. Due diligence does not require an individual acting for the organization to communicate information unless such communication is part of his regular duties or unless he has reason to know of the transaction and that the transaction would be materially affected by the information.

(28) "Organization" includes a corporation, government or governmental subdivision or agency, business trust, estate, trust, partnership or association, two or more persons having a joint or common interest, or any other legal or commercial entity.

(29) "Party", as distinct from "third party", means a person who has engaged in a transaction or made an agreement within this Act.

(30) "Person" includes an individual or an organization (See Section 1—102).

(31) "Presumption" or "presumed" means that the trier of fact must find the existence of the fact presumed unless and until evidence is introduced which would support a finding of its non-existence.

(32) "Purchase" includes taking by sale, discount, negotiation, mortgage, pledge, lien, issue or re-issue, gift or any other voluntary transaction creating an interest in property.

(33) "Purchaser" means a person who takes by purchase.

(34) "Remedy" means any remedial right to which an aggrieved party is entitled with or without resort to a tribunal.

(35) "Representative" includes an agent, an officer of a corporation or association, and a trustee, executor or administrator of an estate, or any other person empowered to act for another.

(36) "Rights" includes remedies.

(37) "Security interest" means an interest in personal property or fixtures which secures payment or performance of an obligation. The retention or reservation of title by a seller of goods notwithstanding shipment or delivery to the buyer (Section 2—401) is limited in effect to a reservation of a "security interest". The term also includes any interest of a buyer of accounts or chattel paper which is subject to Article 9. The special property interest of a buyer of goods on identification of those goods to a contract for sale under Section 2—401 is not a "security interest", but a buyer may also acquire a "security interest" by complying with Article 9. Unless a consignment is intended as security, reservation of title thereunder is not a "security interest," but a consignment is in any event subject to the provisions on consignment sales (Section 2—326).

Whether a transaction creates a lease or security interest is determined by the facts of each case; however, a transaction creates a security interest if the consideration the lessee is to pay the lessor for the right to possession and use of the goods is an obligation for the term of the lease not subject to termination by the lessee, and

    (a) the original term of the lease is equal to or greater than the remaining economic life of the goods,

    (b) the lessee is bound to renew the lease for the remaining economic life of the goods or is bound to become the owner of the goods,

    (c) the lessee has an option to renew the lease for the remaining economic life of the goods for no additional consideration or nominal additional consideration upon compliance with the lease agreement, or

    (d) the lessee has an option to become the owner of the goods for no additional consideration or nominal additional consideration upon compliance with the lease agreement.

A transaction does not create a security interest merely because it provides that

    (a) the present value of the consideration the lessee is obligated to pay the lessor for the right to possession and use of the goods is substantially equal to or is greater than the fair market value of the goods at the time the lease is entered into,

    (b) the lessee assumes risk of loss of the goods, or agrees to pay taxes, insurance, filing, recording, or registration fees, or service or maintenance costs with respect to the goods,

    (c) the lessee has an option to renew the lease or to become the owner of the goods,

    (d) the lessee has an option to renew the lease for a fixed rent that is equal to or greater than the reasonably predictable fair market rent for the use of the goods for the term of the renewal at the time the option is to be performed, or

(e) the lessee has an option to become the owner of the goods for a fixed price that is equal to or greater than the reasonably predictable fair market value of the goods at the time the option is to be performed.

For purposes of this subsection (37):

(x) Additional consideration is not nominal if (i) when the option to renew the lease is granted to the lessee the rent is stated to be the fair market rent for the use of the goods for the term of the renewal determined at the time the option is to be performed, or (ii) when the option to become the owner of the goods is granted to the lessee the price is stated to be the fair market value of the goods determined at the time the option is to be performed. Additional consideration is nominal if it is less than the lessee's reasonably predictable cost of performing under the lease agreement if the option is not exercised;

(y) "Reasonably predictable" and "remaining economic life of the goods" are to be determined with reference to the facts and circumstances at the time the transaction is entered into; and

(z) "Present value" means the amount as of a date certain of one or more sums payable in the future, discounted to the date certain. The discount is determined by the interest rate specified by the parties if the rate is not manifestly unreasonable at the time the transaction is entered into; otherwise, the discount is determined by a commercially reasonable rate that takes into account the facts and circumstances of each case at the time the transaction was entered into.

(38) "Send" in connection with any writing or notice means to deposit in the mail or deliver for transmission by any other usual means of communication with postage or cost of transmission provided for and properly addressed and in the case of an instrument to an address specified thereon or otherwise agreed, or if there be none to any address reasonable under the circumstances. The receipt of any writing or notice within the time at which it would have arrived if properly sent has the effect of a proper sending.

(39) "Signed" includes any symbol executed or adopted by a party with present intention to authenticate a writing.

(40) "Surety" includes guarantor.

(41) "Telegram" includes a message transmitted by radio, teletype, cable, any mechanical method of transmission, or the like.

(42) "Term" means that portion of an agreement which relates to a particular matter.

(43) "Unauthorized" signature means one made without actual, implied or apparent authority and includes a forgery.

(44) "Value". Except as otherwise provided with respect to negotiable instruments and bank collections (Sections 3—303, 4—208 and 4—209) a person gives "value" for rights if he acquires them

(a) in return for a binding commitment to extend credit or for the extension of immediately available credit whether or not drawn upon and whether or not a chargeback is provided for in the event of difficulties in collection; or

(b) as security for or in total or partial satisfaction of a pre-existing claim; or

(c) by accepting delivery pursuant to a preexisting contract for purchase; or

(d) generally, in return for any consideration sufficient to support a simple contract.

(45) "Warehouse receipt" means a receipt issued by a person engaged in the business of storing goods for hire.

(46) "Written" or "writing" includes printing, typewriting or any other intentional reduction to tangible form.

Amended in 1962, 1972, 1977, and 1987.

§ 1—202. **Prima Facie Evidence by Third Party Documents.**

A document in due form purporting to be a bill of lading, policy or certificate of insurance, official weigher's or inspector's certificate, consular invoice, or any other document authorized or required by the contract to be issued by a third party shall be prima facie evidence of its own authenticity and genuineness and of the facts stated in the document by the third party.

§ 1—203. **Obligation of Good Faith.**

Every contract or duty within this Act imposes an obligation of good faith in its performance or enforcement.

§ 1—204. **Time; Reasonable Time; "Seasonably".**

(1) Whenever this Act requires any action to be taken within a reasonable time, any time which is not manifestly unreasonable may be fixed by agreement.

(2) What is a reasonable time for taking any action depends on the nature, purpose and circumstances of such action.

(3) An action is taken "seasonably" when it is taken at or within the time agreed or if no time is agreed at or within a reasonable time.

§ 1—205. **Course of Dealing and Usage of Trade.**

(1) A course of dealing is a sequence of previous conduct between the parties to a particular transaction which is fairly to be regarded as establishing a common basis of understanding for interpreting their expressions and other conduct.

(2) A usage of trade is any practice or method of dealing having such regularity of observance in a place, vocation or trade as to justify an expectation that it will be observed

with respect to the transaction in question. The existence and scope of such a usage are to be proved as facts. If it is established that such a usage is embodied in a written trade code or similar writing the interpretation of the writing is for the court.

(3) A course of dealing between parties and any usage of trade in the vocation or trade in which they are engaged or of which they are or should be aware give particular meaning to and supplement or qualify terms of an agreement.

(4) The express terms of an agreement and an applicable course of dealing or usage of trade shall be construed wherever reasonable as consistent with each other; but when such construction is unreasonable express terms control both course of dealing and usage of trade and course of dealing controls usage trade.

(5) An applicable usage of trade in the place where any part of performance is to occur shall be used in interpreting the agreement as to that part of the performance.

(6) Evidence of a relevant usage of trade offered by one party is not admissible unless and until he has given the other party such notice as the court finds sufficient to prevent unfair surprise to the latter.

§ 1—206. **Statute of Frauds for Kinds of Personal Property Not Otherwise Covered.**

(1) Except in the cases described in subsection (2) of this section a contract for the sale of personal property is not enforceable by way of action or defense beyond five thousand dollars in amount or value of remedy unless there is some writing which indicates that a contract for sale has been made between the parties at a defined or stated price, reasonably identifies the subject matter, and is signed by the party against whom enforcement is sought or by his authorized agent.

(2) Subsection (1) of this section does not apply to contracts for the sale of goods (Section 2—201) nor of securities (Section 8—319) nor to security agreements (Section 9—203).

§ 1—207. **Performance or Acceptance Under Reservation of Rights.**

(1) A party who with explicit reservation of rights performs or promises performance or assents to performance in a manner demanded or offered by the other party does not thereby prejudice the rights reserved. Such words as ''without prejudice'', ''under protest'' or the like are sufficient.

(2) Subsection (1) does not apply to an accord and satisfaction.

§ 1—208. **Option to Accelerate at Will.**

A term providing that one party or his successor in interest may accelerate payment or performance or require collateral or additional collateral ''at will'' or ''when he deems himself insecure'' or in words of similar import shall be construed to mean that he shall have power to do so only if he in good faith believes that the prospect of payment or performance is impaired. The burden of establishing lack of good faith is on the party against whom the power has been exercised.

§ 1—209. **Subordinated Obligations**

An obligation may be issued as subordinated to payment of another obligation of the person obligated, or a creditor may subordinate his right to payment of an obligation by agreement with either the person obligated or another creditor of the person obligated. Such a subordination does not create a security interest as against either the common debtor or a subordinated creditor. This section shall be construed as declaring the law as it existed prior to the enactment of this section and not as modifying it. Added 1966.

Note: *This new section is proposed as an optional provision to make it clear that a subordination agreement does not create a security interest unless so intended.*

Article 2
SALES

Part 1 Short Title, General Construction and Subject Matter

§ 2—101. **Short Title.**

This Article shall be known and may be cited as Uniform Commercial Code—Sales.

§ 2—102. **Scope; Certain Security and Other Transactions Excluded From This Article.**

Unless the context otherwise requires, this Article applies to transactions in goods; it does not apply to any transaction which although in the form of an unconditional contract to sell or present sale is intended to operate only as a security transaction nor does this Article impair or repeal any statute regulating sales to consumers, farmers or other specified classes of buyers.

§ 2—103. **Definitions and Index of Definitions.**

(1) In this Article unless the context otherwise requires

(a) ''Buyer'' means a person who buys or contracts to buy goods.

(b) ''Good faith'' in the case of a merchant means honesty in fact and the observance of reasonable commercial standards of fair dealing in the trade.

(c) ''Receipt'' of goods means taking physical possession of them.

(d) ''Seller'' means a person who sells or contracts to sell goods.

(2) Other definitions applying to this Article or to specified Parts thereof, and the sections in which they appear are:

"Acceptance". Section 2—606.
"Banker's credit". Section 2—325.
"Between merchants". Section 2—104.
"Cancellation". Section 2—106(4).
"Commercial unit". Section 2—105.
"Confirmed credit". Section 2—325.
"Conforming to contract". Section 2—106.
"Contract for sale". Section 2—106.
"Cover". Section 2—712.
"Entrusting". Section 2—403.
"Financing agency". Section 2—104.
"Future goods". Section 2—105.
"Goods". Section 2—105.
"Identification". Section 2—501.
"Installment contract". Section 2—612.
"Letter of Credit". Section 2—325.
"Lot". Section 2—105.
"Merchant". Section 2—104.
"Overseas". Section 2—323.
"Person in position of seller". Section 2—707.
"Present sale". Section 2—106.
"Sale". Section 2—106.
"Sale on approval". Section 2—326.
"Sale or return". Section 2—326.
"Termination". Section 2—106.

(3) The following definitions in other Articles apply to this Article:
"Check". Section 3—104.
"Consignee". Section 7—102.
"Consignor". Section 7—102.
"Consumer goods". Section 9—109.
"Dishonor". Section 3—507.
"Draft". Section 3—104.

(4) In addition Article 1 contains general definitions and principles of construction and interpretation applicable throughout this Article.

§ 2—104. **Definitions: "Merchant"; "Between Merchants"; "Financing Agency".**

(1) "Merchant" means a person who deals in goods of the kind or otherwise by his occupation holds himself out as having knowledge or skill peculiar to the practices or goods involved in the transaction or to whom such knowledge or skill may be attributed by his employment of an agent or broker or other intermediary who by his occupation holds himself out as having such knowledge or skill.

(2) "Financing agency" means a bank, finance company or other person who in the ordinary course of business makes advances against goods or documents of title or who by arrangement with either the seller or the buyer intervenes in ordinary course to make or collect payment due or claimed under the contract for sale, as by purchasing or paying the seller's draft or making advances against it or by merely taking it for collection whether or not documents of title accompany the draft. "Financing agency" includes

also a bank or other person who similarly intervenes between persons who are in the position of seller and buyer in respect to the goods (Section 2—707).

(3) "Between merchants" means in any transaction with respect to which both parties are chargeable with the knowledge or skill of merchants.

§ 2—105. **Definitions: Transferability; "Goods"; "Future" Goods; "Lot"; "Commercial Unit".**

(1) "Goods" means all things (including specially manufactured goods) which are movable at the time of identification to the contract for sale other than the money in which the price is to be paid, investment securities (Article 8) and things in action. "Goods" also includes the unborn young of animals and growing crops and other identified things attached to realty as described in the section on goods to be severed from realty (Section 2—107).

(2) Goods must be both existing and identified before any interest in them can pass. Goods which are not both existing and identified are "future" goods. A purported present sale of future goods or of any interest therein operates as a contract to sell.

(3) There may be a sale of a part interest in existing identified goods.

(4) An undivided share in an identified bulk of fungible goods is sufficiently identified to be sold although the quantity of the bulk is not determined. Any agreed proportion of such a bulk or any quantity thereof agreed upon by number, weight or other measure may to the extent of the seller's interest in the bulk be sold to the buyer who then becomes an owner in common.

(5) "Lot" means a parcel or a single article which is the subject matter of a separate sale or delivery, whether or not it is sufficient to perform the contract.

(6) "Commercial unit" means such a unit of goods as by commercial usage is a single whole for purposes of sale and division of which materially impairs its character or value on the market or in use. A commercial unit may be a single article (as a machine) or a set of articles (as a suite of furniture or an assortment of sizes) or a quantity (as a bale, gross, or carload) or any other unit treated in use or in the relevant market as a single whole.

§ 2—106. **Definitions: "Contract"; "Agreement"; "Contract for Sale"; "Sale"; "Present Sale"; "Conforming" to Contract; "Termination"; "Cancellation".**

(1) In this Article unless the context otherwise requires "contract" and "agreement" are limited to those relating to the present or future sale of goods. "Contract for sale" includes both a present sale of goods and a contract to sell goods at a future time. A "sale" consists in the passing of title from the seller to the buyer for a price (Section 2—401). A "present sale" means a sale which is accomplished by the making of the contract.

(2) Goods or conduct including any part of a performance are "conforming" or conform to the contract when they are in accordance with the obligations under the contract.

(3) "Termination" occurs when either party pursuant to a power created by agreement or law puts an end to the contract otherwise than for its breach. On "termination" all obligations which are still executory on both sides are discharged but any right based on prior breach or performance survives.

(4) "Cancellation" occurs when either party puts an end to the contract for breach by the other and its effect is the same as that of "termination" except that the cancelling party also retains any remedy for breach of the whole contract or any unperformed balance.

§ 2—107. Goods to Be Severed From Realty: Recording.

(1) A contract for the sale of minerals or the like (including oil and gas) or a structure or its materials to be removed from realty is a contract for the sale of goods within this Article if they are to be severed by the seller but until severance a purported present sale thereof which is not effective as a transfer of an interest in land is effective only as a contract to sell.

(2) A contract for the sale apart from the land of growing crops or other things attached to realty and capable of severance without material harm thereto but not described in subsection (1) or of timber to be cut is a contract for the sale of goods within this Article whether the subject matter is to be severed by the buyer or by the seller even though it forms part of the realty at the time of contracting, and the parties can by identification effect a present sale before severance.

(3) The provisions of this section are subject to any third party rights provided by the law relating to realty records, and the contract for sale may be executed and recorded as a document transferring an interest in land and shall then constitute notice to third parties of the buyer's rights under the contract for sale.

Part 2 Form, Formation and Readjustment of Contract

§ 2—201. Formal Requirements; Statute of Frauds.

(1) Except as otherwise provided in this section a contract for the sale of goods for the price of $500 or more is not enforceable by way of action or defense unless there is some writing sufficient to indicate that a contract for sale has been made between the parties and signed by the party against whom enforcement is sought or by his authorized agent or broker. A writing is not insufficient because it omits or incorrectly states a term agreed upon but the contract is not enforceable under this paragraph beyond the quantity of goods shown in such writing.

(2) Between merchants if within a reasonable time a writing in confirmation of the contract and sufficient against the sender is received and the party receiving it has reason to know its contents, its satisfies the requirements of subsection (1) against such party unless written notice of objection to its contents is given within ten days after it is received.

(3) A contract which does not satisfy the requirements of subsection (1) but which is valid in other respects is enforceable

(a) if the goods are to be specially manufactured for the buyer and are not suitable for sale to others in the ordinary course of the seller's business and the seller, before notice of repudiation is received and under circumstances which reasonably indicate that the goods are for the buyer, has made either a substantial beginning of their manufacture or commitments for their procurement; or

(b) if the party against whom enforcement is sought admits in his pleading, testimony or otherwise in court that a contract for sale was made, but the contract is not enforceable under this provision beyond the quantity of goods admitted; or

(c) with respect to goods for which payment has been made and accepted or which have been received and accepted (Sec. 2—606).

§ 2—202. Final Written Expression: Parol or Extrinsic Evidence.

Terms with respect to which the confirmatory memoranda of the parties agree or which are otherwise set forth in a writing intended by the parties as a final expression of their agreement with respect to such terms as are included therein may not be contradicted by evidence of any prior agreement or of a contemporaneous oral agreement but may be explained or supplemented

(a) by course of dealing or usage of trade (Section 1—205) or by course of performance (Section 2—208); and

(b) by evidence of consistent additional terms unless the court finds the writing to have been intended also as a complete and exclusive statement of the terms of the agreement.

§ 2—203. Seals Inoperative.

The affixing of a seal to a writing evidencing a contract for sale or an offer to buy or sell goods does not constitute the writing a sealed instrument and the law with respect to sealed instruments does not apply to such a contract or offer.

§ 2—204. Formation in General.

(1) A contract for sale of goods may be made in any manner suffcent to show agreement, including conduct by both parties which recognizes the existence of such a contract.

(2) An agreement sufficient to constitute a contract for sale

may be found even though the moment of its making is undetermined.

(3) Even though one or more terms are left open a contract for sale does not fail for indefiniteness if the parties have intended to make a contract and there is a reasonably certain basis for giving an appropriate remedy.

§ 2—205. **Firm Offers.**

An offer by a merchant to buy or sell goods in a signed writing which by its terms gives assurance that it will be held open is not revocable, for lack of consideration, during the time stated or if no time is stated for a reasonable time, but in no event may such period of irrevocability exceed three months; but any such term of assurance on a form supplied by the offeree must be separately signed by the offeror.

§ 2—206. **Offer and Acceptance in Formation of Contract.**

(1) Unless other unambiguously indicated by the language or circumstances

    (a) an offer to make a contract shall be construed as inviting acceptance in any manner and by any medium reasonable in the circumstances;

    (b) an order or other offer to buy goods for prompt or current shipment shall be construed as inviting acceptance either by a prompt promise to ship or by the prompt or current shipment of conforming or nonconforming goods, but such a shipment of non-conforming goods does not constitute an acceptance if the seller seasonably notifies the buyer that the shipment is offered only as an accommodation to the buyer.

(2) Where the beginning of a requested performance is a reasonable mode of acceptance an offeror who is not notified of acceptance within a reasonable time may treat the offer as having lapsed before acceptance.

§ 2—207. **Additional Terms in Acceptance or Confirmation.**

(1) A definite and seasonable expression of acceptance or a written confirmation which is sent within a reasonable time operates as an acceptance even though it states terms additional to or different from those offered or agreed upon, unless acceptance is expressly made conditional on assent to the additional or different terms.

(2) The additional terms are to be construed as proposals for addition to the contract. Between merchants such terms become part of the contract unless:

    (a) the offer expressly limits acceptance to the terms of the offer;

    (b) they materially alter it; or

    (c) notification of objection to them has already been given or is given within a reasonable time after notice of them is received.

(3) Conduct by both parties which recognizes the existence of a contract is sufficient to establish a contract for sale although the writings of the parties do not otherwise establish a contract. In such case the terms of the particular contract consist of those terms on which the writings of the parties agree, together with any supplementary terms incorporated under any other provisions of this Act.

§ 2—208. **Course of Performance or Practical Construction.**

(1) Where the contract for sale involves repeated occasions for performance by either party with knowledge of the nature of the performance and opportunity for objection to it by the other, any course of performance accepted or acquiesced in without objection shall be relevant to determine the meaning of the agreement.

(2) The express terms of the agreement and any such course of performance, as well as any course of dealing and usage of trade, shall be construed whenever reasonable as consistent with each other; but when such construction is unreasonable, express terms shall control course of performance and course of performance shall control both course of dealing and usage of trade (Section 1—205).

(3) Subject to the provisions of the next section on modification and waiver, such course of performance shall be relevant to show a waiver or modification of any term inconsistent with such course of performance.

§ 2—209. **Modification, Rescission and Waiver.**

(1) An agreement modifying a contract within this Article needs no consideration to be binding.

(2) A signed agreement which excludes modification or rescission except by a signed writing cannot be otherwise modified or rescinded, but except as between merchants such a requirement on a form supplied by the merchant must be separately signed by the other party.

(3) The requirements of the statute of frauds section of this Article (Section 2—201) must be satisfied if the contract as modified is within its provisions.

(4) Although an attempt at modification or rescission does not satisfy the requirements of subsection (2) or (3) it can operate as a waiver.

(5) A party who has made a waiver affecting an executory portion of the contract may retract the waiver by reasonable notification received by the other party that strict performance will be required of any term waived, unless the retraction would be unjust in view of a material change of position in reliance on the waiver.

§ 2—210. **Delegation of Performance; Assignment of Rights.**

(1) A party may perform his duty through a delegate unless otherwise agreed or unless the other party has a substantial interest in having his original promisor perform or control the acts required by the contract. No delegation of perfor-

mance relieves the party delegating of any duty to perform or any liability for breach.

(2) Unless otherwise agreed all rights of either seller or buyer can be assigned except where the assignment would materially change the duty of the other party, or increase materially the burden or risk imposed on him by his contract, or impair materially his chance of obtaining return performance. A right to damages for breach of the whole contract or a right arising out of the assignor's due performance of his entire obligation can be assigned despite agreement otherwise.

(3) Unless the circumstances indicate the contrary a prohibition of assignment of ''the contract'' is to be construed as barring only the delegation to the assignee of the assignor's performance.

(4) An assignment of ''the contract'' or of ''all my rights under the contract'' or an assignment in similar general terms is an assignment of rights and unless the language or the circumstances (as in an assignment for security) indicate the contrary, it is a delegation of performance of the duties of the assignor and its acceptance by the assignee constitutes a promise by him to perform those duties. This promise is enforceable by either the assignor or the other party to the original contract.

(5) The other party may treat any assignment which delegates performance as creating reasonable grounds for insecurity and may without prejudice to his rights against the assignor demand assurances from the assignee (Section 2—609).

Part 3 General Obligation and Construction of Contract

§ 2—301. **General Obligations of Parties.**

The obligation of the seller is to transfer and deliver and that of the buyer is to accept and pay in accordance with the contract.

§ 2—302. **Unconscionable Contract or Clause.**

(1) If the court as a matter of law finds the contract or any clause of the contract to have been unconscionable at the time it was made the court may refuse to enforce the contract, or it may enforce the remainder of the contract without the unconscionable clause, or it may so limit the application of any unconscionable clause as to avoid any unconscionable result.

(2) When it is claimed or appears to the court that the contract or any clause thereof may be unconscionable the parties shall be afforded a reasonable opportunity to present evidence as to its commercial setting, purpose and effect to aid the court in making the determination.

§ 2—303. **Allocations or Division of Risks.**

Where this Article allocates a risk or a burden as between the parties ''unless otherwise agreed'', the agreement may not only shift the allocation but may also divide the risk or burden.

§ 2—304. **Price Payable in Money, Goods, Realty, or Otherwise.**

(1) The price can be made payable in money or otherwise. If it is payable in whole or in part in goods each party is a seller of the goods which he is to transfer.

(2) Even though all or part of the price is payable in an interest in realty the transfer of the goods and the seller's obligations with reference to them are subject to this Article, but not the transfer of the interest in realty or the transferor's obligations in connection therewith.

§ 2—305. **Open Price Term.**

(1) The parties if they so intend can conclude a contract for sale even though the price is not settled. In such a case the price is a reasonable price at the time for delivery if

   (a) nothing is said as to price; or

   (b) the price is left to be agreed by the parties and they fail to agree; or

   (c) the price is to be fixed in terms of some agreed market or other standard as set or recorded by a third person or agency and it is not so set or recorded.

(2) A price to be fixed by the seller or by the buyer means a price for him to fix in good faith.

(3) When a price left to be fixed otherwise than by agreement of the parties fails to be fixed through fault of one party the other may at his option treat the contract as cancelled or himself fix a reasonable price.

(4) Where, however, the parties intend not to be bound unless the price be fixed or agreed and it is not fixed or agreed there is no contract. In such a case the buyer must return any goods already received or if unable so to do must pay their reasonable value at the time of delivery and the seller must return any portion of the price paid on account.

§ 2—306. **Output, Requirements and Exclusive Dealings.**

(1) A term which measures the quantity by the output of the seller or the requirements of the buyer means such actual output or requirements as may occur in good faith, except that no quantity unreasonably disproportionate to any stated estimate or in the absence of a stated estimate to any normal or otherwise comparable prior output or requirements may be tendered or demanded.

(2) A lawful agreement by either the seller or the buyer for exclusive dealing in the kind of goods concerned imposes unless otherwise agreed an obligation by the seller to use best efforts to supply the goods and by the buyer to use best efforts to promote their sale.

§ 2—307. **Delivery in Single Lot or Several Lots.**

Unless otherwise agreed all goods called for by a contract

for sale must be tendered in a single delivery and payment is due only on such tender but where the circumstances give either party the right to make or demand delivery in lots the price if it can be apportioned may be demanded for each lot.

§ 2—308. **Absence of Specified Place for Delivery.**

Unless otherwise agreed

(a) the place for delivery of goods is the seller's place of business or if he has none his residence; but

(b) in a contract for sale of identified goods which to the knowledge of the parties at the time of contracting are in some other place, that place is the place for their delivery; and

(c) documents of title may be delivered through customary banking channels.

§ 2—309. **Absence of Specific Time Provisions; Notice of Termination.**

(1) The time for shipment or delivery or any other action under a contract if not provided in this Article or agreed upon shall be a reasonable time.

(2) Where the contract provides for successive performances but is indefinite in duration it is valid for a reasonable time but unless otherwise agreed may be terminated at any time by either party.

(3) Termination of a contract by one party except on the happening of an agreed event requires that reasonable notification be received by the other party and an agreement dispensing with notification is invalid if its operation would be unconscionable.

§ 2—310. **Open Time for Payment or Running of Credit; Authority to Ship Under Reservation.**

Unless otherwise agreed

(a) payment is due at the time and place at which the buyer is to receive the goods even though the place of shipment is the place of delivery; and

(b) if the seller is authorized to send the goods he may ship them under reservation, and may tender the documents of title, but the buyer may inspect the goods after their arrival before payment is due unless such inspection is inconsistent with the terms of the contract (Section 2—513); and

(c) if delivery is authorized and made by way of documents of title otherwise than by subsection (b) then payment is due at the time and place at which the buyer is to receive the documents regardless of where the goods are to be received; and

(d) where the seller is required or authorized to ship the goods on credit the credit period runs from the time of shipment but post-dating the invoice or delaying its dispatch will correspondingly delay the starting of the credit period.

§ 2—311. **Options and Cooperation Respecting Performance.**

(1) An agreement for sale which is otherwise sufficiently definite (subsection (3) of Section 2—204) to be a contract is not made invalid by the fact that it leaves particulars of performance to be specified by one of the parties. Any such specification must be made in good faith and within limits set by commercial reasonableness.

(2) Unless otherwise agreed specifications relating to assortment of the goods are at the buyer's option and except as otherwise provided in subsections (1)(c) and (3) of Section 2—319 specifications or arrangements relating to shipment are at the seller's option.

(3) Where such specification would materially affect the other party's performance but is not seasonably made or where one party's cooperation is necessary to the agreed performance of the other but is not seasonably forthcoming, the other party in addition to all other remedies

(a) is excused for any resulting delay in his own performance; and

(b) may also either proceed to perform in any reasonable manner or after the time for a material part of his own performance treat the failure to specify or to cooperate as a breach by failure to deliver or accept the goods.

§ 2—312. **Warranty of Title and Against Infringement; Buyer's Obligation Against Infringement.**

(1) Subject to subsection (2) there is in a contract for sale a warranty by the seller that

(a) the title conveyed shall be good, and its transfer rightful; and

(b) the goods shall be delivered free from any security interest or other lien or encumbrance of which the buyer at the time of contracting has no knowledge.

(2) A warranty under subsection (1) will be excluded or modified only by specific language or by circumstances which give the buyer reason to know that the person selling does not claim title in himself or that he is purporting to sell only such right or title as he or a third person may have.

(3) Unless otherwise agreed a seller who is a merchant regularly dealing in goods of the kind warrants that the goods shall be delivered free of the rightful claim of any third person by way of infringement or the like but a buyer who furnishes specifications to the seller must hold the seller harmless against any such claim which arises out of compliance with the specifications.

§ 2—313. **Express Warranties by Affirmation, Promise, Description, Sample.**

(1) Express warranties by the seller are created as follows:

(a) Any affirmation of fact or promise made by the seller to the buyer which relates to the goods and becomes part of the basis of the bargain creates an express warranty that the goods shall conform to the affirmation or promise.

(b) Any description of the goods which is made part of the basis of the bargain creates an express warranty that the goods shall conform to the description.

(c) Any sample or model which is made part of the basis of the bargain creates an express warranty that the whole of the goods shall conform to the sample or model.

(2) It is not necessary to the creation of an express warranty that the seller use formal words such as ''warrant'' or ''guarantee'' or that he have a specific intention to make a warranty, but an affirmation merely of the value of the goods or a statement purporting to be merely the seller's opinion or commendation of the goods does not create a warranty.

§ 2—314. Implied Warranty: Merchantability; Usage of Trade.

(1) Unless excluded or modified (Section 2—316), a warranty that the goods shall be merchantable is implied in a contract for their sale if the seller is a merchant with respect to goods of that kind. Under this section the serving for value of food or drink to be consumed either on the premises or elsewhere is a sale.

(2) Goods to be merchantable must be at least such as

(a) pass without objection in the trade under the contract description; and

(b) in the case of fungible goods, are of fair average quality within the description; and

(c) are fit for the ordinary purposes for which such goods are used; and

(d) run, within the variations permitted by the agreement, of even kind, quality and quantity within each unit and among all units involved; and

(e) are adequately contained, packaged, and labeled as the agreement may require; and

(f) conform to the promises or affirmations of fact made on the container or label if any.

(3) Unless excluded or modified (Section 2—316) other implied warranties may arise from course of dealing or usage of trade.

§ 2—315. Implied Warranty: Fitness for Particular Purpose.

Where the seller at the time of contracting has reason to know any particular purpose for which the goods are required and that the buyer is relying on the seller's skill or judgment to select or furnish suitable goods, there is unless excluded or modified under the next section an implied warranty that the goods shall be fit for such purpose.

§ 2—316. Exclusion or Modification of Warranties.

(1) Words or conduct relevant to the creation of an express warranty and words or conduct tending to negate or limit warranty shall be construed wherever reasonable as consistent with each other; but subject to the provisions of this Article on parol or extrinsic evidence (Section 2—202) negation or limitation is inoperative to the extent that such construction is unreasonable.

(2) Subject to subsection (3), to exclude or modify the implied warranty of merchantability or any part of it the language must mention merchantability and in case of a writing must be conspicuous, and to exclude or modify any implied warranty of fitness the exclusion must be by a writing and conspicuous. Language to exclude all implied warranties of fitness is sufficient if it states, for example, that ''There are no warranties which extend beyond the description on the face hereof.''

(3) Notwithstanding subsection (2)

(a) unless the circumstances indicate otherwise, all implied warranties are excluded by expressions like ''as is'', ''with all faults'' or other language which in common understanding calls the buyer's attention to the exclusion of warranties and makes plain that there is no implied warranty; and

(b) when the buyer before entering into the contract has examined the goods or the sample or model as fully as he desired or has refused to examine the goods there is no implied warranty with regard to defects which an examination ought in the circumstances to have revealed to him; and

(c) an implied warranty can also be excluded or modified by course of dealing or course of performance or usage of trade.

(4) Remedies for breach of warranty can be limited in accordance with the provisions of this Article on liquidation or limitation of damages and on contractual modification of remedy (Sections 2—718 and 2—719).

§ 2—317. Cumulation and Conflict of Warranties Express or Implied.

Warranties whether express or implied shall be construed as consistent with each other and as cumulative, but if such construction is unreasonable the intention of the parties shall determine which warranty is dominant. In ascertaining that intention the following rules apply:

(a) Exact or technical specifications displace an inconsistent sample or model or general language of description.

(b) A sample from an existing bulk displaces inconsistent general language of description.

(c) Express warranties displace inconsistent implied warranties other than an implied warranty of fitness for a particular purpose.

§ 2—318. **Third Party Beneficiaries of Warranties Express or Implied.**

Note: If this Act is introduced in the Congress of the United States this section should be omitted. (States to select one alternative.)

Alternative A

A seller's warranty whether express or implied extends to any natural person who is in the family or household of his buyer or who is a guest in his home if it is reasonable to expect that such person may use, consume or be affected by the goods and who is injured in person by breach of the warranty. A seller may not exclude or limit the operation of this section.

Alternative B

A seller's warranty whether express or implied extends to any natural person who may reasonably be expected to use, consume or be affected by the goods and who is injured in person by breach of the warranty. A seller may not exclude or limit the operation of this section.

Alternative C

A seller's warranty whether express or implied extends to any person who may reasonably be expected to use, consume or be affected by the goods and who is injured by breach of the warranty. A seller may not exclude or limit the operation of this section with respect to injury to the person of an individual to whom the warranty extends. As amended 1966.

§ 2—319. **F.O.B. and F.A.S. Terms.**

(1) Unless otherwise agreed the term F.O.B. (which means ''free on board'') at a named place, even though used only in connection with the stated price, is a delivery term under which

    (a) when the term is F.O.B. the place of shipment, the seller must at that place ship the goods in the manner provided in this Article (Section 2—504) and bear the expense and risk of putting them into the possession of the carrier; or

    (b) when the term is F.O.B. the place of destination, the seller must at his own expense and risk transport the goods to that place and there tender delivery of them in the manner provided in this Article (Section 2—503);

    (c) when under either (a) or (b) the term is also F.O.B. vessel, car or other vehicle, the seller must in addition at his own expense and risk load the goods on board. If the term is F.O.B. vessel the buyer must name the vessel and in an appropriate case the seller must comply with the provisions of this Article on the form of bill of lading (Section 2—323).

(2) Unless otherwise agreed the term F.A.S. vessel (which means ''free alongside'') at a named port, even though used only in connection with the stated price, is a delivery term under which the seller must

    (a) at his own expense and risk deliver the goods alongside the vessel in the manner usual in that port or on a dock designated and provided by the buyer; and

    (b) obtain and tender a receipt for the goods in exchange for which the carrier is under a duty to issue a bill of lading.

(3) Unless otherwise agreed in any case falling within subsection (1)(a) or (c) or subsection (2) the buyer must seasonably give any needed instructions for making delivery, including when the term is F.A.S. or F.O.B. the loading berth of the vessel and in an appropriate case its name and sailing date. The seller may treat the failure of needed instructions as a failure of cooperation under this Article (Section 2—311). He may also at his option move the goods in any reasonable manner preparatory to delivery or shipment.

(4) Under the term F.O.B. vessel or F.A.S. unless otherwise agreed the buyer must make payment against tender of the required documents and the seller may not tender nor the buyer demand delivery of the goods in substitution for the documents.

§ 2—320. **C.I.F. and C. & F. Terms.**

(1) The term C.I.F. means that the price includes in a lump sum the cost of the goods and the insurance and freight to the named destination. The term C. & F. or C.F. means that the price so includes cost and freight to the named destination.

(2) Unless otherwise agreed and even though used only in connection with the stated price and destination, the term C.I.F. destination or its equivalent requires the seller at his own expense and risk to

    (a) put the goods into the possession of a carrier at the port for shipment and obtain a negotiable bill or bills of lading covering the entire transportation to the named destination; and

    (b) load the goods and obtain a receipt from the carrier (which may be contained in the bill of lading) showing that the freight has been paid or provided for; and

    (c) obtain a policy or certificate of insurance, including any war risk insurance, of a kind and on terms then current at the port of shipment in the usual amount, in the currency of the contract, shown to cover the same goods covered by the bill of lading and providing for payment of loss to the order of the buyer or for the account of whom it may concern; but the seller may add to the price the amount of the premium for any such war risk insurance; and

(d) prepare an invoice of the goods and procure any other documents required to effect shipment or to comply with the contract; and

(e) forward and tender with commercial promptness all the documents in due form and with any indorsement necessary to perfect the buyer's rights.

(3) Unless otherwise agreed the term C. & F. or its equivalent has the same effect and imposes upon the seller the same obligations and risks as a C.I.F. term except the obligation as to insurance.

(4) Under the term C.I.F. or C. & F. unless otherwise agreed the buyer must make payment against tender of the required documents and the seller may not tender nor the buyer demand delivery of the goods in substitution for the documents.

§ 2—321. **C.I.F. or C. & F.: "Net Landed Weights"; "Payment on Arrival"; Warranty of Condition on Arrival.**

Under a contract containing a term C.I.F. or C. & F.

(1) Where the price is based on or is to be adjusted according to "net landed weights", "delivered weights", "out turn" quantity or quality or the like, unless otherwise agreed the seller must reasonably estimate the price. The payment due on tender of the documents called for by the contract is the amount so estimated, but after final adjustment of the price a settlement must be made with commercial promptness.

(2) An agreement described in subsection (1) or any warranty of quality or condition of the goods on arrival places upon the seller the risk of ordinary deterioration, shrinkage and the like in transportation but has no effect on the place or time of identification to the contract for sale or delivery or on the passing of the risk of loss.

(3) Unless otherwise agreed where the contract provides for payment on or after arrival of the goods the seller must before payment allow such preliminary inspection as is feasible; but if the goods are lost delivery of the documents and payment are due when the goods should have arrived.

§ 2—322. **Delivery "Ex-Ship".**

(1) Unless otherwise agreed a term for delivery of goods "ex-ship" (which means from the carrying vessel) or in equivalent language is not restricted to a particular ship and requires delivery from a ship which has reached a place at the named port of destination where goods of the kind are usually discharged.

(2) Under such a term unless otherwise agreed

(a) the seller must discharge all liens arising out of the carriage and furnish the buyer with a direction which puts the carrier under a duty to deliver the goods; and

(b) the risk of loss does not pass to the buyer until the goods leave the ship's tackle or are otherwise properly unloaded.

§ 2—323. **Form of Bill of Lading Required in Overseas Shipment; "Overseas".**

(1) Where the contract contemplates overseas shipment and contains a term C.I.F. or C. & F. or F.O.B. vessel, the seller unless otherwise agreed must obtain a negotiable bill of lading stating that the goods have been loaded on board or, in the case of a term C.I.F. or C. & F., received for shipment.

(2) Where in a case within subsection (1) a bill of lading has been issued in a set of parts, unless otherwise agreed if the documents are not to be sent from abroad the buyer may demand tender of the full set; otherwise only one part of the bill of lading need be tendered. Even if the agreement expressly requires a full set

(a) due tender of a single part is acceptable within the provisions of this Article on cure of improper delivery (subsection (1) of Section 2—508); and

(b) even though the full set is demanded, if the documents are sent from abroad the person tendering an incomplete set may nevertheless require payment upon furnishing an indemnity which the buyer in good faith deems adequate.

(3) A shipment by water or by air or a contract contemplating such shipment is "overseas" insofar as by usage of trade or agreement it is subject to the commercial, financing or shipping practices characteristic of international deep water commerce.

§ 2—324. **"No Arrival, No Sale" Term.**

Under a term "no arrival, no sale" or terms of like meaning, unless otherwise agreed,

(a) the seller must properly ship conforming goods and if they arrive by any means he must tender them on arrival but he assumes no obligation that the goods will arrive unless he has caused the non-arrival; and

(b) where without fault of the seller the goods are in part lost or have so deteriorated as no longer to conform to the contract or arrive after the contract time, the buyer may proceed as if there had been casualty to identified goods (Section 2—613).

§ 2—325. **"Letter of Credit" Term; "Confirmed Credit".**

(1) Failure of the buyer seasonably to furnish an agreed letter of credit is a breach of the contract for sale.

(2) The delivery to seller of a proper letter of credit suspends the buyer's obligation to pay. If the letter of credit is dishonored, the seller may on seasonable notification to the buyer require payment directly from him.

(3) Unless otherwise agreed the term "letter of credit" or "banker's credit" in a contract for sale means an irrevocable credit issued by a financing agency of good repute and, where the shipment is overseas, of good international

repute. The term "confirmed credit" means that the credit must also carry the direct obligation of such an agency which does business in the seller's financial market.

§ 2—326. Sale on Approval and Sale or Return; Consignment Sales and Rights of Creditors.

(1) Unless otherwise agreed, if delivered goods may be returned by the buyer even though they conform to the contract, the transaction is

(a) a "sale on approval" if the goods are delivered primarily for use, and

(b) a "sale or return" if the goods are delivered primarily for resale.

(2) Except as provided in subsection (3), goods held on approval are not subject to the claims of the buyer's creditors until acceptance; goods held on sale or return are subject to such claims while in the buyer's possession.

(3) Where goods are delivered to a person for sale and such person maintains a place of business at which he deals in goods of the kind involved, under a name other than the name of the person making delivery, then with respect to claims of creditors of the person conducting the business the goods are deemed to be on sale or return. The provisions of this subsection are applicable even though an agreement purports to reserve title to the person making delivery until payment or resale or uses such words as "on consignment" or "on memorandum". However, this subsection is not applicable if the person making delivery

(a) complies with an applicable law providing for a consignor's interest or the like to be evidenced by a sign, or

(b) establishes that the person conducting the business is generally known by his creditors to be substantially engaged in selling the goods of others, or

(c) complies with the filing provisions of the Article on Secured Transactions (Article 9).

(4) Any "or return" term of a contract for sale is to be treated as a separate contract for sale within the statute of frauds section of this Article (Section 2—201) and as contradicting the sale aspect of the contract within the provisions of this Article on parol or extrinsic evidence (Section 2—202).

§ 2—327. Special Incidents of Sale on Approval and Sale or Return.

(1) Under a sale on approval unless otherwise agreed

(a) although the goods are identified to the contract the risk of loss and the title do not pass to the buyer until acceptance; and

(b) use of the goods consistent with the purpose of trial is not acceptance but failure seasonably to notify the seller of election to return the goods is acceptance, and

if the goods conform to the contract acceptance of any part is acceptance of the whole; and

(c) after due notification of election to return, the return is at the seller's risk and expense but a merchant buyer must follow any reasonable instructions.

(2) Under a sale or return unless otherwise agreed

(a) the option to return extends to the whole or any commercial unit of the goods while in substantially their original condition, but must be exercised seasonably; and

(b) the return is at the buyer's risk and expense.

§ 2—328. Sale by Auction.

(1) In a sale by auction if goods are put up in lots each lot is the subject of a separate sale.

(2) A sale by auction is complete when the auctioneer so announces by the fall of the hammer or in other customary manner. Where a bid is made while the hammer is falling in acceptance of a prior bid the auctioneer may in his discretion reopen the bidding or declare the goods sold under the bid on which the hammer was falling.

(3) Such a sale is with reserve unless the goods are in explicit terms put up without reserve. In an auction with reserve the auctioneer may withdraw the goods at any time until he announces completion of the sale. In an auction without reserve, after the auctioneer calls for bids on an article or lot, that article or lot cannot be withdrawn unless no bid is made within a reasonable time. In either case a bidder may retract his bid until the auctioneer's announcement of completion of the sale, but a bidder's retraction does not revive any previous bid.

(4) If the auctioneer knowingly receives a bid on the seller's behalf or the seller makes or procures such as bid, and notice has not been given that liberty for such bidding is reserved, the buyer may at his option avoid the sale or take the goods at the price of the last good faith bid prior to the completion of the sale. This subsection shall not apply to any bid at a forced sale.

Part 4 Title, Creditors and Good Faith Purchasers

§ 2—401. Passing of Title; Reservation for Security; Limited Application of This Section.

Each provision of this Article with regard to the rights, obligations and remedies of the seller, the buyer, purchasers or other third parties applies irrespective of title to the goods except where the provision refers to such title. Insofar as situations are not covered by the other provisions of this Article and matters concerning title became material the following rules apply:

(1) Title to goods cannot pass under a contract for sale prior to their identification to the contract (Section 2—501),

and unless otherwise explicitly agreed the buyer acquires by their identification a special property as limited by this Act. Any retention or reservation by the seller of the title (property) in goods shipped or delivered to the buyer is limited in effect to a reservation of a security interest. Subject to these provisions and to the provisions of the Article on Secured Transactions (Article 9), title to goods passes from the seller to the buyer in any manner and on any conditions explicitly agreed on by the parties.

(2) Unless otherwise explicitly agreed title passes to the buyer at the time and place at which the seller completes his performance with reference to the physical delivery of the goods, despite any reservation of a security interest and even though a document of title is to be delivered at a different time or place; and in particular and despite any reservation of a security interest by the bill of lading

(a) if the contract requires or authorizes the seller to send the goods to the buyer but does not require him to deliver them at destination, title passes to the buyer at the time and place of shipment; but

(b) if the contract requires delivery at destination, title passes on tender there.

(3) Unless otherwise explicitly agreed where delivery is to be made without moving the goods,

(a) if the seller is to deliver a document of title, title passes at the time when and the place where he delivers such documents; or

(b) if the goods are at the time of contracting already identified and no documents are to be delivered, title passes at the time and place of contracting.

(4) A rejection or other refusal by the buyer to receive or retain the goods, whether or not justified, or a justified revocation of acceptance revests title to the goods in the seller. Such revesting occurs by operation of law and is not a "sale".

§ 2—402. Rights of Seller's Creditors Against Sold Goods.

(1) Except as provided in subsections (2) and (3), rights of unsecured creditors of the seller with respect to goods which have been identified to a contract for sale are subject to the buyer's rights to recover the goods under this Article (Sections 2—502 and 2—716).

(2) A creditor of the seller may treat a sale or an identification of goods to a contract for sale as void if as against him a retention of possession by the seller is fraudulent under any rule of law of the state where the goods are situated, except that retention of possession in good faith and current course of trade by a merchant-seller for a commercially reasonable time after a sale or identification is not fraudulent.

(3) Nothing in this Article shall be deemed to impair the rights of creditors of the seller

(a) under the provisions of the Article on Secured Transactions (Article 9); or

(b) where identification to the contract or delivery is made not in current course of trade but in satisfaction of or as security for a pre-existing claim for money, security or the like and is made under circumstances which under any rule of law of the state where the goods are situated would apart from this Article constitute the transaction a fraudulent transfer or voidable preference.

§ 2—403. Power to Transfer; Good Faith Purchase of Goods; "Entrusting".

(1) A purchaser of goods acquires all title which his transferor had or had power to transfer except that a purchaser of a limited interest acquires rights only to the extent of the interest purchased. A person with voidable title has power to transfer a good title to a good faith purchaser for value. When goods have been delivered under a transaction of purchase the purchaser has such power even though

(a) the transferor was deceived as to the identity of the purchaser, or

(b) the delivery was in exchange for a check which is later dishonored, or

(c) it was agreed that the transaction was to be a "cash sale", or

(d) the delivery was procured through fraud punishable as larcenous under the criminal law.

(2) Any entrusting of possession of goods to a merchant who deals in goods of that kind gives him power to transfer all rights of the entruster to a buyer in ordinary course of business.

(3) "Entrusting" includes any delivery and any acquiescence in retention of possession regardless of any condition expressed between the parties to the delivery or acquiescence and regardless of whether the procurement of the entrusting or the possessor's disposition of the goods have been such as to be larcenous under the criminal law.

(4) The rights of other purchasers of goods and of lien creditors are governed by the Articles on Secured Transactions (Article 9), Bulk Transfers (Article 6) and Documents of Title (Article 7).

Part 5 Performance

§ 2—501. Insurable Interest in Goods; Manner of Identification of Goods.

(1) The buyer obtains a special property and an insurable interest in goods by identification of existing goods as goods to which the contract refers even though the goods so identified are non-conforming and he has an option to return or reject them. Such identification can be made at any time and in any manner explicitly agreed to by the parties. In the absence of explicit agreement identification occurs

(a) when the contract is made if it is for the sale of goods already existing and identified;

(b) if the contract is for the sale of future goods other than those described in paragraph (c), when goods are shipped, marked or otherwise designated by the seller as goods to which the contract refers;

(c) when the crops are planted or otherwise become growing crops or the young are conceived if the contract is for the sale of unborn young to be born within twelve months after contracting or for the sale of crops to be harvested within twelve months or the next normal harvest season after contracting whichever is longer.

(2) The seller retains an insurable interest in goods so long as title to or any security interest in the goods remains in him and where the identification is by the seller alone he may until default or insolvency or notification to the buyer that the identification is final substitute other goods for those identified.

(3) Nothing in this section impairs any insurable interest recognized under any other statute or rule of law.

§ 2—502. **Buyer's Right to Goods on Seller's Insolvency.**

(1) Subject to subsection (2) and even though the goods have not been shipped a buyer who has paid a part or all of the price of goods in which he has a special property under the provisions of the immediately preceding section may on making and keeping good a tender of any unpaid portion of their price recover them from the seller if the seller becomes insolvent within ten days after receipt of the first installment on their price.

(2) If the identification creating his special property has been made by the buyer he acquires the right to recover the goods only if they conform to the contract for sale.

§ 2—503. **Manner of Seller's Tender of Delivery.**

(1) Tender of delivery requires that the seller put and hold conforming goods at the buyer's disposition and give the buyer any notification reasonably necessary to enable him to take delivery. The manner, time and place for tender are determined by the agreement and this Article, and in particular

(a) tender must be at a reasonable hour, and if it is of goods they must be kept available for the period reasonably necessary to enable the buyer to take possession; but

(b) unless otherwise agreed the buyer must furnish facilities reasonably suited to the receipt of the goods.

(2) Where the case is within the next section respecting shipment tender requires that the seller comply with its provisions.

(3) Where the seller is required to deliver at a particular destination tender requires that he comply with subsection (1) and also in any appropriate case tender documents as described in subsections (4) and (5) of this section.

(4) Where goods are in the possession of a bailee and are to be delivered without being moved

(a) tender requires that the seller either tender a negotiable document of title covering such goods or procure acknowledgment by the bailee of the buyer's right to possession of the goods; but

(b) tender to the buyer of a non-negotiable document of title or of a written direction to the bailee to deliver is sufficient tender unless the buyer seasonably objects, and receipt by the bailee of notification of the buyer's rights fixes those rights as against the bailee and all third persons; but risk of loss of the goods and of any failure by the bailee to honor the non-negotiable document of title or to obey the direction remains on the seller until the buyer has had a reasonable time to present the document or direction, and a refusal by the bailee to honor the document or to obey the direction defeats the tender.

(5) Where the contract requires the seller to deliver documents

(a) he must tender all such documents in correct form, except as provided in this Article with respect to bills of lading in a set (subsection (2) of Section 2—323); and

(b) tender through customary banking channels is sufficient and dishonor of a draft accompanying the documents constitutes non-acceptance or rejection.

§ 2—504. **Shipment by Seller.**

Where the seller is required or authorized to send the goods to the buyer and the contract does not require him to deliver them at a particular destination, then unless otherwise agreed he must

(a) put the goods in the possession of such a carrier and make such a contract for their transportation as may be reasonable having regard to the nature of the goods and other circumstances of the case; and

(b) obtain and promptly deliver or tender in due form any document necessary to enable the buyer to obtain possession of the goods or otherwise required by the agreement or by usage of trade; and

(c) promptly notify the buyer of the shipment.

Failure to notify the buyer under paragraph (c) or to make a proper contract under paragraph (a) is a ground for rejection only if material delay or loss ensues.

§ 2—505. **Seller's Shipment under Reservation.**

(1) Where the seller has identified goods to the contract by or before shipment:

(a) his procurement of a negotiable bill of lading to his own order or otherwise reserves in him a security interest in the goods. His procurement of the bill to the order of a financing agency or of the buyer indicates in addition only the seller's expectation of transferring that interest to the person named.

(b) a non-negotiable bill of lading to himself or his nominee reserves possession of the goods as security but except in a case of conditional delivery (subsection (2) of Section 2—507) a non-negotiable bill of lading naming the buyer as consignee reserves no security interest even though the seller retains possession of the bill of lading.

(2) When shipment by the seller with reservation of a security interest is in violation of the contract for sale it constitutes an improper contract for transportation within the preceding section but impairs neither the rights given to the buyer by shipment and identification of the goods to the contract nor the seller's powers as a holder of a negotiable document.

§ 2—506. **Rights of Financing Agency.**

(1) A financing agency by paying or purchasing for value a draft which relates to a shipment of goods acquires to the extent of the payment or purchase and in addition to its own rights under the draft and any document of title securing it any rights of the shipper in the goods including the right to stop delivery and the shipper's right to have the draft honored by the buyer.

(2) The right to reimbursement of a financing agency which has in good faith honored or purchased the draft under commitment to or authority from the buyer is not impaired by subsequent discovery of defects with reference to any relevant document which was apparently regular on its face.

§ 2—507. **Effect of Seller's Tender; Delivery on Condition.**

(1) Tender of delivery is a condition to the buyer's duty to accept the goods and, unless otherwise agreed, to his duty to pay for them. Tender entitles the seller to acceptance of the goods and to payment according to the contract.

(2) Where payment is due and demanded on the delivery to the buyer of goods or documents of title, his right as against the seller to retain or dispose of them is conditional upon his making the payment due.

§ 2—508. **Cure by Seller of Improper Tender or Delivery; Replacement.**

(1) Where any tender or delivery by the seller is rejected because non-conforming and the time for performance has not yet expired, the seller may seasonably notify the buyer of his intention to cure and may then within the contract time make a conforming delivery.

(2) Where the buyer rejects a non-conforming tender which the seller had reasonable grounds to believe would be acceptable with or without money allowance the seller may

if he seasonably notifies the buyer have a further reasonable time to substitute a conforming tender.

§ 2—509. **Risk of Loss in the Absence of Breach.**

(1) Where the contract requires or authorizes the seller to ship the goods by carrier

(a) if it does not require him to deliver them at a particular destination, the risk of loss passes to the buyer when the goods are duly delivered to the carrier even though the shipment is under reservation (Section 2—505); but

(b) if it does require him to deliver them at a particular destination and the goods are there duly tendered while in the possession of the carrier, the risk of loss passes to the buyer when the goods are there duly so tendered as to enable the buyer to take delivery.

(2) Where the goods are held by a bailee to be delivered without being moved, the risk of loss passes to the buyer

(a) on his receipt of a negotiable document of title covering the goods; or

(b) on acknowledgment by the bailee of the buyer's right to possession of the goods; or

(c) after his receipt of a non-negotiable document of title or other written direction to deliver, as provided in subsection (4)(b) of Section 2—503.

(3) In any case not within subsection (1) or (2), the risk of loss passes to the buyer on his receipt of the goods if the seller is a merchant; otherwise the risk passes to the buyer on tender of delivery.

(4) The provisions of this section are subject to contrary agreement of the parties and to the provisions of this Article on sale on approval (Section 2—327) and on effect of breach on risk of loss (Section 2—510).

§ 2—510. **Effect of Breach on Risk of Loss.**

(1) Where a tender or delivery of goods so fails to conform to the contract as to give a right of rejection the risk of their loss remains on the seller until cure or acceptance.

(2) Where the buyer rightfully revokes acceptance he may to the extent of any deficiency in his effective insurance coverage treat the risk of loss as having rested on the seller from the beginning.

(3) Where the buyer as to conforming goods already identified to the contract for sale repudiates or is otherwise in breach before risk of their loss has passed to him, the seller may to the extent of any deficiency in his effective insurance coverage treat the risk of loss as resting on the buyer for a commercially reasonable time.

§ 2—511. **Tender of Payment by Buyer; Payment by Check.**

(1) Unless otherwise agreed tender of payment is a condition to the seller's duty to tender and complete any delivery.

(2) Tender of payment is sufficient when made by any means or in any manner current in the ordinary course of business unless the seller demands payment in legal tender and gives any extension of time reasonably necessary to procure it.

(3) Subject to the provisions of this Act on the effect of an instrument on an obligation (Section 3—802), payment by check is conditional and is defeated as between the parties by dishonor of the check on due presentment.

§ 2—512. Payment by Buyer Before Inspection.

(1) Where the contract requires payment before inspection non-conformity of the goods does not excuse the buyer from so making payment unless

(a) the non-conformity appears without inspection; or

(b) despite tender of the required documents the circumstances would justify injunction against honor under the provisions of this Act (Section 5—114).

(2) Payment pursuant to subsection (1) does not constitute an acceptance of goods or impair the buyer's right to inspect or any of his remedies.

§ 2—513. Buyer's Right to Inspection of Goods.

(1) Unless otherwise agreed and subject to subsection (3), where goods are tendered or delivered or identified to the contract for sale, the buyer has a right before payment or acceptance to inspect them at any reasonable place and time and in any reasonable manner. When the seller is required or authorized to send the goods to the buyer, the inspection may be after their arrival.

(2) Expenses of inspection must be borne by the buyer but may be recovered from the seller if the goods do not conform and are rejected.

(3) Unless otherwise agreed and subject to the provisions of this Article on C.I.F. contracts (subsection (3) of Section 2—321), the buyer is not entitled to inspect the goods before payment of the price when the contract provides

(a) for delivery "C.O.D." or on other like terms; or

(b) for payment against documents of title, except where such payment is due only after the goods are to become available for inspection.

(4) A place or method of inspection fixed by the parties is presumed to be exclusive but unless otherwise expressly agreed it does not postpone identification or shift the place for delivery or for passing the risk of loss. If compliance becomes impossible, inspection shall be as provided in this section unless the place or method fixed was clearly intended as an indispensable condition failure of which avoids the contract.

§ 2—514. When Documents Deliverable on Acceptance; When on Payment.

Unless otherwise agreed documents against which a draft is drawn are to be delivered to the drawee on acceptance of the draft if it is payable more than three days after presentment; otherwise, only on payment.

§ 2—515. Preserving Evidence of Goods in Dispute.

In furtherance of the adjustment of any claim or dispute

(a) either party on reasonable notification to the other and for the purpose of ascertaining the facts and preserving evidence has the right to inspect, test and sample the goods including such of them as may be in the possession or control of the other; and

(b) the parties may agree to a third party inspection or survey to determine the conformity or condition of the goods and may agree that the findings shall be binding upon them in any subsequent litigation or adjustment.

Part 6 Breach, Repudiation and Excuse

§ 2—601. Buyer's Rights on Improper Delivery.

Subject to the provisions of this Article on breach in installment contracts (Section 2—612) and unless otherwise agreed under the sections on contractual limitations of remedy (Sections 2—718 and 2—719), if the goods or the tender of delivery fail in any respect to conform to the contract, the buyer may

(a) reject the whole; or

(b) accept the whole; or

(c) accept any commercial unit or units and reject the rest.

§ 2—602. Manner and Effect of Rightful Rejection.

(1) Rejection of goods must be within a reasonable time after their delivery or tender. It is ineffective unless the buyer seasonably notifies the seller.

(2) Subject to the provisions of the two following sections on rejected goods (Sections 2—603 and 2—604),

(a) after rejection any exercise of ownership by the buyer with respect to any commercial unit is wrongful as against the seller; and

(b) if the buyer has before rejection taken physical possession of goods in which he does not have a security interest under the provisions of this Article (subsection (3) of Section 2—711), he is under a duty after rejection to hold them with reasonable care at the seller's disposition for a time sufficient to permit the seller to remove them; but

(c) the buyer has no further obligations with regard to goods rightfully rejected.

(3) The seller's rights with respect to goods wrongfully rejected are governed by the provisions of this Article on Seller's remedies in general (Section 2—703).

§ 2—603. Merchant Buyer's Duties as to Rightfully Rejected Goods.

(1) Subject to any security interest in the buyer (subsection (3) of Section 2—711), when the seller has no agent

or place of business at the market of rejection a merchant buyer is under a duty after rejection of goods in his possession or control to follow any reasonable instructions received from the seller with respect to the goods and in the absence of such instructions to make reasonable efforts to sell them for the seller's account if they are perishable or threaten to decline in value speedily. Instructions are not reasonable if on demand indemnity for expenses is not forthcoming.

(2) When the buyer sells goods under subsection (1), he is entitled to reimbursement from the seller or out of the proceeds for reasonable expenses of caring for and selling them, and if the expenses include no selling commission then to such commission as is usual in the trade or if there is none to a reasonable sum not exceeding ten per cent on the gross proceeds.

(3) In complying with this section the buyer is held only to good faith and good faith conduct hereunder is neither acceptance nor conversion nor the basis of an action for damages.

§ 2—604. **Buyer's Options as to Salvage of Rightfully Rejected Goods.**

Subject to the provisions of the immediately preceding section on perishables if the seller gives no instructions within a reasonable time after notification of rejection the buyer may store the rejected goods for the seller's account or reship them to him or resell them for the seller's account with reimbursement as provided in the preceding section. Such action is not acceptance or conversion.

§ 2—605. **Waiver of Buyer's Objections by Failure to Particularize.**

(1) The buyer's failure to state in connection with rejection a particular defect which is ascertainable by reasonable inspection precludes him from relying on the unstated defect to justify rejection or to establish breach

(a) where the seller could have cured it if stated seasonably; or

(b) between merchants when the seller has after rejection made a request in writing for a full and final written statement of all defects on which the buyer proposes to rely.

(2) Payment against documents made without reservation of rights precludes recovery of the payment for defects apparent on the face of the documents.

§ 2—606. **What Constitutes Acceptance of Goods.**

(1) Acceptance of goods occurs when the buyer

(a) after a reasonable opportunity to inspect the goods signifies to the seller that the goods are conforming or that he will take or retain them in spite of their non-conformity; or

(b) fails to make an effective rejection (subsection (1) of Section 2—602), but such acceptance does not occur until the buyer has had a reasonable opportunity to inspect them; or

(c) does any act inconsistent with the seller's ownership; but if such act is wrongful as against the seller it is an acceptance only if ratified by him.

(2) Acceptance of a part of any commercial unit is acceptance of that entire unit.

§ 2—607. **Effect of Acceptance; Notice of Breach; Burden of Establishing Breach After Acceptance; Notice of Claim or Litigation to Person Answerable Over.**

(1) The buyer must pay at the contract rate for any goods accepted.

(2) Acceptance of goods by the buyer precludes rejection of the goods accepted and if made with knowledge of a non-conformity cannot be revoked because of it unless the acceptance was on the reasonable assumption that the non-conformity would be seasonably cured but acceptance does not of itself impair any other remedy provided by this Article for non-conformity.

(3) Where a tender has been accepted

(a) the buyer must within a reasonable time after he discovers or should have discovered any breach notify the seller of breach or be barred from any remedy; and

(b) if the claim is one for infringement or the like (subsection (3) of Section 2—312) and the buyer is sued as a result of such a breach he must so notify the seller within a reasonable time after he receives notice of the litigation or be barred from any remedy over for liability established by the litigation.

(4) The burden is on the buyer to establish any breach with respect to the goods accepted.

(5) Where the buyer is sued for breach of a warranty or other obligation for which his seller is answerable over

(a) he may give his seller written notice of the litigation. If the notice states that the seller may come in and defend and that if the seller does not do so he will be bound in any action against him by his buyer by any determination of fact common to the two litigations, then unless the seller after seasonable receipt of the notice does come in and defend he is so bound.

(b) if the claim is one for infringement or the like (subsection (3) of Section 2—312) the original seller may demand in writing that his buyer turn over to him control of the litigation including settlement or else be barred from any remedy over and if he also agrees to bear all expense and to satisfy any adverse judgment, then unless the buyer after seasonable receipt of the demand does turn over control the buyer is so barred.

(6) The provisions of subsections (3), (4) and (5) apply to any obligation of a buyer to hold the seller harmless against infringement or the like (subsection (3) of Section 2—312).

§ 2—608. **Revocation of Acceptance in Whole or in Part.**

(1) The buyer may revoke his acceptance of a lot or commercial unit whose non-conformity substantially impairs its value to him if he has accepted it

(a) on the reasonable assumption that its non-conformity would be cured and it has not been seasonably cured; or

(b) without discovery of such non-conformity if his acceptance was reasonably induced either by the difficulty of discovery before acceptance or by the seller's assurances.

(2) Revocation of acceptance must occur within a reasonable time after the buyer discovers or should have discovered the ground for it and before any substantial change in condition of the goods which is not caused by their own defects. It is not effective until the buyer notifies the seller of it.

(3) A buyer who so revokes has the same rights and duties with regard to the goods involved as if he had rejected them.

§ 2—609. **Right to Adequate Assurance of Performance.**

(1) A contract for sale imposes an obligation on each party that the other's expectation of receiving due performance will not be impaired. When reasonable grounds for insecurity arise with respect to the performance of either party the other may in writing demand adequate assurance of due performance and until he receives such assurance may if commercially reasonable suspend any performance for which he has not already received the agreed return.

(2) Between merchants the reasonableness of grounds for insecurity and the adequacy of any assurance offered shall be determined according to commercial standards.

(3) Acceptance of any improper delivery or payment does not prejudice the party's right to demand adequate assurance of future performance.

(4) After receipt of a justified demand failure to provide within a reasonable time not exceeding thirty days such assurance of due performance as is adequate under the circumstances of the particular case is a repudiation of the contract.

§ 2—610. **Anticipatory Repudiation.**

When either party repudiates the contract with respect to a performance not yet due the loss of which will substantially impair the value of the contract to the other, the aggrieved party may

(a) for a commercially reasonable time await performance by the repudiating party; or

(b) resort to any remedy for breach (Section 2—703 or Section 2—711), even though he has notified the repudiating party that he would await the latter's performance and has urged retraction; and

(c) in either case suspend his own performance or proceed in accordance with the provisions of this Article on the seller's right to identify goods to the contract notwithstanding breach or to salvage unfinished goods (Section 2—704).

§ 2—611. **Retraction of Anticipatory Repudiation.**

(1) Until the repudiating party's next performance is due he can retract his repudiation unless the aggrieved party has since the repudiation cancelled or materially changed his position or otherwise indicated that he considers the repudiation final.

(2) Retraction may be by any method which clearly indicates to the aggrieved party that the repudiating party intends to perform, but must include any assurance justifiably demanded under the provisions of this Article (Section 2—609).

(3) Retraction reinstates the repudiating party's rights under the contract with due excuse and allowance to the aggrieved party for any delay occasioned by the repudiation.

§ 2—612. **"Installment Contract"; Breach.**

(1) An "installment contract" is one which requires or authorizes the delivery of goods in separate lots to be separately accepted, even though the contract contains a clause "each delivery is a separate contract" or its equivalent.

(2) The buyer may reject any installment which is non-conforming if the non-conformity substantially impairs the value of that installment and cannot be cured or if the non-conformity is a defect in the required documents; but if the non-conformity does not fall within subsection (3) and the seller gives adequate assurance of its cure the buyer must accept that installment.

(3) Whenever non-conformity or default with respect to one or more installments substantially impairs the value of the whole contract there is a breach of the whole. But the aggrieved party reinstates the contract if he accepts a non-conforming installment without seasonably notifying of cancellation or if he brings an action with respect only to past installments or demands performance as to future installments.

§ 2—613. **Casualty to Identified Goods.**

Where the contract requires for its performance goods identified when the contract is made, and the goods suffer casualty without fault of either party before the risk of loss passes to the buyer, or in a proper case under a "no arrival, no sale" term (Section 2—324) then

(a) if the loss is total the contract is avoided; and

(b) if the loss is partial or the goods have so deteriorated as no longer to conform to the contract the buyer may nevertheless demand inspection and at his option either treat the contract as voided or accept the goods with due allowance from the contract price for the deterioration or the deficiency in quantity but without further right against the seller.

§ 2—614. Substituted Performance.

(1) Where without fault of either party the agreed berthing, loading, or unloading facilities fail or an agreed type of carrier becomes unavailable or the agreed manner of delivery otherwise becomes commercially impracticable but a commercially reasonable substitute is available, such substitute performance must be tendered and accepted.

(2) If the agreed means or manner of payment fails because of domestic or foreign governmental regulation, the seller may withhold or stop delivery unless the buyer provides a means or manner of payment which is commercially a substantial equivalent. If delivery has already been taken, payment by the means or in the manner provided by the regulation discharges the buyer's obligation unless the regulation is discriminatory, oppressive or predatory.

§ 2—615. Excuse by Failure of Presupposed Conditions.

Except so far as a seller may have assumed a greater obligation and subject to the preceding section on substituted performance:

(a) Delay in delivery or non-delivery in whole or in part by a seller who complies with paragraphs (b) and (c) is not a breach of his duty under a contract for sale if performance as agreed has been made impracticable by the occurrence of a contingency the nonoccurrence of which was a basic assumption on which the contract was made or by compliance in good faith with any applicable foreign or domestic governmental regulation or order whether or not it later proves to be invalid.

(b) Where the causes mentioned in paragraph (a) affect only a part of the seller's capacity to perform, he must allocate production and deliveries among his customers but may at his option include regular customers not then under contract as well as his own requirements for further manufacture. He may so allocate in any manner which is fair and reasonable.

(c) The seller must notify the buyer seasonably that there will be delay or non-delivery and, when allocation is required under paragraph (b), of the estimated quota thus made available for the buyer.

§ 2—616. Procedure on Notice Claiming Excuse.

(1) Where the buyer receives notification of a material or indefinite delay or an allocation justified under the preceding section he may by written notification to the seller as to any delivery concerned, and where the prospective deficiency substantially impairs the value of the whole contract under the provisions of this Article relating to breach of installment contracts (Section 2—612), then also as to the whole,

> (a) terminate and thereby discharge any unexecuted portion of the contract; or

> (b) modify the contract by agreeing to take his available quota in substitution.

(2) If after receipt of such notification from the seller the buyer fails so to modify the contract within a reasonable time not exceeding thirty days the contract lapses with respect to any deliveries affected.

(3) The provisions of this section may not be negated by agreement except in so far as the seller has assumed a greater obligation under the preceding section.

Part 7 Remedies

§ 2—701. Remedies for Breach of Collateral Contracts Not Impaired.

Remedies for breach of any obligation or promise collateral or ancillary to a contract for sale are not impaired by the provisions of this Article.

§ 2—702. Seller's Remedies on Discovery of Buyer's Insolvency.

(1) Where the seller discovers the buyer to be insolvent he may refuse delivery except for cash including payment for all goods theretofore delivered under the contract, and stop delivery under this Article (Section 2—705).

(2) Where the seller discovers that the buyer has received goods on credit while insolvent he may reclaim the goods upon demand made within ten days after the receipt, but if misrepresentation of solvency has been made to the particular seller in writing within three months before delivery the ten day limitation does not apply. Except as provided in this subsection the seller may not base a right to reclaim goods on the buyer's fraudulent or innocent misrepresentation of solvency or of intent to pay.

(3) The seller's right to reclaim under subsection (2) is subject to the rights of a buyer in ordinary course or other good faith purchaser under this Article (Section 2—403). Successful reclamation of goods excludes all other remedies with respect to them.

§ 2—703. Seller's Remedies in General.

Where the buyer wrongfully rejects or revokes acceptance of goods or fails to make a payment due on or before delivery or repudiates with respect to a part or the whole, then with respect to any goods directly affected and, if the breach is of the whole contract (Section 2—612), then also with respect to the whole undelivered balance, the aggrieved seller may

(a) withhold delivery of such goods;

(b) stop delivery by any bailee as hereafter provided (Section 2—705);

(c) proceed under the next section respecting goods still unidentified to the contract;

(d) resell and recover damages as hereafter provided (Section 2—706);

(e) recover damages for non-acceptance (Section 2—708) or in a proper case the price (Section 2—709);

(f) cancel.

§ 2—704. Seller's Right to Identify Goods to the Contract Notwithstanding Breach or to Salvage Unfinished Goods.

(1) An aggrieved seller under the preceding section may

(a) identify to the contract conforming goods not already identified if at the time he learned of the breach they are in his possession or control;

(b) treat as the subject of resale goods which have demonstrably been intended for the particular contract even though those goods are unfinished.

(2) Where the goods are unfinished an aggrieved seller may in the exercise of reasonable commercial judgment for the purposes of avoiding loss and of effective realization either complete the manufacture and wholly identify the goods to the contract or cease manufacture and resell for scrap or salvage value or proceed in any other reasonable manner.

§ 2—705. Seller's Stoppage of Delivery in Transit or Otherwise.

(1) The seller may stop delivery of goods in the possession of a carrier or other bailee when he discovers the buyer to be insolvent (Section 2—702) and may stop delivery of carload, truckload, planeload or larger shipments of express or freight when the buyer repudiates or fails to make a payment due before delivery or if for any other reason the seller has a right to withhold or reclaim the goods.

(2) As against such buyer the seller may stop delivery until

(a) receipt of the goods by the buyer; or

(b) acknowledgment to the buyer by any bailee of the goods except a carrier that the bailee holds the goods for the buyer; or

(c) such acknowledgment to the buyer by a carrier by reshipment or as warehouseman; or

(d) negotiation to the buyer of any negotiable document of title covering the goods.

(3) (a) To stop delivery the seller must so notify as to enable the bailee by reasonable diligence to prevent delivery of the goods.

(b) After such notification the bailee must hold and deliver the goods according to the directions of the seller but the seller is liable to the bailee for any ensuing charges or damages.

(c) If a negotiable document of title has been issued for goods the bailee is not obliged to obey a notification to stop until surrender of the document.

(d) A carrier who has issued a non-negotiable bill of lading is not obliged to obey a notification to stop received from a person other than the consignor.

§ 2—706. Seller's Resale Including Contract for Resale.

(1) Under the conditions stated in Section 2—703 on seller's remedies, the seller may resell the goods concerned or the undelivered balance thereof. Where the resale is made in good faith and in a commercially reasonable manner the seller may recover the difference between the resale price and the contract price together with any incidental damages allowed under the provisions of this Article (Section 2—710), but less expenses saved in consequence of the buyer's breach.

(2) Except as otherwise provided in subsection (3) or unless otherwise agreed resale may be at public or private sale including sale by way of one or more contracts to sell or of identification to an existing contract of the seller. Sale may be as a unit or in parcels and at any time and place and on any terms but every aspect of the sale including the method, manner, time, place and terms must be commercially reasonable. The resale must be reasonably identified as referring to the broken contract, but it is not necessary that the goods be in existence or that any or all of them have been identified to the contract before the breach.

(3) Where the resale is at private sale the seller must give the buyer reasonable notification of his intention to resell.

(4) Where the resale is at public sale

(a) only identified goods can be sold except where there is a recognized market for a public sale of futures in goods of the kind; and

(b) it must be made at a usual place or market for public sale if one is reasonably available and except in the case of goods which are perishable or threaten to decline in value speedily the seller must give the buyer reasonable notice of the time and place of the resale; and

(c) if the goods are not to be within the view of those attending the sale the notification of sale must state the place where the goods are located and provide for their reasonable inspection by prospective bidders; and

(d) the seller may buy.

(5) A purchaser who buys in good faith at a resale takes the goods free of any rights of the original buyer even though the seller fails to comply with one or more of the requirements of this section.

(6) The seller is not accountable to the buyer for any profit made on any resale. A person in the position of a seller (Section 2—707) or a buyer who has rightfully rejected or justifiably revoked acceptance must account for any excess over the amount of his security interest, as hereinafter defined (subsection (3) of Section 2—711).

§ 2—707. "Person in the Position of a Seller".

(1) A "person in the position of a seller" includes as against a principal an agent who has paid or become responsible for the price of goods on behalf of his principal or anyone who otherwise holds a security interest or other right in goods similar to that of a seller.

(2) A person in the position of a seller may as provided in this Article withhold or stop delivery (Section 2—705) and resell (Section 2—706) and recover incidental damages (Section 2—710).

§ 2—708. Seller's Damages for Non-Acceptance or Repudiation.

(1) Subject to subsection (2) and to the provisions of this Article with respect to proof of market price (Section 2—723), the measure of damages for non-acceptance or repudiation by the buyer is the difference between the market price at the time and place for tender and the unpaid contract price together with any incidental damages provided in this Article (Section 2—710), but less expenses saved in consequence of the buyer's breach.

(2) If the measure of damages provided in subsection (1) is inadequate to put the seller in as good a position as performance would have done then the measure of damages is the profit (including reasonable overhead) which the seller would have made from full performance by the buyer, together with any incidental damages provided in this Article (Section 2—710), due allowance for costs reasonably incurred and due credit for payments or proceeds of resale.

§ 2—709. Action for the Price.

(1) When the buyer fails to pay the price as it becomes due the seller may recover, together with any incidental damages under the next section, the price

(a) of goods accepted or of conforming goods lost or damaged within a commercially reasonable time after risk of their loss has passed to the buyer; and

(b) of goods identified to the contract if the seller is unable after reasonable effort to resell them at a reasonable price or the circumstances reasonably indicate that such effort will be unavailing.

(2) Where the seller sues for the price he must hold for the buyer any goods which have been identified to the contract and are still in his control except that if resale becomes possible he may resell them at any time prior to the collection of the judgment. The net proceeds of any such resale must be credited to the buyer and payment of the judgment entitles him to any goods not resold.

(3) After the buyer has wrongfully rejected or revoked acceptance of the goods or has failed to make a payment due or has repudiated (Section 2—610), a seller who is held not entitled to the price under this section shall nevertheless be awarded damages for non-acceptance under the preceding section.

§ 2—710. Seller's Incidental Damages.

Incidental damages to an aggrieved seller include any commercially reasonable charges, expenses or commissions incurred in stopping delivery, in the transportation, care and custody of goods after the buyer's breach, in connection with return or resale of the goods or otherwise resulting from the breach.

§ 2—711. Buyer's Remedies in General; Buyer's Security Interest in Rejected Goods.

(1) Where the seller fails to make delivery or repudiates or the buyer rightfully rejects or justifiably revokes acceptance then with respect to any goods involved, and with respect to the whole if the breach goes to the whole contract (Section 2—612), the buyer may cancel and whether or not he has done so may in addition to recovering so much of the price as has been paid

(a) "cover" and have damages under the next section as to all the goods affected whether or not they have been identified to the contract; or

(b) recover damages for non-delivery as provided in this Article (Section 2—713).

(2) Where the seller fails to deliver or repudiates the buyer may also

(a) if the goods have been identified recover them as provided in this Article (Section 2—502); or

(b) in a proper case obtain specific performance or replevy the goods as provided in this Article (Section 2—716).

(3) On rightful rejection or justifiable revocation of acceptance a buyer has a security interest in goods in his possession or control for any payments made on their price and any expenses reasonably incurred in their inspection, receipt, transportation, care and custody and may hold such goods and resell them in like manner as an aggrieved seller (Section 2—706).

§ 2—712. "Cover"; Buyer's Procurement of Substitute Goods.

(1) After a breach within the preceding section the buyer may "cover" by making in good faith and without unreasonable delay any reasonable purchase of or contract to purchase goods in substitution for those due from the seller.

(2) The buyer may recover from the seller as damages the difference between the cost of cover and the contract price together with any incidental or consequential damages as hereinafter defined (Section 2—715), but less expenses saved in consequence of the seller's breach.

(3) Failure of the buyer to effect cover within this section does not bar him from any other remedy.

§ 2—713. Buyer's Damages for Non-Delivery or Repudiation.

(1) Subject to the provisions of this Article with respect to proof of market price (Section 2—723), the measure of damages for non-delivery or repudiation by the seller is the difference between the market price at the time when the buyer learned of the breach and the contract price together with any incidental and consequential damages provided in this Article (Section 2—715), but less expenses saved in consequence of the seller's breach.

(2) Market price is to be determined as of the place for tender or, in cases of rejection after arrival or revocation of acceptance, as of the place of arrival.

§ 2—714. Buyer's Damages for Breach in Regard to Accepted Goods.

(1) Where the buyer has accepted goods and given notification (subsection (3) of Section 2—607) he may recover as damages for any non-conformity of tender the loss resulting in the ordinary course of events from the seller's breach as determined in any manner which is reasonable.

(2) The measure of damages for breach of warranty is the difference at the time and place of acceptance between the value of the goods accepted and the value they would have had if they had been as warranted, unless special circumstances show proximate damages of a different amount.

(3) In a proper case any incidental and consequential damages under the next section may also be recovered.

§ 2—715. Buyer's Incidental and Consequential Damages.

(1) Incidental damages resulting from the seller's breach include expenses reasonably incurred in inspection, receipt, transportation and care and custody of goods rightfully rejected, any commercially reasonable charges, expenses or commissions in connection with effecting cover and any other reasonable expense incident to the delay or other breach.

(2) Consequential damages resulting from the seller's breach include

    (a) any loss resulting from general or particular requirements and needs of which the seller at the time of contracting had reason to know and which could not reasonably be prevented by cover or otherwise; and

    (b) injury to person or property proximately resulting from any breach of warranty.

§ 2—716. Buyer's Right to Specific Performance or Replevin.

(1) Specific performance may be decreed where the goods are unique or in other proper circumstances.

(2) The decree for specific performance may include such terms and conditions as to payment of the price, damages, or other relief as the court may deem just.

(3) The buyer has a right of replevin for goods identified to the contract if after reasonable effort he is unable to effect cover for such goods or the circumstances reasonably indicate that such effort will be unavailing or if the goods have been shipped under reservation and satisfaction of the security interest in them has been made or tendered.

§ 2—717. Deduction of Damages From the Price.

The buyer on notifying the seller of his intention to do so may deduct all or any part of the damages resulting from any breach of the contract from any part of the price still due under the same contract.

§ 2—718. Liquidation or Limitation of Damages; Deposits.

(1) Damages for breach by either party may be liquidated in the agreement but only at an amount which is reasonable in the light of the anticipated or actual harm caused by the breach, the difficulties of proof of loss, and the inconvenience or nonfeasibility of otherwise obtaining an adequate remedy. A term fixing unreasonably large liquidated damages is void as a penalty.

(2) Where the seller justifiably withholds delivery of goods because of the buyer's breach, the buyer is entitled to restitution of any amount by which the sum of his payments exceeds

    (a) the amount to which the seller is entitled by virtue of terms liquidating the seller's damages in accordance with subsection (1), or

    (b) in the absence of such terms, twenty per cent of the value of the total performance for which the buyer is obligated under the contract or $500, whichever is smaller.

(3) The buyer's right to restitution under subsection (2) is subject to offset to the extent that the seller establishes

    (a) a right to recover damages under the provisions of this Article other than subsection (1), and

    (b) the amount or value of any benefits received by the buyer directly or indirectly by reason of the contract.

(4) Where a seller has received payment in goods their reasonable value or the proceeds of their resale shall be treated as payments for the purposes of subsection (2); but

if the seller has notice of the buyer's breach before reselling goods received in part performance, his resale is subject to the conditions laid down in this Article on resale by an aggrieved seller (Section 2—706).

§ 2—719. **Contractual Modification or Limitation of Remedy.**

(1) Subject to the provisions of subsections (2) and (3) of this section and of the preceding section on liquidation and limitation of damages,

(a) the agreement may provide for remedies in addition to or in substitution for those provided in this Article and may limit or alter the measure of damages recoverable under this Article, as by limiting the buyer's remedies to return of the goods and repayment of the price or to repair and replacement of non-conforming goods or parts; and

(b) resort to a remedy as provided is optional unless the remedy is expressly agreed to be exclusive, in which case it is the sole remedy.

(2) Where circumstances cause an exclusive or limited remedy to fail of its essential purpose, remedy may be had as provided in this Act.

(3) Consequential damages may be limited or excluded unless the limitation or exclusion is unconscionable. Limitation of consequential damages for injury to the person in the case of consumer goods is prima facie unconscionable but limitation of damages where the loss is commercial is not.

§ 2—720. **Effect of "Cancellation" or "Rescission" on Claims for Antecedent Breach.**

Unless the contrary intention clearly appears, expressions of "cancellation" or "rescission" of the contract or the like shall not be construed as a renunciation or discharge of any claim in damages for an antecedent breach.

§ 2—721. **Remedies for Fraud.**

Remedies for material misrepresentation or fraud include all remedies available under this Article for non-fraudulent breach. Neither rescission or a claim for rescission of the contract for sale nor rejection or return of the goods shall bar or be deemed inconsistent with a claim for damages or other remedy.

§ 2—722. **Who Can Sue Third Parties for Injury to Goods.**

Where a third party so deals with goods which have been identified to a contract for sale as to cause actionable injury to a party to that contract

(a) a right of action against the third party is in either party to the contract for sale who has title to or a security interest or a special property or an insurable interest in the goods; and if the goods have been destroyed or converted a right

of action is also in the party who either bore the risk of loss under the contract for sale or has since the injury assumed that risk as against the other;

(b) if at the time of the injury the party plaintiff did not bear the risk of loss as against the other party to the contract for sale and there is no arrangement between them for disposition of the recovery, his suit or settlement is, subject to his own interest, as a fiduciary for the other party to the contract;

(c) either party may with the consent of the other sue for the benefit of whom it may concern.

§ 2—723. **Proof of Market Price: Time and Place.**

(1) If an action based on anticipatory repudiation comes to trial before the time for performance with respect to some or all of the goods, any damages based on market price (Section 2—708 or Section 2—713) shall be determined according to the price of such goods prevailing at the time when the aggrieved party learned of the repudiation.

(2) If evidence of a price prevailing at the times or places described in this Article is not readily available the price prevailing within any reasonable time before or after the time described or at any other place which in commercial judgment or under usage of trade would serve as a reasonable substitute for the one described may be used, making any proper allowance for the cost of transporting the goods to or from such other place.

(3) Evidence of a relevant price prevailing at a time or place other than the one described in this Article offered by one party is not admissible unless and until he has given the other party such notice as the court finds sufficient to prevent unfair surprise.

§ 2—724. **Admissibility of Market Quotations.**

Whenever the prevailing price or value of any goods regularly bought and sold in any established commodity market is in issue, reports in official publications or trade journals or in newspapers or periodicals of general circulation published as the reports of such market shall be admissible in evidence. The circumstances of the preparation of such a report may be shown to affect its weight but not its admissibility.

§ 2—725. **Statute of Limitations in Contracts for Sale.**

(1) An action for breach of any contract for sale must be commenced within four years after the cause of action has accrued. By the original agreement the parties may reduce the period of limitation to not less than one year but may not extend it.

(2) A cause of action accrues when the breach occurs, regardless of the aggrieved party's lack of knowledge of the breach. A breach of warranty occurs when tender of delivery is made, except that where a warranty explicitly extends to

future performance of the goods and discovery of the breach must await the time of such performance the cause of action accrues when the breach is or should have been discovered.

(3) Where an action commenced within the time limited by subsection (1) is so terminated as to leave available a remedy by another action for the same breach such other action may be commenced after the expiration of the time limited and within six months after the termination of the first action unless the termination resulted from voluntary discontinuance or from dismissal for failure or neglect to prosecute.

(4) This section does not alter the law on tolling of the statute of limitations nor does it apply to causes of action which have accrued before this Act becomes effective.

Article 2A
LEASES

Part 1 General Provisions

§ 2A—101. Short Title.

This Article shall be known and may be cited as the Uniform Commercial Code—Leases.

§ 2A—102. Scope.

This Article applies to any transaction, regardless of form, that creates a lease.

§ 2A—103. Definitions and Index of Definitions.

(1) In this Article unless the context otherwise requires:

(a) "Buyer in ordinary course of business" means a person who in good faith and without knowledge that the sale to him [or her] is in violation of the ownership rights or security interest or leasehold interest of a third party in the goods, buys in ordinary course from a person in the business of selling goods of that kind but does not include a pawnbroker. "Buying" may be for cash or by exchange of other property or on secured or unsecured credit and includes receiving goods or documents of title under a pre-existing contract for sale but does not include a transfer in bulk or as security for or in total or partial satisfaction of a money debt.

(b) "Cancellation" occurs when either party puts an end to the lease contract for default by the other party.

(c) "Commercial unit" means such a unit of goods as by commercial usage is a single whole for purposes of lease and division of which materially impairs its character or value on the market or in use. A commercial unit may be a single article, as a machine, or a set of articles, as a suite of furniture or a line of machinery, or a quantity, as a gross or carload, or any other unit treated in use or in the relevant market as a single whole.

(d) "Conforming" goods or performance under a lease contract means goods or performance that are in accordance with the obligations under the lease contract.

(e) "Consumer lease" means a lease that a lessor regularly engaged in the business of leasing or selling makes to a lessee—who is an individual and who takes under the lease primarily for a personal, family, or household purpose [if the total payments to be made under the lease contract, excluding payments for options to renew or buy, do not exceed $_____].

(f) "Fault" means wrongful act, omission, breach, or default.

(g) "Finance lease" means a lease with respect to which:

(i) the lessor does not select, manufacture or supply the goods;

(ii) the lessor acquires the goods or the right to possession and use of the goods in connection with the lease; and

(iii) one of the following occurs:

(A) the lessee receives a copy of the contract by which the lessor acquired the goods or the right to possession and use of the goods before signing the lease contract;

(B) the lessee's approval of the contract by which the lessor acquired the goods or the right to possession and use of the goods is a condition to effectiveness of the lease contract;

(C) the lessee, before signing the lease contract, receives an accurate and complete statement designating the promises and warranties, and any disclaimers of warranties, limitations or modifications of remedies, or liquidated damages, including those of a third party, such as the manufacturer of the goods, provided to the lessor by the person supplying the goods in connection with or as part of the contract by which the lessor acquired the goods or the right to possession and use of the goods; or

(D) if the lease is not a consumer lease, the lessor, before the lessee signs the lease contract, informs the lessee in writing (a) of the identity of the person supplying the goods to the lessor, unless the lessee has selected that person and directed the lessor to acquire the goods or the right to possession and use of the goods from that person, (b) that the lessee is entitled under this Article to the promises and warranties, including those of any third party, provided to the lessor by the person supplying the goods in connection with or as part of the contract by which the lessor acquired the goods or the right to possession and use of the goods, and (c) that the lessee may communicate with the person supplying the goods to the lessor and receive an accurate and complete statement of those promises and warranties, including any disclaimers and limitations of them or of remedies.

(h) "Goods" means all things that are movable at the time of identification to the lease contract, or are fixtures (Section 2A—309), but the term does not include money, documents, instruments, accounts, chattel paper, general intangibles, or minerals or the like, including oil and gas, before extraction. The term also includes the unborn young of animals.

(i) "Installment lease contract" means a lease contract that authorizes or requires the delivery of goods in separate lots to be separately accepted, even though the lease contract contains a clause "each delivery is a separate lease" or its equivalent.

(j) "Lease" means a transfer of the right to possession and use of goods for a term in return for consideration, but a sale, including a sale on approval or a sale or return, or retention or creation of a security interest is not a lease. Unless the context clearly indicates otherwise, the term includes a sublease.

(k) "Lease agreement" means the bargain, with respect to the lease, of the lessor and the lessee in fact as found in their language or by implication from other circumstances including course of dealing or usage of trade or course of performance as provided in this Article. Unless the context clearly indicates otherwise, the term includes a sublease agreement.

(l) "Lease contract" means the total legal obligation that results from the lease agreement as affected by this Article and any other applicable rules of law. Unless the context clearly indicates otherwise, the term includes a sublease contract.

(m) "Leasehold interest" means the interest of the lessor or the lessee under a lease contract.

(n) "Lessee" means a person who acquires the right to possession and use of goods under a lease. Unless the context clearly indicates otherwise, the term includes a sublessee.

(o) "Lessee in ordinary course of business" means a person who in good faith and without knowledge that the lease to him [or her] is in violation of the ownership rights or security interest or leasehold interest of a third party in the goods leases in ordinary course from a person in the business of selling or leasing goods of that kind but does not include a pawnbroker. "Leasing" may be for cash or by exchange of other property or on secured or unsecured credit and includes receiving goods or documents of title under a pre-existing lease contract but does not include a transfer in bulk or as security for or in total or partial satisfaction of a money debt.

(p) "Lessor" means a person who transfers the right to possession and use of goods under a lease. Unless the context clearly indicates otherwise, the term includes a sublessor.

(q) "Lessor's residual interest" means the lessor's interest in the goods after expiration, termination, or cancellation of the lease contract.

(r) "Lien" means a charge against or interest in goods to secure payment of a debt or performance of an obligation, but the term does not include a security interest.

(s) "Lot" means a parcel or a single article that is the subject matter of a separate lease or delivery, whether or not it is sufficient to perform the lease contract.

(t) "Merchant lessee" means a lessee that is a merchant with respect to goods of the kind subject to the lease.

(u) "Present value" means the amount as of a date certain of one or more sums payable in the future, discounted to the date certain. The discount is determined by the interest rate specified by the parties if the rate was not manifestly unreasonable at the time the transaction was entered into; otherwise, the discount is determined by a commercially reasonable rate that takes into account the facts and circumstances of each case at the time the transaction was entered into.

(v) "Purchase" includes taking by sale, lease, mortgage, security interest, pledge, gift, or any other voluntary transaction creating an interest in goods.

(w) "Sublease" means a lease of goods the right to possession and use of which was acquired by the lessor as a lessee under an existing lease.

(x) "Supplier" means a person from whom a lessor buys or leases goods to be leased under a finance lease.

(y) "Supply contract" means a contract under which a lessor buys or leases goods to be leased.

(z) "Termination" occurs when either party pursuant to a power created by agreement or law puts an end to the lease contract otherwise than for default.

(2) Other definitions applying to this Article and the sections in which they appear are:

"Accessions". Section 2A—310(1).
"Construction mortgage". Section 2A—309(1)(d).
"Encumbrance". Section 2A—309(1)(e).
"Fixtures". Section 2A—309(1)(a).
"Fixture filing". Section 2A—309(1)(b).
"Purchase money lease". Section 2A—309(1)(c).

(3) The following definitions in other Articles apply to this Article:

"Account". Section 9—106.
"Between merchants". Section 2—104(3).

"Buyer". Section 2—103(1)(a).
"Chattel paper". Section 9—105(1)(b).
"Consumer goods". Section 9—109(1).
"Document". Section 9—105(1)(f).
"Entrusting". Section 2—403(3).
"General intangibles". Section 9—106.
"Good faith". Section 2—103(1)(b).
"Instrument". Section 9—105(1)(i).
"Merchant". Section 2—104(1).
"Mortgage". Section 9—105(1)(j).
"Pursuant to commitment". Section 9—105(1)(k).
"Receipt". Section 2—103(1)(c).
"Sale". Section 2—106(1).
"Sale on approval". Section 2—326.
"Sale or return". Section 2—326.
"Seller". Section 2—103(1)(d).

(4) In addition, Article 1 contains general definitions and principles of construction and interpretation applicable throughout this Article.

§ 2A—104. **Leases Subject to Other Law.**

(1) A lease, although subject to this Article, is also subject to any applicable:

(a) certificate of title statute of this State;

(list any certificate of title statutes covering automobiles, trailers, mobile homes, boats, farm tractors, and the like);

(b) certificate of title statute of another jurisdiction (Section 2A—105); or

(c) consumer protection statute of this State, or final consumer protection decision of a court of this State existing on the effective date of this Article.

(2) In case of conflict between this Article, other than Sections 2A—105, 2A—304(3), and 2A—305(3), and a statute or decision referred to in subsection (1), the statute or decision controls.

(3) Failure to comply with an applicable law has only the effect specified therein.

§ 2A—105. **Territorial Application of Article to Goods Covered by Certificate of Title.**

Subject to the provisions of Sections 2A—304(3) and 2A—305(3), with respect to goods covered by a certificate of title issued under a statute of this State or of another jurisdiction, compliance and the effect of compliance or non-compliance with a certificate of title statute are governed by the law (including the conflict of laws rules) of the jurisdiction issuing the certificate until the earlier of (a) surrender of the certificate, or (b) four months after the goods are removed from that jurisdiction and thereafter until a new certificate of title is issued by another jurisdiction.

§ 2A—106. **Limitation on Power of Parties to Consumer Lease to Choose Applicable Law and Judicial Forum.**

(1) If the law chosen by the parties to a consumer lease is that of a jurisdiction other than a jurisdiction in which the lessee resides at the time the lease agreement becomes enforceable or within 30 days thereafter or in which the goods are to be used, the choice is not enforceable.

(2) If the judicial forum chosen by the parties to a consumer lease is a forum that would not otherwise have jurisdiction over the lessee, the choice is not enforceable.

§ 2A—107. **Waiver or Renunciation of Claim or Right After Default.**

Any claim or right arising out of an alleged default or breach of warranty may be discharged in whole or in part without consideration by a written waiver or renunciation signed and delivered by the aggrieved party.

§ 2A—108. **Unconscionability.**

(1) If the court as a matter of law finds a lease contract or any clause of a lease contract to have been unconscionable at the time it was made the court may refuse to enforce the lease contract, or it may enforce the remainder of the lease contract without the unconscionable clause, or it may so limit the application of any unconscionable clause as to avoid any unconscionable result.

(2) With respect to a consumer lease, if the court as a matter of law finds that a lease contract or any clause of a lease contract has been induced by unconscionable conduct or that unconscionable conduct has occurred in the collection of a claim arising from a lease contract, the court may grant appropriate relief.

(3) Before making a finding of unconscionability under subsection (1) or (2), the court, on its own motion or that of a party, shall afford the parties a reasonable opportunity to present evidence as to the setting, purpose, and effect of the lease contract or clause thereof, or of the conduct.

(4) In an action in which the lessee claims unconscionability with respect to a consumer lease:

(a) If the court finds unconscionability under subsection (1) or (2), the court shall award reasonable attorney's fees to the lessee.

(b) If the court does not find unconscionability and the lessee claiming unconscionability has brought or maintained an action he [or she] knew to be groundless, the court shall award reasonable attorney's fees to the party against whom the claim is made.

(c) In determining attorney's fees, the amount of the recovery on behalf of the claimant under subsections (1) and (2) is not controlling.

§ 2A—109. **Option to Accelerate at Will.**

(1) A term providing that one party or his [or her] successor in interest may accelerate payment or performance or require collateral or additional collateral "at will" or "when

he [or she] deems himself [or herself] insecure'' or in words of similar import must be construed to mean that he [or she] has power to do so only if he [or she] in good faith believes that the prospect of payment or performance is impaired.

(2) With respect to a consumer lease, the burden of establishing good faith under subsection (1) is on the party who exercised the power; otherwise the burden of establishing lack of good faith is on the party against whom the power has been exercised.

Part 2 Formation and Construction of Lease Contract

§ 2A—201. **Statute of Frauds.**

(1) A lease contract is not enforceable by way of action or defense unless:

(a) the total payments to be made under the lease contract, excluding payments for options to renew or buy, are less than $1,000; or

(b) there is a writing, signed by the party against whom enforcement is sought or by that party's authorized agent, sufficient to indicate that a lease contract has been made between the parties and to describe the goods leased and the lease term.

(2) Any description of leased goods or of the lease term is sufficient and satisfies subsection (1)(b), whether or not it is specific, if it reasonably identifies what is described.

(3) A writing is not insufficient because it omits or incorrectly states a term agreed upon, but the lease contract is not enforceable under subsection (1)(b) beyond the lease term and the quantity of goods shown in this writing.

(4) A lease contract that does not satisfy the requirements of subsection (1), but which is valid in other respects, is enforceable:

(a) if the goods are to be specially manufactured or obtained for the lessee and are not suitable for lease or sale to others in the ordinary course of the lessor's business, and the lessor, before notice of repudiation is received and under circumstances that reasonably indicate that the goods are for the lessee, has made either a substantial beginning of their manufacture or commitments for their procurement;

(b) if the party against whom enforcement is sought admits in that party's pleading, testimony or otherwise in court that a lease contract was made, but the lease contract is not enforceable under this provision beyond the quantity of goods admitted; or

(c) with respect to goods that have been received and accepted by the lessee.

(5) The lease term under a lease contract referred to in subsection (4) is:

(a) if there is a writing signed by the party against whom enforcement is sought or by that party's authorized agent specifying the lease term, the term so specified;

(b) if the party against whom enforcement is sought admits in that party's pleading, testimony, or otherwise in court a lease term, the term so admitted; or

(c) a reasonable lease term.

§ 2A—202. **Final Written Expression: Parol or Extrinsic Evidence.**

Terms with respect to which the confirmatory memoranda of the parties agree or which are otherwise set forth in a writing intended by the parties as a final expression of their agreement with respect to such terms as are included therein may not be contradicted by evidence of any prior agreement or of a contemporaneous oral agreement but may be explained or supplemented:

(a) by course of dealing or usage of trade or by course of performance; and

(b) by evidence of consistent additional terms unless the court finds the writing to have been intended also as a complete and exclusive statement of the terms of the agreement.

§ 2A—203. **Seals Inoperative.**

The affixing of a seal to a writing evidencing a lease contract or an offer to enter into a lease contract does not render the writing a sealed instrument and the law with respect to sealed instruments does not apply to the lease contract or offer.

§ 2A—204. **Formation in General.**

(1) A lease contract may be made in any manner sufficient to show agreement, including conduct by both parties which recognizes the existence of a lease contract.

(2) An agreement sufficient to constitute a lease contract may be found although the moment of its making is undetermined.

(3) Although one or more terms are left open, a lease contract does not fail for indefiniteness if the parties have intended to make a lease contract and there is a reasonably certain basis for giving an appropriate remedy.

§ 2A—205. **Firm Offers.**

An offer by a merchant to lease goods to or from another person in a signed writing that by its terms gives assurance it will be held open is not revocable, for lack of consideration, during the time stated or, if no time is stated, for a reasonable time, but in no event may the period of irrevocability exceed 3 months. Any such term of assurance on a form supplied by the offeree must be separately signed by the offeror.

§ 2A—206. Offer and Acceptance in Formation of Lease Contract.

(1) Unless otherwise unambiguously indicated by the language or circumstances, an offer to make a lease contract must be construed as inviting acceptance in any manner and by any medium reasonable in the circumstances.

(2) If the beginning of a requested performance is a reasonable mode of acceptance, an offeror who is not notified of acceptance within a reasonable time may treat the offer as having lapsed before acceptance.

§ 2A—207. Course of Performance or Practical Construction.

(1) If a lease contract involves repeated occasions for performance by either party with knowledge of the nature of the performance and opportunity for objection to it by the other, any course of performance accepted or acquiesced in without objection is relevant to determine the meaning of the lease agreement.

(2) The express terms of a lease agreement and any course of performance, as well as any course of dealing and usage of trade, must be construed whenever reasonable as consistent with each other; but if that construction is unreasonable, express terms control course of performance, course of performance controls both course of dealing and usage of trade, and course of dealing controls usage of trade.

(3) Subject to the provisions of Section 2A—208 on modification and waiver, course of performance is relevant to show a waiver or modification of any term inconsistent with the course of performance.

§ 2A—208. Modification, Rescission and Waiver.

(1) An agreement modifying a lease contract needs no consideration to be binding.

(2) A signed lease agreement that excludes modification or rescission except by a signed writing may not be otherwise modified or rescinded, but, except as between merchants, such a requirement on a form supplied by a merchant must be separately signed by the other party.

(3) Although an attempt at modification or rescission does not satisfy the requirements of subsection (2), it may operate as a waiver.

(4) A party who has made a waiver affecting an executory portion of a lease contract may retract the waiver by reasonable notification received by the other party that strict performance will be required of any term waived, unless the retraction would be unjust in view of a material change of position in reliance on the waiver.

§ 2A—209. Lessee under Finance Lease as Beneficiary of Supply Contract.

(1) The benefit of the supplier's promises to the lessor under the supply contract and of all warranties, whether express or implied, including those of any third party provided in connection with or as part of the supply contract, extends to the lessee to the extent of the lessee's leasehold interest under a finance lease related to the supply contract, but is subject to the terms of the warranty and of the supply contract and all defenses or claims arising therefrom.

(2) The extension of the benefit of the supplier's promises and of warranties to the lessee (Section 2A—209(1)) does not: (i) modify the rights and obligations of the parties to the supply contract, whether arising therefrom or otherwise, or (ii) impose any duty or liability under the supply contract on the lessee.

(3) Any modification or rescission of the supply contract by the supplier and the lessor is effective between the supplier and the lessee unless, before the modification or rescission, the supplier has received notice that the lessee has entered into a finance lease related to the supply contract. If the modification or rescission is effective between the supplier and the lessee, the lessor is deemed to have assumed, in addition to the obligations of the lessor to the lessee under the lease contract, promises of the supplier to the lessor and warranties that were so modified or rescinded as they existed and were available to the lessee before modification or rescission.

(4) In addition to the extension of the benefit of the supplier's promises and of warranties to the lessee under subsection (1), the lessee retains all rights that the lessee may have against the supplier which arise from an agreement between the lessee and the supplier or under other law.

§ 2A—210. Express Warranties.

(1) Express warranties by the lessor are created as follows:

(a) Any affirmation of fact or promise made by the lessor to the lessee which relates to the goods and becomes part of the basis of the bargain creates an express warranty that the goods will conform to the affirmation or promise.

(b) Any description of the goods which is made part of the basis of the bargain creates an express warranty that the goods will conform to the description.

(c) Any sample or model that is made part of the basis of the bargain creates an express warranty that the whole of the goods will conform to the sample or model.

(2) It is not necessary to the creation of an express warranty that the lessor use formal words, such as ''warrant'' or ''guarantee,'' or that the lessor have a specific intention to make a warranty, but an affirmation merely of the value of the goods or a statement purporting to be merely the lessor's opinion or commendation of the goods does not create a warranty.

§ 2A—211. Warranties Against Interference and Against Infringement; Lessee's Obligation Against Infringement.

(1) There is in a lease contract a warranty that for the lease term no person holds a claim to or interest in the goods that arose from an act or omission of the lessor, other than a claim by way of infringement or the like, which will interfere with the lessee's enjoyment of its leasehold interest.

(2) Except in a finance lease there is in a lease contract by a lessor who is a merchant regularly dealing in goods of the kind a warranty that the goods are delivered free of the rightful claim of any person by way of infringement or the like.

(3) A lessee who furnishes specifications to a lessor or a supplier shall hold the lessor and the supplier harmless against any claim by way of infringement or the like that arises out of compliance with the specifications.

§ 2A—212. Implied Warranty of Merchantability.

(1) Except in a finance lease, a warranty that the goods will be merchantable is implied in a lease contract if the lessor is a merchant with respect to goods of that kind.

(2) Goods to be merchantable must be at least such as

(a) pass without objection in the trade under the description in the lease agreement;

(b) in the case of fungible goods, are of fair average quality within the description;

(c) are fit for the ordinary purposes for which goods of that type are used;

(d) run, within the variation permitted by the lease agreement, of even kind, quality, and quantity within each unit and among all units involved;

(e) are adequately contained, packaged, and labeled as the lease agreement may require; and

(f) conform to any promises or affirmations of fact made on the container or label.

(3) Other implied warranties may arise from course of dealing or usage of trade.

§ 2A—213. Implied Warranty of Fitness for Particular Purpose.

Except in a finance of lease, if the lessor at the time the lease contract is made has reason to know of any particular purpose for which the goods are required and that the lessee is relying on the lessor's skill or judgment to select or furnish suitable goods, there is in the lease contract an implied warranty that the goods will be fit for that purpose.

§ 2A—214. Exclusion or Modification of Warranties.

(1) Words or conduct relevant to the creation of an express warranty and words or conduct tending to negate or limit a warranty must be construed wherever reasonable as consistent with each other; but, subject to the provisions of Section 2A—202 on parol or extrinsic evidence, negation or limitation is inoperative to the extent that the construction is unreasonable.

(2) Subject to subsection (3), to exclude or modify the implied warranty of merchantability or any part of it the language must mention ''merchantability'', be by a writing, and be conspicuous. Subject to subsection (3), to exclude or modify any implied warranty of fitness the exclusion must be by a writing and be conspicuous. Language to exclude all implied warranties of fitness is sufficient if it is conspicuous and states, for example, ''There is no warranty that the goods will be fit for a particular purpose''.

(3) Notwithstanding subsection (2), but subject to subsection (4),

(a) unless the circumstances indicate otherwise, all implied warranties are excluded by expressions like ''as is'' or ''with all faults'' or by other language that in common understanding calls the lessee's attention to the exclusion of warranties and makes plain that there is no implied warranty, and is conspicuous;

(b) if the lessee before entering into the lease contract has examined the goods or the sample or model as fully as desired or has refused to examine the goods, there is no implied warranty with regard to defects that an examination ought in the circumstances to have revealed; and

(c) an implied warranty may also be excluded or modified by course of dealing, course of performance, or usage of trade.

(4) To exclude or modify a warranty against interference or against infringement (Section 2A—211) or any part of it, the language must be specific, be by a writing, and be conspicuous, unless the circumstances, including course of performance, course of dealing, or usage of trade, give the lessee reason to know that the goods are being leased subject to a claim or interest of any person.

§ 2A—215. Cumulation and Conflict of Warranties Express or Implied.

Warranties, whether express or implied, must be construed as consistent with each other and as cumulative, but if that construction is unreasonable, the intention of the parties determines which warranty is dominant. In ascertaining that intention the following rules apply:

(a) Exact or technical specifications displace an inconsistent sample or model or general language of description.

(b) A sample from an existing bulk displaces inconsistent general language of description.

(c) Express warranties displace inconsistent implied warranties other than an implied warranty of fitness for a particular purpose.

§ 2A—216. Third-Party Beneficiaries of Express and Implied Warranties.

Alternative A

A warranty to or for the benefit of a lessee under this Article, whether express or implied, extends to any natural person who is in the family or household of the lessee or who is a guest in the lessee's home if it is reasonable to expect that such person may use, consume, or be affected by the goods and who is injured in person by breach of the warranty. This section does not displace principles of law and equity that extend a warranty to or for the benefit of a lessee to other persons. The operation of this section may not be excluded, modified, or limited, but an exclusion, modification, or limitation of the warranty, including any with respect to rights and remedies, effective against the lessee is also effective against any beneficiary designated under this section.

Alternative B

A warranty to or for the benefit of a lessee under this Article, whether express or implied, extends to any natural person who may reasonably be expected to use, consume, or be affected by the goods and who is injured in person by breach of the warranty. This section does not displace principles of law and equity that extend a warranty to or for the benefit of a lessee to other persons. The operation of this section may not be excluded, modified, or limited, but an exclusion, modification, or limitation of the warranty, including any with respect to rights and remedies, effective against the lessee is also effective against the beneficiary designated under this section.

Alternative C

A warranty to or for the benefit of a lessee under this Article, whether express or implied, extends to any person who may reasonably be expected to use, consume, or be affected by the goods and who is injured by breach of the warranty. The operation of this section may not be excluded, modified, or limited with respect to injury to the person of an individual to whom the warranty extends, but an exclusion, modification, or limitation of the warranty, including any with respect to rights and remedies, effective against the lessee is also effective against the beneficiary designated under this section.

§ 2A—217. **Identification.**

Identification of goods as goods to which a lease contract refers may be made at any time and in any manner explicitly agreed to by the parties. In the absence of explicit agreement, identification occurs:

(a) when the lease contract is made if the lease contract is for a lease of goods that are existing and identified;

(b) when the goods are shipped, marked, or otherwise designated by the lessor as goods to which the lease contract refers, if the lease contract is for a lease of goods that are not existing and identified; or

(c) when the young are conceived, if the lease contract is for a lease of unborn young of animals.

§ 2A—218. **Insurance and Proceeds.**

(1) A lessee obtains an insurable interest when existing goods are identified to the lease contract even though the goods identified are nonconforming and the lessee has an option to reject them.

(2) If a lessee has an insurable interest only by reason of the lessor's identification of the goods, the lessor, until default or insolvency or notification to the lessee that identification is final, may substitute other goods for those identified.

(3) Notwithstanding a lessee's insurable interest under subsections (1) and (2), the lessor retains an insurable interest until an option to buy has been exercised by the lessee and risk of loss has passed to the lessee.

(4) Nothing in this section impairs any insurable interest recognized under any other statute or rule of law.

(5) The parties by agreement may determine that one or more parties have an obligation to obtain and pay for insurance covering the goods and by agreement may determine the beneficiary of the proceeds of the insurance.

§ 2A—219. **Risk of Loss.**

(1) Except in the case of a finance lease, risk of loss is retained by the lessor and does not pass to the lessee. In the case of a finance lease, risk of loss passes to the lessee.

(2) Subject to the provisions of this Article on the effect of default on risk of loss (Section 2A—220), if risk of loss is to pass to the lessee and the time of passage is not stated, the following rules apply:

(a) If the lease contract requires or authorizes the goods to be shipped by carrier,

(i) and it does not require delivery at a particular destination, the risk of loss passes to the lessee when the goods are duly delivered to the carrier; but

(ii) if it does require delivery at a particular destination and the goods are there duly tendered while in the possession of the carrier, the risk of loss passes to the lessee when the goods are there duly so tendered as to enable the lessee to take delivery.

(b) If the goods are held by a bailee to be delivered without being moved, the risk of loss passes to the lessee on acknowledgment by the bailee of the lessee's right to possession of the goods.

(c) In any case not within subsection (a) or (b), the risk of loss passes to the lessee on the lessee's receipt of the goods if the lessor, or, in the case of a finance lease, the supplier, is a merchant; otherwise the risk passes to the lessee on tender of delivery.

§ 2A—220. **Effect of Default on Risk of Loss.**

(1) Where risk of loss is to pass to the lessee and the time of passage is not stated:

(a) If a tender or delivery of goods so fails to conform to the lease contract as to give a right of rejection, the risk of their loss remains with the lessor, or, in the case of a finance lease, the supplier, until cure or acceptance.

(b) If the lessee rightfully revokes acceptance, he [or she], to the extent of any deficiency in his [or her] effective insurance coverage, may treat the risk of loss as having remained with the lessor from the beginning.

(2) Whether or not risk of loss is to pass to the lessee, if the lessee as to conforming goods already identified to a lease contract repudiates or is otherwise in default under the lease contract, the lessor, or, in the case of a finance lease, the supplier, to the extent of any deficiency in his [or her] effective insurance coverage may treat the risk of loss as resting on the lessee for a commercially reasonable time.

§ 2A—221. Casualty to Identified Goods.

If a lease contract requires goods identified when the lease contract is made, and the goods suffer casualty without fault of the lessee, the lessor or the supplier before delivery, or the goods suffer casualty before risk of loss passes to the lessee pursuant to the lease agreement or Section 2A—219, then:

(a) if the loss is total, the lease contract is avoided; and

(b) if the loss is partial or the goods have so deteriorated as to no longer conform to the lease contract, the lessee may nevertheless demand inspection and at his [or her] option either treat the lease contract as avoided or, except in a finance lease that is not a consumer lease, accept the goods with due allowance from the rent payable for the balance of the lease term for the deterioration or the deficiency in quantity but without further right against the lessor.

Part 3 Effect Of Lease Contract

§ 2A—301. Enforceability of Lease Contract.

Except as otherwise provided in this Article, a lease contract is effective and enforceable according to its terms between the parties, against purchasers of the goods and against creditors of the parties.

§ 2A—302. Title to and Possession of Goods.

Except as otherwise provided in this Article, each provision of this Article applies whether the lessor or a third party has title to the goods, and whether the lessor, the lessee, or a third party has possession of the goods, notwithstanding any statute or rule of law that possession or the absence of possession is fraudulent.

§ 2A—303. Alienability of Party's Interest under Lease Contract or of Lessor's Residual Interest in Goods; Delegation of Performance; Transfer of Rights.

(1) As used in this section, ''creation of a security interest'' includes the sale of a lease contract that is subject to Article 9, Secured Transactions, by reason of Section 9—102(1)(b).

(2) Except as provided in subsections (3) and (4), a provision in a lease agreement which (i) prohibits the voluntary or involuntary transfer, including a transfer by sale, sublease, creation or enforcement of a security interest, or attachment, levy, or other judicial process, of an interest of a party under the lease contract or of the lessor's residual interest in the goods, or (ii) makes such a transfer an event of default, gives rise to the rights and remedies provided in subsection (5), but a transfer that is prohibited or is an event of default under the lease agreement is otherwise effective.

(3) A provision in a lease agreement which (i) prohibits the creation or enforcement of a security interest in an interest of a party under the lease contract or in the lessor's residual interest in the goods, or (ii) makes such a transfer an event of default, is not enforceable unless, and then only to the extent that, there is an actual transfer by the lessee of the lessee's right of possession or use of the goods in violation of the provision or an actual delegation of a material performance of either party to the lease contract in violation of the provision. Neither the granting nor the enforcement of a security interest in (i) the lessor's interest under the lease contract or (ii) the lessor's residual interest in the goods is a transfer that materially impairs the prospect of obtaining return performance by, materially changes the duty of, or materially increases the burden or risk imposed on, the lessee within the purview of subsection (5) unless, and then only to the extent that, there is an actual delegation of a material performance of the lessor.

(4) A provision in a lease agreement which (i) prohibits a transfer of a right to damages for default with respect to the whole lease contract or of a right to payment arising out of the transferor's due performance of the transferor's entire obligation, or (ii) makes such a transfer an event of default, is not enforceable, and such a transfer is not a transfer that materially impairs the prospect of obtaining return performance by, materially changes the duty of, or materially increases the burden or risk imposed on, the other party to the lease contract within the purview of subsection (5).

(5) Subject to subsections (3) and (4):

(a) if a transfer is made which is made an event of default under a lease agreement, the party to the lease contract not making the transfer, unless that party waives the default or otherwise agrees, has the rights and remedies described in Section 2A—501(2);

(b) if paragraph (a) is not applicable and if a transfer is made that (i) is prohibited under a lease agreement or (ii) materially impairs the prospect of obtaining return performance by, materially changes the duty of, or materially increases the burden or risk imposed on, the other party to the lease contract, unless the party not making the transfer agrees at any time to the transfer in the lease contract or otherwise, then, except as limited by contract, (i) the transferor is liable to the party not making the transfer for damages caused by the transfer to the extent that the damages could not reasonably be prevented by the party not making the transfer and (ii) a court having jurisdiction may grant other appropriate relief, including cancellation of the lease contract or an injunction against the transfer.

(6) A transfer of ''the lease'' or of ''all my rights under the lease'', or a transfer in similar general terms, is a transfer of rights and, unless the language or the circumstances, as in a transfer for security, indicate the contrary, the transfer is a delegation of duties by the transferor to the transferee. Acceptance by the transferee constitutes a promise by the transferee to perform those duties. The promise is enforceable by either the transferor or the other party to the lease contract.

(7) Unless otherwise agreed by the lessor and the lessee, a delegation of performance does not relieve the transferor as against the other party of any duty to perform or of any liability for default.

(8) In a consumer lease, to prohibit the transfer of an interest of a party under the lease contract or to make a transfer an event of default, the language must be specific, by a writing, and conspicuous.

§ 2A—304. **Subsequent Lease of Goods by Lessor.**

(1) Subject to Section 2A—303, a subsequent lessee from a lessor of goods under an existing lease contract obtains, to the extent of the leasehold interest transferred, the leasehold interest in the goods that the lessor had or had power to transfer, and except as provided in subsection (2) and Section 2A—527(4), takes subject to the existing lease contract. A lessor with voidable title has power to transfer a good leasehold interest to a good faith subsequent lessee for value, but only to the extent set forth in the preceding sentence. If goods have been delivered under a transaction of purchase, the lessor has that power even though:

(a) the lessor's transferor was deceived as to the identity of the lessor;

(b) the delivery was in exchange for a check which is later dishonored;

(c) it was agreed that the transaction was to be a ''cash sale''; or

(d) the delivery was procured through fraud punishable as larcenous under the criminal law.

(2) A subsequent lessee in the ordinary course of business from a lessor who is a merchant dealing in goods of that kind to whom the goods were entrusted by the existing lessee of that lessor before the interest of the subsequent lessee became enforceable against that lessor obtains, to

the extent of the leasehold interest transferred, all of that lessor's and the existing lessee's rights to the goods, and takes free of the existing lease contract.

(3) A subsequent lessee from the lessor of goods that are subject to an existing lease contract and are covered by a certificate of title issued under a statute of this State or of another jurisdiction takes no greater rights than those provided both by this section and by the certificate of title statute.

§ 2A—305. **Sale or Sublease of Goods by Lessee.**

(1) Subject to the provisions of Section 2A—303, a buyer or sublessee from the lessee of goods under an existing lease contract obtains, to the extent of the interest transferred, the leasehold interest in the goods that the lessee had or had power to transfer, and except as provided in subsection (2) and Section 2A—511(4), takes subject to the existing lease contract. A lessee with a voidable leasehold interest has power to transfer a good leasehold interest to a good faith buyer for value or a good faith sublessee for value, but only to the extent set forth in the preceding sentence. When goods have been delivered under a transaction of lease the lessee has that power even though:

(a) the lessor was deceived as to the identity of the lessee;

(b) the delivery was in exchange for a check which is later dishonored; or

(c) the delivery was procured through fraud punishable as larcenous under the criminal law.

(2) A buyer in the ordinary course of business or a sublessee in the ordinary course of business from a lessee who is a merchant dealing in goods of that kind to whom the goods were entrusted by the lessor obtains, to the extent of the interest transferred, all of the lessor's and lessee's rights to the goods, and takes free of the existing lease contract.

(3) A buyer or sublessee from the lessee of goods that are subject to an existing lease contract and are covered by a certificate of title issued under a statute of this State or of another jurisdiction takes no greater rights than those provided both by this section and by the certificate of title statute.

§ 2A—306. **Priority of Certain Liens Arising by Operation of Law.**

If a person in the ordinary course of his [or her] business furnishes services or materials with respect to goods subject to a lease contract, a lien upon those goods in the possession of that person given by statute or rule of law for those materials or services takes priority over any interest of the lessor or lessee under the lease contract or this Article unless the lien is created by statute and the statute provides otherwise or unless the lien is created by rule of law and the rule of law provides otherwise.

§ 2A—307. **Priority of Liens Arising by Attachment or Levy on, Security Interests in, and Other Claims to Goods.**

(1) Except as otherwise provided in Section 2A—306, a creditor of a lessee takes subject to the lease contract.

(2) Except as otherwise provided in subsections (3) and (4) and in Sections 2A—306 and 2A—308, a creditor of a lessor takes subject to the lease contract unless:

(a) the creditor holds a lien that attached to the goods before the lease contract became enforceable;

(b) the creditor holds a security interest in the goods and the lessee did not give value and receive delivery of the goods without knowledge of the security interest; or

(c) the creditor holds a security interest in the goods which was perfected (Section 9—303) before the lease contract became enforceable.

(3) A lessee in the ordinary course of business takes the leasehold interest free of a security interest in the goods created by the lessor even though the security interest is perfected (Section 9—303) and the lessee knows of its existence.

(4) A lessee other than a lessee in the ordinary course of business takes the leasehold interest free of a security interest to the extent that it secures future advances made after the secured party acquires knowledge of the lease or more than 45 days after the lease contract becomes enforceable, whichever first occurs, unless the future advances are made pursuant to a commitment entered into without knowledge of the lease and before the expiration of the 45-day period.

§ 2A—308. **Special Rights of Creditors.**

(1) A creditor of a lessor in possession of goods subject to a lease contract may treat the lease contract as void if as against the creditor retention of possession by the lessor is fraudulent under any statute or rule of law, but retention of possession in good faith and current course of trade by the lessor for a commercially reasonable time after the lease contract becomes enforceable is not fraudulent.

(2) Nothing in this Article impairs the rights of creditors of a lessor if the lease contract (a) becomes enforceable, not in current course of trade but in satisfaction of or as security for a pre-existing claim for money, security, or the like, and (b) is made under circumstances which under any statute or rule of law apart from this Article would constitute the transaction a fraudulent transfer or voidable preference.

(3) A creditor of a seller may treat a sale or an identification of goods to a contract for sale as void if as against the creditor retention of possession by the seller is fraudulent under any statute or rule of law, but retention of possession of the goods pursuant to a lease contract entered into by the seller as lessee and the buyer as lessor in connection with the sale or identification of the goods is not fraudulent if the buyer bought for value and in good faith.

§ 2A—309. **Lessor's and Lessee's Rights When Goods Become Fixtures.**

(1) In this section:

(a) goods are "fixtures" when they become so related to particular real estate that an interest in them arises under real estate law;

(b) a "fixture filing" is the filing, in the office where a mortgage on the real estate would be filed or recorded, of a financing statement covering goods that are or are to become fixtures and conforming to the requirements of Section 9—402(5);

(c) a lease is a "purchase money lease" unless the lessee has possession or use of the goods or the right to possession or use of the goods before the lease agreement is enforceable;

(d) a mortgage is a "construction mortgage" to the extent it secures an obligation incurred for the construction of an improvement on land including the acquisition cost of the land, if the recorded writing so indicates; and

(e) "encumbrance" includes real estate mortgages and other liens on real estate and all other rights in real estate that are not ownership interests.

(2) Under this Article a lease may be of goods that are fixtures or may continue in goods that become fixtures, but no lease exists under this Article of ordinary building materials incorporated into an improvement on land.

(3) This Article does not prevent creation of a lease of fixtures pursuant to real estate law.

(4) The perfected interest of a lessor of fixtures has priority over a conflicting interest of an encumbrancer or owner of the real estate if:

(a) the lease is a purchase money lease, the conflicting interest of the encumbrancer or owner arises before the goods become fixtures, the interest of the lessor is perfected by a fixture filing before the goods become fixtures or within ten days thereafter, and the lessee has an interest of record in the real estate or is in possession of the real estate; or

(b) the interest of the lessor is perfected by a fixture filing before the interest of the encumbrancer or owner is of record, the lessor's interest has priority over any conflicting interest of a predecessor in title of the encumbrancer or owner, and the lessee has an interest of record in the real estate or is in possession of the real estate.

(5) The interest of a lessor of fixtures, whether or not perfected, has priority over the conflicting interest of an encumbrancer or owner of the real estate if:

(a) the fixtures are readily removable factory or office machines, readily removable equipment that is not primarily used or leased for use in the operation of the real estate, or readily removable replacements of domestic appliances that are goods subject to a consumer lease, and before the goods become fixtures the lease contract is enforceable; or

(b) the conflicting interest is a lien on the real estate obtained by legal or equitable proceedings after the lease contract is enforceable; or

(c) the encumbrancer or owner has consented in writing to the lease or has disclaimed an interest in the goods as fixtures; or

(d) the lessee has a right to remove the goods as against the encumbrancer or owner. If the lessee's right to remove terminates, the priority of the interest of the lessor continues for a reasonable time.

(6) Notwithstanding subsection (4)(a) but otherwise subject to subsections (4) and (5), the interest of a lessor of fixtures, including the lessor's residual interest, is subordinate to the conflicting interest of an encumbrancer of the real estate under a construction mortgage recorded before the goods become fixtures if the goods become fixtures before the completion of the construction. To the extent given to refinance a construction mortgage, the conflicting interest of an encumbrancer of the real estate under a mortgage has this priority to the same extent as the encumbrancer of the real estate under the construction mortgage.

(7) In cases not within the preceding subsections, priority between the interest of a lessor of fixtures, including the lessor's residual interest, and the conflicting interest of an encumbrancer or owner of the real estate who is not the lessee is determined by the priority rules governing conflicting interests in real estate.

(8) If the interest of a lessor of fixtures, including the lessor's residual interest, has priority over all conflicting interests of all owners and encumbrancers of the real estate, the lessor or the lessee may (i) on default, expiration, termination, or cancellation of the lease agreement but subject to the lease agreement and this Article, or (ii) if necessary to enforce other rights and remedies of the lessor or lessee under this Article, remove the goods from the real estate, free and clear of all conflicting interests of all owners and encumbrancers of the real estate, but the lessor or lessee must reimburse any encumbrancer or owner of the real estate who is not the lessee and who has not otherwise agreed for the cost of repair of any physical injury, but not for any diminution in value of the real estate caused by the absence of the goods removed or by any necessity of replacing them. A person entitled to reimbursement may refuse permission to remove until the party seeking removal gives adequate security for the performance of this obligation.

(9) Even though the lease agreement does not create a security interest, the interest of a lessor of fixtures, including the lessor's residual interest, is perfected by filing a financing statement as a fixture filing for leased goods that are or are to become fixtures in accordance with the relevant provisions of the Article on Secured Transactions (Article 9).

§ 2A—310. Lessor's and Lessee's Rights When Goods Become Accessions.

(1) Goods are ''accessions'' when they are installed in or affixed to other goods.

(2) The interest of a lessor or a lessee under a lease contract entered into before the goods became accessions is superior to all interests in the whole except as stated in subsection (4).

(3) The interest of a lessor or a lessee under a lease contract entered into at the time or after the goods became accessions is superior to all subsequently acquired interests in the whole except as stated in subsection (4) but is subordinate to interests in the whole existing at the time the lease contract was made unless the holders of such interests in the whole have in writing consented to the lease or disclaimed an interest in the goods as part of the whole.

(4) The interest of a lessor or a lessee under a lease contract described in subsection (2) or (3) is subordinate to the interest of

(a) a buyer in the ordinary course of business or a lessee in the ordinary course of business of any interest in the whole acquired after the goods became accessions; or

(b) a creditor with a security interest in the whole perfected before the lease contract was made to the extent that the creditor makes subsequent advances without knowledge of the lease contract.

(5) When under subsections (2) or (3) and (4) a lessor or a lessee of accessions holds an interest that is superior to all interests in the whole, the lessor or the lessee may (a) on default, expiration, termination, or cancellation of the lease contract by the other party but subject to the provisions of the lease contract and this Article, or (b) if necessary to enforce his [or her] other rights and remedies under this Article, remove the goods from the whole, free and clear of all interests in the whole, but he [or she] must reimburse any holder of an interest in the whole who is not the lessee and who has not otherwise agreed for the cost of repair of any physical injury but not for any diminution in value of the whole caused by the absence of the goods removed or by any necessity for replacing them. A person entitled to reimbursement may refuse permission to remove until the party seeking removal gives adequate security for the performance of this obligation.

§ 2A—311. Priority Subject to Subordination.

Nothing in this Article prevents subordination by agreement by any person entitled to priority.

Part 4 Performance Of Lease Contract: Repudiated, Substituted And Excused

§ 2A—401. Insecurity: Adequate Assurance of Performance.

(1) A lease contract imposes an obligation on each party that the other's expectation of receiving due performance will not be impaired.

(2) If reasonable grounds for insecurity arise with respect to the performance of either party, the insecure party may demand in writing adequate assurance of due performance. Until the insecure party receives that assurance, if commercially reasonable the insecure party may suspend any performance for which he [or she] has not already received the agreed return.

(3) A repudiation of the lease contract occurs if assurance of due performance adequate under the circumstances of the particular case is not provided to the insecure party within a reasonable time, not to exceed 30 days after receipt of a demand by the other party.

(4) Between merchants, the reasonableness of grounds for insecurity and the adequacy of any assurance offered must be determined according to commercial standards.

(5) Acceptance of any nonconforming delivery or payment does not prejudice the aggrieved party's right to demand adequate assurance of future performance.

§ 2A—402. Anticipatory Repudiation.

If either party repudiates a lease contract with respect to a performance not yet due under the lease contract, the loss of which performance will substantially impair the value of the lease contract to the other, the aggrieved party may:

(a) for a commercially reasonable time, await retraction of repudiation and performance by the repudiating party;

(b) make demand pursuant to Section 2A—401 and await assurance of future performance adequate under the circumstances of the particular case; or

(c) resort to any right or remedy upon default under the lease contract or this Article, even though the aggrieved party has notified the repudiating party that the aggrieved party would await the repudiating party's performance and assurance and has urged retraction. In addition, whether or not the aggrieved party is pursuing one of the foregoing remedies, the aggrieved party may suspend performance or, if the aggrieved party is the lessor, proceed in accordance with the provisions of this Article on the lessor's right to identify goods to the lease contract notwithstanding default or to salvage unfinished goods (Section 2A—524).

§ 2A—403. Retraction of Anticipatory Repudiation.

(1) Until the repudiating party's next performance is due, the repudiating party can retract the repudiation unless, since the repudiation, the aggrieved party has cancelled the lease contract or materially changed the aggrieved party's position or otherwise indicated that the aggrieved party considers the repudiation final.

(2) Retraction may be by any method that clearly indicates to the aggrieved party that the repudiating party intends to perform under the lease contract and includes any assurance demanded under Section 2A—401.

(3) Retraction reinstates a repudiating party's rights under a lease contract with due excuse and allowance to the aggrieved party for any delay occasioned by the repudiation.

§ 2A—404. Substituted Performance.

(1) If without fault of the lessee, the lessor and the supplier, the agreed berthing, loading, or unloading facilities fail or the agreed type of carrier becomes unavailable or the agreed manner of delivery otherwise becomes commercially impracticable, but a commercially reasonable substitute is available, the substitute performance must be tendered and accepted.

(2) If the agreed means or manner of payment fails because of domestic or foreign governmental regulation:

(a) the lessor may withhold or stop delivery or cause the supplier to withhold or stop delivery unless the lessee provides a means or manner of payment that is commercially a substantial equivalent; and

(b) if delivery has already been taken, payment by the means or in the manner provided by the regulation discharges the lessee's obligation unless the regulation is discriminatory, oppressive, or predatory.

§ 2A—405. Excused Performance.

Subject to Section 2A—404 on substituted performance, the following rules apply:

(a) Delay in delivery or nondelivery in whole or in part by a lessor or a supplier who complies with paragraphs (b) and (c) is not a default under the lease contract if performance as agreed has been made impracticable by the occurrence of a contingency the nonoccurrence of which was a basic assumption on which the lease contract was made or by compliance in good faith with any applicable foreign or domestic governmental regulation or order, whether or not the regulation or order later proves to be invalid.

(b) If the causes mentioned in paragraph (a) affect only part of the lessor's or the supplier's capacity to perform, he [or she] shall allocate production and deliveries among his [or her] customers but at his [or her] option may include regular customers not then under contract for sale or lease as well as his [or her] own requirements for further manufacture. He [or she] may so allocate in any manner that is fair and reasonable.

(c) The lessor seasonally shall notify the lessee and in the case of a finance lease the supplier seasonally shall notify

THE UNIFORM COMMERCIAL CODE

the lessor and the lessee, if known, that there will be delay or nondelivery and, if allocation is required under paragraph (b), of the estimated quota thus made available for the lessee.

§ 2A—406. **Procedure on Excused Performance.**

(1) If the lessee receives notification of a material or indefinite delay or an allocation justified under Section 2A—405, the lessee may by written notification to the lessor as to any goods involved, and with respect to all of the goods if under an installment lease contract the value of the whole lease contract is substantially impaired (Section 2A—510):

(a) terminate the lease contract (Section 2A—505(2)); or

(b) except in a finance lease that is not a consumer lease, modify the lease contract by accepting the available quota in substitution, with due allowance from the rent payable for the balance of the lease term for the deficiency but without further right against the lessor.

(2) If, after receipt of a notification from the lessor under Section 2A—405, the lessee fails so to modify the lease agreement within a reasonable time not exceeding 30 days, the lease contract lapses with respect to any deliveries affected.

§ 2A—407. **Irrevocable Promises: Finance Leases.**

(1) In the case of a finance lease that is not a consumer lease the lessee's promises under the lease contract become irrevocable and independent upon the lessee's acceptance of the goods.

(2) A promise that has become irrevocable and independent under subsection (1):

(a) is effective and enforceable between the parties, and by or against third parties including assignees of the parties; and

(b) is not subject to cancellation, termination, modification, repudiation, excuse, or substitution without the consent of the party to whom the promise runs.

(3) This section does not affect the validity under any other law of a covenant in any lease contract making the lessee's promises irrevocable and independent upon the lessee's acceptance of the goods.

Part 5 Default
A. In General

§ 2A—501. **Default: Procedure.**

(1) Whether the lessor or the lessee is in default under a lease contract is determined by the lease agreement and this Article.

(2) If the lessor or the lessee is in default under the lease contract, the party seeking enforcement has rights and rem-

edies as provided in this Article and, except as limited by this Article, as provided in the lease agreement.

(3) If the lessor or the lessee is in default under the lease contract, the party seeking enforcement may reduce the party's claim to judgment, or otherwise enforce the lease contract by self-help or any available judicial procedure or nonjudicial procedure, including administrative proceeding, arbitration, or the like, in accordance with this Article.

(4) Except as otherwise provided in Section 1—106(1) or this Article or the lease agreement, the rights and remedies referred to in subsections (2) and (3) are cumulative.

(5) If the lease agreement covers both real property and goods, the party seeking enforcement may proceed under this Part as to the goods, or under other applicable law as to both the real property and the goods in accordance with that party's rights and remedies in respect of the real property, in which case this Part does not apply.

§ 2A—502. **Notice After Default.**

Except as otherwise provided in this Article or the lease agreement, the lessor or lessee in default under the lease contract is not entitled to notice of default or notice of enforcement from the other party to the lease agreement.

§ 2A—503. **Modification or Impairment of Rights and Remedies.**

(1) Except as otherwise provided in this Article, the lease agreement may include rights and remedies for default in addition to or in substitution for those provided in this Article and may limit or alter the measure of damages recoverable under this Article.

(2) Resort to a remedy provided under this Article or in the lease agreement is optional unless the remedy is expressly agreed to be exclusive. If circumstances cause an exclusive or limited remedy to fail of its essential purpose, or provision for an exclusive remedy is unconscionable, remedy may be had as provided in this Article.

(3) Consequential damages may be liquidated under Section 2A—504, or may otherwise be limited, altered, or excluded unless the limitation, alteration, or exclusion is unconscionable. Limitation, alteration, or exclusion of consequential damages for injury to the person in the case of consumer goods is prima facie unconscionable but limitation, alteration, or exclusion of damages where the loss is commercial is not prima facie unconscionable.

(4) Rights and remedies on default by the lessor or the lessee with respect to any obligation or promise collateral or ancillary to the lease contract are not impaired by this Article.

§ 2A—504. **Liquidation of Damages.**

(1) Damages payable by either party for default, or any other act or omission, including indemnity for loss or dim-

inution of anticipated tax benefits or loss or damage to lessor's residual interest, may be liquidated in the lease agreement but only at an amount or by a formula that is reasonable in light of the then anticipated harm caused by the default or other act or omission.

(2) If the lease agreement provides for liquidation of damages, and such provision does not comply with subsection (1), or such provision is an exclusive or limited remedy that circumstances cause to fail of its essential purpose, remedy may be had as provided in this Article.

(3) If the lessor justifiably withholds or stops delivery of goods because of the lessee's default or insolvency (Section 2A—525 or 2A—526), the lessee is entitled to restitution of any amount by which the sum of his [or her] payments exceeds:

   (a) the amount to which the lessor is entitled by virtue of terms liquidating the lessor's damages in accordance with subsection (1); or

   (b) in the absence of those terms, 20 percent of the then present value of the total rent the lessee was obligated to pay for the balance of the lease term, or, in the case of a consumer lease, the lesser of such amount or $500.

(4) A lessee's right to restitution under subsection (3) is subject to offset to the extent the lessor establishes:

   (a) a right to recover damages under the provisions of this Article other than subsection (1); and

   (b) the amount or value of any benefits received by the lessee directly or indirectly by reason of the lease contract.

§ 2A—505. Cancellation and Termination and Effect of Cancellation, Termination, Rescission, or Fraud on Rights and Remedies.

(1) On cancellation of the lease contract, all obligations that are still executory on both sides are discharged, but any right based on prior default or performance survives, and the cancelling party also retains any remedy for default of the whole lease contract or any unperformed balance.

(2) On termination of the lease contract, all obligations that are still executory on both sides are discharged but any right based on prior default or performance survives.

(3) Unless the contrary intention clearly appears, expressions of ''cancellation,'' ''rescission,'' or the like of the lease contract may not be construed as a renunciation or discharge of any claim in damages for an antecedent default.

(4) Rights and remedies for material misrepresentation or fraud include all rights and remedies available under this Article for default.

(5) Neither rescission nor a claim for rescission of the lease contract nor rejection or return of the goods may bar or be deemed inconsistent with a claim for damages or other right or remedy.

§ 2A—506. Statute of Limitations.

(1) An action for default under a lease contract, including breach of warranty or indemnity, must be commenced within 4 years after the cause of action accrued. By the original lease contract the parties may reduce the period of limitation to not less than one year.

(2) A cause of action for default accrues when the act or omission on which the default or breach of warranty is based is or should have been discovered by the aggrieved party, or when the default occurs, whichever is later. A cause of action for indemnity accrues when the act or omission on which the claim for indemnity is based is or should have been discovered by the indemnified party, whichever is later.

(3) If an action commenced within the time limited by subsection (1) is so terminated as to leave available a remedy by another action for the same default or breach of warranty or indemnity, the other action may be commenced after the expiration of the time limited and within 6 months after the termination of the first action unless the termination resulted from voluntary discontinuance or from dismissal for failure or neglect to prosecute.

(4) This section does not alter the law on tolling of the statute of limitations nor does it apply to causes of action that have accrued before this Article becomes effective.

§ 2A—507. Proof of Market Rent: Time and Place.

(1) Damages based on market rent (Section 2A—519 or 2A—528) are determined according to the rent for the use of the goods concerned for a lease term identical to the remaining lease term of the original lease agreement and prevailing at the times specified in Sections 2A—519 and 2A—528.

(2) If evidence of rent for the use of the goods concerned for a lease term identical to the remaining lease term of the original lease agreement and prevailing at the times or places described in this Article is not readily available, the rent prevailing within any reasonable time before or after the time described or at any other place or for a different lease term which in commercial judgment or under usage of trade would serve as a reasonable substitute for the one described may be used, making any proper allowance for the difference, including the cost of transporting the goods to or from the other place.

(3) Evidence of a relevant rent prevailing at a time or place or for a lease term other than the one described in this Article offered by one party is not admissible unless and until he [or she] has given the other party notice the court finds sufficient to prevent unfair surprise.

(4) If the prevailing rent or value of any goods regularly leased in any established market is in issue, reports in official publications or trade journals or in newspapers or periodicals of general circulation published as the reports

of that market are admissible in evidence. The circumstances of the preparation of the report may be shown to affect its weight but not its admissibility.

B. Default by Lessor

§ 2A—508. **Lessee's Remedies.**

(1) If a lessor fails to deliver the goods in conformity to the lease contract (Section 2A—509) or repudiates the lease contract (Section 2A—402), or a lessee rightfully rejects the goods (Section 2A—509) or justifiably revokes acceptance of the goods (Section 2A—517), then with respect to any goods involved, and with respect to all of the goods if under an installment lease contract the value of the whole lease contract is substantially impaired (Section 2A—510), the lessor is in default under the lease contract and the lessee may:

(a) cancel the lease contract (Section 2A—505(1));

(b) recover so much of the rent and security as has been paid and is just under the circumstances;

(c) cover and recover damages as to all goods affected whether or not they have been identified to the lease contract (Sections 2A—518 and 2A—520), or recover damages for nondelivery (Sections 2A—519 and 2A—520).

(d) exercise any other rights or pursue any other remedies provided in the lease contract.

(2) If a lessor fails to deliver the goods in conformity to the lease contract or repudiates the lease contract, the lessee may also:

(a) if the goods have been identified, recover them (Section 2A—522); or

(b) in a proper case, obtain specific performance or replevy the goods (Section 2A—521).

(3) If a lessor is otherwise in default under a lease contract, the lessee may exercise the rights and pursue the remedies provided in the lease contract, which may include a right to cancel the lease, and in Section 2A—519(3).

(4) If a lessor has breached a warranty, whether express or implied, the lessee may recover damages (Section 2A—519(4)).

(5) On rightful rejection or justifiable revocation of acceptance, a lessee has a security interest in goods in the lessee's possession or control for any rent and security that has been paid and any expenses reasonably incurred in their inspection, receipt, transportation, and care and custody and may hold those goods and dispose of them in good faith and in a commercially reasonable manner, subject to Section 2A—527(5).

(6) Subject to the provisions of Section 2A—407, a lessee, on notifying the lessor of the lessee's intention to do so, may deduct all or any part of the damages resulting from any default under the lease contract from any part of the rent still due under the same lease contract.

§ 2A—509. **Lessee's Rights on Improper Delivery; Rightful Rejection.**

(1) Subject to the provisions of Section 2A—510 on default in installment lease contracts, if the goods or the tender or delivery fail in any respect to conform to the lease contract, the lessee may reject or accept the goods or accept any commercial unit or units and reject the rest of the goods.

(2) Rejection of goods is ineffective unless it is within a reasonable time after tender or delivery of the goods and the lessee seasonably notifies the lessor.

§ 2A—510. **Installment Lease Contracts: Rejection and Default.**

(1) Under an installment lease contract a lessee may reject any delivery that is nonconforming if the nonconformity substantially impairs the value of that delivery and cannot be cured or the nonconformity is a defect in the required documents; but if the nonconformity does not fall within subsection (2) and the lessor or the supplier gives adequate assurance of its cure, the lessee must accept that delivery.

(2) Whenever nonconformity or default with respect to one or more deliveries substantially impairs the value of the installment lease contract as a whole there is a default with respect to the whole. But, the aggrieved party reinstates the installment lease contract as a whole if the aggrieved party accepts a nonconforming delivery without seasonably notifying of cancellation or brings an action with respect only to past deliveries or demands performance as to future deliveries.

§ 2A—511. **Merchant Lessee's Duties as to Rightfully Rejected Goods.**

(1) Subject to any security interest of a lessee (Section 2A—508(5)), if a lessor or a supplier has no agent or place of business at the market of rejection, a merchant lessee, after rejection of goods in his [or her] possession or control, shall follow any reasonable instructions received from the lessor or the supplier with respect to the goods. In the absence of those instructions, a merchant lessee shall make reasonable efforts to sell, lease, or otherwise dispose of the goods for the lessor's account if they threaten to decline in value speedily. Instructions are not reasonable if on demand indemnity for expenses is not forthcoming.

(2) If a merchant lessee (subsection (1)) or any other lessee (Section 2A—512) disposes of goods, he [or she] is entitled to reimbursement either from the lessor or the supplier or out of the proceeds for reasonable expenses of caring for and disposing of the goods and, if the expenses include no disposition commission, to such commission as is usual in the trade, or if there is none, to a reasonable sum not exceeding 10 percent of the gross proceeds.

(3) In complying with this section or Section 2A—512, the lessee is held only to good faith. Good faith conduct hereunder is neither acceptance or conversion nor the basis of an action for damages.

(4) A purchaser who purchases in good faith from a lessee pursuant to this section or Section 2A—512 takes the goods free of any rights of the lessor and the supplier even though the lessee fails to comply with one or more of the requirements of this Article.

§ 2A—512. **Lessee's Duties as to Rightfully Rejected Goods.**

(1) Except as otherwise provided with respect to goods that threaten to decline in value speedily (Section 2A—511) and subject to any security interest of a lessee (Section 2A—508(5)):

(a) the lessee, after rejection of goods in the lessee's possession, shall hold them with reasonable care at the lessor's or the supplier's disposition for a reasonable time after the lessee's seasonable notification of rejection;

(b) if the lessor or the supplier gives no instructions within a reasonable time after notification of rejection, the lessee may store the rejected goods for the lessor's or the supplier's account or ship them to the lessor or the supplier or dispose of them for the lessor's or the supplier's account with reimbursement in the manner provided in Section 2A—511; but

(c) the lessee has no further obligations with regard to goods rightfully rejected.

(2) Action by the lessee pursuant to subsection (1) is not acceptance or conversion.

§ 2A—513. **Cure by Lessor of Improper Tender or Delivery; Replacement.**

(1) If any tender or delivery by the lessor or the supplier is rejected because nonconforming and the time for performance has not yet expired, the lessor or the supplier may seasonably notify the lessee of the lessor's or the supplier's intention to cure and may then make a conforming delivery within the time provided in the lease contract.

(2) If the lessee rejects a nonconforming tender that the lessor or the supplier had reasonable grounds to believe would be acceptable with or without money allowance, the lessor or the supplier may have a further reasonable time to substitute a conforming tender if he [or she] seasonably notifies the lessee.

§ 2A—514. **Waiver of Lessee's Objections.**

(1) In rejecting goods, a lessee's failure to state a particular defect that is ascertainable by reasonable inspection precludes the lessee from relying on the defect to justify rejection or to establish default:

(a) if, stated seasonably, the lessor or the supplier could have cured it (Section 2A—513); or

(b) between merchants if the lessor or the supplier after rejection has made a request in writing for a full and final written statement of all defects on which the lessee proposes to rely.

(2) A lessee's failure to reserve rights when paying rent or other consideration against documents precludes recovery of the payment for defects apparent on the face of the documents.

§ 2A—515. **Acceptance of Goods.**

(1) Acceptance of goods occurs after the lessee has had a reasonable opportunity to inspect the goods and

(a) the lessee signifies or acts with respect to the goods in a manner that signifies to the lessor or the supplier that the goods are conforming or that the lessee will take or retain them in spite of their nonconformity; or

(b) the lessee fails to make an effective rejection of the goods (Section 2A—509(2)).

(2) Acceptance of a part of any commercial unit is acceptance of that entire unit.

§ 2A—516. **Effect of Acceptance of Goods; Notice of Default; Burden of Establishing Default after Acceptance; Notice of Claim or Litigation to Person Answerable Over.**

(1) A lessee must pay rent for any goods accepted in accordance with the lease contract, with due allowance for goods rightfully rejected or not delivered.

(2) A lessee's acceptance of goods precludes rejection of the goods accepted. In the case of a finance lease, if made with knowledge of a nonconformity, acceptance cannot be revoked because of it. In any other case, if made with knowledge of a nonconformity, acceptance cannot be revoked because of it unless the acceptance was on the reasonable assumption that the nonconformity would be seasonably cured. Acceptance does not of itself impair any other remedy provided by this Article or the lease agreement for nonconformity.

(3) If a tender has been accepted:

(a) within a reasonable time after the lessee discovers or should have discovered any default, the lessee shall notify the lessor and the supplier, if any, or be barred from any remedy against the party not notified;

(b) except in the case of a consumer lease, within a reasonable time after the lessee receives notice of litigation for infringement or the like (Section 2A—211) the lessee shall notify the lessor or be barred from any remedy over for liability established by the litigation; and

(c) the burden is on the lessee to establish any default.

(4) If a lessee is sued for breach of a warranty or other obligation for which a lessor or a supplier is answerable over the following apply:

(a) The lessee may give the lessor or the supplier, or both, written notice of the litigation. If the notice states that the person notified may come in and defend and that if the person notified does not do so that person will be bound in any action against that person by the lessee by any determination of fact common to the two litigations, then unless the person notified after seasonable receipt of the notice does come in and defend that person is so bound.

(b) The lessor or the supplier may demand in writing that the lessee turn over control of the litigation including settlement if the claim is one for infringement or the like (Section 2A—211) or else be barred from any remedy over. If the demand states that the lessor or the supplier agrees to bear all expense and to satisfy any adverse judgment, then unless the lessee after seasonable receipt of the demand does turn over control the lessee is so barred.

(5) Subsections (3) and (4) apply to any obligation of a lessee to hold the lessor or the supplier harmless against infringement or the like (Section 2A—211).

§ 2A—517. **Revocation of Acceptance of Goods.**

(1) A lessee may revoke acceptance of a lot or commercial unit whose nonconformity substantially impairs its value to the lessee if the lessee has accepted it:

(a) except in the case of a finance lease, on the reasonable assumption that its nonconformity would be cured and it has not been seasonably cured; or

(b) without discovery of the nonconformity if the lessee's acceptance was reasonably induced either by the lessor's assurances or, except in the case of a finance lease, by the difficulty of discovery before acceptance.

(2) Except in the case of a finance lease that is not a consumer lease, a lessee may revoke acceptance of a lot or commercial unit if the lessor defaults under the lease contract and the default substantially impairs the value of that lot or commercial unit to the lessee.

(3) If the lease agreement so provides, the lessee may revoke acceptance of a lot or commercial unit because of other defaults by the lessor.

(4) Revocation of acceptance must occur within a reasonable time after the lessee discovers or should have discovered the ground for it and before any substantial change in condition of the goods which is not caused by the nonconformity. Revocation is not effective until the lessee notifies the lessor.

(5) A lessee who so revokes has the same rights and duties with regard to the goods involved as if the lessee had rejected them.

§ 2A—518. **Cover; Substitute Goods.**

(1) After a default by a lessor under the lease contract of the type described in Section 2A—508(1), or, if agreed, after other default by the lessor, the lessee may cover by making any purchase or lease of or contract to purchase or lease goods in substitution for those due from the lessor.

(2) Except as otherwise provided with respect to damages liquidated in the lease agreement (Section 2A—504) or otherwise determined pursuant to agreement of the parties (Sections 1—102(3) and 2A—503), if a lessee's cover is by a lease agreement substantially similar to the original lease agreement and the new lease agreement is made in good faith and in a commercially reasonable manner, the lessee may recover from the lessor as damages (i) the present value, as of the date of the commencement of the term of the new lease agreement, of the rent under the new lease agreement applicable to that period of the new lease term which is comparable to the then remaining term of the original lease agreement minus the present value as of the same date of the total rent for the then remaining lease term of the original lease agreement, and (ii) any incidental or consequential damages, less expenses saved in consequence of the lessor's default.

(3) If a lessee's cover is by lease agreement that for any reason does not qualify for treatment under subsection (2), or is by purchase or otherwise, the lessee may recover from the lessor as if the lessee had elected not to cover and Section 2A—519 governs.

§ 2A—519. **Lessee's Damages for Non-Delivery, Repudiation, Default, and Breach of Warranty in Regard to Accepted Goods.**

(1) Except as otherwise provided with respect to damages liquidated in the lease agreement (Section 2A—504) or otherwise determined pursuant to agreement of the parties (Sections 1—102(3) and 2A—503), if a lessee elects not to cover or a lessee elects to cover and the cover is by lease agreement that for any reason does not qualify for treatment under Section 2A—518(2), or is by purchase or otherwise, the measure of damages for non-delivery or repudiation by the lessor or for rejection or revocation of acceptance by the lessee is the present value, as of the date of the default, of the then market rent minus the present value as of the same date of the original rent, computed for the remaining lease term of the original lease agreement, together with incidental and consequential damages, less expenses saved in consequence of the lessor's default.

(2) Market rent is to be determined as of the place for tender or, in cases of rejection after arrival or revocation of acceptance, as of the place of arrival.

(3) Except as otherwise agreed, if the lessee has accepted goods and given notification (Section 2A—516(3)), the measure of damages for non-conforming tender or delivery or other default by a lessor is the loss resulting in the or-

dinary course of events from the lessor's default as determined in any manner that is reasonable together with incidental and consequential damages, less expenses saved in consequence of the lessor's default.

(4) Except as otherwise agreed, the measure of damages for breach of warranty is the present value at the time and place of acceptance of the difference between the value of the use of the goods accepted and the value if they had been as warranted for the lease term, unless special circumstances show proximate damages of a different amount, together with incidental and consequential damages, less expenses saved in consequence of the lessor's default or breach of warranty.

§ 2A—520. **Lessee's Incidental and Consequential Damages.**

(1) Incidental damages resulting from a lessor's default include expenses reasonably incurred in inspection, receipt, transportation, and care and custody of goods rightfully rejected or goods the acceptance of which is justifiably revoked, any commercially reasonable charges, expenses or commissions in connection with effecting cover, and any other reasonable expense incident to the default.

(2) Consequential damages resulting from a lessor's default include:

(a) any loss resulting from general or particular requirements and needs of which the lessor at the time of contracting had reason to know and which could not reasonably be prevented by cover or otherwise; and

(b) injury to person or property proximately resulting from any breach of warranty.

§ 2A—521. **Lessee's Right to Specific Performance or Replevin.**

(1) Specific performance may be decreed if the goods are unique or in other proper circumstances.

(2) A decree for specific performance may include any terms and conditions as to payment of the rent, damages, or other relief that the court deems just.

(3) A lessee has a right of replevin, detinue, sequestration, claim and delivery, or the like for goods identified to the lease contract if after reasonable effort the lessee is unable to effect cover for those goods or the circumstances reasonably indicate that the effort will be unavailing.

§ 2A—522. **Lessee's Right to Goods on Lessor's Insolvency.**

(1) Subject to subsection (2) and even though the goods have not been shipped, a lessee who has paid a part or all of the rent and security for goods identified to a lease contract (Section 2A—217) on making and keeping good a tender of any unpaid portion of the rent and security due under the lease contract may recover the goods identified from the lessor if the lessor becomes insolvent within 10 days after receipt of the first installment of rent and security.

(2) A lessee acquires the right to recover goods identified to a lease contract only if they conform to the lease contract.

C. Default by Lessee

§ 2A—523. **Lessor's Remedies.**

(1) If a lessee wrongfully rejects or revokes acceptance of goods or fails to make a payment when due or repudiates with respect to a part or the whole, then, with respect to any goods involved, and with respect to all of the goods if under an installment lease contract the value of the whole lease contract is substantially impaired (Section 2A—510), the lessee is in default under the lease contract and the lessor may:

(a) cancel the lease contract (Section 2A—505(1));

(b) proceed respecting goods not identified to the lease contract (Section 2A—524);

(c) withhold delivery of the goods and take possession of goods previously delivered (Section 2A—525);

(d) stop delivery of the goods by any bailee (Section 2A—526);

(e) dispose of the goods and recover damages (Section 2A—527), or retain the goods and recover damages (Section 2A—528), or in a proper case recover rent (Section 2A—529);

(f) exercise any other rights or pursue any other remedies provided in the lease contract.

(2) If a lessor does not fully exercise a right or obtain a remedy to which the lessor is entitled under subsection (1), the lessor may recover the loss resulting in the ordinary course of events from the lessee's default as determined in any reasonable manner, together with incidental damages, less expenses saved in consequence of the lessee's default.

(3) If a lessee is otherwise in default under a lease contract, the lessor may exercise the rights and pursue the remedies provided in the lease contract, which may include a right to cancel the lease. In addition, unless otherwise provided in the lease contract:

(a) if the default substantially impairs the value of the lease contract to the lessor, the lessor may exercise the rights and pursue the remedies provided in subsections (1) or (2); or

(b) if the default does not substantially impair the value of the lease contract to the lessor, the lessor may recover as provided in subsection (2).

§ 2A—524. **Lessor's Right to Identify Goods to Lease Contract.**

(1) After default by the lessee under the lease contract of the type described in Section 2A—523(1) or 2A—523(3)(a)

or, if agreed, after other default by the lessee, the lessor may:

(a) identify to the lease contract conforming goods not already identified if at the time the lessor learned of the default they were in the lessor's or the supplier's possession or control; and

(b) dispose of goods (Section 2A—527(1)) that demonstrably have been intended for the particular lease contract even though those goods are unfinished.

(2) If the goods are unfinished, in the exercise of reasonable commercial judgment for the purposes of avoiding loss and of effective realization, an aggrieved lessor or the supplier may either complete manufacture and wholly identify the goods to the lease contract or cease manufacture and lease, sell, or otherwise dispose of the goods for scrap or salvage value or proceed in any other reasonable manner.

§ 2A—525. Lessor's Right to Possession of Goods.

(1) If a lessor discovers the lessee to be insolvent, the lessor may refuse to deliver the goods.

(2) After a default by the lessee under the lease contract of the type described in Section 2A—523(1) or 2A—523(3)(a) or, if agreed, after other default by the lessee, the lessor has the right to take possession of the goods. If the lease contract so provides, the lessor may require the lessee to assemble the goods and make them available to the lessor at a place to be designated by the lessor which is reasonably convenient to both parties. Without removal, the lessor may render unusable any goods employed in trade or business, and may dispose of goods on the lessee's premises (Section 2A—527).

(3) The lessor may proceed under subsection (2) without judicial process if it can be done without breach of the peace or the lessor may proceed by action.

§ 2A—526. Lessor's Stoppage of Delivery in Transit or Otherwise.

(1) A lessor may stop delivery of goods in the possession of a carrier or other bailee if the lessor discovers the lessee to be insolvent and may stop delivery of carload, truckload, planeload, or larger shipments of express or freight if the lessee repudiates or fails to make a payment due before delivery, whether for rent, security or otherwise under the lease contract, or for any other reason the lessor has a right to withhold or take possession of the goods.

(2) In pursuing its remedies under subsection (1) the lessor may stop delivery until

(a) receipt of the goods by the lessee;

(b) acknowledgment to the lessee by any bailee of the goods, except a carrier, that the bailee holds the goods for the lessee; or

(c) such an acknowledgment to the lessee by a carrier via reshipment or as warehouseman.

(3) (a) To stop delivery, a lessor shall so notify as to enable the bailee by reasonable diligence to prevent delivery of the goods.

(b) After notification, the bailee shall hold and deliver the goods according to the directions of the lessor, but the lessor is liable to the bailee for any ensuing charges or damages.

(c) A carrier who has issued a nonnegotiable bill of lading is not obliged to obey a notification to stop received from a person other than the consignor.

§ 2A—527. Lessor's Rights to Dispose of Goods.

(1) After a default by a lessee under the lease contract of the type described in Section 2A—523(1) or 2A—523(3)(a) or after the lessor refuses to deliver or takes possession of goods (Section 2A—525 or 2A—526), or, if agreed, after other default by a lessee, the lessor may dispose of the goods concerned or the undelivered balance thereof by lease, sale, or otherwise.

(2) Except as otherwise provided with respect to damages liquidated in the lease agreement (Section 2A—504) or otherwise determined pursuant to agreement of the parties (Sections 1—102(3) and 2A—503), if the disposition is by lease agreement substantially similar to the original lease agreement and the new lease agreement is made in good faith and in a commercially reasonable manner, the lessor may recover from the lessee as damages (i) accrued and unpaid rent as of the date of the commencement of the term of the new lease agreement, (ii) the present value, as of the same date, of the total rent for the then remaining lease term of the original lease agreement minus the present value, as of the same date, of the rent under the new lease agreement applicable to that period of the new lease term which is comparable to the then remaining term of the original lease agreement, and (iii) any incidental damages allowed under Section 2A—530, less expenses saved in consequence of the lessee's default.

(3) If the lessor's disposition is by lease agreement that for any reason does not qualify for treatment under subsection (2), or is by sale or otherwise, the lessor may recover from the lessee as if the lessor had elected not to dispose of the goods and Section 2A—528 governs.

(4) A subsequent buyer or lessee who buys or leases from the lessor in good faith for value as a result of a disposition under this section takes the goods free of the original lease contract and any rights of the original lessee even though the lessor fails to comply with one or more of the requirements of this Article.

(5) The lessor is not accountable to the lessee for any profit made on any disposition. A lessee who has rightfully rejected or justifiably revoked acceptance shall account to the lessor for any excess over the amount of the lessee's security interest (Section 2A—508(5)).

§ 2A—528. **Lessor's Damages for Non-acceptance, Failure to Pay, Repudiation, or Other Default.**

(1) Except as otherwise provided with respect to damages liquidated in the lease agreement (Section 2A—504) or otherwise determined by pursuant to agreement of the parties (Sections 1—102(3) and 2A—503), if a lessor elects to retain the goods or a lessor elects to dispose of the goods and the disposition is by lease agreement that for any reason does not qualify for treatment under Section 2A—527(2), or is by sale or otherwise, the lessor may recover from the lessee as damages for a default of the type described in Section 2A—523(1) or 2A—523(3)(a), or, if agreed, for other default of the lessee, (i) accrued and unpaid rent as of the date of default if the lessee has never taken possession of the goods, or, if the lessee has taken possession of the goods, as of the date the lessor repossesses the goods or an earlier date on which the lessee makes a tender of the goods to the lessor, (ii) the present value as of the date determined under clause (i) of the total rent for the then remaining lease term of the original lease agreement minus the present value as of the same date of the market rent at the place where the goods are located computed for the same lease term, and (iii) any incidental damages allowed under Section 2A—530, less expenses saved in consequence of the lessee's default.

(2) If the measure of damages provided in subsection (1) is inadequate to put a lessor in as good a position as performance would have, the measure of damages is the present value of the profit, including reasonable overhead, the lessor would have made from full performance by the lessee, together with any incidental damages allowed under Section 2A—530, due allowance for costs reasonably incurred and due credit for payments or proceeds of disposition.

§ 2A—529. **Lessor's Action for the Rent.**

(1) After default by the lessee under the lease contract of the type described in Section 2A—523(1) or 2A—523(3)(a) or, if agreed, after other default by the lessee, if the lessor complies with subsection (2), the lessor may recover from the lessee as damages:

(a) for goods accepted by the lessee and not repossessed by or tendered to the lessor, and for conforming goods lost or damaged within a commercially reasonable time after risk of loss passes to the lessee (Section 2A—219), (i) accrued and unpaid rent as of the date of entry of judgment in favor of the lessor, (ii) the present value as of the same date of the rent for the then remaining lease term of the lease agreement, and (iii) any incidental damages allowed under Section 2A—530, less expenses saved in consequence of the lessee's default; and

(b) for goods identified to the lease contract if the lessor is unable after reasonable effort to dispose of them at a reasonable price or the circumstances reasonably indicate that effort will be unavailing, (i) accrued and unpaid rent as of the date of entry of judgment in favor of the lessor, (ii) the present value as of the same date of the rent for the then remaining lease term of the lease agreement, and (iii) any incidental damages allowed under Section 2A—530, less expenses saved in consequence of the lessee's default.

(2) Except as provided in subsection (3), the lessor shall hold for the lessee for the remaining lease term of the lease agreement any goods that have been identified to the lease contract and are in the lessor's control.

(3) The lessor may dispose of the goods at any time before collection of the judgment for damages obtained pursuant to subsection (1). If the disposition is before the end of the remaining lease term of the lease agreement, the lessor's recovery against the lessee for damages is governed by Section 2A—527 or Section 2A—528, and the lessor will cause an appropriate credit to be provided against a judgment for damages to the extent that the amount of the judgment exceeds the recovery available pursuant to Section 2A—527 or 2A—528.

(4) Payment of the judgment for damages obtained pursuant to subsection (1) entitles the lessee to the use and possession of the goods not then disposed of for the remaining lease term of and in accordance with the lease agreement.

(5) After default by the lessee under the lease contract of the type described in Section 2A—523(1) or Section 2A—523(3)(a) or, if agreed, after other default by the lessee, a lessor who is held not entitled to rent under this section must nevertheless be awarded damages for non-acceptance under Section 2A—527 or Section 2A—528.

§ 2A—530. **Lessor's Incidental Damages.**

Incidental damages to an aggrieved lessor include any commercially reasonable charges, expenses, or commissions incurred in stopping delivery, in the transportation, care and custody of goods after the lessee's default, in connection with return or disposition of the goods, or otherwise resulting from the default.

§ 2A—531. **Standing to Sue Third Parties for Injury to Goods.**

(1) If a third party so deals with goods that have been identified to a lease contract as to cause actionable injury to a party to the lease contract (a) the lessor has a right of action against the third party, and (b) the lessee also has a right of action against the third party if the lessee:

(i) has a security interest in the goods;

(ii) has an insurable interest in the goods; or

(iii) bears the risk of loss under the lease contract or has since the injury assumed that risk as against the lessor and the goods have been converted or destroyed.

(2) If at the time of the injury the party plaintiff did not bear the risk of loss as against the other party to the lease contract and there is no arrangement between them for disposition of the recovery, his [or her] suit or settlement, subject to his [or her] own interest, is as a fiduciary for the other party to the lease contract.

(3) Either party with the consent of the other may sue for the benefit of whom it may concern.

§ 2A—532. Lessor's Rights to Residual Interest.

In addition to any other recovery permitted by this Article or other law, the lessor may recover from the lessee an amount that will fully compensate the lessor for any loss of or damage to the lessor's residual interest in the goods caused by the default of the lessee.

Article 3
COMMERCIAL PAPER

Part 1 Short Title, Form and Interpretation

§ 3—101. Short Title.

This Article shall be known and may be cited as Uniform Commercial Code—Commercial Paper.

§ 3—102. Definitions and Index of Definitions.

(1) In this Article unless the context otherwise requires

(a) "Issue" means the first delivery of an instrument to a holder or a remitter.

(b) An "order" is a direction to pay and must be more than an authorization or request. It must identify the person to pay with reasonable certainty. It may be addressed to one or more such persons jointly or in the alternative but not in succession.

(c) A "promise" is an undertaking to pay and must be more than an acknowledgment of an obligation.

(d) "Secondary party" means a drawer or indorser.

(e) "Instrument" means a negotiable instrument.

(2) Other definitions applying to this Article and the sections in which they appear are:
"Acceptance". Section 3—410.
"Accommodation party". Section 3—415.
"Alteration". Section 3—407.
"Certificate of deposit". Section 3—104.
"Certification". Section 3—411.
"Check". Section 3—104.
"Definite time". Section 3—109.
"Dishonor". Section 3—507.
"Draft". Section 3—104.
"Holder in due course". Section 3—302.
"Negotiation". Section 3—202.
"Note". Section 3—104.

"Notice of dishonor". Section 3—508.
"On demand". Section 3—108.
"Presentment". Section 3—504.
"Protest". Section 3—509.
"Restrictive Indorsement". Section 3—205.
"Signature". Section 3—401.

(3) The following definitions in other Articles apply to this Article:
"Account". Section 4—104.
"Banking Day". Section 4—104.
"Clearing House". Section 4—104.
"Collecting Bank". Section 4—105.
"Customer". Section 4—104.
"Depositary Bank". Section 4—105.
"Documentary Draft". Section 4—104.
"Intermediary Bank". Section 4—105.
"Item". Section 4—104.
"Midnight deadline". Section 4—104.
"Payor Bank". Section 4—105.

(4) In addition Article 1 contains general definitions and principles of construction and interpretation applicable throughout this Article.

§ 3—103. Limitations on Scope of Article.

(1) This Article does not apply to money, documents of title or investment securities.

(2) The provisions of this Article are subject to the provisions of the Article on Bank Deposits and Collections (Article 4) and Secured Transactions (Article 9).

§ 3—104. Form of Negotiable Instruments; "Draft"; "Check"; "Certificate of Deposit"; "Note".

(1) Any writing to be a negotiable instrument within this Article must

(a) be signed by the maker or drawer; and

(b) contain an unconditional promise or order to pay a sum certain in money and no other promise, order, obligation or power given by the maker or drawer except as authorized by this Article; and

(c) be payable on demand or at a definite time; and

(d) be payable to order or to bearer.

(2) A writing which complies with the requirements of this section is

(a) a "draft" ("bill of exchange") if it is an order;

(b) a "check" if it is a draft drawn on a bank and payable on demand;

(c) a "certificate of deposit" if it is an acknowledgment by a bank receipt of money with an engagement to repay it;

(d) a "note" if it is a promise other than a certificate of deposit.

(3) As used in other Articles of this Act, and as the context may require, the terms ''draft'', ''check'', ''certificate of deposit'' and ''note'' may refer to instruments which are not negotiable within this Article as well as to instruments which are so negotiable.

§ 3—105. **When Promise or Order Unconditional.**

(1) A promise or order otherwise unconditional is not made conditional by the fact that the instrument

(a) is subject to implied or constructive conditions; or

(b) states its consideration, whether performed or promised, or the transaction which gave rise to the instrument, or that the promise or order is made or the instrument matures in accordance with or ''as per'' such transaction; or

(c) refers to or states that it arises out of a separate agreement or refers to a separate agreement for rights as to prepayment or acceleration; or

(d) states that it is drawn under a letter of credit; or

(e) states that it is secured, whether by mortgage, reservation of title or otherwise; or

(f) indicates a particular account to be debited or any other fund or source from which reimbursement is expected; or

(g) is limited to payment out of a particular fund or the proceeds of a particular source, if the instrument is issued by a government or governmental agency or unit; or

(h) is limited to payment out of the entire assets of a partnership, unincorporated association, trust or estate by or on behalf of which the instrument is issued.

(2) A promise or order is not unconditional if the instrument

(a) states that it is subject to or governed by any other agreement; or

(b) states that it is to be paid only out of a particular fund or source except as provided in this section.

§ 3—106. **Sum Certain.**

(1) The sum payable is a sum certain even though it is to be paid

(a) with stated interest or by stated installments; or

(b) with stated different rates of interest before and after default or a specified date; or

(c) with a stated discount or addition if paid before or after the date fixed for payment; or

(d) with exchange or less exchange, whether at a fixed rate or at the current rate; or

(e) with costs of collection or an attorney's fee or both upon default.

(2) Nothing in this section shall validate any term which is otherwise illegal.

§ 3—107. **Money.**

(1) An instrument is payable in money if the medium of exchange in which it is payable is money at the time the instrument is made. An instrument payable in ''currency'' or ''current funds'' is payable in money.

(2) A promise or order to pay a sum stated in a foreign currency is for a sum certain in money and, unless a different medium of payment is specified in the instrument, may be satisfied by payment of that number of dollars which the stated foreign currency will purchase at the buying sight rate for that currency on the day on which the instrument is payable or, if payable on demand, on the day of demand. If such an instrument specifies a foreign currency as the medium of payment the instrument is payable in that currency.

§ 3—108. **Payable on Demand.**

Instruments payable on demand include those payable at sight or on presentation and those in which no time for payment is stated.

§ 3—109. **Definite Time.**

(1) An instrument is payable at a definite time if by its terms it is payable

(a) on or before a stated date or at a fixed period after a stated date; or

(b) at a fixed period after sight; or

(c) at a definite time subject to any acceleration; or

(d) at a definite time subject to extension at the option of the holder, or to extension to a further definite time at the option of the maker or acceptor or automatically upon or after a specified act or event.

(2) An instrument which by its terms is otherwise payable only upon an act or event uncertain as to time of occurrence is not payable at a definite time even though the act or event has occurred.

§ 3—110. **Payable to Order.**

(1) An instrument is payable to order when by its terms it is payable to the order or assigns of any person therein specified with reasonable certainty, or to him or his order, or when it is conspicuously designated on its face as ''exchange'' or the like and names a payee. It may be payable to the order of

(a) the maker or drawer; or

(b) the drawee; or

(c) a payee who is not maker, drawer or drawee; or

(d) two or more payees together or in the alternative; or

(e) an estate, trust or fund, in which case it is payable to the order of the representative of such estate, trust or fund or his successors; or

(f) an office, or an officer by his title as such in which case it is payable to the principal but the incumbent of the office or his successors may act as if he or they were the holder; or

(g) a partnership or unincorporated association, in which case it is payable to the partnership or association and may be indorsed or transferred by any person thereto authorized.

(2) An instrument not payable to order is not made so payable by such words as ''payable upon return of this instrument properly indorsed.''

(3) An instrument made payable both to order and to bearer is payable to order unless the bearer words are handwritten or typewritten.

§ 3—111. **Payable to Bearer.**

An instrument is payable to bearer when by its terms it is payable to

(a) bearer or the order of bearer; or

(b) a specified person or bearer; or

(c) ''cash'' or the order of ''cash'', or any other indication which does not purport to designate a specific payee.

§ 3—112. **Terms and Omissions Not Affecting Negotiability.**

(1) The negotiability of an instrument is not affected by

(a) the omission of a statement of any consideration or of the place where the instrument is drawn or payable; or

(b) a statement that collateral has been given to secure obligations either on the instrument or otherwise of an obligor on the instrument or that in case of default on those obligations the holder may realize on or dispose of the collateral; or

(c) a promise or power to maintain or protect collateral or to give additional collateral; or

(d) a term authorizing a confession of judgment on the instrument if it is not paid when due; or

(e) a term purporting to waive the benefit of any law intended for the advantage or protection of any obligor; or

(f) a term in a draft providing that the payee by indorsing or cashing it acknowledges full satisfaction of an obligation of the drawer; or

(g) a statement in a draft drawn in a set of parts (Section 3—801) to the effect that the order is effective only if no other part has been honored.

(2) Nothing in this section shall validate any term which is otherwise illegal.

§ 3—113. **Seal.**

An instrument otherwise negotiable is within this Article even though it is under a seal.

§ 3—114. **Date, Antedating, Postdating.**

(1) The negotiability of an instrument is not affected by the fact that it is undated, antedated or postdated.

(2) Where an instrument is antedated or postdated the time when it is payable is determined by the stated date if the instrument is payable on demand or at a fixed period after date.

(3) Where the instrument or any signature thereon is dated, the date is presumed to be correct.

§ 3—115. **Incomplete Instruments.**

(1) When a paper whose contents at the time of signing show that it is intended to become an instrument is signed while still incomplete in any necessary respect it cannot be enforced until completed, but when it is completed in accordance with authority given it is effective as completed.

(2) If the completion is unauthorized the rules as to material alteration apply (Section 3—407), even though the paper was not delivered by the maker or drawer; but the burden of establishing that any completion is unauthorized is on the party so asserting.

§ 3—116. **Instruments Payable to Two or More Persons.**

An instrument payable to the order of two or more persons

(a) if in the alternative is payable to any one of them and may be negotiated, discharged or enforced by any of them who has possession of it;

(b) if not in the alternative is payable to all of them and may be negotiated, discharged or enforced only by all of them.

§ 3—117. **Instruments Payable With Words of Description.**

An instrument made payable to a named person with the addition of words describing him

(a) as agent or officer of a specified person is payable to his principal but the agent or officer may act as if he were the holder;

(b) as any other fiduciary for a specified person or purpose is payable to the payee and may be negotiated, discharged or enforced by him;

(c) in any other manner is payable to the payee unconditionally and the additional words are without effect on subsequent parties.

§ 3—118. Ambiguous Terms and Rules of Construction.

The following rules apply to every instrument:

(a) Where there is doubt whether the instrument is a draft or a note the holder may treat it as either. A draft drawn on the drawer is effective as a note.

(b) Handwritten terms control typewritten and printed terms, and typewritten control printed.

(c) Words control figures except that if the words are ambiguous figures control.

(d) Unless otherwise specified a provision for interest means interest at the judgment rate at the place of payment from the date of the instrument, or if it is undated from the date of issue.

(e) Unless the instrument otherwise specifies two or more persons who sign as maker, acceptor or drawer or indorser and as a part of the same transaction are jointly and severally liable even though the instrument contains such words as "I promise to pay."

(f) Unless otherwise specified consent to extension authorizes a single extension for not longer than the original period. A consent to extension, expressed in the instrument, is binding on secondary parties and accommodation makers. A holder may not exercise his option to extend an instrument over the objection of a maker or acceptor or other party who in accordance with Section 3—604 tenders full payment when the instrument is due.

§ 3—119. Other Writings Affecting Instrument.

(1) As between the obligor and his immediate obligee or any transferee the terms of an instrument may be modified or affected by any other written agreement executed as a part of the same transaction, except that a holder in due course is not affected by any limitation of his rights arising out of the separate written agreement if he had no notice of the limitation when he took the instrument.

(2) A separate agreement does not affect the negotiability of an instrument.

§ 3—120. Instruments "Payable Through" Bank.

An instrument which states that it is "payable through" a bank or the like designates that bank as a collecting bank to make presentment but does not of itself authorize the bank to pay the instrument.

§ 3—121. Instruments Payable at Bank.

Note: If this Act is introduced in the Congress of the United States this section should be omitted.

(States to select either alternative)

Alternative A—

A note or acceptance which states that it is payable at a bank is the equivalent of a draft drawn on the bank payable when it falls due out of any funds of the maker or acceptor in current account or otherwise available for such payment.

Alternative B—

A note or acceptance which states that it is payable at a bank is not of itself an order or authorization to the bank to pay it.

§ 3—122. Accrual of Cause of Action.

(1) A cause of action against a maker or an acceptor accrues

    (a) in the case of a time instrument on the day after maturity;

    (b) in the case of a demand instrument upon its date or, if no date is stated, on the date of issue.

(2) A cause of action against the obligor of a demand or time certificate of deposit accrues upon demand, but demand on a time certificate may not be made until on or after the date of maturity.

(3) A cause of action against a drawer of a draft or an indorser of any instrument accrues upon demand following dishonor of the instrument. Notice of dishonor is a demand.

(4) Unless an instrument provides otherwise, interest runs at the rate provided by law for a judgment

    (a) in the case of a maker, acceptor or other primary obligor of a demand instrument, from the date of demand;

    (b) in all other cases from the date of accrual of the cause of action.

Part 2 Transfer and Negotiation

§ 3—201. Transfer: Right to Indorsement.

(1) Transfer of an instrument vests in the transferee such rights as the transferor has therein, except that a transferee who has himself been a party to any fraud or illegality affecting the instrument or who as a prior holder had notice of a defense or claim against it cannot improve his position by taking from a later holder in due course.

(2) A transfer of a security interest in an instrument vests the foregoing rights in the transferee to the extent of the interest transferred.

(3) Unless otherwise agreed any transfer for value of an instrument not then payable to bearer gives the transferee the specifically enforceable right to have the unqualified indorsement of the transferor. Negotiation takes effect only when the indorsement is made and until that time there is no presumption that the transferee is the owner.

§ 3—202. Negotiation.

(1) Negotiation is the transfer of an instrument in such form that the transferee becomes a holder. If the instrument is payable to order it is negotiated by delivery with any necessary indorsement; if payable to bearer it is negotiated by delivery.

(2) An indorsement must be written by or on behalf of the holder and on the instrument or on a paper so firmly affixed thereto as to become a part thereof.

(3) An indorsement is effective for negotiation only when it conveys the entire instrument or any unpaid residue. If it purports to be of less it operates only as a partial assignment.

(4) Words of assignment, condition, waiver, guaranty, limitation or disclaimer of liability and the like accompanying an indorsement do not affect its character as an indorsement.

§ 3—203. **Wrong or Misspelled Name.**

Where an instrument is made payable to a person under a misspelled name or one other than his own he may indorse in that name or his own or both; but signature in both names may be required by a person paying or giving value for the instrument.

§ 3—204. **Special Indorsement; Blank Indorsement.**

(1) A special indorsement specifies the person to whom or to whose order it makes the instrument payable. Any instrument specially indorsed becomes payable to the order of the special indorsee and may be further negotiated only by his indorsement.

(2) An indorsement in blank specifies no particular indorsee and may consist of a mere signature. An instrument payable to order and indorsed in blank becomes payable to bearer and may be negotiated by delivery alone until specially indorsed.

(3) The holder may convert a blank indorsement into a special indorsement by writing over the signature of the indorser in blank any contract consistent with the character of the indorsement.

§ 3—205. **Restrictive Indorsements.**

An indorsement is restrictive which either

(a) is conditional; or

(b) purports to prohibit further transfer of the instrument; or

(c) includes the words "for collection", "for deposit", "pay any bank", or like terms signifying a purpose of deposit or collection; or

(d) otherwise states that it is for the benefit or use of the indorser or of another person.

§ 3—206. **Effect of Restrictive Indorsement.**

(1) No restrictive indorsement prevents further transfer or negotiation of the instrument.

(2) An intermediary bank, or a payor bank which is not the depositary bank, is neither given notice nor otherwise affected by a restrictive indorsement of any person except the bank's immediate transferor or the person presenting for payment.

(3) Except for an intermediary bank, any transferee under an indorsement which is conditional or includes the words "for collection", "for deposit", "pay any bank", or like terms (subparagraphs (a) and (c) of Section 3—205) must pay or apply any value given by him for or on the security of the instrument consistently with the indorsement and to the extent that he does so he becomes a holder for value. In addition such transferee is a holder in due course if he otherwise complies with the requirements of Section 3—302 on what constitutes a holder in due course.

(4) The first taker under an indorsement for the benefit of the indorser or another person (subparagraph (d) of Section 3—205) must pay or apply any value given by him for or on the security of the instrument consistently with the indorsement and to the extent that he does so he becomes a holder for value. In addition such taker is a holder in due course if he otherwise complies with the requirements of Section 3—302 on what constitutes a holder in due course. A later holder for value is neither given notice nor otherwise affected by such restrictive indorsement unless he has knowledge that a fiduciary or other person has negotiated the instrument in any transaction for his own benefit or otherwise in breach of duty (subsection (2) of Section 3—304).

§ 3—207. **Negotiation Effective Although It May Be Rescinded.**

(1) Negotiation is effective to transfer the instrument although the negotiation is

(a) made by an infant, a corporation exceeding its powers, or any other person without capacity; or

(b) obtained by fraud, duress or mistake of any kind; or

(c) part of an illegal transaction; or

(d) made in breach of duty.

(2) Except as against a subsequent holder in due course such negotiation is in an appropriate case subject to rescission, the declaration of a constructive trust or any other remedy permitted by law.

§ 3—208. **Reacquisition.**

Where an instrument is returned to or reacquired by a prior party he may cancel any indorsement which is not necessary to his title and reissue or further negotiate the instrument, but any intervening party is discharged as against the reacquiring party and subsequent holders not in due course and if his indorsement has been cancelled is discharged as against subsequent holders in due course as well.

Part 3 Rights of a Holder

§ 3—301. **Rights of a Holder.**

The holder of an instrument whether or not he is the owner may transfer or negotiate it and, except as otherwise provided in Section 3—603 on payment or satisfaction, discharge it or enforce payment in his own name.

§ 3—302. **Holder in Due Course.**

(1) A holder in due course is a holder who takes the instrument

    (a) for value; and

    (b) in good faith; and

    (c) without notice that it is overdue or has been dishonored or of any defense against or claim to it on the part of any person.

(2) A payee may be a holder in due course.

(3) A holder does not become a holder in due course of an instrument:

    (a) by purchase of it at judicial sale or by taking it under legal process; or

    (b) by acquiring it in taking over an estate; or

    (c) by purchasing it as part of a bulk transaction not in regular course of business of the transferor.

(4) A purchaser of a limited interest can be a holder in due course only to the extent of the interest purchased.

§ 3—303. **Taking for Value.**

A holder takes the instrument for value

(a) to the extent that the agreed consideration has been performed or that he acquires a security interest in or a lien on the instrument otherwise than by legal process; or

(b) when he takes the instrument in payment of or as security for an antecedent claim against any person whether or not the claim is due; or

(c) when he gives a negotiable instrument for it or makes an irrevocable commitment to a third person.

§ 3—304. **Notice to Purchaser.**

(1) The purchaser has notice of a claim or defense if

    (a) the instrument is so incomplete, bears such visible evidence of forgery or alteration, or is otherwise so irregular as to call into question its validity, terms or ownership or to create an ambiguity as to the party to pay; or

    (b) the purchaser has notice that the obligation of any party is voidable in whole or in part, or that all parties have been discharged.

(2) The purchaser has notice of a claim against the instrument when he has knowledge that a fiduciary has negotiated the instrument in payment of or as security for his own debt or in any transaction for his own benefit or otherwise in breach of duty.

(3) The purchaser has notice that an instrument is overdue if he has reason to know

    (a) that any part of the principal amount is overdue or that there is an uncured default in payment of another instrument of the same series; or

    (b) that acceleration of the instrument has been made; or

    (c) that he is taking a demand instrument after demand has been made or more than a reasonable length of time after its issue. A reasonable time for a check drawn and payable within the states and territories of the United States and the District of Columbia is presumed to be thirty days.

(4) Knowledge of the following facts does not of itself give the purchaser notice of a defense or claim

    (a) that the instrument is antedated or postdated;

    (b) that it was issued or negotiated in return for an executory promise or accompanied by a separate agreement, unless the purchaser has notice that a defense or claim has arisen from the terms thereof;

    (c) that any party has signed for accommodation;

    (d) that an incomplete instrument has been completed, unless the purchaser has notice of any improper completion;

    (e) that any person negotiating the instrument is or was a fiduciary;

    (f) that there has been default in payment of interest on the instrument or in payment of any other instrument, except one of the same series.

(5) The filing or recording of a document does not of itself constitute notice within the provisions of this Article to a person who would otherwise be a holder in due course.

(6) To be effective notice must be received at such time and in such manner as to give a reasonable opportunity to act on it.

§ 3—305. **Rights of a Holder in Due Course.**

To the extent that a holder is a holder in due course he takes the instrument free from

(1) all claims to it on the part of any person; and

(2) all defenses of any party to the instrument with whom the holder has not dealt except

    (a) infancy, to the extent that it is a defense to a simple contract; and

    (b) such other incapacity, or duress, or illegality of the transaction, as renders the obligation of the party a nullity; and

    (c) such misrepresentation as has induced the party to sign the instrument with neither knowledge nor reasonable opportunity to obtain knowledge of its character or its essential terms; and

    (d) discharge in insolvency proceedings; and

(e) any other discharge of which the holder has notice when he takes the instrument.

§ 3—306. **Rights of One Not Holder in Due Course.**

Unless he has the rights of a holder in due course any person takes the instrument subject to

(a) all valid claims to it on the part of any person; and

(b) all defenses of any party which would be available in an action on a simple contract; and

(c) the defenses of want or failure of consideration, non-performance of any condition precedent, non-delivery, or delivery for a special purpose (Section 3—408); and

(d) the defense that he or a person through whom he holds the instrument acquired it by theft, or that payment or satisfaction to such holder would be inconsistent with the terms of a restrictive indorsement. The claim of any third person to the instrument is not otherwise available as a defense to any party liable thereon unless the third person himself defends the action for such party.

§ 3—307. **Burden of Establishing Signatures, Defenses and Due Course.**

(1) Unless specifically denied in the pleadings each signature on an instrument is admitted. When the effectiveness of a signature is put in issue

(a) the burden of establishing it is on the party claiming under the signature; but

(b) the signature is presumed to be genuine or authorized except where the action is to enforce the obligation of a purported signer who has died or become incompetent before proof is required.

(2) When signatures are admitted or established, production of the instrument entitles a holder to recover on it unless the defendant establishes a defense.

(3) After it is shown that a defense exists a person claiming the rights of a holder in due course has the burden of establishing that he or some person under whom he claims is in all respects a holder in due course.

Part 4 **Liability of Parties**

§ 3—401. **Signature.**

(1) No person is liable on an instrument unless his signature appears thereon.

(2) A signature is made by use of any name, including any trade or assumed name, upon an instrument, or by any word or mark used in lieu of a written signature.

§ 3—402. **Signature in Ambiguous Capacity.**

Unless the instrument clearly indicates that a signature is made in some other capacity it is an indorsement.

§ 3—403. **Signature by Authorized Representative.**

(1) A signature may be made by an agent or other representative, and his authority to make it may be established as in other cases of representation. No particular form of appointment is necessary to establish such authority.

(2) An authorized representative who signs his own name to an instrument

(a) is personally obligated if the instrument neither names the person represented nor shows that the representative signed in a representative capacity;

(b) except as otherwise established between the immediate parties, is personally obligated if the instrument names the person represented but does not show that the representative signed in a representative capacity, or if the instrument does not name the person represented but does show that the representative signed in a representative capacity.

(3) Except as otherwise established the name of an organization preceded or followed by the name and office of an authorized individual is a signature made in a representative capacity.

§ 3—404. **Unauthorized Signatures.**

(1) Any unauthorized signature is wholly inoperative as that of the person whose name is signed unless he ratifies it or is precluded from denying it; but it operates as the signature of the unauthorized signer in favor of any person who in good faith pays the instrument or takes it for value.

(2) Any unauthorized signature may be ratified for all purposes of this Article. Such ratification does not of itself affect any rights of the person ratifying against the actual signer.

§ 3—405. **Impostors; Signature in Name of Payee.**

(1) An indorsement by any person in the name of a named payee is effective if

(a) an impostor by use of the mails or otherwise has induced the maker or drawer to issue the instrument to him or his confederate in the name of the payee; or

(b) a person signing as or on behalf of a maker or drawer intends the payee to have no interest in the instrument; or

(c) an agent or employee of the maker or drawer has supplied him with the name of the payee intending the latter to have no such interest.

(2) Nothing in this section shall affect the criminal or civil liability of the person so indorsing.

§ 3—406. **Negligence Contributing to Alteration or Unauthorized Signature.**

Any person who by his negligence substantially contributes to a material alteration of the instrument or to the making of an unauthorized signature is precluded from asserting the alteration or lack of authority against a holder in due course or against a drawee or other payor who pays the instrument in good faith and in accordance with the reasonable commercial standards of the drawee's or payor's business.

§ 3—407. **Alteration.**

(1) Any alteration of an instrument is material which changes the contract of any party thereto in any respect, including any such change in

>   (a) the number or relations of the parties; or

>   (b) an incomplete instrument, by completing it otherwise than as authorized; or

>   (c) the writing as signed, by adding to it or by removing any part of it.

(2) As against any person other than a subsequent holder in due course

>   (a) alteration by the holder which is both fraudulent and material discharges any party whose contract is thereby changed unless that party assents or is precluded from asserting the defense;

>   (b) no other alteration discharges any party and the instrument may be enforced according to its original tenor, or as to incomplete instruments according to the authority given.

(3) A subsequent holder in due course may in all cases enforce the instrument according to its original tenor, and when an incomplete instrument has been completed, he may enforce it as completed.

§ 3—408. **Consideration.**

Want or failure of consideration is a defense as against any person not having the rights of a holder in due course (Section 3—305), except that no consideration is necessary for an instrument or obligation thereon given in payment of or as security for an antecedent obligation of any kind. Nothing in this section shall be taken to displace any statute outside this Act under which a promise is enforceable notwithstanding lack or failure of consideration. Partial failure of consideration is a defense pro tanto whether or not the failure is in an ascertained or liquidated amount.

§ 3—409. **Draft Not an Assignment.**

(1) A check or other draft does not of itself operate as an assignment of any funds in the hands of the drawee available for its payment, and the drawee is not liable on the instrument until he accepts it.

(2) Nothing in this section shall affect any liability in contract, tort or otherwise arising from any letter of credit or other obligation or representation which is not an acceptance.

§ 3—410. **Definition and Operation of Acceptance.**

(1) Acceptance is the drawee's signed engagement to honor the draft as presented. It must be written on the draft, and may consist of his signature alone. It becomes operative when completed by delivery or notification.

(2) A draft may be accepted although it has not been signed by the drawer or is otherwise incomplete or is overdue or has been dishonored.

(3) Where the draft is payable at a fixed period after sight and the acceptor fails to date his acceptance the holder may complete it by supplying a date in good faith.

§ 3—411. **Certification of a Check.**

(1) Certification of a check is acceptance. Where a holder procures certification the drawer and all prior indorsers are discharged.

(2) Unless otherwise agreed a bank has no obligation to certify a check.

(3) A bank may certify a check before returning it for lack of proper indorsement. If it does so the drawer is discharged.

§ 3—412. **Acceptance Varying Draft.**

(1) Where the drawee's proffered acceptance in any manner varies the draft as presented the holder may refuse the acceptance and treat the draft as dishonored in which case the drawee is entitled to have his acceptance cancelled.

(2) The terms of the draft are not varied by an acceptance to pay at any particular bank or place in the United States, unless the acceptance states that the draft is to be paid only at such bank or place.

(3) Where the holder assents to an acceptance varying the terms of the draft each drawer and indorser who does not affirmatively assent is discharged.

§ 3—413. **Contract of Maker, Drawer and Acceptor.**

(1) The maker or acceptor engages that he will pay the instrument according to its tenor at the time of his engagement or as completed pursuant to Section 3—115 on incomplete instruments.

(2) The drawer engages that upon dishonor of the draft and any necessary notice of dishonor or protest he will pay the amount of the draft to the holder or to any indorser who takes it up. The drawer may disclaim this liability by drawing without recourse.

(3) By making, drawing or accepting the party admits as against all subsequent parties including the drawee the existence of the payee and his then capacity to indorse.

§ 3—414. **Contract of Indorser; Order of Liability.**

(1) Unless the indorsement otherwise specifies (as by such words as "without recourse") every indorser engages that upon dishonor and any necessary notice of dishonor and

protest he will pay the instrument according to its tenor at the time of his indorsement to the holder or to any subsequent indorser who takes it up, even though the indorser who takes it up was not obligated to do so.

(2) Unless they otherwise agree indorsers are liable to one another in the order in which they indorse, which is presumed to be the order in which their signatures appear on the instrument.

§ 3—415. Contract of Accommodation Party.

(1) An accommodation party is one who signs the instrument in any capacity for the purpose of lending his name to another party to it.

(2) When the instrument has been taken for value before it is due the accommodation party is liable in the capacity in which he has signed even though the taker knows of the accommodation.

(3) As against a holder in due course and without notice of the accommodation oral proof of the accommodation is not admissible to give the accommodation party the benefit of discharges dependent on his character as such. In other cases the accommodation character may be shown by oral proof.

(4) An indorsement which shows that it is not in the chain of title is notice of its accommodation character.

(5) An accommodation party is not liable to the party accommodated, and if he pays the instrument has a right of recourse on the instrument against such party.

§ 3—416. Contract of Guarantor.

(1) "Payment guaranteed" or equivalent words added to a signature mean that the signer engages that if the instrument is not paid when due he will pay it according to its tenor without resort by the holder to any other party.

(2) "Collection guaranteed" or equivalent words added to a signature mean that the signer engages that if the instrument is not paid when due he will pay it according to its tenor, but only after the holder has reduced his claim against the maker or acceptor to judgment and execution has been returned unsatisfied, or after the maker or acceptor has become insolvent or it is otherwise apparent that it is useless to proceed against him.

(3) Words of guaranty which do not otherwise specify guarantee payment.

(4) No words of guaranty added to the signature of a sole maker or acceptor affect his liability on the instrument. Such words added to the signature of one of two or more makers or acceptors create a presumption that the signature is for the accommodation of the others.

(5) When words of guaranty are used presentment, notice of dishonor and protest are not necessary to charge the user.

(6) Any guaranty written on the instrument is enforceable notwithstanding any statute of frauds.

§ 3—417. Warranties on Presentment and Transfer.

(1) Any person who obtains payment or acceptance and any prior transferor warrants to a person who in good faith pays or accepts that

(a) he has a good title to the instrument or is authorized to obtain payment or acceptance on behalf of one who has a good title; and

(b) he has no knowledge that the signature of the maker or drawer is unauthorized, except that this warranty is not given by a holder in due course acting in good faith

(i) to a maker with respect to the maker's own signature; or

(ii) to a drawer with respect to the drawer's own signature, whether or not the drawer is also the drawee; or

(iii) to an acceptor of a draft if the holder in due course took the draft after the acceptance or obtained the acceptance without knowledge that the drawer's signature was unauthorized; and

(c) the instrument has not been materially altered, except that this warranty is not given by a holder in due course acting in good faith

(i) to the maker of a note; or

(ii) to the drawer of a draft whether or not the drawer is also the drawee; or

(iii) to the acceptor of a draft with respect to an alteration made prior to the acceptance if the holder in due course took the draft after the acceptance, even though the acceptance provided "payable as originally drawn" or equivalent terms; or

(iv) to the acceptor of a draft with respect to an alteration made after the acceptance.

(2) Any person who transfers an instrument and receives consideration warrants to his transferee and if the transfer is by indorsement to any subsequent holder who takes the instrument in good faith that

(a) he has a good title to the instrument or is authorized to obtain payment or acceptance on behalf of one who has a good title and the transfer is otherwise rightful; and

(b) all signatures are genuine or authorized; and

(c) the instrument has not been materially altered; and

(d) no defense of any party is good against him; and

(e) he has no knowledge of any insolvency proceeding instituted with respect to the maker or acceptor or the drawer of an unaccepted instrument.

(3) By transferring "without recourse" the transferor limits the obligation stated in subsection (2)(d) to a warranty that he has no knowledge of such a defense.

(4) A selling agent or broker who does not disclose the fact that he is acting only as such gives the warranties provided in this section, but if he makes such disclosure warrants only his good faith and authority.

§ 3—418. Finality of Payment or Acceptance.

Except for recovery of bank payments as provided in the Article on Bank Deposits and Collections (Article 4) and except for liability for breach of warranty on presentment under the preceding section, payment or acceptance of any instrument is final in favor of a holder in due course, or a person who has in good faith changed his position in reliance on the payment.

§ 3—419. Conversion of Instrument; Innocent Representative.

(1) An instrument is converted when

(a) a drawee to whom it is delivered for acceptance refuses to return it on demand; or

(b) any person to whom it is delivered for payment refuses on demand either to pay or to return it; or

(c) it is paid on a forged indorsement.

(2) In an action against a drawee under subsection (1) the measure of the drawee's liability is the face amount of the instrument. In any other action under subsection (1) the measure of liability is presumed to be the face amount of the instrument.

(3) Subject to the provisions of this Act concerning restrictive indorsements a representative, including a depositary or collecting bank, who has in good faith and in accordance with the reasonable commercial standards applicable to the business of such representative dealt with an instrument or its proceeds on behalf of one who was not the true owner is not liable in conversion or otherwise to the true owner beyond the amount of any proceeds remaining in his hands.

(4) An intermediary bank or payor bank which is not a depositary bank is not liable in conversion solely by reason of the fact that proceeds of an item indorsed restrictively (Sections 3—205 and 3—206) are not paid or applied consistently with the restrictive indorsement of an indorser other than its immediate transferor.

Part 5 Presentment, Notice of Dishonor and Protest

§ 3—501. When Presentment, Notice of Dishonor, and Protest Necessary or Permissible.

(1) Unless excused (Section 3—511) presentment is necessary to charge secondary parties as follows:

(a) presentment for acceptance is necessary to charge the drawer and indorsers of a draft where the draft so provides, or is payable elsewhere than at the residence or place of business of the drawee, or its date of payment depends upon such presentment. The holder may at his option present for acceptance any other draft payable at a stated date;

(b) presentment for payment is necessary to charge any indorser;

(c) in the case of any drawer, the acceptor of a draft payable at a bank or the maker of a note payable at a bank, presentment for payment is necessary, but failure to make presentment discharges such drawer, acceptor or maker only as stated in Section 3—502(1)(b).

(2) Unless excused (Section 3—511)

(a) notice of any dishonor is necessary to charge any indorser;

(b) in the case of any drawer, the acceptor of a draft payable at a bank or the maker of a note payable at a bank, notice of any dishonor is necessary, but failure to give such notice discharges such drawer, acceptor or maker only as stated in Section 3—502(1)(b).

(3) Unless excused (Section 3—511) protest of any dishonor is necessary to charge the drawer and indorsers of any draft which on its face appears to be drawn or payable outside of the states, territories, dependencies, and possessions of the United States, the District of Columbia and the Commonwealth of Puerto Rico. The holder may at his option make protest of any dishonor of any other instrument and in the case of a foreign draft may on insolvency of the acceptor before maturity make protest for better security.

(4) Notwithstanding any provision of this section, neither presentment nor notice of dishonor nor protest is necessary to charge an indorser who has indorsed an instrument after maturity.

§ 3—502. Unexcused Delay; Discharge.

(1) Where without excuse any necessary presentment or notice of dishonor is delayed beyond the time when it is due

(a) any indorser is discharged; and

(b) any drawer or the acceptor of a draft payable at a bank or the maker of a note payable at a bank who because the drawee or payor bank becomes insolvent during the delay is deprived of funds maintained with the drawee or payor bank to cover the instrument may discharge his liability by written assignment to the holder of his rights against the drawee or payor bank in respect of such funds, but such drawer, acceptor or maker is not otherwise discharged.

(2) Where without excuse a necessary protest is delayed beyond the time when it is due any drawer or indorser is discharged.

§ 3—503. Time of Presentment.

(1) Unless a different time is expressed in the instrument the time for any presentment is determined as follows:

(a) where an instrument is payable at or a fixed period after a stated date any presentment for acceptance must be made on or before the date it is payable;

(b) where an instrument is payable after sight it must either be presented for acceptance or negotiated within a reasonable time after date or issue whichever is later;

(c) where an instrument shows the date on which it is payable presentment for payment is due on that date;

(d) where an instrument is accelerated presentment for payment is due within a reasonable time after the acceleration;

(e) with respect to the liability of any secondary party presentment for acceptance or payment of any other instrument is due within a reasonable time after such party becomes liable thereon.

(2) A reasonable time for presentment is determined by the nature of the instrument, any usage of banking or trade and the facts of the particular case. In the case of an uncertified check which is drawn and payable within the United States and which is not a draft drawn by a bank the following are presumed to be reasonable periods within which to present for payment or to initiate bank collection:

(a) with respect to the liability of the drawer, thirty days after date or issue whichever is later; and

(b) with respect to the liability of an indorser, seven days after his indorsement.

(3) Where any presentment is due on a day which is not a full business day for either the person making presentment or the party to pay or accept, presentment is due on the next following day which is a full business day for both parties.

(4) Presentment to be sufficient must be made at a reasonable hour, and if at a bank during its banking day.

§ 3—504. **How Presentment Made.**

(1) Presentment is a demand for acceptance or payment made upon the maker, acceptor, drawee or other payor by or on behalf of the holder.

(2) Presentment may be made

(a) by mail, in which event the time of presentment is determined by the time of receipt of the mail; or

(b) through a clearing house; or

(c) at the place of acceptance or payment specified in the instrument or if there be none at the place of business or residence of the party to accept or pay. If neither the party to accept or pay nor anyone authorized to act for him is present or accessible at such place presentment is excused.

(3) It may be made

(a) to any one of two or more makers, acceptors, drawees or other payors; or

(b) to any person who has authority to make or refuse the acceptance or payment.

(4) A draft accepted or a note made payable at a bank in the United States must be presented at such bank.

(5) In the cases described in Section 4—210 presentment may be made in the manner and with the result stated in that section.

§ 3—505. **Rights of Party to Whom Presentment Is Made.**

(1) The party to whom presentment is made may without dishonor require

(a) exhibition of the instrument; and

(b) reasonable identification of the person making presentment and evidence of his authority to make it if made for another; and

(c) that the instrument be produced for acceptance or payment at a place specified in it, or if there be none at any place reasonable in the circumstances; and

(d) a signed receipt on the instrument for any partial or full payment and its surrender upon full payment.

(2) Failure to comply with any such requirement invalidates the presentment but the person presenting has a reasonable time in which to comply and the time for acceptance or payment runs from the time of compliance.

§ 3—506. **Time Allowed for Acceptance or Payment.**

(1) Acceptance may be deferred without dishonor until the close of the next business day following presentment. The holder may also in a good faith effort to obtain acceptance and without either dishonor of the instrument or discharge of secondary parties allow postponement of acceptance for an additional business day.

(2) Except as a longer time is allowed in the case of documentary drafts drawn under a letter of credit, and unless an earlier time is agreed to by the party to pay, payment of an instrument may be deferred without dishonor pending reasonable examination to determine whether it is properly payable, but payment must be made in any event before the close of business on the day of presentment.

§ 3—507. **Dishonor; Holder's Right of Recourse; Term Allowing Re-Presentment.**

(1) An instrument is dishonored when

(a) a necessary or optional presentment is duly made and due acceptance or payment is refused or cannot be obtained within the prescribed time or in case of bank collections the instrument is seasonably returned by the midnight deadline (Section 4—301); or

(b) presentment is excused and the instrument is not duly accepted or paid.

(2) Subject to any necessary notice of dishonor and protest, the holder has upon dishonor an immediate right of recourse against the drawers and indorsers.

(3) Return of an instrument for lack of proper indorsement is not dishonor.

(4) A term in a draft or an indorsement thereof allowing a stated time for re-presentment in the event of any dishonor of the draft by nonacceptance if a time draft or by nonpayment if a sight draft gives the holder as against any secondary party bound by the term an option to waive the dishonor without affecting the liability of the secondary party and he may present again up to the end of the stated time.

§ 3—508. **Notice of Dishonor.**

(1) Notice of dishonor may be given to any person who may be liable on the instrument by or on behalf of the holder or any party who has himself received notice, or any other party who can be compelled to pay the instrument. In addition an agent or bank in whose hands the instrument is dishonored may give notice to his principal or customer or to another agent or bank from which the instrument was received.

(2) Any necessary notice must be given by a bank before its midnight deadline and by any other person before midnight of the third business day after dishonor or receipt of notice of dishonor.

(3) Notice may be given in any reasonable manner. It may be oral or written and in any terms which identify the instrument and state that it has been dishonored. A misdescription which does not mislead the party notified does not vitiate the notice. Sending the instrument bearing a stamp, ticket or writing stating that acceptance or payment has been refused or sending a notice of debit with respect to the instrument is sufficient.

(4) Written notice is given when sent although it is not received.

(5) Notice to one partner is notice to each although the firm has been dissolved.

(6) When any party is in insolvency proceedings instituted after the issue of the instrument notice may be given either to the party or to the representative of his estate.

(7) When any party is dead or incompetent notice may be sent to his last known address or given to his personal representative.

(8) Notice operates for the benefit of all parties who have rights on the instrument against the party notified.

§ 3—509. **Protest; Noting for Protest.**

(1) A protest is a certificate of dishonor made under the hand and seal of a United States consul or vice consul or a notary public or other person authorized to certify dishonor by the law of the place where dishonor occurs. It may be made upon information satisfactory to such person.

(2) The protest must identify the instrument and certify either that due presentment has been made or the reason why it is excused and that the instrument has been dishonored by nonacceptance or nonpayment.

(3) The protest may also certify that notice of dishonor has been given to all parties or to specified parties.

(4) Subject to subsection (5) any necessary protest is due by the time that notice of dishonor is due.

(5) If, before protest is due, an instrument has been noted for protest by the officer to make protest, the protest may be made at any time thereafter as of the date of the noting.

§ 3—510. **Evidence of Dishonor and Notice of Dishonor.**

The following are admissible as evidence and create a presumption of dishonor and of any notice of dishonor therein shown:

(a) a document regular in form as provided in the preceding section which purports to be a protest;

(b) the purported stamp or writing of the drawee, payor bank or presenting bank on the instrument or accompanying it stating that acceptance or payment has been refused for reasons consistent with dishonor;

(c) any book or record of the drawee, payor bank, or any collecting bank kept in the usual course of business which shows dishonor, even though there is no evidence of who made the entry.

§ 3—511. **Waived or Excused Presentment, Protest or Notice of Dishonor or Delay Therein.**

(1) Delay in presentment, protest or notice of dishonor is excused when the party is without notice that it is due or when the delay is caused by circumstances beyond his control and he exercises reasonable diligence after the cause of the delay ceases to operate.

(2) Presentment or notice or protest as the case may be is entirely excused when

(a) the party to be charged has waived it expressly or by implication either before or after it is due; or

(b) such party has himself dishonored the instrument or has countermanded payment or otherwise has no reason to expect or right to require that the instrument be accepted or paid; or

(c) by reasonable diligence the presentment or protest cannot be made or the notice given.

(3) Presentment is also entirely excused when

(a) the maker, acceptor or drawee of any instrument except a documentary draft is dead or in insolvency proceedings instituted after the issue of the instrument; or

(b) acceptance or payment is refused but not for want of proper presentment.

(4) Where a draft has been dishonored by nonacceptance a later presentment for payment and any notice of dishonor and protest for nonpayment are excused unless in the meantime the instrument has been accepted.

(5) A waiver of protest is also a waiver of presentment and of notice of dishonor even though protest is not required.

(6) Where a waiver of presentment or notice or protest is embodied in the instrument itself it is binding upon all parties; but where it is written above the signature of an indorser it binds him only.

Part 6 Discharge

§ 3—601. **Discharge of Parties.**

(1) The extent of the discharge of any party from liability on an instrument is governed by the sections on

(a) payment or satisfaction (Section 3—603); or

(b) tender of payment (Section 3—604); or

(c) cancellation or renunciation (Section 3—605); or

(d) impairment of right of recourse or of collateral (Section 3—606); or

(e) reacquisition of the instrument by a prior party (Section 3—208); or

(f) fraudulent and material alteration (Section 3—407); or

(g) certification of a check (Section 3—411); or

(h) acceptance varying a draft (Section 3—412); or

(i) unexcused delay in presentment or notice of dishonor or protest (Section 3—502).

(2) Any party is also discharged from his liability on an instrument to another party by any other act or agreement with such party which would discharge his simple contract for the payment of money.

(3) The liability of all parties is discharged when any party who has himself no right of action or recourse on the instrument

(a) reacquires the instrument in his own right; or

(b) is discharged under any provision of this Article, except as otherwise provided with respect to discharge for impairment of recourse or of collateral (Section 3—606).

§ 3—602. **Effect of Discharge Against Holder in Due Course.**

No discharge of any party provided by this Article is ef-

fective against a subsequent holder in due course unless he has notice thereof when he takes the instrument.

§ 3—603. **Payment or Satisfaction.**

(1) The liability of any party is discharged to the extent of his payment or satisfaction to the holder even though it is made with knowledge of a claim of another person to the instrument unless prior to such payment or satisfaction the person making the claim either supplies indemnity deemed adequate by the party seeking the discharge or enjoins payment or satisfaction by order of a court of competent jurisdiction in an action in which the adverse claimant and the holder are parties. This subsection does not, however, result in the discharge of the liability

(a) of a party who in bad faith pays or satisfies a holder who acquired the instrument by theft or who (unless having the rights of a holder in due course) holds through one who so acquired it; or

(b) of a party (other than an intermediary bank or a payor bank which is not a depositary bank) who pays or satisfies the holder of an instrument which has been restrictively indorsed in a manner not consistent with the terms of such restrictive indorsement.

(2) Payment or satisfaction may be made with the consent of the holder by any person including a stranger to the instrument. Surrender of the instrument to such a person gives him the rights of a transferee (Section 3—201).

§ 3—604. **Tender of Payment.**

(1) Any party making tender of full payment to a holder when or after it is due is discharged to the extent of all subsequent liability for interest, costs and attorney's fees.

(2) The holder's refusal of such tender wholly discharges any party who has a right of recourse against the party making the tender.

(3) Where the maker or acceptor of an instrument payable otherwise than on demand is able and ready to pay at every place of payment specified in the instrument when it is due, it is equivalent to tender.

§ 3—605. **Cancellation and Renunciation.**

(1) The holder of an instrument may even without consideration discharge any party

(a) in any manner apparent on the face of the instrument or the indorsement, as by intentionally cancelling the instrument or the party's signature by destruction or mutilation, or by striking out the party's signature; or

(b) by renouncing his rights by a writing signed and delivered or by surrender of the instrument to the party to be discharged.

(2) Neither cancellation nor renunciation without surrender of the instrument affects the title thereto.

§ 3—606. **Impairment of Recourse or of Collateral.**

(1) The holder discharges any party to the instrument to the extent that without such party's consent the holder

(a) without express reservation of rights releases or agrees not to sue any person against whom the party has to the knowledge of the holder a right of recourse or agrees to suspend the right to enforce against such person the instrument or collateral or otherwise discharges such person, except that failure or delay in effecting any required presentment, protest or notice of dishonor with respect to any such person does not discharge any party as to whom presentment, protest or notice of dishonor is effective or unnecessary; or

(b) unjustifiably impairs any collateral for the instrument given by or on behalf of the party or any person against whom he has a right of recourse.

(2) By express reservation of rights against a party with a right of recourse the holder preserves

(a) all his rights against such party as of the time when the instrument was originally due; and

(b) the right of the party to pay the instrument as of that time; and

(c) all rights of such party to recourse against others.

Part 7 Advice of International Sight Draft

§ 3—701. **Letter of Advice of International Sight Draft.**

(1) A "letter of advice" is a drawer's communication to the drawee that a described draft has been drawn.

(2) Unless otherwise agreed when a bank receives from another bank a letter of advice of an international sight draft the drawee bank may immediately debit the drawer's account and stop the running of interest pro tanto. Such a debit and any resulting credit to any account covering outstanding drafts leaves in the drawer full power to stop payment or otherwise dispose of the amount and creates no trust or interest in favor of the holder.

(3) Unless otherwise agreed and except where a draft is drawn under a credit issued by the drawee, the drawee of an international sight draft owes the drawer no duty to pay an unadvised draft but if it does so and the draft is genuine, may appropriately debit the drawer's account.

Part 8 Miscellaneous

§ 3—801. **Drafts in a Set.**

(1) Where a draft is drawn in a set of parts, each of which is numbered and expressed to be an order only if no other part has been honored, the whole of the parts constitutes one draft but a taker of any part may become a holder in due course of the draft.

(2) Any person who negotiates, indorses or accepts a single part of a draft drawn in a set thereby becomes liable to any holder in due course of that part as if it were the whole set, but as between different holders in due course to whom different parts have been negotiated the holder whose title first accrues has all rights to the draft and its proceeds.

(3) As against the drawee the first presented part of a draft drawn in a set is the part entitled to payment, or if a time draft to acceptance and payment. Acceptance of any subsequently presented part renders the drawee liable thereon under subsection (2). With respect both to a holder and to the drawer payment of a subsequently presented part of a draft payable at sight has the same effect as payment of a check notwithstanding an effective stop order (Section 4—407).

(4) Except as otherwise provided in this section, where any part of a draft in a set is discharged by payment or otherwise the whole draft is discharged.

§ 3—802. **Effect of Instrument on Obligation for Which It Is Given.**

(1) Unless otherwise agreed where an instrument is taken for an underlying obligation

(a) the obligation is pro tanto discharged if a bank is drawer, maker or acceptor of the instrument and there is no recourse on the instrument against the underlying obligor; and

(b) in any other case the obligation is suspended pro tanto until the instrument is due or if it is payable on demand until its presentment. If the instrument is dishonored action may be maintained on either the instrument or the obligation; discharge of the underlying obligor on the instrument also discharges him on the obligation.

(2) The taking in good faith of a check which is not postdated does not of itself so extend the time on the original obligation as to discharge a surety.

§ 3—803. **Notice to Third Party.**

Where a defendant is sued for breach of an obligation for which a third person is answerable over under this Article he may give the third person written notice of the litigation, and the person notified may then give similar notice to any other person who is answerable over to him under this Article. If the notice states that the person notified may come in and defend and that if the person notified does not do so he will in any action against him by the person giving the notice be bound by any determination of fact common to the two litigations, then unless after seasonable receipt of the notice the person notified does come in and defend he is so bound.

§ 3—804. **Lost, Destroyed or Stolen Instruments.**

The owner of an instrument which is lost, whether by destruction, theft or otherwise, may maintain an action in his own name and recover from any party liable thereon upon due proof of his ownership, the facts which prevent his production of the instrument and its terms. The court may require security indemnifying the defendant against loss by reason of further claims on the instrument.

§ 3—805. Instruments Not Payable to Order or to Bearer.

This Article applies to any instrument whose terms do not preclude transfer and which is otherwise negotiable within this Article but which is not payable to order or to bearer, except that there can be no holder in due course of such an instrument.

Revised Article 3
NEGOTIABLE INSTRUMENTS

Part 1 General Provisions and Definitions

§ 3—101. Short Title.

This Article may be cited as Uniform Commercial Code—Negotiable Instruments.

§ 3—102. Subject Matter.

(a) This Article applies to negotiable instruments. It does not apply to money, to payment orders governed by Article 4A, or to securities governed by Article 8.

(b) If there is conflict between this Article and Article 4 or 9, Articles 4 and 9 govern.

(c) Regulations of the Board of Governors of the Federal Reserve System and operating circulars of the Federal Reserve Banks supersede any inconsistent provision of this Article to the extent of the inconsistency.

§ 3—103. Definitions.

(a) In this Article:

(1) ''Acceptor'' means a drawee who has accepted a draft.

(2) ''Drawee'' means a person ordered in a draft to make payment.

(3) ''Drawer'' means a person who signs or is identified in a draft as a person ordering payment.

(4) ''Good faith'' means honesty in fact and the observance of reasonable commercial standards of fair dealing.

(5) ''Maker'' means a person who signs or is identified in a note as a person undertaking to pay.

(6) ''Order'' means a written instruction to pay money signed by the person giving the instruction. The instruction may be addressed to any person, including the person giving the instruction, or to one or more

persons jointly or in the alternative but not in succession. An authorization to pay is not an order unless the person authorized to pay is also instructed to pay.

(7) ''Ordinary care'' in the case of a person engaged in business means observance of reasonable commercial standards, prevailing in the area in which the person is located, with respect to the business in which the person is engaged. In the case of a bank that takes an instrument for processing for collection or payment by automated means, reasonable commercial standards do not require the bank to examine the instrument if the failure to examine does not violate the bank's prescribed procedures and the bank's procedures do not vary unreasonably from general banking usage not disapproved by this Article or Article 4.

(8) ''Party'' means a party to an instrument.

(9) ''Promise'' means a written undertaking to pay money signed by the person undertaking to pay. An acknowledgment of an obligation by the obligor is not a promise unless the obligor also undertakes to pay the obligation.

(10) ''Prove'' with respect to a fact means to meet the burden of establishing the fact (Section 1—201(8)).

(11) ''Remitter'' means a person who purchases an instrument from its issuer if the instrument is payable to an identified person other than the purchaser.

(b);(c) [Other definitions' section references deleted.]

(d) In addition, Article 1 contains general definitions and principles of construction and interpretation applicable throughout this Article.

§ 3—104. Negotiable Instrument.

(a) Except as provided in subsections (c) and (d), ''negotiable instrument'' means an unconditional promise or order to pay a fixed amount of money, with or without interest or other charges described in the promise or order, if it:

(1) is payable to bearer or to order at the time it is issued or first comes into possession of a holder;

(2) is payable on demand or at a definite time; and

(3) does not state any other undertaking or instruction by the person promising or ordering payment to do any act in addition to the payment of money, but the promise or order may contain (i) an undertaking or power to give, maintain, or protect collateral to secure payment, (ii) an authorization or power to the holder to confess judgment or realize on or dispose of collateral, or (iii) a waiver of the benefit of any law intended for the advantage or protection of an obligor.

(b) ''Instrument'' means a negotiable instrument.

(c) An order that meets all of the requirements of subsection (a), except paragraph (1), and otherwise falls within the definition of ''check'' in subsection (f) is a negotiable instrument and a check.

(d) A promise or order other than a check is not an instrument if, at the time it is issued or first comes into possession of a holder, it contains a conspicuous statement, however expressed, to the effect that the promise or order is not negotiable or is not an instrument governed by this Article.

(e) An instrument is a ''note'' if it is a promise and is a ''draft'' if it is an order. If an instrument falls within the definition of both ''note'' and ''draft,'' a person entitled to enforce the instrument may treat it as either.

(f) ''Check'' means (i) a draft, other than a documentary draft, payable on demand and drawn on a bank or (ii) a cashier's check or teller's check. An instrument may be a check even though it is described on its face by another term, such as ''money order.''

(g) ''Cashier's check'' means a draft with respect to which the drawer and drawee are the same bank or branches of the same bank.

(h) ''Teller's check'' means a draft drawn by a bank (i) on another bank, or (ii) payable at or through a bank.

(i) ''Traveler's check'' means an instrument that (i) is payable on demand, (ii) is drawn on or payable at or through a bank, (iii) is designated by the term ''traveler's check'' or by a substantially similar term, and (iv) requires, as a condition to payment, a countersignature by a person whose specimen signature appears on the instrument.

(j) ''Certificate of deposit'' means an instrument containing an acknowledgment by a bank that a sum of money has been received by the bank and a promise by the bank to repay the sum of money. A certificate of deposit is a note of the bank.

§ 3—105. Issue of Instrument.

(a) ''Issue'' means the first delivery of an instrument by the maker or drawer, whether to a holder or nonholder, for the purpose of giving rights on the instrument to any person.

(b) An unissued instrument, or an unissued incomplete instrument that is completed, is binding on the maker or drawer, but nonissuance is a defense. An instrument that is conditionally issued or is issued for a special purpose is binding on the maker or drawer, but failure of the condition or special purpose to be fulfilled is a defense.

(c) ''Issuer'' applies to issued and unissued instruments and means a maker or drawer of an instrument.

§ 3—106. Unconditional Promise or Order.

(a) Except as provided in this section, for the purposes of Section 3—104(a), a promise or order is unconditional unless it states (i) an express condition to payment, (ii) that the promise or order is subject to or governed by another writing, or (iii) that rights or obligations with respect to the promise or order are stated in another writing. A reference to another writing does not of itself make the promise or order conditional.

(b) A promise or order is not made conditional (i) by a reference to another writing for a statement of rights with respect to collateral, prepayment, or acceleration, or (ii) because payment is limited to resort to a particular fund or source.

(c) If a promise or order requires, as a condition to payment, a countersignature by a person whose specimen signature appears on the promise or order, the condition does not make the promise or order conditional for the purposes of Section 3—104(a). If the person whose specimen signature appears on an instrument fails to countersign the instrument, the failure to countersign is a defense to the obligation of the issuer, but the failure does not prevent a transferee of the instrument from becoming a holder of the instrument.

(d) If a promise or order at the time it is issued or first comes into possession of a holder contains a statement, required by applicable statutory or administrative law, to the effect that the rights of a holder or transferee are subject to claims or defenses that the issuer could assert against the original payee, the promise or order is not thereby made conditional for the purposes of Section 3—104(a); but if the promise or order is an instrument, there cannot be a holder in due course of the instrument.

§ 3—107. Instrument Payable in Foreign Money.

Unless the instrument otherwise provides, an instrument that states the amount payable in foreign money may be paid in the foreign money or in an equivalent amount in dollars calculated by using the current bank-offered spot rate at the place of payment for the purchase of dollars on the day on which the instrument is paid.

§ 3—108. Payable on Demand or at Definite Time.

(a) A promise or order is ''payable on demand'' if it (i) states that it is payable on demand or at sight, or otherwise indicates that it is payable at the will of the holder, or (ii) does not state any time of payment.

(b) A promise or order is ''payable at a definite time'' if it is payable on elapse of a definite period of time after sight or acceptance or at a fixed date or dates or at a time or times readily ascertainable at the time the promise or order is issued, subject to rights of (i) prepayment, (ii) acceleration, (iii) extension at the option of the holder, or (iv) extension to a further definite time at the option of the maker or acceptor or automatically upon or after a specified act or event.

(c) If an instrument, payable at a fixed date, is also payable upon demand made before the fixed date, the instrument is payable on demand until the fixed date and, if demand for payment is not made before that date, becomes payable at a definite time on the fixed date.

§ 3—109. **Payable to Bearer or to Order.**

(a) A promise or order is payable to bearer if it:

(1) states that it is payable to bearer or to the order of bearer or otherwise indicates that the person in possession of the promise or order is entitled to payment;

(2) does not state a payee; or

(3) states that it is payable to or to the order of cash or otherwise indicates that it is not payable to an identified person.

(b) A promise or order that is not payable to bearer is payable to order if it is payable (i) to the order of an identified person or (ii) to an identified person or order. A promise or order that is payable to order is payable to the identified person.

(c) An instrument payable to bearer may become payable to an identified person if it is specially indorsed pursuant to Section 3—205(a). An instrument payable to an identified person may become payable to bearer if it is indorsed in blank pursuant to Section 3—205(b).

§ 3—110. **Identification of Person to Whom Instrument Is Payable.**

(a) The person to whom an instrument is initially payable is determined by the intent of the person, whether or not authorized, signing as, or in the name or behalf of, the issuer of the instrument. The instrument is payable to the person intended by the signer even if that person is identified in the instrument by a name or other identification that is not that of the intended person. If more than one person signs in the name or behalf of the issuer of an instrument and all the signers do not intend the same person as payee, the instrument is payable to any person intended by one or more of the signers.

(b) If the signature of the issuer of an instrument is made by automated means, such as a check-writing machine, the payee of the instrument is determined by the intent of the person who supplied the name or identification of the payee, whether or not authorized to do so.

(c) A person to whom an instrument is payable may be identified in any way, including by name, identifying number, office, or account number. For the purpose of determining the holder of an instrument, the following rules apply:

(1) If an instrument is payable to an account and the account is identified only by number, the instrument is payable to the person to whom the account is payable. If an instrument is payable to an account identified by number and by the name of a person, the instrument is payable to the named person, whether or not that person is the owner of the account identified by number.

(2) If an instrument is payable to:

(i) a trust, an estate, or a person described as trustee or representative of a trust or estate, the instrument is payable to the trustee, the representative, or a successor of either, whether or not the beneficiary or estate is also named;

(ii) a person described as agent or similar representative of a named or identified person, the instrument is payable to the represented person, the representative, or a successor of the representative;

(iii) a fund or organization that is not a legal entity, the instrument is payable to a representative of the members of the fund or organization; or

(iv) an office or to a person described as holding an office, the instrument is payable to the named person, the incumbent of the office, or a successor to the incumbent.

(d) If an instrument is payable to two or more persons alternatively, it is payable to any of them and may be negotiated, discharged, or enforced by any or all of them in possession of the instrument. If an instrument is payable to two or more persons not alternatively, it is payable to all of them and may be negotiated, discharged, or enforced only by all of them. If an instrument payable to two or more persons is ambiguous as to whether it is payable to the persons alternatively, the instrument is payable to the persons alternatively.

§ 3—111. **Place of Payment.**

Except as otherwise provided for items in Article 4, an instrument is payable at the place of payment stated in the instrument. If no place of payment is stated, an instrument is payable at the address of the drawee or maker stated in the instrument. If no address is stated, the place of payment is the place of business of the drawee or maker. If a drawee or maker has more than one place of business, the place of payment is any place of business of the drawee or maker chosen by the person entitled to enforce the instrument. If the drawee or maker has no place of business, the place of payment is the residence of the drawee or maker.

§ 3—112. **Interest.**

(a) Unless otherwise provided in the instrument, (i) an instrument is not payable with interest, and (ii) interest on an interest-bearing instrument is payable from the date of the instrument.

(b) Interest may be stated in an instrument as a fixed or variable amount of money or it may be expressed as a fixed or variable rate or rates. The amount or rate of interest may be stated or described in the instrument in any manner and may require reference to information not contained in the instrument. If an instrument provides for interest, but the amount of interest payable cannot be ascertained from the description, interest is payable at the judgment rate in effect at the place of payment of the instrument and at the time interest first accrues.

§ 3—113. **Date of Instrument.**

(a) An instrument may be antedated or postdated. The date stated determines the time of payment if the instrument is payable at a fixed period after date. Except as provided in Section 4—401(c), an instrument payable on demand is not payable before the date of the instrument.

(b) If an instrument is undated, its date is the date of its issue or, in the case of an unissued instrument, the date it first comes into possession of a holder.

§ 3—114. **Contradictory Terms of Instrument.**

If an instrument contains contradictory terms, typewritten terms prevail over printed terms, handwritten terms prevail over both, and words prevail over numbers.

§ 3—115. **Incomplete Instrument.**

(a) "Incomplete instrument" means a signed writing, whether or not issued by the signer, the contents of which show at the time of signing that it is incomplete but that the signer intended it to be completed by the addition of words or numbers.

(b) Subject to subsection (c), if an incomplete instrument is an instrument under Section 3—104, it may be enforced according to its terms if it is not completed, or according to its terms as augmented by completion. If an incomplete instrument is not an instrument under Section 3—104, but, after completion, the requirements of Section 3—104 are met, the instrument may be enforced according to its terms as augmented by completion.

(c) If words or numbers are added to an incomplete instrument without authority of the signer, there is an alteration of the incomplete instrument under Section 3—407.

(d) The burden of establishing that words or numbers were added to an incomplete instrument without authority of the signer is on the person asserting the lack of authority.

§ 3—116. **Joint and Several Liability; Contribution.**

(a) Except as otherwise provided in the instrument, two or more persons who have the same liability on an instrument as makers, drawers, acceptors, indorsers who indorse as joint payees, or anomalous indorsers are jointly and severally liable in the capacity in which they sign.

(b) Except as provided in Section 3—419(e) or by agreement of the affected parties, a party having joint and several liability who pays the instrument is entitled to receive from any party having the same joint and several liability contribution in accordance with applicable law.

(c) Discharge of one party having joint and several liability by a person entitled to enforce the instrument does not affect the right under subsection (b) of a party having the same joint and several liability to receive contribution from the party discharged.

§ 3—117. **Other Agreements Affecting Instrument.**

Subject to applicable law regarding exclusion of proof of contemporaneous or previous agreements, the obligation of a party to an instrument to pay the instrument may be modified, supplemented, or nullified by a separate agreement of the obligor and a person entitled to enforce the instrument, if the instrument is issued or the obligation is incurred in reliance on the agreement or as part of the same transaction giving rise to the agreement. To the extent an obligation is modified, supplemented, or nullified by an agreement under this section, the agreement is a defense to the obligation.

§ 3—118. **Statute of Limitations.**

(a) Except as provided in subsection (e), an action to enforce the obligation of a party to pay a note payable at a definite time must be commenced within six years after the due date or dates stated in the note or, if a due date is accelerated, within six years after the accelerated due date.

(b) Except as provided in subsection (d) or (e), if demand for payment is made to the maker of a note payable on demand, an action to enforce the obligation of a party to pay the note must be commenced within six years after the demand. If no demand for payment is made to the maker, an action to enforce the note is barred if neither principal nor interest on the note has been paid for a continuous period of 10 years.

(c) Except as provided in subsection (d), an action to enforce the obligation of a party to an unaccepted draft to pay the draft must be commenced within three years after dishonor of the draft or 10 years after the date of the draft, whichever period expires first.

(d) An action to enforce the obligation of the acceptor of a certified check or the issuer of a teller's check, cashier's check, or traveler's check must be commenced within three years after demand for payment is made to the acceptor or issuer, as the case may be.

(e) An action to enforce the obligation of a party to a certificate of deposit to pay the instrument must be commenced within six years after demand for payment is made to the maker, but if the instrument states a due date and the maker is not required to pay before that date, the six-year period begins when a demand for payment is in effect and the due date has passed.

(f) An action to enforce the obligation of a party to pay an accepted draft, other than a certified check, must be commenced (i) within six years after the due date or dates stated in the draft or acceptance if the obligation of the acceptor is payable at a definite time, or (ii) within six years after the date of the acceptance if the obligation of the acceptor is payable on demand.

(g) Unless governed by other law regarding claims for indemnity or contribution, an action (i) for conversion of an instrument, for money had and received, or like action based on conversion, (ii) for breach of warranty, or (iii) to enforce an obligation, duty, or right arising under this Article and not governed by this section must be commenced within three years after the [cause of action] accrues.

§ 3—119. **Notice of Right to Defend Action.**

In an action for breach of an obligation for which a third person is answerable over pursuant to this Article or Article 4, the defendant may give the third person written notice of the litigation, and the person notified may then give similar notice to any other person who is answerable over. If the notice states (i) that the person notified may come in and defend and (ii) that failure to do so will bind the person notified in an action later brought by the person giving the notice as to any determination of fact common to the two litigations, the person notified is so bound unless after seasonable receipt of the notice the person notified does come in and defend.

Part 2 Negotiation, Transfer, and Indorsement

§ 3—201. **Negotiation.**

(a) "Negotiation" means a transfer of possession, whether voluntary or involuntary, of an instrument by a person other than the issuer to a person who thereby becomes its holder.

(b) Except for negotiation by a remitter, if an instrument is payable to an identified person, negotiation requires transfer of possession of the instrument and its indorsement by the holder. If an instrument is payable to bearer, it may be negotiated by transfer of possession alone.

§ 3—202. **Negotiation Subject to Rescission.**

(a) Negotiation is effective even if obtained (i) from an infant, a corporation exceeding its powers, or a person without capacity, (ii) by fraud, duress, or mistake, or (iii) in breach of duty or as part of an illegal transaction.

(b) To the extent permitted by other law, negotiation may be rescinded or may be subject to other remedies, but those remedies may not be asserted against a subsequent holder in due course or a person paying the instrument in good faith and without knowledge of facts that are a basis for rescission or other remedy.

§ 3—203. **Transfer of Instrument; Rights Acquired by Transfer.**

(a) An instrument is transferred when it is delivered by a person other than its issuer for the purpose of giving to the person receiving delivery the right to enforce the instrument.

(b) Transfer of an instrument, whether or not the transfer is a negotiation, vests in the transferee any right of the transferor to enforce the instrument, including any right as a holder in due course, but the transferee cannot acquire rights of a holder in due course by a transfer, directly or indirectly, from a holder in due course if the transferee engaged in fraud or illegality affecting the instrument.

(c) Unless otherwise agreed, if an instrument is transferred for value and the transferee does not become a holder because of lack of indorsement by the transferor, the transferee has a specifically enforceable right to the unqualified indorsement of the transferor, but negotiation of the instrument does not occur until the indorsement is made.

(d) If a transferor purports to transfer less than the entire instrument, negotiation of the instrument does not occur. The transferee obtains no rights under this Article and has only the rights of a partial assignee.

§ 3—204. **Indorsement.**

(a) "Indorsement" means a signature, other than that of a signer as maker, drawer, or acceptor, that alone or accompanied by other words is made on an instrument for the purpose of (i) negotiating the instrument, (ii) restricting payment of the instrument, or (iii) incurring indorser's liability on the instrument, but regardless of the intent of the signer, a signature and its accompanying words is an indorsement unless the accompanying words, terms of the instrument, place of the signature, or other circumstances unambiguously indicate that the signature was made for a purpose other than indorsement. For the purpose of determining whether a signature is made on an instrument, a paper affixed to the instrument is a part of the instrument.

(b) "Indorser" means a person who makes an indorsement.

(c) For the purpose of determining whether the transferee of an instrument is a holder, an indorsement that transfers a security interest in the instrument is effective as an unqualified indorsement of the instrument.

(d) If an instrument is payable to a holder under a name that is not the name of the holder, indorsement may be made by the holder in the name stated in the instrument or in the holder's name or both, but signature in both names may be required by a person paying or taking the instrument for value or collection.

§ 3—205. **Special Indorsement; Blank Indorsement; Anomalous Indorsement.**

(a) If an indorsement is made by the holder of an instrument, whether payable to an identified person or payable to bearer, and the indorsement identifies a person to whom it makes the instrument payable, it is a "special indorsement." When specially indorsed, an instrument becomes payable to the identified person and may be negotiated only by the indorsement of that person. The principles stated in Section 3—110 apply to special indorsements.

(b) If an indorsement is made by the holder of an instrument and it is not a special indorsement, it is a "blank indorsement.'' When indorsed in blank, an instrument becomes payable to bearer and may be negotiated by transfer of possession alone until specially indorsed.

(c) The holder may convert a blank indorsement that consists only of a signature into a special indorsement by writing, above the signature of the indorser, words identifying the person to whom the instrument is made payable.

(d) ''Anomalous indorsement'' means an indorsement made by a person who is not the holder of the instrument. An anomalous indorsement does not affect the manner in which the instrument may be negotiated.

§ 3—206. **Restrictive Indorsement.**

(a) An indorsement limiting payment to a particular person or otherwise prohibiting further transfer or negotiation of the instrument is not effective to prevent further transfer or negotiation of the instrument.

(b) An indorsement stating a condition to the right of the indorsee to receive payment does not affect the right of the indorsee to enforce the instrument. A person paying the instrument or taking it for value or collection may disregard the condition, and the rights and liabilities of that person are not affected by whether the condition has been fulfilled.

(c) If an instrument bears an indorsement (i) described in Section 4—201(b), or (ii) in blank or to a particular bank using the words ''for deposit,'' ''for collection,'' or other words indicating a purpose of having the instrument collected by a bank for the indorser or for a particular account, the following rules apply:

(1) A person, other than a bank, who purchases the instrument when so indorsed converts the instrument unless the amount paid for the instrument is received by the indorser or applied consistently with the indorsement.

(2) A depositary bank that purchases the instrument or takes it for collection when so indorsed converts the instrument unless the amount paid by the bank with respect to the instrument is received by the indorser or applied consistently with the indorsement.

(3) A payor bank that is also the depositary bank or that takes the instrument for immediate payment over the counter from a person other than a collecting bank converts the instrument unless the proceeds of the instrument are received by the indorser or applied consistently with the indorsement.

(4) Except as otherwise provided in paragraph (3), a payor bank or intermediary bank may disregard the indorsement and is not liable if the proceeds of the instrument are not received by the indorser or applied consistently with the indorsement.

(d) Except for an indorsement covered by subsection (c), if an instrument bears an indorsement using words to the effect that payment is to be made to the indorsee as agent, trustee, or other fiduciary for the benefit of the indorser or another person, the following rules apply:

(1) Unless there is notice of breach of fiduciary duty as provided in Section 3—307, a person who purchases the instrument from the indorsee or takes the instrument from the indorsee for collection or payment may pay the proceeds of payment or the value given for the instrument to the indorsee without regard to whether the indorsee violates a fiduciary duty to the indorser.

(2) A subsequent transferee of the instrument or person who pays the instrument is neither given notice nor otherwise affected by the restriction in the indorsement unless the transferee or payor knows that the fiduciary dealt with the instrument or its proceeds in breach of fiduciary duty.

(e) The presence on an instrument of an indorsement to which this section applies does not prevent a purchaser of the instrument from becoming a holder in due course of the instrument unless the purchaser is a converter under subsection (c) or has notice or knowledge of breach of fiduciary duty as stated in subsection (d).

(f) In an action to enforce the obligation of a party to pay the instrument, the obligor has a defense if payment would violate an indorsement to which this section applies and the payment is not permitted by this section.

§ 3—207. **Reacquisition.**

Reacquisition of an instrument occurs if it is transferred to a former holder, by negotiation or otherwise. A former holder who reacquires the instrument may cancel indorsements made after the reacquirer first became a holder of the instrument. If the cancellation causes the instrument to be payable to the reacquirer or to bearer, the reacquirer may negotiate the instrument. An indorser whose indorsement is canceled is discharged, and the discharge is effective against any subsequent holder.

Part 3 Enforcement of Instruments

§ 3—301. **Person Entitled to Enforce Instrument.**

''Person entitled to enforce'' an instrument means (i) the holder of the instrument, (ii) a nonholder in possession of the instrument who has the rights of a holder, or (iii) a person not in possession of the instrument who is entitled to enforce the instrument pursuant to Section 3—309 or 3—418(d). A person may be a person entitled to enforce the instrument even though the person is not the owner of the instrument or is in wrongful possession of the instrument.

§ 3—302. **Holder in Due Course.**

(a) Subject to subsection (c) and Section 3—106(d), ''holder in due course'' means the holder of an instrument if:

(1) the instrument when issued or negotiated to the holder does not bear such apparent evidence of forgery or alteration or is not otherwise so irregular or incomplete as to call into question its authenticity; and

(2) the holder took the instrument (i) for value, (ii) in good faith, (iii) without notice that the instrument is overdue or has been dishonored or that there is an uncured default with respect to payment of another instrument issued as part of the same series, (iv) without notice that the instrument contains an unauthorized signature or has been altered, (v) without notice of any claim to the instrument described in Section 3—306, and (vi) without notice that any party has a defense or claim in recoupment described in Section 3—305(a).

(b) Notice of discharge of a party, other than discharge in an insolvency proceeding, is not notice of a defense under subsection (a), but discharge is effective against a person who became a holder in due course with notice of the discharge. Public filing or recording of a document does not of itself constitute notice of a defense, claim in recoupment, or claim to the instrument.

(c) Except to the extent a transferor or predecessor in interest has rights as a holder in due course, a person does not acquire rights of a holder in due course of an instrument taken (i) by legal process or by purchase in an execution, bankruptcy, or creditor's sale or similar proceeding, (ii) by purchase as part of a bulk transaction not in ordinary course of business of the transferor, or (iii) as the successor in interest to an estate or other organization.

(d) If, under Section 3—303(a)(1), the promise of performance that is the consideration for an instrument has been partially performed, the holder may assert rights as a holder in due course of the instrument only to the fraction of the amount payable under the instrument equal to the value of the partial performance divided by the value of the promised performance.

(e) If (i) the person entitled to enforce an instrument has only a security interest in the instrument and (ii) the person obliged to pay the instrument has a defense, claim in recoupment, or claim to the instrument that may be asserted against the person who granted the security interest, the person entitled to enforce the instrument may assert rights as a holder in due course only to an amount payable under the instrument which, at the time of enforcement of the instrument, does not exceed the amount of the unpaid obligation secured.

(f) To be effective, notice must be received at a time and in a manner that gives a reasonable opportunity to act on it.

(g) This section is subject to any law limiting status as a holder in due course in particular classes of transactions.

§ 3—303. **Value and Consideration.**

(a) An instrument is issued or transferred for value if:

(1) the instrument is issued or transferred for a promise of performance, to the extent the promise has been performed;

(2) the transferee acquires a security interest or other lien in the instrument other than a lien obtained by judicial proceeding;

(3) the instrument is issued or transferred as payment of, or as security for, an antecedent claim against any person, whether or not the claim is due;

(4) the instrument is issued or transferred in exchange for a negotiable instrument; or

(5) the instrument is issued or transferred in exchange for the incurring of an irrevocable obligation to a third party by the person taking the instrument.

(b) "Consideration" means any consideration sufficient to support a simple contract. The drawer or maker of an instrument has a defense if the instrument is issued without consideration. If an instrument is issued for a promise of performance, the issuer has a defense to the extent performance of the promise is due and the promise has not been performed. If an instrument is issued for value as stated in subsection (a), the instrument is also issued for consideration.

§ 3—304. **Overdue Instrument.**

(a) An instrument payable on demand becomes overdue at the earliest of the following times:

(1) on the day after the day demand for payment is duly made;

(2) if the instrument is a check, 90 days after its date; or

(3) if the instrument is not a check, when the instrument has been outstanding for a period of time after its date which is unreasonably long under the circumstances of the particular case in light of the nature of the instrument and usage of the trade.

(b) With respect to an instrument payable at a definite time the following rules apply:

(1) If the principal is payable in installments and a due date has not been accelerated, the instrument becomes overdue upon default under the instrument for nonpayment of an installment, and the instrument remains overdue until the default is cured.

(2) If the principal is not payable in installments and the due date has not been accelerated, the instrument becomes overdue on the day after the due date.

(3) If a due date with respect to principal has been accelerated, the instrument becomes overdue on the day after the accelerated due date.

(c) Unless the due date of principal has been accelerated, an instrument does not become overdue if there is default in payment of interest but no default in payment of principal.

§ 3—305. **Defenses and Claims in Recoupment.**

(a) Except as stated in subsection (b), the right to enforce the obligation of a party to pay an instrument is subject to the following:

(1) a defense of the obligor based on (i) infancy of the obligor to the extent it is a defense to a simple contract, (ii) duress, lack of legal capacity, or illegality of the transaction which, under other law, nullifies the obligation of the obligor, (iii) fraud that induced the obligor to sign the instrument with neither knowledge nor reasonable opportunity to learn of its character or its essential terms, or (iv) discharge of the obligor in insolvency proceedings;

(2) a defense of the obligor stated in another section of this Article or a defense of the obligor that would be available if the person entitled to enforce the instrument were enforcing a right to payment under a simple contract; and

(3) a claim in recoupment of the obligor against the original payee of the instrument if the claim arose from the transaction that gave rise to the instrument; but the claim of the obligor may be asserted against a transferee of the instrument only to reduce the amount owing on the instrument at the time the action is brought.

(b) The right of a holder in due course to enforce the obligation of a party to pay the instrument is subject to defenses of the obligor stated in subsection (a)(1), but is not subject to defenses of the obligor stated in subsection (a)(2) or claims in recoupment stated in subsection (a)(3) against a person other than the holder.

(c) Except as stated in subsection (d), in an action to enforce the obligation of a party to pay the instrument, the obligor may not assert against the person entitled to enforce the instrument a defense, claim in recoupment, or claim to the instrument (Section 3—306) of another person, but the other person's claim to the instrument may be asserted by the obligor if the other person is joined in the action and personally asserts the claim against the person entitled to enforce the instrument. An obligor is not obliged to pay the instrument if the person seeking enforcement of the instrument does not have rights of a holder in due course and the obligor proves that the instrument is a lost or stolen instrument.

(d) In an action to enforce the obligation of an accommodation party to pay an instrument, the accommodation party may assert against the person entitled to enforce the instrument any defense or claim in recoupment under subsection (a) that the accommodated party could assert against the person entitled to enforce the instrument, except the defenses of discharge in insolvency proceedings, infancy, and lack of legal capacity.

§ 3—306. **Claims to an Instrument.**

A person taking an instrument, other than a person having rights of a holder in due course, is subject to a claim of a property or possessory right in the instrument or its proceeds, including a claim to rescind a negotiation and to recover the instrument or its proceeds. A person having rights of a holder in due course takes free of the claim to the instrument.

§ 3—307. **Notice of Breach of Fiduciary Duty.**

(a) In this section:

(1) "Fiduciary" means an agent, trustee, partner, corporate officer or director, or other representative owing a fiduciary duty with respect to an instrument.

(2) "Represented person" means the principal, beneficiary, partnership, corporation, or other person to whom the duty stated in paragraph (1) is owed.

(b) If (i) an instrument is taken from a fiduciary for payment or collection or for value, (ii) the taker has knowledge of the fiduciary status of the fiduciary, and (iii) the represented person makes a claim to the instrument or its proceeds on the basis that the transaction of the fiduciary is a breach of fiduciary duty, the following rules apply:

(1) Notice of breach of fiduciary duty by the fiduciary is notice of the claim of the represented person.

(2) In the case of an instrument payable to the represented person or the fiduciary as such, the taker has notice of the breach of fiduciary duty if the instrument is (i) taken in payment of or as security for a debt known by the taker to be the personal debt of the fiduciary, (ii) taken in a transaction known by the taker to be for the personal benefit of the fiduciary, or (iii) deposited to an account other than an account of the fiduciary, as such, or an account of the represented person.

(3) If an instrument is issued by the represented person or the fiduciary as such, and made payable to the fiduciary personally, the taker does not have notice of the breach of fiduciary duty unless the taker knows of the breach of fiduciary duty.

(4) If an instrument is issued by the represented person or the fiduciary as such, to the taker as payee, the taker has notice of the breach of fiduciary duty if the instrument is (i) taken in payment of or as security for a debt known by the taker to be the personal debt of the fiduciary, (ii) taken in a transaction known by the taker to be for the personal benefit of the fiduciary, or (iii) deposited to an account other than an account of the fiduciary, as such, or an account of the represented person.

§ 3—308. **Proof of Signatures and Status as Holder in Due Course.**

(a) In an action with respect to an instrument, the authenticity of, and authority to make, each signature on the instrument is admitted unless specifically denied in the pleadings. If the validity of a signature is denied in the pleadings, the burden of establishing validity is on the person claiming validity, but the signature is presumed to be authentic and authorized unless the action is to enforce the liability of the purported signer and the signer is dead or incompetent at the time of trial of the issue of validity of the signature. If an action to enforce the instrument is brought against a person as the undisclosed principal of a person who signed the instrument as a party to the instrument, the plaintiff has the burden of establishing that the defendant is liable on the instrument as a represented person under Section 3—402(a).

(b) If the validity of signatures is admitted or proved and there is compliance with subsection (a), a plaintiff producing the instrument is entitled to payment if the plaintiff proves entitlement to enforce the instrument under Section 3—301, unless the defendant proves a defense or claim in recoupment. If a defense or claim in recoupment is proved, the right to payment of the plaintiff is subject to the defense or claim, except to the extent the plaintiff proves that the plaintiff has rights of a holder in due course which are not subject to the defense or claim.

§ 3—309. **Enforcement of Lost, Destroyed, or Stolen Instrument.**

(a) A person not in possession of an instrument is entitled to enforce the instrument if (i) the person was in possession of the instrument and entitled to enforce it when loss of possession occurred, (ii) the loss of possession was not the result of a transfer by the person or a lawful seizure, and (iii) the person cannot reasonably obtain possession of the instrument because the instrument was destroyed, its whereabouts cannot be determined, or it is in the wrongful possession of an unknown person or a person that cannot be found or is not amenable to service of process.

(b) A person seeking enforcement of an instrument under subsection (a) must prove the terms of the instrument and the person's right to enforce the instrument. If that proof is made, Section 3—308 applies to the case as if the person seeking enforcement had produced the instrument. The court may not enter judgment in favor of the person seeking enforcement unless it finds that the person required to pay the instrument is adequately protected against loss that might occur by reason of a claim by another person to enforce the instrument. Adequate protection may be provided by any reasonable means.

§ 3—310. **Effect of Instrument on Obligation for Which Taken.**

(a) Unless otherwise agreed, if a certified check, cashier's check, or teller's check is taken for an obligation, the obligation is discharged to the same extent discharge would result if an amount of money equal to the amount of the instrument were taken in payment of the obligation. Discharge of the obligation does not affect any liability that the obligor may have as an indorser of the instrument.

(b) Unless otherwise agreed and except as provided in subsection (a), if a note or an uncertified check is taken for an obligation, the obligation is suspended to the same extent the obligation would be discharged if an amount of money equal to the amount of the instrument were taken, and the following rules apply:

(1) In the case of an uncertified check, suspension of the obligation continues until dishonor of the check or until it is paid or certified. Payment or certification of the check results in discharge of the obligation to the extent of the amount of the check.

(2) In the case of a note, suspension of the obligation continues until dishonor of the note or until it is paid. Payment of the note results in discharge of the obligation to the extent of the payment.

(3) Except as provided in paragraph (4), if the check or note is dishonored and the obligee of the obligation for which the instrument was taken is the person entitled to enforce the instrument, the obligee may enforce either the instrument or the obligation. In the case of an instrument of a third person which is negotiated to the obligee by the obligor, discharge of the obligor on the instrument also discharges the obligation.

(4) If the person entitled to enforce the instrument taken for an obligation is a person other than the obligee, the obligee may not enforce the obligation to the extent the obligation is suspended. If the obligee is the person entitled to enforce the instrument but no longer has possession of it because it was lost, stolen, or destroyed, the obligation may not be enforced to the extent of the amount payable on the instrument, and to that extent the obligee's rights against the obligor are limited to enforcement of the instrument.

(c) If an instrument other than one described in subsection (a) or (b) is taken for an obligation, the effect is (i) that stated in subsection (a) if the instrument is one on which a bank is liable as maker or acceptor, or (ii) that stated in subsection (b) in any other case.

§ 3—311. **Accord and Satisfaction by Use of Instrument.**

(a) If a person against whom a claim is asserted proves that (i) that person in good faith tendered an instrument to the claimant as full satisfaction of the claim, (ii) the amount of the claim was unliquidated or subject to a bona fide dispute, and (iii) the claimant obtained payment of the instrument, the following subsections apply.

(b) Unless subsection (c) applies, the claim is discharged if the person against whom the claim is asserted proves that the instrument or an accompanying written communication contained a conspicuous statement to the effect that the instrument was tendered as full satisfaction of the claim.

(c) Subject to subsection (d), a claim is not discharged under subsection (b) if either of the following applies:

(1) The claimant, if an organization, proves that (i) within a reasonable time before the tender, the claimant sent a conspicuous statement to the person against whom the claim is asserted that communications concerning disputed debts, including an instrument tendered as full satisfaction of a debt, are to be sent to a designated person, office, or place, and (ii) the instrument or accompanying communication was not received by that designated person, office, or place.

(2) The claimant, whether or not an organization, proves that within 90 days after payment of the instrument, the claimant tendered repayment of the amount of the instrument to the person against whom the claim is asserted. This paragraph does not apply if the claimant is an organization that sent a statement complying with paragraph (1)(i).

(d) A claim is discharged if the person against whom the claim is asserted proves that within a reasonable time before collection of the instrument was initiated, the claimant, or an agent of the claimant having direct responsibility with respect to the disputed obligation, knew that the instrument was tendered in full satisfaction of the claim.

§ 3—312. Lost, Destroyed, or Stolen Cashier's Check, Teller's Check, or Certified Check.

(a) In this section:

(1) ''Check'' means a cashier's check, teller's check, or certified check.

(2) ''Claimant'' means a person who claims the right to receive the amount of a cashier's check, teller's check, or certified check that was lost, destroyed, or stolen.

(3) ''Declaration of loss'' means a written statement, made under penalty of perjury, to the effect that (i) the declarer lost possession of a check, (ii) the declarer is the drawer or payee of the check, in the case of a certified check, or the remitter or payee of the check, in the case of a cashier's check or teller's check, (iii) the loss of possession was not the result of a transfer by the declarer or a lawful seizure, and (iv) the declarer cannot reasonably obtain possession of the check because the check was destroyed, its whereabouts cannot be determined, or it is in the wrongful possession of an unknown person or a person that cannot be found or is not amenable to service of process.

(4) ''Obligated bank'' means the issuer of a cashier's check or teller's check or the acceptor of a certified check.

(b) A claimant may assert a claim to the amount of a check by a communication to the obligated bank describing the check with reasonable certainty and requesting payment of the amount of the check, if (i) the claimant is the drawer or payee of a certified check or the remitter or payee of a cashier's check or teller's check, (ii) the communication contains or is accompanied by a declaration of loss of the claimant with respect to the check, (iii) the communication is received at a time and in a manner affording the bank a reasonable time to act on it before the check is paid, and (iv) the claimant provides reasonable identification if requested by the obligated bank. Delivery of a declaration of loss is a warranty of the truth of the statements made in the declaration. If a claim is asserted in compliance with this subsection, the following rules apply:

(1) The claim becomes enforceable at the later of (i) the time the claim is asserted, or (ii) the 90th day following the date of the check, in the case of a cashier's check or teller's check, or the 90th day following the date of the acceptance, in the case of a certified check.

(2) Until the claim becomes enforceable, it has no legal effect and the obligated bank may pay the check or, in the case of a teller's check, may permit the drawee to pay the check. Payment to a person entitled to enforce the check discharges all liability of the obligated bank with respect to the check.

(3) If the claim becomes enforceable before the check is presented for payment, the obligated bank is not obliged to pay the check.

(4) When the claim becomes enforceable, the obligated bank becomes obliged to pay the amount of the check to the claimant if payment of the check has not been made to a person entitled to enforce the check. Subject to Section 4—302(a)(1), payment to the claimant discharges all liability of the obligated bank with respect to the check.

(c) If the obligated bank pays the amount of a check to a claimant under subsection (b)(4) and the check is presented for payment by a person having rights of a holder in due course, the claimant is obliged to (i) refund the payment to the obligated bank if the check is paid, or (ii) pay the amount of the check to the person having rights of a holder in due course if the check is dishonored.

(d) If a claimant has the right to assert a claim under subsection (b) and is also a person entitled to enforce a cashier's check, teller's check, or certified check which is lost, destroyed, or stolen, the claimant may assert rights with respect to the check either under this section or Section 3—309.

Part 4 Liability of Parties

§ 3—401. Signature.

(a) A person is not liable on an instrument unless (i) the person signed the instrument, or (ii) the person is represented by an agent or representative who signed the instrument and the signature is binding on the represented person under Section 3—402.

(b) A signature may be made (i) manually or by means of a device or machine, and (ii) by the use of any name, including a trade or assumed name, or by a word, mark, or symbol executed or adopted by a person with present intention to authenticate a writing.

§ 3—402. Signature by Representative.

(a) If a person acting, or purporting to act, as a representative signs an instrument by signing either the name of the represented person or the name of the signer, the represented person is bound by the signature to the same extent the represented person would be bound if the signature were on a simple contract. If the represented person is bound, the signature of the representative is the "authorized signature of the represented person" and the represented person is liable on the instrument, whether or not identified in the instrument.

(b) If a representative signs the name of the representative to an instrument and the signature is an authorized signature of the represented person, the following rules apply:

(1) If the form of the signature shows unambiguously that the signature is made on behalf of the represented person who is identified in the instrument, the representative is not liable on the instrument.

(2) Subject to subsection (c), if (i) the form of the signature does not show unambiguously that the signature is made in a representative capacity or (ii) the represented person is not identified in the instrument, the representative is liable on the instrument to a holder in due course that took the instrument without notice that the representative was not intended to be liable on the instrument. With respect to any other person, the representative is liable on the instrument unless the representative proves that the original parties did not intend the representative to be liable on the instrument.

(c) If a representative signs the name of the representative as drawer of a check without indication of the representative status and the check is payable from an account of the represented person who is identified on the check, the signer is not liable on the check if the signature is an authorized signature of the represented person.

§ 3—403. Unauthorized Signature.

(a) Unless otherwise provided in this Article or Article 4, an unauthorized signature is ineffective except as the signature of the unauthorized signer in favor of a person who in good faith pays the instrument or takes it for value. An unauthorized signature may be ratified for all purposes of this Article.

(b) If the signature of more than one person is required to constitute the authorized signature of an organization, the signature of the organization is unauthorized if one of the required signatures is lacking.

(c) The civil or criminal liability of a person who makes an unauthorized signature is not affected by any provision of this Article which makes the unauthorized signature effective for the purposes of this Article.

§ 3—404. Impostors; Fictitious Payees.

(a) If an impostor, by use of the mails or otherwise, induces the issuer of an instrument to issue the instrument to the impostor, or to a person acting in concert with the impostor, by impersonating the payee of the instrument or a person authorized to act for the payee, an indorsement of the instrument by any person in the name of the payee is effective as the indorsement of the payee in favor of a person who, in good faith, pays the instrument or takes it for value or for collection.

(b) If (i) a person whose intent determines to whom an instrument is payable (Section 3—110(a) or (b)) does not intend the person identified as payee to have any interest in the instrument, or (ii) the person identified as payee of an instrument is a fictitious person, the following rules apply until the instrument is negotiated by special indorsement:

(1) Any person in possession of the instrument is its holder.

(2) An indorsement by any person in the name of the payee stated in the instrument is effective as the indorsement of the payee in favor of a person who, in good faith, pays the instrument or takes it for value or for collection.

(c) Under subsection (a) or (b), an indorsement is made in the name of a payee if (i) it is made in a name substantially similar to that of the payee or (ii) the instrument, whether or not indorsed, is deposited in a depositary bank to an account in a name substantially similar to that of the payee.

(d) With respect to an instrument to which subsection (a) or (b) applies, if a person paying the instrument or taking it for value or for collection fails to exercise ordinary care in paying or taking the instrument and that failure substantially contributes to loss resulting from payment of the instrument, the person bearing the loss may recover from the person failing to exercise ordinary care to the extent the failure to exercise ordinary care contributed to the loss.

§ 3—405. Employer's Responsibility for Fraudulent Indorsement by Employee.

(a) In this section:

(1) "Employee" includes an independent contractor and employee of an independent contractor retained by the employer.

(2) "Fraudulent indorsement" means (i) in the case of an instrument payable to the employer, a forged indorsement purporting to be that of the employer, or (ii) in the case of an instrument with respect to which the employer is the issuer, a forged indorsement purporting to be that of the person identified as payee.

(3) "Responsibility" with respect to instruments means authority (i) to sign or indorse instruments on

behalf of the employer, (ii) to process instruments received by the employer for bookkeeping purposes, for deposit to an account, or for other disposition, (iii) to prepare or process instruments for issue in the name of the employer, (iv) to supply information determining the names or addresses of payees of instruments to be issued in the name of the employer, (v) to control the disposition of instruments to be issued in the name of the employer, or (vi) to act otherwise with respect to instruments in a responsible capacity. "Responsibility" does not include authority that merely allows an employee to have access to instruments or blank or incomplete instrument forms that are being stored or transported or are part of incoming or outgoing mail, or similar access.

(b) For the purpose of determining the rights and liabilities of a person who, in good faith, pays an instrument or takes it for value or for collection, if an employer entrusted an employee with responsibility with respect to the instrument and the employee or a person acting in concert with the employee makes a fraudulent indorsement of the instrument, the indorsement is effective as the indorsement of the person to whom the instrument is payable if it is made in the name of that person. If the person paying the instrument or taking it for value or for collection fails to exercise ordinary care in paying or taking the instrument and that failure substantially contributes to loss resulting from the fraud, the person bearing the loss may recover from the person failing to exercise ordinary care to the extent the failure to exercise ordinary care contributed to the loss.

(c) Under subsection (b), an indorsement is made in the name of the person to whom an instrument is payable if (i) it is made in a name substantially similar to the name of that person or (ii) the instrument, whether or not indorsed, is deposited in a depositary bank to an account in a name substantially similar to the name of that person.

§ 3—406. Negligence Contributing to Forged Signature or Alteration of Instrument.

(a) A person whose failure to exercise ordinary care substantially contributes to an alteration of an instrument or to the making of a forged signature on an instrument is precluded from asserting the alteration or the forgery against a person who, in good faith, pays the instrument or takes it for value or for collection.

(b) Under subsection (a), if the person asserting the preclusion fails to exercise ordinary care in paying or taking the instrument and that failure substantially contributes to loss, the loss is allocated between the person precluded and the person asserting the preclusion according to the extent to which the failure of each to exercise ordinary care contributed to the loss.

(c) Under subsection (a), the burden of proving failure to exercise ordinary care is on the person asserting the pre-

clusion. Under subsection (b), the burden of proving failure to exercise ordinary care is on the person precluded.

§ 3—407. Alteration.

(a) "Alteration" means (i) an unauthorized change in an instrument that purports to modify in any respect the obligation of a party, or (ii) an unauthorized addition of words or numbers or other change to an incomplete instrument relating to the obligation of a party.

(b) Except as provided in subsection (c), an alteration fraudulently made discharges a party whose obligation is affected by the alteration unless that party assents or is precluded from asserting the alteration. No other alteration discharges a party, and the instrument may be enforced according to its original terms.

(c) A payor bank or drawee paying a fraudulently altered instrument or a person taking it for value, in good faith and without notice of the alteration, may enforce rights with respect to the instrument (i) according to its original terms, or (ii) in the case of an incomplete instrument altered by unauthorized completion, according to its terms as completed.

§ 3—408. Drawee Not Liable on Unaccepted Draft.

A check or other draft does not of itself operate as an assignment of funds in the hands of the drawee available for its payment, and the drawee is not liable on the instrument until the drawee accepts it.

§ 3—409. Acceptance of Draft; Certified Check.

(a) "Acceptance" means the drawee's signed agreement to pay a draft as presented. It must be written on the draft and may consist of the drawee's signature alone. Acceptance may be made at any time and becomes effective when notification pursuant to instructions is given or the accepted draft is delivered for the purpose of giving rights on the acceptance to any person.

(b) A draft may be accepted although it has not been signed by the drawer, is otherwise incomplete, is overdue, or has been dishonored.

(c) If a draft is payable at a fixed period after sight and the acceptor fails to date the acceptance, the holder may complete the acceptance by supplying a date in good faith.

(d) "Certified check" means a check accepted by the bank on which it is drawn. Acceptance may be made as stated in subsection (a) or by a writing on the check which indicates that the check is certified. The drawee of a check has no obligation to certify the check, and refusal to certify is not dishonor of the check.

§ 3—410. Acceptance Varying Draft.

(a) If the terms of a drawee's acceptance vary from the terms of the draft as presented, the holder may refuse the acceptance and treat the draft as dishonored. In that case, the drawee may cancel the acceptance.

(b) The terms of a draft are not varied by an acceptance to pay at a particular bank or place in the United States, unless the acceptance states that the draft is to be paid only at that bank or place.

(c) If the holder assents to an acceptance varying the terms of a draft, the obligation of each drawer and indorser that does not expressly assent to the acceptance is discharged.

§ 3—411. Refusal to Pay Cashier's Checks, Teller's Checks, and Certified Checks.

(a) In this section, "obligated bank" means the acceptor of a certified check or the issuer of a cashier's check or teller's check bought from the issuer.

(b) If the obligated bank wrongfully (i) refuses to pay a cashier's check or certified check, (ii) stops payment of a teller's check, or (iii) refuses to pay a dishonored teller's check, the person asserting the right to enforce the check is entitled to compensation for expenses and loss of interest resulting from the nonpayment and may recover consequential damages if the obligated bank refuses to pay after receiving notice of particular circumstances giving rise to the damages.

(c) Expenses or consequential damages under subsection (b) are not recoverable if the refusal of the obligated bank to pay occurs because (i) the bank suspends payments, (ii) the obligated bank asserts a claim or defense of the bank that it has reasonable grounds to believe is available against the person entitled to enforce the instrument, (iii) the obligated bank has a reasonable doubt whether the person demanding payment is the person entitled to enforce the instrument, or (iv) payment is prohibited by law.

§ 3—412. Obligation of Issuer of Note or Cashier's Check.

The issuer of a note or cashier's check or other draft drawn on the drawer is obliged to pay the instrument (i) according to its terms at the time it was issued or, if not issued, at the time it first came into possession of a holder, or (ii) if the issuer signed an incomplete instrument, according to its terms when completed, to the extent stated in Sections 3—115 and 3—407. The obligation is owed to a person entitled to enforce the instrument or to an indorser who paid the instrument under Section 3—415.

§ 3—413. Obligation of Acceptor.

(a) The acceptor of a draft is obliged to pay the draft (i) according to its terms at the time it was accepted, even though the acceptance states that the draft is payable "as originally drawn" or equivalent terms, (ii) if the acceptance varies the terms of the draft, according to the terms of the draft as varied, or (iii) if the acceptance is of a draft that is an incomplete instrument, according to its terms when completed, to the extent stated in Sections 3—115 and 3—407. The obligation is owed to a person entitled to enforce the

draft or to the drawer or an indorser who paid the draft under Section 3—414 or 3—415.

(b) If the certification of a check or other acceptance of a draft states the amount certified or accepted, the obligation of the acceptor is that amount. If (i) the certification or acceptance does not state an amount, (ii) the amount of the instrument is subsequently raised, and (iii) the instrument is then negotiated to a holder in due course, the obligation of the acceptor is the amount of the instrument at the time it was taken by the holder in due course.

§ 3—414. Obligation of Drawer.

(a) This section does not apply to cashier's checks or other drafts drawn on the drawer.

(b) If an unaccepted draft is dishonored, the drawer is obliged to pay the draft (i) according to its terms at the time it was issued or, if not issued, at the time it first came into possession of a holder, or (ii) if the drawer signed an incomplete instrument, according to its terms when completed, to the extent stated in Sections 3—115 and 3—407. The obligation is owed to a person entitled to enforce the draft or to an indorser who paid the draft under Section 3—415.

(c) If a draft is accepted by a bank, the drawer is discharged, regardless of when or by whom acceptance was obtained.

(d) If a draft is accepted and the acceptor is not a bank, the obligation of the drawer to pay the draft if the draft is dishonored by the acceptor is the same as the obligation of an indorser under Section 3—415(a) and (c).

(e) If a draft states that it is drawn "without recourse" or otherwise disclaims liability of the drawer to pay the draft, the drawer is not liable under subsection (b) to pay the draft if the draft is not a check. A disclaimer of the liability stated in subsection (b) is not effective if the draft is a check.

(f) If (i) a check is not presented for payment or given to a depositary bank for collection within 30 days after its date, (ii) the drawee suspends payments after expiration of the 30-day period without paying the check, and (iii) because of the suspension of payments, the drawer is deprived of funds maintained with the drawee to cover payment of the check, the drawer to the extent deprived of funds may discharge its obligation to pay the check by assigning to the person entitled to enforce the check the rights of the drawer against the drawee with respect to the funds.

§ 3—415. Obligation of Indorser.

(a) Subject to subsections (b), (c), and (d) and to Section 3—419(d), if an instrument is dishonored, an indorser is obliged to pay the amount due on the instrument (i) according to the terms of the instrument at the time it was indorsed, or (ii) if the indorser indorsed an incomplete instrument, according to its terms when completed, to the extent stated in Sections 3—115 and 3—407. The obli-

gation of the indorser is owed to a person entitled to enforce the instrument or to a subsequent indorser who paid the instrument under this section.

(b) If an indorsement states that it is made "without recourse" or otherwise disclaims liability of the indorser, the indorser is not liable under subsection (a) to pay the instrument.

(c) If notice of dishonor of an instrument is required by Section 3—503 and notice of dishonor complying with that section is not given to an indorser, the liability of the indorser under subsection (a) is discharged.

(d) If a draft is accepted by a bank after an indorsement is made, the liability of the indorser under subsection (a) is discharged.

(e) If an indorser of a check is liable under subsection (a) and the check is not presented for payment, or given to a depositary bank for collection, within 30 days after the day the indorsement was made, the liability of the indorser under subsection (a) is discharged.

§ 3—416. **Transfer Warranties.**

(a) A person who transfers an instrument for consideration warrants to the transferee and, if the transfer is by indorsement, to any subsequent transferee that:

(1) the warrantor is a person entitled to enforce the instrument;

(2) all signatures on the instrument are authentic and authorized;

(3) the instrument has not been altered;

(4) the instrument is not subject to a defense or claim in recoupment of any party which can be asserted against the warrantor; and

(5) the warrantor has no knowledge of any insolvency proceeding commenced with respect to the maker or acceptor or, in the case of an unaccepted draft, the drawer.

(b) A person to whom the warranties under subsection (a) are made and who took the instrument in good faith may recover from the warrantor as damages for breach of warranty an amount equal to the loss suffered as a result of the breach, but not more than the amount of the instrument plus expenses and loss of interest incurred as a result of the breach.

(c) The warranties stated in subsection (a) cannot be disclaimed with respect to checks. Unless notice of a claim for breach of warranty is given to the warrantor within 30 days after the claimant has reason to know of the breach and the identity of the warrantor, the liability of the warrantor under subsection (b) is discharged to the extent of any loss caused by the delay in giving notice of the claim.

(d) A [cause of action] for breach of warranty under this section accrues when the claimant has reason to know of the breach.

§ 3—417. **Presentment Warranties.**

(a) If an unaccepted draft is presented to the drawee for payment or acceptance and the drawee pays or accepts the draft, (i) the person obtaining payment or acceptance, at the time of presentment, and (ii) a previous transferor of the draft, at the time of transfer, warrant to the drawee making payment or accepting the draft in good faith that:

(1) the warrantor is, or was, at the time the warrantor transferred the draft, a person entitled to enforce the draft or authorized to obtain payment or acceptance of the draft on behalf of a person entitled to enforce the draft;

(2) the draft has not been altered; and

(3) the warrantor has no knowledge that the signature of the drawer of the draft is unauthorized.

(b) A drawee making payment may recover from any warrantor damages for breach of warranty equal to the amount paid by the drawee less the amount the drawee received or is entitled to receive from the drawer because of the payment. In addition, the drawee is entitled to compensation for expenses and loss of interest resulting from the breach. The right of the drawee to recover damages under this subsection is not affected by any failure of the drawee to exercise ordinary care in making payment. If the drawee accepts the draft, breach of warranty is a defense to the obligation of the acceptor. If the acceptor makes payment with respect to the draft, the acceptor is entitled to recover from any warrantor for breach of warranty the amounts stated in this subsection.

(c) If a drawee asserts a claim for breach of warranty under subsection (a) based on an unauthorized indorsement of the draft or an alteration of the draft, the warrantor may defend by proving that the indorsement is effective under Section 3—404 or 3—405 or the drawer is precluded under Section 3—406 or 4—406 from asserting against the drawee the unauthorized indorsement or alteration.

(d) If (i) a dishonored draft is presented for payment to the drawer or an indorser or (ii) any other instrument is presented for payment to a party obliged to pay the instrument, and (iii) payment is received, the following rules apply:

(1) The person obtaining payment and a prior transferor of the instrument warrant to the person making payment in good faith that the warrantor is, or was, at the time the warrantor transferred the instrument, a person entitled to enforce the instrument or authorized to obtain payment on behalf of a person entitled to enforce the instrument.

(2) The person making payment may recover from any warrantor for breach of warranty an amount equal to the amount paid plus expenses and loss of interest resulting from the breach.

(e) The warranties stated in subsections (a) and (d) cannot be disclaimed with respect to checks. Unless notice of a claim for breach of warranty is given to the warrantor within 30 days after the claimant has reason to know of the breach and the identity of the warrantor, the liability of the warrantor under subsection (b) or (d) is discharged to the extent of any loss caused by the delay in giving notice of the claim.

(f) A [cause of action] for breach of warranty under this section accrues when the claimant has reason to know of the breach.

§ 3—418. **Payment or Acceptance by Mistake.**

(a) Except as provided in subsection (c), if the drawee of a draft pays or accepts the draft and the drawee acted on the mistaken belief that (i) payment of the draft had not been stopped pursuant to Section 4—403 or (ii) the signature of the drawer of the draft was authorized, the drawee may recover the amount of the draft from the person to whom or for whose benefit payment was made or, in the case of acceptance, may revoke the acceptance. Rights of the drawee under this subsection are not affected by failure of the drawee to exercise ordinary care in paying or accepting the draft.

(b) Except as provided in subsection (c), if an instrument has been paid or accepted by mistake and the case is not covered by subsection (a), the person paying or accepting may, to the extent permitted by the law governing mistake and restitution, (i) recover the payment from the person to whom or for whose benefit payment was made or (ii) in the case of acceptance, may revoke the acceptance.

(c) The remedies provided by subsection (a) or (b) may not be asserted against a person who took the instrument in good faith and for value or who in good faith changed position in reliance on the payment or acceptance. This subsection does not limit remedies provided by Section 3—417 or 4—407.

(d) Notwithstanding Section 4—215, if an instrument is paid or accepted by mistake and the payor or acceptor recovers payment or revokes acceptance under subsection (a) or (b), the instrument is deemed not to have been paid or accepted and is treated as dishonored, and the person from whom payment is recovered has rights as a person entitled to enforce the dishonored instrument.

§ 3—419. **Instruments Signed for Accommodation.**

(a) If an instrument is issued for value given for the benefit of a party to the instrument (''accommodated party'') and another party to the instrument (''accommodation party'') signs the instrument for the purpose of incurring liability on the instrument without being a direct beneficiary of the value given for the instrument, the instrument is signed by the accommodation party ''for accommodation.''

(b) An accommodation party may sign the instrument as maker, drawer, acceptor, or indorser and, subject to sub-section (d), is obliged to pay the instrument in the capacity in which the accommodation party signs. The obligation of an accommodation party may be enforced notwithstanding any statute of frauds and whether or not the accommodation party receives consideration for the accommodation.

(c) A person signing an instrument is presumed to be an accommodation party and there is notice that the instrument is signed for accommodation if the signature is an anomalous indorsement or is accompanied by words indicating that the signer is acting as surety or guarantor with respect to the obligation of another party to the instrument. Except as provided in Section 3—605, the obligation of an accommodation party to pay the instrument is not affected by the fact that the person enforcing the obligation had notice when the instrument was taken by that person that the accommodation party signed the instrument for accommodation.

(d) If the signature of a party to an instrument is accompanied by words indicating unambiguously that the party is guaranteeing collection rather than payment of the obligation of another party to the instrument, the signer is obliged to pay the amount due on the instrument to a person entitled to enforce the instrument only if (i) execution of judgment against the other party has been returned unsatisfied, (ii) the other party is insolvent or in an insolvency proceeding, (iii) the other party cannot be served with process, or (iv) it is otherwise apparent that payment cannot be obtained from the other party.

(e) An accommodation party who pays the instrument is entitled to reimbursement from the accommodated party and is entitled to enforce the instrument against the accommodated party. An accommodated party who pays the instrument has no right of recourse against, and is not entitled to contribution from, an accommodation party.

§ 3—420. **Conversion of Instrument.**

(a) The law applicable to conversion of personal property applies to instruments. An instrument is also converted if it is taken by transfer, other than a negotiation, from a person not entitled to enforce the instrument or a bank makes or obtains payment with respect to the instrument for a person not entitled to enforce the instrument or receive payment. An action for conversion of an instrument may not be brought by (i) the issuer or acceptor of the instrument or (ii) a payee or indorsee who did not receive delivery of the instrument either directly or through delivery to an agent or a co-payee.

(b) In an action under subsection (a), the measure of liability is presumed to be the amount payable on the instrument, but recovery may not exceed the amount of the plaintiff's interest in the instrument.

(c) A representative, other than a depositary bank, who has in good faith dealt with an instrument or its proceeds on behalf of one who was not the person entitled to enforce the instrument is not liable in conversion to that person beyond the amount of any proceeds that it has not paid out.

Part 5 Dishonor

§ 3—501. **Presentment.**

(a) ''Presentment'' means a demand made by or on behalf of a person entitled to enforce an instrument (i) to pay the instrument made to the drawee or a party obliged to pay the instrument or, in the case of a note or accepted draft payable at a bank, to the bank, or (ii) to accept a draft made to the drawee.

(b) The following rules are subject to Article 4, agreement of the parties, and clearing-house rules and the like:

(1) Presentment may be made at the place of payment of the instrument and must be made at the place of payment if the instrument is payable at a bank in the United States; may be made by any commercially reasonable means, including an oral, written, or electronic communication; is effective when the demand for payment or acceptance is received by the person to whom presentment is made; and is effective if made to any one of two or more makers, acceptors, drawees, or other payors.

(2) Upon demand of the person to whom presentment is made, the person making presentment must (i) exhibit the instrument, (ii) give reasonable identification and, if presentment is made on behalf of another person, reasonable evidence of authority to do so, and (...) sign a receipt on the instrument for any payment made or surrender the instrument if full payment is made.

(3) Without dishonoring the instrument, the party to whom presentment is made may (i) return the instrument for lack of a necessary indorsement, or (ii) refuse payment or acceptance for failure of the presentment to comply with the terms of the instrument, an agreement of the parties, or other applicable law or rule.

(4) The party to whom presentment is made may treat presentment as occurring on the next business day after the day of presentment if the party to whom presentment is made has established a cut-off hour not earlier than 2 p.m. for the receipt and processing of instruments presented for payment or acceptance and presentment is made after the cut-off hour.

§ 3—502. **Dishonor.**

(a) Dishonor of a note is governed by the following rules:

(1) If the note is payable on demand, the note is dishonored if presentment is duly made to the maker and the note is not paid on the day of presentment.

(2) If the note is not payable on demand and is payable at or through a bank or the terms of the note require presentment, the note is dishonored if presentment is duly made and the note is not paid on the day it becomes payable or the day of presentment, whichever is later.

(3) If the note is not payable on demand and paragraph (2) does not apply, the note is dishonored if it is not paid on the day it becomes payable.

(b) Dishonor of an unaccepted draft other than a documentary draft is governed by the following rules:

(1) If a check is duly presented for payment to the payor bank otherwise than for immediate payment over the counter, the check is dishonored if the payor bank makes timely return of the check or sends timely notice of dishonor or nonpayment under Section 4—301 or 4—302, or becomes accountable for the amount of the check under Section 4—302.

(2) If a draft is payable on demand and paragraph (1) does not apply, the draft is dishonored if presentment for payment is duly made to the drawee and the draft is not paid on the day of presentment.

(3) If a draft is payable on a date stated in the draft, the draft is dishonored if (i) presentment for payment is duly made to the drawee and payment is not made on the day the draft becomes payable or the day of presentment, whichever is later, or (ii) presentment for acceptance is duly made before the day the draft becomes payable and the draft is not accepted on the day of presentment.

(4) If a draft is payable on elapse of a period of time after sight or acceptance, the draft is dishonored if presentment for acceptance is duly made and the draft is not accepted on the day of presentment.

(c) Dishonor of an unaccepted documentary draft occurs according to the rules stated in subsection (b)(2), (3), and (4), except that payment or acceptance may be delayed without dishonor until no later than the close of the third business day of the drawee following the day on which payment or acceptance is required by those paragraphs.

(d) Dishonor of an accepted draft is governed by the following rules:

(1) If the draft is payable on demand, the draft is dishonored if presentment for payment is duly made to the acceptor and the draft is not paid on the day of presentment.

(2) If the draft is not payable on demand, the draft is dishonored if presentment for payment is duly made to the acceptor and payment is not made on the day it becomes payable or the day of presentment, whichever is later.

(e) In any case in which presentment is otherwise required for dishonor under this section and presentment is excused under Section 3—504, dishonor occurs without presentment if the instrument is not duly accepted or paid.

(f) If a draft is dishonored because timely acceptance of the draft was not made and the person entitled to demand acceptance consents to a late acceptance, from the time of acceptance the draft is treated as never having been dishonored.

§ 3—503. **Notice of Dishonor.**

(a) The obligation of an indorser stated in Section 3—415(a) and the obligation of a drawer stated in Section 3—414(d) may not be enforced unless (i) the indorser or drawer is given notice of dishonor of the instrument complying with this section or (ii) notice of dishonor is excused under Section 3—504(b).

(b) Notice of dishonor may be given by any person; may be given by any commercially reasonable means, including an oral, written, or electronic communication; and is sufficient if it reasonably identifies the instrument and indicates that the instrument has been dishonored or has not been paid or accepted. Return of an instrument given to a bank for collection is sufficient notice of dishonor.

(c) Subject to Section 3—504(c), with respect to an instrument taken for collection by a collecting bank, notice of dishonor must be given (i) by the bank before midnight of the next banking day following the banking day on which the bank receives notice of dishonor of the instrument, or (ii) by any other person within 30 days following the day on which the person receives notice of dishonor. With respect to any other instrument, notice of dishonor must be given within 30 days following the day on which dishonor occurs.

§ 3—504. **Excused Presentment and Notice of Dishonor.**

(a) Presentment for payment or acceptance of an instrument is excused if (i) the person entitled to present the instrument cannot with reasonable diligence make presentment, (ii) the maker or acceptor has repudiated an obligation to pay the instrument or is dead or in insolvency proceedings, (iii) by the terms of the instrument presentment is not necessary to enforce the obligation of indorsers or the drawer, (iv) the drawer or indorser whose obligation is being enforced has waived presentment or otherwise has no reason to expect or right to require that the instrument be paid or accepted, or (v) the drawer instructed the drawee not to pay or accept the draft or the drawee was not obligated to the drawer to pay the draft.

(b) Notice of dishonor is excused if (i) by the terms of the instrument notice of dishonor is not necessary to enforce the obligation of a party to pay the instrument, or (ii) the party whose obligation is being enforced waived notice of dishonor. A waiver of presentment is also a waiver of notice of dishonor.

(c) Delay in giving notice of dishonor is excused if the delay was caused by circumstances beyond the control of the person giving the notice and the person giving the notice exercised reasonable diligence after the cause of the delay ceased to operate.

§ 3—505. **Evidence of Dishonor.**

(a) The following are admissible as evidence and create a presumption of dishonor and of any notice of dishonor stated:

   (1) a document regular in form as provided in subsection (b) which purports to be a protest;

   (2) a purported stamp or writing of the drawee, payor bank, or presenting bank on or accompanying the instrument stating that acceptance or payment has been refused unless reasons for the refusal are stated and the reasons are not consistent with dishonor;

   (3) a book or record of the drawee, payor bank, or collecting bank, kept in the usual course of business which shows dishonor, even if there is no evidence of who made the entry.

(b) A protest is a certificate of dishonor made by a United States consul or vice consul, or a notary public or other person authorized to administer oaths by the law of the place where dishonor occurs. It may be made upon information satisfactory to that person. The protest must identify the instrument and certify either that presentment has been made or, if not made, the reason why it was not made, and that the instrument has been dishonored by nonacceptance or nonpayment. The protest may also certify that notice of dishonor has been given to some or all parties.

Part 6 Discharge and Payment

§ 3—601. **Discharge and Effect of Discharge.**

(a) The obligation of a party to pay the instrument is discharged as stated in this Article or by an act or agreement with the party which would discharge an obligation to pay money under a simple contract.

(b) Discharge of the obligation of a party is not effective against a person acquiring rights of a holder in due course of the instrument without notice of the discharge.

§ 3—602. **Payment.**

(a) Subject to subsection (b), an instrument is paid to the extent payment is made (i) by or on behalf of a party obliged to pay the instrument, and (ii) to a person entitled to enforce the instrument. To the extent of the payment, the obligation of the party obliged to pay the instrument is discharged even though payment is made with knowledge of a claim to the instrument under Section 3—306 by another person.

(b) The obligation of a party to pay the instrument is not discharged under subsection (a) if:

   (1) a claim to the instrument under Section 3—306 is enforceable against the party receiving payment and (i)

payment is made with knowledge by the payor that payment is prohibited by injunction or similar process of a court of competent jurisdiction, or (ii) in the case of an instrument other than a cashier's check, teller's check, or certified check, the party making payment accepted, from the person having a claim to the instrument, indemnity against loss resulting from refusal to pay the person entitled to enforce the instrument; or

(2) the person making payment knows that the instrument is a stolen instrument and pays a person it knows is in wrongful possession of the instrument.

§ 3—603. Tender of Payment.

(a) If tender of payment of an obligation to pay an instrument is made to a person entitled to enforce the instrument, the effect of tender is governed by principles of law applicable to tender of payment under a simple contract.

(b) If tender of payment of an obligation to pay an instrument is made to a person entitled to enforce the instrument and the tender is refused, there is discharge, to the extent of the amount of the tender, of the obligation of an indorser or accommodation party having a right of recourse with respect to the obligation to which the tender relates.

(c) If tender of payment of an amount due on an instrument is made to a person entitled to enforce the instrument, the obligation of the obligor to pay interest after the due date on the amount tendered is discharged. If presentment is required with respect to an instrument and the obligor is able and ready to pay on the due date at every place of payment stated in the instrument, the obligor is deemed to have made tender of payment on the due date to the person entitled to enforce the instrument.

§ 3—604. Discharge by Cancellation or Renunciation.

(a) A person entitled to enforce an instrument, with or without consideration, may discharge the obligation of a party to pay the instrument (i) by an intentional voluntary act, such as surrender of the instrument to the party, destruction, mutilation, or cancellation of the instrument, cancellation or striking out of the party's signature, or the addition of words to the instrument indicating discharge, or (ii) by agreeing not to sue or otherwise renouncing rights against the party by a signed writing.

(b) Cancellation or striking out of an indorsement pursuant to subsection (a) does not affect the status and rights of a party derived from the indorsement.

§ 3—605. Discharge of Indorsers and Accommodation Parties.

(a) In this section, the term ''indorser'' includes a drawer having the obligation described in Section 3—414(d).

(b) Discharge, under Section 3—604, of the obligation of a party to pay an instrument does not discharge the obli-gation of an indorser or accommodation party having a right of recourse against the discharged party.

(c) If a person entitled to enforce an instrument agrees, with or without consideration, to an extension of the due date of the obligation of a party to pay the instrument, the extension discharges an indorser or accommodation party having a right of recourse against the party whose obligation is extended to the extent the indorser or accommodation party proves that the extension caused loss to the indorser or accommodation party with respect to the right of recourse.

(d) If a person entitled to enforce an instrument agrees, with or without consideration, to a material modification of the obligation of a party other than an extension of the due date, the modification discharges the obligation of an indorser or accommodation party having a right of recourse against the person whose obligation is modified to the extent the modification causes loss to the indorser or accommodation party with respect to the right of recourse. The loss suffered by the indorser or accommodation party as a result of the modification is equal to the amount of the right of recourse unless the person enforcing the instrument proves that no loss was caused by the modification or that the loss caused by the modification was an amount less than the amount of the right of recourse.

(e) If the obligation of a party to pay an instrument is secured by an interest in collateral and a person entitled to enforce the instrument impairs the value of the interest in collateral, the obligation of an indorser or accommodation party having a right of recourse against the obligor is discharged to the extent of the impairment. The value of an interest in collateral is impaired to the extent (i) the value of the interest is reduced to an amount less than the amount of the right of recourse of the party asserting discharge, or (ii) the reduction in value of the interest causes an increase in the amount by which the amount of the right of recourse exceeds the value of the interest. The burden of proving impairment is on the party asserting discharge.

(f) If the obligation of a party is secured by an interest in collateral not provided by an accommodation party and a person entitled to enforce the instrument impairs the value of the interest in collateral, the obligation of any party who is jointly and severally liable with respect to the secured obligation is discharged to the extent the impairment causes the party asserting discharge to pay more than that party would have been obliged to pay, taking into account rights of contribution, if impairment had not occurred. If the party asserting discharge is an accommodation party not entitled to discharge under subsection (e), the party is deemed to have a right to contribution based on joint and several liability rather than a right to reimbursement. The burden of proving impairment is on the party asserting discharge.

(g) Under subsection (e) or (f), impairing value of an interest in collateral includes (i) failure to obtain or maintain perfection or recordation of the interest in collateral, (ii) release of collateral without substitution of collateral of equal value, (iii) failure to perform a duty to preserve the value of collateral owed, under Article 9 or other law, to a debtor or surety or other person secondarily liable, or (iv) failure to comply with applicable law in disposing of collateral.

(h) An accommodation party is not discharged under subsection (c), (d), or (e) unless the person entitled to enforce the instrument knows of the accommodation or has notice under Section 3—419(c) that the instrument was signed for accommodation.

(i) A party is not discharged under this section if (i) the party asserting discharge consents to the event or conduct that is the basis of the discharge, or (ii) the instrument or a separate agreement of the party provides for waiver of discharge under this section either specifically or by general language indicating that parties waive defenses based on suretyship or impairment of collateral.

ADDENDUM TO REVISED ARTICLE 3
Notes to Legislative Counsel

1. If revised Article 3 is adopted in your state, the reference in Section 2—511 to Section 3—802 should be changed to Section 3—310.

2. If revised Article 3 is adopted in your state and the Uniform Fiduciaries Act is also in effect in your state, you may want to consider amending Uniform Fiduciaries Act § 9 to conform to Section 3—307(b)(2)(iii) and (4)(iii). See Official Comment 3 to Section 3—307.

Article 4
BANK DEPOSITS AND COLLECTIONS

Part 1 General Provisions and Definitions

§ 4—101. **Short Title.**

This Article shall be known and may be cited as Uniform Commercial Code—Bank Deposits and Collections.

§ 4—102. **Applicability.**

(1) To the extent that items within this Article are also within the scope of Articles 3 and 8, they are subject to the provisions of those Articles. In the event of conflict the provisions of this Article govern those of Article 3 but the provisions of Article 8 govern those of this Article.

(2) The liability of a bank for action or non-action with respect to any item handled by it for purposes of presentment, payment or collection is governed by the law of the place where the bank is located. In the case of action or non-action by or at a branch or separate office of a bank, its liability is governed by the law of the place where the branch or separate office is located.

§ 4—103. **Variation by Agreement; Measure of Damages; Certain Action Constituting Ordinary Care.**

(1) The effect of the provisions of this Article may be varied by agreement except that no agreement can disclaim a bank's responsibility for its own lack of good faith or failure to exercise ordinary care or can limit the measure of damages for such lack or failure; but the parties may by agreement determine the standards by which such responsibility is to be measured if such standards are not manifestly unreasonable.

(2) Federal Reserve regulations and operating letters, clearing house rules, and the like, have the effect of agreements under subsection (1), whether or not specifically assented to by all parties interested in items handled.

(3) Action or nonaction approved by this Article or pursuant to Federal Reserve regulations or operating letters constitutes the exercise of ordinary care and, in the absence of special instructions, action or nonaction consistent with clearing house rules and the like or with a general banking usage not disapproved by this Article, prima facie constitutes the exercise of ordinary care.

(4) The specification or approval of certain procedures by this Article does not constitute disapproval of other procedures which may be reasonable under the circumstances.

(5) The measure of damages for failure to exercise ordinary care in handling an item is the amount of the item reduced by an amount which could not have been realized by the use of ordinary care, and where there is bad faith it includes other damages, if any, suffered by the party as a proximate consequence.

§ 4—104. **Definitions and Index of Definitions.**

(1) In this Article unless the context otherwise requires

> (a) ''Account'' means any account with a bank and includes a checking, time, interest or savings account;

> (b) ''Afternoon'' means the period of a day between noon and midnight;

> (c) ''Banking day'' means that part of any day on which a bank is open to the public for carrying on substantially all of its banking functions;

> (d) ''Clearing house'' means any association of banks or other payors regularly clearing items;

> (e) ''Customer'' means any person having an account with a bank or for whom a bank has agreed to collect items and includes a bank carrying an account with another bank;

> (f) ''Documentary draft'' means any negotiable or non-negotiable draft with accompanying documents, se-

curities or other papers to be delivered against honor of the draft;

(g) "Item" means any instrument for the payment of money even though it is not negotiable but does not include money;

(h) "Midnight deadline" with respect to a bank is midnight on its next banking day following the banking day on which it receives the relevant item or notice or from which the time for taking action commences to run, whichever is later;

(i) "Properly payable" includes the availability of funds for payment at the time of decision to pay or dishonor;

(j) "Settle" means to pay in cash, by clearing house settlement, in a charge or credit or by remittance, or otherwise as instructed. A settlement may be either provisional or final;

(k) "Suspends payments" with respect to a bank means that it has been closed by order of the supervisory authorities, that a public officer has been appointed to take it over or that it ceases or refuses to make payments in the ordinary course of business.

(2) Other definitions applying to this Article and the sections in which they appear are:

"Collecting bank" Section 4—105.
"Depositary bank" Section 4—105.
"Intermediary bank" Section 4—105.
"Payor bank" Section 4—105.
"Presenting bank" Section 4—105.
"Remitting bank" Section 4—105.

(3) The following definitions in other Articles apply to this Article:

"Acceptance" Section 3—410.
"Certificate of deposit" Section 3—104.
"Certification" Section 3—411.
"Check" Section 3—104.
"Draft" Section 3—104.
"Holder in due course" Section 3—302.
"Notice of dishonor" Section 3—508.
"Presentment" Section 3—504.
"Protest" Section 3—509.
"Secondary party" Section 3—102.

(4) In addition Article 1 contains general definitions and principles of construction and interpretation applicable throughout this Article.

§ 4—105. **"Depositary Bank"; "Intermediary Bank"; "Collecting Bank"; "Payor Bank"; "Presenting Bank"; "Remitting Bank".**

In this Article unless the context otherwise requires:

(a) "Depositary bank" means the first bank to which an item is transferred for collection even though it is also the payor bank;

(b) "Payor bank" means a bank by which an item is payable as drawn or accepted;

(c) "Intermediary bank" means any bank to which an item is transferred in course of collection except the depositary or payor bank;

(d) "Collecting bank" means any bank handling the item for collection except the payor bank;

(e) "Presenting bank" means any bank presenting an item except a payor bank;

(f) "Remitting bank" means any payor or intermediary bank remitting for an item.

§ 4—106. **Separate Office of a Bank.**

A branch or separate office of a bank [maintaining its own deposit ledgers] is a separate bank for the purpose of computing the time within which and determining the place at or to which action may be taken or notices or orders shall be given under this Article and under Article 3.

Note: *The brackets are to make it optional with the several states whether to require a branch to maintain its own deposit ledgers in order to be considered to be a separate bank for certain purposes under Article 4. In some states "maintaining its own deposit ledgers" is a satisfactory test. In others branch banking practices are such that this test would not be suitable.*

§ 4—107. **Time of Receipt of Items.**

(1) For the purpose of allowing time to process items, prove balances and make the necessary entries on its books to determine its position for the day, a bank may fix an afternoon hour of 2 P.M. or later as a cut-off hour for the handling of money and items and the making of entries on its books.

(2) Any item or deposit of money received on any day after a cut-off hour so fixed or after the close of the banking day may be treated as being received at the opening of the next banking day.

§ 4—108. **Delays.**

(1) Unless otherwise instructed, a collecting bank in a good faith effort to secure payment may, in the case of specific items and with or without the approval of any person involved, waive, modify or extend time limits imposed or permitted by this Act for a period not in excess of an additional banking day without discharge of secondary parties and without liability to its transferor or any prior party.

(2) Delay by a collecting bank or payor bank beyond time limits prescribed or permitted by this Act or by instructions is excused if caused by interruption of communication facilities, suspension of payments by another bank, war, emergency conditions or other circumstances beyond the control of the bank provided it exercises such diligence as the circumstances require.

§ 4—109. **Process of Posting.**

The "process of posting" means the usual procedure followed by a payor bank in determining to pay an item and in recording the payment including one or more of the following or other steps as determined by the bank:

(a) verification of any signature;

(b) ascertaining that sufficient funds are available;

(c) affixing a ''paid'' or other stamp;

(d) entering a charge or entry to a customer's account;

(e) correcting or reversing an entry or erroneous action with respect to the item.

Part 2 Collection of Items: Depositary and Collecting Banks

§ 4—201. Presumption and Duration of Agency Status of Collecting Banks and Provisional Status of Credits; Applicability of Article; Item Indorsed ''Pay Any Bank''.

(1) Unless a contrary intent clearly appears and prior to the time that a settlement given by a collecting bank for an item is or becomes final (subsection (3) of Section 4—211 and Sections 4—212 and 4—213) the bank is an agent or sub-agent of the owner of the item and any settlement given for the item is provisional. This provision applies regardless of the form of indorsement or lack of indorsement and even though credit given for the item is subject to immediate withdrawal as of right or is in fact withdrawn; but the continuance of ownership of an item by its owner and any rights of the owner to proceeds of the item are subject to rights of a collecting bank such as those resulting from outstanding advances on the item and valid rights of setoff. When an item is handled by banks for purposes of presentment, payment and collection, the relevant provisions of this Article apply even though action of parties clearly establishes that a particular bank has purchased the item and is the owner of it.

(2) After an item has been indorsed with the words ''pay any bank'' or the like, only a bank may acquire the rights of a holder

(a) until the item has been returned to the customer initiating collection; or

(b) until the item has been specially indorsed by a bank to a person who is not a bank.

§ 4—202. Responsibility for Collection; When Action Seasonable.

(1) A collecting bank must use ordinary care in

(a) presenting an item or sending it for presentment; and

(b) sending notice of dishonor or non-payment or returning an item other than a documentary draft to the bank's transferor [or directly to the depositary bank under subsection (2) of Section 4—212] *(see note to Section 4—212)* after learning that the item has not been paid or accepted as the case may be; and

(c) settling for an item when the bank receives final settlement; and

(d) making or providing for any necessary protest; and

(e) notifying its transferor of any loss or delay in transit within a reasonable time after discovery thereof.

(2) A collecting bank taking proper action before its midnight deadline following receipt of an item, notice or payment acts seasonably; taking proper action within a reasonably longer time may be seasonable but the bank has the burden of so establishing.

(3) Subject to subsection (1)(a), a bank is not liable for the insolvency, neglect, misconduct, mistake or default of another bank or person or for loss or destruction of an item in transit or in the possession of others.

§ 4—203. Effect of Instructions.

Subject to the provisions of Article 3 concerning conversion of instruments (Section 3—419) and the provisions of both Article 3 and this Article concerning restrictive indorsements only a collecting bank's transferor can give instructions which affect the bank or constitute notice to it and a collecting bank is not liable to prior parties for any action taken pursuant to such instructions or in accordance with any agreement with its transferor.

§ 4—204. Methods of Sending and Presenting; Sending Direct to Payor Bank.

(1) A collecting bank must send items by reasonably prompt method taking into consideration any relevant instructions, the nature of the item, the number of such items on hand, and the cost of collection involved and the method generally used by it or others to present such items.

(2) A collecting bank may send

(a) any item direct to the payor bank;

(b) any item to any non-bank payor if authorized by its transferor; and

(c) any item other than documentary drafts to any non-bank payor, if authorized by Federal Reserve regulation or operating letter, clearing house rule or the like.

(3) Presentment may be made by a presenting bank at a place where the payor bank has requested that presentment be made.

§ 4—205. Supplying Missing Indorsement; No Notice from Prior Indorsement.

(1) A depositary bank which has taken an item for collection may supply any indorsement of the customer which is necessary to title unless the item contains the words ''payee's indorsement required'' or the like. In the absence of such a requirement a statement placed on the item by the depositary bank to the effect that the item was deposited by a customer or credited to his account is effective as the customer's indorsement.

(2) An intermediary bank, or payor bank which is not a depositary bank, is neither given notice nor otherwise affected by a restrictive indorsement of any person except the bank's immediate transferor.

§ 4—206. Transfer Between Banks.

Any agreed method which identifies the transferor bank is sufficient for the item's further transfer to another bank.

§ 4—207. Warranties of Customer and Collecting Bank on Transfer or Presentment of Items; Time for Claims.

(1) Each customer or collecting bank who obtains payment or acceptance of an item and each prior customer and collecting bank warrants to the payor bank or other payor who in good faith pays or accepts the item that

(a) he has a good title to the item or is authorized to obtain payment or acceptance on behalf of one who has a good title; and

(b) he has no knowledge that the signature of the maker or drawer is unauthorized, except that this warranty is not given by any customer or collecting bank that is a holder in due course and acts in good faith

(i) to a maker with respect to the maker's own signature; or

(ii) to a drawer with respect to the drawer's own signature, whether or not the drawer is also the drawee; or

(iii) to an acceptor of an item if the holder in due course took the item after the acceptance or obtained the acceptance without knowledge that the drawer's signature was unauthorized; and

(c) the item has not been materially altered, except that this warranty is not given by any customer or collecting bank that is a holder in due course and acts in good faith

(i) to the maker of a note; or

(ii) to the drawer of a draft whether or not the drawer is also the drawee; or

(iii) to the acceptor of an item with respect to an alteration made prior to the acceptance if the holder in due course took the item after the acceptance, even though the acceptance provided "payable as originally drawn" or equivalent terms; or

(iv) to the acceptor of an item with respect to an alteration made after the acceptance.

(2) Each customer and collecting bank who transfers an item and receives a settlement or other consideration for it warrants to his transferee and to any subsequent collecting bank who takes the item in good faith that

(a) he has a good title to the item or is authorized to obtain payment or acceptance on behalf of one who has a good title and the transfer is otherwise rightful; and

(b) all signatures are genuine or authorized; and

(c) the item has not been materially altered; and

(d) no defense of any party is good against him; and

(e) he has no knowledge of any insolvency proceeding instituted with respect to the maker or acceptor or the drawer of an unaccepted item.

In addition each customer and collecting bank so transferring an item and receiving a settlement or other consideration engages that upon dishonor and any necessary notice of dishonor and protest he will take up the item.

(3) The warranties and the engagement to honor set forth in the two preceding subsections arise notwithstanding the absence of indorsement or words of guaranty or warranty in the transfer or presentment and a collecting bank remains liable for their breach despite remittance to its transferor. Damages for breach of such warranties or engagement to honor shall not exceed the consideration received by the customer or collecting bank responsible plus finance charges and expenses related to the item, if any.

(4) Unless a claim for breach of warranty under this section is made within a reasonable time after the person claiming learns of the breach, the person liable is discharged to the extent of any loss caused by the delay in making claim.

§ 4—208. Security Interest of Collecting Bank in Items, Accompanying Documents and Proceeds.

(1) A bank has a security interest in an item and any accompanying documents or the proceeds of either

(a) in case of an item deposited in an account to the extent to which credit given for the item has been withdrawn or applied;

(b) in case of an item for which it has given credit available for withdrawal as of right, to the extent of the credit given whether or not the credit is drawn upon and whether or not there is a right of charge-back; or

(c) if it makes an advance on or against the item.

(2) When credit which has been given for several items received at one time or pursuant to a single agreement is withdrawn or applied in part the security interest remains upon all the items, any accompanying documents or the proceeds of either. For the purpose of this section, credits first given are first withdrawn.

(3) Receipt by a collecting bank of a final settlement for an item is a realization on its security interest in the item, accompanying documents and proceeds. To the extent and so long as the bank does not receive final settlement for the item or give up possession of the item or accompanying documents for purposes other than collection, the security interest continues and is subject to the provisions of Article 9 except that

(a) no security agreement is necessary to make the security interest enforceable (subsection (1)(a) of Section 9—203); and

(b) no filing is required to perfect the security interest; and

(c) the security interest has priority over conflicting perfected security interests in the item, accompanying documents or proceeds.

§ 4—209. When Bank Gives Value for Purposes of Holder in Due Course.

For purposes of determining its status as a holder in due course, the bank has given value to the extent that it has a security interest in an item provided that the bank otherwise complies with the requirements of Section 3—302 on what constitutes a holder in due course.

§ 4—210. Presentment by Notice of Item Not Payable by, Through or at a Bank; Liability of Secondary Parties.

(1) Unless otherwise instructed, a collecting bank may present an item not payable by, through or at a bank by sending to the party to accept or pay a written notice that the bank holds the item for acceptance or payment. The notice must be sent in time to be received on or before the day when presentment is due and the bank must meet any requirement of the party to accept or pay under Section 3—505 by the close of the bank's next banking day after it knows of the requirement.

(2) Where presentment is made by notice and neither honor nor request for compliance with a requirement under Section 3—505 is received by the close of business on the day after maturity or in the case of demand items by the close of business on the third banking day after notice was sent, the presenting bank may treat the item as dishonored and charge any secondary party by sending him notice of the facts.

§ 4—211. Media of Remittance; Provisional and Final Settlement in Remittance Cases.

(1) A collecting bank may take in settlement of an item

(a) a check of the remitting bank or of another bank on any bank except the remitting bank; or

(b) a cashier's check or similar primary obligation of a remitting bank which is a member of or clears through a member of the same clearing house or group as the collecting bank; or

(c) appropriate authority to charge an account of the remitting bank or of another bank with the collecting bank; or

(d) if the item is drawn upon or payable by a person other than a bank, a cashier's check, certified check or other bank check or obligation.

(2) If before its midnight deadline the collecting bank properly dishonors a remittance check or authorization to charge on itself or presents or forwards for collection a remittance instrument of or on another bank which is of a kind approved by subsection (1) or has not been authorized by it, the collecting bank is not liable to prior parties in the event of the dishonor of such check, instrument or authorization.

(3) A settlement for an item by means of a remittance instrument or authorization to charge is or becomes a final settlement as to both the person making and the person receiving the settlement

(a) if the remittance instrument or authorization to charge is of a kind approved by subsection (1) or has not been authorized by the person receiving the settlement and in either case the person receiving the settlement acts seasonably before its midnight deadline in presenting, forwarding for collection or paying the instrument or authorization,—at the time the remittance instrument or authorization is finally paid by the payor by which it is payable;

(b) if the person receiving the settlement has authorized remittance by a non-bank check or obligation or by a cashier's check or similar primary obligation of or a check upon the payor or other remitting bank which is not of a kind approved by subsection (1)(b),—at the time of the receipt of such remittance check or obligation; or

(c) if in a case not covered by sub-paragraphs (a) or (b) the person receiving the settlement fails to seasonably present, forward for collection, pay or return a remittance instrument or authorization to it to charge before its midnight deadline,—at such midnight deadline.

§ 4—212. Right of Charge-Back or Refund.

(1) If a collecting bank has made provisional settlement with its customer for an item and itself fails by reason of dishonor, suspension of payments by a bank or otherwise to receive a settlement for the item which is or becomes final, the bank may revoke the settlement given by it, charge back the amount of any credit given for the item to its customer's account or obtain refund from its customer whether or not it is able to return the items if by its midnight deadline or within a longer reasonable time after it learns the facts it returns the item or sends notification of the facts. These rights to revoke, charge-back and obtain refund terminate if and when a settlement for the item received by the bank is or becomes final (subsection (3) of Section 4—211 and subsections (2) and (3) of Section 4—213).

[(2) Within the time and manner prescribed by this section and Section 4—301, an intermediary or payor bank, as the case may be, may return an unpaid item directly to the depositary bank and may send for collection a draft on the depositary bank and obtain reimbursement. In such case, if the depositary bank has received provisional settlement for the item, it must reimburse the bank drawing the draft and any provisional credits for the item between banks shall become and remain final.]

Note: *Direct returns is recognized as an innovation that is not yet established bank practice, and therefore, Paragraph 2 has been bracketed. Some lawyers have doubts whether it should be included in legislation or left to development by agreement.*

(3) A depositary bank which is also the payor may charge-back the amount of an item to its customer's account or obtain refund in accordance with the section governing return of an item received by a payor bank for credit on its books (Section 4—301).

(4) The right to charge-back is not affected by

(a) prior use of the credit given for the item; or

(b) failure by any bank to exercise ordinary care with respect to the item but any bank so failing remains liable.

(5) A failure to charge-back or claim refund does not affect other rights of the bank against the customer or any other party.

(6) If credit is given in dollars as the equivalent of the value of an item payable in a foreign currency the dollar amount of any charge-back or refund shall be calculated on the basis of the buying sight rate for the foreign currency prevailing on the day when the person entitled to the charge-back or refund learns that it will not receive payment in ordinary course.

§ 4—213. **Final Payment of Item by Payor Bank; When Provisional Debits and Credits Become Final; When Certain Credits Become Available for Withdrawal.**

(1) An item is finally paid by a payor bank when the bank has done any of the following, whichever happens first:

(a) paid the item in cash; or

(b) settled for the item without reserving a right to revoke the settlement and without having such right under statute, clearing house rule or agreement; or

(c) completed the process of posting the item to the indicated account of the drawer, maker or other person to be charged therewith; or

(d) made a provisional settlement for the item and failed to revoke the settlement in the time and manner permitted by statute, clearing house rule or agreement.

Upon a final payment under subparagraphs (b), (c) or (d) the payor bank shall be accountable for the amount of the item.

(2) If provisional settlement for an item between the presenting and payor banks is made through a clearing house or by debits or credits in an account between them, then to the extent that provisional debits or credits for the item are entered in accounts between the presenting and payor banks or between the presenting and successive prior collecting banks seriatim, they become final upon final payment of the item by the payor bank.

(3) If a collecting bank receives a settlement for an item which is or becomes final (subsection (3) of Section 4—211, subsection (2) of Section 4—213) the bank is accountable to its customer for the amount of the item and any provisional credit given for the item in an account with its customer becomes final.

(4) Subject to any right of the bank to apply the credit to an obligation of the customer, credit given by a bank for an item in an account with its customer becomes available for withdrawal as of right

(a) in any case where the bank has received a provisional settlement for the item,—when such settlement becomes final and the bank has had a reasonable time to learn that the settlement is final;

(b) in any case where the bank is both a depositary bank and a payor bank and the item is finally paid,—at the opening of the bank's second banking day following receipt of the item.

(5) A deposit of money in a bank is final when made but, subject to any right of the bank to apply the deposit to an obligation of the customer, the deposit becomes available for withdrawal as of right at the opening of the bank's next banking day following receipt of the deposit.

§ 4—214. **Insolvency and Preference.**

(1) Any item in or coming into the possession of a payor or collecting bank which suspends payment and which item is not finally paid shall be returned by the receiver, trustee or agent in charge of the closed bank to the presenting bank or the closed bank's customer.

(2) If a payor bank finally pays an item and suspends payments without making a settlement for the item with its customer or the presenting bank which settlement is or becomes final, the owner of the item has a preferred claim against the payor bank.

(3) If a payor bank gives or a collecting bank gives or receives a provisional settlement for an item and thereafter suspends payments, the suspension does not prevent or interfere with the settlement becoming final if such finality occurs automatically upon the lapse of certain time or the happening of certain events (subsection (3) of Section 4—211, subsections (1)(d), (2) and (3) of Section 4—213).

(4) If a collecting bank receives from subsequent parties settlement for an item which settlement is or becomes final and suspends payments without making a settlement for the item with its customer which is or becomes final, the owner of the item has a preferred claim against such collecting bank.

Part 3 Collection of Items: Payor Banks

§ 4—301. Deferred Posting; Recovery of Payment by Return of Items; Time of Dishonor.

(1) Where an authorized settlement for a demand item (other than a documentary draft) received by a payor bank otherwise than for immediate payment over the counter has been made before midnight of the banking day of receipt the payor bank may revoke the settlement and recover any payment if before it has made final payment (subsection (1) of Section 4—213) and before its midnight deadline it

(a) returns the item; or

(b) sends written notice of dishonor or nonpayment if the item is held for protest or is otherwise unavailable for return.

(2) If a demand item is received by a payor bank for credit on its books it may return such item or send notice of dishonor and may revoke any credit given or recover the amount thereof withdrawn by its customer, if it acts within the time limit and in the manner specified in the preceding subsection.

(3) Unless previous notice of dishonor has been sent an item is dishonored at the time when for purposes of dishonor it is returned or notice sent in accordance with this section.

(4) An item is returned:

(a) as to an item received through a clearing house, when it is delivered to the presenting or last collecting bank or to the clearing house or is sent or delivered in accordance with its rules; or

(b) in all other cases, when it is sent or delivered to the bank's customer or transferor or pursuant to his instructions.

§ 4—302. Payor Bank's Responsibility for Late Return of Item.

In the absence of a valid defense such as breach of a presentment warranty (subsection (1) of Section 4— 207), settlement effected or the like, if an item is presented on and received by a payor bank the bank is accountable for the amount of

(a) a demand item other than a documentary draft whether properly payable or not if the bank, in any case where it is not also the depositary bank, retains the item beyond midnight of the banking day of receipt without settling for it or, regardless of whether it is also the depositary bank, does not pay or return the item or send notice of dishonor until after its midnight deadline; or

(b) any other properly payable item unless within the time allowed for acceptance or payment of that item the bank either accepts or pays the item or returns it and accompanying documents.

§ 4—303. When Items Subject to Notice, Stop-Order, Legal Process or Setoff; Order in Which Items May Be Charged or Certified.

(1) Any knowledge, notice or stop-order received by, legal process served upon or setoff exercised by a payor bank, whether or not effective under other rules of law to terminate, suspend or modify the bank's right or duty to pay an item or to charge its customer's account for the item, comes too late to so terminate, suspend or modify such right or duty if the knowledge, notice, stop-order or legal process is received or served and a reasonable time for the bank to act thereon expires or the setoff is exercised after the bank has done any of the following:

(a) accepted or certified the item;

(b) paid the item in cash;

(c) settled for the item without reserving a right to revoke the settlement and without having such right under statute, clearing house rule or agreement;

(d) completed the process of posting the item to the indicated account of the drawer, maker or other person to be charged therewith or otherwise has evidenced by examination of such indicated account and by action its decision to pay the item; or

(e) become accountable for the amount of the item under subsection (1)(d) of Section 4—213 and Section 4—302 dealing with the payor bank's responsibility for late return of items.

(2) Subject to the provisions of subsection (1) items may be accepted, paid, certified or charged to the indicated account of its customer in any order convenient to the bank.

Part 4 Relationship Between Payor Bank and Its Customer

§ 4—401. When Bank May Charge Customer's Account.

(1) As against its customer, a bank may charge against his account any item which is otherwise properly payable from that account even though the charge creates an overdraft.

(2) A bank which in good faith makes payment to a holder may charge the indicated account of its customer according to

(a) the original tenor of his altered item; or

(b) the tenor of his completed item, even though the bank knows the item has been completed unless the bank has notice that the completion was improper.

§ 4—402. Bank's Liability to Customer for Wrongful Dishonor.

A payor bank is liable to its customer for damages proximately caused by the wrongful dishonor of an item. When the dishonor occurs through mistake liability is limited to actual damages proved. If so proximately caused and proved damages may include damages for an arrest or prosecution of the customer or other consequential damages. Whether any consequential damages are proximately caused by the wrongful dishonor is a question of fact to be determined in each case.

§ 4—403. Customer's Right to Stop Payment; Burden of Proof of Loss.

(1) A customer may by order to his bank stop payment of any item payable for his account but the order must be received at such time and in such manner as to afford the bank a reasonable opportunity to act on it prior to any action by the bank with respect to the item described in Section 4—303.

(2) An oral order is binding upon the bank only for fourteen calendar days unless confirmed in writing within that period. A written order is effective for only six months unless renewed in writing.

(3) The burden of establishing the fact and amount of loss resulting from the payment of an item contrary to a binding stop payment order is on the customer.

§ 4—404. Bank Not Obligated to Pay Check More Than Six Months Old.

A bank is under no obligation to a customer having a checking account to pay a check, other than a certified check, which is presented more than six months after its date, but it may charge its customer's account for a payment made thereafter in good faith.

§ 4—405. Death or Incompetence of Customer.

(1) A payor or collecting bank's authority to accept, pay or collect an item or to account for proceeds of its collection if otherwise effective is not rendered ineffective by incompetence of a customer of either bank existing at the time the item is issued or its collection is undertaken if the bank does not know of an adjudication of incompetence. Neither death nor incompetence of a customer revokes such authority to accept, pay, collect or account until the bank knows of the fact of death or of an adjudication of incompetence and has reasonable opportunity to act on it.

(2) Even with knowledge a bank may for 10 days after the date of death pay or certify checks drawn on or prior to that date unless ordered to stop payment by a person claiming an interest in the account.

§ 4—406. Customer's Duty to Discover and Report Unauthorized Signature or Alteration.

(1) When a bank sends to its customer a statement of account accompanied by items paid in good faith in support of the debit entries or holds the statement and items pursuant to a request or instructions of its customer or otherwise in a reasonable manner makes the statement and items available to the customer, the customer must exercise reasonable care and promptness to examine the statement and items to discover his unauthorized signature or any alteration on an item and must notify the bank promptly after discovery thereof.

(2) If the bank establishes that the customer failed with respect to an item to comply with the duties imposed on the customer by subsection (1) the customer is precluded from asserting against the bank

(a) his unauthorized signature or any alteration on the item if the bank also establishes that it suffered a loss by reason of such failure; and

(b) an unauthorized signature or alteration by the same wrongdoer on any other item paid in good faith by the bank after the first item and statement was available to the customer for a reasonable period not exceeding fourteen calendar days and before the bank receives notification from the customer of any such unauthorized signature or alteration.

(3) The preclusion under subsection (2) does not apply if the customer establishes lack of ordinary care on the part of the bank in paying the item(s).

(4) Without regard to care or lack of care of either the customer or the bank a customer who does not within one year from the time the statement and items are made available to the customer (subsection (1)) discover and report his unauthorized signature or any alteration on the face or back of the item or does not within three years from that time discover and report any unauthorized indorsement is precluded from asserting against the bank such unauthorized signature or indorsement or such alteration.

(5) If under this section a payor bank has a valid defense against a claim of a customer upon or resulting from payment of an item and waives or fails upon request to assert the defense the bank may not assert against any collecting bank or other prior party presenting or transferring the item a claim based upon the unauthorized signature or alteration giving rise to the customer's claim.

§ 4—407. Payor Bank's Right to Subrogation on Improper Payment.

If a payor bank has paid an item over the stop payment order of the drawer or maker or otherwise under circumstances giving a basis for objection by the drawer or maker, to prevent unjust enrichment and only to the extent necessary to prevent loss to the bank by reason of its payment of the item, the payor bank shall be subrogated to the rights

(a) of any holder in due course on the item against the drawer or maker; and

(b) of the payee or any other holder of the item against the drawer or maker either on the item or under the transaction out of which the item arose; and

(c) of the drawer or maker against the payee or any other holder of the item with respect to the transaction out of which the item arose.

Part 5 Collection of Documentary Drafts

§ 4—501. Handling of Documentary Drafts; Duty to Send for Presentment and to Notify Customer of Dishonor.

A bank which takes a documentary draft for collection must present or send the draft and accompanying documents for presentment and upon learning that the draft has not been paid or accepted in due course must seasonably notify its customer of such fact even though it may have discounted or bought the draft or extended credit available for withdrawal as of right.

§ 4—502. Presentment of "On Arrival" Drafts.

When a draft or the relevant instructions require presentment "on arrival", "when goods arrive" or the like, the collecting bank need not present until in its judgment a reasonable time for arrival of the goods has expired. Refusal to pay or accept because the goods have not arrived is not dishonor; the bank must notify its transferor of such refusal but need not present the draft again until it is instructed to do so or learns of the arrival of the goods.

§ 4—503. Responsibility of Presenting Bank for Documents and Goods; Report of Reasons for Dishonor; Referee in Case of Need.

Unless otherwise instructed and except as provided in Article 5 a bank presenting a documentary draft

    (a) must deliver the documents to the drawee on acceptance of the draft if it is payable more than three days after presentment; otherwise, only on payment; and

    (b) upon dishonor, either in the case of presentment for acceptance or presentment for payment, may seek and follow instructions from any referee in case of need designated in the draft or if the presenting bank does not choose to utilize his services it must use diligence and good faith to ascertain the reason for dishonor, must notify its transferor of the dishonor and of the results of its effort to ascertain the reasons therefor and must request instructions.

But the presenting bank is under no obligation with respect to goods represented by the documents except to follow any reasonable instructions seasonably received; it has a right to reimbursement for any expense incurred in following instructions and to prepayment of or indemnity for such expenses.

§ 4—504. Privilege of Presenting Bank to Deal With Goods; Security Interest for Expenses.

(1) A presenting bank which, following the dishonor of a documentary draft, has seasonably requested instructions but does not receive them within a reasonable time may store, sell, or otherwise deal with the goods in any reasonable manner.

(2) For its reasonable expenses incurred by action under subsection (1) the presenting bank has a lien upon the goods or their proceeds, which may be foreclosed in the same manner as an unpaid seller's lien.

Revised Article 4
BANK DEPOSITS AND COLLECTIONS

Part 1 General Provisions and Definitions

§ 4—101. Short Title.

This Article may be cited as Uniform Commercial Code—Bank Deposits and Collections.

§ 4—102. Applicability.

(a) To the extent that items within this Article are also within Articles 3 and 8, they are subject to those Articles. If there is conflict, this Article governs Article 3, but Article 8 governs this Article.

(b) The liability of a bank for action or non-action with respect to an item handled by it for purposes of presentment, payment, or collection is governed by the law of the place where the bank is located. In the case of action or non-action by or at a branch or separate office of a bank, its liability is governed by the law of the place where the branch or separate office is located.

§ 4—103. Variation by Agreement; Measure of Damages; Action Constituting Ordinary Care.

(a) The effect of the provisions of this Article may be varied by agreement, but the parties to the agreement cannot disclaim a bank's responsibility for its lack of good faith or failure to exercise ordinary care or limit the measure of damages for the lack or failure. However, the parties may determine by agreement the standards by which the bank's responsibility is to be measured if those standards are not manifestly unreasonable.

(b) Federal Reserve regulations and operating circulars, clearing-house rules, and the like have the effect of agreements under subsection (a), whether or not specifically assented to by all parties interested in items handled.

(c) Action or non-action approved by this Article or pursuant to Federal Reserve regulations or operating circulars is the exercise of ordinary care and, in the absence of special instructions, action or non-action consistent with clearing-house rules and the like or with a general banking usage not disapproved by this Article, is prima facie the exercise of ordinary care.

(d) The specification or approval of certain procedures by this Article is not disapproval of other procedures that may be reasonable under the circumstances.

(e) The measure of damages for failure to exercise ordinary care in handling an item is the amount of the item reduced by an amount that could not have been realized by the exercise of ordinary care. If there is also bad faith it includes any other damages the party suffered as a proximate consequence.

§ 4—104. **Definitions and Index of Definitions.**

(a) In this Article, unless the context otherwise requires:

(1) "Account" means any deposit or credit account with a bank, including a demand, time, savings, passbook, share draft, or like account, other than an account evidenced by a certificate of deposit;

(2) "Afternoon" means the period of a day between noon and midnight;

(3) "Banking day" means the part of a day on which a bank is open to the public for carrying on substantially all of its banking functions;

(4) "Clearing house" means an association of banks or other payors regularly clearing items;

(5) "Customer" means a person having an account with a bank or for whom a bank has agreed to collect items, including a bank that maintains an account at another bank;

(6) "Documentary draft" means a draft to be presented for acceptance or payment if specified documents, certificated securities (Section 8—102) or instructions for uncertificated securities (Section 8—308), or other certificates, statements, or the like are to be received by the drawee or other payor before acceptance or payment of the draft;

(7) "Draft" means a draft as defined in Section 3—104 or an item, other than an instrument, that is an order;

(8) "Drawee" means a person ordered in a draft to make payment;

(9) "Item" means an instrument or a promise or order to pay money handled by a bank for collection or payment. The term does not include a payment order governed by Article 4A or a credit or debit card slip;

(10) "Midnight deadline" with respect to a bank is midnight on its next banking day following the banking day on which it receives the relevant item or notice or from which the time for taking action commences to run, whichever is later;

(11) "Settle" means to pay in cash, by clearing-house settlement, in a charge or credit or by remittance, or otherwise as agreed. A settlement may be either provisional or final;

(12) "Suspends payments" with respect to a bank means that it has been closed by order of the supervisory authorities, that a public officer has been appointed to take it over, or that it ceases or refuses to make payments in the ordinary course of business.

(b);(c) [Other definitions' section references deleted.]

(d) In addition, Article 1 contains general definitions and principles of construction and interpretation applicable throughout this Article.

§ 4—105. **"Bank"; "Depositary Bank"; "Payor Bank"; "Intermediary Bank"; "Collecting Bank"; "Presenting Bank".**

In this Article:

(1) "Bank" means a person engaged in the business of banking, including a savings bank, savings and loan association, credit union, or trust company;

(2) "Depositary bank" means the first bank to take an item even though it is also the payor bank, unless the item is presented for immediate payment over the counter;

(3) "Payor bank" means a bank that is the drawee of a draft;

(4) "Intermediary bank" means a bank to which an item is transferred in course of collection except the depositary or payor bank;

(5) "Collecting bank" means a bank handling an item for collection except the payor bank;

(6) "Presenting bank" means a bank presenting an item except a payor bank.

§ 4—106. **Payable Through or Payable at Bank: Collecting Bank.**

(a) If an item states that it is "payable through" a bank identified in the item, (i) the item designates the bank as a collecting bank and does not by itself authorize the bank to pay the item, and (ii) the item may be presented for payment only by or through the bank.

Alternative A

(b) If an item states that it is "payable at" a bank identified in the item, the item is equivalent to a draft drawn on the bank.

Alternative B

(b) If an item states that it is "payable at" a bank identified in the item, (i) the item designates the bank as a collecting bank and does not by itself authorize the bank to pay the item, and (ii) the item may be presented for payment only by or through the bank.

(c) If a draft names a nonbank drawee and it is unclear whether a bank named in the draft is a co-drawee or a collecting bank, the bank is a collecting bank.

§ 4—107. **Separate Office of Bank.**

A branch or separate office of a bank is a separate bank for the purpose of computing the time within which and determining the place at or to which action may be taken or notices or orders shall be given under this Article and under Article 3.

§ 4—108. Time of Receipt of Items.

(a) For the purpose of allowing time to process items, prove balances, and make the necessary entries on its books to determine its position for the day, a bank may fix an afternoon hour of 2 P.M. or later as a cutoff hour for the handling of money and items and the making of entries on its books.

(b) An item or deposit of money received on any day after a cutoff hour so fixed or after the close of the banking day may be treated as being received at the opening of the next banking day.

§ 4—109. Delays.

(a) Unless otherwise instructed, a collecting bank in a good faith effort to secure payment of a specific item drawn on a payor other than a bank, and with or without the approval of any person involved, may waive, modify, or extend time limits imposed or permitted by this [act] for a period not exceeding two additional banking days without discharge of drawers or indorsers or liability to its transferor or a prior party.

(b) Delay by a collecting bank or payor bank beyond time limits prescribed or permitted by this [act] or by instructions is excused if (i) the delay is caused by interruption of communication or computer facilities, suspension of payments by another bank, war, emergency conditions, failure of equipment, or other circumstances beyond the control of the bank, and (ii) the bank exercises such diligence as the circumstances require.

§ 4—110. Electronic Presentment.

(a) "Agreement for electronic presentment" means an agreement, clearing-house rule, or Federal Reserve regulation or operating circular, providing that presentment of an item may be made by transmission of an image of an item or information describing the item ("presentment notice") rather than delivery of the item itself. The agreement may provide for procedures governing retention, presentment, payment, dishonor, and other matters concerning items subject to the agreement.

(b) Presentment of an item pursuant to an agreement for presentment is made when the presentment notice is received.

(c) If presentment is made by presentment notice, a reference to "item" or "check" in this Article means the presentment notice unless the context otherwise indicates.

§ 4—111. Statute of Limitations.

An action to enforce an obligation, duty, or right arising under this Article must be commenced within three years after the [cause of action] accrues.

Part 2 Collection of Items: Depositary and Collecting Banks

§ 4—201. Status of Collecting Bank As Agent and Provisional Status of Credits; Applicability of Article; Item Indorsed "Pay Any Bank".

(a) Unless a contrary intent clearly appears and before the time that a settlement given by a collecting bank for an item is or becomes final, the bank, with respect to an item, is an agent or sub-agent of the owner of the item and any settlement given for the item is provisional. This provision applies regardless of the form of indorsement or lack of indorsement and even though credit given for the item is subject to immediate withdrawal as of right or is in fact withdrawn; but the continuance of ownership of an item by its owner and any rights of the owner to proceeds of the item are subject to rights of a collecting bank, such as those resulting from outstanding advances on the item and rights of recoupment or setoff. If an item is handled by banks for purposes of presentment, payment, collection, or return, the relevant provisions of this Article apply even though action of the parties clearly establishes that a particular bank has purchased the item and is the owner of it.

(b) After an item has been indorsed with the words "pay any bank" or the like, only a bank may acquire the rights of a holder until the item has been:

(1) returned to the customer initiating collection; or

(2) specially indorsed by a bank to a person who is not a bank.

§ 4—202. Responsibility for Collection or Return; When Action Timely.

(a) A collecting bank must exercise ordinary care in:

(1) presenting an item or sending it for presentment;

(2) sending notice of dishonor or nonpayment or returning an item other than a documentary draft to the bank's transferor after learning that the item has not been paid or accepted, as the case may be;

(3) settling for an item when the bank receives final settlement; and

(4) notifying its transferor of any loss or delay in transit within a reasonable time after discovery thereof.

(b) A collecting bank exercises ordinary care under subsection (a) by taking proper action before its midnight deadline following receipt of an item, notice, or settlement. Taking proper action within a reasonably longer time may constitute the exercise of ordinary care, but the bank has the burden of establishing timeliness.

(c) Subject to subsection (a)(1), a bank is not liable for the insolvency, neglect, misconduct, mistake, or default of another bank or person or for loss or destruction of an item in the possession of others or in transit.

§ 4—203. **Effect of Instructions.**

Subject to Article 3 concerning conversion of instruments (Section 3—420) and restrictive indorsements (Section 3—206), only a collecting bank's transferor can give instructions that affect the bank or constitute notice to it, and a collecting bank is not liable to prior parties for any action taken pursuant to the instructions or in accordance with any agreement with its transferor.

§ 4—204. **Methods of Sending and Presenting; Sending Directly to Payor Bank.**

(a) A collecting bank shall send items by a reasonably prompt method, taking into consideration relevant instructions, the nature of the item, the number of those items on hand, the cost of collection involved, and the method generally used by it or others to present those items.

(b) A collecting bank may send:

(1) an item directly to the payor bank;

(2) an item to a nonbank payor if authorized by its transferor; and

(3) an item other than documentary drafts to a nonbank payor, if authorized by Federal Reserve regulation or operating circular, clearing-house rule, or the like.

(c) Presentment may be made by a presenting bank at a place where the payor bank or other payor has requested that presentment be made.

§ 4—205. **Depositary Bank Holder of Unindorsed Item.**

If a customer delivers an item to a depositary bank for collection:

(1) the depositary bank becomes a holder of the item at the time it receives the item for collection if the customer at the time of delivery was a holder of the item, whether or not the customer indorses the item, and, if the bank satisfies the other requirements of Section 3—302, it is a holder in due course; and

(2) the depositary bank warrants to collecting banks, the payor bank or other payor, and the drawer that the amount of the item was paid to the customer or deposited to the customer's account.

§ 4—206. **Transfer Between Banks.**

Any agreed method that identifies the transferor bank is sufficient for the item's further transfer to another bank.

§ 4—207. **Transfer Warranties.**

(a) A customer or collecting bank that transfers an item and receives a settlement or other consideration warrants to the transferee and to any subsequent collecting bank that:

(1) the warrantor is a person entitled to enforce the item;

(2) all signatures on the item are authentic and authorized;

(3) the item has not been altered;

(4) the item is not subject to a defense or claim in recoupment (Section 3—305(a)) of any party that can be asserted against the warrantor; and

(5) the warrantor has no knowledge of any insolvency proceeding commenced with respect to the maker or acceptor or, in the case of an unaccepted draft, the drawer.

(b) If an item is dishonored, a customer or collecting bank transferring the item and receiving settlement or other consideration is obliged to pay the amount due on the item (i) according to the terms of the item at the time it was transferred, or (ii) if the transfer was of an incomplete item, according to its terms when completed as stated in Sections 3—115 and 3—407. The obligation of a transferor is owed to the transferee and to any subsequent collecting bank that takes the item in good faith. A transferor cannot disclaim its obligation under this subsection by an indorsement stating that it is made "without recourse" or otherwise disclaiming liability.

(c) A person to whom the warranties under subsection (a) are made and who took the item in good faith may recover from the warrantor as damages for breach of warranty an amount equal to the loss suffered as a result of the breach, but not more than the amount of the item plus expenses and loss of interest incurred as a result of the breach.

(d) The warranties stated in subsection (a) cannot be disclaimed with respect to checks. Unless notice of a claim for breach of warranty is given to the warrantor within 30 days after the claimant has reason to know of the breach and the identity of the warrantor, the warrantor is discharged to the extent of any loss caused by the delay in giving notice of the claim.

(e) A cause of action for breach of warranty under this section accrues when the claimant has reason to know of the breach.

§ 4—208. **Presentment Warranties.**

(a) If an unaccepted draft is presented to the drawee for payment or acceptance and the drawee pays or accepts the draft, (i) the person obtaining payment or acceptance, at the time of presentment, and (ii) a previous transferor of the draft, at the time of transfer, warrant to the drawee that pays or accepts the draft in good faith that:

(1) the warrantor is, or was, at the time the warrantor transferred the draft, a person entitled to enforce the draft or authorized to obtain payment or acceptance of the draft on behalf of a person entitled to enforce the draft;

(2) the draft has not been altered; and

(3) the warrantor has no knowledge that the signature of the purported drawer of the draft is unauthorized.

(b) A drawee making payment may recover from a warrantor damages for breach of warranty equal to the amount paid by the drawee less the amount the drawee received or is entitled to receive from the drawer because of the payment. In addition, the drawee is entitled to compensation for expenses and loss of interest resulting from the breach. The right of the drawee to recover damages under this subsection is not affected by any failure of the drawee to exercise ordinary care in making payment. If the drawee accepts the draft (i) breach of warranty is a defense to the obligation of the acceptor, and (ii) if the acceptor makes payment with respect to the draft, the acceptor is entitled to recover from a warrantor for breach of warranty the amounts stated in this subsection.

(c) If a drawee asserts a claim for breach of warranty under subsection (a) based on an unauthorized indorsement of the draft or an alteration of the draft, the warrantor may defend by proving that the indorsement is effective under Section 3—404 or 3—405 or the drawer is precluded under Section 3—406 or 4—406 from asserting against the drawee the unauthorized indorsement or alteration.

(d) If (i) a dishonored draft is presented for payment to the drawer or an indorser or (ii) any other item is presented for payment to a party obliged to pay the item, and the item is paid, the person obtaining payment and a prior transferor of the item warrant to the person making payment in good faith that the warrantor is, or was, at the time the warrantor transferred the item, a person entitled to enforce the item or authorized to obtain payment on behalf of a person entitled to enforce the item. The person making payment may recover from any warrantor for breach of warranty an amount equal to the amount paid plus expenses and loss of interest resulting from the breach.

(e) The warranties stated in subsections (a) and (d) cannot be disclaimed with respect to checks. Unless notice of a claim for breach of warranty is given to the warrantor within 30 days after the claimant has reason to know of the breach and the identity of the warrantor, the warrantor is discharged to the extent of any loss caused by the delay in giving notice of the claim.

(f) A cause of action for breach of warranty under this section accrues when the claimant has reason to know of the breach.

§ 4—209. Encoding and Retention Warranties.

(a) A person who encodes information on or with respect to an item after issue warrants to any subsequent collecting bank and to the payor bank or other payor that the information is correctly encoded. If the customer of a depositary bank encodes, that bank also makes the warranty.

(b) A person who undertakes to retain an item pursuant to an agreement for electronic presentment warrants to any subsequent collecting bank and to the payor bank or other payor that retention and presentment of the item comply with the agreement. If a customer of a depositary bank undertakes to retain an item, that bank also makes this warranty.

(c) A person to whom warranties are made under this section and who took the item in good faith may recover from the warrantor as damages for breach of warranty an amount equal to the loss suffered as a result of the breach, plus expenses and loss of interest incurred as a result of the breach.

§ 4—210. Security Interest of Collecting Bank in Items, Accompanying Documents and Proceeds.

(a) A collecting bank has a security interest in an item and any accompanying documents or the proceeds of either:

(1) in case of an item deposited in an account, to the extent to which credit given for the item has been withdrawn or applied;

(2) in case of an item for which it has given credit available for withdrawal as of right, to the extent of the credit given, whether or not the credit is drawn upon or there is a right of charge-back; or

(3) if it makes an advance on or against the item.

(b) If credit given for several items received at one time or pursuant to a single agreement is withdrawn or applied in part, the security interest remains upon all the items, any accompanying documents or the proceeds of either. For the purpose of this section, credits first given are first withdrawn.

(c) Receipt by a collecting bank of a final settlement for an item is a realization on its security interest in the item, accompanying documents, and proceeds. So long as the bank does not receive final settlement for the item or give up possession of the item or accompanying documents for purposes other than collection, the security interest continues to that extent and is subject to Article 9, but:

(1) no security agreement is necessary to make the security interest enforceable (Section 9—203(1)(a));

(2) no filing is required to perfect the security interest; and

(3) the security interest has priority over conflicting perfected security interests in the item, accompanying documents, or proceeds.

§ 4—211. When Bank Gives Value for Purposes of Holder in Due Course.

For purposes of determining its status as a holder in due course, a bank has given value to the extent it has a security interest in an item, if the bank otherwise complies with the requirements of Section 3—302 on what constitutes a holder in due course.

§ 4—212. **Presentment by Notice of Item Not Payable by, Through, or at Bank; Liability of Drawer or Indorser.**

(a) Unless otherwise instructed, a collecting bank may present an item not payable by, through, or at a bank by sending to the party to accept or pay a written notice that the bank holds the item for acceptance or payment. The notice must be sent in time to be received on or before the day when presentment is due and the bank must meet any requirement of the party to accept or pay under Section 3—501 by the close of the bank's next banking day after it knows of the requirement.

(b) If presentment is made by notice and payment, acceptance, or request for compliance with a requirement under Section 3—501 is not received by the close of business on the day after maturity or, in the case of demand items, by the close of business on the third banking day after notice was sent, the presenting bank may treat the item as dishonored and charge any drawer or indorser by sending it notice of the facts.

§ 4—213. **Medium and Time of Settlement by Bank.**

(a) With respect to settlement by a bank, the medium and time of settlement may be prescribed by Federal Reserve regulations or circulars, clearing-house rules, and the like, or agreement. In the absence of such prescription:

(1) the medium of settlement is cash or credit to an account in a Federal Reserve bank of or specified by the person to receive settlement; and

(2) the time of settlement is:

(i) with respect to tender of settlement by cash, a cashier's check, or teller's check, when the cash or check is sent or delivered;

(ii) with respect to tender of settlement by credit in an account in a Federal Reserve Bank, when the credit is made;

(iii) with respect to tender of settlement by a credit or debit to an account in a bank, when the credit or debit is made or, in the case of tender of settlement by authority to charge an account, when the authority is sent or delivered; or

(iv) with respect to tender of settlement by a funds transfer, when payment is made pursuant to Section 4A—406(a) to the person receiving settlement.

(b) If the tender of settlement is not by a medium authorized by subsection (a) or the time of settlement is not fixed by subsection (a), no settlement occurs until the tender of settlement is accepted by the person receiving settlement.

(c) If settlement for an item is made by cashier's check or teller's check and the person receiving settlement, before its midnight deadline:

(1) presents or forwards the check for collection, settlement is final when the check is finally paid; or

(2) fails to present or forward the check for collection, settlement is final at the midnight deadline of the person receiving settlement.

(d) If settlement for an item is made by giving authority to charge the account of the bank giving settlement in the bank receiving settlement, settlement is final when the charge is made by the bank receiving settlement if there are funds available in the account for the amount of the item.

§ 4—214. **Right of Charge-Back or Refund; Liability of Collecting Bank: Return of Item.**

(a) If a collecting bank has made provisional settlement with its customer for an item and fails by reason of dishonor, suspension of payments by a bank, or otherwise to receive settlement for the item which is or becomes final, the bank may revoke the settlement given by it, charge back the amount of any credit given for the item to its customer's account, or obtain refund from its customer, whether or not it is able to return the item, if by its midnight deadline or within a longer reasonable time after it learns the facts it returns the item or sends notification of the facts. If the return or notice is delayed beyond the bank's midnight deadline or a longer reasonable time after it learns the facts, the bank may revoke the settlement, charge back the credit, or obtain refund from its customer, but it is liable for any loss resulting from the delay. These rights to revoke, charge back, and obtain refund terminate if and when a settlement for the item received by the bank is or becomes final.

(b) A collecting bank returns an item when it is sent or delivered to the bank's customer or transferor or pursuant to its instructions.

(c) A depositary bank that is also the payor may charge back the amount of an item to its customer's account or obtain refund in accordance with the section governing return of an item received by a payor bank for credit on its books (Section 4—301).

(d) The right to charge back is not affected by:

(1) previous use of a credit given for the item; or

(2) failure by any bank to exercise ordinary care with respect to the item, but a bank so failing remains liable.

(e) A failure to charge back or claim refund does not affect other rights of the bank against the customer or any other party.

(f) If credit is given in dollars as the equivalent of the value of an item payable in foreign money, the dollar amount of any charge-back or refund must be calculated on the basis of the bank-offered spot rate for the foreign money prevailing on the day when the person entitled to the charge-back or refund learns that it will not receive payment in ordinary course.

§ 4—215. **Final Payment of Item by Payor Bank; When Provisional Debits and Credits Become Final; When Certain Credits Become Available for Withdrawal.**

(a) An item is finally paid by a payor bank when the bank has first done any of the following:

(1) paid the item in cash;

(2) settled for the item without having a right to revoke the settlement under statute, clearing-house rule, or agreement; or

(3) made a provisional settlement for the item and failed to revoke the settlement in the time and manner permitted by statute, clearing-house rule, or agreement.

(b) If provisional settlement for an item does not become final, the item is not finally paid.

(c) If provisional settlement for an item between the presenting and payor banks is made through a clearing house or by debits or credits in an account between them, then to the extent that provisional debits or credits for the item are entered in accounts between the presenting and payor banks or between the presenting and successive prior collecting banks seriatim, they become final upon final payment of the item by the payor bank.

(d) If a collecting bank receives a settlement for an item which is or becomes final, the bank is accountable to its customer for the amount of the item and any provisional credit given for the item in an account with its customer becomes final.

(e) Subject to (i) applicable law stating a time for availability of funds and (ii) any right of the bank to apply the credit to an obligation of the customer, credit given by a bank for an item in a customer's account becomes available for withdrawal as of right:

(1) if the bank has received a provisional settlement for the item, when the settlement becomes final and the bank has had a reasonable time to receive return of the item and the item has not been received within that time;

(2) if the bank is both the depositary bank and the payor bank, and the item is finally paid, at the opening of the bank's second banking day following receipt of the item.

(f) Subject to applicable law stating a time for availability of funds and any right of a bank to apply a deposit to an obligation of the depositor, a deposit of money becomes available for withdrawal as of right at the opening of the bank's next banking day after receipt of the deposit.

§ 4—216. **Insolvency and Preference.**

(a) If an item is in or comes into the possession of a payor or collecting bank that suspends payment and the item has not been finally paid, the item must be returned by the receiver, trustee, or agent in charge of the closed bank to the presenting bank or the closed bank's customer.

(b) If a payor bank finally pays an item and suspends payments without making a settlement for the item with its customer or the presenting bank which settlement is or becomes final, the owner of the item has a preferred claim against the payor bank.

(c) If a payor bank gives or a collecting bank gives or receives a provisional settlement for an item and thereafter suspends payments, the suspension does not prevent or interfere with the settlement's becoming final if the finality occurs automatically upon the lapse of certain time or the happening of certain events.

(d) If a collecting bank receives from subsequent parties settlement for an item, which settlement is or becomes final and the bank suspends payments without making a settlement for the item with its customer which settlement is or becomes final, the owner of the item has a preferred claim against the collecting bank.

Part 3 Collection of Items: Payor Banks

§ 4—301. **Deferred Posting; Recovery of Payment by Return of Items; Time of Dishonor; Return of Items by Payor Bank.**

(a) If a payor bank settles for a demand item other than a documentary draft presented otherwise than for immediate payment over the counter before midnight of the banking day of receipt, the payor bank may revoke the settlement and recover the settlement if, before it has made final payment and before its midnight deadline, it

(1) returns the item; or

(2) sends written notice of dishonor or nonpayment if the item is unavailable for return.

(b) If a demand item is received by a payor bank for credit on its books, it may return the item or send notice of dishonor and may revoke any credit given or recover the amount thereof withdrawn by its customer, if it acts within the time limit and in the manner specified in subsection (a).

(c) Unless previous notice of dishonor has been sent, an item is dishonored at the time when for purposes of dishonor it is returned or notice sent in accordance with this section.

(d) An item is returned:

(1) as to an item presented through a clearing house, when it is delivered to the presenting or last collecting bank or to the clearing house or is sent or delivered in accordance with clearing-house rules; or

(2) in all other cases, when it is sent or delivered to the bank's customer or transferor or pursuant to instructions.

§ 4—302. **Payor Bank's Responsibility for Late Return of Item.**

(a) If an item is presented to and received by a payor bank, the bank is accountable for the amount of:

(1) a demand item, other than a documentary draft, whether properly payable or not, if the bank, in any case in which it is not also the depositary bank, retains the item beyond midnight of the banking day of receipt without settling for it or, whether or not it is also the depositary bank, does not pay or return the item or send notice of dishonor until after its midnight deadline; or

(2) any other properly payable item unless, within the time allowed for acceptance or payment of that item, the bank either accepts or pays the item or returns it and accompanying documents.

(b) The liability of a payor bank to pay an item pursuant to subsection (a) is subject to defenses based on breach of a presentment warranty (Section 4—208) or proof that the person seeking enforcement of the liability presented or transferred the item for the purpose of defrauding the payor bank.

§ 4—303. **When Items Subject to Notice, Stop-Payment Order, Legal Process, or Setoff; Order in Which Items May Be Charged or Certified.**

(a) Any knowledge, notice, or stop-payment order received by, legal process served upon, or setoff exercised by a payor bank comes too late to terminate, suspend, or modify the bank's right or duty to pay an item or to charge its customer's account for the item if the knowledge, notice, stop-payment order, or legal process is received or served and a reasonable time for the bank to act thereon expires or the setoff is exercised after the earliest of the following:

(1) the bank accepts or certifies the item;

(2) the bank pays the item in cash;

(3) the bank settles for the item without having a right to revoke the settlement under statute, clearing-house rule, or agreement;

(4) the bank becomes accountable for the amount of the item under Section 4—302 dealing with the payor bank's responsibility for late return of items; or

(5) with respect to checks, a cutoff hour no earlier than one hour after the opening of the next banking day after the banking day on which the bank received the check and no later than the close of that next banking day or, if no cutoff hour is fixed, the close of the next banking day after the banking day on which the bank received the check.

(b) Subject to subsection (a), items may be accepted, paid, certified, or charged to the indicated account of its customer in any order.

Part 4 **Relationship Between Payor Bank and its Customer**

§ 4—401. **When Bank May Charge Customer's Account.**

(a) A bank may charge against the account of a customer an item that is properly payable from the account even though the charge creates an overdraft. An item is properly payable if it is authorized by the customer and is in accordance with any agreement between the customer and bank.

(b) A customer is not liable for the amount of an overdraft if the customer neither signed the item nor benefited from the proceeds of the item.

(c) A bank may charge against the account of a customer a check that is otherwise properly payable from the account, even though payment was made before the date of the check, unless the customer has given notice to the bank of the postdating describing the check with reasonable certainty. The notice is effective for the period stated in Section 4—403(b) for stop-payment orders, and must be received at such time and in such manner as to afford the bank a reasonable opportunity to act on it before the bank takes any action with respect to the check described in Section 4—303. If a bank charges against the account of a customer a check before the date stated in the notice of postdating, the bank is liable for damages for the loss resulting from its act. The loss may include damages for dishonor of subsequent items under Section 4—402.

(d) A bank that in good faith makes payment to a holder may charge the indicated account of its customer according to:

(1) the original terms of the altered item; or

(2) the terms of the completed item, even though the bank knows the item has been completed unless the bank has notice that the completion was improper.

§ 4—402. **Bank's Liability to Customer for Wrongful Dishonor; Time of Determining Insufficiency of Account.**

(a) Except as otherwise provided in this Article, a payor bank wrongfully dishonors an item if it dishonors an item that is properly payable, but a bank may dishonor an item that would create an overdraft unless it has agreed to pay the overdraft.

(b) A payor bank is liable to its customer for damages proximately caused by the wrongful dishonor of an item. Liability is limited to actual damages proved and may include damages for an arrest or prosecution of the customer or other consequential damages. Whether any consequential damages are proximately caused by the wrongful dishonor is a question of fact to be determined in each case.

(c) A payor bank's determination of the customer's account balance on which a decision to dishonor for insufficiency of available funds is based may be made at any time between the time the item is received by the payor bank and the time that the payor bank returns the item or gives notice in lieu of return, and no more than one determination need be made. If, at the election of the payor bank, a subsequent balance determination is made for the purpose of reevaluating the bank's decision to dishonor the item, the account balance at that time is determinative of whether a dishonor for insufficiency of available funds is wrongful.

§ 4—403. Customer's Right to Stop Payment; Burden of Proof of Loss.

(a) A customer or any person authorized to draw on the account if there is more than one person may stop payment of any item drawn on the customer's account or close the account by an order to the bank describing the item or account with reasonable certainty received at a time and in a manner that affords the bank a reasonable opportunity to act on it before any action by the bank with respect to the item described in Section 4—303. If the signature of more than one person is required to draw on an account, any of these persons may stop payment or close the account.

(b) A stop-payment order is effective for six months, but it lapses after 14 calendar days if the original order was oral and was not confirmed in writing within that period. A stop-payment order may be renewed for additional six-month periods by a writing given to the bank within a period during which the stop-payment order is effective.

(c) The burden of establishing the fact and amount of loss resulting from the payment of an item contrary to a stop-payment order or order to close an account is on the customer. The loss from payment of an item contrary to a stop-payment order may include damages for dishonor of subsequent items under Section 4—402.

§ 4—404. Bank Not Obliged to Pay Check More Than Six Months Old.

A bank is under no obligation to a customer having a checking account to pay a check, other than a certified check, which is presented more than six months after its date, but it may charge its customer's account for a payment made thereafter in good faith.

§ 4—405. Death or Incompetence of Customer.

(a) A payor or collecting bank's authority to accept, pay, or collect an item or to account for proceeds of its collection, if otherwise effective, is not rendered ineffective by incompetence of a customer of either bank existing at the time the item is issued or its collection is undertaken if the bank does not know of an adjudication of incompetence. Neither death nor incompetence of a customer revokes the authority to accept, pay, collect, or account until the bank knows of the fact of death or of an adjudication of incompetence and has reasonable opportunity to act on it.

(b) Even with knowledge, a bank may for 10 days after the date of death pay or certify checks drawn on or before the date unless ordered to stop payment by a person claiming an interest in the account.

§ 4—406. Customer's Duty to Discover and Report Unauthorized Signature or Alteration.

(a) A bank that sends or makes available to a customer a statement of account showing payment of items for the account shall either return or make available to the customer the items paid or provide information in the statement of account sufficient to allow the customer reasonably to identify the items paid. The statement of account provides sufficient information if the item is described by item number, amount, and date of payment.

(b) If the items are not returned to the customer, the person retaining the items shall either retain the items or, if the items are destroyed, maintain the capacity to furnish legible copies of the items until the expiration of seven years after receipt of the items. A customer may request an item from the bank that paid the item, and that bank must provide in a reasonable time either the item or, if the item has been destroyed or is not otherwise obtainable, a legible copy of the item.

(c) If a bank sends or makes available a statement of account or items pursuant to subsection (a), the customer must exercise reasonable promptness in examining the statement or the items to determine whether any payment was not authorized because of an alteration of an item or because a purported signature by or on behalf of the customer was not authorized. If, based on the statement or items provided, the customer should reasonably have discovered the unauthorized payment, the customer must promptly notify the bank of the relevant facts.

(d) If the bank proves that the customer failed, with respect to an item, to comply with the duties imposed on the customer by subsection (c), the customer is precluded from asserting against the bank:

> (1) the customer's unauthorized signature or any alteration on the item, if the bank also proves that it suffered a loss by reason of the failure; and

> (2) the customer's unauthorized signature or alteration by the same wrongdoer on any other item paid in good faith by the bank if the payment was made before the bank received notice from the customer of the unauthorized signature or alteration and after the customer had been afforded a reasonable period of time, not exceeding 30 days, in which to examine the item or statement of account and notify the bank.

(e) If subsection (d) applies and the customer proves that the bank failed to exercise ordinary care in paying the item and that the failure substantially contributed to loss, the loss is allocated between the customer precluded and the bank asserting the preclusion according to the extent to which the failure of the customer to comply with subsection (c) and the failure of the bank to exercise ordinary care contributed to the loss. If the customer proves that the bank did not pay the item in good faith, the preclusion under subsection (d) does not apply.

(f) Without regard to care or lack of care of either the customer or the bank, a customer who does not within one year after the statement or items are made available to the customer (subsection (a)) discover and report the customer's unauthorized signature on or any alteration on the item is precluded from asserting against the bank the unauthorized signature or alteration. If there is a preclusion under this subsection, the payor bank may not recover for breach or warranty under Section 4—208 with respect to the unauthorized signature or alteration to which the preclusion applies.

§ 4—407. Payor Bank's Right to Subrogation on Improper Payment.

If a payor has paid an item over the order of the drawer or maker to stop payment, or after an account has been closed, or otherwise under circumstances giving a basis for objection by the drawer or maker, to prevent unjust enrichment and only to the extent necessary to prevent loss to the bank by reason of its payment of the item, the payor bank is subrogated to the rights

(1) of any holder in due course on the item against the drawer or maker;

(2) of the payee or any other holder of the item against the drawer or maker either on the item or under the transaction out of which the item arose; and

(3) of the drawer or maker against the payee or any other holder of the item with respect to the transaction out of which the item arose.

Part 5 Collection of Documentary Drafts

§ 4—501. Handling of Documentary Drafts; Duty to Send for Presentment and to Notify Customer of Dishonor.

A bank that takes a documentary draft for collection shall present or send the draft and accompanying documents for presentment and, upon learning that the draft has not been paid or accepted in due course, shall seasonably notify its customer of the fact even though it may have discounted or bought the draft or extended credit available for withdrawal as of right.

§ 4—502. Presentment of "On Arrival" Drafts.

If a draft or the relevant instructions require presentment "on arrival", "when goods arrive" or the like, the collecting bank need not present until in its judgment a reasonable time for arrival of the goods has expired. Refusal to pay or accept because the goods have not arrived is not dishonor; the bank must notify its transferor of the refusal but need not present the draft again until it is instructed to do so or learns of the arrival of the goods.

§ 4—503. Responsibility of Presenting Bank for Documents and Goods; Report of Reasons for Dishonor; Referee in Case of Need.

Unless otherwise instructed and except as provided in Article 5, a bank presenting a documentary draft:

(1) must deliver the documents to the drawee on acceptance of the draft if it is payable more than three days after presentment, otherwise, only on payment; and

(2) upon dishonor, either in the case of presentment for acceptance or presentment for payment, may seek and follow instructions from any referee in case of need designated in the draft or, if the presenting bank does not choose to utilize the referee's services, it must use diligence and good faith to ascertain the reason for dishonor, must notify its transferor of the dishonor and of the results of its effort to ascertain the reasons therefor, and must request instructions.

However, the presenting bank is under no obligation with respect to goods represented by the documents except to follow any reasonable instructions seasonably received; it has a right to reimbursement for any expense incurred in following instructions and to prepayment of or indemnity for those expenses.

§ 4—504. Privilege of Presenting Bank to Deal With Goods; Security Interest for Expenses.

(a) A presenting bank that, following the dishonor of a documentary draft, has seasonably requested instructions but does not receive them within a reasonable time may store, sell, or otherwise deal with the goods in any reasonable manner.

(b) For its reasonable expenses incurred by action under subsection (a) the presenting bank has a lien upon the goods or their proceeds, which may be foreclosed in the same manner as an unpaid seller's lien.

Article 4A
FUNDS TRANSFERS

Part 1 Subject Matter and Definitions

§ 4A—101. Short Title.

This Article may be cited as Uniform Commercial Code—Funds Transfers.

§ 4A—102. Subject Matter.

Except as otherwise provided in Section 4A—108, this Article applies to funds transfers defined in Section 4A—104.

§ 4A—103. **Payment Order—Definitions.**

(1) In this Article:

(a) "Payment order" means an instruction of a sender to a receiving bank, transmitted orally, electronically, or in writing, to pay, or to cause another bank to pay, a fixed or determinable amount of money to a beneficiary if:

(i) the instruction does not state a condition to payment to the beneficiary other than time of payment,

(ii) the receiving bank is to be reimbursed by debiting an account of, or otherwise receiving payment from, the sender, and

(iii) the instruction is transmitted by the sender directly to the receiving bank or to an agent, funds-transfer system, or communication system for transmittal to the receiving bank.

(b) "Beneficiary" means the person to be paid by the beneficiary's bank.

(c) "Beneficiary's bank" means the bank identified in a payment order in which an account of the beneficiary is to be credited pursuant to the order or which otherwise is to make payment to the beneficiary if the order does not provide for payment to an account.

(d) "Receiving bank" means the bank to which the sender's instruction is addressed.

(e) "Sender" means the person giving the instruction to the receiving bank.

(2) If an instruction complying with subsection (1)(a) is to make more than one payment to a beneficiary, the instruction is a separate payment order with respect to each payment.

(3) A payment order is issued when it is sent to the receiving bank.

§ 4A—104. **Funds Transfer—Definitions.**

(1) In this Article:

(a) "Funds transfer" means the series of transactions, beginning with the originator's payment order, made for the purpose of making payment to the beneficiary of the order. The term includes any payment order issued by the originator's bank or an intermediary bank intended to carry out the originator's payment order. A funds transfer is completed by acceptance by the beneficiary's bank of a payment order for the benefit of the beneficiary of the originator's payment order.

(b) "Intermediary bank" means a receiving bank other than the originator's bank or the beneficiary's bank.

(c) "Originator" means the sender of the first payment order in a funds transfer.

(d) "Originator's bank" means (i) the receiving bank to which the payment order of the originator is issued if the originator is not a bank, or (ii) the originator if the originator is a bank.

§ 4A—105. **Other Definitions.**

(1) In this Article:

(a) "Authorized account" means a deposit account of a customer in a bank designated by the customer as a source of payment of payment orders issued by the customer to the bank. If a customer does not so designate an account, any account of the customer is an authorized account if payment of a payment order from that account is not inconsistent with a restriction on the use of that account.

(b) "Bank" means a person engaged in the business of banking and includes a savings bank, savings and loan association, credit union, and trust company. A branch or separate office of a bank is a separate bank for purposes of this Article.

(c) "Customer" means a person, including a bank, having an account with a bank or from whom a bank has agreed to receive payment orders.

(d) "Funds-transfer business day" of a receiving bank means the part of a day during which the receiving bank is open for the receipt, processing, and transmittal of payment orders and cancellations and amendments of payment orders.

(e) "Funds-transfer system" means a wire transfer network, automated clearing house, or other communication system of a clearing house or other association of banks through which a payment order by a bank may be transmitted to the bank to which the order is addressed.

(f) "Good faith" means honesty in fact and the observance of reasonable commercial standards of fair dealing.

(g) "Prove" with respect to a fact means to meet the burden of establishing the fact (Section 1— 201(8)).

(2) Other definitions applying to this Article and the sections in which they appear are:

"Acceptance"	Section 4A—209
"Beneficiary"	Section 4A—103
"Beneficiary's bank"	Section 4A—103
"Executed"	Section 4A—301
"Execution date"	Section 4A—301
"Funds transfer"	Section 4A—104
"Funds-transfer system rule"	Section 4A—501
"Intermediary bank"	Section 4A—104
"Originator"	Section 4A—104
"Originator's bank"	Section 4A—104

"Payment by beneficiary's bank to beneficiary"   Section 4A—405

"Payment by originator to beneficiary"   Section 4A—406

"Payment by sender to receiving bank"   Section 4A—403

"Payment date"   Section 4A—401

"Payment order"   Section 4A—103

"Receiving bank"   Section 4A—103

"Security procedure"   Section 4A—201

"Sender"   Section 4A—103

(3) The following definitions in Article 4 apply to this Article:

"Clearing house"   Section 4—104

"Item"   Section 4—104

"Suspends payments"   Section 4—104

(4) In addition, Article 1 contains general definitions and principles of construction and interpretation applicable throughout this Article.

§ 4A—106. **Time Payment Order Is Received.**

(1) The time of receipt of a payment order or communication cancelling or amending a payment order is determined by the rules applicable to receipt of a notice stated in Section 1—201(27). A receiving bank may fix a cut-off time or times on a funds-transfer business day for the receipt and processing of payment orders and communications cancelling or amending payment orders. Different cut-off times may apply to payment orders, cancellations, or amendments, or to different categories of payment orders, cancellations, or amendments. A cut-off time may apply to senders generally or different cut-off times may apply to different senders or categories of payment orders. If a payment order or communication cancelling or amending a payment order is received after the close of a funds-transfer business day or after the appropriate cut-off time on a funds-transfer business day, the receiving bank may treat the payment order or communication as received at the opening of the next funds-transfer business day.

(2) If this Article refers to an execution date or payment date or states a day on which a receiving bank is required to take action, and the date or day does not fall on a funds-transfer business day, the next day that is a funds-transfer business day is treated as the date or day stated, unless the contrary is stated in this Article.

§ 4A—107. **Federal Reserve Regulations and Operating Circulars.**

Regulations of the Board of Governors of the Federal Reserve System and operating circulars of the Federal Reserve Banks supersede any inconsistent provision of this Article to the extent of the inconsistency.

§ 4A—108. **Exclusion of Consumer Transactions Governed by Federal Law.**

This Article does not apply to a funds transfer any part of which is governed by the Electronic Fund Transfer Act of 1978 (Title XX, Public Law 95—630, 92 Stat. 3728, 15 U.S.C. § 1693 et seq.) as amended from time to time.

Part 2   Issue and Acceptance of Payment Order

§ 4A—201. **Security Procedure.**

"Security procedure" means a procedure established by agreement of a customer and a receiving bank for the purpose of (i) verifying that a payment order or communication amending or cancelling a payment order is that of the customer, or (ii) detecting error in the transmission or the content of the payment order or communication. A security procedure may require the use of algorithms or other codes, identifying words or numbers, encryption, callback procedures, or similar security devices. Comparison of a signature on a payment order or communication with an authorized specimen signature of the customer is not by itself a security procedure.

§ 4A—202. **Authorized and Verified Payment Orders.**

(1) A payment order received by the receiving bank is the authorized order of the person identified as sender if that person authorized the order or is otherwise bound by it under the law of agency.

(2) If a bank and its customer have agreed that the authenticity of payment orders issued to the bank in the name of the customer as sender will be verified pursuant to a security procedure, a payment order received by the receiving bank is effective as the order of the customer, whether or not authorized, if (i) the security procedure is a commercially reasonable method of providing security against unauthorized payment orders, and (ii) the bank proves that it accepted the payment order in good faith and in compliance with the security procedure and any written agreement or instruction of the customer restricting acceptance of payment orders issued in the name of the customer. The bank is not required to follow an instruction that violates a written agreement with the customer or notice of which is not received at a time and in a manner affording the bank a reasonable opportunity to act on it before the payment order is accepted.

(3) Commercial reasonableness of a security procedure is a question of law to be determined by considering the wishes of the customer expressed to the bank, the circumstances of the customer known to the bank, including the size, type, and frequency of payment orders normally issued by the customer to the bank, alternative security procedures

offered to the customer, and security procedures in general use by customers and receiving banks similarly situated. A security procedure is deemed to be commercially reasonable if (i) the security procedure was chosen by the customer after the bank offered, and the customer refused, a security procedure that was commercially reasonable for that customer, and (ii) the customer expressly agreed in writing to be bound by any payment order, whether or not authorized, issued in its name and accepted by the bank in compliance with the security procedure chosen by the customer.

(4) The term ''sender'' in this Article includes the customer in whose name a payment order is issued if the order is the authorized order of the customer under subsection (1), or it is effective as the order of the customer under subsection (2).

(5) This section applies to amendments and cancellations of payment orders to the same extent it applies to payment orders.

(6) Except as provided in this section and in Section 4A—203(1)(a), rights and obligations arising under this section or Section 4A—203 may not be varied by agreement.

§ 4A—203. Unenforceability of Certain Verified Payment Orders.

(1) If an accepted payment order is not, under Section 4A—202(1), an authorized order of a customer identified as sender, but is effective as an order of the customer pursuant to Section 4A—202(2), the following rules apply:

(a) By express written agreement, the receiving bank may limit the extent to which it is entitled to enforce or retain payment of the payment order.

(b) The receiving bank is not entitled to enforce or retain payment of the payment order if the customer proves that the order was not caused, directly or indirectly, by a person (i) entrusted at any time with duties to act for the customer with respect to payment orders or the security procedure, or (ii) who obtained access to transmitting facilities of the customer or who obtained, from a source controlled by the customer and without authority of the receiving bank, information facilitating breach of the security procedure, regardless of how the information was obtained or whether the customer was at fault. Information includes any access device, computer software, or the like.

(2) This section applies to amendments of payment orders to the same extent it applies to payment orders.

§ 4A—204. Refund of Payment and Duty of Customer to Report with Respect to Unauthorized Payment Order.

(1) If a receiving bank accepts a payment order issued in the name of its customer as sender which is (i) not authorized and not effective as the order of the customer under

Section 4A—202, or (ii) not enforceable, in whole or in part, against the customer under Section 4A—203, the bank shall refund any payment of the payment order received from the customer to the extent the bank is not entitled to enforce payment and shall pay interest on the refundable amount calculated from the date the bank received payment to the date of the refund. However, the customer is not entitled to interest from the bank on the amount to be refunded if the customer fails to exercise ordinary care to determine that the order was not authorized by the customer and to notify the bank of the relevant facts within a reasonable time not exceeding 90 days after the date the customer received notification from the bank that the order was accepted or that the customer's account was debited with respect to the order. The bank is not entitled to any recovery from the customer on account of a failure by the customer to give notification as stated in this section.

(2) Reasonable time under subsection (1) may be fixed by agreement as stated in Section 1—204(1), but the obligation of a receiving bank to refund payment as stated in subsection (1) may not otherwise be varied by agreement.

§ 4A—205. Erroneous Payment Orders.

(1) If an accepted payment order was transmitted pursuant to a security procedure for the detection of error and the payment order (i) erroneously instructed payment to a beneficiary not intended by the sender, (ii) erroneously instructed payment in an amount greater than the amount intended by the sender, or (iii) was an erroneously transmitted duplicate of a payment order previously sent by the sender, the following rules apply:

(a) If the sender proves that the sender or a person acting on behalf of the sender pursuant to Section 4A—206 complied with the security procedure and that the error would have been detected if the receiving bank had also complied, the sender is not obliged to pay the order to the extent stated in paragraphs (b) and (c).

(b) If the funds transfer is completed on the basis of an erroneous payment order described in clause (i) or (iii) of subsection (1), the sender is not obliged to pay the order and the receiving bank is entitled to recover from the beneficiary any amount paid to the beneficiary to the extent allowed by the law governing mistake and restitution.

(c) If the funds transfer is completed on the basis of a payment order described in clause (ii) of subsection (1), the sender is not obliged to pay the order to the extent the amount received by the beneficiary is greater than the amount intended by the sender. In that case, the receiving bank is entitled to recover from the beneficiary the excess amount received to the extent allowed by the law governing mistake and restitution.

(2) If (i) the sender of an erroneous payment order described in subsection (1) is not obliged to pay all or part

of the order, and (ii) the sender receives notification from the receiving bank that the order was accepted by the bank or that the sender's account was debited with respect to the order, the sender has a duty to exercise ordinary care, on the basis of information available to the sender, to discover the error with respect to the order and to advise the bank of the relevant facts within a reasonable time, not exceeding 90 days, after the bank's notification was received by the sender. If the bank proves that the sender failed to perform that duty, the sender is liable to the bank for the loss the bank proves it incurred as a result of the failure, but the liability of the sender may not exceed the amount of the sender's order.

(3) This section applies to amendments to payment orders to the same extent it applies to payment orders.

§ 4A—206. **Transmission of Payment Order through Funds-Transfer or Other Communication System.**

(1) If a payment order addressed to a receiving bank is transmitted to a funds-transfer system or other thirdparty communication system for transmittal to the bank, the system is deemed to be an agent of the sender for the purpose of transmitting the payment order to the bank. If there is a discrepancy between the terms of the payment order transmitted to the system and the terms of the payment order transmitted by the system to the bank, the terms of the payment order of the sender are those transmitted by the system. This section does not apply to a funds-transfer system of the Federal Reserve Banks.

(2) This section applies to cancellations and amendments to payment orders to the same extent it applies to payment orders.

§ 4A—207. **Misdescription of Beneficiary.**

(1) Subject to subsection (2), if, in a payment order received by the beneficiary's bank, the name, bank account number, or other identification of the beneficiary refers to a nonexistent or unidentifiable person or account, no person has rights as a beneficiary of the order and acceptance of the order cannot occur.

(2) If a payment order received by the beneficiary's bank identifies the beneficiary both by name and by an identifying or bank account number and the name and number identify different persons, the following rules apply:

    (a) Except as otherwise provided in subsection (3), if the beneficiary's bank does not know that the name and number refer to different persons, it may rely on the number as the proper identification of the beneficiary of the order. The beneficiary's bank need not determine whether the name and number refer to the same person.

    (b) If the beneficiary's bank pays the person identified by name or knows that the name and number identify different persons, no person has rights as beneficiary except the person paid by the beneficiary's bank if that

person was entitled to receive payment from the originator of the funds transfer. If no person has rights as beneficiary, acceptance of the order cannot occur.

(3) If (i) a payment order described in subsection (2) is accepted, (ii) the originator's payment order described the beneficiary inconsistently by name and number, and (iii) the beneficiary's bank pays the person identified by number as permitted by subsection (2)(a), the following rules apply:

    (a) If the originator is a bank, the originator is obliged to pay its order.

    (b) If the originator is not a bank and proves that the person identified by number was not entitled to receive payment from the originator, the originator is not obliged to pay its order unless the originator's bank proves that the originator, before acceptance of the originator's order, had notice that payment of a payment order issued by the originator might be made by the beneficiary's bank on the basis of an identifying or bank account number even if it identifies a person different from the named beneficiary. Proof of notice may be made by any admissible evidence. The originator's bank satisfies the burden of proof it it proves that the originator, before the payment order was accepted, signed a writing stating the information to which the notice relates.

(4) In a case governed by subsection (2)(a), if the beneficiary's bank rightfully pays the person identified by number and that person was not entitled to receive payment from the originator, the amount paid may be recovered from that person to the extent allowed by the law governing mistake and restitution as follows:

    (a) If the originator is obliged to pay its payment order as stated in subsection (3), the originator has the right to recover.

    (b) If the originator is not a bank and is not obliged to pay its payment order, the originator's bank has the right to recover.

§ 4A—208. **Misdescription of Intermediary Bank or Beneficiary's Bank.**

(1) This subsection applies to a payment order identifying an intermediary bank or the beneficiary's bank only by an identifying number.

    (a) The receiving bank may rely on the number as the proper identification of the intermediary or beneficiary's bank and need not determine whether the number identifies a bank.

    (b) The sender is obliged to compensate the receiving bank for any loss and expenses incurred by the receiving bank as a result of its reliance on the number in executing or attempting to execute the order.

(2) This subsection applies to a payment order identifying an intermediary bank or the beneficiary's bank both by

name and an identifying number if the name and number identify different persons.

(a) If the sender is a bank, the receiving bank may rely on the number as the proper identification of the intermediary or beneficiary's bank if the receiving bank, when it executes the sender's order, does not know that the name and number identify different persons. The receiving bank need not determine whether the name and number refer to the same person or whether the number refers to a bank. The sender is obliged to compensate the receiving bank for any loss and expenses incurred by the receiving bank as a result of its reliance on the number in executing or attempting to execute the order.

(b) If the sender is not a bank and the receiving bank proves that the sender, before the payment order was accepted, had notice that the receiving bank might rely on the number as the proper identification of the intermediary or beneficiary's bank even if it identifies a person different from the bank identified by name, the rights and obligations of the sender and the receiving bank are governed by subsection (2)(a), as though the sender were a bank. Proof of notice may be made by any admissible evidence. The receiving bank satisfies the burden of proof if it proves that the sender, before the payment order was accepted, signed a writing stating the information to which the notice relates.

(c) Regardless of whether the sender is a bank, the receiving bank may rely on the name as the proper identification of the intermediary or beneficiary's bank if the receiving bank, at the time it executes the sender's order, does not know that the name and number identify different persons. The receiving bank need not determine whether the name and number refer to the same person.

(d) If the receiving bank knows that the name and number identify different persons, reliance on either the name or the number in executing the sender's payment order is a breach of the obligation stated in Section 4A—302(1)(a).

§ 4A—209. Acceptance of Payment Order.

(1) Subject to subsection (4), a receiving bank other than the beneficiary's bank accepts a payment order when it executes the order.

(2) Subject to subsections (3) and (4), a beneficiary's bank accepts a payment order at the earliest of the following times:

(a) When the bank (i) pays the beneficiary as stated in Section 4A—405(1) or 4A—405(2), or (ii) notifies the beneficiary of receipt of the order or that the account of the beneficiary has been credited with respect to the order unless the notice indicates that the bank is re-

jecting the order or that funds with respect to the order may not be withdrawn or used until receipt of payment from the sender of the order;

(b) When the bank receives payment of the entire amount of the sender's order pursuant to Section 4A—403(1)(a) or 4A—403(1)(b); or

(c) The opening of the next funds-transfer business day of the bank following the payment date of the order if, at that time, the amount of the sender's order is fully covered by a withdrawable credit balance in an authorized account of the sender or the bank has otherwise received full payment from the sender, unless the order was rejected before that time or is rejected within (i) one hour after that time, or (ii) one hour after the opening of the next business day of the sender following the payment date if that time is later. If notice of rejection is received by the sender after the payment date and the authorized account of the sender does not bear interest, the bank is obliged to pay interest to the sender on the amount of the order for the number of days elapsing after the payment date to the day the sender receives notice or learns that the order was not accepted, counting that day as an elapsed day. If the withdrawable credit balance during that period falls below the amount of the order, the amount of interest payable is reduced accordingly.

(3) Acceptance of a payment order cannot occur before the order is received by the receiving bank. Acceptance does not occur under subsection (2)(b) or (2)(c) if the beneficiary of the payment order does not have an account with the receiving bank, the account has been closed, or the receiving bank is not permitted by law to receive credits for the beneficiary's account.

(4) A payment order issued to the originator's bank cannot be accepted until the payment date if the bank is the beneficiary's bank, or the execution date if the bank is not the beneficiary's bank. If the originator's bank executes the originator's payment order before the execution date or pays the beneficiary of the originator's payment order before the payment date and the payment order is subsequently cancelled pursuant to Section 4A—211(2), the bank may recover from the beneficiary any payment received to the extent allowed by the law governing mistake and restitution.

§ 4A—210. Rejection of Payment Order.

(1) A payment order is rejected by the receiving bank by a notice of rejection transmitted to the sender orally, electronically, or in writing. A notice of rejection need not use any particular words and is sufficient if it indicates that the receiving bank is rejecting the order or will not execute or pay the order. Rejection is effective when the notice is given if transmission is by a means that is reasonable in the circumstances. If notice of rejection is given by a means that is not reasonable, rejection is effective when the notice is

received. If an agreement of the sender and receiving bank establishes the means to be used to reject a payment order, (i) any means complying with the agreement is reasonable and (ii) any means not complying is not reasonable unless no significant delay in receipt of the notice resulted from the use of the noncomplying means.

(2) This subsection applies if a receiving bank other than the beneficiary's bank fails to execute a payment order despite the existence on the execution date of a withdrawable credit balance in an authorized account of the sender sufficient to cover the order. If the sender does not receive notice of rejection of the order on the execution date and the authorized account of the sender does not bear interest, the bank is obliged to pay interest to the sender on the amount of the order for the number of days elapsing after the execution date to the earlier of the day the order is cancelled pursuant to Section 4A—211(4) or the day the sender receives notice or learns that the order was not executed, counting the final day of the period as an elapsed day. If the withdrawable credit balance during that period falls below the amount of the order, the amount of interest is reduced accordingly.

(3) If a receiving bank suspends payments, all unaccepted payment orders issued to it are are deemed rejected at the time the bank suspends payments.

(4) Acceptance of a payment order precludes a later rejection of the order. Rejection of a payment order precludes a later acceptance of the order.

§ 4A—211. Cancellation and Amendment of Payment Order.

(1) A communication of the sender of a payment order cancelling or amending the order may be transmitted to the receiving bank orally, electronically, or in writing. If a security procedure is in effect between the sender and the receiving bank, the communication is not effective to cancel or amend the order unless the communication is verified pursuant to the security procedure or the bank agrees to the cancellation or amendment.

(2) Subject to subsection (1), a communication by the sender cancelling or amending a payment order is effective to cancel or amend the order if notice of the communication is received at a time and in a manner affording the receiving bank a reasonable opportunity to act on the communication before the bank accepts the payment order.

(3) After a payment order has been accepted, cancellation or amendment of the order is not effective unless the receiving bank agrees or a funds-transfer system rule allows cancellation or amendment without agreement of the bank.

(a) With respect to a payment order accepted by a receiving bank other than the beneficiary's bank, cancellation or amendment is not effective unless a conforming cancellation or amendment of the payment order issued by the receiving bank is also made.

(b) With respect to a payment order accepted by the beneficiary's bank, cancellation or amendment is not effective unless the order was issued in execution of an unauthorized payment order, or because of a mistake by a sender in the funds transfer which resulted in the issuance of a payment order (i) that is a duplicate of a payment order previously issued by the sender, (ii) that orders payment to a beneficiary not entitled to receive payment from the originator, or (iii) that orders payment in an amount greater than the amount the beneficiary was entitled to receive from the originator. If the payment order is cancelled or amended, the beneficiary's bank is entitled to recover from the beneficiary any amount paid to the beneficiary to the extent allowed by the law governing mistake and restitution.

(4) An unaccepted payment order is cancelled by operation of law at the close of the fifth funds-transfer business day of the receiving bank after the execution date or payment date of the order.

(5) A cancelled payment order cannot be accepted. If an accepted payment order is cancelled, the acceptance is nullified and no person has any right or obligation based on the acceptance. Amendment of a payment order is deemed to be cancellation of the original order at the time of amendment and issue of a new payment order in the amended form at the same time.

(6) Unless otherwise provided in an agreement of the parties or in a funds-transfer system rule, if the receiving bank, after accepting a payment order, agrees to cancellation or amendment of the order by the sender or is bound by a funds-transfer system rule allowing cancellation or amendment without the bank's agreement, the sender, whether or not cancellation or amendment is effective, is liable to the bank for any loss and expenses, including reasonable attorney's fees, incurred by the bank as a result of the cancellation or amendment or attempted cancellation or amendment.

(7) A payment order is not revoked by the death or legal incapacity of the sender unless the receiving bank knows of the death or of an adjudication of incapacity by a court of competent jurisdiction and has reasonable opportunity to act before acceptance of the order.

(8) A funds-transfer system rule is not effective to the extent it conflicts with subsection (3)(b).

§ 4A—212. Liability and Duty of Receiving Bank Regarding Unaccepted Payment Order.

If a receiving bank fails to accept a payment order that it is obliged by express agreement to accept, the bank is liable for breach of the agreement to the extent provided in the agreement or in this Article, but does not otherwise have any duty to accept a payment order or, before acceptance, to take any action, or refrain from taking action, with respect to the order except as provided in this Article or by express agreement. Liability based on acceptance arises only when acceptance occurs as stated in Section 4A—209, and liability is limited to that provided in this Article. A receiving bank is not the agent of the sender or beneficiary of the payment order it accepts, or of any other party to the funds transfer, and the bank owes no duty to any party to the funds transfer except as provided in this Article or by express agreement.

Part 3 Execution of Sender's Payment Order by Receiving Bank

§ 4A—301. **Execution and Execution Date.**

(1) A payment order is "executed" by the receiving bank when it issues a payment order intended to carry out the payment order received by the bank. A payment order received by the beneficiary's bank can be accepted but cannot be executed.

(2) "Execution date" of a payment order means the day on which the receiving bank may properly issue a payment order in execution of the sender's order. The execution date may be determined by instruction of the sender but cannot be earlier than the day the order is received and, unless otherwise determined, is the day the order is received. If the sender's instruction states a payment date, the execution date is the payment date or an earlier date on which execution is reasonably necessary to allow payment to the beneficiary on the payment date.

§ 4A—302. **Obligations of Receiving Bank in Execution of Payment Order.**

(1) Except as provided in subsections (2) through (4), if the receiving bank accepts a payment order pursuant to Section 4A—209(1), the bank has the following obligations in executing the order:

(a) The receiving bank is obliged to issue, on the execution date, a payment order complying with the sender's order and to follow the sender's instructions concerning (i) any intermediary bank or funds-transfer system to be used in carrying out the funds transfer, or (ii) the means by which payment orders are to be transmitted in the funds transfer. If the originator's bank issues a payment order to an intermediary bank, the originator's bank is obliged to instruct the intermediary bank according to the instruction of the originator. An intermediary bank in the funds transfer is similarly bound by an instruction given to it by the sender of the payment order it accepts.

(b) If the sender's instruction states that the funds transfer is to be carried out telephonically or by wire transfer or otherwise indicates that the funds transfer is to be carried out by the most expeditious means, the receiving bank is obliged to transmit its payment order by the most expeditious available means, and to instruct any

intermediary bank accordingly. If a sender's instruction states a payment date, the receiving bank is obliged to transmit its payment order at a time and by means reasonably necessary to allow payment to the beneficiary on the payment date or as soon thereafter as is feasible.

(2) Unless otherwise instructed, a receiving bank executing a payment order may (i) use any funds-transfer system if use of that system is reasonable in the circumstances, and (ii) issue a payment order to the beneficiary's bank or to an intermediary bank through which a payment order conforming to the sender's order can expeditiously be issued to the beneficiary's bank if the receiving bank exercises ordinary care in the selection of the intermediary bank. A receiving bank is not required to follow an instruction of the sender designating a funds-transfer system to be used in carrying out the funds transfer if the receiving bank, in good faith, determines that it is not feasible to follow the instruction or that following the instruction would unduly delay completion of the funds transfer.

(3) Unless subsection (1)(b) applies or the receiving bank is otherwise instructed, the bank may execute a payment order by transmitting its payment order by first class mail or by any means reasonable in the circumstances. If the receiving bank is instructed to execute the sender's order by transmitting its payment order by a particular means, the receiving bank may issue its payment order by the means stated or by any means as expeditious as the means stated.

(4) Unless instructed by the sender, (i) the receiving bank may not obtain payment of its charges for services and expenses in connection with the execution of the sender's order by issuing a payment order in an amount equal to the amount of the sender's order less the amount of the charges, and (ii) may not instruct a subsequent receiving bank to obtain payment of its charges in the same manner.

§ 4A—303. **Erroneous Execution of Payment Order.**

(1) A receiving bank that (i) executes the payment order of the sender by issuing a payment order in an amount greater than the amount of the sender's order, or (ii) issues a payment order in execution of the sender's order and then issues a duplicate order, is entitled to payment of the amount of the sender's order under Section 4A—402(3) if that subsection is otherwise satisfied. The bank is entitled to recover from the beneficiary of the erroneous order the excess payment received to the extent allowed by the law governing mistake and restitution.

(2) A receiving bank that executes the payment order of the sender by issuing a payment order in an amount less than the amount of the sender's order is entitled to payment of the amount of the sender's order under Section 4A—402(3) if (i) that subsection is otherwise satisfied and (ii) the bank corrects its mistake by issuing an additional payment order for the benefit of the beneficiary of the sender's order. If the error is not corrected, the issuer of the erroneous

order is entitled to receive or retain payment from the sender of the order it accepted only to the extent of the amount of the erroneous order. This subsection does not apply if the receiving bank executes the sender's payment order by issuing a payment order in an amount less than the amount of the sender's order for the purpose of obtaining payment of its charges for services and expenses pursuant to instruction of the sender.

(3) If a receiving bank executes the payment order of the sender by issuing a payment order to a beneficiary different from the beneficiary of the sender's order and the funds transfer is completed on the basis of that error, the sender of the payment order that was erroneously executed and all previous senders in the funds transfer are not obliged to pay the payment orders they issued. The issuer of the erroneous order is entitled to recover from the beneficiary of the order the payment received to the extent allowed by the law governing mistake and restitution.

§ 4A—304. Duty of Sender to Report Erroneously Executed Payment Order.

If the sender of a payment order that is erroneously executed as stated in Section 4A—303 receives notification from the receiving bank that the order was executed or that the sender's account was debited with respect to the order, the sender has a duty to exercise ordinary care to determine, on the basis of information available to the sender, that the order was erroneously executed and to notify the bank of the relevant facts within a reasonable time not exceeding 90 days after the notification from the bank was received by the sender. If the sender fails to perform that duty, the bank is not obliged to pay interest on any amount refundable to the sender under Section 4A—402(4) for the period before the bank learns of the execution error. The bank is not entitled to any recovery from the sender on account of a failure by the sender to perform the duty stated in this section.

§ 4A—305. Liability for Late or Improper Execution or Failure to Execute Payment Order.

(1) If a funds transfer is completed but execution of a payment order by the receiving bank in breach of Section 4A—302 results in delay in payment to the beneficiary, the bank is obliged to pay interest to either the originator or the beneficiary of the funds transfer for the period of delay caused by the improper execution. Except as provided in subsection (3), additional damages are not recoverable.

(2) If execution of a payment order by a receiving bank in breach of Section 4A—302 results in (i) noncompletion of the funds transfer, (ii) failure to use an intermediary bank designated by the originator, or (iii) issuance of a payment order that does not comply with the terms of the payment order of the originator, the bank is liable to the originator for its expenses in the funds transfer and for incidental expenses and interest losses, to the extent not covered by

subsection (1), resulting from the improper execution. Except as provided in subsection (3), additional damages are not recoverable.

(3) In addition to the amounts payable under subsections (1) and (2), damages, including consequential damages, are recoverable to the extent provided in an express written agreement of the receiving bank.

(4) If a receiving bank fails to execute a payment order it was obliged by express agreement to execute, the receiving bank is liable to the sender for its expenses in the transaction and for incidental expenses and interest losses resulting from the failure to execute. Additional damages, including consequential damages, are recoverable to the extent provided in an express written agreement of the receiving bank, but are not otherwise recoverable.

(5) Reasonable attorney's fees are recoverable if demand for compensation under subsection (1) or (2) is made and refused before an action is brought on the claim. If a claim is made for breach of an agreement under subsection (4) and the agreement does not provide for damages, reasonable attorney's fees are recoverable if demand for compensation under subsection (4) is made and refused before an action is brought on the claim.

(6) Except as stated in this section, the liability of a receiving bank under subsections (1) and (2) may not be varied by agreement.

Part 4 Payment

§ 4A—401. Payment Date.

''Payment date'' of a payment order means the day on which the amount of the order is payable to the beneficiary by the beneficiary's bank. The payment date may be determined by instruction of the sender but cannot be earlier than the day the order is received by the beneficiary's bank and, unless otherwise determined, is the day the order is received by the beneficiary's bank.

§ 4A—402. Obligation of Sender to Pay Receiving Bank.

(1) This section is subject to Sections 4A—205 and 4A—207.

(2) With respect to a payment order issued to the beneficiary's bank, acceptance of the order by the bank obliges the sender to pay the bank the amount of the order, but payment is not due until the payment date of the order.

(3) This subsection is subject to subsection (5) and to Section 4A—303. With respect to a payment order issued to a receiving bank other than the beneficiary's bank, acceptance of the order by the receiving bank obliges the sender to pay the bank the amount of the sender's order. Payment by the sender is not due until the execution date of the sender's order. The obligation of that sender to pay its

payment order is excused if the funds transfer is not completed by acceptance by the beneficiary's bank of a payment order instructing payment to the beneficiary of that sender's payment order.

(4) If the sender of a payment order pays the order and was not obliged to pay all or part of the amount paid, the bank receiving payment is obliged to refund payment to the extent the sender was not obliged to pay. Except as provided in Sections 4A—204 and 4A—304, interest is payable on the refundable amount from the date of payment.

(5) If a funds transfer is not completed as stated in subsection (3) and an intermediary bank is obliged to refund payment as stated in subsection (4) but is unable to do so because not permitted by applicable law or because the bank suspends payments, a sender in the funds transfer that executed a payment order in compliance with an instruction, as stated in Section 4A—302(1)(a), to route the funds transfer through that intermediary bank is entitled to receive or retain payment from the sender of the payment order that it accepted. The first sender in the funds transfer that issued an instruction requiring routing through that intermediary bank is subrogated to the right of the bank that paid the intermediary bank to refund as stated in subsection (4).

(6) The right of the sender of a payment order to be excused from the obligation to pay the order as stated in subsection (3) or to receive refund under subsection (4) may not be varied by agreement.

§ 4A—403. Payment by Sender to Receiving Bank.

(1) Payment of the sender's obligation under Section 4A—402 to pay the receiving bank occurs as follows:

(a) If the sender is a bank, payment occurs when the receiving bank receives final settlement of the obligation through a Federal Reserve Bank or through a funds-transfer system.

(b) If the sender is a bank and the sender (i) credited an account of the receiving bank with the sender, or (ii) caused an account of the receiving bank in another bank to be credited, payment occurs when the credit is withdrawn or, if not withdrawn, at midnight of the day on which the credit is withdrawable and the receiving bank learns of that fact.

(c) If the receiving bank debits an account of the sender with the receiving bank, payment occurs when the debit is made to the extent the debit is covered by a withdrawable credit balance in the account.

(2) If the sender and receiving bank are members of a funds-transfer system that nets obligations multilaterally among participants, the receiving bank receives final settlement when settlement is complete in accordance with the rules of the system. The obligation of the sender to pay the amount of a payment order transmitted through the funds-transfer system may be satisfied, to the extent per-

mitted by the rules of the system, by setting off and applying against the sender's obligation the right of the sender to receive payment from the receiving bank of the amount of any other payment order transmitted to the sender by the receiving bank through the funds-transfer system. The aggregate balance of obligations owed by each sender to each receiving bank in the funds-transfer system may be satisfied, to the extent permitted by the rules of the system, by setting off and applying against that balance the aggregate balance of obligations owed to the sender by other members of the system. The aggregate balance is determined after the right of setoff stated in the second sentence of this subsection has been exercised.

(3) If two banks transmit payment orders to each other under an agreement that settlement of the obligations of each bank to the other under Section 4A—402 will be made at the end of the day or other period, the total amount owed with respect to all orders transmitted by one bank shall be set off against the total amount owed with respect to all orders transmitted by the other bank. To the extent of the setoff, each bank has made payment to the other.

(4) In a case not covered by subsection (1), the time when payment of the sender's obligation under Section 4A—402(2) or 4A—402(3) occurs is governed by applicable principles of law that determine when an obligation is satisfied.

§ 4A—404. Obligation of Beneficiary's Bank to Pay and Give Notice to Beneficiary.

(1) Subject to Sections 4A—211(5), 4A—405(4), and 4A—405(5), if a beneficiary's bank accepts a payment order, the bank is obliged to pay the amount of the order to the beneficiary of the order. Payment is due on the payment date of the order, but if acceptance occurs on the payment date after the close of the funds-transfer business day of the bank, payment is due on the next funds-transfer business day. If the bank refuses to pay after demand by the beneficiary and receipt of notice of particular circumstances that will give rise to consequential damages as a result of nonpayment, the beneficiary may recover damages resulting from the refusal to pay to the extent the bank had notice of the damages, unless the bank proves that it did not pay because of a reasonable doubt concerning the right of the beneficiary to payment.

(2) If a payment order accepted by the beneficiary's bank instructs payment to an account of the beneficiary, the bank is obliged to notify the beneficiary of receipt of the order before midnight of the next funds-transfer business day following the payment date. If the payment order does not instruct payment to an account of the beneficiary, the bank is required to notify the beneficiary only if notice is required by the order. Notice may be given by first class mail or any other means reasonable in the circumstances. If the bank fails to give the required notice, the bank is obliged to pay

interest to the beneficiary on the amount of the payment order from the day notice should have been given until the day the beneficiary learned of receipt of the payment order by the bank. No other damages are recoverable. Reasonable attorney's fees are also recoverable if demand for interest is made and refused before an action is brought on the claim.

(3) The right of a beneficiary to receive payment and damages as stated in subsection (1) may not be varied by agreement or a funds-transfer system rule. The right of a beneficiary to be notified as stated in subsection (2) may be varied by agreement of the beneficiary or by a funds-transfer system rule if the beneficiary is notified of the rule before initiation of the funds transfer.

§ 4A—405. **Payment by Beneficiary's Bank to Beneficiary.**

(1) If the beneficiary's bank credits an account of the beneficiary of a payment order, payment of the bank's obligation under Section 4A—404(1) occurs when and to the extent (i) the beneficiary is notified of the right to withdraw the credit, (ii) the bank lawfully applies the credit to a debt of the beneficiary, or (iii) funds with respect to the order are otherwise made available to the beneficiary by the bank.

(2) If the beneficiary's bank does not credit an account of the beneficiary of a payment order, the time when payment of the bank's obligation under Section 4A—404(1) occurs is governed by principles of law that determine when an obligation is satisfied.

(3) Except as stated in subsections (4) and (5), if the beneficiary's bank pays the beneficiary of a payment order under a condition to payment or agreement of the beneficiary giving the bank the right to recover payment from the beneficiary if the bank does not receive payment of the order, the condition to payment or agreement is not enforceable.

(4) A funds-transfer system rule may provide that payments made to beneficiaries of funds transfers made through the system are provisional until receipt of payment by the beneficiary's bank of the payment order it accepted. A beneficiary's bank that makes a payment that is provisional under the rule is entitled to refund from the beneficiary if (i) the rule requires that both the beneficiary and the originator be given notice of the provisional nature of the payment before the funds transfer is initiated, (ii) the beneficiary, the beneficiary's bank, and the originator's bank agreed to be bound by the rule, and (iii) the beneficiary's bank did not receive payment of the payment order that it accepted. If the beneficiary is obliged to refund payment to the beneficiary's bank, acceptance of the payment order by the beneficiary's bank is nullified and no payment by the originator of the funds transfer to the beneficiary occurs under Section 4A—406.

(5) This subsection applies to a funds transfer that includes a payment order transmitted over a funds-transfer system

that (i) nets obligations multilaterally among participants, and (ii) has in effect a loss-sharing agreement among participants for the purpose of providing funds necessary to complete settlement of the obligations of one or more participants that do not meet their settlement obligations. If the beneficiary's bank in the funds transfer accepts a payment order and the system fails to complete settlement pursuant to its rules with respect to any payment order in the funds transfer, (i) the acceptance by the beneficiary's bank is nullified and no person has any right or obligation based on the acceptance, (ii) the beneficiary's bank is entitled to recover payment from the beneficiary, (iii) no payment by the originator to the beneficiary occurs under Section 4A—406, and (iv) subject to Section 4A—402(5), each sender in the funds transfer is excused from its obligation to pay its payment order under Section 4A—402(3) because the funds transfer has not been completed.

§ 4A—406. **Payment by Originator to Beneficiary; Discharge of Underlying Obligation.**

(1) Subject to Sections 4A—211(5), 4A—405(4), and 4A—405(5), the originator of a funds transfer pays the beneficiary of the originator's payment order (i) at the time a payment order for the benefit of the beneficiary is accepted by the beneficiary's bank in the funds transfer and (ii) in an amount equal to the amount of the order accepted by the beneficiary's bank, but not more than the amount of the originator's order.

(2) If payment under subsection (1) is made to satisfy an obligation, the obligation is discharged to the same extent discharge would result from payment to the beneficiary of the same amount in money, unless (i) the payment under subsection (1) was made by a means prohibited by the contract of the beneficiary with respect to the obligation, (ii) the beneficiary, within a reasonable time after receiving notice of receipt of the order by the beneficiary's bank, notified the originator of the beneficiary's refusal of the payment, (iii) funds with respect to the order were not withdrawn by the beneficiary or applied to a debt of the beneficiary, and (iv) the beneficiary would suffer a loss that could reasonably have been avoided if payment had been made by a means complying with the contract. If payment by the originator does not result in discharge under this section, the originator is subrogated to the rights of the beneficiary to receive payment from the beneficiary's bank under Section 4A—404(1).

(3) For the purpose of determining whether discharge of an obligation occurs under subsection (2), if the beneficiary's bank accepts a payment order in an amount equal to the amount of the originator's payment order less charges of one or more receiving banks in the funds transfer, payment to the beneficiary is deemed to be in the amount of the originator's order unless upon demand by the beneficiary the originator does not pay the beneficiary the amount of the deducted charges.

(4) Rights of the originator or of the beneficiary of a funds transfer under this section may be varied only by agreement of the originator and the beneficiary.

Part 5 Miscellaneous Provisions

§ 4A—501. **Variation by Agreement and Effect of Funds-Transfer System Rule.**

(1) Except as otherwise provided in this Article, the rights and obligations of a party to a funds transfer may be varied by agreement of the affected party.

(2) "Funds-transfer system rule" means a rule of an association of banks (i) governing transmission of payment orders by means of a funds-transfer system of the association or rights and obligations with respect to those orders, or (ii) to the extent the rule governs rights and obligations between banks that are parties to a funds transfer in which a Federal Reserve Bank, acting as an intermediary bank, sends a payment order to the beneficiary's bank. Except as otherwise provided in this Article, a funds-transfer system rule governing rights and obligations between participating banks using the system may be effective even if the rule conflicts with this Article and indirectly affects another party to the funds transfer who does not consent to the rule. A funds-transfer system rule may also govern rights and obligations of parties other than participating banks using the system to the extent stated in Sections 4A—404(3), 4A—405(4), and 4A—507(3).

§ 4A—502. **Creditor Process Served on Receiving Bank; Setoff by Beneficiary's Bank.**

(1) As used in this section, "creditor process" means levy, attachment, garnishment, notice of lien, sequestration, or similar process issued by or on behalf of a creditor or other claimant with respect to an account.

(2) This subsection applies to creditor process with respect to an authorized account of the sender of a payment order if the creditor process is served on the receiving bank. For the purpose of determining rights with respect to the creditor process, if the receiving bank accepts the payment order the balance in the authorized account is deemed to be reduced by the amount of the payment order to the extent the bank did not otherwise receive payment of the order, unless the creditor process is served at a time and in a manner affording the bank a reasonable opportunity to act on it before the bank accepts the payment order.

(3) If a beneficiary's bank has received a payment order for payment to the beneficiary's account in the bank, the following rules apply:

(a) The bank may credit the beneficiary's account. The amount credited may be set off against an obligation owed by the beneficiary to the bank or may be applied to satisfy creditor process served on the bank with respect to the account.

(b) The bank may credit the beneficiary's account and allow withdrawal of the amount credited unless creditor process with respect to the account is served at a time and in a manner affording the bank a reasonable opportunity to act to prevent withdrawal.

(c) If creditor process with respect to the beneficiary's account has been served and the bank has had a reasonable opportunity to act on it, the bank may not reject the payment order except for a reason unrelated to the service of process.

(4) Creditor process with respect to a payment by the originator to the beneficiary pursuant to a funds transfer may be served only on the beneficiary's bank with respect to the debt owed by that bank to the beneficiary. Any other bank served with the creditor process is not obliged to act with respect to the process.

§ 4A—503. **Injunction or Restraining Order with Respect to Funds Transfer.**

For proper cause and in compliance with applicable law, a court may restrain (i) a person from issuing a payment order to initiate a funds transfer, (ii) an originator's bank from executing the payment order of the originator, or (iii) the beneficiary's bank from releasing funds to the beneficiary or the beneficiary from withdrawing the funds. A court may not otherwise restrain a person from issuing a payment order, paying or receiving payment of a payment order, or otherwise acting with respect to a funds transfer.

§ 4A—504. **Order in Which Items and Payment Orders May Be Charged to Account; Order of Withdrawals from Account.**

(1) If a receiving bank has received more than one payment order of the sender or one or more payment orders and other items that are payable from the sender's account, the bank may charge the sender's account with respect to the various orders and items in any sequence.

(2) In determining whether a credit to an account has been withdrawn by the holder of the account or applied to a debt of the holder of the account, credits first made to the account are first withdrawn or applied.

§ 4A—505. **Preclusion of Objection to Debit of Customer's Account.**

If a receiving bank has received payment from its customer with respect to a payment order issued in the name of the customer as sender and accepted by the bank, and the customer received notification reasonably identifying the order, the customer is precluded from asserting that the bank is not entitled to retain the payment unless the customer notifies the bank of the customer's objection to the payment within one year after the notification was received by the customer.

§ 4A—506. **Rate of Interest.**

(1) If, under this Article, a receiving bank is obliged to pay interest with respect to a payment order issued to the bank, the amount payable may be determined (i) by agreement of the sender and receiving bank, or (ii) by a funds-transfer system rule if the payment order is transmitted through a funds-transfer system.

(2) If the amount of interest is not determined by an agreement or rule as stated in subsection (1), the amount is calculated by multiplying the applicable Federal Funds rate by the amount on which interest is payable, and then multiplying the product by the number of days for which interest is payable. The applicable Federal Funds rate is the average of the Federal Funds rates published by the Federal Reserve Bank of New York for each of the days for which interest is payable divided by 360. The Federal Funds rate for any day on which a published rate is not available is the same as the published rate for the next preceding day for which there is a published rate. If a receiving bank that accepted a payment order is required to refund payment to the sender of the order because the funds transfer was not completed, but the failure to complete was not due to any fault by the bank, the interest payable is reduced by a percentage equal to the reserve requirement on deposits of the receiving bank.

§ 4A—507. **Choice of Law.**

(1) The following rules apply unless the affected parties otherwise agree or subsection (3) applies:

(a) The rights and obligations between the sender of a payment order and the receiving bank are governed by the law of the jurisdiction in which the receiving bank is located.

(b) The rights and obligations between the beneficiary's bank and the beneficiary are governed by the law of the jurisdiction in which the beneficiary's bank is located.

(c) The issue of when payment is made pursuant to a funds transfer by the originator to the beneficiary is governed by the law of the jurisdiction in which the beneficiary's bank is located.

(2) If the parties described in each paragraph of subsection (1) have made an agreement selecting the law of a particular jurisdiction to govern rights and obligations between each other, the law of that jurisdiction governs those rights and obligations, whether or not the payment order or the funds transfer bears a reasonable relation to that jurisdiction.

(3) A funds-transfer system rule may select the law of a particular jurisdiction to govern (i) rights and obligations between participating banks with respect to payment orders transmitted or processed through the system, or (ii) the rights and obligations of some or all parties to a funds transfer any part of which is carried out by means of the system. A choice of law made pursuant to clause (i) is binding on participating banks. A choice of law made pursuant to clause (ii) is binding on the originator, other sender, or a receiving bank having notice that the funds-transfer system might be used in the funds transfer and of the choice of law by the system when the originator, other sender, or receiving bank issued or accepted a payment order. The beneficiary of a funds transfer is bound by the choice of law if, when the funds transfer is initiated, the beneficiary has notice that the funds-transfer system might be used in the funds transfer and of the choice of law by the sytem. The law of a jurisdiction selected pursuant to this subsection may govern, whether or not that law bears a reasonable relation to the matter in issue.

(4) In the event of inconsistency between an agreement under subsection (2) and a choice-of-law rule under subsection (3), the agreement under subsection (2) prevails.

(5) If a funds transfer is made by use of more than one funds-transfer system and there is inconsistency between choice-of-law rules of the systems, the matter in issue is governed by the law of the selected jurisdiction that has the most significant relationship to the matter in issue.

Article 5
LETTERS OF CREDIT

§ 5—101. **Short Title.**

This Article shall be known and may be cited as Uniform Commercial Code—Letters of Credit.

§ 5—102. **Scope.**

(1) This Article applies

(a) to a credit issued by a bank if the credit requires a documentary draft or a documentary demand for payment; and

(b) to a credit issued by a person other than a bank if the credit requires that the draft or demand for payment be accompanied by a document of title; and

(c) to a credit issued by a bank or other person if the credit is not within subparagraphs (a) or (b) but conspicuously states that it is a letter of credit or is conspicuously so entitled.

(2) Unless the engagement meets the requirements of subsection (1), this Article does not apply to engagements to make advances or to honor drafts or demands for payment, to authorities to pay or purchase, to guarantees or to general agreements.

(3) This Article deals with some but not all of the rules and concepts of letters of credit as such rules or concepts have developed prior to this act or may hereafter develop. The fact that this Article states a rule does not by itself require, imply or negate application of the same or a converse rule to a situation not provided for or to a person not specified by this Article.

§ 5—103. **Definitions.**

(1) In this Article unless the context otherwise requires

(a) ''Credit'' or ''letter of credit'' means an engagement by a bank or other person made at the request of a customer and of a kind within the scope of this Article (Section 5—102) that the issuer will honor drafts or other demands for payment upon compliance with the conditions specified in the credit. A credit may be either revocable or irrevocable. The engagement may be either an agreement to honor or a statement that the bank or other person is authorized to honor.

(b) A ''documentary draft'' or a ''documentary demand for payment'' is one honor of which is conditioned upon the presentation of a document or documents. ''Document'' means any paper including document of title, security, invoice, certificate, notice of default and the like.

(c) An ''issuer'' is a bank or other person issuing a credit.

(d) A ''beneficiary'' of a credit is a person who is entitled under its terms to draw or demand payment.

(e) An ''advising bank'' is a bank which gives notification of the issuance of a credit by another bank.

(f) A ''confirming bank'' is a bank which engages either that it will itself honor a credit already issued by another bank or that such a credit will be honored by the issuer or a third bank.

(g) A ''customer'' is a buyer or other person who causes an issuer to issue a credit. The term also includes a bank which procures issuance or confirmation on behalf of that bank's customer.

(2) Other definitions applying to this Article and the sections in which they appear are:
''Notation of Credit''. Section 5—108.
''Presenter''. Section 5—112(3).

(3) Definitions in other Articles applying to this Article and the sections in which they appear are:
''Accept'' or ''Acceptance''. Section 3—410.
''Contract for sale''. Section 2—106.
''Draft''. Section 3—104.
''Holder in due course''. Section 3—302.
''Midnight deadline''. Section 4—104.
''Security''. Section 8—102.

(4) In addition, Article 1 contains general definitions and principles of construction and interpretation applicable throughout this Article.

§ 5—104. **Formal Requirements; Signing.**

(1) Except as otherwise required in subsection (1)(c) of Section 5—102 on scope, no particular form of phrasing is required for a credit. A credit must be in writing and signed by the issuer and a confirmation must be in writing and signed by the confirming bank. A modification of the terms of a credit or confirmation must be signed by the issuer or confirming bank.

(2) A telegram may be a sufficient signed writing if it identifies its sender by an authorized authentication. The authentication may be in code and the authorized naming of the issuer in an advice of credit is a sufficient signing.

§ 5—105. **Consideration.**

No consideration is necessary to establish a credit or to enlarge or otherwise modify its terms.

§ 5—106. **Time and Effect of Establishment of Credit.**

(1) Unless otherwise agreed a credit is established

(a) as regards the customer as soon as a letter of credit is sent to him or the letter of credit or an authorized written advice of its issuance is sent to the beneficiary; and

(b) as regards the beneficiary when he receives a letter of credit or an authorized written advice of its issuance.

(2) Unless otherwise agreed once an irrevocable credit is established as regards the customer it can be modified or revoked only with the consent of the customer and once it is established as regards the beneficiary it can be modified or revoked only with his consent.

(3) Unless otherwise agreed after a revocable credit is established it may be modified or revoked by the issuer without notice to or consent from the customer or beneficiary.

(4) Notwithstanding any modification or revocation of a revocable credit any person authorized to honor or negotiate under the terms of the original credit is entitled to reimbursement for or honor of any draft or demand for payment duly honored or negotiated before receipt of notice of the modification or revocation and the issuer in turn is entitled to reimbursement from its customer.

§ 5—107. **Advice of Credit; Confirmation; Error in Statement of Terms.**

(1) Unless otherwise specified an advising bank by advising a credit issued by another bank does not assume any obligation to honor drafts drawn or demands for payment made under the credit but it does assume obligation for the accuracy of its own statement.

(2) A confirming bank by confirming a credit becomes directly obligated on the credit to the extent of its confirmation as though it were its issuer and acquires the rights of an issuer.

(3) Even though an advising bank incorrectly advises the terms of a credit it has been authorized to advise the credit is established as against the issuer to the extent of its original terms.

(4) Unless otherwise specified the customer bears as against the issuer all risks of transmission and reasonable translation or interpretation of any message relating to a credit.

§ 5—108. "Notation Credit"; Exhaustion of Credit.

(1) A credit which specifies that any person purchasing or paying drafts drawn or demands for payment made under it must note the amount of the draft or demand on the letter or advice of credit is a "notation credit".

(2) Under a notation credit

(a) a person paying the beneficiary or purchasing a draft or demand for payment from him acquires a right to honor only if the appropriate notation is made and by transferring or forwarding for honor the documents under the credit such a person warrants to the issuer that the notation has been made; and

(b) unless the credit or a signed statement that an appropriate notation has been made accompanies the draft or demand for payment the issuer may delay honor until evidence of notation has been procured which is satisfactory to it but its obligation and that of its customer continue for a reasonable time not exceeding thirty days to obtain such evidence.

(3) If the credit is not a notation credit

(a) the issuer may honor complying drafts or demands for payment presented to it in the order in which they are presented and is discharged pro tanto by honor of any such draft or demand;

(b) as between competing good faith purchasers of complying drafts or demands the person first purchasing his priority over a subsequent purchaser even though the later purchased draft or demand has been first honored.

§ 5—109. Issuer's Obligation to Its Customer.

(1) An issuer's obligation to its customer includes good faith and observance of any general banking usage but unless otherwise agreed does not include liability or responsibility

(a) for performance of the underlying contract for sale or other transaction between the customer and the beneficiary; or

(b) for any act or omission of any person other than itself or its own branch or for loss or destruction of a draft, demand or document in transit or in the possession of others; or

(c) based on knowledge or lack of knowledge of any usage of any particular trade.

(2) An issuer must examine documents with care so as to ascertain that on their face they appear to comply with the terms of the credit but unless otherwise agreed assumes no liability or responsibility for the genuineness, falsification or effect of any document which appears on such examination to be regular on its face.

(3) A non-bank issuer is not bound by any banking usage of which it has no knowledge.

§ 5—110. Availability of Credit in Portions; Presenter's Reservation of Lien or Claim.

(1) Unless otherwise specified a credit may be used in portions in the discretion of the beneficiary.

(2) Unless otherwise specified a person by presenting a documentary draft or demand for payment under a credit relinquishes upon its honor all claims to the documents and a person by transferring such draft or demand or causing such presentment authorizes such relinquishment. An explicit reservation of claim makes the draft or demand noncomplying.

§ 5—111. Warranties on Transfer and Presentment.

(1) Unless otherwise agreed the beneficiary by transferring or presenting a documentary draft or demand for payment warrants to all interested parties that the necessary conditions of the credit have been complied with. This is in addition to any warranties arising under Articles 3, 4, 7 and 8.

(2) Unless otherwise agreed a negotiating, advising, confirming, collecting or issuing bank presenting or transferring a draft or demand for payment under a credit warrants only the matters warranted by a collecting bank under Article 4 and any such bank transferring a document warrants only the matters warranted by an intermediary under Articles 7 and 8.

§ 5—112. Time Allowed for Honor or Rejection; Withholding Honor or Rejection by Consent; "Presenter".

(1) A bank to which a documentary draft or demand for payment is presented under a credit may without dishonor of the draft, demand or credit

(a) defer honor until the close of the third banking day following receipt of the documents; and

(b) further defer honor if the presenter has expressly or impliedly consented thereto.

Failure to honor within the time here specified constitutes dishonor of the draft or demand and of the credit [except as otherwise provided in subsection (4) of Section 5—114 on conditional payment].

Note: *The bracketed language in the last sentence of subsection (1) should be included only if the optional provisions of Section 5—114(4) and (5) are included.*

(2) Upon dishonor the bank may unless otherwise instructed fulfill its duty to return the draft or demand and the documents by holding them at the disposal of the presenter and sending him an advice to that effect.

(3) ''Presenter'' means any person presenting a draft or demand for payment for honor under a credit even though that person is a confirming bank or other correspondent which is acting under an issuer's authorization.

§ 5—113. Indemnities.

(1) A bank seeking to obtain (whether for itself or another) honor, negotiation or reimbursement under a credit may give an indemnity to induce such honor, negotiation or reimbursement.

(2) An indemnity agreement inducing honor, negotiation or reimbursement

(a) unless otherwise explicitly agreed applies to defects in the documents but not in the goods; and

(b) unless a longer time is explicitly agreed expires at the end of ten business days following receipt of the documents by the ultimate customer unless notice of objection is sent before such expiration date. The ultimate customer may send notice of objection to the person from whom he received the documents and any bank receiving such notice is under a duty to send notice to its transferor before its midnight deadline.

§ 5—114. Issuer's Duty and Privilege to Honor; Right to Reimbursement.

(1) An issuer must honor a draft or demand for payment which complies with the terms of the relevant credit regardless of whether the goods or documents conform to the underlying contract for sale or other contract between the customer and the beneficiary. The issuer is not excused from honor of such a draft or demand by reason of an additional general term that all documents must be satisfactory to the issuer, but an issuer may require that specified documents must be satisfactory to it.

(2) Unless otherwise agreed when documents appear on their face to comply with the terms of a credit but a required document does not in fact conform to the warranties made on negotiation or transfer of a document of title (Section 7—507) or of a certificated security (Section 8—306) or is forged or fraudulent or there is fraud in the transaction:

(a) the issuer must honor the draft or demand for payment if honor is demanded by a negotiating bank or other holder of the draft or demand which has taken the draft or demand under the credit and under circumstances which would make it a holder in due course (Section 3—302) and in an appropriate case would make it a person to whom a document of title has been duly negotiated (Section 7—502) or a bona fide purchaser of a certificated security (Section 8—302); and

(b) in all other cases as against its customer, an issuer acting in good faith may honor the draft or demand for payment despite notification from the customer of fraud, forgery or other defect not apparent on the face of the documents but a court of appropriate jurisdiction may enjoin such honor.

(3) Unless otherwise agreed an issuer which has duly honored a draft or demand for payment is entitled to immediate reimbursement of any payment made under the credit and to be put in effectively available funds not later than the day before maturity of any acceptance made under the credit.

[(4) When a credit provides for payment by the issuer on receipt of notice that the required documents are in the possession of a correspondent or other agent of the issuer

(a) any payment made on receipt of such notice is conditional; and

(b) the issuer may reject documents which do not comply with the credit if it does so within three banking days following its receipt of the documents; and

(c) in the event of such rejection, the issuer is entitled by charge back or otherwise to return of the payment made.]

[(5) In the case covered by subsection (4) failure to reject documents within the time specified in sub-paragraph (b) constitutes acceptance of the documents and makes the payment final in favor of the beneficiary.]

Note: *Subsections (4) and (5) are bracketed as optional. If they are included the bracketed language in the last sentence of Section 5—112(1) should also be included.*

§ 5—115. Remedy for Improper Dishonor or Anticipatory Repudiation.

(1) When an issuer wrongfully dishonors a draft or demand for payment presented under a credit the person entitled to honor has with respect to any documents the rights of a person in the position of a seller (Section 2—707) and may recover from the issuer the face amount of the draft or demand together with incidental damages under Section 2—710 on seller's incidental damages and interest but less any amount realized by resale or other use or disposition of the subject matter of the transaction. In the event no resale or other utilization is made the documents, goods or other subject matter involved in the transaction must be turned over to the issuer on payment of judgment.

(2) When an issuer wrongfully cancels or otherwise repudiates a credit before presentment of a draft or demand for payment drawn under it the beneficiary has the rights of a seller after anticipatory repudiation by the buyer under Section 2—610 if he learns of the repudiation in time reasonably to avoid procurement of the required documents. Otherwise the beneficiary has an immediate right of action for wrongful dishonor.

§ 5—116. Transfer and Assignment.

(1) The right to draw under a credit can be transferred or assigned only when the credit is expressly designated as transferable or assignable.

(2) Even through the credit specifically states that it is nontransferable or nonassignable the beneficiary may before performance of the conditions of the credit assign his right to proceeds. Such an assignment is an assignment of an account under Article 9 on Secured Transactions and is governed by that Article except that

(a) the assignment is ineffective until the letter of credit or advice of credit is delivered to the assignee which delivery constitutes perfection of the security interest under Article 9; and

(b) the issuer may honor drafts or demands for payment drawn under the credit until it receives a notification of the assignment signed by the beneficiary which reasonably identifies the credit involved in the assignment and contains a request to pay the assignee; and

(c) after what reasonably appears to be such a notification has been received the issuer may without dishonor refuse to accept or pay even to a person otherwise entitled to honor until the letter of credit or advice of credit is exhibited to the issuer.

(3) Except where the beneficiary has effectively assigned his right to draw or his right to proceeds, nothing in this section limits his right to transfer or negotiate drafts or demands drawn under the credit.

§ 5—117. **Insolvency of Bank Holding Funds for Documentary Credit.**

(1) Where an issuer or an advising or confirming bank or a bank which has for a customer procured issuance of a credit by another bank becomes insolvent before final payment under the credit and the credit is one to which this Article is made applicable by paragraphs (a) or (b) of Section 5—102(1) on scope, the receipt or allocation of funds or collateral to secure or meet obligations under the credit shall have the following results:

(a) to the extent of any funds or collateral turned over after or before the insolvency as indemnity against or specifically for the purpose of payment of drafts or demands for payment drawn under the designated credit, the drafts or demands are entitled to payment in preference over depositors or other general creditors of the issuer or bank; and

(b) on expiration of the credit or surrender of the beneficiary's rights under it unused any person who has given such funds or collateral is similarly entitled to return thereof; and

(c) a charge to a general or current account with a bank if specifically consented to for the purpose of indemnity against or payment of drafts or demands for payment drawn under the designated credit falls under the same rules as if the funds had been drawn out in cash and then turned over with specific instructions.

(2) After honor or reimbursement under this section the customer or other person for whose account the insolvent bank has acted is entitled to receive the documents involved.

Article 6
BULK TRANSFERS

§ 6—101. **Short Title.**

This Article shall be known and may be cited as Uniform Commercial Code—Bulk Transfers.

§ 6—102. **"Bulk Transfers"; Transfers of Equipment; Enterprises Subject to This Article; Bulk Transfers Subject to This Article.**

(1) A "bulk transfer" is any transfer in bulk and not in the ordinary course of the transferor's business of a major part of the materials, supplies, merchandise or other inventory (Section 9—109) of an enterprise subject to this Article.

(2) A transfer of a substantial part of the equipment (Section 9—109) of such an enterprise is a bulk transfer if it is made in connection with a bulk transfer of inventory, but not otherwise.

(3) The enterprises subject to this Article are all those whose principal business is the sale of merchandise from stock, including those who manufacture what they sell.

(4) Except as limited by the following section all bulk transfers of goods located within this state are subject to this Article.

§ 6—103. **Transfers Excepted From This Article.**

The following transfers are not subject to this Article:

(1) Those made to give security for the performance of an obligation;

(2) General assignments for the benefit of all the creditors of the transferor, and subsequent transfers by the assignee thereunder;

(3) Transfers in settlement or realization of a lien or other security interests;

(4) Sales by executors, administrators, receivers, trustees in bankruptcy, or any public officer under judicial process;

(5) Sales made in the course of judicial or administrative proceedings for the dissolution or reorganization of a corporation and of which notice is sent to the creditors of the corporation pursuant to order of the court or administrative agency;

(6) Transfers to a person maintaining a known place of business in this State who becomes bound to pay the debts of the transferor in full and gives public notice of that fact, and who is solvent after becoming so bound;

(7) A transfer to a new business enterprise organized to take over and continue the business, if public notice of the

transaction is given and the new enterprise assumes the debts of the transferor and he receives nothing from the transaction except an interest in the new enterprise junior to the claims of creditors;

(8) Transfers of property which is exempt from execution.

Public notice under subsection (6) or subsection (7) may be given by publishing once a week for two consecutive weeks in a newspaper of general circulation where the transferor had its principal place of business in this state an advertisement including the names and addresses of the transferor and transferee and the effective date of the transfer.

§ 6—104. Schedule of Property, List of Creditors.

(1) Except as provided with respect to auction sales (Section 6—108), a bulk transfer subject to this Article is ineffective against any creditor of the transferor unless:

(a) The transferee requires the transferor to furnish a list of his existing creditors prepared as stated in this section; and

(b) The parties prepare a schedule of the property transferred sufficient to identify it; and

(c) The transferee preserves the list and schedule for six months next following the transfer and permits inspection of either or both and copying therefrom at all reasonable hours by any creditor of the transferor, or files the list and schedule in (a public office to be here identified).

(2) The list of creditors must be signed and sworn to or affirmed by the transferor or his agent. It must contain the names and business addresses of all creditors of the transferor, with the amounts when known, and also the names of all persons who are known to the transferor to assert claims against him even though such claims are disputed. If the transferor is the obligor of an outstanding issue of bonds, debentures or the like as to which there is an indenture trustee, the list of creditors need include only the name and address of the indenture trustee and the aggregate outstanding principal amount of the issue.

(3) Responsibility for the completeness and accuracy of the list of creditors rests on the transferor, and the transfer is not rendered ineffective by errors or omissions therein unless the transferee is shown to have had knowledge.

§ 6—105. Notice to Creditors.

In addition to the requirements of the preceding section, any bulk transfer subject to this Article except one made by auction sale (Section 6—108) is ineffective against any creditor of the transferor unless at least ten days before he takes possession of the goods or pays for them, whichever happens first, the transferee gives notice of the transfer in the manner and to the persons hereafter provided (Section 6—107).

[§ 6—106. Application of the Proceeds.

In addition to the requirements of the two preceding sections:

(1) Upon every bulk transfer subject to this Article for which new consideration becomes payable except those made by sale at auction it is the duty of the transferee to assure that such consideration is applied so far as necessary to pay those debts of the transferor which are either shown on the list furnished by the transferor (Section 6—104) or filed in writing in the place stated in the notice (Section 6—107) within thirty days after the mailing of such notice. This duty of the transferee runs to all the holders of such debts, and may be enforced by any of them for the benefit of all.

(2) If any of said debts are in dispute the necessary sum may be withheld from distribution until the dispute is settled or adjudicated.

(3) If the consideration payable is not enough to pay all of the said debts in full distribution shall be made pro rata.]

Note: *This section is bracketed to indicate division of opinion as to whether or not it is a wise provision, and to suggest that this is a point on which State enactments may differ without serious damage to the principle of uniformity. In any State where this section is omitted, the following parts of sections, also bracketed in the text, should also be omitted, namely:*
Section 6—107(2)(e).
6—108(3)(c).
6—109(2).

In any State where this section is enacted, these other provisions should be also.

Optional Subsection (4)

[(4) The transferee may within ten days after he takes possession of the goods pay the consideration into the (specify court) in the county where the transferor had its principal place of business in this state and thereafter may discharge his duty under this section by giving notice by registered or certified mail to all the persons to whom the duty runs that the consideration has been paid into that court and that they should file their claims there. On motion of any interested party, the court may order the distribution of the consideration to the persons entitled to it.]

Note: *Optional subsection (4) is recommended for those states which do not have a general statute providing for payment of money into court.*

§ 6—107. The Notice.

(1) The notice to creditors (Section 6—105) shall state:

(a) that a bulk transfer is about to be made; and

(b) the names and business addresses of the transferor and transferee, and all other business names and addresses used by the transferor within three years last past so far as known to the transferee; and

(c) whether or not all the debts of the transferor are to be paid in full as they fall due as a result of the transaction, and if so, the address to which creditors should send their bills.

(2) If the debts of the transferor are not to be paid in full as they fall due or if the transferee is in doubt on that point then the notice shall state further:

(a) the location and general description of the property to be transferred and the estimated total of the transferor's debts;

(b) the address where the schedule of property and list of creditors (Section 6—104) may be inspected;

(c) whether the transfer is to pay existing debts and if so the amount of such debts and to whom owing;

(d) whether the transfer is for new consideration and if so the amount of such consideration and the time and place of payment; [and]

[(e) if for new consideration the time and place where creditors of the transferor are to file their claims.]

(3) The notice in any case shall be delivered personally or sent by registered or certified mail to all the persons shown on the list of creditors furnished by the transferor (Section 6—104) and to all other persons who are known to the transferee to hold or assert claims against the transferor.

§ 6—108. **Auction Sales; "Auctioneer".**

(1) A bulk transfer is subject to this Article even though it is by sale at auction, but only in the manner and with the results stated in this section.

(2) The transferor shall furnish a list of his creditors and assist in the preparation of a schedule of the property to be sold, both prepared as before stated (Section 6—104).

(3) The person or persons other than the transferor who direct, control or are responsible for the auction are collectively called the "auctioneer". The auctioneer shall:

(a) receive and retain the list of creditors and prepare and retain the schedule of property for the period stated in this Article (Section 6—104);

(b) give notice of the auction personally or by registered or certified mail at least ten days before it occurs to all persons shown on the list of creditors and to all other persons who are known to him to hold or assert claims against the transferor; [and]

[(c) assure that the net proceeds of the auction are applied as provided in this Article (Section 6—106).]

(4) Failure of the auctioneer to perform any of these duties does not affect the validity of the sale or the title of the purchasers, but if the auctioneer knows that the auction constitutes a bulk transfer such failure renders the auctioneer liable to the creditors of the transferor as a class for the sums owing to them from the transferor up to but not exceeding the net proceeds of the auction. If the auctioneer consists of several persons their liability is joint and several.

§ 6—109. **What Creditors Protected; [Credit for Payment to Particular Creditors].**

(1) The creditors of the transferor mentioned in this Article are those holding claims based on transactions or events occurring before the bulk transfer, but creditors who become such after notice to creditors is given (Sections 6—105 and 6—107) are not entitled to notice.

[(2) Against the aggregate obligation imposed by the provisions of this Article concerning the application of the proceeds (Section 6—106 and subsection (3)(c) of 6—108) the transferee or auctioneer is entitled to credit for sums paid to particular creditors of the transferor, not exceeding the sums believed in good faith at the time of the payment to be properly payable to such creditors.]

§ 6—110. **Subsequent Transfers.**

When the title of a transferee to property is subject to a defect by reason of his noncompliance with the requirements of this Article, then:

(1) a purchaser of any of such property from such transferee who pays no value or who takes with notice of such noncompliance takes subject to such defect, but

(2) a purchaser for value in good faith and without such notice takes free of such defect.

§ 6—111. **Limitation of Actions and Levies.**

No action under this Article shall be brought nor levy made more than six months after the date on which the transferee took possession of the goods unless the transfer has been concealed. If the transfer has been concealed, actions may be brought or levies made within six months after its discovery.

Note to Article 6: *Section 6—106 is bracketed to indicate division of opinion as to whether or not it is a wise provision, and to suggest that this is a point on which State enactments may differ without serious damage to the principle of uniformity.*

In any State where Section 6—106 is not enacted, the following parts of sections, also bracketed in the text, should also be omitted, namely:
Sec. 6—107(2)(e).
   6—108(3)(c).
   6—109(2).
In any State where Section 6—106 is enacted, these other provisions should be also.

Article 6
Alternative B*

§ 6—101. **Short Title.**

This Article shall be known and may be cited as Uniform Commercial Code—Bulk Sales.

---

* Approved by the National Conference of Commissioners on Uniform State Laws and The American Law Institute. States have the choice of adopting this alternative to the existing Article 6 or repealing Article 6 entirely (Alternative A).

§ 6—102. **Definitions and Index of Definitions.**

(1) In this Article, unless the context otherwise requires:

(a) ''Assets'' means the inventory that is the subject of a bulk sale and any tangible and intangible personal property used or held for use primarily in, or arising from, the seller's business and sold in connection with that inventory, but the term does not include:

(i) fixtures (Section 9—313(1)(a)) other than readily removable factory and office machines;

(ii) the lessee's interest in a lease of real property; or

(iii) property to the extent it is generally exempt from creditor process under nonbankruptcy law.

(b) ''Auctioneer'' means a person whom the seller engages to direct, conduct, control, or be responsible for a sale by auction.

(c) ''Bulk sale'' means:

(i) in the case of a sale by auction or a sale or series of sales conducted by a liquidator on the seller's behalf, a sale or series of sales not in the ordinary course of the seller's business of more than half of the seller's inventory, as measured by value on the date of the bulk-sale agreement, if on that date the auctioneer or liquidator has notice, or after reasonable inquiry would have had notice, that the seller will not continue to operate the same or a similar kind of business after the sale or series of sales; and

(ii) in all other cases, a sale not in the ordinary course of the seller's business of more than half the seller's inventory, as measured by value on the date of the bulk-sale agreement, if on that date the buyer has notice, or after reasonable inquiry would have had notice, that the seller will not continue to operate the same or a similar kind of business after the sale.

(d) ''Claim'' means a right to payment from the seller, whether or not the right is reduced to judgment, liquidated, fixed, matured, disputed, secured, legal, or equitable. The term includes costs of collection and attorney's fees only to the extent that the laws of this state permit the holder of the claim to recover them in an action against the obligor.

(e) ''Claimant'' means a person holding a claim incurred in the seller's business other than:

(i) an unsecured and unmatured claim for employment compensation and benefits, including commissions and vacation, severance, and sick-leave pay;

(ii) a claim for injury to an individual or to property, or for breach of warranty, unless:

(A) a right of action for the claim has accrued;

(B) the claim has been asserted against the seller; and

(C) the seller knows the identity of the person asserting the claim and the basis upon which the person has asserted it; and
(States to Select One Alternative)

Alternative A
[(iii) a claim for taxes owing to a governmental unit.]

Alternative B
[(iii) a claim for taxes owing to a governmental unit, if:

(A) a statute governing the enforcement of the claim permits or requires notice of the bulk sale to be given to the governmental unit in a manner other than by compliance with the requirements of this Article; and

(B) notice is given in accordance with the statute.]

(f) ''Creditor'' means a claimant or other person holding a claim.

(g)(i) ''Date of the bulk sale'' means:

(A) if the sale is by auction or is conducted by a liquidator on the seller's behalf, the date on which more than ten percent of the net proceeds is paid to or for the benefit of the seller; and

(B) in all other cases, the later of the date on which:

(I) more than ten percent of the net contract price is paid to or for the benefit of the seller; or

(II) more than ten percent of the assets, as measured by value, are transferred to the buyer.

(ii) For purposes of this subsection:

(A) delivery of a negotiable instrument (Section 3—104(1)) to or for the benefit of the seller in exchange for assets constitutes payment of the contract price pro tanto;

(B) to the extent that the contract price is deposited in an escrow, the contract price is paid to or for the benefit of the seller when the seller acquires the unconditional right to receive the deposit or when the deposit is delivered to the seller or for the benefit of the seller, whichever is earlier; and

(C) an asset is transferred when a person holding an unsecured claim can no longer obtain through judicial proceedings rights to the asset that are superior to those of the buyer arising as a result of the bulk sale. A person holding an unsecured claim can obtain those superior rights to a tangible asset at least until the buyer has an unconditional right, under the bulk-sale agreement, to possess the asset, and a person holding an unsecured claim can obtain those superior rights to an intangible asset at least until the buyer has an unconditional right, under the bulk-sale agreement, to use the asset.

(h) "Date of the bulk-sale agreement" means:

(i) in the case of a sale by auction or conducted by a liquidator (subsection (c)(i)), the date on which the seller engages the auctioneer or liquidator; and

(ii) in all other cases, the date on which a bulk-sale agreement becomes enforceable between the buyer and the seller.

(i) "Debt" means liability on a claim.

(j) "Liquidator" means a person who is regularly engaged in the business of disposing of assets for businesses contemplating liquidation or dissolution.

(k) "Net contract price" means the new consideration the buyer is obligated to pay for the assets less:

(i) the amount of any proceeds of the sale of an asset, to the extent the proceeds are applied in partial or total satisfaction of a debt secured by the asset; and

(ii) the amount of any debt to the extent it is secured by a security interest or lien that is enforceable against the asset before and after it has been sold to a buyer. If a debt is secured by an asset and other property of the seller, the amount of the debt secured by a security interest or lien that is enforceable against the asset is determined by multiplying the debt by a fraction, the numerator of which is the value of the new consideration for the asset on the date of the bulk sale and the denominator of which is the value of all property securing the debt on the date of the bulk sale.

(l) "Net proceeds" means the new consideration received for assets sold at a sale by auction or a sale conducted by a liquidator on the seller's behalf less:

(i) commissions and reasonable expenses of the sale;

(ii) the amount of any proceeds of the sale of an asset, to the extent the proceeds are applied in partial or total satisfaction of a debt secured by the asset; and

(iii) the amount of any debt to the extent it is secured by a security interest or lien that is enforceable against the asset before and after it has been sold to a buyer. If a debt is secured by an asset and other property of the seller, the amount of the debt secured by a security interest or lien that is enforceable against the asset is determined by multiplying the debt by a fraction, the numerator of which is the value of the new consideration for the asset on the date of the bulk sale and the denominator of which is the value of all property securing the debt on the date of the bulk sale.

(m) A sale is "in the ordinary course of the seller's business" if the sale comports with usual or customary practices in the kind of business in which the seller is engaged or with the seller's own usual or customary practices.

(n) "United States" includes its territories and possessions and the Commonwealth of Puerto Rico.

(o) "Value" means fair market value.

(p) "Verified" means signed and sworn to or affirmed.

(2) The following definitions in other Articles apply to this Article:

(a)	"Buyer."	Section 2—103(1)(a).
(b)	"Equipment."	Section 9—109(2).
(c)	"Inventory."	Section 9—109(4).
(d)	"Sale."	Section 2—106(1).
(e)	"Seller."	Section 2—103(1)(d).

(3) In addition, Article 1 contains general definitions and principles of construction and interpretation applicable throughout this Article.

§ 6—103. Applicability of Article.

(1) Except as otherwise provided in subsection (3), this Article applies to a bulk sale if:

(a) the seller's principal business is the sale of inventory from stock; and

(b) on the date of the bulk-sale agreement the seller is located in this state or, if the seller is located in a jurisdiction that is not a part of the United States, the seller's major executive office in the United States is in this state.

(2) A seller is deemed to be located at his [or her] place of business. If a seller has more than one place of business, the seller is deemed located at his [or her] chief executive office.

(3) This Article does not apply to:

(a) a transfer made to secure payment or performance of an obligation;

(b) a transfer of collateral to a secured party pursuant to Section 9—503;

(c) a sale of collateral pursuant to Section 9—504;

(d) retention of collateral pursuant to Section 9—505;

(e) a sale of an asset encumbered by a security interest or lien if (i) all the proceeds of the sale are applied in partial or total satisfaction of the debt secured by the security interest or lien or (ii) the security interest or lien is enforceable against the asset after it has been sold to the buyer and the net contract price is zero;

(f) a general assignment for the benefit of creditors or to a subsequent transfer by the assignee;

(g) a sale by an executor, administrator, receiver, trustee in bankruptcy, or any public officer under judicial process;

(h) a sale made in the course of judicial or administrative proceedings for the dissolution or reorganization of an organization;

(i) a sale to a buyer whose principal place of business is in the United States and who:

(i) not earlier than 21 days before the date of the bulk sale, (A) obtains from the seller a verified and dated list of claimants of whom the seller has notice three days before the seller sends or delivers the list to the buyer or (B) conducts a reasonable inquiry to discover the claimants;

(ii) assumes in full the debts owed to claimants of whom the buyer has knowledge on the date the buyer receives the list of claimants from the seller or on the date the buyer completes the reasonable inquiry, as the case may be;

(iii) is not insolvent after the assumption; and

(iv) gives written notice of the assumption not later than 30 days after the date of the bulk sale by sending or delivering a notice to the claimants identified in subparagraph (ii) or by filing a notice in the office of the [Secretary of State];

(j) a sale to a buyer whose principal place of business is in the United States and who:

(i) assumes in full the debts that were incurred in the seller's business before the date of the bulk sale;

(ii) is not insolvent after the assumption; and

(iii) gives written notice of the assumption not later than 30 days after the date of the bulk sale by sending or delivering a notice to each creditor whose debt is assumed or by filing a notice in the office of the [Secretary of State];

(k) a sale to a new organization that is organized to take over and continue the business of the seller and that has its principal place of business in the United States if:

(i) the buyer assumes in full the debts that were incurred in the seller's business before the date of the bulk sale;

(ii) the seller receives nothing from the sale except an interest in the new organization that is subordinate to the claims against the organization arising from the assumption; and

(iii) the buyer gives written notice of the assumption not later than 30 days after the date of the bulk sale by sending or delivering a notice to each creditor whose debt is assumed or by filing a notice in the office of the [Secretary of State];

(l) a sale of assets having:

(i) a value, net of liens and security interests, of less than $10,000. If a debt is secured by assets and other property of the seller, the net value of the assets is determined by subtracting from their value an amount equal to the product of the debt multiplied by a fraction, the numerator of which is the value of the assets on the date of the bulk sale and the denominator of which is the value of all property securing the debt on the date of the bulk sale; or

(ii) a value of more than $25,000,000 on the date of the bulk-sale agreement; or

(m) a sale required by, and made pursuant to, statute.

(4) The notice under subsection (3)(i)(iv) must state: (i) that a sale that may constitute a bulk sale has been or will be made; (ii) the date or prospective date of the bulk sale; (iii) the individual, partnership, or corporate names and the addresses of the seller and buyer; (iv) the address to which inquiries about the sale may be made, if different from the seller's address; and (v) that the buyer has assumed or will assume in full the debts owed to claimants of whom the buyer has knowledge on the date the buyer receives the list of claimants from the seller or completes a reasonable inquiry to discover the claimants.

(5) The notice under subsections (3)(j)(iii) and (3)(k)(iii) must state: (i) that a sale that may constitute a bulk sale has been or will be made; (ii) the date or prospective date of the bulk sale; (iii) the individual, partnership, or corporate names and the addresses of the seller and buyer; (iv) the address to which inquiries about the sale may be made, if different from the seller's address; and (v) that the buyer has assumed or will assume the debts that were incurred in the seller's business before the date of the bulk sale.

(6) For purposes of subsection (3)(l), the value of assets is presumed to be equal to the price the buyer agrees to pay for the assets. However, in a sale by auction or a sale conducted by a liquidator on the seller's behalf, the value of assets is presumed to be the amount the auctioneer or liquidator reasonably estimates the assets will bring at auction or upon liquidation.

§ 6—104. **Obligations of Buyer.**

(1) In a bulk sale as defined in Section 6—102(1)(c)(ii) the buyer shall:

(a) obtain from the seller a list of all business names and addresses used by the seller within three years before the date the list is sent or delivered to the buyer;

(b) unless excused under subsection (2), obtain from the seller a verified and dated list of claimants of whom the seller has notice three days before the seller sends or delivers the list to the buyer and including, to the extent known by the seller, the address of and the amount claimed by each claimant;

(c) obtain from the seller or prepare a schedule of distribution (Section 6—106(1));

(d) give notice of the bulk sale in accordance with Section 6—105;

(e) unless excused under Section 6—106(4), distribute the net contract price in accordance with the undertakings of the buyer in the schedule of distribution; and

(f) unless excused under subsection (2), make available the list of claimants (subsection (1)(b)) by:

(i) promptly sending or delivering a copy of the list without charge to any claimant whose written request is received by the buyer no later than six months after the date of the bulk sale;

(ii) permitting any claimant to inspect and copy the list at any reasonable hour upon request received by the buyer no later than six months after the date of the bulk sale; or

(iii) filing a copy of the list in the office of the [Secretary of State] no later than the time for giving a notice of the bulk sale (Section 6—105(5)). A list filed in accordance with this subparagraph must state the individual, partnership, or corporate name and a mailing address of the seller.

(2) A buyer who gives notice in accordance with Section 6—105(2) is excused from complying with the requirements of subsections (1)(b) and (1)(f).

§ 6—105. Notice to Claimants.

(1) Except as otherwise provided in subsection (2), to comply with Section 6—104(1)(d) the buyer shall send or deliver a written notice of the bulk sale to each claimant on the list of claimants (Section 6—104(1)(b)) and to any other claimant of which the buyer has knowledge at the time the notice of the bulk sale is sent or delivered.

(2) A buyer may comply with Section 6—104(1)(d) by filing a written notice of the bulk sale in the office of the [Secretary of State] if:

(a) on the date of the bulk-sale agreement the seller has 200 or more claimants, exclusive of claimants holding secured or matured claims for employment compensation and benefits, including commissions and vacation, severance, and sick-leave pay; or

(b) the buyer has received a verified statement from the seller stating that, as of the date of the bulk-sale agreement, the number of claimants, exclusive of claimants holding secured or matured claims for employment compensation and benefits, including commissions and vacation, severance, and sick-leave pay, is 200 or more.

(3) The written notice of the bulk sale must be accompanied by a copy of the schedule of distribution (Section 6—106(1)) and state at least:

(a) that the seller and buyer have entered into an agreement for a sale that may constitute a bulk sale under the laws of the State of _____;

(b) the date of the agreement;

(c) the date on or after which more than ten percent of the assets were or will be transferred;

(d) the date on or after which more than ten percent of the net contract price was or will be paid, if the date is not stated in the schedule of distribution;

(e) the name and a mailing address of the seller;

(f) any other business name and address listed by the seller pursuant to Section 6—104(1)(a);

(g) the name of the buyer and an address of the buyer from which information concerning the sale can be obtained;

(h) a statement indicating the type of assets or describing the assets item by item;

(i) the manner in which the buyer will make available the list of claimants (Section 6—104(1)(f)), if applicable; and

(j) if the sale is in total or partial satisfaction of an antecedent debt owed by the seller, the amount of the debt to be satisfied and the name of the person to whom it is owed.

(4) For purposes of subsections (3)(e) and (3)(g), the name of a person is the person's individual, partnership, or corporate name.

(5) The buyer shall give notice of the bulk sale not less than 45 days before the date of the bulk sale and, if the buyer gives notice in accordance with subsection (1), not more than 30 days after obtaining the list of claimants.

(6) A written notice substantially complying with the requirements of subsection (3) is effective even though it contains minor errors that are not seriously misleading.

(7) A form substantially as follows is sufficient to comply with subsection (3):

Notice of Sale

(1) _____, whose address is _____, is described in this notice as the ''seller.''

(2) _____, whose address is _____, is described in this notice as the ''buyer.''

(3) The seller has disclosed to the buyer that within the past three years the seller has used other business names, operated at other addresses, or both, as follows: _____.

(4) The seller and the buyer have entered into an agreement dated _____, for a sale that may constitute a bulk sale under the laws of the State of _____ .

(5) The date on or after which more than ten percent of the assets that are the subject of the sale were or will be transferred is _____, and [if not stated in the schedule of distribution] the date on or after which more than ten percent of the net contract price was or will be paid is _____.

(6) The following assets are the subject of the sale: _____ .

(7) [If applicable] The buyer will make available to claimants of the seller a list of the seller's claimants in the following manner: _____.

(8) [If applicable] The sale is to satisfy $_____ of an antecedent debt owed by the seller to _____.

(9) A copy of the schedule of distribution of the net contract price accompanies this notice.

[End of Notice]

§ 6—106. **Schedule of Distribution.**

(1) The seller and buyer shall agree on how the net contract price is to be distributed and set forth their agreement in a written schedule of distribution.

(2) The schedule of distribution may provide for distribution to any person at any time, including distribution of the entire net contract price to the seller.

(3) The buyer's undertakings in the schedule of distribution run only to the seller. However, a buyer who fails to distribute the net contract price in accordance with the buyer's undertakings in the schedule of distribution is liable to a creditor only as provided in Section 6—107(1).

(4) If the buyer undertakes in the schedule of distribution to distribute any part of the net contract price to a person other than the seller, and, after the buyer has given notice in accordance with Section 6—105, some or all of the anticipated net contract price is or becomes unavailable for distribution as a consequence of the buyer's or seller's having complied with an order of court, legal process, statute, or rule of law, the buyer is excused from any obligation arising under this Article or under any contract with the seller to distribute the net contract price in accordance with the buyer's undertakings in the schedule if the buyer:

(a) distributes the net contract price remaining available in accordance with any priorities for payment stated in the schedule of distribution and, to the extent that the price is insufficient to pay all the debts having a given priority, distributes the price pro rata among those debts shown in the schedule as having the same priority;

(b) distributes the net contract price remaining available in accordance with an order of court;

(c) commences a proceeding for interpleader in a court of competent jurisdiction and is discharged from the proceeding; or

(d) reaches a new agreement with the seller for the distribution of the net contract price remaining available, sets forth the new agreement in an amended schedule of distribution, gives notice of the amended schedule, and distributes the net contract price remaining available in accordance with the buyer's undertakings in the amended schedule.

(5) The notice under subsection (4)(d) must identify the buyer and the seller, state the filing number, if any, of the original notice, set forth the amended schedule, and be given in accordance with subsection (1) or (2) of Section 6—105, whichever is applicable, at least 14 days before the buyer distributes any part of the net contract price remaining available.

(6) If the seller undertakes in the schedule of distribution to distribute any part of the net contract price, and, after the buyer has given notice in accordance with Section 6—105, some or all of the anticipated net contract price is or becomes unavailable for distribution as a consequence of the buyer's or seller's having complied with an order of court, legal process, statute, or rule of law, the seller and any person in control of the seller are excused from any obligation arising under this Article or under any agreement with the buyer to distribute the net contract price in accordance with the seller's undertakings in the schedule if the seller:

(a) distributes the net contract price remaining available in accordance with any priorities for payment stated in the schedule of distribution and, to the extent that the price is insufficient to pay all the debts having a given priority, distributes the price pro rata among those debts shown in the schedule as having the same priority;

(b) distributes the net contract price remaining available in accordance with an order of court;

(c) commences a proceeding for interpleader in a court of competent jurisdiction and is discharged from the proceeding; or

(d) prepares a written amended schedule of distribution of the net contract price remaining available for distribution, gives notice of the amended schedule, and distributes the net contract price remaining available in accordance with the amended schedule.

(7) The notice under subsection (6)(d) must identify the buyer and the seller, state the filing number, if any, of the original notice, set forth the amended schedule, and be given in accordance with subsection (1) or (2) of Section 6—105, whichever is applicable, at least 14 days before the seller

distributes any part of the net contract price remaining available.

§ 6—107. **Liability for Noncompliance.**

(1) Except as provided in subsection (3), and subject to the limitation in subsection (4):

(a) a buyer who fails to comply with the requirements of Section 6—104(1)(e) with respect to a creditor is liable to the creditor for damages in the amount of the claim, reduced by any amount that the creditor would not have realized if the buyer had complied; and

(b) a buyer who fails to comply with the requirements of any other subsection of Section 6—104 with respect to a claimant is liable to the claimant for damages in the amount of the claim, reduced by any amount that the claimant would not have realized if the buyer had complied.

(2) In an action under subsection (1), the creditor has the burden of establishing the validity and amount of the claim, and the buyer has the burden of establishing the amount that the creditor would not have realized if the buyer had complied.

(3) A buyer who:

(a) made a good faith and commercially reasonable effort to comply with the requirements of Section 6—104(1) or to exclude the sale from the application of this Article under Section 6—103(3); or

(b) on or after the date of the bulk-sale agreement, but before the date of the bulk sale, held a good faith and commercially reasonable belief that this Article does not apply to the particular sale

is not liable to creditors for failure to comply with the requirements of Section 6—104. The buyer has the burden of establishing the good faith and commercial reasonableness of the effort or belief.

(4) In a single bulk sale the cumulative liability of the buyer for failure to comply with the requirements of Section 6—104(1) may not exceed an amount equal to:

(a) if the assets consist only of inventory and equipment, twice the net contract price, less the amount of any part of the net contract price paid to or applied for the benefit of the seller or a creditor; or

(b) if the assets include property other than inventory and equipment, twice the net value of the inventory and equipment less the amount of the portion of any part of the net contract price paid to or applied for the benefit of the seller or a creditor which is allocable to the inventory and equipment.

(5) For the purposes of subsection (4)(b), the "net value" of an asset is the value of the asset less (i) the amount of any proceeds of the sale of an asset, to the extent the pro-

ceeds are applied in partial or total satisfaction of a debt secured by the asset and (ii) the amount of any debt to the extent it is secured by a security interest or lien that is enforceable against the asset before and after it has been sold to a buyer. If a debt is secured by an asset and other property of the seller, the amount of the debt secured by a security interest or lien that is enforceable against the asset is determined by multiplying the debt by a fraction, the numerator of which is the value of the asset on the date of the bulk sale and the denominator of which is the value of all property securing the debt on the date of the bulk sale. The portion of a part of the net contract price paid to or applied for the benefit of the seller or a creditor that is "allocable to the inventory and equipment" is the portion that bears the same ratio to that part of the net contract price as the net value of the inventory and equipment bears to the net value of all of the assets.

(6) A payment made by the buyer to a person to whom the buyer is, or believes he [or she] is, liable under subsection (1) reduces pro tanto the buyer's cumulative liability under subsection (4).

(7) No action may be brought under subsection (1)(b) by or on behalf of a claimant whose claim is unliquidated or contingent.

(8) A buyer's failure to comply with the requirements of Section 6—104(1) does not (i) impair the buyer's rights in or title to the assets, (ii) render the sale ineffective, void, or voidable, (iii) entitle a creditor to more than a single satisfaction of his [or her] claim, or (iv) create liability other than as provided in this Article.

(9) Payment of the buyer's liability under subsection (1) discharges pro tanto the seller's debt to the creditor.

(10) Unless otherwise agreed, a buyer has an immediate right of reimbursement from the seller for any amount paid to a creditor in partial or total satisfaction of the buyer's liability under subsection (1).

(11) If the seller is an organization, a person who is in direct or indirect control of the seller, and who knowingly, intentionally, and without legal justification fails, or causes the seller to fail, to distribute the net contract price in accordance with the schedule of distribution is liable to any creditor to whom the seller undertook to make payment under the schedule for damages caused by the failure.

§ 6—108. **Bulk Sales by Auction; Bulk Sales Conducted by Liquidator.**

(1) Sections 6—104, 6—105, 6—106, and 6—107 apply to a bulk sale by auction and a bulk sale conducted by a liquidator on the seller's behalf with the following modifications:

(a) "buyer" refers to auctioneer or liquidator, as the case may be;

(b) "net contract price" refers to net proceeds of the auction or net proceeds of the sale, as the case may be;

(c) the written notice required under Section 6—105(3) must be accompanied by a copy of the schedule of distribution (Section 6—106(1)) and state at least:

(i) that the seller and the auctioneer or liquidator have entered into an agreement for auction or liquidation services that may constitute an agreement to make a bulk sale under the laws of the State of _____;

(ii) the date of the agreement;

(iii) the date on or after which the auction began or will begin or the date on or after which the liquidator began or will begin to sell assets on the seller's behalf;

(iv) the date on or after which more than ten percent of the net proceeds of the sale were or will be paid, if the date is not stated in the schedule of distribution;

(v) the name and a mailing address of the seller;

(vi) any other business name and address listed by the seller pursuant to Section 6—104(1)(a);

(vii) the name of the auctioneer or liquidator and an address of the auctioneer or liquidator from which information concerning the sale can be obtained;

(viii) a statement indicating the type of assets or describing the assets item by item;

(ix) the manner in which the auctioneer or liquidator will make available the list of claimants (Section 6—104(1)(f)), if applicable; and

(x) if the sale is in total or partial satisfaction of an antecedent debt owed by the seller, the amount of the debt to be satisfied and the name of the person to whom it is owed; and

(d) in a single bulk sale the cumulative liability of the auctioneer or liquidator for failure to comply with the requirements of this section may not exceed the amount of the net proceeds of the sale allocable to inventory and equipment sold less the amount of the portion of any part of the net proceeds paid to or applied for the benefit of a creditor which is allocable to the inventory and equipment.

(2) A payment made by the auctioneer or liquidator to a person to whom the auctioneer or liquidator is, or believes he [or she] is, liable under this section reduces pro tanto the auctioneer's or liquidator's cumulative liability under subsection (1)(d).

(3) A form substantially as follows is sufficient to comply with subsection (1)(c):

Notice of Sale

(1) _____, whose address is _____, is described in this notice as the "seller."

(2) _____, whose address is _____, is described in this notice as the "auctioneer" or "liquidator."

(3) The seller has disclosed to the auctioneer or liquidator that within the past three years the seller has used other business names, operated at other addresses, or both, as follows: _____.

(4) The seller and the auctioneer or liquidator have entered into an agreement dated _ for auction or liquidation services that may constitute an agreement to make a bulk sale under the laws of the State of _____.

(5) The date on or after which the auction began or will begin or the date on or after which the liquidator began or will begin to sell assets on the seller's behalf is _____ , and [if not stated in the schedule of distribution] the date on or after which more than ten percent of the net proceeds of the sale were or will be paid is _____.

(6) The following assets are the subject of the sale: _____

(7) [If applicable] The auctioneer or liquidator will make available to claimants of the seller a list of the seller's claimants in the following manner: _____.

(8) [If applicable] The sale is to satisfy $_____ of an antecedent debt owed by the seller to _____ .

(9) A copy of the schedule of distribution of the net proceeds accompanies this notice.

[End of Notice]

(4) A person who buys at a bulk sale by auction or conducted by a liquidator need not comply with the requirements of Section 6—104(1) and is not liable for the failure of an auctioneer or liquidator to comply with the requirements of this section.

§ 6—109. What Constitutes Filing; Duties of Filing Officer; Information from Filing Officer.

(1) Presentation of a notice or list of claimants for filing and tender of the filing fee or acceptance of the notice or list by the filing officer constitutes filing under this Article.

(2) The filing officer shall:

(a) mark each notice or list with a file number and with the date and hour of filing;

(b) hold the notice or list or a copy for public inspection;

(c) index the notice or list according to each name given for the seller and for the buyer; and

(d) note in the index the file number and the addresses of the seller and buyer given in the notice or list.

(3) If the person filing a notice or list furnishes the filing officer with a copy, the filing officer upon request shall note upon the copy the file number and date and hour of the filing of the original and send or deliver the copy to the person.

(4) The fee for filing and indexing and for stamping a copy furnished by the person filing to show the date and place of filing is $_____$ for the first page and $_____$ for each additional page. The fee for indexing each name beyond the first two is $_____$.

(5) Upon request of any person, the filing officer shall issue a certificate showing whether any notice or list with respect to a particular seller or buyer is on file on the date and hour stated in the certificate. If a notice or list is on file, the certificate must give the date and hour of filing of each notice or list and the name and address of each seller, buyer, auctioneer, or liquidator. The fee for the certificate is $_____$ if the request for the certificate is in the standard form prescribed by the [Secretary of State] and otherwise is $_____$. Upon request of any person, the filing officer shall furnish a copy of any filed notice or list for a fee of $_____$.

(6) The filing officer shall keep each notice or list for two years after it is filed.

§ 6—110. Limitation of Actions.

(1) Except as provided in subsection (2), an action under this Article against a buyer, auctioneer, or liquidator must be commenced within one year after the date of the bulk sale.

(2) If the buyer, auctioneer, or liquidator conceals the fact that the sale has occurred, the limitation is tolled and an action under this Article may be commenced within the earlier of (i) one year after the person bringing the action discovers that the sale has occurred or (ii) one year after the person bringing the action should have discovered that the sale has occurred, but no later than two years after the date of the bulk sale. Complete noncompliance with the requirements of this Article does not of itself constitute concealment.

(3) An action under Section 6—107(11) must be commenced within one year after the alleged violation occurs.

Article 7
Warehouse Receipts, Bills of Lading and Other Documents of Title

Part 1 General

§ 7—101. Short Title.
This Article shall be known and may be cited as Uniform Commercial Code—Documents of Title.

§ 7—102. Definitions and Index of Definitions.

(1) In this Article, unless the context otherwise requires:

(a) ''Bailee'' means the person who by a warehouse receipt, bill of lading or other document of title acknowledges possession of goods and contracts to deliver them.

(b) ''Consignee'' means the person named in a bill to whom or to whose order the bill promises delivery.

(c) ''Consignor'' means the person named in a bill as the person from whom the goods have been received for shipment.

(d) ''Delivery order'' means a written order to deliver goods directed to a warehouseman, carrier or other person who in the ordinary course of business issues warehouse receipts or bills of lading.

(e) ''Document'' means document of title as defined in the general definitions in Article 1 (Section 1—201).

(f) ''Goods'' means all things which are treated as movable for the purposes of a contract of storage or transportation.

(g) ''Issuer'' means a bailee who issues a document except that in relation to an unaccepted delivery order it means the person who orders the possessor of goods to deliver. Issuer includes any person for whom an agent or employee purports to act in issuing a document if the agent or employee has real or apparent authority to issue documents, notwithstanding that the issuer received no goods or that the goods were misdescribed or that in any other respect the agent or employee violated his instructions.

(h) ''Warehouseman'' is a person engaged in the business of storing goods for hire.

(2) Other definitions applying to this Article or to specified Parts thereof, and the sections in which they appear are:

''Duly negotiate''. Section 7—501.

''Person entitled under the document''. Section 7—403(4).

(3) Definitions in other Articles applying to this Article and the sections in which they appear are:

''Contract for sale''. Section 2—106.

''Overseas''. Section 2—323.

''Receipt'' of goods. Section 2—103.

(4) In addition Article 1 contains general definitions and principles of construction and interpretation applicable throughout this Article.

§ 7—103. Relation of Article to Treaty, Statute, Tariff, Classification or Regulation.

To the extent that any treaty or statute of the United States, regulatory statute of this State or tariff, classification or regulation filed or issued pursuant thereto is applicable, the provisions of this Article are subject thereto.

§ 7—104. Negotiable and Nonnegotiable Warehouse Receipt, Bill of Lading or Other Document of Title.

(1) A warehouse receipt, bill of lading or other document of title is negotiable

(a) if by its terms the goods are to be delivered to bearer or to the order of a named person; or

(b) where recognized in overseas trade, if it runs to a named person or assigns.

(2) Any other document is nonnegotiable. A bill of lading in which it is stated that the goods are consigned to a named person is not made negotiable by a provision that the goods are to be delivered only against a written order signed by the same or another named person.

§ 7—105. Construction Against Negative Implication.

The omission from either Part 2 or Part 3 of this Article of a provision corresponding to a provision made in the other Part does not imply that a corresponding rule of law is not applicable.

Part 2 Warehouse Receipts: Special Provisions

§ 7—201. Who May Issue a Warehouse Receipt; Storage Under Government Bond.

(1) A warehouse receipt may be issued by any warehouseman.

(2) Where goods including distilled spirits and agricultural commodities are stored under a statute requiring a bond against withdrawal or a license for the issuance of receipts in the nature of warehouse receipts, a receipt issued for the goods has like effect as a warehouse receipt even though issued by a person who is the owner of the goods and is not a warehouseman.

§ 7—202. Form of Warehouse Receipt; Essential Terms; Optional Terms.

(1) A warehouse receipt need not be in any particular form.

(2) Unless a warehouse receipt embodies within its written or printed terms each of the following, the warehouseman is liable for damages caused by the omission to a person injured thereby:

(a) the location of the warehouse where the goods are stored;

(b) the date of issue of the receipt;

(c) the consecutive number of the receipt;

(d) a statement whether the goods received will be delivered to the bearer, to a specified person, or to a specified person or his order;

(e) the rate of storage and handling charges, except that where goods are stored under a field warehousing arrangement a statement of that fact is sufficient on a nonnegotiable receipt;

(f) a description of the goods or of the packages containing them;

(g) the signature of the warehouseman, which may be made by his authorized agent;

(h) if the receipt is issued for goods of which the warehouseman is owner, either solely or jointly or in common with others, the fact of such ownership; and

(i) a statement of the amount of advances made and of liabilities incurred for which the warehouseman claims a lien or security interest (Section 7—209). If the precise amount of such advances made or of such liabilities incurred is, at the time of the issue of the receipt, unknown to the warehouseman or to his agent who issues it, a statement of the fact that advances have been made or liabilities incurred and the purpose thereof is sufficient.

(3) A warehouseman may insert in his receipt any other terms which are not contrary to the provisions of this Act and do not impair his obligation of delivery (Section 7—403) or his duty of care (Section 7—204). Any contrary provisions shall be ineffective.

§ 7—203. Liability for Nonreceipt or Misdescription.

A party to or purchaser for value in good faith of a document of title other than a bill of lading relying in either case upon the description therein of the goods may recover from the issuer damages caused by the nonreceipt or misdescription of the goods, except to the extent that the document conspicuously indicates that the issuer does not know whether any part or all of the goods in fact were received or conform to the description, as where the description is in terms of marks or labels or kind, quantity or condition, or the receipt or description is qualified by ''contents, condition and quality unknown'', ''said to contain'' or the like, if such indication be true, or the party or purchaser otherwise has notice.

§ 7—204. Duty of Care; Contractual Limitation of Warehouseman's Liability.

(1) A warehouseman is liable for damages for loss of or injury to the goods caused by his failure to exercise such care in regard to them as a reasonably careful man would exercise under like circumstances but unless otherwise agreed he is not liable for damages which could not have been avoided by the exercise of such care.

(2) Damages may be limited by a term in the warehouse receipt or storage agreement limiting the amount of liability in case of loss or damage, and setting forth a specific liability per article or item, or value per unit of weight, beyond which the warehouseman shall not be liable; provided, however, that such liability may on written request of the bailor at the time of signing such storage agreement or within a reasonable time after receipt of the warehouse receipt be increased on part or all of the goods thereunder, in which event increased rates may be charged based on such increased valuation, but that no such increase shall be per-

mitted contrary to a lawful limitation of liability contained in the warehouseman's tariff, if any. No such limitation is effective with respect to the warehouseman's liability for conversion to his own use.

(3) Reasonable provisions as to the time and manner of presenting claims and instituting actions based on the bailment may be included in the warehouse receipt or tariff.

(4) This section does not impair or repeal . . .

Note: *Insert in subsection (4) a reference to any statute which imposes a higher responsibility upon the warehouseman or invalidates contractual limitations which would be permissible under this Article.*

§ 7—205. **Title Under Warehouse Receipt Defeated in Certain Cases.**

A buyer in the ordinary course of business of fungible goods sold and delivered by a warehouseman who is also in the business of buying and selling such goods takes free of any claim under a warehouse receipt even though it has been duly negotiated.

§ 7—206. **Termination of Storage at Warehouseman's Option.**

(1) A warehouseman may on notifying the person on whose account the goods are held and any other person known to claim an interest in the goods require payment of any charges and removal of the goods from the warehouse at the termination of the period of storage fixed by the document, or, if no period is fixed, within a stated period not less than thirty days after the notification. If the goods are not removed before the date specified in the notification, the warehouseman may sell them in accordance with the provisions of the section on enforcement of a warehouseman's lien (Section 7—210).

(2) If a warehouseman in good faith believes that the goods are about to deteriorate or decline in value to less than the amount of his lien within the time prescribed in subsection (1) for notification, advertisement and sale, the warehouseman may specify in the notification any reasonable shorter time for removal of the goods and in case the goods are not removed, may sell them at public sale held not less than one week after a single advertisement or posting.

(3) If as a result of a quality or condition of the goods of which the warehouseman had no notice at the time of deposit the goods are a hazard to other property or to the warehouse or to persons, the warehouseman may sell the goods at public or private sale without advertisement on reasonable notification to all persons known to claim an interest in the goods. If the warehouseman after a reasonable effort is unable to sell the goods he may dispose of them in any lawful manner and shall incur no liability by reason of such disposition.

(4) The warehouseman must deliver the goods to any person entitled to them under this Article upon due demand made at any time prior to sale or other disposition under this section.

(5) The warehouseman may satisfy his lien from the proceeds of any sale or disposition under this section but must hold the balance for delivery on the demand of any person to whom he would have been bound to deliver the goods.

§ 7—207. **Goods Must Be Kept Separate; Fungible Goods.**

(1) Unless the warehouse receipt otherwise provides, a warehouseman must keep separate the goods covered by each receipt so as to permit at all times identification and delivery of those goods except that different lots of fungible goods may be commingled.

(2) Fungible goods so commingled are owned in common by the persons entitled thereto and the warehouseman is severally liable to each owner for that owner's share. Where because of overissue a mass of fungible goods is insufficient to meet all the receipts which the warehouseman has issued against it, the persons entitled include all holders to whom overissued receipts have been duly negotiated.

§ 7—208. **Altered Warehouse Receipts.**

Where a blank in a negotiable warehouse receipt has been filled in without authority, a purchaser for value and without notice of the want of authority may treat the insertion as authorized. Any other unauthorized alteration leaves any receipt enforceable against the issuer according to its original tenor.

§ 7—209. **Lien of Warehouseman.**

(1) A warehouseman has a lien against the bailor on the goods covered by a warehouse receipt or on the proceeds thereof in his possession for charges for storage or transportation (including demurrage and terminal charges), insurance, labor, or charges present or future in relation to the goods, and for expenses necessary for preservation of the goods or reasonably incurred in their sale pursuant to law. If the person on whose account the goods are held is liable for like charges or expenses in relation to other goods whenever deposited and it is stated in the receipt that a lien is claimed for charges and expenses in relation to other goods, the warehouseman also has a lien against him for such charges and expenses whether or not the other goods have been delivered by the warehouseman. But against a person to whom a negotiable warehouse receipt is duly negotiated a warehouseman's lien is limited to charges in an amount or at a rate specified on the receipt or if no charges are so specified then to a reasonable charge for storage of the goods covered by the receipt subsequent to the date of the receipt.

(2) The warehouseman may also reserve a security interest against the bailor for a maximum amount specified on the receipt for charges other than those specified in subsec-

tion (1), such as for money advanced and interest. Such a security interest is governed by the Article on Secured Transactions (Article 9).

(3)(a) A warehouseman's lien for charges and expenses under subsection (1) or a security interest under subsection (2) is also effective against any person who so entrusted the bailor with possession of the goods that a pledge of them by him to a good faith purchaser for value would have been valid but is not effective against a person as to whom the document confers no right in the goods covered by it under Section 7—503.

(b) A warehouseman's lien on household goods for charges and expenses in relation to the goods under subsection (1) is also effective against all persons if the depositor was the legal possessor of the goods at the time of deposit. "Household goods" means furniture, furnishings and personal effects used by the depositor in a dwelling.

(4) A warehouseman loses his lien on any goods which he voluntarily delivers or which he unjustifiably refuses to deliver.

§ 7—210. Enforcement of Warehouseman's Lien.

(1) Except as provided in subsection (2), a warehouseman's lien may be enforced by public or private sale of the goods in bloc or in parcels, at any time or place and on any terms which are commercially reasonable, after notifying all persons known to claim an interest in the goods. Such notification must include a statement of the amount due, the nature of the proposed sale and the time and place of any public sale. The fact that a better price could have been obtained by a sale at a different time or in a different method from that selected by the warehouseman is not of itself sufficient to establish that the sale was not made in a commercially reasonable manner. If the warehouseman either sells the goods in the usual manner in any recognized market therefor, or if he sells at the price current in such market at the time of his sale, or if he has otherwise sold in conformity with commercially reasonable practices among dealers in the type of goods sold, he has sold in a commercially reasonable manner. A sale of more goods than apparently necessary to be offered to ensure satisfaction of the obligation is not commercially reasonable except in cases covered by the preceding sentence.

(2) A warehouseman's lien on goods other than goods stored by a merchant in the course of his business may be enforced only as follows:

(a) All persons known to claim an interest in the goods must be notified.

(b) The notification must be delivered in person or sent by registered or certified letter to the last known address of any person to be notified.

(c) The notification must include an itemized statement of the claim, a description of the goods subject to the lien, a demand for payment within a specified time not less than ten days after receipt of the notification, and a conspicuous statement that unless the claim is paid within the time the goods will be advertised for sale and sold by auction at a specified time and place.

(d) The sale must conform to the terms of the notification.

(e) The sale must be held at the nearest suitable place to that where the goods are held or stored.

(f) After the expiration of the time given in the notification, an advertisement of the sale must be published once a week for two weeks consecutively in a newspaper of general circulation where the sale is to be held. The advertisement must include a description of the goods, the name of the person on whose account they are being held, and the time and place of the sale. The sale must take place at least fifteen days after the first publication. If there is no newspaper of general circulation where the sale is to be held, the advertisement must be posted at least ten days before the sale in not less than six conspicuous places in the neighborhood of the proposed sale.

(3) Before any sale pursuant to this section any person claiming a right in the goods may pay the amount necessary to satisfy the lien and the reasonable expenses incurred under this section. In that event the goods must not be sold, but must be retained by the warehouseman subject to the terms of the receipt and this Article.

(4) The warehouseman may buy at any public sale pursuant to this section.

(5) A purchaser in good faith of goods sold to enforce a warehouseman's lien takes the goods free of any rights of persons against whom the lien was valid, despite noncompliance by the warehouseman with the requirements of this section.

(6) The warehouseman may satisfy his lien from the proceeds of any sale pursuant to this section but must hold the balance, if any, for delivery on demand to any person to whom he would have been bound to deliver the goods.

(7) The rights provided by this section shall be in addition to all other rights allowed by law to a creditor against his debtor.

(8) Where a lien is on goods stored by a merchant in the course of his business the lien may be enforced in accordance with either subsection (1) or (2).

(9) The warehouseman is liable for damages caused by failure to comply with the requirements for sale under this section and in case of willful violation is liable for conversion.

Part 3 Bills of Lading: Special Provisions

§ 7—301. Liability for Nonreceipt or Misdescription; "Said to Contain"; "Shipper's Load and Count"; Improper Handling.

(1) A consignee of a nonnegotiable bill who has given value in good faith or a holder to whom a negotiable bill has been duly negotiated relying in either case upon the description therein of the goods, or upon the date therein shown, may recover from the issuer damages caused by the misdating of the bill or the nonreceipt or misdescription of the goods, except to the extent that the document indicates that the issuer does not know whether any part of all of the goods in fact were received or conform to the description, as where the description is in terms of marks or labels or kind, quantity, or condition or the receipt or description is qualified by "contents or condition of contents of packages unknown", "said to contain", "shipper's weight, load and count" or the like, if such indication be true.

(2) When goods are loaded by an issuer who is a common carrier, the issuer must count the packages of goods if package freight and ascertain the kind and quantity if bulk freight. In such cases "shipper's weight, load and count" or other words indicating that the description was made by the shipper are ineffective except as to freight concealed by packages.

(3) When bulk freight is loaded by a shipper who makes available to the issuer adequate facilities for weighing such freight, an issuer who is a common carrier must ascertain the kind and quantity within a reasonable time after receiving the written request of the shipper to do so. In such cases "shipper's weight" or other words of like purport are ineffective.

(4) The issuer may by inserting in the bill the words "shipper's weight, load and count" or other words of like purport indicate that the goods were loaded by the shipper; and if such statement be true the issuer shall not be liable for damages caused by the improper loading. But their omission does not imply liability for such damages.

(5) The shipper shall be deemed to have guaranteed to the issuer the accuracy at the time of shipment of the description, marks, labels, number, kind, quantity, condition and weight, as furnished by him; and the shipper shall indemnify the issuer against damage caused by inaccuracies in such particulars. The right of the issuer to such indemnity shall in no way limit his responsibility and liability under the contract of carriage to any person other than the shipper.

§ 7—302. Through Bills of Lading and Similar Documents.

(1) The issuer of a through bill of lading or other document embodying an undertaking to be performed in part by persons acting as its agents or by connecting carriers is liable to anyone entitled to recover on the document for any breach by such other persons or by a connecting carrier of its obligation under the document but to the extent that the bill covers an undertaking to be performed overseas or in territory not contiguous to the continental United States or an undertaking including matters other than transportation this liability may be varied by agreement of the parties.

(2) Where goods covered by a through bill of lading or other document embodying an undertaking to be performed in part by persons other than the issuer are received by any such person, he is subject with respect to his own performance while the goods are in his possession to the obligation of the issuer. His obligation is discharged by delivery of the goods to another such person pursuant to the document, and does not include liability for breach by any other such persons or by the issuer.

(3) The issuer of such through bill of lading or other document shall be entitled to recover from the connecting carrier or such other person in possession of the goods when the breach of the obligation under the document occurred, the amount it may be required to pay to anyone entitled to recover on the document therefor, as may be evidenced by any receipt, judgment, or transcript thereof, and the amount of any expense reasonably incurred by it in defending any action brought by anyone entitled to recover on the document therefor.

§ 7—303. Diversion; Reconsignment; Change of Instructions.

(1) Unless the bill of lading otherwise provides, the carrier may deliver the goods to a person or destination other than that stated in the bill or may otherwise dispose of the goods on instructions from

(a) the holder of a negotiable bill; or

(b) the consignor on a nonnegotiable bill notwithstanding contrary instructions from the consignee; or

(c) the consignee on a nonnegotiable bill in the absence of contrary instructions from the consignor, if the goods have arrived at the billed destination or if the consignee is in possession of the bill; or

(d) the consignee on a nonnegotiable bill if he is entitled as against the consignor to dispose of them.

(2) Unless such instructions are noted on a negotiable bill of lading, a person to whom the bill is duly negotiated can hold the bailee according to the original terms.

§ 7—304. Bills of Lading in a Set.

(1) Except where customary in overseas transportation, a bill of lading must not be issued in a set of parts. The issuer is liable for damages caused by violation of this subsection.

(2) Where a bill of lading is lawfully drawn in a set of parts, each of which is numbered and expressed to be valid only if the goods have not been delivered against any other part, the whole of the parts constitute one bill.

(3) Where a bill of lading is lawfully issued in a set of parts and different parts are negotiated to different persons, the title of the holder to whom the first due negotiation is made prevails as to both the document and the goods even though any later holder may have received the goods from the carrier in good faith and discharged the carrier's obligation by surrender of his part.

(4) Any person who negotiates or transfers a single part of a bill of lading drawn in a set is liable to holders of that part as if it were the whole set.

(5) The bailee is obliged to deliver in accordance with Part 4 of this Article against the first presented part of a bill of lading lawfully drawn in a set. Such delivery discharges the bailee's obligation on the whole bill.

§ 7—305. **Destination Bills.**

(1) Instead of issuing a bill of lading to the consignor at the place of shipment a carrier may at the request of the consignor procure the bill to be issued at destination or at any other place designated in the request.

(2) Upon request of anyone entitled as against the carrier to control the goods while in transit and on surrender of any outstanding bill of lading or other receipt covering such goods, the issuer may procure a substitute bill to be issued at any place designated in the request.

§ 7—306. **Altered Bills of Lading.**

An unauthorized alteration or filling in of a blank in a bill of lading leaves the bill enforceable according to its original tenor.

§ 7—307. **Lien of Carrier.**

(1) A carrier has a lien on the goods covered by a bill of lading for charges subsequent to the date of its receipt of the goods for storage or transportation (including demurrage and terminal charges) and for expenses necessary for preservation of the goods incident to their transportation or reasonably incurred in their sale pursuant to law. But against a purchaser for value of a negotiable bill of lading a carrier's lien is limited to charges stated in the bill or the applicable tariffs, or if no charges are stated then to a reasonable charge.

(2) A lien for charges and expenses under subsection (1) on goods which the carrier was required by law to receive for transportation is effective against the consignor or any person entitled to the goods unless the carrier had notice that the consignor lacked authority to subject the goods to such charges and expenses. Any other lien under subsection (1) is effective against the consignor and any person who permitted the bailor to have control or possession of the goods unless the carrier had notice that the bailor lacked such authority.

(3) A carrier loses his lien on any goods which he voluntarily delivers or which he unjustifiably refuses to deliver.

§ 7—308. **Enforcement of Carrier's Lien.**

(1) A carrier's lien may be enforced by public or private sale of the goods, in bloc or in parcels, at any time or place and on any terms which are commercially reasonable, after notifying all persons known to claim an interest in the goods. Such notification must include a statement of the amount due, the nature of the proposed sale and the time and place of any public sale. The fact that a better price could have been obtained by a sale at a different time or in a different method from that selected by the carrier is not of itself sufficient to establish that the sale was not made in a commercially reasonable manner. If the carrier either sells the goods in the usual manner in any recognized market therefor or if he sells at the price current in such market at the time of his sale or if he has otherwise sold in conformity with commercially reasonable practices among dealers in the type of goods sold he has sold in a commercially reasonable manner. A sale of more goods than apparently necessary to be offered to ensure satisfaction of the obligation is not commercially reasonable except in cases covered by the preceding sentence.

(2) Before any sale pursuant to this section any person claiming a right in the goods may pay the amount necessary to satisfy the lien and the reasonable expenses incurred under this section. In that event the goods must not be sold, but must be retained by the carrier subject to the terms of the bill and this Article.

(3) The carrier may buy at any public sale pursuant to this section.

(4) A purchaser in good faith of goods sold to enforce a carrier's lien takes the goods free of any rights of persons against whom the lien was valid, despite noncompliance by the carrier with the requirements of this section.

(5) The carrier may satisfy his lien from the proceeds of any sale pursuant to this section but must hold the balance, if any, for delivery on demand to any person to whom he would have been bound to deliver the goods.

(6) The rights provided by this section shall be in addition to all other rights allowed by law to a creditor against his debtor.

(7) A carrier's lien may be enforced in accordance with either subsection (1) or the procedure set forth in subsection (2) of Section 7—210.

(8) The carrier is liable for damages caused by failure to comply with the requirements for sale under this section and in case of willful violation is liable for conversion.

§ 7—309. **Duty of Care; Contractual Limitation of Carrier's Liability.**

(1) A carrier who issues a bill of lading whether negotiable or nonnegotiable must exercise the degree of care in relation to the goods which a reasonably careful man would exercise under like circumstances. This subsection does not repeal

or change any law or rule of law which imposes liability upon a common carrier for damages not caused by its negligence.

(2) Damages may be limited by a provision that the carrier's liability shall not exceed a value stated in the document if the carrier's rates are dependent upon value and the consignor by the carrier's tariff is afforded an opportunity to declare a higher value or a value as lawfully provided in the tariff, or where no tariff is filed he is otherwise advised of such opportunity; but no such limitation is effective with respect to the carrier's liability for conversion to its own use.

(3) Reasonable provisions as to the time and manner of presenting claims and instituting actions based on the shipment may be included in a bill of lading or tariff.

Part 4 Warehouse Receipts and Bills of Lading: General Obligations

§ 7—401. **Irregularities in Issue of Receipt or Bill or Conduct of Issuer.**

The obligations imposed by this Article on an issuer apply to a document of title regardless of the fact that

(a) the document may not comply with the requirements of this Article or of any other law or regulation regarding its issue, form or content; or

(b) the issuer may have violated laws regulating the conduct of his business; or

(c) the goods covered by the document were owned by the bailee at the time the document was issued; or

(d) the person issuing the document does not come within the definition of warehouseman if it purports to be a warehouse receipt.

§ 7—402. **Duplicate Receipt or Bill; Overissue.**

Neither a duplicate nor any other document of title purporting to cover goods already represented by an outstanding document of the same issuer confers any right in the goods, except as provided in the case of bills in a set, overissue of documents for fungible goods and substitutes for lost, stolen or destroyed documents. But the issuer is liable for damages caused by his overissue or failure to identify a duplicate document as such by conspicuous notation on its face.

§ 7—403. **Obligation of Warehouseman or Carrier to Deliver; Excuse.**

(1) The bailee must deliver the goods to a person entitled under the document who complies with subsections (2) and (3), unless and to the extent that the bailee establishes any of the following:

  (a) delivery of the goods to a person whose receipt was rightful as against the claimant;

  (b) damage to or delay, loss or destruction of the goods for which the bailee is not liable [, but the burden of establishing negligence in such cases is on the person entitled under the document];

Note: *The brackets in (1)(b) indicate that State enactments may differ on this point without serious damage to the principle of uniformity.*

  (c) previous sale or other disposition of the goods in lawful enforcement of a lien or on warehouseman's lawful termination of storage;

  (d) the exercise by a seller of his right to stop delivery pursuant to the provisions of the Article on Sales (Section 2—705);

  (e) a diversion, reconsignment or other disposition pursuant to the provisions of this Article (Section 7—303) or tariff regulating such right;

  (f) release, satisfaction or any other fact affording a personal defense against the claimant;

  (g) any other lawful excuse.

(2) A person claiming goods covered by a document of title must satisfy the bailee's lien where the bailee so requests or where the bailee is prohibited by law from delivering the goods until the charges are paid.

(3) Unless the person claiming is one against whom the document confers no right under Sec. 7—503(1), he must surrender for cancellation or notation of partial deliveries any outstanding negotiable document covering the goods, and the bailee must cancel the document or conspicuously note the partial delivery thereon or be liable to any person to whom the document is duly negotiated.

(4) ''Person entitled under the document'' means holder in the case of a negotiable document, or the person to whom delivery is to be made by the terms of or pursuant to written instructions under a nonnegotiable document.

§ 7—404. **No Liability for Good Faith Delivery Pursuant to Receipt or Bill.**

A bailee who in good faith including observance of reasonable commercial standards has received goods and delivered or otherwise disposed of them according to the terms of the document of title or pursuant to this Article is not liable therefor. This rule applies even though the person from whom he received the goods had no authority to procure the document or to dispose of the goods and even though the person to whom he delivered the goods had no authority to receive them.

Part 5 Warehouse Receipts and Bills of Lading: Negotiation and Transfer

§ 7—501. **Form of Negotiation and Requirements of ''Due Negotiation''.**

(1) A negotiable document of title running to the order of a named person is negotiated by his indorsement and delivery. After his indorsement in blank or to bearer any person can negotiate it by delivery alone.

(2)(a) A negotiable document of title is also negotiated by delivery alone when by its original terms it runs to bearer.

(b) When a document running to the order of a named person is delivered to him the effect is the same as if the document had been negotiated.

(3) Negotiation of a negotiable document of title after it has been indorsed to a specified person requires indorsement by the special indorsee as well as delivery.

(4) A negotiable document of title is ''duly negotiated'' when it is negotiated in the manner stated in this section to a holder who purchases it in good faith without notice of any defense against or claim to it on the part of any person and for value, unless it is established that the negotiation is not in the regular course of business or financing or involves receiving the document in settlement or payment of a money obligation.

(5) Indorsement of a nonnegotiable document neither makes it negotiable nor adds to the transferee's rights.

(6) The naming in a negotiable bill of a person to be notified of the arrival of the goods does not limit the negotiability of the bill nor constitute notice to a purchaser thereof of any interest of such person in the goods.

§ 7—502. Rights Acquired by Due Negotiation.

(1) Subject to the following section and to the provisions of Section 7—205 on fungible goods, a holder to whom a negotiable document of title has been duly negotiated acquires thereby:

(a) title to the document;

(b) title to the goods;

(c) all rights accruing under the law of agency or estoppel, including rights to goods delivered to the bailee after the document was issued; and

(d) the direct obligation of the issuer to hold or deliver the goods according to the terms of the document free of any defense or claim by him except those arising under the terms of the document or under this Article. In the case of a delivery order the bailee's obligation accrues only upon acceptance and the obligation acquired by the holder is that the issuer and any indorser will procure the acceptance of the bailee.

(2) Subject to the following section, title and rights so acquired are not defeated by any stoppage of the goods represented by the document or by surrender of such goods by the bailee, and are not impaired even though the negotiation or any prior negotiation constituted a breach of duty or even though any person has been deprived of possession of the document by misrepresentation, fraud, accident, mistake, duress, loss, theft or conversion, or even though a previous sale or other transfer of the goods or document has been made to a third person.

§ 7—503. Document of Title to Goods Defeated in Certain Cases.

(1) A document of title confers no right in goods against a person who before issuance of the document had a legal interest or a perfected security interest in them and who neither

(a) delivered or entrusted them or any document of title covering them to the bailor or his nominee with actual or apparent authority to ship, store or sell or with power to obtain delivery under this Article (Section 7—403) or with power of disposition under this Act (Sections 2—403 and 9—307) or other statute or rule of law; nor

(b) acquiesced in the procurement by the bailor or his nominee of any document of title.

(2) Title to goods based upon an unaccepted delivery order is subject to the rights of anyone to whom a negotiable warehouse receipt or bill of lading covering the goods has been duly negotiated. Such a title may be defeated under the next section to the same extent as the rights of the issuer or a transferee from the issuer.

(3) Title to goods based upon a bill of lading issued to a freight forwarder is subject to the rights of anyone to whom a bill issued by the freight forwarder is duly negotiated; but delivery by the carrier in accordance with Part 4 of this Article pursuant to its own bill of lading discharges the carrier's obligation to deliver.

§ 7—504. Rights Acquired in the Absence of Due Negotiation; Effect of Diversion; Seller's Stoppage of Delivery.

(1) A transferee of a document, whether negotiable or nonnegotiable, to whom the document has been delivered but not duly negotiated, acquires the title and rights which his transferor had or had actual authority to convey.

(2) In the case of a nonnegotiable document, until but not after the bailee receives notification of the transfer, the rights of the transferee may be defeated

(a) by those creditors of the transferor who could treat the sale as void under Section 2—402; or

(b) by a buyer from the transferor in ordinary course of business if the bailee has delivered the goods to the buyer or received notification of his rights; or

(c) as against the bailee by good faith dealings of the bailee with the transferor.

(3) A diversion or other change of shipping instructions by the consignor in a nonnegotiable bill of lading which

causes the bailee not to deliver to the consignee defeats the consignee's title to the goods if they have been delivered to a buyer in ordinary course of business and in any event defeats the consignee's rights against the bailee.

(4) Delivery pursuant to a nonnegotiable document may be stopped by a seller under Section 2—705, and subject to the requirement of due notification there provided. A bailee honoring the seller's instructions is entitled to be indemnified by the seller against any resulting loss or expense.

§ 7—505. Indorser Not a Guarantor for Other Parties.

The indorsement of a document of title issued by a bailee does not make the indorser liable for any default by the bailee or by previous indorsers.

§ 7—506. Delivery Without Indorsement: Right to Compel Indorsement.

The transferee of a negotiable document of title has a specifically enforceable right to have his transferor supply any necessary indorsement but the transfer becomes a negotiation only as of the time the indorsement is supplied.

§ 7—507. Warranties on Negotiation or Transfer of Receipt or Bill.

Where a person negotiates or transfers a document of title for value otherwise than as a mere intermediary under the next following section, then unless otherwise agreed he warrants to his immediate purchaser only in addition to any warranty made in selling the goods

(a) that the document is genuine; and

(b) that he has no knowledge of any fact which would impair its validity or worth; and

(c) that his negotiation or transfer is rightful and fully effective with respect to the title to the document and the goods it represents.

§ 7—508. Warranties of Collecting Bank as to Documents.

A collecting bank or other intermediary known to be entrusted with documents on behalf of another or with collection of a draft or other claim against delivery of documents warrants by such delivery of the documents only its own good faith and authority. This rule applies even though the intermediary has purchased or made advances against the claim or draft to be collected.

§ 7—509. Receipt or Bill: When Adequate Compliance With Commercial Contract.

The question whether a document is adequate to fulfill the obligations of a contract for sale or the conditions of a credit is governed by the Articles on Sales (Article 2) and on Letters of Credit (Article 5).

Part 6 Warehouse Receipts and Bills of Lading: Miscellaneous Provisions

§ 7—601. Lost and Missing Documents.

(1) If a document has been lost, stolen or destroyed, a court may order delivery of the goods or issuance of a substitute document and the bailee may without liability to any person comply with such order. If the document was negotiable the claimant must post security approved by the court to indemnify any person who may suffer loss as a result of non-surrender of the document. If the document was not negotiable, such security may be required at the discretion of the court. The court may also in its discretion order payment of the bailee's reasonable costs and counsel fees.

(2) A bailee who without court order delivers goods to a person claiming under a missing negotiable document is liable to any person injured thereby, and if the delivery is not in good faith becomes liable for conversion. Delivery in good faith is not conversion if made in accordance with a filed classification or tariff or, where no classification or tariff is filed, if the claimant posts security with the bailee in an amount at least double the value of the goods at the time of posting to indemnify any person injured by the delivery who files a notice of claim within one year after the delivery.

§ 7—602. Attachment of Goods Covered by a Negotiable Document.

Except where the document was originally issued upon delivery of the goods by a person who had no power to dispose of them, no lien attaches by virtue of any judicial process to goods in the possession of a bailee for which a negotiable document of title is outstanding unless the document be first surrendered to the bailee or its negotiation enjoined, and the bailee shall not be compelled to deliver the goods pursuant to process until the document is surrendered to him or impounded by the court. One who purchases the document for value without notice of the process or injunction takes free of the lien imposed by judicial process.

§ 7—603. Conflicting Claims; Interpleader.

If more than one person claims title or possession of the goods, the bailee is excused from delivery until he has had a reasonable time to ascertain the validity of the adverse claims or to bring an action to compel all claimants to interplead and may compel such interpleader, either in defending an action for nondelivery of the goods, or by original action, whichever is appropriate.

Article 8
INVESTMENT SECURITIES

Part 1 Short Title and General Matters

§ 8—101. Short Title.

This Article shall be known and may be cited as Uniform Commercial Code—Investment Securities.

§ 8—102. **Definitions and Index of Definitions.**

(1) In this Article, unless the context otherwise requires:

(a) A "certificated security" is a share, participation, or other interest in property of or an enterprise of the issuer or an obligation of the issuer which is

(i) represented by an instrument issued in bearer or registered form;

(ii) of a type commonly dealt in on securities exchanges or markets or commonly recognized in any area in which it is issued or dealt in as a medium for investment; and

(iii) either one of a class or series or by its terms divisible into a class or series of shares, participations, interests, or obligations.

(b) An "uncertificated security" is a share, participation, or other interest in property or an enterprise of the issuer or an obligation of the issuer which is

(i) not represented by an instrument and the transfer of which is registered upon books maintained for that purpose by or on behalf of the issuer;

(ii) of a type commonly dealt in on securities exchanges or markets; and

(iii) either one of a class or series or by its terms divisible into a class or series of shares, participations, interests, or obligations.

(c) A "security" is either a certificated or an uncertificated security. If a security is certificated, the terms "security" and "certificated security" may mean either the intangible interest, the instrument representing that interest, or both, as the context requires. A writing that is a certificated security is governed by this Article and not by Article 3, even though it also meets the requirements of that Article. This Article does not apply to money. If a certificated security has been retained by or surrendered to the issuer or its transfer agent for reasons other than registration of transfer, other temporary purpose, payment, exchange, or acquisition by the issuer, that security shall be treated as an uncertificated security for purposes of this Article.

(d) A certificated security is in "registered form" if

(i) it specifies a person entitled to the security or the rights it represents; and

(ii) its transfer may be registered upon books maintained for that purpose by or on behalf of the issuer, or the security so states.

(e) A certificated security is in "bearer form" if it runs to bearer according to its terms and not by reason of any indorsement.

(2) A "subsequent purchaser" is a person who takes other than by original issue.

(3) A "clearing corporation" is a corporation registered as a "clearing agency" under the federal securities laws or a corporation:

(a) at least 90 percent of whose capital stock is held by or for one or more organizations, none of which, other than a national securities exchange or association, holds in excess of 20 percent of the capital stock of the corporation, and each of which is

(i) subject to supervision or regulation pursuant to the provisions of federal or state banking laws or state insurance laws,

(ii) a broker or dealer or investment company registered under the federal securities laws, or

(iii) a national securities exchange or association registered under the federal securities laws; and

(b) any remaining capital stock of which is held by individuals who have purchased it at or prior to the time of their taking office as directors of the corporation and who have purchased only so much of the capital stock as is necessary to permit them to qualify as directors.

(4) A "custodian bank" is a bank or trust company that is supervised and examined by state or federal authority having supervision over banks and is acting as custodian for a clearing corporation.

(5) Other definitions applying to this Article or to specified Parts thereof and the sections in which they appear are:

"Adverse claim". Section 8—302.
"Bona fide purchaser". Section 8—302.
"Broker". Section 8—303.
"Debtor". Section 9—105.
"Financial intermediary". Section 8—313.
"Guarantee of the signature". Section 8—402.
"Initial transaction statement". Section 8—408.
"Instruction". Section 8—308.
"Intermediary bank". Section 4—105.
"Issuer". Section 8—201.
"Overissue". Section 8—104.
"Secured Party". Section 9—105.
"Security Agreement". Section 9—105.

(6) In addition, Article 1 contains general definitions and principles of construction and interpretation applicable throughout this Article.

§ 8—103. **Issuer's Lien.**

A lien upon a security in favor of an issuer thereof is valid against a purchaser only if:

(a) the security is certificated and the right of the issuer to the lien is noted conspicuously thereon; or

(b) the security is uncertificated and a notation of the right of the issuer to the lien is contained in the initial transaction statement sent to the purchaser or, if his interest is transferred to him other than by registration of transfer, pledge, or release, the initial transaction statement sent to the registered owner or the registered pledgee.

§ 8—104. Effect of Overissue; ''Overissue''.

(1) The provisions of this Article which validate a security or compel its issue or reissue do not apply to the extent that validation, issue, or reissue would result in overissue; but if:

(a) an identical security which does not constitute an overissue is reasonably available for purchase, the person entitled to issue or validation may compel the issuer to purchase the security for him and either to deliver a certificated security or to register the transfer of an uncertificated security to him, against surrender of any certificated security he holds; or

(b) a security is not so available for purchase, the person entitled to issue or validation may recover from the issuer the price he or the last purchaser for value paid for it with interest from the date of his demand.

(2) ''Overissue'' means the issue of securities in excess of the amount the issuer has corporate power to issue.

§ 8—105. Certificated Securities Negotiable; Statements and Instructions Not Negotiable; Presumptions.

(1) Certificated securities governed by this Article are negotiable instruments.

(2) Statements (Section 8—408), notices, or the like, sent by the issuer of uncertificated securities and instructions (Section 8—308) are neither negotiable instruments nor certificated securities.

(3) In any action on a security:

(a) unless specifically denied in the pleadings, each signature on a certificated security, in a necessary indorsement, on an initial transaction statement, or on an instruction, is admitted;

(b) if the effectiveness of a signature is put in issue, the burden of establishing it is on the party claiming under the signature, but the signature is presumed to be genuine or authorized;

(c) if signatures on a certificated security are admitted or established, production of the security entitles a holder to recover on it unless the defendant establishes a defense or a defect going to the validity of the security;

(d) if signatures on an initial transaction statement are admitted or established, the facts stated in the statement are presumed to be true as of the time of its issuance; and

(e) after it is shown that a defense or defect exists, the plaintiff has the burden of establishing that he or some person under whom he claims is a person against whom the defense or defect is ineffective (Section 8—202).

§ 8—106. Applicability.

The law (including the conflict of laws rules) of the jurisdiction of organization of the issuer governs the validity of a security, the effectiveness of registration by the issuer, and the rights and duties of the issuer with respect to:

(a) registration of transfer of a certificated security;

(b) registration of transfer, pledge, or release of an uncertificated security; and

(c) sending of statements of uncertificated securities.

§ 8—107. Securities Transferable; Action for Price.

(1) Unless otherwise agreed and subject to any applicable law or regulation respecting short sales, a person obligated to transfer securities may transfer any certificated security of the specified issue in bearer form or registered in the name of the transferee, or indorsed to him or in blank, or he may transfer an equivalent uncertificated security to the transferee or a person designated by the transferee.

(2) If the buyer fails to pay the price as it comes due under a contract of sale, the seller may recover the price of:

(a) certificated securities accepted by the buyer;

(b) uncertificated securities that have been transferred to the buyer or a person designated by the buyer; and

(c) other securities if efforts at their resale would be unduly burdensome or if there is no readily available market for their resale.

§ 8—108. Registration of Pledge and Release of Uncertificated Securities.

A security interest in an uncertificated security may be evidenced by the registration of pledge to the secured party or a person designated by him. There can be no more than one registered pledge of an uncertificated security at any time. The registered owner of an uncertificated security is the person in whose name the security is registered, even if the security is subject to a registered pledge. The rights of a registered pledgee of an uncertificated security under this Article are terminated by the registration of release.

Part 2 Issue—Issuer

§ 8—201. ''Issuer.''

(1) With respect to obligations on or defenses to a security, ''issuer'' includes a person who:

(a) places or authorizes the placing of his name on a certificated security (otherwise than as authenticating trustee, registrar, transfer agent, or the like) to evidence that it represents a share, participation, or other interest in his property or in an enterprise, or to evidence his duty to perform an obligation represented by the certificated security;

    (b) creates shares, participations, or other interests in his property or in an enterprise or undertakes obligations, which shares, participations, interests, or obligations are uncertificated securities;

    (c) directly or indirectly creates fractional interests in his rights or property, which fractional interests are represented by certificated securities; or

    (d) becomes responsible for or in place of any other person described as an issuer in this section.

(2) With respect to obligations on or defenses to a security, a guarantor is an issuer to the extent of his guaranty, whether or not his obligation is noted on a certificated security or on statements of uncertificated securities sent pursuant to Section 8—408.

(3) With respect to registration of transfer, pledge, or release (Part 4 of this Article), ''issuer'' means a person on whose behalf transfer books are maintained.

§ 8—202. Issuer's Responsibility and Defenses; Notice of Defect or Defense.

(1) Even against a purchaser for value and without notice, the terms of a security include:

    (a) if the security is certificated, those stated on the security;

    (b) if the security is uncertificated, those contained in the initial transaction statement sent to such purchaser or, if his interest is transferred to him other than by registration of transfer, pledge, or release, the initial transaction statement sent to the registered owner or registered pledgee; and

    (c) those made part of the security by reference, on the certificated security or in the initial transaction statement, to another instrument, indenture, or document or to a constitution, statute, ordinance, rule, regulation, order or the like, to the extent that the terms referred to do not conflict with the terms stated on the certificated security or contained in the statement. A reference under this paragraph does not of itself charge a purchaser for value with notice of a defect going to the validity of the security, even though the certificated security or statement expressly states that a person accepting it admits notice.

(2) A certificated security in the hands of a purchaser for value or an uncertificated security as to which an initial transaction statement has been sent to a purchaser for value, other than a security issued by a government or governmental agency or unit, even though issued with a defect going to its validity, is valid with respect to the purchaser if he is without notice of the particular defect unless the defect involves a violation of constitutional provisions, in which case the security is valid with respect to a subsequent purchaser for value and without notice of the defect. This subsection applies to an issuer that is a government or governmental agency or unit only if either there has been substantial compliance with the legal requirements governing the issue or the issuer has received a substantial consideration for the issue as a whole or for the particular security and a stated purpose of the issue is one for which the issuer has power to borrow money or issue the security.

(3) Except as provided in the case of certain unauthorized signatures (Section 8—205), lack of genuineness of a certificated security or an initial transaction statement is a complete defense, even against a purchaser for value and without notice.

(4) All other defenses of the issuer of a certificated or uncertificated security, including nondelivery and conditional delivery of a certificated security, are ineffective against a purchaser for value who has taken without notice of the particular defense.

(5) Nothing in this section shall be construed to affect the right of a party to a ''when, as and if issued'' or a ''when distributed'' contract to cancel the contract in the event of a material change in the character of the security that is the subject of the contract or in the plan or arrangement pursuant to which the security is to be issued or distributed.

§ 8—203. Staleness as Notice of Defects or Defenses.

(1) After an act or event creating a right to immediate performance of the principal obligation represented by a certificated security or that sets a date on or after which the security is to be presented or surrendered for redemption or exchange, a purchaser is charged with notice of any defect in its issue or defense of the issuer if:

    (a) the act or event is one requiring the payment of money, the delivery of certificated securities, the registration of transfer of uncertificated securities, or any of these on presentation or surrender of the certificated security, the funds or securities are available on the date set for payment or exchange, and he takes the security more than one year after that date; and

    (b) the act or event is not covered by paragraph (a) and he takes the security more than 2 years after the date set for surrender or presentation or the date on which performance became due.

(2) A call that has been revoked is not within subsection (1).

§ 8—204. Effect of Issuer's Restrictions on Transfer.

A restriction on transfer of a security imposed by the issuer, even if otherwise lawful, is ineffective against any person without actual knowledge of it unless:

(a) the security is certificated and the restriction is noted conspicuously thereon; or

(b) the security is uncertificated and a notation of the restriction is contained in the initial transaction statement sent to the person or, if his interest is transferred to him other than by registration of transfer, pledge, or release, the initial transaction statement sent to the registered owner or the registered pledgee.

§ 8—205. Effect of Unauthorized Signature on Certificated Security or Initial Transaction Statement.

An unauthorized signature placed on a certificated security prior to or in the course of issue or placed on an initial transaction statement is ineffective, but the signature is effective in favor of a purchaser for value of the certificated security or a purchaser for value of an uncertificated security to whom the initial transaction statement has been sent, if the purchaser is without notice of the lack of authority and the signing has been done by:

(a) an authenticating trustee, registrar, transfer agent, or other person entrusted by the issuer with the signing of the security, of similar securities, or of initial transaction statements or the immediate preparation for signing of any of them; or

(b) an employee of the issuer, or of any of the foregoing, entrusted with responsible handling of the security or initial transaction statement.

§ 8—206. Completion or Alteration of Certificated Security or Initial Transaction Statement.

(1) If a certificated security contains the signatures necessary to its issue or transfer but is incomplete in any other respect:

(a) any person may complete it by filling in the blanks as authorized; and

(b) even though the blanks are incorrectly filled in, the security as completed is enforceable by a purchaser who took it for value and without notice of the incorrectness.

(2) A complete certificated security that has been improperly altered, even though fraudulently, remains enforceable, but only according to its original terms.

(3) If an initial transaction statement contains the signatures necessary to its validity, but is incomplete in any other respect:

(a) any person may complete it by filling in the blanks as authorized; and

(b) even though the blanks are incorrectly filled in, the statement as completed is effective in favor of the person to whom it is sent if he purchased the security referred to therein for value and without notice of the incorrectness.

(4) A complete initial transaction statement that has been improperly altered, even though fraudulently, is effective

in favor of a purchaser to whom it has been sent, but only according to its original terms.

§ 8—207. Rights and Duties of Issuer With Respect to Registered Owners and Registered Pledgees.

(1) Prior to due presentment for registration of transfer of a certificated security in registered form, the issuer or indenture trustee may treat the registered owner as the person exclusively entitled to vote, to receive notifications, and otherwise to exercise all the rights and powers of an owner.

(2) Subject to the provisions of subsections (3), (4), and (6), the issuer or indenture trustee may treat the registered owner of an uncertificated security as the person exclusively entitled to vote, to receive notifications, and otherwise to exercise all the rights and powers of an owner.

(3) The registered owner of an uncertificated security that is subject to a registered pledge is not entitled to registration of transfer prior to the due presentment to the issuer of a release instruction. The exercise of conversion rights with respect to a convertible uncertificated security is a transfer within the meaning of this section.

(4) Upon due presentment of a transfer instruction from the registered pledgee of an uncertificated security, the issuer shall:

(a) register the transfer of the security to the new owner free of pledge, if the instruction specifies a new owner (who may be the registered pledgee) and does not specify a pledgee;

(b) register the transfer of the security to the new owner subject to the interest of the existing pledgee, if the instruction specifies a new owner and the existing pledgee; or

(c) register the release of the security from the existing pledge and register the pledge of the security to the other pledgee, if the instruction specifies the existing owner and another pledgee.

(5) Continuity of perfection of a security interest is not broken by registration of transfer under subsection (4)(b) or by registration of release and pledge under subsection (4)(c), if the security interest is assigned.

(6) If an uncertificated security is subject to a registered pledge:

(a) any uncertificated securities issued in exchange for or distributed with respect to the pledged security shall be registered subject to the pledge;

(b) any certificated securities issued in exchange for or distributed with respect to the pledged security shall be delivered to the registered pledgee; and

(c) any money paid in exchange for or in redemption of part or all of the security shall be paid to the registered pledgee.

(7) Nothing in this Article shall be construed to affect the liability of the registered owner of a security for calls, assessments, or the like.

§ 8—208. Effect of Signature of Authenticating Trustee, Registrar, or Transfer Agent.

(1) A person placing his signature upon a certificated security or an initial transaction statement as authenticating trustee, registrar, transfer agent, or the like, warrants to a purchaser for value of the certificated security or a purchaser for value of an uncertificated security to whom the initial transaction statement has been sent, if the purchaser is without notice of the particular defect, that:

(a) the certificated security or initial transaction statement is genuine;

(b) his own participation in the issue or registration of the transfer, pledge, or release of the security is within his capacity and within the scope of the authority received by him from the issuer; and

(c) he has reasonable grounds to believe the security is in the form and within the amount the issuer is authorized to issue.

(2) Unless otherwise agreed, a person by so placing his signature does not assume responsibility for the validity of the security in other respects.

Part 3 Transfer

§ 8—301. Rights Acquired by Purchaser.

(1) Upon transfer of a security to a purchaser (Section 8—313), the purchaser acquires the rights in the security which his transferor had or had actual authority to convey unless the purchaser's rights are limited by Section 8—302(4).

(2) A transferee of a limited interest acquires rights only to the extent of the interest transferred. The creation or release of a security interest in a security is the transfer of a limited interest in that security.

§ 8—302. "Bona Fide Purchaser"; "Adverse Claim"; Title Acquired by Bona Fide Purchaser.

(1) A "bona fide purchaser" is a purchaser for value in good faith and without notice of any adverse claim:

(a) who takes delivery of a certificated security in bearer form or in registered form, issued or indorsed to him or in blank;

(b) to whom the transfer, pledge, or release of an uncertificated security is registered on the books of the issuer; or

(c) to whom a security is transferred under the provisions of paragraph (c), (d)(i), or (g) of Section 8—313(1).

(2) "Adverse claim" includes a claim that a transfer was

or would be wrongful or that a particular adverse person is the owner of or has an interest in the security.

(3) A bona fide purchaser in addition to acquiring the rights of a purchaser (Section 8—301) also acquires his interest in the security free of any adverse claim.

(4) Notwithstanding Section 8—301(1), the transferee of a particular certificated security who has been a party to any fraud or illegality affecting the security, or who as a prior holder of that certificated security had notice of an adverse claim, cannot improve his position by taking from a bona fide purchaser.

§ 8—303. "Broker".

"Broker" means a person engaged for all or part of his time in the business of buying and selling securities, who in the transaction concerned acts for, buys a security from, or sells a security to, a customer. Nothing in this Article determines the capacity in which a person acts for purposes of any other statute or rule to which the person is subject.

§ 8—304. Notice to Purchaser of Adverse Claims.

(1) A purchaser (including a broker for the seller or buyer, but excluding an intermediary bank) of a certificated security is charged with notice of adverse claims if:

(a) the security, whether in bearer or registered form, has been indorsed "for collection" or "for surrender" or for some other purpose not involving transfer; or

(b) the security is in bearer form and has on it an unambiguous statement that it is the property of a person other than the transferor. The mere writing of a name on a security is not such a statement.

(2) A purchaser (including a broker for the seller or buyer, but excluding an intermediary bank) to whom the transfer, pledge, or release of an uncertificated security is registered is charged with notice of adverse claims as to which the issuer has a duty under Section 8—403(4) at the time of registration and which are noted in the initial transaction statement sent to the purchaser or, if his interest is transferred to him other than by registration of transfer, pledge, or release, the initial transaction statement sent to the registered owner or the registered pledgee.

(3) The fact that the purchaser (including a broker for the seller or buyer) of a certificated or uncertificated security has notice that the security is held for a third person or is registered in the name of or indorsed by a fiduciary does not create a duty of inquiry into the rightfulness of the transfer or constitute constructive notice of adverse claims. However, if the purchaser (excluding an intermediary bank) has knowledge that the proceeds are being used or that the transaction is for the individual benefit of the fiduciary or otherwise in breach of duty, the purchaser is charged with notice of adverse claims.

§ 8—305. Staleness as Notice of Adverse Claims.

An act or event that creates a right to immediate performance of the principal obligation represented by a certificated security or sets a date on or after which a certificated security is to be presented or surrendered for redemption or exchange does not itself constitute any notice of adverse claims except in the case of a transfer:

(a) after one year from any date set for presentment or surrender for redemption or exchange; or

(b) after 6 months from any date set for payment of money against presentation or surrender of the security if funds are available for payment on that date.

§ 8—306. Warranties on Presentment and Transfer of Certificated Securities; Warranties of Originators of Instructions.

(1) A person who presents a certificated security for registration of transfer or for payment or exchange warrants to the issuer that he is entitled to the registration, payment, or exchange. But, a purchaser for value and without notice of adverse claims who receives a new, reissued, or re-registered certificated security on registration of transfer or receives an initial transaction statement confirming the registration of transfer of an equivalent uncertificated security to him warrants only that he has no knowledge of any unauthorized signature (Section 8—311) in a necessary indorsement.

(2) A person by transferring a certificated security to a purchaser for value warrants only that:

(a) his transfer is effective and rightful;

(b) the security is genuine and has not been materially altered; and

(c) he knows of no fact which might impair the validity of the security.

(3) If a certificated security is delivered by an intermediary known to be entrusted with delivery of the security on behalf of another or with collection of a draft or other claim against delivery, the intermediary by delivery warrants only his own good faith and authority, even though he has purchased or made advances against the claim to be collected against the delivery.

(4) A pledgee or other holder for security who redelivers a certificated security received, or after payment and on order of the debtor delivers that security to a third person, makes only the warranties of an intermediary under subsection (3).

(5) A person who originates an instruction warrants to the issuer that:

(a) he is an appropriate person to originate the instruction; and

(b) at the time the instruction is presented to the issuer he will be entitled to the registration of transfer, pledge, or release.

(6) A person who originates an instruction warrants to any person specially guaranteeing his signature (subsection 8—312(3)) that:

(a) he is an appropriate person to originate the instruction; and

(b) at the time the instruction is presented to the issuer

(i) he will be entitled to the registration of transfer, pledge, or release; and

(ii) the transfer, pledge, or release requested in the instruction will be registered by the issuer free from all liens, security interests, restrictions, and claims other than those specified in the instruction.

(7) A person who originates an instruction warrants to a purchaser for value and to any person guaranteeing the instruction (Section 8—312(6)) that:

(a) he is an appropriate person to originate the instruction;

(b) the uncertificated security referred to therein is valid; and

(c) at the time the instruction is presented to the issuer

(i) the transferor will be entitled to the registration of transfer, pledge, or release;

(ii) the transfer, pledge, or release requested in the instruction will be registered by the issuer free from all liens, security interests, restrictions, and claims other than those specified in the instruction; and

(iii) the requested transfer, pledge, or release will be rightful.

(8) If a secured party is the registered pledgee or the registered owner of an uncertificated security, a person who originates an instruction of release or transfer to the debtor or, after payment and on order of the debtor, a transfer instruction to a third person, warrants to the debtor or the third person only that he is an appropriate person to originate the instruction and, at the time the instruction is presented to the issuer, the transferor will be entitled to the registration of release or transfer. If a transfer instruction to a third person who is a purchaser for value is originated on order of the debtor, the debtor makes to the purchaser the warranties of paragraphs (b), (c)(ii) and (c)(iii) of subsection (7).

(9) A person who transfers an uncertificated security to a purchaser for value and does not originate an instruction in connection with the transfer warrants only that:

(a) his transfer is effective and rightful; and

(b) the uncertificated security is valid.

(10) A broker gives to his customer and to the issuer and a purchaser the applicable warranties provided in this section and has the rights and privileges of a purchaser under this section. The warranties of and in favor of the broker,

acting as an agent are in addition to applicable warranties given by and in favor of his customer.

§ 8—307. Effect of Delivery Without Indorsement; Right to Compel Indorsement.

If a certificated security in registered form has been delivered to a purchaser without a necessary indorsement he may become a bona fide purchaser only as of the time the indorsement is supplied; but against the transferor, the transfer is complete upon delivery and the purchaser has a specifically enforceable right to have any necessary indorsement supplied.

§ 8—308. Indorsements; Instructions.

(1) An indorsement of a certificated security in registered form is made when an appropriate person signs on it or on a separate document an assignment or transfer of the security or a power to assign or transfer it or his signature is written without more upon the back of the security.

(2) An indorsement may be in blank or special. An indorsement in blank includes an indorsement to bearer. A special indorsement specifies to whom the security is to be transferred, or who has power to transfer it. A holder may convert a blank indorsement into a special indorsement.

(3) An indorsement purporting to be only of part of a certificated security representing units intended by the issuer to be separately transferable is effective to the extent of the indorsement.

(4) An "instruction" is an order to the issuer of an uncertificated security requesting that the transfer, pledge, or release from pledge of the uncertificated security specified therein be registered.

(5) An instruction originated by an appropriate person is:

(a) a writing signed by an appropriate person; or

(b) a communication to the issuer in any form agreed upon in a writing signed by the issuer and an appropriate person.

If an instruction has been originated by an appropriate person but is incomplete in any other respect, any person may complete it as authorized and the issuer may rely on it as completed even though it has been completed incorrectly.

(6) "An appropriate person" in subsection (1) means the person specified by the certificated security or by special indorsement to be entitled to the security.

(7) "An appropriate person" in subsection (5) means:

(a) for an instruction to transfer or pledge an uncertificated security which is then not subject to a registered pledge, the registered owner; or

(b) for an instruction to transfer or release an uncertificated security which is then subject to a registered pledge, the registered pledgee.

(8) In addition to the persons designated in subsections (6) and (7), "an appropriate person" in subsections (1) and (5) includes:

(a) if the person designated is described as a fiduciary but is no longer serving in the described capacity, either that person or his successor;

(b) if the persons designated are described as more than one person as fiduciaries and one or more are no longer serving in the described capacity, the remaining fiduciary or fiduciaries, whether or not a successor has been appointed or qualified;

(c) if the person designated is an individual and is without capacity to act by virtue of death, incompetence, infancy, or otherwise, his executor, administrator, guardian, or like fiduciary;

(d) if the persons designated are described as more than one person as tenants by the entirety or with right of survivorship and by reason of death all cannot sign, the survivor or survivors;

(e) a person having power to sign under applicable law or controlling instrument; and

(f) to the extent that the person designated or any of the foregoing persons may act through an agent, his authorized agent.

(9) Unless otherwise agreed, the indorser of a certificated security by his indorsement or the originator of an instruction by his origination assumes no obligation that the security will be honored by the issuer but only the obligations provided in Section 8—306.

(10) Whether the person signing is appropriate is determined as of the date of signing and an indorsement made by or an instruction originated by him does not become unauthorized for the purposes of this Article by virtue of any subsequent change of circumstances.

(11) Failure of a fiduciary to comply with a controlling instrument or with the law of the state having jurisdiction of the fiduciary relationship, including any law requiring the fiduciary to obtain court approval of the transfer, pledge, or release, does not render his indorsement or an instruction originated by him unauthorized for the purposes of this Article.

§ 8—309. Effect of Indorsement Without Delivery.

An indorsement of a certificated security, whether special or in blank, does not constitute a transfer until delivery of the certificated security on which it appears or, if the indorsement is on a separate document, until delivery of both the document and the certificated security.

§ 8—310. Indorsement of Certificated Security in Bearer Form.

An indorsement of a certificated security in bearer form may give notice of adverse claims (Section 8—304) but does not otherwise affect any right to registration the holder possesses.

§ 8—311. **Effect of Unauthorized Indorsement or Instruction.**

Unless the owner or pledgee has ratified an unauthorized indorsement or instruction or is otherwise precluded from asserting its ineffectiveness:

(a) he may assert its ineffectiveness against the issuer or any purchaser, other than a purchaser for value and without notice of adverse claims, who has in good faith received a new, reissued, or re-registered certificated security on registration of transfer or received an initial transaction statement confirming the registration of transfer, pledge, or release of an equivalent uncertificated security to him; and

(b) an issuer who registers the transfer of a certificated security upon the unauthorized indorsement or who registers the transfer, pledge, or release of an uncertificated security upon the unauthorized instruction is subject to liability for improper registration (Section 8—404).

§ 8—312. **Effect of Guaranteeing Signature, Indorsement or Instruction.**

(1) Any person guaranteeing a signature of an indorser of a certificated security warrants that at the time of signing:

　(a) the signature was genuine;

　(b) the signer was an appropriate person to indorse (Section 8—308); and

　(c) the signer had legal capacity to sign.

(2) Any person guaranteeing a signature of the originator of an instruction warrants that at the time of signing:

　(a) the signature was genuine;

　(b) the signer was an appropriate person to originate the instruction (Section 8—308) if the person specified in the instruction as the registered owner or registered pledgee of the uncertificated security was, in fact, the registered owner or registered pledgee of the security, as to which fact the signature guarantor makes no warranty;

　(c) the signer had legal capacity to sign; and

　(d) the taxpayer identification number, if any, appearing on the instruction as that of the registered owner or registered pledgee was the taxpayer identification number of the signer or of the owner or pledgee for whom the signer was acting.

(3) Any person specially guaranteeing the signature of the originator of an instruction makes not only the warranties of a signature guarantor (subsection (2)) but also warrants that at the time the instruction is presented to the issuer:

　(a) the person specified in the instruction as the registered owner or registered pledgee of the uncertificated security will be the registered owner or registered pledgee; and

(b) the transfer, pledge, or release of the uncertificated security requested in the instruction will be registered by the issuer free from all liens, security interests, restrictions, and claims other than those specified in the instruction.

(4) The guarantor under subsections (1) and (2) or the special guarantor under subsection (3) does not otherwise warrant the rightfulness of the particular transfer, pledge, or release.

(5) Any person guaranteeing an indorsement of a certificated security makes not only the warranties of a signature guarantor under subsection (1) but also warrants the rightfulness of the particular transfer in all respects.

(6) Any person guaranteeing an instruction requesting the transfer, pledge, or release of an uncertificated security makes not only the warranties of a special signature guarantor under subsection (3) but also warrants the rightfulness of the particular transfer, pledge, or release in all respects.

(7) No issuer may require a special guarantee of signature (subsection (3)), a guarantee of indorsement (subsection (5)), or a guarantee of instruction (subsection (6)) as a condition to registration of transfer, pledge, or release.

(8) The foregoing warranties are made to any person taking or dealing with the security in reliance on the guarantee, and the guarantor is liable to the person for any loss resulting from breach of the warranties.

§ 8—313. **When Transfer to Purchaser Occurs; Financial Intermediary as Bona Fide Purchaser; "Financial Intermediary".**

(1) Transfer of a security or a limited interest (including a security interest) therein to a purchaser occurs only:

　(a) at the time he or a person designated by him acquires possession of a certificated security;

　(b) at the time the transfer, pledge, or release of an uncertificated security is registered to him or a person designated by him;

　(c) at the time his financial intermediary acquires possession of a certificated security specially indorsed to or issued in the name of the purchaser;

　(d) at the time a financial intermediary, not a clearing corporation, sends him confirmation of the purchase and also by book entry or otherwise identifies as belonging to the purchaser

　　(i) a specific certificated security in the financial intermediary's possession;

　　(ii) a quantity of securities that constitute or are part of a fungible bulk of certificated securities in the financial intermediary's possession or of uncertificated securities registered in the name of the financial intermediary; or

(iii) a quantity of securities that constitute or are part of a fungible bulk of securities shown on the account of the financial intermediary on the books of another financial intermediary;

(e) with respect to an identified certificated security to be delivered while still in the possession of a third person, not a financial intermediary, at the time that person acknowledges that he holds for the purchaser;

(f) with respect to a specific uncertificated security the pledge or transfer of which has been registered to a third person, not a financial intermediary, at the time that person acknowledges that he holds for the purchaser;

(g) at the time appropriate entries to the account of the purchaser or a person designated by him on the books of a clearing corporation are made under Section 8—320;

(h) with respect to the transfer of a security interest where the debtor has signed a security agreement containing a description of the security, at the time a written notification, which, in the case of the creation of the security interest, is signed by the debtor (which may be a copy of the security agreement) or which, in the case of the release or assignment of the security interest created pursuant to this paragraph, is signed by the secured party, is received by

(i) a financial intermediary on whose books the interest of the transferor in the security appears;

(ii) a third person, not a financial intermediary, in possession of the security, if it is certificated;

(iii) a third person, not a financial intermediary, who is the registered owner of the security, if it is uncertificated and not subject to a registered pledge; or

(iv) a third person, not a financial intermediary, who is the registered pledgee of the security, if it is uncertificated and subject to a registered pledge;

(i) with respect to the transfer of a security interest where the transferor has signed a security agreement containing a description of the security, at the time new value is given by the secured party; or

(j) with respect to the transfer of a security interest where the secured party is a financial intermediary and the security has already been transferred to the financial intermediary under paragraphs (a), (b), (c), (d), or (g), at the time the transferor has signed a security agreement containing a description of the security and value is given by the secured party.

(2) The purchaser is the owner of a security held for him by a financial intermediary, but cannot be a bona fide purchaser of a security so held except in the circumstances specified in paragraphs (c), (d)(i), and (g) of subsection (1).

If a security so held is part of a fungible bulk, as in the circumstances specified in paragraphs (d)(ii) and (d)(iii) of subsection (1), the purchaser is the owner of a proportionate property interest in the fungible bulk.

(3) Notice of an adverse claim received by the financial intermediary or by the purchaser after the financial intermediary takes delivery of a certificated security as a holder for value or after the transfer, pledge, or release of an uncertificated security has been registered free of the claim to a financial intermediary who has given value is not effective either as to the financial intermediary or as to the purchaser. However, as between the financial intermediary and the purchaser the purchaser may demand transfer of an equivalent security as to which no notice of adverse claim has been received.

(4) A "financial intermediary" is a bank, broker, clearing corporation, or other person (or the nominee of any of them) which in the ordinary course of its business maintains security accounts for its customers and is acting in that capacity. A financial intermediary may have a security interest in securities held in account for its customer.

§ 8—314. **Duty to Transfer, When Completed.**

(1) Unless otherwise agreed, if a sale of a security is made on an exchange or otherwise through brokers:

(a) the selling customer fulfills his duty to transfer at the time he:

(i) places a certificated security in the possession of the selling broker or a person designated by the broker;

(ii) causes an uncertificated security to be registered in the name of the selling broker or a person designated by the broker;

(iii) if requested, causes an acknowledgment to be made to the selling broker that a certificated or uncertificated security is held for the broker; or

(iv) places in the possession of the selling broker or of a person designated by the broker a transfer instruction for an uncertificated security, providing the issuer does not refuse to register the requested transfer if the instruction is presented to the issuer for registration within 30 days thereafter; and

(b) the selling broker, including a correspondent broker acting for a selling customer, fulfills his duty to transfer at the time he:

(i) places a certificated security in the possession of the buying broker or a person designated by the buying broker;

(ii) causes an uncertificated security to be registered in the name of the buying broker or a person designated by the buying broker;

(iii) places in the possession of the buying broker

or of a person designated by the buying broker a transfer instruction for an uncertificated security, providing the issuer does not refuse to register the requested transfer if the instruction is presented to the issuer for registration within 30 days thereafter; or

(iv) effects clearance of the sale in accordance with the rules of the exchange on which the transaction took place.

(2) Except as provided in this section or unless otherwise agreed, a transferor's duty to transfer a security under a contract of purchase is not fulfilled until he:

(a) places a certificated security in form to be negotiated by the purchaser in the possession of the purchaser or of a person designated by the purchaser;

(b) causes an uncertificated security to be registered in the name of the purchaser or a person designated by the purchaser; or

(c) if the purchaser requests, causes an acknowledgment to be made to the purchaser that a certificated or uncertificated security is held for the purchaser.

(3) Unless made on an exchange, a sale to a broker purchasing for his own account is within subsection (2) and not within subsection (1).

§ 8—315. Action Against Transferee Based Upon Wrongful Transfer.

(1) Any person against whom the transfer of a security is wrongful for any reason, including his incapacity, as against anyone except a bona fide purchaser, may:

(a) reclaim possession of the certificated security wrongfully transferred;

(b) obtain possession of any new certificated security representing all or part of the same rights;

(c) compel the origination of an instruction to transfer to him or a person designated by him an uncertificated security constituting all or part of the same rights; or

(d) have damages.

(2) If the transfer is wrongful because of an unauthorized indorsement of a certificated security, the owner may also reclaim or obtain possession of the security or a new certificated security, even from a bona fide purchaser, if the ineffectiveness of the purported indorsement can be asserted against him under the provisions of this Article on unauthorized indorsements (Section 8—311).

(3) The right to obtain or reclaim possession of a certificated security or to compel the origination of a transfer instruction may be specifically enforced and the transfer of a certificated or uncertificated security enjoined and a certificated security impounded pending the litigation.

§ 8—316. Purchaser's Right to Requisites for Registration of Transfer, Pledge, or Release on Books.

Unless otherwise agreed, the transferor of a certificated security or the transferor, pledgor, or pledgee of an uncertificated security on due demand must supply his purchaser with any proof of his authority to transfer, pledge, or release or with any other requisite necessary to obtain registration of the transfer, pledge, or release of the security; but if the transfer, pledge, or release is not for value, a transferor, pledgor, or pledgee need not do so unless the purchaser furnishes the necessary expenses. Failure within a reasonable time to comply with a demand made gives the purchaser the right to reject or rescind the transfer, pledge, or release.

§ 8—317. Creditors' Rights.

(1) Subject to the exceptions in subsections (3) and (4), no attachment or levy upon a certificated security or any share or other interest represented thereby which is outstanding is valid until the security is actually seized by the officer making the attachment or levy, but a certificated security which has been surrendered to the issuer may be reached by a creditor by legal process at the issuer's chief executive office in the United States.

(2) An uncertificated security registered in the name of the debtor may not be reached by a creditor except by legal process at the issuer's chief executive office in the United States.

(3) The interest of a debtor in a certificated security that is in the possession of a secured party not a financial intermediary or in an uncertificated security registered in the name of a secured party not a financial intermediary (or in the name of a nominee of the secured party) may be reached by a creditor by legal process upon the secured party.

(4) The interest of a debtor in a certificated security that is in the possession of or registered in the name of a financial intermediary or in an uncertificated security registered in the name of a financial intermediary may be reached by a creditor by legal process upon the financial intermediary on whose books the interest of the debtor appears.

(5) Unless otherwise provided by law, a creditor's lien upon the interest of a debtor in a security obtained pursuant to subsection (3) or (4) is not a restraint on the transfer of the security, free of the lien, to a third party for new value; but in the event of a transfer, the lien applies to the proceeds of the transfer in the hands of the secured party or financial intermediary, subject to any claims having priority.

(6) A creditor whose debtor is the owner of a security is entitled to aid from courts of appropriate jurisdiction, by injunction or otherwise, in reaching the security or in satisfying the claim by means allowed at law or in equity in regard to property that cannot readily be reached by ordinary legal process.

§ 8—318. **No Conversion by Good Faith Conduct.**

An agent or bailee who in good faith (including observance of reasonable commercial standards if he is in the business of buying, selling, or otherwise dealing with securities) has received certificated securities and sold, pledged, or delivered them or has sold or caused the transfer or pledge of uncertificated securities over which he had control according to the instructions of his principal, is not liable for conversion or for participation in breach of fiduciary duty although the principal had no right so to deal with the securities.

§ 8—319. **Statute of Frauds.**

A contract for the sale of securities is not enforceable by way of action or defense unless:

(a) there is some writing signed by the party against whom enforcement is sought or by his authorized agent or broker, sufficient to indicate that a contract has been made for sale of a stated quantity of described securities at a defined or stated price;

(b) delivery of a certificated security or transfer instruction has been accepted, or transfer of an uncertificated security has been registered and the transferee has failed to send written objection to the issuer within 10 days after receipt of the initial transaction statement confirming the registration, or payment has been made, but the contract is enforceable under this provision only to the extent of the delivery, registration, or payment;

(c) within a reasonable time a writing in confirmation of the sale or purchase and sufficient against the sender under paragraph (a) has been received by the party against whom enforcement is sought and he has failed to send written objection to its contents within 10 days after its receipt; or

(d) the party against whom enforcement is sought admits in his pleading, testimony, or otherwise in court that a contract was made for the sale of a stated quantity of described securities at a defined or stated price.

§ 8—320. **Transfer or Pledge Within Central Depository System.**

(1) In addition to other methods, a transfer, pledge, or release of a security or any interest therein may be effected by the making of appropriate entries on the books of a clearing corporation reducing the account of the transferor, pledgor, or pledgee and increasing the account of the transferee, pledgee, or pledgor by the amount of the obligation or the number of shares or rights transferred, pledged, or released, if the security is shown on the account of a transferor, pledgor, or pledgee on the books of the clearing corporation; is subject to the control of the clearing corporation; and

    (a) if certificated,

        (i) is in the custody of the clearing corporation, another clearing corporation, a custodian bank, or a nominee of any of them; and

        (ii) is in bearer form or indorsed in blank by an appropriate person or registered in the name of the clearing corporation, a custodian bank, or a nominee of any of them; or

    (b) if uncertificated, is registered in the name of the clearing corporation, another clearing corporation, a custodian bank, or a nominee of any of them.

(2) Under this section entries may be made with respect to like securities or interests therein as a part of a fungible bulk and may refer merely to a quantity of a particular security without reference to the name of the registered owner, certificate or bond number, or the like, and, in appropriate cases, may be on a net basis taking into account other transfers, pledges, or releases of the same security.

(3) A transfer under this section is effective (Section 8—313) and the purchaser acquires the rights of the transferor (Section 8—301). A pledge or release under this section is the transfer of a limited interest. If a pledge or the creation of a security interest is intended, the security interest is perfected at the time when both value is given by the pledgee and the appropriate entries are made (Section 8—321). A transferee or pledgee under this section may be a bona fide purchaser (Section 8—302).

(4) A transfer or pledge under this section is not a registration of transfer under Part 4.

(5) That entries made on the books of the clearing corporation as provided in subsection (1) are not appropriate does not affect the validity or effect of the entries or the liabilities or obligations of the clearing corporation to any person adversely affected thereby.

§ 8—321. **Enforceability, Attachment, Perfection and Termination of Security Interests.**

(1) A security interest in a security is enforceable and can attach only if it is transferred to the secured party or a person designated by him pursuant to a provision of Section 8—313(1).

(2) A security interest so transferred pursuant to agreement by a transferor who has rights in the security to a transferee who has given value is a perfected security interest, but a security interest that has been transferred solely under paragraph (i) of Section 8—313(1) becomes unperfected after 21 days unless, within that time, the requirements for transfer under any other provision of Section 8—313(1) are satisfied.

(3) A security interest in a security is subject to the provisions of Article 9, but:

    (a) no filing is required to perfect the security interest; and

(b) no written security agreement signed by the debtor is necessary to make the security interest enforceable, except as provided in paragraph (h), (i), or (j) of Section 8—313(1). The secured party has the rights and duties provided under Section 9—207, to the extent they are applicable, whether or not the security is certificated, and, if certificated, whether or not it is in his possession.

(4) Unless otherwise agreed, a security interest in a security is terminated by transfer to the debtor or a person designated by him pursuant to a provision of Section 8—313(1). If a security is thus transferred, the security interest, if not terminated, becomes unperfected unless the security is certificated and is delivered to the debtor for the purpose of ultimate sale or exchange or presentation, collection, renewal, or registration of transfer. In that case, the security interest becomes unperfected after 21 days unless, within that time, the security (or securities for which it has been exchanged) is transferred to the secured party or a person designated by him pursuant to a provision of Section 8—313(1).

Part 4 Registration

§ 8—401. **Duty of Issuer to Register Transfer, Pledge, or Release.**

(1) If a certificated security in registered form is presented to the issuer with a request to register transfer or an instruction is presented to the issuer with a request to register transfer, pledge, or release, the issuer shall register the transfer, pledge, or release as requested if:

(a) the security is indorsed or the instruction was originated by the appropriate person or persons (Section 8—308);

(b) reasonable assurance is given that those indorsements or instructions are genuine and effective (Section 8—402);

(c) the issuer has no duty as to adverse claims or has discharged the duty (Section 8—403);

(d) any applicable law relating to the collection of taxes has been complied with; and

(e) the transfer, pledge, or release is in fact rightful or is to a bona fide purchaser.

(2) If an issuer is under a duty to register a transfer, pledge, or release of a security, the issuer is also liable to the person presenting a certificated security or an instruction for registration or his principal for loss resulting from any unreasonable delay in registration or from failure or refusal to register the transfer, pledge, or release.

§ 8—402. **Assurance that Indorsements and Instructions Are Effective.**

(1) The issuer may require the following assurance that each necessary indorsement of a certificated security or each instruction (Section 8—308) is genuine and effective:

(a) in all cases, a guarantee of the signature (Section 8—312(1) or (2)) of the person indorsing a certificated security or originating an instruction including, in the case of an instruction, a warranty of the taxpayer identification number or, in the absence thereof, other reasonable assurance of identity;

(b) if the indorsement is made or the instruction is originated by an agent, appropriate assurance of authority to sign;

(c) if the indorsement is made or the instruction is originated by a fiduciary, appropriate evidence of appointment or incumbency;

(d) if there is more than one fiduciary, reasonable assurance that all who are required to sign have done so; and

(e) if the indorsement is made or the instruction is originated by a person not covered by any of the foregoing, assurance appropriate to the case corresponding as nearly as may be to the foregoing.

(2) A "guarantee of the signature" in subsection (1) means a guarantee signed by or on behalf of a person reasonably believed by the issuer to be responsible. The issuer may adopt standards with respect to responsibility if they are not manifestly unreasonable.

(3) "Appropriate evidence of appointment or incumbency" in subsection (1) means:

(a) in the case of a fiduciary appointed or qualified by a court, a certificate issued by or under the direction or supervision of that court or an officer thereof and dated within 60 days before the date of presentation for transfer, pledge, or release; or

(b) in any other case, a copy of a document showing the appointment or a certificate issued by or on behalf of a person reasonably believed by the issuer to be responsible or, in the absence of that document or certificate, other evidence reasonably deemed by the issuer to be appropriate. The issuer may adopt standards with respect to the evidence if they are not manifestly unreasonable. The issuer is not charged with notice of the contents of any document obtained pursuant to this paragraph (b) except to the extent that the contents relate directly to the appointment or incumbency.

(4) The issuer may elect to require reasonable assurance beyond that specified in this section, but if it does so and, for a purpose other than that specified in subsection (3)(b), both requires and obtains a copy of a will, trust, indenture, articles of co-partnership, by-laws, or other controlling instrument, it is charged with notice of all matters contained therein affecting the transfer, pledge, or release.

§ 8—403. **Issuer's Duty as to Adverse Claims.**

(1) An issuer to whom a certificated security is presented for registration shall inquire into adverse claims if:

(a) a written notification of an adverse claim is received at a time and in a manner affording the issuer a reasonable opportunity to act on it prior to the issuance of a new, reissued, or re-registered certificated security, and the notification identifies the claimant, the registered owner, and the issue of which the security is a part, and provides an address for communications directed to the claimant; or

(b) the issuer is charged with notice of an adverse claim from a controlling instrument it has elected to require under Section 8—402(4).

(2) The issuer may discharge any duty of inquiry by any reasonable means, including notifying an adverse claimant by registered or certified mail at the address furnished by him or, if there be no such address, at his residence or regular place of business that the certificated security has been presented for registration of transfer by a named person, and that the transfer will be registered unless within 30 days from the date of mailing the notification, either:

(a) an appropriate restraining order, injunction, or other process issues from a court of competent jurisdiction; or

(b) there is filed with the issuer an indemnity bond, sufficient in the issuer's judgment to protect the issuer and any transfer agent, registrar, or other agent of the issuer involved from any loss it or they may suffer by complying with the adverse claim.

(3) Unless an issuer is charged with notice of an adverse claim from a controlling instrument which it has elected to require under Section 8—402(4) or receives notification of an adverse claim under subsection (1), if a certificated security presented for registration is indorsed by the appropriate person or persons the issuer is under no duty to inquire into adverse claims. In particular:

(a) an issuer registering a certificated security in the name of a person who is a fiduciary or who is described as a fiduciary is not bound to inquire into the existence, extent, or correct description of the fiduciary relationship; and thereafter the issuer may assume without inquiry that the newly registered owner continues to be the fiduciary until the issuer receives written notice that the fiduciary is no longer acting as such with respect to the particular security;

(b) an issuer registering transfer on an indorsement by a fiduciary is not bound to inquire whether the transfer is made in compliance with a controlling instrument or with the law of the state having jurisdiction of the fiduciary relationship, including any law requiring the fiduciary to obtain court approval of the transfer; and

(c) the issuer is not charged with notice of the contents of any court record or file or other recorded or unrecorded document even though the document is in its possession and even though the transfer is made on the indorsement of a fiduciary to the fiduciary himself or to his nominee.

(4) An issuer is under no duty as to adverse claims with respect to an uncertificated security except:

(a) claims embodied in a restraining order, injunction, or other legal process served upon the issuer if the process was served at a time and in a manner affording the issuer a reasonable opportunity to act on it in accordance with the requirements of subsection (5);

(b) claims of which the issuer has received a written notification from the registered owner or the registered pledgee if the notification was received at a time and in a manner affording the issuer a reasonable opportunity to act on it in accordance with the requirements of subsection (5);

(c) claims (including restrictions on transfer not imposed by the issuer) to which the registration of transfer to the present registered owner was subject and were so noted in the initial transaction statement sent to him; and

(d) claims as to which an issuer is charged with notice from a controlling instrument it has elected to require under Section 8—402(4).

(5) If the issuer of an uncertificated security is under a duty as to an adverse claim, he discharges that duty by:

(a) including a notation of the claim in any statements sent with respect to the security under Sections 8—408(3), (6), and (7); and

(b) refusing to register the transfer or pledge of the security unless the nature of the claim does not preclude transfer or pledge subject thereto.

(6) If the transfer or pledge of the security is registered subject to an adverse claim, a notation of the claim must be included in the initial transaction statement and all subsequent statements sent to the transferee and pledgee under Section 8—408.

(7) Notwithstanding subsections (4) and (5), if an uncertificated security was subject to a registered pledge at the time the issuer first came under a duty as to a particular adverse claim, the issuer has no duty as to that claim if transfer of the security is requested by the registered pledgee or an appropriate person acting for the registered pledgee unless:

(a) the claim was embodied in legal process which expressly provides otherwise;

(b) the claim was asserted in a written notification from the registered pledgee;

(c) the claim was one as to which the issuer was charged with notice from a controlling instrument it required under Section 8—402(4) in connection with the pledgee's request for transfer; or

(d) the transfer requested is to the registered owner.

§ 8—404. **Liability and Non-Liability for Registration.**

(1) Except as provided in any law relating to the collection of taxes, the issuer is not liable to the owner, pledgee, or any other person suffering loss as a result of the registration of a transfer, pledge, or release of a security if:

(a) there were on or with a certificated security the necessary indorsements or the issuer had received an instruction originated by an appropriate person (Section 8—308); and

(b) the issuer had no duty as to adverse claims or has discharged the duty (Section 8—403).

(2) If an issuer has registered a transfer of a certificated security to a person not entitled to it, the issuer on demand shall deliver a like security to the true owner unless:

(a) the registration was pursuant to subsection (1);

(b) the owner is precluded from asserting any claim for registering the transfer under Section 8—405(1); or

(c) the delivery would result in overissue, in which case the issuer's liability is governed by Section 8—104.

(3) If an issuer has improperly registered a transfer, pledge, or release of an uncertificated security, the issuer on demand from the injured party shall restore the records as to the injured party to the condition that would have obtained if the improper registration had not been made unless:

(a) the registration was pursuant to subsection (1); or

(b) the registration would result in overissue, in which case the issuer's liability is governed by Section 8—104.

§ 8—405. **Lost, Destroyed, and Stolen Certificated Securities.**

(1) If a certificated security has been lost, apparently destroyed, or wrongfully taken, and the owner fails to notify the issuer of that fact within a reasonable time after he has notice of it and the issuer registers a transfer of the security before receiving notification, the owner is precluded from asserting against the issuer any claim for registering the transfer under Section 8—404 or any claim to a new security under this section.

(2) If the owner of a certificated security claims that the security has been lost, destroyed, or wrongfully taken, the issuer shall issue a new certificated security or, at the option of the issuer, an equivalent uncertificated security in place of the original security if the owner:

(a) so requests before the issuer has notice that the security has been acquired by a bona fide purchaser;

(b) files with the issuer a sufficient indemnity bond; and

(c) satisfies any other reasonable requirements imposed by the issuer.

(3) If, after the issue of a new certificated or uncertificated security, a bona fide purchaser of the original certificated security presents it for registration of transfer, the issuer shall register the transfer unless registration would result in overissue, in which event the issuer's liability is governed by Section 8—104. In addition to any rights on the indemnity bond, the issuer may recover the new certificated security from the person to whom it was issued or any person taking under him except a bona fide purchaser or may cancel the uncertificated security unless a bona fide purchaser or any person taking under a bona fide purchaser is then the registered owner or registered pledgee thereof.

§ 8—406. **Duty of Authenticating Trustee, Transfer Agent, or Registrar.**

(1) If a person acts as authenticating trustee, transfer agent, registrar, or other agent for an issuer in the registration of transfers of its certificated securities or in the registration of transfers, pledges, and releases of its uncertificated securities, in the issue of new securities, or in the cancellation of surrendered securities:

(a) he is under a duty to the issuer to exercise good faith and due diligence in performing his functions; and

(b) with regard to the particular functions he performs, he has the same obligation to the holder or owner of a certificated security or to the owner or pledgee of an uncertificated security and has the same rights and privileges as the issuer has in regard to those functions.

(2) Notice to an authenticating trustee, transfer agent, registrar or other agent is notice to the issuer with respect to the functions performed by the agent.

§ 8—407. **Exchangeability of Securities.**

(1) No issuer is subject to the requirements of this section unless it regularly maintains a system for issuing the class of securities involved under which both certificated and uncertificated securities are regularly issued to the category of owners, which includes the person in whose name the new security is to be registered.

(2) Upon surrender of a certificated security with all necessary indorsements and presentation of a written request by the person surrendering the security, the issuer, if he has no duty as to adverse claims or has discharged the duty (Section 8—403), shall issue to the person or a person designated by him an equivalent uncertificated security subject to all liens, restrictions, and claims that were noted on the certificated security.

THE UNIFORM COMMERCIAL CODE

(3) Upon receipt of a transfer instruction originated by an appropriate person who so requests, the issuer of an uncertificated security shall cancel the uncertificated security and issue an equivalent certificated security on which must be noted conspicuously any liens and restrictions of the issuer and any adverse claims (as to which the issuer has a duty under Section 8—403(4)) to which the uncertificated security was subject. The certificated security shall be registered in the name of and delivered to:

(a) the registered owner, if the uncertificated security was not subject to a registered pledge; or

(b) the registered pledgee, if the uncertificated security was subject to a registered pledge.

§ 8—408. Statements of Uncertificated Securities.

(1) Within 2 business days after the transfer of an uncertificated security has been registered, the issuer shall send to the new registered owner and, if the security has been transferred subject to a registered pledge, to the registered pledgee a written statement containing:

(a) a description of the issue of which the uncertificated security is a part;

(b) the number of shares or units transferred;

(c) the name and address and any taxpayer identification number of the new registered owner and, if the security has been transferred subject to a registered pledge, the name and address and any taxpayer identification number of the registered pledgee;

(d) a notation of any liens and restrictions of the issuer and any adverse claims (as to which the issuer has a duty under Section 8—403(4)) to which the uncertificated security is or may be subject at the time of registration or a statement that there are none of those liens, restrictions, or adverse claims; and

(e) the date the transfer was registered.

(2) Within 2 business days after the pledge of an uncertificated security has been registered, the issuer shall send to the registered owner and the registered pledgee a written statement containing:

(a) a description of the issue of which the uncertificated security is a part;

(b) the number of shares or units pledged;

(c) the name and address and any taxpayer identification number of the registered owner and the registered pledgee;

(d) a notation of any liens and restrictions of the issuer and any adverse claims (as to which the issuer has a duty under Section 8—403(4)) to which the uncertificated security is or may be subject at the time of registration or a statement that there are none of those liens, restrictions, or adverse claims; and

(e) the date the pledge was registered.

(3) Within 2 business days after the release from pledge of an uncertificated security has been registered, the issuer shall send to the registered owner and the pledgee whose interest was released a written statement containing:

(a) a description of the issue of which the uncertificated security is a part;

(b) the number of shares or units released from pledge;

(c) the name and address and any taxpayer identification number of the registered owner and the pledgee whose interest was released;

(d) a notation of any liens and restrictions of the issuer and any adverse claims (as to which the issuer has a duty under Section 8—403(4)) to which the uncertificated security is or may be subject at the time of registration or a statement that there are none of those liens, restrictions, or adverse claims; and

(e) the date the release was registered.

(4) An "initial transaction statement" is the statement sent to:

(a) the new registered owner and, if applicable, to the registered pledgee pursuant to subsection (1);

(b) the registered pledgee pursuant to subsection (2); or

(c) the registered owner pursuant to subsection (3).

Each initial transaction statement shall be signed by or on behalf of the issuer and must be identified as "Initial Transaction Statement".

(5) Within 2 business days after the transfer of an uncertificated security has been registered, the issuer shall send to the former registered owner and the former registered pledgee, if any, a written statement containing:

(a) a description of the issue of which the uncertificated security is a part;

(b) the number of shares or units transferred;

(c) the name and address and any taxpayer identification number of the former registered owner and of any former registered pledgee; and

(d) the date the transfer was registered.

(6) At periodic intervals no less frequent than annually and at any time upon the reasonable written request of the registered owner, the issuer shall send to the registered owner of each uncertificated security a dated written statement containing:

(a) a description of the issue of which the uncertificated security is a part;

(b) the name and address and any taxpayer identification number of the registered owner;

(c) the number of shares or units of the uncertificated security registered in the name of the registered owner on the date of the statement;

(d) the name and address and any taxpayer identification number of any registered pledgee and the number of shares or units subject to the pledge; and

(e) a notation of any liens and restrictions of the issuer and any adverse claims (as to which the issuer has a duty under Section 8—403(4)) to which the uncertificated security is or may be subject or a statement that there are none of those liens, restrictions, or adverse claims.

(7) At periodic intervals no less frequent than annually and at any time upon the reasonable written request of the registered pledgee, the issuer shall send to the registered pledgee of each uncertificated security a dated written statement containing:

(a) a description of the issue of which the uncertificated security is a part;

(b) the name and address and any taxpayer identification number of the registered owner;

(c) the name and address and any taxpayer identification number of the registered pledgee;

(d) the number of shares or units subject to the pledge; and

(e) a notation of any liens and restrictions of the issuer and any adverse claims (as to which the issuer has a duty under Section 8—403(4)) to which the uncertificated security is or may be subject or a statement that there are none of those liens, restrictions, or adverse claims.

(8) If the issuer sends the statements described in subsections (6) and (7) at periodic intervals no less frequent than quarterly, the issuer is not obliged to send additional statements upon request unless the owner or pledgee requesting them pays to the issuer the reasonable cost of furnishing them.

(9) Each statement sent pursuant to this section must bear a conspicuous legend reading substantially as follows: "This statement is merely a record of the rights of the addressee as of the time of its issuance. Delivery of this statement, of itself, confers no rights on the recipient. This statement is neither a negotiable instrument nor a security."

Article 9
SECURED TRANSACTIONS; SALES OF ACCOUNTS AND CHATTEL PAPER

Note: *The adoption of this Article should be accompanied by the repeal of existing statutes dealing with conditional sales, trust receipts, factor's liens where the factor is given a nonpossessory* *lien, chattel mortgages, crop mortgages, mortgages on railroad equipment, assignment of accounts and generally statutes regulating security interests in personal property.*

Where the state has a retail installment selling act or small loan act, that legislation should be carefully examined to determine what changes in those acts are needed to conform them to this Article. This Article primarily sets out rules defining rights of a secured party against persons dealing with the debtor; it does not prescribe regulations and controls which may be necessary to curb abuses arising in the small loan business or in the financing of consumer purchases on credit. Accordingly there is no intention to repeal existing regulatory acts in those fields by enactment or re-enactment of Article 9. See Section 9—203(4) and the Note thereto.

Part 1 Short Title, Applicability and Definitions

§ 9—101. Short Title.

This Article shall be known and may be cited as Uniform Commercial Code—Secured Transactions.

§ 9—102. Policy and Subject Matter of Article.

(1) Except as otherwise provided in Section 9—104 on excluded transactions, this Article applies

(a) to any transaction (regardless of its form) which is intended to create a security interest in personal property or fixtures including goods, documents, instruments, general intangibles, chattel paper or accounts; and also

(b) to any sale of accounts or chattel paper.

(2) This Article applies to security interests created by contract including pledge, assignment, chattel mortgage, chattel trust, trust deed, factor's lien, equipment trust, conditional sale, trust receipt, other lien or title retention contract and lease or consignment intended as security. This Article does not apply to statutory liens except as provided in Section 9—310.

(3) The application of this Article to a security interest in a secured obligation is not affected by the fact that the obligation is itself secured by a transaction or interest to which this Article does not apply.

§ 9—103. Perfection of Security Interest in Multiple State Transactions.

(1) Documents, instruments and ordinary goods.

(a) This subsection applies to documents and instruments and to goods other than those covered by a certificate of title described in subsection (2), mobile goods described in subsection (3), and minerals described in subsection (5).

(b) Except as otherwise provided in this subsection, perfection and the effect of perfection or non-perfection of a security interest in collateral are governed by the law of the jurisdiction where the collateral is when the last event occurs on which is based the assertion that the security interest is perfected or unperfected.

(c) If the parties to a transaction creating a purchase money security interest in goods in one jurisdiction understand at the time that the security interest attaches that the goods will be kept in another jurisdiction, then the law of the other jurisdiction governs the perfection and the effect of perfection or non-perfection of the security interest from the time it attaches until thirty days after the debtor receives possession of the goods and thereafter if the goods are taken to the other jurisdiction before the end of the thirty-day period.

(d) When collateral is brought into and kept in this state while subject to a security interest perfected under the law of the jurisdiction from which the collateral was removed, the security interest remains perfected, but if action is required by Part 3 of this Article to perfect the security interest,

   (i) if the action is not taken before the expiration of the period of perfection in the other jurisdiction or the end of four months after the collateral is brought into this state, whichever period first expires, the security interest becomes unperfected at the end of that period and is thereafter deemed to have been unperfected as against a person who became a purchaser after removal;

   (ii) if the action is taken before the expiration of the period specified in subparagraph (i), the security interest continues perfected thereafter;

   (iii) for the purpose of priority over a buyer of consumer goods (subsection (2) of Section 9—307), the period of the effectiveness of a filing in the jurisdiction from which the collateral is removed is governed by the rules with respect to perfection in subparagraphs (i) and (ii).

(2) Certificate of title.

   (a) This subsection applies to goods covered by a certificate of title issued under a statute of this state or of another jurisdiction under the law of which indication of a security interest on the certificate is required as a condition of perfection.

   (b) Except as otherwise provided in this subsection, perfection and the effect of perfection or non-perfection of the security interest are governed by the law (including the conflict of laws rules) of the jurisdiction issuing the certificate until four months after the goods are removed from that jurisdiction and thereafter until the goods are registered in another jurisdiction, but in any event not beyond surrender of the certificate. After the expiration of that period, the goods are not covered by the certificate of title within the meaning of this section.

   (c) Except with respect to the rights of a buyer described in the next paragraph, a security interest, perfected in another jurisdiction otherwise than by notation on a certificate of title, in goods brought into this state and thereafter covered by a certificate of title issued by this state is subject to the rules stated in paragraph (d) of subsection (1).

   (d) If goods are brought into this state while a security interest therein is perfected in any manner under the law of the jurisdiction from which the goods are removed and a certificate of title is issued by this state and the certificate does not show that the goods are subject to the security interest or that they may be subject to security interests not shown on the certificate, the security interest is subordinate to the rights of a buyer of the goods who is not in the business of selling goods of that kind to the extent that he gives value and receives delivery of the goods after issuance of the certificate and without knowledge of the security interest.

(3) Accounts, general intangibles and mobile goods.

   (a) This subsection applies to accounts (other than an account described in subsection (5) on minerals) and general intangibles (other than uncertificated securities) and to goods which are mobile and which are of a type normally used in more than one jurisdiction, such as motor vehicles, trailers, rolling stock, airplanes, shipping containers, road building and construction machinery and commercial harvesting machinery and the like, if the goods are equipment or are inventory leased or held for lease by the debtor to others, and are not covered by a certificate of title described in subsection (2).

   (b) The law (including the conflict of laws rules) of the jurisdiction in which the debtor is located governs the perfection and the effect of perfection or non-perfection of the security interest.

   (c) If, however, the debtor is located in a jurisdiction which is not a part of the United States, and which does not provide for perfection of the security interest by filing or recording in that jurisdiction, the law of the jurisdiction in the United States in which the debtor has its major executive office in the United States governs the perfection and the effect of perfection or non-perfection of the security interest through filing. In the alternative, if the debtor is located in a jurisdiction which is not a part of the United States or Canada and the collateral is accounts or general intangibles for money due or to become due, the security interest may be perfected by notification to the account debtor. As used in this paragraph, ''United States'' includes its territories and possessions and the Commonwealth of Puerto Rico.

   (d) A debtor shall be deemed located at his place of business if he has one, at his chief executive office if he has more than one place of business, otherwise at his residence. If, however, the debtor is a foreign air carrier under the Federal Aviation Act of 1958, as amended, it shall be deemed located at the designated office of the agent upon whom service of process may be made on behalf of the foreign air carrier.

(e) A security interest perfected under the law of the jurisdiction of the location of the debtor is perfected until the expiration of four months after a change of the debtor's location to another jurisdiction, or until perfection would have ceased by the law of the first jurisdiction, whichever period first expires. Unless perfected in the new jurisdiction before the end of that period, it becomes unperfected thereafter and is deemed to have been unperfected as against a person who became a purchaser after the change.

(4) Chattel paper.

The rules stated for goods in subsection (1) apply to a possessory security interest in chattel paper. The rules stated for accounts in subsection (3) apply to a nonpossessory security interest in chattel paper, but the security interest may not be perfected by notification to the account debtor.

(5) Minerals.

Perfection and the effect of perfection or non-perfection of a security interest which is created by a debtor who has an interest in minerals or the like (including oil and gas) before extraction and which attaches thereto as extracted, or which attaches to an account resulting from the sale thereof at the wellhead or minehead are governed by the law (including the conflict of laws rules) of the jurisdiction wherein the wellhead or minehead is located.

(6) Uncertificated securities.

The law (including the conflict of laws rules) of the jurisdiction of organization of the issuer governs the perfection and the effect of perfection or non-perfection of a security interest in uncertificated securities.

§ 9—104. **Transactions Excluded From Article.**

This Article does not apply

(a) to a security interest subject to any statute of the United States, to the extent that such statute governs the rights of parties to and third parties affected by transactions in particular types of property; or

(b) to a landlord's lien; or

(c) to a lien given by statute or other rule of law for services or materials except as provided in Section 9—310 on priority of such liens; or

(d) to a transfer of a claim for wages, salary or other compensation of an employee; or

(e) to a transfer by a government or governmental subdivision or agency; or

(f) to a sale of accounts or chattel paper as part of a sale of the business out of which they arose, or an assignment of accounts or chattel paper which is for the purpose of

collection only, or a transfer of a right to payment under a contract to an assignee who is also to do the performance under the contract or a transfer of a single account to an assignee in whole or partial satisfaction of a preexisting indebtedness; or

(g) to a transfer of an interest in or claim in or under any policy of insurance, except as provided with respect to proceeds (Section 9—306) and priorities in proceeds (Section 9—312); or

(h) to a right represented by a judgment (other than a judgment taken on a right to payment which was collateral); or

(i) to any right of set-off; or

(j) except to the extent that provision is made for fixtures in Section 9—313, to the creation or transfer of an interest in or lien on real estate, including a lease or rents thereunder; or

(k) to a transfer in whole or in part of any claim arising out of tort; or

(l) to a transfer of an interest in any deposit account (subsection (1) of Section 9—105), except as provided with respect to proceeds (Section 9—306) and priorities in proceeds (Section 9—312).

§ 9—105. **Definitions and Index of Definitions.**

(1) In this Article unless the context otherwise requires:

(a) "Account debtor" means the person who is obligated on an account, chattel paper or general intangible;

(b) "Chattel paper" means a writing or writings which evidence both a monetary obligation and a security interest in or a lease of specific goods, but a charter or other contract involving the use or hire of a vessel is not chattel paper. When a transaction is evidenced both by such a security agreement or a lease and by an instrument or a series of instruments, the group of writings taken together constitutes chattel paper;

(c) "Collateral" means the property subject to a security interest, and includes accounts and chattel paper which have been sold;

(d) "Debtor" means the person who owes payment or other performance of the obligation secured, whether or not he owns or has rights in the collateral, and includes the seller of accounts or chattel paper. Where the debtor and the owner of the collateral are not the same person, the term "debtor" means the owner of the collateral in any provision of the Article dealing with the collateral, the obligor in any provision dealing with the obligation, and may include both where the context so requires;

(e) "Deposit account" means a demand, time, savings, passbook or like account maintained with a bank, savings and loan association, credit union or like organization, other than an account evidenced by a certificate of deposit;

(f) "Document" means document of title as defined in the general definitions of Article 1 (Section 1—201), and a receipt of the kind described in subsection (2) of Section 7—201;

(g) "Encumbrance" includes real estate mortgages and other liens on real estate and all other rights in real estate that are not ownership interests;

(h) "Goods" includes all things which are movable at the time the security interest attaches or which are fixtures (Section 9—313), but does not include money, documents, instruments, accounts, chattel paper, general intangibles, or minerals or the like (including oil and gas) before extraction. "Goods" also includes standing timber which is to be cut and removed under a conveyance or contract for sale, the unborn young of animals, and growing crops;

(i) "Instrument" means a negotiable instrument (defined in Section 3—104), or a certificated security (defined in Section 8—102) or any other writing which evidences a right to the payment of money and is not itself a security agreement or lease and is of a type which is in ordinary course of business transferred by delivery with any necessary indorsement or assignment;

(j) "Mortgage" means a consensual interest created by a real estate mortgage, a trust deed on real estate, or the like;

(k) An advance is made "pursuant to commitment" if the secured party has bound himself to make it, whether or not a subsequent event of default or other event not within his control has relieved or may relieve him from his obligation;

(l) "Security agreement" means an agreement which creates or provides for a security interest;

(m) "Secured party" means a lender, seller or other person in whose favor there is a security interest, including a person to whom accounts or chattel paper have been sold. When the holders of obligations issued under an indenture of trust, equipment trust agreement or the like are represented by a trustee or other person, the representative is the secured party;

(n) "Transmitting utility" means any person primarily engaged in the railroad, street railway or trolley bus business, the electric or electronics communications transmission business, the transmission of goods by pipeline, or the transmission or the production and transmission of electricity, steam, gas or water, or the provision of sewer service.

(2) Other definitions applying to this Article and the sections in which they appear are:

"Account". Section 9—106.
"Attach". Section 9—203.
"Construction mortgage". Section 9—313(1).
"Consumer goods". Section 9—109(1).
"Equipment". Section 9—109(2).
"Farm products". Section 9—109(3).
"Fixture". Section 9—313(1).
"Fixture filing". Section 9—313(1).
"General intangibles". Section 9—106.
"Inventory". Section 9—109(4).
"Lien creditor". Section 9—301(3).
"Proceeds". Section 9—306(1).
"Purchase money security interest". Section 9—107.
"United States". Section 9—103.

(3) The following definitions in other Articles apply to this Article:
"Check". Section 3—104.
"Contract for sale". Section 2—106.
"Holder in due course". Section 3—302.
"Note". Section 3—104.
"Sale". Section 2—106.

(4) In addition Article 1 contains general definitions and principles of construction and interpretation applicable throughout this Article.

§ 9—106. Definitions: "Account"; "General Intangibles".

"Account" means any right to payment for goods sold or leased or for services rendered which is not evidenced by an instrument or chattel paper, whether or not it has been earned by performance. "General intangibles" means any personal property (including things in action) other than goods, accounts, chattel paper, documents, instruments, and money. All rights to payment earned or unearned under a charter or other contract involving the use or hire of a vessel and all rights incident to the charter or contract are accounts.

§ 9—107. Definitions: "Purchase Money Security Interest".

A security interest is a "purchase money security interest" to the extent that it is

(a) taken or retained by the seller of the collateral to secure all or part of its price; or

(b) taken by a person who by making advances or incurring an obligation gives value to enable the debtor to acquire rights in or the use of collateral if such value is in fact so used.

§ 9—108. When After-Acquired Collateral Not Security for Antecedent Debt.

Where a secured party makes an advance, incurs an obligation, releases a perfected security interest, or otherwise gives new value which is to be secured in whole or in part by after-acquired property his security interest in the after-acquired collateral shall be deemed to be taken for new value and not as security for an antecedent debt if the debtor acquires his rights in such collateral either in the ordinary course of his business or under a contract of purchase made pursuant to the security agreement within a reasonable time after new value is given.

§ 9—109. **Classification of Goods; "Consumer Goods"; "Equipment"; "Farm Products"; "Inventory".**

Goods are

(1) "consumer goods" if they are used or bought for use primarily for personal, family or household purposes;

(2) "equipment" if they are used or bought for use primarily in business (including farming or a profession) or by a debtor who is a non-profit organization or a governmental subdivision or agency or if the goods are not included in the definitions of inventory, farm products or consumer goods;

(3) "farm products" if they are crops or livestock or supplies used or produced in farming operations or if they are products of crops or livestock in their unmanufactured states (such as ginned cotton, wool-clip, maple syrup, milk and eggs), and if they are in the possession of a debtor engaged in raising, fattening, grazing or other farming operations. If goods are farm products they are neither equipment nor inventory;

(4) "inventory" if they are held by a person who holds them for sale or lease or to be furnished under contracts of service or if he has so furnished them, or if they are raw materials, work in process or materials used or consumed in a business. Inventory of a person is not to be classified as his equipment.

§ 9—110. **Sufficiency of Description.**

For purposes of this Article any description of personal property or real estate is sufficient whether or not it is specific if it reasonably identifies what is described.

§ 9—111. **Applicability of Bulk Transfer Laws.**

The creation of a security interest is not a bulk transfer under Article 6 (see Section 6—103).

§ 9—112. **Where Collateral Is Not Owned by Debtor.**

Unless otherwise agreed, when a secured party knows that collateral is owned by a person who is not the debtor, the owner of the collateral is entitled to receive from the secured party any surplus under Section 9—502(2) or under Section 9—504(1), and is not liable for the debt or for any deficiency after resale, and he has the same right as the debtor

(a) to receive statements under Section 9—208;

(b) to receive notice of and to object to a secured party's

proposal to retain the collateral in satisfaction of the indebtedness under Section 9—505;

(c) to redeem the collateral under Section 9—506;

(d) to obtain injunctive or other relief under Section 9—507(1); and

(e) to recover losses caused to him under Section 9—208(2).

§ 9—113. **Security Interests Arising Under Article on Sales or Under Article on Leases.**

A security interest arising solely under the Article on Sales (Article 2) or the Article on Leases (Article 2A) is subject to the provisions of this Article except that to the extent that and so long as the debtor does not have or does not lawfully obtain possession of the goods

(a) no security agreement is necessary to make the security interest enforceable; and

(b) no filing is required to perfect the security interest; and

(c) the rights of the secured party on default by the debtor are governed (i) by the Article on Sales (Article 2) in the case of a security interest arising solely under such Article or (ii) by the Article on Leases (Article 2A) in the case of a security interest arising solely under such Article.

§ 9—114. **Consignment.**

(1) A person who delivers goods under a consignment which is not a security interest and who would be required to file under this Article by paragraph (3)(c) of Section 2—326 has priority over a secured party who is or becomes a creditor of the consignee and who would have a perfected security interest in the goods if they were the property of the consignee, and also has priority with respect to identifiable cash proceeds received on or before delivery of the goods to a buyer, if

(a) the consignor complies with the filing provision of the Article on Sales with respect to consignments (paragraph (3)(c) of Section 2—326) before the consignee receives possession of the goods; and

(b) the consignor gives notification in writing to the holder of the security interest if the holder has filed a financing statement covering the same types of goods before the date of the filing made by the consignor; and

(c) the holder of the security interest receives the notification within five years before the consignee receives possession of the goods; and

(d) the notification states that the consignor expects to deliver goods on consignment to the consignee, describing the goods by item or type.

(2) In the case of a consignment which is not a security

interest and in which the requirements of the preceding subsection have not been met, a person who delivers goods to another is subordinate to a person who would have a perfected security interest in the goods if they were the property of the debtor.

Part 2 Validity of Security Agreement and Rights of Parties Thereto

§ 9—201. General Validity of Security Agreement.

Except as otherwise provided by this Act a security agreement is effective according to its terms between the parties, against purchasers of the collateral and against creditors. Nothing in this Article validates any charge or practice illegal under any statute or regulation thereunder governing usury, small loans, retail installment sales, or the like, or extends the application of any such statute or regulation to any transaction not otherwise subject thereto.

§ 9—202. Title to Collateral Immaterial.

Each provision of this Article with regard to rights, obligations and remedies applies whether title to collateral is in the secured party or in the debtor.

§ 9—203. Attachment and Enforceability of Security Interest; Proceeds; Formal Requisites.

(1) Subject to the provisions of Section 4—208 on the security interest of a collecting bank, Section 8—321 on security interests in securities and Section 9—113 on a security interest arising under the Article on Sales, a security interest is not enforceable against the debtor or third parties with respect to the collateral and does not attach unless:

(a) the collateral is in the possession of the secured party pursuant to agreement, or the debtor has signed a security agreement which contains a description of the collateral and in addition, when the security interest covers crops growing or to be grown or timber to be cut, a description of the land concerned;

(b) value has been given; and

(c) the debtor has rights in the collateral.

(2) A security interest attaches when it becomes enforceable against the debtor with respect to the collateral. Attachment occurs as soon as all of the events specified in subsection (1) have taken place unless explicit agreement postpones the time of attaching.

(3) Unless otherwise agreed a security agreement gives the secured party the rights to proceeds provided by Section 9—306.

(4) A transaction, although subject to this Article, is also subject to ....*, and in the case of conflict between the provisions of this Article and any such statute, the provisions of such statute control. Failure to comply with any applicable statute has only the effect which is specified therein.

Note: *At * in subsection (4) insert reference to any local statute regulating small loans, retail installment sales and the like.*

The foregoing subsection (4) is designed to make it clear that certain transactions, although subject to this Article, must also comply with other applicable legislation.

This Article is designed to regulate all the ''security'' aspects of transactions within its scope. There is, however, much regulatory legislation, particularly in the consumer field, which supplements this Article and should not be repealed by its enactment. Examples are small loan acts, retail installment selling acts and the like. Such acts may provide for licensing and rate regulation and may prescribe particular forms of contract. Such provisions should remain in force despite the enactment of this Article. On the other hand if a retail installment selling act contains provisions on filing, rights on default, etc., such provisions should be repealed as inconsistent with this Article except that inconsistent provisions as to deficiencies, penalties, etc., in the Uniform Consumer Credit Code and other recent related legislation should remain because those statutes were drafted after the substantial enactment of the Article and with the intention of modifying certain provisions of this Article as to consumer credit.

§ 9—204. After-Acquired Property; Future Advances.

(1) Except as provided in subsection (2), a security agreement may provide that any or all obligations covered by the security agreement are to be secured by after-acquired collateral.

(2) No security interest attaches under an after-acquired property clause to consumer goods other than accessions (Section 9—314) when given as additional security unless the debtor acquires rights in them within ten days after the secured party gives value.

(3) Obligations covered by a security agreement may include future advances or other value whether or not the advances or value are given pursuant to commitment (subsection (1) of Section 9—105).

§ 9—205. Use or Disposition of Collateral Without Accounting Permissible.

A security interest is not invalid or fraudulent against creditors by reason of liberty in the debtor to use, commingle or dispose of all or part of the collateral (including returned or repossessed goods) or to collect or compromise accounts or chattel paper, or to accept the return of goods or make repossessions, or to use, commingle or dispose of proceeds, or by reason of the failure of the secured party to require the debtor to account for proceeds or replace collateral. This section does not relax the requirements of possession where perfection of a security interest depends upon possession of the collateral by the secured party or by a bailee.

§ 9—206. Agreement Not to Assert Defenses Against Assignee; Modification of Sales Warranties Where Security Agreement Exists.

(1) Subject to any statute or decision which establishes a different rule for buyers or lessees of consumer goods, an agreement by a buyer or lessee that he will not assert against an assignee any claim or defense which he may have against the seller or lessor is enforceable by an assignee who takes his assignment for value, in good faith and without notice of a claim or defense, except as to defenses of a type which may be asserted against a holder in due course of a negotiable instrument under the Article on Commercial Paper (Article 3). A buyer who as part of one transaction signs both a negotiable instrument and a security agreement makes such an agreement.

(2) When a seller retains a purchase money security interest in goods the Article on Sales (Article 2) governs the sale and any disclaimer, limitation or modification of the seller's warranties.

§ 9—207. **Rights and Duties When Collateral is in Secured Party's Possession.**

(1) A secured party must use reasonable care in the custody and preservation of collateral in his possession. In the case of an instrument or chattel paper reasonable care includes taking necessary steps to preserve rights against prior parties unless otherwise agreed.

(2) Unless otherwise agreed, when collateral is in the secured party's possession

(a) reasonable expenses (including the cost of any insurance and payment of taxes or other charges) incurred in the custody, preservation, use or operation of the collateral are chargeable to the debtor and are secured by the collateral;

(b) the risk of accidental loss or damage is on the debtor to the extent of any deficiency in any effective insurance coverage;

(c) the secured party may hold as additional security any increase or profits (except money) received from the collateral, but money so received, unless remitted to the debtor, shall be applied in reduction of the secured obligation;

(d) the secured party must keep the collateral identifiable but fungible collateral may be commingled;

(e) the secured party may repledge the collateral upon terms which do not impair the debtor's right to redeem it.

(3) A secured party is liable for any loss caused by his failure to meet any obligation imposed by the preceding subsections but does not lose his security interest.

(4) A secured party may use or operate the collateral for the purpose of preserving the collateral or its value or pursuant to the order of a court of appropriate jurisdiction or, except in the case of consumer goods, in the manner and to the extent provided in the security agreement.

§ 9—208. **Request for Statement of Account or List of Collateral.**

(1) A debtor may sign a statement indicating what he believes to be the aggregate amount of unpaid indebtedness as of a specified date and may send it to the secured party with a request that the statement be approved or corrected and returned to the debtor. When the security agreement or any other record kept by the secured party identifies the collateral a debtor may similarly request the secured party to approve or correct a list of the collateral.

(2) The secured party must comply with such a request within two weeks after receipt by sending a written correction or approval. If the secured party claims a security interest in all of a particular type of collateral owned by the debtor he may indicate that fact in his reply and need not approve or correct an itemized list of such collateral. If the secured party without reasonable excuse fails to comply he is liable for any loss caused to the debtor thereby; and if the debtor has properly included in his request a good faith statement of the obligation or a list of the collateral or both the secured party may claim a security interest only as shown in the statement against persons misled by his failure to comply. If he no longer has an interest in the obligation or collateral at the time the request is received he must disclose the name and address of any successor in interest known to him and he is liable for any loss caused to the debtor as a result of failure to disclose. A successor in interest is not subject to this section until a request is received by him.

(3) A debtor is entitled to such a statement once every six months without charge. The secured party may require payment of a charge not exceeding $10 for each additional statement furnished.

Part 3 Rights of Third Parties; Perfected and Unperfected Security Interests; Rules of Priority

§ 9—301. **Persons Who Take Priority Over Unperfected Security Interests; Rights of "Lien Creditor".**

(1) Except as otherwise provided in subsection (2), an unperfected security interest is subordinate to the rights of

(a) persons entitled to priority under Section 9—312;

(b) a person who becomes a lien creditor before the security interest is perfected;

(c) in the case of goods, instruments, documents, and chattel paper, a person who is not a secured party and who is a transferee in bulk or other buyer not in ordinary course of business or is a buyer of farm products in ordinary course of business, to the extent that he gives value and receives delivery of the collateral without knowledge of the security interest and before it is perfected;

(d) in the case of accounts and general intangibles, a person who is not a secured party and who is a transferee to the extent that he gives value without knowledge of the security interest and before it is perfected.

(2) If the secured party files with respect to a purchase money security interest before or within ten days after the debtor receives possession of the collateral, he takes priority over the rights of a transferee in bulk or of a lien creditor which arise between the time the security interest attaches and the time of filing.

(3) A ''lien creditor'' means a creditor who has acquired a lien on the property involved by attachment, levy or the like and includes an assignee for benefit of creditors from the time of assignment, and a trustee in bankruptcy from the date of the filing of the petition or a receiver in equity from the time of appointment.

(4) A person who becomes a lien creditor while a security interest is perfected takes subject to the security interest only to the extent that it secures advances made before he becomes a lien creditor or within 45 days thereafter or made without knowledge of the lien or pursuant to a commitment entered into without knowledge of the lien.

§ 9—302. When Filing Is Required to Perfect Security Interest; Security Interests to Which Filing Provisions of This Article Do Not Apply.

(1) A financing statement must be filed to perfect all security interests except the following:

(a) a security interest in collateral in possession of the secured party under Section 9—305;

(b) a security interest temporarily perfected in instruments or documents without delivery under Section 9—304 or in proceeds for a 10 day period under Section 9—306;

(c) a security interest created by an assignment of a beneficial interest in a trust or a decedent's estate;

(d) a purchase money security interest in consumer goods; but filing is required for a motor vehicle required to be registered; and fixture filing is required for priority over conflicting interests in fixtures to the extent provided in Section 9—313;

(e) an assignment of accounts which does not alone or in conjunction with other assignments to the same assignee transfer a significant part of the outstanding accounts of the assignor;

(f) a security interest of a collecting bank (Section 4—208) or in securities (Section 8—321) or arising under the Article on Sales (see Section 9—113) or covered in subsection (3) of this section;

(g) an assignment for the benefit of all the creditors of the transferor, and subsequent transfers by the assignee thereunder.

(2) If a secured party assigns a perfected security interest, no filing under this Article is required in order to continue the perfected status of the security interest against creditors of and transferees from the original debtor.

(3) The filing of a financing statement otherwise required by this Article is not necessary or effective to perfect a security interest in property subject to

(a) a statute or treaty of the United States which provides for a national or international registration or a national or international certificate of title or which specifies a place of filing different from that specified in this Article for filing of the security interest; or

(b) the following statutes of this state; [list any certificate of title statute covering automobiles, trailers, mobile homes, boats, farm tractors, or the like, and any central filing statute.]; but during any period in which collateral is inventory held for sale by a person who is in the business of selling goods of that kind, the filing provisions of this Article (Part 4) apply to a security interest in that collateral created by him as debtor; or

(c) a certificate of title statute of another jurisdiction under the law of which indication of a security interest on the certificate is required as a condition of perfection (subsection (2) of Section 9—103).

(4) Compliance with a statute or treaty described in subsection (3) is equivalent to the filing of a financing statement under this Article, and a security interest in property subject to the statute or treaty can be perfected only by compliance therewith except as provided in Section 9—103 on multiple state transactions. Duration and renewal of perfection of a security interest perfected by compliance with the statute or treaty are governed by the provisions of the statute or treaty; in other respects the security interest is subject to this Article.

§ 9—303. When Security Interest Is Perfected; Continuity of Perfection.

(1) A security interest is perfected when it has attached and when all of the applicable steps required for perfection have been taken. Such steps are specified in Sections 9—302, 9—304, 9—305 and 9—306. If such steps are taken before the security interest attaches, it is perfected at the time when it attaches.

(2) If a security interest is originally perfected in any way permitted under this Article and is subsequently perfected in some other way under this Article, without an intermediate period when it was unperfected, the security interest shall be deemed to be perfected continuously for the purposes of this Article.

§ 9—304. Perfection of Security Interest in Instruments, Documents, and Goods Covered by Documents; Perfection by Permissive Filing; Temporary Perfection Without Filing or Transfer of Possession.

(1) A security interest in chattel paper or negotiable documents may be perfected by filing. A security interest in money or instruments (other than certificated securities or instruments which constitute part of chattel paper) can be perfected only by the secured party's taking possession, except as provided in subsections (4) and (5) of this section and subsections (2) and (3) of Section 9—306 on proceeds.

(2) During the period that goods are in the possession of the issuer of a negotiable document therefor, a security interest in the goods is perfected by perfecting a security interest in the document, and any security interest in the goods otherwise perfected during such period is subject thereto.

(3) A security interest in goods in the possession of a bailee other than one who has issued a negotiable document therefor is perfected by issuance of a document in the name of the secured party or by the bailee's receipt of notification of the secured party's interest or by filing as to the goods.

(4) A security interest in instruments (other than certificated securities) or negotiable documents is perfected without filing or the taking of possession for a period of 21 days from the time it attaches to the extent that it arises for new value given under a written security agreement.

(5) A security interest remains perfected for a period of 21 days without filing where a secured party having a perfected security interest in an instrument (other than a certificated security), a negotiable document or goods in possession of a bailee other than one who has issued a negotiable document therefor

(a) makes available to the debtor the goods or documents representing the goods for the purpose of ultimate sale or exchange or for the purpose of loading, unloading, storing, shipping, transshipping, manufacturing, processing or otherwise dealing with them in a manner preliminary to their sale or exchange, but priority between conflicting security interests in the goods is subject to subsection (3) of Section 9—312; or

(b) delivers the instrument to the debtor for the purpose of ultimate sale or exchange or of presentation, collection, renewal or registration of transfer.

(6) After the 21 day period in subsections (4) and (5) perfection depends upon compliance with applicable provisions of this Article.

§ 9—305. When Possession by Secured Party Perfects Security Interest Without Filing.

A security interest in letters of credit and advices of credit (subsection (2)(a) of Section 5—116), goods, instruments (other than certificated securities), money, negotiable documents, or chattel paper may be perfected by the secured party's taking possession of the collateral. If such collateral other than goods covered by a negotiable document is held by a bailee, the secured party is deemed to have possession from the time the bailee receives notification of the secured party's interest. A security interest is perfected by possession from the time possession is taken without a relation back and continues only so long as possession is retained, unless otherwise specified in this Article. The security interest may be otherwise perfected as provided in this Article before or after the period of possession by the secured party.

§ 9—306. "Proceeds"; Secured Party's Rights on Disposition of Collateral.

(1) "Proceeds" includes whatever is received upon the sale, exchange, collection or other disposition of collateral or proceeds. Insurance payable by reason of loss or damage to the collateral is proceeds, except to the extent that it is payable to a person other than a party to the security agreement. Money, checks, deposit accounts, and the like are "cash proceeds". All other proceeds are "noncash proceeds".

(2) Except where this Article otherwise provides, a security interest continues in collateral notwithstanding sale, exchange or other disposition thereof unless the disposition was authorized by the secured party in the security agreement or otherwise, and also continues in any identifiable proceeds including collections received by the debtor.

(3) The security interest in proceeds is a continuously perfected security interest if the interest in the original collateral was perfected but it ceases to be a perfected security interest and becomes unperfected ten days after receipt of the proceeds by the debtor unless

(a) a filed financing statement covers the original collateral and the proceeds are collateral in which a security interest may be perfected by filing in the office or offices where the financing statement has been filed and, if the proceeds are acquired with cash proceeds, the description of collateral in the financing statement indicates the types of property constituting the proceeds; or

(b) a filed financing statement covers the original collateral and the proceeds are identifiable cash proceeds; or

(c) the security interest in the proceeds is perfected before the expiration of the ten day period.

Except as provided in this section, a security interest in proceeds can be perfected only by the methods or under the circumstances permitted in this Article for original collateral of the same type.

(4) In the event of insolvency proceedings instituted by or against a debtor, a secured party with a perfected security interest in proceeds has a perfected security interest only in the following proceeds:

(a) in identifiable noncash proceeds and in separate deposit accounts containing only proceeds;

(b) in identifiable cash proceeds in the form of money which is neither commingled with other money nor deposited in a deposit account prior to the insolvency proceedings;

(c) in identifiable cash proceeds in the form of checks and the like which are not deposited in a deposit account prior to the insolvency proceedings; and

(d) in all cash and deposit accounts of the debtor in which proceeds have been commingled with other funds, but the perfected security interest under this paragraph (d) is

(i) subject to any right to set-off; and

(ii) limited to an amount not greater than the amount of any cash proceeds received by the debtor within ten days before the institution of the insolvency proceedings less the sum of (I) the payments to the secured party on account of cash proceeds received by the debtor during such period and (II) the cash proceeds received by the debtor during such period to which the secured party is entitled under paragraphs (a) through (c) of this subsection (4).

(5) If a sale of goods results in an account or chattel paper which is transferred by the seller to a secured party, and if the goods are returned to or are repossessed by the seller or the secured party, the following rules determine priorities:

(a) If the goods were collateral at the time of sale, for an indebtedness of the seller which is still unpaid, the original security interest attaches again to the goods and continues as a perfected security interest if it was perfected at the time when the goods were sold. If the security interest was originally perfected by a filing which is still effective, nothing further is required to continue the perfected status; in any other case, the secured party must take possession of the returned or repossessed goods or must file.

(b) An unpaid transferee of the chattel paper has a security interest in the goods against the transferor. Such security interest is prior to a security interest asserted under paragraph (a) to the extent that the transferee of the chattel paper was entitled to priority under Section 9—308.

(c) An unpaid transferee of the account has a security interest in the goods against the transferor. Such security interest is subordinate to a security interest asserted under paragraph (a).

(d) A security interest of an unpaid transferee asserted under paragraph (b) or (c) must be perfected for protection against creditors of the transferor and purchasers of the returned or repossessed goods.

§ 9—307. **Protection of Buyers of Goods.**

(1) A buyer in ordinary course of business (subsection (9) of Section 1—201) other than a person buying farm products from a person engaged in farming operations takes free of a security interest created by his seller even though the security interest is perfected and even though the buyer knows of its existence [subject to the Food Security Act of 1985 (7 U.S.C. Section 1631)].

(2) In the case of consumer goods, a buyer takes free of a security interest even though perfected if he buys without knowledge of the security interest, for value and for his own personal, family or household purposes unless prior to the purchase the secured party has filed a financing statement covering such goods.

(3) A buyer other than a buyer in ordinary course of business (subsection (1) of this section) takes free of a security interest to the extent that it secures future advances made after the secured party acquires knowledge of the purchase, or more than 45 days after the purchase, whichever first occurs, unless made pursuant to a commitment entered into without knowledge of the purchase and before the expiration of the 45 day period.

§ 9—308. **Purchase of Chattel Paper and Instruments.**

A purchaser of chattel paper or an instrument who gives new value and takes possession of it in the ordinary course of his business has priority over a security interest in the chattel paper or instrument

(a) which is perfected under Section 9—304 (permissive filing and temporary perfection) or under Section 9—306 (perfection as to proceeds) if he acts without knowledge that the specific paper or instrument is subject to a security interest; or

(b) which is claimed merely as proceeds of inventory subject to a security interest (Section 9—306) even though he knows that the specific paper or instrument is subject to the security interest.

§ 9—309. **Protection of Purchasers of Instruments, Documents and Securities.**

Nothing in this Article limits the rights of a holder in due course of a negotiable instrument (Section 3—302) or a holder to whom a negotiable document of title has been duly negotiated (Section 7—501) or a bona fide purchaser of a security (Section 8—302) and the holders or purchasers take priority over an earlier security interest even though perfected. Filing under this Article does not constitute notice of the security interest to such holders or purchasers.

§ 9—310. **Priority of Certain Liens Arising by Operation of Law.**

When a person in the ordinary course of his business furnishes services or materials with respect to goods subject to a security interest, a lien upon goods in the possession of such person given by statute or rule of law for such materials or services takes priority over a perfected security interest unless the lien is statutory and the statute expressly provides otherwise.

§ 9—311. **Alienability of Debtor's Rights: Judicial Process.**

The debtor's rights in collateral may be voluntarily or involuntarily transferred (by way of sale, creation of a security interest, attachment, levy, garnishment or other judicial process) notwithstanding a provision in the security agreement prohibiting any transfer or making the transfer constitute a default.

§ 9—312. **Priorities Among Conflicting Security Interests in the Same Collateral.**

(1) The rules of priority stated in other sections of this Part and in the following sections shall govern when applicable: Section 4—208 with respect to the security interests of collecting banks in items being collected, accompanying documents and proceeds; Section 9—103 on security interests related to other jurisdictions; Section 9—114 on consignments.

(2) A perfected security interest in crops for new value given to enable the debtor to produce the crops during the production season and given not more than three months before the crops become growing crops by planting or otherwise takes priority over an earlier perfected security interest to the extent that such earlier interest secures obligations due more than six months before the crops become growing crops by planting or otherwise, even though the person giving new value had knowledge of the earlier security interest.

(3) A perfected purchase money security interest in inventory has priority over a conflicting security interest in the same inventory and also has priority in identifiable cash proceeds received on or before the delivery of the inventory to a buyer if

(a) the purchase money security interest is perfected at the time the debtor receives possession of the inventory; and

(b) the purchase money secured party gives notification in writing to the holder of the conflicting security interest if the holder had filed a financing statement covering the same types of inventory (i) before the date of the filing made by the purchase money secured party, or (ii) before the beginning of the 21 day period where the purchase money security interest is temporarily perfected without filing or possession (subsection (5) of Section 9—304); and

(c) the holder of the conflicting security interest receives the notification within five years before the debtor receives possession of the inventory; and

(d) the notification states that the person giving the notice has or expects to acquire a purchase money se-

curity interest in inventory of the debtor, describing such inventory by item or type.

(4) A purchase money security interest in collateral other than inventory has priority over a conflicting security interest in the same collateral or its proceeds if the purchase money security interest is perfected at the time the debtor receives possession of the collateral or within ten days thereafter.

(5) In all cases not governed by other rules stated in this section (including cases of purchase money security interests which do not qualify for the special priorities set forth in subsections (3) and (4) of this section), priority between conflicting security interests in the same collateral shall be determined according to the following rules:

(a) Conflicting security interests rank according to priority in time of filing or perfection. Priority dates from the time a filing is first made covering the collateral or the time the security interest is first perfected, whichever is earlier, provided that there is no period thereafter when there is neither filing nor perfection.

(b) So long as conflicting security interests are unperfected, the first to attach has priority.

(6) For the purposes of subsection (5) a date of filing or perfection as to collateral is also a date of filing or perfection as to proceeds.

(7) If future advances are made while a security interest is perfected by filing, the taking of possession, or under Section 8—321 on securities, the security interest has the same priority for the purposes of subsection (5) with respect to the future advances as it does with respect to the first advance. If a commitment is made before or while the security interest is so perfected, the security interest has the same priority with respect to advances made pursuant thereto. In other cases a perfected security interest has priority from the date the advance is made.

§ 9—313. **Priority of Security Interests in Fixtures.**

(1) In this section and in the provisions of Part 4 of this Article referring to fixture filing, unless the context otherwise requires

(a) goods are "fixtures" when they become so related to particular real estate that an interest in them arises under real estate law

(b) a "fixture filing" is the filing in the office where a mortgage on the real estate would be filed or recorded of a financing statement covering goods which are or are to become fixtures and conforming to the requirements of subsection (5) of Section 9—402

(c) a mortgage is a "construction mortgage" to the extent that it secures an obligation incurred for the construction of an improvement on land including the acquisition cost of the land, if the recorded writing so indicates.

(2) A security interest under this Article may be created in goods which are fixtures or may continue in goods which become fixtures, but no security interest exists under this Article in ordinary building materials incorporated into an improvement on land.

(3) This Article does not prevent creation of an encumbrance upon fixtures pursuant to real estate law.

(4) A perfected security interest in fixtures has priority over the conflicting interest of an encumbrancer or owner of the real estate where

    (a) the security interest is a purchase money security interest, the interest of the encumbrancer or owner arises before the goods become fixtures, the security interest is perfected by a fixture filing before the goods become fixtures or within ten days thereafter, and the debtor has an interest of record in the real estate or is in possession of the real estate; or

    (b) the security interest is perfected by a fixture filing before the interest of the encumbrancer or owner is of record, the security interest has priority over any conflicting interest of a predecessor in title of the encumbrancer or owner, and the debtor has an interest of record in the real estate or is in possession of the real estate; or

    (c) the fixtures are readily removable factory or office machines or readily removable replacements of domestic appliances which are consumer goods, and before the goods become fixtures the security interest is perfected by any method permitted by this Article; or

    (d) the conflicting interest is a lien on the real estate obtained by legal or equitable proceedings after the security interest was perfected by any method permitted by this Article.

(5) A security interest in fixtures, whether or not perfected, has priority over the conflicting interest of an encumbrancer or owner of the real estate where

    (a) the encumbrancer or owner has consented in writing to the security interest or has disclaimed an interest in the goods as fixtures; or

    (b) the debtor has a right to remove the goods as against the encumbrancer or owner. If the debtor's right terminates, the priority of the security interest continues for a reasonable time.

(6) Notwithstanding paragraph (a) of subsection (4) but otherwise subject to subsections (4) and (5), a security interest in fixtures is subordinate to a construction mortgage recorded before the goods become fixtures if the goods become fixtures before the completion of the construction. To the extent that it is given to refinance a construction mortgage, a mortgage has this priority to the same extent as the construction mortgage.

(7) In cases not within the preceding subsections, a security interest in fixtures is subordinate to the conflicting interest of an encumbrancer or owner of the related real estate who is not the debtor.

(8) When the secured party has priority over all owners and encumbrancers of the real estate, he may, on default, subject to the provisions of Part 5, remove his collateral from the real estate but he must reimburse any encumbrancer or owner of the real estate who is not the debtor and who has not otherwise agreed for the cost of repair of any physical injury, but not for any diminution in value of the real estate caused by the absence of the goods removed or by any necessity of replacing them. A person entitled to reimbursement may refuse permission to remove until the secured party gives adequate security for the performance of this obligation.

§ 9—314. Accessions.

(1) A security interest in goods which attaches before they are installed in or affixed to other goods takes priority as to the goods installed or affixed (called in this section "accessions") over the claims of all persons to the whole except as stated in subsection (3) and subject to Section 9—315(1).

(2) A security interest which attaches to goods after they become part of a whole is valid against all persons subsequently acquiring interests in the whole except as stated in subsection (3) but is invalid against any person with an interest in the whole at the time the security interest attaches to the goods who has not in writing consented to the security interest or disclaimed an interest in the goods as part of the whole.

(3) The security interests described in subsections (1) and (2) do not take priority over

    (a) a subsequent purchaser for value of any interest in the whole; or

    (b) a creditor with a lien on the whole subsequently obtained by judicial proceedings; or

    (c) a creditor with a prior perfected security interest in the whole to the extent that he makes subsequent advances

if the subsequent purchase is made, the lien by judicial proceedings obtained or the subsequent advance under the prior perfected security interest is made or contracted for without knowledge of the security interest and before it is perfected. A purchaser of the whole at a foreclosure sale other than the holder of a perfected security interest purchasing at his own foreclosure sale is a subsequent purchaser within this section.

(4) When under subsections (1) or (2) and (3) a secured party has an interest in accessions which has priority over the claims of all persons who have interests in the whole, he may on default subject to the provisions of Part 5 remove

his collateral from the whole but he must reimburse any encumbrancer or owner of the whole who is not the debtor and who has not otherwise agreed for the cost of repair of any physical injury but not for any diminution in value of the whole caused by the absence of the goods removed or by any necessity for replacing them. A person entitled to reimbursement may refuse permission to remove until the secured party gives adequate security for the performance of this obligation.

§ 9—315. **Priority When Goods Are Commingled or Processed.**

(1) If a security interest in goods was perfected and subsequently the goods or a part thereof have become part of a product or mass, the security interest continues in the product or mass if

(a) the goods are so manufactured, processed, assembled or commingled that their identity is lost in the product or mass; or

(b) a financing statement covering the original goods also covers the product into which the goods have been manufactured, processed or assembled.

In a case to which paragraph (b) applies, no separate security interest in that part of the original goods which has been manufactured, processed or assembled into the product may be claimed under Section 9—314.

(2) When under subsection (1) more than one security interest attaches to the product or mass, they rank equally according to the ratio that the cost of the goods to which each interest originally attached bears to the cost of the total product or mass.

§ 9—316. **Priority Subject to Subordination.**

Nothing in this Article prevents subordination by agreement by any person entitled to priority.

§ 9—317. **Secured Party Not Obligated on Contract of Debtor.**

The mere existence of a security interest or authority given to the debtor to dispose of or use collateral does not impose contract or tort liability upon the secured party for the debtor's acts or omissions.

§ 9—318. **Defenses Against Assignee; Modification of Contract After Notification of Assignment; Term Prohibiting Assignment Ineffective; Identification and Proof of Assignment.**

(1) Unless an account debtor has made an enforceable agreement not to assert defenses or claims arising out of a sale as provided in Section 9—206 the rights of an assignee are subject to

(a) all the terms of the contract between the account debtor and assignor and any defense or claim arising therefrom; and

(b) any other defense or claim of the account debtor against the assignor which accrues before the account debtor receives notification of the assignment.

(2) So far as the right to payment or a part thereof under an assigned contract has not been fully earned by performance, and notwithstanding notification of the assignment, any modification of or substitution for the contract made in good faith and in accordance with reasonable commercial standards is effective against an assignee unless the account debtor has otherwise agreed but the assignee acquires corresponding rights under the modified or substituted contract. The assignment may provide that such modification or substitution is a breach by the assignor.

(3) The account debtor is authorized to pay the assignor until the account debtor receives notification that the amount due or to become due has been assigned and that payment is to be made to the assignee. A notification which does not reasonably identify the rights assigned is ineffective. If requested by the account debtor, the assignee must seasonably furnish reasonable proof that the assignment has been made and unless he does so the account debtor may pay the assignor.

(4) A term in any contract between an account debtor and an assignor is ineffective if it prohibits assignment of an account or prohibits creation of a security interest in a general intangible for money due or to become due or requires the account debtor's consent to such assignment or security interest.

Part 4 **Filing**

§ 9—401. **Place of Filing; Erroneous Filing; Removal of Collateral.**

First Alternative Subsection (1)

(1) The proper place to file in order to perfect a security interest is as follows:

(a) when the collateral is timber to be cut or is minerals or the like (including oil and gas) or accounts subject to subsection (5) of Section 9—103, or when the financing statement is filed as a fixture filing (Section 9—313) and the collateral is goods which are or are to become fixtures, then in the office where a mortgage on the real estate would be filed or recorded;

(b) in all other cases, in the office of the [Secretary of State].

Second Alternative Subsection (1)

(1) The proper place to file in order to perfect a security interest is as follows:

(a) when the collateral is equipment used in farming operations, or farm products, or accounts or general intangibles arising from or relating to the sale of farm products by a farmer, or consumer goods, then in the office of the .... in the county of the debtor's residence or if the debtor is not a resident of this state then in the office of the .... in the county where the goods are kept, and in addition when the collateral is crops growing or to be grown in the office of the .... in the county where the land is located;

(b) when the collateral is timber to be cut or is minerals or the like (including oil and gas) or accounts subject to subsection (5) of Section 9—103, or when the financing statement is filed as a fixture filing (Section 9—313) and the collateral is goods which are or are to become fixtures, then in the office where a mortgage on the real estate would be filed or recorded;

(c) in all other cases, in the office of the [Secretary of State].

Third Alternative Subsection (1)

(1) The proper place to file in order to perfect a security interest is as follows:

(a) when the collateral is equipment used in farming operations, or farm products, or accounts or general intangibles arising from or relating to the sale of farm products by a farmer, or consumer goods, then in the office of the .... in the county of the debtor's residence or if the debtor is not a resident of this state then in the office of the .... in the county where the goods are kept, and in addition when the collateral is crops growing or to be grown in the office of the .... in the county where the land is located;

(b) when the collateral is timber to be cut or is minerals or the like (including oil and gas) or accounts subject to subsection (5) of Section 9—103, or when the financing statement is filed as a fixture filing (Section 9—313) and the collateral is goods which are or are to become fixtures, then in the office where a mortgage on the real estate would be filed or recorded;

(c) in all other cases, in the office of the [Secretary of State] and in addition, if the debtor has a place of business in only one county of this state, also in the office of .... of such county, or, if the debtor has no place of business in this state, but resides in the state, also in the office of .... of the county which he resides.

Note: *One of the three alternatives should be selected as subsection (1).*

(2) A filing which is made in good faith in an improper place or not in all of the places required by this section is nevertheless effective with regard to any collateral as to which the filing complied with the requirements of this Article and is also effective with regard to collateral covered by the financing statement against any person who has knowledge of the contents of such financing statement.

(3) A filing which is made in the proper place in this state continues effective even though the debtor's residence or place of business or the location of the collateral or its use, whichever controlled the original filing, is thereafter changed.

Alternative Subsection (3)

[(3) A filing which is made in the proper county continues effective for four months after a change to another county of the debtor's residence or place of business or the location of the collateral, whichever controlled the original filing. It becomes ineffective thereafter unless a copy of the financing statement signed by the secured party is filed in the new county within said period. The security interest may also be perfected in the new county after the expiration of the four-month period; in such case perfection dates from the time of perfection in the new county. A change in the use of the collateral does not impair the effectiveness of the original filing.]

(4) The rules stated in Section 9—103 determine whether filing is necessary in this state.

(5) Notwithstanding the preceding subsections, and subject to subsection (3) of Section 9—302, the proper place to file in order to perfect a security interest in collateral, including fixtures, of a transmitting utility is the office of the [Secretary of State]. This filing constitutes a fixture filing (Section 9—313) as to the collateral described therein which is or is to become fixtures.

(6) For the purposes of this section, the residence of an organization is its place of business if it has one or its chief executive office if it has more than one place of business.

Note: *Subsection (6) should be used only if the state chooses the Second or Third Alternative Subsection (1).*

§ 9—402. Formal Requisites of Financing Statement; Amendments; Mortgage as Financing Statement.

(1) A financing statement is sufficient if it gives the names of the debtor and the secured party, is signed by the debtor, gives an address of the secured party from which information concerning the security interest may be obtained, gives a mailing address of the debtor and contains a statement indicating the types, or describing the items, of collateral. A financing statement may be filed before a security agreement is made or a security interest otherwise attaches. When the financing statement covers crops growing or to be grown, the statement must also contain a description of the real estate concerned. When the financing statement covers timber to be cut or covers minerals or the like (including oil and gas) or accounts subject to subsection (5) of Section 9—103, or when the financing statement is filed as a fixture filing (Section 9—313) and the collateral is goods which are or are to become fixtures, the statement must also comply with subsection (5). A copy of the security agreement is sufficient as a financing statement if it contains

the above information and is signed by the debtor. A carbon, photographic or other reproduction of a security agreement or a financing statement is sufficient as a financing statement if the security agreement so provides or if the original has been filed in this state.

(2) A financing statement which otherwise complies with subsection (1) is sufficient when it is signed by the secured party instead of the debtor if it is filed to perfect a security interest in

(a) collateral already subject to a security interest in another jurisdiction when it is brought into this state, or when the debtor's location is changed to this state. Such a financing statement must state that the collateral was brought into this state or that the debtor's location was changed to this state under such circumstances; or

(b) proceeds under Section 9—306 if the security interest in the original collateral was perfected. Such a financing statement must describe the original collateral; or

(c) collateral as to which the filing has lapsed; or

(d) collateral acquired after a change of name, identity or corporate structure of the debtor (subsection (7)).

(3) A form substantially as follows is sufficient to comply with subsection (1):

Name of debtor (or assignor) ....
Address ....
Name of secured party (or assignee) ....
Address ....
1. This financing statement covers the following types (or items) of property:
    (Describe) ....
2. (If collateral is crops) The above described crops are growing or are to be grown on:
    (Describe Real Estate) ....
3. (If applicable) The above goods are to become fixtures on *
*Where appropriate substitute either ''The above timber is standing on . . . .'' or ''The above minerals or the like (including oil and gas) or accounts will be financed at the wellhead or minehead of the well or mine located on . . . .''
    (Describe Real Estate) ....
and this financing statement is to be filed [for record] in the real estate records. (If the debtor does not have an interest of record) The name of a record owner is
4. (If products of collateral are claimed) Products of the collateral are also covered.

  (use   ....
whichever   Signature of Debtor (or Assignor)

  is   ....
applicable)   Signature of Secured Party
      (or Assignee)

(4) A financing statement may be amended by filing a writing signed by both the debtor and the secured party. An amendment does not extend the period of effectiveness of a financing statement. If any amendment adds collateral, it is effective as to the added collateral only from the filing date of the amendment. In this Article, unless the context otherwise requires, the term ''financing statement'' means the original financing statement and any amendments.

(5) A financing statement covering timber to be cut or covering minerals or the like (including oil and gas) or accounts subject to subsection (5) of Section 9—103, or a financing statement filed as a fixture filing (Section 9—313) where the debtor is not a transmitting utility, must show that it covers this type of collateral, must recite that it is to be filed [for record] in the real estate records, and the financing statement must contain a description of the real estate [sufficient if it were contained in a mortgage of the real estate to give constructive notice of the mortgage under the law of this state]. If the debtor does not have an interest of record in the real estate, the financing statement must show the name of a record owner.

(6) A mortgage is effective as a financing statement filed as a fixture filing from the date of its recording if

(a) the goods are described in the mortgage by item or type; and

(b) the goods are or are to become fixtures related to the real estate described in the mortgage; and

(c) the mortgage complies with the requirements for a financing statement in this section other than a recital that it is to be filed in the real estate records; and

(d) the mortgage is duly recorded.

No fee with reference to the financing statement is required other than the regular recording and satisfaction fees with respect to the mortgage.

(7) A financing statement sufficiently shows the name of the debtor if it gives the individual, partnership or corporate name of the debtor, whether or not it adds other trade names or names of partners. Where the debtor so changes his name or in the case of an organization its name, identity or corporate structure that a filed financing statement becomes seriously misleading, the filing is not effective to perfect a security interest in collateral acquired by the debtor more than four months after the change, unless a new appropriate financing statement is filed before the expiration of that time. A filed financing statement remains effective with respect to collateral transferred by the debtor even though the secured party knows of or consents to the transfer.

(8) A financing statement substantially complying with the requirements of this section is effective even though it contains minor errors which are not seriously misleading.

Note: *Language in brackets is optional.*

Note: *Where the state has any special recording system for real estate other than the usual grantor-grantee index (as, for instance, a tract system or a title registration or Torrens system) local adaptations of subsection (5) and Section 9—403(7) may be necessary. See Mass.Gen.Laws Chapter 106, Section 9—409.*

§ 9—403. What Constitutes Filing; Duration of Filing; Effect of Lapsed Filing; Duties of Filing Officer.

(1) Presentation for filing of a financing statement and tender of the filing fee or acceptance of the statement by the filing officer constitutes filing under this Article.

(2) Except as provided in subsection (6) a filed financing statement is effective for a period of five years from the date of filing. The effectiveness of a filed financing statement lapses on the expiration of the five year period unless a continuation statement is filed prior to the lapse. If a security interest perfected by filing exists at the time insolvency proceedings are commenced by or against the debtor, the security interest remains perfected until termination of the insolvency proceedings and thereafter for a period of sixty days or until expiration of the five year period, whichever occurs later. Upon lapse the security interest becomes unperfected, unless it is perfected without filing. If the security interest becomes unperfected upon lapse, it is deemed to have been unperfected as against a person who became a purchaser or lien creditor before lapse.

(3) A continuation statement may be filed by the secured party within six months prior to the expiration of the five year period specified in subsection (2). Any such continuation statement must be signed by the secured party, identify the original statement by file number and state that the original statement is still effective. A continuation statement signed by a person other than the secured party of record must be accompanied by a separate written statement of assignment signed by the secured party of record and complying with subsection (2) of Section 9—405, including payment of the required fee. Upon timely filing of the continuation statement, the effectiveness of the original statement is continued for five years after the last date to which the filing was effective whereupon it lapses in the same manner as provided in subsection (2) unless another continuation statement is filed prior to such lapse. Succeeding continuation statements may be filed in the same manner to continue the effectiveness of the original statement. Unless a statute on disposition of public records provides otherwise, the filing officer may remove a lapsed statement from the files and destroy it immediately if he has retained a microfilm or other photographic record, or in other cases after one year after the lapse. The filing officer shall so arrange matters by physical annexation of financing statements to continuation statements or other related filings, or by other means, that if he physically destroys the financing statements of a period more than five years past, those which have been continued by a continuation state-

ment or which are still effective under subsection (6) shall be retained.

(4) Except as provided in subsection (7) a filing officer shall mark each statement with a file number and with the date and hour of filing and shall hold the statement or a microfilm or other photographic copy thereof for public inspection. In addition the filing officer shall index the statement according to the name of the debtor and shall note in the index the file number and the address of the debtor given in the statement.

(5) The uniform fee for filing and indexing and for stamping a copy furnished by the secured party to show the date and place of filing for an original financing statement or for a continuation statement shall be $. . . . . . . if the statement is in the standard form prescribed by the [Secretary of State] and otherwise shall be $. . . . . . ., plus in each case, if the financing statement is subject to subsection (5) of Section 9—402, $. . . . . . . The uniform fee for each name more than one required to be indexed shall be $. . . . . . . The secured party may at his option show a trade name for any person and an extra uniform indexing fee of $. . . . . . . shall be paid with respect thereto.

(6) If the debtor is a transmitting utility (subsection (5) of Section 9—401) and a filed financing statement so states, it is effective until a termination statement is filed. A real estate mortgage which is effective as a fixture filing under subsection (6) of Section 9—402 remains effective as a fixture filing until the mortgage is released or satisfied of record or its effectiveness otherwise terminates as to the real estate.

(7) When a financing statement covers timber to be cut or covers minerals or the like (including oil and gas) or accounts subject to subsection (5) of Section 9—103, or is filed as a fixture filing, [it shall be filed for record and] the filing officer shall index it under the names of the debtor and any owner of record shown on the financing statement in the same fashion as if they were the mortgagors in a mortgage of the real estate described, and, to the extent that the law of this state provides for indexing of mortgages under the name of the mortgagee, under the name of the secured party as if he were the mortgagee thereunder, or where indexing is by description in the same fashion as if the financing statement were a mortgage of the real estate described.

Note: *In states in which writings will not appear in the real estate records and indices unless actually recorded the bracketed language in subsection (7) should be used.*

§ 9—404. Termination Statement.

(1) If a financing statement covering consumer goods is filed on or after . . . ., then within one month or within ten days following written demand by the debtor after there is no outstanding secured obligation and no commitment to make advances, incur obligations or otherwise give value,

the secured party must file with each filing officer with whom the financing statement was filed, a termination statement to the effect that he no longer claims a security interest under the financing statement, which shall be identified by file number. In other cases whenever there is no outstanding secured obligation and no commitment to make advances, incur obligations or otherwise give value, the secured party must on written demand by the debtor send the debtor, for each filing officer with whom the financing statement was filed, a termination statement to the effect that he no longer claims a security interest under the financing statement, which shall be identified by file number. A termination statement signed by a person other than the secured party of record must be accompanied by a separate written statement of assignment signed by the secured party of record complying with subsection (2) of Section 9—405, including payment of the required fee. If the affected secured party fails to file such a termination statement as required by this subsection, or to send such a termination statement within ten days after proper demand therefor, he shall be liable to the debtor for one hundred dollars, and in addition for any loss caused to the debtor by such failure.

(2) On presentation to the filing officer of such a termination statement he must note it in the index. If he has received the termination statement in duplicate, he shall return one copy of the termination statement to the secured party stamped to show the time of receipt thereof. If the filing officer has a microfilm or other photographic record of the financing statement, and of any related continuation statement, statement of assignment and statement of release, he may remove the originals from the files at any time after receipt of the termination statement, or if he has no such record, he may remove them from the files at any time after one year after receipt of the termination statement.

(3) If the termination statement is in the standard form prescribed by the [Secretary of State], the uniform fee for filing and indexing the termination statement shall be $. . . . . . ., and otherwise shall be $. . . . . . ., plus in each case an additional fee of $. . . . . . . for each name more than one against which the termination statement is required to be indexed.

Note: *The date to be inserted should be the effective date of the revised Article 9.*

§ 9—405. Assignment of Security Interest; Duties of Filing Officer; Fees.

(1) A financing statement may disclose an assignment of a security interest in the collateral described in the financing statement by indication in the financing statement of the name and address of the assignee or by an assignment itself or a copy thereof on the face or back of the statement. On presentation to the filing officer of such a financing statement the filing officer shall mark the same as provided in Section 9—403(4). The uniform fee for filing, indexing and furnishing filing data for a financing statement so indicating

an assignment shall be $. . . . . . . if the statement is in the standard form prescribed by the [Secretary of State] and otherwise shall be $. . . . . . ., plus in each case an additional fee of $. . . . . . . for each name more than one against which the financing statement is required to be indexed.

(2) A secured party may assign of record all or part of his rights under a financing statement by the filing in the place where the original financing statement was filed of a separate written statement of assignment signed by the secured party of record and setting forth the name of the secured party of record and the debtor, the file number and the date of filing of the financing statement and the name and address of the assignee and containing a description of the collateral assigned. A copy of the assignment is sufficient as a separate statement if it complies with the preceding sentence. On presentation to the filing officer of such a separate statement, the filing officer shall mark such separate statement with the date and hour of the filing. He shall note the assignment on the index of the financing statement, or in the case of a fixture filing, or a filing covering timber to be cut, or covering minerals or the like (including oil and gas) or accounts subject to subsection (5) of Section 9—103, he shall index the assignment under the name of the assignor as grantor and, to the extent that the law of this state provides for indexing the assignment of a mortgage under the name of the assignee, he shall index the assignment of the financing statement under the name of the assignee. The uniform fee for filing, indexing and furnishing filing data about such a separate statement of assignment shall be $. . . . . if the statement is in the standard form prescribed by the [Secretary of State] and otherwise shall be $. . . . . ., plus in each case an additional fee of $. . . . . for each name more than one against which the statement of assignment is required to be indexed. Notwithstanding the provisions of this subsection, an assignment of record of a security interest in a fixture contained in a mortgage effective as a fixture filing (subsection (6) of Section 9—402) may be made only by an assignment of the mortgage in the manner provided by the law of this state other than this Act.

(3) After the disclosure or filing of an assignment under this section, the assignee is the secured party of record.

§ 9—406. Release of Collateral; Duties of Filing Officer; Fees.

A secured party of record may by his signed statement release all or a part of any collateral described in a filed financing statement. The statement of release is sufficient if it contains a description of the collateral being released, the name and address of the debtor, the name and address of the secured party, and the file number of the financing statement. A statement of release signed by a person other than the secured party of record must be accompanied by a separate written statement of assignment signed by the secured party of record and complying with subsection (2) of Section 9—405, including payment of the required fee.

Upon presentation of such a statement of release to the filing officer he shall mark the statement with the hour and date of filing and shall note the same upon the margin of the index of the filing of the financing statement. The uniform fee for filing and noting such a statement of release shall be $. . . . . if the statement is in the standard form prescribed by the [Secretary of State] and otherwise shall be $. . . . ., plus in each case an additional fee of $. . . . . for each name more than one against which the statement of release is required to be indexed.

§ 9—407. **Information From Filing Officer.**

[(1) If the person filing any financing statement, termination statement, statement of assignment, or statement of release, furnishes the filing officer a copy thereof, the filing officer shall upon request note upon the copy the file number and date and hour of the filing of the original and deliver or send the copy to such person.]

[(2) Upon request of any person, the filing officer shall issue his certificate showing whether there is on file on the date and hour stated therein, any presently effective financing statement naming a particular debtor and any statement of assignment thereof and if there is, giving the date and hour of filing of each such statement and the names and addresses of each secured party therein. The uniform fee for such a certificate shall be $. . . . . if the request for the certificate is in the standard form prescribed by the [Secretary of State] and otherwise shall be $. . . . . . Upon request the filing officer shall furnish a copy of any filed financing statement or statement of assignment for a uniform fee of $. . . . . per page.]

Note: *This section is proposed as an optional provision to require filing officers to furnish certificates. Local law and practices should be consulted with regard to the advisability of adoption.*

§ 9—408. **Financing Statements Covering Consigned or Leased Goods.**

A consignor or lessor of goods may file a financing statement using the terms ''consignor,'' ''consignee,'' ''lessor,'' ''lessee'' or the like instead of the terms specified in Section 9—402. The provisions of this Part shall apply as appropriate to such a financing statement but its filing shall not of itself be a factor in determining whether or not the consignment or lease is intended as security (Section 1—201(37)). However, if it is determined for other reasons that the consignment or lease is so intended, a security interest of the consignor or lessor which attaches to the consigned or leased goods is perfected by such filing.

Part 5 Default

§ 9—501. **Default; Procedure When Security Agreement Covers Both Real and Personal Property.**

(1) When a debtor is in default under a security agreement, a secured party has the rights and remedies provided in this Part and except as limited by subsection (3) those provided in the security agreement. He may reduce his claim to judgment, foreclose or otherwise enforce the security interest by any available judicial procedure. If the collateral is documents the secured party may proceed either as to the documents or as to the goods covered thereby. A secured party in possession has the rights, remedies and duties provided in Section 9—207. The rights and remedies referred to in this subsection are cumulative.

(2) After default, the debtor has the rights and remedies provided in this Part, those provided in the security agreement and those provided in Section 9—207.

(3) To the extent that they give rights to the debtor and impose duties on the secured party, the rules stated in the subsections referred to below may not be waived or varied except as provided with respect to compulsory disposition of collateral (subsection (3) of Section 9—504 and Section 9—505) and with respect to redemption of collateral (Section 9—506) but the parties may by agreement determine the standards by which the fulfillment of these rights and duties is to be measured if such standards are not manifestly unreasonable:

(a) subsection (2) of Section 9—502 and subsection (2) of Section 9—504 insofar as they require accounting for surplus proceeds of collateral;

(b) subsection (3) of Section 9—504 and subsection (1) of Section 9—505 which deal with disposition of collateral;

(c) subsection (2) of Section 9—505 which deals with acceptance of collateral as discharge of obligation;

(d) Section 9—506 which deals with redemption of collateral; and

(e) subsection (1) of Section 9—507 which deals with the secured party's liability for failure to comply with this Part.

(4) If the security agreement covers both real and personal property, the secured party may proceed under this Part as to the personal property or he may proceed as to both the real and the personal property in accordance with his rights and remedies in respect of the real property in which case the provisions of this Part do not apply.

(5) When a secured party has reduced his claim to judgment the lien of any levy which may be made upon his collateral by virtue of any execution based upon the judgment shall relate back to the date of the perfection of the security interest in such collateral. A judicial sale, pursuant to such execution, is a foreclosure of the security interest by judicial procedure within the meaning of this section, and the secured party may purchase at the sale and thereafter hold the collateral free of any other requirements of this Article.

§ 9—502. Collection Rights of Secured Party.

(1) When so agreed and in any event on default the secured party is entitled to notify an account debtor or the obligor on an instrument to make payment to him whether or not the assignor was theretofore making collections on the collateral, and also to take control of any proceeds to which he is entitled under Section 9—306.

(2) A secured party who by agreement is entitled to charge back uncollected collateral or otherwise to full or limited recourse against the debtor and who undertakes to collect from the account debtors or obligors must proceed in a commercially reasonable manner and may deduct his reasonable expenses of realization from the collections. If the security agreement secures an indebtedness, the secured party must account to the debtor for any surplus, and unless otherwise agreed, the debtor is liable for any deficiency. But, if the underlying transaction was a sale of accounts or chattel paper, the debtor is entitled to any surplus or is liable for any deficiency only if the security agreement so provides.

§ 9—503. Secured Party's Right to Take Possession After Default.

Unless otherwise agreed a secured party has on default the right to take possession of the collateral. In taking possession a secured party may proceed without judicial process if this can be done without breach of the peace or may proceed by action. If the security agreement so provides the secured party may require the debtor to assemble the collateral and make it available to the secured party at a place to be designated by the secured party which is reasonably convenient to both parties. Without removal a secured party may render equipment unusable, and may dispose of collateral on the debtor's premises under Section 9—504.

§ 9—504. Secured Party's Right to Dispose of Collateral After Default; Effect of Disposition.

(1) A secured party after default may sell, lease or otherwise dispose of any or all of the collateral in its then condition or following any commercially reasonable preparation or processing. Any sale of goods is subject to the Article on Sales (Article 2). The proceeds of disposition shall be applied in the order following to

(a) the reasonable expenses of retaking, holding, preparing for sale or lease, selling, leasing and the like and, to the extent provided for in the agreement and not prohibited by law, the reasonable attorneys' fees and legal expenses incurred by the secured party;

(b) the satisfaction of indebtedness secured by the security interest under which the disposition is made;

(c) the satisfaction of indebtedness secured by any subordinate security interest in the collateral if written notification of demand therefor is received before distribution of the proceeds is completed. If requested by the secured party, the holder of a subordinate security interest must seasonably furnish reasonable proof of his interest, and unless he does so, the secured party need not comply with his demand.

(2) If the security interest secures an indebtedness, the secured party must account to the debtor for any surplus, and, unless otherwise agreed, the debtor is liable for any deficiency. But if the underlying transaction was a sale of accounts or chattel paper, the debtor is entitled to any surplus or is liable for any deficiency only if the security agreement so provides.

(3) Disposition of the collateral may be by public or private proceedings and may be made by way of one or more contracts. Sale or other disposition may be as a unit or in parcels and at any time and place and on any terms but every aspect of the disposition including the method, manner, time, place and terms must be commercially reasonable. Unless collateral is perishable or threatens to decline speedily in value or is of a type customarily sold on a recognized market, reasonable notification of the time and place of any public sale or reasonable notification of the time after which any private sale or other intended disposition is to be made shall be sent by the secured party to the debtor, if he has not signed after default a statement renouncing or modifying his right to notification of sale. In the case of consumer goods no other notification need be sent. In other cases notification shall be sent to any other secured party from whom the secured party has received (before sending his notification to the debtor or before the debtor's renunciation of his rights) written notice of a claim of an interest in the collateral. The secured party may buy at any public sale and if the collateral is of a type customarily sold in a recognized market or is of a type which is the subject of widely distributed standard price quotations he may buy at private sale.

(4) When collateral is disposed of by a secured party after default, the disposition transfers to a purchaser for value all of the debtor's rights therein, discharges the security interest under which it is made and any security interest or lien subordinate thereto. The purchaser takes free of all such rights and interests even though the secured party fails to comply with the requirements of this Part or of any judicial proceedings

(a) in the case of a public sale, if the purchaser has no knowledge of any defects in the sale and if he does not buy in collusion with the secured party, other bidders or the person conducting the sale; or

(b) in any other case, if the purchaser acts in good faith.

(5) A person who is liable to a secured party under a guaranty, indorsement, repurchase agreement or the like and who receives a transfer of collateral from the secured party

or is subrogated to his rights has thereafter the rights and duties of the secured party. Such a transfer of collateral is not a sale or disposition of the collateral under this Article.

§ 9—505. Compulsory Disposition of Collateral; Acceptance of the Collateral as Discharge of Obligation.

(1) If the debtor has paid sixty per cent of the cash price in the case of a purchase money security interest in consumer goods or sixty per cent of the loan in the case of another security interest in consumer goods, and has not signed after default a statement renouncing or modifying his rights under this Part a secured party who has taken possession of collateral must dispose of it under Section 9—504 and if he fails to do so within ninety days after he takes possession the debtor at his option may recover in conversion or under Section 9—507(1) on secured party's liability.

(2) In any other case involving consumer goods or any other collateral a secured party in possession may, after default, propose to retain the collateral in satisfaction of the obligation. Written notice of such proposal shall be sent to the debtor if he has not signed after default a statement renouncing or modifying his rights under this subsection. In the case of consumer goods no other notice need be given. In other cases notice shall be sent to any other secured party from whom the secured party has received (before sending his notice to the debtor or before the debtor's renunciation of his rights) written notice of a claim of an interest in the collateral. If the secured party receives objection in writing from a person entitled to receive notification within twenty-one days after the notice was sent, the secured party must dispose of the collateral under Section 9—504. In the absence of such written objection the secured party may retain the collateral in satisfaction of the debtor's obligation.

§ 9—506. Debtor's Right to Redeem Collateral.

At any time before the secured party has disposed of collateral or entered into a contract for its disposition under Section 9—504 or before the obligation has been discharged under Section 9—505(2) the debtor or any other secured party may unless otherwise agreed in writing after default redeem the collateral by tendering fulfillment of all obligations secured by the collateral as well as the expenses reasonably incurred by the secured party in retaking, holding and preparing the collateral for disposition, in arranging for the sale, and to the extent provided in the agreement and not prohibited by law, his reasonable attorneys' fees and legal expenses.

§ 9—507. Secured Party's Liability for Failure to Comply With This Part.

(1) If it is established that the secured party is not proceeding in accordance with the provisions of this Part disposition may be ordered or restrained on appropriate terms and conditions. If the disposition has occurred the debtor or any person entitled to notification or whose security interest has been made known to the secured party prior to the disposition has a right to recover from the secured party any loss caused by a failure to comply with the provisions of this Part. If the collateral is consumer goods, the debtor has a right to recover in any event an amount not less than the credit service charge plus ten per cent of the principal amount of the debt or the time price differential plus 10 per cent of the cash price.

(2) The fact that a better price could have been obtained by a sale at a different time or in a different method from that selected by the secured party is not of itself sufficient to establish that the sale was not made in a commercially reasonable manner. If the secured party either sells the collateral in the usual manner in any recognized market therefor or if he sells at the price current in such market at the time of his sale or if he has otherwise sold in conformity with reasonable commercial practices among dealers in the type of property sold he has sold in a commercially reasonable manner. The principles stated in the two preceding sentences with respect to sales also apply as may be appropriate to other types of disposition. A disposition which has been approved in any judicial proceeding or by any bona fide creditors' committee or representative of creditors shall conclusively be deemed to be commercially reasonable, but this sentence does not indicate that any such approval must be obtained in any case nor does it indicate that any disposition not so approved is not commercially reasonable.

Article 10
EFFECTIVE DATE AND REPEALER

§ 10—101. Effective Date.

This Act shall become effective at midnight on December 31st following its enactment. It applies to transactions entered into and events occurring after that date.

§ 10—102. Specific Repealer; Provision for Transition.

(1) The following acts and all other acts and parts of acts inconsistent herewith are hereby repealed:
(Here should follow the acts to be specifically repealed including the following:
    Uniform Negotiable Instruments Act
    Uniform Warehouse Receipts Act
    Uniform Sales Act
    Uniform Bills of Lading Act
    Uniform Stock Transfer Act
    Uniform Conditional Sales Act

Uniform Trust Receipts Act
   Also any acts regulating:
Bank collections
Bulk sales
Chattel mortgages
Conditional sales
Factor's lien acts
Farm storage of grain and similar acts
Assignment of accounts receivable)

(2) Transactions validly entered into before the effective date specified in Section 10—101 and the rights, duties and interests flowing from them remain valid thereafter and may be terminated, completed, consummated or enforced as required or permitted by any statute or other law amended or repealed by this Act as though such repeal or amendment had not occurred.

Note: *Subsection (1) should be separately prepared for each state. The foregoing is a list of statutes to be checked.*

§ 10—103. **General Repealer.**

Except as provided in the following section, all acts and parts of acts inconsistent with this Act are hereby repealed.

§ 10—104. **Laws Not Repealed.**

(1) The Article on Documents of Title (Article 7) does not repeal or modify any laws prescribing the form or contents of documents of title or the services or facilities to be afforded by bailees, or otherwise regulating bailees' businesses in respects not specifically dealt with herein; but the fact that such laws are violated does not affect the status of a document of title which otherwise complies with the definition of a document of title (Section 1—201).

[(2) This Act does not repeal . . . .*, cited as the Uniform Act for the Simplification of Fiduciary Security Transfers, and if in any respect there is any inconsistency between that Act and the Article of this Act on investment securities (Article 8) the provisions of the former Act shall control.]

Note: *At * in subsection (2) insert the statutory reference to the Uniform Act for the Simplification of Fiduciary Security Transfers if such Act has previously been enacted. If it has not been enacted, omit subsection (2).*

Article 11
(REPORTERS' DRAFT)
EFFECTIVE DATE AND
TRANSITION PROVISIONS

This material has been numbered Article 11 to distinguish it from Article 10, the transition provision of the 1962 Code, which may still remain in effect in some states to cover transition problems from pre-Code law to the original Uniform Commercial Code. Adaptation may be necessary in particular states. The terms "[old Code]" and "[new

Code]" and "[old U.C.C.]" and "[new U.C.C.]" are used herein, and should be suitably changed in each state.

Note: *This draft was prepared by the Reporters and has not been passed upon by the Review Committee, the Permanent Editorial Board, the American Law Institute, or the National Conference of Commissioners on Uniform State Laws. It is submitted as a working draft which may be adapted as appropriate in each state.*

§ 11—101. **Effective Date.**

This Act shall become effective at 12:01 A.M. on ———— , 19 ———— .

§ 11—102. **Preservation of Old Transition Provision.**

The provisions of [here insert reference to the original transition provision in the particular state] shall continue to apply to [the new U.C.C.] and for this purpose the [old U.C.C. and new U.C.C.] shall be considered one continuous statute.

§ 11—103. **Transition to [New Code]—General Rule.**

Transactions validly entered into after [effective date of old U.C.C.] and before [effective date of new U.C.C.], and which were subject to the provisions of [old U.C.C.] and which would be subject to this Act as amended if they had been entered into after the effective date of [new U.C.C.] and the rights, duties and interests flowing from such transactions remain valid after the latter date and may be terminated, completed, consummated or enforced as required or permitted by the [new U.C.C.]. Security interests arising out of such transactions which are perfected when [new U.C.C.] becomes effective shall remain perfected until they lapse as provided in [new U.C.C.], and may be continued as permitted by [new U.C.C.], except as stated in Section 11—105.

§ 11—104. **Transition Provision on Change of Requirement of Filing.**

A security interest for the perfection of which filing or the taking of possession was required under [old U.C.C.] and which attached prior to the effective date of [new U.C.C.] but was not perfected shall be deemed perfected on the effective date of [new U.C.C.] if [new U.C.C.] permits perfection without filing or authorizes filing in the office or offices where a prior ineffective filing was made.

§ 11—105. **Transition Provision on Change of Place of Filing.**

(1) A financing statement or continuation statement filed prior to [effective date of new U.C.C.] which shall not have lapsed prior to [the effective date of new U.C.C.] shall remain effective for the period provided in the [old Code], but not less than five years after the filing.

(2) With respect to any collateral acquired by the debtor subsequent to the effective date of [new U.C.C.], any ef-

fective financing statement or continuation statement described in this section shall apply only if the filing or filings are in the office or offices that would be appropriate to perfect the security interests in the new collateral under [new U.C.C.].

(3) The effectiveness of any financing statement or continuation statement filed prior to [effective date of new U.C.C.] may be continued by a continuation statement as permitted by [new U.C.C.], except that if [new U.C.C.] requires a filing in an office where there was no previous financing statement, a new financing statement conforming to Section 11—106 shall be filed in that office.

(4) If the record of a mortgage of real estate would have been effective as a fixture filing of goods described therein if [new U.C.C.] had been in effect on the date of recording the mortgage, the mortgage shall be deemed effective as a fixture filing as to such goods under subsection (6) of Section 9—402 of the [new U.C.C.] on the effective date of [new U.C.C.].

§ 11—106. **Required Refilings.**

(1) If a security interest is perfected or has priority when this Act takes effect as to all persons or as to certain persons without any filing or recording, and if the filing of a financing statement would be required for the perfection or priority of the security interest against those persons under [new U.C.C.], the perfection and priority rights of the security interest continue until 3 years after the effective date of [new U.C.C.]. The perfection will then lapse unless a financing statement is filed as provided in subsection (4) or unless the security interest is perfected otherwise than by filing.

(2) If a security interest is perfected when [new U.C.C.] takes effect under a law other than [U.C.C.] which requires no further filing, refiling or recording to continue its perfection, perfection continues until and will lapse 3 years after [new U.C.C.] takes effect, unless a financing statement is filed as provided in subsection (4) or unless the security interest is perfected otherwise than by filing, or unless under subsection (3) of Section 9—302 the other law continues to govern filing.

(3) If a security interest is perfected by a filing, refiling or recording under a law repealed by this Act which required

further filing, refiling or recording to continue its perfection, perfection continues and will lapse on the date provided by the law so repealed for such further filing, refiling or recording unless a financing statement is filed as provided in subsection (4) or unless the security interest is perfected otherwise than by filing.

(4) A financing statement may be filed within six months before the perfection of a security interest would otherwise lapse. Any such financing statement may be signed by either the debtor or the secured party. It must identify the security agreement, statement or notice (however denominated in any statute or other law repealed or modified by this Act), state the office where and the date when the last filing, refiling or recording, if any, was made with respect thereto, and the filing number, if any, or book and page, if any, of recording and further state that the security agreement, statement or notice, however denominated, in another filing office under the [U.C.C.] or under any statute or other law repealed or modified by this Act is still effective. Section 9—401 and Section 9—103 determine the proper place to file such a financing statement. Except as specified in this subsection, the provisions of Section 9—403(3) for continuation statements apply to such a financing statement.

§ 11—107. **Transition Provisions as to Priorities.**

Except as otherwise provided in [Article 11], [old U.C.C.] shall apply to any questions of priority if the positions of the parties were fixed prior to the effective date of [new U.C.C.]. In other cases questions of priority shall be determined by [new U.C.C.].

§ 11—108. **Presumption that Rule of Law Continues Unchanged.**

Unless a change in law has clearly been made, the provisions of [new U.C.C.] shall be deemed declaratory of the meaning of the [old U.C.C.].

OFFICIAL TEXT—UCC—1992

The preceding articles and sections constitute the official text of the Uniform Commercial Code as of 1992.

Appendix D

The Uniform Partnership Act

(Adopted in forty-nine States [all of the states except Louisiana], the District of Columbia, the Virgin Islands, and Guam. The adoptions by Alabama and Nebraska do not follow the official text in every respect, but are substantially similar, with local variations.)

The Act consists of 7 Parts as follows:

  I. Preliminary Provisions

  II. Nature of Partnership

  III. Relations of Partners to Persons Dealing with the Partnership

  IV. Relations of Partners to One Another

  V. Property Rights of a Partner

  VI. Dissolution and Winding Up

  VII. Miscellaneous Provisions

An Act to make uniform the Law of Partnerships

Be it enacted, etc.:

Part I Preliminary Provisions

Sec. 1. Name of Act

This act may be cited as Uniform Partnership Act.

Sec. 2. Definition of Terms

In this act, "Court" includes every court and judge having jurisdiction in the case.

"Business" includes every trade, occupation, or profession.

"Person" includes individuals, partnerships, corporations, and other associations.

"Bankrupt" includes bankrupt under the Federal Bankruptcy Act or insolvent under any state insolvent act.

"Conveyance" includes every assignment, lease, mortgage, or encumbrance.

"Real property" includes land and any interest or estate in land.

Sec. 3. Interpretation of Knowledge and Notice

(1) A person has "knowledge" of a fact within the meaning of this act not only when he has actual knowledge thereof, but also when he has knowledge of such other facts as in the circumstances shows bad faith.

(2) A person has "notice" of a fact within the meaning of this act when the person who claims the benefit of the notice:

  (a) States the fact to such person, or

  (b) Delivers through the mail, or by other means of communication, a written statement of the fact to such person or to a proper person at his place of business or residence.

Sec. 4. Rules of Construction

(1) The rule that statutes in derogation of the common law are to be strictly construed shall have no application to this act.

(2) The law of estoppel shall apply under this act.

(3) The law of agency shall apply under this act.

(4) This act shall be so interpreted and construed as to effect its general purpose to make uniform the law of those states which enact it.

(5) This act shall not be construed so as to impair the obligations of any contract existing when the act goes into

effect, nor to affect any action or proceedings begun or right accrued before this act takes effect.

Sec. 5. **Rules for Cases Not Provided for in This Act.**

In any case not provided for in this act the rules of law and equity, including the law merchant, shall govern.

Part II Nature of Partnership

Sec. 6. **Partnership Defined**

(1) A partnership is an association of two or more persons to carry on as co-owners a business for profit.

(2) But any association formed under any other statute of this state, or any statute adopted by authority, other than the authority of this state, is not a partnership under this act, unless such association would have been a partnership in this state prior to the adoption of this act; but this act shall apply to limited partnerships except in so far as the statutes relating to such partnerships are inconsistent herewith.

Sec. 7. **Rules for Determining the Existence of a Partnership**

In determining whether a partnership exists, these rules shall apply:

(1) Except as provided by Section 16 persons who are not partners as to each other are not partners as to third persons.

(2) Joint tenancy, tenancy in common, tenancy by the entireties, joint property, common property, or part ownership does not of itself establish a partnership, whether such co-owners do or do not share any profits made by the use of the property.

(3) The sharing of gross returns does not of itself establish a partnership, whether or not the persons sharing them have a joint or common right or interest in any property from which the returns are derived.

(4) The receipt by a person of a share of the profits of a business is prima facie evidence that he is a partner in the business, but no such inference shall be drawn if such profits were received in payment:

(a) As a debt by installments or otherwise,

(b) As wages of an employee or rent to a landlord,

(c) As an annuity to a widow or representative of a deceased partner,

(d) As interest on a loan, though the amount of payment vary with the profits of the business,

(e) As the consideration for the sale of a good-will of a business or other property by installments or otherwise.

Sec. 8. **Partnership Property**

(1) All property originally brought into the partnership stock or subsequently acquired by purchase or otherwise, on account of the partnership, is partnership property.

(2) Unless the contrary intention appears, property acquired with partnership funds is partnership property.

(3) Any estate in real property may be acquired in the partnership name. Title so acquired can be conveyed only in the partnership name.

(4) A conveyance to a partnership in the partnership name, though without words of inheritance, passes the entire estate of the grantor unless a contrary intent appears.

Part III Relations of Partners to Persons Dealing with the Partnership

Sec. 9. **Partner Agent of Partnership as to Partnership Business**

(1) Every partner is an agent of the partnership for the purpose of its business, and the act of every partner, including the execution in the partnership name of any instrument, for apparently carrying on in the usual way the business of the partnership of which he is a member binds the partnership, unless the partner so acting has in fact no authority to act for the partnership in the particular matter, and the person with whom he is dealing has knowledge of the fact that he has no such authority.

(2) An act of a partner which is not apparently for the carrying on of the business of the partnership in the usual way does not bind the partnership unless authorized by the other partners.

(3) Unless authorized by the other partners or unless they have abandoned the business, one or more but less than all the partners have no authority to:

(a) Assign the partnership property in trust for creditors or on the assignee's promise to pay the debts of the partnership,

(b) Dispose of the good-will of the business,

(c) Do any other act which would make it impossible to carry on the ordinary business of a partnership,

(d) Confess a judgment,

(e) Submit a partnership claim or liability to arbitration or reference.

(4) No act of a partner in contravention of a restriction on authority shall bind the partnership to persons having knowledge of the restriction.

Sec. 10. **Conveyance of Real Property of the Partnership**

(1) Where title to real property is in the partnership name, any partner may convey title to such property by a conveyance executed in the partnership name; but the partnership may recover such property unless the partner's act

binds the partnership under the provisions of paragraph (1) of section 9, or unless such property has been conveyed by the grantee or a person claiming through such grantee to a holder for value without knowledge that the partner, in making the conveyance, has exceeded his authority.

(2) Where title to real property is in the name of the partnership, a conveyance executed by a partner, in his own name, passes the equitable interest of the partnership, provided the act is one within the authority of the partner under the provisions of paragraph (1) of section 9.

(3) Where title to real property is in the name of one or more but not all the partners, and the record does not disclose the right of the partnership, the partners in whose name the title stands may convey title to such property, but the partnership may recover such property if the partners' act does not bind the partnership under the provisions of paragraph (1) of section 9, unless the purchaser or his assignee, is a holder for value, without knowledge.

(4) Where the title to real property is in the name of one or more or all the partners, or in a third person in trust for the partnership, a conveyance executed by a partner in the partnership name, or in his own name, passes the equitable interest of the partnership, provided the act is one within the authority of the partner under the provisions of paragraph (1) of section 9.

(5) Where the title to real property is in the names of all the partners a conveyance executed by all the partners passes all their rights in such property.

Sec. 11. **Partnership Bound by Admission of Partner**

An admission or representation made by any partner concerning partnership affairs within the scope of his authority as conferred by this act is evidence against the partnership.

Sec. 12. **Partnership Charged with Knowledge of or Notice to Partner**

Notice to any partner of any matter relating to partnership affairs, and the knowledge of the partner acting in the particular matter, acquired while a partner or then present to his mind, and the knowledge of any other partner who reasonably could and should have communicated it to the acting partner, operate as notice to or knowledge of the partnership, except in the case of a fraud on the partnership committed by or with the consent of that partner.

Sec. 13. **Partnership Bound by Partner's Wrongful Act**

Where, by any wrongful act or omission of any partner acting in the ordinary course of the business of the partnership or with the authority of his co-partners, loss or injury is caused to any person, not being a partner in the partnership, or any penalty is incurred, the partnership is liable therefor to the same extent as the partner so acting or omitting to act.

Sec. 14. **Partnership Bound by Partner's Breach of Trust**

The partnership is bound to make good the loss:

(a) Where one partner acting within the scope of his apparent authority receives money or property of a third person and misapplies it; and

(b) Where the partnership in the course of its business receives money or property of a third person and the money or property so received is misapplied by any partner while it is in the custody of the partnership.

Sec. 15. **Nature of Partner's Liability**

All partners are liable

(a) Jointly and severally for everything chargeable to the partnership under sections 13 and 14.

(b) Jointly for all other debts and obligations of the partnership; but any partner may enter into a separate obligation to perform a partnership contract.

Sec. 16. **Partner by Estoppel**

(1) When a person, by words spoken or written or by conduct, represents himself, or consents to another representing him to any one, as a partner in an existing partnership or with one or more persons not actual partners, he is liable to any such person to whom such representation has been made, who has, on the faith of such representation, given credit to the actual or apparent partnership, and if he has made such representation or consented to its being made in a public manner he is liable to such person, whether the representation has or has not been made or communicated to such person so giving credit by or with the knowledge of the apparent partner making the representation or consenting to its being made.

    (a) When a partnership liability results, he is liable as though he were an actual member of the partnership.

    (b) When no partnership liability results, he is liable jointly with the other persons, if any, so consenting to the contract or representation as to incur liability, otherwise separately.

(2) When a person has been thus represented to be a partner in an existing partnership, or with one or more persons not actual partners, he is an agent of the persons consenting to such representation to bind them to the same extent and in the same manner as though he were a partner in fact, with respect to persons who rely upon the representation. Where all the members of the existing partnership consent to the representation, a partnership act or obligation results; but in all other cases it is the joint act or obligation of the person acting and the persons consenting to the representation.

Sec. 17. **Liability of Incoming Partner**

A person admitted as a partner into an existing partnership is liable for all the obligations of the partnership arising before his admission as though he had been a partner when such obligations were incurred, except that this liability shall be satisfied only out of partnership property.

Part IV Relations of Partners to One Another

Sec. 18. **Rules Determining Rights and Duties of Partners**

The rights and duties of the partners in relation to the partnership shall be determined, subject to any agreement between them, by the following rules:

(a) Each partner shall be repaid his contributions, whether by way of capital or advances to the partnership property and share equally in the profits and surplus remaining after all liabilities, including those to partners, are satisfied; and must contribute towards the losses, whether of capital or otherwise, sustained by the partnership according to his share in the profits.

(b) The partnership must indemnify every partner in respect of payments made and personal liabilities reasonably incurred by him in the ordinary and proper conduct of its business, or for the preservation of its business or property.

(c) A partner, who in aid of the partnership makes any payment or advance beyond the amount of capital which he agreed to contribute, shall be paid interest from the date of the payment or advance.

(d) A partner shall receive interest on the capital contributed by him only from the date when repayment should be made.

(e) All partners have equal rights in the management and conduct of the partnership business.

(f) No partner is entitled to remuneration for acting in the partnership business, except that a surviving partner is entitled to reasonable compensation for his services in winding up the partnership affairs.

(g) No person can become a member of a partnership without the consent of all the partners.

(h) Any difference arising as to ordinary matters connected with the partnership business may be decided by a majority of the partners; but no act in contravention of any agreement between the partners may be done rightfully without the consent of all the partners.

Sec. 19. **Partnership Books**

The partnership books shall be kept, subject to any agreement between the partners, at the principal place of business of the partnership, and every partner shall at all times have access to and may inspect and copy any of them.

Sec. 20. **Duty of Partners to Render Information**

Partners shall render on demand true and full information of all things affecting the partnership to any partner or the legal representative of any deceased partner or partner under legal disability.

Sec. 21. **Partner Accountable as a Fiduciary**

(1) Every partner must account to the partnership for any benefit, and hold as trustee for it any profits derived by him without the consent of the other partners from any transaction connected with the formation, conduct, or liquidation of the partnership or from any use by him of its property.

(2) This section applies also to the representatives of a deceased partner engaged in the liquidation of the affairs of the partnership as the personal representatives of the last surviving partner.

Sec. 22. **Right to an Account**

Any partner shall have the right to a formal account as to partnership affairs:

(a) If he is wrongfully excluded from the partnership business or possession of its property by his co-partners,

(b) If the right exists under the terms of any agreement,

(c) As provided by section 21,

(d) Whenever other circumstances render it just and reasonable.

Sec. 23. **Continuation of Partnership beyond Fixed Term**

(1) When a partnership for a fixed term or particular undertaking is continued after the termination of such term or particular undertaking without any express agreement, the rights and duties of the partners remain the same as they were at such termination, so far as is consistent with a partnership at will.

(2) A continuation of the business by the partners or such of them as habitually acted therein during the term, without any settlement or liquidation of the partnership affairs, is prima facie evidence of a continuation of the partnership.

Part V Property Rights of a Partner

Sec. 24. **Extent of Property Rights of a Partner**

The property rights of a partner are (1) his rights in specific partnership property, (2) his interest in the partnership, and (3) his right to participate in the management.

Sec. 25. **Nature of a Partner's Right in Specific Partnership Property**

(1) A partner is co-owner with his partners of specific partnership property holding as a tenant in partnership.

(2) The incidents of this tenancy are such that:

    (a) A partner, subject to the provisions of this act and to any agreement between the partners, has an equal right with his partners to possess specific partnership property for partnership purposes; but he has no right to possess such property for any other purpose without the consent of his partners.

(b) A partner's right in specific partnership property is not assignable except in connection with the assignment of rights of all the partners in the same property.

(c) A partner's right in specific partnership property is not subject to attachment or execution, except on a claim against the partnership. When partnership property is attached for a partnership debt the partners, or any of them, or the representatives of a deceased partner, cannot claim any right under the homestead or exemption laws.

(d) On the death of a partner his right in specific partnership property vests in the surviving partner or partners, except where the deceased was the last surviving partner, when his right in such property vests in his legal representative. Such surviving partner or partners, or the legal representative of the last surviving partner, has no right to possess the partnership property for any but a partnership purpose.

(e) A partner's right in specific partnership property is not subject to dower, curtesy, or allowances to widows, heirs, or next of kin.

Sec. 26. **Nature of Partner's Interest in the Partnership**

A partner's interest in the partnership is his share of the profits and surplus, and the same is personal property.

Sec. 27. **Assignment of Partner's Interest**

(1) A conveyance by a partner of his interest in the partnership does not of itself dissolve the partnership, nor, as against the other partners in the absence of agreement, entitle the assignee, during the continuance of the partnership, to interfere in the management or administration of the partnership business or affairs, or to require any information or account of partnership transactions, or to inspect the partnership books; but it merely entitles the assignee to receive in accordance with his contract the profits to which the assigning partner would otherwise be entitled.

(2) In case of a dissolution of the partnership, the assignee is entitled to receive his assignor's interest and may require an account from the date only of the last account agreed to by all the partners.

Sec. 28. **Partner's Interest Subject to Charging Order**

(1) On due application to a competent court by any judgment creditor of a partner, the court which entered the judgment, order, or decree, or any other court, may charge the interest of the debtor partner with payment of the unsatisfied amount of such judgment debt with interest thereon; and may then or later appoint a receiver of his share of the profits, and of any other money due or to fall due to him in respect of the partnership, and make all other orders, directions, accounts and inquiries which the debtor partner might have made, or which the circumstances of the case may require.

(2) The interest charged may be redeemed at any time before foreclosure, or in case of a sale being directed by the court may be purchased without thereby causing a dissolution:

(a) With separate property, by any one or more of the partners, or

(b) With partnership property, by any one or more of the partners with the consent of all the partners whose interests are not so charged or sold.

(3) Nothing in this act shall be held to deprive a partner of his right, if any, under the exemption laws, as regards his interest in the partnership.

Part VI Dissolution and Winding up

Sec. 29. **Dissolution Defined**

The dissolution of a partnership is the change in the relation of the partners caused by any partner ceasing to be associated in the carrying on as distinguished from the winding up of the business.

Sec. 30. **Partnership not Terminated by Dissolution**

On dissolution the partnership is not terminated, but continues until the winding up of partnership affairs is completed.

Sec. 31. **Causes of Dissolution**

Dissolution is caused:

(1) Without violation of the agreement between the partners,

(a) By the termination of the definite term or particular undertaking specified in the agreement,

(b) By the express will of any partner when no definite term or particular undertaking is specified,

(c) By the express will of all the partners who have not assigned their interests or suffered them to be charged for their separate debts, either before or after the termination of any specified term or particular undertaking,

(d) By the expulsion of any partner from the business bona fide in accordance with such a power conferred by the agreement between the partners;

(2) In contravention of the agreement between the partners, where the circumstances do not permit a dissolution under any other provision of this section, by the express will of any partner at any time;

(3) By any event which makes it unlawful for the business of the partnership to be carried on or for the members to carry it on in partnership;

(4) By the death of any partner;

(5) By the bankruptcy of any partner or the partnership;

(6) By decree of court under section 32.

Sec. 32. **Dissolution by Decree of Court**

(1) On application by or for a partner the court shall decree a dissolution whenever:

(a) A partner has been declared a lunatic in any judicial proceeding or is shown to be of unsound mind,

(b) A partner becomes in any other way incapable of performing his part of the partnership contract,

(c) A partner has been guilty of such conduct as tends to affect prejudicially the carrying on of the business,

(d) A partner wilfully or persistently commits a breach of the partnership agreement, or otherwise so conducts himself in matters relating to the partnership business that it is not reasonably practicable to carry on the business in partnership with him,

(e) The business of the partnership can only be carried on at a loss,

(f) Other circumstances render a dissolution equitable.

(2) On the application of the purchaser of a partner's interest under sections 28 or 29 [should read 27 or 28];

(a) After the termination of the specified term or particular undertaking,

(b) At any time if the partnership was a partnership at will when the interest was assigned or when the charging order was issued.

Sec. 33. **General Effect of Dissolution on Authority of Partner**

Except so far as may be necessary to wind up partnership affairs or to complete transactions begun but not then finished, dissolution terminates all authority of any partner to act for the partnership,

(1) With respect to the partners,

(a) When the dissolution is not by the act, bankruptcy or death of a partner; or

(b) When the dissolution is by such act, bankruptcy or death of a partner, in cases where section 34 so requires.

(2) With respect to persons not partners, as declared in section 35.

Sec. 34. **Rights of Partner to Contribution from Co-partners after Dissolution**

Where the dissolution is caused by the act, death or bankruptcy of a partner, each partner is liable to his copartners for his share of any liability created by any partner acting for the partnership as if the partnership had not been dissolved unless

(a) The dissolution being by act of any partner, the partner acting for the partnership had knowledge of the dissolution, or

(b) The dissolution being by the death or bankruptcy of a partner, the partner acting for the partnership had knowledge or notice of the death or bankruptcy.

Sec. 35. **Power of Partner to Bind Partnership to Third Persons after Dissolution**

(1) After dissolution a partner can bind the partnership except as provided in Paragraph (3).

(a) By any act appropriate for winding up partnership affairs or completing transactions unfinished at dissolution;

(b) By any transaction which would bind the partnership if dissolution had not taken place, provided the other party to the transaction

(I) Had extended credit to the partnership prior to dissolution and had no knowledge or notice of the dissolution; or

(II) Though he had not so extended credit, had nevertheless known of the partnership prior to dissolution, and, having no knowledge or notice of dissolution, the fact of dissolution had not been advertised in a newspaper of general circulation in the place (or in each place if more than one) at which the partnership business was regularly carried on.

(2) The liability of a partner under paragraph (1b) shall be satisfied out of partnership assets alone when such partner had been prior to dissolution

(a) Unknown as a partner to the person with whom the contract is made; and

(b) So far unknown and inactive in partnership affairs that the business reputation of the partnership could not be said to have been in any degree due to his connection with it.

(3) The partnership is in no case bound by any act of a partner after dissolution

(a) Where the partnership is dissolved because it is unlawful to carry on the business, unless the act is appropriate for winding up partnership affairs; or

(b) Where the partner has become bankrupt; or

(c) Where the partner has no authority to wind up partnership affairs; except by a transaction with one who

(I) Had extended credit to the partnership prior to dissolution and had no knowledge or notice of his want of authority; or

(II) Had not extended credit to the partnership prior to dissolution, and, having no knowledge or notice of his want of authority, the fact of his want of authority has not been advertised in the manner provided for advertising the fact of dissolution in paragraph (1bII).

(4) Nothing in this section shall affect the liability under Section 16 of any person who after dissolution represents himself or consents to another representing him as a partner in a partnership engaged in carrying on business.

Sec. 36. **Effect of Dissolution on Partner's Existing Liability**

(1) The dissolution of the partnership does not of itself discharge the existing liability of any partner.

(2) A partner is discharged from any existing liability upon dissolution of the partnership by an agreement to that effect between himself, the partnership creditor and the person or partnership continuing the business; and such agreement may be inferred from the course of dealing between the creditor having knowledge of the dissolution and the person or partnership continuing the business.

(3) Where a person agrees to assume the existing obligations of a dissolved partnership, the partners whose obligations have been assumed shall be discharged from any liability to any creditor of the partnership who, knowing of the agreement, consents to a material alteration in the nature or time of payment of such obligations.

(4) The individual property of a deceased partner shall be liable for all obligations of the partnership incurred while he was a partner but subject to the prior payment of his separate debts.

Sec. 37. **Right to Wind Up**

Unless otherwise agreed the partners who have not wrongfully dissolved the partnership or the legal representative of the last surviving partner, not bankrupt, has the right to wind up the partnership affairs; provided, however, that any partner, his legal representative or his assignee, upon cause shown, may obtain winding up by the court.

Sec. 38. **Rights of Partners to Application of Partnership Property**

(1) When dissolution is caused in any way, except in contravention of the partnership agreement, each partner, as against his co-partners and all persons claiming through them in respect of their interests in the partnership, unless otherwise agreed, may have the partnership property applied to discharge its liabilities, and the surplus applied to pay in cash the net amount owing to the respective partners. But if dissolution is caused by expulsion of a partner, bona fide under the partnership agreement and if the expelled partner is discharged from all partnership liabilities, either by payment or agreement under section 36(2), he shall re-

ceive in cash only the net amount due him from the partnership.

(2) When dissolution is caused in contravention of the partnership agreement the rights of the partners shall be as follows:

(a) Each partner who has not caused dissolution wrongfully shall have,

(I) All the rights specified in paragraph (1) of this section, and

(II) The right, as against each partner who has caused the dissolution wrongfully, to damages for breach of the agreement.

(b) The partners who have not caused the dissolution wrongfully, if they all desire to continue the business in the same name, either by themselves or jointly with others, may do so, during the agreed term for the partnership and for that purpose may possess the partnership property, provided they secure the payment by bond approved by the court, or pay to any partner who has caused the dissolution wrongfully, the value of his interest in the partnership at the dissolution, less any damages recoverable under clause (2a II) of the section, and in like manner indemnify him against all present or future partnership liabilities.

(c) A partner who has caused the dissolution wrongfully shall have:

(I) If the business is not continued under the provisions of paragraph (2b) all the rights of a partner under paragraph (1), subject to clause (2a II), of this section,

(II) If the business is continued under paragraph (2b) of this section the right as against his co-partners and all claiming through them in respect of their interests in the partnership, to have the value of his interest in the partnership, less any damages caused to his co-partners by the dissolution, ascertained and paid to him in cash, or the payment secured by bond approved by the court, and to be released from all existing liabilities of the partnership; but in ascertaining the value of the partner's interest the value of the good-will of the business shall not be considered.

Sec. 39. **Rights Where Partnership Is Dissolved for Fraud or Misrepresentation**

Where a partnership contract is rescinded on the ground of the fraud or misrepresentation of one of the parties thereto, the party entitled to rescind is, without prejudice to any other right, entitled,

(a) To a lien on, or right of retention of, the surplus of the partnership property after satisfying the partnership liabilities to third persons for any sum of money paid by him for the purchase of an interest in the partnership and for any capital or advances contributed by him; and

(b) To stand, after all liabilities to third persons have been satisfied, in the place of the creditors of the partnership for any payments made by him in respect of the partnership liabilities; and

(c) To be indemnified by the person guilty of the fraud or making the representation against all debts and liabilities of the partnership.

Sec. 40. **Rules for Distribution**

In settling accounts between the partners after dissolution, the following rules shall be observed, subject to any agreement to the contrary:

(a) The assets of the partnership are:

(I) The partnership property,

(II) The contributions of the partners necessary for the payment of all the liabilities specified in clause (b) of this paragraph.

(b) The liabilities of the partnership shall rank in order of payment, as follows:

(I) Those owing to creditors other than partners,

(II) Those owing to partners other than for capital and profits,

(III) Those owing to partners in respect of capital,

(IV) Those owing to partners in respect of profits.

(c) The assets shall be applied in the order of their declaration in clause (a) of this paragraph to the satisfaction of the liabilities.

(d) The partners shall contribute, as provided by section 18(a) the amount necessary to satisfy the liabilities; but if any, but not all, of the partners are insolvent, or, not being subject to process, refuse to contribute, the other partners shall contribute their share of the liabilities, and, in the relative proportions in which they share the profits, the additional amount necessary to pay the liabilities.

(e) An assignee for the benefit of creditors or any person appointed by the court shall have the right to enforce the contributions specified in clause (d) of this paragraph.

(f) Any partner or his legal representative shall have the right to enforce the contributions specified in clause (d) of this paragraph, to the extent of the amount which he has paid in excess of his share of the liability.

(g) The individual property of a deceased partner shall be liable for the contributions specified in clause (d) of this paragraph.

(h) When partnership property and the individual properties of the partners are in possession of a court for distribution, partnership creditors shall have priority on partnership property and separate creditors on individual property, saving the rights of lien or secured creditors as heretofore.

(i) Where a partner has become bankrupt or his estate is insolvent the claims against his separate property shall rank in the following order:

(I) Those owing to separate creditors,

(II) Those owing to partnership creditors,

(III) Those owing to partners by way of contribution.

Sec. 41. **Liability of Persons Continuing the Business in Certain Cases**

(1) When any new partner is admitted into an existing partnership, or when any partner retires and assigns (or the representative of the deceased partner assigns) his rights in partnership property to two or more of the partners, or to one or more of the partners and one or more third persons, if the business is continued without liquidation of the partnership affairs, creditors of the first or dissolved partnership are also creditors of the partnership so continuing the business.

(2) When all but one partner retire and assign (or the representative of a deceased partner assigns) their rights in partnership property to the remaining partner, who continues the business without liquidation of partnership affairs, either alone or with others, creditors of the dissolved partnership are also creditors of the person or partnership so continuing the business.

(3) When any partner retires or dies and the business of the dissolved partnership is continued as set forth in paragraphs (1) and (2) of this section, with the consent of the retired partners or the representative of the deceased partner, but without any assignment of his right in partnership property, rights of creditors of the dissolved partnership and of the creditors of the person or partnership continuing the business shall be as if such assignment had been made.

(4) When all the partners or their representatives assign their rights in partnership property to one or more third persons who promise to pay the debts and who continue the business of the dissolved partnership, creditors of the dissolved partnership are also creditors of the person or partnership continuing the business.

(5) When any partner wrongfully causes a dissolution and the remaining partners continue the business under the provisions of section 38(2b), either alone or with others, and without liquidation of the partnership affairs, creditors of the dissolved partnership are also creditors of the person or partnership continuing the business.

(6) When a partner is expelled and the remaining partners continue the business either alone or with others, without liquidation of the partnership affairs, creditors of the dissolved partnership are also creditors of the person or partnership continuing the business.

(7) The liability of a third person becoming a partner in the partnership continuing the business, under this section, to the creditors of the dissolved partnership shall be satisfied out of partnership property only.

(8) When the business of a partnership after dissolution is continued under any conditions set forth in this section the creditors of the dissolved partnership, as against the separate creditors of the retiring or deceased partner or the representative of the deceased partner, have a prior right to any claim of the retired partner or the representative of the deceased partner against the person or partnership continuing the business, on account of the retired or deceased partner's interest in the dissolved partnership or on account of any consideration promised for such interest or for his right in partnership property.

(9) Nothing in this section shall be held to modify any right of creditors to set aside any assignment on the ground of fraud.

(10) The use by the person or partnership continuing the business of the partnership name, or the name of a deceased partner as part thereof, shall not of itself make the individual property of the deceased partner liable for any debts contracted by such person or partnership.

Sec. 42. **Rights of Retiring or Estate of Deceased Partner When the Business Is Continued**

When any partner retires or dies, and the business is continued under any of the conditions set forth in section 41 (1, 2, 3, 5, 6), or section 38(2b) without any settlement of accounts as between him or his estate and the person or partnership continuing the business, unless otherwise agreed, he or his legal representative as against such persons or partnership may have the value of his interest at the date of dissolution ascertained, and shall receive as an ordinary creditor an amount equal to the value of his interest in the dissolved partnership with interest, or, at his option or at the option of his legal representative, in lieu of interest, the profits attributable to the use of his right in the property of the dissolved partnership; provided that the creditors of the dissolved partnership as against the separate creditors, or the representative of the retired or deceased partner, shall have priority on any claim arising under this section, as provided by section 41(8) of this act.

Sec. 43. **Accrual of Actions**

The right to an account of his interest shall accrue to any partner, or his legal representative, as against the winding up partners or the surviving partners or the person or partnership continuing the business, at the date of dissolution, in the absence of any agreement to the contrary.

Part VII Miscellaneous Provisions

Sec. 44. **When Act Takes Effect**

This act shall take effect on the ___ day of ___ one thousand nine hundred and ___.

Sec. 45. **Legislation Repealed**

All acts or parts of acts inconsistent with this act are hereby repealed.

Appendix E

A Guide to Research in Business Law

A business student who wishes to do research on legal topics can consult many sources. Depending on the focus of the research, different types of sources should be consulted. For example, if the researcher only wants a general overview of the law, he or she could look at a secondary legal source—such as a legal encyclopedia, a *Restatement of the Law,* or a treatise. If the student wants to consult a primary source of law, such as an actual court case, then he or she might look at a judicial reporter. Other primary sources include constitutions, statutes, and regulations. If a researcher wants to look at commentaries on the status of the law today, there are a plethora of law reviews and topical legal journals that provide scholarly articles on current issues of legal interest.

Any person undertaking legal research will want to become familiar with the "finding tools" of legal research—computer data bases, law digests, looseleaf services, bar association publications, weekly bulletins, and so on—that are available today. These services and publications not only assist the researcher in locating legal documents but also keep the student abreast of recent legal developments.

The summary below explains how these and other legal research tools can be used to assist the business student in learning more about the topics discussed in this text.

■ Legal Encyclopedias

Legal encyclopedias cover topics of law in a general manner. They explain subjects, define terms, and offer historical as well as current coverage. They are also helpful in finding primary sources of authority. The two major legal encyclopedias are *Corpus Juris Secundum* (C.J.S.), published by the West Publishing Company, and *American Jurisprudence 2d* (Am.Jur.2d)—"2d" means second edition—published by the Lawyers Co-Operative Publishing Company. Each of these encyclopedias divides the law into more than four hundred topics. Although legal discussions in these encyclopedias give broad statements of accepted law, because the discussions are extensively footnoted, the encyclopedias are valuable sources for research.

Some states also have encyclopedias, such as *Texas Jurisprudence 3d.* A less technical reference is *The Guide to American Law: Everyone's Legal Encyclopedia,* which is published by West Publishing Company.

■ Restatements of the Law

The *Restatements of the Law* are compilations of the common law covering various legal areas. There are *Restatements* of the law of agency, conflict of laws, contracts, judgments, property, restitution, security, torts, trusts, foreign relations law, and landlord-tenant law. A student wishing more information on the law of contracts, for example, might consult the *Restatement (Second) of Contracts.* (The word "second" in parenthesis means second edition.) Similarly, if a student is interested in studying the law of agency in more detail, he or she could look at the *Restatement (Second) of Agency*. The title of each *Restatement* follows this same format. The *Restatements* include a summary of the "black letter" law on a particular topic, an explanatory comment on the general principles underlying that law, and examples of particular cases and variations on the general proposition.

■ Treatises

Treatises are like encyclopedias; they are written by specialists on certain subjects. Longer treatises are frequently published in multiple volumes. There are treatises for virtually all of the major topics of law. When updated, treatises are usually accurate explanations of the law in a particular area, and, at the same time, they are usually easy to read and a good source to turn when beginning one's legal research. For example, *Prosser and Keeton on Torts* would assist a student in researching those topics introduced in Chapters 5, 7, and 8 of this text. *Collier on Bankruptcy* outlines the law presented in Chapters 33 and 34 of this text.

■ Digests of Case Law

Digests are indexes to American case law. There are digests for both the federal and state court systems. Digests consist primarily of case summaries, which are arranged topically, from each jurisdiction. The advantage of a digest is that researchers can review cases from, for example, all appellate courts for a ten-year period. The American Digest System is the master index giving access to all cases published in the National Reporter System. The American Digest System includes the *Decennial Digest Series,* which is published every ten years, and the *General Digest Series* that is issued periodically between publications of the *Decennial Digest Series.*

There are also a number of subject-matter digests and jurisdictional digests, which are simply extractions of digested cases from the master index. When one is researching a relatively narrow legal topic such as patent law, which was presented in Chapter 8 of this text, the *U.S. Patents Quarterly Digest* would be a promising source of information.

■ Judicial Reporters

Judicial reporters are volumes for various jurisdictions that contain reported appellate decisions and opinions. As discussed in Chapter 1 of this text, there are reporters published by jurisdiction (for example, the *Federal Reporter* includes all cases from the federal courts of appeals, and the *Federal Supplement* contains cases selected for publication from the U.S. district courts and other federal courts), and there are also reporters that cover specific geographical regions (for example, the *Southern Reporter* covers state appellate cases for the states of Louisiana, Mississippi, Alabama, and Florida). In these reporters, cases are reported chronologically, according to the date of the decision.

In addition to general reporters, some subject reporters are also published. For example, a student who wishes to learn more about bankruptcy and reorganization (discussed in Chapter 33 of the text) would be able to find cases on that subject in the *American Bankruptcy Reports.*

■ Annotated Statutes

The *United States Code* (U.S.C.) contains the text of the U.S. Constitution and current federal legislation. There are two annotated versions of the U.S. Code: the *United States Code Annotated* (U.S.C.A.) and the *United States Code Service* (U.S.C.S.). The textual arrangement in these annotated volumes is identical to that found in the official U.S. Code. Unlike the U.S. Code itself, however, as explained in Chapter 1, these annotated volumes provide summaries of cases that have interpreted the statutory sections. If there are numerous case annotations, an outline of the annotations is also provided to make the research easier.

■ Looseleaf Services

Looseleaf services collect legal source material in certain subject areas and are kept current by frequent supplementation (often, once a week). They offer another practical means of access to the law in particular areas of interest. Two of the primary publishers of looseleaf services are the Bureau of National Affairs (BNA) and the Commerce Clearing House (CCH). The *BNA Corporate Practice Series* would be useful for a researcher who wants to study those topics introduced in Unit Seven of this text (on business organizations). The *BNA International Trade Reporter* would supplement the materials presented in Chapters 24 and 56 (on international law). The *CCH Employment Practices Guide* would be useful in researching employment and labor relations law (introduced in Chapter 48). The *CCH Congressional Index* would assist research on administrative law (discussed in

Chapter 44). This two-volume set indexes bills, committee reports, and hearings. It also includes sections on pending bills, bill status tables, members of Congress and their voting records, and so on. A final example of a looseleaf service is the *CCH Secured Transactions Guide,* which would help expand the student's knowledge of the concepts presented in Chapter 31 (on secured transactions).

Law Reviews

Law reviews are scholarly publications edited by law students or legal associations. Law reviews are published periodically (some once a year, others two or more times a year) and cover a broad range of legal topics. The contents of most law reviews include (1) commentaries about the law, usually written by law professors, judges, or practicing attorneys; (2) reviews of books recently written about the law; (3) comments by a student writer explaining the meaning of five or six recent cases; and (4) student notes on specific topics of law. Almost every accredited law school publishes a law review. A scholarly article or review can be found on virtually every topic of law in some issue of a law review, and depending on the topics covered in a particular review, it may assist the researcher in finding further information on any of the subjects presented in this book. The *Harvard Law Review* is one of the most prestigious law reviews. There are many more of equal quality.

Topical Law Journals

In addition to the general law reviews, many law schools also publish law journals on specific topics. The contents of the journals are similar to those of the law reviews—scholarly articles, book reviews, case comments, and student notes—but the range of topics is limited to a specified area. The list of topical journals is quite extensive, and there is likely to be an individual journal on almost every topic covered in this text.

For instance, *Environmental Law* focuses on the impact of various laws on the environment; this journal would therefore assist the student in obtaining a more comprehensive understanding of Chapter 46 of this text (on environmental law). The *Antitrust Law Journal* would offer further detail on the materials presented in Chapter 47 (on antitrust). The *Journal of Products Liability* focuses on the materials presented in Chapter 23 (on product liability). A number of law journals focus specifically on international law. Students interested in researching topics in this area might consult the *American Journal of Comparative Law,* the *American Journal of International Law,* or a number of other topical journals on this subject published by law schools.

Weekly Newsletters/Bulletins

To keep abreast of recent developments in the judicial and executive branches of the government, one should consult the following weekly publications:

1. *United States Law Week*—This is a weekly looseleaf service published in two volumes. The first volume is designed specifically to provide coverage of the United States Supreme Court. The second volume covers topics of general law; the items presented concern legal developments that, although they are unrelated to the Supreme Court, are of national significance.

2. *United States Supreme Court Bulletin*—This is a weekly looseleaf set designed specifically to provide coverage of the United States Supreme Court. This set contains a copy of the Supreme Court opinions rendered during the current term. In addition, there are sections that provide subject access to everything on the court's docket and a copy of the docket. Other sections include rules of the Supreme Court and a tentative calendar for arguments before the Court.

3. *Weekly Compilation of Presidential Documents*—This weekly publication includes executive orders, proclamations, reorganization plans, speeches, and press conferences. All official presidential documents, except executive agreements, are included. Everything found in this compilation is arranged in chronological order. A student wishing to learn more about administrative law (covered in Chapter 44 of this text) would find this publication useful.

Computerized Research Assistance

The days of the hunched-over law clerk searching through copious volumes of dusty tomes filled with ancient cases are not completely over, but, as could be expected, computers have streamlined legal research techniques. Today, there are a number of data bases—collections of information useful to anyone doing legal research—that can be accessed through several high-speed data-delivery systems. The two major legal research systems are LEXIS, owned by Mead Data Central, Inc., and WESTLAW, offered by West Publishing Company.

LEXIS and WESTLAW allow for access to the full text of cases, statutes, and regulations—both state and federal—with a minimum of physical effort and time delay. Both systems are kept extremely current, and often the latest cases can be retrieved through these systems before they are available in the printed reporters. The systems also include specialized libraries of materials on specific topics, such as criminal law, legal ethics, and other topics, which can provide assistance to the student researcher.

■ Bar Association Publications

Bar associations also issue legal materials of various kinds, including newletters and periodicals, that may be useful for the researcher. The *American Bar Association Journal* and the *National Bar Journal,* for example, both contain reports on association activities, articles on legal topics, and notices of recent developments in the law. Additionally, many of the specialized sections of the bar publish their own quarterly newsletters, such as *American Patent Law Association Quarterly Journal,* which provides the members of the section with an update of the most recent developments in this area of the law.

■ Form Books

If a business student had to draft a contract or some other document, or wanted to see the "typical language" found in a legal instrument, he or she would want to look at one of the many form books available. These books frequently offer instructions on how to fill in the sample forms included in the books. An example of a form book is *American Jurisprudence Legal Forms 2d,* a twenty-volume set that contains legal forms of every kind for a commercial transaction. The *American Jurisprudence Pleading and Practice Forms,* in contrast, provides forms that are essential to litigation.

■ List of Selected Research Sources

Administrative Law Bulletin
American Bankruptcy Law Journal
American Business Law Journal
American Civil Law Journal

American Journal of Comparative Law
American Journal of Criminal Law
American Journal of International Law
American Journal of Tax Policy
American Journal of Trial Advocacy
American Judicature Society Journal
American Jurisprudence Forms Proof of Facts
American Jurisprudence Legal Forms 2d
American Jurisprudence Pleading and Practice
    Forms
American Lawyer
American Patent Law Association Quarterly
    Journal
American Society of International Law Proceedings
Annals of Air and Space Law
Annual Review of Banking Law
Annual Survey of Bankruptcy Law
Antitrust Law Journal
Arbitration Law
Banking Law Journal
Bender's Uniform Commercial Code Service
BNA Antitrust and Trade Regulation Reporter
BNA Collective Bargaining and Negotiations and
    Contracts
BNA Corporate Practice Series
BNA International Trade Report
BNA Labor Relations Reporter
BNA Media Law Reporter
BNA Patent, Trademark and Copyright Reporter
BNA Securities Regulations and Law Reporter
BNA United States Law Week
Boston University International Law Journal
Business Law Journal
CCH Bankruptcy Law Reporter
CCH Congressional Index
CCH Consumer Products Safety and Health Guide
CCH Contract Cases
CCH Copyright Law Reporter
CCH Employment Practices Decisions
CCH Labor Law Reporter
CCH Products Liability Reporter
CCH Secured Transactions Guide
Chicago Legal Forum
Clearinghouse for Civil Rights Research
Code of Federal Regulations
Computer Law Journal
Congressional Information Service Index
Congressional Record
Criminal Law Bulletin
Decennial Digest
Environmental Law

Federal Register
Federal Reporter
Federal Rules Decisions
Federal Rules of Civil Procedure
Federal Supplement
Federal Trade Commission Reports
General Digest
George Washington Journal of International Law
    and Economics
Harvard Environmental Law Review
Harvard International Law Journal
Harvard Journal of Law and Public Policy
Index to Legal Periodicals
Insurance Law Journal
Intellectual Property Journal
International and Comparative Law Bulletin
International Journal of Medicine and Law
International Journal of Politics
International Journal of the Sociology of Law
International Law Reporter
International Review of Law and Economics
International Social Science Journal
International Trade Reporter
Journal of Contemporary Law
Journal of Corporate Taxation
Journal of Energy and Natural Resources Law
Journal of Law and Commerce
Journal of Law and Economics
Journal of Law and Politics
Journal of Law and Technology
Journal of Products Liability
Journal of Real Estate Taxation
Journal of the American Medical Association
Law and Contemporary Problems
Legal Times of Washington
Loyola Entertainment Law Journal
Maryland Journal of International Law and Trade
Media Law Reporter
Mediation Quarterly
Moore's Federal Practice
National Bar Journal
New Republic
North Atlantic Regional Business Law Review

Northwestern Journal of International Law and
    Business
Notre Dame Journal of Law, Ethics and Public
    Policy
Patent and Trademark Review
Performing Arts Review
Prentice Hall: Securities Regulation
Quarterly Journal of Economics
Real Estate Law Journal
Real Property Probate and Trust Journal
Restatement (Second) of Agency
Restatement (Second) of Contracts
Restatement (Second) of Torts
Restatement (Second) of Trusts
Restatement of Property
Review of Litigation
Rutgers Journal of Computers, Technology and the
    Law
Shepard's Acts and Cases by Popular Names
    Citations
Social Sciences and Humanities Index
Stanford Environmental Law Journal
Stanford Journal of International Law
Student Lawyer
Supreme Court Bulletin
Supreme Court Reporter
Texas International Law Journal
Trademark Law Handbook
U.S. Attorney General Opinions
U.S. Code Annotated
U.S. Code Congressional and Administrative News
U.S. Code Service
U.S. Patents Quarterly Digest
U.S. Statutes at Large
Uniform Commercial Code Series (Callaghan)
Virginia Journal of International Law
Wall Street Journal
West's Bankruptcy Reporter
Women's Law Journal
Yale Journal of International Law
Yale Journal of World Public Order
Yearbook of Law—Computers and Technology

Appendix F

Spanish Equivalents for Important Legal Terms in English

Abandoned property: bienes abandonados

Acceptance: aceptación; consentimiento; acuerdo

Acceptor: aceptante

Accession: toma de posesión; aumento; accesión

Accommodation indorser: avalista de favor

Accommodation party: firmante de favor

Accord: acuerdo; convenio; arregio

Accord and satisfaction: transacción ejecutada

Act of state doctrine: doctrina de acto de gobierno

Administrative law: derecho administrativo

Administrative process: procedimiento o metódo administrativo

Administrator: administrador (-a)

Adverse possession: posesión de hecho susceptible de proscripción adquisitiva

Affirmative action: acción afirmativa

Affirmative defense: defensa afirmativa

After-acquired property: bienes adquiridos con posterioridad a un hecho dado

Agency: mandato; agencia

Agent: mandatorio; agente; representante

Agreement: convenio; acuerdo; contrato

Alien corporation: empresa extranjera

Allonge: hojas adicionales de endosos

Answer: contestación de la demande; alegato

Anticipatory breach: anuncio previo de las partes de su imposibilidad de cumplir con el contrato

Appeal: apelación; recurso de apelación

Appellate jurisdiction: jurisdicción de apelaciones

Appraisal right: derecho de valuación

Arbitration: arbitraje

Arson: incendio intencional

Articles of partnership: contrato social

Artisian's lien: derecho de retención que ejerce al artesano

Assault: asalto; ataque; agresión

Assignment of rights: transmisión; transferencia; cesión

Assumption of risk: no resarcimiento por exposición voluntaria al peligro

Attachment: auto judicial que autoriza el embargo; embargo

Bailee: depositario

Bailment: depósito; constitución en depósito

Bailor: depositante

Bankruptcy trustee: síndico de la quiebra

Battery: agresión; física

Bearer: portador; tenedor

Bearer instrument: documento al portador

Bequest or legacy: legado (de bienes muebles)

Bilateral contract: contrato bilateral

Bill of lading: conocimiento de embarque; carta de porte

Bill of Rights: declaración de derechos

Binder: póliza de seguro provisoria; recibo de pago a cuenta del precio

Blank indorsement: endoso en blanco

Blue sky laws: leyes reguladoras del comercio bursátil

Bond: título de crédito; garantía; caución

Breach of contract: incumplimiento de contrato

Brief: escrito; resumen; informe

Burglary: violación de domicilio

Business judgment rule: regla de juicio comercial

Business tort: agravio comercial

Case law: ley de casos; derecho casuístico

Cashier's check: cheque de caja

Causation in fact: causalidad en realidad

Cease-and-desist order: orden para cesar y desistir

Certificate of deposit: certificado de depósito

Certified check: cheque certificado

Charitable trust: fideicomiso para fines benéficos

Chattel: bien mueble

Check: cheque

Chose in action: derecho inmaterial; derecho de acción

Civil law: derecho civil

Close corporation: sociedad de un solo accionista o de un grupo restringido de accionistas

Closed shop: taller agremiado (emplea solamente a miembros de un gremio)

Closing argument: argumento al final

Codicil: codicilo

Collateral: garantía; bien objeto de la garantía real

Comity: cortesía; cortesía entre naciones

Commercial paper: instrumentos negociables; documentos a valores commerciales

Common law: derecho consuetudinario; derecho común; ley común

Common stock: acción ordinaria

Comparative negligence: negligencia comparada

Compensatory damages: daños y perjuicios reales o compensatorios

Concurrent conditions: condiciones concurrentes

Concurrent jurisdiction: competencia concurrente de varios tribunales para entender en una misma causa

Concurring opinion: opinión concurrente

Condition: condición

Condition precedent: condición suspensiva

Condition subsequent: condición resolutoria

Confiscation: confiscación

Confusion: confusión; fusión

Conglomerate merger: fusión de firmas que operan en distintos mercados

Consequential damages: daños y perjuicios indirectos

Consideration: consideración; motivo; contraprestación

Consolidation: consolidación

Constructive delivery: entrega simbólica

Constructive trust: fideicomiso creado por aplicación de la ley

Consumer-protection law: ley para proteger el consumidor

Contract: contrato

Contract under seal: contrato formal o sellado

Contributory negligence: negligencia de la parte actora

Conversion: usurpación; conversión de valores

Copyright: derecho de autor

Corporation: sociedad anónima; corporación; persona juridica

Co-sureties: cogarantes

Counterclaim: reconvención; contrademanda

Counteroffer: contraoferta

Course of dealing: curso de transacciones

Course of performance: curso de cumplimiento

Covenant: pacto; garantía; contrato

Covenant not to sue: pacto o contrato a no demandar

Covenant of quiet enjoyment: garantía del uso y goce pacífico del inmueble

Creditors' composition agreement: concordato preventivo

Crime: crimen; delito; contravención

Criminal law: derecho penal

Cross-examination: contrainterrogatorio

Cure: cura; cuidado; derecho de remediar un vicio contractual

Customs receipts: recibos de derechos aduaneros

Damages: daños; indemnización por daños y perjuicios

Debtor: deudor

Debt securities: seguridades de deuda

Deceptive advertising: publicidad engañosa

Deed: escritura; título; acta translativa de domino

Defamation: difamación

Delegation of duties: delegación de obligaciones

Demand deposit: depósito a la vista

Depositions: declaración de un testigo fuera del tribunal

Devise: legado; deposición testamentaria (bienes inmuebles)

Directed verdict: veredicto según orden del juez y sin participación activa del jurado

Direct examination: interrogatorio directo; primer interrogatorio

Disaffirmance: repudiación; renuncia; anulación

Discharge: descargo; liberación; cumplimiento

Disclosed principal: mandante revelado

Discovery: descubrimiento; producción de la prueba

Dissenting opinion: opinión disidente

Dissolution: disolución; terminación

Diversity of citizenship: competencia de los tribunales federales para entender en causas cuyas partes intervinientes son cuidadanos de distintos estados

Divestiture: extinción premature de derechos reales

Dividend: dividendo

Docket: orden del día; lista de causas pendientes

Domestic corporation: sociedad local
Draft: orden de pago; letrade cambio
Drawee: girado; beneficiario
Drawer: librador
Duress: coacción; violencia

Easement: servidumbre
Embezzlement: desfalco; malversación
Eminent domain: poder de expropiación
Employment discrimination: discriminación en el empleo
Entrepreneur: empresario
Environmental law: ley ambiental
Equal dignity rule: regla de dignidad egual
Equity security: tipo de participación en una sociedad
Estate: propiedad; patrimonio; derecho
Estop: impedir; prevenir
Ethical issue: cuestión ética
Exclusive jurisdiction: competencia exclusiva
Exculpatory clause: cláusula eximente
Executed contract: contrato ejecutado
Execution: ejecución; cumplimiento
Executor: albacea
Executory contract: contrato aún no completamente consumado
Executory interest: derecho futuro
Express contract: contrato expreso
Expropriation: expropriación

Federal question: caso federal
Fee simple: pleno dominio; dominio absoluto
Fee simple absolute: dominio absoluto
Fee simple defeasible: dominio sujeta a una condición resolutoria
Felony: crimen; delito grave
Fictitious payee: beneficiario ficticio
Fiduciary: fiduciaro
Firm offer: oferta en firme

Fixture: inmueble por destino, incorporación a anexación
Floating lien: gravamen continuado
Foreign corporation: sociedad extranjera; U.S. sociedad constituída en otro estado
Forgery: falso; falsificación
Formal contract: contrato formal
Franchise: privilegio; franquicia; concesión
Franchisee: persona que recibe una concesión
Franchisor: persona que vende una concesión
Fraud: fraude; dolo; engaño
Future interest: bien futuro

Garnishment: embargo de derechos
General partner: socio comanditario
General warranty deed: escritura translativa de domino con garantía de título
Gift: donación
Gift *causa mortis:* donación por causa de muerte
Gift *inter vivos:* donación entre vivos
Good faith: buena fe
Good-faith purchaser: comprador de buena fe

Holder: tenedor por contraprestación
Holder in due course: tenedor legítimo
Holographic will: testamento ológrafico
Homestead exemption laws: leyes que exceptúan las casas de familia de ejecución por duedas generales
Horizontal merger: fusión horizontal

Identification: identificación
Implied-in-fact contract: contrato implícito en realidad
Implied warranty: guarantía implícita
Implied warranty of

merchantability: garantía implícita de vendibilidad
Impossibility of performance: imposibilidad de cumplir un contrato
Imposter: imposter
Incidental beneficiary: beneficiario incidental; beneficiario secundario
Incidental damages: daños incidentales
Indictment: auto de acusación; acusación
Indorsee: endorsatario
Indorsement: endoso
Indorser: endosante
Informal contract: contrato no formal; contrato verbal
Information: acusación hecha por el ministerio público
Injunction: mandamiento; orden de no innovar
Innkeeper's lien: derecho de retención que ejerce el posadero
Installment contract: contrato de pago en cuotas
Insurable interest: interés asegurable
Intended beneficiary: beneficiario destinado
Intentional tort: agravio; cuasi-delito intenciónal
International law: derecho internaciónal
Interrogatories: preguntas escritas sometidas por una parte a la otra o a un testigo
Inter vivos trust: fideicomiso entre vivos
Intestacy laws: leyes de la condición de morir intestado
Intestate: intestado
Investment company: compañia de inversiones
Issue: emisión

Joint tenancy: derechos conjuntos en un bien inmueble
Joint tenancy: derechos conjuntos en un bien inmueble en favor del beneficiario sobreviviente
Judgment *n.o.v.*: juicio no obstante veredicto

Judgment rate of interest: interés de juicio
Judicial process: acto de procedimiento; proceso jurídico
Judicial review: revisión judicial
Jurisdiction: jurisdicción

Larceny: robo; hurto
Law: derecho; ley; jurisprudencia
Lease: contrato de locación; contrato de alquiler
Leasehold estate: bienes forales
Legal rate of interest: interés legal
Legatee: legatario
Letter of credit: carta de crédito
Levy: embargo; comiso
Libel: libelo; difamación escrita
Life estate: usufructo
Limited partner: comanditario
Limited partnership: sociedad en comandita
Liquidation: liquidación; realización
Lost property: objetos perdidos

Majority opinion: opinión de la mayoría
Maker: persona que realiza u ordena; librador
Mechanic's lien: gravamen de constructor
Mediation: mediación; intervención
Merger: fusión
Mirror image rule: fallo de reflejo
Misdemeanor: infracción; contravención
Mislaid property: bienes extraviados
Mitigation of damages: reducción de daños
Mortgage: hypoteca
Motion to dismiss: excepción parentoria
Mutual fund: fondo mutual

Negotiable instrument: instrumento negociable
Negotiation: negociación
Nominal damages: daños y perjuicios nominales
Novation: novación

Nuncupative will: testamento nuncupativo

Objective theory of contracts: teoria objetiva de contratos
Offer: oferta
Offeree: persona que recibe una oferta
Offeror: oferente
Order instrument: instrumento o documento a la orden
Original jurisdiction: jurisdicción de primera instancia
Output contract: contrato de producción

Parol evidence rule: regla relativa a la prueba oral
Partially disclosed principal: mandante revelado en parte
Partnership: sociedad colectiva; asociación; asociación de participación
Past consideration: causa o contraprestación anterior
Patent: patente; privilegio
Pattern or practice: muestra o práctica
Payee: beneficiario de un pago
Penalty: pena; penalidad
Per capita: por cabeza
Perfection: perfeción
Performance: cumplimiento; ejecución
Personal defenses: excepciones personales
Personal property: bienes muebles
Per stirpes: por estirpe
Plea bargaining: regateo por un alegato
Pleadings: alegatos
Pledge: prenda
Police powers: poders de policia y de prevención del crimen
Policy: póliza
Positive law: derecho positivo; ley positiva
Possibility of reverter: posibilidad de reversión
Precedent: precedente
Preemptive right: derecho de prelación
Preferred stock: acciones preferidas

Premium: recompensa; prima
Presentment warranty: garantía de presentación
Price discrimination: discriminación en los precios
Principal: mandante; principal
Privity: nexo jurídico
Privity of contract: relación contractual
Probable cause: causa probable
Probate: verificación; verificación del testamento
Probate court: tribunal de sucesiones y tutelas
Proceeds: resultados; ingresos
Profit: beneficio; utilidad; lucro
Promise: promesa
Promisee: beneficiario de una promesa
Promisor: promtente
Promissory estoppel: impedimento promisorio
Promissory note: pagaré; nota de pago
Promoter: promotor; fundador
Proximate cause: causa inmediata o próxima
Proxy: apoderado; poder
Punitive, or exemplary, damages: daños y perjuicios punitivos o ejemplares

Qualified indorsement: endoso con reservas
Quasi contract: contrato tácito o implícito
Quitclaim deed: acto de transferencia de una propiedad por finiquito, pero sin ninguna garantía sobre la validez del título transferido

Ratification: ratificación
Real property: bienes inmuebles
Reasonable doubt: duda razonable
Rebuttal: refutación
Recognizance: promesa; compromiso; reconocimiento
Recording statutes: leyes estatales sobre registros oficiales
Reformation: rectificación; reforma; corrección
Rejoinder: dúplica; contrarréplica

Release: liberación; renuncia a un derecho

Remainder: substitución; reversión

Remedy: recurso; remedio; reparación

Replevin: acción reivindicatoria; reivindicación

Reply: réplica

Requirements contract: contrato de suministro

Rescission: rescisión

Respondeat superior: responsabilidad del mandante o del maestro

Restitution: restitución

Restrictive indorsement: endoso restrictivo

Resulting trust: fideicomiso implícito

Reversion: reversión; sustitución

Revocation: revocación; derogación

Right of contribution: derecho de contribución

Right of reimbursement: derecho de reembolso

Right of subrogation: derecho de subrogación

Right-to-work law: ley de libertad de trabajo

Robbery: robo

Rule 10b-5: Regla 10b-5

Sale: venta; contrato de compreventa

Sale on approval: venta a ensayo; venta sujeta a la aprobación del comprador

Sale or return: venta con derecho de devolución

Sales contract: contrato de compraventa; boleto de compraventa

Satisfaction: satisfacción; pago

Scienter: a sabiendas

S corporation: S corporación

Secured party: acreedor garantizado

Secured transaction: transacción garantizada

Securities: volares; titulos; seguridades

Security agreement: convenio de seguridad

Security interest: interés en un

bien dado en garantía que permite a quien lo detenta venderlo en caso de incumplimiento

Service mark: marca de identificación de servicios

Shareholder's derivative suit: acción judicial entablada por un accionista en nombre de la sociedad

Signature: firma; rúbrica

Slander: difamación oral; calumnia

Sovereign immunity: immunidad soberana

Special indorsement: endoso especial; endoso a la orden de una person en particular

Specific performance: ejecución precisa, según los términos del contrato

Spendthrift trust: fideicomiso para pródigos

Stale check: cheque vencido

Stare decisis: acatar las decisiones, observar los precedentes

Statutory law: derecho estatutario; derecho legislado; derecho escrito

Stock: acciones

Stock warrant: certificado para la compra de acciones

Stop-payment order: orden de suspensión del pago de un cheque dada por el librador del mismo

Strict liability: responsabilidad unconditional

Summary judgment: fallo sumario

Tangible property: bienes corpóreos

Tenancy at will: inguilino por tiempo indeterminado (según la voluntad del propietario)

Tenancy by sufferance: posesión por tolerancia

Tenancy by the entirety: locación conyugal conjunta

Tenancy for years: inguilino por un término fijo

Tenancy in common: specie de copropiedad indivisa

Tender: oferta de pago; oferta de ejecución

Testamentary trust: fideicomiso testamentario

Testator: testador (-a)

Third party beneficiary contract:

contrato para el beneficio del tercero-beneficiario

Tort: agravio; cuasi-delito

Totten trust: fideicomiso creado por un depósito bancario

Trade acceptance: letra de cambio aceptada

Trade name: nombre comercial; razón social

Trademark: marca registrada

Traveler's check: cheque del viajero

Trespass to land: ingreso no authorizado a las tierras de otro

Trespass to personal property: violación de los derechos posesorios de un tercero con respecto a bienes muebles

Trust: fideicomiso; trust

Ultra vires: ultra vires; fuera de la facultad (de una sociedad anónima)

Unanimous opinion: opinión unámine

Unconscionable contract or clause: contrato leonino; cláusula leonino

Underwriter: subscriptor; asegurador

Unenforceable contract: contrato que no se puede hacer cumplir

Unilateral contract: contrato unilateral

Union shop: taller agremiado; empresa en la que todos los empleados son miembros del gremio o sindicato

Universal defenses: defensas legitimas o legales

Usage of trade: uso comercial

Usury: usura

Valid contract: contrato válido

Venue: lugar; sede del proceso

Vertical merger: fusión vertical de empresas

Void contract: contrato nulo; contrato inválido, sin fuerza legal

Voidable contract: contrato anulable

Voir dire: examen preliminar de un testigo a jurado por el tribunal para determinar su competencia

Voting trust: fideicomiso para ejercer el derecho de voto

Waiver: renuncia; abandono
Warranty of habitability: garantía de habitabilidad
Watered stock: acciones diluídos; capital inflado
White-collar crime: crimen administrativo

Writ of attachment: mandamiento de ejecución; mandamiento de embargo
Writ of *certiorari*: auto de avocación; auto de certiorari

Writ of execution: auto ejecutivo; mandamiento de ejecutión
Writ of mandamus: auto de mandamus; mandamiento; orden judicial

Glossary

A

Abandoned property Property with which the owner has voluntarily parted, with no intention of recovering it.

Abandonment In landlord-tenant law, a tenant's departure from leased premises completely, with no intention of returning before the end of the lease term.

Acceleration clause A clause in an installment contract that provides for all future payments to become due immediately upon the failure to tender timely payments or upon the occurrence of a specified event.

Acceptance (1) In contract law, the offeree's notification to the offeror that the offeree agrees to be bound by the terms of the offeror's proposal. Although historically the terms of acceptance had to be the mirror image of the terms of the offer, the UCC provides that even modified terms of the offer in a definite expression of acceptance constitute a contract. (2) In commercial paper law, the drawee's signed agreement to pay a draft when presented.

Acceptor The person (the drawee) who accepts a draft and who engages to be primarily responsible for its payment.

Accession The changing (for example, through manufacturing) of one good into a new good (for example, flour into bread); the right, upon payment for the original materials, to keep an article manufactured out of goods that were innocently converted.

Accommodation party A person who signs an instrument for the purpose of lending his or her credit to another party on the instrument.

Accord and satisfaction An agreement and payment (or other performance) between two parties, one of whom has a right of action against the other. After the agreement has been made and payment or other performance has been tendered, the "accord and satisfaction" is complete.

Accredited investors In the context of securities offerings, "sophisticated" investors, such as banks, insurance companies, investment companies, the issuer's executive officers and directors, and persons whose income or net worth exceeds certain limits.

Act of state doctrine A doctrine that provides that the judicial branch of one country will not examine the validity of public acts committed by a recognized foreign government within its own territory.

Actual malice Real and demonstrable evil intent. In a defamation suit, a statement made about a public figure normally must be made with actual malice (with either knowledge of its falsity or a reckless disregard of the truth) for liability to be incurred.

Actus reus A guilty (prohibited) act. The commission of a prohibited act is one of the two essential elements required for criminal liability, the other element being the *intent* to commit a crime.

Adequate protection doctrine In bankruptcy law, a doctrine that protects secured creditors from losing their security as a result of an automatic stay on legal proceedings by creditors against the debtor once the debtor petitions for bankruptcy relief. In certain circumstances, the bankruptcy court may provide adequate protection by requiring the debtor or trustee to pay the creditor or provide additional guaranties to protect the creditor against the losses suffered by the creditor as a result of the stay.

Adhesion contract A "standard form" contract, such as that between a large retailer and a consumer, in which the stronger party dictates the terms.

Adjudication The act of rendering a judicial decision. In administrative process, the proceeding in which an administrative law judge hears and decides on issues that arise when an administrative agency charges a person or a firm with violating a law or regulation enforced by the agency.

Administrative law A body of law created by administrative agencies—such as the Securities and Exchange Commission and the Federal Trade Commission—in the form of rules, regulations, orders, and decisions in order to carry out their duties and responsibilities. This law can initially be enforced by these agencies outside the judicial process.

Administrative law judge (ALJ) One who presides over an administrative agency hearing and who has the power to administer oaths, take testimony, rule on questions of evidence, and make determinations of fact.

Administrative process The procedure used by administrative agencies in the administration of law.

Administrator One who is appointed by a court to handle the probate (disposition) of a person's estate if that person dies intestate (without a will).

Adverse possession The acquisition of title to real property by occupying it openly, without the consent of the owner, for a period of time specified by state statutes. The occupation must be actual, open, notorious, exclusive, and in opposition to all others, including the owner.

Affidavit A written or printed voluntary statement of facts, confirmed by the oath or affirmation of the party making it and made before a person having the authority to administer the oath or affirmation.

Affirmative action Job-hiring policies that give special consideration or compensatory treatment to minority groups in an effort to overcome present effects of past discrimination.

Affirmative advertising Providing specific information in an advertisement so as to prevent consumers from being misled. May be required of a firm by the Federal Trade Commission if the FTC, after investigation, decides that the firm has engaged in deceptive advertising.

Affirmative defense A response to a plaintiff's claim that does not deny the plaintiff's facts but attacks the plaintiff's legal right to bring an action. An example is the running of the statute of limitations.

After-acquired property Property of the debtor that is acquired after a secured creditor's interest in the debtor's property has been created.

Agency A relationship between two persons in which, by agreement or otherwise, one is bound by the words and acts of the other. The former is a *principal;* the latter is an *agent.*

Agent A person authorized by another to act for or in place of him or her.

Agreement A meeting of two or more minds. Often used as a synonym for contract.

Alien corporation A designation in the United States for a corporation formed in another country but doing business in the United States.

Allonge A piece of paper firmly attached to a negotiable instrument, upon which transferees can make indorsements if there is no room left on the instrument itself.

Alterations In the context of leaseholds, improvements or changes made that materially affect the condition of the property. Thus, for example, erecting additional structures probably would (and painting interior walls would not) be considered making alterations.

Alternative dispute resolution (ADR) The resolution of disputes in ways other than those involved in the traditional judicial process. Mediation and arbitration are forms of ADR.

Amend To change and improve through a formal procedure.

Analogy In logical reasoning, an assumption that if two things are similar in some respects, they will be similar in other respects also. Often used in legal reasoning to infer the appropriate application of legal principles in a case being decided by referring to previous cases involving different facts but considered to come within the policy underlying the rule.

Annuity An insurance policy that pays the insured fixed, periodic payments for life or for a term of years, as stipulated in the policy, after the insured reaches a specified age.

Answer Procedurally, a defendant's response to the complaint.

Antecedent claim A preexisting claim. In negotiable instruments law, taking an instrument in satisfaction of an antecedent claim is taking the instrument for value—that is, for valid consideration.

Anticipatory breach An assertion or action by a party indicating that he or she will not perform an obligation that the party is contractually obligated to perform at a future time.

Antitrust law The body of federal and state laws and statutes protecting trade and commerce from unlawful restraints, price discrimination, price fixing, and monopolies. The principal federal antitrust statutes are the Sherman Act (1890), the Clayton Act (1914), and the Federal Trade Commission Act (1914).

Apparent authority Authority that is only apparent, not real. In agency law, a person may be deemed to have had the power to act as an agent for another party if the other party's manifestations to a third party led the third party to believe that an agency existed when, in fact, it did not.

Appellant The party who takes an appeal from one court to another; sometimes referred to as the petitioner.

Appellee The party against whom an appeal is taken—that is, the party who opposes setting aside or reversing the judgment; sometimes referred to as the respondent.

Appraisal right A dissenting shareholder's right, if he or she objects to an extraordinary transaction of the corporation (such as a merger or consolidation), to have his or her shares appraised and to be paid the fair market value of his or her shares by the corporation.

Appropriation In tort law, the act of making a thing one's own or exercising or making use of an object to subserve one's own interest. When the act is wrongful, a tort is committed.

Arbitration The settling of a dispute by submitting it to a disinterested third party (other than a court), who renders a legally binding decision.

Arbitration clause A clause in a contract that provides that, in case of a dispute, the parties will determine their rights by arbitration rather than through the judicial system.

Arson The malicious burning of another's dwelling. Some statutes have expanded this to include any real property regardless of ownership and the destruction of property by other means—for example, by explosion.

Articles of partnership A written agreement that sets

forth each partner's rights in, and obligations to, the partnership.

Artisan's lien A possessory lien given to a person who has made improvements and added value to another person's personal property as security for payment for services performed.

Assault Any word or action intended to make another person fearful of immediate physical harm; a reasonably believable threat.

Assignee The person to whom contract rights are assigned.

Assignment of rights The act of transferring to another all or part of one's rights arising under a contract.

Assignor The person who assigns contract rights.

Assumption of risk A doctrine whereby a plaintiff may not recover for injuries or damages suffered from risks he or she knows of and assents to. A defense against negligence that can be used when the plaintiff has knowledge of and appreciates a danger and voluntarily exposes himself or herself to the danger.

Attachment (1) In a secured transaction, the process by which a security interest in the property of another becomes enforceable. (2) The legal process of seizing another's property in accordance with a writ or judicial order for the purpose of securing satisfaction of a judgment yet to be rendered.

Attractive nuisance doctrine A common law doctrine under which a landowner or landlord may be held liable for injuries incurred by children who are lured onto the property by something dangerous and enticing thereon.

Automated teller machine (ATM) An electronic customer-bank communication terminal that, when activated by an access card and a personal identification number, can conduct routine banking transactions.

Automatic stay A suspension of all judicial proceedings upon the occurrence of an independent event. Under the Bankruptcy Code, the moment a petition to commence bankruptcy proceedings is filed, all litigation by creditors against a debtor and the debtor's property is suspended.

Award As a noun, the decision rendered by an arbitrator or other extrajudicial decider of a controversy. As a verb, to give or assign by sentence, judicial determination, or otherwise after a careful weighing of evidence, as when a jury awards damages.

B

Bailee One to whom goods are entrusted by a bailor.

Bailment An agreement in which goods or personal property of one person (a bailor) are entrusted to another (a bailee), who is obligated to return the bailed property to the bailor or dispose of it as directed.

Bailor One who entrusts goods to a bailee.

Bait-and-switch advertising Advertising a product at a very attractive price (the "bait") and then informing the consumer, once he or she is in the store, that the advertised product is either not available or is of poor quality; the customer is then urged to purchase ("switched" to) a more expensive item.

Bank draft A check, draft, or other order for payment of money drawn by a bank on itself (such as a cashier's check) or on another bank.

Barriers to entry Restrictions on the ability to enter into business in a given industry, sometimes resulting from the fact that the market for that industry is controlled by just a few firms with which an entrant into the industry could not compete effectively.

Battery The unprivileged, intentional touching of another.

Bearer A person in the possession of an instrument payable to bearer or indorsed in blank.

Bearer instrument In the law of commercial paper, any instrument that runs to the bearer, including instruments payable to the bearer or to "cash."

Bequest A gift by will of personal property (from the verb *to bequeath*).

Beyond a reasonable doubt The standard used to determine the guilt or innocence of a person criminally charged. To be guilty of a crime, one must be proved guilty "beyond and to the exclusion of every reasonable doubt." A reasonable doubt is one that would cause a prudent person to hesitate before acting in matters important to him or her.

Bilateral contract A contract that includes the exchange of a promise for a promise.

Bill of lading A document that serves both as evidence of the receipt of goods for shipment and as documentary evidence of title to the goods.

Binder A written, temporary insurance policy.

Blank indorsement An indorsement made by the mere writing of the indorser's name on the back of an instrument. Such indorsement causes an instrument, otherwise payable to order, to become payable to bearer and negotiated only by delivery.

Blue sky laws State laws that regulate the offer and sale of securities.

Bona fide occupational qualification Under Title VII of the Civil Rights Act of 1964, identifiable characteristics reasonably necessary to the normal operation of a particular business. These characteristics can include gender, national origin, and religion, but not race.

Bond A certificate that evidences a corporate debt. It is a security that involves no ownership interest in the issuing corporation.

Breach of contract Failure, without legal excuse, of a promisor to perform the obligations of a contract.

Bribery The offering, giving, receiving, or soliciting of anything of value with the aim of influencing an official action or an official's discharge of a legal or public duty—or, in the case of commercial bribery, a business decision.

Brief A written summary or statement prepared by one side in a lawsuit to explain its case to the judge; a typical brief has a facts summary, a law summary, and an argument about how the law applies to the facts.

Burglary The unlawful entry into a building with the intent to commit a felony. (Some state statutes expand this to include the intent to commit any crime.)

Business ethics Ethics in a business context; a consensus of what constitutes right or wrong behavior in the world of business and the application of moral principles to situations that arise in a business setting.

Business judgment rule A rule that immunizes corporate management from liability for actions that are undertaken in good faith, when the actions are within both the power of the corporation and the authority of management to make.

Business necessity defense A showing that an employment practice that discriminates against members of a protected class is related to job performance.

Business tort A tort occurring within the business context; typical business torts are wrongful interference with the business or contractual relationships of others and unfair competition.

Buy-sell agreement A buy-out agreement. In the context of partnerships, an express agreement made at the time of partnership formation for one or more of the partners to buy out the other or others should the situation warrant—and thus provide for the smooth dissolution of the partnership.

C

Case law Rules of law announced in court decisions. Case law includes the aggregate of reported cases that interpret judicial precedents, statutes, regulations, and constitutional provisions.

Cash surrender value The amount that the insurer has agreed to pay to the insured if a life insurance policy is canceled before the insured's death.

Cashier's check A draft drawn by a bank on itself.

Causation in fact An act or omission without which an event would not have occurred.

Cease-and-desist order An administrative or judicial order prohibiting a person or business firm from conducting activities that an agency or court has deemed illegal.

Certificate of deposit (CD) An instrument evidencing a promissory acknowledgment by a bank of a receipt of money with an engagement to repay it.

Certificate of limited partnership A certificate that is required for the establishment of a limited partnership. The certificate must be filed with the designated state official (usually the secretary of state).

Certification mark A mark used by one or more persons, other than the owner, to certify the region, materials, mode of manufacture, quality, or accuracy of the owner's goods or services. When used by members of a cooperative, association, or other organization, such a mark is referred to as a *collective mark*. Examples of certification marks include the "Good Housekeeping Seal of Approval" and "UL Tested."

Certified check A check drawn by an individual on his or her own account but bearing a guaranty (acceptance) by a bank that the bank will pay the check regardless of whether the drawer's account contains adequate funds at the time the check is presented.

Chain-style business franchise A franchise that operates under a franchisor's trade name and is identified as a member of a select group of dealers that engages in the franchisor's business. The franchisee is generally required to follow standardized or prescribed methods of operations. Examples of this type of franchise are McDonald's and most other fast-food chains.

Chancellor An advisor to the king at the time of the early King's Courts of England. Individuals petitioned the king for relief when they could not obtain an adequate remedy in a court of law, and these petitions were decided by the chancellor.

Charging order In partnership law, an order granted by a court to a judgment creditor that entitles the creditor to attach profits or assets of a partner upon dissolution of the partnership.

Charitable trust A trust in which the property held by a trustee must be used for a charitable purpose, such as the advancement of health, education, or religion.

Chattel A tangible piece of personal property or an intangible right therein.

Check A draft drawn by a drawer ordering the drawee bank or financial institution to pay a certain amount of money to the holder on demand.

Choice-of-language clause A clause in a contract designating the official language by which the contract will be interpreted in the event of a future disagreement over the contract's terms.

Choice-of-law clause A clause in a contract designating the law that will govern the contract. For example, two contracting parties from different countries may choose the law of a third country to govern their agreement.

Citation A citation indicates where a particular constitutional provision, statute, reported case, or article may be found; also an order for a defendant to appear in court or indicating that a person has violated a legal rule.

Civil law The branch of law dealing with the definition and enforcement of all private or public rights, as opposed to criminal matters.

Civil law system A system of law derived from that of the Roman Empire and based on a code rather than case law; the predominant system of law in the nations of continental Europe and the nations that were once their colonies. In the United States, Louisiana is the only state that has a civil law system.

Close corporation A corporation whose shareholders are limited to a small group of persons, often including only family members. The rights of shareholders of a close corporation usually are restricted regarding the transfer of shares to others.

Closed shop A firm that requires union membership by its workers as a condition of employment. The closed shop was made illegal by the Taft-Hartley Act of 1947.

Closing The final step in the sale of real estate—also called settlement or closing escrow. The escrow agent coordinates the closing with the recording of deeds, the obtaining of title insurance, and other concurrent closing activities. Several costs must be paid, in cash, at the time of closing, and they can range from several hundred to several thousand dollars, depending on the amount of the mortgage loan and other conditions of sale.

Closing argument An argument made after the plaintiff and defendant have rested their cases. Closing arguments are made prior to the jury charges.

Codicil A written supplement or modification to a will. Codicils must be executed with the same formalities as a will.

Collateral In a broad sense, any property used as security for a loan. Under the UCC, property of a debtor in which a creditor has an interest or a right.

Collateral promise A secondary promise that is ancillary to a principal transaction or primary contractual relationship, such as a promise made by one person to pay the debts or discharge the duties of another if the latter fails to perform. A collateral promise normally must be in writing to be enforceable.

Collecting bank Any bank handling an item for collection, except the payor bank.

Collective mark A mark used by members of a cooperative, association, or other organization to certify the region, materials, mode of manufacture, quality, or accuracy of the specific goods or services. Examples of collective marks include the labor union marks found on tags of certain products and the credits of movies, which indicate the various associations and organizations that participated in the making of the movies.

Comity A deference by which one nation gives effect to the laws and judicial decrees of another nation. This recognition is based primarily upon respect.

Comment period A period of time following an administrative agency's publication of a notice of a proposed rule during which private parties may comment in writing on the agency proposal in an effort to influence agency policy. The agency takes any comments received into consideration when drafting the final version of the regulation.

Commercial impracticability A doctrine under which a seller may be excused from performing a contract when (1) a contingency occurs, (2) the contingency's occurrence makes performance impracticable, and (3) the nonoccurrence of the contingency was a basic assumption on which the contract was made. Despite the fact that UCC 2-615 expressly frees only sellers under this doctrine, courts have not distinguished between buyers and sellers in applying it.

Commercial paper Under UCC Article 3, negotiable instruments (signed writings that contain an unconditional promise or order to pay an exact sum of money, either when demanded or at an exact future time), including drafts, promissory notes, certificates of deposit, and checks.

Common areas In landlord-tenant law, the portion of the premises over which the landlord retains control and maintenance responsibilities. Common areas may include stairs, lobbies, garages, hallways, and other areas in common use.

Common law That body of law developed from custom or judicial decisions in English and U.S. courts, not attributable to a legislature.

Common stock Shares of ownership in a corporation that are lowest in priority with respect to payment of dividends and distribution of the corporation's assets upon dissolution.

Community property A form of concurrent ownership of property in which each spouse owns an undivided one-half interest in property. This type of ownership applies to most property acquired by the husband or wife during the course of marriage. It generally does not apply to property acquired prior to the marriage or to property acquired by gift or inheritance during the marriage. After a divorce, community property is divided equally in some states and according to the discretion of the court in other states.

Comparable worth A doctrine that aims to correct for past employment discrimination against women by advocating comparable pay for comparable work. The concept of comparable worth involves equal pay for different kinds of jobs that require the same degree of education, training, or effort.

Comparative negligence A theory in tort law under which the liability for injuries resulting from negligent acts is shared by all persons who were guilty of negligence (including the injured party), on the basis of each person's proportionate carelessness.

Compensatory damages A money award equivalent to the actual value of injuries or damages sustained by the aggrieved party.

Complaint The pleading made by a plaintiff or a charge made by the state alleging wrongdoing on the part of the defendant.

Computer crime Any wrongful act that is directed against computers and computer parts, or wrongful use or abuse of computers or software.

Concentrated industry An industry in which a large percentage of market sales is controlled by either a single firm or a small number of firms.

Concurrent conditions Conditions that must occur or be performed at the same time; they are mutually dependent. No obligations arise until these conditions are simultaneously performed.

Concurrent jurisdiction Jurisdiction that exists when two different courts have the power to hear a case. For example, some cases can be heard in a federal or state court.

Concurrent ownership Joint ownership.

Condition A qualification, provision, or clause in a contractual agreement, the occurrence of which creates, suspends, or terminates the obligations of the contracting parties.

Condition precedent In a contractual agreement, a condition that must be met before the other party's obligations arise.

Condition subsequent A condition in a contract that, if not met, discharges an existing obligation of the other party.

Confession of judgment A judgment entered against a debtor by a creditor, with the debtor's permission and for an agreed sum, without the use of legal proceedings.

Confiscation A government's taking of privately owned business or personal property without a proper public purpose or an award of just compensation.

Conforming goods Goods that conform to contract specifications.

Confusion The mixing together of goods belonging to two or more owners so that the independent goods cannot be identified.

Conglomerate merger A merger between firms that do not compete with each other because they are in different markets (as opposed to horizontal and vertical mergers).

Consent Voluntary agreement to a proposition or an act of another. A concurrence of wills.

Consequential damages Special damages that compensate for a loss that is not direct or immediate (for example, lost profits). The special damages must have been reasonably foreseeable at the time the breach or injury occurred in order for the plaintiff to collect them.

Consideration That which motivates the exchange of promises or performance in a contractual agreement. The consideration, which must be present to make the contract legally binding, must result in a detriment to the promisee (something of legal value, legally sufficient, and bargained for) or a benefit to the promisor.

Consignment A transaction in which an owner of goods (the consignor) delivers the goods to another (the consignee) for the consignee to sell. The consignee pays the consignor for the goods when the consignee sells the goods.

Consolidation A contractual and statutory process whereby two or more corporations join to become a completely new corporation. The original corporations cease to exist, and the new corporation acquires all their assets and liabilities.

Constructive delivery An act equivalent to the actual, physical delivery of property that cannot be physically delivered because of difficulty or impossibility; to illustrate, the transfer of a key to a safe constructively delivers the contents of the safe.

Constructive eviction Depriving a person of the possession of rental property that he or she leases by rendering the premises unfit or unsuitable for occupancy.

Constructive trust A trust created by operation of law against one who wrongfully has obtained or holds a legal right to property that the person should not, in equity and good conscience, hold and enjoy.

Consumer-debtors Debtors whose debts are primarily consumer debts—that is, debts for purchases that are primarily for household or personal use.

Contingency fees Attorneys' fees that are based on a percentage of the final awards received by their clients as a result of litigation.

Contract A set of promises constituting an agreement between parties, giving each a legal duty to the other and also the right to seek a remedy for the breach of the promises/duties owed to each. The elements of an enforceable contract are competent parties, a proper or legal purpose, consideration (an exchange of promises/duties), and mutuality of agreement and of obligation.

Contract implied in law A contract imposed upon parties by law, in the absence of justice, to prevent unjust enrichment even though the parties never intended to voluntarily enter into a contract; sometimes referred to as a quasi contract.

Contract under seal A formal agreement in which the seal is a substitute for consideration. A court will not invalidate a contract under seal for lack of consideration.

Contractual capacity The threshold mental capacity required by the law for a party who enters into a contract to be bound by that contract.

Contributory negligence A theory in tort law under which a complaining party's own negligence contributed to or caused his or her injuries. Contributory negligence is an absolute bar to recovery in a minority of jurisdictions.

Convenant of the right to convey A grantor's assurance that he or she has sufficient capacity and title to convey the estate that he or she undertakes to convey by deed.

Conversion The wrongful taking or retaining possession of personal property that belongs to another.

Cooperative An association that is organized to provide an economic service to its members (or shareholders). An incorporated cooperative is a nonprofit corporation. It will make distributions of dividends, or profits, to its owners on the basis of their transactions with the cooperative rather than on the basis of the amount of capital they contributed. Examples of cooperatives are consumer purchasing cooperatives, credit cooperatives, and farmers' cooperatives.

Copyright The exclusive right of "authors" to publish, print, or sell an intellectual production for a statutory period of time. A copyright has the same monopolistic nature as a patent or trademark, but it differs in that it applies exclusively to works of art, literature, and other works of authorship (including computer programs).

Corporation A legal entity created under the authority of the laws of a state or the federal government. The entity is distinct from its shareholders/owners.

Correspondent bank A bank in which another bank has an account (and vice versa) for the purpose of facilitating fund transfers.

Cost-benefit analysis A way to reach decisions in which the costs of a given action are compared with the benefits of the action.

Counteradvertising New advertising that is undertaken pursuant to a Federal Trade Commission order for the purpose of correcting earlier false claims that were made about a product.

Counterclaim A claim made by a defendant in a civil lawsuit that in effect sues the plaintiff; it can be based on entirely different grounds than those given in the plaintiff's complaint.

Counteroffer An offeree's response to an offer in which the offeree rejects the original offer and at the same time makes a new offer.

Course of dealing A sequence of previous conduct between the parties to a particular transaction that establishes a common basis for their understanding.

Course of performance The conduct that occurs under the terms of a particular agreement; such conduct indicates what the parties to an agreement intended it to mean.

Court of equity A court that decides controversies and administers justice according to the rules, principles, and precedents of equity.

Court of law A court in which the only remedies that could be granted were things of value, such as money damages. In the early English King's Court, courts of law were distinct from courts of equity.

Covenant against encumbrances A grantor's assurance that on land conveyed there are no encumbrances—that is, that no third parties have rights to, or interests in, the land that would diminish its value to the grantee.

Covenant not to sue An agreement to substitute a contractual obligation for some other type of action.

Covenant of quiet enjoyment A promise by the grantor (or landlord) that the grantee (or tenant) will not be evicted or disturbed by the grantor or a person having a lien or superior title.

Covenant of seisin An assurance to the purchaser that the grantor has the very estate in the quantity and quality that the grantor purports to convey.

Covenant running with the land An executory promise made between a grantor and a grantee to which they

and subsequent owners of the land are bound.

Cover Under the UCC, a remedy of the buyer that allows the buyer, on the seller's breach, to purchase the goods from another seller and substitute them for the goods due under the contract. If the cost of cover exceeds the cost of the contract goods, the breaching seller will be liable to the buyer for the difference.

Crashworthiness doctrine A doctrine that imposes liability for defects in the design or construction of motor vehicles that increase the extent of injuries to passengers if an accident occurs. The doctrine holds even when the defects do not actually cause the accident.

Creditor beneficiary A creditor who has rights in a contract made by the debtor and a third person, in which the terms of the contract obligate the third person to pay the debt owed to the creditor. The creditor beneficiary can enforce the debt against either party.

Creditors' composition agreement An agreement formed between a debtor and his or her creditors in which the creditors agree to accept a lesser sum than that owed by the debtor in full satisfaction of the debt.

Crime A broad term for violations of law that are punishable by the state and are codified by legislatures. The objective of criminal law is to protect the public.

Criminal law Law that governs and defines those actions that are crimes and that subject the convicted offender to punishment imposed by the government.

Cumulative voting A method of shareholder voting designed to allow minority shareholders to be represented on the board of directors. With cumulative voting, the number of members of the board to be elected is multiplied by the total number of voting shares held. The result equals the number of votes a shareholder has, and this total can be cast for one or more nominees for director.

Cure The right of a party who tenders nonconforming performance to correct his or her performance within the contract period [UCC 3-508].

D

Damages Money sought as a remedy for a breach of contract or for a tortious act.

Debtor A person who owes a sum of money or other obligations to another.

Debtor in possession In Chapter 11 bankruptcy proceedings, a debtor who is allowed, for the benefit of all concerned, to continue in possession of the estate in bankruptcy (the business) and to continue business operations.

Deed A document by which title to property (usually real property) is passed.

Defamation Anything published or publicly spoken that causes injury to another's good name, reputation, or character.

Default judgment A judgment entered by a clerk or

court against a party who has failed to appear in court to answer or defend against a claim that has been brought against him or her by another party.

Defendant One against whom a lawsuit is brought; the accused person in a criminal proceeding.

Defense That which a defendant offers and alleges in an action or suit as a reason why the plaintiff should not recover or establish what he or she seeks.

Deficiency judgment A judgment against a debtor for the amount of a debt remaining unpaid after collateral has been repossessed and sold or after foreclosure proceedings.

Delegation of duties The act of transferring to another all or part of one's duties arising under a contract.

Delivery order A written order to deliver goods directed to a warehouser, carrier, or other person who, in the ordinary course of business, issues warehouse receipts or bills of lading [UCC 7-102(1)(d)].

Demand deposit Funds (accepted by a bank) subject to immediate withdrawal, in contrast to a time deposit, which requires that a depositor wait a specific time before withdrawing or pay a penalty for early withdrawal.

Demurrer *See* Motion to dismiss.

Depositary bank The first bank to which an item is transferred for collection, even though it may also be the payor bank.

Deposition A generic term that refers to any evidence verified by oath. As a legal term, it is often limited to the testimony of a witness taken under oath before a trial, with the opportunity of cross-examination.

Deregulation The removal of regulatory restraints; the opposite of regulation.

Devise To make a gift of real property by will.

Disaffirmance The repudiation of an obligation.

Discharge The termination of one's obligation. In contract law, discharge occurs when the parties have fully performed their contractual obligations or when events, conduct of the parties, or operation of the law releases the parties from further performance.

Discharge in bankruptcy The release of a debtor from all debts that are provable, except those specifically excepted from discharge by statute.

Disclosed principal A principal whose identity and existence as a principal is known by a third person at the time a transaction is conducted by an agent.

Discovery A method by which opposing parties may obtain information from each other to prepare for trial. Generally governed by rules of procedure, but may be controlled by the court.

Disparagement of property Economically injurious falsehoods made about another's product or property. A general term for torts that are more specifically referred to as slander of quality or slander of title.

Disparate-impact discrimination In an employment context, discrimination that results from certain employer practices or procedures that, although not dis-

criminatory on their face, have a discriminatory effect. For example, a requirement that all employees have high school diplomas is not necessarily discriminatory, but it may have the *effect* of discriminating against minority groups.

Disparate-treatment discrimination In an employment context, intentional discrimination against individuals on the basis of color, gender, national origin, race, or religion.

Dissolution The formal disbanding of a partnership or a corporation. It can take place by (1) agreement of the parties or the shareholders and board of directors, (2) the death of a partner, (3) the expiration of a time period stated in a partnership agreement or a certificate of incorporation, or (4) court order.

Distribution agreement A contract between a seller and a distributor of the seller's products setting out the terms and conditions of the distributorship.

Distributorship A business arrangement that is established when a manufacturer licenses a dealer to sell its product. An example of a distributorship is an automobile dealership.

Diversity of citizenship Under Article III, Section 2, of the Constitution, a basis for federal court jurisdiction over a lawsuit between citizens of different states.

Divestiture The act of selling one or more of a company's parts, such as a subsidiary or plant; often mandated by the courts in merger or monopolization cases.

Dividend A distribution to corporate shareholders, disbursed in proportion to the number of shares held.

Document of title Paper exchanged in the regular course of business that evidences the right to possession of goods (for example, a bill of lading or warehouse receipt).

Domestic corporation In a given state, a corporation that does business in, and is organized under the laws of, that state.

Domestic relations courts Courts that deal with domestic (household) relationships, such as adoption, divorce, support payments, child custody, and the like.

Donee beneficiary A third party to whom the benefits of a contract flow as a direct result of an intention to make a gift to that person.

Double taxation A feature (and disadvantage) of the corporate form of business. Because a corporation is a separate legal entity, corporate profits are taxed by state and federal governments. Dividends are again taxable as ordinary income to the shareholders receiving them.

Draft Any instrument drawn on a drawee (such as a bank) that orders the drawee to pay a certain sum of money.

Drawee The person who is ordered to pay a draft or check. With a check, a financial institution is always the drawee.

Drawer A person who initiates a draft (including a check), thereby ordering the drawee to pay.

Due diligence A required standard of care that certain professionals, such as accountants, must meet to avoid liability for securities violations. Under securities law, an accountant will be deemed to have exercised due diligence if he or she followed generally accepted accounting principles and generally accepted auditing standards and had, "after reasonable investigation, reasonable grounds to believe and did believe, at the time such part of the registration statement became effective, that the statements therein were true and that there was no omission of a material fact required to be stated therein or necessary to make the statements therein not misleading."

Due negotiation The transfer of a document of title in such form that the transferee becomes a holder [UCC 7-501].

Dumping Selling goods in a foreign country at a price below the price charged for the same goods in the domestic market.

Duress Unlawful pressure brought to bear on a person, overcoming that person's free will and causing him or her to do (or refrain from doing) what he or she otherwise would not (or would) have done.

E

Easement A nonpossessory right to use another's property in a manner established by either express or implied agreement.

Eighty-day cooling-off period A provision of the Taft-Hartley Act that allows federal courts to issue injunctions against strikes that might create a national emergency.

Ejectment The eviction of a tenant from leased premises. A remedy at common law to which the landlord can resort when a tenant fails to pay rent for leased premises. To obtain possession of the premises, the landlord must appear in court and show that the defaulting tenant is in wrongful possession.

Electronic fund transfer A transfer of funds with the use of an electronic terminal, a telephone, a computer, or magnetic tape.

Electronic fund transfer system (EFTS) A system used to transfer funds electronically.

Embezzlement The fraudulent appropriation of money or other property by a person to whom the money or property has been entrusted.

Eminent domain The power of a government to take land for public use from private citizens for just compensation.

Employee A person who works for an employer for salary or wages.

Employment-at-will doctrine A common law doctrine under which employer-employee contracts are considered to be "at will"—that is, either party may terminate an employment contract at any time and for any reason, unless the contract specifies otherwise. Although several states still adhere to the employment-at-will doctrine, exceptions are frequently made on the basis of an implied employment contract or public policy.

Enabling legislation Statutes enacted by Congress that authorize the creation of an administrative agency and specify the name, composition, and powers of the agency being created.

Endowment insurance A type of insurance that combines life insurance with an investment so that if the insured outlives the policy, the face value is paid to him or her; if the insured does not outlive the policy, the face value is paid to his or her beneficiary.

Entrapment In criminal law, a defense in which the defendant claims that he or she was induced by a public official—usually an undercover agent or police officer—to commit a crime that he or she would otherwise not have committed.

Entrepreneur One who initiates and assumes the financial risks of a new enterprise and who undertakes to provide or control its management.

Entrustment The transfer of goods to a merchant who deals in goods of that kind and who may transfer those goods and all rights to them to a buyer in the ordinary course of business [UCC 2-403(2)].

Environmental impact statement (EIS) A statement required by the National Environmental Policy Act for any major federal action that will significantly affect the quality of the environment. The statement must analyze the action's impact on the environment and alternative actions that might be taken.

Environmental law All statutory, regulatory, and common law relating to the protection of the environment.

Equal dignity rule In most states, a rule stating that express authority given to an agent must be in writing if the contract to be made on behalf of the principal is required to be in writing.

Equal protection clause The clause in the Fourteenth Amendment to the Constitution that guarantees that no state will "deny to any person within its jurisdiction the equal protection of the laws." This clause mandates that the state governments treat similarly situated individuals in a similar manner.

Equitable principles and maxims Propositions or general statements of rules of law that are frequently involved in equity jurisdiction.

Equitable servitudes Restrictions on the use of land that are enforceable in a court of equity.

Equity of redemption The right of a mortgagor who has breached the mortgage agreement to redeem or purchase the property prior to foreclosure proceedings.

Escheat The transfer of property to the state when the owner of the property dies without heirs.

Escrow account An account that is generally held in the name of the depositor and escrow agent; the funds in the account are paid to a third person only upon fulfillment of the escrow condition.

Establishment clause The clause in the First Amendment to the Constitution that prohibits Congress from creating any law ''respecting an establishment of religion.''

Estop To bar, impede, or preclude.

Estoppel The principle that a party's own acts prevent him or her from claiming a right to the detriment of another who was entitled to, and did, rely on those acts. *Agency by estoppel* arises when a principal negligently allows an agent to exercise powers not granted to the agent, thus justifying others in believing that the agent possesses the requisite agency authority. *See also* Promissory estoppel.

Estray statutes Statutes dealing with finders' rights in property when the true owners are unknown.

Ethics Moral principles and values applied to social behavior.

Eviction Depriving a person of the possession of land or rental property that he or she owns or leases.

Exclusionary rule In criminal procedure, a rule under which any evidence that is obtained in violation of the accused's constitutional rights guaranteed by the Fourth, Fifth, and Sixth Amendments, as well as any evidence derived from illegally obtained evidence, will not be admissible in court.

Exclusive dealing contract An agreement under which a producer of goods agrees to sell its goods exclusively through one distributor.

Exclusive distributorship A distributorship in which the seller and distributor of the seller's products agree that the distributor has the exclusive right to distribute the seller's products in a certain geographic area.

Exclusive jurisdiction Jurisdiction that exists when a case can be heard only in a particular court.

Exculpatory clause A clause that releases a party (to a contract) from liability for his or her wrongful acts.

Executed contract A contract that has been completely performed by both parties.

Executor A person appointed by a testator to see that his or her will is administered appropriately.

Executory contract A contract that has not as yet been fully performed.

Executory interest A future interest, held by a person other than the grantor, that either cuts short or begins some time after the natural termination of the preceding estate.

Export To sell products to buyers located in other countries.

Express authority Authority expressly given by one party to another. In agency law, an agent has express authority to act for a principal if both parties agree, orally or in writing, that an agency relationship exists in which the agent had the power (authority) to act in the place of, and on behalf of, the principal.

Express contract A contract that is oral and/or written

(as opposed to an implied contract).

Express warranty A promise, ancillary to an underlying sales agreement, that is included in the written or oral terms of the sales agreement under which the promisor assures the quality, description, or performance of the goods.

Expropriation The seizure by a government of privately owned business or personal property for a proper public purpose and with just compensation.

Extension clause A clause in a time instrument extending the instrument's date of maturity. An extension clause is the reverse of an acceleration clause.

Externalities The costs or benefits of an action that are not known or properly accounted for by the parties to that action. An example of an externality is environmental pollution.

F

Federal question A question that pertains to the U.S. Constitution, acts of Congress, or treaties. A federal question provides jurisdiction for federal courts. This jurisdiction arises from Article III, Section 2, of the Constitution.

Fee simple A form of property ownership entitling the property owner to use, possess, or dispose of the property as he or she chooses during his or her lifetime. Upon death, the interest in the property descends to the owner's heirs.

Fee simple absolute An estate or interest in land with no time, disposition, or descendibility limitations.

Fee simple defeasible An estate that can be taken away (by the prior grantor) upon the occurrence or nonoccurrence of a specified event.

Felony A crime—such as arson, murder, rape, or robbery—that carries the most severe sanctions, usually ranging from one year in a state or federal prison to the forfeiture of one's life.

Felony murder A common law doctrine under which the intent to commit a felony unrelated to a resulting homicide was sufficient to meet the *mens rea* requirement for murder. Because of the many new statutory felonies that pose little threat of death or bodily harm to anyone, this doctrine has been limited by courts and legislatures.

Fictitious payee rule A rule under which indorsements by fictitious payees (a payee on a negotiable instrument whom the maker or drawer does not intend to have an interest in the instrument) will not be deemed forgeries.

Fiduciary relationship A relationship founded upon trust and confidence.

Final order The final decision of an administrative agency on an issue. If no appeal is taken, or if the case is not reviewed or considered anew by the agency commission, the administrative law judge's initial order becomes the final order of the agency.

Financial institutions Organizations authorized to do business under state or federal laws relating to financial institutions. For example, under the Electronic Fund Transfer Act, financial institutions include banks, savings and loan associations, credit unions, and any other business entities that directly or indirectly hold accounts belonging to consumers.

Financing statement A document prepared by a secured creditor, and filed with the appropriate state or local official, to give notice to the public that the creditor claims an interest in collateral belonging to a certain named debtor. The financing statement must be signed by the debtor, contain the addresses of both the debtor and creditor, and describe the collateral by type or item.

Firm offer An offer (by a merchant) that is irrevocable without consideration for a period of time (not longer than three months). A firm offer by a merchant must be in writing and must be signed by the offeror.

Fixture A thing that was once personal property but that has become attached to real property in such a way that it takes on the characteristics of real property and becomes part of that real property.

Float time The time between the issuance of a check and the deduction of the amount of the check from the drawer's account.

Floating lien A security interest retained in collateral even when the collateral changes in character, classification, or location.

***Force majeure* clause** A clause in a contract stipulating that certain unforeseen events—such as war, political upheavals, acts of God, or other events—will excuse a party from liability for nonperformance of contractual obligations.

Foreclosure A proceeding in equity whereby a mortgagee either takes title to, or forces the sale of, the mortgagor's property in satisfaction of a debt.

Foreign corporation In a given state, a corporation that does business in the state without being incorporated therein.

Foreign exchange market A worldwide system in which foreign currencies are bought and sold.

Foreign exchange rate The price of a unit of one country's currency in terms of another country's currency. For example, if today's exchange rate is 100 yen for $1, that means that anybody with 100 yen can obtain $1, or that 1 yen equals $0.01.

Foreseeable risk In negligence law, the risk of harm or injury to another that a person of ordinary intelligence and prudence should have reasonably anticipated or foreseen when undertaking an action or refraining from an action.

Forfeiture The termination of a lease, according to its terms or the terms of a statute, when one of the parties fails to fulfill a condition under the lease and thereby breaches it.

Forgery The false or unauthorized signature of a document, or the false making of a document, with the intent to defraud.

Formal contract An agreement or contract that by law requires for its validity a specific form, such as executed under seal.

Formal rulemaking Agency rulemaking that is much more extensive than informal rulemaking and in which a public hearing is conducted in the manner of a trial. After the hearing is concluded, the agency is required to prepare a formal written statement describing its findings based on the evidence presented by both sides. Also referred to as rulemaking-on-a-record.

Forum-selection clause A clause in a contract designating the forum (the nation, state, or jurisdiction) in which a dispute will be litigated.

Franchise A written agreement whereby an owner of a trademark, trade name, or copyright licenses another to use that trademark, trade name, or copyright, under specified conditions or limitations, in the selling of goods and services.

Franchisee One receiving a license to use another's (the franchisor's) trademark, trade name, or copyright in the sale of goods and services.

Franchisor One licensing another (the franchisee) to use his or her trademark, trade name, or copyright in the sale of goods or services.

Fraud Any misrepresentation, either by misstatement or omission of a material fact, knowingly made with the intention of deceiving another and on which a reasonable person would and does rely to his or her detriment.

Free exercise clause The clause in the First Amendment to the Constitution that prohibits Congress from making any law ''prohibiting the free exercise'' of religion.

Frustration of purpose A court-created doctrine under which a party to a contract will be relieved of his or her duty to perform when the objective purpose for performance no longer exists (due to reasons beyond that party's control).

Fungible goods Goods that are alike by physical nature, by agreement, or by trade usage. Examples of fungible goods are wheat, oil, and wine that are identical in type and quality.

Future interest An interest in real property that is not at present possessory but will or may be possessory in the future. Remainders and reversions are future interests.

G

Garnishment A legal process whereby a creditor appropriates the debtor's property or wages that are in the hands of a third party.

General partner In a limited partnership, a partner who assumes responsibility for the management of the partnership and liability for all partnership debts.

Generally accepted accounting principles (GAAP)
The conventions, rules, and procedures necessary to define accepted accounting practices at a particular time. The source of the principles is the Federal Accounting Standards Board.

Generally accepted auditing standards (GAAS)
Standards concerning an auditor's professional qualities and the judgment exercised by him or her in the performance of an examination and report. The source of the standards is the American Institute of Certified Public Accountants.

Genuineness of assent Knowing and voluntary assent to the terms of a contract. If a contract is formed as a result of a mistake, misrepresentation, undue influence, or duress, genuineness of assent is lacking, and the contract will be voidable.

Gift Any voluntary transfer of property made without consideration, past or present.

Gift *causa mortis* A gift made in contemplation of death. If the donor does not die of that ailment, the gift is revoked.

Gift *inter vivos* A gift made during one's lifetime and not in contemplation of imminent death, in contrast to a gift *causa mortis.*

Good faith purchaser A purchaser who buys without notice of any circumstance that would put a person of ordinary prudence on inquiry as to whether the seller has valid title to the goods being sold.

Grand jury In criminal cases, a body of citizens that decides whether a person accused of a crime should be prosecuted. If the jury concludes that the evidence against the individual is sufficient to justify a trial, the individual will be indicted and a trial held. Called a ''grand'' jury because it consists of a greater number of jurors than the ordinary trial jury, or ''petit'' jury.

Grant deed A deed that simply recites words of consideration and conveyance. Under statute, a grant deed may impliedly warrant that at least the grantor has not conveyed the property's title to someone else.

Group boycott The boycott of a particular person or firm by a group of competitors; prohibited under the Sherman Act.

Guarantor One who agrees to satisfy the debt of another (the debtor) *only* if and when the debtor fails to pay the debt. A guarantor's liability is thus secondary.

H

Holder A person ''who is in possession of a document of title or negotiable instrument or a certificated investment security drawn, issued, or indorsed to him or his order or to bearer or in blank'' [UCC 1-201(20)].

Holder in due course Any holder who acquires a negotiable instrument for value; in good faith; and without notice that the instrument is overdue, that it has been dishonored, or that any defense or claim to it exists on the part of any person.

Holographic will A will written entirely in the signer's handwriting and usually not witnessed.

Homestead exemption A law allowing an owner to designate his or her house and adjoining land as a homestead and thus exempt it from liability for his or her general debt.

Horizontal market division A market division that occurs when competitors agree to divide up the market for their products or services among themselves, either geographically or by functional class of customers (such as retailers or wholesalers). Such market division constitutes a *per se* violation of the Sherman Act.

Horizontal merger A merger between two businesses or persons competing in the marketplace.

Horizontal restraint Any agreement that in some way restrains competition between rival firms competing in the same market. Price fixing and horizontal market division are examples of horizontal restraints on competition.

Hot-cargo agreement An agreement in which employers voluntarily agree with unions not to handle, use, or deal in non-union-produced goods of other employers. A type of secondary boycott explicitly prohibited by the Landrum-Griffin Act of 1959.

Hybrid rulemaking A set of loosely defined procedures for agency rulemaking that incorporate advantages of both the formal and informal procedures. As with formal rulemaking, there is an opportunity for direct participation through a public hearing, but the right of interested parties to cross-examine witnesses is much more restricted.

I

Identification Proof that a thing is what it is purported or represented to be. In the sale of goods, the express designation of the goods provided for in the contract.

Immunity A status of being exempt, or free, from certain duties or requirements. In criminal law, the state may grant an accused person immunity from prosecution—or agree to prosecute for a lesser offense—if the accused person agrees to give the state information that would assist the state in prosecuting other individuals for crimes. In tort law, freedom from liability for defamatory speech. *See also* Privilege.

Implied authority Authority that is created not by an explicit oral or written agreement but by implication. In agency law, implied authority (of the agent) can be conferred by custom, inferred from the position the agent occupies, or implied by virtue of being reasonably necessary to carry out express authority.

Implied warranty A warranty that the law implies through either the situation of the parties or the nature of the transaction.

Implied warranty of fitness for a particular

purpose A presumed promise made by a merchant seller of goods that the goods are fit for the particular purpose for which the buyer will use the goods. The seller must know the buyer's purpose and know that the buyer is relying on the seller's skill and judgment to select suitable goods.

Implied warranty of habitability A presumed promise by the landlord that rented residential premises are fit for human habitation—that is, free of violations of building and sanitary codes.

Implied warranty of merchantability A presumed promise by a merchant seller of goods that the goods are reasonably fit for the general purpose for which they are sold, are properly packaged and labeled, and are of proper quality.

Implied-in-fact contract A contract formed in whole or in part from the conduct of the parties (as opposed to an express contract).

Impossibility of performance A doctrine under which a party to a contract is relieved of his or her duty to perform when performance becomes impossible or totally impracticable (through no fault of either party).

Imposter One who, with the intent to deceive, pretends to be somebody else.

In pari delicto At equal fault.

In personam **jurisdiction** Court jurisdiction over the ''person'' involved in a legal action.

In rem **jurisdiction** Court jurisdiction over a defendant's property.

Incidental beneficiary A third party who incidentally benefits from a contract but whose benefit was not the reason the contract was formed; an incidental beneficiary has no rights in a contract and cannot sue the promisor if the contract is breached.

Incidental damages Damages resulting from a breach of contract, including all reasonable expenses incurred because of the breach.

Indemnify To compensate or reimburse another for losses or expenses incurred.

Independent contractor One who works for, and receives payment from, an employer but whose working conditions and methods are not controlled by the employer. An independent contractor is not an employee but may be an agent.

Indictment A charge or written accusation, issued by a grand jury, that a named person has committed a crime.

Indorsee The one to whom a negotiable instrument is transferred by indorsement.

Indorsement A signature placed on an instrument or a document of title for the purpose of transferring one's ownership in the instrument or document of title.

Indorser One who, being the payee or holder of a negotiable instrument, signs his or her name on the back of it.

Industrywide liability Product liability that is imposed on an entire industry when it is unclear which of several sellers within the industry manufactured a particular product.

Informal contract A contract that does not require a specified form or formality for its validity.

Informal rulemaking A procedure in agency rulemaking that requires (1) notice; (2) opportunity for comment; and (3) a general statement of the basis for, and purpose of, the proposed rule. Also referred to as notice-and-comment rulemaking.

Information A formal accusation or complaint (without an indictment) issued in certain types of actions by a prosecuting attorney or other law officer, such as a magistrate. The types of actions are set forth in the rules of states or in the Federal Rules of Criminal Procedure.

Information return A tax return submitted by a partnership that only reports the income earned by the business. The partnership as an entity does not pay taxes on the income received by the partnership. A partner's profit from the partnership (whether distributed or not) is taxed as individual income to the individual partner.

Initial order In the context of administrative law, an agency's disposition in a matter other than a rulemaking. An administrative law judge's initial order becomes final unless it is appealed.

Injunction A court decree ordering a person to do, or refrain from doing, a certain act or activity.

Innkeeper's lien A possessory or statutory lien allowing the innkeeper to take the personal property of a guest, brought into the hotel, as security for nonpayment of the guest's bill (debt).

Innocent misrepresentation A false statement of fact or an act made in good faith that deceives and causes harm or injury to another.

Insider A corporate director or officer, or other employee or agent, with access to confidential information and a duty not to disclose that information in violation of insider-trading laws.

Insider trading Purchasing or selling securities on the basis of information that has not been made available to the public.

Insolvent A term describing a person whose liabilities exceed the value of owned assets *or* a person who ''either has ceased to pay his debts in the ordinary course of business or cannot pay his debts as they come due'' [UCC 1-201(23)].

Installment contract A contract in which payments due are made periodically. Also may allow for delivery of goods in separate lots with payment made for each.

Insurable interest An interest either in a person's life or well-being or in property that is sufficiently substantial that insuring against injury to the person or damage to the property does not amount to a mere wagering (betting) contract.

Insurance A contract in which, for a stipulated consideration, one party agrees to compensate the other for loss on a specific subject by a specified peril.

Intellectual property Property resulting from intellectual, creative processes—the products of an individual's mind.

Intended beneficiary A third party for whose benefit a contract is formed; intended beneficiaries can sue the promisor if such a contract is breached.

Intentional tort A wrongful act knowingly committed.

Inter vivos **gift** *See* Gift *inter vivos.*

Inter vivos **trust** A trust created by the grantor (settlor) and effective during the grantor's lifetime (that is, a trust not established by a will).

Intermediary bank Any bank to which an item is transferred in the course of collection, except the depositary or payor bank.

International law The law that governs relations among nations. International customs and treaties are generally considered to be two of the most important sources of international law.

International organization In international law, a term that generally refers to an organization composed mainly of nations and usually established by treaty. The United States is a member of more than one hundred multilateral and bilateral organizations, including at least twenty through the United Nations.

Interpretative rules Administrative agency rules that are simply statements and opinions issued by an agency explaining how the agency interprets and intends to apply the statutes it enforces. Such rules are not automatically binding on private individuals or organizations.

Interrogatories A series of written questions for which written answers are prepared and then signed under oath by a party to a lawsuit (the plaintiff or the defendant) or a witness.

Intestacy laws State laws determining the division and descent of the property of one who dies intestate (without a will).

Intestate One who has died without having created a valid will.

Investment company A company that acts on behalf of many smaller shareholders/owners by buying a large portfolio of securities and managing that portfolio professionally.

Invitee A person who, either expressly or impliedly, is privileged to enter upon another's land. The inviter owes the invitee (for example, a customer in a store) the duty to exercise reasonable care to protect the invitee from harm.

Irrevocable offer An offer that cannot be revoked or recalled by the offeror without liability. A merchant's firm offer is an example of an irrevocable offer.

Issue The first transfer, or delivery, of an instrument to a holder.

J

Joint and several liability A doctrine under which a plaintiff may sue, and collect a judgment from, any of several jointly liable defendants, regardless of that particular defendant's degree of fault. In partnership law, joint and several liability means a third party may sue one or more of the partners separately or all of them together, at his or her option. This is true even if the partner did not participate in, ratify, or know about whatever it was that gave rise to the cause of action.

Joint liability Shared liability. In partnership law, partners incur joint liability for partnership obligations and debts. For example, if a third party sues a partner on a partnership debt, the partner has the right to insist that the other partners be sued with him or her.

Joint stock company A hybrid form of business organization that combines characteristics of a corporation (shareholder-owners, management by directors and officers of the company, and perpetual existence) and a partnership (it is formed by agreement, not statute; property is usually held in the names of the members; and the shareholders have personal liability for business debts). Usually, the joint stock company is regarded as a partnership for tax and other legally related purposes.

Joint tenancy The ownership interest of two or more co-owners of property whereby each owns an undivided portion of the property. Upon the death of one of the joint tenants, his or her interest automatically passes to the others and cannot be transferred by the will of the deceased.

Joint venture A joint undertaking of a specific commercial enterprise by an association of persons. A joint venture is normally not a legal entity and is treated like a partnership for federal income tax purposes.

Judgment *n.o.v.* A judgment notwithstanding the verdict; may be entered by the court for the plaintiff (or the defendant) after there has been a jury verdict for the defendant (or the plaintiff).

Judgment rate of interest A rate of interest fixed by statute that is applied to a monetary judgment from the moment the judgment is awarded by a court until the judgment is paid or terminated.

Judicial process The procedures relating to, or connected with, the administration of justice through the judicial system.

Judicial review The authority of a court to reexamine a previously considered dispute; the process by which a court decides on the constitutionality of legislative acts.

Jurisdiction The authority of a court to hear and decide a specific action.

Jurisprudence The science or philosophy of law.

Justice of the peace courts Courts of limited civil and criminal jurisdiction, presided over by judicial magistrates of inferior rank (called justices of the peace).

Justiciable Appropriate for court review. A justiciable controversy is one that is not hypothetical or academic but real and substantial.

K

King's Court A medieval English court. The King's Courts, or *Curia Regis,* were established by the Norman conquerors of England. The body of law that developed in these courts was common to the entire English realm and thus became known as the common law.

L

Laches The equitable doctrine that bars a party's right to legal action if the party has neglected for an unreasonable length of time to act upon his or her rights.

Laissez-faire A doctrine advocating government restraint in the regulation of business.

Landlord's lien A landlord's remedy for a tenant's failure to pay rent. When permitted under a statute or the lease agreement, the landlord may take and keep or sell whatever of the defaulting tenant's property is on the leased premises.

Larceny The act of taking another person's personal property unlawfully. Some states classify larceny as either grand or petit, depending on the property's value.

Last clear chance A doctrine under which a plaintiff may recover from a defendant for injuries or damages suffered, notwithstanding the plaintiff's own negligence, when the defendant had the opportunity—a last clear chance—to avoid harming the plaintiff through the exercise of reasonable care but failed to do so.

Lease A transfer by the landlord/lessor of real or personal property to the tenant/lessee for a period of time for consideration (usually the payment of rent). Upon termination of the lease, the property reverts to the lessor.

Lease agreement An agreement between a landlord and tenant setting forth the terms of the lease.

Leasehold estate An estate in realty held by a tenant under a lease. In every leasehold estate, the tenant has a qualified right to possess and/or use the land.

Legacy A gift of personal property under a will.

Legal rate of interest A rate of interest fixed by statute as either the maximum rate of interest allowed by law or a rate of interest applied when the parties to a contract intend, but do not fix, an interest rate in the contract. In the latter case, the rate is frequently the same as the statutory maximum rate permitted.

Legal realism A school of legal thought of the 1920s and 1930s that challenged many existing jurisprudential assumptions, particularly the assumption that subjective elements played no part in judicial reasoning. The legal realists, as the term implies, generally advocated a less abstract and more realistic approach to the law, an approach that would take into account customary practices and the circumstances in which transactions take place. The school left a lasting imprint on American jurisprudence.

Legatee A person who inherits personal property under a will.

Legislative rules Administrative agency rules that carry the same weight as congressionally enacted statutes.

Lender liability The liability of lenders to their borrowers or for the actions of their borrowers.

Lessee A person who pays for the use or possession of another's property.

Lessor A property owner who allows others to use his or her property in exchange for the payment of rent.

Letter of credit A written instrument, usually issued by a bank on behalf of a customer or other person, in which the issuer promises to honor drafts or other demands for payment by third persons in accordance with the terms of the instrument.

Leveraged buy-out (LBO) A corporate takeover financed by loans secured by the acquired corporation's assets or by the issuance of corporate bonds, resulting in a high debt load for the corporation.

Libel A written defamation of one's character, reputation, business, or property rights. To a limited degree, the First Amendment to the Constitution protects the press from libel actions.

License A revocable privilege to use another's intellectual property or to enter onto another's real property.

Licensee One who receives a license to use, or enter onto, another's property.

Lien An encumbrance upon a property to satisfy or protect a claim for payment of a debt.

Lien creditor One whose claim is secured by a lien on particular property, as distinguished from a general creditor, who has no such security.

Life estate An interest in land that exists only for the duration of the life of some person, usually the holder of the estate.

Limited partner In a limited partnership, a partner who contributes capital to the partnership but has no right to participate in the management and operation of the business. The limited partner assumes no liability for partnership debts beyond the capital contributed.

Limited partnership A partnership consisting of one or more general partners (who manage the business and are liable to the full extent of their personal assets for debts of the partnership) and of one or more limited partners (who contribute only assets and are liable only up to the amount contributed by them).

Limited-payment life A type of life insurance for which premiums are payable for a definite period, after which the policy is fully paid.

Liquidated damages An amount, stipulated in the contract, that the parties to a contract believe to be a reasonable estimation of the damages that will occur in the event of a breach.

Liquidation The sale of the assets of a business or an

individual for cash and the distribution of the cash received to creditors, with the balance going to the owner(s).

Litigant A party to a lawsuit.

Loan workout A common law or bankruptcy composition (agreement) with creditors under which a debtor enters into an agreement with a creditor or creditors for a payment or plan to discharge the debtor's debt(s).

Long arm statute A state statute that permits a state to obtain jurisdiction over nonresident individuals and corporations. Individuals or corporations, however, must have certain ''minimum contacts'' with that state for the statute to apply.

Lost property Property with which the owner has involuntarily parted and then cannot find or recover.

M

Mailbox rule A rule providing that an acceptance of an offer becomes effective upon dispatch (upon being placed in a mailbox), if mail is, expressly or impliedly, an authorized means of communication of acceptance to the offeror.

Maker One who issues a promissory note or certificate of deposit (that is, one who promises to pay a certain sum to the holder of the note or CD).

Manufacturing or processing-plant franchise A franchise that is created when the franchisor transmits to the franchisee the essential ingredients or formula to make a particular product. The franchisee then markets the product either at wholesale or at retail in accordance with the franchisor's standards. Examples of this type of franchise are Coca-Cola and other soft-drink bottling companies.

Market concentration A situation that exists when a small number of firms share the market for a particular good or service. For example, if the four largest grocery stores in Chicago accounted for 80 percent of all retail food sales, the market clearly would be concentrated in those four firms.

Market power The power of a firm to control the market for its product. A monopoly has the greatest degree of market power.

Market share test The primary measure of monopoly power. A firm's market share is the percentage of a market that the firm controls.

Marshalling assets The arrangement or ranking of assets in a certain order toward the payment of debts. In equity, when two creditors have recourse to the same property of the debtor, but one has recourse to other property of the debtor, that creditor must resort first to those assets of the debtor not available to the other creditor.

Mask work A series of images related to the pattern formed by the many layers of a semiconductor chip product.

Material facts Those facts to which a reasonable person would attach importance in determining his or her course of action. In regard to tender offers, for example, a fact is material if there is a substantial likelihood that a reasonable shareholder would consider it important in deciding how to vote.

Mechanic's lien A statutory lien upon the real property of another, created to ensure priority of payment for work performed and materials furnished in erecting or repairing a building or other structure.

Mediation A method of settling disputes outside of court by using the services of a neutral third party, who acts as a communicating agent between the parties; a method of dispute settlement that is less formal than arbitration.

Mens rea Mental state, or intent. A wrongful mental state is as necessary as a wrongful act to establish criminal liability. What constitutes a mental state varies according to the wrongful action. Thus, for murder, the *mens rea* is the intent to take life; for theft, the *mens rea* must involve both the knowledge that the property belongs to another and the intent to deprive the owner of it.

Merger A contractual process by which one corporation (the surviving corporation) acquires all the assets and liabilities of another corporation (the merged corporation). The shareholders of the merged corporation receive either payment for their shares or shares in the surviving corporation.

Minimum-contacts requirement The requirement that before a state court can exercise jurisdiction over a foreign corporation, the foreign corporation must have sufficient contacts with the state. A foreign corporation that has its home office within the state or has manufacturing plants in the state meets this requirement.

Mini-trial A private proceeding that assists disputing parties in determining whether to take their case to court. During the proceeding, each party's attorney briefly argues the party's case before the other party and (usually) a neutral third party, who acts as an adviser. If the parties fail to reach an agreement, the adviser renders an opinion as to how a court would likely decide the issue.

Mirror image rule A common law rule that requires, for a valid contractual agreement, that the terms of the offeree's acceptance adhere exactly to the terms of the offeror's offer.

Misdemeanor A lesser crime than a felony, punishable by a fine or imprisonment for up to one year in other than a state or federal penitentiary.

Mislaid property Property that the owner has voluntarily parted with and then cannot find or recover.

Mitigation of damages The rule requiring the party suing to have done whatever was reasonable to minimize the damages caused by the defendant.

Money laundering Falsely reporting income that has been obtained through criminal activity as income obtained through a legitimate business enterprise—in effect, "laundering" the "dirty money."

Monopolization The possession of monopoly power in the relevant market and the willful acquisition or maintenance of the power, as distinguished from growth or development as a consequence of a superior product, business acumen, or historical accident. A violation of Section 2 of the Sherman Act requires that both of these elements be established.

Monopoly A term generally used to describe a market for which there is a single seller.

Monopoly power An extreme amount of market power.

Mortgage A written instrument giving a creditor (the mortgagee) an interest (lien) in the debtor's (mortgagor's) property as security for a debt.

Mortgagee The creditor who takes the security interest under a mortgage agreement.

Mortgagor The debtor who pledges collateral in a mortgage agreement.

Motion for a directed verdict In a jury trial, a motion for the judge to take the decision out of the hands of the jury and direct a verdict for the moving party on the grounds that the other party has not produced sufficient evidence to support his or her claim.

Motion for judgment on the pleadings A motion, which can be brought by either party to a lawsuit after the pleadings are closed, for the court to decide the issue without proceeding to trial. This motion may be used when only questions of law are at issue.

Motion to dismiss A pleading in which a defendant admits the facts as alleged by the plaintiff but asserts that the plaintiff's claim fails to state a cause of action (that is, has no basis in law) or that there are other grounds on which a suit should be dismissed. Also called a demurrer.

Multiple product order An order issued by the Federal Trade Commission to a firm that has engaged in deceptive advertising by which the firm is required to cease and desist from false advertising not only in regard to the product that was the subject of the action but also in regard to all the firm's other products.

Municipal courts City or community courts with criminal jurisdiction over traffic violations and, less frequently, with civil jurisdiction over other minor matters.

Mutual assent The element of agreement in the formation of a contract. The manifestation of contract parties' mutual assent to the same bargain is required to establish a contract.

Mutual fund A specific type of investment company that continually buys or sells to investors shares of ownership in a portfolio.

Mutual rescission An agreement between the parties to cancel their contract, releasing the parties from further obligations under the contract. The object of the agreement is to restore the parties to the positions they would have occupied had no contract ever been formed. *See also* Rescission.

N

National law Law that pertains to a particular nation (as opposed to international law).

Natural law school The oldest and one of the most significant schools of legal thought. Adherents of the natural law school believe that government and the legal system should reflect universal moral and ethical principles that are inherent in human nature.

Negligence The failure to exercise the standard of care that a reasonable person would exercise in similar circumstances.

Negligent misrepresentation Any manifestation through words or conduct that amounts to an untrue statement of fact made in circumstances in which a reasonable and prudent person would not have done (or failed to do) that which led to the misrepresentation. A representation made with an honest belief in its truth may still be negligent due to (1) a lack of reasonable care in ascertaining the facts, (2) the manner of expression, or (3) the absence of the skill or competence required by a particular business or profession.

Negotiable instrument A written and signed unconditional promise or order to pay a specified sum of money on demand or at a definite time to order (to a specific person or entity) or to bearer.

Negotiation The transferring of a negotiable instrument to another in such form that the transferee becomes a holder.

No par shares Corporate shares that have no face value—that is, no specific dollar amount is printed on their face.

Nominal damages A small monetary award (often one dollar) granted to a plaintiff when no actual damage was suffered.

Note A written instrument signed by a maker unconditionally promising to pay a sum certain in money to a payee or a holder on demand or on a specific date [UCC 3-104].

Notice of Proposed Rulemaking A notice published (in the *Federal Register*) by an administrative agency describing a proposed rule. The notice must give the time and place for which agency proceedings on the proposed rule will be held, a description of the nature of the proceedings, the legal authority for the proceedings (which is usually the agency's enabling legislation), and the terms of the proposed rule or the subject matter of the proposed rule.

Notice-and-comment rulemaking A procedure in agency rulemaking that requires (1) notice, (2) opportunity for comment, and (3) a general statement of the basis for, and purpose of, the proposed rule. Also referred to as informal rulemaking.

Novation The substitution, by agreement, of a new contract for an old one, with the rights under the old one being terminated. Typically, there is a substitution of a new person who is responsible for the contract and the removal of the original party's rights and duties under the contract.

Nuisance An act that interferes unlawfully with a person's possession or ability to use his or her property.

Nuncupative will An oral will (often called a deathbed will) made before witnesses; usually limited to transfers of personal property.

O

Objective theory of contracts The view taken by American law that contracting parties shall only be bound by terms that can actually be inferred from promises made. Contract law does not examine a contracting party's subjective intent or underlying motive.

Offer An offeror's proposal to do something, which creates in the offeree accepting the offer a legal power to bind the offeror to the terms of the proposal by accepting the offer.

Offeree A person to whom an offer is made.

Offeror A person who makes an offer.

Omnibus, or other-driver, clause A provision in an automobile insurance policy that protects the vehicle owner who has taken out the insurance policy and anyone who drives the vehicle with the owner's permission.

Opinion A statement by the court expressing the reasons for its decision in a case.

Option contract A contract under which the offeror cannot revoke his or her offer for a stipulated time period, and the offeree can accept or reject the offer during this period without fear of the offer's being made to another person. The offeree must give consideration for the option (the irrevocable offer) to be enforceable.

Order for relief A court's grant of assistance to a complainant. In the context of bankruptcy, relief consists of discharging a complainant's debts.

Order instrument A negotiable instrument that is payable to the order of a specific person.

Output contract A binding agreement in which a seller agrees to deliver/sell the seller's entire output of a good (an unspecified amount at the time of agreement) to a buyer, and the buyer agrees to buy all the goods supplied.

P

Par-value shares Corporate shares that have a specific face value, or formal cash-in value, written on them, such as one penny or one dollar.

Parol evidence rule A substantive rule of contracts under which a court will not receive into evidence prior statements or contemporaneous oral statements that contradict a written agreement when the court finds that the written agreement was intended by the parties to be a final, complete, and unambiguous expression of their agreement.

Partially disclosed principal A principal whose identity is unknown by a third person, but the third person knows that the agent is or may be acting for a principal at the time the contract is made.

Partnership An association of two or more persons to carry on, as co-owners, a business for profit.

Past consideration An act done before the contract is made, which ordinarily, by itself, cannot be consideration for a later promise to pay for the act.

Patent A government grant that gives an inventor the exclusive right or privilege to make, use, or sell his or her invention for a limited time period. The word *patent* usually refers to some invention and designates either the instrument by which patent rights are evidenced or the patent itself.

Payee A person to whom an instrument is made payable.

Payor bank A bank on which an item is payable as drawn (or is payable as accepted).

Penalty A sum inserted into a contract, not as a measure of compensation for its breach but rather as punishment for a default. The agreement as to the amount will not be enforced, and recovery will be limited to actual damages.

Per capita A Latin term meaning *per person*. In the law governing estate distribution, a method of distributing the property of an intestate's estate by which all the heirs receive equal shares.

Per se In itself; inherent.

***Per se* violation** A type of anticompetitive agreement—such as a price-fixing agreement—that is considered to be so injurious to the public that there is no need to determine whether it actually injures market competition; rather, it is in itself (*per se*) a violation of the Sherman Act.

Per stirpes A Latin term meaning *by the roots*. In the law governing estate distribution, a method of distributing an intestate's estate in which a class or group of distributees take the share to which their deceased ancestor would have been entitled.

Perfect tender rule A common law rule under which a seller was required to deliver to the buyer goods that conformed perfectly to the requirements stipulated in the sales contract. A tender of nonconforming goods would automatically constitute a breach of contract. Under the UCC, the rule has been greatly modified.

Perfection The method by which a secured party obtains a priority by notice that his or her security interest in the debtor's collateral is effective against the debtor's subsequent creditors. Usually accomplished by filing a financing statement at a location set out in the state statute.

Performance In contract law, the fulfillment of one's duties arising under a contract with another; the normal way of discharging one's contractual obligations.

Periodic tenancy A lease interest in land for an indefinite period involving payment of rent at fixed intervals, such as week to week, month to month, or year to year.

Personal defenses Defenses that can be used to avoid payment to an ordinary holder of a negotiable instrument. Personal defenses cannot be used to avoid payment to a holder in due course (HDC) or (under the shelter principle) to a holder through an HDC.

Personal identification number (PIN) A number given to the holder of an access card that is used to conduct financial transactions in electronic fund transfer systems. Typically, the card will not provide access to a system without the number, which is meant to be kept secret to inhibit unauthorized use of the card.

Personal property Property that is movable; any property that is not real property.

Personalty Personal property.

Petition in bankruptcy An application to a bankruptcy court for relief in bankruptcy; filing for bankruptcy. The official forms required for a petition in bankruptcy must be completed accurately, sworn to under oath, and signed by the debtor.

Petitioner The party who presents a petition to a court, initiates an equity proceeding, or appeals from a judgment.

Petty offense In criminal law, the least serious kind of wrong, such as a traffic or building-code violation.

Plaintiff One who initiates a lawsuit.

Plea bargaining The process by which the accused and the prosecutor in a criminal case work out a mutually satisfactory disposition of the case, subject to court approval. Usually involves the defendant's pleading guilty to a lesser offense in return for a lighter sentence.

Pleadings Statements by the plaintiff and the defendant that detail the facts, charges, and defenses. Modern rules simplify common law pleading, often requiring only the complaint, an answer, and sometimes a reply to the answer.

Pledge The bailment of personal property to a creditor as security for the payment of a debt.

Point-of-sale system An electronic customer-bank-merchant communication terminal that, when activated by an access card and a personal identification number, can debit the customer's account to cover a purchase from the merchant.

Police powers Powers possessed by states as part of their inherent sovereignty. These powers may be exercised to protect or promote public health, safety, or morals, or the general welfare.

Policy In insurance law, the contract of indemnity against a contingent loss between the insurer and the insured.

Positive law The objective laws legally created by a society, as opposed to natural law or the unwritten laws arising from social customs; also called *black-letter law*.

Positivist school A school of legal thought that holds that there can be no higher law than a nation's positive law—law created by a particular society at a particular point in time. In contrast to the natural law school, the positivist school maintains that there are no "natural" rights; rights come into existence only when there is a sovereign power (government) to confer and enforce those rights.

Possibility of reverter A future interest in land that a grantor retains after conveying property subject to a condition subsequent (for example, if a certain future event occurs, the interest in the estate will terminate automatically).

Potential competition doctrine A doctrine under which a conglomerate merger may be prohibited by law because it would be injurious to potential competition. Potential competition is the competitive effect that a firm has on a market even though the firm does not operate in the market. The firm's effect is felt by its "waiting in the wings"—ready to enter the market if firms already in the market begin to earn supranormal profits by charging noncompetitive prices. This potential competition is lost if the firm that is waiting in the wings merges with a dominant firm in the industry.

Power of attorney A document or instrument authorizing another to act as one's agent or attorney.

Preauthorized transfer A transaction authorized in advance to recur at substantially regular intervals. The terms and procedure for preauthorized electronic fund transfers through certain financial institutions are subject to the Electronic Fund Transfer Act.

Precedent A court decision that furnishes an example or authority for deciding subsequent cases in which identical or similar facts are presented.

Preemptive rights Rights held by shareholders that entitle them to purchase newly issued shares of a corporation's stock, equal in percentage to shares presently held, before the stock is offered to any outside buyers. Preemptive rights enable shareholders to maintain their proportionate ownership and voice in the corporation.

Preference In bankruptcy proceedings, the debtor's favoring of one creditor over others by making payments or transferring property to that creditor at the expense of the rights of other creditors in the bankruptcy estate. The bankruptcy trustee is allowed to recover payments made both voluntarily and involuntarily to one creditor in preference over another.

Preferred stock Classes of stock that have priority over common stock both as to payment of dividends and distribution of assets upon the corporation's dissolution.

Prejudgment interest Interest that accrues on the amount of a court judgment from the time of the filing of the suit to the issuing of the judgment.

Premium In insurance law, the price for insurance protection for a specified period of time.

Presentment warranty An implied warranty, made by

any person who seeks payment or acceptance of a negotiable instrument to any person who in good faith pays or accepts the instrument, that the party presenting the instrument has good title to the instrument or is authorized to obtain payment or acceptance on behalf of a person who has good title, has no knowledge that the signature of the maker or the drawer is unauthorized, and has no knowledge that the instrument has been materially altered [UCC 3-417(1), 3-418].

Pretrial motion A written or oral application to a court for a ruling or order, made before trial.

Price discrimination Setting prices in such a way that two competing buyers pay two different prices for an identical product or service.

Price fixing Fixing—by means of an anticompetitive agreement between competitors—the prices of products or services.

Prima facie case A case in which the plaintiff has produced sufficient evidence of his or her conclusion that the case can go to a jury; a case in which the evidence compels the plaintiff's conclusion if the defendant produces no evidence to rebut it.

Principal In agency law, a person who, by agreement or otherwise, authorizes an agent to act on his or her behalf in such a way that the acts of the agent become binding on the principal.

Private law Law governing the behavior of individual members of society as that behavior affects other individuals. Examples of private law are contract law and tort law.

Privilege In tort law, the ability to act contrary to another person's right without that person's having legal redress for such acts. Privilege is usually raised as a defense.

Privity of contract The relationship that exists between the promisor and the promisee of a contract.

Probable cause Reasonable grounds to believe the existence of facts warranting certain actions, such as the search or arrest of a person.

Probate The process of proving and validating a will and the settling of all matters pertaining to administration, guardianship, and like matters.

Probate court A court having jurisdiction over proceedings concerning the settlement of a person's estate.

Procedural law Rules that define the manner in which the rights and duties of individuals may be enforced.

Proceeds In secured transactions law, whatever is received when the collateral is sold, exchanged, collected, or otherwise disposed of, such as insurance payments for destroyed or lost collateral. Money, checks, and the like are _cash proceeds,_ whereas all other proceeds received are _noncash proceeds._

Product liability The legal liability of manufacturers and sellers to buyers, users, and sometimes bystanders for injuries or damages suffered because of defects in goods purchased. Liability arises when a product has a defective condition that makes it unreasonably dangerous to the user or consumer.

Product misuse A defense against product liability that may be raised when the plaintiff used a product in a manner not intended by the manufacturer. If the misuse is reasonably foreseeable, the seller will not escape liability unless measures were taken to guard against the harm that could result from the misuse.

Professional corporation A corporation formed by professional persons, such as physicians, lawyers, dentists, and accountants, to gain tax benefits. Subject to certain exceptions (when a court may treat a professional corporation as a partnership for liability purposes), the shareholders of a professional corporation have the limited liability characteristic of the corporate form of business.

Profit In real property law, the right to enter upon and remove things from the property of another (for example, the right to enter onto a person's land and remove sand and gravel therefrom).

Promise A declaration that binds the person who makes it (promisor) to do or not to do a certain act. The person to whom the promise is made (promisee) has a right to expect or demand the performance of some particular thing.

Promisee A person to whom a promise is made.

Promisor A person who makes a promise.

Promissory estoppel A doctrine that applies when a promisor reasonably expects a promise to induce definite and substantial action or forbearance by the promisee, and that does induce such action or forbearance in reliance thereon; such a promise is binding if injustice can be avoided only by enforcing the promise. _See also_ Estoppel.

Promissory note A written instrument signed by a maker unconditionally promising to pay a certain sum in money to a payee or a holder on demand or on a specified date.

Promoter An entrepreneur who participates in the organization of a corporation in its formative stage, usually by issuing a prospectus, procuring subscriptions to the stock, making contract purchases, securing a charter, and the like.

Property The legally protected rights and interests a person has in anything with an ascertainable value that is subject to ownership. _See also_ Personal property; Real property.

Protected class A class of persons with identifiable characteristics who historically have been victimized by discriminatory treatment for certain purposes. Depending on the context, these characteristics include age, color, gender, national origin, race, and religion.

Proximate cause The ''next'' or ''substantial'' cause; in tort law, a concept used to determine whether a plaintiff's injury was the natural and continuous result of a defendant's negligent act. If the negligent act of a defendant was the sole cause or a substantial cause of injuries to a plaintiff, the defendant will be liable.

Proxy In corporation law, a written agreement between a stockholder and another under which the stockholder authorizes the other to vote the stockholder's shares in a certain manner.

Public figures Individuals who are thrust into the public limelight. Public figures include government officials and politicians, movie stars, well-known businesspersons, and generally anybody who becomes known to the public because of his or her position or activities.

Public law Law governing the relationships between individuals and their government. Examples of public law are administrative law, constitutional law, and criminal law.

Puffing A salesperson's often exaggerated claims concerning the quality of the goods offered for sale. Such claims involve opinions rather than facts and are not considered to be legally binding promises or warranties.

Punitive damages Compensation in excess of actual or consequential damages. They are awarded in order to punish the wrongdoer and usually will be awarded only in cases involving willful or malicious misconduct.

Purchase-money security interest A security interest to the extent that it is (1) taken or retained by a seller of the collateral to secure all or part of the price of the collateral or (2) taken by a creditor who, by making advances or incurring an obligation, gives value to enable the debtor to acquire rights in, or use of, the collateral, if such value is in fact so used.

Q

Qualified indorsement An indorsement on a negotiable instrument by which the indorser disclaims to subsequent holders secondary liability on the instrument; the most common qualified indorsement is "without recourse."

Quantum meruit Literally, "as much as he deserves"—an expression describing the extent of liability on a contract implied in law (quasi contract). An equitable doctrine based on the concept that one who benefits from another's labor and materials should not be unjustly enriched thereby but should be required to pay a reasonable amount for the benefits received, even absent a contract.

Quasi contract An obligation or contract imposed by law, in the absence of agreement, to prevent unjust enrichment. Sometimes referred to as an implied-in-law contract (a legal fiction) to distinguish it from an implied-in-fact contract.

Questions of fact In lawsuits, issues involving factual disputes that can be decided by a jury.

Questions of law In lawsuits, issues involving the application or interpretation of law; therefore, the judge, and not the jury, decides the issues.

Quitclaim deed A deed intended to pass any title, interest, or claim that the grantor may have in the premises but not professing that such title is valid and not containing any warranty or covenants of title.

R

Ratification The approval or validation of a previous action. In contract law, the confirmation of a voidable act (that is, an act that without ratification would not be an enforceable contractual obligation). In agency law, the confirmation by one person of an act or contract performed or entered into on his or her behalf by another, who assumed, without authority, to act as his or her agent.

Reaffirmation agreement An agreement between a debtor and a creditor in which the debtor reaffirms, or promises to pay, a debt dischargeable in bankruptcy. To be enforceable, the agreement must be made prior to the discharge of the debt by the bankruptcy court.

Real property Immovable property consisting of land and buildings thereupon, as opposed to personal property, which can be moved. In the absence of a contract, real property includes things growing on the land before they are severed (such as timber), as well as fixtures.

Reasonable care The degree of care that a person of ordinary prudence would exercise in the same or similar circumstances.

Reasonable doubt *See* Beyond a reasonable doubt.

Reasonable person standard The standard of behavior expected of a hypothetical "reasonable person." The standard against which negligence is measured and that must be observed to avoid liability for negligence.

Rebuttal The refutation of evidence introduced by an adverse party's attorney.

Receiver A court-appointed person who receives, preserves, and manages a business or other property that is involved in bankruptcy proceedings.

Recording statutes Statutes requiring that deeds, mortgages, and other real property transactions be recorded so as to provide notice to future purchasers, creditors, and encumbrancers of an existing claim on the property.

Red herring A preliminary prospectus that can be distributed to potential investors after the registration statement (for a securities offering) has been filed with the Securities and Exchange Commission. The name derives from the red legend printed across the prospectus stating that the registration has been filed but has not become effective.

Redemption A repurchase, or buying back. In secured transactions law, a debtor's repurchase of collateral securing a debt after a creditor has taken title to the collateral due to the debtor's default but before the secured party disposes of it.

Reformation A court-ordered correction of a written

contract so that it reflects the true intentions of the parties.

Regulation E A set of rules issued by the Federal Reserve System's board of governors under the authority of the Electronic Fund Transfer Act to protect users of electronic fund transfer systems.

Regulation Z A set of rules promulgated by the Federal Reserve System's board of governors to implement the provisions of the Truth-in-Lending Act.

Rejoinder The defendant's answer to the plaintiff's rebuttal.

Release The relinquishment, concession, or giving up of a right, claim, or privilege, by the person in whom it exists or to whom it accrues, to the person against whom it might have been enforced or demanded.

Remainder A future interest in property, held by a person other than the grantor, that occurs at the natural termination of the preceding estate.

Remanded Sent back. If an appellate court disagrees with a lower court's judgment, the case may be remanded to the lower court for further proceedings, in which the lower court's decision should be consistent with the appellate court's opinion on the matter.

Remedy The relief given to innocent parties, by law or by contract, to enforce a right or to prevent or compensate for the violation of a right.

Remedy at law A remedy available in a court of law. Money damages are awarded as a remedy at law.

Remedy in equity A remedy allowed by courts in situations where remedies at law are not appropriate. Remedies in equity are based on settled rules of fairness, justice, and honesty.

Rent escalation An increase in rent during a lease term according to a lease clause.

Repair-and-deduct statutes Statutes providing that a tenant may pay for repairs and deduct the cost of the repairs from the rent, as a remedy for a landlord's failure to maintain leased premises.

Replevin An action brought to recover the possession of personal property unlawfully held by another.

Reply Procedurally, a plaintiff's response to a defendant's answer.

Requirements contract An agreement under which a promisor promises to supply the promisee with all the goods and/or services the promisee might require from period to period.

Res ipsa loquitur A doctrine under which negligence may be inferred simply because an event occurred, if it is the type of event that would not occur absent negligence. Literally, the term means *the thing speaks for itself.*

Resale price maintenance agreement An agreement between a manufacturer and a retailer in which the manufacturer specifies the minimum retail price of its products. Resale price maintenance agreements are illegal *per se* under the Sherman Act.

Rescission A remedy whereby a contract is terminated

and the parties are returned to the positions they occupied before the contract was made; may be effected through the mutual consent of the parties, by their conduct, or by the decree of a court of equity.

Respondeat superior In Latin, ''Let the master respond.'' A principle of law whereby a principal or an employer is held liable for the wrongful acts committed by agents or employees while acting within the scope of their agency or employment.

Respondent In equity practice, the party who answers a bill or other proceeding. In appellate practice, the party against whom an appeal is taken (sometimes referred to as the appellee).

Restitution An equitable remedy under which a person is restored to his or her original position prior to loss or injury, or placed in the position he or she would have been in had the breach not occurred.

Restrictive indorsement Any indorsement of a negotiable instrument that purports to condition or prohibit further transfer of the instrument. As against payor and intermediary banks, such indorsements are usually ineffective.

Resulting trust A trust implied in law from the intentions of the parties to a given transaction. A trust in which a party holds legal title for the benefit of another, although without expressed intent to do so, because the presumption of such intent arises by operation of law.

Retaliatory eviction The eviction of a tenant because of the tenant's complaints, participation in a tenant's union, or similar activity with which the landlord does not agree.

Reversible error An error by a lower court that is sufficiently substantial to justify an appellate court's reversal of the lower court's decision.

Reversion A future interest under which a grantor retains a present right to a future interest in property that the grantor conveys to another; usually the residue of a life estate. The reversion is always a vested property right.

Revocation In contract law, the withdrawal of an offer by an offeror; unless the offer is irrevocable, it can be revoked at any time prior to acceptance without liability.

Right of contribution The right of a co-surety who pays more than his or her proportionate share upon a debtor's default to recover the excess paid from other co-sureties.

Right of entry The right to peaceably take or resume possession of real property.

Right of first refusal The right to purchase personal or real property—such as corporate shares or real estate—before the property is offered for sale to others.

Right of reimbursement The legal right of a person to be restored, repaid, or indemnified for costs, expenses, or losses incurred or expended on behalf of another.

Right of subrogation The right of a person to stand in the place of (be substituted for) another, giving the substituted party the same legal rights that the original party had.

Right-to-work laws State laws generally providing that employees are not to be required to join a union as a condition of receiving or retaining employment.

Risk A specified contingency or peril.

Risk management Planning that is undertaken to protect one's interest should some event threaten to undermine its security. In the context of insurance, transferring certain risks from the insured to the insurance company.

Robbery Theft from a person, accompanied by force or fear of force.

Rule of four A rule of the United States Supreme Court under which the Court will not issue a writ of *certiorari* unless at least four justices approve of the decision to issue the writ.

Rule of reason A test by which a court balances the reasons (such as economic efficiency) for an agreement against its potentially anticompetitive effects. In antitrust litigation, most practices are analyzed under the rule of reason.

Rule 10b-5 A rule of the Securities and Exchange Commission that makes it unlawful, in connection with the purchase or sale of any security, to make any untrue statement of a material fact or to omit a material fact if such omission causes the statement to be misleading.

Rulemaking The actions undertaken by administrative agencies when formally adopting new regulations or amending old ones. Under the Administrative Procedures Act, rulemaking includes notifying the public of proposed rules or changes and receiving and considering the public's comments.

Rulemaking-on-a-record Agency rulemaking that is much more extensive than informal rulemaking and in which a public hearing is conducted in the manner of a trial. After the hearing is concluded, the agency is required to prepare a formal written statement describing its findings based on the evidence presented by both sides. Also referred to as formal rulemaking.

S

S corporation A close business corporation that has met certain requirements as set out by the Internal Revenue Code and thus qualifies for special income-tax treatment. Essentially, an S corporation is taxed the same as a partnership, but its owners enjoy the privilege of limited liability.

Sale The passing of title to property from the seller to the buyer for a price.

Sale on approval A type of conditional sale that becomes absolute only when the buyer approves, or is satisfied with, the good(s) sold. Besides express approval of goods, approval may be inferred if the buyer keeps the goods beyond a reasonable time or uses the goods

in any way that is inconsistent with the seller's ownership.

Sale or return A type of conditional sale wherein title and possession pass from the seller to the buyer; however, the buyer retains the option to rescind or return the goods during a specified period even though the goods conform to the contract.

Scienter Knowledge by the misrepresenting party that material facts have been falsely represented or omitted with an intent to deceive.

Searches and seizures The searching or taking into custody of persons or private property by the government. Unreasonable and unwarranted searches and seizures are prohibited by the Fourth Amendment. In the context of administrative law, searches and seizures may be undertaken by administrative agencies to gather information and necessary evidence to prove that a regulation has been violated.

Secondary boycott A union's refusal to work for, purchase from, or handle the products of a secondary employer, with whom the union has no dispute, with the object of forcing that employer to stop doing business with the primary employer, with whom the union has a labor dispute.

Secured party A lender, seller, or any other person in whose favor there is a security interest, including a person to whom accounts or chattel paper has been sold.

Secured transaction Any transaction, regardless of its form, that is intended to create a security interest in personal property or fixtures, including goods, documents, and other intangibles.

Securities Stock certificates, bonds, notes, debentures, warrants, or other documents given as evidence of an ownership interest in the corporation or as a promise of repayment by the corporation.

Security agreement The agreement that creates or provides for a security interest between the debtor and a secured party.

Security interest Every interest "in *personal property or fixtures* [emphasis added] that secures payment or performance of an obligation" [UCC 1-201(37)].

Self-defense The legally recognized privilege to protect one's self or property against injury by another. The privilege of self-defense only protects acts that are reasonably necessary to protect one's self or property.

Service mark A mark used in the sale or the advertising of services, such as to distinguish the services of one person from the services of others. Titles, character names, and other distinctive features of radio and television programs may be registered as service marks.

Sham transaction A false transaction without substance that is undertaken with the intent to defraud a creditor or the government. An example of a sham transaction is the sale of assets to a friend or relative for the purpose of concealing assets from creditors or a bankruptcy court.

Shareholder's derivative suit A suit brought by a shareholder to enforce a corporate cause of action against a third person.

Shelter principle The principle that the holder of a negotiable instrument who cannot qualify as a holder in due course (HDC), but who derives his or her title through an HDC, acquires the rights of an HDC.

Short-form merger A merger between a subsidiary corporation and a parent corporation that owns at least 90 percent of the outstanding shares of each class of stock issued by the subsidiary corporation. Short-form mergers can be accomplished without the approval of the shareholders of either corporation.

Signature The name or mark of a person, written by that person or at his or her direction. In commercial law, any name, word, or mark used with the intention to authenticate a writing constitutes a signature.

Slander An oral defamation of one's character, reputation, business, or property rights.

Slander of quality Publication of false information about another's product, alleging it is not what its seller claims; also referred to as trade libel.

Slander of title The publication of a statement that denies or casts doubt upon another's legal ownership of any property, causing financial loss to that property's owner.

Small claims courts Special courts in which parties may litigate small claims (usually, claims involving $2,500 or less). Attorneys are not required in small claims courts, and in many states, attorneys are not allowed to represent the parties.

Sole proprietorship The simplest form of business, in which the owner is the business; thus, anyone who does business without creating a formal business entity has a sole proprietorship. The owner of a sole proprietorship reports business income on his or her personal income tax return and is legally responsible for all debts and obligations incurred by the business.

Sovereign immunity A doctrine that immunizes foreign nations from the jurisdiction of U.S. courts when certain conditions are satisfied.

Special indorsement An indorsement on an instrument that specifies to whom or to whose order the instrument is payable.

Special warranty deed A deed in which the grantor only covenants to warrant and defend the title against claims and demands of the grantor and all persons claiming by, through, and under the grantor.

Specific performance An equitable remedy requiring *exactly* the performance that was specified in a contract. Usually granted only when money damages would be an inadequate remedy and the subject matter of the contract is unique (for example, real property).

Spendthrift trust A trust created to protect the beneficiary from spending all the money to which he or she is entitled. Only a certain portion of the total amount is given to the beneficiary at any one time, and most states prohibit creditors from attaching assets of the trust.

Spot zoning Granting a zoning classification to a parcel of land that is different from the classification given to other land in the immediate area.

Stale check A check, other than a certified check, that is presented for payment more than six months after its date.

Standing The requirement that an individual must have a sufficient stake in a controversy before he or she can bring a lawsuit. The plaintiff must demonstrate that he or she either has been injured or threatened with injury.

Stare decisis A flexible doctrine of the courts, recognizing the value of following prior decisions (precedents) in cases similar to the one before the court; the courts' practice of being consistent with prior decisions based on similar facts.

Statute of Frauds A state statute under which certain types of contracts must be in writing to be enforceable.

Statute of limitations A statute of the federal government or state government setting the maximum time period during which certain actions can be brought or rights enforced. After the time period set out in the applicable statute of limitations has run, no legal action can be brought.

Statute of repose Basically, a statute of limitations that is not dependent upon the happening of a cause of action. Statutes of repose generally begin to run at an earlier date and run for a longer period of time than statutes of limitations.

Statutory law Laws enacted by a legislative body (as opposed to constitutional law, administrative law, or case law).

Statutory period of redemption A time period (usually set by state statute) during which the property subject to a defaulted mortgage, land contract, or other contract can be redeemed by the debtor after foreclosure or judicial sale.

Stock In corporation law, an equity or ownership interest in a corporation, measured in units of shares.

Stock certificate A certificate issued by a corporation evidencing the ownership of a specified number of shares at a specified value.

Stock warrant A certificate commonly attached to preferred stock and bonds that grants the owner the right to buy a given number of shares of stock, usually within a set time period.

Stop-payment order An order by the drawer of a draft or check directing the drawer's bank not to pay the check.

Strict liability Liability regardless of fault. In tort law, strict liability is imposed on a merchant who introduces into commerce a good that is unreasonably dangerous when in a defective condition.

Sublease A lease executed by the lessee of real estate to a third person, conveying the same interest that the lessee enjoys, but for a shorter term than that held by the lessee (as compared with an assignment of a lease, in which the lessee transfers the entire unexpired term of the leasehold to a third party).

Subpoena A document commanding a person to appear at a certain time and place to give testimony concerning a certain matter.

Substantive law Law that defines the rights and duties of individuals with respect to each other, as opposed to procedural law, which defines the manner in which these rights and duties may be enforced.

Summary judgment A judgment entered by a trial court prior to trial that is based on the valid assertion by one of the parties that there are no disputed issues of fact that would necessitate a trial.

Summary jury trial A relatively recent method of settling disputes in which a trial is held but the jury's verdict is not binding. The verdict only acts as a guide to both sides in reaching an agreement during the mandatory negotiations that immediately follow the trial. If a settlement is not reached, both sides have the right to a full trial later.

Summons A document informing a person that a legal action has been commenced against him or her and that he or she must appear in court on a certain date to answer the plaintiff's complaint. The document is delivered by a sheriff or other official.

Supremacy clause The clause in Article VI of the Constitution that provides that the Constitution, laws, and treaties of the United States are ''the supreme Law of the Land.'' Under this clause, state laws that directly conflict with federal law will be rendered invalid.

Surety One who agrees to be primarily responsible for the debt of another, such as a cosigner on a note.

Suretyship A contract in which a third party to a debtor-creditor relationship (the surety) promises that the third party will be primarily responsible for the debtor's obligation.

T

Target corporation The acquired corporation in a corporate takeover; a corporation to whose shareholders a tender offer is submitted.

Technology licensing Allowing another to use and profit from intellectual property (patents, copyrights, trademarks, innovative products or processes, and so on) for consideration. In the context of international business transactions, technology licensing sometimes is an attractive alternative to the establishment of foreign production facilities.

Tenancy at sufferance Tenancy by one who, after rightfully being in possession of leased premises, continues (wrongfully) to occupy the property after the lease has been terminated. The tenant has no estate in the land and occupies it only because the person entitled to evict has not done so.

Tenancy at will The right of a tenant to remain in possession of land with permission of the landlord until either the tenant or the landlord chooses to terminate the tenancy.

Tenancy by the entirety The joint ownership of property by husband and wife. Neither party can alienate or encumber the property without the consent of the other. The property is inherited by the survivor of the two, and dissolution of marriage transforms a tenancy by the entirety into a tenancy in common.

Tenancy for years A nonfreehold estate/lease for a specified period of time, after which the interest reverts to the grantor.

Tenancy in common Co-ownership of property in which each party owns an undivided interest that passes to his or her heirs at death.

Tender A timely offer or expression of willingness to pay a debt or perform an obligation.

Term insurance A type of life insurance policy for which premiums are paid for a specified term. Payment on the policy is due only if death occurs within the term period. Premiums are less expensive than for whole life or limited-payment life, and there is usually no cash surrender value.

Testamentary trust A trust that is created by will and therefore does not take effect until the death of the testator.

Testator One who makes and executes a will.

Third party beneficiary contract A contract between two or more parties, the performance of which is intended to benefit a third party directly, thus giving the third party a right to file suit for breach of contract by either of the original contracting parties.

Tippee A person who receives inside information.

Title insurance Insurance commonly purchased by a purchaser of real property to protect against loss in the event that the title to the property is not free from liens or superior ownership claims.

Tombstone ad An advertisement, in a format resembling a tombstone, of a securities offering. The ad informs potential investors of where and how they may obtain a prospectus.

Tort Civil (as opposed to criminal) wrongs not arising from a breach of contract. A breach of a legal duty owed by the defendant to the plaintiff; the breach must be the proximate cause of the harm done to the plaintiff.

Tortfeasor One who commits a tort.

Totten trust A trust created by the deposit of a person's own money in his or her own name as a trustee for another. It is a tentative trust, revocable at will until the depositor dies or completes the gift in his or her lifetime by some unequivocal act or declaration.

Trade libel The publication of false information about another's product, alleging it is not what its seller claims; also referred to as slander of quality.

Trade name A name used in commercial activity to

designate a particular business, a place at which a business is located, or a class of goods. Trade names can be exclusive or nonexclusive. Examples of trade names are Sears, Safeway, and Firestone.

Trade secrets Information or processes that give a business an advantage over competitors who do not know the information or processes.

Trademark A word or symbol that has become sufficiently associated with a good (at common law) or has been registered with a government agency. Once a trademark is established, the owner has exclusive use of it and has the right to bring a legal action against those who infringe upon the protection given the trademark.

Tradeoff A desired result that one must sacrifice (trade off) to obtain another desired result.

Transfer warranties Warranties (guaranties) made by the indorser and transferor of a negotiable instrument to all subsequent transferees and holders who take the instrument in good faith that (1) the transferor has good title to the instrument or is otherwise authorized to obtain payment or acceptance on behalf of one who does have good title; (2) all signatures are genuine or authorized; (3) the instrument has not been materially altered; (4) no defense of any party is good against the transferor; and (5) the transferor has no knowledge of any insolvency proceedings against the maker, the acceptor, or the drawer of an unaccepted instrument.

Transferee In negotiable instruments law, one to whom a negotiable instrument is transferred (delivered).

Transferor In negotiable instruments law, one who transfers (delivers) a negotiable instrument to another.

Traveler's check An instrument purchased from a bank, express company, or the like, in various denominations, that can be used as cash upon a second signature by the purchaser. It has the characteristics of a cashier's check.

Treasure trove Money or coin, gold, silver, or bullion found hidden in the earth or other private place, the owner of which is unknown; literally, treasure found.

Treble damages Damages consisting of single damages determined by a jury and tripled in amount in certain cases as required by statute.

Trespass to land At common law, the intentional or unintentional passing over another person's land uninvited, regardless of whether any physical damage is done to the land. Today a majority of courts find trespass only in cases of intentional intrusion, negligence, or some ''abnormally dangerous activity'' on the part of the defendant.

Trespass to personal property Any wrongful transgression or offense against the personal property of another.

Trust (1) A form of business organization somewhat similar to a corporation. Originally, the trust was a device by which several corporations that were engaged in the same general line of business combined for their mutual advantage to eliminate competition and control the mar-

ket for their products. The term *trust* derived from the transfer of the voting power of the corporations' shareholders to the committee or board that controlled the organization. (2) An arrangement in which title to property is held by one person (a trustee) for the benefit of another (a beneficiary).

Trustee One who holds title to property for the use or benefit of another (the beneficiary).

Tying arrangement An agreement between a buyer and a seller under which the buyer of a specific product or service is obligated to purchase additional products or services from the seller.

U

Ultra vires A Latin term meaning *beyond the powers*. Activities of a corporation's managers that are outside the scope of the power granted them by the corporation's charter or the laws of the state of incorporation are *ultra vires* acts.

Unconscionable contract or clause A contract or clause that is void on the basis of public policy because one party, as a result of his or her disproportionate bargaining power, is forced to accept terms that are unfairly burdensome and that unfairly benefit the dominating party.

Underwriter In insurance law, the one assuming a risk in return for the payment of a premium; the insurer. In securities law, any person, banker, or syndicate that guarantees a definite sum of money to a business or government in return for the issue of stock or bonds, usually for resale purposes.

Undisclosed principal A principal whose identity is unknown by a third person, and the third person has no knowledge that the agent is acting in an agency capacity at the time the contract is made.

Unenforceable contract A valid contract having no legal effect or force in a court action.

Unilateral contract A contract that includes the exchange of a promise for an act.

Union shop A place of employment in which all workers, once employed, must become union members within a specified period of time as a condition of their continued employment.

U.S. trustee A government official who performs appointing and other administrative tasks that a bankruptcy judge would otherwise have to perform.

Universal defenses Defenses that can be used to avoid payment to all holders of a negotiable instrument, including a holder in due course (HDC) or (under the shelter principle) a holder through an HDC. Also called *real defenses.*

Universal life A type of insurance that combines some aspects of term insurance with some aspects of whole life insurance.

Unlawful detainer The unjustifiable retention of the

possession of real property by one whose right to possession has terminated—as when a tenant holds over after the end of the lease term in spite of the landlord's demand for possession.

Unreasonably dangerous product In product liability, a product that is defective to the point of threatening a consumer's health and safety. A product will be considered unreasonably dangerous if it is dangerous beyond the expectation of the ordinary consumer or if a less dangerous alternative was economically feasible for the manufacturer, but the manufacturer failed to produce it.

Usage of trade Any practice or method of dealing having such regularity of observance in a place, vocation, or trade as to justify an expectation that it will be observed with respect to the transaction in question.

Usury Charging an illegal rate of interest.

Utilitarianism An approach to ethical reasoning in which ethically correct behavior is not related to any absolute ethical or moral values but to an evaluation of the consequences of a given action on those who will be affected by it. In utilitarian reasoning, a ''good'' decision is one that results in the greatest good for the greatest number of people affected by the decision.

V

Valid contract A properly constituted contract having legal strength or force.

Venue The geographical district in which an action is tried and from which the jury is selected.

Vertical merger A combining of two firms, one of which purchases goods for resale from the other. If a producer or wholesaler acquires a retailer, it is a *forward* vertical merger. If a retailer or distributor acquires its producer, it is a *backward* vertical merger.

Void contract A contract having no legal force or binding effect.

Voidable contract A contract that may be legally annulled at the option of one of the parties.

Voir dire From the French, meaning ''to speak the truth.'' A phrase denoting the preliminary questions that attorneys for the plaintiff and the defendant ask prospective jurors to determine whether potential jury members are biased or have any connection with a party to the action or with a prospective witness.

Voting trust The transfer of title by stockholders of shares of a corporation to a trustee who is authorized to vote the shares on their behalf.

W

Waiver An intentional, knowing relinquishment of a legal right.

Warranty deed A deed under which the grantor guarantees to the grantee that the grantor has title to the property conveyed in the deed, that there are no encumbrances on the property other than what the grantor has

represented, and that the grantee will enjoy quiet possession.

Waste The abuse or destructive use of real property by one who is in rightful possession of the property but who does not have title to it. Waste does not include ordinary depreciation due to age and normal use.

Watered stock Stock issued by a corporation as if fully paid for, when in fact less than par value has been paid.

Whistleblowing Telling the government or the press that one's employer is engaged in some unsafe or illegal activity.

White-collar crime Nonviolent crime committed by corporations and individuals. Embezzlement and commercial bribery are two examples of white-collar crime.

Whole life A life insurance policy in which the insured pays a level premium for his or her entire life and in which there is a constantly accumulating cash value that can be withdrawn or borrowed against by the borrower. Sometimes referred to as straight life insurance.

Will An instrument directing what is to be done with the testator's property upon his or her death, made by the testator and revocable during his or her lifetime. No interests pass until the testator dies.

Winding up The second of two stages involved in the dissolution of a partnership or corporation. Once the firm is dissolved, it continues to exist legally until the process of winding up all business affairs (collecting and distributing the firm's assets) is complete.

Workers' compensation laws State statutes establishing an administrative procedure for compensating workers' injuries that arise out of, or in the course of, their employment, regardless of fault. Instead of suing the employer, an injured worker files a claim with the administrative agency or board that administers the local workers' compensation claims.

Working papers The various documents used and developed by an accountant during an audit. Working papers include notes, computations, memoranda, copies, and other papers that make up the work product of an accountant's services to a client.

Workout A common law or bankruptcy out-of-court negotiation with creditors in which a debtor enters into an agreement with a creditor or creditors for a payment or plan to discharge the debtor's debt(s).

Workout team Individuals specifically designated by a lending institution to negotiate the terms of a workout arrangement with a major debtor when the debtor is in default. The team normally does not include the loan officer who approved the loan that is in default.

Writ of attachment A writ employed to enforce obedience to an order or judgment of the court. The writ may take the form of taking or seizing property to bring it under the control of the court.

Writ of *certiorari* A writ from a higher court asking the lower court for the record of a case.

Writ of execution A writ that puts in force a court's decree or judgment.

Table of Cases

The principal cases are in bold type. Cases cited or discussed are in roman type. Cases that can also be retrieved on West's LEGAL CLERK Research Software System are indicated by a colored dot. To determine which of the three versions of LEGAL CLERK a particular case appears on, please turn to the text page cited and refer to the color-coded computer symbol printed with the case citation.

A black computer symbol with a white background indicates that the case appears on *Uniform Commercial Code Article 2 Sales-Version 1.0*. A black computer symbol with a grey background indicates that the case is on *Government Regulation and the Legal Environment of Business-Version 1.0*. A black computer symbol with a light green background identifies the case as appearing on *Contracts-Version 1.0*.

C

Index